Baseball America

ALMANAC 2004

A Comprehensive Review of the 2003 Season, Featuring Statistics and Commentary

PUBLISHED BY
Baseball America Inc.

EDITOR
Allan Simpson

ASSISTANT EDITORS
J.J. Cooper, Chris Kline, Will Lingo

CONTRIBUTING EDITORS
Josh Boyd, Will Kimmey,
John Manuel, Gary Martin, Alan Matthews

CONTRIBUTING WRITERS
Jim Callis, John Perrotto, Alan Schwarz

DESIGN & PRODUCTION
Phillip Daquila, Matthew Eddy, Linwood Webb

STATISTICAL CONSULTANT
SportsTicker
Boston

Baseball America

PRESIDENT/CEO Catherine Silver
VICE PRESIDENT/PUBLISHER Lee Folger
EDITOR Allan Simpson
MANAGING EDITOR Will Lingo
DESIGN & PRODUCTION DIRECTOR Phillip Daquila

COVER PHOTOS Josh Beckett after final out of World Series by Denis Bancroft;
Joe Mauer by David Schofield; Rice pitchers by Anthony Neste; Delmon Young by Bill Mitchell.

To order, call **800-845-2726** or send $16.95 (regular) or $19.95 (spiral) each plus $8 shipping and handling
for first copy and $2 for each additional copy to:
Baseball America, P.O. Box 2089, Durham, NC 27702

Distributed by Simon & Schuster

EDITOR'S NOTE

Major league statistics are based on final, unofficial 2003 averages. Minor league statistics are official.

The organization statistics, which begin on Page 55, include all players who participated in at least one game during the 2003 season. Pitchers' batting statistics are not included, nor are the pitching statistics of field players who pitched on rare occasions. For players who played with more than one team in the same league, the player's cumulative statistics appear on the line immediately after the player's last-team statistics.

Innings have been rounded off to the nearest full inning.

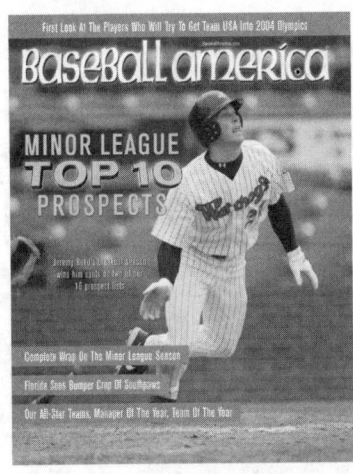

TABLE OF CONTENTS

ANTHONY NESTE

INDEX

MAJOR AND MINOR LEAGUE CLUBS

MAJOR
LEAGUES

2003 IN REVIEW

Game gets a shot in the arm from captivating postseason

BY JOHN PERROTTO

On Oct. 13, the Yankees hosted the Red Sox in Game Five of the American League Championship Series, and the St. Louis Rams hosted the Atlanta Falcons on "Monday Night Football."

When the television numbers came in the next morning, the Yankees-Red Sox game drew an 11.6 rating, meaning the game had been viewed in more than 12.5 million homes across the United States. The football game drew an 8.4 rating on ABC, 38 percent less than the ALCS.

That might not seem like a big deal on the surface, but it was a significant moment for baseball. It marked the third time in network TV history that a baseball telecast went head-to-head with a National Football League telecast and got a better rating. The other times were Game Seven of the 1986 World Series and Game Two of the 1996 World Series.

Baseball needed a shot in the arm in a season when ratings and attendance were down early. In fact, baseball had become such a disappointing ratings performer that Fox did not carry a national game of the week for two Saturday afternoons in September, in the midst of the pennant races, fearing it would have no chance of competing against college football.

Everything changed in October.

Following a regular season with fewer compelling plot lines than recent years, the postseason was riveting from the first day of Division Series play until the last game of the World Series. None of the seven series resulted in sweeps, four went the distance, and 38 of a possible 41 postseason games were played.

A dozen of the 38 games were decided by one run, and 11 were two-run games. Nine games were decided in the winning team's last at-bat, including five of the walk-off variety that included three ending on home runs.

"There's a buzz about baseball that, frankly, I haven't heard for a long time," commissioner Bud Selig said prior to the final game of the World Series.

LARRY GOREN

Bud Selig

"Any time baseball can not only beat, but pound 'Monday Night Football' rating-wise, I don't think you can look at that as anything but a glorious moment for this sport," Fox announcer Joe Buck said.

CBS and NBC yanked new editions of "CSI: Crime Scene Investigation" and "Friends"—television's most popular drama and comedy—to avoid going up against the Yankees and Red Sox in Game Seven of the ALCS.

"We're all running into the buzzsaw of baseball," CBS spokesman Chris Ender said. "Baseball is clearly wreaking havoc with the rollout of our new season."

Baseball started slowly in 2003, hurt by several weeks of cold and stormy weather in the northern part of the United States. Average attendance was down 5 percent at the end of May before rebounding to finish at 28,168 a game. Nevertheless, it was the fourth straight season when attendance declined in the major leagues.

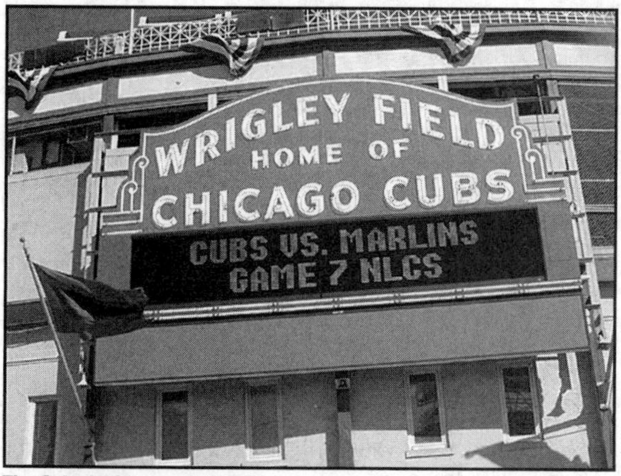

DENIS BANCROFT

The Cubs had 'em watching
TV ratings reached historic levels in 2003 postseason play

The playoffs made everyone forget about that. The four Division Series averaged a 7.5 rating on Fox, up 21 percent from the previous season and the highest rating since 1995, when the first-round games were regional broadcasts through the ill-fated Baseball Network.

The average for both League Championship Series was 10.7, up 65 percent from 2002 and the highest since 1993.

While Fox hoped for a World Series between the Red Sox and Cubs, that didn't happen as both continued their long championship droughts by losing in the LCS. Nevertheless, the Marlins-Yankees matchup drew a 12.8 rating, which was up over the 2002 matchup between the Angels and Giants.

While the World Series was the third-lowest

BONDS A player for the ages; a man on a mission

LARRY GOREN

A season of adversity, offensive feats

Barry Bonds overcame the loss of his father in 2003 to win his sixth NL MVP award

PLAYER of the YEAR

He won his third straight National League MVP award and sixth overall. His team won 100 games and a division title. But it was the saddest of years for Barry Bonds in 2003.

The most devastating offensive presence of his era, Bonds spent most of the year knowing his father, Bobby, was going to die. A former spectacular power-speed package himself, Bobby Bonds had been ill for nearly a year with lung cancer and a brain tumor. He finally succumbed to his illnesses and passed away on Aug. 23.

His death left a gaping hole in Barry Bonds' season, but it didn't stop him from dominating the National League once again, even at the age of 39. He batted .341, third in the league. He tied for second with 45 home runs. He led all of baseball with a .529 on-base percentage and .749 slugging percentage and was rewarded with that sixth MVP. Bonds continued to prove that he remains the best hitter in baseball, probably the best since Ted Williams; he also walked away with Baseball America's Major League Player of the Year award for the second time in three years.

What made Bonds' season even more remarkable, though, was how he persevered through personal tragedy, displaying a humanity his gruff demeanor had obscured for most of his career. The crowning moment came on Aug. 30, when in his first game back after a week of mourning, he hit a home run off fireballer Randy Johnson to beat the Diamondbacks, 2-1.

As he crossed the plate and pointed to the sky, Bonds almost broke down in tears. Said Giants manager Felipe Alou afterward, "That's the closest I've seen a major league guy come to actual crying."

PREVIOUS WINNERS

1998—Mark McGwire, 1b, Cardinals
1999—Pedro Martinez, rhp, Red Sox
2000—Alex Rodriguez, ss, Mariners
2001—Barry Bonds, of, Giants
2002—Alex Rodriguez, ss, Rangers

Bonds' heart began racing, about 150 beats a minute, and he soon had to be removed from the game. "It's tough," Bonds explained somberly. "I lost my dad. It's really tough right now. Emotions just went through me. I got a little light-headed. I couldn't stop my heart from pounding."

Bonds was scratched from the following day's game and spent that night in the hospital for exhaustion. It underscored how important his dad had been to him—not just as a father, but as a coach and baseball confidant. They had always spent hours on the phone talking about hitting. "My dad has been my coach my whole life," said Bonds, who missed four games before his father's death to spend some final days with him. "Everything he ever taught me has to stay in my mental Rolodex now. I've never had to do it alone, ever."

top TEN

1. Barry Bonds, of, Giants
2. Albert Pujols, of, Cardinals
3. Alex Rodriguez, ss, Rangers
4. Eric Gagne, rhp, Dodgers
5. Gary Sheffield, of, Braves
6. Mark Prior, rhp, Cubs
7. Jason Schmidt, rhp, Giants
8. Roy Halladay, rhp, Blue Jays
9. Carlos Delgado, 1b, Blue Jays
10. Javy Lopez, c, Braves

Bonds stands alone as baseball's top offensive force. He enjoyed the finest season ever for a player his age, except perhaps Ted Williams' 1957 season. He finished the year with 658 career home runs, two behind his godfather and hero, Willie Mays; 56 behind Babe Ruth; and 97 behind all-time leader Hank Aaron.

"Barry is a man on a mission," Alou said. "He has been for a long time. But with him and his father, baseball was everything. I think the game will mean even more to him now."

—ALAN SCHWARZ

rated ever, Fox still had a 10.5 rating for the postseason, the highest since 1995 and a good sign for a network that has said it overpaid on the six-year, $2.5 billion contract with MLB that started in 2001. The World Series also gave Fox improved ratings in a fall when ABC, CBS, NBC, the WB and UPN—the other five biggest networks—lost viewers compared to 2002 and the younger viewers that advertisers crave. Baseball did so well for Fox that the network topped the prime-time ratings race for three weeks in a row, the first time that's ever happened.

Exhilarating Theatre

It was little wonder the postseason ratings were up. There were plenty of good things to see.

In the NL Division Series, the Marlins upset the defending league champion Giants in four games. The series ended in dramatic fashion with Marlins catcher Ivan Rodriguez tagging out Giants first baseman J.T. Snow on a play at home to preserve a 7-6 victory.

Meanwhile, the Cubs beat the Braves in an exciting five-game series, giving the Cubs their first postseason series victory since they beat the Tigers in the 1908 World Series.

In the AL, the Yankees dispatched the Twins in four games, while the Red Sox downed the Athletics in a tense five-game series, rallying after losing the first two games.

The League Championship Series were even better, as both went down to the final game with heartbreaking finishes for the Cubs and Red Sox, whose streak of seasons without winning a World Series reached 75, dating to 1918.

The Cubs took a 3-1 series lead over the Marlins before Florida's Josh Beckett threw a shutout in Game Five to keep his team alive. With ace Mark Prior holding a 3-0 lead in Game Six in Chicago, the Cubs looked like they were on the way to their first World Series since 1945.

LARRY GOREN
Moises Alou

But disaster struck in the eighth inning. Cubs left fielder Moises Alou tried to catch a foul ball as it drifted toward the left-field stands at Wrigley Field, but fan Steve Bartman deflected it. Then Cubs shortstop Alex Gonzalez committed an error on a play that could have ended the inning, and the Marlins went on to score eight runs and post an 8-3 win.

The Marlins won 9-6 in the decisive Game Seven, rallying from a 5-3 deficit in the fifth inning. Rodriguez was named the series MVP as he set an NLCS record with nine RBIs while hitting .321 with two home runs.

The Red Sox seemed on their way to their first World Series since 1986 when they led the Yankees 5-2 in the bottom of the eighth inning of Game Seven of the ALCS at Yankee Stadium. Red Sox starter Pedro Martinez began to tire, though he convinced manager Grady Little to stay in the game.

The Yankees rallied with three runs against Martinez in the eighth, and third baseman Aaron Boone hit Tim Wakefield's first pitch of the 11th inning over the left-field fence for a home run, giving New York a 6-5 win and a trip to the World Series. Little was fired 11 days later.

Yankees closer Mariano Rivera was the series MVP with seven scoreless innings in three games, notching one win and one save.

LARRY GOREN
Grady Little

The World Series looked like it might be anticlimactic when the heavily favored Yankees won two of the first three games, but things picked up in a Game Four that went 12 innings before Marlins shortstop Alex Gonzalez won it with a leadoff home run off Jeff Weaver.

That was the turning point. Florida won 6-4 in Game Five, and 23-year-old pitcher Josh Beckett threw a five-hit shutout in Game Six at Yankee Stadium to give the Marlins their second World Series title in seven seasons—their only two winning seasons

TOP 10 MAJOR LEAGUE STORIES OF 2003

1 Cursemongers find more reasons to believe. Both the Cubs and Red Sox made it to the seventh game of their League Championship Series, but both came up short (again) under circumstances that drove their fans to distraction (again).

2 Baseball playoffs provide drama and ratings. While most television networks struggled to hold on to viewers at the beginning of a new TV season, Fox and ESPN found a ratings bonanza in baseball, with compelling series from start to finish grabbing the nation's attention.

3 Flying fish. Doldrums that started right after their World Series title in 1997 continued through the early season for the Marlins. Then an injection of young talent like Dontrelle Willis and an old manager in Jack McKeon sparked an amazing turnaround that gave the franchise another title, renewed fan interest and could lead to a baseball-only park for the team.

4 Clemens goes out in impressive fashion. Roger Clemens put the wraps on a Hall of Fame career with a 17-win season for the Yankees, including a June game against the Cardinals when he got his 300th career win and 4,000th career strikeout. Rumors persisted that he could return in 2004, however.

5 Sosa uncorks memorable season. Sammy Sosa got his 500th career home run and the Cubs made it to the playoffs, but most fans will remember a June corked-bat incident when they think of Sosa and 2003.

6 Disaster in Detroit. They missed the modern record for losses by one, but the Tigers still lost 119 games and piled up unwanted milestones, such as Mike Maroth becoming the first pitcher to lose 20 games since 1980.

7 Bittersweet year for Bonds. Barry Bonds put together another amazing offensive season, becoming baseball's first 500-homer/500-stolen base player, but it was tinged with sorrow because of the death of his father Bobby.

8 Expos play in Puerto Rico, continue searching for a home. The Expos played part of their home schedule in Puerto Rico to generate more money for Major League Baseball, which made no progress in its efforts to find the team a new owner and a permanent home.

9 Gagne closes the door. Dodgers closer Eric Gagne converted all 55 of his save opportunities, setting a new major league record and earning the National League Cy Young Award.

10 Bechler's death highlights potential dangers of supplements. Orioles pitcher Steve Bechler died of heat stroke in spring training, and doctors determined his use of the dietary supplement ephedrine was a factor in his death.

since joining the NL as an expansion franchise in 1993. Beckett was named series MVP after going 1-1, 1.10 in his two starts.

It was fitting end to a wacky postseason as Florida had the 21st-highest payroll in baseball at $54 million. The Yankees' $164 million payroll was the highest in baseball history.

While small-market teams like the Reds and Pirates cut payroll and traded away many of their veterans in July, the Marlins provided hope that anyone could win a World Series. After all, they fired manager Jeff Torborg on May 11, replacing him with 72-year-old Jack McKeon, and were 10 games under .500 on May 22 but still won it all. Their victory came one year after another improbable team, the Angels, also won it all.

"We showed that anything is possible," Marlins third baseman Mike Lowell said, "especially, if you have enough ulcer medicine to get through the postseason."

Milestone Markers

While the 2003 postseason was one to remember, the regular season had its share of special moments, particularly when it came to milestones.

Yankees righthander Roger Clemens reached two heady benchmarks on the same June 13 evening against the Cardinals at Yankee Stadium, recording his 300th win and 4,000th strikeout in a 5-2 win.

300-WINS CLUB

No.	Player	Wins
1.	Cy Young	511
2.	Walter Johnson	417
3.	Grover Alexander	373
	Christy Mathewson	373
5.	Warren Spahn	363
6.	Pud Galvin	361
	Kid Nichols	361
8.	Tim Keefe	342
9.	Steve Carlton	329
10.	John Clarkson	328
11.	Eddie Plank	326
12.	Nolan Ryan	324
	Don Sutton	324
14.	Phil Niekro	318
15.	Gaylord Perry	314
16.	Tom Seaver	311
17.	**Roger Clemens**	**310**
18.	Old Hoss Radbourn	309
19.	Mickey Welch	307
20.	Lefty Grove	300
	Early Wynn	300

Active players in bold type

Clemens allowed two runs in 6⅔ innings and struck out 10 on a cool and damp late spring evening. He became the 21st pitcher to win 300 games and the third to reach 4,000 strikeouts, along with Nolan Ryan and Steve Carlton.

Clemens had to wait for No. 300. He got his 299th win on May 21 at Fenway Park but five days later lost 8-4 to the Red Sox at Yankee Stadium. The bullpen then wasted leads June 1 at Detroit and June 7 against the Cubs in Chicago.

"To have these two milestones I was able to achieve in the same night, it was really special," Clemens said. "Everybody can stop chasing me around the country. It was time to finally get the whole thing over with."

The 500-home run club also grew by two to 19 as Cubs right fielder Sammy Sosa and Rangers first baseman Rafael Palmeiro reached the milestone.

Sosa sat on 499 homers in the offseason, then connected for No. 500 in the Cubs' fourth game of the season, April 4 at Cincinnati's Great American Ball Park off Reds reliever Scott Sullivan.

LARRY GOREN

Two milestones on one night
Roger Clemens reached 300 wins, 4,000 strikeouts

"It's great because I don't have to think about it anymore," Sosa said. "I don't have to go up there every at-bat thinking of hitting the ball out of the park. When I made contact, I knew the ball was gone and I'm like, 'Wow, I got it.' "

Palmeiro hit his 500th on May 11 off Indians reliever David Elder at The Ballpark in Arlington.

"It's not a record of longevity. It's a record of quality," Rangers manager Buck Showalter said.

Only four players had been older than the 38-year-old Palmeiro when reaching 500 homers: Ted Williams, Eddie Murray, Willie McCovey and Ernie Banks.

"I don't put myself in some of those guys' groups," Palmeiro said. "They're the best of all time, and I don't consider myself a player like Ted Williams or Mickey Mantle. Those guys are the best ever."

Giants left fielder Barry Bonds continued to amass amazing numbers despite turning 39 during the 2003 season, as he became the first player in history to hit 500 homers and steal 500 bases in a career.

Bonds reached 500 steals on June 23 against the Dodgers.

While Bonds moved into uncharted territory, the Astros also pulled off a first in their 8-0 win over the Yankees in New York on June 11. Six Astros combined to pitch a no-hitter. The old record for most pitchers in a no-hitter was four.

3,000-K CLUB

No.	Player	Strikeouts
1.	Nolan Ryan	5,714
2.	Steve Carlton	4,136
3.	**Roger Clemens**	**4,099**
4.	**Randy Johnson**	**3,871**
5.	Bert Blyleven	3,701
6.	Tom Seaver	3,640
7.	Don Sutton	3,574
8.	Gaylord Perry	3,534
9.	Walter Johnson	3,508
10.	Phil Niekro	3,342
11.	Ferguson Jenkins	3,192
12.	Bob Gibson	3,117

Active players in bold type

After starting pitcher Roy Oswalt was injured in the second inning, Pete Munro, Kirk Saarloos, Brad Lidge, Octavio Dotel and Billy Wagner finished off the victory.

"One guy usually goes out there and does it," Astros manager Jimy Williams said. "Maybe two, but not six."

Oswalt strained his right groin, and Munro came on and pitched 2⅔ innings, Saarloos 1⅓ and Lidge two innings. Dotel threw the eighth before Wagner finished with a perfect ninth.

Phillies righthander Kevin Millwood pitched a more conventional no-hitter, winning 1-0 over the Giants on April 27 in Philadelphia.

"It was one of those special days, and I don't plan on doing it every time out, but it was a lot of fun," Millwood said.

Millwood threw fastballs on 81 of his 108 pitches, and the crowd at Veterans Stadium, which hadn't seen a no-hitter since Terry Mulholland's gem in 1990, hung on every pitch in the late innings.

Millwood was part of another historic event at Veterans Stadium, but it didn't work out as well when he lost 5-2 to the Braves in the last game at the park Sept. 28. And unlike the reaction to his no-hitter, Millwood was roundly booed this time as a disappointing season ended for the Phillies.

Blue Jays first baseman Carlos Delgado and Braves shortstop Rafael Furcal also put their names into the history books. Delgado became the 15th player to hit four homers in a game on Sept. 25 against the Devil Rays in Toronto, while Furcal became the 12th player to pull off an unassisted triple play, performing the feat Aug. 10 against the Cardinals in St. Louis.

Delgado was only the fifth AL player to hit four homers in a game, along with Lou Gehrig, Pat Seerey, Rocky Colavito and Mike Cameron. Delgado homered in each at-bat. His first homer was the 300th of his career, and fourth tied the score 8-8 in the eighth, putting the Blue Jays in position to pull out a 10-8 win.

"I can't think of any other way to explain it, it just kind of happened," Delgado said. "It seems like everything you hit goes into the air and goes out. I wish I could do it more often."

TOM PRIDDY

Rafael Furcal

St. Louis had runners on first and second with none out in the fifth inning of a 3-2 win when Furcal found himself in the right place at the right time.

Furcal made a leaping grab of pitcher Woody Williams' line drive. The runners were going on a 1-1 pitch and Furcal stepped on second to double up Mike Matheny. Furcal then tagged out Orlando Palmeiro, who made a futile attempt to get back to first.

"I didn't think I had a triple play right away," Furcal said. "I wasn't thinking of trying to get three outs by myself. I was just trying to get outs."

Furcal's teammate, Greg Maddux, became the first pitcher in history to record 16 consecutive 15-win seasons when he beat the Expos on Sept. 21. The only other pitcher to win 15 in 15 straight seasons was Cy Young.

The relief pitching feat of the year was performed by Dodgers closer Eric Gagne, as he converted all 55 save opportunities while leading the NL in that category. Gagne broke the major league record for most saves converted in a row, 54 by Tom Gordon in 1998-99.

In a year when Boston established modern major league records for total bases (2,832) and slugging percentage (.491), Red Sox third baseman Bill Mueller became the first player in history to

LARRY GOREN

Corked bat furor
Sammy Sosa was suspended for seven games

hit a grand slam from both sides of the plate, connecting in consecutive innings against Texas on July 29.

The Cork Heard 'Round The World

Sosa had an eventful season. In addition to his 500th homer and just missing out on his first World Series appearance in the heartbreaking loss to Florida, the veteran outfielder was at the center of the biggest controversy of 2003.

In a 3-2 win over the Devil Rays on June 3 in Chicago, umpires found cork in Sosa's bat. He was suspended for eight games, though the penalty was reduced to seven games on appeal.

Sosa broke his bat on a routine ground ball to the second baseman in the first inning. Umpire crew chief Tim McClelland, who was working home plate, spotted the cork after Tampa Bay catcher Toby Hall flipped the part containing the handle at his feet. Sosa claimed the bat was one he used to put on home run displays in batting practice and it somehow got mixed in with the bats he used in games.

FOUR-HOMER GAMES

Players with four home runs in one game:

Carlos Delgado

Bobby Lowe, Boston (NL)	May 30, 1894
Ed Delahanty, Philadelphia (NL)	July 13, 1896
Lou Gehrig, New York (AL)	June 3, 1932
Chuck Klein, Philadelphia (NL)	July 10, 1936
Pat Seerey, Chicago (AL)	July 18, 1948
Gil Hodges, Brooklyn	Aug. 31, 1950
Joe Adcock, Milwaukee	July 31, 1954
Rocky Colavito, Cleveland	June 10, 1959
Willie Mays, San Francisco	April 30, 1961
Mike Schmidt, Philadelphia	April 17, 1976
Bob Horner, Atlanta	July 6, 1986
Mark Whiten, St. Louis	Sept. 7, 1993
Mike Cameron, Seattle	May 2, 2002
Shawn Green, Los Angeles	May 23, 2002
Carlos Delgado, Toronto	**Sept. 25, 2003**

2003 MAJOR LEAGUE ALL-STARS

Javy Lopez: Hit career-high 43 homers

Jason Schmidt: Led National League with 2.34 ERA

Selected by Baseball America

FIRST TEAM

Pos.	Player, Team	B-T	Ht.	Wt.	Age	AVG	AB	R	H	2B	3B	HR	RBI	SB
C	Javy Lopez, Braves	R-R	6-4	200	32	.328	457	89	150	29	3	43	109	0
1B	Carlos Delgado, Blue Jays	L-R	6-3	230	31	.302	570	117	172	38	1	42	145	0
2B	Bret Boone, Mariners	R-R	5-10	190	34	.294	622	111	183	35	5	35	117	16
3B	Mike Lowell, Marlins	R-R	6-4	200	29	.276	492	76	136	27	1	32	105	3
SS	Alex Rodriguez, Rangers	R-R	6-3	210	28	.298	607	124	181	30	6	47	118	17
OF	Barry Bonds, Giants	L-L	6-2	220	39	.341	390	111	133	22	1	45	90	7
OF	Albert Pujols, Cardinals	R-R	6-3	210	23	.359	591	137	212	51	1	43	124	5
OF	Gary Sheffield, Braves	R-R	6-0	200	34	.330	576	126	190	37	2	39	132	18
DH	Jim Thome, Phillies	L-R	6-4	220	33	.266	578	111	154	30	3	47	131	0
						W	L	ERA	G	SV	IP	H	BB	SO
SP	Roy Halladay, Blue Jays	R-R	6-6	230	26	22	7	3.25	36	0	266	253	32	204
	Esteban Loaiza, White Sox	R-R	6-3	210	31	21	9	2.90	34	0	226	196	56	207
	Mark Prior, Cubs	R-R	6-5	220	22	18	6	2.43	30	0	211	183	50	245
	Jason Schmidt, Giants	R-R	6-5	200	30	17	5	2.34	29	0	208	152	46	208
RP	Eric Gagne, Dodgers	R-R	6-2	190	27	2	3	1.20	77	55	82	37	20	137

SECOND TEAM

Pos.	Player, Team	B-T	Ht.	Wt.	Age	AVG	AB	R	H	2B	3B	HR	RBI	SB
C	Ivan Rodriguez, Marlins	R-R	5-9	200	31	.297	511	90	152	36	3	16	85	10
1B	Todd Helton, Rockies	L-L	6-2	200	29	.358	583	135	209	49	5	33	117	0
2B	Marcus Giles, Braves	R-R	5-8	180	25	.316	551	101	174	49	2	21	69	14
3B	Bill Mueller, Red Sox	B-R	5-10	180	32	.326	524	85	171	45	5	19	85	1
SS	Edgar Renteria, Cardinals	R-R	6-1	180	28	.330	587	96	194	47	1	13	100	34
OF	Carlos Beltran, Royals	B-R	6-1	190	26	.307	521	102	160	14	10	26	100	41
OF	Aubrey Huff, Devil Rays	L-R	6-4	220	26	.311	636	91	198	47	3	34	107	2
OF	Vernon Wells, Blue Jays	R-R	6-1	220	24	.317	678	118	215	49	5	33	117	4
DH	Frank Thomas, White Sox	R-R	6-5	270	35	.267	546	87	146	35	0	42	105	0
						W	L	ERA	G	SV	IP	H	BB	SO
SP	Kevin Brown, Dodgers	R-R	6-4	200	38	14	9	2.39	32	0	211	184	56	185
	Tim Hudson, Athletics	R-R	6-1	160	28	16	7	2.70	34	0	240	197	61	162
	Pedro Martinez, Red Sox	R-R	5-11	180	31	14	4	2.22	29	0	187	147	47	206
	Jamie Moyer, Mariners	L-L	6-0	170	40	21	7	3.27	33	0	215	199	66	129
RP	John Smoltz, Braves	R-R	6-3	220	36	0	2	1.12	62	45	64	48	8	73

Ages as of July 1, 2003

Player of the Year: Barry Bonds, of, Giants. **Pitcher of the Year:** Eric Gagne, rhp, Dodgers. **Rookie of the Year:** Brandon Webb, rhp, Diamondbacks. **Manager of the Year:** Jack McKeon, Marlins. **Executive of the Year:** Brian Sabean, Giants.

Cork inside a wood bat is thought to help players hit the ball farther and is against baseball rules.

"Just to put on a show for the fans," Sosa said. "I like to make people happy and I do that in batting practice. I was just trying to get ready and go out there and get ready for the game, and I just picked the wrong bat. I feel sorry. I just apologize to everybody."

The cork incident brought a cloud of suspicion over all of Sosa's accomplishments during a career that seems certain to land him in the Hall of Fame.

"It's certainly a black mark against his name," Yankees manager Joe Torre said.

All five of Sosa's bats at the Hall of Fame showed no signs of cork or anything else that would violate baseball rules after the hall ran the bats through X-rays. Major League Baseball officials also tested 76 of Sosa's bats they confiscated from his locker and found no cork in any of them.

That was enough to persuade MLB officials to take one game off Sosa's suspension.

"I am convinced of the sincerity of Sosa's explanation and his contrition," MLB chief operating officer Bob DuPuy said. "In my opinion, his candor and the promptness of his apology on the night of June 3 were exemplary.

"However, at the end of the day, each player must be accountable for his own equipment complying with the rules, whether the violation is deliberate or inadvertent."

Cubs general manager Jim Hendry said MLB's action vindicated Sosa, particularly in the face of a slew of negative press and fan reaction following the incident.

"The fact that people want to tarnish what happened in his past has no credence," Hendry said. "He's been shattering bats his whole career. If this had been going on for years, it would have come out a long time ago."

Sosa heard his share of catcalls from fans, particularly on the road. The boos and taunts eventually died down, and the incident seemed all but forgotten by season's end.

"I have to deal with that for the rest of my life, no question," he said. "But I'm only human. I'm not the only guy in this world that made a mistake. Hopefully, they'll forget and just let me continue to make people happy."

Schilling Vs. QuesTec

While the hoopla surrounding Sosa's corked bat died down, the QuesTec controversy was a season-long issue.

The QuesTec Umpire Evaluation System, an electronic device that evaluates umpires' calls on balls and strikes, was installed in 13 ballparks in 2003 including Bank One Ballpark in Phoenix, where the entire situation came to the fore. Diamondbacks righthander Curt Schiling became so fed up during a 5-1 loss to the Padres on May 24 that he smashed one of the QuesTec cameras near the Diamondbacks' dugout.

DAVID SCHOFIELD

Curt Schilling

"I said something to one of the umpires about it and he said, 'Do us a favor and break the other one,' " said Schilling, who was fined $15,000.

The umpires did not like the QuesTec system, and their union filed a grievance contending the system was inaccurate and varied greatly depending on the person operating it.

In a Feb. 14 letter to the World Umpires Association, MLB said umpires whose calls did not match QuesTec at least 90 percent of the time would be judged as not meeting standards. In March, 47 of 68 umpires signed a statement expressing a lack of confidence in the QuesTec system.

"Major League Baseball wants to have everyone conform to the strike zone as this machine says it is," veteran umpire Mike Winters said. "Everybody's working to try to do that. Borderline pitches, this machine says they're balls. If I call them a strike and the machine doesn't, I'm getting downgraded. I've got to worry about my own livelihood."

MLB vice president of baseball operations Sandy Alderson was a staunch supporter of QuesTec in his crusade to get umpires to call a consistent strike zone. He said the experience of operators wasn't a significant factor, and they needed just a working knowledge of baseball and computers.

Alderson was also livid that Schilling damaged the equipment.

"If you are a baseball fan and subscribe to AOL, you can operate the system," Alderson said. "It's not about the system. It's not about the umpires—the umpires have never been more accurate and more consistent about the strike zone and the rulebook than they are today.

"What this is about is Curt Schilling

LARGEST SALARIES

The 25 largest individual player salaries of 2003:

Player, Team	Salary
1. Alex Rodriguez, ss, Rangers	$22,000,000
2. Manny Ramirez, of, Red Sox	20,000,000
3. Carlos Delgado, 1b, Blue Jays	18,700,000
4. Mo Vaughn, 1b, Mets	17,166,667
5. Sammy Sosa, of, Cubs	16,000,000
6. Kevin Brown, rhp, Dodgers	15,714,286
7. Shawn Green, of, Dodgers	15,666,667
8. Derek Jeter, ss, Yankees	15,600,000
9. Mike Piazza, c, Mets	15,571,429
10. Barry Bonds, of, Giants	15,500,000
Pedro Martinez, rhp, Red Sox	15,500,000
12. Randy Johnson, lhp, Diamondbacks	15,000,000
13. Greg Maddux, rhp, Braves	14,750,000
14. Mike Hampton, lhp, Braves	13,625,000
15. Chipper Jones, of, Braves	13,333,333
16. Jeff Bagwell, 1b, Astros	13,000,000
*Albert Belle, of, Orioles	13,000,000
Juan Gonzalez, of, Rangers	13,000,000
Raul Mondesi, of, D'backs/Yankees	13,000,000
Chan Ho Park, rhp, Rangers	13,000,000
21. Larry Walker, of, Rockies	12,666,667
22. Ken Griffey Jr., of, Reds	12,500,000
23. Darren Dreifort, rhp, Dodgers	12,400,000
24. Bernie Williams, of, Yankees	12,357,143
25. Jeromy Burnitz, of, Dodgers/Mets	12,166,667

*Inactive

Alex Rodriguez

Manny Ramirez

Marlins enjoy dramatic turnaround

It's a difficult task, but the Yankees can be defeated—even if they have a payroll nearing $170 million. It doesn't just take a complete team effort, but one that extends throughout the entire organization. Especially when your payroll is the sixth-lowest in the majors.

ORGANIZATION of the YEAR

Sudden change of fortune
Marlins owner Jeffrey Loria

LARRY GOREN

That's just what the Marlins did in 2003, as the franchise excelled in every facet of the game, from the majors to the farm system to the draft. The major league team won 91 games (just the second winning season in club history), pulled off a pair of dramatic upsets against the Giants and Cubs in the National League playoffs, then toppled the mighty Yankees in six games to win their second World Series since 1997. The organization's top three minor league affiliates each made the playoffs, with Double-A Carolina winning the Southern League championship.

Larry Beinfest

The Marlins' extraordinary turnaround began on May 10, when the 16-22 club fired manager Jeff Torborg and pitching coach Brad Arnsberg without noticing that no team had advanced to the playoffs after a midseason manager switch since the 1989 Blue Jays. Two weeks later, with 72-year-old Jack McKeon at the helm, the Marlins fell 10 games below .500.

From there, things were considerably different. Florida posted the best record in baseball the rest of the way. Contributions came from all sides, and virtually every personnel move general manager Larry Beinfest made paid off. Assistant GM Dan Jennings provided a valuable scouting perspective. The changes actually started over the winter, when center fielder Preston Wilson and catcher Charles Johnson went to the Rockies for center fielder Juan Pierre and lefthander Mike Hampton. After agreeing to pick up part of Hampton's salary, Beinfest spun him over to the division rival Braves for reliever Tim Spooneybarger. Then the Marlins signed catcher Ivan Rodriguez to a one-year, $10 million deal. Pierre served as an offensive catalyst by leading the majors with 65 steals, and Rodriguez hit .297-16-85 before driving in 17 runs during the playoffs.

The farm system supplied reinforcements as the playoff race heated up. Dontrelle Willis left Carolina to make his major league debut on May 9. He went 14-6, 3.30 in the big leagues, winning the NL rookie of the year award and leading the club in wins. Miguel Cabrera, who was hitting .365-10-59 for the same Carolina club, made his major league debut June 20 with a walk-off homer. He played left field at the outset—the first time he had played in the outfield—but then moved to his more natural third base when Mike Lowell missed September with a broken bone in his hand. He hit .268-12-62, then proved even more valuable in the playoffs, moving to right field and the cleanup spot in the lineup while producing four homers and 12 RBIs.

The Marlins also used their farm system to augment the big league club, and owner Jeffrey Loria authorized adding salary at midseason for the first time since 1997. They used five prospects, including 2000 No. 1 overall pick Adrian Gonzalez, to add Ugueth Urbina, their closer down the stretch, from the Rangers and original Marlin Jeff Conine from the Orioles.

Dan Jennings

Along with Carolina, Triple-A Albuquerque and high Class A Jupiter also made the playoffs as those three teams combined for a .548 winning percentage and the farm system finished above .500 as a whole. The Marlins also were winners in the 2003 draft. BA High School Player of the Year Jeff Allison fell to them at the 16th overall pick, and they didn't pinch pennies when signing the dominant righthander for $1.85 million. Allison compares to Josh Beckett, the second overall pick in 1999. Beckett, BA's Minor League Player of the Year in 2001, recovered from a sprained ligament in his elbow and recurring blister problems to anchor the staff during the playoffs with a 2.11 ERA in six outings. He tossed the first two complete games of his career in two of his final three playoff starts, including the World Series clincher. Beckett earned MVP honors for his performance, and symbolized the entire organization's year as a homegrown player making a superlative performance to cap a stunning season.

PREVIOUS WINNERS

1982—Oakland Athletics
1983—New York Mets
1984—New York Mets
1985—Milwaukee Brewers
1986—Milwaukee Brewers
1987—Milwaukee Brewers
1988—Montreal Expos
1989—Texas Rangers
1990—Montreal Expos
1991—Atlanta Braves
1992—Cleveland Indians
1993—Toronto Blue Jays
1994—Kansas City Royals
1995—New York Mets
1996—Atlanta Braves
1997—Detroit Tigers
1998—New York Yankees
1999—Oakland Athletics
2000—Chicago White Sox
2001—Houston Astros
2002—Minnesota Twins

400-HOME RUN CLUB

No.	Player	Home Runs
1.	Hank Aaron	755
2.	Babe Ruth	714
3.	Willie Mays	660
4.	**Barry Bonds**	**658**
5.	Frank Robinson	586
6.	Mark McGwire	583
7.	Harmon Killebrew	573
8.	Reggie Jackson	563
9.	Mike Schmidt	548
10.	**Sammy Sosa**	**539**
11.	Mickey Mantle	536
12.	Jimmie Foxx	534
13.	Ted Williams	521
	Willie McCovey	521
15.	**Rafael Palmeiro**	**518**
16.	Eddie Mathews	512
	Ernie Banks	512
18.	Mel Ott	511
19.	Eddie Murray	504
20.	**Sammy Sosa**	**539**
21.	Lou Gehrig	493
22.	**Fred McGriff**	**491**
23.	**Ken Griffey Jr.**	**481**
24.	Stan Musial	475
	Willie Stargell	475
26.	Dave Winfield	465
27.	Jose Canseco	462
28.	Carl Yastrzemski	452
29.	Dave Kingman	442
30.	Andre Dawson	438
31.	Cal Ripken	431
32.	**Juan Gonzalez**	**429**
33.	Billy Williams	426
34.	**Jeff Bagwell**	**419**
35.	**Frank Thomas**	**418**
36.	Darrell Evans	414
37.	Duke Snider	407

LARRY GOREN

Rafael Palmeiro

Bold indicates active player

Waiting in the Wings

No.	Player	Home Runs
43.	Andres Galarraga	398
48.	Jim Thome	381
52.	Gary Sheffield	379
63.	Mike Piazza	358
67.	Ellis Burks	351
67.	Larry Walker	351
71.	Manny Ramirez	347
72.	Alex Rodriguez	345

wanting pitches that are balls called strikes. If that's what he wants, he should go to the rules committee. Otherwise, he should stop whining and go about his business."

Mets pitcher Tom Glavine was also outspoken about QuesTec and wondered if machines might replace the men in blue.

"Why not eliminate umpires altogether and have an electronic strike zone?" Glavine said. "That's almost what it's coming to.

"It's just not the pitchers who are complaining. You can ask the hitters. They don't know what the strike zone is. Nobody knows."

Despite all the criticism, Alderson stood behind the QuesTec system and plans were in place to use it again in 2004.

Power Outage

While pitchers said QuesTec was just another in a long line of factors that work against them and contribute to more offense, the statistics suggested otherwise. For the first full season since 1993, no one hit 50 home runs.

Rangers shortstop Alex Rodriguez paced the AL and Phillies first baseman Jim Thome led the NL with 47 each. Ten players hit 40 or more homers, up from eight in 2002 but below the 16 in 2000. Thirty reached 30 homers, an increase of two from 2002, but down from 47 three years earlier, and 37 had 100 or more RBIs, an increase of one.

One of the theories in the decrease in homers was that baseball started testing for steroids in 2003, part of the collective bargaining agreement between the owners and players a year earlier.

"You look at the home run numbers and you look at the averages that have gone down this year," White Sox DH Frank Thomas said. "I think it's a tell-tale sign that the testing is having a positive effect."

Before the 1994-95 strike, players had hit 50 homers in a season just 18 times in baseball history. Babe Ruth in 1927 was the only one to hit 60 until Roger Maris had 61 in 1961.

Then came an unprecedented power barrage. Since the strike, players have reached 50 homers 18 times. Sosa topped 60 in three seasons and Mark McGwire did it twice, hitting a record 70 in 1998. Then in 2001, Bonds hit 73.

"There was a time when 60 was just an easy thing to do for guys," Giants manager Felipe Alou said.

While the big bashers dropped off, the overall average didn't. There were 2.14 homers a game in 2003, up from 2.09 in 2002. Still, it was below the peak years of 2.28 in 1999, 2.34 in 2000 and 2.25 in 2001.

"Things go in cycles," Cubs manager Dusty Baker said.

Former MVPs Jose Canseco and Ken Caminiti said in published reports in 2002 that many players use steroids. That led to the Major League Baseball Players Association agreeing to testing for the first time, an issue on which executive director Don Fehr had long refused to budge.

All players gave urine samples in 2003 as part of survey testing, with samples taken twice from each player within a given week. In addition, the commissioner's office had the right to test up to 240 players randomly.

LARRY GOREN

Jason Giambi

Under the CBA, no players could be disciplined if they tested positive for steroids in 2003. But if more than five percent of the players tested positive, it could lead to suspensions in 2004.

Officials from MLB and the union downplayed steroid testing as a factor in 50 homers not being reached.

"There's been talk about some guys showing up to camp slimmer, but I think a lot of the talk does players a disservice," said Gene Orza, Fehr's top assistant.

DuPuy said it was simply another cyclical baseball trend and pitching getting better. "There are a number of very good young pitchers who are maturing and having an impact," he said.

On the other end of the spectrum, a previously undetectable steroid, THG, was at the center of a potentially major scandal involving chemists, athletes and coaches. The U.S. Anti-Doping Agency believes the THG came from a laboratory that supplies some of the nation's top sports stars with nutritional supplements.

Dozens of professional athletes, including Bonds and

Webb picks up pieces for Big Two

How is this for a scrapbook moment from your rookie year?

After Brandon Webb threw seven shutout innings, striking out 10, in his first major league start in the opening game of a doubleheader against the New York Mets on April 27, 2003, the Diamondbacks' Game Two starter corralled Webb in the clubhouse.

ROOKIE of the YEAR

"That's a tough act to follow," Randy Johnson said.

When a guy with five Cy Youngs talks, you listen.

"That was cool," Webb said.

Webb proved to be a difficult act to follow all season. He developed into the Diamondbacks No. 1 starter after injuries to Randy Johnson and Curt Schilling, made the jump from Double-A to the major leagues seem effortless and earned BA's 2003 Rookie of the Year award in the process.

Webb finished with 10-9, 2.84 numbers, finishing fourth in the NL in ERA behind Jason Schmidt, Kevin Brown and Mark Prior. He could have won half again as many games with a little more timely run support.

"Everyone talks about the 14 wins Dontrelle Willis has. If we average three runs a game for this guy, he wins 14, 15 games," said Diamondbacks scouting director Mike Rizzo, who made Webb an eighth-round pick in the 2000 draft out of the University of Kentucky. "His other numbers were mind-boggling."

The long season—a month longer than any he had ever pitched—may have finally taken its toll in the final week of the season, when Webb gave up nine runs in eight innings over his final two starts.

ROB CUNI

Diamondbacks' savior
Brandon Webb was the year's top rookie

Webb still ended the season giving up fewer hits than innings—140 hits in 181 innings—while striking out 172 and walking 68. Opponents hit only .212 against him, behind only Schmidt and Kerry Wood.

Webb's primary pitch is a two-seam fastball that seems to get most of its action as it enters the hitting zone. He also features a curveball and a changeup that he became much more comfortable with as the season went along.

"I had an advance scout tell me it almost looked like a split-finger pitch," Rizzo said. "It not only has great sink, it has life at the plate. It is so late and so violent on its drop. And he can throw that thing for strikes."

Webb set the Kentucky single-season strikeout record in 2000, the year that he signed with the Diamondbacks. That record has since been surpassed by 2002 Athletics' first-rounder Joe Blanton.

His signing was a group effort by the Diamondbacks' scouting department in Rizzo's first year on the job. Area scout Scott Jaster saw Webb as a sophomore and made a point to see him early in his junior year. Special assignment scout Phil Rizzo, Mike's father, saw Webb later that year and caught him on a day in which he had great movement on his two-seamer.

The elder Rizzo filed a strong report, as did central regional supervisor Kris Kline. Webb missed a few starts with shoulder tendinitis during the middle of the season, perhaps turning some teams off. But Mike Rizzo and east coast supervisor Ed Durkin made certain to attend Webb's first start in the Southeastern Conference tournament, where Webb handed top-ranked South Carolina one of its 10 defeats that season.

Mental makeup was also part of their evaluation.

"He competes really well," Rizzo said, "and that's a big part of the process. You like guys who are under control—very, very competitive, but under control. It's so easy to lose your cool on the mound when things go wrong, but you have to pitch through that."

Rizzo does not claim to know how quickly Webb would arrive, although he did say the tools were evident.

"We thought he'd be maybe a top three starter on a contending club, and he's doing that right now," Rizzo said. "We did like his stuff, and we did like the total package. We knew he had a good arm. He has turned out to be a top of the rotation starter.

"For several months, this guy was the No. 1 starter for a contender in the NL West. When the two horses came out, he was the main man. He showed as much as anybody in baseball."

Not a bad moment to remember.

—JACK MAGRUDER

PREVIOUS WINNERS

1989—Gregg Olson, rhp, Orioles
1990—Sandy Alomar, c, Indians
1991—Jeff Bagwell, 1b, Astros
1992—Pat Listach, ss, Brewers
1993—Mike Piazza, c, Dodgers
1994—Raul Mondesi, of, Dodgers
1995—Hideo Nomo, rhp, Dodgers
1996—Derek Jeter, ss, Yankees
1997—Nomar Garciaparra, ss, Red Sox
1998—Kerry Wood, rhp, Cubs
1999—Carlos Beltran, of, Royals
2000—Rafael Furcal, ss/2b, Braves
2001—Albert Pujols, of/3b/1b, Cardinals
2002—Eric Hinske, 3b, Blue Jays

top 20 rookies

1. Brandon Webb, rhp, Diamondbacks
2. Dontrelle Willis, lhp, Marlins
3. Angel Berroa, ss, Royals
4. Scott Podsednik, of, Brewers
5. Jody Gerut, of, Indians
6. Mark Teixeira, 1b, Rangers
7. Hideki Matsui, of, Yankees
8. Rocco Baldelli, of, Devil Rays
9. Jerome Williams, rhp, Giants
10. Miguel Cabrera, of, Marlins
11. Jose Reyes, ss, Mets
12. Marlon Byrd, of, Phillies
13. Jose Valverde, rhp, Diamondbacks
14. Brad Lidge, rhp, Astros
15. Oscar Villarreal, rhp, Diamondbacks
16. Jason Phillips, 1b/c, Mets
17. Horacio Ramirez, lhp, Braves
18. Rafael Soriano, rhp, Mariners
19. Francisco Rodriguez, rhp, Angels
20. Adam Everett, ss, Astros

Yankees first baseman Jason Giambi, were subpoenaed in October to testify before a federal grand jury probing the Bay Area Laboratory Co-Operative, or BALCO. BALCO founder Victor Conte had served as Bonds' personal trainer.

Rest In Peace

While steroid testing began in 2003, the cry also started for MLB to ban the supplement ephedrine after it caused Orioles rookie righthander Steve Bechler to collapse and die of multiple organ failure due to heatstroke during a spring training workout.

Bechler, 23, died Feb. 17, one day after collapsing in warm and humid weather in Fort Lauderdale, Fla. The 6-foot-2, 239-pound Bechler had battled weight problems throughout his five-year professional career and reported to camp out of shape after getting married in the offseason.

Bechler was taking the over-the-counter supplement Xenadrine RFA-1 in order to lose weight, and toxicology tests confirmed significant amounts of the substance led to heatstroke, along with other factors.

Ephedra products are legal and marketed in drug stores, convenience stores and gyms as a weight-loss and energy pill made from natural herbs. The Food and Drug Administration has said the drug can be blamed for more than 100 deaths nationwide.

Bechler's widow Kily filed a lawsuit in July against Cytodyne Technologies, the New Jersey-based distributor of Xenadrine RFA-1.

Because ephedrine is legal, the union said it would not follow the lead of the NFL, NCAA and International Olympic Committee and approve an effort to ban the supplement. The union did urge players to stop using ephedrine.

That wasn't enough for Orioles owner Peter Angelos, who called for an immediate ban.

"Unfortunately, we're all human and don't move until something very grim and very tragic like this occurs," Angelos said. "Hopefully, if anything positive can come from this tragedy, it will be that we'll get the kind of movement we need in these circumstances."

Bechler made his major league debut with Baltimore late in the 2002 season, going 0-0, 13.50 in three relief appearances.

RODGER WOOD

Steve Bechler

"Steve was a tough guy," Orioles manager Mike Hargrove said. "He was a competitor. I didn't know him that well, but I knew him enough to learn he loved the game and to compete."

Baseball also lost Hall of Fame outfielder Larry Doby in 2004 when he died June 18 in Montclair, N.J., after a lengthy illness. Doby was 79.

Doby was the first black player in American League history, debuting for the Indians on July 5, 1947, a little more than 11 weeks after Jackie Robinson broke the color barrier with the Brooklyn Dodgers. Doby was also the second black manager in major league history, taking over the White Sox during the 1978 season. Frank Robinson became the first black manager in 1975 with Cleveland.

Doby hit .283-253-970 in 13 major league seasons with the Indians (1947-55, 1958) and the White Sox (1956-57, 1959).

"He was a great guy, a great center fielder and a great teammate," said Hall of Famer Bob Feller, Doby's longtime teammate with the Indians.

Most importantly, Doby was one of the game's great pioneers.

"We talked a little about what things were like when he first came into the game but he never went into details," said Lamar Johshon, who played first base when Doby managed the White Sox. "He said the game had come a long way in some regards and in other regards it hadn't."

Home Away From Home

One thing that didn't change in 2003 was that the Expos' situation was still unsettled and the club remained a ward of Major League Baseball.

For a second straight season, the Expos were a team without an owner. Instead, the other 29 clubs all had an equal share in the club. A new wrinkle was that the Expos played 22 of their home games at Hiram Bithorn Stadium in San Juan, Puerto Rico, as MLB looked at ways to increase attendance and revenue. It was the first time a team called two stadiums home since the late 1960s, when the White Sox played some of their home games in Milwaukee after the Braves left for Atlanta.

The Expos drew an average of 14,222 fans in their 22 games in San Juan, compared to 11,906 in 59 home dates in Montreal. Puerto Rican promoter Antonio Munoz reportedly guaranteed $6.6 million to MLB to bring the games there, with the earnings split between his company and the commissioner's office.

BILL NICHOLS

Brad Wilkerson

"The San Juan experiment worked out beautifully," Selig said.

Nevertheless, the idea of a franchise being run by MLB gave the impression of a conflict of interest, and the Puerto Rico arrangement may have cost the Expos a shot at the second playoff spot in their 35-year history. In a 28-day stretch beginning May 26, the Expos traveled to Miami, Philadelphia, San Juan, Seattle, Oakland and Pittsburgh.

The Expos were 32-18 at the beginning of the six-city, 25-game junket. They went 8-14 on the trip and were never the same.

"It was pretty ludicrous to have us play in two different homes," outfielder Brad Wilkerson said. "If they wanted to give this team the best chance to win, they wouldn't have done it."

The Expos' future was still up in the air at the end of the season. Groups in Northern Virginia, Portland, Ore., and Washington, D.C., had interest in buying the Expos, but none had money in place to build a stadium.

"There are a number of temporary solutions that are still available, but our number-one priority is to get a permanent solution," DuPuy said.

Buying A Champion

While the Expos couldn't find an owner, Arte Moreno took his place in history when he purchased the defending World Series champion Angels for $184 million on May 22 from the Walt Disney Co.

Sabean keeps Giants atop NL West

Just wait till next year, they said.

This was not the battle cry of second-division teams in 2002—it was the howl of detractors after the Giants won the National League pennant. The Giants were losing their manager (Dusty Baker), a former MVP (Jeff Kent), several more position players (David Bell, Kenny Lofton, Reggie Sanders), and a rotation stalwart because of finances (Russ Ortiz). The Giants were sure to fall back to the pack.

EXECUTIVE of the YEAR

But that didn't happen—thanks to Brian Sabean.

BILL NICHOLS

Credit for resourcefulness
Giants GM Brian Sabean

As the Giants' general manager, Sabean reworked his club so quickly, resolutely and resourcefully that San Francisco not only improved in 2003—from 95 to a cool 100 wins—but ran away with the National League West by 15½ games. Even though the Giants lost in the first round of the playoffs to the eventual champion Marlins, Sabean's performance earned him Baseball America's sixth annual Executive of the Year award.

"He moves with conviction, self-confidence and guts," said Billy Beane, Sabean's more recognized counterpart across the Bay in Oakland. "He doesn't need the approval of everyone analyzing the game. He knows what he wants and just does it."

PREVIOUS WINNERS
1998—Doug Melvin, Rangers
1999—Jim Bowden, Reds
2000—Walt Jocketty, Cardinals
2001—Pat Gillick, Mariners
2002—Billy Beane, Athletics

Operating with a payroll budget in the low-$80 million range that was not luxurious for a contender, Sabean enjoyed the luxury of having Barry Bonds under contract but had little else entering 2003. He lured 67-year-old Felipe Alou out of retirement to manage the club. He signed two infielders (Edgardo Alfonzo and Ray Durham) and two outfielders (Marquis Grissom and Jose Cruz Jr.) as free agents. His farm system graduated top pitching prospects Jesse Foppert and Jerome Williams into the rotation. And when that rotation needed a boost at the trading deadline, he acquired Sidney Ponson.

The result was 100 wins and a division title, leaving the Dodgers and Diamondbacks in his dust. Sabean was no longer a secret, though he never minded anyway.

"I don't need to be out front," he said. "At the end of the day, as long as the guys on the team, my co-workers and especially ownership know what I'm doing and how we're doing it, that's the only reinforcement you need."

—ALAN SCHWARZ

McKeon feted for Marlins turnaround

History says it doesn't work. But because a general manager can't fire his whole roster, the manager often gets the ax for his team's poor performance.

MANAGER of the YEAR

It's supposed to serve as a wakeup call, energizing the players and changing the attitude of a losing clubhouse. Entering the 2003 season, however, just three teams in the previous 20 years had advanced to the playoffs after changing managers in midseason and nine since divisional play began in 1969.

Yet Marlins GM Larry Beinfest pulled it off. He let Jeff Torborg go on May 10 after a 16-22 start, picking 72-year-old Jack McKeon to right Florida's ship even though he hadn't set foot in a dugout since the Reds fired him after the 2000 season.

BILL NICHOLS

Jack McKeon: Led team to 91 wins

After the Marlins fell to 10 games below .500, they reeled off the best record in the majors the rest of the way to finish with 91 wins and capture the National League wild card. They continued the magic with three straight playoff upsets en route to the club's second World Series championship in its 11-year history.

In the process, the Marlins became the fifth team to change managers midseason and make the Series since '69, and just the second to win it all. The only other team to accomplish the feat, the Marlins' World Series victims, Yankees, who did it themselves behind new skipper Bob Lemon in 1978. Florida also became the first team to win the World Series in the same year it fell 10 games below .500 since the 1914 Boston Braves.

PREVIOUS WINNERS
1998—Larry Dierker, Astros
1999—Jimy Williams, Red Sox
2000—Dusty Baker, Giants
2001—Lou Piniella, Mariners
2002—Mike Scioscia, Angels

"Nobody gave us a chance and here they are world champions," McKeon said.

Call it one for the ages—or the aged—as McKeon became the oldest manager to advance to the playoffs for the first time and oldest ever to win it all.

—WILL KIMMEY

"Every guy's dream is to own a baseball team," Moreno said. "It's an opportunity I've always dreamed about."

Moreno, who lives in Phoenix and La Jolla, Calif., became the first minority with a controlling stake in a major league team. But he said he doesn't want to be thought of as a minority owner. He is a fourth-generation American.

"The first thing is I'm an American," he said. "I'm proud to be a Mexican-American, but as far as being the first minority, I think most of us are immigrants from someplace, and I think we always try to do our best to be Americans."

While the Mariners' majority interest is owned by Hiroshi Yamauchi, who is Japanese, the team has been controlled by John Ellis and Howard Lincoln.

Disney bought a 25 percent share of the Angels and took control of the team from founding owner Gene Autry in 1996, then purchased the remainder of the team after he died in 1998.

Moreno, the oldest of 11 brothers, once owned a small interest in the Diamondbacks. His net worth has been estimated at $940 million by Forbes magazine, a fortune he made in the billboard industry.

"Since Jackie Robinson, we've expanded diversity of the game on the field; we've expanded diversity in the front office," DuPuy said.

The Angels, beset by injuries in 2003, finished 77-85 after winning their first World Series in 2003.

Meanwhile, the Dodgers were put on the market and Boston land developer Frank McCourt reached a tentative agreement, pending approval by MLB, to buy the team from News Corp. for $430 million.

Almost A New Low

Anaheim might have suffered through a losing season, but it was nothing compared to what the Tigers went through. Detroit lost 17 of its first 18 games and had to finish with a rush to avoid surpassing the 1962 Mets' modern-day record of 120 losses in a season.

The Tigers won five of their final six games to finish 43-119. They averted loss No. 120 in the finale with a seven-run sixth inning to post a 9-4 home win over the Twins, who had already clinched the AL Central title and were resting their regulars for the playoffs.

LARRY GOREN

Mike Maroth

Lefthander Mike Maroth got the win, a rare occurrence for him as he went 9-21 to become the first 20-game loser since Brian Kingman went 8-20 for the Athletics in 1980.

"Believe it or not, I can look back on this year with a smile on my face because of how this season ended," Maroth said. "It's a great feeling to end like this."

With the 18,959 fans at Comerica Park standing and cheering, and Kool & The Gang's "Celebration" playing over the public-address system following the final out, Tigers players hugged each other near the mound as the scoreboard flashed "Victory!" The Tigers then celebrated with postgame beers in the clubhouse.

Detroit manager Alan Trammell, the shortstop on the Tigers' last World Series winner in 1984, knew it really wasn't much of a reason to celebrate.

"I'm very glad we didn't tie or surpass the '62 Mets' record," Trammell said. "But in all honesty, how much better is 119 than 120? It's been a tough year."

Hanging It Up

Roger Clemens had a good year to wrap up a career that will land him in the Hall of Fame. In addition to reaching the 300-win and 4,000-strikeout plateaus, the Yankees righthander went 17-9, 3.91 as a 41-year-old.

Clemens' strong season didn't persuade him to change his mind when it came to retirement. He decided to call it quits before the season started, and even another trip to the World Series with the Yankees apparently couldn't sway him to come back for one more year—though he indicated he would have liked to pitch for the United States in the 2004 Olympics if the U.S. had qualified.

"I have four sons and the time has come to go home, be with them and be a full-time dad," Clemens said.

Clemens' teammates still hoped he would have a change of heart.

"I can't believe he's retiring now with the way he is still pitching," Mariano Rivera said. "Personally, I'd keep on going, but I also respect that he thinks it's time to do other things. It's too bad because I think he could still be a quality pitcher for many more years to come."

Clemens went 310-160, with 3.19 ERA in 20 seasons with the Red Sox (1984-96), Blue Jays (1997-98) and Yankees (1999-2003).

Clemens was one of several notable players who retired, joining first baseman Mark Grace and third baseman Matt Williams of the Diamondbacks, righthander David Cone and shortstop Jay Bell of the Mets and Blue Jays shortstop Mike Bordick.

BILL NICHOLS

Mark Grace

Grace hit .303-176-1,146 in 16 seasons with the Cubs (1988-2000) and Diamondbacks (2001-03). Williams batted .268-378-1,218 in 17 seasons with the Giants (1987-96), Indians (1997) and Diamondbacks (1998-2003).

After sitting out the 2002 season, Cone made a comeback with the Mets in 2003, but it was cut short by an arthritic hip. He finished his career with a 194-126, 3.46 record in 17 seasons with the Royals (1986, 1993-94), Mets (1987-92, 2003), Blue Jays (1992, 1995), Yankees (1995-2000) and Red Sox (2001).

Bell hit .265-195-860 in 17 seasons with the Indians (1986-88), Pirates (1989-96), Royals (1997), Diamondbacks (1998-2002) and Mets (2003). Bordick hit .260-91-626 in 14 seasons with the Athletics (1990-96), Orioles (1997-2002), Mets (2000) and Blue Jays (2003).

Ousted

While Clemens and the others left on their own terms in 2003, five managers didn't.

The Marlins fired Jeff Torborg on May 11, the Reds axed Bob Boone on July 28 and the Orioles' Mike Hargrove and White Sox' Jerry Manuel got pink slips the day after the regular season ended. The Red Sox fired Grady Little 11 days after losing to the Yankees in the ALCS.

Two general managers also didn't survive the season, as the Mets jettisoned Steve Phillips on June 12 and Jim Bowden was fired in Cincinnati at the same time as Boone. Mariners GM Pat Gillick resigned at the end of the season.

The Marlins were foundering under Torborg, with a 16-22 record when he was replaced by Jack McKeon, who hadn't managed since being fired by Cincinnati after the 2000 season and became the third-oldest manager in major league history behind Connie Mack and Casey Stengel. Florida made a dramatic turnaround under McKeon, going 75-49 the rest of the way and scoring a stunning World Series victory over the Yankees.

The Reds were a disappointing 46-58 in their first season in Great American Ball Park—which opened with a 10-1 loss to the Pirates on March 31—when Boone, in his third year, and Bowden, in his 11th, were swept out. Longtime minor league manager Dave Miley replaced Boone and the Reds went 21-35 under his guidance.

Hargrove was axed after four straight losing seasons in Baltimore in which he went 275-372, including 71-91 in 2003.

The White Sox had another inconsistent season in Manuel's sixth season at the helm. They fell 8½ games back in the AL Central in early June, rallied to take a two-game lead on Sept. 9, then collapsed down the stretch as they lost 10 of 15 games while the Twins passed them.

LARRY GOREN

Steve Phillips

Manuel, the 2000 AL manager of the year, had a 500-471 career record, including 86-76 in 2003.

"If you don't get it done, you have to try to find a new plan of action or find out where you have missed the boat," White Sox GM Ken Williams said.

The Mets, despite having the second-highest payroll in the major leagues at the start of the season, got off to a 28-35 start that cost Phillips his job. Phillips, replaced by assistant GM Jim Duquette, took over as GM midway through the 1997 season and assembled the 2000 club that won the NL.

Gillick decided to step down after the Mariners blew an eight-game lead in the AL West and failed to make the playoffs for a second straight season after tying the major league record with 116 wins in 2001. Despite winning 393 games during Gillick's four-year tenure, the Mariners never made it to the World Series.

"I had four kicks at it and I didn't get the job done," Gillick said. "Let's give somebody else a shot. Maybe they can bring a new angle or perspective and get it over the hump."

Speed 'Em Up

For years, MLB talked of finding ways to speed up games that grew longer with each passing season. In 2003, those initiatives finally took hold.

The average time of a nine-inning game dropped six minutes to 2:46, the fastest since 1989. After peaking at 2:58 in 2000, the average fell to 2:54 in 2001 and 2:52 in 2002.

"We started to involve some of the peripheral elements, such as video board, the music, so those kinds of things weren't dictating the pace of the game, rather than the game itself," Alderson said. "And this year we involved the umpires and the players."

Game times also dropped dramatically in the postseason to 3:05, after averaging 3:24 in 2002. That was the lowest mark since an average of 3:04 in 1998.

ALL-STAR GAME

LARRY GOREN

Wins MVP award, home run derby
Angels' Garret Anderson does it all

Angels' Anderson powers AL to 7-6 win over NL

Major League Baseball wanted the All-Star Game to mean something again.

No one was happy that the 2002 Midsummer Classic ended in a 7-7, stopped after 11 innings because both sides ran out of players. That was quite an embarrassment to Commissioner Bud Selig, particularly with the game played in his hometown of Milwaukee.

Thus, MLB implemented a big change for the 2003 All-Star Game—the winning league was given home-field advantage in the World Series.

As it turned out, the player who decided home-field advantage came from a last-place team. Texas Rangers third baseman Hank Blalock's two-run pinch home run off Los Angeles Dodgers closer Eric Gagne in the bottom of the eighth inning lifted the American League to a 7-6 win over the National League at U.S. Cellular Field in Chicago.

"Just because I'm not going to be in the World Series doesn't mean I'm going to turn it down a notch," said Blalock, whose Rangers finished in the AL West cellar.

However, New York Yankees first baseman Jason Giambi certainly appreciated it. Giambi's team eventually made it to the World Series and got an extra game at Yankee Stadium during a season in which the old system of alternating home-field advantage would have benefited the NL.

"I'm sure whoever reaches the World Series in a Game 7 or something like that will send him a 12-pack of something," Giambi said.

The Yankees didn't benefit from home field advantage, as they lost to Florida in six games with the Marlins clinching at Yankee Stadium.

When asked just before the start of the World Series if the Yankees had taken care of him, Blalock laughed and said, "I don't think they've voted me a share."

Blalock's homer off Gagne, who did not blow any of his 55 regular-season save opportunities to set a major-league record, capped the AL's comeback from a 5-1 deficit in the sixth inning. The AL also posted its sixth straight victory, matching its longest winning streak.

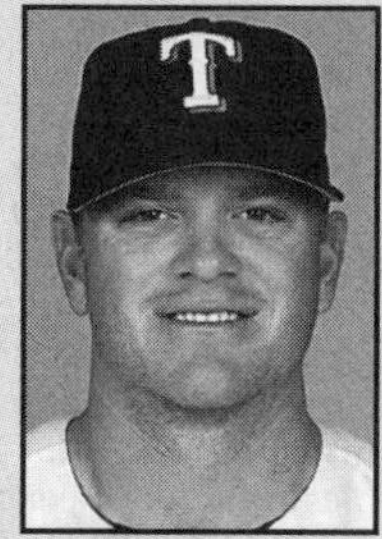
Hank Blalock

Giambi and Anaheim Angels outfielder Garret Anderson, who won the All-Star Home Run Derby two days earlier, also homered during the rally.

Just as MLB had hoped, the outcome was in doubt until the final pitch when Atlanta Braves shortstop Rafael Furcal flied out to the warning track.

"We realize and recognize what was put on us and the stakes that were there," said NL manager Dusty Baker of the Chicago Cubs. "I'm not crazy about the outcome, even though it was a great game to watch and a great game to manage."

Anderson went 3-for-4 and won the first Ted Williams MVP trophy. That award was supposed to have been presented at the 2002 All-Star Game but the tie changed that.

The Colorado Rockies' Todd Helton and the Atlanta Braves' Andruw Jones homered for the NL.

Anaheim's Brendan Donnelly was the winning pitcher with one scoreless relief inning.

—JOHN PERROTTO

TOP VOTE-GETTERS

NATIONAL LEAGUE

CATCHER: 1. Javy Lopez, Braves, 1,287,030; 2. Ivan Rodriguez, Marlins, 911, 828; 3. Mike Matheny, Cardinals, 772,851.

FIRST BASE: 1. Todd Helton, Rockies, 1,202,261; 2. Jeff Bagwell, Astros, 883,085; 3. Tino Martinez, Cardinals, 816,166.

SECOND BASE: 1. Marcus Giles, Braves, 1,103,569; 2. Jeff Kent, Astros, 965,728; 3. Aaron Boone, Reds, 644,310.

THIRD BASE: 1. Scott Rolen, Cardinals, 1,979,936; 2. Mike Lowell, Marlins, 871,059; 3. Vinny Castilla, Braves, 824,189.

SHORTSTOP: 1. Edgar Renteria, Cardinals, 1,669,026; 2. Rafael Furcal, Braves, 1,309,392; 3. Rich Aurilia, Giants, 496,584.

OUTFIELD: 1. Albert Pujols, Cardinals, 2,030,702; 2. Barry Bonds, Giants, 1,919,116; 3. Gary Sheffield, Braves, 1,533,278; 4. Sammy Sosa, Cubs, 1,390,355; 5. Jim Edmonds, Cardinals, 1,211,384; 6. Andruw Jones, Braves, 1,134,959; 7. Chipper Jones, Braves, 894,367; 8. Vladimir Guerrero, Expos, 738,423; 9. Ken Griffey Jr., Reds, 664,038.

AMERICAN LEAGUE

CATCHER: 1. Jorge Posada, Yankees, 1,598,649; 2. Jason Varitek, Red Sox, 638,062; 3. A.J. Pierzynski, Twins, 622,717.

FIRST BASE: 1. Carlos Delgado, Blue Jays, 1,417,087; 2. Jason Giambi, Yankees, 1,080,641; 3. John Olerud, Mariners, 615,495.

SECOND BASE: 1. Alfonso Soriano, Yankees, 1,850,890; 2. Bret Boone, Mariners, 1,498,854; 3. Roberto Alomar, White Sox, 593,088.

THIRD BASE: 1. Troy Glaus, Angels, 944,321; 2. Eric Chavez, Athletics, 740,985; 3. Robin Ventura, Yankees, 683,377.

SHORTSTOP: 1. Alex Rodriguez, Rangers, 1,447,190; 2. Nomar Garciaparra, Red Sox, 1,283,437; 3. Derek Jeter, Yankees, 833,381.

OUTFIELD: 1. Ichiro Suzuki, Mariners, 2,130,708; 2. Manny Ramirez, Red Sox, 1,333,775; 3. Hideki Matsui, Yankees, 1,301,118; 4. Torii Hunter, Twins, 1,146,254; 5. Garret Anderson, Angels, 827,741; 6. Bernie Williams, Yankees, 806,615; 7. Juan Gonzalez, Rangers, 722,772; 8. Mike Cameron, Mariners, 665,072; 9. Vernon Wells, Blue Jays, 641,294.

DESIGNATED HITTER: 1. Edgar Martinez, Mariners, 1,790,016; 2. Carl Everett, Rangers, 596,594; 3. Frank Thomas, White Sox, 501,722.

ROSTERS

NATIONAL LEAGUE

PITCHERS: Armando Benitez, Mets; x-Kevin Brown, Dodgers; x-Shawn Chacon, Rockies; Eric Gagne, Dodgers; Russ Ortiz, Braves; Mark Prior, Cubs; **Jason Schmidt, Giants**; John Smoltz, Braves; Billy Wagner, Astros; Mike Williams, Pirates; Woody Williams, Cardinals; Dontrelle Willis, Marlins; Randy Wolf, Phillies; Kerry Wood, Cubs..

CATCHERS: Paul Lo Duca, Dodgers; **Javy Lopez, Braves.**

INFIELDERS: Aaron Boone, Reds; Luis Castillo, Marlins; Rafael Furcal, Braves; x-Marcus Giles, Braves; **Todd Helton, Rockies (1b)**; Mike Lowell, Marlins; **Edgar Renteria, Cardinals (ss); Scott Rolen, Cardinals (3b)**; Richie Sexson, Brewers; **Jose Vidro, Expos (2b).**

OUTFIELDERS: Barry Bonds, Giants (dh); Jim Edmonds, Cardinals (cf); Luis Gonzalez, Diamondbacks; Andruw Jones; Braves; **Albert Pujols, Cardinals (lf); Gary Sheffield, Braves (rf)**; Rondell White, Padres; Preston Wilson, Rockies.

AMERICAN LEAGUE

PITCHERS: Lance Carter, Devil Rays; Roger Clemens, Yankees; Brendan Donnelly, Angels; Keith Foulke, Athletics; Eddie Guardado, Twins; Roy Halladay, Blue Jays; Shigetoshi Hasegawa, Mariners; **Esteban Loaiza, White Sox**; Mike MacDougal, Royals; Jamie Moyer, Mariners; Mark Mulder, Athletics; C.C. Sabathia, Indians; x-Barry Zito, Athletics.

CATCHERS: Ramon Hernandez, Athletics; **Jorge Posada, Yankees.**

INFIELDERS: Hank Blalock, Rangers; Bret Boone, Mariners; **Carlos Delgado, Blue Jays (1b)**; Nomar Garciaparra, Red Sox; Jason Giambi, Yankees; **Troy Glaus, Angels (3b)**; **Alex Rodriguez, Rangers (ss)**; **Alfonso Soriano, Yankees (2b)**; x-Mike Sweeney, Royals.

OUTFIELDERS: Garret Anderson, Angels (lf); Hideki Matsui, Yankees (cf); Melvin Mora, Orioles; Magglio Ordonez, White Sox; x-Manny Ramirez, Red Sox; **Ichiro Suzuki, Mariners (rf)**; Vernon Wells, Blue Jays; Dmitri Young, Tigers.

DESIGNATED HITTER: Edgar Martinez, Mariners; Carl Everett, White Sox.

Starters in **boldface.**

x-injured, did not play.

July 15 in Chicago
American League 7, National League 6

NATIONAL	ab	r	h	bi	AMERICAN	ab	r	h	bi
Renteria, ss	2	0	0	0	**Suzuki, rf**	1	1	0	0
Furcal, ph-ss	3	1	1	0	Ordonez, ph-rf	1	0	0	0
Edmonds, cf	2	0	1	0	**Soriano, 2b**	3	0	0	0
Jones, ph-cf	2	2	2	3	Giambi, 1b	1	1	1	1
Pujols, lf	3	0	1	1	**Delgado, 1b**	3	0	1	1
Gonzalez, lf	1	0	1	0	Hernandez, c	1	0	0	0
Bonds, dh	3	0	0	0	**Rodriguez, ss**	3	1	1	0
White, dh	1	0	0	0	Garciaparra, ss	1	0	0	0
Sheffield, rf	1	1	0	0	**Anderson, lf**	4	1	3	2
Wilson, rf	2	0	1	0	Mora, pr-lf	0	1	0	0
Helton, 1b	2	1	1	2	**Martinez, dh**	2	0	0	0
Sexson, 1b	2	0	0	0	Everett, ph-dh	1	0	0	0
Rolen, 3b	2	1	1	0	**Matsui, cf**	2	0	1	0
Lowell, 3b	1	0	1	0	Wells, pr-cf	2	1	1	1
Boone, ph-3b	1	0	0	0	**Glaus, 3b**	3	0	0	0
Lopez, c	2	0	0	0	Blalock, ph-3b	1	1	1	2
Lo Duca, ph-c	2	0	1	0	**Posada, c**	2	0	0	0
Vidro, 2b	2	0	0	0	Boone, 2b	2	0	0	0
Castillo, 2b	2	0	0	0					
Totals	**36**	**6**	**11**	**6**	**Totals**	**33**	**7**	**9**	**7**

National	**000**	**050**	**100—6**
American	**010**	**002**	**13x—7**

LOB—National 4, American 5. **2B**—Jones, Lowell, Anderson, Wells. **HR**—Helton, Jones, Anderson, Giambi, Blalock.

National	ip	h	r	er	bb	so	American	ip	h	r	er	bb	so
Schmidt	2	1	0	0	0	3	Loaiza	2	1	0	0	0	1
Wolf	1	1	1	1	1	2	Clemens	1	0	0	0	0	2
Wood	1	1	0	0	0	2	Moyer	1	0	0	0	0	1
Ortiz	1	0	0	0	1	2	Hasegawa	⅔	3	4	4	1	1
Williams	1	2	2	2	0	1	Guardado	⅓	2	1	1	0	0
Wagner	1	1	1	1	0	0	Mulder	2	5	1	1	0	1
Gagne	1	3	3	3	0	1	Donnelly	1	0	0	0	0	1
							Foulke	1	0	0	0	0	0

WP—Wolf. **HBP**—Martinez (by Schmidt).

Umpires: HP—Tim McClelland; **1B**—Larry Young; **2B**—Gary Darling; **3B**—Gary Cederstrom; **LF**—Mark Carlson; **RF**—Bill Welke.

T—2:38. **A**—47,609.

While game times fell, offense increased slightly. Average runs per game rose from 9.24 to 9.46, still well below the 10.58 average in 2000. Home runs increased from an average of 2.09 to 2.14, below the peak of 2.34 three years ago.

The major league batting average rose from .261 to .264, and the ERA increased from 4.27 to 4.39. Strikeouts dropped from 12.94 to 12.68, its lowest average since 1995, when it was 12.61. Walks fell from 6.70 to 6.53.

LARRY GOREN

Jim Bowden

Races At The Plate

While offense dipped slightly, that didn't detract from the batting races in both leagues. Each went down to the final day of the season and the NL saw its closest in history, one that was tinged with a bit of controversy.

Cardinals left fielder Albert Pujols edged Rockies first baseman Todd Helton by .00022, with Pujols finishing at .35871 and Helton finishing at .35849.

LARRY GOREN

Bob Boone

Pujols went 2-for-5 on the final day of the season as St. Louis beat the Diamondbacks 9-5. At the same time, Helton went 2-for-4 with a walk in the Rockies' 10-8 victory over the Padres in the last game at Qualcomm Stadium in San Diego.

"Can you imagine? You get 590 at-bats and it comes down to one at-bat the last day," Pujols said. "This is unbelievable."

After Pujols struck out in the eighth inning in Phoenix, Helton had a chance to move ahead in the eighth at San Diego. But with a runner on second and a 3-0 count, catcher Gary Bennett called for an intentional walk.

"Obviously, I wasn't too pleased with that last at-bat," said Helton, who won the batting crown in 2000. "I'm disappointed at the way it ended. Overall, it was a good year."

San Diego manager Bruce Bochy apologized to Helton.

"I feel terrible for him because that at-bat was the deciding factor in the batting race," Bochy said. "Nobody on this side had any idea of the magnitude of that at-bat. There's no way we would have done that had we known the situation."

Pujols, 23, became the youngest NL batting champion since Tommy Davis won the title at 23 in 1962 for the Dodgers, and was the first righthander to win it since Andres Galarraga in 1993 for the Rockies.

The race was the third-tightest in major league history. In 1945, the Yankees' Snuffy Stirnweiss beat Tony Cuccinello of the White Sox by .00009, and in 1949 the Tigers' George Kell edged the Red Sox' Ted Williams by .00016.

LARRY GOREN

Albert Pujols

The previous closest NL race was a .00028 difference in 1931, when Chick Hafey of St. Louis beat Bill Terry of the New York Giants.

Pujols led the majors with 51 doubles, 137 runs and 394 total bases and also topped the NL with 212 hits.

Boston's Bill Mueller won his first AL batting title. He began the final day one point ahead of the Yankees' Derek Jeter and two ahead of teammate Manny Ramirez.

After Jeter went 0-for-3 against the Orioles and came out of the game with a .324 average, Mueller grounded into a force out as a pinch-hitter at Tampa Bay and finished at .326. Ramirez, who didn't play against the Devil Rays, wound up at .325.

Mueller's average was the lowest for an AL champion since the Twins' Rod Carew hit .318 in 1972, and the lowest in either league since the Braves' Terry Pendleton won the NL title with a .319 average in 1991.

Carlos Delgado hit a grand slam in his final at-bat and finished the year with a major league-leading 145 RBIs, four more than Colorado's Preston Wilson.

BILL NICHOLS

Bill Mueller

Bonds led the major leagues in slugging percentage (.749) and on-base percentage (.529) for the third year in a row. Rangers shortstop Alex Rodriguez topped the AL in slugging percentage (.600) and runs (124), and Ramirez led in on-base percentage (.427).

Toronto's Vernon Wells led the AL with 215 hits and 373 total bases, and Wells and the Angels' Garret Anderson tied for the most doubles with 49.

The Marlins' Juan Pierre led the major leagues with 65 steals, and Tampa Bay's Carl Crawford led the AL with 55.

Toronto's Roy Halladay led the AL in wins with a 22-7 record, while Atlanta's Russ Ortiz led the NL at 21-7.

Pedro Martinez (2.22) led the major leagues in ERA for the second straight season and fourth time in five years. The Giants' Jason Schmidt (2.34) led the NL for the first time.

The Cubs' Kerry Wood led the major leagues in strikeouts for the first time with 266, and Esteban Loaiza of the White Sox led the AL in strikeouts for the first time with 207.

Both leagues had first-time saves leaders. Eric Gagne had 55, two shy of Bobby Thigpen's major league record, and the Athletics' Keith Foulke led the AL with 43.

Newly Enshrined

Two players with divergent per-

MANAGERIAL CHANGES

Five big league teams made managerial changes before, during or after the 2003 season—compared with 16 in 2002. Here are the changes and new managers for 2004:

Team	Original Manager	In-Season Change	Post-Season Change
Baltimore	Mike Hargrove		Lee Mazzilli
Boston	Grady Little		
Chicago (AL)	Jerry Manuel		Ozzie Guillen
Cincinnati	Bob Boone	Dave Miley	
Florida	Jeff Torborg	Jack McKeon	

sonalities were inducted into the Hall of Fame, the taciturn Eddie Murray and the ebullient Gary Carter.

Murray, who played for 21 seasons, became the 38th player elected on the first ballot.

Murray broke in with the Orioles in 1977 and won AL rookie of the year honors after hitting .283-27-88. He played with the Orioles for 12 seasons through 1988 and served another stint with them in 1996. He also played for the Dodgers (1989-91, 1997), Mets (1992-93), Indians (1994-96) and Angels (1997) in his 21-year career.

TOM DiAPCE

LARRY GOREN

Hall of Famers
Gary Carter and Eddie Murray were 2003 inductees

Taught to switch-hit in the minor leagues, Murray quickly became one of the most feared clutch hitters of his generation. He hit 504 homers, including 19 grand slams, second all-time to the 23 of Lou Gehrig. He also drove in at least 75 runs for a major league-record 20 consecutive seasons.

"It's a dream—one of the few things I never dreamed of," Murray said. "When Ted Williams was inducted, he said he must have earned it because he didn't win it because of his friendship with the writers. I guess in that way, I'm proud to be in his company.

"I've never been much on words. I had a job to do."

Carter, whose selection came on his sixth try, was the first inductee to have an Expos hat on his plaque. He thanked the people of Quebec in French, and thanked former President George Bush, who created a stir when he sat down in the audience right before the ceremony got under way.

Carter, nicknamed "Kid" because of his youthful exuberance, broke into the major leagues with the Expos from 1974-84 and returned to Montreal for his final season in 1992. During his 19-year career, Carter also played with the Mets (1985-89), Giants (1990) and Dodgers (1991).

Carter hit .262-324-1,225. He also holds the major league career record for most putouts at catcher (11,785) and most chances accepted at catcher (12,988).

The Brewers' Bob Uecker was honored with the Ford Frick Award for excellence in broadcasting.

PAYROLLS

Following are team payrolls for 2003 (playoff participants in bold):

1. New York Yankees	**$152,749,814**
2. New York Mets	117,176,429
3. Atlanta Braves	**106,243,667**
4. Los Angeles Dodgers	105,872,620
5. Texas Rangers	103,491,667
6. Boston Red Sox	**99,946,500**
7. Seattle Mariners	86,959,167
8. St. Louis Cardinals	83,486,666
9. San Francisco Giants	**82,852,167**
10. Arizona Diamondbacks	80,640,333
11. Chicago Cubs	**79,868,333**
12. Anaheim Angels	79,031,667
13. Baltimore Orioles	73,877,500
14. Houston Astros	71,040,000
15. Philadelphia Phillies	70,780,000
16. Colorado Rockies	67,179,667
17. Cincinnati Reds	59,335,667
18. Minnesota Twins	**55,505,000**
19. Pittsburgh Pirates	54,812,429
20. Montreal Expos	51,948,500
21. Toronto Blue Jays	51,269,000
22. Chicago White Sox	51,010,000
23. Oakland Athletics	**50,260,834**
24. Detroit Tigers	49,168,000
25. Florida Marlins	**49,050,000**
26. Cleveland Indians	48,584,834
27. San Diego Padres	47,928,000
28. Milwaukee Brewers	40,627,000
29. Kansas City Royals	40,518,000
30. Tampa Bay Devil Rays	19,630,000

Hal McCoy of the Dayton Daily News won the J.G. Taylor Spink Award for his excellence as a baseball writer. McCoy covered the Reds for a 31st straight season in 2003 despite suffering a second optic stroke one month before the start of spring training that left him legally blind.

Sausage-Gate

It seems every baseball season has a bizarre story, and none was weirder than what happened on the night of July 9 when the Pirates played the Brewers at Miller Park in Milwaukee.

During the nightly costume sausage race at Miller Park, Randall Simon took a playful tap at the Italian Sausage with his bat as he sat on the top step of the visitor's dugout. Under the heavy weight of the costume, 19-year-old Mandy Block tumbled and fell. Another racer, Veronica Piech, tripped over Block and also hit the ground.

GEORGE GOJKOVICH

Randall Simon

The sausage race, a fan favorite since 1995, features team employees dressed as an oversized bratwurst, hot dog, Italian sausage and Polish sausage.

Simon was arrested by local police after the game and led from the Pirates' clubhouse in handcuffs. He was cited for disorderly conduct and fined $432. Simon said he was just joking when he swatted the sausage and meant no harm.

"I thought at the moment they were trying to play with us. They were running right next to the players," he said. "I'm a fun player, and I've never hurt anyone in my life."

Local prosecutor Jon Reddin decided after reviewing videotape of the incident and interviewing the two women he would not file criminal charges.

"It's such a silly little thing, you know," Block said. "I can see both points of views. From my point of view, it's crazy because I am not used to like being interviewed or anything. I'm like, 'I'm just a sausage, guys. It's not a big deal. I'm fine.'"

Commissioner Bud Selig, the father of Brewers owner Wendy Selig-Prieb, thought it was a big deal. MLB suspended Simon for three days and fined him $2,000.

MAJOR LEAGUE DEBUTS, 2003

AMERICAN LEAGUE

Anaheim Angels

Chris Bootcheck, rhp	Sept. 9
Kevin Gregg, rhp	Aug. 9
Tom Gregorio, c	Sept. 5
Gary Johnson, of	April 26
Greg Jones, rhp	July 30
Robb Quinlan, of	July 28

Baltimore Orioles

Carlos Mendez, c	May 22
Jose Morban, ss	April 6

Boston Red Sox

Matt J. White, lhp	May 27

Chicago White Sox

Jon Adkins, rhp	Aug. 14
Neal Cotts, lhp	Aug. 12
Aaron Miles, 2b	Sept. 11
David Sanders, lhp	April 23
Josh Stewart, lhp	April 6

Cleveland Indians

Rafael Betancourt, rhp	July 13
Jody Gerut, of	April 26
Jhonny Peralta, 3b	June 12
Zach Sorensen, 2b	June 3
Jason Stanford, lhp	July 6
Billy Traber, lhp	April 4

Detroit Tigers

Jeremy Bonderman, rhp	April 2
Wil Ledezma, lhp	April 2
Chris Mears,rhp	June 29
Matt Roney, rhp	April 2
Cody Ross, of	July 4
Brian Schmack, rhp	Aug. 24
Chris Spurling, rhp	April 2

Kansas City Royals

D.J. Carrasco, rhp	April 2
David DeJesus, of	Sept. 2
Jason Gilfillan, rhp	May 16
Jimmy Gobble, rhp	Aug. 3
Rontrez Johnson, of	March 31
Kyle Snyder, rhp	May 1
Les Walrond, lhp	June 8

Minnesota Twins

Rob Bowen, c	Sept. 1
Lew Ford, of	May 29
Justin Morneau, 1b	June 10
Mike Nakamura, rhp	June 7
Alex Prieto, 2b	July 26

New York Yankees

Jason Anderson, rhp	March 31
Brandon Claussen, lhp	June 28
Jose Contreras, rhp	March 31
Jorge DePaula, rhp	Sept. 5
Michel Hernandez, c	Sept. 6
Hideki Matsui, of	March 31

Oakland Athletics

Bobby Crosby, ss	Sept. 2
Mike Edwards, of	Sept. 20
Rich Harden, rhp	July 21
Graham Koonce, 1b	Sept. 20
Mike Neu, rhp	April 9
Mike Wood, rhp	Aug. 21

Seattle Mariners

Aaron Looper, rhp	Aug. 2
J.J. Putz, rhp	Aug. 11
Jamal Strong, of	Sept. 2
Brian Sweeney, rhp	Aug. 16

Tampa Bay Devil Rays

Rocco Baldelli, of	March 31
Matt Diaz, of	July 19
Chad Gaudin, rhp	Aug. 1
Jonny Gomes, of	Sept. 12
Pete LaForest, c	Sept. 2
Mark Malaska, lhp	July 17
Seth McClung, rhp	March 31
Antonio Perez, 2b	May 14
Jon Switzer, lhp	Aug. 2
Doug Waechter, rhp	Aug. 27

Texas Rangers

Juan Dominguez, rhp	Aug. 12
Rosman Garcia, rhp	April 19
Jason Jones, 1b	July 23
Gerald Laird, c	April 30
Tony Mounce, lhp	June 13
Ramon Nivar, 2b	July 30
Laynce Nix, of	July 10
Erasmo Ramirez, lhp	April 30
Mario Ramos, lhp	June 19
Mark Teixeira, 3b	April 1

Toronto Blue Jays

Vinny Chulk, rhp	Sept. 8
Reed Johnson, of	April 17
Aquilino Lopez, rhp	April 2

NATIONAL LEAGUE

Arizona Diamondbacks

Chris Capuano, lhp	May 4
Edgar Gonzalez, rhp	June 1
Andrew Good, rhp	April 18
Robby Hammock, c	April 11
Matt Kata, 2b	June 15
Stephen Randolph, lhp	March 31
Luis Terrero, of	July 10
Jose Valverde, rhp	June 1
Oscar Villarreal, rhp	March 31
Brandon Webb, rhp	April 22

Atlanta Braves

Mike Hessman, 3b	Aug. 22
Horacio Ramirez, lhp	April 2

Chicago Cubs

Dave Kelton, 1b	June 8
Sergio Mitre, rhp	July 22
Felix Sanchez, lhp	Sept. 3
Todd Wellemeyer, rhp	May 15

Cincinnati Reds

Matt Belisle, rhp	Sept. 7
Mark Budzinski, of	Aug. 3
Juan Cerros, rhp	Sept. 8
Jim Chamblee, 3b	Aug. 24
Josh Hall, rhp	Aug. 2
Tim Hummel, 2b	Aug. 26
Ray Olmedo, ss	May 25
Scott Randall, rhp	Aug. 26
Dane Sardinha, c	Sept. 6
Stephen Smitherman, of	July 1
Dernell Stenson, of	Aug. 13
Joe Valentine, rhp	Aug. 24
Ryan Wagner, rhp	July 19

Colorado Rockies

Garrett Atkins, 3b	Aug. 3
Clint Barmes, ss	Sept. 5
Javier Lopez, lhp	April 1
Matt Miller, rhp	June 27
Rene Reyes, of	July 22
Chin-Hui Tsao, rhp	July 25
Jason Young, rhp	May 12

Florida Marlins

Nate Bump, rhp	June 28
Miguel Cabrera, of/3b	June 20
Tommy Phelps, lhp	March 31
Dontrelle Willis, lhp	May 9

Houston Astros

Nate Bland, lhp	May 5
Eric Bruntlett, ss	June 27
Mike Gallo, lhp	July 2
David Matranga, 2b	June 27
Colin Porter, of	May 30
Rodrigo Rosario, rhp	June 21

Los Angeles Dodgers

Steve Colyer, lhp	April 3
Bubba Crosby, of	May 29
Koyie Hill, c	Sept. 5
Edwin Jackson, rhp	Sept. 9

Milwaukee Brewers

Enrique Cruz, 3b	April 2
Matt Ford, lhp	April 2
David Manning, rhp	Aug. 2
Luis Martinez, lhp	Sept. 3
Rickie Weeks, 2b	Sept. 15
Pete Zoccolillo, of	Sept. 5

Montreal Expos

Luis Ayala, rhp	March 31
Ron Calloway, of	March 31
Roy Corcoran, rhp	July 30
Chad Cordero, rhp	Aug. 30
Anthony Ferrari, lhp	June 7
Bryan Hebson, rhp	July 6
Julio Manon, rhp	June 5
Claudio Vargas, rhp	April 26

New York Mets

Edwin Almonte, rhp	July 7
Joe DePastino, c	Aug. 5
Jeff Duncan, of	May 20
Danny Garcia, 2b	Sept. 2
Mike Glavine, 1b	Sept. 14
Jeremy Griffiths, rhp	June 5
Aaron Heilman, rhp	June 26
Prentice Redman, of	Aug. 24
Jose Reyes, ss	June 10
Jason Roach, rhp	June 14
Matt Watson, of	Sept. 12

Philadelphia Phillies

Travis Chapman, 3b	Sept. 9
Geoff Geary, rhp	Aug. 27
Anderson Machado, ss	Sept. 27
Ryan Madson, rhp	Sept. 27
Chase Utley, 3b	April 4

Pittsburgh Pirates

Mike Gonzalez, lhp	Aug. 11
John Grabow, lhp	Sept. 14
J.R. House, c	Sept. 27
Carlos Rivera, 1b	June 22

St. Louis Cardinals

Kiko Calero, rhp	April 2
Dan Haren, rhp	June 30
Bo Hart, 2b	June 19
Jimmy Journell, rhp	June 29
Kevin Ohme, lhp	April 14

San Diego Padres

Jason Bay, of	May 23
Roger Deago, lhp	May 10
Khalil Greene, ss	Sept. 3
Miguel Ojeda, c	May 17
Humberto Quintero, c	Sept. 3
Shane Victorino, of	April 2

San Francisco Giants

Kevin Correia, rhp	July 10
Jason Ellison, of	May 9
Jesse Foppert, rhp	April 14
Todd Linden, of	Aug. 18
Noah Lowry, lhp	Sept. 5
Lance Niekro, 1b	Sept. 5
Deivis Santos, of	June 18
Carlos Valderrama, of	June 21
Jerome Williams, rhp	April 26

WORLD SERIES

BY JOHN PERROTTO

In May, it was hard to imagine the Marlins doing anything but finishing worse than .500 for the 10th time in their 11 seasons of existence.

The Marlins, perennial doormats except for their World Series season in 1997, found themselves with a 16-22 record on May 11. The team raised eyebrows and drew a share of snickers around baseball by firing manager Jeff Torborg and replacing him with Jack McKeon.

McKeon was 72 and had been out of baseball since the Reds fired him as their manager following the 2000 season. In retirement in Elon, N.C., even McKeon was surprised when Marlins owner Jeffrey Loria offered him the job, making him the third-oldest manager in major league history behind Connie Mack and Casey Stengel.

By October, though, McKeon and the Marlins were the kings of baseball as they surprised the favored Giants and Cubs in the National League playoffs, then stunned the high-priced and heavily favored Yankees in six games in the World Series.

"In our mind, it's not an upset at all," outfielder Jeff Conine said. "In everybody else's mind, it's a humongous upset. Nobody gave us a chance."

"We shocked the world," Marlins center fielder Juan Pierre exclaimed over and over in the moments after Florida put away New York in Game Six at Yankee Stadium, becoming the first team to eliminate the Yankees in a postseason series in the Bronx since the Dodgers won the World Series in 1981.

LARRY GOREN

Rags to riches
Marlins overcome slow start to beat Yankees in '03 Classic

The Marlins pulled the upset despite being outspent 3-1 by the Yankees. Florida's payroll was $54 million, 21st among the 30 major league clubs, while the Yankees easily had the highest at $164 million.

Fish Story

It was a shock to see the Marlins even get into the postseason as they fell to 19-29 after a loss in Montreal on May 22. They became the second team in major league history to win a World Series after dipping 10 games below break-even—the 1914 Boston Braves were the other—by going 75-49 for the remainder of the regular season, the best record in the major leagues during that span, to capture the NL wild card.

Florida pulled the biggest shocker of all by knocking off the Yankees in the World Series. After falling behind two games to one, the Marlins won three in a row to capture the series, with 23-year-old Josh Beckett firing a five-hit shutout in a 2-0 victory in Game Six.

"I took this job with the idea I could turn this club around and make it a winner," McKeon said. "I had no idea we would get to the World Series, and I had no idea that we would win the World Series."

"We're a low-revenue team, and we get lost in the shuffle because we don't play on the Game of the Week," Marlins third baseman Mike Lowell said. "We don't have those established veterans who hit 40 home runs every year. A lot of people don't know us."

And a lot of people had also given up on the Marlins after they beat the Indians in the 1997 World Series then immediately were dismantled under orders

WORLD SERIES YEAR-BY-YEAR

Year	Winner	Manager	Loser	Manager	Result	MVP
1903	Boston (AL)	Jimmy Collins	Pittsburgh (NL)	Fred Clarke	5-3	None Selected
1904	NO SERIES					
1905	New York (NL)	John McGraw	Philadelphia (AL)	Connie Mack	4-1	None Selected
1906	Chicago (AL)	Fielder Jones	Chicago (NL)	Frank Chance	4-2	None Selected
1907	Chicago (NL)	Frank Chance	Detroit (AL)	Hugh Jennings	4-0	None Selected
1908	Chicago (NL)	Frank Chance	Detroit (AL)	Hugh Jennings	4-1	None Selected
1909	Pittsburgh (NL)	Fred Clarke	Detroit (AL)	Hugh Jennings	4-3	None Selected
1910	Philadelphia (AL)	Connie Mack	Chicago (NL)	Frank Chance	4-1	None Selected
1911	Philadelphia (AL)	Connie Mack	New York (NL)	John McGraw	4-2	None Selected
1912	Boston (AL)	Jake Stahl	New York (NL)	John McGraw	4-3-1	None Selected
1913	Philadelphia (AL)	Connie Mack	New York (NL)	John McGraw	4-1	None Selected
1914	Boston (NL)	George Stallings	Philadelphia (AL)	Connie Mack	4-0	None Selected
1915	Boston (AL)	Bill Carrigan	Philadelphia (NL)	Pat Moran	4-1	None Selected
1916	Boston (AL)	Bill Carrigan	Brooklyn (NL)	Wilbert Robinson	4-1	None Selected
1917	Chicago (AL)	Pants Rowland	New York (NL)	John McGraw	4-2	None Selected
1918	Boston (AL)	Ed Barrow	Chicago (NL)	Fred Mitchell	4-2	None Selected
1919	Cincinnati (NL)	Pat Moran	Chicago (AL)	Kid Gleason	5-3	None Selected
1920	Cleveland (AL)	Tris Speaker	Brooklyn (NL)	Wilbert Robinson	5-2	None Selected
1921	New York (NL)	John McGraw	New York (AL)	Miller Huggins	5-3	None Selected
1922	New York (NL)	John McGraw	New York (AL)	Miller Huggins	4-0	None Selected
1923	New York (AL)	Miller Huggins	New York (NL)	John McGraw	4-2	None Selected
1924	Washington (AL)	Bucky Harris	New York (NL)	John McGraw	4-3	None Selected
1925	Pittsburgh (NL)	Bill McKechnie	Washington (AL)	Bucky Harris	4-3	None Selected
1926	St. Louis (NL)	Rogers Hornsby	New York (AL)	Miller Huggins	4-3	None Selected
1927	New York (AL)	Miller Huggins	Pittsburgh (NL)	Donie Bush	4-0	None Selected
1928	New York (AL)	Miller Huggins	St. Louis (NL)	Bill McKechnie	4-0	None Selected
1929	Philadelphia (AL)	Connie Mack	Chicago (NL)	Joe McCarthy	4-1	None Selected
1930	Philadelphia (AL)	Connie Mack	St. Louis (NL)	Gabby Street	4-2	None Selected
1931	St. Louis (NL)	Gabby Street	Philadelphia (AL)	Connie Mack	4-3	None Selected
1932	New York (AL)	Joe McCarthy	Chicago (NL)	Charlie Grimm	4-0	None Selected
1933	New York (NL)	Bill Terry	Washington (AL)	Joe Cronin	4-1	None Selected
1934	St. Louis (NL)	Frankie Frisch	Detroit (AL)	Mickey Cochrane	4-3	None Selected
1935	Detroit (AL)	Mickey Cochrane	Chicago (NL)	Charlie Grimm	4-2	None Selected
1936	New York (AL)	Joe McCarthy	New York (NL)	Bill Terry	4-2	None Selected
1937	New York (AL)	Joe McCarthy	New York (NL)	Bill Terry	4-1	None Selected
1938	New York (AL)	Joe McCarthy	Chicago (NL)	Gabby Hartnett	4-0	None Selected
1939	New York (AL)	Joe McCarthy	Cincinnati (NL)	Bill McKechnie	4-0	None Selected
1940	Cincinnati (NL)	Bill McKechnie	Detroit (AL)	Del Baker	4-3	None Selected
1941	New York (AL)	Joe McCarthy	Brooklyn (NL)	Leo Durocher	4-1	None Selected
1942	St. Louis (NL)	Billy Southworth	New York (AL)	Joe McCarthy	4-1	None Selected
1943	New York (AL)	Joe McCarthy	St. Louis (NL)	Billy Southworth	4-1	None Selected
1944	St. Louis (NL)	Billy Southworth	St. Louis (AL)	Luke Sewell	4-2	None Selected
1945	Detroit (AL)	Steve O'Neill	Chicago (NL)	Charlie Grimm	4-3	None Selected
1946	St. Louis (NL)	Eddie Dyer	Boston (AL)	Joe Cronin	4-3	None Selected
1947	New York (AL)	Bucky Harris	Brooklyn (NL)	Burt Shotton	4-3	None Selected
1948	Cleveland (AL)	Lou Boudreau	Boston (NL)	Billy Southworth	4-2	None Selected
1949	New York (AL)	Casey Stengel	Brooklyn (NL)	Burt Shotton	4-1	None Selected
1950	New York (AL)	Casey Stengel	Philadelphia (NL)	Eddie Sawyer	4-0	None Selected
1951	New York (AL)	Casey Stengel	New York (NL)	Leo Durocher	4-2	None Selected
1952	New York (AL)	Casey Stengel	Brooklyn (NL)	Chuck Dressen	4-3	None Selected
1953	New York (AL)	Casey Stengel	Brooklyn (NL)	Chuck Dressen	4-2	None Selected
1954	New York (NL)	Leo Durocher	Cleveland (AL)	Al Lopez	4-0	None Selected
1955	Brooklyn (NL)	Walter Alston	New York (AL)	Casey Stengel	4-3	Johnny Podres, p, Brooklyn
1956	New York (AL)	Casey Stengel	Brooklyn (NL)	Walter Alston	4-3	Don Larsen, p, New York
1957	Milwaukee (NL)	Fred Haney	New York (AL)	Casey Stengel	4-3	Lew Burdette, p, Milwaukee
1958	New York (AL)	Casey Stengel	Milwaukee (NL)	Fred Haney	4-3	Bob Turley, p, New York
1959	Los Angeles (NL)	Walter Alston	Chicago (AL)	Al Lopez	4-2	Larry Sherry, p, Los Angeles
1960	Pittsburgh (NL)	Danny Murtaugh	New York (AL)	Casey Stengel	4-3	Bobby Richardson, 2b, New York
1961	New York (AL)	Ralph Houk	Cincinnati (NL)	Fred Hutchinson	4-1	Whitey Ford, p, New York
1962	New York (AL)	Ralph Houk	San Francisco (NL)	Alvin Dark	4-3	Ralph Terry, p, New York
1963	Los Angeles (NL)	Walter Alston	New York (AL)	Ralph Houk	4-0	Sandy Koufax, p, Los Angeles
1964	St. Louis (NL)	Johnny Keene	New York (AL)	Yogi Berra	4-3	Bob Gibson, p, St. Louis
1965	Los Angeles (NL)	Walter Alston	Minnesota (AL)	Sam Mele	4-3	Sandy Koufax, p, Los Angeles
1966	Baltimore (AL)	Hank Bauer	Los Angeles (NL)	Walter Alston	4-0	Frank Robinson, of, Baltimore
1967	St. Louis (NL)	Red Schoendienst	Boston (AL)	Dick Williams	4-3	Bob Gibson, p, St. Louis
1968	Detroit (AL)	Mayo Smith	St. Louis (NL)	Red Schoendienst	4-3	Mickey Lolich, p, Detroit
1969	New York (NL)	Gil Hodges	Baltimore (AL)	Earl Weaver	4-1	Donn Clendenon, 1b, New York
1970	Baltimore (AL)	Earl Weaver	Cincinnati (NL)	Sparky Anderson	4-1	Brooks Robinson, 3b, Baltimore
1971	Pittsburgh (NL)	Danny Murtaugh	Baltimore (AL)	Earl Weaver	4-3	Roberto Clemente, of, Pittsburgh
1972	Oakland (AL)	Dick Williams	Cincinnati (NL)	Sparky Anderson	4-3	Gene Tenace, c, Oakland
1973	Oakland (AL)	Dick Williams	New York (NL)	Yogi Berra	4-3	Reggie Jackson, of, Oakland
1974	Oakland (AL)	Alvin Dark	Los Angeles (NL)	Walter Alston	4-1	Rollie Fingers, p, Oakland
1975	Cincinnati (NL)	Sparky Anderson	Boston (AL)	Darrell Johnson	4-3	Pete Rose, 3b, Cincinnati
1976	Cincinnati (NL)	Sparky Anderson	New York (AL)	Billy Martin	4-0	Johnny Bench, c, Cincinnati
1977	New York (AL)	Billy Martin	Los Angeles (NL)	Tom Lasorda	4-2	Reggie Jackson, of, New York
1978	New York (AL)	Bob Lemon	Los Angeles (NL)	Tom Lasorda	4-2	Bucky Dent, ss, New York
1979	Pittsburgh (NL)	Chuck Tanner	Baltimore (AL)	Earl Weaver	4-3	Willie Stargell, 1b, Pittsburgh
1980	Philadelphia (NL)	Dallas Green	Kansas City (AL)	Jim Frey	4-2	Mike Schmidt, 3b, Philadelphia
1981	Los Angeles (NL)	Tom Lasorda	New York (AL)	Bob Lemon	4-2	Cey/Guerrero/Yeager, L.A.
1982	St. Louis (NL)	Whitey Herzog	Milwaukee (AL)	Harvey Kuenn	4-3	Darrell Porter, c, St. Louis
1983	Baltimore (AL)	Joe Altobelli	Philadelphia (NL)	Paul Owens	4-1	Rick Dempsey, c, Baltimore
1984	Detroit (AL)	Sparky Anderson	San Diego (NL)	Dick Williams	4-1	Alan Trammell, ss, Detroit
1985	Kansas City (AL)	Dick Howser	St. Louis (NL)	Whitey Herzog	4-3	Bret Saberhagen, p, Kansas City
1986	New York (NL)	Dave Johnson	Boston (AL)	John McNamara	4-3	Ray Knight, 3b, New York
1987	Minnesota (AL)	Tom Kelly	St. Louis (NL)	Whitey Herzog	4-3	Frank Viola, p, Minnesota
1988	Los Angeles (NL)	Tom Lasorda	Oakland (AL)	Tony La Russa	4-1	Orel Hershiser, p, Los Angeles
1989	Oakland (AL)	Tony La Russa	San Francisco (NL)	Roger Craig	4-0	Dave Stewart, p, Oakland
1990	Cincinnati (NL)	Lou Piniella	Oakland (AL)	Tony La Russa	4-0	Jose Rijo, p, Cincinnati
1991	Minnesota (AL)	Tom Kelly	Atlanta (NL)	Bobby Cox	4-3	Jack Morris, p, Minnesota
1992	Toronto (AL)	Cito Gaston	Atlanta (NL)	Bobby Cox	4-2	Pat Borders, c, Toronto
1993	Toronto (AL)	Cito Gaston	Philadelphia (NL)	Jim Fregosi	4-2	Paul Molitor, dh, Toronto
1994	NO SERIES					
1995	Atlanta (NL)	Bobby Cox	Cleveland (AL)	Mike Hargrove	4-2	Tom Glavine, p, Atlanta
1996	New York (AL)	Joe Torre	Atlanta (NL)	Bobby Cox	4-2	John Wetteland, p, New York
1997	Florida (NL)	Jim Leyland	Cleveland (AL)	Mike Hargrove	4-3	Livan Hernandez, p, Florida
1998	New York (AL)	Joe Torre	San Diego (NL)	Bruce Bochy	4-0	Scott Brosius, 3b, New York
1999	New York (AL)	Joe Torre	Atlanta (NL)	Bobby Cox	4-0	Mariano Rivera, p, New York
2000	New York (AL)	Joe Torre	New York (NL)	Bobby Valentine	4-1	Derek Jeter, ss, New York
2001	Arizona (NL)	Bob Brenly	New York (AL)	Joe Torre	4-3	Johnson, p/Schilling, p, Arizona
2002	Anaheim (AL)	Mike Scioscia	San Francisco (NL)	Dusty Baker	4-3	Troy Glaus, 3b, Anaheim
2003	Florida (NL)	Jack McKeon	New York (AL)	Joe Torre	4-2	Josh Beckett, p, Florida

from founding owner Wayne Huizenga.

Huizenga sold the Marlins to John Henry in 1998. Prior to the 2002 season, former Expos owner Jeffrey Loria bought the Marlins, Henry bought the Red Sox and Major League Baseball took over control of the Expos in a controversial three-way transaction.

While Loria tore apart the Expos and was one of the reasons why baseball has all but died in Montreal, he showed more of a willingness to spend in Florida, even though the Marlins drew only 813,111 fans during the 2002 season.

While the Marlins traded catcher Charles Johnson and center fielder Preston Wilson to the Rockies following the 2002 season to rid themselves of their large contracts, they got an offensive catalyst in return in the speedy Pierre. (They took part of the contract burden of lefthander Mike Hampton from the Rockies, immediately sending him to the Braves for righthander Tim Spooneybarger.)

The Marlins also signed free agent catcher Ivan Rodriguez to a one-year, $10 million as a free agent. He became the Marlins' glue with both his clutch hitting and handling of a young pitching staff.

And when Florida got its season turned around and moved into playoff contention, the front office stepped up and got Conine in a trade with the Orioles at the end of August. Conine provided leadership and a much-needed bat when Lowell, who had 32 homers and 105 RBIs in the regular season, broke his hand and didn't return until the last day of the regular season.

"I think Jeffrey made a sound commitment to put a winning ballclub on the field, and it all paid off in the long run," McKeon said.

While the Marlins added players to a good young core of talent, it was McKeon who got much of the credit for turning things around. He set the tone in his first meeting with his new club.

"He sat us all down and told us we were good enough to play in October," Marlins first baseman Derrek Lee said. "He told us just to go out and play hard and have fun. Jack is such an easy guy to play for. Everyone responded to him. He turned out to be the right guy for the situation."

Smart Decision

McKeon did more than just lift morale, though. He made outstanding tactical decisions, including the one prior to Game Six that wound up winning the Marlins a World Series.

LARRY GOREN

Rallying force
Jack McKeon, 72, turned season around for Marlins

MORRIS FOSTOFF

Responding to the challenge
Marlins righthander Josh Beckett blanked Yankees 2-0 in clincher

McKeon decided to buck recent trends by bringing Beckett back to start on short rest, even though Beckett would have been available on full rest for Game Seven.

Pitchers working on three days' rest in the postseason since 1999 had gone 6-20, with a 5.93 ERA in 37 starts. But Beckett was dazzling while pitching on short rest for the first time in his career. He shut down the Yankees, never letting a runner past second base in notching his second big league shutout. Both came in the 2003 postseason, as he also blanked the Cubs on two hits in Game Five of the National League Championship Series.

Beckett became the first pitcher to throw a shutout in a decisive World Series game since the Twins' Jack Morris beat the Braves in 1991. He was the youngest to perform the feat since 21-year-old Bret Saberhagen blanked the Cardinals for the Royals in Game Seven in 1985.

"This guy has got the guts of a burglar," McKeon said. "He's mentally tough. And I knew he had the confidence to go out there and do the job that he did. This guy is going to be something special."

Beckett certainly didn't show any apprehension in facing a Yankees team that had won four of the previous seven World Series and 26 titles in all.

"That kid showed that he is going to be a great one down the road, if he isn't already," Yankees manager Joe Torre said. "When you're that young, you don't know what fear is."

Beckett was the named the series' most valuable player as he went 1-1, 1.10 in his two starts.

In Game Six, Beckett outdueled Yankees lefthander Andy Pettitte, who tied an all-time record earlier in the series with his 13th postseason win. Pettitte allowed two runs in seven innings, but it was all the Marlins needed. They used consecutive singles by Alex Gonzalez, Pierre and Luis Castillo to score in the fifth, and Juan Encarnacion lofted a sacrifice fly in the sixth for the other run.

Beckett seemed oblivious to what he accomplished. He was nonchalant in the postgame celebration and seemed happy just to see the season end.

"I can't believe we don't have a game tomorrow," Beckett said. "Not to say that winning the world championship isn't a big thing. It's kind of relief to get to go deer hunting now."

STEVE MOORE

Champagne celebration
Lenny Harris, right, and Juan Pierre hold World Series trophy aloft

Unfamiliar Territory

While Beckett might have felt relief, the Yankees felt plenty of pain in dropping a World Series on their home field.

After losing the 2001 World Series to the Diamondbacks and being upset in the first round of the 2002 American League Division Series by the Angels, the Yankees were under enormous pressure to win it all this time. Temperamental owner George Steinbrenner promised major changes if the Yankees didn't win, then stomped out of Yankee Stadium without comment following Game Six.

"Nobody had scripted this end," Yankees first baseman Jason Giambi said. "It was supposed to come out different."

"It makes you sick," shortstop and captain Derek Jeter said. "How else can you feel?"

"I feel emptiness," Torre said.

The Yankees outscored the Marlins 21-17 in the six games and had six home runs to the Marlins' two. In the end, though, the Yankees inability to perform in the clutch was their downfall. The Yankees hit just .140 (7-for-50) with runners in scoring position, including 0-for-7 against Beckett in the finale.

"Obviously, in this series we didn't fire on all cylinders for whatever reason," New York general manager Brian Cashman said. "The Marlins had an opportunity and they took advantage of it. I know we're better than what we showed. Typically our guys are better than that."

Alex Gonzalez

The Marlins showed they weren't in awe of New York right from the start, using their advantage in team speed to post a 3-2 win in Game One and snap the Yankees' 10-game home World Series winning streak.

Pierre, who led the major leagues with 65 stolen bases, led off the game with a bunt single and scored on Rodriguez' sacrifice fly. He slapped a two-run single to the opposite field off David Wells in the fifth inning that proved to be the game-winning hit.

The Yankees came back to knot the Series at 1-1 with a 6-1 victory in Game Two. Hideki Matsui got the Yankees going with a three-run home run off Mark Redman in the first inning, and Alfonso Soriano pushed the lead to 6-0 in the fourth with a two-run shot. Pettitte carried a shutout into the ninth inning before losing it on Lee's two-out single, following an error by third baseman Aaron Boone.

The series shifted to Miami for Game Three and the Yankees seemed to gain control with another 6-1 victory. In a driving rain, Beckett and Yankees starter Mike Mussina dueled for seven innings before Matsui put New York ahead 2-1 in the eighth with an RBI single off rookie sensation Dontrelle Willis. The Yankees added four runs in the ninth on a solo homer by Boone and a three-run shot by Bernie Williams.

The Marlins drew even with a 4-3 win in 12 innings in a pivotal and emotional Game Four that saw Yankees pitcher Roger Clemens, who won his 300th game and notched his 4,000th strikeout in June, make what might have been his final big league appearance.

Clemens gave up three runs in the first inning, then blanked the Marlins through the seventh. When he walked off the mound for the last time, the Pro Player Stadium crowd of 65,934 gave him a thunderous ovation and the Marlins tipped their caps.

There was more emotion in the later innings as New York's Ruben Sierra had a pinch-hit, two-run triple with two outs in the top of the ninth to tie the game at 3-3. The score stayed that way until Gonzalez led off the bottom of the 12th with a game-winning homer for the Marlins. The shortstop had been 5-for-53 in the postseason before his blast off Jeff Weaver, a starter who had been relegated to the bullpen late in the season and had pitched just one inning since Sept. 14.

Gonzalez' homer was the obvious momentum shifter in the series. Florida jumped out to a 6-1 lead after five innings in Game Five and held on for a 6-4 win and a 3-2 series lead. Winning pitcher Brad Penny allowed two runs in seven innings and delivered a two-run single in the second inning off reliever Jose Contreras, pressed into emergency duty when Wells left after one inning with back spasms.

That set the stage for Beckett to close it out for the Marlins when the series moved back to New York for Game Six.

"We wanted to come in here to Yankee Stadium and play the Yankees," Beckett said. "If you are going to beat somebody, why not beat the best?"

That's exactly what the Marlins did, overcoming not only the odds of beating the Yankees but a huge early-season hole.

"In my heart of hearts, I kept hearing that this was the little team that could," Loria said.

WORLD SERIES
BOX SCORES

GAME ONE: October 18
Florida 3, New York 2

Florida	ab	r	h	bi	bb	so
Pierre, cf	3	1	2	2	1	0
Castillo, 2b	5	0	1	0	0	0
Rodriguez, c	3	0	0	1	0	0
Cabrera, lf	3	0	0	0	1	0
Lee, 1b	4	0	1	0	0	1
Lowell, 3b	4	0	0	0	0	0
Conine, dh	2	1	1	0	2	0
Encarnacion, rf	4	1	2	0	0	1
Gonzalez, ss	3	0	0	0	0	1
Totals	**31**	**3**	**7**	**3**	**4**	**3**

New York	ab	r	h	bi	bb	so
Soriano, 2b	5	0	1	0	0	1
Johnson, 1b	4	0	0	0	1	1
Jeter, ss	4	0	1	1	0	1
Williams, cf	4	1	2	1	0	0
Matsui, lf	4	0	3	0	0	0
Posada, c	2	0	0	0	2	1
Giambi, dh	3	0	0	0	1	1
Dellucci, pr-dh	0	0	0	0	0	0
Boone, 3b	4	0	0	0	0	1
Garcia, rf	2	1	2	0	0	0
J. Rivera, ph-rf	1	0	0	0	0	1
Sierra, ph	0	0	0	0	1	0
Totals	**33**	**2**	**9**	**2**	**5**	**7**

Florida	**100 020 000—3**
New York	**001 001 000—2**

E—Cabrera (1). **DP**—Florida 2, New York 1. **LOB**—Florida 8, New York 9. **HR**—Williams (1). **SB**—Castillo (1), Pierre (1), Soriano (1), Posada (1). **SH**—Gonzalez. **SF**—Rodriguez.

Florida	ip	h	r	er	bb	so
Penny W	5⅓	7	2	2	3	3
Willis	2⅔	2	0	0	0	2
Urbina S	1⅓	0	0	0	2	2

New York	ip	h	r	er	bb	so
Wells L	7	6	3	3	2	1
Nelson	1	1	0	0	1	0
Contreras	1	0	0	0	1	2

HBP—Pierre (by Wells).

Umpires: HP—Marsh; **1B**—Young; **2B**—Darling; **3B**—Kellogg; **LF**—Rapuano; **RF**— Welke.

T—3:43. **A**—55,769.

GAME TWO: October 19
New York 6, Florida 1

Florida	ab	r	h	bi	bb	so
Pierre, cf	4	0	1	0	0	0
Castillo, 2b	4	1	2	0	0	0
Rodriguez, c	3	0	1	0	0	1
Redmond, c	1	0	0	0	0	0
Cabrera, lf	4	0	0	0	0	0
Lee, 1b	4	0	1	1	0	1
Lowell, 3b	4	0	1	0	0	0
Conine, dh	3	0	0	0	0	2
Encarnacion, rf	2	0	0	0	1	1
Gonzalez, ss	3	0	0	0	0	2
Totals	**32**	**1**	**6**	**1**	**1**	**7**

New York	ab	r	h	bi	bb	so
Soriano, 2b	3	1	1	2	1	2
Jeter, ss	4	0	1	0	0	2
Giambi, dh	3	1	1	0	0	0
Williams, cf	2	1	1	0	2	0
Matsui, lf	4	1	1	3	0	0
Posada, c	3	0	0	0	1	2
Boone, 3b	4	0	1	0	0	2
Johnson, 1b	4	2	3	0	0	1
J. Rivera, rf	4	0	1	1	0	0
Totals	**31**	**6**	**10**	**6**	**4**	**9**

Florida	**000 000 001—1**
New York	**310 200 00x—6**

E—Boone 2 (2). **DP**—Florida 1, New York 3. **LOB**—Florida 5, New York 6. **2B**—J. Rivera (1), Johnson (1), Giambi (1). **HR**—Matsui (1), Soriano (1). **CS**—Castillo (1), Posada (1), Soriano (1).

Florida	ip	h	r	er	bb	so
Redman L	2⅓	5	4	4	2	2
Helling	2⅔	2	2	2	0	2
Fox	1	1	0	0	1	1
Pavano	1	1	0	0	1	2
Looper	1	1	0	0	0	2

New York	ip	h	r	er	bb	so
Pettitte W	8⅔	6	1	0	1	7
Contreras	⅓	0	0	0	0	0

WP—Redman. **HBP**—Giambi (by Redman).

Umpires: HP—Young; **1B**—Darling; **2B**—Kellogg; **3B**—Rapuano; **LF**—Welke; **RF**—Marsh.

T—2:56. **A**—55,750.

GAME THREE: October 21
New York 6, Florida 1

New York	ab	r	h	bi	bb	so
Soriano, 2b	4	1	0	0	1	3
Jeter, ss	4	3	3	0	0	1
Giambi, 1b	2	0	0	0	2	1
Dellucci, pr-rf	1	0	0	0	0	0
Williams, cf	5	1	1	3	0	1
Matsui, lf	3	0	1	1	1	1
Posada, c	2	0	0	1	2	0
Garcia, rf	3	0	0	0	0	0
Sierra, ph	1	0	0	0	0	1
M. Rivera, p	0	0	0	0	0	0
Boone, 3b	4	1	1	1	0	1
Mussina, p	3	0	0	0	0	3
Johnson, 1b	1	0	0	0	0	0
Totals	**33**	**6**	**6**	**6**	**6**	**12**

Florida	ab	r	h	bi	bb	so
Pierre, cf	3	1	2	0	1	0
Castillo, 2b	4	0	0	0	0	3
Rodriguez, c	4	0	1	0	0	0
Cabrera, rf	4	0	2	1	0	2
Lee, 1b	4	0	0	0	0	0
Lowell, 3b	4	0	0	0	0	2
Conine, lf	4	0	2	0	0	0
Gonzalez, ss	3	0	1	0	0	1
Encarnacion, ph	1	0	0	0	0	1
Beckett, p	2	0	0	0	0	2
Willis, p	0	0	0	0	0	0
Fox, p	0	0	0	0	0	0
Looper, p	0	0	0	0	0	0
Hollandsworth, ph	1	0	0	0	0	0
Totals	**34**	**1**	**8**	**1**	**1**	**11**

LARRY GOREN

Swan song
Roger Clemens made his last appearance in Game Four

New York	**000 100 014—6**
Florida	**100 000 000—1**

E—Boone (3). **LOB**—New York 8, Florida 8. **2B**—Jeter 2 (2), Pierre (1), Gonzalez (1), Rodriguez (1). **HR**—Boone (1), Williams (2). **SH**—Beckett. **CS**—Pierre (1). **PB**—Posada (1).

New York	ip	h	r	er	bb	so
Mussina W	7	7	1	1	1	9
Rivera S	2	1	0	0	0	2

Florida	ip	h	r	er	bb	so
Beckett L	7⅓	3	2	2	3	10
Willis	⅓	1	0	0	2	0
Fox	⅔	1	2	2	1	1
Looper	⅔	1	2	2	0	1

IBB—Pierre (by Mussina). **HBP**—Matsui (by Beckett), Jeter (by Looper).

Umpires: HP—Darling; **1B**—Kellogg; **2B**—Rapuano; **3B**—Welke; **LF**—Marsh; **RF**—Young.

T—3:21. **A**—65,731.

GAME FOUR: October 22
Florida 4, New York 3

New York	ab	r	h	bi	bb	so
Soriano, 2b	6	0	1	0	0	2
Jeter, ss	6	0	1	0	0	1
Giambi, 1b	6	0	2	0	0	1
Williams, cf	6	2	4	0	0	0
Matsui, lf	3	0	1	0	2	0
Posada, c	4	0	1	0	0	1
Dellucci, pr-rf	0	1	0	0	0	0
Garcia, rf	3	0	0	0	0	1
Sierra, ph	1	0	1	2	0	0
Contreras, p	0	0	0	0	0	0
J. Rivera, ph	0	0	0	0	1	0
Weaver, p	0	0	0	0	0	0
Boone, 3b	4	0	0	1	0	1
Celmens, p	2	0	1	0	0	0
Johnson, ph	1	0	0	0	0	0
Nelson, p	0	0	0	0	0	0
Flaherty, c	2	0	0	0	0	0
Totals	**44**	**3**	**12**	**3**	**3**	**7**

Florida	ab	r	h	bi	bb	so
Pierre, cf	4	0	0	0	1	0
Castillo, 2b	4	0	0	0	0	2
Rodriguez, c	5	1	2	0	0	1
Cabrera, rf	5	1	1	2	0	2
Looper, p	0	0	0	0	0	0
Conine, lf	5	1	3	0	0	0
Lowell, 3b	5	0	1	0	0	0
Lee, 1b	5	0	2	1	0	1
Gonzalez, ss	5	1	1	1	0	2
Pavano, p	2	0	0	0	0	1
Urbina, p	0	0	0	0	0	0
Hollandsworth, ph	1	0	0	0	0	1
Fox, p	0	0	0	0	0	0
Encarnacion, rf	0	0	0	0	0	0
Totals	**41**	**4**	**10**	**4**	**1**	**10**

New York	**010 000 002 000—3**
Florida	**300 000 000 001—4**

DP—Florida 2. **LOB**—New York 10, Florida 7. **2B**—Jeter (3), Williams (1), Rodriguez (2). **3B**—Sierra (1). **HR**—Cabrera (1), Gonzalez (1). **SH**—Dellucci, Castillo, Pavano. **SF**—Boone.

New York	ip	h	r	er	bb	so
Clemens	7	8	3	3	0	5
Nelson	1	1	0	0	0	1
Contreras	2	0	0	0	1	4
Weaver L	1	1	1	1	0	0

Florida	ip	h	r	er	bb	so
Pavano	8	7	1	1	0	4
Urbina	1	2	2	2	1	0
Fox	1⅓	2	0	0	2	2
Looper W	1⅔	1	0	0	0	1

IBB—J. Rivera (by Fox).

Umpires: HP—Kellogg; **1B**—Rapuano; **2B**—Welke; **3B**—Marsh; **LF**—Young; **RF**—Darling.

T—4:03. **A**—65,934.

GAME FIVE: October 23
Florida 6, New York 4

New York	ab	r	h	bi	bb	so	Florida	ab	r	h	bi	bb	so
Jeter, ss	4	2	3	1	1	0	Pierre, cf	3	0	1	1	1	0
Wilson, 2b	4	0	2	1	1	0	Castillo, 2b	4	0	0	0	0	1
Williams, cf	4	0	1	1	0	0	Rodriguez, c	4	1	1	0	0	2
Matsui, lf	5	0	0	0	0	0	Cabrera, rf	4	0	1	0	0	1
Posada, c	4	0	1	0	0	1	Willis, p	0	0	0	0	0	0
Johnson, 1b	4	1	2	0	0	1	Looper, p	0	0	0	0	0	0
Garcia, rf	3	0	1	0	0	1	Urbina, p	0	0	0	0	0	0
Soriano, ph-rf	1	0	0	0	0	1	Conine, lf	3	1	1	0	1	0
Boone, 3b	4	0	1	0	0	0	Lowell, 3b	3	1	1	2	1	1
Wells, p	0	0	0	0	0	0	Lee, 1b	3	2	1	0	1	1
Dellucci, ph	1	0	0	0	0	0	Gonzalez, ss	4	1	2	1	0	1
Contreras, p	0	0	0	0	0	0	Penny, p	2	0	1	2	0	0
J. Rivera, ph	1	0	0	0	0	0	Encarnacion, rf	1	0	0	0	0	1
Hammond	0	0	0	0	0	0							
Sierra, ph	1	0	0	0	0	1							
Nelson, p	0	0	0	0	0	0							
Giambi, ph	1	1	1	1	0	0							
Totals	**37**	**4**	**12**	**4**	**2**	**5**	**Totals**	**31**	**6**	**9**	**6**	**4**	**8**

New York	**100 000 102—4**
Florida	**030 120 00x—6**

E—Wilson (1), Lee (1). **LOB**—New York 9, Florida 6. **2B**—Wilson (1), Gonzalez (2), Conine (1), Pierre (2). **HR**—Giambi (1). **CS**—Gonzalez (1). **SH**—Penny. **SF**—Williams.

New York	ip	h	r	er	bb	so	Florida	ip	h	r	er	bb	so
Wells	1	0	0	0	0	1	Penny W	7	8	2	1	2	4
Contreras L	3	5	4	4	3	4	Willis	1	1	0	0	0	1
Hammond	2	2	2	0	0	0	Looper	1/3	3	2	2	0	0
Nelson	2	2	0	0	1	4	Urbina	2/3	0	0	0	0	0

Umpires: HP—Rapuano; **1B**—Welke; **2B**—Marsh; **3B**—Young; **LF**—Darling; **RF**—Kellogg.

T—3:05. **A**—65,975.

GAME SIX: October 25
Florida 2, New York 0

Florida	ab	r	h	bi	bb	so	New York	ab	r	h	bi	bb	so
Pierre, cf	4	0	1	0	1	2	Jeter, ss	4	0	0	0	0	2
Castillo, 2b	5	0	1	1	0	1	Johnson, 1b	3	0	0	0	1	0
Rodriguez, c	3	0	1	0	1	0	Williams, cf	4	0	1	0	0	1
Cabrera, lf	4	0	0	0	0	2	Matsui, lf	4	0	0	0	0	1
Conine, dh	4	1	0	0	0	0	Posada, c	4	0	1	0	0	2
Lowell, 3b	3	0	2	0	1	0	Giambi, dh	2	0	0	0	1	0
Lee, 1b	4	0	0	0	0	3	Garcia, rf	3	0	1	0	0	1
Encarnacion, rf	3	0	0	1	0	1	Wilson, 3b	0	0	0	0	0	0
Gonzalez, ss	4	1	2	0	0	0	Boone, 3b	1	0	0	0	0	1
							Sierra, ph-rf	1	0	0	0	0	1
							Soriano, 2b	3	0	2	0	0	0
Totals	**34**	**2**	**7**	**2**	**3**	**9**	**Totals**	**29**	**0**	**5**	**0**	**2**	**9**

Florida	**000 011 000— 2**
New York	**000 000 000— 0**

E—Jeter (1). **DP**—Florida 2. **LOB**—Florida 9, New York 5. **2B**—Lowell (1), Williams (2), Posada (1). **SH**—Boone. **SF**—Encarnacion.

Florida	ip	h	r	er	bb	so	New York	ip	h	r	er	bb	so
Beckett W	9	5	0	0	2	9	Pettitte L	7	6	2	1	3	7
							M.Rivera	2	1	0	0	0	2

IBB—Rodriguez (by Pettitte).

Umpires: HP—Welke; **1B**—Marsh; **2B**—Young; **3B**—Darling; **LF**—Kellogg; **RF**—Rapuano.

T—2:57. **A**—55,773.

COMPOSITE BOX

FLORIDA

Player, Pos.	AVG	G	AB	R	H	2B	3B	HR	RBI	BB	SO	SB
Brad Penny, p	.500	2	2	0	1	0	0	0	2	0	0	0
Jeff Conine, lf-dh	.333	6	21	4	7	1	0	0	0	3	2	0
Juan Pierre, cf	.333	6	21	2	7	2	0	0	3	5	2	1
Ivan Rodriguez, c	.273	6	22	2	6	2	0	0	1	1	4	0
Alex Gonzalez, ss	.273	6	22	3	6	2	0	1	2	0	7	0
Mike Lowell, 3b	.217	6	23	1	5	1	0	0	2	2	3	0
Derrek Lee, 1b	.208	6	24	2	5	0	0	0	2	1	7	0
Juan Encarnacion, rf-ph	.182	6	11	1	2	0	0	0	1	1	5	0
Miguel Cabrera, rf-lf	.167	6	24	1	4	0	0	1	3	1	7	0
Luis Castillo, 2b	.154	6	26	1	4	0	0	0	1	0	7	1
Todd Hollandsworth, ph	.000	2	2	0	0	0	0	0	0	0	1	0
Carl Pavano, p	.000	2	2	0	0	0	0	0	0	0	1	0
Josh Beckett, p	.000	2	2	0	0	0	0	0	0	0	2	0
Mike Redmond, c	.000	1	1	0	0	0	0	0	0	0	0	0
Totals	**.232**	**6**	**203**	**17**	**47**	**8**	**0**	**2**	**17**	**14**	**48**	**2**

Pitcher	W	L	ERA	G	GS	SV	IP	H	R	ER	BB	SO
Dontrelle Willis	0	0	0.00	3	0	0	4	4	0	0	2	3
Carl Pavano	0	0	1.00	2	1	0	9	8	1	1	1	6
Josh Beckett	1	1	1.10	2	2	0	16	8	2	2	5	19
Brad Penny	2	0	2.19	2	2	0	12	15	4	3	5	7
Ugueth Urbina	0	0	6.00	3	0	2	3	2	2	2	3	2
Chad Fox	0	0	6.00	3	0	0	3	4	2	2	4	4
Rick Helling	0	0	6.75	1	0	0	3	2	2	2	0	2
Braden Looper	1	0	9.82	4	0	0	4	6	4	4	0	4
Mark Redman	0	1	15.43	1	1	0	2	5	4	4	2	2
Totals	**4**	**2**	**3.21**	**6**	**6**	**2**	**56**	**54**	**21**	**20**	**22**	**49**

NEW YORK

Player, Pos.	AVG	G	AB	R	H	2B	3B	HR	RBI	BB	SO	SB
Enrique Wilson, 2b-3b	.500	2	4	0	2	1	0	0	1	1	0	0
Roger Clemens, p	.500	1	2	0	1	0	0	0	0	0	0	0
Bernie Williams, cf	.400	6	25	5	10	2	0	2	5	2	2	0
Derek Jeter, ss	.346	6	26	5	9	3	0	0	2	1	7	0
Nick Johnson, 1b-ph	.294	6	17	3	5	1	0	0	0	2	3	0
Karim Garcia, rf	.286	5	14	1	4	0	0	0	0	0	3	0
Hideki Matsui, lf	.261	6	23	1	6	0	0	1	4	3	2	0
Ruben Sierra, ph	.250	5	4	0	1	0	1	0	2	1	3	0
Jason Giambi, dh-1b-ph	.235	6	17	2	4	1	0	1	1	4	3	0
Alfonso Soriano, 2b-rf-ph	.227	6	22	2	5	0	0	1	2	2	9	1
Juan Rivera, ph-rf	.167	4	6	0	1	1	0	0	1	1	1	0
Jorge Posada, c	.158	6	19	0	3	1	0	0	1	5	7	1
Aaron Boone, 3b	.143	6	21	1	3	0	0	1	2	0	6	0
Mike Mussina, p	.000	1	3	0	0	0	0	0	0	0	3	0
John Flaherty, c	.000	1	2	0	0	0	0	0	0	0	0	0
Dave Dellucci, ph-rf	.000	4	2	1	0	0	0	0	0	0	0	0
Totals	**.261**	**6**	**207**	**21**	**54**	**10**	**1**	**6**	**21**	**22**	**49**	**2**

Pitcher	W	L	ERA	G	GS	SV	IP	H	R	ER	BB	SO
Jeff Nelson	0	0	0.00	3	0	0	4	4	0	0	2	5
Mariano Rivera	0	0	0.00	2	0	1	4	2	0	0	0	4
Chris Hammond	0	0	0.00	1	0	0	2	2	2	0	0	0
Andy Pettitte	1	1	0.57	2	2	0	16	12	3	1	4	14
Mike Mussina	1	0	1.29	1	1	0	7	7	1	1	1	9
David Wells	0	1	3.38	2	2	0	8	6	3	3	2	1
Roger Clemens	0	0	3.86	1	1	0	7	8	3	3	0	5
Jose Contreras	0	1	5.68	4	0	0	6	5	4	4	5	10
Jeff Weaver	0	1	9.00	1	0	0	1	1	1	1	0	0
Totals	**2**	**4**	**2.13**	**6**	**6**	**1**	**55**	**47**	**17**	**13**	**14**	**48**

SCORE BY INNINGS	
Florida	**530 151 001 001—17**
New York	**421 301 118 000—21**

E—Boone 3, Cabrera, Lee, Jeter, Wilson. **DP**—Florida 8, New York 6. **LOB**—Florida 43, New York 47. **SB**—Castillo, Pierre, Posada, Soriano. **CS**—Castillo, Gonzalez, Pierre, Soriano, Posada. **SH**—Beckett, Castillo, Gonzalez, Pavano, Penny, Boone, Dellucci. **SF**—Encarnacion, Rodriguez, Boone, Williams. **IBB**—Pierre (by Mussina), J. Rivera (by Fox), Rodriguez (by Pettitte). **HBP**—Pierre (by Wells), Giambi (by Redman), Matsui (by Beckett), Jeter (by Looper). **WP**—Redman. **PB**—Posada.

AMERICAN LEAGUE

BY WILL KIMMEY

The 2002 American League Championship Series pitted a pair of throwback organizations that succeeded with homegrown players and without major trades or free-agent signings. For a moment, it looked like the beginning of a new cycle in baseball.

But that moment was fleeting. Things returned to normal a year later, with two of the six largest payrolls in baseball slugging it out for the 2003 American League pennant in a championship series pitting the league's two most historic and popular teams as the Yankees faced the wild-card Red Sox.

The Red Sox have ratcheted up their payroll every year since 1998 in their quest to catch the Yankees. They haven't wrested the Eastern Division title away from New York since 1995, when Jose Canseco called Boston home. They came closest in 1999, when Boston lost to their rivals in a five-game ALCS.

Things looked like they might turn out different in 2003. The Yankees battled injuries and looked old at times. They suffered through infighting between owner George Steinbrenner and manager Joe Torre, the heights of which hadn't been reached publicly during the organization's seven-year hold on the AL East that began in 1996, the year the Yankees won the first of four World Series titles in six years.

And for the Red Sox, everything was falling into place. The planets were aligning in just the right way under 29-year-old, first-year general manager Theo Epstein. Heck, with Mars making its closest orbit to Earth in the last 60,000 years, the planets *were* aligned for something strange, especially with Boston positioning itself to end a championship drought that its fans felt had gone on for at least that long.

The Red Sox almost got the job done. They fell five outs short of eliminating the Yankees in a stirring seven-game ALCS that New York won with a 6-5 victory in Game Seven, courtesy of an 11th-inning walkoff home run by Aaron Boone. Just three innings earlier, the Red Sox held a 5-2 lead, having knocked former Boston ace Roger Clemens out of what looked like his last career appearance in the fourth inning. Current ace Pedro Martinez took the mound to begin the eighth and retired Nick Johnson, then allowed a double to Derek Jeter, who scored on a base hit by Bernie Williams.

BILL NICHOLS
Grady Little

With his ace tiring, Red Sox manager Grady Little went to the mound and asked Martinez, who had thrown more than 110 pitches, if he wanted to face Hideki Matsui. Martinez stayed in, yielding a double to Matsui and a two-run blooper to Jorge Posada that tied the game. Little was castigated by Boston media and fans for his decision, and was fired 11 days after the season despite guiding the Red Sox to 184 wins in his two years at the helm.

"Right now I am disappointed that evidently some people are judging me on the results of one decision I made—not the decision, but the results of the decision," Little said. "Less than 24 hours before, those same people were hugging and kissing me. If that's the way they operate, I'm not sure I want to be part of it."

LARRY GOREN
Sudden death blow
Aaron Boone's dramatic home run lifts Yankees in ALCS

Boone's home run came off Tim Wakefield, who had already delivered the Sox two wins in the first and fourth games of the series. The Red Sox faced elimination in Game Six, but finally unleashed their record-setting offense in a 9-6 win that forced the deciding game. It marked the only time in the postseason that Boston had produced more than five runs after averaging nearly six runs a game during the regular season.

While Boone's home run was the series' most dramatic moment, the most heated came in Game Three—the first meeting of Clemens and Martinez. Martinez hit Yankees right fielder Karim Garcia in the upper shoulder on a pitch that narrowly missed the outfielder's head. Both benches emptied, with Yankees bench coach Don Zimmer charging Martinez and being thrown to the ground.

Clemens delivered a pitch just off the inside corner to Manny Ramirez in the bottom of the inning, and Ramirez took offense, causing more players to leave their dugouts for the field. Finally, in the ninth inning, Garcia hopped off the field of play in the Yankees bullpen to help reliever Jeff Nelson in a battle with a Fenway Park grounds crew member who New York players said was displaying a little too much home team spirit.

"I know it's the playoffs and a great setting," Clemens told the media, "but, gosh, when I told y'all the other day it was going to be festive, I didn't know it was going to be this festive."

Baseball's Best Rivalry

The festivities only served to toss more life into the Yankees-Red Sox rivalry and the series, one so emotional-

AMERICAN LEAGUE CHAMPIONS, 1901-2003

NO-DIVISION FORMAT

	PENNANT	PCT	GA
1901	Chicago	.610	4
1902	Philadelphia	.610	5
1903	Boston	.659	14½
1904	Boston	.617	1½
1905	Philadelphia	.622	2
1906	Chicago	.616	3
1907	Detroit	.613	1½
1908	Detroit	.588	½
1909	Detroit	.645	3½
1910	Philadelphia	.680	14½
1911	Philadelphia	.669	13½
1912	Boston	.691	14
1913	Philadelphia	.627	6½
1914	Philadelphia	.651	8½
1915	Boston	.669	2½
1916	Boston	.591	2
1917	Chicago	.649	9
1918	Boston	.595	2½
1919	Chicago	.629	3½
1920	Cleveland	.636	2
1921	New York	.641	4½
1922	New York	.610	1
1923	New York	.645	16
1924	Washington	.597	2
1925	Washington	.636	8½
1926	New York	.591	3
1927	New York	.714	19
1928	New York	.656	2½
1929	Philadelphia	.693	18
1930	Philadelphia	.662	8
1931	Philadelphia	.704	13½
1932	New York	.695	13
1933	Washington	.651	7
1934	Detroit	.656	7
1935	Detroit	.616	3
1936	New York	.667	19½
1937	New York	.662	13
1938	New York	.651	9½
1939	New York	.702	17
1940	Detroit	.584	1
1941	New York	.656	17
1942	New York	.669	9
1943	New York	.636	13½
1944	St. Louis	.578	1
1945	Detroit	.575	1½
1946	Boston	.675	12
1947	New York	.630	12
1948	Cleveland	.626	1
1949	New York	.630	1
1950	New York	.636	3
1951	New York	.636	5
1952	New York	.617	2
1953	New York	.656	8½
1954	Cleveland	.721	8
1955	New York	.623	3
1956	New York	.630	9
1957	New York	.636	8
1958	New York	.597	10
1959	Chicago	.610	5
1960	New York	.630	8
1961	New York	.673	8
1962	New York	.593	5
1963	New York	.646	10½
1964	New York	.611	1
1965	Minnesota	.630	7
1966	Baltimore	.606	9
1967	Boston	.568	1
1968	Detroit	.636	12

TWO-DIVISION FORMAT

	EAST	PCT	GA	WEST	PCT	GA	PENNANT		MVP
1969	Baltimore	.673	19	Minnesota	.599	9	Baltimore	3-0	Harmon Killebrew, 1b-3b, Minnesota
1970	Baltimore	.667	15	Minnesota	.605	9	Baltimore	3-0	Boog Powell, 1b, Baltimore
1971	Baltimore	.639	12	Oakland	.627	16	Baltimore	3-0	Vida Blue, lhp, Oakland
1972	Detroit	.551	½	Oakland	.600	5½	Oakland	3-2	Dick Allen, 1b, Chicago
1973	Baltimore	.599	8	Oakland	.580	6	Oakland	3-2	Reggie Jackson, of, Oakland
1974	Baltimore	.562	2	Oakland	.556	5	Oakland	3-1	Jeff Burroughs, of, Texas
1975	Boston	.594	4½	Oakland	.605	7	Boston	3-0	Fred Lynn, of, Boston
1976	New York	.610	10½	Kansas City	.556	2½	New York	3-2	Thurman Munson, c, New York
1977	New York	.617	2½	Kansas City	.630	8	New York	3-2	Rod Carew, 1b, Minnesota
1978	New York	.613	1	Kansas City	.568	5	New York	3-1	Jim Rice, of, Boston
1979	Baltimore	.642	8	California	.543	3	Baltimore	3-1	Don Baylor, dh, California
1980	New York	.636	3	Kansas City	.599	14	Kansas City	3-0	George Brett, 3b, Kansas City
1981	New York*	.607	2	Oakland**	.587	—	New York	3-0	Rollie Fingers, rhp, Milwaukee
	Milwaukee	.585	1½	Kansas City	.566	1			
1982	Milwaukee	.586	1	California	.574	3	Milwaukee	3-2	Robin Yount, ss, Milwaukee
1983	Baltimore	.605	6	Chicago	.611	20	Baltimore	3-1	Cal Ripken, ss, Baltimore
1984	Detroit	.642	15	Kansas City	.519	3	Detroit	3-0	Willie Hernandez, lhp, Detroit
1985	Toronto	.615	2	Kansas City	.562	1	Kansas City	4-3	Don Mattingly, 1b, New York
1986	Boston	.590	5½	California	.568	5	Boston	4-3	Roger Clemens, rhp, Boston
1987	Detroit	.605	2	Minnesota	.525	2	Minnesota	4-1	George Bell, of, Toronto
1988	Boston	.549	1	Oakland	.642	13	Oakland	4-0	Jose Canseco, of, Oakland
1989	Toronto	.549	2	Oakland	.611	7	Oakland	4-1	Robin Yount, of, Milwaukee
1990	Boston	.543	2	Oakland	.636	9	Oakland	4-0	Rickey Henderson, of, Oakland
1991	Toronto	.562	7	Minnesota	.586	8	Minnesota	4-1	Cal Ripken, ss, Baltimore
1992	Toronto	.593	4	Oakland	.593	6	Toronto	4-2	Dennis Eckersley, rhp, Oakland
1993	Toronto	.586	7	Chicago	.580	8	Toronto	4-2	Frank Thomas, 1b, Chicago

* Won first half; defeated Milwaukee 3-2 in best-of-5 playoff.
** Won first half, defeated Kansas City 3-0 in best-of-5 playoff.

THREE-DIVISION FORMAT/WILD CARD

	EAST	PCT	GA	CENTRAL	PCT	GA	WEST	PCT	GA	WILD CARD	PCT	PENNANT	MVP
1994	New York	.619	6½	Chicago	.593	1	Texas	.456	1	None		None (season incomplete)	Frank Thomas, 1b, Chicago
1995	Boston	.597	7	Cleveland	.694	30	Seattle	.545	1	New York (East)	.549	Cleveland def. Seattle 4-2	Mo Vaughn, 1b, Boston
1996	New York	.568	4	Cleveland	.615	14½	Texas	.556	4	Baltimore (East)	.543	New York def. Baltimore 4-1	Juan Gonzalez, of, Texas
1997	Baltimore	.605	2	Cleveland	.534	6	Seattle	.556	6	New York (East)	.593	Cleveland def. Baltimore 4-2	Ken Griffey, of, Seattle
1998	New York	.704	22	Cleveland	.549	9	Texas	.543	3	Boston (East)	.568	New York def. Cleveland 4-2	Juan Gonzalez, of, Texas
1999	New York	.605	4	Cleveland	.599	21½	Texas	.586	8	Boston (East)	.580	New York def. Boston 4-1	Ivan Rodriguez, c, Texas
2000	New York	.540	2½	Chicago	.586	5	Oakland	.565	½	Seattle (West)	.562	New York def. Seattle 4-2	Jason Giambi, 1b, Oakland
2001	New York	.594	13½	Cleveland	.562	6	Seattle	.716	14	Oakland (West)	.630	New York def. Seattle 4-1	Ichiro Suzuki, of, Seattle
2002	New York	.640	10½	Minnesota	.584	13½	Oakland	.636	4	Anaheim (West)	.611	Anaheim def. Minnesota 4-1	Miguel Tejada, ss, Oakland
2003	New York	.623	6	Minnesota	.556	4	Oakland	.593	3	Boston (East)	.586	New York def. Boston 4-3	Alex Rodriguez, ss, Rangers

STANDINGS

Page	EAST	W	L	PCT	GB	Manager	General Manager(s)	Attend.	Avg.	Last Penn.
186	New York Yankees	101	61	.623	—	Joe Torre	Brian Cashman	3,465,599	42,263	2003
85	*Boston Red Sox	95	67	.586	6	Grady Little	Theo Epstein	2,724,165	33,632	1986
267	Toronto Blue Jays	86	76	.531	15	Carlos Tosca	J. P. Ricciardi	1,799,458	22,216	1993
77	Baltimore Orioles	71	91	.438	30	Mike Hargrove	J. Beattie/M. Flanagan	2,425,440	29,944	1983
252	Tampa Bay Devil Rays	63	99	.389	38	Lou Piniella	Chuck LaMar	1,058,695	13,070	None
Page	**CENTRAL**	**W**	**L**	**PCT**	**GB**	**Manager**	**General Manager**	**Attend.**	**Avg.**	**Last Penn.**
172	Minnesota Twins	90	72	.556	—	Ron Gardenhire	Terry Ryan	1,946,012	24,025	1991
93	Chicago White Sox	86	76	.531	4	Jerry Manuel	Ken Williams	1,939,594	23,946	1959
151	Kansas City Royals	83	79	.512	7	Tony. Pena	Allard Baird	1,753,211	21,915	1985
115	Cleveland Indians	68	94	.420	22	Eric Wedge	Mark Shapiro	1,729,911	21,357	1997
130	Detroit Tigers	43	119	.265	47	Alan Trammell	Dave Dombrowski	1,368,245	16,892	1984
Page	**WEST**	**W**	**L**	**PCT**	**GB**	**Manager**	**General Manager**	**Attend.**	**Avg.**	**Last Penn.**
202	Oakland Athletics	96	66	.593	—	Ken Macha	Billy Beane	2,216,414	27,363	1990
245	Seattle Mariners	93	69	.574	3	Bob Melvin	Pat Gillick	3,268,504	40,352	None
56	Anaheim Angels	77	85	.475	19	Mike Scioscia	Bill Stoneman	3,061,093	37,330	2002
259	Texas Rangers	71	91	.438	25	Buck Showalter	John Hart	2,094,394	25,857	None

*Won wild-card playoff berth

NOTE: Team's individual batting, pitching and fielding statistics can be found on page indicated in lefthand column.

ly draining that it ended with series MVP Mariano Rivera lying on the mound weeping after having held Boston at bay for Game Seven's final three innings. It was so close that the Yankees scored just one more run than the Red Sox overall. And counting the postseason, the two teams played 26 times in 2003, with the Yankees winning 14 while the Red Sox ended up outscoring them overall.

STEVE MOORE

Power provider
Jason Giambi paced the Yankees offense with 41 HRs

The rivalry heated up even before the 2003 season started with Red Sox president Larry Lucchino referring to the Yankees as the "Evil Empire" after they outbid Boston for sought-after Cuban defector Jose Contreras.

Epstein was able to use the money not spent on Contreras to supplement his lineup with David Ortiz and Kevin Millar, two players who not only contributed 56 homers and 197 RBIs, but also became the team's clubhouse leaders. With 27 home runs after July 1, Ortiz made a late push for AL MVP after being nontendered by the Twins the previous December.

With baseball historian Bill James as a member of the front office and a mind toward his and Billy Beane's emphasis in on-base and slugging percentage in constructing a lineup, Epstein fashioned the best offense baseball had seen since the 1927 Yankees. In fact, the 2003 Red Sox' .491 team slugging percentage topped that Babe Ruth and Lou Gehrig-fueled team's record as Boston also led the majors in runs and had eight players collect 80 or more RBIs.

Then the Red Sox appeared to have gotten the best of the Yankees at the July 31 trade deadline. Epstein acquired the best reliever on the market, Reds righthander Scott Wiliamson, and then nabbed the best available lefthanded set-up man, Scott Sauerbeck, while also adding starter Jeff Suppan—both from the Pirates.

Pundits agreed the Red Sox improved themselves the most at the deadline, and the moves made Steinbrenner uneasy, so he forced GM Brian Cashman to make deals in retaliation. The Yankees acquired 47-year-old lefty Jesse Orosco, who was later released to make room on the roster for lefty Gabe White, acquired from the Reds. New York made a minor upgrade at third base, getting Aaron Boone from the Reds and shipping Robin Ventura to the Dodgers. The Yankees also acquired Armando Benitez from the Mets, only to swap him to the Mariners for Nelson.

The bullpen was a constant question for the Yankees. They used 20 different relief pitchers and for awhile there were questions about whether Rivera had lost his effectiveness. (He proved he hadn't in the playoffs.) New York also had to make do with a constantly changing lineup as Jeter, Williams and Johnson all missed extended stretches with injuries.

Jeter dislocated his shoulder sliding into third base in the season opener and didn't play again until May 13. Upon his return, he returned to normal, ranking third in the league with a .324 average. Jason Giambi (.250-41-107) and Alfonso Soriano (.290-38-91) again provided the lineup's thump, while catcher Jorge Posada drew MVP consideration for his offensive contribution (.281-30-101) and the way he handled the pitching staff. Hideki Matsui also proved a vital part of the lineup after signing a three-year, $21 million contract to join the Yankees from Japan. After a slow start, Matsui worked his way into rookie of the year consideration by hitting .287-16-106 and subbing in center field while Williams was injured.

Andy Pettitte led the Yankees with 21 wins, but Roger Clemens took center stage by notching his 300th victory and 4,000th career strikeout—on the same night—and finished the year with 17 wins. With a rotation that included four pitchers who won at least 15 games (Mussina 17, Wells 15), the Yankees managed the best record in the AL at 101-61, finishing six games

AL YEAR-BY-YEAR BATTING LEADERS

SINCE 1925

Year	Batting Average		Home Runs		RBIs	
1925	Harry Heilmann, Detroit	.393	Bob Meusel, New York	33	Bob Meusel, New York	138
1926	Heinie Manush, Detroit	.377	Babe Ruth, New York	47	Babe Ruth, New York	145
1927	Harry Heilmann, Detroit	.398	Babe Ruth, New York	60	Lou Gehrig, New York	175
1928	Goose Goslin, Washington	.379	Babe Ruth, New York	54	Two tied at	142
1929	Lew Fonseca, Cleveland	.369	Babe Ruth, New York	46	Al Simmons, Philadelphia	157
1930	Al Simmons, Philadelphia	.381	Babe Ruth, New York	49	Lou Gehrig, New York	174
1931	Al Simmons, Philadelphia	.390	Two tied at	46	Lou Gehrig, New York	184
1932	Dale Alexander, Detroit-Boston	.367	Jimmie Foxx, Philadelphia	58	Jimmie Foxx, Philadelphia	169
1933	Jimmie Foxx, Philadelphia	.356	Jimmie Foxx, Philadelphia	48	Jimmie Foxx, Philadelphia	163
1934	Lou Gehrig, New York	.363	Lou Gehrig, New York	49	Lou Gehrig, New York	165
1935	Buddy Myer, Washington	.349	Two tied at	36	Hank Greenberg, Detroit	170
1936	Luke Appling, Chicago	.388	Lou Gehrig, New York	49	Hal Trosky, Cleveland	162
1937	Charlie Gehringer, Detroit	.371	Joe DiMaggio, New York	46	Hank Greenberg, Detroit	183
1938	Jimmie Foxx, Boston	.349	Hank Greenberg, Detroit	58	Jimmie Foxx, Boston	175
1939	Joe DiMaggio, New York	.381	Jimmie Foxx, Boston	35	Ted Williams, Boston	145
1940	Joe DiMaggio, New York	.352	Hank Greenberg, Detroit	41	Hank Greenberg, Detroit	150
1941	Ted Williams, Boston	.406	Ted Williams, Boston	37	Joe DiMaggio, New York	125
1942	Ted Williams, Boston	.356	Ted Williams, Boston	36	Ted Williams, Boston	137
1943	Luke Appling, Chicago	.328	Rudy York, Detroit	34	Rudy York, Detroit	118
1944	Lou Boudreau, Cleveland	.327	Nick Etten, New York	22	Vern Stephens, St. Louis	109
1945	Snuffy Stirnweiss, New York	.309	Vern Stephens, St. Louis	24	Nick Etten, New York	111
1946	Mickey Vernon, Wash.	.352	Hank Greenberg, Detroit	44	Hank Greenberg, Detroit	127
1947	Ted Williams, Boston	.343	Ted Williams, Boston	32	Ted Williams, Boston	114
1948	Ted Williams, Boston	.369	Joe DiMaggio, New York	39	Joe DiMaggio, New York	155
1949	George Kell, Detroit	.343	Ted Williams, Boston	43	Two tied at	159
1950	Billy Goodman, Boston	.354	Al Rosen, Cleveland	37	Two tied at	144
1951	Ferris Fain, Philadelphia	.344	Gus Zernial, Chicago-Phil.	33	Gus Zernial, Chicago-Philadelphia	129
1952	Ferris Fain, Philadelphia	.327	Larry Doby, Cleveland	32	Al Rosen, Cleveland	105
1953	Mickey Vernon, Washington	.337	Al Rosen, Cleveland	43	Al Rosen, Cleveland	145
1954	Bobby Avila, Cleveland	.341	Larry Doby, Cleveland	32	Larry Doby, Cleveland	126
1955	Al Kaline, Detroit	.340	Mickey Mantle, New York	37	Two tied at	116
1956	Mickey Mantle, New York	.353	Mickey Mantle, New York	52	Mickey Mantle, New York	130
1957	Ted Williams, Boston	.388	Roy Sievers, Washington	42	Roy Sievers, Washington	114
1958	Ted Williams, Boston	.328	Mickey Mantle, New York	42	Jackie Jensen, Boston	122
1959	Harvey Kuenn, Detroit	.353	Two tied at	42	Jackie Jensen, Boston	112
1960	Pete Runnels, Boston	.320	Mickey Mantle, New York	40	Roger Maris, New York	112
1961	Norm Cash, Detroit	.361	Roger Maris, New York	61	Roger Maris, New York	142
1962	Pete Runnels, Boston	.326	Harmon Killebrew, Minnesota	48	Harmon Killebrew, Minnesota	126
1963	Carl Yastrzemski, Boston	.321	Harmon Killebrew, Minnesota	45	Dick Stuart, Boston	118
1964	Tony Oliva, Minnesota	.323	Harmon Killebrew, Minnesota	49	Brooks Robinson, Baltimore	118
1965	Tony Oliva, Minnesota	.321	Tony Conigliaro, Boston	32	Rocky Colavito, Cleveland	108
1966	Frank Robinson, Baltimore	.316	Frank Robinson, Baltimore	49	Frank Robinson, Baltimore	122
1967	Carl Yastrzemski, Boston	.326	Two tied at	44	Carl Yastrzemski, Boston	121
1968	Carl Yastrzemski, Boston	.301	Frank Howard, Washington	44	Ken Harrelson, Boston	109
1969	Rod Carew, Minnesota	.332	Harmon Killebrew, Minnesota	49	Harmon Killebrew, Minnesota	140
1970	Alex Johnson, California	.329	Frank Howard, Washington	44	Frank Howard, Washington	126
1971	Tony Oliva, Minnesota	.337	Bill Melton, Chicago	33	Harmon Killebrew, Minnesota	119
1972	Rod Carew, Minnesota	.318	Dick Allen, Chicago	37	Dick Allen, Chicago	113
1973	Rod Carew, Minnesota	.350	Reggie Jackson, Oakland	32	Reggie Jackson, Oakland	117
1974	Rod Carew, Minnesota	.364	Dick Allen, Chicago	32	Jeff Burroughs, Texas	118
1975	Rod Carew, Minnesota	.359	Two tied at	36	George Scott, Milwaukee	109
1976	George Brett, Kansas City	.333	Graig Nettles, New York	32	Lee May, Baltimore	109
1977	Rod Carew, Minnesota	.388	Jim Rice, Boston	39	Larry Hisle, Minnesota	119
1978	Rod Carew, Minnesota	.333	Jim Rice, Boston	46	Jim Rice, Boston	139
1979	Fred Lynn, Boston	.333	Gorman Thomas, Milwaukee	45	Don Baylor, California	139
1980	George Brett, Kansas City	.390	Two tied at	41	Cecil Cooper, Milwaukee	122
1981	Carney Lansford, Boston	.336	Four tied at	22	Eddie Murray, Baltimore	78
1982	Willie Wilson, Kansas City	.332	Two tied at	39	Hal McRae, Kansas City	133
1983	Wade Boggs, Boston	.361	Jim Rice, Boston	39	Two tied at	126
1984	Don Mattingly, New York	.343	Tony Armas, Boston	43	Tony Armas, Boston	123
1985	Wade Boggs, Boston	.368	Darrell Evans, Detroit	40	Don Mattingly, New York	145
1986	Wade Boggs, Boston	.357	Jesse Barfield, Toronto	40	Joe Carter, Cleveland	121
1987	Wade Boggs, Boston	.363	Mark McGwire, Oakland	49	George Bell, Toronto	134
1988	Wade Boggs, Boston	.366	Jose Canseco, Oakland	42	Jose Canseco, Oakland	124
1989	Kirby Puckett, Minnesota	.339	Fred McGriff, Toronto	36	Ruben Sierra, Texas	119
1990	George Brett, Kansas City	.329	Cecil Fielder, Detroit	51	Cecil Fielder, Detroit	132
1991	Julio Franco, Texas	.341	Two tied at	44	Cecil Fielder, Detroit	133
1992	Edgar Martinez, Seattle	.343	Juan Gonzalez, Texas	43	Cecil Fielder, Detroit	124
1993	John Olerud, Toronto	.363	Juan Gonzalez, Texas	46	Albert Belle, Cleveland	129
1994	Paul O'Neill, New York	.359	Ken Griffey, Seattle	40	Kirby Puckett, Minnesota	112
1995	Edgar Martinez, Seattle	.356	Albert Belle, Cleveland	50	Two tied at	126
1996	Alex Rodriguez, Seattle	.358	Mark McGwire Oakland	52	Albert Belle, Cleveland	148
1997	Frank Thomas, Chicago	.347	Ken Griffey, Seattle	56	Ken Griffey, Seattle	147
1998	Bernie Williams, New York	.339	Ken Griffey, Seattle	56	Juan Gonzalez, Texas	157
1999	Nomar Garciaparra, Boston	.357	Ken Griffey, Seattle	48	Manny Ramirez, Cleveland	165
2000	Nomar Garciaparra, Boston	.372	Troy Glaus, Anaheim	47	Edgar Martinez, Seattle	145
2001	Ichiro Suzuki, Seattle	.350	Alex Rodriguez, Texas	52	Bret Boone, Seattle	141
2002	Manny Ramirez, Boston	.349	Alex Rodriguez, Texas	57	Alex Rodriguez, Texas	142
2003	Bill Mueller, Boston	.326	Alex Rodriguez, Texas	47	Carlos Delgado, Toronto	145

ahead of the Red Sox.

LARRY GOREN

Pivotal acquisition
The Twins took off after trading for Shannon Stewart

West Teams Fall Short Again

The Red Sox outlasted the Mariners for the wild-card, largely on the strength of a four-game sweep of Seattle in Fenway Park at the end of August. It marked the second straight year the Mariners had led the AL West for most of the year before a late-season letdown.

Seattle led the West into late August, but finished three games behind the Athletics and two behind the Red Sox. It was eerily similar to the 2002 season, when the Mariners led the division in mid-August and finished behind both the A's and Angels, six games out of the playoffs. The troubling collapses, combined with management's unwillingness to take on salary in trades, led to GM Pat Gillick resigning his post. In Gillick's four years in Seattle, the club won more games than any team in baseball, including 116 in 2001, but never reached the World Series.

Postseason failures have also become a familiar story for the A's. Though the team captured back-to-back AL West titles in 2002-03 and earned wild-card bids the two previous seasons, Oakland hasn't won a postseason series since advancing to the 1990 World Series. GM Billy Beane has received plenty of recognition for building an annual contender on one of the league's lowest payrolls, and his skills were extolled in 'Moneyball', a revealing book that went behind the scenes with him during the 2002 season, detailing how he ran his club. Beane's A's have collected 300 victories over the past three seasons, including a 96-66 record in 2003.

The A's have slowly morphed from a slugging squad with passable pitching to one with a trio of stud pitchers and an offense that emphasizes on-base percentage and minimizing outs. The loss of Jason Giambi to free agency after the 2001 season played as much a role in the transformation as the rapid development of Tim Hudson, Mark Mulder and Barry Zito, who each won at least 14 games and posted an ERA of 3.30 or better in 2003. Keith Foulke, the A's third different closer in three years, anchored the bullpen with a 9-1, 2.08 record and a league-leading 43 saves after being acquired from the White Sox for Billy Koch.

Oakland laid the foundation for even a greater shift in that direction in 2003, announcing before the season they wouldn't re-sign reigning MVP Miguel Tejada (who hit .278-27-106) after the year, setting him off in a dreadful early season slump, and adding precocious pitching prospect Rich Harden to the rotation just after the all-star break.

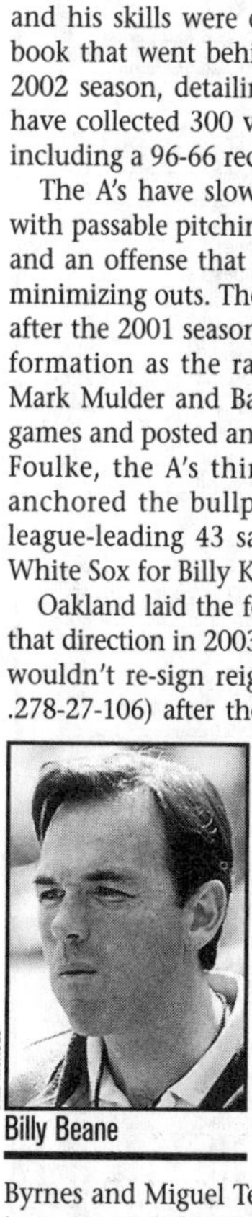
BILL NICHOLS

Billy Beane

A late-season hip injury put Mulder out for the playoffs, and then Hudson came up lame in Game Four of the Division Series against the Red Sox, leaving the A's short on the mound after they built a 2-0 series lead. The A's lost Game Three on a series of bizarre baserunning plays that left Eric Byrnes and Miguel Tejada each tagged out at home plate in a contest the Red Sox won in extra innings on a pinch-hit, walk-off two-run home run by Trot Nixon. The Red Sox took Game Four as well, and then Game Five behind Martinez as the A's fell to 0-8 in series-clinching games over the last four years. They haven't won a postseason series since reaching the World Series in 1990.

Central Shootout

The Central Division didn't quite match up to the East and West in quality, but it didn't lack in drama. The defending champion Twins got off to a poor start, but posted the best second-half record in the majors at 46-23 and came from 7½ games out at the all-star break to win the division.

A midseason trade for Blue Jays outfielder Shannon Stewart ignited the stretch-drive fire for the Twins, as Stewart hit and proved a catalyst atop the lineup by hitting .332 with 43 runs in 65 games in Minnesota. Lefthander Johan Santana gave the rotation a lift in July when injuries forced his move from the bullpen. Santana went 11-2, 2.86 as a starter and 12-3, 3.07 overall. The rotation as a whole improved, trimming the team ERA by almost a run during the second half.

"The way I looked at it was, 'Forget about the whole first half,' " said righthander Kyle Lohse, who went 14-11, 4.61. "I was trying to throw the perfect pitch every time. I put a lot of pressure on myself."

The Twins' biggest strength came at the end of games, where the pressure is always on. Closer Eddie Guardado (41 saves, 2.89 ERA) and set-up man LaTroy Hawkins (nine wins and a team-leading 1.86 ERA) were able to preserve plenty of leads and allow Minnesota to hold off the White Sox and Royals. Though they made the playoffs and took Game One of the ALDS in Yankee Stadium, the Twins couldn't count their season successful as the Yankees rolled in the next three games to end the series. It left Minnesota shy of the ALCS a year after reaching the doorstep of the World Series.

No two teams had more divergent expectation/result pairings than Chicago and Kansas City. The White Sox

AL YEAR-BY-YEAR PITCHING LEADERS

SINCE 1925

Year	Wins		ERA		Strikeouts	
1925	Two tied at	21	Stan Coveleski, Washington	2.84	Lefty Grove, Philadelphia	116
1926	George Uhle, Cleveland	27	Lefty Grove, Philadelphia	2.51	Lefty Grove, Philadelphia	194
1927	Two tied at	22	Wilcy Moore, New York	2.28	Lefty Grove, Philadelphia	174
1928	Two tied at	24	Garland Braxton, Washington	2.52	Lefty Grove, Philadelphia	183
1929	George Earnshaw, Philadelphia	24	Lefty Grove, Philadelphia	2.82	Lefty Grove, Philadelphia	170
1930	Lefty Grove, Philadelphia	28	Lefty Grove, Philadelphia	2.54	Lefty Grove, Philadelphia	209
1931	Lefty Grove, Philadelphia	31	Lefty Grove, Philadelphia	2.05	Lefty Grove, Philadelphia	175
1932	General Crowder, Washington	26	Lefty Grove, Philadelphia	2.84	Red Ruffing, New York	190
1933	Two tied at	24	Monte Pearson, Cleveland	2.33	Lefty Gomez, New York	163
1934	Lefty Gomez, New York	26	Lefty Gomez, New York	2.33	Lefty Gomez, New York	158
1935	Wes Ferrell, Boston	25	Lefty Grove, Boston	2.70	Tommy Bridges, Detroit	163
1936	Tommy Bridges, Detroit	23	Lefty Grove, Boston	2.81	Tommy Bridges, Detroit	175
1937	Lefty Gomez, New York	21	Lefty Gomez, New York	2.33	Lefty Gomez, New York	194
1938	Red Ruffing, New York	21	Lefty Grove, Philadelphia	3.07	Bob Feller, Cleveland	240
1939	Bob Feller, Cleveland	24	Lefty Grove, Philadelphia	2.54	Bob Feller, Cleveland	246
1940	Bob Feller, Cleveland	27	Bob Feller, Cleveland	2.62	Bob Feller, Cleveland	261
1941	Bob Feller, Cleveland	25	Thornton Lee, Chicago	2.37	Bob Feller, Cleveland	260
1942	Tex Hughson, Boston	22	Ted Lyons, Chicago	2.10	Two tied at	113
1943	Two tied at	20	Spud Chandler, New York	1.64	Allie Reynolds, Cleveland	151
1944	Hal Newhouser, Detroit	29	Dizzy Trout, Detroit	2.12	Hal Newhouser, Detroit	187
1945	Hal Newhouser, Detroit	25	Hal Newhouser, Detroit	1.81	Hal Newhouser, Detroit	212
1946	Two tied at	26	Hal Newhouser, Detroit	1.94	Bob Feller, Cleveland	348
1947	Bob Feller, Cleveland	20	Spud Chandler, New York	2.46	Bob Feller, Cleveland	196
1948	Hal Newhouser, Detroit	21	Gene Bearden, Cleveland	2.43	Bob Feller, Cleveland	164
1949	Mel Parnell, Boston	25	Mel Parnell, Boston	2.78	Virgil Trucks, Detroit	153
1950	Bob Lemon, Cleveland	23	Early Wynn, Cleveland	3.20	Bob Lemon, Cleveland	170
1951	Bob Feller, Cleveland	22	Saul Rogovin, Detroit-Chicago	2.78	Vic Raschi, New York	164
1952	Bobby Shantz, Philadelphia	24	Allie Reynolds, New York	2.07	Allie Reynolds, New York	160
1953	Bob Porterfield, Washington	22	Eddie Lopat, New York	2.43	Billy Pierce, Chicago	186
1954	Two tied at	23	Mike Garcia, Cleveland	2.64	Bob Turley, Baltimore	185
1955	Three tied at	18	Billy Pierce, Chicago	1.97	Herb Score, Cleveland	245
1956	Frank Lary, Detroit	21	Whitey Ford, New York	2.47	Herb Score, Cleveland	263
1957	Two tied at	20	Bobby Shantz, New York	2.45	Early Wynn, Cleveland	184
1958	Bob Turley, New York	21	Whitey Ford, New York	2.01	Early Wynn, Chicago	179
1959	Early Wynn, Chicago	22	Hoyt Wilhelm, Baltimore	2.19	Jim Bunning, Detroit	201
1960	Two tied at	18	Frank Baumann, Chicago	2.68	Jim Bunning, Detroit	201
1961	Whitey Ford, New York	25	Dick Donovan, Washington	2.40	Camilo Pascual, Minnesota	221
1962	Ralph Terry, New York	23	Hank Aguirre, Detroit	2.21	Camilo Pascual, Minnesota	206
1963	Whitey Ford, New York	24	Gary Peters, Chicago	2.33	Camilo Pascual, Minnesota	202
1964	Two tied at	20	Dean Chance, Los Angeles	1.65	Al Downing, New York	217
1965	Mudcat Grant, Minnesota	21	Sam McDowell, Cleveland	2.18	Sam McDowell, Cleveland	325
1966	Jim Kaat, Minnesota	25	Gary Peters, Chicago	1.98	Sam McDowell, Cleveland	225
1967	Two tied at	22	Joel Horlen, Chicago	2.06	Jim Lonborg, Boston	246
1968	Denny McLain, Detroit	31	Luis Tiant, Cleveland	1.60	Sam McDowell, Cleveland	283
1969	Denny McLain, Detroit	24	Dick Bosman, Washington	2.19	Sam McDowell, Cleveland	279
1970	Three tied at	24	Diego Segui, Oakland	2.56	Sam McDowell, Cleveland	304
1971	Mickey Lolich, Detroit	25	Vida Blue, Oakland	1.82	Mickey Lolich, Detroit	308
1972	Two tied at	24	Luis Tiant, Boston	1.91	Nolan Ryan, California	329
1973	Wilbur Wood, Chicago	24	Jim Palmer, Baltimore	2.40	Nolan Ryan, California	383
1974	Two tied at	25	Catfish Hunter, Oakland	2.49	Nolan Ryan, California	367
1975	Two tied at	23	Jim Palmer, Baltimore	2.09	Frank Tanana, California	269
1976	Jim Palmer, Baltimore	22	Mark Fidrych, Detroit	2.34	Nolan Ryan, California	327
1977	Three tied at	20	Frank Tanana, California	2.54	Nolan Ryan, California	341
1978	Ron Guidry, New York	25	Ron Guidry, New York	1.74	Nolan Ryan, California	260
1979	Mike Flanagan, Baltimore	23	Ron Guidry, New York	2.78	Nolan Ryan, California	223
1980	Steve Stone, Baltimore	25	Rudy May, New York	2.47	Len Barker, Cleveland	187
1981	Steve McCatty, Oakland	14	Steve McCatty, Oakland	2.32	Len Barker, Cleveland	127
1982	LaMarr Hoyt, Chicago	19	Rick Sutcliffe, Cleveland	2.96	Floyd Bannister, Seattle	209
1983	LaMarr Hoyt, Chicago	21	Rick Honeycutt, Texas	2.42	Jack Morris, Detroit	232
1984	Mike Boddicker, Baltimore	20	Mike Boddicker, Baltimore	2.79	Mark Langston, Seattle	204
1985	Ron Guidry, New York	22	Dave Stieb, Toronto	2.48	Bert Blyleven, Cleve.-Minnesota	206
1986	Roger Clemens, Boston	24	Roger Clemens, Boston	2.48	Mark Langston, Seattle	245
1987	Two tied at	20	Jimmy Key, Toronto	2.76	Mark Langston, Seattle	262
1988	Frank Viola, Minnesota	24	Allan Anderson, Minnesota	2.45	Roger Clemens, Boston	291
1989	Bret Saberhagen, Kansas City	23	Bret Saberhagen, Kansas City	2.16	Nolan Ryan, Texas	301
1990	Bob Welch, Oakland	27	Roger Clemens, Boston	1.93	Nolan Ryan, Texas	232
1991	Two tied at	20	Roger Clemens, Boston	2.62	Roger Clemens, Boston	241
1992	Two tied at	21	Roger Clemens, Boston	2.41	Randy Johnson, Seattle	241
1993	Jack McDowell, Chicago	22	Kevin Appier, Kansas City	2.56	Randy Johnson, Seattle	308
1994	Jimmy Key, New York	17	Steve Ontiveros, Oakland	2.65	Randy Johnson, Seattle	204
1995	Mike Mussina, Baltimore	19	Randy Johnson, Seattle	2.48	Randy Johnson, Seattle	294
1996	Andy Pettitte, New York	21	Juan Guzman, Toronto	2.93	Roger Clemens, Boston	257
1997	Roger Clemens, Toronto	21	Roger Clemens, Toronto	2.05	Roger Clemens, Toronto	292
1998	Three tied at	20	Roger Clemens, Toronto	2.65	Roger Clemens, Toronto	271
1999	Pedro Martinez, Boston	23	Pedro Martinez, Boston	2.07	Pedro Martinez, Boston	313
2000	Two tied at	20	Pedro Martinez, Boston	1.74	Pedro Martinez, Boston	284
2001	Mark Mulder, Oakland	21	Freddy Garcia, Seattle	3.05	Hideo Nomo, Boston	220
2002	Barry Zito, Oakland	23	Pedro Martinez, Boston	2.26	Pedro Martinez, Boston	239
2003	Roy Halladay, Toronto	22	Pedro Martinez, Boston	2.22	Esteban Loaiza, Chicago	207

LARRY GOREN

Pleasant surprise
Esteban Loaiza stepped forward as the Sox' unlikely ace

AL: BEST TOOLS

A Baseball America survey of American League managers, conducted at midseason 2003, ranked AL players with the best tools:

BEST HITTER
1. Ichiro Suzuki, Mariners
2. Manny Ramirez, Red Sox
3. Garret Anderson, Angels

BEST POWER
1. Carlos Delgado, Blue Jays
2. Jason Giambi, Yankees
3. Alex Rodriguez, Rangers

BEST BUNTER
1. Ichiro Suzuki, Mariners
2. Omar Vizquel, Indians
3. David Eckstein, Angels

BEST STRIKE-ZONE JUDGEMENT
1. Jason Giambi, Yankees
2. Frank Thomas, White Sox
3. Edgar Martinez, Mariners

BEST HIT-AND-RUN BATTER
1. David Eckstein, Angels
2. Derek Jeter, Yankees
3. Michael Young, Rangers

BEST BASERUNNER
1. Ichiro Suzuki, Mariners
2. Johnny Damon, Red Sox
3. Carlos Beltran, Royals

FASTEST BASERUNNER
1. Ichiro Suzuki, Mariners
2. Carl Crawford, Devil Rays
3. Rocco Baldelli, Devil Rays

BEST PITCHER
1. Roy Halladay, Blue Jays
2. Mark Mulder, Athletics
3. Pedro Martinez, Red Sox

BEST FASTBALL
1. Bartolo Colon, White Sox
2. Mike MacDougal, Royals
3. Mariano Rivera, Yankees

BEST CURVEBALL
1. Barry Zito, Athletics
2. Roy Halladay, Blue Jays
3. Mike Mussina, Yankees

BEST SLIDER
1. Pedro Martinez, Red Sox
2. Jeff Nelson, Mariners/Yankees
3. Esteban Loaiza, White Sox

BEST CHANGEUP
1. Pedro Martinez, Red Sox
2. Jamie Moyer, Mariners
3. Keith Foulke, Athletics

BEST CONTROL
1. David Wells, Yankees
2. Jamie Moyer, Mariners
3. Mike Mussina, Yankees

BEST PICKOFF MOVE
1. Andy Pettitte, Yankees
2. Brian Anderson Indians/Royals
3. Kenny Rogers, Twins

BEST RELIEVER
1. Mariano Rivera, Yankees
2. Keith Foulke, Athletics
3. Mike MacDougal, Royals

BEST DEFENSIVE C
1. Bengie Molina, Angels
2. Ramon Hernandez, Athletics
3. Jason Varitek, Red Sox

BEST DEFENSIVE 1B
1. Doug Mientkiewicz, Twins
2. John Olerud, Mariners
3. Scott Spiezio, Angels

BEST DEFENSIVE 2B
1. Bret Boone, Mariners
2. Michael Young, Rangers
3. Luis Rivas, Twins

BEST DEFENSIVE 3B
1. Eric Chavez, Athletics
2. Troy Glaus, Angels
3. Corey Koskie, Twins

BEST DEFENSIVE SS
1. Alex Rodriguez, Rangers
2. Omar Vizquel, Indians
3. Derek Jeter, Yankees

BEST INFIELD ARM
1. Alex Rodriguez, Rangers
2. Troy Glaus, Angels
3. Nomar Garciaparra, Red Sox

BEST DEFENSIVE OF
1. Ichiro Suzuki, Mariners
2. Torii Hunter, Twins
3. Mike Cameron, Mariners

BEST OUTFIELD ARM
1. Ichiro Suzuki, Mariners
2. Raul Mondesi, Yankees
3. Torii Hunter, Twins

MOST EXCITING PLAYER
1. Ichiro Suzuki, Mariners
2. Alex Rodriguez, Rangers
3. Alfonso Soriano, Yankees

BEST MANAGER
1. Mike Scioscia, Angels
2. Tony Pena, Royals
3. Bob Melvin, Mariners

beefed up their pitching staff by adding Bartolo Colon in an offseason trade and seemed to have the arms and offense to take the division crown from the Twins. They grabbed the division lead a few different times, including a two-game lead on Sept. 9, but ultimately lost by dropping 10 of their last 15 games to finish four back of the Twins. The collapse cost manager Jerry Manuel his job.

"This wasn't a case of not having talent," said GM Kenny Williams, who traded for Roberto Alomar, Carl Everett, Scott Sullivan and Scott Schoeneweis during the season.

The top performance in Chicago came from an unlikely source, righthander Esteban Loaiza, who was signed as an afterthought free agent heading into spring training. He made a case for the AL Cy Young Award with a 21-9, 2.90 season. A productive offense was led by Frank Thomas, who enjoyed a bounce-back year by hitting 42 home runs; Carlos Lee, who broke out with a team-high 113 RBIs; and the always-steady Magglio Ordoñez, who led the Sox with a .317 average.

Perhaps the biggest surprise of the season, and definitely baseball's biggest story of the first half, was the resurgence of the Royals. No one expected Kansas City to contend in the Central, especially since the team hit the 100-loss mark for the first time in club history in 2002 and trimmed $10 million off the payroll heading into the 2003 campaign.

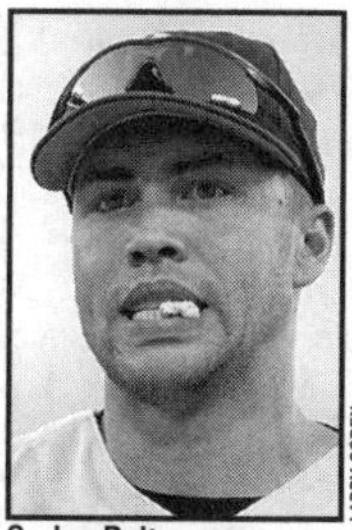

LARRY GOREN

Carlos Beltran

But the Royals led the division for more days than either the Twins or White Sox and finished with 83 wins, a 21-game improvement that ranked as the sixth-best turnaround since 1900. It could have been even greater had injuries and inexperience not derailed their pitching staff down the stretch.

Much of the credit went to manager Tony Pena, who fostered an upbeat environment with a "Believe" mantra that spawned a local marketing scheme. He led the Royals to 16 wins in their first 19 games and the Royals remained in the race until the season's final week. Instead of trading all-star outfielder Carlos Beltran, a free agent after the 2004 season, the club kept him and made trades to strengthen the pitching staff and batting order.

"The team learned that it can win," Pena said. "We learned to have fun and still win. I never doubted that we would compete."

The Blue Jays were another AL success story. They reached 86 wins for the first time since 1998 as GM J.P. Ricciardi's rebuilding process looked ahead of schedule. The team's success was buoyed by righthander Roy Halladay (22-7, 3.25 in a major league-high 266 innings), first baseman Carlos Delgado (.302-42-145, including a four-homer game on Sept. 25) and center fielder Vernon Wells (.317-33-117), who pushed his way into stardom by showing marked improvement for the

AMERICAN LEAGUE DEPARTMENT LEADERS

BATTING

GAMES
Hideki Matsui, Yankees	162
Miguel Tejada, Athletics	162
Aubrey Huff, Devil Rays	162
Carlos Delgado, Blue Jays	161
Alex Rodriguez, Rangers	161
Tony Batista, Orioles	161
Vernon Wells, Blue Jays	161

AT-BATS
Alfonso Soriano, Yankees	682
Ichiro Suzuki, Mariners	679
Vernon Wells, Blue Jays	678
Michael Young, Rangers	666
Nomar Garciaparra, Red Sox	658

RUNS
Alex Rodriguez, Rangers	124
Nomar Garciaparra, Red Sox	120
Vernon Wells, Blue Jays	118
Manny Ramirez, Red Sox	117
Carlos Delgado, Blue Jays	117

HITS
Vernon Wells, Blue Jays	215
Ichiro Suzuki, Mariners	212
Michael Young, Rangers	204
Garret Anderson, Angels	201
Nomar Garciaparra, Red Sox	198
Aubrey Huff, Devil Rays	198
Alfonso Soriano, Yankees	198

TOTAL BASES
Vernon Wells, Blue Jays	373
Alex Rodriguez, Rangers	364
Alfonso Soriano, Yankees	358
Aubrey Huff, Devil Rays	353
Garret Anderson, Angels	345
Nomar Garciaparra, Red Sox	345

EXTRA-BASE HITS
Vernon Wells, Blue Jays	87
Aubrey Huff, Devil Rays	84
Alex Rodriguez, Rangers	83
Garret Anderson, Angels	82
Carlos Delgado, Blue Jays	81

SINGLES
Ichiro Suzuki, Mariners	162
Michael Young, Rangers	148
Carl Crawford, Devil Rays	145
Rocco Baldelli, Devil Rays	135
Vernon Wells, Blue Jays	128

DOUBLES
Garret Anderson, Angels	49
Vernon Wells, Blue Jays	49
Aubrey Huff, Devil Rays	47
Magglio Ordonez, White Sox	46
Bill Mueller, Red Sox	45
Eric Hinske, Blue Jays	45

Vernon Wells: 373 total bases

LARRY GOREN

TRIPLES
Cristian Guzman, Twins	14
Nomar Garciaparra, Red Sox	13
Carlos Beltran, Royals	10
Luis Rivas, Twins	9
Eric Byrnes, Athletics	9
Carl Crawford, Devil Rays	9
Michael Young, Rangers	9

HOME RUNS
Alex Rodriguez, Rangers	47
Frank Thomas, White Sox	42
Carlos Delgado, Blue Jays	42
Jason Giambi, Yankees	41
Rafael Palmeiro, Rangers	38
Alfonso Soriano, Yankees	38

HOME RUN RATIO
(At-Bats per Home Run)

Alex Rodriguez, Rangers	12.9
Frank Thomas, White Sox	13.0
Jason Giambi, Yankees	13.0
Carlos Delgado, Blue Jays	13.5
David Ortiz, Red Sox	14.4

RUNS BATTED IN
Carlos Delgado, Blue Jays	145
Alex Rodriguez, Rangers	118
Bret Boone, Mariners	117
Vernon Wells, Blue Jays	117
Garret Anderson, Angels	116

SACRIFICE BUNTS
Ramon Santiago, Tigers	18
Angel Berroa, Royals	13
Cristian Guzman, Twins	12
David Eckstein, Angels	10
Jerry Hairston, Orioles	10
Luis Matos, Orioles	10

SACRIFICE FLIES
Jeff Conine, Orioles	12
Shannon Stewart, Twins/Blue Jays	11
Raul Ibanez, Royals	10
Todd Walker, Red Sox	10
Nomar Garciaparra, Red Sox	10

HIT BY PITCHES
Jason Giambi, Yankees	21
Reed Johnson, Blue Jays	20
Carlos Delgado, Blue Jays	19
Angel Berroa, Royals	18
Josh Phelps, Blue Jays	17

WALKS
Jason Giambi, Yankees	129
Carlos Delgado, Blue Jays	109
Frank Thomas, White Sox	100
Erubiel Durazo, Athletics	100
Manny Ramirez, Red Sox	97

INTENTIONAL WALKS
Manny Ramirez, Red Sox	28
Carlos Delgado, Blue Jays	23
Aubrey Huff, Devil Rays	17
Dmitri Young, Tigers	16
Erubiel Durazo, Athletics	12
A.J. Pierzynski, Twins	12

STOLEN BASES
Carl Crawford, Devil Rays	55
Alex Sanchez, Tigers	44
Carlos Beltran, Royals	41
Alfonso Soriano, Yankees	35
Ichiro Suzuki, Mariners	34

CAUGHT STEALING
Alex Sanchez, Tigers	18
Michael Tucker, Royals	10
Carl Crawford, Devil Rays	10
Rocco Baldelli, Devil Rays	10
Cristian Guzman, Twins	9
Casey Blake, Indians	9
Adam Kennedy, Angels	9
Coco Crisp, Indians	9

LARRY GOREN

Ichiro Suzuki: 66 multi-hit games

STRIKEOUTS
Jason Giambi, Yankees	140
Carlos Delgado, Blue Jays	137
Mike Cameron, Mariners	137
Dmitri Young, Tigers	130
Alfonso Soriano, Yankees	130

TOUGHEST TO STRIKE OUT
(Plate Appearances per SO)

Todd Walker, Red Sox	11.9
Deivi Cruz, Orioles	11.8
Nomar Garciaparra, Red Sox	11.7
Scott Hatteberg, Athletics	11.7
David Eckstein, Angels	11.4

GROUNDED INTO DOUBLE PLAYS
Paul Konerko, White Sox	28
Hideki Matsui, Yankees	25
Manny Ramirez, Red Sox	22
Bernie Williams, Yankees	21
Vernon Wells, Blue Jays	21

HITTING STREAKS
Nomar Garciaparra, Red Sox	26
Melvin Mora, Orioles	23
Eric Byrnes, Athletics	22
Five tied at	20

MULTIPLE-HIT GAMES
Ichiro Suzuki, Mariners	66
Vernon Wells, Blue Jays	65
Michael Young, Rangers	63
Alfonso Soriano, Yankees	62
Nomar Garciaparra, Red Sox	60

SLUGGING PERCENTAGE
Alex Rodriguez, Rangers	.600
Carlos Delgado, Blue Jays	.593
David Ortiz, Red Sox	.592
Manny Ramirez, Red Sox	.587
Trot Nixon, Red Sox	.578

ON-BASE PERCENTAGE
Manny Ramirez, Red Sox	.427
Carlos Delgado, Blue Jays	.426
Jason Giambi, Yankees	.412
Edgar Martinez, Mariners	.406
Jorge Posada, Yankees	.405

PITCHING

WINS
Roy Halladay, Blue Jays	22

Jamie Moyer, Mariners 21
Andy Pettitte, Yankees 21
Esteban Loaiza, White Sox 21
Roger Clemens, Yankees 17
Mike Mussina, Yankees 17
Derek Lowe, Red Sox 17

LOSSES

Mike Maroth, Tigers 21
Jeremy Bonderman, Tigers 19
Nate Cornejo, Tigers 17
John Lackey, Angels 16
Corey Lidle, Blue Jays 15
Jarrod Washburn, Angels 15

WINNING PERCENTAGE

Pedro Martinez, Red Sox .778
Roy Halladay, Blue Jays .759
Jamie Moyer, Mariners .750
Andy Pettitte, Yankees .724
Derek Lowe, Red Sox .708
Esteban Loaiza, White Sox .700

GAMES

Trever Miller, Blue Jays 79
Jamie Walker, Tigers 78
Jason Grimsley, Royals 76
B.J. Ryan, Orioles 76
LaTroy Hawkins, Twins 74

GAMES STARTED

Roy Halladay, Blue Jays 36
John Thomson, Rangers 35
Barry Zito, Athletics 35
Mark Buehrle, White Sox 35
Esteban Loaiza, White Sox 34
Bartolo Colon, White Sox 34
Tim Hudson, Athletics 34

COMPLETE GAMES

Bartolo Colon, White Sox 9
Roy Halladay, Blue Jays 9
Mark Mulder, Athletics 9
David Wells, Yankees 4
Sidney Ponson, Orioles 4

SHUTOUTS

John Lackey, Angels 2
Roy Halladay, Blue Jays 2
Tim Hudson, Athletics 2
Mark Mulder, Athletics 2
Joel Piniero, Mariners 2

GAMES FINISHED

Keith Foulke, Athletics 67
Mike MacDougal, Royals 61
Eddie Guardado, Twins 60
Mariano Rivera, Yankees 57
Lance Carter, Devil Rays 55

SAVES

Keith Foulke, Athletics 43
Eddie Guardado, Twins 41
Mariano Rivera, Yankees 40
Jorge Julio, Orioles 36
Troy Percival, Angels 33

INNINGS PITCHED

Roy Halladay, Blue Jays 266
Bartolo Colon, White Sox 242
Tim Hudson, Athletics 240
Barry Zito, Athletics 232
Mark Buehrle, White Sox 230

HITS ALLOWED

Roy Halladay, Blue Jays 253
Mark Buehrle, White Sox 250
David Wells, Yankees 242
Brad Radke, Twins 242
Nate Cornejo, Tigers 236

RUNS ALLOWED

Corey Lidle, Blue Jays 133
Mike Maroth, Tigers 131
John Thomson, Rangers 125
Mark Buehrle, White Sox 124
Ramon Ortiz, Angels 121

HOME RUNS ALLOWED

Jarrod Washburn, Angels 34
Ryan Franklin, Mariners 34
Mike Maroth, Tigers 34
Brad Radke, Twins 32

BILL NICHOLS

Keith Foulke: 43 saves

Darrell May, Royals 31
Freddy Garcia, Mariners 31
John Lackey, Angels 31

WALKS

Victor Zambrano, Devil Rays 106
Barry Zito, Athletics 88
Jason Johnson, Orioles 80
Kelvim Escobar, Blue Jays 78
Joel Pineiro, Mariners 76

FEWEST WALKS PER 9 INNINGS

David Wells, Yankees 0.85
Roy Halladay, Blue Jays 1.08
Brad Radke, Twins 1.19
Mike Mussina, Yankees 1.68
Mark Mulder, Athletics 1.93

HIT BATSMEN

Victor Zambrano, Devil Rays 20
Jeremi Gonzalez, Devil Rays 12
Rick Helling, Orioles 12
Ramon Ortiz, Angels 12
Aaron Sele, Angels 12
Tim Wakefield, Red Sox 12
Jake Westbrook, Indians 12

STRIKEOUTS

Esteban Loaiza, White Sox 207
Pedro Martinez, Red Sox 206
Roy Halladay, Blue Jays 204
Mike Mussina, Yankees 195
Roger Clemens, Yankees 190

STRIKEOUTS PER 9 INNINGS

Pedro Martinez, Red Sox 9.93
Esteban Loaiza, White Sox 8.23
Mike Mussina, Yankees 8.18
Roger Clemens, Yankees 8.08
Kelvim Escobar, Blue Jays 7.94

PICKOFFS

Mike Maroth, Tigers 8
Mark Mulder, Athletics 7
Brian Anderson, Indians/Royals 6
Nate Cornejo, Tigers 6
Ryan Franklin, Mariners 6

WILD PITCHES

Victor Zambrano, Devil Rays 15
Jeremy Bonderman, Tigers 12
Freddy Garcia, Mariners 11
John Lackey, Angels 11
Kyle Lohse, Twins 10

BALKS

Kenny Rogers, Twins 4
Ted Lilly, Athletics 4
Bartolo Colon, White Sox 3
Chris George, Royals 3
John Halama, Athletics 3
Victor Zambrano, Devil Rays 3

OPPONENT BATTING AVERAGE

Pedro Martinez, Red Sox .215
Barry Zito, Athletics .219
Tim Hudson, Athletics .223
Esteban Loaiza, White Sox .233
Victor Zambrano, Devil Rays .237

FIELDING

PITCHER

PCT Derek Lowe, Red Sox 1.000
PO Roy Halladay Blue Jays 23
A Tim Hudson, Athletics 54
E Andy Pettitte, Yankees 6
Jason Davis, Indians 6
TC Tim Hudson, Athletics 76
DP Steve Sparks Tigers/Athletics 6

CATCHER

PCT Dan Wilson, Mariners .998
PO Jorge Posada, Yankees 933
A Jorge Posada, Yankees 75
E Three tied at 9
TC Jorge Posada, Yankees 1014
DP Brandon Inge, Tigers 11
PB Doug Mirabelli, Red Sox 14

FIRST BASE

PCT Paul Konerko, White Sox .998
PO Carlos Delgado, Blue Jays 1355
A John Olerud, Mariners 125
E Carlos Pena, Tigers 13
TC Carlos Delgado, Blue Jays 1468
DP Carlos Delgado, Blue Jays 137

SECOND BASE

PCT Adam Kennedy, Angels .990
PO Mark Ellis, Athletics 324
A Orlando Hudson, Blue Jays 477
E Alfonso Soriano, Yankees 19
TC Mark Ellis, Athletics 793
DP Michael Young, Rangers 117

THIRD BASE

PCT Joe Randa, Royals .980
PO Eric Chavez, Athletics 125
A Eric Chavez, Athletics 343
E Eric Hinske, Blue Jays 22
TC Eric Chavez, Athletics 482
DP Tony Batista, Orioles 33
Eric Chavez, Athletics 33

SHORTSTOP

PCT Alex Rodriguez, Rangers .989
PO Angel Berroa, Royals 264
A Miguel Tejada, Athletics 490
E Angel Berroa, Royals 24
TC Angel Berroa, Royals 761
DP Alex Rodriguez, Rangers 111

OUTFIELD

PCT Johnny Damon, Red Sox .997
PO Mike Cameron, Mariners 485
A Rocco Baldelli, Devil Rays 14
E Hideki Matsui, Yankees 8
TC Mike Cameron, Mariners 492
DP Three tied at 4

BILL NICHOLS

Pedro Martinez: 9.93 strikeouts per 9 IP

2003 AMERICAN LEAGUE STATISTICS

CLUB BATTING

	AVG	G	AB	R	H	2B	3B	HR	BB	SO	SB
Boston	.289	162	5769	961	1667	371	40	238	620	943	88
Toronto	.279	162	5661	894	1580	357	33	190	546	1081	37
Minnesota	.277	162	5655	801	1567	318	45	155	512	1027	94
Kansas City	.274	162	5568	836	1526	288	39	162	476	926	120
Seattle	.271	162	5561	795	1509	290	33	139	586	989	108
New York	.271	163	5605	877	1518	304	14	230	684	1042	98
Anaheim	.268	162	5487	736	1473	276	33	150	476	838	129
Baltimore	.268	163	5665	743	1516	277	24	152	431	902	89
Texas	.266	162	5664	826	1506	274	36	239	488	1052	65
Tampa Bay	.265	162	5654	715	1501	298	38	137	420	1030	142
Chicago	.263	162	5487	791	1445	303	19	220	519	916	77
Oakland	.254	162	5497	768	1398	317	24	176	556	898	48
Cleveland	.254	162	5572	699	1413	296	26	158	466	1062	86
Detroit	.240	162	5466	591	1312	201	39	153	443	1099	98

CLUB PITCHING

	ERA	G	CG	SHO	SV	IP	H	R	ER	BB	SO
Oakland	3.63	162	16	14	48	1442	1336	643	582	499	1018
Seattle	3.76	162	8	15	38	1441	1340	637	602	466	1001
New York	4.02	163	8	12	49	1462	1512	716	653	375	1119
Chicago	4.17	162	12	4	36	1431	1364	715	663	518	1056
Cleveland	4.21	162	5	7	34	1459	1477	778	682	501	943
Anaheim	4.27	162	5	9	39	1431	1444	743	680	486	980
Minnesota	4.41	162	7	8	45	1462	1526	758	716	402	997
Boston	4.48	162	5	6	36	1465	1503	809	729	488	1141
Toronto	4.69	162	14	6	36	1435	1560	826	748	485	984
Baltimore	4.76	163	9	3	41	1450	1579	820	767	526	981
Tampa Bay	4.93	162	7	7	30	1437	1454	852	787	639	877
Kansas City	5.05	162	7	10	36	1439	1569	867	808	566	865
Detroit	5.30	162	3	5	27	1439	1616	928	847	557	764
Texas	5.67	162	4	3	43	1433	1625	969	903	603	1009

CLUB FIELDING

	PCT	PO	A	E	DP		PCT	PO	A	E	DP
Seattle	.989	4323	1450	65	159	Anaheim	.982	4294	1517	105	138
Minnesota	.985	4386	1481	87	114	Boston	.982	4394	1679	113	130
Texas	.985	4300	1703	94	168	Kansas City	.982	4316	1704	108	143
Chicago	.984	4293	1588	93	154	New York	.981	4386	1578	114	126
Baltimore	.983	4349	1683	105	164	Toronto	.981	4305	1742	117	161
Oakland	.983	4325	1779	107	145	Cleveland	.980	4378	1780	126	178
Tampa Bay	.983	4310	1580	103	158	Detroit	.978	4316	1813	138	194

INDIVIDUAL BATTING LEADERS

(Minimum 502 Plate Appearances)

	AVG	G	AB	R	H	2B	3B	HR	RBI	BB	SO	SB
Mueller, Bill, Boston	.326	146	524	85	171	45	5	19	85	59	77	1
Ramirez, Manny, Boston	.325	154	569	117	185	36	1	37	104	97	94	3
Jeter, Derek, New York	.342	119	482	87	156	25	3	10	52	43	88	11
Wells, Vernon, Toronto	.317	161	678	118	215	49	5	33	117	42	80	4
Ordonez, Magglio, Chicago	.317	160	606	95	192	46	3	29	99	57	73	9
Anderson, Garret, Anaheim	.315	159	638	80	201	49	4	29	116	31	83	6
Suzuki, Ichiro, Seattle	.312	159	679	111	212	29	8	13	62	36	69	34
Huff, Aubrey, Tampa Bay	.311	162	636	91	198	47	3	34	107	53	80	2
Stewart, Shannon, Minn./Toronto	.307	136	573	90	176	44	2	13	73	52	66	4
Beltran, Carlos, Kansas City	.307	141	521	102	160	14	10	26	100	72	81	41

INDIVIDUAL PITCHING LEADERS

(Minimum 162 Innings)

	W	L	ERA	G	GS	CG	SV	IP	H	R	ER	BB	SO
Martinez, Pedro, Boston	14	4	2.22	29	29	3	0	187	147	52	46	47	206
Hudson, Tim, Oakland	16	7	2.70	34	34	3	0	240	197	84	72	61	162
Loaiza, Esteban, Chicago	21	9	2.90	34	34	1	0	226	196	75	73	56	207
Mulder, Mark, Oakland	15	9	3.13	26	26	9	0	187	180	66	65	40	128
Halladay, Roy, Toronto	22	7	3.25	36	36	9	0	266	253	111	96	32	204
Moyer, Jamie, Seattle	21	7	3.27	33	33	1	0	215	199	83	78	66	129
Zito, Barry, Oakland	14	12	3.30	35	35	4	0	232	186	98	85	88	146
Mussina, Mike, New York	17	8	3.40	31	31	2	0	215	192	86	81	40	195
Franklin, Ryan, Seattle	11	13	3.57	32	32	2	0	212	199	93	84	61	99
Sabathia, C.C., Cleveland	13	9	3.60	30	30	2	0	198	190	85	79	66	141

AWARD WINNERS

Selected by Baseball Writers Association of America

MVP

Player, Team	1st	2nd	3rd	Total
Alex Rodriguez, Texas	6	5	6	242
Carlos Delgado, Toronto	5	8	3	210
Jorge Posada, N.Y.	5	4	4	194
Shannon Stewart, Minn.	3	2	2	140
David Ortiz, Boston	4	3	2	130
Manny Ramirez, Boston	1	3	3	103
Nomar Garciaparra, Bos.	1	2	1	99
Vernon Wells, Toronto	1	0	1	84
Carlos Beltran, K.C.	0	0	1	77
Bret Boone, Seattle	0	0	1	65
Miguel Tejada, Oakland	1	0	1	49
Bill Mueller, Boston	0	0	2	45
Jason Giambi, N.Y.	1	0	0	36
Garret Anderson, Ana.	0	0	0	35
Keith Foulke, Oakland	0	0	1	20
Frank Thomas, Chicago	0	0	0	20
Eric Chavez, Oakland	0	0	0	18
Carlos Lee, Chicago	0	0	0	16
Magglio Ordonez, Chi.	0	0	0	16
Alfonso Soriano, N.Y.	0	0	0	15
Derek Jeter, N.Y.	0	1	0	10
Pedro Martinez, Bos.	0	0	0	7
Ichiro Suzuki, Seattle	0	0	0	6
Esteban Loaiza, Chicago	0	0	0	4
Jason Varitek, Boston	0	0	0	4
Aubrey Huff, Tampa Bay	0	0	0	4
Mariano Rivera, N.Y.	0	0	0	3

CY YOUNG AWARD

Player, Team	1st	2nd	3rd	Total
Roy Halladay, Toronto	26	2	0	136
Esteban Loaiza, Chicago	2	16	5	63
Pedro Martinez, Boston	0	3	11	20
Tim Hudson, Oakland	0	4	3	15
Jamie Moyer, Seattle	0	2	6	12
Andy Pettitte, N.Y.	0	1	1	4
Keith Foulke, Oakland	0	0	1	1
Johan Santana, Minn.	0	0	1	1

ROOKIE OF THE YEAR

Player, Team	1st	2nd	3rd	Total
Angel Berroa, K.C.	12	7	7	88
Hideki Matsui, N.Y.	10	9	7	84
Rocco Baldelli, T.B.	5	5	11	51
Jody Gerut, Cleveland	0	6	2	20
Mark Teixeira, Texas	1	1	1	9

MANAGER OF THE YEAR

Manager, Team	1st	2nd	3rd	Total
Tony Pena, K.C.	24	3	1	130
Ron Gardenhire, Minn.	4	7	3	44
Ken Macha, Oakland	0	7	5	26
Grady Little, Boston	0	4	7	19
Joe Torre, N.Y.	0	2	8	14
Lou Piniella, Tampa Bay	0	4	1	13
Carlos Tosca, Toronto	0	1	0	3
Eric Wedge, Cleveland	0	0	2	2
Alan Trammell, Detroit	0	0	1	1

NOTE: MVP balloting based on 14 points for first-place vote, nine for second, eight for third, etc.; Cy Young Award, Rookie of the Year and Manager of the Year balloting based on five points for first-place vote, three for second and one for third.

GOLD GLOVE AWARDS

Selected by AL managers

C—Bengie Molina, Anaheim. **1B**—John Olerud, Seattle. **2B**—Bret Boone, Seattle. **3B**—Eric Chavez, Oakland. **SS**—Alex Rodriguez, Texas. **OF**—Mike Cameron, Seattle; Torii Hunter, Minnesota; Ichiro Suzuki, Seattle. **P**—Mike Mussina, New York.

SILVER SLUGGER AWARDS

Selected by AL managers, coaches

C—Jorge Posada, New York. **1B**—Carlos Delgado, Toronto. **2B**—Bret Boone, Seattle. **3B**—Bill Mueller, Boston. **SS**—Alex Rodriguez, Texas. **OF**—Vernon Wells, Toronto; Garret Anderson, Anaheim; Manny Ramirez, Boston. **DH**—Edgar Martinez, Seattle.

second straight season.

Shortstop Alex Rodriguez also posted MVP-caliber numbers in Texas, as he hit .298-47-118 and led the AL in homers for a third straight season. But the numbers came for another Rangers outfit heavy on bats but short on arms. The Rangers got encouraging results from a number of young position players including Hank Blalock, Mark Teixeira and Michael Young and got to watch first baseman Rafael Palmiero join the 500-home run club, but posted the worst ERA in the majors at 5.67. As a result, the Rangers finished last in the West for the fourth straight season—Buck Showalter's first year as manager.

Losing Proposition

Losing was the story of the 2003 Tigers. They came within one loss of tying the 1962 Mets' modern-day record of 120 defeats in a season. Detroit did surpass the AL record for losses, topping the Philadelphia A's mark of 117.

It was a long season for a young team whose best and most recognizable player was Dmitri Young (.285-29-87). The team posted losing steaks of one game and 10 games—and every number in between. They had to rally with five wins in their last six contests to finish at 43-119. That was 47 games behind the Twins in the Central and 20 games behind than the Devil Rays, baseball's next-worst team.

Lefthander Mike Maroth went 9-21, 5.73, becoming the first pitcher to lose 20 games since 1980. The team also kept three major league Rule 5 draft picks, as pitchers Chris Spurling, Wil Ledezma and Matt Roney took their lumps with the rest of the staff, which included 20-year-old Jeremy Bonderman (6-19, 5.56) straight from Class A.

"We knew it would be a struggle, but it was a tougher struggle than we thought it would be," Tigers GM Dave Dombrowski said. "And what made it even more difficult was all the attention we drew because of the Mets' record."

The Angels didn't come close to any futility records, but it was still a disappointing season for a club coming off its first World Series victory. A year after the Angels caught all the breaks, Murphy's Law was in full effect in Anaheim. It was almost a complete turnaround from the previous season as the Angels suffered a 22-win dropoff and became the first team since the Marlins' dismantled squad in 1998 to fall below .500 a year after winning it all.

World Series MVP Troy Glaus, the middle-infield combination of David Eckstein and Adam Kennedy, catcher Benji Molina, DH Brad Fullmer and Darin Erstad, the team's emotional heart and soul, all saw time on the disabled list. Not even 2002 World Series hero Francisco Rodriguez was immune. He spent time on the disabled list after a rough start to his season before returning to post strong numbers in his rookie campaign.

"We really didn't play that well in the beginning, and then guys started dropping like flies," lefthander Jarrod Washburn said. "So we weren't able to be the team that we know we're capable of being. I think having won the championship actually makes it easier to deal with this."

The Angels also changed hands during the 2003 season, as the Walt Disney Co. sold the franchise to Arizona businessman Arte Moreno.

AMERICAN LEAGUE DIVISION SERIES

MINNESOTA VS. NEW YORK

COMPOSITE BOX

MINNESOTA

Player, Pos.	AVG	G	AB	R	H	2B	3B	HR	RBI	BB	SO	SB
Torii Hunter, cf	.429	4	14	3	6	0	1	1	2	2	2	0
Shannon Stewart, lf	.400	4	15	0	6	2	0	0	0	2	4	1
Michael Cuddyer, dh	.250	1	4	0	1	0	0	0	1	0	3	0
A.J. Pierzynski, c	.231	4	13	1	3	0	0	1	1	2	0	0
Corey Koskie, 3b	.200	4	15	0	3	1	0	0	0	0	5	0
Cristian Guzman, ss	.154	4	13	1	2	0	0	0	0	1	2	0
Doug Mientkiewicz, 1b	.133	4	15	0	2	0	0	0	0	1	2	0
Jacque Jones, rf	.125	4	16	0	2	0	0	0	0	0	5	0
Matthew LeCroy, dh	.091	3	11	1	1	0	0	0	0	1	4	0
Lew Ford, ph	.000	1	1	0	0	0	0	0	0	0	1	0
Luis Rivas, 2b	.000	4	13	0	0	0	0	0	1	0	4	0
Michael Ryan, ph	.000	1	1	0	0	0	0	0	0	0	1	0
Totals	**.198**	**4**	**131**	**6**	**26**	**3**	**1**	**2**	**5**	**9**	**33**	**1**

Pitcher	W	L	ERA	G	GS	SV	IP	H	R	ER	BB	SO
Eric Milton	0	0	0.00	1	0	0	3	2	0	0	0	2
Rick Reed	0	0	0.00	1	0	0	1	1	0	0	0	0
Juan Rincon	0	0	0.00	3	0	0	2	1	0	0	4	1
Kenny Rogers	0	0	0.00	1	0	0	1	1	0	0	1	3
J.C. Romero	0	0	0.00	3	0	0	3	3	0	0	2	1
Brad Radke	0	1	2.84	1	1	0	6	5	2	2	2	4
Kyle Lohse	0	1	5.40	1	1	0	5	6	3	3	2	5
LaTroy Hawkins	1	0	6.00	3	0	0	3	5	3	2	0	5
Johan Santana	0	1	7.04	2	2	0	8	9	6	6	3	6
Eddie Guardado	0	0	9.00	2	0	1	2	5	2	2	0	2
Totals	**1**	**3**	**3.86**	**4**	**4**	**1**	**35**	**38**	**16**	**15**	**14**	**29**

NEW YORK

Player, Pos.	AVG	G	AB	R	H	2B	3B	HR	RBI	BB	SO	SB
Derek Jeter, ss	.429	4	14	2	6	0	0	1	1	4	2	1
Bernie Williams, cf	.400	4	15	3	6	2	0	0	3	2	2	0
Alfonso Soriano, 2b	.368	4	19	2	7	1	0	0	4	0	6	2
Juan Rivera, rf	.333	4	12	2	4	0	0	0	0	1	0	0
Hideki Matsui, lf	.267	4	15	2	4	1	0	1	3	2	3	0
Jason Giambi, dh	.250	4	16	1	4	2	0	0	2	2	5	0
Aaron Boone, 3b	.200	4	15	1	3	1	0	0	0	0	3	1
Jorge Posada, c	.176	4	17	1	3	1	0	0	0	0	6	0
Nick Johnson, 1b	.077	4	13	2	1	1	0	0	2	3	2	0
Ruben Sierra, ph-rf	.000	1	2	0	0	0	0	0	0	0	0	0
Totals	**.259**	**4**	**138**	**16**	**38**	**9**	**0**	**2**	**16**	**14**	**29**	**4**

Pitcher	W	L	ERA	G	GS	SV	IP	H	R	ER	BB	SO
Felix Heredia	0	0	0.00	1	0	0	2	1	0	0	1	1
Mariano Rivera	0	0	0.00	2	0	2	4	0	0	0	0	4
Gabe White	0	0	0.00	1	0	0	1	1	0	0	0	1

STEVE MOORE

Andy Pettitte: led Yankees in ALDS, ALCS.

Jeff Nelson	0	0	0.00	1	0	0	0	0	0	0	1	0
David Wells	1	0	1.17	1	1	0	8	8	1	1	0	5
Roger Clemens	1	0	1.29	1	1	0	7	5	1	1	1	6
Andy Pettitte	1	0	1.29	1	1	0	7	4	1	1	3	10
Mike Mussina	0	1	3.86	1	1	0	7	7	3	3	3	6
Totals	**3**	**1**	**1.50**	**4**	**4**	**2**	**36**	**26**	**6**	**6**	**9**	**33**

SCORE BY INNINGS

Minnesota	**001 111 200 —6**
New York	**121 600 312 —16**

E—Hawkins (3), Williams, Jeter, Soriano. **DP**—Minnesota 2, New York 2. **LOB**—New York 35, Minnesota 28. **CS**—Koskie. **HBP**—Johnson (by Radke). **IBB**—Rivera (by Santana), Jeter (by Rogers), Williams (by Romero), Pierzynski (by Mussina), Hunter (by Heredia). **WP**—Heredia, Pettitte. **PB**— Pierzynski.

BOSTON VS. OAKLAND

COMPOSITE BOX

BOSTON

Player, Pos.	AVG	G	AB	R	H	2B	3B	HR	RBI	BB	SO	SB
Doug Mirabelli, c	.500	2	4	2	2	1	0	0	0	0	2	0
Johnny Damon, cf	.316	5	19	2	6	2	0	1	3	2	1	2
Todd Walker, 2b-ph	.313	5	16	4	5	0	0	3	4	0	1	0
Nomar Garciaparra, ss	.300	5	20	2	6	1	0	0	0	3	2	0
Jason Varitek, c-ph	.286	5	14	4	4	0	0	2	2	2	2	0
Kevin Millar, 1b	.238	5	21	0	5	0	0	0	0	2	4	0
Trot Nixon, rf-ph	.200	4	10	1	2	0	0	1	2	1	3	0
Manny Ramirez, lf	.200	5	20	2	4	0	0	1	3	3	7	0
Bill Mueller, 3b	.105	5	19	0	2	1	0	0	0	3	4	0
David Ortiz, dh	.095	5	21	0	2	1	0	0	2	2	7	0
Adrian Brown, ph-rf-cf	.000	4	2	0	0	0	0	0	0	0	1	0
Damian Jackson, 2b	000	4	5	0	0	0	0	0	0	0	2	0
Gabe Kapler, ph-rf	.000	4	9	0	0	0	0	0	0	0	3	0
Dave McCarty, ph	.000	1	0	0	0	0	0	0	0	0	0	0
Totals	**.253**	**5**	**180**	**17**	**38**	**6**	**0**	**8**	**16**	**18**	**39**	**2**

Pitcher	W	L	ERA	G	GS	SV	IP	H	R	ER	BB	SO
Alan Embree	0	0	0.00	3	0	0	2	1	0	0	0	0
Mike Timlin	0	0	0.00	3	0	0	4	0	0	0	0	5
Scott Williamson	2	0	0.00	5	0	0	5	2	0	0	3	8
Derek Lowe	0	1	0.93	3	1	1	10	7	2	1	7	6
Tim Wakefield	0	1	3.52	2	1	0	8	6	5	3	3	7
Pedro Martinez	1	0	3.86	2	2	0	14	13	6	6	5	9
John Burkett	0	0	6.75	1	1	0	5	9	4	4	2	1
Byung-Hyun Kim	0	0	13.50	1	0	0	1	0	1	1	1	1
Totals	**3**	**1**	**2.75**	**5**	**5**	**1**	**49**	**38**	**18**	**15**	**21**	**37**

OAKLAND

Player, Pos.	AVG	G	AB	R	H	2B	3B	HR	RBI	BB	SO	SB
Adam Melhuse, c-ph	.600	2	5	1	3	0	1	0	1	0	1	0
Eric Byrnes, ph-lf-cf	.462	5	13	2	6	1	0	0	2	0	5	1
Jose Guillen, lf	.455	4	11	1	5	1	0	0	1	3	2	0
Chris Singleton, cf	.286	2	7	2	2	2	0	0	0	1	1	1
Terrence Long, ph-lf-rf	.250	4	8	0	2	0	0	0	0	1	3	0
Erubiel Durazo, dh	.238	5	21	3	5	2	0	0	3	3	4	0
Jermaine Dye, rf	.231	4	13	2	3	0	0	1	3	0	2	0
Ramon Hernandez, c	.200	4	15	1	3	0	0	0	2	2	1	0
Scott Hatteberg, 1b	.176	5	17	3	3	0	0	0	0	5	3	0
Billy McMillon, ph-lf	.167	3	6	0	1	0	0	0	1	1	1	0
Mark Ellis, 2b	.118	5	17	2	2	0	0	0	0	4	7	0
Miguel Tejada, ss	.087	5	23	0	2	1	0	0	2	0	4	0
Eric Chavez, 3b	.045	5	22	1	1	1	0	0	0	1	3	1
Totals	**.235**	**5**	**178**	**18**	**38**	**8**	**1**	**1**	**15**	**21**	**37**	**2**

Pitcher	W	L	ERA	G	GS	SV	IP	H	R	ER	BB	SO
Chad Bradford	0	0	0.00	4	0	0	4	4	0	0	2	5
Ted Lilly	0	0	0.00	2	1	0	9	2	1	0	2	7
Jim Mecir	0	0	0.00	1	0	0	1	1	0	0	1	0
Barry Zito	1	1	3.46	2	2	0	13	9	5	5	4	13
Tim Hudson	0	0	3.52	2	2	0	8	10	3	3	1	6
Keith Foulke	0	1	3.60	3	0	0	5	4	2	2	2	3
Ricardo Rincon	0	0	4.50	3	0	0	4	4	2	2	1	3
Steve Sparks	0	0	4.50	1	0	0	4	2	2	2	3	1
Rich Harden	1	1	13.50	2	0	0	1	2	2	2	2	1
Totals	**2**	**3**	**2.98**	**5**	**5**	**0**	**49**	**38**	**17**	**16**	**18**	**39**

SCORE BY INNINGS

Boston	**113 015 220 020—17**
Oakland	**063 105 011 001—18**

E—Walker (3), Chavez (2), Tejada, Hernandez, Lowe, Garciaparra, Ellis, Martinez. **DP**—Oakland 4, Boston 2. **LOB**—Oakland 40, Boston 38. **CS**—Hatteberg. **HBP**—Singleton (by Kim), Dye (by Wakefield), Ellis (by Wakefield), Damon (by Lilly), Hernandez (by Martinez), Walker (by Zito).. **IBB**— Chavez (by Lowe), Ortiz (by Bradford), Ramirez (by Mecir), Varitek (by Bradford), Garciaparra (by Foulke), Mueller (by Harden), Long (by Lowe). **WP**— Harden. **PB**— Mirabelli.

CHAMPIONSHIP SERIES

BOSTON VS. NEW YORK

COMPOSITE BOX

BOSTON

Player, Pos.	AVG	G	AB	R	H	2B	3B	HR	RBI	BB	SO	SB
Todd Walker, 2b-ph	.370	7	27	5	10	1	1	2	2	1	2	0
Trot Nixon, rf	.333	7	24	3	8	1	0	3	5	3	7	1
Damian Jackson, 2b	.333	5	3	0	1	0	0	0	1	0	1	0
Manny Ramirez, lf	.310	7	29	6	9	1	0	2	4	1	4	0
Jason Varitek, c-ph	.300	6	20	4	6	2	0	2	3	1	5	0
Doug Mirabelli, c	.286	3	7	0	2	0	0	0	0	0	2	0
David Ortiz, dh	.269	7	26	4	7	1	0	2	6	3	8	0
Nomar Garciaparra, ss	.241	7	29	2	7	0	1	0	1	2	8	0
Kevin Millar, 1b	.241	7	29	3	7	0	0	1	3	1	9	0
Bill Mueller, 3b	.222	7	27	1	6	2	0	0	0	2	7	0
Johnny Damon, cf	.200	5	20	1	4	1	0	0	1	3	3	1
Gabe Kapler, cf-dh	.125	3	8	0	1	0	0	0	0	0	3	0
Dave McCarty, ph	.000	1	1	0	0	0	0	0	0	0	1	0
Totals	**.272**	**7**	**250**	**29**	**68**	**9**	**2**	**12**	**26**	**17**	**60**	**2**

Pitcher	W	L	ERA	G	GS	SV	IP	H	R	ER	BB	SO
Mike Timlin	0	0	0.00	5	0	0	5	1	0	0	2	6
Alan Embree	1	0	0.00	5	0	0	5	3	0	0	0	1
Todd Jones	0	0	0.00	1	0	0	0	1	0	0	1	1
Scott Sauerbeck	0	0	0.00	1	0	0	0	1	0	0	1	0
Tim Wakefield	2	1	2.57	3	2	0	14	8	4	4	6	10
Bronson Arroyo	0	0	2.70	3	0	0	3	2	1	1	2	5
Scott Williamson	0	0	3.00	3	0	3	3	1	1	1	0	6
Pedro Martinez	0	1	5.65	2	2	0	14	16	9	9	2	14
Derek Lowe	0	2	6.43	2	2	0	14	14	10	10	7	5
John Burkett	0	0	7.36	1	1	0	4	7	5	3	0	1
Totals	**3**	**4**	**4.00**	**7**	**7**	**3**	**63**	**54**	**30**	**28**	**21**	**49**

NEW YORK

Player, Pos.	AVG	G	AB	R	H	2B	3B	HR	RBI	BB	SO	SB
Ruben Sierra, ph-rf	.500	3	2	1	1	0	0	1	1	1	0	0
David Dellucci, dh-rf	.333	3	3	2	1	0	0	0	0	0	1	1
Hideki Matsui, lf	.308	7	26	3	8	3	0	0	4	1	3	0
Jorge Posada, c	.296	7	27	5	8	4	0	1	6	3	4	0
Karim Garcia, rf	.250	5	16	1	4	0	0	0	3	2	4	0
Derek Jeter, ss	.233	7	30	3	7	2	0	1	2	2	4	1
Jason Giambi, dh	.231	7	26	4	6	0	0	3	3	4	7	0
Nick Johnson, 1b	.231	7	26	4	6	1	0	1	3	2	4	0
Bernie Williams, cf	.192	7	26	5	5	1	0	0	2	4	3	0
Aaron Boone, 3b-ph	.176	7	17	2	3	0	0	1	2	1	6	1
Enrique Wilson, 3b	.143	2	7	0	1	0	0	0	0	0	1	0
Alfonso Soriano, 2b	.133	7	30	0	4	1	0	0	3	1	11	2
Juan Rivera, rf	.000	2	2	0	0	0	0	0	0	0	1	0
Totals	**.227**	**7**	**238**	**30**	**54**	**12**	**0**	**8**	**29**	**21**	**49**	**5**

Pitcher	W	L	ERA	G	GS	SV	IP	H	R	ER	BB	SO
Mariano Rivera	1	0	1.13	4	0	2	8	5	1	1	0	6
David Wells	1	0	2.35	2	1	0	8	5	2	2	2	5
Felix Heredia	0	0	3.38	5	0	0	3	0	1	1	3	3
Mike Mussina	0	2	4.11	3	2	0	15	16	7	7	4	17
Gabe White	0	0	4.50	2	0	0	2	4	1	1	0	1
Andy Pettitte	1	0	4.63	2	2	0	12	17	6	6	4	10
Roger Clemens	1	0	5.00	2	2	0	9	11	6	5	2	8
Jose Contreras	0	1	5.79	4	0	0	5	6	3	3	2	7
Jeff Nelson	0	0	6.00	4	0	0	3	4	2	2	0	3
Totals	**4**	**3**	**3.94**	**7**	**7**	**2**	**64**	**68**	**29**	**28**	**17**	**60**

SCORE BY INNINGS

Boston	**244 531 622 00—29**
New York	**162 640 541 01—30**

E— Boone (2), Jackson, Soriano, Millar, Garciaparra, Matsui, Wilson. **DP**—New York 12, Boston 5. **LOB**—Boston 46, New York 45. **CS**— Nixon (2), Ramirez, Kapler, Jackson, Boone. **HBP**—Ortiz (by Nelson), Boone (by Lowe), Soriano (by Arroyo), Garcia (by Martinez), Delucci (by Wakefield), Walker (by Heredia), Nixon (by Wells). **IBB**— Mueller (by Mussina), Johnson (by Lowe), Varitek (by Heredia), Sierra (by Timlin). **WP**—- Contreras(2), Heredia. **PB**— Varitek (2), Mirabelli.

NATIONAL LEAGUE

BY CHRIS KLINE

The Florida Marlins won the 2003 National League Championship Series in seven games, but all Chicago fans are ever likely to remember was Game Six.

Leading the series 3-2, the Cubs were just five outs away from claiming their first World Series berth in 58 years, but suddenly the wheels came off in a hurry. Eight-run eighth innings will do that.

Chicago had its best pitcher in Mark Prior on the mound with one out in the eighth and a three-run lead. Florida center fielder Juan Pierre then doubled, and Luis Castillo got new life on a foul ball that was knocked away from Cubs outfielder Moises Alou by a fan. Castillo eventually walked and Ivan Rodriguez singled in the Marlins' first run to make it 3-1.

MORRIS FOSTOFF

World Series bound
The Marlins defeated the Cubs in the NLCS after trailing three games to one

Cubs shortstop Alex Gonzalez booted a routine grounder by rookie sensation Miguel Cabrera that potentially could have been an inning-ending double play. From there, the floodgates opened. Derrek Lee doubled in a pair of runs to knot the game at 3-3. Prior's night was over and the momentum had quickly shifted to Florida.

"We thought we had a ground-ball double play, because Gonzo . . . he has only made 10 errors all year," Cubs manager Dusty Baker said. "That's the stunning part, because he doesn't miss anything. And then after that we couldn't stop the bleeding. They just started hitting the ball all over."

Said Gonzalez of the error: "I was trying to get an out there and the ball ate me up. I didn't expect it to get there that fast. It was an unfortunate inning."

Dusty Baker

Florida went on to rack up five more runs in the frame, and while Chicago fans hung their hopes on righthander Kerry Wood in Game Seven, destiny was with the Marlins, who outslugged the Cubs 9-6 in the deciding game.

Florida was on the way to its second World Series title in 10 years of existence, while the Cubs were left shaking their heads. Chicago became the fourth team in history to lose a League Championship Series after leading 3-1.

Almost overnight, the Marlins put together what became one of the most exciting teams in baseball, made up of homegrown talent, players acquired in astute trades, free-agent acquisitions and 72-year-old manager Jack McKeon.

McKeon, who took over after manager Jeff Torborg was fired in early May, led the Marlins to the wild card after holding off the lethargic Phillies down the stretch.

"I'm a seasoned citizen, in years and baseball experience," McKeon said after he was hired by Marlins owner Jeffrey Loria. "But I'm not a miracle worker. We've got a lot of work to do. Hopefully we can take this club to another level."

The Marlins had already lost pitchers A.J. Burnett, Josh Beckett, Mark Redman and Michael Tejera to injury when McKeon took over, but both Beckett and Redman were healthy and key players for Florida's NLCS run.

So was McKeon's demeanor and ability to get his players to believe in themselves; that and some of his unorthodox moves. No move seemed stranger when he named Carl Pavano, who had five relief appearances but no starts in the postseason, his Game Six starter in the LCS. But that move, like the later decision to start Beckett on short rest in Game Six of the World Series, worked out.

McKeon became the 12th manager to step in at midseason and take a team to the playoffs. The last manager to accomplish the feat was Bill Russell, who took over Tommy Lasorda's Dodgers in 1996.

"I've enjoyed it immensely," McKeon said. "It's probably the most enjoyable year I've had. We have a great bunch of players who have dedicated themselves to winning and are unselfish and fun to be around."

The series brought back shades of the 1992 NLCS, when the Braves had an eight-run eighth inning in Game Six against the Pirates and went on to win Game Seven.

Braves Falter Again

The Braves' formula for success went through a major alteration in 2003, but the end result was still the same: the team won its ninth consecutive NL East title.

The means is what changed for Atlanta, which saw veteran lefthander Tom Glavine leave via free agency and righthander Kevin Millwood depart in a controversial trade. The Braves put an emphasis on hitting in 2003 and bashed their way through the season, blasting an NL-best 235 home runs.

Another troubling part of the end result also remained the same: The Braves couldn't get past two of the top

NATIONAL LEAGUE CHAMPIONS, 1901-2003

NO-DIVISION FORMAT

	PENNANT	PCT	GA
1901	Pittsburgh	.647	1½
1902	Pittsburgh	.741	27½
1903	Pittsburgh	.650	6½
1904	New York	.693	13
1905	New York	.686	9
1906	Chicago	.763	20
1907	Chicago	.704	17
1908	Chicago	.643	1
1909	Pittsburgh	.724	6½
1910	Chicago	.675	13
1911	New York	.647	7½
1912	New York	.682	10
1913	New York	.664	12½
1914	Boston	.614	10½
1915	Philadelphia	.592	7
1916	Brooklyn	.610	2½
1917	New York	.636	10
1918	Chicago	.651	10½
1919	Cincinnati	.686	9
1920	Brooklyn	.604	7
1921	New York	.614	4
1922	New York	.604	7
1923	New York	.621	4½
1924	New York	.608	1½
1925	Pittsburgh	.621	8½
1926	St. Louis	.578	2
1927	Pittsburgh	.610	1½
1928	St. Louis	.617	2
1929	Chicago	.645	10½
1930	St. Louis	.597	2
1931	St. Louis	.656	13
1932	Chicago	.584	4
1933	New York	.599	5
1934	St. Louis	.621	2
1935	Chicago	.649	4
1936	New York	.597	5
1937	New York	.625	3
1938	Chicago	.586	2
1939	Cincinnati	.630	4½
1940	Cincinnati	.654	12
1941	Brooklyn	.649	2½
1942	St. Louis	.688	2
1943	St. Louis	.682	18
1944	St. Louis	.682	14½
1945	Chicago	.636	3
1946	St. Louis	.628	2
1947	Brooklyn	.610	5
1948	Boston	.595	6½
1949	Brooklyn	.630	1
1950	Philadelphia	.591	2
1951	New York	.624	1
1952	Brooklyn	.627	4½
1953	Brooklyn	.682	13
1954	New York	.630	5
1955	Brooklyn	.641	13½
1956	Brooklyn	.604	1
1957	Milwaukee	.617	8
1958	Milwaukee	.597	8
1959	Los Angeles	.564	2
1960	Pittsburgh	.617	7
1961	Cincinnati	.604	4
1962	San Francisco	.624	1
1963	Los Angeles	.611	6
1964	St. Louis	.574	1
1965	Los Angeles	.599	2
1966	Los Angeles	.586	1½
1967	St. Louis	.627	10½
1968	St. Louis	.599	9

TWO-DIVISION FORMAT

	EAST	PCT	GA	WEST	PCT	GA	PENNANT		MVP
1969	New York	.617	8	Atlanta	.574	3	New York	3-0	Willie McCovey, 1b, San Francisco
1970	Pittsburgh	.549	5	Cincinnati	.630	14½	Cincinnati	3-0	Johnny Bench, c, Cincinnati
1971	Pittsburgh	.599	7	San Francisco	.556	1	Pittsburgh	3-1	Joe Torre, 3b, St. Louis
1972	Pittsburgh	.619	11	Cincinnati	.617	10½	Cincinnati	3-2	Johnny Bench, c, Cincinnati
1973	New York	.509	1½	Cincinnati	.611	3½	New York	3-2	Pete Rose, of, Cincinnati
1974	Pittsburgh	.543	1½	Los Angeles	.630	4	Los Angeles	3-1	Steve Garvey, 1b, Los Angeles
1975	Pittsburgh	.571	6½	Cincinnati	.667	20	Cincinnati	3-0	Joe Morgan, 2b, Cincinnati
1976	Philadelphia	.623	9	Cincinnati	.630	10	Cincinnati	3-0	Joe Morgan, 2b, Cincinnati
1977	Philadelphia	.623	5	Los Angeles	.605	10	Los Angeles	3-1	George Foster, of, Cincinnati
1978	Philadelphia	.556	1½	Los Angeles	.586	2½	Los Angeles	3-1	Dave Parker, of, Pittsburgh
1979	Pittsburgh	.605	2	Cincinnati	.559	1½	Pittsburgh	3-0	Hernandez, St. Louis; Stargell, Pittsburgh
1980	Philadelphia	.562	1	Houston	.571	1	Philadelphia	3-2	Mike Schmidt, 3b, Philadelphia
1981	Montreal*	.566	½	Los Angeles**	.632	½	Los Angeles	3-2	Mike Schmidt, 3b, Philadelphia
	Philadelphia	.618	1½	Houston	.623	1			
1982	St. Louis	.568	3	Atlanta	.549	1	St. Louis	3-0	Dale Murphy, of, Atlanta
1983	Philadelphia	.556	6	Los Angeles	.562	3	Philadelphia	3-1	Dale Murphy, of, Atlanta
1984	Chicago	.596	6½	San Diego	.568	12	San Diego	3-2	Ryne Sandberg, 2b, Chicago
1985	St. Louis	.623	3	Los Angeles	.586	5½	St. Louis	4-2	Willie McGee, of, St. Louis
1986	New York	.667	21½	Houston	.593	10	New York	4-2	Mike Schmidt, 3b, Philadelphia
1987	St. Louis	.586	3	San Francisco	.556	6	St. Louis	4-3	Andre Dawson, of, Chicago
1988	New York	.625	15	Los Angeles	.584	7	Los Angeles	4-3	Kirk Gibson, of, Los Angeles
1989	Chicago	.571	6	San Francisco	.568	3	San Francisco	4-1	Kevin Mitchell, of, San Francisco
1990	Pittsburgh	.586	4	Cincinnati	.562	5	Cincinnati	4-2	Barry Bonds, of, Pittsburgh
1991	Pittsburgh	.605	14	Atlanta	.580	1	Atlanta	4-3	Terry Pendleton, 3b, Atlanta
1992	Pittsburgh	.593	9	Atlanta	.605	8	Atlanta	4-3	Barry Bonds, of, Pittsburgh
1993	Philadelphia	.599	3	Atlanta	.642	1	Philadelphia	4-2	Barry Bonds, of, San Francisco

* Won second half; defeated Philadelphia 3-2 in best-of-5 playoff.
** Won first half; defeated Houston 3-2 in best-of-5 playoff.

THREE-DIVISION FORMAT/WILD CARD

	EAST	PCT	GA	CENTRAL	PCT	GA	WEST	PCT	GA	WILD CARD	PCT
1994	Montreal	.649	6	Cincinnati	.593	½	Los Angeles	.509	3½	None	
	PENNANT: None (season incomplete)						**MVP:** Jeff Bagwell, 1b, Houston				
1995	Atlanta	.625	21	Cincinnati	.590	9	Los Angeles	.542	1	Colorado (West)	.535
	PENNANT: Atlanta def. Cincinnati, 4-2						**MVP:** Barry Larkin, ss, Cincinnati				
1996	Atlanta	.593	8	St. Louis	.543	6	San Diego	.562	1	Los Angeles (West)	.556
	PENNANT: Atlanta def. St. Louis 4-3						**MVP:** Ken Caminiti, 3b, Houston				
1997	Atlanta	.623	9	Houston	.519	5	San Francisco	.556	2	Florida (East)	.568
	PENNANT: Florida def. Atlanta 4-2						**MVP:** Larry Walker, of, Colorado				
1998	Atlanta	.654	18	Houston	.630	12½	San Diego	.605	9½	Chicago (Central)	.552
	PENNANT: San Diego def. Atlanta 4-2						**MVP:** Sammy Sosa, of, Chicago				
1999	Atlanta	.636	6½	Houston	.599	1½	Arizona	.617	14	New York (East)	.595
	PENNANT: Atlanta def. New York 4-2						**MVP:** Chipper Jones, 3b, Atlanta				
2000	Atlanta	.586	½	St. Louis	.586	10	San Francisco	.599	11	New York (East)	.580
	PENNANT: New York def. St. Louis 4-1						**MVP:** Jeff Kent, 2b, San Francisco				
2001	Atlanta	543	2	Houston	574	—	Arizona	.568	2	St. Louis (Central)	.574
	PENNANT: Arizona def. Atlanta 4-1						**MVP:** Barry Bonds, of, San Francisco				
2002	Atlanta	.631	19	St. Louis	.599	13	Arizona	.605	2½	San Francisco (West)	.590
	PENNANT: San Francisco def. St. Louis 4-1						**MVP:** Barry Bonds, of, San Francisco				
2003	Atlanta	.623	10	Chicago	.543	1	San Francisco	.621	15½	Florida (East)	.562
	PENNANT: Florida def. Chicago 4-3						**MVP:** Barry Bonds, of, San Francisco				

STANDINGS

Page	EAST	W	L	PCT	GB	Manager(s)	General Manager(s)	Attend.	Avg.	Last Penn.
70	Atlanta Braves	101	61	.623	—	Bobby Cox	John Schuerholz	2,401,084	30,643	1999
137	*Florida Marlins	91	71	.562	10	J. Torborg/J. McKeon	Larry Beinfest	1,302,714	16,083	2003
209	Philadelphia Phillies	86	76	.531	15	Larry Bowa	Ed Wade	2,259,943	27,901	1993
179	Montreal Expos	83	79	.512	18	Frank Robinson	Omar Minaya	1,025,639	12,662	None
194	New York Mets	66	95	.410	34½	Art Howe	S. Phillips/J. Duquette	2,172,771	27,160	2000
Page	**CENTRAL**	**W**	**L**	**PCT**	**GB**	**Manager**	**General Manager**	**Attend.**	**Avg.**	**Last Penn.**
100	Chicago Cubs	88	74	.543	—	Dusty Baker	Jim Hendry	2,952,620	36,452	1945
144	Houston Astros	87	75	.537	1	Jimy Williams	Gerry Hunsicker	2,455,239	30,312	None
223	St. Louis Cardinals	85	77	.525	3	Tony LaRussa	Walt Jocketty	2,910,386	35,931	1987
216	Pittsburgh Pirates	75	87	.463	13	Lloyd McClendon	Dave Littlefield	1,636,752	20,207	1979
107	Cincinnati Reds	69	93	.426	19	B. Boone/D. Miley	J. Bowden	2,355,266	29,077	1990
165	Milwaukee Brewers	68	94	.420	20	Ned Yost	Doug Melvin	1,700,354	20,992	None
Page	**WEST**	**W**	**L**	**PCT**	**GB**	**Manager**	**General Manager**	**Attend.**	**Avg.**	**Last Penn.**
238	San Francisco Giants	100	61	.621	—	Felipe Alou	Brian Sabean	3,264,888	40,307	2002
158	Los Angeles Dodgers	85	77	.525	15½	Jim Tracy	Dan Evans	3,138,626	38,748	1988
63	Arizona Diamondbacks	84	78	.519	16½	Bob Brenly	Joe Garagiola Jr.	2,808,492	34,673	2001
123	Colorado Rockies	74	88	.457	26½	Clint Hurdle	Dan O'Dowd	2,335,424	28,832	None
231	San Diego Padres	64	98	.395	36½	Bruce Bochy	Kevin Towers	2,030,083	25,063	1998

*Won wild-card playoff berth

NOTE: Team's individual batting, pitching and fielding statistics can be found on page indicated in lefthand column.

starters in the game in the Cubs' Prior and Kerry Wood. The Braves bowed out in the first round for the second straight season, losing three games to two.

Wood shut down the Braves bats in a 5-1 clinching victory in Game Five, and Bobby Cox' club faced yet another postseason meltdown.

"We just didn't make any adjustments," closer John Smoltz said. "They pitched the same way the whole series. But they dominated. It's not like they were throwing slop up there."

The powerful Braves lineup managed just 15 runs in the five-game series against the Cubs, as they were eliminated on their home field for the sixth time in the last seven seasons.

"I'm tired of talking about it, but that's what happened," Smoltz said. "I'm man enough to say we got beat, but I don't like it."

The Braves' pitching staff put them in an unfamiliar position heading into the playoffs: win without their regular bounty of quality starters in a short series and rely on outslugging their opponent. Behind 21-game winner Russ Ortiz, the rest of the staff was shaky at times. Righthander Greg Maddux, (16-11, 3.96) was a shadow of his former self, while Mike Hampton (14-8, 3.84) and Shane Reynolds (11-9, 5.43) also weren't what they once were. Rookie Horacio Ramirez (12-4, 4.00) was a nice addition, but was not used in the postseason.

The Atlanta front office did not make any moves to bolster the pitching staff at the trade deadline, but instead settled for what they had and it eventually came back to haunt them.

"I was disappointed, I really was," said GM John Schuerholz after the deadline passed. "We were very aggressive, as aggressive as we've ever been. There was no complacency at all. We tried everything we could to make our team stronger."

The Braves finished the regular season with a 4.10 ERA, ranking ninth in the National League and 12th overall.

JOHN WILLIAMSON

Another postseason disappointment
John Smoltz and the Braves fell in the first round

Giant Disappointment

By the July 31 trade deadline, the Giants seemed poised to defend their NL title. Giants GM Brian Sabean obtained Orioles righthander Sidney Ponson, regarded as the best pitcher available.

The Giants paid top dollar for the 14-game winner, giving up lefthander Damian Moss, promising young righthander Kurt Ainsworth and lefty prospect Ryan Hannaman.

"You have to trade quality to get quality," Sabean said. "We accomplished what we needed to do, which was bring a prize starter and hopefully get some more innings out of a starter than we were getting."

While the Giants got 68 innings in 10 starts from Ponson, the 26-year-old righthander finished just 3-6, 3.71 for San Francisco. In fact, along with ace Jason Schmidt, two rookies helped to carry the rest of the staff to win the not-so-wild West.

Jerome Williams (7-5, 3.30) and Jesse Foppert (8-9, 5.03) showed flashes of brilliance in 2003, with Williams taking center stage. The Hawaiian native finished with 21 starts and two complete games. Foppert looked like he was living up to his minor league promise, but he was sidelined by injuries and eventually succumbed to Tommy John surgery and was expected to miss the 2004 season.

NL YEAR-BY-YEAR BATTING LEADERS

SINCE 1925

Year	Batting Average		Home Runs		RBIs	
1925	Rogers Hornsby, St. Louis	.403	Rogers Hornsby, St. Louis	39	Rogers Hornsby, St. Louis	143
1926	Bubbles Hargrave, Cincinnati	.353	Hack Wilson, Chicago	21	Jim Bottomley, St. Louis	120
1927	Paul Waner, Pittsburgh	.380	Two tied at	30	Paul Waner, Pittsburgh	131
1928	Rogers Hornsby, St. Louis	.370	Two tied at	31	Jim Bottomley, St. Louis	136
1929	Lefty O'Doul, Philadelphia	.398	Chuck Klein, Philadelphia	43	Hack Wilson, Chicago	159
1930	Bill Terry, New York	.401	Hack Wilson, Chicago	56	Hack Wilson, Chicago	190
1931	Chick Hafey, St. Louis	.349	Chuck Klein, Philadelphia	31	Chuck Klein, Philadelphia	121
1932	Lefty O'Doul, Brooklyn	.368	Two tied at	38	Frank Hurst, Philadelphia	143
1933	Chuck Klein, Philadelphia	.368	Chuck Klein, Philadelphia	28	Chuck Klein, Philadelphia	120
1934	Paul Waner, Pittsburgh	.362	Two tied at	35	Mel Ott, New York	135
1935	Arky Vaughan, Pittsburgh	.385	Wally Berger, Boston	34	Wally Berger, Boston	130
1936	Paul Waner, Pittsburgh	.373	Mel Ott, New York	33	Joe Medwick, St. Louis	138
1937	Joe Medwick, St. Louis	.374	Two tied at	31	Joe Medwick, St. Louis	154
1938	Ernie Lombardi, Cincinnati	.342	Mel Ott, New York	36	Joe Medwick, St. Louis	122
1939	Johnny Mize, St. Louis	.349	Johnny Mize, St. Louis	28	Frank McCormick, Cincinnati	128
1940	Debs Garms, Pittsburgh	.355	Johnny Mize, St. Louis	43	Johnny Mize, St. Louis	137
1941	Pete Reiser, Brooklyn	.343	Dolf Camilli, Brooklyn	34	Dolf Camilli, Brooklyn	120
1942	Ernie Lombardi, Boston	.330	Mel Ott, New York	30	Johnny Mize, New York	110
1943	Stan Musial, St. Louis	.357	Bill Nicholson, Chicago	29	Bill Nicholson, Chicago	128
1944	Dixie Walker, Brooklyn	.357	Bill Nicholson, Chicago	33	Bill Nicholson, Chicago	122
1945	Phil Cavarretta, Chicago	.355	Tommy Holmes, Boston	28	Dixie Walker, Brooklyn	124
1946	Stan Musial, St. Louis	.365	Ralph Kiner, Pittsburgh	23	Enos Slaughter, St. Louis	130
1947	Harry Walker, St.Louis-Philadelphia	.363	Two tied at	51	Johnny Mize, New York	138
1948	Stan Musial, St. Louis	.376	Two tied at	40	Stan Musial, St. Louis	131
1949	Jackie Robinson, Brooklyn	.342	Ralph Kiner, Pittsburgh	54	Ralph Kiner, Pittsburgh	127
1950	Stan Musial, St. Louis	.346	Ralph Kiner, Pittsburgh	47	Del Ennis, Philadelphia	126
1951	Stan Musial, St. Louis	.355	Ralph Kiner, Pittsburgh	42	Monte Irvin, New York	121
1952	Stan Musial, St. Louis	.336	Two tied at	37	Hank Sauer, Chicago	121
1953	Carl Furillo, Brooklyn	.344	Eddie Mathews, Milwaukee	47	Roy Campanella, Brooklyn	142
1954	Willie Mays, New York	.345	Ted Kluszewski, Cincinnati	49	Ted Kluszewski, Cincinnati	141
1955	Richie Ashburn, Philadelphia	.338	Willie Mays, New York	51	Duke Snider, Brooklyn	136
1956	Hank Aaron, Milwaukee	.328	Duke Snider, Brooklyn	43	Stan Musial, St. Louis	109
1957	Stan Musial, St. Louis	.351	Hank Aaron, Milwaukee	44	Hank Aaron, Milwaukee	132
1958	Richie Ashburn, Philadelphia	.350	Ernie Banks, Chicago	47	Ernie Banks, Chicago	129
1959	Hank Aaron, Milwaukee	.355	Eddie Mathews, Milwaukee	46	Ernie Banks, Chicago	143
1960	Dick Groat, Pittsburgh	.325	Ernie Banks, Chicago	41	Hank Aaron, Milwaukee	126
1961	Roberto Clemente, Pittsburgh	.351	Orlando Cepeda, San Francisco	46	Orlando Cepeda, San Francisco	142
1962	Tommy Davis, Los Angeles	.346	Willie Mays, San Francisco	49	Tommy Davis, Los Angeles	153
1963	Tommy Davis, Los Angeles	.326	Two tied at	44	Hank Aaron, Milwaukee	130
1964	Roberto Clemente, Pittsburgh	.339	Willie Mays, San Francisco	47	Ken Boyer, St. Louis	119
1965	Roberto Clemente, Pittsburgh	.329	Willie Mays, San Francisco	52	Deron Johnson, Cincinnati	130
1966	Matty Alou, Pittsburgh	.342	Hank Aaron, Atlanta	44	Hank Aaron, Atlanta	127
1967	Roberto Clemente, Pittsburgh	.357	Hank Aaron, Atlanta	39	Orlando Cepeda, San Francisco	111
1968	Pete Rose, Cincinnati	.335	Willie McCovey, San Francisco	36	Willie McCovey, San Francisco	105
1969	Pete Rose, Cincinnati	.348	Willie McCovey, San Francisco	45	Willie McCovey, San Francisco	126
1970	Rico Carty, Atlanta	.366	Johnny Bench, Cincinnati	45	Johnny Bench, Cincinnati	148
1971	Joe Torre, St. Louis	.363	Willie Stargell, Pittsburgh	48	Joe Torre, St. Louis	137
1972	Billy Williams, Chicago	.333	Johnny Bench, Cincinnati	40	Johnny Bench, Cincinnati	125
1973	Pete Rose, Cincinnati	.338	Willie Stargell, Pittsburgh	44	Willie Stargell, Pittsburgh	119
1974	Ralph Garr, Atlanta	.353	Mike Schmidt, Philadelphia	36	Johnny Bench, Cincinnati	129
1975	Bill Madlock, Chicago	.354	Mike Schmidt, Philadelphia	38	Greg Luzinski, Philadelphia	120
1976	Bill Madlock, Chicago	.339	Mike Schmidt, Philadelphia	38	George Foster, Cincinnati	121
1977	Dave Parker, Pittsburgh	.338	George Foster, Cincinnati	52	George Foster, Cincinnati	149
1978	Dave Parker, Pittsburgh	.334	George Foster, Cincinnati	40	George Foster, Cincinnati	120
1979	Keith Hernandez, St. Louis	.344	Dave Kingman, Chicago	48	Dave Winfield, San Diego	118
1980	Bill Buckner, Chicago	.324	Mike Schmidt, Philadelphia	48	Mike Schmidt, Philadelphia	121
1981	Bill Madlock, Pittsburgh	.341	Mike Schmidt, Philadelphia	31	Mike Schmidt, Philadelphia	91
1982	Al Oliver, Montreal	.331	Dave Kingman, New York	37	Two tied at	109
1983	Bill Madlock, Pittsburgh	.323	Mike Schmidt, Philadelphia	40	Dale Murphy, Atlanta	121
1984	Tony Gwynn, San Diego	.351	Two tied at	36	Two tied at	106
1985	Willie McGee, St. Louis	.353	Dale Murphy, Atlanta	37	Dave Parker, Cincinnati	125
1986	Tim Raines, Montreal	.334	Mike Schmidt, Philadelphia	37	Mike Schmidt, Philadelphia	119
1987	Tony Gwynn, San Diego	.370	Andre Dawson, Chicago	49	Andre Dawson, Chicago	137
1988	Tony Gwynn, San Diego	.313	Darryl Strawberry, New York	39	Will Clark, San Francisco	109
1989	Tony Gwynn, San Diego	.336	Kevin Mitchell, San Francisco	47	Kevin Mitchell, San Francisco	125
1990	Willie McGee, St. Louis	.335	Ryne Sandberg, Chicago	40	Matt Williams, San Francisco	122
1991	Terry Pendleton, Atlanta	.319	Howard Johnson, New York	38	Howard Johnson, New York	117
1992	Gary Sheffield, San Diego	.330	Fred McGriff, San Diego	35	Darren Daulton, Philadelphia	109
1993	Andres Galarraga, Colorado	.370	Barry Bonds, San Francisco	46	Barry Bonds, San Francisco	123
1994	Tony Gwynn, San Diego	.394	Matt Williams, San Francisco	43	Jeff Bagwell, Houston	116
1995	Tony Gwynn, San Diego	.368	Dante Bichette, Colorado	40	Dante Bichette, Colorado	128
1996	Tony Gwynn, San Diego	.353	Andres Galarraga, Colorado	47	Andres Galarraga, Colorado	150
1997	Tony Gwynn, San Diego	.372	Larry Walker, Colorado	49	Andres Galarraga, Colorado	140
1998	Larry Walker, Colorado	.363	Mark McGwire, St. Louis	70	Sammy Sosa, Chicago	158
1999	Larry Walker, Colorado	.379	Mark McGwire, St. Louis	65	Mark McGwire, St. Louis	147
2000	Todd Helton, Colorado	.372	Sammy Sosa, Chicago	50	Todd Helton, Colorado	147
2001	Larry Walker, Colorado	.350	Barry Bonds, San Francisco	73	Sammy Sosa, Chicago	160
2002	Barry Bonds, San Francisco	.370	Sammy Sosa, Chicago	49	Lance Berkman, Houston	128
2003	Albert Pujols, St. Louis	.359	Jim Thome, Philadelphia	47	Preston Wilson, Colorado	141

Not surprisingly, outfielder Barry Bonds carried the Giants' offense. Unfortunately for San Francisco's title hopes, he did not have a great supporting cast.

Bonds once again put up MVP-caliber numbers in 2003, even though he battled just about everything mentally and physically that one person could battle. But Bonds proved he is no ordinary player.

He hit .341-45-90 with 148 walks and a .749 slugging percentage for the Giants. He played through the entire season with a nagging hamstring injury, and then his father Bobby died of cancer on Aug. 23. He was just 57.

Bonds missed six games mourning his father's death, then came back and hit his 40th homer of the season against Diamondbacks lefthander Randy Johnson in his second at-bat.

"I didn't even ask him," Giants manager Felipe Alou said. "I just put him in the lineup. We were talking about other stuff, not even about the lineup. He told me he watched every game."

Soon after that, Bonds was hospitalized with exhaustion. He missed a pair of games, then hit a double off the left-field wall in his first at-bat back at Pac Bell Park.

"I have to get back to work," Bonds told reporters a day before his return from exhaustion. "I have to get back in there. I need a vacation where I can take everything in, but I have no choice. I have to wait on it, deal with it and keep playing. I'm not going to walk away from these guys. There's no way."

Bonds' vacation package came sooner than expected as the Giants stumbled in the Division Series against the Marlins, an early look at the trouble Florida gave everyone they faced in the postseason.

"We fought our (butts) off, but they're a better team," Sabean said. "Having said that, I thought we should have won Game Two and we should have won Game Three. I thought we should have won three straight."

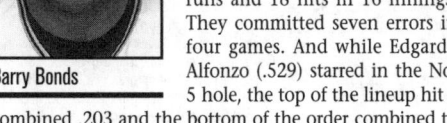

Even though Sabean thought the Giants should have won the series, and even though Marlins pitchers refused to challenge Bonds (they walked him eight times), San Francisco's shaky bullpen, poor defense and lack of hitting spelled doom in the postseason.

Barry Bonds

The Giants' pen gave up 11 runs and 18 hits in 16 innings. They committed seven errors in four games. And while Edgardo Alfonzo (.529) starred in the No. 5 hole, the top of the lineup hit a combined .203 and the bottom of the order combined to hit at a .183 clip.

Thome Delivers

The Phillies opened their checkbooks in 2003, spending nearly $118 million on six free-agent signings, though only one paid major dividends.

First baseman Jim Thome made a splash for the Phillies after leaving Cleveland after 12 seasons. Thome batted .266-47-131 in his debut season, winning the NL home run title in the process.

But the overall play of teammates Pat Burrell, Jimmy Rollins and the disappointing season of free agent David Bell, along with a rocky pitching staff in September, left one of the most promising clubs in the East mired in third place at season's end.

DAVID SCHOFIELD

Pulling his weight
Jim Thome hit 47 home runs for the underachieving Phillies

Burrell signed a six-year, $50 million dollar contract extension in the offseason, after a breakout year in 2002 when he hit 37 homers and drove in 116 runs. But he was a bust in 2003, batting just .209-21-64. Burrell often struggled just to make contact, fanning 142 times in 522 at-bats. Manager Larry Bowa even went so far as to bench Burrell in September, as the team was in the heat of a battle with the Marlins for the wild card.

Rollins had a similar season, batting .263-8-62. He struck out 113 times and lost his leadoff spot to rookie center fielder Marlon Byrd. Bell hit .195 and appeared in just 85 games due to a back injury.

The Phillies had a half-game lead over Florida with eight games to go, but lost back-to-back games to the Reds. They were then eliminated from the wild card race after the Marlins swept them in a three-game series at Pro Player Stadium.

"It's disappointing," Bowa said. "We didn't go where we wanted to go."

It was disappointing for Phillies fans as well, who saw the curtain close on Veterans Stadium, a city landmark since 1971. The Vet was better known for its unruly fans and horrible artificial turf, but the Phillies had their share of good memories there.

But the 2003 season wasn't one of them.

Crazy Central

The only division to have any kind of legitimate race in 2003 was the Central, as the Cubs, Astros and Cardinals all fought their way into contention in September.

Houston seemed to have the division title in its grasp, at least until the final week of the season. That's when the wheels came off for the Astros as the Cubs laid claim to their first division title since 1989.

With both teams playing at home—the Astros hosting

NL YEAR-BY-YEAR PITCHING LEADERS

SINCE 1925

Year	Wins		ERA		Strikeouts	
1925	Dazzy Vance, Brooklyn	22	Dolf Luque, Cincinnati	2.63	Dazzy Vance, Brooklyn	221
1926	Four tied at	20	Ray Kremer, Pittsburgh	2.61	Dazzy Vance, Brooklyn	140
1927	Charlie Root, Chicago	26	Ray Kremer, Pittsburgh	2.47	Dazzy Vance, Brooklyn	184
1928	Two tied at	25	Dazzy Vance, Brooklyn	2.09	Dazzy Vance, Brooklyn	200
1929	Pat Malone, Chicago	22	Bill Walker, New York	3.08	Pat Malone, Chicago	166
1930	Two tied at	20	Dazzy Vance, Brooklyn	2.61	Bill Hallahan, St. Louis	177
1931	Three tied at	19	Bill Walker, New York	2.26	Bill Hallahan, St. Louis	159
1932	Lon Warneke, Chicago	22	Lon Warneke, Chicago	2.37	Dizzy Dean, St. Louis	191
1933	Carl Hubbell, New York	23	Carl Hubbell, New York	1.66	Dizzy Dean, St. Louis	199
1934	Dizzy Dean, St. Louis	30	Carl Hubbell, New York	2.30	Dizzy Dean, St. Louis	195
1935	Dizzy Dean, St. Louis	28	Cy Blanton, Pittsburgh	2.59	Dizzy Dean, St. Louis	182
1936	Carl Hubbell, New York	26	Carl Hubbell, New York	2.31	Van Lingle Mungo, Brooklyn	238
1937	Carl Hubbell, New York	22	Jim Turner, Boston	2.38	Carl Hubbell, New York	159
1938	Bill Lee, Chicago	22	Bill Lee, Chicago	2.66	Clay Bryant, Chicago	135
1939	Bucky Walters, Cincinnati	27	Bucky Walters, Cincinnati	2.29	Two tied at	137
1940	Bucky Walters, Cincinnati	22	Bucky Walters, Cincinnati	2.48	Kirby Higbe, Philadelphia	137
1941	Two tied at	22	Elmer Riddle, Cincinnati	2.24	Johnny Vander Meer, Cincinnati	202
1942	Mort Cooper, St. Louis	22	Mort Cooper, St. Louis	1.77	Johnny Vander Meer, Cincinnati	186
1943	Three tied at	21	Howie Pollet, St. Louis	1.75	Johnny Vander Meer, Cincinnati	174
1944	Bucky Walters, Cincinnati	23	Ed Heusser, Cincinnati	2.38	Bill Voiselle, New York	161
1945	Red Barrett, Boston-St.Louis	23	Hank Borowy, Chicago	2.14	Preacher Roe, Pittsburgh	148
1946	Howie Pollet, St. Louis	21	Howie Pollet, St. Louis	2.10	John Schmitz, Chicago	135
1947	Ewell Blackwell, Cincinnati	22	Warren Spahn, Boston	2.33	Ewell Blackwell, Cincinnati	193
1948	Johnny Sain, Boston	24	Harry Brecheen, St. Louis	2.24	Harry Brecheen, St. Louis	149
1949	Warren Spahn, Boston	21	Dave Koslo, New York	2.50	Warren Spahn, Boston	151
1950	Warren Spahn, Boston	21	Jim Hearn, St.Louis-New York	2.49	Warren Spahn, Boston	191
1951	Two tied at	23	Chet Nichols, Boston	2.88	Two tied at	164
1952	Robin Roberts, Philadelphia	28	Hoyt Wilhelm, New York	2.43	Warren Spahn, Boston	183
1953	Two tied at	23	Warren Spahn, Milwaukee	2.10	Robin Roberts, Philadelphia	198
1954	Robin Roberts, Philadelphia	23	John Antonelli, New York	2.29	Robin Roberts, Philadelphia	185
1955	Robin Roberts, Philadelphia	23	Bob Friend, Pittsburgh	2.84	Sam Jones, Chicago	198
1956	Don Newcombe, Brooklyn	27	Lew Burdette, Milwaukee	2.71	Sam Jones, Chicago	176
1957	Warren Spahn, Milwaukee	21	Johnny Podres, Brooklyn	2.66	Jack Sanford, Philadelphia	188
1958	Two tied at	22	Stu Miller, San Francisco	2.47	Sam Jones, St. Louis	225
1959	Three tied at	21	Sam Jones, San Francisco	2.82	Don Drysdale, Los Angeles	242
1960	Two tied at	21	Mike McCormick, San Francisco	2.70	Don Drysdale, Los Angeles	246
1961	Two tied at	21	Warren Spahn, Milwaukee	3.01	Sandy Koufax, Los Angeles	269
1962	Don Drysdale, Los Angeles	25	Sandy Koufax, Los Angeles	2.54	Don Drysdale, Los Angeles	232
1963	Two tied at	25	Sandy Koufax, Los Angeles	1.88	Sandy Koufax, Los Angeles	306
1964	Larry Jackson, Chicago	24	Sandy Koufax, Los Angeles	1.74	Bob Veale, Pittsburgh	250
1965	Sandy Koufax, Los Angeles	26	Sandy Koufax, Los Angeles	2.04	Sandy Koufax, Los Angeles	382
1966	Sandy Koufax, Los Angeles	27	Sandy Koufax, Los Angeles	1.73	Sandy Koufax, Los Angeles	317
1967	Mike McCormick, San Francisco	22	Phil Niekro, Atlanta	1.87	Jim Bunning, Philadelphia	253
1968	Juan Marichal, San Francisco	26	Bob Gibson, St. Louis	1.12	Bob Gibson, St. Louis	268
1969	Tom Seaver, New York	25	Juan Marichal, San Francisco	2.10	Ferguson Jenkins, Chicago	273
1970	Two tied at	23	Tom Seaver, New York	2.81	Tom Seaver, New York	283
1971	Ferguson Jenkins, Chicago	24	Tom Seaver, New York	1.76	Tom Seaver, New York	289
1972	Steve Carlton, Philadelphia	27	Steve Carlton, Philadelphia	1.98	Steve Carlton, Philadelphia	310
1973	Ron Bryant, San Francisco	24	Tom Seaver, New York	2.08	Tom Seaver, New York	251
1974	Two tied at	20	Buzz Capra, Atlanta	2.28	Steve Carlton, Philadelphia	240
1975	Tom Seaver, New York	23	Randy Jones, San Diego	2.24	Tom Seaver, New York	243
1976	Randy Jones, San Diego	22	John Denny, St. Louis	2.52	Tom Seaver, New York	235
1977	Steve Carlton, Philadelphia	23	John Candelaria, Pittsburgh	2.34	Phil Niekro, Atlanta	252
1978	Gaylord Perry, San Diego	21	Craig Swan, New York	2.43	J.R. Richard, Houston	303
1979	Two tied at	21	J.R. Richard, Houston	2.71	J.R. Richard, Houston	313
1980	Steve Carlton, Philadelphia	24	Don Sutton, Los Angeles	2.21	Steve Carlton, Philadelphia	286
1981	Tom Seaver, Cincinnati	14	Nolan Ryan, Houston	1.69	Fernando Valenzuela, Los Angeles	180
1982	Steve Carlton, Philadelphia	23	Steve Rogers, Montreal	2.40	Steve Carlton, Philadelphia	286
1983	John Denny, Philadelphia	19	Atlee Hammaker, San Francisco	2.25	Steve Carlton, Philadelphia	275
1984	Joaquin Andujar, St. Louis	20	Alejandro Pena, Los Angeles	2.48	Dwight Gooden, New York	276
1985	Dwight Gooden, New York	24	Dwight Gooden, New York	1.53	Dwight Gooden, New York	268
1986	Fernando Valenzuela, Los Angeles	21	Mike Scott, Houston	2.22	Mike Scott, Houston	306
1987	Rick Sutcliffe, Chicago	18	Nolan Ryan, Houston	2.76	Nolan Ryan, Houston	270
1988	Two tied at	23	Joe Magrane, St. Louis	2.18	Nolan Ryan, Houston	228
1989	Mike Scott, Houston	20	Scott Garrelts, San Francisco	2.28	Jose DeLeon, St. Louis	201
1990	Doug Drabek, Pittsburgh	22	Danny Darwin, Houston	2.21	David Cone, New York	233
1991	Two tied at	20	Dennis Martinez, Montreal	2.39	David Cone, New York	241
1992	Two tied at	20	Bill Swift, San Francisco	2.08	John Smoltz, Atlanta	215
1993	Two tied at	22	Greg Maddux, Atlanta	2.36	Jose Rijo, Cincinnati	227
1994	Two tied at	16	Greg Maddux, Atlanta	1.56	Andy Benes, San Diego	189
1995	Greg Maddux, Atlanta	19	Greg Maddux, Atlanta	1.63	Hideo Nomo, Los Angeles	236
1996	John Smoltz, Atlanta	24	Kevin Brown, Florida	1.89	John Smoltz, Atlanta	276
1997	Denny Neagle, Atlanta	20	Pedro Martinez, Montreal	1.90	Curt Schilling, Philadelphia	319
1998	Tom Glavine, Atlanta	20	Greg Maddux, Atlanta	2.22	Curt Schilling, Philadelphia	300
1999	Mike Hampton, Houston	22	Randy Johnson, Arizona	2.48	Randy Johnson, Arizona	364
2000	Tom Glavine, Atlanta	21	Kevin Brown, Los Angeles	2.58	Randy Johnson, Arizona	347
2001	Two tied at	22	Randy Johnson, Arizona	2.49	Randy Johnson, Arizona	372
2002	Randy Johnson, Arizona	24	Randy Johnson, Arizona	2.32	Randy Johnson, Arizona	334
2003	Russ Ortiz, Atlanta	21	Jason Schmidt, San Francisco	2.34	Kerry Wood, Chicago	266

NL: BEST TOOLS

A Baseball America survey of National League managers, conducted at midseason 2003, ranked NL players with the best tools:

BEST HITTER
1. Albert Pujols, Cardinals
2. Barry Bonds, Giants
3. Todd Helton, Rockies

BEST POWER
1. Barry Bonds, Giants
2. Albert Pujols, Cardinals
3. Gary Sheffield, Braves

BEST BUNTER
1. Luis Castillo, Marlins
2. Juan Pierre, Marlins
3. Dave Roberts, Dodgers

BEST STRIKE-ZONE JUDGEMENT
1. Barry Bonds, Giants
2. Albert Pujols, Cardinals
3. Todd Helton, Rockies

BEST HIT-AND-RUN BATTER
1. Placido Polanco, Phillies
2. Jose Vidro, Expos
3. Edgar Renteria, Cardinals

BEST BASERUNNER
1. Larry Walker, Rockies
2. Juan Pierre, Marlins
3. Jeff Bagwell, Astros

FASTEST BASERUNNER
1. Juan Pierre, Marlins
2. Rafael Furcal, Braves
3. Luis Castillo, Marlins

BEST PITCHER
1. Kevin Brown, Dodgers
2. Jason Schmidt, Giants
3. Woody Williams, Cardinals

BEST FASTBALL
1. Billy Wagner, Astros
2. Randy Johnson, Diamondbacks
3. Eric Gagne, Dodgers

BEST CURVEBALL
1. Kerry Wood, Cubs
2. Roy Oswalt, Astros
3. Woody Williams, Cardinals

BEST SLIDER
1. John Smoltz, Braves
2. Randy Johnson, Diamondbacks
3. Jason Schmidt, Giants

BEST CHANGEUP
1. Greg Maddux, Braves
2. Eric Gagne, Dodgers
3. Mark Redman, Marlins

BEST CONTROL
1. Greg Maddux, Braves
2. Curt Schilling, Diamondbacks
3. Woody Williams, Cardinals

BEST PICKOFF MOVE
1. Jeriome Robertson, Astros
2. Kevin Brown, Dodgers
3. Joe Beimel, Pirates

BEST RELIEVER
1. John Smoltz, Braves
2. Eric Gagne, Dodgers
3. Billy Wagner, Astros

BEST DEFENSIVE C
1. Mike Matheny, Cardinals
2. Brad Ausmus, Astros
3. Ivan Rodriguez, Marlins

BEST DEFENSIVE 1B
1. J.T. Snow, Giants
2. Todd Helton, Rockies
3. Derrek Lee, Marlins

BEST DEFENSIVE 2B
1. Jose Vidro, Expos
2. Luis Castillo, Marlins
3. Pokey Reese, Pirates

BEST DEFENSIVE 3B
1. Scott Rolen, Cardinals
2. Mike Lowell, Marlins
3. Aaron Boone, Reds

BEST DEFENSIVE SS
1. Edgar Renteria, Cardinals
2. Orlando Cabrera, Expos
3. Rafael Furcal, Braves

BEST INFIELD ARM
1. Rafael Furcal, Braves
2. Scott Rolen, Cardinals
3. Jimmy Rollins, Phillies

BEST DEFENSIVE OF
1. Andruw Jones, Braves
2. Jim Edmonds, Cardinals
3. Larry Walker, Rockies

BEST OUTFIELD ARM
1. Vladimir Guerrero, Expos
2. Jose Guillen, Reds
3. Andruw Jones, Braves

MOST EXCITING PLAYER
1. Barry Bonds, Giants
2. Albert Pujols, Cardinals
3. Vladimir Guerrero, Expos

BEST MANAGER
1. Bobby Cox, Braves
2. Tony La Russa, Cardinals
3. Dusty Baker, Cubs

BILL NICHOLS

Triple Crown contender
Albert Pujols posted impressive numbers, once again

the Brewers and the Cubs playing the Brian Giles-less Pirates—the race came down to the final weekend. And in essence, it went minute-to-minute on Sept. 27. With the Cubs leading the division by a half-game, they needed to sweep a doubleheader. After they won the day game 4-2 behind Prior, the last-place Brewers put an end to the drama by knocking off Houston for the second straight game, 5-2.

"I guess if I knew what happened, we'd have done something to change it," said Astros second baseman Jeff Kent after the Cubs won the Central. "The Cubbies have played well lately and we haven't. We've just been running on empty."

An early September slump effectively ended the Cardinals' run, even though they had some of the game's best hitters. Outfielders Albert Pujols and Jim Edmonds, shortstop Edgar Renteria, third baseman Scott Rolen and righthander Woody Williams all were in the 2003 All-Star Game, but the team went 4-10 during the first two weeks of September and finished three games back of the Cubs.

"The World Series is a goal and dream," said Cardinals manager Tony La Russa at the season's end. "A failure to get to the World Series does not mean you failed. The tougher question is if you fail to get to the postseason, is your season a failure? I don't think this club could have won more than in the 80's with everything we faced."

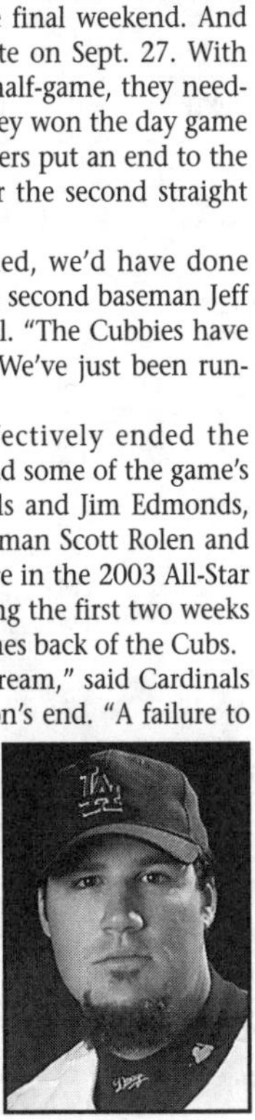

Eric Gagne

The Cardinals had plenty of injuries in 2003, as Fernando Vina, Jason Isringhausen, Matt Morris, Joe Girardi and Edmonds were lost at various times. With Isringhausen gone for nearly half the season, the bullpen took the brunt of the blame for the Cardinals' failure, with good reason: Cardinals relievers accounted for 30 blown saves.

There was one bright spot, which more than likely will be the Cardinals fans' memory of 2003. Pujols put together an MVP-caliber season that featured a 30-game hitting streak and a batting title. He flirted with a triple crown and finished the season batting .359-43-124. He was the first player in history to record 30 homers, 100 RBIs and 100 runs in his first three seasons.

But as the team began its September fade, even Pujols' amazing season wasn't enough to salvage their season. From June 4 on, the club never won more than four games in a row and was never more than eight games above .500.

"Sometimes the lineup hasn't produced, sometimes we've given up runs, sometimes the manager has been clueless," La Russa said. "That's what we are."

Great Gagne, Great Race

A relief pitcher hasn't won a Cy Young Award since Oakland's Dennis Eckersley in 1992, but two legitimate candidates emerged in the NL in 2003 in the Dodgers' Eric Gagne and the Braves' Smoltz.

Gagne was untouchable all season, going 55-for-55 in

NATIONAL LEAGUE DEPARTMENT LEADERS

BATTING

GAMES

Orlando Cabrera, Expos	162
Richie Sexson, Brewers	162
Juan Pierre, Marlins	162
Jeff Bagwell, Astros	160
Shawn Green, Dodgers	160
Todd Helton, Rockies	160

AT-BATS

Juan Pierre, Marlins	668
Rafael Furcal, Braves	664
Craig Biggio, Astros	628
Jimmy Rollins, Phillies	628
Orlando Cabrera, Expos	626

RUNS

Albert Pujols, Cardinals	137
Todd Helton, Rockies	135
Rafael Furcal, Braves	130
Gary Sheffield, Braves	126
Barry Bonds, Giants	111
Jim Thome, Phillies	111

HITS

Albert Pujols, Cardinals	212
Todd Helton, Rockies	209
Juan Pierre, Marlins	204
Edgar Renteria, Cardinals	194
Rafael Furcal, Braves	194

TOTAL BASES

Albert Pujols, Cardinals	394
Todd Helton, Rockies	367
Gary Sheffield, Braves	348
Richie Sexson, Brewers	332
Jim Thome, Phillies	331

EXTRA-BASE HITS

Albert Pujols, Cardinals	95
Todd Helton, Rockies	87
Jim Thome, Phillies	80
Preston Wilson, Rockies	80
Gary Sheffield, Braves	78
Scott Rolen, Cardinals	78

SINGLES

Juan Pierre, Marlins	168
Luis Castillo, Marlins	156
Jason Kendall, Pirates	153
Mark Loretta, Padres	140
Rafael Furcal, Braves	134

DOUBLES

Albert Pujols, Cardinals	51
Shawn Green, Dodgers	49
Scott Rolen, Cardinals	49
Todd Helton, Rockies	49
Marcus Giles, Braves	49

GEORGE GOJKOVICH

Preston Wilson: 141 RBIs

TRIPLES

Steve Finley, Diamondbacks	10
Rafael Furcal, Braves	10
Kenny Lofton, Cubs/Pirates	8
Scott Podsednik, Brewers	8
Four tied at	7

HOME RUNS

Jim Thome, Phillies	47
Barry Bonds, Giants	45
Richie Sexson, Brewers	45
Javy Lopez, Braves	43
Albert Pujols, Cardinals	43

HOME RUN RATIO

(At-Bats per Home Run)

Barry Bonds, Giants	8.6
Javy Lopez, Braves	10.6
Jim Edmonds, Cardinals	11.4
Jim Thome, Phillies	12.2
Sammy Sosa, Cubs	12.9

RUNS BATTED IN

Preston Wilson, Rockies	141
Gary Sheffield, Braves	132
Jim Thome, Phillies	131
Richie Sexson, Brewers	124
Albert Pujols, Cardinals	124

SACRIFICE BUNTS

Jason Schmidt, Giants	15
Luis Castillo, Marlins	15
Juan Pierre, Marlins	15
Matt Morris, Cardinals	12
Javier Vazquez, Expos	12
Wayne Franklin, Brewers	12

SACRIFICE FLIES

Aramis Ramirez, Cubs/Pirates	11
Ryan Klesko, Padres	9
Orlando Cabrera, Expos	9
Timo Perez, Mets	9
Gary Sheffield, Braves	8
Ramon Martinez, Cubs	8

HIT BY PITCHES

Craig Biggio, Astros	27
Jason Kendall, Pirates	25
Jason LaRue, Reds	20
Keith Ginter, Brewers	17
Mike Kinkade, Dodgers	16

WALKS

Barry Bonds, Giants	148
Jim Thome, Phillies	111
Todd Helton, Rockies	111
Bobby Abreu, Phillies	109
Lance Berkman, Astros	107

INTENTIONAL WALKS

Barry Bonds, Giants	61
Vladimir Guerrero, Expos	22
Todd Helton, Rockies	21
Luis Gonzalez, Diamondbacks	17
Mike Matheny, Cardinals	16

STRIKEOUTS

Jim Thome, Phillies	182
Jose Hernandez, Cubs/Pirates/Rockies	177
Brad Wilkerson, Expos	155
Richie Sexson, Brewers	151
Sammy Sosa, Cubs	143

TOUGHEST TO STRIKE OUT

(Plate Appearances per SO)

Juan Pierre, Marlins	21.3
Jason Kendall, Pirates	16.6
Placido Polanco, Phillies	14.5
Edgardo Alfonzo, Giants	14.2
Gary Sheffield, Braves	12.3

LARRY GOREN

Juan Pierre: 65 stolen bases

STOLEN BASES

Juan Pierre, Marlins	65
Scott Podsednik, Brewers	43
Dave Roberts, Dodgers	40
Edgar Renteria, Cardinals	34
Kenny Lofton, Cubs/Pirates	30

CAUGHT STEALING

Juan Pierre, Marlins	20
Luis Castillo, Marlins	19
Dave Roberts, Dodgers	14
Eric Young, Brewers/Giants	12
Jimmy Rollins, Phillies	12

GROUNDED INTO DOUBLE PLAYS

Jay Payton, Rockies	27
Jeff Bagwell, Astros	25
Royce Clayton, Brewers	25
Preston Wilson, Rockies	23
Vinny Castilla, Braves	22

HITTING STREAKS

Albert Pujols, Cardinals	30
Kenny Lofton, Cubs	26
Paul Lo Duca, Dodgers	25
Gary Sheffield, Braves	24
Jason Kendall, Pirates	23

MULTIPLE-HIT GAMES

Albert Pujols, Cardinals	63
Todd Helton, Rockies	61
Edgar Renteria, Cardinals	61
Juan Pierre, Marlins	60
Jason Kendall, Pirates	55
Scott Podsednik, Brewers	55

SLUGGING PERCENTAGE

Barry Bonds, Giants	.749
Albert Pujols, Cardinals	.667
Todd Helton, Rockies	.630
Jim Edmonds, Cardinals	.617
Gary Sheffield, Braves	.604

ON-BASE PERCENTAGE

Barry Bonds, Giants	.529
Todd Helton, Rockies	.458
Albert Pujols, Cardinals	.439
Brian Giles, Padres/Pirates	.427
Larry Walker, Rockies	.422

PITCHING

WINS

Russ Ortiz, Braves ... 21
Woody Williams, Cardinals ... 18
Mark Prior, Cubs ... 18
Jason Schmidt, Giants ... 17
Four tied at ... 16

LOSSES

Jeff D'Amico, Pirates ... 16
Danny Graves, Reds ... 15
Brian Lawrence, Padres ... 15
Tom Glavine, Mets ... 14
Tim Redding, Astros ... 14

WINNING PERCENTAGE

Jason Schmidt, Giants ... .773
Russ Ortiz, Braves ... .750
Mark Prior, Cubs ... .750
Horacio Ramirez, Braves ... .750
Woody Williams, Cardinals ... .667

GAMES

Paul Quantrill, Dodgers ... 89
Oscar Villarreal, Diamondbacks ... 86
Tom Martin, Dodgers ... 80
Ray King, Braves ... 80
Four tied at ... 78

GAMES STARTED

Greg Maddux, Braves ... 36
Kevin Millwood, Phillies ... 35
Wayne Franklin, Brewers ... 34
Tomo Ohka, Expos ... 34
Russ Ortiz, Braves ... 34
Ben Sheets, Brewers ... 34
Javier Vazquez, Expos ... 34

COMPLETE GAMES

Livan Hernandez, Expos ... 8
Jason Schmidt, Giants ... 5
Kevin Millwood, Phillies ... 5
Matt Morris, Cardinals ... 4
Javier Vazquez, Expos ... 4
Kerry Wood, Cubs ... 4

SHUTOUTS

Jason Schmidt, Giants ... 3
Matt Morris, Cardinals ... 3
Kevin Millwood, Phillies ... 3
Seven tied at ... 2

GAMES FINISHED

Billy Wagner, Astros ... 67
Eric Gagne, Dodgers ... 67
Tim Worrell, Giants ... 64
Braden Looper, Marlins ... 64
Joe Borowski, Cubs ... 59

SAVES

Eric Gagne, Dodgers ... 55
John Smoltz, Braves ... 45
Billy Wagner, Astros ... 44
Todd Worrell, Giants ... 38
Rocky Biddle, Expos ... 34

INNINGS PITCHED

Livan Hernandez, Expos ... 233
Javier Vazquez, Expos ... 231
Kevin Millwood, Phillies ... 222
Woody Williams, Cardinals ... 221
Ben Sheets, Brewers ... 221

HITS ALLOWED

Brett Tomko, Cardinals ... 252
Tomo Ohka, Expos ... 233
Ben Sheets, Brewers ... 232
Greg Maddux, Braves ... 225
Livan Hernandez, Expos ... 225

RUNS ALLOWED

Wayne Franklin, Brewers ... 129
Brett Tomko, Cardinals ... 126
Ben Sheets, Brewers ... 122
Matt Kinney, Brewers ... 121
Jason Jennings, Rockies ... 115

HOME RUNS ALLOWED

Wayne Franklin, Brewers ... 36
Brett Tomko, Cardinals ... 35
Jake Peavy, Padres ... 33
Danny Graves, Reds ... 30
Garrett Stephenson, Cardinals ... 30

TOM PRIDDY

Russ Ortiz: 22 wins

WALKS

Russ Ortiz, Braves ... 102
Kazuhisa Ishii, Dodgers ... 101
Kerry Wood, Cubs ... 100
Hideo Nomo, Dodgers ... 98
Al Leiter, Mets ... 94
Wayne Franklin, Brewers ... 94
Carlos Zambrano, Cubs ... 94

FEWEST WALKS PER 9 INNINGS

Greg Maddux, Braves ... 1.36
Curt Schilling, Diamondbacks ... 1.71
Ben Sheets, Brewers ... 1.75
Jason Schmidt, Giants ... 1.99
Tomo Ohka, Expos ... 2.04

HIT BATSMEN

Kerry Wood, Cubs ... 21
Vicente Padilla, Phillies ... 16
Matt Clement, Cubs ... 14
Garrett Stephenson, Cardinals ... 13
Brandon Webb, Diamondbacks ... 13

STRIKEOUTS

Kerry Wood, Cubs ... 266
Mark Prior, Cubs ... 245
Javier Vazquez, Expos ... 241
Jason Schmidt, Giants ... 208
Curt Schilling, Diamondbacks ... 194

STRIKEOUTS PER 9 INNINGS

Kerry Wood, Cubs ... 11.35
Mark Prior, Cubs ... 10.43
Curt Schilling, Diamondbacks ... 10.39
Javier Vazquez, Expos ... 9.40
Jason Schmidt, Giants ... 9.01

PICKOFFS

Joe Beimel, Pirates ... 7
Odalis Perez, Dodgers ... 7
Jeriome Robertson, Astros ... 7
Tom Glavine, Mets ... 5
Al Leiter, Mets ... 5
Steve Trachsel, Mets ... 5

WILD PITCHES

Matt Clement, Cubs ... 13
Zach Day, Expos ... 13
Jaret Wright, Braves/Padres ... 12
Carlos Silva, Phillies ... 12
Jesse Foppert, Giants ... 12

BALKS

Brad Penny, Florida ... 4
Wayne Franklin, Brewers ... 4
Damian Moss, Giants ... 3
Javier Lopez, Rockies ... 3
Eleven tied at ... 2

OPPONENT BATTING AVERAGE

Jason Schmidt, Giants ... .200
Kerry Wood, Cubs ... .203
Brandon Webb, Diamondbacks ... .212
Russ Ortiz, Braves ... .223
Hideo Nomo, Dodgers ... .223

FIELDING

PITCHER

PCT	Brett Tomko, Cardinals	1.000
PO	Ben Sheets, Brewers	22
A	Greg Maddux, Braves	58
E	Kip Wells, Pirates	5
	Curt Schilling, Diamondbacks	5
TC	Greg Maddux, Braves	73
DP	Livan Hernandez, Expos	6
	Shawn Estes, Cubs	6

CATCHER

PCT	Mike Matheny, Cardinals	1.000
PO	Paul Lo Duca, Dodgers	1014
A	Paul Lo Duca, Dodgers	100
E	Paul Lo Duca, Dodgers	15
TC	Paul Lo Duca, Dodgers	1129
DP	Paul Lo Duca, Dodgers	14
PB	Mike Lieberthal, Phillies	11

FIRST BASE

PCT	Tino Martinez, Cardinals	.997
PO	Todd Helton, Rockies	1418
A	Todd Helton, Rockies	156
E	Robert Fick, Braves	14
TC	Todd Helton, Rockies	1585
DP	Todd Helton, Rockies	149

SECOND BASE

PCT	Mark Loretta, Padres	.990
PO	Alex Cora, Dodgers	286
	Luis Castillo, Marlins	286
A	Marcus Giles, Braves	471
E	Eric Young, Brewers/Giants	16
TC	Marcus Giles, Braves	763
DP	Alex Cora, Dodgers	112

THIRD BASE

PCT	Mike Lowell, Marlins	.973
PO	Ty Wigginton, Mets	117
A	Aramis Ramirez, Cubs/Pirates	336
E	Aramis Ramirez, Cubs/Pirates	33
TC	Aramis Ramirez, Cubs/Pirates	466
DP	Adrian Beltre, Dodgers	33

SHORTSTOP

PCT	Alex S. Gonzalez, Cubs	.984
PO	Orlando Cabrera, Expos	258
A	Cesar Izturis, Dodgers	481
	Rafael Furcal, Braves	481
E	Rafael Furcal, Braves	31
TC	Rafael Furcal, Braves	749
DP	Alex Gonzalez, Marlins	109

OUTFIELD

PCT	Juan Encarnacion, Marlins	1.000
PO	Juan Pierre, Marlins	402
A	Richard Hidalgo, Astros	22
E	Adam Dunn, Reds	10
TC	Juan Pierre, Marlins	411
DP	Jose Cruz, Giants	7

STEVE MOORE

Kerry Wood: 266 strikeouts

2003 NATIONAL LEAGUE STATISTICS

CLUB BATTING

	AVG	G	AB	R	H	2B	3B	HR	BB	SO	SB
Atlanta	.284	162	5670	907	1608	321	31	235	545	933	68
St. Louis	.279	162	5672	876	1580	342	32	196	580	952	82
Pittsburgh	.267	162	5581	753	1492	275	45	163	529	1049	86
Colorado	.267	162	5518	853	1472	330	31	198	619	1134	63
Florida	.266	162	5490	751	1459	292	44	157	515	978	150
San Francisco	.264	161	5456	755	1440	281	29	180	593	980	53
Arizona	.263	162	5570	717	1467	303	47	152	531	1006	76
Houston	.263	162	5583	805	1466	308	30	191	557	1021	66
Philadelphia	.261	162	5543	791	1448	325	27	166	651	1155	72
San Diego	.261	162	5531	678	1442	257	32	128	565	1073	76
Chicago	.259	162	5519	724	1431	302	24	172	492	1158	73
Montreal	.258	162	5437	711	1404	294	25	144	522	990	100
Milwaukee	.256	162	5548	714	1423	266	24	196	547	1221	99
New York	.247	161	5341	642	1317	262	24	124	489	1035	70
Cincinnati	.245	162	5509	694	1349	239	21	182	524	1326	80
Los Angeles	.243	162	5458	574	1328	260	25	124	407	985	80

CLUB PITCHING

	ERA	G	CG	SHO	SV	IP	H	R	ER	BB	SO
Los Angeles	3.16	162	3	17	58	1458	1254	556	511	526	1289
San Francisco	3.72	161	7	10	43	1437	1349	638	595	546	1006
Chicago	3.82	162	13	14	36	1456	1304	683	619	617	1404
Arizona	3.84	162	7	11	42	1455	1379	685	621	526	1291
Houston	3.86	162	1	5	50	1450	1350	677	622	565	1139
Montreal	4.01	162	15	10	42	1438	1467	716	640	463	1028
Florida	4.03	162	7	11	36	1445	1415	692	648	530	1132
Philadelphia	4.04	162	9	13	33	1444	1386	697	648	536	1060
Atlanta	4.10	162	4	7	51	1456	1425	740	663	555	992
New York	4.48	161	3	10	38	1413	1497	754	704	576	907
St. Louis	4.60	162	9	10	41	1464	1544	796	748	508	969
Pittsburgh	4.63	162	7	10	44	1444	1527	801	744	502	926
San Diego	4.87	162	2	10	31	1431	1458	831	774	611	1091
Milwaukee	5.02	162	5	3	44	1452	1590	873	810	575	1034
Cincinnati	5.09	162	4	5	38	1446	1578	886	818	590	932
Colorado	5.20	162	3	4	34	1420	1629	892	821	552	866

CLUB FIELDING

	PCT	PO	A	E	DP		PCT	PO	A	E	DP
St. Louis	.987	4391	1644	77	138	Arizona	.983	4365	1693	107	132
Florida	.987	4336	1590	78	162	Milwaukee	.981	4356	1617	114	142
San Francisco	.987	4312	1675	80	163	Colorado	.981	4260	1785	116	165
Houston	.985	4350	1710	95	149	Los Angeles	.981	4373	1810	119	164
Philadelphia	.984	4331	1694	97	146	Atlanta	.981	4369	1884	121	166
Montreal	.983	4313	1733	102	152	Pittsburgh	.980	4333	1844	123	159
San Diego	.983	4294	1634	102	141	New York	.980	4240	1655	118	158
Chicago	.983	4369	1681	106	157	Cincinnati	.977	4339	1700	141	152

INDIVIDUAL BATTING LEADERS

(Minimum 502 Plate Appearances)

	AVG	G	AB	R	H	2B	3B	HR	RBI	BB	SO	SB
Pujols, Albert, St. Louis	.359	157	591	137	212	51	1	43	124	79	65	5
Helton, Todd, Colorado	.358	160	583	135	209	49	5	33	117	111	72	0
Renteria, Edgar, St. Louis	.330	157	587	96	194	47	1	13	100	65	54	34
Sheffield, Gary, Atlanta	.330	155	576	126	190	37	2	39	132	86	55	18
Kendall, Jason, Pittsburgh	.325	150	587	84	191	29	3	6	58	49	40	8
Giles, Marcus, Atlanta	.316	145	551	101	174	49	2	21	69	59	80	14
Castillo, Luis, Florida	.314	152	595	99	187	19	6	6	39	63	60	21
Loretta, Mark, San Diego	.314	154	589	74	185	28	4	13	72	54	62	5
Podsednik, Scott, Milwaukee	.314	154	558	100	175	29	8	9	58	56	91	43
Lieberthal, Mike, Philadelphia	.313	131	508	68	159	30	1	13	81	38	59	0

INDIVIDUAL PITCHING LEADERS

(Minimum 162 Innings)

	W	L	ERA	G	GS	CG	SV	IP	H	R	ER	BB	SO
Schmidt, Jason, San Francisco	17	5	2.34	29	29	5	0	208	152	56	54	46	208
Brown, Kevin, Los Angeles	14	9	2.39	32	32	0	0	211	184	67	56	56	185
Prior, Mark, Chicago	18	6	2.43	30	30	3	0	211	183	67	57	50	245
Webb, Brandon, Arizona	10	9	2.84	29	28	1	0	181	140	65	57	68	172
Schilling, Curt, Arizona	8	9	2.95	24	24	3	0	168	144	58	55	32	194
Nomo, Hideo, Los Angeles	16	13	3.09	33	33	2	0	218	175	82	75	98	177
Zambrano, Carlos, Chicago	13	11	3.11	32	32	3	0	214	188	88	74	94	168
Hernandez, Livan, Montreal	15	10	3.20	33	33	8	0	233	225	92	83	57	187
Wood, Kerry, Chicago	14	11	3.20	32	32	4	0	211	152	77	75	100	266
Vazquez, Javier, Montreal	13	12	3.24	34	34	4	0	231	198	93	83	57	241

AWARD WINNERS

Selected by Baseball Writers Association of America

MVP

Player, Team	1st	2nd	3rd	Total
Barry Bonds, S.F.	28	2	2	426
Albert Pujols, St. Louis	3	29	0	303
Gary Sheffield, Atlanta	1	1	18	247
Jim Thome, Phil.	0	0	5	203
Javy Lopez, Atlanta	0	0	4	159
Eric Gagne, L.A.	0	0	3	143
Todd Helton, Colorado	0	0	0	75
Sammy Sosa, Chicago	0	0	0	53
Mark Prior, Chicago	0	0	0	44
Juan Pierre, Florida	0	0	0	39
Mike Lowell, Florida	0	0	0	30
Richie Sexson, Mil.	0	0	0	21
Andruw Jones, Atlanta	0	0	0	15
Jeff Bagwell, Houston	0	0	0	14
Edgar Renteria, St. Louis	0	0	0	13
Preston Wilson, Col.	0	0	0	12
Vladimir Guerrero, Mon.	0	0	0	10
John Smoltz, Atlanta	0	0	0	9
Marcus Giles, Atlanta	0	0	0	9
Richard Hidalgo, Hou.	0	0	0	9
Luis Castillo, Florida	0	0	0	8
Jason Schmidt, S.F.	0	0	0	7
Ivan Rodriguez, Florida	0	0	0	5
Billy Wagner, Houston	0	0	0	5
Luis Gonzalez, Arizona	0	0	0	4
Chipper Jones, Atlanta	0	0	0	4
Bobby Abreu, Phil.	0	0	0	3
Miguel Cabrera, Florida	0	0	0	3
Jim Edmonds, St. Louis	0	0	0	3
Mark Grudzielanek, Chi.	0	0	0	3
Derrek Lee, Florida	0	0	0	3
Russ Ortiz, Atlanta	0	0	0	3
Rafael Furcal, Atlanta	0	0	0	2
Dontrelle Willis, Florida	0	0	0	1

CY YOUNG AWARD

Player, Team	1st	2nd	3rd	Total
Eric Gagne, L.A.	28	2	0	146
Jason Schmidt, S.F.	2	17	12	73
Mark Prior, Chicago	2	11	17	60
Russ Ortiz, Atlanta	0	2	3	9

ROOKIE OF THE YEAR

Player, Team	1st	2nd	3rd	Total
Dontrelle Willis, Florida	17	9	6	118
Scott Podsednik, Mil.	8	10	11	81
Brandon Webb, Ariz.	7	10	8	73
Marlon Byrd, Phil.	0	1	3	6
Miguel Cabrera, Florida	0	1	0	3
Brad Lidge, Houston	0	1	0	3
Jeriome Robertson, Hou.	0	0	2	2
Jose Reyes, N.Y.	0	0	1	1
Ty Wigginton, N.Y.	0	0	1	1

MANAGER OF THE YEAR

Manager, Team	1st	2nd	3rd	Total
Jack McKeon, Florida	19	6	3	116
Dusty Baker, Chicago	2	15	7	62
Bobby Cox, Atlanta	6	5	11	56
Felipe Alou, S.F.	5	6	8	51
Frank Robinson, Mon.	0	0	3	3

NOTE: MVP balloting based on 14 points for first-place vote, nine for second, eight for third, etc.; Cy Young Award, Rookie of the Year and Manager of the Year balloting based on five points for first-place vote, three for second and one for third.

GOLD GLOVE AWARDS

Selected by NL managers

C—Mike Matheny, St. Louis. **1B**—Derrek Lee, Florida. **2B**—Luis Castillo, Florida. **3B**—Scott Rolen, St. Louis. **SS**—Edgar Renteria, St. Louis. **OF**—Jim Edmonds, St. Louis; Andruw Jones, Atlanta; Jose Cruz, San Francisco. **P**—Mike Hampton, Atlanta.

SILVER SLUGGER AWARDS

Selected by NL managers, coaches

C—Javy Lopez, Atlanta. **1B**—Todd Helton, Colorado. **2B**—Jose Vidro, Montreal. **3B**—Mike Lowell, Florida. **SS**—Edgar Renteria, St. Louis. **OF**—Barry Bonds, San Francisco; Albert Pujols, St. Louis; Gary Sheffield, Atlanta. **P**—Mike Hampton, Atlanta.

save opportunities. He was just as tough against lefthanded hitters (.130) as he was against righties (.135).

Gagne had a 1.20 ERA, struck out 137 and walked just 20. He shut the door consistently for a team that scored fewer runs (574) than the lowly Tigers (591). Los Angeles scored two runs or fewer in 61 games and was shut out or scored one run 40 times.

"He's mixing it up now, which makes him more dangerous," Dodgers outfielder Brian Jordan said. "He's throwing that Bugs Bunny changeup to these guys, where they're looking for 97 mile an hour heat. It's almost like you have no chance. It's just unfair."

On the other side, there is no one more professional than Smoltz, who spent the better part of a month on the disabled list with tendinitis in his elbow but still had a 1.12 ERA with 45 saves. He struck out 73 and issued seven walks.

As good as Smoltz has been at slamming the door on opposing teams since adapting to the role in 2001, he still has the mentality of a starter and would prefer not to pitch out of the bullpen.

"I don't see us winning a championship with me in the closer role," Smoltz said at the end of the season. "I feel my best asset is as a starter in the postseason."

Smoltz has a 12-4 record in the playoffs, though he had notched 100 saves during the past two seasons. The tendinitis grew worse as the season progressed and Smoltz had surgery after the 2003 season, the fourth procedure on his right elbow.

"This will be the last one for me, I guarantee you that," he said. "If I have to have another surgery, it's time to do something else."

NATIONAL LEAGUE DIVISION SERIES

CHICAGO VS. ATLANTA

COMPOSITE BOX

CHICAGO

Player, Pos.	AVG	G	AB	R	H	2B	3B	HR	RBI	BB	SO	SB
Tom Goodwin, cf	1.000	2	1	0	1	1	0	0	2	0	0	0
Moises Alou, lf	.500	5	20	3	10	1	0	0	3	1	4	1
Randall Simon,1b	.429	4	7	1	3	1	0	0	2	0	2	0
Eric Karros, 1b	.375	4	16	4	6	0	0	2	2	0	3	0
Kenny Lofton, cf	.286	5	21	3	6	1	0	0	1	2	2	3
Kerry Wood, p	.286	2	7	1	2	1	0	0	2	0	2	0
Aramis Ramirez, 3b	.278	5	18	2	5	1	0	1	3	2	2	0
Alex Gonzalez, ss	.250	5	12	1	3	0	0	1	1	2	3	0
Sammy Sosa, rf	.188	5	16	1	3	1	0	0	1	6	4	1
Mark Grudzielanek, 2b	.150	5	20	2	3	0	0	0	0	3	4	0
Damian Miller, c	.091	4	11	0	1	1	0	0	1	2	5	0
Paul Bako, c	.000	3	4	0	0	0	0	0	1	2	2	0
Ramon Martinez, 2b-ph	.000	2	4	0	0	0	0	0	0	0	2	0
Mark Prior, p	.000	1	3	0	0	0	0	0	0	0	0	0
Carlos Zambrano, p	.000	1	3	0	0	0	0	0	0	0	2	0
Matt Clement, p	.000	1	2	0	0	0	0	0	0	0	1	0
Doug Glanville, ph	.000	2	1	1	0	0	0	0	0	0	0	0
Troy O'Leary, ph	.000	1	1	0	0	0	0	0	0	0	0	0
Totals	**.257**	**5**	**167**	**19**	**43**	**8**	**0**	**4**	**19**	**20**	**38**	**5**

Pitcher	W	L	ERA	G	GS	SV	IP	H	R	ER	BB	SO
Antonio Alfonseca	0	0	0.00	1	0	0	1	1	0	0	0	0
Joe Borowski	0	0	0.00	2	0	1	2	1	0	0	0	5
Juan Cruz	0	0	0.00	1	0	0	1	0	0	0	1	2
Kyle Farnsworth	0	0	0.00	3	0	0	3	1	0	0	1	2
Mike Remlinger	0	0	0.00	2	0	0	1	0	0	0	1	1
Mark Prior	1	0	1.00	1	1	0	9	2	1	1	4	7
Kerry Wood	2	0	1.76	2	2	0	15	7	3	3	7	18
Carlos Zambrano	0	0	4.76	1	1	0	6	11	3	3	0	4
Matt Clement	0	1	7.71	1	1	0	5	8	4	4	4	3
Dave Veres	0	1	13.50	2	0	0	1	2	2	2	2	0
Mark Guthrie	0	0	27.00	1	0	0	1	2	2	2	1	0
Totals	**3**	**2**	**3.06**	**5**	**5**	**1**	**44**	**35**	**15**	**15**	**21**	**42**

ATLANTA

Player, Pos.	AVG	G	AB	R	H	2B	3B	HR	RBI	BB	SO	SB
Julio Franco, 1b-ph	.500	4	8	1	4	1	0	0	0	2	2	0
Mark DeRosa, ph-2b	.429	4	7	1	3	2	0	0	2	1	2	0
Marcus Giles, 2b	.357	5	14	3	5	0	0	1	3	2	2	0
Javy Lopez, c	.333	5	21	1	7	2	0	0	0	0	6	0
Vinny Castilla, 3b	.250	5	16	0	4	0	0	0	1	3	6	0
Mike Hampton, p	.250	2	4	0	1	0	0	0	0	0	2	0
Rafael Furcal, ss	.211	5	19	3	4	0	0	0	0	3	5	1
Russ Ortiz, p	.200	2	5	0	1	0	0	0	0	0	2	0
Chipper Jones, lf	.167	5	18	3	3	0	0	2	6	3	4	0
Gary Sheffield, rf	.143	4	14	0	2	0	0	0	1	2	0	0
Andruw Jones, cf	.059	5	17	1	1	0	0	0	1	4	7	0
Darren Bragg, ph-rf	.000	2	5	0	0	0	0	0	1	0	1	0
Robert Fick, 1b	.000	4	11	0	0	0	0	0	0	1	2	0
Matt Franco, ph	.000	2	2	1	0	0	0	0	0	0	1	0
Greg Maddux, p	.000	1	2	0	0	0	0	0	0	0	0	0
Jesse Garcia, ph	.000	2	0	1	0	0	0	0	0	0	0	0
Totals	**.215**	**5**	**163**	**15**	**35**	**5**	**0**	**3**	**15**	**21**	**42**	**1**

Pitcher	W	L	ERA	G	GS	SV	IP	H	R	ER	BB	SO
Roberto Hernandez	0	0	0.00	1	0	0	1	1	0	0	0	0
Ray King	0	0	0.00	4	0	0	1	1	0	0	1	0
Kent Mercker	0	0	0.00	1	0	0	1	0	0	0	1	1
Jaret Wright	0	0	0.00	4	0	0	4	0	0	0	2	4
Kevin Gryboski	0	0	3.00	5	0	0	3	2	1	1	2	4
Greg Maddux	0	1	3.00	1	1	0	6	6	2	2	1	1
Mike Hampton	0	1	4.26	2	2	0	13	11	6	6	6	16
Russ Ortiz	1	1	5.06	2	2	0	11	15	6	6	7	9
Will Cunnane	0	0	5.40	2	0	0	2	3	2	1	0	2
John Smoltz	1	0	6.00	2	0	1	3	4	2	2	0	1
Totals	**2**	**3**	**3.68**	**5**	**5**	**1**	**44**	**43**	**19**	**18**	**20**	**38**

SCORE BY INNINGS

Chicago	**511 007 032—19**
Atlanta	**101 232 060—15**

E—Castilla 2, Giles. **DP**—Atlanta 9, Chicago 1. **LOB**—Chicago 37, Atlanta 37. **CS**—Lofton, Gonzalez. **HBP**—Sheffield (by Prior). **IBB**—Gonzalez (by Gryboski), Sosa (by Ortiz), Furcal (by Veres). **WP**—Wood, Clement, Guthrie, Prior, Maddux, Hampton.

FLORIDA VS. SAN FRANCISCO

COMPOSITE BOX

FLORIDA

Player, Pos.	AVG	G	AB	R	H	2B	3B	HR	RBI	BB	SO	SB
Dontrelle Willis, p	1.000	2	3	1	3	0	1	0	0	0	0	0
Brad Penny, p	1.000	2	1	0	1	0	0	0	0	0	0	0
Lenny Harris, ph	.500	2	2	0	1	0	0	0	0	0	0	0
Ivan Rodriguez, c	.353	4	17	3	6	1	0	1	6	3	1	0
Todd Hollandsworth, ph	.333	3	3	1	1	0	0	0	0	0	2	0
Luis Castillo, 2b	.294	4	17	2	5	3	0	0	1	3	3	0
Miguel Cabrera, lf-3b	.286	4	14	1	4	2	0	0	3	1	6	0
Jeff Conine, lf-1b	.267	4	15	2	4	0	0	0	2	2	1	0
Juan Pierre, cf	.263	4	19	5	5	1	0	0	3	1	1	1
Derrek Lee, 1b	.250	4	16	2	4	1	0	0	2	1	2	1
Juan Encarnacion, rf	.133	4	15	1	2	0	0	1	1	2	3	0
Alex Gonzalez, ss	.063	4	16	2	1	0	0	0	0	1	3	0
Brian Banks, ph	.000	2	2	0	0	0	0	0	0	0	0	0
Mike Lowell, 3b-ph	.000	2	3	0	0	0	0	0	0	0	1	0
Josh Beckett, p	.000	1	1	0	0	0	0	0	0	0	1	0
Mark Redman, p	.000	1	2	0	0	0	0	0	0	0	1	0
Totals	**.253**	**4**	**146**	**20**	**37**	**8**	**1**	**2**	**18**	**14**	**25**	**2**

Pitcher	W	L	ERA	G	GS	SV	IP	H	R	ER	BB	SO
Braden Looper	1	0	0.00	2	0	0	2	1	1	0	2	0
Carl Pavano	2	0	0.00	3	0	0	3	1	0	0	1	1
Josh Beckett	0	1	1.29	1	1	0	7	2	1	1	5	9
Chad Fox	0	0	1.80	3	0	0	5	3	1	1	3	3
Mark Redman	0	0	3.00	1	1	0	6	7	2	2	3	4
Ugueth Urbina	0	0	3.00	3	0	1	3	4	1	1	1	2
Brad Penny	0	0	6.35	2	1	0	6	5	4	4	1	6
Dontrelle Willis	0	0	7.94	2	1	0	6	7	5	5	2	3
Rick Helling	0	0	27.00	1	0	0	0	2	1	1	2	0
Totals	**3**	**1**	**3.65**	**4**	**4**	**1**	**37**	**32**	**16**	**15**	**20**	**28**

SAN FRANCISCO

Player, Pos.	AVG	G	AB	R	H	2B	3B	HR	RBI	BB	SO	SB
Pedro Feliz, ph	.667	3	3	1	2	0	1	0	1	0	1	0
Edgardo Alfonzo, 3b	.529	4	17	3	9	4	0	0	5	1	1	0
Kirk Rueter, p	.500	1	2	0	1	0	0	0	0	0	0	0
Jeffrey Hammonds, of	.400	3	5	1	2	0	0	0	0	1	0	0
Neifi Perez, ph-2b	.333	3	3	1	1	1	0	0	0	1	0	0

J.T. Snow, 1b	.313	4	16	0	5	0	0	0	3	0	3	0
Ray Durham, 2b	.235	4	17	2	4	0	0	0	0	1	5	0
Barry Bonds, lf	.222	4	9	3	2	1	0	0	2	8	0	1
Benito Santiago, c	.182	4	11	0	2	0	0	0	0	1	2	0
Marquis Grissom, cf	.143	4	14	1	2	0	0	0	1	2	5	0
Rich Aurilia, ss	.133	4	15	4	2	1	0	0	1	3	3	0
Jose Cruz, rf	.000	4	11	0	0	0	0	0	1	2	4	0
Andres Galarraga, 1b-ph	.000	2	5	0	0	0	0	0	0	0	1	0
Yorvit Torrealba, c	.000	2	3	0	0	0	0	0	1	0	0	0
Jason Schmidt, p	.000	1	3	0	0	0	0	0	0	0	2	0
Sidney Ponson, p	.000	1	1	0	0	0	0	0	0	0	0	0
Jerome Williams, p	.000	1	1	0	0	0	0	0	0	0	1	0
Totals	**.235**	**4**	**136**	**16**	**32**	**7**	**1**	**0**	**15**	**20**	**28**	**1**

Pitcher	W	L	ERA	G	GS	SV	IP	H	R	ER	BB	SO
Scott Eyre	0	0	0.00	1	0	0	0	0	0	0	0	0
Matt Herges	0	0	0.00	3	0	0	4	1	0	0	2	5
Dustin Hermanson	0	0	0.00	1	0	0	1	1	0	0	1	0
Jason Schmidt	1	0	0.00	1	1	0	9	3	0	0	0	5
Tim Worrell	0	1	0.00	2	0	0	3	3	2	0	3	0
Jason Christiansen	0	0	0.00	1	0	0	0	1	0	0	0	0
Felix Rodriguez	0	1	2.25	3	0	0	4	4	3	1	1	5
Kirk Rueter	0	0	3.60	1	1	0	5	3	2	2	2	2
Jim Brower	0	0	6.00	1	0	0	3	5	3	2	3	3
Sidney Ponson	0	0	7.20	1	1	0	5	7	4	4	0	3
Jerome Williams	0	0	13.50	1	1	0	2	5	3	3	1	1
Joe Nathan	0	1	81.00	2	0	0	0	4	3	3	1	1
Totals	**1**	**3**	**3.75**	**4**	**4**	**0**	**36**	**37**	**20**	**15**	**14**	**25**

SCORE BY INNINGS

Florida	**312**	**233**	**130**	**02—20**
San Francisco	**110**	**416**	**011**	**01—16**

E—Snow 3, Aurilia 2, Cruz, Gonzalez, Torrealba, Grissom, Cabrera. **DP**—San Francisco 3. **LOB**—Florida 35, San Francisco 26. **CS**—Grissom. **SF**—Torrealba, Bonds. **HBP**—Lee 2 (by Herges, by Rodriguez), Durham (by Urbina), Hammonds (by Pavano). **IBB**—Bonds 6 (by Fox 2, by Urbina, by Helling, by Beckett, by Pavano), Perez (by Looper), Cruz (by Redman), Pierre (by Worrell), Encarnacion (by Rodriguez), Conine (by Brower).

CHAMPIONSHIP SERIES

FLORIDA VS. CHICAGO

COMPOSITE BOX

FLORIDA

Player, Pos.	AVG	G	AB	R	H	2B	3B	HR	RBI	BB	SO	SB
Todd Hollandsworth, ph	1.000	4	3	2	3	1	0	0	2	1	0	0
Jeff Conine, lf	.458	7	24	4	11	1	1	1	3	4	2	0
Miguel Cabrera, 3b-ss-rf	.333	7	30	9	10	0	0	3	6	2	6	0
Ivan Rodriguez, c	.321	7	28	5	9	2	0	2	10	5	7	0
Juan Pierre, cf	.303	7	33	5	10	1	2	0	1	2	1	1
Juan Encarnacion, rf	.250	5	12	1	3	1	0	1	1	0	4	0
Josh Beckett, p	.250	3	8	0	2	0	0	0	0	1	3	0
Luis Castillo, 2b	.214	7	28	3	6	1	0	0	2	5	2	2
Mike Lowell, ph-3b	.200	7	20	5	4	0	0	2	3	3	4	0
Mike Mordecai, ph-2b-ss	.200	3	5	1	1	1	0	0	3	0	0	0
Derrek Lee, 1b	.188	7	32	2	6	2	0	1	4	1	8	1
Alex Gonzalez, ss	.125	7	24	1	3	2	0	0	4	0	6	0
Lenny Harris, ph	.000	3	2	0	0	0	0	0	0	1	0	0
Carl Pavano, p	.000	3	2	0	0	0	0	0	0	0	1	0
Mark Redman, p	.000	2	2	0	0	0	0	0	0	1	0	0
Rick Helling, p	.000	2	1	0	0	0	0	0	0	0	0	0
Brian Banks,ph	.000	2	1	1	0	0	0	0	0	1	0	0
Brad Penny, p	.000	3	1	0	0	0	0	0	0	1	0	0
Mike Redmond, c	.000	1	0	1	0	0	0	0	0	1	0	0
Totals	**.266**	**7**	**256**	**40**	**68**	**12**	**3**	**10**	**39**	**28**	**44**	**4**

Pitcher	W	L	ERA	G	GS	SV	IP	H	R	ER	BB	SO
Braden Looper	0	0	0.00	2	0	1	2	1	0	0	1	1
Carl Pavano	0	0	2.35	3	1	0	8	8	2	2	1	8
Ugueth Urbina	1	0	2.57	4	0	1	7	2	2	2	0	10
Josh Beckett	1	0	3.26	3	2	0	19	11	7	7	2	19
Chad Fox	1	0	5.40	3	0	0	3	5	2	2	2	2
Nate Bump	0	0	6.00	2	0	0	3	3	2	2	0	3
Rick Helling	0	0	6.35	2	0	0	6	7	5	4	4	5
Mark Redman	0	0	6.52	2	2	0	10	13	7	7	4	4
Michael Tejera	0	1	6.75	2	0	0	1	2	1	1	0	1
Brad Penny	1	1	15.75	3	1	0	4	9	7	7	3	0
Dontrelle Willis	0	1	18.90	2	1	0	3	4	7	7	6	4
Totals	**4**	**3**	**5.59**	**7**	**7**	**2**	**66**	**65**	**42**	**41**	**23**	**57**

CHICAGO

Player, Pos.	AVG	G	AB	R	H	2B	3B	HR	RBI	BB	SO	SB
Doug Glanville, ph-lf	1.000	1	1	0	1	0	1	0	1	0	0	0
Troy O'Leary, ph-lf	.333	3	3	1	1	0	0	1	1	0	0	0
Kerry Wood, p	.333	2	3	1	1	0	0	1	3	0	0	0
Kenny Lofton, cf	.323	7	31	8	10	1	0	0	2	3	4	1
Moises Alou, lf	.310	7	29	4	9	1	0	2	5	2	1	0
Sammy Sosa, rf	.308	7	26	7	8	1	0	2	6	6	9	0
Randall Simon, ph-1b	.294	6	17	3	5	2	0	1	4	0	3	0
Alex S. Gonzalez, ss	.286	7	28	5	8	2	0	3	7	2	7	0
Paul Bako, c	.250	6	16	4	4	1	0	0	1	1	7	0
Tom Goodwin, ph	.250	5	4	1	1	0	1	0	0	0	3	0
Aramis Ramirez, 3b	.231	7	26	4	6	0	1	3	7	5	6	0
Eric Karros, ph-1b	.231	5	13	2	3	0	0	0	0	2	3	0
Mark Grudzielanek, 2b	.200	7	30	2	6	1	1	0	3	0	5	0
Damian Miller, c	.200	4	10	0	2	1	0	0	1	2	2	0
Ramon Martinez, ph-ss	.000	4	4	0	0	0	0	0	0	0	1	0
Matt Clement, p	.000	1	4	0	0	0	0	0	0	0	1	0
Mark Prior, p	.000	2	4	0	0	0	0	0	0	0	2	0
Carlos Zambrano, p	.000	2	3	0	0	0	0	0	0	0	3	0
Totals	**.258**	**7**	**252**	**42**	**65**	**10**	**4**	**13**	**41**	**23**	**57**	**1**

Pitcher	W	L	ERA	G	GS	SV	IP	H	R	ER	BB	SO
Antonio Alfonseca	0	0	0.00	3	0	0	2	2	0	0	2	0
Joe Borowski	1	0	1.59	3	0	0	6	5	2	1	3	1
Mike Remlinger	0	0	2.70	5	0	1	3	3	1	1	1	2
Dave Veres	0	0	3.00	3	0	0	3	4	1	1	1	0
Mark Prior	1	1	3.14	2	2	0	14	14	8	5	5	11
Matt Clement	1	0	3.52	1	1	0	8	5	3	3	2	3
Carlos Zambrano	0	1	5.73	2	2	0	11	14	8	7	5	8
Kerry Wood	0	1	7.30	2	2	0	12	14	10	10	7	13
Mark Guthrie	0	1	9.00	2	0	0	1	1	1	1	0	0
Kyle Farnsworth	0	0	10.13	5	0	0	6	6	6	6	2	7
Totals	**3**	**4**	**4.36**	**7**	**7**	**1**	**66**	**68**	**40**	**32**	**28**	**45**

SCORE BY INNINGS

Florida	**315**	**074**	**5(12)2**	**01—40**
Chicago	**(12)77**	**134**	**322**	**01—42**

E—Grudzielanek 3, A. Gonzalez 2, Conine, Simon, Rodriguez, A.S. Gonzalez. **DP**—Florida 4, Chicago 6. **LOB**—Florida 49, Chicago 45. **CS**—Pierre 3. **SH**—Lofton, Prior 2, Grudzielanek 2, Wood, Pierre, Mordecai, Castillo. **SF**—Conine 2, Wood. **HBP**—Lee (by Clement), Cabrera (by Zambrano), Sosa (by Redman), Ramirez (by Urbina). **IBB**—Rodriguez 2 (by Alfonseca, by Borowski), Sosa 3 (by Helling, by Looper, by Penny), Lowell (by Farnsworth), Hollandsworth (by Farnsworth). **WP**—Willis, Prior, Zambrano, Helling 2, Remlinger, Bump. **PB**—Bako 2.

ORGANIZATION
STATISTICS

ANAHEIM ANGELS

BY BILL SHAIKIN

No one knew it at the time, but the highlight of the Angels' 2003 season came in the middle of May—not on the field, but in a news conference. Arte Moreno, the Angels' new owner, declared the price of beer at Edison Field was too high and decreed that it be cut.

"I can do that, can't I?" asked Moreno.

"You can, um, do anything you want," responded Kevin Uhlich, the Angels' senior vice president of business operations.

Moreno cut other prices—on food, drink, tickets and souvenirs—and eliminated the surcharge slapped on tickets to the most attractive games. Four months before the end of the 2003 season, he pledged not to raise ticket prices in 2004. On the final day of the season, as the Angels celebrated drawing three million fans for the first time, Moreno vowed, "We're going to do it again."

The unprecedented attendance followed the first World Series championship in franchise history, leaving Moreno and the Angels with a tough act to follow.

The Angels became the second team since the introduction of the wild card in 1994 to miss the playoffs the year after winning the series—joining the 1998 Marlins, whose owner took a cost-cutting ax to the roster. On Aug. 20, the Angels fell into a last-place tie, then rallied to finish third in the American League West.

The Angels essentially stood pat after winning. On its way out of ownership, Disney did not mandate that general manager Bill Stoneman keep the championship roster intact, but the company allowed a $16 million payroll increase that made it possible for him to do so.

That experiment will not be repeated. Moreno vowed to pursue free agents, but he also extended the contracts of Stoneman and manager Mike Scioscia through 2007.

The Angels were doomed primarily by poor starting pitching in the first half and injuries in the second. Every starter posted a higher ERA in 2003 and the Angels were so fed up with Kevin Appier that they released him in July, cutting the largest severance check in major league history—$15.67 million. For the second consecutive season, the Angels' bullpen posted the lowest ERA in the league, with closer Troy Percival recording 25 saves for the eighth consecutive year and set-up man Brendan Donnelly elected to the All-Star Game by AL players.

Injuries, which the Angels avoided in 2002, significantly altered the 2003 club. DH Brad Fullmer went out for the year in June, third baseman Troy Glaus in July and center fielder Darin Erstad in August. The only starters to avoid the disabled list were Salmon, infielder Scott Spiezio and left fielder Garret Anderson.

Anderson enjoyed a marvelous season, becoming the third Angel to record a 200-hit season and earning national acclaim by winning the All-Star Game MVP award, one day after winning the home run derby.

The jewels of the minor league system—first baseman Casey Kotchman, catcher Jeff Mathis, third baseman Dallas McPherson and righthander Ervin Santana—all started the season at Class A Rancho Cucamonga. Mathis and Santana went to the Futures Game, and all but Kotchman went to Double-A Arkansas in July.

Though scouting director Donny Rowland selected Kotchman, Mathis and McPherson 1-2-3 in a widely acclaimed 2001 draft, Stoneman fired Rowland in August. The decision had little to do with Rowland's acknowledged eye for talent and much to do with a frayed relationship between the scouting and baseball operations staffs. In October, Stoneman replaced Rowland with former major league pitcher Eddie Bane, who had worked as a special assistant to Tampa Bay GM Chuck LaMar.

Garret Anderson

Dallas McPherson

BILL MITCHELL

PLAYERS of the YEAR

MAJOR LEAGUE: Garret Anderson, of

Anderson topped 200 hits for the first time in his career in 2003 and tied for the American League lead with 49 doubles. He paced the Angels in 10 offensive categories, including average, home runs and RBIs.

MINOR LEAGUE: Dallas McPherson, 3b

McPherson hit .310-23-86 between Class A Rancho Cucamonga and Double-A Arkansas, including a home run against a rehabbing Randy Johnson. McPherson ranked third in the minors with a .596 slugging percentage.

ORGANIZATION LEADERS

BATTING		
*AVG	Warner Madrigal, Provo	.369
R	Jeff Mathis, Arkansas/Rancho Cucamonga	93
H	Alberto Callaspo, Cedar Rapids	168
TB	Nick Gorneault, Arkansas/Rancho Cucamonga	260
2B	Nick Gorneault, Arkansas/Rancho Cucamonga	42
3B	Chone Figgins, Salt Lake	15
HR	Dallas McPherson, Arkansas/Rancho Cucamonga	23
RBI	Nick Gorneault, Arkansas/Rancho Cucamonga	91
BB	Mike O'Keefe, Arkansas	62
SO	Tommy Murphy, Rancho Cucamonga	138
SB	Trent Durrington, Salt Lake	35
*OBP	Dallas McPherson, Arkansas/Rancho Cucamonga	.410
*SLG	Dallas McPherson, Arkansas/Rancho Cucamonga	.596
PITCHING		
W	Jean Toledo, Cedar Rapids	12
	Jake Woods, Rancho Cucamonga	12
L	Billy Stokley, Salt Lake/Arkansas	14
#ERA	Bobby Jenks, Arkansas/AZL Angels	2.07
G	Richard Thompson, Rancho Cuca./Cedar Rapids	55
CG	Chris Bootcheck, Salt Lake	3
SV	Jonathon Rouwenhorst, Rancho Cucamonga	20
	Joel Peralta, Salt Lake/Arkansas	20
IP	Jake Woods, Rancho Cucamonga	171
	Chris Bootcheck, Salt Lake	171
BB	Rafael Rodriguez, Cedar Rapids	59
SO	Ervin Santana, Arkansas/Rancho Cucamonga	153

*Minimum 250 At-Bats #Minimum 75 Innings

ANAHEIM ANGELS

Manager: Mike Scioscia.

2003 Record: 77-85, .475 (3rd, AL West).

BATTING	AVG	G	AB	R	H	2B	3B	HR	RBI	BB	SO	SB	CS	SLG	OBP	B	T	HT	WT	DOB	1st Yr	Resides
Amezaga, Alfredo	.210	37	105	15	22	3	2	2	7	9	23	2	2	.333	.278	S	R	5-10	160	1-16-78	1999	Obregon, Mexico
Anderson, Garret	.315	159	638	80	201	49	4	29	116	31	83	6	3	.541	.345	L	L	6-3	220	6-30-72	1990	Tustin, Calif.
DaVanon, Jeff	.282	123	330	56	93	16	1	12	43	42	59	17	5	.445	.360	S	R	6-0	190	12-8-73	1995	Scottsdale, Ariz.
Delgado, Wilson	.320	19	50	4	16	0	0	0	4	8	8	0	0	.320	.414	S	R	5-11	160	7-15-72	1993	San Cristobal, D.R.
Durrington, Trent	.143	12	14	5	2	0	0	0	1	3	0	1	1	.143	.294	R	R	5-10	190	8-27-75	1994	Broadbeach Waters, Australia
Eckstein, David	.252	120	452	59	114	22	1	3	31	36	45	16	5	.325	.325	R	R	5-7	160	1-20-75	1997	Sanford, Fla.
Erstad, Darin	.252	67	258	35	65	7	1	4	17	18	40	9	1	.333	.309	L	L	6-2	210	6-4-74	1995	Fargo, N.D.
Figgins, Chone	.296	71	240	34	71	9	4	0	27	20	38	13	7	.367	.345	S	R	5-8	160	1-22-78	1997	Seffner, Fla.
Fullmer, Brad	.306	63	206	32	63	9	2	9	35	26	31	5	4	.500	.387	L	R	6-0	220	1-17-75	1994	Henderson, Nevada
Gil, Benji	.192	62	125	12	24	5	1	1	9	4	33	5	1	.272	.214	R	R	6-2	210	10-6-72	1991	Grapevine, Texas
Glaus, Troy	.248	91	319	53	79	17	2	16	50	46	73	7	2	.464	.343	R	R	6-5	240	8-3-76	1997	Corona, Calif.
Gregorio, Tom	.158	12	19	1	3	0	0	0	2	1	8	0	0	.158	.238	R	R	6-2	210	5-5-77	1999	Staten Island, N.Y.
Johnson, Gary	.375	5	8	1	3	1	0	0	0	1	1	0	1	.500	.444	L	L	6-3	210	10-29-75	1999	Atherton, Calif.
Kennedy, Adam	.269	143	449	71	121	17	1	13	49	45	73	22	9	.399	.344	L	R	6-1	180	1-10-76	1997	Yorba Linda, Calif.
Molina, Bengie	.281	119	409	37	115	24	0	14	71	13	31	1	1	.443	.304	R	R	5-11	220	7-20-74	1993	Yuma, Ariz.
Molina, Jose	.184	53	114	12	21	4	0	0	6	1	26	0	0	.219	.210	R	R	6-2	220	6-3-75	1993	Vega Alta, P.R.
Owens, Eric	.270	111	241	29	65	6	0	1	20	10	24	11	8	.307	.300	R	R	6-0	200	2-3-71	1992	Phoenix, Ariz.
Quinlan, Robb	.287	38	94	13	27	4	2	0	4	6	16	1	2	.372	.330	R	R	6-1	200	3-17-77	1999	Maplewood, Minn.
Ramirez, Julio	.000	6	2	1	0	0	0	0	0	0	0	0	0	.000	.000	R	R	5-11	150	8-10-77	1994	Santo Domingo, D.R.
Riggs, Adam	.246	24	61	11	15	4	1	3	5	9	9	3	1	.492	.343	R	R	6-0	190	10-4-72	1994	The Woodlands, Texas
Salmon, Tim	.275	148	528	78	145	35	4	19	72	77	93	3	1	.464	.374	R	R	6-3	230	8-24-68	1989	Scottsdale, Ariz.
Spiezio, Scott	.265	158	521	69	138	36	7	16	83	46	66	6	3	.453	.326	S	R	6-2	220	9-21-72	1993	Morris, Ill.
Wesson, Barry	.182	10	11	2	2	0	0	1	3	0	4	1	0	.455	.182	R	R	6-2	210	4-6-77	1995	Glen Allan, Miss.
Wooten, Shawn	.243	98	272	25	66	8	0	7	32	24	45	0	4	.349	.303	R	R	5-10	230	7-24-72	1993	Covina, Calif.

PITCHING	W	L	ERA	G	GS	CG	SV	IP	H	R	ER	BB	SO	AVG	B	T	HT	WT	DOB	1st Yr	Resides
Appier, Kevin	7	7	5.63	19	19	0	0	93	105	60	58	36	50	.278	R	R	6-2	210	12-6-67	1987	Paola, Kan.
Bootcheck, Chris	0	1	9.58	4	1	0	0	10	16	13	11	6	7	.340	R	R	6-5	200	10-24-78	2001	Phoenix, Ariz.
Callaway, Mickey	1	4	6.81	17	4	0	0	38	57	32	29	16	22	.345	R	R	6-2	200	5-13-75	1996	Memphis, Tenn.
Donnelly, Brendan	2	2	1.58	63	0	0	3	74	55	14	13	24	79	.200	R	R	6-3	240	7-4-71	1992	Hilton Head, S.C.
Glover, Gary	1	0	5.00	18	0	0	0	27	34	15	15	8	14	.314	R	R	6-5	200	12-3-76	1994	Deland, Fla.
2-team (24 Chicago)	2	0	4.74	42	0	0	0	63	77	33	33	22	37	.309							
Gregg, Kevin	2	0	3.28	5	3	0	0	25	18	9	9	8	14	.204	R	R	6-6	220	6-20-78	1996	Corvallis, Ore.
Jones, Greg	0	0	4.88	18	0	0	0	28	29	15	15	14	28	.261	R	R	6-2	190	11-15-76	1997	Seminole, Fla.
Lackey, John	10	16	4.63	33	33	2	0	204	223	117	105	66	151	.278	R	R	6-6	230	10-23-78	1999	Bothell, Wash.
Miadich, Bart	0	0	18.00	1	0	0	0	2	5	4	4	1	3	.500	R	R	6-4	200	2-3-76	1997	Lake Oswego, Ore.
Ortiz, Ramon	16	13	5.20	32	32	1	0	180	209	121	104	63	94	.286	R	R	6-0	170	3-23-73	1995	Cotui, D.R.
Percival, Troy	0	5	3.47	52	0	0	33	49	33	22	19	23	48	.184	R	R	6-3	230	8-9-69	1990	Riverside, Calif.
Rodriguez, Francisco	8	3	3.03	59	0	0	2	86	50	30	29	35	95	.171	R	R	6-0	180	1-7-82	1999	Caracas, Venez.
Rodriguez, Rich	0	0	2.45	3	0	0	0	4	4	1	1	1	3	.307	L	L	6-0	200	3-1-63	1984	Thousand Oaks, Calif.
Schoeneweis, Scott	1	1	3.96	39	0	0	0	39	37	19	17	10	29	.250	L	L	6-0	190	10-2-73	1996	Fountain Hills, Ariz.
Sele, Aaron	7	11	5.77	25	25	0	0	122	135	82	78	58	53	.283	R	R	6-5	230	6-25-70	1991	Bellevue, Wash.
Shields, Scot	5	6	2.85	44	13	0	1	148	138	56	47	38	111	.246	R	R	6-1	170	7-22-75	1997	Livonia, Mich.
Turnbow, Derrick	2	0	0.59	11	0	0	0	15	7	1	1	3	15	.140	R	R	6-3	210	1-25-78	1997	Franklin, Tenn.
Washburn, Jarrod	10	15	4.43	32	32	2	0	207	205	106	102	54	118	.256	L	L	6-1	190	8-13-74	1995	Danbury, Wisc.
Weber, Ben	5	1	2.69	62	0	0	0	80	84	26	24	22	46	.275	R	R	6-4	200	11-17-69	1991	Beaumont, Texas

FIELDING

Catcher	PCT	G	PO	A	E	DP	PB
Gregorio	.979	12	44	2	1	0	3
B. Molina	.993	117	672	63	5	10	4
J. Molina	.996	53	221	17	1	0	3
Wooten	1.000	19	65	4	0	0	1

First Base	PCT	G	PO	A	E	DP
Fullmer	1.000	19	142	11	0	17
Gil	1.000	5	15	4	0	2
Quinlan	.988	33	146	13	2	15
Riggs	.976	10	71	10	2	5
Spiezio	.994	114	722	57	5	61
Wooten	.995	32	207	14	1	21

Second Base	PCT	G	PO	A	E	DP
Delgado	1.000	1	4	3	0	1
Durrington	1.000	5	1	5	0	0
Figgins	.980	14	23	27	1	6
Gil	.979	28	32	62	2	14
Kennedy	.990	140	235	371	6	78
Riggs	1.000	3	3	3	0	0

Third Base	PCT	G	PO	A	E	DP
Amezaga	.941	13	12	20	2	1
Delgado	.867	9	3	10	2	2
Durrington	1.000	4	1	1	0	0
Gil	1.000	4	2	2	0	1
Glaus	.923	87	56	136	16	11
Spiezio	.939	52	31	61	6	10
Wooten	.974	17	12	26	1	1

Shortstop	PCT	G	PO	A	E	DP
Amezaga	.970	24	39	57	3	11
Delgado	.974	9	20	18	1	6
Eckstein	.984	116	193	293	8	67
Figgins	.935	8	11	18	2	4
Gil	.938	20	25	35	4	12

Outfield	PCT	G	PO	A	E	DP
Anderson	.997	144	326	13	1	2
DaVanon	.983	115	229	2	4	0
Durrington	.000	1	0	0	0	0
Erstad	1.000	66	190	2	0	1
Figgins	1.000	47	113	1	0	0
Johnson	1.000	4	6	0	0	0
Owens	.971	97	164	3	5	2
Quinlan	1.000	1	5	0	0	0
Ramirez	.750	5	3	0	1	0
Riggs	1.000	8	13	1	0	1
Salmon	.958	78	133	4	6	1
Spiezio	1.000	10	6	0	0	0
Wesson	1.000	9	9	0	0	0

FARM SYSTEM

Director, Player Development: Tony Reagins

Class	Farm Team	League	W	L	Pct.	Finish*	Manager	First Yr.
AAA	Salt Lake (Utah) Stingers	Pacific Coast	68	75	.476	13th (16)	Mike Brumley	2001
AA	Arkansas Travelers	Texas	70	70	.500	5th (8)	Tyrone Boykin	2001
High A	Rancho Cucamonga (Calif.) Quakes	California	74	66	.529	t-5th (10)	Bobby Meacham	2001
Low A	Cedar Rapids (Iowa) Kernels	Midwest	66	72	.478	9th (14)	Todd Claus	1993
Rookie	Provo (Utah) Angels	Pioneer	54	22	.710	1st (8)	Tom Kotchman	2001
Rookie	Mesa (Ariz.) Angels	Arizona	20	29	.408	7th (9)	Brian Harper	2001

*Finish in overall standings (No. of teams in league)

SALT LAKE STINGERS — Class AAA

PACIFIC COAST LEAGUE

BATTING	AVG	G	AB	R	H	2B	3B	HR	RBI	BB	SO	SB	CS	SLG	OBP	B	T	HT	WT	DOB	1st Yr	Resides
Alviso, Jerome	.228	16	57	4	13	1	0	0	5	3	6	2	0	.246	.267	S	R	6-1	160	9-4-75	1997	Livermore, Calif.
2-team (38 Colo. Spr.)	.283	54	159	16	45	4	0	0	11	7	13	3	2	.308	.315							
Amezaga, Alfredo	.347	75	317	55	110	20	5	3	45	20	39	14	8	.470	.391	S	R	5-10	160	1-16-78	1999	Obregon, Mexico
DaVanon, Jeff	.300	16	60	11	18	4	1	2	14	9	9	4	1	.500	.400	S	R	6-0	190	12-8-73	1995	Scottsdale, Ariz.
Durrington, Trent	.304	117	447	81	136	27	5	7	54	61	75	35	8	.434	.390	R	R	5-10	190	8-27-75	1994	Broadbeach Waters, Australia
Erstad, Darin	.407	7	27	6	11	0	0	0	4	2	1	1	0	.407	.448	L	L	6-2	210	6-4-74	1995	Fargo, N.D.
Figgins, Chone	.312	68	285	55	89	14	15	4	30	29	36	16	6	.509	.379	S	R	5-8	160	1-22-78	1997	Seffner, Fla.
Gomez, Rudy	.000	2	3	0	0	0	0	0	0	1	1	0	0	.000	.250	R	R	5-11	180	9-14-74	1996	Miami, Fla.
Gregorio, Tom	.221	54	181	26	40	10	0	5	24	14	44	0	0	.359	.290	R	R	6-2	210	5-5-77	1999	Staten Island, N.Y.
Guiel, Jeff	.240	94	325	48	78	16	2	13	48	48	80	3	1	.422	.339	L	R	5-11	190	1-12-74	1997	Langley, B.C.
Harrison, Adonis	.292	47	178	23	52	8	2	0	18	22	18	1	2	.360	.363	L	R	5-9	160	9-28-76	1995	Pasadena, Calif.
Haynes, Nathan	.217	28	120	16	26	3	3	1	7	9	20	6	0	.317	.280	L	L	5-9	170	9-7-79	1997	Vallejo, Calif.
Hill, Jason	.206	11	34	5	7	0	1	2	5	4	3	1	0	.441	.282	R	R	6-3	210	3-17-77	1998	Danville, Calif.
Johnson, Gary	.255	121	447	65	114	23	7	12	74	61	112	4	2	.418	.346	L	L	6-3	210	10-29-75	1999	Atherton, Calif.
Johnson, Keith	.286	117	451	51	129	33	2	11	64	19	70	6	6	.441	.317	R	R	5-11	200	4-17-71	1992	Las Vegas, Nevada
Nieves, Wil	.283	102	361	48	102	16	2	4	38	25	53	1	2	.371	.327	R	R	5-11	190	9-25-77	1996	Santurce, P.R.
Pavkovich, Adam	.200	1	5	0	1	0	0	0	0	0	0	0	0	.200	.200	R	R	6-2	185	12-31-81	2003	Venice, Fla.
Quinlan, Robb	.310	95	393	55	122	18	4	9	68	25	59	10	3	.445	.352	R	R	6-1	200	3-17-77	1999	Maplewood, Minn.
Ramirez, Julio	.279	110	402	50	112	17	6	10	48	12	86	16	6	.425	.304	R	R	5-11	150	8-10-77	1994	Santo Domingo, D.R.
Riggs, Adam	.294	103	394	59	116	35	0	14	82	37	67	8	2	.490	.354	R	R	6-0	190	10-4-72	1994	The Woodlands, Texas
Salazar, Oscar	.308	7	26	5	8	2	1	1	4	3	4	0	0	.577	.367	R	R	6-0	170	6-27-78	1994	Maracay, Venez.
Wesson, Barry	.280	123	475	62	133	27	6	8	53	38	86	17	3	.413	.334	R	R	6-2	210	4-6-77	1995	Glen Allan, Miss.

PITCHING	W	L	ERA	G	GS	CG	SV	IP	H	R	ER	BB	SO	AVG	B	T	HT	WT	DOB	1st Yr	Resides
Bergman, Dusty	0	1	20.25	1	0	0	0	1	5	5	3	1	0	.714	L	L	6-5	200	2-1-78	1999	Carson City, Nevada
Bootcheck, Chris	8	9	4.25	28	26	3	0	171	194	103	81	43	82	.289	R	R	6-5	200	10-24-78	2001	Phoenix, Ariz.
Callaway, Mickey	1	0	2.95	7	4	0	0	21	22	8	7	6	10	.285	R	R	6-2	200	5-13-75	1996	Memphis, Tenn.
Cummings, Ryan	1	3	8.36	12	0	0	0	14	22	14	13	7	6	.392	R	R	6-2	220	6-3-76	1997	Marietta, Ga.
Donaldson, Bo	0	0	1.80	3	0	0	0	5	5	1	1	2	5	.263	R	R	6-0	200	10-10-74	1997	Wesley Chapel, Fla.
Duncan, Courtney	0	0	0.00	2	0	0	0	3	2	0	0	2	5	.200	L	R	6-0	190	10-9-74	1996	Huntsville, Ala.
2-team (54 Portland)	2	6	4.38	56	0	0	18	64	68	39	31	39	54	.277							
Dunn, Scott	0	0	11.74	6	0	0	0	8	9	10	10	10	11	.272	R	R	6-3	180	5-23-78	1999	San Antonio, Texas
Emanuel, Brandon	6	10	5.14	29	23	1	2	147	186	93	84	37	71	.315	R	R	6-3	210	4-9-76	1998	Tampa, Fla.
Green, Steve	9	5	4.66	21	21	0	0	110	120	63	57	47	70	.283	R	R	6-2	200	1-26-78	1997	Longueuil, Quebec
Gregg, Kevin	7	4	4.03	15	15	0	0	92	90	47	41	18	75	.256	R	R	6-6	220	6-20-78	1996	Corvallis, Ore.
Hensley, Matt	8	12	4.89	27	27	1	0	158	194	105	86	49	85	.302	R	R	6-2	220	8-18-78	2000	San Diego, Calif.
Jones, Greg	2	3	4.40	33	0	0	4	47	36	24	23	9	56	.206	R	R	6-2	190	11-15-76	1997	Seminole, Fla.
Kroon, Marc	2	1	3.86	9	0	0	2	14	10	6	6	3	10	.192	R	R	6-2	190	4-2-73	1991	Phoenix, Ariz.
Lukasiewicz, Mark	2	2	6.06	40	4	0	1	62	74	47	42	18	52	.293	L	L	6-5	240	3-8-73	1994	Clay, N.Y.
Miadich, Bart	5	5	3.68	46	0	0	16	51	39	23	21	41	65	.209	R	R	6-4	200	2-3-76	1997	Lake Oswego, Ore.
Nickle, Doug	2	2	1.48	34	0	0	4	49	40	8	8	18	23	.225	R	R	6-4	210	10-2-74	1997	Sonoma, Calif.
Peralta, Joel	0	0	0.00	1	0	0	0	0	0	0	0	1	0	.000	R	R	5-11	160	3-23-76	1996	Bonao, D.R.
Rodriguez, Rich	3	2	2.47	34	0	0	1	44	47	14	12	12	18	.283	L	L	6-0	200	3-1-63	1984	Thousand Oaks, Calif.
Secoda, Jason	2	1	5.40	7	0	0	0	13	12	9	8	9	4	.272	R	R	6-1	200	9-2-74	1995	Anaheim, Calif.
Sele, Aaron	1	2	6.43	3	3	0	0	14	16	10	10	9	8	.296	R	R	6-5	230	6-25-70	1991	Bellevue, Wash.
Serrano, Elio	5	4	4.72	46	1	0	2	69	84	43	36	22	46	.304	R	R	6-3	210	12-4-78	1996	Valencia, Venez.
Snyder, John	3	2	4.88	10	10	0	0	55	60	38	30	19	31	.280	R	R	6-3	200	8-16-74	1992	Joliet, Ill.
Stokley, Billy	0	5	6.46	9	9	1	0	47	69	40	34	13	16	.353	L	R	6-4	200	5-13-77	2000	Pasadena, Texas
Turnbow, Derrick	1	2	5.73	35	0	0	2	55	68	36	35	24	63	.299	R	R	6-3	210	1-25-78	1997	Franklin, Tenn.

FIELDING

Catcher	PCT	G	PO	A	E	DP	PB
Durrington	1.000	2	10	1	0	0	1
Gregorio	1.000	53	271	37	0	3	7
Hill	1.000	7	41	3	0	0	0
Nieves	.988	88	510	45	7	5	5

First Base	PCT	G	PO	A	E	DP
Durrington	.980	15	138	11	3	14
Guiel	.983	35	261	20	5	35
Hill	1.000	3	24	1	0	0
Johnson	1.000	3	26	4	0	3
Nieves	.992	15	127	5	1	17
Quinlan	1.000	59	483	46	0	58
Riggs	.989	20	174	14	2	18

Second Base	PCT	G	PO	A	E	DP
Alviso	.962	4	7	18	1	4
Amezaga	.982	10	21	34	1	12
Durrington	.989	57	97	161	3	30
Figgins	.948	35	54	111	9	30
Harrison	.953	15	31	50	4	10
Johnson	.964	11	26	27	2	11
Riggs	.900	8	12	24	4	5
Salazar	.977	7	20	22	1	6

Third Base	PCT	G	PO	A	E	DP
Durrington	.943	28	21	45	4	8
Figgins	1.000	2	1	11	0	1
Guiel	.936	22	9	35	3	5
Hill	.000	1	0	0	0	0
Johnson	.953	96	67	137	10	17

Shortstop	PCT	G	PO	A	E	DP
Alviso	.941	12	16	32	3	12
Amezaga	.982	64	125	206	6	46
Figgins	.938	27	42	78	8	21
Harrison	.964	32	51	83	5	14
Johnson	.936	10	16	28	3	7
Pavkovich	1.000	1	5	6	0	2

Outfield	PCT	G	PO	A	E	DP
DaVanon	.933	15	28	0	2	0
Durrington	1.000	8	6	1	0	0
Erstad	1.000	7	16	0	0	0

Figgins	1.000	5	21	0	0	0
Guiel	.977	18	40	3	1	0
Haynes	.950	26	76	0	4	0
Johnson	.985	86	186	9	3	2

Quinlan	1.000	29	51	3	0	1
Ramirez	.975	103	268	8	7	2
Riggs	.971	23	34	0	1	0
Wesson	.968	118	253	19	9	5

ARKANSAS TRAVELERS — Class AA

TEXAS LEAGUE

BATTING	AVG	G	AB	R	H	2B	3B	HR	RBI	BB	SO	SB	CS	SLG	OBP	B	T	HT	WT	DOB	1st Yr	Resides
Alviso, Jerome	.000	2	8	0	0	0	0	0	0	1	1	0	0	.000	.111	S	R	6-1	160	9-4-75	1997	Livermore, Calif.
Budde, Ryan	.213	96	342	45	73	9	1	10	41	35	76	1	1	.333	.289	R	R	5-11	200	8-15-79	2001	Midwest City, Okla.
Cahill, Jon	.000	1	2	0	0	0	0	0	0	2	0	0	0	.000	.500	R	R	6-0	190	2-21-78	2001	Peabody, Mass.
Del Chiaro, Brent	.162	46	154	18	25	11	2	1	10	9	56	0	0	.279	.222	R	R	6-3	220	6-26-79	2001	Oakley, Calif.
Duncan, Carlos	.244	87	303	33	74	19	3	5	28	12	94	25	4	.376	.282	R	R	6-1	190	6-30-77	1995	San Pedro de Macoris, D.R.
Gorneault, Nick	.345	29	110	19	38	6	4	2	19	8	25	2	0	.527	.395	R	R	6-3	200	4-19-79	2001	Springfield, Mass.
Harrison, Adonis	.309	46	139	18	43	9	4	2	15	20	20	3	5	.475	.398	L	R	5-9	160	9-28-76	1995	Pasadena, Calif.
Haynes, Nathan	.296	91	372	59	110	16	10	5	42	34	74	27	9	.433	.356	L	L	5-9	170	9-7-79	1997	Vallejo, Calif.
Hill, Jason	.239	67	247	21	59	10	0	4	27	3	27	4	1	.328	.256	R	R	6-3	210	3-17-77	1998	Danville, Calif.
James, Kenny	.284	125	447	60	127	23	2	3	46	34	63	13	7	.365	.341	S	R	6-0	190	10-9-76	1995	St. Petersburg, Fla.
Mann, Derek	.211	9	19	2	4	1	0	0	1	4	1	0	1	.263	.348	L	R	6-0	180	3-8-78	1996	Columbus, Ga.
Mathis, Jeff	.284	24	95	19	27	11	0	2	14	12	16	1	2	.463	.364	R	R	6-0	180	3-31-83	2001	Marianna, Fla.
McPherson, Dallas	.314	28	102	22	32	9	1	5	27	19	25	4	0	.569	.426	L	R	6-4	230	7-23-80	2001	Randleman, N.C.
O'Keefe, Mike	.261	122	444	52	116	25	1	10	71	62	71	6	9	.390	.357	L	L	5-10	200	6-28-78	1999	Hamden, Conn.
Pichardo, Maximo	.205	25	88	9	18	6	0	0	8	4	13	3	1	.273	.278	R	R	6-0	150	6-27-79	1999	Santo Domingo, D.R.
Quintero, Edgar	.000	3	8	1	0	0	0	0	0	1	3	0	0	.000	.111	R	R	5-10	180	8-9-77	1997	Mazatlan, Mexico
Salazar, Oscar	.329	39	143	22	47	6	2	4	21	19	20	2	1	.483	.410	R	R	6-0	170	6-27-78	1994	Maracay, Venez.
Smith, Casey	.284	82	324	46	92	10	2	4	32	19	44	5	7	.364	.329	R	R	6-2	200	3-18-79	2001	Ashford, Ala.
Specht, Brian	.253	128	458	62	116	18	4	14	63	46	112	12	8	.402	.327	S	R	5-11	170	10-19-80	1999	Colorado Springs, Colo.
Weber, Jake	.302	136	539	67	163	31	3	5	66	47	45	12	5	.399	.364	L	R	5-11	180	4-22-76	1998	Wappinger Falls, N.Y.
Zamora, Junior	.281	115	430	61	121	24	4	9	54	30	96	3	1	.419	.336	R	R	6-2	190	5-3-76	1994	Church Hill, Tenn.

PITCHING	W	L	ERA	G	GS	CG	SV	IP	H	R	ER	BB	SO	AVG	B	T	HT	WT	DOB	1st Yr	Resides
Andrade, Stephen	5	1	2.65	36	0	0	7	51	26	16	15	19	74	.146	R	R	6-1	220	2-6-78	2001	Woodland, Calif.
Bergman, Dusty	6	5	3.79	50	10	0	0	109	116	54	46	33	82	.272	L	L	6-5	200	2-1-78	1999	Carson City, Nev.
Brunet, Mike	6	8	4.69	32	19	2	0	127	133	78	66	43	87	.268	R	R	6-2	160	3-5-77	1997	Land O'Lakes, Fla.
Cummings, Ryan	1	5	5.26	37	2	0	0	65	86	48	38	23	22	.329	R	R	6-2	220	6-3-76	1997	Marietta, Ga.
Cyr, Eric	6	6	4.96	20	20	0	0	103	91	61	57	52	78	.236	R	L	6-4	200	2-11-79	1999	Ada, Okla.
Dunn, Scott	1	0	0.00	3	0	0	0	5	2	0	0	0	7	.125	R	R	6-3	180	5-23-78	1999	San Antonio, Texas
Fischer, Rich	5	11	4.61	26	26	2	0	154	159	91	79	43	123	.268	R	R	6-3	180	10-21-80	2000	Riverside, Calif.
Garcia, Jose	2	2	4.54	6	6	0	0	34	39	17	17	15	25	.302	R	R	6-3	220	4-29-78	1996	Las Vegas, Nev.
Gregg, Kevin	4	3	3.53	15	11	2	0	66	60	29	26	19	60	.240	R	R	6-6	220	6-20-78	1996	Corvallis, Ore.
Griffith, Dustin	1	0	9.00	1	0	0	0	1	2	1	1	0	0	.500	R	R	6-4	190	9-16-80	2001	Littleton, Colo.
Jenks, Bobby	7	2	2.17	16	16	0	0	83	56	23	20	51	103	.191	R	R	6-3	240	3-14-81	2000	Bothell, Wash.
Kroon, Marc	3	3	3.00	37	1	0	4	45	28	20	15	31	60	.175	R	R	6-2	190	4-2-73	1991	Phoenix, Ariz.
Mendoza, Mario	0	1	11.32	6	0	0	0	10	20	13	13	8	4	.425	R	R	6-3	200	1-19-79	1999	Navojoa, Mexico
Nickoli, Mike	1	2	7.56	4	4	0	0	17	23	19	14	10	11	.315	R	R	6-5	200	3-6-80	2001	Hoover, Ala.
Peralta, Joel	5	4	2.24	47	0	0	20	52	39	13	13	12	48	.205	R	R	5-11	160	3-23-76	1996	Bonao, D.R.
Pine, Chris	2	0	5.11	9	0	0	0	12	12	11	7	7	6	.250	R	R	6-2	200	9-25-76	1998	Hillsboro, Ore.
Rogers, Brian	2	1	3.97	25	2	0	0	34	38	19	15	14	27	.287	R	R	6-6	200	2-13-77	1998	Carthage, N.C.
Santana, Ervin	1	1	3.94	6	6	0	0	30	23	15	13	12	23	.211	R	R	6-2	150	1-10-83	2001	San Cristobal, D.R.
Schneider, Scott	8	4	4.06	33	2	0	0	71	63	39	32	25	51	.228	R	R	6-4	210	5-4-78	2000	Virginia Beach, Va.
Smith, Cliff	1	0	2.60	13	1	0	0	28	20	9	8	15	10	.208	R	R	6-6	200	10-13-79	2001	Haverhill, Mass.
Stokley, Billy	2	9	3.57	26	14	0	1	111	115	66	44	23	58	.266	L	R	6-4	200	5-13-77	2000	Pasadena, Texas
Turnbow, Derrick	1	0	0.00	7	0	0	3	14	4	0	0	5	19	.086	R	R	6-3	210	1-25-78	1997	Franklin, Tenn.
Wilhite, Matt	0	2	8.38	5	0	0	2	10	17	12	9	1	8	.377	R	R	6-1	185	7-3-81	2003	Franklin, Ky.

FIELDING

Catcher	PCT	G	PO	A	E	DP	PB
Budde	.985	73	515	60	9	2	7
Del Chiaro	.982	33	193	28	4	0	9
Hill	.981	18	95	11	2	0	3
Mathis	.995	23	176	16	1	0	5

First Base	PCT	G	PO	A	E	DP
Del Chiaro	1.000	1	5	0	0	0
Hill	.992	25	226	12	2	21
O'Keefe	.984	95	748	68	13	91
Zamora	.995	25	165	20	1	4

Second Base	PCT	G	PO	A	E	DP
Alviso	1.000	1	4	1	0	0
Duncan	.958	19	24	45	3	4
Harrison	.955	20	22	41	3	11
Hill	.000	1	0	0	0	0
Mann	1.000	6	7	23	0	2
Pichardo	.933	3	6	8	1	3
Salazar	.951	25	46	71	6	21
Smith	.955	64	92	186	13	36
Specht	.957	9	14	30	2	8

Third Base	PCT	G	PO	A	E	DP
Cahill	1.000	1	0	1	0	0
Duncan	.800	4	1	7	2	1
Harrison	.950	8	7	12	1	0
Hill	.750	5	0	9	3	1
Mann	1.000	1	0	1	0	0
McPherson	.955	21	17	25	2	2
Pichardo	.946	16	12	23	2	2
Salazar	.714	6	2	3	2	0
Smith	.933	18	8	34	3	3
Zamora	.902	69	44	121	18	10

Shortstop	PCT	G	PO	A	E	DP
Alviso	1.000	1	3	3	0	1
Harrison	.958	16	27	41	3	9
Salazar	.969	7	14	17	1	4
Specht	.936	119	204	294	34	77

Outfield	PCT	G	PO	A	E	DP
Duncan	.932	47	64	4	5	1
Gorneault	.988	29	75	4	1	0
Haynes	.976	90	240	8	6	4
Hill	.000	1	0	0	0	0
James	.980	124	282	7	6	2
O'Keefe	1.000	9	14	0	0	0
Quintero	.000	1	0	0	0	0
Salazar	1.000	3	6	2	0	0
Weber	.980	125	237	10	5	1

RANCHO CUCAMONGA QUAKES — High Class A

CALIFORNIA LEAGUE

BATTING	AVG	G	AB	R	H	2B	3B	HR	RBI	BB	SO	SB	CS	SLG	OBP	B	T	HT	WT	DOB	1st Yr	Resides
Aspito, Jason	.258	117	449	57	116	31	4	12	61	22	94	7	8	.425	.310	L	R	6-0	200	1-3-79	2000	Itasca, Ill.
Budde, Ryan	.240	14	50	6	12	3	1	1	6	2	10	0	0	.400	.259	R	R	5-11	200	8-15-79	2001	Midwest City, Okla.
Corbeil, Al	.254	76	244	22	62	13	0	3	38	14	53	0	1	.344	.303	L	R	6-0	190	12-16-78	2001	Margate, Fla.
Coulie, Jason	.243	38	148	22	36	11	1	1	13	12	32	3	5	.351	.304	R	R	6-2	200	4-13-78	2000	Manchester, N.H.

BATTING	AVG	G	AB	R	H	2B	3B	HR	RBI	BB	SO	SB	CS	SLG	OBP	B	T	HT	WT	DOB	1st Yr	Resides
Del Chiaro, Brent	.227	7	22	2	5	0	0	0	3	3	9	0	0	.227	.370	R	R	6-3	220	6-26-79	2001	Oakley, Calif.
Duenas, Tommy	.071	5	14	0	1	0	0	0	1	1	6	0	0	.071	.133	R	R	5-11	200	7-16-81	2002	Miami, Fla.
Esposito, Brian	.344	9	32	2	11	2	0	0	2	0	5	0	0	.406	.344	R	R	6-1	190	2-24-79	2000	Willington, Conn.
Eylward, Mike	.290	109	389	51	113	27	2	13	61	35	67	1	4	.470	.355	R	R	6-2	210	9-28-79	2001	Clearwater, Fla.
Gates, David	.235	75	264	35	62	17	1	10	42	17	78	3	3	.420	.287	R	R	6-1	200	9-23-80	2001	Huntsville, Ala.
Glaus, Troy	.333	2	6	1	2	0	0	0	1	3	2	0	0	.333	.556	R	R	6-5	240	8-3-76	1997	Corona, Calif.
Gorneault, Nick	.321	97	374	67	120	36	2	14	72	20	82	11	6	.540	.363	R	R	6-3	200	4-19-79	2001	Springfield, Mass.
Kennedy, Adam	.273	3	11	3	3	1	0	1	1	0	2	0	0	.636	.333	L	R	6-1	180	1-10-76	1997	Yorba Linda, Calif.
Kimpton, Nick	.228	109	342	27	78	8	2	1	18	29	63	20	7	.272	.293	L	L	6-1	170	10-27-83	2001	Canberra, Australia
Kotchman, Casey	.350	57	206	42	72	12	0	8	28	30	16	2	0	.524	.441	L	L	6-3	210	2-22-83	2001	Seminole, Fla.
Mann, Derek	.282	11	39	5	11	1	0	0	3	1	4	0	1	.308	.300	L	R	6-0	180	3-8-78	1996	Columbus, Ga.
Mathis, Jeff	.323	97	378	73	122	28	3	11	54	35	74	5	3	.500	.384	R	R	6-0	180	3-31-83	2001	Marianna, Fla.
McPherson, Dallas	.308	77	292	65	90	21	6	18	59	41	79	12	6	.606	.404	L	R	6-4	230	7-23-80	2001	Randleman, N.C.
Melgarejo, Ransel	.261	29	111	15	29	3	1	1	10	11	14	4	2	.333	.331	R	R	6-0	180	8-28-81	2001	Miami, Fla.
Murphy, Tommy	.267	132	565	74	151	25	6	11	43	31	138	24	12	.391	.313	R	R	6-0	180	8-27-79	2000	Boynton Beach, Fla.
Napoli, Michael	.267	47	165	28	44	10	1	4	26	23	32	5	0	.412	.364	R	R	6-0	200	10-31-81	2000	Cooper City, Fla.
Pichardo, Maximo	.223	34	94	11	21	5	0	0	6	8	11	2	1	.277	.291	R	R	6-0	150	6-27-79	1999	Santo Domingo, D.R.
Riera, Zack	.000	3	10	1	0	0	0	0	0	1	4	0	0	.000	.167	S	R	6-0	190	4-16-79	2000	Tallahassee, Fla.
Rodriguez, Javy	.262	32	122	17	32	5	1	2	6	5	21	6	4	.369	.291	R	R	5-11	170	1-16-79	2002	Miami, Fla.
Smith, Casey	.285	37	130	12	37	2	0	3	15	10	11	1	2	.369	.350	R	R	6-2	200	3-18-79	2001	Ashford, Ala.
Sugden, Jason	.000	1	0	1	0	0	0	0	0	0	0	0	0	.000	.000	S	R	6-3	190	10-11-81	2002	Harrisburg, Penn.
Turner, Justin	.260	106	384	46	100	17	9	8	55	28	111	2	7	.414	.310	L	R	6-1	190	12-19-79	2001	Cape Coral, Fla.

PITCHING	W	L	ERA	G	GS	CG	SV	IP	H	R	ER	BB	SO	AVG	B	T	HT	WT	DOB	1st Yr	Resides
Andrade, Stephen	0	0	0.00	3	0	0	1	3	0	0	0	3	7	.000	R	R	6-1	220	2-6-78	2001	Woodland, Calif.
Bilke, Austin	2	1	7.25	14	0	0	0	22	35	22	18	10	16	.364	R	R	6-2	220	8-13-79	2002	Beaver Dam, Wisc.
Bittner, Tim	5	0	0.28	6	6	1	0	33	18	5	1	14	28	.160	L	L	6-2	200	6-9-80	2001	Wilmington, Del.
Buckley, Allen	1	0	6.50	6	4	0	0	18	20	13	13	7	22	.270	R	R	6-6	240	9-18-79	2003	Brandon, Miss.
Bukowski, Stan	0	0	0.57	6	0	0	0	16	8	2	1	4	9	.150	R	R	6-4	220	9-16-81	1999	Clearwater, Fla.
Camp, Rusty	3	1	8.34	17	0	0	0	23	34	25	21	14	21	.357	S	R	6-1	200	7-15-79	2000	Aberdeen, Miss.
D'Amico, Leonardo	0	1	7.00	6	1	0	0	9	8	7	7	3	5	.235	R	R	6-2	170	12-14-81	1999	Mariara,Venez.
Griffith, Dustin	3	2	3.89	36	2	0	2	72	76	33	31	19	53	.274	R	R	6-4	190	9-16-80	2001	Littleton, Colo.
Mendoza, Mario	1	0	11.57	4	0	0	0	7	14	9	9	3	6	.424	R	R	6-3	200	1-19-79	1999	Navojoa, Mexico
Mozingo, Dan	6	7	6.04	20	16	1	0	92	110	72	62	39	55	.301	L	L	6-2	190	6-3-80	1998	Ashtabula, Ohio
Nickoli, Mike	1	0	3.32	4	3	0	0	19	19	8	7	5	8	.267	R	R	6-5	200	3-6-80	2001	Hoover, Ala.
O'Sullivan, Mark	3	2	3.70	52	0	0	2	75	59	34	31	33	56	.211	R	R	6-2	200	10-24-78	2001	Andover, Mass.
Petke, Tim	2	7	4.39	10	10	0	0	55	60	31	27	17	35	.294	R	R	6-3	225	4-17-80	2003	Portland, Ore.
Ramirez, Edward	0	2	8.10	4	4	0	0	17	29	16	15	7	9	.386	R	R	6-3	150	3-28-84	2001	San Juan, D.R.
Reyes, Ramon	0	0	22.50	1	0	0	0	2	5	5	5	5	2	.454	R	R	5-11	160	10-22-81	2002	San Pedro de Macoris, D.R.
Rouwenhorst, Jon	1	5	1.73	52	0	0	20	62	58	27	12	14	52	.244	L	L	6-1	180	9-25-79	2001	Anaheim, Calif.
Santana, Ervin	10	2	2.53	20	20	1	0	125	98	44	35	36	130	.211	R	R	6-2	150	1-10-83	2001	San Cristobal, D.R.
Schneider, Scott	3	2	5.19	17	0	0	3	26	27	17	15	18	21	.267	R	R	6-4	210	5-4-78	2000	Virginia Beach, Va.
Sele, Aaron	0	0	4.50	3	2	0	0	8	12	4	4	3	7	.375	R	R	6-5	230	6-25-70	1991	Bellevue, Wash.
Shell, Steven	6	8	4.24	22	21	1	0	127	123	66	60	26	100	.248	R	R	6-5	190	3-10-83	2001	Cleburne, Texas
Smith, Cliff	2	2	5.79	15	5	0	2	33	38	23	21	9	25	.292	R	R	6-6	200	10-13-79	2001	Haverhill, Mass.
Smith, Jesse	0	4	7.13	5	5	0	0	24	26	19	19	12	7	.279	R	R	6-2	210	7-11-80	2003	Lincoln, Neb.
Thompson, Richard	2	2	4.91	24	0	0	8	29	28	19	16	18	33	.245	R	R	6-1	170	7-1-84	2002	Sydney, Australia
Torres, Joe	3	3	5.88	8	7	0	0	34	47	28	22	20	17	.345	L	L	6-2	180	9-3-82	2000	Kissimmee, Fla.
Williams, Bryan	3	3	6.80	19	2	0	0	42	55	40	32	27	20	.312	R	R	5-11	170	1-26-80	2002	Orlando, Fla.
Wilson, Phil	1	1	3.72	2	2	0	0	10	13	13	4	3	6	.288	R	R	6-8	200	4-1-81	1999	Ramona, Calif.
Wolensky, Dave	4	4	5.87	46	2	0	4	80	89	64	52	46	92	.276	R	R	6-0	190	1-15-80	2000	Atlanta, Ga.
Woods, Jake	12	7	3.99	28	28	2	0	171	178	90	76	54	109	.269	L	L	6-1	190	9-3-81	2001	Kingsburg, Calif.

FIELDING

Catcher	PCT	G	PO	A	E	DP	PB
Budde	.967	12	76	13	3	0	0
Corbeil	.957	10	40	4	2	0	0
Del Chiaro	.982	7	52	3	1	1	0
Duenas	.976	5	37	3	1	0	2
Esposito	1.000	7	52	5	0	0	0
Mathis	.991	82	562	67	6	6	14
Napoli	.986	20	119	20	2	0	2
Riera	.960	3	23	1	1	0	1

First Base	PCT	G	PO	A	E	DP
Corbeil	.980	45	314	26	7	23
Eylward	.991	52	431	27	4	44
Kotchman	.988	48	388	23	5	36
Napoli	1.000	6	51	3	0	7

Second Base	PCT	G	PO	A	E	DP
Kennedy	.923	3	8	4	1	2
Mann	1.000	6	6	13	0	2
Pichardo	.950	9	9	10	1	3
Rodriguez	.925	23	41	57	8	15
Smith	.985	13	29	36	1	11
Turner	.952	93	157	203	18	46

Third Base	PCT	G	PO	A	E	DP
Eylward	.884	31	17	44	8	2
Mann	.900	6	5	13	2	1
McPherson	.926	67	37	137	14	16
Pichardo	.848	18	7	32	7	5
Rodriguez	.833	3	1	4	1	0
Smith	.923	22	18	42	5	2

Shortstop	PCT	G	PO	A	E	DP
Murphy	.942	131	212	375	36	69
Pichardo	.944	3	10	7	1	3
Rodriguez	1.000	4	5	12	0	3
Smith	1.000	2	5	6	0	0

Outfield	PCT	G	PO	A	E	DP
Aspito	.975	111	184	8	5	2
Corbeil	.000	1	0	0	0	0
Coulie	.981	34	52	1	1	0
Eylward	.875	8	14	0	2	0
Gates	.951	55	93	4	5	0
Gorneault	.972	94	237	8	7	1
Kimpton	.983	108	286	9	5	3
Melgarejo	.984	29	61	2	1	1
Sugden	.000	1	0	0	0	0

CEDAR RAPIDS KERNELS — Low Class A

MIDWEST LEAGUE

BATTING	AVG	G	AB	R	H	2B	3B	HR	RBI	BB	SO	SB	CS	SLG	OBP	B	T	HT	WT	DOB	1st Yr	Resides
Abram, Matt	.197	41	132	19	26	7	0	7	24	11	35	1	0	.409	.264	R	R	6-0	180	6-13-80	2001	Scottsdale, Ariz.
Abruzzo, Jared	.271	130	468	64	127	30	1	13	73	59	99	1	0	.423	.352	S	R	6-3	210	11-15-81	2000	La Mesa, Calif.
Aybar, Erick	.308	125	496	83	153	30	10	6	57	17	54	32	9	.446	.346	S	R	5-11	160	1-14-84	2002	Bani, D.R.
Brown, Matt	.207	49	164	22	34	6	1	3	15	19	36	1	0	.311	.307	R	R	6-0	180	8-8-82	2001	Hayden, Idaho
Callaspo, Alberto	.327	133	514	86	168	38	4	2	67	42	28	20	6	.428	.377	S	R	5-10	150	4-19-83	2001	Maracay, Venez.
Contreras, Sergio	.176	12	34	6	6	1	0	0	3	6	7	3	1	.206	.333	L	L	5-10	190	4-30-80	1999	Esperanza, Mexico
Cosby, Quan	.249	104	370	55	92	4	1	0	21	36	79	17	9	.265	.316	S	R	5-10	190	12-23-82	2001	Mart, Texas
Duenas, Tommy	.216	22	51	4	11	2	0	2	10	1	15	0	1	.373	.245	R	R	5-11	200	7-16-81	2002	Miami, Fla.

BATTING	AVG	G	AB	R	H	2B	3B	HR	RBI	BB	SO	SB	CS	SLG	OBP	B	T	HT	WT	DOB	1st Yr	Resides
Dvorsky, Alex	.252	96	302	42	76	10	3	7	36	35	52	2	2	.374	.340	R	R	6-2	200	8-8-79	2002	Marion, Iowa
Gates, David	.250	25	88	11	22	1	1	5	19	5	24	1	1	.455	.295	R	R	6-1	200	9-23-80	2001	Huntsville, Ala.
Hancock, Justin	.161	23	62	3	10	3	0	0	2	6	24	0	0	.210	.246	R	R	6-2	190	3-10-80	2002	Valrico, Fla.
Jenkins, Kevin	.171	50	123	9	21	0	1	1	9	12	37	6	2	.211	.254	L	L	6-0	200	4-6-82	2000	Miami, Fla.
Maher, Caleb	.233	92	335	36	78	13	3	7	46	16	71	2	1	.352	.277	R	R	6-2	200	3-22-83	2002	Ceres, Calif.
Mathis, Jake	.229	104	354	32	81	9	1	4	40	25	104	5	5	.294	.285	L	R	6-3	200	1-24-80	2002	Marianna, Fla.
Melgarejo, Ransel	.262	85	290	43	76	11	1	3	28	28	40	9	5	.338	.333	R	R	6-0	180	8-28-81	2001	Miami, Fla.
Pavkovich, Adam	.320	35	125	20	40	6	0	1	18	13	19	1	1	.392	.382	R	R	6-2	185	12-31-81	2003	Venice, Fla.
Porter, Greg	.305	79	279	48	85	17	5	4	52	30	52	1	2	.444	.381	L	R	6-4	220	8-15-80	2001	Roanoke, Texas
Sugden, Jason	.304	21	56	6	17	0	1	0	7	7	21	0	1	.339	.381	S	R	6-3	190	10-11-81	2002	Harrisburg, Pa.
Weed, B.J.	.264	116	435	45	115	14	3	0	32	16	58	16	12	.310	.292	L	R	5-10	180	11-11-79	2003	Maybrook, N.Y.

PITCHING	W	L	ERA	G	GS	CG	SV	IP	H	R	ER	BB	SO	AVG	B	T	HT	WT	DOB	1st Yr	Resides
Arias, Daniel	2	2	4.39	29	0	0	0	41	41	22	20	21	37	.264	R	R	6-1	220	6-19-82	2000	Bani, D.R.
Astacio, Hector	2	2	4.18	6	6	0	0	28	32	18	13	6	19	.288	R	R	6-0	160	8-10-83	2000	Hato Mayor, D.R.
Bilke, Austin	1	3	5.91	19	0	0	4	21	26	15	14	6	25	.282	R	R	6-2	220	8-13-79	2002	Beaver Dam, Wisc.
Carroll, James	1	2	2.56	23	0	0	5	32	25	12	9	10	19	.215	R	R	6-0	185	2-1-80	2003	Arlington, Texas
Cimorelli, Brett	1	2	7.57	31	5	0	0	69	89	68	58	54	31	.328	R	R	6-4	220	2-22-82	2000	Zephyrhills, Fla.
D'Amico, Leonardo	1	2	5.90	12	5	0	1	29	33	20	19	7	16	.282	R	R	6-2	170	12-14-81	1999	Mariara,Venez.
Gliemmo, Hayden	7	3	3.73	42	0	0	0	63	55	32	26	33	53	.232	L	L	5-10	170	11-20-78	2003	Moultrie, Ga.
Goas, Adrian	0	0	5.06	18	0	0	1	27	28	21	15	17	12	.266	R	R	6-7	210	11-24-79	2002	San Juan, P.R.
Griffith, Dustin	0	0	5.68	4	0	0	0	6	10	4	4	2	3	.357	R	R	6-4	190	9-16-80	2001	Littleton, Colo.
Holcomb, James	2	6	3.91	14	14	0	0	71	68	37	31	36	61	.249	R	R	6-5	190	11-28-80	2002	Reno, Nev.
Jepsen, Kevin	6	3	2.65	10	10	0	0	51	32	24	15	28	42	.179	R	R	6-3	200	7-26-84	2002	Sparks, Nev.
Lincoln, Matt	1	1	3.55	10	0	0	1	13	12	5	5	5	14	.240	R	L	6-1	205	10-11-83	2003	Windsor, Calif.
Lugo, Ozzie	1	2	2.63	52	0	0	10	65	40	20	19	29	79	.175	R	R	6-0	220	12-22-80	2002	Miami, Fla.
Marquez, Jeff	3	4	5.23	45	2	0	0	83	93	60	48	43	51	.274	L	R	6-0	200	11-5-81	2002	Hialeah, Fla.
Morban, Carlos	0	0	5.59	9	0	0	0	10	14	6	6	6	13	.341	R	R	6-6	180	1-29-83	2001	Santo Domingo, D.R.
Moreno, Abel	1	1	1.62	3	3	0	0	17	13	3	3	3	15	.228	R	R	6-2	180	6-15-83	2001	Santo Domingo, D.R.
Posey, Micah	8	6	3.34	20	20	0	0	110	100	48	41	51	68	.241	L	L	6-5	220	10-18-82	2002	Tallahassee, Fla.
Ramirez, Edward	1	1	3.32	6	1	0	0	19	17	7	7	8	15	.232	R	R	6-3	150	3-28-84	2001	San Juan, D.R.
Ray, Ronnie	3	11	5.13	20	20	0	0	100	109	65	57	46	60	.273	R	R	6-3	190	5-11-84	2002	Pacific, Mo.
Reyes, Ramon	2	0	0.00	4	0	0	0	5	2	2	0	3	4	.105	R	R	5-11	160	10-22-81	2002	San Pedro de Macoris, D.R.
Rodriguez , Rafael	10	11	4.31	26	26	1	0	144	129	85	69	59	100	.235	R	R	6-1	170	9-24-84	2001	Santo Domingo, D.R.
Thompson, Richard	1	2	0.24	31	0	0	9	38	18	5	1	13	54	.139	R	R	6-1	170	7-1-84	2002	Sydney, Australia
Toledo, Jean	12	7	2.44	24	24	0	0	136	132	60	37	50	58	.262	R	R	6-1	160	3-6-83	2001	Barcelona, Venez.
Williams, Bryan	0	0	7.94	7	0	0	0	11	11	11	10	12	9	.261	R	R	5-11	170	1-26-80	2002	Orlando, Fla.
Wilson, Phil	0	1	4.09	2	2	1	0	11	10	6	5	3	6	.250	R	R	6-8	200	4-1-81	1999	Ramona, Calif.

FIELDING

Catcher	PCT	G	PO	A	E	DP	PB
Abram	1.000	4	5	0	0	0	0
Abruzzo	.978	94	572	54	14	3	18
Duenas	1.000	20	86	8	0	0	1
Dvorsky	.996	38	224	31	1	1	2

First Base	PCT	G	PO	A	E	DP
Abram	.988	28	233	17	3	22
Brown	1.000	1	7	0	0	2
Contreras	1.000	8	74	7	0	3
Hancock	.975	10	71	6	2	9
Jenkins	.932	10	64	4	5	5
Mathis	.984	94	729	52	13	55

Second Base	PCT	G	PO	A	E	DP
Callaspo	.969	124	234	332	18	68
Pavkovich	1.000	1	1	0	0	0
Weed	.975	29	34	45	2	10

Third Base	PCT	G	PO	A	E	DP
Abram	.667	3	1	1	1	1
Brown	.896	48	37	92	15	8
Hancock	.857	8	9	9	3	1
Mathis	.923	12	5	19	2	1
Pavkovich	.937	26	19	55	5	8
Porter	.938	48	47	88	9	7
Weed	.667	2	0	2	1	0

Shortstop	PCT	G	PO	A	E	DP
Aybar	.944	124	212	324	32	64
Callaspo	.966	7	13	15	1	3
Hancock	.833	6	1	4	1	0
Pavkovich	.905	10	12	26	4	4
Porter	1.000	4	3	1	0	0

Outfield	PCT	G	PO	A	E	DP
Contreras	1.000	4	5	0	0	0
Cosby	.981	101	246	6	5	1
Gates	1.000	18	28	2	0	0
Hancock	.000	1	0	0	0	0
Jenkins	.959	32	46	1	2	0
Maher	.950	69	110	5	6	1
Melgarejo	.994	80	164	1	1	0
Porter	.980	29	47	3	1	1
Sugden	.963	20	23	3	1	1
Weed	.966	94	163	7	6	2

PROVO ANGELS — Rookie

PIONEER LEAGUE

BATTING	AVG	G	AB	R	H	2B	3B	HR	RBI	BB	SO	SB	CS	SLG	OBP	B	T	HT	WT	DOB	1st Yr	Resides
Almonte, Aneury	.259	26	54	13	14	1	0	0	2	12	14	6	3	.278	.403	R	R	5-11	150	9-15-80	2001	San Pedro de Macoris, D.R.
Balkcom, Blake	.290	36	131	20	38	12	0	2	28	10	26	0	0	.427	.345	R	R	6-2	225	8-8-82	2003	Chipley, Fla.
Blanco, Gregory	.333	4	3	0	1	0	0	0	0	0	2	0	0	.333	.500	R	R	5-11	170	12-24-83	2002	Cua, Venez.
Brown, Matt	.292	65	233	58	68	19	0	11	52	42	56	2	3	.515	.412	R	R	6-0	180	8-8-82	2001	Hayden, Idaho
Collins, Mike	.333	37	132	20	44	8	2	1	15	3	19	0	0	.447	.353	R	R	6-3	210	7-18-84	2001	Canberra, Australia
Duenas, Tommy	.267	14	45	10	12	3	0	2	7	12	11	0	0	.467	.421	R	R	5-11	200	7-16-81	2002	Miami, Fla.
Esposito, Brian	.091	3	11	0	1	0	0	0	0	0	4	0	0	.091	.091	R	R	6-1	190	2-24-79	2000	Willington, Conn.
Guzman, Jose	.277	34	94	19	26	7	3	1	14	10	32	3	0	.447	.352	S	R	6-0	160	10-19-83	2001	Santo Domingo, D.R.
Hauseman, Chad	.200	23	65	7	13	2	0	0	11	5	16	1	0	.231	.257	R	R	6-1	205	11-11-79	2003	Neptune Beach, Fla.
Hess, Samuel	.143	3	7	1	1	1	0	0	1	2	1	0	0	.286	.333	R	R	6-2	215	12-5-79	2003	Colbert, Wash.
Kendrick, Howie	.368	63	234	65	86	20	3	3	36	24	28	8	3	.517	.434	R	R	5-10	180	7-12-83	2002	Callahan, Fla.
Kenning, Ryan	.261	55	184	31	48	18	1	10	38	24	70	2	0	.533	.357	L	L	6-0	190	11-10-80	2002	North Vancouver, B.C.
Madrigal, Warner	.369	70	279	75	103	28	2	9	51	12	58	2	0	.581	.394	R	R	6-0	190	3-21-84	2001	San Pedro de Macoris, D.R.
Pali, Matt	.327	64	223	47	73	15	3	8	43	32	44	2	1	.529	.422	L	L	6-1	215	12-10-80	2003	Houston, Texas
Pavkovich, Adam	.283	27	106	17	30	6	0	1	11	14	21	2	1	.368	.381	R	R	6-2	185	12-31-81	2003	Venice, Fla.
Peel, Aaron	.302	65	242	39	73	18	2	6	39	19	57	1	2	.467	.364	R	R	6-1	190	2-8-83	2002	Seminole, Texas
Renz, Jordan	.250	5	20	2	5	1	0	1	5	2	8	0	0	.450	.318	S	R	6-2	200	7-21-83	2002	Broken Arrow, Okla.
Willits, Reggie	.300	59	230	53	69	14	4	4	27	37	52	14	4	.448	.410	S	R	5-11	185	5-30-81	2003	Noble, Okla.
Wilson, Bobby	.284	57	236	36	67	12	0	6	62	18	31	0	0	.411	.329	R	R	6-0	205	4-8-83	2003	Seminole, Fla.
Wood, Brandon	.278	42	162	25	45	13	2	5	31	16	48	1	1	.475	.348	R	R	6-3	185	3-2-85	2003	Scottsdale, Ariz.

GAMES BY POSITION: C—Collins 22, Duenas 13, Esposito 3, Hess 2, Wilson 40. **1B**—Kenning 49, Pali 35, Wilson 1. **2B**—Almonte 23, Guzman 4, Kendrick 63. **3B**—Almonte 1, Brown 63, Pavkovich 3, Wilson 7, Wood 10. **SS**—Guzman 22, Pavkovich 26, Wood 35. **OF**—Balkcom 35, Guzman 7, Hauseman 12, Kenning 2, Madrigal 70, Pali 26, Peel 34, Renz 5, Willits 58.

PITCHING	W	L	ERA	G	GS	CG	SV	IP	H	R	ER	BB	SO	AVG	B	T	HT	WT	DOB	1st Yr	Resides
Astacio, Hector	0	3	11.39	14	3	0	0	28	50	42	35	15	21	.390	R	R	6-0	160	8-10-83	2000	Hato Mayor, D.R.
Austen, David	4	2	1.85	23	3	0	8	44	46	12	9	7	49	.269	R	R	6-1	185	5-21-81	2003	Coconut Creek, Fla.
Carroll, James	0	1	3.24	4	0	0	0	8	9	3	3	2	9	.272	R	R	6-0	185	2-1-80	2003	Arlington, Texas
Cox, Jason	1	1	6.39	9	0	0	1	13	17	12	9	4	7	.303	R	R	6-6	215	4-7-83	2003	Albuquerque, N.M.
Davidson, Daniel	8	2	1.64	15	13	0	0	71	65	17	13	15	50	.239	L	L	6-4	225	1-8-81	2003	Lynn Haven, Fla.
Goas, Adrian	1	0	3.12	7	0	0	4	9	9	3	3	2	4	.257	R	R	6-7	210	11-24-79	2002	San Juan, P.R.
Hedden, Wayne	2	0	2.76	17	0	0	1	33	33	15	10	14	20	.268	R	R	6-2	200	10-27-82	2003	Tampa, Fla.
Hindman, Scott	3	0	4.13	6	4	0	0	24	21	13	11	13	17	.238	L	L	6-4	210	3-6-81	2002	Inverness, Ill.
Morban, Carlos	2	1	3.18	21	0	0	5	23	20	8	8	8	26	.238	R	R	6-6	180	1-29-83	2001	Santo Domingo, D.R.
Moreno, Abel	10	0	2.38	13	10	0	0	68	58	23	18	10	79	.223	R	R	6-2	180	6-15-83	2001	Santo Domingo, D.R.
Pawelczyk, Kyle	3	2	4.03	5	4	0	0	22	19	13	10	8	20	.231	L	L	6-5	180	11-18-81	2002	Elkins, W.Va.
Pullin, Aaron	5	1	3.42	23	0	0	0	47	54	23	18	5	32	.287	R	R	6-3	200	2-17-81	2003	Midland, Texas
Requena, Ricardo	2	2	9.35	9	1	0	0	17	28	28	18	6	14	.337	R	R	6-0	160	5-27-84	2001	Maracay, Venez.
Reyes, Ramon	0	1	7.88	6	0	0	1	8	12	7	7	6	8	.342	R	R	5-11	160	10-22-81	2002	San Pedro de Macoris, D.R.
Rodriguez, Fernando	0	0	1.50	4	0	0	1	6	9	4	1	1	9	.333	R	R	6-3	210	6-18-84	2003	El Paso, Texas
Simard, Michel	4	1	2.08	12	10	0	0	52	42	15	12	12	53	.217	R	R	6-3	200	9-4-81	2003	Charlesburg, Quebec
Smith, Jesse	0	1	2.41	5	3	0	0	19	19	8	5	6	20	.256	R	R	6-2	210	7-11-80	2003	Lincoln, Neb.
Stertzbach, Von	1	1	4.82	22	5	0	0	47	55	31	25	14	51	.277	R	R	6-2	190	5-15-81	2003	Plantation, Fla.
Touchstone, Nick	2	1	3.56	14	10	0	0	48	47	27	19	35	48	.262	L	L	6-5	220	11-19-81	2003	Niceville, Fla.
Wilhite, Matt	2	0	2.63	12	0	0	5	27	23	11	8	5	17	.227	R	R	6-1	185	7-3-81	2003	Franklin, Ky.
Zimmermann, Bob	4	2	4.50	11	10	0	0	48	57	29	24	8	37	.285	R	R	6-5	225	11-17-81	2003	St. Louis, Mo.

MESA ANGELS — Rookie

ARIZONA LEAGUE

BATTING	AVG	G	AB	R	H	2B	3B	HR	RBI	BB	SO	SB	CS	SLG	OBP	B	T	HT	WT	DOB	1st Yr	Resides
Almonte, Aneury	.200	9	30	3	6	0	0	0	2	6	8	3	0	.200	.351	R	R	5-11	150	9-15-80	2001	San Pedro de Macoris, D.R.
Blanco, Gregory	.292	10	24	5	7	1	0	0	1	6	6	0	0	.333	.433	R	R	5-11	170	12-24-83	2002	Cua, Venez.
Boyer, Billy	.291	41	165	24	48	3	5	0	18	13	40	3	3	.370	.337	S	R	6-0	185	3-8-84	2003	Sumner, Wash.
Collins, Mike	.368	11	38	9	14	5	1	0	6	2	5	0	0	.553	.409	R	R	6-3	210	7-18-84	2001	Canberra, Australia
Cowles, Josh	.208	47	154	16	32	8	3	1	18	25	66	2	2	.318	.332	R	R	6-2	185	6-7-84	2003	Redlands, Calif.
Del Orbe, Samuel	.285	46	151	28	43	6	4	2	19	11	42	6	4	.417	.329	R	R	6-0	170	4-18-82	2002	Cotui, D.R.
Harrison, Adonis	.333	1	3	0	1	0	0	0	0	1	0	0	0	.333	.500	L	R	5-9	160	9-28-76	1995	Pasadena, Calif.
Hess, Samuel	.190	7	21	2	4	1	0	0	0	1	5	0	0	.238	.227	R	R	6-2	215	12-5-79	2003	Colbert, Wash.
Jones, J.J.	.235	29	102	13	24	5	0	0	14	3	21	4	1	.284	.271	R	R	6-4	200	6-29-83	2001	Houston, Texas
Kotchman, Casey	.333	7	27	5	9	1	0	2	6	2	3	0	0	.593	.379	L	L	6-3	210	2-22-83	2001	Seminole, Fla.
LePage, Patrice	.213	32	89	18	19	5	2	0	8	14	31	1	2	.315	.324	L	R	6-1	200	7-10-84	2003	St. Catherine, Quebec
Lopez, Baltazar	.301	44	173	26	52	12	3	2	23	16	46	3	0	.439	.360	L	L	6-1	180	11-22-83	2003	Caborca, Mexico
Martinez, Brett	.250	46	148	16	37	1	3	0	15	19	22	9	5	.297	.337	R	R	6-0	174	10-14-83	2003	Redlands, Calif.
Nunez, Felix	.333	30	123	23	41	6	2	0	10	9	15	8	6	.415	.390	R	R	6-1	170	10-9-82	2001	El Tigre, Venez.
Renz, Jordan	.260	52	204	31	53	9	7	5	28	17	59	4	1	.446	.321	S	R	6-2	200	7-21-83	2002	Broken Arrow, Okla.
Rodriguez, Sean	.269	54	216	30	58	8	5	2	25	14	37	11	4	.380	.332	R	R	6-0	180	4-26-85	2003	Miami, Fla.
Walston, Chris	.182	52	198	25	36	7	3	6	36	19	88	1	1	.338	.255	R	R	6-6	230	10-1-84	2002	Lakeside, Calif.
Wood, Brandon	.308	19	78	14	24	8	2	0	13	4	15	3	0	.462	.349	R	R	6-3	185	3-2-85	2003	Scottsdale, Ariz.

GAMES BY POSITION: C—Blanco 6, Collins 8, Hess 6, LePage 17, Martinez 36. **1B**—Blanco 1, Kotchman 4, Lopez 27, Martinez 2, Walston 26. **2B**—Almonte 8, Boyer 41, Del Orbe 8, Rodriguez 4. **3B**—Almonte 2, Cowles 1, Del Orbe 31, Martinez 10, Nunez 1, Rodriguez 12, Wood 4. **SS**—Almonte 1, Del Orbe 6, Harrison 1, Rodriguez 37, Wood 14. **OF**—Cowles 43, Jones 29, Lepage 6, Martinez 1, Nunez 25, Renz 45, Rodriguez 4, Walston 22.

PITCHING	W	L	ERA	G	GS	CG	SV	IP	H	R	ER	BB	SO	AVG	B	T	HT	WT	DOB	1st Yr	Resides
Arnold, Mitchell	1	3	3.86	21	0	0	4	23	17	14	10	19	19	.204	R	R	6-9	230	1-31-82	2002	Saratoga, Wyo.
Benoit, Hector	0	0	27.00	5	0	0	0	5	10	14	14	9	4	.454	R	R	6-5	250	7-1-83	2000	Santiago, D.R.
Brito, Jose	0	0	4.42	13	0	0	0	18	22	15	9	11	12	.285	L	L	6-4	180	6-17-84	2001	San Cristobal, D.R.
Brown, B.J.	2	2	7.71	14	2	0	0	30	38	29	26	19	28	.322	L	L	6-1	195	8-1-80	2003	Niles, Mich.
Buckley, Allen	2	0	0.59	10	0	0	0	15	11	3	1	4	12	.220	R	R	6-6	240	9-18-79	2003	Brandon, Miss.
Bukowski, Stan	1	0	13.50	4	0	0	0	4	11	10	6	1	1	.478	R	R	6-4	220	9-16-81	1999	Clearwater, Fla.
Corbett, Jason	1	2	7.77	20	0	0	0	22	27	21	19	22	29	.296	R	R	6-7	230	1-8-84	2003	Palm Harbor, Fla.
Cox, Jason	3	3	3.81	10	10	0	0	50	58	28	21	11	37	.302	R	R	6-6	215	4-7-83	2003	Albuquerque, N.M.
D'Amico, Leonardo	0	0	0.00	1	0	0	0	1	1	0	0	2	2	.200	R	R	6-2	170	12-14-81	1999	Mariara,Venez.
Gamboa, Felix	0	2	9.95	10	2	0	1	13	15	15	14	17	10	.300	R	R	6-5	170	7-18-85	2002	Barcelona, Venez.
Gelinas, Karl	0	4	6.04	12	7	0	0	45	51	35	30	9	38	.291	R	R	6-4	200	8-6-83	2003	Iberville, Quebec
Green, Steve	1	1	1.29	2	2	0	0	7	4	2	1	2	7	.166	R	R	6-2	200	1-26-78	1997	Longueuil, Quebec
Hartnett, Chris	1	0	6.75	7	0	0	1	11	16	9	8	2	9	.333	R	L	6-3	225	8-2-81	2003	Albany, N.Y.
Hill, Andrew	2	2	2.79	6	5	0	0	19	17	7	6	12	18	.242	R	R	6-4	195	10-31-84	2003	Okanogan, Wash.
Hindman, Scott	2	1	3.13	6	6	0	0	23	22	10	8	8	23	.250	L	L	6-4	210	3-6-81	2002	Inverness, Ill.
Jenks, Bobby	0	0	0.00	1	1	0	0	4	2	0	0	0	5	.153	R	R	6-3	240	3-14-81	2000	Bothell, Wash.
Lincoln, Matt	0	0	1.08	6	0	0	2	8	2	2	1	6	14	.080	R	L	6-1	205	10-11-83	2003	Windsor, Calif.
Pawelczyk, Kyle	0	2	6.49	7	5	0	0	26	32	25	19	19	24	.290	L	L	6-5	180	11-18-81	2002	Elkins, W.Va.
Petke, Tim	1	0	1.69	4	1	0	0	16	11	4	3	5	22	.200	R	R	6-3	225	4-17-80	2003	Portland, Ore.
Requena, Ricardo	0	2	5.85	4	4	0	0	20	25	15	13	6	16	.304	R	R	6-0	160	5-27-84	2001	Maracay, Venez.
Reyes, Ramon	1	3	9.39	9	2	0	0	15	23	21	16	8	10	.328	R	R	5-11	160	10-22-81	2002	San Pedro de Macoris, D.R.
Rodriguez, Fernando	0	2	6.48	15	0	0	0	25	29	24	18	14	27	.284	R	R	6-3	210	6-18-84	2003	El Paso, Texas
Roque, Chris	0	3	6.66	17	0	0	0	24	35	21	18	14	16	.339	R	R	6-3	180	10-13-82	2003	Miami, Fla.
Saladin, John	1	0	3.92	13	0	0	0	21	23	12	9	8	16	.294	R	R	6-3	170	8-21-83	2001	San Pedro De Macoris, D.R.
Smith, Jesse	0	0	5.40	3	1	0	0	7	7	4	4	5	7	.304	R	R	6-2	210	7-11-80	2003	Lincoln, Neb.
Torres, Joe	2	0	0.56	3	3	0	0	16	7	2	1	6	15	.137	L	L	6-2	180	9-3-82	2000	Kissimmee, Fla.
Whittington, Anthony	0	3	8.03	9	5	0	0	25	31	24	22	17	20	.319	R	L	6-5	225	10-9-84	2003	Buffalo, W.Va.

ARIZONA DIAMONDBACKS

BY JACK MAGRUDER

The Diamondbacks thought they had dismissed the popular theory that they were a two-man team, pooh-poohing the notion even as twin aces Randy Johnson and Curt Schilling won 10 postseason games en route to the 2001 World Series title for Arizona and 90 regular season games in 2001-02.

But when Johnson, winner of four National League Cy Young awards, missed 12 weeks of the 2003 season after knee surgery, and Schilling missed another eight weeks because of an emergency appendectomy and a fractured right hand, the Diamondbacks missed the playoffs for only the second time in five years, still a model for expansion franchises.

The numbers suggest the translation is not exact, since the D-backs' pitching staff finished fourth in the National League with a 3.84 ERA. But without their two horses, Arizona often failed to find the extra hit or make the extra defensive play and slid to 84-78, third in the NL West. The 84 victories were the second-fewest in the franchise's six-season history.

Johnson and Schilling are signed through the 2004 season, and they may become focal points again as owner Jerry Colangelo, disappointed at not making the playoffs with an $85 million payroll, says he wants to decrease his payroll to about $50 million in the next two years.

Johnson had torn cartilage removed from his right knee in early May and returned after the all-star break, though it was clear he was never himself. He finished 6-8, 4.25 while allowing more hits than innings, his worst numbers since missing most of the 1996 season in Seattle after back surgery. Schilling pitched well but had only eight wins in 24 starts despite limiting opponents to a .230 average.

Rookies Brandon Webb and Oscar Villarreal and veteran Miguel Batista picked up a lot of the slack while leading the Diamondbacks with 10 wins apiece.

ORGANIZATION LEADERS

BATTING		
*AVG	Billy Martin, Tucson/El Paso	.348
R	Dan Uggla, Lancaster	104
H	Chad Tracy, Tucson	169
TB	Kyle Nichols, Lancaster	278
2B	Josh Kroeger, El Paso/Lancaster	39
3B	Luis Terrero, Tucson	15
HR	Kyle Nichols, Lancaster	31
RBI	Kyle Nichols, Lancaster	108
BB	Jeff Stanek, Lancaster/South Bend	55
SO	Kyle Nichols, Lancaster	118
SB	Marland Williams, Lancaster	57
*SLG	Billy Martin, Tucson/El Paso	.587
*OBP	Billy Martin, Tucson/El Paso	.424
PITCHING		
W	Sam Smith, South Bend	16
L	Matt Henrie, Tucson/El Paso/Lancaster	14
#ERA	Sergio Lizarraga, South Bend	1.78
G	Mark Freed, El Paso	67
CG	Matt Henrie, Tucson/El Paso/Lancaster	4
	Sam Smith, South Bend	4
SV	Matty Wilkinson, South Bend	30
IP	Matt Henrie, Tucson/El Paso/Lancaster	185
BB	Phil Stockman, Tucson/El Paso	68
SO	Phil Stockman, Tucson/El Paso	151

*Minimum 250 At-Bats #Minimum 75 Innings

Luis Gonzalez

Chad Tracy

PLAYERS of the YEAR

MAJOR LEAGUE: Luis Gonzalez, of

Gonzalez, 35, led the injury-ravaged Diamondbacks in almost every key offensive category in 2003. He hit .304 and was tops with 92 runs, 176 hits, 46 doubles, 26 homers and 104 RBIs.

MINOR LEAGUE: Chad Tracy, 3b

Tracy hit .324-10-80 with 31 doubles for Tucson to lead the Pacfic Coast League in average a year after winning the batting title in the Double-A Texas League. His 169 hits ranked seventh in the minors.

It would be hard to overstate the impact of Webb and Villarreal. Webb entered the rotation after Johnson's knee surgery and finished fourth in the NL in ERA, with 21 quality starts among his 28 starts, and was Baseball America's Rookie of the Year. Villarreal provided a bridge between the rotation and closer Matt Mantei, who had 29 saves despite missing a month with a shoulder injury. Villarreal set a major league record for appearances by a rookie with 86.

While veterans Luis Gonzalez and Steve Finley continued to produce, manager Bob Brenly juggled his lineup most of the year with a cast of rookies and role players.

Brenly used 11 cleanup hitters, 14 players in the No. 5 spot, 15 in the No. 6 spot and 18 in the No. 7 spot but nothing seemed to work. Arizona finished 10th in the NL in runs, 12th in home runs and 10th in on-base percentage. Arizona also committed 107 errors, tying a franchise season-high, and turned the NL's fewest double plays.

But as it appears the big league team will need an infusion of youth, the farm system looks like it will be able to provide it. Webb, Villarreal, Jose Valverde, Alex Cintron, Matt Kata and Robby Hammock all made contributions at the major league level in 2003, and the team marketed them as the "Baby 'Backs."

Others seem close. Third baseman Chad Tracy led the Triple-A Pacific Coast League in hitting at .324 and was a postseason all-star for the third straight season. Center fielder Luis Terrero made strides, hitting .287 with 15 triples and 23 stolen bases in his first season at Triple-A.

Righthander Edgar Gonzalez got a taste of the majors, as did lefthander Chris Capuano, who returned from Tommy John surgery and could challenge for a rotation spot in 2004. Closer Brian Bruney led both Tucson and El Paso in saves and features a 95-97 mph fastball.

ARIZONA DIAMONDBACKS

Manager: Bob Brenly.

2003 Record: 84-78, .519 (3rd, NL West).

BATTING	AVG	G	AB	R	H	2B	3B	HR	RBI	BB	SO	SB	CS	SLG	OBP	B	T	HT	WT	DOB	1st Yr	Resides
Baerga, Carlos	.343	105	207	31	71	13	0	4	39	18	20	1	1	.464	.396	S	R	5-11	215	11-4-68	1986	Bayamon, D.R.
Barajas, Rod	.218	80	220	19	48	15	0	3	28	14	43	0	0	.327	.265	R	R	6-2	220	9-5-75	1996	Scottsdale, Ariz.
Bautista, Danny	.275	88	284	29	78	16	3	4	36	21	50	3	2	.394	.330	R	R	5-11	225	5-24-72	1989	Santo Domingo, D.R.
Cintron, Alex	.317	117	448	70	142	26	6	13	51	29	33	2	3	.489	.359	S	R	6-2	200	12-17-78	1997	Yabucoa, P.R.
Counsell, Craig	.234	89	303	40	71	6	3	3	21	41	32	11	4	.304	.328	L	R	6-0	185	8-21-70	1992	Mequon, Wisc.
Dellucci, David	.242	70	165	18	40	11	3	2	19	19	45	9	0	.382	.328	L	L	5-11	190	10-31-73	1995	Baton Rouge, La.
Finley, Steve	.287	147	516	82	148	24	10	22	70	57	94	15	8	.500	.363	L	L	6-2	195	3-12-65	1987	Del Mar, Calif.
Gonzalez, Luis	.304	156	579	92	176	46	4	26	104	94	67	5	3	.532	.402	L	R	6-2	200	9-3-67	1988	Scottsdale, Ariz.
Grace, Mark	.200	66	135	13	27	5	0	3	16	16	15	0	0	.304	.279	L	L	6-2	200	6-28-64	1986	Paradise Valley, Ariz.
Hammock, Rob	.282	65	195	30	55	10	2	8	28	17	44	3	2	.477	.343	R	R	5-10	185	5-13-77	1998	Dacula, Ga.
Hillenbrand, Shea	.267	85	330	40	88	18	1	17	59	17	44	0	0	.482	.302	R	R	6-1	210	7-27-75	1996	Mesa, Ariz.
Jose, Felix	.333	18	18	1	6	1	0	1	6	6	3	0	0	.556	.500	S	R	6-1	220	5-8-65	1984	Boca Raton, Fla.
Kata, Matt	.257	78	288	42	74	16	5	7	29	25	53	3	2	.420	.315	S	R	6-1	185	3-14-78	1999	Cleveland, Ohio
McCracken, Quinton	.227	115	203	17	46	5	2	0	18	15	34	5	1	.271	.276	S	R	5-7	190	8-16-70	1992	Scottsdale, Ariz.
Moeller, Chad	.268	78	239	29	64	17	1	7	29	23	59	1	2	.435	.335	R	R	6-3	215	2-18-75	1996	Scottsdale, Ariz.
Mondesi, Raul	.302	45	162	27	49	8	1	8	22	18	31	5	4	.512	.372	R	R	5-11	230	3-2-71	1988	San Cristobal, D.R.
Overbay, Lyle	.276	86	254	23	70	20	0	4	28	35	67	1	0	.402	.365	L	L	6-2	225	1-28-77	1999	Centralia, Wash.
Spivey, Junior	.255	106	365	52	93	22	2	13	50	33	95	4	3	.433	.326	R	R	6-0	200	1-28-75	1996	Phoenix, Ariz.
Terrero, Luis	.250	5	4	0	1	0	0	0	0	0	1	0	0	.250	.400	R	R	6-2	205	5-18-80	1997	Barahona, D.R.
Williams, Matt	.246	44	134	17	33	9	0	4	16	16	26	0	0	.403	.327	R	R	6-2	210	11-28-65	1986	Scottsdale, Ariz.
Womack, Tony	.237	61	219	30	52	10	3	2	15	8	27	8	3	.338	.270	L	R	5-9	170	9-25-69	1991	Greensboro, N.C.

PITCHING	W	L	ERA	G	GS	CG	SV	IP	H	R	ER	BB	SO	AVG	B	T	HT	WT	DOB	1st Yr	Resides
Batista, Miguel	10	9	3.54	36	29	2	0	193	197	85	76	60	142	.266	R	R	6-1	195	2-19-71	1988	Weston, Fla.
Bottalico, Ricky	1	0	5.40	2	0	0	0	2	3	1	1	2	2	.375	L	R	6-0	220	8-26-69	1991	Rocky Hill, Conn.
Capuano, Chris	2	4	4.64	9	5	0	0	33	27	19	17	11	23	.230	L	L	6-2	220	8-19-78	1999	W. Springfield, Mass.
Dessens, Elmer	8	8	5.07	34	30	0	0	176	212	107	99	57	113	.299	R	R	5-10	200	1-13-71	1993	Hermosillo, Mexico
Gonzalez, Edgar	2	1	4.91	9	2	0	0	18	28	10	10	7	14	.368	R	R	6-0	220	2-23-83	2000	San Nicolas, Mexico
Good, Andrew	4	2	5.29	16	10	0	0	66	74	42	39	16	42	.281	R	R	6-1	210	9-19-79	1998	Rochester Hills, Mich.
Johnson, Randy	6	8	4.26	18	18	1	0	114	125	61	54	27	125	.279	R	L	6-10	230	9-10-63	1985	Scottsdale, Ariz.
Kim, Byung-Hyun	1	5	3.56	7	7	0	0	43	34	17	17	15	33	.213	R	R	5-11	180	1-21-79	1999	Gwangju, Korea
Koplove, Mike	3	0	2.15	31	0	0	0	38	31	11	9	10	27	.224	R	R	5-10	180	8-30-76	1998	Philadelphia, Pa.
Mantei, Matt	5	4	2.62	50	0	0	29	55	37	17	16	18	68	.190	R	R	6-1	200	7-7-73	1991	Sawyer, Mich.
Myers, Mike	0	1	5.70	64	0	0	0	36	38	23	23	21	21	.262	L	L	6-3	220	6-26-69	1990	Highlands Ranch, Colo.
Oropesa, Eddie	3	3	5.82	47	0	0	0	39	38	27	25	27	39	.256	L	L	6-1	205	11-23-71	1993	Miami, Fla.
Patterson, John	1	4	6.05	16	8	0	1	55	61	39	37	30	43	.281	R	R	6-5	210	1-30-78	1996	Scottsdale, Ariz.
Prinz, Bret	0	0	0.00	1	0	0	0	1	1	0	0	1	1	.250	R	R	6-3	210	6-15-77	1998	Peoria, Ariz.
Raggio, Brady	0	0	6.48	10	0	0	1	8	9	6	6	6	8	.290	R	R	6-4	210	9-17-72	1992	Danville, Calif.
Randolph, Stephen	8	1	4.05	50	0	0	0	60	50	28	27	43	50	.226	L	L	6-3	200	5-1-74	1995	Austin, Texas
Reyes, Dennys	0	0	11.57	3	0	0	0	2	5	3	3	1	5	.416	R	L	6-3	240	4-19-77	1994	Zaragoza, Mexico
2-team (12 Pittsburgh)	0	0	10.66	15	0	0	0	13	15	16	15	10	16	.300							
Schilling, Curt	8	9	2.95	24	24	3	0	168	144	58	55	32	194	.230	R	R	6-5	235	11-14-66	1986	Paradise Valley, Ariz.
Service, Scott	0	2	4.91	18	0	0	1	18	21	10	10	2	18	.287	R	R	6-6	250	2-26-67	1986	Cincinnati, Ohio
Valverde, Jose	2	1	2.15	54	0	0	10	50	24	16	12	26	71	.137	R	R	6-4	255	7-24-79	1997	Santo Domingo, D.R.
Villarreal, Oscar	10	7	2.57	86	1	0	0	98	80	40	28	46	80	.221	L	R	6-0	205	11-22-81	1999	Monterrey, Mexico
Webb, Brandon	10	9	2.84	29	28	1	0	181	140	65	57	68	172	.212	R	R	6-2	230	5-9-79	2000	Ashland, Ky.

FIELDING

Catcher	PCT	G	PO	A	E	DP	PB
Baerga	.000	1	0	0	0	0	0
Barajas	1.000	79	543	40	0	6	8
Hammock	.993	36	263	18	2	2	4
Moeller	.987	76	490	37	7	3	3

First Base	PCT	G	PO	A	E	DP
Baerga	.985	19	123	8	2	12
Counsell	1.000	2	3	0	0	1
Grace	.993	39	258	19	2	24
Hillenbrand	.989	56	439	27	5	32
Overbay	.997	75	643	58	2	48

Second Base	PCT	G	PO	A	E	DP
Baerga	.984	15	21	40	1	11
Cintron	1.000	9	14	17	0	5
Counsell	1.000	10	9	22	0	5
Kata	.988	52	106	131	3	27
Spivey	.982	98	169	269	8	54

Third Base	PCT	G	PO	A	E	DP
Baerga	1.000	5	6	7	0	0
Cintron	.923	16	14	22	3	0
Counsell	.986	57	32	105	2	9
Hammock	.930	16	8	45	4	4
Hillenbrand	.908	34	15	54	7	5
Kata	.981	23	10	41	1	3
Williams	.959	42	21	72	4	5

Shortstop	PCT	G	PO	A	E	DP
Cintron	.979	93	138	235	8	56
Counsell	.989	26	23	66	1	9
Kata	1.000	6	7	5	0	1
Womack	.966	58	70	130	7	28

Outfield	PCT	G	PO	A	E	DP
Bautista	.961	79	123	1	5	0
Dellucci	.976	53	79	1	2	0
Finley	.982	140	258	9	5	2
Gonzalez	.989	154	249	9	3	1
Hammock	.933	17	14	0	1	0
Jose	.000	1	0	0	0	0
McCracken	.983	55	58	1	1	1
Mondesi	.964	43	80	1	3	1
Spivey	.000	1	0	0	0	0
Terrero	1.000	3	1	0	0	0

BILL NICHOLS

Curt Schilling

FARM SYSTEM

Director, Player Development: Tommy Jones

Class	Farm Team	League	W	L	Pct.	Finish*	Manager(s)	First Yr.
AAA	Tucson (Ariz.) Sidewinders	Pacific Coast	73	71	.507	7th (16)	Al Pedrique	1998
AA	El Paso (Texas) Diablos	Texas	67	73	.479	6th (8)	Scott Coolbaugh	1999
High A	Lancaster (Calif.) Jet Hawks	California	73	67	.521	7th (10)	Mike Aldrete	2001
Low A	South Bend (Ind.) Silver Hawks	Midwest	72	64	.529	4th (14)	Von Hayes	1997
SS A	Yakima (Wash.) Bears	Northwest	45	31	.592	2nd (8)	Bill Plummer	1999
Rookie	Missoula (Mont.) Osprey	Pioneer	36	40	.474	5th (8)	Tony Perezchica	1999

*Finish in overall standings (No. of teams in league)

TUCSON SIDEWINDERS — Class AAA

PACIFIC COAST LEAGUE

BATTING	AVG	G	AB	R	H	2B	3B	HR	RBI	BB	SO	SB	CS	SLG	OBP	B	T	HT	WT	DOB	1st Yr	Resides
Barajas, Rod	.438	4	16	3	7	1	0	1	4	1	1	0	0	.688	.471	R	R	6-2	220	9-5-75	1996	Scottsdale, Ariz.
Bautista, Danny	.375	8	24	4	9	1	1	1	4	2	2	1	1	.625	.423	R	R	5-11	225	5-24-72	1989	Santo Domingo, D.R.
Bell, Mike	.262	117	416	60	109	26	3	11	70	26	59	1	3	.418	.311	R	R	6-2	210	12-7-74	1993	Chandler, Ariz.
Carvajal, Jhonny	.203	43	123	12	25	7	0	4	13	11	29	0	2	.358	.279	R	R	5-10	180	7-24-73	1993	Barcelona, Venez.
Cintron, Alex	.393	26	107	21	42	11	2	2	21	8	6	1	0	.589	.435	S	R	6-2	200	12-17-78	1997	Yabucoa, P.R.
Counsell, Craig	.435	5	23	8	10	2	0	0	2	1	3	0	0	.522	.458	L	R	6-0	185	8-21-70	1992	Mequon, Wisc.
Cresse, Brad	.229	82	306	40	70	21	1	10	47	18	89	0	0	.402	.282	R	R	6-2	230	7-31-78	2000	Long Beach, Calif.
Devore, Doug	.292	134	462	74	135	29	7	14	75	44	95	5	7	.476	.357	L	L	6-4	215	12-14-77	1999	Dublin, Ohio
Donnels, Chris	.323	36	62	10	20	1	0	2	13	17	6	0	0	.435	.475	L	R	6-0	180	4-21-66	1987	Coto de Caza, Calif.
Gordon, Brian	.265	124	449	58	119	20	7	13	70	33	93	1	3	.428	.314	L	R	6-0	180	8-16-78	1997	Round Rock, Texas
Hairston, Scott	.000	1	0	0	0	0	0	0	1	0	0	0	0	.000	.000	R	R	6-0	190	5-25-80	2001	Oro Valley, Ariz.
Hammock, Rob	.267	33	116	14	31	6	2	2	17	11	24	1	0	.405	.321	R	R	5-10	185	5-13-77	1998	Dacula, Ga.
Hillenbrand, Shea	.300	3	10	0	3	1	0	0	1	0	1	0	0	.400	.300	R	R	6-1	210	7-27-75	1996	Mesa, Ariz.
Kata, Matt	.289	48	201	31	58	13	5	3	25	9	29	2	3	.448	.327	S	R	6-1	185	3-14-78	1999	Cleveland, Ohio
Little, Mark	.316	31	95	13	30	5	4	5	13	3	18	3	1	.611	.369	R	R	6-0	190	7-11-72	1994	Edwardsville, Ill.
Loeb, Bryan	.333	5	15	1	5	2	0	0	0	2	5	0	0	.467	.412	R	R	6-2	200	4-8-78	2000	Sugar Land, Texas
Martin, Billy	.346	53	179	32	62	16	1	12	40	18	43	0	0	.648	.408	R	R	6-2	215	6-10-76	1998	Abilene, Texas
Morales, Willie	.286	11	42	4	12	2	1	1	3	1	9	1	0	.452	.302	R	R	5-10	180	9-7-72	1993	Tucson, Ariz.
Neal, Steve	.246	97	285	32	70	17	2	7	37	23	78	0	1	.393	.306	L	L	6-2	255	2-14-77	1998	Pine Bluff, Ark.
Olson, Tim	.262	115	397	59	104	22	0	6	40	31	77	11	2	.363	.323	R	R	6-2	200	8-1-78	2000	Bismarck, N.D.
Overbay, Lyle	.286	35	119	24	34	11	0	4	16	28	19	0	0	.479	.419	L	L	6-2	225	1-28-77	1999	Centralia, Wash.
Ramirez, Dan	.274	73	230	23	63	4	0	3	22	5	43	14	5	.330	.289	R	R	6-1	195	2-22-74	1992	San Pedro de Macoris, D.R.
Spivey, Junior	.267	4	15	3	4	2	0	0	1	1	1	0	0	.400	.313	R	R	6-0	200	1-28-75	1996	Phoenix, Ariz.
Terrero, Luis	.287	118	467	83	134	20	15	3	46	31	103	23	19	.413	.345	R	R	6-2	205	5-18-80	1997	Barahona, D.R.
Tracy, Chad	.324	133	522	91	169	31	4	10	80	41	52	0	2	.456	.372	L	R	6-2	200	5-22-80	2001	Charlotte, N.C.
Waldron, Jeff	.248	34	101	10	25	4	0	0	11	14	27	0	1	.287	.369	L	R	6-1	220	10-4-76	1999	Lynn, Mass.

PITCHING	W	L	ERA	G	GS	CG	SV	IP	H	R	ER	BB	SO	AVG	B	T	HT	WT	DOB	1st Yr	Resides
Abbott, Paul	3	4	3.95	11	8	1	0	55	63	29	24	12	50	.285	R	R	6-3	200	9-15-67	1985	Fullerton, Calif.
Barber, Scott	1	0	2.05	5	2	1	0	22	19	5	5	5	4	.237	R	R	6-3	205	12-12-78	2000	Belton, S.C.
Bottalico, Ricky	2	2	3.66	31	0	0	0	39	39	24	16	16	28	.258	L	R	6-0	220	8-26-69	1991	Rocky Hill, Conn.
Bruney, Brian	3	1	2.81	32	0	0	12	32	24	12	10	18	32	.206	R	R	6-3	225	2-17-82	2000	Warrenton, Ore.
Capuano, Chris	9	5	3.34	23	23	0	0	143	133	66	53	43	108	.249	L	L	6-2	220	8-19-78	1999	W. Springfield, Mass.
Cervantes, Chris	3	4	4.04	11	7	0	1	42	41	22	19	24	27	.266	L	L	6-1	160	2-4-79	1998	Tucson, Ariz.
Cormier, Lance	1	1	2.60	5	4	0	0	28	26	10	8	5	11	.260	R	R	6-1	190	8-19-80	2002	Lafayette, La.
Ebert, Derrin	0	1	2.63	15	0	0	0	14	21	4	4	6	7	.355	R	L	6-3	200	8-21-76	1994	Hesperia, Calif.
2-team (6 Iowa)	1	1	3.92	21	0	0	0	21	30	9	9	10	11	.340							
Ferns, Robert	0	0	5.40	1	0	0	0	2	2	1	1	1	1	.285	R	R	6-4	230	1-4-81	2002	Troy, Mich.
Gonzalez, Edgar	8	7	3.75	20	19	1	0	130	126	65	54	28	69	.254	R	R	6-0	220	2-23-83	2000	San Nicolas, Mexico
Good, Andrew	4	4	5.00	11	11	0	0	63	78	36	35	13	45	.300	R	R	6-1	210	9-19-79	1998	Rochester Hills, Mich.
Gosling, Mike	9	12	5.61	26	26	0	0	136	190	106	85	56	89	.329	L	L	6-2	210	9-23-80	2001	Las Vegas, Nev.
Henrie, Matt	0	0	3.00	1	1	0	0	6	8	3	2	2	1	.320	L	R	6-3	200	11-28-79	2002	Jupiter, Fla.
Johnson, Randy	0	0	0.00	1	1	0	0	4	0	0	0	0	4	.000	R	L	6-10	230	9-10-63	1985	Scottsdale, Ariz.
Kim, Byung-Hyun	1	1	2.55	3	3	0	0	18	17	5	5	1	8	.269	R	R	5-11	180	1-21-79	1999	Gwangju, Korea
Koplove, Mike	0	1	13.50	3	0	0	1	3	4	4	4	3	2	.333	R	R	5-10	180	8-30-76	1998	Philadelphia, Pa.
Mantei, Matt	0	0	2.25	3	0	0	0	4	2	1	1	0	4	.153	R	R	6-1	200	7-7-73	1991	Sawyer, Mich.
Marshall, Lee	4	6	6.21	50	3	0	1	67	97	52	46	23	43	.345	R	R	6-5	230	9-25-76	1995	Ariton, Ala.
Oropesa, Eddie	0	1	2.35	15	0	0	0	15	14	4	4	4	9	.245	L	L	6-1	205	11-23-71	1993	Miami, Fla.
Patterson, John	10	5	2.63	18	18	2	0	109	100	48	32	43	74	.240	R	R	6-5	210	1-30-78	1996	Scottsdale, Ariz.
Perisho, Matt	0	0	9.82	4	0	0	0	4	4	4	4	2	2	.285	L	L	6-0	200	6-8-75	1993	Chandler, Ariz.
Prinz, Bret	0	1	6.00	10	0	0	0	12	19	9	8	3	7	.345	R	R	6-3	210	6-15-77	1998	Peoria, Ariz.
Raggio, Brady	4	4	3.49	18	7	0	0	57	60	27	22	8	32	.267	R	R	6-4	210	9-17-72	1992	Danville, Calif.
Randolph, Stephen	1	0	3.86	7	0	0	0	9	8	5	4	3	6	.228	L	L	6-3	200	5-1-74	1995	Austin, Texas
Reyes, Dennys	2	1	2.84	33	0	0	2	32	24	16	10	22	30	.206	R	L	6-3	240	4-19-77	1994	Zaragoza, Mexico
Sabel, Erik	2	3	4.94	42	2	0	1	62	79	38	34	18	34	.307	R	R	6-3	190	10-14-74	1996	Indianapolis, Ind.
Scarbery, Chad	0	0	6.75	2	0	0	0	5	7	4	4	2	7	.304	R	R	6-3	215	9-23-80	2003	Clovis, Calif.
Schilling, Curt	1	0	4.50	2	2	0	0	10	10	5	5	3	15	.256	R	R	6-5	235	11-14-66	1986	Paradise Valley, Ariz.
Service, Scott	0	0	0.00	9	0	0	3	12	6	2	0	2	13	.133	R	R	6-6	250	2-26-67	1986	Cincinnati, Ohio
Spradlin, Jerry	0	1	19.80	6	0	0	0	5	13	12	11	1	3	.500	S	R	6-7	240	6-14-67	1988	Anaheim, Calif.
Stockman, Phil	1	1	1.00	2	1	0	0	9	8	1	1	4	5	.258	R	R	6-6	200	1-25-80	1997	Warren Park, Australia
Swindell, Greg	0	1	6.53	8	3	0	0	21	32	15	15	5	8	.376	L	L	6-3	230	1-2-65	1986	Paradise Valley, Ariz.
Valverde, Jose	1	1	3.10	22	0	0	5	29	26	11	10	14	26	.236	R	R	6-4	255	7-24-79	1997	Santo Domingo, D.R.
Villone, Ron	1	1	3.55	15	0	0	1	25	20	14	10	12	22	.232	L	L	6-3	230	1-16-70	1992	River Vale, N.J.
Ward, Jeremy	1	1	6.51	25	0	0	5	28	37	21	20	11	13	.324	R	R	6-2	235	2-24-78	1999	Rocky Mount, N.C.
Webb, Brandon	1	1	6.00	3	3	0	0	18	18	17	12	9	17	.257	R	R	6-2	230	5-9-79	2000	Ashland, Ky.

FIELDING

Catcher	PCT	G	PO	A	E	DP	PB
Barajas	1.000	3	19	2	0	1	0
Cresse	.987	78	490	46	7	1	2
Hammock	.962	21	114	14	5	2	2
Loeb	1.000	5	29	1	0	0	0
Morales	.980	8	44	5	1	0	0
Waldron	.980	34	182	16	4	2	2

First Base	PCT	G	PO	A	E	DP
Bell	.985	17	126	8	2	12
Donnels	1.000	4	26	4	0	1
Hammock	1.000	3	29	5	0	3
Hillenbrand	1.000	2	4	0	0	0
Martin	.992	26	223	14	2	15
Morales	1.000	1	1	1	0	0
Neal	.994	76	594	42	4	64
Overbay	.985	33	294	25	5	19

Second Base	PCT	G	PO	A	E	DP
Bell	.964	78	150	196	13	49
Carvajal	.947	28	27	63	5	9
Cintron	1.000	2	8	8	0	1
Counsell	.889	2	4	4	1	2
Kata	.958	40	70	112	8	23
Olson	1.000	7	15	14	0	5
Spivey	1.000	4	4	13	0	3

Third Base	PCT	G	PO	A	E	DP
Bell	.857	14	20	16	6	4
Carvajal	.750	1	1	2	1	1
Counsell	1.000	1	1	4	0	0
Donnels	1.000	2	2	1	0	0
Hammock	1.000	2	1	4	0	1
Hillenbrand	1.000	2	0	4	0	0
Tracy	.951	125	94	292	20	17

Shortstop	PCT	G	PO	A	E	DP
Carvajal	.984	18	20	40	1	4
Cintron	.966	23	43	70	4	18
Counsell	1.000	2	6	7	0	3
Kata	.957	11	22	22	2	9
Olson	.937	104	141	293	29	50

Outfield	PCT	G	PO	A	E	DP
Bautista	1.000	8	8	1	0	0
Bell	.923	10	12	0	1	0
Devore	.967	126	221	13	8	1
Gordon	.982	113	218	6	4	0
Hammock	1.000	5	5	2	0	0
Little	.951	21	37	2	2	0
Martin	.875	5	6	1	1	0
Olson	1.000	8	14	1	0	0
Ramirez	.966	59	112	2	4	0
Terrero	.968	117	298	8	10	2

EL PASO DIABLOS — Class AA

TEXAS LEAGUE

BATTING	AVG	G	AB	R	H	2B	3B	HR	RBI	BB	SO	SB	CS	SLG	OBP	B	T	HT	WT	DOB	1st Yr	Resides
Ansman, Craig	.324	63	213	46	69	17	1	15	49	31	58	5	3	.624	.421	R	R	6-3	220	3-10-78	2000	West Islip, N.Y.
Barden, Brian	.287	109	383	50	110	24	5	3	57	29	78	10	4	.399	.348	R	R	5-11	195	4-2-81	2002	Corvallis, Ore.
Bautista, Danny	.143	2	7	1	1	0	0	0	1	1	2	0	0	.143	.250	R	R	5-11	225	5-24-72	1989	Santo Domingo, D.R.
Burns, Kevan	.300	12	40	5	12	2	1	1	8	5	9	0	1	.475	.378	L	L	6-0	180	11-10-76	1999	Beloit, Wisc.
Carvajal, Jhonny	.267	35	131	14	35	8	1	2	17	9	16	2	3	.389	.308	R	R	5-10	180	7-24-73	1993	Barcelona, Venez.
Ceriani, Matt	.147	9	34	4	5	1	0	0	0	0	11	0	0	.176	.147	R	R	6-2	220	10-9-76	1998	Vacaville, Calif.
Cota, Jesus	.272	98	364	51	99	16	3	1	37	27	57	2	5	.341	.322	L	R	6-3	220	11-7-81	2001	Tucson, Ariz.
Firlit, Dan	.204	46	147	10	30	2	1	1	12	4	46	3	1	.252	.237	R	R	6-1	190	11-22-78	2000	Orland Park, Ill.
Green, Andy	.302	126	490	70	148	38	2	2	51	38	51	17	9	.400	.366	R	R	5-9	165	7-7-77	2000	Lexington, Ky.
Hairston, Scott	.276	88	337	53	93	21	7	10	47	30	80	6	2	.469	.345	R	R	6-0	190	5-25-80	2001	Oro Valley, Ariz.
Hall, Victor	.300	124	490	76	147	13	12	0	45	51	88	23	19	.376	.370	L	L	5-11	170	9-16-80	1998	Arleta, Calif.
Jones, Jaime	.323	10	31	3	10	0	0	0	2	2	7	0	0	.323	.364	L	L	6-3	190	8-2-76	1995	Temecula, Calif.
Kroeger, Josh	.274	54	208	26	57	9	2	3	22	10	54	3	5	.380	.315	L	L	6-2	200	8-31-82	2000	San Diego, Calif.
Loeb, Bryan	.286	63	182	29	52	10	2	4	27	6	34	3	1	.429	.343	R	R	6-2	200	4-8-78	2000	Sugar Land, Texas
Macha, Erick	.279	19	43	5	12	3	0	0	2	1	12	0	1	.349	.295	R	R	6-1	180	12-13-79	2001	Victoria, Texas
Martin, Billy	.350	44	160	27	56	16	1	3	27	22	40	1	0	.519	.441	R	R	6-2	215	6-10-76	1998	Abilene, Texas
Morales, Willie	.315	26	89	15	28	6	0	1	11	7	14	0	0	.416	.374	R	R	5-10	180	9-7-72	1993	Tucson, Ariz.
Murphy, Nate	.291	79	289	52	84	23	1	8	48	32	68	8	6	.460	.372	L	L	6-0	190	4-15-75	1996	Tucson, Ariz.
Myers, Corey	.290	124	428	63	124	27	3	9	60	42	78	3	3	.430	.354	R	R	6-2	210	6-5-80	1999	Henderson, Nev.
Olson, Tim	.196	14	56	5	11	2	0	2	8	5	19	0	2	.339	.258	R	R	6-2	200	8-1-78	2000	Bismarck, N.D.
Ramirez, Dan	.042	9	24	3	1	1	0	0	2	1	6	0	0	.083	.115	R	R	6-1	195	2-22-74	1992	San Pedro de Macoris, D.R.
Santos, Sergio	.255	37	137	13	35	7	1	2	16	8	25	0	0	.365	.293	R	R	6-3	190	7-4-83	2002	Hacienda Heights, Calif.
Snyder, Chris	.202	53	188	21	38	14	0	4	26	19	29	0	0	.340	.286	R	R	6-3	220	2-12-81	2002	Houston, Texas
Spivey, Junior	.455	4	11	2	5	1	0	0	1	2	1	2	0	.545	.533	R	R	6-0	200	1-28-75	1996	Phoenix, Ariz.
Timmons, Ozzie	.306	63	216	31	66	17	1	6	40	22	31	0	3	.477	.369	R	R	6-2	220	9-18-70	1991	Tampa, Fla.
Waldron, Jeff	.227	27	75	7	17	2	0	2	10	12	17	0	0	.333	.333	L	R	6-1	220	10-4-76	1999	Lynn, Mass.
Womack, Tony	.294	4	17	3	5	0	0	0	2	2	2	3	0	.294	.368	L	R	5-9	170	9-25-69	1991	Greensboro, N.C.

PITCHING	W	L	ERA	G	GS	CG	SV	IP	H	R	ER	BB	SO	AVG	B	T	HT	WT	DOB	1st Yr	Resides
Aquino, Greg	7	3	3.46	20	20	0	0	107	115	43	41	38	91	.278	R	R	6-1	150	1-11-78	1996	Palenque, D.R.
Belflower, Jay	4	2	5.14	53	0	0	2	70	105	51	40	24	35	.352	R	R	6-4	225	11-12-79	2001	Sebring, Fla.
Bruney, Brian	0	2	2.59	28	0	0	14	31	29	17	9	13	28	.233	R	R	6-3	225	2-17-82	2000	Warrenton, Ore.
Cormier, Lance	2	3	6.10	9	8	0	0	41	59	33	28	22	26	.337	R	R	6-1	190	8-19-80	2002	Lafayette, La.
Cramblitt, Joey	1	0	0.00	1	0	0	0	2	2	0	0	0	0	.250	R	R	6-3	230	7-27-78	2000	Meridian, Miss.
Daigle, Casey	11	11	4.59	29	27	1	0	176	219	108	90	51	115	.303	R	R	6-5	215	4-4-81	1999	Vinton, La.
Freed, Mark	4	3	4.81	67	0	0	1	64	75	38	34	37	43	.285	L	L	6-5	210	8-10-78	2000	Pennsville, N.J.
Gonzalez, Edgar	2	2	3.50	6	6	0	0	36	40	18	14	11	30	.281	R	R	6-0	220	2-23-83	2000	San Nicolas, Mexico
Henrie, Matt	5	7	4.13	14	14	2	0	89	112	45	41	17	44	.309	L	R	6-3	200	11-28-79	2002	Jupiter, Fla.
Holsten, Ryan	2	8	6.93	38	12	1	0	101	139	89	78	54	41	.326	R	R	6-4	210	5-5-79	2001	Wilmington, Del.
Johnson, Randy	0	0	0.00	1	1	0	0	4	3	2	0	1	5	.230	R	L	6-10	230	9-10-63	1985	Scottsdale, Ariz.
Krawczyk, Jack	1	1	5.08	12	0	0	0	28	34	16	16	5	18	.314	R	R	6-4	195	8-12-75	1998	Scottsdale, Ariz.
2-team (9 Midland)	1	3	6.80	21	0	0	0	41	56	32	31	11	27	.335							
Leclair, Aric	1	0	0.00	11	0	0	0	12	9	1	0	6	10	.214	L	L	6-0	190	4-12-78	2000	Swanzey, N.H.
Marshall, Lee	1	0	4.15	5	0	0	0	4	7	3	2	2	6	.368	R	R	6-5	230	9-25-76	1995	Ariton, Ala.
Medders, Brandon	5	3	4.41	56	0	0	7	69	65	37	34	26	72	.244	R	R	6-2	195	1-26-80	2001	Duncanville, Ala.
Meyer, Jake	0	1	6.75	3	0	0	0	3	3	2	2	1	2	.272	R	R	6-1	200	1-7-75	1997	San Diego, Calif.
Perez, Beltran	2	11	5.30	29	20	0	0	148	180	94	87	54	88	.309	R	R	6-2	180	10-24-81	1999	San Fran. de Macoris, D.R.
Prinz, Bret	0	0	4.50	2	0	0	0	2	3	1	1	1	2	.333	R	R	6-3	210	6-15-77	1998	Peoria, Ariz.
Silva, Jesus	5	4	5.02	55	0	0	3	66	84	44	37	20	56	.304	R	R	5-11	170	12-24-82	1999	Maracay, Venez.
Stockman, Phil	11	7	3.96	26	26	0	0	148	137	75	65	64	146	.244	R	R	6-6	200	1-25-80	1997	Warren Park, Australia
Wells, Carlton	2	2	10.29	10	0	0	0	7	13	14	8	5	4	.371	L	L	6-2	210	3-25-80	2000	Tampa, Fla.
White, Bill	1	3	6.23	15	6	0	0	39	42	27	27	22	25	.287	L	L	6-3	215	11-20-78	2000	Alexander City, Ala.

FIELDING

Catcher	PCT	G	PO	A	E	DP	PB
Ansman	.979	49	306	23	7	0	4
Ceriani	.977	5	35	8	1	2	1
Loeb	.976	28	149	14	4	2	4
Morales	1.000	3	28	0	0	0	0
Snyder	.991	49	308	35	3	2	16
Waldron	.983	18	105	10	2	1	4

First Base	PCT	G	PO	A	E	DP
Jones	1.000	1	2	1	0	0
Loeb	1.000	7	70	4	0	2
Martin	.993	17	129	9	1	12
Morales	.974	8	73	2	2	5
Myers	.985	112	930	86	15	81
Timmons	.900	1	9	0	1	0

Second Base	PCT	G	PO	A	E	DP
Barden	1.000	2	1	2	0	0
Carvajal	.900	3	6	3	1	1
Green	.983	64	102	188	5	28
Hairston	.960	74	131	227	15	38
Macha	1.000	5	4	9	0	1
Spivey	.909	4	7	3	1	0

Third Base	PCT	G	PO	A	E	DP
Barden	.931	101	80	178	19	12
Carvajal	.929	17	13	26	3	2
Firlit	.750	2	0	3	1	1
Green	.957	10	8	14	1	1
Macha	.882	9	3	12	2	0
Morales	1.000	10	3	15	0	0
Myers	.800	3	1	3	1	0

Shortstop	PCT	G	PO	A	E	DP
Carvajal	.919	16	22	46	6	10
Firlit	.966	42	64	108	6	14
Green	.925	39	79	107	15	23
Olson	.949	12	28	28	3	8
Santos	.924	37	60	98	13	26
Womack	.923	4	4	8	1	2

Outfield	PCT	G	PO	A	E	DP
Bautista	1.000	2	4	0	0	0
Burns	.957	9	22	0	1	0
Cota	.976	89	154	6	4	0
Green	1.000	14	25	2	0	0
Hall	.964	121	287	7	11	2
Jones	.909	8	10	0	1	0
Kroeger	.984	54	118	6	2	1
Loeb	.906	17	27	2	3	0
Macha	.000	1	0	0	0	0
Martin	.833	5	5	0	1	0
Murphy	.990	76	184	14	2	2
Olson	.875	2	6	1	1	0
Ramirez	1.000	8	16	2	0	0
Timmons	.965	37	54	1	2	1

LANCASTER JETHAWKS — High Class A

CALIFORNIA LEAGUE

BATTING	AVG	G	AB	R	H	2B	3B	HR	RBI	BB	SO	SB	CS	SLG	OBP	B	T	HT	WT	DOB	1st Yr	Resides
Barajas, Rod	.417	3	12	2	5	0	0	0	3	1	2	0	0	.417	.462	R	R	6-2	220	9-5-75	1996	Scottsdale, Ariz.
DiRosa, Michael	.226	77	257	22	58	17	0	6	37	30	85	0	2	.362	.313	R	R	5-11	190	1-17-80	2001	Miami, Fla.
Firlit, Dan	.217	21	69	5	15	1	1	1	10	4	15	1	0	.304	.276	R	R	6-1	190	11-22-78	2000	Orland Park, Ill.
Garthwaite, Jay	.297	113	437	82	130	33	2	22	87	30	97	3	5	.533	.351	R	R	6-2	210	11-26-80	2002	Kent, Wash.
Gorman, Jason	.232	42	125	19	29	6	2	3	18	16	34	0	1	.384	.324	R	R	6-0	195	9-9-80	2002	Palmdale, Calif.
Heath, Matt	.163	12	43	6	7	3	0	1	3	4	14	1	0	.302	.250	S	R	6-0	190	3-21-79	2002	Live Oak, Fla.
Johnson, Bryan	.218	35	78	7	17	4	0	0	7	9	16	0	0	.269	.303	S	R	6-1	200	2-23-81	2002	Ephrata, Wash.
Jones, Jaime	.288	97	351	62	101	15	2	12	53	34	62	4	3	.444	.356	L	L	6-3	190	8-2-76	1995	Temecula, Calif.
Kroeger, Josh	.341	78	305	50	104	30	6	5	55	35	58	6	6	.528	.409	L	L	6-2	200	8-31-82	2000	San Diego, Calif.
Macha, Erick	.258	16	31	7	8	3	0	0	3	2	6	1	0	.355	.303	R	R	6-1	180	12-13-79	2001	Victoria, Texas
McAndrews, Travis	.250	37	96	12	24	3	0	1	11	6	18	1	0	.313	.301	L	L	6-1	200	4-5-81	2003	El Segundo, Calif.
Neal, Steve	.300	12	40	2	12	4	0	0	8	8	11	0	0	.400	.417	L	L	6-2	255	2-14-77	1998	Pine Bluff, Ark.
Nichols, Kyle	.312	130	484	82	151	34	0	31	108	51	118	0	0	.574	.378	R	R	6-2	225	3-29-78	2001	Southport, Fla.
Richar, Danny	.304	123	405	51	123	19	9	1	42	14	70	6	3	.402	.331	R	R	5-11	165	6-9-83	2001	La Romana, D.R.
Santana, Mayobanex	.278	54	162	30	45	9	1	1	18	16	25	0	0	.364	.346	R	R	6-3	185	8-23-81	1999	Santo Domingo, D.R.
Santos, Sergio	.287	93	341	55	98	13	2	8	49	41	64	5	4	.408	.368	R	R	6-3	190	7-4-83	2002	Hacienda Heights, Calif.
Snyder, Chris	.314	69	245	53	77	16	2	10	53	35	43	0	1	.518	.414	R	R	6-3	220	2-12-81	2002	Houston, Texas
Stanek, Jeff	.232	20	56	8	13	6	0	0	2	7	21	0	0	.339	.317	L	R	6-3	200	8-18-80	2002	Lockport, Ill.
Thiessen, Mike	.278	85	281	42	78	10	4	5	29	33	55	11	5	.395	.355	R	R	5-11	185	11-10-78	2001	Peoria, Ariz.
Uggla, Dan	.290	134	534	104	155	31	7	23	90	46	105	24	9	.504	.355	R	R	5-11	195	3-11-80	2001	Columbia, Tenn.
Varela, Edgar	.238	40	143	16	34	4	2	2	16	4	19	0	1	.336	.276	L	R	6-1	200	8-9-80	2002	E. Rancho Dominguez, Calif.
Wilkins, Joe	.239	16	46	5	11	2	0	0	5	7	14	0	1	.283	.333	S	R	6-1	185	8-8-79	2002	Grove City, Ohio
Williams, Marland	.287	102	425	85	122	15	1	4	30	31	99	57	7	.355	.340	R	R	5-9	175	6-22-81	2002	Williston, Fla.
Wilson, Andy	.375	3	8	3	3	2	0	0	2	0	1	1	0	.625	.375	R	R	5-6	160	8-12-75	1998	Thousand Oaks, Calif.

PITCHING	W	L	ERA	G	GS	CG	SV	IP	H	R	ER	BB	SO	AVG	B	T	HT	WT	DOB	1st Yr	Resides
Barber, Scott	10	7	5.31	23	23	0	0	134	165	86	79	39	89	.306	R	R	6-3	205	12-12-78	2000	Belton, S.C.
Biggs, Billy	2	5	3.73	54	0	0	8	60	57	38	25	28	46	.251	R	R	6-0	200	9-9-79	2002	Scott Depot, W.Va.
Bulger, Jason	2	1	6.75	4	4	0	0	17	23	13	13	5	20	.310	R	R	6-4	210	12-6-78	2002	Snellville, Ga.
Castellanos, Jon	7	3	4.63	30	13	1	0	117	138	67	60	41	66	.296	R	R	6-0	215	9-17-81	2000	San Nicolas, Mexico
Cormier, Lance	6	5	3.82	15	15	0	0	94	102	55	40	16	59	.280	R	R	6-1	190	8-19-80	2002	Lafayette, La.
Cramblitt, Joey	0	1	1.98	10	0	0	0	14	14	10	3	5	8	.264	R	R	6-3	230	7-27-78	2000	Meridian, Miss.
Griffin, Charles	0	0	5.56	20	2	0	0	34	37	25	21	18	27	.284	R	R	6-3	210	6-9-79	2003	Dallas, Texas
Henrie, Matt	5	7	3.30	14	14	2	0	90	92	39	33	16	60	.263	L	R	6-3	200	11-28-79	2002	Jupiter, Fla.
Holsten, Ryan	1	0	4.66	2	1	0	0	10	10	5	5	3	3	.277	R	R	6-4	210	5-5-79	2001	Wilmington, Del.
Johnson, Randy	0	1	6.00	1	1	0	0	6	11	5	4	0	6	.366	R	L	6-10	230	9-10-63	1985	Scottsdale, Ariz.
Kerbs, Reuben	1	0	11.05	9	0	0	0	15	20	21	18	14	14	.298	L	L	6-2	185	10-19-80	2003	Dodge City, Kan.
Kranawetter, Josh	2	2	4.85	17	0	0	0	30	36	19	16	14	15	.297	R	R	5-10	185	5-21-80	2002	Jacob, Ill.
Krawczyk, Jack	0	0	2.08	3	0	0	0	4	7	1	1	0	6	.388	R	R	6-4	195	8-12-75	1998	Scottsdale, Ariz.
McMachen, Cliff	7	4	3.61	33	5	0	1	85	69	41	34	42	86	.224	L	L	6-1	205	1-14-81	2001	North Las Vegas, Nev.
Medlin, Corbey	2	2	6.27	33	0	0	0	52	62	42	36	27	36	.295	R	R	6-3	195	8-4-81	2001	Katy, Texas
Prinz, Bret	0	0	0.00	1	1	0	0	1	0	0	0	0	2	.000	R	R	6-3	210	6-15-77	1998	Peoria, Ariz.
Schultz, Mike	2	2	4.67	9	9	0	0	44	57	27	23	20	32	.333	R	R	6-7	210	11-28-79	2000	Reseda, Calif.
Sikaras, Pete	3	1	2.83	46	0	0	23	48	44	21	15	27	56	.245	R	R	6-2	200	5-5-79	2000	Niles, Ill.
Slaten, Doug	6	7	6.03	32	19	0	0	119	156	94	80	47	78	.315	L	L	6-5	190	2-4-80	2000	Venice, Calif.
Trejo, Francisco	1	1	5.02	16	1	0	0	29	38	20	16	13	36	.311	L	L	5-11	150	3-6-80	1997	Santo Domingo, D.R.
Vicente, Ruben	0	1	5.19	3	3	0	0	17	22	12	10	5	10	.297	R	R	6-0	160	3-3-80	2000	La Romana, D.R.
Wechsler, Justin	9	11	5.61	27	21	0	0	112	129	79	70	64	88	.289	R	R	6-2	240	4-6-80	2001	Pendleton, Ind.
Wells, Carlton	4	3	2.95	46	0	0	6	73	80	27	24	27	41	.274	L	L	6-2	210	3-25-80	2000	Tampa, Fla.
Whatley, Keith	3	3	5.17	8	8	1	0	47	53	29	27	21	17	.291	L	L	6-2	215	4-23-80	2002	Atlanta, Texas

FIELDING

Catcher	PCT	G	PO	A	E	DP	PB
Barajas	1.000	2	16	1	0	0	1
DiRosa	.979	72	416	48	10	0	12
Heath	.941	4	13	3	1	0	1
Snyder	.984	56	365	54	7	1	11
Wilkins	.980	15	92	8	2	0	1

First Base	PCT	G	PO	A	E	DP
Heath	1.000	2	16	1	0	1
Johnson	.982	20	147	21	3	9
Jones	.500	1	1	0	1	0
Neal	1.000	9	76	7	0	3
Nichols	.984	66	570	43	10	62
Santana	.988	28	155	9	2	17
Stanek	.982	17	146	15	3	9
Thiessen	1.000	1	8	0	0	0
Varela	.980	25	217	28	5	19

Second Base	PCT	G	PO	A	E	DP
Gorman	.965	36	57	81	5	25
Macha	.667	1	1	1	1	0
Richar	.968	87	152	238	13	42
Santana	.000	1	0	0	0	0
Uggla	.977	45	86	127	5	23
Varela	1.000	1	0	1	0	0

Third Base	PCT	G	PO	A	E	DP
Firlit	.500	1	1	0	1	0
Gorman	.923	5	4	8	1	0
Johnson	1.000	3	0	1	0	0
Santana	.990	33	23	73	1	9
Uggla	.941	102	76	212	18	18
Varela	.973	16	7	29	1	1

Shortstop	PCT	G	PO	A	E	DP
Firlit	.980	20	37	60	2	15
Gorman	1.000	1	1	1	0	0
Macha	1.000	5	4	2	0	0
Richar	.948	41	53	110	9	21
Santos	.951	91	133	271	21	58
Wilson	1.000	3	1	4	0	0

Outfield	PCT	G	PO	A	E	DP
Garthwaite	.973	105	213	5	6	1
Gorman	1.000	2	2	0	0	0
Heath	1.000	2	1	0	0	0
Jones	.934	80	106	7	8	0
Kroeger	.953	74	118	5	6	0
Macha	1.000	4	2	0	0	0
McAndrews	.944	30	33	1	2	0
Thiessen	.961	63	98	1	4	0
Williams	.981	95	207	2	4	0

SOUTH BEND SILVER HAWKS — Low Class A

MIDWEST LEAGUE

BATTING	AVG	G	AB	R	H	2B	3B	HR	RBI	BB	SO	SB	CS	SLG	OBP	B	T	HT	WT	DOB	1st Yr	Resides
Avlas, Phil	.203	47	133	14	27	7	0	1	15	16	17	4	1	.278	.283	R	R	5-11	175	12-17-82	2001	North Hills, Calif.
Ball, Jarred	.281	125	463	62	130	23	2	4	52	41	84	32	11	.365	.342	S	R	6-1	170	4-18-83	2001	Tomball, Texas
Barrett, Rich	.207	47	82	6	17	3	0	0	9	6	20	12	2	.244	.264	R	R	6-6	200	8-20-79	2001	Hartsville, Penn.
Brooks, Doc	.270	82	289	53	78	20	5	5	38	25	67	1	7	.426	.344	R	R	5-10	190	1-21-80	2001	Phenix City, Ala.
2-team (29 Ft. Wayne)	.262	111	390	62	102	26	6	5	48	36	104	1	7	.397	.336							
Brown, Neb	.259	133	491	74	127	24	5	7	42	47	59	19	10	.371	.332	L	R	6-0	185	11-7-79	2002	Stillwater, Okla.
Callahan, Dan	.197	22	66	7	13	2	0	0	4	6	8	2	0	.227	.264	L	L	6-4	190	11-5-79	2002	Medfield, Mass.
Cook, Jeff	.279	65	233	30	65	12	3	1	18	26	33	10	2	.369	.358	L	R	5-10	190	10-4-80	2003	Hattiesburg, Miss.
Firlit, Dan	.143	7	21	2	3	1	0	0	0	0	9	0	0	.190	.143	R	R	6-1	190	11-22-78	2000	Orland Park, Ill.
Gil, Jerry	.259	116	429	52	111	16	6	4	58	10	90	19	10	.352	.275	R	R	6-3	180	10-14-82	1999	Santo Domingo, D.R.
Haley, Adam	.125	18	40	2	5	1	0	0	1	3	11	0	1	.150	.222	L	R	6-0	170	9-4-80	2002	Louisville, Ky.
Hutchinson, Burney	.160	10	25	4	4	1	0	0	2	5	7	2	0	.200	.300	L	R	6-0	180	10-12-78	2002	Tupelo, Miss.
Jacobo, Kervin	.234	35	111	9	26	5	0	1	10	8	39	4	1	.306	.286	S	R	6-2	190	9-26-82	1999	Haina, D.R.
Johnson, Bryan	.259	20	58	6	15	2	1	1	5	7	11	0	0	.379	.348	S	R	6-1	200	2-23-81	2002	Ephrata, Wash.
Luellwitz, Sean	.291	128	475	59	138	34	1	18	79	49	82	5	2	.480	.365	R	R	6-5	220	11-16-79	2002	Brookfield, Wisc.
Morgan, Matt	.208	16	48	6	10	1	0	0	4	4	10	0	0	.229	.283	R	R	6-2	170	8-10-81	2002	Orosi, Calif.
Reynolds, Tila	.262	23	61	9	16	0	1	0	6	5	11	1	1	.295	.328	R	R	5-11	180	2-7-81	2003	Renton, Wash.
Santana, Mayobanex	.302	66	248	36	75	11	0	6	33	24	33	4	0	.419	.372	R	R	6-3	185	8-23-81	1999	Santo Domingo, D.R.
Santiago, Rudy	.205	73	215	16	44	6	1	0	13	10	48	6	7	.242	.241	L	R	6-1	180	11-23-79	1999	Santo Domingo, D.R.
Simon, Brandon	.194	17	36	6	7	1	0	0	3	1	2	7	1	.222	.326	L	L	6-0	175	9-9-80	2002	Fresno, Calif.
Sprowl, Jon-Mark	.296	95	321	56	95	22	3	4	42	54	31	5	4	.421	.402	L	R	6-1	200	8-1-80	1999	Panama City, Fla.
Stanek, Jeff	.253	83	245	31	62	13	0	3	37	48	68	2	2	.343	.367	L	R	6-3	200	8-18-80	2002	Lockport, Ill.
Teilon, Nilson	.277	105	358	50	99	16	2	7	55	19	61	7	3	.391	.330	R	R	6-0	180	6-10-80	1998	San Pedro de Macoris, D.R.
Tosca, Daniel	.261	19	46	4	12	2	0	0	4	11	9	0	0	.304	.414	L	R	6-0	180	11-1-80	1999	Seffner, Fla.
Wilkins, Joe	.135	19	52	3	7	1	0	0	4	4	12	1	0	.154	.203	S	R	6-1	185	8-8-79	2002	Grove City, Ohio

PITCHING	W	L	ERA	G	GS	CG	SV	IP	H	R	ER	BB	SO	AVG	B	T	HT	WT	DOB	1st Yr	Resides
Coffin, Ryan	3	9	4.18	29	17	0	0	116	120	72	54	37	58	.260	R	R	6-4	200	8-5-81	2002	Tempe, Ariz.
Davis, Mike	0	4	6.55	23	0	0	1	34	44	34	25	25	20	.312	R	R	6-4	195	7-6-80	1999	Eddyville, Ky.
Doyle, Jared	12	8	2.78	27	26	3	0	149	124	64	46	65	93	.229	L	L	6-0	190	1-30-81	2002	Orlando, Fla.
Garber, Mike	0	0	6.14	6	0	0	0	7	12	6	5	6	4	.352	L	L	6-2	190	1-9-81	2001	Palos Heights, Ill.
Gonzalez, Enrique	4	3	2.13	55	0	0	3	72	58	22	17	29	63	.218	R	R	5-10	195	7-14-82	1999	Bolivar, Venez.
Heiberger, Heath	4	5	3.61	39	2	0	0	52	53	30	21	26	37	.258	L	L	6-4	205	6-20-80	2001	Hennepin, Ill.
Incinelli, Matt	0	1	4.50	2	1	0	0	4	4	2	2	2	2	.307	R	R	6-2	180	2-2-80	2002	Orlando, Fla.
Kinsey, Chris	0	0	6.94	10	0	0	0	12	10	12	9	15	5	.243	R	R	6-3	230	10-18-82	2003	Elk Grove, Calif.
Kranawetter, Josh	1	3	6.96	24	0	0	0	32	43	30	25	20	23	.325	R	R	5-10	185	5-21-80	2002	Jacob, Ill.
Krawczyk, Jack	3	1	1.59	16	0	0	0	28	23	7	5	6	40	.227	R	R	6-4	195	8-12-75	1998	Scottsdale, Ariz.
Lizarraga, Sergio	9	2	1.78	42	9	0	1	96	71	22	19	29	85	.205	R	R	6-4	190	7-23-81	2001	Mazatlan, Mexico
Nippert, Dustin	6	4	2.82	17	17	0	0	96	66	32	30	32	96	.191	R	R	6-7	200	5-6-81	2002	Beallsville, Ohio
Rosario, Adriano	9	5	2.86	27	27	0	0	160	149	69	51	30	119	.246	R	R	6-2	190	5-16-85	2002	San Francisco de Macoris, D.R.
Smith, Sam	16	6	3.83	27	27	4	0	167	185	77	71	38	77	.278	R	R	6-4	210	8-23-79	2002	Rio Rancho, N.M.
Taulli, Sam	1	4	5.66	23	6	0	0	41	51	33	26	24	26	.312	L	L	6-1	190	9-19-79	2001	Mariana, Fla.
Van, Robbie	1	2	3.91	21	0	0	0	25	12	12	11	25	12	.151	L	L	6-2	210	11-3-81	2003	Las Vegas, Nev.
Watson, Mike	0	0	0.78	16	1	0	0	23	15	3	2	14	17	.194	R	R	6-1	180	9-28-80	2002	Altoona, Pa.
Whatley, Keith	0	1	2.93	3	3	0	0	15	18	5	5	3	6	.310	L	L	6-2	215	4-23-80	2002	Atlanta, Texas
Wilkinson, Matty	3	6	2.29	55	0	0	30	63	38	21	16	28	80	.170	L	R	6-3	195	10-25-77	2001	Chicago, Ill.

FIELDING

Catcher	PCT	G	PO	A	E	DP	PB
Avlas	.991	46	311	35	3	1	7
Morgan	1.000	1	1	0	0	0	0
Sprowl	.973	75	386	42	12	0	15
Tosca	.978	15	87	4	2	0	1
Wilkins	.969	17	83	10	3	2	4

First Base	PCT	G	PO	A	E	DP
Johnson	1.000	3	20	2	0	2
Luellwitz	.996	110	912	70	4	75
Santana	1.000	1	2	0	0	0
Stanek	.978	30	256	17	6	22

Second Base	PCT	G	PO	A	E	DP
Brooks	1.000	1	3	2	0	0
Brown	.969	107	211	288	16	58
Haley	.957	10	20	25	2	1
Morgan	1.000	1	1	1	0	0
Teilon	.935	32	51	79	9	12

Third Base	PCT	G	PO	A	E	DP
Brown	.971	26	14	54	2	2
Jacobo	.927	33	17	59	6	3
Morgan	.833	13	9	16	5	1
Reynolds	1.000	7	2	15	0	1
Santana	.944	66	49	138	11	13
Teilon	1.000	4	2	3	0	0

Shortstop	PCT	G	PO	A	E	DP
Firlit	1.000	6	4	17	0	4
Gil	.947	115	225	348	32	58
Haley	.900	6	8	10	2	1
Morgan	.900	2	2	7	1	1
Reynolds	.979	12	22	24	1	6

Outfield	PCT	G	PO	A	E	DP
Ball	.976	125	277	2	7	0
Barrett	.983	40	57	2	1	1
Brooks	.932	70	120	3	9	0
Callahan	.958	16	22	1	1	0
Cook	.974	65	108	5	3	0
Haley	.000	1	0	0	0	0
Hutchinson	.667	3	2	0	1	0
Santiago	.972	70	131	7	4	0
Simon	.895	12	16	1	2	0
Sprowl	.909	8	10	0	1	0
Teilon	.973	47	71	1	2	0

YAKIMA BEARS — Short-Season Class A

NORTHWEST LEAGUE

BATTING	AVG	G	AB	R	H	2B	3B	HR	RBI	BB	SO	SB	CS	SLG	OBP	B	T	HT	WT	DOB	1st Yr	Resides
Avlas, Phil	.333	17	45	7	15	4	1	0	4	6	11	0	1	.467	.412	R	R	5-11	175	12-17-82	2001	North Hills, Calif.
Barrett, Rich	.219	37	114	21	25	2	1	0	12	10	25	16	1	.254	.308	R	R	6-6	200	8-20-79	2001	Hartsville, Penn.
Buchanan, Todd	.262	63	214	36	56	15	1	2	19	36	42	0	0	.369	.372	L	L	6-2	200	9-16-80	2003	Roswell, Ga.
D'Antona, Jamie	.277	70	271	46	75	18	1	15	57	35	60	0	0	.517	.356	R	R	6-2	210	5-12-82	2003	Trumbull, Conn.
Frazier, Alex	.264	70	276	45	73	15	4	8	39	17	58	1	3	.435	.336	R	R	6-4	215	12-21-80	2002	Dunnellon, Fla.
Garcia, Lino	.221	49	154	24	34	6	1	0	18	16	34	13	3	.273	.293	R	R	6-3	180	10-12-83	2001	San Fernando, Venez.
Garrabrants, Steve	.276	55	199	41	55	11	4	1	22	39	58	30	5	.387	.410	R	R	5-10	170	11-18-81	2003	Phoenix, Ariz.
Haley, Adam	.232	69	237	32	55	11	1	2	30	19	42	2	2	.312	.298	L	R	6-0	170	9-4-80	2002	Louisville, Ky.
Heath, Matt	.286	3	7	3	2	1	0	0	1	2	2	0	0	.429	.444	S	R	6-0	190	3-21-79	2002	Live Oak, Fla.
Jackson, Conor	.319	68	257	44	82	35	1	6	60	36	41	3	0	.533	.410	R	R	6-3	205	5-7-82	2003	Austin, Texas
Mathis, Greg	.297	37	128	20	38	7	3	3	20	10	40	3	2	.469	.357	R	R	6-1	215	9-9-80	2003	Steele, Mo.

BATTING	AVG	G	AB	R	H	2B	3B	HR	RBI	BB	SO	SB	CS	SLG	OBP	B	T	HT	WT	DOB	1st Yr	Resides
Moreno, Juan J.	.169	33	71	6	12	4	0	1	5	2	24	0	0	.268	.189	L	R	5-9	180	8-16-81	1999	Santo Domingo, D.R.
Morgan, Matt	.248	58	214	27	53	13	2	0	23	26	36	1	1	.327	.335	R	R	6-2	170	8-10-81	2002	Orosi, Calif.
Reynolds, Tila	.130	8	23	3	3	0	0	0	2	3	8	1	1	.130	.286	R	R	5-11	180	2-7-81	2003	Renton, Wash.
Rose, Brian	.229	53	179	17	41	7	1	1	25	20	43	2	0	.296	.358	R	R	6-2	230	9-17-80	2003	Miami, Fla.
Simon, Brandon	.279	39	147	28	41	3	1	0	15	15	31	24	4	.313	.387	L	L	6-0	175	9-9-80	2002	Fresno, Calif.
Symonds, Grady	.125	10	8	0	1	0	0	0	1	1	1	0	0	.125	.200	R	R	6-2	180	1-15-81	2002	Buffalo Grove, Ill.
Viafore, Brian	.068	19	44	2	3	1	0	0	4	8	24	0	0	.091	.241	R	R	6-4	215	4-30-80	2003	Fircrest, Wash.

GAMES BY POSITION: C—Avlas 17, Heath 1, Morgan 14, Rose 50, Symonds 6. **1B**—Buchanan 58, D'Antona 7, Morgan 5, Viafore 15. **2B**—Garrabrants 54, Haley 4, Moreno 1, Morgan 22. **3B**—D'Antona 58, Moreno 11, Morgan 15. **SS**—Haley 65, Moreno 1, Morgan 7, Reynolds 8. **OF**—Barrett 32, Frazier 56, Garcia 49, Jackson 29, Mathis 36, Moreno 5, Simon 38.

PITCHING	W	L	ERA	G	GS	CG	SV	IP	H	R	ER	BB	SO	AVG	B	T	HT	WT	DOB	1st Yr	Resides
Barrett, Rich	0	1	4.91	4	0	0	0	3	5	5	2	5	6	.000	R	R	6-6	200	8-20-79	2001	Hartsville, Pa.
Bass, Adam	0	0	0.80	27	0	0	3	34	26	4	3	14	34	.209	R	R	6-6	210	7-31-81	2003	Madison, Ala.
Carque, Joe	0	1	5.91	26	0	0	0	32	35	26	21	7	14	.271	R	R	6-2	185	5-20-81	2003	Henderson, Nev.
Chico, Matt	7	4	3.53	17	13	0	0	71	75	28	28	25	71	.273	L	L	5-11	190	6-10-83	2003	Fallbrook, Calif.
Clark, Chad	1	1	4.99	24	0	0	1	31	19	19	17	29	30	.188	R	R	6-6	215	7-30-80	2003	Glendora, Calif.
Corley, Klent	2	1	4.79	5	5	0	0	21	19	12	11	15	12	.246	R	R	6-5	210	6-26-81	2002	Phoenix, Ariz.
Davis, Mike	4	0	0.92	23	0	0	0	29	15	3	3	14	22	.153	R	R	6-4	195	7-6-80	1999	Eddyville, Ky.
Ferns, Robert	1	1	27.00	3	0	0	0	2	10	7	7	2	2	.625	R	R	6-4	230	1-4-81	2002	Troy, Mich.
Glant, Dustin	1	2	1.85	34	0	0	18	34	19	9	7	9	31	.157	R	R	6-2	200	7-20-81	2003	Fort Wayne, Ind.
Goocher, Clint	3	1	2.73	31	0	0	0	33	28	10	10	6	33	.225	L	L	6-2	200	6-15-82	2003	Denton, Texas
Juarez, William	5	3	2.95	15	15	0	0	85	87	48	28	31	72	.255	R	R	6-2	205	4-22-81	2000	Chinandega, Nicaragua
Kerbs, Reuben	1	0	3.54	15	0	0	0	20	17	8	8	12	23	.223	L	L	6-2	185	10-19-80	2003	Dodge City, Kan.
Kinsey, Chris	3	3	4.00	9	9	0	0	45	45	34	20	16	23	.257	R	R	6-3	230	10-18-82	2003	Elk Grove, Calif.
Liebeck, Jered	5	3	2.95	12	10	0	0	64	57	25	21	11	50	.233	R	R	6-1	200	1-27-81	2003	Phoenix, Ariz.
Muegge, Danny	2	3	4.63	21	0	0	0	23	31	13	12	6	22	.322	L	R	6-5	180	3-6-81	2003	Brenham, Texas
Rio, Gabriele	0	0	15.00	5	0	0	0	6	14	11	10	7	5	.424	L	L	6-1	190	6-5-81	2003	New Britain, Conn.
Rosen, Mark	1	1	14.09	2	2	0	0	8	14	12	12	5	8	.388	L	L	5-11	200	6-30-84	2002	Randolph, Mass.
Scarbery, Chad	7	6	4.04	15	15	0	0	82	86	47	37	33	59	.271	R	R	6-3	215	9-23-80	2003	Clovis, Calif.
Schultz, Mike	1	0	4.71	5	5	0	0	29	21	16	15	10	27	.200	R	R	6-7	210	11-28-79	2000	Reseda, Calif.
Van, Robbie	0	0	0.00	1	0	0	0	1	0	0	0	1	0	.000	L	L	6-2	210	11-3-81	2003	Las Vegas, Nev.
Vicente, Ruben	1	0	3.00	10	2	0	0	21	23	12	7	7	14	.277	R	R	6-0	160	3-3-80	2000	La Romana, D.R.

MISSOULA OSPREY — Rookie

PIONEER LEAGUE

BATTING	AVG	G	AB	R	H	2B	3B	HR	RBI	BB	SO	SB	CS	SLG	OBP	B	T	HT	WT	DOB	1st Yr	Resides
Acosta, Johe	.251	65	223	35	56	10	2	10	30	13	75	7	1	.448	.320	R	R	6-5	190	12-19-81	2000	Santo Domingo, D.R.
Belz, Tim	.000	1	2	0	0	0	0	0	0	0	0	0	0	.000	.000	R	R	6-4	210	4-7-80	2002	Westbury, N.Y.
Bonifacio, Emilio	.199	54	146	20	29	1	1	0	16	18	43	15	3	.219	.298	R	R	5-10	160	4-23-85	2002	Santo Domingo, D.R.
Brito, Javier	.258	38	97	11	25	3	0	1	7	6	27	2	1	.320	.324	R	R	6-3	210	3-25-83	2002	Puerto la Cruz, Venez.
Gonzalez, Carlos	.258	72	275	45	71	14	4	6	25	16	61	12	7	.404	.308	L	L	6-1	170	10-17-85	2002	Maracaibo, Venez.
Guerrero, Michael	.183	25	60	3	11	4	0	0	9	4	16	1	0	.250	.242	R	R	6-3	210	10-14-80	2003	Mesa, Ariz.
Kaplan, Jon	.276	69	257	28	71	15	6	4	32	18	34	11	5	.428	.336	R	R	6-9	180	1-11-80	2003	Chesterfield, Mo.
McCreery, Andrew	.280	42	125	23	35	5	0	4	13	15	16	4	2	.416	.368	R	R	6-3	215	11-15-81	2003	Solana Beach, Calif.
McStoots, Jason	.225	59	200	33	45	6	2	1	17	31	42	8	5	.290	.335	L	R	5-10	185	5-10-80	2003	West Brooklyn, Ill.
Melendez, Cristobal	.230	45	122	14	28	3	0	0	9	6	31	5	2	.254	.299	R	R	6-2	185	11-9-80	2003	Patillas, P.R.
Mercado, Orlando	.213	23	47	3	10	3	0	0	4	3	12	0	0	.277	.275	R	R	5-10	195	3-13-85	2003	Arecibo, P.R.
Montero, Miguel	.301	59	196	24	59	10	2	4	32	9	15	2	3	.434	.352	L	R	5-11	195	7-9-83	2001	Caracas, Venez.
Mottram, Allen	.266	68	244	29	65	8	1	7	35	16	34	4	0	.393	.321	R	R	6-1	210	6-24-81	2003	North Andover, Mass.
Murillo, Agustin	.302	74	278	48	84	22	2	5	39	17	34	2	2	.450	.357	R	R	6-3	195	5-5-82	2003	Tijuana, Mexico
Olivares, Juan	.222	54	180	21	40	7	1	3	21	5	45	8	0	.322	.251	R	R	6-2	160	8-2-84	2002	San Pedro de Macoris, D.R.
Santiago, Jayson	.132	23	38	2	5	0	0	0	0	1	16	0	0	.132	.154	L	L	6-1	175	10-9-85	2003	Vega Alta, P.R.
Vanzile, Travis	.106	36	47	8	5	0	0	0	4	6	12	1	0	.106	.250	R	R	5-11	175	4-28-81	2003	Reedsburg, Wisc.

GAMES BY POSITION: C—Belz 1, Mercado 22, Montero 52, Mottram 19. **1B**—Brito 34, Guerrero 1, McCreery 26, Mottram 28. **2B**—Bonifacio 51, McStoots 23, Murillo 10. **3B**—McCreery 16, McStoots 8, Murillo 64, Vanzile 1. **SS**—McStoots 28, Olivares 54. **OF**—Acosta 29, Gonzalez 70, Guerrero 17, Kapaln 69, Melendez 44, Santiago 21, Vanzile 33.

PITCHING	W	L	ERA	G	GS	CG	SV	IP	H	R	ER	BB	SO	AVG	B	T	HT	WT	DOB	1st Yr	Resides
Allender, John	1	4	11.12	17	8	0	0	40	49	57	49	42	38	.295	R	R	6-4	200	2-18-85	2002	Gowrie, Australia
Cremidan, Alexander	2	1	1.40	24	0	0	15	26	17	6	4	12	30	.177	L	R	6-3	210	1-15-81	2003	San Diego, Calif.
Cuevas, Manuel	0	0	8.07	16	1	0	0	29	49	32	26	8	16	.371	R	R	6-0	170	2-28-82	2002	Nigua, D.R.
Dove, Shane	1	1	4.19	19	1	0	1	39	40	23	18	7	34	.264	L	L	6-1	170	7-22-84	2003	Tega Cay, S.C.
Guerrero, Hipolito	0	0	5.40	23	0	0	0	25	27	16	15	6	21	.272	L	L	6-0	140	6-13-83	2000	Santo Domingo, D.R.
Julio, Donald	3	3	7.68	18	5	0	0	43	69	41	37	9	36	.363	R	R	6-1	160	8-12-83	2000	Panama City, Panama
Krantz, Ben	1	2	5.98	17	8	0	0	47	50	36	31	23	32	.268	R	R	6-2	195	7-28-80	2003	Toronto, Ontario
Liebeck, Jered	0	0	3.38	5	0	0	0	8	10	5	3	3	11	.303	R	R	6-1	200	1-27-81	2003	Phoenix, Ariz.
Nippert, Derik	0	0	4.96	13	0	0	0	16	20	14	9	6	9	.298	R	R	6-7	220	5-6-81	2003	Beallsville, Ohio
Novosel, Walt	4	1	0.30	25	0	0	1	30	21	4	1	13	33	.192	L	L	6-3	215	6-16-81	2003	Pulaski, Pa.
Perrault, Josh	3	1	3.47	24	1	0	2	36	38	15	14	11	33	.267	R	R	6-3	205	6-11-82	2003	Mesa, Ariz.
Rocha, Angel	5	8	3.12	15	15	1	0	92	79	43	32	26	82	.228	L	L	6-3	180	11-15-84	2002	Santo Domingo, D.R.
Rosen, Mark	5	5	5.81	13	12	0	0	62	76	48	40	38	56	.305	L	L	5-11	200	6-30-84	2002	Randolph, Mass.
Silva, Erick	3	3	6.82	7	7	1	0	32	50	26	24	10	25	.362	R	R	6-1	170	11-20-82	1999	Maracay, Venez.
Vaillancourt, Tim	0	3	6.41	22	0	0	0	27	33	21	19	16	22	.300	R	R	6-4	195	12-5-81	2003	Bear, Del.
Vicente, Ruben	2	1	5.00	3	3	0	0	18	16	11	10	4	13	.222	R	R	6-0	160	3-3-80	2000	La Romana, D.R.
Yamaguchi, Tetsuya	6	7	4.54	15	15	1	0	83	89	47	42	28	63	.275	L	L	6-0	165	11-11-83	2002	Yokohama, Japan

ATLANTA BRAVES

BY BILL BALLEW

The 2003 season ended much like 11 of the previous 12 seasons for the Braves, which was both good and bad news in Atlanta.

Not only did the Braves finish with the best record in the National League and extend their string to 12 straight division titles—the longest run in the history of professional sports—but the team also reinvented itself again by clubbing opponents after relying on pitching throughout their record-breaking streak.

Yet the entire organization, from general manager John Schuerholz down to the batboy, left Turner Field wondering how something so right could turn out so wrong. In what has become an annual trend since the Braves defeated the Indians to win the 1995 World Series, Atlanta ended the postseason downcast after creating so much hope during the previous six months.

Atlanta led the NL in most offensive categories, including batting (.284), slugging percentage (.475), runs (907), total bases (2,696), RBIs (872) and home runs (235, a franchise record). Outfielders Gary Sheffield, Andruw Jones and Chipper Jones all had at least 27 home runs and 100 RBIs. Catcher Javy Lopez established a new season standard for homers by a catcher (42), while middle infielders Rafael Furcal and Marcus Giles returned to rookie form by setting the table atop the Braves' batting order.

Pitching also remained a forte, if not the dominating force it has been in the recent past. Despite losing such stalwarts as Tom Glavine and Kevin Millwood, the Braves stayed the course by replacing them with Russ Ortiz, who led the league with 21 wins, and 14-game winner Mike Hampton. Greg Maddux became the first pitcher in major league history to win 15 games in 16 straight seasons, and Horacio Ramirez made the jump from the minors to win 12 games in 29 starts. John Smoltz also was as dominant as any closer this side of Eric Gagne, with 45 saves in 49 opportunities.

Even so, after placing no worse than second in the NL in ERA every year since 1992, the Braves fell to ninth in 2003 at 4.10. Atlanta starters also threw only one shutout and four complete games, numbers that show the team's lack of a dominating ace. That weakness was apparent in the NL Division Series. Behind aces Kerry Wood and Mark Prior, the Cubs silenced the Braves' bats and outlasted the Atlanta starters to win their first postseason series in 95 years.

There was a sense of urgency in Atlanta on the eve of the playoffs. With Sheffield, Lopez and Maddux among the major contributors eligible for free agency, the Braves realized 2003 could be their best opportunity to seize their second World Series title since moving to Atlanta in 1966.

While the Braves fell short of the World Series for the fourth straight season, the organization did capture crowns in the lower reaches of the minors. The Braves won the Rookie-level Gulf Coast League championship for the first time since 1964 and the Class A South Atlantic League flag for the first time since 1979.

Individual accomplishments were headed by Class A Myrtle Beach third baseman Andy Marte, who ranked second in the Carolina League with 35 doubles while hitting .285-16-63. Richmond first baseman Adam LaRoche proved he is ready to make the jump to Atlanta by leading the organization with 20 home runs and 72 RBIs and tying for fourth with a .290 average. Pitching remained strong as well, with prospects Bubba Nelson, Adam Wainwright and Macay McBride moving closer to their major league debuts.

Javy Lopez

Adam LaRoche

PLAYERS of the YEAR

MAJOR LEAGUE: Javy Lopez, c

Lopez bounced back from a rough 2002 campaign by hitting 42 home runs as a catcher (43 overall) to break Todd Hundley's major league record for the position. He tied for fourth in the National League in homers, and ranked eighth in RBIs and total bases.

MINOR LEAGUE: Adam LaRoche, 1b

LaRoche hit .292-20-72 between Double-A Greenville and Triple-A Richmond, leading the organization in the latter two categories. Managers voted him the best defensive first baseman in both the International and Southern leagues.

ORGANIZATION LEADERS

BATTING		
*AVG	Johnny Estrada, Richmond	.328
R	Jeff Francoeur, Rome	78
H	Jeff Francoeur, Rome	147
TB	Adam LaRoche, Richmond/Greenville	235
2B	Andy Marte, Myrtle Beach	35
	James Jurries, Greenville	35
3B	Wilson Betemit, Richmond	13
HR	Adam LaRoche, Richmond/ Greenville	20
RBI	Adam LaRoche, Richmond/ Greenville	72
BB	Andy Marte, Myrtle Beach	67
SO	Cory Aldridge, Greenville	134
SB	Gregor Blanco, Myrtle Beach	34
*SLG	Johnny Estrada, Richmond	.494
*OBP	Johnny Estrada, Richmond	.393
PITCHING		
W	Matt Wright, Myrtle Beach/Rome	12
	Blaine Boyer, Rome	12
L	Matt Merricks, Myrtle Beach/Rome	15
ERA	Anthony Lerew, Rome	2.38
G	Three tied at	53
CG	Jason Marquis, Richmond	3
	Daniel Curtis, Greenville/Myrtle Beach	3
SV	Joey Dawley, Richmond	23
IP	Macay McBride, Myrtle Beach	165
BB	Andy Pratt, Richmond	77
SO	Andy Pratt, Richmond	161

*Minimum 250 At-Bats #Minimum 75 Innings

ATLANTA BRAVES

Manager: Bobby Cox.

2003 Record: 101-61, .623 (1st, NL East).

BATTING	AVG	G	AB	R	H	2B	3B	HR	RBI	BB	SO	SB	CS	SLG	OBP	B	T	HT	WT	DOB	1st Yr	Resides
Blanco, Henry	.199	55	151	11	30	8	0	1	13	10	21	0	0	.272	.252	R	R	5-11	220	8-29-71	1990	Guarenas, Venez.
Bragg, Darren	.241	104	162	21	39	5	1	0	9	13	38	2	1	.284	.305	L	R	5-9	180	9-7-69	1991	Roswell, Ga.
Castilla, Vinny	.277	147	542	65	150	28	3	22	76	26	86	1	2	.461	.310	R	R	6-1	200	7-4-67	1990	Littleton, Colo.
DeRosa, Mark	.263	103	266	40	70	14	0	6	22	16	49	1	0	.383	.316	R	R	6-1	200	2-2-75	1996	Atlanta, Ga.
Estrada, Johnny	.306	16	36	2	11	0	0	0	2	0	3	0	0	.306	.359	S	R	5-11	200	6-27-76	1997	Salisbury, N.C.
Fick, Robert	.269	126	409	52	110	26	1	11	80	42	47	1	0	.418	.335	L	R	6-1	200	3-15-74	1996	Manhattan Beach, Calif.
Franco, Julio	.294	103	197	28	58	12	2	5	31	25	43	0	2	.452	.372	R	R	6-1	180	8-23-61	1978	San Pedro de Macoris, D.R.
Franco, Matt	.246	112	134	11	33	5	0	3	15	11	26	0	1	.351	.299	L	R	6-1	210	8-19-69	1987	Thousand Oaks, Calif.
Furcal, Rafael	.292	156	664	130	194	35	10	15	61	60	76	25	2	.443	.352	S	R	5-10	160	10-24-77	1997	Loma de Cabrera, D.R.
Garcia, Jesse	.400	13	10	6	4	0	1	0	2	0	1	0	0	.600	.400	R	R	5-10	170	9-24-73	1993	Robstown, Texas
Giles, Marcus	.316	145	551	101	174	49	2	21	69	59	80	14	4	.526	.390	R	R	5-8	180	5-18-78	1997	El Cajon, Calif.
Hampton, Mike	.183	32	60	6	11	2	1	2	8	5	13	0	0	.350	.246	R	L	5-10	180	9-9-72	1990	Evergreen, Colo.
Hessman, Mike	.286	19	21	2	6	2	0	2	3	5	6	0	0	.667	.423	R	R	6-5	210	3-5-78	1996	Westminster, Calif.
Jones, Andruw	.277	156	595	101	165	28	2	36	116	53	125	4	3	.513	.338	R	R	6-1	180	4-23-77	1994	Willemstad, Curacao
Jones, Chipper	.305	153	555	103	169	33	2	27	106	94	83	2	2	.517	.402	S	R	6-4	210	4-24-72	1990	Alpharetta, Ga.
Langerhans, Ryan	.267	16	15	2	4	0	0	0	0	0	6	0	0	.267	.267	L	L	6-3	190	2-20-80	1998	Round Rock, Texas
Lopez, Javy	.328	129	457	89	150	29	3	43	109	33	90	0	1	.687	.378	R	R	6-3	220	11-5-70	1988	Ponce, P.R.
Ortiz, Russ	.257	35	70	6	18	4	0	2	10	4	17	0	0	.400	.303	R	R	6-1	200	6-5-74	1995	Gilbert, Ariz.
Sheffield, Gary	.330	155	576	126	190	37	2	39	132	86	55	18	4	.604	.419	R	R	6-0	200	11-18-68	1986	St. Petersburg, Fla.

PITCHING	W	L	ERA	G	GS	CG	SV	IP	H	R	ER	BB	SO	AVG	B	T	HT	WT	DOB	1st Yr	Resides
Bong, Jung	6	2	5.05	44	0	0	1	57	56	32	32	31	47	.266	L	L	6-3	170	7-15-80	1997	Norcross, Ga.
Cunnane, Will	2	2	2.70	20	0	0	3	20	14	6	6	6	20	.189	R	R	6-1	200	4-24-74	1993	Rockland, N.Y.
Dawley, Joey	0	0	18.00	5	0	0	0	7	15	14	14	3	8	.405	R	R	6-4	200	9-19-71	1993	Moreno Valley, Calif.
Gryboski, Kevin	6	4	3.86	64	0	0	0	44	44	22	19	23	32	.271	R	R	6-5	230	11-15-73	1995	Plains, Pa.
Hampton, Mike	14	8	3.84	31	31	1	0	190	186	91	81	78	110	.255	R	L	5-10	180	9-9-72	1990	Evergreen, Colo.
Hernandez, Roberto	5	3	4.35	66	0	0	0	60	61	36	29	43	45	.262	R	R	6-4	250	11-11-64	1986	Largo, Fla.
Hodges, Trey	3	3	4.66	52	1	0	0	66	69	38	34	31	66	.268	R	R	6-3	180	6-29-78	2000	Spring, Texas
Holmes, Darren	1	2	4.29	48	0	0	0	42	47	22	20	11	46	.279	R	R	6-0	200	4-25-66	1984	Fletcher, N.C.
King, Ray	3	4	3.51	80	0	0	0	59	46	30	23	27	43	.212	L	L	6-1	240	1-15-74	1995	Franklin, Wisc.
Maddux, Greg	16	11	3.96	36	36	1	0	218	225	112	96	33	124	.267	R	R	6-0	180	4-14-66	1984	Las Vegas, Nev.
Marquis, Jason	0	0	5.53	21	2	0	1	41	43	27	25	18	19	.270	L	R	6-1	210	8-21-78	1996	Staten Island, N.Y.
Mercker, Kent	0	0	1.06	18	0	0	1	17	15	3	2	7	7	.230	L	L	6-2	190	2-1-68	1986	Dublin, Ohio
2-team (49 Cincinnati)	0	2	1.95	67	0	0	1	55	46	16	12	32	48	.226							
Ortiz, Russ	21	7	3.81	34	34	1	0	212	177	101	90	102	149	.223	R	R	6-1	200	6-5-74	1995	Gilbert, Ariz.
Ramirez, Horacio	12	4	4.00	29	29	1	0	182	181	91	81	72	100	.263	L	L	6-1	170	11-24-79	1997	Inglewood, Calif.
Reynolds, Shane	11	9	5.43	30	29	0	0	167	191	104	101	59	94	.293	R	R	6-3	215	3-26-68	1989	Houston, Texas
Smoltz, John	0	2	1.12	62	0	0	45	64	48	9	8	8	73	.204	R	R	6-3	220	5-15-67	1986	Duluth, Ga.
Wright, Jaret	1	0	2.00	11	0	0	0	9	7	2	2	3	9	.225	R	R	6-2	230	12-29-75	1994	Newport Beach, Calif.
2-team (39 San Diego)	2	5	7.35	50	0	0	2	56	76	46	46	31	50	.331							

FIELDING

Catcher	PCT	G	PO	A	E	DP	PB
Blanco	.996	52	255	25	1	4	1
Estrada	1.000	14	47	1	0	0	0
Lopez	.994	120	718	53	5	6	6

First Base	PCT	G	PO	A	E	DP
DeRosa	1.000	1	1	0	0	1
Fick	.987	115	1004	52	14	89
J. Franco	.998	75	432	32	1	47
M. Franco	.977	15	122	6	3	13
Hessman	1.000	4	30	1	0	3

Second Base	PCT	G	PO	A	E	DP
DeRosa	.984	29	49	78	2	21
Garcia	1.000	6	6	4	0	1
Giles	.982	139	278	471	14	85

Third Base	PCT	G	PO	A	E	DP
Castilla	.955	147	98	307	19	28
DeRosa	.933	25	12	44	4	4
Garcia	1.000	2	2	1	0	1
Hessman	1.000	3	0	3	0	0

Shortstop	PCT	G	PO	A	E	DP
DeRosa	1.000	20	21	42	0	9
Furcal	.959	155	237	481	31	108
Garcia	1.000	3	0	1	0	0

Outfield	PCT	G	PO	A	E	DP
Bragg	.988	78	79	1	1	0
DeRosa	1.000	2	2	0	0	0
M. Franco	1.000	3	1	0	0	0
Hessman	.800	8	4	0	1	0
A. Jones	.993	155	390	8	3	1
C. Jones	.968	149	202	9	7	2
Langerhans	1.000	14	12	1	0	0
Sheffield	.986	153	283	7	4	2

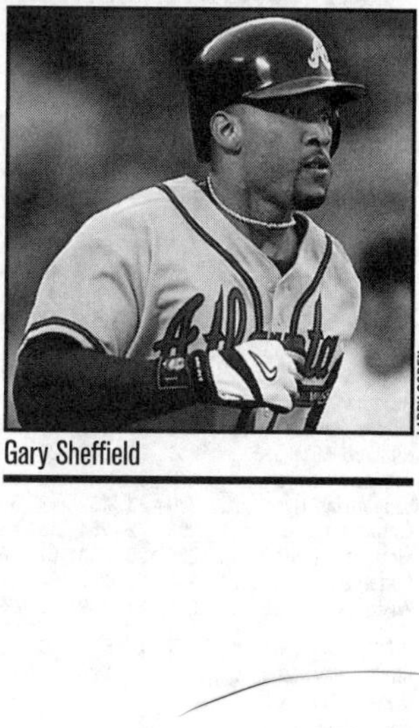
LARRY GOREN

Gary Sheffield

FARM SYSTEM

Director, Player Development: Dayton Moore.

Class	Farm Team	League	W	L	Pct.	Finish*	Manager	First Yr.
AAA	Richmond (Va.) Braves	International	64	79	.448	13th (14)	Pat Kelly	1996
AA	Greenville (S.C.) Braves	Southern	68	70	.493	5th (10)	Brian Snitker	1984
High A	Myrtle Beach (S.C.) Pelicans	Carolina	56	82	.406	8th (8)	Randy Ingle	1999
Low A	Rome (Ga.) Braves	South Atlantic	78	61	.561	+3rd (16)	Rocket Wheeler	2003
Rookie	Danville (Va.) Braves	Appalachian	36	30	.545	4th (10)	Kevin McMullan	1993
Rookie	Kissimmee (Fla.) Braves	Gulf Coast	38	22	.633	+1st (14)	Ralph Henriquez	1998

*Finish in overall standings (No. of teams in league) +League champion

LARRY GOREN

LARRY GOREN

Rafael Furcal and Marcus Giles: Braves double play combination hit .303 overall with 231 runs, 84 doubles and 36 homers

RICHMOND BRAVES Class AAA

INTERNATIONAL LEAGUE

BATTING	AVG	G	AB	R	H	2B	3B	HR	RBI	BB	SO	SB	CS	SLG	OBP	B	T	HT	WT	DOB	1st Yr	Resides
Betemit, Wilson	.262	127	478	55	125	23	13	8	65	38	115	8	5	.414	.315	S	R	6-3	190	11-2-81	1996	Santo Domingo, D.R.
Boscan, Jean	.250	3	12	0	3	2	0	0	1	1	4	0	0	.417	.308	R	R	6-2	160	12-26-79	1996	Maracaibo, Venez.
Castro, Ramon	.155	33	84	11	13	2	0	0	8	10	22	0	0	.179	.242	R	R	6-0	190	10-23-79	1996	Valencia, Venez.
Clapp, Stubby	.217	105	286	43	62	11	9	3	23	46	66	6	2	.350	.333	L	R	5-8	170	2-24-73	1996	Windsor, Ontario
Estrada, Johnny	.328	106	354	40	116	29	0	10	66	30	30	0	0	.494	.393	S	R	5-11	200	6-27-76	1997	Salisbury, N.C.
Evans, Lee	.245	16	53	5	13	0	0	0	3	4	12	0	0	.245	.298	S	R	6-1	180	7-20-77	1996	Northport, Ala.
Fitzgerald, Jason	.209	13	43	2	9	1	0	0	1	0	10	1	1	.233	.227	L	L	6-1	190	9-16-75	1997	Belle Chasse, La.
Garcia, Jesse	.306	110	425	45	130	17	3	2	30	12	50	29	9	.374	.329	R	R	5-10	170	9-24-73	1993	Robstown, Texas
Green, Nick	.248	124	399	40	99	26	1	11	51	26	79	7	5	.401	.303	R	R	6-0	170	9-10-78	1999	Duluth, Ga.
Hessman, Mike	.248	96	359	47	89	15	3	16	52	24	87	3	1	.440	.296	R	R	6-5	210	3-5-78	1996	Westminster, Calif.
Hollins, Damon	.274	91	307	39	84	23	4	11	45	22	62	7	2	.482	.324	R	L	5-11	180	6-12-74	1992	Fairfield, Calif.
Hubbard, Mike	.233	70	206	22	48	12	0	2	15	13	28	0	0	.320	.283	R	R	6-1	220	2-16-71	1992	Madison Heights, Va.
Johnson, Rontrez	.173	31	81	8	14	1	0	0	5	8	15	3	1	.185	.261	R	R	5-10	160	12-8-76	1995	Marshall, Texas
Langerhans, Ryan	.280	38	132	13	37	10	2	4	11	11	29	2	1	.477	.338	L	L	6-3	190	2-20-80	1998	Round Rock, Texas
LaRoche, Adam	.295	72	264	33	78	21	0	8	35	27	58	1	2	.466	.360	L	L	6-3	180	11-6-79	2000	Fort Scott, Kan.
McDonald, Donzell	.254	129	464	61	118	18	9	2	19	62	113	31	10	.345	.345	S	R	5-11	180	2-20-75	1995	Glendale, Colo.
Porter, Bo	.240	79	267	34	64	13	5	5	31	26	78	14	4	.382	.309	R	R	6-2	190	7-5-72	1994	Fresno, Texas
Wilson, Travis	.257	121	409	38	105	26	4	6	39	9	110	5	2	.384	.284	R	R	6-2	180	7-10-77	1996	Christchurch, New Zealand

PITCHING	W	L	ERA	G	GS	CG	SV	IP	H	R	ER	BB	SO	AVG	B	T	HT	WT	DOB	1st Yr	Resides
Aguilar, Ray	1	0	1.80	1	1	0	0	5	2	1	1	2	5	.125	S	L	5-11	200	1-18-80	1999	South El Monte, Calif.
Belisle, Matt	1	1	2.25	3	3	0	0	20	17	6	5	0	10	.229	S	R	6-3	190	6-6-80	1998	Austin, Texas
Bong, Jung	1	2	5.56	3	3	0	0	11	11	7	7	3	15	.239	L	L	6-3	170	7-15-80	1997	Norcross, Ga.
Castillo, Frank	0	1	1.50	4	3	0	0	18	23	5	3	4	14	.306	R	R	6-1	200	4-1-69	1987	Cave Creek, Ariz.
Cunnane, Will	1	0	0.00	15	0	0	2	21	11	2	0	2	19	.159	R	R	6-1	200	4-24-74	1993	Rockland, N.Y.

PITCHING	W	L	ERA	G	GS	CG	SV	IP	H	R	ER	BB	SO	AVG	B	T	HT	WT	DOB	1st Yr	Resides
Dawley, Joey	3	5	3.34	46	4	0	23	57	47	25	21	23	73	.220	R	R	6-4	200	9-19-71	1993	Moreno Valley, Calif.
Emiliano, Jamie	0	7	4.07	53	0	0	1	73	80	41	33	30	40	.280	R	R	5-10	210	8-2-74	1995	Andrews, Texas
Ennis, John	2	11	5.56	28	15	0	0	100	121	70	62	37	76	.304	R	R	6-5	220	10-17-79	1998	Panorama, Calif.
Fussell, Chris	7	11	4.03	29	26	0	0	152	142	77	68	74	130	.254	R	R	6-2	200	5-19-76	1994	Oregon, Ohio
Glynn, Ryan	6	5	2.91	16	16	0	0	93	84	31	30	31	75	.244	R	R	6-3	200	11-1-74	1995	Grand Prairie, Texas
Hernandez, Buddy	4	3	3.42	53	0	0	4	71	65	30	27	31	82	.241	R	R	5-9	170	3-3-79	2000	Birdsboro, Pa.
Hernandez, Roberto	1	1	9.45	6	0	0	0	7	11	9	7	4	10	.333	R	R	6-4	250	11-11-64	1986	Largo, Fla.
Jones, Bobby M.	1	3	3.12	37	0	0	5	35	29	12	12	18	39	.223	R	L	6-0	170	4-11-72	1992	East Rutherford, N.J.
Lewis, Derrick	2	5	7.15	36	5	0	0	62	83	53	49	29	46	.322	R	R	6-5	210	5-7-76	1997	Montgomery, Ala.
Marquis, Jason	8	4	3.35	15	15	3	0	94	93	40	35	34	75	.256	L	R	6-1	210	8-21-78	1996	Staten Island, N.Y.
McConnell, Sam	8	4	2.70	22	13	0	0	93	94	31	28	17	64	.264	L	L	6-1	210	12-31-75	1997	Fairfield, Ohio
Nelson, Bubba	0	1	1.88	11	0	0	0	14	10	3	3	5	7	.222	R	R	6-2	200	8-26-81	2000	Fort Washington, Md.
Phelps, Travis	9	5	3.47	47	8	0	4	93	77	44	36	38	91	.223	R	R	6-2	160	7-25-77	1997	Rocky Comfort, Mo.
Pratt, Andy	7	10	3.40	28	27	1	0	156	146	77	59	77	161	.250	L	L	6-0	180	8-27-79	1998	Chino Valley, Ariz.
Romano, Mike	1	0	0.73	8	0	0	2	12	9	1	1	3	7	.225	R	R	6-2	190	3-3-72	1993	Chalmette, La.
Smith, Chuck	1	0	2.00	3	3	0	0	18	13	5	4	9	13	.203	R	R	6-1	180	10-21-69	1991	Hillside, Ill.
Sylvester, Billy	0	0	3.86	12	1	0	0	19	11	9	8	19	27	.166	R	R	6-5	210	10-1-76	1997	Florence, S.C.
Takeoka, Kazuhiro	0	0	2.31	9	0	0	0	12	10	3	3	5	7	.250	R	R	6-4	190	1-25-75	2001	Shiga, Japan

FIELDING

Catcher	PCT	G	PO	A	E	DP	PB
Boscan	1.000	3	26	3	0	1	0
Estrada	.994	83	627	40	4	8	7
Evans	.987	11	68	7	1	1	3
Hubbard	.995	55	376	28	2	1	1

First Base	PCT	G	PO	A	E	DP
Hessman	.995	54	392	28	2	33
Hubbard	1.000	1	3	0	0	2
LaRoche	.993	72	549	39	4	70
Wilson	.977	24	158	12	4	20

Second Base	PCT	G	PO	A	E	DP
Castro	.973	10	16	20	1	7
Clapp	.957	31	50	60	5	19
Garcia	.938	6	4	11	1	3
Green	.967	108	202	261	16	72
Wilson	1.000	1	0	1	0	1

Third Base	PCT	G	PO	A	E	DP
Betemit	.896	107	62	163	26	18
Castro	.667	4	2	2	2	0
Clapp	.943	19	8	42	3	6
Garcia	1.000	3	1	4	0	1
Hessman	.962	19	12	39	2	2
Wilson	1.000	3	0	5	0	0

Shortstop	PCT	G	PO	A	E	DP
Betemit	.944	9	8	26	2	3
Castro	1.000	11	17	31	0	8
Clapp	.979	30	59	78	3	25
Garcia	.955	94	139	226	17	55
Green	.900	10	15	21	4	7

Outfield	PCT	G	PO	A	E	DP
Clapp	.800	4	4	0	1	0
Evans	1.000	1	1	0	0	0
Fitzgerald	1.000	11	22	1	0	0
Garcia	1.000	6	9	0	0	0
Hessman	.975	24	36	3	1	0
Hollins	.981	89	196	11	4	4
Johnson	1.000	25	50	3	0	1
Langerhans	.949	37	73	2	4	0
McDonald	.993	123	256	9	2	0
Porter	.977	74	122	7	3	1
Wilson	.989	59	91	1	1	0

GREENVILLE BRAVES — Class AA

SOUTHERN LEAGUE

BATTING	AVG	G	AB	R	H	2B	3B	HR	RBI	BB	SO	SB	CS	SLG	OBP	B	T	HT	WT	DOB	1st Yr	Resides
Aldridge, Cory	.234	127	448	55	105	20	2	16	49	37	134	11	3	.395	.298	L	R	6-1	220	6-13-79	1997	Abilene, Texas
Boscan, Jean	.185	41	130	13	24	5	0	2	15	14	35	0	1	.269	.259	R	R	6-2	160	12-26-79	1996	Maracaibo, Venez.
Castro, Ramon	.289	66	204	33	59	9	1	5	20	27	39	4	5	.417	.376	R	R	6-0	190	10-23-79	1996	Valencia, Venez.
De Renne, Keoni	.146	23	41	3	6	0	0	0	0	7	11	0	0	.146	.286	R	R	5-7	160	4-30-79	2000	Honolulu, Hawaii
Evans, Lee	.230	55	183	21	42	9	2	3	16	22	44	3	0	.350	.316	S	R	6-1	180	7-20-77	1996	Northport, Ala.
Fitzgerald, Jason	.259	110	386	45	100	14	3	6	44	41	72	19	7	.358	.330	L	L	6-1	190	9-16-75	1997	Belle Chasse, La.
Jeffcoat, Bryon	.260	37	100	15	26	5	0	0	11	17	24	1	0	.310	.364	R	R	6-1	190	5-14-79	2001	West Columbia, S.C.
Johnson, Kelly	.275	98	334	46	92	22	5	6	45	35	81	10	3	.425	.340	L	R	6-1	180	2-22-82	2000	Austin, Texas
Jurries, James	.284	129	465	73	132	35	4	9	54	48	108	4	2	.434	.354	R	R	6-0	190	4-13-79	2002	Lake Jackson, Texas
Langerhans, Ryan	.253	94	336	42	85	23	2	6	38	46	85	10	10	.387	.348	L	L	6-3	190	2-20-80	1998	Round Rock, Texas
LaRoche, Adam	.283	61	219	42	62	12	1	12	37	34	53	1	2	.511	.381	L	L	6-3	180	11-6-79	2000	Fort Scott, Kan.
Lewis, Richard	.239	129	460	59	110	23	3	6	47	44	101	19	9	.341	.305	R	R	6-1	190	6-29-80	2001	Marietta, Ga.
McCarthy, Bill	.250	86	276	35	69	19	2	6	47	41	59	5	1	.399	.355	R	R	6-2	200	12-2-79	2001	Sewell, N.J.
Miller, Greg	.214	16	42	6	9	0	0	1	6	6	6	2	1	.286	.313	R	R	6-0	180	1-9-79	2001	Sterling, Va.
Orr, Pete	.226	98	257	22	58	10	2	2	31	25	48	14	5	.304	.299	L	R	6-1	170	6-8-79	1999	Newmarket, Ontario
Roat, Kyle	.000	1	1	0	0	0	0	0	0	0	1	0	0	.000	.000	R	R	5-10	200	5-14-80	2001	Coweta, Okla.
Terveen, Bryce	.197	61	178	17	35	7	0	0	16	30	49	1	0	.236	.329	L	R	6-1	200	3-1-78	1999	Modesto, Calif.
Thomas, Charles	.324	47	176	29	57	14	4	0	23	18	25	5	4	.449	.396	L	L	6-0	190	12-26-78	2000	Asheville, N.C.
Waters, Chris	.136	18	22	1	3	0	0	0	1	0	5	0	0	.136	.136	L	L	6-0	170	8-17-80	2000	Lakeland, Fla.

PITCHING	W	L	ERA	G	GS	CG	SV	IP	H	R	ER	BB	SO	AVG	B	T	HT	WT	DOB	1st Yr	Resides
Aguilar, Ray	3	4	2.71	35	7	0	1	93	81	39	28	20	91	.235	S	L	5-11	200	1-18-80	1999	South El Monte, Calif.
Barry, Kevin	4	4	4.95	51	0	0	5	56	54	36	31	32	68	.248	R	R	6-2	210	8-18-78	2001	Princeton Junction, N.J.
Belisle, Matt	6	8	3.52	21	21	1	0	125	128	59	49	42	94	.271	S	R	6-3	190	6-6-80	1998	Austin, Texas
Blank, Matt	0	0	0.00	2	0	0	0	2	0	0	0	0	0	.000	L	L	6-2	190	4-5-76	1997	Arlington, Texas
Byrd, Paul	0	0	8.31	1	1	0	0	4	8	6	4	1	3	.363	R	R	6-1	180	12-3-70	1991	Louisville, Ky.
Collazo, William	6	2	3.66	39	0	0	0	47	41	22	19	21	34	.241	L	L	5-9	170	11-7-79	2001	Miami, Fla.
Colon, Roman	11	3	3.36	39	12	1	2	107	104	48	40	33	58	.260	R	R	6-3	170	8-13-79	1996	Monte Cristi, D.R.
Curtis, Daniel	6	4	2.87	17	12	2	0	78	72	29	25	15	47	.242	R	R	6-3	210	11-3-79	1998	Chattanooga, Tenn.
Digby, Bryan	0	1	5.40	9	1	0	0	12	12	8	7	7	6	.272	R	R	6-2	190	12-31-81	2000	Peachtree City, Ga.
Ennis, John	0	0	2.45	1	1	0	0	4	4	1	1	2	3	.285	R	R	6-5	220	10-17-79	1998	Panorama, Calif.
Evert, Brett	4	9	4.02	33	15	1	1	116	126	57	52	44	103	.283	L	R	6-6	200	10-23-80	1999	Salem, Ore.
Herndon, Eric	0	0	6.23	7	0	0	0	9	14	9	6	2	9	.378	L	R	6-1	190	10-4-76	1998	Upper Marlboro, Md.
Lewis, Derrick	0	0	7.56	3	1	0	0	8	12	7	7	4	6	.352	R	R	6-5	210	5-7-76	1997	Montgomery, Ala.
McConnell, Sam	1	0	4.11	16	0	0	0	15	18	7	7	4	8	.300	L	L	6-1	210	12-31-75	1997	Fairfield, Ohio
Nelson, Bubba	8	10	3.18	23	20	0	0	119	106	47	42	45	77	.240	R	R	6-2	200	8-26-81	2000	Fort Washington, Md.
Smith, Chuck	1	2	3.38	3	3	0	0	19	14	8	7	5	12	.215	R	R	6-1	180	10-21-69	1991	Hillside, Ill.
Sylvester, Billy	1	2	1.51	41	0	0	18	42	22	7	7	25	55	.156	R	R	6-5	210	10-1-76	1997	Florence, S.C.
Takeoka, Kazuhiro	2	1	6.00	20	0	0	1	27	32	19	18	7	9	.304	R	R	6-4	190	1-25-75	2001	Shiga, Japan
Tillery, Josh	0	2	11.57	8	0	0	0	7	13	11	9	5	3	.393	R	R	6-6	250	8-2-78	2000	Laverne, Okla.
Wainwright, Adam	10	8	3.37	27	27	1	0	150	133	59	56	37	128	.241	R	R	6-6	190	8-30-81	2000	St. Simons Island, Ga.
Waters, Chris	3	8	4.41	17	17	0	0	86	104	53	42	26	54	.304	L	L	6-0	170	8-17-80	2000	Lakeland, Fla.
Winkelsas, Joe	1	1	2.93	23	0	0	2	28	26	11	9	8	14	.257	R	R	6-3	180	9-14-73	1996	Buffalo, N.Y.
Zumwalt, Alec	1	1	1.42	11	0	0	0	19	13	3	3	12	19	.191	R	R	6-2	190	1-20-81	1999	Kernersville, N.C.

FIELDING

Catcher	PCT	G	PO	A	E	DP	PB
Boscan	.997	40	286	27	1	2	2
Evans	.988	42	298	24	4	1	10
Terveen	.987	58	355	35	5	3	1

First Base	PCT	G	PO	A	E	DP
Castro	.900	1	7	2	1	0
Evans	.969	9	57	5	2	7
Fitzgerald	1.000	20	164	15	0	13
Jeffcoat	.990	23	178	20	2	9
Jurries	.988	32	234	14	3	15
LaRoche	.996	60	496	39	2	46
Roat	1.000	1	2	0	0	0

Second Base	PCT	G	PO	A	E	DP
Castro	.931	8	10	17	2	5
De Renne	1.000	4	6	10	0	2
Lewis	.979	120	217	302	11	60
Orr	1.000	13	27	29	0	6

Third Base	PCT	G	PO	A	E	DP
Castro	.941	34	27	68	6	4
De Renne	1.000	2	0	2	0	0
Jeffcoat	1.000	8	5	16	0	2
Jurries	.926	88	55	146	16	13
Orr	.932	19	19	22	3	1

Shortstop	PCT	G	PO	A	E	DP
Castro	.938	11	16	29	3	7
Johnson	.959	91	122	249	16	40
Orr	.948	49	53	130	10	21

Outfield	PCT	G	PO	A	E	DP
Aldridge	.971	121	198	3	6	0
Fitzgerald	.963	86	147	9	6	0
Langerhans	.991	89	204	9	2	1
McCarthy	1.000	78	123	3	0	1
Miller	1.000	11	23	0	0	0
Orr	1.000	4	3	0	0	0
Thomas	.983	44	109	4	2	0

MYRTLE BEACH PELICANS — High Class A

CAROLINA LEAGUE

BATTING	AVG	G	AB	R	H	2B	3B	HR	RBI	BB	SO	SB	CS	SLG	OBP	B	T	HT	WT	DOB	1st Yr	Resides
Bernard, Miguel	.000	1	2	0	0	0	0	0	0	0	1	0	0	.000	.000	R	R	5-11	170	1-1-81	1997	San Pedro de Macoris, D.R.
Blanco, Gregor	.271	126	461	66	125	19	7	5	36	54	114	34	16	.375	.357	L	L	5-11	170	12-12-83	2000	Cua, Venez.
Boscan, Jean	.207	28	87	9	18	4	0	1	11	11	33	2	0	.287	.296	R	R	6-2	160	12-26-79	1996	Maracaibo, Venez.
Burrows, Angelo	.252	41	127	14	32	7	1	0	10	5	18	3	4	.323	.286	L	R	5-11	170	7-2-80	1999	Freeport, Bahamas
Duran, Carlos	.224	118	415	45	93	20	6	3	35	17	60	11	10	.323	.257	L	L	6-1	160	12-27-82	1999	Barquisimeto, Venez.
Hanson, Mike	.200	5	15	0	3	1	0	0	0	0	1	0	0	.267	.200	R	R	5-11	175	5-2-81	2003	Smyrna, Ga.
Herr, Aaron	.267	113	416	40	111	17	1	13	46	19	99	5	8	.406	.306	R	R	5-11	180	3-7-81	2000	Lancaster, Pa.
Iorg, Isaac	.268	89	280	34	75	14	2	2	32	21	55	4	6	.354	.325	R	R	6-1	190	6-5-79	2001	Knoxville, Tenn.
Jeffcoat, Bryon	.240	37	96	12	23	4	0	1	9	15	25	1	1	.313	.351	R	R	6-1	190	5-14-79	2001	West Columbia, S.C.
Marte, Andy	.285	130	463	69	132	35	1	16	63	67	109	5	2	.469	.372	R	R	6-1	180	10-21-83	2001	Villa Tapia, D.R.
Miller, Greg	.263	85	297	30	78	12	1	0	37	26	57	11	6	.310	.327	R	R	6-0	180	1-9-79	2001	Sterling, Va.
Pena, Brayan	.294	82	286	24	84	14	1	2	27	11	28	2	5	.371	.320	S	R	5-11	210	1-7-82	2001	San Jose, Costa Rica
Pena, Tony	.259	120	405	43	105	14	1	4	30	24	82	17	12	.328	.304	R	R	6-1	160	3-23-81	1999	Santiago, D.R.
Peters, Yaron	.170	35	112	9	19	3	1	2	5	15	30	0	0	.268	.304	R	R	6-2	220	7-30-79	2002	Sherman Oaks, Calif.
Roat, Kyle	.214	14	42	6	9	2	0	0	5	5	10	0	0	.262	.306	R	R	5-10	200	5-14-80	2001	Coweta, Okla.
Salas, Jose	.243	73	235	20	57	7	0	5	23	15	38	1	2	.336	.294	S	R	6-3	210	2-16-82	1998	Caracas, Venez.
Stern, Adam	.194	28	103	11	20	2	0	0	6	13	21	7	3	.214	.282	L	R	5-11	180	2-12-80	2001	London, Ontario
Thomas, Charles	.242	66	207	30	50	8	1	2	15	29	54	6	2	.319	.357	L	L	6-0	190	12-26-78	2000	Asheville, N.C.
Thorman, Scott	.243	124	445	44	108	26	2	12	56	42	79	0	0	.391	.311	L	R	6-3	200	1-6-82	2000	Cambridge, Ontario

PITCHING	W	L	ERA	G	GS	CG	SV	IP	H	R	ER	BB	SO	AVG	B	T	HT	WT	DOB	1st Yr	Resides
Acosta, Manuel	2	0	6.39	8	0	0	1	13	19	14	9	11	10	.327	R	R	6-4	170	5-1-81	1998	Colon, Panama
Bush, Paul	4	4	3.63	34	2	0	0	62	49	32	25	30	64	.210	R	R	6-1	190	10-5-79	2002	Titusville, Fla.
Butler, Matt	1	4	9.00	10	5	0	0	22	27	23	22	21	14	.303	R	R	6-3	190	9-24-79	1999	Hattiesburg, Miss.
Coenen, Matt	8	10	3.86	28	28	0	0	147	145	74	63	62	90	.263	L	L	6-6	230	3-13-80	2001	St. Michaels, Md.
Collazo, William	0	1	3.07	11	0	0	1	15	12	5	5	4	15	.222	L	L	5-9	170	11-7-79	2001	Miami, Fla.
Curtis, Daniel	3	4	4.04	12	11	1	0	65	77	41	29	23	55	.292	R	R	6-3	210	11-3-79	1998	Chattanooga, Tenn.
David, Brad	0	0	4.57	17	0	0	0	22	24	11	11	11	13	.282	L	L	6-0	190	5-26-80	2002	Baton Rouge, La.
Digby, Bryan	0	1	4.45	21	0	0	0	32	31	20	16	17	21	.254	R	R	6-2	190	12-31-81	2000	Peachtree City, Ga.
Lopez, Gonzalo	0	2	9.00	3	2	0	0	10	12	10	10	4	10	.292	R	R	6-2	170	10-6-83	2000	Managua, Nicaragua
Mabry, Barry	0	0	0.00	1	0	0	0	3	3	0	0	0	2	.250	R	R	6-5	180	11-2-81	2000	Spartanburg, S.C.
McBride, Macay	9	8	2.95	27	27	1	0	165	164	63	54	49	139	.261	L	L	5-11	180	10-24-82	2001	Sylvania, Ga.
McDaniel, Denny	1	0	1.88	11	0	0	1	14	20	5	3	1	13	.333	L	L	6-3	210	8-12-76	1996	Austin, Texas
Mendez, David	0	0	6.75	3	0	0	0	4	5	3	3	5	3	.294	L	L	6-2	190	10-1-79	1996	Pueblo Nuevo, Panama
Merricks, Matt	1	8	3.23	11	8	0	0	47	45	29	17	23	37	.251	L	L	5-11	180	8-6-82	2000	Oxnard, Calif.
Meyer, Dan	3	6	2.87	13	13	0	0	78	69	29	25	17	63	.236	R	L	6-3	190	7-3-81	2002	Mickleton, N.J.
Miller, Matt	0	0	7.20	4	0	0	0	5	6	4	4	4	3	.300	L	L	6-2	200	6-6-78	2000	Devon, Pa.
Miner, Zach	6	10	3.69	27	27	2	0	154	150	74	63	61	88	.261	R	R	6-3	190	3-12-82	2001	Jupiter, Fla.
Roberts, Ralph	3	5	2.92	44	0	0	8	62	50	27	20	23	68	.219	R	R	6-2	200	3-28-80	2001	Cherryville, N.C.
Rodriguez, Jose	0	0	1.08	5	0	0	0	8	7	2	1	3	6	.233	R	R	6-0	170	1-15-82	1998	Carora, Venez.
Tillery, Josh	2	2	2.98	26	0	0	0	45	47	16	15	13	32	.270	R	R	6-6	250	8-2-78	2000	Laverne, Okla.
Vianna, Marcel	5	4	2.96	26	0	0	0	52	36	20	17	29	42	.198	R	R	6-2	170	3-23-81	1997	Sao Paulo, Brazil
Waters, Chris	1	1	2.89	2	2	0	0	9	7	7	3	6	6	.225	L	L	6-0	170	8-17-80	2000	Lakeland, Fla.
Watkins, Dave	0	3	1.92	25	0	0	3	52	31	13	11	18	51	.176	R	R	6-1	190	8-18-81	1999	Leitchfield, Ky.
Wright, Matt	2	7	6.38	13	13	0	0	61	82	47	43	42	58	.326	R	R	6-4	220	3-13-82	2000	Lorena, Texas
Zumwalt, Alec	5	2	2.22	30	0	0	6	45	29	11	11	16	43	.190	R	R	6-2	190	1-20-81	1999	Kernersville, N.C.

FIELDING

Catcher	PCT	G	PO	A	E	DP	PB
Bernard	1.000	1	5	0	0	0	0
Boscan	.977	27	189	26	5	0	4
Pena	.996	62	408	46	2	2	7
Roat	.986	13	68	4	1	1	2
Salas	.982	45	284	45	6	1	10

First Base	PCT	G	PO	A	E	DP
Iorg	1.000	4	35	0	0	4
Jeffcoat	1.000	5	32	1	0	1
Peters	1.000	11	68	6	0	10
Salas	.963	6	49	3	2	3
Thorman	.992	120	999	49	8	96

Second Base	PCT	G	PO	A	E	DP
Hanson	1.000	5	9	8	0	4
Herr	.976	105	170	272	11	70
Iorg	.955	31	51	76	6	15
Jeffcoat	1.000	2	3	5	0	0

Third Base	PCT	G	PO	A	E	DP
Herr	1.000	3	0	4	0	0
Iorg	.944	16	9	25	2	3
Jeffcoat	.923	9	5	7	1	0
Marte	.911	117	71	215	28	20

Shortstop	PCT	G	PO	A	E	DP
Iorg	.941	8	8	24	2	4
Jeffcoat	.958	19	22	47	3	8
Pena	.965	116	186	336	19	76

Outfield	PCT	G	PO	A	E	DP
Blanco	.967	123	260	6	9	0
Burrows	.961	34	72	2	3	0
Duran	.983	111	222	16	4	0
Iorg	1.000	1	1	0	0	0
Jeffcoat	1.000	2	4	0	0	0
Miller	.982	66	105	2	2	0
Stern	1.000	26	66	1	0	0
Thomas	.969	60	121	5	4	0

ROME BRAVES — Low Class A

SOUTH ATLANTIC LEAGUE

BATTING	AVG	G	AB	R	H	2B	3B	HR	RBI	BB	SO	SB	CS	SLG	OBP	B	T	HT	WT	DOB	1st Yr	Resides
Barthel, Cole	.250	10	32	1	8	1	0	0	4	2	3	0	0	.281	.286	R	R	6-2	200	8-11-82	2001	Decatur, Ala.
Bernard, Miguel	.308	35	107	17	33	10	1	0	17	8	9	2	2	.421	.361	R	R	5-11	170	1-1-81	1997	San Pedro de Macoris, D.R.
Burrows, Angelo	.204	22	49	6	10	3	1	1	5	4	8	3	2	.367	.255	L	R	5-11	170	7-2-80	1999	Freeport, Bahamas
Burrus, Josh	.178	16	45	4	8	2	0	1	2	1	12	2	1	.289	.245	R	R	5-11	190	8-20-83	2001	Marietta, Ga.
Donato, Greg	.276	10	29	4	8	1	0	1	3	1	4	0	0	.414	.323	R	R	6-0	180	11-10-80	1998	Clovis, Calif.
Francoeur, Jeff	.281	134	524	78	147	26	9	14	68	30	68	14	6	.445	.325	R	R	6-4	200	1-8-84	2002	Lilburn, Ga.
Grasso, Mike	.263	36	76	14	20	3	1	0	7	3	21	6	0	.329	.288	R	R	6-0	170	12-25-79	2002	Albany, N.Y.
Guzman, Carlos	.229	99	314	40	72	15	3	10	44	27	105	11	3	.392	.303	R	R	6-3	200	7-5-83	1999	La Vega, D.R.
Hernandez, Luis	.231	111	337	27	78	4	1	2	25	24	42	7	3	.267	.287	S	R	5-10	140	6-26-84	2001	Quibor, Venez.
James, Willie	.237	30	59	14	14	2	0	0	3	16	10	10	1	.271	.408	S	R	5-8	160	4-30-81	2002	Moreno Valley, Calif.
Jansen, Ardley	.260	97	373	53	97	13	2	3	29	25	84	18	6	.330	.308	R	R	6-2	190	2-16-83	1999	Willemstad, Curacao
Joseph, Onil	.296	120	483	66	143	16	6	4	47	37	89	32	22	.379	.349	R	R	6-1	150	2-12-82	2000	San Pedro de Macoris, D.R.
McCann, Brian	.290	115	424	40	123	31	3	12	71	24	73	7	4	.462	.329	L	R	6-3	190	2-20-84	2002	Satellite Beach, Fla.
Peters, Yaron	.286	86	318	46	91	27	1	11	47	27	70	0	3	.481	.345	R	R	6-2	220	7-30-79	2002	Sherman Oaks, Calif.
Roat, Kyle	.219	61	187	17	41	5	0	3	15	21	30	1	1	.294	.300	R	R	5-10	200	5-14-80	2001	Coweta, Okla.
Ruelas, Alonzo	.223	64	215	18	48	7	0	1	18	11	30	2	1	.270	.261	R	R	6-1	200	4-2-81	2001	El Paso, Texas
Ruiz, Daniel	.246	48	122	13	30	6	0	1	12	7	26	0	0	.320	.288	R	R	6-4	190	1-1-80	2001	San Luis, Ariz.
Schuerholz, Jon	.251	135	407	52	102	14	3	0	39	59	68	25	7	.300	.356	S	R	5-11	180	6-25-80	2002	Atlanta, Ga.
Timmons, Wes	.282	124	422	67	119	19	4	7	49	52	31	10	4	.396	.376	R	R	6-0	190	7-12-79	2002	Jacksonville Beach, Fla.

PITCHING	W	L	ERA	G	GS	CG	SV	IP	H	R	ER	BB	SO	AVG	B	T	HT	WT	DOB	1st Yr	Resides
Almeida, Brian	0	0	0.93	6	0	0	0	10	4	1	1	9	6	.125	L	R	6-6	220	7-26-81	2000	Englewood, Fla.
Arteaga, Francisco	1	0	7.36	4	0	0	0	7	11	6	6	3	7	.333	R	R	6-2	180	10-4-81	2001	Los Angeles, Calif.
Boyer, Blaine	12	8	3.69	30	26	1	0	137	146	70	56	58	115	.270	R	R	6-3	190	7-11-81	2000	Marietta, Ga.
Capellan, Jose	1	2	3.80	14	12	1	0	47	43	23	20	19	32	.252	R	R	6-3	170	1-13-81	1998	Cotui, D.R.
David, Brad	2	1	2.90	28	0	0	15	31	33	12	10	5	28	.268	L	L	6-0	190	5-26-80	2002	Baton Rouge, La.
Davies, Kyle	8	8	2.89	27	27	1	0	146	128	52	47	53	148	.237	R	R	6-2	210	9-9-83	2001	Dover, Fla.
Ewin, Ryan	5	4	2.38	16	7	0	0	64	55	22	17	20	61	.234	R	R	6-7	180	10-5-81	1999	Spring Valley, Calif.
Jung, Sung	1	4	2.16	53	0	0	18	67	56	21	16	26	83	.228	R	R	5-10	160	8-6-79	2002	Yee Soo, Korea
Lerew, Anthony	7	6	2.38	25	25	0	0	144	112	45	38	43	127	.215	L	R	6-3	210	10-28-82	2001	Wellsville, Penn.
Mabry, Barry	1	1	2.96	14	0	0	0	24	18	9	8	7	19	.197	R	R	6-5	180	11-2-81	2000	Spartanburg, S.C.
Merricks, Matt	5	7	2.82	14	10	0	0	67	58	27	21	19	60	.232	L	L	5-11	180	8-6-82	2000	Oxnard, Calif.
Meyer, Dan	4	4	2.87	15	15	0	0	82	76	35	26	15	95	.248	R	L	6-3	190	7-3-81	2002	Mickleton, N.J.
Mueller, Mike	0	2	5.08	24	4	0	0	44	42	26	25	29	40	.256	R	R	6-5	230	8-22-80	2002	West Bend, Wisc.
Peralta, Efigenio	4	2	2.52	20	0	0	0	39	33	12	11	11	36	.235	R	R	6-2	190	1-31-82	1999	San Cristobal, D.R.
Rodriguez, Jose	4	1	4.20	37	0	0	0	56	61	34	26	30	41	.281	R	R	6-0	170	1-15-82	1998	Carora, Venez.
Rodriguez, Ricardo	8	4	3.45	33	0	0	1	60	51	30	23	38	52	.232	R	R	6-0	140	4-28-81	1998	Caracas, Venez.
Tadefa, Fernando	3	5	2.88	45	0	0	5	50	43	19	16	30	44	.236	L	L	6-0	200	11-2-79	2002	San Antonio, Texas
Watkins, Dave	0	0	0.00	1	0	0	0	1	2	0	0	0	0	.500	R	R	6-1	190	8-18-81	1999	Leitchfield, Ky.
Weichard, Paul	2	0	2.14	22	0	0	2	21	17	8	5	13	15	.217	S	L	5-10	200	11-7-79	1997	Ringwood, Australia
Wright, Matt	10	2	1.65	14	13	1	0	82	53	19	15	32	98	.187	R	R	6-4	220	3-13-82	2000	Lorena, Texas

FIELDING

Catcher	PCT	G	PO	A	E	DP	PB
Bernard	.976	34	216	32	6	1	8
McCann	.995	64	529	47	3	5	10
Roat	.982	27	155	12	3	2	5
Ruelas	1.000	32	229	20	0	2	1

First Base	PCT	G	PO	A	E	DP
Donato	1.000	10	68	3	0	8
Peters	.983	84	589	40	11	43
Roat	.980	20	139	9	3	15
Ruelas	.986	10	66	6	1	6
Ruiz	.994	31	156	3	1	15

Second Base	PCT	G	PO	A	E	DP
Donato	.000	1	0	0	0	0
Grasso	.952	26	40	59	5	10
James	.968	15	23	38	2	9
Schuerholz	.975	103	170	264	11	45
Timmons	1.000	3	5	5	0	2

Third Base	PCT	G	PO	A	E	DP
Barthel	.667	10	3	5	4	0
Grasso	.000	1	0	0	0	0
James	.833	5	1	4	1	0
Ruiz	.792	14	5	14	5	0
Timmons	.960	121	88	152	10	13

Shortstop	PCT	G	PO	A	E	DP
Hernandez	.958	110	165	288	20	58
James	.947	4	8	10	1	2
Schuerholz	.972	30	48	58	3	14

Outfield	PCT	G	PO	A	E	DP
Burrows	1.000	20	33	5	0	2
Burrus	.938	15	14	1	1	0
Donato	1.000	1	1	0	0	0
Francoeur	.986	127	276	10	4	1
Guzman	.975	56	76	3	2	1
Jansen	.975	95	151	7	4	2
Joseph	.971	116	225	12	7	1
Timmons	1.000	1	1	0	0	0

DANVILLE BRAVES — Rookie

APPALACHIAN LEAGUE

BATTING	AVG	G	AB	R	H	2B	3B	HR	RBI	BB	SO	SB	CS	SLG	OBP	B	T	HT	WT	DOB	1st Yr	Resides
Barden, Andy	.133	29	83	3	11	5	0	0	5	7	39	0	1	.193	.215	R	R	6-0	215	11-25-80	2003	Chesterfield, Va.
Barthel, Cole	.238	7	21	1	5	1	0	0	2	4	7	0	1	.286	.346	R	R	6-2	200	8-11-82	2001	Decatur, Ala.
Burrus, Josh	.254	53	189	25	48	11	1	1	16	15	48	10	4	.339	.318	R	R	5-11	190	8-20-83	2001	Marietta, Ga.
Donato, Greg.	.250	24	80	12	20	3	0	2	12	7	13	2	1	.363	.300	R	R	6-0	180	11-10-80	1998	Clovis, Calif.
Esquivel, Matt	.282	61	220	41	62	10	4	11	42	20	72	7	4	.514	.352	R	R	6-2	220	12-17-82	2001	San Antonio, Texas
Foskey, Will	.250	3	8	0	2	0	0	0	3	1	3	0	0	.250	.333	R	R	6-0	200	8-19-80	2002	Dublin, Ga.
Hanson, Mike	.277	57	213	27	59	15	4	2	20	15	32	9	4	.413	.329	R	R	5-11	175	5-2-81	2003	Smyrna, Ga.
Hemingway, Jamie	.272	51	191	25	52	13	1	1	19	13	35	15	5	.366	.338	R	R	6-3	215	10-31-80	2003	Greensboro, N.C.
Hessman, Mike	.067	5	15	1	1	0	0	0	2	2	2	0	0	.067	.200	R	R	6-5	210	3-5-78	1996	Westminster, Calif.
James, Willie	.189	48	148	21	28	3	0	0	5	24	33	10	10	.209	.302	S	R	5-8	160	4-30-81	2002	Moreno Valley, Calif.
Martinez, Edwin	.243	27	70	7	17	3	0	0	6	11	15	1	1	.286	.354	S	R	5-11	170	10-12-82	2001	Caracas, Venez.
Partridge, Dominique	.250	58	208	22	52	8	2	3	30	15	40	10	2	.351	.302	R	R	6-2	210	7-28-83	2001	Palmetto, Ga.
Pyzik, Steve	.215	34	93	5	20	2	0	0	8	9	8	0	1	.237	.282	R	R	5-10	175	5-18-81	2003	Mt. Airy, N.C.
Saltalamacchia, Justin	.214	9	28	3	6	2	0	0	3	2	1	0	0	.286	.267	R	R	5-11	190	5-26-81	2003	Royal Palm Beach, Fla.
Schade, Scott	.256	53	176	20	45	11	1	2	22	16	56	6	2	.364	.316	R	R	6-0	205	2-22-82	2003	Lewisburg, Pa.
Thomas, Ben	.247	66	223	29	55	14	0	0	25	29	40	7	3	.309	.338	L	L	6-0	200	6-30-82	2003	Rapid City, S.D.
White, Dean	.227	54	172	24	39	6	1	0	11	12	56	16	6	.273	.288	R	R	6-2	180	2-12-83	2001	Perth, Australia

GAMES BY POSITION: C—Barden 29, Martinez 14, Pyzik 33. **1B**—Barthel 1, Donato 11, Pyzik 1, Saltalamacchia 5, Schade 51. **2B**—Hanson 46, James 22, Schade 1. **3B**—Barthel 3, James 1, Schade 1, Thomas 62, White 2. **SS**—James 22, White 46. **OF**—Burrus 49, Donato 6, Esquivel 60, Hemingway 37, Hessman 3, James 1, Partridge 48, Saltalamacchia 2.

PITCHING	W	L	ERA	G	GS	CG	SV	IP	H	R	ER	BB	SO	AVG	B	T	HT	WT	DOB	1st Yr	Resides
Basner, Ryan	4	1	1.83	19	0	0	1	44	29	15	9	11	50	.181	R	R	6-3	225	7-15-81	2003	West Chester, Pa.
Blackmon, Cory	3	2	4.11	21	0	0	0	35	29	25	16	19	27	.223	L	L	6-2	200	5-9-80	2003	Conyers, Ga.
Blakeney, Jacob	3	1	1.24	24	0	0	9	36	25	6	5	5	37	.201	R	R	6-1	200	7-26-80	2003	Mendenhall, Miss.
Collins, Danny	1	6	2.87	14	14	0	0	63	63	32	20	19	47	.263	L	L	6-3	175	4-12-83	2003	Fort Pierce, Fla.
Farr, Whitt	4	0	2.19	23	1	0	0	49	46	16	12	10	42	.247	R	R	6-2	180	5-15-81	2002	Danville, Va.
James, Chuck	2	1	1.25	11	11	0	0	50	26	9	7	19	68	.151	L	L	6-0	170	11-9-81	2002	Mableton, Ga.
Mead, Dan	0	1	7.43	24	0	0	0	27	28	26	22	31	21	.277	R	L	6-4	190	8-4-81	2002	Worthington, Ohio
Morton, Charles	2	5	4.67	14	13	0	0	54	65	32	28	25	46	.302	R	R	6-4	190	10-12-83	2002	Redding, Conn.
Nelson, Brad	8	3	4.15	24	0	0	2	39	47	23	18	9	23	.281	R	R	6-3	220	1-5-82	2003	Cary, N.C.
Nieves, Roberto	0	2	5.21	14	7	0	0	38	39	25	22	22	51	.267	S	R	6-2	170	12-25-82	2002	Vega Alta, P.R.
Peralta, Efigenio	0	0	1.13	2	2	0	0	8	4	3	1	2	6	.153	R	R	6-2	190	1-31-82	1999	San Cristobal, D.R.
Redfern, Chad	0	1	10.38	4	0	0	0	4	7	5	5	2	2	.368	R	R	6-3	190	12-27-80	2002	Sylmar, Calif.
Russell, Steve	3	2	3.71	8	8	0	0	34	25	17	14	13	27	.203	R	R	6-6	180	12-20-83	2002	Las Vegas, Nev.
Smith, Dan	0	0	5.40	2	0	0	0	2	3	1	1	3	2	.428	L	L	6-5	225	9-9-83	2003	Fort Myers, Fla.
Tucker, Glen	3	2	3.47	25	0	0	6	36	41	18	14	3	30	.277	R	R	6-3	200	4-9-81	2003	Plantation, Fla.
Weichard, Paul	0	0	0.00	4	0	0	0	5	5	1	0	3	3	.263	S	L	5-10	200	11-7-79	1997	Ringwood, Australia
White, Sean	3	3	2.98	14	10	0	1	51	53	22	17	16	32	.269	R	R	6-4	195	4-25-81	2003	Mercer Island, Wash.

KISSIMMEE BRAVES — Rookie

GULF COAST LEAGUE

BATTING	AVG	G	AB	R	H	2B	3B	HR	RBI	BB	SO	SB	CS	SLG	OBP	B	T	HT	WT	DOB	1st Yr	Resides
Armstrong, Cole	.118	9	17	0	2	0	0	0	0	1	2	0	0	.118	.167	L	R	6-3	210	8-24-83	2003	Surrey, B.C.
Barthel, Cole	.229	13	35	2	8	0	0	0	0	4	7	0	0	.229	.325	R	R	6-2	200	8-11-82	2001	Decatur, Ala.
Cruz, Ramon	.143	18	35	0	5	0	0	0	2	0	9	0	1	.143	.167	R	R	6-1	180	10-22-83	2001	Santo Domingo, D.R.
Doetsch, Steve	.320	60	228	39	73	11	3	8	37	25	49	8	9	.500	.404	R	R	6-2	200	12-2-83	2003	St. Petersburg, Fla.
Eichas, Keith	.345	40	119	18	41	9	0	5	22	9	28	0	0	.546	.406	R	R	6-2	200	6-29-83	2003	Georgetown, Texas
Guerra, Junior	.193	28	57	5	11	5	0	1	9	0	19	0	0	.333	.233	R	R	5-11	180	1-16-85	2002	Guayana, Venez.
Hernandez, Diory	.221	54	190	26	42	9	2	1	12	14	24	2	4	.305	.287	R	R	6-0	170	4-8-84	2002	San Pedro de Macoris, D.R.
Johnson, Kelly	.385	6	26	10	10	1	1	1	3	3	4	1	1	.615	.467	L	R	6-1	180	2-22-82	2000	Austin, Texas
Loadenthal, Carl	.310	58	216	41	67	9	1	1	24	31	38	21	9	.375	.402	L	L	5-11	180	12-27-81	2003	Southampton, Pa.
Martinez, Edwin	.143	7	21	3	3	0	0	0	1	1	4	2	0	.143	.182	S	R	5-11	170	10-12-82	2001	Caracas, Venez.
Moreta, Carlos	.289	60	225	35	65	14	1	8	39	15	56	1	1	.467	.351	R	R	6-2	180	1-5-83	1999	Barahona, D.R.
Ortega, Raul	.231	50	121	15	28	8	2	1	17	13	27	1	0	.355	.297	S	R	6-1	160	5-21-84	2001	Valencia, Venez.
Ponce, Angel	.234	42	137	18	32	5	1	2	16	2	31	5	0	.328	.250	R	R	5-11	187	7-8-82	2003	Veracruz, Mexico
Prado, Martin	.286	59	220	28	63	2	6	0	23	24	30	9	9	.350	.358	R	R	6-1	170	10-27-83	2001	Maracay, Venez.
Romak, Jamie	.176	19	51	5	9	2	0	0	4	9	10	0	0	.216	.300	R	R	6-2	220	9-30-85	2003	London, Ontario
Saltalamacchia, Jarrod	.239	46	134	23	32	11	2	2	14	28	33	0	0	.396	.382	S	R	6-4	195	5-2-85	2003	West Palm Beach, Fla.
Saltalamacchia, Justin	.194	24	36	3	7	2	0	0	6	2	5	0	0	.250	.256	R	R	5-11	190	5-26-81	2003	Royal Palm Beach, Fla.
Stern, Adam	.345	7	29	6	10	1	0	1	6	6	3	2	2	.483	.457	L	R	5-11	180	2-12-80	2001	London, Ontario
Stoecklein, Brian	.263	44	114	14	30	4	1	1	13	7	19	2	2	.342	.311	R	R	6-0	190	5-23-80	2003	Cranberry, Penn.

GAMES BY POSITION: C—Armstrong 6, Cruz 14, Eichas 1, Guerra 26, Martinez 7, Ja. Saltalamacchia 36. **1B**—Eichas 16, Moreta 49. **2B**—Eichas 1, Ortega 1, Prado 47, Stoecklein 19. **3B**—Barthel 9, Hernandez 34, Ortega 2, Prado 14, Romak 16, Ja. Saltalamacchia 1, Ju. Saltalamacchia 5. **SS**—Hernandez 29, Johnson 2, Ortega 43. **OF**—Barthel 5, Doetsch 59, Eichas 1, Hernandez 1, Loadenthal 58, Moreta 11, Ponce 40, Ju. Saltalamacchia 9, Stern 7, Stoecklein 1.

PITCHING	W	L	ERA	G	GS	CG	SV	IP	H	R	ER	BB	SO	AVG	B	T	HT	WT	DOB	1st Yr	Resides
Anderson, Devin	0	1	2.48	18	0	0	3	29	26	8	8	6	30	.236	L	L	6-5	220	1-24-84	2003	Ocoee, Fla.
Ascanio, Jose	4	0	1.37	8	0	0	0	26	26	4	4	5	17	.270	R	R	6-0	150	5-2-85	2002	Maracay, Venez.
Atilano, Luis	3	2	3.83	12	12	1	0	54	61	25	23	7	24	.287	R	R	6-3	180	5-10-85	2003	San Juan, P.R.
Bacot, Paul	4	0	0.95	9	6	0	0	38	23	6	4	4	26	.167	R	R	6-6	205	8-16-84	2003	Atlanta, Ga.
Bale, Manuel	2	0	3.00	19	0	0	2	27	20	10	9	8	13	.217	R	R	6-3	170	6-11-81	1999	La Romana, D.R.
Candelario, Alexis	1	0	0.00	3	0	0	0	4	1	0	0	1	4	.076	R	R	5-11	150	1-1-81	2002	San Pedro de Macoris, D.R.
Capellan, Jose	0	1	2.65	5	5	0	0	17	18	7	5	8	17	.276	R	R	6-3	170	1-13-81	1998	Cotui, D.R.
Demme, Asher	0	1	5.63	4	0	0	0	8	8	8	5	5	3	.266	R	R	6-3	200	11-1-84	2003	Reston, Va.
Dewar, Andrew	2	2	6.00	14	0	0	0	18	19	12	12	9	16	.275	L	L	6-0	190	3-9-84	2001	East Bentleigh, Australia
Harrison, Matt	3	1	3.69	11	6	0	1	39	40	18	16	9	33	.263	L	L	6-5	205	8-16-85	2003	Stem, N.C.
Jimenez, Rodny	1	0	3.94	16	0	0	0	32	25	17	14	24	38	.217	R	R	6-2	170	3-16-82	1999	Santo Domingo, D.R.
Mason, Robert	0	0	0.00	1	1	0	0	1	1	2	0	0	2	.200	L	L	5-11	190	9-5-83	2001	Walnut, Calif.
McClendon, Matt	0	0	4.15	3	3	0	0	4	4	2	2	4	3	.250	R	R	6-6	220	10-13-77	1999	Orlando, Fla.
Nieves, Roberto	1	0	0.00	1	0	0	0	2	1	0	0	1	2	.142	S	R	6-2	170	12-25-82	2002	Vega Alta, P.R.
Payano, Nelson	0	0	6.75	13	0	0	0	13	15	10	10	10	17	.277	L	L	5-11	150	11-13-82	2000	Santo Domingo, D.R.
Reyes, Jo Jo	5	3	2.56	11	10	0	0	46	34	16	13	14	55	.204	L	L	6-2	200	11-20-84	2003	Riverside, Calif.
Rosario, Eduardo	2	5	3.97	12	11	0	0	45	51	25	20	14	37	.298	L	L	6-1	160	6-7-84	2001	Valencia, Venez.
Santiago, Jose	0	2	1.52	16	0	0	3	24	13	5	4	6	28	.160	R	R	6-4	180	8-1-81	2001	Villa Altagracia, D.R.
Smith, Dan	6	0	1.91	13	0	0	1	28	22	7	6	8	35	.209	L	L	6-5	225	9-9-83	2003	Fort Myers, Fla.
Stanley, Adam	1	0	3.96	16	0	0	0	25	35	15	11	15	20	.324	L	L	6-2	195	11-20-84	2003	Raleigh, N.C.
Stevens, Jake	3	4	2.87	14	6	0	0	47	49	23	15	16	47	.262	L	L	6-3	210	3-15-85	2003	Cape Coral, Fla.

BALTIMORE ORIOLES

BY ROCH KUBATKO

Mike Hargrove completed the 2003 season needing four more wins to reach 1,000 for his career. But his inability to lift the Orioles out of fourth place will prevent him from achieving that milestone in Baltimore.

Hargrove was fired one day after the Orioles finished 71-91, a record that kept them ahead of only the Devil Rays in the American League East for the sixth consecutive year. They were four games better than the 2002 season, a modest gain that didn't satisfy club executives Jim Beattie and Mike Flanagan.

"From the pit of my stomach and the depths of my heart, I feel like I did a really good job this year," said Hargrove, who was 275-372 in four seasons with the Orioles. "And I feel like everybody else did, too."

The Orioles were beaten down by injuries again, with pitchers Rodrigo Lopez, Omar Daal and Willis Roberts, and position players David Segui, Marty Cordova, Melvin Mora, B.J. Surhoff and Jerry Hairston missing significant time. Trades took their ace pitcher (Sidney Ponson) and cleanup hitter and emotional leader (Jeff Conine). The Padres claimed center fielder Gary Matthews Jr. on waivers two months after he started on Opening Day.

After ranking second in the AL in ERA in 2002, the Orioles' bullpen tumbled to ninth. Relievers accounted for 29 losses. Buddy Groom lost his job as the lefthanded set-up man, his ERA increasing from 1.60 to 5.36, and his major league record for consecutive seasons with 70 or more appearances ended at seven.

Perhaps nobody disappointed more than Lopez, a 15-game winner as a rookie who went 7-10, 5.82 in 147 innings.

Two key pitching acquisitions, Daal and Rick Helling, didn't pan out. Daal was removed from the rotation and finished 4-11, 6.34 in 94 innings. Helling also fell out of the rotation before being released. Like Conine, he ended up with the Marlins and got a World Series ring.

The Orioles endured losing streaks of eight and nine games in August after Ponson was traded to the Giants. At least they avoided another 4-32 stretch, like the one that ended the 2002 season.

On the bright side, Mora made his first all-star appearance and led the league in batting before a hand injury took him out of the lineup. He batted .317-15-48 while making most of his starts in left field.

Right fielder Jay Gibbons was named the team's most valuable player after batting .277-23-100 and appearing in 160 games. Though his home runs were down from 2002, he reached 100 RBIs for the first time and raised his average 30 points.

More encouragement came from the development of young players such as Luis Matos, Brian Roberts and Larry Bigbie. Matos replaced Matthews in center field and batted .303-13-45. Roberts inherited second base when Hairston broke his right foot on May 20, and batted .270-5-41 with 23 steals as the leadoff hitter. Bigbie, an outfielder, batted .303-9-31.

Lefthander Eric DuBose, a first-round draft pick of the Athletics in 1997, might have sealed a place in the 2004 rotation after going 3-6, 3.79 in 74 innings in his first full season in the majors. And Kurt Ainsworth, a 1999 first-round pick who came over from the Giants in the Ponson trade, has the stuff to be an ace.

Unlike the 2002 season, the minor leagues were a source of pride rather than embarrassment. Baltimore's seven affiliates finished 21 games below .500, compared to 102 games the previous year, and farm director Doc Rodgers was praised for instilling more discipline in the system.

Melvin Mora

RODGER WOOD

Mike Fontenot

PLAYERS of the YEAR

MAJOR LEAGUE: Melvin Mora, of

Mora enjoyed a career year and his first all-star appearance in 2003 before hand and knee injuries cut short his season. Had he qualified, Mora would have ranked third in the American League in on-base percentage and fourth in batting average.

MINOR LEAGUE: Mike Fontenot, 2b

Fontenot reached base in 43 straight games and 74 of his final 84 while posting a .399 on-base percentage. He also hit .325-16-66 with 16 steals and 24 doubles, ranking fourth in the Double-A Eastern League in batting.

ORGANIZATION LEADERS

BATTING

*AVG	Mike Fontenot, Bowie	.325
R	Tim Raines Jr., Ottawa/Bowie	81
H	Mike Fontenot, Bowie	146
TB	Mike Fontenot, Bowie	216
2B	Val Majewski, Frederick/Delmarva	35
3B	Val Majewski, Frederick/Delmarva	11
HR	Three tied at	14
RBI	Mike Huggins, Frederick	74
BB	Jack Cust, Ottawa	80
SO	Neal Stephenson, Delmarva	137
SB	Tim Raines Jr., Ottawa/Bowie	51
*SLG	Val Majewski, Frederick/Delmarva	.541
*OBP	Jack Cust, Ottawa	.422

PITCHING

W	John Maine, Frederick/Delmarva	13
L	Ryan Keefer, Delmarva	12
#ERA	Scott Rice, Frederick/Delmarva	1.83
G	Darwin Cubillan, Ottawa	65
CG	Four tied at	2
SV	Jeff Montani, Delmarva	23
IP	John Stephens, Ottawa	159
BB	Mike Paradis, Bowie	81
SO	John Maine, Frederick/Delmarva	185

*Minimum 250 At-Bats #Minimum 75 Innings

BALTIMORE ORIOLES

Manager: Mike Hargrove.

2003 Record: 71-91, .438 (4th, AL East).

BATTING	AVG	G	AB	R	H	2B	3B	HR	RBI	BB	SO	SB	CS	SLG	OBP	B	T	HT	WT	DOB	1st Yr	Resides
Batista, Tony	.235	161	631	76	148	20	1	26	99	28	102	4	3	.393	.270	R	R	6-0	208	12-9-73	1992	Mao Valverde, D.R.
Bigbie, Larry	.303	83	287	43	87	15	1	9	31	29	60	7	1	.456	.365	L	L	6-4	215	11-4-77	1999	Hobart, Ind.
Conine, Jeff	.290	124	493	75	143	33	3	15	80	37	60	5	0	.460	.338	R	R	6-1	220	6-27-66	1988	Weston, Fla.
Cordova, Marty	.233	9	30	5	7	1	0	1	4	8	5	1	0	.367	.410	R	R	6-0	213	7-10-69	1989	Las Vegas, Nev.
Cruz, Deivi	.250	152	548	61	137	24	2	14	65	13	49	1	2	.378	.269	R	R	6-0	207	11-6-72	1993	Nizao, D.R.
Cust, Jack	.260	27	73	7	19	7	0	4	11	10	25	0	0	.521	.357	L	R	6-1	200	1-16-79	1997	Flemington, N.J.
Escalona, Felix	.185	10	27	2	5	2	0	0	2	2	6	1	0	.259	.241	R	R	6-0	190	3-12-79	1996	Puerto Cabello, Venez.
Fordyce, Brook	.273	108	348	28	95	12	2	6	31	19	44	2	3	.371	.311	R	R	6-0	194	5-7-70	1989	Stuart, Fla.
Gibbons, Jay	.277	160	625	80	173	39	2	23	100	49	89	0	1	.456	.330	L	L	6-0	193	3-2-77	1998	Lakewood, Calif.
Gil, Geronimo	.237	54	169	22	40	4	0	3	16	12	34	0	0	.314	.299	R	R	6-2	227	8-7-75	1996	Oaxaca, Mexico
Hairston, Jerry	.271	58	218	25	59	12	2	2	21	23	25	14	5	.372	.353	R	R	5-10	185	5-29-76	1997	Pikesville, Md.
Leon, Jose	.241	21	54	6	13	1	0	0	0	3	18	0	0	.259	.305	R	R	6-0	210	12-8-76	1994	Cayey, P.R.
Machado, Robert	.265	18	49	8	13	1	0	1	3	6	12	0	0	.347	.345	R	R	6-1	210	6-3-73	1989	Caracas, Venez.
Matos, Luis	.303	109	439	70	133	23	3	13	45	28	90	15	7	.458	.353	R	R	6-0	208	10-30-78	1996	Bayamon, P.R.
Matthews, Gary	.204	41	162	21	33	12	1	2	20	9	29	0	3	.327	.250	S	R	6-3	225	8-25-74	1994	Baltimore, Md.
Mendez, Carlos	.222	26	45	3	10	2	0	0	5	0	12	0	0	.267	.217	R	R	6-0	228	6-18-74	1991	Caracas, Venez.
Mora, Melvin	.317	96	344	68	109	17	1	15	48	49	71	6	3	.503	.418	R	R	5-11	198	2-2-72	1991	Bel Air, Md.
Morban, Jose	.141	61	71	14	10	0	0	2	5	3	21	8	0	.225	.187	R	R	6-1	170	12-2-79	1997	Santiago, D.R.
Raines, Tim	.140	20	43	4	6	1	1	0	2	2	12	0	0	.209	.196	R	R	5-10	189	8-31-79	1998	Heathrow, Fla.
Roberts, Brian	.270	112	460	65	124	22	4	5	41	46	58	23	6	.367	.337	S	R	5-9	172	10-9-77	1999	Chapel Hill, N.C.
Segui, David	.263	67	224	26	59	10	1	5	25	26	47	1	0	.384	.341	S	L	6-1	216	7-19-66	1988	Kansas City, Kan.
Surhoff, B.J.	.295	93	319	32	94	20	0	5	41	29	29	2	2	.404	.353	L	R	6-1	215	8-4-64	1985	Cockeysville, Md.
Swann, Pedro	.214	8	14	3	3	1	0	1	2	1	4	0	0	.500	.267	L	R	6-0	200	10-27-70	1991	Townsend, Del.

PITCHING	W	L	ERA	G	GS	CG	SV	IP	H	R	ER	BB	SO	AVG	B	T	HT	WT	DOB	1st Yr	Resides
Ainsworth, Kurt	0	1	11.57	3	0	0	0	2	6	3	3	1	4	.428	R	R	6-3	190	9-9-78	1999	Baton Rouge, La.
Bauer, Rick	0	0	4.55	35	0	0	0	61	58	36	31	24	43	.255	R	R	6-6	218	1-10-77	1997	Erie, Pa.
Carrasco, Hector	2	6	4.93	40	0	0	1	38	40	22	21	20	27	.270	R	R	6-2	220	10-22-69	1988	San Pedro de Macoris, D.R.
Daal, Omar	4	11	6.34	19	17	0	0	94	134	69	66	30	53	.342	L	L	6-3	193	2-23-72	1990	Weston, Fla.
Douglass, Sean	0	0	13.50	3	0	0	0	8	14	12	12	6	3	.378	R	R	6-6	218	4-28-79	1997	Lancaster, Calif.
Driskill, Travis	3	5	6.00	20	0	0	1	48	62	35	32	9	33	.310	R	R	6-0	215	8-1-71	1993	Austin, Texas
Dubose, Eric	3	6	3.79	17	10	1	0	74	60	33	31	25	44	.222	L	L	6-3	223	5-15-76	1997	Houston, Texas
Groom, Buddy	1	3	5.36	60	0	0	1	45	58	27	27	14	34	.308	L	L	6-2	201	7-10-65	1987	Ovilla, Texas
Helling, Rick	7	8	5.71	24	24	0	0	139	156	90	88	40	86	.286	R	R	6-3	241	12-15-70	1992	Southlake, Texas
Hentgen, Pat	7	8	4.09	28	22	1	1	161	150	74	73	58	100	.246	R	R	6-2	195	11-13-68	1986	Tarpon Springs, Fla.
Johnson, Jason	10	10	4.18	32	32	0	0	190	216	100	88	80	118	.282	R	R	6-6	217	10-27-73	1992	Tampa, Fla.
Julio, Jorge	0	7	4.38	64	0	0	36	62	60	36	30	34	52	.256	R	R	6-1	223	3-3-79	1996	Caracas, Venez.
Ligtenberg, Kerry	4	2	3.34	68	0	0	1	59	60	23	22	14	47	.263	R	R	6-2	222	5-11-71	1994	Inner Grove Heights, Minn.
Lopez, Rodrigo	7	10	5.82	26	26	3	0	147	188	101	95	43	103	.313	R	R	6-1	187	12-14-75	1995	Mexico City, Mexico
Moss, Damian	1	5	6.22	10	9	0	0	51	63	40	35	29	22	.307	R	L	6-0	180	11-24-76	1994	Dublin, Ga.
Parrish, John	0	1	1.90	14	0	0	0	24	17	7	5	8	15	.204	L	L	5-11	176	11-26-77	1996	Owings Mills, Md.
Ponson, Sidney	14	6	3.77	21	21	4	0	148	147	65	62	43	100	.257	R	R	6-1	249	11-2-76	1994	Baltimore, Md.
Riley, Matt	1	0	1.80	2	2	0	0	10	7	2	2	5	8	.194	L	L	6-1	207	8-2-79	1998	Corona, Calif.
Roberts, Willis	3	1	5.72	26	0	0	0	39	41	26	25	16	26	.273	R	R	6-3	240	6-19-75	1992	San Cristobal, D.R.
Ryan, B.J.	4	1	3.40	76	0	0	0	50	42	19	19	27	63	.227	L	L	6-6	240	12-28-75	1998	Bossier City, La.

FIELDING

Catcher	PCT	G	PO	A	E	DP	PB
Fordyce	.996	107	624	41	3	5	6
Gil	.984	53	326	34	6	3	3
Machado	.990	18	83	14	1	3	3

First Base	PCT	G	PO	A	E	DP
Conine	.992	118	1060	80	9	106
Gibbons	.990	13	91	7	1	16
Leon	.979	7	44	2	1	7
Mendez	.939	9	28	3	2	1
Mora	1.000	1	2	0	0	0
Segui	1.000	8	52	6	0	7
Surhoff	.994	22	157	11	1	14

Second Base	PCT	G	PO	A	E	DP
Escalona	1.000	1	3	4	0	3
Hairston	.980	48	103	136	5	34
Mora	1.000	6	14	16	0	6
Morban	.974	12	14	23	1	4
Roberts	.987	107	198	324	7	68

Third Base	PCT	G	PO	A	E	DP
Batista	.950	154	91	292	20	33
Conine	1.000	1	0	4	0	0
Escalona	.000	1	0	0	0	0
Leon	.963	10	10	16	1	3
Morban	.000	1	0	0	0	0

Shortstop	PCT	G	PO	A	E	DP
Cruz	.975	147	222	409	16	96
Escalona	1.000	8	15	21	0	8
Mora	.980	11	19	30	1	5
Morban	1.000	14	13	12	0	7
Roberts	.818	2	1	8	2	1

Outfield	PCT	G	PO	A	E	DP
Bigbie	.994	80	165	5	1	0
Conine	1.000	8	8	0	0	0
Cordova	1.000	4	7	2	0	0
Cust	1.000	1	3	0	0	0
Gibbons	.983	144	283	8	5	1
Matos	.987	107	304	5	4	1
Matthews	1.000	40	99	2	0	0
Mora	.994	79	162	9	1	2
Raines	.974	18	37	1	1	1
Surhoff	.978	27	44	0	1	0
Swann	1.000	6	6	0	0	0

FARM SYSTEM

Director, Minor League Operations: Doc Rodgers.

Class	Farm Team	League	W	L	Pct.	Finish*	Manager	First Yr.
AAA	Ottawa (Ontario) Lynx	International	79	65	.549	3rd (14)	Gary Allenson	2003
AA	Bowie (Md.) Baysox	Eastern	69	72	.489	8th (12)	Dave Trembley	1993
High A	Frederick (Md.) Keys	Carolina	60	75	.444	7th (8)	Tom Lawless	1989

Low A	Delmarva (Md.) Shorebirds	South Atlantic	67	71	.486	10th (16)	Stan Hough	1997
SS A	Aberdeen (Md.) IronBirds	New York-Penn	38	38	.500	t-8th (14)	Joe Almaraz	2002
Rookie	Bluefield (W.Va.) Orioles	Appalachian	23	40	.365	9th (10)	Don Buford	1958
Rookie	Sarasota (Fla.) Orioles	Gulf Coast	32	28	.533	4th (12)	Jesus Alfaro	1991

*Finish in overall standings (No. of teams in league)

OTTAWA LYNX — Class AAA

INTERNATIONAL LEAGUE

BATTING	AVG	G	AB	R	H	2B	3B	HR	RBI	BB	SO	SB	CS	SLG	OBP	B	T	HT	WT	DOB	1st Yr	Resides
Alviso, Jerome	.137	17	51	5	7	1	0	0	1	3	11	2	0	.157	.241	S	R	6-1	160	9-4-75	1997	Livermore, Calif.
Bates, Fletcher	.216	24	74	7	16	7	1	0	10	4	15	1	0	.338	.256	S	R	6-1	190	3-24-74	1994	Rocky Point, N.C.
Bigbie, Larry	.350	30	117	23	41	14	4	3	21	14	31	0	0	.615	.421	L	L	6-4	215	11-4-77	1999	Hobart, Ind.
Calzado, Napoleon	.311	51	196	30	61	7	4	0	15	14	30	9	3	.388	.363	R	R	6-3	181	2-9-77	1996	Santo Domingo, D.R.
Casanova, Raul	.286	26	91	12	26	5	0	3	14	10	15	0	0	.440	.365	S	R	6-0	220	8-23-72	1990	Ponce, P.R.
Cust, Jack	.285	97	333	55	95	18	1	9	58	80	94	5	2	.426	.422	L	R	6-1	200	1-16-79	1997	Flemington, N.J.
Escalona, Felix	.233	9	30	5	7	2	0	0	5	1	5	2	0	.300	.303	R	R	6-0	190	3-12-79	1996	Puerto Cabello, Venez.
Garabito, Eddy	.281	114	459	62	129	28	5	3	56	31	70	14	8	.383	.327	S	R	5-8	186	12-2-76	1996	Manrreza, D.R.
Gil, Geronimo	.351	36	134	15	47	10	0	1	17	7	28	0	3	.448	.386	R	R	6-2	227	8-7-75	1996	Oaxaca, Mexico
Hammond, Joey	.273	103	348	43	95	11	7	0	32	44	60	2	1	.345	.354	R	R	6-1	189	10-27-77	1998	Frederick, Md.
Lemonis, Chris	.234	60	188	28	44	10	0	2	34	17	47	1	2	.319	.303	L	R	5-11	185	8-21-73	1995	New York, N.Y.
Leon, Jose	.265	79	309	33	82	19	2	4	39	15	47	1	1	.379	.305	R	R	6-0	210	12-8-76	1994	Cayey, P.R.
Littleton, B.J.	.252	29	119	12	30	6	0	0	15	5	23	3	3	.303	.282	S	L	5-10	166	10-3-79	2000	Arlington, Texas
Lomasney, Steve	.241	81	253	28	61	10	2	0	19	28	93	2	1	.296	.322	R	R	6-0	207	8-29-77	1995	Peabody, Mass.
Lopez, Luis	.263	52	186	23	49	6	0	5	32	6	24	1	1	.376	.299	S	R	5-11	175	9-4-70	1988	Cidra, P.R.
Machado, Robert	.335	59	221	30	74	17	0	8	38	17	36	0	0	.520	.390	R	R	6-1	210	6-3-73	1989	Caracas, Venez.
Matos, Luis	.303	45	175	28	53	16	4	1	25	13	34	6	1	.457	.347	R	R	6-0	208	10-30-78	1996	Bayamon, P.R.
McDonald, Darnell	.296	40	152	19	45	7	1	0	20	18	27	5	7	.355	.374	R	R	5-11	208	11-17-78	1997	Glendale, Colo.
Mendez, Carlos	.347	61	248	32	86	18	4	4	42	11	28	1	2	.500	.375	R	R	6-0	228	6-18-74	1991	Caracas, Venez.
Molina, Izzy	.000	3	9	0	0	0	0	0	0	0	6	0	0	.000	.000	R	R	6-1	213	6-3-71	1990	Miami, Fla.
Perez, Santiago	.257	13	35	4	9	2	0	0	1	4	9	2	2	.314	.333	S	R	6-2	160	12-30-75	1993	Santo Domingo, D.R.
Quattlebaum, Hugh	.250	3	8	0	2	1	0	0	0	0	2	0	0	.375	.333	R	R	6-4	205	6-26-78	2000	Andover, Mass.
Raines, Tim	.299	52	214	37	64	11	5	3	23	19	37	23	9	.439	.357	R	R	5-10	189	8-31-79	1998	Heathrow, Fla.
Rios, Brian	.200	21	65	3	13	3	1	1	8	2	10	0	0	.323	.229	R	R	6-3	190	7-25-74	1996	Corona, Calif.
Rivera, Ruben	.417	14	48	12	20	3	2	2	7	4	12	2	0	.688	.481	R	R	6-3	200	11-14-73	1992	La Chorrera, Panama
Roberts, Brian	.315	44	178	36	56	13	1	0	15	27	12	19	6	.399	.401	S	R	5-9	172	10-9-77	1999	Chapel Hill, N.C.
Sasser, Rob	.189	53	175	21	33	11	0	1	19	10	30	3	0	.269	.230	R	R	6-3	200	3-9-75	1993	Oakland, Calif.
Seestedt, Mike	.125	4	8	1	1	0	0	0	0	1	0	0	0	.125	.222	R	R	6-0	200	11-10-77	1999	Mt. Pleasant, MI
Swann, Pedro	.280	121	418	62	117	21	2	10	53	35	73	4	6	.411	.338	L	R	6-0	200	10-27-70	1991	Townsend, Del.

PITCHING	W	L	ERA	G	GS	CG	SV	IP	H	R	ER	BB	SO	AVG	B	T	HT	WT	DOB	1st Yr	Resides
Bauer, Rick	3	1	2.45	7	7	0	0	37	31	10	10	13	21	.234	R	R	6-6	218	1-10-77	1997	Erie, Pa.
Beltran, Rigo	5	4	2.71	31	13	2	1	103	77	33	31	41	69	.213	L	L	5-11	215	11-13-69	1991	Delray Beach, Fla.
Carrasco, Hector	4	2	2.22	33	0	0	4	45	32	11	11	20	47	.207	R	R	6-2	220	10-22-69	1988	San Pedro de Macoris, D.R.
Croushore, Rick	0	0	3.00	9	0	0	0	9	7	3	3	7	8	.225	R	R	6-4	210	8-7-70	1993	Benton, Ark.
Cubillan, Darwin	5	6	3.21	65	0	0	20	73	57	29	26	34	77	.212	R	R	6-2	177	11-15-72	1994	Tampa, Fla.
Douglass, Sean	10	8	3.40	27	27	0	0	143	142	67	54	58	118	.256	R	R	6-6	218	4-28-79	1997	Lancaster, Calif.
Driskill, Travis	4	0	2.84	9	9	0	0	51	46	17	16	6	36	.238	R	R	6-0	215	8-1-71	1993	Austin, Texas
Drumright, Mike	4	5	5.55	23	15	0	0	94	106	65	58	41	70	.284	L	R	6-4	217	4-19-74	1995	Valley Center, Kan.
Dubose, Eric	9	5	3.39	19	19	0	0	114	112	49	43	34	107	.261	L	L	6-3	223	5-15-76	1997	Houston, Texas
Garcia, Mike	2	2	2.55	34	0	0	13	35	30	15	10	13	44	.223	R	R	6-2	231	5-11-68	1989	Moreno Valley, Calif.
Harikkala, Tim	5	0	0.81	20	3	0	2	44	27	4	4	7	29	.176	R	R	6-2	180	7-15-71	1992	Lake Worth, Fla.
Mohler, Mike	6	5	3.88	50	1	0	1	72	69	40	31	42	50	.254	R	L	6-2	207	7-26-68	1990	Prairieville, La.
Pina, Rafael	2	5	5.30	7	7	0	0	37	41	24	22	23	20	.294	R	R	6-1	170	8-16-71	1991	Alta Loma, Calif.
Pulsipher, Bill	4	5	5.63	51	0	0	3	54	59	43	34	29	43	.274	S	L	6-3	228	10-9-73	1992	Port St. Lucie, Fla.
Rakers, Aaron	2	4	5.13	21	0	0	1	26	19	18	15	11	26	.202	R	R	6-3	205	1-22-77	1999	Trenton, Ill.
Rakers, Jason	0	0	10.13	2	1	0	0	5	8	6	6	1	6	.333	R	R	6-2	200	6-29-73	1995	Pittsburgh, Pa.
2-team (3 Buffalo)	0	1	8.22	5	1	0	0	8	10	7	7	3	7	.312							
Rijo, Fernando	2	0	2.25	2	2	0	0	12	11	3	3	4	13	.255	R	R	5-11	173	11-15-77	1995	La Romana, D.R.
Riley, Matt	4	2	3.58	13	13	0	0	70	70	30	28	28	77	.261	L	L	6-1	207	8-2-79	1998	Corona, Calif.
Rizzo, Todd	2	4	4.58	47	0	0	0	59	67	36	30	31	36	.285	R	L	6-2	220	5-24-71	1992	Philadelphia, Penn.
Stephens, John	6	7	3.97	27	27	1	0	159	155	76	70	39	132	.255	R	R	6-1	212	11-15-79	1996	Berala, Australia

FIELDING

Catcher	PCT	G	PO	A	E	DP	PB
Casanova	1.000	3	26	4	0	0	0
Gil	.992	29	220	27	2	1	3
Lomasney	.992	68	468	47	4	3	5
Machado	.994	40	278	40	2	6	1
Mendez	1.000	1	4	0	0	0	0
Molina	1.000	3	16	1	0	0	0
Seestedt	1.000	4	16	0	0	1	0

First Base	PCT	G	PO	A	E	DP
Alviso	.900	1	9	0	1	0
Bates	1.000	2	3	1	0	0
Casanova	.900	3	18	0	2	1
Gil	1.000	1	11	0	0	1
Hammond	1.000	14	100	4	0	4
Lemonis	.983	32	225	9	4	22
Leon	.936	5	41	3	3	3
Lomasney	.000	1	0	0	0	0
Mendez	.994	58	470	31	3	46
Quattlebaum	.960	3	21	3	1	1
Rios	1.000	3	16	1	0	3
Sasser	.991	29	210	14	2	22
Swann	1.000	4	22	5	0	3

Second Base	PCT	G	PO	A	E	DP
Alviso	.982	8	22	32	1	5
Escalona	.943	8	18	15	2	4
Garabito	.909	5	11	9	2	3
Hammond	.993	38	58	86	1	19
Lemonis	1.000	6	6	15	0	2
Lopez	.963	32	66	91	6	23
Roberts	.987	38	72	81	2	23
Sasser	.981	16	25	27	1	8

Third Base	PCT	G	PO	A	E	DP
Alviso	1.000	2	1	4	0	0
Calzado	.875	21	20	36	8	7
Hammond	.951	20	11	28	2	3
Lemonis	.889	9	4	12	2	3
Leon	.946	68	51	125	10	13
Lopez	1.000	1	2	1	0	0
Mendez	.000	1	0	0	0	0
Perez	.861	9	3	28	5	2
Rios	.953	16	10	31	2	5
Sasser	.909	8	5	15	2	4

Shortstop	PCT	G	PO	A	E	DP
Alviso	.967	6	9	20	1	3
Calzado	.950	8	19	19	2	4
Escalona	1.000	2	3	2	0	0
Garabito	.942	106	160	280	27	53
Lopez	.984	15	15	46	1	8
Perez	.500	2	0	1	1	1
Roberts	.941	6	17	15	2	2
Sasser	1.000	1	0	4	0	1

Outfield	PCT	G	PO	A	E	DP
Bates	.975	20	36	3	1	1
Bigbie	.974	22	34	3	1	0
Calzado	.976	20	40	0	1	0
Cust	.978	77	126	7	3	1
Hammond	1.000	33	56	0	0	0

	PCT	G	PO	A	E	DP
Littleton	1.000	29	78	1	0	1
Matos	.990	45	95	1	1	1
McDonald	.968	37	90	2	3	0
Raines	.993	52	134	3	1	1
Rivera	.950	14	37	1	2	0
Sasser	1.000	4	2	0	0	0
Swann	.977	86	165	6	4	0

BOWIE BAYSOX — Class AA

EASTERN LEAGUE

BATTING	AVG	G	AB	R	H	2B	3B	HR	RBI	BB	SO	SB	CS	SLG	OBP	B	T	HT	WT	DOB	1st Yr	Resides
Airoso, Kurt	.210	41	119	17	25	5	0	6	19	17	33	2	1	.403	.324	R	R	6-2	190	2-12-75	1996	Tulare, Calif.
Alviso, Jerome	.367	9	30	4	11	1	0	0	0	2	2	2	1	.400	.406	S	R	6-1	160	9-4-75	1997	Livermore, Calif.
Barker, Glen	.237	20	59	5	14	1	1	0	7	5	10	2	2	.288	.297	S	R	5-10	180	5-10-71	1993	Albany, N.Y.
Bates, Fletcher	.240	23	75	14	18	4	1	1	7	8	14	0	0	.360	.310	S	R	6-1	190	3-24-74	1994	Rocky Point, N.C.
Bonilla, Clemente	.000	1	1	0	0	0	0	0	0	0	1	0	0	.000	.000	R	R	5-9	170	2-6-80	2002	Trabuco Canyon, Calif.
Calzado, Napoleon	.265	40	166	16	44	6	1	1	11	5	14	11	3	.331	.293	R	R	6-3	181	2-9-77	1996	Santo Domingo, D.R.
Cates, Gary	.283	19	46	10	13	4	1	0	10	5	3	2	0	.413	.364	R	R	5-7	163	7-3-81	1999	Brandon, Fla.
Coffie, Ivanon	.245	93	319	47	78	20	0	14	42	42	66	1	4	.439	.338	L	R	6-1	190	5-16-77	1995	Willemstad, Curacao
Del Rosario, Manny	.125	9	24	2	3	0	0	0	0	0	1	0	0	.125	.125	S	R	5-11	155	7-8-81	1997	Hato Mayor Del Rey, D.R.
Diaz, Juan	.274	68	248	29	68	22	0	14	55	26	64	1	0	.532	.341	R	R	6-2	260	2-19-74	1996	Santo Domingo, D.R.
Escalona, Felix	.333	1	3	0	1	0	0	0	0	0	1	0	0	.333	.333	R	R	6-0	190	3-12-79	1996	Puerto Cabello, Venez.
Fontenot, Mike	.325	126	449	63	146	24	5	12	66	50	89	16	5	.481	.399	L	R	5-8	160	6-9-80	2002	Slidell, La.
Gredvig, Doug	.220	26	100	5	22	6	0	1	13	5	20	1	0	.310	.252	R	R	6-3	231	8-25-79	2000	Sacramento, Calif.
Hairston, Jerry	.300	6	20	4	6	1	0	1	2	1	4	0	0	.500	.391	R	R	5-10	185	5-29-76	1997	Pikesville, Md.
Hammond, Joey	.333	18	57	7	19	3	0	0	6	11	5	3	1	.386	.435	R	R	6-1	189	10-27-77	1998	Frederick, Md.
Hoffpauir, Josh	.289	108	356	38	103	21	2	2	33	26	24	13	7	.376	.354	L	R	5-10	175	9-21-77	2000	Vidalia, La.
Lemonis, Chris	.206	9	34	4	7	2	0	0	2	0	3	0	0	.265	.200	L	R	5-11	185	8-21-73	1995	New York, N.Y.
Littleton, B.J.	.230	52	135	24	31	9	1	0	12	13	22	6	2	.311	.293	S	L	5-10	166	10-3-79	2000	Arlington, Texas
Mack, Tony	.235	21	68	4	16	1	0	0	4	2	12	1	4	.250	.257	R	R	5-11	200	3-19-79	1998	Orlando, Fla.
Martinez, Octavio	.000	3	4	1	0	0	0	0	0	0	0	0	0	.000	.200	R	R	6-0	185	7-30-79	1999	Bakersfield, Calif.
Martinez, Raul	.000	1	1	0	0	0	0	0	0	0	0	0	0	.000	.000	L	R	6-0	194	10-7-79	2000	San Lorenzo, P.R.
Molina, Izzy	.313	5	16	3	5	1	0	0	2	5	4	0	1	.375	.476	R	R	6-1	213	6-3-71	1990	Miami, Fla.
Mora, Melvin	.286	6	21	3	6	0	0	2	5	2	4	0	0	.571	.348	R	R	5-11	198	2-2-72	1991	Bel Air, Md.
O'Sullivan, Patrick	.250	13	40	4	10	4	0	1	4	1	13	0	0	.425	.286	R	R	6-2	210	3-22-77	1999	Marietta, Ga.
Otanez, Willis	.236	16	55	6	13	3	0	0	9	7	13	0	0	.291	.333	R	R	6-1	210	4-19-73	1990	Las Vega Baja, D.R.
Raines, Tim	.308	66	247	44	76	15	4	4	26	21	40	28	6	.449	.371	R	R	5-10	189	8-31-79	1998	Heathrow, Fla.
Ramos, Kelly	.206	30	97	7	20	4	0	3	12	5	18	0	1	.340	.243	S	R	6-1	215	10-15-76	1994	San Pedro de Macoris, D.R.
Reed, Keith	.258	114	419	63	108	11	1	10	39	31	94	16	9	.360	.314	R	R	6-4	205	10-8-78	1999	Yarmouth Port, Mass.
Rios, Brian	.217	6	23	2	5	0	0	0	3	2	6	0	0	.217	.280	R	R	6-3	190	7-25-74	1996	Corona, Calif.
Rivera, Ruben	.195	41	128	17	25	5	1	6	20	12	35	0	1	.391	.273	R	R	6-3	200	11-14-73	1992	La Chorrera, Panama
Rogers, Ed	.212	97	340	48	72	13	1	6	35	12	64	27	8	.309	.249	R	R	6-1	183	8-29-78	1997	San Pedro de Macoris, D.R.
Romero, Willie	.259	20	81	9	21	3	1	1	7	3	10	4	2	.358	.291	R	R	5-9	190	8-5-74	1991	Maracay, Venez.
Sasser, Rob	.225	12	40	7	9	4	0	1	4	4	8	1	0	.400	.295	R	R	6-3	200	3-9-75	1993	Oakland, Calif.
Seestedt, Mike	.244	46	123	8	30	3	0	0	6	14	17	0	1	.268	.319	R	R	6-0	200	11-10-77	1999	Mt. Pleasant, Mich.
Shier, Peter	.200	1	5	1	1	0	0	0	0	0	1	0	0	.200	.200	R	R	6-2	163	3-16-81	1999	Columbus, Ohio
Whiteside, Eli	.204	81	265	21	54	13	1	1	23	5	44	0	0	.272	.230	R	R	6-2	213	10-22-79	2001	New Albany, Miss.
Wilken, Kris	.263	116	426	40	112	19	1	2	43	26	58	5	1	.326	.303	S	R	5-11	195	4-11-79	2000	Albuquerque, N.M.

PITCHING	W	L	ERA	G	GS	CG	SV	IP	H	R	ER	BB	SO	AVG	B	T	HT	WT	DOB	1st Yr	Resides
Agamennone, Brandon	2	2	4.79	29	3	0	1	56	65	33	30	13	37	.282	R	R	6-2	190	11-6-75	1998	Crofton, Md.
Borkowski, Dave	6	7	3.29	24	19	2	0	120	126	50	44	22	66	.270	R	R	6-1	220	2-7-77	1995	Monroe, Mich.
2-team (6 Erie)	6	8	3.30	30	19	2	0	128	136	54	47	24	70	.274							
Corcoran, Tim	4	1	4.09	26	2	0	3	44	37	22	20	19	33	.231	R	R	6-2	205	4-15-78	1997	Slaughter, La.
Crouthers, Dave	4	2	3.80	9	9	0	0	45	37	20	19	18	29	.220	R	R	6-3	203	12-18-79	2001	Edwardsville, Ill.
Daal, Omar	0	0	12.00	1	1	0	0	3	5	4	4	2	2	.384	L	L	6-3	193	2-23-72	1990	Weston, Fla.
Drumright, Mike	2	1	2.23	6	6	0	0	32	23	13	8	10	39	.191	L	R	6-4	217	4-19-74	1995	Valley Center, Kan.
Edwards, Brad	1	0	10.13	2	0	0	0	3	5	4	3	1	2	.416	R	L	6-3	184	4-10-80	2001	Dumfries, Va.
Forystek, Brian	9	9	3.39	29	21	1	0	125	116	57	47	42	103	.251	L	L	6-1	177	10-30-78	2000	Palos Park, Ill.
Lopez, Rodrigo	1	0	0.00	1	1	0	0	6	3	0	0	0	13	.142	R	R	6-1	187	12-14-75	1995	Mexico City, Mexico
Ormond, Rodney	7	2	2.86	46	0	0	1	85	70	33	27	31	72	.221	R	R	6-4	210	6-17-77	1999	Princeton, N.C.
Paradis, Mike	5	10	5.27	25	25	1	0	125	129	85	73	81	82	.272	R	R	6-3	198	5-3-78	1999	Clemson, S.C.
Parrish, John	3	3	2.00	49	0	0	6	76	58	22	17	33	85	.214	L	L	5-11	176	11-26-77	1996	Owings Mills, Md.
Pina, Rafael	0	1	4.30	6	0	0	1	15	13	7	7	1	7	.240	R	R	6-1	170	8-16-71	1991	Alta Loma, Calif.
Rakers, Aaron	5	0	2.75	31	0	0	8	39	27	12	12	19	42	.195	R	R	6-3	205	1-22-77	1999	Trenton, Ill.
Ramirez, Enrique	1	3	5.64	14	0	0	0	22	20	15	14	19	20	.240	R	R	6-2	210	8-15-76	1996	El Seibo, D.R.
Rijo, Fernando	3	10	5.47	20	19	2	0	100	107	65	61	46	71	.271	R	R	5-11	173	11-15-77	1995	La Romana, D.R.
Riley, Matt	5	2	3.11	14	14	1	0	72	56	27	25	23	73	.209	L	L	6-1	207	8-2-79	1998	Corona, Calif.
Rizzo, Todd	0	0	3.24	7	0	0	0	8	5	3	3	7	6	.185	R	L	6-2	220	5-24-71	1992	Philadelphia, Pa.
Rodriguez, Eddy	3	4	2.34	56	0	0	13	73	49	26	19	35	66	.187	R	R	6-1	194	8-8-81	1999	San Pedro de Macoris, D.R.
Rosario, Juan	0	3	8.68	5	5	0	0	19	25	19	18	10	5	.320	R	R	6-4	229	11-17-75	1993	Perth Amboy, N.J.
Sequea, Jacobo	1	3	5.40	12	8	0	0	40	43	26	24	28	24	.279	R	R	6-1	194	8-31-81	1997	Anaco, Venez.
Sims, Kenny	0	1	27.00	1	1	0	0	2	10	7	7	0	2	.588	R	R	6-4	217	7-24-75	1996	Union, S.C.
Spencer, Sean	2	1	1.53	12	0	0	0	18	19	3	3	7	12	.271	L	L	5-11	180	5-29-75	1996	Port Orchard, Wash.
Wilson, Jeff	5	7	3.78	28	8	0	0	81	84	36	34	24	50	.274	R	L	6-2	194	5-30-76	1997	Greensboro, N.C.

FIELDING

Catcher	PCT	G	PO	A	E	DP	PB
Martinez	1.000	3	13	3	0	0	1
Molina	1.000	2	14	0	0	0	0
Ramos	.982	29	199	21	4	2	1
Seestedt	.996	45	254	24	1	1	3
Whiteside	.989	78	489	55	6	8	14

First Base	PCT	G	PO	A	E	DP
Bates	.962	4	24	1	1	1
Diaz	.985	40	322	16	5	31
Gredvig	.990	23	181	11	2	18
O'Sullivan	1.000	4	34	0	0	2
Otanez	1.000	4	31	5	0	0
Rios	1.000	1	10	0	0	1
Sasser	1.000	3	23	2	0	1
Wilken	.993	66	545	38	4	54

Second Base	PCT	G	PO	A	E	DP
Alviso	1.000	1	2	7	0	0
Cates	1.000	1	0	5	0	0
Del Rosario	.944	3	6	11	1	2
Escalona	1.000	1	1	3	0	1
Fontenot	.968	114	226	317	18	69
Hairston	.941	4	5	11	1	1
Hoffpauir	.977	22	33	53	2	10
Lemonis	1.000	2	3	5	0	2

Third Base	PCT	G	PO	A	E	DP
Alviso	1.000	1	0	2	0	0
Calzado	.950	36	25	70	5	8
Cates	1.000	1	1	5	0	0
Coffie	.951	82	43	151	10	14
Lemonis	.800	2	1	3	1	0
Otanez	1.000	1	1	0	0	0
Sasser	1.000	3	0	6	0	1
Wilken	.852	21	12	34	8	2

Shortstop	PCT	G	PO	A	E	DP
Alviso	.889	7	8	16	3	3
Calzado	.833	1	2	3	1	0
Cates	.882	9	5	10	2	2
Coffie	.978	10	14	30	1	4
Del Rosario	.917	6	4	7	1	1
Hammond	.961	18	22	51	3	10
Hoffpauir	.000	1	0	0	1	0
Rogers	.957	97	139	242	17	58
Shier	1.000	1	0	5	0	1

Outfield	PCT	G	PO	A	E	DP
Airoso	.971	40	65	1	2	0
Barker	1.000	18	33	3	0	0
Bates	.923	10	11	1	1	0
Calzado	1.000	2	5	0	0	0
Cates	1.000	8	9	0	0	0
Hoffpauir	.977	66	123	4	3	0
Lemonis	1.000	1	1	0	0	0
Littleton	.978	45	90	1	2	0
Mack	1.000	21	45	1	0	0
Mora	1.000	6	10	0	0	0
Otanez	1.000	1	1	0	0	0
Raines	.976	56	120	3	3	0
Reed	.979	112	224	11	5	3
Rios	1.000	3	8	0	0	0
Rivera	1.000	37	86	6	0	1
Romero	1.000	20	34	1	0	0
Sasser	1.000	4	5	1	0	0
Wilken	1.000	7	11	0	0	0

FREDERICK KEYS — High Class A

CAROLINA LEAGUE

BATTING	AVG	G	AB	R	H	2B	3B	HR	RBI	BB	SO	SB	CS	SLG	OBP	B	T	HT	WT	DOB	1st Yr	Resides
Arko, Tommy	.186	34	113	13	21	3	0	6	15	8	40	0	0	.372	.244	R	R	6-1	197	7-28-82	2000	Abilene, Texas
Cates, Gary	.315	92	355	50	112	23	3	3	35	21	40	11	12	.423	.361	R	R	5-7	163	7-3-81	1999	Brandon, Fla.
Cliffords, Woody	.282	124	440	70	124	29	1	8	44	71	77	16	10	.407	.390	L	R	6-2	193	12-2-80	2001	West Hills, Calif.
Davies, Gregg	.270	14	37	1	10	2	0	0	3	5	4	0	0	.324	.364	L	L	6-1	200	1-8-80	2002	Olney, Md.
Fahey, Brandon	.233	107	365	41	85	11	3	1	22	22	56	4	2	.288	.279	L	R	6-2	183	1-18-81	2002	Dallas, Texas
Gordon, Alex	.221	69	235	29	52	11	3	3	29	18	85	0	0	.332	.276	L	L	6-4	233	3-3-80	1998	Seattle, Wash.
Gredvig, Doug	.275	12	40	8	11	3	0	1	6	6	6	0	0	.425	.383	R	R	6-3	231	8-25-79	2000	Sacramento, Calif.
Guerrero, Henry	.286	6	21	1	6	1	0	0	0	2	2	0	0	.333	.348	R	R	6-0	180	4-4-82	2000	Valencia,Venez.
Hubele, Ryan	.250	26	92	11	23	6	0	1	12	5	14	0	1	.348	.293	R	R	5-11	190	9-9-80	2002	Paradise Valley, Ariz.
Huggins, Mike	.293	126	454	66	133	32	0	13	74	55	93	3	3	.449	.367	R	R	6-3	212	8-29-80	2002	San Antonio, Texas
Johnson, Tripper	.273	123	417	43	114	25	3	5	50	46	92	7	8	.384	.359	R	R	6-1	200	4-28-82	2000	Bellevue, Wash.
Keylor, Cory	.244	79	270	38	66	15	2	7	39	28	65	2	3	.393	.315	L	R	6-3	194	8-25-79	2001	Westerville, Ohio
Majewski, Val	.289	41	159	15	46	18	1	5	20	7	23	0	0	.509	.321	L	L	6-2	200	6-19-81	2002	Freehold, N.J.
Manley, Adam	.196	82	275	28	54	7	0	10	34	16	82	3	1	.331	.247	L	L	6-2	194	7-18-78	2001	Lakewood, Wash.
Martin, Kyle	.222	19	54	7	12	3	0	0	3	9	6	0	0	.278	.344	R	R	5-11	217	6-12-80	1999	Yakima, Wash.
Martinez, Octavio	.248	42	133	12	33	4	0	0	6	4	19	0	0	.278	.291	R	R	6-0	185	7-30-79	1999	Bakersfield, Calif.
Martinez, Raul	.250	5	12	0	3	0	0	0	0	0	5	0	0	.250	.250	L	R	6-0	194	10-7-79	2000	San Lorenzo, P.R.
O'Sullivan, Patrick	.178	27	90	6	16	2	1	3	12	2	31	1	0	.322	.200	R	R	6-2	210	3-22-77	1999	Marietta, Ga.
Quattlebaum, Hugh	.177	30	79	5	14	1	0	0	4	12	11	0	1	.190	.283	R	R	6-4	205	6-26-78	2000	Andover, Mass.
Rogers, Omar	.292	99	356	49	104	24	0	3	28	42	70	4	5	.385	.374	R	R	6-0	182	10-12-79	1999	San Pedro de Macoris, D.R.
Ruiz, Randy	.250	17	68	7	17	4	1	1	8	4	24	0	0	.382	.301	R	R	6-3	220	10-19-77	1999	Bronx, N.Y.
Seestedt, Mike	.229	13	35	1	8	2	0	0	5	3	6	0	0	.286	.289	R	R	6-0	200	11-10-77	1999	Mt. Pleasant, Mich.
Segui, David	.250	1	4	0	1	0	0	0	0	0	1	0	0	.250	.250	S	L	6-1	216	7-19-66	1988	Kansas City, Kan.
Shanks, Eric	.242	14	33	4	8	3	0	1	3	3	4	0	0	.424	.297	R	R	5-11	180	7-7-78	2001	Charlotte, N.C.
Shier, Peter	.267	74	255	36	68	8	0	8	31	24	51	8	5	.392	.327	R	R	6-2	163	3-16-81	1999	Columbus, Ohio
Wilken, Kris	.143	9	21	0	3	0	0	0	3	1	1	0	0	.143	.174	S	R	5-11	195	4-11-79	2000	Albuquerque, N.M.

PITCHING	W	L	ERA	G	GS	CG	SV	IP	H	R	ER	BB	SO	AVG	B	T	HT	WT	DOB	1st Yr	Resides
Agamennone, Brandon	0	0	6.75	2	1	0	0	4	5	3	3	1	2	.294	R	R	6-2	190	11-6-75	1998	Crofton, Md.
Babula, Shaun	7	1	2.68	37	0	0	1	50	45	20	15	16	46	.234	S	L	6-1	183	5-21-77	1999	Burlington, N.J.
Bartlett, Richard	1	2	9.12	9	6	0	1	26	38	31	26	22	17	.342	R	R	6-3	216	10-6-81	2000	Kennewick, Wash.
Bedard, Erik	0	1	7.36	1	1	0	0	4	5	3	3	1	2	.357	L	L	6-1	191	3-6-79	1999	Navan, Ontario
Berube, Martin	0	0	3.38	3	0	0	0	5	5	2	2	4	3	.263	L	R	6-1	198	9-12-81	1999	Montreal, Quebec
Birkins, Kurt	8	11	4.70	25	25	0	0	126	152	82	66	40	79	.296	L	L	6-2	188	8-11-80	2001	Canoga Park, Calif.
Boughner, Anthony	3	3	7.71	18	2	0	0	28	41	26	24	10	21	.333	L	L	6-3	212	11-1-78	2002	Beallsville, Ohio
Coppinger, Joe	1	0	3.38	1	1	0	0	5	5	2	2	1	6	.238	R	R	6-3	218	7-23-82	2001	El Paso, Texas
Corcoran, Tim	2	5	5.74	22	3	0	0	47	57	38	30	27	41	.293	R	R	6-2	205	4-15-78	1997	Slaughter, La.
Crouthers, Dave	7	5	3.59	18	18	0	0	93	83	47	37	43	82	.242	R	R	6-3	203	12-18-79	2001	Edwardsville, Ill.
Deza, Fredy	0	0	27.00	1	0	0	0	1	4	5	4	3	2	.444	R	R	6-2	167	12-11-82	1999	La Romana, D.R.
Edwards, Brad	0	0	14.73	3	0	0	0	4	5	6	6	2	4	.294	R	L	6-3	184	4-10-80	2001	Dumfries, Va.
Farren, Dave	0	4	5.71	18	10	0	1	69	73	45	44	29	52	.272	R	R	6-1	183	3-20-81	1999	Texarkana, Texas
Hannaman, Ryan	1	3	3.79	5	5	0	0	19	14	9	8	17	22	.205	L	L	6-3	200	8-28-81	2000	Mobile, Ala.
Knapp, Ben	0	3	9.24	9	5	0	0	25	37	28	26	9	15	.355	R	R	6-7	219	11-8-79	1998	Oviedo, Fla.
Lewis, Rommie	4	9	3.34	26	20	1	0	113	108	54	42	60	69	.250	L	L	6-6	203	9-2-82	2001	Bellevue, Wash.
Maine, John	6	1	3.07	12	12	1	0	70	48	27	24	20	77	.190	R	R	6-4	190	5-8-81	2002	Hartwood, Va.
Makowsky, Carl	2	2	4.02	29	0	0	3	40	31	21	18	24	34	.213	R	R	6-1	200	12-13-79	2002	Conroe, Texas
McCurdy, Nick	1	6	4.89	19	18	0	0	92	125	58	50	28	76	.323	R	R	6-3	185	1-24-80	2002	Thomasville, Ala.
Mitchell, Andy	5	4	3.46	60	0	0	1	91	84	41	35	36	49	.250	R	R	6-3	206	9-10-78	2001	Conyers, Ga.
Morris, Cory	3	2	2.61	7	7	0	0	38	32	15	11	16	28	.231	R	R	6-2	189	6-2-79	2001	Beckville, Texas
Ramirez, Enrique	2	0	4.56	13	0	0	0	24	24	12	12	15	17	.269	R	R	6-2	210	8-15-76	1996	El Seibo, D.R.
Rice, Scott	1	3	3.19	25	0	0	0	31	34	12	11	14	27	.285	L	L	6-6	217	9-21-81	1999	Simi Valley, Calif.
Rleal, Sendy	3	5	3.16	44	0	0	11	57	35	20	20	23	59	.176	R	R	6-1	165	6-21-80	1999	San Pedro de Macoris, D.R.
Salazar, Richard	0	0	10.38	6	0	0	0	9	8	11	10	8	4	.266	L	L	5-11	200	1-6-81	2001	Miami, Fla.
Sequea, Jacobo	1	0	2.87	32	0	0	20	31	27	11	10	11	26	.228	R	R	6-1	194	8-31-81	1997	Anaco, Venez.
Sims, Kenny	1	1	5.29	11	0	0	0	17	22	10	10	5	6	.323	R	R	6-4	217	7-24-75	1996	Union, S.C.
Sperring, Jayme	0	3	5.64	15	0	0	2	22	30	20	14	15	21	.319	R	R	6-4	209	11-16-78	2000	Cypress, Texas
Sutton, Zach	0	1	1.29	5	0	0	0	7	5	1	1	0	4	.192	R	R	6-1	185	1-6-79	2002	Lake Wales, Fla.
Tiller, James	0	0	6.23	1	1	0	0	4	4	3	3	0	3	.235	R	R	6-5	194	4-13-83	2001	Elysian Fields, Texas
Wilson, Jeff	1	0	2.00	7	0	0	0	9	6	2	2	3	9	.193	R	L	6-2	194	5-30-76	1997	Greensboro, N.C.

FIELDING

Catcher	PCT	G	PO	A	E	DP	PB
Arko	.981	34	242	19	5	1	8
Guerrero	1.000	6	36	9	0	1	3
Hubele	.973	26	170	12	5	1	13
Martin	.960	19	132	13	6	0	8
Martinez	.976	38	258	30	7	3	3
Martinez	1.000	5	20	1	0	0	1
Seestedt	1.000	13	67	10	0	0	4

First Base	PCT	G	PO	A	E	DP
Gredvig	1.000	3	26	3	0	1
Huggins	.990	115	967	75	10	92
Manley	.973	5	35	1	1	0
O'Sullivan	1.000	5	45	4	0	6
Quattlebaum	1.000	9	69	13	0	6
Ruiz	1.000	1	10	0	0	2
Wilken	1.000	1	4	1	0	0

Second Base	PCT	G	PO	A	E	DP
Cates	.962	39	59	117	7	22
Rogers	.971	88	161	237	12	41
Shanks	.933	3	4	10	1	3
Shier	.925	9	17	20	3	3
Wilken	1.000	1	1	0	0	0

Third Base	PCT	G	PO	A	E	DP
Cates	.000	1	0	0	0	0
Johnson	.940	118	98	202	19	21

	PCT	G	PO	A	E	DP
Quattlebaum	1.000	3	1	4	0	1
Shier	.929	15	15	37	4	8
Wilken	1.000	1	1	2	0	1

Shortstop	PCT	G	PO	A	E	DP
Cates	.700	4	4	3	3	0
Fahey	.962	106	175	307	19	64
Shanks	.900	2	4	5	1	1

	PCT	G	PO	A	E	DP
Shier	.939	25	41	67	7	11
Wilken	1.000	1	0	1	0	1

Outfield	PCT	G	PO	A	E	DP
Cates	.982	36	53	2	1	0
Cliffords	.989	117	261	9	3	0
Davies	1.000	14	26	1	0	0
Gordon	.985	38	62	5	1	1
Keylor	.962	74	123	3	5	1
Majewski	.938	35	60	1	4	0
Manley	.991	65	102	4	1	1
O'Sullivan	1.000	4	6	0	0	0
Ruiz	1.000	4	8	0	0	0
Shanks	1.000	6	8	0	0	0
Shier	.972	27	34	1	1	0
Wilken	.667	4	1	1	1	0

DELMARVA SHOREBIRDS — Low Class A

SOUTH ATLANTIC LEAGUE

BATTING	AVG	G	AB	R	H	2B	3B	HR	RBI	BB	SO	SB	CS	SLG	OBP	B	T	HT	WT	DOB	1st Yr	Resides
Alvarez, Gera	.260	100	331	47	86	21	2	5	43	46	48	18	9	.381	.362	R	R	5-10	182	10-31-79	2002	Vista, Calif.
Arko, Tommy	.204	47	152	19	31	5	0	4	12	20	50	1	2	.316	.316	R	R	6-1	197	7-28-82	2000	Abilene, Texas
Bass, Bryan	.205	60	205	23	42	8	7	0	21	21	58	7	4	.312	.284	S	R	6-1	180	4-12-82	2001	Seminole, Fla.
Bonilla, Clemente	.000	3	4	0	0	0	0	0	0	0	0	0	0	.000	.000	R	R	5-9	170	2-6-80	2002	Trabuco Canyon, Calif.
Carter, Chris	.283	26	92	18	26	4	2	2	11	12	15	6	1	.435	.383	R	R	6-1	195	2-13-79	2002	Conway, S.C.
Clendenin, Morgan	.136	11	22	2	3	1	0	0	4	5	13	0	0	.182	.286	L	R	6-0	201	10-2-81	2003	Ripley, W.Va.
Davies, Gregg	.220	43	141	17	31	4	0	2	18	17	34	5	1	.291	.309	L	L	6-1	200	1-8-80	2002	Olney, Md.
Done, Mike	.252	85	298	37	75	22	1	4	32	33	78	2	1	.372	.331	S	R	5-11	190	7-27-79	2002	Aurora, Colo.
Gonzalez, Patrick	.133	24	60	9	8	1	0	0	3	12	19	3	0	.150	.288	R	R	5-10	170	11-21-79	2002	Ontario, Calif.
Gordon, Alex	.200	8	25	3	5	3	0	1	3	2	13	0	0	.440	.310	L	L	6-4	233	3-3-80	1998	Seattle, Wash.
Harris, Cory	.288	37	139	15	40	11	1	3	22	13	11	6	4	.446	.366	R	R	5-10	180	12-7-79	1999	Davenport, Iowa
Hubele, Ryan	.251	56	195	25	49	6	2	5	22	14	31	0	1	.379	.319	R	R	5-11	190	9-9-80	2002	Paradise Valley, Ariz.
Joyce, Tom	.233	41	150	19	35	11	1	3	12	19	57	5	1	.380	.331	L	L	5-11	168	3-1-82	2000	Macon, Ga.
Littleton, B.J.	.294	34	119	21	35	2	4	0	12	15	19	12	2	.378	.375	S	L	5-10	166	10-3-79	2000	Arlington, Texas
Majewski, Val	.303	56	208	38	63	15	8	7	48	28	20	10	1	.553	.383	L	L	6-2	200	6-19-81	2002	Freehold, N.J.
Martin, Kyle	.250	13	40	10	10	1	1	0	2	3	9	0	0	.325	.302	R	R	5-11	217	6-12-80	1999	Yakima, Wash.
McCurdy, Josh	.087	7	23	0	2	1	0	0	0	1	2	2	0	.130	.125	R	R	6-6	220	12-28-79	2003	Thornhill, Ontario
O'Sullivan, Patrick	.317	10	41	4	13	5	0	1	7	2	12	2	0	.512	.349	R	R	6-2	210	3-22-77	1999	Marietta, Ga.
Ramos, Kelly	.239	34	113	14	27	4	0	5	15	9	12	1	0	.407	.315	S	R	6-1	215	10-15-76	1994	San Pedro de Macoris, D.R.
Rijo, Carlos	.266	111	403	26	107	13	0	1	38	14	60	2	5	.305	.296	R	R	6-0	200	9-11-82	1999	La Romana, D.R.
Rivas, Arturo	.190	44	163	16	31	11	1	1	11	16	42	2	2	.288	.271	R	R	6-0	189	2-2-84	2001	San Francisco, Venez.
Robinson-Pierce, Whit	.188	10	32	1	6	0	0	0	1	1	12	0	0	.188	.212	R	R	6-3	210	3-4-82	2002	Fresno, Calif.
Robinson, Levi	.242	97	281	51	68	18	3	0	17	43	53	12	9	.327	.358	R	R	6-0	180	3-28-80	2002	Anchorage, Alaska
Ruiz, Randy	.310	67	239	33	74	18	2	11	51	29	70	3	3	.540	.391	R	R	6-3	220	10-19-77	1999	Bronx, N.Y.
Russell, Mike	.176	27	74	10	13	5	0	1	3	5	31	0	1	.284	.256	R	R	6-0	193	8-14-81	2000	Bothell, Wash.
Smallwood, Erik	.214	6	14	1	3	0	0	0	2	3	5	0	0	.214	.353	L	R	5-10	185	9-5-79	2002	Robertsdale, Ala.
Stephenson, Neal	.227	124	437	56	99	23	3	10	48	42	137	6	5	.362	.300	L	R	6-1	200	1-15-80	2002	Bryan, Texas
Sultemeier, Eric	.174	7	23	2	4	3	0	0	1	2	3	1	0	.304	.269	R	R	6-2	180	6-28-82	2003	New Braunfels, Texas
Yount, Dustin	.222	122	419	45	93	20	0	8	49	47	115	1	5	.327	.309	L	R	6-1	200	10-27-82	2001	Scottsdale, Ariz.

PITCHING	W	L	ERA	G	GS	CG	SV	IP	H	R	ER	BB	SO	AVG	B	T	HT	WT	DOB	1st Yr	Resides
Bartlett, Richard	1	5	4.33	12	12	0	0	60	58	38	29	26	47	.243	R	R	6-3	216	10-6-81	2000	Kennewick, Wash.
Cabrera, Daniel	5	9	4.24	26	26	1	0	125	105	74	59	78	120	.224	R	R	6-7	220	5-28-81	1999	San Pedro de Macoris, D.R.
Cooney, Jim	0	0	11.25	6	0	0	0	8	14	11	10	6	4	.411	L	L	6-0	180	4-6-80	2002	Boca Raton, Fla.
Coppinger, Joe	2	1	3.94	13	3	0	0	30	31	15	13	14	26	.256	R	R	6-3	218	7-23-82	2001	El Paso, Texas
Farren, Dave	0	0	4.22	7	0	0	1	11	9	7	5	6	10	.219	R	R	6-1	183	3-20-81	1999	Texarkana, Texas
Guzman, Juan	3	2	3.25	31	2	0	1	64	55	25	23	27	52	.233	R	R	6-2	180	4-3-77	1995	San Pedro de Macoris, D.R.
Henry, Paul	4	4	2.76	42	0	0	4	85	70	40	26	18	99	.214	R	R	6-3	190	6-27-81	2002	Chattanooga, Tenn.
Keefer, Ryan	7	12	4.36	26	26	1	0	149	162	88	72	34	94	.277	L	R	6-3	202	8-10-81	2000	Catawissa, Penn.
Knapp, Ben	5	0	2.53	15	4	0	3	46	39	14	13	14	48	.228	L	R	6-7	219	11-8-79	1998	Oviedo, Fla.
Maine, John	7	3	1.53	14	14	1	0	76	43	16	13	18	108	.164	R	R	6-4	190	5-8-81	2002	Hartwood, Va.
Makowsky, Carl	2	2	1.73	22	0	0	3	26	24	6	5	10	28	.235	R	R	6-1	200	12-13-79	2002	Conroe, Texas
McCurdy, Nick	2	4	3.38	6	6	0	0	32	30	17	12	3	27	.238	R	R	6-3	185	1-24-80	2002	Thomasville, Ala.
Montani, Jeff	4	5	3.17	58	0	0	23	60	53	29	21	30	49	.235	R	R	5-11	174	11-22-80	2001	Liverpool, N.Y.
Morris, Cory	5	4	3.19	19	19	1	0	96	74	42	34	45	110	.207	R	R	6-2	189	6-2-79	2001	Beckville, Texas
Patitucci, Mike	0	0	10.80	2	0	0	0	2	4	4	2	1	3	.444	L	L	6-0	195	11-6-80	2002	Uniontown, Penn.
Rice, Scott	4	1	0.94	32	0	0	5	48	21	7	5	12	53	.130	L	L	6-6	217	9-21-81	1999	Simi Valley, Calif.
Salazar, Richard	5	3	1.85	41	0	0	3	63	44	17	13	21	65	.194	L	L	5-11	200	1-6-81	2001	Miami, Fla.
Sperring, Jayme	7	7	4.19	25	12	0	1	82	77	39	38	30	92	.251	R	R	6-4	209	11-16-78	2000	Cypress, Texas
Stahl, Richard	1	3	5.48	28	1	0	1	48	47	41	29	50	46	.261	R	L	6-7	222	4-11-81	1999	Covington, Ga.
Teeter, Travis	0	0	5.68	8	0	0	1	13	15	9	8	3	13	.283	R	R	6-1	210	7-13-80	2002	Cohoes, N.Y.
Tiller, James	3	6	3.51	13	13	0	0	67	78	44	26	13	52	.282	R	R	6-5	194	4-13-83	2001	Elysian Fields, Texas

FIELDING

Catcher	PCT	G	PO	A	E	DP	PB
Arko	.987	46	402	39	6	0	6
Clendenin	.948	11	60	13	4	0	1
Hubele	.986	43	331	23	5	0	9
Martin	.960	13	93	3	4	0	5
Ramos	.986	22	189	19	3	0	4
Robinson-Pierce	.981	10	97	6	2	0	1

First Base	PCT	G	PO	A	E	DP
O'Sullivan	.975	4	36	3	1	5
Ramos	.972	4	34	1	1	3
Ruiz	1.000	12	93	8	0	3
Russell	.983	7	54	3	1	2
Yount	.980	112	911	59	20	55

Second Base	PCT	G	PO	A	E	DP
Alvarez	.971	17	22	45	2	10
Done	.971	43	67	99	5	11
Gonzalez	1.000	3	4	5	0	1
Robinson	.957	85	127	203	15	30

Third Base	PCT	G	PO	A	E	DP
Alvarez	.866	26	14	44	9	4
Done	.873	27	17	45	9	6
Gonzalez	.952	14	8	32	2	3
Rijo	.897	79	46	120	19	2
Russell	.500	2	0	1	1	0

Shortstop	PCT	G	PO	A	E	DP
Alvarez	.956	44	48	103	7	17
Bass	.880	58	84	135	30	21
Bonilla	1.000	1	2	1	0	0
Gonzalez	1.000	5	8	14	0	3
Rijo	.950	33	40	75	6	7
Robinson	1.000	3	1	4	0	0

Outfield	PCT	G	PO	A	E	DP
Alvarez	1.000	13	17	0	0	0
Carter	.971	23	32	2	1	1
Davies	.987	42	71	6	1	0
Harris	.987	36	73	3	1	0
Joyce	1.000	40	64	1	0	1
Littleton	1.000	30	51	2	0	1
Majewski	.980	56	98	2	2	0
McCurdy	1.000	7	9	1	0	0
O'Sullivan	1.000	4	8	1	0	0
Rivas	.970	44	92	4	3	0
Ruiz	1.000	4	1	0	0	0
Russell	.000	1	0	0	1	0
Smallwood	1.000	5	5	0	0	0
Stephenson	.989	118	179	7	2	2
Sultemeier	1.000	7	10	1	0	0

ABERDEEN IRONBIRDS — Short-Season Class A

NEW YORK-PENN LEAGUE

BATTING	AVG	G	AB	R	H	2B	3B	HR	RBI	BB	SO	SB	CS	SLG	OBP	B	T	HT	WT	DOB	1st Yr	Resides
Arko, Tommy	.256	14	43	7	11	3	1	4	7	6	19	0	0	.651	.360	R	R	6-1	197	7-28-82	2000	Abilene, Texas
Ascencion, Quincy	.100	9	30	2	3	2	0	0	3	1	6	0	0	.167	.125	R	R	6-0	215	11-1-82	1999	Willemstad, Curacao
Bass, Bryan	.193	70	254	26	49	11	1	2	14	24	75	11	11	.268	.273	S	R	6-1	180	4-12-82	2001	Seminole, Fla.
Beck, Alan	.083	18	48	3	4	1	0	1	3	3	12	1	1	.167	.135	R	R	6-0	210	10-5-80	2003	Hudson, N.C.
Bock, Brian	.222	43	126	15	28	2	0	0	9	9	19	4	2	.238	.283	R	R	6-1	210	8-24-81	2003	Bakersfield, Calif.
Boudon, Chad	.195	34	87	11	17	5	1	2	10	5	21	1	2	.345	.240	R	R	6-2	215	6-9-81	2003	Seattle, Wash.
Calzado, Napoleon	.188	4	16	5	3	0	0	0	0	2	0	3	0	.188	.278	R	R	6-3	181	2-9-77	1996	Santo Domingo, D.R.
Cenate, Josh	.000	1	1	0	0	0	0	0	0	0	0	0	0	.000	.000	L	L	6-1	211	1-28-81	1999	Charleston, W.Va.
Clendenin, Morgan	.267	17	45	6	12	6	2	1	8	6	20	2	2	.556	.346	L	R	6-0	201	10-2-81	2003	Ripley, W.Va.
Colbert, Eddie	.278	10	18	1	5	1	0	0	0	1	7	1	0	.333	.316	S	R	6-3	205	12-3-81	2002	Baltimore, Md.
Del Rosario, Manny	.240	60	175	21	42	3	0	0	7	15	17	18	5	.257	.300	S	R	5-11	155	7-8-81	1997	Hato Mayor Del Rey, D.R.
Duncan, Jacob	.161	43	118	13	19	3	2	1	7	8	29	3	2	.246	.220	L	L	5-11	190	11-20-81	2003	Marshall, Texas
Gonzalez, Patrick	.091	9	22	0	2	0	0	0	0	2	4	1	0	.091	.200	R	R	5-10	170	11-21-79	2002	Ontario, Calif.
Grimm, Eric	.273	56	165	22	45	11	0	1	18	32	40	2	2	.358	.394	S	R	6-0	185	4-30-81	2003	Parkersburg, W.Va.
Hairston, Jerry	.333	2	3	2	1	0	0	0	0	3	0	1	0	.333	.667	R	R	5-10	185	5-29-76	1997	Pikesville, Md.
Hoffpauir, Josh	.333	3	12	2	4	1	0	0	1	1	1	1	0	.417	.385	L	R	5-10	175	9-21-77	2000	Vidalia, La.
Hubele, Ryan	.385	3	13	1	5	2	0	0	2	0	2	0	0	.538	.385	R	R	5-11	190	9-9-80	2002	Paradise Valley, Ariz.
Jimenez, Luis	.244	53	168	17	41	9	0	1	21	26	40	7	4	.315	.349	L	L	6-4	205	5-7-82	1999	Bobure, Venez.
Joyce, Tom	.222	38	99	12	22	2	2	2	10	22	29	5	2	.343	.361	L	L	5-11	168	3-1-82	2000	Macon, Ga.
Majewski, Val	.375	4	16	2	6	2	2	0	3	1	2	1	0	.750	.412	L	L	6-2	200	6-19-81	2002	Freehold, N.J.
Markakis, Nick	.283	59	205	22	58	14	3	1	28	30	33	13	5	.395	.372	L	L	6-1	175	11-17-83	2003	Woodstock, Ga.
McCurdy, Josh	.276	29	87	17	24	2	2	0	11	2	12	7	3	.345	.292	R	R	6-6	220	12-28-79	2003	Thornhill, Ontario
Molina, Izzy	.203	19	59	6	12	3	1	2	4	12	10	2	1	.390	.347	R	R	6-1	213	6-3-71	1990	Miami, Fla.
Ramos, Kelly	.208	6	24	4	5	1	0	2	6	1	5	1	0	.500	.240	S	R	6-1	215	10-15-76	1994	San Pedro de Macoris, D.R.
Rine, Jarod	.252	67	230	36	58	8	5	2	14	15	44	20	7	.357	.313	L	R	6-1	190	11-14-81	2003	Moundsville, W.Va.
Robinson-Pierce, Whit	.233	10	30	3	7	1	1	0	4	4	8	0	0	.333	.342	R	R	6-3	210	3-4-82	2002	Fresno, Calif.
Rogers, Ed	.357	3	14	2	5	2	0	1	6	0	2	0	0	.714	.333	R	R	6-1	183	8-29-78	1997	San Pedro de Macoris, D.R.
Russell, Mike	.162	58	185	19	30	7	2	4	22	19	49	1	1	.286	.252	R	R	6-0	193	8-14-81	2000	Bothell, Wash.
Sultemeier, Eric	.063	4	16	3	1	0	0	0	1	0	3	0	0	.063	.167	R	R	6-2	180	6-28-82	2003	New Braunfels, Texas
Wareham, Landon	.000	1	3	0	0	0	0	0	0	0	1	0	0	.000	.000	R	R	5-11	180	9-21-81	2003	Delta, Colo.
Whiteside, Eli	.700	2	10	0	7	3	0	0	4	0	1	1	0	1.000	.700	R	R	6-2	213	10-22-79	2001	New Albany, Miss.
Wyrick, Dennis	.234	57	154	14	36	6	2	0	15	17	26	6	2	.299	.324	R	R	6-1	215	2-9-81	2003	Azusa, Calif.

GAMES BY POSITION: C—Arko 14, Bock 37, Clendenin 7, Hubele 2, Molina 8, Ramos 5, Robinson-Pierce 10, Whiteside 2. **1B**—Boudon 18, Jimenez 21, Russell 44, Wyrick 1. **2B**—Del Rosario 37, Grimm 50, Hairston 1, Hoffpauir 3. **3B**—Bass 3, Boudon 1, Del Rosario 10, Gonzalez 9, Grimm 4, Russell 10, Wyrick 55. **SS**—Bass 66, Del Rosario 12, Rogers 3. **OF**—Ascencion 9, Beck 14, Boudon 7, Calzado 4, Colbert 8, Duncan 38, Joyce 35, Majewski 3, Markakis 55, McCurdy 21, Rine 63, Sultemeier 4.

PITCHING	W	L	ERA	G	GS	CG	SV	IP	H	R	ER	BB	SO	AVG	B	T	HT	WT	DOB	1st Yr	Resides
Bedard, Erik	0	0	2.35	2	2	0	0	8	7	2	2	1	13	.233	L	L	6-1	191	3-6-79	1999	Navan, Ontario
Berube, Martin	3	3	4.01	18	3	0	2	52	50	27	23	21	48	.247	L	R	6-1	198	9-12-81	1999	Montreal, Quebec
Boughner, Anthony	1	2	1.90	24	0	0	6	47	40	11	10	15	36	.238	L	R	6-3	212	11-1-78	2002	Beallsville, Ohio
Cierlik, Jason	3	1	3.29	22	0	0	3	38	37	18	14	25	39	.258	L	L	6-0	205	2-21-81	2002	Brooklyn Park, Minn.
Coppinger, Joe	6	4	3.29	14	12	0	0	63	56	29	23	17	59	.234	R	R	6-3	218	7-23-82	2001	El Paso, Texas
Deza, Fredy	3	5	3.25	15	14	1	0	75	75	32	27	20	69	.256	R	R	6-2	167	12-11-82	1999	La Romana, D.R.
Dixon, Zachary	4	3	2.91	14	14	0	0	68	65	26	22	18	70	.250	L	L	6-2	195	11-29-80	2003	Houston, Texas
Finch, Brian	1	3	1.93	8	5	0	0	28	19	9	6	5	29	.182	R	R	6-4	195	9-27-81	2003	Brazoria, Texas
Knapp, Ben	0	0	7.71	2	2	0	0	5	5	4	4	4	2	.263	R	R	6-7	219	11-8-79	1998	Oviedo, Fla.
Loewen, Adam	0	2	2.70	7	7	0	0	23	13	7	7	9	25	.166	L	L	6-6	220	4-9-84	2003	Surrey, B.C.
Mincey, T.W.	1	1	3.52	9	0	0	0	8	7	3	3	4	6	.241	L	L	6-3	194	5-17-80	2001	Winston, Ga.
Neal, Tony	2	1	1.94	19	0	0	1	42	30	15	9	19	43	.212	R	R	6-2	210	9-12-80	2003	Eight Mile, Ala.
Osentowski, Chris	4	5	5.05	19	1	0	0	41	43	30	23	11	33	.265	R	R	6-2	185	3-11-80	2003	Garland, Texas
Patitucci, Mike	0	1	3.75	18	0	0	6	24	21	12	10	9	25	.235	L	L	6-0	195	11-6-80	2002	Uniontown, Pa.
Ray, Chris	2	0	2.82	9	8	0	0	38	32	15	12	10	44	.225	R	R	6-3	200	1-12-82	2003	Tampa, Fla.
Rijo, Fernando	0	0	0.00	2	0	0	0	3	1	0	0	1	4	.125	R	R	5-11	173	11-15-77	1995	La Romana, D.R.
Spillers, Brandon	0	2	2.57	17	0	0	7	14	13	12	4	14	10	.245	R	R	6-3	210	3-12-82	2000	Roberta, Ga.
Tate, Matt	1	1	3.78	10	0	0	0	17	18	9	7	7	12	.290	R	R	6-2	187	9-21-80	1999	Bonifay, Fla.
Teeter, Travis	3	2	3.43	12	6	0	0	45	34	19	17	9	42	.212	R	R	6-1	210	7-13-80	2002	Cohoes, N.Y.
Tiller, James	1	0	2.08	2	2	0	0	9	7	2	2	1	9	.225	R	R	6-5	194	4-13-83	2001	Elysian Fields, Texas
Torres, Carlos	3	2	6.35	16	0	0	0	34	42	26	24	14	18	.300	R	R	6-2	176	7-11-80	1999	Miami, Fla.

BLUEFIELD ORIOLES — Rookie

APPALACHIAN LEAGUE

BATTING	AVG	G	AB	R	H	2B	3B	HR	RBI	BB	SO	SB	CS	SLG	OBP	B	T	HT	WT	DOB	1st Yr	Resides
Ascencion, Quincy	.282	39	131	20	37	8	0	1	18	5	14	5	3	.366	.321	R	R	6-0	215	11-1-82	1999	Willemstad, Curacao
Beck, Alan	.239	16	46	7	11	3	0	1	9	8	11	3	0	.370	.397	R	R	6-0	210	10-5-80	2003	Hudson, N.C.
Blanton, Stephen	.146	23	48	3	7	1	1	0	4	6	15	0	1	.208	.263	L	R	6-4	212	10-14-82	2002	Brooksville, Fla.
Brown, Travis	.315	48	165	27	52	11	0	1	15	15	27	15	5	.400	.383	R	R	5-11	180	8-1-80	2003	Kankakee, Ill.
Cenate, Josh	.000	1	1	0	0	0	0	0	0	0	1	0	0	.000	.000	L	L	6-1	211	1-28-81	1999	Charleston, W.Va.
Colbert, Eddie	.188	27	64	7	12	1	0	0	3	6	21	2	0	.203	.268	S	R	6-3	205	12-3-81	2002	Baltimore, Md.
Costello, Michael	.217	8	23	1	5	0	1	0	7	4	8	0	0	.304	.321	R	R	6-1	210	2-19-81	2003	Baltimore, Md.
Estrada, Robert	.169	18	59	8	10	1	0	2	5	9	10	1	1	.288	.290	R	R	6-2	195	5-31-82	1999	Paracotos, Venez.
George, Kyle	.208	53	168	25	35	7	0	4	16	40	47	3	3	.321	.367	R	R	6-0	195	10-14-81	2003	Miller, Md.
Gilhooly, Tim	.210	46	157	18	33	12	0	5	14	14	71	3	1	.382	.279	R	R	6-3	210	8-31-81	2002	Sugar Land, Texas
Guerrero, Francisco	.250	39	128	13	32	4	1	2	10	3	23	4	2	.344	.274	R	R	6-0	160	5-5-83	2001	San Pedro de Macoris, D.R.
Guerrero, Henry	.216	31	97	13	21	2	0	1	10	8	25	0	0	.268	.274	R	R	6-0	180	4-4-82	2000	Valencia,Venez.
Hadad, Jorge	.163	29	80	8	13	0	0	1	5	5	14	0	0	.200	.212	R	R	6-2	185	5-4-82	2001	Mexico City, Mexico
Houston, Matt	.280	31	100	9	28	4	0	1	6	5	19	1	1	.350	.342	R	R	5-11	195	2-1-82	2003	Oklahoma City, Okla.
Morel, Elvis	.267	58	225	34	60	10	3	3	20	16	30	14	5	.378	.324	R	R	6-0	155	2-25-81	2001	Santo Domingo, D.R.
Rivas, Arturo	.344	9	32	7	11	4	0	0	7	3	6	3	0	.469	.389	R	R	6-0	189	2-2-84	2001	San Francisco, Venez.

BATTING	AVG	G	AB	R	H	2B	3B	HR	RBI	BB	SO	SB	CS	SLG	OBP	B	T	HT	WT	DOB	1st Yr	Resides
Shafer, Corey	.220	60	218	32	48	11	0	7	34	26	60	3	4	.367	.301	L	L	6-2	215	12-17-82	2002	Choctaw, Okla.
Sultemeier, Eric	.200	6	20	1	4	2	0	0	2	1	6	0	1	.300	.273	R	R	6-2	180	6-28-82	2003	New Braunfels, Texas
Thurman, Tim	.250	52	180	18	45	6	1	5	27	18	48	0	4	.378	.332	R	R	6-7	250	12-31-79	2002	Corona Del Mar, Calif.
Wareham, Landon	.211	32	95	12	20	3	0	1	2	9	28	2	1	.274	.286	R	R	5-11	180	9-21-81	2003	Delta, Colo.

GAMES BY POSITION: C—Guerrero 31, Hadad 14, Houston 26. **1B**—Blanton 11, Costello 3, George 3, Thurman 52. **2B**—Brown 2, George 3, Guerrero 3, Morel 33, Wareham 26. **3B**—George 44, Guerrero 23. **SS**—Brown 44, Morel 21. **OF**—Ascencion 35, Beck 7, Colbert 21, Estrada 6, Gilhooly 42, Guerrero 10, Morel 4, Rivas 9, Shafer 58, Sultemeier 6.

PITCHING	W	L	ERA	G	GS	CG	SV	IP	H	R	ER	BB	SO	AVG	B	T	HT	WT	DOB	1st Yr	Resides
Acosta, Richal	2	6	4.06	28	1	0	6	31	32	17	14	7	30	.273	R	R	6-1	145	2-5-84	2001	San Rafael de Yuma, D.R.
Azze, Justin	0	2	3.07	20	1	0	1	29	21	11	10	12	23	.205	L	L	6-3	190	9-14-82	2003	Fountain Valley, Calif.
Brown, Darrius	0	0	27.00	4	0	0	0	2	6	6	6	6	3	.545	L	L	5-11	190	9-10-79	2002	Biloxi, Miss.
Brubaker, Doug	4	3	5.52	22	0	0	0	31	29	20	19	19	33	.241	R	R	6-2	200	1-15-82	2002	Shelton, Wash.
Cahill, Casey	0	0	9.00	2	0	0	0	1	2	1	1	1	3	.400	R	R	6-3	180	3-15-82	2000	New Brunswick, N.J.
Caughey, Trevor	1	7	4.84	13	12	0	0	58	67	41	31	20	64	.281	L	L	6-1	165	11-23-82	2002	San Luis Obispo, Calif.
Hoey, James	2	3	2.79	11	8	0	0	42	33	19	13	19	20	.218	R	R	6-6	200	12-30-82	2003	Hamilton, N.J.
Johnson, James	3	2	3.68	11	11	0	0	51	62	24	21	18	46	.291	R	R	6-5	213	6-27-83	2001	Endicott, N.Y.
McKernan, Richard	0	0	27.00	1	0	0	0	1	2	4	3	3	1	.333	R	R	6-2	225	12-28-80	2003	Newport News, Va.
Mincey, T.W.	0	1	8.10	5	0	0	0	10	15	9	9	3	9	.348	L	L	6-3	194	5-17-80	2001	Winston, Ga.
Penn, Hayden	1	4	4.30	12	11	0	0	52	58	27	25	19	38	.282	R	R	6-3	185	10-13-84	2002	Santee, Calif.
Perez, Carlos	5	5	2.01	12	11	0	0	58	52	23	13	11	58	.232	L	L	6-1	185	5-20-82	2000	San Pedro de Macoris, D.R.
Petrick, Russell	2	0	2.81	22	0	0	0	26	23	13	8	15	27	.227	L	L	6-1	185	2-12-83	2003	Monroe, Wash.
Potter, Josh	1	4	3.11	18	1	0	0	38	35	13	13	16	27	.248	R	R	6-4	170	4-8-83	2001	Philipsburg, Penn.
Reilly, Chris	1	1	4.25	16	7	0	0	42	38	21	20	15	35	.245	R	R	6-6	220	11-17-80	2002	Bound Brook, N.J.
Salas, Marino	1	2	4.89	23	0	0	0	35	36	22	19	9	27	.270	R	R	6-0	181	2-2-81	1998	Hato Mayor, D.R.
Spivey, Melvin	0	0	3.38	5	0	0	1	8	8	4	3	1	9	.242	R	R	6-3	210	12-6-79	2002	Hoover, Ala.
Sutton, Zach	0	0	4.58	18	0	0	2	20	21	11	10	2	14	.256	R	R	6-1	185	1-6-79	2002	Lake Wales, Fla.

SARASOTA ORIOLES — Rookie

GULF COAST LEAGUE

BATTING	AVG	G	AB	R	H	2B	3B	HR	RBI	BB	SO	SB	CS	SLG	OBP	B	T	HT	WT	DOB	1st Yr	Resides
Bigbie, Larry	.333	2	6	1	2	1	0	0	0	0	1	0	0	.500	.333	L	L	6-4	215	11-4-77	1999	Hobart, Ind.
Blanton, Stephen	.077	4	13	1	1	0	0	0	0	1	5	0	0	.077	.143	L	R	6-4	212	10-14-82	2002	Brooksville, Fla.
Cardy, Edwal	.215	22	65	7	14	4	1	0	6	6	16	4	0	.308	.292	R	R	6-3	175	2-4-81	2001	San Pedro de Macoris, D.R.
Costello, Michael	.275	42	120	18	33	6	0	3	26	34	28	1	0	.400	.436	R	R	6-1	210	2-19-81	2003	Baltimore, Md.
Davis, Zach	.222	48	153	21	34	5	1	0	18	21	40	8	4	.268	.311	L	L	6-0	170	2-20-84	2002	Mabelvale, Ark.
Del Carmen, Jose	.222	27	72	4	16	3	0	0	7	2	15	0	0	.264	.240	R	R	6-1	185	8-25-83	2001	San Pedro de Macoris, D.R.
Gredvig, Doug	.238	6	21	2	5	1	0	0	3	4	4	1	0	.286	.346	R	R	6-3	231	8-25-79	2000	Sacramento, Calif.
Guerrero, Francisco	.400	5	15	4	6	1	0	0	1	1	0	0	0	.467	.412	R	R	6-0	160	5-5-83	2001	San Pedro de Macoris, D.R.
Gutierrez, Juan	.335	55	194	29	65	11	4	4	40	27	27	5	2	.495	.422	S	R	6-0	190	8-1-81	2003	Miami, Fla.
Howerton, Matt	.173	42	139	15	24	3	0	2	12	14	45	3	3	.237	.263	R	R	5-11	170	8-29-84	2002	Fort Myers, Fla.
Hummel, Richard	.136	27	59	11	8	0	0	0	3	11	24	4	1	.136	.268	S	R	6-0	160	5-15-85	2003	Sierra Vista, Ariz.
Katotakis, James	.242	19	33	3	8	0	0	0	5	5	10	0	1	.242	.333	L	R	5-11	225	10-27-81	2003	Riverbank, Calif.
Majewski, Val	.333	1	3	0	1	0	0	0	0	1	0	0	0	.333	.500	L	L	6-2	200	6-19-81	2002	Freehold, N.J.
Marmolejos, Hector	.200	33	95	11	19	4	0	1	8	12	27	4	2	.274	.300	R	R	6-4	200	7-29-83	2001	Paraiso, D.R.
Melendez, Alcides	.220	38	100	16	22	5	0	0	4	22	20	6	1	.270	.361	L	R	6-0	165	5-18-83	2001	Valencia, Venez.
Patrick, Sean	.244	31	86	9	21	7	1	1	16	9	15	1	0	.384	.320	R	R	6-1	190	9-14-81	2003	Carterville, Ill.
Piste, Carlos	.140	38	93	18	13	1	0	2	7	13	27	7	1	.215	.283	S	R	6-1	170	3-8-85	2002	Merida, Mexico
Pulley, Matt	.275	48	178	30	49	11	1	2	28	24	51	0	0	.382	.366	L	R	6-3	200	5-15-85	2003	Woodland, Calif.
Scott, Lorenzo	.319	33	116	30	37	8	4	0	24	25	28	11	1	.457	.441	L	L	6-3	210	3-1-82	2003	St. Louis, Mo.
Spears, Nate	.289	56	180	38	52	7	5	1	19	40	32	18	5	.400	.427	L	R	5-11	165	5-3-85	2003	Port Charlotte, Fla.
Whiteside, Eli	.333	1	3	0	1	1	0	0	0	1	1	0	0	.667	.500	R	R	6-2	213	10-22-79	2001	New Albany, Miss.
Zapata, Jose	.177	40	96	14	17	2	1	0	7	11	18	6	0	.219	.273	R	R	6-3	150	4-4-84	2001	Quisqeya, D.R.

GAMES BY POSITION: C—Del Carmen 21, Gutierrez 22, Katotakis 8, Patrick 23, Whiteside 1. **1B**—Blanton 4, Costello 33, Gredvig 2, Gutierrez 18, Patrick 4, Pulley 4, Zapata 3. **2B**—Guerrero 1, Melendez 35, Piste 19, Zapata 15. **3B**—Costello 1, Guerrero 2, Melendez 1, Piste 13, Pulley 45, Zapata 8. **SS**—Piste 7, Spears 48, Zapata 11. **OF**—Bigbie 2, Cardy 20, Davis 42, Guerrero 2, Howerton 41, Hummel 25, Majewski 1, Marmolejos 30, Scott 32.

PITCHING	W	L	ERA	G	GS	CG	SV	IP	H	R	ER	BB	SO	AVG	B	T	HT	WT	DOB	1st Yr	Resides
Azze, Justin	0	0	6.00	2	0	0	0	3	4	3	2	0	1	.333	L	L	6-3	190	9-14-82	2003	Fountain Valley, Calif.
Bartlett, Richard	0	0	0.00	1	1	0	0	3	3	0	0	0	3	.272	R	R	6-3	216	10-6-81	2000	Kennewick, Wash.
Bedard, Erik	0	0	1.13	3	3	0	0	8	4	1	1	2	11	.153	L	L	6-1	191	3-6-79	1999	Navan, Ontario
Bolander, Matt	0	2	9.00	6	3	0	0	11	16	17	11	10	12	.326	R	R	6-2	185	11-2-83	2002	Anderson, Ind.
Brnardic, Ryan	1	1	4.64	12	1	0	1	21	26	12	11	9	17	.295	L	R	6-3	210	11-4-81	2003	Windsor, Ontario
Brocato, Russell	3	3	2.41	13	7	0	1	52	45	19	14	14	30	.229	R	R	6-6	200	11-9-82	2003	New Freedom, Pa.
Burch, Kevin	0	1	4.05	15	0	0	1	20	19	10	9	8	9	.243	R	R	6-0	200	4-18-81	2003	Hollywood, Md.
Camacho, Gustavo	1	6	5.73	10	9	1	0	38	42	32	24	16	27	.285	R	R	6-3	190	10-17-84	2002	Chirgua, Venez.
Childs, Ryan	5	1	1.99	12	7	0	0	54	46	15	12	11	40	.231	L	R	6-3	210	8-16-81	2002	Gaithersburg, Md.
Croushore, Rick	0	0	0.00	1	1	0	0	2	2	0	0	2	1	.222	R	R	6-4	210	8-7-70	1993	Benton, Ark.
Felix, Wilkin	3	2	5.22	16	1	0	1	29	32	20	17	25	30	.296	R	R	6-1	170	3-16-83	1999	San Pedro de Macoris, D.R.
Fleming, Travis	0	0	4.35	9	0	0	5	10	13	7	5	2	6	.295	R	R	6-4	197	9-26-76	1999	McKinleyville, Calif.
Furrow, Jason	1	1	2.33	15	0	0	2	27	28	14	7	10	21	.254	R	L	6-4	184	12-31-84	2003	Converse, Texas
Hernandez, Moises	2	1	4.15	8	4	0	0	22	19	13	10	13	22	.240	R	R	6-1	170	3-18-84	2002	Valencia, Venez.
Lozado, Henry	1	3	3.38	14	1	0	0	29	32	16	11	15	24	.275	R	R	6-3	180	1-19-84	2003	Bayamon, P.R.
Mendez, Wimer	5	1	1.52	12	9	0	0	53	42	13	9	17	41	.214	R	R	6-2	150	1-5-84	2001	Santo Domingo, D.R.
Pascual, Juan	1	2	3.81	14	1	0	0	28	31	21	12	15	19	.271	R	R	6-2	170	12-12-82	1999	San Pedro de Macoris, D.R.
Penn, Hayden	0	0	2.70	1	1	0	0	3	3	1	1	1	4	.272	R	R	6-3	185	10-13-84	2002	Santee, Calif.
Petrick, Russell	0	0	11.57	2	0	0	0	2	3	4	3	2	2	.272	L	L	6-1	185	2-12-83	2003	Monroe, Wash.
Ramirez, Luis	6	4	2.12	12	11	0	0	59	45	17	14	14	76	.208	R	R	6-4	180	6-9-82	2000	Barcelona, Venez.
Sutton, Zach	0	0	0.00	2	0	0	0	2	2	1	0	0	2	.250	R	R	6-1	185	1-6-79	2002	Lake Wales, Fla.
Tate, Matt	3	0	3.26	9	0	0	1	19	14	7	7	10	10	.208	R	R	6-2	187	9-21-80	1999	Bonifay, Fla.

BOSTON RED SOX

BY JOHN TOMASE

The question will be asked by future generations of Red Sox fans. And they may never get a satisfactory answer.

Why didn't Grady lift Pedro?

A magical season derailed in the eighth inning of Game Seven of the American League Championship Series against the Yankees, when manager Grady Little left a spent Pedro Martinez on the mound just five outs from the World Series. A 5-2 lead turned into a 5-5 tie, the Yankees prevailed in 11, and a franchise known for agonizing near-misses had plumbed maybe its deepest depth yet.

The finish marred an otherwise marvelous campaign. Buoyed by baseball's best offense and inspired by their rallying cry of "Cowboy up," the Red Sox earned the American League wild card, overcame a 2-0 deficit to the Athletics in the Division Series and nearly reached their first World Series since 1986.

Rookie general manager Theo Epstein dispelled concerns about his age by sticking to a plan. The 29-year-old weathered early criticism of his refusal to swap Casey Fossum for Bartolo Colon. He passed up marquee acquisitions in favor of lesser-known players who went on to form baseball's most potent offense.

Bill Mueller arrived from San Francisco a lifetime .286 hitter and led the AL in batting at .326. Set free by Minnesota, David Ortiz set career highs in home runs (31) and RBIs (101) and contended for the AL MVP. Two prospects netted second baseman Todd Walker, who set a Red Sox postseason record for home runs (five) and nearly won the ALCS. After a month of international squabbling, Kevin Millar escaped Japan and became a clubhouse leader.

Further buoyed by career years from Jason Varitek and Trot Nixon, the Red Sox scored a league-best 961 runs and slugged .491 to break the 1927 Yankees record of .489. Six players hit at least 25 home runs, and eight drove in at least 85 runs.

Pedro Martinez

DAN HENRICKSON

Kelly Shoppach

PLAYERS of the YEAR

MAJOR LEAGUE: Pedro Martinez, rhp

Martinez worked in only 187 innings, but he led American League pitchers with a 2.22 ERA. He also finished with 206 strikeouts—one behind league leader Esteban Loaiza of the White Sox—while going 14-4.

MINOR LEAGUE: Kelly Shoppach, c

Offseason rotator cuff surgery pushed Shoppach's 2003 season debut back a bit, but he returned to action as good as new, hitting .282-12-60 for Double-A Portland while throwing out 30 percent of basestealers.

ORGANIZATION LEADERS

BATTING		
*AVG	Sean McGowan, Portland/Sarasota	.320
R	Kevin Youkilis, Pawtucket/Portland	83
H	Andy Abad, Pawtucket	153
TB	Andy Abad, Pawtucket	233
2B	Andy Abad, Pawtucket	35
3B	Anton French, Pawtucket	10
HR	Earl Snyder, Pawtucket	22
RBI	Andy Abad, Pawtucket	93
BB	Kevin Youkilis, Pawtucket/Portland	104
SO	Jeremy Owens, Portland	161
SB	Anton French, Pawtucket	40
*SLG	Andy Dominique, Pawtucket/Portland	.508
*OBP	Kevin Youkilis, Pawtucket/Portland	.441
PITCHING		
W	Bronson Arroyo, Pawtucket	12
L	Luis Villarreal, Augusta	11
#ERA	Jamie Brown, Pawtucket	2.95
G	Three tied at	51
CG	Tim Kester, Portland	3
SV	Juan Perez, Portland/Sarasota	18
IP	Charlie Zink, Portland/Sarasota	175
BB	Charlie Zink, Portland/Sarasota	78
SO	Bronson Arroyo, Pawtucket	155

*Minimum 250 At-Bats #Minimum 75 Innings

The offensive explosion was counterbalanced by a bullpen implosion. Red Sox relievers lost a 4-1 ninth inning lead at Tampa Bay on Opening Day, and it got worse from there. Trying to operate without a traditional closer in what pundits viewed as Epstein's biggest gamble, the pen blew 11 saves before July 1. Alan Embree, Chad Fox, rookie Brandon Lyon and even rehabbing Robert Person tried the role before Byung-Hyun Kim stabilized it on July 1. The combustible pen made for a series of exciting finishes. The Red Sox won a league-best 25 games in their last at-bat and lost almost as many in heartbreaking fashion.

Epstein remained active during the season, acquiring Kim for Shea Hillenbrand in May, then landing Scott Sauerbeck, Scott Williamson and Jeff Suppan at the trading deadline. Kim pitched well until late August. Ex-Pirates Sauerbeck and Suppan disappointed. Williamson regained his 96 mph fastball and moxie in the postseason, saving all three ALCS victories.

After blowing Game One of the Division Series, Red Sox relievers experienced a playoff rebirth, posting a 1.31 ERA in 12 games. Mike Timlin retired his first 23 batters and allowed just one hit. Embree pitched seven scoreless innings. Williamson struck out 14 in six innings.

Little will be haunted for not summoning one of them sooner in Game Seven. Until then, he deserved credit for avoiding the controversies that plagued previous outfits.

In the minors, top prospect Kevin Youkilis reached base in 71 straight games between Double-A Trenton and Triple-A Pawtucket on his way to a franchise-best .441 on-base percentage. The season also witnessed the emergence of Trenton lefthander Jorge de la Rosa and Class A Augusta third baseman Chad Spann.

BOSTON RED SOX

Manager: Grady Little.

2003 Record: 95-67, .586 (2nd, AL East).

BATTING	AVG	G	AB	R	H	2B	3B	HR	RBI	BB	SO	SB	CS	SLG	OBP	B	T	HT	WT	DOB	1st Yr	Resides
Abad, Andy	.118	9	17	1	2	0	0	0	0	2	5	0	1	.118	.211	L	L	6-1	180	8-25-72	1993	Jupiter, Fla.
Brown, Adrian	.200	9	15	2	3	0	0	0	1	1	4	2	0	.200	.250	S	R	6-0	200	2-7-74	1992	Summit, Miss.
Collier, Lou	.000	4	1	0	0	0	0	0	0	0	0	0	1	.000	.000	R	R	5-10	190	8-21-73	1993	Chicago, Ill.
Damon, Johnny	.273	145	608	103	166	32	6	12	67	68	74	30	6	.405	.345	L	L	6-2	190	11-5-73	1992	Overland Park, Kan.
Garciaparra, Nomar	.301	156	658	120	198	37	13	28	105	39	61	19	5	.524	.345	R	R	6-0	190	7-23-73	1994	Boston, Mass.
Giambi, Jeremy	.197	50	127	15	25	5	0	5	15	26	42	1	0	.354	.342	L	L	5-11	210	9-30-74	1996	Las Vegas, Nevada
Haselman, Bill	.000	4	3	0	0	0	0	0	0	0	1	0	0	.000	.000	R	R	6-3	220	5-25-66	1987	New Castle, Wash.
Hillenbrand, Shea	.303	49	185	20	56	17	0	3	38	7	26	1	0	.443	.335	R	R	6-1	210	7-27-75	1996	Mesa, Ariz.
Jackson, Damian	.261	109	161	34	42	7	0	1	13	8	28	16	8	.323	.294	R	R	5-11	180	8-16-73	1992	Concord, Calif.
Kapler, Gabe	.291	68	158	29	46	11	1	4	23	14	23	4	2	.449	.349	R	R	6-2	210	7-31-75	1995	Sherman Oaks, Calif.
McCarty, David	.407	16	27	4	11	3	0	1	6	2	7	0	0	.630	.448	R	L	6-5	215	11-23-69	1991	Piedmont, Calif.
2-team (8 Oakland)	.340	24	53	6	18	5	0	1	8	3	14	0	0	.491	.368							
Merloni, Lou	.233	15	30	4	7	1	0	0	1	4	8	0	0	.267	.324	R	R	5-10	200	4-6-71	1993	Framingham, Mass.
Millar, Kevin	.276	148	544	83	150	30	1	25	96	60	108	3	2	.472	.348	R	R	6-0	210	9-24-71	1993	Encino, Calif.
Mirabelli, Doug	.258	62	163	23	42	13	0	6	18	11	36	0	0	.448	.307	R	R	6-1	220	10-18-70	1992	Orlando, Fla.
Mueller, Bill	.326	146	524	85	171	45	5	19	85	59	77	1	4	.540	.398	S	R	5-10	180	3-17-71	1993	Maryland Heights, Mo.
Nixon, Trot	.306	134	441	81	135	24	6	28	87	65	96	4	2	.578	.396	L	L	6-2	210	4-11-74	1993	Wilmington, N.C.
Ortiz, David	.288	128	448	79	129	39	2	31	101	58	83	0	0	.592	.369	L	L	6-4	230	11-18-75	1993	Haina, D.R.
Ramirez, Manny	.325	154	569	117	185	36	1	37	104	97	94	3	1	.587	.427	R	R	6-0	200	5-30-72	1991	Fort Lauderdale, Fla.
Sanchez, Freddy	.235	20	34	6	8	2	0	0	2	0	8	0	0	.294	.235	R	R	5-11	180	12-21-77	2000	Burbank, Calif.
Varitek, Jason	.273	142	451	63	123	31	1	25	85	51	106	3	2	.512	.351	S	R	6-2	230	4-11-72	1995	Suwanee, Ga.
Walker, Todd	.283	144	587	92	166	38	4	13	85	48	54	1	1	.428	.333	L	R	6-0	190	5-25-73	1994	Castle Rock, Colo.

PITCHING	W	L	ERA	G	GS	CG	SV	IP	H	R	ER	BB	SO	AVG	B	T	HT	WT	DOB	1st Yr	Resides
Almonte, Hector	0	1	8.22	7	0	0	0	8	9	7	7	7	6	.310	R	R	6-2	190	10-17-75	1993	Santo Domingo, D.R.
Arroyo, Bronson	0	0	2.08	6	0	0	1	17	10	5	4	4	14	.163	R	R	6-5	190	2-24-77	1995	Brooksville, Fla.
Burkett, John	12	9	5.15	32	30	1	0	182	202	108	104	47	107	.280	R	R	6-3	210	11-28-64	1983	Southlake, Texas
Chen, Bruce	0	1	5.11	5	2	0	0	12	12	8	7	2	12	.255	L	L	6-1	210	6-19-77	1994	Panama City, Panama
Embree, Alan	4	1	4.25	65	0	0	1	55	49	26	26	16	45	.241	L	L	6-2	190	1-23-70	1990	Vancouver, Wash.
Fossum, Casey	6	5	5.47	19	14	0	1	79	82	55	48	34	63	.269	S	L	6-1	160	1-9-78	1999	Waco, Texas
Fox, Chad	1	2	4.50	17	0	0	3	18	19	10	9	17	19	.263	R	R	6-3	190	9-3-70	1992	Houston, Texas
Howry, Bobby	0	0	12.46	4	0	0	0	4	11	6	6	3	4	.478	L	R	6-5	220	8-4-73	1994	Glendale, Ariz.
Jones, Todd	2	1	5.52	26	0	0	0	29	32	19	18	13	31	.268	S	R	6-3	230	4-24-68	1989	Pell City, Ala.
Kim, Byung-Hyun	8	5	3.18	49	5	0	16	79	70	38	28	18	69	.229	R	R	5-11	180	1-21-79	1999	Gwangju, Korea
Lowe, Derek	17	7	4.47	33	33	1	0	203	216	113	101	72	110	.271	R	R	6-6	210	6-1-73	1991	Fort Myers, Fla.
Lyon, Brandon	4	6	4.12	49	0	0	9	59	73	33	27	19	50	.295	R	R	6-1	180	8-10-79	2000	Salt Lake City, Utah
Martinez, Pedro	14	4	2.22	29	29	3	0	187	147	52	46	47	206	.214	R	R	5-11	180	10-25-71	1988	Santo Domingo, D.R.
Mendoza, Ramiro	3	5	6.75	37	5	0	0	67	98	51	50	20	36	.348	R	R	6-2	190	6-15-72	1992	Los Santos, Panama
Person, Robert	0	0	7.71	7	0	0	1	12	11	10	10	8	10	.250	R	R	6-0	190	1-8-69	1989	Clearwater, Fla.
Rupe, Ryan	1	1	6.30	4	1	0	0	10	13	9	7	1	7	.302	R	R	6-5	240	3-31-75	1998	Houston, Texas
Sauerbeck, Scott	0	1	6.48	26	0	0	0	17	17	14	12	18	18	.265	R	L	6-3	200	11-9-71	1994	Cleves, Ohio
Seanez, Rudy	0	1	6.23	9	0	0	0	9	11	7	6	6	9	.297	R	R	5-11	200	10-20-68	1986	El Centro, Calif.
Shiell, Jason	2	0	4.63	17	0	0	1	23	23	13	12	17	23	.252	R	R	6-0	180	10-19-76	1995	Savannah, Ga.
Suppan, Jeff	3	4	5.57	11	10	0	0	63	70	41	39	20	32	.281	R	R	6-2	210	1-2-75	1993	Los Angeles, Calif.
Timlin, Mike	6	4	3.55	72	0	0	2	84	77	37	33	9	65	.239	R	R	6-4	210	3-10-66	1987	Oldsmar, Fla.
Tolar, Kevin	0	0	9.00	6	0	0	0	4	5	5	4	2	3	.312	R	L	6-3	230	1-28-71	1989	Sarasota, Fla.
Wakefield, Tim	11	7	4.09	35	33	0	1	202	193	106	92	71	169	.246	R	R	6-2	210	8-2-66	1988	Melbourne, Fla.
White, Matt	0	1	27.00	3	0	0	0	4	10	11	11	3	0	.526	R	L	6-1	180	8-19-77	1998	Windsor, Mass.
Williamson, Scott	0	1	6.20	24	0	0	0	20	20	15	14	9	21	.253	R	R	6-0	180	2-17-76	1997	Friendswood, Texas
Woodard, Steve	1	0	5.09	7	0	0	0	18	23	10	10	5	12	.310	L	R	6-4	210	5-15-75	1994	Hartselle, Ala.

FIELDING

Catcher	PCT	G	PO	A	E	DP	PB
Haselman	1.000	2	2	0	0	0	0
Mirabelli	.988	55	319	21	4	3	14
Varitek	.990	137	854	43	9	8	6

First Base	PCT	G	PO	A	E	DP
Abad	.973	7	35	1	1	2
Hillenbrand	1.000	28	193	13	0	13
Jackson	1.000	2	4	0	0	0
Kapler	1.000	1	3	0	0	0
McCarty	.962	5	23	2	1	2
Millar	.996	101	858	81	4	80
Mirabelli	.857	2	5	1	1	0
Ortiz	.992	45	342	30	3	20

Second Base	PCT	G	PO	A	E	DP
Jackson	.960	38	18	54	3	6
Merloni	1.000	7	5	5	0	3
Mueller	1.000	10	22	17	0	7
Sanchez	1.000	3	9	2	0	1
Walker	.975	139	235	391	16	78

Third Base	PCT	G	PO	A	E	DP
Collier	1.000	2	1	1	0	0
Hillenbrand	.958	29	26	42	3	3
Jackson	.889	3	1	7	1	0
Merloni	1.000	7	6	14	0	1
Mueller	.951	135	76	235	16	22
Sanchez	1.000	7	4	12	0	0

Shortstop	PCT	G	PO	A	E	DP
Garciaparra	.971	156	216	456	20	83
Jackson	.881	18	19	18	5	4
Mueller	1.000	1	1	0	0	0
Sanchez	1.000	6	2	9	0	1

Outfield	PCT	G	PO	A	E	DP
Abad	.000	1	0	0	0	0
Brown	1.000	9	9	0	0	0
Collier	.000	2	0	0	0	0
Damon	.997	144	362	7	1	2
Giambi	.944	11	17	0	1	0
Jackson	1.000	38	51	4	0	1
Kapler	.932	61	77	5	6	1
McCarty	1.000	8	7	0	0	0
Merloni	.000	1	0	0	0	0
Millar	.981	31	50	3	1	0
Nixon	.983	130	231	4	4	0
Ramirez	.982	128	207	11	4	1

FARM SYSTEM

Director, Player Development: Ben Cherington.

Class	Farm Team	League	W	L	Pct.	Finish*	Manager(s)	First Yr.
AAA	Pawtucket (R.I.) Red Sox	International	83	61	.576	1st (14)	Buddy Bailey	1973
AA	Portland (Me.) Sea Dogs	Eastern	72	70	.507	t-5th (12)	Ron Johnson	2003
High A	Sarasota (Fla.) Red Sox	Florida State	63	67	.485	8th (12)	Tim Leiper	1994
Low A	Augusta (Ga.) GreenJackets	South Atlantic	49	87	.360	16th (16)	Russ Morman	1999
SS A	Lowell (Mass.) Spinners	New York-Penn	39	35	.527	6th (14)	Jon Deeble/Lynn Jones	1996
Rookie	Fort Myers (Fla.) Red Sox	Gulf Coast	33	26	.559	3rd (14)	Ralph Treuel	1993

*Finish in overall standings (No. of teams in league)

PAWTUCKET RED SOX — Class AAA

INTERNATIONAL LEAGUE

BATTING	AVG	G	AB	R	H	2B	3B	HR	RBI	BB	SO	SB	CS	SLG	OBP	B	T	HT	WT	DOB	1st Yr	Resides
Abad, Andy	.304	134	504	78	153	35	3	13	93	55	67	0	3	.462	.372	L	L	6-1	180	8-25-72	1993	Jupiter, Fla.
Brown, Adrian	.282	122	482	81	136	16	3	5	32	48	81	34	11	.359	.347	S	R	6-0	200	2-7-74	1992	Summit, Miss.
Charles, Frank	.194	20	72	9	14	0	0	4	9	1	21	0	0	.361	.213	R	R	6-3	215	2-23-69	1991	Brockport, N.Y.
Collier, Lou	.293	103	392	58	115	19	4	14	69	32	94	8	7	.469	.354	R	R	5-10	190	8-21-73	1993	Chicago, Ill.
Coquillette, Trace	.305	68	233	36	71	21	0	5	30	17	65	3	3	.459	.376	R	R	5-11	180	6-4-74	1993	Orangevale, Calif.
Coste, Chris	.188	29	96	5	18	5	0	1	8	4	18	0	0	.271	.218	R	R	6-1	200	2-4-73	1995	Fargo, N.D.
Crespo, Cesar	.267	132	465	69	124	31	3	9	58	40	93	13	8	.404	.323	S	R	5-10	180	5-23-79	1997	Miami Beach, Fla.
Dominique, Andy	.304	79	289	42	88	18	0	13	57	22	45	2	1	.502	.364	R	R	6-0	220	10-30-75	1997	Granada Hills, Calif.
Dransfeldt, Kelly	.210	66	214	29	45	11	1	6	34	16	53	0	1	.355	.274	R	R	6-2	190	4-16-75	1996	Morris, Ill.
2-team (46 Louisville)	.212	112	354	44	75	20	3	8	46	25	87	0	2	.353	.269							
French, Anton	.293	98	314	51	92	9	10	2	22	30	61	40	12	.404	.357	L	R	5-11	170	7-25-75	1993	St. Louis, Mo.
Giambi, Jeremy	.229	10	35	6	8	4	0	1	4	7	15	0	0	.429	.357	L	L	5-11	210	9-30-74	1996	Las Vegas, Nevada
Goelz, Jim	.154	8	26	1	4	1	0	0	1	0	7	0	0	.192	.154	R	R	5-10	170	2-13-76	1998	St. James, N.Y.
Haselman, Bill	.225	79	280	37	63	6	0	6	24	9	46	1	1	.311	.247	R	R	6-3	220	5-25-66	1987	New Castle, Wash.
Headley, Justin	.237	12	38	4	9	1	0	1	4	0	6	0	0	.342	.262	L	L	6-2	200	4-27-76	1998	Memphis, Tenn.
Leon, Donny	.000	1	4	0	0	0	0	0	0	0	3	0	0	.000	.000	S	R	6-2	180	5-7-76	1995	Ponce, P.R.
Matthews, Lamont	.167	7	18	3	3	1	0	0	2	3	7	1	1	.222	.286	L	L	6-2	210	6-15-78	1999	Petersburg, Va.
Mottola, Chad	.319	21	72	11	23	3	2	3	18	6	10	0	1	.542	.380	R	R	6-3	220	10-15-71	1992	Casselberry, Fla.
2-team (56 Durham)	.274	77	285	35	78	10	3	9	46	25	47	6	4	.425	.334							
Sanchez, Freddy	.341	58	211	46	72	17	0	5	25	31	36	8	0	.493	.430	R	R	5-11	180	12-21-77	2000	Burbank, Calif.
Santos, Angel	.238	70	214	25	51	8	0	5	20	32	50	9	4	.346	.339	S	R	5-11	170	8-14-79	1997	Cayey, P.R.
Snyder, Earl	.255	130	467	61	119	25	1	22	71	24	113	0	0	.454	.299	R	R	6-0	200	5-6-76	1998	New Britain, Conn.
Youkilis, Kevin	.165	32	109	9	18	3	0	2	15	18	21	0	1	.248	.295	R	R	6-1	220	3-15-79	2001	Cincinnati, Ohio
Zuleta, Julio	.275	55	204	28	56	11	0	12	49	13	47	0	0	.505	.336	R	R	6-5	230	3-28-75	1993	Chandler, Ariz.

PITCHING	W	L	ERA	G	GS	CG	SV	IP	H	R	ER	BB	SO	AVG	B	T	HT	WT	DOB	1st Yr	Resides
Aldred, Scott	2	1	4.63	11	0	0	0	12	10	6	6	7	11	.227	L	L	6-4	190	6-12-68	1987	Fenton, Mich.
Almonte, Hector	3	0	1.73	21	0	0	9	26	16	5	5	6	28	.175	R	R	6-2	190	10-17-75	1993	Santo Domingo, D.R.
Arroyo, Bronson	12	6	3.43	24	24	1	0	150	148	66	57	23	155	.251	R	R	6-5	190	2-24-77	1995	Brooksville, Fla.
Brown, Jamie	4	1	2.26	18	3	0	1	52	40	17	13	5	39	.209	R	R	6-2	200	3-31-77	1997	Collinsville, Miss.
2-team (13 Buffalo)	8	5	2.95	31	13	0	1	113	85	43	37	22	65	.207							
Cameron, Ryan	1	3	4.79	27	1	0	1	56	56	32	30	34	46	.256	R	R	6-1	175	9-13-77	1998	Williamstown, Mass.
Chen, Bruce	5	5	4.24	16	15	1	1	85	80	44	40	15	73	.243	L	L	6-1	210	6-19-77	1994	Panama City, Panama
Coste, Chris	0	0	9.00	2	0	0	0	2	2	2	2	1	1	.000	R	R	6-1	200	2-4-73	1995	Fargo, N.D.
Davey, Tom	1	2	3.45	16	0	0	0	29	28	14	11	16	28	.254	R	R	6-7	230	9-11-73	1994	San Diego, Calif.
De La Rosa, Jorge	1	2	3.75	5	5	0	0	24	27	14	10	12	17	.278	L	L	6-1	190	4-5-81	1998	San Nicolas de los Garza, Mexico
Elmore, Chris	2	2	5.24	8	8	0	0	34	37	20	20	18	19	.286	L	L	6-1	190	4-28-77	2000	Virginia Beach, Va.
Fossum, Casey	1	0	3.46	5	4	0	1	13	11	5	5	5	14	.234	S	L	6-1	160	1-9-78	1999	Waco, Texas
Foster, Kris	1	1	7.11	4	0	0	0	6	14	5	5	2	3	.466	R	R	6-1	210	8-30-74	1992	Lehigh Acres, Fla.
Fox, Chad	0	0	13.50	1	0	0	0	1	3	3	2	1	2	.500	R	R	6-3	190	9-3-70	1992	Houston, Texas
Glaser, Eric	2	0	4.82	4	1	0	0	9	9	5	5	5	7	.250	R	R	6-6	230	1-23-78	1997	Fort Thomas, Ky.
Gonzalez, Dicky	8	8	4.04	27	25	1	0	152	180	77	68	29	104	.295	R	R	5-11	170	12-21-78	1996	Bayamon, P.R.
Gonzalez, Mike	0	0	0.00	2	0	0	1	2	2	0	0	1	2	.285	R	L	6-2	210	5-23-78	1997	Pasadena, Texas
Hebson, Bryan	2	1	2.73	18	0	0	0	26	17	9	8	6	22	.177	R	R	6-5	210	3-12-76	1997	Phenix City, Ala.
Howry, Bobby	2	0	1.06	13	0	0	0	17	14	2	2	1	10	.215	L	R	6-5	220	8-4-73	1994	Glendale, Ariz.
Izquierdo, Hansel	0	1	11.48	4	3	0	0	13	21	17	17	6	4	.355	R	R	6-1	200	1-2-77	1995	Miami, Fla.
Johnson, James	0	0	0.00	3	0	0	0	3	0	0	0	0	3	.000	S	L	6-1	170	8-7-76	1998	San Diego, Calif.
Kaye, Justin	2	2	2.49	31	0	0	4	43	37	16	12	19	24	.235	R	R	6-4	190	6-9-76	1995	Fort Lauderdale, Fla.
Lyon, Brandon	0	0	3.24	5	0	0	0	8	7	3	3	2	7	.218	R	R	6-1	180	8-10-79	2000	Salt Lake City, Utah
Martinez, Anastacio	2	1	1.93	8	0	0	0	14	12	3	3	3	15	.226	R	R	6-2	180	11-3-78	1998	Santo Domingo, D.R.
Mendoza, Ramiro	0	0	2.00	4	0	0	1	9	8	2	2	0	8	.242	R	R	6-2	190	6-15-72	1992	Los Santos, Panama
Person, Robert	0	0	4.70	6	1	0	1	8	5	4	4	5	6	.178	R	R	6-0	190	1-8-69	1989	Clearwater, Fla.
Rupe, Ryan	8	4	3.26	20	18	0	0	102	93	50	37	19	77	.237	R	R	6-5	240	3-31-75	1998	Houston, Texas
Seanez, Rudy	2	2	6.10	17	0	0	3	21	20	14	14	10	24	.253	R	R	5-11	200	10-20-68	1986	El Centro, Calif.
Shibilo, Andy	2	1	4.76	38	1	0	1	45	46	26	24	22	49	.261	R	R	6-7	220	9-16-76	1998	Belleville, N.J.
Shiell, Jason	3	2	2.42	20	0	0	2	26	26	11	7	6	22	.262	R	R	6-0	180	10-19-76	1995	Savannah, Ga.
Stewart, Paul	6	8	4.30	27	24	0	0	121	133	79	58	42	76	.275	R	R	6-5	220	10-21-78	1996	Raleigh, N.C.
Tolar, Kevin	5	1	2.27	47	0	0	4	32	19	9	8	17	34	.177	R	L	6-3	230	1-28-71	1989	Sarasota, Fla.
White, Matt	0	0	0.00	2	0	0	0	3	1	1	0	0	5	.083	R	L	6-1	180	8-19-77	1998	Windsor, Mass.
Woodard, Steve	6	7	4.69	31	11	0	2	94	103	55	49	12	58	.279	L	R	6-4	210	5-15-75	1994	Hartselle, Ala.

FIELDING

Catcher	PCT	G	PO	A	E	DP	PB
Charles	.993	19	130	8	1	0	7
Coste	.961	8	46	3	2	1	1
Dominique	.992	51	322	30	3	1	5
Haselman	.989	72	497	39	6	2	3

First Base	PCT	G	PO	A	E	DP
Abad	.995	90	700	36	4	54
Collier	1.000	1	9	1	0	3
Coquillette	.000	1	0	0	0	0
Coste	.978	6	44	0	1	3
Dominique	1.000	3	17	0	0	1
Headley	1.000	3	23	1	0	0
Snyder	1.000	14	92	14	0	5
Zuleta	.979	36	260	22	6	23

Second Base	PCT	G	PO	A	E	DP
Coquillette	.984	50	79	106	3	22
Crespo	.967	42	77	98	6	19
Goelz	.857	1	3	3	1	1
Sanchez	.989	21	36	50	1	9
Santos	.982	37	71	93	3	20

Third Base	PCT	G	PO	A	E	DP
Collier	1.000	1	1	2	0	0
Crespo	.500	2	1	1	2	0
Sanchez	1.000	2	0	6	0	0
Santos	1.000	9	3	9	0	1
Snyder	.957	103	86	161	11	17
Youkilis	.952	29	29	50	4	2
Zuleta	1.000	1	1	2	0	0

Shortstop	PCT	G	PO	A	E	DP
Collier	.961	22	25	49	3	6
Crespo	1.000	2	2	2	0	0
Dransfeldt	.963	65	79	178	10	31
Goelz	1.000	2	3	6	0	1
Sanchez	.979	35	52	89	3	19
Santos	.927	27	28	73	8	12

Outfield	PCT	G	PO	A	E	DP
Abad	.982	27	53	1	1	0
Brown	.983	121	280	4	5	1
Collier	.973	72	137	9	4	1
Coquillette	1.000	11	10	0	0	0
Crespo	.959	79	155	7	7	0
French	.978	92	217	3	5	0
Goelz	1.000	5	7	1	0	0
Headley	1.000	9	17	1	0	1
Matthews	1.000	7	13	0	0	0
Mottola	.966	15	28	0	1	0
Snyder	1.000	14	16	3	0	1

PORTLAND SEA DOGS — Class AA

EASTERN LEAGUE

BATTING	AVG	G	AB	R	H	2B	3B	HR	RBI	BB	SO	SB	CS	SLG	OBP	B	T	HT	WT	DOB	1st Yr	Resides
Blasi, Blake	.182	4	11	1	2	0	0	0	0	1	1	0	0	.182	.250	S	R	5-8	160	3-23-79	2000	Wichita, Kan.
Borowiak, Zach	.182	3	11	0	2	0	0	0	0	0	2	0	0	.182	.182	R	R	6-1	185	5-18-81	2003	Nashville, Ill.
Brisson, Dustin	.223	60	211	23	47	15	0	4	32	14	42	4	1	.351	.274	L	R	6-3	210	3-18-78	2000	West Palm Beach, Fla.
Brown, Tonayne	.228	53	189	25	43	6	2	1	26	13	40	2	2	.296	.284	R	L	5-11	190	8-24-77	1998	Tallahassee, Fla.
Castro, Nelson	.222	16	63	11	14	2	0	0	1	6	14	6	3	.254	.310	S	R	5-10	200	6-4-76	1994	Monte Cristi, D.R.
Catalanotte, Greg	.200	21	65	10	13	6	0	1	10	6	24	1	0	.338	.278	S	R	6-3	210	6-18-77	1999	Glendale, Ariz.
Coquillette, Trace	.247	48	158	23	39	7	1	7	21	22	46	5	5	.437	.365	R	R	5-11	180	6-4-74	1993	Orangevale, Calif.
Dominique, Andy	.361	32	97	18	35	7	0	3	21	16	15	0	0	.526	.454	R	R	6-0	220	10-30-75	1997	Granada Hills, Calif.
Goelz, Jim	.232	56	181	22	42	6	0	0	9	7	25	1	2	.265	.267	R	R	5-10	170	2-13-76	1998	St. James, N.Y.
2-team (6 Buffalo)	.230	62	196	24	45	7	0	0	10	8	26	1	2	.265	.266							
Hattig, John	.219	8	32	3	7	2	0	0	1	2	11	0	0	.281	.265	S	R	6-2	210	2-27-80	1999	Dededo, Guam
Haverbusch, Kevin	.236	59	203	19	48	12	1	5	30	18	44	0	4	.379	.323	R	R	6-3	200	6-16-76	1997	Massapequa, N.Y.
Headley, Justin	.258	116	457	69	118	23	2	9	61	40	68	6	3	.376	.324	L	L	6-2	200	4-27-76	1998	Memphis, Tenn.
Kapler, Gabe	.333	1	3	1	1	1	0	0	0	0	1	0	0	.667	.333	R	R	6-2	210	7-31-75	1995	Sherman Oaks, Calif.
Leon, Carlos	.301	75	259	45	78	10	4	2	23	21	34	10	6	.394	.368	S	R	5-10	160	8-31-79	1997	Cabimas, Venez.
Loyd, Brian	.290	29	100	9	29	6	0	1	11	7	11	1	0	.380	.343	R	R	6-2	200	12-3-73	1996	Yorba Linda, Calif.
McGowan, Sean	.311	79	299	41	93	21	0	6	39	20	38	3	0	.441	.351	R	R	6-6	240	5-15-77	1999	Burlington, Mass.
Nathans, John	.194	25	72	5	14	3	0	0	4	2	25	0	0	.236	.237	R	R	6-1	210	6-10-79	2001	Warwick, N.Y.
Nieves, Raul	.249	71	253	31	63	8	1	0	21	24	28	5	6	.289	.317	S	R	6-2	180	1-1-79	2000	Barranquitas, P.R.
Owens, Jeremy	.263	136	471	63	124	25	8	21	68	41	161	15	7	.484	.326	R	R	6-1	200	12-9-76	1998	Johnson City, Tenn.
Schrager, Tony	.252	117	412	48	104	28	1	9	54	57	85	3	5	.391	.347	R	R	6-1	170	6-14-77	1998	Omaha, Neb.
Sherrod, Justin	.259	127	448	69	116	28	2	15	74	47	143	6	5	.431	.346	R	R	6-2	200	1-11-78	2000	Boynton Beach, Fla.
Shoppach, Kelly	.282	92	340	45	96	30	2	12	60	35	83	0	0	.488	.353	R	R	5-11	210	4-29-80	2001	Fort Worth, Texas
Smith, Jeff	.286	10	35	4	10	2	0	1	5	1	8	0	0	.429	.306	L	R	6-3	210	6-17-74	1995	Naples, Fla.
Youkilis, Kevin	.327	94	312	74	102	23	1	6	37	86	40	7	0	.465	.487	R	R	6-1	220	3-15-79	2001	Cincinnati, Ohio

PITCHING	W	L	ERA	G	GS	CG	SV	IP	H	R	ER	BB	SO	AVG	B	T	HT	WT	DOB	1st Yr	Resides
Adams, Brian	0	1	4.76	7	0	0	0	11	8	6	6	15	7	.210	L	L	6-3	190	10-2-77	2000	Bishopville, S.C.
Aldred, Scott	0	0	0.84	18	0	0	8	21	13	3	2	6	18	.178	L	L	6-4	190	6-12-68	1987	Fenton, Mich.
Cameron, Ryan	2	4	3.14	10	9	1	0	52	49	21	18	17	37	.252	R	R	6-1	175	9-13-77	1998	Williamstown, Mass.
Chapman, Jake	6	1	3.45	35	0	0	0	57	65	35	22	21	49	.283	R	L	6-1	190	1-11-74	1996	Rensselaer, Ind.
De la Rosa, Jorge	6	3	2.80	22	20	0	1	100	87	39	31	36	102	.236	L	L	6-1	190	4-5-81	1998	San Nicolas, Mexico
Elmore, Chris	1	1	3.65	3	3	0	0	12	11	5	5	10	7	.239	L	L	6-1	190	4-28-77	2000	Virginia Beach, Va.
Fossum, Casey	0	1	6.75	3	2	0	0	4	5	3	3	3	7	.294	S	L	6-1	160	1-9-78	1999	Waco, Texas
Fox, Chad	0	0	0.00	1	0	0	0	1	1	0	0	2	2	.200	R	R	6-3	190	9-3-70	1992	Houston, Texas
Gamble, Jerome	2	0	4.91	2	2	0	0	11	10	6	6	1	11	.238	R	R	6-2	200	4-5-80	1998	Alexander City, Ala.
Glaser, Eric	3	3	4.10	29	7	0	0	75	65	38	34	25	52	.230	R	R	6-6	230	1-23-78	1997	Fort Thomas, Ky.
Herndon, Junior	9	8	4.85	25	23	2	0	134	154	79	72	31	69	.288	R	R	6-1	190	9-11-78	1997	Craig, Colo.
Johnson, James	3	5	3.74	38	0	0	5	55	40	24	23	20	66	.202	S	L	6-1	170	8-7-76	1998	San Diego, Calif.
Kaercher, Matt	0	0	27.00	1	0	0	0	0	3	1	1	0	0	.750	R	R	6-3	200	1-2-80	2003	Enid, Okla.
Kester, Tim	10	10	3.78	27	27	3	0	164	193	88	69	21	128	.296	R	R	6-4	190	12-1-71	1993	Coral Springs, Fla.
Kumagai, Ryo	0	0	1.93	3	0	0	0	5	5	1	1	2	4	.263	R	R	6-1	180	8-22-79	2002	Tokyo, Japan
Martinez, Anastacio	3	1	2.25	34	0	0	14	40	31	13	10	24	37	.212	R	R	6-2	180	11-3-78	1998	Santo Domingo, D.R.
Miniel, Rene	0	1	2.45	15	0	0	0	26	27	16	7	12	20	.270	R	R	6-2	170	4-26-79	1998	Santo Domingo, D.R.
Montalbano, Greg	2	1	9.39	6	5	0	0	15	25	17	16	13	8	.373	L	L	6-2	180	8-24-77	2000	Fort Myers, Fla.
Nicolas, Mike	4	2	6.06	20	0	0	0	33	20	26	22	33	37	.175	R	R	6-3	220	9-5-79	2000	Santo Domingo, D.R.
Pahucki, David	0	0	3.27	2	1	0	0	11	9	5	4	5	3	.225	R	R	6-2	210	10-17-80	2002	New Hampton, N.Y.
Perez, Juan	3	3	3.82	18	0	0	0	31	37	19	13	11	24	.305	R	L	6-0	150	2-10-81	1999	Villa Rivas, D.R.
Rudrude, Brett	1	2	4.26	6	6	0	0	32	39	20	15	10	16	.304	R	R	6-3	190	1-23-79	2001	Alta Loma, Calif.
Shibilo, Andy	1	2	1.33	13	0	0	1	20	14	4	3	7	19	.200	R	R	6-7	220	9-16-76	1998	Belleville, N.J.
Stevens, Josh	10	9	3.85	25	24	1	0	154	163	76	66	19	96	.274	R	R	6-4	200	6-6-79	1998	Riverside, Calif.
Villegas, Felix	1	8	6.37	23	5	0	0	54	61	41	38	28	34	.283	R	R	6-2	200	8-8-78	2000	San Juan, P.R.
Weatherby, Charlie	2	2	5.92	30	1	0	1	52	68	41	34	20	25	.330	R	R	6-0	200	12-23-78	2001	Beaufort, N.C.
White, Matt	0	0	0.00	2	1	0	0	3	1	1	0	2	3	.111	R	L	6-1	180	8-19-77	1998	Windsor, Mass.
Zink, Charlie	3	2	3.43	6	6	0	0	39	21	16	15	14	18	.154	R	R	6-1	190	8-26-79	2001	El Dorado Hills, Calif.

FIELDING

Catcher	PCT	G	PO	A	E	DP	PB
Dominique	.986	10	64	4	1	0	1
Loyd	.994	26	161	8	1	2	6
Nathans	.991	22	104	6	1	0	1
Shoppach	.982	82	547	64	11	8	3
Smith	1.000	10	53	3	0	0	2

First Base	PCT	G	PO	A	E	DP
Brisson	.989	40	329	17	4	32
Coquillette	1.000	3	20	1	0	0
Dominique	.981	12	93	10	2	3
Headley	.992	44	331	21	3	42
Kapler	1.000	1	2	0	0	0
McGowan	.981	50	387	33	8	50
Schrager	1.000	1	1	1	0	0

Second Base	PCT	G	PO	A	E	DP
Blasi	1.000	4	8	6	0	2
Coquillette	.980	24	40	59	2	18
Goelz	1.000	9	15	18	0	5
Leon	.956	70	119	166	13	46
Nieves	.961	12	16	33	2	9
Schrager	.950	37	63	90	8	20

Third Base	PCT	G	PO	A	E	DP
Goelz	1.000	3	1	2	0	2
Hattig	.875	8	7	14	3	2
Haverbusch	.818	3	4	5	2	0
Schrager	.913	37	33	72	10	8
Youkilis	.925	93	66	182	20	19

Shortstop	PCT	G	PO	A	E	DP
Borowiak	.842	3	5	11	3	4
Castro	.924	15	23	38	5	10
Coquillette	.889	5	2	6	1	0
Goelz	.968	27	32	58	3	12
Leon	1.000	3	0	1	0	0
Nieves	.974	60	98	162	7	44
Schrager	.959	43	61	102	7	18

Outfield	PCT	G	PO	A	E	DP
Brown	.969	53	93	0	3	0
Catalanotte	.971	20	31	2	1	1
Coquillette	1.000	14	22	0	0	0
Goelz	.917	19	32	1	3	0
Haverbusch	1.000	36	63	2	0	0
Headley	1.000	27	45	3	0	0
Kapler	1.000	1	2	0	0	0
McGowan	1.000	12	11	3	0	0
Nathans	1.000	1	1	0	0	0
Owens	.976	136	352	10	9	1
Sherrod	.973	123	235	17	7	5

SARASOTA RED SOX — High Class A

FLORIDA STATE LEAGUE

BATTING	AVG	G	AB	R	H	2B	3B	HR	RBI	BB	SO	SB	CS	SLG	OBP	B	T	HT	WT	DOB	1st Yr	Resides
Bailie, Stefan	.251	75	267	27	67	14	1	3	29	16	70	7	2	.345	.300	R	R	6-0	210	5-16-80	2001	Mesa, Wash.
Barclay, Mike	.266	31	79	8	21	1	0	1	5	9	18	4	1	.316	.337	R	R	6-3	170	8-6-79	2002	Tampa, Fla.
Blasi, Blake	.215	41	135	15	29	4	1	0	13	25	25	6	4	.259	.345	S	R	5-8	160	3-23-79	2000	Wichita, Kan.
Boran, Patrick	.232	29	95	10	22	4	1	0	3	11	24	1	0	.295	.318	S	R	6-2	200	8-8-80	2002	Pottsville, Pa.
Borowiak, Zach	.183	27	93	2	17	4	0	0	2	7	13	0	2	.226	.248	R	R	6-1	185	5-18-81	2003	Nashville, Ill.
Buckley, James	.236	17	55	5	13	2	0	2	7	7	12	0	0	.382	.323	R	R	6-1	230	9-14-79	2002	Ocean City, N.J.
Calitri, Mike	.264	61	201	32	53	10	4	3	23	38	62	1	4	.398	.383	R	R	6-3	210	3-14-78	2000	Canton, Mass.
Callahan, Dave	.232	20	69	6	16	7	0	0	7	13	12	2	4	.333	.349	L	L	5-11	200	12-7-79	1998	Palm Bay, Fla.
Castillo, Osmar	.155	31	103	14	16	0	0	0	7	24	20	4	2	.155	.328	S	R	5-10	170	1-3-79	2002	Manhattan, Kan.
Catalanotte, Greg	.213	102	342	41	73	14	5	11	40	45	110	16	6	.380	.303	S	R	6-3	210	6-18-77	1999	Glendale, Ariz.
Concepcion, Alberto	.218	56	156	16	34	5	0	0	5	15	40	2	0	.250	.309	R	R	6-1	220	4-18-81	2002	El Segundo, Calif.
Cooper, Matt	.176	44	131	11	23	4	0	4	12	20	53	0	2	.298	.323	R	R	6-3	200	10-10-80	2000	Stillwater, Okla.
Dorta, Melvin	.216	93	324	36	70	7	1	0	27	28	46	20	9	.244	.288	R	R	5-11	160	1-15-82	1999	Guscara, Venez.
Durazo, William	.178	23	73	6	13	1	0	1	7	4	18	2	1	.233	.231	S	R	6-1	210	2-15-79	2002	Los Angeles, Calif.
Esposito, Brian	.000	2	7	0	0	0	0	0	0	0	0	0	0	.000	.000	R	R	6-1	190	2-24-79	2000	Willington, Conn.
Fulse, Sheldon	.272	22	81	14	22	7	1	2	5	13	18	13	2	.457	.368	S	R	6-3	170	11-10-81	1999	Bartow, Fla.
Goelz, Jim	.289	21	83	9	24	4	0	1	8	8	16	1	1	.373	.359	R	R	5-10	170	2-13-76	1998	St. James, N.Y.
Hattig, John	.295	114	400	51	118	29	2	6	70	59	70	9	7	.423	.385	S	R	6-2	210	2-27-80	1999	Dededo, Guam
Martinez, Edgar	.201	66	199	17	40	6	0	0	11	13	24	6	3	.231	.263	R	R	6-0	160	10-23-81	1998	Guigue, Venez.
Matthews, Lamont	.266	57	192	29	51	14	4	5	31	38	59	5	1	.458	.386	L	L	6-2	210	6-15-78	1999	Petersburg, Va.
McGowan, Sean	.358	18	67	12	24	5	1	1	11	6	7	3	2	.507	.411	R	R	6-6	240	5-15-77	1999	Burlington, Mass.
Money, Freddie	.200	16	45	7	9	3	0	2	5	1	9	4	1	.400	.234	R	R	5-11	160	1-11-79	2000	Cowarts, Ala.
Murphy, David	.242	45	153	18	37	5	1	1	18	20	33	6	2	.307	.329	L	L	6-4	192	10-18-81	2003	Spring, Texas
Perez, Kenny	.278	65	230	32	64	17	4	2	39	15	24	11	4	.413	.319	S	R	6-2	190	9-28-81	2000	Miami, Fla.
Ramos, Jason	.300	6	10	2	3	0	0	0	0	6	3	0	0	.300	.563	S	R	5-11	185	8-9-83	2003	Miami, Fla.
Rodriguez, Eladio	.227	57	172	18	39	12	0	2	20	15	36	11	1	.331	.296	R	R	5-11	170	4-4-79	1998	Mao Valverde, D.R.
Schrager, Tony	.294	4	17	1	5	2	0	0	2	2	1	1	0	.412	.368	R	R	6-1	170	6-14-77	1998	Omaha, Neb.
Seiber, Antron	.198	29	106	10	21	1	4	1	6	10	37	6	2	.311	.265	R	R	6-1	180	5-19-80	1999	Independence, La.
Shanks, Eric	.221	33	113	18	25	7	0	0	9	19	19	2	4	.283	.343	R	R	5-11	180	7-7-78	2001	Charlotte, N.C.
Smith, Will	.120	8	25	2	3	1	0	0	2	5	7	1	2	.160	.267	R	R	5-11	180	5-7-77	2000	Prattville, Ala.
Stone, Greg	.231	17	65	9	15	3	0	0	1	6	11	4	1	.277	.296	L	R	5-11	170	2-19-81	2002	Claremore, Okla.
Veracierto, Fernando	.211	6	19	2	4	1	0	0	0	3	4	0	0	.263	.348	R	R	5-11	170	8-18-82	1999	Caracas, Venez.

PITCHING	W	L	ERA	G	GS	CG	SV	IP	H	R	ER	BB	SO	AVG	B	T	HT	WT	DOB	1st Yr	Resides
Byron, Terry	0	1	2.17	32	0	0	9	46	41	13	11	20	39	.246	R	R	6-0	200	3-28-79	1999	St. Croix, V.I.
Carbajal, Alex	2	3	4.17	22	1	0	0	37	40	17	17	16	22	.294	L	L	6-2	190	11-6-77	2000	Rosemead, Calif.
Clelland, James	4	2	3.57	11	10	1	0	58	67	27	23	12	36	.300	R	R	6-4	180	9-28-79	2001	Pasadena, Calif.
DeJesus, Elvis	0	0	3.79	27	0	0	0	40	42	20	17	18	21	.264	R	R	6-3	150	7-12-78	1999	Moca, D.R.
Delcarmen, Manny	1	1	3.13	4	3	0	0	23	16	9	8	7	16	.200	R	R	6-2	190	2-16-82	2000	Hyde Park, Mass.
Dennison, Michael	0	1	2.84	4	0	0	2	6	5	2	2	1	5	.208	R	R	6-0	200	1-9-81	2003	Overland Park, Kan.
Dumatrait, Phillip	7	5	3.02	21	20	0	1	104	74	41	35	59	74	.204	R	L	6-2	170	7-12-81	2000	Bakersfield, Calif.
Elmore, Chris	0	0	1.93	1	1	0	0	5	3	4	1	4	2	.166	L	L	6-1	190	4-28-77	2000	Virginia Beach, Va.
Embree, Alan	0	0	13.50	1	1	0	0	1	2	1	1	0	2	.500	L	L	6-2	190	1-23-70	1990	Vancouver, Wash.
Fox, Chad	0	0	4.50	2	1	0	0	2	2	1	1	1	1	.250	R	R	6-3	190	9-3-70	1992	Houston, Texas
Gabbard, Kason	0	1	10.29	2	2	0	0	7	13	8	8	3	4	.464	L	L	6-4	200	4-8-82	2001	Royal Palm Beach, Fla.
Gamble, Jerome	6	4	3.66	17	14	0	0	76	68	36	31	21	51	.239	R	R	6-2	200	4-5-80	1998	Alexander City, Ala.
Howell, Jason	9	4	2.99	48	0	0	5	75	71	29	25	24	59	.247	L	L	6-2	190	5-25-79	2001	Millers Creek, N.C.
Huang, Kevin	1	0	3.97	4	1	0	1	11	13	8	5	6	9	.288	R	R	6-0	170	4-25-82	2001	Chau Chou, Taiwan
Kaercher, Matt	0	2	3.38	8	0	0	0	11	7	6	4	3	4	.184	R	R	6-3	200	1-2-80	2003	Enid, Okla.
Kumagai, Ryo	0	0	4.50	1	0	0	0	2	2	1	1	0	1	.333	R	R	6-1	180	8-22-79	2002	Tokyo, Japan
Mendoza, Ramiro	1	0	0.00	1	1	0	0	5	2	0	0	1	4	.133	R	R	6-2	190	6-15-72	1992	Los Santos, Panama
Miniel, Rene	3	4	3.34	19	7	0	0	65	62	27	24	27	47	.261	R	R	6-2	170	4-26-79	1998	Santo Domingo, D.R.
Pahucki, David	3	8	4.68	18	17	0	0	85	103	57	44	46	42	.308	R	R	6-2	210	10-17-80	2002	New Hampton, N.Y.
Perez, Juan	3	4	2.37	33	0	0	18	38	34	15	10	12	37	.229	R	L	6-0	150	2-10-81	1999	Villa Rivas, D.R.
Person, Robert	1	1	2.92	7	7	0	0	25	27	12	8	6	17	.281	R	R	6-0	190	1-8-69	1989	Clearwater, Fla.
Reynolds, Josh	3	1	3.53	23	7	0	2	59	61	27	23	8	49	.266	R	R	6-2	190	9-27-79	2000	Holts Summit, Mo.
Rhodes, Shane	3	4	3.39	39	0	0	1	61	61	36	23	29	43	.254	L	L	6-2	200	1-19-80	2001	Monkton, Md.
Rudrude, Brett	4	7	4.22	22	12	0	1	79	82	42	37	18	59	.267	R	R	6-3	190	1-23-79	2001	Alta Loma, Calif.
Smith, Chris	2	0	0.00	2	2	0	0	12	8	2	0	2	9	.186	R	R	6-2	200	4-9-81	2002	Hesperia, Calif.
Thompson, Matt	2	3	4.70	20	0	0	1	31	32	21	16	19	19	.264	R	R	6-2	200	8-28-81	1999	Boise, Idaho
Villegas, Felix	1	2	1.23	10	2	0	0	22	17	3	3	11	15	.215	R	R	6-2	200	8-8-78	2000	San Juan, P.R.
White, Matt	0	0	0.00	2	2	0	0	5	6	1	0	1	2	.285	R	L	6-1	180	8-19-77	1998	Windsor, Mass.
Zink, Charlie	7	9	3.90	24	19	2	0	136	123	69	59	64	94	.245	R	R	6-1	190	8-26-79	2001	El Dorado Hills, Calif.

FIELDING

Catcher	PCT	G	PO	A	E	DP	PB
Buckley	.989	14	79	8	1	1	3
Concepcion	.996	46	246	19	1	3	9
Durazo	1.000	5	18	1	0	0	1
Esposito	.900	1	8	1	1	0	1
Martinez	.984	62	378	54	7	1	9
Rodriguez	.990	17	93	10	1	2	11

First Base	PCT	G	PO	A	E	DP
Bailie	.974	52	448	33	13	50
Calitri	.987	60	486	38	7	56
Callahan	1.000	1	15	0	0	2
Durazo	1.000	11	82	4	0	6
Esposito	1.000	1	3	1	0	0
Hattig	.900	1	8	1	1	0
McGowan	.986	8	63	5	1	9

Second Base	PCT	G	PO	A	E	DP
Blasi	.918	15	18	38	5	8
Borowiak	1.000	1	4	6	0	2
Castillo	1.000	2	6	4	0	0
Dorta	.971	86	176	260	13	61
Goelz	1.000	1	3	1	0	1
Shanks	.965	23	44	65	4	17
Stone	1.000	4	8	12	0	1

Third Base	PCT	G	PO	A	E	DP
Blasi	1.000	9	5	17	0	2
Boran	.846	8	8	14	4	1
Calitri	.500	1	0	1	1	0
Castillo	.926	10	6	19	2	3
Concepcion	.000	1	0	0	0	0
Dorta	.667	2	1	1	1	0
Goelz	1.000	1	0	2	0	0
Hattig	.925	97	71	199	22	21
Stone	.889	4	0	8	1	0

Shortstop	PCT	G	PO	A	E	DP
Blasi	.921	11	13	22	3	9
Boran	.867	10	15	24	6	9
Borowiak	.967	26	56	63	4	20
Castillo	.962	5	11	14	1	5
Dorta	1.000	1	1	3	0	0
Goelz	1.000	4	7	13	0	7
Perez	.972	62	86	155	7	22
Ramos	.960	6	8	16	1	6
Schrager	.900	4	7	11	2	5
Stone	1.000	2	5	1	0	0
Veracierto	.958	6	12	11	1	2

Outfield	PCT	G	PO	A	E	DP
Bailie	.667	1	2	0	1	0
Barclay	1.000	28	39	4	0	0
Blasi	1.000	1	2	0	0	0
Boran	1.000	2	2	0	0	0
Callahan	1.000	11	22	0	0	0
Castillo	1.000	13	18	2	0	0
Catalanotte	.975	92	143	10	4	1
Cooper	.956	33	64	1	3	0
Dorta	.000	1	0	0	0	0
Fulse	.955	22	60	3	3	1
Goelz	.975	16	37	2	1	0
Matthews	.993	57	141	2	1	1
Money	.971	13	31	2	1	0
Murphy	.990	43	93	2	1	1
Rodriguez	.920	25	43	3	4	0
Seiber	.971	28	65	1	2	1
Shanks	1.000	6	8	1	0	0
Smith	1.000	7	20	0	0	0
Stone	1.000	7	16	0	0	0

AUGUSTA GREENJACKETS — Low Class A

SOUTH ATLANTIC LEAGUE

BATTING	AVG	G	AB	R	H	2B	3B	HR	RBI	BB	SO	SB	CS	SLG	OBP	B	T	HT	WT	DOB	1st Yr	Resides
Alcala, Arian	.000	2	7	0	0	0	0	0	0	1	1	0	0	.000	.125	R	R	6-2	200	10-7-79	2002	Hialeah, Fla.
Bonvechio, Brett	.190	75	263	21	50	12	1	4	34	24	54	1	2	.289	.259	L	R	6-1	190	11-13-82	2001	Santa Clara, Calif.
Bowman, Addison	.262	88	298	23	78	14	2	1	32	25	64	3	2	.332	.341	R	R	6-2	200	8-31-79	2002	Dayton, Va.
Brisson, Dustin	.274	34	117	23	32	7	0	5	21	15	22	1	1	.462	.360	L	R	6-3	210	3-18-78	2000	West Palm Beach, Fla.
Brown, Dusty	.263	87	285	27	75	17	6	2	41	37	69	7	1	.386	.358	R	R	6-0	180	6-19-82	2001	Prescott Valley, Ariz.
Bryan, Jason	.105	11	38	3	4	3	0	0	3	3	15	3	0	.184	.190	R	R	6-2	190	11-18-81	1999	Brooklyn, N.Y.
Castillo, Osmar	.333	25	66	12	22	0	1	0	6	17	20	3	1	.364	.476	S	R	5-10	170	1-3-79	2002	Manhattan, Kan.
Coffey, David	.241	63	216	26	52	9	1	0	23	19	25	11	0	.292	.304	L	R	5-11	175	4-15-81	2003	Perry, Ga.
Cooper, Matt	.293	57	188	24	55	15	0	3	30	34	51	1	1	.420	.422	R	R	6-3	200	10-10-80	2000	Stillwater, Okla.
Curtis, Lee	.257	57	179	14	46	8	0	2	10	15	32	2	6	.335	.323	R	R	5-11	187	7-21-81	2003	Greer, S.C.
Durazo, William	.194	23	62	4	12	2	0	0	4	8	13	0	0	.226	.315	S	R	6-1	210	2-15-79	2002	Los Angeles, Calif.
Durbin, Chris	.229	29	96	10	22	4	0	4	10	9	19	1	2	.396	.300	R	R	6-0	180	9-8-81	2003	Wylie, Texas
Goss, Michael	.245	100	319	45	78	9	2	1	28	34	71	29	7	.295	.327	L	L	5-11	180	9-26-80	2002	Louisville, Miss.
Myers, Kenton	.164	21	67	4	11	2	0	0	7	8	19	0	0	.194	.253	R	R	6-1	200	4-14-80	2001	Albuquerque, N.M.
Ontiveros, Jeff	.241	104	344	44	83	24	0	5	50	34	79	1	0	.355	.343	R	R	6-0	220	4-26-79	2002	Round Rock, Texas
Ramirez, Hanley	.275	111	422	69	116	24	3	8	50	32	73	36	13	.403	.327	S	R	6-1	170	12-23-83	2000	Santo Domingo, D.R.
Soto, Jose	.239	55	176	22	42	6	2	2	11	5	48	8	2	.330	.266	S	R	6-2	160	6-18-79	1996	San Cristobal, D.R.
Spann, Chad	.312	116	414	55	129	21	3	5	63	40	64	9	5	.413	.379	R	R	6-1	190	10-25-83	2002	Buena Vista, Ga.
Stone, Greg	.263	97	346	59	91	10	2	0	25	46	60	13	7	.303	.353	L	R	5-11	170	2-19-81	2002	Claremore, Okla.
Veracierto, Fernando	.200	61	155	16	31	5	0	0	8	11	28	4	0	.232	.265	R	R	5-11	170	8-18-82	1999	Caracas, Venez.
West, Eric	.195	70	231	29	45	15	0	0	22	29	51	4	3	.260	.293	R	R	6-1	160	3-24-83	2001	Southside, Ala.

PITCHING	W	L	ERA	G	GS	CG	SV	IP	H	R	ER	BB	SO	AVG	B	T	HT	WT	DOB	1st Yr	Resides
Blaney, Matt	1	2	4.78	16	0	0	0	26	33	17	14	18	10	.311	S	R	6-0	180	5-7-79	2001	Mandalay Beach, Fla.
Cedeno, Juan	7	9	3.02	23	21	0	0	101	87	38	34	44	87	.234	L	L	6-1	160	8-19-83	2001	Higuey, D.R.
Clelland, James	0	0	3.00	2	0	0	0	3	3	4	1	1	3	.214	R	R	6-4	180	9-28-79	2001	Pasadena, Calif.
Dennison, Michael	1	1	1.35	18	0	0	5	20	16	5	3	8	15	.213	R	R	6-0	200	1-9-81	2003	Overland Park, Kan.
Esposito, Brian	1	2	5.33	13	0	0	0	25	27	22	15	13	11	.270	R	R	6-1	190	2-24-79	2000	Willington, Conn.
Friske, Parker	1	2	6.75	14	0	0	0	23	22	19	17	14	18	.258	L	L	6-4	210	5-1-79	2001	Virginia Beach, Va.
Galvez, Willy	0	2	7.71	13	0	0	1	21	28	19	18	10	14	.314	R	R	6-4	160	4-1-80	1998	Cotuy, D.R.
Garber, Mike	2	4	4.40	35	2	0	5	57	66	40	28	23	44	.277	L	L	6-2	190	1-9-81	2001	Palos Heights, Ill.
Generelli, Dan	2	3	7.71	17	1	0	0	33	42	35	28	22	23	.302	R	R	6-2	200	8-25-80	1999	Hubbardston, Mass.
Hertzler, Barry	1	0	0.84	8	0	0	1	11	6	2	1	3	5	.166	R	R	6-2	215	2-15-81	2003	East Providence, R.I.
Huang, Kevin	2	5	3.86	22	12	0	2	72	72	38	31	26	77	.260	R	R	6-0	170	4-25-82	2001	Chau Chou, Taiwan
Kumagai, Ryo	0	3	7.47	20	0	0	0	31	43	31	26	20	33	.313	R	R	6-1	180	8-22-79	2002	Tokyo, Japan
Lester, Jon	6	9	3.65	24	21	0	0	106	102	54	43	44	71	.262	L	L	6-3	200	1-7-84	2002	Puyallup, Wash.
Lundgren, Wayne	0	0	9.00	3	0	0	1	5	6	7	5	0	3	.300	R	R	6-6	180	4-21-82	2000	Baulkham Hills, Australia
MacLane, Thomas	1	3	4.37	21	0	0	1	35	41	19	17	11	28	.288	L	L	6-0	170	2-2-80	2002	Riverside, R.I.
Mateo, Aneudis	0	5	4.89	13	11	0	0	53	62	33	29	16	34	.292	R	R	6-4	180	10-3-82	2000	San Pedro de Macoris, D.R.
Mendoza, Luis	3	3	2.26	13	11	0	0	60	46	19	15	14	29	.210	L	R	6-3	180	10-31-83	2000	Mexico City, Mexico
Morle, Carlos	2	2	5.40	28	0	0	7	40	33	25	24	22	37	.224	R	R	6-0	140	4-15-82	1999	San Pedro de Macoris, D.R.
Pahucki, David	1	1	1.89	5	4	0	0	19	7	4	4	9	17	.107	R	R	6-2	210	10-17-80	2002	New Hampton, N.Y.
Priola, John	0	1	4.09	5	0	0	0	11	13	6	5	5	7	.309	R	R	6-3	190	9-30-79	2002	Jemison, Ala.
Roy, Angus	3	7	5.54	29	3	0	0	67	77	44	41	33	37	.301	L	R	6-2	210	6-27-80	2003	Mississauga, Ontario
Shipman, Andrew	0	1	11.12	4	1	0	0	6	13	10	7	5	6	.433	R	R	6-3	185	10-18-81	2003	Bellevue, Neb.
Smith, Brandon	0	5	9.87	16	4	0	0	35	61	41	38	14	30	.381	R	R	6-2	200	2-18-80	2002	Ballwin, Mo.
Smith, Chris	3	3	4.27	8	8	0	0	46	48	22	22	5	25	.272	R	R	6-2	200	4-9-81	2002	Hesperia, Calif.
Sturge, Justin	2	0	0.56	11	0	0	1	16	13	3	1	5	8	.245	R	L	6-4	200	5-4-81	2003	Syracuse, N.Y.
Tavarez, Milton	1	1	2.86	18	3	0	0	44	43	18	14	13	36	.254	R	R	6-2	190	3-29-82	1999	Higuey, D.R.
Thompson, Matt	2	2	4.78	11	10	0	0	43	45	23	23	19	35	.267	R	R	6-2	200	8-28-81	1999	Boise, Idaho
Villarreal, Luis	7	11	5.17	25	24	0	0	111	140	75	64	31	82	.311	L	L	6-1	210	12-20-79	2002	San Antonio, Texas

FIELDING

Catcher	PCT	G	PO	A	E	DP	PB
Bowman	.973	41	258	35	8	1	3
Brown	.972	66	351	64	12	3	20
Durazo	.985	19	116	14	2	0	2
Myers	.979	21	125	12	3	2	1

First Base	PCT	G	PO	A	E	DP
Bonvechio	.988	42	314	27	4	34
Bowman	1.000	1	7	0	0	0
Brisson	.992	29	229	14	2	21
Durazo	1.000	1	7	0	0	1
Ontiveros	.991	68	517	41	5	32

Second Base	PCT	G	PO	A	E	DP
Alcala	1.000	1	1	1	0	0
Castillo	1.000	20	33	50	0	15
Curtis	.941	47	81	94	11	17
Stone	.982	13	23	33	1	9
Veracierto	.963	19	39	40	3	7
West	.955	44	87	124	10	23

Third Base	PCT	G	PO	A	E	DP
Alcala	1.000	2	1	4	0	0
Bonvechio	.939	21	14	32	3	4
Castillo	1.000	4	5	4	0	0
Curtis	.857	8	5	13	3	1
Spann	.937	102	79	174	17	21
Stone	1.000	1	0	2	0	0
Veracierto	1.000	5	1	9	0	1

Shortstop	PCT	G	PO	A	E	DP
Castillo	1.000	1	0	1	0	1
Ramirez	.926	102	162	286	36	37
Stone	.935	14	16	42	4	5
Veracierto	.600	4	1	5	4	1
West	.910	20	32	39	7	9

Outfield	PCT	G	PO	A	E	DP
Bowman	.973	45	70	3	2	0
Brown	1.000	9	15	1	0	0
Bryan	.913	11	21	0	2	0
Coffey	.973	61	108	2	3	1
Cooper	.952	36	59	1	3	0
Durbin	.984	29	61	2	1	0
Goss	.955	95	210	4	10	1
Roy	.000	1	0	0	0	0
Soto	.960	47	93	4	4	1
Stone	.993	70	143	3	1	2
Veracierto	.950	30	36	2	2	0

LOWELL SPINNERS — Short-Season Class A

NEW YORK-PENN LEAGUE

BATTING	AVG	G	AB	R	H	2B	3B	HR	RBI	BB	SO	SB	CS	SLG	OBP	B	T	HT	WT	DOB	1st Yr	Resides
Arias, Claudio	.262	49	187	29	49	9	1	5	33	7	55	3	3	.401	.293	R	R	6-2	200	5-9-82	2002	Bani, D.R.
Barnowski, Bryan	.077	4	13	1	1	0	0	0	0	1	4	0	0	.077	.200	R	R	6-2	200	9-3-80	1999	Granville, Mass.
Bonvechio, Brett	.190	34	105	14	20	5	0	3	9	13	27	0	0	.324	.298	L	R	6-1	190	11-13-82	2001	Santa Clara, Calif.
Borowiak, Zach	.272	35	125	13	34	5	1	0	7	16	18	12	4	.328	.372	R	R	6-1	185	5-18-81	2003	Nashville, Ill.
Buckley, James	.158	37	114	15	18	9	0	2	13	10	46	1	0	.289	.230	R	R	6-1	230	9-14-79	2002	Ocean City, N.J.
Cloninger, Erich	.263	24	38	4	10	3	0	0	1	8	16	3	0	.342	.383	R	R	5-11	190	11-6-80	2003	Denver, N.C.
Cucinotta, Rob	.224	24	67	7	15	2	1	0	8	1	15	2	1	.284	.246	R	R	6-3	222	3-1-80	2003	Aldan, Pa.
DeVries, Jon	.182	35	99	9	18	3	0	1	9	17	47	0	0	.242	.331	R	R	6-3	200	8-22-82	2001	Irvine, Calif.
Evans, Robert	.265	58	181	33	48	13	4	6	33	20	43	5	4	.481	.346	L	L	5-11	185	3-1-81	2003	Birmingham, Ala.
Jordan, Kevin	.263	63	217	46	57	4	3	0	22	49	50	24	10	.309	.404	L	R	5-8	160	12-15-80	2003	Rowlett, Texas
Kapler, Gabe	.667	1	3	2	2	0	0	0	0	1	0	1	0	.667	.750	R	R	6-2	210	7-31-75	1995	Sherman Oaks, Calif.
Moss, Brandon	.237	65	228	29	54	15	4	7	34	15	53	7	5	.430	.290	L	R	6-0	180	9-16-83	2002	Monroe, Ga.
Murphy, David	.346	21	78	13	27	4	0	0	13	16	9	4	1	.397	.453	L	L	6-4	192	10-18-81	2003	Spring, Texas
Murton, Matt	.286	53	189	30	54	11	2	2	29	27	39	9	3	.397	.374	R	R	6-1	215	10-3-81	2003	Kissimmee, Fla.
Ramos, Jason	.190	28	79	10	15	3	0	0	10	14	17	4	2	.228	.313	S	R	5-11	185	8-9-83	2003	Miami, Fla.
Reyes, Melvin	.259	57	193	28	50	16	3	1	25	12	60	8	2	.389	.300	S	R	5-11	170	3-14-83	2001	Santo Domingo, D.R.
Schartz, Lance	.154	7	13	1	2	0	0	0	1	0	3	0	0	.154	.214	R	R	6-0	215	1-26-83	2003	Larned, Kan.
Suarez, Ignacio	.222	58	207	32	46	13	0	0	19	32	43	12	4	.285	.326	R	R	5-11	165	5-3-81	2003	Corona, N.Y.
West, Jeremy	.280	72	264	32	74	17	1	4	43	31	52	1	3	.398	.369	R	R	6-0	200	11-8-81	2003	Las Vegas, Nev.

GAMES BY POSITION: C—Buckley 36, Cloninger 19, DeVries 34, Schartz 7. **1B**—Barnowski 2, Bonvechio 12, Cucinotta 18, West 46. **2B**—Ramos 11, Reyes 55, Suarez 11. **3B**—Arias 46, Bonvechio 12, Borowiak 11, Ramos 7. **SS**—Borowiak 21, Ramos 10, Suarez 45. **OF**—Evans 50, Jordan 51, Kapler 1, Moss 60, Murphy 20, Murton 47.

PITCHING	W	L	ERA	G	GS	CG	SV	IP	H	R	ER	BB	SO	AVG	B	T	HT	WT	DOB	1st Yr	Resides
Alvarez, Abe	0	0	0.00	9	9	0	0	19	9	2	0	2	19	.138	L	L	6-2	190	10-17-82	2003	Fontana, Calif.
Anderson, Wes	0	0	0.00	3	3	0	0	2	1	0	0	2	1	.125	R	R	6-4	170	9-10-79	1997	Lady Lake, Fla.
Basch, Zach	3	2	4.08	24	0	0	6	29	30	19	13	18	25	.267	R	R	6-3	190	6-22-81	2003	Sylvania, Ohio
Blaney, Matt	0	0	2.08	5	0	0	0	9	6	3	2	4	5	.193	S	R	6-0	180	5-7-79	2001	Mandalay Beach, Fla.
Cochran, Tom	2	3	4.86	20	0	0	2	33	40	26	18	4	20	.300	L	L	6-2	195	10-16-82	2003	Wilmington, Del.
Cooper, Dexter	0	0	5.40	3	0	0	0	5	7	4	3	3	5	.333	R	R	6-2	210	7-14-82	2001	Acworth, Ga.
Corn, Jessie	0	0	0.00	4	0	0	0	4	2	5	0	3	4	.117	R	R	6-0	190	7-16-82	2003	Villa Rica, Ga.
Farley, Chris	1	3	4.70	18	0	0	0	31	30	17	16	9	29	.260	R	R	6-2	180	2-24-83	2001	Orange, Mass.
Gardner, Jarrett	5	3	4.20	14	7	0	0	60	69	34	28	2	29	.286	R	R	6-1	175	3-26-81	2003	Moore, Okla.
Hertzler, Barry	2	2	3.77	12	0	0	1	14	22	9	6	5	8	.333	R	R	6-2	215	2-15-81	2003	East Providence, R.I.
Jackson, Kyle	1	1	0.93	2	2	0	0	10	7	6	1	2	2	.200	R	R	6-3	180	4-9-83	2002	Litchfield, N.H.
Lundgren, Wayne	1	2	3.46	15	2	0	0	39	39	22	15	3	17	.251	R	R	6-6	180	4-21-82	2000	Baulkham Hills, Australia
Marshall, Brian	1	1	1.08	15	0	0	6	17	10	3	2	2	15	.169	L	L	6-5	190	8-30-82	2003	Chesterfield, Va.
Ool, Kevin	3	1	2.56	25	0	0	1	39	37	14	11	5	33	.251	L	L	5-11	185	1-4-81	2003	Middletown, N.Y.
Papelbon, Jon	1	2	6.34	13	6	0	0	33	43	23	23	9	36	.311	R	R	6-4	230	11-23-80	2003	Jacksonville, Fla.
Penny, David	4	1	2.68	12	10	0	0	54	43	22	16	14	36	.215	R	R	6-3	210	9-9-81	2003	Benson, N.C.
Sanders, David	0	1	2.41	9	0	0	1	19	22	11	5	5	14	.289	L	L	6-4	195	1-5-82	2003	Tulsa, Okla.
Santos, Arthur	3	4	1.99	14	13	0	0	59	65	24	13	7	35	.277	R	R	6-0	180	2-20-82	2003	Miami, Fla.
Smith, Brandon	2	5	4.14	10	6	0	0	41	50	26	19	13	21	.303	R	R	6-2	200	2-18-80	2002	Ballwin, Mo.
Sturge, Justin	2	0	1.40	12	0	0	0	26	18	5	4	1	28	.189	R	L	6-4	200	5-4-81	2003	Syracuse, N.Y.
Vaquedano, Jose	7	4	3.30	14	10	0	0	74	67	30	27	15	70	.241	R	R	6-4	170	7-9-81	2002	San Antonio, Texas
Vaughan, Beau	1	0	2.32	11	6	0	0	31	27	8	8	15	30	.234	S	R	6-4	230	6-4-81	2003	Glendale, Ariz.

FORT MYERS RED SOX — Rookie

GULF COAST LEAGUE

BATTING	AVG	G	AB	R	H	2B	3B	HR	RBI	BB	SO	SB	CS	SLG	OBP	B	T	HT	WT	DOB	1st Yr	Resides
Alcala, Arian	.316	6	19	3	6	2	0	0	4	1	3	0	0	.421	.350	R	R	6-2	200	10-7-79	2002	Hialeah, Fla.
Bailie, Stefan	.409	5	22	4	9	0	1	1	7	1	4	0	0	.636	.435	R	R	6-0	210	5-16-80	2001	Mesa, Wash.
Bawden, Thomas	.214	16	42	6	9	2	0	0	3	5	11	0	1	.262	.298	R	R	5-11	175	7-24-84	2003	Chesterfield, Mo.
Bianucci, Anthony	.260	22	73	10	19	2	2	0	6	3	31	1	0	.342	.289	S	R	5-11	180	4-25-81	2002	Annandale, Va.
Boitel, Edwin	.310	29	87	10	27	5	1	0	9	6	13	4	2	.391	.365	R	R	6-1	170	7-6-83	2002	Santiago, D.R.
Boran, Patrick	.000	2	4	0	0	0	0	0	0	1	1	0	0	.000	.200	S	R	6-2	200	8-8-80	2002	Pottsville, Pa.
Castillo, Osmar	.462	5	13	0	6	0	0	0	2	1	1	0	0	.462	.467	S	R	5-10	170	1-3-79	2002	Manhattan, Kan.
Castro, Nelson	.133	4	15	4	2	0	0	1	3	1	3	0	0	.333	.188	S	R	5-10	200	6-4-76	1994	Monte Cristi, D.R.
Chavez, Dirimo	.342	36	111	17	38	4	0	0	7	11	8	4	3	.378	.413	R	R	6-0	170	8-10-83	2001	Cabudare, Venez.
Ciofrone, Peter	.276	38	123	14	34	7	2	0	17	22	13	0	6	.366	.381	L	R	5-11	190	9-28-83	2002	Nesconset, N.Y.

BATTING	AVG	G	AB	R	H	2B	3B	HR	RBI	BB	SO	SB	CS	SLG	OBP	B	T	HT	WT	DOB	1st Yr	Resides
Concepcion, Alberto	.200	5	15	0	3	0	0	0	3	3	3	0	0	.200	.368	R	R	6-1	220	4-18-81	2002	El Segundo, Calif.
Coste, Chris	.233	11	30	3	7	2	1	1	6	7	5	0	0	.467	.378	R	R	6-1	200	2-4-73	1995	Fargo, N.D.
Cronkhite, Ian	.245	33	106	22	26	8	1	1	16	17	21	9	0	.368	.349	L	L	6-1	180	8-11-83	2002	Edmond, Okla.
Cucinotta, Rob	.136	8	22	4	3	0	0	0	2	7	6	0	0	.136	.345	R	R	6-3	222	3-1-80	2003	Aldan, Pa.
De la Cruz, Carlos	.270	44	148	22	40	3	5	0	12	13	24	15	4	.358	.339	S	L	6-0	160	7-2-84	2001	Santo Domingo, D.R.
Fulse, Sheldon	.222	3	9	0	2	1	0	0	3	4	0	0	0	.333	.462	S	R	6-3	170	11-10-81	1999	Bartow, Fla.
Guzman, Heriberto	.248	46	153	26	38	9	5	7	29	14	43	3	4	.510	.322	R	R	6-1	180	1-26-84	2001	Bajo de Haina, D.R.
Hall, Mickey	.227	21	66	7	15	6	0	0	9	19	24	1	3	.318	.400	L	L	6-1	195	5-20-85	2003	Marietta, Ga.
Loyd, Brian	.200	6	20	2	4	2	0	0	3	0	5	0	0	.300	.200	R	R	6-2	200	12-3-73	1996	Yorba Linda, Calif.
Nieves, Raul	.130	6	23	2	3	3	0	0	1	0	5	0	0	.261	.130	S	R	6-2	180	1-1-79	2000	Barranquitas, P.R.
Paniagua, Salvador	.308	39	130	17	40	9	0	3	19	7	20	0	0	.446	.345	R	R	6-1	190	5-21-83	2001	San Juan, D.R.
Penalo, Alexander	.305	32	82	12	25	5	0	1	9	8	15	4	0	.402	.370	S	R	6-1	170	5-2-84	2002	Santo Domingo, D.R.
Perez, Kenny	.273	7	22	4	6	1	1	0	2	1	3	0	0	.409	.304	S	R	6-2	190	9-28-81	2000	Miami, Fla.
Perez, Koby	.250	16	52	7	13	5	0	0	3	2	17	0	0	.346	.278	R	R	6-2	220	9-26-82	2001	Santo Domingo, D.R.
Petersen, Ryan	.000	2	4	0	0	0	0	0	0	0	1	0	0	.000	.200	R	R	5-9	170	10-21-77	2001	Plantsville, Conn.
Ramos, Jason	.200	5	15	4	3	0	0	0	2	2	1	0	0	.200	.333	S	R	5-11	185	8-9-83	2003	Miami, Fla.
Schartz, Lance	.240	9	25	3	6	0	0	1	4	2	4	0	0	.360	.321	R	R	6-0	215	1-26-83	2003	Larned, Kan.
Smith, Jeff	.182	7	22	2	4	0	0	0	2	2	2	0	0	.182	.250	L	R	6-3	210	6-17-74	1995	Naples, Fla.
Turner, Chris	.254	35	126	18	32	8	4	1	15	11	36	3	2	.405	.338	R	R	5-11	195	12-2-83	2003	El Dorado, Ark.
VanKirk, Robert	.188	9	32	0	6	0	0	0	5	2	11	0	0	.188	.235	R	R	5-10	200	2-11-81	2003	Sunshine Ranches, Fla.
West, Eric	.250	6	20	1	5	2	0	0	2	0	5	0	0	.350	.250	R	R	6-1	160	3-24-83	2001	Southside, Ala.
White, Scott	.168	38	131	9	22	1	0	0	11	11	16	0	0	.176	.241	R	R	6-3	190	10-18-83	2002	Pembroke Pines, Fla.
Williams, Devoris	.202	35	124	18	25	5	2	1	8	15	48	3	4	.298	.298	S	R	5-10	180	8-8-83	2002	Greensboro, Ala.

GAMES BY POSITION: C—Concepcion 4, Coste 5, Loyd 6, Paniagua 26, Perez 8, Schartz 8, Smith 7, VanKirk 8. **1B**—Alcala 3, Chavez 3, Ciofrone 11, Concepcion 2, Coste 4, Cucinotta 8, Guzman 14, Ko. Perez 7, White 14. **2B**—Alcala 2, Bawden 13, Castillo 4, Chavez 19, Ciofrone 21, Nieves 1, Petersen 2, Ramos 2, West 5. **3B**—Boran 2, Chavez 3, Guzman 32, White 25. **SS**—Bawden 3, Castillo 1, Castro 4, Chavez 12, Ciofrone 2, Nieves 5, Penalo 32, Ke. Perez 7, Ko. Perez 2, Ramos 3. **OF**—Bianucci 16, Boitel 18, Cronkhite 33, De la Cruz 38, Fulse 3, Hall 16, Turner 29, Williams 33.

PITCHING	W	L	ERA	G	GS	CG	SV	IP	H	R	ER	BB	SO	AVG	B	T	HT	WT	DOB	1st Yr	Resides
Aybar, Ismael	0	0	8.27	10	0	0	0	16	18	15	15	15	11	.310	L	L	6-3	205	11-29-81	2003	Santiago, D.R.
Blackley, Adam	0	0	0.73	7	0	0	1	25	13	3	2	5	24	.156	L	L	6-1	190	2-22-85	2003	Melbourne, Australia
Blanco, Julio	0	0	0.00	2	0	0	0	2	2	1	0	1	2	.250	R	R	6-0	160	1-31-83	2000	Carabobo, Venez.
Borland, Curt	6	0	0.83	13	1	0	1	43	42	11	4	7	38	.253	R	R	6-2	210	10-13-79	2003	Broomfield, Colo.
Elfeldt, Matt	0	2	5.63	8	0	0	0	16	18	13	10	8	12	.290	R	R	6-3	185	1-4-81	2003	Delmar, N.Y.
Fink, Doug	0	1	9.00	1	0	0	0	1	2	1	1	0	2	.400	R	R	6-3	225	12-14-82	2003	Southington, Conn.
Frias, Junior	2	4	6.06	10	8	0	0	33	35	27	22	19	17	.273	R	R	6-3	200	8-26-84	2002	Santo Domingo, D.R.
Galvez, Willy	0	2	5.50	16	0	0	9	18	26	14	11	7	13	.346	R	R	6-4	160	4-1-80	1998	Cotuy, D.R.
Garcia, Harvey	3	0	1.89	9	8	0	0	33	21	11	7	12	32	.179	R	R	6-2	170	3-16-84	2000	Guarenas, Venez.
Guanchez, Argimiro	5	0	1.95	18	0	0	8	32	34	11	7	9	29	.272	L	L	6-0	170	12-30-82	1999	Valencia, Venez.
Hilario, Elpidio	3	3	3.76	14	2	0	0	38	41	21	16	15	21	.280	R	R	6-2	170	12-14-83	2002	San Fran. de Macoris, D.R.
Jackson, Kyle	5	2	1.85	12	12	0	0	58	40	14	12	11	37	.195	R	R	6-3	180	4-9-83	2002	Litchfield, N.H.
Kaercher, Matt	0	1	2.70	6	0	0	0	13	7	4	4	3	10	.152	R	R	6-3	200	1-2-80	2003	Enid, Okla.
Mateo, Aneudis	0	0	1.80	2	2	0	0	5	4	1	1	0	6	.222	R	R	6-4	180	10-3-82	2000	San Pedro de Macoris, D.R.
Mendoza, Luis	0	0	0.00	2	2	0	0	5	4	0	0	0	3	.222	L	R	6-3	180	10-31-83	2000	Mexico City, Mexico
Mendoza, Ramiro	0	0	0.00	2	2	0	0	7	3	0	0	0	4	.130	R	R	6-2	190	6-15-72	1992	Los Santos, Panama
Montalbano, Greg	0	0	3.09	3	3	0	0	12	8	4	4	7	6	.200	L	L	6-2	180	8-24-77	2000	Fort Myers, Fla.
Orozco, Dernier	4	2	6.07	14	0	0	0	30	42	25	20	4	21	.333	R	R	6-1	180	1-22-82	1999	Carabobo, Venez.
Pelland, Tyler	3	4	1.62	11	8	0	0	39	26	12	7	18	34	.185	R	L	6-0	190	10-9-83	2002	Bristol, Vt.
Person, Robert	0	0	0.00	1	1	0	0	3	2	0	0	2	4	.222	R	R	6-0	190	1-8-69	1989	Clearwater, Fla.
Smith, Chris	0	2	6.48	3	2	0	0	8	11	8	6	4	3	.314	R	R	6-2	200	4-9-81	2002	Hesperia, Calif.
Smith, Jason	0	0	3.86	1	1	0	0	2	2	1	1	1	2	.222	R	R	6-3	196	7-12-84	2003	Bourne, Mass.
Soriano, Alexander	2	1	4.07	14	0	0	0	24	19	12	11	14	20	.220	L	L	6-0	160	7-15-82	2002	Santo Domingo, D.R.
Valdez, Argelis	0	0	4.50	2	0	0	0	2	3	2	1	0	1	.300	R	R	6-2	180	8-4-81	2001	Nizao, D.R.
Wilson, Jonathan	0	2	1.76	10	7	0	0	31	30	12	6	10	18	.250	R	R	6-0	210	11-24-82	2003	Aurora, Colo.

CHICAGO WHITE SOX

BY PHIL ROGERS

Poised for a long playoff run in 2003, the White Sox made the most basic of mistakes. They failed to win enough games to get into the field.

Jose Valentin was among those who saw the possibilities for a team that had Cy Young candidate Esteban Loiaza, Bartolo Colon and Mark Buehrle in the starting rotation and added veterans Carl Everett, Roberto Alomar, Scott Sullivan and Scott Schoenweis in midseason trades.

"With the pitching staff we have, we're definitely a lot better than 2000—a lot, lot, lot better than 2000," Valentin said with two weeks left in the season. "If we get in (the playoffs), I think we'll be in for a long time."

But the White Sox finished four games behind the Twins in the American League Central Division, in large part because they went 2-5 in two late-season series against the Twins. That included a three-game sweep at the Metrodome.

Jerry Manuel, who had been the manager since 1998, was fired after the 86-76 season, which marked his fourth second-place finish with the White Sox. The White Sox dug their way out from under a 45-49 first half, but went 10-8 down the stretch, compared to a 14-4 sprint to the wire by the Twins.

Thanks mostly to the contributions of Loaiza and Colon, the White Sox finished fourth in the AL with a 4.17 ERA, their lowest since the strike season of 1994. Paul Konerko and several others got off to slow starts as Chicago averaged only 4.2 runs in the first half. They averaged 5.9 in the second half but finished eighth overall with 791 runs.

Loaiza went from nonroster spring invitee to Cy Young candidate. He won 21 games, tying Fernando Valenzuela's record for Mexican-born pitchers, and finished third in the AL with a 2.90 ERA. Colon, acquired from the Expos in an offseason trade, won 15 games and shared the league lead with nine complete games.

While Magglio Ordonez finished fifth in the AL with a .317 batting average and was an All-Star for the fourth consecutive season, it was 26-year-old outfielder Carlos Lee who had a career year. He hit .291-31-113, leading the team in RBIs.

Frank Thomas turned in his best performance since rupturing a biceps tendon in late April 2001. He tied for second in the AL with 42 homers while driving in 105 runs. He hit .267 but drew 100 walks for the 10th time.

The White Sox had to trade for Everett because of the disappointing play of 2000 first-round pick Joe Borchard. He failed to take advantage of a chance to win a job in center field, hitting .184 during a 16-game trial in the big leagues and .253 with 13 homers and 103 strikeouts at Triple-A Charlotte.

In the meantime, Jeremy Reed, a second-round pick in the 2002 draft, played his way into 2004 consideration by hitting .373-11-95 with 45 steals between Double-A Birmingham and high Class A Winston-Salem.

Led by pitchers Kris Honel and Ryan Wing, manager Razor Shines' Winston-Salem Warthogs won the Carolina League championship. Josh Fields had 20 saves during the regular season and five more in the playoffs, when he didn't allow an earned run.

General manager Ken Williams gave up some highly regarded players to get stretch-run help. He dealt 2002 first-round pick Royce Ring to the New York Mets in the Alomar deal and center fielder Anthony Webster, ranked as the organization's No. 3 prospect, to Texas in the Everett deal. They also saw their latest first-round pick, center fielder Brian Anderson from the University of Arizona, have his first pro season end after 13 games because of wrist surgery.

Esteban Loaiza

RODGER WOOD

Jeremy Reed

PLAYERS of the YEAR

MAJOR LEAGUE: Esteban Loaiza, rhp

After signing for $500,000 in the 2002-03 offseason, Loaiza went from the scrap heap to the top of the heap among American League pitchers in 2003. He ranked first in strikeouts, second in wins and third in ERA.

MINOR LEAGUE: Jeremy Reed, of

Reed also emerged in 2003, vaulting to the top of the organization's prospect charts by leading the minors in batting. He hit .373-11-95 while splitting his season between Class A Winston-Salem and Double-A Birmingham.

ORGANIZATION LEADERS

BATTING		
*AVG	Jeremy Reed, Birmingham/Winston-Salem	.373
R	Jeremy Reed, Birmingham/Winston-Salem	88
H	Jeremy Reed, Birmingham/Winston-Salem	173
TB	Ross Gload, Charlotte	266
2B	Ross Gload, Charlotte	40
3B	Ross Gload, Charlotte	6
HR	Brian Becker, Winston-Salem	19
RBI	Jeremy Reed, Birmingham/Winston-Salem	95
BB	Jeremy Reed, Birmingham/Winston-Salem	70
SO	Charlie Lisk, Kannapolis/Great Falls	104
SB	Ruddy Yan, Winston-Salem	76
*SLG	Jeremy Reed, Birmingham/Winston-Salem	.537
*OBP	Jeremy Reed, Birmingham/Winston-Salem	.453
PITCHING		
W	Brian Cooper, Charlotte	15
L	Three tied at	12
#ERA	Ryan Meaux, Birmingham/Winston-Salem	1.55
G	Josh Fields, Winston-Salem	58
CG	Kris Honel, Birmingham/Winston-Salem	3
SV	Josh Fields, Winston-Salem	20
IP	Brian Cooper, Charlotte	174
BB	Wyatt Allen, Winston-Salem	89
SO	Kris Honel, Birmingham/Winston-Salem	135

*Minimum 250 At-Bats #Minimum 75 Innings

CHICAGO WHITE SOX

Manager: Jerry Manuel.

2003 Record: 87-76, .531 (2nd, AL West).

BATTING	AVG	G	AB	R	H	2B	3B	HR	RBI	BB	SO	SB	CS	SLG	OBP	B	T	HT	WT	DOB	1st Yr	Resides
Alomar, Roberto	.253	67	253	42	64	11	1	3	17	30	37	6	2	.340	.330	S	R	6-0	180	2-5-68	1985	Bradenton, Fla.
Alomar, Sandy	.268	75	194	22	52	12	0	5	26	4	17	0	0	.407	.281	R	R	6-5	230	6-18-66	1984	Chicago, Ill.
Borchard, Joe	.184	16	49	5	9	1	0	1	5	5	18	0	1	.265	.246	S	R	6-5	220	11-25-78	2000	Camarillo, Calif.
Burke, Jamie	.375	6	8	0	3	0	0	0	2	0	0	0	0	.375	.375	R	R	6-0	190	9-24-71	1993	Roseburg, Ore.
Crede, Joe	.261	151	536	68	140	31	2	19	75	32	75	1	1	.433	.308	R	R	6-2	190	4-26-78	1996	Westphalia, Mo.
Daubach, Brian	.230	95	183	26	42	11	0	6	21	34	54	1	0	.388	.352	L	R	6-1	230	2-11-72	1990	Belleville, Ill.
Everett, Carl	.301	73	256	40	77	14	0	10	41	22	36	4	3	.473	.377	S	R	6-0	210	6-3-71	1990	Brandon, Fla.
2-team (64 Texas)	.287	147	526	93	151	27	3	28	92	53	84	8	4	.510	.366							
Graffanino, Tony	.260	90	250	51	65	15	3	7	23	24	37	8	0	.428	.331	R	R	6-1	190	6-6-72	1990	Marietta, Ga.
Harris, Willie	.204	79	137	19	28	3	1	0	5	10	28	12	2	.241	.259	L	R	5-9	170	6-22-78	1999	Cairo, Ga.
Jimenez, D'Angelo	.255	73	271	35	69	11	5	7	26	32	46	4	3	.410	.332	S	R	6-0	190	12-21-77	1995	Santo Domingo, D.R.
Konerko, Paul	.234	137	444	49	104	19	0	18	65	43	50	0	0	.399	.305	R	R	6-2	210	3-5-76	1994	Scottsdale, Ariz.
Lee, Carlos	.291	158	623	100	181	35	1	31	113	37	91	18	4	.499	.331	R	R	6-2	230	6-20-76	1994	Aguadulce, Panama
Miles, Aaron	.333	8	12	3	4	3	0	0	2	0	0	0	0	.583	.333	S	R	5-8	170	12-15-76	1995	Antioch, Calif.
Olivo, Miguel	.237	114	317	37	75	19	1	6	27	19	80	6	4	.360	.287	R	R	6-0	220	7-15-78	1996	Ceres, Calif.
Ordonez, Magglio	.317	160	606	95	192	46	3	29	99	57	73	9	5	.546	.380	R	R	6-0	210	1-28-74	1991	Miami, Fla.
Paul, Josh	.353	13	17	6	6	0	0	0	4	3	3	0	0	.353	.450	R	R	6-1	200	5-19-75	1996	Naperville, Ill.
Rios, Armando	.212	49	104	4	22	3	0	2	11	5	13	0	1	.298	.245	L	L	5-9	190	9-13-71	1994	Pembroke Pines, Fla.
Rowand, Aaron	.287	93	157	22	45	8	0	6	24	7	21	0	0	.452	.327	R	R	6-1	210	8-29-77	1998	Las Vegas, Nev.
Thomas, Frank	.267	153	546	87	146	35	0	42	105	100	115	0	0	.562	.390	R	R	6-5	270	5-27-68	1989	Chicago, Ill.
Valentin, Jose	.237	144	503	79	119	26	2	28	74	54	114	8	3	.463	.313	S	R	5-10	180	10-12-69	1987	Manati, P.R.

PITCHING	W	L	ERA	G	GS	CG	SV	IP	H	R	ER	BB	SO	AVG	B	T	HT	WT	DOB	1st Yr	Resides
Adkins, Jon	0	0	4.82	4	0	0	0	9	8	5	5	7	3	.250	L	R	6-0	200	8-30-77	1998	Wayne, W.Va.
Buehrle, Mark	14	14	4.14	35	35	2	0	230	250	124	106	61	119	.278	L	L	6-2	200	3-23-79	1999	St. Charles, Mo.
Colon, Bartolo	15	13	3.87	34	34	9	0	242	223	107	104	67	173	.248	R	R	5-11	240	5-24-73	1994	Westlake, Ohio
Cotts, Neal	1	1	8.10	4	4	0	0	13	15	12	12	17	10	.294	L	L	6-2	200	3-25-80	2001	Lebanon, Ill.
Garland, Jon	12	13	4.51	32	32	0	0	192	188	103	96	74	108	.260	R	R	6-6	200	9-27-79	1997	Granada Hills, Calif.
Ginter, Matt	0	0	13.50	3	0	0	0	3	2	5	5	1	0	.181	R	R	6-1	220	12-24-77	1999	Winchester, Ky.
Glover, Gary	1	0	4.54	24	0	0	0	36	43	18	18	14	23	.304	R	R	6-5	200	12-3-76	1994	Deland, Fla.
Gordon, Tom	7	6	3.16	66	0	0	12	74	57	29	26	31	91	.212	R	R	5-10	190	11-18-67	1986	Avon Park, Fla.
Koch, Billy	5	5	5.77	55	0	0	11	53	59	36	34	28	42	.280	R	R	6-3	210	12-14-74	1996	Clearwater, Fla.
Loaiza, Esteban	21	9	2.90	34	34	1	0	226	196	75	73	56	207	.232	R	R	6-3	210	12-31-71	1991	Southlake, Texas
Marte, Damaso	4	2	1.58	71	0	0	11	80	50	16	14	34	87	.184	L	L	6-2	200	2-14-75	1993	Santo Domingo, D.R.
Paniagua, Jose	0	0	108.00	1	0	0	0	0	3	4	4	1	0	.750	R	R	6-2	190	8-20-73	1991	Santo Domingo, D.R.
Porzio, Mike	1	1	6.43	3	3	0	0	14	18	10	10	1	9	.321	L	L	6-3	200	8-20-72	1993	Norwalk, Conn.
Sanders, Dave	0	0	6.14	20	0	0	0	22	25	16	15	11	14	.280	L	L	6-0	200	8-29-79	1999	Derby, Kan.
Schoeneweis, Scott	2	1	4.50	20	0	0	0	26	26	16	13	9	27	.254	L	L	6-0	190	10-2-73	1996	Fountain Hills, Ariz.
2-team (39 Anaheim)	3	2	4.18	59	0	0	0	65	63	35	30	19	56	.252							
Stewart, Josh	1	2	5.96	5	5	0	0	26	28	18	17	16	13	.271	L	L	6-3	200	12-5-78	1999	Ledbetter, Ky.
Sullivan, Scott	0	0	3.77	15	0	0	0	14	9	6	6	6	13	.183	R	R	6-3	210	3-13-71	1993	Livingston, Ala.
White, Rick	1	2	6.61	34	0	0	1	48	56	39	35	13	37	.294	R	R	6-4	230	12-23-68	1990	Springfield, Ohio
Wright, Danny	1	7	6.15	20	15	0	1	86	91	63	59	46	47	.276	R	R	6-5	220	12-14-77	1999	Batesville, Ark.
Wunsch, Kelly	0	0	2.75	43	0	0	0	36	17	13	11	25	33	.139	L	L	6-5	220	7-12-72	1993	Houston, Texas

FIELDING

Catcher	PCT	G	PO	A	E	DP	PB
S. Alomar	.997	75	371	16	1	3	3
Burke	1.000	4	7	1	0	0	1
Olivo	.988	113	692	39	9	5	8
Paul	1.000	11	27	4	0	0	1

First Base	PCT	G	PO	A	E	DP
Burke	1.000	1	1	1	0	0
Daubach	.996	45	245	21	1	21
Graffanino	1.000	2	6	0	0	0
Konerko	.998	119	889	80	2	102
Thomas	.995	27	206	9	1	19

Second Base	PCT	G	PO	A	E	DP
R. Alomar	.990	67	119	171	3	37
Graffanino	.977	29	53	77	3	22
Harris	1.000	12	13	24	0	5
Jimenez	.977	68	118	174	7	41
Miles	1.000	3	1	6	0	0

Third Base	PCT	G	PO	A	E	DP
Crede	.964	151	107	264	14	29
Graffanino	.958	20	5	18	1	2
Jimenez	.667	2	0	4	2	0

Shortstop	PCT	G	PO	A	E	DP
Graffanino	.968	36	42	79	4	17
Valentin	.969	143	225	396	20	96

Outfield	PCT	G	PO	A	E	DP
Borchard	1.000	16	32	0	0	0
Daubach	.929	12	13	0	1	0
Everett	.987	68	145	3	2	0
Harris	.977	61	83	3	2	0
Lee	.978	156	307	8	7	1
Ordonez	.994	157	321	7	2	1
Rios	.981	32	51	1	1	0
Rowand	1.000	87	114	6	0	0

RON VESELY

Carlos Lee

FARM SYSTEM

Director, Player Development: Bob Fontaine.

Class	Farm Team	League	W	L	Pct.	Finish*	Manager	First Yr.
AAA	Charlotte (N.C.) Knights	International	74	70	.514	6th (14)	Nick Capra	1999
AA	Birmingham (Ala.) Barons	Southern	73	64	.533	3rd (10)	Wally Backman	1986
High A	Winston-Salem (N.C.) Warthogs	Carolina	71	67	.514	+5th (8)	Razor Shines	1997
Low A	Kannapolis (N.C.) Intimidators	South Atlantic	55	82	.401	15th (16)	John Orton	2001
Rookie	Great Falls (Mont.) White Sox	Pioneer	38	38	.500	4th (7)	Chris Cron	2003
Rookie	Bristol (Va.) Sox	Appalachian	33	33	.500	6th (10)	Jerry Hairston	1995

*Finish in overall standings (No. of teams in league) +League champion

CHARLOTTE KNIGHTS Class AAA

INTERNATIONAL LEAGUE

BATTING	AVG	G	AB	R	H	2B	3B	HR	RBI	BB	SO	SB	CS	SLG	OBP	B	T	HT	WT	DOB	1st Yr	Resides
Acevas, Jon	.360	8	25	3	9	2	0	0	4	2	5	0	0	.440	.448	R	R	6-2	190	3-7-78	1997	Sonora, Mexico
Alomar, Sandy	.267	5	15	2	4	0	0	0	1	1	1	0	0	.267	.313	R	R	6-5	230	6-18-66	1984	Chicago, Ill.
Borchard, Joe	.253	114	435	62	110	20	2	13	53	27	103	2	4	.398	.307	S	R	6-5	220	11-25-78	2000	Camarillo, Calif.
Brumbaugh, Cliff	.309	62	223	33	69	13	2	9	30	23	48	1	3	.507	.371	R	R	6-2	200	4-21-74	1995	New Castle, Del.
Burke, Jamie	.322	94	323	47	104	13	0	6	50	20	39	1	1	.418	.363	R	R	6-0	190	9-24-71	1993	Roseburg, Ore.
Gload, Ross	.315	133	508	72	160	40	6	18	70	29	60	6	3	.524	.349	L	L	6-0	180	4-5-76	1997	East Hampton, N.Y.
Hankins, Ryan	.276	68	239	29	66	16	0	6	33	16	38	2	4	.418	.322	R	R	5-11	200	6-30-76	1997	Simi Valley, Calif.
Harris, Willie	.380	28	100	22	38	6	1	6	13	17	20	9	3	.640	.470	L	R	5-9	170	6-22-78	1999	Cairo, Ga.
Hummel, Tim	.284	128	476	72	135	25	3	15	80	46	83	9	3	.443	.350	R	R	6-2	190	11-18-78	2000	Montgomery, N.Y.
Miles, Aaron	.304	133	546	80	166	34	5	11	50	40	52	8	9	.445	.351	S	R	5-8	170	12-15-76	1995	Antioch, Calif.
Morales, Steve	.189	14	37	4	7	1	0	1	2	1	8	0	0	.297	.211	S	R	5-10	190	5-4-78	1996	Mayaguez, P.R.
Morgan, Scott	.265	110	359	47	95	22	2	9	48	36	100	5	4	.412	.337	R	R	6-7	230	7-19-73	1995	Lompoc, Calif.
Murphy, Nate	.238	42	126	22	30	4	0	8	15	10	29	2	0	.460	.297	L	L	6-0	190	4-15-75	1996	Tucson, Ariz.
Nicholson, Tommy	.140	19	43	1	6	1	0	0	1	6	10	0	1	.163	.245	L	R	5-9	160	8-23-79	2000	Anaheim, Calif.
Nunez, Jorge	.231	112	350	35	81	8	1	1	26	12	80	15	8	.269	.255	R	R	5-10	160	3-5-75	1995	Villa Mella, D.R.
Paul, Josh	.188	19	64	6	12	0	1	2	5	5	14	1	1	.313	.243	R	R	6-1	200	5-19-75	1996	Naperville, Ill.
Rios, Armando	.323	45	155	23	50	9	1	6	30	14	30	5	6	.510	.389	L	L	5-9	190	9-13-71	1994	Pembroke Pines, Fla.
Rivera, Mike	.310	68	245	38	76	11	0	12	52	16	50	0	1	.502	.373	R	R	6-0	210	9-8-76	1997	Bayamon, P.R.
Rowand, Aaron	.242	32	120	15	29	9	0	3	13	11	12	0	0	.392	.316	R	R	6-1	210	8-29-77	1998	Las Vegas, Nev.
Sanders, Anthony	.229	76	245	32	56	10	2	10	40	21	65	5	2	.408	.295	R	R	6-2	200	3-2-74	1993	Tucson, Ariz.
Valenzuela, Mario	.254	31	114	14	29	5	0	3	10	3	25	1	0	.377	.277	R	R	6-2	190	3-10-77	1996	Isla San Marcos, Mexico

PITCHING	W	L	ERA	G	GS	CG	SV	IP	H	R	ER	BB	SO	AVG	B	T	HT	WT	DOB	1st Yr	Resides
Adkins, Jon	7	8	3.96	26	19	1	1	123	119	65	54	34	59	.254	L	R	6-0	200	8-30-77	1998	Wayne, W.Va.
Almonte, Ed	2	6	6.88	30	0	0	14	34	45	27	26	14	24	.330	R	R	6-3	220	12-17-76	1998	New York, N.Y.
Castillo, Carlos	0	1	9.77	6	1	0	0	16	24	19	17	7	9	.342	R	R	6-2	250	4-21-75	1994	Miami, Fla.
Cooper, Brian	15	9	3.98	28	28	2	0	174	195	91	77	35	106	.285	R	R	6-1	180	8-19-74	1995	Upland, Calif.
Diaz, Felix	5	7	3.97	27	18	1	0	116	122	59	51	33	83	.269	R	R	6-1	180	7-27-80	1998	Las Mata de Farfan, D.R.
Eason, Clay	0	0	12.23	8	0	0	0	18	30	24	24	12	14	.375	R	R	5-11	190	9-28-75	1997	Dunn, N.C.
Ginter, Matt	3	5	3.03	49	0	0	14	68	66	27	23	22	52	.249	R	R	6-1	220	12-24-77	1999	Winchester, Ky.
Jacquez, Tom	5	3	4.08	13	1	0	0	29	29	14	13	16	21	.261	L	L	6-2	190	12-29-75	1997	Stockton, Calif.
Koch, Billy	0	1	4.91	4	0	0	0	4	5	2	2	3	2	.312	R	R	6-3	210	12-14-74	1996	Clearwater, Fla.
Kohlmeier, Ryan	7	4	4.71	33	17	1	0	117	129	62	61	20	73	.275	R	R	6-2	220	6-25-77	1996	Cottonwood Falls, Kan.
Majewski, Gary	6	4	3.96	42	1	0	4	73	62	33	32	29	72	.231	R	R	6-2	200	2-26-80	1999	Houston, Texas
Meyer, Jake	1	2	3.42	20	0	0	0	26	26	11	10	10	15	.265	R	R	6-1	200	1-7-75	1997	San Diego, Calif.
Munoz, Arnaldo	4	3	4.75	49	0	0	6	55	52	35	29	27	63	.253	L	L	5-9	170	6-21-82	1999	Mao, D.R.
Nickle, Doug	1	1	2.87	11	0	0	2	16	17	5	5	3	16	.274	R	R	6-4	210	10-2-74	1997	Sonoma, Calif.
Paniagua, Jose	0	0	7.71	3	0	0	0	2	4	2	2	2	2	.400	R	R	6-2	190	8-20-73	1991	Santo Domingo, D.R.
Porzio, Mike	8	6	4.24	26	22	1	0	134	124	70	63	47	115	.248	L	L	6-3	200	8-20-72	1993	Norwalk, Conn.
Rauch, Jon	7	1	4.11	24	23	1	0	125	121	60	57	35	94	.257	R	R	6-11	260	9-27-78	1999	Tucson, Ariz.
Sanders, Dave	1	1	3.68	19	0	0	4	22	23	9	9	6	25	.264	L	L	6-0	200	8-29-79	1999	Derby, Kan.
Stewart, Josh	0	3	6.15	5	5	0	0	26	38	18	18	6	10	.345	L	L	6-3	200	12-5-78	1999	Ledbetter, Ky.
West, Brian	1	0	5.40	1	1	0	0	5	4	3	3	2	2	.210	R	R	6-4	230	8-4-80	1999	West Monroe, La.
Wright, Danny	1	3	4.64	8	7	1	0	33	25	18	17	10	25	.211	R	R	6-5	220	12-14-77	1999	Batesville, Ark.
Wunsch, Kelly	0	1	5.40	3	0	0	0	3	6	3	2	0	4	.428	L	L	6-5	220	7-12-72	1993	Houston, Texas
Yofu, Tetsu	0	1	4.82	3	1	0	0	9	11	5	5	4	13	.289	R	R	6-0	180	6-26-73	2003	Fujisaw City, Japan

FIELDING

Catcher	PCT	G	PO	A	E	DP	PB
Acevas	.962	7	45	6	2	1	1
Alomar	1.000	3	11	2	0	0	0
Burke	.989	72	493	34	6	5	3
Morales	.989	13	87	5	1	0	1
Paul	.982	17	101	8	2	2	0
Rivera	.991	36	216	15	2	1	5

First Base	PCT	G	PO	A	E	DP
Burke	1.000	6	36	2	0	4
Gload	.990	112	770	58	8	63
Hankins	.994	21	150	13	1	21
Morgan	.991	14	106	4	1	5
Rivera	1.000	4	29	1	0	1

Second Base	PCT	G	PO	A	E	DP
Harris	1.000	17	43	44	0	10
Hummel	1.000	6	11	7	0	3
Miles	.973	121	224	310	15	60
Nicholson	1.000	3	2	2	0	1
Paul	1.000	1	1	0	0	0

Third Base	PCT	G	PO	A	E	DP
Brumbaugh	1.000	4	2	3	0	0
Burke	1.000	1	1	1	0	0
Hankins	.960	47	29	67	4	6
Hummel	.955	97	63	150	10	17
Miles	1.000	2	1	3	0	0
Nicholson	1.000	2	0	2	0	0

Shortstop	PCT	G	PO	A	E	DP
Hummel	.966	31	37	48	3	9
Nicholson	.870	10	12	8	3	1
Nunez	.949	110	170	296	25	55

Outfield	PCT	G	PO	A	E	DP
Borchard	.985	114	316	9	5	2
Brumbaugh	.985	30	61	3	1	1
Gload	1.000	28	50	2	0	0
Harris	1.000	10	14	1	0	0
Morgan	.980	64	144	1	3	1
Murphy	1.000	38	57	2	0	1
Rios	.976	36	80	2	2	0
Rowand	.950	32	95	1	5	0
Sanders	.979	74	135	7	3	1
Valenzuela	1.000	20	36	2	0	0

BIRMINGHAM BARONS — Class AA

SOUTHERN LEAGUE

BATTING	AVG	G	AB	R	H	2B	3B	HR	RBI	BB	SO	SB	CS	SLG	OBP	B	T	HT	WT	DOB	1st Yr	Resides
Acevas, Jon	.230	51	126	17	29	7	0	3	16	14	35	0	2	.357	.331	R	R	6-2	190	3-7-78	1997	Sonora, Mexico
Alvarez, Gabe	.310	118	410	60	127	34	0	11	78	58	87	2	5	.473	.401	R	R	6-1	200	3-6-74	1995	San Gabriel, Calif.
Battersby, Eric	.174	24	46	4	8	2	0	0	3	6	11	2	0	.217	.304	R	L	6-1	200	2-28-76	1998	Corpus Christi, Texas
Bikowski, Scott	.312	118	394	53	123	23	3	3	49	50	65	3	7	.409	.391	L	L	6-0	180	2-12-77	1999	Suffield, Conn.
Durham, Chad	.270	119	408	59	110	13	2	1	37	39	81	15	16	.319	.334	R	R	5-8	170	6-23-78	1997	Charlotte, N.C.
Hamilton, Jon	.224	51	170	22	38	4	1	3	18	20	41	10	6	.312	.306	L	L	6-1	200	10-23-77	1997	San Ramon, Calif.
2-team (71 West Tenn)	.241	122	411	51	99	20	2	7	45	44	78	22	10	.350	.316							
Hankins, Ryan	.288	67	243	34	70	20	1	7	36	30	39	5	3	.465	.371	R	R	5-11	200	6-30-76	1997	Simi Valley, Calif.
Holt, Daylan	.000	5	13	1	0	0	0	0	0	2	7	0	0	.000	.133	R	R	6-1	200	10-4-78	2000	Mesquite, Texas
Ingram, Darron	.207	65	227	27	47	3	2	9	28	23	79	2	1	.357	.285	R	R	6-3	220	6-7-76	1994	Lexington, Ky.
Maldonado, Carlos	.262	120	408	50	107	24	1	6	63	43	50	1	1	.370	.335	R	R	6-2	180	1-3-79	1996	Maracaibo, Venez.
Morales, Steve	.244	31	86	6	21	1	1	2	12	5	12	0	0	.349	.287	S	R	5-10	190	5-4-78	1996	Mayaguez, P.R.
Nicholson, Tommy	.280	47	125	14	35	8	1	1	11	16	20	2	1	.384	.372	L	R	5-9	160	8-23-79	2000	Anaheim, Calif.
Piniella, Juan	.292	115	346	45	101	24	2	4	27	28	82	12	5	.408	.352	R	R	5-10	180	3-13-78	1996	Woodbridge, Va.
Reed, Jeremy	.409	66	242	51	99	17	3	7	43	29	19	18	13	.591	.474	L	L	6-0	180	6-15-81	2002	La Verne, Calif.
Reyes, Guillermo	.210	116	376	40	79	10	2	4	34	32	71	15	8	.279	.275	S	R	5-9	160	12-29-81	1999	Villa Vasquez, D.R.
Sandoval, Danny	.287	130	478	62	137	30	2	3	49	43	67	21	11	.377	.343	R	R	5-11	180	4-7-79	1997	Venez.
Saunders, Chris	.191	17	47	4	9	0	0	0	6	11	15	1	0	.191	.345	R	R	6-1	200	7-19-70	1992	Clovis, Calif.
Shaffer, Josh	.204	98	304	17	62	7	2	0	21	17	70	1	2	.240	.252	L	R	6-1	180	6-26-80	1999	Yorba Linda, Calif.

PITCHING	W	L	ERA	G	GS	CG	SV	IP	H	R	ER	BB	SO	AVG	B	T	HT	WT	DOB	1st Yr	Resides
An, Byeong	5	3	3.94	16	14	0	0	80	76	38	35	34	45	.248	L	L	6-2	230	7-1-80	2001	Bu Chun City, Korea
Bajenaru, Jeff	4	2	3.20	50	0	0	14	65	53	29	23	28	62	.224	R	R	6-1	190	3-21-78	2000	Rancho Cucamonga, Calif.
Bullard, Jim	5	3	3.69	53	6	0	3	90	103	51	37	42	61	.288	L	L	6-7	190	12-29-79	2001	West Covina, Calif.
Castillo, Carlos	3	1	3.96	5	4	0	0	25	23	11	11	6	19	.242	R	R	6-2	250	4-21-75	1994	Miami, Fla.
Cotts, Neal	9	7	2.16	21	21	0	0	108	67	32	26	56	133	.177	L	L	6-2	200	3-25-80	2001	Lebanon, Ill.
Dunn, Scott	3	1	1.69	8	0	0	1	11	8	2	2	5	14	.216	R	R	6-3	180	5-23-78	1999	San Antonio, Texas
2-team (31 Chattanooga)	6	3	3.35	39	0	0	9	51	39	23	19	21	68	.211							
Eason, Clay	1	3	3.72	17	1	0	1	36	47	23	15	13	38	.313	R	R	5-11	190	9-28-75	1997	Dunn, N.C.
Honel, Kris	1	0	3.75	2	2	0	0	12	9	6	5	6	13	.204	R	R	6-5	190	11-7-82	2001	Bourbonnais, Ill.
Malone, Corwin	4	2	5.40	8	8	0	0	40	50	26	24	28	28	.304	R	L	6-3	200	7-3-80	1999	Thomasville, Ala.
McWhirter, Kris	3	8	5.64	25	5	1	0	61	60	44	38	44	42	.260	L	R	6-4	190	5-11-79	1999	Goodlettsville, Tenn.
Meaux, Ryan	1	2	2.13	26	0	0	2	38	39	11	9	3	29	.276	R	L	5-11	170	10-5-78	2001	Lamar, Colo.
Meyer, Jake	1	1	3.20	17	0	0	1	25	22	10	9	10	20	.231	R	R	6-1	200	1-7-75	1997	San Diego, Calif.
Murray, Brad	0	0	5.40	5	0	0	0	5	7	3	3	4	1	.333	L	L	5-11	170	8-20-78	2000	La Belle, Fla.
O'Neal, Brandon	0	0	7.20	5	0	0	0	5	6	4	4	4	2	.315	S	R	6-1	210	10-17-78	2000	Olathe, Kan.
Pacheco, Enemencio	12	2	2.56	30	24	0	0	151	131	51	43	51	116	.233	R	R	6-1	170	8-31-78	1997	Santo Domingo, D.R.
Phillips, Heath	0	1	10.50	1	1	0	0	6	14	8	7	1	5	.466	L	L	6-3	200	3-24-82	2001	Evansville, Ind.
Purvis, Rob	0	0	9.47	13	0	0	0	19	27	24	20	14	15	.325	R	R	6-2	200	8-11-77	1999	Tipton, Ind.
Ring, Royce	1	4	2.52	36	0	0	19	36	33	11	10	14	44	.237	L	L	6-0	220	12-21-80	2002	La Mesa, Calif.
Smith, Matt	4	1	3.89	52	0	0	2	69	74	33	30	31	44	.269	R	R	6-5	240	8-14-78	1999	Godfrey, Ill.
Stumm, Jason	0	0	4.50	7	0	0	0	8	8	4	4	6	8	.266	R	R	6-2	210	4-13-81	1999	Centralia, Wash.
Ulacia, Dennis	1	5	4.53	11	10	0	0	50	59	27	25	21	31	.301	L	L	6-1	180	4-2-81	1999	Hialeah, Fla.
West, Brian	3	5	5.80	12	11	1	0	54	70	39	35	28	37	.312	R	R	6-4	230	8-4-80	1999	West Monroe, La.
Wylie, Mitch	3	5	4.40	14	10	1	0	57	53	33	28	17	42	.246	R	R	6-3	190	1-14-77	1998	Princeton, Iowa
Yofu, Tetsu	9	8	3.50	29	20	0	2	131	117	58	51	37	114	.238	R	R	6-0	180	6-26-73	2003	Fujisaw City, Japan

FIELDING

Catcher	PCT	G	PO	A	E	DP	PB
Acevas	.984	23	171	9	3	0	3
Hankins	1.000	1	2	1	0	0	0
Maldonado	.988	94	632	51	8	5	6
Morales	.975	29	181	18	5	2	1

First Base	PCT	G	PO	A	E	DP
Acevas	.980	17	98	1	2	7
Alvarez	.985	87	583	53	10	59
Battersby	.979	20	90	3	2	4
Hamilton	.988	13	77	5	1	3
Hankins	1.000	21	130	18	0	16
Maldonado	1.000	2	10	0	0	2
Sandoval	1.000	2	3	0	0	1
Saunders	1.000	3	23	2	0	4

Second Base	PCT	G	PO	A	E	DP
Hankins	1.000	7	15	14	0	5
Nicholson	.933	20	33	51	6	10
Reyes	1.000	13	28	29	0	7
Sandoval	.975	108	194	227	11	45
Shaffer	.896	8	19	24	5	4

Third Base	PCT	G	PO	A	E	DP
Alvarez	.875	16	6	15	3	2
Hankins	.908	32	16	43	6	1
Nicholson	.931	31	21	33	4	3
Sandoval	.903	12	7	21	3	3
Saunders	.963	12	4	22	1	1
Shaffer	.870	63	36	84	18	14

Shortstop	PCT	G	PO	A	E	DP
Acevas	1.000	1	0	1	0	1
Reyes	.940	104	135	227	23	40
Sandoval	.985	21	24	40	1	12
Shaffer	.911	28	40	52	9	9

Outfield	PCT	G	PO	A	E	DP
Battersby	.846	5	10	1	2	0
Bikowski	.977	84	167	5	4	0
Durham	.982	115	260	8	5	4
Hamilton	.966	38	85	1	3	0
Holt	1.000	4	4	0	0	0
Ingram	1.000	36	58	2	0	0
Piniella	.979	103	181	4	4	0
Reed	1.000	60	150	5	0	0

WINSTON-SALEM WARTHOGS — High Class A

CAROLINA LEAGUE

BATTING	AVG	G	AB	R	H	2B	3B	HR	RBI	BB	SO	SB	CS	SLG	OBP	B	T	HT	WT	DOB	1st Yr	Resides
Amador, Chris	.197	26	66	6	13	1	1	0	3	4	18	8	0	.242	.250	R	R	5-10	160	12-14-82	2000	Camuy, P.R.
Barnett, Dan	.111	9	18	1	2	1	0	0	1	1	6	0	0	.167	.150	R	R	5-10	180	3-31-80	2002	Wauchula, Fla.
Becker, Brian	.257	115	408	47	105	24	1	19	72	27	98	3	3	.461	.299	R	R	6-7	230	5-26-75	1996	Tempe, Ariz.
Ciraco, Darren	.286	2	7	0	2	1	0	0	0	0	1	0	0	.429	.286	R	R	6-2	200	4-6-81	2000	New Rochelle, N.Y.
Holt, Daylan	.259	112	340	50	88	28	0	11	58	35	68	8	4	.438	.326	R	R	6-1	200	10-4-78	2000	Mesquite, Texas
Lackaff, John	.263	28	80	14	21	5	0	2	11	4	11	3	0	.400	.344	R	R	5-11	190	5-3-79	2000	Downers Grove, Ill.
Lopez, Pedro	.231	4	13	1	3	0	0	0	0	1	0	0	0	.231	.286	R	R	6-1	160	4-28-84	2001	Moca, D.R.
Martel, Normand	.273	117	348	36	95	13	4	3	36	22	32	9	5	.359	.318	L	R	6-0	180	8-4-78	2001	Newport News, Va.
Morse, Michael	.245	122	432	45	106	30	2	10	55	25	91	4	4	.394	.296	R	R	6-4	180	3-22-82	2000	Plantation, Fla.
Nicholson, Tommy	.289	26	90	16	26	7	1	2	9	5	18	1	1	.456	.340	L	R	5-9	160	8-23-79	2000	Anaheim, Calif.
Reed, Jeremy	.333	65	222	37	74	18	1	4	52	41	17	27	6	.477	.431	L	L	6-0	180	6-15-81	2002	La Verne, Calif.

BATTING	AVG	G	AB	R	H	2B	3B	HR	RBI	BB	SO	SB	CS	SLG	OBP	B	T	HT	WT	DOB	1st Yr	Resides
Rogowski, Casey	.246	116	357	46	88	20	1	7	38	53	73	18	4	.367	.354	L	L	6-3	230	5-1-81	1999	Livonia, Mich.
Rosa, Wally	.211	69	199	17	42	7	0	1	13	15	40	1	2	.261	.274	R	R	6-1	180	11-28-81	2000	Hialeah, Fla.
Salvo, Andrew	.143	5	14	1	2	0	0	0	0	2	1	0	0	.143	.250	L	R	5-10	170	8-27-79	2001	East Islip, N.Y.
Spidale, Mike	.262	120	393	61	103	21	5	1	42	57	76	25	7	.349	.362	R	R	6-1	180	3-12-82	2000	Broadview, Ill.
Stewart, Chris	.207	76	217	18	45	8	2	2	27	27	29	1	0	.290	.294	R	R	6-4	200	2-19-82	2001	Moreno Valley, Calif.
Storey, Eric	.272	111	331	48	90	25	1	9	31	49	98	10	5	.435	.369	R	R	6-0	170	10-12-77	2000	Indianapolis, Ind.
Welsh, Eric	.240	96	308	45	74	17	0	15	51	28	74	2	1	.442	.307	L	L	6-3	200	9-17-76	1997	Tinley Park, Ill.
Yan, Ruddy	.264	130	485	85	128	11	3	2	24	47	73	76	13	.311	.328	S	R	6-0	160	1-13-81	1999	Santo Domingo, D.R.

PITCHING	W	L	ERA	G	GS	CG	SV	IP	H	R	ER	BB	SO	AVG	B	T	HT	WT	DOB	1st Yr	Resides
Allen, Wyatt	6	8	4.39	28	25	0	0	139	128	79	68	89	86	.251	R	R	6-4	200	4-12-80	2001	Brentwood, Tenn.
An, Byeong	8	4	3.16	12	12	1	0	68	66	29	24	27	45	.262	L	L	6-2	230	7-1-80	2001	Bu Chun City, Korea
Bittner, Tim	3	3	3.60	17	0	0	1	30	18	13	12	12	23	.176	L	L	6-2	200	6-9-80	2001	Wilmington, Del.
Castillo, Carlos	0	2	7.20	2	2	0	0	10	15	8	8	3	4	.365	R	R	6-2	250	4-21-75	1994	Miami, Fla.
Castro, Julio	3	1	1.01	26	0	0	2	36	25	7	4	13	26	.195	R	R	6-1	160	6-30-81	1998	San Pedro de Macoris, D.R.
Fields, Josh	6	7	3.10	58	0	0	20	73	54	29	25	25	68	.203	R	R	6-1	170	1-20-80	2001	Hungry Horse, Mont.
Francisco, Frank	7	3	3.56	16	16	1	0	78	59	40	31	36	67	.207	R	R	6-2	180	9-11-79	1997	Santo Domingo, D.R.
Garza, Rolando	1	0	5.93	17	0	0	0	14	12	10	9	21	14	.240	R	R	6-4	210	12-14-79	1997	Coachella, Calif.
Honel, Kris	9	7	3.11	24	24	3	0	133	122	51	46	42	122	.247	R	R	6-5	190	11-7-82	2001	Bourbonnais, Ill.
Hummel, Rick	1	1	3.27	19	0	0	1	22	30	12	8	4	9	.326	R	R	6-2	190	9-12-80	2002	Wonder Lake, Ill.
Kirkland, Aaron	1	0	4.07	16	0	0	0	24	32	17	11	16	16	.326	R	R	6-5	200	3-1-79	2001	Chatom, Ala.
LaMura, B.J.	0	2	9.00	4	2	0	0	13	19	14	13	6	8	.372	R	R	6-1	200	1-1-81	2002	Ronkonkoma, N.Y.
Lubisich, Nik	1	0	3.18	3	0	0	0	6	6	3	2	2	2	.272	L	L	6-2	190	4-19-79	2001	Portland, Ore.
McWhirter, Kris	0	3	3.27	11	5	0	1	33	21	14	12	18	36	.179	L	R	6-4	190	5-11-79	1999	Goodlettsville, Tenn.
Meaux, Ryan	1	3	1.15	32	0	0	10	55	49	14	7	3	43	.239	R	L	5-11	170	10-5-78	2001	Lamar, Colo.
O'Neal, Brandon	2	3	3.47	35	5	0	1	62	58	40	24	42	28	.252	S	R	6-1	210	10-17-78	2000	Olathe, Kan.
Patten, Scott	1	1	4.82	10	1	0	0	19	29	17	10	10	14	.349	R	R	6-3	210	11-26-80	1999	Tecumseh, Okla.
Phillips, Heath	2	7	3.58	13	13	0	0	75	84	37	30	7	51	.288	L	L	6-3	200	3-24-82	2001	Evansville, Ind.
Pollok, Dwayne	0	1	3.92	14	0	0	0	21	25	12	9	2	14	.297	R	R	6-3	195	11-12-80	2003	San Antonio, Texas
Purvis, Rob	4	3	2.14	12	7	0	0	42	34	15	10	20	30	.222	R	R	6-2	200	8-11-77	1999	Tipton, Ind.
Stumm, Jason	1	0	3.60	20	0	0	0	25	28	10	10	11	23	.294	R	R	6-2	210	4-13-81	1999	Centralia, Wash.
Ulacia, Dennis	3	1	0.42	12	0	0	0	22	12	6	1	12	13	.151	L	L	6-1	180	4-2-81	1999	Hialeah, Fla.
Wing, Ryan	9	7	2.98	26	26	0	0	145	116	62	48	67	107	.227	L	L	6-2	170	2-1-82	2001	Murrieta, Calif.
Wylie, Mitch	2	0	3.38	4	0	0	0	8	7	3	3	3	7	.233	R	R	6-3	190	1-14-77	1998	Princeton, Iowa

FIELDING

Catcher	PCT	G	PO	A	E	DP	PB
Barnett	1.000	2	2	0	0	0	0
Rosa	.982	69	379	46	8	0	13
Stewart	.976	76	500	68	14	3	8
Storey	1.000	1	1	0	0	0	1

First Base	PCT	G	PO	A	E	DP
Becker	.995	23	172	19	1	13
Rogowski	.997	104	826	62	3	66
Storey	1.000	2	5	3	0	0
Welsh	.992	16	109	12	1	12

Second Base	PCT	G	PO	A	E	DP
Amador	.963	6	10	16	1	1
Lopez	1.000	2	4	6	0	0
Nicholson	1.000	4	6	6	0	1
Salvo	1.000	1	0	2	0	0
Storey	1.000	2	4	4	0	1
Yan	.975	129	250	326	15	65

Third Base	PCT	G	PO	A	E	DP
Amador	.909	12	11	9	2	0
Lackaff	.948	27	18	37	3	4
Nicholson	.905	19	11	27	4	2
Spidale	.000	1	0	0	1	0
Storey	.896	91	62	153	25	13

Shortstop	PCT	G	PO	A	E	DP
Amador	.792	6	7	12	5	3
Lopez	.867	2	5	8	2	3
Morse	.959	120	164	285	19	51
Nicholson	1.000	4	8	14	0	3
Salvo	1.000	4	6	7	0	1
Storey	.833	4	5	10	3	1

Outfield	PCT	G	PO	A	E	DP
Ciraco	1.000	2	3	0	0	0
Holt	.977	106	165	8	4	0
Martel	.979	112	184	6	4	0
Reed	.979	64	135	6	3	0
Spidale	.989	120	272	1	3	1
Welsh	.958	51	67	2	3	0

KANNAPOLIS INTIMIDATORS — Low Class A

SOUTH ATLANTIC LEAGUE

BATTING	AVG	G	AB	R	H	2B	3B	HR	RBI	BB	SO	SB	CS	SLG	OBP	B	T	HT	WT	DOB	1st Yr	Resides
Acevas, Jon	.284	24	81	14	23	9	0	5	15	9	15	0	0	.580	.359	R	R	6-2	190	3-7-78	1997	Sonora, Mexico
Amador, Chris	.250	5	16	1	4	1	0	0	1	1	3	2	0	.313	.294	R	R	5-10	160	12-14-82	2000	Camuy, P.R.
Barnett, Dan	.265	23	68	9	18	5	0	1	11	7	22	0	0	.382	.342	R	R	5-10	180	3-31-80	2002	Wauchula, Fla.
Brice, Thomas	.280	120	397	50	111	21	2	1	49	43	63	8	7	.350	.355	L	L	6-5	210	8-24-81	2002	Mile End, Australia
Cavin, Jonathan	.221	45	131	16	29	3	0	0	7	20	47	0	1	.244	.327	L	R	6-3	220	3-19-80	2000	Stilwell, Okla.
Christensen, Mike	.235	70	243	34	57	16	0	7	36	22	58	0	0	.387	.302	R	R	6-2	190	5-24-76	1998	Fort Myers, Fla.
Ciraco, Darren	.228	100	338	32	77	19	4	4	54	24	69	7	1	.343	.276	R	R	6-2	200	4-6-81	2000	New Rochelle, N.Y.
Cook, David	.162	40	136	14	22	5	0	0	7	13	36	4	0	.199	.233	R	R	5-11	195	7-21-81	2003	Columbus, Ohio
Gillikin, Joey	.202	35	104	14	21	9	0	2	14	26	34	3	0	.346	.359	R	R	5-10	200	3-17-77	2000	Yukon, Okla.
Gonzalez, Andy	.231	123	429	58	99	17	1	1	39	69	82	22	10	.282	.347	R	R	6-2	180	12-15-81	2001	Rio Piedras, P.R.
Hickman, Brian	.125	9	16	1	2	0	0	0	1	4	7	0	0	.125	.286	R	R	6-2	200	2-7-78	2001	Yuba City, Calif.
Ivy, Bjorn	.174	42	115	10	20	1	1	0	6	14	25	10	5	.200	.275	R	R	5-10	170	9-20-81	2000	Shannon, Miss.
Lackaff, John	.180	19	61	9	11	4	0	2	8	10	10	1	0	.344	.311	R	R	5-11	190	5-3-79	2000	Downers Grove, Ill.
Lebron, Freddie	.229	15	48	4	11	0	0	0	4	4	11	3	1	.229	.288	S	R	5-9	170	1-23-82	2001	Humacao, P.R.
Lisk, Charlie	.190	42	126	20	24	8	1	3	17	18	41	0	2	.341	.301	R	R	6-3	200	1-3-83	2001	Fort Mill, S.C.
Lopez, Pedro	.264	109	390	40	103	23	0	0	33	26	43	24	14	.323	.314	R	R	6-1	160	4-28-84	2001	Moca, D.R.
Luna, Leonardo	.177	19	62	4	11	2	0	1	6	3	9	0	0	.258	.227	R	R	6-0	160	2-14-82	1999	Santiago, D.R.
Molina, Gustavo	.229	96	315	30	72	15	1	5	41	17	56	5	3	.330	.287	R	R	6-2	180	2-24-82	2000	La Guaira, Venez.
Reyes, Julio	.256	90	336	35	86	17	1	2	32	9	75	1	1	.330	.278	L	R	6-2	180	6-30-80	1999	San Luis, Mexico
Salvo, Andrew	.235	37	98	19	23	4	0	1	6	19	17	1	2	.306	.359	L	R	5-10	170	8-27-79	2001	East Islip, N.Y.
Terrell, Jim	.273	52	172	18	47	8	0	1	12	19	31	8	3	.337	.342	L	R	6-1	170	9-8-77	1996	Blue Springs, Mo.
Varela, Edgar	.230	72	248	17	57	12	0	1	29	19	37	0	0	.290	.290	L	R	6-1	200	8-9-80	2002	E. Rancho Dominguez, Calif.
Webster, Anthony	.289	94	363	68	105	18	1	2	33	31	58	20	12	.361	.353	L	R	6-0	190	4-10-83	2001	Parsons, Tenn.
Young, Eddie	.231	22	65	7	15	1	0	0	7	5	10	1	3	.246	.286	R	R	6-2	190	2-6-82	2000	Macon, Ga.

PITCHING	W	L	ERA	G	GS	CG	SV	IP	H	R	ER	BB	SO	AVG	B	T	HT	WT	DOB	1st Yr	Resides
Arellan, Felix	1	3	5.03	31	0	0	0	54	55	34	30	42	45	.276	L	L	6-2	170	2-23-81	1997	Maracay, Venez.
Bittner, Tim	4	4	3.40	10	10	1	0	50	45	24	19	26	45	.241	L	L	6-2	200	6-9-80	2001	Wilmington, Del.
Castro, Fabio	0	2	3.27	2	2	0	0	11	8	5	4	5	16	.200	L	L	5-8	150	1-20-85	2002	Monte Cristi, D.R.

PITCHING	W	L	ERA	G	GS	CG	SV	IP	H	R	ER	BB	SO	AVG	B	T	HT	WT	DOB	1st Yr	Resides
Castro, Julio	1	3	3.38	14	0	0	0	29	26	11	11	11	44	.236	R	R	6-1	160	6-30-81	1998	San Pedro de Macoris, D.R.
Deininger, Todd	6	4	3.65	32	14	0	0	111	90	63	45	56	103	.218	R	R	6-3	200	9-4-81	2002	Joliet, Ill.
Fryson, Andrew	1	4	3.24	21	5	1	0	58	52	30	21	27	37	.236	R	R	6-7	200	10-13-80	2001	Tallahassee, Fla.
Garza, Rolando	1	1	2.89	21	0	0	1	28	20	11	9	30	30	.210	R	R	6-4	210	12-14-79	1997	Coachella, Calif.
Hudson, Jeremy	0	0	0.00	1	0	0	0	1	1	0	0	0	0	.250	R	R	6-7	210	3-15-80	2002	Cullman, Ala.
Hummel, Rick	2	3	1.47	27	0	0	10	37	27	13	6	16	33	.201	R	R	6-2	190	9-12-80	2002	Wonder Lake, Ill.
Larson, Adam	2	4	3.62	39	1	0	7	75	74	35	30	13	66	.254	R	R	6-3	230	12-6-79	2002	Terre Haute, Ind.
LaMura, B.J.	6	10	3.58	24	21	2	0	128	125	69	51	62	101	.263	R	R	6-1	200	1-1-81	2002	Ronkonkoma, N.Y.
Lubisich, Nik	2	2	3.09	16	7	0	1	67	68	27	23	17	31	.265	L	L	6-2	190	4-19-79	2001	Portland, Ore.
Malone, Corwin	0	3	5.11	5	5	1	0	25	27	19	14	10	29	.272	R	L	6-3	200	7-3-80	1999	Thomasville, Ala.
Miller, Brian	8	12	5.30	25	25	1	0	126	124	85	74	61	93	.258	R	R	6-3	200	10-18-82	2001	Charlotte, Mich.
Murray, Brad	1	1	0.54	11	0	0	3	17	13	2	1	8	12	.232	L	L	5-11	170	8-20-78	2000	La Belle, Fla.
Perez, Armando	4	6	4.41	34	5	0	0	82	82	51	40	40	56	.261	L	L	6-2	190	12-26-80	2000	San Ysidro, Calif.
Phillips, Heath	2	0	1.71	3	3	0	0	21	13	4	4	5	11	.178	L	L	6-3	200	3-24-82	2001	Evansville, Ind.
Reynoso, Paulino	5	7	3.16	22	21	1	0	108	81	46	38	55	86	.213	L	L	6-3	190	8-10-80	1999	Santiago, D.R.
Rupe, Josh	5	5	3.02	26	7	2	6	66	50	27	22	36	69	.211	R	R	6-2	180	8-18-82	2002	Chesapeake, Va.
Tisch, Tim	1	0	1.93	3	2	0	0	14	11	5	3	8	11	.211	L	L	6-5	190	4-11-80	2002	Santee, Calif.
Tracey, Sean	2	7	9.50	14	9	0	0	42	51	54	44	46	28	.305	L	R	6-3	210	11-14-80	2002	Upland, Calif.
Wasserman, Ehren	1	1	1.00	6	0	0	0	9	8	1	1	3	10	.266	S	R	6-0	185	12-6-80	2003	Birmingham, Ala.

FIELDING

Catcher	PCT	G	PO	A	E	DP	PB
Acevas	.991	15	89	17	1	1	3
Barnett	.994	22	139	19	1	0	10
Hickman	1.000	8	40	5	0	0	1
Lisk	.976	31	257	22	7	0	21
Molina	.983	71	465	55	9	1	17
Reyes	1.000	1	1	0	0	0	0

First Base	PCT	G	PO	A	E	DP
Acevas	.986	8	66	4	1	3
Brice	.971	15	97	5	3	7
Christensen	1.000	6	32	2	0	3
Luna	.000	1	0	0	0	0
Molina	1.000	26	176	21	0	9
Reyes	.990	73	539	33	6	20
Terrell	.984	8	58	5	1	5
Varela	1.000	17	95	7	0	2

Second Base	PCT	G	PO	A	E	DP
Amador	1.000	2	4	5	0	1
Lebron	.947	14	23	31	3	8
Lopez	.974	92	171	211	10	19
Luna	.974	14	35	40	2	6
Molina	.000	1	0	0	0	0
Salvo	.983	22	28	30	1	1

Third Base	PCT	G	PO	A	E	DP
Amador	1.000	3	0	4	0	0
Christensen	.957	49	34	98	6	3
Gonzalez	.000	1	0	0	0	0
Lackaff	.954	18	14	48	3	3
Lebron	.000	1	0	0	0	0
Lopez	1.000	1	1	0	0	0
Luna	1.000	2	1	2	0	0
Molina	.000	1	0	0	0	0
Salvo	.900	15	5	13	2	0
Varela	.950	58	46	126	9	2

Shortstop	PCT	G	PO	A	E	DP
Gonzalez	.935	121	236	307	38	37
Lopez	.955	16	22	42	3	4
Luna	1.000	3	0	5	0	0
Molina	1.000	1	0	1	0	0
Salvo	1.000	1	2	1	0	0

Outfield	PCT	G	PO	A	E	DP
Brice	.968	94	142	8	5	0
Cavin	.938	40	61	0	4	0
Ciraco	.945	94	143	11	9	0
Cook	.980	37	95	2	2	0
Ivy	.981	37	50	3	1	0
Molina	1.000	1	2	0	0	0
Reyes	1.000	7	7	0	0	0
Salvo	.000	1	0	0	0	0
Terrell	.906	13	29	0	3	0
Webster	.984	91	185	3	3	0
Young	.971	19	34	0	1	0

BRISTOL SOX — Rookie

APPALACHIAN LEAGUE

BATTING	AVG	G	AB	R	H	2B	3B	HR	RBI	BB	SO	SB	CS	SLG	OBP	B	T	HT	WT	DOB	1st Yr	Resides
Arias, Angel	.239	30	92	6	22	6	1	0	5	4	12	1	2	.326	.271	R	R	5-11	170	9-8-82	1999	Azua, D.R.
Bohlander, Mike	.224	41	98	18	22	5	2	1	9	11	20	1	0	.347	.303	L	R	6-1	230	11-8-80	2002	Katonah, N.Y.
Castillo, Cesar	.222	41	99	10	22	3	0	1	8	14	19	0	2	.283	.336	R	R	5-10	180	6-26-79	2002	Yuma, Ariz.
Collaro, Tom	.226	45	146	17	33	9	1	8	28	4	46	1	0	.466	.252	R	R	6-4	210	4-4-83	2002	Sunrise, Fla.
Herring, Matt	.234	46	128	17	30	4	2	4	22	16	41	0	0	.391	.322	L	L	6-2	210	9-24-80	2002	Valdosta, Ga.
Lebron, Freddie	.250	37	116	19	29	6	1	2	13	8	17	10	4	.371	.307	S	R	5-9	170	1-23-82	2001	Humacao, P.R.
Lenderman, Matt	.204	22	49	5	10	1	0	1	6	2	29	0	0	.286	.235	R	R	5-11	205	4-18-84	2003	Plano, Texas
Luna, Leonardo	.321	26	109	21	35	8	0	1	12	4	19	1	0	.422	.348	R	R	6-0	160	2-14-82	1999	Santiago, D.R.
Martin, Scott	.185	43	108	13	20	6	1	2	14	2	31	0	0	.315	.219	R	R	6-1	205	5-16-81	2003	Middletown, Del.
Perez, Melvin	.262	62	221	27	58	16	4	3	33	13	64	2	3	.412	.313	R	R	6-1	170	2-2-84	2001	San Cristobal, D.R.
Ramirez, Estevinson	.280	29	50	9	14	3	0	0	5	7	16	1	6	.340	.368	S	R	5-11	160	8-6-81	2000	La Cienaga, D.R.
Rivera, Jhonny	.259	49	139	19	36	11	1	0	13	2	41	13	5	.353	.288	R	R	6-1	170	7-4-83	2000	Guarenas, Venez.
Rodriguez, Manuel	.154	29	78	8	12	3	1	2	10	4	30	0	1	.295	.214	R	R	6-2	180	5-24-83	2001	Chitre, Panama
Schmidt, Jeff	.200	26	70	5	14	4	0	0	10	3	15	0	1	.257	.230	R	R	6-3	210	8-15-85	2003	San Diego, Calif.
Sweeney, Ryan	.313	19	67	11	21	3	0	2	5	7	10	3	0	.448	.387	L	L	6-4	200	2-20-85	2003	Cedar Rapids, Iowa
Valido, Robert	.307	58	215	39	66	15	2	6	31	17	28	17	6	.479	.364	R	R	6-2	180	5-16-85	2003	Miami, Fla.
Young, Chris	.290	64	238	47	69	18	3	7	28	23	40	21	7	.479	.357	R	R	6-2	170	9-5-83	2001	Houston, Texas
Young, Eddie	.241	26	83	12	20	5	1	1	11	8	13	5	2	.361	.330	R	R	6-2	190	2-6-82	2000	Macon, Ga.

GAMES BY POSITION: C—Arias 25, Castillo 39, Lenderman 18. **1B**—Bohlander 34, Castillo 1, Collaro 23, Herring 1, Perez 9, Rodriguez 10. **2B**—Lebron 29, Luna 22, Perez 2, Ramirez 18. **3B**—Lebron 2, Luna 1, Perez 49, Schmidt 17. **SS**—Lebron 7, Luna 3, Valido 58. **OF**—Bohlander 1, Collaro 19, Martin 28, Rivera 49, Rodriguez 17, Sweeney 13, C. Young 64, E. Young 26.

PITCHING	W	L	ERA	G	GS	CG	SV	IP	H	R	ER	BB	SO	AVG	B	T	HT	WT	DOB	1st Yr	Resides
Banks, Demetrius	1	1	6.85	15	0	0	0	22	25	22	17	18	28	.265	L	L	6-0	160	5-23-83	2002	Austell, Ga.
Casey, James	2	2	4.28	10	6	0	1	40	35	19	19	15	41	.239	R	R	6-4	215	9-22-84	2003	Azle, Texas
Castro, Fabio	6	2	1.72	19	0	0	2	47	29	14	9	19	59	.172	L	L	5-8	150	1-20-85	2002	Monte Cristi, D.R.
Curreri, Joe	0	0	12.27	3	0	0	0	4	6	5	5	2	3	.400	R	R	6-1	190	6-29-77	1999	Pomona, N.Y.
De Aza, Fernando	2	2	3.42	12	9	0	0	47	51	22	18	16	28	.281	R	R	6-3	200	8-30-80	2003	Carolina, P.R.
Flores, Rafael	3	5	3.27	16	5	0	0	41	49	27	15	12	34	.275	R	R	6-7	220	4-26-84	2002	El Paso, Texas
Gomez, Rafael	0	0	0.00	1	0	0	0	0	3	4	4	1	0	1.000	R	R	6-1	190	9-26-83	2001	Miami, Fla.
Huchingson, Jamin	0	1	16.43	7	0	0	0	8	14	16	14	11	2	.378	R	R	6-7	190	2-2-84	2002	Fayetteville, Ark.
Little, Jeff	1	1	12.60	3	0	0	0	5	9	8	7	3	9	.375	R	R	6-3	200	4-30-80	2003	West Lafayette, Ind.
Lopez, Orionny	5	3	2.37	17	0	0	2	49	38	18	13	18	53	.213	R	R	6-2	170	4-1-84	2002	West Palm Beach, Fla.
Malone, Corwin	0	0	5.14	4	4	0	0	14	17	8	8	3	15	.298	R	L	6-3	200	7-3-80	1999	Thomasville, Ala.
Marshall, Jay	2	0	2.61	10	10	0	0	41	38	15	12	13	42	.243	L	L	6-5	185	2-25-83	2003	Manchester, Mo.
McGary, Gerron	1	0	4.82	11	0	0	0	9	4	6	5	6	9	.133	L	L	6-0	180	2-14-82	2002	Texarkana, Texas
Morales, Ruddy	1	0	3.46	5	0	0	2	13	9	6	5	5	9	.200	R	R	6-5	180	1-20-82	1999	La Romana, D.R.
Murray, Brad	0	0	1.69	5	0	0	1	5	4	1	1	0	4	.210	L	L	5-11	170	8-20-78	2000	La Belle, Fla.

PITCHING	W	L	ERA	G	GS	CG	SV	IP	H	R	ER	BB	SO	AVG	B	T	HT	WT	DOB	1st Yr	Resides
Novoa, Yunior	4	4	5.49	11	11	0	0	41	48	27	25	16	35	.294	L	L	6-3	170	9-11-84	2003	Santo Domingo, D.R.
Ortiz, Dario	0	0	5.40	7	0	0	1	8	10	6	5	4	8	.270	R	R	6-4	190	12-19-82	2002	San Pedro de Macoris, D.R.
Pollok, Dwayne	0	0	3.12	11	0	0	3	9	8	3	3	4	8	.266	R	R	6-3	195	11-12-80	2003	San Antonio, Texas
Sager, Brian	0	1	9.00	1	1	0	0	3	3	5	3	2	4	.230	R	R	6-5	230	10-30-79	2002	Branford, Conn.
Stewart, Josh	0	0	0.00	2	2	0	0	6	5	0	0	2	5	.227	L	L	6-3	200	12-5-78	1999	Ledbetter, Ky.
Suarez, Sony	2	4	3.70	16	6	0	1	56	49	26	23	16	59	.230	R	R	6-0	160	5-8-83	1999	Monte Cristi, D.R.
Thompson, Sean	0	1	3.24	6	1	0	0	17	21	6	6	8	21	.313	L	L	6-2	190	1-3-81	2003	Goleta, Calif.
Tisch, Tim	3	5	3.13	11	11	1	0	60	52	21	21	21	44	.235	L	L	6-5	190	4-11-80	2002	Santee, Calif.
Wasserman, Ehren	0	1	14.73	4	0	0	0	4	9	6	6	3	4	.473	S	R	6-0	185	12-6-80	2003	Birmingham, Ala.

GREAT FALLS WHITE SOX — Rookie

PIONEER LEAGUE

BATTING	AVG	G	AB	R	H	2B	3B	HR	RBI	BB	SO	SB	CS	SLG	OBP	B	T	HT	WT	DOB	1st Yr	Resides
Anderson, Brian	.388	13	49	6	19	2	1	2	13	9	10	3	1	.592	.492	R	R	6-2	205	3-11-82	2003	Tucson, Ariz.
Bounds, Brandon	.326	72	279	51	91	20	5	9	47	18	58	3	3	.530	.362	L	R	6-5	190	8-10-81	2001	Arlington, Texas
Cook, David	.273	6	22	5	6	0	0	0	2	2	8	0	0	.273	.333	R	R	5-11	195	7-21-81	2003	Columbus, Ohio
Deuchler, Matt	.300	27	80	14	24	5	0	2	9	7	24	1	0	.438	.356	R	R	5-11	205	4-6-81	2003	Ellicott City, Md.
Gray, Antoin	.292	69	277	63	81	20	0	8	43	49	62	4	1	.451	.406	R	R	5-9	195	5-19-81	2003	Hattiesburg, Miss.
Haggerty, Cory	.244	60	156	35	38	9	3	1	16	25	40	4	6	.359	.368	L	R	6-0	180	8-25-81	2003	Manilus, N.Y.
Hodges, Brent	.056	9	18	1	1	0	0	0	0	0	5	0	1	.056	.105	R	R	5-11	193	4-29-81	2003	Anderson, Ind.
Huson, Tim	.154	5	13	1	2	0	0	0	0	2	5	0	0	.154	.267	L	R	6-2	200	4-8-80	2001	Cottonwood, Ariz.
Ivy, Bjorn	.222	4	9	1	2	0	0	0	0	1	6	1	0	.222	.300	R	R	5-10	170	9-20-81	2000	Shannon, Miss.
Kelly, Chris	.245	54	200	25	49	15	1	4	40	11	44	3	0	.390	.292	R	R	6-1	195	2-23-82	2003	Las Vegas, Nev.
King, Clint	.305	59	223	41	68	10	4	3	29	26	55	6	5	.426	.384	L	R	5-11	205	8-6-82	2003	Pearl, Miss.
Lee, Carlos	.300	47	180	25	54	11	1	3	33	10	22	1	0	.422	.344	R	R	6-1	220	9-29-81	2000	Aguadulce, Panama
Lisk, Charlie	.271	54	203	40	55	11	1	9	34	16	63	5	0	.468	.335	R	R	6-3	200	1-3-83	2001	Fort Mill, S.C.
Morris, Seth	.250	53	204	31	51	12	0	9	29	18	79	3	2	.441	.311	R	R	6-2	200	8-25-80	2002	Hamilton, Ohio
Myers, Mike	.301	69	249	38	75	11	4	3	47	37	59	18	9	.414	.410	R	R	6-1	190	12-11-79	2002	St. Petersburg, Fla.
Nanita, Ricardo	.384	47	185	38	71	7	4	5	37	17	28	11	6	.546	.445	L	L	6-1	180	6-12-81	2003	Santo Domingo, D.R.
Schnurstein, Micah	.264	50	193	35	51	9	1	1	16	11	39	0	1	.337	.313	R	R	6-1	200	7-18-84	2002	Henderson, Nev.
Sweeney, Ryan	.353	10	34	0	12	2	0	0	4	2	3	0	2	.412	.389	L	L	6-4	200	2-20-85	2003	Cedar Rapids, Iowa
Valenzuela, Mario	.355	17	62	13	22	4	0	3	20	7	16	0	0	.565	.434	R	R	6-2	190	3-10-77	1996	Isla San Marcos, Mexico
Young, Chris	.176	10	34	5	6	3	0	0	0	1	10	0	0	.265	.200	R	R	6-2	170	9-5-83	2001	Houston, Texas

GAMES BY POSITION: C—Deuchler 24, Lee 15, Lisk 44. **1B**—Bounds 60, Haggerty 1, Huson 1, Kelly 21, Lee 2. **2B**—Gray 49, Haggerty 26, Hodges 8, Huson 1. **3B**—Gray 20, Huson 1, Kelly 10, Lee 1, Schnurstein 49. **SS**—Haggerty 30, Myers 53. **OF**—Anderson 13, Cook 5, Ivy 3, Kelly 25, King 57, Morris 44, Myers 20, Nanita 46, Sweeney 10, Valenzuela 12, Young 10.

PITCHING	W	L	ERA	G	GS	CG	SV	IP	H	R	ER	BB	SO	AVG	B	T	HT	WT	DOB	1st Yr	Resides
Dizard, Fraser	3	0	4.02	12	6	0	0	40	49	22	18	16	30	.302	L	L	6-0	195	8-6-81	2003	Edmonds, Wash.
Hernandez, Fernando	1	3	2.70	24	0	0	7	23	23	10	7	10	14	.261	R	R	5-11	190	7-31-84	2003	Miami, Fla.
Hudson, Jeremy	1	0	5.14	2	1	0	0	7	11	4	4	1	2	.379	R	R	6-7	210	3-15-80	2002	Cullman, Ala.
Hurd, John	0	0	13.50	7	0	0	0	6	11	10	9	4	6	.392	R	R	5-11	185	1-29-83	2003	Fruitvale, B.C.
Jacquez, Tom	0	0	2.45	6	4	0	0	11	12	3	3	3	9	.292	L	L	6-2	190	12-29-75	1997	Stockton, Calif.
Johnson, J.D.	2	4	4.46	19	0	0	0	42	47	25	21	10	47	.274	R	R	6-5	190	12-10-82	2002	Moriarty, N.M.
Kane, Kyle	0	1	5.14	5	5	0	0	7	6	4	4	2	3	.230	L	R	6-3	210	2-4-76	1997	Reno, Nev.
Little, Jeff	1	0	3.66	12	0	0	0	20	26	11	8	7	23	.309	R	R	6-3	200	4-30-80	2003	West Lafayette, Ind.
Logan, Boone	3	3	6.58	16	14	0	0	67	76	60	49	31	48	.279	R	L	6-5	200	8-13-84	2003	Helotes, Texas
McCarthy, Brandon	9	4	3.65	16	15	1	0	101	105	49	41	15	125	.262	R	R	6-7	180	7-7-83	2002	Colorado Springs, Colo.
McGary, Gerron	0	0	13.50	2	0	0	0	4	5	6	6	5	8	.312	L	L	6-0	180	2-14-82	2002	Texarkana, Texas
Moat, Mike	2	0	3.99	18	0	0	2	38	34	20	17	10	28	.229	R	R	6-1	190	10-25-81	2003	Boulder, Colo.
Moviel, Paul	0	3	7.48	14	0	0	0	22	31	22	18	8	20	.322	R	R	6-6	220	9-28-82	2003	Berea, Ohio
Nachreiner, Matt	2	4	11.25	13	5	0	0	28	50	45	35	20	23	.373	L	R	6-2	190	11-17-84	2003	Cedar Park, Texas
Payne, Matt	0	0	0.00	4	0	0	1	3	0	0	0	5	4	.000	R	R	6-2	190	12-25-78	2002	San Francisco, Calif.
Reed, Rylan	1	3	5.75	14	2	0	0	36	47	24	23	18	26	.333	R	R	6-7	260	11-18-81	2000	Round Rock, Texas
Russ, John	0	3	4.58	16	2	0	4	35	43	25	18	13	29	.300	R	R	6-3	185	10-11-82	2003	Westlake, La.
Suarez, Sony	0	1	18.90	2	1	0	0	3	7	7	7	2	4	.466	R	R	6-0	160	5-8-83	1999	Monte Cristi, D.R.
Surratt, Randy	4	1	2.25	23	0	0	1	36	32	15	9	13	34	.242	L	L	6-2	190	8-17-81	2003	Roseville, Mich.
Thompson, Sean	1	1	5.90	10	5	0	0	29	40	24	19	8	28	.312	L	L	6-2	190	1-3-81	2003	Goletia, Calif.
Tracey, Sean	8	5	3.69	16	12	1	0	93	90	45	38	22	74	.258	L	R	6-3	210	11-14-80	2002	Upland, Calif.
Ulacia, Dennis	0	2	6.39	4	4	0	0	13	13	10	9	3	14	.250	L	L	6-1	180	4-2-81	1999	Hialeah, Fla.

CHICAGO CUBS

BY JEFF VORVA

In Dusty Baker's first year as Cubs manager, he guided the team to their seventh winning season in 31 years and fourth postseason in 57 years. His team was five outs away from a World Series bid.

Pretty good stuff, right? Well, it wasn't good enough for everyone.

Days after the Cubs were eliminated by the Marlins in seven games in the National League Championship Series, an ex-fan sent Baker his Cubs hat and jacket and wrote to the skipper that he "just couldn't take it anymore."

"I'm thinking, 'man, don't do that,' " Baker said. "As far as I'm concerned, this is only the beginning of something for the Cubs, not the end."

And that will be the key. Baker has three years left on his contract and many thought the first year would be more of a feeling-out process filled with growing pains after the team won just 67 games in 2002. Instead, the Cubs nipped Houston by a game in the NL Central with an 88-74 mark and knocked out the powerhouse Braves in five games in the Division Series to set up a wild NLCS in which the Cubs had a 3-1 lead in the best-of-seven series before dropping the final three games.

Expectations will be high for Chicago in 2004. But they could be met if the starting pitching quartet of Kerry Wood (14-11, 3.20, a major-league best 266 strikeouts), Mark Prior (18-6, 2.43, 245 strikeouts), Carlos Zambrano (13-11, 3.11 and nine homers allowed in 214 innings) and Matt Clement (14-12, 4.11) continues to improve.

Prior lived up to his hype in his first full season and went 10-1, 1.52 in 11 starts after coming back from a shoulder injury that sidelined him for three weeks. He also outdueled Greg Maddux in an NLDS game at Wrigley Field.

The bullpen, which was a disaster in 2002, was improved in 2003 thanks in part to Joe Borowski's surprising development as a closer after Antonio Alfonseca went down with a hamstring injury in spring training. The 32-year-old Borowski, who had just two saves in his major league career before the 2003 season, racked up a team-high 33, which was the best by a Cubs reliever since Rod Beck in 1998.

The Cubs' offense was a weakness for much of 2003, but general manager Jim Hendry did his best to "Buc" that trend when he made a pair of midseason deals with the Pirates to bring center fielder Kenny Lofton, third baseman Aramis Ramirez and first baseman Randall Simon to town.

Those deals paid off handsomely as the three ex-Bucs were instrumental to the Cubs reaching the postseason. Lofton hit .327, scored 39 runs and stole 12 bases in 56 games. Ramirez pounded 15 homers and drove in 39 runs in 63 games. And Simon drove in 21 runs in 33 games.

Right fielder Sammy Sosa missed 17 games with a toe injury and seven more when he was suspended for using a corked bat. But he still hit 40 homers and drove in 103 runs. Center fielder Corey Patterson looked like he was enjoying a breakout season (.298-13-55) before suffering a season-ending knee injury July 7. And left fielder Moises Alou (.280-22-91) improved over a disastrous 2002 campaign. Second baseman Mark Grudzielanek also provided some welcome consistent offense with his .314 average.

The Cubs minor league system had a rough year as only one team—Class A Lansing—posted a winning record.

The Lugnuts qualified for the Midwest League playoffs and went 7-0 en route to the title. Outfielder Felix Pie, who was named to the Futures Game, was one of the Lugnuts leaders throughout 2003.

Class A Daytona pitchers Carmen Pignatiello and Jared Blasdell combined for a no-hitter on July 17. That was the first no-hitter by Daytona since Kerry Wood and two relievers combined for one in 1996.

Mark Prior

Chadd Blasko

PLAYERS of the YEAR

MAJOR LEAGUE: Mark Prior, rhp

In his first full major league season, Prior thrust himself squarely into the Cy Young Award debate in 2003 by ranking second in the National League in wins and strikeouts and placing third in ERA.

MINOR LEAGUE: Chadd Blasko, rhp

A supplemental first-round pick out of Purdue in 2002, Blasko went 10-5 with a Florida State League-leading 1.98 ERA in his first full pro season. He allowed three homers in 136 innings, with 131 strikeouts and 43 walks.

ORGANIZATION LEADERS

BATTING		
*AVG	Trenidad Hubbard, Iowa	.319
R	Three tied at	72
H	Felix Pie, Lansing	144
TB	Phil Hiatt, Iowa	242
2B	Phil Hiatt, Iowa	35
3B	Alberto Garcia, AZL Cubs	10
HR	Phil Hiatt, Iowa	25
RBI	Phil Hiatt, Iowa	89
BB	Dwaine Bacon, West Tenn/Daytona	66
SO	Mike Mallory, Daytona	136
SB	Dwaine Bacon, West Tenn/Daytona	74
*SLG	Phil Hiatt, Iowa	.506
*OBP	Trenidad Hubbard, Iowa	.405
PITCHING		
W	Anderson Tavarez, Lansing	12
L	Carlos Vasquez, Lansing	13
#ERA	Chadd Blasko, Daytona/Lansing	1.95
G	Mark Carter, Daytona/Lansing	61
CG	Andy Sisco, Lansing	3
SV	Jason Wylie, Lansing	29
IP	Carmen Pignatiello, West Tenn/Daytona	162
BB	Steve Smyth, Iowa	72
SO	Mike Nannini, West Tenn	158

*Minimum 250 At-Bats #Minimum 75 Innings

CHICAGO CUBS

Manager: Dusty Baker.

2003 Record: 88-74, .543 (1st, NL West).

BATTING	AVG	G	AB	R	H	2B	3B	HR	RBI	BB	SO	SB	CS	SLG	OBP	B	T	HT	WT	DOB	1st Yr	Resides
Alou, Moises	.280	151	565	83	158	35	1	22	91	63	67	3	1	.462	.357	R	R	6-3	220	7-3-66	1986	Santo Domingo, D.R.
Bako, Paul	.229	70	188	19	43	13	3	0	17	22	47	0	1	.330	.311	L	R	6-2	210	6-20-72	1993	Lafayette, La.
Bellhorn, Mark	.209	51	139	15	29	7	1	2	22	29	46	3	3	.317	.341	S	R	6-1	200	8-23-74	1995	Oviedo, Fla.
Choi, Hee Seop	.218	80	202	31	44	17	0	8	28	37	71	1	1	.421	.350	L	L	6-5	240	3-16-79	1999	Vancouver, Wash.
Glanville, Doug	.235	28	51	2	12	0	0	1	2	2	4	0	1	.294	.259	R	R	6-2	170	8-25-70	1991	Philadelphia, Pa.
Gonzalez, Alex	.228	152	536	71	122	37	0	20	59	47	123	3	3	.409	.295	R	R	6-0	200	4-8-73	1991	Coral Gables, Fla.
Goodwin, Tom	.287	87	171	26	49	10	0	1	12	11	33	19	5	.363	.328	L	R	6-0	180	7-27-68	1989	Grapevine, Texas
Grudzielanek, Mark	.314	121	481	73	151	38	1	3	38	30	64	6	2	.416	.366	R	R	6-1	190	6-30-70	1991	West Palm Beach, Fla.
Harris, Lenny	.183	75	131	11	24	3	0	1	7	13	20	1	0	.229	.255	L	R	5-10	220	10-28-64	1983	Miami, Fla.
Hernandez, Jose	.188	23	69	6	13	3	1	2	9	3	26	0	0	.348	.222	R	R	6-1	190	7-14-69	1987	Dorado, P.R.
Hill, Bobby	.250	5	4	0	1	0	0	0	0	1	2	0	0	.250	.400	S	R	5-10	180	4-3-78	2000	San Jose, Calif.
Hubbard, Trenidad	.250	10	16	2	4	1	0	0	2	4	3	1	0	.313	.429	R	R	5-9	200	5-11-66	1986	Houston, Texas
Karros, Eric	.286	114	336	37	96	16	1	12	40	28	46	1	1	.446	.340	R	R	6-4	220	11-4-67	1988	Los Angeles, Calif.
Kelton, Dave	.167	10	12	1	2	1	0	0	1	0	5	0	0	.250	.167	R	R	6-3	200	12-17-79	1998	La Grange, Ga.
Lofton, Kenny	.327	56	208	39	68	13	4	3	20	18	22	12	4	.471	.381	L	L	6-0	180	5-31-67	1988	Tucson, Ariz.
2-team (84 Pittsburgh)	.296	140	547	97	162	32	8	12	46	46	51	30	9	.450	.352							
Martinez, Ramon E.	.283	108	293	30	83	16	1	3	34	24	50	0	1	.375	.333	R	R	6-1	190	10-10-72	1993	Toa Alta, P.R.
Miller, Damian	.233	114	352	34	82	19	1	9	36	39	91	1	0	.369	.310	R	R	6-3	220	10-13-69	1990	La Crosse, Wisc.
O'Leary, Troy	.218	93	174	18	38	9	0	5	28	14	31	3	0	.356	.275	L	L	6-0	200	8-4-69	1987	Phoenix, Ariz.
Ojeda, Augie	.120	12	25	2	3	0	0	0	0	1	5	0	0	.120	.185	S	R	5-8	170	12-20-74	1996	South Gate, Calif.
Patterson, Corey	.298	83	329	49	98	17	7	13	55	15	77	16	5	.511	.329	L	R	5-9	180	8-13-79	1999	Marietta, Ga.
Paul, Josh	.000	3	6	0	0	0	0	0	0	0	3	0	0	.000	.000	R	R	6-1	200	5-19-75	1996	Naperville, Ill.
Prior, Mark	.250	32	72	6	18	4	0	1	6	2	27	0	0	.347	.270	R	R	6-5	230	9-7-80	2002	Chicago, Ill.
Ramirez, Aramis	.259	63	232	31	60	7	1	15	39	17	31	1	1	.491	.314	R	R	6-1	210	6-25-78	1994	Santo Domingo, D.R.
2-team (96 Pittsburgh)	.272	159	607	75	165	32	2	27	106	42	99	2	2	.465	.324							
Simon, Randall	.282	33	103	13	29	3	0	6	21	4	7	0	0	.485	.318	L	L	6-0	240	5-26-75	1993	Willemstad, Curacao
2-team (91 Pittsburgh)	.276	124	410	47	113	17	0	16	72	16	37	0	0	.434	.309							
Sosa, Sammy	.279	137	517	99	144	22	0	40	103	62	143	0	1	.553	.358	R	R	6-0	220	11-12-68	1986	Santo Domingo, D.R.
Womack, Tony	.235	21	51	4	12	2	1	0	2	1	11	2	1	.314	.250	L	R	5-9	170	9-25-69	1991	Greensboro, N.C.
2-team (82 Arizona)	.226	103	349	43	79	14	4	2	22	9	47	13	5	.307	.251							

PITCHING	W	L	ERA	G	GS	CG	SV	IP	H	R	ER	BB	SO	AVG	B	T	HT	WT	DOB	1st Yr	Resides
Alfonseca, Antonio	3	1	5.83	60	0	0	0	66	76	43	43	27	51	.290	R	R	6-5	250	4-16-72	1990	La Romana, D.R.
Benes, Alan	0	0	2.16	3	0	0	1	8	8	2	2	6	9	.266	R	R	6-5	240	1-21-72	1993	St. Louis, Mo.
Borowski, Joe	2	2	2.63	68	0	0	33	68	53	23	20	19	66	.207	R	R	6-2	220	5-4-71	1989	Bayonne, N.J.
Clement, Matt	14	12	4.11	32	32	2	0	202	169	100	92	79	171	.226	R	R	6-3	210	8-12-74	1994	Butler, Penn.
Cruz, Juan	2	7	6.05	25	6	0	0	61	66	44	41	28	65	.275	R	R	6-2	160	10-15-78	1997	Bonao, D.R.
Estes, Shawn	8	11	5.73	29	28	1	0	152	182	113	97	83	103	.304	R	L	6-2	200	2-18-73	1991	San Francisco, Calif.
Farnsworth, Kyle	3	2	3.30	77	0	0	0	76	53	31	28	36	92	.195	R	R	6-4	230	4-14-76	1995	Canton, Ga.
Guthrie, Mark	2	3	2.74	65	0	0	0	43	40	14	13	22	24	.259	R	L	6-4	210	9-22-65	1987	Sarasota, Fla.
Mitre, Sergio	0	1	8.31	3	2	0	0	9	15	8	8	4	3	.394	R	R	6-4	210	2-16-81	2001	San Ysidro, Calif.
Norton, Phil	0	0	5.40	4	0	0	0	3	2	2	2	3	0	.181	R	L	6-0	210	2-1-76	1996	Texarkana, Texas
Prior, Mark	18	6	2.43	30	30	3	0	211	183	67	57	50	245	.230	R	R	6-5	230	9-7-80	2002	Chicago, Ill.
Remlinger, Mike	6	5	3.65	73	0	0	0	69	54	30	28	39	83	.210	L	L	6-1	210	3-23-66	1987	Paradise Valley, Ariz.
Sanchez, Felix	0	0	10.80	3	0	0	0	2	2	2	2	3	2	.333	R	L	6-3	180	8-3-81	1999	Puerto Plata, D.R.
Veres, Dave	2	1	4.68	31	0	0	1	33	36	17	17	5	26	.290	R	R	6-2	220	10-19-66	1986	Castle Rock, Colo.
Wellemeyer, Todd	1	1	6.51	15	0	0	1	28	25	22	20	19	30	.245	R	R	6-3	200	8-30-78	2000	Louisville, Ky.
Wood, Kerry	14	11	3.20	32	32	4	0	211	152	77	75	100	266	.202	R	R	6-5	220	6-16-77	1995	Scottsdale, Ariz.
Zambrano, Carlos	13	11	3.11	32	32	3	0	214	188	88	74	94	168	.239	S	R	6-5	240	6-1-81	1997	Puerto Cabello,Venez.

FIELDING

Catcher	PCT	G	PO	A	E	DP	PB
Bako	.987	69	440	33	6	2	4
Miller	.997	114	940	73	3	6	8
Paul	1.000	3	20	2	0	1	0

First Base	PCT	G	PO	A	E	DP
Choi	.991	69	523	40	5	46
Karros	.992	97	675	47	6	80
Martinez	1.000	2	1	0	0	0
Simon	.991	29	197	20	2	16

Second Base	PCT	G	PO	A	E	DP
Grudzielanek	.986	121	231	331	8	94
Hill	1.000	2	1	0	0	0
Martinez	.979	42	56	84	3	26
Ojeda	1.000	5	8	9	0	2
Womack	1.000	14	20	25	0	4

Third Base	PCT	G	PO	A	E	DP
Bellhorn	.938	42	18	72	6	4
Hernandez	.968	17	5	25	1	5
Martinez	.923	37	12	48	5	6
Ojeda	.000	1	0	0	0	0
Ramirez	.939	63	35	120	10	14

Shortstop	PCT	G	PO	A	E	DP
Gonzalez	.984	150	193	422	10	95
Hernandez	1.000	5	2	10	0	1
Martinez	.977	32	29	57	2	15
Ojeda	1.000	7	8	9	0	2
Womack	.000	1	0	0	0	0

Outfield	PCT	G	PO	A	E	DP
Alou	.972	142	203	4	6	1
Glanville	1.000	18	30	1	0	1
Goodwin	1.000	57	66	0	0	0
Harris	.000	2	0	0	0	0
Hubbard	1.000	4	5	0	0	0
Kelton	1.000	2	4	0	0	0
Lofton	.974	55	111	3	3	0
O'Leary	1.000	51	58	3	0	0
Patterson	.975	82	152	3	4	1
Sosa	.977	137	212	2	5	1
Womack	1.000	1	1	0	0	0

FARM SYSTEM

Director, Player Development: Oneri Fleita.

Class	Farm Team	League	W	L	Pct.	Finish*	Manager	First Yr.
AAA	Iowa (Des Moines, Iowa) Cubs	Pacific Coast	70	72	.493	t-9th (16)	Mike Quade	1981
AA	West Tenn (Jackson, Tenn.) Diamond Jaxx	Southern	65	73	.471	9th (10)	Bobby Dickerson	1998
High A	Daytona (Fla.) Cubs	Florida State	66	71	.482	9th (12)	Rick Kranitz	1993
Low A	Lansing (Mich.) Lugnuts	Midwest	69	66	.511	+t-6th (14)	Julio Garcia	1999
SS A	Boise (Idaho) Hawks	Northwest	27	49	.355	8th (8)	Steve McFarland	2001
Rookie	Mesa (Ariz.) Cubs	Arizona	25	24	.510	t-5th (9)	Carmelo Martinez	1997

*Finish in overall standings (No. of teams in league) +League champion

IOWA CUBS — Class AAA

PACIFIC COAST LEAGUE

BATTING	AVG	G	AB	R	H	2B	3B	HR	RBI	BB	SO	SB	CS	SLG	OBP	B	T	HT	WT	DOB	1st Yr	Resides
Alexander, Chad	.077	9	13	2	1	0	0	0	0	2	3	0	0	.077	.200	R	R	6-1	190	5-22-74	1995	Norfolk, Va.
Arteaga, Joshua	.265	30	83	14	22	6	0	0	9	2	11	0	0	.337	.295	R	R	5-9	170	3-14-80	2001	Homestead, Fla.
Choi, Hee Seop	.258	18	66	12	17	4	1	6	16	9	19	0	1	.621	.351	L	L	6-5	240	3-16-79	1999	Vancouver, Wash.
Cummings, Midre	.255	114	385	53	98	22	2	19	54	40	86	1	3	.470	.328	L	R	6-0	190	10-14-71	1990	Tarpon Springs, Fla.
Donnels, Chris	.243	31	74	11	18	5	0	4	8	17	11	0	0	.473	.398	L	R	6-0	180	4-21-66	1987	Coto de Caza, Calif.
Dzurilla, Mike	.227	7	22	4	5	3	0	1	5	3	1	0	0	.500	.320	R	R	6-0	190	5-4-78	1999	Bayside, N.Y.
Evans, Tom	.200	6	10	1	2	1	0	0	0	1	0	0	0	.300	.273	R	R	6-1	200	7-9-74	1992	Issaquah, Wash.
Frese, Nate	.243	99	309	37	75	14	2	6	32	38	64	0	0	.359	.328	R	R	6-3	200	7-10-77	1998	Walford, Iowa
Grudzielanek, Mark	.500	2	10	1	5	0	0	0	1	1	1	0	0	.500	.545	R	R	6-1	190	6-30-70	1991	West Palm Beach, Fla.
Hiatt, Phil	.272	134	478	72	130	35	1	25	89	45	110	10	2	.506	.335	R	R	6-3	210	5-1-69	1990	Pensacola, Fla.
Hill, Bobby	.288	92	361	53	104	23	4	6	40	37	65	8	7	.424	.365	S	R	5-10	180	4-3-78	2000	San Jose, Calif.
Hubbard, Trenidad	.319	91	348	65	111	16	2	5	27	47	29	24	7	.420	.405	R	R	5-9	200	5-11-66	1986	Houston, Texas
Jackson, Nic	.253	125	458	56	116	19	4	11	44	35	102	17	9	.384	.315	L	R	6-3	200	9-25-79	2000	Richmond, Va.
Kelton, Dave	.269	121	442	62	119	24	3	16	67	46	115	8	2	.446	.338	R	R	6-3	200	12-17-79	1998	La Grange, Ga.
Leon, Donny	.300	90	350	45	105	26	2	14	55	10	51	2	1	.506	.320	S	R	6-2	180	5-7-76	1995	Ponce, P.R.
Mahoney, Mike	.258	65	190	19	49	12	1	2	18	11	32	0	1	.363	.302	R	R	6-1	200	12-5-72	1995	Des Moines, Iowa
McDonald, Keith	.239	94	280	31	67	15	0	14	45	30	44	0	0	.443	.330	R	R	6-2	230	2-8-73	1994	Anaheim Hills, Calif.
Melian, Jackson	.178	43	129	7	23	4	0	3	9	8	27	4	0	.279	.226	R	R	6-2	200	1-7-80	1996	Barcelona, Venez.
Ojeda, Augie	.251	106	283	42	71	10	3	2	23	34	25	4	0	.329	.351	S	R	5-8	170	12-20-74	1996	South Gate, Calif.
Paul, Josh	.253	47	146	12	37	4	0	2	15	8	30	0	2	.322	.297	R	R	6-1	200	5-19-75	1996	Naperville, Ill.
Pritchett, Chris	.157	43	102	8	16	4	0	3	14	13	21	0	0	.284	.254	L	R	6-4	210	1-31-70	1991	Carlsbad, Calif.
Rojas, Carlos	1.000	1	1	0	1	0	0	0	1	0	0	0	0	1.000	1.000	R	R	6-1	170	1-11-84	2001	Altagracia, Venez.

PITCHING	W	L	ERA	G	GS	CG	SV	IP	H	R	ER	BB	SO	AVG	B	T	HT	WT	DOB	1st Yr	Resides
Alfonseca, Antonio	0	1	4.91	3	0	0	0	4	6	2	2	1	5	.352	R	R	6-5	250	4-16-72	1990	La Romana, D.R.
Banks, Willie	2	0	2.03	25	0	0	17	31	24	7	7	7	29	.210	R	R	6-1	200	2-27-69	1987	Miami, Fla.
Beck, Rod	1	1	0.59	21	0	0	4	31	25	3	2	7	26	.227	R	R	6-1	230	8-3-68	1986	Scottsdale, Ariz.
Beltran, Francis	6	2	2.96	31	2	0	4	49	46	17	16	19	33	.247	R	R	6-6	230	11-29-79	1997	Santo Domingo, D.R.
Benes, Alan	7	7	5.37	19	17	2	0	114	129	74	68	44	81	.293	R	R	6-5	240	1-21-72	1993	St. Louis, Mo.
Brown, Eric	0	0	0.00	3	0	0	0	4	3	0	0	1	6	.200	R	R	6-3	210	12-5-78	2001	Basking Ridge, N.J.
Bruback, Matt	6	8	3.96	20	19	1	0	125	120	65	55	33	90	.252	R	R	6-7	210	1-12-79	1998	Sarasota, Fla.
Chavez, Wilton	11	7	4.24	26	22	1	0	140	144	69	66	51	113	.268	R	R	6-2	160	6-13-78	1998	Monte Cristi, D.R.
Cruz, Juan	4	0	1.95	9	9	0	0	51	37	12	11	11	47	.206	R	R	6-2	160	10-15-78	1997	Bonao, D.R.
Cunnane, Will	0	1	2.20	12	0	0	0	16	17	5	4	8	16	.274	R	R	6-1	200	4-24-74	1993	Rockland, N.Y.
Davis, Kane	2	1	2.35	22	0	0	2	31	21	8	8	12	24	.198	R	R	6-3	190	6-25-75	1993	Reedy, W.Va.
Dingman, Craig	1	0	2.00	11	0	0	0	18	14	4	4	7	12	.212	R	R	6-4	210	3-12-74	1994	Wichita, Kan.
Ebert, Derrin	1	0	6.43	6	0	0	0	7	9	5	5	4	4	.310	R	L	6-3	200	8-21-76	1994	Hesperia, Calif.
Evans, Keith	1	0	3.98	10	1	0	0	20	22	10	9	7	10	.282	R	R	6-5	220	11-2-75	1996	San Pedro, Calif.
2-team (12 Edmonton)	2	2	5.01	22	1	0	1	41	50	25	23	13	16	.303							
Jongejan, Ferenc	2	1	5.59	29	0	0	1	29	34	20	18	15	23	.290	L	L	6-2	170	10-20-78	2001	Utrecht, Netherlands
Karnuth, Jason	0	1	4.74	13	0	0	1	19	23	12	10	12	7	.310	R	R	6-2	190	5-15-76	1997	Memphis, Tenn.
Kaye, Justin	1	4	7.20	20	0	0	0	30	33	26	24	18	21	.277	R	R	6-4	190	6-9-76	1995	Fort Lauderdale, Fla.
Leicester, Jon	0	0	7.20	1	1	0	0	5	6	4	4	2	4	.315	R	R	6-2	220	2-7-79	2000	Huntington Beach, Calif.
Meyers, Mike	5	2	4.60	30	9	0	0	74	77	42	38	36	45	.271	R	R	6-2	210	10-18-77	1997	Molina, Ill.
Norton, Phil	4	2	3.78	48	1	0	1	48	44	26	20	24	43	.241	R	L	6-0	210	2-1-76	1996	Texarkana, Texas
Rodgers, Bobby	0	1	19.50	5	0	0	0	6	16	13	13	7	5	.500	R	R	6-3	220	7-22-74	1996	St. Charles, Mo.
2-team (8 Edmonton)	0	1	12.00	13	0	0	0	15	30	20	20	18	15	.416							
Seanez, Rudy	1	2	3.46	13	0	0	2	13	12	10	5	9	13	.235	R	R	5-11	200	10-20-68	1986	El Centro, Calif.
2-team (5 Oklahoma)	1	3	3.12	18	0	0	2	17	15	14	6	14	20	.220							
Silva, Jose	0	2	7.71	3	0	0	0	5	8	4	4	4	2	.400	R	R	6-6	235	12-19-73	1991	Sarasota, Fla.
3-team (7 Sacra., 17 Port.)	1	5	5.29	24	7	0	0	51	64	35	30	22	32	.307							
Sinclair, Steve	0	0	4.00	6	0	0	0	9	6	5	4	3	9	.181	L	L	6-2	190	8-2-71	1991	Victoria, B.C.
Smyth, Steve	6	11	5.23	25	24	0	0	131	143	85	76	72	98	.287	L	L	6-1	200	6-3-78	1999	Temecula, Calif.
Sonnier, Shawn	0	0	13.50	3	0	0	0	2	4	3	3	1	1	.444	R	R	6-5	220	7-5-76	1998	Carencro, La.
Stanifer, Rob	1	0	3.86	3	0	0	0	7	8	3	3	4	5	.285	R	R	6-2	220	3-10-72	1994	Largo, Fla.
Szuminski, Jason	0	0	3.55	3	2	0	0	13	11	5	5	1	5	.234	R	R	6-5	220	12-11-78	2000	San Antonio, Texas
Teut, Nate	0	3	11.17	3	3	0	0	10	15	14	12	4	7	.333	R	L	6-7	220	3-11-76	1997	Des Moines, Iowa
2-team (2 Albuquerque)	0	4	9.50	5	5	0	0	18	29	23	19	9	13	.358							
Veres, Dave	0	1	2.81	11	4	0	0	16	15	5	5	1	13	.241	R	R	6-2	220	10-19-66	1986	Castle Rock, Colo.
Wellemeyer, Todd	5	5	5.18	13	12	0	0	66	68	39	38	33	56	.272	R	R	6-3	200	8-30-78	2000	Louisville, Ky.
Wuertz, Mike	3	9	4.57	43	16	0	1	124	140	70	63	35	92	.288	R	R	6-3	200	12-15-78	1997	Burnsville, Minn.

FIELDING

Catcher	PCT	G	PO	A	E	DP	PB
Mahoney	.988	51	291	31	4	2	3
McDonald	.997	77	532	43	2	4	4
Paul	1.000	25	146	20	0	5	3

First Base	PCT	G	PO	A	E	DP
Choi	1.000	18	125	14	0	13
Donnels	1.000	11	73	6	0	7
Hiatt	.993	91	672	60	5	82
Kelton	1.000	1	9	0	0	1
Leon	1.000	3	15	2	0	2
Mahoney	1.000	4	22	0	0	4
Paul	.900	1	9	0	1	0
Pritchett	.978	27	204	17	5	14

Second Base	PCT	G	PO	A	E	DP
Arteaga	.984	17	29	31	1	8
Donnels	.967	10	16	13	1	3
Dzurilla	.972	7	19	16	1	5
Evans	.909	2	4	6	1	2
Grudzielanek	1.000	1	2	1	0	0
Hiatt	1.000	6	12	12	0	3
Hill	.977	87	187	194	9	52
Ojeda	.983	26	51	66	2	17

Third Base	PCT	G	PO	A	E	DP
Arteaga	1.000	3	3	4	0	0
Donnels	.667	4	1	1	1	0
Evans	1.000	1	0	1	0	0
Hiatt	.800	3	2	2	1	0
Hill	.818	6	4	5	2	0
Hubbard	1.000	9	4	11	0	2
Kelton	.855	34	23	42	11	5
Leon	.930	83	54	146	15	16
Ojeda	.975	17	13	26	1	0

Shortstop	PCT	G	PO	A	E	DP
Arteaga	.938	7	13	17	2	3
Frese	.971	96	136	267	12	55
Ojeda	.975	57	75	161	6	36

Outfield	PCT	G	PO	A	E	DP
Alexander	1.000	4	8	0	0	0
Cummings	.987	89	146	1	2	1
Hiatt	1.000	29	48	2	0	2
Hubbard	.970	87	181	12	6	2
Jackson	.994	122	306	6	2	4
Kelton	.973	74	138	6	4	1
Leon	1.000	2	6	1	0	1
Melian	1.000	37	69	1	0	0
Paul	1.000	15	17	1	0	0

WEST TENN DIAMOND JAXX — Class AA

SOUTHERN LEAGUE

BATTING	AVG	G	AB	R	H	2B	3B	HR	RBI	BB	SO	SB	CS	SLG	OBP	B	T	HT	WT	DOB	1st Yr	Resides
Arteaga, Josh	.245	59	147	20	36	7	0	1	8	7	27	1	1	.313	.282	R	R	5-9	170	3-14-80	2001	Homestead, Fla.
Bacon, Dwaine	.149	12	47	7	7	2	0	0	2	3	11	3	0	.191	.200	S	R	6-0	180	4-11-79	2001	Fort Washington, Md.
Barbier, Blair	.226	50	137	8	31	2	0	1	16	16	19	0	3	.263	.313	R	R	5-10	200	2-13-78	2000	Harvey, La.
Cardona, Javier	.152	10	33	4	5	1	0	1	2	1	5	0	1	.273	.200	R	R	6-1	210	9-15-75	1994	Dorado, P.R.
Creighton, Matt	.221	28	68	8	15	5	0	1	10	10	7	0	2	.338	.321	R	R	6-0	190	2-22-79	2002	Weldon, Calif.
Dubois, Jason	.269	130	443	57	119	31	4	15	73	57	118	2	4	.458	.367	R	R	6-5	220	3-26-79	2000	Virginia Beach, Va.
Dzurilla, Mike	.264	104	337	50	89	22	3	11	44	22	66	4	3	.445	.313	R	R	6-0	190	5-4-78	1999	Bayside, N.Y.
Hamilton, Jon	.253	71	241	29	61	16	1	4	27	24	37	12	4	.378	.323	L	L	6-1	200	10-23-77	1997	San Ramon, Calif.
Harris, Brendan	.280	120	435	56	122	34	7	5	52	51	72	6	7	.425	.364	R	R	6-1	190	8-26-80	2001	Queensbury, N.Y.
Hood, Donnie	.273	48	154	16	42	16	1	1	12	6	41	3	0	.409	.305	R	R	6-1	180	12-30-78	2002	Powder Springs, Ga.
Kopitzke, Casey	.261	106	318	27	83	10	1	0	25	29	45	3	5	.299	.335	R	R	6-2	200	5-31-78	1999	DePere, Wisc.
Leon, Donny	.299	23	77	11	23	8	0	1	8	7	16	0	0	.442	.353	S	R	6-2	180	5-7-76	1995	Ponce, P.R.
Liriano, Pedro	.324	10	37	4	12	1	1	0	4	2	6	4	2	.405	.350	R	R	5-11	160	2-20-77	1999	Pimentel, D.R.
McKnight, Lukas	.196	42	112	7	22	1	0	0	11	10	26	2	0	.205	.266	L	R	6-0	200	2-19-80	2000	Libertyville, Ill.
Melian, Jackson	.258	79	252	28	65	8	3	7	28	20	47	8	7	.397	.318	R	R	6-2	200	1-7-80	1996	Barcelona, Venez.
Ortiz, Nick	.297	43	148	18	44	10	0	3	17	13	30	0	1	.426	.352	R	R	6-0	180	7-9-73	1991	Cidra, P.R.
Powers, John	.235	34	102	11	24	3	1	0	10	22	18	3	0	.284	.371	L	R	5-10	170	6-2-74	1996	San Diego, Calif.
Sadler, Ray	.291	110	412	56	120	31	5	6	42	33	81	17	7	.434	.352	R	R	6-1	200	9-19-80	2000	Waco, Texas
Schrager, Tony	.163	18	49	1	8	1	1	0	3	5	11	1	1	.224	.241	R	R	6-1	170	6-14-77	1998	Omaha, Neb.
Sing, Brandon	.209	42	139	15	29	7	0	5	23	10	39	2	1	.367	.256	R	R	6-5	210	3-13-81	1999	Joliet, Ill.
Spearman, Jemel	.351	15	57	11	20	2	1	1	9	6	6	5	2	.474	.413	R	R	6-0	190	12-27-80	2002	Lawrenceville, Ga.
Theriot, Ryan	.236	53	178	20	42	3	0	1	9	29	21	9	8	.270	.351	S	R	5-11	170	12-7-79	2001	Baton Rouge, La.
Velazquez, Jose	.239	54	138	11	33	3	0	1	22	21	22	1	1	.283	.331	L	L	6-2	220	8-24-75	1994	Guayama, P.R.
Weston, Aron	.201	56	194	27	39	6	2	3	14	13	54	12	4	.299	.261	L	L	6-5	190	11-5-80	1999	Solon, Ohio

PITCHING	W	L	ERA	G	GS	CG	SV	IP	H	R	ER	BB	SO	AVG	B	T	HT	WT	DOB	1st Yr	Resides
Anderson, Travis	2	3	4.37	14	5	0	0	35	37	17	17	13	25	.272	R	R	6-4	240	3-18-78	1999	Bellevue, Wash.
Arteaga, Josh	0	0	3.86	3	0	0	1	2	3	1	1	2	0	.000	R	R	5-9	170	3-14-80	2001	Homestead, Fla.
Benik, B.J.	0	1	1.42	3	0	0	0	6	6	1	1	3	4	.260	R	R	6-1	190	9-13-78	2001	Delray Beach, Fla.
Brown, Eric	6	1	3.71	44	0	0	1	51	59	25	21	14	40	.289	R	R	6-3	210	12-5-78	2001	Basking Ridge, N.J.
Cash, David	2	5	4.98	50	0	0	11	60	64	37	33	27	80	.268	R	R	6-1	180	7-25-79	2001	Modesto, Calif.
Chavez, Wilton	0	0	2.25	2	1	0	0	8	5	2	2	2	15	.172	R	R	6-2	160	6-13-78	1998	Montecristi, D.R.
Dingman, Craig	0	1	6.00	4	0	0	0	6	6	4	4	5	5	.272	R	R	6-4	210	3-12-74	1994	Wichita, Kan.
Guzman, Angel	3	3	2.81	15	15	0	0	90	83	30	28	26	87	.249	R	R	6-3	180	12-14-81	1999	Caracas, Venez.
Karnuth, Jason	3	5	3.35	45	0	0	13	48	53	21	18	11	36	.276	R	R	6-2	190	5-15-76	1997	Memphis, Tenn.
Koronka, John	0	0	0.00	1	1	0	0	7	3	0	0	1	3	.136	L	L	6-1	180	7-3-80	1998	Clermont, Fla.
2-team (25 Chattanooga)	7	13	4.20	26	26	0	0	163	180	88	76	61	118	.292							
Krawiec, Aaron	3	4	3.25	8	8	0	0	44	50	19	16	9	24	.285	L	L	6-6	220	3-17-79	2000	Hamburg, N.Y.
Leicester, Jon	6	7	3.89	45	9	1	6	106	89	54	46	53	106	.227	R	R	6-2	220	2-7-79	2000	Huntington Beach, Calif.
Mitchell, Nathan	0	0	3.18	4	0	0	0	6	5	2	2	2	4	.227	R	R	6-0	190	5-2-80	2002	Houston, Texas
Mitre, Sergio	7	9	3.34	25	24	0	0	146	162	75	54	41	128	.282	R	R	6-4	210	2-16-81	2001	San Ysidro, Calif.
Nannini, Mike	10	9	3.62	31	24	1	0	154	155	70	62	47	158	.262	R	R	5-11	190	8-9-80	1998	Las Vegas, Nevada
Pignatiello, Carmen	1	0	1.50	1	1	0	0	6	3	1	1	2	11	.150	R	L	6-0	180	9-12-82	2000	Mokena, Ill.
Ramirez, Emmanuel	3	1	2.01	22	0	0	0	31	25	9	7	20	34	.219	R	R	6-3	190	11-2-79	1999	Santo Domingo, D.R.
Rohlicek, Russ	2	3	9.77	13	2	0	0	16	22	17	17	13	12	.343	R	L	6-6	230	12-26-79	2001	Pleasant Hill, Calif.
Ryu, Jae-Kuk	2	5	5.43	11	11	1	0	58	63	37	35	25	45	.280	R	R	6-3	210	5-30-83	2001	Seoul, Korea
Sanchez, Felix	2	2	3.23	30	8	0	0	64	57	30	23	31	55	.234	R	L	6-3	180	8-3-81	1999	Puerto Plata, D.R.
Sonnier, Shawn	0	0	3.44	12	0	0	0	18	11	8	7	11	16	.186	R	R	6-5	220	7-5-76	1998	Carencro, La.
Szuminski, Jason	7	4	2.26	29	3	0	2	60	51	19	15	19	45	.232	R	R	6-5	220	12-11-78	2000	San Antonio, Texas
Waligora, T.P.	0	0	10.54	11	0	0	0	14	18	17	16	11	12	.310	R	R	6-8	250	8-7-76	1997	Richmond, Va.
Webb, John	5	8	4.50	30	22	0	1	132	135	74	66	52	85	.270	R	R	6-3	220	5-23-79	1999	Pensacola, Fla.
Wellemeyer, Todd	1	1	5.48	4	4	0	0	21	19	13	13	10	34	.237	R	R	6-3	200	8-30-78	2000	Louisville, Ky.

FIELDING

Catcher	PCT	G	PO	A	E	DP	PB
Cardona	.979	10	84	9	2	2	0
Kopitzke	.993	100	761	92	6	2	3
McKnight	.992	34	240	14	2	1	3

First Base	PCT	G	PO	A	E	DP
Arteaga	1.000	1	10	1	0	0
Creighton	1.000	2	20	1	0	0
Dubois	.972	16	103	3	3	6
Dzurilla	.995	50	366	25	2	31
Hood	.985	20	122	13	2	10
Leon	1.000	2	16	1	0	1
Powers	1.000	2	6	0	0	0
Sing	.993	38	284	18	2	29
Velazquez	1.000	20	149	17	0	13

Second Base	PCT	G	PO	A	E	DP
Arteaga	1.000	17	22	30	0	8
Barbier	1.000	12	19	17	0	2
Creighton	.932	20	28	41	5	7
Dzurilla	.993	33	57	79	1	11
Harris	1.000	20	22	39	0	3
Hood	1.000	1	2	1	0	0
Kopitzke	1.000	1	1	0	0	0

	PCT	G	PO	A	E	DP
Liriano	.875	3	3	4	1	0
Powers	.985	27	50	84	2	17
Schrager	1.000	11	18	16	0	1
Spearman	.984	14	26	37	1	5

Third Base	PCT	G	PO	A	E	DP
Barbier	.900	25	14	40	6	1
Creighton	1.000	1	0	1	0	0
Dzurilla	.667	2	1	3	2	0
Harris	.921	103	60	138	17	13
Hood	.923	4	5	7	1	0
Leon	.962	13	7	18	1	1
Spearman	.667	1	0	4	2	0

Shortstop	PCT	G	PO	A	E	DP
Arteaga	.951	26	37	60	5	15
Harris	1.000	1	0	1	0	0
Hood	.910	16	25	36	6	7
Liriano	.929	8	6	20	2	4
Ortiz	.940	41	67	105	11	20
Schrager	.931	7	13	14	2	5
Theriot	.953	50	83	121	10	19

Outfield	PCT	G	PO	A	E	DP
Bacon	.920	12	22	1	2	1
Barbier	.000	1	0	0	0	0
Dubois	.969	108	177	12	6	2
Dzurilla	1.000	8	12	1	0	0
Hamilton	.982	65	104	3	2	1
Leon	1.000	9	8	1	0	0
Melian	.990	64	96	4	1	0
Sadler	.988	107	231	8	3	2
Velazquez	.933	14	14	0	1	0
Weston	.982	53	104	5	2	1

DAYTONA CUBS — High Class A

FLORIDA STATE LEAGUE

BATTING	AVG	G	AB	R	H	2B	3B	HR	RBI	BB	SO	SB	CS	SLG	OBP	B	T	HT	WT	DOB	1st Yr	Resides
Bacon, Dwaine	.269	106	350	65	94	12	6	4	22	63	100	71	12	.371	.392	S	R	6-0	180	4-11-79	2001	Fort Washington, Md.
Bouras, Brad	.258	62	233	21	60	10	0	5	26	19	31	0	1	.365	.323	R	R	6-3	230	8-10-79	2001	Lilburn, Ga.
Cedeno, Ronny	.211	107	380	43	80	18	1	4	36	21	82	19	6	.295	.257	R	R	6-0	180	2-2-83	1999	Carabobo, Venez.
Craig, Matt	.285	119	442	56	126	25	2	11	66	46	87	4	4	.425	.357	S	R	6-3	200	4-16-81	2002	Dallas, Texas
Creighton, Matt	.354	16	48	9	17	5	0	2	7	6	5	0	0	.583	.446	R	R	6-0	190	2-22-79	2002	Weldon, Calif.
Greenberg, Adam	.299	72	271	42	81	11	5	3	27	38	46	26	9	.410	.387	L	L	5-9	180	2-21-81	2002	Sparta, N.J.
Hoffpauir, Micah	.254	124	477	59	121	33	2	8	58	44	96	2	1	.382	.323	L	L	6-3	180	3-1-80	2002	Jacksonville, Texas
Mallory, Mike	.229	122	411	59	94	29	0	11	50	55	136	15	3	.380	.336	R	R	6-4	210	12-8-80	1999	Dinwiddie, Va.
McKnight, Lukas	.208	6	24	0	5	5	0	0	6	1	5	0	0	.417	.240	L	R	6-0	200	2-19-80	2000	Libertyville, Ill.
Miller, Chris	.250	49	180	17	45	12	0	4	23	9	22	0	1	.383	.289	R	R	6-2	210	9-12-80	2002	Long Beach, Calif.
Monahan, Joey	.200	27	90	10	18	3	0	1	15	17	23	4	2	.267	.327	R	R	6-0	180	1-14-81	2002	Marietta, Ga.
Montanez, Luis	.253	126	486	51	123	18	3	5	38	33	89	11	4	.333	.305	R	R	6-2	180	12-15-81	2000	Miami, Fla.
O'Toole, Paul	.185	49	124	11	23	4	0	0	11	19	25	3	0	.218	.308	L	R	6-1	200	2-24-80	2002	South Bend, Ind.
Sing, Brandon	.235	39	136	20	32	6	0	4	23	17	29	0	3	.368	.318	R	R	6-5	210	3-13-81	1999	Joliet, Ill.
Soto, Geovany	.242	89	297	26	72	12	2	2	38	31	58	0	0	.316	.313	R	R	6-1	230	1-20-83	2001	San Juan, P.R.
Spearman, Jemel	.274	100	365	53	100	13	1	2	47	39	71	15	11	.332	.349	R	R	6-0	190	12-27-80	2002	Lawrenceville, Ga.
Weston, Aron	.280	58	207	32	58	11	4	1	23	20	50	14	3	.386	.351	L	L	6-5	190	11-5-80	1999	Solon, Ohio

PITCHING	W	L	ERA	G	GS	CG	SV	IP	H	R	ER	BB	SO	AVG	B	T	HT	WT	DOB	1st Yr	Resides
Anderson, Travis	2	0	0.00	12	0	0	2	23	10	1	0	1	23	.129	R	R	6-4	240	3-18-78	1999	Bellevue, Wash.
Benik, B.J.	4	2	3.61	25	2	0	0	47	59	25	19	14	32	.310	R	R	6-1	190	9-13-78	2001	Delray Beach, Fla.
Blasdell, Jared	3	4	3.20	56	0	0	27	59	52	25	21	34	84	.229	R	R	6-3	180	5-14-79	2001	Las Vegas, Nevada
Blasko, Chadd	10	5	1.98	24	24	1	0	136	100	33	30	43	131	.204	R	R	6-7	220	3-9-81	2003	Mishawaka, Ind.
Brownlie, Bobby	5	4	3.00	13	13	1	0	66	48	26	22	24	59	.200	R	R	6-0	210	10-5-80	2003	Edison, N.J.
Carter, Mark	0	1	5.60	16	0	0	0	18	20	12	11	8	17	.289	L	L	6-4	220	8-27-80	2001	Oneonta, Ala.
Christensen, Ben	0	2	5.27	14	3	0	0	27	32	18	16	11	21	.293	R	R	6-4	210	2-7-78	1999	Wichita, Kan.
Fahrner, Evan	1	2	0.46	13	0	0	0	20	13	4	1	7	28	.183	R	R	6-2	200	3-4-78	1999	Peoria, Ill.
Fernley, Nate	2	2	5.76	17	0	0	0	30	40	20	19	10	29	.317	R	R	6-3	160	1-13-77	2001	Long Beach, Calif.
Ferreras, Yorkin	0	2	6.86	11	0	0	0	21	26	16	16	15	19	.292	L	L	6-1	180	1-28-81	1998	Santo Domingo, D.R.
Foli, Daniel	1	1	8.10	6	0	0	0	10	12	11	9	8	7	.300	R	R	6-1	180	3-30-81	2001	Kodak, Tenn.
Martin, Nick	6	10	4.20	33	17	0	0	116	121	71	54	41	85	.264	L	L	6-3	190	3-5-80	2001	Houston, Texas
Mejia, Anderson	0	0	4.50	1	0	0	0	2	2	1	1	2	1	.285	R	R	6-2	200	6-15-82	1999	Hato Mayor, D.R.
Mitchell, Nathan	3	4	3.21	42	3	0	0	70	66	29	25	33	66	.249	R	R	6-0	190	5-2-80	2002	Houston, Texas
Nolasco, Ricky	11	5	2.96	26	26	1	0	149	129	58	49	48	136	.232	R	R	6-2	220	12-13-82	2001	Rialto, Calif.
Pignatiello, Carmen	8	11	4.38	26	26	1	0	156	144	87	76	55	140	.240	R	L	6-0	180	9-12-82	2000	Mokena, Ill.
Pinto, Renyel	3	8	3.22	20	19	0	0	115	91	47	41	45	104	.220	L	L	6-4	190	7-8-82	1999	Cupira, Venez.
Ramirez, Emmanuel	2	0	3.14	11	0	0	0	14	11	5	5	6	13	.207	R	R	6-3	190	11-2-79	1999	Santo Domingo, D.R.
Rohlicek, Russ	2	3	2.40	41	0	0	0	49	34	13	13	21	50	.197	R	L	6-6	230	12-26-79	2001	Pleasant Hill, Calif.
Ryu, Jae-Kuk	0	1	3.05	4	4	0	0	21	14	14	7	11	22	.186	R	R	6-3	210	5-30-83	2001	Seoul, Korea
Szuminski, Jason	2	1	3.65	13	0	0	0	25	29	12	10	9	23	.295	R	R	6-5	220	12-11-78	2000	San Antonio, Texas
Wynegar, Adam	1	3	5.40	19	0	0	1	25	21	21	15	27	14	.244	L	L	6-1	190	9-11-80	2001	Centreville, Va.

FIELDING

Catcher	PCT	G	PO	A	E	DP	PB
McKnight	.983	6	53	4	1	2	1
Miller	.980	38	325	17	7	3	3
O'Toole	.986	20	126	15	2	2	3
Soto	.987	79	617	61	9	5	7

First Base	PCT	G	PO	A	E	DP
Bouras	.978	29	209	9	5	16
Creighton	1.000	10	70	3	0	7
Hoffpauir	.993	95	775	44	6	68
O'Toole	1.000	6	45	2	0	1
Sing	1.000	2	16	0	0	1

Second Base	PCT	G	PO	A	E	DP
Cedeno	.935	28	53	77	9	13
Creighton	.923	2	6	6	1	1
Monahan	.966	7	10	18	1	3
Montanez	.952	82	163	213	19	50
Spearman	.968	19	36	54	3	14

Third Base	PCT	G	PO	A	E	DP
Craig	.917	105	70	194	24	20
Monahan	.750	5	1	8	3	2
O'Toole	.667	1	2	0	1	0
Soto	1.000	1	0	2	0	0
Spearman	.921	30	12	58	6	3

Shortstop	PCT	G	PO	A	E	DP
Cedeno	.944	77	121	217	20	46
Craig	1.000	1	1	3	0	0
Monahan	.867	11	8	18	4	2
Montanez	.921	33	44	84	11	12
Spearman	.909	19	31	39	7	7

Outfield	PCT	G	PO	A	E	DP
Bacon	.969	101	185	5	6	1
Bouras	1.000	1	1	0	0	0
Creighton	.000	1	0	0	0	0
Greenberg	1.000	69	127	6	0	1
Hoffpauir	.853	24	28	1	5	0
Mallory	.992	121	248	9	2	1
O'Toole	1.000	6	7	1	0	0
Sing	.945	32	49	3	3	0
Spearman	1.000	9	13	0	0	0
Weston	.964	56	103	4	4	2

LANSING LUGNUTS — Low Class A

MIDWEST LEAGUE

BATTING	AVG	G	AB	R	H	2B	3B	HR	RBI	BB	SO	SB	CS	SLG	OBP	B	T	HT	WT	DOB	1st Yr	Resides
Butler, Keith	.250	121	432	47	108	27	0	5	56	38	51	21	4	.347	.311	R	R	5-10	180	8-11-80	2002	Marietta, Ga.
Chirinos, Robinson	.232	108	362	51	84	27	1	7	39	28	82	10	2	.370	.298	R	R	6-1	180	6-5-84	2000	Punto Fijo, Venez.
Coats, Buck	.277	132	488	64	135	25	7	1	59	64	93	32	15	.363	.364	L	R	6-3	190	6-9-82	2000	Hahira, Ga.
Collins, Kevin	.225	89	306	40	69	19	1	14	43	39	116	1	3	.431	.314	L	L	6-2	210	5-6-81	2000	Land O' Lakes, Fla.

BATTING	AVG	G	AB	R	H	2B	3B	HR	RBI	BB	SO	SB	CS	SLG	OBP	B	T	HT	WT	DOB	1st Yr	Resides
Creighton, Matt	.230	43	135	21	31	7	3	4	15	10	28	4	2	.415	.297	R	R	6-0	190	2-22-79	2002	Weldon, Calif.
Dopirak, Brian	.269	19	78	8	21	3	0	2	10	2	22	0	0	.385	.305	R	R	6-4	230	12-20-83	2002	Crystal Beach, Fla.
Fox, Jake	.260	29	100	13	26	8	0	5	12	8	19	0	0	.490	.330	R	R	5-11	210	7-20-82	2003	Greenfield, Ind.
Fransz, Jason	.262	77	267	27	70	10	1	9	42	23	67	4	4	.408	.328	R	R	6-3	210	2-5-81	2002	Corona, Calif.
Hickman, Chuck	.200	9	30	3	6	1	0	0	1	0	7	1	0	.233	.200	R	R	5-11	175	5-24-81	2003	Mandeville, La.
Hood, Donnie	.317	49	186	36	59	16	1	9	32	15	46	0	2	.559	.371	R	R	6-1	180	12-30-78	2002	Powder Springs, Ga.
Johnson, J.J.	.241	104	361	40	87	10	2	3	41	33	55	6	2	.305	.305	R	R	6-2	210	11-3-81	2000	Appling, Ga.
Jones, Nick	.193	42	119	11	23	6	1	0	6	2	19	3	2	.261	.230	R	R	6-1	185	3-29-82	2003	Roanoke, Va.
Lopaze, Daniel	.226	10	31	2	7	3	0	0	2	4	11	0	0	.323	.306	L	R	6-3	200	12-13-80	2003	Lake Ridge, Va.
McGehee, Casey	.272	64	243	24	66	18	1	3	23	10	46	2	3	.391	.302	R	R	6-1	190	10-12-82	2003	Aptos, Calif.
Medlin, C.J.	.100	12	30	2	3	1	0	0	0	1	12	0	0	.133	.156	R	R	6-2	200	3-3-82	2002	Broken Arrow, Okla.
Miller, Chris	.250	5	12	2	3	1	0	0	3	1	2	0	1	.333	.375	R	R	6-2	210	9-12-80	2002	Long Beach, Calif.
Monahan, Joey	.111	5	18	3	2	0	0	0	3	2	1	1	1	.111	.200	R	R	6-0	180	1-14-81	2002	Marietta, Ga.
O'Toole, Paul	.360	8	25	3	9	1	0	0	3	3	3	2	0	.400	.429	L	R	6-1	200	2-24-80	2002	South Bend, Ind.
Pie, Felix	.285	124	505	72	144	22	9	4	47	41	98	19	13	.388	.346	L	L	6-2	170	2-8-85	2001	La Romana, D.R.
Reyes, Jose	.239	70	234	18	56	9	0	0	20	16	37	2	1	.278	.295	S	R	5-11	180	2-26-84	1999	Barahona, D.R.
Richie, Tony	.175	21	57	6	10	2	0	0	4	6	12	0	0	.211	.266	R	R	6-1	215	2-9-82	2003	Jacksonville, Fla.
Salas, Francisco	.269	52	175	27	47	12	2	7	28	10	24	2	4	.480	.335	R	R	5-9	190	7-25-82	2001	Tijuana, Mexico
Theriot, Ryan	.259	58	220	29	57	8	1	1	17	31	34	21	5	.318	.353	S	R	5-11	170	12-7-79	2001	Baton Rouge, La.
Wells, Randy	.149	24	67	5	10	0	0	0	1	7	14	0	0	.149	.227	R	R	6-4	200	8-28-82	2002	Lebanon, Ill.

PITCHING	W	L	ERA	G	GS	CG	SV	IP	H	R	ER	BB	SO	AVG	B	T	HT	WT	DOB	1st Yr	Resides
Baez, Federico	4	3	3.38	51	0	0	1	67	72	39	25	20	46	.265	R	R	6-2	190	8-4-81	2001	Dorado, P.R.
Benik, B.J.	2	0	3.20	18	0	0	1	25	25	10	9	8	30	.250	R	R	6-1	190	9-13-78	2001	Delray Beach, Fla.
Blasko, Chadd	0	1	1.64	2	2	0	0	11	10	3	2	5	6	.256	R	R	6-7	220	3-9-81	2003	Mishawaka, Ind.
Carter, Mark	4	1	2.25	45	0	0	0	52	32	14	13	11	54	.173	L	L	6-4	220	8-27-80	2001	Oneonta, Ala.
Cherry, Rocky	2	0	2.76	8	4	0	0	29	23	10	9	7	18	.216	R	R	6-5	210	8-19-79	2003	Coppell, Texas
Ferreras, Yorkin	4	1	3.56	10	9	1	0	56	50	22	22	15	62	.238	L	L	6-1	180	1-28-81	1998	Santo Domingo, D.R.
Foli, Daniel	6	9	4.08	34	13	0	0	104	93	57	47	64	84	.240	R	R	6-1	180	3-30-81	2001	Kodak, Tenn.
Green, Craig	0	0	7.94	6	0	0	0	11	14	14	10	7	5	.274	R	R	6-3	210	11-8-81	2003	Bakersfield, Calif.
Hill, Richard	0	1	2.76	15	4	0	0	29	14	12	9	36	50	.141	L	L	6-5	190	3-11-80	2002	Milton, Mass.
Jones, Justin	3	5	2.28	16	16	0	0	71	56	29	18	32	87	.214	L	L	6-4	190	9-25-84	2002	Virginia Beach, Va.
Marshall, Sean	1	0	0.00	1	1	0	0	7	5	1	0	0	11	.192	L	L	6-5	185	8-30-82	2003	Chesterfield, Va.
Mendez, Adalberto	0	0	4.38	9	1	0	0	12	15	9	6	6	11	.288	R	R	6-2	160	2-22-82	2001	Azua, D.R.
O'Brien, Wes	1	5	3.20	55	0	0	0	65	48	32	23	32	77	.203	R	R	6-6	250	10-4-82	2001	Chino, Calif.
O'Malley, Ryan	6	4	2.88	40	3	0	0	81	85	34	26	17	55	.268	R	L	6-1	190	4-9-80	2002	Springfield, Ill.
Rapada, Clayton	1	2	5.31	21	4	0	0	42	46	29	25	19	24	.273	R	L	6-5	180	3-9-81	2002	Chesapeake, Va.
Ryu, Jae-Kuk	6	1	1.75	11	11	0	0	72	59	19	14	19	57	.225	R	R	6-3	210	5-30-83	2001	Seoul, Korea
Sisco, Andy	6	8	3.54	19	19	3	0	94	76	44	37	31	99	.220	L	L	6-9	260	1-13-83	2001	Scottsdale, Ariz.
Tavares, Anderson	12	9	3.24	26	25	1	0	153	154	69	55	25	100	.262	R	R	6-1	170	2-14-82	2001	Santiago, D.R.
Vasquez, Carlos	10	13	3.74	24	23	0	0	137	136	74	57	47	87	.251	L	L	6-2	210	12-6-82	2000	Sucre, Venez.
Wylie, Jason	1	2	1.38	57	0	0	29	59	36	13	9	22	54	.171	R	R	6-5	230	5-27-81	2002	West Jordan, Utah

FIELDING

Catcher	PCT	G	PO	A	E	DP	PB
Fox	.981	22	133	22	3	1	5
Medlin	.957	12	84	4	4	0	2
Miller	1.000	4	25	4	0	0	0
O'Toole	.968	3	29	1	1	0	2
Reyes	.990	64	443	60	5	1	10
Richie	.987	19	138	11	2	0	3
Wells	.989	20	162	19	2	0	3

First Base	PCT	G	PO	A	E	DP
Collins	.979	71	626	38	14	45
Creighton	.984	24	172	13	3	15
Dopirak	.992	13	119	4	1	7
Hood	.966	15	138	6	5	13
Lopaze	1.000	10	82	5	0	5
Salas	1.000	11	61	13	0	9
Wells	1.000	2	2	0	0	1

Second Base	PCT	G	PO	A	E	DP
Chirinos	.978	54	115	153	6	42
Creighton	.976	10	13	27	1	1
Hickman	.955	9	19	23	2	3
Jones	.892	11	12	21	4	2
Monahan	1.000	4	10	12	0	3
Salas	.964	7	10	17	1	2
Theriot	.967	51	111	152	9	22

Third Base	PCT	G	PO	A	E	DP
Chirinos	.917	43	23	88	10	5
Creighton	.667	2	0	2	1	1
Hood	.882	6	2	13	2	1
Jones	1.000	3	0	2	0	0
McGehee	.944	64	40	130	10	6
Salas	.917	24	15	51	6	4

Shortstop	PCT	G	PO	A	E	DP
Chirinos	.906	9	7	22	3	0
Coats	.912	122	206	323	51	59
Hickman	1.000	1	3	1	0	1
Salas	1.000	1	0	1	0	0
Theriot	.909	7	7	23	3	4

Outfield	PCT	G	PO	A	E	DP
Butler	.981	110	153	3	3	1
Fransz	.959	60	67	4	3	0
Johnson	.941	103	162	14	11	3
Jones	1.000	18	22	0	0	0
O'Toole	1.000	6	4	0	0	0
Pie	.981	123	257	5	5	1
Reyes	.000	1	0	0	0	0

BOISE HAWKS — Short-Season Class A

NORTHWEST LEAGUE

BATTING	AVG	G	AB	R	H	2B	3B	HR	RBI	BB	SO	SB	CS	SLG	OBP	B	T	HT	WT	DOB	1st Yr	Resides
Banks, Gary	.247	28	81	8	20	0	1	0	8	5	25	2	1	.272	.303	S	R	6-1	190	11-4-81	2000	Gilbertown, Ala.
Boyer, Kyle	.271	47	170	28	46	6	5	9	27	17	57	2	1	.524	.344	R	R	6-1	210	11-23-81	2003	Temecula, Calif.
Dawkins, Lance	.158	32	95	9	15	5	0	0	3	10	32	2	2	.211	.257	R	R	6-3	190	1-31-82	2003	Columbus, Miss.
Dopirak, Brian	.240	52	192	25	46	4	0	13	37	24	58	0	2	.464	.330	R	R	6-4	230	12-20-83	2002	Crystal Beach, Fla.
Francisco, Alfredo	.154	14	52	3	8	2	0	0	0	0	15	0	0	.192	.170	R	R	6-3	200	8-27-84	2002	San Pedro de Macoris, D.R.
Garcia, Alberto	.263	5	19	3	5	2	0	0	3	0	3	0	0	.368	.333	R	R	6-1	180	6-5-83	2001	Bonao, D.R.
Gresky, David	.216	49	167	16	36	6	3	3	11	17	53	3	1	.341	.303	L	L	6-3	210	6-8-82	2003	North Royalton, Ohio
Hickman, Chuck	.228	45	158	16	36	10	3	1	14	7	29	9	2	.348	.260	R	R	5-11	175	5-24-81	2003	Mandeville, La.
Larsen, Andrew	.259	69	266	29	69	12	1	6	23	11	64	10	3	.380	.303	R	R	6-0	190	3-9-83	2003	South Jordan, Utah
Lopaze, Daniel	.209	44	148	12	31	6	1	3	9	13	37	0	2	.324	.280	L	R	6-3	200	12-13-80	2003	Lake Ridge, Va.
Marquez, Uriak	.239	52	201	21	48	10	1	6	19	10	38	2	4	.388	.276	S	R	6-0	170	8-17-83	2001	Caracas, Venez.
McIntyre, Patrick	.154	14	39	2	6	1	0	0	2	5	12	0	1	.179	.267	R	R	6-0	200	10-5-82	2003	Caldwell, Idaho
McQuade, Tony	.232	52	190	19	44	8	1	6	25	15	40	4	2	.379	.302	S	R	6-2	205	12-24-81	2003	Gainesville, Fla.
Medlin, C.J.	.195	29	87	7	17	6	0	1	7	3	22	0	0	.299	.237	R	R	6-2	200	3-3-82	2002	Broken Arrow, Okla.
Monahan, Joey	.247	23	85	9	21	5	0	0	11	3	19	8	2	.306	.301	R	R	6-0	180	1-14-81	2002	Marietta, Ga.
Reyes, Jose	.278	11	36	4	10	0	0	0	5	1	4	0	1	.278	.297	S	R	5-11	180	2-26-84	1999	Barahona, D.R.
Rick, Alan	.257	50	171	20	44	7	0	6	20	18	47	2	1	.404	.339	L	R	6-3	210	9-8-83	2002	Palatka, Fla.
Rosario, Samuel	.261	30	111	13	29	4	2	0	6	7	23	4	6	.333	.322	R	R	6-0	170	2-13-80	2002	Maria Sanchez, D.R.

BATTING	AVG	G	AB	R	H	2B	3B	HR	RBI	BB	SO	SB	CS	SLG	OBP	B	T	HT	WT	DOB	1st Yr	Resides
Tidball, Adam	.053	8	19	0	1	0	0	0	0	1	7	0	0	.053	.100	R	R	6-4	218	4-22-82	2003	Bethesda, Md.
Walker, Chris	.235	68	247	25	58	5	1	0	14	8	51	25	9	.263	.267	R	R	5-8	170	7-3-80	2002	Alpharetta, Ga.

GAMES BY POSITION: C—Garcia 3, McIntyre 3, Medlin 24, Reyes 9, Rick 39, Tidball 7. **1B**—Dopirak 41, Larsen 2, Lopaze 24, McIntyre 11, Medlin 1. **2B**—Hickman 9, Marquez 39, Monahan 23, Rosario 12. **3B**—Dawkins 10, Francisco 14, Larsen 48, Lopaze 2, Rosario 2. **SS**—Dawkins 19, Hickman 32, Larsen 4, Marquez 12, Rosario 15. **OF**—Banks 27, Boyer 40, Gresky 45, Hickman 4, Lopaze 7, Marquez 1, McQuade 42, Rosario 1, Walker 67.

PITCHING	W	L	ERA	G	GS	CG	SV	IP	H	R	ER	BB	SO	AVG	B	T	HT	WT	DOB	1st Yr	Resides
Bay, Ronald	1	2	3.74	4	4	0	0	22	17	9	9	7	24	.212	R	R	6-2	160	8-7-83	2003	Houston, Texas
Carter, Brian	2	4	5.35	26	0	0	2	39	47	31	23	23	21	.291	L	L	6-5	220	11-21-81	2003	Gig Harbor, Wash.
Cherry, Rocky	5	2	2.17	10	10	0	0	54	36	21	13	18	55	.180	R	R	6-5	210	8-19-79	2003	Coppell, Texas
Cuevas, Alvin	1	1	3.97	19	0	0	4	23	13	12	10	15	17	.164	R	R	6-1	200	9-24-80	1999	Santo Domingo, D.R.
Green, Craig	0	1	2.70	11	0	0	0	13	15	11	4	6	8	.254	R	R	6-3	210	11-8-81	2003	Bakersfield, Calif.
Gross, Kris	1	1	3.04	13	0	0	0	24	19	10	8	7	23	.208	R	R	6-2	185	12-28-80	2003	Lee's Summit, Mo.
Guerrero, Aneury	0	1	9.72	5	0	0	0	8	10	9	9	7	10	.303	L	L	6-3	190	3-16-83	2000	San Pedro de Macoris, D.R.
Hill, Rich	1	6	4.35	14	14	0	0	68	57	40	33	32	99	.232	L	L	6-5	190	3-11-80	2002	Milton, Mass.
Hines, Matthew	1	3	4.89	24	0	0	1	39	43	23	21	26	44	.275	R	R	6-7	220	5-13-81	2002	Coal City, Ill.
Marshall, Sean	5	6	2.57	14	14	0	0	74	66	31	21	23	88	.236	L	L	6-5	185	8-30-82	2003	Chesterfield, Va.
Mejia, Anderson	1	5	5.23	19	10	0	1	64	64	42	37	47	22	.265	R	R	6-2	200	6-15-82	1999	Hato Mayor, D.R.
Mendez, Adalberto	0	4	4.09	15	5	0	7	33	29	18	15	15	33	.237	R	R	6-2	160	2-22-82	2001	Azua, D.R.
Overholt, Sean	3	1	0.49	10	0	0	0	18	18	9	1	7	17	.246	R	R	6-1	195	5-20-82	2003	Sandy, Utah
Petrick, Billy	2	5	4.76	14	14	0	0	64	60	49	34	27	64	.240	S	R	6-6	240	4-29-84	2002	Morris, Ill.
Rapada, Clayton	0	0	0.00	1	0	0	0	3	2	0	0	1	3	.200	R	L	6-5	180	3-9-81	2002	Chesapeake, Va.
Sonnier, Shawn	0	1	7.16	8	0	0	2	16	20	13	13	8	15	.298	R	R	6-5	220	7-5-76	1998	Carencro, La.
Valdez, Richard	0	0	6.34	22	0	0	0	33	43	34	23	15	32	.313	R	R	6-3	170	7-11-81	2001	Nizao, D.R.
Willett, Reid	4	5	4.63	20	5	0	1	56	54	31	29	23	49	.246	R	R	6-5	205	3-25-82	2003	Nashua, N.H.
Wynegar, Adam	0	1	2.16	21	0	0	0	17	12	8	4	10	10	.190	L	L	6-1	190	9-11-80	2001	Centreville, Va.

MESA CUBS — Rookie

ARIZONA LEAGUE

BATTING	AVG	G	AB	R	H	2B	3B	HR	RBI	BB	SO	SB	CS	SLG	OBP	B	T	HT	WT	DOB	1st Yr	Resides
Balcom, Jasha	.329	24	85	17	28	1	2	0	6	12	21	2	2	.388	.414	L	R	5-11	180	7-7-82	2003	Dublin, Ga.
Bernard, Oscar	.226	26	84	15	19	5	1	0	9	6	11	1	2	.310	.278	R	R	6-2	170	6-27-83	2001	San Pedro de Macoris, D.R.
Davidson, Matt	.207	12	29	2	6	1	0	0	1	3	5	0	0	.241	.303	L	R	6-1	225	11-20-80	2003	Republic, Mo.
Fitzgerald, Ryan	.381	54	202	37	77	14	8	7	44	18	43	9	3	.634	.431	R	R	6-2	195	11-29-80	2003	West Des Moines, Iowa
Fox, Jake	.240	15	50	4	12	5	0	1	6	5	14	0	1	.400	.321	R	R	5-11	210	7-20-82	2003	Greenfield, Ind.
Francisco, Alfredo	.263	41	160	14	42	9	2	1	19	4	42	1	4	.363	.289	R	R	6-3	200	8-27-84	2002	San Pedro de Macoris, D.R.
Garcia, Alberto	.319	48	182	34	58	15	10	0	34	13	30	5	3	.511	.385	R	R	6-1	180	6-5-83	2001	Bonao, D.R.
Harvey, Ryan	.235	14	51	9	12	3	2	1	7	6	21	0	0	.431	.339	R	R	6-5	220	8-30-84	2003	Palm Harbor, Fla.
Jackson, Noah	.208	31	106	9	22	4	1	0	8	11	22	0	1	.264	.292	R	R	6-1	220	9-2-81	2003	Mill Valley, Calif.
Johnston, Trey	.185	28	81	10	15	3	0	1	9	11	27	1	3	.259	.287	R	R	5-11	190	7-4-85	2003	Bradenton, Fla.
Jones, Nick	.269	6	26	5	7	3	0	0	3	0	5	0	0	.385	.321	R	R	6-1	185	3-29-82	2003	Roanoke, Va.
McIntyre, Patrick	.132	18	53	7	7	0	1	0	3	8	14	0	0	.170	.270	R	R	6-0	200	10-5-82	2003	Caldwell, Idaho
Mejia, Carlos	.262	49	202	27	53	11	8	4	30	2	32	1	3	.455	.276	R	R	6-3	170	5-16-83	2002	San Pedro de Macoris, D.R.
Rios, Jose	.279	38	165	27	46	5	2	0	17	5	16	0	2	.333	.297	R	R	6-1	160	4-6-84	2003	Barranquitas, P.R.
Rojas, Carlos	.235	47	187	38	44	7	3	0	15	18	20	9	3	.305	.308	R	R	6-1	170	1-11-84	2001	Altagracia, Venez.
Rosario, Samuel	.303	22	76	21	23	6	3	0	14	17	14	8	2	.461	.436	R	R	6-0	170	2-13-80	2002	Maria Sanchez, D.R.
Tidball, Adam	.324	12	37	5	12	3	1	0	3	2	4	0	1	.459	.366	R	R	6-4	218	4-22-82	2003	Bethesda, Md.
Valdez, Jesus	.320	48	175	20	56	8	5	0	29	7	31	7	2	.423	.364	R	R	6-2	170	11-2-84	2002	Santo Domingo, D.R.
Welsch, Travis	.233	9	30	5	7	2	1	0	8	4	5	0	0	.367	.306	R	R	5-11	180	11-30-79	2002	Muscatine, Iowa

GAMES BY POSITION: C—Bernard 22, Davidson 4, Fox 8, Garcia 10, McIntyre 12, Tidball 9. **1B**—Bernard 1, Davidson 1, Francisco 3, Garcia 31, Jackson 16, McIntyre 5, Tidball 1, Welsch 6. **2B**—Balcom 5, Johnston 8, Jones 5, Rios 24, Rojas 6, Rosario 7, Welsch 3. **3B**—Francisco 40, Garcia 6, Johnston 9, Jones 1, Rosario 6, Welsch 1. **SS**—Fox 1, Rios 15, Rojas 41, Rosario 1. **OF**—Balcom 16, Fitzgerald 50, Garcia 3, Harvey 8, Jackson 7, Mejia 43, Rosario 6, Valdez 44.

PITCHING	W	L	ERA	G	GS	CG	SV	IP	H	R	ER	BB	SO	AVG	B	T	HT	WT	DOB	1st Yr	Resides
Alvarez, Jose	1	1	6.04	14	0	0	0	28	34	21	19	13	10	.306	R	R	6-3	180	3-6-85	2002	Yaritagua, Venez.
Bay, Ronald	7	1	2.50	10	6	0	0	58	51	18	16	9	69	.237	R	R	6-2	160	8-7-83	2003	Houston, Texas
Blanton, Jason	0	1	2.70	6	3	0	0	7	7	4	2	9	8	.280	R	R	6-4	240	9-10-79	2001	Raleigh, N.C.
Brito, Luis	1	0	5.17	5	1	0	0	16	16	13	9	2	15	.258	R	R	6-3	180	10-19-83	2001	Monagas, Venez.
Campusano, Emmanuel	1	1	4.91	6	3	0	0	22	30	12	12	9	14	.322	L	L	6-4	170	3-2-85	2001	San Pedro de Macoris, D.R.
Chiasson, Scott	0	0	3.38	2	2	0	0	3	3	1	1	0	5	.300	R	R	6-3	200	8-14-77	1998	Norwich, Conn.
Christensen, Ben	0	0	2.70	2	2	0	0	3	3	2	1	1	4	.230	R	R	6-4	210	2-7-78	1999	Wichita, Kan.
Clanton, Matt	0	0	0.00	1	1	0	0	2	2	0	0	2	0	.285	S	R	6-3	220	4-16-81	2002	Fountain Valley, Calif.
Downs, Darin	0	2	6.57	13	11	0	0	38	48	30	28	17	32	.317	R	L	6-3	176	12-26-84	2003	Boynton Beach, Fla.
Green, Craig	0	2	10.80	4	0	0	0	5	9	7	6	2	5	.375	R	R	6-3	210	11-8-81	2003	Bakersfield, Calif.
Gross, Kris	1	1	2.91	9	0	0	1	22	19	7	7	6	16	.256	R	R	6-2	185	12-28-80	2003	Lee's Summit, Mo.
Kalita, Ryan	0	0	40.50	1	0	0	0	1	5	3	3	1	0	.714	R	R	6-2	210	2-2-81	2003	Oak Park, Ill.
Laird, Matt	2	0	0.45	14	0	0	5	20	13	3	1	7	25	.180	R	R	6-0	185	11-23-80	2003	Houston, Texas
Marmol, Carlos	3	5	4.19	14	9	0	0	62	54	38	29	37	74	.225	R	R	6-2	190	10-14-82	1999	Bonao, D.R.
Mateo, Juan	4	1	4.46	18	0	0	2	36	42	25	18	14	35	.287	R	R	6-2	180	12-17-82	2001	Bani, D.R.
Ortiz, Jose	1	1	1.52	7	3	0	0	24	19	9	4	10	16	.211	R	R	6-2	160	11-17-83	2003	San Fran. de Macoris, D.R.
Overholt, Sean	1	0	5.40	9	1	0	0	17	19	15	10	6	15	.275	R	R	6-1	195	5-20-82	2003	Sandy, Utah
Polanco, Alfredo	1	1	7.80	6	5	0	0	15	18	14	13	8	19	.295	R	R	6-1	160	3-16-82	2001	Bonao, D.R.
Rodriguez, Pedro	2	4	8.84	14	6	0	0	39	58	46	38	19	31	.341	R	R	6-7	200	11-20-84	2001	Anoco, Venez.
Sanchez, Felix	0	0	0.00	1	1	0	0	2	2	0	0	0	3	.250	R	L	6-3	180	8-3-81	1999	Puerto Plata, D.R.
Santana, Andy	1	5	5.89	13	4	0	0	37	47	41	24	27	25	.326	L	L	6-3	160	8-17-83	2001	San Pedro de Macoris, D.R.
Urena, Jose	0	1	4.74	16	0	0	4	25	24	21	13	22	25	.263	R	R	6-3	160	6-8-81	1998	San Francisco de Macoris, D.R.
Weber, Matthew	0	2	4.05	7	0	0	1	13	14	10	6	3	13	.259	R	R	6-3	200	5-5-85	2003	Roscoe, Ill.
Wells, Randy	0	0	3.60	3	0	0	0	5	5	2	2	4	4	.250	R	R	6-4	200	8-28-82	2002	Lebanon, Ill.

CINCINNATI REDS

BY CHRIS HAFT

Record-setting is usually a flattering term. That wasn't the case with the 2003 Reds, however.

Cincinnati set franchise marks for home runs allowed (209), strikeouts by batters (1,326), runs and earned runs allowed (886, 818) and ERA (5.09). Cincinnati used more players (57), pitchers (30) and starting pitchers (17) than ever, a plethora of transactions and injuries that precipitated the club's 69-93, fifth-place finish in the National League Central Division.

The Reds demonstrated that their greatest ability was unpredictability. They led the majors in last at-bat victories (29) and extra-inning wins (15). Living on the edge in the standings as well as on the field, they spent 10 days with a record above .500, yet stood only 2½ games out of first place as late as July 2.

But faulty starting pitching—Cincinnati's perennial shortcoming—and various injuries began to conspire against the Reds. Austin Kearns' right shoulder, which he hurt in a home-plate collision with Atlanta reliever Ray King while sliding headfirst on May 21, never recovered.

Ken Griffey Jr. prompted a brief stir of excitement when he homered in five consecutive games before the all-star break. Then he ruptured a tendon in his right ankle on July 17, ending his season. Since joining the Reds in 2000, Griffey has played in 379 of the Reds' 649 games, a mere 58 percent.

"Nobody's more frustrated than me," Griffey said. "If (others) think I want to get hurt and not want to get out there and hit home runs and rob people—that's what coming to the ballpark is, that's what it's about. It makes it tough when you can't do them."

Cincinnati lost eight of its first nine games after the break, spurring a tumultuous succession of changes. General manager Jim Bowden, who had held his job since October 1992, and manager Bob Boone were fired on July 28. Promoted from Triple-A Louisville, interim manager Dave Miley had a dramatically altered team to guide. In the few days between the firings and the trading deadline, Cincinnati dealt closer Scott Williamson, outfielder Jose Guillen, lefthander Gabe White and third baseman Aaron Boone, a charismatic force on the field and in the clubhouse.

Transactions continued past the deadline. Relievers Kent Mercker and Scott Sullivan were traded. Lefty Felix Heredia was waived and claimed by the Yankees. Season-ending injuries to Jimmy Haynes (back) and Ryan Dempster (elbow), coupled with Paul Wilson's shutdown and Danny Graves' return to the bullpen, left Cincinnati without a single member of its season-opening rotation by early September.

The upheaval crested as shortstop Barry Larkin turned down a $500,000 contract for 2004, complaining about management's refusal to negotiate from that figure. Then Larkin agreed to a one-year, $700,000 deal that will extend his Reds career into a 19th season.

First-round pick Ryan Wagner should help sustain the team's traditional bullpen strength. The 21-year-old from the University of Houston became the first player from the 2003 draft to reach the majors and the only Reds' first pick to make his big league debut the year he was drafted. In 17 outings, he was 2-0, 1.66 with 25 strikeouts in 22 innings. His opponents' batting average was a mere .173, and he didn't allow a run in his final eight appearances.

Just two of Cincinnati's six minor league affiliates finished above .500, but both reached the postseason. Billings captured the Pioneer League championship, defeating Provo in the title game as righthander Jim Paduch threw a no-hitter.

Jose Guillen

Stephen Smitherman

PLAYERS of the YEAR

MAJOR LEAGUE: Jose Guillen, of

Guillen didn't start the 2003 season with the Reds—he was in Triple-A—nor did he end it with them after being traded to the A's. But while in Cincinnati, he was the most productive player, hitting .337-23-63 in 315 at-bats.

MINOR LEAGUE: Stephen Smitherman, of

As if the Reds weren't already crowed in the outfield, Smitherman emerged in 2003, leading the Southern League in on-base percentage, ranking second in slugging and third in home runs and batting average.

ORGANIZATION LEADERS

BATTING		
*AVG	Brandon Larson, Louisville	.323
R	Luis Bolivar, Dayton/Billings	83
H	Kevin Howard, Dayton	145
TB	Jesse Gutierrez, Chattanooga/Potomac	230
2B	Jesse Gutierrez, Chattanooga/Potomac	34
3B	Three tied at	5
HR	Brandon Larson, Louisville	20
	Jesse Gutierrez, Chattanooga/Potomac	20
RBI	Jesse Gutierrez, Chattanooga/Potomac	96
BB	Joey Votto, Dayton/Billings	90
SO	Mark Schramek, Chatt./Potomac/Dayton	155
SB	William Bergolla, Potomac	52
*SLG	Brandon Larson, Louisville	.617
*OBP	Joey Votto, Dayton/Billings	.406
PITCHING		
W	Eddy Valdez, Potomac/Dayton	16
L	Daylan Childress, Chattanooga/Potomac	13
#ERA	Todd Coffey, Potomac/Dayton	2.16
G	Todd Coffey, Potomac/Dayton	50
CG	Three tied at	2
SV	Nathan Cotton, Chattanooga/Potomac	28
IP	Eddy Valdez, Potomac/Dayton	169
BB	Daylan Childress, Chattanooga/Potomac	71
SO	Daylan Childress, Chattanooga/Potomac	124

*Minimum 250 At-Bats #Minimum 75 Innings

CINCINNATI REDS

Managers: Bob Boone/Dave Miley. **2003 Record:** 69-93, .426 (5th, NL Central).

BATTING	AVG	G	AB	R	H	2B	3B	HR	RBI	BB	SO	SB	CS	SLG	OBP	B	T	HT	WT	DOB	1st Yr	Resides
Boone, Aaron	.273	106	403	61	110	19	3	18	65	35	74	15	3	.469	.339	R	R	6-2	200	3-9-73	1994	Villa Park, Calif.
Branyan, Russell	.216	74	176	22	38	12	0	9	26	27	69	0	0	.438	.322	L	R	6-3	195	12-19-75	1994	Kathleen, Ga.
Budzinski, Mark	.000	4	7	0	0	0	0	0	0	0	4	0	0	.000	.000	L	L	6-2	180	8-26-73	1995	Richmond, Va.
Casey, Sean	.291	147	573	71	167	19	3	14	80	51	58	4	0	.408	.350	L	R	6-4	225	7-2-74	1995	Jupiter, Fla.
Castro, Juan	.253	113	320	28	81	14	1	9	33	18	58	2	3	.388	.290	R	R	5-11	195	6-20-72	1991	Glendale, Ariz.
Chamblee, Jim	.000	2	2	0	0	0	0	0	0	0	2	0	0	.000	.000	R	R	6-4	185	5-6-75	1995	Denton, Texas
Dunn, Adam	.215	116	381	70	82	12	1	27	57	74	126	8	2	.465	.354	L	R	6-6	240	11-9-79	1998	Porter, Texas
Freel, Ryan	.285	43	137	23	39	6	1	4	12	9	13	9	4	.431	.344	R	R	5-10	180	3-8-76	1995	Jacksonville, Fla.
Griffey, Ken	.247	53	166	34	41	12	1	13	26	27	44	1	0	.566	.370	L	L	6-3	205	11-21-69	1987	Orlando, Fla.
Guillen, Jose	.337	91	315	52	106	21	1	23	63	17	63	1	3	.629	.385	R	R	5-11	190	5-17-76	1993	San Cristobal, D.R.
Hummel, Tim	.226	26	84	9	19	5	0	2	10	8	13	0	0	.357	.290	R	R	6-2	190	11-18-78	2000	Montgomery, N.Y.
Jimenez, D'Angelo	.290	73	290	34	84	13	2	7	31	34	43	7	4	.421	.365	S	R	6-0	190	12-21-77	1995	Santo Domingo, D.R.
Kearns, Austin	.264	82	292	39	77	11	0	15	58	41	68	5	2	.455	.364	R	R	6-3	220	5-20-80	1998	Lexington, Ky.
Larkin, Barry	.282	70	241	39	68	16	1	2	18	22	32	2	0	.382	.345	R	R	6-0	185	4-28-64	1985	Orlando, Fla.
Larson, Brandon	.101	32	89	6	9	1	0	1	9	13	31	2	2	.146	.212	R	R	6-0	210	5-24-76	1997	San Antonio, Texas
LaRue, Jason	.230	118	379	52	87	23	1	16	50	33	111	3	3	.422	.321	R	R	5-11	200	3-19-74	1995	San Antonio, Texas
Lopez, Felipe	.213	59	197	28	42	7	2	2	13	28	59	8	5	.299	.313	S	R	6-1	185	5-12-80	1998	Altamonte Springs, Fla.
Mateo, Ruben	.242	74	207	16	50	9	0	3	18	12	53	0	0	.329	.290	R	R	6-0	185	2-10-78	1995	San Cristobal, D.R.
Miller, Corky	.267	14	30	4	8	0	0	0	1	5	7	0	0	.267	.395	R	R	6-1	225	3-18-76	1998	Calimesa, Calif.
Olmedo, Rainer	.239	79	230	24	55	6	1	0	17	13	46	1	1	.274	.280	S	R	5-11	155	5-31-81	1999	Maracay, Venez.
Pena, Wily Mo	.218	80	165	20	36	6	1	5	16	12	53	3	2	.358	.283	R	R	6-3	215	1-23-82	1998	Tampa, Fla.
Sardinha, Dane	.000	1	2	0	0	0	0	0	0	0	1	0	0	.000	.000	R	R	6-0	215	4-8-79	2001	Gulfport, Fla.
Smitherman, Stephen	.159	21	44	3	7	2	0	1	6	3	9	1	0	.273	.213	R	R	6-4	235	9-1-78	2000	Hartshorne, Okla.
Stenson, Dernell	.247	37	81	14	20	5	0	3	13	11	24	0	0	.420	.333	L	L	6-1	230	6-17-78	1996	La Grange, Ga.
Stinnett, Kelly	.229	60	179	14	41	13	0	3	19	13	51	0	0	.352	.294	R	R	5-11	220	2-4-70	1990	Mesa, Ariz.
Taylor, Reggie	.217	100	180	17	39	5	2	5	19	11	68	7	0	.350	.266	L	R	6-1	180	1-12-77	1995	Newberry, S.C.
Valent, Eric	.214	18	42	3	9	0	0	0	1	2	9	0	0	.214	.250	L	L	5-11	190	4-4-77	1998	Anaheim, Calif.

PITCHING	W	L	ERA	G	GS	CG	SV	IP	H	R	ER	BB	SO	AVG	B	T	HT	WT	DOB	1st Yr	Resides
Acevedo, Jose	2	0	2.67	5	4	1	0	27	17	8	8	6	23	.182	R	R	6-0	185	12-18-77	1997	Santiago, D.R.
Anderson, Jimmy	1	5	8.84	8	7	0	0	39	60	39	38	14	13	.359	L	L	6-1	210	1-22-76	1994	Chesapeake, Va.
Austin, Jeff	2	3	8.58	7	7	0	0	28	28	27	27	21	22	.254	R	R	6-0	180	10-19-76	1999	Kingwood, Texas
Bale, John	1	2	4.47	10	9	0	0	46	50	24	23	12	37	.280	L	L	6-4	210	5-22-74	1996	Crestview, Fla.
Belisle, Matt	1	1	5.19	6	0	0	0	9	10	5	5	2	6	.303	S	R	6-3	190	6-6-80	1998	Austin, Texas
Cerros, Juan	0	0	4.85	11	0	0	0	13	11	7	7	5	9	.224	R	R	6-1	200	9-25-76	1996	Monterrey, Mexico
Dempster, Ryan	3	7	6.54	22	20	0	0	116	134	89	84	70	84	.293	R	R	6-3	215	5-3-77	1995	Denver, Colo.
Etherton, Seth	2	4	6.90	7	7	0	0	30	39	23	23	15	17	.322	R	R	6-1	200	10-17-76	1998	Monarch Beach, Calif.
Graves, Danny	4	15	5.33	30	26	2	2	169	204	108	100	41	60	.298	R	R	6-0	185	8-7-73	1995	Lake Mary, Fla.
Hall, Josh	0	2	6.57	6	5	0	0	25	33	22	18	15	18	.314	R	R	6-2	190	12-16-80	1998	Lynchburg, Va.
Hamilton, Joey	0	0	12.66	3	0	0	0	11	21	15	15	5	7	.403	R	R	6-4	240	9-9-70	1991	Norcross, Ga.
Harang, Aaron	4	3	5.28	9	9	0	0	46	48	28	27	10	26	.271	R	R	6-7	240	5-9-78	1999	San Diego, Calif.
Haynes, Jimmy	2	12	6.30	18	18	1	0	94	118	74	66	57	49	.311	R	R	6-4	220	9-5-72	1991	La Grange, Ga.
Heredia, Felix	5	2	3.00	57	0	0	1	72	61	27	24	28	41	.228	L	L	6-0	180	6-18-75	1993	Miami, Fla.
Manzanillo, Josias	0	2	12.66	9	0	0	0	11	21	20	15	4	12	.388	R	R	6-0	200	10-16-67	1983	Hyde Park, Mass.
Mercker, Kent	0	2	2.35	49	0	0	0	38	31	13	10	25	41	.224	L	L	6-2	190	2-1-68	1986	Dublin, Ohio
Norton, Phil	0	0	2.45	17	0	0	0	15	7	4	4	6	7	.148	R	L	6-0	210	2-1-76	1996	Texarkana, Texas
2-team (4 Chicago)	0	0	3.00	21	0	0	0	18	9	6	6	9	7	.155							
Randall, Scott	2	5	6.51	15	2	0	0	28	34	20	20	11	25	.303	R	R	6-3	225	10-29-75	1995	Goleta, Calif.
Reith, Brian	2	3	4.11	42	1	0	1	61	61	32	28	36	39	.262	R	R	6-5	220	2-28-78	1996	Ft. Wayne, Ind.
Reitsma, Chris	9	5	4.29	57	3	0	12	84	92	41	40	19	53	.281	R	R	6-5	235	12-31-77	1996	Calgary, Alberta
Riedling, John	2	3	4.90	55	8	0	1	101	107	61	55	47	65	.269	R	R	5-11	190	8-29-75	1994	Wellington, Fla.
Serafini, Dan	1	3	5.40	10	4	0	0	30	41	23	18	14	13	.336	L	L	6-1	190	1-25-74	1992	San Bruno, Calif.
Sullivan, Scott	6	0	3.62	50	0	0	0	50	39	22	20	26	43	.210	R	R	6-3	210	3-13-71	1993	Livingston, Ala.
Valentine, Joe	0	0	18.00	2	0	0	0	2	5	4	4	1	1	.454	R	R	6-2	195	12-24-79	1999	Pensacola, Fla.
Van Poppel, Todd	2	1	4.54	9	4	0	0	36	31	18	18	6	25	.227	R	R	6-5	230	12-9-71	1990	Southlake, Texas
Wagner, Ryan	2	0	1.66	17	0	0	0	22	13	4	4	12	25	.173	R	R	6-4	210	7-15-82	2003	Yoakum, Texas
Watson, Mark	0	0	4.50	2	0	0	0	2	2	1	1	1	2	.250	R	L	6-3	240	1-23-74	1996	Atlanta, Ga.
White, Gabe	3	0	3.93	34	0	0	0	34	36	15	15	6	23	.274	L	L	6-2	200	11-20-71	1990	Sebring, Fla.
Williamson, Scott	5	3	3.19	42	0	0	21	42	34	15	15	25	53	.213	R	R	6-0	180	2-17-76	1997	Friendswood, Texas
Wilson, Paul	8	10	4.64	28	28	0	0	167	190	97	86	50	93	.285	R	R	6-5	215	3-28-73	1994	Palm City, Fla.

FIELDING

Catcher	PCT	G	PO	A	E	DP	PB
LaRue	.984	114	649	46	11	8	6
Miller	1.000	11	60	5	0	0	0
Sardinha	1.000	1	2	0	0	0	0
Stinnett	.993	50	262	21	2	3	3

First Base	PCT	G	PO	A	E	DP
Branyan	.991	14	98	7	1	13
Casey	.996	144	1257	75	6	112
Castro	.000	1	0	0	0	0
Dunn	.989	19	81	8	1	10
LaRue	1.000	1	7	1	0	0
Stenson	1.000	1	1	0	0	0

Second Base	PCT	G	PO	A	E	DP
Boone	1.000	19	43	63	0	14
Castro	.984	56	100	154	4	33
Freel	.971	11	14	20	1	2
Hummel	1.000	1	2	3	0	1
Jimenez	.990	73	164	214	4	56
Lopez	.875	3	3	4	1	1
Olmedo	1.000	18	35	36	0	9

Third Base	PCT	G	PO	A	E	DP
Boone	.945	83	62	180	14	20
Branyan	.968	20	12	49	2	5
Castro	.983	30	17	42	1	7
Chamblee	.000	1	0	0	0	0
Freel	1.000	2	0	2	0	2
Hummel	.894	20	10	32	5	0

	PCT	G	PO	A	E	DP
Jimenez	1.000	2	0	2	0	0
Larson	.943	24	18	48	4	7
Lopez	1.000	8	3	4	0	0
Pena	1.000	1	0	1	0	0

Shortstop	PCT	G	PO	A	E	DP
Boone	.857	5	3	15	3	1
Castro	1.000	24	28	43	0	14
Hummel	1.000	2	1	4	0	0
Larkin	.962	60	71	159	9	36

	PCT	G	PO	A	E	DP
Lopez	.928	50	60	132	15	20
Olmedo	.929	51	60	122	14	21

Outfield	PCT	G	PO	A	E	DP
Branyan	1.000	17	30	0	0	0
Budzinski	1.000	1	3	0	0	0
Dunn	.955	102	208	5	10	2
Freel	1.000	24	58	2	0	0
Griffey	.989	43	89	3	1	0
Guillen	.957	78	169	9	8	1

	PCT	G	PO	A	E	DP
Kearns	.990	80	199	5	2	0
Larson	1.000	3	9	1	0	0
LaRue	.000	1	0	0	0	0
Mateo	.982	54	106	2	2	1
Pena	.977	47	85	1	2	1
Smitherman	1.000	14	17	0	0	0
Stenson	.979	22	44	2	1	0
Taylor	.990	60	98	2	1	0
Valent	1.000	8	20	1	0	0

FARM SYSTEM

Director, Player Development: Tim Naehring.

Class	Farm Team	League	W	L	Pct.	Finish*	Manager(s)	First Yr.
AAA	Louisville (Ky.) RiverBats	International	79	64	.552	2nd (14)	Dave Miley/Rick Burleson	2000
AA	Chattanooga (Tenn.) Lookouts	Southern	66	74	.471	8th (10)	Phillip Wellman	1988
High A	Potomac (Va.) Cannons	Carolina	62	77	.446	6th (8)	Jayhawk Owens	2003
Low A	Dayton (Ohio) Dragons	Midwest	61	78	.439	13th (14)	Donnie Scott	2000
Rookie	Billings (Mont.) Mustangs	Pioneer	41	35	.539	+3rd (8)	Rick Burleson/Jay Sorg	1974
Rookie	Sarasota (Fla.) Reds	Gulf Coast	26	34	.433	10th (12)	Edgar Caceres	1999

*Finish in overall standings (No. of teams in league) + League champion

LOUISVILLE RIVERBATS — Class AAA

INTERNATIONAL LEAGUE

BATTING	AVG	G	AB	R	H	2B	3B	HR	RBI	BB	SO	SB	CS	SLG	OBP	B	T	HT	WT	DOB	1st Yr	Resides
Baez, Kevin	.172	10	29	2	5	0	0	0	3	1	5	0	0	.172	.200	R	R	5-11	170	1-10-67	1988	Brooklyn, N.Y.
Beattie, Andrew	.233	9	30	5	7	1	1	1	6	1	4	0	0	.433	.258	S	R	5-10	165	2-28-78	1998	Sarasota, Fla.
Branyan, Russell	.327	14	49	5	16	5	0	1	3	9	15	0	0	.490	.441	L	R	6-3	195	12-19-75	1994	Kathleen, Ga.
Brown, Emil	.295	97	369	58	109	20	3	12	63	27	76	18	3	.463	.343	R	R	6-2	200	12-29-74	1994	Chicago, Ill.
Budzinski, Mark	.274	74	259	53	71	15	3	1	15	37	56	10	4	.367	.370	L	L	6-2	180	8-26-73	1995	Richmond, Va.
2-team (46 Indy)	.273	120	418	80	114	22	4	2	27	53	95	17	6	.359	.358							
Caceres, Wilmy	.000	4	7	1	0	0	0	0	2	0	1	0	0	.000	.000	S	R	6-0	160	10-2-73	1997	Moca, D.R.
Cairns, Troy	.000	2	1	1	0	0	0	0	0	0	0	0	0	.000	.000	R	R	6-0	160	9-29-80	2002	Blue Springs, Mo.
Castro, Juan	.219	9	32	3	7	0	0	1	5	2	3	0	1	.313	.257	R	R	5-11	195	6-20-72	1991	Glendale, Ariz.
Chamblee, Jim	.285	85	263	31	75	13	4	5	35	29	59	2	0	.422	.366	R	R	6-4	185	5-6-75	1995	Denton, Texas
Clapinski, Chris	.345	7	29	8	10	0	0	1	3	2	9	1	0	.448	.387	S	R	6-0	170	8-20-71	1992	Cape Canaveral, Fla.
Coleman, Michael	.254	18	63	12	16	4	0	3	19	6	12	1	0	.460	.315	R	R	5-11	210	8-16-75	1994	Antioch, Tenn.
Crespo, Felipe	.244	107	360	43	88	20	0	6	48	43	54	9	5	.350	.330	S	R	5-11	200	3-5-73	1991	Caguas, P.R.
Cruz, Jacob	.348	36	132	25	46	8	0	7	29	14	22	3	0	.568	.409	L	L	6-0	210	1-28-73	1994	Gilbert, Ariz.
Darula, Bobby	.300	13	40	4	12	4	0	0	8	4	6	1	1	.400	.364	L	R	5-10	185	10-29-74	1996	Greenwich, Conn.
Dransfeldt, Kelly	.214	46	140	15	30	9	2	2	12	9	34	0	1	.350	.263	R	R	6-2	190	4-16-75	1996	Morris, Ill.
Foreman, JuJu	.333	2	3	1	1	0	0	0	0	0	0	0	0	.333	.333	L	R	5-8	160	2-18-79	2000	Girard, Ga.
Freel, Ryan	.274	54	215	38	59	11	1	3	12	21	32	25	6	.377	.336	R	R	5-10	180	3-8-76	1995	Jacksonville, Fla.
Guerrero, Wilton	.277	126	476	68	132	20	1	1	29	26	58	30	9	.330	.315	S	R	6-0	175	10-24-74	1992	Nizao, D.R.
Guillen, Jose	.333	4	15	4	5	1	0	0	3	1	3	1	0	.400	.353	R	R	5-11	190	5-17-76	1993	San Cristobal, D.R.
Hanigan, Ryan	.333	1	3	1	1	0	0	0	0	0	1	0	0	.333	.500	R	R	6-1	185	8-16-80	2002	Andover, Mass.
Hill, Jason	.667	3	3	0	2	1	0	0	0	1	1	0	0	1.000	.750	R	R	6-3	210	3-17-77	1998	Danville, Calif.
Jennings, Robin	.210	64	219	23	46	12	1	1	15	18	43	3	2	.288	.278	L	L	6-2	210	4-11-72	1992	Springfield, Va.
Larson, Brandon	.323	72	282	51	91	19	2	20	74	28	70	3	0	.617	.384	R	R	6-0	210	5-24-76	1997	San Antonio, Texas
Lopez, Felipe	.280	35	143	22	40	11	0	2	18	12	38	2	5	.399	.333	S	R	6-1	185	5-12-80	1998	Altamonte Springs, Fla.
Mateo, Ruben	.327	57	217	36	71	15	1	9	50	26	34	3	1	.530	.408	R	R	6-0	185	2-10-78	1995	San Cristobal, D.R.
Maxwell, Jason	.260	103	361	52	94	17	1	8	46	29	57	2	1	.380	.314	R	R	6-1	175	3-26-72	1993	Franklin, Tenn.
Miller, Corky	.249	103	354	49	88	28	0	11	43	35	58	0	0	.421	.326	R	R	6-1	225	3-18-76	1998	Calimesa, Calif.
Mitchell, Keith	.192	18	52	5	10	2	1	0	5	10	16	0	0	.269	.323	R	R	5-10	190	8-6-69	1987	San Diego, Calif.
Olmedo, Rainer	.240	9	25	4	6	1	0	1	4	2	6	0	0	.400	.296	S	R	5-11	155	5-31-81	1999	Maracay, Venez.
Pena, Wily Mo	.373	14	51	16	19	3	0	4	14	5	13	0	0	.667	.450	R	R	6-3	215	1-23-82	1998	Tampa, Fla.
Perez, Santiago	.125	6	16	1	2	0	0	1	1	4	2	1	0	.313	.300	S	R	6-2	160	12-30-75	1993	Santo Domingo, D.R.
2-team (13 Ottawa)	.216	19	51	5	11	2	0	1	2	8	11	3	2	.314	.322							
Pickering, Calvin	.284	26	81	10	23	3	0	4	18	17	31	0	0	.469	.422	L	L	6-5	260	9-29-76	1995	Temple Terrace, Fla.
Smitherman, Stephen	.127	17	63	1	8	0	0	0	5	4	19	0	0	.127	.188	R	R	6-4	235	9-1-78	2000	Hartshorne, Okla.
Stefanski, Mike	.218	64	202	20	44	7	1	3	20	13	30	1	1	.307	.266	R	R	6-2	210	9-12-69	1991	Farmington, Mich.
Stenson, Dernell	.237	17	59	9	14	3	0	5	14	5	10	0	0	.542	.292	L	L	6-1	230	6-17-78	1996	La Grange, Ga.
Thomas, Juan	.161	9	31	3	5	1	0	0	2	2	12	0	0	.194	.235	R	R	6-4	295	4-17-72	1991	Lilburn, Ga.

PITCHING	W	L	ERA	G	GS	CG	SV	IP	H	R	ER	BB	SO	AVG	B	T	HT	WT	DOB	1st Yr	Resides
Acevedo, Jose	6	2	3.43	29	3	0	0	60	56	26	23	20	57	.245	R	R	6-0	185	12-18-77	1997	Santiago, D.R.
Adkins, Tim	0	1	3.46	12	1	0	0	26	23	10	10	11	21	.244	L	L	6-0	190	5-12-74	1992	Huntington, W.Va.
Almanzar, Carlos	2	2	3.50	42	0	0	23	46	47	19	18	3	54	.251	R	R	6-2	165	11-6-73	1991	Santo Domingo, D.R.
Anderson, Jimmy	6	1	3.12	9	9	0	0	61	61	26	21	14	30	.265	L	L	6-1	210	1-22-76	1994	Chesapeake, Va.
Austin, Jeff	4	2	4.34	9	9	0	0	46	46	24	22	19	37	.265	R	R	6-0	180	10-19-76	1999	Kingwood, Texas
Bale, John	4	1	3.30	26	2	0	4	44	36	17	16	13	43	.220	L	L	6-4	210	5-22-74	1996	Crestview, Fla.
2-team (8 Norfolk)	4	2	3.30	34	2	0	4	57	47	22	21	16	58	.220							
Belisle, Matt	1	3	3.81	4	4	0	0	26	31	15	11	5	15	.303	S	R	6-3	190	6-6-80	1998	Austin, Texas
2-team (3 Richmond)	2	4	3.13	7	7	0	0	46	48	21	16	5	25	.272							
Bevel, Bobby	0	0	18.00	2	0	0	0	1	5	3	2	0	0	.714	L	L	5-10	180	10-10-73	1995	West Plains, Mo.
Cerros, Juan	0	0	4.50	4	0	0	0	4	6	2	2	0	1	.352	R	R	6-1	200	9-25-76	1996	Monterrey, Mexico
Claussen, Brandon	0	1	7.47	3	3	0	0	16	17	13	13	6	16	.293	R	L	6-2	200	5-1-79	1999	Roswell, N.M.
2-team (11 Columbus)	2	2	3.63	14	14	1	0	84	70	41	34	24	55	.228							
Cortes, Jorge	0	0	0.00	1	0	0	0	1	0	0	0	0	0	.000	R	R	6-4	190	9-4-72	1995	Panama City, Panama

PITCHING	W	L	ERA	G	GS	CG	SV	IP	H	R	ER	BB	SO	AVG	B	T	HT	WT	DOB	1st Yr	Resides
Croushore, Rick	1	0	1.93	5	0	0	0	5	3	1	1	7	5	.200	R	R	6-4	210	8-7-70	1993	Benton, Ark.
2-team (9 Ottawa)	1	0	2.63	14	0	0	0	14	10	4	4	14	13	.217							
Davis, Lance	8	9	4.55	26	22	1	0	138	166	75	70	42	62	.299	R	L	6-0	170	9-1-76	1995	Polk City, Fla.
Dempster, Ryan	1	1	3.29	2	2	1	0	14	13	5	5	3	9	.254	R	R	6-3	215	5-3-77	1995	Denver, Colo.
DePaula, Sean	0	0	6.17	10	0	0	0	12	15	10	8	7	8	.312	R	R	6-4	210	11-7-73	1996	Derry, N.H.
Etherton, Seth	7	7	4.31	21	21	2	0	123	144	62	59	26	69	.296	R	R	6-1	200	10-17-76	1998	Monarch Beach, Calif.
Gil, David	0	1	3.38	16	2	0	0	32	33	14	12	7	20	.268	R	R	6-4	215	10-1-78	2000	Miami, Fla.
Hamilton, Joey	8	3	3.23	33	8	0	1	86	103	38	31	18	45	.305	R	R	6-4	240	9-9-70	1991	Norcross, Ga.
Harang, Aaron	0	1	15.00	1	1	0	0	3	5	5	5	2	4	.357	R	R	6-7	240	5-9-78	1999	San Diego, Calif.
Harnisch, Pete	0	4	10.06	8	8	0	0	34	59	39	38	11	17	.393	R	R	6-0	220	9-23-66	1987	Lake Mary, Fla.
Haynes, Jimmy	1	1	2.53	2	2	0	0	11	10	4	3	3	7	.243	R	R	6-4	220	9-5-72	1991	La Grange, Ga.
Keller, Kris	0	1	9.00	2	0	0	0	1	1	1	1	2	0	.333	R	R	6-2	260	3-1-78	1996	Atlantic Beach, Fla.
Manzanillo, Josias	1	1	4.18	22	0	0	0	28	25	17	13	11	16	.250	R	R	6-0	200	10-16-67	1983	Hyde Park, Mass.
Michalak, Chris	2	1	5.13	9	3	0	0	26	35	15	15	5	18	.336	L	L	6-2	195	1-4-71	1993	Keller, Texas
Miller, Travis	1	0	0.00	4	0	0	0	4	4	0	0	1	4	.266	R	L	6-3	210	11-2-72	1994	Eaton, Ohio
Moseley, Dustin	2	3	2.70	8	8	0	0	50	46	19	15	14	27	.244	R	R	6-4	190	12-26-81	2001	Texarkana, Texas
Mottl, Ryan	0	2	5.63	3	3	0	0	16	20	10	10	8	12	.322	S	R	6-3	200	12-9-77	2000	Florissant, Mo.
Navarro, Jaime	0	1	2.70	2	2	0	0	10	11	3	3	2	4	.289	R	R	6-4	250	3-27-68	1986	Milwaukee, Wisc.
Randall, Scott	10	4	4.63	30	20	0	3	136	170	76	70	39	86	.309	R	R	6-3	225	10-29-75	1995	Goleta, Calif.
Reith, Brian	3	1	1.96	16	0	0	1	23	12	9	5	9	28	.151	R	R	6-5	220	2-28-78	1996	Fort Wayne, Ind.
Reitsma, Chris	1	2	4.00	4	4	0	0	18	22	10	8	5	11	.293	R	R	6-5	235	12-31-77	1996	Calgary, Alberta
Service, Scott	0	0	2.45	4	0	0	0	4	3	1	1	0	7	.214	R	R	6-6	250	2-26-67	1986	Cincinnati, Ohio
Shackelford, Brian	1	0	2.30	12	0	0	0	16	15	4	4	7	10	.258	L	L	6-1	190	8-30-76	1998	Norman, Okla.
Valentine, Joe	1	0	0.79	9	0	0	1	11	5	1	1	3	8	.131	R	R	6-2	195	12-24-79	1999	Pensacola, Fla.
Van Poppel, Todd	4	3	3.17	20	5	0	1	54	49	23	19	11	45	.247	R	R	6-5	230	12-9-71	1990	Southlake, Texas
Wagner, Ryan	0	1	4.50	4	0	0	0	4	5	2	2	0	4	.312	R	R	6-4	210	7-15-82	2003	Yoakum, Texas
Watson, Mark	4	4	4.36	44	0	0	4	54	53	30	26	14	46	.267	R	L	6-3	240	1-23-74	1996	Atlanta, Ga.
White, Gabe	0	0	9.00	1	1	0	0	1	2	1	1	1	0	.400	L	L	6-2	200	11-20-71	1990	Sebring, Fla.

FIELDING

Catcher	PCT	G	PO	A	E	DP	PB
Hanigan	1.000	1	5	1	0	1	0
Hill	1.000	1	7	2	0	0	0
Miller	.989	98	608	51	7	5	5
Stefanski	.987	50	270	31	4	4	2

First Base	PCT	G	PO	A	E	DP
Branyan	.958	2	22	1	1	1
Chamblee	.995	26	185	14	1	18
Crespo	.991	61	494	30	5	55
Cruz	.945	6	44	8	3	4
Jennings	.991	37	325	19	3	36
Larson	.800	1	8	0	2	1
Pickering	.991	14	104	5	1	9
Smitherman	1.000	1	2	0	0	1
Stefanski	.965	10	53	2	2	10
Thomas	1.000	4	24	3	0	6

Second Base	PCT	G	PO	A	E	DP
Beattie	1.000	7	12	23	0	8
Chamblee	.981	11	27	26	1	7
Freel	.989	39	74	110	2	31
Guerrero	.992	30	54	73	1	17
Lopez	.972	7	20	15	1	4
Maxwell	.983	59	105	177	5	44
Olmedo	.958	4	9	14	1	6

Third Base	PCT	G	PO	A	E	DP
Branyan	1.000	2	1	3	0	0
Chamblee	.982	39	18	89	2	9
Crespo	.000	1	0	0	0	0
Dransfeldt	.929	7	4	9	1	0
Freel	1.000	4	3	9	0	0
Guerrero	.853	15	9	20	5	2
Larson	.942	70	51	175	14	19
Maxwell	.941	13	5	27	2	1

Shortstop	PCT	G	PO	A	E	DP
Baez	.931	8	11	16	2	3
Caceres	.800	1	2	2	1	0
Castro	.950	9	11	27	2	9
Clapinski	1.000	7	6	18	0	6
Dransfeldt	.948	37	67	98	9	21
Guerrero	.988	18	31	54	1	14
Lopez	.930	28	36	70	8	19
Maxwell	.962	32	42	84	5	21
Olmedo	1.000	6	13	21	0	6
Perez	.966	6	8	20	1	2

Outfield	PCT	G	PO	A	E	DP
Beattie	1.000	2	5	1	0	0
Branyan	1.000	3	3	0	0	0
Brown	.979	91	223	9	5	2
Budzinski	.987	72	153	3	2	1
Chamblee	1.000	9	17	0	0	0
Coleman	1.000	16	25	1	0	0
Crespo	.975	18	37	2	1	0
Cruz	.962	25	48	2	2	1
Darula	1.000	7	16	0	0	0
Foreman	.000	1	0	0	0	0
Freel	1.000	8	10	1	0	0
Guerrero	1.000	55	84	2	0	0
Guillen	1.000	4	5	0	0	0
Jennings	1.000	25	45	0	0	0
Larson	1.000	1	1	0	0	0
Mateo	.984	57	117	3	2	0
Mitchell	1.000	14	26	1	0	0
Pena	.933	14	28	0	2	0
Smitherman	.969	15	29	2	1	1
Stenson	.960	17	24	0	1	0

CHATTANOOGA LOOKOUTS — Class AA

SOUTHERN LEAGUE

BATTING	AVG	G	AB	R	H	2B	3B	HR	RBI	BB	SO	SB	CS	SLG	OBP	B	T	HT	WT	DOB	1st Yr	Resides
Anderson, Bryan	.208	44	101	12	21	8	0	1	14	13	30	0	1	.317	.317	R	R	6-2	170	7-10-78	2000	San Antonio, Texas
Bannon, Jeff	.104	13	48	4	5	1	0	0	2	5	8	0	0	.125	.189	R	R	6-4	185	8-21-79	2001	Camarillo, Calif.
Beattie, Andrew	.251	116	423	52	106	28	0	6	38	48	87	5	9	.359	.328	S	R	5-10	165	2-28-78	1998	Sarasota, Fla.
Caceres, Wilmy	.275	108	357	56	98	12	2	4	27	26	39	22	9	.353	.322	S	R	6-0	160	10-2-73	1997	Moca, D.R.
Cairns, Troy	.190	19	42	4	8	3	0	1	5	7	10	0	0	.333	.300	R	R	6-0	160	9-29-80	2002	Blue Springs, Mo.
Cesar, Dionys	.413	12	46	7	19	4	0	0	8	4	2	1	1	.500	.460	S	R	5-10	150	9-27-76	1994	Santo Domingo, D.R.
Chamblee, Jim	.333	28	102	16	34	7	0	4	16	9	27	3	1	.520	.414	R	R	6-4	185	5-6-75	1995	Denton, Texas
Conley, Evan	.176	8	17	2	3	1	0	0	2	2	5	0	0	.235	.263	R	R	6-1	200	2-25-81	2003	Bradenton, Fla.
Correll, Brad	.230	22	74	8	17	1	2	2	11	1	12	3	3	.378	.237	R	R	6-2	205	6-17-81	2002	Gastonia, N.C.
Darula, Bobby	.333	1	3	1	1	0	0	1	2	0	0	0	0	1.333	.333	L	R	5-10	185	10-29-74	1996	Greenwich, Conn.
Dellaero, Jason	.231	22	65	7	15	4	1	2	13	5	20	2	0	.415	.278	R	R	6-2	190	12-17-76	1997	Brewster, N.Y.
Diaz, Alejandro	.269	105	360	44	97	18	3	4	33	19	56	16	10	.369	.304	R	R	5-9	195	7-9-75	1999	Constanza, D.R.
Encarnacion, Edwin	.272	67	254	40	69	13	1	5	36	22	44	8	3	.390	.331	R	R	6-1	195	1-7-83	2000	La Romana, D.R.
Gubanich, Creighton	.227	42	119	13	27	7	0	2	14	7	26	0	0	.336	.273	R	R	6-3	230	3-27-72	1991	Phoenixville, Pa.
Gutierrez, Jesse	.215	27	107	12	23	8	1	4	20	9	16	0	0	.421	.288	R	R	6-2	195	6-16-78	2001	McAllen, Texas
Haas, Chris	.256	32	90	12	23	8	2	1	14	15	33	1	1	.422	.364	L	R	6-1	200	10-15-76	1995	Paducah, Ky.
Hill, Jason	.067	6	15	0	1	0	0	0	2	2	2	0	0	.067	.222	R	R	6-3	210	3-17-77	1998	Danville, Calif.
Jennings, Robin	.333	8	30	5	10	3	1	1	2	3	7	0	0	.600	.394	L	L	6-2	210	4-11-72	1992	Springfield, Va.
Kearns, Austin	.200	3	5	2	1	0	0	0	1	2	2	0	0	.200	.500	R	R	6-3	220	5-20-80	1998	Lexington, Ky.
Lewis, Kenny	.118	6	17	4	2	1	0	0	0	4	9	3	2	.176	.318	L	L	5-9	195	10-13-84	2003	Danville, Va.
Mitchell, Keith	.291	20	55	11	16	4	1	2	8	14	8	1	0	.509	.435	R	R	5-10	190	8-6-69	1987	San Diego, Calif.
Moseley, Dustin	.351	19	37	6	13	1	0	1	9	1	6	1	0	.459	.368	R	R	6-4	190	12-26-81	2001	Texarkana, Texas
Olmedo, Rainer	.294	49	160	23	47	11	0	2	15	14	29	3	3	.400	.349	S	R	5-11	155	5-31-81	1999	Maracay, Venez.
Owens, Ryan	.200	20	50	6	10	3	0	2	4	3	18	0	0	.380	.255	R	R	6-2	200	3-18-78	1999	Anaheim Hills, Calif.
Perez, Santiago	.303	62	234	45	71	12	5	4	30	31	68	19	9	.449	.382	S	R	6-2	160	12-30-75	1993	Santo Domingo, D.R.

BATTING	AVG	G	AB	R	H	2B	3B	HR	RBI	BB	SO	SB	CS	SLG	OBP	B	T	HT	WT	DOB	1st Yr	Resides
Peterson, Brian	.240	36	100	15	24	7	0	0	4	10	22	3	1	.310	.315	R	R	6-2	205	10-22-78	1999	Greencastle, Penn.
Sardinha, Dane	.256	72	246	21	63	15	0	3	32	22	61	5	3	.354	.313	R	R	6-0	215	4-8-79	2001	Gulfport, Fla.
Schramek, Mark	.177	42	141	14	25	9	0	0	10	8	55	2	1	.241	.242	L	R	6-3	230	6-2-80	2003	San Antonio, Texas
Secrist, Reed	.241	17	54	9	13	3	0	3	9	5	14	1	1	.463	.317	L	R	6-0	220	5-7-70	1992	Farmington, Utah
Senjem, Guye	.265	123	351	75	93	21	1	15	61	56	81	9	3	.459	.373	L	R	6-0	210	5-2-75	1997	Kenyon, Minn.
Smitherman, Stephen	.310	105	365	60	113	21	2	19	73	54	95	11	3	.534	.402	R	R	6-4	235	9-1-78	2000	Hartshorne, Okla.
Stenson, Dernell	.306	101	356	51	109	28	0	14	76	39	74	4	5	.503	.371	L	L	6-1	230	6-17-78	1996	La Grange, Ga.

PITCHING	W	L	ERA	G	GS	CG	SV	IP	H	R	ER	BB	SO	AVG	B	T	HT	WT	DOB	1st Yr	Resides
Adkins, Tim	0	2	1.86	9	0	0	0	10	8	5	2	4	11	.222	L	L	6-0	190	5-12-74	1992	Huntington, W.Va.
Andrews, Clayton	0	1	3.48	2	2	0	0	10	14	8	4	3	3	.358	R	L	6-0	180	5-15-78	1996	Largo, Fla.
Barreto, Joel	0	1	3.70	15	0	0	0	24	19	10	10	9	15	.220	R	R	5-11	150	10-14-80	1997	La Guaria, Venez.
Basham, Bobby	5	10	5.17	17	17	0	0	94	133	72	54	24	56	.330	R	R	6-3	205	3-7-80	2001	Hardy, Va.
Bevel, Bobby	2	1	1.63	16	1	0	1	28	20	12	5	9	28	.194	L	L	5-10	180	10-10-73	1995	West Plains, Mo.
Bludau, Frank	0	1	12.00	3	0	0	0	3	7	4	4	5	2	.437	R	R	6-0	200	11-19-76	2000	Hallettsville, Texas
Childress, Daylan	2	4	6.75	9	9	0	0	48	53	41	36	26	35	.292	R	R	6-1	200	7-31-78	2001	Floresville, Texas
Cortes, Jorge	1	2	5.84	9	0	0	0	12	15	8	8	4	9	.306	R	R	6-4	190	9-4-72	1995	Panama City, Panama
Cotton, Nathan	0	0	0.00	1	0	0	0	1	2	0	0	1	1	.400	L	R	6-2	195	7-19-79	2000	Southside, Ala.
Cyr, Eric	0	0	13.50	1	0	0	0	2	6	3	3	0	0	.500	R	L	6-4	200	2-11-79	1999	Ada, Okla.
Darnell, Paul	0	0	6.50	15	0	0	2	18	25	17	13	13	14	.333	R	L	6-6	200	6-4-76	1999	Hubbard, Texas
DeHart, Casey	3	2	3.86	41	4	0	2	75	78	35	32	43	50	.276	L	L	6-1	180	11-1-77	1998	Burleson, Texas
Devey, Phil	1	0	5.06	12	0	0	1	16	15	10	9	2	11	.238	L	L	6-0	170	5-31-77	1999	Lachute, Quebec
Dunn, Scott	3	2	3.79	31	0	0	8	40	31	21	17	16	54	.210	R	R	6-3	180	5-23-78	1999	San Antonio, Texas
Gil, David	1	2	3.14	30	4	0	11	49	45	22	17	16	39	.239	R	R	6-4	215	10-1-78	2000	Miami, Fla.
Gray, Brett	5	3	3.94	43	2	0	1	64	76	34	28	14	57	.302	R	R	6-0	190	8-19-76	1998	Vandalia, Mich.
Hall, Josh	8	10	3.47	26	25	2	0	153	152	73	59	53	114	.259	R	R	6-2	190	12-16-80	1998	Lynchburg, Va.
Howington, Ty	0	2	6.91	4	4	0	0	14	15	12	11	20	16	.272	S	L	6-5	205	11-4-80	1999	Vancouver, Wash.
Keller, Kris	2	1	2.35	35	0	0	12	38	34	11	10	15	28	.236	R	R	6-2	260	3-1-78	1996	Atlantic Beach, Fla.
Kelly, Steve	4	2	2.09	6	6	0	0	39	34	11	9	12	30	.253	R	R	6-1	195	9-30-79	2001	Hamilton, Ohio
Koronka, John	7	13	4.39	25	25	0	0	156	177	88	76	60	115	.298	L	L	6-1	180	7-3-80	1998	Clermont, Fla.
Miller, Travis	0	1	40.50	1	0	0	0	1	3	4	3	0	1	.500	R	L	6-3	210	11-2-72	1994	Eaton, Ohio
Moseley, Dustin	5	6	3.83	18	18	0	0	113	116	55	48	28	73	.264	R	R	6-4	190	12-26-81	2001	Texarkana, Texas
Mottl, Ryan	6	5	3.94	23	19	0	0	114	116	57	50	47	101	.263	S	R	6-3	200	12-9-77	2000	Florissant, Mo.
Rice, Leonard	0	0	0.00	2	0	0	0	5	4	0	0	0	4	.235	L	L	6-3	215	6-15-81	2003	Angleton, Texas
Salmon, Brad	4	0	5.11	10	1	0	1	25	27	14	14	9	21	.278	L	R	6-4	220	1-3-80	1999	Cantonment, Fla.
Shackelford, Brian	3	2	6.30	13	1	0	1	20	26	18	14	14	19	.313	L	L	6-1	190	8-30-76	1998	Norman, Okla.
Therneau, Dave	1	0	3.72	9	0	0	0	10	13	4	4	4	8	.351	R	R	6-5	190	12-23-75	1998	Denton, Texas
Thompson, Travis	2	0	2.89	9	2	0	1	28	27	11	9	5	21	.257	R	R	6-5	225	7-3-77	1999	Matthews, N.C.
Wagner, Ryan	1	0	0.00	5	0	0	0	5	2	1	0	2	6	.125	R	R	6-4	210	7-15-82	2003	Yoakum, Texas

FIELDING

Catcher	PCT	G	PO	A	E	DP	PB
Gubanich	1.000	23	126	15	0	1	2
Gutierrez	.960	4	21	3	1	0	1
Hill	.933	3	10	4	1	1	0
Peterson	.991	28	204	25	2	0	2
Sardinha	.985	70	476	67	8	8	2
Secrist	.993	16	133	10	1	1	3

First Base	PCT	G	PO	A	E	DP
Chamblee	1.000	3	26	1	0	3
Conley	1.000	3	30	1	0	2
Dellaero	1.000	1	9	1	0	0
Gubanich	.935	8	55	3	4	2
Gutierrez	.995	24	190	17	1	21
Haas	.994	21	146	10	1	13
Jennings	.984	8	56	5	1	2
Owens	.989	9	79	7	1	4
Peterson	.000	1	0	0	0	0
Smitherman	.974	5	36	2	1	3
Stenson	.983	64	535	29	10	42

Second Base	PCT	G	PO	A	E	DP
Anderson	1.000	3	12	8	0	3
Beattie	.981	104	192	264	9	54
Caceres	1.000	11	18	30	0	4
Cairns	.962	7	12	13	1	0
Cesar	.966	11	21	36	2	6
Dellaero	1.000	1	2	0	0	0
Diaz	1.000	1	3	1	0	0
Olmedo	1.000	1	1	1	0	0
Owens	.800	1	1	3	1	0
Perez	.971	7	19	15	1	2

Third Base	PCT	G	PO	A	E	DP
Anderson	1.000	1	0	1	0	0
Caceres	.947	7	3	15	1	1
Cairns	.800	2	2	6	2	0
Chamblee	.973	13	10	26	1	3
Conley	1.000	1	2	2	0	0
Encarnacion	.897	62	63	119	21	8
Haas	1.000	5	3	12	0	0
Owens	1.000	2	0	4	0	0
Perez	.852	7	14	9	4	0
Schramek	.947	41	22	68	5	7

Shortstop	PCT	G	PO	A	E	DP
Anderson	.954	17	27	35	3	9
Bannon	.955	13	29	35	3	12
Caceres	.919	41	64	106	15	16
Dellaero	.979	11	23	24	1	6
Encarnacion	.667	2	2	2	2	0
Olmedo	.950	45	66	125	10	29
Perez	.907	20	29	39	7	5

Outfield	PCT	G	PO	A	E	DP
Anderson	1.000	9	18	0	0	0
Beattie	1.000	5	10	1	0	0
Caceres	.972	31	67	3	2	0
Chamblee	1.000	11	20	1	0	0
Correll	.927	21	34	4	3	0
Darula	1.000	1	3	0	0	0
Diaz	.996	93	224	5	1	1
Kearns	1.000	2	2	1	0	0
Lewis	1.000	5	6	1	0	0
Mitchell	.870	17	20	0	3	0
Owens	1.000	1	2	0	0	0
Perez	.929	24	51	1	4	0
Senjem	.970	88	151	13	5	3
Smitherman	.994	98	166	7	1	2
Stenson	.957	32	43	1	2	0

POTOMAC CANNONS — High Class A

CAROLINA LEAGUE

BATTING	AVG	G	AB	R	H	2B	3B	HR	RBI	BB	SO	SB	CS	SLG	OBP	B	T	HT	WT	DOB	1st Yr	Resides
Anderson, Bryan	.245	60	200	20	49	17	0	2	26	17	41	3	0	.360	.301	R	R	6-2	170	7-10-78	2000	San Antonio, Texas
Bannon, Jeff	.295	104	366	45	108	26	2	8	42	35	67	7	8	.443	.360	R	R	6-4	185	8-21-79	2001	Camarillo, Calif.
Bergolla, William	.272	128	523	77	142	25	3	2	31	29	59	52	18	.342	.309	R	R	6-0	175	2-4-83	1999	Valencia,Venez.
Blanco, Tony	.266	69	241	33	64	17	2	10	49	26	62	0	0	.477	.338	R	R	6-1	175	11-10-81	1998	Haina, D.R.
Calitri, Mike	.222	55	171	22	38	10	1	6	26	21	48	3	1	.398	.308	R	R	6-3	210	3-14-78	2000	Canton, Mass.
Campana, Wandel	.083	5	12	2	1	0	0	1	1	1	2	0	0	.333	.154	R	R	6-0	175	6-6-78	1998	Santo Domingo, D.R.
Correll, Brad	.287	38	143	19	41	11	1	5	24	15	22	2	1	.483	.358	R	R	6-2	205	6-17-81	2002	Gastonia, N.C.
Davis, Justin	.149	30	67	6	10	2	0	0	3	12	15	0	1	.179	.278	L	L	6-3	195	7-17-78	2001	Diamond Bar, Calif.
Denorfia, Chris	.236	128	470	60	111	10	5	4	39	54	106	20	7	.304	.317	R	R	6-1	185	7-15-80	2002	Southington, Conn.
Encarnacion, Edwin	.321	58	215	40	69	15	1	6	29	24	32	7	1	.484	.387	R	R	6-1	195	1-7-83	2000	La Romana, D.R.
Gutierrez, Jesse	.278	108	400	52	111	26	0	16	76	22	52	1	2	.463	.325	R	R	6-2	195	6-16-78	2001	McAllen, Texas
Hawes, B.J.	.244	59	172	14	42	6	1	0	9	9	36	3	3	.291	.284	R	R	6-0	170	6-2-79	1999	Appling, Ga.
Hernandez, Habelito	.250	8	28	2	7	0	0	0	1	1	7	0	0	.250	.267	R	R	6-0	180	1-11-81	2000	Bonao, D.R.
Honeycutt, Heath	.259	57	197	22	51	15	2	2	22	18	42	1	3	.386	.326	R	R	6-4	210	7-30-76	1998	Alpharetta, Ga.
Martinez, Candido	.129	13	31	3	4	2	0	0	0	5	9	2	2	.194	.250	R	R	6-2	170	1-10-78	1996	Yakima, Wash.

BATTING	AVG	G	AB	R	H	2B	3B	HR	RBI	BB	SO	SB	CS	SLG	OBP	B	T	HT	WT	DOB	1st Yr	Resides
Motooka, Rafael	.171	14	35	3	6	0	0	0	4	4	12	0	0	.171	.244	R	R	6-0	200	8-18-82	2000	Sao Paulo, Brazil
Patchett, Gary	.239	47	113	11	27	1	0	1	6	10	24	0	2	.274	.323	R	R	6-2	180	9-25-78	2000	Gardena, Calif.
Peterson, Brian	.268	49	142	16	38	6	1	0	8	12	30	4	0	.324	.327	R	R	6-2	205	10-22-78	1999	Greencastle, Penn.
Prince, Bryan	.248	47	145	14	36	3	0	4	15	20	30	0	0	.352	.343	R	R	6-2	200	11-4-78	2001	Smyrna, Ga.
Rios, Fernando	.272	36	125	13	34	5	1	1	21	21	17	4	4	.352	.372	R	R	6-2	190	12-15-78	1997	Glendale, Calif.
Ruiz, Junior	.281	41	139	22	39	10	1	1	17	19	17	12	1	.388	.375	L	R	5-10	195	6-7-80	2001	Manteca, Calif.
Schramek, Mark	.203	36	128	9	26	4	0	2	12	6	42	0	0	.281	.261	L	R	6-3	230	6-2-80	2003	San Antonio, Texas
Shanks, Eric	.357	4	14	0	5	0	0	0	0	0	1	0	2	.357	.357	R	R	5-11	180	7-7-78	2001	Charlotte, N.C.
2-team (14 Frederick)	.277	18	47	4	13	3	0	1	3	3	5	0	2	.404	.314							
Sulbaran, Orlando	.333	2	3	0	1	0	0	0	0	0	2	0	0	.333	.333	R	R	6-2	160	11-16-81	1998	Maracaibo, Venez.
Williamson, Chris	.197	102	319	31	63	20	0	2	30	33	113	1	0	.279	.272	L	L	6-5	225	8-21-78	2000	Houston, Texas
Wong, Travis	.171	21	76	7	13	2	0	2	12	4	21	0	0	.276	.217	R	R	6-6	235	8-28-81	2002	Boise, Idaho

PITCHING	W	L	ERA	G	GS	CG	SV	IP	H	R	ER	BB	SO	AVG	B	T	HT	WT	DOB	1st Yr	Resides
Andrews, Clayton	5	6	4.62	18	18	1	0	101	95	66	52	43	46	.254	R	L	6-0	180	5-15-78	1996	Largo, Fla.
Barreto, Joel	0	0	0.00	3	0	0	0	8	5	0	0	2	15	.178	R	R	5-11	150	10-14-80	1997	La Guaira, Venez.
Basham, Bobby	0	1	2.70	1	1	0	0	7	5	3	2	1	1	.200	R	R	6-3	205	3-7-80	2001	Hardy, Va.
Brannon, Nick	4	5	3.29	40	0	0	0	52	53	21	19	30	55	.271	L	L	6-5	190	4-23-78	2001	Sevierville, Tenn.
Bruksch, Jeff	1	3	4.50	6	6	0	0	30	29	16	15	21	16	.256	R	R	6-4	215	4-29-80	2002	Los Angeles, Calif.
Childress, Daylan	5	9	3.00	17	16	2	0	96	78	44	32	45	89	.224	R	R	6-1	200	7-31-78	2001	Floresville, Texas
Coffey, Todd	0	2	1.96	11	0	0	2	23	16	6	5	3	21	.207	R	R	6-5	230	9-9-80	1998	Forest City, N.C.
Cortes, Jorge	0	0	6.43	5	0	0	0	7	7	5	5	6	4	.291	R	R	6-4	190	9-4-72	1995	Panama City, Panama
Cotton, Nathan	2	4	4.24	48	0	0	28	47	39	26	22	7	51	.221	L	R	6-2	195	7-19-79	2000	Southside, Ala.
Culp, Brandon	3	6	3.56	31	11	0	0	99	92	48	39	38	74	.246	R	R	6-6	250	8-27-77	2000	Jemison, Ala.
Daws, Josh	0	2	7.71	18	0	0	1	19	35	16	16	5	13	.432	R	R	5-10	190	12-8-78	2001	Fort Myers, Fla.
DeHart, Casey	0	1	5.06	6	0	0	0	11	11	7	6	3	6	.261	L	L	6-1	180	11-1-77	1998	Burleson, Texas
Dumatrait, Phillip	4	1	3.35	7	7	1	0	38	36	17	14	14	32	.248	R	L	6-2	170	7-12-81	2000	Bakersfield, Calif.
Edens, Kyle	0	5	4.91	28	2	0	3	55	73	39	30	16	45	.321	R	R	5-10	190	1-25-80	2003	San Antonio, Texas
Granado, Jan	3	6	4.66	15	11	0	1	68	76	37	35	33	46	.286	L	L	6-0	190	9-26-82	1999	Barcelona, Venez.
Gray, Brett	1	0	0.96	2	2	0	0	9	12	2	1	0	9	.333	R	R	6-0	190	8-19-76	1998	Vandalia, Mich.
Howington, Ty	7	7	3.53	19	19	0	0	99	103	44	39	34	86	.271	S	L	6-5	205	11-4-80	1999	Vancouver, Wash.
Kelly, Steve	7	5	3.87	17	17	0	0	95	105	52	41	28	69	.283	R	R	6-1	195	9-30-79	2001	Hamilton, Ohio
Manning, Charlie	5	0	1.19	6	6	0	0	38	24	7	5	11	31	.181	L	L	6-2	180	3-31-79	2001	Winter Haven, Fla.
Reed, Chris	0	0	2.08	8	0	0	0	13	12	4	3	6	13	.240	R	R	6-2	220	8-25-73	1991	Huntington Beach, Calif.
Salmon, Brad	3	2	4.56	32	1	0	1	49	55	27	25	18	53	.283	L	R	6-4	220	1-3-80	1999	Cantonment, Fla.
Shackelford, Brian	0	1	1.98	18	0	0	1	27	17	6	6	8	20	.180	L	L	6-1	190	8-30-76	1998	Norman, Okla.
Sobkowiak, Scott	1	2	5.91	4	4	0	0	21	19	19	14	9	21	.234	R	R	6-5	230	10-26-77	1998	Orlando, Fla.
Stanton, Kyle	1	3	3.38	20	0	0	1	35	32	15	13	6	35	.244	R	R	6-2	200	2-19-77	2000	Coshocton, Ohio
Thompson, Travis	5	4	3.30	17	11	1	0	79	77	30	29	17	62	.259	R	R	6-5	225	7-3-77	1999	Matthews, N.C.
Valdez, Edward	5	2	3.40	8	7	0	0	56	55	22	21	11	41	.258	R	R	6-1	190	2-8-80	1999	Nizao, D.R.

FIELDING

Catcher	PCT	G	PO	A	E	DP	PB
Gutierrez	.988	37	221	26	3	2	2
Motooka	.964	14	72	9	3	0	4
Peterson	.965	49	313	49	13	7	7
Prince	.992	47	347	40	3	2	1
Sulbaran	1.000	2	5	1	0	0	1

First Base	PCT	G	PO	A	E	DP
Blanco	.971	15	129	7	4	8
Calitri	1.000	30	231	29	0	23
Correll	1.000	5	49	2	0	4
Gutierrez	.973	19	168	11	5	14
Williamson	.985	55	434	38	7	56
Wong	.995	19	175	8	1	16

Second Base	PCT	G	PO	A	E	DP
Anderson	1.000	4	6	4	0	1
Bergolla	.959	127	244	380	27	76
Campana	1.000	1	6	3	0	1
Hernandez	.944	4	5	12	1	3
Patchett	.889	3	2	6	1	0
Ruiz	1.000	2	1	3	0	1
Shanks	.875	2	3	4	1	1

Third Base	PCT	G	PO	A	E	DP
Anderson	.889	15	13	19	4	4
Bannon	1.000	3	2	7	0	1
Calitri	.929	25	18	47	5	4
Correll	1.000	1	1	0	0	0
Encarnacion	.879	57	34	89	17	4
Honeycutt	.867	3	4	9	2	0
Schramek	.928	36	24	66	7	6

Shortstop	PCT	G	PO	A	E	DP
Anderson	.950	3	8	11	1	5
Bannon	.950	99	168	247	22	58
Bergolla	1.000	2	0	1	0	0
Hernandez	1.000	4	5	12	0	3
Patchett	.939	35	44	79	8	24
Shanks	1.000	2	4	1	0	0

Outfield	PCT	G	PO	A	E	DP
Anderson	.985	41	62	3	1	1
Correll	.944	33	48	3	3	0
Davis	.909	13	10	0	1	0
Denorfia	.982	126	263	15	5	2
Hawes	.991	58	104	5	1	2
Honeycutt	.984	46	60	3	1	0
Martinez	.800	11	12	0	3	0
Rios	.955	36	60	3	3	1
Ruiz	.985	39	65	1	1	0
Williamson	.957	36	43	1	2	0

DAYTON DRAGONS — Low Class A

MIDWEST LEAGUE

BATTING	AVG	G	AB	R	H	2B	3B	HR	RBI	BB	SO	SB	CS	SLG	OBP	B	T	HT	WT	DOB	1st Yr	Resides
Araque, Tulio	.086	12	35	2	3	1	0	0	1	1	12	0	0	.114	.158	R	R	6-2	170	10-17-81	1999	Maracaibo, Venez.
Bassett, Mike	.293	28	82	9	24	4	0	2	19	7	21	1	0	.415	.341	L	L	6-2	205	2-10-80	2002	Paramus, N.J.
Bolivar, Luis	.230	57	183	26	42	8	1	2	14	17	42	6	5	.317	.304	S	R	6-1	150	2-15-81	1999	Aragua, Venez.
Boone, Matt	.195	55	210	21	41	9	0	2	16	17	70	2	0	.267	.261	R	R	6-2	175	7-18-79	1997	Villa Park, Calif.
Booth, Steve	.200	4	10	0	2	1	0	0	3	0	7	0	0	.300	.308	R	R	6-1	190	8-14-79	2002	San Jose, Calif.
Cairns, Troy	.208	18	72	8	15	3	0	0	7	3	8	0	0	.250	.240	R	R	6-0	160	9-29-80	2002	Blue Springs, Mo.
Campos, Tiago	.194	64	211	18	41	9	1	4	11	7	56	2	1	.303	.226	R	R	6-2	170	3-18-81	2000	Sao Paulo, Brazil
Correll, Brad	.283	78	276	50	78	20	1	8	48	30	44	9	2	.449	.358	R	R	6-2	205	6-17-81	2002	Gastonia, N.C.
Davis, Justin	.242	38	120	14	29	6	0	3	24	23	19	1	1	.367	.363	L	L	6-3	195	7-17-78	2001	Diamond Bar, Calif.
Foreman, JuJu	.220	12	50	6	11	1	0	0	2	6	9	0	1	.240	.304	L	R	5-8	160	2-18-79	2000	Girard, Ga.
Fry, Ryan	.234	59	214	30	50	4	1	15	42	13	80	1	0	.472	.290	R	R	6-1	200	5-11-80	2001	Stockertown, Penn.
Hanigan, Ryan	.277	92	311	43	86	12	0	1	31	40	44	3	4	.325	.363	R	R	6-1	185	8-16-80	2002	Andover, Mass.
Hawes, B.J.	.227	11	44	6	10	2	0	2	4	0	8	1	0	.409	.227	R	R	6-0	170	6-2-79	1999	Appling, Ga.
Howard, Kevin	.285	134	509	80	145	26	3	9	75	50	67	12	5	.401	.355	L	R	6-2	180	6-25-81	2003	Thousand Oaks, Calif.
Keown, Clint	.255	17	55	6	14	0	0	0	0	8	15	1	2	.255	.349	R	R	6-2	190	2-25-80	2003	Evansville, Ind.
Lewis, Domonique	.284	46	155	25	44	8	0	1	19	9	31	10	2	.355	.339	R	R	5-9	160	8-6-79	2001	Channelview, Texas
Martinez, Freddy	.154	4	13	2	2	2	0	0	1	0	3	0	0	.308	.154	R	R	5-10	180	4-3-79	2000	Santo Domingo, D.R.
Paula, Manuel	.173	48	162	16	28	1	1	0	9	11	61	7	2	.191	.242	R	R	6-2	205	1-25-81	1999	Bonao, D.R.
Perez, Miguel	.172	20	58	3	10	0	0	0	3	4	19	1	0	.172	.273	R	R	6-3	190	9-25-83	2001	Guatire, Venez.

BATTING	AVG	G	AB	R	H	2B	3B	HR	RBI	BB	SO	SB	CS	SLG	OBP	B	T	HT	WT	DOB	1st Yr	Resides
Reyes, Ivan	.145	26	76	8	11	1	0	1	3	6	25	1	0	.197	.207	R	R	6-2	180	6-6-81	1999	Toa Baja, P.R.
Ruiz, Junior	.276	71	250	38	69	10	4	2	22	38	32	2	4	.372	.383	L	R	5-10	195	6-7-80	2001	Manteca, Calif.
Schmidt, Jarrod	.283	69	254	28	72	15	1	6	33	21	61	3	1	.421	.343	R	R	6-2	215	10-2-80	2002	Marietta, Ga.
Schramek, Mark	.296	57	206	29	61	18	2	3	37	19	58	2	1	.447	.368	L	R	6-3	230	6-2-80	2003	San Antonio, Texas
Sulbaran, Orlando	.205	11	39	1	8	0	0	0	1	0	7	1	0	.205	.244	R	R	6-2	160	11-16-81	1998	Maracaibo, Venez.
Tiburcio, Hector	.229	114	407	53	93	9	2	0	22	36	90	22	8	.260	.295	S	R	6-0	150	6-11-81	1999	San Cristobal, D.R.
Vavao, Jason	.224	60	219	25	49	9	0	5	32	18	49	3	2	.333	.290	R	R	6-4	205	5-5-81	2001	Carson, Calif.
Votto, Joey	.231	60	195	19	45	8	0	1	20	34	64	2	5	.287	.348	L	R	6-3	200	9-10-83	2002	Toronto, Ontario
Wong, Travis	.186	48	177	14	33	8	0	3	26	8	48	0	0	.282	.255	R	R	6-6	235	8-28-81	2002	Boise, Idaho

PITCHING	W	L	ERA	G	GS	CG	SV	IP	H	R	ER	BB	SO	AVG	B	T	HT	WT	DOB	1st Yr	Resides
Barreto, Joel	4	3	1.93	29	0	0	4	56	28	17	12	32	72	.148	R	R	5-11	150	10-14-80	1997	La Guaira, Venez.
Batista, Gorky	1	3	3.69	8	8	0	0	46	46	25	19	11	30	.270	R	R	6-0	190	3-20-81	2000	Sarasota, Fla.
Berry, Jon	2	2	5.79	12	0	0	0	19	24	13	12	9	20	.303	R	R	6-1	190	11-17-77	1999	Branchville, S.C.
Booker, Chris	0	0	9.00	5	0	0	0	5	4	5	5	4	6	.210	R	R	6-3	230	12-9-76	1995	Monroeville, Ala.
Coffey, Todd	3	3	2.25	39	0	0	9	56	61	20	14	14	53	.289	R	R	6-5	230	9-9-80	1998	Forest City, N.C.
Daws, Josh	0	1	1.74	18	0	0	11	21	11	7	4	12	24	.152	R	R	5-10	190	12-8-78	2001	Fort Myers, Fla.
Edens, Kyle	0	0	1.80	6	0	0	1	10	9	2	2	3	6	.236	R	R	5-10	190	1-25-80	2003	San Antonio, Texas
Farfan, Alexander	5	3	3.73	40	0	0	4	80	73	35	33	30	43	.245	R	R	6-3	175	1-6-83	2000	Maracay, Venez.
Frias, Juan	10	10	3.54	25	25	0	0	140	140	68	55	53	94	.266	L	L	5-11	170	8-7-79	1999	Santo Domingo, D.R.
Gemmell, Don	1	2	5.24	22	2	0	0	45	53	26	26	12	33	.297	R	R	6-1	215	7-15-79	2002	Manteca, Calif.
George, Brad	2	2	3.38	24	1	0	1	51	42	22	19	21	39	.224	R	R	6-5	210	5-31-82	2000	New Braunfels, Texas
Gillman, Justin	0	3	3.96	7	7	0	0	36	33	23	16	16	22	.234	R	R	6-2	175	6-27-83	2001	Panama City, Fla.
Granado, Jan	4	4	4.39	13	13	0	0	70	77	38	34	20	45	.277	L	L	6-0	190	9-26-82	1999	Barcelona, Venez.
Gruler, Chris	0	2	27.00	3	3	0	0	6	10	19	17	12	6	.370	R	R	6-3	200	9-11-83	2002	Freemont, Mich.
Guevara, Carlos	0	1	3.43	12	3	0	0	39	37	17	15	14	39	.246	R	R	6-0	175	3-18-82	2003	Uvalde, Texas
Haynes, Jimmy	1	0	0.00	1	1	0	0	7	2	1	0	2	6	.086	R	R	6-4	220	9-5-72	1991	La Grange, Ga.
Jumelles, Edduar	2	2	6.56	16	0	0	1	23	22	20	17	21	15	.250	R	R	6-4	195	12-23-77	1998	Santo Domingo, D.R.
King, O.J.	0	1	3.55	4	4	0	0	13	10	5	5	6	9	.222	R	R	6-3	205	9-12-79	2002	Tahlequah, Okla.
Lucas, Kyle	4	9	4.53	25	15	0	2	115	140	69	58	33	79	.303	R	R	6-5	210	8-31-79	2002	Lancaster, S.C.
McWilliams, Matt	5	3	2.48	36	0	0	2	54	38	18	15	31	49	.201	L	L	6-3	210	4-27-79	2001	Lawrenceburg, Ky.
Medina, Julio	0	1	6.23	1	1	0	0	4	5	3	3	1	2	.312	R	R	6-3	180	4-25-83	2003	Elk Grove, Ill.
Pauly, Thomas	2	5	4.02	12	12	0	0	47	45	26	21	10	36	.247	R	R	6-1	195	7-28-81	2003	Atlantic, Fla.
Thigpen, Josh	3	9	5.10	28	14	0	2	85	96	53	48	50	66	.284	R	R	6-4	205	6-27-82	2000	Killen, Ala.
Ursin, Damian	0	2	7.50	13	0	0	2	18	25	16	15	11	15	.342	R	R	6-0	197	11-27-82	2003	Gramercy, La.
Valdez, Edward	11	3	3.72	19	19	0	0	114	111	54	47	28	67	.256	R	R	6-1	190	2-8-80	1999	Nizao, D.R.
Vazquez, Camilo	1	4	5.93	13	11	0	0	44	54	37	29	28	47	.296	L	L	6-0	180	10-3-83	2003	Hialeah, Fla.

FIELDING

Catcher	PCT	G	PO	A	E	DP	PB
Booth	1.000	4	20	3	0	0	0
Fry	1.000	2	13	2	0	0	0
Hanigan	.987	82	580	48	8	3	8
Martinez	1.000	3	15	4	0	1	2
Perez	.950	18	121	12	7	0	3
Schmidt	.960	24	134	9	6	0	4
Sulbaran	.987	11	66	8	1	0	2

First Base	PCT	G	PO	A	E	DP
Fry	1.000	1	7	0	0	2
Reyes	.967	9	56	2	2	5
Ruiz	.929	3	13	0	1	2
Vavao	.991	48	402	36	4	40
Votto	.980	48	404	40	9	37
Wong	.988	36	313	18	4	36

Second Base	PCT	G	PO	A	E	DP
Bolivar	.964	9	18	35	2	11
Cairns	1.000	2	4	6	0	0
Howard	.970	126	249	369	19	69
Lewis	1.000	2	2	4	0	2
Reyes	1.000	4	10	14	0	5

Third Base	PCT	G	PO	A	E	DP
Bolivar	.875	21	16	26	6	3
Boone	.924	51	25	97	10	8
Cairns	.950	7	5	14	1	2
Correll	1.000	2	1	2	0	0
Reyes	.846	6	3	8	2	1
Schramek	.927	56	28	111	11	6

Shortstop	PCT	G	PO	A	E	DP
Bolivar	.949	29	43	68	6	17
Cairns	.750	1	1	2	1	0
Reyes	.929	3	7	6	1	0
Tiburcio	.932	113	203	317	38	70

Outfield	PCT	G	PO	A	E	DP
Araque	1.000	11	18	0	0	0
Bassett	.900	7	9	0	1	0
Campos	.985	60	131	4	2	0
Correll	.963	71	96	9	4	2
Davis	.925	38	47	2	4	0
Foreman	1.000	12	24	3	0	0
Fry	.941	39	58	6	4	0
Hawes	.941	11	15	1	1	0
Keown	1.000	17	31	2	0	0
Lewis	.963	40	74	3	3	0
Paula	.983	48	112	5	2	0
Ruiz	.992	53	118	5	1	1
Schmidt	1.000	26	44	4	0	0

BILLINGS MUSTANGS — Rookie

PIONEER LEAGUE

BATTING	AVG	G	AB	R	H	2B	3B	HR	RBI	BB	SO	SB	CS	SLG	OBP	B	T	HT	WT	DOB	1st Yr	Resides
Acevedo, Juan	.295	24	88	15	26	5	2	2	12	5	38	1	0	.466	.333	S	R	6-2	200	8-4-81	1999	San Cristobal, D.R.
Beale, David	.209	58	191	28	40	5	2	1	23	21	46	5	3	.272	.290	R	R	6-1	175	10-21-80	2003	Tifton, Ga.
Bolivar, Luis	.349	55	235	57	82	20	3	9	42	17	32	12	6	.574	.405	S	R	6-1	150	2-15-81	1999	Aragua, Venez.
Cairns, Troy	.295	34	132	17	39	5	0	1	11	8	17	2	2	.356	.340	R	R	6-0	160	9-29-80	2002	Blue Springs, Mo.
Campos, Tiago	.250	7	28	6	7	2	0	4	10	0	10	0	1	.750	.250	R	R	6-2	170	3-18-81	2000	Sao Paulo, Brazil
Cleveland, Clay	.118	9	34	3	4	0	0	0	6	4	14	0	0	.118	.231	R	R	6-4	250	9-21-80	2003	Daphne, Ala.
Dickerson, Chris	.244	58	201	36	49	6	4	6	38	39	66	9	4	.403	.376	L	L	6-4	212	4-10-82	2003	Van Nuys, Calif.
Gentry, Philip	.226	56	186	21	42	14	1	1	22	13	50	1	3	.328	.275	L	R	6-1	195	9-2-80	2003	DeSoto, Texas
Gutierrez, Tonys	.200	3	10	1	2	1	0	0	1	0	1	0	0	.300	.200	L	L	6-2	180	8-18-83	2001	Aragua, Venez.
Hernandez, Habelito	.377	36	162	42	61	14	5	8	32	1	22	5	0	.673	.392	R	R	6-0	180	1-11-81	2000	Bonao, D.R.
Himes, Ben	.317	62	246	40	78	11	1	7	42	19	87	4	3	.455	.369	L	R	6-4	210	3-9-81	2003	Austin, Texas
Hudson, Will	.192	19	52	6	10	2	1	0	7	11	12	1	3	.269	.338	S	R	6-2	190	1-26-81	2002	Fountain Valley, Calif.
Mosby, Robert	.223	55	179	24	40	7	1	9	34	20	76	0	0	.425	.300	R	R	6-3	240	4-9-82	2002	Belleville, Ill.
Motooka, Rafael	.000	3	4	1	0	0	0	0	0	2	1	0	0	.000	.333	R	R	6-0	200	8-18-82	2000	Sao Paulo, Brazil
Olmstead, Walter	.277	70	264	42	73	14	2	12	48	13	82	2	3	.481	.324	S	R	6-6	240	12-5-80	2002	San Antonio, Texas
Paula, Manuel	.321	7	28	2	9	0	1	0	3	1	10	3	0	.393	.345	R	R	6-2	205	1-25-81	1999	Bonao, D.R.
Perez, Miguel	.339	60	227	46	77	11	2	1	25	18	27	1	1	.419	.410	R	R	6-3	190	9-25-83	2001	Guatire, Venez.
Reyes, Ivan	.133	9	15	1	2	0	0	0	0	3	6	0	0	.133	.278	R	R	6-2	180	6-6-81	1999	Toa Baja, P.R.
Ronda, Jose	.667	1	3	2	2	0	0	0	0	1	1	1	0	.667	.750	S	R	6-2	175	6-8-85	2003	San Juan, P.R.
Smith, Kyle	.262	13	42	3	11	4	0	2	9	1	18	0	0	.500	.273	R	R	6-2	205	5-17-81	2003	Houston, Texas
Urgelles, Jeff	.130	7	23	2	3	0	0	0	2	0	8	0	0	.130	.167	R	R	6-1	200	6-19-82	2003	Miami, Fla.
Votto, Joey	.317	70	240	47	76	17	3	6	38	56	80	4	0	.488	.452	L	R	6-3	200	9-10-83	2002	Toronto, Ontario
Ziemendorf, Chad	.180	22	50	9	9	5	0	0	4	3	20	0	1	.280	.293	R	R	5-11	195	4-9-81	2003	Los Altos, Calif.

GAMES BY POSITION: C—Motooka 3, Perez 60, Urgelles 3, Ziemendorf 20. **1B**—Gutierrez 1, Mosby 11, Olmstead 7, Votto 64. **2B**—Beale 35, Bolivar 10, Cairns 2, Hernandez 29, Hudson 2, Reyes 2. **3B**—Bolivar 10, Cairns 31, Hernandez 8, Hudson 2, Olmstead 28, Reyes 4. **SS**—Beale 25, Bolivar 39, Hudson 14, Reyes 3, Ronda 1. **OF**—Acevedo 17, Campos 6, Dickerson 57, Gentry 44, Gutierrez 1, Himes 62, Olmstead 34, Paula 7, Smith 11.

PITCHING	W	L	ERA	G	GS	CG	SV	IP	H	R	ER	BB	SO	AVG	B	T	HT	WT	DOB	1st Yr	Resides
Bohorquez, Carlos	1	3	3.41	19	0	0	1	37	34	27	14	16	46	.237	R	R	5-11	165	10-6-81	1999	Maracaibo, Venez.
Cabrera, Walin	4	5	5.00	16	9	0	0	54	58	40	30	27	36	.271	R	R	6-0	190	3-28-82	1999	Puerto Plata, D.R.
Escorcha, Orlando	5	1	2.20	17	2	0	0	41	39	15	10	19	44	.246	L	L	6-2	175	1-20-82	1999	Valencia,Venez.
George, Jon	2	2	3.77	6	6	0	0	29	38	19	12	13	25	.308	R	R	6-4	220	7-6-84	2002	Pennsauken, N.J.
Groeger, Jeff	1	2	7.33	12	2	0	2	27	34	25	22	17	23	.317	R	R	6-5	220	9-5-80	2002	Diamond Bar, Calif.
Guevara, Carlos	1	0	0.82	2	2	0	0	11	4	1	1	3	14	.108	R	R	6-0	175	3-18-82	2003	Uvalde, Texas
Hawk, Derek	5	3	2.97	14	12	0	1	70	70	30	23	16	53	.260	R	R	6-5	190	11-13-82	2003	Ukiah, Calif.
Hendley, Blake	1	4	4.97	6	6	0	0	29	37	22	16	11	18	.289	R	R	6-3	195	9-1-81	2003	Edmond, Okla.
Knoff, Justin	7	4	2.83	14	11	0	0	76	76	32	24	19	53	.259	R	R	6-4	195	6-22-81	2002	Burlington, N.J.
Medina, Julio	0	0	1.69	4	0	0	0	5	1	2	1	5	1	.055	R	R	6-3	180	4-25-83	2003	Elk Grove, Ill.
Medlock, Calvin	1	0	1.88	19	0	0	1	29	25	7	6	9	31	.233	R	R	5-10	175	11-8-82	2003	Houston, Texas
Paduch, Jim	7	1	1.94	15	15	0	0	79	72	28	17	20	65	.241	R	R	6-3	185	11-2-82	2003	Elmwood Park, Ill.
Shafer, David	0	3	3.04	25	0	0	13	24	25	13	8	3	32	.252	R	R	6-2	180	3-7-82	2002	Flagstaff, Ariz.
Talamantez, David	2	1	5.35	16	1	0	0	34	35	22	20	7	30	.271	R	R	6-3	230	7-4-81	2003	Austin, Texas
Till, Brock	1	1	2.48	18	0	0	2	29	23	16	8	21	23	.209	R	R	5-10	195	7-1-80	2003	Lewistown, Ill.
Trepkowski, Matt	0	0	5.14	9	0	0	0	7	4	5	4	17	5	.166	L	L	6-6	235	4-1-81	2003	San Antonio, Texas
Ursin, Damian	0	0	0.00	7	0	0	4	9	3	0	0	1	13	.096	R	R	6-0	197	11-27-82	2003	Gramercy, La.
Vazquez, Camilo	2	3	3.03	9	8	0	0	36	35	20	12	15	33	.255	L	L	6-0	180	10-3-83	2003	Hialeah, Fla.
Wachman, Corey	0	1	7.50	2	2	0	0	6	11	5	5	5	5	.407	R	R	6-0	185	10-16-80	2002	Valdosta, Ga.
Wells, Mark	1	1	1.97	23	0	0	1	32	31	14	7	7	29	.248	R	R	6-4	190	6-14-80	2002	Charlotte, N.C.

SARASOTA REDS — Rookie

GULF COAST LEAGUE

BATTING	AVG	G	AB	R	H	2B	3B	HR	RBI	BB	SO	SB	CS	SLG	OBP	B	T	HT	WT	DOB	1st Yr	Resides
Araque, Tulio	.167	6	18	1	3	0	0	0	0	0	4	0	2	.167	.250	R	R	6-2	170	10-17-81	1999	Maracaibo, Venez.
Avila, Denny	.192	27	52	5	10	0	0	0	1	4	13	1	1	.192	.263	R	R	5-11	180	8-31-83	2003	La Romana, D.R.
Belcher, Jordan	.274	53	190	23	52	11	1	0	17	17	27	6	1	.342	.329	R	R	6-2	185	2-17-84	2003	Grovetown, Ga.
Boone, Matt	.286	5	21	2	6	2	0	0	2	0	6	0	0	.381	.273	R	R	6-2	175	7-18-79	1997	Villa Park, Calif.
Coffey, Josh	.133	7	15	1	2	1	0	0	6	1	5	0	0	.200	.158	R	R	6-2	180	8-4-83	2001	Mechanicsville, Va.
Conley, Evan	.284	57	194	25	55	14	2	2	21	23	45	1	2	.407	.369	R	R	6-1	200	2-25-81	2003	Bradenton, Fla.
Dennis, Billy	.143	3	7	0	1	0	0	0	0	0	1	0	0	.143	.143	L	L	6-2	180	9-29-80	2002	Bigfoot, Texas
Ellis, Jason	.267	21	45	7	12	4	0	0	5	2	6	0	0	.356	.365	R	R	5-11	190	9-22-79	2002	Batavia, Ohio
Esparragoza, Eyoxy	.217	44	138	21	30	10	0	3	14	4	44	10	4	.355	.267	R	R	6-0	185	9-9-84	2002	El Sombrero, Venez.
Franco, Ambiorix	.180	19	61	1	11	3	0	0	6	3	21	0	0	.230	.219	R	R	6-3	190	12-21-82	2003	Villa Mella, D.R.
Gray, Matthew	.188	55	186	25	35	5	3	2	21	21	32	6	6	.280	.295	L	L	6-2	205	4-18-84	2003	Overland Park, Kan.
Gutierrez, Tonys	.303	46	155	21	47	12	4	3	18	20	22	1	4	.490	.399	L	L	6-2	180	8-18-83	2001	Aragua, Venez.
Hawes, Don	.128	12	39	3	5	1	0	1	2	2	12	0	0	.231	.171	R	R	5-11	180	2-11-80	2002	Tremonton, Utah
Hernandez, Habelito	.200	3	10	1	2	0	0	0	0	0	2	0	0	.200	.200	R	R	6-0	180	1-11-81	2000	Bonao, D.R.
Keown, Clint	.188	5	16	1	3	0	0	0	1	1	2	2	0	.188	.235	R	R	6-2	190	2-25-80	2003	Evansville, Ind.
Lewis, Kenny	.242	55	194	40	47	8	4	0	14	29	66	37	8	.325	.345	L	L	5-9	195	10-13-84	2003	Danville, Va.
Ronda, Jose	.301	47	173	25	52	16	2	2	26	13	40	5	2	.451	.353	S	R	6-2	175	6-8-85	2003	San Juan, P.R.
Sanchez, Carlos	.223	36	94	15	21	2	0	0	7	6	25	3	2	.245	.298	R	R	6-1	180	9-19-84	2003	Culiacan, Mexico
Sandoval, Mayker	.315	14	54	8	17	3	1	0	4	4	9	3	1	.407	.373	R	R	5-11	170	2-9-84	2002	Barquisimeto, Venez.
Sulbaran, Orlando	.342	10	38	5	13	3	0	0	5	5	5	1	0	.421	.419	R	R	6-2	160	11-16-81	1998	Maracaibo, Venez.
Urgelles, Jeff	.270	56	185	21	50	20	0	2	28	22	32	0	1	.411	.357	R	R	6-1	200	6-19-82	2003	Miami, Fla.
Wong, Travis	.233	11	43	6	10	2	0	2	6	3	13	0	0	.419	.283	R	R	6-6	235	8-28-81	2002	Boise, Idaho

GAMES BY POSITION: C—Coffey 5, Ellis 16, Hawes 8, Urgelles 40. **1B**—Araque 1, Avila 1, Conley 3, Gutierrez 40, Sanchez 4, Sulbaran 9, Urgelles 3, Wong 5. **2B**—Avila 24, Conley 33, Keown 1, Sanchez 4, Sandoval 14. **3B**—Boone 4, Conley 7, Esparragoza 9, Franco 19, Hernandez 2, Sanchez 27. **SS**—Avila 1, Conley 21, Ronda 42, Sanchez 2. **OF**—Araque 4, Belcher 52, Esparragoza 25, Gray 53, Gutierrez 3, Hawes 1, Keown 2, Lewis 48.

PITCHING	W	L	ERA	G	GS	CG	SV	IP	H	R	ER	BB	SO	AVG	B	T	HT	WT	DOB	1st Yr	Resides
Batista, Gorky	2	2	4.05	5	4	0	0	27	26	13	12	6	12	.257	R	R	6-0	190	3-20-81	2000	Sarasota, Fla.
Bernal, Christian	0	0	8.10	2	0	0	0	3	6	3	3	1	4	.400	R	R	6-0	180	11-30-80	2003	Los Mochis, Mexico
Booker, Chris	0	2	8.49	12	0	0	2	12	17	11	11	8	11	.326	R	R	6-3	230	12-9-76	1995	Monroeville, Ala.
Borsa, B.J.	1	1	2.74	18	0	0	2	23	22	7	7	4	16	.258	R	R	6-3	195	3-21-81	2003	Union City, Pa.
Bryant, Michael	0	3	3.86	13	0	0	1	23	25	13	10	5	18	.280	R	R	6-6	205	11-9-83	2003	Pasadena, Texas
Castro, Randy	0	1	9.60	9	1	0	0	15	20	16	16	16	11	.317	R	R	6-4	180	9-7-81	2002	Pimentel, D.R.
Cortes, Jorge	0	1	0.00	2	1	0	0	7	6	4	0	1	6	.230	R	R	6-4	190	9-4-72	1995	Panama City, Panama
Craig, Jonathan	1	1	8.53	5	0	0	0	6	14	7	6	4	5	.451	R	R	6-5	245	1-31-81	2003	Bethlehem, Ga.
Feliz, Ranier	2	2	3.20	10	10	0	0	45	39	17	16	13	36	.239	R	R	6-5	170	3-22-83	2001	Villa Altagracia, D.R.
George, Jon	4	2	4.91	7	7	0	0	33	40	19	18	8	22	.298	R	R	6-4	220	7-6-84	2002	Pennsauken, N.J.
Gillman, Justin	1	0	0.00	3	3	0	0	18	7	0	0	3	16	.118	R	R	6-2	175	6-27-83	2001	Panama City, Fla.
Golden, Michael	0	1	9.53	6	0	0	0	6	6	6	6	2	5	.260	R	R	6-0	196	2-4-83	2003	Ontario, Calif.
Jumelles, Edduar	0	0	6.00	3	0	0	0	6	3	4	4	3	7	.142	R	R	6-4	195	12-23-77	1998	Santo Domingo, D.R.
Mallett, Justin	0	2	8.35	12	1	0	0	18	26	21	17	16	20	.325	R	R	6-7	215	11-11-81	2003	East St. Louis, Ill.
Medina, Julio	2	2	2.84	12	1	0	2	32	24	12	10	9	27	.203	R	R	6-3	180	4-25-83	2003	Elk Grove, Ill.
Medlock, Calvin	0	0	0.00	3	0	0	0	5	5	1	0	0	3	.263	R	R	5-10	175	11-8-82	2003	Houston, Texas
Meque, Jacobo	0	0	2.25	2	2	0	0	4	2	1	1	2	3	.153	L	L	6-2	200	10-1-83	2000	Villa Altagracia, D.R.
Noriega, Luis	3	4	3.24	9	9	0	0	42	30	17	15	20	42	.206	R	R	6-3	140	7-5-82	1999	Sucre, Venez.
Pelland, Tyler	0	0	0.00	1	1	0	0	3	3	0	0	0	1	.272	R	L	6-0	190	10-9-83	2002	Bristol, Vt.
2-team (11 Red Sox)	3	4	1.51	12	9	0	0	42	29	12	7	18	35	.192							
Perez, Aneudy	3	1	5.06	13	0	0	0	27	36	23	15	17	17	.327	R	R	6-2	175	12-2-81	2001	Santo Domingo, D.R.
Rice, Trey	2	3	2.61	13	6	0	1	41	36	15	12	11	45	.232	L	L	6-3	215	6-15-81	2003	Angleton, Texas
Segovia, Omar	3	1	3.83	10	10	0	0	45	44	29	19	19	34	.251	L	L	6-2	210	5-28-83	1999	Cagua, Venez.
Skinner, Andrew	1	2	4.86	13	0	0	1	17	27	10	9	8	8	.397	R	R	6-2	210	8-3-81	2003	Santa Rosa, Fla.
Soriano, Wally	0	0	0.00	3	0	0	0	4	2	0	0	4	3	.153	R	R	6-2	165	2-11-83	2002	San Cristobal, D.R.
Valera, Luis	0	1	0.00	7	0	0	1	8	10	1	0	3	7	.322	R	R	5-11	175	1-30-82	1999	Maracaibo, Venez.
White, Scott	1	2	4.91	12	4	0	1	33	31	21	18	14	28	.252	R	R	6-3	180	4-6-81	2003	Syracuse, Kan.

CLEVELAND INDIANS

BY JIM INGRAHAM

Indians officials went into the 2003 season with the idea of rebuilding, but this was ridiculous.

By midseason, the few veterans on the team were all sidelined with season-ending injuries. As a result, the Indians played most of the second half of the season with seven, eight and sometimes nine rookies in the lineup. By the end of the season there were an almost unheard-of 18 rookies on the major league roster.

That's not including rookie manager Eric Wedge. "I don't think anyone has ever been through what Eric went through, managing a team with that many young players," general manager Mark Shapiro said.

The bad news was all the inexperience led to a record of 68-94, the eighth-highest loss total since 1900. The good news was that Indians officials were able to accelerate the development and evaluation of the many young players they brought to the major leagues in 2003.

"We accomplished most everything we set out to accomplish," Wedge said. "At the very least, I'd say we're right on schedule, but we're probably a lot further ahead in this thing than most people believe."

The young player who clearly made the most progress and had the biggest impact was outfielder Jody Gerut, who hit .279-22-75 in becoming the first rookie in 23 years to lead the Indians in home runs and RBIs.

Gerut was the point man in a platoon of young outfielders who made good use of their opportunities at the major league level. Coco Crisp hit a combined .299, with 35 stolen bases at Cleveland and Triple-A Buffalo. Alex Escobar hit 24 homers with 78 RBIs at Buffalo before adding five more homers and 14 RBIs in Cleveland. And Ryan Ludwick, acquired from Texas in a mid-season trade for righthander Ricardo Rodriguez, hit seven home runs, with 26 RBIs, and had a .383 average with runners in scoring position in just 47 games, before missing the last month of the season with a knee injury.

Jody Gerut

RICH ABEL

Fausto Carmona

PLAYERS of the YEAR

MAJOR LEAGUE: Jody Gerut, of

Gerut forced his way into a crowded Cleveland outfield picture and into the 2003 American League Rookie of the Year race by leading all first-year players in slugging percentage and ranking second with 22 home runs.

MINOR LEAGUE: Fausto Carmona, rhp

The 2003 South Atlantic League's pitcher of the year led the loop in wins and ERA at 17-4, 2.06. Carmona posted an 83-14 strikeout-walk ratio in 148 innings, allowing just 117 hits.

Catchers Victor Martinez and Josh Bard both split their seasons at Buffalo and Cleveland, Martinez hitting a combined .314-8-61 and Bard .268-13-57.

Travis Hafner and Ben Broussard split playing time at first base on the big league club, and combined to hit .251-30-95. Jhonny Peralta, 21, started more games at shortstop than the injured Omar Vizquel, and drew raves from Wedge for the progress he made, despite being unavoidably rushed to the big leagues.

In a season devoted to what was mostly the successful development of their top prospects, however, Indians officials were faced with regression by the club's No.1 prospect at the start of the season. Second baseman Brandon Phillips struggled offensively all season, hitting .208-6-33 and Shapiro called him "our only failure developmentally."

The Indians also were riddled by injuries in 2003, finishing the season with 11 players on the disabled list, including two lefthanders, Billy Traber and Brian Tallet, being counted on as members of the club's nucleus for the future. Both had Tommy John surgery, and will miss most, if not all of the 2004 season.

One of the few non-rookies on the roster was center fielder Milton Bradley, who lived up to his reputation as a magnet for controversy. Bradley had several such moments on and off the field in 2003, in addition to making two trips onto the disabled list.

In the minor leagues, the Indians' prospect-heavy system produced three teams that made it to the postseason, led by the low Class A Lake County Captains, who won a minor league-high 97 games. Double-A Akron outfielder Grady Sizemore, the MVP of the Futures Game, hit .304-13-78, with an Eastern League-leading 13 triples.

ORGANIZATION LEADERS

BATTING		
*AVG	Victor Martinez, Buffalo/Akron	.329
R	Grady Sizemore, Akron	96
H	Grady Sizemore, Akron	151
TB	Jason Cooper, Kinston/Lake County	260
2B	Jason Cooper, Kinston/Lake County	34
3B	Grady Sizemore, Akron	11
HR	Alex Escobar, Buffalo	24
RBI	Luke Scott, Akron/ Kinston	81
BB	Shaun Larkin, Lake County	73
SO	Alex Escobar, Buffalo	133
SB	Willy Taveras, Kinston	57
*SLG	Jason Cooper, Kinston/Lake County	.542
*OBP	Joe Inglett, Kinston/Akron	.396
PITCHING		
W	Fausto Carmona, Akron/Lake County	17
L	Jeremy Guthrie, Buffalo/Akron	11
#ERA	Shea Douglas, Akron/Lake County	1.42
G	Lee Gronkiewicz, Kinston	51
CG	Francisco Cruceta, Akron	6
SV	Lee Gronkiewicz, Kinston	37
IP	Francisco Cruceta, Akron	163
BB	Jim Ed Warden, Akron/Kinston/Lake County	74
SO	Francisco Cruceta, Akron	134

*Minimum 250 At-Bats #Minimum 75 Innings

CLEVELAND INDIANS

Manager: Eric Wedge. **2003 Record:** 68-94, .420 (4th, AL Central).

BATTING	AVG	G	AB	R	H	2B	3B	HR	RBI	BB	SO	SB	CS	SLG	OBP	B	T	HT	WT	DOB	1st Yr	Resides
Bard, Josh	.244	91	303	25	74	13	1	8	36	22	53	0	2	.373	.293	S	R	6-3	210	3-30-78	1999	Chandler, Ariz.
Blake, Casey	.257	152	557	80	143	35	0	17	67	38	109	7	9	.411	.312	R	R	6-2	210	8-23-73	1996	Indianola, Iowa
Bradley, Milton	.321	101	377	61	121	34	2	10	56	64	73	17	7	.501	.421	S	R	6-0	190	4-15-78	1996	Long Beach, Calif.
Broussard, Ben	.249	116	386	53	96	21	3	16	55	32	75	5	2	.443	.312	L	L	6-2	220	9-24-76	1999	Beaumont, Texas
Burks, Ellis	.263	55	198	27	52	11	1	6	28	27	46	1	1	.419	.360	R	R	6-2	200	9-11-64	1983	Englewood, Colo.
Crisp, Coco	.266	99	414	55	110	15	6	3	27	23	51	15	9	.353	.302	S	R	6-0	180	11-1-79	1999	Desert Hot Springs, Calif.
Escobar, Alex	.273	28	99	16	27	2	0	5	14	7	33	1	0	.444	.324	R	R	6-1	190	9-6-78	1996	Valencia, Venez.
Garcia, Karim	.194	24	93	8	18	1	0	5	14	5	20	0	0	.366	.238	L	L	6-0	210	10-29-75	1992	Ciudad. Obregon, Mexico
Gerut, Jody	.279	127	480	66	134	33	2	22	75	35	70	4	5	.494	.336	L	L	6-0	200	9-18-77	1998	Lombard, Ill.
Gutierrez, Ricky	.260	16	50	2	13	3	0	0	3	3	5	0	0	.320	.309	R	R	6-1	190	5-23-70	1988	Pembroke Pines, Fla.
Hafner, Travis	.254	91	291	35	74	19	3	14	40	22	81	2	1	.485	.327	L	R	6-3	240	6-3-77	1997	Sykeston, N.D.
Laker, Tim	.241	52	162	17	39	11	0	3	21	9	38	2	2	.364	.281	R	R	6-3	220	11-27-69	1988	Simi Valley, Calif.
Lawton, Matt	.249	99	374	57	93	19	0	15	53	47	47	10	3	.420	.343	L	R	5-10	190	11-3-71	1991	Saucier, Miss.
LaRocca, Greg	.333	5	9	3	3	1	0	0	0	1	1	0	0	.444	.400	R	R	5-11	180	11-10-72	1994	Bedford, N.H.
Ludwick, Ryan	.265	39	136	14	36	7	1	7	26	8	39	2	0	.485	.306	R	L	6-3	200	7-13-78	1999	Las Vegas, Nevada
2-team (8 Texas)	.247	47	162	17	40	8	1	7	26	12	48	2	0	.438	.299							
Magruder, Chris	.346	9	26	3	9	2	1	1	3	3	6	0	1	.615	.433	S	R	5-11	200	4-26-77	1998	Mesa, Ariz.
Martinez, Victor	.289	49	159	15	46	4	0	1	16	13	21	1	1	.333	.345	S	R	6-2	170	12-23-78	1997	Ciudad Bolivar, Venez.
McDonald, John	.215	82	214	21	46	9	1	1	14	11	31	3	3	.280	.258	R	R	5-11	170	9-24-74	1996	East Lyme, Conn.
Peralta, John	.227	77	242	24	55	10	1	4	21	20	65	1	3	.326	.295	R	R	6-1	180	5-28-82	1999	Santiago, D.R.
Phillips, Brandon	.208	112	370	36	77	18	1	6	33	14	77	4	5	.311	.242	R	R	5-11	190	6-28-81	1999	Stone Mountain, Ga.
Rodriguez, Ricardo	.000	15	3	0	0	0	0	0	0	0	1	0	0	.000	.000	R	R	6-3	190	5-21-78	1996	Guayubin, D.R.
Sabathia, C.C.	.500	31	6	1	3	0	0	0	0	0	1	0	0	.500	.500	L	L	6-7	290	7-21-80	1998	Vallejo, Calif.
Santos, Angel	.224	32	76	9	17	3	1	3	6	3	18	1	1	.408	.253	S	R	5-11	170	8-14-79	1997	Cayey, P.R.
Selby, Bill	.103	27	39	3	4	1	0	0	5	3	11	0	0	.128	.163	L	R	5-10	190	6-11-70	1992	Southhaven, Miss.
Sorensen, Zach	.135	36	37	2	5	1	0	1	2	7	13	0	3	.243	.273	S	R	6-0	190	1-3-77	1998	St. George, Utah
Spencer, Shane	.271	64	210	23	57	10	0	8	26	18	52	2	0	.433	.328	R	R	6-0	220	2-20-72	1990	Tampa, Fla.
Vizquel, Omar	.244	64	250	43	61	13	2	2	19	29	20	8	3	.336	.321	S	R	5-9	180	4-24-67	1984	Issaquah, Wash.

PITCHING	W	L	ERA	G	GS	CG	SV	IP	H	R	ER	BB	SO	AVG	B	T	HT	WT	DOB	1st Yr	Resides
Anderson, Brian	9	10	3.71	25	24	0	0	148	162	88	61	32	72	.281	R	L	6-1	180	4-26-72	1993	Bratenahl, Ohio
Baez, Danys	2	9	3.81	73	0	0	25	76	65	36	32	23	66	.228	R	R	6-3	220	9-10-77	2000	Miami, Fla.
Bere, Jason	0	0	4.05	2	2	0	0	7	5	3	3	2	1	.208	R	R	6-3	220	5-26-71	1990	North Andover, Mass.
Betancourt, Rafael	2	2	2.13	33	0	0	1	38	27	11	9	13	36	.195	R	R	6-2	170	4-29-75	1994	Cumana, Venez.
Bierbrodt, Nick	0	0	6.75	5	0	0	0	8	5	6	6	4	9	.185	L	L	6-5	210	5-16-78	1996	Tierra Verde, Fla.
2-team (13 Tampa Bay)	0	2	9.14	18	5	0	0	43	64	47	44	27	29	.347							
Boyd, Jason	3	1	4.30	44	0	0	0	52	38	25	25	26	31	.200	R	R	6-3	180	2-23-73	1994	Edwardsville, Ill.
Cortes, David	0	0	12.00	2	0	0	0	3	8	5	4	0	1	.470	R	R	5-11	190	10-15-73	1996	El Centro, Calif.
Cressend, Jack	2	1	2.51	33	0	0	0	43	40	12	12	9	28	.251	R	R	6-1	190	5-13-75	1996	Mandeville, La.
Davis, Jason	8	11	4.68	27	27	1	0	165	172	101	86	47	85	.272	R	R	6-6	190	5-8-80	2000	Charleston, Tenn.
Durbin, Chad	0	1	7.27	3	1	0	0	9	18	12	7	3	8	.428	R	R	6-2	200	12-3-77	1996	Baton Rouge, La.
Elder, Dave	1	1	19.29	4	0	0	0	2	5	5	5	4	3	.416	R	R	6-0	180	9-23-75	1997	Conyers, Ga.
Herrera, Alex	0	0	9.00	10	0	0	0	7	7	7	7	8	6	.250	L	L	5-11	190	11-5-76	1997	Maracaibo, Venez.
Lee, Cliff	3	3	3.61	9	9	0	0	52	41	28	21	20	44	.220	L	L	6-3	190	8-30-78	2000	Benton, Ark.
Lee, Dave	1	0	4.70	8	0	0	0	8	4	4	4	6	7	.142	R	R	6-1	200	3-12-73	1995	Pittsburgh, Pa.
Miceli, Danny	1	1	1.20	13	0	0	0	15	9	4	2	6	19	.163	R	R	6-0	225	9-9-70	1990	Winter Springs, Fla.
Mulholland, Terry	3	4	4.91	45	3	0	0	99	117	60	54	37	42	.295	R	L	6-3	220	3-9-63	1984	Scottsdale, Ariz.
Myette, Aaron	0	0	23.63	2	0	0	0	3	7	7	7	2	1	.466	R	R	6-4	210	9-26-77	1997	Gig Harbor, Wash.
Paronto, Chad	0	2	9.45	6	0	0	0	7	7	8	7	3	6	.291	R	R	6-5	250	7-28-75	1996	Pittsfield, Mass.
Phillips, Jason	0	1	9.00	3	0	0	0	5	9	5	5	2	2	.409	R	R	6-6	220	3-22-74	1992	Montoursville, Penn.
Riggan, Jerrod	0	0	9.00	2	0	0	0	4	7	4	4	1	2	.411	R	R	6-3	190	5-16-74	1996	Brewster, Wash.
Riske, David	2	2	2.29	68	0	0	8	75	52	21	19	20	82	.196	R	R	6-2	180	10-23-76	1997	Kent, Wash.
Rodriguez, Ricardo	3	9	5.73	15	15	0	0	81	89	57	52	28	41	.000	R	R	6-3	190	5-21-78	1996	Guayubin, D.R.
Sabathia, C.C.	13	9	3.60	30	30	2	0	198	190	85	79	66	141	.254	L	L	6-7	290	7-21-80	1998	Vallejo, Calif.
Sadler, Carl	0	0	1.86	18	0	0	0	10	11	2	2	5	10	.305	L	L	6-2	190	10-11-76	1996	Perry, Fla.
Santiago, Jose	1	3	2.84	25	0	0	0	32	37	11	10	14	15	.298	R	R	6-3	220	11-5-74	1994	Loiza, P.R.
Stanford, Jason	1	3	3.60	13	8	0	0	50	48	20	20	16	30	.246	L	L	6-2	200	1-23-77	1999	Tucson, Ariz.
Tallet, Brian	0	2	4.74	5	3	0	0	19	23	14	10	8	9	.302	L	L	6-7	200	9-21-77	2000	Bethany, Okla.
Traber, Billy	6	9	5.24	33	18	1	0	112	132	67	65	40	88	.292	L	L	6-5	200	9-18-79	2001	El Segundo, Calif.
Westbrook, Jake	7	10	4.33	34	22	1	0	133	142	70	64	56	58	.281	R	R	6-3	200	9-29-77	1996	Danielsville, Ga.

FIELDING

Catcher	PCT	G	PO	A	E	DP	PB
Bard	.991	87	486	55	5	7	4
Laker	.983	50	265	19	5	6	4
Martinez	.996	40	231	23	1	2	3
Sorensen	.000	1	0	0	0	0	0

First Base	PCT	G	PO	A	E	DP
Blake	1.000	31	131	12	0	22
Broussard	.991	114	957	63	9	85
Hafner	.985	42	369	18	6	47
Selby	.000	1	0	0	0	0

Second Base	PCT	G	PO	A	E	DP
McDonald	.980	37	49	95	3	27
Phillips	.981	109	236	325	11	76
Santos	.981	28	39	64	2	17
Selby	1.000	1	0	1	0	0
Sorensen	.944	14	14	20	2	5

Third Base	PCT	G	PO	A	E	DP
Blake	.952	140	91	289	19	29
Gutierrez	1.000	7	5	5	0	0
LaRocca	1.000	2	0	6	0	0
McDonald	.900	23	10	17	3	2
Peralta	1.000	6	2	6	0	1
Santos	1.000	4	0	3	0	0
Selby	.926	10	6	19	2	2
Sorensen	.000	1	0	0	0	0

Shortstop	PCT	G	PO	A	E	DP
Bard	.000	1	0	0	0	0

	PCT	G	PO	A	E	DP
Gutierrez	.929	9	13	26	3	4
McDonald	.959	27	39	54	4	17
Peralta	.976	72	104	222	8	43
Sorensen	1.000	3	2	6	0	1
Vizquel	.978	64	114	203	7	59

Outfield	PCT	G	PO	A	E	DP
Bradley	.992	93	245	6	2	3
Burks	1.000	2	5	0	0	0
Crisp	.995	90	213	5	1	2
Escobar	.969	25	59	3	2	2
Garcia	.905	23	36	2	4	0
Gerut	.984	113	234	9	4	2
Lawton	.993	74	133	4	1	0
Ludwick	1.000	32	70	2	0	0
Magruder	1.000	8	11	0	0	0
Selby	1.000	1	1	0	0	0
Sorensen	.000	1	0	0	0	0
Spencer	.987	43	75	2	1	1

LARRY GOREN

C.C. Sabathia: Led the Indians with 13 wins

STEVE MOORE

Alex Escobar: Slugged a system-high 24 homers

FARM SYSTEM

Director, Player Development: John Farrell.

Class	Farm Team	League	W	L	Pct.	Finish*	Manager	First Yr.
AAA	Buffalo (N.Y.) Bisons	International	73	70	.510	t-7th (14)	Marty Brown	1995
AA	Akron (Ohio) Aeros	Eastern	88	53	.624	+1st (12)	Brad Komminsk	1997
High A	Kinston (N.C.) Indians	Carolina	73	66	.525	4th (8)	Torey Lovullo	1987
Low A	Lake County (Ohio) Captains	South Atlantic	97	43	.693	1st (16)	Luis Rivera	2003
SS A	Mahoning Valley (Ohio) Indians	New York-Penn	38	36	.514	7th (14)	Ted Kubiak	1999
Rookie	Burlington (N.C.) Indians	Appalachian	37	31	.544	5th (10)	Rouglas Odor	1986

*Finish in overall standings (No. of teams in league) +League champion

BUFFALO BISONS Class AAA

INTERNATIONAL LEAGUE

BATTING	AVG	G	AB	R	H	2B	3B	HR	RBI	BB	SO	SB	CS	SLG	OBP	B	T	HT	WT	DOB	1st Yr	Resides
Bard, Josh	.330	35	115	14	38	7	0	5	21	14	17	1	2	.522	.408	S	R	6-3	210	3-30-78	1999	Chandler, Ariz.
Broussard, Ben	.250	32	120	17	30	2	1	3	15	9	29	3	0	.358	.303	L	L	6-2	220	9-24-76	1999	Beaumont, Texas
Crisp, Coco	.360	56	225	42	81	19	6	1	24	26	24	20	8	.511	.434	S	R	6-0	180	11-1-79	1999	Desert Hot Springs, Calif.
DeCinces, Tim	.125	3	8	1	1	0	0	0	1	3	3	1	0	.125	.364	L	R	6-2	190	4-26-74	1996	Newport Beach, Calif.
Escobar, Alex	.251	118	439	63	110	21	2	24	78	24	133	8	3	.472	.296	R	R	6-1	190	9-6-78	1996	Valencia, Venez.
Garcia, Karim	.267	14	60	6	16	6	0	0	7	2	17	2	1	.367	.290	L	L	6-0	210	10-29-75	1992	Ciudad. Obregon, Mexico
Garcia, Luis	.215	122	432	41	93	27	1	7	51	22	97	2	4	.331	.260	R	R	6-4	190	11-5-78	1997	Guadalajara, Mexico
Gerut, Jody	.277	17	65	13	18	5	0	5	19	11	11	4	0	.585	.377	L	L	6-0	200	9-18-77	1998	Lombard, Ill.
Gil, Benji	.139	9	36	4	5	1	0	2	6	0	10	0	0	.333	.139	R	R	6-2	210	10-6-72	1991	Grapevine, Texas
Grindell, Nate	.223	46	130	14	29	9	0	2	14	12	23	2	4	.338	.320	R	R	6-1	180	4-9-77	1998	Carrollton, Texas
Gutierrez, Ricky	.292	16	65	8	19	2	1	0	5	4	5	4	1	.354	.338	R	R	6-1	190	5-23-70	1988	Pembroke Pines, Fla.
Hafner, Travis	.270	29	100	15	27	4	0	2	10	25	26	2	1	.370	.421	L	R	6-3	240	6-3-77	1997	Sykeston, N.D.
Izturis, Maicer	.262	85	301	43	79	16	4	2	29	24	28	14	6	.362	.317	S	R	5-8	150	9-12-80	1998	Barquisimeto, Venez.
LaRocca, Greg	.290	132	500	63	145	33	2	10	68	40	53	5	3	.424	.346	R	R	5-11	180	11-10-72	1994	Bedford, N.H.
Little, Mark	.281	45	146	20	41	5	1	2	16	5	45	4	2	.370	.329	R	R	6-0	190	7-11-72	1994	Edwardsville, Ill.
Lucca, Lou	.222	9	27	5	6	3	0	0	1	0	10	1	1	.333	.250	R	R	5-11	210	10-13-70	1992	So. San Francisco, Calif.
Magruder, Chris	.328	41	137	20	45	7	2	3	15	15	27	5	1	.474	.391	S	R	5-11	200	4-26-77	1998	Mesa, Ariz.
Martinez, Victor	.328	73	274	42	90	19	0	7	45	26	32	3	5	.474	.395	S	R	6-2	170	12-23-78	1997	Ciudad Bolivar, Venez.
Mouton, Lyle	.282	49	170	21	48	10	1	10	30	13	36	1	1	.529	.330	R	R	6-4	230	5-13-69	1991	Tarpon Springs, Fla.
3-team (47 Norf., 10 Scr.)	.281	106	352	48	99	22	2	14	58	37	93	8	2	.474	.354							
Peralta, John	.257	63	237	25	61	12	1	1	21	15	45	1	3	.329	.310	R	R	6-1	180	5-28-82	1999	Santiago, D.R.

BATTING	AVG	G	AB	R	H	2B	3B	HR	RBI	BB	SO	SB	CS	SLG	OBP	B	T	HT	WT	DOB	1st Yr	Resides
Phillips, Brandon	.175	43	154	14	27	7	0	3	13	12	22	7	3	.279	.247	R	R	5-11	190	6-28-81	1999	Stone Mountain, Ga.
Pratt, Scott	.246	108	357	43	88	11	5	4	31	14	70	18	9	.339	.272	L	R	5-10	180	2-4-77	1998	Gilbert, Ariz.
Santos, Angel	.239	13	46	10	11	2	0	2	8	5	8	5	0	.413	.314	S	R	5-11	170	8-14-79	1997	Cayey, P.R.
2-team (70 Pawtucket)	.238	83	260	35	62	10	0	7	28	37	58	14	4	.358	.334							
Secrist, Reed	.246	27	69	12	17	6	0	3	7	6	14	0	1	.464	.316	L	R	6-0	220	5-7-70	1992	Farmington, Utah
Sorensen, Zach	.239	61	238	39	57	12	3	3	29	22	42	12	5	.353	.299	S	R	6-0	190	1-3-77	1998	St. George, Utah
Valencia, Vic	.314	10	35	5	11	2	0	1	1	0	14	0	0	.457	.314	R	R	6-2	180	5-30-77	1994	Maracay, Venez.
Wakeland, Chris	.222	16	45	2	10	1	0	1	6	2	17	0	0	.311	.250	L	L	6-0	190	6-15-74	1996	St. Helens, Ore.
Wathan, Dusty	.277	61	188	21	52	7	0	2	15	18	31	3	0	.346	.355	R	R	6-4	210	8-22-73	1994	Peoria, Ariz.
White, Derrick	.243	10	37	3	9	1	0	1	7	0	13	1	0	.351	.263	R	R	6-1	220	10-12-69	1991	Marin City, Calif.

PITCHING	W	L	ERA	G	GS	CG	SV	IP	H	R	ER	BB	SO	AVG	B	T	HT	WT	DOB	1st Yr	Resides
Bere, Jason	1	0	0.61	3	3	0	0	15	9	1	1	3	17	.180	R	R	6-3	220	5-26-71	1990	North Andover, Mass.
Betancourt, Rafael	0	0	4.05	4	0	0	1	7	6	3	3	2	6	.240	R	R	6-2	170	4-29-75	1994	Cumana, Venez.
Bierbrodt, Nick	2	2	3.00	16	1	0	0	27	22	10	9	18	31	.222	L	L	6-5	210	5-16-78	1996	Tierra Verde, Fla.
Boyd, Jason	1	0	1.23	9	0	0	3	15	12	3	2	2	14	.222	R	R	6-3	180	2-23-73	1994	Edwardsville, Ill.
Brown, Jamie	4	4	3.52	13	10	0	0	61	45	26	24	17	26	.206	R	R	6-2	200	3-31-77	1997	Collinsville, Miss.
Burba, Dave	1	3	2.05	4	4	0	0	22	18	6	5	5	10	.227	R	R	6-4	240	7-7-66	1987	Gilbert, Ariz.
Caraccioli, Lance	4	8	5.10	34	13	0	2	101	123	61	57	35	83	.308	L	L	6-4	200	12-14-77	1998	Walker, La.
Cortes, David	1	0	2.70	5	0	0	1	7	4	3	2	0	9	.153	R	R	5-11	190	10-15-73	1996	El Centro, Calif.
Cressend, Jack	1	0	1.23	8	0	0	0	15	7	2	2	6	12	.148	R	R	6-1	190	5-13-75	1996	Mandeville, La.
Denney, Kyle	2	1	5.28	6	6	0	0	31	35	18	18	10	26	.275	R	R	6-2	190	7-27-77	1999	Prague, Okla.
Durbin, Chad	3	6	4.60	10	10	1	0	59	51	30	30	16	64	.232	R	R	6-2	200	12-3-77	1996	Baton Rouge, La.
Elder, Dave	0	0	0.00	8	0	0	6	13	5	0	0	6	17	.121	R	R	6-0	180	9-23-75	1997	Conyers, Ga.
Fyhrie, Mike	1	5	5.80	8	8	1	0	45	55	30	29	12	31	.303	R	R	6-2	200	12-9-69	1991	Coto de Caza, Calif.
Guthrie, Jeremy	4	9	6.52	18	18	1	0	97	129	75	70	30	62	.320	S	R	6-1	200	4-8-79	2003	Las Vegas, Nev.
Herrera, Alex	4	6	5.30	34	0	0	1	56	51	40	33	45	46	.240	L	L	5-11	190	11-5-76	1997	Maracaibo, Venez.
Kleine, Victor	0	0	1.80	1	1	0	0	5	4	2	1	4	4	.200	L	L	6-4	180	9-12-79	2000	Florence, Ky.
Lee, Cliff	6	1	3.27	11	11	0	0	63	62	24	23	31	61	.260	L	L	6-3	190	8-30-78	2000	Benton, Ark.
Miceli, Danny	0	1	3.00	5	0	0	0	6	7	2	2	1	6	.280	R	R	6-0	225	9-9-70	1990	Winter Springs, Fla.
Myette, Aaron	0	0	4.59	23	1	0	1	33	33	21	17	23	25	.261	R	R	6-4	210	9-26-77	1997	Gig Harbor, Wash.
Paronto, Chad	3	5	4.34	49	0	0	18	56	64	36	27	22	48	.274	R	R	6-5	250	7-28-75	1996	Pittsfield, Mass.
Phillips, Jason	10	1	2.12	13	12	1	0	85	68	24	20	19	56	.222	R	R	6-6	220	3-22-74	1992	Montoursville, Pa.
Rakers, Jason	0	1	3.86	3	0	0	0	2	2	1	1	2	1	.250	R	R	6-2	200	6-29-73	1995	Pittsburgh, Pa.
Rayborn, Kenny	1	0	3.00	1	1	0	0	6	6	2	2	1	2	.250	R	R	6-4	210	11-22-74	1997	Purvis, Miss.
Riggan, Jerrod	2	1	2.20	9	0	0	0	16	14	5	4	5	14	.237	R	R	6-3	190	5-16-74	1996	Brewster, Wash.
Rodriguez, Ricardo	0	1	4.32	2	2	0	0	8	6	4	4	3	7	.200	R	R	6-3	190	5-21-78	1996	Guayubin, D.R.
Sadler, Carl	2	1	6.28	31	0	0	3	53	62	41	37	31	32	.298	L	L	6-2	190	10-11-76	1996	Perry, Fla.
Santiago, Jose	3	3	2.43	25	4	0	2	67	79	25	18	22	33	.298	R	R	6-3	220	11-5-74	1994	Loiza, P.R.
Stanford, Jason	10	4	3.43	20	20	1	0	126	124	57	48	25	108	.260	L	L	6-2	200	1-23-77	1999	Tucson, Ariz.
Sturkie, Scott	0	0	0.00	1	0	0	0	2	1	0	0	0	1	.166	R	R	6-3	210	6-12-79	2001	West Columbia, S.C.
Tadano, Kazuhito	0	0	3.86	2	0	0	0	7	6	3	3	4	6	.230	R	R	6-0	180	4-25-80	2003	Tokyo, Japan
Tallet, Brian	4	4	5.14	15	15	0	0	84	89	50	48	34	67	.269	L	L	6-7	200	9-21-77	2000	Bethany, Okla.
Vargas, Jose	0	0	16.20	1	0	0	0	2	6	5	3	2	2	.600	R	R	6-1	150	2-18-83	2001	Puerto Cabello, Venez.
Westbrook, Jake	1	0	0.00	2	2	0	0	10	0	0	0	4	7	.000	R	R	6-3	200	9-29-77	1996	Danielsville, Ga.
White, Matt	2	3	2.13	19	1	0	0	42	36	12	10	16	34	.230	R	L	6-1	180	8-19-77	1998	Windsor, Mass.
2-team (2 Pawtucket)	2	3	1.97	21	1	0	0	46	37	13	10	16	39	.220							

FIELDING

Catcher	PCT	G	PO	A	E	DP	PB
Bard	.995	30	201	16	1	3	2
DeCinces	1.000	2	9	0	0	0	0
LaRocca	.000	1	0	0	0	0	0
Martinez	.995	56	393	27	2	5	5
Secrist	1.000	1	0	1	0	0	0
Valencia	1.000	8	55	3	0	0	1
Wathan	.992	54	336	24	3	6	3

First Base	PCT	G	PO	A	E	DP
Broussard	.990	24	190	18	2	22
L. Garcia	.984	73	592	38	10	57
Gil	1.000	3	18	3	0	3
Grindell	1.000	2	1	1	0	0
Hafner	.986	24	197	14	3	23
LaRocca	1.000	4	27	1	0	3
Lucca	.900	1	9	0	1	0
Martinez	.982	14	104	8	2	7
Secrist	1.000	8	42	1	0	4
Wathan	1.000	2	9	1	0	1

Second Base	PCT	G	PO	A	E	DP
Gil	1.000	3	4	11	0	2
Gutierrez	1.000	3	7	3	0	1
Izturis	.991	20	40	65	1	19
LaRocca	.952	12	29	31	3	9
Phillips	.985	43	99	102	3	30
Pratt	.968	28	48	74	4	10
Santos	.946	8	17	18	2	5
Sorensen	.973	30	70	74	4	25

Third Base	PCT	G	PO	A	E	DP
Gil	.667	1	0	2	1	0
Grindell	.960	8	4	20	1	1
Gutierrez	1.000	7	4	13	0	2
LaRocca	.932	106	66	195	19	18
Lucca	.750	5	3	3	2	0
Peralta	1.000	3	3	7	0	1
Pratt	.868	16	7	26	5	3
Santos	1.000	2	2	2	0	0
Secrist	1.000	3	3	0	0	0
Sorensen	.900	4	3	6	1	2

Shortstop	PCT	G	PO	A	E	DP
Gil	1.000	1	1	2	0	0
Gutierrez	1.000	4	3	11	0	3
Izturis	.959	66	84	195	12	37
Peralta	.968	60	98	201	10	49
Pratt	1.000	1	1	2	0	0
Santos	1.000	3	2	8	0	0
Sorensen	.917	9	13	20	3	3

Outfield	PCT	G	PO	A	E	DP
Crisp	.982	56	155	6	3	2
Escobar	.975	103	191	8	5	1
K. Garcia	1.000	12	22	1	0	0
L. Garcia	.976	22	38	3	1	0
Gerut	1.000	16	36	1	0	0
Grindell	1.000	32	47	0	0	0
Little	.982	42	101	6	2	2
Magruder	1.000	40	73	2	0	0
Mouton	.972	18	31	4	1	1
Pratt	.980	54	95	5	2	0
Secrist	1.000	11	18	2	0	0
Sorensen	.951	18	39	0	2	0
Wakeland	.941	15	16	0	1	0
White	1.000	7	12	1	0	0

AKRON AEROS — Class AA

EASTERN LEAGUE

BATTING	AVG	G	AB	R	H	2B	3B	HR	RBI	BB	SO	SB	CS	SLG	OBP	B	T	HT	WT	DOB	1st Yr	Resides
Chauncey, Clinton	.000	5	13	0	0	0	0	0	0	0	7	0	0	.000	.000	R	R	6-1	180	1-1-81	2000	Jacksonville, Fla.
Church, Ryan	.261	99	371	47	97	17	3	13	52	32	64	4	3	.429	.325	L	L	6-1	190	10-14-78	2000	Lompoc, Calif.
Cotto, Luis	.250	1	4	0	1	0	0	0	0	0	2	0	0	.250	.250	R	R	5-10	180	7-9-81	2000	Rio Piedras, P.R.
Crozier, Eric	.245	108	347	52	85	10	3	19	52	51	92	5	3	.455	.344	L	L	6-4	200	8-11-78	2000	Columbus, Ohio
Goelz, Jim	.200	6	15	2	3	1	0	0	1	1	1	0	0	.267	.250	R	R	5-10	170	2-13-76	1998	St. James, N.Y.
Gonzalez, Luis	.318	116	431	72	137	22	4	7	62	46	41	1	0	.436	.385	R	R	5-11	170	6-26-79	1997	El Tigre, Venez.
Grindell, Nate	.232	42	142	24	33	12	2	3	22	20	24	0	0	.408	.323	R	R	6-1	180	4-9-77	1998	Carrollton, Texas

BATTING	AVG	G	AB	R	H	2B	3B	HR	RBI	BB	SO	SB	CS	SLG	OBP	B	T	HT	WT	DOB	1st Yr	Resides
Inglett, Joe	.283	71	276	41	78	16	1	4	25	37	36	1	2	.391	.377	L	R	5-10	170	6-29-78	2000	Citrus Heights, Calif.
Izturis, Maicer	.280	53	218	31	61	11	5	1	20	24	23	14	6	.390	.351	S	R	5-8	150	9-12-80	1998	Barquisimeto, Venez.
Lawton, Matt	.053	5	19	1	1	0	0	0	1	2	6	0	0	.053	.143	L	R	5-10	190	11-3-71	1991	Saucier, Miss.
Luderer, Brian	.241	76	245	29	59	12	2	4	34	24	33	0	1	.355	.320	R	R	5-11	190	8-19-78	1996	Tarzana, Calif.
Luna, Hector	.297	127	462	87	137	19	2	2	38	48	64	17	5	.359	.368	R	R	6-1	170	2-1-80	1999	Monte Cristi, D.R.
Magruder, Chris	.462	3	13	0	6	0	0	0	3	1	2	1	0	.462	.500	S	R	5-11	200	4-26-77	1998	Mesa, Ariz.
Martinez, Victor	.333	3	12	1	4	2	0	0	2	0	1	0	0	.500	.333	S	R	6-2	170	12-23-78	1997	Ciudad Bolivar, Venez.
Minges, Tyler	.223	122	422	49	94	18	5	10	44	27	65	6	4	.360	.270	R	R	6-0	180	11-15-79	1998	Hamilton, Ohio
Panther, Nathan	.000	3	9	0	0	0	0	0	1	0	3	0	0	.000	.000	L	L	6-2	180	7-12-81	2002	Muscatine, Iowa
Requena, Alex	.180	50	150	18	27	2	2	1	5	10	39	6	3	.240	.245	S	R	5-11	150	8-13-80	1998	Maracay, Venez.
Scott, Luke	.273	50	183	21	50	13	1	7	37	11	37	0	1	.470	.317	L	R	6-0	210	6-25-78	2001	Deleon Springs, Fla.
Sizemore, Grady	.304	128	496	96	151	26	11	13	78	46	73	10	9	.480	.373	L	L	6-2	200	8-2-82	2000	Mill Creek, Wash.
Smith, Corey	.271	127	473	51	128	27	3	9	64	50	99	7	2	.397	.340	R	R	6-1	200	4-15-82	2000	Piscataway, N.J.
Valencia, Vic	.251	58	207	22	52	11	1	9	33	20	49	2	1	.444	.319	R	R	6-2	180	5-30-77	1994	Maracay, Venez.
Wathan, Dusty	.273	9	33	3	9	2	0	0	4	0	4	0	0	.333	.257	R	R	6-4	210	8-22-73	1994	Peoria, Ariz.
Wright, Ron	.261	50	176	25	46	9	0	9	38	29	39	0	1	.466	.376	R	R	6-1	230	1-21-76	1994	St. George, Utah

PITCHING	W	L	ERA	G	GS	CG	SV	IP	H	R	ER	BB	SO	AVG	B	T	HT	WT	DOB	1st Yr	Resides
Alvarez, Oscar	2	2	4.09	13	6	0	0	33	33	19	15	13	20	.257	L	L	6-0	160	9-17-80	1997	Barcelona, Venez.
Betancourt, Rafael	0	0	1.39	31	0	0	16	45	33	10	7	13	75	.195	R	R	6-2	170	4-29-75	1994	Cumana, Venez.
Cabrera, Fernando	9	4	2.97	36	15	0	5	109	96	41	36	40	115	.237	R	R	6-4	170	11-16-81	1999	Toa Baja, P.R.
Carmona, Fausto	0	0	4.50	1	1	0	0	6	8	3	3	0	3	.307	R	R	6-4	180	12-7-83	2001	Santo Domingo, D.R.
Cressend, Jack	2	0	0.00	8	0	0	1	16	15	4	0	2	10	.234	R	R	6-1	190	5-13-75	1996	Mandeville, La.
Cruceta, Francisco	13	9	3.09	27	25	6	0	163	141	70	56	66	134	.232	R	R	6-2	180	7-4-81	1999	La Vega, D.R.
Denney, Kyle	7	3	2.42	18	18	1	0	104	97	34	28	24	87	.243	R	R	6-2	190	7-27-77	1999	Prague, Okla.
Douglas, Shea	0	1	2.70	2	0	0	0	3	3	1	1	1	2	.230	L	L	6-1	190	2-3-81	2002	Vicksburg, Miss.
Durbin, Chad	2	0	1.50	3	3	0	0	12	7	2	2	1	11	.162	R	R	6-2	200	12-3-77	1996	Baton Rouge, La.
Evans, Kyle	9	5	3.59	28	19	0	1	133	140	72	53	37	69	.268	R	R	6-3	190	10-10-78	2000	Waco, Texas
Guthrie, Jeremy	6	2	1.44	10	9	2	0	63	44	11	10	14	35	.196	S	R	6-1	200	4-8-79	2003	Las Vegas, Nevada
Larson, Ryan	2	6	3.84	40	0	0	2	63	78	36	27	18	29	.307	R	R	5-10	190	5-13-79	2000	Rocklin, Calif.
Lee, Cliff	1	0	1.50	2	2	0	0	12	7	2	2	4	13	.166	L	L	6-3	190	8-30-78	2000	Benton, Ark.
Martin, Kevin	0	0	4.50	2	0	0	0	2	3	1	1	2	3	.375	R	R	6-2	180	1-3-79	2001	Las Vegas, Nevada
Mendoza, Marcos	1	0	10.67	9	0	0	0	14	16	21	17	13	14	.266	L	L	5-10	180	10-31-80	2001	El Cajon, Calif.
Montano, Ignacio	0	0	9.00	1	0	0	0	1	3	1	1	0	0	.500	L	L	5-8	150	3-8-80	2001	Veracruz, Mexico
Myette, Aaron	0	0	0.00	3	0	0	0	5	0	0	0	2	7	.000	R	R	6-4	210	9-26-77	1997	Gig Harbor, Wash.
Neil, Dan	0	0	7.71	5	0	0	0	7	10	6	6	1	4	.357	L	L	6-0	180	8-8-78	1999	Bardonia, N.Y.
Pennington, Todd	1	0	3.60	7	0	0	0	10	8	4	4	6	9	.228	R	R	6-2	210	4-6-80	2001	McClure, Ill.
Pinales, Aquiles	1	1	7.00	6	0	0	0	9	5	7	7	8	8	.156	R	R	5-11	190	9-5-74	1996	La Romana, D.R.
Rakers, Jason	1	1	1.08	4	0	0	1	8	7	2	1	1	9	.233	R	R	6-2	200	6-29-73	1995	Pittsburgh, Pa.
Ramsey, Keith	1	0	6.35	2	2	0	0	11	15	8	8	3	4	.312	L	L	6-1	170	3-5-80	2002	Los Angeles, Calif.
Rayborn, Kenny	4	1	2.05	5	4	0	0	26	28	7	6	5	20	.271	R	R	6-4	210	11-22-74	1997	Purvis, Miss.
Rigdon, Paul	3	0	3.23	6	6	0	0	31	27	12	11	5	16	.230	R	R	6-5	240	11-2-75	1996	Jacksonville, Fla.
Robbins, Jake	6	3	2.16	34	0	0	8	58	44	18	14	24	38	.217	R	R	6-5	190	5-23-76	1994	Charlotte, N.C.
Stein, Blake	0	1	27.00	2	0	0	0	3	6	8	8	4	4	.461	R	R	6-7	240	8-3-73	1994	Folsom, La.
Tadano, Kazuhito	4	1	1.24	31	0	0	3	73	62	15	10	15	78	.226	R	R	6-0	180	4-25-80	2003	Tokyo, Japan
Van Dusen, Derrick	10	8	4.92	28	26	1	0	139	183	100	76	51	77	.317	L	L	6-3	180	6-6-81	2000	Fontana, Calif.
Vargas, Jose	3	2	1.92	37	0	0	8	52	52	21	11	27	52	.258	R	R	6-1	150	2-18-83	2001	Puerto Cabello, Venez.
Wallace, Shane	0	2	4.82	10	1	0	1	19	23	11	10	12	3	.306	L	L	6-2	200	12-29-80	1999	Carrollton, Texas
Warden, Jim Ed	0	1	9.00	1	1	0	0	4	6	4	4	5	1	.400	R	R	6-7	190	5-7-79	2001	Murfreesboro, Tenn.
Wickman, Bob	0	0	16.20	2	2	0	0	2	3	3	3	1	2	.428	R	R	6-1	240	2-6-69	1990	Wausaukee, Wisc.
Wohlers, Mark	0	0	5.40	2	1	0	0	2	5	1	1	2	0	.625	R	R	6-4	210	1-23-70	1988	Alpharetta, Ga.

FIELDING

Catcher	PCT	G	PO	A	E	DP	PB
Chauncey	1.000	5	26	2	0	0	0
Luderer	.996	73	462	41	2	5	11
Martinez	1.000	1	5	0	0	0	0
Valencia	.994	57	441	30	3	3	5
Wathan	1.000	9	59	9	0	1	0

First Base	PCT	G	PO	A	E	DP
Crozier	.986	100	771	66	12	62
Gonzalez	.995	43	362	27	2	34
Grindell	.889	2	7	1	1	1
Luderer	1.000	1	3	0	0	0
Wright	1.000	2	12	0	0	1

Second Base	PCT	G	PO	A	E	DP
Cotto	.857	1	2	4	1	0
Goelz	1.000	2	3	4	0	0
Gonzalez	.977	32	57	71	3	17
Inglett	.966	66	112	172	10	33
Izturis	.951	41	66	110	9	19
Luna	1.000	1	2	3	0	0

Third Base	PCT	G	PO	A	E	DP
Gonzalez	.871	12	9	18	4	1
Grindell	.950	11	3	16	1	2
Smith	.865	122	77	204	44	9

Shortstop	PCT	G	PO	A	E	DP
Goelz	1.000	1	1	4	0	1
Gonzalez	1.000	6	8	15	0	3
Izturis	.921	9	15	20	3	0
Luna	.935	126	188	319	35	73
Smith	.000	1	0	0	1	0

Outfield	PCT	G	PO	A	E	DP
Church	.977	98	245	11	6	2
Crozier	1.000	2	3	0	0	0
Goelz	1.000	2	1	0	0	0
Gonzalez	1.000	15	21	1	0	0
Grindell	.974	21	33	4	1	0
Inglett	1.000	2	2	0	0	0
Magruder	1.000	1	5	0	0	0
Minges	.979	118	268	18	6	5
Panther	1.000	2	6	1	0	0
Requena	.984	35	57	3	1	2
Scott	.947	17	34	2	2	0
Sizemore	.986	125	283	6	4	0

KINSTON INDIANS — High Class A

CAROLINA LEAGUE

BATTING	AVG	G	AB	R	H	2B	3B	HR	RBI	BB	SO	SB	CS	SLG	OBP	B	T	HT	WT	DOB	1st Yr	Resides
Camacaro, Armando	.236	58	182	19	43	7	0	2	17	9	29	2	3	.308	.299	R	R	5-11	170	4-6-79	1998	Guarenas, Venez.
Choy Foo, Rodney	.257	125	444	57	114	17	2	11	65	53	95	22	8	.378	.342	S	R	6-1	180	12-12-81	2000	Waimanalo, Hawaii
Cooper, Jason	.307	61	218	36	67	17	2	9	36	25	46	3	0	.528	.380	L	L	6-2	220	12-6-80	2002	Moses Lake, Wash.
Cotto, Luis	.153	39	111	6	17	4	0	0	6	9	37	1	1	.189	.248	R	R	5-10	180	7-9-81	2000	Rio Piedras, P.R.
2-team (17 Wilmington)	.160	56	163	14	26	4	0	0	11	16	52	1	1	.184	.254							
Dyson, Trey	.364	7	22	5	8	1	0	1	3	6	6	1	0	.545	.533	L	L	6-4	220	3-11-80	2002	Blythewood, S.C.
2-team (128 Wilmington)	.279	135	480	69	134	32	0	15	75	66	98	7	2	.440	.373							
Elder, Rick	.221	42	136	15	30	7	0	6	21	20	55	0	1	.404	.319	L	L	6-6	250	2-24-80	1998	Marietta, Ga.
Inglett, Joe	.329	28	85	21	28	10	1	0	15	20	14	1	0	.471	.454	L	R	5-10	170	6-29-78	2000	Citrus Heights, Calif.
Jenkins, Brian	.257	27	105	15	27	6	1	1	16	6	17	0	3	.362	.289	R	R	5-11	210	10-11-78	1997	Port St. Joe, Fla.

BATTING	AVG	G	AB	R	H	2B	3B	HR	RBI	BB	SO	SB	CS	SLG	OBP	B	T	HT	WT	DOB	1st Yr	Resides
Kirby, Brian	.184	40	103	6	19	1	0	3	7	6	39	0	0	.282	.241	L	R	6-2	190	8-3-79	2001	North Little Rock, Ark.
Knox, Matt	.248	61	230	26	57	10	1	4	27	9	41	0	2	.352	.280	R	R	6-4	210	12-29-79	2001	Lebanon, Pa.
Malave, Dennis	.179	41	112	6	20	1	0	0	12	8	31	3	3	.188	.238	L	L	5-9	160	1-6-80	1997	Caracas, Venez.
Margalski, Ben	.154	41	117	11	18	4	0	0	6	21	40	2	1	.188	.286	L	R	6-2	210	9-2-79	2001	High Ridge, Mo.
Ochoa, Ivan	.253	82	296	42	75	12	3	0	23	31	67	28	10	.314	.336	R	R	5-10	140	12-16-82	2000	Guacara, Venez.
Osborn, Pat	.254	60	205	24	52	16	0	1	24	23	42	1	2	.346	.333	R	R	6-3	210	2-27-81	2002	Gainesville, Fla.
Peavey, Bill	.229	42	140	14	32	9	0	1	23	22	30	0	0	.314	.343	L	L	6-4	250	1-16-79	2002	Brisbane, Calif.
Quintana, Miguel	.283	99	343	33	97	18	2	4	35	17	71	3	6	.382	.318	L	R	6-1	190	6-29-79	2001	Miami, Fla.
Scott, Luke	.278	67	241	37	67	12	1	13	44	27	62	6	3	.498	.360	L	R	6-0	210	6-25-78	2001	Deleon Springs, Fla.
Sherrill, J.J.	.249	46	173	21	43	7	4	3	22	16	50	5	1	.387	.309	S	R	5-7	170	8-11-80	1999	Seaside, Calif.
Taveras, Willy	.282	113	397	64	112	9	6	2	35	52	68	57	12	.350	.381	R	R	6-0	160	12-25-81	1999	Tenares, D.R.
Torres, Eider	.248	124	447	63	111	13	0	1	39	39	73	43	14	.284	.314	S	R	5-8	160	1-16-83	2000	Maracaibo, Venez.
Wallace, David	.224	44	147	20	33	13	0	2	14	16	43	1	0	.354	.321	R	R	6-4	220	10-17-79	2001	Brentwood, Tenn.
Wright, Brian	.263	54	194	29	51	11	2	4	28	24	35	4	2	.402	.348	L	R	6-1	200	4-6-80	2002	Ramseur, N.C.

PITCHING	W	L	ERA	G	GS	CG	SV	IP	H	R	ER	BB	SO	AVG	B	T	HT	WT	DOB	1st Yr	Resides
Alvarez, Oscar	1	1	2.78	4	3	0	0	23	18	7	7	7	19	.216	L	L	6-0	160	9-17-80	1997	Barcelona, Venez.
Arthurs, Shane	1	0	4.58	12	0	0	0	20	19	10	10	7	15	.256	R	R	6-5	180	8-30-79	1997	Round Rock, Texas
Casey, Reid	0	0	27.00	1	0	0	0	1	4	3	3	0	1	.571	R	R	6-1	170	2-1-80	2002	Kingsport, Tenn.
Cooper, Chris	2	4	3.71	40	0	0	2	68	67	30	28	23	51	.256	L	L	5-11	190	10-31-78	2001	Sewickley, Pa.
Cressend, Jack	0	1	12.46	2	0	0	0	4	9	6	6	0	4	.428	R	R	6-1	190	5-13-75	1996	Mandeville, La.
Denham, Dan	5	5	4.50	14	14	1	0	72	82	42	36	27	39	.298	R	R	6-2	190	12-24-82	2001	Stateline, Nev.
Dittler, Jake	5	1	2.40	8	8	1	0	49	47	17	13	11	32	.256	R	R	6-4	220	11-24-82	2001	Henderson, Nev.
Fernley, Nate	1	1	3.57	15	0	0	0	23	24	12	9	14	6	.279	R	R	6-3	160	1-13-77	2001	Long Beach, Calif.
Foley, Travis	10	10	3.69	24	24	1	0	127	115	54	52	54	96	.253	R	R	6-1	180	3-11-83	2001	Louisville, Ky.
Gomez, Mariano	6	4	3.67	18	18	1	0	101	91	49	41	38	69	.242	L	L	6-5	170	9-12-82	1999	San Pedro, Honduras
Gronkiewicz, Lee	2	3	2.41	51	0	0	37	56	50	19	15	14	46	.239	R	R	5-11	180	8-21-78	2001	Lancaster, S.C.
Hernandez, Michael	6	3	3.73	19	0	0	0	31	31	17	13	8	37	.256	L	L	6-4	190	4-8-81	2002	Fresno, Calif.
Kleine, Victor	6	5	2.56	28	16	0	1	116	114	42	33	35	79	.260	L	L	6-4	180	9-12-79	2000	Florence, Ky.
Lantz, Doug	3	3	3.66	27	0	0	1	52	53	27	21	19	32	.262	R	R	6-1	180	8-26-79	2001	Southlake, Texas
Lee, Cliff	0	0	0.00	1	1	0	0	4	0	1	0	3	4	.000	L	L	6-3	190	8-30-78	2000	Benton, Ark.
Martin, J.D.	5	3	4.27	16	16	0	0	86	95	50	41	30	57	.281	R	R	6-4	170	1-2-83	2001	Ridgecrest, Calif.
Martin, Kevin	0	1	2.70	1	0	0	0	3	5	1	1	1	1	.384	R	R	6-2	180	1-3-79	2001	Las Vegas, Nev.
Mattison, Kieran	0	0	4.91	2	0	0	0	4	3	2	2	2	3	.214	L	R	6-0	200	6-21-80	2002	Greenville, N.C.
2-team (7 Wilmington)	3	1	3.86	9	7	0	0	37	41	18	16	11	32	.284							
Mendoza, Marcos	2	3	3.25	28	2	0	0	53	51	24	19	26	34	.256	L	L	5-10	180	10-31-80	2001	El Cajon, Calif.
Moran, Nick	4	0	3.55	6	6	0	0	33	32	14	13	7	20	.244	R	R	6-5	190	1-3-80	2001	Elk Grove, Calif.
Navarro, Rodolfo	0	1	6.23	2	0	0	0	4	5	5	3	2	4	.263	R	R	6-2	170	12-17-82	2002	Juarez, Mexico
Prahm, Ryan	1	3	4.21	9	2	0	0	26	23	12	12	14	16	.244	R	R	6-5	210	5-17-79	2000	Cedar Rapids, Iowa
Slocum, Brian	6	7	4.46	22	21	0	1	107	112	61	53	41	66	.266	R	R	6-4	190	3-27-81	2002	East Chester, N.Y.
Sturkie, Scott	4	2	2.76	40	0	0	1	78	73	27	24	27	44	.245	R	R	6-3	210	6-12-79	2001	West Columbia, S.C.
Tadano, Kazuhito	2	1	1.89	7	1	0	0	19	13	5	4	3	28	.191	R	R	6-0	180	4-25-80	2003	Tokyo, Japan
Warden, Jim Ed	0	4	7.52	7	7	1	0	26	32	23	22	25	21	.301	R	R	6-7	190	5-7-79	2001	Murfreesboro, Tenn.

FIELDING

Catcher	PCT	G	PO	A	E	DP	PB
Camacaro	.990	58	358	30	4	3	7
Kirby	1.000	5	10	0	0	0	2
Margalski	.985	41	237	26	4	3	7
Wallace	.986	43	261	22	4	1	14

First Base	PCT	G	PO	A	E	DP
Dyson	.941	1	14	2	1	0
Elder	.987	28	218	18	3	17
Kirby	1.000	18	134	8	0	15
Knox	.988	55	469	33	6	42
Peavey	.982	42	361	27	7	33

Second Base	PCT	G	PO	A	E	DP
Choy Foo	.986	43	91	126	3	31
Cotto	.000	1	0	0	0	0
Inglett	.979	17	37	58	2	10
Torres	.987	84	139	240	5	42

Third Base	PCT	G	PO	A	E	DP
Choy Foo	.932	60	39	99	10	8
Cotto	.935	20	13	45	4	7
Kirby	1.000	3	1	6	0	0
Knox	.000	2	0	0	0	0
Osborn	.940	60	45	111	10	8

Shortstop	PCT	G	PO	A	E	DP
Choy Foo	1.000	4	6	10	0	1
Cotto	.927	18	30	46	6	11
Ochoa	.968	81	134	225	12	40
Torres	.927	39	51	114	13	26

Outfield	PCT	G	PO	A	E	DP
Cooper	1.000	36	67	1	0	0
Dyson	1.000	4	9	1	0	0
Jenkins	.947	20	34	2	2	0
Malave	1.000	39	60	12	0	1
Quintana	.977	83	152	16	4	1
Scott	.989	45	85	2	1	0
Sherrill	.970	46	92	5	3	1
Taveras	.978	109	267	5	6	0
Wright	1.000	51	70	5	0	0

LAKE COUNTY CAPTAINS — Low Class A

MIDWEST LEAGUE

BATTING	AVG	G	AB	R	H	2B	3B	HR	RBI	BB	SO	SB	CS	SLG	OBP	B	T	HT	WT	DOB	1st Yr	Resides
Aubrey, Michael	.348	38	138	22	48	13	0	5	19	14	22	0	0	.551	.409	L	L	6-0	195	4-15-82	2003	Shreveport, La.
Bastardo, Angel	.294	8	17	3	5	1	0	1	1	5	3	0	0	.529	.478	R	R	6-0	170	4-2-77	1997	Monroeville, Ohio
Colmenter, Jesus	.157	19	51	6	8	0	0	0	4	8	14	1	0	.157	.262	S	R	5-10	150	12-1-81	1998	Barquisimeto, Venez.
Cooper, Jason	.297	69	263	50	78	17	7	12	36	32	52	3	2	.551	.385	L	L	6-2	220	12-6-80	2002	Moses Lake, Wash.
De la Cruz, Chris	.264	108	402	44	106	9	2	0	49	37	55	6	7	.296	.327	S	R	6-0	160	5-3-82	2001	Monte Plata, D.R.
Francisco, Ben	.287	80	289	57	83	21	1	11	48	31	50	15	6	.481	.359	R	R	6-1	180	10-23-81	2002	Anaheim, Calif.
Garcia, Julio	.231	4	13	2	3	0	0	0	1	0	5	0	0	.231	.231	S	R	5-11	160	10-18-84	2002	Santo Domingo, D.R.
Herrera, Javier	.240	46	154	15	37	14	0	1	22	17	32	0	2	.351	.324	R	R	6-1	195	1-8-81	2003	Miami, Fla.
Johnson, Eric	.216	45	167	23	36	3	2	5	17	15	41	9	4	.347	.276	R	R	6-1	210	8-14-77	1999	Shallotte, N.C.
Kent, Bryan	.215	85	274	33	59	11	0	4	33	19	53	7	0	.299	.267	R	R	6-0	190	6-27-78	2001	Waco, Texas
Kirby, Brian	.213	17	61	10	13	5	0	4	6	6	22	0	0	.492	.284	L	R	6-2	190	8-3-79	2001	North Little Rock, Ark.
Knox, Matt	.245	68	237	33	58	17	2	10	43	25	35	0	2	.460	.332	R	R	6-4	210	12-29-79	2001	Lebanon, Pa.
Larkin, Shaun	.266	128	448	79	119	26	3	20	80	73	70	5	3	.471	.373	L	R	5-9	170	9-7-79	2002	Cypress, Calif.
McCullough, Clayton	.165	45	109	6	18	1	0	0	6	17	25	0	1	.174	.281	L	R	5-10	180	12-27-79	2002	Greenville, N.C.
McDonald, John	.000	1	3	0	0	0	0	0	0	0	0	0	0	.000	.000	R	R	5-11	170	9-24-74	1996	East Lyme, Conn.
Panther, Nathan	.285	108	428	88	122	22	6	13	52	45	75	38	11	.456	.356	L	L	6-2	180	7-12-81	2002	Muscatine, Iowa
Peavey, Bill	.260	22	77	10	20	1	0	5	14	15	19	0	0	.468	.376	L	L	6-4	250	1-16-79	2002	Brisbane, Calif.
Pinckney, Brandon	.429	3	7	2	3	0	0	0	1	2	1	0	0	.429	.600	R	R	5-10	165	4-12-82	2003	Elk Grove, Calif.
Rojas, Ricardo	.232	105	379	48	88	19	5	5	42	23	98	29	11	.348	.277	R	R	6-0	160	2-2-83	2000	Puerto Plata, D.R.

BATTING	AVG	G	AB	R	H	2B	3B	HR	RBI	BB	SO	SB	CS	SLG	OBP	B	T	HT	WT	DOB	1st Yr	Resides
Schilling, Micah	.231	109	360	53	83	15	5	0	43	55	92	6	6	.300	.336	L	R	5-11	180	12-27-82	2002	Clinton, La.
Sherrill, J.J.	.259	60	216	44	56	20	2	8	31	36	59	12	4	.481	.374	S	R	5-7	170	8-11-80	1999	Seaside, Calif.
Van Every, Jon	.193	59	197	22	38	9	2	5	24	12	89	15	5	.335	.261	L	L	6-1	190	11-27-79	2001	Brandon, Miss.
Vizquel, Omar	.071	4	14	0	1	0	0	0	0	1	2	1	0	.071	.133	S	R	5-9	180	4-24-67	1984	Issaquah, Wash.
Wallace, David	.291	64	223	39	65	14	2	6	36	37	52	5	1	.453	.413	R	R	6-4	220	10-17-79	2001	Brentwood, Tenn.

PITCHING	W	L	ERA	G	GS	CG	SV	IP	H	R	ER	BB	SO	AVG	B	T	HT	WT	DOB	1st Yr	Resides
Allen, Blake	6	3	2.24	36	0	0	5	76	65	23	19	25	74	.228	L	L	6-2	200	7-17-81	2002	Humboldt, Tenn.
Bere, Jason	0	0	6.75	1	1	0	0	4	7	3	3	0	1	.388	R	R	6-3	220	5-26-71	1990	North Andover, Mass.
Carmona, Fausto	17	4	2.06	24	24	1	0	148	117	48	34	14	83	.213	R	R	6-4	180	12-7-83	2001	Santo Domingo, D.R.
Casey, Reid	1	0	3.00	7	0	0	1	9	9	3	3	3	10	.272	R	R	6-1	170	2-1-80	2002	Kingsport, Tenn.
De la Cruz, Carlos	8	1	3.66	32	3	0	3	76	67	34	31	30	94	.230	R	R	6-1	160	1-14-82	1999	Santo Domingo, D.R.
Denham, Dan	5	2	3.08	14	14	0	0	73	75	28	25	22	63	.263	R	R	6-2	190	12-24-82	2001	Stateline, Nev.
Dittler, Jake	6	4	2.63	17	17	1	0	89	86	39	26	20	82	.243	R	R	6-4	220	11-24-82	2001	Henderson, Nev.
Douglas, Shea	5	3	1.37	34	0	0	10	86	46	14	13	30	104	.155	L	L	6-1	190	2-3-81	2002	Vicksburg, Miss.
Eisentrager, Dan	12	3	1.72	32	6	0	6	105	79	20	20	19	99	.210	R	R	6-3	170	12-30-80	2002	Elk Grove, Calif.
Hiraldo, Nelson	1	1	3.14	3	2	0	0	14	11	5	5	2	14	.211	R	R	6-0	160	9-17-83	2001	Puerto Plata, D.R.
Lara, Juan	1	4	5.00	16	3	0	1	45	51	31	25	26	37	.278	R	L	6-2	190	1-26-81	1999	Bani, D.R.
Martin, Kevin	1	1	1.07	28	0	0	4	34	27	5	4	7	29	.216	R	R	6-2	180	1-3-79	2001	Las Vegas, Nev.
Montano, Ignacio	2	0	3.38	21	0	0	2	40	45	20	15	8	36	.281	L	L	5-8	150	3-8-80	2001	Mopnterrey, Mexico
Pennington, Todd	2	1	0.72	36	0	0	20	37	14	3	3	17	65	.112	R	R	6-2	210	4-6-80	2001	McClure, Ill.
Perez, Randy	1	2	4.05	5	4	0	0	27	31	15	12	6	17	.298	L	L	6-1	170	4-13-80	1998	Sarasota, Fla.
Prahm, Ryan	1	1	1.32	5	1	0	0	14	5	3	2	7	14	.108	R	R	6-5	210	5-17-79	2000	Cedar Rapids, Iowa
Ramsey, Keith	13	6	2.99	24	24	3	0	145	146	54	48	15	108	.258	L	L	6-1	170	3-5-80	2002	Los Angeles, Calif.
Smith, Sean	11	4	3.71	26	26	0	0	121	100	62	50	67	101	.228	R	R	6-4	180	10-13-83	2002	Zephyr Cove, N.Y.
Southerland, Chip	0	0	0.00	1	0	0	0	1	2	0	0	0	2	.285	R	R	6-3	230	5-3-82	2002	Santa Ana, Calif.
Warden, Jim Ed	4	3	2.86	14	13	0	0	69	49	30	22	44	61	.196	R	R	6-7	190	5-7-79	2001	Murfreesboro, Tenn.
Wickman, Bob	0	0	0.00	2	2	0	0	2	1	0	0	0	4	.142	R	R	6-1	240	2-6-69	1990	Wausaukee, Wisc.

FIELDING

Catcher	PCT	G	PO	A	E	DP	PB
Bastardo	1.000	2	6	0	0	0	2
Herrera	.983	44	323	25	6	1	7
McCullough	.991	42	279	37	3	1	5
Wallace	.998	60	486	46	1	1	18

First Base	PCT	G	PO	A	E	DP
Aubrey	.994	37	331	30	2	30
Bastardo	.971	5	32	2	1	2
Colmenter	.986	9	66	4	1	6
Kent	.991	12	105	6	1	11
Kirby	.991	12	99	6	1	4
Knox	.986	64	574	39	9	26
Peavey	1.000	6	31	5	0	2

Second Base	PCT	G	PO	A	E	DP
Colmenter	1.000	6	9	17	0	2
Garcia	.941	4	9	7	1	3
Kent	1.000	23	41	54	0	14
Pinckney	.900	2	6	3	1	0
Schilling	.948	109	159	275	24	44

Third Base	PCT	G	PO	A	E	DP
Colmenter	.714	2	2	3	2	0
Kent	.962	19	12	39	2	2
Larkin	.924	120	55	200	21	7

Shortstop	PCT	G	PO	A	E	DP
Colmenter	.000	1	0	0	0	0
De La Cruz	.943	106	148	285	26	46
Kent	.963	33	43	87	5	11
McDonald	1.000	1	2	1	0	0
Pinckney	1.000	1	0	1	0	1
Vizquel	1.000	4	4	16	0	4

Outfield	PCT	G	PO	A	E	DP
Cooper	.966	58	85	1	3	0
Francisco	.993	65	131	4	1	0
Johnson	.981	32	49	3	1	0
Panther	.973	96	173	9	5	0
Rojas	.971	94	192	6	6	1
Sherrill	.971	37	67	0	2	0
Van Every	.964	41	53	1	2	0

MAHONING VALLEY SCRAPPERS — Short-Season Class A

NEW YORK-PENN LEAGUE

BATTING	AVG	G	AB	R	H	2B	3B	HR	RBI	BB	SO	SB	CS	SLG	OBP	B	T	HT	WT	DOB	1st Yr	Resides
Chauncey, Clint	.241	24	83	16	20	2	0	0	6	9	18	3	0	.265	.330	R	R	6-1	180	1-1-81	2000	Jacksonville, Fla.
Colmenter, Jesus	.249	65	249	25	62	9	1	1	29	18	39	2	3	.305	.298	S	R	5-10	150	12-1-81	1998	Barquisimebo, Venez.
Conroy, Mike	.292	73	288	34	84	12	6	7	44	17	47	4	3	.448	.330	L	L	6-3	190	10-3-82	2001	Fort Myers, Wash.
Cotto, Luis	.120	9	25	3	3	0	0	0	0	6	7	0	0	.120	.313	R	R	5-10	180	7-9-81	2000	Rio Piedras, P.R.
Garcia, Julio	.000	1	4	0	0	0	0	0	0	0	3	0	0	.000	.000	S	R	5-11	160	10-18-84	2002	Santo Domingo, D.R.
Garko, Ryan	.273	45	165	23	45	8	1	4	16	12	19	1	1	.406	.337	R	R	6-2	225	1-2-81	2003	Walnut, Calif.
Goldfield, Josh	.000	2	3	0	0	0	0	0	0	1	1	0	0	.000	.250	L	R	6-1	190	7-11-79	1999	Thousand Oaks, Calif.
Goleski, Ryan	.296	64	243	39	72	15	2	8	37	21	66	3	5	.473	.358	R	R	6-3	225	3-19-82	2003	Lake Orion, Mich.
Herrera, Javier	.289	12	45	9	13	3	0	0	8	5	11	0	0	.356	.353	R	R	6-1	195	1-8-81	2003	Miami, Fla.
Johnson, Eric	.281	14	57	14	16	3	1	2	7	6	16	10	1	.474	.397	R	R	6-1	210	8-14-77	1999	Shallotte, N.C.
Kouzmanoff, Kevin	.272	54	206	31	56	8	1	8	33	21	36	2	1	.437	.342	R	R	6-1	200	7-25-81	2003	Evergreen, Colo.
Lunetta, Anthony	.249	58	201	31	50	16	0	3	29	16	38	1	1	.373	.307	R	R	5-9	185	1-9-80	2003	Riverside, Calif.
Magruder, Chris	.182	3	11	5	2	2	0	0	0	2	1	2	0	.364	.357	S	R	5-11	200	4-26-77	1998	Mesa, Ariz.
McDonald, John	.000	1	2	1	0	0	0	0	0	1	0	0	0	.000	.333	R	R	5-11	170	9-24-74	1996	East Lyme, Conn.
Mulhern, Ryan	.279	59	229	32	64	25	1	5	30	19	68	6	2	.463	.340	R	R	6-2	195	11-29-80	2003	Highlands Ranch, Colo.
Noviskey, Josh	.256	38	125	17	32	7	2	2	20	16	28	0	1	.392	.343	S	R	6-4	210	3-15-83	2001	Newton, N.J.
Osborn, Pat	.625	2	8	1	5	1	0	0	0	2	0	1	0	.750	.727	R	R	6-3	210	2-27-81	2002	Gainesville, Fla.
Parker, Brett	.185	7	27	3	5	0	0	1	3	2	7	1	0	.296	.241	R	R	6-0	190	8-27-80	2003	Mobile, Ala.
Snyder, Brad	.284	62	225	52	64	11	6	6	31	41	82	14	5	.467	.393	L	L	6-3	200	5-25-82	2003	Bellevue, Ohio
Suarez, Cesar	.236	48	165	10	39	6	1	0	19	7	22	4	3	.285	.264	R	R	5-11	170	8-17-83	2000	Maracaibo, Venez.
Threinen, Scott	.222	17	45	6	10	3	0	0	3	11	9	0	0	.289	.379	R	R	6-0	190	8-23-81	2001	Mantorville, Minn.
Van Every, Jon	.262	22	65	13	17	6	1	1	9	9	23	7	4	.431	.367	L	L	6-1	190	11-27-79	2001	Brandon, Miss.

GAMES BY POSITION: C—Chauncey 23, Garko 34, Herrera 12, Noviskey 5. **1B**—Colmenter 5, Goldfield 1, Mulhern 47, Noviskey 15, Suarez 6, Threinen 3. **2B**—Colmenter 30, Cotto 1, Lunetta 26, Suarez 24. **3B**—Kouzmanoff 52, Noviskey 1, Osborn 1, Suarez 16, Threinen 7. **SS**—Colmenter 32, Cotto 8, Garcia 1, Lunetta 32, McDonald 1, Parker 7. **OF**—Conroy 71, Goleski 58, Johnson 11, Magruder 2, Mulhern 2, Noviskey 1, Snyder 62, Suarez 1, Van Every 15.

PITCHING	W	L	ERA	G	GS	CG	SV	IP	H	R	ER	BB	SO	AVG	B	T	HT	WT	DOB	1st Yr	Resides
Brandenburg, Adam	1	4	5.13	11	11	0	0	47	58	29	27	11	26	.300	L	L	6-5	225	8-17-81	2003	Snellville, Ga.
Burton, T.J.	4	2	6.79	14	14	0	0	64	83	52	48	28	39	.316	R	R	6-3	170	7-30-83	2001	Ottawa, Ontario
Casey, Reid	1	2	3.06	16	0	0	7	18	18	6	6	5	20	.268	R	R	6-1	170	2-1-80	2002	Kingsport, Tenn.
Cevette, Dan	0	2	8.22	2	2	0	0	8	14	11	7	5	3	.368	L	L	6-3	180	10-19-83	2002	Elkland, Pa.
Davis, Matt	4	4	1.54	23	0	0	0	47	34	17	8	11	40	.198	R	R	6-2	205	11-19-81	2003	Mason, Ohio
Durbin, Chad	1	1	2.25	2	2	0	0	12	9	4	3	3	8	.219	R	R	6-2	200	12-3-77	1996	Baton Rouge, La.
Garza, Alberto	0	0	0.00	1	0	0	0	1	0	0	0	0	2	.000	R	R	6-3	190	5-25-77	1996	Wapato, Wash.
Hanson, Adam	3	2	2.45	21	0	0	0	40	38	15	11	6	33	.246	R	R	6-2	195	8-6-81	2003	Medford, N.J.

PITCHING	W	L	ERA	G	GS	CG	SV	IP	H	R	ER	BB	SO	AVG	B	T	HT	WT	DOB	1st Yr	Resides
Harris, Mark	2	2	4.22	16	0	0	0	21	21	10	10	10	9	.256	R	R	6-3	205	2-17-81	2003	Loveland, Ohio
Hernandez, Michael	3	0	0.00	4	0	0	0	10	2	0	0	3	14	.060	L	L	6-4	190	4-8-81	2002	Fresno, Calif.
Lara, Juan	3	3	3.50	12	12	0	0	62	54	29	24	18	54	.234	R	L	6-2	190	1-26-81	1999	Bani, D.R.
Lincoln, Roger	3	0	2.64	17	4	0	0	44	43	13	13	11	41	.254	L	L	5-10	175	7-19-80	2003	Northford, Conn.
Montano, Ignacio	0	1	15.43	5	0	0	0	5	9	8	8	3	3	.391	L	L	5-8	150	3-8-80	2001	Monterrey, Mexico
Pereyra, Honeudis	1	1	2.59	21	0	0	1	42	32	16	12	27	51	.217	R	R	5-11	160	3-3-81	2001	Santo Domingo, D.R.
Perez, Randy	1	1	4.26	7	5	0	0	32	34	21	15	12	20	.276	L	L	6-1	170	4-13-80	1998	Sarasota, Fla.
Prahm, Ryan	2	0	2.89	3	1	0	0	9	5	4	3	4	14	.151	R	R	6-5	210	5-17-79	2000	Cedar Rapids, Iowa
Rich, Dan	1	1	1.61	18	0	0	4	22	15	5	4	5	20	.192	L	L	6-2	230	8-31-79	2002	Rocky River, Ohio
Rickert, Brandon	0	1	6.35	5	0	0	0	6	8	4	4	7	4	.320	R	R	6-3	200	1-23-81	2003	Deland, Fla.
Rigdon, Paul	0	0	3.60	3	3	0	0	10	11	4	4	3	8	.297	R	R	6-5	240	11-2-75	1996	Jacksonville, Fla.
Roehl, Scott	5	6	3.64	14	14	0	0	64	63	35	26	28	50	.264	R	R	6-1	195	8-19-81	2003	Somers, Wisc.
Southerland, Chip	0	0	4.09	8	0	0	3	11	6	5	5	4	20	.153	R	R	6-3	230	5-3-82	2002	Santa Ana, Calif.
Wallace, Shane	1	2	5.40	8	0	0	0	12	12	9	7	5	13	.260	L	L	6-2	200	12-29-80	1999	Carrollton, Texas
Weaver, Joe	1	0	2.91	13	6	0	0	34	36	20	11	11	21	.268	R	R	6-4	205	8-17-81	2003	Stillwater, Okla.
White, Chris	1	1	4.87	14	0	0	0	20	23	13	11	9	23	.283	L	L	6-1	190	9-11-80	2002	Frankfort, Ohio

BURLINGTON INDIANS

Rookie

APPALACHIAN LEAGUE

BATTING	AVG	G	AB	R	H	2B	3B	HR	RBI	BB	SO	SB	CS	SLG	OBP	B	T	HT	WT	DOB	1st Yr	Resides
Brock, Caleb	.288	33	118	19	34	3	2	1	15	10	13	3	1	.373	.361	R	R	5-11	200	3-30-80	2003	Lexington, Ky.
Casillas, Omar	.174	17	46	6	8	1	0	1	4	8	6	0	2	.261	.309	R	R	6-1	170	9-17-83	2002	Cidra, P.R.
Clem, Chris	.273	48	154	22	42	11	0	1	18	23	27	6	4	.364	.386	R	R	6-0	190	2-3-84	2002	Brisbane, Australia
Colin, Matt	.228	27	79	10	18	1	0	2	15	14	16	0	1	.316	.380	R	R	6-0	200	5-5-80	2003	Anaheim, Calif.
Cruz, Jose	.253	48	166	26	42	10	4	3	27	24	25	7	2	.416	.358	S	R	6-1	180	10-21-82	2001	Rio Piedras, P.R.
Encarnacion, Teodoro	.272	54	184	24	50	8	0	4	28	14	44	1	2	.380	.330	R	R	6-2	190	3-26-83	2001	Santo Domingo, D.R.
Garcia, Julio	.220	30	100	11	22	2	1	0	7	11	24	5	0	.260	.297	S	R	5-11	160	10-18-84	2002	Santo Domingo, D.R.
Garcia, Junior	.256	37	129	21	33	4	4	3	17	6	44	11	2	.419	.294	R	R	6-0	170	1-1-83	2000	Villa Altagracia, D.R.
Hodge, Luis	.235	51	196	23	46	7	3	4	29	10	46	2	2	.362	.283	R	R	6-1	170	2-13-82	2000	San Pedro de Macoris, D.R.
Longworth, Chad	.206	35	107	25	22	4	3	3	7	14	29	7	0	.383	.295	R	R	6-3	190	6-11-83	2002	Wise, Va.
Munsey, Tanner	.111	9	9	0	1	0	0	0	1	3	4	0	0	.111	.385	R	R	6-2	200	12-29-81	2003	Durham, N.H.
Pacheco, Fernando	.208	53	183	19	38	13	0	3	19	15	60	0	0	.328	.272	L	L	6-1	190	10-1-84	2002	San Ysidro, Calif.
Pinckney, Brandon	.276	62	257	41	71	11	0	1	27	23	23	8	2	.331	.337	R	R	5-10	165	4-12-82	2003	Elk Grove, Calif.
Reyes, Argenis	.278	39	151	26	42	2	0	0	9	7	23	14	1	.291	.321	S	R	5-10	160	9-25-82	2001	Santiago, D.R.
Valdes, Juan	.223	39	130	14	29	3	1	1	14	10	33	5	3	.285	.275	S	R	6-0	150	6-22-85	2003	Manati, P.R.
Vasquez, Domingo	.222	60	221	18	49	10	0	2	29	17	44	0	1	.294	.279	R	R	6-1	200	9-16-83	2000	Guarcara,Venez.
Woodson, Mike	.214	26	84	11	18	5	0	1	7	5	24	1	0	.310	.272	R	R	5-11	180	12-11-84	2002	Salinas, P.R.

GAMES BY POSITION: C—Brock 32, Casillas 13, Munsey 7, Woodson 26. **1B**—Pacheco 53, Vasquez 19. **2B**—Clem 16, Jul. Garcia 20, Reyes 39. **3B**—Clem 30, Jul. Garcia 4, Vasquez 41. **SS**—Clem 1, Jul. Garcia 6, Pinckney 62. **OF**—Colin 6, Cruz 39, Encarnacion 40, Jul. Garcia 1, Jun. Garcia 31, Hodge 44, Longworth 23, Munsey 1, Valdes 34.

PITCHING	W	L	ERA	G	GS	CG	SV	IP	H	R	ER	BB	SO	AVG	B	T	HT	WT	DOB	1st Yr	Resides
Amador, Jonathan	0	0	4.26	16	0	0	0	19	16	10	9	14	22	.222	R	R	6-0	170	1-1-83	2002	Barahona, D.R.
Ashabraner, Bo	2	1	6.06	17	0	0	2	16	20	11	11	7	18	.294	R	R	6-7	230	2-19-81	2003	Yorba Linda, Calif.
Cevette, Dan	2	5	3.45	13	13	0	0	57	58	27	22	29	48	.261	L	L	6-3	180	10-19-83	2002	Elkland, Pa.
De los Santos, Richard	3	4	6.41	12	0	0	1	39	45	32	28	10	40	.284	R	R	6-1	170	6-1-84	2001	Elias Pina, D.R.
Guzman, Dan	1	1	3.00	17	0	0	1	30	26	11	10	17	36	.224	R	R	6-1	180	2-5-82	1999	Caracas, Venez.
Haynes, Matt	1	0	2.50	17	0	0	2	36	25	11	10	29	57	.190	L	R	6-3	180	4-18-83	2002	Maroochydore, Australia
Hiraldo, Nelson	6	1	3.81	12	6	0	0	52	48	23	22	11	52	.241	R	R	6-0	160	9-17-83	2001	Puerto Plata, D.R.
Laffey, Aaron	3	1	2.91	9	4	0	0	34	22	13	11	15	46	.183	L	L	6-0	170	4-15-85	2003	Cumberland, Md.
Miller, Adam	0	4	4.96	10	10	0	0	33	30	20	18	9	23	.250	R	R	6-4	175	11-26-84	2003	McKinney, Texas
Mujica, Ed	2	6	4.37	14	10	0	0	56	57	31	27	20	41	.275	R	R	6-2	180	5-10-84	2002	Yagua, Venez.
Navarro, Rodolfo	3	2	5.79	14	0	0	1	23	36	20	15	3	10	.352	R	R	6-2	170	12-17-82	2002	Juarez, Mexico
Perez, Rafael	9	3	1.70	13	12	0	0	69	56	23	13	16	63	.220	L	L	6-3	170	5-15-82	2002	Santo Domingo, D.R.
Pesco, Nick	3	1	1.82	13	13	0	0	54	36	16	11	22	55	.187	R	R	6-6	200	9-17-83	2003	Lodi, Calif.
Santana, Hector	0	2	7.40	13	0	0	1	21	23	19	17	11	18	.277	R	R	6-0	160	7-13-82	2000	San Pedro de Macoris, D.R.
Santos, Reid	1	0	4.40	14	0	0	2	29	29	15	14	6	25	.263	L	L	6-1	170	8-24-82	2003	Kaneohe, Hawaii
Schultz, Jimmy	1	0	4.76	13	0	0	1	17	25	10	9	7	14	.328	R	R	6-3	170	9-12-82	2001	Houston, Texas
Southerland, Chip	0	0	0.53	12	0	0	4	17	10	1	1	3	24	.163	R	R	6-3	230	5-3-82	2002	Santa Ana, Calif.

COLORADO ROCKIES

BY BARNEY HUTCHINSON

The Rockies increased their number of wins from 73 in 2002 to 74 in 2003, yet it did not feel like improvement at all.

In fact, the prevailing feeling in Colorado was how the 2003 season had more negatives than positives. The Rockies had their third consecutive losing season and their fifth in the last six seasons. Attendance declined for the seventh consecutive season as 2.3 million fans came out to Coors Field, which brought on the organization's new financial constraints.

"We need to get better," Rockies manager Clint Hurdle said. "This is an active sports town. I've been at other venues (in Denver). I watched the Avalanche games and the success they've had; they fill the can over there. That place is loud and electric. Invesco (Field, home of the Broncos), loud and electric. This place has been loud and electric. It echoes now.

"That's what we have to look to, to find ways to get the rear ends back in the seats. That's the biggest challenge. That's the thing I'm looking forward to, that I will be here when this place gets loud and electric again."

Adding Preston Wilson from the Marlins in the trade of Mike Hampton and Juan Pierre put a solid cleanup hitter in the lineup. Wilson led the National League in RBIs with 141. Left fielder Jay Payton gave the Rockies a .300 hitter with 28 home runs.

Among the winter of 2002-03's bargains, veteran lefthander Darren Oliver turned into the staff's leading winner with a 13-11 record. Third baseman Chris Stynes displayed the hard-nosed attitude the team loved and a solid glove, but his batting average faded to .255. The Rockies have two young lefthanded relief pitchers in Brian Fuentes and Javier Lopez. For the first half of the season, righthander Shawn Chacon turned himself into the best starting pitcher the Rockies have had.

ORGANIZATION LEADERS

BATTING

*AVG	Rene Reyes, Colorado Springs	.343
R	Jeff Salazar, Visalia/Asheville	110
H	Cory Sullivan, Tulsa	167
TB	Jayson Nix, Visalia	267
2B	Jayson Nix, Visalia	46
3B	Sandy Almonte, Tri-City	9
HR	Jeff Salazar, Visalia/Asheville	29
RBI	Jeff Salazar, Visalia/Asheville	98
BB	Jeff Salazar, Visalia/Asheville	77
SO	Justin Lincoln, Visalia	151
SB	K.J. Hendricks, Asheville	50
*SLG	Andy Tracy, Tulsa	.563
*OBP	Ryan Shealy, Visalia	.391

PITCHING

W	Justin Hampson, Tulsa/Visalia	14
L	Ben Crockett, Visalia/Asheville	12
#ERA	Steve Reba, Asheville	2.66
G	Jentry Beckstead, Asheville	63
CG	Cory Vance, Colorado Springs	3
SV	Brad Clontz, Colorado Springs	30
IP	Ben Crockett, Visalia/Asheville	184
BB	Ubaldo Jimenez, Visalia/Asheville	68
SO	Jeff Francis, Visalia	153

*Minimum 250 At-Bats #Minimum 75 Innings

Todd Helton

Jeff Salazar

PLAYERS of the YEAR

MAJOR LEAGUE: Todd Helton, 1b

Helton hit .358 in 2003, narrowly missing out on the National League batting title. He also finished among league leaders in runs (135), hits (209), total bases (367), doubles (49), walks (111), slugging percentage (.630) and on-base percentage (.458).

MINOR LEAGUE: Jeff Salazar, of

Known more for his speed and defensive ability, Salazar took advantage of McCormick Field's 300-foot right-field fence to lead the South Atlantic League with 29 home runs and 98 RBIs. He also swiped 28 bases for Class A Asheville.

What went wrong is a longer list. Larry Walker had an off year, hitting .284-16-79 and playing the whole season with injuries. Walker had shoulder surgery after the season, and doctors also repaired damaged meniscus in his right knee. The Rockies hope a repaired Walker, 37, will return to form in 2004. He is the highest-paid player on the team at $12.5 million.

Injuries also ruined $11 million lefty Denny Neagle's season, limiting him to seven starts and a 2-4 record. Todd Jones and Jose Jimenez were supposed to hold down the back end of the bullpen, but Jones' ineffectiveness led to his release and Jimenez lost his closer job in July.

Young pitchers Jason Jennings, Denny Stark, Aaron Cook, Jason Young and Chin-hui Tsao did not enjoy as much success as expected, and the Rockies need improvement from all of them to have a better team.

The Rockies had their second-best home record (49-32) but their worst-ever road record (25-56), further evidence that the more they tailor their team for Coors Field, the worse they do outside Denver.

"We have regained some home-field dominance," Hurdle said. "I think we have cracked some hard rock in some different areas about who we are, what we are, what we need to become."

The farm system produced both in the standings and in talent. Rene Reyes, Clint Barmes, Tsao and Garrett Atkins all received a taste of the major leagues with an eye toward bigger contributions in 2004. The system has solid talent on the way with lefthander Jeff Francis, second baseman Jayson Nix and third baseman Ian Stewart making strong showings at the lower levels. Francis was the team's 2002 first-round pick, while Stewart was the 2003 top choice.

COLORADO ROCKIES

Manager: Clint Hurdle.

2003 Record: 74-88, .457 (4th, NL West).

BATTING	AVG	G	AB	R	H	2B	3B	HR	RBI	BB	SO	SB	CS	SLG	OBP	B	T	HT	WT	DOB	1st Yr	Resides
Allen, Luke	.000	2	2	0	0	0	0	0	0	0	0	0	0	.000	.000	L	R	6-2	220	8-4-78	1996	Covington, Ga.
Atkins, Garrett	.159	25	69	6	11	2	0	0	4	3	14	0	0	.188	.205	R	R	6-3	210	12-12-79	2000	Irvine, Calif.
Barmes, Clint	.320	12	25	2	8	2	0	0	2	0	10	0	0	.400	.357	R	R	6-0	175	3-6-79	2000	Vincennes, Ind.
Bellhorn, Mark	.236	48	110	12	26	3	0	0	4	21	32	2	3	.264	.368	S	R	6-1	200	8-23-74	1995	Oviedo, Fla.
2-team (51 Chicago)	.221	99	249	27	55	10	1	2	26	50	78	5	6	.293	.353							
Belliard, Ron	.277	116	447	73	124	31	2	8	50	49	71	7	2	.409	.351	R	R	5-8	190	4-7-75	1994	Miami, Fla.
Butler, Brent	.211	37	90	13	19	3	1	1	4	7	13	1	0	.300	.276	R	R	6-0	180	2-11-78	1996	Laurinburg, N.C.
Estalella, Bobby	.200	46	140	17	28	7	0	7	21	19	55	2	0	.400	.294	R	R	6-1	225	8-23-74	1993	Weston, Fla.
Helton, Todd	.358	160	583	135	209	49	5	33	117	111	72	0	4	.630	.458	L	L	6-2	205	8-20-73	1995	Thornton, Colo.
Hernandez, Jose	.237	69	257	33	61	6	1	8	27	27	95	1	1	.362	.308	R	R	6-1	190	7-14-69	1987	Dorado, P.R.
Jennings, Jason	.222	33	54	3	12	3	0	0	3	5	16	0	0	.278	.283	L	R	6-2	245	7-17-78	1999	Rockwall, Texas
Johnson, Charles	.230	108	356	49	82	20	0	20	61	49	84	1	3	.455	.320	R	R	6-3	250	7-20-71	1992	Plantation Acres, Fla.
Kapler, Gabe	.224	39	67	10	15	2	0	0	4	8	18	2	0	.254	.307	R	R	6-2	210	7-31-75	1995	Sherman Oaks, Calif.
Norton, Greg	.263	114	179	19	47	15	0	6	31	16	47	2	1	.447	.325	S	R	6-1	200	7-6-72	1993	Denver, Colo.
Oliver, Darren	.254	35	67	6	17	3	0	1	8	3	17	0	0	.343	.296	R	L	6-2	220	10-6-70	1988	Southlake, Texas
Ozuna, Pablo	.200	17	40	5	8	1	0	0	2	2	6	3	0	.225	.273	R	R	5-10	185	8-25-74	1996	Boca Chica, D.R.
Payton, Jay	.302	157	600	93	181	32	5	28	89	43	77	6	4	.512	.354	R	R	5-10	185	11-22-72	1994	Zanesville, Ohio
Pellow, Kit	.444	11	18	6	8	3	1	1	4	0	4	0	0	.889	.476	R	R	6-1	205	8-28-73	1996	Olathe, Kan.
Petrick, Ben	.000	3	2	0	0	0	0	0	0	0	1	0	0	.000	.000	R	R	6-0	200	4-7-77	1996	Hillsboro, Ore.
Reyes, Rene	.259	53	116	13	30	7	1	2	7	5	19	2	1	.388	.287	S	R	5-11	215	2-21-78	1996	Margarita, Venez.
Richard, Chris	.222	19	27	3	6	1	1	1	3	3	6	0	1	.444	.300	L	L	6-2	200	6-7-74	1995	San Diego, Calif.
Romero, Mandy	.429	3	7	2	3	1	0	0	0	0	1	0	0	.571	.556	S	R	5-11	195	10-19-67	1988	Miami, Fla.
Stynes, Chris	.255	138	443	71	113	31	3	11	73	48	76	3	1	.413	.335	R	R	5-10	205	1-19-73	1991	Deerfield Beach, Fla.
Sweeney, Mark	.258	67	97	13	25	9	0	2	14	9	27	0	1	.412	.321	L	L	6-1	215	10-26-69	1991	Scottsdale, Ariz.
Uribe, Juan	.253	87	316	45	80	19	3	10	33	17	60	7	2	.427	.297	R	R	5-11	175	7-22-79	1997	Palenque, D.R.
Vaughn, Greg	.189	22	37	8	7	3	0	3	5	8	13	0	0	.514	.326	R	R	6-0	200	7-3-65	1986	Elk Grove, Calif.
Walker, Larry	.284	143	454	86	129	25	7	16	79	98	87	7	4	.476	.422	L	R	6-3	335	12-1-66	1985	Evergreen, Colo.
Wilson, Preston	.282	155	600	94	169	43	1	36	141	54	139	14	7	.537	.343	R	R	6-2	210	7-19-74	1993	Miami, Fla.
Womack, Tony	.190	21	79	9	15	2	0	0	5	0	9	3	1	.215	.200	L	R	5-9	170	9-25-69	1991	Greensboro, N.C.
Zaun, Greg	.261	15	46	6	12	1	0	3	8	5	7	0	1	.478	.333	S	R	5-10	190	4-14-71	1989	Houston, Texas
2-team (59 Houston)	.229	74	166	15	38	8	0	4	21	19	21	1	1	.349	.309							

PITCHING	W	L	ERA	G	GS	CG	SV	IP	H	R	ER	BB	SO	AVG	B	T	HT	WT	DOB	1st Yr	Resides
Bernero, Adam	0	2	5.23	31	0	0	0	33	33	22	19	13	26	.266	R	R	6-4	210	11-28-76	1999	Elk Grove, Calif.
Chacon, Shawn	11	8	4.60	23	23	0	0	137	124	73	70	58	93	.242	R	R	6-3	210	12-23-77	1996	Greeley, Colo.
Cook, Aaron	4	6	6.02	43	16	1	0	124	160	89	83	57	43	.317	R	R	6-3	170	2-8-79	1997	Hamilton, Ohio
Cruz, Nelson	3	5	7.21	20	7	0	0	54	65	43	43	11	38	.300	R	R	6-1	185	9-13-72	1989	Washington, D.C.
Darensbourg, Vic	0	0	0.00	3	0	0	0	2	4	1	0	0	0	.333	L	L	5-8	170	11-13-70	1992	Henderson, Nev.
Elarton, Scott	4	4	6.27	11	10	0	0	52	73	46	36	20	20	.328	R	R	6-8	240	2-23-76	1994	Denver, Colo.
Fuentes, Brian	3	3	2.75	75	0	0	4	75	64	24	23	34	82	.231	L	L	6-4	220	8-9-75	1996	Merced, Calif.
Jennings, Jason	12	13	5.11	32	32	1	0	181	212	115	103	88	119	.298	L	R	6-2	245	7-17-78	1999	Rockwall, Texas
Jimenez, Jose	2	10	5.22	63	7	0	20	102	137	62	59	32	45	.321	R	R	6-3	230	7-7-73	1992	Boca China, D.R.
Jones, Todd	1	4	8.24	33	1	0	0	39	61	39	36	18	28	.360	S	R	6-3	230	4-24-68	1989	Pell City, Ala.
Lopez, Javier	4	1	3.70	75	0	0	1	58	58	25	24	12	40	.257	L	L	6-4	200	7-11-77	1998	Fairfax, Va.
Miceli, Danny	0	2	5.66	14	0	0	0	21	24	13	13	9	18	.285	R	R	6-0	225	9-9-70	1990	Winter Springs, Fla.
Miller, Matt	0	0	2.08	4	0	0	0	4	5	1	1	2	5	.312	R	R	6-3	215	11-23-71	1997	Greenville, Miss.
Neagle, Denny	2	4	7.90	7	7	0	0	35	47	31	31	12	21	.319	L	L	6-3	225	9-13-68	1989	Morrison, Colo.
Oliver, Darren	13	11	5.04	33	32	1	0	180	201	108	101	61	88	.283	R	L	6-2	220	10-6-70	1988	Southlake, Texas
Reed, Steve	5	3	3.27	67	0	0	0	63	59	24	23	26	39	.254	R	R	6-2	210	3-11-66	1988	Golden, Colo.
Roa, Joe	0	0	4.05	4	0	0	0	7	7	3	3	0	4	.269	R	R	6-2	200	10-11-71	1989	Royal Oak, Mich.
Sanchez, Jesus	0	0	9.00	9	0	0	0	8	11	8	8	4	2	.323	L	L	5-10	165	10-11-74	1992	Nizao Bani, D.R.
Speier, Justin	3	1	4.05	72	0	0	9	73	73	37	33	23	66	.257	R	R	6-4	205	11-6-73	1995	Paradise Valley, Ariz.
Stark, Denny	3	3	5.83	17	13	0	0	79	98	57	51	33	30	.305	R	R	6-2	210	10-27-74	1996	Edgerton, Ohio
Tsao, Chin-Hui	3	3	6.02	9	8	0	0	43	48	30	29	20	29	.284	R	R	6-2	175	6-2-81	1999	Hualien, Taiwan
Vance, Cory	1	3	5.60	9	3	0	0	27	31	19	17	10	12	.287	L	L	6-1	195	6-20-79	2000	Vandalia, Ohio
Young, Jason	0	2	8.44	8	3	0	0	21	34	22	20	9	18	.354	R	R	6-5	215	9-28-79	2001	Bodega, Calif.

FIELDING

Catcher	PCT	G	PO	A	E	DP	PB
Estalella	.985	46	248	19	4	2	3
Johnson	.993	107	561	34	4	5	6
Pellow	1.000	7	14	0	0	0	1
Petrick	.000	1	0	0	0	0	0
Romero	.938	2	13	2	1	0	0
Zaun	.973	14	71	2	2	0	1

First Base	PCT	G	PO	A	E	DP
Bellhorn	1.000	1	1	1	0	0
Helton	.993	159	1418	156	11	149
Norton	1.000	9	20	2	0	0
Pellow	1.000	1	9	0	0	0
Richard	1.000	1	3	1	0	1
Sweeney	1.000	8	12	0	0	2

Second Base	PCT	G	PO	A	E	DP
Bellhorn	.973	20	31	41	2	6
Belliard	.973	113	224	311	15	79
Butler	.988	20	32	51	1	10
Ozuna	.981	8	22	31	1	9
Stynes	1.000	5	7	10	0	3
Uribe	.985	11	25	40	1	10
Womack	1.000	7	12	14	0	4

Third Base	PCT	G	PO	A	E	DP
Atkins	.850	19	9	25	6	0
Bellhorn	.966	15	6	22	1	1
Butler	.714	8	1	4	2	0
Norton	.924	34	24	49	6	3
Stynes	.972	119	92	225	9	22

Shortstop	PCT	G	PO	A	E	DP
Barmes	.958	12	19	27	2	6
Bellhorn	1.000	6	1	9	0	1
Butler	1.000	4	4	7	0	2
Hernandez	.983	69	116	181	5	49
Ozuna	.900	3	3	6	1	0
Uribe	.972	74	143	242	11	57
Womack	.959	14	16	31	2	5

Outfield	PCT	G	PO	A	E	DP
Bellhorn	1.000	5	2	0	0	0
Kapler	.970	29	29	3	1	1

Norton	.000	3	0	0	0	0
Ozuna	1.000	5	1	0	0	0
Payton	.987	151	306	6	4	1
Pellow	1.000	1	1	0	0	0
Petrick	1.000	2	2	1	0	0
Reyes	.964	36	50	3	2	0
Richard	1.000	3	5	0	0	0
Sweeney	1.000	17	18	0	0	0
Uribe	1.000	1	3	0	0	0
Vaughn	1.000	7	12	0	0	0
Walker	.983	131	229	8	4	2
Wilson	.980	155	331	8	7	1

FARM SYSTEM

Director, Player Development: Bill Geivett.

Class	Farm Team	League	W	L	Pct.	Finish*	Manager	First Yr.
AAA	Colorado Springs (Colo.) Sky Sox	Pacific Coast	73	70	.510	6th (16)	Rick Sofield	1993
AA	Tulsa (Okla.) Drillers	Texas	74	64	.536	2nd (8)	Marv Foley	2003
High A	Visalia (Calif.) Oaks	California	79	61	.564	1st (10)	Stu Cole	2003
Low A	Asheville (N.C.) Tourists	South Atlantic	74	65	.532	6th (16)	Joe Mikulik	1994
SS A	Tri-City (Wash.) Dust Devils	Northwest	33	43	.434	6th (8)	Ron Gideon	2001
Rookie	Casper (Wyo.) Rockies	Pioneer	28	48	.368	7th (8)	P.J. Carey	2001

*Finish in overall standings (No. of teams in league)

COLORADO SPRINGS SKY SOX — Class AAA

PACIFIC COAST LEAGUE

BATTING	AVG	G	AB	R	H	2B	3B	HR	RBI	BB	SO	SB	CS	SLG	OBP	B	T	HT	WT	DOB	1st Yr	Resides
Allen, Luke	.274	127	438	65	120	21	3	6	45	51	78	9	12	.377	.346	L	R	6-2	220	8-4-78	1996	Covington, Ga.
Alviso, Jerome	.314	38	102	12	32	3	0	0	6	4	7	1	2	.343	.343	S	R	6-1	160	9-4-75	1997	Livermore, Calif.
Atkins, Garrett	.319	118	439	80	140	30	1	13	67	45	52	2	4	.481	.382	R	R	6-3	210	12-12-79	2000	Irvine, Calif.
Barmes, Clint	.276	136	493	63	136	35	1	7	54	22	63	12	7	.394	.316	R	R	6-0	175	3-6-79	2000	Vincennes, Ind.
Bellhorn, Mark	.389	16	54	11	21	5	1	4	16	11	10	2	0	.741	.485	S	R	6-1	200	8-23-74	1995	Oviedo, Fla.
Belliard, Ron	.263	6	19	2	5	1	0	0	0	0	1	0	0	.316	.263	R	R	5-8	190	4-7-75	1994	Miami, Fla.
Butler, Brent	.332	54	205	37	68	19	1	6	27	19	20	0	1	.522	.399	R	R	6-0	180	2-11-78	1996	Laurinburg, N.C.
Casanova, Raul	.301	60	193	25	58	20	0	4	36	14	21	0	0	.466	.349	S	R	6-0	220	8-23-72	1990	Ponce, P.R.
Evans, Tom	.111	5	9	1	1	0	0	0	1	0	2	0	0	.111	.111	R	R	6-1	200	7-9-74	1992	Issaquah, Wash.
2-team (6 Iowa)	.158	11	19	2	3	1	0	0	1	1	2	0	0	.211	.200							
Freeman, Choo	.254	103	327	44	83	9	4	7	36	23	71	2	8	.370	.315	R	R	6-2	200	10-20-79	1998	Dallas, Texas
Kapler, Gabe	.171	13	35	5	6	2	1	0	2	8	10	4	0	.286	.333	R	R	6-2	210	7-31-75	1995	Sherman Oaks, Calif.
Lopez, Luis	.207	47	140	14	29	10	0	3	18	9	29	0	1	.343	.265	S	R	5-11	175	9-4-70	1988	Cidra, P.R.
Magee, Wendell	.328	38	134	15	44	10	0	3	21	5	22	1	2	.470	.357	R	R	6-0	220	8-3-72	1994	Hattiesburg, Miss.
Matos, Pascual	.231	10	26	5	6	1	0	2	5	2	11	0	0	.500	.276	R	R	6-2	180	12-23-74	1992	Barahona, D.R.
Morales, Willie	.208	21	77	11	16	3	0	6	18	0	17	0	1	.481	.208	R	R	5-10	180	9-7-72	1993	Tucson, Ariz.
3-team (11 Tuc., 16 Mem.)	.236	48	174	19	41	9	2	9	31	5	42	1	1	.466	.264							
Newhan, David	.348	72	244	43	85	17	2	3	28	16	36	6	4	.471	.392	L	R	5-10	180	9-7-73	1995	Yorba Linda, Calif.
Ozuna, Pablo	.269	56	219	30	59	13	7	1	17	9	23	12	6	.406	.300	R	R	5-10	185	8-25-74	1996	Boca Chica, D.R.
Pellow, Kit	.291	89	320	48	93	15	1	19	57	25	75	2	1	.522	.363	R	R	6-1	205	8-28-73	1996	Olathe, Kan.
Petrick, Ben	.259	80	228	38	59	16	3	11	40	26	53	4	4	.500	.333	R	R	6-0	200	4-7-77	1996	Hillsboro, Ore.
Post, Dave	.259	12	27	2	7	0	1	0	2	3	2	1	0	.333	.333	R	R	5-11	170	9-3-73	1992	Kingston, N.Y.
Reyes, Rene	.343	98	370	60	127	23	3	6	50	22	56	12	8	.470	.380	S	R	5-11	215	2-21-78	1996	Margarita, Venez.
Romero, Mandy	.296	81	250	30	74	11	1	4	31	18	38	0	0	.396	.341	S	R	5-11	195	10-19-67	1988	Miami, Fla.
Sakamoto, Mitsuru	.000	1	1	0	0	0	0	0	0	0	0	0	0	.000	.000	L	R	6-2	170	10-7-80	2002	Fukuoka, Japan
Sullivan, Kevin	.167	4	12	1	2	1	0	0	2	0	5	0	0	.250	.154	R	R	6-1	210	10-4-77	2000	Stevens Point, Wisc.
Sweeney, Mark	.297	51	165	24	49	10	1	5	35	34	32	1	4	.461	.407	L	L	6-1	215	10-26-69	1991	Scottsdale, Ariz.
Vaughn, Greg	.302	35	116	26	35	7	1	12	35	16	28	1	0	.690	.388	R	R	6-0	200	7-3-65	1986	Elk Grove, Calif.

PITCHING	W	L	ERA	G	GS	CG	SV	IP	H	R	ER	BB	SO	AVG	B	T	HT	WT	DOB	1st Yr	Resides
Belitz, Todd	0	0	10.80	3	0	0	0	5	9	6	6	2	3	.409	L	L	6-3	200	10-23-75	1997	Spokane, Wash.
Bevel, Bobby	1	2	3.60	26	0	0	0	30	31	18	12	12	20	.267	L	L	5-10	180	10-10-73	1995	West Plains, Mo.
Chacon, Shawn	0	0	6.00	1	1	0	0	3	5	2	2	0	2	.384	R	R	6-3	210	12-23-77	1996	Greeley, Colo.
Clontz, Brad	3	2	3.42	57	0	0	30	55	54	31	21	26	63	.252	R	R	6-1	195	4-25-71	1992	Alpharetta, Ga.
Cook, Aaron	1	1	2.25	2	2	1	0	16	10	4	4	4	12	.175	R	R	6-3	170	2-8-79	1997	Hamilton, Ohio
Cruz, Nelson	1	2	7.20	4	4	0	0	15	24	18	12	3	10	.369	R	R	6-1	185	9-13-72	1989	Washington, D.C.
Darensbourg, Vic	2	2	3.57	20	0	0	0	23	24	13	9	5	15	.272	L	L	5-8	170	11-13-70	1992	Henderson, Nev.
Darnell, Paul	0	1	0.00	1	0	0	0	2	1	1	0	2	1	.200	R	L	6-6	200	6-4-76	1999	Hubbard, Texas
Elarton, Scott	6	8	5.31	20	20	0	0	119	146	81	70	39	92	.297	R	R	6-8	240	2-23-76	1994	Denver, Colo.
Esslinger, Cam	0	1	9.82	6	0	0	0	7	10	9	8	12	8	.344	R	R	5-11	180	12-28-76	1999	Hewitt, N.J.
Flores, Randy	10	8	4.98	28	24	0	0	143	156	89	79	67	116	.278	L	L	6-0	180	7-31-75	1997	Pico Rivera, Calif.
Gissell, Chris	8	4	3.55	38	10	0	1	109	96	53	43	35	82	.232	R	R	6-5	210	1-4-78	1996	Vancouver, Wash.
Looney, Brian	2	1	7.53	3	3	0	0	14	23	17	12	6	11	.365	L	L	5-10	180	9-26-69	1991	Cheshire, Conn.
Michalak, Chris	7	9	4.41	24	18	0	1	120	138	76	59	44	72	.289	L	L	6-2	195	1-4-71	1993	Keller, Texas
Miller, Matt	5	0	2.13	61	0	0	3	63	46	17	15	23	83	.204	R	R	6-3	215	11-23-71	1997	Greenville, Miss.
Neagle, Denny	3	0	3.38	4	4	0	0	24	28	10	9	4	16	.291	L	L	6-3	225	9-13-68	1989	Morrison, Colo.
Pena, Jesus	0	2	4.50	11	1	0	0	12	15	8	6	9	9	.300	L	L	6-0	170	3-8-75	1993	Santo Domingo, D.R.
Perisho, Matt	1	1	3.42	8	4	0	0	24	25	16	9	14	15	.260	L	L	6-0	200	6-8-75	1993	Chandler, Ariz.
2-team (4 Tucson)	1	1	4.28	12	4	0	0	27	29	20	13	16	17	.263							
Sanchez, Jesus	2	0	3.98	46	3	0	2	63	61	28	28	26	52	.257	L	L	5-10	165	10-11-74	1992	Nizao Bani, D.R.
Smith, Brian	0	4	10.45	9	0	0	0	10	21	16	12	5	9	.403	R	R	5-10	190	7-19-72	1994	Toney, Ala.
Stark, Denny	0	2	5.95	4	4	0	0	20	22	14	13	9	10	.275	R	R	6-2	210	10-27-74	1996	Edgerton, Ohio
Thompson, Doug	1	1	6.32	10	0	0	0	16	13	12	11	11	11	.220	R	R	6-0	190	7-22-76	1998	Biloxi, Miss.
Vance, Cory	9	11	4.63	24	24	3	0	157	179	89	81	50	96	.293	L	L	6-1	195	6-20-79	2000	Vandalia, Ohio
Ward, Bryan	0	1	16.39	9	0	0	0	9	19	17	17	6	6	.422	L	L	6-2	200	1-25-72	1993	Mt. Holly, N.J.
Whiteside, Matt	3	0	4.66	21	0	0	1	29	26	16	15	8	15	.238	R	R	6-0	200	8-8-67	1990	Arlington, Texas
Young, Jason	6	7	3.95	23	21	2	0	116	128	63	51	37	99	.271	R	R	6-5	215	9-28-79	2001	Bodega, Calif.
Young, Tim	2	0	2.49	29	0	0	0	25	21	8	7	8	27	.228	L	L	5-9	170	10-15-73	1996	Bristol, Fla.

FIELDING

Catcher	PCT	G	PO	A	E	DP	PB
Casanova	.977	36	231	19	6	2	1
Matos	.984	8	56	7	1	0	1
Morales	1.000	11	82	5	0	0	0
Pellow	.994	24	143	15	1	1	7
Petrick	.955	20	82	2	4	0	0
Romero	.983	59	386	22	7	4	3
Sullivan	1.000	2	6	0	0	0	1

First Base	PCT	G	PO	A	E	DP
Alviso	1.000	8	35	5	0	2
Atkins	1.000	3	22	1	0	2
Butler	.989	12	84	2	1	5
Casanova	.980	11	95	3	2	9
Lopez	1.000	5	20	1	0	1
Morales	1.000	3	29	1	0	1
Newhan	.981	17	143	11	3	9
Pellow	.990	55	449	30	5	38
Petrick	.984	23	184	4	3	23
Post	1.000	6	30	1	0	2
Romero	1.000	8	37	2	0	4
Sweeney	.976	11	77	3	2	9
Vaughn	.947	10	68	4	4	7

Second Base	PCT	G	PO	A	E	DP
Alviso	.990	23	34	65	1	15
Barmes	.833	2	2	3	1	1
Bellhorn	1.000	4	7	8	0	2
Belliard	1.000	6	2	15	0	1
Butler	.979	42	78	109	4	28
Lopez	.968	31	61	61	4	10
Newhan	.943	33	72	77	9	17
Ozuna	.988	21	30	52	1	7
Post	1.000	3	5	3	0	3

Third Base	PCT	G	PO	A	E	DP
Alviso	.000	1	0	0	0	0
Atkins	.938	110	70	232	20	18
Bellhorn	.974	12	10	28	1	2
Evans	.750	2	0	3	1	0
Lopez	1.000	4	1	4	0	2
Morales	1.000	5	3	9	0	1
Ozuna	.947	7	6	12	1	0
Pellow	.941	10	2	14	1	0

Shortstop	PCT	G	PO	A	E	DP
Alviso	.833	7	1	9	2	0
Barmes	.953	132	177	385	28	70
Butler	1.000	1	0	2	0	0
Lopez	.897	9	7	19	3	5
Ozuna	.964	14	20	34	2	6

Outfield	PCT	G	PO	A	E	DP
Allen	.971	120	222	11	7	2
Alviso	.000	1	0	0	0	0
Freeman	.936	92	174	1	12	1
Kapler	.955	11	20	1	1	0
Magee	1.000	34	56	4	0	1
Newhan	.920	15	21	2	2	0
Ozuna	.949	20	37	0	2	0
Pellow	1.000	3	1	0	0	0
Petrick	.971	33	31	3	1	2
Post	.000	3	0	0	0	0
Reyes	.970	93	153	7	5	1
Sullivan	1.000	1	2	0	0	0
Sweeney	1.000	37	54	0	0	0
Vaughn	.944	13	17	0	1	0

TULSA DRILLERS — Class AA

TEXAS LEAGUE

BATTING	AVG	G	AB	R	H	2B	3B	HR	RBI	BB	SO	SB	CS	SLG	OBP	B	T	HT	WT	DOB	1st Yr	Resides
Burford, Kevin	.258	90	271	39	70	15	1	7	35	45	48	5	1	.399	.372	L	L	6-1	215	11-7-77	1997	Westminster, Calif.
Closser, J.D.	.283	118	410	62	116	28	5	13	54	47	79	3	2	.471	.359	S	R	5-10	175	1-15-80	1998	Alexandria, Ind.
Colina, Javier	.278	95	388	61	108	26	2	17	60	13	59	7	0	.487	.303	R	R	6-1	190	2-15-79	1997	Cocorote, Venez.
Hawpe, Brad	.277	93	346	52	96	27	0	17	68	31	84	1	3	.503	.338	L	L	6-3	200	6-22-79	2000	Fort Worth, Texas
Holliday, Matt	.253	135	522	65	132	28	5	12	72	43	74	15	9	.395	.313	R	R	6-4	230	1-10-80	1998	Chico, Texas
Joffrion, Jack	.250	38	124	16	31	5	0	3	13	4	35	2	0	.363	.279	R	R	5-11	170	9-19-75	1997	Seabrook, Texas
Loggins, Josh	.148	9	27	0	4	1	0	0	2	1	12	0	0	.185	.179	R	R	6-1	190	11-29-76	1998	West Lafayette, Ind.
Merrill, Ronnie	.181	62	199	32	36	8	4	2	20	19	40	2	2	.291	.257	S	R	6-1	180	11-13-78	2000	Seffner, Fla.
Ozuna, Pablo	.254	12	59	4	15	3	0	0	4	2	5	4	2	.305	.279	R	R	5-10	185	8-25-74	1996	Boca Chica, D.R.
Piedra, Jorge	.275	96	357	56	98	17	7	18	52	31	50	5	2	.513	.342	L	L	6-0	190	4-17-79	1997	Van Nuys, Calif.
Polanco, Enohel	.252	42	135	16	34	10	1	1	16	6	29	1	1	.363	.288	R	R	5-11	160	8-11-75	1992	Puerto Plata, D.R.
Sanchez, Tino	.233	96	313	33	73	12	2	2	33	26	31	4	1	.304	.292	S	R	6-0	175	2-2-79	1997	Yauco, P.R.
Sullivan, Cory	.300	135	557	81	167	34	8	5	61	39	83	17	13	.417	.347	L	L	6-0	180	8-20-79	2001	Evanston, Wyo.
Sullivan, Kevin	.239	52	142	9	34	5	0	0	12	6	34	2	0	.275	.278	R	R	6-1	210	10-4-77	2000	Stevens Point, Wisc.
Taylor, Seth	.261	90	322	50	84	16	3	10	50	22	55	10	2	.422	.315	R	R	6-1	180	8-23-77	1999	Louisville, Miss.
Tracy, Andy	.299	106	384	75	115	24	1	25	62	41	116	3	3	.563	.371	L	R	6-3	220	12-11-73	1996	Columbus, Ohio
Uribe, Juan	.250	5	20	3	5	2	0	1	4	0	2	0	0	.500	.238	R	R	5-11	175	7-22-79	1997	Palenque, D.R.
Warren, Chris	.183	21	60	9	11	2	0	1	2	11	20	1	0	.267	.315	R	R	6-0	170	11-24-76	1999	Athens, Ga.

PITCHING	W	L	ERA	G	GS	CG	SV	IP	H	R	ER	BB	SO	AVG	B	T	HT	WT	DOB	1st Yr	Resides
Anderson, Travis	1	5	4.56	17	8	0	0	51	50	30	26	23	46	.251	R	R	6-4	240	3-18-78	1999	Bellevue, Wash.
Bouknight, Kip	10	7	4.04	26	26	1	0	158	153	84	71	57	101	.256	R	R	6-0	190	11-16-78	2001	Gaston, S.C.
Buglovsky, Chris	10	10	4.83	28	28	0	0	158	204	111	85	60	75	.320	L	R	6-2	165	11-22-79	2000	Iselin, N.J.
Bumatay, Mike	4	1	2.60	40	0	0	1	55	42	20	16	29	69	.210	L	L	6-0	170	10-9-79	1998	Clovis, Calif.
DiFelice, Mark	7	6	3.72	21	21	0	0	114	121	61	47	24	75	.272	R	R	6-1	180	8-23-76	1998	Havertown, Penn.
Dohmann, Scott	9	4	4.13	50	4	0	4	94	94	47	43	29	102	.258	R	R	6-1	180	2-13-78	2000	Morgan City, La.
Dotel, Melido	4	6	4.46	49	0	0	1	67	71	39	33	37	59	.278	R	R	6-3	215	4-20-77	1993	San Cristobal, D.R.
Esslinger, Cam	0	0	2.61	15	0	0	0	21	21	9	6	8	11	.272	R	R	5-11	180	12-28-76	1999	Hewitt, N.J.
Hampson, Justin	0	1	13.50	1	1	0	0	4	8	6	6	3	0	.421	L	L	6-1	180	5-24-80	2000	Worden, Ill.
Huisman, Justin	7	2	1.75	57	0	0	26	62	55	22	12	7	46	.234	R	R	6-1	195	4-16-79	2000	Thornton, Ill.
Martin, Chandler	0	0	3.93	5	2	0	0	18	17	10	8	4	12	.239	R	R	6-1	195	10-23-73	1995	Salem, Ore.
Parrish, Wade	4	6	5.52	24	10	0	0	73	91	49	45	37	33	.317	L	L	6-1	190	11-13-77	1999	Othello, Wash.
Ramirez, Emmanuel	0	0	0.00	4	0	0	0	6	2	0	0	4	7	.111	R	R	6-3	190	11-2-79	1999	Santo Domingo, D.R.
Sampson, Benj	5	6	3.68	18	18	1	0	108	117	49	44	25	61	.277	R	L	6-2	210	4-27-75	1993	Plymouth, Minn.
Stark, Denny	0	1	6.23	1	1	0	0	4	4	5	3	4	3	.250	R	R	6-2	210	10-27-74	1996	Edgerton, Ohio
Thompson, Doug	0	3	4.55	29	2	0	1	61	68	34	31	21	47	.278	R	R	6-0	190	7-22-76	1998	Biloxi, Miss.
Tsao, Chin-Hui	11	4	2.46	18	18	0	0	113	88	34	31	26	125	.214	R	R	6-2	175	6-2-81	1999	Hualien, Taiwan
Young, Colin	2	2	2.40	40	0	0	2	45	36	15	12	19	44	.216	L	L	6-0	185	8-1-77	1999	West Newbury, Mass.

FIELDING

Catcher	PCT	G	PO	A	E	DP	PB
Closser	.978	94	670	69	17	7	8
Sanchez	.986	43	250	24	4	1	2
K. Sullivan	.931	5	25	2	2	0	1

First Base	PCT	G	PO	A	E	DP
Burford	.994	77	612	44	4	58
Hawpe	.980	18	140	10	3	11
Loggins	.987	8	74	0	1	13
Sanchez	.953	6	36	5	2	3
K. Sullivan	.965	15	98	12	4	12
Tracy	.989	23	170	17	2	18

Second Base	PCT	G	PO	A	E	DP
Colina	.963	71	178	210	15	57
Joffrion	.848	13	19	20	7	0
Ozuna	.923	7	12	12	2	1
Taylor	.974	37	77	109	5	26
Uribe	1.000	2	4	3	0	2
Warren	.891	17	27	55	10	9

Third Base	PCT	G	PO	A	E	DP
Colina	.939	30	23	39	4	4
Loggins	.000	1	0	0	0	0
Ozuna	1.000	3	1	3	0	0
Polanco	.800	7	0	4	1	0
Sanchez	1.000	6	1	13	0	1
Taylor	.910	28	17	44	6	3
Tracy	.940	75	46	125	11	12
Uribe	1.000	1	0	2	0	0

Shortstop	PCT	G	PO	A	E	DP
Joffrion	.920	23	29	63	8	13
Merrill	.933	62	101	162	19	37
Ozuna	.957	4	9	13	1	6
Polanco	.938	35	36	99	9	16
Taylor	.961	20	27	47	3	12
Uribe	1.000	1	4	5	0	2
Warren	1.000	1	1	0	0	0

Outfield	PCT	G	PO	A	E	DP
Burford	.000	1	0	0	0	0
Closser	.000	1	0	0	1	0
Hawpe	.970	49	93	3	3	0
Holliday	.991	126	211	15	2	0
Piedra	.973	78	170	10	5	1
Sanchez	1.000	20	37	4	0	0
C. Sullivan	.994	133	328	13	2	2
K. Sullivan	1.000	12	26	0	0	0
Uribe	1.000	1	3	0	0	0
Warren	1.000	1	1	0	0	0

VISALIA OAKS

High Class A

CALIFORNIA LEAGUE

BATTING	AVG	G	AB	R	H	2B	3B	HR	RBI	BB	SO	SB	CS	SLG	OBP	B	T	HT	WT	DOB	1st Yr	Resides
Barker, Sean	.280	104	378	61	106	24	4	10	41	25	71	6	3	.444	.334	R	R	6-3	220	5-26-80	2002	Bakersfield, Calif.
Barre, Brian	.244	39	123	21	30	4	4	6	18	29	31	2	2	.488	.388	L	L	5-9	180	5-26-80	2002	Garden Grove, Calif.
Bernier, Doug	.201	84	268	50	54	5	0	0	21	64	63	12	2	.220	.358	S	R	5-11	170	6-24-80	2002	Santa Maria, Calif.
Conway, Dan	.292	86	319	42	93	17	3	5	43	23	59	1	2	.411	.353	R	R	6-2	190	10-13-79	2000	Delmar, N.Y.
Frome, Jason	.230	35	126	18	29	8	1	2	16	9	47	1	2	.357	.275	L	L	6-0	190	7-3-79	2001	Appleton, Wisc.
Fuller, Casey	.000	1	3	0	0	0	0	0	0	0	3	0	0	.000	.000	L	L	6-6	215	2-9-79	2002	Marysville, Calif.
Lambert, Casey	.250	1	4	0	1	0	0	0	0	0	0	0	0	.250	.250	R	R	5-9	165	8-31-79	2001	St. Amant, La.
Lincoln, Justin	.224	121	428	47	96	22	5	11	59	36	151	0	3	.376	.297	R	R	6-3	205	4-4-79	1999	Sarasota, Fla.
Miller, Tony	.248	67	266	47	66	14	5	4	31	40	58	11	7	.383	.349	R	R	5-9	180	8-18-80	2001	Lorain, Ohio
Nix, Jayson	.281	137	562	107	158	46	0	21	86	54	131	24	8	.475	.351	R	R	5-11	180	8-26-82	2001	Midland, Texas
Ozuna, Pablo	.625	2	8	1	5	0	0	0	1	1	1	1	1	.625	.667	R	R	5-10	185	8-25-74	1996	Boca Chica, D.R.
Peck, Bryan	.259	35	116	15	30	9	1	2	24	22	24	3	0	.405	.375	R	R	5-11	195	8-9-77	2000	Athens, Tenn.
Phillips, Dan	.262	119	484	68	127	32	3	18	73	20	115	13	8	.452	.306	R	R	6-3	190	8-23-78	1999	Northridge, Calif.
Rosario, Melvin	.234	97	338	36	79	13	3	0	24	28	87	7	7	.290	.293	L	L	6-1	170	9-22-78	1998	Carolina, P.R.
Salazar, Jeff	.000	1	5	1	0	0	0	0	0	0	0	0	0	.000	.000	L	L	6-0	180	11-24-80	2002	Port Bolivar, Texas
Shealy, Ryan	.299	93	341	70	102	31	1	14	73	42	72	0	0	.519	.391	R	R	6-5	240	8-29-79	2002	Fort Lauderdale, Fla.
Slavik, Corey	.321	109	392	66	126	27	1	14	75	40	67	1	5	.503	.390	L	R	6-0	190	3-24-80	2001	St. Petersburg, Fla.
Sullivan, Kevin	.333	4	12	1	4	0	0	1	2	0	1	0	0	.583	.333	R	R	6-1	210	10-4-77	2000	Stevens Point, Wisc.
Tena, Hector	.211	84	298	32	63	12	1	1	16	16	55	4	2	.268	.259	R	R	6-0	155	6-20-82	1999	San Cristobal, D.R.
Uribe, Juan	.556	2	9	4	5	1	0	0	1	1	0	0	0	.667	.600	R	R	5-11	175	7-22-79	1997	Palenque, D.R.
Winchester, Jeff	.252	83	302	33	76	18	0	8	37	14	51	1	3	.391	.304	R	R	5-11	210	1-21-80	1998	Metairie, La.

PITCHING	W	L	ERA	G	GS	CG	SV	IP	H	R	ER	BB	SO	AVG	B	T	HT	WT	DOB	1st Yr	Resides
Bumatay, Mike	0	0	.00	8	0	0	2	9	1	0	0	5	16	.037	L	L	6-0	170	10-9-79	1998	Clovis, Calif.
Crockett, Ben	2	3	4.50	5	5	0	0	32	35	18	16	7	26	.277	R	R	6-3	200	12-19-79	2002	Topsfield, Mass.
Darnell, Paul	1	1	4.63	23	1	0	1	35	40	21	18	11	30	.289	R	L	6-6	200	6-4-76	1999	Hubbard, Texas
Edwards, John	0	0	0.00	1	0	0	0	1	1	0	0	0	1	.333	R	R	6-1	180	6-27-78	1998	Melton, Australia
Esposito, Mike	12	6	3.75	27	27	1	0	161	173	83	67	55	116	.276	R	R	6-0	190	9-27-81	2003	Las Vegas, Nev.
Esslinger, Cam	2	1	5.52	11	0	0	0	15	16	9	9	10	13	.301	R	R	5-11	180	12-28-76	1999	Hewitt, N.J.
Francis, Jeff	12	9	3.47	27	27	2	0	161	135	66	62	45	153	.229	L	L	6-5	200	1-8-81	2002	Sammamish, Wash.
Green, Sean	3	4	4.84	46	2	0	0	80	90	54	43	38	56	.281	R	R	6-6	230	4-20-79	2000	Louisville, Ky.
Hampson, Justin	14	7	3.68	26	26	1	0	159	153	73	65	51	150	.252	L	L	6-1	180	5-24-80	2000	Worden, Ill.
Jimenez, Ubaldo	1	0	0.00	1	0	0	0	5	3	0	0	1	7	.176	R	R	6-2	165	1-22-84	2001	San Cristobal, D.R.
Neagle, Denny	1	0	0.00	2	2	0	0	10	4	0	0	2	13	.117	L	L	6-3	225	9-13-68	1989	Morrison, Colo.
Parker, Zach	5	5	3.69	16	16	1	0	90	85	38	37	27	52	.250	R	L	6-2	205	8-19-81	2001	Austin, Texas
Pavlik, Isaac	3	3	4.94	51	0	0	1	55	65	33	30	19	50	.288	R	L	5-8	170	5-19-80	2002	Rutherford, N.J.
Price, Ryan	0	0	7.47	7	0	0	0	16	20	13	13	10	13	.327	R	R	6-3	200	1-31-78	1997	Roswell, N.M.
Serrano, Alex	4	5	3.09	49	0	0	4	76	74	34	26	13	71	.253	R	R	6-1	200	2-18-81	1998	Barcelona, Venez.
Simpson, Gerrit	11	10	5.37	27	27	1	0	158	188	103	94	56	84	.300	R	R	6-3	200	12-18-79	2001	Austin, Texas
Songster, Judd	0	1	5.40	9	0	0	3	8	13	5	5	3	9	.361	R	R	6-3	195	12-26-79	2001	North Platte, Neb.
Speier, Ryan	4	2	1.53	56	0	0	18	59	50	14	10	17	73	.226	R	R	6-7	200	7-24-79	2001	Springfield, Va.
Stanton, Kyle	1	1	6.05	14	0	0	0	19	24	13	13	7	14	.303	R	R	6-2	200	2-19-77	2000	Coshocton, Ohio
Stark, Denny	0	0	0.00	1	1	0	0	4	2	0	0	1	5	.142	R	R	6-2	210	10-27-74	1996	Edgerton, Ohio
Webb, Nick	3	2	4.81	25	6	0	1	73	98	45	39	29	65	.320	L	L	6-3	205	7-8-79	2000	Houston, Texas
Wrigley, Jase	0	1	10.13	5	0	0	1	5	10	6	6	3	3	.434	R	R	6-3	210	11-6-75	1998	Atlanta, Ga.

FIELDING

Catcher	PCT	G	PO	A	E	DP	PB
Conway	.991	76	529	38	5	4	15
Sullivan	1.000	2	8	0	0	0	1
Winchester	.994	63	493	40	3	7	10

First Base	PCT	G	PO	A	E	DP
Lincoln	.991	12	108	4	1	17
Peck	.982	20	154	11	3	12
Shealy	.993	76	677	54	5	79
Slavik	.997	34	318	21	1	32

Second Base	PCT	G	PO	A	E	DP
Bernier	1.000	3	5	12	0	2
Nix	.972	135	273	460	21	120
Ozuna	1.000	1	1	4	0	1
Uribe	1.000	1	4	2	0	0

Third Base	PCT	G	PO	A	E	DP
Bernier	.955	16	7	35	2	6
Lambert	1.000	1	1	1	0	0
Lincoln	.923	92	49	180	19	20
Slavik	.901	35	11	62	8	8

Shortstop	PCT	G	PO	A	E	DP
Bernier	.948	61	92	182	15	46
Ozuna	1.000	1	1	5	0	2
Tena	.935	83	127	246	26	54
Uribe	1.000	1	0	1	0	0

Outfield	PCT	G	PO	A	E	DP
Barker	.971	92	125	10	4	1
Barre	.976	30	36	4	1	1
Bernier	1.000	4	3	0	0	0
Frome	.980	32	48	0	1	0
Miller	.961	67	144	3	6	0
Phillips	.965	115	188	6	7	0
Rosario	1.000	95	208	15	0	5
Salazar	1.000	1	2	0	0	0
Sullivan	1.000	1	2	0	0	0

ASHEVILLE TOURISTS

Low Class A

SOUTH ATLANTIC LEAGUE

BATTING	AVG	G	AB	R	H	2B	3B	HR	RBI	BB	SO	SB	CS	SLG	OBP	B	T	HT	WT	DOB	1st Yr	Resides
Anderson, Scott	.111	20	63	5	7	3	0	0	6	4	8	0	1	.159	.211	R	R	5-10	175	5-23-81	2003	Arroyo Grande, Calif.
Baker, Jeff	.289	70	263	44	76	17	0	11	44	30	79	4	2	.479	.377	R	R	6-2	210	6-21-81	2003	Woodbridge, Va.
Bibee, Hal	.239	26	88	5	21	4	0	1	12	6	14	0	1	.318	.302	R	R	6-0	190	5-8-79	2002	Knoxville, Tenn.
Brand, Kevin	.065	12	31	2	2	0	0	1	4	2	8	0	1	.161	.121	S	R	5-10	170	1-24-80	2001	Mesa, Ariz.
Bushey, Andrew	.000	4	8	2	0	0	0	0	1	3	1	0	0	.000	.273	L	R	5-11	190	8-30-79	2002	Boardman, Ohio
Colina, Alvin	.266	72	256	26	68	20	1	4	23	20	53	5	4	.398	.329	R	R	6-3	210	12-26-81	1999	Puerto Cabello, Venez.
Freeman, Ashley	.249	89	333	41	83	20	1	5	32	28	53	5	10	.360	.314	R	R	6-1	195	1-27-79	2001	Town Creek, Ala.
Frome, Jason	.336	36	131	33	44	7	1	6	26	21	37	10	1	.542	.429	L	L	6-0	190	7-3-79	2001	Appleton, Wisc.
Gentry, Garett	.326	44	175	29	57	8	4	7	34	13	18	3	2	.537	.381	L	R	5-10	210	6-27-81	1999	Victorville, Calif.
George, Trey	.193	25	83	9	16	3	1	0	9	8	16	0	1	.253	.277	R	R	6-0	200	1-26-83	2001	Houston, Texas
Gonzalez, Bernie	.284	129	504	70	143	38	4	11	81	43	100	17	9	.440	.351	R	R	6-2	200	5-10-80	2002	Miami, Fla.
Gretz, Nick	.272	87	327	33	89	16	1	15	62	32	70	1	2	.465	.337	L	R	5-11	205	1-28-78	2001	Apple Valley, Minn.
Guance, Walkill	.241	108	369	47	89	18	4	6	37	38	93	21	11	.360	.314	R	R	5-9	160	3-6-82	1999	Sabana Grande, D.R.
Hendricks, K.J.	.253	106	376	69	95	11	3	3	20	52	53	50	11	.322	.344	S	R	5-7	160	2-20-81	2002	Killeen, Texas

BATTING	AVG	G	AB	R	H	2B	3B	HR	RBI	BB	SO	SB	CS	SLG	OBP	B	T	HT	WT	DOB	1st Yr	Resides
Materano, Oscar	.251	82	339	48	85	14	1	4	30	17	78	8	3	.333	.292	R	R	6-1	170	11-18-81	1998	Valencia, Venez.
Mills, Rock	.232	21	56	11	13	6	0	1	13	12	10	2	1	.393	.397	R	R	6-1	210	7-11-80	2002	Westlake, Ohio
Pellow, Kit	.450	6	20	3	9	2	0	1	8	5	5	0	0	.700	.571	R	R	6-1	205	8-28-73	1996	Olathe, Kan.
Salazar, Jeff	.284	129	486	109	138	23	4	29	98	77	74	28	14	.527	.387	L	L	6-0	180	11-24-80	2002	Port Bolivar, Texas
Santiago, Rudy	.133	5	15	0	2	1	0	0	2	0	5	0	0	.200	.133	L	R	6-1	180	11-23-79	1999	Santo Domingo, D.R.
Sardinha, Duke	.285	42	158	23	45	18	0	5	27	15	36	0	1	.494	.356	R	R	6-0	200	12-9-80	2002	Kailua, Hawaii
Spilborghs, Ryan	.281	119	434	78	122	22	2	15	61	63	96	10	11	.445	.379	R	R	6-1	190	9-5-79	2002	Santa Barbara, Calif.
Street, Dan	.381	12	42	7	16	6	0	0	9	3	5	2	0	.524	.435	R	R	6-2	200	10-27-80	2002	Purcellville, Va.
Sweeney, James	.149	21	67	5	10	2	0	1	7	8	20	3	1	.224	.247	R	R	6-1	195	6-13-83	2001	Austin, Texas
Todd, Jeremy	.087	7	23	0	2	0	0	0	0	2	12	0	0	.087	.160	L	R	6-2	210	1-30-78	2000	Maylene, Ala.
Welsch, Travis	.222	20	63	8	14	0	0	0	4	9	18	1	2	.222	.333	R	R	5-11	180	11-30-79	2002	Muscatine, Iowa

PITCHING	W	L	ERA	G	GS	CG	SV	IP	H	R	ER	BB	SO	AVG	B	T	HT	WT	DOB	1st Yr	Resides
Beckstead, Jentry	3	5	4.09	63	0	0	29	62	52	31	28	37	66	.234	R	R	5-11	165	6-9-80	2001	Sandy, Utah
Cartier, Richard	12	5	4.11	30	20	0	0	140	132	81	64	43	104	.243	R	R	6-1	180	10-9-79	2002	Simi Valley, Calif.
Clarke, Darren	8	6	3.83	27	25	1	0	157	155	80	67	59	107	.259	R	R	6-8	230	3-18-81	2001	Tampa, Fla.
Crockett, Ben	10	9	2.49	23	23	2	0	152	152	60	42	32	117	.259	R	R	6-3	200	12-19-79	2002	Topsfield, Mass.
Dannemiller, Beau	4	3	4.58	42	0	0	1	55	52	33	28	18	42	.242	R	R	6-0	210	12-26-79	2001	Munroe Falls, Ohio
Davies, Michael	1	5	3.92	10	10	0	0	57	61	30	25	12	34	.269	L	L	6-3	190	3-29-81	2000	Beaverton, Ore.
Dooley, Jason	0	2	11.08	11	0	0	0	13	27	19	16	9	10	.428	R	R	6-3	180	2-4-80	2002	Danville, Va.
Dunkle, Peter	0	0	22.50	4	0	0	0	4	8	11	10	9	1	.444	R	R	6-5	210	8-7-80	2002	Alamo, Calif.
Gallagher, Buddy	0	1	3.21	11	0	0	0	14	16	8	5	6	9	.285	L	L	5-11	175	1-3-79	2001	Billings, Mont.
Jimenez, Ubaldo	10	6	3.46	27	27	0	0	154	129	67	59	67	138	.229	R	R	6-2	165	1-22-84	2001	San Cristobal, D.R.
Johnson, Doug	12	8	4.09	29	28	0	0	167	182	85	76	45	88	.277	R	R	6-1	180	12-1-80	2002	Pelham, N.H.
Johnston, Rikki	4	3	5.03	29	2	0	0	48	45	32	27	31	46	.247	L	L	6-4	180	4-2-81	1998	Vicoria, Australia
Jones, Chris	0	1	5.40	16	0	0	0	18	22	13	11	6	26	.289	L	L	6-3	180	8-29-79	1998	Charlotte, N.C.
Mitchell, Jay	0	1	7.71	2	2	0	0	7	6	7	6	14	3	.272	R	R	6-7	205	1-5-83	2001	La Grange, Ga.
Reba, Steve	6	3	2.66	47	2	0	3	81	81	31	24	15	81	.257	R	R	6-3	190	3-23-80	2002	Ft. Wayne, Ind.
Vazquez, Will	0	0	0.00	3	0	0	0	6	9	11	0	1	2	.333	R	R	6-0	140	12-26-79	2000	Guayama, P.R.
Watson, Mike	1	3	5.02	17	0	0	0	29	31	18	16	11	29	.284	R	R	6-1	180	9-28-80	2002	Altoona, Pa.
Young, Chris	3	4	2.73	59	0	0	9	69	59	26	21	21	63	.230	R	R	6-4	205	4-19-81	2002	Stow, Ohio

FIELDING

Catcher	PCT	G	PO	A	E	DP	PB
Bibee	1.000	26	190	18	0	2	6
Bushey	1.000	3	12	2	0	0	1
Colina	.987	70	483	64	7	4	10
Gentry	1.000	13	82	6	0	0	1
Mills	1.000	13	80	9	0	0	0
Sweeney	.973	21	133	12	4	2	6

First Base	PCT	G	PO	A	E	DP
Brand	.986	9	64	5	1	7
Bushey	1.000	1	8	0	0	0
Freeman	.995	42	344	27	2	21
Gretz	.986	46	398	24	6	36
Mills	1.000	2	15	1	0	3
Pellow	1.000	3	24	2	0	4
Sardinha	.974	33	281	19	8	24
Street	1.000	4	42	0	0	4
Todd	1.000	7	57	5	0	5

Second Base	PCT	G	PO	A	E	DP
Anderson	.952	9	22	18	2	5
Brand	1.000	1	0	1	0	0
Freeman	.923	2	3	9	1	2
Guance	.955	106	192	317	24	53
Hendricks	.982	13	23	33	1	8
Sardinha	.897	5	9	17	3	5
Welsch	.974	7	16	22	1	6

Third Base	PCT	G	PO	A	E	DP
Baker	.902	61	43	104	16	6
Brand	1.000	1	0	4	0	0
Freeman	.922	42	38	81	10	7
Hendricks	.944	22	14	37	3	6
Pellow	.750	2	1	2	1	0
Street	.833	3	5	5	2	2
Welsch	.968	9	9	21	1	1

Shortstop	PCT	G	PO	A	E	DP
Anderson	.925	10	13	36	4	7
Hendricks	.975	55	77	153	6	28
Materano	.930	73	113	230	26	44
Welsch	.957	4	7	15	1	2

Outfield	PCT	G	PO	A	E	DP
Freeman	1.000	4	7	0	0	0
Frome	.976	24	39	1	1	1
George	1.000	22	38	2	0	1
Gonzalez	.967	120	227	7	8	1
Hendricks	.750	3	3	0	1	0
Salazar	.987	126	292	21	4	4
Santiago	1.000	4	7	1	0	0
Sardinha	1.000	2	2	0	0	0
Spilborghs	.982	116	211	12	4	1
Street	1.000	1	3	0	0	0

TRI-CITY DUST DEVILS

Short-Season Class A

NORTHWEST LEAGUE

BATTING	AVG	G	AB	R	H	2B	3B	HR	RBI	BB	SO	SB	CS	SLG	OBP	B	T	HT	WT	DOB	1st Yr	Resides
Almonte, Sandy	.211	68	270	28	57	10	9	3	20	18	72	9	5	.348	.268	S	R	5-11	150	11-16-82	2000	Puerto Plata, D.R.
Anderson, Scott	.143	13	35	4	5	0	0	0	2	13	10	0	3	.143	.375	R	R	5-10	175	5-23-81	2003	Arroyo Grande, Calif.
Blood, Randy	.257	68	265	28	68	12	2	3	35	23	69	2	2	.351	.319	L	R	5-10	180	1-7-81	2003	Costa Mesa, Calif.
Brinson, Matt	.181	37	144	15	26	5	0	3	18	13	43	0	0	.278	.247	L	L	6-5	230	9-9-80	2003	Brandon, Miss.
Bushey, Andrew	.224	39	147	18	33	4	0	0	9	16	16	2	1	.252	.305	L	R	5-11	190	8-30-79	2002	Boardman, Ohio
Colonel, Christian	.245	56	208	21	51	8	1	1	21	19	31	9	3	.308	.331	R	R	6-2	210	12-25-81	2003	Pocatello, Idaho
Czarniecki, Jordan	.245	51	184	19	45	9	0	1	16	14	38	4	4	.310	.304	R	R	6-1	175	10-4-80	2003	Anderson, Ind.
Fox, Ryan	.175	58	194	26	34	8	1	8	26	22	82	1	1	.351	.281	R	R	6-3	220	10-13-80	2003	Rogers, Ark.
Gaetti, Joe	.276	34	116	15	32	7	2	4	9	14	38	1	2	.474	.348	R	R	5-11	205	10-16-81	2003	Raleigh, N.C.
George, Trey	.228	60	219	23	50	16	0	4	23	20	50	3	0	.356	.298	R	R	6-0	200	1-26-83	2001	Houston, Texas
Guarno, Rick	.234	37	137	16	32	8	2	1	9	11	29	3	0	.343	.293	R	R	6-0	185	8-16-82	2003	Rochester, N.Y.
Lynam, Guy	.400	3	10	3	4	0	0	0	0	1	2	1	0	.400	.455	R	R	5-11	190	10-27-80	2001	Williamstown, N.J.
Sakamoto, Mitsuru	.196	16	56	7	11	2	0	0	5	7	11	0	0	.232	.286	L	R	6-2	170	10-7-80	2002	Fukuoka, Japan
Sardinha, Duke	.235	26	98	11	23	7	0	4	16	12	23	2	2	.429	.324	R	R	6-0	200	12-9-80	2002	Kailua, Hawaii
Spivey, Brett	.277	14	47	7	13	3	2	1	12	7	12	0	1	.489	.370	L	R	5-9	185	6-4-81	2003	Charleston, S.C.
Street, Dan	.325	33	123	12	40	10	1	0	16	12	22	0	1	.423	.387	R	R	6-2	200	10-27-80	2002	Purcellville, Va.
Swearingen, Jonathan	.186	20	70	9	13	3	0	0	2	3	13	0	0	.229	.250	R	R	6-1	210	12-10-80	2003	Marianna, Fla.
Sweeney, James	.187	59	203	27	38	8	0	3	15	26	70	5	1	.271	.298	R	R	6-1	195	6-13-83	2001	Austin, Texas

GAMES BY POSITION: C—Bushey 8, Guarno 9, Lynam 3, Sweeney 56. **1B**—Brinson 35, Bushey 22, Colonel 1, Sardinha 8, Street 11. **2B**—Almonte 19, Anderson 3, Blood 48, Sardinha 8. **3B**—Anderson 1, Blood 8, Bushey 8, Colonel 43, Sardinha 8, Street 8, Swearingen 1. **SS**—Almonte 50, Anderson 9, Blood 5, Swearingen 14. **OF**—Czarniecki 49, Fox 53, Gaetti 31, George 58, Sakamoto 13, Spivey 14, Street 14.

PITCHING	W	L	ERA	G	GS	CG	SV	IP	H	R	ER	BB	SO	AVG	B	T	HT	WT	DOB	1st Yr	Resides
Arakawa, Yusuke	3	1	3.18	30	0	0	2	34	31	13	12	11	38	.234	R	R	6-0	160	3-26-78	2003	Saitama, Japan
Castleman, Stephen	0	2	4.55	18	0	0	0	28	30	19	14	16	20	.275	R	R	6-4	195	11-6-79	2003	Biloxi, Miss.
Corpas, Manuel	5	6	5.79	15	15	0	0	84	98	61	54	22	47	.291	R	R	6-3	170	12-3-82	1999	Panama City, Panama
Dunkle, Peter	2	1	3.21	22	0	0	0	34	31	17	12	17	22	.236	R	R	6-5	210	8-7-80	2002	Alamo, Calif.

PITCHING	W	L	ERA	G	GS	CG	SV	IP	H	R	ER	BB	SO	AVG	B	T	HT	WT	DOB	1st Yr	Resides
Edwards, John	3	2	3.06	22	0	0	0	35	32	15	12	13	27	.253	R	R	6-1	180	6-27-78	1998	Melton, Australia
Gagne, J.P.	1	2	3.63	32	0	0	16	35	35	16	14	8	21	.275	R	R	6-1	200	10-27-80	2003	Bloomington, Minn.
Gallagher, Buddy	0	0	0.00	2	0	0	0	2	0	0	0	1	1	.000	L	L	5-11	175	1-3-79	2001	Billings, Mont.
Kaiser, Marc	3	3	0.49	7	7	0	0	37	30	10	2	8	16	.220	R	R	6-2	205	5-7-82	2003	Reno, Nev.
Lo, Ching-Lung	3	7	2.85	14	14	0	0	76	66	27	24	27	48	.237	R	R	6-6	190	8-20-85	2002	Tainan, Taiwan
Lynch, Brian	4	3	2.84	14	14	0	0	70	66	30	22	20	48	.250	R	R	6-2	195	9-21-80	2003	Connersville, Ind.
Marsden, Aaron	4	3	2.79	13	10	0	1	61	49	21	19	18	46	.216	L	L	6-5	225	11-18-81	2003	Grand Forks, N.D.
Salas, Pedro	2	7	5.56	11	11	0	0	57	67	42	35	21	20	.305	R	R	6-3	170	7-14-82	1999	Barinas, Venez.
Santiago, Tomas	1	4	4.50	21	3	0	0	46	44	28	23	19	32	.255	R	R	6-4	210	10-30-81	2002	Cidra, P.R.
Shartzer, Bryan	2	1	3.68	24	0	0	0	37	33	17	15	18	23	.244	R	R	6-0	190	6-17-80	2002	Louisville, Ky.
Smith, Brandon	0	0	31.50	2	0	0	0	2	7	7	7	2	2	.538	R	R	6-2	200	2-18-80	2002	Ballwin, Mo.
Valcarcel, Jonathan	0	0	0.00	1	0	0	0	1	1	0	0	0	1	.333	L	L	6-3	180	11-23-83	2002	Bayamon, P.R.
Vargas, Reynaldo	0	1	5.40	17	2	0	0	38	47	25	23	16	27	.311	R	R	6-1	160	11-13-82	1999	Santo Domingo, D.R.

CASPER ROCKIES

Rookie

PIONEER LEAGUE

BATTING	AVG	G	AB	R	H	2B	3B	HR	RBI	BB	SO	SB	CS	SLG	OBP	B	T	HT	WT	DOB	1st Yr	Resides
Brinson, Matt	.257	9	35	3	9	2	0	1	8	6	5	0	1	.400	.366	L	L	6-5	230	9-9-80	2003	Brandon, Miss.
Fuller, Casey	.290	49	183	27	53	5	3	12	43	9	61	5	1	.546	.325	L	L	6-6	215	2-9-79	2002	Marysville, Calif.
Ghutzman, Stephen	.304	28	102	11	31	8	1	1	14	13	25	1	2	.431	.383	S	R	6-0	210	12-2-80	2003	Spring, Texas
Herrera, Jonathan	.308	39	159	27	49	7	1	1	25	10	25	12	3	.384	.355	S	R	5-9	150	11-3-84	2002	Maracaibo, Venez.
Mosqueda, Juan	.273	51	172	20	47	5	4	1	19	17	60	7	6	.366	.339	R	R	5-10	160	2-25-82	1999	Estado, Venez.
Nunez, Florentino	.263	55	209	34	55	12	6	1	27	16	37	6	6	.392	.322	S	R	6-0	165	3-23-84	2001	Villa Mella, D.R.
Restrepo, John	.315	54	222	37	70	14	3	2	13	18	53	13	8	.432	.378	L	L	6-1	185	7-27-82	2003	Santa Ana, Calif.
Reynolds, Gene	.304	50	204	33	62	6	1	1	10	13	31	15	4	.358	.341	R	R	5-10	165	12-29-80	2003	Brandon, Fla.
Robledo, Nelson	.241	54	203	23	49	9	1	3	29	13	43	3	2	.340	.305	R	R	6-1	180	6-13-84	2001	Panama City, Panama
Stewart, Ian	.317	57	224	40	71	14	5	10	43	29	54	4	1	.558	.401	L	R	6-3	205	4-5-85	2003	Garden Grove, Calif.
Strop, Pedro	.172	40	128	13	22	4	1	1	11	15	43	1	3	.242	.284	R	R	6-0	160	6-13-85	2002	San Cristobal, D.R.
Tejeda, Francisco	.203	43	148	17	30	3	2	0	6	2	25	5	3	.250	.212	R	R	6-1	150	12-19-80	2002	Santo Domingo, D.R.
Underwood, Daniel	.316	67	266	54	84	15	0	7	40	15	78	12	3	.451	.359	R	R	6-1	200	3-4-81	2003	Bedford, Ind.
Valdez, Angel	.237	52	177	19	42	3	0	1	15	9	50	7	1	.271	.275	R	R	6-0	140	8-2-84	2001	La Romana, D.R.
Valdez, Jose	.254	39	142	16	36	4	2	3	15	15	20	2	3	.373	.321	L	R	6-1	150	9-6-83	2002	La Vega, D.R.
Vasquez, Jose	.194	8	31	2	6	2	0	0	3	1	17	0	0	.258	.265	L	L	6-3	220	12-28-82	2000	Sarasota, Fla.
Wilson, Neil	.295	23	78	13	23	6	1	2	12	19	15	3	0	.474	.439	R	R	6-1	190	12-7-83	2002	Vero Beach, Fla.

GAMES BY POSITION: C—Ghutzman 12, Robledo 31, Underwood 28, Valdez 1, Wilson 15. **1B**—Brinson 9, Fuller 2, Ghutzman 8, Robledo 11, Tejeda 1, Underwood 33, Valdez 19. **2B**—Herrera 39, Reynolds 8, Tejeda 30, Valdez 4. **3B**—Reynolds 1, Robledo 1, Stewart 51, Strop 1, Tejeda 8, Valdez 15. **SS**—Reynolds 42, Strop 36. **OF**—Fuller 30, Ghutzman 1, Mosqueda 50, Nunez 46, Restrepo 54, Underwood 4, Valdez 51, Vasquez 4.

PITCHING	W	L	ERA	G	GS	CG	SV	IP	H	R	ER	BB	SO	AVG	B	T	HT	WT	DOB	1st Yr	Resides
Arias, Alberto	4	4	3.58	13	13	1	0	73	69	45	29	23	64	.244	R	R	5-11	150	10-14-83	2000	Santo Domingo, D.R.
Beerer, Scott	0	2	7.71	5	3	0	1	14	23	13	12	5	10	.359	R	R	6-1	200	7-4-82	2003	Mission, Texas
Bright, Adam	2	2	4.29	33	0	0	0	42	46	27	20	22	25	.275	L	L	6-0	180	8-11-84	2002	Perth, Australia
Diangelo, Jason	2	3	4.71	17	9	0	0	65	82	41	34	13	47	.307	R	R	6-1	200	9-9-80	2003	McMurray, Penn.
Guzman, Carlos	0	1	14.73	4	1	0	0	7	11	12	12	11	6	.366	R	R	6-1	170	5-7-83	2001	San Pedro de Macoris, D.R.
Harrelson, Paul	1	0	1.69	5	0	0	0	11	13	8	2	3	14	.295	R	R	6-2	185	7-24-81	2003	Pauline, S.C.
Ion, Mark	1	3	3.00	27	0	0	11	27	26	15	9	13	25	.242	R	R	6-2	220	1-8-81	2003	Plantation, Fla.
Kerschen, Josh	0	1	5.40	4	0	0	0	7	8	4	4	2	6	.320	R	R	6-4	180	11-21-81	2002	Merriam, Kan.
Merino, Josh	0	2	7.50	3	3	0	0	12	17	15	10	4	10	.314	R	R	6-6	205	7-31-82	2003	Vinton, Iowa
Merrell, Darric	4	4	5.10	13	11	0	0	60	77	40	34	14	39	.314	R	R	6-4	210	1-22-82	2003	Temecula, Calif.
Mitchell, Jay	2	3	9.35	22	5	0	0	42	56	49	44	33	33	.307	R	R	6-7	205	1-5-83	2001	La Grange, Ga.
Morillo, Juan	1	6	5.91	15	15	0	0	64	85	73	42	40	44	.318	R	R	6-1	160	11-5-83	2001	San Pedro de Macoris, D.R.
Riley, Kenny	0	1	7.43	23	0	0	0	36	61	37	30	17	29	.367	R	R	6-2	200	4-15-80	2002	Sparks, Nevada
Robles, Larry	3	7	5.87	16	16	0	0	80	114	68	52	21	58	.331	R	R	6-2	205	10-29-80	2003	San Pedro, Calif.
Silva, Doug	2	5	2.85	27	0	0	0	41	27	15	13	12	52	.182	R	R	6-0	190	2-7-81	2003	Roseville, Calif.
Watchko, Jeff	5	3	1.75	31	0	0	3	46	38	17	9	11	41	.223	R	R	6-3	195	11-7-80	2003	Canton, Ga.
Wiley, Mike	1	1	5.26	32	0	0	0	38	46	34	22	23	41	.283	L	L	6-1	190	1-27-81	2003	Orlando, Fla.

DETROIT TIGERS

BY PAT CAPUTO

It was a mistaken notion that entering the 2003 season the Tigers had nowhere to go but up.

Though they had already hit rock bottom with 106 losses in 2002, the Tigers somehow managed to drill even deeper.

In the end, the Tigers won five of their final six games to avoid becoming the losingest team in major league history. Yet, their legacy as one of the worst major league teams ever was sealed. A 43-119 record speaks volumes of just how far a climb general manager Dave Dombrowski has to lead the Tigers in order to make it back merely to respectability, let alone contention.

Dombrowski turned to the Tigers' minor league system in earnest. He didn't tender contracts to or traded arbitration eligible veteran players such as Robert Fick, Randall Simon and Mark Redman. And as he did with Florida, Dombrowski continued trying to gather good, young arms for the pitching staff.

Jeremy Bonderman, 20, jumped from high Class A in 2002 to the majors. He learned a lot from a 6-17, 5.56 season and has a chance to be No.1 starter in the future. He touches 94 mph consistently with movement and has an excellent breaking ball. The command and makeup are also there.

Lefthander Mike Maroth became the first 20-game loser in almost a quarter of a century, while Nate Cornejo also took the ball every fifth day. Both grinded through the season, but there are questions about their long-term chances because neither throws hard enough to miss a bat when necessary.

The Tigers carried three Rule 5 pitchers the entire season, lefthander Wilfredo Ledezma and righthanders Matt Roney and Chris Spurling. As expected, they had their ups and mostly downs. But each displayed enough arm strength and command to project as possible mainstays in the future.

ORGANIZATION LEADERS

BATTING

*AVG	Donald Kelly, Erie/Lakeland	.306
R	Cody Ross, Toledo	74
H	Curtis Granderson, Lakeland	136
TB	Cody Ross, Toledo	242
2B	Brant Ust, Toledo/Erie	36
3B	Three tied at	11
HR	Ernie Young, Toledo	21
RBI	Ernie Young, Toledo	84
BB	Brent Clevlen, West Michigan	72
SO	Neil Jenkins, Lakeland	150
SB	Nook Logan, Erie	37
*SLG	Cody Ross, Toledo	.515
*OBP	Donald Kelly, Erie/Lakeland	.396

PITCHING

W	Jon Connolly, West Michigan	16
L	Preston Larrison, Toledo/Erie	13
#ERA	Jon Connolly, West Michigan	1.41
G	Ian Ostlund, Lakeland/West Michigan	61
CG	Jon Connolly, West Michigan	5
SV	Brian Schmack, Erie	29
IP	Pat Ahearne, Toledo/Erie	184
BB	Humberto Sanchez, West Michigan	78
SO	Joel Zumaya, West Michigan	126

*Minimum 250 At-Bats #Minimum 75 Innings

Dmitri Young

DAN ARNOLD

Jon Connolly

PLAYERS of the YEAR

MAJOR LEAGUE: Dmitri Young, of

Young was one of the few bright spots in an otherwise dismal 2003 season in Detroit. He led the team in virtually every offensive category. The big man even legged out seven triples, which tied for 10th in the American League.

MINOR LEAGUE: Jon Connolly, lhp

The crafty lefty used excellent command to lead the minors with a 1.41 ERA. Connolly also won 16 games, and one more victory would have thrust him into a five-way tie for the minor league lead in that category as well.

The Tigers positional prospects did not fare as well. After much anticipation, the Tigers moved Omar Infante in at shortstop and Ramon Santiago at second base as their every day middle-infield combination. Both players struggled mightily both in the field and at the plate. Because young position players such as Infante, Santiago, catcher Brandon Inge, first baseman Carlos Pena and outfielder Andres Torres did not live up to expectations, the Tigers turned to their Triple-A Toledo team to fill spots with minor league free agents such as Warren Morris, Kevin Witt, A.J. Hinch and Matt Walbeck.

It did not help that outfielder Bobby Higginson, making $11.83 million on the third year of a five-year, $36 million contract, hit .235-14-52.

Center fielder Alex Sanchez, acquired from the Brewers early in the season, did some good things, especially with his speed, but was also inconsistent.

Veteran Dmitri Young hit .297-29-85 and displayed uncommon professionalism under the most trying of circumstances.

The best of the Tigers' younger players was 1999 first-round pick Eric Munson, who hit 18 home runs and made a surprising transition from first base to third base.

As bad as things went at the major league level for the Tigers, they weren't much better in the minor leagues. The Tigers have been praised for their recent drafts, but most of their top prospects from those drafts did not perform as anticipated in 2003.

Particularly disappointing were the seasons put together by righthander Preston Larrison, second baseman Michael Woods and third baseman Jack Hannahan. All were selected within the first three rounds of the 2001 draft and expected to move swiftly, but each took a step back in 2003.

DETROIT TIGERS

Manager: Alan Trammell.

2003 Record: 43-119, .265 (5th, AL Central).

BATTING	AVG	G	AB	R	H	2B	3B	HR	RBI	BB	SO	SB	CS	SLG	OBP	B	T	HT	WT	DOB	1st Yr	Resides
Bocachica, Hiram	.045	6	22	1	1	1	0	0	0	0	7	0	0	.091	.045	R	R	5-11	180	3-4-76	1994	Toa Alta, P.R.
Halter, Shane	.217	114	360	33	78	5	2	12	30	27	77	2	3	.342	.269	R	R	6-0	190	11-8-69	1991	Overland Park, Kan.
Higginson, Bob	.235	130	469	61	110	13	4	14	52	59	73	8	8	.369	.320	L	R	5-11	190	8-18-70	1992	Bloomfield Hills, Mich.
Hinch, A.J.	.203	27	74	7	15	3	1	3	11	3	18	0	0	.392	.247	R	R	6-1	200	5-15-74	1996	Scottsdale, Ariz.
Infante, Omar	.222	69	221	24	49	6	1	0	8	18	37	6	3	.258	.278	R	R	6-0	170	12-26-81	1999	Guanta, Venez.
Inge, Brandon	.203	104	330	32	67	15	3	8	30	24	79	4	4	.339	.265	R	R	5-11	190	5-19-77	1998	Ann Arbor, Mich.
Kingsale, Eugene	.208	39	120	11	25	3	1	1	8	10	17	1	3	.275	.265	S	R	6-3	190	8-20-76	1994	Oranjestad, Aruba
Klassen, Danny	.247	22	73	9	18	3	1	1	7	4	26	0	1	.356	.286	R	R	6-0	190	9-22-75	1993	Stuart, Fla.
Monroe, Craig	.240	128	425	51	102	18	1	23	70	27	89	4	2	.449	.287	R	R	6-1	210	2-27-77	1995	Texarkana, Texas
Morris, Warren	.272	97	346	37	94	13	2	6	37	23	42	4	2	.373	.316	L	R	5-11	180	1-11-74	1996	Alexandria, La.
Munson, Eric	.240	99	313	28	75	9	0	18	50	35	61	3	0	.441	.312	L	R	6-3	220	10-3-77	1999	Chandler, Ariz.
Palmer, Dean	.140	26	86	3	12	2	0	0	6	9	28	0	0	.163	.235	R	R	6-1	210	12-27-68	1986	Tallahassee, Fla.
Paquette, Craig	.152	11	33	2	5	0	0	0	0	0	5	0	0	.152	.152	R	R	6-0	210	3-28-69	1989	Wildwood, Mo.
Pena, Carlos	.248	131	452	51	112	21	6	18	50	53	123	4	5	.440	.332	L	L	6-2	210	5-17-78	1998	Haverhill, Mass.
Petrick, Ben	.225	43	120	18	27	6	0	4	12	8	30	0	0	.375	.273	R	R	6-0	200	4-7-77	1996	Hillsboro, Ore.
Ross, Cody	.211	6	19	1	4	1	0	1	5	1	3	0	0	.421	.286	R	L	5-11	180	12-23-80	1999	Carlsbad, N.M.
Sanchez, Alex	.289	101	394	43	114	13	5	1	22	18	46	44	18	.355	.320	L	L	5-10	150	8-26-76	1996	Coral Gables, Fla.
Santiago, Ramon	.225	141	444	41	100	18	1	2	29	33	66	10	4	.284	.292	S	R	5-11	160	8-31-79	1998	Las Matas de Farfan, D.R.
Torres, Andres	.220	59	168	23	37	4	3	1	9	10	35	5	5	.298	.263	R	R	5-10	190	1-26-78	1998	Aguada, P.R.
Walbeck, Matt	.174	59	138	11	24	4	1	1	6	3	26	0	1	.239	.197	S	R	5-11	190	10-2-69	1987	Fair Oaks, Calif.
Witt, Kevin	.263	93	270	25	71	9	0	10	26	15	68	1	1	.407	.301	L	R	6-4	220	1-5-76	1994	Bellaire, Texas
Young, Dmitri	.297	155	562	78	167	34	7	29	85	58	130	2	1	.537	.372	S	R	6-2	240	10-11-73	1991	Parkland, Fla.
Young, Ernie	.182	5	11	0	2	0	0	0	0	4	5	0	2	.182	.400	R	R	6-1	230	7-8-69	1990	Gilbert, Ariz.

PITCHING	W	L	ERA	G	GS	CG	SV	IP	H	R	ER	BB	SO	AVG	B	T	HT	WT	DOB	1st Yr	Resides
Anderson, Matt	0	1	5.40	23	0	0	3	23	25	17	14	9	13	.271	R	R	6-4	200	8-17-76	1997	Louisville, Ky.
Avery, Steve	2	0	5.63	19	0	0	0	16	19	11	10	7	6	.301	L	L	6-4	200	4-14-70	1988	Dearborn, Mich.
Bernero, Adam	1	12	6.08	18	17	0	0	101	104	68	68	41	54	.266	R	R	6-4	210	11-28-76	1999	Elk Grove, Calif.
Bonderman, Jeremy	6	19	5.56	33	28	0	0	162	193	118	100	58	108	.294	R	R	6-2	210	10-28-82	2001	Pasco, Wash.
Cornejo, Nate	6	17	4.67	32	32	2	0	195	236	111	101	58	46	.307	R	R	6-5	240	9-24-79	1998	Wellington, Kan.
Eckenstahler, Eric	0	0	2.87	20	0	0	0	16	9	6	5	15	12	.166	L	L	6-7	220	12-17-76	2000	Lake Villa, Ill.
German, Franklyn	2	4	6.04	45	0	0	5	45	47	32	30	45	41	.273	R	R	6-4	260	1-20-80	1996	San Cristobal, D.R.
Knotts, Gary	3	8	6.04	20	18	0	0	95	111	70	64	47	51	.287	R	R	6-4	230	2-12-77	1996	Decatur, Ala.
Ledezma, Wil	3	7	5.79	34	8	0	0	84	99	55	54	35	49	.297	L	L	6-3	150	1-21-81	1998	Maracay, Venez.
Loux, Shane	1	1	7.12	11	4	0	0	30	37	24	24	12	8	.303	R	R	6-2	230	8-31-79	1997	Gilbert, Ariz.
Maroth, Mike	9	21	5.73	33	33	1	0	193	231	131	123	50	87	.298	L	L	6-0	190	8-17-77	1998	Orlando, Fla.
Mears, Chris	1	3	5.44	29	3	0	5	41	50	28	25	11	21	.306	R	R	6-4	190	1-20-78	1996	Victoria, B.C.
Patterson, Danny	0	0	4.08	19	0	0	3	18	15	8	8	4	19	.227	R	R	6-0	190	2-17-71	1989	Colleyville, Texas
Robertson, Nate	1	2	5.44	8	8	0	0	45	55	27	27	23	33	.305	R	L	6-2	210	9-3-77	1999	Valley Center, Kan.
Rodney, Fernando	1	3	6.07	27	0	0	3	30	35	20	20	17	33	.294	R	R	5-11	200	3-18-77	1997	Santo Domingo, D.R.
Roney, Matt	1	9	5.45	45	11	0	0	101	102	67	61	48	47	.262	R	R	6-3	230	1-10-80	1998	Edmond, Okla.
Schmack, Brian	1	0	3.46	11	0	0	0	13	14	6	5	4	4	.291	R	R	6-2	190	12-7-73	1996	Barrington, Ill.
Sparks, Steve	0	6	4.72	42	0	0	2	90	95	57	47	34	49	.277	R	R	6-0	190	7-2-65	1987	Sugar Land, Texas
Spurling, Chris	1	3	4.68	66	0	0	3	77	78	42	40	22	38	.266	R	R	6-6	240	6-28-77	1998	Tampa, Fla.
Walker, Jamie	4	3	3.32	78	0	0	3	65	61	30	24	17	45	.246	L	L	6-2	190	7-1-71	1992	Overland Park, Kan.

FIELDING

Catcher	PCT	G	PO	A	E	DP	PB
Hinch	.983	27	110	6	2	0	2
Inge	.996	104	500	67	2	11	5
Petrick	1.000	6	25	0	0	0	0
Walbeck	.979	55	172	16	4	1	4

First Base	PCT	G	PO	A	E	DP
Halter	.978	12	84	4	2	13
Palmer	1.000	1	9	1	0	0
Paquette	1.000	5	42	1	0	4
Pena	.990	128	1135	91	13	130
Petrick	1.000	2	3	0	0	0
Witt	1.000	27	214	20	0	31
Young	1.000	1	5	0	0	0

Second Base	PCT	G	PO	A	E	DP
Halter	1.000	24	40	74	0	12
Infante	1.000	2	3	3	0	2
Klassen	.966	4	12	16	1	4
Morris	.987	89	182	271	6	83
Santiago	.963	53	105	153	10	45

Third Base	PCT	G	PO	A	E	DP
Halter	.985	50	36	98	2	12
Infante	.900	4	1	8	1	1
Klassen	1.000	13	15	24	0	3
Munson	.920	91	68	150	19	13
Palmer	1.000	1	0	4	0	0
Witt	1.000	5	1	4	0	0
Young	.849	16	8	37	8	5

Shortstop	PCT	G	PO	A	E	DP
Halter	.950	27	33	62	5	14
Infante	.962	63	117	211	13	53
Klassen	.867	3	5	8	2	0
Santiago	.975	85	141	248	10	68

Outfield	PCT	G	PO	A	E	DP
Bocachica	1.000	6	11	1	0	0
Halter	.000	2	0	0	0	0
Higginson	.981	118	249	4	5	0
Kingsale	.985	30	66	0	1	0
Monroe	.970	108	221	8	7	1
Paquette	1.000	5	10	0	0	0
Petrick	.969	32	61	2	2	1
Ross	.882	6	15	0	2	0
Sanchez	.979	99	278	1	6	0
Torres	.991	50	102	4	1	1
Witt	1.000	13	20	0	0	0
Young	.985	61	125	5	2	2

BILL NICHOLS

Mike Maroth

FARM SYSTEM

Director, Player Development: Steve Boros.

Class	Farm Team	League	W	L	Pct.	Finish*	Manager	First Yr.
AAA	Toledo (Ohio) Mud Hens	International	65	78	.455	11th (14)	Larry Parrish	1987
AA	Erie (Pa.) Sea Wolves	Eastern	72	70	.507	t-5th (12)	Kevin Bradshaw	2001
High A	Lakeland (Fla.) Tigers	Florida State	55	78	.414	11th (12)	Gary Green	1967
Low A	West Michigan (Grand Rapids, Mich.) Whitecaps	Midwest	67	73	.479	9th (14)	Phil Regan	1997
SS A	Oneonta (N.Y.) Tigers	New York-Penn	45	30	.600	4th (14)	Randy Ready	1999
Rookie	Lakeland (Fla.) Tigers	Gulf Coast	28	29	.491	5th (12)	Howard Bushong	1995

*Finish in overall standings (No. of teams in league)

BILL NICHOLS

Alex Sanchez: Second in the AL with 44 steals

MICHAEL WALBY

Cody Ross: Led the organization in runs and total bases

TOLEDO MUD HENS — Class AAA

INTERNATIONAL LEAGUE

BATTING	AVG	G	AB	R	H	2B	3B	HR	RBI	BB	SO	SB	CS	SLG	OBP	B	T	HT	WT	DOB	1st Yr	Resides
Bocachica, Hiram	.242	95	322	48	78	19	3	12	37	24	57	11	6	.432	.313	R	R	5-11	180	3-4-76	1994	Toa Alta, P.R.
Evans, Tom	.153	38	118	17	18	4	1	3	6	14	36	5	0	.280	.270	R	R	6-1	200	7-9-74	1992	Issaquah, Wash.
Hinch, A.J.	.259	55	185	20	48	15	1	4	23	13	38	0	1	.416	.320	R	R	6-1	200	5-15-74	1996	Scottsdale, Ariz.
Infante, Omar	.223	64	224	28	50	10	0	2	18	22	32	22	4	.295	.299	R	R	6-0	170	12-26-81	1999	Guanta, Venez.
Inge, Brandon	.275	39	142	15	39	9	0	5	15	11	23	3	1	.444	.327	R	R	5-11	190	5-19-77	1998	Ann Arbor, Mich.
Jordan, Kevin	.225	46	160	10	36	7	0	2	17	8	17	1	1	.306	.269	R	R	6-1	200	10-9-69	1990	Birkdale, Australia
Kingsale, Eugene	.244	46	160	19	39	6	5	0	12	11	24	9	5	.344	.297	S	R	6-3	190	8-20-76	1994	Oranjestad, Aruba
Klassen, Danny	.246	112	407	63	100	19	4	11	48	28	110	12	5	.393	.303	R	R	6-0	190	9-22-75	1993	Stuart, Fla.
Lennon, Pat	.246	62	203	26	50	10	1	9	32	23	56	2	1	.438	.326	R	R	6-2	200	4-27-68	1986	Whiteville, N.C.
Magee, Wendell	.214	53	192	13	41	7	2	2	18	9	46	0	3	.302	.248	R	R	6-0	220	8-3-72	1994	Hattiesburg, Miss.
2-team (25 Scranton)	.253	78	285	24	72	15	3	3	30	17	62	1	6	.358	.296							
Monroe, Craig	.404	14	47	14	19	4	1	2	6	4	.10	1	0	.660	.451	R	R	6-1	210	2-27-77	1995	Texarkana, Texas
Morris, Warren	.277	56	206	26	57	13	4	2	19	16	26	4	1	.408	.330	L	R	5-11	180	1-11-74	1996	Alexandria, La.
Munoz, Billy	.000	2	6	0	0	0	0	0	0	2	0	0	0	.000	.250	L	L	6-2	220	6-30-75	1998	Mesa, Ariz.
Nicholson, Derek	.224	23	67	9	15	2	0	2	9	12	17	1	0	.343	.338	L	R	6-0	200	6-17-76	1998	Redondo Beach, Calif.
Peeples, Mike	.190	23	79	4	15	4	0	0	11	5	14	0	1	.241	.230	R	R	6-0	170	9-3-76	1994	Green Cove Springs, Fla.
Pena, Carlos	.333	8	30	4	10	4	1	0	5	4	7	0	0	.533	.429	L	L	6-2	210	5-17-78	1998	Haverhill, Mass.
Perez, Jhonny	.223	72	215	22	48	8	1	2	17	7	37	14	4	.298	.256	R	R	5-10	180	10-23-76	1994	Santo Domingo, D.R.
Ross, Cody	.287	124	470	74	135	35	6	20	61	32	86	15	6	.515	.333	R	L	5-11	180	12-23-80	1999	Carlsbad, N.M.
Taveras, Luis	.128	16	39	3	5	1	0	1	1	4	8	0	0	.231	.209	R	R	5-10	180	8-1-75	1995	Santiago, D.R.
Torres, Andres	.255	70	271	36	69	13	3	2	16	18	61	27	11	.347	.301	R	R	5-10	190	1-26-78	1998	Aguada, P.R.
Ust, Brant	.253	86	296	26	75	25	2	5	31	14	61	1	3	.402	.297	R	R	6-2	200	7-17-78	1999	Redmond, Wash.
Valera, Yohanny	.197	65	188	20	37	12	0	3	18	10	63	1	1	.309	.252	R	R	6-1	200	8-17-76	1993	Virginia Beach, Va.
Walbeck, Matt	.417	4	12	2	5	0	0	0	1	3	2	0	0	.417	.533	S	R	5-11	190	10-2-69	1987	Fair Oaks, Calif.
Witt, Kevin	.316	39	133	22	42	10	0	9	28	16	36	0	0	.594	.391	L	R	6-4	220	1-5-76	1994	Bellaire, Texas
Wright, Ron	.176	5	17	0	3	0	0	0	3	1	6	0	0	.176	.263	R	R	6-1	230	1-21-76	1994	St. George, Utah
Young, Ernie	.264	128	454	56	120	22	0	21	84	50	119	10	6	.452	.342	R	R	6-1	230	7-8-69	1990	Gilbert, Ariz.

PITCHING	W	L	ERA	G	GS	CG	SV	IP	H	R	ER	BB	SO	AVG	B	T	HT	WT	DOB	1st Yr	Resides
Ahearne, Pat	4	5	3.36	15	15	1	0	102	97	43	38	26	57	.251	R	R	6-3	190	12-10-69	1992	Atascadero, Calif.
Anderson, Matt	1	3	3.79	23	5	0	3	38	50	23	16	8	31	.314	R	R	6-4	200	8-17-76	1997	Louisville, Ky.
Avery, Steve	1	4	3.15	22	2	0	0	34	37	16	12	10	14	.284	L	L	6-4	200	4-14-70	1988	Dearborn, Mich.
Brittan, Corey	5	5	3.73	44	1	0	1	63	74	36	26	23	24	.302	R	R	6-6	200	2-23-75	1996	Scott City, Kan.
De la Cruz, Fernando	0	0	13.50	2	0	0	0	3	6	5	5	2	4	.352	R	R	6-0	170	1-25-71	1993	La Romana, D.R.
Eckenstahler, Eric	3	6	3.16	39	0	0	0	43	32	21	15	25	40	.213	L	L	6-7	220	12-17-76	2000	Lake Villa, Ill.
Ennis, John	1	0	5.17	3	3	0	0	16	22	9	9	5	9	.354	R	R	6-5	220	10-17-79	1998	Panorama, Calif.
2-team (28 Richmond)	3	11	5.51	31	18	0	0	116	143	79	71	42	85	.311							
German, Franklyn	1	4	2.45	24	0	0	4	29	21	9	8	9	32	.212	R	R	6-4	260	1-20-80	1996	San Cristobal, D.R.
Greisinger, Seth	6	9	3.97	25	21	2	0	136	154	77	60	23	80	.284	R	R	6-3	190	7-29-75	1996	Falls Church, Va.
Jimenez, Jason	1	2	4.04	47	0	0	2	49	42	23	22	29	35	.235	R	L	6-2	200	1-10-76	1997	Elk Grove, Calif.
Knotts, Gary	4	6	5.13	13	13	0	0	79	98	54	45	28	63	.304	R	R	6-4	230	2-12-77	1996	Decatur, Ala.
Larrison, Preston	0	1	3.38	1	1	0	0	5	3	3	2	2	3	.157	R	R	6-4	230	11-19-80	2001	Aurora, Ill.
Loux, Shane	11	6	3.02	21	20	2	0	128	129	53	43	30	58	.265	R	R	6-2	230	8-31-79	1997	Gilbert, Ariz.
Mears, Chris	5	1	2.78	25	5	0	2	58	53	20	18	19	28	.245	R	R	6-4	190	1-20-78	1996	Victoria, B.C.
Patterson, Danny	1	0	2.45	10	0	0	0	11	8	3	3	5	6	.210	R	R	6-0	190	2-17-71	1989	Colleyville, Texas
Pearson, Terry	5	3	4.34	45	0	0	2	48	61	36	23	20	27	.305	R	R	6-0	200	11-10-71	1995	Carrollton, Ala.
Robertson, Nate	9	7	3.14	24	23	3	0	155	145	62	54	47	102	.249	R	L	6-2	210	9-3-77	1999	Valley Center, Kan.
Rodney, Fernando	1	1	1.33	38	0	0	23	41	22	6	6	13	58	.162	R	R	5-11	200	3-18-77	1997	Santo Domingo, D.R.
Van Hekken, Andy	4	6	5.88	13	12	1	0	72	93	47	47	18	25	.322	R	L	6-3	180	7-31-79	1998	Holland, Mich.
Walker, Tyler	2	9	4.45	26	22	1	0	131	139	73	65	47	117	.270	R	R	6-3	230	5-15-76	1997	Ross, Calif.

FIELDING

Catcher	PCT	G	PO	A	E	DP	PB
Hinch	.991	48	299	22	3	5	3
Inge	1.000	35	207	28	0	2	4
Taveras	.974	14	68	8	2	1	1
Valera	.980	54	265	31	6	4	1
Walbeck	1.000	1	7	1	0	0	1
Witt	.983	24	226	9	4	27	
Young	.981	7	48	4	1	6	

First Base	PCT	G	PO	A	E	DP
Evans	1.000	2	6	0	0	1
Hinch	1.000	2	17	0	0	2
Jordan	1.000	17	165	14	0	15
Lennon	.985	47	413	35	7	49
Morris	1.000	1	5	1	0	0
Munoz	1.000	2	19	1	0	4
Nicholson	.990	13	94	5	1	14
Peeples	.990	21	186	10	2	21
Pena	.986	7	65	5	1	9
Perez	1.000	2	6	0	0	0
Ust	1.000	2	8	2	0	2
Valera	.987	7	72	2	1	7

Second Base	PCT	G	PO	A	E	DP
Bocachica	.938	20	29	61	6	17
Jordan	.978	22	39	51	2	14
Klassen	.989	30	67	106	2	35
Morris	.983	44	107	125	4	49
Perez	.969	32	69	88	5	17
Ust	1.000	1	2	4	0	0

Third Base	PCT	G	PO	A	E	DP
Bocachica	1.000	2	2	3	0	0
Evans	.960	34	17	102	5	14
Hinch	.000	1	0	0	0	0
Klassen	.667	3	0	2	1	1
Magee	.000	1	0	0	0	0
Morris	.920	9	6	17	2	0
Perez	1.000	3	0	6	0	0
Ust	.944	83	47	188	14	26
Witt	.839	13	3	23	5	3

Shortstop	PCT	G	PO	A	E	DP
Infante	.942	64	101	191	18	48
Klassen	.949	76	119	237	19	57
Perez	.938	6	11	19	2	4
Ust	1.000	1	1	2	0	0

Outfield	PCT	G	PO	A	E	DP
Bocachica	.964	69	129	4	5	1
Evans	1.000	2	1	0	0	0
Jordan	.000	1	0	0	0	0
Kingsale	1.000	46	84	1	0	0
Lennon	.917	7	11	0	1	0
Magee	.987	43	73	2	1	0
Monroe	1.000	13	24	0	0	0
Nicholson	1.000	2	4	0	0	0
Peeples	.857	4	6	0	1	0
Perez	1.000	21	28	4	0	0
Ross	.977	119	243	15	6	0
Torres	.973	70	181	2	5	1
Young	.978	51	84	6	2	3

ERIE SEAWOLVES — Class AA

EASTERN LEAGUE

BATTING	AVG	G	AB	R	H	2B	3B	HR	RBI	BB	SO	SB	CS	SLG	OBP	B	T	HT	WT	DOB	1st Yr	Resides
Bautista, Rayner	.286	115	398	44	114	18	4	11	48	18	96	4	3	.435	.322	R	R	5-11	150	9-17-78	1995	Nizao, D.R.
Brown, Tonayne	.276	72	275	39	76	19	5	3	34	15	52	2	1	.415	.324	R	L	5-11	190	8-24-77	1998	Tallahassee, Fla.
2-team (53 Portland)	.256	125	464	64	119	25	7	4	60	28	92	4	3	.366	.308							
Daigle, Leo	.238	118	412	59	98	25	1	13	54	41	82	3	1	.398	.317	R	R	6-3	220	9-18-79	1997	Spring Valley, Calif.
Hannahan, Jack	.257	135	471	64	121	18	0	9	45	48	78	2	0	.352	.328	L	R	6-2	200	3-4-80	2001	St. Paul, Minn.
Kelly, Donald	.265	22	83	14	22	5	1	1	13	15	9	0	0	.386	.378	L	R	6-4	190	2-15-80	2001	Pittsburgh, Pa.
Knoedler, Jason	.143	5	14	0	2	0	0	0	0	2	6	1	0	.143	.294	S	R	6-1	190	7-17-80	2001	Springfield, Ill.
Kropf, Andy	.190	16	42	5	8	0	0	0	4	1	9	0	0	.190	.205	S	R	6-1	190	7-19-78	2000	Roswell, Ga.
Logan, Nook	.251	136	514	71	129	16	7	4	38	51	103	37	13	.333	.316	S	R	6-2	180	11-28-79	2000	Natchez, Miss.
Munoz, Billy	.280	110	378	49	106	15	3	17	61	45	83	4	0	.471	.357	L	L	6-2	220	6-30-75	1998	Mesa, Ariz.
Nicholson, Derek	.269	80	279	35	75	16	1	3	31	39	56	3	2	.366	.362	L	R	6-0	200	6-17-76	1998	Redondo Beach, Calif.
Perez, Jhonny	.265	20	68	8	18	6	1	1	12	8	9	4	0	.426	.354	R	R	5-10	180	10-23-76	1994	Santo Domingo, D.R.
Richardson, Corey	.172	49	128	14	22	5	1	1	11	9	28	2	2	.250	.226	S	R	6-0	160	3-9-77	1999	Lone Star, Texas
Romprey, Ed	.292	17	24	2	7	3	0	0	2	3	3	0	0	.417	.370	R	R	6-0	180	4-13-80	2002	Victorville, Calif.
St. Pierre, Maxim	.236	115	399	50	94	16	0	11	54	33	66	2	0	.358	.299	R	R	6-0	170	4-17-80	1997	Montreal, Quebec
Taveras, Luis	.253	44	146	19	37	6	1	3	22	16	20	1	0	.370	.325	R	R	5-10	180	8-1-75	1995	Santiago, D.R.
Tousa, Scott	.245	130	437	56	107	17	8	5	51	70	81	10	3	.355	.357	L	R	5-11	180	8-3-79	2001	St. George, Utah
Ust, Brant	.286	45	161	24	46	11	2	5	25	7	26	2	0	.472	.320	R	R	6-2	200	7-17-78	1999	Redmond, Wash.
Varner, Noochie	.303	44	175	25	53	6	2	3	30	14	29	0	0	.411	.353	R	R	6-0	180	12-7-80	2000	Cynthiana, Ky.
Walker, Matt	.268	87	291	43	78	18	0	9	44	21	60	2	2	.423	.324	R	R	6-2	200	12-3-77	2000	Gibsonia, Penn.

PITCHING	W	L	ERA	G	GS	CG	SV	IP	H	R	ER	BB	SO	AVG	B	T	HT	WT	DOB	1st Yr	Resides
Ahearne, Pat	4	1	2.07	12	12	2	0	83	61	23	19	20	53	.203	R	R	6-3	190	12-10-69	1992	Atascadero, Calif.
Alvarado, Carlo	3	2	3.14	37	1	0	0	66	56	29	23	28	55	.228	R	R	6-4	210	1-24-78	1995	Arecibo, P.R.
Baugh, Kenny	7	9	4.60	19	19	1	0	110	111	71	56	32	58	.262	R	R	6-4	190	2-5-79	2001	Houston, Texas
Birtwell, John	1	0	3.93	11	0	0	0	18	22	8	8	3	26	.314	R	R	6-2	220	9-4-79	2001	Walpole, Mass.
Borkowski, Dave	0	1	3.38	6	0	0	0	8	10	4	3	2	4	.333	R	R	6-1	220	2-7-77	1995	Monroe, Mich.
Burnside, Adrian	2	4	6.28	15	11	0	2	67	81	57	47	27	46	.296	R	L	6-3	210	3-15-77	1996	Bradenton, Fla.
Cordova, Jorge	1	1	4.53	30	0	0	0	48	47	28	24	16	31	.262	R	R	6-0	200	1-13-78	1998	La Asuncion, Venez.
De la Cruz, Fernando	1	0	8.25	7	0	0	0	12	18	12	11	3	6	.346	R	R	6-0	170	1-25-71	1993	La Romana, D.R.
Farnsworth, Jeff	3	3	3.21	8	8	2	0	53	59	21	19	10	35	.286	R	R	6-2	190	10-6-75	1996	Pensacola, Fla.
Henkel, Rob	9	3	3.38	16	16	0	0	83	67	33	31	27	70	.219	R	L	6-2	210	8-3-78	2001	La Mesa, Calif.
Johnson, Jeremy	5	3	2.82	10	10	0	0	61	52	23	19	15	31	.234	R	R	6-3	170	7-19-82	2000	Mooresville, N.C.
Johnson, Mark	8	3	3.59	48	3	0	4	88	87	39	35	19	54	.262	R	R	6-3	220	5-2-75	1997	Leesburg, Fla.
Kalita, Tim	0	5	7.15	15	10	0	0	50	75	43	40	23	29	.344	R	L	6-2	220	11-21-78	1999	Oak Park, Ill.

PITCHING	W	L	ERA	G	GS	CG	SV	IP	H	R	ER	BB	SO	AVG	B	T	HT	WT	DOB	1st Yr	Resides
Larrison, Preston	4	12	5.61	24	24	0	0	127	161	89	79	59	53	.322	R	R	6-4	230	11-19-80	2001	Aurora, Ill.
Pearson, Terry	1	0	3.55	9	0	0	0	13	12	5	5	0	11	.255	R	R	6-0	200	11-10-71	1995	Carrollton, Ala.
Pettyjohn, Adam	1	4	4.00	19	10	1	0	81	87	39	36	18	49	.276	R	L	6-3	190	6-11-77	1998	Exeter, Calif.
Rivera, Homero	13	4	2.97	54	0	0	1	73	76	26	24	22	36	.278	R	L	5-10	160	8-13-77	1995	Nizao, D.R.
Schmack, Brian	3	3	2.05	53	0	0	29	57	53	15	13	10	47	.252	R	R	6-2	190	12-7-73	1996	Barrington, Ill.
Spiegel, Mike	0	5	3.07	24	3	0	0	44	43	25	15	20	28	.260	L	L	6-5	200	11-24-75	1996	Carmichael, Calif.
Van Hekken, Andy	5	6	4.02	13	13	0	0	81	89	41	36	18	32	.280	R	L	6-3	180	7-31-79	1998	Holland, Mich.
Woodyard, Mark	1	0	5.56	2	2	0	0	11	14	7	7	5	6	.325	R	R	6-2	190	12-19-78	2000	Grand Bay, Ala.

FIELDING

Catcher	PCT	G	PO	A	E	DP	PB
Kropf	.980	12	46	2	1	0	3
St. Pierre	.984	104	545	76	10	7	5
Taveras	.981	35	193	18	4	2	8
Ust	1.000	1	1	0	0	0	0

First Base	PCT	G	PO	A	E	DP
Daigle	.991	90	832	46	8	92
Kelly	1.000	1	7	0	0	1
Munoz	.986	60	504	45	8	58
Nicholson	1.000	2	7	2	0	0

Second Base	PCT	G	PO	A	E	DP
Bautista	1.000	2	3	3	0	3
Perez	1.000	3	7	11	0	1
Tousa	.986	129	265	388	9	118
Ust	.981	13	17	35	1	8

Third Base	PCT	G	PO	A	E	DP
Hannahan	.928	132	103	334	34	41
Perez	.857	4	1	5	1	0
Romprey	.857	5	1	5	1	1
Ust	.947	5	0	18	1	2

Shortstop	PCT	G	PO	A	E	DP
Bautista	.954	107	140	300	21	69
Kelly	.959	20	28	66	4	14
Perez	.909	5	4	16	2	2
Romprey	.955	5	10	11	1	8
Ust	.911	14	16	35	5	9

Outfield	PCT	G	PO	A	E	DP
Brown	.992	72	128	4	1	1
Knoedler	1.000	5	8	0	0	0
Kropf	.000	2	0	0	0	0
Logan	.991	134	340	9	3	2
Munoz	1.000	2	2	0	0	0
Nicholson	.952	59	96	4	5	0
Perez	1.000	7	12	0	0	0
Richardson	.987	44	75	2	1	0
Romprey	.000	1	0	0	0	0
Ust	1.000	8	10	0	0	0
Varner	1.000	44	80	6	0	1
Walker	.974	75	147	3	4	0

LAKELAND TIGERS — High Class A

FLORIDA STATE LEAGUE

BATTING	AVG	G	AB	R	H	2B	3B	HR	RBI	BB	SO	SB	CS	SLG	OBP	B	T	HT	WT	DOB	1st Yr	Resides
Cleveland, Russ	.192	20	73	6	14	3	0	0	6	3	18	0	0	.233	.224	R	R	6-3	210	12-26-79	1998	Las Vegas, Nev.
Espinosa, David	.271	92	350	57	95	18	7	4	46	50	78	13	10	.397	.359	S	R	6-2	190	12-16-81	2001	Miami, Fla.
Granderson, Curtis	.286	127	476	71	136	29	10	11	51	49	91	10	7	.458	.365	L	R	6-1	180	3-16-81	2002	Lynwood, Ill.
Hernandez, Anderson	.229	106	380	47	87	11	4	2	28	27	69	15	7	.295	.278	S	R	5-9	160	10-30-82	2001	Santo Domingo, D.R.
Jenkins, Neil	.221	88	321	28	71	21	1	14	55	22	150	1	0	.424	.270	R	R	6-5	200	7-17-80	1999	Jupiter, Fla.
Kelly, Donald	.317	87	303	48	96	17	4	1	38	45	25	15	2	.409	.401	L	R	6-4	190	2-15-80	2001	Pittsburgh, Pa.
Kropf, Andy	.284	44	148	16	42	5	1	0	13	19	32	0	2	.331	.359	S	R	6-1	190	7-19-78	2000	Roswell, Ga.
Lugo, Alfredo	.254	88	287	34	73	11	1	2	19	28	63	2	2	.321	.325	R	R	6-2	190	7-18-79	2001	Caracas, Venez.
Mattle, David	.227	102	365	41	83	16	3	8	52	25	69	6	3	.353	.277	L	R	6-0	200	12-21-79	2001	Barberton, Ohio
McDonald, Kevin	.133	5	15	1	2	0	0	0	0	0	6	0	0	.133	.133	L	R	6-1	210	3-8-80	2002	Rockaway, N.J.
Raburn, Ryan	.222	95	325	52	72	14	3	12	56	45	89	2	1	.394	.332	R	R	6-0	180	4-17-81	2001	Plant City, Fla.
Roughton, Jody	.196	14	51	4	10	1	0	0	3	7	10	0	0	.216	.317	L	R	6-1	190	5-6-81	2002	Carthage, Mo.
Sanchez, Danilo	.105	12	38	4	4	1	0	0	3	5	13	0	0	.132	.227	R	R	5-11	210	10-25-80	1997	Santo Domingo, D.R.
Tejeda, Juan	.280	125	461	63	129	28	4	10	76	56	68	6	3	.423	.360	R	R	6-2	190	1-26-82	1999	Santiago, D.R.
Tress, Irving	.200	3	5	0	1	0	0	0	0	1	2	0	0	.200	.333	R	R	6-2	200	12-18-80	2003	Cordoba, Mexico
Trezza, Alex	.266	74	267	16	71	19	1	3	27	18	65	0	1	.378	.309	L	R	6-3	210	9-1-80	2001	Middletown, N.Y.
Watson, Rob	.219	31	114	14	25	9	0	3	7	5	23	1	0	.377	.260	R	R	5-10	180	12-31-79	2002	Riverside, Calif.
Woods, Michael	.205	116	361	38	74	12	4	0	27	52	92	10	8	.260	.304	R	R	6-1	200	9-11-80	2001	Baton Rouge, La.

PITCHING	W	L	ERA	G	GS	CG	SV	IP	H	R	ER	BB	SO	AVG	B	T	HT	WT	DOB	1st Yr	Resides
Alvarado, Carlo	0	0	3.68	4	0	0	0	7	5	3	3	6	12	.185	R	R	6-4	210	1-24-78	1995	Arecibo, P.R.
Baugh, Kenny	3	0	3.86	4	4	0	0	21	21	14	9	11	12	.262	R	R	6-4	190	2-5-79	2001	Houston, Texas
Birtwell, John	3	3	1.74	35	0	0	3	41	35	11	8	11	41	.233	R	R	6-2	220	9-4-79	2001	Walpole, Mass.
Cuello, Felix	0	1	6.23	14	2	0	0	26	31	21	18	27	17	.295	R	R	6-3	180	9-17-79	2000	Santo Domingo, D.R.
Diaz, Luis	2	1	4.12	10	0	0	0	20	16	11	9	7	13	.225	S	R	6-0	160	4-16-78	1997	Nizao, D.R.
Hamman, Corey	6	5	3.32	46	0	0	1	60	63	30	22	21	46	.275	L	L	6-2	200	4-12-80	2002	Flanders, N.J.
Howell, Michael	0	4	5.57	5	5	0	0	21	27	19	13	10	13	.317	R	R	6-4	200	11-9-79	2001	Binghamton, N.Y.
Kieninger, Billy	0	2	7.46	21	0	0	0	35	56	33	29	7	20	.366	R	R	6-4	200	12-31-79	2002	Xenia, Ohio
Kirsten, Rick	1	1	3.60	2	2	0	0	10	11	4	4	2	8	.289	R	R	6-0	180	7-23-78	1996	Rolling Meadows, Ill.
Kobow, Mike	5	1	1.05	32	0	0	15	34	24	8	4	14	28	.195	R	R	6-4	190	4-9-79	2001	Hutchinson, Minn.
Leu, Trevor	5	6	3.24	33	14	0	0	108	121	54	39	42	84	.284	L	L	6-2	200	12-29-78	2001	Bartlesville, Okla.
McDowell, Kevin	5	12	4.99	24	22	0	0	126	139	77	70	47	75	.286	L	L	6-2	200	11-20-78	2001	Cheswick, Penn.
Moates, Jason	4	6	3.61	31	13	2	2	92	83	41	37	50	84	.247	R	R	6-2	210	8-22-78	2001	Columbia, Tenn.
Myers, Damien	2	3	2.93	26	0	0	3	43	40	15	14	14	35	.251	L	L	6-0	180	11-3-80	2002	New York, N.Y.
Novoa, Roberto	4	5	3.73	19	15	2	0	99	93	45	41	25	71	.242	R	R	6-5	200	8-15-79	1999	Santo Domingo, D.R.
Ostlund, Ian	0	1	8.59	17	0	0	0	22	35	21	21	5	17	.350	R	L	6-1	200	10-17-78	2001	Singers Glen, Va.
Petty, Chad	3	4	4.40	10	10	0	0	57	66	35	28	10	36	.286	L	L	6-4	200	2-17-82	2000	West Farmington, Ohio
Rodney, Lee	6	12	4.26	27	23	0	0	133	150	69	63	44	103	.289	R	R	6-2	180	11-6-77	2000	Dacula, Ga.
Stockman, Landon	2	3	5.20	44	0	0	7	54	54	41	31	37	31	.271	R	R	6-2	190	8-28-79	2001	Dickson, Tenn.
Woodyard, Mark	4	8	4.53	23	23	1	0	117	133	69	59	53	84	.287	R	R	6-2	190	12-19-78	2000	Grand Bay, Ala.

FIELDING

Catcher	PCT	G	PO	A	E	DP	PB
Cleveland	.992	20	113	13	1	1	2
Kropf	.982	25	152	12	3	2	1
McDonald	1.000	5	26	4	0	1	1
Sanchez	1.000	12	95	5	0	1	3
Trezza	.980	74	456	44	10	5	8

First Base	PCT	G	PO	A	E	DP
Kelly	1.000	15	135	17	0	18
Kropf	1.000	4	25	3	0	3
Lugo	1.000	1	5	1	0	1
Roughton	1.000	5	36	0	0	4
Tejeda	.985	110	895	67	15	102

Second Base	PCT	G	PO	A	E	DP
Kelly	1.000	2	1	5	0	2
Lugo	.983	12	26	33	1	10
Watson	.982	9	22	32	1	10
Woods	.964	114	232	309	20	74

Third Base	PCT	G	PO	A	E	DP
Kelly	.957	34	30	58	4	9
Lugo	.942	19	6	43	3	6
Raburn	.911	84	53	163	21	20
Watson	1.000	1	1	3	0	0

Shortstop	PCT	G	PO	A	E	DP
Hernandez	.947	102	160	304	26	62
Kelly	.967	20	32	56	3	18
Watson	.968	16	31	61	3	10

Outfield	PCT	G	PO	A	E	DP
Espinosa	.984	91	188	2	3	1
Granderson	.984	126	292	15	5	3
Jenkins	.976	33	40	0	1	0
Kropf	1.000	1	4	1	0	0
Lugo	.989	53	83	5	1	0
Mattle	.965	99	183	12	7	0
Tress	.500	3	1	0	1	0

WEST MICHIGAN WHITECAPS — Low Class A

SOUTH ATLANTIC LEAGUE

BATTING	AVG	G	AB	R	H	2B	3B	HR	RBI	BB	SO	SB	CS	SLG	OBP	B	T	HT	WT	DOB	1st Yr	Resides
Brito, Angel	.087	9	23	0	2	0	0	0	0	0	4	0	0	.087	.125	R	R	6-0	180	4-7-78	1995	San Cristobal, D.R.
Clevlen, Brent	.260	138	481	67	125	22	7	12	63	72	111	6	3	.410	.359	R	R	6-2	190	10-27-83	2002	Cedar Park, Texas
Francia, Juan	.240	118	405	49	97	7	6	0	27	42	78	31	14	.286	.316	S	R	5-9	150	1-4-82	1998	San Antonio, Venez.
Gonzalez, Juan	.249	126	453	65	113	16	6	4	39	65	81	24	10	.338	.346	S	R	6-0	160	2-23-82	1999	Valencia, Venez.
Heath, Demetrius	.256	73	195	34	50	6	2	1	24	26	39	5	3	.323	.348	R	R	5-10	170	1-23-81	2001	Bethel, N.C.
Kennedy, Jason	.103	19	39	2	4	1	1	0	2	8	11	0	0	.179	.255	R	R	6-3	200	7-14-79	2002	Minneapolis, Minn.
Knoedler, Jason	.210	91	248	36	52	10	0	4	25	29	75	14	2	.298	.298	S	R	6-1	190	7-17-80	2001	Springfield, Ill.
Maples, Chris	.187	85	235	23	44	11	0	4	27	21	47	1	2	.285	.258	R	R	5-10	180	10-31-79	2002	Hillsborough, N.C.
Mejia, Gilberto	.200	34	115	14	23	2	1	1	9	8	31	0	1	.261	.252	S	R	5-9	160	9-1-82	2000	Bani, D.R.
Mendez, Victor	.236	137	471	64	111	20	11	9	63	47	85	14	8	.382	.307	S	R	5-11	180	6-28-80	1998	Las Matos de Farfan, D.R.
Moore, Scott	.239	107	372	40	89	16	6	6	45	41	110	2	4	.363	.325	L	R	6-2	180	11-17-83	2002	Long Beach, Calif.
Oakes, Matt	.230	42	87	8	20	3	0	1	7	3	17	0	2	.299	.264	R	R	5-11	180	8-30-79	2002	Taloga, Okla.
Rabelo, Mike	.274	123	394	41	108	16	0	5	40	31	62	9	4	.353	.328	S	R	6-1	200	1-17-80	2001	New Port Richey, Fla.
Raburn, Ryan	.351	16	57	14	20	7	0	3	12	6	14	1	1	.632	.431	R	R	6-0	180	4-17-81	2001	Plant City, Fla.
Reynolds, Wilton	.267	102	359	39	96	17	6	8	44	33	86	7	6	.415	.338	R	R	6-4	190	3-5-80	2002	Sacramento, Calif.
Romprey, Ed	.045	9	22	1	1	1	0	0	0	0	4	0	0	.091	.045	R	R	6-0	180	4-13-80	2002	Victorville, Calif.
Roughton, Jody	.255	106	380	41	97	28	4	4	46	32	72	0	2	.382	.316	L	R	6-1	190	5-6-81	2002	Carthage, Mo.
Watson, Rob	.251	58	191	32	48	5	0	3	22	32	38	5	1	.325	.383	R	R	5-10	180	12-31-79	2002	Riverside, Calif.

PITCHING	W	L	ERA	G	GS	CG	SV	IP	H	R	ER	BB	SO	AVG	B	T	HT	WT	DOB	1st Yr	Resides
Connolly, Jon	16	3	1.41	25	25	5	0	166	128	37	26	38	104	.211	R	L	6-0	200	8-24-83	2001	Oneonta, N.Y.
Diaz, Luis	0	0	3.97	4	2	0	0	11	12	5	5	2	5	.266	S	R	6-0	160	4-16-78	1997	Nizao, D.R.
Figueroa, Juan	2	5	6.44	55	0	0	13	50	51	43	36	38	55	.262	R	R	6-0	180	10-8-81	2001	Carolina, P.R.
Gerk, Jordan	2	5	3.07	55	1	0	2	67	69	26	23	12	68	.260	L	L	6-1	180	7-6-79	2000	Kelowna, B.C.
Graham, Jason	2	1	4.23	28	0	0	0	45	51	24	21	25	20	.298	R	R	6-3	190	9-24-79	2002	Atlantis, Fla.
Howell, Michael	7	3	2.09	11	9	1	0	78	52	22	18	12	50	.188	R	R	6-4	200	11-9-79	2001	Binghamton, N.Y.
Kieninger, Billy	2	2	3.00	26	0	0	0	48	63	25	16	17	31	.318	R	R	6-4	200	12-31-79	2002	Xenia, Ohio
Koenig, Ross	0	1	7.83	20	0	0	0	23	25	24	20	20	22	.268	R	R	6-3	170	5-4-80	2001	Festus, Mo.
Lewis, Lavon	0	1	13.50	1	1	0	0	2	2	4	3	5	1	.285	R	R	6-4	205	12-17-83	2003	Warrensburg, Mo.
Ostlund, Ian	3	0	1.59	44	0	0	19	45	31	10	8	14	56	.192	R	L	6-1	200	10-17-78	2001	Singers Glen, Va.
Parris, Matt	6	6	3.21	32	15	0	0	126	127	56	45	38	80	.260	R	R	6-4	200	10-4-82	2000	Ventura, Calif.
Pender, Matt	2	10	5.65	17	17	0	0	86	95	60	54	42	51	.290	R	R	6-5	210	6-11-81	2002	Kathleen, Ga.
Pickford, Troy	5	7	2.66	16	16	1	0	98	97	41	29	26	71	.261	R	R	6-8	220	8-9-79	2002	Fresno, Calif.
Rodriguez, Jermy	3	6	3.81	41	0	0	0	52	54	30	22	28	32	.268	R	R	5-10	160	1-10-80	2002	Esperanza, D.R.
Sanchez, Humberto	7	7	4.42	23	23	0	0	116	107	71	57	78	96	.249	R	R	6-6	230	5-28-83	2002	Bronx, N.Y.
Smith, Dan	1	1	4.91	12	0	0	1	15	17	10	8	9	16	.288	R	R	6-4	225	11-29-78	2001	Bonne Terre, Mo.
Smith, Dustin	1	4	5.35	7	7	0	0	39	34	23	23	14	30	.234	R	R	6-4	220	7-5-80	2003	Clarksville, Tenn.
Steinborn, Chris	1	6	6.39	18	5	0	0	44	62	37	31	16	19	.328	L	L	6-4	210	3-23-82	2002	Akron, Ohio
Zumaya, Joel	7	5	2.79	19	19	0	0	90	69	35	28	38	126	.209	R	R	6-3	210	11-9-84	2002	Chula Vista, Calif.

FIELDING

Catcher	PCT	G	PO	A	E	DP	PB
Oakes	.980	42	186	12	4	0	8
Rabelo	.994	118	773	84	5	4	7

First Base	PCT	G	PO	A	E	DP
Brito	1.000	9	44	5	0	5
Maples	.980	51	319	19	7	23
Roughton	.990	99	750	58	8	56

Second Base	PCT	G	PO	A	E	DP
Francia	.948	70	129	162	16	36
Heath	1.000	3	7	2	0	0
Maples	1.000	12	11	23	0	4
Mejia	.970	25	39	58	3	14
Romprey	.938	6	4	11	1	3
Watson	.965	42	94	98	7	21

Third Base	PCT	G	PO	A	E	DP
Gonzalez	.867	13	8	18	4	2
Maples	.895	17	5	29	4	3
Moore	.887	102	64	156	28	11
Raburn	.889	7	4	12	2	1
Watson	.903	15	8	20	3	0

Shortstop	PCT	G	PO	A	E	DP
Francia	.921	30	33	83	10	13
Gonzalez	.972	116	165	326	14	51
Romprey	1.000	3	3	5	0	2

Outfield	PCT	G	PO	A	E	DP
Clevlen	.966	134	271	16	10	3
Heath	.973	23	35	1	1	0
Kennedy	1.000	4	1	0	0	0
Knoedler	.975	72	112	7	3	1
Mendez	.977	135	329	7	8	2
Reynolds	.943	77	138	10	9	1

ONEONTA TIGERS — Short-Season Class A

NEW YORK-PENN LEAGUE

BATTING	AVG	G	AB	R	H	2B	3B	HR	RBI	BB	SO	SB	CS	SLG	OBP	B	T	HT	WT	DOB	1st Yr	Resides
Blue, Vincent	.288	70	233	47	67	7	8	2	26	38	56	13	3	.412	.388	L	R	6-2	180	2-8-83	2001	Houston, Texas
Brown, Michael	.266	45	169	18	45	5	4	1	10	8	19	5	1	.361	.315	R	R	6-0	195	11-25-80	2003	Richmond, Va.
Burgos, Richie	.288	34	125	11	36	4	4	2	22	10	31	0	1	.432	.333	R	R	6-0	190	4-18-82	2003	Glendora, Calif.
Cotto, Pedro	.273	30	99	11	27	5	0	0	3	5	7	1	3	.323	.314	L	L	5-11	170	5-26-82	2002	San Juan, P.R.
Doyle, Nathan	.190	29	79	16	15	5	0	0	12	12	27	2	1	.253	.320	R	R	6-1	195	1-30-81	2003	Wilmington, Del.
Flowers, Bo	.177	37	124	17	22	1	2	0	9	9	42	5	1	.218	.244	R	R	6-0	190	11-12-83	2002	Maywood, Ill.
Ford, Jake	.216	28	97	8	21	7	0	2	14	6	18	0	0	.351	.278	R	R	6-1	220	2-18-81	2003	Louisville, Ky.
Giarratano, Tony	.328	47	189	31	62	11	4	3	27	12	22	9	4	.476	.369	S	R	6-0	180	11-29-82	2003	Marlboro, N.J.
Graham, Andrew	.182	20	55	6	10	3	0	0	8	3	11	0	0	.236	.233	R	R	6-4	215	4-22-82	2003	Sydney, Australia
Huddleston, Bobby	.208	38	120	10	25	4	0	0	10	9	18	0	0	.242	.289	R	R	6-1	235	3-20-80	2003	Montgomery, Ala.
Hunt, Kelly	.257	47	179	18	46	13	0	2	21	16	42	0	0	.363	.322	R	R	6-5	240	4-15-81	2003	Bowling Green, Ohio
Kirkland, Kody	.303	67	254	46	77	15	11	4	49	25	60	14	5	.496	.390	R	R	6-4	200	6-9-83	2002	Pocatello, Idaho
McGorty, John	.172	32	93	10	16	2	0	0	5	9	24	0	1	.194	.250	L	L	6-1	195	11-20-80	2003	West Sayville, N.Y.
McIntyre, Nick	.245	33	102	12	25	3	0	0	9	11	24	4	5	.275	.325	S	R	5-10	185	3-11-81	2003	Lafayette, Ind.
McKinney, Garth	.224	54	196	27	44	6	4	4	19	12	61	6	1	.357	.285	R	R	6-3	210	5-7-82	2002	Johnson City, Tenn.
Mejia, Gilberto	.238	6	21	4	5	1	1	0	5	3	3	1	1	.381	.333	S	R	5-9	160	9-1-82	2000	Bani, D.R.
Piantek, Kurt	1.000	1	1	0	1	0	0	0	0	1	0	0	0	1.000	1.000	R	R	6-3	215	6-19-81	2003	Wallingford, Conn.
Rodland, Eric	.328	57	244	43	80	15	8	0	27	17	25	13	2	.455	.377	L	R	6-1	180	2-23-80	2003	Snohomish, Wash.
Romprey, Ed	.179	8	28	1	5	1	0	0	3	3	9	0	0	.214	.250	R	R	6-0	180	4-13-80	2002	Victorville, Calif.
Sanchez, Danilo	.264	38	121	16	32	9	0	5	23	15	16	0	1	.463	.348	R	R	5-11	210	10-25-80	1997	Santo Domingo, D.R.

GAMES BY POSITION: C—Graham 20, Huddleston 27, Sanchez 38. **1B**—Burgos 24, Hunt 32, McGorty 23, Piantek 1. **2B**—McIntyre 19, Mejia 3, Rodland 55. **3B**—Doyle 2, Ford 9, Kirkland 65, McIntyre 3, Romprey 1. **SS**—Doyle 23, Giarratano 47, McIntyre 2, Romprey 7. **OF**—Blue 70, Brown 42, Cotto 26, Flowers 35, McGorty 7, McKinney 51.

PITCHING	W	L	ERA	G	GS	CG	SV	IP	H	R	ER	BB	SO	AVG	B	T	HT	WT	DOB	1st Yr	Resides
Baez, Reese	0	1	7.20	5	0	0	0	5	5	4	4	5	0	.277	R	R	5-11	190	5-1-81	2003	Garland, Texas
Baldwin, Andy	4	2	2.76	9	9	0	0	42	41	16	13	16	27	.259	R	R	6-2	190	2-28-82	2003	Campbellsville, Ky.
Contreras, Manuel	3	0	3.28	17	0	0	1	25	29	12	9	14	16	.284	R	R	6-0	170	3-20-81	2002	Villa Altagracia, D.R.
Dean, Herman	0	0	6.75	1	0	0	0	1	1	2	1	1	1	.200	R	R	6-3	190	11-25-80	2001	Monrovia, Calif.
Delacruz, Eulogio	0	0	10.80	2	0	0	0	3	6	4	4	1	4	.400	R	R	5-11	170	3-12-84	2002	Santo Domingo, D.R.
Diaz, Luis	1	0	2.70	2	2	0	0	10	11	3	3	3	12	.289	S	R	6-0	160	4-16-78	1997	Nizao, D.R.
Graham, Jason	0	1	9.82	7	0	0	0	11	15	12	12	8	7	.312	R	R	6-3	190	9-24-79	2002	Atlantis, Fla.
Homer, Chris	2	1	2.60	26	0	0	15	28	17	9	8	10	30	.178	R	R	6-1	190	3-6-81	2003	Jamesville, N.Y.
Howell, Michael	2	0	1.35	4	3	0	0	20	13	4	3	4	12	.175	R	R	6-4	200	11-9-79	2001	Binghamton, N.Y.
Lyons, Tom	2	5	4.41	12	4	0	0	35	38	20	17	10	22	.277	R	R	6-2	200	3-22-83	2001	Downers Grove, Ill.
Pender, Matt	0	2	3.47	7	4	0	0	23	16	10	9	8	19	.197	R	R	6-5	210	6-11-81	2002	Kathleen, Ga.
Perez, Ezequiel	2	2	2.64	21	0	0	1	44	37	15	13	13	27	.221	R	R	6-1	185	9-10-81	2003	San Juan, P.R.
Rogers, Brian	3	2	3.34	12	12	0	0	57	49	23	21	18	66	.232	R	R	6-4	190	7-17-82	2003	Marietta, Ga.
Ronz, Kenon	4	1	2.10	25	0	0	3	30	19	11	7	8	44	.175	L	L	5-11	185	4-30-81	2003	Scottsdale, Ariz.
Santo, Brian	4	0	2.20	23	0	0	0	41	32	14	10	16	35	.220	R	R	6-8	240	10-26-80	2003	Oberlin, Pa.
Spring, Daniel	4	2	4.89	23	0	0	1	39	37	24	21	19	21	.262	R	R	6-1	190	12-15-80	2003	Potomac, Md.
Steinborn, Chris	3	0	0.64	6	3	0	0	28	26	4	2	9	19	.252	L	L	6-4	210	3-23-82	2002	Akron, Ohio
Tata, Jordan	4	3	2.58	16	12	0	1	73	64	32	21	20	60	.236	R	R	6-6	220	9-20-81	2003	Dallas, Texas
Tomey, Anthony	3	2	5.43	20	7	0	0	53	46	38	32	34	56	.237	R	R	6-4	245	8-17-81	2003	Northville, Mich.
Vasquez, Matt	3	4	6.92	11	11	0	0	53	76	43	41	10	35	.327	R	R	6-3	205	6-7-82	2003	Santa Barbara, Calif.
Zell, Danny	1	2	4.65	8	8	0	0	31	32	18	16	18	19	.275	L	L	6-5	210	11-27-81	2003	Cypress, Texas

LAKELAND TIGERS — Rookie

GULF COAST LEAGUE

BATTING	AVG	G	AB	R	H	2B	3B	HR	RBI	BB	SO	SB	CS	SLG	OBP	B	T	HT	WT	DOB	1st Yr	Resides
Barnes, Justin	.239	31	71	6	17	2	0	0	9	7	17	0	0	.268	.325	R	R	6-3	210	10-13-80	2003	Gallion, Ala.
Billmaier, Kris	.205	32	78	13	16	3	0	1	11	13	14	2	2	.282	.347	R	R	5-10	185	10-16-80	2003	Woodinville, Wash.
Castro, Francisco	.260	47	173	33	45	6	3	1	21	25	34	15	1	.347	.353	S	R	5-10	170	6-13-83	2001	Santo Domingo, D.R.
Flowers, Bo	.182	15	44	3	8	3	1	0	2	2	12	2	1	.295	.234	R	R	6-0	190	11-12-83	2002	Maywood, Ill.
Gil, Luis	.200	36	105	15	21	4	3	0	10	6	26	6	1	.295	.257	R	R	6-1	170	2-12-84	2002	Castillo, D.R.
Laster, Jeramy	.240	42	121	27	29	4	1	1	17	10	35	9	2	.314	.295	R	R	6-1	185	4-5-85	2003	Nashville, Tenn.
Lee, Jonathan	.200	13	20	1	4	2	0	0	1	6	8	1	0	.300	.385	R	R	5-11	190	2-7-80	2003	Coconut Creek, Fla.
McDonald, Kevin	.235	5	17	1	4	0	0	0	2	0	4	0	0	.235	.222	L	R	6-1	210	3-8-80	2002	Rockaway, N.J.
McRae, Aaron	.286	7	14	2	4	0	0	0	0	3	7	1	0	.286	.412	L	R	6-2	203	4-11-80	2003	Delta, B.C.
Mejia, Gilberto	.360	44	175	36	63	11	9	5	29	13	29	23	5	.611	.400	S	R	5-9	160	9-1-82	2000	Bani, D.R.
Mendez, Rafael	.207	47	150	27	31	5	2	7	25	27	56	8	3	.407	.337	R	R	6-0	200	4-24-84	2002	Caguas, P.R.
Patino, Jorge	.215	29	65	7	14	0	0	0	1	2	8	3	1	.215	.250	R	R	5-10	150	1-25-86	2002	Puerto la Cruz, Venez.
Piantek, Kurt	.279	32	111	16	31	10	0	4	22	8	16	1	0	.477	.336	R	R	6-3	215	6-19-81	2003	Wallingford, Conn.
Ramirez, Wilkin	.275	54	200	34	55	6	7	5	35	13	51	6	1	.450	.321	R	R	6-2	190	10-25-85	2003	Bani, D.R.
Roa, Joel	.267	34	90	14	24	10	0	0	12	8	28	1	1	.378	.347	R	R	6-0	170	1-2-84	2001	Santo Domingo, D.R.
Sabino, Luis	.240	52	171	27	41	5	4	5	28	22	39	11	2	.404	.323	S	R	6-2	190	5-24-83	2003	Canovanas, P.R.
Sovie, Robbie	.200	41	130	23	26	5	1	1	13	7	33	9	2	.277	.255	R	R	6-1	180	11-24-83	2002	Jacksonville, Fla.
Williams, Matt	.143	42	98	11	14	2	0	0	6	9	26	5	4	.163	.213	S	R	6-2	170	11-18-83	2001	Los Angeles, Calif.

GAMES BY POSITION: C—Barnes 28, Lee 11, McDonald 4, Roa 34, Williams 1. **1B**—Mendez 43, Piantek 16, **2B**—Castro 43, Mejia 8, Patino 7. **3B**—Castro 2, Mejia 2, Ramirez 48, Williams 10. **SS**—Gil 27, Mejia 23, Patino 21. **OF**—Barnes 1, Billmaier 30, Flowers 9, Laster 37, Sabino 50, Sovie 38, Williams 30.

PITCHING	W	L	ERA	G	GS	CG	SV	IP	H	R	ER	BB	SO	AVG	B	T	HT	WT	DOB	1st Yr	Resides
Caraballo, Jesse	1	3	9.67	16	0	0	0	22	27	31	24	22	15	.290	R	R	6-1	190	7-17-86	2003	San Cristobal, D.R.
Contreras, Manuel	1	1	5.06	4	2	0	1	16	15	12	9	1	11	.230	R	R	6-0	170	3-20-81	2002	Villa Altagracia, D.R.
Cordova, Jorge	0	0	0.00	3	1	0	0	3	1	0	0	0	3	.100	R	R	6-0	200	1-13-78	1998	La Asuncion, Venez.
Dean, Herman	2	0	2.45	7	0	0	0	15	11	7	4	15	10	.211	R	R	6-3	190	11-25-80	2001	Monrovia, Calif.
Delacruz, Eulogio	2	2	2.59	22	0	0	7	24	18	10	7	15	30	.204	R	R	5-11	170	3-12-84	2002	Santo Domingo, D.R.
Dolsi, Freddy	1	1	4.70	8	2	0	0	23	27	20	12	12	19	.281	R	R	6-0	160	1-9-83	2003	San Pedro de Macoris, D.R.
Eugenio, Mario	0	2	8.54	17	0	0	1	26	33	32	25	30	23	.300	R	R	6-0	170	9-24-81	2002	Santo Domingo, D.R.
Garcia, Felipe	3	4	4.77	11	10	1	0	60	66	40	32	28	43	.272	R	R	5-11	160	9-20-82	2001	San Pedro de Macoris, D.R.
Gonzalez, Jose	1	0	7.50	8	0	0	0	6	5	7	5	11	8	.217	R	R	6-3	190	4-9-83	1999	Santo Domingo, D.R.
Herrera, Jose	2	3	3.05	15	2	1	1	38	39	24	13	16	24	.260	R	R	6-5	190	9-2-82	2003	Santo Domingo, D.R.
Jurrjens, Jair	2	1	3.21	7	2	0	0	28	33	16	10	3	20	.292	R	R	6-1	160	1-29-86	2003	Willemstad, Curacao
Kirsten, Rick	1	1	2.00	4	3	0	0	9	7	2	2	1	11	.212	R	R	6-0	180	7-23-78	1996	Rolling Meadows, Ill.
Lewis, Lavon	3	3	3.17	11	8	0	0	54	53	29	19	18	37	.257	R	R	6-4	205	12-17-83	2003	Warrensburg, Mo.
Martinez, Cristhian	3	2	5.86	9	5	0	0	35	34	25	23	11	39	.242	R	R	6-1	160	3-6-82	2003	San Cristobal, D.R.
Rainwater, Josh	1	2	4.78	10	9	0	0	38	41	23	20	20	40	.273	R	R	6-1	220	4-9-85	2003	DeRidder, La.
Sborz, Jay	0	2	4.85	8	7	0	0	26	20	18	14	14	35	.206	R	R	6-4	210	1-24-85	2003	Riverview, Fla.
Smith, Dustin	3	0	1.82	6	5	1	0	35	17	8	7	6	39	.137	R	R	6-4	220	7-5-80	2003	Clarksville, Tenn.
Vasquez, Sendy	2	2	7.47	11	1	0	0	16	18	13	13	11	12	.290	S	R	6-1	160	8-10-82	2003	Hato Mayor del Rey, D.R.

FLORIDA MARLINS

BY MIKE BERARDINO

OK, raise your hand if you saw this coming.

The eventual World Series champion would begin the 2003 season with a $48 million payroll, sixth-lowest in the majors. It would lose its best pitcher (A.J. Burnett) after one month to Tommy John surgery. It would later lose its top set-up man (Tim Spooneybarger) to the same procedure.

One of its key free-agent signings (Todd Hollandsworth) would lose his starting job by the middle of June, giving way to a 20-year-old Venezuelan (Miguel Cabrera) called up from Double-A. Oh, and Cabrera had only three games in the minors at his new position, left field.

Six weeks before Cabrera arrived, one of his Carolina Mudcats teammates beat him to South Florida. Some kid named Dontrelle Willis. Big lefthander with a goofy windup. Maybe you've heard of him.

The eventual World Series MVP (Josh Beckett) would miss two months during the first half with a sprained ligament in his throwing elbow. He would finish the year with eight wins, a career big league mark of 17-17 and zero complete games in his professional career.

Beckett would then toss complete games in two of his last three starts in the postseason, including the clinching Game Six at Yankee Stadium.

Among the players tossed aside the winter before by the eventual champs: National League RBI leader Preston Wilson and Red Sox team leader Kevin Millar.

Among the players brought in were fading catcher Ivan Rodriguez, punchless center fielder Juan Pierre and supposedly soft lefthander Mark Redman.

More reinforcements came in July and August: veteran relievers Ugueth Urbina and Chad Fox, pinch-hit leader Lenny Harris, and after two-time all-star Mike Lowell broke his left hand, the erstwhile Mr. Marlin, Jeff Conine.

ORGANIZATION LEADERS

BATTING		
***AVG**	Miguel Cabrera, Carolina	.365
R	Eric Reed, Jupiter	86
H	Eric Reed, Jupiter	154
TB	Jason Wood, Albuquerque	222
2B	Jason Stokes, Jupiter	31
3B	Chip Ambres, Carolina	8
	Eric Reed, Jupiter	8
HR	Rob Stratton, Albuquerque	32
RBI	Jason Stokes, Jupiter	89
BB	Jeremy Hermida, Albuquerque/Greensboro	80
SO	Rob Stratton, Albuquerque	175
SB	Eric Reed, Jupiter	53
***SLG**	Miguel Cabrera, Carolina	.609
***OBP**	Matt Erickson, Albuquerque	.442
PITCHING		
W	Phil Akens, Jupiter/Greensboro	13
L	Justin Wayne, Albuquerque/Jupiter	12
#ERA	Chris Key, Carolina/Jupiter	1.66
G	Ozwaldo Mairena, Albuquerque	61
CG	Yorman Bazardo, Greensboro	4
SV	Mike Flannery, Carolina	23
	Kevin Cave, Jupiter	23
IP	Nick Ungs, Carolina/Jupiter	170
BB	Three tied at	70
SO	Denny Bautista, Carolina/Jupiter	138

*Minimum 250 At-Bats #Minimum 75 Innings

Mike Lowell

Miguel Cabrera

PLAYERS of the YEAR

MAJOR LEAGUE: Mike Lowell, 3b

Always a steady major league player, Lowell enjoyed a breakout year in 2003, setting career-highs and team-leading totals with 32 home runs and 105 RBIs despite a broken left hand that forced him to miss the last month of the season.

MINOR LEAGUE: Miguel Cabrera, 3b

He played just half the minor league season, but Cabrera's numbers were still better than what most produced over the whole year. He hit .365-10-59 with 29 doubles in 266 at-bats for Carolina before joining the Marlins in late June.

The team that wound up as the best in baseball would fire its manager (Jeff Torborg) and pitching coach (Brad Arnsberg) on May 10. The Marlins brought in 72-year-old Jack McKeon, who hadn't worked in baseball for more than two seasons and who had been watching television and puttering in the yard at his North Carolina home. Less than two weeks after taking over, McKeon had guided the Marlins from a 16-22 mark to a full 10 games under .500.

The Marlins had baseball's best record after May 23. They went nearly three full months without a three-game losing streak and steadily climbed the standings. They finally overtook the Phillies for the wild card in the final week of the season and finished with 91 wins.

That, of course, matched the Opening Day eve prediction of team president David Samson, last seen attending the Marlins' World Series victory parade wearing a Marlins No. 91 jersey with "Sparky" on the back.

No fewer than three World Series parades were held in South Florida, which after ignoring the franchise for nearly six seasons flocked back to Pro Player Stadium for the playoffs. Crowds of 65,000 filled the stadium throughout the three rounds against the Giants, Cubs and Yankees.

By the end of the whole crazy ride, there was even a plan to build a new 38,000-seat baseball stadium in Miami. The stadium would have a retractable roof and cost $325 million, but no one was sure where the final $115 million would come from.

No matter. No one saw this Marlins World Series title coming either.

Despite the loss of Willis, Cabrera and others used in the Urbina deal, Double-A Carolina rolled to the Southern League title under first-year manager Tracy Woodson. Triple-A Albuquerque and Class A Jupiter also reached the playoffs.

FLORIDA MARLINS

Managers: Jeff Torborg/Jack McKeon.

2003 Record: 91-71, .562 (2nd, NL East).

BATTING	AVG	G	AB	R	H	2B	3B	HR	RBI	BB	SO	SB	CS	SLG	OBP	B	T	HT	WT	DOB	1st Yr	Resides
Allen, Chad	.208	12	24	2	5	1	1	0	0	0	5	0	0	.333	.240	R	R	6-1	200	2-6-75	1996	Dallas, Texas
Banks, Brian	.235	92	149	14	35	6	2	4	23	25	38	2	1	.383	.348	S	R	6-3	220	9-28-70	1993	Mesa, Ariz.
Cabrera, Miguel	.268	87	314	39	84	21	3	12	62	25	84	0	2	.468	.325	R	R	6-2	185	4-18-83	1999	Maracay, Venez.
Castillo, Luis	.314	152	595	99	187	19	6	6	39	63	60	21	19	.397	.381	S	R	5-11	190	9-12-75	1993	Santo Domingo, D.R.
Castro, Ramon	.283	40	53	6	15	2	0	5	8	4	11	0	0	.604	.333	R	R	6-3	235	3-1-76	1994	Vega Baja, P.R.
Conine, Jeff	.238	25	84	13	20	3	0	5	15	13	10	0	0	.452	.337	R	R	6-1	220	6-27-66	1988	Weston, Fla.
Encarnacion, Juan	.270	156	601	80	162	37	6	19	94	37	82	19	8	.446	.313	R	R	6-3	215	3-8-76	1992	Santo Domingo, D.R.
Fox, Andy	.194	70	108	12	21	5	1	0	8	7	29	1	2	.259	.269	L	R	6-4	200	1-12-71	1989	Fair Oaks, Calif.
Gonzalez, Alex	.256	150	528	52	135	33	6	18	77	33	106	0	4	.443	.313	R	R	6-0	200	2-15-77	1994	Miami Lakes, Fla.
Harris, Lenny	.286	13	14	3	4	0	0	0	1	3	1	0	0	.286	.412	L	R	5-10	220	10-28-64	1983	Miami, Fla.
2-team (75 Chicago)	.193	88	145	14	28	3	0	1	8	16	21	1	0	.234	.272	L	R	5-10	220	10-28-64	1983	Miami, Fla.
Hollandsworth, Todd	.254	93	228	32	58	23	3	3	20	22	55	2	3	.421	.317	L	L	6-2	225	4-20-73	1991	Castle Rock, Colo.
Lee, Derrek	.271	155	539	91	146	31	2	31	92	88	131	21	8	.508	.379	R	R	6-5	250	9-6-75	1993	El Dorado Hills, Calif.
Lowell, Mike	.276	130	492	76	136	27	1	32	105	56	78	3	1	.530	.350	R	R	6-3	215	2-24-74	1995	Miami, Fla.
Mordecai, Mike	.213	65	89	11	19	4	0	2	8	8	21	3	0	.326	.276	R	R	5-10	185	12-13-67	1989	Kennesaw, Ga.
Pierre, Juan	.305	162	668	100	204	28	7	1	41	55	35	65	20	.373	.361	L	L	6-0	180	8-14-77	1998	Lone Tree, Colo.
Redmond, Mike	.240	59	125	12	30	7	1	0	11	7	16	0	0	.312	.302	R	R	5-11	210	5-5-71	1993	Veradale, Wash.
Rodriguez, Ivan	.297	144	511	90	152	36	3	16	85	55	92	10	6	.474	.369	R	R	5-9	220	11-30-71	1989	Miami, Fla.
Williams, Gerald	.129	27	31	5	4	1	0	0	3	2	5	3	0	.161	.182	R	R	6-2	185	8-10-66	1987	Tampa, Fla.

PITCHING	W	L	ERA	G	GS	CG	SV	IP	H	R	ER	BB	SO	AVG	B	T	HT	WT	DOB	1st Yr	Resides
Almanza, Armando	4	5	6.08	51	0	0	0	50	59	37	34	25	49	.296	L	L	6-3	240	10-26-72	1993	El Paso, Texas
Alvarez, Juan	0	0	3.09	9	0	0	0	12	8	4	4	8	6	.216	L	L	6-0	170	8-9-73	1995	Miami, Fla.
Beckett, Josh	9	8	3.04	24	23	0	0	142	132	54	48	56	152	.245	R	R	6-5	220	5-15-80	2000	Spring, Texas
Borland, Toby	0	0	1.86	7	0	0	0	10	3	3	2	8	4	.096	R	R	6-6	210	5-29-69	1989	Quitman, La.
Bump, Nate	4	0	4.71	32	0	0	0	36	34	21	19	20	17	.246	R	R	6-2	180	7-24-76	1998	Jupiter, Fla.
Burnett, A.J.	0	2	4.70	4	4	0	0	23	18	13	12	18	21	.216	R	R	6-4	230	1-3-77	1995	Miramar, Fla.
Fox, Chad	2	1	2.13	21	0	0	0	25	16	6	6	14	27	.190	R	R	6-3	190	9-3-70	1992	Houston, Texas
Helling, Rick	1	0	0.55	11	0	0	0	16	11	1	1	5	12	.192	R	R	6-3	241	12-15-70	1992	Southlake, Texas
Levrault, Allen	1	0	3.86	19	0	0	0	28	38	12	12	15	21	.333	R	R	6-3	240	8-15-77	1996	Westport, Mass.
Looper, Braden	6	4	3.68	74	0	0	28	81	82	34	33	29	56	.263	R	R	6-3	220	10-28-74	1996	Pembroke Pines, Fla.
Neal, Blaine	0	0	8.14	18	0	0	0	21	38	20	19	9	10	.413	L	R	6-5	240	4-6-78	1996	Haddon Heights, N.J.
Nunez, Vladimir	0	3	16.03	14	0	0	0	11	21	21	19	7	10	.396	R	R	6-4	240	3-15-75	1996	Miami, Fla.
Olsen, Kevin	0	0	12.75	7	0	0	0	12	25	18	17	4	12	.431	R	R	6-2	195	7-26-76	1998	Norco, Calif.
Pavano, Carl	12	13	4.30	33	32	2	0	201	204	99	96	49	133	.264	R	R	6-5	235	1-8-76	1994	Palm Beach Gardens, Fla.
Penny, Brad	14	10	4.13	32	32	0	0	196	195	96	90	56	138	.263	R	R	6-4	250	5-24-78	1996	Broken Arrow, Okla.
Phelps, Tommy	3	2	4.00	27	7	0	0	63	70	32	28	23	43	.282	L	L	6-3	190	3-4-74	1993	Tampa, Fla.
Redman, Mark	14	9	3.59	29	29	3	0	191	172	82	76	61	151	.238	L	L	6-5	245	1-5-74	1995	Catoosa, Okla.
Spooneybarger, Tim	1	2	4.07	33	0	0	0	42	27	21	19	11	32	.190	R	R	6-3	190	10-21-79	1999	Pensacola, Fla.
Tejera, Mike	3	4	4.67	50	6	0	2	81	82	44	42	36	58	.267	L	L	5-9	190	10-18-76	1995	Miami, Fla.
Urbina, Ugueth	3	0	1.41	33	0	0	6	38	23	6	6	13	37	.174	R	R	6-0	200	2-15-74	1991	Ocumare Del Tuy, Venez.
Wayne, Justin	0	2	11.81	2	2	0	0	5	9	7	7	5	1	.375	R	R	6-3	205	4-16-79	2000	Jupiter, Fla.
Willis, Dontrelle	14	6	3.30	27	27	2	0	161	148	61	59	58	142	.245	L	L	6-4	200	1-12-82	2000	Alameda, Calif.

FIELDING

Catcher	PCT	G	PO	A	E	DP	PB
Castro	.982	18	51	3	1	0	1
Redmond	.995	37	195	10	1	2	0
Rodriguez	.992	138	915	47	8	9	10

First Base	PCT	G	PO	A	E	DP
Banks	1.000	12	72	2	0	11
Fox	1.000	2	14	1	0	3
Harris	1.000	2	5	1	0	0
Lee	.996	155	1279	97	5	132
Mordecai	1.000	1	10	0	0	1
Redmond	1.000	1	1	0	0	1

Second Base	PCT	G	PO	A	E	DP
Castillo	.986	152	286	433	10	99
Fox	.923	15	14	22	3	6
Mordecai	.938	12	5	10	1	4

Third Base	PCT	G	PO	A	E	DP
Cabrera	.986	34	17	53	1	2
Fox	.900	5	4	5	1	1
Harris	.948	35	10	45	3	4
Lowell	.973	128	84	243	9	27
Mordecai	.889	12	5	3	1	0
Redmond	.000	1	0	0	0	0

Shortstop	PCT	G	PO	A	E	DP
Fox	1.000	9	5	10	0	3
Gonzalez	.976	150	237	426	16	109
Mordecai	.976	14	14	26	1	7

Outfield	PCT	G	PO	A	E	DP
Allen	1.000	8	13	1	0	0
Banks	.975	33	38	1	1	0
Cabrera	.972	55	99	5	3	1
Conine	1.000	25	44	3	0	3
Encarnacion	1.000	155	329	7	0	3
Fox	1.000	2	1	0	0	0
Harris	1.000	4	5	0	0	0
Hollandsworth	.983	64	114	5	2	0
Pierre	.993	161	402	6	3	5
Williams	.941	16	16	0	1	0

LARRY GOREN

Mike Lowell

FARM SYSTEM

Director, Player Development: Jim Fleming.

Class	Farm Team	League	W	L	Pct.	Finish*	Manager	First Yr.
AAA	Albuquerque (N.M.) Isotopes	Pacific Coast	74	70	.514	5th (16)	Dean Treanor	2003
AA	Carolina (Zebulon, N.C.) Mudcats	Southern	80	58	.580	+1st (10)	Tracy Woodson	2003
High A	Jupiter (Fla.) Hammerheads	Florida State	76	62	.551	3rd (12)	Luis Dorante	2002
Low A	Greensboro (N.C.) Hornets	South Atlantic	67	69	.493	9th (16)	Steve Phillips	2003
SS A	Jamestown (N.Y.) Jammers	New York-Penn	22	51	.301	13th (14)	Benny Castillo	2002
Rookie	Jupiter (Fla.) Marlins	Gulf Coast	26	32	.448	11th (12)	Tim Cossins	1992

*Finish in overall standings (No. of teams in league) +League champion

ALBUQUERQUE ISOTOPES — Class AAA

PACIFIC COAST LEAGUE

BATTING	AVG	G	AB	R	H	2B	3B	HR	RBI	BB	SO	SB	CS	SLG	OBP	B	T	HT	WT	DOB	1st Yr	Resides
Allen, Chad	.323	91	337	45	109	30	2	8	53	18	48	11	10	.496	.364	R	R	6-1	200	2-6-75	1996	Dallas, Texas
Ashby, Chris	.338	20	68	9	23	3	0	1	11	7	10	3	0	.426	.400	R	R	6-3	190	12-15-74	1993	Boca Raton, Fla.
Barker, Kevin	.167	10	24	1	4	0	0	0	1	7	5	0	0	.167	.355	L	L	6-3	200	7-26-75	1996	Mendota, Va.
Donnels, Chris	.299	42	127	23	38	7	0	7	21	20	24	1	1	.520	.396	L	R	6-0	180	4-21-66	1987	Coto de Caza, Calif.
Erickson, Matt	.342	98	298	43	102	22	4	2	35	43	42	14	9	.463	.442	L	R	5-11	190	7-30-75	1997	Appleton, Wisc.
Gonzalez, Adrian	.216	39	139	17	30	5	1	1	18	14	25	1	0	.288	.286	L	L	6-2	190	5-8-82	2000	Bonita, Calif.
Harris, Lenny	.167	8	24	3	4	1	0	0	1	4	3	0	0	.208	.286	L	R	5-10	220	10-28-64	1983	Miami, Fla.
Hermida, Jeremy	.000	1	3	0	0	0	0	0	0	0	3	0	0	.000	.000	L	R	6-4	200	1-30-84	2002	Marietta, Ga.
Hooper, Kevin	.266	130	493	77	131	9	4	1	54	35	62	25	9	.306	.325	R	R	5-10	160	12-7-76	1999	Lawrence, Kan.
Hoover, Paul	.270	81	256	35	69	22	2	5	40	18	62	10	3	.430	.321	R	R	6-1	210	4-14-76	1997	Steubenville, Ohio
Iapoce, Anthony	.227	52	128	16	29	7	1	0	12	16	21	6	2	.297	.322	R	L	5-10	170	8-23-73	1994	Ridgewood, N.Y.
Medrano, Jesus	.228	31	114	22	26	3	1	1	12	14	26	7	2	.298	.310	R	R	6-0	180	9-11-78	1997	La Puente, Calif.
Nunez, Abraham	.311	59	212	35	66	13	2	11	38	32	56	9	4	.547	.398	S	R	6-3	210	2-5-77	1996	Haina, D.R.
Stratton, Rob	.212	110	372	63	79	12	2	32	82	36	175	6	4	.513	.283	R	R	6-2	250	10-7-77	1996	Santa Barbara, Calif.
Treanor, Matt	.273	98	315	45	86	18	1	11	40	39	44	9	4	.441	.380	R	R	6-2	220	3-3-76	1994	Anaheim, Calif.
Valdez, Wilson	.287	90	338	45	97	12	4	0	18	19	37	33	9	.346	.326	R	R	5-11	160	5-20-78	1997	Nizao, D.R.
Wakeland, Chris	.283	65	219	32	62	12	2	7	30	17	62	2	2	.452	.343	L	L	6-0	190	6-15-74	1996	St. Helens, Ore.
Wathan, Derek	.296	116	409	54	121	24	7	4	55	34	56	21	8	.418	.350	S	R	6-3	190	12-13-76	1998	Blue Springs, Mo.
Williams, Gerald	.303	85	327	59	99	22	5	14	50	24	45	15	11	.529	.356	R	R	6-2	185	8-10-66	1987	Tampa, Fla.
Wood, Jason	.296	128	473	80	140	26	4	16	83	45	96	5	1	.469	.358	R	R	6-1	200	12-16-69	1991	Fresno, Calif.

PITCHING	W	L	ERA	G	GS	CG	SV	IP	H	R	ER	BB	SO	AVG	B	T	HT	WT	DOB	1st Yr	Resides
Alvarez, Juan	3	2	5.88	51	0	0	0	52	69	38	34	24	43	.328	L	L	6-0	170	8-9-73	1995	Miami, Fla.
Belitz, Todd	1	0	5.93	13	0	0	0	14	20	12	9	4	8	.333	L	L	6-3	200	10-23-75	1997	Spokane, Wash.
2-team (3 Colo. Springs)	1	0	7.23	16	0	0	0	19	29	18	15	6	11	.353							
Bergman, Sean	8	11	4.69	28	28	2	0	171	193	99	89	44	101	.286	R	R	6-4	220	4-11-70	1991	Joliet, Ill.
Bochtler, Doug	5	3	5.37	23	5	0	1	54	61	33	32	18	40	.289	L	R	6-3	200	7-5-70	1989	West Palm Beach, Fla.
Borland, Toby	1	1	3.72	9	0	0	3	10	6	5	4	6	12	.176	R	R	6-6	210	5-29-69	1989	Quitman, La.
Bump, Nate	6	5	4.43	15	15	0	0	85	89	48	42	24	52	.267	R	R	6-2	180	7-24-76	1998	Jupiter, Fla.
Croushore, Rick	0	0	0.00	3	0	0	0	3	0	0	0	1	2	.000	R	R	6-4	210	8-7-70	1993	Benton, Ark.
Fesh, Sean	1	0	10.80	6	0	0	0	7	12	9	8	5	4	.387	L	L	6-2	180	11-3-72	1991	Bethel, Conn.
Fox, Chad	0	0	3.86	3	0	0	0	2	4	1	1	1	5	.363	R	R	6-3	190	9-3-70	1992	Houston, Texas
Fuell, Jerrod	0	0	3.60	3	0	0	0	5	6	3	2	0	2	.285	R	R	6-4	210	10-3-80	1999	Tucson, Ariz.
Fyhrie, Mike	1	0	2.53	5	0	0	0	11	7	3	3	3	8	.189	R	R	6-2	200	12-9-69	1991	Coto De Caza, Calif.
2-team (15 Omaha)	8	4	4.05	20	14	0	0	109	110	55	49	41	72	.269							
Grilli, Jason	6	2	3.38	12	12	0	0	67	64	30	25	30	38	.260	R	R	6-4	180	11-11-76	1997	Orlando, Fla.
House, Craig	0	0	19.64	7	0	0	0	7	14	16	16	13	8	.400	R	R	6-2	220	7-8-77	1999	Nashville, Tenn.
2-team (5 Tacoma)	0	0	11.85	12	0	0	0	14	20	18	18	18	12	.350							
Iapoce, Anthony	0	0	0.00	2	0	0	0	2	0	0	0	0	1	.000	R	L	5-10	170	8-23-73	1994	Ridgewood, N.Y.
Judd, Mike	4	9	6.05	30	8	0	4	58	58	44	39	30	54	.260	R	R	6-1	210	6-30-75	1995	San Diego, Calif.
Keagle, Greg	0	2	14.85	3	2	0	0	7	14	13	11	8	6	.451	R	R	6-2	190	6-28-71	1993	Horseheads, N.Y.
Levrault, Allen	3	0	1.40	21	0	0	0	26	12	5	4	9	18	.142	R	R	6-3	240	8-15-77	1996	Westport, Mass.
Mairena, Ozwaldo	6	4	5.86	61	0	0	1	86	110	62	56	28	55	.320	L	L	5-11	165	6-30-74	1996	Chinandega, Nicaragua
McLeary, Marty	1	1	4.32	20	1	0	0	33	40	22	16	18	17	.294	R	R	6-5	220	10-26-74	1997	Mansfield, Ohio
Neal, Blaine	3	2	2.33	40	0	0	21	46	55	22	12	16	32	.303	L	R	6-5	240	4-6-78	1996	Haddon Heights, N.J.
Nunez, Vladimir	4	1	4.76	46	3	0	5	68	67	36	36	20	54	.258	R	R	6-4	240	3-15-75	1996	Miami, Fla.
Olsen, Kevin	2	1	2.11	7	7	0	0	38	36	12	9	7	28	.253	R	R	6-2	195	7-26-76	1998	Norco, Calif.
Phelps, Tommy	0	0	1.17	5	0	0	0	8	5	1	1	3	13	.217	L	L	6-3	190	3-4-74	1993	Tampa, Fla.
Sanders, Scott	7	5	3.92	19	19	2	0	117	124	57	51	32	110	.274	R	R	6-4	220	3-25-69	1990	Poway, Calif.
Secoda, Jason	1	0	29.25	3	0	0	0	4	12	13	13	8	3	.545	R	R	6-1	200	9-2-74	1995	Anaheim, Calif.
2-team (7 Salt Lake)	3	1	10.90	10	0	0	0	17	24	22	21	17	7	.363							
Small, Aaron	6	4	4.63	14	14	0	0	89	95	50	46	18	56	.269	R	R	6-5	220	11-23-71	1989	Loudon, Tenn.
Sodowsky, Clint	0	3	11.05	3	3	0	0	15	31	18	18	1	8	.442	L	R	6-4	200	7-13-72	1991	Lamont, Okla.
Teut, Nate	0	1	7.56	2	2	0	0	8	14	9	7	5	6	.388	R	L	6-7	220	3-11-76	1997	Des Moines, Iowa
Wayne, Justin	4	12	4.24	23	23	2	0	136	138	81	64	40	82	.265	R	R	6-3	205	4-16-79	2000	Jupiter, Fla.
Wilkins, Marc	1	1	6.75	20	2	0	1	36	46	28	27	17	27	.326	R	R	5-11	210	10-21-70	1992	Palmetto, Fla.

FIELDING

Catcher	PCT	G	PO	A	E	DP	PB
Ashby	1.000	1	1	0	0	0	0
Hoover	.986	59	330	29	5	4	6
Treanor	.984	96	602	54	11	3	7

First Base	PCT	G	PO	A	E	DP
Ashby	1.000	1	6	1	0	0
Barker	.981	7	49	4	1	2
Donnels	.988	30	238	16	3	29
Gonzalez	.997	38	330	28	1	40
Harris	.977	4	41	2	1	2
Hoover	.986	10	63	6	1	3
Wathan	.986	47	406	28	6	49
Wood	.977	22	160	11	4	17

Second Base	PCT	G	PO	A	E	DP
Erickson	.972	33	57	83	4	17
Hooper	.986	79	144	219	5	63
Medrano	.992	29	50	82	1	21
Valdez	.975	6	21	18	1	6

	PCT	G	PO	A	E	DP
Wathan	1.000	4	2	9	0	0

Third Base	PCT	G	PO	A	E	DP
Erickson	.941	48	25	86	7	7
Harris	1.000	1	1	2	0	0
Hoover	1.000	4	0	6	0	0
Wathan	.889	5	3	5	1	0
Wood	.972	101	71	204	8	23

Shortstop	PCT	G	PO	A	E	DP
Hooper	.975	48	64	169	6	39
Valdez	.974	82	143	237	10	56
Wathan	.953	19	18	63	4	15
Wood	.000	1	0	0	0	0

Outfield	PCT	G	PO	A	E	DP
Allen	.993	82	145	5	1	1
Ashby	.973	16	32	4	1	0
Erickson	1.000	3	3	0	0	0
Hermida	1.000	1	1	0	0	0
Hoover	1.000	1	2	0	0	0
Iapoce	.963	40	70	7	3	0
Nunez	.979	57	139	3	3	0
Stratton	.973	90	172	6	5	0
Wakeland	.972	52	65	4	2	1
Wathan	.957	34	65	1	3	0
Williams	.972	79	200	9	6	2

CAROLINA MUDCATS — Class AA

SOUTHERN LEAGUE

BATTING	AVG	G	AB	R	H	2B	3B	HR	RBI	BB	SO	SB	CS	SLG	OBP	B	T	HT	WT	DOB	1st Yr	Resides
Aguila, Chris	.320	93	337	58	108	21	3	11	55	36	67	6	2	.499	.384	R	R	5-11	180	2-23-79	1997	Reno, Nev.
Ambres, Chip	.258	127	380	75	98	23	8	10	55	72	81	9	6	.439	.376	R	R	6-1	190	12-19-79	1998	Beaumont, Texas
Anderson, Dennis	.282	15	39	2	11	6	0	0	8	4	5	1	0	.436	.364	S	R	6-0	200	2-1-78	1999	Tucson, Ariz.
Ashby, Chris	.263	72	240	21	63	12	1	4	31	6	34	4	2	.371	.284	R	R	6-3	190	12-15-74	1993	Boca Raton, Fla.
Bost, Tom	.214	47	126	15	27	2	3	2	11	17	31	2	1	.325	.309	L	R	6-2	220	10-5-75	1998	Columbia, Tenn.
Cabrera, Miguel	.365	69	266	46	97	29	3	10	59	31	49	9	4	.609	.429	R	R	6-2	185	4-18-83	1999	Maracay, Venez.
Clute, Kris	.143	4	7	1	1	0	0	0	0	3	2	0	0	.143	.400	R	R	5-10	170	4-20-79	2001	Miami, Fla.
Gonzalez, Adrian	.307	36	137	15	42	9	1	1	16	14	25	1	1	.409	.368	L	L	6-2	190	5-8-82	2000	Bonita, Calif.
Hall, Billy	.245	114	367	59	90	10	3	3	33	34	47	45	4	.313	.313	S	R	5-9	180	6-17-69	1991	Wichita, Kan.
Harper, Brandon	.241	67	195	18	47	12	0	2	20	24	34	2	0	.333	.327	R	R	6-4	200	4-29-76	1997	Hobbs, N.M.
Jorgensen, Ryan	.242	67	211	28	51	16	0	6	34	30	53	1	0	.403	.337	R	R	6-2	200	5-4-79	2000	Kingwood, Texas
Magness, Pat	.227	52	132	10	30	7	0	3	18	24	36	0	1	.348	.350	L	R	6-3	230	1-19-78	2000	Overland Park, Kan.
Medrano, Jesus	.251	73	251	36	63	15	2	2	28	41	48	18	6	.351	.356	R	R	6-0	180	9-11-78	1997	La Puente, Calif.
Niles, Drew	.262	118	390	64	102	17	3	3	37	38	79	1	3	.344	.329	S	R	6-1	175	3-17-77	1998	Irmo, S.C.
Padgett, Matt	.277	129	462	65	128	29	1	17	76	43	104	2	3	.455	.337	L	L	6-2	215	7-22-77	1998	Lexington, S.C.
Polcovich, Kevin	.143	13	42	4	6	0	0	0	5	0	7	2	1	.143	.163	R	R	5-9	180	6-28-70	1992	Auburn, N.Y.
Smith, Will	.293	34	123	23	36	5	1	1	13	11	23	1	0	.374	.346	L	R	6-1	180	10-23-81	2000	Tucson, Ariz.
Valdez, Wilson	.313	37	144	28	45	6	2	0	14	15	17	16	5	.382	.373	R	R	5-11	160	5-20-78	1997	Nizao, D.R.
Willingham, Josh	.299	22	67	15	20	2	1	5	14	13	20	0	0	.582	.434	R	R	6-1	200	2-17-79	2000	Florence, Ala.
Wilson, Josh	.253	118	434	53	110	30	6	3	58	27	70	6	5	.371	.294	R	R	6-1	160	3-26-81	1999	Pittsburgh, Pa.

PITCHING	W	L	ERA	G	GS	CG	SV	IP	H	R	ER	BB	SO	AVG	B	T	HT	WT	DOB	1st Yr	Resides
Ashby, Chris	0	1	2.21	9	0	0	0	20	15	6	5	11	12	.000	R	R	6-3	190	12-15-74	1993	Boca Raton, Fla.
Baker, Ryan	5	2	2.95	44	1	0	4	64	54	28	21	38	56	.232	R	R	6-0	200	3-20-78	2000	Linthicum, Md.
Barnett, Marty	0	2	5.68	5	5	0	0	19	29	20	12	5	12	.362	R	R	6-3	210	3-10-74	1995	Harlan, Iowa
Bautista, Denny	4	5	3.71	11	11	0	0	53	45	33	22	35	61	.226	R	R	6-5	170	10-23-82	2000	Santo Domingo, D.R.
Beckett, Josh	0	0	4.50	1	1	0	0	4	4	2	2	0	7	.266	R	R	6-5	220	5-15-80	2000	Spring, Texas
Bridges, Donnie	10	2	2.81	31	19	1	0	135	85	47	42	70	109	.185	R	R	6-4	220	12-10-78	1997	Purvis, Miss.
Cueto, Jose	5	3	3.22	35	2	0	1	59	49	23	21	35	43	.234	R	R	6-2	190	9-13-76	1996	San Pedro de Macoris, D.R.
Fesh, Sean	9	1	1.87	49	0	0	7	77	58	20	16	21	71	.210	L	L	6-2	180	11-3-72	1991	Bethel, Conn.
Flannery, Mike	7	3	2.31	56	0	0	23	58	42	20	15	26	50	.199	R	R	6-1	195	9-20-79	2000	Collings Lakes, N.J.
Fuell, Jerrod	1	0	3.38	6	0	0	0	11	12	4	4	2	7	.292	R	R	6-4	210	10-3-80	1999	Tucson, Ariz.
Gracesqui, Frank	3	3	2.48	44	0	0	5	58	44	19	16	43	75	.210	S	L	6-5	210	8-20-79	1998	New York, N.Y.
House, Craig	1	1	4.35	8	0	0	1	10	7	5	5	6	8	.200	R	R	6-2	220	7-8-77	1999	Nashville, Tenn.
Hutchinson, Trevor	3	3	3.86	8	6	0	0	35	32	21	15	13	18	.244	R	R	6-5	220	10-8-79	2003	Irving, Texas
Kent, Steve	4	5	5.37	37	2	0	0	59	58	36	35	36	30	.260	L	L	5-11	170	10-3-78	1999	Killeen, Texas
Key, Chris	0	0	0.00	1	0	0	0	2	3	0	0	0	1	.428	R	L	6-3	210	10-30-77	2000	Reno, Nev.
Marchbanks, David	0	1	3.00	1	1	1	0	6	4	2	2	5	3	.222	L	L	6-3	205	2-3-82	2003	Simpsonville, S.C.
McLeary, Marty	1	1	1.80	11	2	0	0	30	22	8	6	15	22	.207	R	R	6-5	220	10-26-74	1997	Mansfield, Ohio
McNutt, Mike	0	1	9.00	1	1	0	0	5	8	5	5	2	6	.363	R	R	6-2	190	10-18-79	2000	Cincinnati, Ohio
Messenger, Randy	5	7	5.46	29	23	0	0	114	137	83	69	51	78	.295	R	R	6-0	220	8-13-81	1999	Sparks, Nev.
Moser, Todd	6	4	3.41	18	18	0	0	98	107	42	37	29	78	.274	L	L	6-5	180	10-28-76	1999	Davie, Fla.
Ortiz, Omar	0	1	6.08	8	0	0	0	13	16	9	9	8	12	.320	S	R	6-1	210	9-11-77	1999	Brownsville, Texas
Saucedo, Matthew	0	0	0.00	1	0	0	0	2	1	0	0	0	1	.142	R	R	5-11	170	5-17-80	2003	Highland, Calif.
Small, Aaron	3	4	4.83	8	7	0	0	41	47	23	22	14	24	.290	R	R	6-5	220	11-23-71	1989	Loudon, Tenn.
Snare, Ryan	5	4	3.67	18	18	0	0	103	98	46	42	37	77	.253	L	L	6-0	190	2-8-79	2000	Palm Harbor, Fla.
Sodowsky, Clint	1	0	2.70	5	5	0	0	27	22	8	8	4	27	.220	L	R	6-4	200	7-13-72	1991	Lamont, Okla.
Ungs, Nic	3	4	3.53	10	10	0	0	59	61	30	23	8	37	.272	R	R	6-2	220	9-3-79	2001	Dyersville, Iowa
Willis, Dontrelle	4	0	1.49	6	6	0	0	36	24	6	6	9	32	.193	L	L	6-4	200	1-12-82	2000	Alameda, Calif.

FIELDING

Catcher	PCT	G	PO	A	E	DP	PB
Anderson	.988	12	80	5	1	1	2
Ashby	1.000	5	11	3	0	1	0
Harper	.994	64	437	26	3	4	4
Jorgensen	.988	65	439	42	6	6	3
Willingham	1.000	4	24	3	0	0	0

First Base	PCT	G	PO	A	E	DP
Ashby	.988	52	374	37	5	44
Gonzalez	.987	36	291	21	4	24
Harper	.000	1	0	0	0	0
Magness	.975	39	252	24	7	17
Niles	.988	17	77	6	1	8
Padgett	.976	7	33	7	1	4
Willingham	1.000	9	51	4	0	4

Second Base	PCT	G	PO	A	E	DP
Clute	1.000	2	2	5	0	0
Hall	.967	16	23	35	2	11
Medrano	.955	72	139	180	15	37
Niles	.982	30	47	60	2	11
Valdez	.981	32	82	74	3	26
Wilson	1.000	1	4	3	0	3

Third Base	PCT	G	PO	A	E	DP
Anderson	.000	1	0	0	0	0
Cabrera	.924	64	45	137	15	22
Hall	.864	25	10	28	6	3
Niles	.932	55	33	104	10	17
Willingham	1.000	3	3	6	0	0

Shortstop	PCT	G	PO	A	E	DP
Niles	.932	14	19	22	3	5
Polcovich	.927	13	13	38	4	5
Valdez	.947	5	3	15	1	3
Wilson	.952	114	150	290	22	47

Outfield	PCT	G	PO	A	E	DP
Aguila	.989	88	161	11	2	1
Ambres	1.000	117	265	4	0	0
Ashby	1.000	6	11	1	0	0
Bost	1.000	35	70	2	0	0
Cabrera	1.000	3	7	0	0	0
Hall	1.000	58	89	5	0	1
Padgett	.987	111	221	12	3	2
Smith	1.000	30	44	2	0	0
Willingham	1.000	3	9	0	0	0

JUPITER HAMMERHEADS — High Class A

FLORIDA STATE LEAGUE

BATTING	AVG	G	AB	R	H	2B	3B	HR	RBI	BB	SO	SB	CS	SLG	OBP	B	T	HT	WT	DOB	1st Yr	Resides
Anderson, Dennis	.239	68	197	22	47	6	1	0	18	24	20	2	5	.279	.352	S	R	6-0	200	2-1-78	1999	Tucson, Ariz.
Aponte, Jose	.207	13	29	3	6	1	1	0	3	1	8	2	0	.310	.233	L	R	5-10	160	1-4-83	2000	Aragua, Venez.
Bost, Tom	.255	59	200	26	51	7	3	1	16	21	53	10	5	.335	.332	L	R	6-2	220	10-5-75	1998	Columbia, Tenn.
Clute, Kris	.147	15	34	1	5	1	0	0	3	4	12	2	1	.176	.256	R	R	5-10	170	4-20-79	2001	Miami, Fla.
Demarco, Matt	.240	114	375	36	90	10	2	2	43	24	44	4	7	.293	.293	L	R	5-10	160	1-24-80	1999	Clayton, N.J.
Easterday, Matt	.207	78	213	23	44	4	1	1	15	20	35	2	3	.249	.283	R	R	6-1	180	5-3-79	2000	Covington, Ga.
Frazier, Charles	.211	63	194	25	41	5	2	1	17	15	43	17	5	.273	.280	R	R	6-3	185	7-6-80	1999	Tom's River, N.J.
Grzecka, Casey	.132	14	38	1	5	1	0	0	2	3	9	0	0	.158	.214	R	R	6-2	200	11-12-79	2002	Laguna Niguel, Calif.
Hicks, Scott	.207	56	150	20	31	5	1	1	14	23	53	0	4	.273	.322	L	R	6-4	210	6-6-80	2000	Altamonte Springs, Fla.
Kavourias, Jim	.247	108	389	54	96	19	1	20	65	34	97	10	1	.455	.307	R	R	6-4	230	10-4-79	2000	Strongsville, Ohio
Lopez, Angel	.250	43	132	9	33	6	2	2	14	9	40	0	1	.371	.306	R	R	5-11	200	4-17-73	2002	Miami Beach, Fla.
Lynam, Guy	.231	6	13	2	3	1	0	0	2	2	3	0	0	.308	.333	R	R	5-11	190	10-27-80	2001	Williamstown, N.J.
Nunez, Abraham	.276	8	29	6	8	3	0	0	2	4	9	1	0	.379	.364	S	R	6-3	210	2-5-77	1996	Haina, D.R.
Reed, Eric	.300	134	514	86	154	15	8	0	25	52	83	53	18	.360	.367	L	L	5-11	170	12-2-80	2002	College Station, Texas
Rigsby, Randy	.275	40	131	11	36	8	1	1	12	5	28	1	2	.374	.299	L	L	6-0	190	8-7-76	1998	Goldsboro, N.C.
Rundgren, Rex	.231	119	415	44	96	15	2	0	31	19	76	5	2	.277	.270	R	R	6-1	170	11-20-80	2001	Sacramento, Calif.
Santos, Jose	.258	94	314	31	81	16	1	5	36	42	74	2	3	.363	.363	R	R	5-10	195	3-1-74	1995	Santiago, D.R.
Smith, Will	.083	3	12	0	1	1	0	0	2	0	2	0	0	.167	.083	L	R	6-1	180	10-23-81	2000	Tucson, Ariz.
Stokes, Jason	.258	121	462	67	119	31	3	17	89	36	135	6	4	.448	.312	R	R	6-4	225	1-23-82	2000	Coppell, Texas
Tucker, Michael	.276	107	384	36	106	22	2	5	51	32	92	2	2	.383	.336	R	R	6-3	205	11-7-79	2001	Lakeland, Fla.
Willingham, Josh	.264	59	193	46	51	17	1	12	34	46	42	9	2	.549	.422	R	R	6-1	200	2-17-79	2000	Florence, Ala.

PITCHING	W	L	ERA	G	GS	CG	SV	IP	H	R	ER	BB	SO	AVG	B	T	HT	WT	DOB	1st Yr	Resides
Akens, Phil	6	3	2.88	11	11	1	0	66	67	24	21	14	45	.271	R	R	6-6	200	8-9-82	2000	Bel Air, Md.
Asahina, Jon	1	2	2.70	12	4	0	0	37	36	16	11	18	21	.270	S	R	5-11	185	12-31-80	2001	Fresno, Calif.
Baez, Benito	1	0	1.42	3	2	0	0	6	3	1	1	1	6	.150	L	L	6-0	160	5-6-77	1994	Bonao, D.R.
Bautista, Denny	8	4	3.21	14	14	0	0	84	68	32	30	35	77	.219	R	R	6-5	170	10-23-82	2000	Santo Domingo, D.R.
Beckett, Josh	0	0	0.00	1	1	0	0	3	2	0	0	0	5	.181	R	R	6-5	220	5-15-80	2000	Spring, Texas
Belizario, Ronald	1	2	4.91	6	4	0	0	18	20	10	10	8	13	.277	R	R	6-2	150	12-31-82	1999	Aragua, Venez.
Blalock, Casey	1	0	0.00	2	0	0	1	3	0	0	0	1	1	.000	R	R	5-11	180	1-25-80	2002	Shreveport, La.
Cave, Kevin	2	2	1.60	39	0	0	23	45	36	11	8	14	43	.216	R	R	6-2	220	5-25-80	2001	Levittown, Pa.
Demontel, Jimmy	0	1	1.93	2	0	0	0	5	5	3	1	2	4	.263	R	R	6-4	240	6-7-80	2002	Wichita Falls, Texas
Florian, Frailyn	3	3	4.95	10	5	0	0	36	37	24	20	15	17	.276	L	L	6-2	170	7-25-82	1999	Santiago, D.R.
Fuell, Jerrod	3	1	2.68	46	0	0	6	50	48	19	15	10	43	.248	R	R	6-4	210	10-3-80	1999	Tucson, Ariz.
Fulchino, Jeff	2	4	4.04	17	16	1	0	78	76	41	35	32	47	.257	R	R	6-4	235	11-26-79	2001	Hollis, N.H.
Greusel, Evan	4	3	3.95	24	0	0	1	41	39	21	18	17	36	.243	R	R	6-3	210	8-22-79	2002	Norman, Okla.
Grilli, Jason	4	2	2.53	7	7	0	0	43	38	13	12	6	30	.236	R	R	6-4	180	11-11-76	1997	Orlando, Fla.
Haynes, Brad	0	0	7.79	13	0	0	0	17	20	17	15	18	10	.294	R	R	6-5	185	9-29-81	1999	Glasgow, Ky.
Holdzkom, Lincoln	0	2	3.07	13	0	0	2	14	9	6	5	7	20	.000	R	R	6-4	240	3-23-82	2001	Yuma, Ariz.
Hutchinson, Trevor	9	2	2.77	14	13	2	0	84	77	30	26	16	58	.242	R	R	6-5	220	10-8-79	2003	Irving, Texas
Kent, Steve	2	2	2.93	5	4	0	0	28	25	9	9	10	13	.240	L	L	5-11	170	10-3-78	1999	Killeen, Texas
Key, Chris	4	2	1.70	45	0	0	2	74	78	27	14	15	40	.265	R	L	6-3	210	10-30-77	2000	Reno, Nev.
Levinski, Donald	4	11	4.03	21	21	0	0	87	75	48	39	70	77	.235	R	R	6-4	200	10-20-82	2001	Weimar, Texas
McNutt, Mike	7	4	2.45	33	8	0	1	96	80	35	26	22	83	.226	R	R	6-2	190	10-18-79	2000	Cincinnati, Ohio
Moser, Todd	3	0	1.50	5	5	0	0	30	25	5	5	7	24	.240	L	L	6-5	180	10-28-76	1999	Davie, Fla.
Olsen, Kevin	0	0	0.00	1	1	0	0	4	1	0	0	0	3	.083	R	R	6-2	195	7-26-76	1998	Norco, Calif.
Overman, Matt	0	2	3.38	11	2	0	0	27	35	10	10	11	15	.339	R	R	6-0	185	9-10-80	2003	Casper, Wyo.
Phelps, Tommy	0	0	6.00	2	1	0	0	3	5	2	2	0	3	.357	L	L	6-3	190	3-4-74	1993	Tampa, Fla.
Russ, James	0	1	3.60	1	1	0	0	5	6	4	2	3	4	.315	R	R	6-4	210	10-24-80	2003	Concord, N.C.
Russell, Eddie	1	1	3.78	10	0	0	1	17	19	10	7	15	9	.311	R	R	6-2	190	6-20-78	2001	San Francisco, Calif.
Sloan, Brandon	2	5	5.38	41	0	0	5	72	83	54	43	33	57	.289	S	R	6-2	190	10-26-77	2000	Wichita, Kan.
Ungs, Nic	8	3	1.99	18	17	1	0	113	92	28	25	14	80	.221	R	R	6-2	220	9-3-79	2001	Dyersville, Iowa
Wayne, Justin	0	0	0.00	1	1	0	0	6	6	0	0	0	4	.250	R	R	6-3	205	4-16-79	2000	Jupiter, Fla.

FIELDING

Catcher	PCT	G	PO	A	E	DP	PB
Anderson	.988	62	373	39	5	2	9
Grzecka	.988	13	81	4	1	0	0
Lopez	.987	32	205	20	3	3	1
Lynam	.962	5	21	4	1	0	0
Willingham	1.000	36	232	27	0	3	19

First Base	PCT	G	PO	A	E	DP
Anderson	1.000	1	10	1	0	4
Hicks	.989	12	82	8	1	6
Stokes	.987	101	878	68	12	93
Tucker	1.000	21	174	11	0	21
Willingham	.976	9	72	8	2	5

Second Base	PCT	G	PO	A	E	DP
Clute	1.000	14	21	32	0	5
Demarco	.980	78	142	248	8	69
Easterday	.976	60	96	144	6	28

Third Base	PCT	G	PO	A	E	DP
Demarco	1.000	20	8	32	0	5
Santos	.943	42	19	80	6	7
Tucker	.922	86	50	152	17	14
Willingham	1.000	2	3	1	0	0

Shortstop	PCT	G	PO	A	E	DP
Demarco	.976	23	27	55	2	14
Rundgren	.956	119	204	387	27	84

Outfield	PCT	G	PO	A	E	DP
Aponte	.958	12	22	1	1	0
Bost	.934	50	80	5	6	0
Easterday	.941	12	15	1	1	0
Frazier	.965	48	79	4	3	1
Hicks	.983	42	55	3	1	0
Holdzkom	1.000	1	1	1	0	1
Kavourias	.988	100	149	12	2	3
Nunez	1.000	5	12	0	0	0
Reed	.986	129	335	10	5	2
Rigsby	.966	27	55	1	2	0
Smith	.000	2	0	0	0	0
Willingham	1.000	3	4	0	0	0

GREENSBORO BATS — Low Class A

SOUTH ATLANTIC LEAGUE

BATTING	AVG	G	AB	R	H	2B	3B	HR	RBI	BB	SO	SB	CS	SLG	OBP	B	T	HT	WT	DOB	1st Yr	Resides
Andino, Robert	.188	119	416	45	78	17	2	2	27	46	128	6	5	.252	.266	R	R	6-0	170	4-25-84	2002	Miami, Fla.
Aponte, Jose	.298	53	218	28	65	10	3	1	19	14	45	9	9	.385	.345	L	R	5-10	160	1-4-83	2000	Aragua, Venez.
Arlis, Patrick	.203	74	246	26	50	8	1	1	21	17	61	10	3	.256	.262	R	R	6-0	210	12-18-80	2002	Glendale Heights, Ill.
Arroyo, William	.200	7	20	4	4	2	0	0	2	5	4	0	1	.300	.360	S	R	5-10	170	11-8-81	1999	Cabudare, Venez.
Brewer, Anthony	.198	87	248	30	49	6	4	2	18	28	92	11	1	.278	.282	R	R	6-0	165	8-2-82	2000	Chicago, Ill.
Clute, Kris	.202	65	198	19	40	4	0	0	19	17	46	9	7	.222	.277	R	R	5-10	170	4-20-79	2001	Miami, Fla.

BATTING	AVG	G	AB	R	H	2B	3B	HR	RBI	BB	SO	SB	CS	SLG	OBP	B	T	HT	WT	DOB	1st Yr	Resides
Grzecka, Casey	.276	27	76	13	21	5	0	1	12	10	15	0	0	.382	.378	R	R	6-2	200	11-12-79	2002	Laguna Niguel, Calif.
Hermida, Jeremy	.284	133	468	73	133	23	5	6	49	80	100	28	2	.393	.387	L	R	6-4	200	1-30-84	2002	Marietta, Ga.
Lynam, Guy	.000	3	7	1	0	0	0	0	0	0	4	0	0	.000	.000	R	R	5-11	190	10-27-80	2001	Williamstown, N.J.
Merkle, Tom	.278	88	295	39	82	14	2	9	35	40	75	0	1	.431	.369	R	R	6-1	190	8-4-80	2002	East Meadow, N.Y.
Mitchell, Lee	.228	23	79	7	18	4	0	2	7	6	17	1	1	.354	.282	R	R	6-1	198	4-21-82	2003	Carterville, Ga.
Molina, Angel	.252	79	258	34	65	16	3	8	48	25	72	3	0	.430	.322	R	R	6-2	200	11-4-81	2000	Santa Isabel, P.R.
Ordorica, Eric	.216	105	371	35	80	21	1	1	43	29	54	9	4	.286	.282	R	R	5-9	170	5-28-80	2002	West Covina, Calif.
Ortiz, Juan	.200	9	20	2	4	1	0	0	2	2	7	0	0	.250	.273	R	R	5-10	210	2-26-79	1998	Brooklyn, N.Y.
Randel, Kevin	.216	124	449	66	97	21	3	13	54	63	96	30	7	.363	.331	L	R	6-1	180	6-11-81	2002	Montclair, Calif.
Resop, Chris	.191	37	89	6	17	4	1	1	8	1	29	0	0	.292	.209	R	R	6-3	200	11-4-82	2001	Naples, Fla.
Rohleder, Andy	.249	128	457	64	114	22	1	13	64	61	93	11	3	.387	.349	R	R	6-0	190	2-27-80	2002	Ferdinand, Ind.
Tucker, Michael	.254	17	63	9	16	8	0	0	7	9	6	0	0	.381	.342	R	R	6-3	205	11-7-79	2001	Lakeland, Fla.
Word, Robert	.201	112	388	41	78	19	1	9	44	17	120	1	1	.325	.242	L	L	6-2	220	9-16-80	2002	Charlottesville, Va.

PITCHING	W	L	ERA	G	GS	CG	SV	IP	H	R	ER	BB	SO	AVG	B	T	HT	WT	DOB	1st Yr	Resides
Akens, Phil	7	6	3.15	16	16	2	0	100	89	38	35	28	70	.239	R	R	6-6	200	8-9-82	2000	Bel Air, Md.
Asahina, Jon	1	0	0.00	5	0	0	0	8	4	0	0	2	11	.142	S	R	5-11	185	12-31-80	2001	Fresno, Calif.
Bazardo, Yorman	9	8	3.12	21	21	4	0	130	132	56	45	26	70	.260	R	R	6-2	170	7-11-84	2000	Maracay, Venez.
Belizario, Ronald	5	1	3.00	10	8	1	0	48	41	23	16	18	45	.229	R	R	6-2	150	12-31-82	1999	Aragua, Venez.
Blalock, Casey	5	3	1.75	56	0	0	18	67	47	17	13	15	75	.190	R	R	5-11	180	1-25-80	2002	Shreveport, La.
Bostick, Adam	0	1	3.77	7	1	0	0	14	12	6	6	12	15	.230	L	L	6-1	220	3-17-83	2001	Greensburg, Pa.
Demontel, Jimmy	1	2	5.73	31	1	0	2	38	46	26	24	15	29	.308	R	R	6-4	240	6-7-80	2002	Wichita Falls, Texas
Eazor, Kyle	0	0	3.97	9	0	0	0	11	22	16	5	10	6	.400	L	L	6-0	200	8-17-81	2002	Phoenix, Ariz.
Esquivia, Manuel	10	5	4.24	42	13	0	0	115	113	60	54	40	91	.252	R	R	6-0	165	5-30-80	1997	Cartagena, Colombia
Florian, Frailyn	0	0	4.73	14	1	0	0	27	29	18	14	16	19	.268	L	L	6-2	170	7-25-82	1999	Santiago, D.R.
Fulchino, Jeff	1	2	4.01	5	4	0	0	25	28	14	11	7	16	.277	R	R	6-4	235	11-26-79	2001	Hollis, N.H.
Greusel, Evan	2	0	1.52	12	1	0	2	30	24	6	5	3	31	.212	R	R	6-3	210	8-22-79	2002	Norman, Okla.
Griffin, Daniel	3	1	6.13	36	0	0	0	47	53	45	32	45	31	.281	R	R	6-3	190	2-21-78	1997	San Pedro de Macoris, D.R.
Holdzkom, Lincoln	1	4	2.84	43	0	0	4	57	36	24	18	27	74	.181	R	R	6-4	240	3-23-82	2001	Yuma, Ariz.
Johnson, Josh	4	7	3.61	17	17	0	0	82	69	44	33	29	59	.223	L	R	6-7	220	1-31-84	2002	Tulsa, Okla.
Kensing, Logan	0	2	4.50	4	4	0	0	20	18	10	10	5	11	.243	R	R	6-1	185	7-3-82	2003	Boerne, Texas
Marchbanks, David	0	1	2.12	3	3	0	0	17	16	5	4	1	15	.250	L	L	6-3	205	2-3-82	2003	Simpsonville, S.C.
Martinez, Carlos	0	3	2.95	15	0	0	1	18	18	7	6	4	15	.250	R	R	6-2	170	5-26-82	2001	Villa Vasquez, D.R.
Mildren, Paul	4	10	4.43	27	21	0	0	102	94	70	50	54	83	.248	R	L	6-1	160	5-3-84	2001	Adelaide, Australia
Nickerson, Jon-Michael	0	0	1.80	1	1	0	0	5	3	1	1	1	2	.187	L	L	6-5	180	12-4-84	2003	Millbrook, Ala.
Olsen, Scott	7	9	2.81	25	24	0	0	128	101	51	40	59	129	.220	L	L	6-4	170	1-12-84	2002	Lake in the Hills, Ill.
Resop, Chris	0	1	4.97	11	0	0	0	12	11	7	7	5	15	.000	R	R	6-3	200	11-4-82	2001	Naples, Fla.
Reynolds, Eric	0	1	3.00	3	0	0	0	3	1	1	1	2	1	.100	L	L	6-3	210	4-20-80	2000	Guntown, Miss.
Russell, Eddie	1	1	3.77	9	0	0	0	14	12	8	6	14	15	.226	R	R	6-2	190	6-20-78	2001	San Francisco, Calif.
Wolf, Ross	6	1	1.61	27	0	0	2	50	32	10	9	10	26	.182	R	R	6-0	180	10-18-82	2002	Wheeler, Ill.

FIELDING

Catcher	PCT	G	PO	A	E	DP	PB
Arlis	.987	74	486	57	7	3	10
Grzecka	.974	19	135	17	4	0	2
Lynam	1.000	3	20	1	0	0	1
Molina	.989	48	318	29	4	0	12

First Base	PCT	G	PO	A	E	DP
Clute	.976	5	37	4	1	1
Grzecka	1.000	1	3	0	0	3
Merkle	.988	75	632	33	8	49
Ordorica	1.000	2	9	0	0	1
Randel	1.000	1	3	0	0	0
Tucker	1.000	7	41	2	0	2
Word	.974	54	426	27	12	27

Second Base	PCT	G	PO	A	E	DP
Arroyo	.875	6	7	14	3	2
Clute	.967	14	22	37	2	10
Ordorica	.979	22	33	60	2	10
Randel	.954	96	200	255	22	40

Third Base	PCT	G	PO	A	E	DP
Arroyo	1.000	1	1	2	0	0
Clute	.926	43	39	87	10	7
Merkle	.795	13	6	25	8	2
Mitchell	.958	23	19	49	3	5
Ordorica	.952	49	28	112	7	11
Tucker	.960	11	5	19	1	1

Shortstop	PCT	G	PO	A	E	DP
Andino	.945	119	164	315	28	49
Ordorica	.955	18	26	37	3	6

Outfield	PCT	G	PO	A	E	DP
Aponte	.957	51	84	6	4	1
Brewer	.991	86	222	1	2	0
Hermida	.964	129	209	7	8	0
Ordorica	.800	4	3	1	1	0
Ortiz	1.000	8	9	0	0	0
Randel	1.000	1	1	0	0	0
Resop	.933	21	27	1	2	0
Rohleder	.991	124	222	2	2	1

JAMESTOWN JAMMERS — Short-Season Class A

NEW YORK-PENN LEAGUE

BATTING	AVG	G	AB	R	H	2B	3B	HR	RBI	BB	SO	SB	CS	SLG	OBP	B	T	HT	WT	DOB	1st Yr	Resides
Alen, Luis	.278	25	54	3	15	3	0	1	6	2	13	0	1	.389	.298	R	R	6-1	170	4-16-85	2002	Puerto Ordaz, Venez.
Allan, Joshua	.246	24	69	12	17	7	0	3	12	8	13	1	0	.478	.321	R	R	6-0	210	1-4-82	2003	Boca Raton, Fla.
Arroyo, Xavier	.159	35	132	15	21	5	0	0	5	14	47	13	3	.197	.250	S	R	6-1	170	8-9-84	2002	San Juan, P.R.
Bastardo, Frederick	.222	15	45	6	10	1	0	0	0	5	11	1	1	.244	.314	R	R	5-11	160	8-8-81	1998	Maracay, Venez.
Bear, Ryan	.296	70	240	42	71	12	5	6	37	24	36	15	2	.463	.367	R	R	6-2	220	1-26-81	2003	Panama City, Fla.
Blake, Ryan	.285	46	137	22	39	7	2	7	18	15	40	4	1	.518	.385	R	R	6-1	206	1-2-80	2003	Kernersville, N.C.
Brown, Greg	.211	13	19	2	4	0	0	0	1	1	4	0	0	.211	.318	R	R	5-11	195	5-4-80	2003	Pembroke Pines, Fla.
Dierks, Scott	.211	60	180	33	38	7	0	6	18	19	60	6	4	.350	.342	R	R	5-10	200	9-3-80	2003	Los Gatos, Calif.
Ewen, Nick	.213	25	94	9	20	3	1	3	9	13	20	4	0	.362	.306	L	R	6-4	210	3-8-83	2003	Roselle, Ill.
Mattison, Justin	.211	52	161	16	34	7	2	1	9	13	46	3	2	.298	.287	L	L	6-0	190	6-24-81	2003	Dominguez Hills, Calif.
Mazzuca, Joe	.167	16	48	7	8	3	0	1	6	4	14	1	0	.292	.241	R	R	6-0	185	5-21-81	2003	Elmwood Park, Ill.
Miller, Jai	.233	11	43	5	10	3	0	0	6	3	15	1	1	.302	.292	R	R	6-4	195	1-17-85	2003	Selma, Ala.
Mitchell, Lee	.308	46	169	21	52	5	2	2	19	16	39	3	0	.396	.365	R	R	6-1	198	4-21-82	2003	Carterville, Ga.
Olsen, Mikela	.206	47	155	14	32	5	1	0	21	13	45	1	2	.252	.266	S	L	6-0	210	11-2-81	2003	Oakhurst, Calif.
Schade, Ryan	.304	47	125	11	38	3	1	1	15	13	21	8	2	.368	.376	R	R	5-9	170	11-21-78	2003	Lewisburg, Pa.
Schroeder, Ben	.205	55	200	17	41	7	1	0	13	16	70	11	6	.250	.266	L	R	6-0	185	9-8-80	2003	Dubuque, Iowa
Seifrig, Cole	.261	11	46	3	12	3	0	0	8	2	12	2	0	.326	.286	R	R	6-3	190	9-10-84	2003	Santa Claus, Ind.
Sosa, Pablo	.243	35	136	10	33	7	2	0	8	2	27	1	2	.324	.262	R	R	6-1	180	8-11-82	2001	San Cristobal, D.R.
Thedorf, Chris	.144	34	90	10	13	0	1	0	7	10	31	6	0	.167	.245	L	L	5-10	190	1-21-83	2003	St. Charles, Ill.
Wyman, Spencer	.192	26	73	8	14	5	1	0	7	14	29	0	0	.288	.330	L	R	6-0	205	5-10-82	2003	Vista, Calif.
Young, Dustin	.244	50	160	16	39	5	0	0	16	10	25	6	2	.275	.291	R	R	5-11	175	8-10-80	2003	Albuquerque, N.M.

GAMES BY POSITION: C—Alen 22, Allan 10, Blake 35, Brown 12, Wyman 18. **1B**—Bastardo 1, Bear 65, Olsen 10. **2B**—Bastardo 4, Dierks 43, Schade 11, Seifrig 11, Young 8. **3B**—Bastardo 2, Dierks 9, Mitchell 27, Schade 5, Sosa 35, Young 1. **SS**—Mazzuca 5, Mitchell 19, Schade 12, Young 41. **OF**—Allan 2,

Arroyo 27, Bastardo 7, Dierks 1, Ewen 25, Mattison 46, Miller 11, Olsen 29, Schade 12, Schroeder 54, Thedorf 26.

PITCHING	W	L	ERA	G	GS	CG	SV	IP	H	R	ER	BB	SO	AVG	B	T	HT	WT	DOB	1st Yr	Resides
Bostick, Adam	4	6	5.12	15	15	0	0	77	77	49	44	39	76	.262	L	L	6-1	220	3-17-83	2001	Greensburg, Pa.
Chick, Travis	1	2	5.71	13	10	0	0	52	63	41	33	26	48	.301	R	R	6-3	220	6-10-84	2002	Tyler, Texas
Cillo, Cody	3	1	2.86	17	0	0	1	22	23	8	7	9	27	.277	R	R	6-2	200	7-17-80	2003	Longmont, Colo.
Eazor, Kyle	0	0	11.25	2	0	0	0	4	6	6	5	5	2	.375	L	L	6-0	200	8-17-81	2002	Phoenix, Ariz.
Humen, David	1	1	11.57	7	0	0	0	9	15	13	12	11	10	.384	R	R	6-2	210	6-11-81	2003	Bedford, Texas
Iehl, Jason	1	2	9.00	4	4	0	0	18	22	18	18	5	16	.305	R	R	6-2	180	4-23-84	2002	Woodridge, Ill.
Kensing, Logan	2	4	5.73	8	6	0	0	33	48	23	21	6	20	.333	R	R	6-1	185	7-3-82	2003	Boerne, Texas
Kupper, Dustin	3	6	5.43	14	8	0	0	56	57	35	34	32	49	.270	R	R	6-6	195	2-22-81	2001	Tucson, Ariz.
Lovato, Nick	2	6	8.06	20	0	0	0	26	37	28	23	18	21	.333	L	L	6-4	215	12-20-80	2003	Anaheim, Calif.
Marchbanks, David	0	0	1.23	5	3	0	0	15	11	2	2	3	12	.203	L	L	6-3	205	2-3-82	2003	Simpsonville, S.C.
Martinez, Carlos	0	1	5.40	1	0	0	0	2	2	1	1	1	4	.250	R	R	6-2	170	5-26-82	2001	Villa Vasquez, D.R.
McCormack, Zach	0	2	4.56	17	0	0	4	26	24	18	13	26	35	.252	L	L	6-3	210	1-18-82	2003	Fairfield, Calif.
Nowicki, Nate	0	2	5.46	18	0	0	3	28	32	18	17	13	18	.299	R	R	6-4	190	4-25-82	2003	Littleton, Colo.
O'Connor, Shaun	0	0	11.25	3	0	0	0	4	7	6	5	5	3	.411	R	R	6-10	260	5-6-79	2002	Stafford, Va.
Ohalek, Corey	1	0	5.68	3	0	0	0	6	9	5	4	2	6	.321	L	L	5-11	185	2-17-80	2003	Steubenville, Ohio
Orozco, Antonio	0	1	9.00	1	0	0	0	4	9	4	4	0	2	.473	L	R	6-5	220	12-20-80	2003	Riverside, Calif.
Pawelk, Reed	0	0	7.11	18	0	0	0	25	34	23	20	10	21	.311	S	R	6-5	225	6-13-80	2003	Plymouth, Minn.
Pillsbury, Chris	1	4	4.97	18	8	0	0	54	56	35	30	26	54	.256	R	R	6-4	190	10-13-81	2003	Orange Park, Fla.
Prieto, Victor	0	6	5.52	13	11	0	0	46	40	29	28	40	45	.242	R	R	6-2	175	4-24-83	1999	Villa de Cura, Venez.
Primus, Carl	2	3	6.25	18	4	0	0	40	40	29	28	20	35	.254	R	R	6-3	180	7-1-80	2002	Greenwell Springs, La.
Russell, Eddie	0	1	2.08	4	0	0	0	9	8	2	2	5	6	.275	R	R	6-2	190	6-20-78	2001	San Francisco, Calif.
Saucedo, Matt	1	1	4.71	17	0	0	4	29	32	18	15	18	24	.285	R	R	5-11	170	5-17-80	2003	Highland, Calif.
Wood, Tim	0	2	5.35	16	4	0	2	39	44	33	23	28	32	.289	R	R	6-1	185	11-16-82	2003	Tucson, Ariz.

JUPITER MARLINS — Rookie

GULF COAST LEAGUE

BATTING	AVG	G	AB	R	H	2B	3B	HR	RBI	BB	SO	SB	CS	SLG	OBP	B	T	HT	WT	DOB	1st Yr	Resides
Aguila, Chris	.750	1	4	1	3	0	0	1	2	0	1	0	0	1.500	.750	R	R	5-11	180	2-23-79	1997	Reno, Nev.
Alen, Luis	.111	6	18	1	2	1	0	0	2	0	3	0	0	.167	.158	R	R	6-1	170	4-16-85	2002	Puerto Ordaz, Venez.
Arroyo, Xavier	.282	20	71	12	20	4	3	0	6	8	15	5	0	.423	.354	S	R	6-1	170	8-9-84	2002	San Juan, P.R.
Baker, Jordan	.206	46	141	12	29	6	1	0	11	32	42	8	3	.262	.364	L	L	6-1	170	9-15-83	2002	Chillicothe, Ohio
Bastardo, Frederick	.200	31	95	14	19	4	0	2	10	12	18	10	1	.305	.294	R	R	5-11	160	8-8-81	1998	Maracay, Venez.
Berkenbosch, Kenny	.244	43	127	12	31	6	0	0	13	16	22	3	4	.291	.326	R	R	6-2	200	3-17-85	2002	Flevoland, Netherlands
Brown, Greg	.194	12	36	0	7	0	0	0	1	5	6	1	0	.194	.286	R	R	5-11	195	5-4-80	2003	Pembroke Pines, Fla.
Encarnacion, Salvador	.103	11	29	1	3	1	0	0	2	1	11	0	1	.138	.161	R	R	6-4	215	8-26-82	2003	Orange Park, Fla.
Ewen, Nick	.221	27	104	8	23	2	2	1	8	6	24	2	3	.308	.265	L	R	6-4	210	3-8-83	2003	Roselle, Ill.
Franco, Luis	.241	14	29	4	7	0	0	0	2	6	5	1	0	.241	.389	S	R	6-0	180	9-27-84	2003	Barquisimeto, Venez.
Fulton, Jonathan	.196	46	168	9	33	9	0	1	13	9	51	0	3	.268	.247	R	R	6-4	200	12-1-83	2003	Danville, Va.
Lambis, Alberto	.216	23	74	7	16	2	0	0	4	2	11	0	1	.243	.247	R	R	5-11	170	4-1-83	2000	Cartagena, Colombia
Lindesey, Juan	.197	36	117	12	23	3	0	0	8	4	28	3	0	.222	.221	R	R	6-3	180	11-1-81	2003	San Pedro de Macoris, D.R.
Magness, Pat	.000	1	1	0	0	0	0	0	0	2	0	0	0	.000	.667	L	R	6-3	230	1-19-78	2000	Overland Park, Kan.
Mazzuca, Joe	.321	20	56	13	18	5	1	0	5	12	18	0	2	.446	.449	R	R	6-0	185	5-21-81	2003	Elmwood Park, Ill.
Miller, Jai	.199	45	146	17	29	4	1	1	15	15	45	9	3	.260	.279	R	R	6-4	195	1-17-85	2003	Selma, Ala.
Restko, J.T.	.249	48	177	15	44	6	0	4	19	16	43	0	2	.350	.320	R	R	6-5	190	12-15-84	2003	Tinley Park, Ill.
Rigsby, Randy	.538	3	13	5	7	1	0	1	7	1	2	0	0	.846	.571	L	L	6-0	190	8-7-76	1998	Goldsboro, N.C.
Rogers, Tanner	.181	32	94	5	17	2	0	2	8	10	29	1	1	.266	.255	R	R	6-0	180	1-11-85	2003	Littleton, Colo.
Seifrig, Cole	.285	49	186	27	53	7	2	2	7	10	44	11	3	.376	.335	R	R	6-3	190	9-10-84	2003	Santa Claus, Ind.
Sosa, Pablo	.296	21	71	10	21	2	1	0	5	4	9	2	3	.352	.333	R	R	6-1	180	8-11-82	2001	San Cristobal, D.R.
Veloz, Vladimil	.183	23	60	5	11	5	0	0	3	2	13	1	0	.267	.231	R	R	6-1	170	1-19-85	2003	San Juan Maguana, D.R.
Willingham, Josh	.429	2	7	3	3	1	0	1	3	1	2	0	0	1.000	.500	R	R	6-1	200	2-17-79	2000	Florence, Ala.

GAMES BY POSITION: C—Alen 6, Baker 1, Brown 12, Lambis 23, Rogers 19. **1B**—Baker 37, Magness 1, Restko 22. **2B**—Bastardo 4, Franco 9, Rogers 5, Seifrig 47. **3B**—Bastardo 22, Franco 2, Restko 17, Seifrig 2, Sosa 19. **SS**—Bastardo 4, Franco 4, Fulton 46, Rogers 4. **OF**—Aguila 1, Arroyo 19, Baker 4, Berkenbosch 37, Encarnacion 5, Ewen 25, Lindesey 33, Miller 43, Rigsby 1, Veloz 20.

PITCHING	W	L	ERA	G	GS	CG	SV	IP	H	R	ER	BB	SO	AVG	B	T	HT	WT	DOB	1st Yr	Resides
Allison, Jeff	0	2	1.00	3	3	0	0	9	7	2	1	4	11	.205	R	R	6-2	195	11-7-84	2003	Peabody, Mass.
Bartlett, Greg	1	1	6.45	15	0	0	1	22	29	17	16	5	17	.315	L	L	6-2	205	1-31-83	2003	Phoenix, Ariz.
Berger, Garrett	1	2	9.15	14	0	0	0	20	27	23	20	24	14	.337	R	R	6-3	240	5-11-83	2001	Carmel, Ind.
Brito, Joel	2	4	2.89	12	8	0	1	47	36	20	15	20	50	.209	R	R	6-1	175	3-23-84	2001	Santiago, D.R.
Cillo, Cody	0	0	0.00	3	0	0	3	6	2	0	0	0	9	.105	R	R	6-2	200	7-17-80	2003	Longmont, Colo.
Davis, Lance	0	0	0.00	1	0	0	0	1	0	0	0	0	0	.000	R	R	6-2	190	1-18-83	2001	Lucedale, Miss.
Fernandez, Rodney	0	0	13.50	2	0	0	0	2	4	3	3	2	2	.400	R	R	6-1	215	1-12-79	2003	New York, N.Y.
Friesen, Roy	0	0	108.00	1	0	0	0	0	2	4	4	2	0	.666	R	R	6-1	205	2-17-82	2003	Wasilla, Alaska
Glynn, Josh	0	3	1.29	10	2	0	0	35	22	7	5	7	20	.176	R	R	6-2	195	4-28-81	2003	Marysville, Calif.
Humen, David	1	0	1.08	12	0	0	3	17	7	2	2	14	19	.137	R	R	6-2	210	6-11-81	2003	Bedford, Texas
Iehl, Jason	3	2	3.22	7	7	1	0	36	38	17	13	11	27	.271	R	R	6-2	180	4-23-84	2002	Woodridge, Ill.
Kamimura, Soichi	2	0	3.07	5	0	0	0	15	13	5	5	5	8	.224	R	R	6-1	190	1-6-83	2003	Hyogo, Japan
Lybarger, Craig	2	1	5.73	7	0	0	0	11	15	8	7	3	15	.312	L	L	6-0	190	10-7-82	2003	Birmingham, Ala.
Martinez, Carlos	1	0	0.00	3	0	0	1	6	1	0	0	1	2	.052	R	R	6-2	170	5-26-82	2001	Villa Vasquez, D.R.
McCormack, Zach	0	0	0.00	4	0	0	0	6	1	1	0	1	6	.052	L	L	6-3	210	1-18-82	2003	Fairfield, Calif.
Miner, Josh	0	3	7.58	11	1	0	1	19	32	18	16	9	11	.390	R	R	6-1	175	4-6-84	2003	Jupiter, Fla.
Nestor, Scott	4	1	2.49	12	0	0	0	25	20	11	7	16	27	.210	R	R	6-4	225	8-20-84	2003	Glendora, Calif.
Nickerson, Jon-Michael	5	1	1.87	12	12	1	0	53	36	15	11	23	50	.191	L	L	6-5	180	12-4-84	2003	Millbrook, Ala.
Ohalek, Corey	0	1	5.32	14	0	0	1	22	28	15	13	2	22	.301	L	L	5-11	185	2-17-80	2003	Steubenville, Ohio
Orozco, Antonio	0	2	1.57	4	4	0	0	23	16	4	4	3	16	.197	L	R	6-5	220	12-20-80	2003	Riverside, Calif.
Overman, Matt	1	1	1.71	6	3	0	0	21	13	5	4	5	21	.173	R	R	6-0	185	9-10-80	2003	Casper, Wyo.
Reynolds, Eric	0	0	2.45	4	1	0	0	7	6	2	2	4	10	.222	L	L	6-3	210	4-20-80	2000	Guntown, Miss.
Russ, James	1	2	1.63	11	7	0	1	50	33	12	9	15	46	.190	R	R	6-4	210	10-24-80	2003	Concord, N.C.
Russell, Eddie	0	0	2.25	2	0	0	0	4	4	2	1	1	1	.250	R	R	6-2	190	6-20-78	2001	San Francisco, Calif.
Vanden Hurk, Henricus	2	6	5.35	11	10	0	0	39	49	30	23	20	30	.308	R	R	6-5	190	5-22-85	2003	Eindhover, Holland

HOUSTON ASTROS

BY TOM HALLIBURTON

The Astros entered the year armed with the highest payroll ever at $71 million and excited by the offseason acquisition of former Giants second baseman Jeff Kent.

Steeped in expectations, the Astros won a disappointing 87 games and finished one game behind the Cubs in the National League Central.

The Astros failed to consistently produce the kind of explosiveness expected from an everyday lineup of stalwarts Kent, Jeff Bagwell, Craig Biggio, Lance Berkman and Richard Hidalgo. The team tied for seventh in NL team batting at .263 and ranked fifth in the league with 191 home runs despite playing in homer-friendly Minute Maid Park.

Hidalgo received team MVP honors, leading the regulars with a .309 average and a .572 slugging percentage. Hidalgo had been shot in the forearm during a carjacking incident in Venezuela in November 2002, but the right fielder rebounded with a career season. Hidalgo also led the major leagues with 22 outfield assists.

Bagwell knocked a club-best 39 home runs and 100 RBIs but his average dipped to .278. Bothered off and on by a tender wrist, Kent occupied the cleanup spot most of the season, finishing at .299-22-93. Berkman did not deliver all-star caliber numbers (.288-25-93) but improved as a left fielder. Biggio surprised many pundits by playing admirably in center field, but his offensive numbers continued their recent decline (.264-15-62).

A pair of young infielders produced the lineup's most pleasant surprises. Failures at the start of the 2002 season, Morgan Ensberg and Adam Everett bloomed a year later. Ensberg batted .291-25-60 to earn outright the third base chores he shared with Geoff Blum early on.

Everett replaced Julio Lugo as the starting shortstop in early May. From the time Everett was inserted as Houston's everyday shortstop, the Astros fashioned a 75-59 record.

ORGANIZATION LEADERS

BATTING		
*AVG	Colin Porter, New Orleans	.320
R	Chris Burke, Round Rock	88
H	Chris Burke, Round Rock	165
TB	Henri Stanley, New Orleans	225
2B	T.J. Soto, Salem/Lexington	29
	Brooks Conrad, Salem/Lexington	29
3B	Three tied at	8
HR	John Fagan, Lexington	18
RBI	T.J. Soto, Salem/Lexington	82
BB	Todd Self, Salem	87
SO	Freddy Acevedo, Lexington	132
SB	Chris Burke, Round Rock	34
*SLG	Colin Porter, New Orleans	.511
*OBP	Todd Self, Salem	.433
PITCHING		
W	Fernando Nieve, Lexington	14
L	Ruddy Lugo, Round Rock	15
#ERA	Chris Sampson, Salem/Lexington	1.90
G	Kirk Bullinger, New Orleans	55
	Miguel Saladin, New Orleans	55
CG	Chad Qualls, Round Rock	3
SV	Juan Campos, Round Rock/Salem	24
IP	Chad Qualls, Round Rock	175
BB	Jailen Peguero, Lexington	69
SO	D.J. Houlton, New Orleans/Round Rock	149

*Minimum 250 At-Bats #Minimum 75 Innings

Richard Hidalgo

Chris Burke

PLAYERS of the YEAR

MAJOR LEAGUE: Richard Hidalgo, of

Despite the presence of the Killer B's—Bagwell, Berkman and Biggio—and addition of Jeff Kent, Hidalgo was Houston's most productive hitter in 2003. He led the team in average, on-base percentage and slugging percentage.

MINOR LEAGUE: Chris Burke, 2b/ss

Burke struggled in his first try at Double-A in 2002, but bounced back a year later, hitting .301-3-41. He showed the potential to be a quality leadoff hitter, registering a .379 on-base percentage and 34 steals.

There was an unlikely leader on the mound as well. Lefthander Jeriome Robertson became the first rookie in franchise history to lead the Astros in wins but that would hint of the struggles encountered by pitching aces Roy Oswalt and Wade Miller.

Robertson had an unimpressive 5.10 ERA but his run support helped the young lefthander to finish 15-9.

The Astros simply lacked enough starting pitching to win the Central championship. Houston's starting rotation worked fewer innings than any National League staff. Manager Jimy Williams drew public criticism for his frequent pulling of pitchers. The Astros were last in the majors with one complete game. Part of that strategy could be explained because Houston's bullpen belonged among baseball's finest. Houston received superb years from the trio of Brad Lidge, Octavio Dotel and the club's lone all-star selection Billy Wagner, who ranked third in the league with 44 saves.

The Astros' bullpen depth helped to make major league history during the club's first-ever visit to Yankee Stadium. Six pitchers combined on a June 11 no-hitter. Oswalt and relievers Pete Munro, Kirk Saarloos, Lidge, Dotel and Wagner were the most pitchers to ever combine on a no-hitter.

While Houston's minor league franchises did not enjoy superior team performances as in previous years, prospects such as Double-A Round Rock second baseman Chris Burke and Class A pitchers Jared Gothreaux and Jesse Carlson were superb.

Burke was a Texas League all-star, batting .301 with the league's second-most hits (165) and stolen bases (34).

Gothreaux was 13-4, 2.62 for Salem of the Carolina League while lefty Carlson compiled a 1.56 ERA with a string of 35 consecutive scoreless innings as a reliever.

HOUSTON ASTROS

Manager: Jimy Williams.

2003 Record: 87-75, .537 (2nd, NL Central).

BATTING	AVG	G	AB	R	H	2B	3B	HR	RBI	BB	SO	SB	CS	SLG	OBP	B	T	HT	WT	DOB	1st Yr	Resides
Ausmus, Brad	.229	143	450	43	103	12	2	4	47	46	66	5	3	.291	.303	R	R	5-11	200	4-14-69	1987	San Diego, Calif.
Bagwell, Jeff	.278	160	605	109	168	28	2	39	100	88	119	11	4	.524	.373	R	R	6-0	210	5-27-68	1989	Houston, Texas
Berkman, Lance	.288	153	538	110	155	35	6	25	93	107	108	5	3	.515	.412	S	L	6-1	220	2-10-76	1997	Houston, Texas
Biggio, Craig	.264	153	628	102	166	44	2	15	62	57	116	8	4	.412	.350	R	R	5-11	180	12-14-65	1987	Houston, Texas
Blum, Geoff	.262	123	420	51	110	19	0	10	52	20	50	0	0	.379	.295	S	R	6-3	200	4-26-73	1994	Los Angeles, Calif.
Bruntlett, Eric	.259	31	54	3	14	3	0	1	4	0	10	0	0	.370	.255	R	R	6-0	200	3-29-78	2000	Lafayette, Ind.
Chavez, Raul	.270	19	37	5	10	1	1	1	4	1	6	0	0	.432	.289	R	R	5-11	210	3-18-73	1990	Valencia, Venez.
Cromer, Tripp	.250	3	4	0	1	0	1	0	1	0	0	0	0	.750	.250	R	R	6-2	165	11-21-67	1989	Columbia, S.C.
Ensberg, Morgan	.291	127	385	69	112	15	1	25	60	48	60	7	2	.530	.377	R	R	6-2	220	8-26-75	1998	Orlando, Fla.
Everett, Adam	.256	128	387	51	99	18	3	8	51	28	66	8	1	.380	.320	R	R	6-0	160	2-5-77	1998	Kennesaw, Ga.
Hidalgo, Richard	.309	141	514	91	159	43	4	28	88	58	104	9	7	.572	.385	R	R	6-3	220	7-2-75	1991	Guarenas, Venez.
Hunter, Brian L.	.235	56	98	13	23	6	1	0	13	6	21	0	0	.316	.278	R	R	6-3	180	3-25-71	1989	Vancouver, Wash.
Kent, Jeff	.297	130	505	77	150	39	1	22	93	39	85	6	2	.509	.351	R	R	6-1	215	3-7-68	1989	Foster City, Calif.
Lane, Jason	.296	18	27	5	8	2	0	4	10	0	2	0	0	.815	.296	R	L	6-2	210	12-22-76	1999	Sebastopol, Calif.
Lugo, Julio	.246	22	65	6	16	3	0	0	2	9	12	2	1	.292	.338	R	R	6-1	170	11-16-75	1995	Brooklyn, N.Y.
Matranga, Dave	.200	6	5	1	1	0	0	1	1	0	2	0	0	.800	.200	R	R	6-0	170	1-8-77	1998	Aliso Viejo, Calif.
Meluskey, Mitch	.111	12	9	1	1	1	0	0	2	2	2	0	0	.222	.250	S	R	6-0	200	9-18-73	1992	Yakima, Wash.
Merced, Orlando	.231	123	212	20	49	17	2	3	26	15	33	3	2	.373	.283	L	R	6-1	195	11-2-66	1985	Cortez, Fla.
Porter, Colin	.188	24	32	5	6	0	0	0	0	1	17	1	0	.188	.212	L	L	6-2	210	11-23-75	1998	Tucson, Ariz.
Vizcaino, Jose	.249	91	189	14	47	7	3	3	26	8	22	0	1	.365	.281	S	R	6-1	180	3-26-68	1986	Poway, Calif.
Zaun, Greg	.217	59	120	9	26	7	0	1	13	14	14	1	0	.300	.299	S	R	5-10	190	4-14-71	1989	Houston, Texas

PITCHING	W	L	ERA	G	GS	CG	SV	IP	H	R	ER	BB	SO	AVG	B	T	HT	WT	DOB	1st Yr	Resides
Bland, Nate	1	2	5.75	22	0	0	0	20	22	13	13	12	18	.285	L	L	6-5	190	12-27-74	1993	Birmingham, Ala.
Bullinger, Kirk	0	0	6.75	7	0	0	0	8	7	6	6	1	5	.218	R	R	6-2	170	10-28-69	1992	Gretna, La.
Chen, Bruce	0	0	6.00	11	0	0	0	12	14	8	8	8	8	.311	L	L	6-1	210	6-19-77	1994	Panama City, Panama
Dotel, Octavio	6	4	2.48	76	0	0	4	87	53	25	24	31	97	.171	R	R	6-0	200	11-25-73	1993	Santo Domingo, D.R.
Fernandez, Jared	3	3	3.99	12	6	0	0	38	37	17	17	12	19	.258	R	R	6-1	225	2-2-72	1994	Ogden, Utah
Gallo, Mike	1	0	3.00	32	0	0	0	30	28	10	10	10	16	.266	L	L	6-0	175	4-2-77	1999	Long Beach, Calif.
Johnson, Jonathan	0	1	5.87	4	3	0	0	15	20	11	10	15	7	.322	R	R	6-0	180	7-16-74	1995	Irmo, S.C.
Lidge, Brad	6	3	3.60	78	0	0	1	85	60	36	34	42	97	.202	R	R	6-5	210	12-23-76	1998	Englewood, Colo.
Linebrink, Scott	1	1	4.26	9	6	0	0	32	38	15	15	14	17	.316	R	R	6-2	200	8-4-76	1997	Taylor, Texas
Miceli, Danny	1	1	2.10	23	0	0	0	30	22	7	7	7	20	.207	R	R	6-0	225	9-9-70	1990	Winter Springs, Fla.
2-team (12 Colorado)	1	3	3.55	37	0	0	0	51	46	20	20	16	38	.242							
Miller, Wade	14	13	4.13	33	33	1	0	187	168	96	86	77	161	.241	R	R	6-2	210	9-13-76	1996	Douglassville, Pa.
Moehler, Brian	0	0	7.90	3	3	0	0	14	22	12	12	6	5	.379	R	R	6-3	235	12-31-71	1993	Marietta, Ga.
Munro, Pete	3	4	4.67	40	2	0	0	54	63	30	28	26	27	.294	R	R	6-3	210	6-14-75	1994	Little Neck, N.Y.
Oswalt, Roy	10	5	2.97	21	21	0	0	127	116	48	42	29	108	.245	R	R	6-0	175	8-29-77	1997	Weir, Miss.
Puffer, Brandon	0	0	5.14	13	0	0	0	21	24	13	12	16	10	.300	R	R	6-3	190	10-5-75	1994	Round Rock, Texas
Redding, Tim	10	14	3.68	33	32	0	0	176	179	85	72	65	116	.260	R	R	6-0	195	2-12-78	1998	Churchville, N.Y.
Robertson, Jeriome	15	9	5.10	32	31	0	0	161	180	98	91	64	99	.286	L	L	6-1	200	3-30-77	1996	Exeter, Calif.
Rosario, Rodrigo	1	0	1.13	2	2	0	0	8	5	2	1	3	6	.172	R	R	6-2	165	3-14-78	1996	La Romana, D.R.
Saarloos, Kirk	2	1	4.93	36	4	0	0	49	55	31	27	17	43	.280	R	R	6-0	180	5-23-79	2001	Houston, Texas
Stone, Ricky	6	4	3.69	65	0	0	1	83	76	36	34	31	47	.246	R	R	6-1	190	2-28-75	1994	Hamilton, Ohio
Villone, Ron	6	6	4.13	19	19	0	0	107	91	51	49	48	91	.233	L	L	6-3	230	1-16-70	1992	River Vale, N.J.
Wagner, Billy	1	4	1.78	78	0	0	44	86	52	18	17	23	105	.168	L	L	5-11	195	7-25-71	1993	Charlottesville, Va.
White, Rick	0	0	3.72	15	0	0	0	19	18	9	8	8	17	.243	R	R	6-4	230	12-23-68	1990	Springfield, Ohio

FIELDING

Catcher	PCT	G	PO	A	E	DP	PB
Ausmus	.997	143	982	76	3	13	3
Chavez	1.000	16	55	3	0	0	0
Zaun	.976	31	152	8	4	0	1

First Base	PCT	G	PO	A	E	DP
Bagwell	.994	158	1290	112	9	125
Blum	1.000	6	11	0	0	1
Merced	.982	12	50	4	1	6
Vizcaino	1.000	1	6	0	0	0

Second Base	PCT	G	PO	A	E	DP
Blum	.987	25	34	42	1	8
Bruntlett	1.000	9	13	14	0	4
Cromer	1.000	1	1	2	0	1
Kent	.983	128	278	354	11	83
Matranga	1.000	2	2	0	0	0
Vizcaino	.975	20	35	44	2	9

Third Base	PCT	G	PO	A	E	DP
Blum	.971	83	32	135	5	18
Bruntlett	.000	1	0	0	0	0
Ensberg	.967	111	77	184	9	18
Merced	1.000	2	0	1	0	0
Vizcaino	.000	2	0	0	0	0

Shortstop	PCT	G	PO	A	E	DP
Blum	.955	11	3	18	1	6
Bruntlett	.963	10	12	14	1	3
Everett	.970	128	207	344	17	71
Lugo	.966	22	30	55	3	10
Vizcaino	.963	32	31	48	3	12

Outfield	PCT	G	PO	A	E	DP
Berkman	.989	153	254	10	3	0
Biggio	.997	150	326	9	1	1
Blum	1.000	2	0	1	0	0
Bruntlett	.000	2	0	0	0	0
Hidalgo	.987	137	277	22	4	5
Hunter	.944	32	33	1	2	0
Lane	1.000	10	7	0	0	0
Merced	.959	31	43	4	2	1
Porter	1.000	14	17	0	0	0

LARRY GOREN

Jeff Bagwell

ORGANIZATION STATISTICS

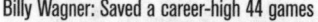

Billy Wagner: Saved a career-high 44 games

Adam Everett: Steadying defensive presence at shortstop

FARM SYSTEM

Assistant GM/Director, Player Development: Tim Purpura

Class	Farm Team	League	W	L	Pct.	Finish*	Manager	First Yr.
AAA	New Orleans (La.) Zephyrs	Pacific Coast	71	73	.493	8th(16)	Chris Maloney	1997
AA	Round Rock (Texas) Express	Texas	46	94	.329	8th (8)	Jackie Moore	2000
High A	Salem (Va.) Avalanche	Carolina	73	65	.529	3rd (8)	John Massarelli	2003
Low A	Lexington (Ky.) Legends	South Atlantic	75	63	.543	5th (16)	Russ Nixon	2001
SS A	Tri-City (Troy, N.Y.) Valley Cats	New York-Penn	44	32	.579	5th (14)	Ivan DeJesus	2001
Rookie	Martinsville (Va.) Astros	Appalachian	42	23	.646	1st (10)	Jorge Orta	1999

*Finish in overall standings (No. of teams in league)

NEW ORLEANS ZEPHYRS — Class AAA

PACIFIC COAST LEAGUE

BATTING	AVG	G	AB	R	H	2B	3B	HR	RBI	BB	SO	SB	CS	SLG	OBP	B	T	HT	WT	DOB	1st Yr	Resides
Alfaro, Jason	.296	105	361	45	107	20	4	9	49	30	53	2	3	.449	.354	R	R	5-10	185	11-29-77	1997	Ft. Worth, Texas
Bruntlett, Eric	.259	84	324	48	84	10	0	2	27	35	51	9	4	.309	.332	R	R	6-0	200	3-29-78	2000	Lafayette, Ind.
Buck, John	.255	78	274	32	70	18	2	2	39	14	53	1	0	.358	.301	R	R	6-3	210	7-7-80	1998	Salt Lake City, Utah
Chavez, Raul	.273	101	355	47	97	28	1	6	47	13	43	0	2	.408	.315	R	R	5-11	210	3-18-73	1990	Valencia, Venez.
Cole, Eric	.210	32	81	4	17	4	0	1	6	3	13	1	1	.296	.238	R	R	6-0	180	11-15-75	1995	Gerome, Idaho
Cromer, Tripp	.252	84	242	29	61	15	3	4	36	17	41	0	0	.388	.303	R	R	6-2	165	11-21-67	1989	Columbia, S.C.
Everett, Adam	.250	25	100	23	25	6	1	1	9	7	16	3	1	.360	.306	R	R	6-0	160	2-5-77	1998	Kennesaw, Ga.
Fatheree, Danny	.200	19	15	1	3	1	0	0	0	1	5	0	0	.267	.250	R	R	5-11	230	8-25-78	1997	Grand Prairie, Texas
Hernandez, Carlos	.225	17	40	6	9	2	0	0	2	2	12	0	0	.275	.256	R	R	5-9	170	12-12-75	1993	Caracas, Venez.
2-eam (73 Fresno)	.211	90	256	23	54	5	0	1	16	17	50	4	1	.242	.264							
Huffman, Royce	.289	128	460	49	133	20	2	2	60	43	68	7	3	.354	.353	R	R	6-0	200	1-11-77	1999	Missouri City, Texas
Lane, Jason	.298	71	248	37	74	17	0	7	39	30	26	2	1	.452	.374	R	L	6-2	210	12-22-76	1999	Sebastopol, Calif.
Logan, Kyle	.257	134	460	43	118	25	2	5	44	22	88	14	8	.352	.294	L	R	6-0	195	7-11-75	1997	Hattiesburg, Miss.
Matranga, Dave	.241	102	315	34	76	16	4	3	25	21	71	3	3	.346	.296	R	R	6-0	170	1-8-77	1998	Aliso Viejo, Calif.
Moriarty, Mike	.250	58	172	19	43	9	1	5	17	16	30	3	1	.401	.319	R	R	6-0	180	3-8-74	1995	Mount Laurel, N.J.
Norris, Dax	.158	9	19	1	3	1	0	0	1	0	2	0	0	.211	.150	R	R	5-10	190	1-14-73	1996	La Grange, Ga.
Porter, Colin	.320	102	356	52	114	23	6	11	50	22	80	22	6	.511	.361	L	L	6-2	210	11-23-75	1998	Tucson, Ariz.
Stanley, Henri	.292	135	506	85	148	28	8	11	48	60	93	15	7	.445	.368	L	L	5-10	185	12-15-77	2000	Columbia, S.C.
Topolski, Jon	.364	5	11	1	4	0	0	1	1	0	2	0	0	.636	.364	L	R	5-10	200	12-28-76	1999	Houston, Texas
Vizcaino, Jose	.250	2	8	1	2	0	0	1	1	1	0	0	0	.625	.333	S	R	6-1	180	3-26-68	1986	Poway, Calif.
Zinter, Alan	.254	114	342	48	87	17	0	17	57	36	77	1	0	.453	.333	S	R	6-2	195	5-19-68	1989	Oro Valley, Ariz.

PITCHING	W	L	ERA	G	GS	CG	SV	IP	H	R	ER	BB	SO	AVG	B	T	HT	WT	DOB	1st Yr	Resides
Bland, Nate	0	1	2.84	17	0	0	1	19	15	6	6	9	23	.217	L	L	6-5	190	12-27-74	1993	Birmingham, Ala.
Bullinger, Kirk	3	3	1.94	55	0	0	20	65	56	18	14	14	46	.230	R	R	6-2	170	10-28-69	1992	Gretna, La.
Cammack, Eric	0	0	1.93	4	0	0	0	5	4	2	1	2	3	.235	R	R	6-1	180	8-14-75	1997	Port Neches, Texas
Fernandez, Jared	7	10	3.81	26	23	2	0	156	164	73	66	37	51	.270	R	R	6-1	225	2-2-72	1994	Ogden, Utah
Gallo, Mike	3	0	2.08	16	0	0	0	17	13	4	4	3	11	.216	L	L	6-0	175	4-2-77	1999	Long Beach, Calif.
Houlton, D.J.	3	4	5.40	11	11	0	0	62	70	39	37	19	48	.288	R	R	6-4	220	8-12-79	2001	Yorba Linda, Calif.

PITCHING	W	L	ERA	G	GS	CG	SV	IP	H	R	ER	BB	SO	AVG	B	T	HT	WT	DOB	1st Yr	Resides
Johnson, Jonathan	5	4	3.92	13	13	1	0	78	74	38	34	27	62	.247	R	R	6-0	180	7-16-74	1995	Irmo, S.C.
Keisler, Randy	2	3	4.28	9	9	0	0	48	53	24	23	21	27	.289	L	L	6-3	190	2-24-76	1998	Richards, Texas
3-team (8 Port., 5 Okla.)	7	6	4.13	22	17	0	0	102	107	49	47	38	60	.274							
Linebrink, Scott	0	2	2.70	2	2	0	0	10	8	3	3	5	6	.222	R	R	6-2	200	8-4-76	1997	Taylor, Texas
Miller, Greg	0	3	7.02	9	7	0	0	41	59	37	32	22	16	.349	L	L	6-5	210	9-30-79	1997	Aurora, Ill.
Moehler, Brian	0	0	4.50	1	1	0	0	2	3	1	1	0	3	.375	R	R	6-3	235	12-31-71	1993	Marietta, Ga.
Munro, Pete	0	4	6.04	5	4	0	0	22	28	16	15	12	12	.307	R	R	6-3	210	6-14-75	1994	Little Neck, N.Y.
Oswalt, Roy	0	0	3.00	1	1	0	0	3	3	1	1	0	2	.250	R	R	6-0	175	8-29-77	1997	Weir, Miss.
Puffer, Brandon	7	3	2.91	44	0	0	5	53	50	23	17	16	41	.252	R	R	6-3	190	10-5-75	1994	Round Rock, Texas
Ramirez, Santiago	4	0	4.26	10	0	0	0	13	7	7	6	9	9	.175	R	R	5-11	200	8-15-78	1997	Bonao, D.R.
Robertson, Jeriome	1	0	6.75	1	1	0	0	7	7	5	5	2	6	.269	L	L	6-1	200	3-30-77	1996	Exeter, Calif.
Rosario, Rodrigo	5	7	4.03	15	15	1	0	87	71	40	39	32	68	.221	R	R	6-2	165	3-14-78	1996	La Romana, D.R.
Saarloos, Kirk	5	0	3.08	13	7	2	0	61	54	22	21	11	34	.242	R	R	6-0	180	5-23-79	2001	Houston, Texas
Saladin, Miguel	5	6	2.99	55	0	0	3	84	75	35	28	33	60	.237	R	R	5-11	200	5-22-75	1996	San Pedro de Macoris, D.R.
Scanlan, Bob	1	9	3.75	32	14	0	0	98	95	47	41	34	49	.260	R	R	6-8	220	8-9-66	1984	San Diego, Calif.
Sessions, Doug	9	5	2.92	31	25	1	1	157	149	57	51	43	92	.247	R	R	6-1	205	9-28-76	1998	Orange Park, Fla.
Stanifer, Rob	3	2	3.97	41	0	0	4	57	55	27	25	13	38	.255	R	R	6-2	220	3-10-72	1994	Largo, Fla.
2-team (3 Iowa)	4	2	3.96	44	0	0	4	64	63	30	28	17	43	.259							
Venafro, Mike	2	1	3.54	23	0	0	0	28	35	11	11	5	11	.309	L	L	5-10	180	8-2-73	1995	Fort Myers, Fla.
Villone, Ron	3	1	1.23	5	5	0	0	29	24	5	4	10	18	.233	L	L	6-3	230	1-16-70	1992	River Vale, N.J.
2-team (15 Tucson)	4	2	2.30	20	5	0	1	55	44	19	14	22	40	.232							
Vining, Ken	3	5	5.20	41	6	0	1	64	75	41	37	22	30	.297	L	L	6-0	180	12-5-74	1996	Hopkins, S.C.

FIELDING

Catcher	PCT	G	PO	A	E	DP	PB
Buck	.993	71	385	36	3	2	9
Chavez	.983	58	305	45	6	6	2
Fatheree	1.000	6	5	0	0	0	0
Norris	1.000	9	36	4	0	0	1
Zinter	1.000	20	74	5	0	0	1

First Base	PCT	G	PO	A	E	DP
Cromer	1.000	3	3	0	0	0
Huffman	.990	92	828	60	9	81
Lane	.987	7	71	6	1	7
Zinter	.996	60	429	33	2	38

Second Base	PCT	G	PO	A	E	DP
Bruntlett	.971	30	42	92	4	20
Cromer	.984	49	103	136	4	37
Everett	.938	3	4	11	1	3
Hernandez	.974	9	14	24	1	6
Huffman	.952	15	27	32	3	5
Matranga	.982	51	122	147	5	24
Vizcaino	.889	2	1	7	1	0

Third Base	PCT	G	PO	A	E	DP
Alfaro	.947	47	29	79	6	11
Chavez	.956	40	26	82	5	7
Cromer	.972	13	14	21	1	1
Hernandez	1.000	2	0	1	0	0
Huffman	1.000	1	0	1	0	0
Matranga	.967	15	9	20	1	5
Moriarty	.927	42	37	90	10	10
Zinter	.000	1	0	0	1	0

Shortstop	PCT	G	PO	A	E	DP
Alfaro	.961	44	65	131	8	24
Bruntlett	.964	47	93	149	9	39
Everett	.990	22	39	57	1	13
Matranga	.976	22	42	40	2	14
Moriarty	.981	14	17	35	1	6
Vizcaino	.000	1	0	0	0	0

Outfield	PCT	G	PO	A	E	DP
Alfaro	1.000	11	21	1	0	0
Bruntlett	1.000	3	5	0	0	0
Cole	.980	22	49	0	1	0
Huffman	.933	17	26	2	2	0
Lane	.966	53	86	0	3	0
Logan	.979	128	230	6	5	0
Matranga	1.000	2	4	0	0	0
Porter	.989	97	255	6	3	2
Stanley	.980	125	235	4	5	1
Topolski	.667	1	4	0	2	0

ROUND ROCK EXPRESS — Class AA

TEXAS LEAGUE

BATTING	AVG	G	AB	R	H	2B	3B	HR	RBI	BB	SO	SB	CS	SLG	OBP	B	T	HT	WT	DOB	1st Yr	Resides
Acevedo, Anthony	.283	130	459	62	130	22	2	11	56	56	101	10	4	.412	.363	L	L	6-5	195	5-5-78	2000	Bakersfield, Calif.
Alfaro, Jason	.148	22	81	6	12	3	0	0	9	5	20	0	1	.185	.198	R	R	5-10	185	11-29-77	1997	Fort Worth, Texas
Burke, Chris	.301	137	549	88	165	23	8	3	41	57	57	34	10	.388	.379	R	R	5-11	180	3-11-80	2001	Knoxville, Tenn.
Cole, Eric	.266	87	327	43	87	14	1	6	33	17	52	17	7	.370	.305	R	R	6-0	180	11-15-75	1995	Gerome, Idaho
Coolbaugh, Mike	.259	42	147	24	38	6	0	7	29	22	43	1	0	.442	.349	R	R	6-1	190	6-5-72	1990	San Antonio, Texas
Fatheree, Danny	.000	1	2	0	0	0	0	0	0	0	0	0	0	.000	.000	R	R	5-11	230	8-25-78	1997	Grand Prairie, Texas
German, Ramon	.217	35	115	5	25	1	0	1	8	12	26	0	1	.252	.291	S	R	6-1	210	1-15-80	1997	Santo Domingo, D.R.
Hernandez, Carlos	.258	16	62	9	16	1	0	1	9	3	8	4	0	.323	.299	R	R	5-9	170	12-12-75	1993	Caracas, Venez.
Hill, Mike	.245	45	159	16	39	4	2	3	21	8	36	2	1	.352	.284	R	R	6-4	200	9-30-76	1999	Lawton, Okla.
Kent, Jeff	.300	3	10	1	3	0	0	1	6	1	1	0	1	.600	.333	R	R	6-1	215	3-7-68	1989	Foster City, Calif.
Landry, Jacques	.247	68	259	34	64	15	3	9	31	17	75	5	2	.432	.309	R	R	6-3	200	8-15-73	1996	LaMarque, Texas
Lentini, Fehlandt	.217	17	23	4	5	1	1	0	1	2	8	0	0	.348	.280	R	R	6-0	185	8-12-77	2001	Santa Rosa, Calif.
Meluskey, Mitch	.265	13	49	5	13	2	0	1	6	5	9	1	0	.367	.327	S	R	6-0	200	9-18-73	1992	Yakima, Wash.
Norris, Dax	.245	77	265	22	65	12	0	6	45	21	35	0	0	.358	.301	R	R	5-10	190	1-14-73	1996	La Grange, Ga.
Rosamond, Mike	.273	127	455	55	124	24	2	11	43	31	124	7	8	.407	.320	R	R	6-5	230	4-18-78	1999	Madison, Miss.
Tamargo, John	.226	83	288	25	65	4	1	2	27	34	38	5	2	.267	.311	L	R	5-9	180	5-3-75	1996	Tampa, Fla.
Topolski, Jon	.227	82	207	31	47	6	5	5	31	29	53	9	6	.377	.321	L	R	5-10	200	12-28-76	1999	Houston, Texas
Tremie, Chris	.243	93	301	33	73	11	1	9	35	26	50	0	1	.375	.309	R	R	6-0	210	10-17-69	1992	New Waverly, Texas
Whiteman, Tommy	.261	133	532	65	139	18	2	13	70	35	102	3	8	.376	.310	R	R	6-3	180	7-14-79	2000	Edmond, Okla.
Wright, Gavin	.247	111	372	38	92	15	1	2	29	22	78	8	8	.309	.292	R	R	6-2	190	5-6-79	1999	Lufkin, Texas

PITCHING	W	L	ERA	G	GS	CG	SV	IP	H	R	ER	BB	SO	AVG	B	T	HT	WT	DOB	1st Yr	Resides
Burns, Mike	2	13	6.13	38	14	0	0	106	129	80	72	30	89	.296	R	R	6-1	190	7-14-78	2000	Diamond Bar, Calif.
Cammack, Eric	0	1	0.59	26	0	0	5	30	21	6	2	13	27	.192	R	R	6-1	180	8-14-75	1997	Port Neches, Texas
Campos, Juan	0	0	8.53	9	0	0	0	13	19	12	12	3	17	.333	R	R	6-0	180	3-28-80	1997	Edo Monagas, Venez.
Coughenour, Jory	2	5	7.09	34	1	0	3	53	71	46	42	30	34	.324	R	R	6-1	200	6-17-78	2000	Dunbar, Pa.
Gallo, Mike	1	1	1.37	17	0	0	2	20	17	3	3	6	22	.246	L	L	6-0	175	4-2-77	1999	Long Beach, Calif.
Houlton, D.J.	5	4	3.47	18	18	1	0	109	93	45	42	28	101	.225	R	R	6-4	220	8-12-79	2001	Yorba Linda, Calif.
Ireland, Eric	1	5	5.21	32	6	0	0	67	85	51	39	30	55	.306	R	R	6-1	170	3-11-77	1996	Long Beach, Calif.
Janke, Cheyenne	2	4	4.45	28	3	0	1	55	63	29	27	22	42	.285	R	R	6-5	230	2-16-77	1999	Elk Mound, Wisc.
Lira, James	0	5	6.04	18	5	0	1	48	67	33	32	18	39	.331	R	R	6-1	175	5-19-78	1998	Bishop, Texas
Lugo, Ruddy	4	15	6.01	41	15	1	1	118	133	93	79	53	112	.283	R	R	6-0	190	5-22-80	1999	Brooklyn, N.Y.
McClaskey, Tim	5	4	4.66	15	9	0	1	66	69	39	34	15	56	.267	R	R	5-10	170	1-11-76	1996	Melbourne, Fla.
Miller, Greg	3	4	5.49	27	10	1	0	77	80	56	47	38	63	.272	L	L	6-5	210	9-30-79	1997	Aurora, Ill.
Powell, Greg	7	9	3.89	36	18	1	0	141	155	75	61	39	80	.280	R	R	6-4	200	8-26-78	2001	Holland, Pa.
Qualls, Chad	8	11	3.85	28	28	3	0	175	174	85	75	61	132	.264	R	R	6-5	220	8-17-78	2000	Reno, Nev.
Ramirez, Santiago	0	0	0.00	6	1	0	1	5	5	0	0	4	3	.277	R	R	5-11	200	8-15-78	1997	Bonao, D.R.

PITCHING	W	L	ERA	G	GS	CG	SV	IP	H	R	ER	BB	SO	AVG	B	T	HT	WT	DOB	1st Yr	Resides
Roberts, Nick	2	8	4.95	13	12	0	0	73	77	47	40	26	51	.275	R	R	6-2	185	11-6-76	1999	Annabella, Utah
Santillan, Manny	0	0	15.00	4	0	0	0	3	6	5	5	5	2	.461	R	R	6-0	215	8-20-79	1996	La Romana, D.R.
Scanlan, Bob	0	0	0.00	4	0	0	0	3	2	1	0	1	4	.181	R	R	6-8	220	8-9-66	1984	San Diego, Calif.
Tremblay, Max	2	3	5.91	41	0	0	0	32	37	27	21	14	35	.286	L	L	6-0	210	6-18-76	1998	San Dimas, Calif.
Wade, Travis	2	2	4.70	28	0	0	3	31	39	20	16	15	17	.314	R	R	6-3	210	7-8-75	1997	Climax, Mich.

FIELDING

Catcher	PCT	G	PO	A	E	DP	PB
Fatheree	1.000	1	2	0	0	0	0
Meluskey	1.000	8	62	3	0	0	2
Norris	.989	65	422	39	5	3	8
Tremie	.991	75	508	54	5	8	3

First Base	PCT	G	PO	A	E	DP
Acevedo	1.000	1	11	0	0	2
Cole	.977	44	323	21	8	30
Coolbaugh	.978	12	81	7	2	15
German	1.000	4	33	1	0	4
Landry	.973	28	199	16	6	21
Norris	1.000	3	21	2	0	1
Topolski	.990	47	362	23	4	27
Tremie	.972	12	94	11	3	11

Second Base	PCT	G	PO	A	E	DP
Burke	.983	93	205	269	8	50
Coolbaugh	1.000	8	8	21	0	3
Hernandez	1.000	9	20	17	0	8
Kent	.875	2	2	5	1	0
Tamargo	.981	32	66	87	3	26

Third Base	PCT	G	PO	A	E	DP
Alfaro	.882	22	9	36	6	2
Coolbaugh	.919	13	6	28	3	3
German	.905	30	25	51	8	5
Hernandez	.909	6	8	12	2	2
Landry	.923	4	2	10	1	0
Tamargo	.944	35	21	47	4	1
Tremie	1.000	5	0	2	0	0
Whiteman	.905	34	21	55	8	10

Shortstop	PCT	G	PO	A	E	DP
Burke	.932	42	79	98	13	28
Whiteman	.932	100	136	249	28	52

Outfield	PCT	G	PO	A	E	DP
Acevedo	.965	114	185	6	7	3
Alfaro	.000	1	0	0	0	0
Burke	1.000	1	4	0	0	0
Cole	.990	41	94	3	1	1
Hill	1.000	7	14	0	0	0
Landry	.957	28	64	2	3	0
Lentini	1.000	6	6	0	0	0
Meluskey	.667	1	2	0	1	0
Rosamond	.967	123	255	9	9	0
Topolski	1.000	13	12	2	0	0
Wright	.968	103	237	6	8	2

SALEM AVALANCHE — High Class A

CAROLINA LEAGUE

BATTING	AVG	G	AB	R	H	2B	3B	HR	RBI	BB	SO	SB	CS	SLG	OBP	B	T	HT	WT	DOB	1st Yr	Resides
Canales, Josh	.162	71	142	18	23	0	0	0	3	20	42	3	1	.162	.265	R	R	5-11	170	1-15-79	2001	Carson, Calif.
Caraway, Brandon	.252	123	436	74	110	21	2	2	50	49	65	17	9	.323	.331	S	R	6-0	175	10-6-77	2000	Houston, Texas
Checksfield, Steven	.238	79	252	29	60	16	2	7	37	21	54	2	0	.401	.301	R	R	6-3	240	6-11-79	2001	Hurley, N.Y.
Conrad, Brooks	.284	99	345	50	98	24	3	11	61	42	60	4	2	.467	.369	S	R	5-11	190	1-16-80	2001	Spring Valley, Calif.
Gimenez, Hector	.247	109	381	41	94	17	1	7	54	29	75	2	0	.352	.304	S	R	5-10	180	9-28-82	1999	San Felipe, Venez.
Helquist, Jon	.183	28	93	14	17	3	1	2	11	10	25	1	1	.301	.264	R	R	6-0	170	8-17-80	1999	Jacksonville, Fla.
Jimerson, Charlton	.265	97	336	53	89	19	3	12	55	25	109	27	4	.446	.317	R	R	6-3	210	9-22-79	2001	Hayward, Calif.
Lentini, Fehlandt	.279	100	369	45	103	21	4	3	48	25	58	19	7	.382	.326	R	R	6-0	185	8-12-77	2001	Santa Rosa, Calif.
Likely, Cameron	.097	11	31	1	3	0	0	0	1	1	13	1	2	.097	.121	R	R	5-10	160	2-2-78	2001	Port St. Joe, Fla.
Lucas, Matt	.133	7	15	1	2	1	0	0	1	1	4	0	0	.200	.188	R	R	6-1	185	11-21-78	2000	Fullerton, Calif.
Lydic, Joe	.203	58	153	11	31	6	0	2	12	9	40	0	0	.281	.253	R	R	6-4	190	2-20-79	2000	Bethel Park, Pa.
Mote, Trevor	.235	125	426	55	100	20	2	2	50	55	81	6	1	.305	.321	S	R	6-1	205	7-22-79	2001	Kingman, Ariz.
Rodriguez, Mike	.278	113	443	78	123	22	8	5	42	50	50	23	9	.397	.356	L	L	5-10	180	10-15-80	2001	Cooper City, Fla.
Ruiz, Reinaldo	.170	53	147	13	25	8	0	2	20	9	26	0	0	.265	.230	R	R	6-0	200	2-4-80	1996	Falcon, Venez.
Self, Todd	.318	126	431	84	137	27	2	6	57	87	93	2	1	.432	.433	L	R	6-5	215	11-9-78	2000	Stonewall, La.
Soto, T.J.	.153	30	111	8	17	4	1	3	21	6	37	2	1	.288	.195	R	R	5-11	190	8-31-77	2000	Ruston, La.
Stegall, Ryan	.227	128	366	36	83	11	2	3	36	41	72	5	3	.292	.327	R	R	6-1	190	11-13-79	2001	Liberty, Mo.

PITCHING	W	L	ERA	G	GS	CG	SV	IP	H	R	ER	BB	SO	AVG	B	T	HT	WT	DOB	1st Yr	Resides
Astacio, Andres	0	1	13.00	3	3	0	0	9	15	15	13	8	3	.365	R	R	6-2	160	8-5-80	1999	La Romana, D.R.
Barrett, Jimmy	7	10	5.33	26	26	0	0	138	160	87	82	56	75	.291	R	R	6-2	190	6-7-81	1999	Cumberland, Md.
Barzilla, Philip	8	3	3.10	52	0	0	5	93	86	39	32	41	51	.253	L	L	6-0	180	1-25-79	2001	Sugar Land, Texas
Campos, Juan	3	0	1.84	45	0	0	24	68	51	15	14	16	68	.208	R	R	6-0	180	3-28-80	1997	Edo Monagas, Venez.
Coughenour, Jory	1	0	2.08	10	0	0	1	17	20	8	4	7	11	.298	R	R	6-1	200	6-17-78	2000	Dunbar, Pa.
Gothreaux, Jared	13	4	2.82	29	22	1	1	147	144	54	46	26	85	.258	R	R	6-0	200	1-27-80	2002	Lake Charles, La.
Hamilton, Mark	0	4	5.13	34	2	0	1	60	57	37	34	25	47	.251	L	L	6-3	200	4-23-78	2000	Hurst, Texas
Ireland, Eric	1	0	0.00	1	0	0	0	4	3	0	0	1	5	.200	R	R	6-1	170	3-11-77	1996	Long Beach, Calif.
Mansfield, Monte	1	1	4.30	13	0	0	0	23	24	16	11	12	24	.266	R	R	6-4	215	3-22-81	2000	Hesperia, Calif.
McDaniel, Denny	5	1	4.54	34	0	0	1	42	46	23	21	11	39	.273	L	L	6-3	210	8-12-76	1996	Austin, Texas
2-team (11 Myrtle Beach)	6	1	3.86	45	0	0	2	56	66	28	24	12	52	.289	L	L	6-3	210	8-12-76	1996	Austin, Texas
Pena, Francisco	5	9	3.80	33	12	0	0	95	89	51	40	44	64	.252	R	R	5-11	175	3-9-79	1997	Bonao, D.R.
Pluta, Anthony	0	1	5.84	3	3	0	0	12	13	8	8	8	14	.270	R	R	6-2	210	10-28-82	2000	Las Vegas, Nevada
Roberson, Brandon	8	5	3.72	38	18	2	0	126	134	58	52	24	78	.278	R	R	6-3	190	4-26-78	2001	Aledo, Texas
Roberts, Nick	0	2	9.00	3	3	0	0	12	18	12	12	2	8	.360	R	R	6-2	185	11-6-76	1999	Annabella, Utah
Rodaway, Brian	5	9	3.99	26	25	2	0	140	156	68	62	35	82	.287	L	L	6-3	190	9-11-78	2001	Lincoln, Neb.
Rodriguez, Wandy	8	7	3.49	20	20	1	0	111	102	51	43	41	72	.239	S	L	5-11	160	1-18-79	1999	Santiago Rodriguez, D.R.
Sampson, Chris	1	1	5.91	9	0	0	1	11	14	8	7	5	6	.325	R	R	6-0	170	5-23-78	1999	Lubbock, Texas
Santillan, Manny	3	5	6.00	36	4	0	0	51	56	39	34	41	33	.287	R	R	6-0	215	8-20-79	1996	La Romana, D.R.
Sinclair, Ernnie	0	0	12.38	6	0	0	0	8	15	12	11	5	4	.384	R	R	6-0	190	4-2-79	1998	Bluefields, Nicaragua
Tremblay, Max	4	2	3.44	13	0	0	1	18	20	11	7	11	13	.273	L	L	6-0	210	6-18-76	1998	San Dimas, Calif.

FIELDING

Catcher	PCT	G	PO	A	E	DP	PB
Gimenez	.991	101	574	77	6	7	19
Lucas	.952	7	19	1	1	0	2
Ruiz	1.000	45	210	14	0	2	2

First Base	PCT	G	PO	A	E	DP
Checksfield	.971	22	184	15	6	6
Lydic	.977	32	239	17	6	18
Mote	1.000	2	12	0	0	1
Self	.994	95	839	60	5	64
Soto	.960	2	22	2	1	3

Second Base	PCT	G	PO	A	E	DP
Canales	.964	13	22	31	2	6
Conrad	.970	97	170	315	15	50
Helquist	.960	28	56	111	7	16
Mote	.900	2	4	5	1	2
Soto	.933	2	6	8	1	1

Third Base	PCT	G	PO	A	E	DP
Canales	.979	28	14	33	1	4
Lydic	1.000	14	9	17	0	2
Mote	.932	116	75	211	21	15
Soto	.909	5	1	9	1	2

Shortstop	PCT	G	PO	A	E	DP
Canales	.976	25	24	57	2	7
Mote	.000	1	0	0	0	0
Stegall	.959	127	203	354	24	65

Outfield	PCT	G	PO	A	E	DP
Canales	1.000	1	2	0	0	0
Caraway	.987	113	206	19	3	1
Checksfield	1.000	3	4	0	0	0
Jimerson	.985	91	196	4	3	1
Lentini	.987	72	145	8	2	3
Likely	1.000	10	18	0	0	0
Rodriguez	.972	101	163	8	5	0
Self	.976	26	41	0	1	0
Soto	1.000	15	22	0	0	0

LEXINGTON LEGENDS — Low Class A

SOUTH ATLANTIC LEAGUE

BATTING	AVG	G	AB	R	H	2B	3B	HR	RBI	BB	SO	SB	CS	SLG	OBP	B	T	HT	WT	DOB	1st Yr	Resides
Acevedo, Freddy	.237	110	405	51	96	28	4	10	46	34	132	11	6	.400	.307	R	R	6-2	200	8-23-81	1999	La Romana, D.R.
Alvarez, Wilner	.215	91	260	27	56	13	0	3	14	24	51	9	4	.300	.299	R	R	6-0	165	7-14-82	2001	Caracas, Venez.
Cespedes, Robinson	.229	88	310	41	71	11	1	3	33	38	46	7	2	.300	.330	R	R	6-0	170	7-30-80	1998	Palmarejo, Venez.
Checksfield, Steven	.241	32	116	19	28	4	2	7	21	14	35	1	1	.491	.326	R	R	6-3	240	6-11-79	2001	Hurley, N.Y.
Conrad, Brooks	.186	38	140	20	26	5	2	3	11	17	25	7	1	.314	.288	S	R	5-11	190	1-16-80	2001	Spring Valley, Calif.
Davidson, Kevin	.333	1	3	1	1	0	0	1	2	0	1	0	0	1.333	.333	R	R	5-9	185	7-21-80	2002	Port Richey, Fla.
Fagan, John	.251	116	346	53	87	17	1	18	57	52	115	0	0	.462	.372	R	R	6-5	200	8-8-79	2001	San Jose, Calif.
Fernando, Osvaldo	.226	129	451	58	102	17	1	1	36	33	81	17	7	.275	.290	R	R	6-0	175	10-15-80	2000	San Pedro de Macoris, D.R.
Hawkins, Dustin	.196	95	336	40	66	11	3	0	26	48	72	7	3	.247	.296	L	L	6-0	180	11-22-79	2002	Ogden, Utah
Humphries, Justin	.269	102	338	39	91	21	2	14	50	54	83	0	1	.467	.376	R	R	6-4	220	2-24-83	2001	Richmond, Texas
Kochen, Ryan	.248	123	475	65	118	28	1	11	53	30	96	5	2	.381	.306	R	R	6-2	195	6-13-79	2001	Batavia, Ill.
Likely, Cameron	.262	46	164	26	43	4	2	1	17	19	26	11	2	.329	.335	R	R	5-10	160	2-2-78	2001	Port St. Joe, Fla.
Melendez, German	.218	59	179	16	39	6	0	0	16	15	35	3	0	.251	.294	R	R	6-0	180	9-13-80	1998	Mariara,Venez.
Obradovich, Mark	.218	84	275	28	60	13	1	2	25	39	51	4	2	.295	.320	S	R	6-2	175	10-26-80	2001	Tuscaloosa, Ala.
Peavey, Pat	.238	104	369	43	88	19	0	11	49	45	60	0	2	.379	.332	R	R	6-1	195	5-5-80	2002	Brisbane, Calif.
Pedrique, Franmig	.000	1	0	0	0	0	0	0	0	1	0	0	0	.000	1.000	R	R	5-10	195	11-27-78	2003	Tucson, Ariz.
Soto, T.J.	.295	86	325	60	96	25	5	12	62	37	77	16	5	.514	.369	R	R	5-11	190	8-31-77	2000	Ruston, La.

PITCHING	W	L	ERA	G	GS	CG	SV	IP	H	R	ER	BB	SO	AVG	B	T	HT	WT	DOB	1st Yr	Resides
Barrios, Angel	0	0	4.50	3	0	0	0	6	6	5	3	6	4	.285	R	R	6-2	160	8-6-81	1998	Ciudad Bolivar, Venez.
Carlson, Jesse	3	0	1.56	53	0	0	13	63	37	11	11	16	84	.168	L	L	6-1	160	12-31-80	2002	Kensington, Conn.
Davis, Brendon	1	0	3.78	10	0	0	0	17	15	10	7	10	13	.223	R	R	6-5	196	4-18-80	2003	Cedar Park, Texas
De Leon, Juan	2	0	1.83	26	0	0	2	39	24	11	8	22	45	.180	R	R	5-11	160	6-24-81	2001	Santo Domingo, D.R.
Doyne, Cory	3	1	2.14	9	9	0	0	55	34	18	13	19	48	.177	R	R	6-2	210	8-13-81	2000	Lutz, Fla.
Escobar, Rodrigo	1	0	5.63	25	0	0	1	46	49	32	29	22	41	.270	R	R	5-11	165	2-11-83	1999	Cartagena, Colombia
Freeman, Daniel	4	2	1.64	44	0	0	21	55	46	17	10	18	63	.220	R	R	6-2	215	8-3-82	2002	Jonesboro, La.
Grigsby, Derick	2	2	4.79	12	9	0	0	36	40	19	19	14	21	.294	R	R	6-0	190	6-30-82	2002	Marshall, Texas
Hamilton, Mark	0	0	0.96	4	0	0	0	9	5	2	1	3	17	.142	L	L	6-3	200	4-23-78	2000	Hurst, Texas
Hansack, Devern	10	6	4.52	22	16	0	0	92	100	53	46	32	76	.278	R	R	6-2	180	2-5-78	1999	Pearl Lagoon, Nicaragua
Heitzman, Aaron	12	10	4.35	28	28	0	0	157	165	87	76	60	75	.274	L	L	6-0	180	11-21-79	2002	New Ulm, Minn.
McLemore, Mark	2	11	4.58	36	7	0	0	92	84	57	47	55	101	.243	L	L	6-2	220	10-9-80	2002	Granite Bay, Calif.
Nieve, Fernando	14	9	3.65	28	28	1	0	150	133	69	61	65	144	.237	R	R	6-0	195	7-15-82	1999	San Felipe, Venez.
Peguero, Jailen	5	13	3.64	31	21	0	1	146	110	74	59	69	111	.209	R	R	6-0	195	1-4-81	2000	Azua, D.R.
Salazar, Julio	1	0	2.81	8	0	0	1	16	7	6	5	9	11	.129	L	L	6-0	180	6-24-83	2000	Rubio, Venez.
Sampson, Chris	4	3	1.39	22	14	0	1	84	66	17	13	14	66	.212	R	R	6-0	170	5-23-78	1999	Lubbock, Texas
Sinclair, Ernnie	5	3	3.15	21	6	0	0	54	45	22	19	28	47	.226	R	R	6-0	190	4-2-79	1998	Bluefields, Nicaragua
Westhoff, Billy	6	2	3.10	45	0	0	2	90	84	44	31	48	59	.246	L	R	6-0	195	1-18-80	2002	Frisco, Texas

FIELDING

Catcher	PCT	G	PO	A	E	DP	PB
Davidson	1.000	1	9	0	0	0	1
Melendez	.988	58	435	51	6	6	19
Obradovich	.994	84	593	61	4	2	27

First Base	PCT	G	PO	A	E	DP
Checksfield	1.000	1	9	0	0	1
Fagan	.985	114	867	79	14	75
Humphries	.997	39	307	16	1	24

Second Base	PCT	G	PO	A	E	DP
Conrad	.966	38	74	126	7	27
Peavey	.979	26	30	62	2	7
Pedrique	.000	1	0	0	0	0
Soto	.956	75	132	192	15	35

Third Base	PCT	G	PO	A	E	DP
Kochen	.912	81	43	155	19	21
Peavey	.925	59	31	130	13	12

Shortstop	PCT	G	PO	A	E	DP
Fernando	.951	129	205	355	29	56
Kochen	.897	10	18	34	6	5

Outfield	PCT	G	PO	A	E	DP
Acevedo	.951	110	201	11	11	1
Alvarez	.974	84	179	9	5	3
Cespedes	.965	84	159	8	6	0
Checksfield	1.000	19	35	0	0	0
Fagan	.000	1	0	0	0	0
Hawkins	.981	90	151	8	3	1
Likely	.986	39	69	2	1	1

TRI-CITY VALLEY CATS — Short-Season Class A

NEW YORK-PENN LEAGUE

BATTING	AVG	G	AB	R	H	2B	3B	HR	RBI	BB	SO	SB	CS	SLG	OBP	B	T	HT	WT	DOB	1st Yr	Resides
Anderson, Josh	.286	74	297	44	85	11	4	3	30	16	53	26	9	.380	.339	L	R	6-2	195	8-10-82	2003	Eubank, Ky.
Fair, Kerry	.185	57	119	21	22	3	0	0	10	8	20	9	2	.210	.259	R	R	5-11	190	2-20-82	2003	Vincent, Ala.
Hearod, Beau	.228	52	162	17	37	9	2	5	20	13	44	0	0	.401	.317	R	R	5-10	205	4-3-81	2003	Jennings, La.
Koman, Brock	.267	72	266	30	71	25	3	3	39	16	32	3	0	.417	.327	R	R	6-0	205	10-11-80	2003	Pueblo West, Colo.
Mackor, Jeff	.250	40	132	22	33	11	1	1	14	9	21	1	2	.371	.301	R	R	6-1	215	6-17-80	2002	Salem, N.H.
Maysonet, Edwin	.275	45	138	30	38	7	1	1	13	29	28	9	1	.362	.411	R	R	6-1	180	10-17-81	2003	Vega Baja, P.R.
McGarvey, Randy	.238	36	84	8	20	2	1	1	7	19	14	1	2	.321	.390	L	R	6-3	195	2-6-79	2002	Hilton Head, S.C.
O'Brien, Patrick	.203	26	74	6	15	1	0	0	7	6	19	0	0	.216	.256	R	R	6-1	200	1-17-81	2003	Cincinnati, Ohio
Pedrique, Franmig	.227	17	44	6	10	1	0	1	9	1	13	1	0	.318	.292	R	R	5-10	195	11-27-78	2003	Tucson, Ariz.
Prosser, Chad	.243	45	144	22	35	10	1	0	16	13	28	7	1	.326	.315	R	R	5-6	155	5-11-81	2003	Austell, Ga.
Reuss, Jason	.098	12	41	3	4	1	1	0	3	5	19	0	0	.171	.191	R	R	6-6	210	11-2-79	2002	Anaheim, Calif.
Robinson, Chris	.306	58	209	36	64	8	2	3	29	9	28	4	2	.407	.332	L	R	6-2	165	1-12-81	2003	Bastrop, La.
Robinson, Scott	.253	73	277	36	70	23	0	4	36	17	32	4	4	.379	.297	L	S	6-1	185	10-14-83	2003	San Diego, Calif.
Salmela, Andy	.202	41	124	16	25	4	1	3	18	12	34	2	0	.323	.284	R	R	6-3	210	2-14-80	2002	Cottage Grove, Minn.
Seuss, Adam	.278	73	255	34	71	17	1	6	40	32	50	3	1	.424	.365	L	R	6-0	185	8-31-80	2002	La Quinta, Calif.
Skaug, Brian	.278	14	36	5	10	2	1	0	4	1	10	0	2	.389	.297	R	R	6-1	190	4-13-81	2003	Moses Lake, Wash.
Walls, Michael	.192	34	99	13	19	3	2	0	6	11	18	0	1	.263	.270	R	R	6-1	190	8-9-81	2003	Hockessin, Del.

GAMES BY POSITION: C—Mackor 39, McGarvey 21, O'Brien 26.**1B**—S. Robinson 55, Salmela 22. **2B**—Maysonet 32, Pedrique 7, Prosser 42. **3B**—Koman 69, Pedrique 7, Skaug 3, Walls 3. **SS**—Maysonet 13, Pedrique 2, C. Robinson 58, Skaug 8. **OF**—Anderson 74, Fair 55, Hearod 22, Reuss 10, Seuss 71, Walls 22.

PITCHING	W	L	ERA	G	GS	CG	SV	IP	H	R	ER	BB	SO	AVG	B	T	HT	WT	DOB	1st Yr	Resides
Albers, Matt	5	4	2.92	15	14	0	0	86	69	37	28	25	94	.214	L	R	6-0	205	1-20-83	2002	Sugar Land, Texas
Astacio, Andres	0	1	5.68	3	1	0	0	6	7	4	4	4	6	.291	R	R	6-2	160	8-5-80	1999	La Romana, D.R.

PITCHING	W	L	ERA	G	GS	CG	SV	IP	H	R	ER	BB	SO	AVG	B	T	HT	WT	DOB	1st Yr	Resides
Beltre, Jonathan	2	1	3.43	21	0	0	3	45	32	18	17	20	51	.201	L	L	6-0	160	7-7-80	2000	Azua, D.R.
Collar, Mike	2	3	4.11	14	3	0	5	35	29	18	16	9	26	.216	R	R	6-3	210	10-16-81	2003	Scarborough, Me.
Davis, Brendon	1	1	2.19	12	0	0	1	25	25	12	6	10	23	.252	R	R	6-5	196	4-18-80	2003	Cedar Park, Texas
DeLeon, Joey	5	3	2.47	17	14	0	0	87	67	30	24	26	68	.214	R	R	5-11	190	10-21-82	2001	Nixon, Texas
Edmiston, Bo	3	2	4.61	18	0	0	1	27	29	17	14	21	21	.290	R	R	6-5	220	8-1-81	2003	Greenville, Miss.
Escobar, Rodrigo	4	1	2.97	15	1	0	1	36	35	13	12	8	38	.251	R	R	5-11	165	2-11-83	1999	Cartagena, Colombia
Fischer, Sam	2	3	3.94	22	0	0	2	30	19	15	13	28	43	.184	R	R	6-0	170	9-20-80	2002	Orland Park, Ill.
Grigsby, Derick	5	5	4.86	15	15	0	0	76	73	44	41	32	62	.251	R	R	6-0	190	6-30-82	2002	Marshall, Texas
Hirsh, Jason	3	1	1.95	10	8	0	0	32	22	10	7	7	33	.189	R	R	6-8	250	2-20-82	2003	Las Vegas, Nev.
Mansfield, Monte	1	1	2.79	10	0	0	4	10	6	3	3	9	11	.181	R	R	6-4	215	3-22-81	2000	Hesperia, Calif.
Merchant, Jamie	5	1	3.44	16	8	0	1	55	36	22	21	25	56	.184	R	R	6-4	260	3-19-81	2003	Colchester, Vt.
Muecke, Josh	3	3	4.14	14	11	0	0	54	58	28	25	25	43	.284	L	L	6-3	195	1-9-82	2003	San Diego, Calif.
Ramsey, Rob	3	2	1.38	20	0	0	3	39	21	6	6	27	47	.161	R	R	6-2	185	9-26-81	2003	Austin, Texas
Shortell, Rory	0	0	9.00	1	0	0	0	1	2	1	1	0	0	.500	R	R	6-3	205	6-3-81	2002	Portland, Ore.
Stiehl, Rob	0	0	16.88	4	1	0	0	3	7	5	5	1	1	.500	R	R	6-3	205	12-9-80	2000	Torrance, Calif.
Yurek, Ryan	0	0	5.14	12	0	0	0	14	9	9	8	13	8	.191	R	R	6-3	200	4-3-81	2003	Great Falls, Mont.

MARTINSVILLE ASTROS — Rookie

APPALACHIAN LEAGUE

BATTING	AVG	G	AB	R	H	2B	3B	HR	RBI	BB	SO	SB	CS	SLG	OBP	B	T	HT	WT	DOB	1st Yr	Resides
Acosta, Jose	.260	27	100	15	26	11	1	2	20	5	21	0	0	.450	.299	R	R	6-2	170	4-18-83	2001	Bonao, D.R.
Alcantara, Ervin	.344	54	195	25	67	18	0	2	33	19	39	1	4	.467	.407	R	R	6-2	175	10-3-80	2001	San Pedro de Macoris, D.R.
Babilonia, Edgar	.253	40	146	19	37	6	1	1	13	3	28	5	2	.329	.268	R	R	5-10	160	8-5-83	1999	Cartagena, Colombia
Batista, Ariel	.258	10	31	4	8	0	0	1	4	1	8	0	0	.355	.281	R	R	6-0	170	8-28-80	1999	Chitre, Panama
Caraballo, Francisco	.286	52	206	28	59	18	3	4	31	14	55	1	2	.461	.327	R	R	6-1	185	10-21-83	2001	Anaco, Venez.
Corapci, Jason	.220	11	41	3	9	1	0	0	2	2	4	0	0	.244	.273	R	R	5-8	170	10-11-81	2003	Orange, Calif.
Davidson, Kevin	.331	39	130	23	43	11	1	4	29	30	25	6	2	.523	.454	R	R	5-9	185	7-21-80	2002	Port Richey, Fla.
Garcia, Antonio	.295	28	95	12	28	5	0	3	22	13	21	2	1	.442	.380	S	R	6-5	235	8-21-82	1999	Panama City, Panama
Garcia, Winfield	.271	49	210	37	57	9	1	0	16	11	19	6	1	.324	.319	R	R	6-1	160	1-17-82	2000	Palmarejo, Venez.
Garza, Mario	.295	24	78	19	23	6	0	5	16	15	18	2	0	.564	.412	L	R	6-0	202	5-26-81	2003	Melbourne, Fla.
Hudgson, Maximiliano	.233	35	116	10	27	8	0	1	15	8	34	2	1	.328	.281	S	R	5-11	160	8-7-80	2000	Cali, Colombia
Koenig, Lance	.275	44	131	21	36	11	1	0	13	18	30	4	2	.374	.375	R	R	6-3	190	12-10-80	2003	Brielle, N.J.
Mendez, Valentin	.395	11	38	7	15	2	0	1	6	1	7	1	0	.526	.439	R	R	6-0	170	2-14-81	1999	San Pedro de Macoris, D.R.
Saccomanno, Mark	.324	34	136	25	44	5	1	3	21	9	18	1	1	.441	.367	R	R	6-4	200	4-30-80	2003	Spring, Texas
Sarabia, Hamilton	.260	47	150	22	39	4	0	1	15	17	31	6	4	.307	.339	L	R	5-11	185	6-11-82	1999	Cartagena, Colombia
Torres, Saul	.318	57	214	40	68	19	3	0	25	27	33	3	1	.435	.406	R	R	6-3	200	2-18-82	1999	Curarigua, Venez.
Vital, Kevin	.232	46	155	25	36	12	0	2	22	32	49	3	0	.348	.366	L	R	6-0	245	2-9-80	2003	Loreauville, La.

GAMES BY POSITION: C—Acosta 27, Davidson 39, Garza 1. **1B**—A. Garcia 26, Vital 41. **2B**—Babilonia 21, Corapci 3, Koenig 43, Mendez 2. **3B**—Babilonia 3, Corapci 6, Torres 56. **SS**—Babilonia 15, Corapci 2, W. Garcia 49. **OF**—Alcantara 54, Batista 9, Caraballo 52, Garza 4, Hudgson 35, Sarabia 45.

PITCHING	W	L	ERA	G	GS	CG	SV	IP	H	R	ER	BB	SO	AVG	B	T	HT	WT	DOB	1st Yr	Resides
Arguello, Douglas	4	0	5.26	17	0	0	2	26	25	16	15	10	17	.252	L	L	6-1	175	11-21-84	2002	Managua, Nicaragua
Barthmaier, James	1	1	2.49	8	3	0	0	22	19	9	6	7	18	.226	R	R	6-4	210	1-6-84	2003	Roswell, Ga.
Davis, Cliff	1	0	7.50	12	1	0	0	18	13	15	15	17	13	.213	R	R	6-5	205	12-31-84	2003	Europa, Miss.
Diaz, Raymar	4	0	0.90	19	0	0	5	30	17	4	3	13	29	.161	R	R	6-7	190	11-13-83	2003	Canovanas, P.R.
Douglass, Chance	5	1	2.34	10	10	0	0	58	50	17	15	10	48	.241	R	R	6-1	200	2-24-84	2002	Amarillo, Texas
Estrada, Paul	1	0	5.48	12	1	0	1	21	19	17	13	22	25	.234	R	R	6-1	215	9-10-82	1999	Ciudad Bolivar, Venez.
Gutierrez, Juan	1	2	4.76	16	3	0	2	34	42	22	18	13	30	.302	R	R	6-3	200	7-14-83	2001	Puerto la Cruz, Venez.
Marte, Violenny	0	2	5.06	12	0	0	2	16	18	9	9	6	19	.268	R	R	6-2	165	2-27-81	2001	Azua, D.R.
Martinez, Ronnie	6	4	2.39	12	12	0	0	64	61	29	17	11	56	.244	R	R	5-11	180	7-6-83	2001	Cotui, D.R.
McKeller, Ryan	3	0	3.58	15	4	0	3	38	33	16	15	19	46	.240	R	R	6-5	210	7-8-83	2003	Pflugerville, Texas
Paulino, Felipe	2	2	5.61	16	0	0	1	26	23	20	16	19	27	.234	R	R	6-2	180	10-5-83	2001	Los Teques, Venez.
Romero, Levi	2	2	4.66	16	0	0	3	29	29	16	15	14	24	.261	R	R	6-4	170	4-12-84	2001	El Tigre, Venez.
Salazar, Julio	5	2	1.83	10	9	0	0	44	42	18	9	18	34	.248	L	L	6-0	180	6-24-83	2000	Rubio, Venez.
Soler, Jose	0	0	4.12	14	0	0	2	20	17	10	9	15	21	.232	R	R	6-3	185	8-25-82	1999	La Romana, D.R.
Talbot, Mitch	4	4	2.83	12	12	0	0	54	45	26	17	11	46	.223	R	R	6-2	175	10-17-83	2002	Cedar City, Utah
Vergara, Alan	3	3	4.21	15	10	0	4	58	59	30	27	10	54	.264	R	R	5-11	170	6-24-84	2001	Panama City, Panama

KANSAS CITY ROYALS

BY ALAN ESKEW

After losing a franchise-record 100 games in 2002, the Royals moved their spring training site from Florida for the first time in 2003 to a new complex in Surprise, Ariz.

The Royals ended up having a surprisingly good season as manager Tony Pena's "believe" slogan in spring training carried over throughout the season.

The Royals had been notorious slow starters, not having a winning April since 1989, but they began the season 9-0 and won 16 of their first 19 games.

The club finished 83-79 for their first winning season since 1994. The 83 victories tied for the sixth most wins for a club coming off a 100-loss season, and it marked a 21-win improvement over 2002. With the turnaround, the Royals had a significant increase of more than 400,000 in attendance from 1.3 million in 2002 to 1.7 million in 2003.

The Royals remained in first place for most of the summer and had a seven-game lead in the American League Central at the all-star break before fading to third. The Royals were not officially eliminated until five games remained in the season. Keeping that team together, however, may be difficult, as 14 Royals were eligible for free agency after the season.

The Royals had to overcome a glut of injuries, as they used the disabled list 17 times with players missing 619 games, 54 by four-time all-star selection Mike Sweeney, who suffered a herniated disc that kept him out the entire month of July.

After going 4-0, 1.10 in his first five starts, Opening Day starter Runelvys Hernandez finished 7-5, 4.61 in 16 starts before elbow problems ended his season prematurely. He had Tommy John surgery and will likely miss the entire 2004 season.

Injuries also sidelined other significant contributors including Jose Lima, Carlos Beltran, Miguel Asencio, Michael Tucker, Joe Randa, Kyle Snyder and Kevin Appier.

Lefthander Darrell May, who did not pick up his first win until June 27, led the team with 10 wins and was the only starter who remained in the rotation the entire season.

Lima was signed June 15 out of the independent Atlantic League and turned out to be a breath of fresh air to the beleaguered rotation. Lima won seven straight starts and had a 2.17 ERA before hurting his groin. He tried to come back too soon and wound up 1-3, 4.91 in his final six starts.

Beltran again demonstrated he is a five-tool player and one of the best in the game. Beltran hit .307-26-100 with 102 runs and 41 stolen bases in 45 attempts. He became only the sixth player since 1900 to log three seasons with 100 RBIs, 100 runs and 30 stolen bases. Only Beltran, Barry Bonds and George Sisler accomplished that in three consecutive seasons.

Shortstop Angel Berroa had one of the best rookie campaigns in the American League, hitting .287-17-73 with 52 extra-base hits and 21 stolen bases, while playing solid defense.

Righthander Zack Greinke, a 2002 first-round round pick, was the top pitching prospect in the minors, finishing second to Twins catcher Joe Mauer for player of the year honors. Greinke, 19, went a combined 15-4, 1.93 for Double-A Wichita and High Class A Wilmington.

Outfielder Chris Lubanski and catcher Mitch Maier, the Royals' two first-round picks in 2003, had outstanding seasons in the Rookie-level Arizona League. Lubanski, who has plus speed, hit .326-4-27 and was selected the top prospect in the league, while Maier, who hit .350-2-45, was ranked No. 4 on the league's prospect list.

Carlos Beltran

Zack Greinke

STEVE MOORE

PLAYERS of the YEAR

MAJOR LEAGUE: Carlos Beltran, of

A true five-tool player, Beltran ranked third in the American League in triples and stolen bases (a career-high 41) in 2003, while hitting .308-26-100 to lead the Royals in the triple crown categories.

MINOR LEAGUE: Zack Greinke, rhp

Greinke enjoyed an amazing year in his first full pro season. He went 15-4, 1.93 between Class A Wilmington and Double-A Wichita, ranking third among minor leaguers in ERA and finishing two victories shy of the lead in wins.

ORGANIZATION LEADERS

BATTING

*AVG	Donald Murphy, Burlington	.313
R	Mel Stocker, Wilmington/Burlington	91
H	Donald Murphy, Burlington	158
TB	Byron Gettis, Wichita	241
2B	Jarrod Patterson, Omaha	33
3B	Brandon Powell, Royals I	15
HR	Jarrod Patterson, Omaha	18
RBI	Byron Gettis, Wichita	103
BB	Chris Fallon, Wilmington	84
SO	Chad Santos, Wichita	116
SB	Mel Stocker, Wilmington/Burlington	41
*SLG	Mike Kelly, Omaha	.495
*OBP	David DeJesus, Omaha/Wichita	.414

PITCHING

W	Zack Greinke, Wichita/Wilmington	15
L	Danny Tamayo, Wichita	14
#ERA	Zack Greinke, Wichita/Wilmington	1.93
G	Jorge Vasquez, Wichita/Wilmington	53
CG	Jamey Wright, Omaha	3
	Zack Greinke, Wichita/Wilmington	3
SV	Jorge Vasquez, Wichita/Wilmington	29
IP	Kyle Middleton, Wilmington	160
BB	Colt Griffin, Wilmington/Burlington	97
SO	Jonah Bayliss, Burlington	133

*Minimum 250 At-Bats #Minimum 75 Innings

KANSAS CITY ROYALS

Manager: Tony Pena. **2003 Record:** 83-79, .512 (3rd, AL Central).

BATTING	AVG	G	AB	R	H	2B	3B	HR	RBI	BB	SO	SB	CS	SLG	OBP	B	T	HT	WT	DOB	1st Yr	Resides
Abernathy, Brent	.074	10	27	2	2	0	0	0	0	1	3	0	0	.074	.107	R	R	6-0	190	9-23-77	1996	Marietta, Ga.
2-team (2 Tampa Bay)	.059	12	34	3	2	0	0	0	0	1	3	1	0	.059	.086							
Beltran, Carlos	.307	141	521	102	160	14	10	26	100	72	81	41	4	.522	.389	S	R	6-1	190	4-24-77	1995	Manati, P.R.
Berger, Brandon	.219	13	32	3	7	0	0	0	3	5	4	0	0	.219	.324	R	R	5-11	200	2-21-75	1996	Fort Mitchell, Ky.
Berroa, Angel	.287	158	567	92	163	28	7	17	73	29	100	21	5	.451	.338	R	R	6-0	170	1-27-78	1997	Santo Domingo, D.R.
Brown, Dee	.227	50	132	16	30	7	0	2	14	8	37	1	1	.326	.280	L	R	6-0	220	3-27-78	1996	Orlando, Fla.
Burkhart, Morgan	.200	6	15	1	3	0	0	0	1	1	2	0	0	.200	.250	S	L	5-11	220	1-29-72	1995	St. Louis, Mo.
Dawkins, Gookie	.000	3	2	0	0	0	0	0	0	1	2	0	0	.000	.333	R	R	6-1	180	5-12-79	1997	Chappells, S.C.
DeJesus, David	.286	12	7	0	2	0	1	0	0	1	2	0	0	.571	.444	L	L	6-0	170	12-20-79	2000	Manalapan, N.J.
DiFelice, Mike	.254	62	189	29	48	16	1	3	25	9	30	1	0	.397	.299	R	R	6-2	200	5-28-69	1991	Safety Harbor, Fla.
Febles, Carlos	.235	74	196	31	46	5	0	0	11	13	30	8	2	.260	.299	R	R	5-11	180	5-24-76	1994	La Romana, D.R.
Guiel, Aaron	.277	99	354	63	98	30	0	15	52	27	63	3	5	.489	.346	L	R	5-10	200	10-5-72	1993	Langley, B.C.
Harvey, Ken	.266	135	485	50	129	30	0	13	64	29	94	2	3	.408	.313	R	R	6-2	240	3-1-78	1999	Cerritos, Calif.
Ibanez, Raul	.294	157	608	95	179	33	5	18	90	49	81	8	4	.454	.345	L	R	6-2	200	6-2-72	1992	Miami, Fla.
Johnson, Rontrez	.333	8	3	3	1	0	0	0	0	0	2	0	0	.333	.333	R	R	5-10	160	12-8-76	1995	Marshall, Texas
Lopez, Mendy	.277	52	94	13	26	5	1	3	11	4	28	2	0	.447	.306	R	R	6-2	200	10-15-73	1992	Santo Domingo, D.R.
Matos, Julius	.263	28	57	7	15	1	0	2	7	1	12	1	0	.386	.276	R	R	5-11	170	12-12-74	1994	Racine, Wisc.
Mayne, Brent	.245	113	372	39	91	17	1	6	36	32	59	0	2	.344	.307	L	R	6-1	190	4-19-68	1989	Corona Del Mar, Calif.
Patterson, Jarrod	.182	13	22	3	4	0	0	0	0	3	6	0	0	.182	.280	L	R	6-1	190	9-7-73	1993	Clanton, Ala.
Prince, Tom	.250	8	8	0	2	0	0	0	1	0	0	0	0	.250	.250	R	R	5-11	200	8-13-64	1984	Bradenton, Fla.
2-team (24 Minnesota)	.208	32	48	5	10	2	0	2	6	5	7	1	0	.375	.309							
Randa, Joe	.291	131	502	80	146	31	1	16	72	41	61	1	0	.452	.348	R	R	5-11	190	12-18-69	1991	Overland Park, Kan.
Relaford, Desi	.254	141	500	70	127	27	5	8	59	40	70	20	4	.376	.315	S	R	5-9	170	9-16-73	1991	Jacksonville, Fla.
Sweeney, Mike	.293	108	392	62	115	18	1	16	83	64	56	3	2	.467	.391	R	R	6-3	220	7-22-73	1991	Overland Park, Kan.
Tucker, Michael	.262	104	389	61	102	20	5	13	55	39	88	8	10	.440	.331	L	R	6-2	190	6-25-71	1992	Lehigh Acres, Fla.
White, Rondell	.347	22	75	13	26	6	1	4	21	6	8	0	0	.613	.400	R	R	6-1	220	2-23-72	1990	Gray, Ga.

PITCHING	W	L	ERA	G	GS	CG	SV	IP	H	R	ER	BB	SO	AVG	B	T	HT	WT	DOB	1st Yr	Resides
Abbott, Paul	1	2	5.29	10	8	0	0	48	47	29	28	26	32	.256	R	R	6-3	200	9-15-67	1985	Fullerton, Calif.
Affeldt, Jeremy	7	6	3.93	36	18	0	4	126	126	58	55	38	98	.260	L	L	6-4	210	6-6-79	1997	Medical Lake, Wash.
Anderson, Brian	5	1	3.99	7	7	2	0	50	50	22	22	11	15	.271	R	L	6-1	180	4-26-72	1993	Bratenahl, Ohio
2-team (25 Cleveland)	14	11	3.78	32	31	2	0	198	212	110	83	43	87	.279							
Appier, Kevin	1	2	4.26	4	4	0	0	19	15	9	9	7	5	.217	R	R	6-2	210	12-6-67	1987	Paola, Kan.
2-team (19 Anaheim)	8	9	5.40	23	23	0	0	112	120	69	67	43	55	.269							
Asencio, Miguel	2	1	5.21	8	8	1	0	48	54	29	28	21	27	.295	R	R	6-2	190	9-29-80	1998	La Victoria, D.R.
Bukvich, Ryan	1	0	9.58	9	0	0	0	10	12	11	11	9	8	.292	R	R	6-2	250	5-13-78	2000	Brandon, Miss.
Carrasco, Dan	6	5	4.82	50	2	0	2	80	82	44	43	40	57	.270	R	R	6-1	210	4-12-77	1997	Safford, Ariz.
DeHart, Rick	0	2	13.50	4	0	0	0	4	8	6	6	2	1	.421	L	L	6-1	180	3-21-70	1992	Topeka, Kan.
Field, Nathan	1	1	4.15	19	0	0	0	22	19	10	10	14	19	.234	R	R	6-2	200	12-11-75	1998	Littleton, Colo.
George, Chris	9	6	7.11	18	18	0	0	94	120	75	74	44	39	.309	L	L	6-2	200	9-16-79	1998	Spring, Texas
Gilfillan, Jason	2	0	7.71	13	0	0	0	16	22	14	14	10	12	.309	R	R	6-5	220	8-31-76	1997	Blacksburg, S.C.
Gobble, Jimmy	4	5	4.61	9	9	0	0	53	56	32	27	15	31	.270	L	L	6-3	190	7-19-81	1999	Bristol, Va.
Grimsley, Jason	2	6	5.16	76	0	0	0	75	88	47	43	36	58	.299	R	R	6-3	200	8-7-67	1985	Lafayette, La.
Hernandez, Runelvys	7	5	4.61	16	16	0	0	92	87	51	47	37	48	.249	R	R	6-1	200	4-27-78	1998	Santo Domingo, D.R.
Hill, Jeremy	0	0	0.00	1	0	0	0	1	1	0	0	0	0	.250	R	R	5-11	200	8-8-77	1996	Dallas, Texas
Leskanic, Curt	1	0	1.73	27	0	0	2	26	16	7	5	11	22	.179	R	R	6-0	185	4-2-68	1990	Longwood, Fla.
Levine, Alan	0	1	2.53	18	0	0	1	21	22	6	6	11	5	.268	L	R	6-3	190	5-22-68	1991	Gilbert, Ariz.
2-team (36 Tampa Bay)	3	6	2.79	54	0	0	1	71	67	29	22	29	30	.250							
Lima, Jose	8	3	4.91	14	14	0	0	73	80	40	40	26	32	.279	R	R	6-2	200	9-30-72	1989	Houston, Texas
Lloyd, Graeme	0	2	10.95	16	0	0	0	12	29	18	15	7	8	.453	L	L	6-7	220	4-9-67	1988	Palm Harbor, Fla.
Lopez, Albie	4	2	12.71	15	0	0	0	23	41	32	32	17	15	.383	R	R	6-2	240	8-18-71	1991	Gilbert, Ariz.
Lowe, Sean	1	1	6.25	28	0	0	0	45	55	32	31	21	28	.300	R	R	6-2	220	3-29-71	1992	Royse City, Texas
MacDougal, Mike	3	5	4.08	68	0	0	27	64	64	36	29	32	57	.266	S	R	6-4	190	3-5-77	1999	Marco Island, Fla.
May, Darrell	10	8	3.77	35	32	2	0	210	197	98	88	53	115	.245	L	L	6-2	180	6-13-72	1992	Rogue River, Ore.
Mullen, Scott	0	0	16.62	2	0	0	0	4	11	8	8	5	3	.458	R	L	6-2	190	1-17-75	1996	Beaufort, S.C.
Snyder, Kyle	1	6	5.17	15	15	0	0	85	94	52	49	21	39	.283	S	R	6-8	220	9-9-77	1999	Sarasota, Fla.
Voyles, Brad	0	2	7.18	11	3	0	0	31	47	29	25	18	24	.348	R	R	6-1	190	12-30-76	1998	Green Bay, Wisc.
Walrond, Les	0	2	10.13	7	0	0	0	8	11	9	9	7	6	.323	L	L	6-0	190	11-7-76	1998	Brentwood, Tenn.
Wilson, Kris	6	3	5.33	29	4	0	0	73	92	49	43	16	42	.304	R	R	6-4	220	8-6-76	1997	Palm Harbor, Fla.
Wright, Jamey	1	2	4.26	4	4	2	0	25	23	14	12	11	19	.244	R	R	6-5	230	12-24-74	1993	Phoenix, Ariz.

FIELDING

Catcher	PCT	G	PO	A	E	DP	PB
DiFelice	.994	58	304	35	2	1	2
Mayne	.994	112	593	43	4	5	5
Prince	a1.000	7	8	1	0	0	1
Sweeney	.000	1	0	0	0	0	0

First Base	PCT	G	PO	A	E	DP
Burkhart	1.000	2	10	0	0	2
Harvey	.988	99	805	80	11	78
Ibanez	.995	22	164	19	1	15
Lopez	1.000	17	59	9	0	3
Patterson	1.000	2	8	1	0	0
Sweeney	.990	45	379	35	4	30

Second Base	PCT	G	PO	A	E	DP
Abernathy	1.000	9	12	20	0	4
Dawkins	1.000	3	3	4	0	0
Febles	.989	67	98	162	3	34
Lopez	1.000	11	22	15	0	5
Matos	.971	11	10	24	1	4
Relaford	.981	89	183	223	8	50

Third Base	PCT	G	PO	A	E	DP
Lopez	1.000	13	3	15	0	0
Matos	1.000	13	3	9	0	0
Patterson	.000	4	0	0	1	0
Randa	.980	129	102	238	7	12
Relaford	.922	33	11	60	6	5

Shortstop	PCT	G	PO	A	E	DP
Berroa	.968	158	264	473	24	108
Febles	.000	1	0	0	0	0
Lopez	.900	4	2	7	1	1
Matos	1.000	2	0	1	0	0
Relaford	1.000	6	6	11	0	2

Outfield	PCT	G	PO	A	E	DP
Beltran	.987	130	371	10	5	3
Berger	1.000	11	16	1	0	0
Brown	.985	33	62	2	1	1
DeJesus	1.000	9	2	0	0	0
Guiel	.985	89	190	9	3	2
Ibanez	.988	131	243	9	3	2
Johnson	.000	6	0	0	1	0
Lopez	1.000	3	5	0	0	0
Matos	.000	1	0	0	0	0
Relaford	.953	20	37	4	2	2
Tucker	.989	85	173	7	2	0
White	.978	17	45	0	1	0

FARM SYSTEM

Assistant GM, Player Personnel: Muzzy Jackson.

Class	Farm Team	League	W	L	Pct.	Finish*	Manager	First Yr.
AAA	Omaha (Neb.) Royals	Pacific Coast	70	73	.490	11th (16)	Mike Jirschele	1969
AA	Wichita (Kan.) Wranglers	Texas	71	69	.507	4th (8)	Keith Bodie	1995
High A	Wilmington (Del.) Blue Rocks	Carolina	80	60	.571	1st (8)	Billy Gardner	1993
Low A	Burlington (Iowa) Bees	Midwest	64	74	.464	14th (16)	Joe Szekely	2001
Rookie	Surprise (Ariz.) Royals I	Arizona	31	18	.633	+2nd (9)	Lloyd Simmons	2003
Rookie	Surprise (Ariz.) Royals II	Arizona	32	22	.593	4th (9)	Kevin Boles	2003

*Finish in overall standings (No. of teams in league) +League champion

OMAHA ROYALS — Class AAA

PACIFIC COAST LEAGUE

BATTING	AVG	G	AB	R	H	2B	3B	HR	RBI	BB	SO	SB	CS	SLG	OBP	B	T	HT	WT	DOB	1st Yr	Resides
Abernathy, Brent	.291	92	368	60	107	22	0	7	40	34	38	13	7	.408	.354	R	R	6-0	190	9-23-77	1996	Marietta, Ga.
Agbayani, Benny	.237	88	299	49	71	8	0	16	45	53	61	0	2	.425	.359	R	R	6-0	220	12-28-71	1993	Aiea, Hawaii
Berger, Brandon	.270	62	226	43	61	16	3	12	53	31	58	6	1	.527	.367	R	R	5-11	200	2-21-75	1996	Fort Mitchell, Ky.
Brito, Juan	.238	36	122	14	29	2	0	2	12	3	25	0	2	.303	.262	R	R	5-11	200	11-7-79	1996	Santiago Rodriguez, D.R.
Brown, Dee	.277	12	47	6	13	2	0	2	9	4	9	1	0	.447	.340	L	R	6-0	220	3-27-78	1996	Orlando, Fla.
Burkhart, Morgan	.251	104	382	54	96	18	0	17	57	50	67	2	0	.432	.361	S	L	5-11	220	1-29-72	1995	St. Louis, Mo.
Dawkins, Gookie	.259	33	112	18	29	6	0	2	18	7	24	2	3	.366	.303	R	R	6-1	180	5-12-79	1997	Chappells, S.C.
2-team (32 Las Vegas)	.211	65	227	23	48	11	1	2	30	16	50	5	4	.295	.263							
DeJesus, David	.298	59	215	49	64	16	3	5	23	34	30	8	4	.470	.412	L	L	6-0	170	12-20-79	2000	Manalapan, N.J.
Febles, Carlos	.313	9	32	7	10	4	0	0	6	3	6	0	0	.438	.389	R	R	5-11	180	5-24-76	1994	La Romana, D.R.
Gomez, Alexis	.269	121	457	49	123	23	8	8	58	26	92	4	5	.407	.307	L	L	6-2	180	8-6-80	1997	Loma de Cabrera, D.R.
Guiel, Aaron	.279	52	190	38	53	9	2	8	30	33	43	3	0	.474	.408	L	R	5-10	200	10-5-72	1993	Langley, B.C.
Hansen, Jed	.252	93	337	50	85	25	2	10	44	47	81	8	7	.427	.350	R	R	6-1	190	8-19-72	1994	Olympia, Wash.
2-team (10 Memphis)	.248	103	359	54	89	25	2	11	45	57	88	9	8	.421	.357							
Harris, Brian	.259	72	243	37	63	11	4	3	19	32	38	2	2	.374	.352	S	R	5-10	170	4-28-75	1997	Carmel, Ind.
Kelly, Mike	.296	100	368	63	109	29	1	14	65	50	80	6	1	.495	.382	R	R	6-4	190	6-2-70	1991	Los Alamitos, Calif.
Lunar, Fernando	.211	75	251	28	53	9	0	6	24	11	34	0	0	.319	.256	R	R	6-1	230	5-25-77	1994	Alamogordo, NM
Martinez, Sandy	.247	24	73	12	18	1	0	3	13	5	15	0	1	.384	.313	L	R	6-2	210	10-8-70	1990	Santo Domingo, D.R.
Matos, Julius	.289	92	370	44	107	19	0	7	48	13	31	10	5	.397	.325	R	R	5-11	170	12-12-74	1994	Racine, Wisc.
Ordaz, Luis	.242	49	178	15	43	13	0	0	21	11	19	3	0	.315	.284	R	R	5-11	170	8-12-75	1993	Maracaibo, Venez.
Patterson, Jarrod	.257	123	478	74	123	33	2	18	91	51	92	4	1	.448	.329	L	R	6-1	190	9-7-73	1993	Clanton, Ala.
Prince, Tom	.308	29	91	16	28	10	0	1	6	14	15	0	1	.451	.418	R	R	5-11	200	8-13-64	1984	Bradenton, Fla.
Sasser, Rob	.279	17	61	6	17	3	1	1	5	1	13	4	1	.410	.290	R	R	6-3	200	3-9-75	1993	Oakland, Calif.
Sweeney, Mike	.250	2	8	3	2	1	0	1	1	1	1	0	0	.750	.333	R	R	6-3	220	7-22-73	1991	Overland Park, Kan.
Ullery, Dave	.400	2	5	1	2	1	0	0	1	0	1	0	0	.600	.400	L	R	6-3	220	12-16-74	1997	Brazil, Ind.

PITCHING	W	L	ERA	G	GS	CG	SV	IP	H	R	ER	BB	SO	AVG	B	T	HT	WT	DOB	1st Yr	Resides
Baerlocher, Ryan	4	7	4.65	19	19	1	0	120	115	68	62	42	73	.257	R	R	6-5	220	8-6-77	1999	Lewiston, Idaho
Baldwin, James	3	2	4.08	8	8	0	0	46	48	25	21	13	24	.265	R	R	6-3	230	7-15-71	1990	Southern Pines, N.C.
Bukvich, Ryan	1	2	4.91	34	0	0	5	37	39	21	20	25	44	.272	R	R	6-2	250	5-13-78	2000	Brandon, Miss.
Carlyle, Buddy	0	1	5.40	2	0	0	0	5	5	3	3	1	4	.263	L	R	6-3	170	12-21-77	1996	Bellevue, Neb.
DeHart, Rick	1	3	4.82	25	0	0	1	28	38	15	15	7	17	.333	L	L	6-1	180	3-21-70	1992	Topeka, Kan.
Ferguson, Ian	0	2	6.39	3	3	0	0	13	14	9	9	13	5	.280	R	R	6-4	220	8-23-79	2000	Bellingham, Wash.
Field, Nate	2	2	3.18	19	0	0	4	23	15	8	8	4	17	.187	R	R	6-2	200	12-11-75	1998	Littleton, Colo.
Flury, Pat	0	0	4.50	7	0	0	0	10	11	5	5	3	7	.268	R	R	6-2	210	3-14-73	1993	Sparks, Nev.
2-team (7 Portland)	0	0	5.19	14	0	0	0	17	19	12	10	15	16	.275							
Fyhrie, Mike	7	4	4.21	15	14	0	0	98	103	52	46	38	64	.277	R	R	6-2	200	12-9-69	1991	Coto De Caza, Calif.
George, Chris	3	5	7.29	10	10	0	0	54	71	49	44	22	28	.314	L	L	6-2	200	9-16-79	1998	Spring, Texas
Gilfillan, Jason	6	0	2.05	35	0	0	7	53	46	14	12	12	33	.239	R	R	6-5	220	8-31-76	1997	Blacksburg, S.C.
Hernandez, Runelvys	1	0	1.80	1	1	0	0	5	3	1	1	2	5	.176	R	R	6-1	200	4-27-78	1998	Santo Domingo, D.R.
Hill, Jeremy	1	3	7.81	26	1	0	1	40	42	38	35	42	41	.274	R	R	5-11	200	8-8-77	1996	Dallas, Texas
Jones, Bobby M.	1	2	3.65	20	1	0	1	37	28	15	15	20	27	.210	R	L	6-0	170	4-11-72	1992	East Rutherford, N.J.
Lopez, Albie	0	0	0.00	4	0	0	0	5	3	0	0	0	2	.166	R	R	6-2	240	8-18-71	1991	Gilbert, Ariz.
Lowe, Sean	4	0	3.25	14	7	0	0	53	54	22	19	19	27	.272	R	R	6-2	220	3-29-71	1992	Royse City, Texas
Mullen, Scott	5	3	3.88	20	9	0	1	70	75	35	30	22	50	.281	R	L	6-2	190	1-17-75	1996	Beaufort, S.C.
Obermueller, Wes	10	5	4.40	17	17	2	0	106	108	61	52	42	62	.262	R	R	6-2	190	12-22-76	1999	North Liberty, Iowa
Osting, Jimmy	1	4	5.66	9	9	1	0	49	48	31	31	23	26	.253	R	L	6-5	190	4-7-77	1995	Louisville, Ky.
Sedlacek, Shawn	4	11	6.45	27	13	0	0	96	137	75	69	25	52	.340	R	R	6-4	200	6-29-77	1998	Cedar Rapids, Iowa
Serrano, Jim	3	2	3.21	19	0	0	3	28	25	12	10	11	28	.245	R	R	5-10	170	5-9-76	1998	Grand Junction, Colo.
Snyder, Kyle	3	0	2.79	5	5	0	0	29	28	9	9	6	15	.259	S	R	6-8	220	9-9-77	1999	Sarasota, Fla.
Turman, Jason	2	5	3.87	31	5	0	4	74	68	34	32	35	45	.250	R	R	6-10	210	11-10-75	1996	Gordo, Ala.
Voyles, Brad	2	2	2.99	29	9	1	2	81	68	27	27	24	69	.231	R	R	6-1	190	12-30-76	1998	Green Bay, Wisc.
Walrond, Les	3	1	2.45	18	0	0	2	26	19	9	7	9	20	.195	L	L	6-0	190	11-7-76	1998	Brentwood, Tenn.
2-team (10 Memphis)	3	1	1.88	28	1	0	2	43	31	11	9	16	34	.194							
Wilson, Kris	0	2	8.03	5	0	0	0	12	21	12	11	3	9	.381	R	R	6-4	220	8-6-76	1997	Palm Harbor, Fla.
Wright, Jamey	3	5	3.64	13	12	1	0	77	70	35	31	38	65	.245	R	R	6-5	230	12-24-74	1993	Phoenix, Ariz.
2-team (7 Oklahoma)	5	6	3.80	20	19	3	0	116	108	53	49	59	105	.250							

FIELDING

Catcher	PCT	G	PO	A	E	DP	PB
Brito	1.000	36	238	21	0	4	5
Lunar	.984	73	423	55	8	5	1
Martinez	1.000	15	62	8	0	0	3
Prince	1.000	28	174	16	0	2	1
Ullery	1.000	2	9	1	0	0	0

First Base	PCT	G	PO	A	E	DP
Berger	.917	2	22	0	2	5
Burkhart	.997	96	817	63	3	89
Hansen	.984	18	161	19	3	22
Patterson	.988	28	240	14	3	24
Sasser	1.000	1	12	1	0	1

Second Base	PCT	G	PO	A	E	DP
Abernathy	.981	87	178	241	8	66
Febles	1.000	5	9	15	0	5
Hansen	.979	19	42	53	2	9
Harris	.970	30	72	88	5	24
Matos	1.000	2	4	7	0	0
Ordaz	1.000	8	20	21	0	8

Third Base	PCT	G	PO	A	E	DP
Abernathy	.750	4	3	6	3	1
Dawkins	.923	4	2	10	1	1
Hansen	.920	26	21	48	6	11
Harris	1.000	12	7	26	0	2
Matos	1.000	1	0	1	0	1
Ordaz	.936	21	10	34	3	1
Patterson	.928	71	36	169	16	9
Sasser	1.000	10	8	16	0	1

Shortstop	PCT	G	PO	A	E	DP
Abernathy	.000	1	0	0	1	0
Dawkins	.986	28	54	89	2	25
Febles	.933	4	6	8	1	3
Hansen	1.000	1	2	4	0	0
Harris	.958	24	44	70	5	14
Matos	.949	68	109	207	17	45
Ordaz	.982	23	35	75	2	22

Outfield	PCT	G	PO	A	E	DP
Agbayani	.984	35	59	1	1	0
Berger	.978	39	85	6	2	1
Brown	.955	9	19	2	1	0
DeJesus	1.000	56	114	2	0	1
Gomez	.970	120	278	11	9	1
Guiel	.962	52	121	6	5	0
Hansen	1.000	31	68	2	0	1
Kelly	.986	82	132	5	2	1
Matos	.946	19	33	2	2	0
Patterson	1.000	2	2	1	0	1

WICHITA WRANGLERS — Class AA

TEXAS LEAGUE

BATTING	AVG	G	AB	R	H	2B	3B	HR	RBI	BB	SO	SB	CS	SLG	OBP	B	T	HT	WT	DOB	1st Yr	Resides
Arnerich, Tony	.200	3	10	1	2	0	0	0	0	1	1	0	0	.200	.273	R	R	6-0	190	12-14-79	2001	Santa Rosa, Calif.
Beltran, Carlos	.333	3	9	3	3	2	0	0	1	2	3	1	0	.556	.455	S	R	6-1	190	4-24-77	1995	Manati, P.R.
Bledsoe, Hunter	.255	31	110	16	28	3	0	2	10	6	18	1	1	.336	.295	R	R	6-4	210	1-24-76	1999	Nashville, Tenn.
Cunningham, Marco	.276	104	319	60	88	12	2	6	35	29	50	13	9	.382	.364	R	R	5-10	180	8-3-77	2000	Lubbock, Texas
Dellaero, Jason	.000	1	4	0	0	0	0	0	0	0	0	0	0	.000	.000	R	R	6-2	190	12-17-76	1997	Brewster, N.Y.
DeJesus, David	.338	17	71	14	24	4	0	2	10	9	8	1	3	.479	.422	L	L	6-0	170	12-20-79	2000	Manalapan, N.J.
Fenster, Darren	.133	5	15	2	2	1	0	0	2	1	3	0	0	.200	.188	R	R	5-9	170	9-11-78	2000	Middletown, N.J.
Gemoll, Justin	.275	117	382	52	105	19	0	1	34	46	58	15	5	.332	.360	R	R	6-2	200	11-19-77	2000	San Jose, Calif.
Gettis, Byron	.302	140	510	80	154	31	4	16	103	55	110	15	11	.473	.377	R	R	6-0	240	3-13-80	1998	East St. Louis, Ill.
Guzman, Jacob	.000	1	1	0	0	0	0	0	0	0	0	0	0	.000	.000	R	R	6-0	210	8-2-82	2001	Santee, Calif.
Harris, Brian	.255	37	145	16	37	6	2	2	16	15	28	5	4	.366	.329	S	R	5-10	170	4-28-75	1997	Carmel, Ind.
Hart, Corey	.275	93	334	40	92	9	0	4	47	49	69	12	4	.338	.369	S	R	6-0	190	9-5-75	1998	Oklahoma City, Okla.
Hopper, Norris	.300	115	424	56	127	14	2	0	40	27	58	24	10	.342	.346	R	R	5-9	200	3-24-79	1998	Passaic, N.J.
Lora, Tom	.233	16	43	6	10	2	0	0	2	5	7	2	1	.279	.313	S	R	5-10	180	10-14-77	1997	Monte Cristi, D.R.
Machado, Alejandro	.287	78	289	59	83	13	5	1	31	34	45	19	9	.377	.368	S	R	6-0	160	4-26-82	1998	Caracas, Venez.
Meadows, Tydus	.290	114	421	60	122	27	4	17	79	41	75	14	8	.494	.368	R	R	6-2	210	9-5-77	1998	Evans, Ga.
Medrano, Steve	.321	10	28	4	9	1	0	0	3	1	6	1	0	.357	.367	S	R	5-11	150	10-8-77	1996	West Covina, Calif.
Ortiz, Nick	.230	35	126	15	29	4	0	1	7	9	32	1	2	.286	.287	R	R	6-0	180	7-9-73	1991	Cidra, P.R.
Rodriguez, Victor	.326	47	184	32	60	11	0	1	26	14	13	2	1	.402	.372	R	R	6-2	190	10-25-76	1994	Aguirre, P.R.
Salazar, Oscar	.279	78	287	34	80	15	2	7	43	24	48	4	4	.418	.331	R	R	6-0	170	6-27-78	1994	Maracay, Venez.
2-team (39 Arkansas)	.295	117	430	56	127	21	4	11	64	43	68	6	5	.440	.358							
Santos, Chad	.270	111	396	48	107	21	3	11	49	35	116	3	0	.422	.332	L	L	5-11	220	4-28-81	1999	Kaneohe, Hawaii
Tonis, Mike	.238	87	307	34	73	18	0	2	24	23	52	3	1	.316	.296	R	R	6-3	220	2-9-79	2000	Elk Grove, Calif.
Ullery, Dave	.202	37	119	12	24	3	0	0	12	8	30	0	0	.227	.250	L	R	6-3	220	12-16-74	1997	Brazil, Ind.
Walter, Scott	.269	48	167	21	45	13	1	5	21	7	36	1	1	.449	.324	R	R	6-2	200	12-28-78	2000	Manhattan Beach, Calif.

PITCHING	W	L	ERA	G	GS	CG	SV	IP	H	R	ER	BB	SO	AVG	B	T	HT	WT	DOB	1st Yr	Resides
Asencio, Miguel	0	0	0.00	1	1	0	0	4	1	0	0	1	3	.076	R	R	6-2	190	9-29-80	1998	La Victoria, D.R.
Baerlocher, Ryan	2	1	4.93	12	2	0	0	35	40	25	19	14	36	.283	R	R	6-5	220	8-6-77	1999	Lewiston, Idaho
Carlyle, Buddy	3	2	1.98	15	0	0	3	27	19	6	6	7	41	.191	L	R	6-3	170	12-21-77	1996	Bellevue, Neb.
Douglass, Ryan	0	3	4.77	28	7	0	1	66	94	43	35	16	38	.336	R	R	6-3	210	12-3-78	1997	Pittsburgh, Pa.
Ferguson, Ian	2	1	7.52	13	3	0	0	26	37	23	22	17	15	.333	R	R	6-4	220	8-23-79	2000	Bellingham, Wash.
Field, Nate	1	0	3.60	15	0	0	3	20	20	9	8	8	20	.256	R	R	6-2	200	12-11-75	1998	Littleton, Colo.
Flury, Pat	2	0	3.04	17	0	0	0	27	24	11	9	12	25	.247	R	R	6-2	210	3-14-73	1993	Sparks, Nev.
Gobble, Jimmy	12	8	3.19	22	22	2	0	133	128	57	47	40	100	.253	L	L	6-3	190	7-19-81	1999	Bristol, Va.
Greinke, Zack	4	3	3.23	9	9	0	0	53	58	20	19	5	34	.285	R	R	6-2	190	10-21-83	2002	Apopka, Fla.
Hernandez, Runelvys	0	2	3.86	2	2	0	0	9	9	4	4	5	5	.257	R	R	6-1	200	4-27-78	1998	Santo Domingo, D.R.
Hill, Jeremy	0	0	0.00	2	0	0	0	2	0	1	0	3	3	.000	R	R	5-11	200	8-8-77	1996	Dallas, Texas
Lee, Garrett	5	9	5.02	30	13	1	1	118	146	72	66	33	74	.311	R	R	6-5	210	8-17-76	1996	Montrose, Calif.
Luque, Roger	0	1	9.64	5	0	0	0	5	10	5	5	2	2	.400	L	L	6-1	170	1-8-80	1997	Charallave, Venez.
Natale, Mike	1	2	2.79	20	0	0	4	39	32	12	12	19	28	.230	R	R	6-0	190	9-2-79	2000	Whittier, Calif.
Rose, Brian	0	4	5.40	7	5	0	0	25	27	17	15	12	11	.287	R	R	6-3	210	2-13-76	1995	Dartmouth, Mass.
Sanches, Brian	1	5	3.16	38	6	0	2	85	84	38	30	17	73	.260	R	R	6-0	190	8-8-78	1999	Nederland, Texas
Sedlacek, Shawn	1	2	5.60	5	5	0	0	27	32	17	17	7	15	.296	R	R	6-4	200	6-29-77	1998	Cedar Rapids, Iowa
Shiery, Shaun	0	1	9.00	3	0	0	0	3	3	3	3	2	3	.272	L	L	6-4	180	12-8-78	2001	Katy, Texas
Snyder, Kyle	0	0	0.00	1	1	0	0	5	2	0	0	0	2	.125	S	R	6-8	220	9-9-77	1999	Sarasota, Fla.
Stiles, Brad	0	0	10.64	8	0	0	0	11	21	14	13	7	7	.437	L	L	6-5	230	2-9-81	1999	Lamar, Colo.
Tamayo, Danny	11	14	4.56	27	26	1	0	154	159	84	78	56	95	.266	R	R	6-1	240	6-3-79	2001	Miami, Fla.
Thompson, Eric	11	0	2.11	20	13	0	1	94	76	26	22	29	57	.226	R	R	6-2	195	9-7-77	1998	Fairborn, Ohio
2-team (5 Midland)	11	3	2.92	25	18	0	1	108	93	40	35	41	65	.237							
Vasquez, Jorge	3	1	1.92	36	0	0	22	52	39	12	11	18	52	.211	R	R	6-1	160	7-16-78	1999	Nagua, D.R.
Walrond, Les	2	0	3.27	2	2	0	0	11	7	4	4	2	9	.170	L	L	6-0	190	11-7-76	1998	Brentwood, Tenn.
Wilkerson, Wes	6	6	4.80	32	13	0	1	105	117	65	56	46	35	.285	R	R	6-3	200	9-11-76	2000	Nashville, Tenn.
Wrightsman, Dusty	4	4	6.07	20	10	0	1	76	98	55	51	17	51	.314	R	R	6-4	220	12-7-79	2000	Terre Haute, Ind.
Young, Doug	0	0	9.00	6	0	0	0	6	7	6	6	6	3	.333	R	R	6-2	200	1-23-76	1997	Roseville, Calif.

FIELDING

Catcher	PCT	G	PO	A	E	DP	PB
Arnerich	.889	3	16	0	2	0	3
Guzman	1.000	1	1	0	0	0	0
Tonis	.987	83	482	60	7	4	4
Ullery	.994	24	147	22	1	0	2
Walter	.991	35	200	18	2	1	4

First Base	PCT	G	PO	A	E	DP
Bledsoe	.971	8	62	5	2	7
Hart	.959	20	154	10	7	13
Santos	.986	107	861	63	13	92
Ullery	.976	10	78	5	2	9

Second Base	PCT	G	PO	A	E	DP
Fenster	1.000	4	9	5	0	0
Harris	.984	36	69	113	3	25
Hart	1.000	6	14	16	0	4
Hopper	.000	1	0	0	0	0
Lora	1.000	2	2	1	0	1
Machado	.990	75	167	214	4	51
Medrano	1.000	1	3	1	0	0
Rodriguez	1.000	1	1	3	0	1
Salazar	1.000	21	42	53	0	12

Third Base	PCT	G	PO	A	E	DP
Fenster	1.000	1	0	2	0	0
Gemoll	.952	108	78	178	13	16
Hart	.960	18	14	34	2	4
Medrano	.000	2	0	0	0	0
Salazar	.919	16	8	26	3	2

Shortstop	PCT	G	PO	A	E	DP
Dellaero	1.000	1	1	2	0	0
Hart	.956	36	53	98	7	19
Lora	.956	13	16	27	2	10
Machado	.000	1	0	0	0	0
Medrano	.941	7	15	17	2	5
Ortiz	.971	33	50	86	4	24
Rodriguez	.968	43	63	117	6	22
Salazar	.971	17	33	34	2	12

Outfield	PCT	G	PO	A	E	DP
Beltran	1.000	2	3	0	0	0
Cunningham	.995	100	213	8	1	3
DeJesus	.980	17	48	0	1	0
Gettis	.980	135	289	5	6	1
Hart	.000	1	0	0	0	0
Hopper	.981	112	250	8	5	1
Meadows	.965	63	133	5	5	1
Salazar	.900	9	9	0	1	0

WILMINGTON BLUE ROCKS — High Class A

CAROLINA LEAGUE

BATTING	AVG	G	AB	R	H	2B	3B	HR	RBI	BB	SO	SB	CS	SLG	OBP	B	T	HT	WT	DOB	1st Yr	Resides
Alleva, J.D.	.250	58	184	20	46	7	0	2	17	16	28	0	4	.321	.311	L	R	5-11	190	11-2-78	2001	Durham, N.C.
Arnerich, Tony	.196	53	148	13	29	8	1	1	20	24	28	0	0	.284	.326	R	R	6-0	190	12-14-79	2001	Santa Rosa, Calif.
Blanco, Andres	.244	113	394	61	96	11	3	0	25	44	50	13	7	.287	.330	S	R	5-10	150	4-11-84	2000	Moron,Venez.
Boruff, Gabriel	.000	1	4	0	0	0	0	0	0	0	1	0	0	.000	.000	S	R	6-1	210	11-17-79	2003	Ephrata, Wash.
Costa, Shane	.143	3	7	1	1	1	0	0	0	2	1	0	0	.286	.400	L	R	6-0	200	12-12-81	2003	Visalia, Calif.
Cotto, Luis	.173	17	52	8	9	0	0	0	5	7	15	0	0	.173	.267	R	R	5-10	180	7-9-81	2000	Rio Piedras, P.R.
Cowan, Justin	.274	119	438	52	120	23	6	7	52	25	66	2	0	.402	.334	R	R	5-10	190	11-24-77	2000	Canon City, Colo.
Dorsey, Ryan	.000	2	2	1	0	0	0	0	0	3	0	0	0	.000	.600	R	R	6-1	160	8-29-81	1999	Wheaton, Md.
Draper, John	.234	127	441	42	103	15	1	2	47	41	80	9	2	.286	.313	R	R	6-2	190	8-11-80	2001	Whittier, Calif.
Dyson, Trey	.275	128	458	64	126	31	0	14	72	60	92	6	2	.434	.364	L	L	6-4	220	3-11-80	2002	Blythewood, S.C.
Fallon, Chris	.272	135	471	69	128	28	0	11	79	84	99	4	2	.401	.386	L	R	6-2	180	3-9-79	2001	Bayonne, N.J.
Fenster, Darren	.237	88	312	39	74	10	0	0	33	51	40	0	2	.269	.350	R	R	5-9	170	9-11-78	2000	Middletown, N.J.
Gotay, Ruben	.261	134	502	68	131	31	2	9	72	60	97	8	1	.384	.343	S	R	5-11	160	12-25-82	2001	Fajardo, P.R.
Groves, Brett	.256	66	180	28	46	7	1	1	14	26	41	1	2	.322	.363	R	R	6-0	180	10-1-78	2002	Tampa, Fla.
Keim, Adam	.225	63	213	13	48	9	2	2	12	20	46	1	0	.315	.291	R	R	6-0	180	1-5-81	2002	Lebanon, Penn.
Lytle, Derrik	.273	43	132	20	36	2	2	1	11	21	39	3	1	.341	.381	L	L	6-2	180	12-1-81	2002	Mesa, Ariz.
Phillips, Paul	.239	13	46	1	11	1	0	0	6	1	6	0	1	.261	.271	R	R	5-11	180	4-15-77	1998	Bailey, Miss.
Shanks, James	.301	85	346	54	104	15	2	2	23	28	71	21	8	.373	.359	R	R	6-0	180	1-26-79	1998	Appling, Ga.
Stocker, Mel	.232	20	56	6	13	0	1	0	8	3	12	5	0	.268	.267	S	R	5-10	160	8-15-80	2001	Tucson, Ariz.
Walter, Scott	.272	52	191	29	52	12	0	5	34	13	27	0	0	.414	.324	R	R	6-2	200	12-28-78	2000	Manhattan Beach, Calif.

PITCHING	W	L	ERA	G	GS	CG	SV	IP	H	R	ER	BB	SO	AVG	B	T	HT	WT	DOB	1st Yr	Resides
Armitage, Barry	0	2	6.27	30	0	0	0	37	44	29	26	24	36	.293	R	R	6-4	250	5-11-79	2000	Durban, South Africa
Bass, Brian	9	8	2.84	26	26	2	0	152	129	59	48	43	119	.229	R	R	6-0	190	1-6-82	2000	Montgomery, Ala.
Burch, Matt	1	2	2.70	13	1	0	1	23	24	8	7	10	16	.272	R	R	6-2	190	12-21-76	1998	Horseheads, N.Y.
Douglass, Ryan	4	0	1.93	8	5	0	0	33	22	8	7	5	28	.188	R	R	6-3	210	12-3-78	1997	Pittsburgh, Pa.
Greinke, Zack	11	1	1.14	14	14	3	0	87	56	16	11	13	78	.178	R	R	6-2	190	10-21-83	2002	Apopka, Fla.
Griffin, Colt	1	0	0.00	1	1	0	0	6	3	1	0	0	5	.142	R	R	6-4	200	9-29-82	2001	Marshall, Texas
Keppinger, Billy	6	2	2.25	34	0	0	2	52	41	16	13	16	34	.222	L	L	6-0	190	12-15-78	2000	Auburn, Ga.
Leclair, Aric	1	2	3.03	32	0	0	5	39	32	17	13	30	53	.225	L	L	6-0	190	4-12-78	2000	Swanzey, N.H.
Lord, Justin	0	2	4.09	13	1	0	0	22	17	10	10	5	18	.212	R	R	6-4	210	11-15-79	2001	Marianna, Fla.
Mattison, Kieran	3	1	3.74	7	7	0	0	34	38	16	14	9	29	.292	L	R	6-0	200	6-21-80	2002	Greenville, N.C.
McClellan, Robbie	0	0	0.00	1	0	0	1	1	1	0	0	0	1	.250	R	R	6-1	170	1-31-81	2003	Liberal, Kan.
McClellan, Zach	8	8	2.84	30	23	1	0	133	101	51	42	39	100	.212	R	R	6-5	190	11-25-78	2000	Toledo, Ohio
McGill, Trae	0	0	1.35	6	0	0	0	13	10	2	2	2	7	.217	R	R	6-0	190	8-7-77	2001	Mobile, Ala.
Middleton, Kyle	11	8	2.41	27	27	1	0	160	155	59	43	35	75	.256	R	R	6-6	230	6-13-80	2000	Pensacola, Fla.
Morrison, Robbie	4	3	3.54	42	0	0	11	53	39	22	21	18	65	.202	R	R	6-0	210	12-7-76	1998	Valrico, Fla.
Natale, Mike	2	2	2.79	27	0	0	7	39	35	14	12	13	57	.230	R	R	6-0	190	9-2-79	2000	Whittier, Calif.
Stiles, Brad	2	2	2.41	26	0	0	2	37	32	12	10	18	40	.226	L	L	6-5	230	2-9-81	1999	Lamar, Colo.
Stodolka, Mike	2	1	3.00	5	5	0	0	21	15	8	7	9	10	.208	L	L	6-2	210	9-24-81	2000	Corona, Calif.
Tierney, Chris	5	11	4.38	26	26	0	0	127	160	77	62	48	73	.312	L	L	6-6	200	9-1-83	2001	Lockport, Ill.
Vasquez, Jorge	1	2	1.96	17	0	0	7	23	19	7	5	14	31	.223	R	R	6-1	160	7-16-78	1999	Nagua, D.R.
Villacis, Eduardo	6	2	2.82	42	4	0	2	93	78	36	29	28	64	.226	R	R	6-2	170	8-29-79	1998	Aragua, Venez.
Wrightsman, Dusty	3	1	4.42	10	0	0	0	18	21	9	9	7	11	.304	R	R	6-4	220	12-7-79	2000	Terre Haute, Ind.

FIELDING

Catcher	PCT	G	PO	A	E	DP	PB
Alleva	.993	48	269	24	2	0	3
Arnerich	.990	45	282	23	3	1	7
Phillips	.988	11	77	8	1	0	1
Walter	.986	44	338	23	5	4	4

First Base	PCT	G	PO	A	E	DP
Alleva	1.000	1	2	0	0	1
Cowan	.957	2	22	0	1	0
Dyson	.992	26	217	25	2	19
Fallon	.990	114	988	82	11	98

Second Base	PCT	G	PO	A	E	DP
Cotto	1.000	3	9	13	0	4
Fenster	.933	3	5	9	1	0
Gotay	.973	128	199	379	16	82
Groves	1.000	11	22	31	0	6

Third Base	PCT	G	PO	A	E	DP
Cotto	1.000	1	0	2	0	0
Fenster	.959	74	47	142	8	14
Groves	.976	18	10	30	1	3
Keim	.970	56	37	93	4	13

Shortstop	PCT	G	PO	A	E	DP
Blanco	.947	110	157	305	26	65
Cotto	.875	2	1	6	1	1
Fenster	.977	9	15	28	1	9
Groves	.899	26	33	65	11	12

Outfield	PCT	G	PO	A	E	DP
Costa	1.000	3	3	0	0	0
Cowan	.981	70	100	4	2	0
Draper	.974	126	258	7	7	1
Dyson	.988	100	162	7	2	1
Lytle	.962	29	49	1	2	0
Shanks	.967	84	176	2	6	0
Stocker	.976	18	40	0	1	0

BURLINGTON BEES — Low Class A

MIDWEST LEAGUE

BATTING	AVG	G	AB	R	H	2B	3B	HR	RBI	BB	SO	SB	CS	SLG	OBP	B	T	HT	WT	DOB	1st Yr	Resides
Alexander, Alexis	.140	16	50	2	7	0	1	0	7	2	24	1	0	.180	.182	R	R	5-11	200	11-18-82	2001	Spokane, Wash.
Dean, Erik	.265	64	223	35	59	9	1	3	42	24	37	3	1	.354	.340	L	R	6-0	190	2-7-82	2001	Santa Clara, Calif.

BATTING	AVG	G	AB	R	H	2B	3B	HR	RBI	BB	SO	SB	CS	SLG	OBP	B	T	HT	WT	DOB	1st Yr	Resides
Espino, Damaso	.285	130	480	58	137	25	3	3	88	69	76	8	4	.369	.377	S	R	6-1	190	5-8-83	1999	Panama City, Panama
Frend, Tim	.267	120	453	57	121	22	3	11	55	39	75	8	5	.402	.328	R	R	6-2	180	5-20-80	2002	Charlotte, N.C.
Gonzalez, Luis	.171	64	210	15	36	3	0	3	15	12	58	0	1	.229	.251	R	R	6-2	210	11-8-82	1999	Guanta, Venez.
Graham, Bryan	.233	15	60	7	14	2	0	0	3	4	11	0	0	.267	.281	L	L	6-1	185	6-8-81	2003	Medford, N.J.
Guzman, Jacob	.167	1	6	0	1	0	0	0	0	0	1	0	0	.167	.167	R	R	6-0	210	8-2-82	2001	Santee, Calif.
Jensen, Dave	.205	105	371	32	76	10	1	1	21	46	90	3	2	.245	.295	L	L	6-3	210	12-16-79	2002	Henderson, Nevada
Kaaihue, Kila	.238	114	395	53	94	21	1	11	63	67	87	1	3	.380	.355	L	R	6-3	210	3-29-84	2002	Kailua, Hawaii
Lonnquist, Eric	.217	55	175	30	38	3	0	0	8	29	29	6	0	.234	.348	R	R	6-0	180	6-20-80	2002	Rosemount, Minn.
Lytle, Derrik	.223	47	157	27	35	6	1	1	9	16	43	3	2	.293	.298	L	L	6-2	180	12-1-81	2002	Mesa, Ariz.
Murphy, Donald	.313	132	504	77	158	29	6	5	98	65	78	15	6	.425	.397	R	R	5-10	180	3-10-83	2002	Anaheim, Calif.
Sanchez, Angel	.270	106	408	54	110	8	1	2	35	28	52	14	5	.309	.321	R	R	6-1	170	9-20-83	2001	Las Piedras, P.R.
Stephens, Bernard	.245	121	432	64	106	15	5	2	34	41	106	24	12	.317	.314	L	R	6-0	190	11-11-79	2002	North Augusta, S.C.
Stocker, Mel	.273	103	403	85	110	16	9	3	33	46	48	36	5	.380	.367	S	R	5-10	160	8-15-80	2001	Tucson, Ariz.
Tupman, Matt	.223	81	296	32	66	12	3	2	38	27	41	1	2	.304	.288	L	R	5-11	180	11-25-79	2002	Concord, N.H.

PITCHING	W	L	ERA	G	GS	CG	SV	IP	H	R	ER	BB	SO	AVG	B	T	HT	WT	DOB	1st Yr	Resides
Ackerman, Eric	9	5	4.69	26	25	0	0	150	156	87	78	62	74	.273	L	L	6-0	190	10-19-79	2002	Denver, Pa.
Armitage, Barry	0	1	6.52	8	0	0	1	10	14	7	7	4	5	.358	R	R	6-4	250	5-11-79	2000	Durban, South Africa
Atencio, Greg	0	1	12.38	2	0	0	0	8	15	12	11	5	7	.384	R	R	6-3	210	7-15-81	2002	Albuquerque, N.M.
Bayliss, Jonah	7	12	3.86	26	26	2	0	140	129	78	60	69	133	.242	R	R	6-2	200	8-13-80	2002	Williamstown, Mass.
Burch, Matt	0	1	2.20	8	0	0	1	16	16	4	4	5	13	.258	R	R	6-2	190	12-21-76	1998	Horseheads, N.Y.
Burgos, Ambiorix	0	1	5.40	2	2	0	0	5	3	3	3	6	4	.200	R	R	6-0	180	4-19-84	2001	Nagua, D.R.
Carter, Ramsey	0	0	1.29	2	0	0	0	7	5	2	1	2	6	.200	S	R	6-2	190	11-26-80	2001	El Paso, Texas
Chamberlain, Steve	3	7	3.38	33	0	0	10	75	54	29	28	23	57	.198	L	R	6-3	200	7-20-80	2002	Pullman, Wash.
Christensen, Danny	1	12	5.92	17	16	0	0	79	83	62	52	31	46	.268	L	L	6-2	200	8-10-83	2002	Vero Beach, Fla.
Colton, Kyle	0	0	6.35	2	0	0	0	6	5	4	4	6	3	.250	R	R	6-2	170	11-16-80	1999	Longwood, Fla.
De la Cruz, Andres	2	0	4.60	21	0	0	0	29	23	18	15	21	9	.209	R	R	6-4	190	12-5-79	1996	Santo Domingo, D.R.
Endicott, Drew	7	5	3.73	32	11	1	5	116	125	55	48	29	60	.277	R	R	6-3	180	3-30-81	2002	Carthage, Mo.
Griffin, Colt	9	11	3.91	27	27	0	0	150	127	80	65	97	107	.233	R	R	6-4	200	9-29-82	2001	Marshall, Texas
Hoelscher, Nate	2	4	4.22	34	0	0	3	60	68	33	28	16	53	.280	L	L	6-2	190	11-11-79	2002	St. Joseph, Minn.
Kaanoi, Jason	2	3	6.06	31	0	0	2	52	58	38	35	29	30	.277	L	R	5-11	170	8-19-82	2000	Kaneohe, Hawaii
Keppinger, Billy	0	0	0.00	3	0	0	0	5	2	0	0	1	5	.133	L	L	6-0	190	12-15-78	2000	Auburn, Ga.
Lord, Justin	3	1	3.92	19	0	0	1	44	36	20	19	8	33	.222	R	R	6-4	210	11-15-79	2001	Marianna, Fla.
Lowery, Devon	6	4	3.36	26	10	0	5	96	78	39	36	34	74	.222	L	R	6-1	190	3-24-83	2001	Belmont, N.C.
Mattison, Kieran	8	5	2.50	17	17	2	0	108	82	32	30	26	89	.209	L	R	6-0	200	6-21-80	2002	Greenville, N.C.
McGill, Trae	3	1	3.27	16	2	0	2	44	46	17	16	10	49	.261	R	R	6-0	190	8-7-77	2001	Mobile, Ala.
Metzger, Jon	0	0	16.88	3	0	0	0	3	8	5	5	5	0	.571	L	L	6-2	200	10-27-78	2000	Fairfax Station, Va.
Shiery, Shaun	2	0	1.32	2	2	0	0	14	16	6	2	3	7	.280	L	L	6-4	180	12-8-78	2001	Katy, Texas

FIELDING

Catcher	PCT	G	PO	A	E	DP	PB
Gonzalez	.987	64	397	46	6	8	18
Guzman	1.000	1	17	2	0	0	0
Tupman	.984	78	478	63	9	8	14

First Base	PCT	G	PO	A	E	DP
Jensen	.989	67	582	52	7	47
Kaaihue	.985	72	669	31	11	53

Second Base	PCT	G	PO	A	E	DP
Dean	.967	29	45	74	4	14
Espino	.000	1	0	0	0	0
Lonnquist	.989	19	39	51	1	10
Murphy	.984	82	172	250	7	55
Sanchez	.957	9	18	27	2	3

Third Base	PCT	G	PO	A	E	DP
Dean	.860	19	14	35	8	3
Espino	.899	115	71	188	29	19
Lonnquist	.818	5	2	7	2	0

Shortstop	PCT	G	PO	A	E	DP
Dean	1.000	1	1	3	0	1
Lonnquist	1.000	1	1	3	0	1
Murphy	.963	41	64	116	7	19
Sanchez	.953	97	138	286	21	53

Outfield	PCT	G	PO	A	E	DP
Alexander	1.000	16	29	1	0	0
Frend	.981	111	199	4	4	1
Graham	.909	15	17	3	2	0
Lonnquist	.944	9	16	1	1	0
Lytle	1.000	46	96	4	0	1
Stephens	.973	121	235	17	7	2
Stocker	.992	101	250	6	2	1

SURPRISE ROYALS-1 — Rookie

ARIZONA LEAGUE

BATTING	AVG	G	AB	R	H	2B	3B	HR	RBI	BB	SO	SB	CS	SLG	OBP	B	T	HT	WT	DOB	1st Yr	Resides
Aviles, Mike	.363	52	212	51	77	19	5	6	39	13	28	11	5	.585	.404	R	R	5-11	193	3-13-81	2003	Middletown, N.Y.
Batista, Alexander	.367	48	180	37	66	10	2	1	21	7	30	6	4	.461	.394	R	R	6-0	180	8-11-83	2001	Puerto Plata, D.R.
Brown, Dee	.714	2	7	4	5	2	0	0	3	0	2	0	0	1.000	.750	L	R	6-0	220	3-27-78	1996	Orlando, Fla.
Caballero, Carlos	.203	30	64	17	13	2	0	1	6	7	18	5	2	.281	.333	R	R	6-0	170	12-5-83	2002	San Juan, P.R.
Donachie, Adam	.222	20	63	8	14	3	1	0	7	9	12	0	1	.302	.338	R	R	6-2	180	3-3-84	2002	Orlando, Fla.
2-team (2 Royals-2)	.250	22	72	11	18	4	1	0	7	10	16	0	1	.333	.357							
Grana, Robert	.333	6	21	3	7	1	1	0	3	3	8	2	0	.476	.440	R	R	6-3	200	8-4-83	2003	Las Vegas, Nev.
Lopez, Mendy	.250	7	20	9	5	1	0	3	6	4	5	0	0	.750	.400	R	R	6-2	200	10-15-73	1992	Santo Domingo, D.R.
Lubanski, Chris	.326	53	221	41	72	4	6	4	27	18	50	9	10	.452	.382	L	L	6-3	185	3-24-85	2003	Oldsmar, Fla.
Maier, Mitch	.350	51	203	41	71	14	6	2	45	18	25	7	3	.507	.403	L	R	6-2	200	6-30-82	2003	Howell, Mich.
McDonald, Chamar	.297	22	74	17	22	5	0	3	13	12	30	1	0	.486	.404	R	R	6-4	200	6-18-83	2001	Madison, Miss.
2-team (7 Royals-2)	.302	29	106	24	32	8	0	3	17	14	36	1	0	.462	.390							
McFall, Brian	.220	51	191	34	42	9	4	6	36	17	50	1	0	.403	.296	R	R	6-3	205	6-17-84	2003	Flagstaff, Ariz.
Oriental, Rene	.247	47	166	27	41	4	3	5	27	14	40	6	4	.398	.302	R	R	6-3	200	5-4-84	2001	San Pedro de Macoris, D.R.
Phillips, Paul	.462	4	13	3	6	2	0	1	2	1	0	0	0	.846	.500	R	R	5-11	180	4-15-77	1998	Bailey, Miss.
Powell, Brandon	.326	52	215	47	70	12	15	4	46	27	39	15	6	.577	.399	L	R	6-0	185	8-15-80	2003	Johnsonville, S.C.
Solis, Eddie	.259	27	58	12	15	5	2	3	9	6	14	1	0	.569	.338	R	R	5-11	185	9-19-84	2003	San Diego, Calif.
Springer, Kenard	.346	49	182	35	63	15	1	3	39	10	20	7	4	.489	.388	R	R	6-0	210	9-18-83	2002	Nettleton, Miss.
Vega, Miguel	.222	25	81	12	18	5	0	2	11	2	25	0	0	.358	.238	R	R	6-3	205	7-31-85	2003	Arroyo, P.R.
Weitz, Konrad	.125	7	8	0	1	1	0	0	0	0	2	0	0	.250	.125	R	R	6-2	200	7-16-85	2001	Cape Town, South Africa

GAMES BY POSITION: C—Donachie 18, Grana 4, Maier 32, Phillips 3, Weitz 5. **1B**—McDonald 18, McFall 41. **2B**—Batista 4, Lopez 3, Powell 48, Solis 3. **3B**—Batista 25, Lopez 2, Solis 18, Vega 25. **SS**—Aviles 52, Lopez 2, Solis 4. **OF**—Batista 13, Brown 2, Caballero 26, Lubanski 53, Oriental 46, Springer 42.

PITCHING	W	L	ERA	G	GS	CG	SV	IP	H	R	ER	BB	SO	AVG	B	T	HT	WT	DOB	1st Yr	Resides
Alleva, Jeff	1	1	3.00	11	0	0	0	18	20	6	6	3	15	.277	R	R	6-2	180	8-22-80	2003	Durham, N.C.
Asencio, Miguel	0	0	2.84	3	3	0	0	6	11	3	2	1	3	.366	R	R	6-2	190	9-29-80	1998	La Victoria, D.R.
Blanco, Carlos	0	0	0.00	1	0	0	0	1	1	0	0	0	1	.250	R	L	6-1	160	6-20-82	2000	La Vega, D.R.

PITCHING	W	L	ERA	G	GS	CG	SV	IP	H	R	ER	BB	SO	AVG	B	T	HT	WT	DOB	1st Yr	Resides
Braun, Ryan	0	0	2.95	18	0	0	3	21	15	9	7	10	25	.185	R	R	6-2	205	7-29-80	2003	Mooresville, N.C.
Burgos, Ambiorix	3	2	4.00	9	7	0	0	36	37	22	16	16	43	.260	R	R	6-0	180	4-19-84	2001	Nagua, D.R.
Christensen, Danny	0	0	2.25	4	2	0	0	12	8	4	3	5	12	.177	L	L	6-2	200	8-10-83	2002	Vero Beach, Fla.
Coughlin, Chris	1	3	6.75	12	0	0	1	16	28	15	12	2	16	.383	R	R	6-0	190	9-30-80	2003	Southport, N.C.
Damico, Vovany	2	1	3.32	11	0	0	0	19	25	8	7	3	20	.320	R	R	6-1	170	8-18-84	2003	Mariara, Venez.
Encarnacion, Alexis	2	0	1.71	14	0	0	1	21	17	4	4	2	19	.220	R	R	6-0	160	9-26-82	1999	Santo Domingo, D.R.
Fingers, Jason	0	0	6.00	2	0	0	0	3	2	2	2	1	1	.181	R	R	6-5	180	8-17-78	2000	Las Vegas, Nev.
Goodman, Chris	3	1	4.09	11	7	0	0	44	48	24	20	11	42	.275	R	R	6-0	180	8-30-81	2003	Marietta, Ga.
Guzman, Jonathan	1	2	5.09	10	0	0	1	18	22	11	10	4	9	.297	R	R	6-1	170	8-28-78	1998	Santiago, D.R.
Hughes, Dustin	5	2	2.84	11	6	0	0	51	38	21	16	18	54	.206	L	L	5-9	195	6-29-83	2003	Horn Lake, Miss.
McCleland, Bruce	2	2	6.04	10	3	0	0	22	24	17	15	11	15	.275	R	R	6-5	210	12-16-84	2002	Capetown, South Africa
Palmer, Lucas	6	0	3.62	14	7	0	1	55	55	28	22	17	50	.258	R	R	6-3	200	5-7-83	2002	Baker, Ore.
Rosa, Carlos	5	3	3.63	15	11	0	0	69	79	36	28	18	54	.288	R	R	6-2	170	9-21-84	2002	San Francisco de Macoris, D.R.
Rosario, Julio	1	0	11.49	13	0	0	0	16	18	24	20	13	8	.281	R	R	6-0	160	6-12-82	2002	La Romana, D.R.
Rose, Brian	1	0	0.00	2	0	0	0	6	3	0	0	0	5	.150	R	R	6-3	210	2-13-76	1995	Dartmouth, Mass.
Sherman, Justin	3	2	4.41	12	8	0	1	49	51	24	24	10	40	.269	R	R	6-4	195	12-6-80	2003	Las Vegas, Nev.
Snyder, Kyle	0	0	4.50	1	1	0	0	2	3	1	1	0	1	.375	S	R	6-8	220	9-9-77	1999	Sarasota, Fla.
Taveras, Nelson	0	0	3.00	1	0	0	1	3	2	1	1	1	0	.200	R	R	6-2	180	2-6-83	1999	Dajabon, D.R.

SURPRISE ROYALS-2 — Rookie

ARIZONA LEAGUE

BATTING	AVG	G	AB	R	H	2B	3B	HR	RBI	BB	SO	SB	CS	SLG	OBP	B	T	HT	WT	DOB	1st Yr	Resides
Alexander, Alexis	.288	25	73	17	21	4	3	4	10	11	26	6	0	.589	.395	R	R	5-11	200	11-18-82	2001	Spokane, Wash.
Barry, Jeff	.306	46	183	38	56	7	2	1	12	27	45	15	4	.383	.409	R	R	6-0	185	8-1-81	2003	Essex Junction, Vt.
Boruff, Gabriel	.234	21	64	11	15	4	0	0	10	11	24	0	0	.297	.351	S	R	6-1	210	11-17-79	2003	Ephrata, Wash.
Costa, Shane	.386	23	88	22	34	6	4	1	24	6	7	4	3	.580	.444	L	R	6-0	200	12-12-81	2003	Visalia, Calif.
Del Rosario, Felipe	.248	34	117	18	29	9	1	0	7	15	29	0	1	.342	.348	R	R	5-10	180	9-8-84	2001	La Romana, D.R.
Donachie, Adam	.444	2	9	3	4	1	0	0	0	1	4	0	0	.556	.500	R	R	6-2	180	3-3-84	2002	Orlando, Fla.
Dorsey, Ryan	.333	1	3	2	1	0	0	0	0	1	1	0	0	.333	.500	R	R	6-1	160	8-29-81	1999	Wheaton, Md.
Eusebio, Juan	.286	11	28	4	8	0	1	0	2	6	7	3	0	.357	.429	R	R	5-11	150	2-4-84	2001	Hato Mayor, D.R.
Falu, Irving	.259	36	139	26	36	6	2	1	11	24	22	8	6	.353	.387	S	R	6-0	174	6-6-83	2003	Carolina, P.R.
Ferrara, Matt	.217	40	143	15	31	7	2	3	23	13	52	3	2	.357	.298	R	R	6-1	200	9-27-82	2001	Miramar, Fla.
Figuereo, Anibal	.284	25	102	18	29	4	1	3	18	7	15	3	1	.431	.336	R	R	6-2	200	1-21-82	1999	Barahona, D.R.
Gaffney, Michael	.275	39	149	15	41	6	1	0	25	21	17	4	2	.329	.368	R	R	6-1	185	11-11-81	2003	Westbury, N.Y.
Graham, Bryan	.363	28	113	19	41	11	2	4	28	13	17	0	0	.602	.433	L	L	6-1	185	6-8-81	2003	Medford, N.J.
Guzman, Jacob	.217	18	60	6	13	4	0	1	13	7	16	0	0	.333	.282	R	R	6-0	210	8-2-82	2001	Santee, Calif.
McDonald, Chamar	.313	7	32	7	10	3	0	0	4	2	6	0	0	.406	.353	R	R	6-4	200	6-18-83	2001	Madison, Miss.
Salazar, Darwinson	.262	44	141	21	37	7	2	1	18	18	45	5	4	.362	.355	R	R	6-3	190	12-12-82	2000	Higuerote, Venez.
Saunches, Mike	.255	44	161	15	41	14	0	1	23	27	35	1	0	.360	.361	L	L	6-3	250	7-6-81	2002	Decatur, Ill.
Sevilla, Walter	.257	40	148	28	38	8	3	0	10	18	22	11	0	.351	.353	R	R	5-8	170	8-24-81	2003	Miami, Fla.
Valentin, Geraldo	.352	32	122	25	43	12	1	2	23	11	16	3	2	.516	.413	R	R	6-0	175	9-8-82	2003	Rio Piedras, P.R.

GAMES BY POSITION: C—Boruff 3, Del Rosario 34, Donachie 2, Guzman 17. **1B**—Ferrara 1, Figuereo 19, Gaffney 1, McDonald 3, Saunches 33. **2B**—Falu 19, Sevilla 34, Valentin 1. **3B**—Ferrara 39, Figuereo 1, Gaffney 16. **SS**—Dorsey 1, Falu 16, Gaffney 22, Sevilla 3, Valentin 15. **OF**—Alexander 24, Barry 46, Boruff 9, Costa 19, Eusebio 10, Graham 25, Salazar 44.

PITCHING	W	L	ERA	G	GS	CG	SV	IP	H	R	ER	BB	SO	AVG	B	T	HT	WT	DOB	1st Yr	Resides
Atencio, Greg	2	5	3.91	12	12	0	0	71	62	40	31	17	62	.235	R	R	6-3	210	7-15-81	2002	Albuquerque, N.M.
Blanco, Carlos	0	1	18.41	8	0	0	0	7	14	15	15	8	9	.388	R	L	6-1	160	6-20-82	2000	La Vega, D.R.
2-team (1 Royals-1)	0	1	16.20	9	0	0	0	8	15	15	15	8	10	.375							
Bray, Stephen	4	2	3.38	14	0	0	3	40	41	17	15	7	32	.284	R	R	6-1	190	12-22-80	2003	Branford, Conn.
Brown, Ira	4	2	4.96	15	11	0	0	62	57	45	34	50	66	.244	R	R	6-4	210	8-3-82	2001	Conroe, Texas
Bryan, Bobby	0	1	10.72	15	0	0	1	23	40	28	27	12	17	.380	R	R	6-0	190	5-31-80	2002	Richmond, Texas
Colton, Kyle	2	1	8.00	5	0	0	0	9	12	10	8	9	8	.285	R	R	6-2	170	11-16-80	1999	Longwood, Fla.
Dossett, Dusty	2	1	1.80	21	0	0	6	25	30	12	5	3	23	.288	R	R	6-2	170	4-11-80	2001	Athens, Texas
Ferguson, Ian	3	1	2.70	5	5	0	0	23	16	9	7	6	26	.186	R	R	6-4	220	8-23-79	2000	Bellingham, Wash.
Gragg, John	3	2	3.45	13	13	0	0	60	63	27	23	10	55	.259	L	L	5-10	185	5-9-81	2003	Beaumont, Texas
McClellan, Robbie	4	3	4.00	18	0	0	2	45	44	24	20	7	51	.247	R	R	6-1	170	1-31-81	2003	Liberal, Kan.
McConiga, Jacob	1	0	4.15	9	0	0	1	9	9	5	4	5	11	.257	L	L	5-10	180	1-21-81	2003	Elverta, Calif.
Mullis, Jacob	4	3	3.82	13	13	0	0	64	75	34	27	7	57	.297	R	R	6-2	215	1-22-81	2003	Arden, N.C.
Nendza, Brian	3	0	3.41	16	0	0	2	32	31	13	12	6	36	.248	L	L	6-6	200	12-9-80	2003	Palos Park, Ill.
Smith, Michael	0	0	6.75	5	0	0	1	9	14	7	7	3	6	.411	L	L	6-6	200	7-8-81	2002	Valdosta, Ga.

LOS ANGELES DODGERS

BY CHRIS COCOLES

If you're into nostalgia and cling to the "pitching is 75 percent of baseball" theories, the Dodgers should have gotten by with decent production from its offense.

Surely they need not send out a lineup full of sluggers with a pitching staff highlighted by a league-low 3.12 ERA and a dominating 55-saves-in-55-chances effort from closer Eric Gagne, who could turn out to be the best of the decade at his position.

But oh those bats. The Dodgers' 85-77 final record and exclusion from the postseason for a seventh consecutive October was attributed to anemic hitting that couldn't be overcome. The lack of production was most glaring when the Dodgers plummeted from a first-place tie to 13½ games off the pace. The swoon spanned most of June-through-August, though the Dodgers hung around the wild-card race until the final week.

That's what made 2003 such a tease. The Dodgers couldn't decide if they were a legitimate contender or one-dimensional. A club gasping to score runs played the game like the old fellas, relying on pitching, and it was almost enough to steal a berth.

"You need to give a lot of credit to this club," manager Jim Tracy told reporters after L.A. was mathematically eliminated from consideration. "The fact that we scored 562 runs and we were three days before the end of the season before we were eliminated, that says a lot about the character of this club. We were trying to do a miraculous thing, and we damn near pulled it off."

But there were too many setbacks to get it done. The Dodgers ranked last in the National League in hitting (.243), runs scored (571), walks (403) and slugging percentage (.368).

For every pleasant surprise on the mound—Kevin Brown's relatively stable health, Wilson Alvarez's second-half heroics, Tom Martin's unsung bullpen work—there were major disappointments elsewhere.

The offseason trade of the infield's right side had to sting when Mark Grudzielanek and Eric Karros helped the Cubs to the NL Central title. The key acquisition for the Dodgers, catcher Todd Hundley, was injured and a non-factor.

Other medical setbacks contributing to the hitting drought included: left fielder Brian Jordan (knee), center fielder Dave Roberts (hamstring), first baseman Fred McGriff (groin) and right fielder Shawn Green (shoulder). Green, whose .285-42-114 performance in 2002 was MVP-worthy, slipped to .280-19-84 playing in pain.

Trade deadline deals for Robin Ventura and Jeromy Burnitz caused little impact. Nor did the signing of Rickey Henderson. Those and other failures continued to add pressure for general manager Dan Evans to make more positive moves.

Aside from the pitching, the Dodgers' other feel-good story was the minor league system. Farm director Bill Bavasi and scouting director Logan White are forming an efficient team that is rebuilding nicely, with depth on the mound. Righthander Edwin Jackson will have to wait for another year to legally purchase a beer with his Dodger Dog, but in his big league debut he beat Randy Johnson on his 20th birthday and could challenge for a 2004 rotation spot.

Lefthander Greg Miller, just 19 but already having reached Double-A, leads a promising stable of arms compiled mostly over the previous two drafts, which also included 2003 first-rounder Chad Billingsley and 2002 picks Jonathan Broxton and Mike Megrew.

The organization's only playoff team was Rookie-level Ogden, which lost in three games to Provo in the Pioneer League's opening round.

Eric Gagne

Greg Miller

PLAYERS of the YEAR

MAJOR LEAGUE: Eric Gagne, rhp

Gagne converted all 55 of his save opportunities in 2003, leading the majors in saves and success ratio while nailing down 65 percent of his team's wins. He fanned 132 batters in 82 innings, while posting a 1.20 ERA.

MINOR LEAGUE: Greg Miller, lhp

Miller advanced to Double-A before his 19th birthday and ranked sixth in the minors with 9.6 strikeouts per nine innings. At 12-5, 2.21 between Double-A Jacksonville and Class A Vero Beach, Miller posted the 10th best ERA in the minors.

ORGANIZATION LEADERS

BATTING		
*AVG	Bubba Crosby, Las Vegas	.361
R	Chin-Feng Chen, Las Vegas	84
H	Joe Thurston, Las Vegas	156
TB	Franklin Gutierrez, Jacksonville/Vero Beach	258
2B	Delwyn Young, South Georgia	38
3B	Bubba Crosby, Las Vegas	8
HR	Chin-Feng Chen, Las Vegas	26
RBI	Chin-Feng Chen, Las Vegas	86
BB	Tarrik Brock, Las Vegas/Jacksonville	62
SO	Reggie Abercrombie, Jacksonville	164
SB	Wilkin Ruan, Las Vegas	41
*SLG	Bubba Crosby, Las Vegas	.635
*OBP	Bubba Crosby, Las Vegas	.410
PITCHING		
W	Brian Pilkington, Jacksonville/Vero Beach	13
L	Heath Totten, Jacksonville	12
#ERA	Greg Miller, Jacksonville/Vero Beach	2.21
G	Bryan Corey, Las Vegas	60
CG	Heath Totten, Jacksonville	2
	T.J. Nall, Vero Beach	2
SV	Steve Colyer, Las Vegas	23
	Jason Frasor, Jacksonville/Vero Beach	23
IP	Heath Totten, Jacksonville	181
BB	Joel Hanrahan, Las Vegas/Jacksonville	73
SO	Edwin Jackson, Jacksonville	157

*Minimum 250 At-Bats #Minimum 75 Innings

LOS ANGELES DODGERS

Manager: Jim Tracy.

2003 Record: 85-77, .525 (2nd, NL West).

BATTING	AVG	G	AB	R	H	2B	3B	HR	RBI	BB	SO	SB	CS	SLG	OBP	B	T	HT	WT	DOB	1st Yr	Resides
Barnes, Larry	.211	30	38	2	8	2	0	0	2	1	9	0	0	.263	.231	L	L	6-1	190	7-23-74	1995	Bakersfield, Calif.
Beltre, Adrian	.240	158	559	50	134	30	2	23	80	37	103	2	2	.424	.290	R	R	5-11	220	4-7-79	1994	Santo Domingo, D.R.
Burnitz, Jeromy	.204	61	230	25	47	4	0	13	32	14	57	4	0	.391	.252	L	R	6-0	210	4-14-69	1990	Poway, Calif.
2-team (65 New York)	.239	126	464	63	111	22	0	31	77	35	112	5	4	.487	.299							
Cabrera, Jolbert	.282	128	347	43	98	32	2	6	37	17	62	6	4	.438	.332	R	R	6-1	195	12-8-72	1991	Cartagena, Colombia
Chen, Chin-Feng	.000	1	1	0	0	0	0	0	0	0	0	0	0	.000	.000	R	R	6-1	189	10-28-77	1999	Tainan City, Taiwan
Coomer, Ron	.240	69	125	11	30	4	0	4	15	10	19	0	0	.368	.299	R	R	6-0	210	11-18-66	1987	Chicago, Ill.
Cora, Alex	.249	148	477	39	119	24	3	4	34	16	59	4	2	.338	.287	L	R	6-0	200	10-18-75	1996	Caguas, P.R.
Crosby, Bubba	.083	9	12	0	1	0	0	0	1	0	3	0	0	.083	.083	L	L	5-11	185	8-11-76	1998	Bellaire, Texas
Green, Shawn	.280	160	611	84	171	49	2	19	85	68	112	6	2	.460	.355	L	L	6-4	200	11-10-72	1991	Newport Beach, Calif.
Henderson, Rickey	.208	30	72	7	15	1	0	2	5	11	16	3	0	.306	.321	R	L	5-10	190	12-25-58	1976	Hillsborough, Calif.
Hermansen, Chad	.160	11	25	2	4	1	0	0	2	2	9	0	0	.200	.222	R	R	6-2	190	9-10-77	1995	Las Vegas, Nev.
Hill, Koyie	.333	3	3	0	1	1	0	0	0	0	2	0	0	.667	.333	S	R	6-0	190	3-9-79	2000	Lawton, Okla.
Hundley, Todd	.182	21	33	2	6	1	0	2	11	8	13	0	1	.394	.341	S	R	5-11	200	5-27-69	1987	Port St. Lucie, Fla.
Izturis, Cesar	.251	158	558	47	140	21	6	1	40	25	70	10	5	.315	.282	S	R	5-9	180	2-10-80	1996	Barquisimeto, Venez.
Jordan, Brian	.299	66	224	28	67	9	0	6	28	23	30	1	1	.420	.372	R	R	6-1	225	3-29-67	1988	Alpharetta, Ga.
Kinkade, Mike	.216	88	162	25	35	7	0	5	14	13	38	1	3	.352	.335	R	R	6-1	210	5-6-73	1995	Pullman, Wash.
LoDuca, Paul	.273	147	568	64	155	34	2	7	52	44	54	0	2	.377	.335	R	R	5-10	185	4-12-72	1993	San Antonio, Texas
McGriff, Fred	.249	86	297	32	74	14	0	13	40	31	66	0	0	.428	.322	L	L	6-3	225	10-31-63	1981	Tampa, Fla.
Roberts, Dave	.250	107	388	56	97	6	5	2	16	43	39	40	14	.307	.331	L	L	5-10	180	5-31-72	1994	Oceanside, Calif.
Romano, Jason	.083	37	36	3	3	0	0	0	0	1	8	2	0	.083	.108	R	R	6-0	185	6-24-79	1997	Tampa, Fla.
Ross, David	.258	40	124	19	32	7	0	10	18	13	42	0	0	.556	.336	R	R	6-2	205	3-19-77	1998	Tallahassee, Fla.
Ruan, Wilkin	.220	21	41	2	9	2	1	0	2	0	7	1	0	.317	.220	R	R	6-0	182	9-18-78	1996	Guaymate, D.R.
Thurston, Joe	.200	12	10	2	2	0	0	0	0	1	1	0	0	.200	.273	L	R	5-11	190	9-29-79	1999	Vallejo, Calif.
Ventura, Robin	.220	49	109	11	24	5	1	5	13	18	25	0	0	.422	.331	L	R	6-1	200	7-14-67	1989	Greenwich, Conn.
Ward, Daryle	.183	52	109	6	20	1	0	0	9	3	19	0	0	.193	.211	L	L	6-2	240	6-27-75	1994	Riverside, Calif.

PITCHING	W	L	ERA	G	GS	CG	SV	IP	H	R	ER	BB	SO	AVG	B	T	HT	WT	DOB	1st Yr	Resides
Alvarez, Victor	0	1	12.71	5	0	0	0	6	9	8	8	6	3	.391	L	L	5-10	155	11-8-76	1997	Culiacan, Mexico
Alvarez, Wilson	6	2	2.37	21	12	1	1	95	80	27	25	23	82	.231	L	L	6-1	250	3-24-70	1987	Bradenton, Fla.
Ashby, Andy	3	10	5.18	21	12	0	0	73	90	42	42	17	41	.311	R	R	6-1	195	7-11-67	1986	Pittston, Pa.
Brohawn, Troy	2	0	3.86	12	0	0	0	12	10	6	5	4	13	.227	L	L	6-1	190	1-14-73	1994	Woolford, Md.
Brown, Kevin	14	9	2.39	32	32	0	0	211	184	67	56	56	185	.235	R	R	6-4	220	3-14-65	1986	Macon, Ga.
Colyer, Steve	0	0	2.75	13	0	0	0	20	22	6	6	9	16	.297	L	L	6-4	205	2-22-79	1998	St. Peters, Mo.
Dreifort, Darren	4	4	4.03	10	10	0	0	60	58	29	27	25	67	.250	R	R	6-2	211	5-3-72	1993	Wichita, Kan.
Gagne, Eric	2	3	1.20	77	0	0	55	82	37	12	11	20	137	.132	R	R	6-2	234	1-7-76	1995	Montreal, Quebec
Ishii, Kasuhisa	9	7	3.86	27	27	0	0	147	129	72	63	101	140	.238	L	L	6-0	215	9-9-73	2002	Tokyo, Japan
Jackson, Edwin	2	1	2.45	4	3	0	0	22	17	6	6	11	19	.220	R	R	6-3	190	9-9-83	2001	Columbus, Ga.
Kida, Masao	0	1	3.00	3	2	0	0	12	15	5	4	3	8	.300	R	R	6-3	210	9-12-68	1998	Tokyo, Japan
Martin, Tom	1	2	3.53	80	0	0	0	51	36	21	20	24	51	.197	L	L	6-1	200	5-21-70	1989	Panama City, Fla.
Mota, Guillermo	6	3	1.97	76	0	0	1	105	78	23	23	26	99	.205	R	R	6-4	210	7-25-73	1991	San Pedro de Macoris, D.R.
Mullen, Scott	0	0	9.00	1	1	0	0	3	2	3	3	5	1	.200	R	L	6-2	190	1-17-75	1996	Beaufort, S.C.
Myers, Rodney	0	0	6.00	4	0	0	0	9	10	7	6	4	5	.270	R	R	6-1	200	6-26-69	1990	Chandler, Ariz.
Nomo, Hideo	16	13	3.09	33	33	2	0	218	175	82	75	98	177	.223	R	R	6-2	235	8-31-68	1995	Tokyo, Japan
Perez, Odalis	12	12	4.52	30	30	0	0	185	191	98	93	46	141	.267	L	L	6-0	222	6-11-77	1994	Las Matas de Farfan, D.R.
Quantrill, Paul	2	5	1.75	89	0	0	1	77	61	18	15	15	44	.226	L	R	6-1	198	11-3-68	1989	Tarpon Springs, Fla.
Shuey, Paul	6	4	3.00	62	0	0	0	69	50	24	23	33	60	.206	R	R	6-2	235	9-16-70	1992	Wake Forest, N.C.

FIELDING

Catcher	PCT	G	PO	A	E	DP	PB
Hundley	.981	10	49	3	1	0	0
LoDuca	.987	123	1014	100	15	14	6
Ross	.986	38	259	26	4	2	2

First Base	PCT	G	PO	A	E	DP
Barnes	1.000	8	43	2	0	4
Cabrera	1.000	8	25	2	0	2
Coomer	1.000	24	106	10	0	10
Kinkade	1.000	13	72	10	0	7
LoDuca	.994	22	158	11	1	14
McGriff	.989	79	667	41	8	66
Ventura	.993	42	252	17	2	26
Ward	.992	13	108	10	1	14

Second Base	PCT	G	PO	A	E	DP
Cabrera	.995	59	93	95	1	24
Cora	.978	141	286	377	15	112
Romano	.000	1	0	0	0	0
Thurston	.857	3	2	4	1	2

Third Base	PCT	G	PO	A	E	DP
Beltre	.957	157	112	309	19	33
Cabrera	1.000	5	1	7	0	2
Coomer	1.000	11	4	10	0	2
Kinkade	.000	2	0	0	1	0
Ventura	.667	3	1	1	1	0

Shortstop	PCT	G	PO	A	E	DP
Beltre	.000	1	0	0	0	0
Cabrera	.900	9	7	11	2	4
Cora	1.000	15	10	18	0	4
Izturis	.977	158	198	481	16	94

Outfield	PCT	G	PO	A	E	DP
Barnes	1.000	2	2	0	0	0
Burnitz	.946	60	84	3	5	0
Cabrera	.967	63	55	3	2	0
Crosby	.667	1	2	0	1	0
Green	.982	157	261	9	5	1
Henderson	.955	18	20	1	1	1
Hermansen	1.000	6	8	0	0	0
Jordan	.990	62	98	2	1	0
Kinkade	.914	36	32	0	3	0
LoDuca	1.000	6	10	1	0	0
Roberts	.976	105	202	4	5	1
Romano	1.000	28	18	0	0	0
Ruan	1.000	20	22	1	0	0
Ward	1.000	11	10	0	0	0

MICHAEL WALBY

Kevin Brown

FARM SYSTEM

Director, Player Development: Bill Bavasi.

Class	Farm Team	League	W	L	Pct.	Finish*	Manager	First Yr.
AAA	Las Vegas (Nev.) 51s	Pacific Coast	76	66	.535	3rd (16)	John Shoemaker	2001
AA	Jacksonville (Fla.) Suns	Southern	66	73	.475	6th (10)	Dino Ebel	2002
High A	Vero Beach (Fla.) Dodgers	Florida State	62	69	.473	10th (12)	Scott Little	1980
Low A	South Georgia (Columbus, Ga.) Waves	South Atlantic	64	72	.471	11th (16)	Dann Bilardello	2002
Rookie	Ogden (Utah) Raptors	Pioneer	35	41	.461	6th (8)	Travis Barbary	2003
Rookie	Vero Beach (Fla.) Dodgers	Gulf Coast	29	31	.483	6th (12)	Luis Salazar	2001

*Finish in overall standings (No. of teams in league)

LAS VEGAS 51s — Class AAA

PACIFIC COAST LEAGUE

BATTING	AVG	G	AB	R	H	2B	3B	HR	RBI	BB	SO	SB	CS	SLG	OBP	B	T	HT	WT	DOB	1st Yr	Resides
Barnes, Larry	.275	82	302	43	83	20	3	15	57	23	61	4	1	.510	.326	L	L	6-1	190	7-23-74	1995	Bakersfield, Calif.
Bell, Rick	.294	91	343	49	101	25	7	5	49	16	44	2	2	.452	.331	R	R	6-2	180	4-5-79	1997	Scottsdale, Ariz.
Brock, Tarrik	.125	15	32	2	4	0	0	0	0	6	10	0	0	.125	.263	L	L	6-3	170	12-25-73	1991	Tarzana, Calif.
Chen, Chin-Feng	.281	133	474	84	133	30	5	26	86	59	106	6	4	.530	.360	R	R	6-1	189	10-28-77	1999	Tainan City, Taiwan
Clapinski, Chris	.317	96	278	43	88	18	5	10	59	25	44	5	2	.525	.377	S	R	6-0	170	8-20-71	1992	Cape Canaveral, Fla.
Crosby, Bubba	.361	76	277	57	100	24	8	12	57	25	47	8	0	.635	.410	L	L	5-11	185	8-11-76	1998	Bellaire, Texas
Dawkins, Gookie	.165	32	115	5	19	5	1	0	12	9	26	3	1	.226	.224	R	R	6-1	180	5-12-79	1997	Chappells, S.C.
Hermansen, Chad	.353	68	235	43	83	15	1	9	31	19	38	4	1	.540	.405	R	R	6-2	190	9-10-77	1995	Las Vegas, Nev.
Hill, Koyie	.314	85	312	48	98	18	0	3	36	15	39	5	0	.401	.345	S	R	6-0	190	3-9-79	2000	Lawton, Okla.
Kellner, Ryan	.209	48	153	9	32	11	0	0	14	8	49	1	0	.281	.262	R	R	6-2	205	12-9-77	1997	Morganton, N.C.
Malloy, Marty	.350	7	20	3	7	2	0	0	2	0	6	0	0	.450	.381	L	R	5-10	160	7-6-72	1992	Trenton, Fla.
Murray, Calvin	.260	102	312	45	81	18	6	3	40	27	50	13	4	.385	.322	R	R	5-11	180	7-30-71	1993	Spring, Texas
Riggs, Eric	.280	125	410	70	115	31	6	8	58	49	73	3	1	.444	.362	S	R	6-2	190	8-19-76	1998	Miami, Fla.
Roberts, Dave	.000	2	5	2	0	0	0	0	0	1	0	0	0	.000	.167	L	L	5-10	180	5-31-72	1994	Oceanside, Calif.
Romano, Jason	.306	57	216	45	66	18	4	4	23	11	32	10	6	.481	.336	R	R	6-0	185	6-24-79	1997	Tampa, Fla.
Ross, David	.221	24	86	12	19	4	0	5	16	11	27	0	2	.442	.313	R	R	6-2	205	3-19-77	1998	Tallahassee, Fla.
Ruan, Wilkin	.308	108	403	58	124	6	3	0	40	10	38	41	7	.337	.334	R	R	6-0	182	9-18-78	1996	Guaymate, D.R.
Theodorou, Nick	.188	23	32	6	6	1	0	0	4	6	11	0	0	.219	.316	S	R	5-11	182	6-7-75	1998	Rialto, Calif.
Thurston, Joe	.290	132	538	77	156	27	6	7	68	31	48	1	12	.401	.345	L	R	5-11	190	9-29-79	1999	Vallejo, Calif.
Victorino, Shane	.390	11	41	6	16	1	2	1	9	1	5	0	1	.585	.395	R	R	5-9	160	11-30-80	1999	Wailuku, Hawaii
Ward, Daryle	.297	34	128	16	38	9	0	4	24	10	22	0	0	.461	.343	L	L	6-2	240	6-27-75	1994	Riverside, Calif.

PITCHING	W	L	ERA	G	GS	CG	SV	IP	H	R	ER	BB	SO	AVG	B	T	HT	WT	DOB	1st Yr	Resides
Alvarez, Victor	4	4	2.70	22	7	0	1	63	53	25	19	15	47	.224	L	L	5-10	155	11-8-76	1997	Culiacan, Mexico
Alvarez, Wilson	5	1	1.34	8	8	0	0	47	36	9	7	6	33	.215	L	L	6-1	250	3-24-70	1987	Bradenton, Fla.
Brohawn, Troy	1	0	4.50	1	0	0	0	4	3	2	2	0	1	.200	L	L	6-1	190	1-14-73	1994	Woolford, Md.
Colyer, Steve	2	3	3.21	44	0	0	23	48	44	18	17	22	50	.243	L	L	6-4	205	2-22-79	1998	St. Peters, Mo.
Corey, Bryan	4	5	2.97	60	0	0	3	91	94	40	30	29	46	.267	R	R	6-0	170	10-21-73	1993	Phoenix, Ariz.
Devey, Phil	0	2	9.82	3	1	0	0	7	9	8	8	6	4	.310	L	L	6-0	170	5-31-77	1999	Lachute, Quebec
Farmer, Tom	2	2	2.54	5	5	0	0	28	30	12	8	9	14	.275	R	R	6-3	185	7-27-79	2001	Miami, Fla.
Gonzalez, Alfredo	1	0	1.13	2	2	0	0	8	6	2	1	3	5	.200	S	R	5-11	165	9-17-79	1997	Nagua, D.R.
Gulin, Lindsay	10	10	4.85	28	27	1	0	154	153	97	83	63	127	.258	L	L	6-3	170	11-22-76	1995	Issaquah, Wash.
Hanrahan, Joel	1	2	10.08	5	5	0	0	25	36	28	28	20	13	.342	R	R	6-3	215	10-6-81	2000	Norwalk, Iowa
Kida, Masao	2	4	5.02	21	12	0	1	84	89	53	47	23	57	.270	R	R	6-3	210	9-12-68	1998	Tokyo, Japan
Langone, Steve	0	0	8.31	6	0	0	0	9	14	11	8	0	9	.358	R	R	6-2	205	1-12-78	2000	Reading, Mass.
Lee, Dave	3	2	3.13	56	0	0	9	60	47	22	21	36	61	.211	R	R	6-1	200	3-12-73	1995	Pittsburgh, Pa.
Lorraine, Andrew	8	9	4.16	30	27	0	0	158	211	86	73	39	77	.319	L	L	6-3	200	8-11-72	1993	Scottsdale, Ariz.
Mallette, Brian	0	0	4.50	1	1	0	0	4	4	2	2	0	1	.266	R	R	6-0	180	1-19-75	1997	Glenwood, Ga.
McKnight, Tony	2	0	3.31	4	3	0	0	16	20	7	6	5	6	.298	L	R	6-5	200	6-29-77	1995	Texarkana, Ark.
Montero, Agustin	2	2	4.97	35	0	0	1	51	57	32	28	31	30	.298	R	R	6-3	212	8-26-77	1995	San Pedro de Macoris, D.R.
Mullen, Scott	4	2	3.95	7	7	0	0	41	50	22	18	14	23	.314	R	L	6-2	190	1-17-75	1996	Beaufort, S.C.
2-team (20 Omaha)	9	5	3.90	27	16	0	1	111	125	57	48	36	73	.294							
Myers, Rodney	9	1	3.30	46	1	0	1	71	66	32	26	22	48	.246	R	R	6-1	200	6-26-69	1990	Chandler, Ariz.
Proctor, Scott	4	2	3.66	24	0	0	1	39	35	17	16	13	35	.246	R	R	6-1	198	1-2-77	1998	Jensen Beach, Fla.
Roberts, Rick	0	0	13.50	2	0	0	0	1	0	2	2	5	2	.000	L	L	6-1	180	5-20-79	1997	Summer Hill, Pa.
Saipe, Mike	6	5	4.99	21	18	0	0	101	123	67	56	35	63	.303	R	R	6-1	190	9-10-73	1994	San Diego, Calif.
Shuey, Paul	0	1	27.00	1	1	0	0	1	2	3	3	1	1	.400	R	R	6-2	235	9-16-70	1992	Wake Forest, N.C.
Simas, Bill	4	0	1.96	26	3	0	0	46	46	12	10	9	25	.267	L	R	6-3	230	11-28-71	1992	Fresno, Calif.
Winchester, Scott	2	9	5.95	19	14	1	0	88	134	63	58	18	38	.362	R	R	6-2	210	4-20-73	1995	Midland, Mich.

FIELDING

Catcher	PCT	G	PO	A	E	DP	PB
Hill	.982	77	448	36	9	1	9
Kellner	.989	45	245	19	3	4	4
Ross	.989	24	160	14	2	2	1

First Base	PCT	G	PO	A	E	DP
Barnes	.989	65	583	39	7	49
Bell	.993	22	141	9	1	19
Brock	.970	10	62	3	2	5
Chen	.954	13	92	11	5	9
Clapinski	1.000	7	56	5	0	7
Hermansen	1.000	1	8	0	0	1
Hill	1.000	1	1	0	0	0
Riggs	.973	3	31	5	1	3
Theodorou	1.000	1	3	2	0	0
Ward	.992	30	220	36	2	29

Second Base	PCT	G	PO	A	E	DP
Clapinski	.833	2	0	5	1	2
Malloy	1.000	1	2	2	0	1
Riggs	1.000	7	22	17	0	5
Romano	.975	9	18	21	1	4
Theodorou	1.000	1	1	2	0	1
Thurston	.980	125	277	360	13	85

Third Base	PCT	G	PO	A	E	DP
Bell	.905	70	44	118	17	8
Clapinski	.938	4	3	12	1	0
Malloy	1.000	1	1	4	0	1
Riggs	.925	66	42	131	14	12
Romano	.944	8	8	9	1	2
Theodorou	1.000	4	2	3	0	1

Shortstop	PCT	G	PO	A	E	DP
Clapinski	.974	62	94	171	7	36
Dawkins	.928	32	43	85	10	15
Malloy	.833	2	1	4	1	3
Riggs	.942	48	62	116	11	27
Romano	1.000	2	4	5	0	0
Thurston	.929	6	8	18	2	4

Outfield	PCT	G	PO	A	E	DP
Barnes	.973	15	36	0	1	0
Brock	1.000	1	1	0	0	0
Chen	.969	104	179	8	6	0
Crosby	.991	57	108	7	1	1
Hermansen	.988	41	80	1	1	0
Murray	.995	82	201	7	1	2
Roberts	.000	2	0	0	0	0
Romano	.981	39	101	3	2	0
Ruan	.992	104	242	11	2	2
Theodorou	1.000	5	5	0	0	0
Victorino	.966	10	28	0	1	0

JACKSONVILLE SUNS — Class AA

SOUTHERN LEAGUE

BATTING	AVG	G	AB	R	H	2B	3B	HR	RBI	BB	SO	SB	CS	SLG	OBP	B	T	HT	WT	DOB	1st Yr	Resides
Abercrombie, Reggie	.261	116	448	59	117	25	7	15	54	16	164	28	9	.449	.298	R	R	6-3	210	7-15-80	2000	Columbus, Ga.
Alvarez, Nick	.274	101	292	39	80	16	2	5	46	21	47	19	10	.394	.325	R	R	6-3	205	2-8-77	2000	Miami, Fla.
Bellorin, Edwin	.193	17	57	2	11	2	1	0	3	2	13	0	0	.263	.220	R	R	5-11	170	2-21-82	1998	Edo Bolivar, Venez.
Brock, Tarrik	.272	98	305	52	83	23	6	11	57	56	96	4	7	.495	.386	L	L	6-3	170	12-25-73	1991	Tarzana, Calif.
Collins, Mike	.237	83	279	19	66	5	0	0	24	16	28	1	4	.254	.278	R	R	5-9	166	1-29-77	1998	Phoenix, Ariz.
Dawkins, Gookie	.265	35	113	12	30	6	0	4	20	10	12	3	2	.425	.333	R	R	6-1	180	5-12-79	1997	Chappells, S.C.
Detienne, Dave	.191	32	94	14	18	6	0	0	3	8	29	3	1	.255	.260	R	R	6-3	190	8-16-79	1997	Dartmouth, N.S.
Diaz, Victor	.291	85	316	42	92	20	2	10	55	27	60	8	10	.462	.353	R	R	6-0	200	12-10-81	2001	Chicago, Ill.
Duplissea, Bill	.071	7	14	0	1	0	0	0	2	5	5	0	1	.071	.316	R	R	6-0	200	9-27-77	1999	San Carlos, Calif.
Feliciano, Jesus	.148	37	81	7	12	0	0	1	4	11	16	2	3	.185	.255	L	L	5-11	150	6-6-79	1997	Bayamon, P.R.
Gutierrez, Franklin	.313	18	67	12	21	3	2	4	12	7	20	3	3	.597	.387	R	R	6-2	175	2-21-83	2001	Caracas, Venez.
Hill, Koyie	.228	25	101	9	23	7	0	0	7	6	19	2	1	.297	.271	S	R	6-0	190	3-9-79	2000	Lawton, Okla.
King, Brennan	.242	124	434	47	105	15	1	9	43	44	92	0	3	.343	.315	R	R	6-3	180	1-20-81	1999	Murfreesboro, Tenn.
Matthews, Lamont	.200	12	30	2	6	2	1	0	3	4	12	0	0	.333	.314	L	L	6-2	210	6-15-78	1999	Petersburg, Va.
Michaelis, Derek	.267	120	378	56	101	28	2	13	50	51	123	9	0	.455	.358	L	L	6-7	230	12-2-78	2000	Waco, Texas
Repko, Jason	.240	119	416	62	100	14	5	10	23	42	89	21	8	.370	.317	R	R	5-11	175	12-27-80	1999	West Richland, Wash.
Rodriguez, Victor	.253	45	154	12	39	8	0	3	17	6	19	1	1	.364	.284	R	R	6-2	190	10-25-76	1994	Aguirre, P.R.
Rogers, Brandon	.400	6	10	2	4	1	0	1	1	4	3	0	0	.800	.571	R	R	6-0	200	3-1-78	2000	El Cajon, Calif.
Socarras, Tony	.203	66	182	22	37	8	2	5	31	18	50	1	0	.352	.290	L	R	6-0	200	11-8-78	2000	Miami, Fla.
Theodorou, Nick	.294	36	119	18	35	7	0	0	7	22	19	1	2	.353	.414	S	R	5-11	182	6-7-75	1998	Rialto, Calif.
Van Buizen, Rodney	.217	20	46	3	10	0	0	0	2	5	11	1	0	.217	.308	R	R	6-0	190	9-25-80	1998	Sydney, Australia
Victorino, Shane	.282	66	266	37	75	9	4	2	15	21	41	16	7	.368	.340	R	R	5-9	160	11-30-80	1999	Wailuku, Hawaii
Ward, Daryle	.125	4	16	0	2	0	0	0	1	0	3	0	0	.125	.125	L	L	6-2	240	6-27-75	1994	Riverside, Calif.
Waszgis, B.J.	.181	40	116	7	21	3	0	1	9	27	35	1	1	.233	.336	R	R	6-2	210	8-24-70	1991	Camilla, Ga.

PITCHING	W	L	ERA	G	GS	CG	SV	IP	H	R	ER	BB	SO	AVG	B	T	HT	WT	DOB	1st Yr	Resides
Bauer, Greg	6	6	2.93	46	3	0	2	86	92	34	28	41	61	.280	R	R	6-1	195	11-30-77	2000	Tulsa, Okla.
Brown, Andrew	0	0	0.00	1	1	0	0	1	0	0	0	0	1	.000	R	R	6-6	230	2-17-81	1999	Deltona, Fla.
Diaz, Joselo	1	0	0.00	5	0	0	0	8	5	1	0	3	7	.185	R	R	6-0	225	4-13-80	1996	San Pedro de Macoris, D.R.
Farmer, Tom	5	8	3.45	20	19	0	0	117	116	51	45	26	69	.260	R	R	6-3	185	7-27-79	2001	Miami, Fla.
Frasor, Jason	1	0	2.95	35	0	0	17	37	33	14	12	14	50	.240	R	R	5-10	170	8-9-77	1999	Oak Forest, Ill.
Gonzalez, Alfredo	4	4	5.47	10	10	0	0	49	65	33	30	17	37	.315	S	R	5-11	165	9-17-79	1997	Nagua, D.R.
Hanrahan, Joel	10	4	2.43	23	23	1	0	133	117	44	36	53	130	.238	R	R	6-3	215	10-6-81	2000	Norwalk, Iowa
Jackson, Edwin	7	7	3.70	27	27	0	0	148	121	68	61	53	157	.219	R	R	6-3	190	9-9-83	2001	Columbus, Ga.
Langone, Steve	3	0	1.98	22	0	0	1	50	38	15	11	12	51	.207	R	R	6-2	205	1-12-78	2000	Reading, Mass.
McCrotty, Will	3	5	4.06	32	11	0	1	93	88	52	42	41	67	.249	R	R	6-2	195	6-23-79	1997	Russellville, Ark.
Miller, Greg	1	1	1.01	4	4	0	0	27	15	5	3	7	40	.156	L	L	6-5	190	11-3-84	2002	Yorba Linda, Calif.
Minor, Ryan	1	2	5.19	15	0	0	0	17	21	12	10	4	9	.313	R	R	6-7	240	1-5-74	1996	Edmond, Okla.
Montero, Agustin	2	1	3.04	16	0	0	0	27	24	10	9	13	22	.247	R	R	6-3	212	8-26-77	1995	San Pedro de Macoris, D.R.
Nina, Elvin	1	0	2.77	8	1	0	0	13	7	4	4	10	10	.166	R	R	6-0	180	11-25-75	1997	Tempe, Ariz.
Pilkington, Brian	3	0	3.34	5	5	0	0	32	31	13	12	2	24	.250	R	R	6-5	210	9-17-82	2001	Garden Grove, Calif.
Pineda, Luis	1	1	4.09	9	0	0	0	11	13	5	5	6	11	.317	R	R	6-1	170	10-17-74	1995	San Cristobal, D.R.
Proctor, Scott	1	2	1.00	17	0	0	0	27	20	6	3	7	24	.208	R	R	6-1	198	1-2-77	1998	Jensen Beach, Fla.
Reina, Dimas	0	0	9.64	4	0	0	0	5	9	10	5	6	4	.391	R	R	6-0	170	2-23-82	1998	Caracas, Venez.
Rodriguez, Orlando	1	2	3.75	11	0	0	0	12	10	5	5	7	14	.232	L	L	5-10	155	11-28-80	2000	Santiago, D.R.
Ruhl, Nathan	0	1	4.00	5	0	0	0	9	9	4	4	6	7	.281	R	R	6-4	230	7-16-76	1996	Lee's Summit, Mo.
Steffek, Brian	1	5	7.92	24	0	0	1	31	41	28	27	23	31	.325	R	R	6-2	195	3-2-78	2000	Stafford, Texas
Stults, Eric	3	4	4.97	9	7	0	1	38	46	23	21	13	14	.304	L	L	6-3	215	12-9-79	2002	Mishawaka, Ind.
Totten, Heath	11	12	3.42	28	28	2	0	181	196	83	69	17	114	.273	R	R	6-3	210	9-30-78	2000	Lumberton, Texas
Urdaneta, Lino	0	8	4.29	44	0	0	6	65	68	37	31	24	42	.279	R	R	6-1	168	11-20-79	1996	Guarenas, Venez.

FIELDING

Catcher	PCT	G	PO	A	E	DP	PB
Bellorin	.981	17	137	19	3	5	0
Duplissea	.977	7	33	9	1	0	2
Hill	.989	24	170	17	2	5	3
Rogers	.957	4	22	0	1	0	0
Socarras	.994	60	422	37	3	3	4
Waszgis	1.000	37	241	18	0	1	9

First Base	PCT	G	PO	A	E	DP
Alvarez	1.000	30	232	31	0	24
Brock	1.000	9	64	9	0	4
Michaelis	.982	106	789	64	16	80
Ward	1.000	2	13	4	0	1

Second Base	PCT	G	PO	A	E	DP
Collins	.975	27	55	63	3	16
Diaz	.962	77	145	207	14	51
Rodriguez	.989	22	38	50	1	13
Theodorou	1.000	7	15	18	0	5
Van Buizen	.949	11	18	19	2	6

Third Base	PCT	G	PO	A	E	DP
Collins	.871	11	8	19	4	1
Detienne	.941	7	5	11	1	1
King	.924	120	67	223	24	27
Van Buizen	.846	4	3	8	2	0

Shortstop	PCT	G	PO	A	E	DP
Collins	.969	38	50	104	5	18
Dawkins	.953	34	54	89	7	23
Detienne	.941	20	26	54	5	13
Rodriguez	1.000	23	23	75	0	14
Theodorou	.950	29	33	62	5	13

Outfield	PCT	G	PO	A	E	DP
Abercrombie	.939	115	256	7	17	1
Alvarez	.962	29	47	3	2	1
Brock	.976	60	119	4	3	1
Feliciano	1.000	19	28	2	0	0
Gutierrez	1.000	18	31	1	0	0
Matthews	.944	10	17	0	1	0
Minor	.000	1	0	0	0	0
Repko	.980	109	229	12	5	3
Victorino	.978	65	172	7	4	3
Ward	.667	2	2	0	1	0

VERO BEACH DODGERS — High Class A

FLORIDA STATE LEAGUE

BATTING	AVG	G	AB	R	H	2B	3B	HR	RBI	BB	SO	SB	CS	SLG	OBP	B	T	HT	WT	DOB	1st Yr	Resides
Abreu, Etanislao	.000	3	10	0	0	0	0	0	0	1	2	0	0	.000	.091	R	R	5-11	160	11-13-84	2003	Puerto Plata, D.R.
Aybar, Willy	.274	119	445	47	122	29	3	11	74	41	70	9	9	.427	.336	S	R	6-0	175	3-9-83	2000	Bani, D.R.

BATTING	AVG	G	AB	R	H	2B	3B	HR	RBI	BB	SO	SB	CS	SLG	OBP	B	T	HT	WT	DOB	1st Yr	Resides
Bellorin, Edwin	.245	67	233	19	57	9	0	3	28	10	32	0	2	.322	.287	R	R	5-11	170	2-21-82	1998	Edo Bolivar, Venez.
Cabrera, Ruben	.200	6	15	0	3	0	0	0	1	0	4	0	0	.200	.200	R	R	5-10	170	7-7-81	2000	Edo Bolivar, Venez.
Castro, Nelson	.141	25	85	14	12	4	0	3	8	2	23	1	0	.294	.189	S	R	5-10	200	6-4-76	1994	Monte Cristi, D.R.
Comfort, Geoff	.235	4	17	2	4	2	0	0	0	1	5	0	1	.353	.278	R	R	6-0	210	3-27-80	2002	Burlingame, Calif.
Coomer, Ron	.500	3	10	1	5	1	0	0	2	0	1	0	0	.600	.455	R	R	6-0	210	11-18-66	1987	Chicago, Ill.
Detienne, Dave	.264	30	106	14	28	4	1	0	8	10	24	5	3	.321	.333	R	R	6-3	190	8-16-79	1997	Dartmouth, N.S.
Ferrer, Simon	.204	20	49	4	10	2	1	0	4	5	14	1	3	.286	.304	R	R	5-10	175	6-24-80	2002	Santa Ynez, Calif.
Garcia, Sergio	.218	64	188	27	41	6	0	1	19	24	25	8	3	.266	.320	R	R	5-9	175	3-29-80	2002	Paramount, Calif.
Gillitzer, Scott	.230	107	379	41	87	16	0	5	42	22	41	9	6	.311	.282	R	R	6-1	185	6-11-79	2001	Prairie du Chien, Wisc.
Gutierrez, Franklin	.282	110	425	65	120	28	5	20	68	39	111	17	5	.513	.345	R	R	6-2	175	2-21-83	2001	Caracas, Venez.
Guzman, Joel	.246	62	240	30	59	13	1	5	24	11	60	0	4	.371	.279	R	R	6-4	198	11-24-84	2001	San Pedro de Macoris, D.R.
Hermansen, Chad	.238	17	63	12	15	4	0	1	7	6	7	0	1	.349	.296	R	R	6-2	190	9-10-77	1995	Las Vegas, Nev.
Herrera, Christian	.206	40	126	12	26	3	0	0	9	12	18	0	4	.230	.275	R	R	5-11	169	4-9-82	2001	Aguascalientes, Mexico
Hoorelbeke, Jesse	.280	57	200	27	56	6	0	10	29	11	43	1	3	.460	.327	R	R	6-3	225	10-13-77	2002	Hansen, Idaho
Hundley, Todd	.083	7	24	2	2	0	0	0	1	3	5	0	0	.083	.214	S	R	5-11	200	5-27-69	1987	Port St. Lucie, Fla.
Langill, Eric	.246	27	69	5	17	2	0	0	9	1	11	0	1	.275	.288	R	R	5-9	190	4-4-79	2000	Kirkland, Quebec
Langs, Ronte	.217	60	203	35	44	8	1	2	21	35	58	5	3	.296	.348	R	R	5-10	200	1-29-79	2000	Southaven, Tenn.
Loney, James	.276	125	468	64	129	31	3	7	46	43	80	9	4	.400	.337	L	L	6-3	200	5-7-84	2002	Missouri City, Texas
McGriff, Fred	.167	2	6	0	1	0	0	0	0	1	2	0	0	.167	.286	L	L	6-3	225	10-31-63	1981	Tampa, Fla.
Pierce, Sean	.250	22	60	9	15	2	0	0	4	16	18	2	2	.283	.430	R	R	5-9	190	11-26-78	2001	Covina, Calif.
Price, Jared	.181	32	105	21	19	4	0	5	13	8	38	3	0	.362	.259	R	R	6-1	190	3-18-82	2000	Rupert, Idaho
Rogers, Brandon	.241	20	54	4	13	3	0	0	1	5	11	1	1	.296	.305	R	R	6-0	200	3-1-78	2000	El Cajon, Calif.
Rohan, Jimmy	.250	7	24	3	6	1	0	0	0	0	0	0	0	.292	.250	R	R	6-1	190	5-13-84	2002	Valencia, Calif.
Story-Harden, Thomari	.255	51	165	21	42	10	0	5	14	15	47	2	3	.406	.346	R	R	6-5	204	4-6-80	1998	Reno, Nev.
Thomas, Charles	.237	108	338	53	80	19	0	4	37	61	84	30	15	.328	.359	R	R	6-0	200	6-10-80	1998	Fresno, Calif.
Van Buizen, Rodney	.326	52	187	19	61	6	0	0	29	12	24	6	6	.358	.376	R	R	6-0	190	9-25-80	1998	Sydney, Australia

PITCHING	W	L	ERA	G	GS	CG	SV	IP	H	R	ER	BB	SO	AVG	B	T	HT	WT	DOB	1st Yr	Resides
Campbell, Dayle	0	0	0.00	1	0	0	0	1	0	0	0	1	0	.000	R	R	6-7	200	9-30-78	1999	Carson, Calif.
Diaz, Joselo	5	2	3.50	15	11	0	1	62	39	25	24	48	69	.180	R	R	6-0	225	4-13-80	1996	San Pedro de Macoris, D.R.
Dougherty, Kevin	0	0	3.52	7	0	0	0	8	13	5	3	7	5	.361	L	L	6-5	200	3-4-78	1997	Voorhees, N.J.
Frasor, Jason	1	0	1.85	15	0	0	6	24	16	7	5	4	36	.181	R	R	5-10	170	8-9-77	1999	Oak Forest, Ill.
Gonzalez, Luis	2	3	1.48	21	0	0	3	30	25	6	5	11	19	.231	L	L	6-0	190	2-27-83	2001	Carolina, P.R.
Hamilton, Jamaal	0	0	0.00	4	0	0	0	9	3	0	0	2	7	.107	L	L	6-3	220	9-13-83	2002	Lubbock, Texas
Hee, Aaron	0	0	4.91	9	0	0	0	11	8	6	6	18	7	.205	L	L	6-0	190	3-4-79	1998	Las Vegas, Nev.
Hosford, Clint	1	5	5.48	8	8	0	0	43	57	31	26	12	30	.314	R	R	6-2	185	8-8-80	1998	Vancouver, B.C.
Hull, Eric	3	5	2.68	31	14	1	1	111	82	37	33	40	105	.211	R	R	5-11	185	12-3-79	2002	Selah, Wash.
Keirstead, Mike	4	5	3.84	10	10	1	0	59	53	29	25	18	34	.236	R	R	6-3	210	1-26-81	2000	Musquash, N.B.
Kennedy, Casey	0	3	6.18	8	5	0	0	28	31	23	19	10	8	.281	R	R	6-1	195	10-29-78	2000	Fort Lauderdale, Fla.
Lopez, Arturo	1	1	4.32	11	0	0	0	17	11	8	8	3	16	.189	L	L	5-10	165	2-22-83	2001	Culiacan, Mexico
McCracken, Vance	0	1	6.75	8	0	0	0	16	15	17	12	7	11	.241	R	R	6-7	220	4-16-79	2001	St. Albans, W.Va.
McCrotty, Will	1	1	3.98	4	4	0	0	20	19	10	9	11	13	.263	R	R	6-2	195	6-23-79	1997	Russellville, Ark.
Miller, Greg	11	4	2.49	21	21	1	0	116	103	40	32	41	111	.239	L	L	6-5	190	11-3-84	2002	Yorba Linda, Calif.
Minor, Ryan	0	0	1.59	6	0	0	0	6	7	3	1	0	2	.304	R	R	6-7	240	1-5-74	1996	Edmond, Okla.
Nall, T.J.	6	7	3.42	29	16	2	1	116	118	56	44	23	73	.257	R	R	6-1	175	11-4-80	1999	Schaumburg, Ill.
Nelson, Steve	0	2	2.08	4	3	1	0	17	12	4	4	5	20	.196	L	R	6-3	200	11-10-82	2001	Dartmouth, N.S.
Nina, Elvin	0	0	3.60	4	0	0	0	5	6	5	2	1	7	.285	R	R	6-0	180	11-25-75	1997	Tempe, Ariz.
O'Flaherty, Liam	0	1	0.00	1	0	0	0	1	0	1	0	2	0	.000	R	L	6-0	165	1-18-85	2002	Castle Hill, Australia
Obispo, Jose	0	0	2.40	4	4	0	0	15	7	4	4	20	17	.137	R	R	6-1	160	5-11-84	2002	Sabana De La Mar, D.R.
Ojeda, Alvis	0	1	12.00	1	1	0	0	3	5	4	4	4	1	.384	R	R	6-0	170	9-23-83	2002	Maracaibo, Venez.
Osoria, Franquelis	3	6	3.00	33	3	0	6	75	69	34	25	19	53	.243	R	R	6-0	165	9-12-81	2000	Santiago, D.R.
Pilkington, Brian	10	6	3.88	21	21	1	0	125	136	55	54	16	74	.275	R	R	6-5	210	9-17-82	2001	Garden Grove, Calif.
Reina, Dimas	1	0	6.88	15	0	0	0	17	23	13	13	9	16	.315	R	R	6-0	170	2-23-82	1998	Caracas, Venez.
Rodriguez, Osvaldo	0	1	4.50	1	1	0	0	4	3	2	2	3	3	.230	R	R	5-10	168	6-10-84	2002	Hatillo Palma, D.R.
Rojas, Jose	3	4	5.00	14	6	0	0	36	34	23	20	27	29	.255	R	R	5-10	150	3-20-82	1999	San Pedro de Macoris, D.R.
Santiago, Victor	2	2	6.56	10	2	0	1	23	28	23	17	17	15	.291	R	R	5-11	178	8-10-81	1998	Santiago, D.R.
Silva, Efrain	0	1	2.54	16	0	0	0	28	19	8	8	17	37	.190	R	R	6-7	240	7-25-78	2002	Elk Grove, Calif.
Steffek, Brian	0	1	0.99	23	0	0	10	27	16	6	3	13	32	.170	R	R	6-2	195	3-2-78	2000	Stafford, Texas
Stewart, James	0	0	11.57	4	0	0	0	5	7	6	6	2	2	.368	R	R	6-2	190	5-9-82	2001	Vail, Ariz.
Strayhorn, Kole	5	2	2.93	30	0	0	7	46	42	17	15	13	44	.235	R	R	6-0	185	10-1-82	2001	Shawnee, Okla.
Stults, Eric	0	1	6.00	1	1	0	0	3	6	2	2	1	1	.500	L	L	6-3	215	12-9-79	2002	Mishawaka, Ind.
Tequida, Mauricio	0	0	0.00	3	0	0	0	9	4	0	0	3	3	.129	R	R	6-1	180	2-5-82	2003	Obregon, Mexico
Williams, Ryan	3	4	4.03	19	0	0	1	29	32	20	13	15	18	.280	R	R	6-4	210	11-10-80	2002	Virginia Beach, Va.

FIELDING

Catcher	PCT	G	PO	A	E	DP	PB
Bellorin	.980	61	430	48	10	6	4
Cabrera	.917	6	28	5	3	0	3
Hundley	1.000	2	8	0	0	0	0
Langill	.986	24	125	14	2	3	1
Price	.988	32	237	17	3	1	3
Rogers	.991	18	100	14	1	2	3

First Base	PCT	G	PO	A	E	DP
Coomer	1.000	2	19	0	0	4
Gillitzer	1.000	4	12	2	0	2
Hoorelbeke	.979	11	88	4	2	2
Loney	.994	110	871	89	6	80
McGriff	1.000	1	1	1	0	0
Story-Harden	1.000	10	90	5	0	10

Second Base	PCT	G	PO	A	E	DP
Abreu	1.000	3	2	5	0	0
Aybar	1.000	1	4	7	0	2
Castro	.966	13	19	38	2	6
Detienne	1.000	3	8	4	0	3
Ferrer	.974	17	27	48	2	5
Garcia	.963	45	83	124	8	24
Gillitzer	.975	57	108	122	6	35
Van Buizen	.957	12	20	24	2	7

Third Base	PCT	G	PO	A	E	DP
Aybar	.944	110	87	199	17	29
Coomer	1.000	1	1	1	0	0
Detienne	1.000	6	3	8	0	0
Ferrer	.500	2	1	0	1	0
Gillitzer	.824	9	6	8	3	0
Hoorelbeke	.900	3	0	9	1	2
Rohan	.933	5	3	11	1	1
Van Buizen	.875	2	1	6	1	1

Shortstop	PCT	G	PO	A	E	DP
Aybar	1.000	1	1	3	0	0
Castro	1.000	3	8	4	0	1
Detienne	.875	15	14	35	7	8
Ferrer	.000	1	0	0	0	0
Garcia	.947	17	24	47	4	5
Guzman	.921	60	77	155	20	34
Herrera	.926	40	72	102	14	22

Outfield	PCT	G	PO	A	E	DP
Castro	1.000	11	12	1	0	0
Comfort	1.000	2	2	0	0	0
Detienne	.900	5	9	0	1	0
Ferrer	1.000	1	2	1	0	0
Garcia	1.000	4	5	0	0	0
Gillitzer	1.000	50	68	5	0	2
Gutierrez	.984	106	240	4	4	1
Hermansen	.952	13	19	1	1	0
Hoorelbeke	1.000	4	4	0	0	0
Langs	.992	55	117	2	1	1
Loney	.833	2	5	0	1	0
Pierce	.950	22	37	1	2	0
Rogers	1.000	1	4	0	0	0
Rohan	.750	3	3	0	1	0
Thomas	.957	100	174	4	8	0
Van Buizen	.985	40	64	1	1	0

SOUTH GEORGIA WAVES — Low Class A

SOUTH ATLANTIC LEAGUE

BATTING	AVG	G	AB	R	H	2B	3B	HR	RBI	BB	SO	SB	CS	SLG	OBP	B	T	HT	WT	DOB	1st Yr	Resides
Bagley, David	.265	60	204	33	54	8	0	3	19	28	44	3	1	.348	.379	R	R	6-2	200	12-26-80	2002	Poway, Calif.
Bok, Matt	.195	31	77	11	15	3	1	1	8	11	23	1	2	.299	.337	L	R	5-11	200	10-5-79	2002	Akron, Ohio
Denker, Travis	.227	8	22	2	5	2	0	0	1	2	6	0	1	.318	.292	R	R	5-9	170	8-5-85	2003	Brea, Calif.
Ellis, A.J.	.000	3	6	0	0	0	0	0	0	0	0	0	1	.000	.143	R	R	6-3	240	4-9-81	2003	Lexington, Ky.
Ezi, Travis	.259	120	451	51	117	10	4	7	42	33	136	33	14	.346	.314	S	L	6-0	175	9-5-81	2000	Baltimore, Md.
Garcia, Sergio	.260	49	177	23	46	4	1	1	18	26	20	10	9	.311	.374	R	R	5-9	175	3-29-80	2002	Paramount, Calif.
Goelz, Bryan	.272	110	367	54	100	14	2	2	42	47	61	14	9	.338	.360	L	L	6-1	180	4-10-80	2002	St. James, N.Y.
Guzman, Joel	.235	58	217	33	51	13	0	8	29	9	62	4	4	.406	.263	R	R	6-4	198	11-24-84	2001	San Pedro de Macoris, D.R.
Herrera, Christian	.155	17	58	8	9	1	0	0	2	4	8	2	0	.172	.246	R	R	5-11	169	4-9-82	2001	Aguascalientes, Mexico
Hoorelbeke, Jesse	.326	52	190	35	62	11	0	12	39	22	44	4	1	.574	.403	R	R	6-3	225	10-13-77	2002	Hansen, Idaho
Martin, Russell	.286	25	98	15	28	4	1	3	14	9	11	5	2	.439	.343	R	R	5-11	202	2-15-83	2002	Chelsea, Quebec
Montague, Ed	.231	113	377	52	87	19	2	5	48	26	75	5	9	.332	.290	L	R	6-0	195	3-23-80	2002	San Mateo, Calif.
Nixon, Mike	.274	102	390	58	107	20	1	1	38	33	76	13	5	.338	.334	R	R	6-3	210	8-17-83	2002	Phoenix, Ariz.
Owen, Ryan	.246	24	65	9	16	3	0	1	8	5	19	2	1	.338	.338	R	R	6-0	200	9-15-80	2002	Wichita, Kan.
Perozo, Hector	.235	108	353	43	83	15	1	6	49	31	109	10	6	.334	.306	R	R	6-2	190	9-20-83	2000	Caracas, Venez.
Pierce, Sean	.242	33	124	15	30	6	3	0	12	26	25	11	3	.339	.377	R	R	5-9	190	11-26-78	2001	Covina, Calif.
Rogers, Brandon	.260	15	50	5	13	1	0	2	6	2	12	0	2	.400	.302	R	R	6-0	200	3-1-78	2000	El Cajon, Calif.
Story-Harden, Thomari	.200	51	165	23	33	9	1	4	22	24	55	2	1	.339	.316	R	R	6-5	204	4-6-80	1998	Reno, Nev.
Testa, Chris	.276	113	387	56	107	22	4	11	69	29	72	4	3	.439	.334	L	L	6-2	180	5-23-81	1999	Palmdale, Calif.
Wayne, Brett	.268	88	272	30	73	8	1	2	29	14	58	8	4	.327	.307	R	R	6-0	175	4-28-80	2002	Simi Valley, Calif.
Young, Delwyn	.323	119	443	67	143	38	7	15	73	36	87	5	2	.542	.381	S	R	5-10	180	6-30-82	2002	Santa Barbara, Calif.

PITCHING	W	L	ERA	G	GS	CG	SV	IP	H	R	ER	BB	SO	AVG	B	T	HT	WT	DOB	1st Yr	Resides
Alvarez, Gabriel	0	1	8.31	8	0	0	2	9	12	8	8	6	12	.315	R	R	5-11	178	8-10-84	2002	Guadalupe, Mexico
Broxton, Jonathan	4	2	3.13	9	8	0	0	37	27	15	13	22	30	.207	R	R	6-4	240	6-16-84	2002	Waynesboro, Ga.
Campbell, Dayle	3	0	3.98	21	0	0	8	43	40	22	19	13	36	.243	R	R	6-7	200	9-30-78	1999	Carson, Calif.
Cuen, David	2	2	4.11	9	7	0	0	35	38	22	16	18	23	.277	L	L	6-4	180	8-4-83	2001	Somerton, Ariz.
De los Santos, Omar	1	2	6.16	22	1	0	1	50	40	37	34	32	39	.223	R	R	6-0	162	8-13-81	1998	San Pedro de Macoris, D.R.
Diaz, Jose	0	1	7.04	5	5	0	0	15	21	14	12	6	8	.313	R	R	6-4	230	2-27-84	2001	La Romana, D.R.
Figueroa, Jonathan	1	8	4.94	17	17	0	0	78	79	60	43	42	74	.264	L	L	6-5	205	9-15-83	2002	Acarigua, Venez.
Gonzalez, Luis	2	2	3.30	19	0	0	3	30	25	13	11	11	31	.221	L	L	6-0	190	2-27-83	2001	Carolina, P.R.
Hamilton, Jamaal	4	4	3.82	14	14	0	0	73	84	37	31	11	46	.285	L	L	6-3	220	9-13-83	2002	Lubbock, Texas
Hammes, Zach	7	11	5.54	25	24	0	0	117	138	91	72	65	75	.294	R	R	6-6	225	5-15-84	2002	Iowa City, Iowa
Hawley, Ross	0	1	23.14	3	0	0	0	2	6	8	6	4	3	.461	R	R	6-0	180	12-14-79	2002	Wentworth, S.D.
Hosford, Clint	1	3	5.56	4	4	0	0	23	21	16	14	9	10	.241	R	R	6-2	185	8-8-80	1998	Vancouver, B.C.
Kennedy, Casey	5	1	2.11	23	2	0	2	60	58	17	14	15	26	.255	R	R	6-1	195	10-29-78	2000	Fort Lauderdale, Fla.
LaSalle, Julio	2	4	6.34	34	1	0	1	61	71	51	43	36	66	.285	R	R	6-3	215	9-14-81	2002	Brooklyn, N.Y.
Lopez, Arturo	1	4	8.68	20	4	0	0	37	48	40	36	15	27	.305	L	L	5-10	165	2-22-83	2001	Culiacan, Mexico
McCracken, Vance	1	2	3.28	21	0	0	0	47	56	22	17	19	31	.296	R	R	6-7	220	4-16-79	2001	St. Albans, W.Va.
Nelson, Steve	4	8	4.33	22	15	0	0	87	85	56	42	45	58	.250	L	R	6-3	200	11-10-82	2001	Dartmouth, N.S.
Neuage, Leigh	1	5	6.69	9	9	0	0	35	44	27	26	14	37	.303	R	R	6-4	210	7-6-83	2001	Adelaide, Australia
Plummer, Jarod	1	2	4.34	9	0	0	2	19	12	10	9	10	21	.187	R	R	6-5	200	1-27-84	2002	Garland, Texas
Reina, Dimas	8	0	3.02	23	0	0	4	51	37	19	17	22	42	.206	R	R	6-0	170	2-23-82	1998	Caracas, Venez.
Rodriguez, Mike	1	4	10.61	9	5	0	0	19	23	26	22	25	19	.302	R	R	6-1	180	8-31-82	2002	Roseville, Calif.
Rodriguez, Osvaldo	3	0	1.80	10	7	0	0	40	30	9	8	23	30	.217	R	R	5-10	168	6-10-84	2002	Hatillo Palma, D.R.
Santiago, Victor	4	0	3.35	23	2	0	3	51	45	22	19	14	52	.240	R	R	5-11	178	8-10-81	1998	Santiago, D.R.
Silva, Efrain	1	0	2.31	7	0	0	0	12	9	4	3	7	13	.204	R	R	6-7	240	7-25-78	2002	Elk Grove, Calif.
Testa, Chris	0	0	0.53	14	0	0	2	17	9	1	1	11	19	.000	L	L	6-2	180	5-23-81	1999	Palmdale, Calif.
Warriax, Brandon	6	5	5.13	30	11	0	0	100	124	70	57	31	53	.300	R	R	6-0	160	6-23-79	1997	Maxton, N.C.
Wayne, Brett	1	0	10.80	5	0	0	0	3	5	4	4	5	3	.000	R	R	6-0	175	4-28-80	2002	Simi Valley, Calif.
Williams, Ryan	0	0	3.09	11	0	0	5	12	7	4	4	5	11	.170	R	R	6-4	210	11-10-80	2002	Virginia Beach, Va.

FIELDING

Catcher	PCT	G	PO	A	E	DP	PB
Bok	1.000	1	2	0	0	0	0
Ellis	.929	2	12	1	1	1	0
Martin	.964	14	101	7	4	0	4
Nixon	.994	89	607	49	4	4	14
Owen	.994	23	139	15	1	0	6
Rogers	.974	12	68	8	2	1	3

First Base	PCT	G	PO	A	E	DP
Bagley	1.000	1	1	0	0	0
Bok	.983	8	54	5	1	9
Ellis	1.000	1	1	1	0	0
Hoorelbeke	.991	46	412	20	4	33
Nixon	1.000	2	1	0	0	0
Story-Harden	.982	51	404	29	8	27
Testa	.988	41	314	25	4	33

Second Base	PCT	G	PO	A	E	DP
Denker	.947	5	8	10	1	5
Pierce	.000	1	0	0	0	0
Wayne	.941	29	39	56	6	5
Young	.942	110	206	315	32	54

Third Base	PCT	G	PO	A	E	DP
Denker	1.000	2	1	2	0	0
Guzman	1.000	1	1	3	0	0
Martin	.500	1	1	0	1	0
Montague	.000	1	0	0	0	0
Perozo	.910	103	70	184	25	15
Wayne	.910	32	14	57	7	7

Shortstop	PCT	G	PO	A	E	DP
Garcia	.923	48	69	135	17	25
Guzman	.928	57	75	170	19	27
Herrera	.944	17	25	43	4	6
Perozo	1.000	2	3	4	0	1
Wayne	.953	16	17	44	3	6

Outfield	PCT	G	PO	A	E	DP
Bok	.950	18	18	1	1	0
Ezi	.966	118	304	9	11	3
Goelz	.985	106	186	11	3	1
Martin	1.000	2	0	1	0	0
Montague	.930	91	140	7	11	4
Nixon	1.000	8	2	0	0	0
Pierce	.974	29	33	4	1	0
Testa	.955	56	80	5	4	0
Wayne	1.000	10	8	0	0	0

OGDEN RAPTORS — Rookie

PIONEER LEAGUE

BATTING	AVG	G	AB	R	H	2B	3B	HR	RBI	BB	SO	SB	CS	SLG	OBP	B	T	HT	WT	DOB	1st Yr	Resides
Bok, Matt	.375	4	8	2	3	1	0	0	2	1	1	0	0	.500	.400	L	R	5-11	200	10-5-79	2002	Akron, Ohio
Cardona, Dave	.292	38	137	15	40	8	0	1	14	4	39	2	2	.372	.333	R	R	6-2	175	11-7-82	2001	San Juan, P.R.
Carter, Ryan	.313	49	179	32	56	13	5	7	35	14	49	8	1	.559	.394	R	R	6-2	175	1-4-83	2001	Fort Myers, Fla.
Castillo, Luis	.285	67	260	46	74	22	2	7	48	24	69	0	0	.465	.349	R	R	6-3	175	1-18-84	2001	Estado Guarico, Venez.
Comfort, Geoff	.256	49	172	36	44	12	2	4	21	24	46	5	2	.419	.356	R	R	6-0	210	3-27-80	2002	Burlingame, Calif.
Crissotomo, Miguel	.237	33	93	16	22	4	2	0	9	10	20	2	0	.323	.314	S	R	5-11	155	1-3-81	2001	Bayaguana, D.R.
De Aza, Alejandro	.231	55	208	36	48	11	1	2	24	23	34	15	6	.322	.336	L	L	6-0	174	4-11-84	2001	La Romana, D.R.

BATTING	AVG	G	AB	R	H	2B	3B	HR	RBI	BB	SO	SB	CS	SLG	OBP	B	T	HT	WT	DOB	1st Yr	Resides
Dowdy, Brett	.276	29	105	11	29	4	3	0	11	6	27	1	0	.371	.330	R	R	6-0	189	2-22-82	2003	Bradenton, Fla.
Ferrer, Simon	.250	8	28	4	7	3	0	0	2	2	9	0	0	.357	.290	R	R	5-10	175	6-24-80	2002	Santa Ynez, Calif.
Gonzalez, Juan	.244	38	135	20	33	1	1	1	11	10	26	2	4	.289	.297	R	R	5-9	165	8-21-82	2001	Carolina, P.R.
Hu, Chin-Lung	.305	53	220	34	67	9	5	3	23	14	33	5	4	.432	.343	R	R	5-9	150	2-2-84	2003	Tainan City, Taiwan
LaRoche, Andy	.211	6	19	1	4	1	0	0	5	1	4	0	0	.263	.238	R	R	5-11	185	9-13-83	2003	Fort Scott, Kan.
Laurin, Dominique	.204	30	93	12	19	6	2	1	11	15	35	1	1	.344	.330	R	R	6-0	185	10-7-82	2003	North Vancouver, B.C.
Ludwig, Michael	.269	28	104	9	28	4	1	0	9	4	26	0	1	.327	.303	R	R	6-6	210	4-30-81	2003	Blaine, Minn.
Lynch, Michael	.186	28	102	8	19	3	0	0	12	11	29	0	0	.216	.261	R	R	6-3	220	10-31-82	2002	Oak Forest, Ill.
Martin, Russell	.271	52	188	25	51	13	0	6	36	26	26	3	1	.436	.368	R	R	5-11	202	2-15-83	2002	Chelsea, Quebec
Milons, Jereme	.308	51	195	37	60	7	5	1	23	19	47	10	3	.410	.369	R	R	6-2	205	2-5-83	2002	Starkville, Miss.
Paul, Xavier	.307	69	264	60	81	15	6	7	47	34	58	11	4	.489	.384	L	R	6-0	200	2-25-85	2003	Slidell, La.
Piazza, Thomas	.087	6	23	1	2	1	0	0	3	0	15	0	0	.130	.087	L	R	6-0	200	10-9-81	2003	Boynton Beach, Fla.
Roberts, Dave	.400	3	10	4	4	0	0	0	0	1	0	1	0	.400	.455	L	L	5-10	180	5-31-72	1994	Oceanside, Calif.
Slimak, Taylor	.300	20	60	7	18	6	0	0	9	3	21	0	0	.400	.323	L	R	6-1	190	10-2-80	2003	Moorpark, Calif.

GAMES BY POSITION: C—Lynch 21, Martin 49, Slimak 9. **1B**—Comfort 46, Ludwig 28, Lynch 4. **2B**—Crissotomo 19, Dowdy 16, Ferrer 8, Gonzalez 16, Laurin 20. **3B**—Castillo 55, Dowdy 9, Gonzalez 14. **SS**—Crissotomo 5, Dowdy 2, Gonzalez 8, Hu 53, Laurin 10. **OF**—Cardona 34, Carter 41, De Aza 52, Milons 48, Paul 55, Roberts 3.

PITCHING	W	L	ERA	G	GS	CG	SV	IP	H	R	ER	BB	SO	AVG	B	T	HT	WT	DOB	1st Yr	Resides
Ahumada, Edgar	1	5	4.91	12	8	0	0	44	56	36	24	23	33	.306	L	L	6-1	180	11-17-82	2002	Culiacan, Mexico
Alvarez, Gabriel	3	2	4.25	19	0	0	1	42	44	26	20	22	58	.258	R	R	5-11	178	8-10-84	2002	Guadalupe, Mexico
Bailey, Chad	1	2	2.57	14	2	0	2	42	38	17	12	19	43	.248	L	L	6-4	190	6-24-83	2003	Ewa Beach, Hawaii
Billingsley, Chad	5	4	2.83	11	11	0	0	54	49	24	17	15	62	.242	R	R	6-2	215	7-29-84	2003	Defiance, Ohio
Carvajal, Marcos	2	1	3.08	23	0	0	2	38	32	16	13	22	50	.223	R	R	6-4	175	8-19-84	2001	Ciudad Bolivar, Venez.
Cuen, David	3	8	8.11	15	15	0	0	64	102	68	58	20	44	.361	L	L	6-4	180	8-4-83	2001	Somerton, Ariz.
De los Santos, Omar	0	0	0.00	5	2	0	0	13	7	0	0	5	13	.159	R	R	6-0	162	8-13-81	1998	San Pedro de Macoris, D.R.
Diaz, Jose	0	0	3.86	2	0	0	0	2	2	1	1	1	2	.200	R	R	6-4	230	2-27-84	2001	La Romana, D.R.
Dumesnil, Bryan	1	0	8.05	16	0	0	0	19	17	17	17	21	24	.229	R	L	6-3	210	9-19-83	2002	Nanaimo, B.C.
Megrew, Mike	5	3	3.40	14	14	0	0	77	64	40	29	24	99	.222	L	L	6-6	210	1-29-84	2002	Hope Valley, R.I.
Parker, David	2	1	3.76	18	0	0	1	41	38	20	17	15	47	.246	R	R	6-4	185	4-18-83	2002	Winnipeg, Manitoba
Pratt, Jordan	0	9	7.69	16	8	0	0	46	65	54	39	18	31	.325	R	R	6-3	195	5-17-85	2003	Monmouth, Ore.
Rodriguez, Mike	1	0	3.27	2	2	0	0	11	13	4	4	2	6	.295	R	R	6-1	180	8-31-82	2002	Roseville, Calif.
Schmoll, Stephen	3	1	3.68	24	1	0	7	37	27	23	15	15	53	.200	R	R	6-2	200	2-4-80	2003	Rockville, Md.
Sobkow, Phil	5	3	6.08	14	12	0	1	53	70	49	36	30	48	.324	R	R	6-5	210	6-17-81	2003	Calder, Sask.
Stewart, James	2	1	3.65	18	1	0	0	44	56	28	18	8	34	.307	R	R	6-2	190	5-9-82	2001	Vail, Ariz.
Tiffany, Chuck	0	0	10.13	3	0	0	0	3	4	4	3	2	4	.363	L	L	6-1	195	1-25-85	2003	Covina, Calif.
White, Michael	1	1	3.95	19	0	0	1	27	31	22	12	13	39	.267	L	L	6-2	215	9-12-82	2002	Clearwater, Fla.

VERO BEACH DODGERS — Rookie

GULF COAST LEAGUE

BATTING	AVG	G	AB	R	H	2B	3B	HR	RBI	BB	SO	SB	CS	SLG	OBP	B	T	HT	WT	DOB	1st Yr	Resides
Abreu, Etanislao	.294	44	163	30	48	7	5	0	20	11	24	9	3	.399	.358	R	R	5-11	160	11-13-84	2003	Puerto Plata, D.R.
Arias, Hector	.222	38	126	10	28	4	1	0	15	9	33	11	0	.270	.277	R	R	6-3	200	9-5-84	2003	Bani, D.R.
Cabrera, Ruben	.156	28	77	2	12	0	0	0	3	6	17	0	2	.156	.233	R	R	5-10	170	7-7-81	2000	Edo Blivar, Venez.
Denker, Travis	.270	38	122	17	33	8	1	3	13	20	16	2	0	.426	.382	R	R	5-9	170	8-5-85	2003	Brea, Calif.
Golindano, Jesus	.239	28	71	11	17	3	0	0	8	7	12	1	1	.282	.316	S	R	5-11	165	1-13-84	2001	Maturin, Venez.
Kemp, Matthew	.270	42	159	11	43	5	2	1	17	7	25	2	1	.346	.298	R	R	6-4	210	9-23-84	2003	Midwest City, Okla.
Laurin, Dominique	.160	9	25	4	4	0	1	0	2	6	7	1	1	.240	.371	R	R	6-0	185	10-7-82	2003	North Vancouver, B.C.
Marcos, Emilio	.240	45	154	20	37	8	0	3	16	7	35	9	5	.351	.285	R	R	6-2	160	3-21-81	2003	Villa Altagracia, D.R.
May, Lucas	.252	48	159	19	40	8	0	0	10	19	38	11	1	.302	.350	R	R	6-0	190	10-24-84	2003	Chesterfield, Mo.
McGriff, Fred	.667	1	3	1	2	1	0	0	0	0	0	0	0	1.000	.667	L	L	6-3	225	10-31-63	1981	Tampa, Fla.
Mitchell, Russell	.338	26	77	13	26	8	1	1	9	12	5	2	1	.506	.441	R	R	6-1	182	2-15-85	2003	Cartersville, Ga.
Ndungidi, Sambu	.248	32	109	11	27	6	1	2	15	9	35	8	1	.376	.322	S	R	6-3	200	5-9-85	2002	Pierre Fonds, Quebec
Nowak, David	.252	31	103	17	26	6	1	0	7	20	34	5	4	.330	.394	L	L	6-3	190	6-29-81	2003	Phoenix, Ariz.
Owen, Ryan	.143	4	7	1	1	0	0	1	1	0	4	0	0	.571	.143	R	R	6-0	200	9-15-80	2002	Wichita, Kan.
Piazza, Thomas	.000	3	11	1	0	0	0	0	0	0	8	0	0	.000	.000	L	R	6-0	200	10-9-81	2003	Boynton Beach, Fla.
Pierce, Sean	.250	7	16	2	4	0	0	0	2	5	5	0	2	.250	.409	R	R	5-9	190	11-26-78	2001	Covina, Calif.
Rohan, Jimmy	.257	47	171	17	44	4	2	0	15	10	12	5	5	.304	.309	R	R	6-1	190	5-13-84	2002	Valencia, Calif.
Rohena, Angel	.290	24	62	11	18	2	1	1	7	4	22	2	0	.403	.338	R	R	6-3	200	1-5-83	2003	Carolina, P.R.
Sapp, Steven	.248	38	121	12	30	6	1	0	7	8	38	10	3	.314	.336	R	R	6-3	190	11-17-85	2003	Los Angeles, Calif.
Sutherland, David	.236	51	191	12	45	5	1	0	20	12	19	1	2	.272	.281	L	L	6-6	175	5-2-85	2003	Ferny Grove, Australia
Tatum, John	.103	10	29	1	3	0	0	0	0	4	13	0	0	.103	.212	R	R	6-2	270	1-28-78	2003	West Palm Beach, Fla.

GAMES BY POSITION: C—Cabrera 27, Golindano 25, Owen 3, Rohena 22. **1B**—McGriff 1, Rohan 11, Sutherland 51. **2B**—Abreu 36, Denker 15, Golindano 2, Laurin 3, Mitchell 10, Rohan 2. **3B**—Denker 19, Laurin 6, Mitchell 9, Rohan 27. **SS**—Abreu 7, May 46, Mitchell 2, Rohan 7. **OF**—Arias 29, Kemp 37, Marcos 42, Ndungidi 21, Nowak 22, Pierce 6, Sapp 36.

PITCHING	W	L	ERA	G	GS	CG	SV	IP	H	R	ER	BB	SO	AVG	B	T	HT	WT	DOB	1st Yr	Resides
Alvarez, Carlos	2	2	2.05	22	0	0	3	26	19	11	6	12	26	.204	L	L	5-9	160	3-31-85	2002	Maracaibo, Venez.
Castillo, Albenis	2	1	2.72	19	1	0	0	36	35	13	11	8	35	.248	R	R	6-4	178	12-24-83	2001	Cocle, Panama
Garcia, Javier	4	5	2.34	14	11	0	0	62	61	21	16	8	41	.264	R	R	6-5	175	1-5-84	2001	Aragua, Venez.
Garrison, Kale	2	2	7.04	15	1	0	0	23	23	22	18	18	24	.258	L	L	6-1	175	3-1-82	2003	Gilbert, Ariz.
Hayes, Alvin	1	1	4.05	6	2	0	0	13	11	8	6	16	9	.234	R	R	6-6	195	8-19-83	2003	Century, Fla.
Langone, Steve	0	0	3.00	2	1	0	0	3	4	1	1	0	2	.333	R	R	6-2	205	1-12-78	2000	Reading, Mass.
Lugo, Jorge	0	0	9.00	1	0	0	0	1	1	1	1	0	1	.333	L	L	5-11	160	7-15-83	2001	Zulia, Venez.
McDonald, James	2	4	3.33	12	9	0	0	49	39	20	18	15	47	.220	L	R	6-5	195	10-19-84	2003	Long Beach, Calif.
O'Flaherty, Liam	3	1	1.55	15	2	0	2	41	33	13	7	12	24	.227	R	L	6-0	165	1-18-85	2002	Castle Hill, Australia
Obispo, Jose	2	3	3.83	9	8	0	0	40	32	23	17	21	42	.217	R	R	6-1	160	5-11-84	2002	Sabana de la Mar, D.R.
Ojeda, Alvis	4	0	1.81	21	1	0	2	45	39	14	9	10	35	.237	R	R	6-0	170	9-23-83	2002	Maracaibo, Venez.
Plummer, Jarod	0	0	2.25	2	2	0	0	4	3	2	1	1	4	.200	R	R	6-5	200	1-27-84	2002	Garland, Texas
Potoczny, Mike	2	5	2.79	16	7	0	1	52	45	25	16	26	29	.239	R	R	6-1	190	12-27-83	2002	Worthington, W.Va.
Rodriguez, Osvaldo	0	0	1.17	6	6	0	0	23	12	5	3	7	27	.150	R	R	5-10	168	6-10-84	2002	Hatillo Palma, D.R.
Simas, Bill	0	0	4.50	1	1	0	0	2	1	1	1	1	1	.142	L	R	6-3	230	11-28-71	1992	Fresno, Calif.
Soto, Reyes	2	2	2.80	14	3	0	2	35	20	15	11	23	29	.166	R	R	6-2	195	4-19-81	2003	Santo Domingo, D.R.
Tequida, Mauricio	0	4	2.49	13	0	0	6	22	22	7	6	2	16	.255	R	R	6-1	180	2-5-82	2003	Obregon, Mexico
Wright, Wesley	3	1	3.58	14	5	0	0	38	37	15	15	19	26	.270	R	L	5-11	160	1-28-85	2003	Grady, Ala.

MILWAUKEE BREWERS

BY TOM HAUDRICOURT

It's not often that players on a last-place team go home for the winter feeling better about themselves, but that was the case for the Brewers at the end of the 2003 season.

After bumbling through a franchise-worst 106 losses the previous year, the Brewers regrouped under new management and came out with a new, fighting spirit. The result was an 11th consecutive losing season and another last-place finish, but that did not tell the entire story.

With 68 victories, the Brewers improved by 12 games. More important, however, was the never-say-die approach and renewed focus that first-year manager Ned Yost fostered.

"Our guys fought hard until the very end," said Yost, who learned at the hand of venerable Braves manager Bobby Cox. "That's the one thing we promised our fans, and I was determined to live up to that."

What the Brewers couldn't overcome was a lack of talent, particularly on the pitching staff. When veteran free agent Todd Ritchie was lost in the first month of the season with a shoulder injury and Glendon Rusch began an unexpected descent to a 1-12 record, the rotation was thrown into turmoil.

Ben Sheets (11-13, 4.45), Wayne Franklin (10-13, 5.50) and Matt Kinney (10-13, 5.19) took regular turns but the other two rotation spots became a revolving door.

One positive development in the bullpen was the emergence of Dan Kolb as closer. Released by the Rangers early in the year, Kolb joined the Brewers in July and converted 21 of 23 save opportunities after incumbent Mike DeJean lost the job and later was traded to the Cardinals.

Keeping the ball in the ballpark was a major problem for the pitching staff, which allowed a franchise-record 219 long balls. Brewers pitchers often pointed to the homer-friendly nature of Miller Park but they also surrendered 95 blasts in 81 road games.

On the offensive end, the Brewers were too reliant on the all-star duo of left fielder Geoff Jenkins and first baseman Richie Sexson. Sexson hit 45 homers and drove in 124 runs, and Jenkins finished with 28 home runs and 95 RBIs despite missing the final month of the season with a broken thumb.

At the top of the list of positive developments was the emergence of centerfielder Scott Podsednik as a rookie of the year candidate. Acquired on waivers from the Mariners the previous winter, Podsednik waited for his chance, which came when Alex Sanchez played his way out of the lineup (and eventually off the team) in mid-May.

Podsednik became one of only four rookies in big league history to bat .300 with 40 stolen bases and 100 runs scored. He also made a memorable exit by socking a home run in his final at-bat of the season.

"I think we're headed in the right direction," Yost said. "We are a team that provides opportunities. It's up to the players to come in and take advantage of them."

Giving the Brewers added hope for the future is a flourishing farm system that was a vast wasteland as recently as four years ago. As proof of the influx of top prospects, the system produced three league MVPs—Double-A Huntsville third baseman Corey Hart, Class A Beloit first baseman Prince Fielder and Rookie-level Helena catcher Lou Palmisano, a third-round draft pick in 2003.

Boosting their talent level, the Brewers grabbed consensus college player of the year Rickie Weeks with the second pick in the draft. Weeks, a second baseman from Southern University, spent the final weeks of the season with the Brewers, getting a taste of life in the big leagues.

Richie Sexson

BILL MITCHELL

Prince Fielder

PLAYERS of the YEAR

MAJOR LEAGUE: Richie Sexson, 1b

Sexson was as durable in 2003 as he was prolific. He tied for second in the National League in home runs and ranked fourth in RBIs while becoming the first Brewer ever to play every inning of every game, and the first major leaguer to do so since 1995.

MINOR LEAGUE: Prince Fielder, 1b

The Class A Midwest League MVP made a run at the circuit's triple crown before finishing the 2003 season at .313-27-112 with 71 walks. Fielder ranked first in RBIs, third in average and second in homers, on-base percentage and slugging percentage.

ORGANIZATION LEADERS

BATTING		
*AVG	Terry Trofholz, Helena	.349
R	Kennard Bibbs, Beloit	85
H	Prince Fielder, Beloit	157
TB	Prince Fielder, Beloit	264
2B	Corey Hart, Huntsville	40
3B	Dave Krynzel, Huntsville	11
HR	Prince Fielder, Beloit	27
RBI	Prince Fielder, Beloit	112
BB	Rich Paz, Indianapolis/Huntsville	74
SO	Jeff Eure, Beloit	128
SB	Chris Morris, High Desert	67
*SLG	Prince Fielder, Beloit	.526
*OBP	Rich Paz, Indianapolis/Huntsville	.422
PITCHING		
W	Derek Lee, Indianapolis /Huntsville	13
L	Dan Hall, High Desert	14
#ERA	Luis Martinez, Indianapolis/Huntsville	2.13
G	Rob Giron, Indianapolis	52
	Josh Alliston, Beloit	52
CG	Several tied at	1
SV	Rob Giron, Indianapolis	15
IP	Luis Martinez, Indianapolis/Huntsville	161
BB	Luis Martinez, Indianapolis/Huntsville	73
SO	Luis Martinez, Indianapolis/Huntsville	162

*Minimum 250 At-Bats #Minimum 75 Innings

MILWAUKEE BREWERS

Manager: Ned Yost. **2003 Record:** 68-94, .420 (6th, NL Central).

BATTING	AVG	G	AB	R	H	2B	3B	HR	RBI	BB	SO	SB	CS	SLG	OBP	B	T	HT	WT	DOB	1st Yr	Resides
Clark, Brady	.273	128	315	33	86	21	1	6	40	21	40	13	2	.403	.330	R	R	6-2	190	4-18-73	1996	Beaverton, Ore.
Clayton, Royce	.228	146	483	49	110	16	1	11	39	49	92	5	2	.333	.301	R	R	6-0	185	1-2-70	1988	Scottsdale, Ariz.
Conti, Jason	.229	30	48	3	11	2	0	2	7	2	18	0	1	.396	.255	L	R	5-11	180	1-27-75	1996	Phoenix, Ariz.
Cruz, Enrique	.085	60	71	6	6	1	0	0	2	4	30	0	0	.099	.145	R	R	6-1	180	11-21-81	1998	Santo Domingo, D.R.
Ginter, Keith	.257	127	358	51	92	15	2	14	44	37	87	1	1	.427	.352	R	R	5-10	195	5-5-76	1998	Fullerton, Calif.
Hall, Bill	.261	52	142	23	37	9	2	5	20	7	28	1	2	.458	.298	R	R	6-0	170	12-28-79	1998	Nettleton, Miss.
Hammonds, Jeffrey	.158	10	38	2	6	2	0	1	3	3	7	0	0	.289	.220	R	R	6-0	200	3-5-71	1992	Cincinnati, Ohio
Helms, Wes	.261	134	476	56	124	21	0	23	67	43	131	0	1	.450	.330	R	R	6-4	230	5-12-76	1994	Atlanta, Ga.
Jenkins, Geoff	.296	124	487	81	144	30	2	28	95	58	120	0	0	.538	.375	L	R	6-1	215	7-21-74	1996	Scottsdale, Ariz.
Kieschnick, Brooks	.300	70	70	12	21	1	0	7	12	6	13	0	0	.614	.355	L	R	6-4	220	6-6-72	1993	Caldwell, Texas
Osik, Keith	.249	80	241	22	60	12	0	2	21	31	44	0	1	.324	.342	R	R	6-0	200	10-22-68	1990	Shoreham, N.Y.
Perez, Eddie	.271	107	350	26	95	17	1	11	45	17	47	0	1	.420	.304	R	R	6-1	220	5-4-68	1987	Duluth, Ga.
Podsednik, Scott	.314	154	558	100	175	29	8	9	58	56	91	43	10	.443	.379	L	L	6-0	170	3-18-76	1994	West, Texas
Sanchez, Alex	.282	43	163	15	46	10	3	0	10	7	28	8	6	.380	.316	L	L	5-10	150	8-26-76	1996	Coral Gables, Fla.
Sexson, Richie	.272	162	606	97	165	28	2	45	124	98	151	2	3	.548	.379	R	R	6-7	235	12-29-74	1993	Vancouver, Wash.
Smith, Mark	.238	33	63	8	15	4	0	3	10	4	13	0	0	.444	.275	R	R	6-3	220	5-7-70	1991	Flower Mound, Texas
Vander Wal, John	.257	117	327	50	84	25	1	14	45	46	104	1	2	.468	.350	L	L	6-1	210	4-29-66	1987	Grand Rapids, Mich.
Weeks, Rickie	.167	7	12	1	2	1	0	0	0	1	6	0	0	.250	.286	R	R	6-0	195	9-13-82	2003	Altamonte Springs, Fla.
Young, Eric	.260	109	404	71	105	18	1	15	31	48	34	25	7	.421	.344	R	R	5-8	185	5-18-67	1989	Atlanta, Ga.
Zoccolillo, Peter	.108	20	37	0	4	1	0	0	3	2	13	0	0	.135	.154	L	R	6-2	200	2-6-77	1999	White Plains, N.Y.

PITCHING	W	L	ERA	G	GS	CG	SV	IP	H	R	ER	BB	SO	AVG	B	T	HT	WT	DOB	1st Yr	Resides
Burba, Dave	1	1	3.53	17	2	0	0	43	42	19	17	19	35	.250	R	R	6-4	240	7-7-66	1987	Gilbert, Ariz.
Crudale, Mike	0	0	2.89	9	0	0	0	9	1	3	3	6	7	.035	R	R	6-0	200	1-3-77	1999	Danville, Calif.
2-team (13 St. Louis)	0	1	2.61	22	0	0	0	21	12	8	6	18	13	.166							
Davis, Doug	3	2	2.58	8	8	1	0	52	49	18	15	21	35	.247	R	L	6-4	190	9-21-75	1996	Cedar Hill, Texas
De Jean, Mike	4	7	4.87	58	0	0	18	65	69	38	35	27	58	.270	R	R	6-2	220	9-28-70	1992	Castle Rock, Colo.
De Los Santos, Valerio	3	3	4.13	45	0	0	1	48	38	24	22	22	35	.224	L	L	6-2	220	10-6-72	1993	Santo Domingo, D.R.
Durocher, Jayson	2	0	11.05	6	0	0	0	7	9	9	9	2	7	.300	R	R	6-3	230	8-18-74	1993	Scottsdale, Ariz.
Estrella, Leo	7	3	4.36	58	0	0	3	66	75	32	32	21	25	.289	R	R	6-1	180	2-20-75	1994	Port St. Lucie, Fla.
Ford, Matt	0	3	4.33	25	4	0	0	44	46	23	21	21	26	.264	S	L	6-1	175	4-8-81	1999	Tamarac, Fla.
Foster, John	2	0	4.71	23	0	0	0	21	30	11	11	8	16	.340	L	L	6-0	200	5-17-78	1999	Stockton, Calif.
Franklin, Wayne	10	13	5.50	36	34	1	0	195	201	129	119	94	116	.267	L	L	6-2	210	3-9-74	1996	Rising Sun, Md.
Kieschnick, Brooks	1	1	5.26	42	0	0	0	53	66	32	31	13	39	.298	L	R	6-4	220	6-6-72	1993	Caldwell, Texas
Kinney, Matt	10	13	5.19	33	31	1	0	191	201	121	110	80	152	.271	R	R	6-5	220	12-16-76	1995	Bangor, Me.
Kolb, Dan L.	1	2	1.96	37	0	0	21	41	34	10	9	19	39	.220	R	R	6-4	210	3-29-75	1995	Walnut, Ill.
Leskanic, Curt	4	0	2.70	26	0	0	0	27	22	8	8	18	28	.226	R	R	6-0	185	4-2-68	1990	Longwood, Fla.
Manning, David	0	2	16.20	2	2	0	0	7	11	13	12	8	2	.392	R	R	6-3	210	8-14-72	1992	West Palm Beach, Fla.
Martinez, Luis	0	3	9.92	4	4	0	0	16	25	18	18	15	10	.373	L	L	6-6	200	1-20-80	1997	Boca Chica, D.R.
Nance, Shane	0	2	4.81	26	0	0	0	24	34	16	13	10	25	.326	L	L	5-8	180	9-7-77	2000	Houston, Texas
Obermueller, Wes	2	5	5.07	12	11	0	0	66	81	40	37	25	34	.301	R	R	6-2	190	12-22-76	1999	North Liberty, Iowa
Quevedo, Ruben	1	4	6.75	9	8	0	0	43	53	32	32	23	19	.313	R	R	6-1	255	1-5-79	1996	Valencia, Venez.
Ritchie, Todd	1	2	5.08	5	5	0	0	28	36	17	16	10	15	.318	R	R	6-3	210	11-7-71	1990	Kerens, Texas
Rusch, Glendon	1	12	6.42	32	19	1	1	123	171	93	88	45	93	.330	L	L	6-1	225	11-7-74	1993	Tujunga, Calif.
Sheets, Ben	11	13	4.45	34	34	1	0	221	232	122	109	43	157	.268	R	R	6-1	220	7-18-78	1999	St. Amant, La.
Vizcaino, Luis	4	3	6.39	75	0	0	0	62	64	45	44	25	61	.263	R	R	5-11	180	8-6-74	1995	Bani, D.R.

FIELDING

Catcher	PCT	G	PO	A	E	DP	PB
Osik	.991	78	479	44	5	5	6
Perez	.991	102	613	32	6	6	8

First Base	PCT	G	PO	A	E	DP
Sexson	.993	162	1363	130	11	131

Second Base	PCT	G	PO	A	E	DP
Cruz	1.000	6	3	7	0	0
Ginter	.991	53	103	128	2	35
Hall	.956	18	41	46	4	14
Weeks	.667	4	1	1	1	0
Young	.968	99	196	251	15	55

Third Base	PCT	G	PO	A	E	DP
Cruz	.667	2	0	2	1	0
Ginter	.921	40	19	51	6	6
Hall	.000	1	0	0	1	0
Helms	.945	130	88	236	19	20

Shortstop	PCT	G	PO	A	E	DP
Clayton	.977	141	193	396	14	76
Cruz	1.000	13	8	20	0	3
Ginter	1.000	2	4	3	0	1
Hall	.951	18	30	48	4	10

Outfield	PCT	G	PO	A	E	DP
Clark	.973	105	174	5	5	3
Conti	.909	20	29	1	3	0
Ginter	1.000	2	1	0	0	0
Hammonds	1.000	10	17	0	0	0
Jenkins	1.000	123	222	11	0	1
Kieschnick	.667	3	2	0	1	0
Podsednik	.992	139	345	5	3	1
Sanchez	.990	36	99	3	1	1
Smith	.960	15	24	0	1	0
Vander Wal	.984	89	176	4	3	2
Zoccolillo	1.000	7	16	0	0	0

LARRY GOREN

Geoff Jenkins

FARM SYSTEM

Director, Player Development: Reid Nichols.

Class	Farm Team	League	W	L	Pct.	Finish*	Manager(s)	First Yr.
AAA	Indianapolis (Ind.) Indians	International	64	78	.451	12th (14)	Cecil Cooper	2000
AA	Huntsville (Ala.) Stars	Southern	75	63	.543	2nd (10)	Frank Kremblas	1999
High A	High Desert (Calif.) Mavericks	California	42	98	.300	10th (10)	Tim Blackwell	2001
Low A	Beloit (Wis.) Snappers	Midwest	75	61	.551	2nd (14)	Don Money	1982
Rookie	Helena (Mont.) Brewers	Pioneer	48	28	.632	2nd (8)	Ed Sedar	2003
Rookie	Phoenix (Ariz.) Brewers	Arizona	15	34	.306	9th (9)	Hector Torres	2001

*Finish in overall standings (No. of teams in league)

INDIANAPOLIS INDIANS — Class AAA

INTERNATIONAL LEAGUE

BATTING	AVG	G	AB	R	H	2B	3B	HR	RBI	BB	SO	SB	CS	SLG	OBP	B	T	HT	WT	DOB	1st Yr	Resides
Budzinski, Mark	.270	46	159	27	43	7	1	1	12	16	39	7	2	.346	.339	L	L	6-2	180	8-26-73	1995	Richmond, Va.
Clark, Brady	.265	9	34	4	9	3	0	0	3	2	6	1	0	.353	.306	R	R	6-2	190	4-18-73	1996	Beaverton, Ore.
Conti, Jason	.248	121	456	57	113	17	3	10	40	24	120	13	8	.364	.295	L	R	5-11	180	1-27-75	1996	Phoenix, Ariz.
Delgado, Alex	.298	41	131	10	39	6	0	2	10	7	12	2	0	.389	.333	R	R	6-0	160	1-11-71	1988	Palmarejo, Venez.
Hall, Bill	.282	89	354	57	100	25	2	5	32	27	79	10	11	.407	.335	R	R	6-0	170	12-28-79	1998	Nettleton, Miss.
Hansen, Jed	.000	3	5	0	0	0	0	0	0	0	1	0	0	.000	.000	R	R	6-1	190	8-19-72	1994	Olympia, Wash.
Helms, Wes	.400	2	5	0	2	0	0	0	0	1	1	0	0	.400	.500	R	R	6-4	230	5-12-76	1994	Atlanta, Ga.
Jennings, Doug	.260	59	169	17	44	13	1	5	23	17	48	1	1	.438	.357	L	L	5-10	190	9-30-64	1984	Boca Raton, Fla.
Kieschnick, Brooks	.000	11	10	0	0	0	0	0	0	1	4	0	0	.000	.091	L	R	6-4	220	6-6-72	1993	Caldwell, Texas
Knox, Ryan	.275	36	131	18	36	8	0	0	5	7	20	17	3	.336	.321	R	R	6-1	190	6-28-77	1999	Peoria, Ill.
Lawrence, Joe	.204	43	137	19	28	7	0	2	8	23	33	2	2	.299	.317	R	R	6-2	190	2-13-77	1996	Lake Charles, La.
Luuloa, Keith	.259	109	359	50	93	26	3	11	54	35	45	3	3	.440	.323	R	R	6-0	180	12-24-74	1994	Menifee, Calif.
McKay, Cody	.232	109	371	32	86	15	1	6	43	26	50	2	2	.326	.294	L	R	6-0	210	1-11-74	1996	Scottsdale, Ariz.
Paz, Rich	.351	36	131	13	46	8	0	0	5	16	19	1	2	.412	.422	R	R	5-8	170	7-30-77	1994	Los Teques, Venez.
Rushford, Jim	.311	99	373	43	116	12	0	9	50	30	33	4	3	.416	.371	L	L	6-1	190	3-24-74	1996	San Diego, Calif.
Scarborough, Steve	.241	127	428	46	103	25	7	8	43	28	115	4	6	.388	.290	R	R	6-0	160	3-10-78	1999	College Station, Texas
Seabol, Scott	.235	25	81	6	19	1	2	0	9	4	18	0	1	.296	.264	R	R	6-4	200	5-17-75	1996	McKeesport, Penn.
Smith, Mark	.294	103	388	46	114	25	2	15	62	21	58	3	2	.485	.337	R	R	6-3	220	5-7-70	1991	Flower Mound, Texas
Stevens, Lee	.281	18	64	8	18	2	0	2	8	6	17	0	0	.406	.343	L	L	6-4	230	10-3-67	1986	Highland Ranch, Colo.
Veras, Wilton	.221	119	402	35	89	14	1	2	23	23	36	2	4	.276	.267	R	R	6-2	200	1-19-78	1995	Santo Domingo, D.R.
Zoccolillo, Peter	.280	132	443	57	124	36	1	12	73	51	70	3	5	.447	.360	L	R	6-2	200	2-6-77	1999	White Plains, N.Y.

PITCHING	W	L	ERA	G	GS	CG	SV	IP	H	R	ER	BB	SO	AVG	B	T	HT	WT	DOB	1st Yr	Resides
Buddie, Mike	0	4	3.75	18	2	0	0	36	32	16	15	12	18	.244	R	R	6-3	210	12-12-70	1992	Lutz, Fla.
Burba, Dave	5	4	5.33	10	9	0	0	51	65	37	30	16	34	.315	R	R	6-4	240	7-7-66	1987	Gilbert, Ariz.
2-team (4 Buffalo)	6	7	4.33	14	13	0	0	73	83	43	35	21	44	.291							
Campos, Francisco	2	4	5.72	8	8	0	0	39	53	30	25	12	28	.321	R	R	6-0	175	8-12-72	1991	Guaymas, Mexico
Childers, Jason	5	4	2.29	46	0	0	10	63	50	22	16	20	47	.217	R	R	6-0	160	1-13-75	1997	Douglas, Ga.
Childers, Matt	3	0	0.47	11	0	0	0	19	15	2	1	6	19	.223	R	R	6-5	190	12-3-78	1997	Augusta, Ga.
Coco, Pasqual	10	9	4.80	27	27	1	0	146	168	91	78	46	100	.291	R	R	6-1	180	9-8-77	1995	Santo Domingo, D.R.
Crudale, Mike	0	0	0.00	2	0	0	0	2	1	0	0	0	1	.142	R	R	6-0	200	1-3-77	1999	Danville, Calif.
Davis, Doug	1	2	4.15	5	5	0	0	35	33	16	16	10	19	.250	R	L	6-4	190	9-21-75	1996	Cedar Hill, Texas
Durocher, Jayson	0	0	2.57	7	3	0	0	7	7	2	2	1	9	.241	R	R	6-3	230	8-18-74	1993	Scottsdale, Ariz.
Ebert, Derrin	0	2	4.50	4	1	0	0	10	11	5	5	3	6	.323	R	L	6-3	200	8-21-76	1994	Hesperia, Calif.
Estrella, Leo	1	0	1.20	7	0	0	0	15	9	2	2	6	12	.169	R	R	6-1	180	2-20-75	1994	Port St. Lucie, Fla.
Ford, Ben	5	4	3.00	26	9	1	1	84	80	32	28	18	72	.253	R	R	6-7	230	8-15-75	1994	Cedar Rapids, Iowa
Foster, John	2	2	3.70	27	0	0	0	41	44	21	17	13	37	.271	L	L	6-0	200	5-17-78	1999	Stockton, Calif.
Giron, Roberto	1	5	4.73	52	0	0	15	59	65	37	31	28	56	.286	R	R	6-2	170	3-24-76	1994	Villa Mella, D.R.
Guerra, Mark	0	3	5.47	5	4	0	0	25	24	16	15	6	13	.260	R	R	6-2	200	11-4-71	1994	Grand Ridge, Fla.
Kieschnick, Brooks	1	0	8.56	8	0	0	0	14	17	15	13	10	14	.303	L	R	6-4	220	6-6-72	1993	Caldwell, Texas
Kolb, Dan L.	0	1	1.37	26	0	0	4	39	26	10	6	13	46	.183	R	R	6-4	210	3-29-75	1995	Walnut, Ill.
Lee, Derek	2	4	3.75	14	8	0	0	60	55	30	25	19	55	.238	L	L	6-4	180	8-20-74	1997	Fort Worth, Texas
Manning, David	6	8	4.91	23	17	0	0	99	103	57	54	60	76	.268	R	R	6-3	210	8-14-72	1992	West Palm Beach, Fla.
Marquez, Rob	0	2	3.99	30	1	0	0	56	55	31	25	25	44	.264	R	R	6-0	200	4-21-73	1995	Houston, Texas
Martinez, Luis	4	0	0.99	7	7	0	0	46	37	5	5	19	46	.237	L	L	6-6	200	1-20-80	1997	Boca Chica, D.R.
Miller, Travis	5	2	5.33	16	8	0	0	51	74	32	30	9	33	.337	R	L	6-3	210	11-2-72	1994	Eaton, Ohio
2-team (4 Louisville)	6	2	4.94	20	8	0	0	55	78	32	30	10	37	.333							
Nance, Shane	2	4	1.38	35	1	0	3	52	34	10	8	13	53	.184	L	L	5-8	180	9-7-77	2000	Houston, Texas
Obermueller, Wes	0	2	4.70	3	3	0	0	15	18	9	8	6	11	.300	R	R	6-2	190	12-22-76	1999	North Liberty, Iowa
Quevedo, Ruben	2	1	2.10	5	5	0	0	26	24	7	6	8	23	.250	R	R	6-1	255	1-5-79	1996	Valencia, Venez.
Roa, Joe	2	2	4.74	5	4	0	0	25	32	15	13	3	18	.323	R	R	6-2	200	10-11-71	1989	Royal Oak, Mich.
Rusch, Glendon	1	1	3.86	4	3	1	0	21	17	9	9	4	20	.217	L	L	6-1	225	11-7-74	1993	Tujunga, Calif.
Teut, Nate	3	5	4.41	18	13	0	0	84	92	47	41	20	47	.280	R	L	6-7	220	3-11-76	1997	Des Moines, Iowa
Wright, Jamey	1	3	7.36	7	4	0	0	22	32	21	18	10	17	.344	R	R	6-5	230	12-24-74	1993	Phoenix, Ariz.

FIELDING

Catcher	PCT	G	PO	A	E	DP	PB
Delgado	.996	37	239	29	1	7	3
Lawrence	1.000	17	89	9	0	0	5
Luuloa	1.000	1	4	0	0	0	0
McKay	.986	92	660	62	10	6	10

First Base	PCT	G	PO	A	E	DP
Hansen	1.000	2	12	0	0	0
Jennings	1.000	12	101	6	0	13
Luuloa	.993	36	286	15	2	23
McKay	1.000	5	49	4	0	7
Rushford	.993	67	552	52	4	63
Seabol	.991	11	105	5	1	8
Smith	1.000	4	30	1	0	1
Stevens	.990	12	99	5	1	7
Veras	1.000	1	8	0	0	1

Second Base	PCT	G	PO	A	E	DP
Hall	.967	51	118	142	9	33
Lawrence	.973	11	15	21	1	2
Luuloa	1.000	27	41	67	0	18
Paz	.983	35	83	93	3	25
Scarborough	.962	23	42	60	4	17

Third Base	PCT	G	PO	A	E	DP
Hansen	1.000	1	0	1	0	0

	PCT	G	PO	A	E	DP
Helms	1.000	2	2	5	0	1
Lawrence	.889	7	3	13	2	3
Luuloa	.937	31	15	59	5	6
McKay	1.000	2	2	6	0	0
Seabol	1.000	5	7	11	0	0
Veras	.936	105	75	204	19	15

Shortstop	PCT	G	PO	A	E	DP
Hall	.946	36	60	98	9	28
Luuloa	.833	1	1	4	1	0
Scarborough	.965	105	158	286	16	68
Veras	1.000	4	5	9	0	0

Outfield	PCT	G	PO	A	E	DP
Budzinski	1.000	45	86	1	0	0
Clark	1.000	7	14	0	0	0
Conti	.976	116	266	21	7	3
Hall	.750	3	3	0	1	0
Jennings	1.000	9	10	2	0	0
Knox	.973	33	67	4	2	2
Lawrence	.889	8	8	0	1	0
Rushford	1.000	29	31	0	0	0
Seabol	.875	5	7	0	1	0
Smith	.982	65	106	3	2	2
Zoccolillo	.986	122	200	8	3	0

HUNTSVILLE STARS — Class AA

SOUTHERN LEAGUE

BATTING	AVG	G	AB	R	H	2B	3B	HR	RBI	BB	SO	SB	CS	SLG	OBP	B	T	HT	WT	DOB	1st Yr	Resides
Alvarado, Joel	.154	14	39	1	6	0	0	0	5	7	7	0	4	.154	.292	R	R	6-2	190	6-30-80	2001	Cayey, P.R.
Barnwell, Chris	.246	102	313	39	77	7	0	3	25	27	47	6	6	.297	.322	R	R	5-10	180	3-1-79	2001	Jacksonville, Fla.
Clark, Daryl	.233	72	202	27	47	11	1	2	17	40	62	6	1	.327	.363	L	R	6-2	210	9-25-79	2000	Boalsburg, Pa.
Cosbey, Chris	.171	33	70	9	12	4	0	0	6	13	21	9	1	.229	.314	L	L	5-9	160	11-14-74	1998	Arcadia, Calif.
Gemoll, Brandon	.272	128	456	52	124	32	3	11	65	50	105	7	9	.428	.344	L	L	6-2	210	9-15-80	2001	San Jose, Calif.
Gripp, Ryan	.285	67	144	22	41	5	0	5	22	22	36	1	0	.424	.391	R	R	6-1	210	4-20-78	1999	Indianola, Iowa
Guerrero, Cristian	.195	32	123	8	24	6	0	0	7	4	29	3	1	.244	.220	R	R	6-5	200	7-12-80	1997	Bani, D.R.
Hardy, J.J.	.279	114	416	67	116	26	0	12	62	58	54	6	4	.428	.368	R	R	6-2	180	8-19-82	2001	Tucson, Ariz.
Hart, Corey	.302	130	493	70	149	40	1	13	94	28	101	25	8	.467	.340	R	R	6-6	200	3-24-82	2000	Bowling Green, Ky.
Jenkins, Geoff	.250	6	20	6	5	0	0	2	3	1	7	1	0	.550	.286	L	R	6-1	215	7-21-74	1996	Scottsdale, Ariz.
Johnson, Kade	.192	65	213	26	41	8	1	4	31	21	65	5	3	.296	.271	R	R	6-1	205	9-28-78	1999	Baytown, Texas
Knox, Ryan	.238	96	340	58	81	18	4	2	21	24	76	29	9	.332	.296	R	R	6-1	190	6-28-77	1999	Peoria, Ill.
Kremblas, Mike	.192	68	198	23	38	7	0	4	19	26	53	5	3	.288	.321	R	R	6-0	190	10-1-75	1998	Sevierville, Tenn.
Krynzel, Dave	.267	124	457	72	122	13	11	2	34	60	119	43	21	.357	.357	L	L	6-1	180	11-7-81	2000	Henderson, Nev.
Machado, Alejandro	.226	45	155	14	35	4	1	0	13	15	24	11	1	.265	.302	S	R	6-0	160	4-26-82	1998	Caracas, Venez.
Moon, Brian	.227	6	22	3	5	3	0	1	3	0	1	0	0	.500	.227	S	R	6-0	190	7-15-77	1997	Mansfield, Ga.
Nelson, Brad	.210	39	143	15	30	12	0	1	14	11	34	2	2	.315	.274	L	R	6-2	220	12-23-82	2001	Algona, Iowa
Paz, Rich	.246	73	228	39	56	14	0	1	24	58	36	6	3	.320	.406	R	R	5-8	170	7-30-77	1994	Los Teques, Venez.
Varner, Noochie	.270	80	293	30	79	12	2	6	47	14	52	7	3	.386	.304	R	R	6-0	180	12-7-80	2000	Cynthiana, Ky.

PITCHING	W	L	ERA	G	GS	CG	SV	IP	H	R	ER	BB	SO	AVG	B	T	HT	WT	DOB	1st Yr	Resides
Adams, Brian	3	1	2.95	32	0	0	3	61	57	30	20	36	32	.252	L	L	6-3	190	10-2-77	2000	Bishopville, S.C.
Adams, Mike	3	7	3.15	45	2	0	14	74	58	30	26	33	83	.207	R	R	6-5	190	7-29-78	2001	Sinton, Texas
Bruso, Greg	1	1	3.60	2	2	0	0	10	13	5	4	6	5	.351	R	R	6-3	190	5-5-80	2002	South Lake Tahoe, Calif.
Childers, Matt	1	0	2.93	36	1	0	8	74	67	32	24	24	44	.239	R	R	6-5	190	12-3-78	1997	Augusta, Ga.
Crabtree, Tim	0	0	9.82	6	0	0	0	7	11	8	8	4	3	.354	R	R	6-4	220	10-13-69	1992	Colleyville, Texas
Davis, Doug	1	0	3.00	1	1	0	0	6	5	2	2	3	6	.227	R	L	6-4	190	9-21-75	1996	Cedar Hill, Texas
Diggins, Ben	3	2	2.36	8	8	0	0	46	41	18	12	16	32	.235	R	R	6-7	230	6-13-79	2000	Tucson, Ariz.
Hammons, Matt	0	1	4.30	13	0	0	0	15	14	9	7	11	16	.264	R	R	6-3	200	4-9-77	1995	San Diego, Calif.
Hendrickson, Ben	7	6	3.45	17	16	0	0	78	82	35	30	28	56	.277	R	R	6-4	190	2-4-81	1999	Eden Prairie, Minn.
Housman, Jeff	3	2	3.30	8	8	1	0	46	49	21	17	17	26	.273	L	L	6-3	180	8-4-81	2002	Visalia, Calif.
Hundley, Jeff	1	1	1.59	9	1	0	2	17	15	3	3	4	11	.238	L	L	6-2	200	2-19-77	1998	Warren, Ohio
Jones, Mike	7	2	2.40	17	17	0	0	98	87	35	26	47	63	.238	R	R	6-4	200	4-23-83	2001	Phoenix, Ariz.
Lee, Derek	11	3	3.30	20	13	1	0	87	85	36	32	28	59	.267	L	L	6-4	180	8-20-74	1997	Fort Worth, Texas
Liriano, Pedro	9	13	3.79	27	26	0	0	143	138	77	60	62	116	.255	R	R	6-2	170	10-23-80	1999	Cotui, D.R.
Martinez, Luis	8	5	2.58	20	20	1	0	115	93	46	33	54	116	.223	L	L	6-6	200	1-20-80	1997	Boca Chica, D.R.
Miller, Ryan	1	8	3.84	50	1	0	4	87	80	46	37	46	82	.247	R	R	6-1	200	2-12-78	2000	Newburgh, Ind.
Nolasco, Dave	3	2	3.58	9	5	0	0	33	34	17	13	13	15	.276	R	R	6-2	200	4-3-79	2001	Rialto, Calif.
Parker, Matt	8	6	3.10	42	5	0	6	96	96	40	33	36	72	.263	R	R	6-3	210	12-13-78	1999	Hartsfield, Ga.
Ray, Ken	2	1	2.93	31	0	0	4	61	65	25	20	25	49	.286	R	R	6-2	200	11-27-74	1993	Dawsonville, Ga.
Robinson, Jeff	0	0	6.10	3	3	0	0	10	11	7	7	4	7	.268	R	R	6-4	220	6-2-77	1999	Broussard, La.
Saenz, Chris	0	0	1.50	1	0	0	0	6	4	2	1	3	6	.200	R	R	6-3	200	8-14-81	2001	Tucson, Ariz.
Shelley, Jason	3	2	2.63	9	9	1	0	55	38	18	16	21	53	.203	R	R	6-2	190	3-19-77	1999	Plainfield, Ill.

FIELDING

Catcher	PCT	G	PO	A	E	DP	PB
Alvarado	.992	14	116	16	1	1	5
Johnson	.987	63	401	40	6	3	9
Kremblas	.987	62	412	54	6	4	13
Moon	.961	6	36	13	2	1	3

First Base	PCT	G	PO	A	E	DP
Barnwell	.944	2	17	0	1	2
Gemoll	.990	118	1025	77	11	100
Gripp	.984	15	115	10	2	11
Nelson	1.000	6	36	3	0	6

Second Base	PCT	G	PO	A	E	DP
Barnwell	.946	35	72	102	10	23
Kremblas	1.000	1	1	0	0	0
Machado	.985	40	94	105	3	30
Paz	.976	67	145	187	8	37

Third Base	PCT	G	PO	A	E	DP
Barnwell	.929	18	17	48	5	3
Gripp	.808	6	3	18	5	1
Hart	.897	119	74	206	32	23

Shortstop	PCT	G	PO	A	E	DP
Barnwell	.967	34	70	78	5	17
Hardy	.970	108	167	321	15	58

Outfield	PCT	G	PO	A	E	DP
Barnwell	.500	1	1	0	1	0
Clark	.946	55	82	5	5	1
Cosbey	1.000	17	27	0	0	0
Gripp	1.000	5	8	0	0	0
Guerrero	.984	31	57	3	1	1
Hart	.000	1	0	0	0	0
Jenkins	1.000	6	7	0	0	0
Knox	.973	88	176	7	5	2
Kremblas	1.000	1	2	0	0	0
Krynzel	.963	120	273	14	11	3
Nelson	.956	32	42	1	2	0
Paz	.667	3	2	0	1	0
Varner	.965	77	125	11	5	3

HIGH DESERT MAVERICKS — High Class A

CALIFORNIA LEAGUE

BATTING	AVG	G	AB	R	H	2B	3B	HR	RBI	BB	SO	SB	CS	SLG	OBP	B	T	HT	WT	DOB	1st Yr	Resides
Alvarado, Joel	.162	67	198	23	32	10	0	0	20	17	32	1	0	.212	.233	R	R	6-2	190	6-30-80	2001	Cayey, P.R.
Belcher, Jason	.320	91	350	43	112	23	3	5	54	26	35	4	6	.446	.370	L	R	6-1	190	1-13-82	2000	Walnut Ridge, Ark.
Boyd, Dan	.294	37	143	30	42	16	0	1	14	16	29	3	2	.427	.380	R	R	5-11	190	9-28-78	2001	Dade City, Fla.
Candelaria, Scott	.288	115	455	54	131	28	5	3	52	14	65	5	3	.391	.318	R	R	6-2	190	11-2-78	2000	Albuquerque, N.M.
Chavez, Ozzie	.224	81	272	29	61	2	6	3	25	23	52	5	9	.309	.283	S	R	6-1	150	7-13-83	1999	Villa Mella, D.R.
Clark, Daryl	.314	50	191	38	60	6	5	14	35	32	51	1	2	.618	.412	L	R	6-2	210	9-25-79	2000	Boalsburg, Pa.

BATTING	AVG	G	AB	R	H	2B	3B	HR	RBI	BB	SO	SB	CS	SLG	OBP	B	T	HT	WT	DOB	1st Yr	Resides
Ernster, Mark	.288	46	163	28	47	12	2	2	29	14	31	6	1	.423	.339	R	R	6-0	190	12-10-77	1999	Glendale, Ariz.
Foster, Brian	.190	88	294	47	56	12	3	17	46	20	108	2	2	.425	.252	R	R	6-2	200	8-21-81	1999	Burlington, N.C.
Frost, Jeremy	.241	55	195	27	47	14	0	10	35	12	58	2	1	.467	.279	R	R	6-3	210	11-19-79	2002	Oviedo, Fla.
Guerrero, Cristian	.333	3	12	3	4	1	1	0	2	1	4	0	0	.583	.385	R	R	6-5	200	7-12-80	1997	Bani, D.R.
Johnson, Kade	.321	32	134	28	43	11	1	9	31	6	28	3	0	.619	.372	R	R	6-1	205	9-28-78	1999	Baytown, Texas
Lozada, Charlie	.370	7	27	3	10	1	0	0	4	3	6	1	0	.407	.433	R	R	5-11	190	6-28-83	2003	Caracas, Venez.
Morris, Chris	.265	128	486	81	129	26	4	2	52	55	107	67	18	.348	.345	S	R	5-8	180	7-1-79	2000	Andrews, S.C.
Nelson, Brad	.311	41	167	23	52	9	1	1	18	12	22	2	2	.395	.363	L	R	6-2	220	12-23-82	2001	Algona, Iowa
Raburn, Johnny	.288	121	448	68	129	12	6	0	42	58	71	26	12	.342	.368	S	R	6-1	160	2-16-79	2000	Plant City, Fla.
Santana, Ralph	.286	112	419	60	120	11	4	2	41	29	58	42	16	.346	.338	L	R	6-1	170	9-30-80	2001	Orlando, Fla.
Toner, John	.218	20	78	9	17	5	2	2	9	5	18	4	0	.410	.265	R	R	6-3	210	9-22-79	2001	St. Joseph, Mich.
Villanueva, Froilan	.294	112	439	46	129	23	4	10	76	15	66	4	3	.433	.330	R	R	6-2	150	10-5-78	1997	Santo Domingo, D.R.
West, Todd	.239	109	389	47	93	21	2	0	41	28	62	13	7	.303	.287	R	R	5-11	160	3-2-79	2000	El Paso, Texas

PITCHING	W	L	ERA	G	GS	CG	SV	IP	H	R	ER	BB	SO	AVG	B	T	HT	WT	DOB	1st Yr	Resides
Backsmeyer, Justin	1	9	6.33	40	0	0	4	70	77	52	49	24	55	.278	R	R	6-4	200	1-24-80	1998	Rhinelander, Wisc.
Bystrowski, Bobby	0	4	5.53	48	0	0	13	54	56	35	33	21	41	.267	R	R	6-1	190	9-27-76	1997	Fair Oaks, Calif.
Candelaria, Scott	0	0	22.50	2	0	0	0	2	7	5	5	1	1	.000	R	R	6-2	190	11-2-78	2000	Albuquerque, N.M.
Dean, Aaron	5	5	6.87	38	1	0	1	90	108	72	69	54	82	.292	R	R	6-4	190	4-9-79	1999	Pleasanton, Calif.
Ebert, Derrin	2	1	6.19	3	3	0	0	16	20	11	11	1	11	.307	R	L	6-3	200	8-21-76	1994	Hesperia, Calif.
Gold, J.M.	1	1	6.65	11	3	0	0	23	29	20	17	5	21	.298	R	R	6-5	220	4-10-80	1998	Toms River, N.J.
Gordon, Justin	1	4	5.51	38	1	0	5	83	90	63	51	56	72	.271	L	L	6-5	220	5-26-79	1999	Taunton, Mass.
Hall, Dan	6	14	7.10	26	26	0	0	123	169	116	97	47	79	.330	R	R	6-3	220	6-18-79	2000	Roper, N.C.
Hundley, Jeff	0	1	4.29	23	1	0	1	36	32	18	17	12	34	.240	L	L	6-2	200	2-19-77	1998	Warren, Ohio
Kolb, Dan J.	6	12	6.42	27	27	0	0	150	194	118	107	51	110	.311	R	R	6-1	190	6-5-80	2001	Palmetto, Fla.
Marx, Tommy	0	5	12.15	21	4	0	0	33	43	48	45	49	21	.328	R	L	6-7	200	9-5-79	1998	West Bloomfield, Mich.
Mazone, Brian	0	7	9.31	13	13	0	0	59	97	66	61	27	49	.368	L	L	6-4	200	7-26-76	1998	Cardiff, Calif.
Nolasco, Dave	3	5	5.44	21	7	0	0	81	103	56	49	28	63	.315	R	R	6-2	200	4-3-79	2001	Rialto, Calif.
Petty, Chad	0	10	7.41	17	16	1	0	81	112	76	67	38	55	.334	L	L	6-4	200	2-17-82	2000	West Farmington, Ohio
Pruett, Hubert	1	0	7.20	1	1	0	0	5	8	4	4	3	2	.400	R	R	6-2	220	3-16-83	2001	Pearl City, Hawaii
Raburn, Johnny	0	0	0.00	2	0	0	0	0	0	0	0	1	1	.000	S	R	6-1	160	2-16-79	2000	Plant City, Fla.
Ray, Ken	1	1	7.71	7	0	0	0	14	22	13	12	6	18	.349	R	R	6-2	200	11-27-74	1993	Dawsonville, Ga.
Robinson, Jeff	1	1	2.16	7	4	0	1	25	26	8	6	9	20	.270	R	R	6-4	220	6-2-77	1999	Broussard, La.
Saenz, Chris	9	9	5.20	26	26	1	0	128	121	80	74	56	136	.250	R	R	6-3	200	8-14-81	2001	Tucson, Ariz.
Schaub, Greg	0	1	2.08	8	0	0	0	17	19	4	4	9	21	.271	R	R	6-1	185	3-30-77	1995	Willow Street, Penn.
Smart, Pete	1	3	9.00	5	5	0	0	22	33	22	22	9	23	.366	R	L	6-7	200	11-22-77	2001	Lawrence, Kan.
Stavros, Tony	2	3	4.46	46	1	0	3	85	87	49	42	39	101	.267	R	R	6-2	180	8-7-80	2001	Eugene, Ore.
Stout, Danny	2	2	7.07	12	1	0	0	28	38	23	22	10	22	.327	R	R	6-2	210	2-16-78	2001	Pensacola, Fla.

FIELDING

Catcher	PCT	G	PO	A	E	DP	PB
Alvarado	.982	64	456	47	9	6	12
Candelaria	.000	1	0	0	0	0	0
Foster	.984	51	279	37	5	2	14
Frost	.981	7	48	5	1	0	4
Johnson	.972	20	153	23	5	1	1
Lozada	.976	4	39	2	1	0	0
Raburn	1.000	1	0	1	0	0	0
Villanueva	1.000	14	76	9	0	0	2

First Base	PCT	G	PO	A	E	DP
Alvarado	1.000	1	13	0	0	0
Candelaria	.986	44	314	27	5	25
Ernster	.970	6	29	3	1	1
Frost	.989	22	168	20	2	19
Nelson	.988	31	239	15	3	21
Raburn	1.000	1	1	0	0	0
Santana	1.000	2	3	0	0	1
Villanueva	.997	44	323	25	1	27

Second Base	PCT	G	PO	A	E	DP
Candelaria	1.000	5	8	10	0	4
Ernster	1.000	1	0	2	0	0
Raburn	.981	25	45	57	2	11
Santana	.976	62	138	145	7	29
West	1.000	55	102	124	0	34

Third Base	PCT	G	PO	A	E	DP
Candelaria	.929	51	31	99	10	4
Ernster	.904	28	12	35	5	1
Raburn	.875	31	15	48	9	4
Santana	.714	3	1	4	2	0
Villanueva	.929	40	36	68	8	7

Shortstop	PCT	G	PO	A	E	DP
Candelaria	.833	2	2	3	1	0
Chavez	.955	79	124	219	16	44
Ernster	1.000	1	1	0	0	0
Raburn	.968	9	9	21	1	4
West	.980	53	96	143	5	25

Outfield	PCT	G	PO	A	E	DP
Belcher	.938	77	127	9	9	2
Boyd	1.000	34	50	0	0	0
Candelaria	.944	12	16	1	1	0
Clark	.974	45	69	5	2	3
Ernster	1.000	1	1	0	0	0
Foster	1.000	2	2	0	0	0
Frost	.929	9	12	1	1	0
Guerrero	1.000	3	6	0	0	0
Morris	.974	124	324	9	9	3
Nelson	1.000	10	13	0	0	0
Raburn	.918	53	84	5	8	0
Santana	.961	46	110	12	5	2
Toner	.939	19	28	3	2	0
Villanueva	1.000	2	1	0	0	0

BELOIT SNAPPERS — Low Class A

MIDWEST LEAGUE

BATTING	AVG	G	AB	R	H	2B	3B	HR	RBI	BB	SO	SB	CS	SLG	OBP	B	T	HT	WT	DOB	1st Yr	Resides
Bibbs, Kennard	.302	124	497	87	150	14	1	0	40	52	63	55	18	.334	.369	L	L	5-9	160	3-5-80	2002	Houston, Texas
Bohanan, Keith	.181	38	94	9	17	0	0	0	6	8	32	3	0	.181	.260	R	R	6-2	190	3-25-81	2002	Fremont, Calif.
Carter, Nic	.145	62	200	17	29	3	1	0	18	12	50	6	4	.170	.192	R	R	6-3	190	9-17-80	2002	Parkersburg, W.Va.
Crabbe, Callix	.260	129	465	79	121	25	6	1	46	68	52	25	9	.346	.356	S	R	5-8	190	2-14-83	2002	Lithonia, Ga.
Ernster, Mark	.229	9	35	7	8	2	0	1	5	2	11	1	0	.371	.270	R	R	6-0	190	12-10-77	1999	Glendale, Ariz.
Esparragoza, Pedro	.244	75	254	36	62	9	1	2	23	21	48	14	3	.311	.304	R	R	5-11	160	3-16-82	1999	Caracas, Venez.
Eure, Jeff	.244	123	475	69	116	21	4	11	53	35	128	29	4	.375	.313	R	R	6-1	200	8-17-80	2001	Pillow, Pa.
Fielder, Prince	.313	137	502	81	157	22	2	27	112	71	80	2	1	.526	.409	L	R	6-0	260	5-9-84	2002	Melbourne, Fla.
Gwynn, Anthony	.280	61	236	35	66	8	0	1	33	32	31	14	2	.326	.364	L	R	6-0	185	10-4-82	2003	Poway, Calif.
Heether, Adam	.228	47	171	28	39	12	1	2	22	18	28	4	4	.345	.313	R	R	6-0	200	1-14-82	2003	Ripon, Calif.
Hinton, Travis	.231	103	372	37	86	21	1	9	58	27	72	1	1	.366	.290	L	L	6-1	210	11-21-80	2001	Chandler, Ariz.
Mendez, Mario	.246	111	350	38	86	13	4	2	30	24	81	6	5	.323	.294	R	R	6-0	170	8-21-81	1999	Azua, D.R.
Moss, Steve	.290	57	186	25	54	8	3	1	22	32	44	7	5	.382	.398	R	R	6-2	180	1-12-84	2002	Sherman Oaks, Calif.
Murray, Josh	.188	10	32	4	6	2	0	0	4	2	11	0	0	.250	.278	R	R	6-2	180	8-12-84	2002	Lutz, Fla.
Terni, Chas	.239	106	352	37	84	12	1	2	36	33	81	1	1	.295	.317	R	R	5-10	170	10-1-78	1997	Uncasville, Conn.
Vanden Berg, John	.297	76	276	37	82	12	0	7	39	20	56	2	2	.417	.351	R	R	6-2	210	2-5-80	2002	Cedarburg, Wisc.
Weeks, Rickie	.349	20	63	13	22	8	1	1	16	15	9	2	0	.556	.494	R	R	6-0	195	9-13-82	2003	Altamonte Springs, Fla.

PITCHING	W	L	ERA	G	GS	CG	SV	IP	H	R	ER	BB	SO	AVG	B	T	HT	WT	DOB	1st Yr	Resides
Alliston, Josh	4	6	3.33	52	0	0	10	70	67	34	26	18	75	.248	R	R	6-5	230	2-29-80	2002	Long Beach, Calif.
Baker, Jason	5	4	4.08	21	6	0	0	57	70	35	26	18	35	.295	R	R	6-0	200	9-18-80	2002	Accokeek, Md.
Ballouli, Khalid	5	4	4.15	15	8	0	2	56	60	34	26	14	45	.267	R	R	6-2	190	3-20-80	2002	Austin, Texas
Bausher, Tim	1	2	3.33	19	0	0	3	27	19	12	10	12	39	.193	R	R	6-4	200	4-23-79	2001	Bechtelsville, Pa.
Bohanan, Keith	0	0	0.00	3	0	0	0	2	0	0	0	0	0	.000	R	R	6-2	190	3-25-81	2002	Fremont, Calif.
Breslow, Craig	3	4	5.12	33	0	0	2	65	64	43	37	27	80	.253	L	L	6-1	180	8-8-80	2002	Trumbull, Conn.
Carpenter, Calvin	3	6	3.86	16	12	0	0	61	53	40	26	50	46	.227	R	R	6-2	190	9-23-82	2001	Natchitoches, La.
Gabriel, Justin	2	0	4.23	21	0	0	1	45	54	25	21	19	44	.301	L	L	5-9	160	3-2-79	2002	Las Vegas, Nev.
Hall, Bo	8	4	2.59	46	0	0	11	73	52	27	21	29	76	.200	R	R	6-0	180	9-5-80	2002	Ormond Beach, Fla.
Henderson, Eric	4	2	4.53	10	10	0	0	54	61	29	27	23	23	.308	L	L	6-4	210	9-5-79	2000	Litchfield Park, Ariz.
Housman, Jeff	2	7	1.81	20	15	0	0	89	79	40	18	26	50	.230	L	L	6-3	180	8-4-81	2002	Visalia, Calif.
Huizinga, Jon	4	0	4.32	23	0	0	2	42	56	34	20	13	30	.311	R	R	6-3	220	10-16-79	2002	Wayland, Mich.
Martin, Forrest	0	0	6.48	4	0	0	0	8	12	6	6	0	3	.352	R	R	6-2	190	1-8-80	2003	Talihina, Okla.
Mendez, Mario	0	0	29.45	5	0	0	0	3	10	12	12	8	3	.000	R	R	6-0	170	8-21-81	1999	Azua, D.R.
Mendoza, Gabriel	1	2	4.13	18	0	0	2	33	34	24	15	16	38	.255	L	L	6-2	160	1-13-82	1999	Barinitas, Venez.
Parra, Manny	11	2	2.73	23	23	1	0	139	127	50	42	24	117	.243	L	L	6-3	200	10-30-82	2002	Citrus Heights, Calif.
Pena, Luismar	2	6	3.90	23	18	1	0	90	92	51	39	46	53	.267	R	R	6-5	160	1-10-83	1999	La Victoria, Venez.
Sarfate, Dennis	12	2	2.84	26	26	0	0	140	114	50	44	66	140	.226	R	R	6-4	210	4-9-81	2001	Chandler, Ariz.
Steitz, Jon	0	1	5.79	4	0	0	0	9	12	9	6	5	5	.300	R	R	6-3	200	9-5-80	2001	Branford, Conn.
Trytten, Ryan	3	4	6.33	28	4	0	1	58	81	53	41	29	31	.336	R	R	6-3	200	5-10-81	2001	Agency, Iowa
Wilhelmsen, Tom	5	5	2.76	15	15	1	0	88	78	35	27	27	63	.240	R	R	6-6	190	12-16-83	2002	Tucson, Ariz.

FIELDING

Catcher	PCT	G	PO	A	E	DP	PB
Esparragoza	.977	75	528	77	14	2	10
Vanden Berg	.987	65	492	33	7	2	18
Ernster	1.000	1	2	3	0	1	
Heether	1.000	2	1	4	0	0	
Weeks	.923	19	31	53	7	6	

First Base	PCT	G	PO	A	E	DP
Bohanan	1.000	2	16	1	0	3
Eure	.989	10	86	2	1	5
Fielder	.984	126	1030	67	18	83

Second Base	PCT	G	PO	A	E	DP
Bohanan	.875	9	10	18	4	3
Crabbe	.946	113	232	328	32	64

Third Base	PCT	G	PO	A	E	DP
Bohanan	1.000	3	0	1	0	0
Ernster	.900	5	3	6	1	0
Eure	.951	93	63	171	12	7
Heether	.869	38	23	50	11	2

Shortstop	PCT	G	PO	A	E	DP
Bohanan	.889	13	16	32	6	8
Crabbe	.846	6	11	11	4	3
Eure	.833	8	10	20	6	5
Murray	.868	10	16	17	5	4
Terni	.932	105	188	279	34	51

Outfield	PCT	G	PO	A	E	DP
Bibbs	.991	122	216	12	2	1
Carter	.950	62	73	3	4	0
Gwynn	.988	61	158	6	2	3
Hinton	.952	36	58	1	3	0
Mendez	.969	100	182	4	6	1
Moss	1.000	57	125	9	0	0

HELENA BREWERS — Rookie

PIONEER LEAGUE

BATTING	AVG	G	AB	R	H	2B	3B	HR	RBI	BB	SO	SB	CS	SLG	OBP	B	T	HT	WT	DOB	1st Yr	Resides
Anderson, Drew	.318	61	214	33	68	11	3	2	38	35	39	9	5	.425	.420	L	R	6-2	195	6-9-81	2003	Kearney, Neb.
Barnes, Justin	.241	56	195	29	47	10	1	5	34	12	49	3	2	.379	.283	R	R	6-3	205	8-21-82	2003	Port St. Lucie, Fla.
Carter, Nic	.260	24	50	5	13	1	0	0	1	3	14	4	2	.280	.302	R	R	6-3	190	9-17-80	2002	Parkersburg, W.Va.
Corporan, Carlos	.222	10	27	4	6	1	0	0	4	4	7	0	0	.259	.353	S	R	6-3	212	1-7-84	2003	Catano, P.R.
Deevers, Robby	.326	64	221	49	72	14	3	4	41	17	51	9	3	.471	.384	R	R	5-10	190	6-23-80	2003	Elgin, Okla.
Frost, Jeremy	.200	7	25	2	5	1	0	0	2	0	7	1	0	.240	.200	R	R	6-3	210	11-19-79	2002	Oviedo, Fla.
Gomez, Andri	.225	52	151	23	34	7	0	2	13	2	20	8	5	.311	.250	S	R	5-11	160	10-31-81	1999	Cabral, D.R.
Lewis, William	.000	1	3	0	0	0	0	0	0	0	0	0	0	.000	.000	R	R	5-10	180	8-18-81	2003	Texarkana, Ark.
Lozada, Charlie	.182	8	22	1	4	1	0	0	4	1	4	0	0	.227	.217	R	R	5-11	190	6-28-83	2003	Caracas, Venez.
Melo, Manuel	.255	46	141	26	36	4	1	0	11	12	28	11	3	.298	.314	S	R	6-1	160	9-28-81	1999	Guarico, Venez.
Palmisano, Louis	.391	47	174	32	68	13	2	6	43	18	29	13	2	.592	.458	R	R	6-1	185	9-16-82	2003	Fort Lauderdale, Fla.
Ramirez, Manuel	.330	63	218	36	72	19	1	11	52	23	48	0	1	.578	.400	R	R	6-0	165	9-7-82	2000	Acarigua, Venez.
Rodriguez, Guilder	.224	69	255	51	57	1	1	0	25	47	35	29	3	.235	.345	S	R	6-1	160	7-24-83	2001	Barquisimeto, Venez.
Rottino, Vinny	.311	64	222	42	69	10	0	1	20	28	25	5	2	.369	.404	R	R	6-0	195	4-7-80	2003	Racine, Wisc.
Segura Cornier, Alberto	.325	28	80	10	26	1	1	1	11	7	11	3	0	.400	.407	R	R	5-11	180	11-9-83	2000	Los Llanos, D.R.
Septimo, Agustin	.214	56	182	29	39	3	1	0	19	22	51	8	2	.242	.308	S	R	6-1	160	5-27-84	2003	Santo Domingo, D.R.
Trofholz, Terry	.349	68	261	60	91	10	3	0	22	19	39	39	6	.410	.396	R	R	6-2	190	9-11-80	2003	Plano, Texas
Whitney, Barrett	.273	56	176	24	48	18	1	1	28	23	35	0	1	.403	.356	L	R	6-2	205	4-6-81	2003	Edmond, Okla.

GAMES BY POSITION: C—Corporan 9, Lozada 7, Palmisano 40, Ramirez 1, Rottino 11, Segura Cornier 23. **1B**—Ramirez 18, Rottino 30, Whitney 38. **2B**—Gomez 16, Lewis 1, Rodriguez 69. **3B**—Barnes 54, Frost 2, Gomez 1, Rottino 25. **SS**—Gomez 29, Rottino 2, Septimo 51. **OF**—Anderson 54, Carter 17, Deevers 63, Frost 5, Melo 41, Ramirez 1, Rottino 5, Trofholz 67.

PITCHING	W	L	ERA	G	GS	CG	SV	IP	H	R	ER	BB	SO	AVG	B	T	HT	WT	DOB	1st Yr	Resides
Beresford, Simon	2	4	5.28	17	0	0	1	29	32	28	17	14	19	.283	R	R	6-6	215	1-2-83	2003	Glen Waverley, Australia
Carter, Nic	1	0	4.97	8	0	0	0	12	15	12	7	10	11	.000	R	R	6-3	190	9-17-80	2002	Parkersburg, W.Va.
Dillard, Tim	0	0	0.00	3	0	0	0	5	5	0	0	2	6	.250	S	R	6-4	200	7-19-83	2003	Saltillo, Miss.
Durost, Ken	3	5	5.26	17	8	0	0	51	67	34	30	16	42	.320	R	R	6-4	190	10-10-81	2003	Palmdale, Calif.
Eveland, Dana	2	1	2.08	19	0	0	14	26	30	9	6	8	41	.285	L	L	6-1	220	10-29-83	2003	Palmdale, Calif.
Gelatka, Todd	0	0	3.00	3	0	0	0	6	5	2	2	1	5	.217	L	R	6-3	180	8-2-81	2001	Lake Forest, Calif.
Grybash, Daniel	2	1	2.82	17	6	0	0	38	37	19	12	12	31	.260	R	R	6-1	205	12-26-80	2003	Palatine, Ill.
Henderson, Eric	3	0	3.26	4	2	0	0	19	14	8	7	2	14	.205	L	L	6-4	210	9-5-79	2000	Litchfield Park, Ariz.
Hendrix, Phillip	2	1	6.38	16	0	0	0	24	34	18	17	7	23	.326	R	R	5-11	175	6-5-81	2003	Richmond, Va.
Kloosterman, Greg	6	1	3.28	14	14	0	0	69	68	28	25	23	76	.257	L	L	6-3	205	6-21-82	2003	Bristol, Ind.
McKenna, Daniel	1	1	5.60	13	0	0	0	18	20	12	11	7	21	.273	R	R	6-5	210	1-30-81	2003	Marlton, N.J.
Mendoza, Gabriel	0	1	12.46	5	0	0	0	4	9	6	6	5	4	.391	L	L	6-2	160	1-13-82	1999	Barinitas, Venez.
Montalbo, Brian	2	1	3.18	13	4	0	1	45	51	26	16	12	30	.278	S	R	6-4	210	11-22-81	2003	Anchorage, Alaska
Moreira, Greg	2	2	4.33	17	7	0	0	44	57	33	21	14	22	.322	R	R	6-5	210	5-29-83	2001	Apopka, Fla.
Ramirez, Carlos	7	3	3.46	15	15	1	0	78	78	34	30	17	60	.261	L	L	6-3	160	8-12-84	2001	Azua, D.R.
Richardson, Judd	2	1	5.18	14	12	0	0	40	49	27	23	22	30	.306	L	R	6-4	200	2-13-80	2001	Terra Cotta, Ontario
Slack, Nick	1	1	2.19	19	0	0	10	25	13	6	6	6	37	.147	R	R	6-1	215	1-5-83	2003	Deltona, Fla.
Stetter, Mitch	6	2	3.95	15	8	0	0	55	55	34	24	12	63	.252	L	L	6-4	195	1-16-81	2003	Huntingburg, Ind.
Stover, Ricky	0	2	6.56	16	0	0	0	23	25	24	17	15	21	.290	L	L	6-6	205	1-26-82	2003	Rockwall, Texas
Taubenheim, Ty	6	1	2.15	14	0	0	1	50	47	13	12	3	44	.251	R	R	6-5	200	11-17-82	2003	Lynden, Wash.

ARIZONA LEAGUE

BATTING	AVG	G	AB	R	H	2B	3B	HR	RBI	BB	SO	SB	CS	SLG	OBP	B	T	HT	WT	DOB	1st Yr	Resides
Acosta, Gilberto	.349	50	189	43	66	8	4	1	26	20	30	30	3	.450	.413	S	R	6-1	150	10-5-82	1999	Valencia,Venez.
Bates, Dallas	.250	38	148	17	37	8	0	0	15	18	35	2	4	.304	.339	L	L	5-8	170	7-20-84	2002	Chandler, Ariz.
Bates, Nick	.143	3	7	2	1	0	0	0	2	2	1	0	0	.143	.333	R	R	6-4	210	2-28-80	2003	Blissfield, Mich.
Corporan, Carlos	.250	34	120	13	30	6	0	2	9	3	22	0	1	.350	.278	S	R	6-3	212	1-7-84	2003	Catano, P.R.
DePaula, Bartolo	.217	37	115	20	25	5	1	0	11	7	26	6	4	.278	.268	S	R	6-0	150	1-24-84	2001	Villa Mella, D.R.
Fermaint, Charlie	.300	25	100	16	30	3	3	1	9	3	19	6	3	.420	.327	R	R	5-10	170	10-11-85	2003	Vega Alta, P.R.
Guhring, Simon	.281	21	57	7	16	1	1	0	8	5	11	2	0	.333	.359	R	R	6-1	200	7-14-83	2002	Leonberg, Germany
Heether, Adam	.000	3	11	1	0	0	0	0	0	2	1	0	0	.000	.214	R	R	6-0	200	1-14-82	2003	Ripon, Calif.
Lewis, William	.242	25	99	16	24	5	3	0	19	7	16	3	4	.354	.327	R	R	5-10	180	8-18-81	2003	Texarkana, Ark.
Lozada, Charlie	.358	24	67	10	24	4	1	0	10	6	10	0	1	.448	.400	R	R	5-11	190	6-28-83	2003	Caracas, Venez.
Mannon, Adam	.274	47	179	26	49	13	4	3	37	21	53	6	2	.441	.353	R	R	6-3	200	12-12-83	2003	Queen Creek, Ariz.
McCormack, Taylor	.260	42	146	24	38	9	1	2	19	14	41	1	2	.377	.333	R	R	6-2	190	10-20-82	2001	Palm Harbor, Fla.
Mejia, Fausto	.308	32	107	12	33	6	1	0	13	5	19	3	1	.383	.345	R	R	6-1	160	11-13-83	2001	Azua, D.R.
Olayemi, Gbenga	.170	24	53	7	9	1	0	0	3	3	17	1	0	.189	.224	R	R	6-1	190	9-8-82	2002	Ilorin, Nigeria
Opdyke, Bryan	.272	32	103	16	28	8	2	0	10	16	25	1	0	.388	.364	L	R	6-2	190	8-7-84	2003	Tucson, Ariz.
Phillips, Jonathan	.191	26	68	7	13	1	0	0	7	8	12	0	1	.206	.286	R	R	5-10	160	4-16-86	2003	Capetown, South Africa
Pijuan, Ricky	.200	41	145	16	29	5	3	1	12	10	62	1	0	.297	.261	L	L	6-1	210	7-6-82	2003	Pomona, Calif.
Plasencia, Francisco	.283	47	187	30	53	11	3	2	21	19	43	14	6	.406	.356	L	L	6-2	150	6-19-84	2000	Barinas, Venez.
Weeks, Rickie	.500	1	4	0	2	0	0	0	4	0	2	1	0	.500	.600	R	R	6-0	195	9-13-82	2003	Altamonte Springs, Fla.
Willis, Lendon	.667	2	6	1	4	2	0	0	3	1	2	2	0	1.000	.625	R	R	6-1	170	10-17-82	2002	Millington, Tenn.

GAMES BY POSITION: C—Corporan 16, Guhring 15, Lozada 10, Olayemi 16, Opdyke 21. **1B**—Corporan 15, Guhring 3, Pijuan 39. **2B**—Acosta 1, DePaula 27, Lewis 22, Phillips 13. **3B**—DePaula 2, Guhring 1, Heether 2, Lozada 6, McCormack 40, Phillips 8. **SS**—Acosta 48, DePaula 11, Heether 1, McCormack 2, Phillips 2. **OF**—D. Bates 36, N. Bates 1, Fermaint 22, Mannon 45, Mejia 25, Plasencia 44.

PITCHING	W	L	ERA	G	GS	CG	SV	IP	H	R	ER	BB	SO	AVG	B	T	HT	WT	DOB	1st Yr	Resides
Carpenter, Calvin	0	0	0.00	1	0	0	0	3	3	1	0	0	1	.250	R	R	6-2	190	9-23-82	2001	Natchitoches, La.
Castillo, Ruben	0	2	13.50	6	0	0	0	8	10	14	12	13	7	.312	R	R	5-11	160	6-5-83	2000	Barinita, Venez.
Cedeno , Jonathan	0	4	8.75	14	0	0	0	24	39	26	23	17	23	.375	R	R	6-2	170	1-25-84	2002	Caracas, Venez.
Correa, Alexander	0	0	12.46	9	0	0	1	13	28	26	18	13	10	.405	L	L	6-4	170	7-17-82	1999	Valle la Pascua, Venez.
Dillard, Tim	1	2	3.79	11	4	0	0	36	36	19	15	5	32	.260	S	R	6-4	200	7-19-83	2003	Saltillo, Miss.
Durocher, Jayson	0	0	0.00	2	2	0	0	2	0	0	0	0	3	.000	R	R	6-3	230	8-18-74	1993	Scottsdale, Ariz.
Flandes, Wington	0	1	4.50	11	0	0	1	20	26	13	10	1	7	.298	R	R	6-4	170	4-27-83	2000	La Romana, D.R.
Garcia, Miguel	1	5	7.59	12	7	0	0	43	65	46	36	21	27	.353	R	R	6-2	160	6-29-85	2001	Barinas, Venez.
Gittings, Chris	2	2	4.84	13	0	0	1	22	22	14	12	5	10	.278	R	R	6-3	190	11-1-82	2001	Louisville, Ky.
Hawk, Tommy	2	1	2.31	12	6	0	0	47	47	17	12	17	30	.261	R	R	6-3	210	2-7-85	2003	Lompoc, Calif.
Marion, Ryan	2	1	4.55	9	4	0	0	28	28	18	14	9	29	.264	R	R	6-1	200	9-23-84	2003	Kernersville, N.C.
Martin, Forrest	2	1	2.78	11	0	0	2	23	25	13	7	12	34	.265	R	R	6-2	190	1-8-80	2003	Talihina, Okla.
Martinez Sosa, Alvaro	1	5	5.54	12	6	0	1	39	38	29	24	35	47	.251	R	R	6-6	190	7-29-85	2002	Caracas, Venez.
Morrison, Tyler	1	4	6.02	10	8	0	0	40	58	34	27	9	30	.353	R	R	6-0	200	5-1-85	2003	Glendora, Calif.
Pruett, Hubert	2	3	5.85	10	5	0	0	40	46	30	26	17	31	.287	R	R	6-2	220	3-16-83	2001	Pearl City, Hawaii
Rauch, Brian	2	3	4.01	11	3	0	1	34	30	20	15	8	21	.238	R	R	6-4	220	11-30-80	2003	Rockledge, Fla.
Walker, Edwin	0	2	5.54	9	5	0	0	26	27	17	16	9	22	.272	R	L	6-3	190	10-26-83	2002	San Antonio, Texas
Wilhelmsen, Tom	0	1	4.50	2	2	0	0	4	5	2	2	4	4	.312	R	R	6-6	190	12-16-83	2002	Tucson, Ariz.
Wooley, Robbie	2	0	2.49	7	3	0	0	22	21	8	6	7	18	.259	R	R	6-1	190	12-7-84	2003	Kokomo, Ind.

MINNESOTA TWINS

BY JOHN MILLEA

Coming off a surprising Central Division title and trip to the American League Championship Series in 2002, the Twins opened 2003 with high expectations. Their season closed with a disappointing defeat to the Yankees in the divisional playoffs, ending a year of alternating highs and lows.

The Twins were so-so in April, very good in May, swooned in June and July and got back on track in August and September.

What looked like a lost season at the all-star break turned around dramatically on July 16 when Minnesota acquired veteran leadoff hitter Shannon Stewart from the Blue Jays for outfielder Bobby Kielty.

The deal wasn't heralded with hosannas for general manager Terry Ryan. Kielty was viewed by many as a player who had great potential for the future, including the ability to hit in the leadoff spot.

But Stewart made everyone forget about that.

The Twins were 44-49 at the break, 7½ games behind the Royals in the division. But Stewart helped them finish 46-23, the best record in the major leagues after the all-star break.

Their 90-win season was four fewer than in 2002, but at midseason few would have guessed they would have close to that many victories. The first omen may have come in spring training, when starting pitcher Eric Milton was lost to knee surgery (he returned for three late-season appearances). Kenny Rogers was signed to replace Milton and finished the year 13-8, 4.57.

Another starter, Joe Mays, struggled all season and had an 8-8, 6.30 record when he was lost to elbow surgery in the final weeks (he is expected to miss the 2004 season). But Brad Radke and Kyle Lohse each won 14 games and Johan Santana won 12, including going 11-2, 2.86 after moving into the rotation.

The biggest key on the mound down the stretch was the combo of LaTroy Hawkins and Eddie Guardado. Hawkins continued to establish himself as a top-level set-up guy, going 9-3, 1.86, and Guardado had 41 saves.

The arrival of Stewart helped solidify the outfield, with Jacque Jones making room for his new teammate by moving from left to right and Torii Hunter continuing to play a splendid center field. That eased the pain of trying many young players in right field; Kielty, Dustan Mohr, Michael Cuddyer, Michael Restovich and Michael Ryan all had a shot.

Hitting for power continued to be a problem for the Twins, who, of course, play in a ballpark that makes sluggers drool. Hunter hit 26 homers (driving in a career-high 102 runs), and seven others hit between 10 and 17.

The Twins had gone 0-6 in Anaheim and Texas immediately preceding the All-Star Game, by which time they had lost eight straight. But with Stewart on board they won five in a row after the break and then went 4-2 on an Anaheim-Texas swing.

They flirted with the White Sox during the final month of the season, locking up the division crown with an 11-game winning streak.

In the minors, Double-A New Britain and high A Fort Myers reached their league's playoffs, and Rookie-level Elizabethton won the Appalachian League title.

Fort Myers and New Britain each won 73 games, and it's probably not a coincidence that catcher Joe Mauer played at both levels in 2003. The 20-year-old Minnesota native, who was the first player selected in the 2001 June draft, hit .339-5-85 between Fort Myers and New Britain on his way to becoming Minor League Player of the Year. He may get his first taste of the big leagues sometime in 2004.

Johan Santana

Joe Mauer

PLAYERS of the YEAR

MAJOR LEAGUE: Johan Santana, lhp

At 12-3, 3.07 overall, Santana was even more impressive after moving into the rotation in July. He went 11-2, 2.86 as a starter, leading the Twins' second-half surge to a second straight division total.

MINOR LEAGUE: Joe Mauer, c

Baseball America's Minor League Player of the Year hit .339-5-85 between Class A Fort Myers and Double-A New Britain, leading both clubs to half-season division titles. He also threw out better than 50 percent of basestealers.

ORGANIZATION LEADERS

BATTING		
*AVG	Joe Mauer, New Britain/Fort Myers	.338
R	Jason Bartlett, New Britain	96
H	Joe Mauer, New Britain/Fort Myers	172
TB	Jeff Deardorff, Rochester/New Britain	249
2B	Kevin West, New Britain	41
3B	Jason Bartlett, New Britain	8
	Trent Oeltjen, Quad City	8
HR	Justin Morneau, Rochester/New Britain	22
RBI	Terry Tiffee, New Britain	93
BB	Jason Bartlett, New Britain	58
SO	Jeff Deardorff, Rochester/New Britain	130
	Dusty Gomon, Quad City/Elizabethton	130
SB	Jason Bartlett, New Britain	41
*SLG	Justin Morneau, Rochester/New Britain	.526
*OBP	Joe Mauer, New Britain/Fort Myers	.398
PITCHING		
W	J.D. Durbin, New Britain/Fort Myers	15
L	Scott Tyler, Quad City	12
#ERA	Jesse Crain, Rochester/New Britain/Fort Myers	1.93
G	Beau Kemp, New Britain/Fort Myers	58
CG	Four tied at	2
SV	Beau Kemp, New Britain/Fort Myers	22
IP	J.D. Durbin, New Britain/Fort Myers	182
BB	Scott Tyler, Quad City	82
SO	J.D. Durbin, New Britain/Fort Myers	139

*Minimum 250 At-Bats #Minimum 75 Innings

MINNESOTA TWINS

Manager: Ron Gardenhire.

2003 Record: 90-72, .556 (1st, AL Central).

BATTING	AVG	G	AB	R	H	2B	3B	HR	RBI	BB	SO	SB	CS	SLG	OBP	B	T	HT	WT	DOB	1st Yr	Resides
Bowen, Rob	.100	7	10	0	1	0	0	0	1	0	4	0	0	.100	.091	S	R	6-3	220	2-24-81	1999	Fort Myers, Fla.
Cuddyer, Michael	.245	35	102	14	25	1	3	4	8	12	19	1	1	.431	.325	R	R	6-2	220	3-27-79	1997	Fort Myers, Fla.
Ford, Lew	.329	34	73	16	24	7	1	3	15	8	9	2	0	.575	.402	R	R	6-0	190	8-12-76	1999	Lufkin, Texas
Gomez, Chris	.251	58	175	14	44	9	3	1	15	7	13	2	1	.354	.279	R	R	6-1	180	6-16-71	1992	Carlsbad, Calif.
Guzman, Cristian	.268	143	534	78	143	15	14	3	53	30	79	18	9	.365	.311	S	R	6-0	190	3-21-78	1995	Santo Domingo, D.R.
Hocking, Denny	.239	83	188	22	45	10	2	3	22	15	37	0	1	.362	.291	S	R	5-10	180	4-2-70	1989	Tustin, Calif.
Hunter, Torii	.250	154	581	83	145	31	4	26	102	50	106	6	7	.451	.312	R	R	6-2	210	7-18-75	1993	The Colony, Texas
Jones, Jacque	.304	136	517	76	157	33	1	16	69	21	105	13	1	.464	.333	L	L	5-10	200	4-25-75	1996	San Diego, Calif.
Kielty, Bobby	.252	75	238	40	60	13	0	9	32	42	56	6	2	.420	.370	S	R	6-1	220	8-5-76	1999	Fort Myers, Fla.
Koskie, Corey	.292	131	469	76	137	29	2	14	69	77	113	11	5	.452	.393	L	R	6-3	220	6-28-73	1994	Fort Myers, Fla.
LeCroy, Matthew	.287	107	345	39	99	19	0	17	64	25	82	0	1	.490	.342	R	R	6-2	220	12-13-75	1997	Belton, S.C.
Mientkiewicz, Doug	.300	142	487	67	146	38	1	11	65	74	55	4	1	.450	.393	L	R	6-2	200	6-19-74	1995	Estero, Fla.
Mohr, Dustan	.250	121	348	50	87	22	0	10	36	33	106	5	2	.399	.314	R	R	6-1	210	6-19-76	1997	Hattiesburg, Miss.
Morneau, Justin	.226	40	106	14	24	4	0	4	16	9	30	0	0	.377	.287	L	R	6-4	220	5-15-81	1999	Fort Myers, Fla.
Pierzynski, A.J.	.312	137	487	63	152	35	3	11	74	24	55	3	1	.464	.360	L	R	6-3	220	12-30-76	1994	Fort Myers, Fla.
Prieto, Alex	.091	8	11	1	1	0	0	0	0	0	4	0	0	.091	.091	R	R	5-11	200	6-19-76	1993	Wichita, Kan.
Prince, Tom	.200	24	40	5	8	2	0	2	5	5	7	1	0	.400	.319	R	R	5-11	200	8-13-64	1984	Bradenton, Fla.
Restovich, Michael	.283	24	53	10	15	3	2	0	4	10	12	0	0	.415	.406	R	R	6-4	240	1-3-79	1997	Fort Myers, Fla.
Rivas, Luis	.259	135	475	69	123	16	9	8	43	30	65	17	7	.381	.308	R	R	5-11	190	8-30-79	1995	La Guaira, Venez.
Ryan, Michael	.393	27	61	13	24	7	0	5	13	6	12	2	1	.754	.441	L	R	6-0	180	7-6-77	1996	Indiana, Pa.
Sears, Todd	.246	24	65	7	16	2	0	2	11	7	15	0	0	.369	.324	R	R	6-5	210	10-23-75	1997	Ankeny, Iowa
Stewart, Shannon	.322	65	270	43	87	22	0	6	38	25	36	3	4	.470	.384	R	R	6-1	210	2-25-74	1992	Miami, Fla.
2-team (71 Toronto)	.307	136	573	90	176	44	2	13	73	52	66	4	6	.459	.364							

PITCHING	W	L	ERA	G	GS	CG	SV	IP	H	R	ER	BB	SO	AVG	B	T	HT	WT	DOB	1st Yr	Resides
Baldwin, James	0	1	5.40	10	0	0	1	15	21	10	9	4	7	.333	R	R	6-3	230	7-15-71	1990	Southern Pines, N.C.
Balfour, Grant	1	0	4.15	17	1	0	0	26	23	12	12	14	30	.234	R	R	6-2	190	12-30-77	1997	Sydney, Australia
Fetters, Mike	0	0	0.00	5	0	0	0	6	2	0	0	1	1	.100	R	R	6-4	230	12-19-64	1986	Chandler, Ariz.
Fiore, Tony	1	1	5.50	21	0	0	0	36	32	25	22	21	23	.242	R	R	6-4	220	10-12-71	1992	Tampa, Fla.
Guardado, Eddie	3	5	2.89	66	0	0	41	65	50	22	21	14	60	.207	R	L	6-0	200	10-2-70	1990	Stockton, Calif.
Hawkins, LaTroy	9	3	1.86	74	0	0	2	77	69	20	16	15	75	.238	R	R	6-5	210	12-21-72	1991	Frisco, Texas
Johnson, Adam	0	1	47.25	2	0	0	0	1	8	8	7	1	0	.666	R	R	6-2	210	7-12-79	2000	Fort Myers, Fla.
Lohse, Kyle	14	11	4.61	33	33	2	0	201	211	107	103	45	130	.268	R	R	6-2	200	10-4-78	1997	Fort Myers, Fla.
Mays, Joe	8	8	6.30	31	21	0	0	130	159	92	91	39	50	.301	S	R	6-1	190	12-10-75	1995	Sarasota, Fla.
Milton, Eric	1	0	2.65	3	3	0	0	17	15	5	5	1	7	.234	L	L	6-3	220	8-4-75	1996	Fort Myers, Fla.
Nakamura, Micheal	0	0	7.82	12	0	0	1	13	20	11	11	2	14	.338	R	R	5-10	170	9-6-76	1997	Ferntree Gully, Australia
Orosco, Jesse	1	1	5.79	8	0	0	0	5	4	3	3	5	3	.235	R	L	6-2	205	4-21-57	1978	San Diego, Calif.
2-team (15 New York)	1	1	8.00	23	0	0	0	9	8	9	8	11	7	.242							
Pulido, Carlos	0	1	4.02	7	1	0	0	16	15	9	7	3	6	.254	L	L	6-0	180	8-5-71	1989	Caracas, Venez.
Radke, Brad	14	10	4.49	33	33	3	0	212	242	111	106	28	120	.288	R	R	6-2	180	10-27-72	1991	Largo, Fla.
Reed, Rick	6	12	5.07	27	21	2	0	135	155	80	76	29	71	.285	R	R	6-1	190	8-16-65	1986	Proctorville, Ohio
Rincon, Juan	5	6	3.68	58	0	0	0	86	74	38	35	38	63	.230	R	R	5-11	190	1-23-79	1996	Maracaibo, Venez.
Rogers, Kenny	13	8	4.57	33	31	0	0	195	227	108	99	50	116	.291	L	L	6-1	210	11-10-64	1982	Southlake, Texas
Romero, J.C.	2	0	5.00	73	0	0	0	63	66	37	35	42	50	.271	S	L	5-11	190	6-4-76	1997	San Juan, P.R.
Santana, Johan	12	3	3.07	45	18	0	0	158	127	56	54	47	169	.215	L	L	6-0	190	3-13-79	1996	Tovar, Venez.
Thomas, Brad	0	1	7.71	3	0	0	0	5	6	4	4	3	2	.315	L	L	6-4	220	10-12-77	1995	Sydney, Australia

FIELDING

Catcher	PCT	G	PO	A	E	DP	PB
Bowen	.944	7	15	2	1	0	1
LeCroy	.980	22	95	4	2	0	2
Pierzynski	.993	135	843	45	6	6	5
Prince	1.000	22	83	5	0	0	2

First Base	PCT	G	PO	A	E	DP
Cuddyer	.969	5	30	1	1	2
Hocking	.980	10	44	4	1	3
LeCroy	.990	17	99	3	1	7
Mientkiewicz	.997	139	1091	68	4	86
Morneau	.971	7	29	4	1	1
Sears	.990	14	93	7	1	7

Second Base	PCT	G	PO	A	E	DP
Cuddyer	.000	1	0	0	0	0
Gomez	.989	23	37	50	1	10
Hocking	1.000	26	31	36	0	9
Mientkiewicz	.000	1	0	0	0	0
Prieto	1.000	5	5	6	0	1
Rivas	.982	134	218	325	10	64

Third Base	PCT	G	PO	A	E	DP
Cuddyer	1.000	7	2	7	0	0
Gomez	.978	18	14	31	1	3
Hocking	.963	24	19	33	2	1
Koskie	.973	131	91	234	9	15
Mientkiewicz	.000	1	0	0	0	0

Shortstop	PCT	G	PO	A	E	DP
Gomez	.971	17	13	21	1	3
Guzman	.980	141	195	352	11	67
Hocking	1.000	17	23	41	0	8
Prieto	1.000	1	1	1	0	0

Outfield	PCT	G	PO	A	E	DP
Cuddyer	1.000	18	24	1	0	0
Ford	.923	25	35	1	3	1
Hocking	1.000	8	10	0	0	0
Hunter	.991	151	425	5	4	1
Jones	.977	101	211	2	5	0
Kielty	.972	36	68	1	2	0
Mientkiewicz	1.000	3	3	0	0	0
Mohr	.976	110	239	2	6	0
Restovich	1.000	17	29	1	0	0
Ryan	1.000	16	33	2	0	1
Stewart	.993	58	136	4	1	0

LARRY GOREN

Torii Hunter

FARM SYSTEM

Director, Baseball Operations: Jim Rantz.

Class	Farm Team	League	W	L	Pct.	Finish*	Manager	First Yr.
AAA	Rochester (N.Y.) Red Wings	International	68	75	.476	9th (14)	Phil Roof	2003
AA	New Britain (Conn.) Rock Cats	Eastern	73	68	.518	4th (12)	Stan Cliburn	1995
High A	Fort Myers (Fla.) Miracle	Florida State	73	63	.537	5th (12)	Jose Marzan	1993
Low A	Quad City (Iowa) River Bandits	Midwest	59	78	.431	14th (14)	Jeff Carter	1999
Rookie	Elizabethton (Tenn.) Twins	Appalachian	42	24	.636	+2nd (10)	Ray Smith	1974
Rookie	Fort Myers (Fla.) Twins	Gulf Coast	28	31	.475	7th (14)	Rudy Hernandez	1989

*Finish in overall standings (No. of teams in league) +League champion

ROCHESTER RED WINGS — Class AAA

INTERNATIONAL LEAGUE

BATTING	AVG	G	AB	R	H	2B	3B	HR	RBI	BB	SO	SB	CS	SLG	OBP	B	T	HT	WT	DOB	1st Yr	Resides
Andrews, Shane	.256	126	445	50	114	31	2	11	59	43	126	2	2	.409	.324	R	R	6-1	220	8-28-71	1990	Carlsbad, N.M.
Bowen, Rob	.257	30	105	14	27	7	0	6	17	11	25	0	0	.495	.333	S	R	6-3	220	2-24-81	1999	Fort Myers, Fla.
Connacher, Kevin	.221	61	145	14	32	5	2	2	15	15	50	4	3	.324	.294	R	R	5-9	180	4-6-75	1997	West Palm Beach, Fla.
Cuddyer, Michael	.306	53	186	25	57	17	0	3	34	25	49	5	4	.446	.381	R	R	6-2	220	3-27-79	1997	Fort Myers, Fla.
Deardorff, Jeff	.299	20	67	9	20	6	2	2	8	3	20	2	1	.537	.324	R	R	6-3	220	8-14-78	1997	Clermont, Fla.
Ford, Lew	.303	53	211	33	64	18	2	3	31	10	28	4	5	.450	.357	R	R	6-0	190	8-12-76	1999	Lufkin, Texas
Green, Chad	.252	106	397	50	100	24	3	9	29	22	85	12	7	.395	.294	S	R	5-10	200	6-28-75	1996	Lexington, Ky.
Kennedy, Bryan	.308	5	13	1	4	0	0	0	3	0	3	0	0	.308	.357	L	R	6-2	210	10-4-78	2001	Riverside, Calif.
Lamb, David	.259	120	405	45	105	15	2	2	31	49	60	2	6	.321	.346	S	R	6-2	200	6-6-75	1993	Newbury Park, Calif.
Marsters, Brandon	.242	103	359	39	87	24	0	10	45	17	99	0	2	.393	.276	R	R	5-11	210	3-14-75	1996	Fort Myers, Fla.
McGuire, Ryan	.303	24	76	10	23	6	0	1	9	9	23	0	1	.421	.386	L	L	6-0	210	11-23-71	1993	Coto de Caza, Calif.
2-team (65 Columbus)	.251	89	267	27	67	13	1	3	28	32	59	0	1	.341	.334	L	L	6-0	210	11-23-71	1993	Coto de Caza, Calif.
Morneau, Justin	.268	71	265	39	71	11	1	16	42	28	56	0	2	.498	.344	L	R	6-4	220	5-15-81	1999	Fort Myers, Fla.
Prieto, Alex	.265	69	234	27	62	9	1	5	21	12	49	6	3	.376	.298	R	R	5-11	200	6-19-76	1993	Wichita, Kan.
Rabe, Josh	.237	38	131	15	31	6	0	5	11	11	22	2	1	.397	.301	R	R	6-2	210	10-15-78	2000	Mendon, Ill.
Restovich, Michael	.275	119	454	75	125	34	2	16	72	47	117	10	3	.465	.346	R	R	6-4	240	1-3-79	1997	Fort Myers, Fla.
Rodriguez, Luis	.295	131	518	65	153	35	2	1	44	46	46	6	8	.376	.354	S	R	5-9	180	6-27-80	1997	Cojedes, Venez.
Ryan, Michael	.225	115	408	56	92	20	4	15	60	38	89	6	1	.404	.289	L	R	6-0	180	7-6-77	1996	Indiana, Pa.
Sears, Todd	.254	80	283	35	72	12	1	7	41	37	90	6	1	.378	.347	R	R	6-5	210	10-23-75	1997	Ankeny, Iowa
Torres, Gabby	.182	21	55	4	10	1	0	0	2	2	8	0	0	.200	.224	R	R	5-10	200	3-22-78	1995	Acarigua, Venez.
Young, Kevin	.143	4	7	0	1	1	0	0	1	3	3	0	0	.286	.400	R	R	6-3	230	6-16-69	1990	Phoenix, Ariz.

PITCHING	W	L	ERA	G	GS	CG	SV	IP	H	R	ER	BB	SO	AVG	B	T	HT	WT	DOB	1st Yr	Resides
Baldwin, James	0	2	2.43	5	5	0	0	30	25	11	8	3	18	.225	R	R	6-3	230	7-15-71	1990	Southern Pines, N.C.
Balfour, Grant	5	2	2.41	21	11	0	5	71	48	21	19	16	87	.187	R	R	6-2	190	12-30-77	1997	Sydney, Australia
Carnes, Matt	2	7	5.28	25	20	0	0	119	141	74	70	26	70	.300	R	R	6-3	210	8-18-75	1997	Miami, Okla.
Crain, Jesse	3	1	3.12	23	0	0	10	26	24	10	9	10	33	.244	R	R	6-1	200	7-5-81	2002	Austin, Texas
Duvall, Mike	1	4	5.48	24	6	0	0	44	59	32	27	15	29	.312	R	L	6-0	200	10-11-74	1995	Windham, Me.
Erdos, Todd	2	2	4.54	29	0	0	11	34	42	20	17	5	16	.315	R	R	6-1	200	11-21-73	1992	Meadville, Pa.
Eyre, Willie	0	2	6.00	6	5	0	0	24	30	18	16	16	23	.309	R	R	6-2	200	7-21-78	1999	Taylorsville, Utah
Fiore, Tony	5	6	3.95	16	11	2	1	84	80	43	37	21	48	.248	R	R	6-4	220	10-12-71	1992	Tampa, Fla.
Flohr, Adam	0	0	9.39	2	0	0	0	8	12	9	8	4	6	.342	L	L	6-2	200	3-29-77	1998	Liberty Lake, Wash.
Hoard, Brent	3	5	5.35	13	12	0	0	66	88	46	39	15	31	.317	R	L	6-4	210	11-3-76	1998	Los Gatos, Calif.
Johnson, Adam	6	11	5.35	28	17	1	0	114	128	73	68	48	78	.292	R	R	6-2	210	7-12-79	2000	Fort Myers, Fla.
Mills, Ryan	5	1	4.11	32	0	0	0	61	62	37	28	31	51	.271	R	L	6-5	190	7-21-77	1998	Scottsdale, Ariz.
Nakamura, Micheal	6	6	2.99	43	0	0	2	78	71	28	26	28	95	.243	R	R	5-10	170	9-6-76	1997	Ferntree Gully, Australia
Padilla, Juan	7	4	3.36	57	0	0	6	91	94	40	34	17	68	.265	R	R	6-0	200	2-17-77	1998	Levittown, P.R.
Palki, Jeromy	7	6	4.10	47	7	1	1	101	105	50	46	31	91	.268	R	R	6-0	200	4-14-76	1995	Oakland, Ore.
Pulido, Carlos	12	5	3.56	25	25	1	0	149	145	65	59	40	87	.261	L	L	6-0	180	8-5-71	1989	Caracas, Venez.
Rincon, Juan	0	2	7.56	2	2	0	0	8	12	7	7	5	8	.363	R	R	5-11	190	1-23-79	1996	Maracaibo, Venez.
Rodriguez, Jose	0	0	5.87	6	0	0	0	8	9	5	5	6	6	.281	L	L	6-1	200	12-18-74	1997	Cayey, P.R.
Stull, Everett	4	6	5.97	11	11	1	0	57	68	41	38	20	36	.298	R	R	6-3	210	8-24-71	1992	Stone Mountain, Ga.
Thomas, Brad	0	3	3.53	15	11	0	0	59	68	23	23	10	50	.291	L	L	6-4	220	10-12-77	1995	Sydney, Australia

FIELDING

Catcher	PCT	G	PO	A	E	DP	PB
Boscan	1.000	3	26	3	0	1	0
Estrada	.994	83	627	40	4	8	7
Evans	.987	11	68	7	1	1	3
Hubbard	.995	55	376	28	2	1	1

First Base	PCT	G	PO	A	E	DP
Hessman	.995	54	392	28	2	33
Hubbard	1.000	1	3	0	0	2
LaRoche	.993	72	549	39	4	70
Wilson	.977	24	158	12	4	20

Second Base	PCT	G	PO	A	E	DP
Castro	.973	10	16	20	1	7
Clapp	.957	31	50	60	5	19
Garcia	.938	6	4	11	1	3
Green	.967	108	202	261	16	72
Wilson	1.000	1	0	1	0	1

Third Base	PCT	G	PO	A	E	DP
Betemit	.896	107	62	163	26	18
Castro	.667	4	2	2	2	0
Clapp	.943	19	8	42	3	6
Garcia	1.000	3	1	4	0	1
Hessman	.962	19	12	39	2	2
Wilson	1.000	3	0	5	0	0

Shortstop	PCT	G	PO	A	E	DP
Betemit	.944	9	8	26	2	3
Castro	1.000	11	17	31	0	8
Clapp	.979	30	59	78	3	25
Garcia	.955	94	139	226	17	55
Green	.900	10	15	21	4	7

Outfield	PCT	G	PO	A	E	DP
Clapp	.800	4	4	0	1	0
Evans	1.000	1	1	0	0	0
Fitzgerald	1.000	11	22	1	0	0
Garcia	1.000	6	9	0	0	0
Hessman	.975	24	36	3	1	0
Hollins	.981	89	196	11	4	4
Johnson	1.000	25	50	3	0	1
Langerhans	.949	37	73	2	4	0
McDonald	.993	123	256	9	2	0
Porter	.977	74	122	7	3	1
Wilson	.989	59	91	1	1	0

NEW BRITAIN ROCK CATS — Class AA

EASTERN LEAGUE

BATTING	AVG	G	AB	R	H	2B	3B	HR	RBI	BB	SO	SB	CS	SLG	OBP	B	T	HT	WT	DOB	1st Yr	Resides
Baron, Brian	.254	98	276	34	70	11	2	0	34	20	17	1	4	.308	.300	L	R	5-11	200	9-12-78	2001	Santa Clarita, Calif.
Bartlett, Jason	.296	139	548	96	162	31	8	8	48	58	67	41	24	.425	.380	R	R	6-0	170	10-30-79	2001	Norman, Okla.
Bowen, Rob	.306	42	134	17	41	13	0	1	16	13	24	0	0	.425	.376	S	R	6-3	220	2-24-81	1999	Fort Myers, Fla.
Christensen, Mike	.133	6	15	0	2	1	0	0	0	0	6	0	0	.200	.133	R	R	6-2	190	5-24-76	1998	Fort Myers, Fla.
Connacher, Kevin	.278	6	18	2	5	1	0	0	0	1	4	0	1	.333	.316	R	R	5-9	180	4-6-75	1997	West Palm Beach, Fla.
Davidson, Seth	.263	12	38	2	10	1	0	0	3	1	3	0	1	.289	.275	R	R	6-0	180	2-26-79	2001	San Diego, Calif.
Deardorff, Jeff	.316	108	412	66	130	28	2	17	73	41	110	16	5	.517	.377	R	R	6-3	220	8-14-78	1997	Clermont, Fla.
Garbe, B.J.	.178	66	225	27	40	9	1	3	21	16	60	5	3	.267	.241	R	R	6-2	190	2-3-81	1999	Moses Lake, Wash.
Gulledge, Kelley	.250	33	80	12	20	6	0	1	7	9	23	1	0	.363	.358	R	R	6-1	200	1-25-79	2000	Arlington, Texas
Lorenzo, Juan	.241	37	83	12	20	5	1	0	4	5	13	0	0	.325	.297	S	R	5-11	180	11-10-78	1995	Cambita, D.R.
Mauer, Joe	.341	73	276	48	94	17	1	4	41	25	25	0	0	.453	.400	L	R	6-4	220	4-19-83	2001	Fort Myers, Minn.
Morneau, Justin	.329	20	79	14	26	3	1	6	13	7	14	0	0	.620	.384	L	R	6-4	220	5-15-81	1999	Fort Myers, Fla.
Owens, Ryan	.252	96	301	49	76	16	2	7	39	41	74	1	5	.389	.342	R	R	6-2	200	3-18-78	1999	Anaheim Hills, Calif.
Rabe, Josh	.303	94	366	63	111	15	2	11	72	30	63	19	3	.445	.361	R	R	6-2	210	10-15-78	2000	Mendon, Ill.
Renick, Josh	.241	102	328	57	79	8	3	0	38	29	51	13	5	.284	.313	R	R	5-9	170	12-28-78	2001	Sarasota, Fla.
Scanlon, Matt	.249	115	358	45	89	22	3	6	43	41	71	10	8	.377	.343	L	R	5-11	180	6-19-78	1999	Richfield, Minn.
Tiffee, Terry	.315	139	530	77	167	31	3	14	93	31	49	4	1	.464	.351	S	R	6-3	210	4-21-79	1999	No. Little Rock, Ark.
Torres, Gabby	.323	48	155	26	50	14	3	1	18	12	23	1	0	.471	.387	R	R	5-10	200	3-22-78	1995	Acarigua, Venez.
West, Kevin	.279	136	494	54	138	41	1	14	79	27	110	3	5	.451	.318	R	R	6-2	210	1-1-80	1999	Redwood Valley, Calif.

PITCHING	W	L	ERA	G	GS	CG	SV	IP	H	R	ER	BB	SO	AVG	B	T	HT	WT	DOB	1st Yr	Resides
Abbott, Jim	4	2	2.60	10	8	1	0	45	44	17	13	14	35	.258	R	R	6-3	190	10-12-79	1999	Caledonia, Mich.
Bonilla, Henry	9	7	3.36	26	20	1	0	142	143	58	53	37	77	.263	R	R	6-0	190	8-16-78	2000	Reno, Nev.
Carnes, Matt	1	3	4.15	6	6	0	0	30	32	15	14	11	26	.268	R	R	6-3	210	8-18-75	1997	Miami, Okla.
Corona, Ronnie	0	1	3.46	4	3	0	0	13	8	6	5	12	12	.181	R	R	6-0	180	1-27-79	2000	Apple Valley, Calif.
Crain, Jesse	1	1	0.69	22	0	0	9	39	13	4	3	10	56	.099	R	R	6-1	200	7-5-81	2002	Austin, Texas
Durbin, J.D.	6	3	3.14	14	14	2	0	95	102	39	33	29	70	.277	R	R	6-0	190	2-24-82	2000	Scottsdale, Ariz.
Estrada, Horacio	2	1	3.34	5	5	1	0	30	26	14	11	5	19	.232	L	L	6-0	160	10-19-75	1992	San Joaquin, Venez.
Eyre, Willie	6	5	3.46	29	10	1	0	96	93	42	37	38	66	.252	R	R	6-2	200	7-21-78	1999	Taylorsville, Utah
Fisher, Pete	4	1	4.60	8	8	0	0	45	56	23	23	11	22	.307	R	R	6-3	220	7-7-77	1998	Stoneham, Mass.
Flohr, Adam	2	1	4.88	43	2	0	0	63	61	35	34	35	41	.260	L	L	6-2	200	3-29-77	1998	Liberty Lake, Wash.
Hoard, Brent	0	0	0.00	3	2	0	0	5	3	0	0	3	4	.187	R	L	6-4	210	11-3-76	1998	Los Gatos, Calif.
Hodge, Kevin	6	8	3.86	56	0	0	9	93	87	45	40	28	66	.250	R	R	5-11	180	10-28-76	1998	Bryan, Texas
Kemp, Beau	5	6	3.98	36	0	0	11	52	63	32	23	23	38	.305	R	R	6-0	190	10-31-80	2000	Tulsa, Okla.
McDonald, Jon	0	0	11.30	8	2	0	0	14	26	19	18	13	4	.406	R	R	6-3	190	10-16-77	2000	Orlando, Fla.
Moreno, Victor	1	1	6.95	24	0	0	0	34	37	27	26	22	27	.280	R	R	6-0	200	6-10-79	1997	Puerto Cabello, Venez.
Neshek, Pat	1	1	5.87	5	1	0	1	8	7	5	5	3	5	.233	S	R	6-2	200	9-4-80	2002	Brooklyn Park, Minn.
Pridie, Jon	6	9	5.19	27	17	1	0	111	136	72	64	35	65	.301	R	R	6-5	240	12-7-79	1998	Prescott, Ariz.
Romero, Josmir	2	5	5.37	27	7	0	0	64	80	40	38	25	50	.311	R	R	6-2	200	11-18-80	1997	Guarenas, Venez.
Schoening, Brent	12	6	3.98	26	26	0	0	147	141	67	65	43	105	.256	R	R	6-1	180	4-7-78	1999	Houston, Texas
Wolfe, Brian	5	7	6.42	30	10	1	3	83	111	65	59	24	42	.325	R	R	6-2	200	11-29-80	1999	Fullerton, Calif.

FIELDING

Catcher	PCT	G	PO	A	E	DP	PB
Bowen	.992	41	222	28	2	3	5
Gulledge	.975	25	147	10	4	1	1
Mauer	.992	60	351	29	3	3	2
Torres	.993	24	131	3	1	0	2

First Base	PCT	G	PO	A	E	DP
Christensen	.969	3	28	3	1	2
Deardorff	.993	98	791	64	6	81
Morneau	1.000	20	157	26	0	12
Owens	.984	17	109	13	2	11
Tiffee	.972	8	58	12	2	8

Second Base	PCT	G	PO	A	E	DP
Connacher	1.000	4	7	7	0	2
Davidson	1.000	11	12	27	0	9
Lorenzo	.902	12	18	19	4	4
Owens	.987	40	62	94	2	23
Renick	.970	85	156	196	11	43

Third Base	PCT	G	PO	A	E	DP
Christensen	.000	1	0	0	0	0
Deardorff	.947	10	3	15	1	4
Lorenzo	.800	12	3	9	3	0
Tiffee	.947	126	89	252	19	28

Shortstop	PCT	G	PO	A	E	DP
Bartlett	.969	139	249	380	20	74
Lorenzo	1.000	3	5	6	0	3

Outfield	PCT	G	PO	A	E	DP
Baron	.982	37	53	3	1	0
Garbe	.995	66	201	3	1	0
Owens	.951	24	37	2	2	0
Rabe	.982	94	221	3	4	0
Scanlon	.965	81	135	3	5	0
West	.964	135	283	13	11	4

FORT MYERS MIRACLE — High Class A

FLORIDA STATE LEAGUE

BATTING	AVG	G	AB	R	H	2B	3B	HR	RBI	BB	SO	SB	CS	SLG	OBP	B	T	HT	WT	DOB	1st Yr	Resides
Alvarez, Renyel	.259	92	293	28	76	9	1	1	24	22	42	1	2	.307	.319	L	L	6-0	200	6-17-78	2003	Hialeah Gardens, Fla.
Blum, Greg	.209	76	230	25	48	11	1	5	21	25	45	1	0	.330	.300	R	R	6-1	200	8-7-78	2000	Chino, Calif.
Christensen, Mike	.215	21	79	10	17	4	0	2	16	6	16	1	0	.342	.273	R	R	6-2	190	5-24-76	1998	Fort Myers, Fla.
Gulledge, Kelley	.097	8	31	0	3	1	0	0	2	1	9	0	0	.129	.125	R	R	6-1	200	1-25-79	2000	Arlington, Texas
Jones, Garrett	.220	117	404	52	89	12	5	18	67	32	98	5	4	.408	.280	L	L	6-4	220	6-21-81	1999	Tinley Park, Ill.
Kennedy, Bryan	.213	25	89	9	19	4	0	0	5	5	19	0	0	.258	.265	L	R	6-2	210	10-4-78	2001	Riverside, Calif.
Kubel, Jason	.298	116	420	56	125	20	4	5	82	48	54	4	6	.400	.361	L	R	5-11	190	5-25-82	2000	Palmdale, Calif.
Kuhaulua, Kaulana	.250	33	108	13	27	7	0	0	8	7	19	10	1	.315	.302	R	R	6-0	160	1-30-80	2001	Waianae, Hawaii
Mauer, Jake	.279	109	340	39	95	8	0	0	17	28	32	11	5	.303	.352	R	R	6-2	180	12-20-78	2001	St. Paul, Minn.
Mauer, Joe	.335	62	233	25	78	13	1	1	44	24	24	3	0	.412	.395	L	R	6-4	220	4-19-83	2001	Fort Myers, Minn.
Maza, Luis	.290	111	410	70	119	18	6	5	61	34	79	1	1	.400	.368	R	R	5-9	180	6-22-80	1997	Cumana, Venez.
Mendez, Jose	.267	8	30	3	8	0	0	1	3	0	2	0	0	.367	.267	R	R	5-8	180	7-17-83	1999	Bejuma, Venez.
Morales, Jose	.357	12	42	6	15	3	1	0	2	1	5	0	2	.476	.372	S	R	5-11	180	2-20-83	2001	San Juan, P.R.
Phillips, Kyle	.500	1	2	0	1	0	0	0	0	0	0	0	0	.500	.500	L	R	6-2	190	4-3-84	2002	El Cajon, Calif.
Sandoval, Michael	.294	74	248	34	73	14	0	2	34	31	37	2	4	.375	.385	R	R	5-10	200	7-8-81	1997	Puerto Cabello, Venez.
Tamburrino, Brett	.256	75	238	36	61	8	5	2	28	33	42	15	3	.357	.354	S	R	5-11	190	11-10-81	1998	Sunbury, Australia
Tomlin, James	.303	122	498	88	151	17	2	2	42	36	51	24	10	.357	.351	R	R	6-1	170	8-12-82	2000	Los Angeles, Calif.
Tope, Stephen	.258	93	302	42	78	19	2	4	33	31	73	0	3	.374	.341	R	R	6-0	200	1-12-82	1999	Perth, Australia
Velazquez, Juan	.221	60	172	18	38	3	1	0	17	23	36	2	2	.250	.317	S	R	5-11	150	8-22-78	1997	San Lorenzo, P.R.
Watkins, Tommy	.259	104	347	53	90	9	2	1	35	34	44	11	5	.305	.332	R	R	5-8	200	6-18-80	1998	Fort Myers, Fla.

PITCHING	W	L	ERA	G	GS	CG	SV	IP	H	R	ER	BB	SO	AVG	B	T	HT	WT	DOB	1st Yr	Resides
Abbott, Jim	5	3	2.31	17	8	0	0	58	43	15	15	19	52	.206	R	R	6-3	190	10-12-79	1999	Caledonia, Mich.
Bonilla, Henry	1	2	4.91	10	0	0	3	11	14	6	6	3	11	.311	R	R	6-0	190	8-16-78	2000	Reno, Nev.
Bowyer, Travis	5	2	3.83	45	0	0	1	80	68	43	34	56	70	.243	R	R	6-3	220	8-3-81	1999	Big Island, Va.
Contreras, Jean	0	2	6.23	14	3	0	1	22	29	17	15	12	19	.318	L	L	6-0	150	4-24-82	1998	Caracas, Venez.
Crain, Jesse	2	1	2.84	10	0	0	0	19	10	6	6	5	25	.153	R	R	6-1	200	7-5-81	2002	Austin, Texas
Daws, Josh	0	1	3.86	11	0	0	5	14	11	7	6	6	11	.229	R	R	5-10	190	12-8-78	2001	Fort Myers, Fla.
Durbin, J.D.	9	2	3.09	14	14	0	0	87	73	35	30	22	69	.223	R	R	6-0	190	2-24-82	2000	Scottsdale, Ariz.
Foote, Joe	0	3	9.37	5	4	0	0	16	31	17	17	5	4	.413	R	R	6-4	200	8-30-79	1997	Bradenton, Fla.
Gutierrez, Jannio	2	3	3.53	40	0	0	10	51	46	23	20	26	56	.233	R	R	5-10	200	5-3-82	2001	Maracaibo, Venez.
Holubec, Ken	4	5	4.59	26	11	2	0	82	96	44	42	35	49	.302	L	L	6-0	210	9-1-78	2000	Houma, La.
Kemp, Beau	1	2	3.76	22	0	0	11	26	30	14	11	7	16	.275	R	R	6-0	190	10-31-80	2000	Tulsa, Okla.
Lincoln, Jeff	0	0	1.17	6	0	0	0	8	8	2	1	5	4	.258	R	R	6-2	180	4-30-78	2000	Citrus Heights, Calif.
Lohse, Eric	0	2	4.05	15	0	0	0	27	28	12	12	9	22	.269	R	R	6-0	200	6-5-80	2001	Glenn, Calif.
Miller, Colby	9	6	2.71	26	26	1	0	156	139	58	47	43	114	.241	R	R	6-2	190	3-19-82	2000	Weatherford, Okla.
Miller, Jason	3	4	4.24	13	10	0	0	51	60	30	24	21	39	.300	L	L	6-1	200	7-20-82	2000	Sarasota, Fla.
Milton, Eric	0	0	0.00	1	1	0	0	2	1	0	0	2	2	.142	L	L	6-3	220	8-4-75	1996	Fort Myers, Fla.
Moreno, Victor	3	1	2.03	16	0	0	0	27	21	9	6	14	32	.212	R	R	6-0	200	6-10-79	1997	Puerto Cabello, Venez.
Neshek, Pat	4	1	2.15	20	0	0	2	29	22	8	7	6	29	.201	S	R	6-2	200	9-4-80	2002	Brooklyn Park, Minn.
Olson, Justin	2	0	2.25	6	0	0	1	8	9	2	2	5	6	.290	R	R	6-3	215	4-5-80	2003	Oak Park, Ill.
Randazzo, Jeff	5	6	4.66	20	17	0	0	87	95	53	45	40	35	.285	R	L	6-7	200	8-12-81	1999	Broomall, Pa.
Richardson, Jason	4	2	3.78	46	2	0	0	88	77	38	37	42	60	.243	R	R	6-3	220	6-11-80	1999	Lakeland, Fla.
Romero, Josmir	2	2	2.40	5	2	0	0	15	12	8	4	4	6	.214	R	R	6-2	200	11-18-80	1997	Guarenas, Venez.
Tejada, Manny	1	0	1.88	8	6	0	0	24	9	5	5	20	20	.118	R	R	6-3	210	4-16-82	1998	Center Point, Iowa
Vorwald, Matt	3	1	5.40	15	0	0	0	15	16	14	9	6	13	.266	S	R	6-2	190	11-29-79	2001	Freeport, Ill.
Watkins, Tommy	0	0	0.00	2	0	0	0	2	0	0	0	0	1	.000	R	R	5-8	200	6-18-80	1998	Fort Myers, Fla.
Wolfe, Brian	2	1	2.53	7	7	0	0	46	41	15	13	6	22	.231	R	R	6-2	200	11-29-80	1999	Fullerton, Calif.
Yeatman, Matt	6	11	5.16	25	25	0	0	129	134	79	74	64	100	.266	R	R	6-4	200	8-2-82	2000	Tomball, Texas

FIELDING

Catcher	PCT	G	PO	A	E	DP	PB
Blum	.990	64	355	38	4	4	10
Gulledge	1.000	5	38	3	0	1	1
Kennedy	.981	21	141	13	3	1	4
Mauer	1.000	1	5	0	0	0	0
Mauer	1.000	39	294	29	0	3	3
Mendez	1.000	8	54	3	0	0	3
Morales	.957	5	22	0	1	0	2
Phillips	1.000	1	5	0	0	0	0
Watkins	1.000	8	51	6	0	3	

First Base	PCT	G	PO	A	E	DP
Blum	1.000	1	10	0	0	2
Jones	.994	110	889	84	6	95
Mauer	1.000	4	28	3	0	3
Mauer	1.000	1	1	0	0	1
Tope	1.000	19	127	20	0	8

Second Base	PCT	G	PO	A	E	DP
Kuhaulua	.963	7	12	14	1	5
Mauer	.978	17	12	32	1	7
Maza	.973	104	194	269	13	66
Tamburrino	1.000	9	12	20	0	4
Watkins	.980	9	20	28	1	6

Third Base	PCT	G	PO	A	E	DP
Christensen	.982	21	15	40	1	4
Kuhaulua	.000	1	0	0	0	0
Mauer	1.000	16	9	21	0	2
Morales	.800	3	2	2	1	0
Sandoval	.924	69	48	98	12	6
Tamburrino	1.000	8	7	16	0	2
Watkins	.887	28	17	46	8	4

Shortstop	PCT	G	PO	A	E	DP
Kuhaulua	1.000	1	2	5	0	1
Mauer	.983	68	111	185	5	36
Velazquez	.956	59	102	138	11	35
Watkins	.914	17	20	54	7	9

Outfield	PCT	G	PO	A	E	DP
Alvarez	.979	29	44	2	1	0
Jones	1.000	1	2	0	0	0
Kubel	.991	109	207	15	2	1
Kuhaulua	1.000	19	36	1	0	0
Mauer	1.000	2	1	0	0	0
Tamburrino	.979	55	94	0	2	0
Tomlin	.986	120	269	8	4	4
Tope	1.000	63	115	5	0	1
Watkins	.951	38	73	5	4	2

QUAD CITY RIVER BANDITS — Low Class A

MIDWEST LEAGUE

BATTING	AVG	G	AB	R	H	2B	3B	HR	RBI	BB	SO	SB	CS	SLG	OBP	B	T	HT	WT	DOB	1st Yr	Resides
Burgos, Omar	.224	127	456	45	102	13	1	2	33	31	99	4	1	.270	.288	R	R	6-2	210	11-11-82	2000	Maturin, Venez.
Davidson, Seth	.266	109	428	52	114	26	1	4	58	18	32	7	6	.360	.315	R	R	6-0	180	2-26-79	2001	San Diego, Calif.
Geiger, Kyle	.139	11	36	4	5	1	0	0	1	2	7	0	0	.167	.184	R	R	6-3	215	5-8-82	2003	Greenwood, Ind.
Gomon, Dusty	.153	42	150	19	23	9	0	2	18	11	45	2	1	.253	.218	R	R	6-4	210	9-3-82	2001	Jacksonville, Fla.
Guzman, Garrett	.282	82	298	44	84	18	4	3	33	23	22	2	1	.399	.343	L	L	5-10	170	2-7-83	2001	Henderson, Nev.
Huether, J.D.	.248	35	125	11	31	4	0	0	14	10	11	0	1	.280	.307	R	R	6-0	200	5-17-80	2002	Fort Myers, Fla.
Johnson, Josh	.176	12	34	2	6	0	0	0	0	3	9	0	0	.176	.243	R	R	5-11	190	11-3-82	2001	Ridgway, Pa.
Kennedy, Bryan	.296	63	223	26	66	10	2	5	36	28	33	0	0	.426	.395	L	R	6-2	210	10-4-78	2001	Riverside, Calif.
Kuhaulua, Kaulana	.230	57	196	24	45	12	1	1	21	16	38	5	2	.316	.294	R	R	6-0	160	1-30-80	2001	Waianae, Hawaii
Lebron, Edgardo	.195	53	195	16	38	4	0	2	12	2	57	0	0	.246	.202	S	R	6-1	180	8-16-82	2000	Las Piedras, P.R.
Liz, Jose	.218	34	101	5	22	3	0	0	6	2	24	1	1	.248	.238	R	R	6-3	200	5-16-81	1999	El Brisal, D.R.
Matienzo, Danny	.275	90	349	45	96	20	3	15	59	22	77	1	0	.479	.324	R	R	5-11	190	9-3-80	2002	Miami, Fla.
Merchan, Jesus	.296	101	392	60	116	16	3	5	53	31	18	8	6	.390	.362	R	R	5-11	180	3-26-81	1999	Maracay Venez.
Molina, Felix	.243	79	268	33	65	11	0	2	31	19	33	3	6	.306	.299	S	R	5-8	170	5-5-83	2001	Mayaguez, P.R.
Morales, Jose	.271	48	170	14	46	10	1	2	25	5	32	0	1	.376	.302	S	R	5-11	180	2-20-83	2001	San Juan, P.R.
Oeltjen, Trent	.298	123	466	73	139	12	8	4	44	37	57	29	14	.384	.371	L	L	6-1	180	2-28-83	2001	Sydney, Australia
Pattee, Ben	.286	5	14	0	4	0	0	0	2	1	3	0	1	.286	.375	R	R	6-0	184	9-24-81	2003	Ukiah, Calif.
Perodin, Ron	.272	35	92	16	25	2	0	0	4	7	27	8	4	.293	.320	L	L	5-9	170	10-13-80	2002	Los Angeles, Calif.
Romero, Alex	.296	120	423	50	125	16	3	4	40	43	43	11	8	.376	.359	S	R	6-0	170	9-9-83	2000	Maracaibo, Venez.
Whitrock, Scott	.230	91	274	34	63	13	2	3	20	16	96	13	2	.325	.302	R	R	6-1	190	12-18-80	2001	Wisconsin Rapids, Wisc.

PITCHING	W	L	ERA	G	GS	CG	SV	IP	H	R	ER	BB	SO	AVG	B	T	HT	WT	DOB	1st Yr	Resides
Baker, Scott	3	1	2.49	11	11	0	0	51	45	16	14	8	47	.234	R	R	6-4	190	9-19-81	2003	Shreveport, La.
Barrett, Ricky	0	1	3.29	3	3	0	0	14	13	5	5	11	4	.254	L	L	5-11	180	3-9-81	2002	West Sacramento, Calif.
Blackburn, Nick	2	9	4.86	16	10	2	1	76	78	44	41	18	40	.268	R	R	6-4	210	2-24-82	2002	Norman, Okla.
Cameron, Kevin	1	5	3.92	39	0	0	2	62	57	30	27	33	58	.237	R	R	6-1	180	12-15-79	2001	Joliet, Ill.
Crawford, Tristan	2	2	5.45	19	0	0	1	35	45	27	21	17	17	.306	R	R	6-2	180	7-22-82	2000	Browns Plains, Australia
Fischer, Eric	2	5	5.02	11	11	0	0	57	57	36	32	28	42	.263	S	L	6-7	200	2-19-80	1998	Cincinnati, Ohio
Gray, Josh	3	3	4.19	10	10	0	0	54	59	27	25	15	29	.279	L	L	6-4	195	11-20-80	2003	Orange, Texas
Harben, Adam	5	6	4.33	16	15	0	0	87	91	54	42	35	77	.258	R	R	6-5	210	8-19-83	2002	Maumelle, Ark.
Hill, Josh	7	4	3.95	26	21	1	0	137	135	63	60	57	132	.260	R	R	6-3	210	3-27-83	2001	Warilla, Australia
Keeling, Justin	0	1	6.75	4	0	0	0	5	5	4	4	3	3	.294	L	L	5-10	190	3-29-81	2002	Oceanside, Calif.
Kuhaulua, Kaulana	0	0	0.00	2	0	0	0	2	2	0	0	1	0	.000	R	R	6-0	160	1-30-80	2001	Waianae, Hawaii

PITCHING	W	L	ERA	G	GS	CG	SV	IP	H	R	ER	BB	SO	AVG	B	T	HT	WT	DOB	1st Yr	Resides
Lohse, Eric	6	5	3.32	28	1	0	1	62	65	31	23	15	51	.277	R	R	6-0	200	6-5-80	2001	Glenn, Calif.
Mauer, Bill	0	0	3.52	4	0	0	0	8	6	6	3	4	2	.200	R	R	6-4	200	5-6-80	2003	St. Paul, Minn.
Miller, Jason	5	1	2.36	13	12	0	0	69	67	25	18	21	50	.263	L	L	6-1	200	7-20-82	2000	Sarasota, Fla.
Murray, Steve	3	1	4.57	47	0	0	1	61	56	33	31	11	54	.242	L	L	6-1	200	6-29-80	1998	Ennismore, Ontario
Neshek, Pat	3	2	0.52	28	0	0	14	34	20	3	2	11	53	.165	S	R	6-2	200	9-4-80	2002	Brooklyn Park, Minn.
Oakes, Gerry	2	5	9.45	24	5	0	1	53	61	62	56	60	33	.291	L	R	6-4	170	4-29-82	2000	Upper Darby, Pa.
Olson, Justin	1	0	2.33	14	0	0	5	19	17	5	5	8	23	.242	R	R	6-3	215	4-5-80	2003	Oak Park, Ill.
Prunty, T.J.	4	10	4.97	30	19	0	0	127	142	82	70	46	81	.288	R	R	6-3	210	7-5-81	2002	Inver Grove Heights, Minn.
Smith, Ryan	0	0	3.86	11	0	0	0	16	20	9	7	7	17	.294	S	R	6-2	220	10-21-80	2001	West Covina, Calif.
Tautor, Peter	4	5	4.60	43	0	0	3	63	64	36	32	27	48	.262	L	R	6-4	210	6-26-81	2003	Wantina South, Australia
Tyler, Scott	6	12	5.50	30	20	0	0	106	93	70	65	82	110	.233	R	R	6-5	230	8-20-82	2001	Downingtown, Pa.
Williams, Aaron	0	0	12.19	5	0	0	0	10	17	14	14	1	7	.361	R	R	6-1	180	10-7-80	2002	Oakfield, N.Y.

FIELDING

Catcher	PCT	G	PO	A	E	DP	PB
Geiger	.976	10	77	5	2	0	3
Huether	.974	12	66	8	2	0	6
Johnson	.984	11	55	8	1	0	2
Kennedy	.988	54	367	45	5	2	7
Matienzo	.988	31	210	27	3	0	5
Morales	.976	28	181	20	5	0	10

First Base	PCT	G	PO	A	E	DP
Burgos	.989	25	168	14	2	19
Gomon	.992	40	330	28	3	28
Huether	1.000	19	156	16	0	17
Kennedy	1.000	3	22	3	0	2
Lebron	.988	20	158	12	2	12
Liz	1.000	2	5	1	0	1
Matienzo	.982	37	321	14	6	23

Second Base	PCT	G	PO	A	E	DP
Davidson	.973	8	16	20	1	5
Kuhaulua	.970	27	60	71	4	17
Merchan	.979	36	71	72	3	18
Molina	.955	67	103	197	14	34
Morales	1.000	4	9	7	0	0
Pattee	.882	3	10	5	2	1

Third Base	PCT	G	PO	A	E	DP
Burgos	.930	101	61	164	17	18
Kuhaulua	.947	14	12	24	2	1
Lebron	.667	5	4	4	4	0
Merchan	.960	21	12	36	2	3
Morales	1.000	1	0	1	0	0

Shortstop	PCT	G	PO	A	E	DP
Davidson	.964	99	158	291	17	60
Kuhaulua	.929	3	3	10	1	3
Merchan	.934	41	61	109	12	12
Molina	.917	2	4	7	1	2

Outfield	PCT	G	PO	A	E	DP
Guzman	.979	73	132	5	3	0
Kuhaulua	1.000	8	11	0	0	0
Liz	.964	19	26	1	1	0
Oeltjen	.968	114	240	4	8	1
Perodin	.962	25	48	2	2	0
Romero	.982	115	271	8	5	1
Whitrock	.957	71	124	8	6	0

ELIZABETHTON TWINS — Rookie

APPALACHIAN LEAGUE

BATTING	AVG	G	AB	R	H	2B	3B	HR	RBI	BB	SO	SB	CS	SLG	OBP	B	T	HT	WT	DOB	1st Yr	Resides
Arneson, Justin	.256	49	160	31	41	5	2	3	29	24	45	10	3	.369	.370	R	R	5-11	160	12-17-81	2002	Fergus Falls, Minn.
Collins, Jesse	.215	31	107	15	23	9	0	1	16	21	25	1	0	.327	.354	S	R	5-10	200	3-28-81	2003	Palm Beach Gardens, Fla.
Fermin, Angelo	.275	42	131	22	36	7	3	1	15	23	36	14	1	.397	.381	S	R	5-8	160	11-6-83	2000	Santo Domingo, D.R.
Geiger, Kyle	.212	9	33	1	7	2	0	0	4	2	6	0	0	.273	.257	R	R	6-3	215	5-8-82	2003	Greenwood, Ind.
Gomon, Dusty	.262	61	233	36	61	14	0	15	46	27	85	0	1	.515	.342	R	R	6-4	210	9-3-82	2001	Jacksonville, Fla.
Johnson, Josh	.164	27	67	7	11	1	0	1	12	6	25	0	1	.224	.278	R	R	5-11	190	11-3-82	2001	Ridgway, Pa.
Molina, Felix	.352	20	88	15	31	10	3	0	14	3	10	3	1	.534	.383	S	R	5-8	170	5-5-83	2001	Mayaguez, P.R.
Perodin, Ron	.335	50	170	35	57	8	3	0	23	19	34	15	3	.418	.405	L	L	5-9	170	10-13-80	2002	Los Angeles, Calif.
Peterson, Brock	.290	61	207	53	60	9	1	9	31	32	48	5	1	.473	.404	R	R	6-3	200	11-20-83	2003	Chehalis, Wash.
Phillips, Kyle	.289	63	246	36	71	12	0	8	49	26	34	1	0	.435	.358	L	R	6-2	190	4-3-84	2002	El Cajon, Calif.
Pospishil, Jason	.209	29	86	13	18	4	1	0	12	3	26	0	1	.279	.250	S	R	5-8	160	1-28-83	2001	Werrington, Australia
Sims, Justin	.197	25	76	10	15	1	0	2	8	4	18	1	1	.289	.241	L	R	5-9	180	12-18-80	2002	Knoxville, Tenn.
Span, Denard	.271	50	207	34	56	5	1	1	18	23	34	14	5	.319	.355	L	L	6-1	180	2-27-84	2002	Tampa, Fla.
Spataro, Ryan	.239	57	205	42	49	5	0	4	22	34	42	12	3	.322	.349	L	R	5-10	180	9-1-82	2001	Barrie, Ontario
Taylor, Sam	.261	52	188	35	49	9	2	2	26	27	26	7	5	.362	.358	S	R	5-7	160	11-6-82	2001	San Leandro, Calif.

GAMES BY POSITION: C—Collins 25, Geiger 4, Johnson 25, Phillips 18. **1B**—Gomon 49, Peterson 1, Phillips 17. **2B**—Arneson 39, Fermin 16, Molina 11, Pospishil 1. **3B**—Fermin 5, Molina 8, Peterson 53, Taylor 1. **SS**—Fermin 18, Taylor 49. **OF**—Arneson 8, Fermin 1, Perodin 45, Pospishil 23, Sims 18, Span 50, Spataro 57, Taylor 1.

PITCHING	W	L	ERA	G	GS	CG	SV	IP	H	R	ER	BB	SO	AVG	B	T	HT	WT	DOB	1st Yr	Resides
Brandon, Eric	1	1	2.14	20	0	0	0	34	28	10	8	8	31	.222	R	R	6-1	220	2-18-81	2003	Nashville, Tenn.
Culpepper, Kevin	4	1	3.86	16	5	0	0	42	37	19	18	18	44	.245	R	L	6-5	190	6-28-82	2003	Toccoa, Ga.
DePaula, Julio	2	3	1.71	22	0	0	5	26	19	7	5	8	24	.200	R	R	6-0	170	12-31-82	1999	Santo Domingo, D.R.
Garcia, Angel	2	1	2.89	9	9	0	0	37	37	18	12	18	44	.256	R	R	6-7	210	10-28-83	2001	Dorado, P.R.
Gray, Josh	0	0	0.00	6	0	0	0	11	3	1	0	2	10	.085	L	L	6-4	195	11-20-80	2003	Orange, Texas
Hader, Ryan	1	2	2.89	19	0	0	0	28	15	11	9	24	39	.154	R	L	6-3	230	3-3-83	2002	Peculiar, Mo.
Henkenjohann, Tim	0	0	8.22	8	0	0	0	8	6	7	7	10	11	.206	L	R	6-5	210	9-3-80	2001	Wilhelmshaven, Germany
Iida, Hiroyuki	1	0	4.80	18	1	0	0	30	36	22	16	9	25	.283	R	R	6-2	180	8-19-80	2003	Yamaguchi, Japan
Lynch, John	0	2	3.22	18	0	0	2	22	21	11	8	5	21	.250	L	L	6-1	190	5-23-81	2002	Rogers, Minn.
Marini, Chris	3	1	3.21	13	7	0	0	34	34	15	12	17	27	.259	L	L	6-1	190	2-11-83	2003	Glendale, Ariz.
Medina, Dennis	3	2	5.88	10	7	0	0	34	30	23	22	12	33	.240	R	R	6-3	190	1-17-83	2001	Cabimas, Venez.
Meek, Evan	7	1	2.47	14	8	0	1	51	33	15	14	24	47	.178	R	R	6-1	190	5-12-83	2003	Bothell, Wash.
Mutch, Paul	0	1	3.33	18	1	0	0	24	26	16	9	18	19	.260	R	R	6-5	220	1-15-83	2001	Chermside, Australia
Schutt, Chris	5	2	1.98	11	10	0	0	55	37	23	12	21	72	.184	R	R	6-1	200	2-8-82	2003	Park Ridge, Ill.
Simonitsch, Errol	5	1	1.76	10	8	0	0	46	39	13	9	6	57	.220	L	L	6-4	225	8-24-82	2003	Glendale, Calif.
Speigner, Jimmy	5	2	3.94	22	0	0	4	30	31	13	13	4	35	.264	R	R	5-11	170	9-24-80	2003	Thomasville, Ga.
Uhl, Jon	3	4	3.92	11	10	0	0	44	38	20	19	15	42	.240	R	R	6-2	190	10-6-80	2003	Tampa, Fla.

FORT MYERS TWINS — Rookie

GULF COAST LEAGUE

BATTING	AVG	G	AB	R	H	2B	3B	HR	RBI	BB	SO	SB	CS	SLG	OBP	B	T	HT	WT	DOB	1st Yr	Resides
Anderson, Heath	.244	30	82	6	20	3	0	1	5	12	11	1	0	.317	.357	R	R	6-4	190	4-29-84	2003	Panama City, Fla.
Campusano, Luis	.237	16	38	6	9	0	1	0	2	2	8	1	1	.289	.275	R	R	6-0	160	8-31-84	2001	Santo Domingo, D.R.
Cuddyer, Michael	.800	2	5	1	4	0	0	1	3	1	0	0	1	1.400	.857	R	R	6-2	220	3-27-79	1997	Fort Myers, Fla.
Deeds, Doug	.333	5	15	1	5	0	0	0	4	1	2	1	0	.333	.375	L	L	6-2	180	6-2-81	2002	Columbus, Ohio
Garbe, B.J.	.206	8	34	1	7	2	0	0	4	1	7	1	1	.265	.250	R	R	6-2	190	2-3-81	1999	Moses Lake, Wash.
Hughes, Luke	.305	54	190	22	58	9	4	2	25	15	22	5	5	.426	.361	R	R	5-11	160	8-2-84	2002	Morley, Australia

BATTING	AVG	G	AB	R	H	2B	3B	HR	RBI	BB	SO	SB	CS	SLG	OBP	B	T	HT	WT	DOB	1st Yr	Resides
Jones, Larry	.239	28	71	10	17	5	0	0	5	8	21	1	0	.310	.333	R	R	6-1	210	9-19-84	2003	Stockton, Ala.
Kalin, Travis	.234	23	47	5	11	3	0	0	7	2	10	1	0	.298	.275	R	R	6-3	180	7-30-84	2003	Lake Mary, Fla.
Lebron, Edgardo	.154	11	39	6	6	3	0	0	3	1	11	0	0	.231	.175	S	R	6-1	180	8-16-82	2000	Las Piedras, P.R.
Lopez, Javier	.234	53	197	25	46	2	2	0	18	11	33	8	3	.264	.291	R	R	6-2	190	10-19-83	2002	Juana Diaz, P.R.
Marin, Daniel	.000	1	4	0	0	0	0	0	0	0	1	0	0	.000	.000	R	R	5-11	190	3-2-83	1999	Valencia, Venez.
Mendez, Jose	.200	26	60	4	12	3	0	1	7	5	6	0	1	.300	.262	R	R	5-8	180	7-17-83	1999	Bejuma, Venez.
Moses, Matt	.385	18	65	6	25	5	1	0	11	5	9	0	1	.492	.417	L	R	6-0	210	2-20-85	2003	Richmond, Va.
Najac, Greg	.190	25	63	8	12	1	1	0	6	7	15	0	0	.238	.282	L	R	6-0	210	4-28-85	2003	Nanuet, N.Y.
Ortiz, Patrick	.208	31	77	11	16	3	0	0	5	6	16	3	0	.247	.265	S	R	5-11	165	7-30-85	2003	Maunabo, P.R.
Pattee, Ben	.308	36	117	12	36	7	1	0	17	4	9	6	1	.385	.344	R	R	6-0	184	9-24-81	2003	Ukiah, Calif.
Patterson, Tarrence	.308	49	169	32	52	9	5	2	23	9	19	15	7	.456	.343	R	R	5-8	170	6-12-84	2002	Bartow, Fla.
Rumsey, John	.261	50	161	26	42	7	6	1	25	20	31	8	1	.398	.342	R	R	5-10	190	7-20-80	2003	Imperial Beach, Calif.
Rutgers, Paul	.353	56	201	35	71	12	3	0	21	9	15	16	7	.443	.388	R	R	5-10	170	1-17-84	2001	Melbourne, Australia
Tintor, Eli	.266	25	64	4	17	3	0	0	5	6	14	0	2	.313	.338	R	R	6-2	195	12-24-84	2003	Hibbing, Minn.
Winfree, David	.129	23	70	4	9	1	2	0	3	2	16	0	0	.200	.164	R	R	6-3	215	8-5-85	2003	Virginia Beach, Va.
Woodard, Johnny	.238	52	172	19	41	6	1	1	15	22	42	1	1	.302	.330	L	R	6-4	208	9-15-84	2003	Fairfield, Calif.

GAMES BY POSITION: C—Anderson 20, Marin 1, Mendez 26, Najac 15, Tintor 18. **1B**—Campusano 1, Lopez 9, Winfree 17, Woodard 36. **2B**—Kalin 21, Pattee 11, Rutgers 44. **3B**—Hughes 23, Lebron 10, Lopez 11, Moses 14, Rutgers 6. **SS**—Hughes 32, Kalin 1, Ortiz 28, Rutgers 9. **OF**—Campusano 14, Cuddyer 1, Deeds 3, Garbe 8, Jones 26, Lopez 34, Pattee 17, Patterson 45, Rumsey 40, Winfree 1, Woodard 5.

PITCHING	W	L	ERA	G	GS	CG	SV	IP	H	R	ER	BB	SO	AVG	B	T	HT	WT	DOB	1st Yr	Resides
Barrett, Ricky	0	1	1.29	5	1	0	0	7	10	1	1	3	5	.312	L	L	5-11	180	3-9-81	2002	West Sacramento, Calif.
Bowlin, Jason	1	0	2.28	20	0	0	6	24	18	10	6	6	14	.202	R	R	6-0	185	8-4-82	2003	Fairfield, Ohio
Contreras, J.C.	0	0	0.00	1	0	0	0	2	1	0	0	0	2	.142	L	L	6-0	150	4-24-82	1998	Caracas, Venez.
Duguay, Steven	1	4	4.79	16	8	0	4	47	45	26	25	7	36	.258	R	R	6-1	200	10-29-82	2003	Fleetwood, N.C.
Fischer, Eric	0	1	16.88	2	1	0	0	3	5	5	5	3	4	.454	S	L	6-7	200	2-19-80	1998	Cincinnati, Ohio
Fisher, Pete	0	0	16.20	1	1	0	0	2	6	6	3	1	2	.545	R	R	6-3	220	7-7-77	1998	Stoneham, Mass.
Gault, Joe	2	1	3.66	14	0	0	1	20	17	12	8	12	13	.226	R	R	6-5	190	12-28-84	2003	Canyon Country, Calif.
Jones, K.C.	0	3	7.22	15	4	0	0	34	50	31	27	23	15	.349	R	R	6-6	200	6-30-84	2002	Coral, Fla.
Killion, Terry	0	1	9.60	16	0	0	0	15	18	21	16	22	7	.295	R	R	6-5	240	4-27-84	2003	Austin, Texas
Koch, Jonathon	2	3	2.73	12	2	0	3	26	29	8	8	6	18	.295	R	R	6-2	180	4-7-83	2003	Berrien Springs, Mich.
Lankford, Kris	3	1	3.99	15	4	0	0	29	32	15	13	12	22	.290	S	R	6-3	195	7-15-82	2003	Altus, Okla.
Martinez, Javier	3	3	2.03	12	10	0	0	62	43	19	14	21	54	.191	L	L	5-11	160	6-13-84	2001	Maracaibo, Venez.
Mauer, Bill	3	1	1.71	15	0	0	0	21	13	6	4	10	18	.168	R	R	6-4	200	5-6-80	2003	St. Paul, Minn.
McConnell, Brandon	3	3	4.60	11	9	0	0	43	53	31	22	22	40	.306	R	R	6-4	205	2-8-85	2003	Red Bluff, Calif.
Merricks, Alex	0	2	10.80	15	1	0	0	15	13	21	18	37	14	.232	L	L	5-11	180	12-23-83	2002	Oxnard, Calif.
Nunez, Francisco	5	1	0.31	20	0	0	1	29	21	4	1	3	28	.203	R	R	5-11	160	5-12-82	2002	Bonao, D.R.
Ramirez, Wandar	1	0	6.43	17	0	0	1	21	20	17	15	14	20	.250	R	R	6-0	160	12-31-80	2002	Las Matas de Farfan, D.R.
Samuels, Matt	0	0	6.41	18	0	0	0	20	30	19	14	7	10	.340	R	R	6-2	210	9-17-81	2003	Terre Haute, Ind.
Shinskie, David	1	4	7.41	5	5	0	0	17	20	18	14	10	13	.294	R	R	6-4	205	5-4-84	2003	Kulpmont, Pa.
Smit, Alexander	3	0	1.18	8	7	0	0	38	19	8	5	20	40	.155	L	L	6-3	190	10-2-85	2002	Eindhoven, Netherlands
Thomas, Brad	0	0	0.00	2	2	0	0	10	6	0	0	1	12	.166	L	L	6-4	220	10-12-77	1995	Sydney, Australia
Wheldon, Rhys	0	2	8.15	5	4	0	0	18	26	18	16	6	14	.333	R	R	6-2	200	2-12-84	2001	Perth, Australia

MONTREAL EXPOS

BY MICHAEL LEVESQUE

For the past five years, the end of a baseball season began the questions about whether the Expos would be back the following spring. While the franchise will still be in Montreal in 2004, its long-term future of the team reminds muddled as ever.

Owned and operated by Major League Baseball, the Expos played three homestands in Puerto Rico in 2003 season in an effort to generate more revenue. The extra travel sapped the team, and Expos players voted against a similar arrangement for the 2004 season, though officials were trying to work out a compromise plan.

Also rearing its ugly head was the pending arbitration case filed against commissioner Bud Selig, Marlins owner Jeffery Loria and his son David Samson by the Expos' former limited partners. The process dragged on for more than a year and could continue as the plaintiffs seek damages from Loria's purchase and sale of the team.

On the field, the Expos had postseason aspirations in 2003. They stayed in contention and led the wild-card race in late August, only to wilt in September as the grueling schedule and injuries took a toll. The Expos played 103 games on the road, 22 in Puerto Rico, and went through one stretch when they played 22 road games in 25 days. They ended 2003 the same way they ended 2002, with a record of 83-79, but slipped to fourth in the National League East after claiming second place the pervious year.

After a lackluster 2002 campaign, shortstop Orlando Cabrera rebounded with his best season and emerged as a leader on the club. The 28-year-old played in all 162 games for the second time in his career, as he hit .297 with 17 home runs, 80 RBIs and 24 stolen bases in 26 tries. He led the Expos in hits, doubles, extra-base hits, stolen bases, runs and multi-hit games.

Vladimir Guerrero continued to rewrite the franchise record book despite missing 40 games with a herniated disc in his lower back. He ended up batting .330 with 25 home runs and 79 RBIs, and would have placed fourth in the league in batting if he had enough appearances to qualify. He moved past Andre Dawson into first place on the Expos' all-time homer list, and became the sixth Expo to hit for the cycle on Sept. 14 against the Mets. But like Dawson, Guerrero is probably headed out of Montreal, as he became a free agent after the season.

On the mound, the Expos lost two key members of the rotation when Orlando Hernandez and Tony Armas went down for the year in April. An astute trade by general manager Omar Minaya brought Livan Hernandez over from the Giants, however, and the rotation was solid.

Hernandez helped anchor the staff, going 15-10, 3.20 and proving to be a workhorse with 233 innings and eight complete games. Righthander Javier Vazquez rebounded from a poor 2002 and went 13-10, 3.24 while striking out a career high 241 batters. Rookie reliever Luis Ayala blossomed into a quality set-up man, winning 10 games with a 2.96 ERA. He ranked third in the NL by stranding 83.3 percent of inherited runners.

In the minors, Triple-A Edmonton made the playoffs, but it was a rough year for the system otherwise as the Trappers were the only affiliate with a record better than .500. Expos affiliates had a combined record of 300-386, a .437 winning percentage, which was worst among the 30 major league organizations.

Chad Cordero, the Expos' first-round pick in the draft, had a quick ascent to the majors. He made his major league debut Aug. 29, less than two months after being drafted. The hard-throwing righthander out of Cal State Fullerton was 1-0, 1.64 in 12 appearances, and looks like a lock for the big league bullpen in 2004.

Livan Hernandez

MORRIS FOSTOFF

Terrmel Sledge

PLAYERS of the YEAR

MAJOR LEAGUE: Livan Hernandez, rhp

Hernandez was the National League's most durable pitcher, leading the senior circuit in innings pitched and complete games. He also ranked seventh in strikeouts and ninth in ERA and wins.

MINOR LEAGUE: Terrmel Sledge, of

Sledge broke out the hammer in 2003, leading the organization in the triple crown categories by hitting .324-22-92 for Edmonton. He led the Pacific Coast league in runs, tied for third in batting and finished second in triples and slugging percentage.

ORGANIZATION LEADERS

BATTING		
***AVG**	Terrmel Sledge, Edmonton	.324
R	Terrmel Sledge, Edmonton	95
H	Brandon Watson, Harrisburg	180
TB	Terrmel Sledge, Edmonton	271
2B	Larry Broadway, Harrisburg/Savannah/Brevard County	35
3B	Terrmel Sledge, Edmonton	9
HR	Terrmel Sledge, Edmonton	22
RBI	Terrmel Sledge, Edmonton	92
BB	Val Pascucci, Edmonton	101
SO	Val Pascucci, Edmonton	132
SB	Reggie Fitzpatrick, Savannah	36
***SLG**	Terrmel Sledge, Edmonton	.545
***OBP**	Noah Hall, Harrisburg	.434
PITCHING		
W	Mike Hinckley, Brevard County/Savannah	13
L	Nick Long, Savannah/Vermont	16
#ERA	Nehomar Ochoa, Vermont/GCL Expos	2.04
G	Chad Bentz, Harrisburg	52
CG	Scott Downs, Edmonton	3
	Mike Hinckley, Brevard County/Savannah	3
SV	Chad Bentz, Harrisburg	16
IP	Shawn Hill, Harrisburg/Brevard County	147
BB	Nick Long, Savannah/Vermont	67
SO	Mike Hinckley, Brevard County/Savannah	134

*Minimum 250 At-Bats #Minimum 75 Innings

MONTREAL EXPOS

Manager: Frank Robinson.

2003 Record: 83-79, .512 (4th, NL East).

BATTING	AVG	G	AB	R	H	2B	3B	HR	RBI	BB	SO	SB	CS	SLG	OBP	B	T	HT	WT	DOB	1st Yr	Resides
Barrett, Michael	.208	70	226	33	47	9	2	10	30	21	37	0	0	.398	.280	R	R	6-2	200	10-22-76	1995	Alpharetta, Ga.
Cabrera, Orlando	.297	162	626	95	186	47	2	17	80	52	64	24	2	.460	.347	R	R	5-9	180	11-2-74	1994	Cartagena, Colombia
Calloway, Ron	.238	126	340	36	81	17	1	9	52	20	80	9	2	.374	.282	L	L	6-1	210	9-4-76	1997	Los Banos, Calif.
Carroll, Jamey	.260	105	227	31	59	10	1	1	10	19	39	5	2	.326	.323	R	R	5-9	170	2-18-74	1996	Evansville, Ind.
Cepicky, Matt	.250	5	8	0	2	1	0	0	0	0	2	0	0	.375	.250	L	R	6-2	220	11-10-77	1999	Sun City Center, Fla.
Chavez, Endy	.251	141	483	66	121	25	5	5	47	31	59	18	7	.354	.294	L	L	5-9	170	2-7-78	1996	Valencia, Venez.
Cordero, Wil	.278	130	436	57	121	27	0	16	71	49	90	1	1	.450	.354	R	R	6-2	210	10-3-71	1988	Westlake, Ohio
Guerrero, Vladimir	.330	112	394	71	130	20	3	25	79	63	53	9	5	.586	.426	R	R	6-3	220	2-9-76	1993	Nizao Bani, D.R.
Guzman, Edwards	.240	52	146	15	35	5	0	1	14	5	17	0	0	.295	.263	L	R	5-11	200	9-11-76	1996	Naranjito, P.R.
Liefer, Jeff	.193	35	88	6	17	3	0	3	18	3	26	0	1	.330	.217	L	R	6-3	210	8-17-74	1996	Costa Mesa, Calif.
Macias, Jose	.239	111	272	31	65	15	2	4	22	11	45	4	3	.353	.273	S	R	5-8	190	1-25-72	1992	Panama City, Panama
Mateo, Henry	.240	100	154	29	37	3	1	0	7	11	38	11	1	.273	.304	S	R	5-11	180	10-14-76	1995	Santo Domingo, D.R.
Schneider, Brian	.230	108	335	34	77	26	1	9	46	37	75	0	2	.394	.309	L	R	6-0	200	11-26-76	1995	West Palm Beach, Fla.
Tatis, Fernando	.194	53	175	15	34	6	0	2	15	18	40	2	1	.263	.281	R	R	5-10	180	1-1-75	1993	San Pedro de Macoris, D.R.
Vidro, Jose	.310	144	509	77	158	36	0	15	65	69	50	3	2	.470	.397	S	R	5-11	190	8-27-74	1992	Sabana Grande, P.R.
Vitiello, Joe	.342	38	76	12	26	6	0	3	13	7	14	0	0	.539	.407	R	R	6-3	230	4-11-70	1991	Stoneham, Mass.
Wilkerson, Brad	.268	146	504	78	135	34	4	19	77	89	155	13	10	.464	.380	L	L	6-0	200	6-1-77	1999	Owensboro, Ky.
Zeile, Todd	.257	34	113	11	29	2	2	5	19	10	18	1	0	.442	.331	R	R	6-1	200	9-9-65	1986	Thousand Oaks, Calif.

PITCHING	W	L	ERA	G	GS	CG	SV	IP	H	R	ER	BB	SO	AVG	B	T	HT	WT	DOB	1st Yr	Resides
Almonte, Hector	1	1	6.83	28	0	0	0	29	34	22	22	17	26	.290	R	R	6-2	190	10-17-75	1993	Santo Domingo, D.R.
Armas, Tony	2	1	2.61	5	5	0	0	31	25	9	9	8	23	.225	R	R	6-4	220	4-29-78	1994	Puerto Piritu, Venez.
Ayala, Luis	10	3	2.92	65	0	0	5	71	65	27	23	13	46	.244	R	R	6-2	170	1-12-78	1997	Los Mochis, Mexico
Biddle, Rocky	5	8	4.65	73	0	0	34	72	71	43	37	40	54	.254	R	R	6-3	230	5-21-76	1997	San Dimas, Calif.
Corcoran, Roy	0	0	1.23	5	0	0	0	7	7	2	1	3	2	.250	R	R	5-10	170	5-11-80	2001	Slaughter, La.
Cordero, Chad	1	0	1.64	12	0	0	1	11	4	2	2	3	12	.111	R	R	6-0	195	3-18-82	2003	Chino, Calif.
Darensbourg, Vic	0	0	10.80	6	0	0	0	7	13	8	8	1	4	.406	L	L	5-8	170	11-13-70	1992	Henderson, Nevada
Day, Zach	9	8	4.18	23	23	1	0	131	132	64	61	59	61	.261	R	R	6-4	210	6-15-78	1996	Cincinnati, Ohio
Downs, Scott	0	1	15.00	1	1	0	0	3	5	5	5	3	4	.357	L	L	6-2	190	3-17-76	1997	Lexington, Ky.
Drew, Tim	0	2	12.46	6	1	0	0	9	12	12	12	8	3	.342	R	R	6-1	190	8-31-78	1997	Hahira, Ga.
Eischen, Joey	2	2	3.06	70	0	0	1	53	57	27	18	13	40	.282	L	L	6-0	210	5-25-70	1989	Rotonda West, Fla.
Ferrari, Anthony	0	0	6.75	4	0	0	0	4	4	3	3	5	1	.266	L	L	5-9	160	6-22-78	2000	Greenbrae, Calif.
Hebson, Bryan	0	0	13.50	2	0	0	0	2	4	3	3	1	1	.444	R	R	6-5	210	3-12-76	1997	Phenix City, Ala.
Hernandez, Livan	15	10	3.20	33	33	8	0	233	225	92	83	57	178	.252	R	R	6-2	240	2-20-75	1996	Miami Beach, Fla.
Kim, Sun-Woo	0	1	8.36	4	3	0	0	14	24	13	13	8	5	.406	R	R	6-1	180	9-4-77	1997	Seoul, South Korea
Knott, Eric	1	2	5.12	13	1	0	0	19	23	12	11	6	17	.294	L	L	6-1	180	9-23-74	1997	Sebring, Fla.
Manon, Julio	1	2	4.13	23	0	0	1	28	26	13	13	17	15	.252	L	R	6-0	200	6-10-73	1992	Santo Domingo, D.R.
Mercedes, Jose	0	0	0.00	5	0	0	0	7	6	3	0	5	3	.230	R	R	6-1	180	3-5-71	1992	La Romana, D.R.
Ohka, Tomo	10	12	4.16	34	34	2	0	199	233	106	92	45	118	.291	R	R	6-1	180	3-18-76	1999	Kyoto, Japan
Reames, Britt	0	0	27.00	2	0	0	0	1	4	4	4	2	1	.500	R	R	5-10	180	8-19-73	1995	Seneca, S.C.
Smith, Dan	2	2	5.26	32	0	0	0	38	42	23	22	18	35	.280	R	R	6-3	230	9-15-75	1993	Carl Junction, Kan.
Stewart, Scott	3	1	3.98	51	0	0	0	43	52	22	19	13	29	.305	R	L	6-2	220	8-14-75	1994	Mt. Holly, N.C.
Tucker, T.J.	2	3	4.73	45	7	0	0	80	90	49	42	20	47	.277	R	R	6-3	260	8-20-78	1997	New Port Richey, Fla.
Vargas, Claudio	6	8	4.34	23	20	0	0	114	111	59	55	41	62	.254	R	R	6-3	220	6-19-78	1996	Santiago, D.R.
Vazquez, Javier	13	12	3.24	34	34	4	0	231	198	93	83	57	241	.228	R	R	6-2	200	7-25-76	1994	Ponce, P.R.

FIELDING

Catcher	PCT	G	PO	A	E	DP	PB
Barrett	.998	68	391	21	1	5	7
Guzman	1.000	4	23	0	0	0	1
Schneider	.996	98	661	45	3	12	3

First Base	PCT	G	PO	A	E	DP
Cordero	.996	123	1065	66	5	90
Guzman	.973	13	68	3	2	7
Liefer	.980	21	142	7	3	18
Vitiello	.976	12	74	8	2	7
Wilkerson	1.000	27	148	9	0	8

Second Base	PCT	G	PO	A	E	DP
Carroll	1.000	11	12	15	0	5
Macias	1.000	4	0	2	0	0
Mateo	.970	43	49	82	4	23
Vidro	.983	137	199	396	10	76

Third Base	PCT	G	PO	A	E	DP
Carroll	.969	67	43	115	5	8
Guzman	.956	28	6	37	2	3
Macias	.936	25	9	35	3	1
Tatis	.968	49	32	88	4	9
Zeile	.947	34	22	67	5	4

Shortstop	PCT	G	PO	A	E	DP
Cabrera	.975	162	258	456	18	101
Carroll	1.000	14	7	15	0	4
Mateo	1.000	2	1	1	0	1

Outfield	PCT	G	PO	A	E	DP
Calloway	.983	97	166	4	3	0
Cepicky	1.000	4	1	0	0	0
Chavez	.990	135	279	9	3	2
Cordero	.000	1	0	0	0	0
Guerrero	.970	112	217	10	7	1
Macias	.977	62	82	4	2	2
Mateo	1.000	10	9	0	0	0
Vitiello	1.000	15	14	0	0	0
Wilkerson	.982	135	257	11	5	1

FARM SYSTEM

Director, Player Development: Adam Wogan.

Class	Farm Team	League	W	L	Pct.	Finish*	Manager	First Yr.
AAA	Edmonton (Alberta) Trappers	Pacific Coast	73	69	.514	4th (16)	Dave Huppert	2003
AA	Harrisburg (Pa.) Senators	Eastern	60	82	.423	12th (12)	Dave Machemer	1991
High A	Brevard County (Fla.) Manatees	Florida State	65	66	.496	7th (12)	Doug Sisson	2002
Low A	Savannah (Ga.) Sand Gnats	South Atlantic	58	80	.420	13th (16)	Joey Cora	2003

SS A	Vermont (Burlington, Vt.) Expos	New York-Penn	19	56	.253	14th (14)	Dave Barnett	1994
Rookie	Melbourne (Fla.) Expos	Gulf Coast	25	33	.431	10th (12)	Bobby Henley	1998

*Finish in overall standings (No. of teams in league)

EDMONTON TRAPPERS — Class AAA

PACIFIC COAST LEAGUE

BATTING	AVG	G	AB	R	H	2B	3B	HR	RBI	BB	SO	SB	CS	SLG	OBP	B	T	HT	WT	DOB	1st Yr	Resides
Bailey, Jeff	.412	5	17	5	7	3	0	1	6	3	5	0	0	.765	.524	R	R	6-2	200	11-19-78	1997	Kelso, Wash.
Balfe, Ryan	.295	54	183	33	54	13	0	6	30	18	40	0	0	.464	.358	S	R	6-1	180	11-11-75	1994	Cornwall, N.Y.
Barrett, Michael	.333	2	6	2	2	1	0	0	0	0	2	1	0	.500	.333	R	R	6-2	200	10-22-76	1995	Alpharetta, Ga.
Bergeron, Pete	.302	110	388	62	117	19	7	1	32	37	64	12	3	.394	.360	L	R	6-0	190	11-9-77	1996	St. Petersburg, Fla.
Brown, Jason	.400	4	10	2	4	0	0	0	2	0	4	0	0	.400	.417	R	R	6-2	200	5-22-74	1997	Rolling Hills Estates, Calif.
Buford, Damon	.150	15	20	3	3	1	0	0	1	5	6	1	2	.200	.308	R	R	5-10	180	6-12-70	1990	Dallas, Texas
Cepicky, Matt	.301	122	442	61	133	23	4	7	64	31	82	7	2	.419	.349	L	R	6-2	220	11-10-77	1999	Sun City Center, Fla.
Cesar, Dionys	.304	21	56	8	17	6	0	0	11	4	11	0	0	.411	.355	S	R	5-10	150	9-27-76	1994	Santo Domingo, D.R.
Encarnacion, Mario	.313	16	48	8	15	2	0	1	6	7	11	0	1	.417	.400	R	R	6-2	210	9-24-75	1994	Bani, D.R.
Figueroa, Luis	.317	126	480	66	152	30	2	2	44	36	31	7	7	.400	.364	S	R	5-9	140	2-16-74	1997	Vega Alta, P.R.
Guzman, Edwards	.352	55	213	26	75	12	1	3	27	8	18	5	1	.460	.372	L	R	5-11	200	9-11-76	1996	Naranjito, P.R.
Hodges, Scott	.288	126	482	67	139	21	3	12	66	29	93	5	2	.419	.327	L	R	6-0	190	12-26-78	1997	Lexington, Ky.
Knorr, Randy	.304	88	316	37	96	19	1	7	48	29	57	1	0	.437	.364	R	R	6-2	210	11-12-68	1986	Tampa, Fla.
Medrano, Anthony	.245	125	425	63	104	18	3	2	46	50	49	5	4	.315	.335	R	R	5-10	170	12-8-74	1993	Long Beach, Calif.
Ortiz, Luis	.305	59	190	30	58	13	0	10	39	14	26	1	0	.532	.357	R	R	6-0	180	5-25-70	1991	North Richland, Texas
Pascucci, Val	.281	138	459	80	129	29	1	15	85	101	132	3	2	.447	.419	R	R	6-6	230	11-17-78	1999	Cerritos, Calif.
Sandusky, Scott	.284	39	109	10	31	5	0	0	8	8	27	0	1	.330	.347	R	R	6-0	200	3-6-76	1998	Arvada, Colo.
Sledge, Terrmel	.324	131	497	95	161	26	9	22	92	61	93	13	5	.545	.397	L	L	6-0	180	3-18-77	1999	Granada Hills, Calif.
Thrower, Jake	.224	51	143	12	32	5	0	2	15	6	18	0	1	.301	.248	S	R	5-11	180	11-19-75	1997	Yuma, Ariz.
2-team (28 Portland)	.243	79	226	23	55	13	0	3	28	13	26	1	1	.341	.283							
Vitiello, Joe	.271	27	96	11	26	7	0	2	14	10	17	0	0	.406	.333	R	R	6-3	230	4-11-70	1991	Stoneham, Mass.
2-team (23 Fresno)	.246	50	171	20	42	12	0	2	17	18	26	0	0	.351	.314							
Ware, Jeremy	.300	12	20	3	6	0	0	1	1	1	4	0	0	.450	.333	R	R	6-0	200	10-23-75	1995	Guelph, Ontario

PITCHING	W	L	ERA	G	GS	CG	SV	IP	H	R	ER	BB	SO	AVG	B	T	HT	WT	DOB	1st Yr	Resides
Agamennone, Brandon	1	2	6.94	5	1	0	0	12	16	10	9	7	9	.333	R	R	6-2	190	11-6-75	1998	Crofton, Md.
Blank, Matt	1	1	4.26	5	5	0	0	25	29	14	12	9	22	.292	L	L	6-2	190	4-5-76	1997	Arlington, Texas
Chiavacci, Ron	4	6	5.46	23	15	1	0	97	112	65	59	41	81	.291	R	R	6-2	220	9-5-77	1998	Scranton, Pa.
Colon, Jose	1	1	5.85	13	0	0	0	20	25	13	13	6	14	.308	R	R	6-0	170	11-24-74	1996	Puerto Plata, D.R.
Corcoran, Roy	0	0	0.00	2	0	0	0	2	0	0	0	0	1	.000	R	R	5-10	170	5-11-80	2001	Slaughter, La.
Crumpton, Chuck	2	1	4.79	19	2	0	4	47	42	25	25	21	19	.244	R	R	6-4	210	12-30-76	1999	Mesquite, Texas
Darensbourg, Vic	1	1	1.98	11	0	0	0	14	12	3	3	7	11	.235	L	L	5-8	170	11-13-70	1992	Henderson, Nev.
2-team (20 Colo. Springs)	3	3	2.97	31	0	0	0	36	36	16	12	12	26	.258							
Donaldson, Bo	0	0	4.34	9	1	0	0	19	20	12	9	14	12	.263	R	R	6-0	200	10-10-74	1997	Wesley Chapel, Fla.
2-team (3 Salt Lake)	0	0	3.80	12	1	0	0	24	25	13	10	16	17	.263							
Downs, Scott	8	9	4.29	21	21	3	0	122	119	67	58	39	54	.262	L	L	6-2	190	3-17-76	1997	Lexington, Ky.
Drew, Tim	5	9	7.23	27	15	0	2	93	128	80	75	35	54	.334	R	R	6-1	190	8-31-78	1997	Hahira, Ga.
Evans, Keith	1	2	6.00	12	0	0	1	21	28	15	14	6	6	.321	R	R	6-5	220	11-2-75	1996	San Pedro, Calif.
Ferrari, Anthony	5	2	4.89	28	0	0	0	50	63	29	27	18	17	.316	L	L	5-9	160	6-22-78	2000	Greenbrae, Calif.
Hebson, Bryan	6	0	4.36	30	0	0	6	43	44	23	21	22	44	.260	R	R	6-5	210	3-12-76	1997	Phenix City, Ala.
Izquierdo, Hansel	2	2	7.41	17	5	0	3	51	73	42	42	19	37	.337	R	R	6-1	200	1-2-77	1995	Miami, Fla.
Joseph, Kevin	1	2	9.39	7	1	0	1	15	25	16	16	7	8	.362	R	R	6-4	200	8-1-76	1997	Dallas, Texas
2-team (22 Memphis)	2	7	5.40	29	6	0	1	75	96	50	45	28	38	.314							
Kim, Sun-Woo	10	8	5.03	22	22	3	0	132	147	83	74	53	83	.280	R	R	6-1	180	9-4-77	1997	Seoul, South Korea
Knott, Eric	6	5	4.32	24	10	1	0	77	102	40	37	13	38	.314	L	L	6-1	180	9-23-74	1997	Sebring, Fla.
Lewis, Richie	0	0	6.08	7	0	0	0	13	17	9	9	7	7	.314	R	R	5-10	170	1-25-66	1987	Muncie, Ind.
Manon, Julio	3	1	2.14	35	0	0	14	42	33	12	10	19	48	.204	R	R	6-0	200	6-10-73	1992	Santo Domingo, D.R.
Mattes, Troy	1	0	1.50	1	1	0	0	6	5	1	1	4	3	.227	R	R	6-8	230	8-26-75	1994	Sarasota, Fla.
Reames, Britt	5	13	5.42	25	20	0	0	118	146	80	71	46	86	.299	R	R	5-10	180	8-19-73	1995	Seneca, S.C.
Rodgers, Bobby	0	0	7.00	8	0	0	0	9	14	7	7	11	10	.350	R	R	6-3	220	7-22-74	1996	St. Charles, Mo.
Rodriguez, Jose	0	1	5.32	13	0	0	1	24	26	16	14	10	15	.270	L	L	6-1	200	12-18-74	1997	Cayey, P.R.
Song, Seung	7	2	3.79	13	13	1	0	74	69	34	31	33	40	.253	R	R	6-1	190	6-29-80	1999	Stanley, N.C.
Stein, Blake	2	1	5.16	15	5	1	2	52	60	32	30	18	34	.283	R	R	6-7	240	8-3-73	1994	Folsom, La.
Tucker, T.J.	1	0	2.76	3	3	0	0	16	16	5	5	7	6	.262	R	R	6-3	260	8-20-78	1997	New Port Richey, Fla.
Ulloa, Enmanuel	0	0	11.05	3	0	0	0	7	14	10	9	2	5	.388	R	R	6-2	170	11-26-78	1997	New York, N.Y.
Vargas, Claudio	0	0	2.79	2	2	0	0	10	7	3	3	5	12	.189	R	R	6-3	220	6-19-78	1996	Santiago, D.R.

FIELDING

Catcher	PCT	G	PO	A	E	DP	PB
Barrett	1.000	2	3	1	0	0	0
Brown	1.000	4	26	1	0	1	0
Guzman	.985	21	124	11	2	1	5
Knorr	.994	86	465	27	3	4	5
Sandusky	1.000	36	176	15	0	2	3

First Base	PCT	G	PO	A	E	DP
Bailey	1.000	2	24	2	0	2
Balfe	.990	38	281	25	3	33
Cepicky	.875	2	14	0	2	4
Encarnacion	.852	4	21	2	4	4
Guzman	.993	16	132	10	1	10
Knorr	1.000	1	5	0	0	0
Ortiz	.997	36	307	15	1	21
Pascucci	.980	29	229	16	5	33
Sledge	1.000	1	5	0	0	1
Thrower	1.000	4	35	2	0	3
Vitiello	.995	21	166	18	1	21

Second Base	PCT	G	PO	A	E	DP
Cesar	.955	10	17	25	2	6
Figueroa	.981	102	213	291	10	73
Guzman	.965	11	19	36	2	7
Thrower	.984	30	58	62	2	10

Third Base	PCT	G	PO	A	E	DP
Balfe	.913	8	6	15	2	4
Cesar	1.000	2	2	3	0	1
Guzman	.968	9	11	19	1	1
Hodges	.945	122	74	235	18	31
Thrower	.941	9	4	12	1	2

Shortstop	PCT	G	PO	A	E	DP
Figueroa	.957	28	43	69	5	12
Medrano	.975	123	178	358	14	80

Outfield	PCT	G	PO	A	E	DP
Bailey	1.000	1	1	0	0	0
Balfe	1.000	1	1	0	0	0
Bergeron	.981	97	243	10	5	2
Buford	.889	9	8	0	1	0
Cepicky	.954	93	187	1	9	0
Cesar	.667	2	2	0	1	0
Encarnacion	.889	7	8	0	1	0
Ortiz	1.000	4	4	0	0	0
Pascucci	.981	109	197	15	4	5
Sledge	.971	121	258	11	8	1
Ware	1.000	5	9	2	0	1

HARRISBURG SENATORS — Class AA

EASTERN LEAGUE

BATTING	AVG	G	AB	R	H	2B	3B	HR	RBI	BB	SO	SB	CS	SLG	OBP	B	T	HT	WT	DOB	1st Yr	Resides
Ackerman, Scott	.223	88	292	30	65	11	4	7	43	17	43	0	2	.360	.263	R	R	6-1	210	4-23-79	1997	Oregon City, Ore.
Bailey, Jeff	.246	109	362	54	89	18	3	13	57	35	74	2	1	.420	.321	R	R	6-2	200	11-19-78	1997	Kelso, Wash.
Balfe, Ryan	.295	26	78	9	23	4	0	1	13	12	17	0	0	.385	.391	S	R	6-1	180	11-11-75	1994	Cornwall, N.Y.
Broadway, Larry	.321	21	78	13	25	3	0	5	18	7	15	0	0	.551	.371	L	L	6-4	230	12-17-80	2002	Scotts Hill, Tenn.
Brown, Jason	.320	13	50	5	16	4	0	4	12	1	13	0	0	.640	.333	R	R	6-2	200	5-22-74	1997	Rolling Hills Estates, Calif.
Carroll, Wes	.318	7	22	1	7	1	0	0	3	2	3	0	1	.364	.375	R	R	5-11	180	1-5-79	2001	Evansville, Ind.
Davis, Glenn	.210	101	333	34	70	19	2	8	46	32	93	1	2	.351	.280	S	L	6-1	200	11-25-75	1997	Aston, Pa.
Diaz, Felix	.195	57	185	17	36	4	4	7	19	14	79	1	1	.373	.259	S	R	6-2	200	8-1-77	1996	Bani, D.R.
Foster, Quincy	.292	88	216	34	63	7	2	2	18	12	26	22	6	.370	.328	L	R	6-2	170	10-30-74	1996	Hendersonville, N.C.
Gingrich, Troy	.267	20	45	5	12	2	0	2	4	2	5	2	1	.444	.298	L	L	5-10	170	1-17-77	2000	Apache Junction, Ariz.
Gutierrez, Vic	.240	90	262	33	63	9	1	1	19	16	42	8	2	.294	.286	R	R	5-9	170	12-23-77	1994	Santo Domingo, D.R.
Hall, Noah	.307	131	449	94	138	23	4	10	70	91	67	33	9	.443	.434	R	R	5-11	200	6-9-77	1996	Aptos, Calif.
Labandeira, Josh	.239	60	238	25	57	18	2	2	26	20	38	0	2	.357	.298	R	R	5-7	180	2-25-79	2001	Porterville, Calif.
Lane, Rich	.213	56	207	19	44	3	2	4	24	7	40	1	0	.304	.240	L	L	6-3	190	1-4-80	1999	Tustin, Calif.
Machado, Albenis	.215	110	339	46	73	13	0	0	25	52	52	3	3	.254	.318	S	R	6-0	170	3-20-79	1996	Caracas, Venez.
McKinley, Josh	.288	126	458	82	132	33	2	15	75	60	86	17	5	.467	.367	S	R	6-2	200	9-14-79	1998	Windermere, Fla.
Nunnari, Talmadge	.194	12	31	4	6	0	0	0	4	10	11	0	0	.194	.372	L	L	6-1	200	4-9-75	1997	Pensacola, Fla.
Sandusky, Scott	.241	26	83	7	20	5	1	1	11	8	14	2	0	.361	.315	R	R	6-0	200	3-6-76	1998	Arvada, Colo.
Thrower, Jake	.283	15	53	11	15	3	1	0	5	8	6	3	1	.377	.377	S	R	5-11	180	11-19-75	1997	Yuma, Ariz.
Urquhart, Derick	.176	4	17	2	3	1	0	0	3	1	3	1	0	.235	.222	L	L	5-8	180	12-20-75	1998	Florence, S.C.
Ware, Jeremy	.280	68	254	33	71	10	1	12	52	16	41	1	0	.469	.320	R	R	6-0	200	10-23-75	1995	Guelph, Ontario
Watson, Brandon	.319	139	565	86	180	17	6	1	39	38	60	18	17	.375	.362	L	R	6-1	170	9-30-81	1999	Inglewood, Calif.

PITCHING	W	L	ERA	G	GS	CG	SV	IP	H	R	ER	BB	SO	AVG	B	T	HT	WT	DOB	1st Yr	Resides
Bentz, Chad	1	4	2.55	52	0	0	16	85	72	31	24	39	56	.240	R	L	6-2	210	5-5-80	2001	Juneau, Alaska
Casadiego, Gerardo	1	4	6.64	22	7	0	1	61	71	46	45	41	31	.299	R	R	6-0	180	12-19-80	1998	Barquisimeto, Venez.
Chiavacci, Ron	1	4	6.02	8	8	0	0	40	41	27	27	19	38	.259	R	R	6-2	220	9-5-77	1998	Scranton, Pa.
Collins, Pat	2	3	7.12	25	0	0	0	43	46	37	34	31	30	.278	R	R	6-5	230	3-3-78	1999	Union, N.J.
Corcoran, Roy	1	1	0.38	14	0	0	3	24	14	4	1	7	26	.166	R	R	5-10	170	5-11-80	2001	Slaughter, La.
Crumpton, Chuck	4	6	3.57	26	5	0	3	63	72	34	25	24	30	.290	R	R	6-4	210	12-30-76	1999	Mesquite, Texas
Dequin, Benji	2	4	4.69	22	0	0	0	40	47	34	21	20	44	.284	R	L	5-10	170	6-2-80	2000	Gilroy, Calif.
Ferrari, Anthony	2	0	0.56	14	0	0	5	16	13	1	1	6	9	.224	L	L	5-9	160	6-22-78	2000	Greenbrae, Calif.
Gutierrez, Vic	0	0	0.00	2	0	0	0	2	2	2	0	2	0	.000	R	R	5-9	170	12-23-77	1994	Santo Domingo, D.R.
Hill, Shawn	3	1	3.54	4	4	0	0	20	23	12	8	11	12	.280	R	R	6-2	180	4-28-81	2000	Georgetown, Ontario
Karp, Josh	4	10	4.99	23	23	1	0	123	126	76	68	49	77	.265	R	R	6-5	210	9-21-79	2002	Bothell, Wash.
Lockwood, Luke	8	11	5.16	26	26	2	0	145	175	89	83	41	64	.303	L	L	6-3	170	7-21-81	1999	Victorville, Calif.
Mata, Gustavo	6	8	4.95	22	22	0	0	107	141	67	59	39	42	.320	R	R	6-1	190	5-20-83	2001	Carupano, Venez.
Mattes, Troy	0	1	5.68	5	3	0	0	19	21	15	12	3	8	.269	R	R	6-8	230	8-26-75	1994	Sarasota, Fla.
Maust, David	3	6	2.70	17	9	0	1	67	58	24	20	21	33	.231	L	L	6-2	200	11-6-78	2001	Morgantown, W.Va.
Puello, Ignacio	1	0	7.32	18	0	0	0	36	40	31	29	28	21	.289	R	R	6-1	170	10-16-80	1998	San Pedro de Macoris, D.R.
Rodriguez, Cristobal	0	0	54.00	1	0	0	0	1	4	6	6	2	1	.571	R	R	6-4	210	1-27-79	1996	Chichiriviche, Venez.
Schroder, Chris	9	2	2.84	49	0	0	4	82	68	29	26	47	81	.231	R	R	6-3	210	8-20-78	2001	Okarche, Okla.
Seale, Dustin	1	2	4.82	26	1	0	1	47	47	29	25	23	23	.262	L	L	6-1	190	12-2-77	1997	Safford, Ariz.
Song, Seung	5	2	2.35	13	13	1	0	73	55	26	19	24	44	.207	R	R	6-1	190	6-29-80	1999	Stanley, N.C.
Stein, Blake	1	3	6.63	4	3	0	0	19	24	15	14	11	10	.315	R	R	6-7	240	8-3-73	1994	Folsom, La.
2-team (2 Akron)	1	4	9.14	6	3	0	0	22	30	23	22	15	14	.337							
Torres, Luis	0	4	4.80	11	0	0	0	15	11	10	8	10	20	.211	R	R	6-4	200	3-12-81	1999	Caracas, Venez.
Ulloa, Enmanuel	0	2	10.95	6	1	0	1	12	19	15	15	9	12	.351	R	R	6-2	170	11-26-78	1997	New York, N.Y.
Vargas, Claudio	1	0	0.75	2	2	0	0	12	7	1	1	3	13	.170	R	R	6-3	220	6-19-78	1996	Santiago, D.R.
Young, Chris	4	4	4.01	15	15	0	0	83	83	39	37	22	64	.259	R	R	6-10	250	5-25-79	2001	Dallas, Texas

FIELDING

Catcher	PCT	G	PO	A	E	DP	PB
Ackerman	.994	77	416	53	3	7	8
Bailey	.981	28	141	11	3	0	3
Balfe	1.000	8	34	1	0	0	1
Brown	.962	13	92	8	4	1	0
Sandusky	.987	23	140	7	2	0	1

First Base	PCT	G	PO	A	E	DP
Bailey	.988	31	247	8	3	24
Balfe	1.000	1	5	0	0	0
Broadway	.988	20	153	11	2	19
Davis	.995	73	568	62	3	57
Lane	.995	23	184	15	1	15
Nunnari	.947	2	15	3	1	0

Second Base	PCT	G	PO	A	E	DP
Carroll	1.000	5	3	9	0	2
Gutierrez	.957	16	37	30	3	7
Hall	.889	3	5	3	1	0
Machado	.929	6	8	18	2	3
McKinley	.967	119	255	325	20	76
Thrower	1.000	1	2	1	0	1

Third Base	PCT	G	PO	A	E	DP
Bailey	.923	5	2	10	1	1
Balfe	.875	4	3	4	1	0
Carroll	1.000	1	3	2	0	1
Diaz	.874	50	21	83	15	7
Gutierrez	.921	53	38	67	9	9
Machado	.963	35	26	52	3	7
McKinley	1.000	2	0	4	0	0
Thrower	1.000	7	4	10	0	0

Shortstop	PCT	G	PO	A	E	DP
Gutierrez	.931	12	11	16	2	2
Labandeira	.953	60	91	175	13	34
Machado	.975	69	100	209	8	49
Thrower	.957	8	6	16	1	2

Outfield	PCT	G	PO	A	E	DP
Bailey	.977	23	41	2	1	0
Balfe	1.000	2	1	0	0	0
Carroll	1.000	1	2	0	0	0
Diaz	.000	1	0	0	0	0
Foster	.973	62	104	5	3	0
Gingrich	.935	19	28	1	2	0
Gutierrez	.800	4	3	1	1	0
Hall	.989	120	253	5	3	1
Lane	1.000	18	31	1	0	0
Nunnari	.933	8	14	0	1	0
Thrower	1.000	1	1	0	0	0
Urquhart	1.000	2	3	0	0	0
Ware	.994	60	148	6	1	3
Watson	.983	139	389	8	7	2

BREVARD COUNTY MANATEES — High Class A

FLORIDA STATE LEAGUE

BATTING	AVG	G	AB	R	H	2B	3B	HR	RBI	BB	SO	SB	CS	SLG	OBP	B	T	HT	WT	DOB	1st Yr	Resides
Ambrosini, Anthony	.238	52	143	13	34	4	0	0	6	9	23	2	1	.266	.292	R	R	5-9	180	9-22-78	2001	Ronkonkoma, N.Y.
Ambrosini, Dominick	.261	114	383	35	100	26	3	5	45	25	98	7	2	.384	.307	L	L	5-10	180	2-21-81	1999	Ronkonkoma, N.Y.
Apodaca, Luis	.333	2	3	0	1	0	0	0	0	0	0	0	0	.333	.333	R	R	5-11	170	7-15-82	1999	Caracas, Venez.
Balfe, Ryan	.291	30	110	10	32	10	0	4	27	7	27	0	1	.491	.350	S	R	6-1	180	11-11-75	1994	Cornwall, N.Y.
Berroa, Cristian	.310	9	29	6	9	1	1	0	2	1	3	1	0	.414	.355	S	R	5-11	150	4-29-79	1996	Haina, D.R.

BATTING	AVG	G	AB	R	H	2B	3B	HR	RBI	BB	SO	SB	CS	SLG	OBP	B	T	HT	WT	DOB	1st Yr	Resides
Broadway, Larry	.224	25	76	8	17	7	1	1	7	18	20	0	1	.382	.367	L	L	6-4	230	12-17-80	2002	Scotts Hill, Tenn.
Brown, Jason	.171	44	111	5	19	3	1	1	9	9	31	0	0	.243	.236	R	R	6-2	200	5-22-74	1997	Rolling Hills Estates, Calif.
Carroll, Wes	.231	99	338	29	78	12	0	1	36	26	50	6	3	.275	.287	R	R	5-11	180	1-5-79	2001	Evansville, Ind.
Cavin, Jonathan	.100	11	30	5	3	2	0	0	1	3	11	1	0	.167	.206	L	R	6-3	220	3-19-80	2000	Stilwell, Okla.
Diaz, Felix	.121	21	66	3	8	0	0	1	3	3	29	0	0	.167	.194	S	R	6-2	200	8-1-77	1996	Bani, D.R.
Ellerson, Brian	.219	12	32	4	7	2	0	1	2	2	6	0	0	.375	.286	R	R	6-1	190	9-18-79	2002	Bayonne, N.J.
Emmerick, Josh	.231	6	13	1	3	0	0	1	4	0	6	0	0	.462	.231	R	R	6-4	190	2-22-81	1999	Oceanside, Calif.
Gingrich, Troy	.217	94	318	45	69	14	3	1	14	38	63	16	6	.289	.308	L	L	5-10	170	1-17-77	2000	Apache Junction, Ariz.
Guerrero, Vladimir	.500	3	6	2	3	0	0	1	1	0	0	0	0	1.000	.571	R	R	6-3	220	2-9-76	1993	Nizao Bani, D.R.
Labandeira, Josh	.324	62	238	41	77	13	4	0	25	24	35	6	5	.412	.386	R	R	5-7	180	2-25-79	2001	Porterville, Calif.
Lane, Rich	.300	67	247	39	74	8	3	7	44	29	40	7	0	.441	.384	L	L	6-3	190	1-4-80	1999	Tustin, Calif.
McMillan, Drew	.191	53	157	8	30	7	0	1	16	13	50	1	1	.255	.277	R	R	6-3	200	10-25-80	1999	Yorba Linda, Calif.
Norris, Shawn	.196	57	194	28	38	9	1	2	14	37	49	1	2	.284	.331	L	R	6-2	170	8-1-80	2001	Draper, Utah
Rodriguez, Robert	.238	11	21	3	5	1	0	0	1	6	9	0	1	.286	.407	R	R	5-10	180	12-17-80	2002	Miami, Fla.
Rombley, Danny	.239	107	376	52	90	16	5	0	23	37	95	22	15	.309	.319	R	R	6-1	180	11-26-79	1999	Amersfoort, Netherlands
Rooi, Vince	.254	97	319	34	81	19	0	7	52	36	70	3	9	.379	.334	R	R	6-1	190	12-13-81	1999	Amsterdam, Netherlands
Schnabel, Nick	.170	61	147	11	25	3	0	0	12	12	25	2	0	.190	.247	R	R	5-9	170	3-16-78	2000	Greenville, N.C.
Sucre, Antonio	.000	1	2	0	0	0	0	0	0	0	2	0	0	.000	.000	R	R	6-2	180	8-13-83	2000	Puerto la Cruz, Venez.
Thissen, Greg	.178	89	275	33	49	6	2	0	13	34	65	10	4	.215	.269	R	R	6-4	180	6-1-81	2001	Davenport, Iowa
Urquhart, Derick	.213	58	160	13	34	5	2	1	12	20	24	2	4	.288	.304	L	L	5-8	180	12-20-75	1998	Florence, S.C.
Williams, Clyde	.241	118	382	38	92	19	4	14	51	34	106	3	1	.421	.300	L	L	6-2	190	7-7-79	1998	Sanford, Fla.

PITCHING	W	L	ERA	G	GS	CG	SV	IP	H	R	ER	BB	SO	AVG	B	T	HT	WT	DOB	1st Yr	Resides
Caputo, Rob	4	6	4.31	21	20	0	0	94	110	62	45	42	57	.290	R	R	6-6	200	11-7-79	2001	New Fairfield, Conn.
Casadiego, Gerardo	0	3	3.20	7	2	0	0	20	23	7	7	4	12	.294	R	R	6-0	180	12-19-80	1998	Barquisimeto, Venez.
Cerezo, Hector	0	0	27.00	1	0	0	0	0	2	1	1	0	0	.666	L	L	6-2	170	2-28-82	2000	Miranda, Venez.
Corcoran, Roy	5	3	1.91	28	0	0	12	33	19	8	7	11	35	.171	R	R	5-10	170	5-11-80	2001	Slaughter, La.
Cordero, Chad	1	1	2.05	19	0	0	6	26	17	8	6	10	17	.197	R	R	6-0	195	3-18-82	2003	Chino, Calif.
Davis, Stockton	3	2	3.82	42	0	0	1	68	74	36	29	28	51	.274	L	R	6-3	210	9-8-79	2002	Owasso, Okla.
Day, Zach	0	0	1.69	1	1	0	0	5	3	1	1	1	3	.166	R	R	6-4	210	6-15-78	1996	Cincinnati, Ohio
Dequin, Benji	6	3	2.63	17	2	0	0	41	34	13	12	18	38	.228	R	L	5-10	170	6-2-80	2000	Gilroy, Calif.
Hernandez, Orlando	0	1	10.80	2	2	0	0	5	5	6	6	4	7	.250	R	R	6-2	220	10-11-69	1998	Miami, Fla.
Hill, Shawn	9	4	2.56	22	21	2	0	127	118	47	36	26	66	.247	R	R	6-2	180	4-28-81	2000	Georgetown, Ontario
Hinckley, Mike	4	0	0.72	4	4	1	0	25	14	2	2	1	23	.159	R	L	6-3	170	10-5-82	2001	Moore, Okla.
Martin, Greg	0	0	6.35	7	0	0	0	6	9	4	4	4	1	.375	L	L	6-1	190	4-10-80	2002	Scranton, Pa.
Mata, Gustavo	2	0	0.60	5	5	0	0	30	20	3	2	4	15	.192	R	R	6-1	190	5-20-83	2001	Carupano, Venez.
Maust, David	1	2	1.31	31	0	0	4	48	36	12	7	8	41	.203	L	L	6-2	200	11-6-78	2001	Morgantown, W.Va.
McAdam, Scott	0	0	36.00	1	0	0	0	1	5	4	4	2	1	.625	R	R	5-11	170	6-5-83	2001	Glenmore Park, Australia
Meyer, Todd	0	0	40.50	1	0	0	0	1	3	3	3	2	0	.750	R	R	6-3	180	8-2-79	2002	York, Pa.
Morales, Alex	0	0	0.00	2	0	0	1	5	3	0	0	3	8	.157	R	R	5-11	170	12-8-82	2003	Mt. Prospect, Ill.
Nicolas, Mike	0	2	3.65	8	0	0	1	12	8	5	5	4	12	.186	R	R	6-3	220	9-5-79	2000	Santo Domingo, D.R.
Norderum, Jason	4	11	5.29	25	18	0	0	99	117	66	58	33	59	.296	L	L	6-3	220	11-21-81	2000	Redding, Calif.
Puello, Ignacio	2	5	6.45	18	9	0	1	53	57	40	38	24	27	.276	R	R	6-1	170	10-16-80	1998	San Pedro de Macoris, D.R.
Rodriguez, Cristobal	0	0	3.86	2	0	0	0	2	2	1	1	0	3	.222	R	R	6-4	210	1-27-79	1996	Chichiriviche, Venez.
Rodriguez, Jose	0	0	0.00	1	0	0	1	1	0	0	0	0	1	.000	L	L	6-1	200	12-18-74	1997	Cayey, P.R.
Rundles, Rich	5	6	2.95	19	19	2	0	107	111	44	35	24	76	.268	L	L	6-5	180	6-3-81	1999	Livingston, Ala.
Seale, Dustin	1	0	4.12	9	1	0	2	20	24	11	9	7	9	.307	L	L	6-1	190	12-2-77	1997	Safford, Ariz.
Searles, Jon	2	3	2.93	18	0	0	2	28	28	9	9	15	17	.277	R	R	6-3	200	1-18-81	1999	Huntington, N.Y.
Stevenson, Jason	9	6	2.62	36	11	0	0	113	88	36	33	33	60	.215	L	L	6-1	170	8-8-81	2001	Redding, Calif.
Stewart, Scott	0	0	0.00	2	2	0	0	4	1	0	0	1	4	.083	R	L	6-2	220	8-14-75	1994	Mt. Holly, N.C.
Torres, Luis	1	3	5.55	30	3	0	3	58	71	36	36	24	40	.300	R	R	6-4	200	3-12-81	1999	Caracas, Venez.
Ulloa, Enmanuel	0	2	2.21	5	3	0	0	20	17	6	5	6	15	.229	R	R	6-2	170	11-26-78	1997	New York, N.Y.
Urquhart, Derick	0	0	13.50	2	0	0	0	1	2	2	2	0	1	.000	L	L	5-8	180	12-20-75	1998	Florence, S.C.
Washburn, Ben	1	1	2.77	8	0	0	0	13	15	7	4	3	5	.267	R	R	6-2	200	5-17-79	2000	Redlands, Calif.
Young, Chris	5	2	1.62	8	8	0	0	50	26	9	9	5	39	.150	R	R	6-10	250	5-25-79	2001	Dallas, Texas

FIELDING

Catcher	PCT	G	PO	A	E	DP	PB
Ambrosini	.996	45	230	20	1	4	6
Apodaca	1.000	1	1	0	0	0	0
Balfe	1.000	7	37	4	0	0	0
Brown	.987	31	142	11	2	0	1
Ellerson	.000	1	0	0	0	0	0
Emmerick	.979	6	39	7	1	1	3
McMillan	.983	51	264	30	5	3	2
Rodriguez	.982	10	49	5	1	0	5

First Base	PCT	G	PO	A	E	DP
Ambrosini	.973	7	64	7	2	7
Broadway	1.000	20	178	17	0	19
Carroll	1.000	1	2	0	0	0
Lane	.986	32	255	20	4	14
Williams	.990	79	673	55	7	55

Second Base	PCT	G	PO	A	E	DP
Carroll	.865	13	21	24	7	4
Norris	.987	30	63	84	2	16
Schnabel	.975	39	63	90	4	19
Thissen	.959	68	114	188	13	37

Third Base	PCT	G	PO	A	E	DP
Berroa	1.000	4	5	9	0	0
Carroll	.902	19	16	39	6	2
Diaz	.778	2	2	5	2	0
Ellerson	.800	1	0	4	1	0
Norris	.909	20	11	49	6	5
Rooi	.920	90	55	176	20	13
Schnabel	.000	2	0	0	0	0
Thissen	1.000	2	1	7	0	2

Shortstop	PCT	G	PO	A	E	DP
Berroa	1.000	4	10	9	0	3
Carroll	.954	44	47	118	8	21
Labandeira	.949	57	77	146	12	23
Norris	.947	5	5	13	1	4
Schnabel	.929	18	23	42	5	9
Thissen	.938	9	16	29	3	7

Outfield	PCT	G	PO	A	E	DP
Ambrosini	.971	92	160	5	5	1
Carroll	1.000	21	35	1	0	0
Cavin	.938	9	14	1	1	0
Diaz	1.000	7	18	0	0	0
Ellerson	.900	6	8	1	1	0
Gingrich	.989	90	171	4	2	0
Guerrero	1.000	2	5	0	0	0
Lane	.983	31	56	2	1	0
Rombley	.992	105	228	10	2	2
Sucre	1.000	1	1	0	0	0
Thissen	.818	6	8	1	2	0
Urquhart	1.000	52	90	1	0	0

SAVANNAH SAND GNATS — Low Class A

SOUTH ATLANTIC LEAGUE

BATTING	AVG	G	AB	R	H	2B	3B	HR	RBI	BB	SO	SB	CS	SLG	OBP	B	T	HT	WT	DOB	1st Yr	Resides
Bernadina, Rogearvin	.237	77	278	36	66	12	3	4	39	19	53	11	4	.345	.292	L	L	6-0	170	6-12-84	2002	Den Haag, Netherlands
Berroa, Cristian	.211	5	19	1	4	2	0	1	1	0	4	1	0	.474	.250	S	R	5-11	150	4-29-79	1996	Haina, D.R.
Broadway, Larry	.307	83	290	56	89	25	4	14	51	44	70	3	4	.566	.400	L	L	6-4	230	12-17-80	2002	Scotts Hill, Tenn.
Brown, Tony	.222	34	126	11	28	1	1	0	4	6	38	6	2	.246	.263	L	R	6-0	180	9-5-79	2002	Hockessin, Del.

BATTING	AVG	G	AB	R	H	2B	3B	HR	RBI	BB	SO	SB	CS	SLG	OBP	B	T	HT	WT	DOB	1st Yr	Resides
Cavin, Jonathan	.171	14	41	5	7	1	0	1	8	6	12	1	1	.268	.292	L	R	6-3	220	3-19-80	2000	Stilwell, Okla.
2-team (45 Kannapolis)	.209	59	172	21	36	4	0	1	15	26	59	1	2	.250	.318							
Chop, Chad	.322	131	485	55	156	26	5	11	77	32	75	10	8	.464	.368	L	L	6-4	210	3-21-80	2002	Santa Ana, Calif.
Clanton, Ja'Mar	.202	37	104	9	21	2	0	0	10	12	36	1	1	.221	.282	R	R	6-0	170	7-14-81	2002	Bellwood, Ill.
Conlisk, Jason	.199	92	306	30	61	13	1	1	29	32	70	8	3	.258	.280	S	R	5-10	180	7-8-81	2002	Ridgewood, N.Y.
Diaz, Frank	.270	122	440	63	119	28	4	7	49	15	73	19	4	.400	.298	R	R	6-2	180	10-6-83	2000	Valencia, Venez.
Ellerson, Brian	.277	61	202	35	56	5	2	5	23	22	27	7	3	.396	.365	R	R	6-1	190	9-18-79	2002	Bayonne, N.J.
Emmerick, Josh	.224	46	152	20	34	7	0	3	23	20	23	2	2	.329	.331	R	R	6-4	190	2-22-81	1999	Oceanside, Calif.
Encarnacion, Henry	.167	4	12	1	2	0	0	0	2	1	0	0	1	.167	.231	S	R	6-0	170	5-20-82	1999	Santo Domingo, D.R.
Fitzpatrick, Reggie	.223	113	430	48	96	9	7	1	26	23	101	36	11	.284	.273	L	L	5-11	180	2-28-83	2001	Atlanta, Ga.
Louisa, Lorvin	.034	12	29	2	1	0	0	0	1	1	13	0	1	.034	.097	R	R	6-4	200	2-7-83	1999	Willemstad, Curacao
Manriquez, Salomon	.239	37	117	14	28	12	0	3	22	4	25	0	0	.419	.280	R	R	6-1	190	9-15-82	1999	Guacara, Venez.
Margalski, Ben	.255	37	110	15	28	5	1	2	14	26	30	3	2	.373	.406	L	R	6-2	210	9-2-79	2001	High Ridge, Mo.
Noboa, Joel	.177	32	96	14	17	2	5	2	10	8	47	1	0	.365	.250	R	R	6-1	180	11-27-79	1997	Santo Domingo, D.R.
Norris, Shawn	.287	67	223	38	64	19	2	2	35	31	42	4	2	.417	.375	L	R	6-2	170	8-1-80	2001	Draper, Utah
Rodriguez, Robert	.183	40	115	9	21	2	0	0	8	6	32	3	0	.200	.254	R	R	5-10	180	12-17-80	2002	Miami, Fla.
St. Martine, Michael	.173	32	104	6	18	2	0	1	11	7	28	2	2	.221	.223	L	R	5-11	195	4-17-82	2003	Levittown, Pa.
Sweeney, Tim	.227	24	75	8	17	2	0	0	4	5	13	1	2	.253	.275	R	R	6-3	190	8-3-80	2002	Sparta, N.J.
Thede, Matt	.216	14	51	4	11	2	0	0	3	2	14	0	1	.255	.245	R	R	6-1	180	6-21-78	2001	Reinbeck, Iowa
Webb, Trey	.238	58	214	32	51	13	2	2	20	10	29	6	4	.346	.278	R	R	6-1	170	2-11-82	2003	Mansfield, Texas
Yepez, Marcos	.264	108	401	56	106	13	5	3	41	35	113	28	10	.344	.335	S	R	5-10	160	12-29-81	1999	Caracas, Venez.
York, Larry	.000	2	7	0	0	0	0	0	0	2	2	0	0	.000	.222	S	R	5-10	180	3-17-80	2003	Ramseur, N.C.

PITCHING	W	L	ERA	G	GS	CG	SV	IP	H	R	ER	BB	SO	AVG	B	T	HT	WT	DOB	1st Yr	Resides
Barlow, Chris	6	10	3.99	29	20	1	3	133	146	78	59	38	65	.281	R	R	6-6	210	11-11-80	2002	Cazenovia, N.Y.
Bergmann, Jason	6	11	4.29	23	22	1	0	109	108	57	52	53	82	.264	R	R	6-4	190	9-25-81	2002	Manalapan, N.J.
Diaz, Eddie	0	0	6.52	7	0	0	0	10	8	10	7	10	17	.216	R	R	6-0	170	1-25-83	2001	Orlando, Fla.
Everts, Clint	0	3	3.46	5	5	0	0	26	23	13	10	10	21	.230	R	R	6-2	170	8-10-84	2002	Cypress, Texas
Fiedler, Erik	1	5	4.56	35	0	0	0	53	56	41	27	27	36	.274	R	R	6-4	190	11-27-78	2002	Placerville, Calif.
Girdley, Josh	2	5	4.76	12	11	0	0	51	49	32	27	27	38	.253	L	L	6-3	180	8-29-80	1999	Jasper, Texas
Hinckley, Mike	9	5	3.64	23	23	2	0	121	124	54	49	41	111	.271	R	L	6-3	170	10-5-82	2001	Moore, Okla.
Long, Nick	2	7	3.92	15	12	0	0	60	53	29	26	29	43	.237	R	R	6-3	180	11-24-82	2001	Columbus, Ga.
Marceau, Pierre-Luc	5	4	4.30	36	5	0	3	92	99	50	44	27	65	.278	L	L	6-2	190	4-11-81	1999	Fleurimont, Quebec
Martin, Greg	1	1	5.65	20	0	0	0	29	32	18	18	19	17	.296	L	L	6-1	190	4-10-80	2002	Scranton, Pa.
Martinez, Roberto	1	1	8.03	17	0	0	0	25	33	23	22	18	14	.305	R	R	6-3	180	5-2-81	1998	Bonao, D.R.
Martinez, Samuel	2	6	5.81	12	11	0	0	48	41	34	31	30	34	.239	R	R	6-2	160	3-22-79	1999	Santo Domingo, D.R.
Maruffi, Joe	0	0	7.88	4	0	0	1	8	15	7	7	4	4	.405	R	R	6-0	215	10-15-79	2003	Albuquerque, N.M.
Meyer, Todd	1	5	6.05	25	1	0	1	39	45	28	26	26	24	.286	R	R	6-3	180	8-2-79	2002	York, Pa.
Mitchell, Tom	1	1	7.79	19	0	0	2	35	46	34	30	33	9	.335	R	R	6-2	180	11-20-80	2000	Bladenboro, N.C.
O'Connor, Michael	8	3	3.86	42	0	0	1	70	56	36	30	35	83	.215	L	L	6-3	170	8-17-80	2002	Ellicott City, Md.
Rasner, Darrell	7	7	4.19	22	22	2	0	105	106	53	49	36	90	.268	R	R	6-3	210	1-13-81	2002	Carson City, Nev.
Rodriguez, Jose	0	1	6.75	7	0	0	0	13	15	10	10	11	5	.294	R	R	6-2	200	2-9-81	1998	Peoria, Ariz.
Rueckel, Danny	1	3	4.06	40	1	0	14	69	68	38	31	16	64	.259	R	R	6-0	170	9-25-79	2002	Dunwoody, Ga.
Seale, Dustin	2	0	3.66	4	3	1	1	20	17	8	8	7	13	.242	L	L	6-1	190	12-2-77	1997	Safford, Ariz.
Searles, Jon	3	2	3.66	20	2	0	5	39	35	19	16	12	36	.234	R	R	6-3	200	1-18-81	1999	Huntington, N.Y.

FIELDING

Catcher	PCT	G	PO	A	E	DP	PB
Emmerick	.978	39	236	32	6	1	8
Manriquez	.990	27	166	26	2	1	3
Margalski	.979	25	175	16	4	1	6
Rodriguez	.978	22	121	14	3	0	2
St. Martine	.975	28	185	13	5	0	7
Thede	1.000	2	10	3	0	0	0

First Base	PCT	G	PO	A	E	DP
Broadway	.993	80	688	57	5	70
Chop	.986	43	330	19	5	25
Manriquez	1.000	1	2	0	0	1
Margalski	1.000	1	3	0	0	1
Noboa	.992	18	122	3	1	8
Yepez	1.000	4	33	0	0	3

Second Base	PCT	G	PO	A	E	DP
Conlisk	.969	91	158	252	13	55
Encarnacion	.846	3	2	9	2	2
Sweeney	.968	7	16	14	1	5
Yepez	.974	39	65	85	4	17

Third Base	PCT	G	PO	A	E	DP
Berroa	.000	1	0	0	0	0
Ellerson	.908	55	29	79	11	3
Noboa	.906	10	7	22	3	3
Norris	.950	64	40	113	8	11
Sweeney	.950	8	4	15	1	2
Thede	1.000	3	8	5	0	1
Yepez	.714	3	1	4	2	0

Shortstop	PCT	G	PO	A	E	DP
Clanton	.916	36	52	101	14	16
Sweeney	.944	4	6	11	1	2
Webb	.930	54	71	155	17	25
Yepez	.970	48	74	152	7	33

Outfield	PCT	G	PO	A	E	DP
Bernadina	.979	67	90	3	2	0
Brown	.943	30	65	1	4	0
Cavin	.957	10	20	2	1	0
Chop	.984	80	118	4	2	0
Diaz	.980	119	218	21	5	2
Fitzpatrick	.967	109	260	3	9	0
Louisa	1.000	10	20	2	0	1
Noboa	.000	1	0	0	0	0
Rodriguez	.000	1	0	0	0	0

VERMONT EXPOS — Short-Season Class A

NEW YORK-PENN LEAGUE

BATTING	AVG	G	AB	R	H	2B	3B	HR	RBI	BB	SO	SB	CS	SLG	OBP	B	T	HT	WT	DOB	1st Yr	Resides
Bernazard, Oscar	.198	32	91	9	18	4	0	0	7	19	30	0	1	.242	.345	S	R	5-10	195	3-23-81	2003	Caguas, P.R.
Blanco, Luis	.167	12	42	3	7	2	0	2	4	0	17	0	0	.357	.167	R	R	6-3	200	7-6-81	1999	Caracas, Venez.
Brown, Tony	.154	9	26	4	4	0	0	0	1	1	4	0	0	.154	.185	L	R	6-0	180	9-5-79	2002	Hockessin, Del.
Casto, Kory	.239	71	259	26	62	14	2	4	28	30	47	1	1	.355	.322	L	R	6-1	200	12-8-81	2003	Aurora, Ore.
Clanton, Ja'Mar	.176	58	176	13	31	3	1	0	11	14	44	11	3	.205	.247	R	R	6-0	170	7-14-81	2002	Bellwood, Ill.
Cloar, Jason	.118	5	17	1	2	0	0	0	1	3	4	0	0	.118	.250	R	L	6-0	195	5-1-81	2003	Ormond Beach, Fla.
Ditter, Brad	.271	64	214	27	58	7	3	1	16	28	41	6	0	.346	.366	L	R	6-0	180	7-22-80	2003	Redmond, Wash.
Encarnacion, Henry	.151	22	73	5	11	2	1	0	4	11	20	0	3	.205	.267	S	R	6-0	170	5-20-82	1999	Santo Domingo, D.R.
Jimenez, Franklyn	.253	58	217	23	55	7	0	2	17	10	43	8	2	.313	.294	R	R	6-2	180	2-23-82	2002	Bayamon, P.R.
Kahr, Danny	.073	27	82	6	6	2	0	1	1	1	41	0	1	.134	.136	S	R	6-3	180	9-25-82	2001	Las Vegas, Nev.
Louisa, Lorvin	.206	62	218	17	45	5	1	5	24	14	73	2	0	.307	.258	R	R	6-4	200	2-7-83	1999	Willemstad, Curacao
Lutz, David	.156	13	32	2	5	2	0	0	1	6	5	0	0	.219	.308	L	R	6-3	190	9-25-81	1999	Spring Valley, Calif.
Manriquez, Salomon	.196	45	168	14	33	4	0	2	11	10	41	0	0	.256	.243	R	R	6-1	190	9-15-82	1999	Guacara, Venez.
Noboa, Joel	.087	9	23	0	2	0	0	0	0	0	12	0	0	.087	.160	R	R	6-1	180	11-27-79	1997	Santo Domingo, D.R.
Owens, Jerry	.125	2	8	0	1	0	0	0	0	0	2	1	0	.125	.125	L	L	6-3	195	2-16-81	2003	Newhall, Calif.
Pignatiello, Bret	.258	9	31	4	8	1	1	0	3	3	8	0	0	.355	.324	L	R	6-1	195	4-4-81	2003	Tinley Park, Ill.
St. Martine, Michael	.300	3	10	1	3	1	0	0	1	1	1	0	0	.400	.364	L	R	5-11	195	4-17-82	2003	Levittown, Pa.

BATTING	AVG	G	AB	R	H	2B	3B	HR	RBI	BB	SO	SB	CS	SLG	OBP	B	T	HT	WT	DOB	1st Yr	Resides
Sweeney, Tim	.202	36	114	10	23	5	0	0	12	17	26	1	1	.246	.319	R	R	6-3	190	8-3-80	2002	Sparta, N.J.
Tuttle, Jason	.281	51	203	23	57	7	1	0	17	15	19	17	4	.325	.333	L	L	5-8	160	11-27-79	2002	Winston-Salem, N.C.
Vroman, Doug	.153	29	72	7	11	1	1	0	4	10	26	2	2	.194	.262	R	R	6-1	195	2-9-81	2003	Westport, Conn.
Webb, Trey	.250	6	24	2	6	1	0	0	1	1	2	2	0	.292	.280	R	R	6-1	170	2-11-82	2003	Mansfield, Texas
Whitesell, Josh	.246	49	167	13	41	10	1	5	19	28	53	0	0	.407	.365	L	L	6-3	220	4-14-82	2003	Redlands, Calif.
York, Larry	.208	32	125	5	26	3	0	0	10	7	15	4	6	.232	.261	S	R	5-10	180	3-17-80	2003	Ramseur, N.C.

GAMES BY POSITION: C—Bernazard 1, Kahr 24, Lutz 4, Manriquez 42, Pignatiello 4, St. Martine 3. **1B**—Blanco 8, Jimenez 8, Lutz 7, Noboa 1, Pignatiello 1, Sweeney 5, Whitesell 46. **2B**—Bernazard 7, Clanton 1, Ditter 24, Encarnacion 13, Jimenez 3, Sweeney 2, York 29. **3B**—Ditter 31, Jimenez 19, Noboa 5, Sweeney 24. **SS**—Clanton 56, Encarnacion 10, Sweeney 5, Webb 6, York 1. **OF**—Brown 9, Casto 65, Cloar 1, Jimenez 21, Louisa 58, Owens 2, Sweeney 1, Tuttle 51, Vroman 25.

PITCHING	W	L	ERA	G	GS	CG	SV	IP	H	R	ER	BB	SO	AVG	B	T	HT	WT	DOB	1st Yr	Resides
Caceres, Carlos	0	2	5.12	12	3	0	1	32	28	22	18	15	15	.229	R	R	6-0	170	12-4-80	2000	Santo Domingo, D.R.
Diaz, Eddie	1	2	3.38	13	1	0	2	27	22	13	10	17	32	.222	R	R	6-0	170	1-25-83	2001	Orlando, Fla.
Dixon, Jeff	1	1	1.69	7	1	0	0	11	7	3	2	2	9	.184	R	R	6-8	260	2-7-81	2003	Brattleboro, Vt.
Everts, Clint	2	4	4.17	10	10	0	0	54	49	26	25	35	50	.247	R	R	6-2	170	8-10-84	2002	Cypress, Texas
Generelli, Daniel	0	3	10.18	13	3	0	1	20	34	29	23	15	8	.377	R	R	6-2	200	8-25-80	1999	Hubbardston, Mass.
Gomez, Warmar	1	2	1.82	16	0	0	2	30	19	11	6	10	13	.177	R	R	6-2	210	5-8-83	2001	Rio Grande, P.R.
Goodman, Chris	3	0	0.84	6	3	0	0	32	18	3	3	5	23	.169	S	R	6-1	180	11-9-81	2003	Benson, Ariz.
Henderson, Jim	1	1	6.93	15	0	0	0	25	32	28	19	15	13	.304	L	R	6-5	190	10-21-82	2003	Calgary, Alberta
Kirkman, Ty	0	3	7.66	21	0	0	0	25	39	31	21	21	9	.364	L	L	6-3	180	12-21-82	2001	Mt. Carmel, Ill.
Little, Chris	0	4	5.88	21	0	0	2	34	41	38	22	25	28	.294	R	R	6-3	180	11-18-81	2001	University City, Mo.
Long, Nick	3	9	7.34	14	14	1	0	69	77	65	56	36	63	.278	R	R	6-3	180	11-24-82	2001	Columbus, Ga.
Martin, Greg	0	1	7.94	3	0	0	0	6	6	5	5	4	3	.250	L	L	6-1	190	4-10-80	2002	Scranton, Pa.
Martinez, Roberto	0	0	4.63	8	0	0	1	12	13	8	6	3	7	.276	R	R	6-3	180	5-2-81	1998	Bonao, D.R.
Maruffi, Joe	0	0	4.91	3	0	0	0	4	4	4	2	1	1	.250	R	R	6-0	215	10-15-79	2003	Albuquerque, N.M.
Nyquist, Brett	0	3	3.15	5	5	0	0	20	16	8	7	6	19	.210	L	L	6-7	200	5-7-81	2003	Duluth, Minn.
Ochoa, Nehomar	2	1	1.80	5	5	0	0	30	26	8	6	8	13	.230	R	R	6-3	170	9-18-82	1999	Tacarigua, Venez.
Pearson, Anthony	0	11	6.90	15	10	0	0	59	57	52	45	54	48	.251	R	R	6-3	190	8-14-81	2002	Baton Rouge, La.
Perrin, Devin	2	4	3.27	11	11	0	0	52	47	23	19	23	36	.251	R	R	6-7	225	5-14-81	2003	Glendale, Ariz.
Plexico, Jeremy	3	3	2.69	17	9	0	1	70	59	26	21	16	49	.227	L	L	6-4	210	2-24-80	2003	Chapin, S.C.
Reid, Brett	0	2	4.76	19	0	0	1	23	24	15	12	16	35	.269	R	R	6-0	175	10-18-79	2003	Liberty, Mo.
Russell, James	0	0	3.24	5	0	0	0	8	7	9	3	11	4	.225	R	R	6-6	240	12-21-80	2003	Rochester, N.Y.

MELBOURNE EXPOS — Rookie

GULF COAST LEAGUE

BATTING	AVG	G	AB	R	H	2B	3B	HR	RBI	BB	SO	SB	CS	SLG	OBP	B	T	HT	WT	DOB	1st Yr	Resides
Apodaca, Luis	.340	43	156	20	53	7	2	0	19	15	18	1	2	.410	.408	R	R	5-11	170	7-15-82	1999	Caracas, Venez.
Baez, Edgardo	.274	34	117	12	32	7	1	3	15	9	31	1	1	.427	.323	R	R	6-2	190	7-12-85	2003	Dorado, P.R.
Batista, Rafael	.189	30	74	10	14	1	0	0	9	5	20	1	3	.203	.241	S	R	5-8	150	2-20-82	2003	Santo Domingo, D.R.
Castro, Ofilio	.152	39	125	8	19	3	0	0	6	11	29	0	1	.176	.226	R	R	6-0	160	8-18-83	2001	Managua, Nicaragua
Cobb, Maurice	.211	41	128	17	27	10	0	0	6	4	42	3	2	.289	.252	R	R	6-1	190	5-23-84	2002	Rocky Mount, N.C.
Contreras, Jose	.197	47	137	19	27	3	1	0	7	18	42	6	5	.234	.304	S	R	6-0	170	4-26-85	2001	Miranda, Venez.
Corro, Abdiel	.160	29	81	4	13	4	0	0	4	5	26	0	0	.210	.244	R	R	6-2	160	3-23-84	2003	Chitre, Panama
Desena, Francis	.280	9	25	7	7	1	1	0	0	5	5	1	1	.400	.419	R	R	6-1	150	6-30-80	2000	Mendoza, D.R.
Fox, Chad	.186	23	70	8	13	2	0	2	9	9	21	0	0	.300	.318	R	R	6-2	205	4-14-81	2003	Poteau, Okla.
Hamisevicz, Victor	.226	47	146	11	33	10	1	1	17	17	27	0	0	.329	.310	L	L	6-4	205	12-4-84	2003	Dunn Loring, Va.
Montz, Luke	.223	32	103	8	23	0	0	2	9	9	21	1	1	.282	.286	R	R	6-2	205	7-7-83	2003	Lafayette, La.
Nunez, Eduardo	.273	33	99	17	27	1	0	1	5	12	15	8	2	.313	.357	R	R	6-2	170	9-21-85	2003	San Sebastian, P.R.
Nunez, Tirzon	.230	26	87	7	20	5	1	0	10	6	10	0	3	.310	.274	R	R	5-11	185	9-26-79	2003	Brooklyn, N.Y.
Ovalles, Jose	.208	36	101	9	21	1	0	0	7	13	17	2	2	.218	.297	R	R	5-10	170	7-7-84	2003	Santo Domingo, D.R.
Pignatiello, Bret	.270	22	63	10	17	1	0	2	6	15	18	1	0	.381	.418	L	R	6-1	195	4-4-81	2003	Tinley Park, Ill.
Sandora, Robert	.218	22	55	4	12	2	0	0	5	9	10	0	0	.255	.323	L	R	6-0	200	8-5-81	2003	West Babylon, N.Y.
Sucre, Antonio	.229	48	166	28	38	10	2	4	28	13	45	1	3	.386	.309	R	R	6-2	180	8-13-83	2000	Puerto la Cruz, Venez.
Wong, Ivanosky	.241	16	54	6	13	1	0	0	3	7	2	0	0	.259	.328	R	R	5-11	170	11-26-83	2001	Bolivar, Venez.

GAMES BY POSITION: C—Apodaca 32, Montz 17, Pignatiello 10, Wong 7. **1B**—Corro 4, Fox 6, Hamisevicz 46, Pignatiello 6. **2B**—Batista 1, Castro 3, Contreras 6, E. Nunez 19, T. Nunez 2, Ovalles 32. **3B**—Apodaca 1, Castro 26, Corro 2, E. Nunez 4, T. Nunez 24, Sandora 5. **SS**—Castro 11, Contreras 38, Corro 1, Desena 9, E. Nunez 8. **OF**—Baez 32, Batista 25, Cobb 39, Corro 22, Fox 5, Sandora 17, Sucre 47.

PITCHING	W	L	ERA	G	GS	CG	SV	IP	H	R	ER	BB	SO	AVG	B	T	HT	WT	DOB	1st Yr	Resides
Ayala, Luis	0	0	0.00	2	2	0	0	4	2	0	0	2	2	.153	R	R	6-2	170	1-12-78	1997	Los Mochis, Mexico
Caceres, Carlos	2	0	0.75	2	2	0	0	12	8	2	1	0	7	.200	R	R	6-0	170	12-4-80	2000	Santo Domingo, D.R.
Centeno, Jhan	0	0	0.00	1	0	0	0	0	1	2	2	2	0	1.000	R	R	6-1	180	3-11-82	1999	Caracas, Venez.
Cerezo, Hector	1	1	1.73	14	1	0	2	26	23	6	5	5	18	.247	L	L	6-2	170	2-28-82	2000	Miranda, Venez.
Day, Zach	0	0	3.86	1	1	0	0	2	3	3	1	1	3	.300	R	R	6-4	210	6-15-78	1996	Cincinnati, Ohio
Galarraga, Armando	1	1	1.80	5	5	0	0	15	13	5	3	5	7	.240	R	R	6-4	170	1-15-82	1999	Caracas, Venez.
Goodman, Chris	3	1	4.23	10	2	0	2	28	31	15	13	3	14	.276	S	R	6-1	180	11-9-81	2003	Benson, Ariz.
Henderson, Jim	0	0	2.25	4	0	0	1	8	6	3	2	1	3	.193	L	R	6-5	190	10-21-82	2003	Calgary, Alberta
Hlebovy, Gus	1	2	2.60	12	0	0	1	28	26	11	8	8	20	.250	R	R	5-11	165	7-6-82	2003	Campbell, Ohio
Jenkins, Clyde	2	1	4.85	14	2	0	3	26	30	20	14	8	30	.277	R	R	6-3	200	6-12-82	2003	North Charleston, S.C.
Lehman, James	1	3	10.19	12	0	0	0	18	34	30	20	12	6	.395	R	R	6-2	185	3-14-85	2003	Brampton, Ontario
Martinez, Samuel	0	1	10.80	3	0	0	1	3	2	4	4	3	3	.166	R	R	6-2	160	3-22-79	1999	Santo Domingo, D.R.
Maruffi, Joe	0	0	0.00	3	0	0	2	3	0	0	0	0	4	.000	R	R	6-0	215	10-15-79	2003	Albuquerque, N.M.
McAdam, Scott	3	2	4.76	16	1	0	0	23	29	18	12	9	12	.325	R	R	5-11	170	6-5-83	2001	Glenmore Park, Australia
Morales, Alex	1	1	0.90	6	0	0	1	10	10	4	1	1	10	.256	R	R	5-11	170	12-8-82	2003	Mt. Prospect, Ill.
Ochoa, Nehomar	2	2	2.19	9	9	0	0	49	37	15	12	19	29	.206	R	R	6-3	170	9-18-82	1999	Tacarigua, Venez.
Rodriguez, Cristobal	0	0	0.00	2	0	0	0	3	1	0	0	0	3	.111	R	R	6-4	210	1-27-79	1996	Chichiriviche, Venez.
Rodriguez, Jose	0	1	4.50	3	0	0	0	6	6	3	3	0	9	.250	R	R	6-2	200	2-9-81	1998	Peoria, Ariz.
Russell, James	0	1	6.00	9	0	0	0	15	17	12	10	9	15	.288	R	R	6-6	240	12-21-80	2003	Rochester, N.Y.
Sandoval, Francisco	3	3	4.20	13	3	0	1	41	43	22	19	15	23	.275	R	R	6-1	170	3-11-84	2001	Valencia, Venez.
Sosa, Gabriel	1	4	3.80	12	6	0	0	45	38	26	19	19	38	.220	L	L	5-9	170	9-27-85	2003	Vega Baja, P.R.
Thompson, Daryl	1	2	2.15	12	10	0	0	46	49	16	11	11	18	.288	R	R	6-1	170	11-2-85	2003	Mechanicsville, Md.
Wideman, Aaron	2	4	2.01	10	8	0	1	40	37	13	9	7	37	.248	R	L	5-11	190	6-8-85	2003	Mississauga, Ontario
Wright, Isaiah	1	3	5.40	11	6	0	1	33	38	22	20	16	12	.304	R	R	6-1	170	7-21-83	2002	Dover, Del.

NEW YORK YANKEES

BY GEORGE KING

There is no truth to the perception that the Yankees finished five games behind the Devil Rays in the American League East. Even if the owner and many of the teams' fans behaved that way after the Yankees lost the 2003 World Series to the Marlins in six games.

People harp on the fatalistic tendencies of Red Sox fans, but Yankees supporters have become George Steinbrenner clones when it comes to their club's chances. And after the Yankees didn't win the World Series for the third straight season, you would have thought they turned into the Mets.

"Disappointing, but not unsuccessful," Joe Torre said of his eighth season at the helm of the Yankees.

Disappointing because the Yankees led the Marlins two games to one and had a big chance to go up 3-1 in Game Four and didn't do it. Disappointing because Alfonso Soriano and Jason Giambi had miserable World Series. Disappointing because David Wells left Game Five after just one inning due to a back problem that could require surgery.

Still, the Yankees won 101 games. Giambi hit 41 homers and had 107 RBIs. Derek Jeter came back from injury to hit .324 and led the team through the playoffs, as usual. Andy Pettitte won 21 games, and Roger Clemens closed out his career with 17 wins, getting No. 300 and passing 4,000 strikeouts. They went to the sixth game of the World Series. That's not good enough for Steinbrenner. Watching the Yankees after they clinched the AL East in Chicago, eliminated the Twins in an AL Division Series and beat the Red Sox in Game Seven of the AL Championship Series on Aaron Boone's walk-off homer, and it was more like they exhaled than celebrated.

Not long after Josh Beckett tagged Jorge Posada for the final out of the World Series, Steinbrenner vowed changes to make sure the Yankees didn't suffer the indignity of having their season end in the sixth game of the World Series again.

"Of course, I was disappointed," he said. "But we will be meeting soon to make whatever changes needed to bring back a stronger and better team for New York and our fans. You can count on it."

Steinbrenner fired hitting coach Rick Down and hired Yankees great Don Mattingly to replace him, even though Mattingly had no experience as a hitting coach. Steinbrenner chaired the organizational meetings in Tampa and heard from Torre that he didn't want certain things repeated next year, the final year of his three-year deal.

"I didn't have a one-on-one. I was in a room with Mr. Steinbrenner, (team president) Randy Levine and (general manager) Brian (Cashman)," said Torre, who made a rare appearance at the organizational meetings. "I talked about some of the things that I didn't appreciate as far as some of the statements that went on all year. It was basically a one-sided conversation. I said something that I needed to say and I would like to believe in a diplomatic way."

Torre admitted in September the 2003 season wasn't fun. Steinbrenner's second-guessing wore on him and prompted trusted bench coach and friend Don Zimmer to tell Steinbrenner to stuff the job after the World Series.

As for the minor league system, one team, low Class A Battle Creek, made the playoffs. Top pitching prospect Brandon Claussen, deemed untouchable in June, was dealt in July for Aaron Boone. Drew Henson didn't make much progress and his baseball future was questioned at every turn. There was a bright spot, as catcher Dioner Navarro cemented his status as a top prospect with a stellar season at high Class A Tampa and Double-A Trenton.

Jorge Posada

Dioner Navarro

DAVID SCHOFIELD

PLAYERS of the YEAR

MAJOR LEAGUE: Jorge Posada, c

Posada moved into the elite class of the game's catchers, hitting .281-30-101. He played solid defense and was one of three Yankees players to hit at least 30 home runs and drive in at least 100 runs.

MINOR LEAGUE: Dioner Navarro, c

Navarro, 19, hit .321-7-65 between Double-A Trenton and Class A Tampa. His average ranked fourth among all minor league catchers and fifth among switch-hitters. He also displayed an above-average arm behind the plate.

ORGANIZATION LEADERS

BATTING		
*AVG	Fernando Seguignol, Columbus/Trenton	.342
R	Brian Myrow, Trenton	99
H	Mike Vento, Columbus/Trenton	151
TB	Jayson Drobiak, Battle Creek	279
2B	Drew Henson, Columbus	40
3B	Three tied at	8
HR	Jayson Drobiak, Battle Creek	30
RBI	Mitch Jones, Trenton	91
BB	Brian Myrow, Trenton	107
SO	Mitch Jones, Trenton	131
SB	Kevin Thompson, Trenton/Tampa	63
*SLG	Fernando Seguignol, Columbus/Tampa	.617
*OBP	Brian Myrow, Trenton	.447
PITCHING		
W	Brad Halsey, Trenton/Tampa	17
L	Jeremy King, Tampa/Battle Creek	13
#ERA	Rik Currier, Trenton/Tampa	2.16
G	David Shepard, Columbus/Trenton	61
CG	Jose Garcia, Tampa/Battle Creek	4
SV	Matt Brumit, Tampa/Battle Creek	24
IP	Brad Halsey, Trenton/Tampa	175
BB	Javier Ortiz, Trenton	71
SO	Brad Halsey, Trenton/Tampa	134

*Minimum 250 At-Bats #Minimum 75 Innings

NEW YORK YANKEES

Manager: Joe Torre.

2003 Record: 101-61, .623 (1st, AL East).

BATTING	AVG	G	AB	R	H	2B	3B	HR	RBI	BB	SO	SB	CS	SLG	OBP	B	T	HT	WT	DOB	1st Yr	Resides
Almonte, Erick	.260	31	100	17	26	6	0	1	11	8	24	1	0	.350	.321	R	R	6-2	180	2-1-78	1996	Santo Domingo, D.R.
Boone, Aaron	.254	54	189	31	48	13	0	6	31	11	30	8	0	.418	.302	R	R	6-2	200	3-9-73	1994	Villa Park, Calif.
Dellucci, David	.176	21	51	8	9	1	0	1	4	4	13	3	0	.255	.263	L	L	5-11	190	10-31-73	1995	Baton Rouge, La.
Flaherty, John	.267	40	105	16	28	8	0	4	14	4	19	0	0	.457	.297	R	R	6-1	200	10-21-67	1988	Lutz, Fla.
Garcia, Karim	.305	52	151	17	46	5	0	6	21	9	32	0	2	.457	.342	L	L	6-0	210	10-29-75	1992	Ciudad Obregon, Mexico
2-team (24 Cleveland)	.262	76	244	25	64	6	0	11	35	14	52	0	2	.422	.302							
Giambi, Jason	.250	156	535	97	134	25	0	41	107	129	140	2	1	.527	.412	L	R	6-3	235	1-8-71	1992	Covina, Calif.
Gipson, Charles	.200	18	10	3	2	0	0	0	2	1	2	2	1	.200	.273	R	R	6-0	190	12-16-72	1992	Orange, Calif.
Henson, Drew	.125	5	8	2	1	0	0	0	0	0	2	0	0	.125	.125	R	R	6-5	220	2-13-80	1998	Brighton, Mich.
Hernandez, Michel	.250	5	4	0	1	0	0	0	0	1	1	0	0	.250	.400	R	R	6-0	210	8-12-78	1998	Caracas, Venez.
Jeter, Derek	.324	119	482	87	156	25	3	10	52	43	88	11	5	.450	.393	R	R	6-3	195	6-26-74	1992	Tampa, Fla.
Johnson, Nick	.284	96	324	60	92	19	0	14	47	70	57	5	2	.472	.422	L	L	6-3	225	9-19-78	1996	Sacramento, Calif.
Latham, Chris	1.000	4	2	3	2	0	0	0	0	0	0	1	0	1.000	1.000	S	R	6-0	200	5-26-73	1991	Las Vegas, Nev.
Matsui, Hideki	.287	163	623	82	179	42	1	16	106	63	86	2	2	.435	.353	L	R	6-2	210	6-12-74	2003	Tokyo, Japan
Mondesi, Raul	.258	98	361	56	93	23	3	16	49	38	66	17	7	.471	.330	R	R	5-11	230	3-2-71	1988	San Cristobal, D.R.
Posada, Jorge	.281	142	481	83	135	24	0	30	101	93	110	2	4	.518	.405	S	R	6-2	205	8-17-71	1991	Tampa, Fla.
Pride, Curtis	.083	4	12	1	1	0	0	1	1	0	2	0	0	.333	.083	L	R	6-0	210	12-17-68	1986	West Palm Beach, Fla.
Rivera, Juan	.266	57	173	22	46	14	0	7	26	10	27	0	0	.468	.304	R	R	6-2	170	7-3-78	1996	Guarenas, Venez.
Seguignol, Fernando	.143	5	7	0	1	0	0	0	0	1	3	0	0	.143	.250	S	R	6-5	230	1-19-75	1993	Panama City, Panama
Sierra, Ruben	.276	63	174	19	48	8	1	6	31	13	20	1	0	.437	.323	S	R	6-1	210	10-6-65	1983	Miami, Fla.
2-team (43 Texas)	.270	106	307	33	83	17	1	9	43	27	47	2	1	.420	.327							
Sojo, Luis	.000	3	4	0	0	0	0	0	0	0	0	0	0	.000	.000	R	R	5-11	170	1-3-66	1987	Barquisimeto, Venez.
Soriano, Alfonso	.290	156	682	114	198	36	5	38	91	38	130	35	8	.525	.338	R	R	6-1	180	1-7-78	1999	San Pedro de Macoris, D.R.
Trammell, Bubba	.200	22	55	4	11	5	0	0	5	6	10	0	0	.291	.279	R	R	6-2	220	11-6-71	1994	Clearwater, Fla.
Ventura, Robin	.251	89	283	31	71	13	0	9	42	40	62	0	0	.392	.344	L	R	6-1	200	7-14-67	1989	Greenwich, Conn.
Williams, Bernie	.263	119	445	77	117	19	1	15	64	71	61	5	0	.411	.367	S	R	6-2	205	9-13-68	1986	Armonk, N.Y.
Wilson, Enrique	.230	63	135	18	31	9	0	3	15	7	14	3	1	.363	.276	S	R	5-11	195	7-27-73	1992	Santo Domingo, D.R.
Zeile, Todd	.210	66	186	29	39	8	0	6	23	24	36	0	0	.349	.294	R	R	6-1	200	9-9-65	1986	Thousand Oaks, Calif.

PITCHING	W	L	ERA	G	GS	CG	SV	IP	H	R	ER	BB	SO	AVG	B	T	HT	WT	DOB	1st Yr	Resides
Acevedo, Juan	0	3	7.71	25	0	0	6	26	34	24	22	10	19	.314	R	R	6-2	220	5-5-70	1992	Algonguin, Il
Anderson, Jason	1	0	4.79	22	0	0	0	21	23	13	11	14	9	.280	L	R	6-0	190	6-9-79	2000	Danville, Ill.
Benitez, Armando	1	1	1.93	9	0	0	0	9	8	4	2	6	10	.235	R	R	6-4	220	11-3-72	1990	San Pedro de Macoris, D.R.
Choate, Randy	0	0	7.36	5	0	0	0	4	7	3	3	1	0	.466	L	L	6-2	195	9-5-75	1997	Tampa, Fla.
Claussen, Brandon	1	0	1.42	1	1	0	0	6	8	2	1	1	5	.296	R	L	6-2	200	5-1-79	1999	Roswell, N.M.
Clemens, Roger	17	9	3.91	33	33	1	0	212	199	99	92	58	190	.246	R	R	6-4	235	8-4-62	1983	Houston, Texas
Contreras, Jose	7	2	3.30	18	9	0	0	71	52	27	26	30	72	.202	R	R	6-4	230	12-6-71	2003	Managua, Nicaragua
De Paula, Jorge	0	0	0.79	4	1	0	0	11	3	1	1	1	7	.083	R	R	6-1	160	11-10-78	1997	Santo Domingo, D.R.
Hammond, Chris	3	2	2.86	62	0	0	1	63	65	23	20	11	45	.269	L	L	6-1	210	1-21-66	1986	Wedowee, Ala.
Heredia, Felix	0	1	1.20	12	0	0	0	15	13	5	2	5	4	.228	L	L	6-0	180	6-18-75	1993	Miami, Fla.
Hitchcock, Sterling	1	3	5.44	27	1	0	0	50	57	33	30	18	36	.285	L	L	6-0	205	4-29-71	1989	Tampa, Fla.
Miceli, Danny	0	0	5.79	7	0	0	1	5	4	3	3	3	1	.210	R	R	6-0	225	9-9-70	1990	Winter Springs, Fla.
2-team (13 Cleveland)	1	1	2.29	20	0	0	1	20	13	7	5	9	20	.175							
Mussina, Mike	17	8	3.40	31	31	2	0	215	192	86	81	40	195	.237	L	R	6-2	185	12-8-68	1990	Montoursville, Penn.
Nelson, Jeff	1	0	4.58	24	0	0	1	18	17	9	9	10	21	.246	R	R	6-8	220	11-17-66	1984	Issaquah, Wash.
2-team (46 Seattle)	4	2	3.74	70	0	0	8	55	51	25	23	24	68	.247							
Orosco, Jesse	0	0	10.38	15	0	0	0	4	4	6	5	6	4	.250	R	L	6-2	205	4-21-57	1978	San Diego, Calif.
Osuna, Antonio	2	5	3.73	48	0	0	0	51	58	22	21	20	47	.281	R	R	5-11	205	4-12-73	1991	Juan Jose Rios, Mexico
Pettitte, Andy	21	8	4.02	33	33	1	0	208	227	109	93	50	180	.271	L	L	6-5	225	6-15-72	1991	Deer Park, Texas
Prinz, Bret	0	0	18.00	2	0	0	0	2	6	4	4	3	2	.500	R	R	6-3	210	6-15-77	1998	Peoria, Ariz.
Reyes, Al	0	0	3.18	13	0	0	0	17	13	7	6	9	9	.203	R	R	6-1	200	4-10-70	1988	Santo Domingo, D.R.
Rivera, Mariano	5	2	1.66	64	0	0	40	71	61	15	13	10	63	.234	R	R	6-2	185	11-29-69	1990	La Chorrera, Panama
Weaver, Jeff	7	9	5.99	32	24	0	0	159	211	113	106	47	93	.320	R	R	6-5	200	8-22-76	1998	Simi Valley, Calif.
Wells, David	15	7	4.14	31	30	4	0	213	242	101	98	20	101	.286	L	L	6-4	235	5-20-63	1982	Clearwater, Fla.
White, Gabe	2	1	4.38	12	0	0	0	12	8	7	6	2	6	.181	L	L	6-2	200	11-20-71	1990	Sebring, Fla.

FIELDING

Catcher	PCT	G	PO	A	E	DP	PB
Flaherty	.991	40	200	10	2	0	0
Hernandez	1.000	5	10	0	0	0	0
Posada	.994	137	933	75	6	4	13

First Base	PCT	G	PO	A	E	DP
Giambi	.995	85	748	19	4	63
Johnson	.991	60	512	34	5	44
Seguignol	1.000	3	9	3	0	0
Sojo	.000	1	0	0	0	0
Zeile	.995	23	181	15	1	11

Second Base	PCT	G	PO	A	E	DP
Sojo	1.000	1	0	3	0	0
Soriano	.975	155	293	445	19	88
Ventura	1.000	1	0	2	0	0
Wilson	1.000	10	14	20	0	2

Third Base	PCT	G	PO	A	E	DP
Boone	.961	54	36	111	6	7
Henson	1.000	3	4	3	0	0
Ventura	.974	80	44	146	5	9
Wilson	.941	17	6	26	2	4
Zeile	.917	30	17	49	6	8

Shortstop	PCT	G	PO	A	E	DP
Almonte	.906	31	49	67	12	13
Jeter	.968	118	159	271	14	51
Wilson	.987	33	32	45	1	8

Outfield	PCT	G	PO	A	E	DP
Dellucci	1.000	18	31	1	0	1
Garcia	.981	50	99	5	2	0
Gipson	1.000	8	8	0	0	0
Latham	1.000	2	3	0	0	0
Matsui	.977	159	320	13	8	4
Mondesi	.986	97	198	7	3	1
Pride	1.000	3	5	0	0	0
Rivera	.979	56	90	3	2	0
Sierra	1.000	17	20	0	0	0
Trammell	1.000	3	9	0	0	0
Williams	.997	115	290	3	1	1

DENTON HANNA

Derek Jeter: Finished two points shy of the batting title

STEVE MOORE

Andy Pettitte: Tied for second in the AL with 21 wins

FARM SYSTEM

Director, Player Development: Rob Thomson

Class	Farm Team	League	W	L	Pct.	Finish*	Manager	First Yr.
AAA	Columbus (Ohio) Clippers	International	76	68	.528	4th (14)	Bucky Dent	1979
AA	Trenton (N.J.) Thunder	Eastern	70	71	.496	7th (12)	Stump Merrill	2003
High A	Tampa (Fla.) Yankees	Florida State	68	64	.515	6th (12)	Bill Masse	1994
Low A	Battle Creek (Mich.) Yankees	Midwest	73	64	.533	3rd (14)	Mitch Seoane	2003
SS A	Staten Island (N.Y.) Yankees	New York-Penn	29	43	.403	11th (14)	Andy Stankiewicz	1999
Rookie	Tampa (Fla.) Yankees	Gulf Coast	26	31	.456	8th (12)	Dan Radison	1980

*Finish in overall standings (No. of teams in league)

COLUMBUS CLIPPERS — Class AAA

INTERNATIONAL LEAGUE

BATTING	AVG	G	AB	R	H	2B	3B	HR	RBI	BB	SO	SB	CS	SLG	OBP	B	T	HT	WT	DOB	1st Yr	Resides
Almonte, Erick	.240	48	179	26	43	11	1	4	26	17	46	4	3	.380	.310	R	R	6-2	180	2-1-78	1996	Santo Domingo, D.R.
Crosby, Bubba	.302	16	63	9	19	2	1	2	8	6	12	3	0	.460	.366	L	L	5-11	185	8-11-76	1998	Bellaire, Texas
Elwood, Brad	.133	5	15	1	2	0	0	0	1	0	4	0	0	.133	.133	R	R	6-1	195	10-22-75	1998	Clear Spring, Md.
Gipson, Charles	.275	31	120	17	33	6	1	0	5	9	18	5	6	.342	.351	R	R	6-0	190	12-16-72	1992	Orange, Calif.
Henson, Drew	.234	133	483	60	113	40	2	14	78	32	122	8	4	.412	.291	R	R	6-5	220	2-13-80	1998	Brighton, Mich.
Hernandez, Michel	.280	89	282	39	79	14	0	4	30	37	35	0	2	.372	.367	R	R	6-0	210	8-12-78	1998	Caracas, Venez.
Jensen, Marcus	.224	66	196	20	44	8	0	3	15	36	53	0	0	.311	.348	S	R	6-4	200	12-14-72	1990	Scottsdale, Ariz.
Johnson, Nick	.500	3	10	1	5	2	0	1	3	2	2	0	0	1.000	.583	L	L	6-3	225	9-19-78	1996	Sacramento, Calif.
McGuire, Ryan	.230	65	191	17	44	7	1	2	19	23	36	0	0	.309	.313	L	L	6-0	210	11-23-71	1993	Coto de Caza, Calif.
Mendez, Deivi	.000	5	13	1	0	0	0	0	0	1	4	0	0	.000	.071	R	R	6-1	160	6-24-83	1999	Santo Domingo, D.R.
Nieves, Jose	.218	44	147	20	32	2	5	2	16	10	22	1	1	.340	.286	R	R	6-0	180	6-16-75	1992	Carabobo, Venez.
Olivares, Teuris	.333	5	12	0	4	0	0	0	1	0	1	0	0	.333	.333	R	R	6-0	165	12-15-78	1996	San Pedro de Macoris, D.R.
Phillips, Andy	.209	17	67	7	14	4	0	2	5	5	17	0	0	.358	.264	R	R	6-0	205	4-6-77	1999	Demopolis, Ala.
Post, Dave	.222	72	248	36	55	12	2	4	28	30	35	3	3	.335	.315	R	R	5-11	170	9-3-73	1992	Kingston, N.Y.
Pride, Curtis	.289	55	225	44	65	11	4	7	34	20	48	7	7	.467	.357	L	R	6-0	210	12-17-68	1986	West Palm Beach, Fla.
Reese, Kevin	.218	15	55	11	12	1	0	1	3	6	8	1	0	.291	.295	L	L	5-11	195	3-11-78	2000	San Diego, Calif.
Rivera, Juan	.325	79	308	47	100	21	0	7	37	26	37	1	3	.461	.374	R	R	6-2	170	7-3-78	1996	Guarenas, Venez.
Robinson, Bo	.143	2	7	0	1	0	0	0	1	0	1	0	0	.143	.143	R	R	6-2	190	8-21-75	1998	Charlotte, N.C.
Rodriguez, John	.263	79	232	35	61	9	2	10	33	24	50	6	0	.448	.333	L	L	6-0	185	1-20-78	1997	New York, N.Y.
Rolison, Nate	.247	113	385	54	95	17	2	16	55	48	113	0	3	.426	.330	L	R	6-6	240	3-27-77	1995	Petal, Miss.
Seguignol, Fernando	.341	106	402	78	137	28	1	28	87	34	81	0	0	.624	.401	S	R	6-5	230	1-19-75	1993	Panama City, Panama
Smith, Bobby	.282	119	458	68	129	36	5	8	69	40	74	4	4	.434	.341	R	R	6-3	190	4-10-74	1992	Oakland, Calif.
Thames, Marcus	.278	52	194	26	54	15	2	2	28	17	48	3	4	.407	.332	R	R	6-2	205	3-6-77	1997	Louisville, Miss.
Vento, Mike	.304	51	184	28	56	14	1	5	31	14	36	1	2	.473	.363	R	R	6-0	195	5-25-78	1998	Corrales, N.M.
Wilson, Craig	.266	103	403	52	107	17	0	7	40	38	54	1	2	.360	.332	R	R	6-0	180	9-3-70	1992	Phoenix, Ariz.

PITCHING	W	L	ERA	G	GS	CG	SV	IP	H	R	ER	BB	SO	AVG	B	T	HT	WT	DOB	1st Yr	Resides
Adkins, Tim	3	2	5.57	28	0	0	0	32	30	20	20	24	22	.254	L	L	6-0	190	5-12-74	1992	Huntington, WV
2-team (12 Louisville)	3	3	4.63	40	1	0	0	58	53	30	30	35	43	.250							

PITCHING	W	L	ERA	G	GS	CG	SV	IP	H	R	ER	BB	SO	AVG	B	T	HT	WT	DOB	1st Yr	Resides
Anderson, Jason	0	0	0.00	6	0	0	3	8	3	0	0	2	13	.115	L	R	6-0	190	6-9-79	2000	Danville, Ill.
Arrojo, Rolando	1	0	2.00	4	1	0	0	9	5	2	2	5	10	.161	R	R	6-4	230	7-18-68	1997	St. Petersburg, Fla.
Banks, Willie	2	3	3.89	31	0	0	3	39	42	21	17	19	26	.283	R	R	6-1	200	2-27-69	1987	Miami, Fla.
Beal, Andy	1	6	7.45	8	8	0	0	39	51	35	32	11	25	.318	L	L	6-2	185	10-31-78	2000	Paducah, Ky.
Bean, Colter	4	2	2.87	50	0	0	4	69	53	33	22	27	70	.210	R	R	6-6	255	1-16-77	2000	Anniston, Ala.
Beech, Matt	0	0	0.00	2	0	0	0	3	2	0	0	2	4	.222	L	L	6-2	180	1-20-72	1994	Clearwater, Fla.
Borrell, Danny	4	2	2.93	10	10	0	0	55	55	24	18	22	30	.259	L	L	6-3	200	1-24-79	2000	Sanford, N.C.
Choate, Randy	3	5	3.91	54	3	0	1	71	75	35	31	24	56	.270	L	L	6-2	195	9-5-75	1997	Tampa, Fla.
Claussen, Brandon	2	1	2.75	11	11	1	0	69	53	28	21	18	39	.212	R	L	6-2	200	5-1-79	1999	Roswell, N.M.
Contreras, Jose	2	0	1.20	3	3	0	0	15	10	2	2	2	18	.188	R	R	6-4	230	12-6-71	2003	Managua, Nicaragua
De Paula, Jorge	10	11	4.35	27	27	3	0	168	168	90	81	57	125	.262	R	R	6-1	160	11-10-78	1997	Santo Domingo, D.R.
Graman, Alex	9	10	4.48	26	26	0	0	143	135	77	71	63	110	.250	L	L	6-4	200	11-17-77	1999	Huntingburg, Ind.
Hansell, Greg	0	0	6.32	9	0	0	0	16	25	11	11	2	12	.357	R	R	6-5	220	3-12-71	1989	La Palma, Calif.
Hernandez, Adrian	8	5	3.21	32	9	0	1	101	92	47	36	49	103	.240	R	R	6-1	180	3-25-75	2000	Tampa, Fla.
Marsonek, Sam	4	4	4.84	54	2	0	18	84	84	52	45	31	57	.258	R	R	6-6	225	7-10-78	1997	Tampa, Fla.
Parker, Christian	7	6	4.90	19	19	0	0	108	135	63	59	44	41	.313	R	R	6-1	200	7-3-75	1996	Albuquerque, N.M.
Prinz, Bret	0	1	8.03	10	0	0	0	12	20	11	11	1	13	.363	R	R	6-3	210	6-15-77	1998	Peoria, Ariz.
Proctor, Scott	2	0	1.42	10	0	0	0	19	13	3	3	3	26	.196	R	R	6-1	198	1-2-77	1998	Jensen Beach, Fla.
Ramirez, Ramon	0	1	4.50	2	1	0	0	6	5	5	3	1	5	.208	R	R	5-11	170	8-31-81	1997	Santiago, D.R.
Reyes, Al	1	1	3.71	15	0	0	2	17	16	7	7	5	21	.238	R	R	6-1	200	4-10-70	1988	Santo Domingo, D.R.
Rogers, Brian	0	0	0.00	2	0	0	1	8	5	1	0	1	5	.178	R	R	6-6	200	2-13-77	1998	Carthage, N.C.
Schmitt, Eric	6	0	4.19	13	12	1	0	69	78	35	32	16	45	.289	R	R	6-4	210	7-23-78	2000	Fairfax, Va.
Shepard, David	0	1	5.74	8	0	0	0	16	19	11	10	3	14	.296	R	R	6-1	190	2-6-74	1996	Sarasota, Fla.
Thurman, Mike	7	7	4.79	26	12	0	1	94	115	56	50	23	74	.304	R	R	6-5	220	7-22-73	1994	West Palm Beach, Fla.

FIELDING

Catcher	PCT	G	PO	A	E	DP	PB
Elwood	1.000	5	24	2	0	0	0
Hernandez	.993	83	563	43	4	6	5
Jensen	.995	62	411	19	2	2	3

First Base	PCT	G	PO	A	E	DP
Johnson	.952	2	19	1	1	2
McGuire	.992	31	228	22	2	20
Post	1.000	3	16	1	0	1
Robinson	1.000	2	16	1	0	2
Rolison	.993	86	659	45	5	72
Seguignol	.992	26	226	17	2	22
Smith	1.000	2	17	1	0	1

Second Base	PCT	G	PO	A	E	DP
Gipson	1.000	1	2	3	0	0
Mendez	1.000	1	1	0	0	0
Nieves	.889	4	6	2	1	0
Olivares	.000	1	0	0	0	0
Phillips	.955	12	17	25	2	6
Post	.931	29	38	57	7	16
Smith	.958	6	8	15	1	4
Wilson	.991	102	174	287	4	65

Third Base	PCT	G	PO	A	E	DP
Almonte	1.000	1	1	1	0	1
Gipson	.909	4	4	6	1	2
Henson	.918	132	98	216	28	16
Post	.833	1	1	4	1	0
Smith	1.000	6	2	14	0	1

Shortstop	PCT	G	PO	A	E	DP
Almonte	.960	46	79	136	9	35
Mendez	.947	4	7	11	1	3
Nieves	.955	40	43	106	7	26
Olivares	.750	2	1	5	2	0
Post	.917	4	7	4	1	2
Smith	.965	54	81	140	8	31

Outfield	PCT	G	PO	A	E	DP
Crosby	1.000	16	42	1	0	0
Gipson	.978	26	83	5	2	1
McGuire	1.000	22	39	0	0	0
Post	.969	37	60	2	2	0
Pride	.991	48	101	4	1	0
Reese	.963	13	24	2	1	0
Rivera	.982	79	160	6	3	0
Rodriguez	.981	70	150	4	3	0
Smith	.953	42	77	5	4	0
Thames	.977	52	123	5	3	0
Vento	.992	49	122	4	1	1

TRENTON THUNDER — Class AA

EASTERN LEAGUE

BATTING	AVG	G	AB	R	H	2B	3B	HR	RBI	BB	SO	SB	CS	SLG	OBP	B	T	HT	WT	DOB	1st Yr	Resides
Boone, Doug	.400	4	5	0	2	1	0	0	1	0	1	0	0	.600	.400	R	R	6-1	200	5-16-79	2002	Sellersburg, Ind.
Bozanich, Sam	.197	30	71	13	14	5	1	0	7	13	21	2	1	.296	.326	R	R	5-9	190	11-10-78	2000	Bakersfield, Calif.
Brown, Andy	.172	18	58	7	10	5	0	1	5	6	20	0	0	.310	.250	L	L	6-6	190	4-14-80	1998	Richmond, Ind.
Cannizaro, Andy	.276	108	369	50	102	23	1	1	39	26	24	9	4	.352	.337	R	R	5-10	170	12-19-78	2001	Mandeville, La.
Cano, Robinson	.280	46	164	21	46	9	1	1	13	9	16	0	0	.366	.341	L	R	6-0	170	10-22-82	2001	San Pedro de Macoris, D.R.
De Renne, Keoni	.240	37	96	5	23	4	0	1	7	5	13	0	1	.313	.275	R	R	5-7	160	4-30-79	2000	Honolulu, Hawaii
Fernandez, Alejandro	.333	4	6	0	2	0	0	0	1	0	3	0	0	.333	.333	R	R	6-2	175	12-19-80	1997	Maracaibo, Venez.
Fuentes, Omar	.236	84	250	29	59	16	0	5	27	27	39	0	0	.360	.319	R	R	6-1	175	4-6-80	1996	Maracay, Venez.
Grove, Jason	.287	76	244	28	70	12	0	5	28	23	48	0	2	.398	.356	L	L	6-2	200	8-15-78	2000	Walla Walla, Wash.
Jeter, Derek	.444	5	18	2	8	1	1	0	5	3	0	0	0	.611	.545	R	R	6-3	195	6-26-74	1992	Tampa, Fla.
Johnson, Nick	.417	4	12	3	5	1	0	0	1	5	0	0	0	.500	.611	L	L	6-3	225	9-19-78	1996	Sacramento, Calif.
Jones, Mitch	.242	136	463	76	112	18	0	23	91	58	131	5	4	.430	.338	R	R	6-2	215	10-15-77	2000	Orem, Utah
Maule, Jason	.274	42	117	20	32	3	0	0	13	22	17	5	1	.299	.393	L	R	6-0	170	7-1-77	1999	East Berlin, Conn.
Mendez, Deivi	.091	5	11	1	1	0	0	1	1	1	1	1	0	.364	.167	R	R	6-1	160	6-24-83	1999	Santo Domingo, D.R.
Myrow, Brian	.306	137	461	99	141	31	8	18	78	107	113	6	3	.525	.447	L	R	5-11	190	9-4-76	1999	Fort Worth, Texas
Navarro, Dioner	.341	58	208	28	71	15	0	4	37	18	26	2	3	.471	.388	S	R	5-10	190	2-9-84	2000	Caracas, Venez.
Olivares, Teuris	.231	65	208	26	48	8	0	6	33	20	35	3	4	.356	.294	R	R	6-0	165	12-15-78	1996	San Pedro de Macoris, D.R.
Parrish, David	.223	32	103	16	23	4	1	1	15	10	18	2	0	.311	.296	R	R	6-3	220	6-13-79	2000	Yorba Linda, Calif.
Reese, Kevin	.272	86	309	42	84	13	2	4	21	25	58	27	5	.366	.328	L	L	5-11	195	3-11-78	2000	San Diego, Calif.
Rifkin, Aaron	.269	137	510	71	137	29	1	19	90	49	104	5	6	.441	.335	L	L	6-3	220	3-12-79	2001	Upland, Calif.
Robinson, Bo	.241	76	228	29	55	17	0	2	19	23	42	2	1	.342	.328	R	R	6-2	190	8-21-75	1998	Charlotte, N.C.
Thompson, Kevin	.226	86	328	48	74	16	2	5	20	37	57	47	8	.332	.310	R	R	5-10	185	9-18-79	2000	Fort Worth, Texas
Vento, Michael	.303	81	314	46	95	19	3	9	56	22	52	4	4	.468	.354	R	R	6-0	195	5-25-78	1998	Corrales, N.M.
Williams, Bernie	.333	5	15	4	5	2	0	0	4	4	1	0	1	.467	.476	S	R	6-2	205	9-13-68	1986	Armonk, N.Y.

PITCHING	W	L	ERA	G	GS	CG	SV	IP	H	R	ER	BB	SO	AVG	B	T	HT	WT	DOB	1st Yr	Resides
Beal, Andy	6	0	3.51	17	12	2	0	74	76	35	29	20	64	.256	L	L	6-2	185	10-31-78	2000	Paducah, Ky.
Bean, Colter	0	0	0.00	3	0	0	0	5	2	0	0	2	9	.125	R	R	6-6	255	1-16-77	2000	Anniston, Ala.
Brazoban, Yhency	2	2	7.81	20	0	0	3	28	33	25	24	14	19	.314	R	R	6-1	170	6-11-80	1997	Santo Domingo, D.R.
Candelario, Eddie	8	5	4.52	28	13	0	1	94	94	51	47	47	69	.265	R	R	6-0	175	11-3-77	1998	La Carmelita, D.R.
Contreras, Jose	0	0	0.00	1	1	0	0	2	1	0	0	2	3	.166	R	R	6-4	230	12-6-71	2003	Managua, Nicaragua
Cooksey, Wes	1	2	16.20	3	0	0	0	5	13	9	9	1	5	.500	L	R	6-3	210	5-22-78	2001	Port Arthur, Texas
Currier, Rik	1	0	2.60	7	5	0	0	35	22	11	10	15	33	.183	R	R	5-10	180	5-26-78	2001	Aliso Viejo, Calif.
Garza, Alberto	0	1	4.00	5	0	0	0	9	5	6	4	11	6	.161	R	R	6-3	190	5-25-77	1996	Wapato, Wash.
Glick, David	4	0	5.31	45	0	0	0	41	58	34	24	24	31	.345	L	L	6-1	190	4-2-76	1995	Palmdale, Calif.

PITCHING	W	L	ERA	G	GS	CG	SV	IP	H	R	ER	BB	SO	AVG	B	T	HT	WT	DOB	1st Yr	Resides
Grace, Bryan	1	2	8.04	7	6	0	0	31	54	29	28	10	14	.394	R	R	6-1	190	4-1-76	1999	Baton Rouge, La.
Halsey, Brad	7	5	4.93	15	15	0	0	91	123	51	50	22	78	.324	L	L	6-1	180	2-14-81	2002	Austin, Texas
Hansell, Greg	0	2	1.89	17	1	0	1	19	19	5	4	5	21	.260	R	R	6-5	220	3-12-71	1989	La Palma, Calif.
Hernandez, Adrian	0	0	3.86	1	1	0	0	5	5	4	2	2	7	.238	R	R	6-1	180	3-25-75	2000	Tampa, Fla.
Isaacson, Charlie	1	3	6.12	14	0	0	1	25	37	17	17	11	15	.370	R	R	6-2	190	5-5-80	2002	Overland Park, Kan.
Kennard, Jeff	1	0	3.86	10	0	0	0	19	16	9	8	14	8	.242	R	R	6-2	195	7-26-81	2001	Centerville, Ohio
Knowles, Mike	0	1	7.59	8	0	0	0	11	16	9	9	2	6	.347	R	R	6-5	215	7-15-79	1997	Daytona Beach, Fla.
Kremer, John	0	0	13.50	3	0	0	0	3	8	6	5	0	3	.421	R	R	6-1	220	11-19-76	1999	Indianapolis, Ind.
Manning, Charlie	0	2	6.26	23	6	0	0	46	53	34	32	35	34	.302	L	L	6-2	180	3-31-79	2001	Winter Haven, Fla.
Ortiz, Javier	6	11	5.76	28	26	1	0	150	181	105	96	71	91	.298	R	R	6-0	155	11-28-79	1996	Cartagena, Colombia
Parker, Christian	1	2	2.83	5	5	2	0	29	17	11	9	11	9	.171	R	R	6-1	200	7-3-75	1996	Albuquerque, N.M.
Ramirez, Ramon	1	1	1.69	4	3	0	0	21	18	8	4	8	21	.230	R	R	5-11	170	8-31-81	1997	Santiago, D.R.
Reynoso, Edison	8	8	6.87	22	12	1	0	77	109	69	59	22	43	.328	R	R	6-1	170	11-10-75	1993	Monte Cristi, D.R.
Rogers, Brian	1	3	5.97	13	2	1	0	35	40	27	23	21	16	.310	R	R	6-6	200	2-13-77	1998	Carthage, N.C.
Roller, Adam	4	3	2.90	36	0	0	10	40	49	19	13	15	36	.295	R	R	6-3	210	6-27-78	1997	Lakeland, Fla.
Schmitt, Eric	0	2	2.76	21	1	0	1	42	44	17	13	15	48	.268	R	R	6-4	210	7-23-78	2000	Fairfax, Va.
Shepard, David	8	7	2.82	53	0	0	12	67	55	22	21	18	65	.220	R	R	6-1	190	2-6-74	1996	Sarasota, Fla.
Smith, Matt	2	3	4.26	9	9	0	0	51	57	29	24	24	36	.290	L	L	6-5	225	6-15-79	2000	Henderson, Nev.
Villegas, Francisco	0	0	1.74	6	0	0	0	10	6	2	2	11	10	.162	R	R	5-10	180	3-23-78	1993	San Luis, Ariz.
Wang, Chien-Ming	7	6	4.65	21	21	2	0	122	143	71	63	32	84	.293	R	R	6-3	200	3-31-80	2000	Tampa, Fla.
White, Gabe	0	0	7.71	2	2	0	0	2	3	2	2	0	2	.300	L	L	6-2	200	11-20-71	1990	Sebring, Fla.

FIELDING

Catcher	PCT	G	PO	A	E	DP	PB
Boone	1.000	4	12	0	0	0	0
Cano	1.000	1	1	0	0	0	0
Fernandez	1.000	4	3	0	0	0	0
Fuentes	.988	75	449	52	6	3	9
Navarro	.986	41	260	23	4	3	3
Parrish	.991	30	189	29	2	2	6

First Base	PCT	G	PO	A	E	DP
Johnson	1.000	4	43	3	0	7
Rifkin	.989	128	1034	84	12	116
Robinson	1.000	10	64	9	0	7

Second Base	PCT	G	PO	A	E	DP
Bozanich	.953	26	35	47	4	9
Cannizaro	.971	43	91	113	6	42
Cano	.977	44	100	108	5	33
De Renne	1.000	3	3	6	0	2
Maule	.908	14	35	34	7	7
Myrow	.956	24	45	63	5	11

Third Base	PCT	G	PO	A	E	DP
De Renne	1.000	9	3	12	0	1
Mendez	1.000	2	0	3	0	0
Myrow	.891	86	50	129	22	14
Robinson	.981	52	27	75	2	7

Shortstop	PCT	G	PO	A	E	DP
Cannizaro	.959	65	81	179	11	36
Cano	1.000	1	0	1	0	0
De Renne	.962	15	18	32	2	7
Jeter	.957	5	9	13	1	5
Mendez	.800	3	0	4	1	0
Olivares	.963	64	110	201	12	55

Outfield	PCT	G	PO	A	E	DP
Brown	.975	17	37	2	1	0
De Renne	1.000	3	7	0	0	0
Grove	1.000	23	34	1	0	0
Jones	.991	116	209	9	2	2
Maule	.941	24	32	0	2	0
Myrow	.972	16	32	3	1	0
Reese	.980	82	191	3	4	0
Thompson	.963	84	151	6	6	0
Vento	.966	69	138	5	5	2
Williams	1.000	4	6	0	0	0

TAMPA YANKEES — High Class A

FLORIDA STATE LEAGUE

BATTING	AVG	G	AB	R	H	2B	3B	HR	RBI	BB	SO	SB	CS	SLG	OBP	B	T	HT	WT	DOB	1st Yr	Resides
Bledsoe, Hunter	.311	61	222	29	69	16	1	0	17	25	16	1	1	.392	.390	R	R	6-4	210	1-24-76	1999	Nashville, Tenn.
Brown, Andy	.239	85	285	29	68	17	3	7	37	28	89	7	1	.393	.307	L	L	6-6	190	4-14-80	1998	Richmond, Ind.
Cano, Robinson	.276	90	366	50	101	16	3	5	50	17	49	1	1	.377	.313	L	R	6-0	170	10-22-82	2001	San Pedro de Macoris, D.R.
Corporan, Elvis	.246	116	410	48	101	15	4	4	47	54	91	9	3	.332	.331	S	R	6-3	200	6-9-80	1999	Catano, P.R.
Duncan, Shelley	.264	91	330	42	87	19	2	8	47	35	83	5	1	.406	.336	R	R	6-5	215	9-29-79	2001	Tucson, Ariz.
Fernandez, Alejandro	.242	42	157	11	38	7	0	1	9	2	45	0	0	.306	.270	R	R	6-2	175	12-19-80	1997	Maracaibo, Venez.
Fowler, Maleke	.272	45	158	24	43	9	1	2	9	25	39	7	2	.380	.373	R	R	5-11	180	8-11-75	1996	Baton Rouge, La.
Grove, Jason	.270	18	63	7	17	7	0	0	13	6	17	1	0	.381	.329	L	L	6-2	200	8-15-78	2000	Walla Walla, Wash.
Koutnik, Jared	.270	87	282	38	76	14	1	4	29	19	62	1	1	.369	.330	R	R	6-3	190	11-9-79	2002	Milwaukee, Wisc.
Macha, Erick	.170	19	53	7	9	2	0	0	3	2	5	1	2	.208	.196	R	R	6-1	180	12-13-79	2001	Victoria, Texas
Madera, Sandy	.250	7	20	2	5	2	0	1	3	0	7	0	0	.500	.238	R	R	6-2	210	8-11-80	1998	Haina, Santo Domingo, D.R.
Mendez, Deivi	.228	30	92	7	21	5	0	0	8	3	16	0	0	.283	.250	R	R	6-1	160	6-24-83	1999	Santo Domingo, D.R.
Navarro, Dioner	.299	52	197	28	59	16	4	3	28	17	27	1	0	.467	.364	S	R	5-10	190	2-9-84	2000	Caracas, Venez.
Parrish, David	.228	18	57	7	13	3	0	0	3	4	10	0	0	.281	.313	R	R	6-3	220	6-13-79	2000	Yorba Linda, Calif.
Rojas, Tommy	.292	11	24	2	7	2	0	1	6	5	6	0	1	.500	.452	R	R	6-1	185	3-31-82	2001	Henderson, Nevada
Sardinha, Bronson	.193	59	212	23	41	8	2	1	17	24	57	8	2	.264	.279	L	R	6-1	195	4-6-83	2001	Kahuku, Hawaii
Segar, Jeff	.223	111	403	49	90	29	1	6	59	29	66	10	2	.345	.280	R	R	6-3	210	11-1-78	2000	Syracuse, N.Y.
Seguignol, Fernando	.385	3	13	1	5	0	0	0	1	0	2	0	0	.385	.385	S	R	6-5	230	1-19-75	1993	Panama City, Panama
Sterner, George	.182	17	44	6	8	1	0	0	3	4	13	0	0	.205	.265	R	R	6-0	190	6-20-80	2003	Jonesboro, Ark.
Tejeda, Ferdin	.295	51	217	33	64	9	5	0	20	6	38	4	3	.382	.320	R	R	5-11	170	9-15-82	2000	Santo Domingo, D.R.
Thompson, Kevin	.331	44	163	42	54	13	4	5	25	32	27	16	5	.552	.433	R	R	5-10	185	9-18-79	2000	Fort Worth, Texas
Tosca, Daniel	.281	22	64	10	18	3	0	0	13	11	11	0	0	.328	.382	L	R	6-0	180	11-1-80	1999	Seffner, Fla.
Turner, Jason	.215	21	65	7	14	0	1	1	9	12	9	0	2	.292	.346	L	L	6-3	205	7-30-77	2000	Versailles, Ohio
Vasquez, Willie	.233	21	73	7	17	4	0	0	7	9	20	0	2	.288	.318	S	R	6-0	150	7-26-83	1999	Piritu, Venez.
Winrow, Gary	.248	111	407	53	101	16	8	7	47	29	80	11	3	.378	.299	L	L	6-2	185	7-12-80	1999	Fort Myers, Fla.

PITCHING	W	L	ERA	G	GS	CG	SV	IP	H	R	ER	BB	SO	AVG	B	T	HT	WT	DOB	1st Yr	Resides
Artiles, Carlos	2	3	3.86	24	0	0	1	47	48	29	20	26	39	.260	L	L	5-11	165	1-21-81	1997	Santo Domingo, D.R.
Bell, Gary	3	3	4.04	22	7	0	0	62	58	31	28	31	52	.248	L	L	6-1	190	9-14-79	2002	Ponce Inlet, Fla.
Bicondoa, Ryan	3	2	3.54	15	5	0	0	48	48	23	19	20	30	.269	R	R	6-3	190	1-26-79	2002	Lovelock, Nev.
Blankenship, Jon	0	0	1.35	10	0	0	3	20	13	3	3	5	12	.178	L	L	5-10	180	11-6-78	2000	Logan, Ala.
Brazoban, Yhency	0	2	2.83	24	0	0	15	29	27	13	9	12	34	.245	R	R	6-1	170	6-11-80	1997	Santo Domingo, D.R.
Brumit, Matt	0	2	4.15	9	0	0	1	13	11	9	6	6	5	.220	R	R	6-4	220	10-28-79	2002	Akron, Ohio
Clark, Ray	2	1	3.76	5	5	0	0	26	37	15	11	8	15	.318	R	R	6-2	180	10-27-80	2002	Grapevine, Texas
Claussen, Brandon	2	0	1.64	4	4	0	0	22	16	5	4	3	26	.197	R	L	6-2	200	5-1-79	1999	Roswell, N.M.
Contreras, Jose	0	0	4.50	1	1	0	0	4	4	2	2	3	5	.285	R	R	6-4	230	12-6-71	2003	Managua, Nicaragua
Cooksey, Wes	2	1	4.34	18	0	0	0	29	29	14	14	14	8	.266	L	R	6-3	210	5-22-78	2001	Port Arthur, Texas
Currier, Rik	4	3	1.95	29	5	0	1	74	53	22	16	30	86	.197	R	R	5-10	180	5-26-78	2001	Aliso Viejo, Calif.
Garcia, Jose	1	0	1.74	4	4	0	0	21	13	4	4	4	14	.173	R	R	6-1	160	6-2-81	1999	Barcelona, Venez.
Halsey, Brad	10	4	3.43	14	13	1	0	84	96	36	32	14	56	.287	L	L	6-1	180	2-14-81	2002	Austin, Texas

PITCHING	W	L	ERA	G	GS	CG	SV	IP	H	R	ER	BB	SO	AVG	B	T	HT	WT	DOB	1st Yr	Resides
Henn, Sean	4	3	3.61	16	16	0	0	72	69	31	29	37	52	.259	R	L	6-5	200	4-23-81	2001	Fort Worth, Texas
Hernandez, Adrian	0	0	0.00	1	0	0	0	2	1	0	0	0	4	.166	R	R	6-1	180	3-25-75	2000	Tampa, Fla.
Isaacson, Charlie	0	0	2.53	7	0	0	4	11	9	3	3	5	4	.243	R	R	6-2	190	5-5-80	2002	Overland Park, Kan.
Kemlo, Chris	3	0	1.74	4	0	0	0	10	6	3	2	2	8	.176	R	R	6-5	200	9-23-83	2002	Oshawa, Ontario
Kennard, Jeff	6	3	2.15	26	1	0	2	54	34	17	13	29	34	.184	R	R	6-2	195	7-26-81	2001	Centerville, Ohio
King, Jeremy	0	7	4.50	11	9	0	0	52	45	33	26	19	45	.228	R	R	6-2	210	11-12-81	2000	Nocatee, Fla.
Knowles, Mike	0	0	3.52	4	0	0	1	8	8	3	3	3	4	.258	R	R	6-5	215	7-15-79	1997	Daytona Beach, Fla.
Knox, Michael	1	1	3.72	3	1	0	0	10	8	6	4	6	5	.235	R	R	6-4	195	9-19-83	2003	Plano, Texas
Kremer, John	2	2	2.98	20	0	0	1	42	29	18	14	13	38	.193	R	R	6-1	220	11-19-76	1999	Indianapolis, Ind.
Lieber, Jon	0	0	13.50	1	1	0	0	2	5	3	3	0	4	.454	L	R	6-2	230	4-2-70	1992	Mobile, Ala.
Manning, Charlie	2	4	3.45	6	6	0	0	31	27	14	12	15	25	.232	L	L	6-2	180	3-31-79	2001	Winter Haven, Fla.
Martinez, Dave	5	4	4.79	14	12	1	0	56	64	40	30	34	41	.277	L	L	6-1	165	6-7-80	1997	Ciudad Bolivar, Venez.
Mendoza, Cristian	0	1	2.82	10	1	0	0	22	16	12	7	18	14	.200	R	R	6-3	160	5-1-82	1998	Cartagena, Colombia
Moore, Ben	0	0	5.52	12	0	0	3	15	17	10	9	5	13	.303	R	R	6-1	170	6-10-81	2003	St. Croix Falls, Wisc.
Osuna, Antonio	0	0	0.00	2	2	0	0	4	1	0	0	1	5	.083	R	R	5-11	205	4-12-73	1991	Juan Jose Rios, Mexico
Parker, Christian	0	0	1.80	1	1	0	0	5	6	1	1	1	6	.352	R	R	6-1	200	7-3-75	1996	Albuquerque, N.M.
Phillips, Mark	6	6	5.76	16	13	0	0	70	63	48	45	51	50	.249	L	L	6-3	200	12-30-81	2000	Hanover, Pa.
Pope, Justin	2	0	0.96	2	0	0	0	9	7	3	1	1	3	.212	S	R	6-0	180	11-8-79	2001	Lake Worth, Fla.
2-team (20 Palm Beach)	6	11	4.60	22	18	1	0	115	130	71	59	34	72	.283							
Ramirez, Ramon	2	8	5.21	14	14	0	0	74	88	47	43	20	70	.291	R	R	5-11	170	8-31-81	1997	Santiago, D.R.
Smith, Jason	0	0	2.19	6	1	0	0	12	7	4	3	7	4	.179	S	R	6-5	205	3-7-82	2000	Kennewick, Wash.
Smith, Matt	2	3	2.23	6	6	0	0	32	20	11	8	12	25	.175	L	L	6-5	225	6-15-79	2000	Henderson, Nevada
Valdez, Jose	1	1	4.02	3	3	0	0	16	11	7	7	4	9	.200	R	R	6-4	185	1-22-83	2001	Santo Domingo, D.R.
Villegas, Francisco	3	0	3.22	22	0	0	3	36	28	15	13	21	34	.213	R	R	5-10	180	3-23-78	1993	San Luis, Ariz.
White, Gabe	0	0	0.00	1	1	0	0	1	1	0	0	0	0	.333	L	L	6-2	200	11-20-71	1990	Sebring, Fla.

FIELDING

Catcher	PCT	G	PO	A	E	DP	PB
Fernandez	.993	38	239	28	2	2	10
Navarro	.992	50	344	28	3	2	6
Parrish	.992	18	110	17	1	1	1
Rojas	1.000	11	51	5	0	1	1
Tosca	.977	21	156	15	4	1	2

First Base	PCT	G	PO	A	E	DP
Bledsoe	.992	42	339	19	3	26
Fernandez	.889	1	8	0	1	1
Segar	.986	76	656	41	10	59
Seguignol	1.000	2	18	2	0	2
Turner	.985	13	127	8	2	12

Second Base	PCT	G	PO	A	E	DP
Cano	.970	88	165	250	13	54
Koutnik	.959	15	27	43	3	6
Macha	.980	11	16	32	1	2
Mendez	.955	4	10	11	1	1
Sterner	.917	14	19	25	4	13
Vasquez	.889	3	4	12	2	1

Third Base	PCT	G	PO	A	E	DP
Corporan	.913	114	63	198	25	6
Koutnik	.941	18	9	39	3	0
Macha	.667	1	0	2	1	0
Sterner	.000	1	0	0	0	0

Shortstop	PCT	G	PO	A	E	DP
Koutnik	.960	46	52	114	7	26
Mendez	.976	26	45	77	3	13
Sterner	1.000	2	0	1	0	0
Tejeda	.956	48	67	174	11	34
Vasquez	.905	16	17	40	6	7

Outfield	PCT	G	PO	A	E	DP
Brown	.980	80	136	8	3	3
Duncan	1.000	3	3	0	0	0
Fowler	1.000	44	94	3	0	0
Grove	1.000	17	28	1	0	0
Koutnik	.933	7	13	1	1	0
Macha	1.000	5	8	0	0	0
Sardinha	.971	58	131	3	4	1
Segar	.983	34	54	3	1	0
Thompson	1.000	44	91	4	0	0
Turner	1.000	6	9	1	0	0
Vasquez	1.000	2	3	0	0	0
Winrow	.978	108	215	5	5	2

BATTLE CREEK YANKEES

Low Class A

MIDWEST LEAGUE

BATTING	AVG	G	AB	R	H	2B	3B	HR	RBI	BB	SO	SB	CS	SLG	OBP	B	T	HT	WT	DOB	1st Yr	Resides
Andrus, Erold	.286	35	140	20	40	5	1	1	6	6	20	1	2	.357	.315	S	L	6-2	170	7-16-84	2000	Maracay, Venez.
Arias, Joaquin	.266	130	481	60	128	12	8	3	48	26	44	12	5	.343	.306	R	R	6-2	160	9-21-84	2001	Santo Domingo, D.R.
Blase, Blake	.063	8	16	2	1	0	0	0	0	5	12	0	0	.063	.286	L	R	6-3	220	1-31-81	2002	Columbia, Mo.
Camacho, Juan	.220	78	273	16	60	12	0	3	37	12	39	1	0	.297	.261	S	R	6-2	175	1-13-81	1997	San Carlos, Venez.
Carson, Matt	.259	119	432	61	112	20	1	11	52	37	100	1	1	.387	.322	R	R	6-2	200	7-1-81	2002	Yucaipa, Calif.
Drobiak, Jayson	.293	128	499	83	146	35	4	30	86	42	120	18	6	.559	.349	L	R	6-2	190	3-3-79	1999	Jewett City, Conn.
Guillen, Rudy	.260	133	493	64	128	29	4	13	79	32	87	13	6	.414	.311	R	R	6-3	185	11-23-83	2000	Santo Domingo, D.R.
Lopez, Gabe	.270	121	426	58	115	21	2	5	41	47	52	7	3	.364	.351	R	R	5-8	170	3-11-80	2002	Pico Rivera, Calif.
Madera, Sandy	.299	48	144	25	43	8	0	5	23	18	30	0	0	.458	.380	R	R	6-2	210	8-11-80	1998	Haina, D.R.
Nunez, Andres	.177	41	113	5	20	2	1	0	6	3	22	0	0	.212	.203	R	R	6-2	190	7-20-82	1999	Valencia,Venez.
Rojas, Tommy	.210	52	162	13	34	9	1	1	18	21	43	0	1	.296	.309	R	R	6-1	185	3-31-82	2001	Henderson, Nev.
Santa, Alexander	.252	31	103	12	26	3	1	0	7	3	19	3	5	.301	.280	L	L	6-0	175	12-27-82	1999	Santo Domingo, D.R.
Santos, Omir	.235	82	277	35	65	11	0	2	30	25	36	0	0	.296	.297	R	R	6-1	200	4-29-81	2001	Toa Baja, P.R.
Sardinha, Bronson	.275	71	269	54	74	16	0	8	41	40	40	5	3	.424	.374	L	R	6-1	195	4-6-83	2001	Kahuku, Hawaii
Sprowl, Jon-Mark	.402	29	97	21	39	8	0	1	20	17	8	0	1	.515	.500	L	R	6-1	200	8-1-80	1999	Panama City, Fla.
2-team (95 South Bend)	.321	124	418	77	134	30	3	5	62	71	39	5	5	.443	.425							
Summerville, Kaazim	.188	23	32	11	6	1	0	1	2	10	9	6	3	.313	.395	R	R	5-10	185	9-18-78	2001	Hayward, Calif.
Vasquez, Willie	.223	66	229	29	51	16	1	5	26	30	64	3	3	.367	.313	S	R	6-0	150	7-26-83	1999	Piritu, Venez.
Verbryke, Eric	.271	113	358	59	97	22	4	9	38	51	63	6	1	.430	.373	L	L	6-2	220	8-6-81	2002	Santa Maria, Calif.

PITCHING	W	L	ERA	G	GS	CG	SV	IP	H	R	ER	BB	SO	AVG	B	T	HT	WT	DOB	1st Yr	Resides
Acosta, Manuel	0	8	6.64	15	11	0	0	61	80	58	45	29	45	.322	R	R	6-4	170	5-1-81	1998	Colon, Panama
Beam, T.J.	2	1	5.82	5	5	0	0	22	27	16	14	8	19	.300	R	R	6-7	215	8-28-80	2003	Scottsdale, Ariz.
Bell, Gary	1	3	3.08	10	6	0	0	38	31	17	13	20	27	.223	L	L	6-1	190	9-14-79	2002	Ponce Inlet, Fla.
Brumit, Matt	5	3	2.47	43	0	0	23	47	48	15	13	13	29	.263	R	R	6-4	220	10-28-79	2002	Akron, Ohio
Clark, Ray	8	7	3.55	22	19	1	0	127	127	57	50	26	92	.262	R	R	6-2	180	10-27-80	2002	Grapevine, Texas
DeSalvo, Matt	2	0	0.82	3	3	0	0	22	15	5	2	5	21	.194	R	R	6-0	170	9-11-80	2003	New Castle, Pa.
Garcia, Anderson	3	6	3.32	16	11	1	0	76	57	35	28	36	62	.208	R	R	6-2	170	3-23-81	2001	Santo Domingo, D.R.
Garcia, Jose	9	8	2.64	21	21	4	0	136	111	46	40	33	90	.223	R	R	6-1	160	6-2-81	1999	Barcelona, Venez.
Harmsen, Brandon	1	3	4.71	8	7	0	0	36	55	30	19	18	17	.348	R	R	6-3	200	12-13-81	2002	Jenison, Mich.
Isaacson, Charlie	3	0	0.54	27	0	0	4	33	18	4	2	13	33	.159	R	R	6-2	190	5-5-80	2002	Overland Park, Kan.
Julianel, Ben	0	0	1.69	4	0	0	0	5	6	1	1	2	10	.272	S	L	6-2	180	9-4-79	2001	Belmont, Calif.
2-team (51 Peoria)	4	2	1.11	55	0	0	9	57	47	12	7	27	88	.220							
King, Jeremy	4	6	3.36	14	14	0	0	83	73	35	31	24	75	.238	R	R	6-2	210	11-12-81	2000	Nocatee, Fla.
Markray, Thad	4	4	2.91	34	0	0	0	59	56	22	19	16	49	.250	R	R	6-4	220	9-20-79	1997	Springhill, La.
Mendoza, Cristian	4	0	3.80	32	0	0	2	47	33	23	20	28	28	.200	R	R	6-3	160	5-1-82	1998	Cartagena, Colombia

PITCHING	W	L	ERA	G	GS	CG	SV	IP	H	R	ER	BB	SO	AVG	B	T	HT	WT	DOB	1st Yr	Resides
Mosley, Eric	0	0	10.29	4	0	0	0	7	14	8	8	4	6	.424	R	R	6-3	180	5-27-81	2000	Tulsa, Okla.
Neitz, Josh	2	1	7.94	31	0	0	1	45	63	44	40	17	31	.331	R	R	6-1	180	7-2-79	2002	Tampa, Fla.
Quezada, Elvys	2	0	1.38	2	2	0	0	13	5	2	2	3	10	.119	R	R	6-1	210	12-15-81	2003	New York, N.Y.
Saldana, Jaime	4	1	3.65	41	0	0	1	49	42	22	20	22	43	.224	L	L	5-9	160	10-30-80	2002	Chiriqui, Panama
Skaggs, Jon	4	3	5.25	14	14	0	0	72	65	49	42	40	55	.246	R	R	6-5	225	3-27-78	2001	Houston, Texas
Valdez, Jose	11	7	3.64	22	22	0	0	134	132	67	54	42	76	.258	R	R	6-4	185	1-22-83	2001	Santo Domingo, D.R.
Villegas, Francisco	1	1	3.00	6	0	0	1	6	2	2	2	4	8	.100	R	R	5-10	180	3-23-78	1993	San Luis, Ariz.
Wiseman, Steven	2	1	4.41	35	0	0	1	51	46	29	25	29	48	.244	R	R	5-11	170	4-23-80	2002	Winchester, Tenn.
Wright, Chase	1	1	6.43	7	2	0	0	14	12	11	10	16	10	.226	L	L	6-2	190	2-8-83	2001	Iowa Park, Texas

FIELDING

Catcher	PCT	G	PO	A	E	DP	PB
Madera	.973	11	65	6	2	0	1
Rojas	.994	42	282	24	2	3	13
Santos	.984	71	436	50	8	4	5
Sprowl	.992	18	119	7	1	1	3

First Base	PCT	G	PO	A	E	DP
Blase	.000	1	0	0	0	0
Drobiak	.984	93	768	48	13	64
Madera	.980	12	91	5	2	6
Nunez	1.000	3	10	0	0	1
Rojas	1.000	3	17	1	0	1
Vasquez	1.000	1	7	2	0	1
Verbryke	.982	34	262	12	5	36

Second Base	PCT	G	PO	A	E	DP
Lopez	.969	119	256	341	19	90
Nunez	.889	11	17	23	5	2
Vasquez	.967	15	23	36	2	6

Third Base	PCT	G	PO	A	E	DP
Camacho	.943	73	42	91	8	6
Drobiak	.880	35	19	62	11	9
Nunez	.933	20	9	19	2	4
Vasquez	.939	21	7	24	2	3

Shortstop	PCT	G	PO	A	E	DP
Arias	.946	130	183	415	34	78
Nunez	1.000	4	3	3	0	0
Vasquez	.885	8	7	16	3	4

Outfield	PCT	G	PO	A	E	DP
Andrus	1.000	29	62	1	0	1
Carson	.985	114	253	5	4	0
Guillen	.966	130	272	12	10	3
Nunez	1.000	3	6	0	0	0
Santa	1.000	28	55	4	0	1
Sardinha	.955	60	102	5	5	0
Summerville	.885	13	23	0	3	0
Vasquez	1.000	12	22	2	0	0
Verbryke	.961	34	71	3	3	1

STATEN ISLAND YANKEES — Short-Season Class A

NEW YORK-PENN LEAGUE

BATTING	AVG	G	AB	R	H	2B	3B	HR	RBI	BB	SO	SB	CS	SLG	OBP	B	T	HT	WT	DOB	1st Yr	Resides
Cabrera, Melky	.283	67	279	34	79	10	2	2	31	23	36	13	5	.355	.345	S	L	5-11	170	8-11-84	2002	Santo Domingo, D.R.
Caradonna, Troy	.071	7	14	0	1	0	0	0	0	0	4	0	0	.071	.071	S	R	6-3	219	4-13-81	2003	Tampa, Fla.
Covarrubias, Nic	.266	24	79	9	21	3	1	0	8	8	18	3	1	.329	.348	R	R	6-2	205	6-12-80	2002	West Covina, Calif.
Cruz, Enrique	.285	32	130	23	37	7	3	0	14	14	20	4	2	.385	.363	R	R	5-10	185	7-13-81	2003	Houston, Texas
Duncan, Eric	.373	14	59	11	22	5	4	2	13	2	11	1	0	.695	.413	L	R	6-3	195	12-7-84	2003	Florham Park, N.J.
Frank, Kyle	.167	15	30	2	5	0	0	0	1	2	4	0	1	.167	.242	L	L	5-10	180	9-18-79	2003	Wolfeboro, N.H.
Gonzalez, Edwar	.229	61	231	25	53	12	3	2	22	10	72	4	0	.333	.275	R	R	5-10	200	1-1-83	2002	Miami, Fla.
Hanish, Tyson	.136	25	66	6	9	3	0	0	2	10	18	2	0	.182	.266	R	R	6-3	200	3-10-81	2003	Melissa, Texas
Kartler, Bryce	.291	42	110	16	32	5	2	3	10	18	31	5	0	.455	.391	L	L	6-2	215	6-9-80	2003	Phoenix, Ariz.
Lawrence, Horace	.211	26	71	4	15	4	0	0	12	7	13	0	1	.268	.288	L	L	6-4	215	1-6-81	2003	Richmond, Calif.
Made, Hector	.259	7	27	4	7	1	0	1	1	0	5	3	0	.407	.259	R	R	6-1	155	12-18-84	2001	Santo Domingo, D.R.
Parrish, David	.000	6	16	1	0	0	0	0	0	1	6	0	0	.000	.111	R	R	6-3	220	6-13-79	2000	Yorba Linda, Calif.
Randolph, Andre	.174	11	23	0	4	0	0	0	1	2	6	0	1	.174	.240	L	R	5-7	160	12-28-80	2003	Franklin Lake, N.J.
Robles, Luis	.232	30	82	8	19	3	0	1	12	8	13	2	0	.305	.298	R	R	6-4	180	3-2-82	2002	Rialto, Calif.
Rosario, Carlos	.157	57	204	19	32	3	2	3	16	6	60	3	0	.235	.185	R	R	5-10	180	2-23-84	2001	Santo Domingo, D.R.
Santa, Alex	.193	33	114	10	22	4	1	0	10	9	32	7	1	.246	.256	L	L	6-0	175	12-27-82	1999	Santo Domingo, D.R.
Shorts, Adam	.208	55	202	22	42	12	0	3	27	26	55	10	3	.312	.309	R	R	6-0	190	5-19-80	2003	Land O' Lakes, Fla.
Slevin, David	.222	44	144	20	32	6	1	1	6	10	33	3	0	.299	.280	R	R	5-11	175	5-23-81	2003	Port St. Lucie, Fla.
Treadway, Jared	.274	52	164	20	45	4	1	4	18	10	56	16	7	.384	.343	R	R	6-0	180	12-21-79	2002	Bay Village, Ohio
Urick, John	.226	59	186	18	42	9	0	0	16	36	36	2	2	.274	.345	L	L	6-2	210	2-22-82	2003	Blue Springs, Mo.
Zamora, Hector	.253	63	225	29	57	10	2	7	27	31	56	5	3	.409	.371	L	R	6-1	210	10-19-81	2002	Culver City, Calif.

GAMES BY POSITION: C—Caradonna 3, Parrish 5, Robles 16, Rosario 57. **1B**—Robles 12, Shorts 8, Urick 59. **2B**—Cruz 30, Randolph 8, Shorts 35, Slevin 5. **3B**—Covarrubias 9, Duncan 13, Shorts 1, Zamora 52. **SS**—Cruz 1, Hanish 22, Made 7, Shorts 6, Slevin 41, Zamora 1. **OF**—Cabrera 67, Covarrubias 6, Frank 10, Gonzalez 55, Kartler 12, Lawrence 6, Santa 31, Shorts 1, Treadway 44.

PITCHING	W	L	ERA	G	GS	CG	SV	IP	H	R	ER	BB	SO	AVG	B	T	HT	WT	DOB	1st Yr	Resides
Beam, T.J.	2	1	2.70	9	5	0	1	33	25	14	10	9	31	.200	R	R	6-7	215	8-28-80	2003	Scottsdale, Ariz.
Blackwell, Brad	0	3	4.79	13	0	0	0	21	20	14	11	13	22	.246	R	R	6-2	215	5-8-82	2003	Bixby, Okla.
Caraballo, Angel	0	0	18.00	1	0	0	0	1	2	2	2	1	0	.500	R	R	6-4	175	6-5-80	1998	Anzoategui, Venez.
Castle, Heath	2	2	6.75	13	0	0	0	13	20	14	10	5	11	.338	L	L	6-0	200	1-6-82	2003	Lomansville, Ky.
Contreras, Jose	0	0	0.00	1	1	0	0	7	2	0	0	0	15	.086	R	R	6-4	230	12-6-71	2003	Managua, Nicaragua
DeSalvo, Matt	3	3	1.84	10	10	1	0	49	42	18	10	19	52	.232	R	R	6-0	170	9-11-80	2003	New Castle, Penn.
Gardner, Michael	1	4	1.93	23	0	0	5	37	31	14	8	11	29	.219	R	R	6-0	190	5-23-81	2003	Louisville, Ky.
Hacker, Eric	0	0	1.00	2	2	0	0	9	10	2	1	1	5	.263	S	R	6-1	210	3-26-83	2002	Duncanville, Texas
Harmsen, Brandon	3	6	3.14	15	15	0	0	86	95	47	30	23	54	.272	R	R	6-3	200	12-13-81	2002	Jenison, Mich.
Karstens, Jeff	4	2	2.54	14	10	0	0	67	63	22	19	16	53	.256	R	R	6-3	175	9-24-82	2003	San Diego, Calif.
Kartler, Bryce	0	3	5.89	14	0	0	1	18	20	15	12	11	19	.000	L	L	6-2	215	6-9-80	2003	Phoenix, Ariz.
Kerschen, Josh	0	2	5.56	8	0	0	0	11	17	15	7	3	7	.346	R	R	6-4	180	11-21-81	2002	Merriam, Kan.
Meccage, Justin	0	0	108.00	1	0	0	0	0	6	4	4	1	0	1.000	R	R	6-5	220	2-10-80	2002	San Antonio, Texas
Picco, John	4	3	6.75	15	0	0	0	19	13	17	14	21	12	.188	L	L	6-1	190	7-9-83	2001	La Salle, Ontario
Quezada, Elvys	3	0	1.83	8	8	0	0	39	23	10	8	20	39	.175	R	R	6-1	210	12-15-81	2003	New York, N.Y.
Smith, Josh	1	2	4.55	11	0	0	1	32	31	23	16	16	31	.252	R	R	6-4	225	11-15-81	2003	McGregor, Texas
Thorp, Paul	1	2	1.98	20	0	0	6	36	29	10	8	9	23	.218	R	R	6-0	200	9-23-80	2002	Carrollton, Texas
Tribe, Phillip	1	0	2.32	17	0	0	0	31	35	17	8	7	32	.286	R	R	6-5	210	10-15-79	2002	Katy, Texas
Weeden, Brandon	0	2	3.72	5	5	0	0	19	14	13	8	14	17	.191	R	R	6-4	190	10-14-83	2002	Oklahoma City, Okla.
Wheeler, Adam	1	3	1.80	14	2	0	0	40	33	14	8	21	24	.234	R	R	6-6	180	4-26-83	2001	Smyrna, Ga.
Wright, Chase	3	5	3.56	14	14	1	0	81	82	42	32	30	68	.268	L	L	6-2	190	2-8-83	2001	Iowa Park, Texas

TAMPA YANKEES — Rookie

GULF COAST LEAGUE

BATTING	AVG	G	AB	R	H	2B	3B	HR	RBI	BB	SO	SB	CS	SLG	OBP	B	T	HT	WT	DOB	1st Yr	Resides
Almonte, Erick	.286	6	21	4	6	0	0	0	0	5	9	0	0	.286	.423	R	R	6-2	180	2-1-78	1996	Santo Domingo, D.R.

BATTING	AVG	G	AB	R	H	2B	3B	HR	RBI	BB	SO	SB	CS	SLG	OBP	B	T	HT	WT	DOB	1st Yr	Resides
Amador, Anderson	.061	19	66	7	4	2	0	0	4	3	34	1	0	.091	.125	R	R	6-2	180	11-4-84	2002	Azua, D.R.
Andrus, Erold	.333	5	21	3	7	2	1	0	6	2	4	0	0	.524	.400	S	L	6-2	170	7-16-84	2000	Maracay, Venez.
Battle, Tim	.208	27	106	14	22	5	0	0	5	7	33	5	1	.255	.270	R	R	6-2	185	9-10-85	2003	Riverdale, Ga.
Boone, Doug	.281	20	57	7	16	6	0	1	12	9	21	0	0	.439	.382	R	R	6-1	200	5-16-79	2002	Sellersburg, Ind.
Cabrera, Edwin	.246	50	175	31	43	9	0	5	26	18	39	3	2	.383	.327	S	R	6-0	170	8-14-83	2001	Santo Domingo, D.R.
De los Santos, Edinson	.258	28	93	14	24	7	1	2	11	9	25	4	0	.419	.327	R	R	5-11	180	10-24-83	2002	Santo Domingo, D.R.
Duncan, Eric	.278	47	180	24	50	12	2	2	28	18	33	0	2	.400	.348	L	R	6-3	195	12-7-84	2003	Florham Park, N.J.
Frank, Kyle	.258	16	62	7	16	2	0	0	4	4	8	3	1	.290	.313	L	L	5-10	180	9-18-79	2003	Wolfeboro, N.H.
Gonzalez, Hector	.322	28	87	8	28	2	1	0	6	10	15	1	2	.368	.398	S	R	6-2	180	2-23-85	2003	Estado, Venez.
Harris, Estee	.277	27	101	18	28	7	1	6	18	14	28	4	0	.545	.368	L	R	5-11	170	1-8-85	2003	Central Islip, N.Y.
Made, Hector	.236	52	178	28	42	6	2	5	18	20	19	8	4	.376	.314	R	R	6-1	155	12-18-84	2001	Santo Domingo, D.R.
Mattingly, Taylor	.224	24	58	4	13	0	0	0	7	12	10	0	0	.224	.387	R	R	6-0	190	3-17-85	2003	Evansville, Ind.
Mendez, Deivi	.000	4	14	0	0	0	0	0	1	2	5	0	0	.000	.118	R	R	6-1	160	6-24-83	1999	Santo Domingo, D.R.
Michelsen, Ross	.100	10	30	2	3	0	0	0	0	5	11	1	0	.100	.250	L	L	6-4	190	2-2-84	2002	Arlington, Texas
Nelson, Kevin	.159	18	44	4	7	3	0	0	4	6	12	0	0	.227	.288	R	R	6-3	215	4-8-81	2003	Arlington Heights, Ill.
Perez, Jose	.186	41	118	16	22	3	0	0	9	30	40	5	2	.212	.355	L	L	6-1	185	9-15-85	2003	Oceanside, Calif.
Rodriguez, Rafael	.258	51	190	23	49	11	3	4	29	8	27	2	1	.411	.295	R	R	5-11	160	1-11-84	2001	San Pedro de Macoris, D.R.
Romero, Luis	.216	34	102	9	22	3	0	0	8	23	21	0	0	.245	.372	S	R	6-1	195	9-8-83	2001	Maturin, Venez.
Santos, Omir	.000	1	0	0	0	0	0	0	0	0	0	0	0	.000	.000	R	R	6-1	200	4-29-81	2001	Toa Baja, P.R.
Schwab, Daniel	.164	23	67	8	11	3	0	0	7	7	17	0	0	.209	.247	L	L	6-5	220	7-14-83	2002	Arvada, Colo.
Sterner, George	.300	6	20	3	6	0	0	0	2	3	4	1	1	.300	.391	R	R	6-0	190	6-20-80	2003	Jonesboro, Ark.
Summerville, Kaazim	.667	3	3	1	2	0	0	0	2	1	1	0	0	.667	.750	R	R	5-10	185	9-18-78	2001	Hayward, Calif.
Tejeda, Ferdin	.393	8	28	4	11	2	0	0	3	2	4	1	0	.464	.433	R	R	5-11	170	9-15-82	2000	Santo Domingo, D.R.
Unger, Adam	.083	16	24	2	2	0	0	0	0	4	8	0	1	.083	.214	S	R	5-8	150	3-29-85	2003	Great Neck, N.Y.

GAMES BY POSITION: C—Boone 16, De los Santos 26, Nelson 18, Romero 4. **1B**—Boone 1, Mattingly 12, Michelsen 9, Romero 30, Schwab 15. **2B**—Gonzalez 8, Made 2, Rodriguez 44, Sterner 2, Unger 9. **3B**—Almonte 2, Duncan 40, Gonzalez 15, Made 2, Sterner 2. **SS**—Almonte 2, Gonzalez 1, Made 49, Mendez 4, Sterner 3, Tejeda 5, Unger 1. **OF**—Amador 17, Andrus 3, Battle 27, Cabrera 45, Frank 15, Gonzalez 2, Harris 21, Mattingly 1, Perez 41, Rodriguez 3, Summerville 2, Unger 2.

PITCHING	W	L	ERA	G	GS	CG	SV	IP	H	R	ER	BB	SO	AVG	B	T	HT	WT	DOB	1st Yr	Resides
Aguero, Miguel	1	3	3.38	10	4	0	0	35	33	14	13	14	36	.251	R	R	6-0	150	2-10-81	2001	Santo Domingo, D.R.
Antigua, Erick	0	0	3.00	2	1	0	0	6	4	2	2	2	9	.181	R	R	6-1	170	8-9-83	2002	Santo Domingo, D.R.
Blankenship, Jon	0	1	3.86	7	0	0	0	7	11	4	3	2	9	.379	L	L	5-10	180	11-6-78	2000	Logan, Ala.
Bonecio, Ryan	1	0	6.59	10	0	0	0	14	16	10	10	1	11	.280	L	L	6-2	205	5-10-81	2003	Carrollton, Texas
Brazoban, Yhency	0	0	6.00	3	0	0	0	3	5	3	2	1	5	.384	R	R	6-1	170	6-11-80	1997	Santo Domingo, D.R.
Caraballo, Angel	1	1	3.86	6	1	0	0	9	11	5	4	3	12	.282	R	R	6-4	175	6-5-80	1998	Anzoategui, Venez.
Clark, Ryan	0	0	4.50	2	0	0	0	2	3	3	1	0	2	.272	L	L	6-3	210	8-3-79	2001	North Baltimore, Ohio
Clippard, Tyler	3	3	2.89	11	5	0	0	44	33	16	14	5	56	.211	R	R	6-4	170	2-14-85	2003	Trinity, Fla.
Coke, Phillip	0	0	3.75	10	0	0	0	12	13	7	5	3	5	.265	L	L	6-1	210	7-19-82	2003	Sugarpine, Calif.
Cowan, Richard	1	2	5.71	13	0	0	1	17	19	14	11	7	11	.271	R	R	6-2	200	5-24-83	2003	Grapevine, Texas
Cruz, Juan	2	1	1.23	12	0	0	0	22	9	6	3	11	27	.123	R	R	6-1	170	1-2-83	2002	Santo Domingo, D.R.
De La Rosa, Dane	0	0	3.00	5	1	0	0	9	5	3	3	6	12	.161	R	R	6-6	220	2-1-83	2003	Wildomar, Calif.
Gomez, Abel	2	2	2.63	11	7	1	0	38	19	14	11	26	43	.157	L	L	6-0	170	11-29-84	2002	Santo Domingo, D.R.
Hacker, Eric	3	2	2.86	7	5	0	0	28	25	9	9	7	26	.233	S	R	6-1	210	3-26-83	2002	Duncanville, Texas
Henn, Sean	1	1	2.25	2	1	0	0	8	5	3	2	3	10	.166	R	L	6-5	200	4-23-81	2001	Fort Worth, Texas
Kemlo, Chris	1	2	2.79	13	0	0	3	19	18	6	6	6	27	.260	R	R	6-5	200	9-23-83	2002	Oshawa, Ontario
Knox, Michael	2	2	1.48	10	1	0	2	24	13	6	4	7	16	.154	R	R	6-4	195	9-19-83	2003	Plano, Texas
Lara, Toni	2	4	3.57	11	6	0	0	40	45	24	16	22	42	.279	L	L	6-0	155	1-31-84	2002	Santo Domingo, D.R.
Lieber, Jon	0	0	4.50	2	2	0	0	6	8	3	3	0	6	.307	L	R	6-2	230	4-2-70	1992	Mobile, Ala.
Moore, Ben	1	0	1.42	4	0	0	0	6	4	2	1	2	9	.173	R	R	6-1	170	6-10-81	2003	St. Croix Falls, Wisc.
Osuna, Antonio	0	0	0.00	1	1	0	0	1	1	0	0	0	2	.250	R	R	5-11	205	4-12-73	1991	Juan Jose Rios, Mexico
Polanco, Dionicio	0	1	81.00	1	0	0	0	0	3	4	3	3	1	.750	R	R	6-3	200	3-5-82	2001	Santo Domingo, D.R.
Smith, Jason	1	0	0.00	3	0	0	0	4	2	0	0	1	5	.153	S	R	6-5	205	3-7-82	2000	Kennewick, Wash.
Soto, Edgar	1	2	3.31	10	7	0	0	35	35	18	13	13	40	.250	L	L	5-11	175	12-28-84	2002	Maracaibo, Venez.
Stephens, Jason	0	2	4.55	10	3	1	1	32	42	20	16	9	25	.333	R	R	6-4	190	10-10-84	2003	Tallmadge, Ohio
Stuart, Cory	0	0	0.00	1	1	0	0	2	2	0	0	0	3	.250	R	R	6-2	185	3-15-82	2003	Surrey, B.C.
Villalona, Guillermo	1	2	3.94	8	5	0	0	30	35	18	13	9	20	.277	R	R	6-2	170	9-15-82	2002	Santo Domingo, D.R.
Wang, Chien-ming	0	0	0.00	1	1	0	0	3	2	0	0	0	2	.181	R	R	6-3	200	3-31-80	2000	Tampa, Fla.
Weeden, Brandon	2	0	1.73	7	4	0	0	26	17	10	5	9	21	.184	R	R	6-4	190	10-14-83	2002	Oklahoma City, Okla.
White, Gabe	0	0	0.00	1	1	0	0	1	0	0	0	1	1	.000	L	L	6-2	200	11-20-71	1990	Sebring, Fla.

NEW YORK METS

BY MARTY NOBLE

Injuries, losses and despair mounted. They gained squatters rights on last place and had reserved seats in the infirmary. They endured public ridicule and scorn. So went the Mets' 2003, a season stripped of hope well before its midpoint and eventually lost to Murphy's Law and too many superior opponents.

The circumstances were similar to what had developed 10 years earlier, a season of greater collapse and an even worse aura.

The Mets needed three seasons to affect a remedy after that, three more seasons of inferior performance, ridicule and significant personnel change. This time, though, the club is intent on a quicker recovery.

So they view their 2003 season, at least a portion of it, as a beginning and not the absolute failure that the record suggests. They balance the disappointing performance of Tom Glavine with the emergence of Jose Reyes, the dismal work of the bullpen with the production of Jason Phillips, the offensive shortfall of their outfield with encouraging work of Jae-Weong Seo. They point out that a team that was the oldest in the game ended the season with a cast of young players and the second-most starting appearances by rookies.

And as the Mets crawled from the wreckage of a 66-95 season, they were hopeful injury wouldn't be so formidable an adversary in 2004. Chances are the 2004 team won't lose the middle of its batting order—whatever it turns out to be—for extended periods as in 2003, when Mike Piazza missed three months because a groin pull, Cliff Floyd shut down Aug. 18 for surgery on his Achilles tendon and Mo Vaughn played in 27 games, probably the last 27 of his career. Chances are two veteran members of the rotation will pitch more than David Cone and Pedro Astacio did—55 innings combined.

ORGANIZATION LEADERS

BATTING		
*AVG	Mike Jacobs, Binghamton	.329
R	Wayne Lydon, St. Lucie	83
H	Aaron Baldiris, Capital City/Brooklyn	155
TB	Rodney Nye, Norfolk/Binghamton	229
2B	Rodney Nye, Norfolk/Binghamton	41
3B	Tyler Davidson, Brooklyn/Kingsport	8
HR	Mike Jacobs, Binghamton	17
	Craig Brazell, Norfolk/Binghamton	17
RBI	Aaron Baldiris, Capital City/Brooklyn	86
BB	Jon Slack, Capital City/Brooklyn	77
SO	Blake Whealy, Capital City/Brooklyn	148
SB	Wayne Lydon, St. Lucie	75
*SLG	Mike Jacobs, Binghamton	.548
*OBP	Aaron Baldiris, Capital City/ Brooklyn	.406
PITCHING		
W	Miguel Pinango, Capital City	13
L	Jason Roach, Norfolk	11
	Lenny Dinardo, Binghamton/St. Lucie	11
#ERA	Blake McGinley, St. Lucie	1.02
G	Pete Zamora, Norfolk	55
CG	Miguel Pinango, Capital City	3
SV	Robert Paulk, St.Lucie/Capital City/Brooklyn	22
IP	Kevin Deaton, Capital City	135
BB	Mike Cox, Binghamton/St.Lucie	63
SO	Scott Kazmir, St Lucie/Capital City	145

*Minimum 250 At-Bats #Minimum 75 Innings

Cliff Floyd

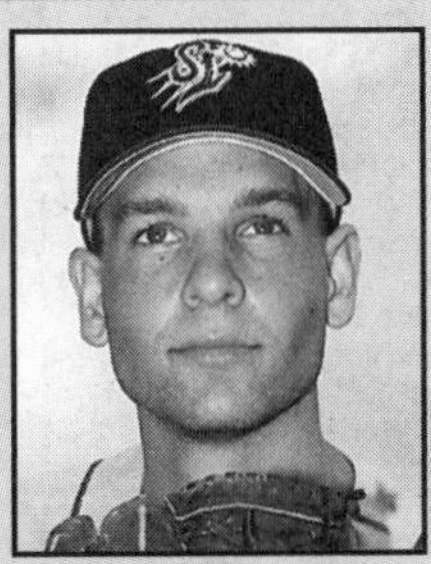
Matt Peterson

MORRIS FOSTOFF

PLAYERS of the YEAR

MAJOR LEAGUE: Cliff Floyd, of

Floyd was one of the few veterans remaining after the Mets headed into rebuilding mode midway through 2003. He led the club in home runs, and on-base and slugging percentage despite a nagging achilles injury that ended his season in mid-August.

MINOR LEAGUE: Matt Peterson, rhp

Scott Kazmir led the minors in strikeouts per nine innings, but Peterson's 15 wins and 2.12 ERA between Class A St. Lucie and Double-A Binghamton was a bit more impressive. Peterson allowed just 94 hits in 115 innings.

The Mets relied too much on older players when 2003 began, so frequent disabled list assignments weren't unlikely. But their on-field failures were equaled by their medical misfortune. First-year manager Art Howe is a lookalike for McLean Stevenson, the actor who played Henry Blake in "M*A*S*H," the old television sitcom. "Sometimes," Howe said, "I feel like the head of a MASH unit."

His lament came two days after Reyes, the brilliant rookie shortstop, sprained his ankle, ending his season. It was Reyes, primarily, who brightened the summer after Piazza's injury, Vaughn's disability, the indifference of eventually discarded Roberto Alomar, dreadful relief and Glavine's failure made it clear the season was lost. After a period of adjustment, Reyes provided the defense the Mets hoped for, more offense than they expected and energy.

But as compelling a player as Reyes is, he doesn't address the Mets' dire need for power and run production. Floyd led the team with 18 home runs, while rookie third baseman Ty Wigginton led the team with 71 RBIs.

When owner Fred Wilpon fired general Steve Phillips June 12, he spoke of the need for a blend of young and veteran talent. Reyes, catcher/first baseman Phillips, Seo and Wigginton provide the youth, while Piazza, likely to play first base often in 2004, Floyd and the rotation veterans of Glavine, Al Leiter and Steve Trachsel are expected to provide the other half in 2004.

The plan was to fill in around them. But with what? When the 2003 season ended without a definite plan for a closer, a leadoff man, a center fielder, a second baseman or a right fielder. The minor league system had fed the major league team throughout the summer and seemed unlikely to provide immediate help other than lefthanded reliever Royce Ring in 2004.

NEW YORK METS

Manager: Art Howe.

2003 Record: 66-95, .410 (5th, NL East).

BATTING	AVG	G	AB	R	H	2B	3B	HR	RBI	BB	SO	SB	CS	SLG	OBP	B	T	HT	WT	DOB	1st Yr	Resides
Alomar, Roberto	.262	73	263	34	69	17	1	2	22	29	40	6	0	.357	.336	S	R	6-0	180	2-5-68	1985	Bradenton, Fla.
Bell, Jay	.181	72	116	11	21	1	0	0	3	22	38	0	0	.190	.319	R	R	6-0	180	12-11-65	1984	Phoenix, Ariz.
Burnitz, Jeromy	.274	65	234	38	64	18	0	18	45	21	55	1	4	.581	.344	L	R	6-0	210	4-14-69	1990	Poway, Calif.
Cedeno, Roger	.267	148	484	70	129	25	4	7	37	38	86	14	9	.378	.320	S	R	6-1	205	8-16-74	1992	Valencia, Venez.
Clark, Tony	.232	125	254	29	59	13	0	16	43	24	73	0	0	.472	.300	S	R	6-7	240	6-15-72	1990	Glendale, Ariz.
DePastino, Joe	.000	2	2	0	0	0	0	0	0	0	1	0	0	.000	.000	R	R	6-2	210	9-4-73	1992	Sarasota, Fla.
Duncan, Jeff	.194	56	139	13	27	0	2	1	10	17	41	4	2	.245	.291	L	L	6-2	190	12-9-78	2000	Frankfort, Ill.
Floyd, Cliff	.290	108	365	57	106	25	2	18	68	51	66	3	0	.518	.376	L	R	6-4	230	12-5-72	1991	Plantation, Fla.
Garcia, Daniel	.214	19	56	5	12	2	0	2	6	2	11	0	0	.357	.274	R	R	6-1	175	4-12-80	2001	Anaheim, Calif.
Glavine, Mike	.143	6	7	0	1	0	0	0	0	0	2	0	0	.143	.143	L	L	6-3	210	1-24-73	1995	Billerica, Mass.
Gonzalez, Raul	.230	107	217	28	50	12	2	2	21	27	34	3	0	.332	.317	R	R	5-9	190	12-27-73	1991	Carolina, P.R.
McEwing, Joe	.241	119	278	31	67	11	0	1	16	25	57	3	0	.291	.309	R	R	5-11	210	10-19-72	1992	Yardley, Penn.
Perez, Timo	.269	127	346	32	93	21	0	4	42	18	29	5	6	.364	.301	L	L	5-9	170	4-8-75	2000	San Cristobal, D.R.
Phillips, Jason	.298	119	403	45	120	25	0	11	58	39	50	0	1	.442	.373	R	R	6-1	175	9-27-76	1997	El Cajon, Calif.
Piazza, Mike	.286	68	234	37	67	13	0	11	34	35	40	0	0	.483	.377	R	R	6-3	215	9-4-68	1989	Boynton Beach, Fla.
Redman, Prentice	.125	15	24	3	3	1	0	1	2	1	9	2	0	.292	.192	R	R	6-3	185	8-23-79	1999	Duncanville, Ala.
Reyes, Jose	.307	69	274	47	84	12	4	5	32	13	36	13	3	.434	.334	S	R	6-0	160	6-11-83	1999	Santiago, D.R.
Sanchez, Rey	.207	56	174	11	36	3	1	0	12	8	18	1	1	.236	.240	R	R	5-9	170	10-5-67	1986	Trujillo Alto, P.R.
Scutaro, Marcos	.213	48	75	10	16	4	0	2	6	13	14	2	0	.347	.333	R	R	5-10	170	10-30-75	1995	San Felipe, Venez.
Shinjo, Tsuyoshi	.193	62	114	10	22	3	0	1	7	6	12	0	1	.246	.238	R	R	6-1	185	1-28-72	2001	Osaka, Japan
Vaughn, Mo	.190	27	79	10	15	2	0	3	15	14	22	0	0	.329	.323	L	R	6-1	275	12-15-67	1989	Columbus, Ohio
Velandia, Jorge	.190	23	58	6	11	3	1	0	8	10	15	0	0	.276	.304	R	R	5-9	180	1-12-75	1992	Roadhouse, Ill.
Watson, Matt	.174	15	23	0	4	2	0	0	2	1	5	0	0	.261	.208	L	R	5-11	200	9-5-78	1999	Lancaster, Penn.
Wigginton, Ty	.255	156	573	73	146	36	6	11	71	46	124	12	2	.396	.318	R	R	6-0	200	10-11-77	1998	Chula Vista, Calif.
Wilson, Vance	.243	96	268	28	65	9	1	8	39	15	56	1	2	.373	.293	R	R	5-11	190	3-17-73	1994	Springdale, Ark.

PITCHING	W	L	ERA	G	GS	CG	SV	IP	H	R	ER	BB	SO	AVG	B	T	HT	WT	DOB	1st Yr	Resides
Almonte, Ed	0	0	11.12	12	0	0	0	11	21	15	14	5	7	.411	R	R	6-3	220	12-17-76	1998	New York, N.Y.
Anderson, Jason	0	0	5.06	6	0	0	0	11	10	6	6	5	7	.256	L	R	6-0	190	6-9-79	2000	Danville, Ill.
Astacio, Pedro	3	2	7.36	7	7	0	0	37	47	30	30	18	20	.311	R	R	6-2	210	11-28-69	1988	Hato Mayor, D.R.
Bacsik, Mike	1	2	10.19	5	3	0	0	18	28	21	20	8	12	.368	L	L	6-3	190	11-11-77	1996	Duncanville, Texas
Benitez, Armando	3	3	3.10	45	0	0	21	49	41	18	17	24	50	.222	R	R	6-4	220	11-3-72	1990	San Pedro de Macoris, D.R.
Cerda, Jaime	1	1	5.85	27	0	0	0	32	32	21	21	20	19	.266	L	L	6-0	175	10-26-78	1999	Selma, Calif.
Cone, David	1	3	6.50	5	4	0	0	18	20	13	13	13	13	.281	L	R	6-1	200	1-2-63	1981	Greenwich, Conn.
Feliciano, Pedro	0	0	3.35	23	0	0	0	48	52	21	18	21	43	.269	L	L	5-10	185	8-25-76	1995	Dorado, P.R.
Franco, John	0	3	2.62	38	0	0	2	34	35	11	10	13	16	.265	L	L	5-10	185	9-17-60	1981	Staten Island, N.Y.
Glavine, Tom	9	14	4.52	32	32	0	0	183	205	94	92	66	82	.287	L	L	6-0	180	3-25-66	1984	Alpharetta, Ga.
Griffiths, Jeremy	1	4	7.02	9	6	0	0	41	57	34	32	19	25	.327	R	R	6-6	240	3-22-78	1999	Avon Lakes, Ohio
Heilman, Aaron	2	7	6.75	14	13	0	0	65	79	53	49	41	51	.300	R	R	6-5	220	11-12-78	2001	Logansport, Ind.
Leiter, Al	15	9	3.99	30	30	1	0	181	176	83	80	94	139	.259	L	L	6-3	220	10-23-65	1984	Weston, Fla.
Lloyd, Graeme	1	2	3.31	36	0	0	0	35	39	16	13	7	17	.280	L	L	6-7	220	4-9-67	1988	Palm Harbor, Fla.
Middlebrook, Jason	0	0	10.29	5	0	0	0	7	13	8	8	4	3	.433	R	R	6-3	215	6-26-75	1996	Grass Lake, Mich.
Moreno, Orber	0	0	7.88	7	0	0	0	8	10	7	7	3	5	.312	R	R	6-3	200	4-27-77	1994	Los Altos, Venez.
Roach, Jason	0	2	12.00	2	2	0	0	9	14	12	12	4	2	.350	R	R	6-4	205	4-20-76	1997	Kinston, N.C.
Roberts, Grant	0	3	3.79	18	0	0	1	19	19	9	8	3	10	.256	R	R	6-3	205	9-13-77	1995	El Cajon, Calif.
Seo, Jae-Weong	9	12	3.82	32	31	0	0	188	193	94	80	46	110	.260	R	R	6-1	215	5-24-77	1997	La Canada, Calif.
Stanton, Mike	2	7	4.57	50	0	0	5	45	37	25	23	19	34	.218	L	L	6-1	215	6-2-67	1987	Houston, Texas
Strange, Pat	0	0	11.00	6	0	0	0	9	13	11	11	11	5	.351	R	R	6-5	245	8-23-80	1998	Springfield, Mass.
Strickland, Scott	0	2	2.25	19	0	0	0	20	16	6	5	10	16	.219	R	R	5-11	180	4-26-76	1997	Spring, Texas
Trachsel, Steve	16	10	3.78	33	33	2	0	205	204	90	86	65	111	.263	R	R	6-4	205	10-31-70	1991	Mesa, Ariz.
Weathers, David	1	6	3.08	77	0	0	7	88	87	33	30	40	75	.263	R	R	6-3	230	9-25-69	1988	Loretto, Tenn.
Wheeler, Dan	1	3	3.71	35	0	0	2	51	49	23	21	17	35	.252	R	R	6-3	220	12-10-77	1997	Warwick, R.I.

FIELDING

Catcher	PCT	G	PO	A	E	DP	PB
DePastino	1.000	1	1	0	0	0	0
Phillips	.994	29	148	6	1	0	0
Piazza	.982	64	346	31	7	7	1
Redman	.000	1	0	0	0	0	0
Wilson	.990	89	442	43	5	5	4

First Base	PCT	G	PO	A	E	DP
Bell	.971	13	33	0	1	3
Clark	.992	80	466	25	4	42
Glavine	1.000	3	10	1	0	1
McEwing	1.000	5	8	0	0	1
Phillips	.990	84	667	44	7	72
Piazza	1.000	1	3	0	0	0
Vaughn	.974	24	179	8	5	21

Second Base	PCT	G	PO	A	E	DP
Alomar	.981	72	138	171	6	50
Bell	.952	14	15	25	2	7
Garcia	.950	17	36	40	4	9
McEwing	.995	55	100	101	1	26
Sanchez	.951	12	16	23	2	8
Scutaro	.981	39	52	52	2	13

Third Base	PCT	G	PO	A	E	DP
Bell	.952	14	7	13	1	2
McEwing	1.000	2	2	5	0	1
Wigginton	.962	155	117	293	16	27

Shortstop	PCT	G	PO	A	E	DP
Bell	.968	12	11	19	1	6
McEwing	.966	42	51	92	5	26
Reyes	.973	69	107	215	9	42
Sanchez	.989	42	57	116	2	23
Scutaro	1.000	1	1	1	0	0
Velandia	.972	23	39	66	3	13

Outfield	PCT	G	PO	A	E	DP
Burnitz	.986	65	138	2	2	0
Cedeno	.987	128	231	5	3	0
Clark	1.000	1	1	0	0	0
Duncan	1.000	52	136	0	0	0
Floyd	.971	95	159	8	5	4
Garcia	.000	1	0	0	0	0
Gonzalez	.993	88	134	4	1	1
McEwing	1.000	18	21	0	0	0
Perez	.989	104	180	6	2	1
Redman	1.000	10	16	0	0	0
Shinjo	.972	54	98	5	3	1
Watson	.846	5	11	0	2	0

STEVE MOORE

Cliff Floyd: Led the Mets in on-base and slugging percentage

ED WOLFSTEIN

Jose Reyes: Hit .307 in a stellar debut season

FARM SYSTEM

Director, Minor League Operations: Kevin Morgan.

Class	Farm Team	League	W	L	Pct.	Finish*	Manager	First Yr.
AAA	Norfolk (Va.) Tides	International	67	76	.469	10th (14)	Bobby Floyd	1969
AA	Binghamton (N.Y.) Mets	Eastern	63	78	.447	9th (12)	John Stearns	1992
High A	St. Lucie (Fla.) Mets	Florida State	77	62	.554	+2nd (12)	Ken Oberkfell	1988
Low A	Capital City (Columbia, S.C.) Bombers	South Atlantic	73	65	.529	7th (16)	Tony Tijerina	1983
SS A	Brooklyn (N.Y.) Cyclones	New York-Penn	47	28	.627	2nd (14)	Tim Teufel	2001
Rookie	Kingsport (Tenn.) Mets	Appalachian	25	39	.391	8th (10)	Mookie WIlson	1980

*Finish in overall standings (No. of teams in league) +League champion

NORFOLK TIDES Class AAA

INTERNATIONAL LEAGUE

BATTING	AVG	G	AB	R	H	2B	3B	HR	RBI	BB	SO	SB	CS	SLG	OBP	B	T	HT	WT	DOB	1st Yr	Resides
Basak, Chris	.239	19	71	10	17	6	0	0	8	7	24	3	3	.324	.316	R	R	6-2	190	12-6-78	2000	Joliet, Ill.
Brazell, Craig	.261	12	46	4	12	3	0	0	1	1	8	1	0	.326	.292	L	R	6-3	210	5-10-80	1998	Montgomery, Ala.
Chevalier, Virgil	.159	42	107	8	17	0	0	1	11	19	16	2	0	.187	.283	R	R	6-2	220	10-31-73	1995	Scotia, N.Y.
DePastino, Joe	.267	84	277	26	74	16	0	2	22	20	51	2	1	.347	.320	R	R	6-2	210	9-4-73	1992	Sarasota, Fla.
Duncan, Jeff	.267	4	15	2	4	1	0	2	4	1	7	1	0	.733	.313	L	L	6-2	190	12-9-78	2000	Frankfort, Ill.
Garcia, Daniel	.263	101	388	45	102	23	3	4	54	22	60	11	1	.369	.313	R	R	6-1	175	4-12-80	2001	Anaheim, Calif.
Glavine, Mike	.266	79	169	15	45	11	0	5	17	25	36	0	0	.420	.357	L	L	6-3	210	1-24-73	1995	Billerica, Mass.
Gonzalez, Raul	.358	32	120	18	43	3	1	3	19	16	23	5	2	.475	.431	R	R	5-9	190	12-27-73	1991	Carolina, P.R.
Johnson, Russ	.284	100	349	37	99	16	0	3	39	44	45	6	5	.355	.362	R	R	5-10	180	2-22-73	1994	Denham Springs, La.
Kelly, Kenny	.261	30	92	15	24	6	2	4	8	6	25	5	0	.500	.306	R	R	6-3	180	1-26-79	1997	Lutz, Fla.
McEwing, Joe	.316	5	19	3	6	0	0	1	3	2	2	3	0	.474	.435	R	R	5-11	210	10-19-72	1992	Yardley, Pa.
Mouton, Lyle	.278	47	151	24	42	10	1	4	24	18	49	6	1	.437	.371	R	R	6-4	230	5-13-69	1991	Tarpon Springs, Fla.
Nye, Rodney	.000	2	7	1	0	0	0	0	0	2	4	0	0	.000	.222	R	R	6-4	215	12-2-76	1999	Cameron, Okla.
Perez, Timo	.222	3	9	2	2	0	0	1	1	1	0	0	0	.556	.300	L	L	5-9	170	4-8-75	2000	San Cristobal, D.R.
Phillips, Jason	.346	22	78	13	27	5	0	4	20	11	9	0	0	.564	.435	R	R	6-1	175	9-27-76	1997	El Cajon, Calif.
Piazza, Mike	.176	5	17	2	3	0	0	1	2	1	3	0	0	.353	.222	R	R	6-3	215	9-4-68	1989	Boynton Beach, Fla.
Pressley, Josh	.148	19	61	9	9	2	0	0	4	11	13	0	1	.180	.274	L	R	6-6	220	4-2-80	1998	Fort Lauderdale, Fla.
Redman, Prentice	.254	128	433	60	110	29	2	11	48	40	96	24	8	.406	.326	R	R	6-3	185	8-23-79	1999	Duncanville, Ala.
Reyes, Jose	.269	42	160	28	43	6	4	0	13	15	25	26	5	.356	.333	S	R	6-0	160	6-11-83	1999	Santiago, D.R.
Scutaro, Marcos	.311	70	244	42	76	18	3	9	32	33	34	11	6	.520	.401	R	R	5-10	170	10-30-75	1995	San Felipe, Venez.
Shinjo, Tsuyoshi	.324	36	111	12	36	5	2	3	9	9	17	0	1	.486	.377	R	R	6-1	185	1-28-72	2001	Osaka, Japan
Shipp, Brian	.263	6	19	1	5	0	0	0	2	3	7	0	0	.263	.364	R	R	6-1	210	8-15-78	1999	Zachary, La.
Snead, Esix	.220	137	472	64	104	14	6	3	31	41	83	61	7	.294	.287	S	R	5-10	170	6-7-76	1998	Williston, Fla.
Toca, Jorge	.274	115	424	38	116	30	0	7	52	17	71	7	1	.394	.301	R	R	6-3	220	1-7-75	1999	Miami, Fla.
Velandia, Jorge	.235	111	374	45	88	22	2	11	48	37	90	2	5	.393	.306	R	R	5-9	180	1-12-75	1992	Roadhouse, Ill.
Velazquez, Gil	.250	5	16	0	4	0	0	0	2	0	5	0	1	.250	.250	R	R	6-3	180	10-17-79	1998	Paramount, Calif.
Watson, Matt	.295	74	254	40	75	18	1	11	55	23	23	2	2	.504	.366	L	R	5-11	200	9-5-78	1999	Lancaster, Penn.
Wilson, John	.190	37	100	6	19	3	0	0	6	7	13	0	0	.220	.255	R	R	6-1	210	9-29-78	2000	Newbury Park, Calif.

PITCHING	W	L	ERA	G	GS	CG	SV	IP	H	R	ER	BB	SO	AVG	B	T	HT	WT	DOB	1st Yr	Resides
Almonte, Ed	1	1	2.55	16	0	0	6	18	16	5	5	6	14	.235	R	R	6-3	220	12-17-76	1998	New York, N.Y.
2-team (30 Charlotte)	3	7	5.40	46	0	0	20	52	61	32	31	20	38	.299							
Anderson, Jason	1	3	2.70	10	5	0	4	23	18	8	7	7	9	.214	L	R	6-0	190	6-9-79	2000	Danville, Ill.
2-team (6 Columbus)	1	3	2.03	16	5	0	7	31	21	8	7	9	22	.190							
Bacsik, Mike	2	9	4.97	22	21	0	0	118	129	70	65	34	62	.287	L	L	6-3	190	11-11-77	1996	Duncanville, Texas
Bale, John	0	1	3.29	8	0	0	0	14	11	5	5	3	15	.220	L	L	6-4	210	5-22-74	1996	Crestview, Fla.
Bell, Heath	2	3	4.71	40	0	0	3	50	54	26	26	8	54	.284	R	R	6-3	230	9-29-77	1998	Tustin, Calif.
Bevis, P.J.	1	0	0.00	4	0	0	0	8	2	0	0	2	8	.074	R	R	6-3	175	7-28-80	1998	Capalaba, Australia
Cammack, Eric	0	0	4.50	5	0	0	1	8	6	4	4	1	7	.200	R	R	6-1	180	8-14-75	1997	Port Neches, Texas
Cerda, Jaime	3	0	1.67	22	0	0	0	32	29	7	6	10	35	.245	L	L	6-0	175	10-26-78	1999	Selma, Calif.
Feliciano, Pedro	3	2	3.97	15	0	0	1	23	20	10	10	6	18	.238	L	L	5-10	185	8-25-76	1995	Dorado, P.R.
Franco, John	0	0	0.00	2	0	0	0	2	1	0	0	1	2	.166	L	L	5-10	185	9-17-60	1981	Staten Island, N.Y.
Griffiths, Jeremy	7	6	2.74	21	19	1	1	115	94	43	35	26	78	.224	R	R	6-6	240	3-22-78	1999	Avon Lakes, Ohio
Heilman, Aaron	6	4	3.24	16	16	0	0	94	99	37	34	32	71	.274	R	R	6-5	220	11-12-78	2001	Logansport, Ind.
Joseph, Jake	5	6	5.93	19	11	0	0	71	97	51	47	21	42	.335	R	R	6-1	220	1-24-78	1999	Citrus Heights, Calif.
Lavigne, Tim	0	0	0.00	1	0	0	0	1	1	0	0	2	0	.333	R	R	5-10	210	7-4-78	2000	Virginia Beach, Va.
Middlebrook, Jason	7	10	4.49	23	23	0	0	118	121	64	59	33	91	.266	R	R	6-3	215	6-26-75	1996	Grass Lake, Mich.
Moreno, Orber	5	1	1.90	38	0	0	12	52	36	11	11	17	58	.191	R	R	6-3	200	4-27-77	1994	Los Altos, Venez.
Riggan, Jerrod	0	0	2.84	5	0	0	1	6	7	2	2	1	11	.280	R	R	6-3	190	5-16-74	1996	Brewster, Wash.
2-team (9 Buffalo)	2	1	2.38	14	0	0	1	23	21	7	6	6	25	.250							
Roach, Jason	5	11	5.07	31	20	2	0	121	140	74	68	36	98	.291	R	R	6-4	205	4-20-76	1997	Kinston, N.C.
Roberts, Grant	0	0	3.52	8	0	0	0	8	7	3	3	5	6	.233	R	R	6-3	205	9-13-77	1995	El Cajon, Calif.
Scobie, Jason	1	3	6.83	8	4	0	0	28	37	24	21	10	15	.330	R	R	6-1	195	9-1-78	2001	Austin, Texas
Seibel, Phil	2	3	6.03	11	5	0	0	34	38	25	23	17	25	.281	L	L	6-1	195	1-28-79	2000	Austin, Texas
Serrano, Jim	1	2	2.39	27	0	0	0	49	38	13	13	19	47	.223	R	R	5-10	170	5-9-76	1998	Grand Junction, Colo.
Strange, Pat	5	4	5.74	31	10	0	1	89	111	61	57	44	64	.312	R	R	6-5	245	8-23-80	1998	Springfield, Mass.
Wheeler, Dan	4	2	3.94	22	5	0	4	46	48	20	20	16	44	.265	R	R	6-3	220	12-10-77	1997	Warwick, R.I.
Yates, Tyler	1	2	4.05	4	4	0	0	20	22	9	9	9	15	.289	R	R	6-4	220	8-7-77	1998	Koloa, Hawaii
Zamora, Pete	5	3	3.49	55	0	0	1	90	94	42	35	32	53	.274	L	L	6-3	180	8-13-75	1997	Mission Viejo, Calif.

FIELDING

Catcher	PCT	G	PO	A	E	DP	PB
Chevalier	1.000	23	152	5	0	0	2
Depastino	.995	78	512	53	3	6	5
Phillips	1.000	16	125	8	0	2	1
Piazza	1.000	4	20	0	0	1	1
Wilson	.983	30	164	13	3	1	3

First Base	PCT	G	PO	A	E	DP
Brazell	1.000	12	105	13	0	11
Chevalier	1.000	5	26	2	0	0
Depastino	1.000	1	1	0	0	0
Glavine	.990	27	175	17	2	21
Johnson	1.000	4	23	1	0	0
McEwing	1.000	1	9	0	0	0
Phillips	1.000	5	33	4	0	4
Piazza	1.000	1	1	0	0	1
Pressley	.971	8	64	3	2	10
Toca	.991	94	728	75	7	91
Wilson	1.000	1	1	0	0	0

Second Base	PCT	G	PO	A	E	DP
Garcia	.972	98	196	254	13	66
Johnson	.929	4	5	8	1	3
McEwing	1.000	1	0	2	0	0
Scutaro	.982	23	46	63	2	11
Shipp	.967	4	17	12	1	5
Velandia	1.000	16	27	39	0	8

Third Base	PCT	G	PO	A	E	DP
Basak	1.000	7	3	10	0	3
Chevalier	1.000	3	1	6	0	0
Johnson	.948	86	41	158	11	18
McEwing	1.000	1	1	4	0	2
Nye	1.000	2	1	3	0	0
Scutaro	.947	36	24	65	5	5
Shipp	1.000	1	1	4	0	0
Velandia	1.000	9	2	19	0	4
Velazquez	1.000	5	6	11	0	2
Wilson	1.000	3	1	7	0	0

Shortstop	PCT	G	PO	A	E	DP
Basak	.966	11	17	39	2	12
Johnson	1.000	6	12	11	0	2
Reyes	.969	40	52	105	5	24
Scutaro	1.000	9	7	15	0	6
Velandia	.951	85	117	236	18	51

Outfield	PCT	G	PO	A	E	DP
Chevalier	1.000	5	7	0	0	0
Duncan	1.000	4	7	0	0	0
Glavine	1.000	3	2	0	0	0
Gonzalez	1.000	30	56	7	0	1
Kelly	.981	25	47	5	1	0
McEwing	1.000	2	2	0	0	0
Mouton	1.000	30	44	4	0	1
Perez	1.000	3	3	1	0	0
Redman	.978	120	207	12	5	3
Scutaro	1.000	4	7	0	0	0
Shinjo	.983	27	58	1	1	0
Snead	.989	132	335	9	4	1
Toca	1.000	13	19	1	0	0
Watson	.939	60	119	5	8	2

BINGHAMTON METS — Class AA

EASTERN LEAGUE

BATTING	AVG	G	AB	R	H	2B	3B	HR	RBI	BB	SO	SB	CS	SLG	OBP	B	T	HT	WT	DOB	1st Yr	Resides
Acuna, Ron	.304	125	474	70	144	28	3	2	50	34	88	24	12	.388	.350	R	R	6-0	215	6-30-79	1996	Valencia, Venez.
Asche, Kirk	.143	19	42	7	6	1	0	1	8	7	20	2	1	.238	.280	R	R	6-2	190	7-10-77	1999	Brandon, Fla.
Bacani, David	.243	52	103	13	25	3	0	0	7	22	19	5	3	.272	.383	R	R	5-7	165	7-30-79	2001	Long Beach, Calif.
Basak, Chris	.272	113	404	59	110	25	2	7	42	35	101	18	10	.396	.332	R	R	6-2	190	12-6-78	2000	Joliet, Ill.
Brazell, Craig	.292	111	432	58	126	23	2	17	76	23	97	2	1	.472	.331	L	R	6-3	210	5-10-80	1998	Montgomery, Ala.
Burnitz, Jeromy	.231	3	13	1	3	0	0	1	3	0	4	1	0	.462	.231	L	R	6-0	210	4-14-69	1990	Poway, Calif.
Calabrese, Tony	.255	43	110	9	28	6	0	2	16	8	28	1	0	.364	.305	R	R	6-4	190	11-5-78	2000	Riverside, Conn.
Chevalier, Virgil	.241	50	174	22	42	14	0	4	18	18	26	2	2	.391	.313	R	R	6-2	220	10-31-73	1995	Scotia, N.Y.
Corr, Frank	.276	48	170	24	47	13	0	4	17	12	32	1	6	.424	.321	R	R	5-11	205	9-19-78	2001	Deltona, Fla.
Deschenes, Pat	.275	44	80	9	22	1	0	0	4	13	10	1	1	.288	.376	L	R	6-0	210	4-26-78	1999	Quebec City, Quebec
Diaz, Victor	.354	45	175	29	62	11	0	6	23	8	32	7	5	.520	.382	R	R	6-0	200	12-10-81	2001	Chicago, Ill.
Duncan, Jeff	.288	76	278	49	80	11	5	4	23	36	59	24	10	.406	.376	L	L	6-2	190	12-9-78	2000	Frankfort, Ill.
Garcia, Daniel	.333	32	117	22	39	12	1	3	22	10	20	2	2	.530	.391	R	R	6-1	175	4-12-80	2001	Anaheim, Calif.
Hietpas, Joe	.100	5	10	1	1	1	0	0	0	0	2	0	0	.200	.100	R	R	6-3	220	5-1-79	2001	Appleton, Wisc.
Huber, Justin	.264	55	193	16	51	13	0	6	36	19	54	0	2	.425	.350	R	R	6-5	190	7-1-82	2000	Emerald, Australia
Jacobs, Mike	.329	119	407	56	134	36	1	17	81	28	87	0	3	.548	.376	L	R	6-2	200	10-30-80	1999	San Diego, Calif.
Nye, Rodney	.312	138	474	77	148	41	5	10	70	58	72	3	5	.483	.387	R	R	6-4	215	12-2-76	1999	Cameron, Okla.
Pressley, Josh	.265	30	98	9	26	6	0	1	10	5	16	0	0	.357	.298	L	R	6-6	220	4-2-80	1998	Fort Lauderdale, Fla.
Sanchez, Rey	.111	3	9	1	1	0	0	0	0	1	1	0	0	.111	.200	R	R	5-9	170	10-5-67	1986	Trujillo Alto, P.R.
Seale, Marvin	.223	120	345	36	77	12	2	5	30	28	102	13	9	.313	.281	S	R	6-0	210	6-16-79	1998	La Canada, Calif.
Shipp, Brian	.189	63	164	21	31	6	1	7	23	10	62	5	0	.366	.249	R	R	6-1	210	8-15-78	1999	Zachary, La.
Velazquez, Gil	.227	59	141	17	32	6	0	3	19	15	30	1	3	.333	.299	R	R	6-3	180	10-17-79	1998	Paramount, Calif.
Watson, Matt	.393	8	28	6	11	3	0	1	1	2	2	1	1	.607	.452	L	R	5-11	200	9-5-78	1999	Lancaster, Pa.
Wilson, John	.324	43	108	19	35	5	0	1	11	14	21	2	1	.398	.417	R	R	6-1	210	9-29-78	2000	Newbury Park, Calif.

PITCHING	W	L	ERA	G	GS	CG	SV	IP	H	R	ER	BB	SO	AVG	B	T	HT	WT	DOB	1st Yr	Resides
Bennett, Steve	1	3	6.90	28	0	0	0	46	68	42	35	34	42	.357	R	R	6-4	250	10-1-76	2000	Helena, Mont.
Bevis, P.J.	4	7	4.18	46	0	0	6	71	55	37	33	30	100	.209	R	R	6-3	175	7-28-80	1998	Capalaba, Australia
Cammack, Eric	1	1	4.50	10	0	0	0	18	19	10	9	4	17	.263	R	R	6-1	180	8-14-75	1997	Port Neches, Texas
Cole, Joey	8	7	4.83	25	20	0	0	114	122	76	61	59	77	.276	L	R	6-8	225	9-15-77	1999	Nacogdoches, Texas
Cox, Mike	1	0	4.12	11	1	0	1	20	10	9	9	25	27	.149	L	L	5-11	205	11-3-78	2000	Pasadena, Texas
Dinardo, Lenny	1	3	3.60	7	7	1	0	40	35	19	16	13	36	.236	L	L	6-4	195	9-19-79	2001	High Springs, Fla.
Elliott, Chad	2	0	8.71	7	0	0	0	10	14	10	10	5	8	.318	R	L	6-1	195	1-28-78	2000	Yorba Linda, Calif.
Hee, Aaron	2	2	5.85	22	3	0	0	40	27	31	26	43	38	.194	L	L	6-0	190	3-4-79	1998	Las Vegas, Nev.
Hill, Jeremy	0	2	10.38	11	0	0	0	13	14	15	15	15	10	.269	R	R	5-11	200	8-8-77	1996	Dallas, Texas
Joseph, Jake	2	4	5.57	11	11	0	0	53	68	40	33	15	30	.311	R	R	6-1	220	1-24-78	1999	Citrus Heights, Calif.
Keppel, Bob	7	4	3.04	18	17	2	0	95	92	36	32	27	46	.264	R	R	6-5	205	6-11-82	2000	Chesterfield, Mo.
Lavigne, Tim	3	5	4.42	46	0	0	11	71	85	42	35	39	50	.310	R	R	5-10	210	7-4-78	2000	Virginia Beach, Va.
Maness, Nick	0	1	10.50	8	1	0	0	12	20	15	14	4	4	.377	R	R	6-3	210	10-17-78	1997	Robbins, N.C.
Mattioni, Nick	0	3	3.58	42	0	0	4	75	75	31	30	40	68	.266	R	R	6-2	205	3-14-79	2000	Deerfield Beach, Fla.
Mattox, David	8	7	3.49	21	20	0	0	113	103	50	44	40	86	.246	R	R	6-2	195	5-24-80	2001	Spartanburg, S.C.
Moreno, Orber	2	0	1.69	4	0	0	1	5	4	1	1	1	7	.200	R	R	6-3	200	4-27-77	1994	Los Altos, Venez.
Musser, Neal	5	9	4.57	20	20	0	0	100	108	57	51	39	76	.281	L	L	6-1	215	8-25-80	1999	Otterbein, Ind.
Orloski, Joe	0	3	10.95	10	0	0	0	12	18	16	15	6	5	.346	R	R	6-3	180	5-17-79	1998	Las Vegas, Nev.
Peterson, Matt	1	2	3.45	6	6	0	0	31	29	18	12	20	23	.247	R	R	6-5	210	2-11-82	2000	Alexandria, La.
Ring, Royce	3	0	1.66	18	0	0	7	22	13	4	4	11	18	.175	L	L	6-0	220	12-21-80	2002	La Mesa, Calif.
Saenz, Jason	4	3	4.30	32	0	0	2	59	58	35	28	40	36	.267	L	L	6-2	205	2-13-77	1998	Santa Ana, Calif.
Scobie, Jason	2	4	4.14	9	9	0	0	50	50	29	23	13	24	.261	R	R	6-1	195	9-1-78	2001	Austin, Texas
Seibel, Phil	5	5	3.59	17	17	0	0	83	79	48	33	32	71	.253	L	L	6-1	195	1-28-79	2000	Austin, Texas
Stanton, Mike	0	1	9.00	1	1	0	0	1	6	3	1	0	1	.750	L	L	6-1	215	6-2-67	1987	Houston, Texas
Yates, Tyler	1	2	4.35	8	8	0	0	39	33	21	19	17	36	.222	R	R	6-4	220	8-7-77	1998	Koloa, Hawaii

FIELDING

Catcher	PCT	G	PO	A	E	DP	PB
Chevalier	1.000	3	6	0	0	0	0
Hietpas	1.000	5	26	2	0	0	1
Huber	.979	43	259	23	6	4	5
Jacobs	.986	65	449	34	7	1	6
Wilson	.985	41	240	24	4	0	5

First Base	PCT	G	PO	A	E	DP
Brazell	.989	108	895	78	11	104
Calabrese	.971	5	28	5	1	5
Deschenes	1.000	3	11	0	0	0
Jacobs	1.000	6	53	4	0	5
Nye	1.000	8	46	5	0	6
Pressley	.985	17	122	7	2	12
Velazquez	1.000	2	4	0	0	0

Second Base	PCT	G	PO	A	E	DP
Bacani	.981	32	43	63	2	16
Basak	.923	3	5	7	1	3
Calabrese	.972	10	14	21	1	5
Diaz	.968	43	80	104	6	30
Garcia	.967	29	58	58	4	18
Shipp	.952	28	35	64	5	18
Velazquez	1.000	13	12	27	0	7

Third Base	PCT	G	PO	A	E	DP
Bacani	.833	4	0	5	1	0
Calabrese	1.000	4	1	7	0	0
Deschenes	.857	6	4	2	1	1
Nye	.935	130	85	276	25	30
Shipp	.857	7	1	11	2	1
Velazquez	1.000	4	1	9	0	1

Shortstop	PCT	G	PO	A	E	DP
Bacani	.800	5	0	4	1	0
Basak	.969	112	160	306	15	75
Calabrese	.944	8	6	11	1	1
Sanchez	.900	3	6	3	1	1
Velazquez	.956	32	47	84	6	19

Outfield	PCT	G	PO	A	E	DP
Acuna	.986	124	256	21	4	4
Asche	1.000	9	12	0	0	0
Burnitz	1.000	3	2	1	0	0
Calabrese	.947	10	18	0	1	0
Chevalier	.977	50	81	4	2	0
Corr	.949	48	85	8	5	1
Deschenes	1.000	6	3	0	0	0
Duncan	.987	76	150	6	2	1
Pressley	.833	9	5	0	1	0
Seale	.975	113	181	11	5	1
Watson	1.000	6	8	0	0	0

ST. LUCIE METS — High Class A

FLORIDA STATE LEAGUE

BATTING	AVG	G	AB	R	H	2B	3B	HR	RBI	BB	SO	SB	CS	SLG	OBP	B	T	HT	WT	DOB	1st Yr	Resides
Bacani, David	.260	44	131	14	34	4	0	0	12	21	16	6	2	.290	.365	R	R	5-7	165	7-30-79	2001	Long Beach, Calif.
Calabrese, Tony	.211	26	76	7	16	1	1	1	8	13	25	2	1	.289	.330	R	R	6-4	190	11-5-78	2000	Riverside, Conn.
Chavez, Ender	.200	29	105	9	21	2	0	0	8	10	14	5	4	.219	.282	L	L	6-0	185	3-9-81	1999	Valencia, Venez.
Clark, Tony	.250	1	4	0	1	0	0	0	0	0	1	0	0	.250	.250	S	R	6-7	240	6-15-72	1990	Glendale, Ariz.
Corr, Frank	.236	85	318	31	75	18	1	6	41	16	50	5	4	.355	.280	R	R	5-11	205	9-19-78	2001	Deltona, Fla.
Devarez, Noel	.167	3	12	1	2	1	1	0	1	0	4	0	0	.417	.167	R	R	6-0	190	12-24-78	1998	San Francisco de Macoris, D.R.
Galante, Matt	.164	20	61	6	10	2	0	0	4	7	11	1	1	.197	.250	R	R	5-7	160	10-10-78	2000	Staten Island, N.Y.
Harper, Brett	.205	13	44	5	9	2	0	0	4	5	13	1	0	.250	.308	L	R	6-4	180	7-31-81	2001	Scottsdale, Ariz.
Hietpas, Joe	.159	63	195	12	31	8	1	1	19	14	60	3	1	.226	.220	R	R	6-3	220	5-1-79	2001	Appleton, Wisc.
Housel, David	.250	17	44	4	11	1	0	0	1	2	16	3	1	.273	.298	S	R	6-1	160	9-6-81	2001	DeBary, Fla.
Huber, Justin	.284	50	183	26	52	15	0	9	36	17	30	1	1	.514	.370	R	R	6-5	190	7-1-82	2000	Emerald, Australia
Jiannetti, Joe	.207	56	188	23	39	10	1	3	20	17	33	6	1	.319	.273	R	R	6-0	185	9-25-81	2001	St. Petersburg, Fla.
Kay, Brett	.251	64	195	25	49	14	0	3	19	21	30	5	1	.369	.327	R	R	6-1	190	10-31-79	2001	Orange, Calif.
Lambin, Chase	.289	118	401	58	116	27	2	5	49	46	81	13	8	.404	.366	S	R	6-1	180	7-7-79	2002	Houston, Texas
Lawson, Forrest	.274	57	186	17	51	5	1	2	15	20	38	6	3	.344	.360	R	R	6-2	185	11-9-80	1999	Federal Way, Wash.
Lydon, Wayne	.264	133	488	83	129	14	7	4	44	52	96	75	20	.346	.342	R	R	6-2	190	4-17-81	1999	Jessup, Pa.
Malek, Bobby	.280	79	286	45	80	20	1	2	36	30	50	17	7	.378	.354	L	R	6-3	205	7-6-81	2002	Canton, Mich.
McIntyre, Robert	.247	85	271	31	67	12	0	5	47	19	68	8	5	.347	.317	R	R	5-10	175	12-8-80	1999	Tampa, Fla.
Pagan, Angel	.249	113	441	64	110	15	5	1	33	35	80	35	15	.313	.307	S	R	6-1	180	7-2-81	2000	Rio Piedras, P.R.
Pressley, Josh	.256	61	234	27	60	13	1	2	30	15	34	3	0	.346	.307	L	R	6-6	220	4-2-80	1998	Fort Lauderdale, Fla.
Toner, John	.045	7	22	1	1	0	0	0	0	2	6	1	1	.045	.192	R	R	6-3	210	9-22-79	2001	St. Joseph, Mich.
Velazquez, Gil	.211	19	57	6	12	3	0	1	6	6	5	0	0	.316	.286	R	R	6-3	180	10-17-79	1998	Paramount, Calif.
Watson, Matt	.286	2	7	2	2	0	1	0	2	1	2	1	0	.571	.333	L	R	5-11	200	9-5-78	1999	Lancaster, Pa.
Wright, David	.270	133	466	69	126	39	2	15	75	72	98	19	5	.459	.369	R	R	6-0	200	12-20-82	2001	Chesapeake, Va.

PITCHING	W	L	ERA	G	GS	CG	SV	IP	H	R	ER	BB	SO	AVG	B	T	HT	WT	DOB	1st Yr	Resides
Astacio, Pedro	0	2	2.08	4	4	0	0	17	15	6	4	3	15	.230	R	R	6-2	210	11-28-69	1988	Hato Mayor, D.R.
Bennett, Steve	0	0	0.00	3	0	0	1	2	1	0	0	1	2	.125	R	R	6-4	250	10-1-76	2000	Helena, Mont.
Bicondoa, Ryan	1	1	3.42	5	4	0	1	26	30	12	10	10	16	.280	R	R	6-3	190	1-26-79	2002	Lovelock, Nevada
2-team (15 Tampa)	4	3	3.50	20	9	0	1	75	78	35	29	30	46	.273							
Byard, David	1	1	1.46	27	0	0	4	37	20	8	6	24	32	.157	R	R	6-2	245	6-1-78	2000	Mt. Vernon, Ohio
Castro, Rafael	1	0	1.42	2	0	0	0	6	5	1	1	5	5	.227	R	R	6-1	180	2-5-81	2000	Cotui, D.R.
Chenard, Ken	7	4	4.04	17	16	0	0	76	65	36	34	32	83	.231	R	R	6-3	195	8-30-78	1999	Victorville, Calif.
Cone, David	0	1	2.84	3	3	0	0	13	10	4	4	3	6	.212	L	R	6-1	200	1-2-63	1981	Greenwich, Conn.

PITCHING	W	L	ERA	G	GS	CG	SV	IP	H	R	ER	BB	SO	AVG	B	T	HT	WT	DOB	1st Yr	Resides
Cox, Mike	6	0	3.32	27	2	0	4	57	35	22	21	38	72	.182	L	L	5-11	205	11-3-78	2000	Pasadena, Texas
Diaz, Joselo	2	2	2.97	11	2	0	1	30	16	12	10	25	41	.161	R	R	6-0	225	4-13-80	1996	San Pedro de Macoris, D.R.
2-team (15 Vero Beach)	7	4	3.33	26	13	0	2	92	55	37	34	73	110	.174							
Dinardo, Lenny	3	8	2.01	19	13	1	1	85	64	27	19	14	93	.210	L	L	6-4	195	9-19-79	2001	High Springs, Fla.
Eckert, Harold	7	3	2.93	17	13	0	0	77	72	30	25	38	50	.255	R	R	6-3	220	7-18-77	1999	Edison, N.J.
Elliott, Chad	4	5	3.03	22	3	1	3	71	64	30	24	26	46	.250	R	L	6-1	195	1-28-78	2000	Yorba Linda, Calif.
Franco, John	0	1	6.23	4	3	0	0	4	6	3	3	1	5	.315	L	L	5-10	185	9-17-60	1981	Staten Island, N.Y.
Kazmir, Scott	1	2	3.27	7	7	0	0	33	29	15	12	16	40	.239	L	L	6-0	170	1-24-84	2002	Houston, Texas
Lopez, Rafael	4	4	3.13	37	0	0	10	60	52	25	21	29	50	.232	R	R	6-6	220	10-24-78	1997	Hato Mayor Del Rey, D.R.
Maness, Nick	0	0	4.26	7	0	0	0	13	10	8	6	6	8	.200	R	R	6-3	210	10-17-78	1997	Robbins, N.C.
McGinley, Blake	9	1	1.02	37	0	0	7	79	51	11	9	20	86	.183	R	L	6-1	175	8-2-78	2001	Bakersfield, Calif.
Musser, Neal	3	0	4.67	7	6	0	0	35	41	20	18	9	16	.292	L	L	6-1	215	8-25-80	1999	Otterbein, Ind.
Ough, Wayne	7	5	2.86	22	14	1	1	104	84	37	33	37	97	.221	R	R	6-2	210	11-27-78	2000	Manly, Australia
Paulk, Robert	1	1	13.50	2	0	0	0	2	3	5	3	2	3	.300	R	R	5-11	170	3-14-81	2002	Madison, Fla.
Peeples, Ross	1	5	5.31	14	7	0	1	58	69	43	34	21	30	.291	L	L	6-4	200	2-20-80	2000	Cordele, Ga.
Peterson, Matt	9	2	1.71	15	15	1	0	84	65	24	16	24	73	.211	R	R	6-5	210	2-11-82	2000	Alexandria, La.
Portobanco, Luz	2	5	5.69	16	10	0	1	62	63	47	39	36	38	.264	R	R	6-3	210	9-15-79	2000	Miami, Fla.
Roberts, Grant	1	0	0.00	5	2	0	0	9	5	4	0	3	5	.156	R	R	6-3	205	9-13-77	1995	El Cajon, Calif.
Roman, Orlando	3	5	3.94	28	0	0	1	62	56	41	27	30	53	.238	R	R	6-1	210	11-28-78	1999	Vega Baja, P.R.
Scobie, Jason	2	1	1.31	4	4	0	0	21	19	4	3	4	20	.243	R	R	6-1	195	9-1-78	2001	Austin, Texas
Strayhorn, Kole	1	1	1.17	16	0	0	10	15	7	2	2	9	16	.140	R	R	6-0	185	10-1-82	2001	Shawnee, Okla.
2-team (30 Vero Beach)	6	3	2.49	46	0	0	17	61	49	19	17	22	60	.214							
Yates, Tyler	1	2	4.31	14	11	0	0	48	41	28	23	24	49	.231	R	R	6-4	220	8-7-77	1998	Koloa, Hawaii

FIELDING

Catcher	PCT	G	PO	A	E	DP	PB
Hietpas	.981	63	454	53	10	6	4
Huber	.982	34	256	24	5	0	4
Kay	.995	47	352	30	2	3	4

First Base	PCT	G	PO	A	E	DP
Calabrese	1.000	8	50	2	0	8
Clark	1.000	1	8	2	0	0
Corr	.977	61	520	28	13	47
Harper	.989	11	83	8	1	5
Kay	1.000	8	57	6	0	3
Lambin	1.000	1	7	1	0	1
Pressley	.987	55	446	26	6	46

Second Base	PCT	G	PO	A	E	DP
Bacani	1.000	2	2	1	0	0
Calabrese	1.000	1	2	3	0	1
Galante	.958	20	26	65	4	11
Housel	.981	12	26	26	1	10
Jiannetti	.933	45	66	128	14	20
Lambin	.960	55	112	152	11	37
McIntyre	.956	7	16	27	2	6

Third Base	PCT	G	PO	A	E	DP
Calabrese	.875	5	1	6	1	0
McIntyre	.900	6	3	6	1	0
Wright	.951	130	70	243	16	17

Shortstop	PCT	G	PO	A	E	DP
Bacani	.976	22	22	58	2	7
Calabrese	.917	4	6	5	1	1
Jiannetti	1.000	1	1	1	0	1
Lambin	.927	49	73	131	16	38
McIntyre	.917	50	74	126	18	36
Velazquez	.948	19	27	46	4	8

Outfield	PCT	G	PO	A	E	DP
Calabrese	1.000	8	10	0	0	0
Chavez	1.000	29	43	3	0	0
Corr	1.000	5	12	2	0	1
Housel	1.000	2	3	0	0	0
Lawson	.957	54	84	6	4	1
Lydon	.974	132	220	9	6	0
Malek	1.000	75	125	7	0	2
Pagan	.967	112	221	10	8	1
Pressley	.000	2	0	0	0	0
Toner	1.000	3	6	0	0	0
Watson	1.000	2	2	0	0	0

CAPITAL CITY BOMBERS — Low Class A

SOUTH ATLANTIC LEAGUE

BATTING	AVG	G	AB	R	H	2B	3B	HR	RBI	BB	SO	SB	CS	SLG	OBP	B	T	HT	WT	DOB	1st Yr	Resides
Anderson, Jimmy	.276	38	116	19	32	9	0	3	17	4	22	3	0	.431	.356	R	R	6-2	200	8-3-81	2002	Riverside, Calif.
Baldiris, Aaron	.313	107	393	55	123	19	4	6	68	51	55	13	5	.427	.396	R	R	6-2	195	1-5-83	1999	St. Lucia , Venez.
Chavez, Ender	.302	34	139	20	42	1	0	0	14	9	25	10	8	.309	.347	L	L	6-0	185	3-9-81	1999	Valencia, Venez.
Clements, Zachary	.190	50	121	13	23	2	1	0	16	19	29	7	3	.223	.301	R	R	6-0	215	4-17-80	2002	Memphis, Tenn.
Galante, Matt	.171	38	105	7	18	2	0	0	7	9	26	1	0	.190	.235	R	R	5-7	160	10-10-78	2000	Staten Island, N.Y.
Garcia, Travis	.288	17	59	14	17	4	0	0	2	6	12	2	0	.356	.348	R	R	6-2	205	4-18-82	2003	Bronx, N.Y.
Harper, Brett	.329	23	79	5	26	6	0	1	9	4	20	1	1	.443	.376	L	R	6-4	180	7-31-81	2001	Scottsdale, Ariz.
Harvey, Ryan	.277	38	119	15	33	2	0	0	15	10	20	3	3	.294	.363	R	R	6-0	190	12-17-79	2003	Riverside, Calif.
Hill, Jamar	.300	8	20	0	6	1	0	0	1	1	6	0	2	.350	.364	R	R	6-4	200	9-20-82	2002	Juneau, Alaska
Hudson, William	.183	32	82	10	15	4	0	0	4	11	13	3	1	.232	.280	S	R	6-2	190	1-26-81	2002	Fountain Valley, Calif.
Jiannetti, Joe	.285	38	137	16	39	8	2	3	19	5	20	6	1	.438	.315	R	R	6-0	185	9-25-81	2001	St. Petersburg, Fla.
Lawson, Forrest	.256	37	133	14	34	7	1	1	20	15	30	4	5	.346	.349	R	R	6-2	185	11-9-80	1999	Federal Way, Wash.
Malek, Bobby	.262	43	149	20	39	11	0	1	26	26	22	11	3	.356	.369	L	R	6-3	205	7-6-81	2002	Canton, Mich.
Parker, Rashad	.197	18	61	15	12	2	0	1	8	13	24	9	1	.279	.351	R	R	5-11	180	9-1-79	2002	Westchester, Calif.
Paulk, Barry	.000	2	3	2	0	0	0	0	0	1	1	2	0	.000	.250	L	R	5-10	180	3-20-79	2001	Miami, Fla.
Ragsdale, Corey	.180	105	355	50	64	11	4	3	27	46	133	31	8	.259	.297	R	R	6-4	185	11-10-82	2001	Jonesboro, Ark.
Rodriguez, Andres	.258	127	461	54	119	26	2	5	54	22	94	6	5	.356	.299	R	R	6-4	220	2-14-79	1998	San Cristobal, D.R.
Rodriguez, Edgar	.263	80	251	39	66	30	0	7	32	7	67	7	5	.466	.288	R	R	6-0	185	11-29-79	1996	San Pedro de Macoris, D.R.
Salvo, Andrew	.260	40	104	11	27	2	0	1	11	21	27	6	4	.308	.384	L	R	5-10	170	8-27-79	2001	East Islip, N.Y.
2-team (37 Kannapolis)	.248	77	202	30	50	6	0	2	17	40	44	7	6	.307	.372							
Slack, Jon	.273	69	238	47	65	9	2	3	27	42	60	21	6	.366	.387	L	L	6-0	175	12-4-81	2002	Henderson, Nev.
Toner, John	.219	34	114	15	25	6	0	2	13	13	24	3	1	.325	.302	R	R	6-3	210	9-22-79	2001	St. Joseph, Mich.
Turay, Alhaji	.236	85	314	44	74	19	3	6	45	28	94	14	6	.373	.324	R	R	6-1	205	9-22-82	2001	Auburn, Wash.
Watts, Derran	.243	111	395	64	96	22	3	4	45	44	136	30	11	.344	.336	R	R	6-3	185	6-28-80	2001	Brampton, Ontario
Whealy, Blake	.257	71	241	47	62	13	3	12	41	34	85	9	4	.485	.352	R	R	6-1	180	5-27-80	2002	River Forest, Ill.
Wilson, Brandon	.181	70	221	16	40	7	0	1	19	23	71	1	1	.226	.267	R	R	6-4	180	9-1-82	2000	Baton Rouge, La.

PITCHING	W	L	ERA	G	GS	CG	SV	IP	H	R	ER	BB	SO	AVG	B	T	HT	WT	DOB	1st Yr	Resides
Acosta, Anthony	3	3	2.50	32	0	0	3	68	61	25	19	22	51	.244	R	R	6-3	185	10-5-80	2001	New York, N.Y.
Anez, Omar	7	7	3.83	26	18	1	2	127	113	72	54	52	105	.234	R	R	6-5	240	2-1-81	1997	Gustiro , Venez.
Bowen, Chad	0	1	5.59	13	0	0	0	19	22	17	12	16	14	.285	R	R	6-5	225	4-28-82	2000	Hendersonville, Tenn.
Cabrera, Yunior	3	5	3.16	18	15	0	1	85	76	40	30	36	81	.247	L	L	6-0	170	10-25-79	1996	San Pedro de Macoris, D.R.
Deaton, Kevin	7	5	3.86	26	25	0	0	135	128	66	58	56	121	.252	R	R	6-5	235	8-7-81	2000	Merritt Island, Fla.
DeLeon, Maikel	1	0	0.00	2	0	0	0	4	2	0	0	0	3	.142	R	R	6-3	180	10-26-79	1998	Azua, D.R.
Devarez, Noel	0	0	5.40	6	0	0	0	6	8	4	4	5	5	.000	R	R	6-0	190	12-24-78	1998	San Francisco de Macoris, D.R.
Garcia, Anderson	0	1	4.26	5	2	0	0	13	10	6	6	2	12	.217	R	R	6-2	170	3-23-81	2001	Santo Domingo, D.R.
Kazmir, Scott	4	4	2.36	18	18	0	0	76	50	26	20	28	105	.185	L	L	6-0	170	1-24-84	2002	Houston, Texas

PITCHING	W	L	ERA	G	GS	CG	SV	IP	H	R	ER	BB	SO	AVG	B	T	HT	WT	DOB	1st Yr	Resides
Kentner, Brandon	1	0	6.92	9	0	0	0	13	15	10	10	4	11	.300	R	R	6-3	200	8-7-81	2000	Benton, Ark.
King, Bryan	3	4	3.74	23	0	0	3	43	39	18	18	24	44	.242	R	R	6-1	185	5-20-81	2002	Englewood, Colo.
Krause, Lukas	0	2	6.45	10	0	0	0	22	28	18	16	15	11	.311	R	L	6-3	200	9-19-78	2003	Naperville, Ill.
Lindstrom, Matt	2	3	2.86	12	11	0	0	57	46	21	18	33	50	.227	R	R	6-4	205	2-11-80	2002	Rexburg, Idaho
McNab, Tim	9	9	3.16	43	0	0	11	74	63	30	26	23	56	.228	R	R	6-0	170	6-4-80	2002	Hollywood, Fla.
Ochoa, Javier	0	1	3.15	14	0	0	0	20	9	8	7	15	24	.132	R	R	6-2	200	1-8-79	1996	Maracay, Venez.
Olson, Ryan	7	2	2.89	36	1	0	2	75	60	30	24	26	94	.219	S	L	6-5	195	1-16-80	2001	Oakhurst, Calif.
Paulk, Robert	2	1	1.55	18	0	0	7	29	22	9	5	17	23	.205	R	R	5-11	170	3-14-81	2002	Madison, Fla.
Peeples, Ross	1	4	6.35	11	3	0	0	40	51	31	28	14	32	.307	L	L	6-4	200	2-20-80	2000	Cordele, Ga.
Pinango, Miguel	13	6	3.47	24	23	3	0	132	140	62	51	25	106	.268	R	R	6-1	160	1-20-83	1999	St. Teresa, Venez.
Rengel, Orlando	0	0	4.50	1	0	0	0	2	3	1	1	1	1	.428	R	R	6-1	170	5-11-83	2001	Piritu, Venez.
Roman, Orlando	2	2	3.34	7	6	0	0	30	29	14	11	20	35	.271	R	R	6-1	210	11-28-78	1999	Vega Baja, P.R.
Walker, Brian	8	5	3.77	24	16	1	2	107	117	52	45	29	94	.277	L	L	6-3	210	2-20-80	2001	Miami, Fla.

FIELDING

Catcher	PCT	G	PO	A	E	DP	PB
Anderson	.973	34	208	11	6	0	6
Clements	.991	47	285	29	3	2	7
Devarez	1.000	1	5	1	0	0	0
Hudson	1.000	1	0	1	0	0	0
Wilson	.982	70	596	51	12	1	10

First Base	PCT	G	PO	A	E	DP
Baldiris	.990	15	96	6	1	4
Harper	1.000	8	52	3	0	3
Hudson	1.000	1	1	0	0	1
Ragsdale	1.000	1	3	0	0	0
A. Rodriguez	.989	122	1054	72	12	67
E. Rodriguez	1.000	2	15	0	0	0

Second Base	PCT	G	PO	A	E	DP
Galante	.987	38	61	94	2	21
Hudson	1.000	11	22	32	0	4
Salvo	.934	29	54	60	8	9
Whealy	.937	68	119	165	19	24

Third Base	PCT	G	PO	A	E	DP
Baldiris	.949	85	60	181	13	12
Garcia	.885	8	6	17	3	0
E. Rodriguez	.915	50	28	112	13	8
Salvo	.000	1	0	0	0	0

Shortstop	PCT	G	PO	A	E	DP
Garcia	.979	9	16	31	1	6
Hudson	.914	18	16	37	5	1
Ragsdale	.946	104	134	336	27	38
Salvo	.917	12	8	25	3	5

Outfield	PCT	G	PO	A	E	DP
Chavez	.961	33	43	6	2	0
Harvey	.923	28	34	2	3	0
Hill	1.000	7	12	0	0	0
Jiannetti	.974	22	34	4	1	0
Lawson	1.000	33	45	2	0	1
Malek	.974	25	33	4	1	0
Parker	1.000	17	40	0	0	0
Paulk	1.000	2	2	0	0	0
E. Rodriguez	.667	7	3	1	2	0
Slack	1.000	67	93	9	0	1
Toner	1.000	20	39	2	0	0
Turay	.957	65	104	8	5	0
Watts	.969	106	147	9	5	0

BROOKLYN CYCLONES — Short-Season Class A

NEW YORK-PENN LEAGUE

BATTING	AVG	G	AB	R	H	2B	3B	HR	RBI	BB	SO	SB	CS	SLG	OBP	B	T	HT	WT	DOB	1st Yr	Resides
Baldiris, Aaron	.364	26	88	20	32	5	2	0	18	14	13	2	2	.466	.451	R	R	6-2	195	1-5-83	1999	St. Lucia, Venez.
Batista, Wilson	.000	3	6	0	0	0	0	0	0	0	3	0	0	.000	.000	S	R	6-0	170	2-7-81	2000	Vietnan los Mina, D.R.
Bennett, Charles	.216	35	88	10	19	6	0	1	9	11	33	3	3	.318	.310	L	R	6-2	200	4-2-82	2003	Watkinsville, Ga.
Bladergroen, Ian	.285	74	274	33	78	12	3	6	36	21	51	0	2	.416	.354	L	L	6-5	210	2-23-83	2003	Albuquerque, N.M.
Bowman, Shawn	.203	42	138	10	28	7	1	0	5	10	49	2	1	.268	.260	R	R	6-2	190	12-9-84	2002	Coquitlam, B.C.
Chavez, Ender	.180	40	122	14	22	2	1	0	9	14	17	9	6	.213	.268	L	L	6-0	185	3-9-81	1999	Valencia, Venez.
Clements, Zachary	.200	5	15	1	3	0	0	0	1	1	3	2	0	.200	.250	R	R	6-0	215	4-17-80	2002	Memphis, Tenn.
Coles, Corey	.167	15	36	5	6	0	1	0	3	3	4	3	3	.222	.231	L	L	6-1	170	1-30-82	2003	Lafayette, La.
Davidson, Tyler	.304	15	46	7	14	2	0	1	5	2	14	4	2	.413	.347	R	R	6-5	240	9-23-80	2002	Edmonds, Wash.
Garcia, Travis	.194	12	36	4	7	0	0	0	1	0	6	3	0	.194	.194	R	R	6-2	205	4-18-82	2003	Bronx, N.Y.
Garcia, Yunir	.177	37	96	11	17	5	0	1	12	18	33	1	0	.260	.304	R	R	6-1	200	8-3-82	1999	San Pablo, Venez.
Gonzalez, Humberto	.227	24	22	4	5	0	0	0	3	5	4	1	1	.227	.393	R	R	5-9	160	3-5-81	2003	Quincy, Calif.
Harper, Brett	.299	28	87	5	26	8	0	1	18	5	12	1	0	.425	.337	L	R	6-4	180	7-31-81	2001	Scottsdale, Ariz.
Harvey, Ryan	.304	16	46	5	14	2	0	1	2	4	5	3	0	.413	.385	R	R	6-0	190	12-17-79	2003	Riverside, Calif.
Housel, David	.258	11	31	3	8	3	0	0	4	1	8	0	0	.355	.273	S	R	6-1	160	9-6-81	2001	DeBary, Fla.
Linares, Jesus	.173	28	52	4	9	2	1	1	6	6	21	0	1	.308	.254	S	R	6-0	190	6-7-82	1999	El Tocuyo, Venez.
Parker, Rashad	.288	60	208	36	60	8	1	2	17	14	46	16	4	.365	.351	R	R	5-11	180	9-1-79	2002	Westchester, Calif.
Piazza, Tony	.210	53	162	13	34	6	1	2	19	19	46	3	0	.296	.294	R	R	6-2	215	6-22-80	2003	Cody, Wyo.
Pietsch, Seth	.183	42	120	18	22	2	0	3	9	12	22	7	4	.275	.285	R	R	5-9	197	9-16-81	2003	Grants Pass, Ore.
Reaver, David	.234	64	205	15	48	8	1	0	25	13	34	11	8	.283	.294	R	R	6-1	200	5-16-81	2003	Union Bridge, Md.
Slack, Jon	.256	59	211	30	54	7	1	0	13	35	47	17	10	.299	.361	L	L	6-0	175	12-4-81	2002	Henderson, Nevada
Watson, Matt	.143	4	14	0	2	1	0	0	0	2	3	2	1	.214	.294	L	R	5-11	200	9-5-78	1999	Lancaster, Penn.
Watts, Derran	.100	9	20	4	2	0	0	0	0	3	7	4	0	.100	.217	R	R	6-3	185	6-28-80	2001	Brampton, Ontario
Whealy, Blake	.247	55	182	24	45	11	2	2	26	20	63	7	6	.363	.329	R	R	6-1	180	5-27-80	2002	River Forest, Ill.
Wilson, Andrew	.250	31	96	15	24	8	0	4	13	13	19	2	0	.458	.342	R	R	6-2	210	11-20-80	2003	Vero Beach, Fla.

GAMES BY POSITION: C—Bennett 1, Clements 5, Y. Garcia 36, Piazza 44. **1B**—Bladergroen 72, Davidson 1, Harper 4, Piazza 1, Whealy 1. **2B**—Gonzalez 12, Housel 10, Linares 10, Whealy 51, Wilson 4. **3B**—Baldiris 25, Bennett 2, Bowman 42, Harper 3, Linares 6, Wilson 6. **SS**—Batista 1, T. Garcia 8, Gonzalez 1, Linares 4, Reaver 64, Wilson 3. **OF**—Bennett 7, Chavez 38, Coles 12, Davidson 12, Gonzalez 3, Harvey 7, Parker 58, Piazza 1, Pietsch 37, Slack 59, Watson 3, Watts 7, Wilson 9.

PITCHING	W	L	ERA	G	GS	CG	SV	IP	H	R	ER	BB	SO	AVG	B	T	HT	WT	DOB	1st Yr	Resides
Bannister, Brian	4	1	2.15	12	9	0	1	46	27	12	11	18	42	.173	R	R	6-1	205	2-28-81	2003	Paradise Valley, Ariz.
Castro, Rafael	3	2	2.17	20	1	0	0	37	25	9	9	11	40	.187	R	R	6-1	180	2-5-81	2000	Cotui, D.R.
Cordova, Vincent	3	2	2.65	9	8	0	0	37	38	13	11	7	41	.260	R	R	6-3	210	4-16-82	2003	Whittier, Calif.
Correa, Stephen	1	1	7.16	13	0	0	0	16	18	13	13	13	19	.268	L	L	6-5	255	5-24-80	2003	Sacramento, Calif.
Danly, Ryan	2	2	3.29	13	11	0	0	55	51	24	20	15	29	.252	L	L	6-8	195	6-23-81	2001	Cedar Rapids, Iowa
George, Taylor	5	3	1.40	26	0	0	3	39	23	7	6	9	29	.174	R	R	6-2	185	8-14-82	2002	Long Beach, Calif.
Hawk, Shane	0	0	0.00	6	3	0	0	13	6	1	0	4	12	.142	R	L	6-5	185	9-10-81	2003	Cibolo, Texas
Keppel, Bob	2	0	2.51	3	3	0	0	14	10	5	4	2	13	.188	R	R	6-5	205	6-11-82	2000	Chesterfield, Mo.
King, Bryan	2	2	2.67	17	0	0	3	30	25	10	9	7	30	.223	R	R	6-1	185	5-20-81	2002	Englewood, Colo.
Lindstrom, Matt	7	3	3.44	14	14	0	0	65	61	28	25	27	52	.250	R	R	6-4	205	2-11-80	2002	Rexburg, Idaho
MacLane, Evan	1	0	0.00	1	1	0	0	6	3	0	0	1	5	.136	L	L	6-2	185	11-4-82	2003	Quincy, Calif.
Maldonado, Ivan	5	2	4.06	18	4	0	1	51	50	23	23	12	34	.255	R	R	6-3	210	6-7-80	2002	Cayey, P.R.
Miramontes, Mateo	0	0	18.00	1	1	0	0	1	0	2	2	5	1	.000	R	R	6-4	200	12-24-81	2003	Pleasanton, Calif.
Muniz, Carlos	0	0	0.45	19	0	0	13	20	12	1	1	5	23	.179	R	R	6-1	180	3-12-81	2003	Wilmington, Calif.
Nunez, Franklin	0	0	5.06	7	0	0	0	5	5	4	3	4	8	.250	R	R	6-0	175	1-18-77	1995	Rincon, D.R.
Ochoa, Javier	3	1	6.23	6	0	0	0	9	10	8	6	11	7	.294	R	R	6-2	200	1-8-79	1996	Maracay, Venez.

PITCHING	W	L	ERA	G	GS	CG	SV	IP	H	R	ER	BB	SO	AVG	B	T	HT	WT	DOB	1st Yr	Resides
Orloski, Joe	3	0	1.08	11	0	0	0	17	12	3	2	4	14	.203	R	R	6-3	180	5-17-79	1998	Las Vegas, Nev.
Osberg, Tanner	1	3	3.00	8	6	0	0	33	30	13	11	6	17	.241	L	R	6-3	185	9-10-82	2000	Red Deer, Alberta
Paulk, Robert	1	1	2.53	27	0	0	15	32	18	12	9	10	38	.165	R	R	5-11	170	3-14-81	2002	Madison, Fla.
Petit, Yusmeiro	1	0	2.19	2	2	0	0	12	5	3	3	2	20	.119	R	R	6-0	180	11-22-84	2002	Maracaibo, Venez.
Ramirez, Greg	1	3	2.96	18	5	0	1	52	51	19	17	17	48	.255	R	R	6-4	205	9-12-80	2003	Oxnard, Calif.
Scobie, Jason	0	0	0.00	1	1	0	0	1	0	0	0	0	0	.000	R	R	6-1	195	9-1-78	2001	Austin, Texas
Smith, David	0	0	7.71	8	0	0	0	9	15	9	8	5	2	.394	L	L	6-2	185	3-12-82	2003	Asheboro, N.C.
Stanton, Mike	0	0	0.00	1	1	0	0	2	1	0	0	0	1	.166	L	L	6-1	215	6-2-67	1987	Houston, Texas
Walker, Adam	0	2	4.86	8	4	0	0	17	12	9	9	9	10	.203	L	L	6-7	200	5-28-76	1997	Albuquerque, N.M.
Worthington, Timothy	2	0	3.49	17	1	0	0	39	39	16	15	10	26	.274	R	R	6-2	200	7-29-80	2003	Redwood City, Calif.

KINGSPORT METS — Rookie

APPALACHIAN LEAGUE

BATTING	AVG	G	AB	R	H	2B	3B	HR	RBI	BB	SO	SB	CS	SLG	OBP	B	T	HT	WT	DOB	1st Yr	Resides
Anderson, Jimmy	.300	15	50	9	15	10	0	2	7	2	10	0	0	.620	.327	R	R	6-2	200	8-3-81	2002	Riverside, Calif.
Batista, Wilson	.258	19	62	6	16	3	1	0	7	11	10	2	1	.339	.370	S	R	6-0	170	2-7-81	2000	Vietnan los Mina, D.R.
Bennett, Charles	.333	4	15	2	5	0	0	0	3	0	4	0	0	.333	.313	L	R	6-2	200	4-2-82	2003	Watkinsville, Ga.
Bowman, Shawn	.121	10	33	2	4	1	0	0	3	1	13	0	0	.152	.216	R	R	6-2	190	12-9-84	2002	Coquitlam, B.C.
Brinkley, Dante	.303	44	142	23	43	7	3	0	17	16	28	9	7	.394	.399	R	R	5-10	180	8-21-81	2003	Fairview Heights, Ill.
Cabral, Marcos	.198	43	131	15	26	5	1	0	9	21	25	4	2	.252	.316	R	R	6-0	180	4-4-84	2003	Miami, Fla.
Camacho, Johan	.243	51	177	15	43	8	1	1	16	15	44	1	0	.316	.310	S	R	6-3	245	8-13-83	2000	Barquisimeto, Venez.
Coles, Corey	.333	27	96	19	32	5	1	0	6	8	17	6	0	.406	.396	L	L	6-1	170	1-30-82	2003	Lafayette, La.
Davidson, Tyler	.337	50	172	29	58	11	8	10	35	15	36	3	0	.669	.394	R	R	6-5	240	9-23-80	2002	Edmonds, Wash.
Dulaney, Todd	.242	35	99	18	24	2	0	0	5	20	10	7	5	.263	.372	R	R	5-10	170	12-20-83	2003	Maywood, Ill.
Gamero, Jesus	.196	13	46	6	9	3	0	0	3	6	8	1	0	.261	.288	R	R	6-1	170	1-24-84	2001	Higuerote, Venez.
Garcia, Miguel	.189	15	37	3	7	1	0	0	2	3	13	1	0	.216	.262	L	L	6-1	180	4-8-82	1999	Santo Domingo, D.R.
Garcia, Travis	.208	22	77	11	16	2	1	1	9	6	13	0	2	.299	.279	R	R	6-2	205	4-18-82	2003	Bronx, N.Y.
Gonzalez, Humberto	.129	12	31	2	4	0	0	0	0	2	7	0	1	.129	.182	R	R	5-9	160	3-5-81	2003	Quincy, Calif.
Harper, Brett	.429	11	35	6	15	8	0	2	10	3	9	0	0	.829	.500	L	R	6-4	180	7-31-81	2001	Scottsdale, Ariz.
Hill, Jamar	.241	44	170	22	41	12	0	6	26	10	45	14	4	.418	.280	R	R	6-4	200	9-20-82	2002	Juneau, Alaska
Mannix, Brendan	.250	19	64	6	16	3	1	1	12	5	18	0	1	.375	.304	S	R	6-3	210	3-20-80	2002	Crofton, Md.
Milledge, Lastings	.231	7	26	4	6	2	0	0	2	3	4	5	1	.308	.323	R	R	6-1	185	4-5-85	2003	Palmetto, Fla.
Pietsch, Seth	.200	10	40	3	8	2	0	0	5	3	10	4	0	.250	.273	R	R	5-9	197	9-16-81	2003	Grants Pass, Ore.
Purkey, Bryan	.333	3	3	2	1	1	0	0	1	3	1	0	0	.667	.667	R	R	6-0	200	8-28-81	2003	Port St. Lucie, Fla.
Reynoso, Danilo	.244	39	131	8	32	11	1	4	13	6	46	0	1	.435	.279	R	R	5-11	205	4-5-82	1997	San Cristobal, D.R.
Rios, Kevin	.231	34	108	6	25	6	0	0	6	5	28	1	1	.287	.272	R	R	6-2	180	7-21-81	2003	Santa Ana, Calif.
Solano, Roberto	.214	45	168	22	36	8	3	0	19	9	35	10	4	.298	.256	R	R	6-2	180	10-15-83	2000	Santo Domingo, D.R.
Wallace, James	.200	21	65	8	13	3	0	3	5	10	30	0	0	.385	.316	R	R	6-3	220	3-27-81	2003	Reno, Nev.
Wells, Cory	.139	15	36	5	5	1	0	0	2	4	8	4	2	.167	.225	R	R	6-0	185	11-18-84	2003	Plant City, Fla.
Wilson, Andrew	.343	10	35	5	12	3	0	1	7	2	5	0	1	.514	.395	R	R	6-2	210	11-20-80	2003	Vero Beach, Fla.
Wilson, Laron	.273	3	11	2	3	1	0	0	1	0	5	0	0	.364	.333	R	R	6-0	200	9-2-81	2002	Mechanicsville, Va.

GAMES BY POSITION: C—Anderson 12, Bennett 3, Purkey 2, Reynoso 39, Wallace 15. **1B**—Camacho 51, Davidson 7, Harper 2, Mannix 2, Rios 1, L. Wilson 2. **2B**—Cabral 17, Dulaney 33, Garcia 5, Gonzalez 8, Mannix 3, Rios 4. **3B**—Bennett 1, Bowman 10, Garcia 7, Harper 8, Mannix 13, Rios 21, A. Wilson 9. **SS**—Batista 19, Cabral 26, Garcia 11, Gonzalez 2, Rios 8. **OF**—Brinkley 39, Coles 26, Davidson 9, Gamero 11, Garcia 12, Hill 38, Pietsch 9, Solano 44, Wells 11.

PITCHING	W	L	ERA	G	GS	CG	SV	IP	H	R	ER	BB	SO	AVG	B	T	HT	WT	DOB	1st Yr	Resides
Alfonzo, Edgar	0	0	3.48	8	0	0	0	10	12	4	4	3	4	.279	L	L	5-10	160	12-14-84	2002	Estado , Venez.
Almenar, Aristides	3	5	4.59	13	9	0	0	49	56	30	25	18	34	.293	R	R	6-0	170	12-27-83	2001	Valencia, Venez.
Beltre, Elvin	0	0	8.31	4	0	0	0	4	5	4	4	5	2	.294	R	R	6-3	190	1-19-80	1999	San Cristobal, D.R.
Brewer, Jeff	0	2	7.71	5	0	0	0	5	6	4	4	4	4	.315	R	R	6-3	190	10-5-80	2002	Fredericton, N.B.
Elliott, Adam	1	0	15.75	5	0	0	0	8	16	14	14	6	9	.432	S	R	6-1	200	3-27-84	2002	Concord, Calif.
Freites, Julio	2	2	3.54	13	0	0	1	20	23	12	8	10	22	.277	R	R	6-1	190	5-30-82	2000	Clarines, Venez.
Fry, Troy	2	1	4.00	16	0	0	1	27	34	20	12	8	22	.295	R	R	6-5	220	6-23-81	2003	Wind Gap, Pa.
Garay, Kelvin	0	0	3.60	5	0	0	0	5	5	3	2	4	4	.263	L	L	6-5	230	1-18-85	2002	Trujillo Alto, P.R.
Gomez, Jose	0	4	5.10	11	7	0	0	30	28	21	17	18	34	.250	R	R	6-3	240	12-16-80	1998	Brooksville, Fla.
Gonzalez, Marino	0	2	8.56	8	2	0	0	14	19	15	13	10	17	.339	R	R	6-4	190	11-4-82	1999	Puerto Plata, D.R.
Krause, Lukas	0	0	0.00	3	0	0	0	5	4	3	0	2	6	.210	R	L	6-3	200	9-19-78	2003	Naperville, Ill.
MacLane, Evan	4	1	2.88	14	6	0	0	56	59	20	18	8	57	.270	L	L	6-2	185	11-4-82	2003	Quincy, Calif.
Meyers, Ryan	1	0	4.50	15	0	0	0	24	29	15	12	4	12	.305	L	R	6-5	195	7-17-85	2003	Springville, Ariz.
Miramontes, Mateo	1	4	8.44	6	5	0	0	21	23	22	20	13	16	.280	R	R	6-4	200	12-24-81	2003	Pleasanton, Calif.
Petit, Yusmeiro	3	3	2.32	12	12	0	0	62	47	19	16	8	65	.218	R	R	6-0	180	11-22-84	2002	Maracaibo, Venez.
Rengel, Orlando	1	5	5.76	12	12	0	0	50	57	42	32	22	38	.282	R	R	6-1	170	5-11-83	2001	Piritu, Venez.
Rondon, Celso	2	2	4.10	19	0	0	11	26	19	13	12	11	44	.197	R	R	6-0	215	4-7-84	2001	Cumana Sucre, Venez.
Sides, Andrew	0	3	3.61	10	10	0	0	42	32	21	17	9	39	.206	L	R	6-7	215	8-5-84	2003	DeSoto, Mo.
Smith, David	0	1	4.15	5	0	0	0	4	2	2	2	2	5	.142	L	L	6-2	185	3-12-82	2003	Asheboro, N.C.
Stefano, Frank	4	2	4.98	15	0	0	0	22	28	18	12	8	14	.297	L	L	6-10	205	3-23-79	2003	Rochester, Ill.
Torres, David	1	2	3.33	15	0	0	1	27	26	13	10	7	25	.240	R	R	6-1	205	3-23-81	2003	Orlando, Fla.
Weitzman, Billy	0	0	4.63	17	1	0	2	23	19	14	12	10	16	.228	R	R	6-3	195	11-29-83	2003	Oceanside, N.Y.

OAKLAND ATHLETICS

BY CASEY TEFERTILLER

In the end, all the talk concerning the Athletics' 2003 season came down to a discussion of futility. Over a four-year period, Oakland has lost nine consecutive opportunities to clinch the deciding game of an American League Division Series. Nine tries, nine failures. Three came in 2003 after the A's won the first two games against Boston, only to falter in succession and again go home without advancing.

It was a sour finish, and one that ached at the very souls of the A's themselves.

"We definitely don't want to be labeled (losers)," lefthander Ted Lilly said. "The Buffalo Bills got to the Super Bowl and lost—unfortunately, we haven't even gotten to the World Series and lost. We're trying to win a (first-round) series here. I think we're frustrated, even angry, especially with the expectations we had coming into this series. Winning the first two games in Oakland and not getting it done is kind of maddening."

The Bills label may haunt the A's until they break the string of frustration. However, in 2003, it masked a truly remarkable season for the organization. Under first-year manager Ken Macha, the A's made the playoffs for the fourth consecutive year, with their third AL West title during that period. They did it with an offense that misfired through most of the season and wound up ranking ninth in the AL in runs scored

Right fielder Jermaine Dye missed half the season with injuries and provided little offense when he did play. DH Erubial Durazo nearly disappeared from May through August and first baseman Scott Hatteberg barely passed .250 and double figures in home runs. Internal strife also plagued the team, as hitting coach Thad Bosley was fired in midseason after publicly expressing dissatisfaction over private criticism of his work.

The organization also became the focus of controversy after the publication of Michael Lewis' "Moneyball," crediting general manager Billy Beane with outsmarting his competition, which raised the ire of many in baseball.

Somehow the A's found a way to overcome all their obstacles. It was never easy. After a struggle through the first half, the A's trailed Seattle by eight games on June 8, then wobbled back to close in on the Mariners over the next two months. By Aug. 19, the A's had closed within three games, but then came a season-ending hip injury to lefthander Mark Mulder, who had a stress fracture in his hip.

The A's are built around three dynamic starting pitchers—Mulder, Tim Hudson and Barry Zito, and the loss of any one would seem to bury the team. Instead, the A's came on strong. On Aug. 27, Oakland took over the division lead and never relinquished it as the Mariners faded down the stretch. Shortstop Miguel Tejada didn't repeat his 2002 MVP season, but he and third baseman Eric Chavez ignited the long-dormant offense.

"We just expect to be in the postseason every year," Hudson said. "It's almost like whatever we need to do, we do it."

The minor leagues continued to funnel talent to the majors, sending starters Rich Harden and Justin Duchscherer to Oakland to fill the rotation. Triple-A Sacramento won the Pacific Coast League championship in dominating form, with a 92-52 regular-season mark and a playoff sweep to earn Baseball America's Team of the Year award.

Both Class A stops, Modesto and new affiliate Kane County, reached the playoffs. Shortstop Bobby Crosby, who may have to replace the free-agent Tejada in Oakland in 2004, and righthander Joe Blanton emerged as premier prospects.

Tim Hudson

Bobby Crosby

PLAYERS of the YEAR

MAJOR LEAGUE: Tim Hudson, rhp

Teammates Barry Zito and Mark Mulder generally get more ink, but Hudson's skill and durability can't be overlooked. Despite poor run support, Hudson won a team-high 16 games in 2003, posted the American League's second-best ERA and ranked third in innings pitched.

MINOR LEAGUE: Bobby Crosby, ss

Miguel Tejada's heir apparent at shortstop lived up to expectations in 2003 by winning the Pacific Coast League's rookie of the year award after hitting .308-22-90 with 32 doubles and 24 steals for Sacramento.

ORGANIZATION LEADERS

BATTING		
***AVG**	Bobby Crosby, Sacramento	.308
R	Gary Thomas, Modesto	95
	Mark Kiger, Modesto	95
H	Dan Johnson, Sacramento/Midland	157
TB	Dan Johnson, Sacramento/Midland	273
2B	Mark Kiger, Modesto	38
	Nick Swisher, Midland/Modesto	38
3B	Freddie Bynum, Midland	9
HR	Graham Koonce, Sacramento	34
RBI	Graham Koonce, Sacramento	115
BB	Graham Koonce, Sacramento	98
SO	Matt Allegra, Midland	156
SB	Esteban German, Sacramento	32
***SLG**	Bobby Crosby, Sacramento	.544
***OBP**	Graham Koonce, Sacramento	.403
PITCHING		
W	Brad Weis, Modesto	15
L	Derell McCall, Modesto/Kane County	13
#ERA	Kyle Crowell, Midland/Modesto	2.19
G	Justin Lehr, Sacramento	53
CG	Drew Dickinson, Kane County	5
SV	Chad Harville, Sacramento	18
IP	Drew Dickinson, Kane County	191
BB	Brad Weis, Modesto	60
SO	Joe Blanton, Midland/Kane County	174

*Minimum 250 At-Bats #Minimum 75 Innings

OAKLAND ATHLETICS

Manager: Ken Macha. **2003 Record:** 96-66, .593 (1st, AL West).

BATTING	AVG	G	AB	R	H	2B	3B	HR	RBI	BB	SO	SB	CS	SLG	OBP	B	T	HT	WT	DOB	1st Yr	Resides
Byrnes, Eric	.263	121	414	64	109	27	9	12	51	42	71	10	2	.459	.333	R	R	6-2	210	2-16-76	1998	Woodside, Calif.
Chavez, Eric	.282	156	588	94	166	39	5	29	101	62	89	8	3	.514	.350	L	R	6-1	200	12-7-77	1996	Walnut Creek, Calif.
Crosby, Bobby	.000	11	12	1	0	0	0	0	0	1	5	0	0	.000	.143	R	R	6-3	195	1-12-80	2001	Cypress, Calif.
Durazo, Erubiel	.259	154	537	92	139	29	0	21	77	100	105	1	1	.430	.374	L	L	6-3	240	1-23-75	1997	Hermosillo, Mexico
Dye, Jermaine	.172	65	221	28	38	6	0	4	20	25	42	1	0	.253	.261	R	R	6-5	220	1-28-74	1993	Phoenix, Ariz.
Edwards, Mike	.250	4	4	0	1	0	0	0	0	2	1	0	0	.250	.500	R	R	6-1	185	11-24-76	1995	Mechanicsburg, Pa.
Ellis, Mark	.248	154	553	78	137	31	5	9	52	48	94	6	2	.371	.313	R	R	5-11	180	6-6-77	1999	Rapid City, S.D.
Gant, Ron	.146	17	41	4	6	0	0	1	4	2	9	0	0	.220	.182	R	R	6-0	190	3-2-65	1983	Alpharetta, Ga.
German, Franklyn	.250	5	4	0	1	0	0	0	1	0	1	0	0	.250	.250	R	R	6-4	260	1-20-80	1996	San Cristobal, D.R.
Grabowski, Jason	.000	8	8	0	0	0	0	0	0	1	5	0	0	.000	.111	L	R	6-3	200	5-24-76	1997	Clinton, Conn.
Guillen, Jose	.265	45	170	25	45	7	1	8	23	7	32	0	0	.459	.311	R	R	5-11	190	5-17-76	1993	San Cristobal, D.R.
Hatteberg, Scott	.253	147	541	63	137	34	0	12	61	66	53	0	1	.383	.342	L	R	6-1	210	12-14-69	1991	Salem, Ore.
Hernandez, Ramon	.273	140	483	70	132	24	1	21	78	33	79	0	0	.458	.331	R	R	6-0	210	5-20-76	1994	Aragua, Venez.
Johnson, Mark	.111	13	27	3	3	1	0	0	3	3	4	0	0	.148	.219	L	R	6-0	180	9-12-75	1994	Warner Robins, Ga.
Koonce, Graham	.125	6	8	0	1	1	0	0	0	0	6	0	0	.250	.125	L	L	6-4	220	5-15-75	1994	Julian, Calif.
Long, Terrence	.245	140	486	64	119	22	2	14	61	31	67	4	1	.385	.293	L	L	6-1	200	2-29-76	1994	Montgomery, Ala.
McCarty, David	.269	8	26	2	7	2	0	0	2	1	7	0	0	.346	.286	R	L	6-5	215	11-23-69	1991	Piedmont, Calif.
McMillon, Billy	.268	66	153	15	41	11	0	6	26	19	36	0	0	.458	.354	L	L	5-11	195	11-17-71	1993	Columbia, S.C.
Melhuse, Adam	.299	40	77	13	23	7	0	5	14	9	19	0	0	.584	.372	S	R	6-2	200	3-27-72	1993	San Luis Obispo, Calif.
Menechino, Frank	.193	43	83	10	16	0	0	2	9	19	16	0	0	.265	.364	R	R	5-8	190	1-7-71	1993	Staten Island, N.Y.
Piatt, Adam	.240	47	100	6	24	10	0	4	15	6	30	1	2	.460	.280	R	R	6-2	205	2-8-76	1997	Missouri City, Texas
Singleton, Chris	.245	120	306	38	75	24	1	1	36	26	55	7	2	.340	.301	L	L	6-2	215	8-15-72	1993	Atlanta, Ga.
Tejada, Miguel	.278	162	636	98	177	42	0	27	106	53	65	10	0	.472	.336	R	R	5-9	200	5-25-76	1994	Santo Domingo, D.R.

PITCHING	W	L	ERA	G	GS	CG	SV	IP	H	R	ER	BB	SO	AVG	B	T	HT	WT	DOB	1st Yr	Resides
Bowie, Micah	0	1	7.56	6	0	0	0	8	13	7	7	2	4	.361	L	L	6-4	205	11-10-74	1993	New Braunfels, Texas
Bradford, Chad	7	4	3.04	72	0	0	2	77	67	28	26	30	62	.235	R	R	6-5	205	9-14-74	1996	Raymond, Miss.
Duchscherer, Justin	1	1	3.31	4	3	0	0	16	17	7	6	3	15	.261	R	R	6-3	190	11-19-77	1996	Colleyville, Texas
Fikac, Jeremy	0	1	4.50	14	0	0	0	16	14	8	8	11	9	.245	R	R	6-2	180	4-8-75	1998	Shiner, Texas
Foulke, Keith	9	1	2.08	72	0	0	43	87	57	21	20	20	88	.184	R	R	6-0	210	10-19-72	1994	Huffman, Texas
Halama, John	3	5	4.22	35	13	0	0	109	117	68	51	36	51	.268	L	L	6-5	210	2-22-72	1994	Brooklyn, N.Y.
Harang, Aaron	1	3	5.34	7	6	0	0	30	41	19	18	9	16	.330	R	R	6-7	240	5-9-78	1999	San Diego, Calif.
Harden, Rich	5	4	4.46	15	13	0	0	75	72	38	37	40	67	.258	L	R	6-1	180	11-30-81	2001	Victoria, B.C.
Harville, Chad	1	0	5.82	21	0	0	1	22	25	15	14	17	18	.294	R	R	5-9	180	9-16-76	1997	Savannah, Tenn.
Hudson, Tim	16	7	2.70	34	34	3	0	240	197	84	72	61	162	.223	R	R	6-1	165	7-14-75	1997	Apollo Beach, Fla.
Lilly, Ted	12	10	4.34	32	31	0	0	178	179	92	86	58	147	.254	L	L	6-1	190	1-4-76	1996	Oakhurst, Calif.
Mecir, Jim	2	3	5.59	41	0	0	1	37	40	25	23	16	25	.279	S	R	6-1	230	5-16-70	1991	Kildeer, Ill.
Mulder, Mark	15	9	3.13	26	26	9	0	187	180	66	65	40	128	.258	L	L	6-6	210	8-5-77	1999	Scottsdale, Ariz.
Neu, Mike	0	0	3.64	32	0	0	1	42	43	18	17	26	20	.260	S	R	5-10	190	3-9-78	1999	Napa, Calif.
Rincon, Ricardo	8	4	3.25	64	0	0	0	55	45	21	20	32	40	.229	L	L	5-10	190	4-13-70	1997	Veracruz, Mexico
Sparks, Steve	0	0	5.71	9	0	0	0	17	19	11	11	3	5	.271	R	R	6-0	190	7-2-65	1987	Sugar Land, Texas
2-team (42 Detroit)	0	6	4.88	51	0	0	2	107	114	68	58	37	54	.276							
Wood, Mike	2	1	10.54	7	1	0	0	14	24	17	16	7	15	.387	R	R	6-3	180	4-26-80	2001	West Palm Beach, Fla.
Zito, Barry	14	12	3.30	35	35	4	0	232	186	98	85	88	146	.219	L	L	6-4	215	5-13-78	1999	Van Nuys, Calif.

FIELDING

Catcher	PCT	G	PO	A	E	DP	PB
Hernandez	.991	139	864	53	8	10	8
Johnson	1.000	13	65	4	0	0	0
Melhuse	.993	33	129	10	1	1	1

First Base	PCT	G	PO	A	E	DP
Durazo	.981	33	298	9	6	26
Hatteberg	.992	128	1177	81	10	101
Koonce	1.000	5	22	3	0	3
McCarty	.964	3	26	1	1	2
McMillon	1.000	3	5	0	0	0
Melhuse	1.000	1	2	0	0	0

Second Base	PCT	G	PO	A	E	DP
Ellis	.982	153	324	455	14	95
German	1.000	5	5	6	0	1
Menechino	.986	22	30	42	1	11

Third Base	PCT	G	PO	A	E	DP
Chavez	.971	154	125	343	14	33
Grabowski	.000	1	0	0	0	0
Melhuse	.500	2	0	1	1	0
Menechino	.931	19	6	21	2	2

Shortstop	PCT	G	PO	A	E	DP
Crosby	.889	9	5	11	2	2
Menechino	.667	3	1	1	1	1
Tejada	.972	162	240	490	21	95

Outfield	PCT	G	PO	A	E	DP
Byrnes	.991	117	212	5	2	1
Dye	1.000	61	106	1	0	0
Edwards	.000	2	0	0	0	0
Gant	1.000	9	9	0	0	0
Grabowski	1.000	3	3	0	0	0
Guillen	.942	44	65	0	4	0
Long	.984	137	239	3	4	0
McCarty	1.000	5	5	0	0	0
McMillon	.979	36	47	0	1	0
Piatt	.978	38	43	2	1	1
Singleton	.969	113	187	1	6	1

LARRY GOREN

Miguel Tejada

LARRY GOREN

Eric Chavez: Paced the A's in homers and doubles

LARRY GOREN

Graham Koonce: Led all minor leaguers with 34 homers

FARM SYSTEM

Director, Player Development: Keith Lieppman.

Class	Farm Team	League	W	L	Pct.	Finish*	Manager	First Yr.
AAA	Sacramento (Calif.) RiverCats	Pacific Coast	92	52	.639	+1st (16)	Tony DeFrancesco	2000
AA	Midland (Texas) RockHounds	Texas	69	70	.496	6th (8)	Greg Sparks	1999
High A	Modesto (Calif.) A's	California	74	66	.529	t-5th (10)	Rick Rodriguez	1975
Low A	Kane County (Geneva, Ill.) Cougars	Midwest	80	59	.576	1st (14)	Webster Garrison	2003
SS A	Vancouver (B.C.) Canadians	Northwest	35	41	.461	5th (8)	Dennis Rogers	2000
Rookie	Phoenix (Ariz.) Athletics	Arizona	15	33	.313	8th (9)	Ruben Escalera	1988

*Finish in overall standings (No. of teams in league)   +League champion

SACRAMENTO RIVERCATS — Class AAA

PACIFIC COAST LEAGUE

BATTING	AVG	G	AB	R	H	2B	3B	HR	RBI	BB	SO	SB	CS	SLG	OBP	B	T	HT	WT	DOB	1st Yr	Resides
Crosby, Bobby	.308	127	465	86	143	32	6	22	90	63	110	24	4	.544	.395	R	R	6-3	195	1-12-80	2001	Cypress, Calif.
Dye, Jermaine	.286	13	49	9	14	2	0	2	9	11	11	0	0	.449	.417	R	R	6-5	220	1-28-74	1993	Phoenix, Ariz.
Edwards, Mike	.298	125	436	78	130	23	4	14	95	60	78	5	2	.466	.387	R	R	6-1	185	11-24-76	1995	Mechanicsburg, Pa.
Flores, Jose	.273	107	370	72	101	12	2	2	38	62	48	16	2	.332	.377	R	R	5-11	180	6-28-73	1994	Corpus Christi, Texas
German, Esteban	.306	115	467	86	143	20	8	3	51	56	64	32	8	.403	.379	R	R	5-9	165	1-26-78	1996	Santo Domingo, D.R.
Grabowski, Jason	.292	67	250	44	73	13	2	9	40	31	46	7	2	.468	.364	L	R	6-3	200	5-24-76	1997	Clinton, Conn.
Johnson, Dan	.250	1	4	0	1	1	0	0	0	0	0	0	0	.500	.250	L	R	6-2	220	8-10-79	2001	Coon Rapids, Minn.
Johnson, Mark	.228	51	162	28	37	11	1	3	30	35	23	0	1	.364	.369	L	R	6-0	180	9-12-75	1994	Warner Robins, Ga.
Koonce, Graham	.277	138	480	82	133	23	1	34	115	98	119	0	0	.542	.403	L	L	6-4	220	5-15-75	1994	Julian, Calif.
Lockwood, Mike	.304	83	263	45	80	11	3	8	33	19	28	1	2	.460	.353	L	L	6-0	190	12-27-76	1999	Powell, Ohio
Lopez, Luis	.245	131	498	67	122	28	0	18	72	40	68	0	1	.410	.303	R	R	6-0	205	10-5-73	1996	Corpus Christi, Texas
McCarty, David	.270	91	352	69	95	23	2	15	72	44	71	4	1	.474	.351	R	L	6-5	215	11-23-69	1991	Piedmont, Calif.
McMillon, Billy	.333	38	153	31	51	10	0	8	35	17	30	1	1	.556	.401	L	L	5-11	195	11-17-71	1993	Columbia, S.C.
Melhuse, Adam	.286	45	147	26	42	9	0	3	17	26	32	0	1	.408	.394	S	R	6-2	200	3-27-72	1993	San Luis Obispo, Calif.
Meluskey, Mitch	.143	4	14	0	2	2	0	0	4	1	3	0	0	.286	.188	S	R	6-0	200	9-18-73	1992	Yakima, Wash.
Neufeld, Andy	.120	17	25	5	3	1	0	0	1	5	9	0	0	.160	.267	L	R	5-11	175	2-21-79	2001	Winter Springs, Fla.
Prieto, Chris	.282	111	390	70	110	12	7	4	54	48	40	5	3	.379	.366	L	L	5-11	180	8-24-72	1993	Fontana, Calif.
Rose, Mike	.262	70	221	44	58	10	1	8	30	44	50	2	1	.425	.390	S	R	6-1	185	8-25-76	1995	Elk Grove, Calif.
Rouse, Michael	.429	2	7	2	3	0	0	0	1	0	0	0	0	.429	.429	L	R	5-11	185	4-25-80	2001	San Jose, Calif.
Sellier, Brian	.211	30	90	15	19	3	0	0	10	13	15	0	1	.244	.305	L	R	6-0	200	1-12-78	2000	Phoenix, Ariz.

PITCHING	W	L	ERA	G	GS	CG	SV	IP	H	R	ER	BB	SO	AVG	B	T	HT	WT	DOB	1st Yr	Resides
Bowie, Micah	0	0	0.00	5	0	0	2	4	2	1	0	1	3	.133	L	L	6-4	205	11-10-74	1993	New Braunfels, Texas
Castillo, Frank	5	4	4.13	19	16	0	0	96	104	47	44	34	59	.279	R	R	6-1	200	4-1-69	1987	Cave Creek, Ariz.
Duchscherer, Justin	14	2	3.25	24	23	0	0	155	151	59	56	18	117	.254	R	R	6-3	190	11-19-77	1996	Colleyville, Texas
Enochs, Chris	6	3	5.23	37	4	0	0	62	76	40	36	30	49	.301	R	R	6-3	225	10-11-75	1997	Newell, W.Va.
Fikac, Jeremy	3	3	2.25	42	0	0	4	56	40	19	14	13	50	.197	R	R	6-2	180	4-8-75	1998	Shiner, Texas
Flores, Ron	2	0	6.59	12	0	0	0	14	16	10	10	3	10	.301	L	L	5-11	190	8-9-79	2000	Pico Rivera, Calif.

PITCHING	W	L	ERA	G	GS	CG	SV	IP	H	R	ER	BB	SO	AVG	B	T	HT	WT	DOB	1st Yr	Resides
Galva, Claudio	0	0	0.00	1	0	0	0	0	1	2	2	1	0	1.000	L	L	6-2	180	3-28-77	1996	Santo Domingo, D.R.
Harang, Aaron	8	2	2.71	12	12	0	0	70	62	24	21	17	60	.233	R	R	6-7	240	5-9-78	1999	San Diego, Calif.
Harden, Rich	9	4	3.15	16	14	0	0	89	72	34	31	35	91	.225	L	R	6-1	180	11-30-81	2001	Victoria, B.C.
Harville, Chad	3	5	2.05	48	0	0	18	57	42	16	13	21	57	.201	R	R	5-9	180	9-16-76	1997	Savannah, Tenn.
Hiljus, Erik	11	10	4.69	29	29	2	0	175	174	106	91	52	129	.254	R	R	6-6	220	12-25-72	1991	Northridge, Calif.
Kusiewicz, Mike	3	1	4.13	27	0	0	0	28	21	16	13	10	20	.203	R	L	6-2	185	11-1-76	1995	Nepean, Ontario
Lehr, Justin	3	2	3.72	53	0	0	4	75	74	34	31	27	64	.258	R	R	6-1	200	8-3-77	1999	West Covina, Calif.
Mecir, Jim	0	0	5.40	3	2	0	0	3	5	4	2	2	3	.312	S	R	6-1	230	5-16-70	1991	Kildeer, Ill.
O'Brien, Matt	1	0	4.82	10	0	0	0	9	10	5	5	6	2	.277	L	L	6-0	180	2-22-77	2000	Seattle, Wash.
Rheinecker, John	2	0	3.79	6	6	0	0	38	47	19	16	12	26	.303	L	L	6-2	215	5-29-79	2001	Waterloo, Ill.
Robertson, Luke	0	1	12.71	1	1	0	0	6	8	8	8	3	2	.320	R	R	6-4	220	6-30-79	2001	Valley Center, Kan.
Silva, Jose	1	2	5.04	7	5	0	0	25	32	18	14	9	18	.307	R	R	6-6	235	12-19-73	1991	Sarasota, Fla.
Smith, Roy	7	4	5.23	52	3	0	3	72	77	49	42	48	47	.270	R	R	6-6	230	5-18-76	1994	Pinellas Park, Fla.
Snow, Bert	1	0	5.28	12	0	0	0	15	18	9	9	4	5	.285	R	R	6-1	200	3-23-77	1998	Brooksville, Fla.
Thompson, Eric	0	0	6.23	3	0	0	0	4	2	3	3	3	3	.133	R	R	6-2	195	9-7-77	1998	Fairborn, Ohio
Valentine, Joe	1	3	4.82	40	0	0	4	52	44	33	28	37	53	.222	R	R	6-2	195	12-24-79	1999	Pensacola, Fla.
Wood, Mike	9	3	3.05	16	16	0	0	91	87	34	31	23	59	.256	R	R	6-3	180	4-26-80	2001	West Palm Beach, Fla.
Yarnall, Ed	3	3	3.76	18	13	0	0	65	72	28	27	30	46	.279	L	L	6-3	235	12-4-75	1997	Baton Rouge, La.

FIELDING

Catcher	PCT	G	PO	A	E	DP	PB
Grabowski	.958	7	45	1	2	0	1
Johnson	.992	50	343	27	3	0	9
Melhuse	.996	27	202	21	1	4	2
Rose	.982	63	404	35	8	0	3

First Base	PCT	G	PO	A	E	DP
Grabowski	1.000	3	26	1	0	0
Johnson	1.000	1	8	1	0	0
Koonce	.995	81	683	55	4	54
Lopez	1.000	1	10	0	0	0
McCarty	.993	62	510	42	4	42

Second Base	PCT	G	PO	A	E	DP
Flores	.966	27	56	84	5	14
German	.976	115	218	318	13	55
Neufeld	.969	10	11	20	1	4

Third Base	PCT	G	PO	A	E	DP
Edwards	.833	3	1	4	1	0
Flores	.800	12	2	14	4	2
Grabowski	1.000	1	1	4	0	0
Lopez	.959	129	72	212	12	12
Melhuse	1.000	3	2	4	0	0
Neufeld	1.000	2	0	2	0	1
Rouse	1.000	1	1	1	0	0

Shortstop	PCT	G	PO	A	E	DP
Crosby	.973	125	186	349	15	59
Edwards	1.000	2	3	3	0	0
Flores	.933	19	33	51	6	11
Lockwood	1.000	1	1	0	0	0
Neufeld	.900	4	6	3	1	1
Rouse	1.000	1	0	1	0	0

Outfield	PCT	G	PO	A	E	DP
Dye	1.000	6	13	0	0	0
Edwards	.989	98	177	2	2	0
Flores	.964	46	76	4	3	0
Grabowski	.964	49	78	2	3	1
Lockwood	.986	75	141	2	2	0
McCarty	1.000	10	18	0	0	0
McMillon	.966	36	55	1	2	1
Melhuse	.944	12	17	0	1	0
Meluskey	1.000	1	2	0	0	0
Prieto	1.000	105	253	7	0	3
Rose	.000	1	0	0	0	0
Sellier	1.000	23	44	1	0	0

MIDLAND ROCKHOUNDS — Class AA

TEXAS LEAGUE

BATTING	AVG	G	AB	R	H	2B	3B	HR	RBI	BB	SO	SB	CS	SLG	OBP	B	T	HT	WT	DOB	1st Yr	Resides
Allegra, Matt	.239	128	452	55	108	22	2	14	69	33	156	5	2	.389	.296	R	R	6-3	195	7-10-81	2000	Lake Mary, Fla.
Baker, John	.240	43	150	16	36	3	0	1	21	14	46	0	0	.280	.316	L	R	6-1	215	1-20-81	2002	Walnut Creek, Calif.
Brown, Jeremy	.275	66	233	37	64	10	1	5	37	41	38	3	0	.391	.388	R	R	5-10	210	10-25-79	2002	Hueytown, Ala.
Bynum, Freddie	.263	132	510	84	134	18	9	5	58	56	135	22	8	.363	.344	L	R	6-1	180	3-15-80	2000	Stantonsburg, N.C.
Campo, Mike	.263	100	304	45	80	10	2	5	38	34	71	7	4	.359	.362	L	R	5-10	185	11-14-76	2000	Absecon, N.J.
Craig, Beau	.000	2	6	0	0	0	0	0	0	0	3	0	0	.000	.000	S	R	5-10	170	2-12-79	2000	Santee, Calif.
Jackson, Steve	.266	81	274	36	73	13	2	9	48	27	73	1	1	.427	.339	R	R	6-5	235	12-13-77	2000	Yakima, Wash.
Johnson, Dan	.290	139	538	90	156	26	4	27	114	68	82	7	4	.504	.365	L	R	6-2	220	8-10-79	2001	Coon Rapids, Minn.
Lockwood, Mike	.247	28	93	11	23	8	0	1	7	15	17	0	1	.366	.345	L	L	6-0	190	12-27-76	1999	Powell, Ohio
Morrissey, Adam	.267	125	469	66	125	27	2	5	65	50	99	9	1	.365	.335	R	R	5-11	180	6-8-81	1999	Ourimbah, Australia
Rouse, Michael	.300	129	457	75	137	33	3	3	53	63	83	7	2	.405	.392	L	R	5-11	185	4-25-80	2001	San Jose, Calif.
Schneidmiller, Gary	.160	31	81	16	13	2	0	1	10	19	20	0	0	.222	.324	R	R	6-1	185	1-26-80	1998	Chino, Calif.
Sellier, Brian	.303	72	271	51	82	17	4	6	44	43	54	9	3	.461	.395	L	R	6-0	200	1-12-78	2000	Phoenix, Ariz.
Stanley, Steve	.296	124	479	68	142	10	3	0	39	56	65	13	7	.330	.370	L	L	5-8	155	12-23-79	2002	Columbus, Ohio
Stotts, J.T.	.307	46	176	24	54	8	0	0	14	18	41	4	2	.352	.377	R	R	5-11	185	1-21-80	2001	Valencia, Calif.
Swisher, Nick	.230	76	287	36	66	24	2	5	43	37	76	0	1	.380	.324	S	L	6-0	190	11-25-80	2002	Parkersburg, W.Va.

PITCHING	W	L	ERA	G	GS	CG	SV	IP	H	R	ER	BB	SO	AVG	B	T	HT	WT	DOB	1st Yr	Resides
Bazzell, Shane	3	6	4.61	34	1	0	1	57	57	36	29	25	42	.262	L	R	6-2	180	3-2-79	1998	Columbus, Miss.
Blanton, Joe	3	1	1.26	7	5	1	1	36	21	6	5	7	30	.173	R	R	6-3	225	12-11-80	2002	Bowling Green, Ky.
Cabaniel, Tomas	1	0	0.79	3	2	0	0	11	5	1	1	1	5	.142	R	R	6-1	165	2-10-83	2000	Caracas, Venez.
Crowell, Kyle	0	1	3.12	9	0	0	1	17	17	8	6	5	12	.269	R	R	6-0	190	6-16-79	2000	Webster, Texas
Cullen, Ryan	2	1	3.38	30	1	0	2	45	54	19	17	13	25	.303	L	L	6-2	170	1-20-80	1999	Satellite Beach, Fla.
Fischer, Steve	0	0	5.40	10	1	0	0	15	20	10	9	11	3	.338	R	R	6-0	200	6-20-78	2000	Benicia, Calif.
Flores, Ron	3	2	2.88	39	0	0	6	59	44	19	19	15	66	.203	L	L	5-11	190	8-9-79	2000	Pico Rivera, Calif.
Frick, Mike	1	2	5.05	28	0	0	0	36	47	22	20	9	21	.324	R	R	6-3	230	3-18-80	2001	Ventura, Calif.
Garcia, Sonny	3	5	6.79	10	10	0	0	50	76	44	38	20	26	.351	R	R	6-3	215	9-10-76	1998	Houston, Texas
Gwyn, Marc	1	1	5.00	9	0	0	0	9	9	5	5	2	12	.264	R	R	6-3	230	11-4-77	2000	The Woodlands, Texas
Harden, Rich	2	0	0.00	2	2	0	0	13	0	0	0	0	17	.000	L	R	6-1	180	11-30-81	2001	Victoria, B.C.
Hooten, Dave	7	8	4.43	39	14	0	0	112	122	59	55	32	76	.275	R	R	6-0	185	5-8-75	1996	Shreveport, La.
Komine, Shane	4	6	3.75	19	18	1	0	103	108	51	43	30	75	.270	R	R	5-9	175	10-18-80	2002	Honolulu, Hawaii
Krawczyk, Jack	0	2	10.66	9	0	0	0	13	22	16	15	6	9	.372	R	R	6-4	195	8-12-75	1998	Scottsdale, Ariz.
Kusiewicz, Mike	0	1	4.30	18	0	0	1	23	25	14	11	8	21	.263	R	L	6-2	185	11-1-76	1995	Nepean, Ontario
Mabeus, Chris	1	3	3.52	32	0	0	13	38	37	20	15	9	40	.255	R	R	6-3	210	2-11-79	2001	Soldotna, Alaska
Murphy, Bill	3	3	4.09	11	11	0	0	55	44	25	25	26	34	.220	L	L	6-0	190	5-9-81	2002	Riverside, Calif.
O'Brien, Matt	6	1	4.92	36	0	0	0	53	56	31	29	23	55	.275	L	L	6-0	180	2-22-77	2000	Seattle, Wash.
Rheinecker, John	9	6	4.74	23	23	1	0	142	186	90	75	32	89	.313	L	L	6-2	215	5-29-79	2001	Waterloo, Ill.
Snow, Bert	1	5	6.08	32	0	0	13	37	34	27	25	27	41	.239	R	R	6-1	200	3-23-77	1998	Brooksville, Fla.
Thompson, Eric	0	3	8.36	5	5	0	0	14	17	14	13	12	8	.303	R	R	6-2	195	9-7-77	1998	Fairborn, Ohio
Withers, Darvin	7	4	5.45	23	22	1	0	119	160	83	72	34	69	.321	R	R	6-2	190	5-31-80	2000	Aiken, S.C.
Ziegler, Mike	12	9	4.04	27	25	2	0	165	185	81	74	29	105	.285	R	R	6-3	220	7-25-79	2000	Glen Burnie, Md.

FIELDING

Catcher	PCT	G	PO	A	E	DP	PB
Baker	.997	42	275	17	1	2	3
Brown	.983	63	388	28	7	3	6
Craig	.929	2	11	2	1	0	0
Jackson	.980	37	224	19	5	1	2

First Base	PCT	G	PO	A	E	DP
Allegra	1.000	1	1	0	0	0
Jackson	.993	31	274	26	2	24
Johnson	.992	111	952	100	8	94
Lockwood	1.000	2	1	0	0	1
Morrissey	1.000	1	4	0	0	1
Schneidmiller	1.000	1	2	0	0	0
Swisher	1.000	2	13	0	0	3

Second Base	PCT	G	PO	A	E	DP
Bynum	.954	116	249	367	30	75
Morrissey	.922	20	31	52	7	11
Stotts	.964	13	18	35	2	9

Third Base	PCT	G	PO	A	E	DP
Allegra	.833	5	2	3	1	0
Bynum	1.000	2	0	2	0	0
Morrissey	.929	105	62	211	21	12
Schneidmiller	.926	26	15	35	4	3
Stotts	.947	11	5	13	1	1

Shortstop	PCT	G	PO	A	E	DP
Bynum	.917	8	11	22	3	6
Morrissey	1.000	1	0	1	0	0
Rouse	.967	122	179	374	19	81
Stotts	.983	13	17	41	1	9

Outfield	PCT	G	PO	A	E	DP
Allegra	.951	123	210	22	12	3
Campo	1.000	50	77	3	0	1
Johnson	.000	1	0	0	0	0
Lockwood	1.000	22	37	4	0	2
Morrissey	.000	1	0	0	0	0
Sellier	1.000	59	88	1	0	0
Stanley	.985	117	254	13	4	1
Swisher	.969	65	154	3	5	0

MODESTO A's — High Class A

CALIFORNIA LEAGUE

BATTING	AVG	G	AB	R	H	2B	3B	HR	RBI	BB	SO	SB	CS	SLG	OBP	B	T	HT	WT	DOB	1st Yr	Resides
Bowser, Matt	.294	112	429	60	126	29	5	7	57	57	83	1	1	.434	.382	L	L	6-3	205	3-8-79	2000	Palm Harbor, Fla.
Christy, Jeff	.248	79	282	48	70	12	3	1	24	48	50	9	3	.323	.362	L	R	5-9	180	10-3-79	2001	Tampa, Fla.
Craig, Beau	.375	4	16	4	6	2	0	0	1	1	5	0	0	.500	.412	S	R	5-10	170	2-12-79	2000	Santee, Calif.
Garcia, Isaac	.241	84	307	36	74	10	1	4	41	24	80	3	1	.319	.292	R	R	6-1	165	11-6-78	1998	Las Matos, D.R.
Harriman, David	.244	33	119	14	29	3	0	2	12	6	26	0	0	.319	.278	R	R	6-0	200	10-15-80	2002	Surrey, B.C.
Kiger, Mark	.281	131	526	95	148	38	3	8	73	77	106	3	0	.411	.375	R	R	5-11	180	5-30-80	2002	San Diego, Calif.
McBeth, Marcus	.130	15	54	7	7	0	0	0	5	5	20	2	0	.130	.210	R	R	6-1	185	8-23-80	2001	Enoree, S.C.
Morris, Jed	.281	101	367	57	103	26	1	13	75	47	58	1	0	.463	.366	L	R	5-11	185	3-4-80	2002	Ripon, Calif.
Myers, Casey	.301	45	166	21	50	5	0	1	25	16	18	0	0	.349	.376	R	R	5-11	210	10-23-78	2001	Phoenix, Ariz.
Neufeld, Andy	.234	63	218	38	51	13	1	4	30	30	50	4	1	.358	.337	L	R	5-11	175	2-21-79	2001	Winter Springs, Fla.
Perry, Jason	.305	50	190	28	58	9	1	4	26	21	46	0	1	.426	.393	L	R	6-0	200	8-18-80	2002	Jonesboro, Ga.
Quintanilla, Omar	.417	8	36	9	15	3	0	2	6	3	6	0	0	.667	.462	L	R	5-9	190	10-24-81	2003	El Paso, Texas
Saenz, Olmedo	.000	1	4	0	0	0	0	0	1	0	1	0	0	.000	.200	R	R	5-11	220	10-8-70	1990	Chitre Herrera, Panama
Schneidmiller, Gary	.254	60	205	31	52	14	1	1	25	24	38	4	0	.346	.336	R	R	6-1	185	1-26-80	1998	Chino, Calif.
Soto, Jorge	.147	35	116	12	17	4	0	3	8	11	56	0	0	.259	.237	R	R	6-0	210	4-14-78	1999	Patillas, P.R.
Stotts, J.T.	.284	75	292	34	83	16	1	2	37	31	37	11	4	.366	.363	R	R	5-11	185	1-21-80	2001	Valencia, Calif.
Swisher, Nick	.296	51	189	38	56	14	2	10	43	41	49	0	2	.550	.418	S	L	6-0	190	11-25-80	2002	Parkersburg, W.Va.
Teahen, Mark	.283	121	453	68	128	27	4	3	71	66	113	4	0	.380	.377	L	R	6-3	210	9-6-81	2002	Yucaipa, Calif.
Thomas, Gary	.303	117	498	95	151	30	3	12	68	41	83	22	7	.448	.374	R	R	5-7	175	9-6-79	1997	Houma, La.
Tritle, Chris	.203	42	153	16	31	6	0	3	16	11	47	2	0	.301	.265	R	R	6-3	195	6-22-82	2000	Center Point, Iowa
Turner, Lloyd	.231	30	104	20	24	2	0	0	5	12	9	0	1	.250	.339	R	R	6-1	180	4-11-80	2002	Hephzibah, Ga.
Weber, Jon	.361	35	147	28	53	10	4	7	38	9	26	2	0	.626	.394	L	L	5-11	180	1-20-78	1999	Lakewood, Calif.

PITCHING	W	L	ERA	G	GS	CG	SV	IP	H	R	ER	BB	SO	AVG	B	T	HT	WT	DOB	1st Yr	Resides
Avendano, Elvis	2	2	5.19	6	3	0	0	26	37	25	15	9	20	.316	R	R	6-1	165	2-8-83	1999	El Guayabo, Venez.
Bazzell, Shane	1	0	2.79	9	0	0	1	19	17	7	6	4	23	.226	L	R	6-2	180	3-2-79	1998	Columbus, Miss.
Bowie, Micah	0	0	0.00	2	2	0	0	2	0	0	0	0	3	.000	L	L	6-4	205	11-10-74	1993	New Braunfels, Texas
Bruksch, Jeff	10	8	5.13	23	23	0	0	126	144	84	72	54	87	.292	R	R	6-4	215	4-29-80	2002	Los Angeles, Calif.
Coleman, Jeff	2	2	5.00	37	0	0	5	67	72	40	37	26	86	.268	R	R	5-11	190	10-6-80	2001	San Dimas, Calif.
Crowell, Kyle	2	2	1.93	30	0	0	4	61	46	16	13	19	61	.209	R	R	6-0	190	6-16-79	2000	Webster, Texas
Cullen, Ryan	1	0	2.83	15	0	0	3	29	21	10	9	11	24	.198	L	L	6-2	170	1-20-80	1999	Satellite Beach, Fla.
Fischer, Steve	7	5	3.39	24	13	0	5	98	109	47	37	24	73	.275	R	R	6-0	200	6-20-78	2000	Benicia, Calif.
France, Ryan	0	0	18.00	1	0	0	0	2	6	4	4	2	0	.500	R	R	6-2	205	1-21-79	2003	Norco, Calif.
Fritz, Ben	4	7	4.91	15	15	0	0	77	83	49	42	34	77	.277	R	R	6-4	225	3-29-81	2002	Clovis, Calif.
Gonzalez, Cristian	5	2	3.29	8	7	0	0	52	37	27	19	15	26	.191	R	R	6-0	190	6-17-77	1996	Santo Domingo, D.R.
Gwyn, Marc	1	1	3.18	32	1	0	7	51	46	20	18	24	61	.248	R	R	6-3	230	11-4-77	2000	The Woodlands, Texas
Mabeus, Chris	2	0	1.52	18	0	0	2	24	19	6	4	6	30	.206	R	R	6-3	210	2-11-79	2001	Soldotna, Alaska
McCall, Derell	3	12	5.87	19	19	0	0	103	127	80	67	46	64	.299	R	R	6-3	205	9-22-81	2000	Cantonment, Fla.
Mowday, Chris	2	1	8.00	9	0	0	0	9	13	8	8	5	18	.325	R	R	6-4	210	8-24-81	1997	Strathpine, Australia
Obenchain, Stephen	3	4	5.15	9	9	0	0	44	56	36	25	20	19	.309	R	R	6-5	210	7-29-81	2002	Henderson, Ky.
Price, Brett	2	1	2.98	41	0	0	1	54	41	25	18	38	64	.205	L	L	5-10	165	12-7-79	2001	Leesville, S.C.
Robertson, Luke	7	7	6.39	29	17	0	0	120	167	104	85	33	83	.321	R	R	6-4	220	6-30-79	2001	Valley Center, Kan.
Sanchez, Adiel	0	0	4.50	4	0	0	0	4	4	2	2	1	2	.266	L	L	6-1	165	8-27-82	2000	Santo Domingo, D.R.
Sauer, Marc	4	3	3.94	22	7	1	2	75	86	43	33	15	58	.286	R	R	6-2	190	6-30-80	1999	Gloucester, N.J.
Shank, Chris	1	2	4.14	26	0	0	3	41	49	21	19	12	43	.298	R	R	6-2	185	1-31-81	2002	Westminster, Mass.
Weis, Brad	15	7	2.82	30	24	3	0	160	132	66	50	60	145	.224	L	L	5-11	180	11-29-77	1999	Winter Park, Fla.

FIELDING

Catcher	PCT	G	PO	A	E	DP	PB
Craig	.964	4	21	6	1	0	0
Harriman	.985	33	248	16	4	1	7
Morris	.984	74	580	51	10	2	22
Myers	.968	17	118	3	4	1	1
Soto	.979	18	130	9	3	1	5

First Base	PCT	G	PO	A	E	DP
Bowser	.980	94	713	56	16	43
Garcia	1.000	2	16	2	0	0
Myers	.971	13	92	7	3	5
Schneidmiller	.972	18	128	9	4	13
Soto	1.000	16	106	5	0	14
Swisher	1.000	3	19	2	0	4

Second Base	PCT	G	PO	A	E	DP
Garcia	.960	34	51	94	6	13
Kiger	.958	75	170	197	16	38
Neufeld	.915	19	36	50	8	11
Stotts	1.000	2	2	2	0	1
Turner	.938	10	23	22	3	3

Third Base	PCT	G	PO	A	E	DP
Garcia	.922	20	16	31	4	4
Kiger	1.000	2	0	3	0	0
Neufeld	.786	5	1	10	3	2
Teahen	.931	116	100	197	22	11

Shortstop	PCT	G	PO	A	E	DP
Garcia	.926	17	29	46	6	10
Kiger	.968	48	85	124	7	24
Quintanilla	.902	8	15	22	4	5
Stotts	.916	68	88	162	23	21

Outfield	PCT	G	PO	A	E	DP
Bowser	.900	7	9	0	1	0
Christy	.983	79	170	4	3	0
McBeth	.973	15	35	1	1	0
Neufeld	1.000	7	14	0	0	0
Perry	.942	38	60	5	4	0
Schneidmiller	.960	36	47	1	2	1
Swisher	.964	43	104	2	4	0
Thomas	.969	112	274	8	9	2
Tritle	.947	38	89	1	5	0
Turner	.935	18	24	5	2	0
Weber	1.000	35	61	2	0	0

KANE COUNTY COUGARS — Low Class A

MIDWEST LEAGUE

BATTING	AVG	G	AB	R	H	2B	3B	HR	RBI	BB	SO	SB	CS	SLG	OBP	B	T	HT	WT	DOB	1st Yr	Resides
Baker, John	.309	82	304	42	94	23	2	6	49	47	77	1	0	.457	.414	L	R	6-1	215	1-20-81	2002	Walnut Creek, Calif.
Basil, Jason	.242	105	343	37	83	13	1	3	36	50	64	4	1	.312	.343	R	R	6-3	225	8-5-78	2001	Cincinnati, Ohio
Colamarino, Brant	.259	133	498	68	129	26	0	19	80	59	101	1	0	.426	.350	L	L	5-11	205	12-4-80	2002	Pittsburgh, Pa.
Craig, Beau	.211	25	76	9	16	2	0	2	11	16	21	0	0	.316	.348	S	R	5-10	170	2-12-79	2000	Santee, Calif.
Cruz, Nelson	.238	119	470	65	112	26	2	20	85	29	128	10	5	.430	.292	R	R	6-3	175	7-1-80	1998	Montecristi, D.R.
Ethier, Andre	.272	40	162	23	44	10	0	0	11	19	25	2	2	.333	.355	L	L	6-3	195	4-10-82	2003	Phoenix, Ariz.
Gomez, Francis	.265	128	483	65	128	18	3	5	53	29	74	21	9	.346	.323	R	R	6-1	165	9-2-81	1999	La Romana, D.R.
Majewski, Dustin	.167	4	18	2	3	1	0	0	2	1	9	0	0	.222	.211	L	L	5-11	190	8-16-81	2003	Brenham, Texas
McBeth, Marcus	.256	68	234	30	60	9	3	4	26	28	57	8	4	.372	.349	R	R	6-1	185	8-23-80	2001	Enoree, S.C.
McCurdy, John	.274	130	515	64	141	33	1	4	52	34	86	22	5	.365	.331	R	R	6-2	195	4-17-81	2002	Crofton, Md.
Nordness, Kirk	.217	38	129	17	28	6	0	0	15	12	25	1	1	.264	.285	R	R	6-0	200	12-20-79	2002	Beaverton, Ore.
Rogers, Nick	.241	89	307	42	74	12	1	5	34	34	82	15	12	.336	.318	R	R	6-1	210	12-12-79	2002	Ponte Vedra Beach, Fla.
Schmidt, J.P.	.153	44	137	21	21	5	0	0	11	17	32	8	0	.190	.250	L	R	6-1	160	1-4-80	1998	Palmdale, Calif.
Stavisky, Brian	.266	98	331	54	88	20	2	6	35	62	74	4	1	.393	.396	L	R	6-3	230	7-6-80	2002	Port Allegheny, Pa.
Suomi, John	.257	69	241	29	62	19	1	1	28	14	34	4	2	.357	.298	L	R	5-11	180	10-5-80	2000	Toronto, Ontario
Tritle, Chris	.174	42	132	11	23	2	1	1	10	6	48	6	2	.227	.209	R	R	6-3	195	6-22-82	2000	Center Point, Iowa
Turner, Lloyd	.333	4	12	2	4	0	0	0	1	0	0	0	0	.333	.333	R	R	6-1	180	4-11-80	2002	Hephzibah, Ga.
Wayment, Kory	.247	115	316	55	78	6	0	5	30	47	92	16	7	.313	.350	R	R	6-1	165	2-18-81	2001	Ogden, Utah

PITCHING	W	L	ERA	G	GS	CG	SV	IP	H	R	ER	BB	SO	AVG	B	T	HT	WT	DOB	1st Yr	Resides
Blanton, Joe	8	7	2.57	21	21	2	0	133	110	47	38	19	144	.219	R	R	6-3	225	12-11-80	2002	Bowling Green, Ky.
Burton, Jared	2	1	2.27	15	2	0	1	32	19	9	8	7	33	.174	R	R	6-5	220	6-2-81	2002	Westminster, S.C.
Dickinson, Drew	11	11	3.15	28	28	5	0	191	168	75	67	42	114	.236	L	L	6-2	170	12-13-79	2002	Freeport, Ill.
Dunwell, Chris	4	0	3.21	30	0	0	2	53	44	23	19	21	53	.220	R	R	6-1	200	1-29-80	2002	El Cajon, Calif.
Garcia, Jairo	0	1	2.55	14	9	0	0	42	40	14	12	19	28	.250	R	R	6-0	165	3-7-83	2000	Juan Baron, D.R.
Gonzalez, Cristian	7	8	4.47	19	14	3	0	93	99	51	46	26	52	.275	R	R	6-0	190	6-17-77	1996	Santo Domingo, D.R.
Kohn, Shawn	6	4	2.54	45	4	0	2	89	71	27	25	15	69	.217	R	R	6-2	200	1-28-80	2002	Snohomish, Wash.
Komine, Shane	6	0	1.82	8	8	1	0	54	45	12	11	9	50	.222	R	R	5-9	175	10-18-80	2002	Honolulu, Hawaii
Landeros, Leonard	1	0	1.48	15	0	0	0	24	25	7	4	4	12	.268	L	L	6-3	170	12-12-80	2001	Hanford, Calif.
Leon, Brigmer	2	1	3.82	30	5	0	2	64	71	31	27	20	44	.282	R	R	6-3	165	4-7-81	1997	Cumana, Venez.
Lynch, Matt	4	4	4.53	13	11	0	0	60	84	33	30	11	43	.340	L	L	6-1	195	1-14-81	2003	Fort Pierce, Fla.
McCall, Derell	3	1	2.66	8	7	1	1	47	47	18	14	7	24	.250	R	R	6-3	205	9-22-81	2000	Cantonment, Fla.
Mowday, Chris	4	3	6.49	21	8	0	0	51	60	45	37	42	48	.289	R	R	6-4	210	8-24-81	1997	Strathpine, Australia
Muessig, Jeff	0	1	2.60	22	0	0	10	28	26	9	8	8	37	.242	R	R	6-2	185	2-27-82	2001	Mt. Sinai, N.Y.
Murphy, Bill	7	4	2.25	14	14	1	0	92	61	27	23	32	87	.188	L	L	6-0	190	5-9-81	2002	Riverside, Calif.
Obenchain, Stephen	3	5	2.57	11	8	0	0	49	48	16	14	13	30	.255	R	R	6-5	210	7-29-81	2002	Henderson, Ky.
Rodriguez, Manuel	3	3	7.42	33	0	0	0	44	56	41	36	20	22	.301	R	R	6-2	165	5-2-81	1999	Estrin, Venez.
Shank, Chris	5	0	2.86	12	0	0	0	22	15	7	7	2	15	.200	R	R	6-2	185	1-31-81	2002	Westminster, Mass.
Sierra, Edwardo	3	5	2.09	51	0	0	17	60	46	23	14	24	52	.204	R	R	6-3	185	4-15-82	1999	San Cristobal, D.R.
Sullivan, Brad	1	0	3.18	6	0	0	0	11	9	4	4	7	9	.225	R	R	6-0	195	9-12-81	2003	Nederland, Texas

FIELDING

Catcher	PCT	G	PO	A	E	DP	PB
Baker	.985	60	417	30	7	2	4
Basil	1.000	12	78	15	0	0	3
Craig	.985	18	117	12	2	1	1
Rogers	.000	1	0	0	0	0	0
Suomi	.982	55	354	34	7	1	8

First Base	PCT	G	PO	A	E	DP
Basil	1.000	11	73	6	0	3
Colamarino	.991	133	1184	66	11	74
Suomi	1.000	1	2	0	0	0

Second Base	PCT	G	PO	A	E	DP
Gomez	.977	118	237	354	14	44
Schmidt	.889	3	3	5	1	0
Turner	.857	2	3	3	1	1
Wayment	.965	25	49	61	4	9

Third Base	PCT	G	PO	A	E	DP
Basil	.895	73	46	99	17	4
Schmidt	.875	5	2	5	1	0
Turner	.000	1	0	0	0	0
Wayment	.936	90	45	144	13	6

Shortstop	PCT	G	PO	A	E	DP
Gomez	.941	9	12	20	2	4
McCurdy	.950	130	182	371	29	59

Outfield	PCT	G	PO	A	E	DP
Basil	.933	8	13	1	1	1
Cruz	.979	119	271	8	6	1
Ethier	.973	40	109	0	3	0
Majewski	.875	4	7	0	1	0
McBeth	.986	67	141	2	2	2
Nordness	.960	33	46	2	2	0
Rogers	.977	77	128	2	3	0
Schmidt	.949	33	55	1	3	0
Stavisky	.958	16	22	1	1	0
Tritle	.959	36	70	1	3	0

VANCOUVER CANADIANS — Short-Season Class A

NORTHWEST LEAGUE

BATTING	AVG	G	AB	R	H	2B	3B	HR	RBI	BB	SO	SB	CS	SLG	OBP	B	T	HT	WT	DOB	1st Yr	Resides
Appert, Luke	.193	58	192	25	37	4	0	1	16	49	29	3	7	.229	.359	L	R	6-0	185	7-14-80	2003	Cottage Grove, Minn.
Bubalo, Ty	.261	7	23	3	6	2	1	0	1	2	8	0	0	.435	.320	R	R	6-3	205	8-8-83	2002	Beaverton, Ore.
Castillo, David	.257	51	144	25	37	9	0	1	14	29	14	0	2	.340	.379	R	R	5-9	185	9-15-81	2003	Corpus Christi, Texas
Corder, Gordon	.244	44	135	14	33	7	0	3	14	11	24	0	0	.363	.331	R	R	6-2	240	12-2-80	2003	Moses Lake, Wash.
Cornejo, Eduardo	.227	41	141	15	32	8	1	0	16	19	13	4	4	.298	.319	L	R	5-10	175	11-19-81	2003	Mira Loma, Calif.
Ethier, Andre	.390	10	41	7	16	4	1	1	7	3	3	2	1	.610	.444	L	L	6-3	195	4-10-82	2003	Phoenix, Ariz.
Farrell, Sean	.223	59	215	24	48	17	0	1	28	28	55	3	1	.316	.319	R	R	5-11	205	4-3-81	2003	Charlotte, N.C.
Francois, Francisco	.261	47	134	21	35	2	0	1	16	12	29	4	2	.299	.340	R	R	6-1	155	11-30-82	2000	La Romana, D.R.
Gibbons, Danny	.240	63	221	28	53	13	0	3	27	19	51	2	0	.339	.306	L	R	6-3	205	10-21-80	2002	Toronto, Ontario
Harriman, David	.170	19	47	3	8	0	0	0	1	7	15	0	0	.170	.291	R	R	6-0	200	10-15-80	2002	Surrey, B.C.
Ingram, Brian	.221	43	104	15	23	5	1	0	13	18	28	0	1	.288	.336	L	R	5-10	175	3-29-81	2003	Rural Hall, N.C.
Kim, Eddie	.305	65	239	26	73	17	0	4	39	35	52	1	0	.427	.394	L	R	6-3	260	4-16-81	2003	Fairfax, Va.
Klippenstein, Tyler	.364	4	11	1	4	0	0	1	1	1	2	0	0	.636	.417	R	R	6-4	210	4-11-81	2002	Okotoks, Alberta
Majewski, Dustin	.291	46	175	33	51	13	2	3	19	28	35	6	5	.440	.390	L	L	5-11	190	8-16-81	2003	Brenham, Texas
Mejia, Jorge	.150	7	20	1	3	0	0	0	1	2	11	1	1	.150	.261	R	R	6-1	165	8-15-82	1999	Santo Domingo, D.R.
Nordness, Kirk	.105	12	38	1	4	1	0	1	4	3	8	0	0	.211	.190	R	R	6-0	200	12-20-79	2002	Beaverton, Ore.
Perez, Luis	.273	66	245	31	67	14	3	1	24	23	30	11	5	.367	.344	R	R	6-0	160	8-17-83	2000	Los Teques, Venez.
Quintanilla, Omar	.341	32	129	22	44	5	4	0	14	12	20	7	1	.442	.401	L	R	5-9	190	10-24-81	2003	El Paso, Texas
Ramirez, Juan	.185	10	27	2	5	2	0	0	3	1	6	0	0	.259	.214	R	R	5-11	185	9-16-83	2001	Monte Plata, D.R.

BATTING	AVG	G	AB	R	H	2B	3B	HR	RBI	BB	SO	SB	CS	SLG	OBP	B	T	HT	WT	DOB	1st Yr	Resides
Snyder, Brian	.253	44	146	14	37	6	0	1	17	39	36	9	2	.315	.409	R	R	6-0	195	3-17-82	2003	Wellington, Fla.
Sutton, Don	.302	13	43	4	13	3	0	0	7	2	16	0	0	.372	.348	R	R	6-1	220	11-21-83	2003	No. Las Vegas, Nev.
Turner, Lloyd	.301	23	83	11	25	4	1	0	12	4	20	1	1	.373	.344	R	R	6-1	180	4-11-80	2002	Hephzibah, Ga.

GAMES BY POSITION: C—Bubalo 3, Castillo 50, Corder 7, Harriman 19, Ramirez 10. **1B**—Appert 1, Corder 25, Cornejo 2, Kim 48, Klippenstein 2, Sutton 1, Turner 3. **2B**—Appert 51, Cornejo 9, Francois 11, Ingram 12, Mejia 2. **3B**—Cornejo 19, Francois 11, Ingram 5, Mejia 1, Perez 1, Snyder 36, Turner 14. **SS**—Cornejo 15, Francois 20, Ingram 19, Mejia 2, Quintanilla 29. **OF**—Ethier 10, Farrell 38, Francois 5, Gibbons 55, Ingram 1, Majewski 45, Mejia 1, Nordness 12, Perez 60, Turner 8.

PITCHING	W	L	ERA	G	GS	CG	SV	IP	H	R	ER	BB	SO	AVG	B	T	HT	WT	DOB	1st Yr	Resides
Barnett, Danny	0	0	5.06	15	0	0	0	21	28	20	12	14	14	.311	R	R	6-1	190	1-22-83	2002	Kearns, Utah
Bondurant, Steven	0	4	3.53	14	8	0	2	59	51	30	23	20	54	.226	L	L	6-0	185	3-3-80	2003	Matthews, N.C.
Burris, Robert	1	3	1.89	15	0	0	1	33	24	12	7	12	47	.196	R	R	6-1	175	11-17-79	2003	Jacksonville, Fla.
Corchado, Jose	0	1	5.93	19	2	0	2	44	49	36	29	16	50	.267	R	R	6-0	195	4-5-84	2002	Isabela, P.R.
Fyvie, Dan	4	2	2.45	26	0	0	4	40	33	15	11	17	35	.218	R	R	6-1	200	8-12-82	2002	Flint, Mich.
Howay, Chris	2	2	5.32	19	0	0	2	44	55	31	26	20	37	.297	R	R	6-3	210	8-17-79	2001	New Westminster, B.C.
Knox, Brad	6	3	2.06	15	12	0	0	70	55	21	16	18	63	.208	R	R	6-3	210	5-27-82	2002	Houston, Texas
Landeros, Leonard	0	2	9.64	8	0	0	1	9	13	11	10	2	11	.325	L	L	6-3	170	12-12-80	2001	Hanford, Calif.
McGirr, Mike	7	5	4.40	16	16	0	0	76	86	44	37	21	58	.285	R	R	6-0	180	3-9-81	2003	Lexington, Mass.
Peterson, John	3	4	3.25	14	9	0	1	61	64	26	22	15	55	.264	R	L	6-1	180	11-16-81	2003	Tallahassee, Fla.
Pickens, J.R.	6	2	3.07	23	4	0	5	44	40	19	15	14	40	.238	L	R	6-1	210	6-22-80	2002	Liberty, Texas
Reynolds, Grant	1	3	5.47	11	4	0	0	26	28	18	16	15	23	.269	R	R	5-10	185	2-2-80	2003	Wentworthville, Australia
Schilsky, Stephen	0	2	7.43	16	0	0	0	27	40	24	22	17	23	.336	R	R	6-2	215	1-3-81	2002	Springfield, Ill.
Trout, Jared	4	4	3.50	16	13	0	0	80	87	39	31	24	49	.282	R	R	6-0	175	1-15-82	2003	Gilbertsville, Pa.
Zambotti, Anthony	1	4	5.89	10	8	0	0	37	37	27	24	15	26	.262	R	R	6-1	200	9-11-80	2003	Shelocta, Pa.

PHOENIX ATHLETICS — Rookie

ARIZONA LEAGUE

BATTING	AVG	G	AB	R	H	2B	3B	HR	RBI	BB	SO	SB	CS	SLG	OBP	B	T	HT	WT	DOB	1st Yr	Resides
Acosta, Jesse	.242	46	178	28	43	4	0	0	15	23	33	2	0	.264	.328	R	R	5-9	185	11-19-80	2003	Kerman, Calif.
Arias, Roberto	.242	12	33	8	8	1	1	0	1	9	9	0	0	.333	.405	R	R	6-1	170	1-2-83	2002	San Jose de Ocoa, D.R.
Beauregard, Joshua	.282	48	177	32	50	10	3	2	30	20	26	4	3	.407	.358	L	L	6-0	195	3-7-81	2003	Deltona, Fla.
Bubalo, Ty	.250	8	32	4	8	1	1	2	9	3	9	0	0	.531	.314	R	R	6-3	205	8-8-83	2002	Beaverton, Ore.
Garcia, Jose	.291	44	151	37	44	11	5	2	31	29	40	2	0	.470	.424	R	R	6-3	190	9-23-82	2001	Santo Domingo, D.R.
Grabowski, Jason	.333	2	6	1	2	1	0	0	1	3	0	0	0	.500	.556	L	R	6-3	200	5-24-76	1997	Clinton, Conn.
Herrera, Javier	.230	17	61	12	14	3	1	2	13	7	19	3	1	.410	.329	R	R	5-10	160	4-9-85	2001	Caracas, Venez.
Klippenstein, Tyler	.239	42	163	17	39	8	1	0	26	11	37	0	2	.301	.291	R	R	6-4	210	4-11-81	2002	Okotoks, AB, Canada
Macha, Eric	.162	43	148	18	24	1	0	0	9	14	28	0	1	.169	.251	R	R	6-4	210	1-22-81	2003	Export, Penn.
Maldonado, Pedro	.221	25	77	8	17	1	0	1	11	6	26	2	3	.273	.291	R	R	6-0	180	11-2-84	2002	Santo Domingo, D.R.
Mejia, Jorge	.377	50	223	48	84	17	6	7	30	15	46	7	9	.601	.409	R	R	6-1	165	8-15-82	1999	Santo Domingo, D.R.
Ogando, Alexi	.342	48	190	33	65	13	1	7	36	7	42	5	6	.532	.379	R	R	6-4	160	10-5-83	2002	San Pedro de Macoris, D.R.
Petit, Gregorio	.265	32	117	13	31	6	0	0	12	10	22	3	5	.316	.323	R	R	5-10	160	12-10-84	2001	Santa Teresa, Venez.
Ramirez, Juan	.256	29	90	13	23	6	0	4	12	8	21	0	0	.456	.333	R	R	5-11	185	9-16-83	2001	Monte Plata, D.R.
Saenz, Olmedo	.333	13	45	13	15	2	0	2	8	8	6	1	0	.511	.455	R	R	5-11	220	10-8-70	1990	Chitre Herrera, Panama
Spanos, Vasili	.278	5	18	3	5	0	0	0	2	1	2	1	1	.278	.350	R	R	6-1	225	2-25-81	2003	River Forest, Ill.
Sutton, Don	.333	40	156	33	52	16	0	7	35	18	31	1	1	.571	.408	R	R	6-1	220	11-21-83	2003	North Las Vegas, Nevada
Winslow, Ben	.280	27	75	12	21	3	0	3	9	9	17	1	0	.440	.360	R	R	6-2	192	10-16-79	2003	Prescott, Ariz.

GAMES BY POSITION: C—Arias 12, Bubalo 2, Maldonado 14, Ramirez 27, Sutton 8. **1B**—Bubalo 1, Klippenstein 14, Macha 10, Maldonado 1, Ramirez 2, Saenz 5, Sutton 30. **2B**—Acosta 5, Mejia 48, Petit 3, Winslow 4. **3B**—Acosta 9, Macha 23, Perez 1, Petit 5, Saenz 4, Spanos 4, Winslow 19. **SS**—Acosta 35, Petit 22, Winslow 2. **OF**—Beauregard 47, Bubalo 5, Garcia 41, Herrera 16, Klippenstein 16, Ogando 47, Winslow 2.

PITCHING	W	L	ERA	G	GS	CG	SV	IP	H	R	ER	BB	SO	AVG	B	T	HT	WT	DOB	1st Yr	Resides
Acevedo, Danielin	0	5	5.94	10	8	0	0	36	46	36	24	20	22	.312	R	R	6-3	170	4-2-83	2001	Puerto Plata, D.R.
Avendano, Elvis	1	3	5.45	7	6	0	1	33	44	25	20	5	33	.328	R	R	6-1	165	2-8-83	1999	El Guayabo, Venez.
Bost, Heath	0	0	9.00	1	0	0	0	1	3	1	1	0	1	.600	R	R	6-3	205	10-13-74	1995	Taylorsville, N.C.
Cabaniel, Tomas	4	3	4.53	11	9	0	0	48	62	31	24	14	33	.308	R	R	6-1	165	2-10-83	2000	Caracas, Venez.
France, Ryan	0	0	9.82	3	0	0	1	7	12	9	8	3	7	.375	R	R	6-2	205	1-21-79	2003	Norco, Calif.
Granado, Julian	0	1	8.15	15	0	0	0	18	28	18	16	13	13	.354	L	L	6-2	170	11-15-82	2000	Barquisimeto, Venez.
Heuser, James	0	1	10.54	14	0	0	2	14	19	17	16	13	16	.365	L	L	6-5	200	3-30-84	2003	Peru, Ill.
Mola, Heydin	1	3	6.59	14	0	0	3	27	40	26	20	8	22	.338	R	R	6-2	160	3-25-84	2002	San Cristobal, D.R.
Montas, Ipolito	1	2	5.15	16	0	0	0	37	50	23	21	10	25	.328	R	R	6-1	160	9-8-81	2002	Santo Domingo, D.R.
Perez, Keith	1	5	5.80	17	4	0	2	35	61	38	23	23	34	.000	R	R	6-2	200	1-18-80	2003	Holly, Mich.
Reynolds, Grant	0	0	6.57	4	2	0	0	12	15	10	9	0	13	.300	R	R	5-10	185	2-2-80	2003	Wentworthville, Australia
Sanchez, Adiel	2	6	5.68	11	9	0	0	52	64	37	33	11	49	.301	L	L	6-1	165	8-27-82	2000	Santo Domingo, D.R.
Santana, Braulio	6	1	4.50	15	13	0	0	74	88	40	37	12	57	.296	R	R	5-11	130	4-3-85	2002	San Pedro de Macoris, D.R.
Santana, Roberto	2	1	5.33	16	1	0	0	27	38	28	16	20	24	.330	L	L	6-0	160	10-13-81	1999	Sabana Perdida, D.R.
Tovar, Miguel	0	2	9.86	14	0	0	1	21	37	26	23	15	15	.389	R	R	6-1	160	2-24-84	2001	Aragua, Venez.
Zorrilla, Junior	1	3	3.76	17	3	0	1	41	37	23	17	20	39	.240	R	R	6-3	170	9-11-80	2001	Hato Mayor, D.R.

PHILADELPHIA PHILLIES

BY JIM SALISBURY

Jim Thome lived up to expectations, and the Phillies closed Veterans Stadium with their third winning season in 17 years. Still, 2003 was a bitter disappointment.

The Phillies spent lavishly before the season, signing free agents Thome and David Bell and trading for pitcher Kevin Millwood, adding three playoff-tested talents to a ripening nucleus of pitchers and hitters.

The expectation was a postseason berth, and the prospects looked good as the Phillies led a tight National League wild-card race for much of the second half. But their starting pitching, which had been reliable for much of the season, faltered late and the Phillies were overtaken by the Marlins down the stretch.

The Marlins won four of six meetings between the teams over the final two weeks, and the Phillies had little margin for error after losing two of three to both Pittsburgh and Cincinnati.

Pat Burrell became the symbol of the Phillies' disappointing season. So much was expected. So little was delivered. After hitting .282 with 37 homers and 116 RBIs in 2002, Burrell signed a $50 million contract extension. The Phillies envisioned him and Thome being towers of power and run production. Thome led the NL with 47 homers and drove in 131 runs, but Burrell suffered through a season-long slump and hit just .209 with 21 homers and 64 RBIs. He frequently was benched late in the season.

Bell and Millwood also illustrated the Phillies' woes. Bell, limited to 85 games by a back injury, hit just .195. Millwood pitched a no-hitter against San Francisco on April 27 and was 7-1 on May 23. After that, however, he was just 7-11 with a 4.55 ERA in 24 starts. Overall, the Phillies were 17-18 in his starts. In the heat of a pennant race, Millwood won just one of his final six starts. He started the last game at Veterans Stadium, gave up 11 hits and four runs against his old Atlanta team, and was booed off the mound.

While the Marlins were active at the trade deadline, the Phillies made few changes. They did acquire reliever Mike Williams from Pittsburgh as insurance for closer Jose Mesa. But Williams was ineffective and could not fill the role when Mesa failed, and the Phillies were basically without a closer for the final two months.

Third-year manager Larry Bowa came under fire late in the season as the annual clubhouse whispers about how difficult it is to play for him almost reached mutiny level. Burrell refused to shake Bowa's hand after hitting a home run on Aug. 29. Management backed Bowa, and he will take the Phillies into their new stadium in 2004, but he no longer seems bulletproof in a town where he has enjoyed immense popularity.

There were pluses. Four starters—Millwood, Randy Wolf, Vicente Padilla and Brett Myers—won at least 14 games. Lefty Rheal Cormier bounced back from two disastrous seasons and was one of the game's best relievers. Catcher Mike Lieberthal hit .313.

Thome was hugely popular. He carried an inconsistent offense down the stretch—20 homers, 51 RBIs over the final two months—and helped the team draw two million fans for the first time since 1995.

As the Phillies got ready to move into their new ballpark, they felt good about the state of the minor league pitching. Lefty Cole Hamels and righthander Gavin Floyd both project as No. 1 starters. Hamels, 19, struck out 147 in 101 innings at low Class A Lakewood. First baseman Ryan Howard was the organization's player of the year, winning the Florida State League batting (.304) and home run (23) titles with high Class A Clearwater.

Jim Thome

DAVID SCHOFIELD

Cole Hamels

PLAYERS of the YEAR

MAJOR LEAGUE: Jim Thome, 1b

After 10 years in Cleveland, Thome had no trouble adjusting to the National League as he led the circuit in home runs with 47. He also tied for second in walks and ranked third in RBIs in his first season with the Phillies.

MINOR LEAGUE: Cole Hamels, lhp

Hamels, the team's first-round pick in 2002, struck out 147 batters in 101 innings during his pro debut season. He split the season between Class A Lakewood and Clearwater, going 6-3, 1.34 while allowing just 15 earned runs all season.

ORGANIZATION LEADERS

BATTING		
*AVG	Chase Utley, Scranton	.323
R	Jeff Inglin, Reading	86
H	Jeff Inglin, Reading	153
TB	Jeff Inglin, Reading	254
2B	Travis Chapman, Scranton	36
3B	Jake Blalock, Batavia	7
HR	Jeff Inglin, Reading	24
RBI	Jeff Inglin, Reading	103
BB	Andy Machado, Reading	108
SO	Ryan Howard, Clearwater	151
SB	Chris Roberson, Lakewood	59
*SLG	Chase Utley, Scranton	.517
*OBP	Chase Utley, Scranton	.390
PITCHING		
W	Ezequiel Astacio, Clearwater	15
L	Francisco Butto, Lakewood	12
	Matt Sweeney, Lakewood	12
#ERA	Cole Hamels, Clearwater/Lakewood	1.34
G	Jim Crowell, Scranton	54
CG	Amaury Telemaco, Scranton	3
	Layne Dawson, Reading/Clearwater	3
SV	Bobby Korecky, Clearwater	25
IP	Josh Hancock, Scranton	166
BB	Nick Bourgeois, Lakewood	62
SO	Cole Hamels, Clearwater/Lakewood	147
	Ryan Madson, Scranton/Clearwater	147

*Minimum 250 At-Bats #Minimum 75 Innings

PHILADELPHIA PHILLIES

Manager: Larry Bowa.

2003 Record: 86-76, .531 (3rd, NL East).

BATTING	AVG	G	AB	R	H	2B	3B	HR	RBI	BB	SO	SB	CS	SLG	OBP	B	T	HT	WT	DOB	1st Yr	Resides
Abreu, Bob	.300	158	577	99	173	35	1	20	101	109	126	22	9	.468	.409	L	R	6-0	200	3-11-74	1991	Aragua, Venez.
Bell, David	.195	85	297	32	58	14	0	4	37	41	40	0	0	.283	.296	R	R	5-10	190	9-14-72	1990	Seattle, Wash.
Burrell, Pat	.209	146	522	57	109	31	4	21	64	72	142	0	0	.404	.309	R	R	6-4	220	10-10-76	1998	Clearwater, Fla.
Byrd, Marlon	.303	135	495	86	150	28	4	7	45	44	94	11	1	.418	.366	R	R	6-0	220	8-30-77	1999	San Diego, Calif.
Chapman, Travis	.000	1	1	0	0	0	0	0	0	0	0	0	0	.000	.000	R	R	6-2	180	6-5-78	2000	Dayton, Ohio
Houston, Tyler	.278	54	97	7	27	6	0	2	14	6	19	0	0	.402	.320	L	R	6-1	210	1-17-71	1989	Henderson, Nev.
Ledee, Ricky	.247	121	255	37	63	15	2	13	46	34	59	0	0	.475	.334	L	L	6-1	200	11-22-73	1990	Salinas, P.R.
Lieberthal, Mike	.313	131	508	68	159	30	1	13	81	38	59	0	0	.453	.373	R	R	6-0	190	1-18-72	1990	Westlake Village, Calif.
Michaels, Jason	.330	76	109	20	36	11	0	5	17	15	22	0	0	.569	.416	R	R	6-0	200	5-4-76	1998	Tampa, Fla.
Perez, Tomas	.265	125	298	39	79	18	1	5	33	23	54	0	1	.383	.316	S	R	5-11	180	12-29-73	1991	Barquisimeto, Venez.
Polanco, Placido	.289	122	492	87	142	30	3	14	63	42	38	14	2	.447	.352	R	R	5-10	180	10-10-75	1994	Miami, Fla.
Pratt, Todd	.272	43	125	16	34	10	1	4	20	22	38	0	0	.464	.400	R	R	6-3	230	2-9-67	1985	Deerfield, Fla.
Punto, Nick	.217	64	92	14	20	2	0	1	4	7	22	2	1	.272	.273	S	R	5-9	170	11-8-77	1998	Mission Viejo, Calif.
Rollins, Jimmy	.263	156	628	85	165	42	6	8	62	54	113	20	12	.387	.320	S	R	5-8	160	11-27-78	1996	Alameda, Calif.
Stinnett, Kelly	.429	7	7	0	3	0	0	0	0	1	1	0	0	.429	.500	R	R	5-11	220	2-4-70	1990	Mesa, Ariz.
2-team (60 Cincinnati)	.237	67	186	14	44	13	0	3	19	14	52	0	0	.355	.302							
Thome, Jim	.266	159	578	111	154	30	3	47	131	111	182	0	3	.573	.385	L	R	6-4	240	8-27-70	1989	Aurora, Ohio
Utley, Chase	.239	43	134	13	32	10	1	2	21	11	22	2	0	.373	.322	L	R	6-1	170	12-17-78	2000	Las Vegas, Nev.

PITCHING	W	L	ERA	G	GS	CG	SV	IP	H	R	ER	BB	SO	AVG	B	T	HT	WT	DOB	1st Yr	Resides
Adams, Terry	1	4	2.65	66	0	0	0	68	68	22	20	23	51	.267	R	R	6-3	220	3-6-73	1991	Semmes, Ala.
Cormier, Rheal	8	0	1.70	65	0	0	1	85	54	18	16	25	67	.181	L	L	5-10	190	4-23-67	1989	Voorhees, N.J.
De los Santos, Valerio	1	0	9.00	6	0	0	0	4	7	7	4	3	4	.388	L	L	6-2	220	10-6-72	1993	Santo Domingo, D.R.
2-team (45 Milwaukee)	4	3	4.50	51	0	0	1	52	45	31	26	25	39	.240							
Duckworth, Brandon	4	7	4.94	24	18	0	0	93	98	58	51	44	68	.272	R	R	6-2	190	1-23-76	1997	Kearns, Utah
Geary, Geoff	0	0	4.50	5	0	0	0	6	8	3	3	3	3	.333	R	R	6-0	170	8-26-76	1998	El Cajon, Calif.
Hancock, Josh	0	0	3.00	2	0	0	0	3	2	1	1	0	4	.181	R	R	6-3	210	4-11-78	1998	Tupelo, Miss.
Junge, Eric	0	0	3.52	6	0	0	0	8	5	3	3	1	5	.185	R	R	6-5	210	1-5-77	1999	New York, N.Y.
Madson, Ryan	0	0	0.00	1	0	0	0	2	0	0	0	0	0	.000	L	R	6-6	180	8-28-80	1998	Moreno Valley, Calif.
Mercado, Hector	0	0	5.79	13	0	0	1	19	18	12	12	12	15	.253	L	L	6-3	230	4-29-74	1992	Dorado, P.R.
Mesa, Jose	5	7	6.52	61	0	0	24	58	71	44	42	31	45	.295	R	R	6-3	230	5-22-66	1982	West Lake, Ohio
Millwood, Kevin	14	12	4.01	35	35	5	0	222	210	103	99	68	169	.249	R	R	6-4	220	12-24-74	1993	Duluth, Ga.
Myers, Brett	14	9	4.43	32	32	1	0	193	205	99	95	76	143	.271	R	R	6-4	210	8-17-80	1999	Jacksonville, Fla.
Padilla, Vicente	14	12	3.62	32	32	1	0	209	196	94	84	62	133	.251	R	R	6-2	210	9-27-77	1998	Chinandega, Nicaragua
Plesac, Dan	2	1	2.70	58	0	0	2	33	29	12	10	11	37	.228	L	L	6-5	210	2-4-62	1983	Valparaiso, Ind.
Roa, Joe	0	2	6.05	6	3	0	0	19	28	13	13	4	16	.341	R	R	6-2	200	10-11-71	1989	Royal Oak, Mich.
Silva, Carlos	3	1	4.43	62	1	0	1	87	92	43	43	37	48	.279	R	R	6-4	220	4-23-79	1996	Bolivar, Venez.
Telemaco, Amaury	1	4	3.97	8	8	0	0	45	41	22	20	11	29	.238	R	R	6-3	220	1-19-74	1991	La Romana, D.R.
Wendell, Turk	3	3	3.38	56	0	0	1	64	54	24	24	28	27	.234	L	R	6-2	200	5-19-67	1988	Castle Rock, Colo.
Williams, Mike	0	4	5.96	28	0	0	3	26	24	18	17	19	19	.247	R	R	6-2	200	7-29-68	1990	Pembroke, Va.
2-team (40 Pittsburgh)	1	7	6.14	68	0	0	28	63	66	44	43	41	39	.268							
Wolf, Randy	16	10	4.23	33	33	2	0	200	176	101	94	78	177	.233	L	L	6-0	190	8-22-76	1997	West Hills, Calif.

FIELDING

Catcher	PCT	G	PO	A	E	DP	PB
Lieberthal	.990	131	868	44	9	2	11
Pratt	.996	35	231	9	1	4	5
Stinnett	1.000	1	6	0	0	0	0

First Base	PCT	G	PO	A	E	DP
Houston	1.000	1	6	0	0	1
Perez	1.000	9	35	3	0	5
Pratt	1.000	6	44	2	0	3
Thome	.997	156	1372	86	5	132

Second Base	PCT	G	PO	A	E	DP
Bell	1.000	3	3	8	0	1
Perez	.981	26	52	54	2	11
Polanco	.992	99	213	301	4	69
Punto	.985	16	36	28	1	6
Utley	.983	37	65	107	3	31

Third Base	PCT	G	PO	A	E	DP
Bell	.966	85	62	168	8	17
Chapman	.000	1	0	0	0	0
Houston	.936	21	15	29	3	0
Perez	.953	58	37	86	6	12
Polanco	.959	21	10	37	2	5
Punto	.917	9	5	6	1	0

Shortstop	PCT	G	PO	A	E	DP
Perez	.917	4	4	7	1	3
Punto	1.000	7	5	17	0	2
Rollins	.979	154	203	463	14	92

Outfield	PCT	G	PO	A	E	DP
Abreu	.981	158	304	6	6	0
Burrell	.976	140	234	7	6	0
Byrd	.984	131	295	5	5	1
Ledee	1.000	71	98	5	0	0
Michaels	.976	38	37	3	1	0

BILL NICHOLS

Bobby Abreu

FARM SYSTEM

Director, Minor Leagues: Steve Noworyta.

Class	Farm Team	League	W	L	Pct.	Finish*	Manager	First Yr.
AAA	Scranton/W-B (Pa.) Red Barons	International	73	70	.510	t-7th (14)	Marc Bombard	1989
AA	Reading (Pa.) Phillies	Eastern	62	79	.440	t-10th (12)	Greg Legg	1967
High A	Clearwater (Fla.) Phillies	Florida State	72	61	.541	4th (12)	Roly deArmas	1985
Low A	Lakewood (N.J.) Blue Claws	South Atlantic	57	81	.413	14th (16)	Buddy Biancalana	2001
SS A	Batavia (N.Y.) Muckdogs	New York-Penn	30	45	.400	12th (14)	Luis Melendez	1988
Rookie	Clearwater (Fla.) Phillies	Gulf Coast	23	33	.411	12th (12)	Ruben Amaro Sr.	1999

*Finish in overall standings (No. of teams in league)

SCRANTON/WILKES-BARRE RED BARONS — Class AAA

INTERNATIONAL LEAGUE

BATTING	AVG	G	AB	R	H	2B	3B	HR	RBI	BB	SO	SB	CS	SLG	OBP	B	T	HT	WT	DOB	1st Yr	Resides
Byrd, Marlon	.750	1	4	1	3	1	0	0	0	0	1	0	0	1.000	.750	R	R	6-0	220	8-30-77	1999	San Diego, Calif.
Camilo, Juan	.333	5	18	7	6	2	0	0	0	1	3	0	0	.444	.368	L	R	6-0	200	6-24-76	1996	Santo Domingo, D.R.
Casillas, Uriel	.317	13	41	4	13	4	0	0	3	5	3	0	0	.415	.404	R	R	5-11	160	8-22-75	1997	Downey, Calif.
Chapman, Travis	.272	134	478	62	130	36	0	12	82	44	97	2	2	.423	.348	R	R	6-2	180	6-5-78	2000	Dayton, Ohio
Christensen, McKay	.238	47	181	26	43	10	1	4	13	14	48	7	2	.370	.294	L	L	5-11	180	8-14-75	1995	Alpine, Utah
Francia, Dave	.111	9	18	2	2	0	0	0	1	0	4	1	0	.111	.111	L	L	6-0	160	4-16-75	1996	Mobile, Ala.
Hitchcox, Brian	.222	15	45	2	10	1	0	1	2	0	3	0	1	.311	.222	L	R	5-11	170	7-21-78	1999	Clearwater, Fla.
Hollins, Dave	.204	29	98	12	20	2	2	2	12	11	16	1	0	.327	.301	S	R	6-1	210	5-25-66	1987	Orchard Park, N.Y.
Houston, Tyler	.174	6	23	2	4	1	1	0	0	1	1	0	0	.304	.208	L	R	6-1	210	1-17-71	1989	Henderson, Nev.
Knupfer, Jason	.214	111	398	49	85	20	0	2	21	46	89	13	1	.279	.298	R	R	6-0	180	9-21-74	1996	Redwood City, Calif.
Levis, Jesse	.279	79	265	26	74	16	0	0	30	18	18	1	0	.340	.328	L	R	5-9	200	4-14-68	1989	Elkins Park, Pa.
Maddox, Garry	.214	18	56	4	12	3	0	0	8	1	12	0	1	.268	.237	L	R	6-3	180	10-24-74	1996	Philadelphia, Pa.
Magee, Wendell	.333	25	93	11	31	8	1	1	12	8	16	1	3	.473	.390	R	R	6-0	220	8-3-72	1994	Hattiesburg, Miss.
Minor, Damon	.232	91	328	45	76	17	1	16	65	27	60	1	2	.436	.305	L	L	6-7	230	1-5-74	1996	Edmond, Okla.
Mouton, Lyle	.290	10	31	3	9	2	0	0	4	6	8	1	0	.355	.395	R	R	6-4	230	5-13-69	1991	Tarpon Springs, Fla.
Perez, Josue	.220	32	123	6	27	5	0	0	8	7	31	2	5	.260	.265	S	R	6-0	180	8-12-77	1998	Santo Domingo, D.R.
Punto, Nick	.315	25	111	19	35	7	1	0	9	7	13	7	1	.396	.353	S	R	5-9	170	11-8-77	1998	Mission Viejo, Calif.
Roberge, J.P.	.266	101	338	40	90	22	2	4	35	23	55	3	0	.379	.320	R	R	6-0	180	9-12-72	1994	Arcadia, Calif.
Salazar, Jeremy	.182	71	231	16	42	7	0	3	25	15	51	0	0	.251	.232	R	R	6-0	190	3-18-76	1998	Breaux Bridge, La.
Sefcik, Kevin	.280	133	492	75	138	32	4	10	66	40	47	10	4	.423	.333	R	R	5-10	180	2-10-71	1993	Orland Park, Ill.
Simmons, Brian	.275	42	178	26	49	9	1	5	13	7	45	2	2	.421	.303	S	R	6-2	190	9-4-73	1995	McMurray, Pa.
Sosa, Juan	.252	91	298	30	75	11	1	3	26	12	39	10	2	.326	.283	R	R	6-1	170	8-19-75	1993	San Francisco de Macoris, D.R.
Utley, Chase	.323	113	431	80	139	26	2	18	77	41	75	10	4	.517	.390	L	R	6-1	170	12-17-78	2000	Las Vegas, Nev.
Valent, Eric	.218	134	450	62	98	27	2	12	51	60	102	0	0	.367	.308	L	L	5-11	190	4-4-77	1998	Anaheim, Calif.

PITCHING	W	L	ERA	G	GS	CG	SV	IP	H	R	ER	BB	SO	AVG	B	T	HT	WT	DOB	1st Yr	Resides
Cabrera, Jose	3	4	2.76	25	1	0	1	46	45	16	14	10	33	.267	R	R	6-0	200	3-24-72	1991	Santiago, D.R.
Coggin, Dave	0	0	1.50	4	3	0	0	6	4	1	1	1	3	.200	R	R	6-4	200	10-30-76	1995	Upland, Calif.
Crowell, Jim	0	8	4.12	54	0	0	9	55	63	31	25	23	42	.288	R	L	6-4	230	5-14-74	1995	Valparaiso, Ind.
Duckworth, Brandon	2	1	3.38	3	3	0	0	19	21	11	7	4	14	.280	R	R	6-2	190	1-23-76	1997	Kearns, Utah
Geary, Geoff	9	4	2.16	46	3	0	5	88	73	26	21	13	80	.228	R	R	6-0	170	8-26-76	1998	El Cajon, Calif.
Giese, Dan	2	0	3.17	34	0	0	0	48	37	19	17	10	49	.210	R	R	6-3	200	5-19-77	1999	San Clemente, Calif.
Gomes, Wayne	4	2	2.59	46	0	0	14	49	31	17	14	24	43	.180	R	R	6-2	220	1-15-73	1993	Cherry Hill, N.J.
Hancock, Josh	10	9	3.86	28	27	2	0	166	147	78	71	46	122	.238	R	R	6-3	210	4-11-78	1998	Tupelo, Miss.
Hernandez, Yoel	0	0	6.00	2	0	0	0	3	5	2	2	0	3	.357	R	R	6-2	170	4-15-80	1999	Ciudad Bolivar, Venez.
Hiles, Cary	0	1	3.71	13	0	0	0	27	31	11	11	11	11	.298	R	R	5-10	170	11-29-75	1998	Memphis, Tenn.
Junge, Eric	1	0	3.06	10	8	0	0	47	38	20	16	16	42	.215	R	R	6-5	210	1-5-77	1999	New York, N.Y.
Kubes, Greg	6	3	4.26	37	10	0	3	95	117	49	45	16	62	.306	R	L	6-6	200	11-10-76	1998	East Bernard, Texas
Lee, Seung	0	2	23.63	2	1	0	0	5	18	15	14	0	5	.580	R	R	6-4	220	6-2-79	2001	Pusan, South Korea
Madson, Ryan	12	8	3.50	26	26	0	0	157	157	70	61	42	138	.262	L	R	6-6	180	8-28-80	1998	Moreno Valley, Calif.
Mercado, Hector	0	3	1.41	14	2	0	0	32	34	12	5	11	20	.283	L	L	6-3	230	4-29-74	1992	Dorado, P.R.
Myette, Aaron	5	4	4.27	11	10	0	0	59	50	28	28	20	54	.229	R	R	6-4	210	9-26-77	1997	Gig Harbor, Wash.
2-team (23 Buffalo)	5	4	4.39	34	11	0	1	92	83	49	45	43	79	.241							
Powell, Brian	2	4	4.61	8	7	2	0	53	57	33	27	12	36	.275	R	R	6-2	200	10-10-73	1995	Bainbridge, Ga.
Pumphrey, Ken	5	7	7.41	17	17	1	0	81	108	75	67	32	46	.323	R	R	6-6	200	9-10-76	1994	Glen Burnie, Md.
Santana, Julio	1	1	3.64	19	0	0	3	30	29	12	12	12	26	.261	R	R	6-0	220	1-20-73	1992	Santo Domingo, D.R.
Telemaco, Amaury	10	9	3.24	25	24	3	0	155	125	59	56	22	116	.221	R	R	6-3	220	1-19-74	1991	La Romana, D.R.
Wedel, Jeremy	1	0	3.76	17	1	0	0	26	28	12	11	9	18	.271	R	R	6-0	190	11-27-76	1998	Wasco, Calif.

FIELDING

Catcher	PCT	G	PO	A	E	DP	PB
Levis	.996	77	514	41	2	3	4
Salazar	.984	70	469	32	8	1	3

First Base	PCT	G	PO	A	E	DP
Hollins	.994	23	169	10	1	19
Houston	1.000	2	14	1	0	2
Knupfer	1.000	14	80	9	0	11
Minor	.991	41	309	34	3	34
Roberge	.990	71	575	46	6	51
Valent	1.000	3	7	0	0	0

Second Base	PCT	G	PO	A	E	DP
Casillas	1.000	3	3	9	0	3
Hitchcox	1.000	12	24	38	0	14
Knupfer	.929	14	25	40	5	6
Sosa	1.000	5	5	9	0	0
Utley	.978	113	260	326	13	67

Third Base	PCT	G	PO	A	E	DP
Casillas	.500	1	0	1	1	0
Chapman	.962	131	75	228	12	17
Houston	1.000	1	0	2	0	0
Knupfer	1.000	3	3	6	0	2
Roberge	.960	7	6	18	1	1
Sosa	.500	1	1	0	1	0

Shortstop	PCT	G	PO	A	E	DP
Casillas	.875	2	4	3	1	1
Knupfer	.948	76	99	209	17	38
Punto	.969	25	37	90	4	19
Roberge	.857	1	3	3	1	0
Sosa	.933	42	59	107	12	30

Outfield	PCT	G	PO	A	E	DP
Byrd	1.000	1	5	1	0	0
Camilo	.909	4	9	1	1	0
Christensen	.992	42	119	2	1	1
Francia	1.000	4	11	0	0	0
Maddox	.956	13	43	0	2	0
Magee	1.000	21	38	2	0	0
Mouton	1.000	5	6	1	0	0
Perez	.989	29	87	2	1	0
Sefcik	.978	121	162	13	4	1
Simmons	.979	40	91	3	2	0
Sosa	.983	26	57	0	1	0
Valent	.973	132	283	10	8	2

READING PHILLIES — Class AA

EASTERN LEAGUE

BATTING	AVG	G	AB	R	H	2B	3B	HR	RBI	BB	SO	SB	CS	SLG	OBP	B	T	HT	WT	DOB	1st Yr	Resides
Avila, Rob	.174	10	23	1	4	0	0	0	2	0	4	0	0	.174	.167	R	R	5-11	200	9-4-78	1999	Fresno, Calif.
Byrd, Marlon	.313	3	16	3	5	0	0	1	3	0	3	0	0	.500	.313	R	R	6-0	220	8-30-77	1999	San Diego, Calif.
Camilo, Juan	.172	21	64	6	11	1	0	2	10	7	13	1	1	.281	.254	L	R	6-0	200	6-24-76	1996	Santo Domingo, D.R.
Casillas, Uriel	.250	76	200	22	50	7	0	2	25	22	22	6	1	.315	.326	R	R	5-11	160	8-22-75	1997	Downey, Calif.
Cruz, Edgar	.221	62	213	18	47	11	0	4	23	11	37	0	0	.329	.259	R	R	6-3	190	8-12-78	1997	Juncos, P.R.
Deschaine, Jim	.295	67	217	32	64	8	0	13	40	16	24	0	3	.512	.347	R	R	6-0	200	9-18-77	1999	Bristol, Conn.
2-team (16 New Haven)	.291	83	258	36	75	11	0	13	46	24	30	0	3	.484	.354							
Espy, Nate	.242	119	347	49	84	14	0	9	49	54	78	10	6	.360	.350	R	R	6-3	210	4-24-78	1998	Pensacola, Fla.
Hannahan, Buzz	.261	117	380	61	99	15	1	3	26	56	74	25	4	.329	.365	R	R	6-2	180	6-29-76	1998	St. Paul, Minn.
Hitchcox, Brian	.250	92	304	36	76	13	4	5	27	41	54	8	5	.368	.351	L	R	5-11	170	7-21-78	1999	Clearwater, Fla.
Inglin, Jeff	.284	141	539	86	153	27	1	24	103	45	58	7	3	.471	.346	R	R	5-11	180	10-8-75	1996	Petaluma, Calif.
Jacobson, Russ	.275	37	109	9	30	4	0	1	5	7	16	1	1	.339	.339	R	R	6-3	210	10-14-77	1999	Scottsdale, Ariz.
Machado, Andy	.196	123	423	80	83	19	4	5	20	108	120	49	15	.296	.360	S	R	5-11	160	1-25-81	1998	Caracas, Venez.
Maddox, Garry	.289	50	180	28	52	8	1	12	38	19	43	3	6	.544	.376	L	R	6-3	180	10-24-74	1996	Philadelphia, Pa.
McNeal, Aaron	.254	118	421	40	107	20	1	13	71	24	103	0	1	.399	.289	R	R	6-3	230	4-28-78	1996	Castro Valley, Calif.
Nonemaker, Karl	.147	14	34	4	5	1	0	0	1	2	7	1	1	.176	.194	L	L	6-0	190	1-7-80	2002	Flanders, N.J.
Padilla, Jorge	.295	46	173	21	51	13	1	2	23	18	29	11	8	.416	.363	R	R	6-2	200	8-11-79	1998	Carolina, P.R.
Perez, Josue	.306	48	183	26	56	7	0	2	21	14	24	10	4	.377	.350	S	R	6-0	180	8-12-77	1998	Santo Domingo, D.R.
Richardson, Juan	.270	65	248	37	67	9	0	15	34	17	69	2	1	.488	.327	R	R	6-1	170	1-27-79	1998	Bani, D.R.
Ruiz, Carlos	.266	52	169	22	45	6	0	2	16	12	15	1	1	.337	.321	R	R	5-10	180	1-22-79	1999	Chiriqui, Panama
Sitzman, Jay	.277	72	249	23	69	13	0	1	9	15	56	9	1	.341	.336	L	L	6-3	190	3-13-78	1999	Scottsdale, Ariz.
Tucker, Mamon	.263	10	38	0	10	0	1	0	6	2	6	0	0	.316	.300	R	R	6-3	180	10-18-79	1998	Austin, Texas
Youngbauer, Scott	.310	16	42	2	13	1	0	1	5	6	7	1	0	.405	.392	S	R	6-1	170	1-14-79	2000	Powder Springs, Ga.

PITCHING	W	L	ERA	G	GS	CG	SV	IP	H	R	ER	BB	SO	AVG	B	T	HT	WT	DOB	1st Yr	Resides
Adams, Daniel	1	1	5.40	10	0	0	0	15	17	9	9	6	11	.293	R	R	6-0	190	2-21-78	2000	Burlington, Wash.
Billingsley, Brent	0	1	10.03	4	2	0	0	12	14	14	13	8	10	.304	L	L	6-2	200	4-19-75	1996	Chino Hills, Calif.
1Brooks, Frank	3	4	2.30	34	0	0	9	59	40	16	15	13	71	.194	L	L	6-1	190	9-6-78	1999	Brooklyn, N.Y.
Buchholz, Taylor	9	11	3.55	25	24	1	0	145	136	62	57	33	114	.248	R	R	6-4	220	10-13-81	2000	Springfield, Pa.
Bucktrot, Keith	3	1	2.56	7	7	0	0	46	34	17	13	15	30	.216	L	R	6-2	180	11-27-80	2000	Claremore, Okla.
Cable, Taft	0	1	2.51	4	3	0	0	14	8	4	4	4	13	.163	R	R	6-2	200	7-25-80	2001	Browns Summit, N.C.
Carter, Ryan	2	7	6.00	17	17	0	0	75	105	61	50	32	47	.334	L	L	6-7	240	8-1-79	2000	Riverbank, Calif.
Dawson, Layne	1	9	7.42	14	14	2	0	74	102	65	61	27	45	.326	R	R	6-2	180	9-13-79	2001	Somerville, Tenn.
Duckworth, Brandon	0	0	4.50	1	1	0	0	2	1	1	1	0	2	.142	R	R	6-2	190	1-23-76	1997	Kearns, Utah
Franco, Martire	4	7	5.71	28	13	1	4	87	116	66	55	25	47	.316	R	R	6-0	170	2-25-78	1998	Bani, D.R.
Giese, Dan	2	1	1.46	9	0	0	1	12	8	2	2	1	16	.186	R	R	6-3	200	5-19-77	1999	San Clemente, Calif.
Glen, Willie	3	6	3.83	31	14	0	0	103	100	61	44	53	79	.255	R	R	6-1	180	10-30-77	2001	Plainfield, Ind.
Guy, Brad	2	6	4.96	31	3	0	3	69	75	43	38	18	33	.283	R	R	6-2	190	10-25-75	1997	Eureka, Calif.
2-team (8 Altoona)	3	8	5.10	39	4	0	3	83	91	52	47	20	42	.283							
Harvey, Ian	4	1	3.75	11	0	0	1	24	22	10	10	11	22	.244	R	R	6-1	190	10-11-76	1999	Oakville, Ontario
Hernandez, Yoel	6	3	4.26	43	1	0	2	74	100	43	35	31	46	.335	R	R	6-2	170	4-15-80	1999	Ciudad Bolivar, Venez.
Hutchison, Ryan	3	2	3.76	34	0	0	5	53	54	23	22	17	17	.268	R	R	6-0	200	8-9-78	2001	Vincennes, Ind.
Lee, Seung	11	6	4.96	26	25	0	0	147	140	85	81	47	109	.248	R	R	6-4	220	6-2-79	2001	Pusan, South Korea
Mercado, Hector	0	0	0.00	1	1	0	0	2	0	0	0	1	0	.000	L	L	6-3	230	4-29-74	1992	Dorado, P.R.
Miller, Josh	0	3	5.36	43	2	0	1	84	98	52	50	19	40	.294	R	R	6-1	200	2-7-79	2001	Melbourne, Fla.
Outlaw, Mark	0	0	5.40	12	0	0	0	12	11	8	7	11	9	.244	L	L	5-11	180	1-2-77	1999	Waco, Texas
Pautz, Brad	4	5	7.69	29	1	0	1	48	60	44	41	20	34	.312	R	R	6-3	190	1-3-77	1999	Reedsville, Wisc.
Smith, Bud	1	1	5.35	8	8	0	0	37	40	23	22	15	24	.275	L	L	6-0	170	10-23-79	1998	Lakewood, Calif.
Weaver, Eric	1	1	6.57	10	0	0	2	12	12	9	9	10	9	.272	R	R	6-5	240	8-4-73	1991	Springfield, Ill.
Wilson, Mike	2	2	3.93	9	6	0	0	34	35	20	15	20	18	.277	R	R	6-7	230	6-12-80	1998	El Cajon, Calif.

FIELDING

Catcher	PCT	G	PO	A	E	DP	PB
Avila	.980	10	45	5	1	1	0
Cruz	.990	61	360	42	4	1	15
Jacobson	.986	32	201	18	3	1	4
Ruiz	.994	49	279	33	2	1	6

First Base	PCT	G	PO	A	E	DP
Deschaine	1.000	1	1	0	0	0
Espy	.994	88	611	54	4	52
McNeal	.991	68	525	44	5	51

Second Base	PCT	G	PO	A	E	DP
Casillas	.973	25	42	66	3	7
Hannahan	.991	27	51	57	1	13
Hitchcox	.986	89	195	218	6	54
Youngbauer	.957	16	19	26	2	4

Third Base	PCT	G	PO	A	E	DP
Casillas	.940	26	22	41	4	6
Deschaine	.912	50	36	57	9	5
Hannahan	.950	13	12	7	1	2
Richardson	.916	63	63	112	16	11

Shortstop	PCT	G	PO	A	E	DP
Casillas	.913	8	8	13	2	2
Hannahan	1.000	19	25	43	0	9
Machado	.951	122	186	318	26	60

Outfield	PCT	G	PO	A	E	DP
Byrd	.800	3	4	0	1	0
Camilo	1.000	20	37	0	0	0
Casillas	1.000	7	8	0	0	0
Deschaine	1.000	11	12	1	0	0
Espy	.000	1	0	0	0	0
Hannahan	.993	64	135	8	1	0
Inglin	1.000	122	249	12	0	1
Maddox	1.000	46	123	4	0	0
Nonemaker	1.000	12	30	0	0	0
Padilla	.990	44	94	2	1	0
Perez	.981	48	100	5	2	1
Ruiz	1.000	2	1	1	0	0
Sitzman	.975	67	152	5	4	2
Tucker	1.000	9	16	2	0	1

CLEARWATER PHILLIES — High Class A

FLORIDA STATE LEAGUE

BATTING	AVG	G	AB	R	H	2B	3B	HR	RBI	BB	SO	SB	CS	SLG	OBP	B	T	HT	WT	DOB	1st Yr	Resides
Acevedo, Carlos	.156	15	45	4	7	2	0	0	1	5	9	1	1	.200	.240	R	R	6-1	160	1-31-79	1997	Santo Domingo, D.R.
Avila, Rob	.225	51	160	11	36	6	0	1	14	11	19	0	1	.281	.276	R	R	5-11	200	9-4-78	1999	Fresno, Calif.
Camilo, Juan	.256	103	387	45	99	17	6	6	49	36	91	11	5	.377	.323	L	R	6-0	200	6-24-76	1996	Santo Domingo, D.R.
Cosbey, Chris	.246	65	240	31	59	9	2	0	16	26	27	8	7	.300	.321	L	L	5-9	160	11-14-74	1998	Arcadia, Calif.
Cruz, Edgar	.162	11	37	3	6	3	0	0	3	3	5	0	0	.243	.220	R	R	6-3	190	8-12-78	1997	Juncos, P.R.
Deschaine, Jim	.313	27	96	13	30	9	0	0	15	13	11	0	1	.406	.396	R	R	6-0	200	9-18-77	1999	Bristol, Conn.
Gonzalez, Daniel	.271	113	436	62	118	22	5	0	34	49	56	5	2	.344	.348	S	R	6-0	180	11-20-81	2000	Trujillo Alto, P.R.
Howard, Ryan	.304	130	490	67	149	32	1	23	82	50	151	0	0	.514	.374	L	L	6-4	230	11-19-79	2001	Wildwood, Mo.

BATTING	AVG	G	AB	R	H	2B	3B	HR	RBI	BB	SO	SB	CS	SLG	OBP	B	T	HT	WT	DOB	1st Yr	Resides
Jarvis, Andy	.333	3	9	0	3	1	0	0	2	1	1	0	0	.444	.400	L	L	6-5	225	9-5-80	2003	Renton, Wash.
Maddox, Garry	.273	7	22	3	6	2	0	1	7	4	6	0	1	.500	.393	L	R	6-3	180	10-24-74	1996	Philadelphia, Pa.
Martinez, Casey	.190	7	21	1	4	0	0	0	0	0	7	0	0	.190	.190	R	R	5-11	200	8-31-77	2000	Clearwater, Fla.
Michaels, Jason	.000	4	14	1	0	0	0	0	0	2	4	0	0	.000	.125	R	R	6-0	200	5-4-76	1998	Tampa, Fla.
Perez, Josue	.286	13	56	8	16	4	0	0	7	5	12	3	1	.357	.344	S	R	6-0	180	8-12-77	1998	Santo Domingo, D.R.
Perry, Rod	.133	9	30	3	4	0	0	0	0	2	5	1	0	.133	.212	R	R	5-10	190	2-1-79	2001	Carlsbad, Calif.
Phelps, Jeff	.263	85	297	39	78	20	1	5	33	31	55	1	2	.387	.335	R	R	6-0	190	11-20-78	2001	Yuma, Ariz.
Pratt, Trent	.217	78	253	31	55	13	1	0	25	26	50	1	0	.277	.297	R	R	6-2	210	8-25-79	2002	Wichita, Kan.
Ruiz, Carlos	.315	15	54	5	17	0	0	2	9	2	5	2	2	.426	.339	R	R	5-10	180	1-22-79	1999	Chiriqui, Panama
Tempesta, Nick	.067	11	30	0	2	0	0	0	2	1	6	0	0	.067	.147	R	R	5-10	180	11-20-78	2001	Brockton, Mass.
Tucker, Mamon	.280	109	418	62	117	21	2	2	45	35	66	14	4	.354	.337	R	R	6-3	180	10-18-79	1998	Austin, Texas
Vukovich, Vince	.258	106	361	31	93	14	1	1	42	32	56	7	5	.310	.317	L	R	6-0	170	5-6-80	2001	Voorhees, N.J.
Walsh, Sean	.265	106	359	58	95	29	1	6	47	43	81	11	2	.401	.369	R	R	6-4	220	11-15-79	2001	Aiken, S.C.
Wardinsky, Ryan	.200	61	195	15	39	5	0	1	18	21	52	3	3	.241	.286	S	R	6-1	180	11-28-79	2002	Kalispell, Mont.
Youngbauer, Scott	.237	97	358	36	85	18	6	5	36	28	70	7	4	.363	.303	S	R	6-1	170	1-14-79	2000	Powder Springs, Ga.

PITCHING	W	L	ERA	G	GS	CG	SV	IP	H	R	ER	BB	SO	AVG	B	T	HT	WT	DOB	1st Yr	Resides
Astacio, Ezequiel	15	5	3.29	25	22	2	0	148	140	60	54	29	83	.247	R	R	6-3	150	11-4-79	1998	Hato Mayor, D.R.
Baisley, Brad	0	1	0.00	1	1	0	0	2	1	1	0	0	1	.166	R	R	6-9	200	8-24-79	1998	Tampa, Fla.
Brito, Eude	4	3	3.09	36	0	0	6	58	50	21	20	27	54	.231	L	L	5-11	160	8-19-78	1998	Sabana de la Mar, D.R.
Bucktrot, Keith	7	7	3.33	19	17	0	0	111	104	50	41	29	68	.250	L	R	6-2	180	11-27-80	2000	Claremore, Okla.
Cable, Taft	4	3	3.41	31	5	0	1	71	61	29	27	25	42	.241	R	R	6-2	200	7-25-80	2001	Browns Summit, N.C.
Coggin, Dave	0	0	2.25	3	3	0	0	4	3	1	1	2	2	.214	R	R	6-4	200	10-30-76	1995	Upland, Calif.
Dawson, Layne	6	3	3.24	14	10	1	2	67	77	33	24	13	31	.288	R	R	6-2	180	9-13-79	2001	Somerville, Tenn.
Doble, Clemente	0	1	6.75	1	1	0	0	4	5	3	3	3	1	.333	R	R	6-2	170	1-23-82	2001	Villa Mella, D.R.
Duckworth, Brandon	0	0	1.00	2	2	0	0	9	3	1	1	2	11	.100	R	R	6-2	190	1-23-76	1997	Kearns, Utah
Encarnacion, Luis	0	0	0.00	1	0	0	0	1	1	0	0	0	1	.250	R	R	6-2	170	11-30-82	2002	Los Alcarrizos, D.R.
Floyd, Gavin	7	8	3.00	24	20	1	0	138	128	61	46	45	115	.247	R	R	6-5	210	1-27-83	2001	Severna Park, Md.
Franco, Martire	0	0	2.25	1	1	0	0	4	4	3	1	1	3	.250	R	R	6-0	170	2-25-78	1998	Bani, D.R.
Glen, Willie	1	2	1.29	7	0	0	1	14	13	4	2	5	8	.250	R	R	6-1	180	10-30-77	2001	Plainfield, Ind.
Hamels, Cole	0	2	2.73	5	5	0	0	26	29	9	8	14	32	.298	L	L	6-3	170	12-27-83	2003	San Diego, Calif.
Hutchison, Ryan	0	0	0.96	8	0	0	5	9	7	1	1	0	9	.212	R	R	6-0	200	8-9-78	2001	Vincennes, Ind.
Korecky, Bobby	5	4	2.26	49	0	0	25	60	52	19	15	9	46	.236	R	R	5-11	180	9-16-79	2002	Saline, Mich.
Madson, Ryan	0	0	5.63	2	2	0	0	8	11	5	5	2	9	.323	L	R	6-6	180	8-28-80	1998	Moreno Valley, Calif.
Mayfield, Brandon	3	5	5.33	25	0	0	0	52	67	32	31	15	24	.316	R	R	6-7	220	10-17-78	2000	Birmingham, Ala.
Miller, Josh	0	0	0.00	1	0	0	0	1	0	0	0	0	0	.000	R	R	6-1	200	2-7-79	2001	Melbourne, Fla.
Paddock, Josh	0	1	5.55	20	1	0	1	36	45	30	22	13	17	.300	R	R	6-2	200	10-15-80	2002	Covington, Ind.
Ramirez, Elizardo	13	9	3.78	27	25	1	0	157	181	85	66	33	101	.289	R	R	6-0	140	1-28-83	1999	Santo Domingo, D.R.
Schultz, Cory	0	1	4.41	9	0	0	1	16	21	8	8	2	13	.333	R	R	6-1	205	9-26-80	2003	Dubuque, Iowa
Smith, Bud	1	0	1.47	4	2	0	0	18	10	3	3	4	12	.161	L	L	6-0	170	10-23-79	1998	Lakewood, Calif.
Squires, Matt	4	2	1.86	41	0	0	2	63	61	14	13	23	52	.259	L	L	5-10	200	1-24-79	2001	Lewiston, Idaho
Tejeda, Rob	2	4	3.20	11	11	1	0	65	53	25	23	23	42	.220	R	R	6-3	180	3-24-82	1999	Bani, D.R.
Wendell, Turk	0	0	0.00	5	5	0	0	6	3	0	0	0	5	.142	L	R	6-2	200	5-19-67	1988	Castle Rock, Colo.

FIELDING

Catcher	PCT	G	PO	A	E	DP	PB
Avila	.990	32	187	11	2	0	9
Cruz	1.000	9	43	7	0	1	3
Martinez	.972	7	33	2	1	0	1
Pratt	.991	78	493	45	5	4	7
Ruiz	1.000	10	62	6	0	0	1

First Base	PCT	G	PO	A	E	DP
Avila	1.000	2	17	2	0	2
Deschaine	1.000	1	7	0	0	1
Howard	.991	116	1044	89	10	102
Jarvis	1.000	3	26	9	0	5
Phelps	1.000	2	7	0	0	0
Walsh	1.000	14	119	8	0	10

Second Base	PCT	G	PO	A	E	DP
Deschaine	.957	5	9	13	1	3
Phelps	.000	1	0	0	0	0
Tempesta	1.000	5	1	7	0	0
Walsh	1.000	3	3	5	0	0
Wardinsky	.970	34	51	113	5	25
Youngbauer	.964	90	147	279	16	56

Third Base	PCT	G	PO	A	E	DP
Avila	.875	3	2	5	1	0
Phelps	.894	71	50	136	22	12
Tempesta	.000	1	0	0	0	0
Walsh	.935	60	40	89	9	6
Wardinsky	1.000	2	0	2	0	0

Shortstop	PCT	G	PO	A	E	DP
Gonzalez	.964	113	175	358	20	85
Tempesta	1.000	4	5	12	0	1
Wardinsky	.933	20	28	42	5	9

Outfield	PCT	G	PO	A	E	DP
Acevedo	.963	11	23	3	1	1
Avila	1.000	1	1	0	0	0
Camilo	.957	90	167	10	8	4
Cosbey	.985	64	134	1	2	0
Deschaine	.963	11	26	0	1	0
Maddox	1.000	7	14	1	0	0
Michaels	1.000	4	10	0	0	0
Perez	1.000	13	24	0	0	0
Perry	.900	7	17	1	2	0
Tucker	.984	92	179	2	3	0
Vukovich	.984	87	174	8	3	0
Walsh	1.000	18	33	3	0	0

LAKEWOOD BLUE CLAWS — Low Class A

SOUTH ATLANTIC LEAGUE

BATTING	AVG	G	AB	R	H	2B	3B	HR	RBI	BB	SO	SB	CS	SLG	OBP	B	T	HT	WT	DOB	1st Yr	Resides
Barthelemy, Ryan	.221	90	312	23	69	14	1	1	26	21	88	4	3	.282	.272	L	R	6-3	220	5-19-80	2002	Miami, Fla.
Borgo, Alex	.200	17	50	3	10	3	0	0	1	7	19	0	0	.260	.310	R	R	6-0	205	8-5-80	2003	Cookstown, Ontario
Bramasco, Omar	.138	24	58	3	8	1	0	0	4	10	23	3	0	.155	.311	R	R	6-0	180	10-28-81	2002	Huntington Park, Calif.
Delos Santos, Esteban	.161	9	31	1	5	0	1	0	1	1	10	0	4	.226	.188	S	R	6-1	160	12-26-82	1999	Santo Domingo, D.R.
Gradoville, Tim	.197	64	193	17	38	4	0	0	6	15	58	13	5	.218	.265	R	R	6-3	190	1-30-80	2002	Aurora, Colo.
Hansen, Bryan	.200	55	175	11	35	6	0	2	12	20	44	5	3	.269	.291	L	L	6-2	170	5-8-83	2001	Coram, N.Y.
Hopper, Matt	.188	32	96	9	18	3	1	1	5	19	34	0	1	.271	.333	R	R	6-4	210	11-6-79	2003	Golden, Colo.
Isenhower, Jeremy	.245	102	326	43	80	17	4	3	39	40	84	14	4	.350	.346	L	R	5-11	180	4-12-80	2002	Osawatomie, Kan.
Italiano, Nick	.222	3	9	1	2	0	1	0	1	0	1	0	0	.444	.200	L	R	5-9	185	5-31-81	2003	Marlton, N.J.
Jarvis, Andy	.267	21	75	10	20	2	0	3	11	8	22	0	2	.413	.333	L	L	6-5	225	9-5-80	2003	Renton, Wash.
Jones, Terry	.240	129	454	57	109	27	4	11	66	43	111	11	9	.390	.306	R	R	6-2	190	3-20-83	2001	Upland, Calif.
Marshall, Andre	.179	98	273	35	49	7	3	3	18	37	116	12	6	.260	.279	S	R	6-5	200	10-2-80	2001	Oak Harbor, Wash.
Martinez, Casey	.253	32	87	8	22	8	1	0	11	5	20	0	2	.368	.302	R	R	5-11	200	8-31-77	2000	Clearwater, Fla.
McRoberts, Mark	.177	103	322	40	57	14	1	17	38	51	120	7	4	.385	.294	R	R	6-3	190	1-15-82	2000	El Cajon, Calif.
Nonemaker, Karl	.213	48	141	20	30	5	0	0	9	18	25	12	2	.248	.300	L	L	6-0	190	1-7-80	2002	Flanders, N.J.
Nulton, Kevin	.123	26	73	4	9	0	0	1	4	4	18	3	1	.164	.167	R	R	6-0	180	8-16-82	2000	Lakeside, Calif.
Oliva, Chad	.240	30	100	11	24	3	0	2	12	16	43	5	2	.330	.350	R	R	5-11	210	8-27-80	2002	Riviera Beach, Fla.

BATTING	AVG	G	AB	R	H	2B	3B	HR	RBI	BB	SO	SB	CS	SLG	OBP	B	T	HT	WT	DOB	1st Yr	Resides
Perry, Rod	.245	23	53	8	13	1	2	0	3	7	10	2	2	.340	.333	R	R	5-10	190	2-1-79	2001	Carlsbad, Calif.
Roberson, Chris	.234	132	470	64	110	19	5	2	32	57	108	59	16	.309	.331	R	R	6-2	180	8-23-79	2001	San Pablo, Calif.
Rodriguez, Carlos	.196	93	322	27	63	10	3	0	24	30	63	18	10	.245	.270	S	R	6-0	170	10-4-83	2001	Santo Domingo, D.R.
Santora, Jack	.245	17	53	7	13	2	0	1	2	10	7	5	2	.340	.385	S	R	5-9	160	10-6-76	1999	Monterey, Calif.
Sato, G.G.	.247	96	312	40	77	28	3	6	42	22	90	19	5	.413	.313	R	R	6-2	220	8-9-78	2001	Chiba, Japan
Tempesta, Nick	.257	39	136	11	35	4	0	1	21	7	18	2	6	.309	.303	R	R	5-10	180	11-20-78	2001	Brockton, Mass.
Tugwell, Marc	.213	27	80	7	17	7	0	0	5	4	23	0	1	.300	.267	R	R	6-0	190	4-16-81	2003	Springfield, Va.
Walsh, Sean	.214	6	14	3	3	1	1	0	1	2	1	2	0	.429	.313	R	R	6-4	220	11-15-79	2001	Aiken, S.C.
Wardinsky, Ryan	.000	2	4	1	0	0	0	0	0	1	3	0	0	.000	.200	S	R	6-1	180	11-28-79	2002	Kalispell, Mont.

PITCHING	W	L	ERA	G	GS	CG	SV	IP	H	R	ER	BB	SO	AVG	B	T	HT	WT	DOB	1st Yr	Resides
Baisley, Brad	0	2	6.91	6	6	0	0	14	18	15	11	5	8	.281	R	R	6-9	200	8-24-79	1998	Tampa, Fla.
Bourgeois, Nick	7	10	4.42	26	24	0	0	110	92	64	54	61	108	.228	L	L	6-4	210	10-26-80	2002	Lake Charles, La.
Butto, Francisco	10	12	3.03	27	25	2	0	149	134	65	50	59	104	.243	R	R	6-1	200	5-11-80	1999	Maturin, Venez.
Cerrato, Justin	0	1	4.42	9	0	0	0	18	22	10	9	7	15	.297	R	R	6-2	205	6-14-82	2003	Clearwater, Fla.
DeChristofaro, Vinny	0	2	6.65	6	4	0	0	23	24	19	17	23	17	.275	L	L	6-2	160	4-2-82	2001	Richmond Hill, Ga.
Gwaltney, Lee	8	8	3.06	22	22	1	0	118	92	48	40	49	72	.220	R	R	6-5	210	5-6-80	2002	Willow Park, Texas
Hamels, Cole	6	1	0.84	13	13	1	0	75	32	8	7	25	115	.135	L	L	6-3	170	12-27-83	2003	San Diego, Calif.
Hodges, Daniel	2	0	0.82	14	0	0	3	22	16	2	2	7	13	.205	L	L	6-0	180	3-6-81	2003	Tallahassee, Fla.
Lawson, Jarrod	1	0	2.60	12	0	0	4	28	13	8	8	17	29	.138	R	R	6-4	190	4-2-79	1998	Potosi, Mo.
Menocal, Victor	2	7	4.69	22	4	0	3	79	95	50	41	39	37	.309	R	R	6-4	210	8-7-79	2002	Wilmington, N.C.
Minor, Zach	2	3	5.09	25	0	0	1	41	46	24	23	14	28	.283	R	R	6-6	210	8-4-79	2002	Walnut Creek, Calif.
Read, Robby	2	4	5.61	33	2	0	2	77	79	63	48	51	73	.256	R	R	6-1	190	7-12-81	2002	Tallahassee, Fla.
Richardson, Beau	6	5	2.66	47	0	0	16	91	82	34	27	29	55	.244	L	L	6-2	200	9-23-79	2002	San Francisco, Calif.
Rupert, Chris	1	2	5.59	23	0	0	0	37	39	27	23	16	27	.267	R	L	6-0	190	6-19-80	2002	Bozeman, Mont.
Sanchez, Emilio	0	3	4.98	11	0	0	1	22	29	17	12	5	18	.315	R	R	6-3	180	7-20-80	1999	Puerto Plata, D.R.
Segovia, Zach	1	5	3.99	11	10	0	0	50	63	25	22	14	27	.307	R	R	6-2	220	4-11-83	2002	Forney, Texas
Simon, Alfredo	5	0	3.79	14	7	0	2	71	59	32	30	25	66	.224	R	R	6-4	170	5-8-81	1999	Santiago, D.R.
Sweeney, Matt	4	12	4.00	26	17	1	0	115	116	66	51	61	74	.267	R	R	6-2	180	2-25-83	2001	Yardville, N.J.
Tejeda, Robinson	0	3	5.30	5	4	0	0	19	17	11	11	16	20	.246	R	R	6-3	180	3-24-82	1999	Bani, D.R.
Urrutia, Carlos	0	1	7.94	9	0	0	1	11	12	11	10	9	4	.279	R	R	6-3	210	9-3-81	1999	Mariara,Venez.

FIELDING

Catcher	PCT	G	PO	A	E	DP	PB
Gradoville	.992	61	424	43	4	5	13
Martinez	.986	31	199	18	3	1	10
McRoberts	1.000	9	44	4	0	0	3
Sato	.982	49	276	49	6	1	19

First Base	PCT	G	PO	A	E	DP
Barthelemy	.994	63	486	43	3	40
Hansen	.967	34	262	29	10	28
Hopper	.987	20	141	14	2	14
Jarvis	.984	21	175	7	3	10
McRoberts	1.000	3	14	2	0	1
Tempesta	1.000	1	10	1	0	0
Walsh	.000	1	0	0	0	0

Second Base	PCT	G	PO	A	E	DP
Bramasco	1.000	9	25	21	0	2
Isenhower	.960	71	125	161	12	36
Italiano	1.000	1	1	3	0	0
Nulton	.982	15	30	25	1	6
Tempesta	.965	24	34	49	3	12
Tugwell	.991	26	48	58	1	14
Wardinsky	1.000	1	1	0	0	0

Third Base	PCT	G	PO	A	E	DP
Barthelemy	.000	1	0	0	0	0
Bramasco	1.000	1	0	2	0	0
Jones	.944	123	82	188	16	15
Nulton	1.000	6	5	7	0	1
Tempesta	1.000	7	2	17	0	3
Tugwell	1.000	1	0	3	0	1
Walsh	1.000	3	0	3	0	0

Shortstop	PCT	G	PO	A	E	DP
Bramasco	.982	14	16	40	1	11
Delos Santos	.838	9	16	15	6	3
Jones	.000	1	0	0	0	0
Nulton	.900	3	7	11	2	5
Rodriguez	.929	92	116	252	28	39
Santora	.952	17	32	27	3	6
Tempesta	1.000	9	12	17	0	4
Wardinsky	1.000	1	0	3	0	1

Outfield	PCT	G	PO	A	E	DP
Borgo	.963	17	26	0	1	0
Isenhower	1.000	18	25	0	0	0
Marshall	.972	95	198	10	6	2
McRoberts	.950	81	132	2	7	0
Nonemaker	.989	43	82	4	1	0
Oliva	.960	26	46	2	2	0
Perry	.903	20	25	3	3	0
Roberson	.980	132	323	20	7	3
Walsh	1.000	2	2	2	0	0

BATAVIA MUCKDOGS — Short-Season Class A

NEW YORK-PENN LEAGUE

BATTING	AVG	G	AB	R	H	2B	3B	HR	RBI	BB	SO	SB	CS	SLG	OBP	B	T	HT	WT	DOB	1st Yr	Resides
Blalock, Jake	.245	72	261	36	64	23	7	5	31	30	81	9	4	.444	.323	R	R	6-4	210	8-6-83	2002	San Diego, Calif.
Borgo, Alex	.255	14	47	8	12	3	0	3	5	7	18	1	0	.511	.407	R	R	6-0	205	8-5-80	2003	Cookstown, Ontario
Bourn, Michael	.280	35	125	12	35	0	1	0	4	23	28	23	5	.296	.404	L	R	5-11	180	12-27-82	2003	Humble, Texas
Bramasco, Omar	.216	48	148	19	32	7	2	4	10	27	57	3	2	.372	.356	R	R	6-0	180	10-28-81	2002	Huntington Park, Calif.
Brito, Henry	.118	15	51	3	6	0	0	0	1	1	13	0	2	.118	.151	R	R	6-2	170	7-26-80	1999	Maiquetia, Venez.
Brunink, Joseph	.195	42	154	16	30	6	1	2	14	15	50	5	3	.286	.272	L	R	6-2	200	10-24-81	2003	Holland, Mich.
Cortez, Jose	.169	41	142	9	24	2	0	1	17	12	34	0	1	.204	.237	S	R	6-1	215	12-15-80	2003	Chino, Calif.
De los Santos, Esteban	.183	47	153	15	28	4	1	1	8	9	52	5	4	.242	.260	S	R	6-1	160	12-26-82	1999	Santo Domingo, D.R.
Diaz, Jeury	.209	15	43	4	9	2	0	0	3	7	16	1	1	.256	.314	S	R	6-1	170	2-16-81	1999	Bonao, D.R.
Fisher, Kiel	.340	26	97	12	33	4	2	1	11	13	26	3	1	.454	.420	L	R	6-4	190	9-29-83	2002	Riverside, Calif.
Foust, Justin	.227	37	128	13	29	5	0	0	16	9	31	4	1	.266	.286	R	R	6-4	200	5-7-81	2003	Norwood, Ohio
Hansen, Bryan	.214	67	248	29	53	18	4	3	33	30	45	4	2	.355	.304	L	L	6-2	170	5-8-83	2001	Coram, N.Y.
Headley, Jack	.272	48	180	19	49	6	4	1	22	12	13	10	10	.367	.340	R	R	5-11	200	12-19-79	2003	Gilroy, Calif.
Moran, Javon	.284	60	250	33	71	9	3	1	12	16	32	27	11	.356	.326	R	R	5-11	175	9-30-82	2003	Valdosta, Ga.
Moss, Tim	.150	43	160	10	24	5	2	1	11	11	47	5	5	.225	.220	S	R	5-9	150	1-26-82	2003	Lancaster, Texas
Norman, Zach	.155	31	110	8	17	2	0	3	14	7	27	3	0	.255	.225	R	R	6-0	210	1-20-82	2003	Napoleon, Mo.
Riley, Justin	.261	8	23	1	6	2	0	0	1	1	5	0	2	.348	.320	R	R	5-11	205	9-15-80	2003	Crestview, Fla.
Tugwell, Marc	.248	28	121	13	30	6	1	1	20	3	27	3	0	.339	.278	R	R	6-0	190	4-16-81	2003	Springfield, Va.
VonTungeln, Cory	.286	18	56	6	16	3	0	0	6	4	13	1	0	.339	.344	R	R	6-1	180	7-7-81	2003	Bethany, Okla.

GAMES BY POSITION: C—Cortez 41, Diaz 15, Riley 7, VonTungeln 17. **1B**—Brunink 17, Hansen 59. **2B**—Bramasco 11, Headley 6, Moss 43, Tugwell 15. **3B**—Blalock 7, Bramasco 5, Fisher 25, Norman 29, Tugwell 11. **SS**—Bramasco 31, De los Santos 45. **OF**—Blalock 54, Borgo 9, Bourn 34, Brito 15, Brunink 4, Foust 23, Headley 31, Moran 60.

PITCHING	W	L	ERA	G	GS	CG	SV	IP	H	R	ER	BB	SO	AVG	B	T	HT	WT	DOB	1st Yr	Resides
De la Cruz, Julio	1	6	4.37	12	12	0	0	56	44	33	27	22	50	.213	R	R	6-1	170	10-7-80	2001	Cotui, D.R.
DeChristofaro, Vinny	4	0	4.62	15	3	0	0	37	36	21	19	20	32	.251	L	L	6-2	160	4-2-82	2001	Richmond Hill, Ga.
Diefenderfer, Joseph	6	8	5.50	16	13	1	0	74	85	49	45	14	58	.287	L	L	6-0	170	1-7-81	2003	San Luis Obispo, Calif.
Echarry, Nelson	0	0	4.50	2	0	0	0	4	4	3	2	4	4	.266	R	R	6-4	190	2-16-82	1998	Naiguata Vargas, Venez.

PITCHING	W	L	ERA	G	GS	CG	SV	IP	H	R	ER	BB	SO	AVG	B	T	HT	WT	DOB	1st Yr	Resides
Hodges, Daniel	0	0	1.26	8	0	0	1	14	12	3	2	3	13	.230	L	L	6-0	180	3-6-81	2003	Tallahassee, Fla.
Libey, Justin	4	4	2.78	17	9	0	1	68	68	31	21	24	63	.261	R	R	6-5	215	1-14-81	2003	Angola, Ind.
Machi, Jean	2	4	4.78	8	8	0	0	32	30	21	17	13	19	.258	R	R	6-0	160	2-1-83	2001	Guarico, Venez.
Mathieson, Scott	0	0	0.00	2	0	0	1	6	0	0	0	0	7	.000	R	R	6-3	190	2-27-84	2002	Aldergrove, B.C.
McConnell, Caleb	0	4	4.08	23	0	0	2	46	54	22	21	13	32	.293	R	R	6-4	220	5-14-81	2003	West Monroe, La.
Menocal, Victor	3	0	1.61	5	5	0	0	28	14	7	5	12	14	.155	R	R	6-4	210	8-7-79	2002	Wilmington, N.C.
Minor, Zach	0	2	1.25	15	0	0	1	36	22	10	5	14	15	.181	R	R	6-6	210	8-4-79	2002	Walnut Creek, Calif.
Naatjes, Darin	1	3	3.62	8	7	0	0	27	23	15	11	10	24	.219	L	R	6-7	240	7-27-80	2002	Alvord, Iowa
Overton, Brad	2	1	3.19	19	0	0	2	42	37	20	15	19	25	.238	R	R	6-2	190	4-27-81	2003	Winston-Salem, N.C.
Padilla, Matt	1	2	2.70	25	0	0	2	43	44	27	13	21	33	.263	R	R	6-2	230	8-30-81	2003	Roseville, Calif.
Parcus, Kyle	2	4	4.01	13	11	0	0	61	59	28	27	13	36	.254	L	L	6-2	190	10-7-81	2003	Rosebud, Texas
Rupert, Chris	0	4	3.38	17	0	0	3	29	26	15	11	16	29	.245	R	L	6-0	190	6-19-80	2002	Bozeman, Mont.
Urrutia, Carlos	0	0	9.00	1	0	0	0	1	1	1	1	1	0	.333	R	R	6-3	210	9-3-81	1999	Mariara,Venez.
Wilson, Joe	1	1	2.40	3	2	0	0	15	11	4	4	7	14	.211	L	L	6-3	195	8-2-82	2003	Fairfield, Conn.
Woodrow, C.J.	2	2	2.94	17	5	0	2	52	51	22	17	3	39	.252	R	R	6-3	200	8-21-81	2003	Plymouth, Minn.
Ziegler, Brad	1	0	1.50	3	0	0	0	6	5	1	1	1	6	.227	R	R	6-4	190	10-10-79	2003	Springfield, Mo.

CLEARWATER PHILLIES — Rookie

GULF COAST LEAGUE

BATTING	AVG	G	AB	R	H	2B	3B	HR	RBI	BB	SO	SB	CS	SLG	OBP	B	T	HT	WT	DOB	1st Yr	Resides
Aguilar, Trino	.241	24	79	14	19	7	2	0	8	3	20	2	1	.380	.279	R	R	5-10	170	7-27-83	2001	Guarico, Venez.
Alvarado, Wellington	.186	43	129	13	24	6	1	1	8	16	49	1	0	.271	.305	R	R	6-3	190	2-1-82	2002	Hato Mayor, D.R.
Aybar, Francisco	.213	41	122	15	26	5	1	1	12	5	37	7	2	.295	.281	R	R	6-1	176	12-2-83	2003	Bani, D.R.
Baez, Welinson	.246	41	142	20	35	6	1	3	17	12	37	3	1	.366	.319	R	R	6-3	190	7-7-84	2003	Bani, D.R.
Barnett, Toby	.173	18	52	2	9	2	0	0	4	2	19	1	1	.212	.246	R	R	6-2	205	8-4-79	2003	Kallaroo, Australia
Cespedes, Osvaldo	.178	45	118	18	21	3	2	2	11	17	39	7	3	.288	.297	S	R	6-0	160	3-22-85	2002	Azua, D.R.
Crosland, Jason	.263	44	152	20	40	6	2	6	22	12	43	4	3	.447	.337	R	R	6-2	215	8-30-82	2003	Lamar, Colo.
Cuevas, Phillip	.208	22	77	7	16	2	1	0	1	4	23	0	2	.260	.265	R	R	5-11	160	6-30-85	2003	Santo Domingo, D.R.
Durand, Alexander	.257	32	109	13	28	4	2	0	9	11	33	1	1	.330	.336	R	R	6-2	170	7-9-83	2001	Valencia, Venez.
Fisher, Kiel	.323	29	96	16	31	6	3	1	13	18	21	4	1	.479	.429	L	R	6-4	190	9-29-83	2002	Riverside, Calif.
Italiano, Nick	.349	37	129	28	45	9	3	0	21	16	22	5	3	.465	.412	L	R	5-9	185	5-31-81	2003	Marlton, N.J.
Jarvis, Andy	.261	35	115	13	30	4	1	5	20	19	18	2	0	.443	.366	L	L	6-5	225	9-5-80	2003	Renton, Wash.
Karlsen, Grant	.134	23	67	5	9	2	0	0	10	7	23	0	0	.164	.224	R	R	6-2	187	2-21-85	2003	Wheelers Hill, Australia
Klemm, Chris	.336	42	143	20	48	8	2	2	23	18	43	3	3	.462	.415	L	L	6-2	185	4-25-81	2003	Whittier, Calif.
Lopez, Mauber	.282	25	71	2	20	5	0	0	6	5	5	1	0	.352	.329	R	R	5-10	170	6-30-81	2000	Carabobo, Venez.
Moni-Erigbali, Timi	.226	44	155	27	35	10	3	2	18	17	47	12	3	.368	.328	R	R	6-1	200	6-11-82	2002	Irvington, N.J.
Perry, Rod	.000	1	2	0	0	0	0	0	0	1	0	0	1	.000	.333	R	R	5-10	190	2-1-79	2001	Carlsbad, Calif.
Torborg, Jesse	.268	13	41	8	11	1	0	0	3	6	17	2	0	.293	.375	R	R	6-1	210	1-27-83	2003	Ronkonkoma, N.Y.

GAMES BY POSITION: C—Barnett 18, Karlsen 23, Lopez 25. **1B**—Alvarado 39, Crosland 6, Jarvis 17. **2B**—Aguilar 18, Cuevas 17, Italiano 29. **3B**—Aguilar 1, Baez 32, Crosland 6, Durand 1, Fisher 22. **SS**—Aguilar 7, Alvarado 1, Aybar 41, Baez 6, Cuevas 7. **OF**—Cespedes 40, Crosland 23, Durand 30, Klemm 38, Moni-Erigbali 41, Perry 1, Torborg 11.

PITCHING	W	L	ERA	G	GS	CG	SV	IP	H	R	ER	BB	SO	AVG	B	T	HT	WT	DOB	1st Yr	Resides
Cabrera, Nathan	0	1	5.56	5	3	1	0	11	9	8	7	5	9	.200	R	R	6-5	235	1-25-83	2003	Arvada, Colo.
Cerrato, Justin	0	0	3.00	2	1	0	0	3	2	1	1	1	2	.181	R	R	6-2	205	6-14-82	2003	Clearwater, Fla.
Cespedes, Osvaldo	0	1	3.00	2	0	0	0	3	5	1	1	2	3	.000	S	R	6-0	160	3-22-85	2002	Azua, D.R.
Doble, Clemente	5	4	3.00	10	9	1	0	57	57	27	19	9	44	.257	R	R	6-2	170	1-23-82	2001	Villa Mella, D.R.
Echarry, Nelson	1	0	3.65	6	1	0	1	12	11	8	5	9	10	.244	R	R	6-4	190	2-16-82	1998	Naiguata Vargas, Venez.
Encarnacion, Luis	1	2	5.50	12	6	0	0	38	41	29	23	19	19	.277	R	R	6-2	170	11-30-82	2002	Los Alcarrizos, D.R.
Gwaltney, Lee	0	0	0.00	1	1	0	0	2	3	2	0	0	1	.272	R	R	6-5	210	5-6-80	2002	Willow Park, Texas
Harrand, Rob	0	0	3.60	2	1	0	0	5	7	2	2	0	7	.333	R	R	6-5	200	1-11-80	2002	Regina, Sask.
Honsa, Chris	1	2	3.00	11	0	0	4	24	24	17	8	9	17	.247	R	R	6-3	185	8-13-83	2003	Chandler, Ariz.
Jarvis, Andy	1	0	2.25	2	0	0	0	4	2	1	1	1	0	.000	L	L	6-5	225	9-5-80	2003	Renton, Wash.
Jimenez, Elvis	0	1	5.45	16	2	0	1	35	44	31	21	19	19	.309	R	R	6-1	190	8-30-85	2003	Caracas, Venez.
Kendrick, Kyle	0	4	5.46	9	5	0	0	31	40	24	19	12	26	.305	R	R	6-3	185	8-26-84	2003	Mt. Vernon, Wash.
Lawson, Jarrod	0	1	9.00	4	0	0	1	5	3	11	5	11	6	.157	R	R	6-4	190	4-2-79	1998	Potosi, Mo.
Linder, Matt	0	0	3.60	3	0	0	0	5	4	2	2	6	4	.235	R	R	6-5	195	9-15-84	2003	Thunder Bay, Ontario
Mathieson, Scott	2	7	5.52	11	11	0	0	59	59	42	36	13	51	.246	R	R	6-3	190	2-27-84	2002	Aldergrove, B.C.
Ochoa, Harry	4	2	2.65	15	1	0	0	37	35	15	11	14	29	.243	L	L	6-2	180	2-3-83	2002	Guarenas, Venez.
Quijada, Fernando	2	4	6.23	17	0	0	3	35	48	29	24	18	33	.333	R	R	6-3	160	10-9-84	2002	La Asuncion, Venez.
Santander, Nelson	1	0	6.00	5	2	0	0	18	27	15	12	6	11	.341	R	R	6-2	180	11-2-82	2001	Caracas, Venez.
Schultz, Cory	1	1	1.04	11	0	0	5	17	9	4	2	2	13	.147	R	R	6-1	205	9-26-80	2003	Dubuque, Iowa
Segovia, Zach	0	1	4.00	5	4	0	0	9	8	5	4	0	6	.235	R	R	6-2	220	4-11-83	2002	Forney, Texas
Wilson, Joe	4	2	2.24	11	9	0	0	52	44	20	13	17	58	.222	L	L	6-3	195	8-2-82	2003	Fairfield, Conn.

PITTSBURGH PIRATES

BY JOHN PERROTTO

The Pittsburgh Pirates were struck by a case of schizophrenia in 2003.

"It was a tale of two halves, two different seasons," manager Lloyd McClendon said. "It's almost like we had one team and then we had a second team."

Indeed, the Pirates did wind up with two distinctively different rosters. At the start of the season, the organization had more optimism than at any time since the Pirates' last playoff year in 1992. The Pirates looked like possible dark horse contenders in the National League Central following an offseason when they found bargains like righthanders Jeff D'Amico, Jeff Suppan and Julian Tavarez and outfielders Kenny Lofton, Reggie Sanders and Matt Stairs on the free-agent market, while also trading for first baseman Randall Simon.

With the team underachieving at 42-52 on July 20, however, and under orders from owner Kevin McClatchy to cut the payroll to make up for a claimed $30 million loss since moving into PNC Park in 2001, general manager Dave Littlefield began overhauling the roster. He started by trading closer Mike Williams to the Phillies, just five days after the righthander represented the Pirates at the All-Star Game for a second straight year.

Within a month, Suppan, Lofton and Simon were gone, as were lefthanded reliever Scott Sauerbeck and third baseman Aramis Ramirez. The biggest move of all came Aug. 26 when the Pirates dealt their best player for the past five seasons, left fielder Brian Giles, to the Padres in a four-player trade.

The Pirates actually played better after Littlefield began tearing apart the team. After the Williams trade, they went 33-35 the rest of the way to finish with a 75-87 record, fourth in the Central and 13 games behind the first-place Cubs.

While the Pirates again failed to reach .500, extending the franchise record for futility to 11 seasons, they bettered their record of 72-89 in 2002 and were 13 games better than their 62-100 mark of 2001.

"It really was a season of mixed emotions," McClendon said. "Everyone was disappointed with the way we played at the start of the season because we felt we had a better team.

"On the other hand, I think we were all happy with the way we finished the season. I think a lot of people on the outside expected things to fall apart after all the trades but we were able to keep it together and play pretty good baseball."

The Pirates were undermined by their bullpen, which finished last in the NL with a 4.84 ERA, as the trio of Williams, Sauerbeck and righthander Brian Boehringer didn't come close to matching their outstanding 2002 performance. Williams had 25 saves in 40 games before being traded, but his ERA was 6.27. Sauerbeck went 3-4, 4.05 in 53 games before being dealt to Boston.

Sanders was the Pirates' best player, batting .285-31-87 with 15 steals in 130 games despite missing the final 11 games with a strained muscle in his left side.

Catcher Jason Kendall had a comeback year after two subpar seasons because of a torn ligament in his left thumb. He finished sixth in the NL batting race at .325.

While the Pirates continue to lose at the major league level, the news is better down on the farm. Each of their six farm clubs qualified for the playoffs in 2003, and their combined .581 winning percentage was the best among the 30 major league organizations. Short-season Williamsport won the New York-Penn League championship. Pittsburgh's entry in the Dominican Summer League also won the championship.

LARRY GOREN

Reggie Sanders

JOHN SPEAR

Ian Oquendo

PLAYERS of the YEAR

MAJOR LEAGUE: Reggie Sanders, of

Signed for the bargain price of $1 million just before the 2003 season started, Sanders was the Pirates most consistent hitter, leading the club in home runs, RBIs and slugging percentage while chipping in 15 steals and a .285 average.

MINOR LEAGUE: Ian Oquendo, rhp

Former first-round draft picks John VanBenschoten, Sean Burnett and Bryan Bullington all had fine seasons, but Oquendo was a touch better. He went 14-3, 3.00 between Class A Lynchburg and Double-A Altoona, striking out 145 batters in 143 innings.

ORGANIZATION LEADERS

BATTING		
*AVG	Nyjer Morgan, Williamsport	.343
R	Chris Shelton, Altoona/Lynchburg	88
H	Chris Shelton, Altoona/Lynchburg	147
TB	Chris Shelton, Altoona/Lynchburg	248
2B	Ryan Doumit, Lynchburg	38
3B	Three tied at	7
HR	Brad Eldred, Hickory	28
RBI	Walter Young, Lynchburg	87
BB	Chris Shelton, Altoona/Lynchburg	76
SO	Brad Eldred, Hickory	142
SB	Tike Redman, Nashville	42
*SLG	Chris Shelton, Altoona/Lynchburg	.568
*OBP	Chris Shelton, Altoona/Lynchburg	.441
PITCHING		
W	Sean Burnett, Altoona	14
	Ian Oquendo, Altoona/Lynchburg	14
L	Landon Jacobsen, Altoona	11
#ERA	Brady Borner, Altoona/Lynchburg	2.25
G	Three tied at	51
CG	Jonathan Albaladejo, Hickory	5
SV	Mark Corey, Nashville	30
IP	Landon Jacobsen, Altoona	163
BB	Alex Hart, Lynchburg/Hickory	62
SO	Ryan Vogelsong, Nashville	146

*Minimum 250 At-Bats #Minimum 75 Innings

PITTSBURGH PIRATES

Manager: Lloyd McClendon.

2003 Record: 75-87, .463 (4th, NL Central).

BATTING	AVG	G	AB	R	H	2B	3B	HR	RBI	BB	SO	SB	CS	SLG	OBP	B	T	HT	WT	DOB	1st Yr	Resides
Bay, Jason	.291	27	79	13	23	6	1	3	12	18	28	3	1	.506	.423	R	R	6-2	200	9-20-78	2000	Trail, B.C.
2-team (3 San Diego)	.287	30	87	15	25	7	1	4	14	19	29	3	1	.529	.421							
Cota, Humberto	.250	10	16	1	4	1	0	0	1	1	5	0	0	.313	.294	R	R	6-0	210	2-7-79	1995	Rio Colorado, Mexico
Davis, J.J.	.200	19	35	1	7	0	0	1	4	3	13	0	1	.286	.263	R	R	6-5	240	10-25-78	1997	Charlotte, N.C.
Giles, Brian	.299	105	388	70	116	30	4	16	70	85	48	0	3	.521	.430	L	L	5-10	200	1-20-71	1989	San Diego, Calif.
Hernandez, Jose	.223	58	193	19	43	9	1	3	21	16	56	1	0	.326	.282	R	R	6-1	190	7-14-69	1987	Dorado, P.R.
3-team (23 Chi., 69 Colo.)	.225	150	519	58	117	18	3	13	57	46	177	2	1	.347	.287							
Hill, Bobby	.333	1	3	1	1	0	0	0	0	1	0	0	0	.333	.500	S	R	5-10	180	4-3-78	2000	San Jose, Calif.
2-team (5 Chicago)	.286	6	7	1	2	0	0	0	0	2	2	0	0	.286	.444							
House, J.R.	1.000	1	1	0	1	0	0	0	0	0	0	0	0	1.000	1.000	R	R	5-10	200	11-11-79	1999	Ormond Beach, Fla.
Hyzdu, Adam	.206	51	63	16	13	5	0	1	8	10	21	0	0	.333	.320	R	R	6-2	220	12-6-71	1990	Mesa, Ariz.
Kendall, Jason	.325	150	587	84	191	29	3	6	58	49	40	8	7	.416	.399	R	R	6-0	190	6-26-74	1992	Manhattan Beach, Calif.
Lofton, Kenny	.277	84	339	58	94	19	4	9	26	28	29	18	5	.437	.333	L	L	6-0	180	5-31-67	1988	Tucson, Ariz.
Mackowiak, Rob	.270	77	174	20	47	4	4	6	19	15	53	6	0	.443	.342	L	R	5-10	190	6-20-76	1996	Sarasota, Fla.
Nunez, Abraham	.248	118	311	37	77	8	7	4	35	26	53	9	3	.357	.310	S	R	5-11	180	3-16-76	1994	Santo Domingo, D.R.
Ramirez, Aramis	.280	96	375	44	105	25	1	12	67	25	68	1	1	.448	.330	R	R	6-1	210	6-25-78	1994	Santo Domingo, D.R.
Reboulet, Jeff	.241	93	261	37	63	10	2	3	25	27	47	2	1	.330	.321	R	R	6-0	170	4-30-64	1986	Dayton, Ohio
Redman, Tike	.330	56	230	36	76	16	5	3	19	14	18	7	3	.483	.374	L	L	5-11	170	3-10-77	1996	Duncanville, Ala.
Reese, Pokey	.215	37	107	9	23	2	0	1	12	9	31	6	0	.262	.271	R	R	5-11	180	6-10-73	1991	Charlotte, N.C.
Rivera, Carlos	.221	78	95	12	21	5	0	3	10	8	28	0	0	.368	.283	L	L	5-11	230	6-10-78	1996	Rio Grande, P.R.
Sanders, Reggie	.285	130	453	74	129	27	4	31	87	38	110	15	5	.567	.345	R	R	6-1	200	12-1-67	1988	Phoenix, Ariz.
Simon, Randall	.274	91	307	34	84	14	0	10	51	12	30	0	0	.417	.305	L	L	6-0	240	5-26-75	1993	Willemstad, Curacao
Stairs, Matt	.292	121	305	49	89	20	1	20	57	45	64	0	1	.561	.389	L	R	5-9	210	2-27-68	1989	Bangor, Maine
Wilson, Craig	.262	116	309	49	81	15	4	18	48	35	89	3	1	.511	.360	R	R	6-2	210	11-30-76	1995	Huntington Beach, Calif.
Wilson, Jack	.256	150	558	58	143	21	3	9	62	36	74	5	5	.353	.303	R	R	6-0	190	12-29-77	1998	Thousand Oaks, Calif.
Young, Kevin	.202	52	84	8	17	4	0	2	7	12	25	1	0	.321	.302	R	R	6-3	230	6-16-69	1990	Phoenix, Ariz.

PITCHING	W	L	ERA	G	GS	CG	SV	IP	H	R	ER	BB	SO	AVG	B	T	HT	WT	DOB	1st Yr	Resides
Beimel, Joe	1	3	5.05	69	0	0	0	62	69	35	35	33	42	.298	L	L	6-3	220	4-19-77	1998	Cranberry Township, Pa.
Benson, Kris	5	9	4.97	18	18	0	0	105	127	67	58	36	68	.294	R	R	6-4	190	11-7-74	1996	Wexford, Pa..
Boehringer, Brian	5	4	5.49	62	0	0	0	62	64	39	38	30	47	.266	S	R	6-2	190	1-8-70	1991	Fenton, Mo.
Corey, Mark	1	2	5.34	22	0	0	0	30	29	19	18	11	27	.252	R	R	6-3	220	11-16-74	1995	Austin, Pa.
D'Amico, Jeff	9	16	4.77	29	29	2	0	175	204	104	93	42	100	.291	R	R	6-7	250	12-27-75	1993	Palm Harbor, Fla.
Figueroa, Nelson	2	1	3.31	12	3	0	0	35	28	13	13	13	23	.220	S	R	6-1	170	5-18-74	1995	Brooklyn, N.Y.
Fogg, Josh	10	9	5.26	26	26	1	0	142	166	90	83	40	71	.293	R	R	6-0	200	12-13-76	1998	Riverview, Fla.
Gonzalez, Mike	0	1	7.56	16	0	0	0	8	7	7	7	6	6	.233	R	L	6-2	210	5-23-78	1997	Pasadena, Texas
Grabow, John	0	0	3.60	5	0	0	0	5	6	3	2	0	9	.272	L	L	6-2	190	11-4-78	1997	San Gabriel, Calif.
Lincoln, Mike	3	4	5.20	36	0	0	5	36	38	22	21	13	28	.277	R	R	6-2	210	4-10-75	1996	Citrus Heights, Calif.
Mahomes, Pat	0	1	4.84	9	1	0	0	22	19	13	12	12	13	.240	R	R	6-4	220	8-9-70	1988	Lindale, Texas
Mann, Jim	0	0	10.80	2	0	0	0	2	5	4	2	1	1	.454	R	R	6-3	220	11-17-74	1994	Holbrook, Mass.
Meadows, Brian	2	1	4.72	34	7	0	1	76	91	45	40	11	38	.289	R	R	6-3	230	11-21-75	1994	Troy, Ala.
Perez, Oliver	0	3	5.87	5	5	0	0	23	26	15	15	12	24	.282	L	L	6-3	160	8-15-81	1999	Culiacan, Mexico
2-team (19 San Diego)	4	10	5.47	24	24	0	0	127	129	80	77	77	141	.262							
Reyes, Dennys	0	0	10.45	12	0	0	0	10	10	13	12	9	11	.263	R	L	6-3	240	4-19-77	1994	Zaragoza, Mexico
Sanchez, Duaner	1	0	16.50	6	0	0	0	6	15	11	11	1	3	.500	R	R	6-0	190	10-14-79	1996	Cotui, D.R.
Sauerbeck, Scott	3	4	4.05	53	0	0	0	40	30	20	18	25	32	.206	R	L	6-3	200	11-9-71	1994	Cleves, Ohio
Suppan, Jeff	10	7	3.57	21	21	3	0	141	147	57	56	31	78	.268	R	R	6-2	210	1-2-75	1993	Los Angeles, Calif.
Tavarez, Julian	3	3	3.66	64	0	0	11	84	75	37	34	27	39	.243	L	R	6-2	190	5-22-73	1990	Broadview, Ohio
Torres, Salomon	7	5	4.76	41	16	0	2	121	128	65	64	42	84	.275	R	R	5-11	210	3-11-72	1990	San Pedro de Macoris, D.R.
Vogelsong, Ryan	2	2	6.55	6	5	0	0	22	30	19	16	9	15	.322	R	R	6-3	210	7-22-77	1998	Carlisle, Pa.
Wells, Kip	10	9	3.28	31	31	1	0	197	171	77	72	76	147	.232	R	R	6-3	200	4-21-77	1999	Houston, Texas
Williams, Mike	1	3	6.27	40	0	0	25	37	42	26	26	22	20	.281	R	R	6-2	200	7-29-68	1990	Pembroke, Va.

FIELDING

Catcher	PCT	G	PO	A	E	DP	PB
Cota	1.000	4	18	0	0	0	0
Kendall	.989	146	841	48	10	3	9
C. Wilson	.990	21	87	11	1	1	1

First Base	PCT	G	PO	A	E	DP
Hernandez	1.000	1	8	1	0	0
Rivera	.984	60	229	15	4	22
Simon	.994	80	655	52	4	55
Stairs	.991	31	212	10	2	16
C. Wilson	.988	36	229	20	3	31
Young	.995	44	202	18	1	25

Second Base	PCT	G	PO	A	E	DP
Hernandez	.000	1	0	0	0	0
Hill	1.000	1	0	2	0	0
Mackowiak	1.000	15	21	30	0	3
Nunez	.979	71	125	198	7	42
Reboulet	.989	76	134	215	4	51
Reese	.969	33	66	119	6	24
Sanders	.000	1	0	0	0	0

Third Base	PCT	G	PO	A	E	DP
Hernandez	.955	58	35	133	8	14
Mackowiak	.946	19	11	24	2	4
Nunez	1.000	1	0	1	0	0
Ramirez	.924	96	62	216	23	10
Reboulet	1.000	7	3	3	0	1

Shortstop	PCT	G	PO	A	E	DP
Nunez	.986	23	29	44	1	9
J. Wilson	.975	149	218	454	17	104

Outfield	PCT	G	PO	A	E	DP
Bay	.976	26	40	1	1	0
Davis	1.000	10	13	1	0	0
Giles	.992	105	233	4	2	0
Hernandez	1.000	2	1	0	0	0
Hyzdu	1.000	34	37	1	0	0
Lofton	1.000	81	203	5	0	2
Mackowiak	1.000	30	30	0	0	0
Redman	.985	54	127	1	2	0
Sanders	.983	120	222	6	4	2
Stairs	.987	55	73	4	1	0
C. Wilson	.978	46	87	3	2	0
Young	.500	1	1	0	1	0

FARM SYSTEM

Director, Player Development: Brian Graham.

Class	Farm Team	League	W	L	Pct.	Finish*	Manager	First Yr.
AAA	Nashville (Tenn.) Sounds	Pacific Coast	81	62	.566	2nd (16)	Trent Jewett	1998
AA	Altoona (Pa.) Curve	Eastern	78	63	.553	3rd (12)	Dale Sveum	1999
High A	Lynchburg (Va.) Hillcats	Carolina	76	59	.563	2nd (8)	Dave Clark	1995
Low A	Hickory (N.C.) Crawdads	South Atlantic	82	54	.603	2nd (16)	Tony Beasley	1999
SS A	Williamsport (Pa.) Crosscutters	New York-Penn	46	30	.605	3rd (14)	Andy Stewart	1999
Rookie	Bradenton (Fla.) Pirates	Gulf Coast	36	20	.643	2nd (12)	Woody Huyke	1967

*Finish in overall standings (No. of teams in league)

NASHVILLE SOUNDS — Class AAA

PACIFIC COAST LEAGUE

BATTING	AVG	G	AB	R	H	2B	3B	HR	RBI	BB	SO	SB	CS	SLG	OBP	B	T	HT	WT	DOB	1st Yr	Resides
Alvarez, Tony	.298	106	349	50	104	27	3	9	53	28	69	22	9	.470	.361	R	R	6-1	200	5-10-78	1995	Los Teques, Venez.
Barnes, John	.323	120	402	61	130	32	2	13	69	28	41	15	7	.510	.369	R	R	6-2	210	4-24-76	1996	Mesa, Ariz.
Barthol, Blake	.225	38	102	15	23	5	0	2	12	9	22	1	1	.333	.308	R	R	5-11	200	4-7-73	1995	Schnecksville, Pa.
Cota, Humberto	.205	62	200	23	41	9	0	8	27	20	59	2	0	.370	.284	R	R	6-0	210	2-7-79	1995	Rio Colorado, Mexico
Davis, J.J.	.284	122	426	68	121	29	4	26	67	35	85	23	6	.554	.342	R	R	6-5	240	10-25-78	1997	Charlotte, N.C.
De la Rosa, Tomas	.247	101	263	33	65	12	1	4	30	25	38	6	2	.346	.318	R	R	5-10	180	1-28-78	1996	Santo Domingo, D.R.
Doster, Dave	.276	122	456	68	126	32	5	12	57	20	55	4	5	.447	.307	R	R	5-10	170	10-8-70	1993	Fort Wayne, Ind.
Gilbert, Shawn	.154	18	39	2	6	1	0	0	3	3	10	0	2	.179	.205	R	R	5-9	180	3-12-65	1987	Fresno, Calif.
Gulan, Mike	.293	110	417	53	122	29	3	10	59	26	105	6	4	.448	.334	R	R	6-1	200	12-18-70	1992	Steubenville, Ohio
Hill, Bobby	.167	17	66	5	11	2	1	1	4	8	8	1	2	.273	.257	S	R	5-10	180	4-3-78	2000	San Jose, Calif.
2-team (92 Iowa)	.269	109	427	58	115	25	5	7	44	45	73	9	9	.400	.349							
Holbert, Aaron	.270	116	397	57	107	20	7	3	37	19	78	29	13	.378	.314	R	R	6-1	190	1-9-73	1990	Wesley Chapel, Fla.
Hyzdu, Adam	.281	40	135	22	38	10	1	6	18	18	28	2	2	.504	.365	R	R	6-2	220	12-6-71	1990	Mesa, Ariz.
King, Brad	.213	79	197	27	42	8	0	2	21	42	45	0	3	.284	.360	R	R	6-2	210	12-3-74	1996	Long Grove, Ill.
Mackowiak, Rob	.230	59	217	21	50	11	1	2	23	18	51	7	3	.318	.286	L	R	5-10	190	6-20-76	1996	Sarasota, Fla.
Perry, Chan	.241	11	29	1	7	1	0	0	1	2	4	1	0	.276	.290	R	R	6-2	200	9-13-72	1994	Mayo, Fla.
Reboulet, Jeff	.224	17	49	6	11	1	0	0	2	10	11	0	3	.245	.356	R	R	6-0	170	4-30-64	1986	Dayton, Ohio
Redman, Tike	.294	100	360	60	106	12	7	4	29	36	32	42	9	.400	.357	L	L	5-11	170	3-10-77	1996	Duncanville, Ala.
Rivera, Carlos	.263	72	262	28	69	18	0	9	31	13	38	3	1	.435	.300	L	L	5-11	230	6-10-78	1996	Rio Grande, P.R.
Sanchez, Freddy	.400	1	5	1	2	1	0	0	0	0	1	0	0	.600	.400	R	R	5-11	180	12-21-77	2000	Burbank, Calif.
Simon, Randall	.375	2	8	3	3	1	0	1	2	0	0	0	0	.875	.375	L	L	6-0	240	5-26-75	1993	Willemstad, Curacao
Snusz, Chris	.333	6	9	2	3	1	0	0	2	0	1	0	0	.444	.333	R	R	6-0	210	11-8-72	1995	West Seneca, N.Y.
Stairs, Matt	.167	7	18	4	3	0	0	2	3	7	2	0	0	.500	.444	L	R	5-9	210	2-27-68	1989	Bangor, Me.
Thompson, Rich	.257	35	109	17	28	3	2	0	11	9	21	22	3	.321	.333	L	R	6-3	180	4-23-79	2000	Montrose, Pa.
Toca, Jorge	.294	10	34	7	10	2	0	2	10	2	8	0	1	.529	.333	R	R	6-3	220	1-7-75	1999	Miami, Fla.

PITCHING	W	L	ERA	G	GS	CG	SV	IP	H	R	ER	BB	SO	AVG	B	T	HT	WT	DOB	1st Yr	Resides
Bennett, Jeff	1	3	6.56	9	5	0	0	23	26	21	17	12	16	.276	R	R	6-3	200	6-10-80	1998	Brush Creek, Tenn.
Brooks, Frank	2	0	2.54	16	0	0	0	28	22	9	8	11	22	.217	L	L	6-1	190	9-6-78	1999	Brooklyn, N.Y.
Bruback, Matt	2	2	4.91	4	4	0	0	22	18	12	12	12	16	.233	R	R	6-7	210	1-12-79	1998	Sarasota, Fla.
Camp, Shawn	0	1	4.98	33	1	0	0	43	50	26	24	15	36	.289	R	R	6-1	200	11-18-75	1997	Fairfax, Va.
Corey, Mark	1	3	4.34	46	0	0	30	46	37	23	22	18	63	.213	R	R	6-3	220	11-16-74	1995	Austin, Pa.
Figueroa, Nelson	12	5	2.97	23	23	3	0	151	144	54	50	37	121	.251	S	R	6-1	170	5-18-74	1995	Brooklyn, N.Y.
Fogg, Josh	0	1	5.40	2	2	0	0	10	12	6	6	1	7	.324	R	R	6-0	200	12-13-76	1998	Riverview, Fla.
Fordham, Tom	2	2	6.87	13	4	1	0	37	51	29	28	21	20	.331	L	L	6-2	200	2-20-74	1993	El Cajon, Calif.
Gonzalez, Mike	0	0	4.50	7	0	0	2	10	9	5	5	4	10	.230	R	L	6-2	210	5-23-78	1997	Pasadena, Texas
Grabow, John	0	2	4.74	17	0	0	0	25	31	17	13	7	26	.298	L	L	6-2	190	11-4-78	1997	San Gabriel, Calif.
Guerrier, Matt	4	6	4.53	20	19	0	0	105	108	56	53	18	78	.261	R	R	6-3	180	8-2-78	1999	Birmingham, Ala.
Holtz, Mike	3	2	4.91	45	0	0	0	44	45	25	24	19	49	.266	L	L	5-9	180	10-10-72	1994	Hollidaysburg, Pa.
King, Brad	0	0	18.00	3	0	0	0	3	8	6	6	1	0	.000	R	R	6-2	210	12-3-74	1996	Long Grove, Ill.
Lincoln, Mike	1	1	0.71	8	0	0	0	13	8	2	1	4	9	.186	R	R	6-2	210	4-10-75	1996	Citrus Heights, Calif.
Mahomes, Pat	8	4	2.67	38	2	0	2	64	55	20	19	21	28	.235	R	R	6-4	220	8-9-70	1988	Lindale, Texas
Mann, Jim	3	2	3.06	51	0	0	5	62	38	23	21	20	48	.175	R	R	6-3	220	11-17-74	1994	Holbrook, Mass.
Meadows, Brian	7	0	1.41	9	8	1	0	51	32	11	8	0	40	.177	R	R	6-3	230	11-21-75	1994	Troy, Ala.
Prieto, Ariel	0	1	2.55	4	4	0	0	18	17	6	5	8	22	.246	R	R	6-3	240	10-22-66	1995	Miami, Fla.
Reid, Justin	3	7	4.81	34	8	0	1	82	90	52	44	23	51	.276	R	R	6-5	210	6-30-77	1999	Folsom, Calif.
Sanchez, Duaner	4	4	3.69	41	1	0	1	61	63	28	25	27	34	.264	R	R	6-0	190	10-14-79	1996	Cotui, D.R.
Shaffar, Ben	0	0	2.31	4	1	0	0	12	11	4	3	6	12	.255	S	R	6-3	190	9-28-77	1999	Leitchfield, Ky.
Torres, Salomon	1	0	1.80	1	1	0	0	5	2	1	1	1	4	.117	R	R	5-11	210	3-11-72	1990	San Pedro de Macoris, D.R.
Vogelsong, Ryan	12	8	4.29	26	26	1	0	149	142	75	71	54	146	.249	R	R	6-3	210	7-22-77	1998	Carlisle, Pa.
Wasdin, John	8	4	3.04	18	18	3	0	112	101	46	38	24	116	.238	R	R	6-2	190	8-5-72	1993	Jacksonville, Fla.
Williams, Dave	7	4	4.19	16	16	0	0	77	78	44	36	30	56	.260	L	L	6-2	210	3-12-79	1998	Tampa, Fla.

FIELDING

Catcher	PCT	G	PO	A	E	DP	PB
Barthol	.995	34	196	14	1	1	3
Cota	1.000	59	417	23	0	1	3
King	.983	63	421	30	8	4	4
Snusz	1.000	4	14	1	0	1	0

First Base	PCT	G	PO	A	E	DP
Gilbert	.889	2	7	1	1	0
Gulan	.959	7	44	3	2	2
Hyzdu	.963	9	51	1	2	5
King	1.000	9	55	3	0	4
Mackowiak	.989	41	339	18	4	25
Perry	.983	8	54	5	1	2
Rivera	.997	70	544	52	2	40
Simon	1.000	2	10	1	0	2
Stairs	1.000	2	12	2	0	0
Toca	1.000	7	40	6	0	3

Second Base	PCT	G	PO	A	E	DP
De la Rosa	.972	26	41	62	3	12
Doster	.994	85	138	208	2	36
Gilbert	.800	1	3	1	1	0
Gulan	1.000	4	5	7	0	0
Hill	1.000	16	37	37	0	7
Holbert	.970	17	25	39	2	6
Mackowiak	1.000	5	6	2	0	0
Reboulet	1.000	3	2	1	0	0
Sanchez	1.000	1	4	2	0	2

Third Base	PCT	G	PO	A	E	DP
De la Rosa	.852	15	4	19	4	0
Doster	.941	24	9	39	3	3
Gilbert	.909	7	3	7	1	0

Second Base (cont.)	PCT	G	PO	A	E	DP
Gulan	.951	96	60	154	11	12
Holbert	1.000	3	1	4	0	0
King	.000	1	0	0	0	0
Mackowiak	.853	14	7	22	5	3
Reboulet	.833	2	3	2	1	1

Shortstop	PCT	G	PO	A	E	DP
De la Rosa	.954	49	67	99	8	15
Gilbert	1.000	1	1	3	0	0
Gulan	.000	1	0	0	0	0
Holbert	.953	94	126	235	18	39
Reboulet	1.000	9	14	20	0	3

Outfield	PCT	G	PO	A	E	DP
Alvarez	.984	91	178	10	3	2
Barnes	.973	93	137	5	4	1
Brooks	.000	1	0	0	0	0
Davis	.964	114	239	3	9	1
De la Rosa	.000	1	0	0	0	0
Doster	.950	11	18	1	1	1
Gulan	.000	3	0	0	1	0
Hyzdu	1.000	32	52	0	0	0
Mackowiak	1.000	3	5	0	0	0
Redman	.987	94	226	3	3	0
Reid	.000	1	0	0	0	0
Stairs	1.000	4	6	0	0	0
Thompson	1.000	27	59	1	0	0
Toca	1.000	2	7	0	0	0

ALTOONA CURVE — Class AA

EASTERN LEAGUE

BATTING	AVG	G	AB	R	H	2B	3B	HR	RBI	BB	SO	SB	CS	SLG	OBP	B	T	HT	WT	DOB	1st Yr	Resides
Barns, B.J.	.184	22	38	3	7	0	0	0	2	4	11	0	2	.184	.262	L	L	6-4	210	7-21-77	1999	Loysville, Pa.
Bonifay, Josh	.285	114	386	51	110	30	0	11	56	39	106	1	4	.448	.348	R	R	6-0	190	7-30-78	1999	Bradenton, Fla.
Caruso, Joe	.196	83	224	28	44	6	0	2	29	28	43	3	1	.250	.300	R	R	5-9	190	12-30-74	1997	Memphis, Tenn.
Castillo, Jose	.287	126	498	68	143	24	6	5	66	40	81	19	10	.390	.339	R	R	6-1	200	3-19-81	1997	Las Mercedes, Venez.
Duffy, Chris	.273	137	494	84	135	23	6	1	42	44	78	34	12	.350	.355	L	L	5-10	170	4-20-80	2001	Glendale, Ariz.
Garrett, Shawn	.288	124	468	68	135	29	6	13	67	36	96	20	7	.459	.340	S	R	6-3	210	11-2-78	1998	Kinmundy, Ill.
Heintz, Chris	.258	78	271	28	70	12	4	2	26	19	24	0	0	.354	.313	R	R	6-1	200	8-6-74	1996	Clearwater, Fla.
House, J.R.	.333	20	63	12	21	6	0	2	11	5	11	0	0	.524	.382	R	R	5-10	200	11-11-79	1999	Ormond Beach, Fla.
Navarrete, Ray	.256	92	285	32	73	20	1	5	35	15	40	1	5	.386	.297	R	R	6-0	190	5-20-78	2000	Colts Neck, N.J.
Nicholson, Kevin	.294	114	405	63	119	31	5	7	45	41	44	8	8	.447	.358	S	R	5-10	190	3-29-76	1997	Surrey, B.C.
Paulino, Ronny	.226	46	159	19	36	6	1	6	19	12	35	0	2	.390	.283	R	R	6-3	210	4-21-81	1997	Santo Domingo, D.R.
Perry, Chan	.285	109	386	46	110	24	1	7	63	28	38	4	2	.407	.329	R	R	6-2	200	9-13-72	1994	Mayo, Fla.
Roneberg, Brett	.281	125	442	60	124	29	4	10	61	40	56	12	6	.432	.338	L	L	6-2	210	2-5-79	1996	Cairns, Australia
Sadler, Ray	.264	14	53	8	14	5	0	1	7	3	16	0	0	.415	.310	R	R	6-1	200	9-19-80	2000	Waco, Texas
Shelton, Chris	.279	35	122	17	34	10	1	0	14	8	23	0	1	.377	.331	R	R	6-0	220	6-26-80	2001	Salt Lake City, Utah
Skrehot, Shaun	.276	89	304	41	84	15	3	1	33	27	48	12	7	.355	.344	R	R	5-10	180	12-5-75	1998	Spring, Texas
Snusz, Chris	.053	6	19	0	1	0	0	0	0	0	6	0	0	.053	.053	R	R	6-0	210	11-8-72	1995	West Seneca, N.Y.

PITCHING	W	L	ERA	G	GS	CG	SV	IP	H	R	ER	BB	SO	AVG	B	T	HT	WT	DOB	1st Yr	Resides
Bennett, Jeff	4	4	2.72	33	2	0	1	60	45	22	18	23	62	.200	R	R	6-3	200	6-10-80	1998	Brush Creek, Tenn.
Borner, Brady	3	2	3.96	17	0	0	0	25	24	11	11	10	19	.250	L	L	5-10	190	4-12-79	2001	Chaska, Minn.
Brooks, Frank	0	0	7.71	1	0	0	0	2	3	2	2	0	4	.300	L	L	6-1	190	9-6-78	1999	Brooklyn, N.Y.
2-team (34 Reading)	3	4	2.51	35	0	0	9	61	43	18	17	13	75	.199							
Burnett, Sean	14	6	3.21	27	27	2	0	160	158	60	57	29	86	.265	L	L	6-1	170	9-17-82	2000	Wellington, Fla.
Camp, Shawn	0	2	4.34	18	0	0	0	29	26	14	14	11	35	.236	R	R	6-1	200	11-18-75	1997	Fairfax, Va.
Chrysler, Clint	2	1	10.46	16	1	0	0	27	43	33	31	18	14	.377	L	L	6-0	190	11-4-75	1997	St. Petersburg, Fla.
Connolly, Mike	7	8	3.39	25	23	0	0	127	123	55	48	38	90	.252	L	L	6-0	180	6-2-82	2000	Oneonta, N.Y.
Fordham, Tom	5	2	3.17	13	12	0	0	71	71	27	25	18	59	.264	L	L	6-2	200	2-20-74	1993	El Cajon, Calif.
Gonzalez, Mike	0	0	1.23	5	0	0	1	7	4	1	1	2	10	.153	R	L	6-2	210	5-23-78	1997	Pasadena, Texas
Grabow, John	6	1	3.36	24	9	0	1	83	87	34	31	19	73	.280	L	L	6-2	190	11-4-78	1997	San Gabriel, Calif.
Guy, Brad	1	2	5.79	8	1	0	0	14	16	9	9	2	9	.285	R	R	6-2	190	10-25-75	1997	Eureka, Calif.
Jacobsen, Landon	9	11	2.93	27	27	1	0	163	156	60	53	40	80	.260	R	R	6-3	210	5-4-79	1999	Canova, SD
Johnston, Mike	6	2	2.12	46	0	0	7	72	49	17	17	27	65	.199	L	L	6-3	200	3-30-79	1998	Colwyn, Penn.
Martinez, Anastacio	0	0	2.25	3	0	0	0	4	6	1	1	1	1	.400	R	R	6-2	180	11-3-78	1998	Santo Domingo, D.R.
2-team (34 Portland)	3	1	2.25	37	0	0	14	44	37	14	11	25	38	.229							
McDade, Neal	1	6	2.72	38	0	0	4	73	75	32	22	18	48	.264	R	R	6-2	180	6-16-76	1995	Orange Park, Fla.
Oquendo, Ian	4	0	1.96	6	6	0	0	37	36	13	8	10	23	.251	R	R	5-11	160	10-30-81	2000	Dover, Del.
Ozias, Todd	2	2	1.62	51	0	0	21	61	47	14	11	17	52	.212	R	R	6-1	190	8-19-76	1998	Coral Springs, Fla.
Palma, Rick	6	5	3.67	35	5	0	0	69	70	35	28	24	61	.262	L	L	6-1	160	9-26-79	1996	Maracay, Venez.
Shaffar, Ben	1	3	4.48	13	11	0	0	64	68	38	32	20	50	.279	S	R	6-3	190	9-28-77	1999	Leitchfield, Ky.
VanBenschoten, John	7	6	3.69	17	17	1	0	90	95	46	37	34	78	.268	R	R	6-4	210	4-14-80	2001	Milford, Ohio

FIELDING

Catcher	PCT	G	PO	A	E	DP	PB
Heintz	.991	76	508	37	5	0	3
House	.983	9	57	0	1	0	1
Paulino	.988	43	285	35	4	1	2
Shelton	.987	10	66	8	1	0	0
Snusz	1.000	6	29	9	0	1	0

First Base	PCT	G	PO	A	E	DP
Navarrete	1.000	6	40	5	0	7
Perry	.992	53	435	34	4	35
Roneberg	.988	70	611	55	8	72
Shelton	.995	22	166	29	1	13

Second Base	PCT	G	PO	A	E	DP
Bonifay	.833	1	2	3	1	1
Caruso	.961	20	32	66	4	16
Castillo	.973	74	170	185	10	56
Navarrete	.989	45	77	111	2	20
Nicholson	.978	11	13	31	1	6
Skrehot	1.000	5	5	9	0	2

Third Base	PCT	G	PO	A	E	DP
Caruso	.964	42	26	80	4	7
Navarrete	.971	29	20	47	2	6
Nicholson	.934	81	40	173	15	17

Shortstop	PCT	G	PO	A	E	DP
Caruso	.833	5	2	3	1	0
Castillo	.949	52	82	162	13	40
Navarrete	.000	1	0	0	0	0
Nicholson	.976	10	13	27	1	4
Skrehot	.972	81	115	228	10	44

Outfield	PCT	G	PO	A	E	DP
Barns	.933	13	14	0	1	0
Bonifay	.964	103	155	7	6	1
Caruso	1.000	10	14	0	0	0
Duffy	.987	135	305	8	4	1
Garrett	.979	120	229	6	5	4
Roneberg	.989	49	83	7	1	1
Sadler	1.000	13	29	2	0	0
Skrehot	1.000	1	1	0	0	0

LYNCHBURG HILLCATS — High Class A

CAROLINA LEAGUE

BATTING	AVG	G	AB	R	H	2B	3B	HR	RBI	BB	SO	SB	CS	SLG	OBP	B	T	HT	WT	DOB	1st Yr	Resides
Asprilla, Avelino	.208	33	106	12	22	6	0	0	17	3	24	0	2	.264	.225	R	R	5-11	170	1-1-81	1998	Panama City, Panama
Bautista, Jose	.242	51	165	28	40	14	2	4	20	27	48	1	5	.424	.359	R	R	6-0	190	10-19-80	2001	Santo Domingo, D.R.
Berroa, Cristian	.220	39	123	11	27	4	1	0	10	2	18	1	0	.268	.230	S	R	5-11	150	4-29-79	1996	Haina, D.R.
Bozanich, Sam	.231	40	117	15	27	6	0	2	12	16	32	2	0	.333	.336	R	R	5-9	190	11-10-78	2000	Bakersfield, Calif.
Buttler, Vic	.285	117	382	49	109	18	5	3	44	37	47	22	5	.382	.360	L	L	6-0	170	8-12-80	2000	Hawthorne, Calif.
Chaves, Brandon	.262	121	443	62	116	23	6	3	49	40	82	13	8	.361	.327	S	R	6-3	180	8-5-79	2000	Hilo, Hawaii
Cockrell, Michael	.458	7	24	3	11	3	0	0	3	2	1	0	0	.583	.500	R	R	5-10	160	7-25-81	2001	Wilmington, Calif.

BATTING	AVG	G	AB	R	H	2B	3B	HR	RBI	BB	SO	SB	CS	SLG	OBP	B	T	HT	WT	DOB	1st Yr	Resides
Cortes, Jorge	.264	37	129	17	34	6	0	1	15	11	25	1	1	.333	.315	L	L	6-0	180	10-17-80	1997	Barranquilla, Colombia
De Caster, Yurendell	.230	97	330	50	76	24	1	13	56	22	86	3	2	.427	.283	R	R	6-1	200	9-26-79	1996	Willemstad, Curacao
Doumit, Ryan	.275	127	458	75	126	38	1	11	77	45	79	4	0	.434	.351	S	R	6-0	190	4-3-81	1999	Moses Lake, Wash.
Harts, Jeremy	.221	91	272	31	60	11	2	5	39	15	74	4	2	.331	.267	S	L	6-1	190	6-6-80	1998	Decatur, Ga.
Hernandez, Jose	.500	3	4	0	2	0	0	0	0	0	1	0	0	.500	.500	R	R	6-1	200	11-3-80	1998	Valencia, Venez.
Keppinger, Jeff	.325	92	342	55	111	21	2	3	51	23	28	3	2	.424	.365	R	R	6-0	180	4-21-80	2001	Auburn, Ga.
McLouth, Nathan	.300	117	440	85	132	27	2	6	33	55	68	40	4	.411	.386	L	R	5-11	170	10-28-81	2000	Whitehall, Mich.
Meath, Matt	.107	12	28	1	3	0	0	0	0	5	8	0	1	.107	.242	S	R	6-0	170	10-6-79	2001	Boca Raton, Fla.
Paulino, Ronny	.235	23	81	8	19	3	0	1	12	8	8	1	0	.309	.308	R	R	6-3	210	4-21-81	1997	Santo Domingo, D.R.
Pena, Rodolfo	.133	12	30	0	4	2	0	0	2	1	7	0	0	.200	.161	R	R	6-0	190	3-7-79	1997	Monte Cristi, D.R.
Ravelo, Manny	.222	57	171	21	38	2	0	0	6	16	46	11	6	.234	.298	R	R	5-10	160	8-8-79	1997	Santo Domingo, D.R.
Shelton, Chris	.359	95	315	71	113	24	1	21	69	68	67	1	4	.641	.478	R	R	6-0	220	6-26-80	2001	Salt Lake City, Utah
Young, Walter	.278	117	431	76	120	15	2	20	87	35	88	2	4	.462	.348	L	R	6-5	290	2-18-80	1999	Purvis, Miss.

PITCHING	W	L	ERA	G	GS	CG	SV	IP	H	R	ER	BB	SO	AVG	B	T	HT	WT	DOB	1st Yr	Resides
Alcala, Jason	2	0	3.81	15	0	0	1	28	29	13	12	9	22	.266	R	R	6-2	210	9-18-80	1997	Cumana, Venez.
Borner, Brady	4	1	1.68	20	6	0	0	75	63	21	14	12	62	.226	L	L	5-10	190	4-12-79	2001	Chaska, Minn.
Bradley, Bobby	3	2	3.40	12	12	0	0	50	43	21	19	28	36	.232	R	R	6-1	180	12-15-80	1999	Wellington, Fla.
Bullington, Bryan	8	4	3.05	17	17	2	0	97	101	39	33	27	67	.270	R	R	6-5	220	9-30-80	2003	Indianapolis, Ind.
Capps, Matt	0	0	5.40	1	1	0	0	5	3	3	3	4	5	.166	R	R	6-3	220	9-3-83	2002	Douglasville, Ga.
Cedeno, Blas	0	2	5.79	4	4	0	0	23	24	17	15	7	14	.266	R	R	6-0	160	11-15-72	1991	Campo, Venez.
Chrysler, Clint	1	0	2.08	7	0	0	1	9	11	3	2	3	6	.333	L	L	6-0	190	11-4-75	1997	St. Petersburg, Fla.
De los santos, Carlos	0	1	8.36	10	0	0	0	14	13	13	13	18	17	.250	R	R	6-0	180	4-11-78	1998	Santo Domingo, D.R.
Fitch, Steve	2	3	5.26	12	1	0	0	26	26	17	15	9	9	.268	R	R	6-1	180	2-15-78	2000	West Chester, Penn.
Gonzalez, Mike	0	1	5.14	5	0	0	0	7	7	9	4	5	9	.269	R	L	6-2	210	5-23-78	1997	Pasadena, Texas
Guerrero, Julio	4	1	3.90	16	0	0	0	32	37	17	14	6	20	.274	R	R	6-4	180	1-4-81	1999	San Pedro de Macoris, D.R.
Hart, Alex	4	5	4.60	11	11	1	0	59	55	34	30	24	44	.244	R	R	6-6	210	1-10-80	2002	Indian Harbor Beach, Fla.
Harts, Jeremy	0	0	6.75	3	2	0	1	2	3	2	2	4	3	.000	S	L	6-1	190	6-6-80	1998	Decatur, Ga.
Higgins, Josh	7	2	2.37	37	0	0	0	61	56	19	16	12	48	.251	R	R	6-5	180	6-16-79	2000	Santee, Calif.
Lopez, Jose	5	6	3.48	20	19	0	0	106	99	55	41	42	46	.251	R	R	5-11	200	1-28-76	1999	Corpus Christi, Texas
Miller, Jeff	5	6	4.88	27	7	1	0	76	89	51	41	25	59	.301	R	R	6-4	220	2-1-80	2001	Springfield, N.J.
O'Brien, Patrick	2	6	5.47	12	10	0	0	49	64	38	30	18	16	.326	R	R	6-4	200	11-20-80	1999	Bath, Ohio
Oquendo, Ian	10	3	3.33	20	20	1	0	116	105	46	43	33	122	.244	R	R	5-11	160	10-30-81	2000	Dover, Del.
Owens, Henry	1	2	2.45	13	0	0	5	15	9	6	4	11	21	.176	R	R	6-3	230	4-23-79	2001	Miami, Fla.
Sharber, Jason	5	6	4.74	21	16	0	1	95	97	63	50	38	88	.260	R	R	6-3	220	2-24-82	2000	Murfreesboro, Tenn.
Shumaker, Casey	1	3	3.65	33	0	0	4	44	34	22	18	20	45	.215	R	R	6-3	190	7-12-80	2002	Jacksonville, Fla.
Torres, Melqui	2	5	4.23	47	0	0	25	55	55	31	26	25	57	.251	R	R	6-2	200	5-27-77	1996	San Pedro de Macoris, D.R.
VanBenschoten, John	6	0	2.22	9	9	0	0	49	33	14	12	18	49	.191	R	R	6-4	210	4-14-80	2001	Milford, Ohio
Waligora, T.P.	3	0	3.93	21	0	0	0	34	36	19	15	11	36	.264	R	R	6-8	250	8-7-76	1997	Richmond, Va.
Withelder, Greg	1	0	7.59	7	0	0	0	11	17	12	9	7	7	.361	R	L	6-3	200	5-11-79	2000	Wallingford, Pa.

FIELDING

Catcher	PCT	G	PO	A	E	DP	PB
Doumit	.985	86	526	65	9	5	23
Hernandez	1.000	3	10	0	0	0	0
Paulino	.983	14	105	11	2	1	4
Pena	.974	11	69	5	2	0	3
Shelton	.987	28	208	19	3	0	5

First Base	PCT	G	PO	A	E	DP
De Caster	.995	23	169	15	1	10
Keppinger	1.000	1	2	0	0	0
Shelton	.997	41	323	23	1	34
Young	.977	77	570	74	15	44

Second Base	PCT	G	PO	A	E	DP
Asprilla	.957	6	11	11	1	3
Bautista	.889	7	12	12	3	3
Berroa	.966	8	13	15	1	4
Bozanich	.967	30	34	54	3	6
Cockrell	.962	5	11	14	1	1
Keppinger	.971	87	148	224	11	47

Third Base	PCT	G	PO	A	E	DP
Asprilla	.906	11	6	23	3	2
Bautista	.946	44	36	86	7	8
Berroa	.875	16	6	29	5	1
Bozanich	.750	12	6	9	5	0
De Caster	.953	63	49	94	7	8
Keppinger	1.000	3	2	5	0	0

Shortstop	PCT	G	PO	A	E	DP
Asprilla	.914	9	10	22	3	3
Berroa	.944	12	13	21	2	9
Chaves	.952	118	183	291	24	54
Cockrell	1.000	2	0	1	0	0

Outfield	PCT	G	PO	A	E	DP
Asprilla	1.000	7	17	1	0	0
Buttler	.988	114	242	7	3	2
Cortes	.957	36	58	8	3	1
De Caster	.938	10	14	1	1	0
Harts	.920	88	121	5	11	2
McLouth	.979	116	228	4	5	1
Meath	1.000	12	21	0	0	0
Ravelo	.979	53	89	4	2	0

HICKORY CRAWDADS — Low Class A

SOUTH ATLANTIC LEAGUE

BATTING	AVG	G	AB	R	H	2B	3B	HR	RBI	BB	SO	SB	CS	SLG	OBP	B	T	HT	WT	DOB	1st Yr	Resides
Asprilla, Avelino	.344	10	32	5	11	5	0	1	4	3	8	1	1	.594	.417	R	R	5-11	170	1-1-81	1998	Panama City, Panama
Bass, Chris	.265	123	456	59	121	23	3	16	79	34	81	4	1	.434	.320	R	R	6-2	190	10-18-81	2000	Madison, Ind.
Bocchino, Anthony	.163	15	49	5	8	2	0	0	4	2	6	0	0	.204	.196	L	L	5-10	180	5-15-80	2002	Brooklyn, N.Y.
Chapman, Travis	.235	64	217	23	51	12	1	4	19	17	34	0	3	.355	.290	R	R	6-1	190	9-6-80	2001	Fort Walton Beach, Fla.
Collum, Mike	.269	10	26	5	7	1	0	1	2	0	3	1	0	.423	.296	R	R	6-3	180	7-16-81	2001	Wellington, Fla.
Cortes, Jorge	.325	98	345	55	112	24	2	8	66	56	47	9	5	.475	.427	L	L	6-0	180	10-17-80	1997	Barranquilla, Colombia
Davis, Rajai	.305	125	478	84	146	21	7	6	54	55	65	40	13	.416	.383	S	R	5-11	180	10-19-80	2001	New London, Conn.
De la Cruz, Miguel	.252	78	266	24	67	10	1	3	26	20	54	1	3	.331	.307	R	R	6-2	220	10-18-79	1997	Santo Domingo, D.R.
Eldred, Brad	.250	115	420	62	105	22	0	28	80	38	142	7	1	.502	.326	R	R	6-6	240	7-12-80	2002	Coconut Creek, Fla.
Hernandez, Jose	.256	61	227	15	58	5	1	2	18	8	37	2	3	.313	.289	R	R	6-1	200	11-3-80	1998	Valencia, Venez.
Hudnall, Joshua	.222	11	27	5	6	2	1	0	2	4	9	1	0	.370	.323	R	R	6-3	180	2-22-80	1999	Monroe, La.
Kingsbury, Bobby	.223	108	367	44	82	16	6	11	48	37	87	15	9	.390	.300	L	L	6-1	180	8-30-80	2002	Lyndhurst, Ohio
Lee, Taber	.247	115	356	59	88	19	5	3	29	51	62	7	3	.354	.349	S	R	6-1	180	10-18-80	2002	Olympia, Wash.
Lytle, Chaz	.335	101	364	55	122	11	3	0	42	26	39	22	2	.382	.387	L	L	6-0	190	10-27-80	2002	Lake Mary, Fla.
Meath, Matt	.259	48	143	27	37	7	2	2	17	28	39	10	2	.378	.381	S	R	6-0	170	10-6-79	2001	Boca Raton, Fla.
Mercedes, Victor	.285	126	456	76	130	22	5	7	53	36	87	22	15	.401	.341	R	R	5-11	170	4-15-79	1999	Santo Domingo, D.R.
Newman, Ryan	.190	50	142	16	27	0	0	0	13	10	36	1	1	.190	.247	R	R	5-11	160	2-25-79	2002	Scottsdale, Ariz.
Nino, Denny	.000	1	4	0	0	0	0	0	0	0	1	0	0	.000	.000	R	R	6-1	200	6-4-83	2001	Caracas, Venez.
Pena, Rodolfo	.091	3	11	2	1	0	0	0	2	0	0	0	0	.091	.231	R	R	6-0	190	3-7-79	1997	Monte Cristi, D.R.
Reyes, Milver	.091	11	33	1	3	0	0	1	1	1	9	0	0	.182	.118	R	R	5-11	180	9-3-82	1999	San Felipe, Yaracuy, Venez.

PITCHING	W	L	ERA	G	GS	CG	SV	IP	H	R	ER	BB	SO	AVG	B	T	HT	WT	DOB	1st Yr	Resides
Albaladejo, Jonathan	12	5	3.11	29	20	5	1	139	114	53	48	19	110	.225	R	R	6-5	230	10-30-82	2001	Vega Alta, P.R.
Bayer, Russ	1	0	3.60	3	0	0	0	5	6	2	2	0	2	.315	L	L	6-4	200	12-19-79	2002	York, S.C.
Beigh, David	0	0	3.38	14	0	0	2	27	26	12	10	11	20	.254	R	R	6-5	240	2-2-81	2000	Battle Ground, Ind.
Berry, Jon	2	0	4.11	22	0	0	3	31	27	15	14	14	21	.241	R	R	6-1	190	11-17-77	1999	Branchville, S.C.
Bullington, Bryan	5	1	1.39	8	7	0	0	45	25	10	7	11	46	.155	R	R	6-5	220	9-30-80	2003	Indianapolis, Ind.
Cedeno, Blas	0	0	6.75	4	0	0	0	4	6	5	3	0	3	.352	R	R	6-0	160	11-15-72	1991	Campo, Venez.
Davila, Marcus	6	7	1.94	36	0	0	1	65	65	25	14	17	47	.261	R	R	6-1	190	8-14-81	2002	Key West, Fla.
De los Santos, Carlos	2	2	2.04	24	0	0	13	40	23	10	9	15	47	.163	R	R	6-0	180	4-11-78	1998	Santo Domingo, D.R.
Duke, Zach	8	7	3.11	26	26	1	0	142	124	66	49	46	113	.236	L	L	6-2	200	4-19-83	2001	Waco, Texas
Gravelle, Nick	11	5	3.38	26	26	2	0	149	121	61	56	47	103	.224	L	L	6-4	190	2-14-80	2001	Kelso, Wash.
Guerrero, Julio	5	3	3.42	18	3	0	1	50	46	21	19	9	25	.242	R	R	6-4	180	1-4-81	1999	San Pedro de Macoris, D.R.
Hart, Alex	9	1	2.66	15	15	0	0	81	50	27	24	38	68	.183	R	R	6-6	210	1-10-80	2002	Indian Harbor Beach, Fla.
Johnson, Blair	1	1	8.71	2	2	0	0	10	11	10	10	3	7	.282	R	R	6-4	210	3-25-84	2002	Topeka, Kan.
Keirstead, Mike	0	5	6.75	13	12	0	0	61	87	53	46	32	38	.350	R	R	6-3	210	1-26-81	2000	Musquash, N.B.
Lissir, Alexander	1	2	4.55	18	0	0	3	30	37	15	15	8	20	.324	R	R	6-0	190	12-29-82	1999	Tucacas, Venez.
Nunez, Leo	2	1	5.59	13	7	0	0	48	59	34	30	14	37	.304	R	R	6-1	150	8-14-83	2000	Bonao, D.R.
O'Brien, Patrick	6	4	2.59	12	12	1	0	73	69	26	21	28	58	.253	R	R	6-4	200	11-20-80	1999	Bath, Ohio
Owens, Henry	2	1	2.91	22	0	0	9	34	21	14	11	17	52	.176	R	R	6-3	230	4-23-79	2001	Miami, Fla.
Rodriguez, Juan	0	0	2.08	2	0	0	0	4	5	2	1	2	5	.277	R	R	6-1	190	6-10-81	1999	Monte Cristi, D.R.
Shafer, Kurt	3	1	3.80	19	0	0	2	43	46	19	18	5	22	.272	R	R	6-4	190	12-4-81	2000	Land O'Lakes, Fla.
Shortslef, Josh	0	5	7.50	5	5	0	0	18	21	15	15	6	14	.295	R	L	6-4	220	2-1-82	2000	Hannibal, N.Y.
Withelder, Greg	0	0	4.63	12	0	0	0	12	11	6	6	11	7	.255	R	L	6-3	200	5-11-79	2000	Wallingford, Pa.
Youman, Shane	6	3	4.65	40	1	0	12	50	51	31	26	35	58	.262	L	L	6-4	200	10-11-79	2001	New Iberia, La.

FIELDING

Catcher	PCT	G	PO	A	E	DP	PB
Chapman	.990	64	431	46	5	4	8
Hernandez	.993	61	390	48	3	3	9
Nino	1.000	1	9	0	0	0	1
Pena	1.000	3	19	0	0	0	0
Reyes	.977	11	77	8	2	0	1

First Base	PCT	G	PO	A	E	DP
Bass	.993	17	133	14	1	13
De la Cruz	.977	17	123	6	3	14
Eldred	.990	105	851	62	9	62

Second Base	PCT	G	PO	A	E	DP
Asprilla	1.000	2	2	1	0	0
Hudnall	1.000	1	2	4	0	1
Mercedes	.971	125	278	329	18	78
Newman	.954	16	27	35	3	6

Third Base	PCT	G	PO	A	E	DP
Asprilla	1.000	4	3	7	0	0
Bass	.945	68	50	106	9	11
Collum	1.000	4	3	7	0	1
De la Cruz	.853	50	29	99	22	16
Hudnall	1.000	1	0	1	0	0
Newman	.957	18	12	33	2	3

Shortstop	PCT	G	PO	A	E	DP
Asprilla	.900	3	8	10	2	3
Collum	1.000	2	0	1	0	0
Hudnall	.867	5	6	7	2	1
Lee	.939	115	121	308	28	44
Newman	.959	15	13	34	2	8

Outfield	PCT	G	PO	A	E	DP
Bocchino	1.000	2	2	1	0	0
Cortes	.970	93	179	13	6	1
Davis	.975	117	260	15	7	2
Hudnall	1.000	2	3	0	0	0
Kingsbury	.982	97	209	6	4	2
Lytle	.992	69	120	3	1	0
Meath	.952	35	59	1	3	0

WILLIAMSPORT CROSSCUTTERS — Short-Season Class A

NEW YORK-PENN LEAGUE

BATTING	AVG	G	AB	R	H	2B	3B	HR	RBI	BB	SO	SB	CS	SLG	OBP	B	T	HT	WT	DOB	1st Yr	Resides
Arbinger, Mike	.248	41	141	21	35	7	3	2	23	7	25	1	0	.383	.295	L	R	5-10	180	4-21-80	2002	Toledo, Ohio
Bocchino, Anthony	.326	59	215	26	70	13	6	0	29	15	28	5	2	.442	.369	L	L	5-10	180	5-15-80	2002	Brooklyn, N.Y.
Boeve, Adam	.250	39	132	20	33	9	1	3	16	15	39	6	1	.402	.353	R	R	6-1	205	6-20-80	2003	Doon, Iowa
Brown, Tim	.253	50	158	24	40	10	0	2	16	21	44	0	1	.354	.385	L	L	6-3	220	2-21-83	2001	Eugene, Ore.
Chance, Andrew	.221	43	149	22	33	4	2	4	20	8	42	2	1	.356	.278	R	R	6-2	210	9-12-80	2003	Brews Bridge, La.
Cockrell, Michael	.277	70	274	47	76	23	5	3	41	15	25	7	6	.431	.332	R	R	5-10	160	7-25-81	2001	Wilmington, Calif.
Collum, Mike	.184	12	38	5	7	2	1	0	6	2	9	1	0	.289	.244	R	R	6-3	180	7-16-81	2001	Wellington, Fla.
Guzman, Javier	.243	47	173	19	42	9	2	2	24	10	26	4	3	.353	.283	R	R	5-11	160	5-4-84	2001	Santo Domingo, D.R.
Harris, Justin	.234	50	171	18	40	6	0	0	18	3	15	1	2	.269	.249	R	R	6-0	165	5-25-81	2003	Longwood, Fla.
Holmes, Brett	.253	34	87	16	22	3	1	0	6	4	21	3	0	.310	.290	R	R	6-2	190	3-13-81	2003	Springfield, Mo.
Madrid, Mike	.273	57	198	24	54	10	0	2	34	18	20	2	1	.354	.347	L	L	6-0	230	6-8-80	2002	Silver City, N.M.
McCuistion, Mike	.206	41	136	19	28	3	1	0	10	15	24	1	0	.243	.292	L	R	6-2	210	5-14-82	2001	Yucaipa, Calif.
Morgan, Nyjer	.343	72	268	49	92	7	4	0	23	33	44	26	17	.399	.439	L	L	6-0	180	7-2-80	2002	Willits, Calif.
Ohtsuka, Yoshiyuki	.209	16	43	4	9	3	0	0	5	1	5	0	1	.279	.261	R	R	5-10	190	6-19-80	2002	Kanagawa, Japan
Ramos, Victor	.286	8	14	1	4	1	0	0	2	2	2	0	0	.357	.375	R	R	6-3	200	10-4-81	2000	Cayey, P.R.
Reyes, Milver	.216	40	125	13	27	6	0	0	12	3	22	0	0	.264	.252	R	R	5-11	180	9-3-82	1999	San Felipe, Venez.
Smith, John	.000	1	3	1	0	0	0	0	0	1	1	0	0	.000	.250	L	R	5-10	180	1-18-82	2002	Hawkinsville, Ga.
Smith, Sean	.208	16	48	6	10	4	1	0	6	2	10	1	0	.333	.269	R	R	5-10	180	8-24-82	2000	Joliet, Ill.
Stansberry, Craig	.307	45	166	19	51	9	3	2	21	13	25	5	3	.434	.370	R	R	6-0	185	3-8-82	2003	Plano, Texas

GAMES BY POSITION: C—McCuistion 37, Ramos 8, Reyes 40. **1B**—Brown 45, Madrid 36. **2B**—Cockrell 59, Guzman 5, Harris 13, Ohtsuka 3, J. Smith 1. **3B**—Cockrell 11, Collum 9, Harris 1, Ohtsuka 12, Stansberry 45. **SS**—Cockrell 1, Collum 2, Guzman 42, Harris 37. **OF**—Arbinger 26, Bocchino 48, Boeve 25, Chance 28, Holmes 25, Morgan 71, S. Smith 15.

PITCHING	W	L	ERA	G	GS	CG	SV	IP	H	R	ER	BB	SO	AVG	B	T	HT	WT	DOB	1st Yr	Resides
Bayer, Russ	1	3	2.21	21	2	0	0	57	51	18	14	21	46	.246	L	L	6-4	200	12-19-79	2002	York, S.C.
Bimeal, Matt	4	2	1.91	27	0	0	1	47	35	13	10	13	37	.208	R	R	6-3	220	8-17-80	1999	Davidsville, Pa.
De Maria, Chris	6	3	2.68	25	1	0	3	47	36	15	14	10	48	.209	R	R	6-3	210	9-28-80	2002	Torrance, Calif.
Gorzelanny, Tom	1	2	1.78	8	8	0	0	30	23	6	6	10	22	.214	S	L	6-2	200	7-12-82	2003	Orland Park, Ill.
Hernandez, Chris	1	2	1.64	20	0	0	3	38	28	8	7	16	41	.204	R	R	6-0	200	8-3-80	2003	Redlands, Calif.
Kiley, Jason	0	1	4.73	10	1	0	0	13	16	10	7	8	8	.296	R	R	6-4	220	10-15-82	2001	St. Charles, Ill.
Lissir, Alexander	5	4	3.72	15	14	0	0	73	77	40	30	24	49	.271	R	R	6-0	190	12-29-82	1999	Tucacas, Venez.
Maholm, Paul	2	1	1.83	8	8	0	0	34	25	11	7	10	32	.196	L	L	6-2	215	6-25-82	2003	Holly Springs, Miss.
Nunez, Leo	4	3	3.05	8	8	0	0	38	31	14	13	12	41	.210	R	R	6-1	150	8-14-83	2000	Bonao, D.R.
Schneider, Jonathan	1	0	0.00	12	0	0	6	12	7	1	0	6	4	.159	R	R	6-7	210	10-28-79	2002	Springfield, Va.
Shafer, Kurt	7	3	3.15	14	9	1	2	66	54	29	23	18	35	.224	R	R	6-4	190	12-4-81	2000	Land O'Lakes, Fla.
Sharpless, Josh	1	1	2.59	22	0	0	5	31	19	9	9	17	45	.172	R	R	6-5	225	1-26-81	2003	Freedom, Pa.
Silva, Sergio	6	3	2.17	12	11	0	0	58	45	18	14	19	49	.213	R	R	6-4	210	12-22-81	2003	Lindsay, Calif.
Torrealba, Yoann	6	1	2.04	14	14	0	0	75	61	24	17	15	60	.221	R	R	5-11	170	6-24-82	2000	Veroe, Venez.
Tower, Scott	1	1	5.20	15	0	0	0	28	25	20	16	17	29	.242	L	L	6-1	170	8-19-81	2002	Lometa, Texas
White, Brian	0	0	4.61	11	0	0	1	14	12	8	7	9	4	.235	R	R	5-11	170	4-23-82	2002	Valrico, Fla.

GULF COAST LEAGUE

BATTING	AVG	G	AB	R	H	2B	3B	HR	RBI	BB	SO	SB	CS	SLG	OBP	B	T	HT	WT	DOB	1st Yr	Resides
Arias, Garvi	.148	23	61	9	9	1	0	1	7	6	12	5	2	.213	.246	R	R	6-0	170	8-11-83	1999	Santo Domingo, D.R.
Asprilla, Avelino	.429	9	35	11	15	2	1	2	11	2	5	3	1	.714	.462	R	R	5-11	170	1-1-81	1998	Panama City, Panama
Bautista, Jose	.348	7	23	5	8	1	0	1	3	4	7	0	0	.522	.429	R	R	6-0	190	10-19-80	2001	Santo Domingo, D.R.
Carlin, Michael	.186	34	113	14	21	2	4	1	15	15	14	2	1	.301	.285	R	R	6-0	205	7-6-81	2003	Pittsburgh, Pa.
Fulton, Josh	.236	41	161	39	38	6	0	1	13	14	22	8	2	.292	.317	S	R	5-10	185	12-11-79	2003	Olympia, Wash.
Hart, Randall	.182	7	22	2	4	1	0	0	3	0	6	0	0	.227	.182	R	R	5-10	180	4-2-81	2003	Seminole, Fla.
Hicks, Joe	.256	44	168	19	43	6	5	4	25	9	48	2	2	.423	.302	R	R	5-11	170	4-22-84	2002	Houston, Texas
House, J.R.	.400	20	65	16	26	9	0	4	23	12	5	0	0	.723	.476	R	R	5-10	200	11-11-79	1999	Ormond Beach, Fla.
Macia, Wanell	.293	52	191	25	56	8	4	1	28	5	40	6	2	.393	.307	L	L	5-11	170	7-20-82	2001	La Romana, D.R.
Morales, Leonardo	.167	6	18	1	3	0	0	0	1	2	4	0	0	.167	.250	R	R	6-1	180	6-28-83	2000	Guarena, Venez.
Nino, Denny	.316	24	79	9	25	5	1	0	9	4	16	1	1	.405	.345	R	R	6-1	200	6-4-83	2001	Caracas, Venez.
Poni, Francis	.088	23	80	7	7	1	0	0	6	2	26	0	1	.100	.140	R	R	6-0	200	8-1-83	2003	Carson, Calif.
Powell, Pedro	.291	26	79	13	23	3	0	0	5	5	10	5	3	.329	.364	R	R	5-7	150	5-20-84	2003	Hawkinsville, Ga.
Ramirez, Rafael	.143	17	56	5	8	1	0	2	5	2	21	0	0	.268	.169	R	R	6-2	180	6-12-82	2003	San Pedro de Macoris, D.R.
Rea, Brad	.366	36	134	18	49	7	0	2	24	10	15	0	1	.463	.407	R	R	6-4	220	7-29-79	2002	Gibsonia, Pa.
Santiago, John	.279	37	140	22	39	9	2	0	16	9	23	1	1	.371	.329	R	R	6-1	170	12-26-84	2003	Trujillo Alto, P.R.
Smith, John	.279	41	147	21	41	11	1	1	20	21	14	3	1	.388	.363	L	R	5-10	180	1-18-82	2002	Hawkinsville, Ga.
Solano, Solamdi	.319	44	166	38	53	4	1	3	20	18	27	12	4	.410	.386	R	R	6-0	160	8-18-83	2000	San Cristobal, D.R.
Stevens, Anthony	.073	17	41	4	3	2	0	0	2	1	14	1	0	.122	.136	R	R	6-0	180	8-27-84	2003	Knoxville, Tenn.
Wulf, Kent	.231	31	117	8	27	5	0	0	15	6	25	7	1	.274	.286	R	R	5-11	175	4-26-85	2003	Leona Valley, Calif.

GAMES BY POSITION: C—Hart 7, House 9, Nino 24, Poni 20. **1B**—Carlin 27, Rea 31. **2B**—Smith 21, Solano 35. **3B**—Asprilla 4, Bautista 5, Ramirez 17, Santiago 31, Solano 3, Stevens 1. **SS**—Asprilla 3, Fulton 41, Santiago 1, Solano 3, Stevens 12. **OF**—Arias 22, Carlin 4, Hicks 44, Macia 52, Morales 6, Powell 22, Wulf 30.

PITCHING	W	L	ERA	G	GS	CG	SV	IP	H	R	ER	BB	SO	AVG	B	T	HT	WT	DOB	1st Yr	Resides
Alcala, Jason	0	0	7.20	2	0	0	0	5	9	4	4	1	4	.391	R	R	6-2	210	9-18-80	1997	Cumana, Venez.
Bradley, Bobby	0	0	0.00	1	1	0	0	3	1	0	0	1	4	.111	R	R	6-1	180	12-15-80	1999	Wellington, Fla.
Capps, Matt	5	1	1.87	10	10	1	0	63	40	16	13	9	54	.177	R	R	6-3	220	9-3-83	2002	Douglasville, Ga.
Cedeno, Blas	1	0	0.00	9	0	0	6	12	7	0	0	3	11	.175	R	R	6-0	160	11-15-72	1991	Campo, Venez.
Chrysler, Clint	1	1	3.00	2	1	0	0	6	6	3	2	2	7	.250	L	L	6-0	190	11-4-75	1997	St. Petersburg, Fla.
Contreras, Omar	0	0	10.13	2	0	0	0	3	4	4	3	1	5	.285	R	R	6-1	170	12-3-82	2000	Valencia, Venez.
Cuffman, Jacob	2	1	4.98	8	3	0	0	22	29	17	12	16	27	.325	R	R	6-4	185	3-3-85	2003	Butler, Pa.
Davidson, David	0	2	12.91	7	0	0	0	8	10	12	11	7	8	.357	L	L	6-1	180	4-23-84	2002	Thorold, Ontario
Garavito, Jean	0	1	7.88	7	0	0	0	8	12	7	7	3	6	.315	R	R	5-11	160	1-11-85	2002	San Felipe, Venez.
Holliday, Brian	3	2	3.83	10	10	1	0	52	50	24	22	22	52	.255	L	L	6-2	180	6-1-84	2002	Moon Township, Pa.
Hummel, John	3	3	3.18	10	0	0	1	34	26	16	12	9	15	.204	L	L	6-5	210	4-18-84	2002	Hoffman Estates, Ill.
Johnson, Blair	4	1	1.34	9	9	0	0	47	32	9	7	11	42	.188	R	R	6-4	210	3-25-84	2002	Topeka, Kan.
Johnson, Russell	0	0	0.00	1	1	0	0	3	0	0	0	0	4	.000	L	R	6-2	200	1-6-85	2003	Alexander City, Ala.
Marquetti, Agustin	0	1	8.25	8	0	0	0	12	13	14	11	12	9	.270	S	R	6-6	220	2-24-78	2002	Caracas, Venez.
Michael, Mark	1	0	2.10	13	0	0	6	26	14	7	6	7	32	.166	R	R	6-3	185	1-20-81	2003	Lexington, Ky.
Molleken, Dustin	0	0	5.68	3	1	0	0	6	6	4	4	1	1	.285	L	R	6-4	220	8-21-84	2003	Regina, Sask.
Munoz, Luis	2	1	4.89	9	5	2	0	39	38	23	21	11	29	.246	R	R	6-2	150	1-10-82	2000	San Pedro de Macoris, D.R.
Ortega, Joel	4	1	1.54	10	0	0	0	23	19	5	4	7	22	.208	R	R	6-1	150	2-4-84	2000	Aguadulce, Panama
Pearson, Kyle	3	2	2.05	7	4	0	0	26	26	9	6	10	25	.252	R	R	6-1	180	10-8-84	2003	Panama City, Fla.
Rodriguez, Juan	1	0	0.96	5	0	0	3	9	3	1	1	2	15	.093	R	R	6-1	190	6-10-81	1999	Monte Cristi, D.R.
Shaffar, Ben	1	0	3.27	5	0	0	0	11	12	5	4	1	12	.260	S	R	6-3	190	9-28-77	1999	Leitchfield, Ky.
Starling, Wardell	4	1	3.94	11	11	0	0	48	47	23	21	13	52	.247	R	R	6-4	200	3-14-83	2003	Missouri City, Texas
Tejada, Luis	1	2	9.15	7	0	0	1	21	37	26	21	8	4	.402	R	R	6-4	170	8-22-83	2002	Monte Cristi, D.R.

ST. LOUIS CARDINALS

BY DAVE WILHELM

It was a season of unfulfilled dreams for the Cardinals. Built to win the 2003 World Series with a payroll of $83 million, the Cardinals instead ran into repeated speed bumps and finished third in the National League Central, three games behind the Cubs.

The Cardinals' season fell apart Sept. 1-4 at Wrigley Field, where they dropped four of five games to the Cubs. Two weekends later, they were swept in a three-game series in Houston. The two series led to a 13-13 record in September. In the three previous Septembers, the Cardinals were 58-20 and made the playoffs each year.

Most of the Cardinals' problems centered on their pitching staff, which had a 4.60 ERA and surrendered a franchise-record 210 home runs. Five pitchers—Brett Tomko (35), Garrett Stephenson (30), Jason Simontacchi (21), Matt Morris (20) and Woody Williams (20)—allowed at least 20, and veteran reliever Jeff Fassero permitted 17 homers in just 78 innings.

Despite a powerful lineup capable of hitting as many home runs as the pitching staff allowed, the Cardinals still lacked clutch hitting and were 14-25 in one-run games. For the third straight year, left fielder Albert Pujols was the focal point of the offense. Pujols won his first NL batting championship and finished at .359-43-124 with 51 doubles. Edgar Renteria (.330-13-100, 34 steals) became the first Cardinals shortstop to drive in 100 runs, and third baseman Scott Rolen finished at .286-28-104. Center fielder Jim Edmonds played his typically strong defense and batted .275-39-89. Catcher Mike Matheny (.252-8-47) didn't commit an error all season.

The offense was also hurt by health problems. Injuries hampered the seasons of outfielder J.D. Drew (.289-15-42), second baseman Fernando Vina (.251-4-23) and outfielder-catcher Eli Marrero (.224-2-20). Rookie second baseman Bo Hart (.277-4-28), however, did help offset Vina's extended loss.

Pitching injuries also played a role in the Cardinals' demise. Closer Jason Isringhausen, who had offseason shoulder surgery, was expected to be ready by late April. Instead, he didn't pitch until June and didn't register his first save until June 19. He finished with 22 saves—10 fewer than in 2002. Without Isringhausen (0-1, 2.36), the Cardinals bullpen was in shambles. It blew 30 of 70 save opportunities.

Other than Isringhausen, Cal Eldred (7-4, 3.74), Steve Kline (5-5, 3.82) and rookie Kiko Calero (1-1. 2.82) were the Cardinals' most reliable arms out of the bullpen. Calero's season, however, ended when he suffered a knee injury in late June. Two other pitchers, Sterling Hitchcock (5-1, 3.79) and Mike DeJean (1-1, 4.00) pitched well after coming to St. Louis in separate trades.

Williams (18-9, 3.87) anchored the rotation, making a team-high 33 starts and recording a career high in wins. Morris (11-8, 3.76) had a sore shoulder and suffered a broken right hand, but he finished strong. Tomko (13-9, 5.28), acquired in the offseason, was hit hard most of the year but enjoyed a fine stretch run. Stephenson (7-13, 4.59) also had his moments—good and bad.

Simontacchi, a rookie success story in 2002, was unable to duplicate that form, going 9-5, 5.66. Rookie righthander Dan Haren (3-7, 5.08) impressed manager Tony La Russa after being recalled at midseason. Haren was a combined 8-1, 2.68 at Triple-A Memphis and Double-A Tennessee before his promotion to the Cardinals on July 19.

The Tennessee affiliate was the Cardinals' only minor league team to finish better than .500, and the Smokies made the Southern League playoffs as a wild card. Memphis hosted the Triple-A all-star game.

Albert Pujols

Dan Haren

STEVE MOORE

PLAYERS of the YEAR

MAJOR LEAGUE: Albert Pujols, of

Pujols became the first major leaguer to produce three straight seasons with a .300 average, 30 homers and 100 RBIs. At. 359, he won his first batting title and also led the National League in runs, hits, doubles and total bases.

MINOR LEAGUE: Dan Haren, rhp

Haren began the 2003 season by going 6-0, 0.82 in Double-A, moved to Triple-A and went 2-1, 4.93 and ended his year in the St. Louis rotation. He allowed 86 hits in 101 minor league innings, registering 84 strikeouts against 14 walks.

ORGANIZATION LEADERS

BATTING		
*AVG	John Gall, Memphis/Tennessee	.314
R	Bucky Jacobsen, Tennessee	84
H	John Gall, Memphis/Tennessee	161
TB	Bucky Jacobsen, Tennessee	252
2B	Caonabo Cosme, Tennessee	35
3B	Reid Gorecki, Peoria	8
HR	Bucky Jacobsen, Tennessee	31
RBI	John Gall, Memphis/Tennessee	85
BB	Jon Nunnally, Memphis	98
SO	Jon Nunnally, Memphis	126
SB	Matt Lemanczyk, Tennessee /Peoria	57
*SLG	Bucky Jacobsen, Tennessee	.564
*OBP	Jon Nunnally, Memphis	.408
PITCHING		
W	Jeremy Cummings, Memphis/Tennessee	15
L	Tyler Adamczyk, Peoria	12
	Rhett Parrott, Memphis/Tennessee	12
#ERA	Josh Kinney, Tennessee/Palm Beach	1.11
G	Carmen Cali, Palm Beach	62
CG	Don Graves, Palm Beach/Peoria	2
SV	Mike Lyons, Tennessee	31
IP	Jason Ryan, Memphis	190
BB	Chance Caple, Palm Beach	63
SO	Rhett Parrott, Memphis/Tennessee	137

*Minimum 250 At-Bats #Minimum 75 Innings

ST. LOUIS CARDINALS

Manager: Tony La Russa.

2003 Record: 85-77, .525 (3rd, NL Central).

BATTING	AVG	G	AB	R	H	2B	3B	HR	RBI	BB	SO	SB	CS	SLG	OBP	B	T	HT	WT	DOB	1st Yr	Resides
Cairo, Miguel	.245	92	261	41	64	15	2	5	32	13	30	4	1	.375	.289	R	R	6-1	210	5-4-74	1991	Bakersfield, Calif.
Delgado, Wilson	.169	43	77	8	13	3	0	0	3	3	10	0	0	.208	.207	S	R	5-11	160	7-15-72	1993	San Cristobal, D.R.
Drew, J.D.	.289	100	287	60	83	13	3	15	42	36	48	2	2	.512	.374	L	R	6-1	200	11-20-75	1997	Hahira, Ga.
Edmonds, Jim	.275	137	447	89	123	32	2	39	89	77	127	1	3	.617	.385	L	L	6-1	210	6-27-70	1988	Orange, Calif.
Girardi, Joe	.130	16	23	1	3	0	0	0	1	3	4	0	0	.130	.231	R	R	5-11	200	10-14-64	1986	Chicago, Ill.
Hart, Bo	.277	77	296	46	82	13	5	4	28	12	64	3	1	.395	.317	R	R	5-11	175	9-27-76	1999	Laselva Beach, Calif.
Marrero, Eli	.224	41	107	10	24	4	2	2	20	7	18	0	1	.355	.267	R	R	6-1	180	11-17-73	1993	Miami, Fla.
Martinez, Tino	.273	138	476	66	130	25	2	15	69	53	71	1	1	.429	.352	L	R	6-2	230	12-7-67	1989	Tampa, Fla.
Matheny, Mike	.252	141	441	43	111	18	2	8	47	44	81	1	1	.356	.320	R	R	6-3	220	9-22-70	1991	St. Charles, Mo.
Palmeiro, Orlando	.271	141	317	37	86	13	1	3	33	32	31	3	3	.347	.336	L	L	5-11	180	1-19-69	1991	Miami, Fla.
Perez, Eduardo	.285	105	253	47	72	16	0	11	41	29	53	5	2	.478	.365	R	R	6-4	240	9-11-69	1991	Santurce, P.R.
Pujols, Albert	.359	157	591	137	212	51	1	43	124	79	65	5	1	.667	.439	R	R	6-3	225	1-16-80	1999	St. Louis, Mo.
Renteria, Edgar	.330	157	587	96	194	47	1	13	100	65	54	34	7	.480	.394	R	R	6-1	200	8-7-75	1992	Pembroke Pines, Fla.
Robinson, Kerry	.250	116	208	19	52	6	3	1	16	8	27	6	1	.322	.281	L	L	6-0	175	10-3-73	1994	Chesterfield, Mo.
Rolen, Scott	.286	154	559	98	160	49	1	28	104	82	104	13	3	.528	.382	R	R	6-4	240	4-4-75	1993	Holmes Beach, Fla.
Taguchi, So	.259	43	54	9	14	3	1	3	13	4	11	0	0	.519	.310	R	R	5-10	165	7-2-69	2002	Nishinomiya, Japan
Vina, Fernando	.251	61	259	35	65	14	4	4	23	11	24	4	4	.382	.309	L	R	5-9	180	4-16-69	1991	Stateline, Nevada
Widger, Chris	.235	44	102	9	24	9	0	0	14	6	20	0	0	.324	.279	R	R	6-2	210	5-21-71	1992	Pennsville, N.J.

PITCHING	W	L	ERA	G	GS	CG	SV	IP	H	R	ER	BB	SO	AVG	B	T	HT	WT	DOB	1st Yr	Resides
Borbon, Pedro	0	1	20.25	7	0	0	0	4	14	9	9	2	0	.560	L	L	6-1	230	11-15-67	1988	Houston, Texas
Calero, Kiko	1	1	2.82	26	1	0	1	38	29	12	12	20	51	.211	R	R	6-1	185	1-9-75	1996	Rio Piedras, P.R.
Crudale, Mike	0	1	2.38	13	0	0	0	11	11	5	3	12	6	.250	R	R	6-0	200	1-3-77	1999	Danville, Calif.
De Jean, Mike	1	1	4.00	18	0	0	1	18	17	8	8	12	13	.261	R	R	6-2	220	9-28-70	1992	Castle Rock, Colo.
2-team (58 Milwaukee)	5	8	4.68	76	0	0	19	83	86	46	43	39	71	.268							
Eldred, Cal	7	4	3.74	62	0	0	8	67	62	32	28	31	67	.248	R	R	6-4	240	11-24-67	1989	Chandler, Ariz.
Fassero, Jeff	1	7	5.68	62	6	0	3	78	93	51	49	34	55	.296	L	L	6-1	200	1-5-63	1984	Paradise Valley, Ariz.
Haren, Danny	3	7	5.08	14	14	0	0	73	84	44	41	22	43	.292	R	R	6-5	220	9-17-80	2001	West Covina, Calif.
Hermanson, Dustin	1	2	5.46	23	0	0	1	30	35	18	18	14	12	.315	R	R	6-2	200	12-21-72	1994	Phoenix, Ariz.
Hitchcock, Sterling	5	1	3.79	8	6	0	0	38	34	17	16	14	32	.237	L	L	6-0	205	4-29-71	1989	Tampa, Fla.
Isringhausen, Jason	0	1	2.36	40	0	0	22	42	31	14	11	18	41	.200	R	R	6-3	230	9-7-72	1992	Tarpon Springs, Fla.
Journell, Jimmy	0	0	6.00	7	0	0	0	9	10	7	6	11	8	.277	R	R	6-4	210	12-29-77	1999	Springfield, Ohio
Kline, Steve	5	5	3.82	78	0	0	3	64	56	29	27	30	31	.237	S	L	6-1	215	8-22-72	1993	Winfield, Pa.
Molina, Gabe	0	0	13.50	3	0	0	0	3	5	4	4	1	1	.384	R	R	5-11	205	5-3-75	1996	Denver, Colo.
Morris, Matt	11	8	3.76	27	27	5	0	172	164	76	72	39	120	.251	R	R	6-5	220	8-9-74	1995	Jupiter, Fla.
Ohme, Kevin	0	0	0.00	2	0	0	0	4	3	0	0	1	2	.200	L	L	6-1	185	4-13-71	1993	Brandon, Fla.
Painter, Lance	0	1	5.50	22	0	0	0	18	17	12	11	7	11	.246	L	L	6-1	200	7-21-67	1990	Highland Ranch, Colo.
Pearce, Josh	0	0	3.00	7	0	0	0	9	11	3	3	2	4	.305	R	R	6-3	220	8-20-77	1999	Yakima, Wash.
Pearson, Jason	0	0	63.00	2	0	0	0	1	4	7	7	3	1	.571	L	L	6-0	190	12-29-75	1998	Freeport, Ill.
Simontacchi, Jason	9	5	5.56	46	16	1	1	126	153	82	78	41	74	.299	R	R	6-2	190	11-13-73	1996	Santa Clara, Calif.
Springer, Russ	1	1	8.31	17	0	0	0	17	19	16	16	6	11	.271	R	R	6-4	215	11-7-68	1989	Pollack, La.
Stephenson, Garrett	7	13	4.59	32	27	1	0	174	167	94	89	60	91	.255	R	R	6-5	215	1-2-72	1992	Kimberly, Idaho
Tomko, Brett	13	9	5.28	33	32	2	0	203	252	126	119	57	114	.305	R	R	6-4	215	4-7-73	1995	San Diego, Calif.
Williams, Woody	18	9	3.87	34	33	0	0	221	220	101	95	55	153	.255	R	R	6-0	200	8-19-66	1988	Fresno, Texas
Yan, Esteban	2	0	6.02	39	0	0	1	43	53	29	29	16	28	.308	R	R	6-4	250	6-22-75	1991	San Pedro de Marocos, D.R.

FIELDING

Catcher	PCT	G	PO	A	E	DP	PB
Girardi	.958	13	23	0	1	0	0
Marrero	1.000	6	29	4	0	0	0
Matheny	1.000	138	774	49	0	7	5
Widger	.995	41	185	14	1	1	2

First Base	PCT	G	PO	A	E	DP
Cairo	1.000	3	9	0	0	1
Marrero	1.000	2	6	0	0	0
Martinez	.997	126	1026	85	3	92
Matheny	1.000	4	7	0	0	1
Perez	1.000	5	9	2	0	1
Pujols	.997	62	340	33	1	34
Widger	1.000	1	2	1	0	0

Second Base	PCT	G	PO	A	E	DP
Cairo	.986	40	58	88	2	17
Delgado	1.000	12	12	20	0	3
Hart	.989	69	167	180	4	35
Taguchi	.000	1	0	0	0	0
Vina	.974	60	147	158	8	44

Third Base	PCT	G	PO	A	E	DP
Cairo	.818	12	3	6	2	1
Delgado	1.000	11	2	6	0	0
Perez	.769	12	3	7	3	1
Rolen	.969	153	109	298	13	23

Shortstop	PCT	G	PO	A	E	DP
Cairo	.938	7	5	10	1	2
Delgado	.947	11	5	13	1	1
Hart	1.000	3	2	5	0	1
Renteria	.975	156	191	439	16	83

Outfield	PCT	G	PO	A	E	DP
Cairo	.970	27	31	1	1	1
Drew	.994	75	154	7	1	1
Edmonds	.986	129	335	12	5	5
Marrero	.980	31	49	1	1	0
Palmeiro	1.000	112	165	6	0	1
Perez	.966	71	113	1	4	0
Pujols	.986	113	198	7	3	0
Robinson	1.000	88	93	0	0	0
Taguchi	1.000	38	30	2	0	1
Widger	1.000	1	1	0	0	0

LARRY GOREN

Woody Williams

Edgar Renteria: Fourth in NL in steals and batting average

John Gall: Led Cardinals farmhands with a .314 average

FARM SYSTEM

Director, Player Development: Bruce Manno.

Class	Farm Team	League	W	L	Pct.	Finish*	Manager(s)	First Yr.
AAA	Memphis (Tenn.) Redbirds	Pacific Coast	64	79	.448	15th (16)	Tom Spencer/Danny Sheaffer	1998
AA	Tennessee (Sevierville, Tenn.) Smokies	Southern	72	67	.518	4th (10)	Mark DeJohn	2003
High A	Palm Beach (Fla.) Cardinals	Florida State	54	84	.391	12th (12)	Tom Nieto	2003
Low A	Peoria (Ill.) Chiefs	Midwest	65	73	.471	11th (14)	Joe Cunningham	1995
SS A	New Jersey (Augusta, N.J.) Cardinals	New York-Penn	31	42	.425	10th (14)	Tommy Shields	1994
Rookie	Johnson City (Tenn.) Cardinals	Appalachian	27	36	.429	7th (10)	Ron Warner	1974

*Finish in overall standings (No. of teams in league)

MEMPHIS REDBIRDS — Class AAA

PACIFIC COAST LEAGUE

BATTING	AVG	G	AB	R	H	2B	3B	HR	RBI	BB	SO	SB	CS	SLG	OBP	B	T	HT	WT	DOB	1st Yr	Resides
Abbott, Kurt	.226	21	62	2	14	5	0	0	6	4	21	0	0	.306	.265	R	R	6-0	200	6-2-69	1989	Davie, Fla.
Bowers, Jason	.246	117	415	42	102	15	7	7	34	24	69	7	6	.366	.299	R	R	5-11	170	1-27-78	1998	Uniontown, Pa.
Cairo, Miguel	.231	3	13	2	3	1	0	0	0	0	3	0	0	.308	.231	R	R	6-1	210	5-4-74	1991	Bakersfield, Calif.
Coffie, Ivanon	.206	12	34	3	7	1	0	2	5	3	3	0	0	.412	.263	L	R	6-1	190	5-16-77	1995	Willemstad, Curacao
Delgado, Alex	.375	8	24	2	9	1	0	0	5	2	5	0	0	.417	.429	R	R	6-0	160	1-11-71	1988	Palmarejo, Venez.
Delgado, Wilson	.233	26	86	11	20	2	0	2	12	10	15	2	1	.326	.313	S	R	5-11	160	7-15-72	1993	San Cristobal, D.R.
Dunwoody, Todd	.225	102	334	39	75	26	2	10	39	18	77	13	4	.404	.261	L	L	6-1	210	4-11-75	1993	West Lafayette, Ind.
Encarnacion, Mario	.143	6	21	1	3	0	0	0	0	0	5	0	0	.143	.143	R	R	6-2	210	9-24-75	1994	Bani, D.R.
2-team (16 Edmonton)	.261	22	69	9	18	2	0	1	6	7	16	0	1	.333	.329							
Espada, Joe	.269	8	26	3	7	0	2	1	1	0	5	0	0	.538	.269	R	R	5-10	170	8-30-75	1996	Carolina, P.R.
Gall, John	.312	123	461	62	144	24	1	16	73	39	56	5	2	.473	.368	R	R	6-0	195	4-2-78	2000	Portola Valley, Calif.
Girardi, Joe	.292	18	65	3	19	1	0	0	4	5	6	0	0	.308	.352	R	R	5-11	200	10-14-64	1986	Chicago, Ill.
Hansen, Jed	.182	10	22	4	4	0	0	1	1	10	7	1	1	.318	.438	R	R	6-1	190	8-19-72	1994	Olympia, Wash.
Hart, Bo	.297	67	266	30	79	14	2	7	31	15	55	4	2	.444	.331	R	R	5-11	175	9-27-76	1999	Laselva Beach, Calif.
Haynes, Dee	.252	125	441	53	111	24	3	18	70	15	50	3	1	.442	.279	R	R	6-0	205	2-22-78	2000	Columbus, Miss.
Krause, Scott	.400	3	10	4	4	0	0	0	0	0	0	0	0	.400	.400	R	R	6-1	180	8-16-73	1994	Willowick, Ohio
Lesher, Brian	.276	10	29	4	8	2	0	0	2	4	5	0	0	.345	.364	R	L	6-5	210	3-5-71	1992	Scottsdale, Ariz.
Malloy, Marty	.246	85	244	28	60	12	2	2	19	22	33	7	2	.336	.312	L	R	5-10	160	7-6-72	1992	Trenton, Fla.
2-team (7 Las Vegas)	.254	92	264	31	67	14	2	2	21	22	39	7	2	.345	.317							
Marrero, Eli	.250	5	12	2	3	1	0	1	1	1	0	0	0	.583	.357	R	R	6-1	180	11-17-73	1993	Miami, Fla.
Morales, Willie	.236	16	55	4	13	4	1	2	10	4	16	0	0	.455	.306	R	R	5-10	180	9-7-72	1993	Tucson, Ariz.
Nieves, Jose	.200	23	70	4	14	2	1	0	1	1	6	3	0	.257	.233	R	R	6-0	180	6-16-75	1992	Carabobo, Venez.
Nunnally, Jon	.269	134	428	81	115	20	5	25	53	98	126	19	11	.514	.408	L	R	5-10	205	11-9-71	1992	Keeling, Va.
Paquette, Craig	.265	11	49	3	13	1	0	0	4	2	12	0	0	.286	.288	R	R	6-0	210	3-28-69	1989	Wildwood, Mo.
Peeples, Mike	.214	30	84	7	18	3	0	0	3	3	16	1	1	.250	.261	R	R	6-0	170	9-3-76	1994	Green Cove Springs, Fla.
Robinson, Kerry	.344	16	61	14	21	2	1	0	3	1	7	5	0	.410	.355	L	L	6-0	175	10-3-73	1994	Chesterfield, Mo.
Rodriguez, Luis	.216	75	199	19	43	6	2	2	9	17	46	2	0	.296	.280	R	R	5-11	195	1-3-74	1991	Tampa, Fla.
Rodriguez, Nerio	.000	13	18	0	0	0	0	0	0	1	10	0	0	.000	.053	R	R	6-1	200	3-4-71	1991	San Pedro de Macoris, D.R.

BATTING	AVG	G	AB	R	H	2B	3B	HR	RBI	BB	SO	SB	CS	SLG	OBP	B	T	HT	WT	DOB	1st Yr	Resides
Ryan, Jason	.109	32	46	1	5	2	0	0	1	0	13	0	0	.152	.109	S	R	6-3	185	1-23-76	1994	Charlotte, N.C.
Seabol, Scott	.300	88	307	40	92	22	1	16	58	32	64	2	0	.534	.376	R	R	6-4	200	5-17-75	1996	McKeesport, Penn.
Selby, Bill	.262	76	279	33	73	12	6	9	41	24	32	5	1	.444	.319	L	R	5-10	190	6-11-70	1992	Southhaven, Miss.
Taguchi, So	.256	90	258	31	66	8	2	2	24	22	36	14	5	.326	.318	R	R	5-10	165	7-2-69	2002	Nishinomiya, Japan
Torrealba, Steve	.274	46	117	16	32	9	1	2	18	16	20	1	1	.419	.370	R	R	6-0	220	2-24-78	1995	Barquisimeto, Venez.
Vina, Fernando	.176	5	17	1	3	0	0	0	1	2	2	0	0	.176	.250	L	R	5-9	180	4-16-69	1991	Stateline, Nev.
Widger, Chris	.239	23	71	8	17	7	0	2	10	7	12	1	0	.423	.304	R	R	6-2	210	5-21-71	1992	Pennsville, N.J.

PITCHING	W	L	ERA	G	GS	CG	SV	IP	H	R	ER	BB	SO	AVG	B	T	HT	WT	DOB	1st Yr	Resides
Borbon, Pedro	0	1	3.12	7	0	0	1	9	6	3	3	0	6	.200	L	L	6-1	230	11-15-67	1988	Houston, Texas
Carpenter, Chris	0	0	5.40	3	3	0	0	8	11	5	5	2	4	.333	R	R	6-6	230	4-27-75	1994	Bedford, N.H.
Cook, B.R.	0	1	9.31	13	0	0	0	19	29	20	20	14	7	.353	R	R	6-4	200	3-2-78	1999	Salem, Ore.
Crudale, Mike	5	5	5.52	32	0	0	6	29	34	19	18	11	23	.283	R	R	6-0	200	1-3-77	1999	Danville, Calif.
Cummings, Jeremy	7	3	4.81	13	13	0	0	73	73	40	39	20	37	.259	R	R	6-2	215	11-7-76	1999	Hurricane, W.Va.
Duff, Matt	4	2	2.62	32	0	0	3	34	28	12	10	14	33	.220	R	R	6-1	215	10-6-74	1997	Alligator, Miss.
Haren, Dan	2	1	4.93	8	8	0	0	46	50	25	25	8	35	.271	R	R	6-5	220	9-17-80	2001	West Covina, Calif.
Joseph, Kevin	1	5	4.37	22	5	0	0	60	71	34	29	21	30	.300	R	R	6-4	200	8-1-76	1997	Dallas, Texas
Journell, Jimmy	6	6	3.92	40	7	0	5	78	80	38	34	32	70	.267	R	R	6-4	210	12-29-77	1999	Springfield, Ohio
Lambert, Jeremy	1	0	3.86	12	0	0	0	12	11	5	5	5	9	.250	R	R	6-1	220	1-10-79	1997	Taylorsville, Utah
Layfield, Scotty	0	3	4.33	22	0	0	2	27	29	13	13	16	17	.287	R	R	6-2	210	9-13-76	1999	Montezuma, Ga.
Molina, Gabe	2	9	5.09	57	0	0	9	64	73	40	36	31	47	.292	R	R	5-11	205	5-3-75	1996	Denver, Colo.
Ohme, Kevin	5	5	4.32	49	0	0	1	67	77	34	32	21	32	.285	L	L	6-1	185	4-13-71	1993	Brandon, Fla.
Painter, Lance	0	0	0.00	3	0	0	0	3	2	0	0	0	1	.200	L	L	6-1	200	7-21-67	1990	Highland Ranch, Colo.
Parrott, Rhett	2	3	3.54	7	7	0	0	41	39	16	16	19	25	.256	R	R	6-2	190	11-12-79	2001	Dalton, Ga.
Pearce, Josh	3	3	4.08	10	9	0	0	46	51	22	21	8	27	.280	R	R	6-3	220	8-20-77	1999	Yakima, Wash.
Pearson, Jason	4	4	3.10	44	0	0	3	52	41	21	18	9	36	.211	L	L	6-0	190	12-29-75	1998	Freeport, Ill.
Rodriguez, Nerio	5	1	1.89	11	11	1	0	76	57	19	16	12	54	.207	R	R	6-1	200	3-4-71	1991	San Pedro de Macoris, D.R.
Ryan, Jason	8	6	2.70	29	28	0	0	190	195	63	57	45	110	.273	S	R	6-3	185	1-23-76	1994	Charlotte, N.C.
Serafini, Dan	0	1	9.00	3	2	0	0	8	19	9	8	2	2	.475	L	L	6-1	190	1-25-74	1992	San Bruno, Calif.
Springer, Russ	0	0	1.42	7	0	0	0	6	2	1	1	4	5	.105	R	R	6-4	215	11-7-68	1989	Pollack, La.
Stemle, Steve	6	11	3.46	26	26	1	0	156	155	71	60	36	89	.259	R	R	6-4	200	5-20-77	1998	New Albany, Ind.
Walrond, Les	0	0	1.04	10	1	0	0	17	12	2	2	7	14	.193	L	L	6-0	190	11-7-76	1998	Brentwood, Tenn.
Weibl, Clint	3	6	4.53	20	16	0	1	95	102	56	48	33	59	.273	R	R	6-3	180	3-17-75	1996	Dawson, Pa.
Yennaco, Jay	0	3	6.62	8	7	0	0	34	41	25	25	18	15	.310	R	R	6-1	220	11-17-75	1996	Windham, N.H.

FIELDING

Catcher	PCT	G	PO	A	E	DP	PB
A. Delgado	1.000	5	36	3	0	0	0
Girardi	1.000	18	73	14	0	3	0
Morales	.989	16	89	5	1	1	0
L. Rodriguez	.985	67	298	40	5	1	5
Torrealba	.996	40	207	15	1	0	2
Widger	.968	19	110	10	4	3	1

First Base	PCT	G	PO	A	E	DP
Dunwoody	.986	9	64	4	1	5
Encarnacion	.889	1	8	0	1	1
Gall	.993	120	1010	48	7	81
Paquette	1.000	2	13	2	0	0
Peeples	.990	14	95	5	1	8
Seabol	.961	6	46	3	2	7
Widger	1.000	1	5	0	0	1

Second Base	PCT	G	PO	A	E	DP
Abbott	1.000	3	6	5	0	0
Bowers	.986	18	31	40	1	8
Cairo	1.000	2	5	3	0	1
Coffie	1.000	2	8	6	0	2
W. Delgado	1.000	1	0	1	0	0
Hart	.979	45	72	113	4	25
Malloy	.993	63	134	151	2	38
Nieves	1.000	2	3	3	0	0
Selby	.980	20	41	56	2	15
Vina	1.000	4	1	12	0	1

Third Base	PCT	G	PO	A	E	DP
Abbott	.881	13	9	28	5	4
Bowers	.905	9	4	15	2	0
Coffie	.846	7	3	8	2	0
Hansen	.941	8	6	10	1	1
Hart	.906	13	5	24	3	4
Morales	1.000	1	0	1	0	0
Nieves	.500	4	0	1	1	0
Paquette	.870	10	5	15	3	2
Peeples	.750	1	0	6	2	0
Seabol	.948	81	63	157	12	16
Selby	.970	13	6	26	1	3

Shortstop	PCT	G	PO	A	E	DP
Bowers	.968	89	129	258	13	53
Coffie	1.000	1	1	4	0	0
A. Delgado	1.000	2	2	4	0	0
W. Delgado	.991	25	43	70	1	9
Espada	1.000	7	8	18	0	1
Hart	1.000	9	10	24	0	4
Malloy	.958	3	7	16	1	3
Nieves	.944	14	25	26	3	5

Outfield	PCT	G	PO	A	E	DP
Dunwoody	.987	79	144	5	2	1
Encarnacion	1.000	3	12	1	0	0
Gall	1.000	6	8	1	0	0
Haynes	.983	113	224	9	4	3
Krause	1.000	2	2	1	0	0
Lesher	1.000	6	12	0	0	0
Marrero	1.000	3	3	0	0	0
Nunnally	.987	119	302	7	4	3
Peeples	1.000	7	13	0	0	0
Robinson	.979	16	46	0	1	0
L. Rodriguez	1.000	1	4	0	0	0
Selby	.987	34	69	5	1	0
Taguchi	.994	70	170	3	1	1
Widger	1.000	2	4	0	0	0

TENNESSEE SMOKIES — Class AA

SOUTHERN LEAGUE

BATTING	AVG	G	AB	R	H	2B	3B	HR	RBI	BB	SO	SB	CS	SLG	OBP	B	T	HT	WT	DOB	1st Yr	Resides
Abreu, Dennis	.250	18	52	6	13	1	1	1	8	4	13	2	2	.365	.298	R	R	6-0	165	4-22-78	1995	Tumero, Venez.
Ankiel, Rick	.240	30	25	2	6	1	0	1	5	1	2	0	0	.400	.269	L	L	6-1	215	7-19-79	1997	Fort Pierce, Fla.
Benjamin, Al	.177	33	79	10	14	4	0	3	11	0	11	1	2	.342	.193	R	R	6-1	200	9-9-77	1996	Houston, Texas
Bolivar, Papo	.278	133	474	56	132	24	3	4	52	46	73	30	11	.367	.344	R	R	5-10	170	10-18-78	1995	Catia La Mar, Venez.
Boyd, Shaun	.273	27	88	9	24	6	0	0	6	4	12	2	2	.341	.305	R	R	5-10	175	8-15-81	2000	Las Vegas, Nevada
Burns, Kevan	.287	87	272	39	78	14	6	3	29	24	66	8	2	.415	.346	L	L	6-0	180	11-10-76	1999	Beloit, Wisc.
Cosme, Caonabo	.273	132	495	63	135	35	3	6	45	32	112	9	6	.392	.320	R	R	6-2	160	3-18-79	1996	La Vega, D.R.
Dodson, Jeremy	.223	41	112	14	25	6	0	3	10	13	30	6	2	.357	.315	L	R	6-2	200	5-3-77	1998	Sherman, Texas
Duncan, Chris	.200	10	25	1	5	1	0	1	3	0	6	0	0	.360	.200	L	R	6-5	210	5-5-81	1999	Tucson, Ariz.
Erickson, Corey	.206	100	311	45	64	21	0	16	50	39	82	5	1	.428	.299	R	R	5-11	190	1-10-77	1995	Springfield, Ill.
Gall, John	.327	12	52	6	17	1	0	3	12	3	4	0	1	.519	.357	R	R	6-0	195	4-2-78	2000	Portola Valley, Calif.
Girardi, Joe	.400	3	10	0	4	0	0	0	1	0	0	0	1	.400	.455	R	R	5-11	200	10-14-64	1986	Chicago, Ill.
Jacobsen, Bucky	.298	131	447	84	133	24	1	31	84	56	91	3	1	.564	.388	R	R	6-4	220	8-30-75	1997	Hermiston, Ore.
Krause, Scott	.294	73	201	30	59	17	2	5	23	19	36	5	3	.473	.376	R	R	6-1	180	8-16-73	1994	Willowick, Ohio
Lemanczyk, Matt	.167	7	12	1	2	0	0	0	0	0	1	1	1	.167	.231	R	R	6-2	195	10-5-80	2002	Rockville Centre, N.Y.
Molina, Yadier	.275	104	364	32	100	13	1	2	51	25	45	0	1	.332	.327	R	R	5-11	185	7-13-82	2001	Vega Alta, P.R.
Moylan, Dan	.275	64	182	21	50	3	1	2	23	29	28	1	0	.335	.377	L	R	6-0	190	4-24-79	2000	Keene, N.H.
Nelson, John	.237	136	506	60	120	22	1	5	42	44	117	10	5	.314	.301	R	R	6-1	190	3-3-79	2001	Denton, Texas
Netwall, Chris	.200	3	10	0	2	0	0	0	3	1	2	0	0	.200	.273	R	R	6-1	205	11-17-79	2001	Allentown, Pa.
Roman, Jesse	.167	16	48	3	8	2	0	1	4	3	16	0	0	.271	.231	L	L	6-0	190	4-21-79	2001	Woodhaven, N.Y.

BATTING	AVG	G	AB	R	H	2B	3B	HR	RBI	BB	SO	SB	CS	SLG	OBP	B	T	HT	WT	DOB	1st Yr	Resides
Schumaker, Skip	.251	91	342	43	86	20	3	2	22	37	54	6	6	.345	.330	L	R	5-10	175	2-3-80	2001	Laguna Niguel, Calif.
Weekly, Chris	.254	111	279	27	71	13	0	3	31	39	53	5	1	.333	.347	L	R	6-2	190	12-4-76	1999	Mesa, Ariz.

PITCHING	W	L	ERA	G	GS	CG	SV	IP	H	R	ER	BB	SO	AVG	B	T	HT	WT	DOB	1st Yr	Resides
Ankiel, Rick	2	6	6.29	20	10	1	0	54	45	42	38	49	64	.231	L	L	6-1	215	7-19-79	1997	Fort Pierce, Fla.
Axelson, Josh	4	2	2.76	27	8	0	0	75	68	26	23	19	58	.247	R	R	6-1	200	12-4-78	2000	Brooklyn, Mich.
Carpenter, Chris	0	1	13.50	1	1	0	0	3	7	5	5	2	2	.437	R	R	6-6	230	4-27-75	1994	Bedford, N.H.
Collins, Pat	1	2	5.96	5	5	0	0	23	26	20	15	18	14	.282	R	R	6-5	230	3-3-78	1999	Union, N.J.
Cook, B.R.	1	0	2.43	29	0	0	1	33	26	15	9	18	23	.222	R	R	6-4	200	3-2-78	1999	Salem, Ore.
Cook, Jeremy	0	3	4.74	10	2	0	0	25	28	14	13	3	14	.280	R	R	6-6	235	5-11-78	2000	Yuba City, Calif.
Cummings, Jeremy	8	6	3.34	15	14	0	0	89	69	36	33	22	63	.216	R	R	6-2	215	11-7-76	1999	Hurricane, W.Va.
Figueroa, Juan	5	2	2.92	34	0	0	2	37	30	15	12	15	44	.218	R	R	6-3	240	6-24-75	1996	Santo Domingo, D.R.
Haren, Dan	6	0	0.82	8	8	0	0	55	36	8	5	6	49	.180	R	R	6-5	220	9-17-80	2001	West Covina, Calif.
Isringhausen, Jason	0	0	0.00	2	2	0	0	2	1	0	0	0	3	.142	R	R	6-3	230	9-7-72	1992	Tarpon Springs, Fla.
Janke, Cheyenne	0	1	4.34	9	1	0	0	19	15	10	9	7	21	.205	R	R	6-5	230	2-16-77	1999	Elk Mound, Wisc.
Johnson, Tyler	1	0	1.65	20	0	0	0	27	16	7	5	15	39	.168	S	L	6-2	180	6-7-81	2001	Newbury Park, Calif.
Kinney, Josh	2	1	0.68	29	0	0	2	40	19	4	3	12	48	.141	R	R	6-1	195	3-31-79	2001	Port Allegany, Pa.
Lambert, Jeremy	0	2	2.18	33	0	0	2	41	31	14	10	15	56	.212	R	R	6-1	220	1-10-79	1997	Taylorsville, Utah
Lyons, Mike	3	4	3.38	57	0	0	31	53	50	27	20	23	63	.234	R	R	6-3	205	5-20-75	1996	Altamonte Springs, Fla.
Narveson, Chris	4	3	3.00	10	10	0	0	57	56	21	19	26	34	.261	L	L	6-3	180	12-20-81	2000	Arden, N.C.
Novinsky, John	2	0	4.38	18	0	0	3	25	32	13	12	13	15	.320	R	R	6-3	190	4-25-79	2001	Hauppauge, N.Y.
Parrott, Rhett	8	9	3.27	21	21	1	0	124	122	52	45	40	112	.259	R	R	6-2	190	11-12-79	2001	Dalton, Ga.
Pearce, Josh	2	1	4.09	5	5	0	0	33	34	15	15	3	20	.269	R	R	6-3	220	8-20-77	1999	Yakima, Wash.
Pearson, Jason	0	0	0.00	9	0	0	0	11	7	0	0	2	11	.179	L	L	6-0	190	12-29-75	1998	Freeport, Ill.
Pena, Juan	6	5	3.49	29	14	0	0	95	101	47	37	44	69	.278	L	L	6-3	200	12-4-77	1996	Santo Domingo, D.R.
Sprague, Kevin	3	4	5.26	53	0	0	2	63	67	43	37	38	61	.270	L	L	6-4	215	3-10-77	1999	Kansas City, Kan.
Stocks, Nick	10	8	4.77	27	26	0	0	151	160	86	80	58	109	.275	R	R	6-2	185	8-27-78	1999	Tampa, Fla.
Villalon, Julio	4	7	4.61	12	12	0	0	66	72	39	34	23	48	.284	R	R	6-2	170	5-11-78	2000	San Jose, Costa Rica
Walrond, Les	0	0	2.70	4	0	0	0	7	4	2	2	4	7	.166	L	L	6-0	190	11-7-76	1998	Brentwood, Tenn.

FIELDING

Catcher	PCT	G	PO	A	E	DP	PB
Girardi	1.000	3	17	2	0	1	1
Molina	.991	100	775	72	8	8	11
Moylan	.993	40	259	20	2	2	7
Netwall	1.000	3	14	3	0	0	1

First Base	PCT	G	PO	A	E	DP
Gall	1.000	2	17	0	0	1
Jacobsen	.985	114	963	58	16	80
Krause	1.000	14	112	3	0	6
Moylan	.964	3	26	1	1	5
Roman	1.000	10	79	6	0	5
Weekly	.974	5	35	2	1	5

Second Base	PCT	G	PO	A	E	DP
Abreu	.714	2	1	4	2	0
Cosme	.978	129	253	373	14	79
Weekly	.988	22	30	49	1	8

Third Base	PCT	G	PO	A	E	DP
Abreu	.833	7	1	9	2	0
Erickson	.940	94	53	151	13	16
Krause	.765	8	1	12	4	1
Weekly	.933	50	19	78	7	7

Shortstop	PCT	G	PO	A	E	DP
Abreu	1.000	3	6	6	0	1
Cosme	1.000	7	10	13	0	0
Nelson	.960	134	159	391	23	67

Outfield	PCT	G	PO	A	E	DP
Abreu	.833	2	4	1	1	0
Benjamin	.975	23	36	3	1	1
Bolivar	.985	128	187	7	3	0
Boyd	.983	26	56	2	1	0
Burns	.992	70	117	3	1	0
Dodson	.981	33	50	3	1	0
Duncan	.889	5	8	0	1	0
Gall	1.000	10	12	0	0	0
Krause	1.000	39	59	5	0	2
Lemanczyk	.600	4	2	1	2	0
Moylan	.875	4	7	0	1	0
Roman	1.000	3	4	1	0	0
Schumaker	.994	88	171	5	1	1
Weekly	.966	29	26	2	1	0

PALM BEACH CARDINALS — High Class A

FLORIDA STATE LEAGUE

BATTING	AVG	G	AB	R	H	2B	3B	HR	RBI	BB	SO	SB	CS	SLG	OBP	B	T	HT	WT	DOB	1st Yr	Resides
Abreu, Dennis	.216	32	116	12	25	5	1	2	8	6	21	3	1	.328	.264	R	R	6-0	165	4-22-78	1995	Tumero, Venez.
Asadoorian, Rick	.192	44	130	11	25	3	1	1	10	10	35	3	1	.254	.262	R	R	6-2	180	7-23-80	1999	Whitinsville, Mass.
Asche, Kirk	.098	14	41	5	4	3	0	0	2	5	15	1	0	.171	.260	R	R	6-2	190	7-10-77	1999	Brandon, Fla.
Benjamin, Al	.275	24	91	13	25	7	0	1	12	7	18	2	0	.385	.330	R	R	6-1	200	9-9-77	1996	Houston, Texas
Blasi, Blake	.259	68	263	42	68	14	1	2	24	30	40	7	4	.342	.337	S	R	5-8	160	3-23-79	2000	Wichita, Kan.
2-team (41 Sarasota)	.244	109	398	57	97	18	2	2	37	55	65	13	8	.314	.340							
Boyd, Shaun	.257	110	416	59	107	17	2	5	35	54	70	28	14	.344	.343	R	R	5-10	175	8-15-81	2000	Las Vegas, Nev.
Brown, Kevin	.280	7	25	2	7	1	0	1	1	3	4	0	0	.440	.357	R	R	6-2	230	4-21-73	1994	Mt. Vernon, Ind.
Coulie, Jason	.125	28	72	5	9	0	0	1	3	5	18	2	0	.167	.213	R	R	6-2	200	4-13-78	2000	Manchester, N.H.
Dodson, Jeremy	.188	53	170	11	32	8	1	3	12	16	49	0	1	.300	.261	L	R	6-2	200	5-3-77	1998	Sherman, Texas
Drew, J.D.	.368	8	19	4	7	0	0	1	3	7	4	0	0	.526	.556	L	R	6-1	200	11-20-75	1997	Hahira, Ga.
Duncan, Chris	.254	121	425	26	108	20	0	2	42	44	115	4	4	.315	.322	L	R	6-5	210	5-5-81	1999	Tucson, Ariz.
Eickhorst, Chris	.196	64	194	14	38	6	0	1	17	27	59	0	1	.242	.323	R	R	6-3	200	12-29-79	2002	New Brunswick, N.J.
Espada, Joe	.236	47	178	17	42	7	0	0	9	20	13	10	4	.275	.317	R	R	5-10	170	8-30-75	1996	Carolina, P.R.
Garcia, Tony	.215	110	377	41	81	13	0	2	30	48	62	5	4	.265	.320	R	R	5-10	170	6-17-80	2001	Temecula, Calif.
Hamill, Ryan	.159	12	44	0	7	0	0	0	2	4	9	0	0	.159	.229	R	R	6-0	200	10-3-78	2000	Woodland Hills, Calif.
Hernandez, Johnny	.167	14	42	4	7	3	0	0	2	6	7	0	0	.238	.271	S	L	6-1	180	9-11-79	1999	Brooklyn, N.Y.
Hileman, Jutt	.292	25	89	17	26	5	0	1	7	12	23	0	1	.382	.390	R	R	6-1	180	7-13-81	2000	Palmyra, Pa.
Jaramillo, Milko	.190	35	121	11	23	4	1	0	5	10	24	0	1	.240	.258	S	R	5-11	165	1-21-80	1996	Caracas, Venez.
Johnson, Gabe	.213	107	385	50	82	12	3	8	40	52	104	5	3	.322	.308	R	R	6-1	195	9-21-79	1998	Delray Beach, Fla.
Johnson, Gary	.189	23	90	6	17	2	0	1	9	5	16	0	1	.244	.255	R	R	6-4	210	9-6-76	1997	Rancho Cucamonga, Calif.
Kirkpatrick, Michael	.133	14	30	1	4	0	0	0	4	2	8	1	0	.133	.206	L	L	6-0	180	11-12-77	1996	New Castle, Del.
Lafferty, Will	.000	2	3	0	0	0	0	0	0	0	1	0	0	.000	.000	R	R	6-2	200	4-18-79	2001	Pine Bluff, Ark.
Lemon, Tim	.149	54	168	17	25	9	1	4	10	9	66	0	2	.286	.204	R	R	6-1	180	9-23-80	1998	La Mirada, Calif.
Moore, Jason	.287	25	94	14	27	3	0	2	10	15	24	6	2	.383	.382	S	R	6-0	180	1-4-78	1999	Miami, Fla.
Morrow, Alvin	.154	4	13	3	2	1	0	0	0	1	5	0	0	.231	.214	R	R	6-4	240	4-28-78	1997	St. Louis, Mo.
Netwall, Chris	.169	65	178	10	30	3	1	1	7	24	57	4	2	.213	.282	R	R	6-1	205	11-17-79	2001	Allentown, Pa.
Rodgers, Albert	.213	26	94	5	20	1	0	2	7	6	25	0	1	.287	.265	R	R	6-2	190	6-8-79	2000	Long Beach, Calif.
Roman, Jesse	.283	99	364	24	103	27	2	7	53	36	62	1	5	.426	.350	L	L	6-0	190	4-21-79	2001	Woodhaven, N.Y.
Schutzenhofer, Andy	.326	13	46	11	15	3	1	0	10	11	5	0	0	.435	.456	L	L	6-0	195	1-24-81	2003	Swansea, Ill.
Urueta, Luis	.067	8	15	4	1	0	0	0	0	1	4	0	0	.067	.222	S	R	6-2	210	1-9-81	1998	Barranquilla, Colombia

BATTING	AVG	G	AB	R	H	2B	3B	HR	RBI	BB	SO	SB	CS	SLG	OBP	B	T	HT	WT	DOB	1st Yr	Resides
Voshell, Chase	.252	42	155	9	39	7	1	1	18	9	32	0	2	.329	.297	R	R	6-2	185	3-29-79	2000	Milford, Ohio
Williams, Matt	.172	9	29	1	5	1	0	0	2	4	15	0	0	.207	.286	R	R	6-1	210	3-24-79	2001	Signal Hill, Calif.

PITCHING	W	L	ERA	G	GS	CG	SV	IP	H	R	ER	BB	SO	AVG	B	T	HT	WT	DOB	1st Yr	Resides
Axelson, Josh	0	2	3.12	9	1	0	0	26	21	9	9	4	23	.218	R	R	6-1	200	12-4-78	2000	Brooklyn, Mich.
Cali, Carmen	2	1	4.99	62	0	0	3	70	72	49	39	32	70	.264	L	L	5-10	185	11-4-78	2000	Naples, Fla.
Caple, Chance	2	6	4.85	20	17	1	0	91	83	53	49	63	45	.247	R	R	6-6	240	8-9-78	1999	Southlake, Texas
Carpenter, Chris	0	1	1.29	4	4	0	0	7	6	3	1	1	6	.222	R	R	6-6	230	4-27-75	1994	Bedford, N.H.
Collins, Pat	1	2	2.17	10	3	0	0	29	20	9	7	18	27	.188	R	R	6-5	230	3-3-78	1999	Union, N.J.
Cook, Jeremy	4	3	3.62	45	0	0	2	60	52	24	24	10	33	.238	R	R	6-6	235	5-11-78	2000	Yuba City, Calif.
Correa, Cristobal	4	9	5.19	21	18	0	0	95	100	64	55	49	49	.274	R	R	6-1	175	12-5-79	1998	Guarico, Venez.
Dodson, Jeremy	0	0	0.00	2	0	0	0	2	1	0	0	2	2	.000	L	R	6-2	200	5-3-77	1998	Sherman, Texas
Estes, Jonathan	1	0	3.31	15	0	0	0	33	36	13	12	7	15	.272	L	R	6-4	210	5-13-80	2002	St. Charles, Mo.
Flynn, Brian	2	1	5.91	7	0	0	0	11	18	10	7	3	5	.367	R	R	6-1	205	6-27-79	2002	Park Ridge, N.J.
Galbraith, Jason	0	1	4.70	5	0	0	0	8	6	5	4	5	5	.214	L	L	6-3	215	7-18-80	2002	Lake Peekskill, N.Y.
Graves, Don	1	0	4.26	3	3	0	0	19	23	9	9	3	8	.298	R	R	6-4	205	1-3-81	1999	Boonville, Mo.
Hammons, Matt	2	2	1.25	21	0	0	8	22	11	4	3	9	32	.150	R	R	6-3	200	4-9-77	1995	San Diego, Calif.
Hawksworth, Blake	1	3	3.94	6	6	0	0	32	28	14	14	11	32	.235	R	R	6-3	195	3-1-83	2002	Sammamish, Wash.
Johnson, Tyler	5	5	3.08	22	10	0	0	79	79	29	27	38	81	.261	S	L	6-2	180	6-7-81	2001	Newbury Park, Calif.
Kinney, Josh	3	0	1.52	31	0	0	3	41	38	7	7	10	35	.245	R	R	6-1	195	3-31-79	2001	Port Allegany, Penn.
Lambert, Jeremy	0	0	2.57	7	0	0	0	7	8	4	2	0	8	.258	R	R	6-1	220	1-10-79	1997	Taylorsville, Utah
Martinez, Miguel	1	1	4.50	8	5	0	0	30	43	17	15	8	17	.352	R	R	6-1	170	9-29-81	1999	Monte Cristi, D.R.
Mejia, Juan	3	0	5.68	8	5	0	0	32	39	21	20	13	14	.307	R	R	6-2	165	12-11-79	1996	Azua, D.R.
Narveson, Chris	7	7	2.86	15	14	1	0	91	83	34	29	19	65	.241	L	L	6-3	180	12-20-81	2000	Arden, N.C.
Novinsky, John	2	3	3.18	37	0	0	16	45	41	16	16	16	36	.244	R	R	6-3	190	4-25-79	2001	Hauppauge, N.Y.
Painter, Lance	0	0	0.00	1	1	0	0	1	0	0	0	0	1	.000	L	L	6-1	200	7-21-67	1990	Highland Ranch, Colo.
Pearce, Josh	1	4	3.21	6	5	0	0	28	28	10	10	2	15	.274	R	R	6-3	220	8-20-77	1999	Yakima, Wash.
Pope, Justin	4	11	4.92	20	18	1	0	106	123	68	58	33	69	.289	S	R	6-0	180	11-8-79	2001	Lake Worth, Fla.
Rawson, Anthony	0	4	3.78	25	0	0	0	33	34	16	14	19	26	.261	L	L	5-11	180	7-31-80	2001	Kosciusko, Miss.
Runyon, Bob	0	2	9.00	5	1	0	0	11	19	12	11	5	3	.380	R	R	6-2	200	6-9-80	2002	Atwater, Calif.
Russelburg, Aaron	1	3	6.52	6	4	0	0	19	19	19	14	7	12	.256	R	R	6-4	215	10-17-79	2001	Hawesville, Ky.
Scalamandre, Rich	1	0	2.45	4	0	0	0	4	6	1	1	0	2	.352	R	R	5-11	195	8-20-80	2002	Brooklyn, N.Y.
Smith, Jared	2	3	3.09	45	5	0	1	76	63	28	26	44	70	.234	L	R	6-2	200	12-1-78	2001	Birmingham, Ala.
Teekel, Josh	0	0	13.50	1	0	0	0	1	2	2	1	0	0	.666	R	R	6-5	200	9-18-80	1999	Greenwell Springs, La.
Thompson, Bradley	1	0	0.00	2	1	0	0	6	3	0	0	0	4	.157	R	R	6-1	190	1-31-82	2002	Las Vegas, Nev.
Villalon, Julio	1	0	1.50	1	1	0	0	6	3	1	1	1	7	.142	R	R	6-2	170	5-11-78	2000	San Jose, Costa Rica
Williams, Blake	2	10	4.36	20	16	0	1	85	81	55	41	33	56	.245	R	R	6-5	210	2-22-79	2000	San Marcos, Texas

FIELDING

Catcher	PCT	G	PO	A	E	DP	PB
Brown	1.000	4	32	9	0	1	1
Eickhorst	.991	64	405	34	4	1	12
Hamill	.977	12	75	11	2	1	2
Lafferty	.900	2	8	1	1	1	0
Netwall	.988	64	370	56	5	6	9

First Base	PCT	G	PO	A	E	DP
Abreu	1.000	2	11	2	0	1
Duncan	.987	116	984	63	14	87
Roman	1.000	14	83	8	0	9
Schutzenhofer	.992	13	117	8	1	10
Williams	1.000	1	8	0	0	0

Second Base	PCT	G	PO	A	E	DP
Abreu	1.000	1	1	0	0	0
Blasi	.957	59	109	178	13	35
Boyd	.918	42	94	107	18	23
Garcia	.984	37	76	110	3	30

Third Base	PCT	G	PO	A	E	DP
Abreu	1.000	9	8	23	0	2
Garcia	.951	12	8	31	2	5
Gabe Johnson	.918	99	82	163	22	17
Rodgers	.824	13	6	22	6	3
Voshell	.667	1	0	2	1	0
Williams	.917	7	10	12	2	4

Shortstop	PCT	G	PO	A	E	DP
Espada	.946	46	81	145	13	28
Garcia	.936	38	62	98	11	22
Jaramillo	.954	35	43	101	7	18
Moore	.954	19	22	61	4	13

Outfield	PCT	G	PO	A	E	DP
Abreu	1.000	1	1	0	0	0
Asadoorian	.979	42	90	4	2	0
Asche	.967	14	27	2	1	0
Benjamin	.981	24	50	2	1	0
Boyd	.979	50	137	3	3	0
Coulie	.971	24	30	3	1	2
Dodson	1.000	42	86	3	0	1
Drew	1.000	6	2	1	0	1
Garcia	.000	1	0	0	0	0
Hernandez	1.000	11	19	1	0	0
Hileman	.940	25	47	0	3	0
Gary Johnson	1.000	23	51	4	0	0
Kirkpatrick	1.000	3	5	0	0	0
Lemon	.979	49	89	4	2	1
Rodgers	.968	14	29	1	1	1
Roman	.992	74	119	8	1	0
Urueta	.941	7	16	0	1	0
Voshell	.983	31	53	5	1	0

PEORIA CHIEFS — Low Class A

MIDWEST LEAGUE

BATTING	AVG	G	AB	R	H	2B	3B	HR	RBI	BB	SO	SB	CS	SLG	OBP	B	T	HT	WT	DOB	1st Yr	Resides
Belz, Tim	.000	9	15	0	0	0	0	0	1	0	6	0	1	.000	.063	R	R	6-4	210	4-7-80	2002	Westbury, N.Y.
Boyer, Kyle	.174	36	121	18	21	5	1	0	8	10	28	7	1	.231	.244	R	R	6-0	185	3-5-80	2002	Ogden, Utah
Chauncey, Clint	.294	15	34	5	10	3	0	0	7	6	12	2	0	.382	.415	R	R	6-1	180	1-1-81	2000	Jacksonville, Fla.
Durham, Tyler	.226	55	133	10	30	2	0	4	17	13	32	1	1	.331	.295	R	R	6-0	190	10-8-79	2002	Fort Worth, Texas
Ehrnsberger, Chad	.377	21	77	16	29	6	0	5	19	8	13	2	2	.649	.425	R	R	5-10	210	11-29-77	2002	Ottawa, Ohio
2-team (25 Wisconsin)	.287	46	167	24	48	8	1	6	28	19	36	3	3	.455	.361							
Eickhorst, Chris	.200	10	30	7	6	2	1	0	2	7	10	0	0	.333	.351	R	R	6-3	200	12-29-79	2002	New Brunswick, N.J.
Evans, Terry	.246	104	382	35	94	28	1	10	41	19	86	13	6	.403	.286	R	R	6-3	200	1-19-82	2002	Dublin, Ga.
Ginther, Andy	.250	3	8	1	2	0	0	0	1	1	3	0	0	.250	.333	R	R	6-1	195	9-22-80	2003	Carrollton, Ga.
Girardi, Joe	.111	3	9	0	1	0	0	0	1	0	2	0	0	.111	.200	R	R	5-11	200	10-14-64	1986	Chicago, Ill.
Gorecki, Reid	.267	128	480	77	128	19	8	15	61	51	90	23	11	.433	.338	R	R	6-1	180	12-22-80	2002	East Rockaway, N.Y.
Hanson, Travis	.277	136	527	70	146	31	5	9	78	35	104	3	4	.406	.325	L	R	6-2	195	1-24-81	2002	Port Orchard, Wash.
Hileman, Jutt	.250	37	120	20	30	4	0	1	11	16	24	3	2	.308	.341	R	R	6-1	180	7-13-81	2000	Palmyra, Pa.
Jaramillo, Milko	.228	96	329	37	75	10	3	3	16	18	53	7	6	.304	.287	S	R	5-11	165	1-21-80	1996	Caracas, Venez.
Lafferty, Will	.174	17	46	4	8	0	0	1	4	2	13	0	0	.239	.240	R	R	6-2	200	4-18-79	2001	Pine Bluff, Ark.
Lemanczyk, Matt	.273	125	477	74	130	12	1	1	32	41	83	56	13	.308	.333	R	R	6-2	195	10-5-80	2002	Rockville Centre, N.Y.
Lemon, Tim	.186	48	156	15	29	6	0	2	12	13	46	9	2	.263	.256	R	R	6-1	180	9-23-80	1998	La Mirada, Calif.
McCoy, Mike	.252	131	464	67	117	16	5	5	46	51	77	24	10	.341	.345	R	R	5-9	175	4-2-81	2002	El Cajon, Calif.
Monette, Daylon	.180	23	61	4	11	2	0	0	4	3	8	0	0	.213	.231	S	L	6-3	205	7-24-81	2002	Colton, Calif.
Motte, Jason	.203	48	133	8	27	1	0	0	10	10	44	1	1	.211	.257	R	R	6-0	195	6-22-82	2003	Johnson City, Tenn.
Parker, Tyler	.222	55	189	16	42	8	2	4	35	12	54	9	2	.349	.274	R	R	6-3	210	5-13-81	2002	Marietta, Ga.
Rodriguez, Marcos	.267	16	60	8	16	2	2	0	6	3	14	0	0	.367	.302	L	L	6-0	180	4-7-83	2001	Lara, Venez.

BATTING	AVG	G	AB	R	H	2B	3B	HR	RBI	BB	SO	SB	CS	SLG	OBP	B	T	HT	WT	DOB	1st Yr	Resides
Santor, John	.268	133	474	57	127	28	2	9	71	54	105	4	5	.392	.348	S	R	6-1	215	11-16-81	2000	Palmdale, Calif.
Voshell, Chase	.240	68	217	22	52	9	0	2	21	19	45	7	5	.309	.307	R	R	6-2	185	3-29-79	2000	Milford, Ohio
Williams, Matt	.286	2	7	0	2	0	0	0	0	1	2	0	0	.286	.375	R	R	6-1	210	3-24-79	2001	Signal Hill, Calif.

PITCHING	W	L	ERA	G	GS	CG	SV	IP	H	R	ER	BB	SO	AVG	B	T	HT	WT	DOB	1st Yr	Resides
Adamczyk, Tyler	7	12	4.49	26	26	1	0	140	158	81	70	48	93	.287	R	R	6-6	190	11-9-82	2001	Westlake, Calif.
Batista, Roberto	3	1	9.19	13	0	0	2	16	23	16	16	10	5	.338	R	R	6-1	165	3-10-82	1999	Guaymate, D.R.
Blair, Buddy	2	2	1.66	7	6	0	0	43	35	9	8	11	17	.222	L	L	6-1	206	7-2-81	2003	Tulsa, Okla.
Burch, Jason	0	2	4.85	13	0	0	2	13	13	7	7	3	9	.254	R	R	6-5	215	10-15-82	2003	Papillion, Neb.
Cavazos, Andy	5	4	3.99	36	13	0	10	104	106	51	46	40	56	.268	R	R	6-3	185	1-5-81	1999	Clute, Texas
Ciprian, Wilson	0	1	2.45	5	0	0	1	7	6	2	2	3	2	.206	R	R	5-11	160	11-14-82	2000	Villa Mella, D.R.
DeJaynes, Brandon	0	0	0.00	2	0	0	0	3	3	0	0	0	2	.300	R	R	6-2	190	9-10-80	2003	Quincy, Ill.
Drown, Erik	1	2	4.74	5	5	0	0	25	27	16	13	12	15	.284	R	R	6-2	200	2-21-80	2003	Ipswich, Mass.
Estes, Jonathan	2	2	3.93	26	0	0	1	37	38	21	16	13	19	.271	L	R	6-4	210	5-13-80	2002	St. Charles, Mo.
Flynn, Brian	2	5	4.24	30	0	0	2	34	30	18	16	17	19	.238	R	R	6-1	205	6-27-79	2002	Park Ridge, N.J.
Galbraith, Jason	0	0	21.60	2	0	0	0	2	4	4	4	2	1	.444	L	L	6-3	215	7-18-80	2002	Lake Peekskill, N.Y.
Graves, Don	8	7	3.22	22	22	2	0	129	137	56	46	24	59	.271	R	R	6-4	205	1-3-81	1999	Boonville, Mo.
Hawksworth, Blake	5	1	2.30	10	10	0	0	55	37	16	14	12	57	.186	R	R	6-3	195	3-1-83	2002	Sammamish, Wash.
Jordan, B.J.	0	1	6.00	2	0	0	0	3	4	2	2	0	3	.363	L	L	6-0	190	4-24-81	2003	Austin, Texas
Julianel, Ben	4	2	1.05	51	0	0	9	52	41	11	6	25	78	.214	S	L	6-2	180	9-4-79	2001	Belmont, Calif.
Knowles, Mike	0	1	0.00	1	0	0	0	0	2	2	2	2	0	1.000	R	R	6-5	215	7-15-79	1997	Daytona Beach, Fla.
Martinez, Miguel	6	6	3.39	20	20	1	0	117	112	55	44	32	60	.256	R	R	6-1	170	9-29-81	1999	Monte Cristi, D.R.
Mejia, Juan	2	3	3.88	30	0	0	0	53	50	24	23	25	27	.261	R	R	6-2	165	12-11-79	1996	Azua, D.R.
Plancich, Nick	0	0	0.00	2	0	0	0	1	2	4	0	2	1	.285	R	R	6-2	190	9-12-78	2001	Redondo Beach, Calif.
Rawson, Anthony	0	2	4.09	20	0	0	6	22	22	11	10	7	17	.265	L	L	5-11	180	7-31-80	2001	Kosciusko, Miss.
Rogers, Joe	2	1	2.30	37	0	0	0	43	30	15	11	12	46	.197	L	L	6-2	175	7-19-81	2001	Fullerton, Calif.
Runyon, Bob	4	6	4.23	11	11	1	0	62	68	43	29	20	23	.273	R	R	6-2	200	6-9-80	2002	Atwater, Calif.
Russelburg, Aaron	1	2	4.05	6	5	0	0	27	31	13	12	14	13	.310	R	R	6-4	215	10-17-79	2001	Hawesville, Ky.
Scalamandre, Rich	0	0	1.88	18	0	0	2	24	18	5	5	9	23	.222	R	R	5-11	195	8-20-80	2002	Brooklyn, N.Y.
Schweitzer, Scott	0	1	13.50	10	0	0	0	7	11	10	10	4	6	.392	L	L	6-3	235	5-4-80	2002	Alexandria, Ky.
Teekel, Josh	6	6	2.36	26	16	0	1	118	107	43	31	39	85	.242	R	R	6-5	200	9-18-80	1999	Greenwell Springs, La.
Thompson, Bradley	5	3	2.91	30	4	0	0	65	70	23	21	10	43	.273	R	R	6-1	190	1-31-82	2002	Las Vegas, Nevada

FIELDING

Catcher	PCT	G	PO	A	E	DP	PB
Belz	1.000	8	28	5	0	0	1
Chauncey	.987	15	62	14	1	2	3
Durham	1.000	1	2	0	0	0	0
Eickhorst	1.000	10	54	7	0	0	1
Ginther	.875	3	14	0	2	0	1
Girardi	1.000	2	8	1	0	0	0
Lafferty	1.000	17	72	12	0	0	0
Motte	.987	48	262	47	4	4	5
Parker	.973	51	287	35	9	2	4

First Base	PCT	G	PO	A	E	DP
Durham	.976	11	75	5	2	8
Evans	1.000	1	8	1	0	0
Rodriguez	1.000	1	1	1	0	0
Santor	.991	133	1277	98	13	104

Second Base	PCT	G	PO	A	E	DP
Boyer	.000	2	0	0	0	0
Durham	.986	18	24	47	1	7
Ehrnsberger	.905	7	14	24	4	6
McCoy	.966	125	252	382	22	74

Third Base	PCT	G	PO	A	E	DP
Durham	.917	6	4	7	1	1
Hanson	.940	135	92	268	23	21
Voshell	.000	1	0	0	0	0

Shortstop	PCT	G	PO	A	E	DP
Boyer	.903	35	43	106	16	19
Durham	1.000	2	1	8	0	0
Jaramillo	.966	96	174	343	18	63
McCoy	.942	11	17	32	3	3

Outfield	PCT	G	PO	A	E	DP
Belz	.000	1	0	0	0	0
Ehrnsberger	1.000	2	1	0	0	0
Evans	.977	82	120	10	3	1
Gorecki	.957	128	271	17	13	4
Hileman	.952	32	57	3	3	1
Lemanczyk	.979	125	228	5	5	1
Lemon	.980	25	43	6	1	1
Monette	1.000	6	7	0	0	0
Rodriguez	.905	14	18	1	2	0
Voshell	1.000	3	4	0	0	0
Williams	1.000	2	3	0	0	0

NEW JERSEY CARDINALS — Short-Season Class A

NEW YORK-PENN LEAGUE

BATTING	AVG	G	AB	R	H	2B	3B	HR	RBI	BB	SO	SB	CS	SLG	OBP	B	T	HT	WT	DOB	1st Yr	Resides
Bridges, Josh	.143	3	7	0	1	0	0	0	1	0	1	0	0	.143	.143	R	R	6-3	200	10-21-79	2002	Centreville, Ala.
Estrada, Kevin	.292	64	236	42	69	9	2	1	24	25	33	21	6	.360	.358	S	R	6-2	185	10-1-80	2003	El Segundo, Calif.
Falu, Melvin	.249	57	213	25	53	9	5	5	28	12	22	6	0	.408	.295	S	R	6-0	185	8-28-80	2002	Carolina, P.R.
Frisella, Paul	.136	7	22	3	3	0	1	0	0	1	8	1	0	.227	.208	R	R	6-1	215	4-10-81	2003	Sunset Hills, Mo.
Ginther, Andy	.235	15	34	4	8	4	0	0	3	2	10	0	0	.353	.278	R	R	6-1	195	9-22-80	2003	Carrollton, Ga.
Grimm, Casey	.286	68	224	29	64	9	4	1	33	25	36	1	1	.375	.385	L	L	6-1	205	2-9-81	2003	Morristown, N.J.
Mather, Joe	.230	65	196	23	45	12	1	2	22	18	38	4	4	.332	.314	R	R	6-4	190	7-23-82	2001	Phoenix, Ariz.
Monette, Daylon	.233	52	176	19	41	9	1	1	32	16	49	4	2	.313	.296	S	L	6-3	205	7-24-81	2002	Colton, Calif.
Obrey, Kainoa	.217	41	120	4	26	3	0	0	11	15	39	1	1	.242	.309	R	R	6-3	225	10-6-80	2003	Honolulu, Hawaii
Pagnozzi, Matt	.178	59	152	13	27	4	1	1	19	23	42	3	2	.237	.302	R	R	6-2	205	11-10-82	2003	Mesa, Ariz.
Pena, Omar	.236	63	212	21	50	12	1	0	13	13	55	6	0	.302	.288	R	R	5-11	175	3-2-82	2003	Haverhill, Mass.
Ryan, Brendan	.311	53	193	20	60	14	4	0	13	14	25	11	3	.425	.363	R	R	6-2	195	3-26-82	2003	Los Angeles, Calif.
Schmitt, Billy	.191	42	131	15	25	5	2	1	10	6	31	1	0	.282	.230	R	R	6-1	200	8-16-82	2000	Henderson, Nev.
Smithlin, Zach	.164	44	67	5	11	0	0	0	2	9	17	3	2	.164	.263	S	R	5-10	165	10-12-80	2003	Fair Lawn, N.H.
Thomas, Tee	.200	6	20	4	4	1	0	0	0	0	7	2	1	.250	.304	R	R	5-11	187	6-13-81	2003	Starkville, Miss.
Tolotti, Jeff	.000	4	13	0	0	0	0	0	1	2	6	0	0	.000	.133	L	L	6-2	200	5-20-80	2002	Reno, Nev.
Tuttle, Chris	.222	47	153	25	34	3	1	0	6	21	26	4	5	.255	.320	L	R	5-10	170	5-25-81	2003	Lagrange, Ohio
Urueta, Luis	.133	4	15	0	2	0	0	0	1	0	6	2	0	.133	.133	S	R	6-2	210	1-9-81	1998	Barranquilla, Colombia
Virgil, Jose	.231	66	242	30	56	12	6	3	36	25	47	11	1	.368	.314	S	R	6-0	205	3-28-81	2003	Glendale, Ariz.

GAMES BY POSITION: C—Bridges 3, Ginther 15, Pagnozzi 58, Schmitt 14. **1B**—Mather 63, Obrey 14, Schmitt 7. **2B**—Estrada 50, Falu 3, Pena 21, Thomas 2. **3B**—Estrada 4, Falu 48, Mather 3, Obrey 12, Pena 1, Ryan 1, Schmitt 12. **SS**—Estrada 5, Falu 5, Pena 38, Ryan 31. **OF**—Falu 4, Frisella 7, Grimm 41, Monette 39, Smithlin 39, Thomas 4, Tolotti 3, Tuttle 44, Urueta 3, Virgil 63.

PITCHING	W	L	ERA	G	GS	CG	SV	IP	H	R	ER	BB	SO	AVG	B	T	HT	WT	DOB	1st Yr	Resides
Aguero, Miguel	1	0	6.75	1	1	0	0	5	7	4	4	2	4	.333	R	R	6-0	180	5-19-82	2001	Venez.
Batista, Roberto	3	1	0.88	26	0	0	11	31	23	8	3	11	22	.205	R	R	6-1	165	3-10-82	1999	Guaymate, D.R.
Blair, Buddy	1	2	3.58	8	6	0	0	38	30	18	15	11	32	.227	L	L	6-1	206	7-2-81	2003	Tulsa, Okla.
Blanton, Matt	0	0	3.00	2	2	0	0	12	14	4	4	2	11	.311	L	L	6-4	210	5-10-81	2003	Clearwater, Fla.
Bonnell, Jared	1	0	5.91	6	0	0	0	11	10	7	7	2	7	.243	R	R	6-2	210	12-9-80	2002	Las Vegas, Nevada
Brey, Josh	3	3	3.24	14	9	0	1	58	59	27	21	18	36	.266	R	L	6-0	185	8-26-79	2001	Allentown, Penn.

PITCHING	W	L	ERA	G	GS	CG	SV	IP	H	R	ER	BB	SO	AVG	B	T	HT	WT	DOB	1st Yr	Resides
Dove, Dennis	1	3	3.51	7	7	0	0	26	29	15	10	15	15	.284	R	R	6-4	205	8-31-81	2003	Ocilla, Ga.
Drown, Erik	3	2	2.96	10	8	0	0	46	26	19	15	22	34	.169	R	R	6-2	200	2-21-80	2003	Ipswich, Mass.
Galbraith, Jason	1	1	1.86	17	0	0	2	19	8	6	4	8	17	.123	L	L	6-3	215	7-18-80	2002	Lake Peekskill, N.Y.
Garza, Justin	0	0	0.00	2	0	0	1	3	1	0	0	0	5	.090	R	R	6-1	190	7-13-82	2003	Frederick, Okla.
John, Jason	1	3	5.84	21	3	0	0	49	81	41	32	23	39	.382	R	R	6-5	230	11-3-81	2003	Corpus Christi, Texas
Jordan, B.J.	4	1	2.08	27	0	0	1	30	30	12	7	11	27	.258	L	L	6-0	190	4-24-81	2003	Austin, Texas
Michael, Mark	1	2	3.17	11	10	0	0	54	50	23	19	20	56	.248	R	R	6-4	215	8-25-82	2003	Gibbstown, N.J.
Mondesir, James	0	4	6.66	7	7	0	0	24	34	22	18	10	19	.346	S	R	6-4	210	6-10-79	2002	Jamaica, N.Y.
Morales, Juan	1	2	2.09	30	0	0	1	39	22	10	9	13	38	.165	R	R	6-4	170	12-1-82	2000	Bonao, D.R.
Pals, Jordan	2	4	6.93	6	5	0	0	25	34	23	19	8	13	.333	R	R	6-8	205	10-18-80	2003	Effingham, Ill.
Roper, Derek	3	3	3.32	17	8	0	0	65	70	26	24	18	43	.278	R	R	6-6	205	12-31-80	2003	Elk City, Okla.
Runyon, Bob	0	2	3.72	4	1	0	0	10	15	4	4	2	8	.375	R	R	6-2	200	6-9-80	2002	Atwater, Calif.
Scalamandre, Rich	1	0	2.25	8	0	0	0	12	8	4	3	2	12	.186	R	R	5-11	195	8-20-80	2002	Brooklyn, N.Y.
Schmitt, Billy	0	0	0.00	2	0	0	0	3	0	0	0	2	1	.000	R	R	6-1	200	8-16-82	2000	Henderson, Nevada
Soteropoulos, Peter	1	1	4.37	15	0	0	0	23	29	13	11	11	16	.325	L	L	6-1	210	8-5-81	2003	Peabody, Mass.
Tamulionis, Mike	2	1	2.30	18	1	0	0	27	23	8	7	11	22	.232	R	R	6-2	190	8-10-80	2003	West Bridgewater, Mass.
Van Gorder, Joe	0	2	6.32	8	1	0	0	16	20	11	11	7	16	.303	L	L	6-2	180	3-10-81	2002	Ithaca, N.Y.
Williamson, Willie	1	5	9.90	17	4	0	0	20	15	26	22	34	16	.211	L	L	6-1	185	5-13-80	2002	Manchester, N.H.

JOHNSON CITY CARDINALS — Rookie

APPALACHIAN LEAGUE

BATTING	AVG	G	AB	R	H	2B	3B	HR	RBI	BB	SO	SB	CS	SLG	OBP	B	T	HT	WT	DOB	1st Yr	Resides
Barton, Daric	.294	54	170	29	50	10	0	4	29	37	48	0	3	.424	.420	L	R	6-0	205	8-16-85	2003	Huntington Beach, Calif.
Capellan, Domingo	.286	14	35	5	10	4	0	2	4	2	9	0	0	.571	.359	R	R	5-10	180	12-12-82	1999	Cotui, D.R.
Colina, Luis	.184	53	158	15	29	3	0	1	13	10	50	0	1	.222	.238	R	R	5-11	170	6-23-83	2001	Caracas, Venez.
Davie, Andrew	.260	50	169	28	44	11	0	8	24	17	48	1	1	.467	.330	L	R	6-5	230	1-5-83	2001	Little Rock, Ark.
Diaz, Sandy	.042	12	24	2	1	0	0	0	0	2	10	0	0	.042	.179	R	R	6-0	185	1-1-84	2001	Azua, D.R.
Frisella, Paul	.337	60	175	36	59	13	0	8	37	24	51	1	5	.549	.434	R	R	6-1	215	4-10-81	2003	Sunset Hills, Mo.
Gary, Tavaris	.225	38	102	14	23	4	0	2	7	9	22	2	2	.324	.295	L	L	6-1	185	3-6-82	2003	Fort Myers, Fla.
Haerther, Cody	.332	63	226	31	75	12	6	3	39	22	30	2	1	.478	.390	L	R	6-0	190	7-14-83	2002	Chatsworth, Calif.
Hayes, Calvin	.304	35	125	25	38	5	0	2	11	14	20	16	2	.392	.387	R	R	5-9	190	3-21-84	2002	Salisbury, N.C.
House, Kevin	.209	33	91	14	19	3	1	0	10	13	21	1	1	.264	.305	R	R	5-11	185	7-27-82	2003	Memphis, Tenn.
Motte, Jason	.310	9	29	2	9	3	0	0	5	0	9	1	1	.414	.300	R	R	6-0	195	6-22-82	2003	Johnson City, Tenn.
Perez, Angel	.186	28	70	11	13	1	0	0	5	10	23	1	0	.200	.321	S	R	5-11	155	8-5-83	2000	Sabana Perdida, D.R.
Rodriguez, Marcos	.297	28	74	8	22	2	2	1	9	3	14	2	0	.419	.333	L	L	6-0	180	4-7-83	2001	Lara, Venez.
Schutzenhofer, Andy	.316	41	136	28	43	11	1	2	19	15	12	1	1	.456	.396	L	L	6-0	195	1-24-81	2003	Swansea, Ill.
Thomas, Tee	.192	36	125	21	24	1	4	3	9	6	37	3	0	.336	.271	R	R	5-11	187	6-13-81	2003	Starkville, Miss.
Webber, Levi	.188	47	160	19	30	6	0	4	23	17	48	1	0	.300	.265	R	R	6-5	220	2-27-82	2003	Glide, Ore.
Wootan, Tanner	.271	53	207	27	56	8	0	4	28	14	39	0	3	.367	.311	S	R	6-1	180	10-14-82	2003	Mesa, Ariz.
Yarbrough, Brandon	.238	13	42	1	10	2	1	0	10	2	17	0	0	.333	.273	L	R	6-2	180	11-9-84	2003	Ellerbee, N.C.

GAMES BY POSITION: C—Barton 37, Capellan 7, Diaz 8, Motte 9, Yarbrough 13. **1B**—Davie 24, Schutzenhofer 37, Webber 6. **2B**—Colina 42, Perez 12, Thomas 13, Webber 1, Wootan 10. **3B**—Barton 6, Colina 12, Haerther 12, Wootan 40. **SS**—Colina 1, Hayes 32, Perez 17, Thomas 20. **OF**—Davie 4, Frisella 56, Gary 35, Haerther 45, House 31, Rodriguez 23, Thomas 1, Webber 23.

PITCHING	W	L	ERA	G	GS	CG	SV	IP	H	R	ER	BB	SO	AVG	B	T	HT	WT	DOB	1st Yr	Resides
Aguero, Miguel	4	5	3.69	12	12	1	0	71	76	39	29	25	46	.279	R	R	6-0	180	5-19-82	2001	Aragua, Venez.
Blanton, Matt	5	5	5.14	13	10	0	0	56	65	38	32	14	44	.290	L	L	6-4	210	5-10-81	2003	Clearwater, Fla.
Bonnell, Jared	0	0	6.23	4	0	0	0	4	5	4	3	3	3	.357	R	R	6-2	210	12-9-80	2002	Las Vegas, Nev.
Burch, Jason	0	1	1.53	17	0	0	10	18	13	7	3	1	25	.188	R	R	6-5	215	10-15-82	2003	Papillion, Neb.
Chavez, Miguel	0	3	7.71	17	3	0	1	30	45	32	26	16	14	.346	R	R	6-0	160	12-12-81	2000	Caracas, Venez.
DeJaynes, Brandon	5	1	1.10	25	0	0	1	33	24	9	4	13	27	.201	R	R	6-2	190	9-10-80	2003	Quincy, Ill.
Garza, Justin	3	0	1.71	21	0	0	2	26	21	10	5	6	25	.225	R	R	6-1	190	7-13-82	2003	Frederick, Okla.
Gomez, Luis	0	1	11.37	17	0	0	1	19	31	34	24	12	15	.352	R	R	6-0	170	11-5-82	2001	Sincerin, Colombia
Hoffmann, Brett	0	4	5.32	15	6	1	0	47	59	36	28	17	24	.302	R	R	6-4	220	3-26-81	2002	Little Rock, Ark.
Kopszywa, Nate	1	1	5.94	12	2	0	0	17	20	13	11	11	6	.289	R	R	6-6	220	12-14-81	2003	D'Iberville, Miss.
Markham, Josh	1	0	6.94	10	0	0	0	12	19	19	9	6	8	.333	L	L	6-2	185	11-19-84	2003	Decatur, Ala.
McClellan, Kyle	3	6	3.99	12	12	0	0	68	74	34	30	16	44	.269	R	R	6-2	185	6-12-84	2002	Florissant, Mo.
Mendez, Orlin	1	1	4.50	17	0	0	0	24	25	17	12	18	15	.268	R	R	6-0	170	6-11-83	2000	Guacara, Venez.
Pals, Jordan	2	2	2.16	8	8	1	0	42	35	13	10	9	24	.224	R	R	6-8	205	10-18-80	2003	Effingham, Ill.
Pomeranz, Stuart	1	1	6.14	4	3	0	0	15	13	10	10	4	14	.236	R	R	6-7	220	12-17-84	2003	Collierville, Tenn.
Reedy, Shane	1	0	2.70	2	2	0	0	10	9	3	3	9	3	.257	R	R	6-2	200	6-2-82	2002	West Jordan, Utah
Soteropoulos, Peter	0	1	0.00	9	0	0	0	10	9	2	0	1	5	.250	L	L	6-1	210	8-5-81	2003	Peabody, Mass.
Van Gorder, Joe	0	3	10.21	11	4	0	0	27	43	37	31	14	30	.355	L	L	6-2	180	3-10-81	2002	Ithaca, N.Y.
Weagle, Matt	0	1	11.25	5	2	0	0	8	15	10	10	5	5	.375	R	R	6-4	210	7-11-82	2003	Charlton, Mass.

SAN DIEGO PADRES

BY JOHN MAFFEI

The 2003 season was over before it began for the Padres.

Shoulder surgery in September 2002 cost Trevor Hoffman, among the best closers ever, most of the 2003 season and turned the bullpen upside down.

A diving catch in a spring training game wiped out left fielder Phil Nevin's shoulder, tearing the heart out of the lineup. Elbow surgery cost Kevin Jarvis, a 12-game winner in 2001, half the season. Throw in shoulder surgery that knocked first baseman Ryan Klesko out for September and a balky back that limited center fielder Mark Kotsay's ability to run and swing the bat, and the results were predictable.

The Padres finished 64-98, the worst record in the National League, and nailed down the first overall pick in the 2004 draft.

Hoffman finally took the mound in September, appeared in nine games and posted a 2.00 ERA. But the team didn't have a save opportunity the last month of the season, so he's stuck at 352 career saves. Nevin returned for the season's final 59 games, hitting .279-13-46. He appeared in only a handful of games with Klesko, who slumped to .252-21-67 in 121 games.

When they were both in the lineup, Nevin played right field and Klesko was at first. That will change in 2004 with Nevin staying at first and Klesko going to the outfield.

"It was a rough year, a real rough year," manager Bruce Bochy said. "But we were able to find some things out about our club. We got to see some of our kids, and that's going to help us down the road."

In 2004, that road will take the Padres about 10 miles south of Qualcomm Stadium to the team's new downtown Petco Park. And with that move comes hope. The Padres started to look to 2004 when they acquired outfielder Brian Giles from the Pirates in August.

Sean Burroughs earned the starting job at third base and hit .286-7-58, and he performed admirably in the leadoff spot the last month of the season. Veteran second baseman Mark Loretta (.314-12-71) had an all-star season and set a club record for hits by an infielder with 185.

The top target of general manager Kevin Towers in the offseason was a starting catcher, one or two starting pitchers and bullpen help.

The Padres want to at least be competitive in their new ballpark in 2004. And Towers will have money to spend, perhaps as much as $60 million. The payroll was about half that in 2003.

"We're more than one or two players away from where we want to be," Towers said. "There are areas we need to address. It's safe to say we might spend more on the bullpen than starting pitching."

There doesn't figure to be much immediate help coming from the minor leagues, particularly on the mound, though righthander Ben Howard (1-3, 3.63 in six starts) could earn a spot. Khalil Greene, the team's first-round pick in 2002, split most of the year between Double-A Mobile and Triple-A Portland. He will have a chance to be the shortstop in 2004.

Several position players did emerge, such as Double-A Mobile catcher Humberto Quintero (.298-3-52), the best defensive catcher in the Southern League. Outfielder Freddy Guzman hit .288 and stole 90 bases while playing at three levels.

But Class A Lake Elsinore second baseman Josh Barfield (.337-16-128) had the best season and was named the California League's player of the year.

"The key to any organization is player development, and we're committed to scouting and development," Towers said. "And we're committed to putting a great product on the field in 2004."

Mark Loretta

BILL MITCHELL

Josh Barfield

PLAYERS of the YEAR

MAJOR LEAGUE: Mark Loretta, 2b

Loretta was the subject of trade rumors all year, but in the end the Padres decided to keep him and he emerged as their best player in 2003. He led the team in hits, runs, doubles, RBIs, batting average and on-base percentage.

MINOR LEAGUE: Josh Barfield, 2b

Barfield led all minor leaguers with 185 hits and 128 RBIs, and his 46 doubles tied for the lead. His .337 average at Class A Lake Elsinore led the California League, and he added 16 steals.

ORGANIZATION LEADERS

BATTING

*AVG	Josh Barfield, Lake Elsinore	.337
R	Josh Barfield, Lake Elsinore	99
H	Josh Barfield, Lake Elsinore	185
TB	Josh Barfield, Lake Elsinore	291
2B	Josh Barfield, Lake Elsinore	46
3B	J.J. Furmaniak, Mobile/Lake Elsinore	9
HR	Jon Knott, Portland/Mobile	28
RBI	Josh Barfield, Lake Elsinore	128
BB	Jon Knott, Portland/Mobile	86
SO	Jake Gautreau, Mobile	131
SB	Freddy Guzman, Portland/Mobile/Lake Elsinore	90
*SLG	Jason Bay, Portland	.541
*OBP	Jason Bay, Portland	.410

PITCHING

W	Gabe Ribas, Lake Elsinore/Fort Wayne	17
L	Mike Bynum, Portland	12
#ERA	Brian Whitaker, Fort Wayne	2.09
G	Three tied at	64
CG	Brian Whitaker, Fort Wayne	3
SV	Rusty Tucker, Mobile	28
IP	Justin Germano, Mobile/Lake Elsinore	169
BB	Dennis Tankersley, Portland	67
SO	Gabe Ribas, Lake Elsinore/Fort Wayne	152

*Minimum 250 At-Bats #Minimum 75 Innings

SAN DIEGO PADRES

Manager: Bruce Bochy.

2003 Record: 64-98, .395 (5th, NL West).

BATTING	AVG	G	AB	R	H	2B	3B	HR	RBI	BB	SO	SB	CS	SLG	OBP	B	T	HT	WT	DOB	1st Yr	Resides
Bay, Jason	.250	3	8	2	2	1	0	1	2	1	1	0	0	.750	.400	R	R	6-2	200	9-20-78	2000	Trail, B.C.
Bennett, Gary	.238	96	307	26	73	15	0	2	42	24	48	3	0	.306	.296	R	R	6-0	210	4-17-72	1990	Waukegan, Ill.
Buchanan, Brian	.263	115	198	29	52	10	2	8	29	24	51	6	2	.455	.346	R	R	6-4	230	7-21-73	1994	Fort Myers, Fla.
Burroughs, Sean	.286	146	517	62	148	27	6	7	58	44	75	7	2	.402	.352	L	R	6-2	200	9-12-80	1999	Long Beach, Calif.
Clark, Jermaine	.000	1	2	0	0	0	0	0	1	0	1	0	1	.000	.000	L	R	5-10	170	9-29-76	1997	Vacaville, Calif.
Giles, Brian	.298	29	104	23	31	4	2	4	18	20	10	4	0	.490	.414	L	L	5-10	200	1-20-71	1989	San Diego, Calif.
2-team (95 Pittsburgh)	.299	134	492	93	147	34	6	20	88	105	58	4	3	.514	.427							
Gonzalez, Wiki	.200	24	65	1	13	5	0	0	10	5	13	0	0	.277	.264	R	R	5-11	205	5-17-74	1992	Palo Negro, Venez.
Greene, Khalil	.215	20	65	8	14	4	1	2	6	4	19	0	1	.400	.271	R	R	5-11	210	10-21-79	2002	Key West, Fla.
Hansen, Dave	.244	110	135	13	33	4	1	2	15	23	25	1	0	.333	.358	L	R	6-0	195	11-24-68	1986	San Juan Capistrano, Calif.
Klesko, Ryan	.252	121	397	47	100	18	0	21	67	65	83	2	5	.456	.354	L	L	6-3	220	6-12-71	1989	Couington, Ga.
Kotsay, Mark	.266	128	482	64	128	28	4	7	38	56	82	6	3	.384	.343	L	L	6-0	200	12-2-75	1996	Pembroke Pines, Fla.
Lockhart, Keith	.242	62	95	18	23	5	1	3	8	13	19	0	1	.411	.339	L	R	5-10	170	11-10-64	1986	Overland Park, Kan.
Loretta, Mark	.314	154	589	74	185	28	4	13	72	54	62	5	4	.441	.372	R	R	6-0	185	8-14-71	1993	Scottsdale, Ariz.
Matthews, Gary	.271	103	306	50	83	19	1	4	22	34	66	12	5	.379	.346	S	R	6-3	225	8-25-74	1994	Baltimore, Md.
Mendez, Donaldo	.226	26	84	10	19	6	0	2	9	7	32	1	0	.369	.298	R	R	6-1	155	6-7-78	1996	Barquisimeto, Venez.
Merloni, Lou	.272	65	151	20	41	7	2	1	17	22	33	2	3	.364	.362	R	R	5-10	200	4-6-71	1993	Framingham, Mass.
Nady, Xavier	.267	110	371	50	99	17	1	9	39	24	74	6	2	.391	.321	R	R	6-2	205	11-14-78	2001	Salinas, Calif.
Nevin, Phil	.279	59	226	30	63	8	0	13	46	21	44	2	0	.487	.339	R	R	6-2	230	1-19-71	1992	San Diego, Calif.
Ojeda, Miguel	.234	61	141	13	33	6	0	4	22	18	26	1	1	.362	.331	R	R	6-2	190	1-29-75	1993	Sonora, Mexico
Quintero, Humberto	.217	12	23	1	5	0	0	0	2	1	6	0	0	.217	.250	R	R	6-1	190	8-2-79	1997	Maracaibo, Venez.
Rivera, Mike	.170	19	53	2	9	1	0	1	2	5	11	0	0	.245	.241	R	R	6-0	210	9-8-76	1997	Bayamon, P.R.
Sears, Todd	.250	9	8	2	2	1	0	0	0	0	3	0	0	.375	.250	R	R	6-5	210	10-23-75	1997	Ankeny, Iowa
Vazquez, Ramon	.261	116	422	56	110	17	4	3	30	52	88	10	3	.341	.342	L	R	5-11	170	8-21-76	1995	Cayey, P.R.
Victorino, Shane	.151	36	73	8	11	2	0	0	4	7	17	7	2	.178	.232	R	R	5-9	160	11-30-80	1999	Wailuku, Hawaii
White, Rondell	.278	115	413	49	115	17	3	18	66	25	71	1	4	.465	.330	R	R	6-1	220	2-23-72	1990	Gray, Ga.

PITCHING	W	L	ERA	G	GS	CG	SV	IP	H	R	ER	BB	SO	AVG	B	T	HT	WT	DOB	1st Yr	Resides
Beck, Rod	3	2	1.78	36	0	0	20	35	25	7	7	11	32	.196	R	R	6-1	230	8-3-68	1986	Scottsdale, Ariz.
Bynum, Mike	1	4	8.75	13	5	0	0	36	44	35	35	15	35	.297	L	L	6-4	200	3-20-78	1999	Middleburg, Fla.
Condrey, Clay	1	2	8.47	9	6	0	0	34	43	32	32	21	25	.304	R	R	6-3	195	11-19-75	1998	Navasota, Texas
Deago, Roger	0	1	7.84	2	2	0	0	10	11	9	9	8	10	.282	R	L	5-10	180	6-21-77	2003	Chitre, Panama
Eaton, Adam	9	12	4.08	31	31	1	0	183	173	91	83	68	146	.245	R	R	6-2	190	11-23-77	1996	Snohomish, Wash.
Hackman, Luther	2	2	5.17	65	0	0	0	77	78	51	44	36	48	.260	R	R	6-4	195	10-10-74	1994	Columbus, Miss.
Herges, Matt	2	2	2.86	40	0	0	3	44	40	16	14	20	40	.243	L	R	6-0	200	4-1-70	1992	Champaign, Ill.
Hoffman, Trevor	0	0	2.00	9	0	0	0	9	7	2	2	3	11	.212	R	R	6-0	215	10-13-67	1989	Del Mar, Calif.
Howard, Ben	1	3	3.63	6	6	0	0	35	31	17	14	15	24	.234	R	R	6-2	190	1-15-79	1997	Jackson, Tenn.
Jarvis, Kevin	4	8	5.87	16	16	0	0	92	113	65	60	32	49	.303	R	R	6-2	200	8-1-69	1991	Lexington, Ky.
Keisler, Randy	0	1	12.00	2	2	0	0	6	7	9	8	7	5	.291	L	L	6-3	190	2-24-76	1998	Richards, Texas
Lawrence, Brian	10	15	4.19	33	33	1	0	211	206	106	98	57	116	.257	R	R	6-0	195	5-14-76	1998	Linden, Texas
Linebrink, Scott	2	1	2.82	43	0	0	0	61	55	22	19	22	51	.244	R	R	6-2	200	8-4-76	1997	Taylor, Texas
2-team (9 Houston)	3	2	3.31	52	6	0	0	92	93	37	34	36	68	.269							
Loewer, Carlton	1	2	6.65	5	5	0	0	22	35	17	16	8	11	.368	S	R	6-6	210	9-24-73	1995	Eunice, La.
Matthews, Mike	6	4	4.45	77	0	0	0	65	65	34	32	29	44	.270	L	L	6-2	170	10-24-73	1992	Woodbridge, Va.
Nagy, Charles	0	2	4.38	5	0	0	0	12	15	7	6	3	7	.312	L	R	6-3	200	5-5-67	1989	Westlake, Ohio
Orosco, Jesse	1	1	7.56	42	0	0	2	25	33	22	21	10	22	.317	R	L	6-2	205	4-21-57	1978	San Diego, Calif.
Peavy, Jake	12	11	4.11	32	32	0	0	195	173	94	89	82	156	.237	R	R	6-1	180	5-31-81	1999	Semmes, Ala.
Perez, Oliver	4	7	5.38	19	19	0	0	104	103	65	62	65	117	.258	L	L	6-3	160	8-15-81	1999	Culiacan, Mexico
Roa, Joe	1	1	6.75	18	1	0	0	25	34	20	19	6	18	.314	R	R	6-2	200	10-11-71	1989	Royal Oak, MI
2-team (6 Philadelphia)	1	3	6.14	28	4	0	0	51	69	36	35	10	38	.319							
Tankersley, Dennis	0	1	0.00	1	1	0	0	0	3	7	7	4	0	1.000	R	R	6-2	185	2-24-79	1999	St. Charles, Mo.
Tollberg, Brian	0	2	6.97	3	3	0	0	10	9	11	8	4	2	.230	R	R	6-3	195	9-16-72	1994	Bradenton, Fla.
Villafuerte, Brandon	0	2	4.20	31	0	0	2	41	39	20	19	26	34	.251	R	R	5-11	195	12-17-75	1995	Morgan Hill, Calif.
Walker, Kevin	0	0	5.40	11	0	0	0	7	5	4	4	5	5	.200	L	L	6-4	190	9-20-76	1995	Glen Rose, Texas
Witasick, Jay	3	7	4.53	46	0	0	2	46	42	24	23	25	42	.244	R	R	6-4	230	8-28-72	1993	Bel Air, Md.
Wright, Jaret	1	5	8.37	39	0	0	2	47	69	44	44	28	41	.348	R	R	6-2	230	12-29-75	1994	Newport Beach, Calif.

FIELDING

Catcher	PCT	G	PO	A	E	DP	PB
Bennett	.996	91	535	25	2	5	6
Gonzalez	.993	23	128	7	1	0	1
Hansen	.000	1	0	0	0	0	0
Ojeda	.981	48	293	14	6	1	4
Quintero	.982	11	52	2	1	1	2
Rivera	.986	19	133	7	2	0	2

First Base	PCT	G	PO	A	E	DP
Buchanan	.986	24	137	9	2	19
Hansen	1.000	20	105	10	0	14
Klesko	.994	111	849	84	6	67
Merloni	1.000	2	5	0	0	1
Nevin	.996	31	239	21	1	26

Ojeda	1.000	2	12	0	0	1	
Rivera	1.000	1	2	0	0	0	
Sears	1.000	1	1	0	0	1	

Second Base	PCT	G	PO	A	E	DP
Hansen	.000	1	0	0	0	0
Lockhart	.986	27	37	33	1	8
Loretta	.990	150	273	412	7	84
Merloni	.950	10	9	10	1	1
Vazquez	1.000	3	6	9	0	5

Third Base	PCT	G	PO	A	E	DP
Burroughs	.966	137	105	239	12	26
Hansen	.957	11	6	16	1	0
Lockhart	.889	3	2	6	1	0
Merloni	.925	25	12	37	4	3
Vazquez	.833	4	2	3	1	0

Shortstop	PCT	G	PO	A	E	DP
Greene	.963	20	27	51	3	11
Loretta	1.000	3	2	0	0	0
Mendez	.951	26	26	71	5	10
Merloni	.987	23	35	43	1	11
Vazquez	.969	108	131	274	13	57

Outfield	PCT	G	PO	A	E	DP
Bay	1.000	3	8	0	0	0
Buchanan	1.000	43	47	2	0	1

Clark	1.000	1	2	0	0	0
Giles	.966	29	55	2	2	0
Kotsay	.991	126	324	13	3	4
Matthews	.993	92	150	2	1	0
Merloni	1.000	2	2	0	0	0
Nady	.968	105	170	12	6	2
Nevin	.980	29	47	1	1	0
Victorino	1.000	32	42	3	0	0
White	.978	104	173	6	4	2

FARM SYSTEM

Director, Player Development: Tye Waller.

Class	Farm Team	League	W	L	Pct.	Finish*	Manager	First Yr.
AAA	Portland (Ore.) Beavers	Pacific Coast	69	75	.479	12th (16)	Rick Sweet	2001
AA	Mobile (Ala.) BayBears	Southern	61	77	.442	10th (10)	Craig Colbert	1997
High A	Lake Elsinore (Calif.) Storm	California	75	65	.536	4th (10)	Jeff Gardner	2001
Low A	Fort Wayne (Ind.) Wizards	Midwest	71	66	.518	5th (14)	Gary Jones	1999
SS A	Eugene (Ore.) Emeralds	Northwest	39	37	.513	4th (8)	Roy Howell	2001
Rookie	Idaho Falls (Idaho) Padres	Pioneer	24	52	.316	8th (8)	Carlos Lezcano	1995

*Finish in overall standings (No. of teams in league)

PORTLAND BEAVERS — Class AAA

PACIFIC COAST LEAGUE

BATTING	AVG	G	AB	R	H	2B	3B	HR	RBI	BB	SO	SB	CS	SLG	OBP	B	T	HT	WT	DOB	1st Yr	Resides
Anderson, Brady	.294	23	68	15	20	1	1	0	7	18	15	5	1	.338	.455	L	L	6-1	200	1-18-64	1985	Lake Tahoe, Nev.
Bay, Jason	.303	91	307	64	93	11	1	20	59	55	71	23	4	.541	.410	R	R	6-2	200	9-20-78	2000	Trail, B.C.
Bozied, Tagg	.273	119	450	59	123	25	2	14	59	38	80	1	0	.431	.331	R	R	6-3	210	7-24-79	2001	Sioux Falls, S.D.
Castro, Bernie	.311	105	425	57	132	17	5	2	24	25	43	49	13	.388	.349	S	R	5-10	160	7-14-79	1997	Santo Domingo, D.R.
Clark, Jermaine	.250	50	160	27	40	2	2	4	10	22	24	14	3	.363	.342	L	R	5-10	170	9-29-76	1997	Vacaville, Calif.
Clements, Jason	.000	1	1	0	0	0	0	0	0	0	1	0	0	.000	.000	S	R	5-11	170	3-1-78	1999	Arlington, Texas
DeHaan, Kory	.202	54	183	26	37	7	1	2	11	17	34	8	1	.284	.276	L	R	6-2	185	7-16-76	1997	Pella, Iowa
Fernandez, Alex	.303	105	379	49	115	23	2	10	52	13	53	16	6	.454	.327	L	L	6-1	200	5-15-81	1998	Cotui, D.R.
Gomez, Rich	.304	80	227	33	69	8	1	11	44	18	36	21	1	.493	.363	R	R	5-11	190	7-19-76	1996	San Francisco de Macoris, D.R.
Gonzalez, Wiki	.282	44	149	17	42	8	1	4	20	21	12	1	0	.430	.379	R	R	5-11	205	5-17-74	1992	Palo Negro, Venez.
Greene, Khalil	.288	76	319	42	92	19	0	10	47	20	52	5	4	.442	.346	R	R	5-11	210	10-21-79	2002	Key West, Fla.
Guzman, Freddy	.300	2	10	1	3	0	0	0	0	0	1	3	0	.300	.300	S	R	5-10	165	1-20-81	2000	Santo Domingo, D.R.
Haad, Yamid	.233	80	258	24	60	13	1	10	34	15	55	3	2	.407	.278	R	R	6-2	210	9-2-77	1994	Cartagena, Colombia
Knott, Jon	.346	7	26	5	9	1	0	1	5	4	3	0	0	.500	.433	R	R	6-3	220	8-4-78	2002	Nokomis, Fla.
Lockhart, Keith	.182	4	11	0	2	0	0	0	4	1	0	0	0	.182	.308	L	R	5-10	170	11-10-64	1986	Overland Park, Kan.
Mendez, Donaldo	.226	102	358	49	81	17	0	6	36	25	83	10	7	.324	.288	R	R	6-1	155	6-7-78	1996	Barquisimeto, Venez.
Nady, Xavier	.265	37	136	19	36	7	0	7	23	12	28	0	0	.471	.329	R	R	6-2	205	11-14-78	2001	Salinas, Calif.
Nevin, Phil	.111	6	18	0	2	0	0	0	1	1	1	0	0	.111	.158	R	R	6-2	230	1-19-71	1992	San Diego, Calif.
Pelaez, Alex	.288	76	292	36	84	16	0	7	49	12	31	0	0	.414	.312	R	R	5-9	190	4-6-76	1998	Chula Vista, Calif.
Quinn, Mark	.272	55	180	28	49	13	0	8	29	24	36	0	0	.478	.362	R	R	6-1	190	5-21-74	1995	West Covina, Calif.
Risinger, Ben	.252	86	278	32	70	18	0	5	35	23	30	3	2	.371	.321	R	R	6-1	170	11-25-77	1999	Perth, Australia
Rivera, Mike	.160	13	50	0	8	1	0	0	2	1	21	0	1	.180	.176	R	R	6-0	210	9-8-76	1997	Bayamon, P.R.
Scales, Bobby	.372	11	43	8	16	7	0	0	2	7	6	3	0	.535	.460	S	R	6-0	170	10-4-77	1999	Roswell, Ga.
Simmons, Brian	.100	10	20	0	2	0	0	0	3	1	4	0	0	.100	.136	S	R	6-2	190	9-4-73	1995	McMurray, Penn.
Thrower, Jake	.277	28	83	11	23	8	0	1	13	7	8	1	0	.410	.340	S	R	5-11	180	11-19-75	1997	Yuma, Ariz.
Valdez, Mario	.270	90	226	23	61	16	0	5	24	34	42	0	0	.407	.366	L	R	6-2	210	11-19-74	1994	Obregon, Mexico
Washington, Rico	.224	17	58	11	13	2	1	3	10	10	14	0	1	.448	.343	L	R	5-9	190	5-30-78	1997	Gray, Ga.

PITCHING	W	L	ERA	G	GS	CG	SV	IP	H	R	ER	BB	SO	AVG	B	T	HT	WT	DOB	1st Yr	Resides
Bartosh, Cliff	2	5	4.29	64	0	0	10	71	67	36	34	22	51	.249	L	L	6-2	175	9-5-79	1998	Duncanville, Texas
Bausher, Andy	1	0	8.25	7	1	0	0	12	17	11	11	3	6	.320	R	L	6-2	200	8-17-76	1997	Bechtelsville, Pa.
Bruback, Matt	2	0	2.61	2	2	0	0	10	12	3	3	4	6	.272	R	R	6-7	210	1-12-79	1998	Sarasota, Fla.
3-team (20 Iowa, 4 Nash.)	10	10	4.00	26	25	1	0	157	150	80	70	49	112	.251							
Bynum, Mike	7	12	4.81	24	23	0	0	125	130	76	67	60	106	.270	L	L	6-4	200	3-20-78	1999	Middleburg, Fla.
Condrey, Clay	3	3	4.14	11	11	0	0	63	64	34	29	12	46	.263	R	R	6-3	195	11-19-75	1998	Navasota, Texas
Cumberland, Chris	0	0	3.68	4	0	0	0	7	7	3	3	2	5	.241	R	L	6-1	180	1-15-73	1993	Mandeville, La.
Duncan, Courtney	2	6	4.57	54	0	0	18	61	66	39	31	37	49	.280	L	R	6-0	190	10-9-74	1996	Huntsville, Ala.
Flury, Pat	0	0	6.14	7	0	0	0	7	8	7	5	12	9	.285	R	R	6-2	210	3-14-73	1993	Sparks, Nevada
Gaal, Bryan	0	1	4.50	2	0	0	0	2	2	1	1	0	1	.250	R	R	6-4	205	12-17-76	1999	Syracuse, N.Y.
Giese, Dan	1	0	13.50	3	0	0	0	6	12	9	9	3	6	.413	R	R	6-3	200	5-19-77	1999	San Clemente, Calif.
Hampton, Matt	1	3	5.83	33	0	0	0	46	51	32	30	22	36	.293	R	L	6-4	220	6-20-77	2001	Wenatchee, Wash.
Herges, Matt	0	0	1.80	4	0	0	0	5	1	1	1	2	5	.062	L	R	6-0	200	4-1-70	1992	Champaign, Ill.
Howard, Ben	7	9	4.55	22	22	0	0	131	118	69	66	49	68	.242	R	R	6-2	190	1-15-79	1997	Jackson, Tenn.
Hunter, Johnny	2	2	6.29	11	3	0	1	24	31	21	17	17	21	.322	R	R	6-1	190	6-14-75	1997	Mansfield, Texas
Keisler, Randy	5	1	2.61	8	6	0	0	41	33	12	12	12	24	.215	L	L	6-3	190	2-24-76	1998	Richards, Texas
Keller, Kris	1	1	5.63	18	1	0	0	24	34	19	15	11	11	.343	R	R	6-2	260	3-1-78	1996	Atlantic Beach, Fla.
Loewer, Carlton	7	8	5.40	23	23	0	0	125	161	84	75	28	57	.320	S	R	6-6	210	9-24-73	1995	Eunice, La.
Nagy, Charles	1	0	1.23	3	1	0	1	7	8	1	1	0	5	.000	L	R	6-3	200	5-5-67	1989	Westlake, Ohio
Perez, Oliver	3	3	3.02	8	8	0	0	48	44	20	16	12	48	.245	L	L	6-3	160	8-15-81	1999	Culiacan, Mexico
Ramsay, Rob	0	0	12.00	2	0	0	0	3	5	4	4	0	1	.416	L	L	6-5	215	12-3-73	1996	Issaquah, Wash.
Silva, Jose	0	3	5.54	17	2	0	0	26	32	17	16	13	14	.307	R	R	6-6	235	12-19-73	1991	Sarasota, Fla.
Steidlmayer, Luke	1	0	1.80	1	0	0	0	5	4	1	1	0	3	.235	R	R	6-5	190	8-13-80	2002	Colusa, Calif.
Tankersley, Dennis	8	11	4.65	27	27	0	0	151	149	82	78	67	148	.257	R	R	6-2	185	2-24-79	1999	St. Charles, Mo.
Tollberg, Brian	5	3	5.25	20	12	0	0	82	94	52	48	13	45	.283	R	R	6-3	195	9-16-72	1994	Bradenton, Fla.
Trujillo, J.J.	1	1	5.63	27	0	0	3	32	32	22	20	10	22	.260	R	R	6-0	180	10-9-75	1999	Corpus Christi, Texas
Villafuerte, Brandon	3	1	1.84	37	0	0	12	44	42	10	9	14	40	.257	R	R	5-11	195	12-17-75	1995	Morgan Hill, Calif.
Walker, Kevin	3	1	4.08	34	1	0	0	46	53	24	21	10	43	.291	L	L	6-4	190	9-20-76	1995	Glen Rose, Texas
Watkins, Steve	1	0	3.08	14	0	0	0	26	20	11	9	12	23	.206	R	R	6-4	190	7-19-78	1998	Lubbock, Texas
Webb, Alan	0	0	0.00	1	0	0	0	2	0	0	0	1	1	.000	L	L	5-10	160	9-26-79	1997	Las Vegas, Nevada
Witasick, Jay	0	0	3.00	5	0	0	1	6	4	2	2	1	8	.181	R	R	6-4	230	8-28-72	1993	Bel Air, Md.
Wright, Jaret	2	1	1.42	12	1	0	0	19	16	7	3	7	21	.222	R	R	6-2	230	12-29-75	1994	Newport Beach, Calif.

FIELDING

Catcher	PCT	G	PO	A	E	DP	PB
Gonzalez	.987	42	278	19	4	3	2
Haad	.984	74	463	40	8	2	12
Risinger	.993	23	133	10	1	2	4
Rivera	.990	13	96	7	1	0	4

First Base	PCT	G	PO	A	E	DP
Bozied	.991	111	911	77	9	87
Haad	1.000	1	1	0	0	0
Knott	1.000	7	56	6	0	5
Nevin	1.000	2	12	0	0	1
Pelaez	1.000	7	38	5	0	6
Risinger	1.000	1	3	0	0	1
Valdez	1.000	24	196	10	0	17
Washington	1.000	2	12	2	0	1

Second Base	PCT	G	PO	A	E	DP
Castro	.970	95	185	261	14	59
Clark	.939	9	11	20	2	7
Lockhart	1.000	1	0	1	0	0
Mendez	.977	20	34	51	2	11
Pelaez	.986	14	23	45	1	9
Scales	1.000	2	5	2	0	0
Thrower	.980	12	19	30	1	7

Third Base	PCT	G	PO	A	E	DP
Clark	1.000	2	4	1	0	0
Mendez	.950	22	17	40	3	8
Pelaez	.966	60	44	97	5	14
Risinger	.973	47	36	73	3	4
Scales	1.000	3	3	4	0	0
Thrower	.909	7	4	6	1	1
Valdez	1.000	1	0	2	0	0
Washington	.943	15	12	38	3	4

Shortstop	PCT	G	PO	A	E	DP
Clark	.917	6	9	13	2	3
Greene	.967	76	96	230	11	42
Mendez	.956	58	98	139	11	35
Risinger	1.000	2	1	8	0	0
Thrower	1.000	6	8	15	0	5

Outfield	PCT	G	PO	A	E	DP
Anderson	1.000	18	29	1	0	0
Bay	.995	90	195	10	1	1
Bozied	.000	1	0	0	0	0
Clark	1.000	35	63	1	0	0
DeHaan	.992	51	131	1	1	1
Fernandez	.976	99	185	15	5	3
Gomez	.971	60	99	3	3	1
Guzman	1.000	2	4	0	0	0
Nady	.954	32	60	2	3	1
Nevin	1.000	2	4	0	0	0
Quinn	.971	37	62	4	2	1
Risinger	1.000	7	3	1	0	0
Scales	1.000	6	13	1	0	0
Simmons	1.000	4	8	0	0	0
Valdez	1.000	28	33	1	0	0

MOBILE BAYBEARS — Class AA

SOUTHERN LEAGUE

BATTING	AVG	G	AB	R	H	2B	3B	HR	RBI	BB	SO	SB	CS	SLG	OBP	B	T	HT	WT	DOB	1st Yr	Resides
Benick, Jon	.203	37	123	11	25	7	0	1	9	8	32	0	1	.285	.258	S	R	6-1	210	9-26-79	2001	Glen Lyon, Pa.
Bravo, Danny	.230	113	365	41	84	16	0	3	38	48	52	0	1	.299	.320	S	R	5-11	170	5-27-77	1996	Maracaibo, Venez.
Clements, Jason	.167	18	42	1	7	0	0	0	2	5	11	1	0	.167	.271	S	R	5-11	170	3-1-78	1999	Arlington, Texas
Donovan, Todd	.202	112	420	61	85	11	7	8	32	47	80	31	11	.319	.288	R	R	6-1	175	8-12-78	1999	East Lyme, Conn.
Faison, Vince	.230	119	392	41	90	15	0	4	28	47	116	13	2	.298	.318	L	R	6-0	180	1-22-81	1999	Lyons, Ga.
Fernandez, Alex	.307	21	75	7	23	5	1	1	10	4	16	2	3	.440	.342	L	L	6-1	200	5-15-81	1998	Cotui, D.R.
Furmaniak, J.J.	.262	31	103	10	27	4	1	3	11	8	27	0	0	.408	.336	R	R	6-0	190	7-31-79	2000	Bolingbrook, Ill.
Gautreau, Jake	.242	122	438	48	106	24	0	14	55	50	131	1	4	.393	.324	L	R	6-0	185	11-14-79	2001	South Padre Island, Texas
Gerber, Joe	.217	24	69	9	15	4	0	3	10	8	34	0	0	.406	.295	L	L	6-1	210	8-27-78	2000	Portland, Ore.
Gomez, Rich	.247	30	93	15	23	4	0	4	14	10	22	8	0	.419	.333	R	R	5-11	190	7-19-76	1996	San Francisco de Macoris, D.R.
Greene, Khalil	.275	59	229	20	63	17	2	3	20	16	55	2	3	.406	.327	R	R	5-11	210	10-21-79	2002	Key West, Fla.
Guzman, Freddy	.271	46	177	30	48	5	2	1	11	26	34	38	7	.339	.368	S	R	5-10	165	1-20-81	2000	Santo Domingo, D.R.
Haad, Yamid	.276	9	29	3	8	2	0	1	5	3	4	0	0	.448	.344	R	R	6-2	210	9-2-77	1994	Cartagena, Colombia
Hastings, Joseph	.083	4	12	0	1	1	0	0	1	2	6	0	0	.167	.214	L	R	6-3	205	6-25-78	2001	Connelly Springs, N.C.
Johnson, Ben	.181	44	127	8	23	5	0	1	7	10	36	0	1	.244	.252	R	R	6-1	200	6-18-81	1999	Memphis, Tenn.
Knott, Jon	.252	127	432	83	109	32	0	27	82	82	117	5	3	.514	.387	R	R	6-3	220	8-4-78	2002	Nokomis, Fla.
Lorenzana, Luis	.186	18	43	6	8	0	0	0	3	9	7	0	0	.186	.321	R	R	6-2	195	11-9-78	1996	San Diego, Calif.
Quintero, Humberto	.298	110	386	37	115	26	0	3	52	19	41	0	0	.389	.343	R	R	6-1	190	8-2-79	1997	Maracaibo, Venez.
Reinking, Kevin	.125	14	40	5	5	1	0	1	6	3	20	0	0	.225	.234	R	R	6-1	190	1-25-79	2001	Long Beach, N.Y.
Scales, Bobby	.282	100	301	41	85	22	3	3	37	36	63	8	2	.405	.361	S	R	6-0	170	10-4-77	1999	Roswell, Ga.
Smith, Ryan	.152	11	33	1	5	0	0	1	3	3	11	0	0	.242	.243	R	R	5-10	190	6-20-79	1998	Mufflinburg, Penn.
Washington, Rico	.244	111	402	60	98	19	2	14	60	44	73	2	2	.405	.329	L	R	5-9	190	5-30-78	1997	Gray, Ga.

PITCHING	W	L	ERA	G	GS	CG	SV	IP	H	R	ER	BB	SO	AVG	B	T	HT	WT	DOB	1st Yr	Resides
Baker, Brad	1	6	5.68	17	9	0	0	51	50	34	32	36	53	.263	R	R	6-2	180	11-6-80	1999	Leyden, Mass.
Bumstead, Mike	1	2	2.88	37	1	0	0	69	65	23	22	28	44	.254	R	R	6-3	210	7-8-77	2001	Big Bear Lake, Calif.
Deago, Roger	8	7	4.03	26	20	0	0	118	127	64	53	51	109	.280	R	L	5-10	180	6-21-77	2003	Chitre, Panama
Gaal, Bryan	3	5	3.10	62	0	0	3	73	64	26	25	29	78	.236	R	R	6-4	205	12-17-76	1999	Syracuse, N.Y.
Germano, Justin	2	5	4.34	9	9	1	0	58	60	34	28	13	44	.267	R	R	6-2	190	8-6-82	2000	Claremont, Calif.
Giese, Dan	1	0	2.25	2	0	0	0	4	1	1	1	0	4	.076	R	R	6-3	200	5-19-77	1999	San Clemente, Calif.
Harvey, Ian	2	0	4.66	6	0	0	0	10	13	6	5	1	10	.317	R	R	6-1	190	10-11-76	1999	Oakville, Ontario
Hunter, Johnny	0	1	9.00	1	1	0	0	4	5	5	4	3	5	.294	R	R	6-1	190	6-14-75	1997	Mansfield, Texas
McAdoo, Duncan	6	8	4.14	30	19	0	0	130	128	70	60	31	110	.263	R	R	6-1	200	4-15-78	2000	Houston, Texas
Miniel, Rene	0	0	0.00	1	0	0	0	1	0	0	0	0	2	.000	R	R	6-2	170	4-26-79	1998	Santo Domingo, D.R.
Nicolas, Mike	0	1	8.10	5	0	0	1	7	6	6	6	7	11	.240	R	R	6-3	220	9-5-79	2000	Santo Domingo, D.R.
Nunez, Jose	1	2	6.00	9	0	0	0	12	11	10	8	4	11	.234	L	L	6-2	175	3-14-79	1996	Monte Cristi, D.R.
Oxspring, Chris	10	6	2.92	40	18	1	0	136	106	47	44	62	129	.210	L	R	6-1	180	5-13-77	2000	Labrador, Australia
Rojas, Chris	5	10	4.27	32	19	1	0	110	94	62	52	53	92	.230	R	R	6-2	180	3-30-77	1998	Glendale, N.Y.
Spiehs, R.D.	0	2	5.30	15	0	0	0	19	17	12	11	7	17	.250	R	R	6-3	210	10-18-79	2001	Grand Island, Neb.
Stewart, Cory	12	7	3.72	24	24	0	0	126	104	60	52	50	133	.222	L	L	6-4	180	11-14-79	1999	Boerne, Texas
Trujillo, J.J.	1	2	3.70	28	0	0	3	41	35	20	17	12	33	.233	R	R	6-0	180	10-9-75	1999	Corpus Christi, Texas
Tucker, Rusty	2	6	3.74	51	0	0	28	53	49	26	22	31	63	.240	R	L	6-1	190	7-15-80	2001	Gloucester, Mass.
Watkins, Steve	5	4	4.17	18	18	0	0	101	100	50	47	34	75	.259	R	R	6-4	190	7-19-78	1998	Lubbock, Texas
Webb, Alan	1	3	3.30	58	0	0	2	85	58	39	31	47	79	.189	L	L	5-10	160	9-26-79	1997	Las Vegas, Nev.

FIELDING

Catcher	PCT	G	PO	A	E	DP	PB
Haad	.944	3	16	1	1	0	0
Quintero	.995	109	857	93	5	5	6
Reinking	.991	13	104	2	1	0	1
Smith	.988	11	79	6	1	2	0
Washington	.985	10	61	6	1	0	2

First Base	PCT	G	PO	A	E	DP
Benick	.986	32	257	18	4	27
Bravo	.992	35	218	23	2	11
Gerber	.992	16	125	7	1	8
Haad	.952	5	39	1	2	5
Hastings	1.000	3	23	0	0	1
Knott	.983	53	394	23	7	40
Washington	1.000	5	36	2	0	2

Second Base	PCT	G	PO	A	E	DP
Bravo	1.000	1	1	3	0	1
Clements	.909	2	5	5	1	2
Donovan	1.000	1	1	2	0	1
Gautreau	.968	112	167	257	14	50
Lorenzana	1.000	7	18	21	0	5
Scales	.957	19	28	38	3	14
Washington	1.000	1	0	1	0	0

Third Base	PCT	G	PO	A	E	DP
Bravo	.852	23	10	42	9	3
Clements	1.000	1	1	2	0	0
Lorenzana	1.000	1	1	1	0	0
Scales	.878	29	23	42	9	3
Washington	.932	91	52	153	15	7

Shortstop	PCT	G	PO	A	E	DP
Benick	1.000	1	1	1	0	0
Bravo	.959	52	71	138	9	33
Clements	.909	1	4	6	1	1
Furmaniak	.929	31	48	69	9	10
Greene	.949	54	50	119	9	30
Lorenzana	.960	7	8	16	1	1

Outfield	PCT	G	PO	A	E	DP
Clements	1.000	6	6	0	0	0

Donovan	.982	107	262	8	5	1
Faison	.952	111	184	16	10	1
Fernandez	.970	19	32	0	1	0
Gerber	1.000	3	7	0	0	0
Gomez	.977	27	41	2	1	0
Guzman	.984	46	120	2	2	0
Johnson	.984	35	60	0	1	0
Knott	.968	72	116	4	4	0
Scales	.957	18	21	1	1	0

LAKE ELSINORE STORM — High Class A

CALIFORNIA LEAGUE

BATTING	AVG	G	AB	R	H	2B	3B	HR	RBI	BB	SO	SB	CS	SLG	OBP	B	T	HT	WT	DOB	1st Yr	Resides
Barfield, Josh	.337	135	549	99	185	46	6	16	128	50	122	16	4	.530	.389	R	R	6-0	185	12-17-82	2001	Spring, Texas
Benick, Jon	.300	82	327	50	98	24	1	9	47	27	53	1	0	.462	.356	S	R	6-1	210	9-26-79	2001	Glen Lyon, Pa.
Bravo, Danny	.291	15	55	13	16	4	1	3	17	8	7	2	1	.564	.375	S	R	5-11	170	5-27-77	1996	Maracaibo, Venez.
Carter, Josh	.300	96	357	58	107	18	3	6	56	32	53	8	3	.417	.362	R	R	6-2	210	11-5-80	2001	Fallbrook, Calif.
Clements, Jason	.299	55	174	28	52	7	3	4	31	19	30	2	2	.443	.374	S	R	5-11	170	3-1-78	1999	Arlington, Texas
Furmaniak, J.J.	.314	78	309	65	97	22	8	9	54	36	55	10	4	.524	.397	R	R	6-0	190	7-31-79	2000	Bolingbrook, Ill.
Gerber, Joe	.278	76	284	47	79	20	1	11	56	27	81	0	2	.472	.351	L	L	6-1	210	8-27-78	2000	Portland, Ore.
Guzman, Freddy	.285	70	281	64	80	12	3	2	22	40	60	49	10	.370	.375	S	R	5-10	165	1-20-81	2000	Santo Domingo, D.R.
Hastings, Joseph	.236	79	267	34	63	16	0	8	51	17	69	1	1	.386	.288	L	R	6-3	205	6-25-78	2001	Connelly Springs, N.C.
Jacobo, Kervin	.313	4	16	2	5	2	0	0	0	1	2	0	0	.438	.353	S	R	6-2	190	9-26-82	1999	Haina, D.R.
Johnson, Ben	.266	52	184	30	49	9	0	8	29	20	49	6	1	.446	.354	R	R	6-1	200	6-18-81	1999	Memphis, Tenn.
Johnson, Michael	.275	46	178	22	49	17	1	5	24	17	48	0	1	.466	.343	L	R	6-3	215	6-25-80	2003	Georgetown, S.C.
Jones, Kennard	.250	17	76	16	19	3	2	0	5	4	11	3	2	.342	.288	L	L	5-11	180	9-8-81	2002	Beltsville, Md.
Lima, Joseph	.217	17	46	6	10	2	0	0	1	2	19	1	0	.261	.265	R	R	6-1	190	7-16-79	2002	San Diego, Calif.
Merloni, Lou	.474	5	19	3	9	3	0	1	7	1	0	0	0	.789	.476	R	R	5-10	200	4-6-71	1993	Framingham, Mass.
Nettles, Marcus	.232	120	423	71	98	9	7	1	30	50	122	32	10	.293	.322	L	L	5-11	180	5-15-80	2001	Chicago, Ill.
Nevin, Phil	.267	5	15	1	4	1	0	0	5	2	2	0	0	.333	.300	R	R	6-2	230	1-19-71	1992	San Diego, Calif.
Reinking, Kevin	.193	18	57	7	11	4	0	1	10	6	20	0	0	.316	.309	R	R	6-1	190	1-25-79	2001	Long Beach, N.Y.
Richardson, Mike	.243	71	206	27	50	14	3	5	29	34	60	1	0	.413	.350	R	R	5-10	210	7-11-79	2002	Inverness, Calif.
Sain, Greg	.274	123	467	74	128	35	0	19	100	43	119	3	1	.471	.336	R	R	6-2	200	12-26-79	2001	Torrance, Calif.
Santora, Jack	.322	47	174	38	56	10	2	1	11	28	24	10	0	.420	.424	S	R	5-9	160	10-6-76	1999	Monterey, Calif.
Serrano, Eddie	.143	5	14	3	2	0	0	0	0	2	5	0	0	.143	.250	R	R	6-0	170	10-26-81	2000	Chiriqui, Panama
Stonard, Peter	.200	1	5	1	1	0	0	0	1	0	2	0	0	.200	.200	L	R	6-0	195	12-31-81	2003	St. Louis, Mo.
Trzesniak, Nick	.245	109	375	59	92	10	0	8	45	49	88	17	4	.336	.340	R	R	6-0	210	11-19-80	1999	Tinley Park, Ill.
Vazquez, Ramon	.188	5	16	3	3	0	0	1	4	3	3	0	1	.375	.350	L	R	5-11	170	8-21-76	1995	Cayey, P.R.

PITCHING	W	L	ERA	G	GS	CG	SV	IP	H	R	ER	BB	SO	AVG	B	T	HT	WT	DOB	1st Yr	Resides
Baker, Brad	3	0	2.01	27	4	0	12	45	31	13	10	14	69	.186	R	R	6-2	180	11-6-80	1999	Leyden, Mass.
Beavers, Kevin	4	3	3.66	42	2	0	0	64	74	32	26	21	42	.290	L	L	6-5	190	10-22-79	2002	Irvine, Calif.
Bumstead, Mike	1	1	5.55	5	5	0	0	24	31	19	15	13	19	.306	R	R	6-3	210	7-8-77	2001	Big Bear Lake, Calif.
Cassel, Jack	5	4	3.59	64	0	0	3	73	69	34	29	18	52	.251	R	R	6-2	190	8-8-79	2000	Northridge, Calif.
Craker, Justin	4	1	5.08	50	0	0	0	67	70	41	38	45	56	.269	R	R	6-0	215	9-11-78	2001	Superior, Wisc.
Garvin, Robert	3	5	4.24	61	0	0	1	68	75	36	32	19	43	.278	R	R	6-0	180	3-14-79	1997	Charleston, S.C.
Germano, Justin	9	5	4.23	19	19	1	0	111	127	61	52	25	78	.286	R	R	6-2	190	8-6-82	2000	Claremont, Calif.
Hensley, Clay	3	4	3.45	8	8	0	0	44	50	24	17	14	40	.285	R	R	5-11	190	8-31-79	2002	Pearland, Texas
2-team (5 San Jose)	5	7	4.40	13	13	0	0	74	88	44	36	23	65	.305							
Hoffman, Trevor	0	0	0.00	3	0	0	0	3	2	0	0	0	4	.181	R	R	6-0	215	10-13-67	1989	Del Mar, Calif.
Huber, Jon	3	5	5.18	12	11	0	0	57	69	41	33	31	43	.300	R	R	6-2	190	7-7-81	2000	North Fort Myers, Fla.
Jarvis, Kevin	2	1	4.09	3	3	0	0	22	18	11	10	4	19	.222	R	R	6-2	200	8-1-69	1991	Lexington, Ky.
Jones, Geoffrey	2	2	3.89	25	2	0	0	35	29	18	15	13	32	.219	L	L	6-6	230	8-10-79	1999	Dolores, Colo.
Kozol, Anthony	2	0	4.24	15	0	0	1	17	19	8	8	1	9	.271	R	R	6-2	190	12-28-77	2000	Dudley, N.C.
Lipari, Thomas	0	4	6.32	12	7	0	0	37	55	37	26	19	28	.339	L	L	6-5	180	4-23-79	2002	Omaha, Neb.
Martinez, Javier	6	3	3.23	16	16	0	0	84	76	35	30	23	70	.233	S	R	6-3	170	12-9-82	2000	Merida, Mexico
Morel, Eudy	0	0	4.00	5	0	0	0	9	12	5	4	4	7	.307	R	R	5-10	160	8-31-79	2000	Monte Cristi, D.R.
Nunez, Jose	0	0	1.04	8	0	0	0	9	7	2	1	2	3	.205	L	L	6-2	175	3-14-79	1996	Monte Cristi, D.R.
Ramsay, Rob	3	1	3.57	27	4	0	0	68	77	37	27	19	44	.289	L	L	6-5	215	12-3-73	1996	Issaquah, Wash.
Reynolds, Josh	0	0	8.22	3	1	0	0	8	13	10	7	4	5	.361	R	R	6-2	190	9-27-79	2000	Holts Summit, Mo.
Ribas, Gabe	4	5	5.81	9	9	0	0	48	63	35	31	14	36	.315	R	R	6-4	220	2-3-80	2002	Brunswick, Me.
Richards, John	0	0	10.54	10	0	0	0	14	26	16	16	4	8	.400	L	L	6-4	200	11-12-78	2001	Coos Bay, Ore.
Richardson, Mike	1	0	5.40	2	0	0	0	1	2	1	1	2	0	.000	R	R	5-10	210	7-11-79	2002	Inverness, Calif.
Thompson, Mike	10	11	4.42	28	22	0	0	136	163	78	67	31	75	.297	R	R	6-4	200	11-6-80	1999	Lamar, Colo.
Tierney, Chris	1	0	1.50	1	1	0	0	6	4	1	1	3	4	.210	L	L	6-6	200	9-1-83	2001	Lockport, Ill.
Villafuerte, Brandon	0	0	0.00	2	0	0	2	2	1	0	0	1	2	.142	R	R	5-11	195	12-17-75	1995	Morgan Hill, Calif.
Walker, Kevin	0	0	13.50	4	0	0	0	4	6	6	6	2	3	.333	L	L	6-4	190	9-20-76	1995	Glen Rose, Texas
Wiedmeyer, Jason	7	3	5.38	14	13	0	0	72	99	49	43	13	32	.331	L	L	6-3	200	10-15-78	2001	West Bend, Wisc.
Witasick, Jay	0	0	5.79	4	0	0	0	5	6	4	3	0	7	.300	R	R	6-4	230	8-28-72	1993	Bel Air, Md.
Wodnicki, Mike	2	5	3.90	43	10	1	13	88	81	45	38	20	53	.240	R	R	6-3	210	1-17-80	2001	Southington, Conn.
Yoshida, Nobuaki	0	2	7.11	3	3	0	0	13	20	15	10	10	6	.370	L	L	6-1	170	8-10-81	2000	Sendai, Japan

FIELDING

Catcher	PCT	G	PO	A	E	DP	PB
Reinking	.992	18	119	10	1	2	1
Richardson	.962	10	43	8	2	0	1
Sain	.989	15	83	11	1	0	1
Trzesniak	.991	104	672	75	7	7	10

First Base	PCT	G	PO	A	E	DP
Benick	.985	66	572	39	9	55
Gerber	.983	23	215	10	4	16
Hastings	.953	12	94	7	5	9
Johnson	.970	34	281	12	9	26
Sain	.964	9	50	4	2	2

Second Base	PCT	G	PO	A	E	DP
Barfield	.971	130	304	368	20	83
Clements	1.000	5	10	10	0	3
Jacobo	1.000	1	3	5	0	1
Lima	1.000	5	11	10	0	1
Merloni	1.000	2	3	3	0	1
Serrano	1.000	1	1	0	0	0

Third Base	PCT	G	PO	A	E	DP
Benick	1.000	1	0	1	0	0
Bravo	.968	11	4	26	1	1
Clements	.887	28	11	36	6	3
Furmaniak	1.000	1	1	3	0	0
Jacobo	.857	2	1	5	1	0
Lima	.905	6	5	14	2	0
Merloni	1.000	2	0	7	0	0
Sain	.882	94	68	194	35	20
Serrano	1.000	2	0	4	0	0
Stonard	.000	1	0	0	0	0

Shortstop	PCT	G	PO	A	E	DP
Bravo	1.000	1	2	2	0	0
Clements	.893	11	16	34	6	7
Furmaniak	.945	76	127	250	22	47
Jacobo	1.000	1	1	2	0	0
Lima	.625	3	0	5	3	0
Merloni	1.000	1	2	1	0	0
Santora	.935	46	68	147	15	18
Serrano	1.000	1	1	0	0	0
Vazquez	.950	5	6	13	1	3

Outfield	PCT	G	PO	A	E	DP
Carter	.985	94	195	7	3	1
Clements	.929	12	23	3	2	0
Gerber	.968	37	57	4	2	1
Guzman	.962	48	121	5	5	4
Hastings	.833	16	14	1	3	0
Johnson	.969	48	122	4	4	0
Jones	.957	17	44	0	2	0
Lima	1.000	2	1	0	0	0
Nettles	.959	115	206	5	9	0
Richardson	.965	52	76	7	3	0

FORT WAYNE WIZARDS — Low Class A

MIDWEST LEAGUE

BATTING	AVG	G	AB	R	H	2B	3B	HR	RBI	BB	SO	SB	CS	SLG	OBP	B	T	HT	WT	DOB	1st Yr	Resides
Agosto, Rolando	.167	9	24	1	4	1	0	0	1	2	5	2	0	.208	.231	R	R	6-0	180	1-10-81	2002	Bayamon, P.R.
Baker, Steve	.241	127	464	53	112	16	3	8	51	32	117	11	8	.341	.306	R	R	6-3	200	4-20-80	2002	Rome, N.Y.
Biernbaum, L.J.	.236	124	444	55	105	16	6	10	66	56	91	3	2	.367	.319	L	L	6-3	200	7-30-79	2002	Newtown, Pa.
Brooks, Doc	.238	29	101	9	24	6	1	0	10	11	37	0	0	.317	.316	R	R	5-10	190	1-21-80	2001	Phenix City, Ala.
Burgamy, Brian	.222	130	455	69	101	20	2	4	35	78	98	17	4	.301	.335	S	R	5-10	190	6-27-81	2002	Lawton, Okla.
Carlin, Luke	.240	17	50	2	12	0	0	0	4	4	11	0	1	.240	.296	S	R	5-11	180	12-20-80	2002	Aylmer, Quebec
Cruz, Luis	.231	129	481	55	111	24	1	8	53	30	55	2	2	.335	.279	R	R	6-1	180	2-10-84	2000	Sonora, Mexico
De Leon, Virgilio	.235	49	166	21	39	8	0	1	8	12	54	5	2	.301	.294	R	R	6-2	170	4-3-80	1998	San Pedro de Macoris, D.R.
DiBetta, John	.188	14	48	8	9	3	0	0	6	6	15	0	1	.250	.268	R	R	6-1	190	10-19-80	2001	Las Vegas, Nev.
Falcon, Omar	.182	12	33	5	6	2	0	0	4	10	15	0	0	.242	.372	R	R	6-0	190	9-1-82	2000	Miami, Fla.
Garcia, Alex	.153	23	59	8	9	2	1	0	1	6	14	2	2	.220	.227	S	R	6-1	150	1-16-82	2001	Nizao, Bani, D.R.
Jacobo, Kervin	.173	40	127	5	22	4	0	0	11	12	37	0	3	.205	.246	S	R	6-2	190	9-26-82	1999	Haina, D.R.
2-team (35 South Bend)	.202	75	238	14	48	9	0	1	21	20	76	4	4	.252	.264							
Jones, Kennard	.307	81	306	61	94	13	4	1	30	50	52	20	19	.386	.407	L	L	5-11	180	9-8-81	2002	Beltsville, Md.
Lima, Joseph	.206	20	63	6	13	3	0	1	5	6	15	0	0	.302	.275	R	R	6-1	190	7-16-79	2002	San Diego, Calif.
Macias, Andres	.000	1	2	0	0	0	0	0	0	0	1	0	0	.000	.000	L	L	6-3	175	3-7-83	2003	Rancho Cucamonga, Calif.
Martinez, Domingo	.176	8	17	1	3	1	0	0	1	1	6	0	0	.235	.222	R	R	5-11	170	8-28-80	2000	Santo Domingo, D.R.
McAnulty, Paul	.273	133	455	48	124	27	0	7	73	67	82	5	3	.378	.370	L	R	5-10	220	2-24-81	2002	Oxnard, Calif.
Morton, Colt	.171	22	76	5	13	4	0	2	7	5	28	0	0	.303	.222	R	R	6-5	230	4-10-82	2003	Loxahatchee, Fla.
Pagan, Andres	.187	95	315	28	59	2	0	0	15	22	66	1	0	.194	.241	R	R	6-4	180	3-18-81	1999	Yauco, P.R.
Richardson, Mike	.188	7	16	6	3	0	0	0	1	6	4	0	0	.188	.409	R	R	5-10	210	7-11-79	2002	Inverness, Calif.
Serrano, Eddie	.227	38	110	11	25	2	0	0	3	9	28	0	5	.245	.298	R	R	6-0	170	10-26-81	2000	Chiriqui, Panama
Shirley, Steve	.195	60	190	17	37	8	0	2	19	8	32	0	1	.268	.229	R	R	6-1	190	7-30-79	2002	Tampa, Fla.
Shorsher, Adam	.000	1	2	0	0	0	0	0	0	1	0	0	0	.000	.333	R	R	6-2	200	10-8-80	2002	San Jose, Calif.
Smith, Rashad	.208	35	106	11	22	5	0	0	5	7	23	3	0	.255	.252	L	R	6-4	200	1-20-80	2002	Bolivar, Tenn.
Stonard, Peter	.293	64	239	22	70	10	0	0	27	18	25	4	5	.335	.338	L	R	6-0	195	12-31-81	2003	St. Louis, Mo.
Tranum, Josh	.218	36	119	13	26	5	1	3	19	21	21	0	0	.353	.333	L	L	6-3	210	5-26-78	2002	Middleton, Tenn.

PITCHING	W	L	ERA	G	GS	CG	SV	IP	H	R	ER	BB	SO	AVG	B	T	HT	WT	DOB	1st Yr	Resides
Beavers, Kevin	1	0	0.00	10	0	0	0	19	4	0	0	3	12	.070	L	L	6-5	190	10-22-79	2002	Irvine, Calif.
Bechtel, Chuck	2	0	1.48	17	0	0	0	24	21	14	4	12	28	.235	R	R	6-4	215	11-12-79	2003	Royersford, Pa.
Coonrod, Aaron	0	0	0.00	4	0	0	0	7	6	1	0	3	9	.214	R	R	6-4	210	5-17-80	2002	Fremont, Ohio
Corona, Andrew	3	3	4.94	21	1	0	0	31	37	20	17	15	22	.291	R	R	6-1	180	9-27-79	2003	New Orleans, La.
Doyne, Cory	4	6	4.21	12	12	0	0	47	44	31	22	29	37	.245	R	R	6-2	210	8-13-81	2000	Lutz, Fla.
Dulkowski, Marc	2	2	6.66	16	0	0	3	24	29	22	18	17	14	.284	S	R	6-0	200	5-28-82	2000	Tinley Park, Ill.
Edwards, Bryan	4	7	2.40	39	10	0	2	112	104	41	30	29	79	.244	R	R	5-11	170	8-21-79	2000	Pflugerville, Texas
Gregg, Grant	0	0	0.00	5	0	0	0	8	4	1	0	2	5	.148	L	L	6-3	230	6-4-80	2003	Abilene, Texas
Huber, Jon	1	1	3.76	7	7	0	0	38	31	18	16	11	34	.226	R	R	6-2	190	7-7-81	2000	North Fort Myers, Fla.
Lipari, Thomas	7	6	2.52	19	15	0	0	96	89	33	27	21	59	.238	L	L	6-5	180	4-23-79	2002	Omaha, Neb.
Morel, Eudy	4	4	4.65	40	0	0	1	60	63	34	31	18	64	.273	R	R	5-10	160	8-31-79	2000	Monte Cristi, D.R.
Pauley, David	7	7	3.29	22	21	0	1	118	109	51	43	38	117	.244	R	R	6-2	170	6-17-83	2001	Longmont, Colo.
Ribas, Gabe	13	3	2.25	19	19	0	0	116	86	36	29	26	116	.201	R	R	6-4	220	2-3-80	2002	Brunswick, Me.
Richards, John	0	3	4.50	9	6	0	0	34	40	25	17	10	22	.283	L	L	6-4	200	11-12-78	2001	Coos Bay, Ore.
Seibert, Kevin	1	2	3.72	19	3	0	0	46	52	22	19	21	42	.285	R	R	6-3	210	9-3-79	2001	Canyon, Texas
Soto, Darwin	7	1	2.64	53	0	0	9	65	53	24	19	26	72	.218	R	R	6-2	180	1-15-82	1998	Bani, D.R.
Steidlmayer, Luke	2	5	4.20	11	11	0	0	56	51	32	26	12	43	.237	R	R	6-5	190	8-13-80	2002	Colusa, Calif.
Thayer, Dale	1	3	2.06	45	0	0	25	48	31	15	11	15	72	.182	R	R	6-0	190	12-17-80	2003	Huntington Beach, Calif.
Villatoro, Wilmer	3	2	2.62	39	0	0	2	55	31	20	16	28	77	.164	R	R	6-0	150	6-27-83	2000	San Salvador, El Salvador
Whitaker, Brian	7	6	2.09	26	26	3	0	164	149	60	38	20	121	.239	R	R	6-4	200	11-5-79	2002	Salisbury, N.C.
Yoshida, Nobuaki	1	5	6.03	10	7	0	0	31	46	29	21	16	18	.328	L	L	6-1	170	8-10-81	2000	Sendai, Japan

FIELDING

Catcher	PCT	G	PO	A	E	DP	PB
Brooks	1.000	1	6	1	0	0	2
Carlin	.989	15	81	13	1	1	2
Falcon	1.000	12	107	5	0	0	2
Martinez	1.000	5	22	2	0	0	0
Morton	.992	17	117	15	1	0	2
Pagan	.987	95	722	61	10	5	11
Richardson	1.000	1	9	2	0	1	0

First Base	PCT	G	PO	A	E	DP
McAnulty	.986	123	1039	56	16	92
Shirley	.959	18	155	10	7	10
Tranum	1.000	3	14	1	0	0

Second Base	PCT	G	PO	A	E	DP
Agosto	.857	4	4	8	2	0
Burgamy	.966	27	50	64	4	9
Cruz	.981	18	33	69	2	12
Lima	.945	18	42	44	5	12
Serrano	.944	16	18	33	3	7
Stonard	.967	63	128	199	11	41

Third Base	PCT	G	PO	A	E	DP
Burgamy	.888	61	35	92	16	5
Carlin	.667	1	1	1	1	0
Dibetta	.914	14	7	25	3	1
Jacobo	.857	40	26	70	16	7
Richardson	1.000	1	3	1	0	0
Serrano	.917	10	4	18	2	0
Shirley	.781	15	6	19	7	2

Shortstop	PCT	G	PO	A	E	DP
Agosto	.909	4	3	7	1	1
Cruz	.927	111	160	345	40	61
Garcia	.914	20	25	60	8	11
Serrano	.958	6	7	16	1	3
Stonard	1.000	1	1	0	0	0

Outfield	PCT	G	PO	A	E	DP
Baker	.984	126	243	7	4	2
Biernbaum	.964	118	175	12	7	1
Brooks	.967	20	29	0	1	0
Burgamy	1.000	37	58	4	0	0
De Leon	.892	31	56	2	7	0
Jones	.954	80	158	8	8	2
Lima	.000	5	0	0	0	0
Macias	.000	1	0	0	0	0
McAnulty	1.000	4	1	0	0	0
Richardson	1.000	2	3	0	0	0
Tranum	1.000	3	3	0	0	0

EUGENE EMERALDS — Short-Season Class A

NORTHWEST LEAGUE

BATTING	AVG	G	AB	R	H	2B	3B	HR	RBI	BB	SO	SB	CS	SLG	OBP	B	T	HT	WT	DOB	1st Yr	Resides
Baker, Casey	.258	43	128	21	33	4	4	0	14	8	25	11	1	.352	.312	R	R	5-9	160	8-7-80	1999	Wysox, Penn.
Bochy, Greg	.162	31	105	11	17	1	0	0	5	4	37	1	0	.171	.219	R	R	6-2	200	8-26-79	2002	Poway, Calif.
Carlin, Luke	.250	28	100	14	25	7	0	0	7	14	25	1	0	.320	.353	S	R	5-11	180	12-20-80	2002	Aylmer, Quebec
Fabrizio, Tom	.242	11	33	5	8	0	0	0	2	1	8	1	0	.242	.286	L	L	5-11	185	10-10-80	2003	Oak Forest, Ill.
Falcon, Omar	.191	32	110	16	21	2	0	5	14	9	37	2	2	.345	.268	R	R	6-0	190	9-1-82	2000	Miami, Fla.
Garcia, Alex	.271	51	192	25	52	3	2	0	15	16	45	14	8	.307	.343	S	R	6-1	150	1-16-82	2001	Nizao, Bani, D.R.
Hogan, Billy	.256	22	78	6	20	7	0	1	10	8	21	0	0	.385	.333	R	R	6-3	210	5-20-83	2003	Scottsdale, Ariz.

BATTING	AVG	G	AB	R	H	2B	3B	HR	RBI	BB	SO	SB	CS	SLG	OBP	B	T	HT	WT	DOB	1st Yr	Resides
Jacobo, Kervin	.190	21	79	6	15	3	0	1	8	8	21	2	0	.266	.261	S	R	6-2	190	9-26-82	1999	Haina, D.R.
Johanning, Ben	.111	7	18	1	2	1	0	0	0	3	6	0	0	.167	.238	L	L	6-3	220	5-2-80	2002	Kissimmee, Fla.
Johnson, Ryan	.275	41	149	18	41	5	1	4	20	13	26	1	2	.403	.341	L	L	6-2	205	1-11-81	2003	Laguna Hills, Calif.
Lauderdale, Matt	.231	12	39	7	9	3	0	1	7	7	15	0	0	.385	.400	R	R	5-10	200	4-14-81	2003	Roswell, Ga.
Leise, Jeff	.211	60	185	26	39	3	2	1	16	18	25	8	3	.265	.289	L	L	5-9	165	9-18-80	2003	Omaha, Neb.
Martinez, Domingo	.000	7	22	0	0	0	0	0	0	2	11	0	0	.000	.083	R	R	5-11	170	8-28-80	2000	Santo Domingo, D.R.
Mora, Ruben	.222	19	63	10	14	3	0	0	6	9	12	4	0	.270	.319	S	R	6-0	170	10-1-82	2000	Colon, Panama
Morton, Colt	.278	25	97	14	27	6	0	7	20	10	29	0	0	.557	.346	R	R	6-5	230	4-10-82	2003	Loxahatchee, Fla.
Pickens, Jordan	.280	29	107	16	30	10	0	5	20	13	31	2	0	.514	.358	R	R	6-2	190	6-10-81	2001	Atascadero, Calif.
Ramos, Peeter	.231	74	290	34	67	8	6	1	36	22	55	16	5	.310	.283	R	R	5-11	150	3-18-82	2001	Caracas, Venez.
Shorsher, Adam	.133	10	30	1	4	2	0	0	0	2	6	0	0	.200	.188	R	R	6-2	200	10-8-80	2002	San Jose, Calif.
Smith, Rashad	.311	11	45	7	14	1	2	1	5	5	4	5	0	.489	.392	L	R	6-4	200	1-20-80	2002	Bolivar, Tenn.
Smyres, Justin	.280	53	186	27	52	7	1	0	14	8	42	11	4	.328	.333	R	R	6-0	175	5-8-81	2003	Paso Robles, Calif.
Valenzuela, Fernando	.248	73	262	36	65	11	0	5	46	43	47	1	0	.347	.372	L	L	5-10	210	9-30-82	2003	Los Angeles, Calif.
Wahlbrink, Brian	.300	69	270	45	81	17	4	4	34	28	82	19	4	.437	.382	R	R	6-3	200	3-19-80	2003	Anaheim, Calif.

GAMES BY POSITION: C—Carlin 28, Falcon 20, Lauderdale 9, Martinez 7, Morton 15. **1B**—Johanning 3, Pickens 4, Valenzuela 72. **2B**—Baker 1, Ramos 74, Smyres 3. **3B**—Baker 1, Bochy 24, Hogan 22, Jacobo 15, Smyres 23. **SS**—Baker 4, Garcia 49, Jacobo 1, Smyres 27. **OF**—Baker 35, Garcia 2, Jacobo 7, Johnson 41, Leise 56, Mora 19, Pickens 1, Smith 11, Wahlbrink 69.

PITCHING	W	L	ERA	G	GS	CG	SV	IP	H	R	ER	BB	SO	AVG	B	T	HT	WT	DOB	1st Yr	Resides
Bechtel, Chuck	0	0	1.80	4	0	0	1	5	4	1	1	5	9	.200	R	R	6-4	215	11-12-79	2003	Royersford, Pa.
Bonine, Eddie	1	2	3.78	31	0	0	14	33	32	15	14	10	33	.250	R	R	6-5	220	6-6-81	2003	Glendale, Ariz.
Coonrod, Aaron	3	3	5.37	13	10	0	0	52	48	32	31	33	45	.255	R	R	6-4	210	5-17-80	2002	Fremont, Ohio
Darby, James	2	4	3.34	33	0	0	0	35	33	21	13	18	36	.248	R	R	6-3	185	1-5-84	2002	Camden, Australia
Girardeau, Clark	4	2	3.74	20	7	0	0	53	47	23	22	27	53	.233	R	R	6-5	210	4-12-82	2003	Mobile, Ala.
Gregg, Grant	0	0	4.76	15	0	0	0	17	15	15	9	6	17	.217	L	L	6-3	230	6-4-80	2003	Abilene, Texas
Hayhurst, Dirk	4	3	3.82	25	1	0	0	38	38	23	16	12	49	.251	L	R	6-3	200	3-24-81	2003	Canton, Ohio
Moore, Daniel	2	3	6.14	12	8	0	0	48	63	35	33	14	43	.308	R	L	6-5	225	6-24-82	2003	Spencer, N.C.
Oyervidez, Jose	1	4	3.07	31	0	0	1	41	25	15	14	17	55	.174	R	R	6-1	180	2-18-82	2002	McAllen, Texas
Pence, Howard	0	0	54.00	1	0	0	0	0	3	2	2	0	1	.750	R	R	6-5	210	10-1-79	2003	Arlington, Texas
Perez, Henry	4	2	4.25	15	15	0	0	72	61	40	34	31	54	.227	R	R	6-3	210	10-27-82	1999	Santo Domingo, D.R.
Prensa, Carlos	0	0	4.09	9	0	0	0	11	8	6	5	9	9	.200	R	R	6-0	190	6-29-80	2000	La Victoria, D.R.
Robinson, Ronnie	2	6	4.71	19	5	0	1	50	44	30	26	21	35	.239	R	R	6-3	195	4-22-81	2003	Atlanta, Ga.
Rosales, Leonel	3	1	2.09	36	0	0	3	43	32	13	10	16	58	.201	R	R	6-1	185	5-28-81	2003	Los Angeles, Calif.
Thompson, Sean	7	1	2.48	15	15	0	0	80	58	28	22	39	97	.203	L	L	5-11	160	10-13-82	2002	La Junta, Colo.
Wells, Jared	4	6	2.75	14	14	0	0	79	77	34	24	32	53	.255	R	R	6-4	200	10-31-81	2003	Brazoria, Texas
Yoshida, Nobuaki	2	0	1.21	17	1	0	0	22	17	6	3	17	7	.223	L	L	6-1	170	8-10-81	2000	Sendai, Japan

IDAHO FALLS PADRES — Rookie

PIONEER LEAGUE

BATTING	AVG	G	AB	R	H	2B	3B	HR	RBI	BB	SO	SB	CS	SLG	OBP	B	T	HT	WT	DOB	1st Yr	Resides
Baker, Casey	.148	9	27	6	4	0	0	1	5	5	11	2	0	.259	.294	R	R	5-9	160	8-7-80	1999	Wysox, Pa.
Burnham, Brett	.290	50	176	24	51	17	1	0	20	25	25	2	2	.398	.380	R	R	5-10	195	1-1-81	2003	South Windsor, Conn.
Ciriaco, Juan	.223	49	157	21	35	6	4	0	19	9	39	8	0	.312	.267	R	R	6-0	160	8-15-83	2003	Santo Domingo, D.R.
Cruceta, Julio	.234	46	171	26	40	7	2	0	15	6	22	4	2	.298	.260	R	R	6-1	170	5-13-83	2001	La Vega, D.R.
Dale, Lachlan	.250	41	132	20	33	10	1	2	20	10	44	0	1	.386	.308	R	R	6-3	190	6-22-83	2002	Kalamunda, Australia
Edwards, Brian	.259	49	185	21	48	7	2	0	10	19	23	11	0	.319	.332	R	R	6-3	190	5-28-81	2003	Littleton, Colo.
Etheridge, Chad	.069	10	29	3	2	2	0	0	0	2	13	0	0	.138	.129	S	R	6-0	205	1-3-83	2003	Old Hickory, Tenn.
Figueroa, Baudilio	.243	40	111	13	27	1	1	0	6	8	30	2	0	.270	.300	S	R	6-2	160	6-28-83	2001	Puerto Plata, D.R.
Garay, Ernesto	.263	46	156	17	41	4	3	1	13	17	28	5	2	.346	.343	L	L	6-1	160	2-17-82	2001	Managua, Nicaragua
Hogan, Billy	.344	45	163	22	56	17	1	3	33	15	36	3	3	.515	.419	R	R	6-3	210	5-20-83	2003	Scottsdale, Ariz.
Johnson, Ryan	.280	20	75	10	21	7	0	1	12	13	12	0	0	.413	.386	L	L	6-2	205	1-11-81	2003	Laguna Hills, Calif.
Kaye, Brandon	.273	52	161	25	44	10	0	10	30	8	30	0	0	.522	.335	L	L	6-2	215	7-1-80	2003	Salts Spring Island, B.C.
Kottaras, George	.259	42	143	27	37	8	1	7	24	19	36	1	1	.476	.348	L	R	6-0	180	5-16-83	2003	Markham, Ontario
Lauderdale, Matt	.170	18	53	6	9	4	0	0	3	8	20	1	0	.245	.302	R	R	5-10	200	4-14-81	2003	Roswell, Ga.
Lobaton, Jose	.272	56	191	22	52	15	0	1	32	22	50	0	1	.366	.352	S	R	6-0	170	10-21-84	2002	Portuguesa, Venez.
Lopez, Luis	.000	2	5	0	0	0	0	0	0	0	2	0	0	.000	.000	R	R	6-2	180	1-8-84	2000	Santiago, Panama
Macias, Andres	.251	61	239	41	60	10	4	2	13	19	32	15	4	.351	.318	L	L	6-3	175	3-7-83	2003	Rancho Cucamonga, Calif.
Martinez, Domingo	.182	8	22	0	4	2	0	0	2	0	6	0	0	.273	.182	R	R	5-11	170	8-28-80	2000	Santo Domingo, D.R.
Martinez, Thomas	.293	25	92	8	27	2	1	2	12	0	10	1	0	.402	.301	R	R	5-11	180	2-27-83	2000	Villa Altagracia, D.R.
Moore, Mewelde	.091	4	11	0	1	0	0	0	0	1	4	0	0	.091	.167	R	R	6-0	195	7-24-82	2001	Baton Rouge, La.
Ramirez, Yordany	.266	22	79	7	21	3	0	0	5	3	17	7	0	.304	.301	R	R	6-1	160	7-31-84	2001	Boca Chica, D.R.
Sencion, Henry	.211	31	95	10	20	3	0	0	8	10	20	3	2	.242	.283	R	R	6-0	160	5-12-83	2001	San Pedro de Macoris, D.R.
Vincent, Tom	.200	36	110	12	22	3	0	3	11	8	35	3	2	.309	.261	L	R	6-3	215	3-3-82	2003	McKellar, Australia

GAMES BY POSITION: C—Kottaras 26, Lauderdale 15, Lobaton 22, Lopez 2, D. Martinez 6, T. Martinez 11. **1B**—Burnham 5, Dale 23, Kaye 45, Kottaras 5, D. Martinez 2, T. Martinez 7. **2B**—Baker 2, Burnham 37, Cruceta 14, Figueroa 1, Sencion 28. **3B**—Ciriaco 1, Cruceta 27, Dale 19, Figueroa 3, Hogan 30, Vincent 4. **SS**—Burnham 1, Ciriaco 45, Figueroa 33, **OF**—Baker 5, Edwards 48, Etheridge 9, Garay 45, Johnson 17, Macias 60, Moore 4, Ramirez 22, Vincent 28.

PITCHING	W	L	ERA	G	GS	CG	SV	IP	H	R	ER	BB	SO	AVG	B	T	HT	WT	DOB	1st Yr	Resides
Baca, Daniel	0	1	6.30	5	0	0	0	10	14	12	7	9	9	.304	R	R	5-10	170	10-17-85	2003	Guadalupe, Mexico
Colbert, Henry	0	1	4.15	16	0	0	1	30	38	23	14	12	37	.301	R	R	6-3	180	12-10-81	2003	Yakima, Wash.
Conden, Greg	4	3	3.94	15	15	0	0	80	78	37	35	29	96	.259	R	R	6-3	220	7-24-80	2003	California, Md.
De La O, Danny	3	1	4.50	31	2	0	3	48	47	26	24	14	56	.250	L	L	6-0	185	8-25-83	2003	Marina del Ray, Calif.
De Montigny, Mat	0	1	9.00	18	0	0	0	23	39	32	23	11	23	.357	R	R	6-1	170	9-22-84	2003	Quebec, Quebec
Fernandez, Alfredo	0	5	6.25	11	11	0	0	45	61	37	31	23	38	.331	R	R	6-4	205	9-15-84	2002	Maracaibo, Venez.
Garcia, Geivy	0	2	4.41	24	3	0	0	49	52	29	24	24	53	.266	R	R	6-1	175	7-8-82	2001	LaGuna Salada, D.R.
Geraldo, Jose	1	3	5.97	21	2	0	0	35	47	33	23	10	25	.315	R	R	6-3	180	9-22-83	2001	Azua, D.R.
Klatt, Ryan	2	3	2.12	32	0	0	12	30	24	9	7	3	51	.212	R	R	6-0	185	9-30-81	2003	Midland, Texas
Larson, Brett	2	5	6.57	26	0	0	0	38	40	32	28	26	26	.275	R	R	6-1	190	2-13-81	2003	Paso Robles, Calif.
Mora, Yency	4	3	4.50	19	9	0	0	72	76	44	36	31	58	.268	R	R	6-1	180	8-19-80	2001	Santo Domingo, D.R.
Pence, Howard	2	2	5.91	27	0	0	0	35	46	26	23	15	19	.319	R	R	6-5	210	10-1-79	2003	Arlington, Texas
Ponce, William	1	11	7.07	15	15	0	0	70	98	65	55	34	54	.337	R	R	6-1	190	2-9-84	2002	San Salvador, El Salvador
Rogers, Nathan	0	6	10.31	9	8	0	0	30	43	38	34	18	19	.335	L	L	6-4	215	10-11-82	2003	Broken Arrow, Okla.
Santo, Joel	5	5	6.71	16	11	0	0	56	66	53	42	23	44	.277	R	R	6-3	180	6-4-84	2002	San Cristobal, D.R.

SAN FRANCISCO GIANTS

BY JOSH SUCHON

The Giants' formula for winning the 2003 National League West will not be copied, stolen, mimicked or bottled up and saved by the Giants or any of their competitors.

In fact, when you examine the details from the season, you would think it's a list of reasons why the team *didn't* win the division. Instead the team somehow ran away with the division by 15½ games, won 100 games, became the ninth wire-to-wire division winner in baseball history, and sent the franchise to the playoffs in consecutive years for the first time since 1933-34.

"I believe with all the obstacles, and being in first place all year, it's extra satisfying," first-year manager Felipe Alou said. "We knew we had a pretty good team. But always being in first place was not something anybody was predicting. I know that I wasn't expecting it."

Nor was Alou expecting a first-round playoff exit. But after Jason Schmidt pitched a three-hit shutout to win Game One, the wild-card Marlins won three straight games, rallying in extra innings to win Game Three, and winning Game Four in dramatic fashion, with J.T. Snow getting thrown at the plate to end the series.

"To me, (the season) is a failure," shortstop Rich Aurilia said. "We have a lot of things to be proud of. We proved a lot of people wrong by winning our division and winning 100 games. But at the same time, we knew what kind of club we had. We knew we could get back to where we were last year—and hopefully win.

"But the bottom line is, we're going home losers and they are going on."

The Giants' obstacles were absurd. Half the starting lineup was new and 60 percent of the rotation was different after a roster overhaul that included the departure of manager Dusty Baker and second baseman Jeff Kent.

ORGANIZATION LEADERS

BATTING

*AVG	Brian Dallimore, Fresno	.352
R	Todd Linden, Fresno	75
H	Alejandro Freire, Norwich	155
TB	Alejandro Freire, Norwich	242
2B	Daniel Ortmeier, San Jose	32
3B	Fred Lewis, Hagerstown	8
	Jose Yens, AZL Giants	8
HR	Dan Trumble, San Jose	21
RBI	Mike Cervenak, Norwich	91
BB	Travis Ishikawa, Hagerstown/Salem-Keizer	77
SO	Travis Ishikawa, Hagerstown/Salem-Keizer	146
SB	Pat Hallmark, Norwich	31
*SLG	Alejandro Freire, Norwich	.486
*OBP	Brian Dallimore, Fresno	.427

PITCHING

W	Greg Bruso, Norwich /San Jose	13
L	Mitch Walk, Norwich	13
#ERA	Merkin Valdez, Hagerstown	2.25
G	Joe Horgan, Fresno	55
CG	Greg Bruso, Norwich /San Jose	3
	Clay Hensley, Hagerstown	3
SV	Matt Palmer, Norwich/Hagerstown	25
IP	Greg Bruso, Norwich/San Jose	170
BB	Boof Bonser, Fresno/Norwich	75
SO	Merkin Valdez, Hagerstown	166

*Minimum 250 At-Bats #Minimum 75 Innings

Barry Bonds

RODGER WOOD

Merkin Valdez

PLAYERS of the YEAR

MAJOR LEAGUE: Barry Bonds, of

Bonds became the first player in major league history to post an on-base percentage better than .500 in three straight seasons and the first since Babe Ruth to have a .700 slugging percentage in three straight years. He also had more intentional walks (60) than strikeouts (55).

MINOR LEAGUE: Merkin Valdez, rhp

Known as Manuel Mateo before he was traded from the Braves to the Giants, Valdez earned the nickname "Magic," or "El Mago" in Spanish, as he went 9-5, 2.25 for Class A Hagerstown in 2003. He led the South Atlantic League with 166 strikeouts.

Cancer took the lives of Barry Bonds' father, Schmidt's mother and general manager Brian Sabean's father.

"We kept everything together," Bonds said. "We've got true professionals here . . . The whole team went through a lot of sorrow. It shows the character of this ballclub. Basically, we all held each other together."

"Seemingly every week, we had to face some kind of problem or another," Sabean said. "Certain guys stepped up. It showed the depth of the organization."

Bonds again saw few pitches to hit, leading the league with 148 walks (61 intentional). He still managed 45 home runs, a .341 average, a .749 slugging and .529 on-base percentage. He stole his 500th base, raised his career home run total to 658 and walked past Babe Ruth into second on the all-time walk list with 2,070—just 120 behind all-time leader Rickey Henderson.

Schmidt emerged as one of the best starters in the National League. He went 17-5 with a league-best 2.34 ERA. Even more impressive, as people learned after the season, Schmidt pitched the last nine weeks of the season with a part of a tendon in his pitching elbow completely off the bone.

Only one of the minor league affiliates reached the playoffs and they posted an aggregate 243-316 (.435) season, but the organization's depth filled many holes in the majors.

Four Giants rookie righthanders—Kurt Ainsworth, Kevin Correia, top prospect Jesse Foppert and Jerome Williams—contributed to the big league club. Ainsworth was traded to the Orioles in the Sidney Ponson deal, while Williams stepped forward and went 7-5, 3.30 over 21 starts.

SAN FRANCISCO GIANTS

Manager: Felipe Alou.

2003 Record: 1001-61, .621 (1st, NL West).

BATTING	AVG	G	AB	R	H	2B	3B	HR	RBI	BB	SO	SB	CS	SLG	OBP	B	T	HT	WT	DOB	1st Yr	Resides
Alfonzo, Edgardo	.259	142	514	56	133	25	2	13	81	58	41	5	2	.391	.334	R	R	5-11	185	11-8-73	1991	Little Neck, N.Y.
Aurilia, Rich	.277	129	505	65	140	26	1	13	58	36	82	2	2	.410	.325	R	R	6-1	190	9-2-71	1992	Phoenix, Ariz.
Benard, Marvin	.197	46	71	5	14	3	1	0	4	4	9	1	0	.268	.237	L	L	5-09	190	1-20-70	1992	Richland, Wash.
Bonds, Barry	.341	130	390	111	133	22	1	45	90	148	58	7	0	.749	.529	L	L	6-2	230	7-24-64	1985	San Carlos, Calif.
Castillo, Alberto	.188	11	16	2	3	1	0	1	4	0	5	0	0	.438	.188	R	R	6-0	200	2-10-70	1987	Port St. Lucie, Fla.
Cruz, Jose	.250	158	539	90	135	26	1	20	68	102	121	5	8	.414	.366	S	R	6-0	210	4-19-74	1995	Coral Gables, Fla.
Durham, Ray	.285	110	410	61	117	30	5	8	33	50	82	7	7	.441	.366	S	R	5-8	180	11-30-71	1990	Charlotte, N.C.
Ellison, Jason	.100	7	10	1	1	0	0	0	0	0	1	0	0	.100	.100	R	R	5-10	180	4-4-78	2000	Lewiston, Idaho
Feliz, Pedro	.247	95	235	31	58	9	3	16	48	10	53	2	2	.515	.278	R	R	6-1	200	4-27-75	1994	Azua, D.R.
Galarraga, Andres	.301	110	272	36	82	15	0	12	42	19	61	1	3	.489	.352	R	R	6-3	265	6-18-61	1979	West Palm Beach, Fla.
Grissom, Marquis	.300	149	587	82	176	33	3	20	79	20	82	11	3	.468	.322	R	R	5-11	190	4-17-67	1988	Fairburn, Ga.
Hammonds, Jeffrey	.277	36	94	20	26	10	0	3	10	13	21	1	0	.479	.370	R	R	6-0	200	3-5-71	1992	Cincinnati, Ohio
2-team (10 Milwaukee)	.242	46	132	22	32	12	0	4	13	16	28	1	0	.424	.329							
Linden, Todd	.211	18	38	2	8	1	0	1	6	1	8	0	0	.316	.231	S	R	6-3	210	6-30-80	2002	Bremerton, Wash.
Lunsford, Trey	.000	1	1	0	0	0	0	0	0	0	0	0	0	.000	.000	R	R	6-1	195	5-25-79	2000	South Haven, Miss.
Niekro, Lance	.200	5	5	2	1	1	0	0	2	0	1	0	0	.400	.200	R	R	6-3	210	1-29-79	2000	Lakeland, Fla.
Perez, Neifi	.256	120	328	27	84	19	4	1	31	14	23	3	2	.348	.285	S	R	6-0	175	6-2-73	1993	Santo Domingo, D.R.
Ransom, Cody	.222	20	27	7	6	1	0	1	1	1	11	0	0	.370	.250	R	R	6-2	190	2-17-76	1998	Chandler, Ariz.
Rivera, Ruben	.180	31	50	6	9	2	0	2	4	5	14	1	0	.340	.255	R	R	6-3	200	11-14-73	1992	La Chorrera, Panama
Santiago, Benito	.280	108	400	53	112	21	2	11	56	29	69	0	1	.425	.330	R	R	6-1	200	3-9-65	1983	Pembroke Pines, Fla.
Santos, Deivis	.200	8	15	2	3	2	0	1	1	0	3	0	0	.533	.200	L	L	6-1	170	3-9-74	1997	Santo Domingo, D.R.
Snow, J.T.	.273	103	330	48	90	18	3	8	51	55	55	1	2	.418	.387	L	L	6-2	210	2-26-68	1989	San Mateo, Calif.
Torcato, Tony	.188	14	16	0	3	1	0	0	1	0	4	0	0	.250	.235	L	R	6-1	195	10-25-79	1998	Woodland, Calif.
Torrealba, Yorvit	.260	66	200	22	52	10	2	4	29	14	39	1	0	.390	.312	R	R	5-11	190	7-19-78	1995	Guarenas, Venez.
Valderrama, Carlos	.143	7	7	0	1	0	0	0	0	0	3	1	0	.143	.143	R	R	5-11	175	11-30-77	1995	Bachaquero, Venez.
Young, Eric	.197	26	71	9	14	2	0	0	3	9	10	3	5	.225	.293	R	R	5-8	185	5-18-67	1989	Atlanta, Ga.
2-team (89 Milwaukee)	.251	135	475	80	119	20	1	15	34	57	44	28	12	.392	.336							

PITCHING	W	L	ERA	G	GS	CG	SV	IP	H	R	ER	BB	SO	AVG	B	T	HT	WT	DOB	1st Yr	Resides
Ainsworth, Kurt	5	4	3.82	11	11	0	0	66	66	31	28	26	48	.261	R	R	6-3	190	9-9-78	1999	Baton Rouge, La.
Aybar, Manny	0	0	6.00	3	0	0	0	3	4	2	2	3	2	.333	R	R	6-1	170	5-4-72	1991	Tampa, Fla.
Brower, Jim	8	5	3.96	51	5	0	2	100	90	48	44	39	65	.248	R	R	6-3	210	12-29-72	1994	Sarasota, Fla.
Christiansen, Jason	0	0	5.19	40	0	0	0	26	25	15	15	11	22	.242	R	L	6-5	240	9-21-69	1991	Mesa, Ariz.
Correia, Kevin	3	1	3.66	10	7	0	0	39	41	16	16	18	28	.275	R	R	6-3	200	8-24-80	2002	San Diego, Calif.
Eyre, Scott	2	1	3.32	74	0	0	1	57	60	23	21	26	35	.267	L	L	6-1	200	5-30-72	1991	Bradenton, Fla.
Foppert, Jesse	8	9	5.03	23	21	0	0	111	103	69	62	69	101	.248	R	R	6-6	210	7-10-80	2001	San Rafael, Calif.
Herges, Matt	1	0	2.31	27	0	0	0	35	28	11	9	9	28	.218	L	R	6-0	200	4-1-70	1992	Champaign, Ill.
2-team (40 San Diego)	3	2	2.62	67	0	0	3	79	68	27	23	29	68	.232							
Hermanson, Dustin	2	1	3.00	9	6	0	0	39	35	14	13	10	27	.238	R	R	6-2	200	12-21-72	1994	Phoenix, Ariz.
2-team (23 St. Louis)	3	3	4.06	32	6	0	1	69	70	32	31	24	39	.271							
Jensen, Ryan	0	0	10.80	6	2	0	0	13	21	16	16	5	3	.403	R	R	6-0	205	9-17-75	1996	West Valley, Utah
Lowry, Noah	0	0	0.00	4	0	0	0	6	1	0	0	2	5	.047	L	L	6-2	190	10-10-80	2001	Ojai, Nev.
Moss, Damian	9	7	4.70	21	20	0	0	115	121	62	60	63	57	.273	R	L	6-0	180	11-24-76	1994	Dublin, Ga.
Nathan, Joe	12	4	2.96	78	0	0	0	79	51	26	26	33	83	.186	R	R	6-4	205	11-22-74	1995	Chandler, Ariz.
Ponson, Sidney	3	6	3.71	10	10	0	0	68	64	29	28	18	34	.254	R	R	6-1	249	11-2-76	1994	Baltimore, Md.
Powell, Brian	0	1	13.50	1	1	0	0	5	8	7	7	1	3	.380	R	R	6-2	200	10-10-73	1995	Bainbridge, Ga.
Rodriguez, Felix	8	2	3.10	68	0	0	2	61	59	21	21	29	46	.258	R	R	6-1	190	9-9-72	1990	Monte Cristi, D.R.
Rueter, Kirk	10	5	4.53	27	27	0	0	147	170	77	74	47	41	.296	L	L	6-2	210	12-1-70	1991	Nashville, Ill.
Schmidt, Jason	17	5	2.34	29	29	5	0	208	152	56	54	46	208	.200	R	R	6-5	205	1-29-73	1991	Longview, Wash.
Williams, Jerome	7	5	3.30	21	21	2	0	131	116	54	48	49	88	.241	R	R	6-3	180	12-4-81	1999	Waipahu, Hawaii
Worrell, Tim	4	4	2.87	76	0	0	38	78	74	35	25	28	65	.245	R	R	6-4	230	7-5-67	1990	Glendale, Ariz.
Zerbe, Chad	1	1	4.71	33	1	0	0	50	60	26	26	14	17	.310	L	L	6-0	190	4-27-72	1991	Highland, Calif.

FIELDING

Catcher	PCT	G	PO	A	E	DP	PB
Castillo	.975	10	37	2	1	0	0
Lunsford	.000	1	0	0	0	0	0
Santiago	.993	106	629	34	5	3	8
Torrealba	.997	66	365	29	1	3	0

First Base	PCT	G	PO	A	E	DP
Feliz	1.000	12	82	4	0	9
Galarraga	.994	69	503	29	3	56
Niekro	1.000	3	4	0	0	1
Santos	1.000	1	5	0	0	2
Snow	.994	97	814	74	5	82

Second Base	PCT	G	PO	A	E	DP
Alfonzo	1.000	6	11	14	0	3
Durham	.990	105	185	309	5	66
Perez	.987	57	97	134	3	36
Young	.989	18	34	55	1	12

Third Base	PCT	G	PO	A	E	DP
Alfonzo	.966	133	79	233	11	17
Feliz	.972	49	24	82	3	8
Perez	.000	2	0	0	0	0
Young	.000	1	0	0	0	0

Shortstop	PCT	G	PO	A	E	DP
Aurilia	.974	123	173	316	13	80
Perez	.990	45	71	129	2	33
Ransom	.963	12	9	17	1	7

Outfield	PCT	G	PO	A	E	DP
Benard	1.000	21	37	2	0	0
Bonds	.992	123	236	5	2	2
Cruz	.994	158	340	18	2	7
Ellison	1.000	4	3	0	0	0
Feliz	.957	15	22	0	1	0
Grissom	.977	148	343	3	8	1
Hammonds	1.000	30	49	1	0	0
Linden	.929	13	13	0	1	0
Rivera	1.000	27	42	0	0	0
Santos	1.000	3	3	0	0	0
Torcato	.833	6	5	0	1	0
Torrealba	.000	1	0	0	0	0
Valderrama	1.000	5	6	0	0	0
Young	1.000	2	2	0	0	0

FARM SYSTEM

Vice President, Player Personnel: Dick Tidrow.

Class	Farm Team	League	W	L	Pct.	Finish*	Manager	First Yr.
AAA	Fresno (Calif.) Grizzlies	Pacific Coast	55	88	.385	16th (16)	Fred Stanley	1998
AA	Norwich (Conn.) Navigators	Eastern	62	79	.440	t-10th (12)	Shane Turner	2003
High A	San Jose (Calif.) Giants	California	58	82	.414	9th (10)	Jack Lind	1988
Low AA	Hagerstown (Md.) Suns	South Atlantic	68	67	.504	8th (16)	Mike Ramsey	2001
SS A	Salem-Keizer (Ore.) Volcanoes	Northwest	43	33	.566	3rd (8)	Joe Strain	1997
Rookie	Scottsdale (Ariz.) Giants	Arizona	25	24	.510	t-5th (9)	Bert Hunter	2000

*Finish in overall standings (No. of teams in league)

FRESNO GRIZZLIES — Class AAA

PACIFIC COAST LEAGUE

BATTING	AVG	G	AB	R	H	2B	3B	HR	RBI	BB	SO	SB	CS	SLG	OBP	B	T	HT	WT	DOB	1st Yr	Resides
Anderson, Keith	.273	4	11	2	3	1	0	1	3	0	3	0	0	.636	.250	R	R	6-1	205	1-6-79	2001	Escondido, Calif.
Bellinger, Clay	.268	117	377	55	101	18	3	16	54	25	72	2	2	.459	.319	R	R	6-3	190	11-18-68	1989	Chandler, Ariz.
Benard, Marvin	.220	14	50	8	11	3	0	1	8	1	4	2	0	.340	.250	L	L	5-09	190	1-20-70	1992	Richland, Wash.
Castillo, Alberto	.235	12	34	2	8	1	0	0	7	8	8	0	0	.265	.381	R	R	6-0	200	2-10-70	1987	Port St. Lucie, Fla.
Clark, Doug	.238	13	21	4	5	0	0	0	0	2	3	0	1	.238	.304	L	R	6-2	205	3-5-76	1998	Springfield, Mass.
Dallimore, Brian	.352	91	330	53	116	16	2	4	46	37	37	6	4	.448	.427	R	R	6-1	180	11-15-73	1996	Las Vegas, Nev.
Ellison, Jason	.295	119	461	74	136	22	4	6	39	39	52	21	13	.399	.356	R	R	5-10	180	4-4-78	2000	Lewiston, Idaho
Hammonds, Jeffrey	.333	11	36	7	12	1	0	2	2	3	3	1	0	.528	.385	R	R	6-0	200	3-5-71	1992	Cincinnati, Ohio
Hernandez, Carlos	.208	73	216	17	45	3	0	1	14	15	38	4	1	.236	.265	R	R	5-9	170	12-12-75	1993	Caracas, Venez.
Holst, Micah	.333	7	3	2	1	0	0	0	0	0	1	0	1	.333	.333	R	R	6-2	205	3-5-77	1999	Independence, Mo.
Kuzmic, Craig	.280	47	143	16	40	5	4	1	17	18	46	5	2	.392	.362	S	R	6-0	180	5-2-77	1998	Fountain Valley, Calif.
2-team (54 Tacoma)	.244	101	303	41	74	12	4	9	40	40	94	6	4	.399	.334							
Linden, Todd	.278	125	471	75	131	24	3	11	56	40	105	14	4	.412	.356	S	R	6-3	210	6-30-80	2002	Bremerton, Wash.
Lunsford, Trey	.286	69	206	20	59	10	1	2	20	17	33	0	1	.374	.341	R	R	6-1	195	5-25-79	2000	South Haven, Miss.
Mendoza, Carlos	.250	9	24	3	6	2	0	0	0	0	4	0	0	.333	.250	S	R	6-0	165	11-27-79	1996	Barquisimeto, Venez.
Minor, Damon	.234	37	141	16	33	2	1	8	21	6	29	0	0	.433	.278	L	L	6-7	230	1-5-74	1996	Edmond, Okla.
Niekro, Lance	.302	98	381	43	115	15	2	4	41	19	39	3	3	.383	.334	R	R	6-3	210	1-29-79	2000	Lakeland, Fla.
Pecci, Jay	.303	11	33	4	10	0	0	0	2	1	2	2	0	.303	.324	S	R	5-11	180	9-26-76	1998	Novato, Calif.
2-team (14 Tacoma)	.205	25	73	7	15	0	0	0	5	4	5	3	0	.205	.272							
Pernalete, Marco	.000	4	2	0	0	0	0	0	0	1	1	0	0	.000	.333	S	R	6-0	155	10-12-78	1996	Barquisimeto, Venez.
Ransom, Cody	.253	112	396	56	100	16	4	12	50	45	91	14	4	.404	.331	R	R	6-2	190	2-17-76	1998	Chandler, Ariz.
Rodriguez, Guillermo	.276	78	239	31	66	8	4	5	36	14	25	1	0	.406	.328	R	R	5-11	195	5-15-78	1996	Barquisimeto, Venez.
Ryan, Rob	.241	49	108	15	26	5	2	1	14	13	22	0	1	.352	.317	L	L	5-11	190	6-24-73	1996	Renton, Wash.
Santos, Francisco	.239	87	301	23	72	15	5	6	42	10	38	1	0	.382	.261	L	L	6-1	170	3-9-74	1997	Santo Domingo, D.R.
Torcato, Tony	.296	106	423	36	125	18	2	3	48	6	33	4	0	.369	.304	L	R	6-1	195	10-25-79	1998	Woodland, Calif.
Valderrama, Carlos	.277	54	202	20	56	5	0	3	10	12	28	7	8	.347	.324	R	R	5-11	175	11-30-77	1995	Bachaquero, Venez.
Vitiello, Joe	.213	23	75	9	16	5	0	0	3	8	9	0	0	.280	.289	R	R	6-3	230	4-11-70	1991	Stoneham, Mass.

PITCHING	W	L	ERA	G	GS	CG	SV	IP	H	R	ER	BB	SO	AVG	B	T	HT	WT	DOB	1st Yr	Resides
Ainsworth, Kurt	0	0	4.50	1	1	0	0	2	2	1	1	2	1	.250	R	R	6-3	190	9-9-78	1999	Baton Rouge, La.
Anderson, Jimmy	1	4	6.44	8	8	0	0	43	65	36	31	15	17	.351	L	L	6-1	210	1-22-76	1994	Chesapeake, Va.
Aybar, Manny	2	4	4.08	52	0	0	17	57	55	27	26	23	45	.253	R	R	6-1	170	5-4-72	1991	Tampa, Fla.
Barcelo, Lorenzo	0	3	6.49	20	0	0	0	26	33	19	19	4	16	.317	R	R	6-4	230	8-10-77	1994	San Pedro de Macoris, D.R.
Blank, Matt	1	2	4.19	8	8	0	0	43	49	22	20	12	30	.291	L	L	6-2	190	4-5-76	1997	Arlington, Texas
2-team (5 Edmonton)	2	3	4.21	13	13	0	0	68	78	36	32	21	52	.292							
Bonser, Boof	1	2	3.13	4	4	0	0	23	17	13	8	8	28	.195	R	R	6-4	230	10-14-81	2000	Pinellas Park, Fla.
Brown, Elliot	3	3	4.62	12	5	0	0	37	37	21	19	13	12	.266	S	R	6-2	190	6-7-75	1996	Metairie, La.
Christiansen, Jason	0	0	5.40	4	1	0	0	5	5	3	3	1	2	.263	R	L	6-5	240	9-21-69	1991	Mesa, Ariz.
Connelly, Steve	3	4	7.43	38	1	0	0	59	97	54	49	24	29	.375	R	R	6-4	210	4-27-74	1995	Long Beach, Calif.
Correia, Kevin	1	0	2.84	3	3	0	0	19	16	8	6	2	23	.222	R	R	6-3	200	8-24-80	2002	San Diego, Calif.
Estrella, Luis	2	9	5.56	51	6	0	5	89	104	62	55	41	52	.294	R	R	6-1	220	10-7-74	1996	Santa Ana, Calif.
Foppert, Jesse	0	0	1.80	1	1	0	0	5	3	1	1	0	9	.166	R	R	6-6	210	7-10-80	2001	San Rafael, Calif.
Garcia, James	1	3	4.18	7	4	0	0	23	23	12	11	12	22	.000	R	R	6-2	210	2-3-80	2002	Torrance, Calif.
Hermanson, Dustin	0	1	4.85	4	4	0	0	26	29	16	14	3	17	.290	R	R	6-2	200	12-21-72	1994	Phoenix, Ariz.
Horgan, Joe	7	7	5.67	55	0	0	3	75	80	51	47	30	65	.275	L	L	6-1	200	6-7-77	1996	Rancho Cordova, Calif.
Jarvis, Matt	1	2	4.35	23	1	0	0	31	42	15	15	11	17	.344	R	L	6-4	180	2-22-72	1991	Albuquerque, N.M.
Jensen, Ryan	1	10	5.30	27	18	0	0	104	114	70	61	36	50	.285	R	R	6-0	205	9-17-75	1996	West Valley, Utah
Johnson, Mike	4	3	3.72	30	4	0	1	65	58	31	27	26	56	.234	L	R	6-2	180	10-3-75	1993	Jupiter, Fla.
Lowry, Noah	1	0	2.37	4	4	0	0	19	15	5	5	6	13	.227	L	L	6-2	190	10-10-80	2001	Ojai, Calif.
Montgomery, Matt	2	2	4.58	24	0	0	1	39	40	25	20	14	35	.261	R	R	6-3	210	5-13-76	1997	Anaheim, Calif.
Pickford, Kevin	9	8	5.09	25	25	0	0	145	169	91	82	56	64	.295	L	L	6-4	200	3-12-75	1993	Fresno, Calif.
Powell, Brian	7	8	4.19	23	15	0	0	101	118	57	47	32	59	.291	R	R	6-2	200	10-10-73	1995	Bainbridge, Ga.
Rueter, Kirk	0	0	0.00	1	1	0	0	5	1	0	0	2	6	.071	L	L	6-2	210	12-1-70	1991	Nashville, Ill.
Urban, Jeff	3	10	5.24	29	19	0	0	127	166	83	74	47	87	.317	R	L	6-8	215	1-25-77	1998	Alexandria, Ind.
Vent, Kevin	0	0	14.90	6	0	0	0	10	20	17	16	6	7	.416	R	R	6-0	185	6-1-77	1999	Maumelle, Ark.
Williams, Jerome	4	2	2.68	10	10	1	0	57	52	19	17	16	40	.237	R	R	6-3	180	12-4-81	1999	Waipahu, Hawaii
Zerbe, Chad	1	1	2.61	7	0	0	2	10	11	6	3	1	7	.275	L	L	6-0	190	4-27-72	1991	Highland, Calif.

FIELDING

Catcher	PCT	G	PO	A	E	DP	PB
Anderson	1.000	3	14	1	0	0	1
Bellinger	1.000	3	17	3	0	1	0
Castillo	1.000	11	100	5	0	0	0
Kuzmic	1.000	11	59	7	0	0	1
Lunsford	.989	65	341	28	4	2	9
Rodriguez	.977	60	303	36	8	2	2

First Base	PCT	G	PO	A	E	DP
Bellinger	1.000	17	112	9	0	11
Minor	.995	20	194	20	1	21
Niekro	.993	17	123	11	1	12
Santos	.989	23	175	11	2	12
Torcato	.983	58	492	36	9	46
Vitiello	.986	14	136	7	2	11

Second Base	PCT	G	PO	A	E	DP
Bellinger	.941	5	7	9	1	0
Dallimore	.973	68	146	176	9	45
Hernandez	.969	50	82	139	7	31
Kuzmic	.959	20	24	46	3	9
Mendoza	.000	1	0	0	1	0
Pecci	.981	11	24	29	1	9

Third Base	PCT	G	PO	A	E	DP
Bellinger	.959	37	24	69	4	7
Dallimore	.984	20	20	43	1	3
Kuzmic	.966	12	8	20	1	3
Niekro	.926	76	51	125	14	12
Torcato	.842	6	8	8	3	3

Shortstop	PCT	G	PO	A	E	DP
Bellinger	.942	10	16	33	3	7
Garcia	1.000	1	1	0	0	0
Hernandez	.988	16	27	52	1	14
Mendoza	.971	7	12	21	1	4
Ransom	.959	112	155	317	20	53

Outfield	PCT	G	PO	A	E	DP
Bellinger	.978	22	43	1	1	0
Benard	.967	13	28	1	1	1
Clark	1.000	5	5	0	0	0
Dallimore	1.000	1	1	0	0	0
Ellison	.974	117	320	16	9	3
Hammonds	1.000	9	26	0	0	0
Holst	1.000	2	1	0	0	0
Linden	.985	120	251	7	4	0
Lunsford	1.000	1	2	0	0	0
Ryan	.982	28	54	1	1	0
Santos	.978	47	84	5	2	0
Torcato	1.000	36	75	0	0	0
Valderrama	.969	51	94	1	3	0
Vitiello	1.000	4	7	0	0	0

NORWICH NAVIGATORS — Class AA

EASTERN LEAGUE

BATTING	AVG	G	AB	R	H	2B	3B	HR	RBI	BB	SO	SB	CS	SLG	OBP	B	T	HT	WT	DOB	1st Yr	Resides
Athas, Jamie	.275	128	444	59	122	14	2	3	41	47	82	12	10	.336	.363	L	R	6-2	190	10-14-79	2001	Winston-Salem, N.C.
Cervenak, Mike	.270	137	511	74	138	26	1	20	91	36	80	2	1	.442	.329	R	R	5-11	180	8-17-76	1999	New Boston, Mich.
Clark, Doug	.301	113	396	47	119	23	4	4	49	45	67	8	5	.409	.371	L	R	6-2	205	3-5-76	1998	Springfield, Mass.
Curry, Chris	.260	73	219	23	57	11	0	4	19	13	50	0	0	.365	.320	R	R	6-1	190	11-17-77	1999	Conway, Ark.
Erickson, Corey	.229	16	48	5	11	4	0	0	5	8	13	0	0	.313	.333	R	R	5-11	190	1-10-77	1995	Springfield, Ill.
Freire, Alejandro	.311	137	498	71	155	31	1	18	80	48	87	1	0	.486	.383	R	R	6-2	185	8-23-74	1992	Caracas, Venez.
Hallmark, Pat	.235	135	485	55	114	22	2	6	58	40	88	31	12	.326	.305	R	R	6-0	170	12-31-73	1995	Houston, Texas
Jester, Joe	.223	40	121	19	27	7	0	2	11	18	26	6	2	.331	.338	R	R	5-10	180	7-17-78	1999	Ashdown, Ark.
LaBarbera, Anthony	.174	9	23	4	4	0	0	0	1	2	8	0	0	.174	.240	R	R	5-10	190	3-17-80	2003	Whittier, Calif.
Mendoza, Carlos	.233	58	180	22	42	10	0	5	19	13	28	1	1	.372	.282	S	R	6-0	165	11-27-79	1996	Barquisimeto, Venez.
Pachot, John	.266	90	320	31	85	28	0	4	36	9	42	2	1	.391	.284	R	R	6-2	210	11-11-74	1993	Ponce, P.R.
Pecci, Jay	.236	35	110	11	26	5	0	0	8	11	15	1	2	.282	.312	S	R	5-11	180	9-26-76	1998	Novato, Calif.
Pernalete, Marco	.208	57	173	22	36	6	1	5	29	19	39	0	0	.341	.284	S	R	6-0	155	10-12-78	1996	Barquisimeto, Venez.
Shabala, Adam	.267	132	513	71	137	22	6	9	54	46	99	10	7	.386	.328	L	R	6-1	190	2-6-78	2000	Streator, Ill.
Soler, Ramon	.255	66	184	27	47	4	1	0	12	16	32	10	2	.288	.320	S	R	6-0	170	9-19-77	1997	Elias Pina, D.R.
Turco, Anthony	.000	1	1	0	0	0	0	0	0	0	1	0	0	.000	.000	L	R	5-9	175	10-8-79	2000	Sarasota, Fla.
Valderrama, Carlos	.308	65	240	37	74	15	3	1	18	25	34	13	6	.408	.375	R	R	5-11	175	11-30-77	1995	Bachaquero, Venez.

PITCHING	W	L	ERA	G	GS	CG	SV	IP	H	R	ER	BB	SO	AVG	B	T	HT	WT	DOB	1st Yr	Resides
Anderson, Luke	0	0	4.38	6	0	0	0	12	9	6	6	4	13	.209	R	R	6-5	210	4-9-78	2000	Las Vegas, Nev.
Begg, Chris	2	1	4.38	4	4	0	0	25	31	14	12	13	13	.322	R	R	6-4	195	9-12-79	2001	Sutherland, Sask.
Bonser, Boof	7	10	4.00	24	24	1	0	135	122	80	60	67	103	.244	R	R	6-4	230	10-14-81	2000	Pinellas Park, Fla.
Brown, Elliot	1	2	6.85	4	4	0	0	24	29	21	18	6	7	.305	S	R	6-2	190	6-7-75	1996	Metairie, La.
Bruso, Greg	5	4	3.42	11	11	2	0	76	72	32	29	11	45	.254	R	R	6-3	190	5-5-80	2002	South Lake Tahoe, Calif.
Clark, Jeff	2	4	4.58	7	7	0	0	37	45	25	19	5	32	.298	R	R	6-6	240	5-6-80	2000	Ledyard, Conn.
Correia, Kevin	6	6	3.65	16	14	0	0	86	80	38	35	30	73	.248	R	R	6-3	200	8-24-80	2002	San Diego, Calif.
Cox, Ryan	1	3	7.46	26	4	0	0	60	89	54	50	28	37	.334	R	R	6-3	195	12-25-76	1999	Stewardson, Ill.
Cozier, Vance	6	7	4.14	26	13	2	0	100	117	54	46	36	36	.291	R	R	6-6	245	9-26-77	1999	Ajax, Ontario
Lira, James	1	1	7.04	6	3	0	0	15	21	12	12	11	11	.328	R	R	6-1	175	5-19-78	1998	Bishop, Texas
Lowry, Noah	9	6	4.72	23	23	2	0	118	127	66	62	47	97	.284	L	L	6-2	190	10-10-80	2001	Ojai, Calif.
Montes, Albert	3	1	4.43	36	0	0	5	63	74	40	31	18	30	.297	R	R	6-2	210	12-11-79	2001	El Paso, Texas
Montgomery, Matt	4	3	2.68	28	0	0	13	37	35	11	11	13	39	.241	R	R	6-3	210	5-13-76	1997	Anaheim, Calif.
Palmer, Matt	0	0	13.50	5	0	0	0	7	12	11	10	5	5	.363	R	R	6-2	200	3-21-79	2002	Caruthersville, Mo.
Spiehs, R.D.	2	5	3.28	39	0	0	7	60	57	31	22	29	51	.252	R	R	6-3	210	10-18-79	2001	Grand Island, Neb.
Taschner, Jack	0	6	5.71	34	12	0	0	76	78	53	48	45	46	.268	L	L	6-3	190	4-21-78	1999	Racine, Wisc.
Threets, Erick	0	0	15.88	11	0	0	0	11	15	20	20	21	16	.306	L	L	6-5	240	11-4-81	2000	Livermore, Calif.
Vent, Kevin	6	5	3.50	37	0	0	1	75	72	36	29	30	47	.257	R	R	6-0	185	6-1-77	1999	Maumelle, Ark.
Wade, Travis	0	2	7.33	19	0	0	2	23	35	20	19	10	13	.360	R	R	6-3	210	7-8-75	1997	Climax, Mich.
Walk, Mitch	6	13	4.12	36	20	2	7	138	147	75	63	55	76	.280	L	L	6-2	185	4-7-78	2000	Mattoon, Ill.
Wilson, Mike	1	0	7.50	2	2	0	0	6	10	5	5	1	5	.370	R	R	6-7	230	6-12-80	1998	El Cajon, Calif.
2-team (9 Reading)	3	2	4.46	11	8	0	0	40	45	25	20	21	23	.294							

FIELDING

Catcher	PCT	G	PO	A	E	DP	PB
Curry	.970	59	326	34	11	2	5
Pachot	.993	85	494	66	4	6	8

First Base	PCT	G	PO	A	E	DP
Cervenak	.988	50	371	24	5	50
Curry	1.000	7	57	5	0	8
Freire	.991	87	687	43	7	75

Second Base	PCT	G	PO	A	E	DP
Athas	1.000	1	1	0	0	0
Jester	.962	38	78	98	7	22
LaBarbera	.882	4	7	8	2	4
Mendoza	.992	29	48	69	1	17
Pecci	.975	33	69	88	4	19
Pernalete	.976	9	21	19	1	6
Soler	.987	35	69	85	2	35

Third Base	PCT	G	PO	A	E	DP
Cervenak	.944	83	53	149	12	18
Erickson	.895	15	11	23	4	1
Mendoza	.951	18	3	36	2	1
Pernalete	.927	29	24	52	6	4

Shortstop	PCT	G	PO	A	E	DP
Athas	.938	127	210	365	38	101
LaBarbera	.917	4	3	8	1	2
Mendoza	.956	12	18	25	2	3
Pernalete	1.000	1	3	2	0	1

Outfield	PCT	G	PO	A	E	DP
Clark	1.000	89	194	9	0	1
Curry	.000	1	0	0	0	0
Freire	1.000	3	1	0	0	0
Hallmark	.985	134	326	7	5	1
Pachot	.000	1	0	0	0	0
Pernalete	.944	6	17	0	1	0
Shabala	.990	129	283	16	3	4
Soler	1.000	3	3	0	0	0
Valderrama	.983	64	115	2	2	0

SAN JOSE GIANTS — High Class A

CALIFORNIA LEAGUE

BATTING	AVG	G	AB	R	H	2B	3B	HR	RBI	BB	SO	SB	CS	SLG	OBP	B	T	HT	WT	DOB	1st Yr	Resides
Anderson, Keith	.220	56	173	24	38	5	0	1	22	20	44	1	2	.266	.301	R	R	6-1	205	1-6-79	2001	Escondido, Calif.
Benard, Marvin	.222	3	9	2	2	0	0	0	0	0	2	0	0	.222	.300	L	L	5-09	190	1-20-70	1992	Richland, Wash.
Benavidez, Julian	.205	58	200	18	41	8	2	3	22	16	57	1	1	.310	.268	R	R	6-2	215	4-14-82	2001	Oakland, Calif.
Carter, Bryan	.253	131	471	68	119	26	3	8	66	37	114	28	11	.372	.337	L	L	6-0	194	2-25-78	2000	Frostproof, Fla.

BATTING	AVG	G	AB	R	H	2B	3B	HR	RBI	BB	SO	SB	CS	SLG	OBP	B	T	HT	WT	DOB	1st Yr	Resides
Chavez, Angel	.280	120	478	69	134	23	6	10	58	22	60	20	11	.416	.314	R	R	6-1	180	7-22-81	1999	David Chiriqui, Panama
Cordido, Julio	.265	122	464	49	123	20	7	3	43	20	75	6	5	.358	.299	R	R	6-1	190	7-30-80	1997	Caracas, Venez.
Florence, Branden	.294	101	405	46	119	26	7	7	58	12	34	8	3	.444	.322	R	R	6-0	200	4-3-78	2001	Boise, Idaho
Holst, Micah	.268	99	366	58	98	24	1	1	32	20	51	17	5	.347	.332	R	R	6-2	205	3-5-77	1999	Independence, Mo.
Knoedler, Justin	.257	101	354	48	91	25	2	10	43	35	78	13	3	.424	.326	R	R	6-2	210	7-17-80	2001	Springfield, Ill.
Knowlton, Jay	.265	24	83	10	22	6	0	1	8	7	18	2	0	.373	.365	R	R	6-1	195	12-8-79	2003	Milwaukie, Ore.
Lunsford, Trey	.286	2	7	1	2	0	0	1	1	0	4	0	0	.714	.286	R	R	6-1	195	5-25-79	2000	South Haven, Miss.
McMains, Derin	.248	25	109	14	27	2	1	1	12	7	8	3	2	.312	.303	S	R	6-0	180	11-3-79	2001	Little Rock, Ark.
Ortmeier, Daniel	.304	115	408	62	124	32	6	8	56	39	89	13	6	.471	.378	S	L	6-4	220	5-11-81	2002	Highland Village, Texas
Sobieraj, Aaron	.219	17	64	10	14	4	0	1	5	8	13	1	0	.328	.315	R	R	6-2	170	6-3-81	2002	Clearwater, Fla.
Soler, Ramon	.280	46	164	24	46	4	2	2	13	14	35	15	6	.366	.353	S	R	6-0	170	9-19-77	1997	Elias Pina, D.R.
Strong, Zach	.241	115	361	40	87	22	1	3	35	68	91	1	6	.332	.363	S	R	6-3	200	6-3-81	2003	Olympia, Wash.
Trumble, Dan	.206	97	296	45	61	12	0	21	43	31	120	3	6	.459	.291	R	R	6-2	205	9-29-79	2000	Nampa, Idaho
Turco, Anthony	.193	24	57	3	11	1	0	0	2	3	21	0	0	.211	.233	L	R	5-9	175	10-8-79	2000	Sarasota, Fla.
Von Schell, Tyler	.243	70	268	29	65	17	0	10	46	9	63	0	0	.418	.265	R	R	6-3	215	7-7-79	2001	Goleta, Calif.

PITCHING	W	L	ERA	G	GS	CG	SV	IP	H	R	ER	BB	SO	AVG	B	T	HT	WT	DOB	1st Yr	Resides
Aardsma, David	1	1	1.96	18	0	0	8	18	14	4	4	7	28	.212	R	R	6-5	200	12-27-81	2003	The Woodlands, Texas
Alvarez, Tim	0	2	7.36	8	0	0	0	11	13	9	9	6	7	.302	L	L	6-4	235	1-5-81	2003	Central Point, Ore.
Anderson, Keith	0	0	3.86	4	0	0	0	4	6	2	2	0	4	.000	R	R	6-1	205	1-6-79	2001	Escondido, Calif.
Begg, Chris	4	1	1.15	7	5	1	0	39	30	5	5	4	21	.212	R	R	6-4	195	9-12-79	2001	Sutherland, Sask.
Brown, Elliot	2	7	6.53	15	12	0	1	61	84	57	44	21	32	.315	S	R	6-2	190	6-7-75	1996	Metairie, La.
Bruso, Greg	7	5	3.11	14	13	1	0	84	69	34	29	11	77	.218	R	R	6-3	190	5-5-80	2002	South Lake Tahoe, Calif.
Burres, Brian	3	3	3.86	39	0	0	1	61	55	33	26	36	64	.239	L	L	6-1	175	4-8-81	2001	Clackamas, Ore.
Christiansen, Jason	0	0	1.93	5	1	0	0	5	5	1	1	3	2	.312	R	L	6-5	240	9-21-69	1991	Mesa, Ariz.
Clark, Jeff	2	2	3.04	9	9	0	0	53	49	23	18	11	43	.241	R	R	6-6	240	5-6-80	2000	Ledyard, Conn.
Cram, Josh	2	4	3.92	31	0	0	1	57	55	30	25	27	29	.263	R	R	6-2	200	8-22-80	2001	Edmonds, Wash.
Foppert, Jesse	0	1	9.00	1	1	0	0	3	5	3	3	0	3	.384	R	R	6-6	210	7-10-80	2001	San Rafael, Calif.
Garcia, James	5	4	4.16	33	3	0	7	71	67	37	33	35	105	.243	R	R	6-2	210	2-3-80	2002	Torrance, Calif.
George, Chris	1	0	7.00	4	0	0	0	9	12	7	7	2	6	.315	R	R	6-1	180	10-13-80	2003	Santa Cruz, Calif.
Gross, Kyle	0	0	4.50	2	0	0	0	2	2	1	1	4	3	.250	R	R	6-4	210	12-11-78	2000	Danville, Calif.
Hannaman, Ryan	4	4	4.71	13	13	1	0	63	66	41	33	32	77	.259	L	L	6-3	200	8-28-81	2000	Mobile, Ala.
Hensley, Clay	2	3	5.83	5	5	0	0	29	38	20	19	9	25	.336	R	R	5-11	190	8-31-79	2002	Pearland, Texas
Hutchison, Wes	3	6	7.04	39	2	0	3	54	78	50	42	36	48	.349	R	R	6-1	195	5-31-79	2001	Lewiston, Idaho
Liriano, Francisco	0	1	54.00	1	1	0	0	1	5	4	4	2	0	.714	L	L	6-2	185	10-26-83	2001	San Cristobal, D.R.
Markert, Jackson	0	2	4.18	13	4	0	1	28	31	15	13	12	23	.276	R	R	6-6	215	2-9-79	2000	Tulsa, Okla.
Martin, Sean	0	0	3.09	5	0	0	0	12	13	6	4	2	14	.276	R	R	6-1	190	3-27-80	2003	Tucson, Ariz.
Padgett, Daniel	0	1	18.47	11	0	0	0	13	22	29	26	16	7	.392	L	L	6-0	170	1-7-78	2000	Littleton, Colo.
Pannone, Anthony	3	10	5.45	22	19	0	0	111	118	73	67	51	89	.274	R	R	6-3	220	7-7-81	2001	Olympia, Wash.
Pavon, Julio	5	4	3.54	41	8	0	2	112	106	48	44	26	103	.249	R	R	6-2	165	6-14-76	1999	Granada, Nicaragua
Rigueiro, Rafael	0	2	13.19	17	0	0	0	29	55	50	43	34	26	.392	R	R	6-6	200	5-20-77	2000	Riverside, Calif.
Schmidt, Jeremy	0	0	6.52	5	0	0	0	10	10	9	7	8	14	.263	R	R	6-2	190	11-15-79	2002	Sarasota, Fla.
Thomas, J.T.	5	12	3.45	33	19	0	3	125	134	64	48	35	104	.266	L	L	6-2	190	7-24-81	1999	Orcutt, Calif.
Treadway, Brion	8	7	4.11	29	22	0	2	134	136	66	61	53	100	.267	R	R	6-4	205	4-1-79	2000	Oxford, Ohio
Vent, Kevin	1	0	11.05	4	1	0	0	7	14	11	9	5	7	.400	R	R	6-0	185	6-1-77	1999	Maumelle, Ark.
Washburn, Ben	0	0	8.10	4	0	0	0	7	9	6	6	8	8	.346	R	R	6-2	200	5-17-79	2000	Redlands, Calif.
Zerbe, Chad	0	0	0.00	2	2	0	0	3	3	2	0	2	1	.250	L	L	6-0	190	4-27-72	1991	Highland, Calif.

FIELDING

Catcher	PCT	G	PO	A	E	DP	PB
Anderson	.985	38	296	28	5	1	10
Knoedler	.989	98	755	60	9	6	16
Lunsford	1.000	1	7	1	0	0	0
Turco	.920	10	41	5	4	0	3

First Base	PCT	G	PO	A	E	DP
Anderson	1.000	13	98	9	0	8
Benavidez	.979	56	403	23	9	34
Cordido	1.000	5	29	1	0	2
Strong	.969	4	29	2	1	5
Von Schell	.992	67	558	30	5	52

Second Base	PCT	G	PO	A	E	DP
Cordido	.970	36	63	100	5	22
Knowlton	.962	23	34	42	3	12
McMains	1.000	25	44	69	0	17
Sobieraj	.949	16	30	26	3	11
Soler	.948	46	63	102	9	20

Third Base	PCT	G	PO	A	E	DP
Benavidez	.857	2	1	5	1	1
Cordido	.920	51	32	95	11	7
Strong	.883	95	44	144	25	14

Shortstop	PCT	G	PO	A	E	DP
Chavez	.957	117	213	344	25	66
Cordido	.942	28	32	65	6	10

Outfield	PCT	G	PO	A	E	DP
Benard	1.000	2	4	0	0	0
Carter	.987	130	298	6	4	3
Cordido	1.000	11	15	1	0	0
Florence	.990	62	103	1	1	0
Holst	.959	81	129	11	6	1
Ortmeier	.979	72	138	2	3	2
Trumble	.950	83	128	6	7	1

HAGERSTOWN SUNS — Low Class A

SOUTH ATLANTIC LEAGUE

BATTING	AVG	G	AB	R	H	2B	3B	HR	RBI	BB	SO	SB	CS	SLG	OBP	B	T	HT	WT	DOB	1st Yr	Resides
Alexander, Kevin	.271	72	255	37	69	14	1	1	25	45	38	6	5	.345	.384	R	R	5-10	160	9-15-80	2000	Eugene, Ore.
Benavidez, Julian	.238	66	227	25	54	11	2	3	24	31	42	0	1	.344	.336	R	R	6-2	215	4-14-82	2001	Oakland, Calif.
Buller, Dayton	.200	11	30	2	6	1	0	1	3	5	8	1	0	.333	.351	R	R	6-0	190	6-22-81	2002	Oakhurst, Calif.
Buscher, Brian	.275	54	200	19	55	7	1	0	26	10	25	0	0	.320	.318	L	R	6-0	201	4-18-81	2003	Jacksonville, Fla.
Columbus, Jason	.211	64	232	26	49	12	0	5	27	21	72	0	0	.328	.287	R	R	6-6	230	9-27-79	2002	Alamogordo, N.M.
Holm, Steve	.220	55	173	12	38	10	1	1	17	8	32	3	1	.306	.265	R	R	6-0	195	10-21-79	2001	Tulsa, Okla.
Hornostaj, Aaron	.207	50	184	19	38	4	1	1	18	18	39	2	1	.255	.280	L	R	6-1	180	5-19-83	2002	Waterloo, Ontario
Ishikawa, Travis	.206	57	194	20	40	5	0	3	22	33	69	3	4	.278	.329	L	L	6-3	190	9-24-83	2002	Federal Way, Wash.
Jernigan, Karl	.197	70	223	28	44	4	3	1	18	15	40	12	0	.256	.279	R	R	6-2	190	4-15-79	2002	Navarre, Fla.
Kelly, Kevin	.247	86	324	39	80	14	0	6	33	20	75	0	1	.346	.294	R	R	6-1	200	3-21-80	2002	Brooklawn, N.J.
Knowlton, Jay	.263	12	38	4	10	1	0	0	4	5	10	1	1	.289	.378	R	R	6-1	195	12-8-79	2003	Milwaukie, Ore.
LaBarbera, A.J.	.239	22	88	13	21	3	2	1	6	9	12	2	0	.352	.316	R	R	5-10	190	3-17-80	2003	Whittier, Calif.
Lewis, Fred	.250	114	420	61	105	17	8	1	27	68	112	30	15	.336	.361	L	R	6-2	190	12-9-80	2002	Wiggins, Miss.
McMains, Derin	.289	54	194	31	56	14	3	0	27	39	21	18	2	.392	.406	S	R	6-0	180	11-3-79	2001	Little Rock, Ark.
Miranda, Miguel	.170	15	47	2	8	0	0	0	4	6	6	1	0	.170	.264	S	R	6-0	170	6-10-79	2001	Little Rock, Ark.
Munhall, Brian	.249	89	293	32	73	16	2	1	30	38	59	3	3	.328	.337	R	R	6-0	190	6-17-80	2002	Spokane, Wash.
Sosa, Carlos	.235	125	460	51	108	16	4	10	63	52	134	9	3	.352	.315	R	R	6-1	170	10-20-81	2001	Santo Domingo, D.R.

BATTING	AVG	G	AB	R	H	2B	3B	HR	RBI	BB	SO	SB	CS	SLG	OBP	B	T	HT	WT	DOB	1st Yr	Resides
Wald, Jake	.217	114	391	39	85	19	2	4	27	41	123	7	6	.307	.302	R	R	6-2	180	2-8-81	2002	Alexandria, Va.
Walter, Randy	.251	121	395	45	99	26	4	5	46	38	91	11	9	.375	.327	R	R	6-2	210	4-14-81	2002	Ballantine, Mont.

PITCHING	W	L	ERA	G	GS	CG	SV	IP	H	R	ER	BB	SO	AVG	B	T	HT	WT	DOB	1st Yr	Resides
Cain, Matt	4	4	2.55	14	14	0	0	74	57	24	21	24	90	.208	R	R	6-3	180	10-1-84	2002	Collierville, Tenn.
Cozier, Vance	0	2	3.38	4	1	0	0	11	13	9	4	5	3	.302	R	R	6-6	245	9-26-77	1999	Ajax, Ontario
Cram, Josh	1	2	4.02	13	0	0	1	31	25	15	14	6	18	.213	R	R	6-2	200	8-22-80	2001	Edmonds, Wash.
Habel, Josh	11	7	2.36	37	16	1	2	122	90	36	32	35	127	.203	L	L	6-1	190	9-10-80	2002	Durango, Iowa
Hennessey, Brad	3	9	4.20	15	15	1	0	79	81	49	37	27	44	.264	R	R	6-2	185	2-7-80	2001	Toledo, Ohio
Hensley, Clay	4	3	3.18	12	12	3	0	68	56	26	24	20	74	.223	R	R	5-11	190	8-31-79	2002	Pearland, Texas
Munter, Scott	3	5	2.36	40	0	0	5	69	61	28	18	28	47	.230	R	R	6-6	235	3-7-80	2001	Wichita, Kan.
Palmer, Matt	5	0	1.20	44	0	0	25	52	21	7	7	15	56	.120	R	R	6-2	200	3-21-79	2002	Caruthersville, Mo.
Portorreal, Daniel	1	4	3.16	6	6	0	0	26	21	18	9	19	20	.233	R	R	6-2	160	1-29-82	2002	Santo Domingo, D.R.
Ransom, Troy	3	0	5.40	29	0	0	0	48	57	34	29	8	22	.295	R	R	6-2	180	7-9-78	1999	Chandler, Ariz.
Rigueiro, Rafael	0	1	1.35	5	0	0	0	7	3	3	1	2	12	.125	R	R	6-6	200	5-20-77	2000	Riverside, Calif.
Sadler, Billy	0	0	4.80	12	0	0	1	15	15	8	8	13	10	.263	R	R	6-0	190	9-21-81	2003	Pensacola, Fla.
Schmidt, Jeremy	1	4	5.85	24	0	0	0	32	43	29	21	19	26	.328	R	R	6-2	190	11-15-79	2002	Sarasota, Fla.
Serrato, Juan	0	2	3.71	6	3	0	0	17	12	8	7	6	21	.206	R	R	6-2	200	11-4-81	2001	Riverside, Calif.
Stirm, Brian	8	5	2.86	17	15	0	0	85	63	30	27	23	80	.205	R	R	6-6	200	3-13-82	2002	Saratoga, Calif.
Threets, Erick	2	3	3.26	22	0	0	0	50	26	20	18	42	47	.158	L	L	6-5	240	11-4-81	2000	Livermore, Calif.
Valdez, Merkin	9	5	2.25	26	26	2	0	156	119	42	39	49	166	.212	R	R	6-3	170	11-5-81	1999	San Cristobal, D.R.
Waddell, Jason	4	2	3.52	36	2	0	0	61	52	32	24	21	54	.231	R	L	6-2	180	6-11-81	2001	Riverside, Calif.
Washburn, Ben	1	0	2.75	11	0	0	0	20	15	6	6	4	12	.208	R	R	6-2	200	5-17-79	2000	Redlands, Calif.
Woolard, Glenn	8	9	3.44	26	25	2	0	144	126	63	55	43	135	.235	R	R	6-1	200	4-18-81	2002	Lititz, Penn.

FIELDING

Catcher	PCT	G	PO	A	E	DP	PB
Buller	.977	11	76	9	2	0	4
Holm	.991	39	281	32	3	1	2
Munhall	.978	88	724	69	18	2	10

First Base	PCT	G	PO	A	E	DP
Alexander	1.000	6	50	4	0	3
Benavidez	.987	60	487	34	7	41
Columbus	.970	12	91	6	3	9
Holm	1.000	1	2	0	0	0
Ishikawa	.990	57	481	38	5	22
Knowlton	.962	3	23	2	1	2

Second Base	PCT	G	PO	A	E	DP
Alexander	1.000	3	5	10	0	1
Hornostaj	.949	43	70	98	9	15
Kelly	.974	46	79	106	5	23
Knowlton	1.000	1	1	6	0	2
LaBarbera	.974	8	12	26	1	6
McMains	1.000	23	38	59	0	7
Miranda	1.000	11	17	18	0	1

Third Base	PCT	G	PO	A	E	DP
Alexander	.871	14	6	21	4	1
Buscher	.964	53	30	104	5	9
Holm	1.000	10	7	7	0	1
Kelly	.878	34	21	51	10	3
Knowlton	1.000	1	0	3	0	0
McMains	.937	27	20	54	5	3

Shortstop	PCT	G	PO	A	E	DP
Alexander	1.000	1	1	3	0	2
Hornostaj	1.000	6	6	18	0	1
Knowlton	1.000	1	1	1	0	0
LaBarbera	.963	6	6	20	1	4
McMains	1.000	4	3	10	0	2
Miranda	.955	4	10	11	1	1
Wald	.944	113	177	330	30	41

Outfield	PCT	G	PO	A	E	DP
Alexander	.971	21	29	4	1	1
Jernigan	.966	65	111	3	4	0
Knowlton	1.000	5	2	1	0	0
Lewis	.986	111	206	5	3	1
Sosa	.965	100	159	5	6	0
Wald	.000	1	0	0	0	0
Walter	.981	117	200	8	4	2

SALEM-KEIZER VOLCANOES — Short-Season Class A

NORTHWEST LEAGUE

BATTING	AVG	G	AB	R	H	2B	3B	HR	RBI	BB	SO	SB	CS	SLG	OBP	B	T	HT	WT	DOB	1st Yr	Resides
Barrows, Derek	.211	33	109	17	23	3	0	2	12	12	14	1	1	.294	.293	R	R	6-1	187	11-20-80	2003	Sarasota, Fla.
Boyer, Brett	.270	47	100	16	27	5	2	0	9	8	29	3	1	.360	.327	R	R	6-0	170	8-8-80	1999	Indian Rocks Beach, Fla.
Ciesluk, Chris	.167	4	12	1	2	0	0	1	2	0	4	0	0	.417	.167	R	R	6-2	215	2-6-83	2001	Taunton, Mass.
Coutlangus, Jon	.301	51	176	34	53	7	3	1	24	25	31	7	4	.392	.394	L	L	6-1	180	10-21-80	2003	St. Lucie, Fla.
D'Jesus, Francisco	.234	23	64	5	15	0	0	0	2	2	9	0	0	.234	.269	R	R	6-0	195	4-12-81	2000	Santo Domingo, D.R.
Diaz, Randor	.000	2	4	1	0	0	0	0	0	0	3	0	0	.000	.333	R	R	6-0	190	9-13-82	2000	Santo Domingo, D.R.
Dobson, Patrick	.231	15	52	2	12	4	1	0	3	6	18	2	0	.346	.322	R	R	6-3	210	12-8-80	2003	Santa Barbara, Calif.
Garrido, Tomas	.226	37	124	7	28	5	1	0	11	6	23	5	0	.282	.261	R	R	6-2	155	8-27-81	1999	Valencia,Venez.
Hornostaj, Aaron	.311	64	257	38	80	9	1	2	33	19	30	10	3	.377	.359	L	R	6-1	180	5-19-83	2002	Waterloo, Ontario
Hutting, Tim	.218	64	248	29	54	7	0	1	31	25	32	4	2	.258	.300	R	R	6-0	190	10-29-81	2003	Newhall, Calif.
Ishikawa, Travis	.254	66	248	53	63	17	4	3	31	44	77	0	0	.391	.376	L	L	6-3	190	9-24-83	2002	Federal Way, Wash.
Jennings, Jeffery	.296	59	233	27	69	9	2	3	32	15	36	5	3	.391	.346	R	R	6-0	190	12-10-81	2003	Orangevale, Calif.
Knowlton, Jay	.310	8	29	4	9	0	0	0	3	2	5	1	0	.310	.375	R	R	6-1	195	12-8-79	2003	Milwaukie, Ore.
LaBarbera, A.J.	.216	11	37	6	8	3	0	0	2	5	5	3	0	.297	.318	R	R	5-10	190	3-17-80	2003	Whittier, Calif.
Lunsford, Trey	.300	3	10	0	3	0	0	0	3	2	1	0	0	.300	.429	R	R	6-1	195	5-25-79	2000	South Haven, Miss.
Schierholtz, Nathan	.306	35	124	23	38	6	2	3	29	12	15	0	1	.460	.382	L	R	6-2	215	2-15-84	2003	Danville, Calif.
Schmidt, Jesse	.261	64	211	31	55	11	0	5	27	29	50	8	2	.384	.354	S	R	6-1	200	10-27-81	2003	Carlsbad, Calif.
Vericker, Brad	.284	70	243	47	69	19	0	15	47	48	58	0	1	.547	.404	L	L	6-2	210	5-8-81	2003	Marana, Ariz.
Wagner, Michael	.276	64	257	42	71	14	4	5	44	17	46	2	0	.420	.348	R	R	6-3	210	9-13-81	2003	Woodinville, Wash.
Williams, Jon	.260	35	100	14	26	7	0	0	12	14	19	0	0	.330	.348	L	R	5-10	190	5-18-79	2001	Columbia, Mo.

GAMES BY POSITION: **C**—D'Jesus 16, Jennings 48, Lunsford 3, Williams 19. **1B**—Ishikawa 66, Vericker 11. **2B**—Boyer 1, Hornostaj 61, Hutting 12, LaBarbera 5. **3B**—Barrows 30, Ciesluk 4, Garrido 10, Knowlton 5, LaBarbera 1, Schierholtz 33. **SS**—Garrido 27, Hutting 50. **OF**—Boyer 46, Coutlangus 48, Diaz 1, Dobson 15, Schmidt 62, Vericker 26, Wagner 61.

PITCHING	W	L	ERA	G	GS	CG	SV	IP	H	R	ER	BB	SO	AVG	B	T	HT	WT	DOB	1st Yr	Resides
Alvarez, Tim	2	1	2.38	14	0	0	1	23	20	8	6	8	18	.240	L	L	6-4	235	1-5-81	2003	Central Point, Ore.
Anderson, Luke	1	0	1.59	3	0	0	0	6	4	1	1	4	8	.190	R	R	6-5	210	4-9-78	2000	Las Vegas, Nev.
Bateman, Jamie	3	2	6.63	26	2	0	4	38	47	31	28	10	30	.305	R	R	6-2	170	5-6-80	2002	Pittsfield, Mass.
Floyd, Jesse	6	4	1.73	14	14	0	0	83	67	18	16	19	76	.215	R	R	6-5	185	1-2-81	2003	Nederland, Texas
George, Chris	0	0	8.24	13	0	0	0	20	25	20	18	14	24	.301	R	R	6-1	180	10-13-80	2003	Santa Cruz, Calif.
Jefferson, Drew	1	3	4.38	26	0	0	13	25	24	13	12	6	26	.244	L	L	5-10	190	4-27-80	2002	Normal, Ill.
Kunes, Michael	1	0	4.60	18	0	0	1	31	31	16	16	7	23	.252	L	L	6-1	205	9-16-81	2003	Chatsworth, Calif.
Ludwig, Kellen	1	1	3.38	17	0	0	0	21	21	9	8	10	24	.256	R	R	6-5	225	11-19-82	2003	Leesburg, Ga.
Martin, Sean	0	0	3.46	10	0	0	0	13	8	5	5	8	12	.173	R	R	6-1	190	3-27-80	2003	Tucson, Ariz.
McNiven, Brooks	7	5	3.62	16	11	0	0	70	74	40	28	16	45	.273	R	R	6-5	180	6-19-81	2003	Vernon, B.C.
Misch, Pat	7	5	2.18	14	14	0	0	87	78	33	21	20	61	.246	R	L	6-2	170	8-18-81	2003	Northbrook, Ill.
Moreno, Anthony	0	1	7.94	4	4	0	0	17	27	18	15	8	6	.375	R	R	6-1	190	5-4-83	2002	Mesa, Ariz.

PITCHING	W	L	ERA	G	GS	CG	SV	IP	H	R	ER	BB	SO	AVG	B	T	HT	WT	DOB	1st Yr	Resides
Musgrave, Mike	1	2	3.51	15	9	0	1	49	51	26	19	19	54	.268	R	R	6-2	185	4-10-84	2003	Ocala, Fla.
Nesmith, Travis	1	0	4.08	14	0	0	0	18	16	10	8	17	21	.250	L	L	6-3	225	4-26-82	2003	Miami, Fla.
Petersen, Jeff	2	1	4.19	17	1	0	1	34	36	18	16	11	26	.257	R	R	6-4	225	10-16-81	2003	Covington, Wash.
Portorreal, Daniel	4	4	5.60	12	12	0	0	53	61	37	33	48	16	.311	R	R	6-2	160	1-29-82	2002	Santo Domingo, D.R.
Reina, Jesus	0	1	9.82	3	0	0	0	4	5	5	4	4	2	.416	L	L	6-0	140	4-20-84	2002	Maracay, Venez.
Sadowski, Ryan	1	2	3.16	15	3	0	0	31	22	11	11	22	26	.203	R	R	6-4	185	10-4-82	2003	Davie, Fla.
Sanchez, Jose	0	1	12.15	4	0	0	0	7	9	9	9	8	9	.321	R	R	6-2	190	10-11-81	2002	Santo Domingo, D.R.
Thurmond, Ben	5	0	1.93	14	6	0	2	51	44	15	11	9	45	.231	R	R	6-0	190	10-2-81	2003	Tempe, Ariz.

SCOTTSDALE GIANTS — Rookie

ARIZONA LEAGUE

BATTING	AVG	G	AB	R	H	2B	3B	HR	RBI	BB	SO	SB	CS	SLG	OBP	B	T	HT	WT	DOB	1st Yr	Resides
Abreu, Johany	.318	50	198	32	63	10	6	0	27	13	33	18	5	.429	.363	S	R	6-0	160	4-3-84	2002	San Cristobal, D.R.
Alexander, Kevin	.455	3	11	6	5	0	1	0	4	3	3	1	0	.636	.571	R	R	5-10	160	9-15-80	2000	Eugene, Ore.
Bozarth, Dustin	.000	2	4	1	0	0	0	0	0	1	3	1	0	.000	.200	L	R	6-0	215	9-17-79	2003	Arlington, Texas
Buller, Dayton	.256	36	125	14	32	3	4	2	15	5	40	0	0	.392	.295	R	R	6-0	190	6-22-81	2002	Oakhurst, Calif.
Conte, Nick	.222	18	45	3	10	1	0	0	0	8	15	1	2	.244	.340	R	R	5-10	175	1-18-82	2003	San Carlos, Calif.
Disla, Lisandro	.254	49	169	28	43	11	3	0	19	21	39	6	3	.355	.352	R	R	6-0	170	4-6-84	2001	Mao, D.R.
Felix, Maximo	.202	29	89	16	18	4	0	4	10	11	28	3	0	.382	.339	R	R	6-0	190	11-9-82	2001	Santo Domingo, D.R.
German, Carlos	.164	43	152	20	25	5	3	0	16	9	62	4	3	.237	.216	R	R	6-3	180	3-12-84	2001	Nizao, D.R.
Hammonds, Jeffrey	.500	4	10	4	5	1	1	3	6	1	1	0	0	1.700	.545	R	R	6-0	200	3-5-71	1992	Cincinnati, Ohio
Lunsford, Trey	.462	5	13	5	6	0	1	0	3	7	3	1	1	.615	.619	R	R	6-1	195	5-25-79	2000	South Haven, Miss.
Mooney, Michael	.290	56	221	30	64	15	6	1	39	18	55	9	2	.425	.346	R	R	6-1	205	6-8-83	2003	Hillsborough, Calif.
Morillo, Roberto	.283	37	120	17	34	5	2	1	16	10	26	6	2	.383	.346	S	R	6-0	155	7-24-84	2001	Maracaibo, Venez.
Paulino, Adalberto	.261	13	46	4	12	2	2	0	6	1	7	3	1	.391	.277	R	R	5-11	150	9-6-82	2000	Nizao, D.R.
Schierholtz, Nathan	.400	11	45	5	18	0	2	0	5	3	8	4	0	.489	.449	L	R	6-2	215	2-15-84	2003	Danville, Calif.
Strain, Ryan	.302	49	182	39	55	10	2	0	15	41	26	7	7	.379	.434	S	R	5-9	180	10-15-80	2003	Englewood, Colo.
Ventura, Robert	.181	41	127	13	23	7	0	0	10	15	44	7	0	.236	.273	R	R	6-2	160	11-26-81	2002	Santiago, D.R.
Yens, Jose	.313	53	208	32	65	10	8	1	26	4	37	9	5	.452	.338	R	R	6-1	190	10-16-82	2002	Santo Domingo, D.R.
Zbacnik, Billy	.206	34	131	12	27	5	0	2	16	19	36	1	2	.290	.311	L	L	6-5	235	4-20-81	2003	San Diego, Calif.

FIELDING: C—Buller 30, Conte 11, Felix 24, Lunsford 2. **1B**—Schierholtz 1, Ventura 22, Zbacnik 34. **2B**—Abreu 3, Disla 6, Morillo 13, Strain 35. **3B**—Abreu 4, Alexander 1, Disla 37, Morillo 7, Schierholtz 10. **SS**—Abreu 28, Disla 6, Morillo 7, Ventura 17. **OF**—Abreu 15, Alexander 1, German 38, Hammonds 4, Mooney 54, Paulino 12, Yens 52.

PITCHING	W	L	ERA	G	GS	CG	SV	IP	H	R	ER	BB	SO	AVG	B	T	HT	WT	DOB	1st Yr	Resides
Acosta, Kelyn	3	4	4.40	10	8	0	0	45	56	28	22	16	35	.314	R	R	6-1	170	4-24-85	2002	Azua, D.R.
Anderson, Luke	0	0	6.75	5	0	0	0	5	8	4	4	0	7	.333	R	R	6-5	210	4-9-78	2000	Las Vegas, Nev.
English, Jesse	0	1	3.98	7	6	0	0	20	11	11	9	19	31	.161	L	L	6-3	220	9-13-84	2002	Vista, Calif.
Gross, Kyle	0	0	31.50	5	0	0	0	4	5	16	14	15	6	.312	R	R	6-4	210	12-11-78	2000	Danville, Calif.
Hannaman, Ryan	1	1	4.38	4	4	0	0	12	8	6	6	7	14	.190	L	L	6-3	200	8-28-81	2000	Mobile, Ala.
Hernandez, Armando	0	1	4.24	17	0	0	0	34	38	16	16	12	27	.285	R	R	6-3	190	11-7-81	2001	Diria, Nicaragua
Liriano, Francisco	0	1	4.32	4	4	0	0	8	5	4	4	6	9	.192	L	L	6-2	185	10-26-83	2001	San Cristobal, D.R.
Lundwall, Todd	1	1	6.35	12	0	0	3	11	8	10	8	14	12	.190	R	R	6-2	205	12-24-80	2003	Los Angeles, Calif.
Markert, Jackson	1	0	1.59	4	0	0	0	6	3	1	1	0	6	.157	R	R	6-6	215	2-9-79	2000	Tulsa, Okla.
Matos, Osiris	2	2	4.67	9	6	0	0	35	35	21	18	10	28	.261	R	R	6-1	180	11-6-84	2002	Santo Domingo, D.R.
McGovern, Ryan	0	0	6.26	14	0	0	0	23	36	21	16	8	18	.339	L	L	6-1	185	6-23-84	2003	Abbotsford, B.C.
Millikan, Bryan	5	1	2.35	11	10	0	0	46	42	16	12	22	32	.248	R	R	6-5	190	8-13-83	2003	Olympia, Wash.
Moreno, Anthony	6	1	2.83	10	4	0	0	35	27	11	11	12	39	.212	R	R	6-1	190	5-4-83	2002	Mesa, Ariz.
Nacar, Leslie	0	1	0.95	20	0	0	9	19	9	4	2	3	31	.136	R	R	6-1	150	7-20-83	1999	Libertad, Venez.
Reina, Jesus	1	1	3.38	11	0	0	0	16	18	9	6	11	22	.285	L	L	6-0	140	4-20-84	2002	Maracay, Venez.
Rondon, Yosy	2	2	8.46	16	0	0	0	22	32	25	21	16	23	.333	L	L	5-10	170	2-3-83	2001	La Romana, D.R.
Sanchez, Jose	2	0	2.04	12	0	0	0	35	28	13	8	12	35	.218	R	R	6-2	190	10-11-81	2002	Santo Domingo, D.R.
Smiley, Jermaine	0	0	2.57	10	0	0	0	14	12	6	4	14	20	.230	L	L	6-2	200	3-5-80	1999	Seattle, Wash.
Solis, Hairo	1	4	7.16	15	3	0	1	33	49	29	26	8	33	.355	R	R	6-1	170	3-3-84	2001	Las Matas de Farfan, D.R.
Villanueva, Carlos	3	6	3.97	12	10	0	0	59	64	31	26	13	67	.277	S	R	6-2	190	11-28-83	2002	Santo Domingo, D.R.
Whitaker, Craig	0	1	1.69	3	1	0	0	5	2	2	1	4	8	.105	R	R	6-4	170	11-19-84	2003	Lufkin, Texas

SEATTLE MARINERS

BY COREY BROCK

Winning 93 games in 2003 wasn't good enough for the Mariners for the second consecutive year, as another second-half meltdown kept the team from getting the playoff berth it once seemed destined for.

The Mariners spent 118 days in first place in the American League West but fell from contention when the team's hitting couldn't keep pace with the Mariners' pitching. The results weren't very pretty—the Mariners went 35-34 in the second half and just 27-27 over the final two months of the season. The slow slide frustrated everyone.

"We didn't play well coming down the stretch—and we didn't play well in the second half at all," first baseman John Olerud said. "We have lost a lot of close games and haven't beaten a lot of teams that we really felt like we should have beat during the year."

This was a vexing predicament for first-year manager Bob Melvin, the man who replaced Lou Piniella. Melvin didn't see this coming. "The second half . . . is something we have got to look at," Melvin said. "We played OK through July and the first half of August but you have to turn it around offensively and play better than .500."

Hitting was just one of the Mariners problems in 2003. During the second half of the season, the Mariners batted only .261. Only two Mariners hit more than 20 home runs—Edgar Martinez (24) and Bret Boone (35). The 139 home runs Seattle hit proved to be the second-fewest in the league, just two ahead of last-place Tampa Bay.

"I think one area we've got to improve is we've got to score a few more runs," general manager Pat Gillick said. "We have got to improve on our power."

Some think that the Mariners downfall began when the team didn't make a significant trade by the July 31 trading deadline. The team did add infielder Rey Sanchez but the team's ownership refused to make a deal to improve the team's chances of making the playoffs. The lack of a deal, his ties to the East Coast and other factors contributed to Gillick's resignation following the season.

"I was saying at the trading deadline that I didn't think we needed to make any moves because I really liked our team," Olerud said. "So maybe that shows that I don't know what I am talking about."

Despite their second-half slump, the Mariners had some highlights, especially with their pitching and defense.

Seattle finished with the fewest errors in major league history (65); the 1999 Mets (68) set the previous record. The Mariners recorded a fielding percentage of .988.

The rotation of Freddy Garcia, Gil Meche, Jamie Moyer, Ryan Franklin and Joel Piniero proved to be successful as well as durable. Seattle was only the fifth team in major league history—the second since 1904—to use only five starters all season.

Moyer set a franchise record with 21 victories. Meche pitched his first full season since 1999. Two shoulder surgeries sidelined his progress but he bounced back with a 15-13 record and displayed dominating stuff.

Seattle had minor league highlights as well. Double-A San Antonio won its second straight Texas League title behind Baseball America's Minor League Manager of the Year, Dave Brundage. Class A Inland Empire won the California League playoffs as well. Missions lefthander Travis Blackley tied for the minor league lead with 17 victories, and 17-year-old righthander Felix Hernandez was named the top prospect in the short-season Northwest League.

Jamie Moyer

Travis Blackley

PLAYERS of the YEAR

MAJOR LEAGUE: Jamie Moyer, lhp

Moyer kept getting better with age in 2003. At age 40, he made his first All-Star Game appearance and won more games than he had in any prior season of his career. At 21-7, 3.27, Moyer ranked second in the American League in wins and sixth in ERA.

MINOR LEAGUE: Travis Blackley, lhp

No minor leaguer won more games in 2003 than Blackley, who at 17-3, 2.61 was one of four pitchers to lead the minors in wins. No Texas League pitcher had won that many games since Jeff Reardon in 1978. Blackley allowed two earned runs or fewer in 21 of his 27 starts.

ORGANIZATION LEADERS

BATTING		
*AVG	Greg Jacobs, San Antonio/Inland Empire	.345
R	Justin Leone, San Antonio	103
H	Greg Jacobs, San Antonio/Inland Empire	163
TB	A.J. Zapp, San Antonio	262
2B	Greg Jacobs, San Antonio/Inland Empire	42
3B	Shin-Soo Choo, Inland Empire	13
HR	A.J. Zapp, San Antonio	26
RBI	Justin Leone, San Antonio	92
	A.J. Zapp, San Antonio	92
BB	Justin Leone, San Antonio	92
SO	A.J. Zapp, San Antonio	178
SB	Mike Curry, San Antonio	58
*SLG	Justin Leone, San Antonio	.541
*OBP	Greg Jacobs, San Antonio/Inland Empire	.412
PITCHING		
W	Travis Blackley, San Antonio	17
L	Jeff Heaverlo, Tacoma	12
	Chris Wright, Tacoma/San Antonio	12
#ERA	T.A. Fullmer, Wisconsin	2.58
G	Jared Hoerman, San Antonio	56
CG	T.A. Fullmer, Wisconsin	5
SV	Jared Hoerman, San Antonio	36
IP	Bobby Livingston, Wisconsin	178
BB	Bobby Madritsch, San Antonio	67
	Clint Nageotte, San Antonio	67
SO	Ryan Ketchner, Inland Empire	159
	Troy Cate, Tacoma/Inland Empire	159

*Minimum 250 At-Bats #Minimum 75 Innings

SEATTLE MARINERS

Manager: Bob Melvin.

2003 Record: 93-69, .574 (2nd, AL West).

BATTING	AVG	G	AB	R	H	2B	3B	HR	RBI	BB	SO	SB	CS	SLG	OBP	B	T	HT	WT	DOB	1st Yr	Resides
Bloomquist, Willie	.250	89	196	30	49	7	2	1	14	19	39	4	1	.321	.317	R	R	5-11	180	11-27-77	1999	Port Orchard, Wash.
Boone, Bret	.294	159	622	111	183	35	5	35	117	68	125	16	3	.535	.366	R	R	5-10	190	4-6-69	1990	Orlando, Fla.
Borders, Pat	.143	12	14	1	2	1	0	0	1	1	5	0	0	.214	.200	R	R	6-2	200	5-14-63	1982	Lake Wales, Fla.
Cameron, Mike	.253	147	534	74	135	31	5	18	76	70	137	17	7	.431	.344	R	R	6-2	200	1-8-73	1991	McDonough, Ga.
Cirillo, Jeff	.205	87	258	24	53	11	0	2	23	24	32	1	1	.271	.284	R	R	6-1	200	9-23-69	1991	Redmond, Wash.
Colbrunn, Greg	.276	22	58	7	16	1	1	3	7	4	16	0	1	.483	.323	R	R	6-0	210	7-26-69	1988	Mount Pleasant, S.C.
Davis, Ben	.236	80	246	25	58	18	0	6	42	18	61	0	0	.382	.284	S	R	6-4	220	3-10-77	1995	West Chester, Penn.
Guillen, Carlos	.276	109	388	63	107	19	3	7	52	52	64	4	4	.394	.359	S	R	6-1	200	9-30-75	1993	Maracay, Venez.
Mabry, John	.212	64	104	12	22	6	0	3	16	15	21	0	0	.356	.328	L	R	6-4	210	10-17-70	1991	St. Louis, Mo.
Martinez, Edgar	.294	145	497	72	146	25	0	24	98	92	95	0	1	.489	.406	R	R	5-11	200	1-2-63	1983	Kirkland, Wash.
McLemore, Mark	.233	99	309	34	72	15	2	2	37	38	71	5	5	.314	.318	S	R	5-11	200	10-4-64	1982	Southlake, Texas
Meyers, Chad	.000	9	1	1	0	0	0	0	0	0	0	1	0	.000	.000	R	R	5-11	190	8-8-75	1996	Omaha, Neb.
Olerud, John	.269	152	539	64	145	35	0	10	83	84	67	0	1	.390	.372	L	L	6-5	220	8-5-68	1989	Fall City, Wash.
Sanchez, Rey	.294	46	170	22	50	5	1	0	11	8	21	1	0	.335	.330	R	R	5-9	170	10-5-67	1986	Trujillo Alto, P.R.
Strong, Jamal	.000	12	2	2	0	0	0	0	0	0	0	0	0	.000	.000	R	R	5-10	180	8-5-78	2000	Altadena, Calif.
Suzuki, Ichiro	.312	159	679	111	212	29	8	13	62	36	69	34	8	.436	.352	L	R	5-9	170	10-22-73	2001	Kobe, Japan
Ugueto, Luis	.200	12	5	4	1	0	0	0	1	1	0	2	0	.200	.333	S	R	5-11	190	2-15-79	1996	Maracay, Venez.
Wilson, Dan	.241	96	316	32	76	15	2	4	43	15	52	0	0	.339	.272	R	R	6-3	210	3-25-69	1990	Seattle, Wash.
Winn, Randy	.295	157	600	103	177	37	4	11	75	41	108	23	5	.425	.346	S	R	6-2	190	6-9-74	1995	Danville, Calif.

PITCHING	W	L	ERA	G	GS	CG	SV	IP	H	R	ER	BB	SO	AVG	B	T	HT	WT	DOB	1st Yr	Resides
Benitez, Armando	0	0	3.14	15	0	0	0	14	10	5	5	11	15	.188	R	R	6-4	220	11-3-72	1990	San Pedro de Macoris, D.R.
2-team (9 New York)	1	1	2.66	24	0	0	0	24	18	9	7	17	25	.206							
Carrara, Giovanni	2	0	6.83	23	0	0	0	29	40	22	22	14	13	.333	R	R	6-2	230	3-4-68	1990	Edo, Venez.
Franklin, Ryan	11	13	3.57	32	32	2	0	212	199	93	84	61	99	.250	R	R	6-3	180	3-5-73	1993	Spiro, Okla.
Garcia, Freddy	12	14	4.51	33	33	1	0	201	196	109	101	71	144	.254	R	R	6-4	240	6-10-76	1994	Baruta, Venez.
Hasegawa, Shigetoshi	2	4	1.48	63	0	0	16	73	62	12	12	18	32	.234	R	R	5-11	180	8-1-68	1997	Newport Beach, Calif.
Looper, Aaron	0	0	5.14	6	0	0	0	7	7	4	4	2	6	.269	R	R	6-2	180	9-7-76	1998	Ada, Okla.
Mateo, Julio	4	0	3.15	50	0	0	1	86	69	32	30	13	71	.219	R	R	6-0	170	8-2-77	1996	Bani, D.R.
Meche, Gil	15	13	4.59	32	32	1	0	186	187	97	95	63	130	.263	R	R	6-3	200	9-8-78	1996	Scott, La.
Moyer, Jamie	21	7	3.27	33	33	1	0	215	199	83	78	66	129	.245	L	L	6-0	180	11-18-62	1984	Seattle, Wash.
Nelson, Jeff	3	2	3.35	46	0	0	7	38	34	16	14	14	47	.248	R	R	6-8	220	11-17-66	1984	Issaquah, Wash.
Pineiro, Joel	16	11	3.78	32	32	3	0	212	192	94	89	76	151	.241	R	R	6-1	200	9-25-78	1997	Rio Piedras, P.R.
Putz, J.J.	0	0	4.91	3	0	0	0	4	4	2	2	3	3	.266	R	R	6-5	220	2-22-77	1999	Trenton, Mich.
Rhodes, Arthur	3	3	4.17	67	0	0	3	54	53	25	25	18	48	.256	L	L	6-2	210	10-24-69	1988	Baltimore, Md.
Sasaki, Kazuhiro	1	2	4.05	35	0	0	10	33	31	17	15	15	29	.238	R	R	6-4	220	2-22-68	2001	Yokohama, Japan
Soriano, Rafael	3	0	1.53	40	0	0	1	53	30	9	9	12	68	.162	R	R	6-1	170	12-19-79	1996	San Jose, D.R.
Sweeney, Brian	0	0	1.93	5	0	0	0	9	7	2	2	1	7	.212	R	R	6-2	180	6-13-74	1996	Yonkers, N.Y.
Taylor, Aaron	0	0	8.53	10	0	0	0	13	17	12	12	6	9	.314	R	R	6-8	240	8-20-77	1996	Hahira, Ga.
White, Matt	0	0	13.50	3	0	0	0	2	3	3	3	2	0	.375	R	L	6-1	180	8-19-77	1998	Windsor, Mass.
2-team (3 Boston)	0	1	22.24	6	0	0	0	6	13	14	14	5	0	.481							

FIELDING

Catcher	PCT	G	PO	A	E	DP	PB
Borders	1.000	7	29	1	0	0	0
Davis	.991	73	421	24	4	9	8
Wilson	.998	96	587	20	1	4	4

First Base	PCT	G	PO	A	E	DP
Bloomquist	1.000	3	6	1	0	0
Cirillo	1.000	1	2	0	0	1
Colbrunn	.989	14	83	5	1	5
Mabry	1.000	9	44	8	0	7
Olerud	.998	152	1096	125	3	126

Second Base	PCT	G	PO	A	E	DP
Bloomquist	1.000	7	3	3	0	0
Boone	.990	158	268	426	7	107
McLemore	.952	6	9	11	1	3
Ugueto	1.000	4	2	3	0	2

Third Base	PCT	G	PO	A	E	DP
Bloomquist	.970	37	21	44	2	3
Borders	1.000	2	0	1	0	0
Cirillo	.977	85	65	108	4	7
Guillen	.965	32	38	45	3	3
McLemore	.970	29	16	48	2	8
Ugueto	.000	1	0	0	0	0

Shortstop	PCT	G	PO	A	E	DP
Bloomquist	.968	18	24	37	2	8
Guillen	.963	76	122	162	11	56
McLemore	.972	38	46	95	4	26
Sanchez	.979	46	77	109	4	33
Ugueto	.000	1	0	0	0	0

Outfield	PCT	G	PO	A	E	DP
Bloomquist	1.000	11	18	0	0	0
Cameron	.992	147	485	3	4	2
Mabry	.957	22	21	1	1	0
McLemore	1.000	16	28	1	0	0
Meyers	.000	3	0	0	0	0
Strong	.000	2	0	0	0	0
Suzuki	.994	159	337	12	2	4
Winn	.992	157	363	3	3	1

LARRY GOREN

Bret Boone

FARM SYSTEM

Director, Player Development: Benny Looper.

Class	Farm Team	League	W	L	Pct.	Finish*	Manager	First Yr.
AAA	Tacoma (Wash.) Rainiers	Pacific Coast	66	78	.458	14th (16)	Dan Rohn	1995
AA	San Antonio (Texas) Missions	Texas	88	51	.633	+1st (8)	Dave Brundage	2001
High A	Inland Empire (Calif.) 66ers	California	78	62	.557	+2nd (10)	Steve Roadcap	2001
Low A	Wisconsin Timber Rattlers	Midwest	69	66	.511	t-6th (14)	Daren Brown	1993
SS A	Everett (Wash.) Aquasox	Northwest	32	44	.421	7th (8)	Pedro Grifol	1995
Rookie	Peoria (Ariz.) Mariners	Arizona	29	19	.604	3rd (9)	Scott Steinmann	2001

*Finish in overall standings (No. of teams in league) +League champion

TACOMA RAINIERS Class AAA

PACIFIC COAST LEAGUE

BATTING	AVG	G	AB	R	H	2B	3B	HR	RBI	BB	SO	SB	CS	SLG	OBP	B	T	HT	WT	DOB	1st Yr	Resides
Abbott, Jeff	.133	4	15	1	2	1	0	0	0	0	2	0	0	.200	.133	R	L	6-2	200	8-17-72	1994	Dunwoody, Ga.
Barkett, Andy	.242	112	401	40	97	21	1	13	60	38	81	4	3	.397	.310	L	L	6-1	200	9-5-74	1995	Raleigh, N.C.
Borders, Pat	.314	79	293	36	92	27	1	12	51	20	54	1	2	.536	.363	R	R	6-2	200	5-14-63	1982	Lake Wales, Fla.
Castillo, Ruben	.211	111	337	34	71	14	0	0	15	22	71	17	10	.252	.263	R	R	6-2	150	8-16-78	1996	San Pedro de Macoris, D.R.
Cirillo, Jeff	.353	5	17	7	6	3	0	2	6	3	3	0	0	.882	.476	R	R	6-1	200	9-23-69	1991	Redmond, Wash.
Colbrunn, Greg	.273	3	11	3	3	0	0	1	2	1	1	0	0	.545	.333	R	R	6-0	210	7-26-69	1988	Mount Pleasant, S.C.
Connors, Greg	.239	32	113	14	27	4	0	4	13	5	28	0	1	.381	.277	R	R	6-2	180	8-22-74	1996	Smithtown, N.Y.
Figueroa, Luis	.281	123	423	40	119	18	0	3	50	45	35	1	5	.345	.350	R	R	6-0	170	3-2-77	1995	Carolina, P.R.
Gandolfo, Rob	.184	13	38	7	7	2	0	0	4	1	8	1	0	.237	.225	L	R	5-9	170	8-24-77	1999	Dumont, N.J.
Guillen, Carlos	.357	4	14	2	5	1	0	2	4	0	1	0	0	.857	.400	S	R	6-1	200	9-30-75	1993	Maracay, Venez.
Horner, Jim	.167	2	6	0	1	0	0	0	0	2	1	0	0	.167	.375	R	R	6-0	210	11-11-73	1996	Twin Falls, Idaho
Kelly, Kenny	.246	96	341	42	84	15	5	13	37	29	79	20	7	.434	.313	R	R	6-3	180	1-26-79	1997	Lutz, Fla.
Kuzmic, Craig	.213	54	160	25	34	7	0	8	23	22	48	1	2	.406	.310	S	R	6-0	180	5-2-77	1998	Fountain Valley, Calif.
Landry, Jacques	.248	44	153	24	38	11	0	7	24	17	46	6	2	.458	.343	R	R	6-3	200	8-15-73	1996	LaMarque, Texas
Leach, Jalal	.292	70	250	25	73	8	2	6	28	22	51	5	5	.412	.352	L	L	6-2	220	3-14-69	1990	Novato, Calif.
Lopez, Mickey	.275	129	455	68	125	23	4	7	41	47	50	20	12	.389	.346	S	R	5-9	170	11-17-73	1995	Miami, Fla.
Mabry, John	.364	3	11	1	4	0	0	0	0	2	1	0	0	.364	.462	L	R	6-4	210	10-17-70	1991	St. Louis, Mo.
Maduro, Jorge	.000	5	18	0	0	0	0	0	0	0	5	0	0	.000	.000	R	R	6-2	200	3-11-81	1999	Miami, Fla.
Meyers, Chad	.300	97	377	50	113	20	3	4	34	30	46	37	12	.401	.361	R	R	5-11	190	8-8-75	1996	Omaha, Neb.
Mosquera, Julio	.285	85	291	35	83	16	1	4	22	11	42	6	4	.388	.332	R	R	6-0	190	1-29-72	1991	Clearwater, Fla.
Myers, Adrian	.269	117	428	57	115	25	3	5	47	34	75	23	11	.376	.322	R	R	5-10	170	5-10-75	1996	Hattiesburg, Miss.
Pecci, Jay	.125	14	40	3	5	0	0	0	3	3	3	1	0	.125	.234	S	R	5-11	180	9-26-76	1998	Novato, Calif.
Phillips, J.R.	.297	81	310	35	92	20	0	14	54	17	74	4	3	.497	.334	L	L	6-1	180	4-29-70	1988	Moreno Valley, Calif.
Rogelstad, Matt	.000	5	4	1	0	0	0	0	0	0	0	0	0	.000	.000	L	R	6-3	185	9-13-82	2003	Hammond, La.
Snelling, Chris	.269	18	67	11	18	2	0	3	10	5	12	1	0	.433	.333	L	L	5-10	160	12-3-81	1999	Gorokan, Australia
Strong, Jamal	.305	56	210	38	64	6	1	2	19	25	38	26	11	.371	.390	R	R	5-10	180	8-5-78	2000	Altadena, Calif.
Ugueto, Luis	.308	8	26	9	8	3	0	2	4	5	4	2	0	.654	.419	S	R	5-11	190	2-15-79	1996	Maracay, Venez.

PITCHING	W	L	ERA	G	GS	CG	SV	IP	H	R	ER	BB	SO	AVG	B	T	HT	WT	DOB	1st Yr	Resides
Anderson, Craig	13	11	3.56	28	27	4	0	177	187	93	70	46	67	.269	L	L	6-3	180	10-30-80	1999	Ourimbah, Australia
Atchison, Scott	6	9	4.31	39	7	0	1	109	114	57	52	37	83	.268	R	R	6-2	180	3-29-76	1999	Fort Worth, Texas
Carrara, Giovanni	1	1	4.23	18	0	0	5	28	28	14	13	9	27	.264	R	R	6-2	230	3-4-68	1990	Edo, Venez.
Cate, Troy	1	0	1.69	1	1	0	0	5	4	3	1	2	6	.190	L	L	6-1	200	10-21-80	2002	Temecula, Calif.
Cloude, Ken	4	4	5.95	21	17	0	0	76	88	56	50	37	39	.290	R	R	6-1	200	1-9-75	1994	Baltimore, Md.
Falkenborg, Brian	4	2	2.94	17	14	0	0	80	66	28	26	26	62	.220	R	R	6-6	190	1-18-78	1996	Redmond, Wash.
Fruto, Emiliano	1	0	0.00	1	0	0	0	4	1	0	0	2	2	.083	R	R	6-3	170	6-6-84	2000	Bolivar, Colombia
Hamulack, Tim	1	0	3.86	10	0	0	0	14	16	6	6	8	12	.301	L	L	6-4	210	11-14-76	1996	Edgewood, Md.
Heaverlo, Jeff	5	12	5.39	24	24	0	0	124	150	80	74	38	75	.304	R	R	6-1	210	1-13-78	1999	Moses Lake, Wash.
House, Craig	0	0	2.84	5	0	0	0	6	6	2	2	5	4	.272	R	R	6-2	220	7-8-77	1999	Nashville, Tenn.
Johnson, Rett	5	2	2.15	11	10	1	0	71	63	26	17	18	49	.241	L	R	6-2	210	7-6-79	2000	Aynor, S.C.
Kuzmic, Craig	0	0	4.50	2	0	0	0	2	4	1	1	1	0	.000	S	R	6-0	180	5-2-77	1998	Fountain Valley, Calif.
Looper, Aaron	5	2	3.11	46	0	0	5	75	72	27	26	26	67	.246	R	R	6-2	180	9-7-76	1998	Ada, Okla.
Putz, J.J.	0	3	2.51	41	0	0	11	86	69	30	24	34	60	.224	R	R	6-5	220	2-22-77	1999	Trenton, Mich.
Sasaki, Kazuhiro	0	1	9.82	3	2	0	1	4	5	4	4	1	5	.312	R	R	6-4	220	2-22-68	2001	Yokohama, Japan
Simpson, Allan	2	5	4.16	43	0	0	1	63	60	30	29	42	69	.251	R	R	6-4	180	8-26-77	1997	Las Vegas, Nev.
Soriano, Rafael	4	3	3.19	11	10	0	0	62	43	24	22	12	63	.191	R	R	6-1	170	12-19-79	1996	San Jose, D.R.
Stitt, Brian	0	0	2.45	4	0	0	0	7	9	3	2	1	1	.290	R	R	6-0	180	8-26-82	2002	Wellington, Fla.
Sweeney, Brian	11	10	4.28	29	21	0	0	141	165	80	67	32	115	.288	R	R	6-2	180	6-13-74	1996	Yonkers, N.Y.
Taylor, Aaron	1	3	2.45	33	0	0	16	40	30	11	11	13	34	.208	R	R	6-8	240	8-20-77	1996	Hahira, Ga.
Thornton, Matt	0	2	8.00	2	2	0	0	9	14	11	8	3	5	.358	L	L	6-6	220	9-15-76	1998	Allendale, Mich.
Wear, Greg	0	0	0.00	2	0	0	0	2	1	0	0	0	1	.142	R	R	6-5	220	7-7-79	2002	Orland Park, Ill.
Williams, Randy	2	2	5.26	18	0	0	1	26	25	17	15	11	19	.252	L	L	6-3	190	9-18-75	1997	Houston, Texas
Wright, Chris	0	6	6.36	9	9	0	0	47	53	33	33	27	33	.291	R	R	6-2	190	6-6-77	1997	Tampa, Fla.

FIELDING

Catcher	PCT	G	PO	A	E	DP	PB
Borders	.987	66	433	31	6	4	2
Horner	1.000	2	15	0	0	0	0
Kuzmic	1.000	7	32	4	0	0	1
Maduro	1.000	5	35	2	0	0	0
Mosquera	.989	71	421	33	5	3	9

First Base	PCT	G	PO	A	E	DP
Barkett	.991	79	607	51	6	65
Borders	1.000	1	2	0	0	0
Colbrunn	1.000	1	8	2	0	0
Kuzmic	.987	19	146	9	2	11
Meyers	1.000	2	10	0	0	2
Phillips	.990	48	380	29	4	37

Second Base	PCT	G	PO	A	E	DP
Figueroa	1.000	13	22	32	0	6
Gandolfo	.978	11	19	25	1	4
Kuzmic	.967	8	15	14	1	2
Lopez	.987	100	192	270	6	63
Meyers	.933	13	26	30	4	7
Pecci	.969	13	26	37	2	7
Rogelstad	.000	1	0	0	0	0

Third Base	PCT	G	PO	A	E	DP
Cirillo	1.000	3	3	6	0	1
Connors	.941	14	9	23	2	3
Figueroa	.932	110	82	190	20	16
Guillen	1.000	3	3	9	0	1
Kuzmic	.923	9	4	8	1	1

	PCT	G	PO	A	E	DP
Mosquera	.931	13	7	20	2	0
Pecci	1.000	1	0	3	0	0
Rogelstad	.000	1	0	0	0	0

Shortstop	PCT	G	PO	A	E	DP
Castillo	.950	110	179	295	25	66
Gandolfo	1.000	2	0	1	0	0
Lopez	.979	35	50	88	3	13
Ugueto	.936	8	14	30	3	12

Outfield	PCT	G	PO	A	E	DP
Barkett	.964	14	24	3	1	1
Connors	1.000	10	21	0	0	0
Kelly	.981	85	197	11	4	1
Kuzmic	.000	1	0	0	0	0
Landry	.986	38	64	4	1	1
Leach	.962	51	74	1	3	1
Lopez	1.000	1	2	0	0	0
Meyers	.967	74	177	1	6	1
Myers	.992	105	235	6	2	0
Rogelstad	1.000	3	1	0	0	0
Snelling	1.000	13	27	1	0	0
Strong	.958	55	136	2	6	1

SAN ANTONIO MISSIONS — Class AA

TEXAS LEAGUE

BATTING	AVG	G	AB	R	H	2B	3B	HR	RBI	BB	SO	SB	CS	SLG	OBP	B	T	HT	WT	DOB	1st Yr	Resides
Bubela, Jaime	.277	128	473	60	131	29	7	4	61	31	108	26	11	.393	.323	L	R	6-1	200	6-6-78	2000	Houston, Texas
Castellano, John	.133	6	15	1	2	0	0	0	2	1	4	0	0	.133	.188	R	R	5-11	180	9-8-77	1997	Boynton Beach, Fla.
Curry, Mike	.276	134	518	89	143	30	10	3	52	67	116	58	11	.390	.361	L	R	5-10	190	2-15-77	1998	Jacksonville, Fla.
Dobbs, Greg	.333	2	6	0	2	2	0	0	0	0	1	0	0	.667	.333	L	R	6-1	200	7-2-78	2001	Moreno Valley, Calif.
Gandolfo, Rob	.293	54	157	18	46	6	1	0	12	9	25	10	5	.344	.339	L	R	5-9	170	8-24-77	1999	Dumont, N.J.
Guzman, Elpidio	.276	129	475	60	131	13	8	4	53	21	66	28	10	.362	.306	L	L	6-0	160	2-24-77	1996	Santo Domingo, D.R.
Horner, Jim	.311	71	254	37	79	11	1	5	43	12	37	4	1	.421	.348	R	R	6-0	210	11-11-73	1996	Twin Falls, Idaho
Jacobs, Greg	.310	34	126	11	39	7	0	1	14	8	14	1	3	.389	.351	L	L	5-10	180	10-9-76	1998	Anaheim Hills, Calif.
Leone, Justin	.288	135	455	103	131	38	7	21	92	92	104	20	6	.541	.405	R	R	6-1	210	3-9-77	1999	Las Vegas, Nev.
Lindsey, John	.296	88	307	40	91	22	1	8	43	22	81	9	1	.453	.363	R	R	6-2	230	1-30-77	1995	Hattiesburg, Miss.
Lopez, Chuck	.275	13	40	1	11	0	0	0	7	3	1	1	1	.275	.318	L	L	6-1	190	11-29-76	2000	Huntington Beach, Calif.
Lopez, Jose	.258	132	538	82	139	35	2	13	69	27	56	18	8	.403	.303	R	R	6-2	170	11-24-83	2000	Barcelona, Venez.
Maynard, Scott	.207	71	237	28	49	6	2	1	18	20	63	0	2	.262	.268	R	R	6-2	210	8-28-77	1995	Laguna Niguel, Calif.
Merritt, Tim	.205	13	44	7	9	2	2	0	5	3	6	2	0	.341	.271	R	R	6-0	180	2-7-80	2001	Cantonment, Fla.
Pecci, Jay	.300	10	40	3	12	1	0	0	1	4	7	0	1	.325	.364	S	R	5-11	180	9-26-76	1998	Novato, Calif.
Snelling, Chris	.333	47	186	24	62	12	2	3	25	8	30	1	7	.468	.371	L	L	5-10	160	12-3-81	1999	Gorokan, Australia
Udy, Nicholas	.222	6	9	0	2	0	0	0	0	1	2	0	0	.222	.300	L	R	6-0	205	3-12-79	2003	Brigham City, Utah
Ugueto, Luis	.260	89	350	53	91	12	2	1	40	27	75	25	10	.314	.312	S	R	5-11	190	2-15-79	1996	Maracay, Venez.
Wilson, Dan	.000	2	7	0	0	0	0	0	0	0	3	0	0	.000	.000	R	R	6-3	210	3-25-69	1990	Seattle, Wash.
Zapp, A.J.	.278	137	528	84	147	35	1	26	92	47	178	7	8	.496	.346	L	R	6-3	190	4-24-78	1996	Greenwood, Ind.

PITCHING	W	L	ERA	G	GS	CG	SV	IP	H	R	ER	BB	SO	AVG	B	T	HT	WT	DOB	1st Yr	Resides
Baek, Cha-Sueng	3	3	2.57	9	9	0	0	56	49	18	16	17	46	.237	R	R	6-4	190	5-29-80	1999	Olympia, Wash.
Blackley, Travis	17	3	2.61	27	27	0	0	162	125	55	47	62	144	.215	L	L	6-3	190	11-4-82	2001	Chelienham, Australia
Hamulack, Tim	0	1	2.09	40	0	0	1	47	32	13	11	15	54	.191	L	L	6-4	210	11-14-76	1996	Edgewood, Md.
Hoerman, Jared	3	6	3.84	56	0	0	36	59	62	32	25	23	56	.268	R	R	6-4	210	4-25-77	1999	Ardmore, Okla.
House, Craig	1	0	2.75	14	0	0	1	20	14	7	6	16	17	.215	R	R	6-2	220	7-8-77	1999	Nashville, Tenn.
Johnson, Rett	6	2	3.04	14	14	1	0	83	74	31	28	21	63	.237	L	R	6-2	210	7-6-79	2000	Aynor, S.C.
Lamber, Justin	3	2	3.39	39	0	0	0	58	65	35	22	15	36	.285	R	L	6-0	210	5-22-76	1997	Hackensack, N.J.
Madritsch, Bobby	13	7	3.63	27	27	2	0	159	133	75	64	67	154	.226	L	L	6-2	190	2-28-76	1998	Burbank, Ill.
Martinez, Gustavo	7	6	3.13	35	9	0	0	92	76	36	32	50	74	.224	R	R	6-0	170	11-9-75	1998	Santo Domingo, D.R.
Matos, Josue	7	2	2.24	48	0	0	4	88	58	23	22	37	104	.187	R	R	6-4	190	3-15-78	1997	Cabo Rojo, P.R.
Nageotte, Clint	11	7	3.10	27	27	2	0	154	127	60	53	67	157	.223	R	R	6-3	200	10-25-80	1999	New Port Richey, Fla.
Olore, Kevin	0	2	5.67	13	5	0	0	40	52	26	25	17	39	.311	L	R	6-2	200	9-21-78	1999	Southington, Conn.
Sherrill, George	3	0	0.33	16	0	0	0	27	19	2	1	12	31	.197	L	L	6-0	210	4-19-77	1999	Memphis, Tenn.
Strelitz, Brian	0	2	3.32	11	1	0	1	19	18	10	7	7	11	.250	R	R	6-2	200	1-8-80	2001	Temple City, Calif.
Thornton, Matt	3	0	0.36	4	4	0	0	25	8	3	1	9	18	.103	L	L	6-6	220	9-15-76	1998	Allendale, Mich.
Ulloa, Enmanuel	0	1	9.28	8	0	0	0	11	14	12	11	11	9	.311	R	R	6-2	170	11-26-78	1997	New York, N.Y.
Williams, Randy	4	1	1.73	29	0	0	2	42	33	9	8	7	38	.212	L	L	6-3	190	9-18-75	1997	Houston, Texas
Wright, Chris	7	6	3.76	20	16	0	0	96	112	56	40	38	80	.295	R	R	6-2	190	6-6-77	1997	Tampa, Fla.

FIELDING

Catcher	PCT	G	PO	A	E	DP	PB
Castellano	1.000	2	6	2	0	0	0
Horner	.997	66	575	39	2	6	5
Maynard	.993	71	541	45	4	6	8
Udy	1.000	6	15	1	0	0	0
Wilson	.941	2	15	1	1	0	0

First Base	PCT	G	PO	A	E	DP
Leone	1.000	2	11	0	0	0
Lindsey	.959	7	38	9	2	4
Zapp	.988	133	1082	113	15	107

Second Base	PCT	G	PO	A	E	DP
Gandolfo	.976	38	69	97	4	18
Leone	1.000	1	3	3	0	0
Lopez	.978	34	81	97	4	23
Merritt	.980	13	19	29	1	10
Pecci	.979	10	18	28	1	10
Ugueto	.980	45	82	118	4	24

Third Base	PCT	G	PO	A	E	DP
Castellano	1.000	1	0	2	0	0
Dobbs	1.000	2	0	6	0	1
Gandolfo	.909	5	3	7	1	0
Horner	1.000	1	0	1	0	0
Leone	.942	123	74	251	20	18
Lopez	.926	10	4	21	2	0
Ugueto	1.000	1	1	1	0	0
Zapp	1.000	1	1	1	0	0

Shortstop	PCT	G	PO	A	E	DP
Leone	.972	9	12	23	1	3
Lopez	.946	88	147	235	22	55
Ugueto	.925	44	55	131	15	26

Outfield	PCT	G	PO	A	E	DP
Bubela	.971	119	217	15	7	3
Castellano	1.000	3	3	0	0	0
Curry	.974	130	263	3	7	1
Gandolfo	1.000	4	6	0	0	0
Guzman	.965	121	216	6	8	2
Jacobs	.895	13	15	2	2	0
Lopez	1.000	9	9	0	0	0
Snelling	1.000	28	41	2	0	0

INLAND EMPIRE 66ers — High Class A

CALIFORNIA LEAGUE

BATTING	AVG	G	AB	R	H	2B	3B	HR	RBI	BB	SO	SB	CS	SLG	OBP	B	T	HT	WT	DOB	1st Yr	Resides
Balet, Pichi	.310	21	84	14	26	3	1	2	14	5	12	1	0	.440	.372	R	R	6-0	210	11-11-77	2001	West Palm Beach, Fla.
Bastida-Martinez, Evel	.274	87	288	44	79	14	2	5	32	23	31	6	6	.389	.330	L	R	6-0	190	2-28-79	2002	Hialeah, Fla.
Bone, Blake	.229	27	83	11	19	7	0	4	16	8	24	0	1	.458	.298	L	R	6-1	190	1-12-79	2000	Southside, Ala.
Brown, Hunter	.248	126	452	84	112	34	3	15	68	67	102	9	6	.436	.353	R	R	6-2	200	10-24-79	2002	Houston, Texas
Castellano, John	.306	114	461	61	141	34	2	12	80	32	50	11	3	.466	.354	R	R	5-11	180	9-8-77	1997	Boynton Beach, Fla.
Castro, Ismael	.275	98	327	46	90	19	2	3	25	12	33	9	7	.373	.314	S	R	5-9	160	8-14-83	1999	Cartagena, Colombia
Choo, Shin-Soo	.286	110	412	62	118	18	13	9	55	44	84	18	10	.459	.365	L	L	5-11	170	7-13-82	2000	Pusan, South Korea
Cirillo, Jeff	.200	5	15	1	3	1	0	0	1	3	1	0	0	.267	.333	R	R	6-1	200	9-23-69	1991	Redmond, Wash.
Collins, Chris	.281	70	199	16	56	12	0	1	29	20	24	0	1	.357	.350	R	R	5-11	190	8-14-81	2001	Phoenix, Ariz.
Delucchi, Dustin	.327	77	312	61	102	19	5	3	32	36	35	15	2	.449	.401	L	L	6-0	180	12-23-77	2000	Burlingame, Calif.

BATTING	AVG	G	AB	R	H	2B	3B	HR	RBI	BB	SO	SB	CS	SLG	OBP	B	T	HT	WT	DOB	1st Yr	Resides
Fulse, Sheldon	.280	49	157	19	44	10	2	2	14	26	35	16	5	.408	.396	S	R	6-3	170	11-10-81	1999	Bartow, Fla.
Guerrero, Cristian	.278	83	299	52	83	9	6	9	38	19	58	12	7	.438	.327	R	R	6-5	200	7-12-80	1997	Bani, D.R.
2-team (3 High Desert)	.280	86	311	55	87	10	7	9	40	20	62	12	7	.444	.329							
Jacobs, Greg	.357	95	347	67	124	35	7	9	64	42	43	4	5	.576	.433	L	L	5-10	180	10-9-76	1998	Anaheim Hills, Calif.
Menchaca, Eddie	.230	116	331	28	76	8	2	0	33	16	60	3	1	.266	.268	R	R	6-0	190	2-7-81	2001	Phoenix, Ariz.
Merritt, Tim	.081	11	37	4	3	0	0	0	3	4	13	1	0	.081	.171	R	R	6-0	180	2-7-80	2001	Cantonment, Fla.
Oliveros, Luis	.286	93	322	43	92	19	0	5	41	18	24	2	3	.391	.333	R	R	6-1	180	6-18-83	2000	Guarenas, Venez.
Pagan, Carlos	.222	6	18	5	4	2	0	1	4	1	4	0	0	.500	.263	R	R	5-9	190	11-2-75	1997	Vega Baja, P.R.
Pecci, Jay	.297	10	37	4	11	1	0	0	4	4	0	0	0	.324	.381	S	R	5-11	180	9-26-76	1998	Novato, Calif.
Pohle, Richard	.257	48	148	15	38	15	1	0	19	14	20	2	1	.372	.327	L	R	5-10	190	5-30-79	2001	Buena Park, Calif.
Quintero, Cesar	.300	3	10	3	3	0	0	0	1	0	2	0	0	.300	.300	R	R	6-1	200	11-16-82	2001	Monagrillo, Panama
Rogelstad, Matt	.395	9	38	8	15	4	1	0	1	0	0	2	1	.553	.395	L	R	6-3	185	9-13-82	2003	Hammond, La.
Sandel, George	.286	3	7	1	2	0	0	0	2	1	0	0	0	.286	.375	L	R	5-10	175	12-4-80	2003	Palm Beach, Fla.
Van Meetren, Jason	.241	100	290	40	70	14	2	2	32	38	74	9	4	.324	.340	R	R	6-3	200	10-4-79	2001	Henderson, Nev.
Williamson, John	.228	22	57	7	13	2	1	1	9	11	14	0	1	.351	.348	S	R	6-1	200	8-23-78	2001	Louisburg, N.C.
Willingham, Phil	.214	11	28	3	6	0	0	1	3	3	9	1	0	.321	.290	L	R	6-1	220	12-29-78	2002	Mobile, Ala.

PITCHING	W	L	ERA	G	GS	CG	SV	IP	H	R	ER	BB	SO	AVG	B	T	HT	WT	DOB	1st Yr	Resides
Baek, Cha-Sueng	5	1	3.65	13	10	0	1	57	55	27	23	9	50	.248	R	R	6-4	190	5-29-80	1999	Olympia, Wash.
Blood, Justin	5	2	3.07	50	0	0	2	59	48	20	20	27	77	.218	L	L	6-3	210	11-20-79	2001	Swanzey, N.H.
Bott, Glenn	7	7	3.16	31	21	0	1	142	131	55	50	38	143	.241	L	L	6-0	170	9-17-81	2001	Houston, Texas
Cate, Troy	9	11	4.11	27	25	0	0	160	165	79	73	37	153	.264	L	L	6-1	200	10-21-80	2002	Temecula, Calif.
Cortez, Renee	0	1	1.66	15	0	0	3	22	10	5	4	6	16	.133	R	R	6-4	170	12-9-82	2000	Valencia, Venez.
Done, Juan	3	4	4.85	30	11	0	2	69	77	50	37	31	46	.284	R	R	6-2	220	10-2-80	1999	Miami, Fla.
Dorman, Rich	5	0	2.65	13	5	0	1	37	29	11	11	21	40	.218	R	R	6-2	210	9-30-78	2000	Medford, Ore.
Fruto, Emiliano	7	8	3.78	42	4	0	7	79	80	43	33	38	83	.266	R	R	6-3	170	6-6-84	2000	Bolivar, Colombia
Gray, Rusty	0	0	12.27	3	0	0	0	4	5	5	5	1	0	.294	R	R	6-2	190	9-2-77	2000	Salt Lake City, Utah
Ketchner, Ryan	14	7	3.45	31	22	2	1	157	133	63	60	33	159	.227	L	L	6-1	190	4-19-82	2000	Lantana, Fla.
Morgan, Russ	1	1	8.10	15	0	0	0	20	36	22	18	10	17	.395	R	L	6-1	200	11-20-77	2000	New Hartford, N.Y.
Olore, Kevin	1	2	5.03	8	8	0	0	39	37	24	22	18	37	.245	L	R	6-2	200	9-21-78	1999	Southington, Conn.
Perez, Elvis	5	5	3.72	13	12	0	0	65	55	30	27	16	58	.224	R	R	6-4	228	7-4-79	1996	Orlando, Fla.
Perez, Jeffrey	1	1	7.65	12	0	0	0	20	23	18	17	15	15	.283	R	R	6-0	180	11-21-78	2002	Tucson, Ariz.
Rall, Tim	2	3	3.65	10	4	0	0	37	34	16	15	9	30	.250	R	L	6-0	200	9-30-79	2003	Lynbrook, N.Y.
Rowland-Smith, Ryan	0	1	3.20	15	0	0	0	20	12	9	7	8	15	.181	L	L	6-3	200	1-26-83	2001	Newcastle, Australia
Sasaki, Kazuhiro	0	0	0.00	1	1	0	0	1	0	0	0	1	2	.000	R	R	6-4	220	2-22-68	2001	Yokohama, Japan
Steele, Mike	2	2	2.56	33	0	0	16	39	29	14	11	8	26	.211	R	R	6-2	200	8-22-78	2000	Midland, Mich.
Strelitz, Brian	4	2	3.48	29	1	0	1	54	51	25	21	11	29	.251	R	R	6-2	200	1-8-80	2001	Temple City, Calif.
Thomas, Jared	5	3	3.61	41	7	0	3	87	67	39	35	46	108	.214	L	L	6-3	220	7-28-80	2002	Grand Blanc, Mich.
Thornton, Matt	0	0	4.00	2	2	0	0	9	9	4	4	4	14	.264	L	L	6-6	220	9-15-76	1998	Allendale, Mich.
Ulloa, Enmanuel	1	1	3.20	17	7	0	1	51	49	20	18	6	61	.252	R	R	6-2	170	11-26-78	1997	New York, N.Y.
Wear, Greg	0	0	36.00	1	0	0	0	1	4	4	4	1	1	.571	R	R	6-5	220	7-7-79	2002	Orland Park, Ill.

FIELDING

Catcher	PCT	G	PO	A	E	DP	PB
Castellano	1.000	2	12	1	0	0	0
Collins	.993	59	402	30	3	2	11
Oliveros	.994	89	770	52	5	2	10
Pagan	.941	3	14	2	1	0	0

First Base	PCT	G	PO	A	E	DP
Balet	1.000	9	59	8	0	3
Bone	.988	12	73	12	1	7
Brown	.750	1	3	0	1	0
Castellano	.990	87	629	44	7	48
Oliveros	1.000	1	8	0	0	0
Van Meetren	.989	36	238	22	3	16

Second Base	PCT	G	PO	A	E	DP
Bastida-Martinez	.968	75	131	138	9	30
Bone	.000	1	0	0	0	0
Castro	.962	77	94	131	9	30
Merritt	1.000	8	10	11	0	2
Pohle	.857	3	6	0	1	0
Rogelstad	1.000	6	12	14	0	3
Sandel	1.000	3	6	1	0	0

Third Base	PCT	G	PO	A	E	DP
Bastida-Martinez	.824	4	6	8	3	0
Bone	.800	3	2	2	1	0
Brown	.925	122	88	207	24	14
Castellano	.875	3	2	5	1	0
Castro	.333	3	0	1	2	0
Cirillo	.833	3	2	3	1	0
Collins	1.000	4	1	3	0	0
Menchaca	.000	1	0	0	0	0
Merritt	1.000	2	1	3	0	0

Shortstop	PCT	G	PO	A	E	DP
Bastida-Martinez	.000	1	0	0	0	0
Brown	.800	2	2	2	1	0
Castro	.990	33	35	65	1	14
Menchaca	.970	115	147	246	12	44
Merritt	1.000	2	1	1	0	0
Pecci	.963	10	12	14	1	3
Rogelstad	.923	3	5	7	1	0

Outfield	PCT	G	PO	A	E	DP
Balet	.667	4	2	0	1	0
Bone	.000	1	0	0	0	0
Castro	1.000	2	2	0	0	0
Choo	.980	104	183	9	4	1
Delucchi	1.000	77	182	2	0	1
Fulse	.983	48	108	5	2	2
Guerrero	.967	71	142	3	5	2
Jacobs	.969	88	153	5	5	2
Van Meetren	1.000	26	37	0	0	0
Williamson	1.000	17	28	1	0	0
Willingham	1.000	4	5	0	0	0

WISCONSIN TIMBER RATTLERS — Low Class A

MIDWEST LEAGUE

BATTING	AVG	G	AB	R	H	2B	3B	HR	RBI	BB	SO	SB	CS	SLG	OBP	B	T	HT	WT	DOB	1st Yr	Resides
Aoki, Tomoshi	.224	53	134	21	30	8	1	1	10	19	40	2	1	.321	.329	R	R	6-1	200	9-10-79	2003	Kanagawa, Japan
Arroyo, Carlos	.273	101	359	47	98	11	2	3	40	34	49	18	8	.340	.334	L	L	5-11	170	5-30-81	1999	Cartagena, Colombia
Bohn, T.J.	.272	128	471	75	128	31	2	13	70	70	131	16	8	.429	.371	R	R	6-5	200	1-17-80	2002	Otsego, Minn.
Bone, Blake	.229	12	35	5	8	4	0	0	4	6	7	0	0	.343	.364	L	R	6-1	190	1-12-79	2000	Southside, Ala.
Cordova, Roman	.227	23	75	10	17	1	0	0	5	2	10	1	1	.240	.247	S	R	6-1	180	9-2-84	2001	Aragua, Venez.
Delucchi, Dustin	.266	43	143	22	38	9	0	2	15	29	28	2	2	.371	.393	L	L	6-0	180	12-23-77	2000	Burlingame, Calif.
Ehrnsberger, Chad	.211	25	90	8	19	2	1	1	9	11	23	1	1	.289	.308	R	R	5-10	210	11-29-77	2002	Ottawa, Ohio
Garcia, Cip	.240	20	50	4	12	2	0	1	8	2	19	0	0	.340	.278	R	R	6-0	200	10-23-78	1997	Albuquerque, N.M.
Garciaparra, Michael	.243	122	440	55	107	12	1	2	38	38	80	14	4	.289	.314	R	R	6-1	160	4-2-83	2001	Harbor Heights, Calif.
Griffin, Brock	.000	1	3	0	0	0	0	0	0	0	1	0	0	.000	.000	L	R	6-0	200	10-4-79	2003	Portland, Ore.
Hagen, Matt	.220	126	450	65	99	28	0	21	65	56	129	8	6	.422	.309	R	R	6-4	210	1-3-80	2002	Greeley, Colo.
Harrington, Corey	.258	93	353	55	91	18	7	2	31	29	69	20	9	.365	.332	R	R	6-1	180	5-6-80	2002	Lincoln, Neb.
Harris, Gary	.284	127	525	80	149	25	7	4	52	36	75	36	13	.381	.336	L	R	5-10	180	9-9-79	2002	Resaca, Ga.
McNulty, Josh	.217	11	23	3	5	1	0	0	1	2	1	0	0	.261	.280	L	R	6-5	210	11-12-80	2003	Magee, Miss.
Merritt, Tim	.257	84	339	44	87	12	4	2	26	22	62	24	6	.333	.304	R	R	6-0	180	2-7-80	2001	Cantonment, Fla.
Metheny, Brenton	.221	24	86	7	19	1	0	0	7	9	17	1	1	.233	.295	L	R	6-0	205	10-3-80	2003	Old Fields, W.Va.
Nelson, Jon	.264	134	537	71	142	38	2	16	91	16	168	13	3	.432	.292	R	R	6-5	210	1-16-80	2001	Orem, Utah

BATTING	AVG	G	AB	R	H	2B	3B	HR	RBI	BB	SO	SB	CS	SLG	OBP	B	T	HT	WT	DOB	1st Yr	Resides
Phillips, Chris	.250	32	92	4	23	4	0	0	12	4	19	0	1	.293	.289	R	R	5-11	210	6-15-79	2003	Shreveport, La.
Rivera, Rene	.275	116	407	39	112	19	0	9	54	38	81	2	2	.388	.344	R	R	5-10	190	7-31-83	2001	Bayamon, P.R.
Udy, Nicholas	.130	10	23	3	3	0	0	0	0	4	5	0	0	.130	.259	L	R	6-0	205	3-12-79	2003	Brigham City, Utah

PITCHING	W	L	ERA	G	GS	CG	SV	IP	H	R	ER	BB	SO	AVG	B	T	HT	WT	DOB	1st Yr	Resides
Cortez, Renee	4	2	2.91	28	0	0	4	46	40	20	15	16	51	.236	R	R	6-4	170	12-9-82	2000	Valencia, Venez.
Delgado, Danny	0	0	4.50	4	0	0	0	4	4	2	2	3	5	.266	R	R	6-2	180	2-10-78	1997	Miami Lakes, Fla.
Delgado, Oscar	3	3	3.88	40	0	0	3	58	55	26	25	28	47	.255	L	L	5-11	170	4-5-81	1999	Maracay, Venez.
Dorman, Rich	1	2	2.80	25	1	0	4	45	36	19	14	24	62	.222	R	R	6-2	210	9-30-78	2000	Medford, Ore.
Dowdy, Justin	2	3	5.92	10	1	0	0	24	25	18	16	7	23	.265	L	L	6-1	160	8-13-83	2001	Chula Vista, Calif.
Fulmer, T.A.	9	8	2.58	27	27	5	0	168	154	60	48	37	130	.243	R	R	6-3	200	1-14-80	2002	Charleston, S.C.
Heaston, Bryan	2	2	2.87	41	0	0	8	53	53	20	17	26	21	.267	R	R	6-3	210	6-9-80	2002	Farmington, N.M.
Hernandez, Felix	0	0	1.93	2	2	0	0	14	9	4	3	3	18	.176	R	R	6-3	170	4-8-86	2002	Valencia, Venez.
Hintz, Beau	0	4	8.39	6	6	0	0	25	37	24	23	6	21	.345	L	L	6-4	210	5-12-80	2001	Stockton, Calif.
Jimenez, Cesar	8	11	2.94	28	20	0	0	126	134	61	41	46	76	.273	L	L	5-11	180	11-12-84	2001	Cumana Sucre, Venez.
Livingston, Bobby	15	7	2.73	26	26	1	0	178	176	72	54	28	105	.259	L	L	6-3	190	9-3-82	2001	Lubbock, Texas
Martinez, Miguel	2	1	1.13	24	3	0	2	56	41	9	7	17	69	.209	L	L	6-2	190	10-22-82	2002	Carolina, P.R.
Moorhead, Brandon	0	2	9.00	5	0	0	3	4	7	4	4	5	5	.368	R	R	6-2	215	1-23-80	2003	Bowersville, Ga.
Morrow, David	0	0	6.48	6	0	0	0	8	7	7	6	7	9	.233	R	R	6-1	200	6-28-81	2002	Sherman, Texas
Ovalles, Juan	0	0	3.00	2	0	0	0	3	3	1	1	1	4	.272	R	R	6-1	160	5-15-82	1999	Caracas, Venez.
Rowland-Smith, Ryan	3	0	1.11	13	0	0	1	32	22	13	4	14	37	.181	L	L	6-3	200	1-26-83	2001	Newcastle, Australia
Sandoval, Juan	11	10	4.46	27	27	0	0	157	190	97	78	58	73	.299	R	R	6-1	170	1-13-81	2000	Santo Domingo, D.R.
Viane, David	3	4	3.12	34	0	0	6	61	59	24	21	18	45	.261	R	R	6-1	210	7-15-79	2002	Farmington Hills, Mich.
Watson, Tanner	6	7	4.58	23	23	1	0	116	142	79	59	53	80	.306	R	R	6-3	190	6-14-82	2000	Arnprior, Ontario
Wear, Greg	0	0	3.15	17	0	0	0	20	22	9	7	6	8	.282	R	R	6-5	220	7-7-79	2002	Orland Park, Ill.

FIELDING

Catcher	PCT	G	PO	A	E	DP	PB
Garcia	1.000	5	26	1	0	0	0
Griffin	1.000	1	13	2	0	1	0
Phillips	.972	24	134	7	4	1	6
Rivera	.987	109	727	114	11	6	15
Udy	1.000	7	25	2	0	0	0

First Base	PCT	G	PO	A	E	DP
Bone	.952	2	19	1	1	2
Garcia	1.000	2	3	0	0	0
Hagen	1.000	1	2	0	0	1
McNulty	1.000	4	30	4	0	2
Metheny	.981	22	184	21	4	11
Nelson	.980	111	957	70	21	81

Second Base	PCT	G	PO	A	E	DP
Cordova	.956	22	43	65	5	17
Ehrnsberger	1.000	5	10	15	0	0
Harrington	.960	43	84	110	8	24
Merritt	.969	71	153	186	11	45

Third Base	PCT	G	PO	A	E	DP
Cordova	1.000	1	1	0	0	0
Hagen	.905	126	92	241	35	21
Harrington	.895	12	9	25	4	4
Metheny	1.000	1	1	6	0	1

Shortstop	PCT	G	PO	A	E	DP
Garciaparra	.915	122	178	358	50	67
Harrington	1.000	5	3	4	0	1
Merritt	.980	12	12	36	1	7

Outfield	PCT	G	PO	A	E	DP
Aoki	1.000	35	51	0	0	0
Arroyo	.983	68	108	6	2	2
Bohn	.980	117	270	20	6	5
Delucchi	.949	26	51	5	3	0
Ehrnsberger	1.000	13	20	1	0	0
Harrington	.887	34	50	5	7	0
Harris	.976	118	229	12	6	2
Nelson	1.000	12	19	0	0	0

EVERETT AQUA SOX — Short-Season Class A

NORTHWEST LEAGUE

BATTING	AVG	G	AB	R	H	2B	3B	HR	RBI	BB	SO	SB	CS	SLG	OBP	B	T	HT	WT	DOB	1st Yr	Resides
Blakeley, Eric	.303	59	195	31	59	9	2	3	24	19	36	13	2	.415	.371	R	R	6-2	180	9-8-79	2002	Greenville, Ohio
Bradford, Sam	.239	55	184	36	44	6	2	5	21	27	57	13	6	.375	.340	S	R	6-1	185	10-15-81	2003	Smyrna, Ga.
Colbrunn, Greg	.667	1	3	0	2	1	0	0	0	1	0	0	0	1.000	.750	R	R	6-0	210	7-26-69	1988	Mount Pleasant, S.C.
Colton, Chris	.260	71	250	33	65	12	1	5	32	38	60	16	9	.376	.359	R	R	6-1	190	9-21-82	2002	Newnan, Ga.
Cordova, Roman	.208	16	53	2	11	2	0	0	2	2	5	2	0	.245	.276	S	R	6-1	180	9-2-84	2001	Aragua, Venez.
Cox, Michael	.194	55	175	22	34	9	0	4	20	23	55	3	2	.314	.292	R	R	6-0	188	11-11-80	2003	Sarasota, Fla.
Cruz, Elvis	.115	7	26	1	3	0	0	0	3	0	10	0	0	.115	.115	R	R	6-3	180	11-23-83	2001	Santo Domingo, D.R.
Dutton, Jeremy	.269	66	245	29	66	6	2	2	32	31	37	11	4	.335	.352	L	R	5-11	195	11-15-80	2003	Durham, N.C.
Ellison, Josh	.269	49	182	26	49	4	2	4	26	16	42	12	4	.379	.337	R	R	5-10	200	7-24-83	2001	West Palm Beach, Fla.
Griffin, Brock	.135	23	52	6	7	0	0	1	7	10	25	0	1	.192	.270	L	R	6-0	200	10-4-79	2003	Portland, Ore.
Jones, Adamq	.462	3	13	2	6	1	0	0	4	1	3	0	0	.538	.467	R	R	6-2	180	8-1-85	2003	San Diego, Calif.
Kroski, Chris	.189	14	37	3	7	2	1	0	2	8	10	0	1	.297	.333	L	R	6-2	220	5-15-82	2002	Clearwater, Fla.
Lahair, Bryan	.244	57	201	26	49	14	0	2	20	11	40	4	3	.343	.286	L	R	6-5	215	11-5-82	2003	Worcester, Mass.
Lentz, Brian	.217	35	106	15	23	4	0	1	12	9	19	3	1	.283	.298	R	R	6-12	015	1-23-80	2003	Manchester, Mass.
Maduro, Jorge	.250	15	56	5	14	1	0	2	9	4	15	0	0	.375	.290	R	R	6-2	200	3-11-81	1999	Miami, Fla.
Navarro, Oswaldo	.258	61	233	42	60	12	1	0	23	10	39	16	3	.318	.302	S	R	6-0	150	10-2-84	2001	Maracay, Venez.
Orlandos, Nick	.317	69	265	41	84	13	4	2	31	12	22	14	7	.419	.361	R	R	6-0	180	7-8-80	2002	Mission Viejo, Calif.
Rogelstad, Matt	.276	16	58	7	16	2	0	0	13	0	9	1	0	.310	.311	L	R	6-3	185	9-13-82	2003	Hammond, La.
Ruchti, Justin	.276	21	76	9	21	2	0	1	8	3	13	1	0	.342	.305	R	R	6-2	200	12-11-80	2003	Houston, Texas
Womack, Josh	.297	41	155	25	46	9	4	3	18	19	40	8	5	.465	.374	L	L	6-1	190	1-5-84	2002	San Diego, Calif.

GAMES BY POSITION: C—Griffin 20, Kroski 5, Lentz 34, Maduro 8, Ruchti 18. **1B**—Blakeley 34, Cox 6, Griffin 1, Kroski 6, Lahair 44, Maduro 1. **2B**—Blakeley 16, Cordova 5, Cox 1, Dutton 19, Orlandos 37, Rogelstad 3. **3B**—Cordova 1, Cox 44, Dutton 30, Orlandos 3, Rogelstad 1. **SS**—Blakeley 4, Cordova 7, Cox 1, Jones 3, Navarro 61, Orlandos 1, Rogelstad 4. **OF**—Blakeley 2, Bradford 53, Colton 69, Cruz 6, Dutton 3, Ellison 38, Lahair 3, Orlandos 23, Rogelstad 3, Womack 37.

PITCHING	W	L	ERA	G	GS	CG	SV	IP	H	R	ER	BB	SO	AVG	B	T	HT	WT	DOB	1st Yr	Resides
Abrams, Casey	0	0	7.11	4	0	0	0	6	5	5	5	7	7	.227	L	L	6-4	200	7-17-81	2003	Lebanon, Ohio
Acosta, Nibaldo	0	0	3.60	10	0	0	0	15	14	6	6	6	10	.237	R	R	6-1	180	3-6-83	2001	Maracaibo, Venez.
Alcantara, Audy	0	4	8.67	19	4	0	0	36	40	37	35	26	34	.281	R	R	6-0	170	5-21-81	2000	San Pedro de Macoris, D.R.
Chang, Kenly	0	0	2.97	24	0	0	1	36	37	13	12	16	37	.260	R	R	6-1	170	8-25-82	2001	Bluefields, Nicaragua
Forbes, Terry	0	0	3.52	6	0	0	0	8	14	7	3	3	2	.424	L	R	6-3	200	6-27-84	2002	Dartmouth, N.S.
Frye, Randall	5	4	4.79	13	12	0	0	62	73	40	33	33	53	.285	R	R	6-5	210	9-11-83	2002	Lake Orion, Mich.
Hays, Sam	2	3	4.89	18	7	0	0	42	44	29	23	37	31	.269	L	L	6-5	210	10-7-81	2000	Waco, Texas
Hernandez, Felix	7	2	2.29	11	7	0	0	55	43	17	14	24	73	.218	R	R	6-3	170	4-8-86	2002	Valencia, Venez.
Hintz, Beau	5	7	4.20	14	14	0	0	81	75	43	38	35	62	.237	L	L	6-4	210	5-12-80	2001	Stockton, Calif.
Moorhead, Michael	0	1	1.57	21	0	0	13	23	27	7	4	6	28	.296	R	R	6-2	215	1-23-80	2003	Bowersville, Ga.
Morrow, David	0	2	10.03	5	4	0	0	12	12	13	13	15	9	.272	R	R	6-1	200	6-28-81	2002	Sherman, Texas

PITCHING	W	L	ERA	G	GS	CG	SV	IP	H	R	ER	BB	SO	AVG	B	T	HT	WT	DOB	1st Yr	Resides
O'Flaherty, Eric	1	0	3.38	3	1	0	0	11	8	5	4	3	7	.235	L	L	6-2	195	2-5-85	2003	Walla Walla, Wash.
Ockerman, Justin	1	2	4.88	22	0	0	0	31	24	25	17	31	24	.206	L	R	6-10	250	1-8-83	2001	Garden City, Mich.
Oldham, Thomas	5	3	2.86	13	11	0	0	63	48	27	20	23	63	.209	L	L	6-2	210	5-18-82	2003	Fremont, Neb.
Ovalles, Juan	1	2	5.40	21	0	0	3	27	29	18	16	10	40	.281	R	R	6-1	160	5-15-82	1999	Caracas, Venez.
Perez, Elvis	0	0	1.29	2	2	0	0	7	5	1	1	0	10	.192	R	R	6-4	228	7-4-79	1996	Orlando, Fla.
Perry, Brandon	0	2	1.29	3	0	0	0	7	4	3	1	6	11	.148	L	L	6-1	180	9-27-84	2002	Graham, N.C.
Ramirez, Victor	4	7	5.29	16	10	0	0	68	79	49	40	31	70	.285	L	L	6-5	180	1-11-83	2000	Aragua, Venez.
Rose, Brad	0	3	5.11	20	2	0	0	44	54	32	25	17	24	.300	R	R	6-4	180	7-24-83	2003	Knoxville, Tenn.
Sasaki, Kazuhiro	0	1	22.50	2	2	0	0	2	5	5	5	0	5	.454	R	R	6-4	220	2-22-68	2001	Yokohama, Japan
Stitt, Brian	1	1	4.50	15	0	0	2	26	28	14	13	10	19	.266	R	R	6-0	180	8-26-82	2002	Wellington, Fla.

PEORIA MARINERS — Rookie

ARIZONA LEAGUE

BATTING	AVG	G	AB	R	H	2B	3B	HR	RBI	BB	SO	SB	CS	SLG	OBP	B	T	HT	WT	DOB	1st Yr	Resides
Balentien, Wladimir	.283	50	187	42	53	12	5	16	52	22	55	4	2	.658	.363	R	R	6-2	160	7-2-84	2000	Willemstad, Curacao
Bradford, Sam	.250	4	16	2	4	2	0	0	3	1	3	0	0	.375	.333	S	R	6-1	185	10-15-81	2003	Smyrna, Ga.
Christianson, Ryan	.200	4	10	0	2	0	0	0	2	2	3	0	0	.200	.333	R	R	6-2	210	4-21-81	1999	Riverside, Calif.
Cirillo, Jeff	.300	6	20	2	6	0	0	0	0	4	1	0	1	.300	.440	R	R	6-1	200	9-23-69	1991	Redmond, Wash.
Connors, Greg	.259	7	27	7	7	2	0	0	6	4	2	0	0	.333	.355	R	R	6-2	180	8-22-74	1996	Smithtown, N.Y.
Craig, Casey	.331	35	142	27	47	11	2	1	21	13	27	10	2	.458	.385	L	R	6-1	185	1-12-85	2003	La Mesa, Calif.
Cruz, Elvis	.231	40	156	20	36	3	2	2	19	15	33	4	1	.314	.297	R	R	6-3	180	11-23-83	2001	Santo Domingo, D.R.
Denny, John	.417	3	12	3	5	2	1	0	2	2	0	0	2	.750	.500	L	R	6-3	210	2-14-80	2002	Tucson, Ariz.
Hern, Craig	.222	3	9	1	2	0	0	0	0	0	1	2	1	.222	.364	R	R	6-2	190	10-15-79	2002	Bindloss, Alberta
Hymon, James	.153	38	118	17	18	1	2	0	8	20	52	8	2	.195	.287	R	R	6-0	170	4-22-80	2003	Chicago, Ill.
Jones, Adamq	.284	28	109	18	31	5	1	0	8	5	19	5	1	.349	.368	R	R	6-2	180	8-1-85	2003	San Diego, Calif.
Metheny, Brenton	.379	24	95	21	36	7	5	2	22	16	16	7	3	.621	.465	L	R	6-0	205	10-3-80	2003	Old Fields, W.Va.
Ozoria, Pedro	.262	39	141	17	37	7	2	1	12	14	34	1	2	.362	.338	R	R	6-3	160	2-22-84	2002	San Pedro de Macoris, D.R.
Quintero, Cesar	.323	28	96	16	31	6	1	1	16	7	23	1	1	.438	.377	R	R	6-1	200	11-16-82	2001	Monagrillo, Panama
Rogelstad, Matt	.393	15	61	11	24	4	1	0	11	1	5	1	0	.492	.403	L	R	6-3	185	9-13-82	2003	Hammond, La.
Sandel, George	.263	50	205	36	54	11	1	0	20	34	27	14	5	.327	.369	L	R	5-10	175	12-4-80	2003	Palm Beach, Fla.
Schweiger, Brian	.287	42	129	21	37	9	1	1	15	18	24	0	0	.395	.377	R	R	6-0	195	8-21-82	2003	Rialto, Calif.
Soto, Luis	.305	32	118	22	36	6	1	3	24	7	18	1	1	.449	.368	R	R	6-0	190	7-30-83	2001	Peravia, D.R.
Strong, Jamal	.714	2	7	5	5	0	1	0	4	3	1	3	0	1.000	.692	R	R	5-10	180	8-5-78	2000	Altadena, Calif.
Udy, Nicholas	1.000	1	2	2	2	0	0	0	0	1	0	1	0	1.000	1.000	L	R	6-0	205	3-12-79	2003	Brigham City, Utah
Ware, Matt	.533	5	15	5	8	0	1	0	2	1	1	2	0	.667	.563	R	R	6-3	200	12-2-82	2002	Malibu, Calif.
Wilson, Michael	.311	48	177	33	55	9	3	3	25	20	46	6	6	.446	.391	S	R	6-2	240	6-29-83	2001	Tulsa, Okla.
Wu, Chao	.279	29	86	12	24	3	2	1	11	5	18	1	0	.395	.326	L	R	6-3	180	5-25-84	2003	Kaohsiung City, Taiwan

GAMES BY POSITION: C—Christianson 4, Connors 1, Quintero 16, Schweiger 32, Soto 6, Udy 1, Wu 17. **1B**—Connors 2, Cruz 5, Denny 2, Metheny 6, Quintero 6, Schweiger 8, Soto 24, Wu 5. **2B**—Craig 3, Hymon 5, Metheny 7, Rogelstad 2, Sandel 42. **3B**—Cirillo 2, Connors 1, Hern 2, Hymon 9, Metheny 7, Ozoria 36. **SS**—Hern 1, Hymon 12, Jones 27, Rogelstad 12, Sandel 5. **OF**—Balentien 44, Bradford 4, Connors 1, Craig 24, Cruz 31, Hrynio 1, Hymon 18, Ozoria 1, Strong 2, Ware 5, Wilson 45.

PITCHING	W	L	ERA	G	GS	CG	SV	IP	H	R	ER	BB	SO	AVG	B	T	HT	WT	DOB	1st Yr	Resides
Bello, Cibney	1	1	6.56	11	5	0	0	36	42	27	26	19	27	.300	L	R	6-5	180	9-10-82	2000	Vargas, Venez.
Bergdall, Kendall	3	4	5.87	9	8	0	0	31	40	25	20	20	27	.314	R	L	6-3	190	11-26-82	2002	Lahoma, Okla.
Bernat, David	1	2	9.89	14	0	0	0	24	35	28	26	12	17	.343	R	R	6-3	180	2-17-84	2002	Miami, Fla.
Cuevas, Alvin	0	0	4.50	1	0	0	0	2	3	1	1	0	1	.375	R	R	6-1	200	9-24-80	1999	Santo Domingo, D.R.
Dorn, Tim	0	0	9.00	6	1	0	0	11	17	11	11	6	8	.377	R	R	6-8	245	12-30-82	2003	Monrovia, Calif.
Fagan, Paul	1	2	4.36	9	7	0	0	33	40	22	16	6	24	.289	L	L	6-5	195	4-13-85	2003	Jacksonville, Fla.
Falconer, Kenny	1	1	8.64	7	0	0	0	8	8	8	8	11	4	.275	L	R	6-6	203	9-27-82	2003	Lethbridge, Alberta
Feierabend, Ryan	2	3	2.61	6	5	0	1	21	23	11	6	6	12	.287	L	L	6-3	190	8-22-85	2003	Grafton, Ohio
Flores, Ruben	2	2	3.73	9	7	0	0	31	28	18	13	12	26	.233	R	R	6-4	165	5-19-84	2003	El Paso, Texas
Forbes, Terry	4	0	5.18	11	6	0	0	40	42	29	23	14	20	.260	L	R	6-3	200	6-27-84	2002	Dartmouth, N.S.
Hall, Vance	2	2	4.89	9	9	0	0	46	42	26	25	20	31	.248	L	L	6-2	210	11-24-83	2002	Pittsburgh, Pa.
Hrynio, Mike	2	3	4.07	14	0	0	0	24	31	20	11	9	20	.310	R	R	6-2	190	11-18-82	2001	Mine Hill, N.J.
James, Craig	2	0	3.81	14	0	0	2	26	28	12	11	4	19	.277	R	R	6-1	170	3-10-83	2001	Miami, Fla.
Leaist, Ryan	1	1	5.14	11	0	0	0	14	12	12	8	12	19	.222	L	R	6-3	200	5-22-82	2003	Hamilton, Ontario
Martinez, Roman	0	1	6.86	12	0	0	0	21	34	20	16	12	24	.357	R	R	6-3	160	8-9-84	2001	Puerto Plata, D.R.
Morrow, David	1	2	2.19	8	4	0	0	25	18	8	6	16	19	.202	R	R	6-1	200	6-28-81	2002	Sherman, Texas
Nottingham, Shawn	1	0	3.72	12	0	0	0	19	17	10	8	8	17	.226	L	L	6-1	190	1-22-85	2003	Massillon, Ohio
O'Flaherty, Eric	3	0	1.95	13	1	0	0	28	17	10	6	7	20	.173	L	L	6-2	195	2-5-85	2003	Walla Walla, Wash.
Perry, Brandon	1	0	2.55	17	0	0	8	18	15	8	5	4	24	.217	L	L	6-1	180	9-27-84	2002	Graham, N.C.
Sundstrom, Matt	0	0	9.00	1	0	0	0	1	1	1	1	3	1	.250	R	R	6-3	160	6-7-84	2002	Sydney, Australia
Tucker, Cordoza	1	1	5.50	12	1	0	1	18	20	16	11	7	11	.281	R	R	6-2	180	11-11-84	2003	Fresno, Calif.
Wang, Chao	0	0	0.00	1	0	0	0	2	3	0	0	0	1	.375	R	R	6-4	160	3-25-83	2001	Beijing, China
Woerman, Joe	1	0	5.06	7	1	0	0	11	14	6	6	5	9	.333	R	R	6-3	200	12-12-82	2003	Coronado, Calif.

TAMPA BAY DEVIL RAYS

The Devil Rays won eight more games in 2003 than the year before, but the feeling in the organization was that it was a much more successful season.

In Lou Piniella's first year on the job, the 99 losses and sixth straight last-place finish were overshadowed by the emergence of a core of talented young players and a new commitment from ownership.

The Rays decided to use 2003 to evaluate as many young players as they could, allowing Piniella and his staff a chance to figure out what they had and what they need. They looked at 51 players, including 24 pitchers.

With a plan to spend $10 million to $15 million to bring in more veterans, Piniella expects the Rays to improve to the .500 range in 2004 and compete for a playoff spot in 2005.

Part of the reason for their optimism is the number of close games the Rays played in 2003. A major league-high 90 were decided by one or two runs (the Rays were 39-51), including an American League-high 51 one-run games (23-28), 29 games decided in the ninth inning or later (16-13) and 19 games decided on the final pitch (10-9).

Among the young players, the biggest to emerge was Aubrey Huff, who in his first full big league season blossomed into an offensive standout. He batted .311-34-107 to join Vernon Wells, Albert Pujols and Gary Sheffield as the only major leaguers to rank in their league's top 10 in the triple crown categories.

Second-year left fielder Carl Crawford won the AL stolen-base title with 55 and improved so much in the second half that Piniella said he could someday win a batting title and a Gold Glove. Rookie center fielder Rocco Baldelli, who spent most of 2002 at Class A, turned out to be more than ready for the big leagues, combining speed, athleticism and ability in all facets of the game to be a strong candidate for the AL rookie of the year award.

Crawford, Baldelli and Huff had the most hits (559) of any outfield trio in the majors.

Pitchers who took advantage of their opportunity include Doug Waechter, Chad Gaudin and Seth McClung (who should be back in May after Tommy John surgery).

The Rays will need more power, as Huff was the only Devil Ray to hit more than 17 homers. Damian Rolls, who may end up starting at third, hit only seven. Catcher Toby Hall has power potential but hit only 12.

Jeremi Gonzalez returned to the majors after a five-year injury odyssey to lead the rotation, but the Rays could use more pitching help. They were the first team since the 1981 Blue Jays to lead the AL in walks, hit batters and wild pitches.

Righthander Lance Carter, a 28-year-old rookie, quietly had a strong season, representing the Rays in the All-Star Game and finishing with 26 saves and seven wins.

Triple-A Durham won a second consecutive International League championship, a tribute to manager Bill Evers as much as anything given the hefty amount of roster turnover he had to deal with.

Most of the organization's advanced prospects made it to the majors in 2003. Those who could make it sometime in 2004 include outfielder Joey Gathright, who probably would have been a September callup if he didn't dislocate his left shoulder; shortstop B.J. Upton, the team's top pick in the 2002 draft; and reliever Evan Rust.

The Double-A team left Orlando and will play in a new stadium in Montgomery, Ala., in 2004.

Aubrey Huff

RICK BATTLE

B.J. Upton

PLAYERS of the YEAR

MAJOR LEAGUE: Aubrey Huff, of

Huff might be the new Brian Giles, one of the best-kept offensive secrets in the game. He played in all 162 games for the Devil Rays in 2003, ranking second in the American League in extra-base hits, and among the league's top 10 in seven other offensive categories.

MINOR LEAGUE: B.J. Upton, ss

The No. 2 pick in the 2002 draft, Upton hit .297-8-62 with 40 steals overall in his first full season, split between Class A Charleston and Double-A Orlando. He also walked 73 times, compiling a .379 on-base percentage.

ORGANIZATION LEADERS

BATTING

*AVG	Matt Diaz, Durham/Orlando	.391
R	John-Paul Davis, Orlando/Charleston, S.C.	86
H	Matt Diaz, Durham/Orlando	170
TB	Matt Diaz, Durham/Orlando	254
2B	Ryan Jackson, Durham	45
3B	Jason Smith, Durham	14
HR	Vince Harrison, Charleston, S.C.	19
RBI	Matt Diaz, Durham/Orlando	86
BB	B.J. Upton, Orlando/Charleston, S.C.	73
SO	Jonny Gomes, Durham/Orlando	153
SB	Joey Gathright, Orlando/Bakersfield	69
*SLG	Pete LaForest, Durham/Orlando	.546
*OBP	Matt Diaz, Durham/Orlando	.419

PITCHING

W	Scott Autrey, Orlando/Charleston, S.C.	14
L	Jason Cromer, Orlando/Charleston, S.C.	14
#ERA	Chad Gaudin, Orlando/Bakersfield	1.81
G	Lee Gardner, Durham	57
	Carlos Hines, Orlando/Bakersfield/Charleston, S.C.	57
CG	Five tied at	2
SV	Lee Gardner, Durham	30
IP	Scott Autrey, Orlando/Charleston, S.C.	171
BB	Jim Magrane, Durham/Orlando	55
SO	Jose Veras, Durham/Orlando	121

*Minimum 250 At-Bats #Minimum 75 Innings

TAMPA BAY DEVIL RAYS

Manager: Lou Piniella.

2003 Record: 63-99, .389 (5th, AL East).

BATTING	AVG	G	AB	R	H	2B	3B	HR	RBI	BB	SO	SB	CS	SLG	OBP	B	T	HT	WT	DOB	1st Yr	Resides
Abernathy, Brent	.000	2	7	1	0	0	0	0	0	0	0	1	0	.000	.000	R	R	6-0	190	9-23-77	1996	Marietta, Ga.
Anderson, Marlon	.270	145	482	59	130	27	3	6	67	41	60	19	3	.376	.328	L	R	5-11	200	1-6-74	1995	Vorhees, N.J.
Baldelli, Rocco	.289	156	637	89	184	32	8	11	78	30	128	27	10	.416	.326	R	R	6-4	190	9-25-81	2000	Cumberland, R.I.
Crawford, Carl	.281	151	630	80	177	18	9	5	54	26	102	55	10	.362	.309	L	L	6-2	210	8-5-81	1999	Houston, Texas
Diaz, Matt	.111	4	9	2	1	0	0	0	0	1	3	0	0	.111	.200	R	R	6-1	200	3-3-78	1999	Winter Haven, Fla.
Easley, Damion	.187	36	107	8	20	3	1	1	7	2	18	0	0	.262	.202	R	R	5-11	180	11-11-69	1988	Glendale, Ariz.
Gomes, Jonny	.133	8	15	1	2	1	0	0	0	0	6	0	0	.200	.188	R	R	6-1	200	11-22-80	2001	Petaluma, Calif.
Grieve, Ben	.230	55	165	28	38	7	0	4	17	32	41	0	0	.345	.371	L	R	6-4	210	5-4-76	1994	Flower Mound, Texas
Hall, Toby	.253	130	463	50	117	23	0	12	47	23	40	0	1	.380	.295	R	R	6-3	240	10-21-75	1997	Tampa, Fla.
Huff, Aubrey	.311	162	636	91	198	47	3	34	107	53	80	2	3	.555	.367	L	R	6-4	230	12-20-76	1998	Gulfport, Fla.
LaForest, Pete	.167	19	48	0	8	2	0	0	6	1	14	0	0	.208	.196	L	R	6-2	200	1-27-78	1995	Montebello, Quebec
Lee, Travis	.275	145	542	75	149	37	3	19	70	64	97	6	2	.459	.348	L	L	6-3	220	5-26-75	1997	Henderson, Nevada
Liefer, Jeff	.120	9	25	4	3	1	0	1	3	3	13	0	0	.280	.214	L	R	6-3	210	8-17-74	1996	Costa Mesa, Calif.
Lombard, George	.216	13	37	8	8	1	0	1	4	0	6	1	0	.324	.237	L	R	6-0	210	9-14-75	1994	Atlanta, Ga.
Lugo, Julio	.275	117	433	58	119	13	4	15	53	35	88	10	3	.427	.333	R	R	6-1	170	11-16-75	1995	Brooklyn, N.Y.
Martin, Al	.252	100	238	19	60	12	2	3	26	17	51	2	2	.357	.306	L	L	6-2	210	11-24-67	1985	Scottsdale, Ariz.
Ordonez, Rey	.316	34	117	14	37	11	0	3	22	2	12	0	2	.487	.328	R	R	5-9	150	1-11-71	1993	Parkland, Fla.
Perez, Antonio	.248	48	125	19	31	6	1	2	12	18	34	4	1	.360	.345	R	R	5-11	170	1-26-80	1998	Bani, D.R.
Piatt, Adam	.188	14	32	5	6	3	0	2	3	3	16	0	0	.469	.250	R	R	6-2	205	2-8-76	1997	Missouri City, Texas
2-team (47 Oakland)	.227	61	132	11	30	13	0	6	18	9	46	1	2	.462	.273							
Rolls, Damian	.255	107	373	43	95	20	0	7	46	19	84	11	3	.365	.301	R	R	6-2	210	9-15-77	1996	Tampa, Fla.
Sandberg, Jared	.213	55	136	15	29	10	1	6	23	16	52	0	0	.434	.305	R	R	6-3	210	3-2-78	1996	Seattle, Wash.
Shumpert, Terry	.190	59	84	14	16	5	2	2	7	10	17	1	0	.369	.289	R	R	6-0	200	8-16-66	1987	Lone Tree, Colo.
Smith, Jason	.250	1	4	0	1	0	0	0	0	0	0	0	0	.250	.250	L	R	6-3	190	7-24-77	1997	Coatopa, Ala.
Truby, Chris	.279	13	43	4	12	3	0	0	3	5	13	0	0	.349	.354	R	R	6-2	210	12-9-73	1993	Noblesville, Ind.
Tyner, Jason	.278	46	90	12	25	7	0	0	6	10	12	2	1	.356	.350	L	L	6-1	160	4-23-77	1998	Beaumont, Texas
Valentin, Javier	.222	49	135	13	30	7	1	3	15	5	31	0	0	.356	.254	S	R	5-10	190	9-19-75	1993	Manati, P.R.

PITCHING	W	L	ERA	G	GS	CG	SV	IP	H	R	ER	BB	SO	AVG	B	T	HT	WT	DOB	1st Yr	Resides
Backe, Brandon	1	1	5.44	28	0	0	0	45	40	28	27	25	36	.246	R	R	6-0	180	4-5-78	1998	Texas City, Texas
Bell, Rob	5	4	5.52	19	18	0	0	101	103	64	62	39	44	.262	R	R	6-5	220	1-17-77	1995	Marlboro, N.Y.
Bierbrodt, Nick	0	2	9.68	13	5	0	0	35	59	41	38	23	20	.375	L	L	6-5	210	5-16-78	1996	Tierra Verde, Fla.
Brazelton, Dewon	1	6	6.89	10	10	0	0	48	57	49	37	23	24	.292	R	R	6-4	210	6-16-80	2002	Tullahoma, Tenn.
Carter, Lance	7	5	4.33	62	0	0	26	79	72	39	38	19	47	.241	R	R	6-1	190	12-18-74	1994	Bradenton, Fla.
Colome, Jesus	3	7	4.50	54	0	0	2	74	69	37	37	46	69	.247	R	R	6-2	200	12-23-77	1996	San Pedro de Macoris, D.R.
Gaudin, Chad	2	0	3.60	15	3	0	0	40	37	18	16	16	23	.240	R	R	5-10	160	3-24-83	2002	Harahan, La.
Gonzalez, Jeremi	6	11	3.91	25	25	2	0	156	131	71	68	69	97	.227	R	R	6-0	220	1-8-75	1992	Maracaibo, Venez.
Harper, Travis	4	8	3.77	61	0	0	1	93	86	45	39	31	64	.252	L	R	6-4	190	5-21-76	1997	Riverton, W.Va.
Kennedy, Joe	3	12	6.13	32	22	1	1	134	167	101	91	47	77	.302	R	L	6-4	230	5-24-79	1998	Indian Shores, Fla.
Levine, Alan	3	5	2.90	36	0	0	0	50	45	23	16	18	25	.243	L	R	6-3	190	5-22-68	1991	Gilbert, Ariz.
Malaska, Mark	2	1	2.81	22	0	0	0	16	13	7	5	12	17	.232	L	L	6-3	190	1-17-78	2000	Youngstown, Ohio
McClung, Seth	4	1	5.35	12	5	0	0	39	33	23	23	25	25	.240	R	R	6-6	230	2-7-81	1999	Lewisburg, W.Va.
Parque, Jim	1	1	11.94	5	5	0	0	17	27	23	23	16	8	.350	L	L	5-11	170	2-8-76	1997	Puyallup, Wash.
Parris, Steve	0	3	6.18	10	7	0	0	44	60	32	30	13	14	.327	R	R	6-0	190	12-17-67	1989	Plainfield, Ill.
Reyes, Carlos	0	3	5.22	10	3	0	0	40	40	23	23	5	13	.264	S	R	6-0	190	4-4-69	1991	Tampa, Fla.
Rocker, John	0	0	9.00	2	0	0	0	1	2	1	1	3	0	.500	R	L	6-4	220	10-17-74	1994	Macon, Ga.
Seay, Bobby	0	0	3.00	12	0	0	0	9	7	3	3	6	5	.225	L	L	6-2	230	6-20-78	1996	West Gulfport, Miss.
Sosa, Jorge	5	12	4.62	29	19	1	0	129	137	71	66	60	72	.277	S	R	6-2	170	4-28-77	1995	San Jose, D.R.
Standridge, Jason	0	5	6.37	8	7	1	0	35	38	25	25	16	20	.275	R	R	6-4	230	11-9-78	1997	Pinson, Ala.
Switzer, Jon	0	0	7.45	5	0	0	0	10	13	8	8	3	7	.342	L	L	6-3	190	8-13-79	2001	Houston, Texas
Venafro, Mike	1	0	4.74	24	0	0	0	19	24	10	10	3	9	.307	L	L	5-10	180	8-2-73	1995	Fort Myers, Fla.
Waechter, Doug	3	2	3.31	6	5	1	0	35	29	13	13	15	29	.224	R	R	6-4	200	1-28-81	1999	St. Petersburg, Fla.
Zambrano, Victor	12	10	4.21	34	28	1	0	188	165	97	88	106	132	.236	R	R	6-0	200	8-6-75	1994	Valencia, Venez.

FIELDING

Catcher	PCT	G	PO	A	E	DP	PB
Hall	.988	130	685	60	9	10	7
LaForest	1.000	4	16	1	0	0	1
Valentin	1.000	42	212	13	0	1	1

First Base	PCT	G	PO	A	E	DP
Huff	1.000	22	166	12	0	23
Lee	.998	142	1223	100	3	117
Martin	1.000	1	2	0	0	0
Piatt	1.000	1	6	0	0	1
Sandberg	1.000	1	7	0	0	0

Second Base	PCT	G	PO	A	E	DP
Abernathy	.900	2	1	8	1	0
Anderson	.973	134	194	350	15	91
Easley	1.000	4	4	7	0	1
Perez	.990	31	35	65	1	11
Rolls	.000	2	0	0	0	0
Shumpert	.978	14	21	24	1	3

Third Base	PCT	G	PO	A	E	DP
Easley	.922	23	12	35	4	2
Huff	.833	8	7	8	3	2
Liefer	.929	6	5	8	1	0
Perez	.889	6	1	7	1	0
Rolls	.972	73	75	135	6	16
Sandberg	.956	50	34	75	5	4
Shumpert	1.000	11	1	1	0	0
Smith	.500	1	0	2	2	1
Truby	.976	13	9	32	1	4

Shortstop	PCT	G	PO	A	E	DP
Lugo	.970	117	211	336	17	75
Ordonez	.970	34	61	102	5	31
Perez	1.000	6	13	13	0	2
Sandberg	1.000	1	1	1	0	0
Shumpert	1.000	1	0	3	0	0

Outfield	PCT	G	PO	A	E	DP
Anderson	1.000	3	4	0	0	0
Baldelli	.989	154	437	14	5	4
Crawford	.992	146	352	10	3	1
Diaz	.857	1	6	0	1	0
Grieve	.947	10	17	1	1	1
Huff	.970	102	190	5	6	1
Liefer	1.000	1	2	0	0	0
Lombard	.964	13	26	1	1	0
Martin	1.000	13	23	0	0	0
Piatt	1.000	7	7	0	0	0
Rolls	.984	37	63	0	1	0
Shumpert	.944	14	17	0	1	0
Tyner	.962	32	49	1	2	1

FARM SYSTEM

Director, Player Personnel: Cam Bonifay.

Class	Farm Team	League	W	L	Pct.	Finish*	Manager	First Yr.
AAA	Durham (N.C.) Bulls	International	73	67	.521	+5th (14)	Bill Evers	1998
AA	Orlando (Fla.) Rays	Southern	65	72	.474	7th (10)	Charlie Montoyo	1999
High A	Bakersfield (Calif.) Blaze	California	70	70	.500	8th (10)	Omer Munoz	2001
Low A	Charleston (S.C.) RiverDogs	South Atlantic	77	62	.554	4th (16)	Mako Oliveras	1997
SS A	Hudson Valley (N.Y.) Renegades	New York-Penn	37	37	.500	t-8th (14)	David Howard	1996
Rookie	Princeton (W.Va.) Devil Rays	Appalachian	23	41	.359	10th (10)	Jamie Nelson	1997

*Finish in overall standings (No. of teams in league) + League champion

DURHAM BULLS — Class AAA

INTERNATIONAL LEAGUE

BATTING	AVG	G	AB	R	H	2B	3B	HR	RBI	BB	SO	SB	CS	SLG	OBP	B	T	HT	WT	DOB	1st Yr	Resides
Abernathy, Brent	.600	1	5	0	3	0	0	0	1	0	0	0	0	.600	.600	R	R	6-0	190	9-23-77	1996	Marietta, Ga.
Badeaux, Brooks	.224	73	245	27	55	13	0	1	13	17	46	0	2	.290	.283	S	R	5-10	170	10-20-76	1998	Scott, La.
Canizaro, Jay	.239	26	92	13	22	7	0	4	13	9	19	2	0	.446	.301	R	R	5-9	190	7-4-73	1993	Spring, Texas
Cantu, Jorge	.295	60	200	26	59	16	1	4	30	8	21	2	1	.445	.319	R	R	6-1	170	1-30-82	1998	Mission, Mexico
Diaz, Matt	.328	67	253	35	83	18	3	8	45	16	45	6	2	.518	.382	R	R	6-1	200	3-3-78	1999	Winter Haven, Fla.
Fabregas, Jorge	.300	42	140	13	42	7	0	2	18	10	10	1	0	.393	.344	L	R	6-3	220	3-13-70	1991	Miami Beach, Fla.
Gomes, Jonny	.316	5	19	2	6	2	1	0	1	2	5	0	0	.526	.435	R	R	6-1	200	11-22-80	2001	Petaluma, Calif.
Greene, Charlie	.077	6	13	2	1	0	0	0	0	2	4	0	0	.077	.250	R	R	6-2	170	1-23-71	1991	Miami, Fla.
Grummitt, Dan	.239	15	46	3	11	3	0	1	5	2	16	0	0	.370	.300	R	R	6-5	230	6-16-76	1998	Twinsburg, Ohio
Jackson, Ryan	.303	131	519	78	157	45	4	13	71	30	85	2	4	.480	.339	L	L	6-2	200	11-15-71	1994	Sarasota, Fla.
LaForest, Pete	.269	61	201	40	54	14	2	14	38	36	56	2	1	.567	.382	L	R	6-2	200	1-27-78	1995	Montebello, Quebec
Liefer, Jeff	.261	44	157	20	41	10	3	7	24	14	49	0	0	.497	.326	L	R	6-3	210	8-17-74	1996	Costa Mesa, Calif.
Lombard, George	.267	112	438	57	117	25	4	17	64	45	143	23	6	.459	.342	L	R	6-0	210	9-14-75	1994	Atlanta, Ga.
Martinez, Gabby	.295	12	44	5	13	2	0	1	2	1	6	2	2	.409	.311	R	R	6-2	190	1-7-74	1992	Santurce, P.R.
Moore, Frank	.105	13	38	0	4	0	0	0	2	2	11	0	0	.105	.150	L	R	6-2	200	7-2-78	1998	Douglas, Ga.
Mottola, Chad	.258	56	213	24	55	7	1	6	28	19	37	6	3	.385	.319	R	R	6-3	220	10-15-71	1992	Casselberry, Fla.
Neuberger, Scott	.268	62	205	29	55	12	0	5	20	19	42	0	4	.400	.341	R	R	6-3	210	8-14-77	1997	Tallahassee, Fla.
Ortiz, Hector	.244	68	221	26	54	14	0	0	25	20	23	0	1	.308	.310	R	R	6-0	200	10-14-69	1988	Canovanas, P.R.
Perez, Antonio	.284	34	134	27	38	12	2	6	20	10	38	3	1	.537	.345	R	R	5-11	170	1-26-80	1998	Bani, D.R.
Quinn, Mark	.167	15	60	7	10	3	1	0	3	3	17	0	0	.250	.206	R	R	6-1	190	5-21-74	1995	West Covina, Calif.
Rolls, Damian	.247	18	77	11	19	4	1	0	9	4	15	4	2	.325	.284	R	R	6-2	210	9-15-77	1996	Tampa, Fla.
Sandberg, Jared	.232	74	272	40	63	17	1	12	37	30	95	1	0	.434	.313	R	R	6-3	210	3-2-78	1996	Seattle, Wash.
Smith, Jason	.285	130	515	76	147	20	14	15	71	11	128	14	9	.466	.304	L	R	6-3	190	7-24-77	1997	Coatopa, Ala.
Thompson, Ryan	.125	2	8	0	1	0	0	0	0	0	3	0	0	.125	.125	R	R	6-3	210	11-4-67	1987	Edesville, Md.
Truby, Chris	.263	112	430	57	113	27	0	16	48	44	77	4	6	.437	.339	R	R	6-2	210	12-9-73	1993	Noblesville, Ind.
Tyner, Jason	.324	65	275	34	89	11	5	0	24	22	25	10	7	.400	.372	L	L	6-1	160	4-23-77	1998	Beaumont, Texas

PITCHING	W	L	ERA	G	GS	CG	SV	IP	H	R	ER	BB	SO	AVG	B	T	HT	WT	DOB	1st Yr	Resides
Backe, Brandon	2	1	4.64	16	2	0	0	33	33	21	17	13	27	.250	R	R	6-0	180	4-5-78	1998	Texas City, Texas
Belitz, Todd	2	1	3.38	24	1	0	0	32	27	14	12	7	25	.236	L	L	6-3	200	10-23-75	1997	Spokane, Wash.
Bell, Rob	6	4	4.02	12	12	0	0	72	72	33	32	15	48	.259	R	R	6-5	220	1-17-77	1995	Marlboro, N.Y.
Bowers, Cedrick	4	3	4.41	32	8	0	2	84	75	46	41	39	80	.244	R	L	6-2	220	2-10-78	1996	Chiefland, Fla.
Brazelton, Dewon	2	2	4.21	5	5	0	0	26	23	14	12	11	18	.234	R	R	6-4	210	6-16-80	2002	Tullahoma, Tenn.
De Los Santos, Luis	1	3	5.57	4	4	0	0	21	28	15	13	1	3	.329	R	R	6-2	210	11-1-77	1995	San Pedro de Macoris, D.R.
Fortunato, Bartolome	1	2	3.32	5	4	0	0	22	15	11	8	11	20	.192	R	R	6-1	170	8-24-74	1996	Santo Domingo, D.R.
Garcia, Gerardo	2	2	4.13	6	6	0	0	28	28	15	13	10	15	.252	R	R	6-0	160	2-13-80	1998	San Nicolas, Mexico
Gardner, Lee	3	7	3.73	57	0	0	30	63	68	29	26	14	56	.273	R	R	6-0	210	1-16-75	1998	Hartland, Mich.
Gonzalez, Jeremi	1	0	2.53	7	6	0	0	32	24	11	9	6	33	.201	R	R	6-0	220	1-8-75	1992	Maracaibo, Venez.
Haines, Talley	5	3	2.53	50	0	0	2	68	57	19	19	11	64	.227	R	R	6-5	200	11-16-76	1998	Jackson, Mo.
James, Delvin	5	10	5.23	34	21	0	0	138	172	91	80	36	65	.307	R	R	6-4	240	1-3-78	1996	Nacogdoches, Texas
Kennedy, Joe	1	0	1.42	1	1	0	0	6	6	1	1	0	4	.250	R	L	6-4	230	5-24-79	1998	Indian Shores, Fla.
Magrane, Jim	0	1	7.50	2	2	0	0	12	15	10	10	4	4	.312	R	R	6-2	200	7-23-78	1999	Ottumwa, Iowa
Malaska, Mark	1	1	4.30	15	0	0	0	23	24	12	11	8	22	.269	L	L	6-3	190	1-17-78	2000	Youngstown, Ohio
Parque, Jim	5	7	4.08	21	21	1	0	121	132	62	55	47	49	.285	L	L	5-11	170	2-8-76	1997	Puyallup, Wash.
Perisho, Matt	7	4	6.52	34	0	0	1	39	43	29	28	12	41	.275	L	L	6-0	200	6-8-75	1993	Chandler, Ariz.
Reyes, Carlos	10	3	2.86	22	21	1	0	132	124	47	42	14	78	.246	S	R	6-0	190	4-4-69	1991	Tampa, Fla.
Rust, Evan	2	2	3.25	26	0	0	1	36	32	13	13	10	26	.244	R	R	6-1	200	5-4-78	2000	Ben Lomond, Calif.
Seay, Bobby	3	0	2.10	25	0	0	0	30	23	10	7	15	29	.205	L	L	6-2	230	6-20-78	1996	West Gulfport, Miss.
Sosa, Jorge	1	1	5.47	4	4	0	0	25	32	15	15	9	17	.313	S	R	6-2	170	4-28-77	1995	San Jose, D.R.
Standridge, Jason	2	4	4.50	12	10	0	1	60	62	32	30	28	37	.269	R	R	6-4	230	11-9-78	1997	Pinson, Ala.
Switzer, Jon	1	0	1.80	1	1	0	0	5	6	1	1	0	3	.315	L	L	6-3	190	8-13-79	2001	Houston, Texas
Veras, Jose	0	0	8.44	3	0	0	0	5	9	5	5	1	3	.360	R	R	6-5	230	10-20-80	1998	Santo Domingo, D.R.
Waechter, Doug	3	3	3.33	10	10	0	0	51	51	25	19	12	35	.261	R	R	6-4	200	1-28-81	1999	St. Petersburg, Fla.
Williams, Todd	3	2	1.55	56	0	0	4	70	55	12	12	14	36	.214	R	R	6-3	210	2-13-71	1991	Land O'Lakes, Fla.
Zambrano, Victor	0	1	4.50	1	1	0	0	4	4	6	2	2	6	.222	R	R	6-0	200	8-6-75	1994	Valencia, Venez.

FIELDING

Catcher	PCT	G	PO	A	E	DP	PB
Fabregas	.987	33	202	18	3	0	2
Greene	1.000	5	25	0	0	0	0
LaForest	.990	50	272	19	3	5	6
Ortiz	.993	60	384	21	3	0	3

First Base	PCT	G	PO	A	E	DP
Fabregas	1.000	1	5	0	0	1
Grummitt	1.000	9	73	4	0	6
Jackson	.997	91	860	61	3	88
Liefer	1.000	4	34	3	0	2
Ortiz	.978	5	42	2	1	5
Sandberg	.959	8	62	9	3	3
Truby	.992	28	236	15	2	17

Second Base	PCT	G	PO	A	E	DP
Abernathy	.000	1	0	0	0	0
Badeaux	.977	57	114	189	7	52
Canizaro	.952	18	28	32	3	4
Martinez	1.000	2	0	3	0	0
Moore	1.000	5	8	7	0	0
Perez	.958	33	73	111	8	22

Third Base	PCT	G	PO	A	E	DP
Sandberg	1.000	5	3	12	0	2
Smith	.961	28	52	72	5	17

Third Base	PCT	G	PO	A	E	DP
Badeaux	.941	4	2	14	1	2
Cantu	1.000	2	0	5	0	1
Liefer	.667	1	2	0	1	0
Sandberg	.973	60	48	133	5	11
Smith	.960	10	4	20	1	2
Truby	.959	66	44	164	9	12

Shortstop	PCT	G	PO	A	E	DP
Badeaux	1.000	2	1	6	0	2
Canizaro	1.000	2	0	6	0	0
Cantu	.948	53	79	141	12	22
Martinez	1.000	2	0	7	0	1
Smith	.959	87	128	268	17	61

Outfield	PCT	G	PO	A	E	DP
Badeaux	1.000	1	1	0	0	0
Diaz	.993	64	131	8	1	2
Gomes	1.000	3	3	2	0	0
Jackson	.983	29	56	1	1	0
Liefer	1.000	26	43	3	0	0
Lombard	.989	108	246	13	3	2
Martinez	.941	7	16	0	1	0
Moore	1.000	6	12	1	0	0
Mottola	.988	40	76	3	1	0
Neuberger	.969	58	93	1	3	0
Quinn	1.000	8	15	0	0	0
Rolls	.913	14	21	0	2	0
Sandberg	1.000	1	2	0	0	0
Thompson	.500	1	1	0	1	0
Tyner	.993	64	147	5	1	1

ORLANDO RAYS — Class AA

SOUTHERN LEAGUE

BATTING	AVG	G	AB	R	H	2B	3B	HR	RBI	BB	SO	SB	CS	SLG	OBP	B	T	HT	WT	DOB	1st Yr	Resides
Badeaux, Brooks	.286	13	42	7	12	1	2	1	3	9	6	2	1	.476	.412	S	R	5-10	170	10-20-76	1998	Scott, La.
Barns, B.J.	.244	54	164	21	40	9	0	0	22	27	41	0	1	.299	.354	L	L	6-4	210	7-21-77	1999	Loysville, Penn.
Brewer, Jace	.221	86	281	25	62	17	1	4	19	12	60	1	1	.331	.251	R	R	6-0	170	6-6-79	2000	Norman, Okla.
Cantu, Jorge	.215	43	158	15	34	10	0	3	17	9	27	0	3	.335	.259	R	R	6-1	170	1-30-82	1998	Mission, Mexico
Cortez, Fernando	.316	30	114	15	36	3	1	1	6	3	22	1	2	.386	.333	L	R	6-1	170	8-10-81	2001	San Diego, Calif.
Davis, John-Paul	.245	34	110	21	27	9	0	1	17	15	28	0	0	.355	.359	R	R	6-4	220	12-20-78	2001	Russellville, Ark.
Deck, Ronnie	.143	3	7	0	1	0	0	0	0	0	4	0	0	.143	.143	R	R	6-2	220	10-24-77	1999	Fort Worth, Texas
DeMent, Dan	.255	96	349	41	89	22	1	3	34	39	62	2	2	.350	.331	R	R	5-10	170	6-17-78	2000	Birmingham, Ala.
Diaz, Matt	.383	60	227	32	87	21	0	5	41	19	24	9	5	.542	.444	R	R	6-1	200	3-3-78	1999	Winter Haven, Fla.
Escalona, Felix	.244	22	90	11	22	7	0	1	8	5	14	0	0	.356	.320	R	R	6-0	190	3-12-79	1996	Puerto Cabello, Venez.
Feliciano, Jesus	.279	72	251	31	70	11	0	1	21	15	25	7	1	.335	.326	L	L	5-11	150	6-6-79	1997	Bayamon, P.R.
2-team (37 Jacksonville)	.247	109	332	38	82	11	0	2	25	26	41	9	4	.298	.308							
Gathright, Joey	.376	22	85	12	32	1	0	0	5	5	15	12	3	.388	.419	L	R	5-10	170	4-22-82	2002	La Place, La.
German, Amado	.271	111	395	40	107	25	3	4	48	33	83	5	5	.380	.329	S	R	6-2	170	3-30-78	1997	San Pedro de Macoris, D.R.
Gomes, Jonny	.249	120	442	68	110	28	3	17	56	53	148	23	2	.441	.348	R	R	6-1	200	11-22-80	2001	Petaluma, Calif.
Grummitt, Dan	.248	93	303	33	75	18	1	11	51	30	95	1	2	.422	.354	R	R	6-5	230	6-16-76	1998	Twinsburg, Ohio
Isenia, Chairon	.218	46	142	13	31	5	0	0	11	8	11	0	0	.254	.279	R	R	5-11	210	1-23-79	1996	Willemstad, Curacao
Kelly, Heath	.267	14	45	7	12	1	0	2	8	2	15	0	0	.422	.298	R	R	6-1	180	2-16-76	1998	Pensacola, Fla.
LaForest, Pete	.250	21	72	9	18	8	0	3	15	16	17	0	0	.486	.385	L	R	6-2	200	1-27-78	1995	Montebello, Quebec
Martinez, Gabby	.361	25	108	16	39	5	0	2	7	5	9	6	0	.463	.389	R	R	6-2	190	1-7-74	1992	Santurce, P.R.
Massiatte, Danny	.213	58	169	18	36	7	0	2	14	16	37	0	1	.290	.282	R	R	5-11	180	7-25-78	2000	Houston, Texas
Merritt, Graig	.197	26	71	9	14	1	0	0	4	8	16	0	0	.211	.278	R	R	6-1	190	7-2-78	2001	Pitt Meadows, B.C.
Moore, Frank	.277	100	354	38	98	16	6	5	34	25	78	9	1	.398	.324	L	R	6-2	200	7-2-78	1998	Douglas, Ga.
Perez, Antonio	.272	24	81	16	22	5	1	2	10	18	18	3	1	.432	.423	R	R	5-11	170	1-26-80	1998	Bani, D.R.
Rico, Matt	.143	2	7	2	1	1	0	0	0	0	2	0	0	.286	.250	R	R	6-3	200	10-8-81	2001	Visalia, Calif.
Riggans, Shawn	.274	22	62	7	17	6	0	1	11	4	14	0	0	.419	.319	R	R	6-2	190	7-25-80	2001	Fort Lauderdale, Fla.
Salas, Juan	.272	75	279	30	76	8	2	3	41	10	43	1	2	.348	.297	R	R	6-2	190	11-7-78	1998	Santo Domingo, D.R.
Shumpert, Terry	.222	2	9	1	2	0	0	0	1	0	2	0	0	.222	.300	R	R	6-0	200	8-16-66	1987	Lone Tree, Colo.
Upton, B.J.	.276	29	105	14	29	8	0	1	16	16	25	2	4	.381	.376	R	R	6-3	170	8-21-84	2003	Chesapeake, Va.

PITCHING	W	L	ERA	G	GS	CG	SV	IP	H	R	ER	BB	SO	AVG	B	T	HT	WT	DOB	1st Yr	Resides
Andersen, Derek	2	1	4.29	22	0	0	0	21	22	12	10	3	13	.265	L	L	6-3	180	10-6-77	1999	Lynnwood, Wash.
Autrey, Scott	5	4	2.99	12	12	2	0	78	79	31	26	15	37	.257	R	R	6-2	210	1-26-81	2002	Arlington, Texas
Benedetti, John	5	5	3.72	42	1	0	3	65	69	28	27	25	51	.274	R	R	6-0	180	6-27-78	2000	Palatine, Ill.
Brazelton, Dewon	2	0	2.53	2	2	0	0	11	8	6	3	8	5	.200	R	R	6-4	210	6-16-80	2002	Tullahoma, Tenn.
Campbell, Jarrett	0	1	7.71	4	0	0	0	5	6	4	4	3	2	.285	R	R	6-2	190	9-6-79	1998	Corpus Christi, Texas
Coose, Austin	0	0	1.80	3	0	0	0	5	2	1	1	1	4	.117	R	R	6-2	230	1-27-79	2001	Kokomo, Ind.
Cromer, Jason	1	5	5.71	6	6	0	0	35	39	27	22	14	16	.280	R	L	6-4	220	12-11-80	1999	Des Moines, Iowa
Flinn, Chris	1	2	2.57	7	4	0	0	21	15	11	6	6	16	.194	R	R	6-2	180	8-18-80	2001	Levittown, N.Y.
Fortunato, Bartolome	4	2	3.06	35	1	0	1	53	48	25	18	20	63	.242	R	R	6-1	170	8-24-74	1996	Santo Domingo, D.R.
Garcia, Gerardo	0	0	3.00	4	3	0	0	12	13	4	4	3	8	.265	R	R	6-0	160	2-13-80	1998	San Nicolas, Mexico
Gaudin, Chad	2	0	0.47	3	3	1	0	19	8	1	1	3	23	.131	R	R	5-10	160	3-24-83	2002	Harahan, La.
Guillory, Dan	2	2	3.92	23	0	0	0	41	39	21	18	18	30	.251	R	R	6-3	200	5-12-76	1998	Baton Rouge, La.
Hines, Carlos	0	1	9.00	2	0	0	0	3	5	3	3	1	2	.416	R	R	6-3	190	9-26-80	1999	Selma, N.C.
Kennedy, Joe	0	0	8.10	1	1	0	0	3	6	3	3	1	3	.400	R	L	6-4	230	5-24-79	1998	Indian Shores, Fla.
Magrane, Jim	10	6	3.26	25	24	0	0	144	147	69	52	51	87	.260	R	R	6-2	200	7-23-78	1999	Ottumwa, Iowa
Malaska, Mark	1	1	2.16	19	0	0	1	25	21	6	6	4	22	.235	L	L	6-3	190	1-17-78	2000	Youngstown, Ohio
Minix, Travis	5	3	3.86	44	6	0	0	79	86	40	34	14	70	.273	R	R	6-1	190	8-8-77	1999	Hamlet, Ind.
O'Connor, Brian	0	1	5.19	8	0	0	0	9	14	6	5	4	5	.350	L	L	6-2	200	1-4-77	1995	Franklin, Tenn.
Parker, Josh	0	3	3.10	24	0	0	12	29	29	13	10	7	19	.256	R	R	6-5	220	1-12-81	2001	Louisville, Ky.
Rocker, John	0	1	9.15	17	0	0	0	20	23	23	20	26	20	.294	R	L	6-4	220	10-17-74	1994	Macon, Ga.
Rust, Evan	1	3	2.65	30	0	0	11	34	28	13	10	15	35	.212	R	R	6-1	200	5-4-78	2000	Ben Lomond, Calif.
Santos, Alex	3	2	6.02	25	1	0	0	40	52	29	27	15	23	.319	R	R	6-1	200	8-9-77	1999	Lake Worth, Fla.
Stokes, Brian	2	5	3.20	10	10	0	0	51	55	26	18	13	33	.273	R	R	6-1	200	9-7-79	1999	River City, Calif.
Switzer, Jon	8	8	3.43	22	22	2	0	126	117	63	48	32	100	.245	L	L	6-3	190	8-13-79	2001	Houston, Texas
Veras, Jose	6	9	3.45	27	22	1	0	130	108	59	50	53	118	.222	R	R	6-5	230	10-20-80	1998	Santo Domingo, D.R.
Waechter, Doug	5	3	4.13	13	12	0	0	76	74	39	35	19	45	.256	R	R	6-4	200	1-28-81	1999	St. Petersburg, Fla.
White, Matt	0	4	7.47	7	7	0	0	31	40	34	26	23	18	.310	R	R	6-5	230	8-13-78	1996	Largo, Fla.

FIELDING

Catcher	PCT	G	PO	A	E	DP	PB
Deck	1.000	3	10	0	0	0	1
Isenia	.972	37	221	23	7	1	3
LaForest	.981	9	48	4	1	1	3
Massiatte	.990	56	346	50	4	2	7
Merritt	.981	23	145	14	3	2	5
Riggans	1.000	21	117	7	0	0	3

First Base	PCT	G	PO	A	E	DP
Brewer	1.000	6	48	1	0	5
Davis	.991	26	208	14	2	14
Grummitt	.994	81	625	47	4	52
Moore	.989	30	257	21	3	21

Second Base	PCT	G	PO	A	E	DP
Badeaux	1.000	2	7	3	0	1
Brewer	1.000	2	5	9	0	2
Cantu	1.000	2	3	4	0	0

	PCT	G	PO	A	E	DP
Cortez	.963	28	37	67	4	8
DeMent	.972	28	33	71	3	8
Escalona	.974	6	16	21	1	6
Martinez	.977	9	18	24	1	5
Moore	.972	40	83	92	5	22
Perez	.967	21	40	49	3	13
Shumpert	1.000	1	1	3	0	0

Third Base	PCT	G	PO	A	E	DP
Badeaux	.955	10	6	15	1	0
Brewer	.500	2	1	0	1	0
Cantu	.924	36	19	54	6	5
DeMent	.846	22	5	39	8	3
Escalona	.864	6	4	15	3	2
LaForest	.000	1	0	0	0	0
Moore	.667	3	1	1	1	0
Salas	.924	64	55	127	15	4

Shortstop	PCT	G	PO	A	E	DP
Badeaux	1.000	2	2	3	0	0
Brewer	.940	73	83	199	18	34
Cantu	1.000	5	7	7	0	1
Escalona	.848	9	11	28	7	5
Kelly	.882	14	15	30	6	9
Martinez	1.000	1	1	3	0	0
Moore	.906	14	26	32	6	4
Upton	.879	27	41	61	14	11

Outfield	PCT	G	PO	A	E	DP
Barns	1.000	28	50	0	0	0
DeMent	1.000	2	1	1	0	0
Diaz	.994	60	147	7	1	3
Feliciano	.980	71	143	3	3	2
Gathright	.983	18	56	2	1	0
German	.981	107	294	8	6	1
Gomes	.977	105	167	6	4	1
Martinez	1.000	7	9	0	0	0
Massiatte	.000	1	0	0	0	0
Moore	.947	14	18	0	1	0
Rico	1.000	2	3	0	0	0
Salas	1.000	11	15	1	0	0

BAKERSFIELD BLAZE — High Class A

CALIFORNIA LEAGUE

BATTING	AVG	G	AB	R	H	2B	3B	HR	RBI	BB	SO	SB	CS	SLG	OBP	B	T	HT	WT	DOB	1st Yr	Resides
Arhart, Josh	.255	88	286	43	73	15	1	4	28	26	70	1	3	.357	.330	R	R	6-1	220	9-13-79	2002	Garden Grove, Calif.
Bonner, Adam	.282	23	85	20	24	7	1	6	19	13	30	1	2	.600	.378	L	R	6-5	200	3-11-81	2000	Hueytown, Ala.
Centeno, Irwin	.234	71	218	28	51	6	0	0	12	16	61	9	2	.261	.304	R	R	6-2	170	6-1-81	1997	Maracay, Venez.
Clark, Aaron	.254	136	527	57	134	26	1	15	83	43	146	6	4	.393	.315	L	L	6-1	190	2-17-79	2001	Ennis, Texas
Cortez, Fernando	.281	102	384	53	108	19	0	1	53	41	61	32	9	.339	.346	L	R	6-1	170	8-10-81	2001	San Diego, Calif.
De Paula, Luis	.258	119	419	50	108	20	0	3	46	23	99	9	8	.327	.301	R	R	5-11	160	12-11-82	1999	Santo Domingo, D.R.
Deck, Ronnie	.222	5	9	1	2	0	0	0	0	1	2	1	0	.222	.300	R	R	6-2	220	10-24-77	1999	Fort Worth, Texas
Gathright, Joey	.324	89	340	65	110	6	3	0	23	41	54	57	13	.359	.406	L	R	5-10	170	4-22-82	2002	La Place, La.
Gomes, Joey	.269	105	401	67	108	26	2	9	55	41	88	2	4	.411	.350	R	R	6-2	210	11-2-79	2002	Petaluma, Calif.
Gonzalez, Edgar	.298	100	349	51	104	34	3	6	62	45	82	8	7	.464	.381	R	R	6-0	170	6-14-78	2000	Chula Vista, Calif.
Isenia, Chairon	.272	24	92	16	25	9	0	2	11	9	19	0	0	.435	.355	R	R	5-11	210	1-23-79	1996	Willemstad, Curacao
Kelly, Heath	.161	31	118	12	19	1	0	2	10	2	47	0	0	.220	.200	R	R	6-1	180	2-16-76	1998	Pensacola, Fla.
Maduro, Jorge	.222	11	36	3	8	1	0	1	2	0	10	0	0	.333	.222	R	R	6-2	200	3-11-81	1999	Miami, Fla.
Martin, Brian	.276	129	478	73	132	26	4	11	65	35	147	19	3	.416	.342	R	R	6-2	220	6-14-80	1998	El Centro, Calif.
Mateo, Luis	.280	107	400	45	112	26	0	11	46	8	130	1	3	.428	.299	R	R	6-2	190	8-9-81	1999	San Pedro de Macoris, D.R.
Merritt, Graig	.218	24	78	4	17	3	0	0	7	4	12	0	1	.256	.253	R	R	6-1	190	7-2-78	2001	Pitt Meadows, B.C.
Reece, Eric	.278	90	324	44	90	22	3	15	52	24	75	1	0	.503	.328	L	R	6-3	210	6-16-78	2001	El Dorado Hills, Calif.
Riley, Ryan	.256	24	82	10	21	3	0	0	9	7	15	2	0	.293	.322	R	R	5-10	180	11-10-78	2001	Seattle, Wash.
Salas, Juan	.321	37	137	26	44	6	1	6	30	7	30	1	0	.511	.365	R	R	6-2	190	11-7-78	1998	Santo Domingo, D.R.
Williams, Brady	.222	5	9	0	2	0	0	0	1	0	5	0	0	.222	.222	R	R	6-1	180	10-18-79	1999	Dunedin, Fla.

PITCHING	W	L	ERA	G	GS	CG	SV	IP	H	R	ER	BB	SO	AVG	B	T	HT	WT	DOB	1st Yr	Resides
Andersen, Derek	1	1	2.82	17	0	0	1	22	18	7	7	5	13	.230	L	L	6-3	180	10-6-77	1999	Lynnwood, Wash.
Brazelton, Dewon	1	5	5.26	9	9	0	0	50	62	33	29	19	42	.298	R	R	6-4	210	6-16-80	2002	Tullahoma, Tenn.
Campbell, Jarrett	5	4	2.65	32	4	0	1	78	79	32	23	21	64	.258	R	R	6-2	190	9-6-79	1998	Corpus Christi, Texas
Coose, Austin	5	5	3.44	50	0	0	2	65	69	30	25	41	66	.272	R	R	6-2	230	1-27-79	2001	Kokomo, Ind.
Cramer, Bob	0	0	3.55	5	0	0	0	13	10	6	5	5	10	.217	L	L	6-1	190	10-28-79	2003	Anaheim, Calif.
Crawford, Chris	6	6	4.16	47	0	0	2	89	96	53	41	36	59	.275	L	L	6-3	210	10-14-77	1999	Marietta, Ga.
Dukeman, Greg	3	4	4.50	28	5	0	0	76	94	44	38	25	47	.310	R	R	6-7	220	12-6-78	1997	Costa Mesa, Calif.
Ellis, Rob	0	0	15.00	2	0	0	0	3	4	5	5	5	0	.333	L	L	6-3	190	1-31-80	2002	Oakland, Calif.
Flinn, Chris	8	6	4.57	24	17	2	0	100	116	65	51	35	79	.290	R	R	6-2	180	8-18-80	2001	Levittown, N.Y.
Gaudin, Chad	5	3	2.13	14	14	1	0	80	63	23	19	23	70	.213	R	R	5-10	160	3-24-83	2002	Harahan, La.
Hines, Carlos	1	1	2.77	25	0	0	8	26	22	10	8	13	23	.220	R	R	6-3	190	9-26-80	1999	Selma, N.C.
Little, Joe	0	1	4.82	2	2	0	0	9	10	5	5	4	8	.285	L	L	6-1	170	3-10-82	2003	Arvada, Colo.
Lockwood, Brian	6	6	4.97	27	17	0	0	118	152	79	65	31	72	.319	R	R	6-2	170	2-20-81	2001	Torrance, Calif.
Matthews, Jarod	8	7	4.02	23	21	1	0	121	131	62	54	27	109	.269	R	R	6-2	190	11-10-82	2001	Olympia, Wash.
O'Connor, Brian	0	0	4.91	2	1	0	0	7	9	4	4	2	4	.310	L	L	6-2	200	1-4-77	1995	Franklin, Tenn.
Parker, Josh	0	0	1.38	31	0	0	16	33	32	6	5	4	42	.253	R	R	6-5	220	1-12-81	2001	Louisville, Ky.
Pruett, Jason	2	0	3.78	48	0	0	1	48	54	23	20	16	34	.281	L	L	6-3	180	1-21-79	1999	Princeton, Texas
Seddon, Chris	9	11	5.00	26	26	0	0	133	147	93	74	54	95	.279	L	L	6-3	170	10-13-83	2001	Canyon Country, Calif.
Shields, Jamie	10	10	4.45	26	24	0	1	144	161	85	71	38	119	.279	R	R	6-3	190	12-20-81	2000	Valencia, Calif.

FIELDING

Catcher	PCT	G	PO	A	E	DP	PB
Arhart	.992	70	461	37	4	4	17
Deck	1.000	4	14	1	0	0	0
Isenia	.995	24	180	19	1	2	1
Maduro	.982	9	51	5	1	0	3
Merritt	.977	24	150	20	4	0	4
Reece	.993	20	124	9	1	0	8

First Base	PCT	G	PO	A	E	DP
Arhart	1.000	1	4	1	0	1
Clark	.993	113	883	73	7	84
Gomes	.882	6	30	0	4	4
Reece	.995	25	182	11	1	20
Williams	1.000	1	2	0	0	0

Second Base	PCT	G	PO	A	E	DP
Centeno	.750	3	2	1	1	0
Cortez	.955	100	234	235	22	59
De Paula	.959	23	52	66	5	19
Gonzalez	.953	10	18	23	2	3
Kelly	1.000	1	1	2	0	1
Riley	.966	6	8	20	1	2
Williams	.875	2	3	4	1	1

Third Base	PCT	G	PO	A	E	DP
Centeno	.500	1	0	1	1	0
Gonzalez	.897	79	42	166	24	10
Reece	.905	36	19	57	8	5
Riley	.857	5	1	5	1	0
Salas	.930	27	20	33	4	3
Williams	1.000	1	0	3	0	0

Shortstop	PCT	G	PO	A	E	DP
Cortez	.900	3	3	6	1	0
De Paula	.923	95	128	234	30	62
Kelly	.909	30	55	94	15	22
Riley	.943	13	26	40	4	12

Outfield	PCT	G	PO	A	E	DP
Bonner	.981	23	49	4	1	0
Centeno	.955	63	97	9	5	0
Clark	.980	26	47	2	1	1
Gathright	.981	63	150	7	3	1
Gomes	.984	30	58	3	1	2
Martin	.987	128	285	11	4	3
Mateo	.934	96	173	11	13	2
Salas	.895	12	16	1	2	0

CHARLESTON RIVERDOGS — Low Class A

SOUTH ATLANTIC LEAGUE

BATTING	AVG	G	AB	R	H	2B	3B	HR	RBI	BB	SO	SB	CS	SLG	OBP	B	T	HT	WT	DOB	1st Yr	Resides
Bankston, Wes	.256	103	375	46	96	18	1	12	60	53	94	2	3	.405	.346	R	R	6-4	200	11-23-83	2002	Plano, Texas

BATTING	AVG	G	AB	R	H	2B	3B	HR	RBI	BB	SO	SB	CS	SLG	OBP	B	T	HT	WT	DOB	1st Yr	Resides
Bonner, Adam	.231	69	216	41	50	14	1	8	38	46	74	4	2	.417	.363	L	R	6-5	200	3-11-81	2000	Hueytown, Ala.
Cordell, Brent	.229	97	323	42	74	20	1	12	48	49	74	1	2	.409	.352	S	R	6-3	210	5-22-80	2001	Reno, Nev.
Davis, John-Paul	.296	97	355	65	105	24	1	15	52	47	59	14	2	.496	.385	R	R	6-4	220	12-20-78	2001	Russellville, Ark.
Deck, Ronnie	.156	17	45	6	7	1	0	0	4	4	12	0	0	.178	.224	R	R	6-2	220	10-24-77	1999	Fort Worth, Texas
Dion, Nate	.282	39	124	16	35	3	1	3	14	5	34	9	3	.395	.313	R	R	6-3	170	11-13-81	2000	Torrance, Okla.
Dukes, Elijah	.245	117	383	51	94	17	4	7	53	45	130	33	11	.366	.338	S	R	6-2	220	6-26-84	2002	Tampa, Fla.
Duncan, Trae	.221	62	199	22	44	9	0	7	22	18	47	3	1	.372	.283	R	R	6-0	220	11-27-80	2002	Baton Rouge, La.
Gomes, Joey	.349	26	86	12	30	9	1	2	10	17	15	6	2	.547	.456	R	R	6-2	210	11-2-79	2002	Petaluma, Calif.
Harrison, Vince	.275	132	488	75	134	20	4	19	79	53	90	16	7	.449	.348	R	R	5-11	200	11-29-79	2001	Springdale, Ohio
Johnson, Elliot	.212	54	151	22	32	4	0	0	15	38	32	8	5	.238	.370	S	R	6-0	160	3-9-84	2002	Thatcher, Ariz.
Maniscalco, Matthew	.259	62	205	31	53	10	1	0	18	23	46	9	7	.317	.339	R	R	5-10	180	2-18-81	2003	Oxford, Ala.
Merritt, Graig	.157	23	70	6	11	0	0	1	6	9	17	1	2	.200	.263	R	R	6-1	190	7-2-78	2001	Pitt Meadows, B.C.
Nikolic, Adam	.205	14	39	2	8	0	1	0	5	0	7	1	0	.256	.205	L	L	5-9	190	9-16-81	2002	Redondo Beach, Calif.
Pridie, Jason	.260	128	530	75	138	28	10	7	48	30	113	26	17	.391	.302	L	R	6-1	180	10-9-83	2002	Prescott, Ariz.
Reames, Joe Don	.000	13	17	3	0	0	0	0	1	3	8	0	1	.000	.190	R	R	5-11	190	9-26-79	2002	Seneca, S.C.
Rico, Matt	.160	10	25	3	4	0	0	0	2	2	11	1	0	.160	.214	R	R	6-3	200	10-8-81	2001	Visalia, Calif.
Riggans, Shawn	.280	68	232	33	65	17	0	3	34	19	35	3	4	.392	.340	R	R	6-2	190	7-25-80	2001	Fort Lauderdale, Fla.
Riley, Ryan	.273	64	187	29	51	7	0	0	12	26	35	13	4	.310	.374	R	R	5-10	180	11-10-78	2001	Seattle, Wash.
Serrano, Ray	.286	13	35	6	10	4	0	0	6	5	4	1	0	.400	.357	R	R	5-9	180	1-19-81	1999	Ponce, P.R.
St. Clair, Jason	.148	9	27	1	4	0	0	0	3	0	3	1	0	.148	.148	R	R	5-10	170	9-27-82	2001	Phoenix, Ariz.
Upton, B.J.	.302	101	384	70	116	22	6	7	46	57	80	38	17	.445	.394	R	R	6-3	170	8-21-84	2003	Chesapeake, Va.

PITCHING	W	L	ERA	G	GS	CG	SV	IP	H	R	ER	BB	SO	AVG	B	T	HT	WT	DOB	1st Yr	Resides
Allen, Brian	6	5	2.89	50	0	0	3	72	63	28	23	12	53	.239	R	R	6-3	180	9-15-79	2002	Cairo, Ga.
Autrey, Scott	9	3	2.61	14	14	0	0	93	77	29	27	10	54	.219	R	R	6-2	210	1-26-81	2002	Arlington, Texas
Bartz, Jason	3	0	4.74	13	0	0	0	19	17	13	10	10	15	.239	R	R	6-2	200	11-25-79	2002	Bradenton, Fla.
Bulger, Brian	11	9	5.21	25	25	0	0	130	145	86	75	53	94	.285	R	R	6-4	200	12-2-80	2002	Snellville, Ga.
Cromer, Jason	2	9	3.32	21	21	0	0	119	164	67	44	30	62	.331	R	L	6-4	220	12-11-80	1999	Des Moines, Iowa
Cromer, Nathan	3	2	3.47	43	1	0	3	62	71	29	24	17	54	.285	L	L	6-4	200	12-11-80	1999	Des Moines, Iowa
DeBarr, Nick	11	7	4.15	27	20	2	0	139	149	77	64	40	105	.272	R	R	6-4	220	8-24-83	2002	Pleasanton, Calif.
Dischiavo, John	1	0	9.00	4	0	0	0	9	14	11	9	6	4	.333	R	R	6-4	150	1-1-82	2000	Las Vegas, Nev.
Ellis, Rob	1	0	3.52	8	0	0	0	15	15	7	6	2	14	.250	L	L	6-3	190	1-31-80	2002	Oakland, Calif.
Hammel, Jason	6	2	3.40	14	12	1	0	77	70	32	29	27	50	.245	R	R	6-6	200	9-2-82	2002	Port Orchard, Wash.
Henderson, Brian	2	0	2.51	24	0	0	2	32	31	11	9	12	27	.250	L	L	5-11	195	5-19-82	2003	Sugar Land, Texas
Hines, Carlos	1	0	1.46	30	0	0	16	37	25	6	6	9	25	.195	R	R	6-3	190	9-26-80	1999	Selma, N.C.
Lopez, Aleurys	1	1	6.91	8	1	0	1	14	17	12	11	6	7	.298	R	R	6-0	170	8-20-83	2002	Puerto Plata, D.R.
McCally, Ryan	0	0	4.50	2	0	0	0	4	4	2	2	1	5	.266	R	R	6-1	195	2-27-81	2003	Phoenix, Ariz.
Navaroli, Michael	0	1	2.67	21	0	0	0	27	38	16	8	5	26	.324	R	R	6-3	220	11-17-80	2001	North Palm Beach, Fla.
Prochaska, Mike	9	7	2.98	29	20	0	0	124	111	49	41	35	76	.242	L	L	6-1	200	5-23-80	2002	Raleigh, N.C.
Ridgway, Jeff	5	8	4.17	24	19	0	0	99	102	63	46	41	74	.268	R	L	6-3	180	8-17-80	1999	Port Angeles, Wash.
Vandermeer, Scott	3	2	4.55	6	6	0	0	32	34	16	16	15	18	.283	R	R	6-4	180	2-16-81	1999	New Orleans, La.
Volquez, Bolivar	0	0	6.53	10	0	0	0	21	28	16	15	10	5	.341	R	R	6-3	180	7-3-80	1998	Santo Domingo, D.R.
Yarbrough, Joe	3	6	1.99	56	0	0	22	72	52	21	16	20	69	.205	L	L	6-3	210	4-16-80	2002	Bessemer, Ala.

FIELDING

Catcher	PCT	G	PO	A	E	DP	PB
Cordell	.989	44	241	34	3	3	6
Deck	.985	14	60	6	1	0	3
Merritt	.985	23	172	20	3	2	7
Riggans	.988	55	294	35	4	4	9
Serrano	1.000	12	83	4	0	1	1

First Base	PCT	G	PO	A	E	DP
Bankston	1.000	5	41	2	0	0
Cordell	.994	38	322	36	2	36
Davis	.990	84	720	65	8	60
Duncan	1.000	14	109	4	0	11
Harrison	.923	2	9	3	1	0

Second Base	PCT	G	PO	A	E	DP
Harrison	.960	17	30	42	3	7
Johnson	.971	49	84	117	6	34
Maniscalco	.985	26	52	79	2	22
Riley	.976	51	94	153	6	21
St. Clair	.903	8	10	18	3	4

Third Base	PCT	G	PO	A	E	DP
Duncan	.854	28	27	43	12	6
Harrison	.936	113	81	226	21	21
Pridie	.667	2	0	2	1	0
Riley	.800	3	0	8	2	1

Shortstop	PCT	G	PO	A	E	DP
Johnson	.800	1	2	2	1	0
Maniscalco	.975	36	51	103	4	24
Riley	.962	10	22	29	2	3
Upton	.907	95	154	255	42	55

Outfield	PCT	G	PO	A	E	DP
Bankston	.976	88	163	3	4	0
Bonner	.985	44	65	2	1	0
Dion	.949	32	72	3	4	0
Dukes	.966	110	190	7	7	1
Gomes	.938	7	15	0	1	0
Johnson	.000	1	0	0	0	0
Nikolic	1.000	8	7	0	0	0
Pridie	.987	122	305	10	4	2
Reames	1.000	12	13	1	0	0
Rico	.917	8	11	0	1	0

HUDSON VALLEY RENEGADES — Short-Season Class A

NEW YORK-PENN LEAGUE

BATTING	AVG	G	AB	R	H	2B	3B	HR	RBI	BB	SO	SB	CS	SLG	OBP	B	T	HT	WT	DOB	1st Yr	Resides
Ayala, Abraham	.200	38	130	9	26	3	0	0	10	6	13	0	0	.223	.248	R	R	6-1	190	10-5-80	2000	Bayamon, P.R.
Cooper, Chad	.214	8	28	2	6	0	1	0	3	2	6	2	0	.286	.290	R	R	6-1	185	1-31-81	2003	Picture Rocks, Pa.
Cuevas, Aneudi	.260	68	223	31	58	17	6	4	25	23	77	5	2	.444	.335	R	R	6-1	160	10-6-81	1999	Nizao, D.R.
Dion, Nate	.243	39	144	21	35	4	10	0	8	12	43	7	0	.410	.319	R	R	6-3	170	11-13-81	2000	Torrance, Okla.
Dufner, Kris	.216	59	218	27	47	5	1	5	14	25	74	1	4	.317	.305	S	R	6-2	185	2-15-80	2003	Philadelphia, Pa.
Jaso, John	.227	47	154	20	35	7	0	2	20	25	26	2	0	.312	.344	L	R	6-2	205	9-19-83	2003	McKinleyville, Calif.
Jones, Mitch	.194	71	273	37	53	10	1	0	16	26	78	13	4	.238	.271	R	R	6-2	185	8-20-81	2003	Birmingham, Ala.
Kendrick, Josh	.233	63	219	22	51	13	0	4	24	8	68	2	3	.347	.282	R	R	6-3	230	6-29-80	2003	Monroeville, Ala.
Martinez, Gabriel	.292	70	243	27	71	21	2	2	43	22	52	0	1	.420	.354	L	R	6-2	160	5-17-83	2002	Sabana Grande, P.R.
Nikolic, Adam	.210	40	143	14	30	2	1	2	9	8	32	6	2	.280	.255	L	L	5-9	190	9-16-81	2002	Redondo Beach, Calif.
Puebla, Fernando	.195	56	164	16	32	3	0	0	9	25	25	3	2	.213	.300	R	R	6-0	180	8-8-80	2003	Baton Rouge, La.
Reames, Joe Don	.095	10	21	1	2	0	0	0	2	3	6	0	0	.095	.208	R	R	5-11	190	9-26-79	2002	Seneca, S.C.
Rico, Matt	.281	72	278	35	78	12	1	9	47	18	70	2	2	.428	.331	R	R	6-3	200	10-8-81	2001	Visalia, Calif.
Schleicher, Mark	.225	12	40	5	9	0	0	1	3	4	10	1	1	.300	.326	R	R	6-1	180	1-1-82	2003	Matthews, N.C.
Serrano, Ray	.182	23	77	4	14	3	0	0	5	6	10	0	1	.221	.247	R	R	5-9	180	1-19-81	1999	Ponce, P.R.
St. Clair, Jason	.291	25	79	9	23	5	2	0	6	5	14	5	1	.405	.356	R	R	5-10	170	9-27-82	2001	Phoenix, Ariz.
Woodruff, Ernest	.333	3	6	1	2	1	0	0	0	0	3	0	0	.500	.333	R	R	6-4	200	9-23-82	2002	Tuscaloosa, Ala.

GAMES BY POSITION: C—Ayala 31, Jaso 38, Serrano 10, Woodruff 1. **1B**—Ayala 2, Kendrick 16, Martinez 63, Rico 1. **2B**—Cooper 8, Dufner 6, Puebla 43, St. Clair 22. **3B**—Dufner 53, Martinez 9, Puebla 4, Schleicher 12. **SS**—Cuevas 68, Puebla 11. **OF**—Dion 38, Jones 70, Kendrick 17, Martinez 1, Nikolic 33, Reames 7, Rico 66.

PITCHING	W	L	ERA	G	GS	CG	SV	IP	H	R	ER	BB	SO	AVG	B	T	HT	WT	DOB	1st Yr	Resides
Basilio, Manuel	1	0	1.69	15	0	0	2	21	17	4	4	8	16	.220	R	R	6-3	190	10-20-79	1998	San Pedro de Macoris, D.R.
Cramer, Bob	0	1	1.69	5	2	0	1	11	9	2	2	1	6	.230	L	L	6-1	190	10-28-79	2003	Anaheim, Calif.
Dischiavo, John	1	4	6.56	7	6	0	0	23	29	21	17	10	15	.308	R	R	6-4	150	1-1-82	2000	Las Vegas, Nev.
Ellis, Rob	1	0	1.29	11	0	0	1	28	22	8	4	2	21	.213	L	L	6-3	190	1-31-80	2002	Oakland, Calif.
Farrell, Jarrod	3	3	3.70	13	12	1	0	73	71	32	30	13	44	.250	R	R	6-6	180	1-25-84	2002	Boutte, La.
Fernandez, Carlos	1	3	3.12	23	0	0	0	35	31	15	12	14	24	.233	R	R	6-1	195	12-26-80	2003	Miami Lakes, Fla.
Gangi, Aaron	5	2	2.63	14	14	0	0	75	75	33	22	10	59	.256	L	L	6-3	190	12-7-81	2003	Ashland, Ohio
Gonzalez, Jino	0	1	4.50	3	3	0	0	12	11	7	6	6	11	.244	L	L	6-2	210	9-5-82	2003	Las Vegas, Nev.
Gosch, Kirk	0	1	3.86	8	0	0	0	14	13	9	6	7	15	.236	R	L	6-0	210	11-26-80	2003	Hayden Lake, Idaho
Haught, Dallas	0	0	9.00	5	0	0	0	6	11	7	6	5	3	.379	R	R	6-1	195	9-12-79	2003	Gilbert, Ariz.
Little, Joe	4	0	0.29	5	5	0	0	31	17	1	1	10	25	.165	L	L	6-1	170	3-10-82	2003	Arvada, Colo.
Lopez, Aleurys	5	1	2.50	11	2	0	1	40	28	15	11	17	22	.197	R	R	6-0	170	8-20-83	2002	Puerto Plata, D.R.
Mann, Brandon	0	2	6.97	2	2	0	0	10	8	8	8	5	7	.235	L	L	6-2	160	5-16-84	2002	Des Moines, Wash.
McCally, Ryan	1	2	3.35	9	8	0	0	46	47	21	17	11	31	.265	R	R	6-1	195	2-27-81	2003	Phoenix, Ariz.
Navaroli, Michael	1	0	0.73	8	0	0	1	12	9	3	1	4	11	.209	R	R	6-3	220	11-17-80	2001	North Palm Beach, Fla.
Orvella, Chad	0	0	0.00	10	0	0	8	12	6	0	0	1	15	.139	R	R	5-11	190	10-1-80	2003	Sammamish, Wash.
Peguero, Tony	4	6	3.34	12	12	0	0	57	60	26	21	15	55	.273	R	R	6-3	170	2-17-81	1999	San Pedro de Macoris, D.R.
Perez, Antonio	4	7	5.23	28	0	0	3	31	32	19	18	14	30	.280	S	L	5-9	165	6-12-81	2003	Chula Vista, Calif.
Rohr, Charles	4	0	3.33	16	0	0	1	27	30	14	10	13	25	.285	R	R	6-1	185	4-16-80	2003	Upland, Calif.
Travis, Matt	0	0	0.00	3	0	0	1	3	2	0	0	1	2	.200	R	L	6-0	200	12-26-80	2003	Glendora, Calif.
Vandermeer, Scott	2	2	3.05	8	8	0	0	41	36	20	14	20	21	.236	R	R	6-4	180	2-16-81	1999	New Orleans, La.
Weimer, Andrew	0	2	4.21	23	0	0	2	36	41	21	17	11	29	.282	R	R	6-2	180	3-20-81	2003	New Hartford, N.Y.

PRINCETON DEVIL RAYS — Rookie

APPALACHIAN LEAGUE

BATTING	AVG	G	AB	R	H	2B	3B	HR	RBI	BB	SO	SB	CS	SLG	OBP	B	T	HT	WT	DOB	1st Yr	Resides
Beech, Travis	.217	48	166	21	36	6	1	2	16	7	32	6	2	.301	.250	L	R	5-11	170	4-22-81	2003	Birmingham, Ala.
Bolen, Josh	.214	43	126	24	27	5	0	2	13	22	37	8	2	.302	.363	R	R	6-3	225	5-5-80	2003	Pekin, Ill.
Cooper, Chad	.264	55	201	38	53	5	2	1	22	21	35	25	5	.323	.358	R	R	6-1	185	1-31-81	2003	Picture Rocks, Pa.
Cumberland, Shaun	.252	62	218	28	55	11	5	1	32	19	41	12	3	.362	.314	L	R	6-2	185	8-1-84	2003	Pace, Fla.
Dufner, Kris	.213	13	47	4	10	2	1	1	10	6	14	2	1	.362	.315	S	R	6-2	185	2-15-80	2003	Philadelphia, Pa.
Frias, Fernando	.260	41	127	20	33	7	4	1	14	12	47	5	3	.402	.324	R	R	6-1	160	9-27-81	1999	San Pedro de Macoris, D.R.
Gustafson, Chris	.151	24	53	4	8	0	0	0	4	5	19	3	0	.151	.246	L	R	6-1	170	11-2-84	2003	Granite Falls, Wash.
Irvin, Blair	.307	34	75	13	23	0	0	0	6	9	20	4	1	.307	.381	L	R	6-2	170	5-16-83	2002	Patterson, La.
Krga, Mike	.154	7	13	1	2	0	0	0	0	2	3	0	0	.154	.267	R	R	6-2	170	9-19-82	2000	Chicago, Ill.
Nichols, Thomas	.266	55	203	21	54	12	1	1	34	17	55	7	2	.350	.329	R	R	6-4	190	8-27-83	2001	Fairfield, Calif.
Paredes, Salvador	.241	63	199	33	48	4	0	2	19	15	61	7	8	.291	.305	R	R	6-1	160	6-16-84	2001	Santo Domingo, D.R.
Schlichting, Travis	.226	46	146	18	33	2	2	0	9	14	38	6	4	.267	.298	R	R	6-4	188	10-19-84	2003	Round Rock, Texas
Shelley, Shane	.290	39	93	18	27	2	1	1	13	13	28	7	3	.366	.405	S	R	5-11	170	4-17-84	2003	Belle Chasse, La.
Simmons, Colt	.274	50	146	19	40	9	1	0	15	28	18	4	5	.349	.424	R	R	6-0	190	12-4-83	2002	Las Vegas, Nev.
Speigner, Brent	.292	37	96	6	28	7	0	0	9	9	27	2	5	.365	.387	R	R	6-1	200	4-3-81	2003	Vestavia Hills, Ala.
Woodruff, Ernest	.235	34	102	13	24	4	0	1	12	10	29	1	1	.304	.298	R	R	6-4	200	9-23-82	2002	Tuscaloosa, Ala.

GAMES BY POSITION: C—Schlichting 1, Simmons 27, Speigner 13, Woodruff 34. **1B**—Beech 1, Bolen 5, Nichols 49, Simmons 5, Speigner 8. **2B**—Beech 14, Cooper 51, Krga 1, Paredes 1, Schlichting 1. **3B**—Beech 17, Dufner 11, Krga 4, Schlichting 37. **SS**—Beech 7, Paredes 61. **OF**—Bolen 39, Cooper 1, Cumberland 55, Frias 38, Gustafson 16, Irvin 29, Shelley 34.

PITCHING	W	L	ERA	G	GS	CG	SV	IP	H	R	ER	BB	SO	AVG	B	T	HT	WT	DOB	1st Yr	Resides
Cobb, Matt	2	1	3.34	18	1	0	1	35	34	15	13	15	39	.255	L	L	6-3	180	7-30-83	2003	Prattville, Ala.
De la Cruz, Jose	0	2	1.33	15	1	0	1	27	25	8	4	9	15	.247	R	R	6-6	180	9-23-83	2003	Haina, D.R.
De la Cruz, Eduardo	1	3	5.66	9	4	0	0	21	22	15	13	13	14	.285	R	R	6-3	170	10-20-83	2000	Pueblo Nuevo, D.R.
Dupas, Greg	2	2	5.06	10	2	0	0	21	20	14	12	13	22	.259	R	R	6-6	230	1-31-84	2003	Riverside, Calif.
Geddes, Michael	1	0	4.91	8	0	0	1	11	8	10	6	5	15	.186	R	R	6-4	218	10-21-83	2003	Hudsonville, Mich.
Gonzalez, Jino	2	1	2.00	3	1	0	0	9	5	6	2	1	10	.142	L	L	6-2	210	9-5-82	2003	Las Vegas, Nevada
Guzman, Henry	0	0	23.14	2	0	0	0	2	3	6	6	5	0	.333	L	L	6-4	170	7-25-84	2002	Santo Domingo, D.R.
Houser, James	0	4	3.73	10	10	0	0	41	43	23	17	13	44	.262	L	L	6-4	185	12-15-84	2003	Sarasota, Fla.
King, Tim	0	5	5.65	14	5	0	0	37	37	31	23	25	30	.268	L	L	6-3	200	8-22-83	2001	Deer Park, Texas
Lavergne, Jarrad	4	2	4.28	11	10	0	0	55	69	35	26	19	23	.315	L	L	6-2	200	2-18-83	2002	New Iberia, La.
Lopez, Romelio	2	6	4.37	11	11	0	0	58	63	40	28	21	48	.275	S	R	6-7	230	10-10-83	2003	Ciudad Piar Campo, Venez.
Mann, Brandon	4	2	4.29	11	11	1	0	63	61	34	30	28	46	.253	L	L	6-2	160	5-16-84	2002	Des Moines, Wash.
Olson, Jordan	2	1	3.18	17	0	0	0	28	20	14	10	20	32	.215	L	L	6-3	190	2-19-81	2003	La Crescenta, Calif.
Rodriguez, Claudio	0	1	8.36	15	1	0	0	14	13	15	13	20	12	.260	R	R	6-5	220	6-29-83	2003	Bonao, D.R.
Rodriguez, Joan	0	0	5.51	10	0	0	0	16	16	18	10	14	4	.246	R	R	6-2	180	10-3-85	2002	San Francisco de Macoris, D.R.
Rohr, Charles	2	1	3.46	6	0	0	2	13	14	7	5	5	10	.285	R	R	6-1	185	4-16-80	2003	Upland, Calif.
Smith, Cole	1	6	5.57	8	7	0	0	32	34	28	20	17	23	.274	R	R	6-4	170	10-30-83	2002	Rockwall, Texas
Travis, Matt	0	4	2.94	20	0	0	5	34	48	22	11	4	24	.315	R	L	6-0	200	12-26-80	2003	Glendora, Calif.
Van Ruiten, Danny	0	0	11.57	5	0	0	0	7	14	9	9	1	4	.411	R	R	6-4	190	9-16-83	2002	Corona, Calif.

TEXAS RANGERS

BY GERRY FRALEY

The Rangers of 2003 produced a moment rich with irony.

The lowest point of the woeful season could become the time that broke the cycle of bad decisions and last-place finishes and eventually turn the franchise into a winner again.

The Rangers dropped to the bottom of the American League West during a 2-20 drought that ran through late June. When the horrid stretch ended, the Rangers were 20 games under .500, 21 games out of first place and ready for a change.

Owner Tom Hicks finally accepted what former general manager Doug Melvin started telling him three years earlier. The Rangers needed to tear it down and start over.

Quit wasting throwing away money and draft picks on veteran free agents. Focus on the farm system. Take a step back to go forward in the future.

"That 2-20 may have been the best thing to happen to us," general manager John Hart said. "It showed everyone what we need to do."

The old way has not worked.

The Rangers went 71-91 to become the first non-expansion team to have four consecutive last-place finishes since Atlanta in 1976-79. The Rangers had a winning record for one day all season: after an Opening-Day win.

After hitting bottom, the Rangers went young in a hurry. Hart unloaded veterans Ugueth Urbina, Carl Everett and Doug Glanville in a series of deals that brought in seven minor leaguers. The best of the bunch could be first baseman Adrian Gonzalez, whom the Marlins took with the No. 1 overall pick of the 2000 draft. The Rangers also picked up righthander Ricardo Rodriguez in a deal with the Indians. Rodriguez opened the season as the Indians' No. 2 starter but fell from favor. Both players were slowed in 2003 by injuries—Gonzalez had wrist surgery, while Rodriguez battled a hip ailment.

Hart wanted to deal two other veterans: Juan Gonzalez and Rafael Palmeiro. Both twice balked, invoking the no-trade protection in their contracts. That was a setback in the Rangers' new plan.

The Rangers are not starting from scratch. Five of their minor league affiliates reached the playoffs. Rather than import older players to make those clubs win, the Rangers pushed younger players through the system.

The major league club responded to the infusion of new blood by playing well. The Rangers played .500 ball for their final 86 games. The Rangers led the AL in homers and finished fifth in scoring. Shortstop Alex Rodriguez had his sixth consecutive season of more than 40 homers, and young corner infielders Hank Blalock and Mark Teixeira showed they will be legitimate power hitters. Add second baseman Michael Young, a defensive whiz who became a .300 hitter by using the opposite field, and the Rangers have an infield upon which they can build a team around.

The Rangers also led the league in homers allowed, gave up at least 10 runs in 28 games and had an AL-high 5.67 ERA. The fact remains that until the Rangers find a way to pitch better, they will be an entertaining but losing team.

Texas used 27 pitchers overall. That included 16 starters, who participated in the league's worst rotation.

The Rangers used the final months to audition inexperienced starting pitchers. Righthanders Colby Lewis (10-9, 7.30), R.A. Dickey (9-8, 5.09) and Joaquin Benoit (8-5, 5.49) all figure in the 2004 plans.

"You can have all the big strong guys in the world," manager Buck Showalter said. "But you have to pitch. That's what we're trying to do here. We have a plan, and we'll get it done."

Alex Rodriguez

Ramon Nivar

PLAYERS of the YEAR

MAJOR LEAGUE: Alex Rodriguez, ss

Rodriguez produced another MVP-type year in 2003, tying for the major league lead in home runs with 47. He also led the American League in runs scored and slugging percentage, while ranking second in RBIs and total bases.

MINOR LEAGUE: Ramon Nivar, of/2b

Nivar won the Texas League batting title with a .347 average for Double-A Frisco, and after moving to Triple-A Oklahoma, his .345 overall average ranked eighth in the minors. The leadoff hitter stole 15 bases and scored 64 runs.

ORGANIZATION LEADERS

BATTING		
*AVG	Ramon Nivar, Oklahoma/Frisco	.345
R	Jason Bourgeois, Frisco/Stockton	103
H	Drew Meyer, Frisco/Stockton	143
TB	Jason Hart, Oklahoma	214
2B	Nate Gold, Clinton	35
	G.J. Raymundo, Oklahoma/Stockton	35
3B	Drew Meyer, Frisco/Stockton	10
HR	Jason Hart, Oklahoma	21
RBI	Jason Botts, Frisco/Stockton	88
BB	Craig Ringe, Clinton	82
SO	Juan Senreiso, Clinton	117
SB	Cameron Coughlan, Clinton	47
*SLG	Ryan Ludwick, Oklahoma	.558
*OBP	Andrew Wishy, Spokane	.416
PITCHING		
W	Erik Thompson, Stockton/Clinton	13
L	John Barnett, Stockton	14
#ERA	Kameron Loe, Stockton/Clinton	1.67
G	Erick Burke, Frisco	64
CG	Robert Ellis, Oklahoma	2
	Tony Mounce, Oklahoma/Frisco	2
SV	Spike Lundberg, Oklahoma/Frisco	31
IP	Mario Ramos, Oklahoma/Frisco	154
BB	Justin Echols, Frisco/Stockton	69
SO	Juan Dominguez, Oklahoma/Frisco/Stockton	140

*Minimum 250 At-Bats #Minimum 75 Innings

TEXAS RANGERS

Manager: Buck Showalter. **2003 Record:** 71-91, .438 (4th, AL West).

BATTING	AVG	G	AB	R	H	2B	3B	HR	RBI	BB	SO	SB	CS	SLG	OBP	B	T	HT	WT	DOB	1st Yr	Resides
Blalock, Hank	.300	143	567	89	170	33	3	29	90	44	97	2	3	.522	.350	L	R	6-1	190	11-21-80	1999	Carlsbad, Calif.
Christenson, Ryan	.176	60	165	22	29	7	0	2	16	15	44	2	2	.255	.255	R	R	6-0	190	3-28-74	1995	Apple Valley, Calif.
Clark, Jermaine	.174	24	46	2	8	2	0	0	6	6	4	2	1	.217	.264	L	R	5-10	170	9-29-76	1997	Vacaville, Calif.
Diaz, Einar	.257	101	334	30	86	14	1	4	35	9	32	3	1	.341	.294	R	R	5-10	190	12-28-72	1991	Chesnee, S.C.
Everett, Carl	.274	74	270	53	74	13	3	18	51	31	48	4	1	.544	.356	S	R	6-0	210	6-3-71	1990	Brandon, Fla.
Glanville, Doug	.272	52	195	22	53	5	0	4	14	6	25	4	0	.359	.294	R	R	6-2	170	8-25-70	1991	Philadelphia, Pa.
Gonzalez, Juan	.294	82	327	49	96	17	1	24	70	14	73	1	1	.572	.329	R	R	6-3	220	10-16-69	1986	Levitown, P.R.
Greene, Todd	.229	62	205	25	47	10	1	10	20	2	47	0	0	.434	.243	R	R	5-10	200	5-8-71	1993	Alpharetta, Ga.
Jones, Jason	.215	40	107	11	23	6	0	3	11	10	21	0	1	.355	.298	S	R	6-3	210	10-17-76	1999	Marietta, Ga.
Kreuter, Chad	.111	7	18	0	2	1	0	0	0	3	2	0	0	.167	.238	S	R	6-2	200	8-26-64	1985	La Quinta, Calif.
Laird, Gerald	.273	19	44	9	12	2	1	1	4	5	11	0	0	.432	.360	R	R	6-2	190	11-13-79	1999	Garden Grove, Calif.
Lamb, Mike	.132	28	38	3	5	0	0	0	2	2	7	1	0	.132	.190	L	R	6-1	190	8-9-75	1997	Valinda, Calif.
Ludwick, Ryan	.154	8	26	3	4	1	0	0	0	4	9	0	0	.192	.267	R	L	6-3	200	7-13-78	1999	Las Vegas, Nev.
Mench, Kevin	.320	38	125	15	40	12	0	2	11	10	17	1	1	.464	.381	R	R	6-0	230	1-7-78	1999	Newark, Del.
Nivar, Ramon	.211	28	90	9	19	1	2	0	7	4	10	4	2	.267	.253	R	R	5-10	170	2-22-80	1998	San Cristobal, D.R.
Nix, Laynce	.255	53	184	25	47	10	0	8	30	9	53	3	0	.440	.289	L	L	6-0	190	10-30-80	2000	Midland, Texas
Palmeiro, Rafael	.260	154	561	92	146	21	2	38	112	84	77	2	0	.508	.359	L	L	6-0	190	9-24-64	1985	Colleyville, Texas
Perry, Herbert	.167	11	24	1	4	1	0	0	2	0	3	0	0	.208	.167	R	R	6-2	230	9-15-69	1991	Mayo, Fla.
Rodriguez, Alex	.298	161	607	124	181	30	6	47	118	87	126	17	3	.600	.396	R	R	6-3	210	7-27-75	1994	Dallas, Texas
Sadler, Donnie	.198	77	131	27	26	5	2	1	5	13	34	4	3	.290	.277	R	R	5-6	170	6-17-75	1994	Waco, Texas
Sierra, Ruben	.263	43	133	14	35	9	0	3	12	14	27	1	1	.398	.333	S	R	6-1	210	10-6-65	1983	Miami, Fla.
Spencer, Shane	.227	55	185	16	42	10	0	4	23	27	40	0	0	.346	.329	R	R	6-0	220	2-20-72	1990	Tampa, Fla.
2-team (64 Cleveland)	.251	119	395	39	99	20	0	12	49	45	92	2	0	.392	.328							
Teixeira, Mark	.259	146	529	66	137	29	5	26	84	44	120	1	2	.480	.331	S	R	6-3	220	4-11-80	2002	Arlington, Texas
Thames, Marcus	.205	30	73	12	15	2	0	1	4	8	18	0	1	.274	.298	R	R	6-2	205	3-6-77	1997	Louisville, Miss.
Young, Mike	.306	160	666	106	204	33	9	14	72	36	103	13	2	.446	.339	R	R	6-1	190	10-19-76	1997	Los Angeles, Calif.

PITCHING	W	L	ERA	G	GS	CG	SV	IP	H	R	ER	BB	SO	AVG	B	T	HT	WT	DOB	1st Yr	Resides
Benes, Alan	0	3	11.40	4	4	0	0	15	29	20	19	8	11	.414	R	R	6-5	240	1-21-72	1993	St. Louis, Mo.
Benoit, Joaquin	8	5	5.49	25	17	0	0	105	99	67	64	51	87	.245	R	R	6-3	200	7-26-77	1996	Santiago, D.R.
Callaway, Mickey	3	3	6.45	6	3	0	0	22	27	18	16	8	19	.313	R	R	6-2	200	5-13-75	1996	Memphis, Tenn.
2-team (17 Anaheim)	1	7	6.68	23	7	0	0	61	84	50	45	24	41	.334							
Cordero, Francisco	5	8	2.94	73	0	0	15	83	70	33	27	38	90	.229	R	R	6-2	200	5-11-75	1994	Santo Domingo, D.R.
Davis, Doug	0	0	12.00	1	1	0	0	3	4	4	4	4	2	.307	R	L	6-4	190	9-21-75	1996	Cedar Hill, Texas
Dickey, R.A.	9	8	5.09	38	13	1	1	117	135	68	66	38	94	.291	R	R	6-3	200	10-29-74	1997	Nashville, Tenn.
Dominguez, Juan	0	2	7.16	6	3	0	0	16	16	14	13	12	13	.271	R	R	6-2	180	5-18-80	2000	Valverde Mao, D.R.
Drese, Ryan	2	4	6.85	11	8	0	0	46	61	42	35	24	26	.314	R	R	6-3	220	4-5-76	1998	Oakland, Calif.
Ellis, Robert	1	1	8.35	4	4	0	0	18	26	17	17	10	8	.342	R	R	6-5	220	12-15-70	1991	Carthage, Texas
Fultz, Aaron	1	3	5.21	64	0	0	0	67	75	43	39	27	53	.287	L	L	6-0	200	9-4-73	1992	Fayette, Ala.
Garcia, Reynaldo	0	0	9.00	17	0	0	0	18	19	18	18	14	15	.275	R	R	6-3	170	4-15-74	1997	Mayua, D.R.
Garcia, Rosman	1	2	6.02	46	0	0	0	46	63	33	31	23	25	.319	R	R	6-2	160	1-3-79	1996	San Joaquin, Venez.
Lewis, Colby	10	9	7.30	26	26	0	0	127	163	104	103	70	88	.316	R	R	6-4	230	8-2-79	1999	Bakersfield, Calif.
Mahay, Ron	3	3	3.18	35	0	0	0	45	33	19	16	20	38	.195	L	L	6-2	190	6-28-71	1991	Manalapan, N.J.
Mounce, Tony	1	5	7.11	11	11	0	0	51	65	42	40	25	30	.317	L	L	6-2	170	2-8-75	1994	Kennewick, Wash.
Nitkowski, C.J.	0	0	7.45	6	0	0	0	10	17	8	8	8	5	.414	L	L	6-3	200	3-9-73	1994	Houston, Texas
Park, Chan Ho	1	3	7.58	7	7	0	0	30	34	26	25	25	16	.306	R	R	6-2	200	6-30-73	1994	Arlington, Texas
Powell, Jay	3	0	7.82	51	0	0	0	59	75	58	51	34	40	.317	R	R	6-4	220	1-9-72	1993	Madison, Miss.
Ramirez, Erasmo	3	1	3.86	34	0	0	0	49	46	21	21	9	28	.251	L	L	6-0	180	4-29-76	1998	Santa Ana, Calif.
Ramos, Mario	1	1	6.23	3	3	0	0	13	11	9	9	13	8	.224	L	L	5-11	180	10-19-77	1999	Pflugerville, Texas
Santos, Victor	0	2	7.01	8	4	0	0	26	29	21	20	16	15	.295	R	R	6-3	190	10-2-76	1995	San Pedro de Macoris, D.R.
Shouse, Brian	0	1	3.10	62	0	0	1	61	62	24	21	14	40	.267	L	L	5-11	180	9-26-68	1990	Peoria, Ill.
Thomson, John	13	14	4.85	35	35	3	0	217	234	125	117	49	136	.275	R	R	6-3	190	10-1-73	1993	Sulphur, La.
Urbina, Ugueth	0	4	4.19	39	0	0	26	39	33	19	18	18	41	.232	R	R	6-0	200	2-15-74	1991	Ocumare Del Tuy, Venez.
Valdes, Ismael	8	8	6.10	22	22	0	0	115	148	83	78	29	47	.317	R	R	6-4	220	8-21-73	1991	Victoria, Mexico
Van Poppel, Todd	1	0	8.53	7	1	0	0	13	20	14	12	9	9	.344	R	R	6-5	230	12-9-71	1990	Southlake, Texas
Yan, Esteban	0	1	6.94	15	0	0	0	23	31	19	18	7	25	.306	R	R	6-4	250	6-22-75	1991	San Pedro de Marocos, D.R.

FIELDING

Catcher	PCT	G	PO	A	E	DP	PB
Diaz	.989	101	650	50	8	9	4
Greene	.987	51	287	26	4	4	6
Kreuter	1.000	7	31	3	0	0	0
Laird	.986	16	65	8	1	2	1

First Base	PCT	G	PO	A	E	DP
Greene	1.000	2	5	3	0	0
Jones	1.000	3	3	0	0	0
Lamb	1.000	5	6	1	0	0
Palmeiro	.996	55	445	49	2	53
Perry	1.000	5	18	3	0	2
Spencer	1.000	11	66	1	0	3
Teixeira	.996	116	931	71	4	95

Second Base	PCT	G	PO	A	E	DP
Blalock	.900	4	2	7	1	1
Clark	1.000	7	5	6	0	2
Sadler	1.000	1	1	0	0	0
Young	.987	159	305	471	10	117

Third Base	PCT	G	PO	A	E	DP
Blalock	.959	141	110	238	15	32
Lamb	.000	1	0	0	0	0
Perry	1.000	2	2	2	0	1
Sadler	.957	23	15	30	2	3
Teixeira	.811	15	10	20	7	0

Shortstop	PCT	G	PO	A	E	DP
Rodriguez	.989	158	227	464	8	111
Sadler	.917	19	7	15	2	3
Young	1.000	7	4	5	0	1

Outfield	PCT	G	PO	A	E	DP
Christenson	1.000	59	134	0	0	0
Clark	1.000	17	29	2	0	0
Everett	.986	72	137	6	2	2
Glanville	1.000	52	117	1	0	0
Gonzalez	1.000	57	98	10	0	2
Jones	.978	27	41	3	1	0
Lamb	1.000	2	1	0	0	0
Ludwick	1.000	8	16	0	0	0

Mench	.984	35	59	1	1	0
Nivar	.961	26	70	3	3	1
Nix	.963	52	130	1	5	0
Sadler	1.000	41	43	2	0	0
Sierra	.962	23	24	1	1	0
Spencer	.982	54	105	2	2	1
Teixeira	.967	25	29	0	1	0
Thames	1.000	24	37	1	0	0

LARRY GOREN

Rafael Palmeiro: Joined 500 home run club

LARRY GOREN

Mark Teixeira: Led all major league rookies with 26 homers

FARM SYSTEM

Director, Minor League Operations: John Lombardo.

Class	Farm Team	League	W	L	Pct.	Finish*	Manager	First Yr.
AAA	Oklahoma RedHawks	Pacific Coast	70	72	.493	t-9th (16)	Bobby Jones	1983
AA	Frisco (Texas) RoughRiders	Texas	73	67	.521	3rd (8)	Tim Ireland	2003
High A	Stockton (Calif.) Ports	California	77	63	.550	3rd (10)	Arnie Beyeler	2003
Low A	Clinton (Iowa) LumberKings	Midwest	69	66	.511	t-6th (14)	Carlos Subero	2003
SS A	Spokane (Wash.) Indians	Northwest	50	26	.658	+1st (8)	Darryl Kennedy	2003
Rookie	Surprise (Ariz.) Rangers	Arizona	35	14	.714	1st (9)	Pedro Lopez	2003

*Finish in overall standings (No. of teams in league) +League champion

OKLAHOMA REDHAWKS Class AAA

PACIFIC COAST LEAGUE

BATTING	AVG	G	AB	R	H	2B	3B	HR	RBI	BB	SO	SB	CS	SLG	OBP	B	T	HT	WT	DOB	1st Yr	Resides
Alexander, Manny	.258	120	450	52	116	17	6	4	48	30	75	27	10	.349	.309	R	R	5-10	180	3-20-71	1988	San Pedro de Macoris, D.R.
Ardoin, Danny	.243	74	239	35	58	11	2	7	35	21	58	0	2	.393	.311	R	R	6-0	220	7-8-74	1995	Ville Platte, La.
Burkhart, Lance	.143	3	7	1	1	0	0	0	0	2	4	0	0	.143	.333	R	R	5-9	220	12-16-74	1997	Florissant, Mo.
Christenson, Ryan	.313	52	195	30	61	15	1	5	24	28	45	11	1	.477	.400	R	R	6-0	190	3-28-74	1995	Apple Valley, Calif.
Clark, Jermaine	.222	49	171	24	38	6	4	6	24	16	26	11	1	.409	.291	L	R	5-10	170	9-29-76	1997	Vacaville, Calif.
2-team (50 Portland)	.236	99	331	51	78	8	6	10	34	38	50	25	4	.387	.316							
Glanville, Doug	.162	9	37	4	6	0	0	0	3	2	3	1	0	.162	.225	R	R	6-2	170	8-25-70	1991	Philadelphia, Pa.
Hart, Jason	.252	137	512	65	129	22	0	21	82	54	106	2	1	.418	.325	R	R	6-4	230	9-5-77	1998	Springfield, Mo.
Johnson, Rontrez	.224	70	241	35	54	10	3	5	20	19	29	14	6	.353	.296	R	R	5-10	160	12-8-76	1995	Marshall, Texas
Jones, Jason	.288	100	375	52	108	29	0	9	55	50	80	7	2	.437	.374	S	R	6-3	210	10-17-76	1999	Marietta, Ga.
Laird, Gerald	.260	99	338	50	88	20	5	9	42	37	61	9	3	.429	.344	R	R	6-2	190	11-13-79	1999	Garden Grove, Calif.
Lamb, Mike	.288	73	274	45	79	19	4	9	46	42	45	1	1	.485	.383	L	R	6-1	190	8-9-75	1997	Valinda, Calif.
Liniak, Cole	.248	62	210	26	52	12	2	6	29	15	32	2	3	.410	.300	R	R	6-1	190	8-23-76	1995	Encinitas, Calif.
Ludwick, Ryan	.303	81	317	51	96	24	3	17	63	33	71	1	1	.558	.372	R	L	6-3	200	7-13-78	1999	Las Vegas, Nev.
McDougall, Marshall	.270	30	111	11	30	4	2	2	9	13	21	1	1	.396	.341	R	R	6-1	200	12-19-78	2000	Tampa, Fla.
Meliah, Dave	.249	56	185	22	46	7	0	5	19	10	42	0	0	.368	.289	L	R	6-3	180	3-11-77	1998	Walla Walla, Wash.
Mench, Kevin	.267	29	105	16	28	8	0	4	21	19	15	2	0	.457	.366	R	R	6-0	230	1-7-78	1999	Newark, Del.
Nivar, Ramon	.337	23	89	11	30	2	2	2	12	5	5	6	1	.472	.368	R	R	5-10	170	2-22-80	1998	San Cristobal, D.R.
Ottavinia, Paul	.258	50	178	13	46	5	0	0	13	12	23	5	1	.287	.304	L	L	6-1	190	4-22-73	1994	Drakestown, N.J.
Pickler, Jeff	.222	125	486	68	108	20	5	2	36	64	74	32	5	.296	.315	L	R	5-10	180	1-6-76	1998	Santa Ana, Calif.
Powers, John	.000	3	11	0	0	0	0	0	0	0	1	0	0	.000	.000	L	R	5-10	170	6-2-74	1996	San Diego, Calif.
Raymundo, G.J.	.120	9	25	4	3	1	0	0	4	5	4	0	0	.160	.250	R	R	6-1	190	3-3-77	1999	Clovis, Calif.
Rushford, Jim	.190	24	84	8	16	4	1	0	9	8	11	2	0	.262	.271	L	L	6-1	190	3-24-74	1996	San Diego, Calif.
Sadler, Donnie	.303	19	66	14	20	4	1	1	6	10	9	6	1	.439	.405	R	R	5-6	170	6-17-75	1994	Waco, Texas
Thames, Marcus	.258	18	66	9	17	4	0	2	7	8	12	1	0	.409	.338	R	R	6-2	205	3-6-77	1997	Louisville, Miss.

PITCHING	W	L	ERA	G	GS	CG	SV	IP	H	R	ER	BB	SO	AVG	B	T	HT	WT	DOB	1st Yr	Resides
Beasley, Ray	5	5	4.59	43	0	0	4	51	57	28	26	20	29	.295	R	L	5-11	160	10-26-76	1996	Lake City, Fla.
Benoit, Joaquin	2	1	3.82	6	6	0	0	33	28	17	14	11	31	.231	R	R	6-3	200	7-26-77	1996	Santiago, D.R.
Callaway, Mickey	2	0	1.59	4	4	0	0	17	16	6	3	5	9	.253	R	R	6-2	200	5-13-75	1996	Memphis, Tenn.
2-team (7 Salt Lake)	3	0	2.35	11	8	0	0	38	38	14	10	11	19	.271							
Davis, Doug	3	0	3.25	4	4	0	0	28	29	10	10	1	18	.271	R	L	6-4	190	9-21-75	1996	Cedar Hill, Texas
Dickey, R.A.	1	1	1.20	3	2	0	0	15	14	3	2	3	4	.259	R	R	6-3	200	10-29-74	1997	Nashville, Tenn.
Dominguez, Juan	1	0	3.50	3	3	0	0	18	15	7	7	3	14	.227	R	R	6-2	180	5-18-80	2000	Valverde Mao, D.R.
Drese, Ryan	8	6	4.65	20	20	0	0	122	143	70	63	39	68	.300	R	R	6-3	220	4-5-76	1998	Oakland, Calif.
Ellis, Robert	3	10	4.94	27	15	2	3	118	128	68	65	35	49	.279	R	R	6-5	220	12-15-70	1991	Carthage, Texas
Fultz, Aaron	0	0	27.00	1	0	0	0	1	2	3	3	1	2	.400	L	L	6-0	200	9-4-73	1992	Fayette, Ala.
Garcia, Reynaldo	4	3	3.69	39	3	0	9	61	64	27	25	19	64	.268	R	R	6-3	170	4-15-74	1997	Mayua, D.R.
Garcia, Rosman	1	2	1.91	17	2	0	10	28	20	7	6	6	21	.196	R	R	6-2	160	1-3-79	1996	San Joaquin, Venez.
Graham, Tom	3	1	5.27	22	0	0	1	41	39	24	24	12	28	.260	R	R	6-7	250	1-26-78	2000	Modesto, Calif.
Hughes, Travis	1	3	5.46	11	11	0	0	58	79	41	35	27	36	.329	R	R	6-5	230	5-25-78	1998	Beaver City, Neb.
Keisler, Randy	0	2	8.53	5	2	0	0	13	21	13	12	5	9	.388	L	L	6-3	190	2-24-76	1998	Richards, Texas
Lewis, Colby	5	1	3.02	7	7	0	0	48	36	16	16	19	43	.208	R	R	6-4	230	8-2-79	1999	Bakersfield, Calif.
Lundberg, Spike	1	0	2.08	2	0	0	0	4	5	1	1	2	2	.312	S	R	6-1	180	5-4-77	1997	San Diego, Calif.
Mahay, Ron	4	2	4.22	26	0	0	3	43	36	21	20	10	51	.223	L	L	6-2	190	6-28-71	1991	Manalapan, N.J.
Mounce, Tony	2	4	3.39	11	11	2	0	66	60	25	25	26	51	.242	L	L	6-2	170	2-8-75	1994	Kennewick, Wash.
Murray, Dan	5	9	5.86	41	6	0	2	81	108	56	53	35	49	.323	R	R	6-1	190	11-21-73	1995	Garden Grove, Calif.
Nitkowski, C.J.	5	4	4.09	33	6	0	2	81	88	40	37	31	53	.281	L	L	6-3	200	3-9-73	1994	Houston, Texas
Park, Chan Ho	1	0	5.89	3	3	0	0	18	27	12	12	8	12	.346	R	R	6-2	200	6-30-73	1994	Arlington, Texas
Ramirez, Erasmo	2	1	1.53	22	0	0	4	35	36	8	6	2	20	.257	L	L	6-0	180	4-29-76	1998	Santa Ana, Calif.
Ramos, Mario	0	3	6.40	5	5	0	0	32	39	24	23	12	22	.304	L	L	5-11	180	10-19-77	1999	Pflugerville, Texas
Rivard, Reggie	0	1	7.11	4	0	0	0	6	8	5	5	6	7	.307	L	R	6-2	190	3-13-78	2000	Bonnyville, Alberta
Santos, Victor	5	4	3.41	20	16	1	1	108	112	54	41	35	65	.263	R	R	6-3	190	10-2-76	1995	San Pedro de Macoris, D.R.
Seanez, Rudy	0	1	2.08	5	0	0	0	4	3	4	1	5	7	.176	R	R	5-11	200	10-20-68	1986	El Centro, Calif.
Shouse, Brian	0	1	3.68	6	0	0	1	7	8	3	3	3	2	.285	L	L	5-11	180	9-26-68	1990	Peoria, Ill.
Snare, Ryan	4	5	3.46	9	9	0	0	55	59	26	21	13	28	.276	L	L	6-0	190	2-8-79	2000	Palm Harbor, Fla.
Stamler, Keith	0	1	4.50	7	0	0	0	10	8	5	5	3	3	.216	R	R	6-2	170	10-20-79	2000	Stockholm, N.J.
Wright, Jamey	2	1	4.12	7	7	2	0	39	38	18	18	21	40	.260	R	R	6-5	230	12-24-74	1993	Phoenix, Ariz.

FIELDING

Catcher	PCT	G	PO	A	E	DP	PB
Ardoin	.980	52	295	40	7	3	2
Burkhart	1.000	3	12	0	0	0	0
Laird	.983	89	552	71	11	5	8

First Base	PCT	G	PO	A	E	DP
Hart	.997	130	1102	70	4	107
Jones	.990	12	97	3	1	12
Lamb	1.000	5	34	1	0	7

Second Base	PCT	G	PO	A	E	DP
Alexander	.981	11	20	31	1	5
Clark	1.000	6	8	18	0	1
Liniak	1.000	1	3	0	0	0
Meliah	1.000	8	14	21	0	3
Nivar	.944	4	9	8	1	0
Pickler	.982	112	243	344	11	85
Powers	1.000	1	4	2	0	1
Raymundo	1.000	2	2	4	0	0
Sadler	1.000	1	2	3	0	1

Third Base	PCT	G	PO	A	E	DP
Alexander	1.000	5	1	6	0	0
Ardoin	.900	10	11	16	3	2
Lamb	.944	66	62	124	11	16
Liniak	.945	31	27	42	4	3
McDougall	.909	7	5	15	2	1
Meliah	.851	24	21	42	11	4
Powers	1.000	2	0	3	0	0
Raymundo	.864	8	3	16	3	1

Shortstop	PCT	G	PO	A	E	DP
Alexander	.972	104	185	305	14	80
Liniak	.864	6	10	9	3	1
McDougall	.955	13	18	45	3	9
Meliah	.917	7	8	14	2	0
Sadler	.952	16	32	47	4	8

Outfield	PCT	G	PO	A	E	DP
Christenson	1.000	52	136	2	0	0
Clark	.975	43	73	5	2	1
Glanville	1.000	8	10	0	0	0
Hart	1.000	7	6	0	0	0
Johnson	.981	70	155	2	3	0
Jones	.990	55	89	6	1	1
Liniak	1.000	14	23	1	0	0
Ludwick	.975	50	116	3	3	2
McDougall	.882	7	14	1	2	0
Meliah	1.000	9	8	2	0	0
Mench	1.000	29	54	0	0	0
Nivar	1.000	20	56	2	0	0
Ottavinia	.979	38	88	4	2	1
Pickler	1.000	2	0	1	0	0
Rushford	.977	23	40	3	1	1
Sadler	1.000	1	2	0	0	0
Thames	.968	17	30	0	1	0

FRISCO ROUGHRIDERS — Class AA

TEXAS LEAGUE

3BATTING	AVG	G	AB	R	H	2B	3B	HR	RBI	BB	SO	SB	CS	SLG	OBP	B	T	HT	WT	DOB	1st Yr	Resides
Airoso, Kurt	.247	76	235	36	58	9	3	11	38	33	68	2	2	.451	.342	R	R	6-2	190	2-12-75	1996	Tulare, Calif.
Beinbrink, Andrew	.266	133	451	67	120	24	1	10	65	60	90	26	11	.390	.358	R	R	6-3	200	9-24-76	1999	San Diego, Calif.
Botts, Jason	.263	55	194	26	51	11	1	4	27	21	45	6	1	.392	.341	S	R	6-6	240	7-26-80	2000	Paso Robles, Calif.
Bourgeois, Jason	.252	55	202	28	51	5	4	4	21	16	45	3	1	.376	.308	R	R	5-9	170	1-4-82	2000	Houston, Texas
Boyd, Patrick	.194	46	160	21	31	5	3	3	9	16	39	9	3	.319	.278	S	R	6-3	200	9-7-78	2002	Palm Harbor, Fla.
Burkhart, Lance	.202	40	109	12	22	6	1	4	12	17	42	0	1	.385	.323	R	R	5-9	220	12-16-74	1997	Florissant, Mo.
Dewey, Jason	.196	81	225	25	44	8	1	6	20	19	81	0	2	.320	.256	R	R	6-1	200	4-18-77	1997	Valrico, Fla.
Espada, Joe	.220	13	41	4	9	0	0	0	1	3	7	0	0	.220	.273	R	R	5-10	170	8-30-75	1996	Carolina, P.R.
Fleming, Ryan	.270	119	423	60	114	23	5	0	24	42	50	14	12	.348	.339	L	L	5-11	180	2-11-76	1998	Ashville, Ohio
Glanville, Doug	.133	4	15	2	2	0	0	0	0	1	4	0	0	.133	.188	R	R	6-2	170	8-25-70	1991	Philadelphia, Pa.
Goldbach, Jeff	.178	36	73	10	13	2	0	2	7	8	24	0	0	.288	.259	R	R	6-0	210	12-20-79	1998	Princeton, Ind.
Gonzalez, Adrian	.283	45	173	16	49	6	2	3	17	11	27	0	0	.393	.326	L	L	6-2	190	5-8-82	2000	Bonita, Calif.
Greene, Todd	.333	3	9	3	3	0	0	2	4	2	2	0	0	1.000	.455	R	R	5-10	200	5-8-71	1993	Alpharetta, Ga.
Liniak, Cole	.214	19	56	7	12	2	0	0	8	3	10	1	2	.250	.258	R	R	6-1	190	8-23-76	1995	Encinitas, Calif.
Martin, Tyler	.190	43	121	13	23	2	1	3	10	16	30	2	1	.298	.295	S	R	6-2	180	8-31-77	2000	West Melbourne, Fla.
McDougall, Marshall	.258	110	418	61	108	16	3	13	69	43	68	18	3	.404	.328	R	R	6-1	200	12-19-78	2000	Tampa, Fla.
Mench, Kevin	.091	3	11	1	1	0	0	0	0	1	2	0	0	.091	.167	R	R	6-0	230	1-7-78	1999	Newark, Del.
Mensik, Todd	.208	70	197	20	41	9	0	3	14	24	46	2	2	.299	.304	L	L	6-2	190	2-27-75	1996	Orland Park, Ill.
Meyer, Drew	.316	26	98	14	31	1	1	0	6	11	23	9	1	.347	.385	L	R	5-10	180	8-29-81	2002	Charleston, S.C.
Nivar, Ramon	.347	79	317	53	110	17	4	4	37	20	23	9	9	.464	.387	R	R	5-10	170	2-22-80	1998	San Cristobal, D.R.
Nix, Laynce	.284	87	335	52	95	23	0	15	63	34	68	9	2	.487	.344	L	L	6-0	190	10-30-80	2000	Midland, Texas
Ottavinia, Paul	.267	75	255	29	68	9	5	3	36	27	36	12	5	.376	.340	L	L	6-1	190	4-22-73	1994	Drakestown, N.J.
Perry, Herbert	.324	9	34	5	11	2	0	1	6	3	3	0	0	.471	.410	R	R	6-2	230	9-15-69	1991	Mayo, Fla.
Powers, John	.148	13	27	4	4	1	0	0	0	3	5	0	2	.185	.233	L	R	5-10	170	6-2-74	1996	San Diego, Calif.
Smith, Jeff	.255	31	102	5	26	2	1	1	10	6	14	1	0	.324	.315	L	R	6-3	210	6-17-74	1995	Naples, Fla.
Smith, Will	.200	37	130	11	26	6	1	4	15	5	28	0	0	.354	.226	L	R	6-1	180	10-23-81	2000	Tucson, Ariz.

BATTING	AVG	G	AB	R	H	2B	3B	HR	RBI	BB	SO	SB	CS	SLG	OBP	B	T	HT	WT	DOB	1st Yr	Resides
Soules, Ryan	.266	73	229	33	61	13	1	7	33	28	61	0	1	.424	.349	L	R	6-2	190	2-27-76	1997	Seattle, Wash.
Vaz, Roberto	.000	8	14	1	0	0	0	0	0	2	1	0	0	.000	.125	L	L	5-9	190	3-15-75	1997	Tuscaloosa, Ala.

PITCHING	W	L	ERA	G	GS	CG	SV	IP	H	R	ER	BB	SO	AVG	B	T	HT	WT	DOB	1st Yr	Resides
Beasley, Ray	0	0	2.25	3	0	0	3	4	4	1	1	0	5	.250	R	L	5-11	160	10-26-76	1996	Lake City, Fla.
Brink, Jim	0	0	32.40	4	0	0	0	3	14	13	12	4	0	.583	R	R	6-0	180	9-11-76	1998	Stockton, Calif.
Burke, Erick	4	4	2.59	64	0	0	3	59	51	22	17	27	51	.236	L	L	6-4	230	8-14-77	1999	Houston, Texas
Dominguez, Juan	5	0	2.60	9	9	0	0	55	35	17	16	21	54	.177	R	R	6-2	180	5-18-80	2000	Valverde Mao, D.R.
Drese, Ryan	1	1	4.00	2	2	0	0	9	10	4	4	0	8	.277	R	R	6-3	220	4-5-76	1998	Oakland, Calif.
Echols, Justin	1	3	4.91	8	8	0	0	44	32	25	24	26	33	.205	R	R	6-3	180	10-6-80	1999	Roby, Mo.
Francisco, Frank	2	3	8.41	7	6	0	0	35	43	33	33	18	22	.304	R	R	6-2	180	9-11-79	1997	Santo Domingo, D.R.
Fultz, Aaron	0	0	9.00	1	0	0	0	1	2	1	1	0	0	.333	L	L	6-0	200	9-4-73	1992	Fayette, Ala.
Gardner, Hayden	4	1	4.50	33	0	0	0	52	63	28	26	25	29	.300	R	R	6-2	200	10-7-80	2000	Stafford, Va.
Graham, Tom	2	1	4.84	16	0	0	2	22	23	12	12	8	21	.273	R	R	6-7	250	1-26-78	2000	Modesto, Calif.
Hughes, Travis	4	8	4.99	24	10	1	0	74	81	47	41	26	58	.277	R	R	6-5	230	5-25-78	1998	Beaver City, Neb.
Kozlowski, Ben	3	2	5.43	11	10	0	0	55	71	38	33	27	29	.312	L	L	6-6	220	8-16-80	1999	Seminole, Fla.
Luna, Brandon	0	0	36.00	1	0	0	0	1	1	4	4	3	1	.250	R	R	6-5	210	6-13-79	2001	Lompoc, Calif.
Lundberg, Spike	3	5	2.48	57	0	0	31	65	63	21	18	15	57	.260	S	R	6-1	180	5-4-77	1997	San Diego, Calif.
Moore, Darin	0	3	5.94	22	1	0	1	36	37	31	24	24	26	.270	R	R	6-0	190	12-19-76	1999	Acampo, Calif.
Moreno, Edwin	6	5	3.29	29	15	0	0	112	105	50	41	33	74	.248	R	R	6-1	170	7-30-80	1998	El Mojan, Venez.
Mounce, Tony	7	1	1.43	9	7	0	0	50	41	13	8	12	31	.226	L	L	6-2	170	2-8-75	1994	Kennewick, Wash.
Murray, A.J.	10	4	3.63	27	25	0	0	144	134	68	58	63	90	.254	S	L	6-3	200	3-17-82	2001	Vernal, Utah
Park, Chan Ho	1	0	2.45	2	2	0	0	11	10	5	3	4	6	.238	R	R	6-2	200	6-30-73	1994	Arlington, Texas
Powell, Jay	0	0	2.70	4	0	0	1	7	5	2	2	5	8	.208	R	R	6-4	220	1-9-72	1993	Madison, Miss.
Ramirez, Erasmo	1	0	6.00	3	0	0	0	3	4	2	2	1	4	.285	L	L	6-0	180	4-29-76	1998	Santa Ana, Calif.
Ramos, Mario	8	7	3.86	19	19	0	0	121	130	59	52	28	103	.276	L	L	5-11	180	10-19-77	1999	Pflugerville, Texas
Regilio, Nick	0	1	21.60	1	0	0	0	2	5	4	4	1	2	.555	R	R	6-2	180	9-4-78	1999	Deltona, Fla.
Rivard, Reggie	0	1	4.86	31	0	0	1	54	76	39	29	22	40	.333	L	R	6-2	190	3-13-78	2000	Bonnyville, Alberta
Stamler, Keith	4	6	3.75	44	0	0	1	70	69	31	29	18	37	.259	R	R	6-2	170	10-20-79	2000	Stockholm, N.J.
Valdes, Ismael	1	2	2.03	3	3	0	0	13	12	5	3	2	6	.235	R	R	6-4	220	8-21-73	1991	Victoria, Mexico
Van Poppel, Todd	0	0	2.00	2	2	0	0	9	8	2	2	2	7	.235	R	R	6-5	230	12-9-71	1990	Southlake, Texas
Wilson, C.J.	6	9	5.05	22	21	0	0	123	135	79	69	38	89	.275	L	L	6-2	190	11-18-80	2001	Huntington Beach, Calif.

FIELDING

Catcher	PCT	G	PO	A	E	DP	PB
Burkhart	1.000	29	172	16	0	0	3
Dewey	.984	79	454	49	8	4	7
Goldbach	.994	29	135	18	1	3	4
Greene	1.000	2	7	0	0	0	0
Smith	.988	26	148	14	2	1	1

First Base	PCT	G	PO	A	E	DP
Beinbrink	1.000	2	13	1	0	5
Botts	.983	10	114	3	2	8
Gonzalez	.983	45	364	53	7	35
Greene	1.000	1	5	2	0	1
Martin	.981	12	92	11	2	7
Mensik	.966	4	26	2	1	3
Ottavinia	.990	15	94	8	1	5
Perry	1.000	1	4	0	0	0
Soules	.997	65	533	42	2	39

Second Base	PCT	G	PO	A	E	DP
Beinbrink	.978	33	54	79	3	8
Bourgeois	.965	54	101	149	9	33
Espada	1.000	2	3	7	0	1
McDougall	1.000	1	0	2	0	0
Nivar	.989	54	108	162	3	37
Powers	.900	2	4	5	1	0

Third Base	PCT	G	PO	A	E	DP
Beinbrink	.921	100	54	180	20	16
Espada	1.000	3	1	3	0	0
Liniak	.900	14	8	28	4	4
Martin	.947	15	15	21	2	2
McDougall	.936	16	10	34	3	6
Powers	1.000	5	2	8	0	0
Smith	1.000	1	0	1	0	0

Shortstop	PCT	G	PO	A	E	DP
Espada	1.000	5	10	20	0	3
McDougall	.965	94	135	275	15	45
Meyer	.966	26	48	93	5	20
Nivar	.920	17	23	69	8	3
Powers	1.000	2	2	4	0	1

Outfield	PCT	G	PO	A	E	DP
Airoso	.966	63	110	5	4	2
Botts	.951	27	57	1	3	0
Boyd	.993	46	136	3	1	0
Fleming	.982	113	211	10	4	1
Glanville	.875	4	7	0	1	0
Liniak	.000	1	0	0	0	0
Mench	1.000	3	4	1	0	0
Mensik	.905	16	18	1	2	0
Nivar	.962	8	24	1	1	0
Nix	.984	81	186	3	3	1
Ottavinia	.960	47	70	2	3	0
Smith	1.000	33	62	2	0	0

STOCKTON PORTS — High Class A

CALIFORNIA LEAGUE

BATTING	AVG	G	AB	R	H	2B	3B	HR	RBI	BB	SO	SB	CS	SLG	OBP	B	T	HT	WT	DOB	1st Yr	Resides
Asadoorian, Rick	.185	31	108	14	20	2	2	4	17	5	31	3	1	.352	.235	R	R	6-2	180	7-23-80	1999	Whitinsville, Mass.
Ayala, Odannys	.198	24	81	15	16	3	1	0	9	12	16	0	2	.259	.313	R	R	5-11	170	7-2-80	2000	Carolina, P.R.
Botts, Jason	.314	76	283	58	89	14	2	9	61	45	59	12	3	.473	.409	S	R	6-6	240	7-26-80	2000	Paso Robles, Calif.
Bourgeois, Jason	.329	69	277	75	91	22	3	4	34	36	33	16	3	.473	.416	R	R	5-9	170	1-4-82	2000	Houston, Texas
Boyd, Patrick	.294	58	221	48	65	17	0	13	50	29	68	11	1	.548	.381	S	R	6-3	200	9-7-78	2002	Palm Harbor, Fla.
Delgado, Gabriel	.306	41	144	13	44	8	0	0	18	15	17	8	7	.361	.366	S	R	5-10	180	10-21-78	2003	Carolina, P.R.
Dill, Jason	.259	87	286	34	74	11	2	6	35	45	80	3	0	.374	.356	L	L	6-1	200	9-22-78	2001	Punta Gorda, Fla.
Eldridge, Rashad	.288	130	462	74	133	23	6	7	69	56	110	20	9	.409	.364	S	R	6-1	180	10-16-81	2000	Macon, Ga.
Gulledge, Kelley	.278	26	97	15	27	6	1	3	14	5	22	1	0	.454	.333	R	R	6-1	200	1-25-79	2000	Arlington, Texas
Heard, Scott	.243	79	267	30	65	10	0	4	28	40	56	1	2	.326	.340	L	R	6-2	190	9-2-81	2000	San Diego, Calif.
Meyer, Drew	.281	94	398	59	112	16	9	5	53	32	92	24	10	.405	.330	L	R	5-10	180	8-29-81	2002	Charleston, S.C.
Mirizzi, Marc	.307	29	114	17	35	7	1	4	18	14	17	2	0	.491	.388	S	R	6-1	190	6-17-75	1997	Los Gatos, Calif.
Moore, Jason	.195	67	221	32	43	11	1	1	18	34	52	4	1	.267	.305	S	R	6-0	180	1-4-78	1999	Miami, Fla.
Pack, Branden	.216	45	148	14	32	6	2	2	18	17	44	1	2	.324	.295	S	R	6-3	210	1-22-79	2000	Salt Lake City, Utah
Quero, Pedro	.262	41	168	19	44	6	2	1	15	6	26	7	1	.339	.286	R	R	6-4	210	11-17-77	1995	Caracas, Venez.
Raymundo, G.J.	.303	103	396	64	120	34	5	5	67	44	68	3	3	.452	.374	R	R	6-1	190	3-3-77	1999	Clovis, Calif.
Roper, Zach	.255	111	412	55	105	32	0	7	68	40	101	3	2	.383	.328	R	R	6-2	200	9-26-77	2000	Pompano Beach, Fla.
Sinisi, Vincent	.258	14	62	9	16	1	0	1	5	3	8	1	1	.323	.288	L	L	6-0	195	11-7-81	2003	The Woodlands, Texas
Smith, Dustin	.302	41	129	17	39	9	0	1	18	15	21	1	1	.395	.388	R	R	6-2	210	5-8-81	2001	Girard, Kan.
Soules, Ryan	.277	25	101	15	28	7	0	4	18	9	23	0	0	.465	.342	L	R	6-2	190	2-27-76	1997	Seattle, Wash.
Stringfellow, Chris	.291	116	416	59	121	15	3	3	46	54	72	9	7	.363	.373	R	R	5-10	170	11-14-80	2002	Vista, Calif.

PITCHING	W	L	ERA	G	GS	CG	SV	IP	H	R	ER	BB	SO	AVG	B	T	HT	WT	DOB	1st Yr	Resides
Abraham, Paul	6	1	4.06	47	0	0	2	58	60	33	26	33	41	.277	R	R	6-1	200	1-10-80	2001	Centreville, Va.
Andrew, Jason	8	7	3.51	31	15	0	1	118	127	66	46	31	94	.276	R	R	6-1	160	1-29-80	2002	Tacoma, Wash.

PITCHING	W	L	ERA	G	GS	CG	SV	IP	H	R	ER	BB	SO	AVG	B	T	HT	WT	DOB	1st Yr	Resides
Barnett, John	4	14	4.95	34	18	0	4	124	149	82	68	36	102	.294	S	R	6-2	190	1-30-81	2002	Fort Meade, Fla.
Bengochea, Kiki	10	8	5.51	34	18	0	1	119	127	84	73	60	94	.273	R	R	6-2	190	12-4-80	2002	Miami, Fla.
Dominguez, Juan	4	0	2.84	16	9	0	1	63	55	27	20	16	72	.226	R	R	6-2	180	5-18-80	2000	Valverde Mao, D.R.
Echols, Justin	4	6	2.85	25	13	0	0	98	74	42	31	43	98	.206	R	R	6-3	180	10-6-80	1999	Roby, Mo.
Gardner, Hayden	1	0	0.00	4	0	0	2	7	4	0	0	1	6	.181	R	R	6-2	200	10-7-80	2000	Stafford, Va.
Gilbert, Rich	6	2	4.26	51	0	0	5	61	63	34	29	36	52	.261	L	L	6-2	180	11-14-79	2000	Clyde Park, Mont.
Jimenez, Kelvin	6	5	4.73	34	18	0	2	131	135	81	69	43	101	.265	R	R	6-2	150	10-27-80	2000	Santo Domingo, D.R.
Keiter, Ben	1	6	5.96	25	13	0	3	83	92	64	55	44	53	.280	R	R	6-3	210	4-23-80	2001	Arvada, Colo.
Loe, Kameron	3	0	0.96	9	4	0	1	38	26	7	4	6	31	.183	R	R	6-8	220	9-10-81	2002	Chatsworth, Calif.
Mead, David	1	3	7.18	24	0	0	0	26	29	23	21	23	29	.278	R	R	6-5	180	3-21-81	1999	Sale Creek, Tenn.
Moore, Darin	0	4	4.26	21	5	0	0	44	44	28	21	33	30	.255	R	R	6-0	190	12-19-76	1999	Acampo, Calif.
Narron, Sam	10	4	3.48	26	14	0	0	103	107	48	40	19	75	.275	L	L	6-7	210	7-12-81	2002	Goldsboro, N.C.
Rowe, Steven	5	0	1.28	48	0	0	15	63	42	18	9	23	63	.182	R	R	6-4	210	7-17-80	2002	Lubbock, Texas
Thompson, Erik	8	3	2.91	19	9	0	0	80	74	28	26	13	62	.242	R	R	5-11	180	6-23-82	2002	Pensacola, Fla.
Valdez, Domingo	0	0	4.94	9	4	0	0	24	21	19	13	20	19	.253	R	R	6-3	220	6-27-80	1998	Corpus Christi, Texas

FIELDING

Catcher	PCT	G	PO	A	E	DP	PB
Gulledge	.991	15	98	11	1	0	1
Heard	.982	68	453	38	9	0	18
Pack	.968	23	184	26	7	1	3
Smith	.990	40	280	27	3	2	7

First Base	PCT	G	PO	A	E	DP
Botts	.977	73	656	34	16	51
Dill	.975	11	71	7	2	7
Moore	1.000	1	2	1	0	0
Pack	.978	4	41	4	1	9
Quero	.994	34	287	29	2	30
Roper	1.000	2	19	1	0	3
Sinisi	1.000	2	17	1	0	3
Soules	.983	18	166	10	3	12

Second Base	PCT	G	PO	A	E	DP
Bourgeois	.943	51	97	150	15	32
Delgado	.970	39	70	92	5	22
Meyer	1.000	2	6	4	0	2
Moore	.964	35	56	105	6	22
Raymundo	.959	19	28	42	3	7

Third Base	PCT	G	PO	A	E	DP
Bourgeois	1.000	1	0	1	0	0
Moore	.952	25	17	42	3	2
Pack	.750	1	1	2	1	0
Raymundo	.972	51	33	104	4	7
Roper	.860	70	35	106	23	5

Shortstop	PCT	G	PO	A	E	DP\
Bourgeois	.923	14	25	35	5	6
Delgado	1.000	2	1	3	0	0
Meyer	.944	92	137	336	28	69
Mirizzi	.953	29	46	96	7	18
Moore	1.000	5	9	16	0	3
Pack	.000	1	0	0	0	0

Outfield	PCT	G	PO	A	E	DP
Asadoorian	.988	30	77	3	1	1
Ayala	.957	21	43	2	2	0
Boyd	.984	57	122	5	2	2
Dill	.976	56	82	1	2	0
Eldridge	.975	128	234	4	6	0
Quero	.000	1	0	0	1	0
Roper	1.000	13	22	1	0	0
Sinisi	.857	8	18	0	3	0
Stringfellow	.987	112	217	5	3	0

CLINTON LUMBER KINGS — Low Class A

MIDWEST LEAGUE

BATTING	AVG	G	AB	R	H	2B	3B	HR	RBI	BB	SO	SB	CS	SLG	OBP	B	T	HT	WT	DOB	1st Yr	Resides
Agustin, Hugo	.241	17	58	8	14	4	0	1	6	4	22	1	2	.362	.281	R	R	6-1	160	9-4-80	1999	Santo Domingo, D.R.
Asadoorian, Rick	.273	45	176	35	48	7	1	5	22	18	43	12	6	.409	.344	R	R	6-2	180	7-23-80	1999	Whitinsville, Mass.
Ayala, Odannys	.091	3	11	1	1	0	0	0	0	1	4	0	0	.091	.167	R	R	5-11	170	7-2-80	2000	Carolina, P.R.
Baez, Fleming	.000	2	2	0	0	0	0	0	0	0	2	0	0	.000	.000	R	R	6-0	170	6-10-81	1999	Santo Domingo, D.R.
Burkhart, Lance	.222	3	9	0	2	0	0	0	1	1	4	0	0	.222	.333	R	R	5-9	220	12-16-74	1997	Florissant, Mo.
Coughlan, Cameron	.273	113	352	67	96	9	7	0	24	66	88	47	13	.338	.387	S	R	5-11	180	8-12-81	2002	Malibu, Calif.
Cruz, Orlando	.222	51	117	19	26	3	0	0	11	15	32	4	1	.248	.326	R	R	6-0	188	10-5-81	1999	Juncos, P.R.
Delgado, Gabriel	.246	42	142	17	35	7	2	0	14	15	13	4	4	.324	.316	S	R	5-10	180	10-21-78	2003	Carolina, P.R.
Fransz, Jason	.256	12	39	5	10	3	0	1	4	7	6	0	0	.410	.375	R	R	6-3	210	2-5-81	2002	Corona, Calif.
2-team (77 Lansing)	.261	89	306	32	80	13	1	10	46	30	73	4	4	.408	.334							
Gold, Nate	.268	107	369	58	99	35	3	12	71	59	76	4	2	.477	.370	R	R	6-3	220	6-12-80	2002	Centerville, Utah
Gonzalez, Jose	.195	27	82	9	16	2	0	0	4	14	17	4	3	.220	.327	S	R	5-10	140	2-11-81	1998	Cumana, Venez.
Grayson, Larry	.207	75	208	29	43	14	2	5	28	29	71	6	3	.365	.304	R	R	5-10	180	7-28-82	2002	Orlando, Fla.
Hamblen, Chris	.259	8	27	3	7	2	1	0	3	3	5	0	2	.407	.333	S	R	6-1	190	2-17-80	2002	Fort Thomas, Ky.
Jaile, Chris	.239	90	289	29	69	12	0	3	30	47	60	1	2	.311	.346	R	R	6-3	190	2-20-81	1999	Miami, Fla.
Lebron, Hector	.305	91	351	40	107	17	4	5	45	24	56	6	5	.419	.346	L	R	6-3	220	7-22-77	1997	Catano, P.R.
O'Riordan, Chris	.326	48	172	26	56	10	1	1	26	26	21	8	3	.413	.429	R	R	5-9	180	1-29-80	2002	La Jolla, Calif.
Quero, Pedro	.257	81	303	45	78	13	1	9	47	26	47	14	3	.396	.318	R	R	6-4	210	11-17-77	1995	Caracas, Venez.
Richardson, Kevin	.164	22	67	4	11	0	0	0	4	10	22	0	1	.164	.296	R	R	6-3	230	9-12-80	2002	Bellingham, Wash.
Ringe, Craig	.217	119	419	62	91	19	3	3	36	82	102	16	7	.298	.360	R	R	5-10	180	3-16-80	2002	Warrensburg, Mo.
Santana, Manny	.251	75	255	24	64	8	0	5	33	24	47	4	0	.341	.319	L	R	6-0	210	8-4-80	1998	Vega Alta, P.R.
Senreiso, Juan	.216	121	473	48	102	18	4	5	58	30	117	45	8	.302	.265	R	R	6-1	170	8-4-81	2000	Guaymate, D.R.
Shelley, Randall	.224	114	348	44	78	18	0	9	49	59	103	7	2	.353	.349	R	R	6-4	200	1-12-80	2001	Trabuco Canyon, Calif.
Webster, Anthony	.270	18	74	11	20	7	0	1	9	0	8	4	1	.405	.286	L	R	6-0	190	4-10-83	2001	Parsons, Tenn.

PITCHING	W	L	ERA	G	GS	CG	SV	IP	H	R	ER	BB	SO	AVG	B	T	HT	WT	DOB	1st Yr	Resides
Beltre, Omar	3	3	2.39	16	5	0	1	49	46	19	13	11	27	.250	R	R	6-3	190	8-24-81	2000	Santo Domingo, D.R.
Bright, Nathan	2	1	6.75	5	0	0	0	4	7	7	3	2	3	.368	R	R	6-3	180	10-6-79	2001	Byers, Colo.
Cedeno, Jovanny	1	0	2.00	8	0	0	1	18	7	4	4	6	20	.111	R	R	6-0	190	10-25-79	1997	La Romana, D.R.
Corrado, Rob	2	2	6.86	6	4	0	0	21	33	18	16	6	17	.354	R	R	6-6	230	9-13-80	2002	Dayton, Ohio
Devenney, Nick	0	2	8.36	6	2	0	0	14	13	18	13	16	13	.240	R	R	6-3	240	7-31-80	2001	Denham Springs, La.
Herrera, Cesar	10	9	4.20	31	19	0	1	129	145	72	60	41	70	.287	R	R	6-0	170	6-5-81	1999	La Romana, D.R.
Hogan, Gary	6	5	4.03	32	17	0	4	116	121	63	52	53	64	.267	R	R	6-4	200	6-20-81	2002	North Little Rock, Ark.
Hudgins, John	0	0	0.00	1	0	0	0	2	1	0	0	0	4	.142	R	R	6-2	195	8-31-81	2003	Mission Viejo, Calif.
Keiter, Ben	1	0	1.71	5	2	0	1	21	14	5	4	7	14	.189	R	R	6-3	210	4-23-80	2001	Arvada, Colo.
Kirsten, Joel	2	2	5.79	9	5	0	1	28	42	23	18	7	13	.344	L	L	6-1	180	5-9-81	2002	Reseda, Calif.
Loe, Kameron	4	3	1.95	23	11	0	2	97	78	34	21	19	94	.217	R	R	6-8	220	9-10-81	2002	Chatsworth, Calif.
Luna, Brandon	2	1	3.30	20	0	0	0	30	29	16	11	18	13	.258	R	R	6-5	210	6-13-79	2001	Lompoc, Calif.
Marcano, Luis	2	2	1.88	39	0	0	13	53	46	15	11	17	27	.231	R	R	6-0	170	1-12-81	1998	Cumana, Venez.
Masset, Nick	7	7	4.08	30	20	0	2	124	144	75	56	43	63	.292	R	R	6-4	190	5-17-82	2001	Largo, Fla.
Mead, David	0	2	10.57	3	2	0	0	8	14	9	9	4	0	.411	R	R	6-5	180	3-21-81	1999	Sale Creek, Tenn.
Ortiz, Omar	1	1	2.03	9	0	0	0	13	13	5	3	8	7	.265	S	R	6-1	210	9-11-77	1999	Brownsville, Texas
Pezely, Franco	4	4	3.16	44	0	0	8	63	64	32	22	19	51	.262	R	L	5-11	190	1-24-80	2002	Riverton, Utah
Rodriguez, Luis	2	0	6.75	14	2	0	0	27	38	20	20	9	20	.333	R	R	6-2	180	7-24-81	1998	Caracas, Venez.
Rupe, Josh	4	1	3.90	6	5	0	0	28	29	14	12	7	23	.266	R	R	6-2	180	8-18-82	2002	Chesapeake, Va.

PITCHING	W	L	ERA	G	GS	CG	SV	IP	H	R	ER	BB	SO	AVG	B	T	HT	WT	DOB	1st Yr	Resides
Schara, Zack	1	1	7.47	12	0	0	0	16	21	13	13	4	12	.308	R	R	6-0	200	8-25-80	2002	Verona, Wisc.
Scheffel, Dustin	0	7	6.66	15	9	0	0	49	66	42	36	19	24	.323	R	R	6-5	200	5-6-81	2002	Cameron Park, Calif.
Smiley, Gerald	4	2	3.74	13	6	0	0	46	40	20	19	17	23	.238	R	R	6-0	200	10-1-82	2001	Seattle, Wash.
Smith, Cody	1	0	0.00	2	1	0	0	8	5	1	0	1	1	.178	R	R	6-3	200	4-20-82	2003	Santa Maria, Calif.
Thompson, Erik	5	2	2.81	14	7	0	2	58	49	24	18	5	52	.224	R	R	5-11	180	6-23-82	2002	Pensacola, Fla.
Truselo, Randy	0	0	9.00	2	1	0	0	4	6	4	4	1	5	.352	R	R	6-3	190	1-11-81	2000	New Castle, Del.
Urena, Sixto	3	5	5.00	38	8	0	1	81	89	54	45	30	59	.278	R	R	6-1	180	6-25-79	1997	Santiago, D.R.
Valdez, Domingo	2	4	4.20	14	9	1	2	56	57	29	26	23	49	.266	R	R	6-3	220	6-27-80	1998	Corpus Christi, Texas
Watts, Joldy	0	0	0.00	1	0	0	0	1	0	0	0	1	1	.000	R	R	6-2	190	6-12-82	2002	St. Anthony, Idaho

FIELDING

Catcher	PCT	G	PO	A	E	DP	PB
Burkhart	1.000	2	11	1	0	0	0
Jaile	.984	87	499	69	9	0	12
Santana	.984	52	280	25	5	2	6

First Base	PCT	G	PO	A	E	DP
Gold	.990	87	697	65	8	63
Jaile	.938	2	14	1	1	3
Lebron	.991	29	207	15	2	17
Quero	.989	20	169	16	2	10
Richardson	.983	6	56	2	1	1

Second Base	PCT	G	PO	A	E	DP
Agustin	.900	10	16	29	5	6
Coughlan	.964	39	80	134	8	26
Delgado	.944	38	66	102	10	17
Gonzalez	.947	12	36	35	4	11
O'Riordan	.973	38	67	110	5	14

Third Base	PCT	G	PO	A	E	DP
Agustin	.818	5	1	8	2	0
Gold	.870	23	16	24	6	2
Gonzalez	.000	2	0	0	0	0
Ringe	.833	1	2	3	1	0
Shelley	.934	114	104	177	20	12

Shortstop	PCT	G	PO	A	E	DP
Agustin	1.000	2	7	2	0	0
Delgado	1.000	2	2	3	0	0
Gonzalez	.925	13	23	39	5	9
Ringe	.928	118	191	338	41	66

Outfield	PCT	G	PO	A	E	DP
Asadoorian	.991	45	109	3	1	2
Ayala	.000	1	0	0	0	0
Coughlan	.962	69	126	0	5	0
Cruz	1.000	51	79	5	0	0
Fransz	1.000	8	17	0	0	0
Grayson	.940	71	118	7	8	1
Lebron	.933	44	83	1	6	0
Richardson	.909	11	10	0	1	0
Senreiso	.955	121	278	20	14	5
Webster	.923	15	33	3	3	0

SPOKANE INDIANS — Short-Season Class A

NORTHWEST LEAGUE

BATTING	AVG	G	AB	R	H	2B	3B	HR	RBI	BB	SO	SB	CS	SLG	OBP	B	T	HT	WT	DOB	1st Yr	Resides
Alexander, Chris	.252	55	206	24	52	14	0	5	30	20	59	0	0	.393	.338	R	R	6-5	225	9-17-80	2003	Albuquerque, N.M.
Ayala, Odannys	.222	3	9	3	2	0	1	0	0	4	1	0	0	.444	.462	R	R	5-11	170	7-2-80	2000	Carolina, P.R.
Benjamin, Casey	.272	32	103	19	28	4	0	1	14	18	26	0	0	.340	.385	R	R	6-2	190	8-1-80	2003	Cookeville, Tenn.
Bourassa, Adam	.220	59	205	40	45	6	1	0	22	45	31	6	5	.259	.358	L	L	5-8	165	3-31-81	2003	Apple Valley, Minn.
Bubela, Dane	.323	62	229	51	74	18	5	4	35	46	62	7	4	.498	.436	L	R	5-10	190	5-31-80	2003	Houston, Texas
Clark, Cody	.209	38	129	22	27	7	0	2	12	9	21	0	0	.310	.287	R	R	6-2	170	9-14-81	2003	Fayetteville, Ark.
Cleveland, Jeremy	.322	64	245	64	79	20	3	7	53	40	50	5	1	.514	.432	R	R	6-2	185	9-10-81	2003	Fairfax Station, Va.
Fox, Adam	.217	65	235	35	51	13	1	4	38	27	45	3	2	.332	.301	R	R	6-0	195	11-23-81	2003	St. Mary's, Pa.
Furtado, Micah	.250	2	8	1	2	0	0	0	1	0	1	0	0	.250	.222	L	R	5-7	170	6-9-82	2003	Kapaa, Hawaii
Gonzalez, Jose	.241	9	29	4	7	1	0	0	2	1	5	0	0	.276	.267	S	R	5-10	140	2-11-81	1998	Cumana, Venez.
Grayson, Larry	.310	8	29	4	9	0	1	0	4	3	7	1	0	.379	.364	R	R	5-10	180	7-28-82	2002	Orlando, Fla.
Kinsler, Ian	.277	51	188	32	52	10	6	1	15	20	34	11	3	.410	.352	R	R	6-0	175	6-22-82	2003	Tucson, Ariz.
Kreuzer, Josh	.226	55	199	35	45	8	0	6	40	29	35	1	0	.357	.350	R	R	6-6	240	9-28-82	2002	San Jose, Calif.
Mann, Jason	.250	1	4	1	1	1	0	0	0	0	1	0	0	.500	.250	L	R	6-4	190	7-30-82	2002	Millbrook, Ala.
Richardson, Kevin	.304	32	112	19	34	10	0	6	26	18	34	0	0	.554	.405	R	R	6-3	230	9-12-80	2002	Bellingham, Wash.
Sandoval, Abigail	.285	67	253	32	72	6	0	1	39	23	38	7	5	.320	.343	R	R	5-11	160	1-23-82	2001	Bolivar, Venez.
Shields, Nick	.279	29	104	18	29	4	0	1	11	10	30	0	1	.346	.353	R	R	6-4	220	5-29-80	2002	Rockford, Ill.
Welch, Scott	.220	16	50	4	11	2	0	0	3	8	13	1	0	.260	.322	L	R	6-0	185	11-16-79	2003	Missoula, Mont.
Wishy, Andrew	.285	72	260	46	74	14	7	6	55	54	58	3	2	.462	.416	L	R	6-3	210	9-27-82	2003	Kansas City, Mo.

GAMES BY POSITION: C—Clark 38, Mann 1, Richardson 16, Shields 28. **1B**—Alexander 54, Cleveland 1, Kreuzer 20, Richardson 7. **2B**—Benjamin 6, Furtado 1, Sandoval 61, Welch 13. **3B**—Benjamin 8, Fox 65, Furtado 1, Sandoval 5. **SS**–Benjamin 18, Gonzalez 7, Kinsler 50, Welch 3. **OF**—Ayala 3, Bourassa 59, Bubela 50, Cleveland 56, Grayson 8, Wishy 61.

PITCHING	W	L	ERA	G	GS	CG	SV	IP	H	R	ER	BB	SO	AVG	B	T	HT	WT	DOB	1st Yr	Resides
Bowman, Charles	0	0	5.40	4	0	0	0	3	4	4	2	4	0	.266	R	R	6-6	220	8-16-80	2003	Pell City, Ala.
Chavez, Jesse	2	2	4.55	17	8	0	1	55	63	30	28	31	48	.286	R	R	6-2	153	8-21-83	2003	Riverside, Calif.
Corrado, Rob	8	2	3.52	23	0	0	0	54	47	21	21	11	34	.239	R	R	6-6	230	9-13-80	2002	Dayton, Ohio
Cunningham, Tim	0	4	8.14	9	5	0	1	21	27	22	19	21	17	.329	L	L	6-2	185	10-19-80	2003	Rocklin, Calif.
Danks, John	0	2	8.53	5	5	0	0	13	12	12	12	7	13	.266	L	L	6-2	190	4-15-85	2003	Round Rock, Texas
Devenney, Nick	1	3	3.29	23	0	0	0	38	32	19	14	23	26	.225	R	R	6-3	240	7-31-80	2001	Denham Springs, La.
Farnum, Matt	5	1	2.39	17	13	0	0	75	70	22	20	17	57	.250	R	R	6-2	195	6-1-81	2003	Littleton, Colo.
Frydendall, Craig	5	4	3.36	17	13	0	0	64	52	34	24	23	41	.219	L	L	6-4	190	5-25-82	2002	Elkhart, Kan.
Kirsten, Joel	4	0	1.44	15	0	0	1	31	27	7	5	8	25	.219	L	L	6-1	180	5-9-81	2002	Reseda, Calif.
Littleton, Wes	6	0	1.56	12	8	0	0	52	36	9	9	8	47	.197	R	R	6-3	200	9-2-82	2003	Oceanside, Calif.
Lorenzo, Matt	5	1	2.53	16	12	0	0	57	43	19	16	22	54	.216	L	R	6-3	205	6-21-82	2003	Hartville, Ohio
Mattoon, Brian	1	2	5.81	9	6	0	0	26	35	17	17	9	16	.339	L	L	6-3	210	9-15-80	2003	Liverpool, N.Y.
Mazurek, David	1	3	2.03	25	0	0	10	31	25	11	7	8	20	.235	R	R	6-5	235	7-23-80	2003	Indian Head Park, Ill.
Ramirez, Victor	4	0	3.44	11	0	0	2	18	14	7	7	7	20	.208	R	R	6-1	170	10-25-80	1997	La Romana, D.R.
Schara, Zack	1	1	9.82	4	0	0	0	7	12	8	8	7	5	.375	R	R	6-0	200	8-25-80	2002	Verona, Wisc.
Scheffel, Dustin	0	0	4.50	1	0	0	0	2	3	1	1	1	3	.428	R	R	6-5	200	5-6-81	2002	Cameron Park, Calif.
Thompson, Justin	2	0	1.24	23	0	0	0	29	15	5	4	8	21	.153	L	L	6-4	210	3-8-73	1991	Spring, Texas
Truselo, Randy	3	0	3.40	15	6	0	2	50	48	19	19	22	27	.256	R	R	6-3	190	1-11-81	2000	New Castle, Del.
Watts, Joldy	2	1	3.94	25	0	0	9	48	44	22	21	21	39	.240	R	R	6-2	190	6-12-82	2002	St. Anthony, Idaho

SURPRISE RANGERS — Rookie

ARIZONA LEAGUE

BATTING	AVG	G	AB	R	H	2B	3B	HR	RBI	BB	SO	SB	CS	SLG	OBP	B	T	HT	WT	DOB	1st Yr	Resides
Baez, Lizahio	.327	53	223	36	73	17	1	7	55	20	31	4	5	.507	.385	S	R	6-2	190	11-2-83	2001	San Cristobal, D.R.
Baldwin, Ryan	.281	18	64	13	18	2	0	0	17	9	13	3	0	.313	.363	R	R	5-9	180	11-23-80	2003	Tulsa, Okla.
Bilezikjian, Charlie	.182	3	11	0	2	0	0	0	2	1	2	1	0	.182	.231	R	R	5-11	180	11-12-80	2002	Staten Island, N.Y.

BATTING	AVG	G	AB	R	H	2B	3B	HR	RBI	BB	SO	SB	CS	SLG	OBP	B	T	HT	WT	DOB	1st Yr	Resides
Cashman, Brandon	.278	50	169	39	47	11	6	2	28	20	36	24	4	.450	.411	R	R	5-11	190	10-31-79	2003	Eagan, Minn.
Charles, Larry	.292	34	120	23	35	13	0	2	13	15	31	7	6	.450	.372	R	R	6-1	190	12-29-83	2001	La Romana, D.R.
Furtado, Micah	.342	49	193	44	66	9	4	0	23	33	33	17	9	.430	.446	L	R	5-7	170	6-9-82	2003	Kapaa, Hawaii
Gac, Ian	.242	46	182	22	44	8	0	3	19	16	59	2	3	.335	.324	R	R	6-3	210	8-10-85	2003	Seattle, Wash.
Grayson, Larry	.444	7	27	3	12	4	0	0	6	3	4	2	0	.593	.500	R	R	5-10	180	7-28-82	2002	Orlando, Fla.
Guerra, Alex	.300	20	80	16	24	5	0	0	17	11	16	10	2	.363	.376	S	R	6-1	170	1-22-83	2000	Maturin Monagas, Venez.
Guzman, Juan	.182	22	77	9	14	4	0	1	9	3	36	1	2	.273	.229	S	R	6-3	190	5-17-84	2003	Caracas, Venez.
Hamblen, Chris	.350	15	60	11	21	3	4	0	15	6	10	2	1	.533	.412	S	R	6-1	190	2-17-80	2002	Fort Thomas, Ky.
Hatcher, Justin	.268	30	97	17	26	5	1	0	8	11	21	5	4	.340	.356	R	R	5-10	200	5-12-80	2003	Fort Worth, Texas
Jacobsen, Brock	.374	24	91	18	34	1	5	2	18	22	23	9	1	.560	.500	S	R	6-2	195	12-31-79	2003	Santa Clara, Utah
Liniak, Cole	.429	2	7	2	3	2	0	0	0	0	2	0	0	.714	.429	R	R	6-1	190	8-23-76	1995	Encinitas, Calif.
Mann, Jason	.168	30	101	13	17	2	1	1	10	14	24	4	0	.238	.283	L	R	6-4	190	7-30-82	2002	Millbrook, Ala.
Martinez, Eduardo	.284	34	134	25	38	6	4	2	12	13	34	11	5	.433	.356	R	R	6-1	160	12-9-82	2001	San Cristobal, D.R.
O'Riordan, Chris	.474	7	19	7	9	1	1	1	3	7	2	0	1	.789	.630	R	R	5-9	180	1-29-80	2002	La Jolla, Calif.
O'Sullivan, Steve	.125	2	8	1	1	1	0	0	0	0	2	0	0	.250	.125	R	R	6-0	170	3-8-80	2002	Bronx, N.Y.
Pena, Antonio	.229	43	157	36	36	7	3	0	23	18	39	9	3	.312	.313	R	R	5-11	160	9-16-84	2001	Monte Cristi, D.R.
Swope, Tobin	.383	14	47	11	18	5	1	0	5	7	7	2	0	.532	.482	R	R	5-10	185	1-15-81	2003	Dallas, Texas
Washington, Johnny	.222	21	63	11	14	2	0	1	8	9	15	4	2	.302	.320	R	R	5-11	165	5-6-84	2003	Compton, Calif.

GAMES BY POSITION: C—Baldwin 10, Hatcher 21, Mann 27. **1B**—Baez 4, Gac 44, Hamblen 4, Jacobsen 4, Mann 1. **2B**—Furtado 36, O'Riordan 7, Swope 1, Washington 18. **3B**—Furtado 9, Guerra 20, Liniak 2, Martinez 23, Swope 6. **SS**—Martinez 10, O'Sullivan 2, Pena 43, Swope 2, Washington 1. **OF**—Baez 45, Bilezikjian 3, Cashman 50, Charles 29, Grayson 7, Guzman 21, Jacobsen 17.

PITCHING	W	L	ERA	G	GS	CG	SV	IP	H	R	ER	BB	SO	AVG	B	T	HT	WT	DOB	1st Yr	Resides
Altman, Kevin	3	0	3.86	11	4	0	0	35	27	18	15	14	26	.204	R	R	6-2	160	12-24-84	2003	Riverside, Calif.
Bannister, John	2	4	4.22	13	7	0	1	43	47	31	20	16	28	.283	R	R	6-4	180	1-20-84	2002	Tucson, Ariz.
Bowman, Charles	0	2	5.00	12	0	0	1	18	24	12	10	4	6	.333	R	R	6-6	220	8-16-80	2003	Pell City, Ala.
Bright, Nathan	0	1	1.93	3	0	0	0	5	5	5	1	1	3	.250	R	R	6-3	180	10-6-79	2001	Byers, Colo.
Cedeno, Jovanny	3	0	1.84	8	0	0	0	15	9	3	3	4	14	.169	R	R	6-0	190	10-25-79	1997	La Romana, D.R.
Cordeiro, Chris	4	0	5.87	12	4	0	0	38	63	28	25	9	19	.364	R	R	6-3	175	4-3-82	2003	Thousand Oaks, Calif.
Cunningham, Tim	0	0	0.00	3	2	0	1	7	2	0	0	5	7	.095	L	L	6-2	185	10-19-80	2003	Rocklin, Calif.
Danks, John	1	0	0.69	5	3	0	0	13	6	3	1	4	22	.136	L	L	6-2	190	4-15-85	2003	Round Rock, Texas
Espinal, Willy	5	2	5.06	14	7	0	1	53	57	32	30	12	38	.270	R	R	6-1	160	12-8-82	1999	Villa Mella, D.R.
Feldman, Scott	1	1	4.26	3	1	0	0	6	4	6	3	1	7	.137	L	R	6-5	210	2-7-83	2003	Burlington, Calif.
Figuereo, Victor	4	3	4.29	14	5	0	0	50	64	37	24	13	35	.303	R	R	6-0	160	12-24-84	2000	Las Matas de Farfan, D.R.
Herrera, Marcos	1	1	4.63	11	1	0	0	23	28	16	12	9	13	.288	R	R	6-5	160	2-24-82	2000	Santo Domingo, D.R.
Hill, Seth	1	2	2.66	10	0	0	3	20	16	9	6	4	27	.210	L	L	6-4	225	5-6-81	2003	Sandwich, Ill.
Mendoza, Jorge	0	0	7.88	5	0	0	0	8	13	7	7	1	2	.393	R	R	6-2	180	2-22-82	1999	Quibor, Venez.
Moye, Jeff	0	0	9.00	1	0	0	0	2	4	2	2	1	1	.400	R	R	6-3	170	8-13-80	2002	Kountz, Texas
Ramirez, Victor	1	0	4.26	10	0	0	3	13	18	8	6	2	19	.305	R	R	6-1	170	10-25-80	1997	La Romana, D.R.
Ramos, Jonathan	1	0	5.17	11	0	0	0	16	17	13	9	13	9	.274	R	R	6-3	182	10-18-84	2003	Bayamon, P.R.
Regilio, Nick	0	0	0.00	2	2	0	0	5	4	2	0	1	7	.235	R	R	6-2	180	9-4-78	1999	Deltona, Fla.
Rodriguez, Luis	0	0	0.00	4	0	0	1	3	3	0	0	1	6	.200	R	R	6-2	180	7-24-81	1998	Caracas, Venez.
Russ, Chris	1	0	3.38	5	0	0	0	5	5	2	2	1	4	.250	L	L	6-3	180	10-26-79	2000	Laurel, Md.
Sarmiento, Williams	6	1	4.36	14	7	0	2	54	61	31	26	14	46	.277	R	R	6-2	190	10-15-83	2002	Estado, Venez.
Smith, Cody	2	0	2.91	12	6	0	2	43	31	15	14	10	27	.198	R	R	6-3	200	4-20-82	2003	Santa Maria, Calif.
Volquez, Edison	2	1	4.00	10	4	0	1	27	24	14	12	11	28	.244	R	R	6-1	160	7-3-83	2002	La Segunua, D.R.
Zimmerman, Jeff	0	0	0.00	3	3	0	0	3	0	0	0	0	2	.000	R	R	6-1	200	8-9-72	1997	Bedford, Texas

TORONTO BLUE JAYS

BY LARRY MILLSON

Before Carlos Tosca embarked on his first full season as Blue Jays manager, he said that 85 wins was a reasonable goal. That total would indicate progress over 2002, when the Blue Jays won 78 games.

There were times like the first month (10-18) when it looked as if the target was beyond the team's reach. There were other times, like the magnificent month of May (21-8) that included a four-game sweep at Yankee Stadium, when the goal seemed too low. The roller-coaster season included a stumbling 21-32 July-August and a 19-7 September.

In the end Tosca's goal was just right, though, as the team finished 86-76, thanks to solid hitting that made up for a patchwork pitching staff.

The Jays finished the season ranked second in the American League behind the Red Sox with a .279 average and 894 runs. They were third in on-base percentage at .349.

But the Jays ranked ninth in the AL with a 4.69 ERA, as the bullpen struggled to maintain leads.

They do have someone to build a pitching staff around in Roy Halladay. Halladay went 22-7, 3.25 with nine complete games and a major league-leading 266 innings. Halladay's 22 wins broke the team record of 21, held by Jack Morris (1992) and Roger Clemens (1997). After starting 0-2, Halladay won 15 consecutive decisions.

The Blue Jays had plenty of offensive help for Halladay. First baseman Carlos Delgado hit .302-42-145 with a .426 on-base percentage, while center fielder Vernon Wells batted .317-34-117 with a .359 on-base percentage.

Delgado also became the fifth AL player and 15th major leaguer to hit four home runs in a game. Delgado hit his in four at-bats on Sept. 25 against the Devil Rays, and in his final at-bat of the season hit a first-inning grand slam, the 304th homer of his career.

Wells, the fifth Blue Jay to reach 200 hits in a season, finished with a club-record 215, snapping Tony Fernandez' record of 213 set in 1986.

Righthander Kelvim Escobar, who began the season as the closer, returned to the rotation in May and went 13-9, 4.29. When Cliff Politte went on the disabled list and struggled on his return, it was a closer-by-matchup situation. Rookie Aquilino Lopez, a major league Rule 5 pick from the Mariners, was used frequently in the role and had 14 saves to lead the club.

Outfielder Reed Johnson, who was not on the 40-man roster in spring training, played his way onto the team and batted .294-10-52 to finish the season as the leadoff hitter.

In the minors, the Blue Jays had plenty of successful team and individual performances. Double-A New Haven made the Eastern League finals, and outfielder Alexis Rios was league MVP after batting .352-11-82 with 181 hits. Marty Pevey was the league's manager of the year after leading New Haven to a 79-63 record.

Mike Basso was manager of the year in the Class A Florida State League as he took Dunedin to the league's championship series.

Dennis Holmberg was New York-Penn League manager of the year after guiding short-season Auburn to a 56-18 record, the most wins in franchise history and three shy of the league record. Williamsport eliminated the Doubledays in the first round of the playoffs. First baseman Vito Chiaravallotti, a 15th-round pick in the 2003 draft, batted .351-12-67 to become the NY-P's first triple crown winner since 1972 and the league MVP.

Roy Halladay

RICH ABEL

Alexis Rios

PLAYERS of the YEAR

MAJOR LEAGUE: Roy Halladay, rhp

In a tough call, Halladay's Cy Young-caliber year narrowly edges out Carlos Delgado's and Vernon Wells' MVP-worthy ones. Halladay led the majors in wins, innings pitched and tied for first in complete games. He ranked fifth in the American League in ERA.

MINOR LEAGUE: Alexis Rios, of

Rios ranked second in the minors in hits and third in batting average as he enjoyed a breakout season at Double-A New Haven. He hit 11 home runs during the year, surpassing his career output to this point, and led the Eastern League with 11 triples.

ORGANIZATION LEADERS

BATTING

*AVG	Alexis Rios, New Haven	.352
R	Russ Adams, New Haven/Dunedin	92
H	Alexis Rios, New Haven	181
TB	Alexis Rios, New Haven	268
2B	Gabe Gross, Syracuse/New Haven	39
3B	Alexis Rios, New Haven	11
HR	Guillermo Quiroz, New Haven	20
RBI	Simon Pond, Syracuse/New Haven	85
BB	Gabe Gross, Syracuse/New Haven	83
SO	Raul Tablado, Dunedin/Charleston	116
SB	Rich Thompson, Syracuse/New Haven	26
	Tyrell Godwin, New Haven/Dunedin	26
*SLG	Alexis Rios, New Haven	.521
*OBP	Gabe Gross, Syracuse/New Haven	.422

PITCHING

W	David Bush, New Haven/Dunedin	14
L	Three tied at	10
#ERA	Andy Torres, Dunedin	2.16
G	Scott Cassidy, Syracuse	57
CG	Three tied at	2
SV	Mark Comolli, Dunedin/Charleston	24
IP	Cameron Reimers, New Haven	164
BB	Vince Perkins, Dunedin/Charleston	75
SO	David Bush, New Haven/Dunedin	148

*Minimum 250 At-Bats #Minimum 75 Innings

TORONTO BLUE JAYS

Manager: Carlos Tosca.

2003 Record: 86-76, .531 (3rd, AL East).

BATTING	AVG	G	AB	R	H	2B	3B	HR	RBI	BB	SO	SB	CS	SLG	OBP	B	T	HT	WT	DOB	1st Yr	Resides
Berg, Dave	.255	61	161	26	41	6	1	4	18	11	34	0	1	.379	.301	R	R	5-11	180	9-3-70	1993	Pembroke Pines, Fla.
Bordick, Mike	.274	102	343	39	94	18	2	5	54	33	60	3	1	.382	.340	R	R	5-11	170	7-21-65	1986	Ruxton, Md.
Cash, Kevin	.142	34	106	10	15	3	0	1	8	4	22	0	0	.198	.179	R	R	6-0	180	12-6-77	1999	Lutz, Fla.
Catalanotto, Frank	.299	133	489	83	146	34	6	13	59	35	62	2	2	.472	.351	L	R	5-11	190	4-27-74	1992	Southlake, Texas
Clark, Howie	.357	38	70	9	25	3	1	0	7	3	6	0	1	.429	.400	L	R	5-10	190	2-13-74	1992	Lake Charles, La.
Delgado, Carlos	.302	161	570	117	172	38	1	42	145	109	137	0	0	.593	.426	L	R	6-3	230	6-25-72	1989	Aguadilla, P.R.
Hinske, Eric	.243	124	449	74	109	45	3	12	63	59	104	12	2	.437	.329	L	R	6-2	220	8-5-77	1998	Menasha, Wisc.
Huckaby, Ken	.182	5	11	1	2	1	0	0	2	0	2	0	0	.273	.182	R	R	6-1	200	1-27-71	1991	Philadelphia, Penn.
Hudson, Orlando	.268	142	474	54	127	21	6	9	57	39	87	5	4	.395	.328	S	R	6-0	180	12-12-77	1998	Darlington, S.C.
Johnson, Reed	.294	114	412	79	121	21	2	10	52	20	67	5	3	.427	.353	R	R	5-10	180	12-8-76	1999	Temecula, Calif.
Kielty, Bobby	.233	62	189	31	44	13	1	4	25	29	36	2	1	.376	.342	S	R	6-1	220	8-5-76	1999	Fort Myers, Fla.
2-team (75 Minnesota)	.244	137	427	71	104	26	1	13	57	71	92	8	3	.400	.358							
Myers, Greg	.307	121	329	51	101	19	0	15	52	37	57	0	3	.502	.374	L	R	6-2	220	4-14-66	1984	Riverside, Calif.
Phelps, Josh	.268	119	396	57	106	18	1	20	66	39	115	1	2	.470	.358	R	R	6-3	220	5-12-78	1996	Rathdrum, Idaho
Stewart, Shannon	.294	71	303	47	89	22	2	7	35	27	30	1	2	.449	.347	R	R	6-1	210	2-25-74	1992	Miami, Fla.
Wells, Vernon	.317	161	678	118	215	49	5	33	117	42	80	4	1	.550	.359	R	R	6-1	220	12-8-78	1997	Arlington, Texas
Werth, Jayson	.208	26	48	7	10	4	0	2	10	3	22	1	0	.417	.255	R	R	6-5	210	5-20-79	1997	Chatham, Ill.
Wilson, Tom	.258	96	256	37	66	19	0	5	35	28	80	0	0	.391	.331	R	R	6-3	220	12-19-70	1991	Lake Havasu City, Ariz.
Woodward, Chris	.261	104	349	49	91	22	2	7	45	28	72	1	2	.395	.316	R	R	6-0	180	6-27-76	1995	Chino, Calif.

PITCHING	W	L	ERA	G	GS	CG	SV	IP	H	R	ER	BB	SO	AVG	B	T	HT	WT	DOB	1st Yr	Resides
Acevedo, Juan	1	2	4.26	14	0	0	0	13	18	8	6	8	9	.327	R	R	6-2	220	5-5-70	1992	Algonguin, Il
2-team (25 New York)	1	5	6.57	39	0	0	6	38	52	32	28	18	28	.319							
Bowles, Brian	0	0	2.57	5	0	0	0	7	8	4	2	2	2	.266	R	R	6-5	220	8-18-76	1995	Manhattan Beach, Calif.
Chulk, Vinny	0	0	5.06	3	0	0	0	5	6	3	3	3	2	.272	R	R	6-2	180	12-19-78	2000	Miami, Fla.
Creek, Doug	0	0	3.29	21	0	0	0	14	14	6	5	12	11	.264	L	L	6-0	200	3-1-69	1991	Palm Harbor, Fla.
Davis, Doug	4	6	5.00	12	11	0	0	54	70	33	30	26	25	.318	R	L	6-4	190	9-21-75	1996	Cedar Hill, Texas
2-team (1 Texas)	4	6	5.37	13	12	0	0	57	74	37	34	30	27	.317							
Escobar, Kelvim	13	9	4.29	41	26	1	4	180	189	94	86	78	159	.270	R	R	6-1	210	4-11-76	1992	Caracas, Venez.
Halladay, Roy	22	7	3.25	36	36	9	0	266	253	111	96	32	204	.253	R	R	6-6	230	5-14-77	1995	Palm Harbor, Fla.
Hendrickson, Mark	9	9	5.51	30	30	1	0	158	207	111	97	40	76	.316	L	L	6-9	230	6-23-74	1998	Mt. Vernon, Wash.
Kershner, Jason	3	3	3.17	40	0	0	0	54	43	21	19	15	32	.217	L	L	6-2	160	12-19-76	1995	Scottsdale, Ariz.
Lidle, Cory	12	15	5.75	31	31	2	0	193	216	133	123	60	112	.282	R	R	5-11	190	3-22-72	1991	Las Vegas, Nevada
Linton, Doug	0	0	3.00	7	0	0	0	9	7	3	3	4	7	.225	R	R	6-1	190	9-2-65	1987	Overland Park, Kan.
Lopez, Aquilino	1	3	3.42	72	0	0	14	74	58	31	28	34	64	.212	R	R	6-3	160	4-21-75	1997	Villa Altagracia, D.R.
Miller, Trever	2	2	4.61	79	0	0	4	53	46	30	27	28	44	.231	R	L	6-3	200	5-29-73	1991	Mt. Washington, Ky.
Politte, Cliff	1	5	5.66	54	0	0	12	49	52	32	31	17	40	.268	R	R	5-11	180	2-27-74	1995	St. Louis, Mo.
Reichert, Dan	0	0	6.06	15	0	0	0	16	28	12	11	8	13	.388	R	R	6-3	170	7-12-76	1997	Turlock, Calif.
Service, Scott	0	0	4.50	15	0	0	0	16	17	8	8	6	17	.274	R	R	6-6	250	2-26-67	1986	Cincinnati, Ohio
Sturtze, Tanyon	7	6	5.94	40	8	0	0	89	107	67	59	43	54	.296	R	R	6-5	200	10-12-70	1990	St. Petersburg, Fla.
Tam, Jeff	0	4	5.64	44	0	0	1	45	58	30	28	25	26	.313	R	R	6-1	210	8-19-70	1993	Melbourne, Fla.
Thurman, Corey	1	1	6.46	6	3	0	0	15	21	11	11	9	11	.313	R	R	6-1	210	11-5-78	1996	Wake Village, Texas
Towers, Josh	8	1	4.48	14	8	1	1	64	67	34	32	7	42	.265	R	R	6-1	180	2-26-77	1996	Owings Mills, Md.
Walker, Pete	2	2	4.88	23	7	0	0	55	59	31	30	24	29	.276	R	R	6-2	190	4-8-69	1990	Waterford, Conn.
Wasdin, John	0	1	23.40	3	2	0	0	5	16	13	13	4	5	.533	R	R	6-2	190	8-5-72	1993	Jacksonville, Fla.

FIELDING

Catcher	PCT	G	PO	A	E	DP	PB
Cash	.995	34	179	13	1	0	1
Huckaby	1.000	4	17	3	0	1	0
Myers	.982	81	404	22	8	4	2
Wilson	.991	76	401	26	4	4	7

First Base	PCT	G	PO	A	E	DP
Berg	1.000	2	15	1	0	2
Catalanotto	.920	5	20	3	2	3
Clark	1.000	2	4	0	0	1
Delgado	.993	147	1355	103	10	137
Kielty	1.000	3	19	2	0	2
Phelps	.967	8	55	4	2	2
Wilson	.980	14	46	4	1	4

Second Base	PCT	G	PO	A	E	DP
Berg	.978	24	38	53	2	8
Bordick	1.000	13	30	37	0	6
Catalanotto	.000	1	0	0	0	0
Clark	.944	3	4	13	1	1
Hudson	.984	139	268	477	12	99

Third Base	PCT	G	PO	A	E	DP
Berg	.941	17	8	24	2	0
Bordick	.981	22	20	32	1	4
Clark	.957	13	2	20	1	4
Hinske	.930	124	80	214	22	13

Shortstop	PCT	G	PO	A	E	DP
Berg	.000	1	0	0	0	0
Bordick	.987	69	113	180	4	53
Clark	.000	1	0	0	0	0
Myers	.000	1	0	0	0	0
Woodward	.964	103	159	300	17	69

Outfield	PCT	G	PO	A	E	DP
Berg	.833	6	5	0	1	0
Catalanotto	.993	100	146	4	1	0
Clark	1.000	5	4	0	0	0
Johnson	.977	111	163	6	4	1
Kielty	.989	60	87	2	1	0
Stewart	.974	69	145	3	4	0
Wells	.990	161	383	3	4	0
Werth	1.000	20	27	1	0	0
Wilson	1.000	2	1	0	0	0

LARRY GOREN

Vernon Wells

FARM SYSTEM

Director, Player Development: Dick Scott.

Class	Farm Team	League	W	L	Pct.	Finish*	Manager	First Yr.
AAA	Syracuse (N.Y.) SkyChiefs	International	62	79	.440	14th (14)	Omar Malave	1978
AA	New Haven (Conn.) Ravens	Eastern	79	63	.556	2nd (12)	Marty Pevey	2003
High A	Dunedin (Fla.) Blue Jays	Florida State	78	62	.557	1st (12)	Mike Basso	1987
Low A	Charleston (W.Va.) Alley Cats	South Atlantic	57	76	.429	12th (16)	Mark Meleski	2001
SS A	Auburn (N.Y.) Doubledays	New York-Penn	56	18	.757	1st (14)	Dennis Holmberg	2001
Rookie	Pulaski (Va.) Blue Jays	Appalachian	38	29	.567	3rd (10)	Paul Elliott	2003

*Finish in overall standings (No. of teams in league) + League champion

SYRACUSE SKYCHIEFS — Class AAA

INTERNATIONAL LEAGUE

BATTING	AVG	G	AB	R	H	2B	3B	HR	RBI	BB	SO	SB	CS	SLG	OBP	B	T	HT	WT	DOB	1st Yr	Resides
Alvarez, Jimmy	.257	99	342	45	88	13	7	4	25	45	92	11	5	.371	.342	S	R	5-10	160	10-4-79	1996	Santo Domingo, D.R.
Aven, Bruce	.214	56	192	21	41	5	0	3	17	26	44	1	1	.286	.309	R	R	5-9	180	3-4-72	1994	Orange, Texas
Berg, Dave	.250	6	20	3	5	1	0	0	0	1	2	0	0	.300	.318	R	R	5-11	180	9-3-70	1993	Pembroke Pines, Fla.
Burnham, Gary	.269	91	349	44	94	25	1	9	51	25	54	0	1	.424	.328	L	L	5-11	200	10-13-74	1997	South Windsor, Conn.
Cash, Kevin	.270	93	326	37	88	28	2	8	37	29	81	1	0	.442	.331	R	R	6-0	180	12-6-77	1999	Lutz, Fla.
Chiaffredo, Paul	.333	5	15	2	5	2	0	0	0	3	3	0	0	.467	.444	R	R	6-2	200	5-30-76	1997	Campbell, Calif.
Clark, Howie	.258	66	252	29	65	14	1	4	30	21	20	1	0	.369	.316	L	R	5-10	190	2-13-74	1992	Lake Charles, La.
Colangelo, Mike	.281	94	310	42	87	20	3	5	45	37	74	5	2	.413	.375	R	R	6-1	180	10-22-76	1997	Dumfries, Va.
Dragicevich, Scott	.289	11	38	1	11	1	0	0	1	3	13	0	0	.316	.341	R	R	6-3	200	6-28-80	2002	Westlake, Calif.
Fagan, Shawn	.207	17	58	7	12	3	0	0	5	2	22	1	0	.259	.230	R	R	5-11	200	3-2-78	2000	Levittown, N.Y.
Galloway, Mike	.333	3	9	2	3	1	0	0	0	0	3	0	0	.444	.333	R	R	6-2	210	5-9-81	2002	St. Thomas, Ontario
Gross, Gabe	.264	53	182	22	48	16	2	5	23	31	56	1	1	.456	.380	L	R	6-3	200	10-21-79	2001	Dothan, Ala.
Hinske, Eric	.500	2	8	2	4	1	0	1	2	0	0	0	0	1.000	.500	L	R	6-2	220	8-5-77	1998	Menasha, Wisc.
Huckaby, Ken	.292	75	267	24	78	14	0	3	25	15	30	1	1	.378	.326	R	R	6-1	200	1-27-71	1991	Philadelphia, Pa.
Johnson, Reed	.327	26	101	14	33	4	1	2	16	3	13	3	1	.446	.369	R	R	5-10	180	12-8-76	1999	Temecula, Calif.
Keene, Kurt	.236	42	140	20	33	6	1	1	14	13	28	0	1	.314	.299	R	R	6-0	190	8-22-77	2000	Chattanooga, Tenn.
Moriarty, Mike	.233	55	176	25	41	6	0	3	14	21	30	4	1	.318	.317	R	R	6-0	180	3-8-74	1995	Mount Laurel, N.J.
Patrick, Brian	.080	7	25	2	2	1	0	0	0	0	9	0	0	.120	.115	S	R	5-10	185	11-29-80	2003	Fort Lauderdale, Fla.
Phelps, Josh	.455	4	11	2	5	0	0	2	4	1	3	0	0	1.000	.500	R	R	6-3	220	5-12-78	1996	Rathdrum, Idaho
Pond, Simon	.306	63	248	33	76	21	1	5	36	16	42	1	1	.460	.353	L	R	6-1	190	10-27-76	1994	North Vancouver, B.C.
Ryan, Rob	.249	50	181	30	45	17	0	6	20	21	24	3	2	.442	.333	L	L	5-11	190	6-24-73	1996	Renton, Wash.
Schneider, John	.083	3	12	0	1	0	0	0	0	0	7	0	0	.083	.083	R	R	6-3	220	2-14-80	2002	Lawrenceville, N.J.
Sequea, Jorge	.255	73	271	43	69	15	4	3	31	30	45	7	5	.373	.341	R	R	5-10	160	10-1-80	1998	Anaco, Venez.
Stewart, Shannon	.000	1	3	0	0	0	0	0	0	1	0	0	0	.000	.250	R	R	6-1	210	2-25-74	1992	Miami, Fla.
Thompson, Rich	.295	28	112	13	33	2	1	0	7	9	10	11	1	.330	.373	L	R	6-3	180	4-23-79	2000	Montrose, Pa.
Umbria, Jose	.087	7	23	1	2	0	0	0	5	1	6	0	0	.087	.115	R	R	6-2	210	1-20-78	1996	Barquisimeto, Venez.
Werth, Jayson	.237	64	236	37	56	19	1	9	34	15	68	11	1	.441	.285	R	R	6-5	210	5-20-79	1997	Chatham, Ill.
Williams, Glenn	.233	59	210	27	49	10	3	3	24	12	56	2	1	.352	.277	S	R	6-2	190	7-18-77	1994	Wattle Grove, Australia
Wise, Dewayne	.218	80	285	37	62	11	4	10	37	17	72	11	3	.389	.262	L	L	6-1	180	2-24-78	1997	Chapin, S.C.
Zuniga, Tony	.295	71	261	33	77	20	0	12	41	27	47	0	2	.510	.362	R	R	6-0	200	1-13-75	1996	Anaheim, Calif.

PITCHING	W	L	ERA	G	GS	CG	SV	IP	H	R	ER	BB	SO	AVG	B	T	HT	WT	DOB	1st Yr	Resides
Abbott, David	1	0	6.00	1	1	0	0	6	7	4	4	1	2	.318	R	R	6-4	230	10-19-77	2000	Tucson, Ariz.
Arnold, Jason	4	8	4.33	21	20	1	0	121	121	69	58	46	82	.261	R	R	6-3	210	5-2-79	2001	Palm Bay, Fla.
Baker, Chris	0	1	10.80	2	2	0	0	7	11	8	8	4	4	.392	R	R	6-1	200	8-24-77	1999	Valencia, Calif.
Bowles, Brian	2	3	2.66	41	0	0	14	47	47	23	14	21	32	.256	R	R	6-5	220	8-18-76	1995	Manhattan Beach, Calif.
Cassidy, Scott	3	4	3.24	57	0	0	4	81	75	31	29	46	75	.252	R	R	6-2	170	10-3-75	1998	Clay, N.Y.
Chulk, Vinny	8	10	4.22	23	21	1	0	119	118	70	56	46	90	.255	R	R	6-2	180	12-19-78	2000	Miami, Fla.
File, Bob	0	0	4.22	11	0	0	0	11	10	5	5	2	7	.250	R	R	6-4	210	1-28-77	1998	Morrisville, Pa.
Frederick, Kevin	1	3	8.06	24	0	0	2	26	40	28	23	12	20	.357	L	R	6-1	210	11-4-76	1998	Prairie View, Ill.
Gassner, Dave	1	0	1.80	1	1	0	0	5	5	1	1	1	4	.250	R	L	6-2	190	12-14-78	2001	Hortonville, Wisc.
Hendrickson, Mark	0	0	4.50	1	1	0	0	6	8	4	3	1	5	.333	L	L	6-9	230	6-23-74	1998	Mt. Vernon, Wash.
Kershner, Jason	6	1	2.36	24	0	0	0	46	42	15	12	9	30	.254	L	L	6-2	160	12-19-76	1995	Scottsdale, Ariz.
Kingrey, Jarrod	0	0	9.00	3	0	0	0	3	4	3	3	3	3	.400	R	R	6-1	200	8-23-76	1998	Forston, Ga.
Lidle, Cory	0	0	0.00	1	1	0	0	4	5	0	0	0	3	.312	R	R	5-11	190	3-22-72	1991	Las Vegas, Nev.
Linton, Doug	2	10	5.28	32	13	1	0	109	133	67	64	19	79	.303	R	R	6-1	190	9-2-65	1987	Overland Park, Kan.
Pena, Juan	0	1	7.56	8	0	0	3	8	7	7	7	6	7	.225	R	R	6-5	210	6-27-77	1995	Carol City, Fla.
Politte, Cliff	0	0	0.00	1	0	0	0	1	0	0	0	0	1	.000	R	R	5-11	180	2-27-74	1995	St. Louis, Mo.
Reichert, Dan	4	3	3.57	41	0	0	0	58	55	26	23	35	60	.254	R	R	6-3	170	7-12-76	1997	Turlock, Calif.
Smith, Mike	8	9	5.00	26	21	2	0	131	140	80	73	58	89	.277	R	R	5-11	190	9-19-77	2000	Westwood, Mass.
Tam, Jeff	1	0	1.53	17	0	0	4	18	16	3	3	3	11	.231	R	R	6-1	210	8-19-70	1993	Melbourne, Fla.
Thomas, Evan	4	8	5.15	20	18	1	0	94	108	57	54	29	63	.287	R	R	5-10	170	6-14-74	1996	Pembroke Pines, Fla.
Thurman, Corey	6	4	4.27	17	16	0	0	86	90	45	41	26	72	.267	R	R	6-1	210	11-5-78	1996	Wake Village, Texas
Towers, Josh	5	7	3.32	21	20	1	0	133	133	55	49	20	76	.258	R	R	6-1	180	2-26-77	1996	Owings Mills, Md.
Walker, Pete	0	1	6.75	5	5	0	0	13	15	10	10	3	8	.277	R	R	6-2	190	4-8-69	1990	Waterford, Conn.
Wasdin, John	2	1	5.23	10	1	0	0	21	28	13	12	1	21	.318	R	R	6-2	190	8-5-72	1993	Jacksonville, Fla.
Wiggins, Scott	2	2	6.62	35	0	0	1	35	47	29	26	22	22	.319	L	L	6-3	200	3-24-76	1997	Newport, Ky.
Young, Tim	2	3	6.75	19	0	0	1	27	23	22	20	25	25	.232	L	L	5-9	170	10-15-73	1996	Bristol, Fla.

FIELDING

Catcher	PCT	G	PO	A	E	DP	PB
Cash	.998	90	521	77	1	12	10
Chiaffredo	1.000	5	28	2	0	0	1
Huckaby	.988	46	308	17	4	2	9
Schneider	1.000	3	31	1	0	0	0
Umbria	1.000	4	26	2	0	0	0

First Base	PCT	G	PO	A	E	DP
Burnham	.988	67	551	37	7	53
Clark	1.000	5	43	2	0	6
Fagan	.995	17	166	16	1	19
Huckaby	.991	23	198	19	2	18
Pond	1.000	16	133	13	0	9

First Base (cont.)	PCT	G	PO	A	E	DP
Williams	.979	12	83	12	2	7
Zuniga	1.000	1	6	1	0	1

Second Base	PCT	G	PO	A	E	DP
Alvarez	.944	27	37	65	6	15
Berg	1.000	4	8	14	0	1
Clark	.961	53	85	138	9	27
Keene	1.000	3	4	5	0	1
Sequea	.955	50	105	130	11	29
Williams	1.000	8	15	22	0	8

Third Base	PCT	G	PO	A	E	DP
Berg	1.000	1	1	2	0	0
Cash	1.000	1	0	1	0	0
Clark	1.000	1	1	4	0	0
Dragicevich	1.000	10	9	18	0	2
Hinske	1.000	2	1	1	0	0
Huckaby	.750	2	1	2	1	0
Keene	.500	2	0	1	1	0
Moriarty	.955	8	4	17	1	1
Pond	.962	31	26	50	3	7
Sequea	.944	10	6	11	1	0
Williams	.966	19	10	46	2	5
Zuniga	.934	61	46	109	11	11

Shortstop	PCT	G	PO	A	E	DP
Alvarez	.958	64	76	172	11	33
Dragicevich	1.000	1	1	5	0	0
Keene	.953	17	23	38	3	8
Moriarty	.960	48	77	138	9	37
Sequea	.926	10	20	30	4	7
Williams	1.000	5	4	15	0	4

Outfield	PCT	G	PO	A	E	DP
Aven	.957	42	65	1	3	1
Clark	1.000	7	16	0	0	0
Colangelo	.971	59	98	1	3	0
Galloway	1.000	3	3	0	0	0
Gross	.985	53	129	5	2	1
Johnson	1.000	26	60	2	0	1
Keene	.929	15	26	0	2	0
Patrick	.933	7	12	2	1	0
Pond	1.000	11	18	0	0	0
Ryan	.964	33	53	1	2	0
Stewart	1.000	1	2	0	0	0
Thompson	.988	28	82	3	1	0
Werth	.954	61	136	10	7	1
Williams	1.000	11	14	1	0	1
Wise	.974	76	183	2	5	0

NEW HAVEN RAVENS — Class AA

EASTERN LEAGUE

BATTING	AVG	G	AB	R	H	2B	3B	HR	RBI	BB	SO	SB	CS	SLG	OBP	B	T	HT	WT	DOB	1st Yr	Resides
Adams, Russ	.277	65	271	42	75	10	4	4	26	30	37	8	1	.387	.349	L	R	6-1	180	8-30-80	2002	Laurinburg, N.C.
Chiaffredo, Paul	.267	66	202	28	54	8	1	7	29	21	59	1	1	.421	.345	R	R	6-2	200	5-30-76	1997	Campbell, Calif.
Deschaine, Jim	.268	16	41	4	11	3	0	0	6	8	6	0	0	.341	.388	R	R	6-0	200	9-18-77	1999	Bristol, Conn.
Fagan, Shawn	.314	115	421	78	132	14	3	5	50	62	82	4	2	.397	.402	R	R	5-11	200	3-2-78	2000	Levittown, N.Y.
Godwin, Tyrell	.309	33	123	20	38	6	3	1	13	3	27	6	1	.431	.328	L	R	6-0	200	7-10-79	2001	Council, N.C.
Griffin, John-Ford	.279	104	373	48	104	23	3	13	75	49	85	2	0	.461	.361	L	L	6-2	210	11-19-79	2001	Sarasota, Fla.
Gross, Gabe	.319	84	310	52	99	23	3	7	51	52	53	3	2	.481	.423	L	R	6-3	200	10-21-79	2001	Dothan, Ala.
Keene, Kurt	.281	43	153	18	43	7	0	2	23	10	12	2	1	.366	.327	R	R	6-0	190	8-22-77	2000	Chattanooga, Tenn.
Kratz, Erik	.000	1	4	0	0	0	0	0	0	0	1	0	0	.000	.000	R	R	6-4	240	6-15-80	2002	Harrisonburg, Va.
Logan, Matt	.268	92	299	45	80	14	1	3	36	39	37	3	2	.351	.360	L	R	6-3	210	7-22-79	1997	Brampton, Ontario
Patrick, Brian	.240	14	25	1	6	0	0	0	1	2	5	0	0	.240	.321	S	R	5-10	185	11-29-80	2003	Fort Lauderdale, Fla.
Pond, Simon	.338	61	228	44	77	17	1	7	49	39	33	1	1	.513	.440	L	R	6-1	190	10-27-76	1994	North Vancouver, B.C.
Quiroz, Guillermo	.282	108	369	63	104	27	0	20	79	45	83	0	0	.518	.372	R	R	6-1	200	11-29-81	1999	Maracaibo, Venez.
Rich, Dominic	.259	108	390	49	101	22	2	3	46	30	48	1	4	.349	.326	L	R	5-10	190	8-22-79	2000	Herndon, Pa.
Rios, Alexis	.352	127	514	86	181	32	11	11	82	39	85	11	3	.521	.402	R	R	6-5	180	2-18-81	1999	Guaynabo, P.R.
Sanders, Anthony	.280	28	107	20	30	8	1	3	15	8	24	0	0	.458	.336	R	R	6-2	200	3-2-74	1993	Tucson, Ariz.
Sequea, Jorge	.342	33	111	17	38	7	0	2	13	11	21	0	4	.459	.400	R	R	5-10	160	10-1-80	1998	Anaco, Venez.
Singleton, Justin	.254	84	244	41	62	11	4	3	31	22	73	4	0	.369	.313	L	R	6-1	190	4-10-79	2001	Sparks, Md.
Solano, Danny	.263	123	396	54	104	30	4	2	43	49	65	3	2	.374	.347	R	R	5-9	150	12-3-75	1997	Santo Domingo, D.R.
Thompson, Rich	.313	49	182	39	57	5	1	0	9	10	24	15	3	.352	.373	L	R	6-3	180	4-23-79	2000	Montrose, Pa.
Umbria, Jose	.316	7	19	3	6	0	0	0	5	3	0	0	0	.316	.409	R	R	6-2	210	1-20-78	1996	Barquisimeto, Venez.
Whittaker, Tim	.000	5	10	0	0	0	0	0	0	1	2	0	0	.000	.091	R	R	6-0	200	1-4-79	2001	Conway, S.C.

PITCHING	W	L	ERA	G	GS	CG	SV	IP	H	R	ER	BB	SO	AVG	B	T	HT	WT	DOB	1st Yr	Resides
Abbott, David	0	1	9.00	3	1	0	0	7	8	8	7	4	4	.307	R	R	6-4	230	10-19-77	2000	Tucson, Ariz.
Arnold, Jason	3	1	1.53	6	6	0	0	35	18	7	6	11	33	.152	R	R	6-3	210	5-2-79	2001	Palm Bay, Fla.
Baker, Chris	9	6	3.90	25	25	1	0	148	158	74	64	37	95	.273	R	R	6-1	200	8-24-77	1999	Valencia, Calif.
Bauer, Peter	5	6	4.96	29	13	1	0	103	116	59	57	45	60	.291	L	R	6-7	250	11-6-78	2000	Hagerstown, Md.
Bush, David	7	3	2.78	14	14	1	0	81	73	26	25	19	73	.239	R	R	6-2	210	11-9-79	2002	Devon, Pa.
Castellanos, Hugo	3	7	5.13	21	0	0	0	33	41	25	19	13	28	.305	R	R	6-4	200	6-30-80	1996	Nuevo Laredo, Mexico
Chacin, Gustavo	3	4	4.15	46	2	0	2	69	78	39	32	29	55	.282	L	L	5-11	190	12-4-80	1998	Maracaibo, Venez.
DeJong, Jordan	4	5	3.58	27	0	0	1	28	27	16	11	17	29	.264	R	R	6-2	170	4-12-79	2002	Yorba Linda, Calif.
Frederick, Kevin	2	2	3.38	25	0	0	7	29	32	16	11	14	27	.271	L	R	6-1	210	11-4-76	1998	Prairie View, Ill.
Gassner, Dave	10	4	2.79	35	19	1	1	145	139	54	45	28	92	.253	R	L	6-2	190	12-14-78	2001	Hortonville, Wisc.
Hamann, Rob	0	2	11.91	6	0	0	0	11	22	17	15	5	3	.400	R	R	6-7	210	12-15-76	1999	Escondido, Calif.
Jackson, Dan	5	1	4.02	33	0	0	2	47	46	23	21	24	38	.258	R	R	5-11	210	7-12-78	2000	Lyons, Ill.
Kegley, Chuck	0	0	9.00	12	0	0	0	14	12	19	14	20	7	.240	R	R	6-3	200	12-17-79	1999	Orange Park, Fla.
Markwell, Diego	5	7	7.04	28	19	0	0	110	146	96	86	54	69	.324	L	L	6-2	190	8-8-80	1996	Willemstad, Curacao
McGowan, Dustin	7	0	3.17	14	14	1	0	77	78	28	27	19	72	.260	R	R	6-3	190	3-24-82	2000	Ludowici, Ga.
Nin, Sandy	0	1	2.57	1	1	0	0	7	5	2	2	0	9	.200	R	R	6-0	170	8-13-80	2000	Estebania, Azua, D.R.
Ogiltree, John	4	4	3.38	45	0	0	2	61	55	29	23	31	38	.236	R	R	6-6	220	6-3-78	2001	Mississauga, Ontario
Pena, Juan	0	0	2.45	7	0	0	5	7	5	2	2	5	10	.185	R	R	6-5	210	6-27-77	1995	Carol City, Fla.
Peterson, Adam	2	2	4.88	24	0	0	9	24	24	13	13	7	24	.260	R	R	6-3	220	5-18-79	2002	Abrams, Wisc.
Reimers, Cameron	10	5	3.08	28	26	0	0	164	170	68	56	38	96	.269	R	R	6-5	200	9-15-78	1999	Missoula, Mont.
Walker, Pete	0	1	9.00	2	2	0	0	2	3	2	2	0	1	.375	R	R	6-2	190	4-8-69	1990	Waterford, Conn.
Wiggins, Scott	0	1	4.00	17	0	0	0	18	19	10	8	2	13	.279	L	L	6-3	200	3-24-76	1997	Newport, Ky.

FIELDING

Catcher	PCT	G	PO	A	E	DP	PB
Chiaffredo	1.000	38	233	16	0	1	4
Kratz	1.000	1	5	1	0	0	0
Quiroz	.994	100	605	57	4	6	10
Umbria	.981	7	45	8	1	0	1
Whittaker	1.000	4	16	2	0	2	1

First Base	PCT	G	PO	A	E	DP
Chiaffredo	1.000	1	1	1	0	0
Deschaine	.986	12	68	5	1	7
Fagan	.986	44	385	27	6	37
Keene	1.000	2	12	1	0	3
Logan	.994	86	732	54	5	65
Pond	1.000	6	42	6	0	4

Second Base	PCT	G	PO	A	E	DP
Keene	.973	18	37	36	2	9
Rich	.981	101	214	289	10	75
Sequea	.981	11	19	34	1	7
Solano	.989	17	35	54	1	14

Third Base	PCT	G	PO	A	E	DP
Deschaine	1.000	1	2	0	0	0
Fagan	.915	31	20	55	7	4
Keene	.929	22	9	56	5	1
Logan	1.000	1	0	1	0	1
Pond	.890	53	34	127	20	12
Sequea	.875	8	3	11	2	1
Solano	.978	34	17	71	2	9

Shortstop	PCT	G	PO	A	E	DP
Adams	.944	64	95	175	16	36
Keene	1.000	1	2	1	0	0
Sequea	.911	13	14	27	4	7
Solano	.961	69	98	225	13	43

Outfield	PCT	G	PO	A	E	DP
Fagan	.962	14	23	2	1	0
Godwin	.940	32	46	1	3	0
Griffin	.977	66	125	3	3	0
Gross	.980	77	139	10	3	2
Keene	1.000	3	2	1	0	0
Logan	.000	1	0	0	0	0
Patrick	.765	11	12	1	4	0
Rios	.990	123	277	8	3	1
Sanders	1.000	25	47	2	0	0
Singleton	.953	72	114	7	6	2
Solano	1.000	1	1	0	0	0
Thompson	.952	29	56	4	3	1

DUNEDIN BLUE JAYS — High Class A

FLORIDA STATE LEAGUE

BATTING	AVG	G	AB	R	H	2B	3B	HR	RBI	BB	SO	SB	CS	SLG	OBP	B	T	HT	WT	DOB	1st Yr	Resides
Adams, Russ	.279	68	258	50	72	9	5	3	16	38	27	9	2	.388	.380	L	R	6-1	180	8-30-80	2002	Laurinburg, N.C.
Bernhardt, Joe	.118	9	34	2	4	1	0	0	1	2	8	0	0	.147	.167	R	R	6-1	180	9-22-80	1996	San Pedro de Macoris, D.R.
Carter, Shannon	.228	32	101	18	23	4	0	0	7	4	13	3	1	.267	.257	L	L	6-0	180	3-23-79	1997	El Reno, Okla.
Cosby, Rob	.277	133	476	53	132	34	2	4	52	46	61	3	5	.382	.343	R	R	6-2	200	4-2-81	1999	Rio Piedras, P.R.
Davenport, Ron	.276	119	421	39	116	27	2	5	57	32	74	6	7	.385	.330	L	R	6-2	190	10-16-81	2000	Raleigh, N.C.
Delfino, Lee	.155	62	161	13	25	3	0	1	11	16	38	2	0	.193	.243	R	R	6-0	180	5-21-80	2001	Richmond Hill, Ontario
Galloway, Mike	.333	1	3	1	1	1	0	0	1	0	2	0	0	.667	.333	R	R	6-2	210	5-9-81	2002	St. Thomas, Ontario
Godwin, Tyrell	.273	97	322	52	88	16	0	1	33	29	39	20	7	.332	.348	L	R	6-0	200	7-10-79	2001	Council, N.C.
Hill, Aaron	.286	32	119	26	34	7	0	0	11	11	10	1	0	.345	.343	R	R	5-11	195	3-21-82	2003	Visalia, Calif.
Jova, Maikel	.271	64	240	34	65	12	0	5	24	6	42	0	1	.383	.291	R	R	6-0	190	3-5-81	1999	San Jose, Costa Rica
Keene, Kurt	.341	36	135	20	46	9	1	2	16	7	19	2	2	.467	.388	R	R	6-0	190	8-22-77	2000	Chattanooga, Tenn.
Mayorson, Manuel	.229	106	363	39	83	14	0	0	30	25	36	6	7	.267	.282	R	R	5-10	160	3-10-83	1999	La Romana, D.R.
McEachran, Aaron	.231	61	182	18	42	9	0	2	17	26	40	0	0	.313	.332	L	R	6-0	200	1-28-79	2001	St. Louis Park, Minn.
Medina, Rodney	.250	2	8	1	2	1	0	1	3	0	0	0	0	.750	.250	S	R	6-1	180	10-17-81	1999	Maracaibo, Venez.
Perry, Jason	.304	39	135	17	41	11	1	1	17	10	32	1	0	.422	.356	L	R	6-0	200	8-18-80	2002	Jonesboro, Ga.
Rico, Erik	.286	13	35	1	10	0	0	0	2	2	3	2	1	.286	.324	L	L	6-2	190	1-21-80	2002	Miami, Fla.
Snyder, Mike	.268	137	496	70	133	24	0	9	75	66	113	6	0	.371	.356	L	R	6-5	230	2-11-81	1999	Chino Hills, Calif.
Tablado, Raul	.258	54	182	27	47	9	3	5	19	17	47	1	2	.423	.328	R	R	6-2	170	3-3-82	2000	Miami, Fla.
Umbria, Jose	.220	42	127	3	28	5	0	0	15	10	26	0	0	.260	.284	R	R	6-2	210	1-20-78	1996	Barquisimeto, Venez.
Waugh, Jason	.273	79	286	32	78	14	2	7	38	32	61	0	5	.409	.344	R	R	6-1	190	3-12-80	2002	Bakersfield, Calif.
Werth, Jayson	.371	18	62	10	23	5	0	4	18	3	14	1	0	.645	.388	R	R	6-5	210	5-20-79	1997	Chatham, Ill.
Whittaker, Tim	.282	86	287	34	81	22	0	1	41	28	65	1	2	.369	.353	R	R	6-0	200	1-4-79	2001	Conway, S.C.
Yepez, Jose	.216	40	116	13	25	2	0	1	10	12	23	0	0	.259	.321	R	R	6-0	170	6-19-81	1997	Lara, Venez.

PITCHING	W	L	ERA	G	GS	CG	SV	IP	H	R	ER	BB	SO	AVG	B	T	HT	WT	DOB	1st Yr	Resides
Abbott, David	1	2	5.87	8	3	0	0	23	34	16	15	5	11	.350	R	R	6-4	230	10-19-77	2000	Tucson, Ariz.
Bush, David	7	3	2.81	14	14	0	0	77	64	29	24	9	75	.222	R	R	6-2	210	11-9-79	2002	Devon, Pa.
Cardwell, Brian	1	0	3.60	8	0	0	0	10	6	6	4	8	5	.166	R	R	6-10	210	12-30-80	1999	Jacksonville, Fla.
Comolli, Mark	1	3	3.43	21	0	0	11	21	16	9	8	13	24	.216	R	R	6-0	190	3-11-79	2001	Millville, Del.
DeJong, Jordan	2	3	2.79	28	0	0	17	29	23	10	9	18	30	.212	R	R	6-2	170	4-12-79	2002	Yorba Linda, Calif.
Esarey, Brad	0	0	11.81	6	0	0	0	5	8	8	7	5	8	.347	L	L	6-3	170	9-20-78	2001	Concord, N.C.
File, Bob	0	0	3.00	3	2	0	0	3	3	1	1	0	0	.272	R	R	6-4	210	1-28-77	1998	Morrisville, Pa.
Flores, Neomar	7	8	4.78	29	18	1	0	111	108	61	59	44	78	.254	R	R	6-2	180	3-12-82	1998	Guarenas, Venez.
Hamann, Rob	1	0	2.08	4	0	0	0	9	7	2	2	3	4	.233	R	R	6-7	210	12-15-76	1999	Escondido, Calif.
Harper, Jesse	13	4	2.54	26	24	1	0	131	112	41	37	31	100	.229	R	R	6-4	200	11-11-80	2000	Clute, Texas
Hendrickson, Mark	1	0	1.59	1	1	0	0	6	5	2	1	4	3	.227	L	L	6-9	230	6-23-74	1998	Mt. Vernon, Wash.
Houston, Ryan	1	2	2.66	26	4	0	3	51	36	15	15	30	54	.198	R	R	6-4	190	9-22-79	1999	Pensacola, Fla.
Jackson, Dan	1	0	1.88	9	0	0	0	14	12	4	3	4	17	.226	R	R	5-11	210	7-12-78	2000	Lyons, Ill.
Kegley, Chuck	5	0	3.20	19	0	0	0	25	26	9	9	12	23	.265	R	R	6-3	200	12-17-79	1999	Orange Park, Fla.
League, Brandon	4	3	4.75	13	12	0	0	66	76	40	35	20	34	.287	R	R	6-2	180	3-16-83	2001	Honolulu, Hawaii
Maureau, Justin	3	4	4.84	38	3	0	0	48	55	34	26	28	35	.291	R	L	6-1	170	12-17-80	2002	Highlands Ranch, Colo.
McGowan, Dustin	5	6	2.85	14	14	1	0	76	62	29	24	25	66	.223	R	R	6-3	190	3-24-82	2000	Ludowici, Ga.
Miller, Justin	0	1	4.50	1	1	0	0	6	3	3	3	2	5	.166	R	R	6-2	200	8-27-77	1997	Torrance, Calif.
Nunley, Derrick	3	2	2.20	42	0	0	1	57	41	17	14	36	64	.200	R	R	6-1	180	9-13-80	1999	Jacksonville, Fla.
Ozuna, Francisco	0	0	5.79	11	0	0	0	14	16	13	9	8	8	.290	L	L	6-2	180	5-17-81	1997	Santo Domingo, D.R.
Perkins, Vince	7	6	2.45	18	17	0	0	84	58	32	23	53	69	.200	L	R	6-5	220	9-27-81	2001	Victoria, B.C.
Peterson, Adam	1	0	0.71	9	0	0	1	13	5	1	1	0	13	.116	R	R	6-3	220	5-18-79	2002	Abrams, Wisc.
Pleiness, Chad	7	8	3.41	25	24	0	0	129	124	60	49	60	89	.257	R	R	6-6	230	3-5-80	2002	Scottville, Mich.
Sandoval, Marcos	0	0	0.00	1	0	0	0	1	1	0	0	1	0	.500	R	R	6-1	180	12-29-80	1997	Carabobo, Venez.
Torres, Andy	4	3	2.16	43	0	0	5	75	62	24	18	23	67	.227	R	R	5-9	160	4-12-78	2002	Bell Gardens, Calif.
Valdez, Santo	2	2	4.90	41	3	0	1	79	96	46	43	25	46	.299	R	R	6-1	170	3-30-82	1999	Bani, D.R.
Vermilyea, Jamie	0	2	2.49	9	0	0	2	22	21	6	6	2	25	.253	R	R	6-4	195	2-10-82	2003	Tucson, Ariz.

FIELDING

Catcher	PCT	G	PO	A	E	DP	PB
McEachran	1.000	11	57	3	0	0	2
Umbria	.988	36	229	16	3	0	4
Whittaker	.996	71	473	42	2	2	13
Yepez	.992	31	214	21	2	3	4

First Base	PCT	G	PO	A	E	DP
Bernhardt	1.000	4	44	6	0	1
Keene	1.000	2	20	1	0	0
McEachran	1.000	3	25	2	0	0
Snyder	.983	131	1055	82	20	96
Tablado	1.000	2	12	1	0	0

Second Base	PCT	G	PO	A	E	DP
Delfino	.971	40	66	104	5	17
Keene	1.000	5	7	15	0	0
Mayorson	.990	87	139	262	4	45
Tablado	1.000	13	19	41	0	11

Third Base	PCT	G	PO	A	E	DP
Bernhardt	.667	1	0	2	1	0
Cosby	.957	122	82	185	12	18
Delfino	.941	12	5	11	1	2
Keene	.929	6	6	7	1	0
Tablado	1.000	3	3	4	0	1
Whittaker	.000	1	0	0	0	0

Shortstop	PCT	G	PO	A	E	DP
Adams	.941	66	114	187	19	34
Hill	.930	30	41	65	8	16
Keene	1.000	1	3	0	0	0
Mayorson	.959	20	25	45	3	8
Tablado	.920	25	34	70	9	12

Outfield	PCT	G	PO	A	E	DP
Carter	.954	30	60	2	3	0
Cosby	.938	11	14	1	1	0
Davenport	1.000	109	184	4	0	0
Galloway	.000	1	0	0	0	0
Godwin	.982	94	216	4	4	1
Jova	.981	57	100	6	2	0
Keene	.964	14	26	1	1	0
McEachran	1.000	1	1	0	0	0
Medina	.875	2	7	0	1	0
Perry	1.000	15	15	0	0	0
Rico	1.000	13	12	0	0	0
Waugh	.979	78	135	8	3	3
Werth	1.000	16	26	1	0	0

CHARLESTON ALLEY CATS — Low Class A

SOUTH ATLANTIC LEAGUE

BATTING	AVG	G	AB	R	H	2B	3B	HR	RBI	BB	SO	SB	CS	SLG	OBP	B	T	HT	WT	DOB	1st Yr	Resides
Arnold, Eric	.206	39	126	15	26	10	0	3	16	13	43	1	2	.357	.281	R	R	6-1	190	7-9-80	2002	La Porte, Texas
Chourio, Junior	.167	11	42	3	7	1	0	0	2	0	11	0	0	.190	.186	R	R	6-3	170	3-23-83	1999	Maracaibo, Venez.
Corrente, David	.214	67	224	19	48	8	0	2	18	19	55	2	1	.277	.296	R	R	6-2	200	10-13-83	2001	Chatham, Ontario
Dragicevich, Scott	.246	108	382	56	94	23	0	1	37	43	88	3	4	.314	.335	R	R	6-3	200	6-28-80	2002	Westlake, Calif.
Hassey, Brad	.189	98	338	34	64	17	0	0	25	32	62	2	1	.240	.272	R	R	5-10	170	11-28-79	2002	Tucson, Ariz.

BATTING	AVG	G	AB	R	H	2B	3B	HR	RBI	BB	SO	SB	CS	SLG	OBP	B	T	HT	WT	DOB	1st Yr	Resides
Johnston, Clint	.203	23	74	10	15	3	0	5	14	10	23	0	0	.446	.294	L	L	6-2	210	7-2-77	1998	Nashville, Tenn.
Jova, Maikel	.292	53	216	19	63	15	2	1	28	8	21	6	2	.394	.320	R	R	6-0	190	3-5-81	1999	San Jose, Costa Rica
Knicely, Jeremy	.316	7	19	4	6	2	0	0	1	2	7	0	0	.421	.381	R	R	6-0	195	2-11-81	2003	Elkton, Va.
Kratz, Erik	.316	8	19	0	6	3	0	0	2	1	7	0	0	.474	.409	R	R	6-4	240	6-15-80	2002	Harrisonburg, Va.
Medina, Rodney	.283	119	452	69	128	23	8	11	45	45	44	6	4	.442	.349	S	R	6-1	180	10-17-81	1999	Maracaibo, Venez.
Negron, Miguel	.303	30	109	13	33	8	1	1	11	2	16	6	2	.422	.330	L	L	6-2	170	8-22-82	2000	Caguas, P.R.
Owens, Justin	.236	111	373	41	88	16	5	4	52	62	106	6	3	.338	.348	L	L	6-3	190	9-28-79	2002	Myrtle Beach, S.C.
Rico, Erik	.228	49	158	18	36	5	1	0	7	20	36	3	3	.272	.315	L	L	6-2	190	1-21-80	2002	Miami, Fla.
Rivera, Willie	.242	116	409	51	99	15	1	4	37	57	86	8	2	.313	.338	L	R	6-0	150	12-28-81	2000	Caguas, P.R.
Salas, Jose	.150	8	20	1	3	1	0	0	3	1	6	0	0	.200	.190	S	R	6-0	180	8-26-81	2002	Caracas, Venez.
Schneider, John	.195	56	174	10	34	11	0	0	14	32	42	3	0	.259	.324	R	R	6-3	220	2-14-80	2002	Lawrenceville, N.J.
Siriveaw, Nom	.115	15	52	4	6	2	0	0	4	5	17	0	0	.154	.193	S	R	6-3	190	12-9-80	2000	Surrey, B.C.
Smith, David	.243	86	342	44	83	13	2	8	29	32	67	7	1	.363	.318	R	R	6-1	190	1-12-81	2002	Charleston, W.Va.
Tablado, Raul	.190	61	226	29	43	10	1	6	26	25	69	2	1	.323	.272	R	R	6-2	170	3-3-82	2000	Miami, Fla.
Waugh, Jason	.209	36	139	18	29	7	1	1	8	10	30	2	0	.295	.262	R	R	6-1	190	3-12-80	2002	Bakersfield, Calif.
Yepez, Jose	.227	21	66	4	15	5	0	1	7	6	12	0	0	.348	.289	R	R	6-0	170	6-19-81	1997	Lara, Venez.
Zinsman, Zeph	.204	110	378	28	77	22	1	2	43	36	115	0	3	.283	.276	L	L	6-3	210	12-4-78	2002	Cupertino, Calif.

PITCHING	W	L	ERA	G	GS	CG	SV	IP	H	R	ER	BB	SO	AVG	B	T	HT	WT	DOB	1st Yr	Resides
Comolli, Mark	1	0	2.51	26	0	0	13	29	20	8	8	8	25	.206	R	R	6-0	190	3-11-79	2001	Millville, Del.
Costello, Ryan	4	4	4.29	45	0	0	3	65	67	34	31	32	60	.269	R	L	6-6	210	7-13-79	2001	Marlton, N.J.
Esarey, Brad	0	5	3.77	31	0	0	7	45	47	24	19	28	37	.270	L	L	6-3	170	9-20-78	2001	Concord, N.C.
Fuller, Brendan	2	3	8.56	41	0	0	0	55	51	53	52	59	61	.255	R	R	6-1	200	9-13-80	2001	Clearwater, Fla.
Hanson, D.J.	10	10	2.54	25	25	2	0	138	110	51	39	56	113	.224	R	R	5-11	170	8-7-80	1999	Richland, Wash.
Houston, Ryan	2	4	2.67	13	3	0	2	30	22	14	9	12	38	.201	R	R	6-4	190	9-22-79	1999	Pensacola, Fla.
League, Brandon	2	3	1.91	12	12	0	0	71	58	15	15	18	61	.230	R	R	6-2	180	3-16-83	2001	Honolulu, Hawaii
Mora, Ramon	4	4	3.92	36	6	0	4	78	85	38	34	28	73	.281	R	R	6-2	210	3-18-81	1998	Maturin, Venez.
Nin, Sandy	7	8	2.89	23	23	1	0	131	124	50	42	19	87	.250	R	R	6-0	170	8-13-80	2000	Estebania, D.R.
Ozuna, Francisco	2	2	4.88	5	5	0	0	24	36	13	13	9	7	.375	L	L	6-2	180	5-17-81	1997	Santo Domingo, D.R.
Perkins, Vince	3	1	1.83	8	8	0	0	44	19	9	9	22	60	.135	L	R	6-5	220	9-27-81	2001	Victoria, B.C.
Peterson, Adam	2	4	2.19	10	0	0	1	25	15	8	6	13	19	.189	R	R	6-3	220	5-18-79	2002	Abrams, Wisc.
Ramirez, Ismael	6	5	3.02	24	22	1	0	119	110	51	40	31	70	.242	R	R	6-3	200	3-3-81	1998	El Tigre, Venez.
Romero, Felix	2	3	3.89	42	0	0	0	69	63	37	30	25	77	.239	R	R	6-2	160	6-18-80	1997	San Pedro de Macoris, D.R.
Sandoval, Marcos	1	4	5.34	16	3	0	0	29	34	23	17	17	17	.293	R	R	6-1	180	12-29-80	1997	Carabobo, Venez.
Sheffield, Chris	0	0	2.08	7	0	0	0	9	7	4	2	11	7	.241	R	R	6-3	210	12-13-79	2001	Richmond, Texas
Stephenson, Eric	4	4	4.38	18	8	0	0	62	67	43	30	36	47	.287	R	L	6-4	180	9-3-82	2000	Benson, N.C.
Talanoa, Charles	2	5	3.71	9	9	0	0	44	49	23	18	21	37	.278	R	R	6-5	230	12-29-80	2001	Hawthorne, Calif.
Thorpe, Tracy	1	2	6.68	20	1	0	0	32	37	26	24	22	21	.289	R	R	6-4	250	12-15-80	2000	Melbourne, Fla.
Wesley, John	2	5	3.48	8	8	0	0	41	38	21	16	13	32	.255	R	R	6-6	230	10-14-80	2002	Westbury, N.Y.

FIELDING

Catcher	PCT	G	PO	A	E	DP	PB
Corrente	.977	67	450	59	12	4	14
Knicely	1.000	4	17	0	0	0	0
Kratz	1.000	3	15	1	0	0	1
Schneider	.989	51	409	29	5	0	6
Yepez	.988	12	77	8	1	0	0

First Base	PCT	G	PO	A	E	DP
Arnold	1.000	1	1	0	0	0
Dragicevich	.987	19	145	12	2	12
Johnston	.972	5	31	4	1	7
Kratz	1.000	4	41	1	0	3
Siriveaw	1.000	5	32	4	0	8
Yepez	1.000	2	8	2	0	0
Zinsman	.984	106	856	76	15	91

Second Base	PCT	G	PO	A	E	DP
Arnold	1.000	8	10	19	0	3
Hassey	.960	15	25	47	3	14
Rivera	.984	112	222	317	9	85

Third Base	PCT	G	PO	A	E	DP
Arnold	.917	27	26	40	6	2
Dragicevich	.958	92	62	167	10	17
Hassey	1.000	8	3	14	0	2
Salas	.846	6	4	7	2	0
Schneider	1.000	1	1	1	0	0
Siriveaw	.750	4	3	6	3	0

Shortstop	PCT	G	PO	A	E	DP
Hassey	.971	69	125	207	10	40
Rivera	.706	4	6	6	5	1
Tablado	.950	61	113	190	16	51

Outfield	PCT	G	PO	A	E	DP
Chourio	.941	11	16	0	1	0
Johnston	.943	19	30	3	2	1
Jova	1.000	53	82	4	0	0
Knicely	.000	1	0	0	0	0
Medina	.935	119	193	9	14	1
Negron	1.000	27	47	3	0	0
Rico	.959	48	67	4	3	0
Siriveaw	1.000	4	6	0	0	0
Smith	.963	86	153	4	6	1
Waugh	.985	35	63	4	1	0

AUBURN DOUBLEDAYS — Short-Season Class A

NEW YORK-PENN LEAGUE

BATTING	AVG	G	AB	R	H	2B	3B	HR	RBI	BB	SO	SB	CS	SLG	OBP	B	T	HT	WT	DOB	1st Yr	Resides
Arnold, Eric	.167	4	12	2	2	0	0	0	4	4	5	1	0	.167	.375	R	R	6-1	190	7-9-80	2002	La Porte, Texas
Blackburn, Alex	.176	23	34	3	6	1	0	0	3	0	8	0	0	.206	.194	R	R	6-1	200	12-30-82	2000	London, Ontario
Chiaravolloti, Vito	.351	68	228	47	80	20	1	12	67	47	48	0	0	.605	.469	R	R	6-3	225	10-26-80	2003	Middletown, N.J.
Cota, Carlo	.320	51	169	31	54	13	3	5	34	27	45	3	2	.521	.416	R	R	5-10	180	9-18-80	2002	Calexico, Calif.
Davis, Morrin	.235	36	81	7	19	4	0	0	8	7	34	2	1	.284	.295	R	R	6-2	190	12-11-82	2000	Tampa, Fla.
Galloway, Mike	.302	52	172	36	52	12	3	4	33	20	47	3	1	.477	.379	R	R	6-2	210	5-9-81	2002	St. Thomas, Ontario
Hill, Aaron	.361	33	122	22	44	4	0	4	34	16	20	1	1	.492	.446	R	R	5-11	195	3-21-82	2003	Visalia, Calif.
Johnston, Clint	.318	23	66	17	21	8	0	1	6	14	12	0	0	.485	.438	L	L	6-2	210	7-2-77	1998	Nashville, Tenn.
Knicely, Jeremy	.000	8	15	0	0	0	0	0	0	1	9	0	0	.000	.118	R	R	6-0	195	2-11-81	2003	Elkton, Va.
Kratz, Erik	.312	49	157	25	49	15	0	5	26	21	31	0	1	.503	.411	R	R	6-4	240	6-15-80	2002	Harrisonburg, Va.
Mangioni, Jarad	.226	42	106	12	24	9	0	0	19	14	32	0	0	.311	.315	R	R	6-3	180	2-8-84	2002	Sydney, Australia
Patrick, Brian	.301	28	83	17	25	3	0	1	16	7	14	2	0	.373	.366	S	R	5-10	185	11-29-80	2003	Fort Lauderdale, Fla.
Peralta, Juan	.247	71	288	62	71	14	1	3	30	43	50	14	7	.333	.346	S	R	6-0	170	6-24-83	2000	Santiago Rodriguez, D.R.
Porfirio, A.J.	.286	71	273	49	78	8	4	7	40	30	63	4	2	.421	.357	R	R	6-2	190	12-3-79	2002	Houston, Texas
Richmond, Paul	.266	48	169	37	45	8	2	5	34	41	36	3	1	.426	.408	L	R	6-2	210	5-30-80	2002	Crockett, Texas
Roberts, Ryan	.278	66	248	52	69	10	3	8	36	35	63	7	3	.440	.374	R	R	5-11	190	9-19-80	2003	North Richland Hills, Texas
Siriveaw, Nom	.143	4	7	3	1	0	0	0	0	5	2	0	0	.143	.538	S	R	6-3	190	12-9-80	2000	Surrey, B.C.
Snavely, Christian	.255	64	208	25	53	9	2	0	22	24	54	6	2	.317	.332	L	R	6-3	200	5-7-82	2003	Defiance, Ohio
Tingler, Jayce	.238	7	21	5	5	1	0	0	1	4	0	0	0	.286	.360	L	L	5-8	155	11-28-80	2003	Smithville, Mo.
Vancamper, Eugenio	.192	7	26	2	5	2	0	1	7	1	10	0	0	.385	.222	S	R	6-1	160	5-16-82	2001	San Pedro de Macoris, D.R.

GAMES BY POSITION: **C**—Blackburn 22, Knicely 5, Kratz 33, Richmond 36. **1B**—Chiaravolloti 58, Johnston 13, Kratz 12. **2B**—Arnold 3, Cota 37, Patrick 5, Peralta 31, Vancamper 5. **3B**—Arnold 1, Cota 13, Mangioni 2, Roberts 62, Siriveaw 2. **SS**—Cota 1, Hill 32, Patrick 1, Peralta 41, Roberts 1, Vancamper 2. **OF**—Cota 1, Davis 31, Galloway 43, Mangioni 26, Patrick 12, Porfirio 71, Siriveaw 1, Snavely 59, Tingler 7.

PITCHING	W	L	ERA	G	GS	CG	SV	IP	H	R	ER	BB	SO	AVG	B	T	HT	WT	DOB	1st Yr	Resides
Banks, Josh	7	2	2.43	15	15	0	0	67	58	21	18	10	81	.232	R	R	6-3	195	7-18-82	2003	Arnold, Md.
Buzachero, Bubbie	1	1	1.54	30	0	0	13	35	25	8	6	7	47	.200	R	R	5-11	180	6-13-81	2002	Livingston, Tenn.
Canizal, Joaquin	0	1	2.08	3	0	0	0	4	1	1	1	2	4	.071	R	R	6-4	200	1-5-81	2003	Trujillo Alto, P.R.
Colson, Jason	0	0	0.00	3	0	0	0	6	3	1	0	4	6	.142	L	R	6-2	220	11-19-78	2001	Weirton, W.Va.
Core, Danny	6	2	3.14	16	4	0	1	52	41	22	18	17	34	.222	R	R	6-1	195	7-17-81	2003	Pembroke Pines, Fla.
Day, Dewon	0	0	0.00	2	0	0	0	1	1	0	0	0	1	.200	R	R	6-4	210	9-29-80	2003	Jackson, Miss.
Harper, Jeremy	5	1	3.79	19	1	0	0	40	28	18	17	18	36	.198	R	R	6-2	190	10-31-80	2003	Seneca Rocks, W.Va.
Isenberg, Kurt	7	2	1.63	13	13	0	0	61	40	17	11	19	57	.183	R	L	6-0	190	1-15-82	2003	Virginia Beach, Va.
James, Justin	2	1	3.20	13	8	0	0	39	34	14	14	11	42	.237	R	R	6-3	215	9-13-81	2003	Yukon, Okla.
Marcum, Shaun	1	0	1.32	21	0	0	8	34	15	6	5	7	47	.129	R	R	6-0	180	12-14-81	2003	Excelsior Springs, Mo.
Mastny, Tom	8	0	2.26	14	14	0	0	64	56	19	16	12	68	.237	R	R	6-6	220	2-4-81	2003	Zionsville, Ind.
Mulholland, Chad	1	0	2.78	8	5	0	0	23	23	10	7	7	14	.264	R	R	6-3	210	1-14-82	2003	Herrin, Ill.
Reed, Brian	1	2	1.99	28	0	0	1	41	29	14	9	11	53	.192	R	R	6-1	210	3-6-81	2003	Amory, Miss.
Roga, Mike	0	0	6.75	2	0	0	0	4	6	3	3	2	3	.333	R	R	6-4	210	5-13-81	2002	Pickering, Ontario
Romero, Davis	4	1	2.38	30	0	0	2	42	31	13	11	8	53	.198	L	L	5-10	140	3-30-83	1999	Aguadulce, Panama
Sandoval, Marcos	2	1	2.55	4	4	0	0	18	8	5	5	7	13	.137	R	R	6-1	180	12-29-80	1997	Carabobo, Venez.
Sopko, Mark	3	0	2.10	18	0	0	0	34	20	8	8	14	29	.170	R	R	5-11	190	12-16-81	2003	Joliet, Ill.
Talanoa, Charles	2	2	4.22	5	5	0	0	21	19	11	10	8	25	.231	R	R	6-5	230	12-29-80	2001	Hawthorne, Calif.
Templet, Jordy	1	0	1.04	8	3	0	0	17	15	3	2	8	13	.230	R	R	6-2	180	8-19-81	2003	Gonzales, La.
Vermilyea, Jamie	5	1	2.37	9	2	0	0	30	22	10	8	5	53	.203	R	R	6-4	195	2-10-82	2003	Tucson, Ariz.
Wheeler, Billy	0	1	6.88	10	0	0	0	17	18	13	13	11	19	.260	R	R	5-11	180	2-20-81	2003	Crown Point, Ind.

PULASKI BLUE JAYS

Rookie

APPALACHIAN LEAGUE

BATTING	AVG	G	AB	R	H	2B	3B	HR	RBI	BB	SO	SB	CS	SLG	OBP	B	T	HT	WT	DOB	1st Yr	Resides
Acey, Jermy	.294	56	214	45	63	16	0	3	28	31	32	11	3	.411	.414	S	R	5-11	185	5-24-81	2003	Elk Grove, Calif.
Braun, Randy	.181	40	144	13	26	4	2	1	18	8	26	0	3	.257	.222	L	L	6-4	190	4-19-84	2002	Belton, Mo.
Chourio, Junior	.176	20	74	4	13	3	0	0	8	0	26	0	0	.216	.171	R	R	6-3	170	3-23-83	1999	Maracaibo, Venez.
Diaz, Robinzon	.374	48	182	33	68	20	2	1	44	10	14	1	4	.522	.407	R	R	5-11	180	9-19-83	2001	Monte Plata, D.R.
Esposito, Vincent	.299	39	127	20	38	11	0	3	23	20	36	2	1	.457	.405	L	R	6-0	195	8-22-80	2003	Middletown, N.J.
Hetherington, Luke	.266	46	143	27	38	8	5	1	24	22	50	2	1	.413	.384	R	R	6-1	190	4-13-83	2001	Covington, Wash.
Ponce, Arnoldo	.256	39	117	18	30	4	0	1	11	12	31	3	2	.316	.353	S	R	6-2	160	12-19-81	1999	El Tigre, Venez.
Reiman, Joey	.301	59	206	47	62	18	2	1	35	32	46	1	3	.422	.416	R	R	6-1	200	12-20-80	2003	Phoenix, Ariz.
Rodriquez, Yuber	.282	41	131	18	37	11	0	2	15	5	41	1	1	.412	.333	S	R	6-1	170	11-17-83	2001	Maracay, Venez.
Salas, Jose	.278	19	54	7	15	4	0	0	7	3	20	0	0	.352	.317	S	R	6-0	180	8-26-81	2002	Caracas, Venez.
Sena, Emmanuel	.191	45	136	15	26	4	0	1	12	19	38	4	1	.243	.299	S	R	6-1	150	10-15-84	2001	Santo Domingo, D.R.
Thomas, Nick	.290	50	186	36	54	14	1	7	39	30	47	0	0	.489	.389	L	R	6-3	195	2-2-83	2003	Elk Grove, Calif.
Tingler, Jayce	.287	62	223	49	64	13	1	1	23	46	14	6	2	.368	.416	L	L	5-8	155	11-28-80	2003	Smithville, Mo.
Vancamper, Eugenio	.258	50	186	20	48	7	2	2	24	8	49	3	4	.349	.291	S	R	6-1	160	5-16-82	2001	San Pedro de Macoris, D.R.
Wolfe, Joey	.314	32	102	20	32	6	0	6	28	21	21	0	1	.549	.457	L	R	5-9	205	10-10-80	2003	Saratoga, Calif.

GAMES BY POSITION: C—Diaz 33, Reiman 14, Wolfe 24. **1B**—Ponce 14, Reiman 38, Thomas 18. **2B**—Acey 26, Sena 39, Vancamper 4. **3B**—Esposito 32, Ponce 24, Salas 18. **SS**—Acey 17, Ponce 1, Salas 1, Sena 5, Vancamper 45. **OF**—Acey 1, Braun 22, Chourio 19, Dalton 1, Hetherington 45, Rodriquez 40, Thomas 25, Tingler 62.

PITCHING	W	L	ERA	G	GS	CG	SV	IP	H	R	ER	BB	SO	AVG	B	T	HT	WT	DOB	1st Yr	Resides
Berroa, Yesson	6	2	3.86	13	13	0	0	63	72	36	27	20	39	.292	R	R	6-4	200	7-20-83	2000	San Pedro de Macoris, D.R.
Canizal, Joaquin	2	3	4.38	27	0	0	2	39	39	30	19	19	32	.258	R	R	6-4	200	1-5-81	2003	Trujillo Alto, P.R.
Dalton, Matthew	3	1	3.00	18	0	0	1	27	36	10	9	5	27	.000	R	R	6-4	200	9-21-79	2003	Monroeville, Pa.
Day, Dewon	2	0	1.80	26	0	0	12	30	21	8	6	9	26	.184	R	R	6-4	210	9-29-80	2003	Jackson, Miss.
Foster, Matt	1	0	4.05	3	0	0	0	7	3	3	3	3	10	.120	L	L	6-3	205	9-4-81	2003	Arnold, Md.
Grant, Brian	2	5	4.80	13	13	0	0	54	64	40	29	27	40	.286	R	R	6-4	190	8-16-84	2002	Goldsboro, N.C.
Grimes, Sean	0	0	2.70	4	0	0	0	3	4	1	1	0	0	.307	R	L	6-4	200	5-31-83	2001	London, Ontario
Harrison, Ben	1	0	10.80	12	0	0	1	17	17	23	20	21	13	.246	L	L	6-1	175	4-14-84	2003	Colleyville, Texas
Mumma, Brad	2	1	5.06	5	4	0	0	21	25	14	12	7	21	.290	L	L	6-4	230	4-1-81	2003	La Porte, Ind.
Neylan, Chris	5	2	4.25	12	8	0	0	53	67	32	25	13	45	.310	R	L	6-6	200	9-27-82	2001	Tampa, Fla.
Perez, Juan	4	6	4.48	13	13	0	0	64	71	37	32	12	35	.287	R	R	6-4	170	12-27-81	2000	San Pedro de Macoris, D.R.
Pidutti, James	1	3	5.61	16	1	0	0	26	40	23	16	9	8	.357	R	L	6-2	205	11-22-81	2002	Coniston, Ontario
Rider, Michael	4	0	6.52	22	0	0	2	39	44	30	28	14	28	.280	R	R	6-3	210	11-21-83	2003	Fairfield, Calif.
Rodriguez, Jayson	1	1	5.94	17	3	0	1	36	42	28	24	19	29	.289	R	R	6-0	175	5-1-83	2003	Tampa, Fla.
Sanchez , Raymon	1	2	5.68	17	1	0	0	38	45	31	24	18	21	.294	L	L	6-0	170	1-7-84	2002	Santo Domingo, D.R.
Savickas, Russell	3	3	4.28	12	12	1	0	55	52	40	26	22	39	.241	R	R	6-4	170	7-30-83	2002	Johnston, R.I.

MINOR LEAGUES

Minor leagues move to suburbs, spur more gains in attendance

BY WILL LINGO

Writer Joel Garreau coined the term "edge cities" in 1991 to describe the suburban communities that were growing on the fringes of larger cities and becoming more than just bedroom communities. Suddenly the suburbs were legitimate cities unto themselves.

Such cities are the latest transformation in how Americans live and work over the last 50 years. After people moved to the suburbs, slowly commercial growth and jobs followed them. Now many places have gone from rural suburbs to centers of work and play. Minor league baseball has become a key component in many of these cities, and its move to these cities has continued an attendance boom that began 25 years ago.

The Texas League moved from Shreveport, La., to Frisco, Texas, in 2003, for instance, and set an attendance record thanks in part to the 666,977 fans who turned out in the city on the outskirts of Dallas-Fort Worth.

As minor league franchises continue to follow the fans, attendance in 2003 increased by 430,565 fans over 2002 and went over the 39 million mark (39,069,707) for the second-largest total attendance in the 102-year history of the minors. The total came from 176 teams in 15 leagues. The all-time record of 39,782,717 occurred in 1949, when there were 448 teams in 59 leagues. Five of the 15 leagues that Minor League Baseball includes in its official attendance numbers (which includes the Mexican League) established new attendance records.

The attendance gains were made in spite of bad weather in much of the northern part of the country and South Atlantic League territory. In all of the minors, there were 236 fewer playing dates than in 2002.

Records were set by the Pacific Coast League with 6,998,344 fans; the Texas with 2,767,854; the Midwest with 3,375,898; the South Atlantic with 3,129,212; and the Pioneer with 628,265. The PCL was paced by Sacramento (766,326) and Memphis (749,446), which finished 1-2 in the minors for the fourth year in a row. The Midwest was led by Dayton, with 590,382 fans, a Class A record that topped its own mark set in 2000.

The Texas League had a 1-2 punch in Round Rock (685,973) and Frisco. Thanks to Frisco, the league had the biggest attendance jump in the minors, and the Express and the RoughRiders each drew more than all but two Triple-A franchises, Sacramento and Memphis.

BALLPARK

Suburban success story
Frisco helped the Texas League set an attendance record in 2003

Just a year after averaging 431 fans a game in Shreveport in 2002, Frisco was a huge success.

"It's worked out extremely well," Texas League president Tom Kayser said. "To be able to move into a metropolitan area the size of Dallas was an unexpected move and one you don't always get to make."

Kayser lamented losing Shreveport, a longtime league member, but said the move was inevitable after the franchise's recent struggles. Minor League Baseball president Mike Moore agreed. "I hate to see us as an industry leaving the Shreveports of the world," he said. "But opportunities like this don't come along very often. It always bothers me to leave towns that have supported us for a long time. But so far, the move looks like a good one."

"The move to Frisco has exceeded all expectations," Frisco team president and general manager Mike McCall said. "The franchise is now located in one of the fastest-growing cities in America, and the fan base from the surrounding counties is phenomenal. The team is great, the fans are happy and the ballpark is gorgeous."

Frisco had a population of 6,138 in 1990, and its 2003 population was estimated at 58,787. It's expected to grow to 75,000 by January 2005. A similar city, and even bigger success story, has been the Round Rock Express, which broke the Double-A attendance record for the fourth straight year, breaking the 2002 record of 670,176 despite the team's 46-94 record.

Round Rock has grown with the success of computer maker Dell Inc., which has brought roughly 9,400 jobs to the city. Overall, Round Rock's population nearly doubled between 1990 and 2000 to 61,000.

The success of the Express prompted ownership to pursue a Triple-A franchise, and team president Reid Ryan announced after the season that the

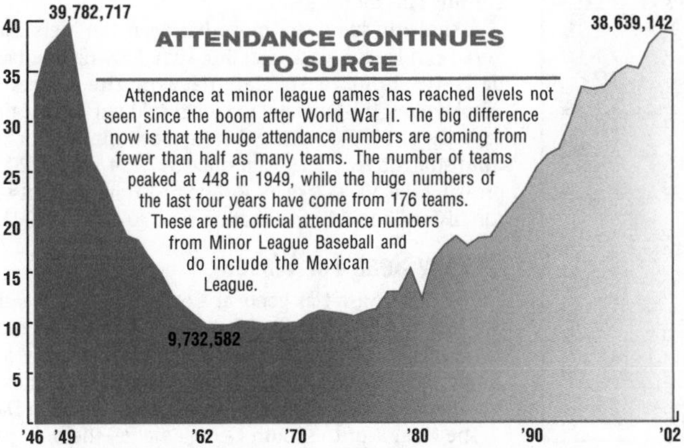

ATTENDANCE CONTINUES TO SURGE
Attendance at minor league games has reached levels not seen since the boom after World War II. The big difference now is that the huge attendance numbers are coming from fewer than half as many teams. The number of teams peaked at 448 in 1949, while the huge numbers of the last four years have come from 176 teams. These are the official attendance numbers from Minor League Baseball and do include the Mexican League.
39,782,717
38,639,142
9,732,582
IN MILLIONS
40
35
30
25
20
15
10
5
'46
'49
'62
'70
'80
'90
'02

MINOR LEAGUES

team purchased the Edmonton Trappers, clearing the way for Round Rock to move up to the PCL in 2005. A new Corpus Christi, Texas, franchise will replace Round Rock in the TL. Round Rock will spend $1.6 million to expand Dell Diamond, which now has 7,816 permanent seats and room for 3,500 more fans on a grass berm. "The Austin/Round Rock area has dictated that we are a Triple-A market," Ryan said. "Now we will be competing on the field with the same cities that we are competing against for economic development."

Edmonton has been in the Pacific Coast League since 1981. The Trappers drew 333,792 in 2003.

"Although we are sorry to part ways with the first-class operation in Edmonton, the PCL gains outstanding leadership and a very positive and successful atmosphere in Round Rock," PCL president Branch Rickey said.

The changes have trickled down to the lower levels of the minors as well. The South Atlantic League drew more than three million fans after moving franchises to Rome, Ga., and Lake County, Ohio, a suburb of Cleveland.

While the Lakewood BlueClaws led the league in attendance for the third consecutive year with 445,838 fans, it was the Lake County Captains (437,515) and Rome Braves (246,718) that pushed the league over three million. Columbus and Macon, the franchises' previous homes, combined to draw 136,000 in 2002.

"To say we have been overwhelmed by the enthusiasm with which we've been received is very accurate," said Captains general manager Mike Edwards.

The Captains weren't worried about playing within a short drive of Jacobs Field.

"I don't think we're competing with them for fans, and I don't think they are competing with us," Edwards said. "In the minor leagues, we are marketing a full entertainment experience. In some ways, we are aiming at fans who may not be hardcore baseball fans."

That's another trend that has paid dividends for both the majors and minors, as officials have discovered that having an affiliate nearby is a good way to raise interest in both teams. The most significant success story to follow this model has been the Dayton Dragons.

"The atmosphere here is as close to the big leagues as any I've been around," said Donnie Scott, in his third season managing the Dragons. "I think at times it can be a little intimidating when you first get here. But once you get comfortable with it, it's a blast."

The Dragons, who have been the Reds' low Class A affiliate since 2000, have sold out every game since the team began playing at the 7,230-seat stadium. Dayton is considered by the Reds to be their most valuable market outside of Cincinnati, but neither club sees the other as competition.

"I definitely think it's an added benefit from a marketing standpoint for the Cincinnati Reds to have their team this close," Dragons president Bob Murphy said. "We're creating fans for the Reds."

A similarly successful move has been the Mets' New York-Penn League affiliate in Brooklyn. Proving that baseball still holds a special place in the hearts of Brooklynites, the Brooklyn Cyclones sold out their season capacity of 285,000 tickets before Opening Day for the third straight year. The team drew 317,124 fans in 2002, breaking the 300,000 mark for the first time in short-season history, and followed that up with 307,383 in 2003.

Choppy Seas For Waves

The news wasn't as good in Columbus, Ga., the city the Lake County Captains left behind. A year after moving from Wilmington, N.C., to Albany, Ga., three weeks before the 2002 season, the South Georgia Waves moved 80 miles northwest about two weeks before Opening Day.

The team kept the South Georgia name, the only part

TOP 10 MINOR LEAGUE STORIES OF 2003

1. **Making new history.** The minor leagues pass the 39 million mark in attendance for just the second time, in spite of worse-than-usual weather in many regions.
2. **More new markets, new ballparks.** Franchises move into hot new markets like Frisco, and new stadiums spark new interest in such cities as Jacksonville and Albuquerque.
3. **Megafranchises keep rolling along.** Sacramento and Memphis in Triple-A, Round Rock in Double-A and Dayton in Class A continue setting attendance records.
4. **Waves of trouble.** The South Georgia Waves move on the eve of Opening Day for the second year in a row, but seek to make Columbus, Ga., a more permanent home.
5. **Royals come up short.** Unable to find a new advanced short-season affiliate, the Royals are forced to field two teams in the Arizona League for one year.
6. **Mauer makes his move.** Joe Mauer's outstanding offensive and defensive skills take him to Double-A and BA's Minor League Player of the Year award.
7. **Reed lights up pitchers.** Unheralded White Sox prospect Jeremy Reed hits .409 after a promotion to Double-A and leads the minors with a .373 average.
8. **Road goes on forever.** Forced on the road by the Cal Ripken World Series, the Aberdeen Ironbirds go on a 17-day, 16-game road trip.
9. **Cruel and unusual.** Cubs prospect Jae-Kuk Ryu is suspended and demoted after he hits an osprey with a thrown ball, and the osprey dies a week later.
10. **Just awful.** Minor league franchises uphold their tradition of promotional innovation with Altoona's Awful Night, which features the worst of everything.

ORGANIZATION STANDINGS

Cumulative farm club records for the 30 major league organizations, with winning percentages going back five years. Every organization has six affiliates except the Orioles, who have seven:

	2003			2002	2001	2000	1999
	W	L	Pct.	Pct.	Pct.	Pct.	Pct.
Pittsburgh	399	288	.581	.571	.467	.491	.487
Cleveland	406	299	.576	.577	.543	.517	.500
Texas	377	312	.547	.498	.478	.530	.541
Oakland	369	324	.532	.509	.480	.551	.573
Toronto	370	327	.531	.480	.460	.529	.534
Seattle	363	326	.527	.471	.560	.577	.483
Kansas City	353	317	.527	.521	.469	.457	.545
Arizona	365	346	.513	.454	.477	.466	.483
Anaheim	353	339	.510	.472	.499	.426	.486
Colorado	361	350	.508	.473	.478	.502	.472
Minnesota	343	339	.503	.540	.541	.537	.496
New York-NL	352	348	.503	.496	.524	.509	.516
Florida	345	342	.502	.491	.539	.496	.477
New York-AL	342	341	.501	.530	.543	.517	.558
Houston	350	350	.500	.535	.598	.526	.499
Tampa Bay	345	349	.497	.445	.474	.478	.508
Atlanta	340	344	.497	.512	.489	.493	.496
Boston	339	345	.496	.454	.468	.522	.526
Chicago-AL	344	353	.494	.466	.495	.483	.520
Baltimore	368	389	.486	.434	.445	.481	.453
Los Angeles	331	352	.485	.563	.538	.527	.457
Detroit	332	358	.481	.509	.508	.478	.480
Cincinnati	334	362	.480	.528	.567	.486	.521
San Diego	338	372	.476	.513	.470	.485	.505
Chicago-NL	324	360	.474	.529	.512	.513	.480
Milwaukee	322	364	.469	.462	.496	.495	.442
Philadelphia	317	369	.462	.525	.504	.568	.523
San Francisco	314	377	.454	.463	.528	.444	.502
St. Louis	313	381	.451	.509	.423	.472	.442
Montreal	300	386	.437	.477	.435	.453	.493

Mauer moves closer to Metrodome

Joe Mauer's aunt and uncle held tickets to see the Twins face the Braves in Game Six of the 1991 World Series, and wanted to take his parents. But with three boys under 12, Jake and Teresa Mauer declined the invitation because they could not find a babysitter.

PLAYER of the YEAR

Instead, the two older boys—Jake III and Bill—got to go see their hero Kirby Puckett rob Ron Gant of extra bases with a catch against the outfield wall, then hit a homer in the 11th to force a deciding Game Seven that the Twins would win. Eight-year-old Joe got to stay home with mom and dad.

Though Mauer's home in St. Paul was just five to 10 minutes on the freeway from the Metrodome, Joe never felt farther away. Now 20, Mauer has a unique chance to avenge the slight.

"He doesn't have to improve any of his tools or skills to jump in and impact the game at the major league level," Twins scouting director Mike Radcliff says. "He's not a normal prospect. Improvement is a different word with a guy like that. He's good enough with his present abilities. He fits into a category with (Cubs righthander Mark) Prior and guys like that who make an impact as soon as they get there."

RICH ABEL

Flashy skills on offense and defense
Twins prospect Joe Mauer

While Prior, the No. 2 pick in the 2001 draft, shot through the minors and already has appeared in the All-Star Game, Mauer, the top pick that year, is developing into a Gold Glove-caliber catcher who could challenge for a batting title.

Mauer hit .339-5-85 between New Britain and high Class A Fort Myers in 2003, posting the highest average of any minor leaguer not yet old enough to order a beer and the best of any minor league catcher. Managers voted Mauer the best defensive catcher in his league for the second straight year—he threw out better than 50 percent of basestealers, and New Britain's team ERA was 0.61 better with him behind the plate. He served as a team leader to a roster including players as much as seven years his senior.

Mauer's contributions in every aspect of the game earned plenty of accolades during the year, and help him garner one more at season's end: Baseball America's 2003 Minor League Player of the Year.

Twins officials weren't sure how Mauer would handle the transition to Double-A at midseason. They knew he'd be fine defensively, but they wondered how his bat would hold up. Mauer was hitting .335 in the Florida State League, so farm director Jim Rantz felt Mauer was ready for a challenge. He quickly showed they had little reason to worry. After going hitless in his first two games for New Britain, Mauer registered at least one hit in 55 of his final 71 games. He hit .341 and would have ranked second in the Eastern League if he had enough at-bats to qualify.

Mauer's mere presence often translates into wins. When the Twins promoted him, along with righthanders J.D. Durbin and Jim Abbott, to New Britain, the RockCats were 25-37 and in the Northern Division cellar. Their arrival sparked a five-game winning streak and led to other spurts of 15 wins in 18 games, 11 of 13 and nine in a row as the RockCats went 48-31 the rest of the way to earn a playoff berth.

"It's unbelievable," Cliburn says. "You don't like to give the credit to one man, but he deserves the credit because people fed off him. They built around him. Joe Mauer at 20 years old, what he's doing here—there is something special. And he's going to do it for a long time wherever he goes."

He did it in Fort Myers during the first half. At 44-26, the Miracle won the first-half title in the Florida State League's Western Division and set a franchise record for wins in a half. Without Mauer and company, Fort Myers went 29-37 in the second half, falling into last place.

The award serves as another reminder that the Twins chose wisely in tabbing the hometown kid first overall in the 2001 draft. He starred in baseball, football and basketball in high school, and could have played for a Division I college in any sport. Rated the top quarterback prospect in the country as well as the best catcher, Mauer spurned his commitment to Florida State in order to sign with the Twins for a club-record $5.15 million bonus.

—WILL KIMMEY

PREVIOUS WINNERS

1981—Mike Marshall, 1b, Albuquerque (Dodgers)
1982—Ron Kittle, of, Edmonton (White Sox)
1983—Dwight Gooden, rhp, Lynchburg (Mets)
1984—Mike Bielecki, rhp, Hawaii (Pirates)
1985—Jose Canseco, of, Huntsville/Tacoma (Athletics)
1986—Gregg Jefferies, ss, Columbia/Lynchburg/Jackson (Mets)
1987—Gregg Jefferies, ss, Jackson/Tidewater (Mets)
1988—Tom Gordon, rhp, Appleton/Memphis/Omaha (Royals)
1989—Sandy Alomar, c, Las Vegas (Padres)
1990—Frank Thomas, 1b, Birmingham (White Sox)
1991—Derek Bell, of, Syracuse (Blue Jays)
1992—Tim Salmon, of, Edmonton (Angels)
1993—Manny Ramirez, of, Canton/Charlotte (Indians)
1994—Derek Jeter, ss, Tampa/Albany/Columbus (Yankees)
1995—Andruw Jones, of, Macon (Braves)
1996—Andruw Jones, of, Durham/Greenville/Richmond (Braves)
1997—Paul Konerko, 1b, Albuquerque (Dodgers)
1998—Eric Chavez, 3b, Huntsville/Edmonton (Athletics)
1999—Rick Ankiel, lhp, Arkansas/Memphis (Cardinals)
2000—Jon Rauch, rhp, Winston-Salem/Birmingham (White Sox)
2001—Josh Beckett, rhp, Brevard County/Portland (Marlins)
2002—Rocco Baldelli, of, Bakersfield/Orlando/Durham (Devil Rays)

of the switch that was easy. Waves owner David Heller applied for the move after getting into a dispute with the city of Albany over a utility bill, stadium renovations and the team's lease. The team's departure was acrimonious on both sides.

"Albany was never a viable long-term option," Heller said. "We said we would play there two, maybe three years at the most. We played one, and we would have played a second if the city hadn't refused to negotiate with us for this year."

The Waves planned to move to Evansville, Ind., for the 2004 season and had a hard time building fan support. Sally League commissioner John Moss said the decision made the best of a bad situation. After the team got to Columbus, a stadium initiative in Evansville fell through, so Heller signed a two-year lease to keep the Waves in Georgia through 2005.

"The project is dead," Evansville mayor Russ Lloyd Jr. said after the project came in as much as $3 million over the original price tag of $25.5 million. Lloyd said extra money would have come from Evansville taxpayers, an idea he wasn't willing to propose. Before signing the lease, the city pushed for improvements in the team's marketing. The Waves' attendance was easily the worst in the full-season minors, with 30,565 fans. Heller said the team will increase its marketing and the size of its front office. The team hired former Memphis general manager Dan Madden as the new GM, along with a new ticket manager and a director of group sales. "With Evansville off the table, we've hired the best people we can find to turn the situation around," Heller said.

Chris Rounds, the new ticket manager, took it upon himself to generate excitement and made himself a shut-in. Just a couple of weeks after taking the job, Rounds laid down a challenge to Waves fans: He wouldn't leave Golden Park until the team drew 1,500 fans to a game. "I've heard too many excuses why the Waves don't draw more fans," Rounds said. "You name it, I've heard it."

When the Waves drew 2,552 fans on Aug. 4, the largest crowd of the season won Rounds his freedom. He had not left the park for three weeks, but the crowd on 75th Ranger Regiment Night made sure he wouldn't spend the entire winter at the park.

Royal Mess

When the music stopped in the game of affiliation musical chairs after the 2002 season, the Royals were left without a short-season seat.

The Royals had an affiliate in Spokane of the Northwest League since 1995, but the Indians sought a new big league affiliate and chose the Rangers. With all the other shuffling at the short-season level, the Royals were left without an opening. They already were moving their Rookie-level team from the Gulf Coast League to the Arizona League because their spring training base

Sacramento's chemistry paves way to victory

TEAM of the YEAR

Sacramento manager Tony DeFrancesco had no trouble pinpointing the reason his club set a franchise record with 92 wins in 2003: chemistry. "It was a special group of guys from the beginning of the season all the way to the end," DeFrancesco said. "All of them had their own personal goals, but at 7 o'clock the team came first."

That's becoming a rarity in Triple-A these days, when rosters are a combination of prospects on the way to the majors and seasoned veterans working for a return trip.

"I've had Triple-A teams that are totally selfish," Sacramento general manager Gary Arthur said. "They don't care if it's a seven-game losing streak as long as they get their two hits."

Losses never came in seven-game streaks for Sacramento. The River Cats lost three consecutive games just twice and were never swept in a series. At 92-52, Sacramento was one of two minor league teams with more than 90 wins (The Indians' Class A Lake County affiliate won 97). The winning didn't stop in the postseason, as Sacramento won six straight playoff games to take home the PCL title and Baseball America's 2003 Minor League Team of the Year award.

Sacramento's veteran character players helped foster a team-first attitude. David McCarty, Billy McMillon and Adam Melhuse all eventually earned their tickets back to the majors, but not before instilling a sense of camaraderie and hard work in the clubhouse. With rising shortstop Bobby Crosby slated to take over for Miguel Tejada in the Athletics lineup in 2004, the veterans playfully dubbed him "the franchise," kidding with him about his status but also reminding the 23-year-old that he needed to improve before reaching the majors.

"With a more veteran-type club mixed with some younger guys, it helps them better understand the situation," Athletics farm director Keith Lieppman said.

The motivation worked, as Crosby began the season batting ninth but quickly moved to the three-hole by hitting .308-22-90 to earn the PCL's rookie of the year award. Crosby teamed with first baseman Graham Koonce, the league MVP who led the minors with 34 home runs and the PCL with 115 RBIs, and outfielder Mike Edwards (.298-14-95) to key an explosive offense.

Sacramento fared well on the mound as well. Righthanders Rich Harden, Justin Duchscherer, Mike Wood, Eric Hiljus and Aaron Harang formed a durable rotation that helped the River Cats post a 3.90 ERA, which ranked fourth in the league. Harden grabbed most of the headlines and left for Oakland in mid-July. Duchscherer continued to excel in Harden's absence, winning 11 straight decisions to finish with a league-leading 14 wins and a 3.25 ERA as he captured the PCL pitcher of the year award.

—WILL KIMMEY

PREVIOUS WINNERS

1993—Harrisburg/Eastern (Expos)
1994—Wilmington/Carolina (Royals)
1995—Norfolk/International (Mets)
1996—Edmonton/Pacific Coast (Athletics)
1997—West Michigan/Midwest (Tigers)
1998—Mobile/Southern (Padres)
1999—Trenton/Eastern (Red Sox)
2000—Round Rock/Texas (Astros)
2001—Lake Elsinore/California (Padres)
2002—Akron Aeros/Eastern (Indians)

switched from Florida to Surprise, Ariz., so the Royals had to go with two Arizona League affiliates for 2003.

And so the AZL standings for 2003 show "Royals 1" and "Royals 2". The first team featured many of the team's top draft picks, including first-round picks Chris Lubanski and Mitch Maier. The other squad had older players and was not eligible for the playoffs because it exceeded the league's age limit. Royals 1 finished 31-18 and won the league title, while Royals 2 was 32-22.

Though the two teams shared the same Surprise complex and stayed in the same hotel, the Kansas City player-development staff handled them as separate entities. Each had its own coaching staff, and players were promoted and demoted between the two clubs.

While the Royals accentuated the positives, the situation was not ideal. First, the competition wasn't rigorous enough for advanced college draft choices like Maier, drafted 30th overall out of Toledo. It was no surprise that four members of Royals 1, including Maier, were among the league's top seven batting leaders, and three pitchers were among the top seven in ERA.

Mercifully, the situation proved to be a one-year arrangement. The commissioner's office kept its promise to deliver a non-complex short-season club to the Royals, and Idaho Falls of the Rookie-level Pioneer League signed a one-year player-development contract and ended its nine-year association with the Padres.

The arrangement should work out well for the Royals, Idaho Falls and the Padres, who will field an AZL team in 2004. Idaho Falls hasn't come close to posting a winning record since winning the PL title in 2000, the last year the Padres used the club as their top short-season team. In 2001, the Padres dropped out of the AZL and affiliated with short-season Eugene of the Northwest League.

As part of the new affiliation, Idaho Falls will change its nickname, which has been the name of the team's major league affiliate almost exclusively since 1946.

Long, Strange Trips

How immersed were the Aberdeen IronBirds, the spawn of Cal Ripken, in road-trip culture?

Their bus driver shagged grounders in batting practice.

Brundage blends development, wins

MANAGER of the YEAR

Dave Brundage knows all about the versatility it takes to be a manager. In 1993, as his playing career was winding down, he was a player/coach at Triple-A Calgary, a righthander who as a coach was responsible for the outfielders.

Brundage was actually suited for the job. He was a two-way player in college at Oregon State, and after spending the first seven years of his professional career as an outfielder and first baseman, the Mariners moved him to the mound in 1992.

Brundage did it all to try to get to the big leagues, a goal he never reached as a player. But it proved invaluable as he builds his resume as a manager, and it's looking more and more likely that he will eventually find himself in a big league dugout as a manager or coach.

CREDIT

Playoff regular
Dave Brundage

In his six seasons as a manager in the Mariners organization, Brundage has taken four of his teams to the playoffs, including all three of his Double-A San Antonio squads. The Missions lost in the first round in 2001 but won back-to-back Texas League titles in 2002 and '03.

Minor league teams change not only from season to season, but also within a season. Brundage, 39, credits his success to the steady stream of talented players the Mariners have sent to San Antonio. He handled them all well enough to lead San Antonio to an 88-51 record and make himself Baseball America's 2003 Minor League Manager of the Year.

Brundage's first managerial job was for the Mariners' California League affiliate in 1995, and except for spending 1998-2000 as the hitting coach at Triple-A Tacoma, he's been managing ever since. It shouldn't be a surprise that his San Antonio team won big. It's a point of emphasis for the Mariners—with whom Brundage has spent most of his professional life—and a particular motivator for him.

"When things aren't going well, you're 'developing,' " he said. "But my philosophy has been the same for quite a while. We love to develop talent, but why do you want to develop losers? I'd rather develop winners."

His 2003 San Antonio team was the embodiment of that approach. After a 3-7 start the Missions went on a tear, easily winning both half-season division titles, putting together an 18-game winning streak and losing just one game in the playoffs.

Brundage blended talented veteran players with such prospects as shortstop Jose Lopez and staff ace Travis Blackley. They all performed and improved as the season went on.

"He has had talent, but he gets a lot out of his ballclub," Texas League president Tom Kayser said. "Players seem to enjoy playing for him. They could have gotten stale in the second half, but they won big and the team stayed sharp."

—WILL LINGO

PREVIOUS WINNERS

1981—Ed Nottle, Tacoma (Athletics)
1982—Eddie Haas, Richmond (Braves)
1983—Bill Dancy, Reading (Phillies)
1984—Sam Perlozzo, Jackson (Mets)
1985—Jim Lefebvre, Phoenix (Giants)
1986—Brad Fischer, Huntsville (Athletics)
1987—Dave Trembley, Harrisburg (Pirates)
1988—Joe Sparks, Indianapolis (Expos)
1989—Buck Showalter, Albany (Yankees)
1990—Kevin Kennedy, Albuquerque (Dodgers)
1991—Butch Hobson, Pawtucket (Red Sox)
1992—Grady Little, Greenville (Braves)
1993—Terry Francona, Birmingham (White Sox)
1994—Tim Ireland, El Paso (Brewers)
1995—Marc Bombard, Indianapolis (Reds)
1996—Carlos Tosca, Portland (Marlins)
1997—Gary Jones, Edmonton (Athletics)
1998—Terry Kennedy, Iowa (Cubs)
1999—John Mizerock, Wichita (Royals)
2000—Joel Skinner, Buffalo (Indians)
2001—Jackie Moore, Round Rock (Astros)
2002—John Russell, Edmonton (Twins)

MINOR LEAGUE ALL-STARS

Selected by Baseball America

LARRY GOREN

Dallas McPherson

TOPPS CO.

Franklin Gutierrez

ROBERT GURGANUS

Travis Blackley

BRIAN WESTERHOLT

Zack Greinke

FIRST TEAM

Pos.	Player, Team (League)	AVG	AB	R	H	2B	3B	HR	RBI	BB	SO	SB
C	Joe Mauer, Fort Myers (FSL)/New Britain (Eastern)	.340	506	73	172	30	2	5	85	49	49	3
1B	Prince Fielder, Beloit (Midwest)	.313	502	81	157	22	2	27	112	71	80	2
2B	Josh Barfield, Lake Elsinore (California)	.337	549	99	185	46	6	16	128	50	122	16
3B	Dallas McPherson, Rancho Cuca. (Cal)/Arkansas (TL)	.310	394	87	122	30	7	23	86	60	104	16
SS	Bobby Crosby, Sacramento (Pacific Coast)	.308	465	86	143	32	6	22	90	63	110	24
OF	Franklin Gutierrez, Vero Beach (FSL)/Jacksonville (SL)	.287	492	76	141	31	7	24	80	46	131	20
OF	Jeremy Reed, Winston-Salem (CL)/Birmingham (SL)	.373	464	88	173	35	4	11	95	70	36	45
OF	Alexis Rios, New Haven (Eastern)	.352	514	86	181	32	11	11	82	39	85	11
DH	Graham Koonce, Sacramento (Pacific Coast)	.277	480	82	133	23	1	34	115	98	119	0

Pos.	Player, Team (League)	W	L	ERA	G	GS	CG	SV	IP	H	BB	SO
SP	Travis Blackley, San Antonio (Texas)	17	3	2.61	27	27	0	0	162	125	62	144
SP	David Bush, Dunedin (FSL)/New Haven (Eastern)	14	6	2.79	28	28	1	0	158	137	28	148
SP	Zack Greinke, Wilmington (CL)/Wichita (Texas)	15	4	1.93	23	23	3	0	140	114	18	112
SP	Greg Miller, Vero Beach (FSL)/Jacksonville (SL)	12	5	2.20	25	25	1	0	143	118	48	151
RP	Fernando Rodney, Toledo (International)	1	1	1.33	38	0	0	23	41	22	13	58

SECOND TEAM

Pos.	Player, Team (League)	AVG	AB	R	H	2B	3B	HR	RBI	BB	SO	SB
C	Jeff Mathis, Rancho Cucamonga (Cal)/Arkansas (TL)	.315	473	93	149	39	3	13	68	47	90	6
1B	Ryan Howard, Clearwater (Florida State)	.304	490	67	149	32	1	23	82	50	151	0
2B	Chase Utley, Scranton/Wilkes-Barre (International)	.323	431	80	139	26	2	18	77	41	75	10
3B	Corey Hart, Huntsville (Southern)	.302	493	70	149	40	1	13	94	28	101	25
SS	Jason Bartlett, New Britain (Eastern)	.296	548	96	162	31	8	8	48	58	67	24
OF	Joey Gathright, Bakersfield (Cal)/Orlando (SL)	.334	425	77	142	7	3	0	28	46	69	69
OF	Ramon Nivar, Frisco (Texas)/Oklahoma (Pacific Coast)	.345	406	64	140	19	6	6	49	25	28	15
OF	Grady Sizemore, Akron (Eastern)	.304	496	96	151	26	11	13	78	46	73	10
DH	Matt Diaz, Orlando (Southern)/Durham (International)	.354	480	67	170	39	3	13	86	35	69	15

Pos.	Player, Team (League)	W	L	ERA	G	GS	CG	SV	IP	H	BB	SO
SP	Jon Connolly, West Michigan (Midwest)	16	3	1.41	25	25	5	0	166	128	38	104
SP	Justin Duchscherer, Sacramento (Pacific Coast)	14	2	3.25	24	23	0	0	155	151	18	117
SP	John Maine, Delmarva (SAL)/Frederick (CL)	13	4	2.27	26	26	2	0	147	91	38	185
SP	Luis Martinez, Huntsville (SL)/Indianapolis (IL)	12	5	2.13	27	27	1	0	161	130	73	162
RP	Jesse Crain, Ft. Myers (FSL)/New Britain (EL)/Rochester (IL)	6	3	1.93	55	0	0	19	84	47	25	114

They watched "Bull Durham" twice on midnight rides from ballpark to ballpark. They lost track of what town they were in, knowing only they were a long way from their home, Ripken Stadium (located appropriately enough at 873 Long Drive).

The New York-Penn League's southernmost team, the IronBirds went on a 17-day, 16-game road trip that took them from 25 miles north of Baltimore on a cross-state medley of backwater towns and big cities in Pennsylvania, New York, Vermont and New Jersey.

"Some guy got on the bus the other day and didn't know where he was; he thought he was in 'Vermont, New Jersey,' " IronBirds manager Joe Almaraz said.

The IronBirds had to take the trip because of the Cal Ripken World Series, which opened Ripken's Aberdeen complex to 12-and-under teams from across the world in August. Almaraz said like everything else in the minor leagues, the trip is something the players can learn from.

At least Aberdeen's trip went smoothly. Imagine taking a bus trip that would normally translate into a six- to six-and-a-half-hour ride from Kinston, N.C., up Interstate 95 to the Washington, D.C., area. Now imagine being five solid hours into that trip and seeing one of a sign that read, "GREENVILLE (N.C.) 26." It could only happen in minor league baseball—in this case to the Class A Kinston Indians as they made their way to a game against the Potomac Cannons.

The Indians' bus left from Grainger Stadium at 7:30 a.m. and pulled into Pfitzner Stadium in Woodbridge, Va., a little after 6 p.m. Apparently, the bus driver got lost not far out of Kinston and drove southeast instead of north. "When I saw all this water, I figured it was just the biggest lake I had ever seen," reliever Nate Fernley said. "Then someone was like, uh, no—that's the Atlantic Ocean."

The long ride didn't throw the K-Tribe off, however. They went out and took it to the Potomac for a 7-3 win, their first of the season.

No league faces more travel problems than the Pacific Coast League, however, just because the leagues stretches across two-thirds of the country. The 2003 lowlight came when a game in Tacoma had to be postponed because, though the Sacramento River Cats showed up, the home team didn't. Mechanical trouble grounded the Rainiers' flight from Edmonton, so the two teams were forced to play a doubleheader the next day.

Minor Leaguers Misbehaving

Cubs pitching prospect Jae-Kuk Ryu created a major stir in the Florida State League when he beaned an osprey that was perched at Jackie Robinson Ballpark in Daytona.

Two ospreys, nicknamed Ozzy and Harriet by Daytona Cubs grounds crew workers, nested on the top of an outfield light pole along with their chicks. Ryu hit Ozzy on April 21, and Ozzy died a week later.

On the same night, Ryu won his first start at Lansing, where the Cubs demoted him after the incident. Ryu was charged by the Florida Fish and Wildlife Conservation Commission with a second-degree misdemeanor.

The incident took place during batting practice, and witnesses said Ryu had thrown several baseballs at the osprey before hitting it. It was a public-relations nightmare for Daytona, so the team scheduled a fund-raiser, with proceeds going to the animal clinic that treated the osprey. Ozzy and Harriet Night raised more than $5,000.

■ Lakewood BlueClaws (South Atlantic) groundskeeper Bill Butler is well known in turf circles and has won groundskeeper of year awards on three separate occasions. But that was behind-the-scenes work. In late May, Butler got his 15 minutes of fame after he was ejected for arguing the decision to continue playing during a steady rain. The team couldn't find another instance when a groundskeeper was ejected from a game. "I'm sure a few years from now, there's very few people who will believe

ALL-STAR FUTURES GAME

Grady Sizemore wrestled with a decision whether to play football or baseball coming out of high school. At the 2003 Futures Game, Sizemore once again proved he made the right choice.

Sizemore, an outfielder in the Indians system, led the U.S. team to a 3-2 win over the World squad with an RBI single and a solo homer in three at-bats. Reds outfielder Stephen Smitherman's homer off Mariners lefthander Travis Blackley in the bottom of the sixth was the decisive blow, but Sizemore won the Larry Doby award as the MVP of the fifth annual game, played during all-star weekend at Chicago's U.S. Cellular Field.

ROB CUNI

Grady Sizemore

Sizemore's homer came off righthander Seung Song of the Expos, the organization that drafted Sizemore out of Cascade High in Everett, Wash., in the third round of the 2000 draft. He also was a blue-chip quarterback recruit who had signed with Washington.

Montreal's $2 million bonus offer helped Sizemore make up his mind, but he said his heart always was with baseball. "In the end, I loved baseball more," said Sizemore, 20. "It's just kind of what I wanted to do. Football is a great sport, and I loved playing it, but there's nothing like baseball."

Sizemore described his Futures Game performance as the highlight of his pro career.

Smitherman's homer came after Blackley made him look silly on consecutive changeups, then tried to fool him with a third. Blackley said his initial thought was to finish Smitherman off with a fastball. But batterymate Huber, who caught him for years back in Australia, signaled for another offspeed pitch. "If that pitch was where it should have been," Huber said, "it would have been strike three."

Song became the first player to make three Futures Game appearances. The lone Korean in the 2003 contest, Song represented the Red Sox twice before they traded him to Montreal in July 2002 in a deal for outfielder Cliff Floyd.

UNITED STATES ROSTER

Pitchers: Neal Cotts (White Sox), J.D. Durbin (Twins), Gavin Floyd (Phillies), Zack Greinke (Royals), Edwin Jackson (Dodgers), Preston Larrison (Tigers), John Maine (Orioles), Clint Nageotte (Mariners), Chris Narveson (Cardinals), Royce Ring (Mets), John VanBenschoten (Pirates).

Catchers: Jeff Mathis (Angels), Joe Mauer (Twins).

Infielders: Josh Barfield (Padres), Chris Burke (Astros), Khalil Greene (Padres), J.J. Hardy (Brewers), Ryan Howard (Phillies), Adam LaRoche (Braves), Chad Tracy (Diamondbacks), Kevin Youkilis (Red Sox)

Outfielders:.David Kelton (Cubs), Dave Krynzel (Brewers), Grady Sizemore (Indians), Stephen Smitherman (Reds).

WORLD ROSTER

Pitchers: Denny Bautista (Marlins), Travis Blackley (Mariners), Jorge de la Rosa (Red Sox), Edgar Gonzalez (Diamondbacks), Rich Harden (Athletics), Shawn Hill (Expos), Ervin Santana (Angels), Seung Song (Expos), Chin-Hui Tsao (Rockies), Merkin Valdez (Giants), Chien-Ming Wang (Yankees).

Catchers: Justin Huber (Mets), Guillermo Quiroz (Blue Jays).

Infielders: Robinson Cano (Yankees), Jose Castillo (Pirates), Edwin Encarnacion (Reds), Pete LaForest (Devil Rays), Andy Marte (Braves), Ramon Nivar (Rangers), Rene Reyes (Rockies), Scott Thorman (Braves)

Outfielders: Alexis Gomez (Royals), Franklin Gutierrez (Dodgers), Felix Pie (Cubs), Alexis Rios (Blue Jays).

USA 3, World 2

WORLD	ab	r	h	bi	USA	ab	r	h	bi
Nivar, 2b	2	1	1	0	Krynzel, cf	2	1	0	0
Cano, 2b	2	0	0	0	Sizemore, lf	3	1	2	2
Gomez, rf	2	0	0	0	Tracy, 3b	2	0	0	0
Pie, rf	1	0	0	0	Youkilis, 3b	0	0	0	0
Reyes, 1b	3	0	0	0	LaRoche, 1b	2	0	1	0
LaForest, dh	2	0	0	0	Howard, 1b	1	0	0	0
Gutierrez, lf	3	0	2	1	Kelton, dh	2	0	0	0
Quiroz, c	2	0	0	0	Smitherman, rf	3	1	2	1
Huber, c	1	0	0	0	Mauer, c	2	0	0	0
Rios, cf	3	1	1	1	Mathis, c	1	0	0	0
Marte, 3b	1	0	0	0	Burke, 2b	2	0	0	0
Encarnacion, 3b	1	0	0	0	Barfield, 2b	1	0	0	0
Castillo, ss	2	0	0	0	Hardy, ss	2	0	1	0
Thorman, ph	1	0	1	0	Greene, ss	1	0	0	0
Totals	**26**	**2**	**5**	**2**	**Totals**	**24**	**3**	**6**	**3**

World	**100**	**010**	**0—2**
USA	**101**	**001**	**x—3**

E—Castillo. **LOB**—World 5, USA 6. **2B**—Nivar, Smitherman. **HR**—Rios, Sizemore, Smitherman. **SB**—Nivar, Krynzel, Youkilis. **CS**—Hardy.

WORLD	ip	h	r	er	bb	so	USA	ip	h	r	er	bb	so
Harden	1	1	1	1	2	3	Cotts	1	2	1	1	1	2
Gonzalez	1	0	0	0	0	0	VanBenschoten	1	0	0	0	0	1
Song	1	3	1	1	0	1	Floyd	1	0	0	0	0	2
Tsao	1	1	0	0	0	1	Greinke	1	0	0	0	0	2
Bautista	1	0	0	0	1	2	Nageotte	⅔	1	1	1	1	2
Blackley L	⅓	1	1	1	0	0	Durbin	⅓	0	0	0	0	1
de la Rosa	⅔	0	0	0	0	1	Maine	⅔	0	0	0	0	0
							Larrison W	⅓	1	0	0	0	0
							Narveson	⅔	0	0	0	0	1
							Ring S	⅓	1	0	0	0	0

WP—Floyd, Larrison. **PB**—Huber. **T**—2:14.

MINOR LEAGUES

CLASSIFICATION ALL-STARS

Selected by Baseball America

TRIPLE-A
International League, Pacific Coast League

Pos.	Player, Team (League)	AVG	AB	R	H	2B	3B	HR	RBI	BB	SO	SB
C	Johnny Estrada, Richmond (International)	.328	354	40	116	29	0	10	66	30	30	0
1B	Graham Koonce, Sacramento (Pacific Coast)	.277	480	82	133	23	1	34	115	98	119	0
2B	Chase Utley, Scranton/Wilkes-Barre (International)	.323	431	80	139	26	2	18	77	41	75	10
3B	Chad Tracy, Tucson (Pacific Coast)	.324	522	91	169	31	4	10	80	41	52	0
SS	Bobby Crosby, Sacramento (Pacific Coast)	.308	465	86	143	32	6	22	90	63	110	24
OF	Chin-Feng Chen, Las Vegas (Pacific Coast)	.281	474	84	133	30	5	26	86	59	106	6
OF	Cody Ross, Toledo (International)	.287	470	74	135	35	6	20	61	32	86	15
OF	Terrmel Sledge, Edmonton (Pacific Coast)	.324	497	95	161	26	9	22	92	61	93	13
DH	Fernando Seguignol, Columbus (International)	.341	402	78	137	28	1	28	87	34	81	0

Pos.	Player, Team (League)	W	L	ERA	G	GS	CG	SV	IP	H	BB	SO
SP	Bronson Arroyo, Pawtucket (International)	12	6	3.43	24	24	1	0	150	148	23	155
SP	Justin Duchscherer, Sacramento (Pacific Coast)	14	2	3.25	24	23	0	0	155	151	18	117
SP	Nelson Figueroa, Nashville (Pacific Coast)	12	5	2.97	23	23	3	0	151	144	37	121
SP	Rich Harden, Sacramento (Pacific Coast)	9	4	3.15	16	14	0	0	89	72	35	91
RP	Fernando Rodney, Toledo (International)	1	1	1.33	38	0	0	23	41	22	13	58

Player of the Year: Bobby Crosby, ss, Sacramento (Pacific Coast). **Manager of the Year:** Bill Evers, Durham (International). **Team of the Year:** Sacramento (Pacific Coast).

BILL MITCHELL

PLAYER of the YEAR
Bobby Crosby, ss
Sacramento

DOUBLE-A
Eastern League, Southern League, Texas League

Pos.	Player, Team (League)	AVG	AB	R	H	2B	3B	HR	RBI	BB	SO	SB
C	Guillermo Quiroz, New Haven (Eastern)	.282	369	63	104	27	0	20	79	45	83	0
1B	Dan Johnson, Midland (Texas)	.290	538	90	156	26	4	27	114	68	82	7
2B	Victor Diaz, Jack. (Southern)/Bing. (Eastern)	.314	491	71	154	31	2	16	77	35	92	15
3B	Corey Hart, Huntsville (Southern)	.302	493	70	149	40	1	13	94	28	101	25
SS	Jason Bartlett, New Britain (Eastern)	.296	548	96	162	31	8	8	48	58	67	41
OF	Jeremy Reed, Birmingham (Southern)	.409	242	51	99	17	3	7	43	29	19	18
OF	Alexis Rios, New Haven (Eastern)	.352	514	86	181	32	11	11	82	39	85	11
OF	Grady Sizemore, Akron (Eastern)	.304	496	96	151	26	11	13	78	46	73	10
DH	Justin Leone, San Antonio (Texas)	.288	455	103	131	38	7	21	92	92	104	20

Pos.	Player, Team (League)	W	L	ERA	G	GS	CG	SV	IP	H	BB	SO
SP	Travis Blackley, San Antonio (Texas)	17	3	2.61	27	27	0	0	162	125	62	144
SP	Sean Burnett, Altoona (Eastern)	14	6	3.21	27	27	2	0	160	158	29	86
SP	Joel Hanrahan, Jacksonville (Southern)	10	4	2.43	23	23	1	0	133	117	53	130
SP	Chin-Hui Tsao, Tulsa (Texas)	11	4	2.46	18	18	0	0	113	88	26	125
RP	Justin Huisman, Tulsa (Texas)	7	2	1.75	57	0	0	26	62	55	7	46

Player of the Year: Alexis Rios, of, New Haven (Eastern). **Manager of the Year:** Dave Brundage, San Antonio (Texas). **Team of the Year:** San Antonio (Texas).

RICH ABEL

PLAYER of the YEAR
Alexis Rios, of
New Haven

HIGH CLASS A
California League, Carolina League, Florida State League

Pos.	Player, Team (League)	AVG	AB	R	H	2B	3B	HR	RBI	BB	SO	SB
C	Jeff Mathis, Rancho Cucamonga (California)	.323	378	74	122	28	3	11	54	35	74	5
1B	Ryan Howard, Clearwater (Florida State)	.304	490	67	149	32	1	23	82	50	151	0
2B	Josh Barfield, Lake Elsinore (California)	.337	549	99	185	46	6	16	128	50	122	16
3B	Andy Marte, Myrtle Beach (Carolina)	.285	463	69	132	35	1	16	63	67	109	5
SS	Angel Chavez, San Jose (California)	.280	478	69	134	23	6	10	58	22	60	20
OF	Franklin Gutierrez, Vero Beach (Florida State)	.282	425	65	120	28	5	20	68	39	111	17
OF	Greg Jacobs, Inland Empire (California)	.357	347	67	124	35	7	9	64	42	43	4
OF	Jason Kubel, Fort Myers (Florida State)	.298	420	56	125	20	4	5	82	48	54	4
DH	Chris Shelton, Lynchburg (Carolina)	.359	315	71	113	24	1	21	69	68	67	1

Pos.	Player, Team (League)	W	L	ERA	G	GS	CG	SV	IP	H	BB	SO
SP	Chadd Blasko, Daytona (Florida State)	10	5	1.98	24	24	1	0	136	100	43	131
SP	Zack Greinke, Wilmington (Carolina)	11	1	1.14	14	14	3	0	87	56	13	78
SP	Greg Miller, Vero Beach (Florida State)	11	4	2.49	21	21	1	0	116	103	41	111
SP	Ervin Santana, Rancho Cucamonga (California)	10	2	2.53	20	20	1	0	125	98	36	130
RP	Lee Gronkiewicz, Kinston (Carolina)	2	3	2.41	51	0	0	37	56	50	14	46

Player of the Year: Josh Barfield, 2b, Lake Elsinore (California). **Manager of the Year:** Mike Basso, Dunedin (Florida State). **Team of the Year:** St. Lucie (Florida State).

BILL MITCHELL

PLAYER of the YEAR
Josh Barfield, 2b
Lake Elsinore

this," Butler said. "I'm not sure I do right now."

The BlueClaws were in the third day of a seven-game homestand when it rained every day, and it rained steadily through the first five innings of the third game. Butler was concerned about the condition of the field and talked to the umpires, but they determined the game could continue.

A half-inning later, Butler returned to the field, bringing with him a printout of weather radar showing the rain wasn't going to let up. After arguing with the umpires about whether the tarp should be brought out, Butler was ejected.

The tarp was brought out shortly after the argument, and the game was called after an hourlong delay.

■ The Mariners suspended Inland Empire 66ers second baseman Evel Bastida-Martinez for the rest of the season, and he faced criminal charges after hitting a Lancaster JetHawks pitcher with a bat in an August incident.

In the top of the 15th inning, shortly after the 66ers took a 7-4 lead, Bastida-Martinez was hit in the back by a pitch from Josh Kranawetter. Bastida-Martinez charged the mound wielding his bat. Kranawetter jumped up to try to avoid the bat, but it hit him in the back. "From all accounts I heard, it looked like he was taking a full swing like he was trying to hit a home run," Lancaster director of business operations Joe Reinsch said.

CLASSIFICATION ALL-STARS

LOW CLASS A — Midwest League, South Atlantic League

Pos.	Player, Team (League)	AVG	AB	R	H	2B	3B	HR	RBI	BB	SO	SB
C	Jon-Mark Sprowl, Battle Creek (Midwest)	.321	418	77	134	30	3	5	62	71	39	5
1B	Prince Fielder, Beloit (Midwest)	.313	502	81	157	22	2	27	112	71	80	2
2B	Alberto Callaspo, Cedar Rapids (Midwest)	.327	514	86	168	38	4	2	67	42	28	20
3B	Aaron Baldiris, Capital City (South Atlantic)	.313	393	55	123	19	4	6	68	51	55	13
SS	Erick Aybar, Cedar Rapids (Midwest)	.308	496	83	153	30	10	6	57	17	54	32
OF	Chad Chop, Savannah (Midwest)	.322	485	55	156	26	5	11	77	32	75	10
OF	Jorge Cortes, Hickory (South Atlantic)	.325	345	55	112	24	2	8	66	56	47	9
OF	Jeff Salazar, Asheville (South Atlantic)	.284	486	109	138	23	4	29	98	77	74	28
DH	Jayson Drobiak, Battle Creek (Midwest)	.293	499	83	146	35	4	30	86	42	120	18

Pos.	Player, Team (League)	W	L	ERA	G	GS	CG	SV	IP	H	BB	SO
SP	Fausto Carmona, Lake County (South Atlantic)	17	4	2.06	24	24	1	0	148	117	14	83
SP	Jon Connolly, West Michigan (Midwest)	16	3	1.41	25	25	5	0	166	128	38	104
SP	Cole Hamels, Lakewood (South Atlantic)	6	1	0.84	13	13	1	0	75	32	25	115
SP	Merkin Valdez, Hagerstown (South Atlantic)	9	5	2.25	26	26	2	0	156	119	49	166
RP	Todd Pennington, Lake County (South Atlantic)	2	1	0.72	36	0	0	20	37	14	17	65

Player of the Year: Prince Fielder, 1b, Beloit (Midwest). **Manager of the Year:** Tony Beasley, Hickory (South Atlantic). **Team of the Year:** Lake County (South Atlantic).

MIKE JANES

PLAYER of the **YEAR**

Prince Fielder, 1b
Beloit

SHORT-SEASON A — New York-Penn League, Northwest League

Pos.	Player, Team (League)	AVG	AB	R	H	2B	3B	HR	RBI	BB	SO	SB
C	Todd Jennings, Salem-Keizer (Northwest)	.296	233	27	69	9	2	3	32	15	36	5
1B	Vito Chiaravalloti, Auburn (New York-Penn)	.351	228	47	80	20	1	12	67	47	48	0
2B	Nick Orlandos, Everett (Northwest)	.317	265	41	84	13	4	2	31	12	22	14
3B	Kody Kirkland, Oneonta (New York-Penn)	.303	254	46	77	15	11	4	49	25	60	14
SS	Aaron Hill, Auburn (New York-Penn)	.361	122	22	44	4	0	4	34	16	20	1
OF	Jeremy Cleveland, Spokane (Northwest)	.322	245	64	79	20	3	7	53	40	50	5
OF	Conor Jackson, Yakima (Northwest)	.319	257	44	82	35	1	6	60	36	41	3
OF	Brian Wahlbrink, Eugene (Northwest)	.300	270	45	81	17	4	4	34	28	82	19
DH	Jamie D'Antona, Yakima (Northwest)	.277	271	46	75	18	1	15	57	35	60	0

Pos.	Player, Team (League)	W	L	ERA	G	GS	CG	SV	IP	H	BB	SO
SP	Josh Banks, Auburn (New York-Penn)	7	2	2.43	15	15	0	0	67	58	10	81
SP	Felix Hernandez, Everett (Northwest)	7	2	2.29	11	7	0	0	55	43	24	73
SP	Tom Mastny, Auburn (New York-Penn)	8	0	2.26	14	14	0	0	64	56	12	68
SP	Sean Thompson, Eugene (Northwest)	7	1	2.48	15	15	0	0	80	58	39	97
RP	Bubby Buzachero, Auburn (New York-Penn)	1	1	1.54	30	0	0	13	35	25	7	47

Player of the Year: Vito Chiaravalloti, 1b, Auburn (New York-Penn). **Manager of the Year:** Darryl Kennedy, Spokane (Northwest). **Team of the Year:** Auburn (New York-Penn).

MIKE JANES

PLAYER of the **YEAR**

Vito Chiaravalloti, 1b
Auburn

ROOKIE — Appalachian League, Arizona League, Gulf Coast League, Pioneer League

Pos.	Player, Team (League)	AVG	AB	R	H	2B	3B	HR	RBI	BB	SO	SB
C	Lou Palmisano, Helena (Pioneer)	.391	174	32	68	13	2	6	43	18	29	13
1B	Joey Votto, Billings (Pioneer)	.317	240	47	76	17	3	6	37	56	80	4
2B	Habelito Hernandez, Billings (Pioneer)	.377	162	42	61	14	5	8	32	1	22	5
3B	Ian Stewart, Casper (Pioneer)	.317	224	40	71	14	5	10	43	29	54	4
SS	Robert Valido, Bristol (Appalachian)	.307	215	39	66	15	2	6	31	17	28	17
OF	Warner Madrigal, Provo (Pioneer)	.369	279	75	103	28	2	9	51	12	58	2
OF	Ricardo Nanita, Great Falls (Pioneer)	.384	185	38	71	7	4	5	37	17	28	11
OF	Xavier Paul, Ogden (Pioneer)	.307	264	60	81	15	6	7	47	34	58	11
DH	Tyler Davidson, Kingsport (Appalachian)	.337	172	29	58	11	8	10	35	15	36	3

Pos.	Player, Team (League)	W	L	ERA	G	GS	CG	SV	IP	H	BB	SO
SP	Abel Moreno, Provo (Pioneer)	10	0	2.38	13	10	0	0	68	58	10	79
SP	James Paduch, Billings (Pioneer)	7	1	1.94	15	15	0	0	79	72	20	65
SP	Rafael Perez, Burlington (Appalachian)	9	3	1.70	13	12	0	0	69	56	16	63
SP	Chris Schutt, Elizabethton (Appalachian)	5	2	1.98	11	10	0	0	55	37	21	72
RP	Nick Slack, Helena (Pioneer)	1	1	2.19	19	0	0	10	25	13	6	37

Player of the Year: Lou Palmisano, c, Helena (Pioneer). **Manager of the Year:** Ed Sedar, Helena (Pioneer). **Team of the Year:** Provo (Pioneer).

PLAYER of the **YEAR**

Lou Palmisano, c
Helena

Umpires suspended the game, and Lancaster ultimately decided to forfeit because of a lack of players, as well as the team's desire to move on.

Bastida-Martinez, 24, cleaned out his locker and was placed on a flight back to his home near Miami on Aug. 19. "His actions are those that the entire Mariners organization (does) not condone in any shape or form," 66ers media-relations director Ryan Seeberg said.

Bastida-Martinez also faced assault charges stemming from the incident. The California League suspended eight players and a coach from each team and fined them $150. In addition to being suspended for the rest of the season, Bastida-Martinez was fined $300.

■ The Pacific Coast League suspended and fined 19 Portland Beavers for entering the stands after a game in Las Vegas in August. Every Portland player at the game, except pitcher Clay Condrey, was penalized. Tagg Bozied, the main player involved in the altercation, was suspended for eight games.

Portland players followed a fan into the stands and onto the concourse after he threw a soft baseball on the field. The fan heckled Bozied after the first baseman didn't throw a ball to the fan and his friends. The heckling continued until the game ended and came to a head when the fan tossed the giveaway item after exchanging words with Bozied.

The suspensions were to be served on a rotating basis, as decided by Portland manager Rick Sweet, and some will carry over to 2004. Sweet had just nine offensive players available for one late-season game, when the club's five game winning streak came to an end.

Minors Find More Innovative Promotions

With teams trying to come up with better promotions, the Altoona Curve (Eastern) went the other way in one of the most inventive nights of the season. The Curve hosted Awful Night for a game against Akron, with an awful giveaway (a swath of bubble wrap), awful between-innings music (Milli Vanilli and William Shatner), awful contests (bald guys racing for a toupee and bobbing for onions) and awful concessions (Tang and Spam).

"You won't believe the amount of people excited by a 12-by-12 piece of bubble wrap," Altoona general manager Todd Parnell said. "And I don't know if you've ever heard Shatner sing, but there's only one word for it."

The team also had an awful fireworks extravaganza after the game (interns holding sparklers) and awful stats (a .300 batting average was presented as a .700 fail average). The reaction was anything but awful, as fans loved it. It also got the Curve national publicity, and the team drew about 750 more fans for Awful Night than a typical Monday night crowd. Parnell also said he got more positive e-mail from season-ticket holders than he had for any promotion he can remember, which makes it likely that Awful Night will return.

"Anything that awful you have give it another chance," Parnell said.

■ A year after Nobody Night made national news, the Charleston River Dogs (South Atlantic) had Silent Night, when fans were encouraged to remain silent until the end of the fifth inning. Golf marshals patrolled the dugouts with "Quiet Please" signs, while librarians served as ushers. Instead of yelling, fans were handed placards to give their opinions. Fans were also given a piece of tape to help them keep their mouths shut. To keep the park silent, radio announcer Dan Lehv broadcast the game from a cherry picker beyond the outfield fence.

■ The best promotion of the season for the independent Brockton Rox (Northeast) was one the team had to keep under wraps. A release in mid-July announced simply that the Rox had signed James Henderson. Henderson struck out in a four-pitch at-bat, wandered back to the dugout and was replaced before the top of the second.

But for anyone in attendance that night, it was clear Henderson was not your normal player. For one thing, teams don't often suit up a middle-aged man who makes Babe Ruth look svelte. And there aren't many players in Brockton who have a CBS camera crew following them.

When Henderson was announced before his at-bat, the crowd was let in on the joke. Biff Henderson, the stage manager for "The Late Show with David Letterman," was getting his chance to take a swing at playing in the minor leagues. CBS had asked the Rox not to publicize Henderson's appearance before then. A couple of weeks later, the rest of the country found out, when Henderson showed off his summer trip to Brockton on a six-minute segment on the Letterman show. The result was a huge bit of free publicity for the Rox.

Not every big idea was a hit, though. In late April, the Des Moines Register published photos of Iowa State basketball coach Larry Eustachy at a postgame party on the Missouri campus after the Cyclones lost to the Tigers, drinking beer and cozying up to coeds.

Quad City (Midwest) GM Dave Ziedelis got together with his staff and come up with Eustachy Night, which would feature discounted beer and a kissing booth. But 24 hours after Eustachy Night was announced, the coach called announced that he was an alcoholic and was seeking treatment for his disease. Eustachy also lost his job.

Just as quickly as the team had planned the promotion, they pulled the plug. "We had one local sports editor say it was Veeckian in concept," Ziedelis said. "But when Eustachy had the press conference, it got very serious at that point."

Of course, showing the fickle nature of the minors, the Wichita Wranglers (Texas) held a Eustachy Night of their own that came off without a whisper of protest.

Around The Minors

■ The Jacksonville Suns easily broke the all-time Jacksonville baseball attendance in its first year playing at the new Baseball Grounds of Jacksonville.

The Suns 2003 attendance figure surged to 359,979, for an average of 5,454 fans a game. The previous record was 254,882, set in 1998.

"We couldn't be happier with the turnout of the fans this season," Suns general manager Peter Bragan Jr. said. "The new ballpark has been very well supported by the people of Jacksonville and the fact that we broke this record so easily is a testament to our fans and just how special the Baseball Grounds are."

A similar success story unfolded in Albuquerque, which returned to the PCL, though Isotopes GM Mel Kowalchuk stepped down at the end of the season, citing personal reasons. The Isotopes' director of business operations, John Traub, was promoted to replace Kowalchuk.

The Isotopes drew 576,876 fans, third-best in the PCL, while Isotopes merchandise quickly became minor league baseball's top seller. The team returned to Albuquerque after a two-year absence caused by the former Dukes' move to Portland. The city renovated Albuquerque Sports Stadium, and Ken Young bought the Calgary Cannons and brought them to New Mexico.

■ Few people realized that Major League Baseball and Minor League Baseball were talking about making changes to the Professional Baseball Agreement, the document that governs their relationship.

But changes were approved in May by a mail vote. Sylvia Lind, the senior manager of minor league operations for MLB, said the amendments tie up a few loose ends and keep MLB from reopening the entire negotiation process. The current PBA runs through the 2007 season, but MLB had the right to opt out after 2003.

Among the changes, it's now crystal clear that MLB can eliminate the Appalachian, Arizona and Gulf Coast leagues (as well as the Dominican and Venezuela summer leagues) at any time. Also, anyone who is thinking about moving into a major league team's territory now must let the team know in advance. The current rule requires a franchise only to get written permission to move into a territory once they decide to move. Finally, no major or minor league club can ask for extra benefits (read: money) from its affiliate, other than what is laid out in a standard player-development contract. Current rules just prohibit this as part of the affiliation process, and the new rule makes it clear it's always against the rules.

■ Just when minor league nicknames and logos were swinging back toward sanity, the Montgomery Biscuits announced their presence. The Southern League franchise is moving to Montgomery from Orlando in 2004.

Tom Dickson and Sherrie Myers, the new owners of the team and also the owners of the Lansing Lugnuts, chose the winning name from more than 3,000 entries in a name-the-team contest. Montgomery resident John (Tripp) Vickers chose the name Biscuits and wrote with his entry, "It's playful and fun, plus who doesn't like Biscuits? All Alabamians like 'em."

The goofy name was accompanied by a goofy logo. The public response when the nickname was announced at a city festival was lukewarm at best. In spite of protests, though, the merchandise was a hot seller. "The minute they walk into the store, they say: 'I can't believe it,' " said Monte Meyers, retail manager of the Biscuit Basket. "But then they walk out with a bag full of clothes."

■ The Tacoma Rainiers finally found a new owner. David Hersh reportedly paid slightly less than $11 million for the PCL club. George Foster bought the team in 1991 for $5.5 million from local owners. Hersh said he wanted to keep the team in Tacoma but would likely require a new or renovated stadium.

Hersh said he might consider moving the team if plans for a new or renovated stadium weren't in the works by the time the team's lease with Pierce County and the City of Tacoma expires following the 2005 season.

■ In a sport that has featured players traded for cash, players to be named and occasionally a bag of baseballs, the Hudson Valley Renegades (New York-Penn) and the Fort Myers Miracle pulled off an unusual swap, even by baseball standards.

Hudson Valley general manager Steve Gliner was sent to Fort Myers for GM Dave Burke and his golden retriever Rutgers, who had been serving as the Miracle's mascot. Both teams are owned by the Goldklang Group, so the GM's did't be change employers. Burke had been the Miracle's GM for three years, while Gliner had been the GM in Hudson Valley since 1998.

■ After battling illness for several years, Salt Lake Stingers owner Joe Buzas died just before Opening Day.

Buzas, 83, lived his entire life in baseball, as a player, manager or owner for more than 60 years. In 47 years as an owner, he operated 82 minor league franchises.

Buzas was the Opening Day shortstop for the Yankees in 1945, playing 30 games in the major leagues. After a severe shoulder injury cut short his playing career, Joe became one of the youngest managers in professional baseball history at 26. But his mark in baseball was as an owner, beginning with taking over a bankrupt Syracuse franchise in 1956. Even when minor league baseball was struggling in the 1960s and 1970s, Buzas was able to run teams successfully.

"During the leaner days of minor league baseball, he was one of the few guys who could turn a profit," minor league entrepreneur Miles Wolff said.

■ Ria Cortesio became the first female umpire in Southern League history when she was promoted from the Class A Florida State League just before the season began. Cortesio began her fifth season as the only female umpire in Organized Baseball and just the fifth female umpire in the history of baseball.

"I know I'm not doing anything different from any other umpire out here," said the 26-year-old Cortesio. "Even though, yes, it can be a little annoying for me. Because there haven't been many women before me, maybe it means a little something."

TRIPLE-A ALL-STAR GAME

The conventional wisdom was that the Braves gave Kevin Millwood away for nothing. But when Atlanta's 2003 budget forced general manager John Schuerholz to send the arbitration-eligible Millwood to the Phillies, the Braves did receive catcher Johnny Estrada in return.

Because Estrada spent most of 2003 with Triple-A Richmond, many Braves fans noticed no return from the Millwood trade until they tuned in to the Triple-A all-star game. Estrada collected an RBI in each of his three at-bats, delivering a home run, single and double to capture the most valuable hitter award as well as the International League MVP award. The IL defeated the Pacific Coast League 13-9.

A standing-room crowd of 15,214 packed into AutoZone Park in Memphis to see the teams combine for a record 22 runs, as the IL registered its first all-star victory since an 8-4 win in 1998. Seven of the first nine half-innings featured at least one run, and Columbus righthander Sam Marsonek recorded the game's first 1-2-3 inning in the bottom of the fifth after 14 runs had scored. Marsonek, who replaced teammate Brandon Claussen on the IL roster, earned the most valuable pitcher award for his efforts.

The IL scored in seven of nine innings, including three each in the fourth, fifth and sixth innings. By the bottom of the sixth, a three-run home run by Oklahoma outfielder Jason Jones cut the PCL's deficit to 11-9. Jones' homer earned him the PCL MVP honor and broke the record for the most runs scored in the 16-year history of the Triple-A all-star game.

That mark was set in 1993 when National League affiliates defeated the American Leaguers 14-3 in Albuquerque. The first 10 games featured that format before shifting to the IL/PCL arrangement when Triple-A baseball realigned after the 1997 season, eliminating the American Association.

Triple-A All-Star Game
July 16 at Memphis
International League 13, Pacific Coast League 9

IL	ab	r	h	bi	PCL	ab	r	h	bi
French, cf	5	3	3	1	Castro, 2b	3	1	1	0
Collier, lf	5	3	3	2	Bell, 2b	2	0	1	0
Utley, 2b	3	0	0	0	Amezaga, ss	3	2	1	0
Miles, 2b	2	1	1	1	Bowers, ss	1	1	0	0
Larson, dh	2	0	1	1	Sledge, cf	1	1	1	0
M. Smith, dh	2	1	1	0	Kelton, cf	2	1	0	0
Gload, 1b	3	2	2	1	Stratton, dh	3	0	1	2
Jackson, 1b	2	0	0	0	Crosby, rf	2	0	0	1
Estrada, c	3	2	3	3	Jones, rf	2	1	1	3
Cash, c	1	0	1	0	Atkins, 3b	2	0	0	1
Escobar, rf	2	0	0	1	Tracy, 3b	2	0	0	0
Restovich, rf	1	0	0	0	Bozied, 1b	5	0	1	0
J. Smith, ss	3	1	1	2	Borders, c	3	1	1	0
Garcia, ss	2	0	0	0	Hill, c	1	0	1	0
Chapman, 3b	4	0	0	0	Reyes, lf	3	1	1	2
LaRocca, ph	1	0	0	0	Kelly, lf	2	0	0	0
Totals	**41**	**13**	**16**	**12**	**Totals**	**37**	**9**	**10**	**9**

International League	**110 333 101—13**
Pacific Coast League	**102 303 000— 9**

E—Chapman, Gload, J.Smith. **DP**—IL 1, PCL 1. **LOB**—IL 9, PCL 9. **2B**—Amezaga, Bozied, Estrada, Gload, Miles. **HR**—Collier, Estrada, French, Jones, Reyes, J.Smith. **SF**—Atkins, Escobar, Stratton. **SB**—Collier, French.

IL	ip	h	r	er	bb	so	PCL	ip	h	r	er	bb	so
Madson	1	0	1	0	1	2	Duchscherer	2	2	2	2	0	1
Stanford	1	1	0	0	0	1	Sessions	2	4	3	3	0	3
Arroyo	1	2	2	0	0	1	Ryan L	1	3	3	3	1	0
Pratt	1	4	3	3	2	0	Vance	1	3	3	3	2	2
Marsonek W	1	0	0	0	0	0	Duff	1	1	1	1	2	1
Beltran	1	1	3	0	1	1	Corey	1	1	0	0	0	0
Griffiths	1	1	0	0	1	1	Clontz	1	2	1	1	0	2
Gomes	1	0	0	0	0	0							
Gardner	1	1	0	0	0	1							

WP—Arroyo, Griffiths, Sessions. **HBP**—Cash (by Duchscherer), Collier (by Vance), Sledge (by Madson). **PB**—Hill. **T**—3:07. **A**—15,214.

MINOR LEAGUE DEPARTMENT LEADERS

*Full-season teams only

TEAM

WINS

Lake County (South Atlantic)	97
Sacramento (Pacific Coast)	92
Akron (Eastern)	88
San Antonio (Texas)	88
Pawtucket (International)	83

LONGEST WINNING STREAK

San Antonio (Texas)	18
Lake County (South Atlantic)	13
Louisville (International)	12
Visalia (California)	12
Provo (Pioneer)	12

LOSSES

High Desert (California)	98
Round Rock (Texas)	94
Fresno (Pacific Coast)	88
Augusta (South Atlantic)	87
Palm Beach (Florida State)	84

LONGEST LOSING STREAK

Orlando (Southern)	12
Memphis (Pacific Coast)	12
Vermont (New York-Penn)	12
Syracuse (International)	10
Delmarva (South Atlantic)	10
San Jose (California)	10
Binghamton (Eastern)	10

BATTING AVERAGE*

New Haven (Eastern)	.293
Edmonton (Pacific Coast)	.292
Colorado Springs (Pacific Coast)	.287
Las Vegas (Pacific Coast)	.286
Lancaster (California)	.285

RUNS

Sacramento (Pacific Coast)	859
Lake Elsinore (California)	821
Lancaster (California)	810
Modesto (California)	759
New Haven (Eastern)	752

HOME RUNS

Sacramento (Pacific Coast)	153
Omaha (Pacific Coast)	143
Iowa (Pacific Coast)	140
Charlotte (International)	139
Lancaster (California)	136

STOLEN BASES

St. Lucie (Florida State)	216
San Antonio (Texas)	210
Capital City (South Atlantic)	203
Winston-Salem (Carolina)	196
Lakewood (South Atlantic)	196

LARRY GOREN

Graham Koonce

DANNY PARKER

Jeremy Reed

EARNED RUN AVERAGE*

Lake County (South Atlantic)	2.67
Wilmington (Carolina)	2.92
Rome (South Atlantic)	2.95
Fort Wayne (Midwest)	3.02
San Antonio (Texas)	3.03

STRIKEOUTS

Inland Empire (California)	1,180
Delmarva (South Atlantic)	1,148
San Antonio (Texas)	1,131
Rome (South Atlantic)	1,107
Daytona (Florida State)	1,105

INDIVIDUAL BATTING

BATTING AVERAGE

(Minimum 378 Plate Appearances)

Jeremy Reed, Birmingham/Winston-Salem	.373
Matt Diaz, Durham/Orlando	.354
Alexis Rios, New Haven	.352
Brian Dallimore, Fresno	.352
Bubba Crosby, Las Vegas/Columbus	.350
Billy Martin, Tucson/El Paso	.348
Greg Jacobs, San Antonio/Inland Empire	.345
Ramon Nivar, Oklahoma/Frisco	.345
Rene Reyes, Colorado Springs	.343
Fernando Seguignol, Columbus/Tampa	.342

RUNS

Jeff Salazar, Visalia/Asheville	110
Jayson Nix, Visalia	107
Dan Uggla, Lancaster	104
Justin Leone, San Antonio	103
Jason Bourgeois, Frisco/Stockton	103

HITS

Josh Barfield, Lake Elsinore	185
Alexis Rios, New Haven	181
Brandon Watson, Harrisburg	180
Jeremy Reed, Birmingham/Winston-Salem	173
Joe Mauer, New Britain/Fort Myers	172

TOP HITTING STREAKS

Ricardo Nanita, Great Falls	30
Brandon Larson, Louisville	26
Kenard Springer, AZL Royals-1	26
John Castellano, Inland Empire	24
Lou Palmisano, Helena	23

MOST HITS, ONE GAME

Travis Hanson, Peoria	6
Peter Bergeron, Edmonton	6
Pat Borders, Tacoma	6
Mark Budzinski, Louisville	6
Brandon Watson, Harrisburg	6

TOTAL BASES

Josh Barfield, Lake Elsinore	291
Jayson Drobiak, Battle Creek	279
Kyle Nichols, Lancaster	278
Dan Johnson, Sacramento/Midland	273
Terrmel Sledge, Edmonton	271

EXTRA-BASE HITS

Jayson Drobiak, Battle Creek	69
Josh Barfield, Lake Elsinore	68
Jayson Nix, Visalia	67
Justin Leone, San Antonio	66
Kyle Nichols, Lancaster	65

DOUBLES

Josh Barfield, Lake Elsinore	46
Jayson Nix, Visalia	46
Ryan Jackson, Durham	45
Nick Gorneault, Arkansas/Rancho Cucamonga	42
Greg Jacobs, San Antonio/Inland Empire	42

TRIPLES

Chone Figgins, Salt Lake	15
Luis Terrero, Tucson	15
Jason Smith, Durham	14
Nathan Haynes, Salt Lake/Arkansas	13
Shin-Soo Choo, Inland Empire	13
Wilson Betemit, Richmond	13

HOME RUNS

Graham Koonce, Sacramento	34
Rob Stratton, Albuquerque	32
Bucky Jacobsen, Tennessee	31
Kyle Nichols, Lancaster	31
Jayson Drobiak, Battle Creek	30

RUNS BATTED IN

Josh Barfield, Lake Elsinore	128
Graham Koonce, Sacramento	115
Dan Johnson, Sacramento/Midland	114
Prince Fielder, Beloit	112
Kyle Nichols, Lancaster	108

MOST RBIs, ONE GAME

Nelson Cruz, Kane County	8
Brent Cordell, Charleston, S.C.	8
Derin McMains, Hagerstown	8
Matt Knox, Lake County	8
Adam Seuss, Tri-City, N.Y.	8
Gerald Williams, Albuquerque	8
Dallas McPherson, Arkansas	8
Chris Kelly, Great Falls	8

STOLEN BASES

Freddy Guzman, Portland/Mobile/Lake Elsinore	90
Ruddy Yan, Winston-Salem	76
Wayne Lydon, St. Lucie	75
Dwaine Bacon, West Tenn/Daytona	74
Joey Gathright, Orlando/Bakersfield	69

CAUGHT STEALING

Jason Bartlett, New Britain	24
Onil Joseph, Rome	22
Dave Krynzel, Huntsville	21
Kennard Jones, Lake Elsinore/Fort Wayne	21
B.J. Upton, Orlando/Charleston, S.C.	21

HIT BY PITCHES

Bryan Carter, San Jose	26
Dan Grummitt, Durham/Orlando	24
Trace Coquillette, Pawtucket/Portland (EL)	21
Jeff Ontiveros, Augusta	20
Trent Oeltjen, Quad City	20
Jason Bartlett, New Britain	20
Chris Duffy, Altoona	20

WALKS
- Andy Machado, Reading 108
- Brian Myrow, Trenton 107
- Kevin Youkilis, Pawtucket/Portland (EL) 104
- Val Pascucci, Edmonton 101
- Jon Nunnally, Memphis 98
- Graham Koonce, Sacramento 98

STRIKEOUTS
- A.J. Zapp, San Antonio 178
- Rob Stratton, Albuquerque 175
- Jon Nelson, Wisconsin 168
- Reggie Abercrombie, Jacksonville 164
- Jeremy Owens, Portland (EL) 161

SACRIFICE FLIES
- Jason Kubel, Fort Myers 13
- Graham Koonce, Sacramento 12
- G.J. Raymundo, Oklahoma/Stockton 12
- Greg Sain, Lake Elsinore 12
- Four tied at 11

SACRIFICE BUNTS
- Andres Blanco, Wilmington (CL) 21
- Osvaldo Fernando, Lexington 21
- Matt Demarco, Jupiter 20
- Wilton Guerrero, Louisville 19
- Wilson Valdez, Albuquerque/Carolina 19
- Eric Reed, Jupiter 19

SLUGGING PERCENTAGE
- Fernando Seguignol, Columbus/Tampa .. .617
- Bubba Crosby, Las Vegas/Columbus .... .603
- Dallas McPherson, Ark./Rancho Cuca. .... .596
- Billy Martin, Tucson/El Paso .... .587
- Kyle Nichols, Lancaster .... .574

ON-BASE PERCENTAGE
- Jeremy Reed, Birmingham/Winston-Salem .. .453
- Brian Myrow, Trenton .... .447
- Kevin Youkilis, Pawtucket/Portland (EL) .. .441
- Chris Shelton, Altoona/Lynchburg .... .441
- Noah Hall, Harrisburg .... .434

BATTING AVERAGE
By Position

(Minimum 383 Plate Appearances)

Catchers
- Joe Mauer, New Britain/Fort Myers .... .338
- Mike Jacobs, Binghamton .... .329
- Johnny Estrada, Richmond .... .328
- Dioner Navarro, Trenton/Tampa .... .321
- Jon-Mark Sprowl, South Bend/Battle Creek .. .321

First Basemen
- Billy Martin, Tucson/El Paso .... .348
- Chris Shelton, Altoona/Lynchburg .... .336
- Sean McGowan, Portland (EL)/Sarasota .. .320
- Luis Gonzalez, Akron .... .318
- Todd Self, Salem .... .318

Second Basemen
- Brian Dallimore, Fresno .... .352
- Josh Barfield, Lake Elsinore .... .337
- Alberto Callaspo, Cedar Rapids .... .327
- Mike Fontenot, Bowie .... .325
- Delwyn Young, South Georgia .... .323
- Chase Utley, Scranton/Wilkes-Barre .... .323

Third Basemen
- Chad Tracy, Tucson .... .324
- Simon Pond, Syracuse/New Haven .... .321
- Garrett Atkins, Colorado Springs .... .319
- Terry Tiffee, New Britain .... .315
- Aaron Baldiris, Capital City/Brooklyn .... .313

Shortstops
- Erick Aybar, Cedar Rapids .... .308
- Bobby Crosby, Sacramento .... .308
- Jesse Garcia, Richmond .... .306
- Donald Kelly, Erie/Lakeland .... .306
- J.J. Furmaniak, Mobile/Lake Elsinore ...... .301

Outfielders
- Jeremy Reed, Birmingham/Winston-Salem .. .373
- Matt Diaz, Durham/Orlando .... .354
- Alexis Rios, Hew Haven .... .352
- Bubba Crosby, Las Vegas/Columbus ...... .350
- Ramon Nivar, Oklahoma/Frisco .... .345

DAN ARNOLD

Jon Connolly

INDIVIDUAL PITCHING

EARNED RUN AVERAGE
(Minimum 112 Innings)
- Jon Connolly, West Michigan 1.41
- Kameron Loe, Stockton/Clinton 1.67
- Zack Greinke, Wichita/Wilmington (CL) .. 1.93
- Chadd Blasko, Daytona/Lansing 1.95
- Brian Whitaker, Fort Wayne 2.09
- David Maust, Harrisburg/Brevard County .. 2.12
- Luis Martinez, Indianapolis/Huntsville 2.13
- Fausto Carmona, Akron/Lake County 2.16
- Matt Peterson, Binghamton/St. Lucie 2.18
- Greg Miller, Jacksonville/Vero Beach 2.21

WORST ERA
- Dan Hall, High Desert 7.10
- Luke Robertson, Sacramento/Modesto 6.68
- Dan Kolb, High Desert 6.42
- Shawn Sedlacek, Omaha/Wichita 6.26
- Chad Petty, Lakeland/High Desert 6.17

WINS
- Fausto Carmona, Akron/Lake County 17
- Brad Halsey, Trenton/Tampa 17
- Travis Blackley, San Antonio 17
- Gabe Ribas, Lake Elsinore/Fort Wayne 17
- Jon Connolly, West Michigan 16
- Edward Valdez, Potomac/Dayton 16
- Sam Smith, South Bend 16

LOSSES
- Ruddy Lugo, Round Rock 15
- Matt Merricks, Myrtle Beach 15
- Seven tied at 14

GAMES
- Mark Freed, El Paso 67
- Darwin Cubillan, Ottawa 65
- Erick Burke, Frisco 64
- Jack Cassel, Lake Elsinore 64
- Cliff Bartosh, Portland (PCL) 64
- Bryan Gaal, Portland (PCL)/Mobile 64

COMPLETE GAMES
- Francisco Cruceta, Akron 6
- Jon Connolly, West Michigan 5
- Drew Dickinson, Kane County 5
- T.A. Fulmer, Wisconsin 5
- Jonathan Albaladejo, Hickory 5

SAVES
- Lee Gronkiewicz, Kinston 37
- Jared Hoerman, San Antonio 36
- Spike Lundberg, Oklahoma/Frisco 31
- Mike Lyons, Tennessee 31
- Brad Clontz, Colorado Springs 30
- Mark Corey, Nashville 30
- Matty Wilkinson, South Bend 30
- Lee Gardner, Durham 30

SHUTOUTS
- Drew Dickinson, Kane County 3
- Sam Smith, South Bend 3
- Twenty tied at 2

INNINGS
- Drew Dickinson, Kane County 191
- Jason Ryan, Memphis 190
- Matt Henrie, Tucson/El Paso/Lancaster 185
- Pat Ahearne, Toledo/Erie 184
- Ben Crockett, Visalia/Asheville 184

WALKS
- Colt Griffin, Wilmington (CL)/Burlington (MWL) 97
- Wyatt Allen, Winston-Salem 89
- Scott Tyler, Quad City 82
- Mike Paradis, Bowie 81
- Daniel Cabrera, Delmarva 78
- Humberto Sanchez, West Michigan 78
- Charlie Zink, Portland (PCL)/Sarasota.......... 78

STRIKEOUTS
- John Maine, Frederick/Delmarva 185
- Joe Blanton, Midland/Kane County 174
- Merkin Valdez, Hagerstown 166
- Luis Martinez, Indianapolis/Huntsville 162
- Andy Pratt, Richmond 161

HITS
- John Rheinecker, Sacramento/Midland 233
- Brad Halsey, Trenton/Tampa 219
- Casey Daigle, El Paso 219
- Matt Henrie, Tucson/El Paso/Lancaster 212
- Andrew Lorraine, Las Vegas 211

STRIKEOUTS PER NINE INNINGS
(Starters)
- Scott Kazmir, St. Lucie/Capital City 11.94
- John Maine, Frederick/Delmarva 11.35
- Neal Cotts, Birmingham 11.05
- Matt Wright, Myrtle Beach/Rome 9.84
- Merkin Valdez, Hagerstown 9.58

STRIKEOUTS PER NINE INNINGS
(Relivers)
- Todd Pennington, Akron/Lake County .. 14.07
- Rafael Betancourt, Buffalo/Akron 14.02
- Ben Julianel, Peoria/Battle Creek 13.89
- Stephen Andrade, Arkansas/Rancho Cucamonga 13.50
- Henry Owens, Lynchburg/Hickory 13.50
- Dale Thayer, Fort Wayne 13.50

BATTING AVERAGE AGAINST
(Starters)
- John Maine, Frederick/Delmarva .... .177
- Neal Cotts, Birmingham .... .178
- Vince Perkins, Dunedin/Charleston, W.Va. .179
- Bill Murphy, Midland/Kane County.......... .200
- Scott Kazmir, St. Lucie/Capital City .... .202

BATTING AVERAGE AGAINST
(Relievers)
- Todd Pennington, Akron/Lake County ..... .138
- Stephen Andrade, Arkansas/Rancho Cucamonga.. .139
- Allen Levrault, Albuquerque .... .142
- Robbie Van, South Bend .... .151
- David Byard, St. Lucie .... .157

MOST STRIKEOUTS, ONE GAME
- John Wasdin, Nashville 15
- Jose Contreras, Staten Island 15
- Joel Zumaya, West Michigan 14
- Clint Nageotte, San Antonio 14
- Joe Blanton, Kane County 14
- Greg Miller, Jacksonville 14
- D.J. Hanson, Charleston, W.Va. 14
- Troy Cate, Inland Empire 14

BALKS
- Cory Vance, Colorado Springs 10
- Bill Murphy, Midland/Kane County 6
- Pasqual Coco, Indianapolis 6
- Joselo Diaz, Jacksonville/Vero Beach/St. Lucie .. 6
- Five tied at 5

INDIVIDUAL FIELDING

MOST ERRORS
- B.J. Upton, Orlando/Charleston, S.C. 56
- Buck Coats, Lancaster 51
- Michael Garciaparra, Wisconsin 50
- Corey Smith, Akron 45
- Luis Cruz, Fort Wayne 42
- Craig Ringe, Clinton 42

MINOR LEAGUE BEST TOOLS

Full season leagues only

	International/AAA	Pacific Coast/AAA	Eastern/AA	Southern/AA	Texas/AA	California/A	Carolina/A	Florida State/A	Midwest/A	South Atlantic/A
Best Batting Prospect	Chase Utley Scranton/W-B	Garrett Atkins Colorado Springs	Alexis Rios New Haven	Miguel Cabrera Carolina	Ramon Nivar Frisco	Josh Barfield Lake Elsinore	Chris Shelton Lynchburg	Joe Mauer Fort Myers	Prince Fielder Beloit	Larry Broadway Savannah
Best Power Prospect	Justin Morneau Rochester	Rob Stratton Albuquerque	Juan Richardson Reading	Stephen Smitherman Chattanooga	Dan Johnson Midland	Jason Botts Stockton	Walter Young Lynchburg	Ryan Howard Clearwater	Prince Fielder Beloit	Larry Broadway Savannah
Best Strike-Zone Judgment	Coco Crisp Buffalo	Val Pascucci Edmonton	Kevin Youkilis Portland	Miguel Cabrera Carolina	Steve Stanley Midland	Joey Gathright Bakersfield	Todd Self Salem	Donald Kelly Lakeland	Prince Fielder Beloit	Jorge Cortes Hickory
Best Baserunner	Esix Snead Norfolk	Tike Redman Nashville	Tim Raines Jr. Bowie	Dave Krynzel Huntsville	Mike Curry San Antonio	Joey Gathright Bakersfield	Willy Taveras Kinston	Wayne Lydon St. Lucie	Matt Lemanczyk Peoria	B.J. Upton Charleston, S.C.
Fastest Baserunner	Jose Reyes Norfolk	Bernie Castro Portland	Nook Logan Erie	Dave Krynzel Huntsville	Nathan Haynes Arkansas	Joey Gathright Bakersfield	Willy Taveras Kinston	Wayne Lydon St. Lucie	Matt Lemanczyk Peoria	Travis Ezi South Georgia
Best Pitching Prospect	Ryan Madson Scranton/W-B	Rich Harden Sacramento	Sean Burnett Altoona	Edwin Jackson Jacksonville	Chin-Hui Tsao Tulsa	Ervin Santana Rancho Cucamonga	Zack Greinke Wilmington	Gavin Floyd Clearwater	Joel Zumaya West Michigan	Scott Kazmir Capital City
Best Fastball	Fernando Rodney Toledo	Rich Harden Sacramento	Jesse Crain New Britain	Edwin Jackson Jacksonville	Bobby Jenks Arkansas	Ervin Santana Rancho Cucamonga	Franklin Francisco Winston-Salem	J.D. Durbin Fort Myers	Joel Zumaya West Michigan	Brandon League Charleston, W.V.
Best Breaking Pitch	Andy Pratt Richmond	Doug Sessions New Orleans	Taylor Buchholz Reading	Joel Hanrahan Jacksonville	Clint Nageotte San Antonio	Ervin Santana Rancho Cucamonga	Ian Oquendo Lynchburg	Gavin Floyd Clearwater	Joe Blanton Kane County	Cole Hamels Lakewood
Best Control	Carlos Reyes Durham	Justin Duchscherer Sacramento	Kyle Denney Akron	Angel Guzman West Tenn	Chin-Hui Tsao Tulsa	Ryan Ketchner Inland Empire	Zack Greinke Wilmington	Nick Ungs Jupiter	Jon Connolly West Michigan	Fausto Carmona Lake County
Best Reliever	Fernando Rodney Toledo	Mark Corey Nashville	Jesse Crain New Britain	Royce Ring Birmingham	Brian Bruney El Paso	Josh Parker Bakersfield	Lee Gronkiewicz Kinston	Kevin Cave Jupiter	Dale Thayer Fort Wayne	Carlos Hines Charleston, S.C.
Best Defensive Catcher	Corky Miller Louisville	John Buck New Orleans	Kelly Shoppach Portland	Humberto Quintero Mobile	Ryan Budde Arkansas	Jeff Mathis Rancho Cucamonga	Hector Gimenez Salem	Joe Mauer Fort Myers	Rene Rivera Wisconsin	Shawn Riggans Charleston, S.C.
Best Defensive First Baseman	Adam LaRoche Richmond	Carlos Rivera Nashville	Craig Brazell Binghamton	Adam LaRoche Greenville	A.J. Zapp San Antonio	Casey Kotchman Rancho Cucamonga	Mike Huggins Frederick	James Loney Vero Beach	Sean Luellwitz South Bend	Larry Broadway Savannah
Best Defensive Second Baseman	Aaron Miles Charlotte	Brent Abernathy Omaha	Danny Garcia Binghamton	Caonabo Cosme Tennessee	Chris Burke Round Rock	Jayson Nix Visalia	Ruddy Yan Winston-Salem	Robinson Cano Tampa	Alberto Callaspo Cedar Rapids	Victor Mercedes Hickory
Best Defensive Third Baseman	Travis Chapman Scranton/W-B	Chad Tracy Tucson	Rodney Nye Binghamton	Miguel Cabrera Carolina	Justin Leone San Antonio	Mark Teahen Modesto	Andy Marte Myrtle Beach	David Wright St. Lucie	Travis Hanson Peoria	Chad Spann Augusta
Best Defensive Shortstop	Jose Reyes Norfolk	Alfredo Amezaga Salt Lake	Anderson Machado Reading	J.J. Hardy Huntsville	Mike Rouse Midland	Eddie Menchaca Inland Empire	Andres Blanco Wilmington	Danny Gonzalez Clearwater	Erick Aybar Cedar Rapids	Corey Ragsdale Capital City
Best Infield Arm	Jose Reyes Norfolk	Ruben Castillo Tacoma	Corey Smith Akron	Miguel Cabrera Carolina	Jose Lopez San Antonio	Drew Meyer Stockton	Tony Pena Myrtle Beach	Ferdin Tejeda Tampa	Jerry Gil South Bend	B.J. Upton Charleston, S.C.
Best Defensive Outfielder	Coco Crisp Buffalo	Tike Redman Nashville	Jeremy Owens Portland	Dave Krynzel Huntsville	Nathan Haynes Arkansas	Gary Thomas Modesto	Willy Taveras Kinston	Eric Reed Jupiter	Felix Pie Lansing	Jeff Salazar Asheville
Best Outfield Arm	Alex Escobar Buffalo	Luke Allen Colorado Springs	Tyler Minges Akron	Reggie Abercrombie Jacksonville	Cory Sullivan Tulsa	Shin-Soo Choo Inland Empire	Jeremy Harts Lynchburg	Jason Kubel Fort Myers	Marcus McBeth Kane County	Angelo Burrows Rome
Most Exciting Player	Jose Reyes Norfolk	Bubba Crosby Las Vegas	Alexis Rios New Haven	Miguel Cabrera Carolina	Ramon Nivar Frisco	Joey Gathright Bakersfield	Andy Marte Myrtle Beach	Franklin Gutierrez Vero Beach	Prince Fielder Beloit	B.J. Upton Charleston, S.C.
Best Managerial Prospect	Marc Bombard Scranton/W-B	Tony DeFrancesco Sacramento	Dale Sveum Altoona	Phillip Wellman Chattanooga	Dave Brundage San Antonio	Jeff Gardner Lake Elsinore	Torey Lovullo Kinston	Mike Basso Dunedin	Webster Garrison Kane County	Luis Rivera Lake County

Selected at midseason 2003, by Baseball America in consultation with minor league managers

FREITAS AWARDS

Baseball America's annual Bob Freitas Awards are presented to franchises that show sustained excellence in the business of minor league baseball.

They were first presented in 1989, shortly after the death of Freitas, a longtime minor league operator, promoter and ambassador. Franchises must be in operation for at least five seasons before they're eligible, but that requirement was not a problem for 2003's group of winners, all of which have proven themselves over the long haul.

■ The **Pawtucket Red Sox** occupy almost as big a place in Rhode Island's sports culture as their parent club does in all of New England. Pawtucket, a repeat Freitas winner that also won in 1990, is an old-school franchise that has continued to update itself to remain vibrant.

McCoy Stadium, for instance, opened in 1946 but was almost completely rebuilt before the 1999 season. One thing that hasn't changed, however, is the fan support and interest. The team is consistently near the top of the International League attendance list, and has drawn more than 10 million fans since Ben Mondor bought the franchise in 1977.

That kind of stability is another hallmark in Pawtucket. Mondor's longtime ownership is surpassed by the Red Sox affiliation, which has been in place since the team debuted in the IL in 1973.

■ A few years ago, the **New Britain Rock Cats** might have been as unlikely to win the Freitas Award as any franchise in the minor leagues. But the team has made a remarkable turnaround and continues to move ahead in the Eastern League.

The turnaround actually began in 1994, when former owner Joe Buzas made an emotional address to the fans of New Britain and resisted efforts to move the team, winning a new stadium for the ballclub. But the team took a quantum leap when a local investment group headed by Coleman Levy bought the team before the 2000 season.

The new ownership brought new energy to the franchise, and attendance and interest have jumped, with overall crowds increasing from 177,026 in 1999 to 271,143 in 2003. Prospects for the future are even brighter, as the nearby New Haven Ravens will move to New Hampshire, giving the Rock Cats more potential fans.

■ You'd be hard-pressed to find any minor league franchise as stable as the **Modesto A's**. Not only are the A's a charter member of the California League—they joined in 1946 and have missed just one season, 1965, since then—but they also have been affiliated with Oakland since 1975. That's one of the longest continuous affiliations in the minors, particularly for a franchise that isn't owned by its major league parent.

Like Pawtucket, Modesto plays in an old stadium (John Thurman Field, opened in 1952) that has been significantly renovated. The team also continues to draw well, and while its attendance doesn't rank among the best in the minors, its last two seasons are the best in local history.

■ The **Spokane Indians** celebrated the 100th anniversary of baseball in Spokane in 2003, much the same way they've celebrated throughout their time in the Northwest League: by leading the league in attendance. The Indians had a new major league affiliate, the Rangers, after eight years with the Royals, but otherwise their successful recipe remained the same.

Spokane has had a team either in the NWL or the Pacific Coast League since 1955. Illustrating the team's relationship with its fans, it held a "100 People for 100 Years" promotion on Opening Night to honor 100 people connected to Spokane baseball history. Players, broadcasters and team officials were included, of course, but fans also had an important place in the ceremonies. That included one fan who had been a season-ticket holder since 1958, and another who had not missed an Indians game since 1973.

PREVIOUS **WINNERS**

Triple-A

1989—Columbus (International)
1990—Pawtucket (International)
1991—Buffalo (American Association)
1992—Iowa (American Association)
1993—Richmond (International)
1994—Norfolk (International)
1995—Albuquerque (Pacific Coast)
1996—Indianapolis (American Association)
1997—Rochester (International)
1998—Salt Lake (Pacific Coast)
1999—Louisville (International)
2000—Edmonton (Pacific Coast)
2001—Buffalo (International)
2002—Memphis (Pacific Coast)

Double-A

1989—El Paso (Texas)
1990—Arkansas (Texas)
1991—Reading (Eastern)
1992—Tulsa (Texas)
1993—Harrisburg (Eastern)
1994—San Antonio (Texas)
1995—Midland (Texas)
1996—Carolina (Southern)
1997—Bowie (Eastern)
1998—Trenton (Eastern)
1999—Portland (Eastern)
2000—Reading (Eastern)
2001—Mobile (Southern)
2002—Chattanooga (Southern)

Class A

1989—Durham (Carolina)
1990—San Jose (California)
1991—Asheville (South Atlantic)
1992—Springfield (Midwest)
1993—South Bend (Midwest)
1994—Kinston (Carolina)
1995—Kane County (Midwest)
1996—Wisconsin (Midwest)
1997—Rancho Cucamonga (California)
1998—West Michigan (Midwest)
1999—Wilmington (Carolina)
2000—Charleston, S.C. (South Atlantic)
2001—Delmarva (South Atlantic)
2002—Fort Myers (Florida State)

Short-Season

1989—Eugene (Northwest)
1990—Salt Lake City (Pioneer)
1991—Spokane (Northwest)
1992—Boise (Northwest)
1993—Billings (Pioneer)
1994—Everett (Northwest)
1995—Great Falls (Pioneer)
1996—Bluefield (Appalachian)
1997—Oneonta (New York-Penn)
1998—Hudson Valley (New York-Penn)
1999—Portland (Northwest)
2000—Lowell (New York-Penn)
2001—Salem-Keizer (Northwest)
2002—Ogden (Northwest

INTERNATIONAL LEAGUE

TRIPLE-A

DURHAM BULLS

Celebrating for the second straight year
Durham Bulls won back-to-back Governors' Cup titles with a dominating 12-1 playoff record in 2002 and 2003

BY DAVID BORGES

If the Tampa Bay Devil Rays remain a doormat in the American League Eastern Division, the same cannot be said of their Triple-A affiliate.

The Durham Bulls continued their reign as the closest thing to a dynasty in the International League with a second straight Governors' Cup championship in 2003. After dusting the Louisville Bats three games to one in the semifinals, the Bulls swept the Pawtucket Red Sox in three straight games to become the first repeat champion in the IL since the 1991-92 Columbus Clippers.

Durham, which also claimed its fifth Southern Division title in six years as a Devil Rays affiliate, has posted a remarkable 12-1 playoff record over the past two seasons. The Bulls won the 2002 title without losing a postseason game.

"It's definitely tough to win a division, then to win a championship," said manager Bill Evers, who became the 13th IL skipper to win at least two Governors' Cup crowns and now boasts a .697 winning percentage in Governors' Cup play. "You've got to get some bounces here and there, some big hits. The guys rose to the occasion."

DURHAM BULLS

Bill Evers

There were plenty of heroes in the tidy sweep of Pawtucket. In Game One, a pair of two-run homers by Jonny Gomes and Chris Truby did the bulk of the damage in a 5-3 Bulls victory. In just his third Triple-A start, left-hander Jon Switzer struck out 11—the most for a Bulls pitcher since the team moved from high Class A to Triple-A in 1998. In Game Two, it was another two-run homer—this one off the bat of Jeff Liefer—that snapped a 3-3 tie and paved the way to another 5-3 Durham victory.

The series shifted to Pawtucket's McCoy Stadium for Game Three. The PawSox were looking to win three straight, just like they did the last time they won a Governors' Cup crown in 1984. But thanks to shortstop Jorge Cantu's two-out, solo home run in the sixth that snapped a 2-2 tie, it wasn't to be. Durham held on for a 3-2 victory to become the first of the IL's 10 repeat champs to do it in successive sweeps.

"It's nice to run out onto someone else's home field and win it, especially against a good team like Pawtucket," said infielder Brooks Badeaux, one of seven Bulls players to participate in the two straight championships.

"We've played well in the playoffs," Evers said. "This year, we started out losing the first game (to Louisville), but the guys came back out and got it done. And the good thing about it was it wasn't one guy. We got contributions from everybody."

Pawsox Foiled Again

For Pawtucket, which was bidding to become the league's 10th different champion over the past 10 years, the finals sweep could best be described as an imperfect ending to a season full of perfection.

It was never more so than on Aug. 10, when right-hander Bronson Arroyo fired just the fourth perfect game in the 120-year history of the International League in Pawtucket's 7-0 win over Buffalo. Arroyo struck out nine and needed 101 pitches to achieve perfection.

The team posted a franchise-record 83 wins in the regular season, won a division title for the first time in seven years, earned a trip to the playoffs for the first time in six years and a berth in the finals for the first time in 12.

Buddy Bailey was IL manager of the year for the second time, just the fourth skipper to do so. First baseman Andy Abad won the RBI title with 93 before getting a September callup to Boston and missing out on the playoffs.

Pawtucket also had three representatives in the Triple-A all-star game (Arroyo, Lou Collier and Anton French) and three players on the league's postseason all-star team

(Arroyo, Collier and Abad). Arroyo (12-6, 3.43) was the league's pitcher of the year and finished second in the loop with 155 strikeouts despite missing the final two weeks of the season after earning a promotion to Boston.

The league's MVP went to Columbus first baseman/DH Fernando Seguignol, who came close to becoming the IL's first triple crown winner since Pawtucket's Jim Rice in 1974. Seguignol led the league in batting (.341) and home runs (28), but his 87 RBIs were second to Abad.

Seguignol's Clipper teammate, Drew Henson, garnered more headlines, despite inferior statistics (.234-14-78). Rumors circulated that Henson would abandon his baseball career for the NFL, but he got a September callup from the Yankees, which squelched the talk momentarily. Henson starred as a quarterback at Michigan and was selected in the 2003 NFL draft by the Houston Texans.

STAN DENNY

Bronson Arroyo

Seguignol and Henson were part of a remarkable turnaround for Bucky Dent's Clippers. With six weeks left in the season, Columbus was 14 games out of first place, but it won 24 of its last 33 games and climbed to within a half-game of first-place Louisville before settling for second place, 3½ games behind the Bats.

Shakeup in Louisville

Louisville survived a shakeup that saw manager Dave Miley promoted on July 29 to become interim manager of the parent Reds. Ex-big leaguer Rick Burleson came from the Rookie-level Billings club to take over in Louisville, and the Bats held on to win the division.

Like Columbus, the Ottawa Lynx had a tremendous August, including a club-record 10-game winning streak. Ottawa was in its first year as an affiliate of the Orioles, who left Rochester after a 41-year relationship, and settled for the IL wild-card berth. The Lynx made their first playoff appearance since 1995.

The league's rookie of the year was Charlotte second baseman Aaron Miles, who led the league with 166 hits and was tops among newcomers with a .304 average.

LEAGUE CHAMPIONS

Last 30 Years

Year	Regular Season*	Pct.	Playoff
1973	Charleston (Pirates)	.586	Pawtucket (Red Sox)
1974	Memphis (Expos)	.613	Rochester (Orioles)
1975	Tidewater (Mets)	.607	Tidewater (Mets)
1976	Rochester (Orioles)	.638	Syracuse (Yankees)
1977	Pawtucket (Red Sox)	.571	Charleston (Astros)
1978	Charleston (Astros)	.607	Richmond (Braves)
1979	Columbus (Yankees)	.612	Columbus (Yankees)
1980	Columbus (Yankees)	.593	Columbus (Yankees)
1981	Columbus (Yankees)	.633	Columbus (Yankees)
1982	Richmond (Braves)	.590	Tidewater (Mets)
1983	Columbus (Yankees)	.593	Tidewater (Mets)
1984	Columbus (Yankees)	.590	Pawtucket (Red Sox)
1985	Syracuse (Blue Jays)	.564	Tidewater (Mets)
1986	Richmond (Braves)	.571	Richmond (Braves)
1987	Tidewater (Mets)	.579	Columbus (Yankees)
1988	Tidewater (Mets)	.546	Rochester (Orioles)
	Rochester (Orioles)	.546	
1989	Syracuse (Blue Jays)	.572	Richmond (Braves)
1990	Rochester (Orioles)	.614	Rochester (Orioles)
1991	Columbus (Yankees)	.590	Columbus (Yankees)
1992	Columbus (Yankees)	.660	Columbus (Yankees)
1993	Charlotte (Indians)	.610	Charlotte (Indians)
1994	Richmond (Braves)	.567	Richmond (Braves)
1995	Norfolk (Mets)	.606	Ottawa (Expos)
1996	Columbus (Yankees)	.599	Columbus (Yankees)
1997	Rochester (Orioles)	.589	Rochester (Orioles)
1998	Buffalo (Indians)	.566	Buffalo (Indians)
1999	Columbus (Yankees)	.589	Charlotte (White Sox)
2000	Buffalo (Indians)	.593	Indianapolis (Brewers)
2001	Buffalo (Indians)	.641	Louisville (Reds)
2002	Scranton/W-B (Phillies)	.632	Durham (Devil Rays)
2003	Pawtucket (Red Sox)	.576	Durham (Devil Rays)

*Best overall record

Norfolk produced one of the game's most promising new stars in 20-year-old Jose Reyes, who earned a June promotion to the Mets. He was selected the IL's top prospect in a survey of managers.

Other standout hitting performances included Louisville outfielder Mark Budzinksi recording the league's only six-hit game on June 6 and Indianapolis outfielder Jason Conti (July 10) and Charlotte first baseman Ross Gload (Aug. 27) each hitting for the cycle.

Louisville led the IL in attendance for the second year in a row, drawing 651,510 fans, and the league's average attendance of 6,833 led the minors. The Lynx averaged 2,551 fans, the worst in the league by nearly 2,000, but planned to return to Ottawa for at least the 2004 season.

STANDINGS

Page	NORTH	W	L	PCT	GB	Manager	Attendance	Avg.	Last Penn.
87	Pawtucket Red Sox (Red Sox)	83	61	.576	—	Buddy Bailey	550,157	8,211	1984
79	Ottawa Lynx (Orioles)	79	65	.549	4	Gary Allenson	176,002	2,551	1995
211	Scranton/W-B Red Barons (Phillies)	73	70	.510	9½	Marc Bombard	427,445	6,476	None
117	Buffalo Bisons (Indians)	73	70	.510	9½	Marty Brown	551,916	8,761	1998
174	Rochester Red Wings (Twins)	68	75	.476	14½	Phil Roof	418,014	6,334	1997
269	Syracuse SkyChiefs (Blue Jays)	62	79	.440	19½	Omar Malave	356,303	5,399	1976
Page	**WEST**	**W**	**L**	**PCT**	**GB**	**Manager(s)**	**Attendance**	**Avg.**	**Last Penn.**
109	Louisville RiverBats (Reds)	79	64	.552	—	Dave Miley/Rick Burleson	651,510	9,307	2001
188	Columbus Clippers (Yankees)	76	68	.528	3½	Bucky Dent	480,445	6,963	1996
132	Toledo Mud Hens (Tigers)	65	78	.455	14	Larry Parrish	517,331	7,608	1967
167	Indianapolis Indians (Brewers)	64	78	.451	14½	Cecil Cooper	550,319	7,976	2000
Page	**SOUTH**	**W**	**L**	**PCT**	**GB**	**Manager**	**Attendance**	**Avg.**	**Last Penn.**
254	Durham Bulls (Devil Rays)	73	67	.521	—	Bill Evers	493,138	6,946	2003
95	Charlotte Knights (White Sox)	74	70	.514	1	Nick Capra	268,374	4,473	1999
196	Norfolk Tides (Mets)	67	76	.469	7½	Bobby Floyd	480,963	7,399	1985
72	Richmond Braves (Braves)	64	79	.448	10½	Pat Kelly	446,882	7,093	1994

GOVERNORS' CUP PLAYOFFS—Semifinals: Durham defeated Louisville 3-1 and Pawtucket defeated Ottawa 3-2 in best-of-5 series. **Finals**: Durham defeated Pawtucket 3-0 in best-of-5 series.

NOTE: Team's individual batting and pitching statistics can be found on page indicated in lefthand column.

2003 INTERNATIONAL LEAGUE STATISTICS

CLUB BATTING

	AVG	G	AB	R	H	2B	3B	HR	BB	SO	SB
Ottawa	.281	144	4842	666	1363	277	46	60	440	909	108
Charlotte	.281	144	4748	659	1332	249	26	139	356	872	72
Durham	.272	140	4820	652	1312	289	43	132	376	1016	82
Pawtucket	.271	144	4739	689	1282	245	27	129	408	959	119
Columbus	.267	144	4880	697	1304	277	30	129	475	958	48
Buffalo	.266	143	4756	626	1264	257	30	106	369	902	129
Louisville	.264	143	4788	690	1265	256	22	113	447	937	116
Indianapolis	.263	142	4736	553	1244	251	25	90	369	859	75
Rochester	.262	143	4766	607	1250	282	24	114	429	1049	67
Richmond	.260	143	4716	544	1228	253	55	89	372	994	117
Syracuse	.260	141	4663	598	1213	276	32	98	425	954	75
Norfolk	.260	143	4689	581	1218	250	27	90	435	875	178
Scranton/W-B	.255	143	4803	614	1226	272	19	93	398	868	72
Toledo	.248	143	4646	577	1154	259	35	119	361	994	139

CLUB PITCHING

	ERA	G	CG	SHO	SV	IP	H	R	ER	BB	SO
Richmond	3.64	143	4	13	41	1237	1191	582	500	495	1086
Ottawa	3.65	144	3	6	45	1243	1166	579	505	482	1029
Toledo	3.72	143	10	8	37	1241	1286	619	513	389	813
Scranton/W-B	3.79	143	8	15	35	1246	1218	597	525	334	963
Pawtucket	3.83	144	3	12	32	1239	1225	616	527	350	993
Durham	3.90	140	2	6	41	1238	1245	602	536	350	844
Indianapolis	3.93	142	3	10	33	1241	1273	627	542	416	974
Buffalo	4.01	143	5	8	38	1245	1242	623	554	456	969
Louisville	4.08	143	4	7	38	1244	1357	630	564	349	846
Norfolk	4.10	143	3	8	35	1239	1277	614	565	398	943
Columbus	4.18	144	5	7	34	1269	1294	674	589	458	964
Rochester	4.26	143	6	5	36	1234	1312	653	584	367	931
Syracuse	4.39	141	7	7	29	1217	1290	675	594	439	892
Charlotte	4.40	144	8	11	45	1228	1279	662	600	377	899

CLUB FIELDING

	PCT	PO	A	E	DP		PCT	PO	A	E	DP
Rochester	.982	3702	1462	93	144	Columbus	.977	3808	1403	122	133
Norfolk	.981	3717	1486	99	146	Louisville	.977	3731	1515	123	152
Durham	.979	3713	1558	112	129	Buffalo	.976	3734	1439	129	138
Scranton/W-B	.978	3737	1428	114	124	Ottawa	.975	3729	1395	131	123
Pawtucket	.978	3717	1296	113	96	Syracuse	.974	3650	1424	135	130
Charlotte	.978	3683	1281	114	105	Richmond	.973	3711	1355	138	137
Indianapolis	.977	3724	1488	122	136	Toledo	.972	3723	1616	154	168

INDIVIDUAL BATTING LEADERS

(Minimum 389 Plate Appearances)

	AVG	G	AB	R	H	2B	3B	HR	RBI	BB	SO	SB
Seguignol, Fernando, Columbus	.341	106	402	78	137	28	1	28	87	34	81	0
Estrada, Johnny, Richmond	.328	106	354	40	116	29	0	10	66	30	30	0
Utley, Chase, Scranton/W-B	.323	113	431	80	139	26	2	18	77	41	75	10
Gload, Ross, Charlotte	.315	133	508	72	160	40	6	18	70	29	60	6
Rushford, Jim, Indianapolis	.311	99	373	43	116	12	0	9	50	30	33	4
Garcia, Jesse, Richmond	.306	110	425	45	130	17	3	2	30	12	50	29
Miles, Aaron, Charlotte	.304	133	546	80	166	34	5	11	50	40	52	8
Abad, Andy, Pawtucket	.304	134	504	78	153	35	3	13	93	55	67	0
Jackson, Ryan, Durham	.303	131	519	78	157	45	4	13	71	30	85	2
Brown, Emil, Louisville	.295	97	369	58	109	20	3	12	63	27	76	18

INDIVIDUAL PITCHING LEADERS

(Minimum 115 Innings)

	W	L	ERA	G	GS	CG	SV	IP	H	R	ER	BB	SO
Griffiths, Jeremy, Norwich	7	6	2.74	21	19	1	1	115	94	43	35	26	78
Reyes, Carlos, Durham	10	3	2.86	22	21	1	0	132	124	47	42	14	78
Loux, Shane, Toledo	11	6	3.02	21	20	2	0	128	129	53	43	30	58
Robertson, Nate, Toledo	9	7	3.14	24	23	3	0	155	145	62	54	47	102
Telemaco, Amaury, Scranton	10	9	3.24	25	24	3	0	155	125	59	56	22	116
Towers, Josh, Syracuse	5	7	3.32	21	20	1	0	133	133	55	49	20	76
Douglass, Sean, Ottawa	10	8	3.40	27	27	0	0	143	142	67	54	58	118
Pratt, Andy, Richmond	7	10	3.40	28	27	1	0	156	146	77	59	77	161
Arroyo, Bronson, Pawtucket	12	6	3.43	24	24	1	0	150	148	66	57	23	155
Stanford, Jason, Buffalo	10	4	3.43	20	20	1	0	126	124	57	48	25	108

ALL-STAR TEAM

C—Johnny Estrada, Richmond. **1B**—Ross Gload, Charlotte. **2B**—Chase Utley, Scranton/Wilkes-Barre. **3B**—Brandon Larson, Louisville. **SS**—Jason Smith, Durham. **OF**—Andy Abad, Pawtucket; Lou Collier, Pawtucket; Alex Escobar, Buffalo. **DH**—Fernando Seguignol, Columbus. **Util**—Ryan Jackson, Durham. **SP**—Bronson Arroyo, Pawtucket. **RP**—Fernando Rodney, Toledo.

Most Valuable Player: Fernando Seguignol, Columbus. **Most Valuable Pitcher:** Bronson Arroyo, Pawtucket. **Rookie of the Year:** Aaron Miles, Charlotte. **Manager of the Year:** Buddy Bailey, Pawtucket

DEPARTMENT LEADERS

BATTING

G	Esix Snead, Norfolk	137
AB	Aaron Miles, Charlotte	546
R	Adrian Brown, Pawtucket	81
H	Aaron Miles, Charlotte	166
TB	Ross Gload, Charlotte	266
XBH	Ross Gload, Charlotte	64
2B	Ryan Jackson, Durham	45
3B	Jason Smith, Durham	14
HR	Fernando Seguignol, Columbus	28
RBI	Andy Abad, Pawtucket	93
SH	Wilton Guerrero, Louisville	19
SF	Drew Henson, Columbus	10
	Peter Zoccolillo, Indianapolis	10
BB	Jack Cust, Ottawa	80
IBB	Andy Abad, Pawtucket	8
HBP	Travis Chapman, Scranton/W-B	15
SO	George Lombard, Durham	143
SB	Esix Snead, Norfolk	61
CS	Anton French, Pawtucket	12
GIDP	Jorge Toca, Norfolk	21
OBP	Jack Cust, Ottawa	.422
SLG	Fernando Seguignol, Columbus	.624

PITCHING

G	Darwin Cubillan, Ottawa	65
GS	Brian Cooper, Charlotte	28
CG	Four tied at	3
ShO	Three tied at	2
GF	Lee Gardner, Durham	49
SV	Lee Gardner, Durham	30
W	Brian Cooper, Charlotte	15
L	Five tied at	11
IP	Brian Cooper, Charlotte	174
H	Brian Cooper, Charlotte	195
R	Three tied at	91
ER	Jorge De Paula, Columbus	81
HR	Jorge De Paula, Columbus	22
HB	Chris Fussell, Richmond	19
BB	Andy Pratt, Richmond	77
SO	Andy Pratt, Richmond	161
WP	Mike Smith, Syracuse	16
BK	Pasqual Coco, Indianapolis	6

FIELDING

C	AVG	Kevin Cash, Syracuse	.998
	PO	Cody McKay, Indianapolis	660
	A	Kevin Cash, Syracuse	77
	E	Cody McKay, Indianapolis	10
	DP	Kevin Cash, Syracuse	12
	PB	Kevin Cash, Syracuse	10
		Cody McKay, Indianapolis	10
1B	AVG	Ross Gload, Charlotte	.990
	PO	Ryan Jackson, Durham	860
	A	Jorge Toca, Norfolk	75
	E	Luis Garcia, Buffalo	10
	DP	Jorge Toca, Norfolk	91
2B	AVG	Craig Wilson, Columbus	.991
	PO	Chase Utley, Scranton/W-B	260
	A	Chase Utley, Scranton/W-B	326
	E	Nick Green, Richmond	16
	DP	Luis Rodriguez, Rochester	85
3B	AVG	Shane Andrews, Rochester	.963
	PO	Drew Henson, Columbus	98
	A	Travis Chapman, Scr./W-B	228
	E	Drew Henson, Columbus	28
	DP	Brant Ust, Toledo	26
SS	AVG	Steve Scarborough, Indy	.965
	PO	Jorge Nunez, Charlotte	170
	A	Jorge Nunez, Charlotte	296
	E	Eddy Garabito, Ottawa	27
	DP	Steve Scarborough, Indy	68
OF	AVG	Chad Green, Rochester	.996
	PO	Esix Snead, Norfolk	335
	A	Jason Conti, Indianapolis	21
	E	Eric Valent, Scranton/W-B	8
		Matt Watson, Norfolk	8
	DP	Damon Hollins, Richmond	4
		Michael Restovich, Rochester	4

PACIFIC COAST LEAGUE

TRIPLE-A

BY COREY BROCK

Consider the 2003 Pacific Coast League season a clean sweep for the Sacramento River Cats, who rolled to the league title and took almost every team and individual award along the way. Sacramento won a franchise-record 92 games and then went 6-0 in the playoffs, including a three-game sweep of Nashville to give the fourth-year franchise its first PCL championship.

"These guys play a team game," River Cats' first-year manager Tony DeFrancesco said. "From the 11 position players to the pitchers, everybody understands their role and what has to be done to go out there and win a game. These guys execute like no other team I've seen."

BILL MITCHELL

Graham Koonce

DeFrancesco, who managed Oakland's Double-A Midland team in 2002, won the PCL manager of the year award. He led Sacramento to the league's best regular record (92-52, .639) in 13 years. The River Cats led the minors in runs (859), home runs (153) and walks (673), bludgeoning opponents all season long and into the playoffs, where their average score was 8-2.

Sacramento third baseman Luis Lopez was the postseason MVP. Lopez hit .346 in the six postseason games with three home runs and 14 RBIs. The River Cats made a living of getting players on base, and driving them in. First baseman Graham Koonce, who led the minors in home runs (34) and paced the league in RBIs (115), was the league's MVP. He hit three home runs in a game on Aug. 31 to secure the home run title.

"Graham has been our most consistent power hitter from day one," DeFrancesco said. "His personality, work-ethic and ability have enabled him to be that player that can carry a club throughout the season."

DERRICK DODSON

Sacramento won even without him

Rich Harden was one of several River Cats called up to Oakland

Koonce was the third Sacramento player to win a postseason award in 2003, joining shortstop Bobby Crosby

MINOR LEAGUES

STANDINGS

AMERICAN CONFERENCE

Page	EAST	W	L	PCT	GB	Manager(s)	Attendance	Avg.	Last Penn.
218	Nashville Sounds (Pirates)	81	62	.566	—	Trent Jewett	387,345	5,781	None
146	New Orleans Zephyrs (Astros)	71	73	.493	10½	Chris Maloney	379,819	5,426	2001
261	Oklahoma RedHawks (Rangers)	70	72	.493	10½	Bobby Jones	380,051	5,508	None
225	Memphis Redbirds (Cardinals)	64	79	.448	17	Tom Spencer/Danny Sheaffer	749,446	10,409	2000
Page	**NORTH**	**W**	**L**	**PCT**	**GB**	**Manager**	**Attendance**	**Avg.**	**Last Penn.**
181	Edmonton Trappers (Expos)	73	69	.514	—	Dave Huppert	333,792	5,472	2002
233	Portland Beavers (Padres)	69	75	.479	5	Rick Sweet	438,931	6,270	1994
58	Salt Lake Stingers (Angels)	68	75	.479	5½	Mike Brumley	474,647	6,980	1979
247	Tacoma Rainiers (Mariners)	66	78	.458	8	Dan Rohn	327,927	4,685	2001

PACIFIC CONFERENCE

Page	CENTRAL	W	L	PCT	GB	Manager	Attendance	Avg.	Last Penn.
139	Albuquerque Isotopes (Marlins)	74	70	.514	—	Dean Treanor	576,867	8,125	None
125	Colorado Springs Sky Sox (Rockies)	73	70	.510	½	Rick Sofield	253,548	3,962	1995
102	Iowa Cubs (Cubs)	70	72	.493	3	Mike Quade	490,150	7,104	None
153	Omaha Royals (Royals)	70	73	.490	3½	Mike Jirschele	304,421	4,412	None
Page	**SOUTH**	**W**	**L**	**PCT**	**GB**	**Manager**	**Attendance**	**Avg.**	**Last Penn.**
204	Sacramento River Cats (Athletics)	92	52	.639	—	Tony DeFrancesco	766,326	10,643	2003
160	Las Vegas 51's (Dodgers)	76	66	.535	15	John Shoemaker	326,243	4,531	1988
65	Tucson Sidewinders (Diamondbacks)	73	71	.507	19	Al Pedrique	286,657	3,981	1993
240	Fresno Grizzlies (Giants)	55	88	.385	36½	Fred Stanley	522,174	7,355	None

PLAYOFFS—Semifinals: Sacramento defeated Edmonton 3-0 and Nashville defeated Albuquerque 3-1 in best-of -5 series. **Final**: Sacramento defeated Nashville 3-0 in best-of-5 series.

NOTE: Team's individual batting and pitching statistics can be found on page indicated in lefthand column.

(.308-22-90), named the PCL's rookie of the year, and righthander Justin Duchscherer (14-2, 3.25), the league's pitcher of the year.

Possibly the most impressive aspect of the River Cats' success in 2003 wasn't their gaudy offensive statistics but how they kept winning despite key players being promoted to Oakland or traded away.

The River Cats lost Crosby and Duchscherer to the parent A's just before the playoffs, and finished the season without outfielders David McCarty (.270-15-72) and Billy McMillon (.333-8-35), righthanders Aaron Harang (8-2, 2.71) and Rich Harden (9-4, 3.15), and closer Chad Harville (3-5, 2.05, 18 saves).

BILL MITCHELL

Bobby Crosby

With a total of 766,326 fans in 72 dates, the River Cats also led the minors in attendance for the fourth straight year.

The organization was rewarded for all its accomplishments in 2003 by being selected Baseball America's Minor League Team of the Year.

Three No-Hitters

In addition to all of Sacramento's achievements, there were several other notable individual accomplishments in the PCL in 2003.

Nashville righthander John Wasdin tossed a perfect game in a 4-0 victory over Albuquerque on April 7. The 30-year-old Wasdin needed just 100 pitches in the second nine-inning perfecto in the 100-year history of the PCL.

Las Vegas' Lindsay Gulin no-hit Tacoma on June 13 in a 7-0 victory, while Colorado Springs pitchers Chris Gissell and Jesus Sanchez combined for the first no-hitter in Sky Sox history on Aug. 2 in a 3-0 win over Nashville.

There were plenty of big hitting performances in the PCL as well. Omaha third baseman Jarrod Patterson was the first of two players to hit for the cycle. Albuquerque outfielder Gerald Williams had to work a little harder to get his. Willams' home run was unconventional—a fourth inning inside-the-park home run, not an easy feat for the 36-year-old veteran. In the eighth inning, Williams needed a bunt single to complete the cycle.

By most accounts, Williams didn't have anything on Tacoma catcher Pat Borders—the 40-year-old ageless wonder. Borders went 6-for-6 in a 15-10 victory over Colorado Springs on May 8. Borders was also the Rainiers lone representative in the Triple-A all-star game in July. Edmonton outfielder Peter Bergeron also enjoyed a six-hit game.

Albuquerque's Rob Stratton hit 32 homers, second in the league to Koonce, but he also had 175 strikeouts—35 more than his closest competitor. He hit only .212.

Isotopes GM Steps Down After Big Debut

The PCL set an attendance record for the fourth consecutive year, as 6,998,344 fans attended PCL games, an average of 6,322 fans a game.

As usual, Sacramento (10,643) and Memphis (10,409) dominated. The two franchises have run 1-2 in the league (and the minors) since 2000, when Sacramento moved from Vancouver into new Raley Field, and Memphis opened AutoZone Park.

Triple-A baseball returned to Albuquerque in 2003 after a two-year absence caused by the former Dukes' move to Portland, Ore. The city renovated Albuquerque Sports Stadium, and Ken Young bought the Calgary Cannons and brought them to New Mexico.

LEAGUE CHAMPIONS

Last 30 Years

Year	Regular Season*	Pct.	Playoff
1973	Tucson (Athletics)	.583	Spokane (Rangers)
1974	Spokane (Rangers)	.549	Spokane (Rangers)
1975	Hawaii (Padres)	.611	Hawaii (Padres)
1976	Salt Lake City (Angels)	.625	Hawaii (Padres)
1977	Phoenix (Giants)	.579	Phoenix (Giants)
1978	Tacoma (Yankees)	.584	Tacoma (Yankees)#
			Albuquerque (Dodgers)#
1979	Albuquerque (Dodgers)	.581	Salt Lake City (Angels)
1980	Tucson (Astros)	.595	Albuquerque (Dodgers)
1981	Albuquerque (Dodgers)	.712	Albuquerque (Dodgers)
1982	Albuquerque (Dodgers)	.594	Albuquerque (Dodgers)
1983	Albuquerque (Dodgers)	.594	Portland (Phillies)
1984	Hawaii (Pirates)	.621	Edmonton (Angels)
1985	Hawaii (Pirates)	.587	Vancouver (Brewers)
1986	Vancouver (Brewers)	.616	Las Vegas (Padres)
1987	Calgary (Mariners)	.596	Albuquerque (Dodgers)
1988	Albuquerque (Dodgers)	.605	Las Vegas (Padres)
1989	Albuquerque (Dodgers)	.563	Vancouver (White Sox)
1990	Albuquerque (Dodgers)	.641	Albuquerque (Dodgers)
1991	Albuquerque (Dodgers)	.580	Tucson (Astros)
1992	Colo. Springs (Indians)	.596	Colo. Springs (Indians)
1993	Portland (Twins)	.608	Tucson (Astros)
1994	Albuquerque (Dodgers)	.597	Albuquerque (Dodgers)
1995	Tucson (Astros)	.608	Colo. Springs (Rockies)
1996	Edmonton (Athletics)	.592	Edmonton (Athletics)
1997	Phoenix (Giants)	.615	Edmonton (Athletics)
1998	Iowa (Cubs)	.590	New Orleans (Astros)
1999	Vancouver (Athletics)	.592	Vancouver (Athletics)
2000	Salt Lake (Twins)	.629	Memphis (Cardinals)
2001	New Orleans (Astros)	.590	New Orleans (Astros)#
	Tacoma (Mariners)	.590	Tacoma (Mariners)#
2002	Las Vegas (Dodgers)	.590	Edmonton (Twins)
2003	Sacramento (Athletics)	.639	Sacramento (Athletics)

*Best overall record #Co-champions

The Isotopes' inaugural season was a big success, as the team drew 576,876 fans, third-best in the league, and Isotopes merchandise quickly became one of minor league baseball's top sellers. The team sold more than $1 million in merchandise.

RODGER WOOD

Tagg Bozied

But after a successful first season, Isotopes general manager Mel Kowalchuk stepped down at the end of the season, citing personal reasons. The Isotopes promoted director of business operations John Traub to replace him.

"We made huge money," Kowalchuk said. "I probably achieved the pinnacle of success in this league and went as far as anybody could go. But for what I was putting into it and the way I thought it was going, I felt maybe it was time for me to go."

Confrontation Sours Season

Not all the news was good in the PCL in 2003. Consider what happened during Portland's visit to Cashman Field in Las Vegas on Aug. 18. After a Las Vegas fan had heckled Portland's Tagg Bozied throughout the game, the two had words after the game and the fan threw a soft baseball—a Cashman Field giveaway that night—at Bozied. A throng of Beavers then rushed into the stands and got into a scrum with the fan on a concourse. The league fined and suspended 19 players after the incident.

2003 PACIFIC COAST LEAGUE STATISTICS

CLUB BATTING

	AVG	G	AB	R	H	2B	3B	HR	BB	SO	SB
Edmonton	.292	142	4799	706	1401	261	31	94	463	834	62
Colorado Springs	.287	143	4856	707	1396	292	32	122	392	819	72
Las Vegas	.286	142	4873	733	1396	287	57	112	375	838	107
Salt Lake	.284	143	4988	725	1417	274	62	106	442	869	145
Sacramento	.281	144	4843	859	1360	246	37	153	673	845	97
Tucson	.278	144	4971	721	1380	276	55	114	392	978	64
Albuquerque	.277	144	4884	721	1351	254	42	123	449	971	178
Fresno	.273	143	4874	607	1333	201	37	90	352	776	89
Tacoma	.267	144	4809	608	1286	247	21	112	406	859	176
Portland	.267	144	4907	651	1310	250	18	132	432	852	166
Nashville	.266	143	4756	651	1265	275	37	116	392	880	186
Omaha	.266	143	4913	736	1306	281	26	143	514	873	76
New Orleans	.265	144	4886	609	1294	260	34	88	375	890	83
Iowa	.258	142	4743	620	1223	249	25	140	444	928	78
Oklahoma	.258	142	4772	646	1230	244	41	116	503	852	141
Memphis	.254	143	4765	567	1211	228	39	127	409	882	95

CLUB PITCHING

	ERA	G	CG	SHO	SV	IP	H	R	ER	BB	SO
New Orleans	3.71	144	7	10	35	1267	1247	582	522	401	766
Nashville	3.88	143	9	16	41	1253	1198	601	540	394	1030
Memphis	3.89	143	2	10	31	1251	1288	593	541	388	787
Sacramento	3.90	144	2	10	35	1262	1237	618	547	439	973
Tacoma	3.96	144	5	6	41	1258	1273	636	553	433	899
Tucson	4.10	144	5	11	32	1268	1375	698	578	422	856
Las Vegas	4.17	142	2	9	40	1246	1362	672	577	424	816
Oklahoma	4.21	142	7	8	40	1246	1328	643	583	418	838
Iowa	4.35	142	4	3	33	1245	1280	667	602	493	945
Omaha	4.40	143	6	1	31	1277	1303	686	624	501	859
Colorado Springs	4.47	143	6	5	38	1231	1332	733	612	468	956
Portland	4.54	144	0	10	46	1262	1317	710	637	456	929
Salt Lake	4.66	143	6	5	34	1252	1404	747	648	420	813
Albuquerque	4.80	144	6	3	36	1264	1402	770	674	433	893
Fresno	4.88	143	1	6	29	1248	1421	765	677	444	810
Edmonton	5.08	142	10	7	34	1212	1392	746	684	479	776

CLUB FIELDING

	PCT	PO	A	E	DP		PCT	PO	A	E	DP
Memphis	.980	3752	1430	104	118	Tacoma	.977	3773	1413	123	127
New Orleans	.980	3800	1574	111	140	Oklahoma	.977	3737	1483	125	140
Sacramento	.980	3785	1442	109	102	Edmonton	.977	3635	1456	122	147
Portland	.979	3787	1464	113	134	Salt Lake	.975	3755	1488	132	159
Iowa	.979	3736	1399	111	133	Las Vegas	.975	3739	1483	136	130
Nashville	.978	3760	1316	113	96	Fresno	.974	3743	1443	136	121
Albuquerque	.978	3792	1576	120	153	Colo. Springs	.969	3694	1537	168	123
Omaha	.978	3830	1604	124	156	Tucson	.968	3805	1564	175	121

INDIVIDUAL BATTING LEADERS

(Minimum 389 Plate Appearances)

	AVG	G	AB	R	H	2B	3B	HR	RBI	BB	SO	SB
Dallimore, Brian, Fresno	.352	91	330	53	116	16	2	4	46	37	37	6
Reyes, Rene, Colo. Springs	.343	98	370	60	127	23	3	6	50	22	56	12
Sledge, Terrmel, Edmonton	.324	131	497	95	161	26	9	22	92	61	93	13
Tracy, Chad, Tucson	.324	133	522	91	169	31	4	10	80	41	52	0
Barnes, John, Nashville	.323	120	402	61	130	32	2	13	69	28	41	15
Hubbard, Trenidad, Iowa	.319	91	348	65	111	16	2	5	27	47	29	24
Atkins, Garrett, Colo. Springs	.319	118	439	80	140	30	1	13	67	45	52	2
Figueroa, Luis, Edmmonton	.317	126	480	66	152	30	2	2	44	36	31	7
Gall, John, Memphis	.312	123	461	62	144	24	1	16	73	39	56	5
Castro, Bernie, Portland	.311	105	425	57	132	17	5	2	24	25	43	49

INDIVIDUAL PITCHING LEADERS

(Minimum 115 Innings)

	W	L	ERA	G	GS	CG	SV	IP	H	R	ER	BB	SO
Ryan, Jason, Memphis	8	6	2.70	29	28	0	0	190	195	63	57	45	110
Sessions, Doug, New Orleans	9	5	2.92	31	25	1	1	157	149	57	51	43	92
Figueroa, Nelson, Nashville	12	5	2.97	23	23	3	0	151	144	54	50	37	121
Duchscherer, Justin, Sacramento	14	2	3.25	24	23	0	0	155	151	59	56	18	117
Capuano, Chris, Tucson	9	5	3.34	23	23	0	0	143	133	66	53	43	108
Stemle, Steve, Memphis	6	11	3.46	26	26	1	0	156	155	71	60	36	89
Anderson, Craig, Tacoma	13	11	3.56	28	27	4	0	177	187	93	70	46	67
Gonzalez, Edgar, Tucson	8	7	3.75	20	19	1	0	130	126	65	54	28	69
Wright, Jamey, Omaha	5	6	3.80	20	19	3	0	116	108	53	49	59	105
Fernandez, Jared, New Orleans	7	10	3.81	26	23	2	0	156	164	73	66	37	51

ALL-STAR TEAM

C—Koyie Hill, Las Vegas. **1B**—Graham Koonce, Sacramento. **2B**—Bernie Castro, Portland. **3B**—Chad Tracy, Tucson. **SS**—Bobby Crosby, Sacramento. **OF**—John Barnes, Nashville; Rene Reyes, Colorado Springs; Terrmel Sledge, Edmonton. **DH**—Robert Stratton, Albuquerque. **RHP**—Justin Duchscherer, Sacramento. **LHP**—Chris Capuano, Tucson. **RP**—Mark Corey, Nashville.

Most Valuable Player: Graham Koonce, Sacramento. **Pitcher of the Year:** Justin Duchscherer, Sacramento. **Rookie of the Year:** Bobby Crosby, Sacramento. **Manger of the Year:** Tony DeFrancesco, Sacramento.

DEPARTMENT LEADERS

BATTING

G	Craig Kuzmic, Fresno	148
AB	Joe Thurston, Las Vegas	538
R	Terrmel Sledge, Edmonton	95
H	Chad Tracy, Tucson	169
TB	Terrmel Sledge, Edmonton	271
XBH	Chin-Feng Chen, Las Vegas	61
	Phil Hiatt, Iowa	61
2B	Three tied at	35
3B	Chone Figgins, Salt Lake	15
	Luis Terrero, Tucson	15
HR	Graham Koonce, Sacramento	34
RBI	Graham Koonce, Sacramento	115
SH	Ruben Castillo, Tacoma	13
	Esteban German, Sacramento	13
SF	Graham Koonce, Sacramento	12
BB	Val Pascucci, Edmonton	101
IBB	Jon Nunnally, Memphis	7
HBP	Joe Thurston, Las Vegas	18
SO	Rob Stratton, Albuquerque	175
SB	Bernie Castro, Portland	49
CS	Luis Terrero, Tucson	19
GIDP	Tagg Bozied, Portland	19
OBP	Brian Dallimore, Fresno	.427
SLG	J.J. Davis, Nashville	.554

PITCHING

G	Cliff Bartosh, Portland	64
GS	Erik Hiljus, Sacramento	29
CG	Craig Anderson, Tacoma	4
ShO	Three tied at	2
GF	Brad Clontz, Colo. Springs	49
SV	Brad Clontz, Colo. Springs	30
	Mark Corey, Nashville	30
W	Justin Duchscherer, Sacramento	14
L	Britt Reames, Edmonton	13
IP	Jason Ryan, Memphis	190
H	Andrew Lorraine, Las Vegas	211
R	Mike Gosling, Tucson	106
	Erik Hiljus, Sacramento	106
ER	Erik Hiljus, Sacramento	91
HR	Erik Hiljus, Sacramento	28
HB	Matt Bruback, Iowa/Nashville/Port.	19
BB	Steve Smyth, Iowa	72
SO	Dennis Tankersley, Portland	148
WP	Mike Gosling, Tucson	13
BK	Cory Vance, Colo. Springs	10

FIELDING

C	AVG	Keith McDonald, Iowa	.997
	PO	Matt Treanor, Albuquerque	602
	A	Gerald Laird, Oklahoma	71
	E	Gerald Laird, Oklahoma	11
		Matt Treanor, Albuquerque	11
	DP	Raul Chavez, New Orleans	6
	PB	Yamid Haad, Portland	12
1B	AVG	Morgan Burkhart, Omaha	.997
	PO	Jason Hart, Oklahoma	1102
	A	Tagg Bozied, Portland	77
	E	Three tied at	9
	DP	Jason Hart, Oklahoma	107
2B	AVG	Mickey Lopez, Tacoma	.987
	PO	Joe Thurston, Las Vegas	277
	A	Joe Thurston, Las Vegas	360
	E	Bernie Castro, Portland	14
	DP	Jeff Pickler, Oklahoma	85
		Joe Thurston, Las Vegas	85
3B	AVG	Jason Wood, Albuquerque	.972
	PO	Chad Tracy, Tucson	94
	A	Chad Tracy, Tucson	292
	E	Three tied at	20
	DP	Scott Hodges, Edmonton	31
SS	AVG	Anthony Medrano, Edmonton	.975
	PO	Bobby Crosby, Sacramento	186
	A	Clint Barmes, Colo. Springs	385
	E	Tim Olson, Tucson	29
	DP	Manny Alexander, Oklahoma	80
		Anthony Medrano, Edmonton	80
OF	AVG	Chris Prieto, Sacramento	1.000
	PO	Jason Ellison, Fresno	320
	A	Barry Wesson, Salt Lake	19
	E	Choo Freeman, Colo. Springs	12
	DP	Val Pascucci, Edmonton	5
		Barry Wesson, Salt Lake	5

EASTERN LEAGUE

DOUBLE-A

BY KEN LIPSHEZ

The 81st Eastern League season was a yearlong celebration of sweet redemption for the Akron Aeros.

The Indians affiliate won 93 games in 2002, only to lose in the playoffs to the Harrisburg Senators. In 2003, the Aeros fell two wins short of becoming the first EL team to win 90 games in successive seasons (88-55) but won six of seven postseason games to claim their first league title.

ROB CUNI

Grady Sizemore

The Aeros, managed again by Brad Komminsk, defeated the Altoona Curve in the semifinals, three games to one, then swept the New Haven Ravens. The Ravens completed their final season in New Haven by beating the New Britain Rock Cats three games to two in the North. The franchise will move to Manchester, N.H., in 2004.

Offensive production paved the way for the Aeros. Left fielder Tyler Minges batted .483, drove in 11 runs and hit two homers in the postseason. Center fielder Grady Sizemore, who was also the MVP of the Futures Game, hit .412 with a homer and seven RBIs. The Aeros batted .358 as a team.

The Aeros also were winners at the gate, drawing 445,603 fans, but settled for second behind the Reading Phillies (465,717). The Ravens were at the opposite end of the attendance spectrum (last at 140,922) but had no less an exciting season. At the forefront was center fielder Alexis Rios, Toronto's first-round pick in the 1999 draft.

Rios won the batting title by hitting .352, 23 points ahead of second-place Mike Jacobs of the Binghamton Mets. Rios also led the league in hits (181) despite missing the first two weeks of the season.

The Ravens were powered by five former first-rounders. Flanking Rios in the outfield were Gabe Gross (Jays, 2001) and John-Ford Griffin (Yankees, 2001). Righthander Dustin McGowan (Jays, 2001) and shortstop Russ Adams (Jays, 2002) joined the team down the stretch.

The Eastern League also saw five no-hitters in 2003. The season was just six days old when the Aeros trio of Fernando Cabrera, Aaron Myette and Jose Vargas shackled Harrisburg, 15-0. Harrisburg's Seung Song notched the first no-hitter in Senators history in a 2-1 win over Erie April 28.

The Aeros recorded another when Chad Durbin and Oscar Alvarez blanked the Bowie Baysox on July 7. Binghamton righthander Bob Keppel zipped the Portland Sea Dogs Aug. 2. Former major league lefthander Horacio Estrada turned the trick for New Britain on Aug. 24 in Reading.

Joe McEacharn became the 11th EL president on Jan. 1, replacing his former mentor Bill Troubh.

Four new affiliates began play in 2003. The Blue Jays replaced the Cardinals in New Haven and the Giants moved from Shreveport (Texas) to Norwich. The Red Sox replaced the Marlins in Portland, and the Sea Dogs paid homage to their new parent club by erecting a replica of Fenway Park's Green Monster at Hadlock Field. The Yankees, formerly in Norwich, replaced the Red Sox by signing a working agreement with Trenton.

The league mourned on March 19 when former New Britain and Reading owner Joe Buzas died at 84. Buzas owned more than 80 minor league teams at one time or another over 47 years.

RICH ABEL

Alexis Rios

The league's all-star game made a gala return in New Britain, with the demise of the combined Double-A all-star game. Terry Tiffee, third baseman for the hometown Rock Cats, earned the MVP trophy by delivering a one-out RBI single in the bottom of the ninth to give the North a 6-5 win before a New Britain-record 7,168.

But the biggest event at an EL venue may have occurred in New Britain June 12. Air Force One delivered President George W. Bush to the New Britain Stadium parking lot, where he received a Rock Cats jersey before a speech at New Britain General Hospital.

STANDINGS

Page	NORTH	W	L	PCT	GB	Manager	Attendance	Avg.	Last Penn.
270	New Haven Ravens (Blue Jays)	79	63	.556	—	Marty Pevey	141,366	2,280	2000
175	New Britain Rock Cats (Twins)	73	68	.518	5½	Stan Cliburn	271,143	4,304	2001
88	Portland Sea Dogs (Red Sox)	72	70	.507	7	Ron Johnson	405,021	6,231	None
189	Trenton Thunder (Yankees)	70	71	.496	8½	Stump Merrill	427,567	6,108	None
197	Binghamton Mets (Mets)	63	78	.447	15½	John Stearns	211,533	3,254	1994
241	Norwich Navigators (Giants)	62	79	.440	16½	Shane Turner	158,622	2,689	2002
Page	**SOUTH**	**W**	**L**	**PCT**	**GB**	**Manager**	**Attendance**	**Avg.**	**Last Penn.**
118	Akron Aeros (Indians)	88	53	.624	—	Brad Komminsk	445,603	6,651	2003
219	Altoona Curve (Pirates)	78	63	.553	10	Dale Sveum	365,376	5,621	None
133	Erie Seawolves (Tigers)	72	70	.507	16½	Kevin Bradshaw	197,693	3,189	None
80	Bowie Baysox (Orioles)	69	72	.489	19	Dave Trembley	329,679	5,072	None
212	Reading Phillies (Phillies)	62	79	.440	26	Greg Legg	465,717	6,849	2001
182	Harrisburg Senators (Expos)	60	82	.423	28½	Dave Machemer	257,989	3,794	1999

PLAYOFFS—Semifinals: Akron defeated Altoona 3-1 and New Haven defeated New Britain 3-2 in best-of-5 series. **Final:** Akron defeated New Haven 3-0 in best-of-5 series.

NOTE: Team's individual batting and pitching statistics can be found on page indicated in lefthand column.

2003 EASTERN LEAGUE STATISTICS

CLUB BATTING

	AVG	G	AB	R	H	2B	3B	HR	BB	SO	SB
New Haven	.293	142	4792	752	1402	267	42	93	533	862	64
New Britain	.282	141	4717	701	1330	273	33	93	408	808	115
Binghamton	.280	141	4621	637	1292	281	22	102	412	1010	115
Altoona	.270	141	4739	636	1278	274	38	73	397	811	114
Akron	.267	141	4717	672	1259	230	45	111	479	804	74
Trenton	.267	141	4568	664	1219	252	21	106	513	840	120
Portland	.265	142	4682	660	1240	271	25	103	486	989	75
Norwich	.264	141	4563	583	1206	229	21	81	401	834	97
Harrisburg	.259	142	4725	653	1225	209	35	96	467	866	116
Erie	.258	142	4695	621	1213	220	37	99	456	896	79
Bowie	.257	142	4640	577	1192	228	22	89	368	817	142
Reading	.255	142	4677	610	1193	198	14	117	499	900	145

CLUB PITCHING

	ERA	G	CG	SHO	SV	IP	H	R	ER	BB	SO
Akron	3.19	141	10	11	46	1238	1208	555	439	420	952
Altoona	3.32	141	4	10	35	1241	1205	525	457	363	920
Bowie	3.85	142	7	16	33	1214	1135	589	519	491	945
Portland	3.98	142	7	7	30	1212	1225	644	536	408	899
Erie	4.02	142	6	9	36	1233	1283	639	551	379	761
New Haven	4.02	142	5	5	29	1222	1275	633	546	422	876
New Britain	4.20	141	8	11	33	1208	1269	625	564	421	830
Harrisburg	4.43	142	4	8	35	1234	1280	700	608	532	789
Binghamton	4.44	141	3	13	32	1195	1207	696	590	573	936
Norwich	4.61	141	9	9	35	1186	1277	705	608	488	797
Reading	4.74	142	4	3	29	1240	1328	738	654	437	846
Trenton	4.77	141	9	2	29	1189	1357	717	630	485	886

CLUB FIELDING

	PCT	PO	A	E	DP
Reading	.979	3720	1361	111	111
Altoona	.976	3722	1558	128	135
New Britain	.976	3624	1410	123	123
Erie	.974	3700	1626	140	165
New Haven	.974	3665	1535	137	129
Harrisburg	.974	3703	1421	136	127
Norwich	.974	3559	1410	133	146
Trenton	.974	3568	1424	134	139
Bowie	.973	3643	1415	139	121
Binghamton	.971	3584	1498	151	142
Portland	.971	3637	1396	152	139
Akron	.969	3715	1384	164	109

INDIVIDUAL BATTING LEADERS

(Minimum 383 Plate Appearances)

	AVG	G	AB	R	H	2B	3B	HR	RBI	BB	SO	SB
Rios, Alexis, New Haven	.352	127	514	86	181	32	11	11	82	39	85	11
Jacobs, Mike, Binghamton	.329	119	407	56	134	36	1	17	81	28	87	0
Youkilis, Kevin, Portland	.327	94	312	74	102	23	1	6	37	86	40	7
Fontenot, Mike, Bowie	.325	126	449	63	146	24	5	12	66	50	89	16
Watson, Brandon, Harrisburg	.319	139	565	86	180	17	6	1	39	38	60	18
Gonzalez, Luis, Akron	.318	116	431	72	137	22	4	7	62	46	41	1
Deardorff, Jeff, New Britain	.316	108	412	66	130	28	2	17	73	41	110	16
Tiffee, Terry, New Britain	.315	139	530	77	167	31	3	14	93	31	49	4
Fagan, Shawn, New Haven	.314	115	421	78	132	14	3	5	50	62	82	4
Nye, Rodney, Binghamton	.312	138	474	77	148	41	5	10	70	58	72	3

INDIVIDUAL PITCHING LEADERS

(Minimum 114 Innings)

	W	L	ERA	G	GS	CG	SV	IP	H	R	ER	BB	SO
Gassner, Dave, New Haven	10	4	2.79	35	19	1	1	145	139	54	45	28	92
Jacobsen, Landon, Altoona	9	11	2.93	27	27	1	0	163	156	60	53	40	80
Reimers, Cam, New Haven	10	5	3.08	28	26	0	0	164	170	68	56	38	96
Cruceta, Francisco, Akron	13	9	3.09	27	25	6	0	163	141	70	56	66	134
Burnett, Sean, Altoona	14	6	3.21	27	27	2	0	160	158	60	57	29	86
Borkowski, Dave, Bowie	6	8	3.30	30	19	2	0	128	136	54	47	24	70
Bonilla, Henry, New Britain	9	7	3.36	26	20	1	0	142	143	58	53	37	77
Connolly, Mike, Altoona	7	8	3.39	25	23	0	0	127	123	55	48	38	90
Forystek, Brian, Bowie	9	9	3.39	29	21	1	0	125	116	57	47	42	103
Buchholz, Taylor, Reading	9	11	3.55	25	24	1	0	145	136	62	57	33	114

ALL-STAR TEAM

C—Guillermo Quiroz, New Haven. **1B**—Craig Brazell, Binghamton. **2B**—Mike Fontenot, Bowie. **3B**—Terry Tiffee, New Britain. **SS**—Jason Bartlett, New Britain. **OF**—Jeff Inglin, Reading; Alexis Rios, New Haven; Grady Sizemore, Akron. **DH**—Alejandro Freire, Norwich. **Util**—Kevin Youkilis, Portland. **RHP**—Kyle Denney, Akron. **LHP**—Sean Burnett, Altoona. **RP**—Brian Schmack, Erie.

Most Valuable Player: Alexis Rios, New Haven. **Pitcher of the Year:** Sean Burnett, Altoona. **Rookie of the Year:** Grady Sizemore, Akron. **Manager of the Year:** Marty Pevey, New Haven.

DEPARTMENT LEADERS

BATTING

G	Jeff Inglin, Reading	141
AB	Brandon Watson, Harrisburg	565
R	Brian Myrow, Trenton	99
H	Alexis Rios, New Haven	181
TB	Alexis Rios, New Haven	268
XBH	Brian Myrow, Trenton	57
2B	Rodney Nye, Binghamton	41
	Kevin West, New Britain	41
3B	Alexis Rios, New Haven	11
	Grady Sizemore, Akron	11
HR	Jeff Inglin, Reading	24
RBI	Jeff Inglin, Reading	103
SH	Nook Logan, Erie	12
	Raul Nieves, Portland	12
SF	Mitch Jones, Trenton	10
BB	Andy Machado, Reading	108
IBB	Jeff Inglin, Reading	8
	Brian Myrow, Trenton	8
HBP	Jason Bartlett, New Britain	20
	Chris Duffy, Altoona	20
SO	Jeremy Owens, Portland	161
SB	Andy Machado, Reading	49
CS	Jason Bartlett, New Britain	24
GIDP	Alexis Rios, New Haven	22
OBP	Kevin Youkilis, Portland	.487
SLG	Mike Jacobs, Binghamton	.548

PITCHING

G	Kevin Hodge, New Britain	56
	Eddy Rodriguez, Bowie	56
GS	Three tied at	27
CG	Francisco Cruceta, Akron	6
ShO	Five tied at	2
GF	Brian Schmack, Erie	48
SV	Brian Schmack, Erie	29
W	Sean Burnett, Altoona	14
L	Mitch Walk, Norwich	13
IP	Tim Kester, Portland	164
H	Tim Kester, Portland	193
R	Javier Ortiz, Trenton	105
ER	Javier Ortiz, Trenton	96
HR	Seung Lee, Reading	21
HB	Mitch Walk, Norwich	14
BB	Mike Paradis, Bowie	81
SO	Francisco Cruceta, Akron	134
WP	Derrick Van Dusen, Akron	13
BK	Francisco Cruceta, Akron	4

FIELDING

C	AVG	Brian Luderer, Akron	.996
	PO	Guillermo Quiroz, New Haven	605
	A	Max St. Pierre, Erie	76
	E	Chris Curry, Norwich	11
		Kelly Shoppach, Portland	11
	DP	Kelly Shoppach, Portland	8
		Eli Whiteside, Bowie	8
	PB	Edgar Cruz, Reading	15
1B	AVG	Jeff Deardorff, New Britain	.993
	PO	Aaron Rifkin, Trenton	1034
	A	Aaron Rifkin, Trenton	84
	E	Eric Crozier, Akron	12
		Aaron Rifkin, Trenton	12
	DP	Aaron Rifkin, Trenton	116
2B	AVG	Scott Tousa, Erie	.986
	PO	Scott Tousa, Erie	265
	A	Scott Tousa, Erie	388
	E	Josh McKinley, Harrisburg	20
	DP	Scott Tousa, Erie	118
3B	AVG	Terry Tiffee, New Britain	.947
	PO	Jack Hannahan, Erie	103
	A	Jack Hannahan, Erie	334
	E	Corey Smith, Akron	44
	DP	Jack Hannahan, Erie	41
SS	AVG	Jason Bartlett, New Britain	.969
	PO	Jason Bartlett, New Britain	249
	A	Jason Bartlett, New Britain	380
	E	Jamie Athas, Norwich	38
	DP	Jamie Athas, Norwich	101
OF	AVG	Jeff Inglin, Reading	1.000
	PO	Brandon Watson	389
	A	Ron Acuna, Binghamton	21
	E	Kevin West, New Britain	11
	DP	Tyler Minges, Akron	5
		Justin Sherrod, Portland	5

SOUTHERN LEAGUE

DOUBLE-A

BY MARK McCARTER

Cigar smoke filled the air, the grass was wet with sprayed champagne and it seemed one endless photo opportunity. The Carolina Mudcats were on the field after clinching the 2003 Southern League championship sharing their celebration with fans and family.

It wouldn't have been inappropriate if there were handshakes of introduction as much as congratulations. The postseason Carolina roster bore little resemblance to the one that began the season. Four of the starters had played fewer than 75 games for the Mudcats.

ED WOLFSTEIN
Miguel Cabrera

The degree of changes—and star power lost—made it more impressive that the Mudcats, a Marlins affiliate, would finish with a league-best 80-58 overall record and 3-2 series edge over Huntsville in a riveting SL championship series. The Mudcats accomplished it all with nary a postseason league all-star selection.

"The Marlins are strong in the minor leagues and they proved it to us," Mudcats general manager Joe Kremer said amid the champage celebration. "(Manager) Tracy Woodson did a great job keeping the chemistry going."

The Mudcats were raided early, with the promotion of phenom Dontelle Willis to the majors. (Willis actually phoned Mudcats outfielder Chip Ambres during the championship game for updates.) Then, after 69 games, third baseman and organization top prospect Miguel Cabrera was called up.

Then, calamaity. The versatile Josh Willingham, developing into the best catcher in the system, hurt his knee four games after his promotion. Chris Aguila, who returned to the lineup just in time to qualify for the league batting title (.320), missed nearly two months with a right wrist injury.

If that wasn't enough, Carolina had to finish the season with seven games in four days at Orlando, winning four to clinch the second-half East title and home-field edge in the playoffs against division runner-up Tennessee.

Carolina was in its first season as a Marlins affiliate; ditto Tennessee with the Cardinals. Both paid immediate dividends, with Carolina capturing its second title in franchise history and the Smokies reaching the playoffs for the first time in three years.

In Florida, there was a hello and a goodbye. Jacksonville moved into the gorgeous new Baseball Grounds of Jacksonville, spiking the Suns' attendance by some 2,000 fans a game. Orlando said farewell to the league after 29 years. The franchise is moving to Montgomery, Ala., for 2004, where it will be known as the Biscuits.

The Suns also said hello to phenomenal pitching prospects. Most noteworthy were Joel Hanrahan(10-4, 2.43, 130 K's in 133 innings), voted the league's best pitcher, and teenage phenom Edwin Jackson (7-7, 3.70, 157 K's in 148 innings), who finished the season in the majors.

League runner-up Huntsville had the most prospects, with eight of the Brewers' preseason top dozen spending at least part of the season with the Stars. Third baseman Corey Hart was the league's MVP, winning the RBI crown with 94 and collecting a league-best 149 hits. Center fielder David Krynzel was runner-up to Hall for the stolen-base title and led with 11 triples. Shortstop J.J. Hardy may have been the most consistent of the group and was superb on defense. But it was pitching that carried Huntsville, behind Luis Martinez (8-5, 2.58), veteran Derek Lee (11 wins in a half-season) and first-round draft pick Mike Jones (7-2, 2.40).

A former Huntsville player, Bucky Jacobsen, led the league with 31 homers and made a strong case for MVP with his 84 RBIs and .298 average for Tennessee.

But Birmingham's Jeremy Reed had the most eye-popping numbers of all. He batted .409 in 66 games at Birmingham, and a minor league-best .373 overall, including a half-season at Class A Winston-Salem.

STANDINGS: SPLIT SEASON

FIRST HALF

EAST	W	L	PCT	GB
Carolina	42	26	.618	—
Greenville	36	32	.529	6
Tennessee	35	35	.500	8
Orlando	32	37	.464	10½
Jacksonville	31	38	.449	11½
WEST	**W**	**L**	**PCT**	**GB**
Huntsville	40	28	.588	—
West Tenn	34	36	.486	7
Birmingham	33	35	.485	7
Chattanooga	32	38	.457	9
Mobile	29	39	.426	11

SECOND HALF

EAST	W	L	PCT	GB
Carolina	38	32	.543	—
Tennessee	37	32	.536	½
Jacksonville	35	35	.500	3
Orlando	33	35	.485	4
Greenville	32	38	.457	6
WEST	**W**	**L**	**PCT**	**GB**
Birmingham	40	29	.580	—
Huntsville	35	35	.500	5½
Chattanooga	34	36	.486	6½
Mobile	32	38	.457	8½
West Tenn	31	37	.456	8½

PLAYOFFS—Semifinals: Carolina defeated Tennessee 3-1 and Huntsville defeated Birmingham 3-2 in best-of-5 series. **Final**: Carolina defeated Huntsville 3-2 in best-of-5 series.

STANDINGS: OVERALL

Page		W	L	PCT	GB	Manager	Attendance	Avg.	Last Penn.
140	Carolina Mudcats (Marlins)	80	58	.580	—	Tracy Woodson	204,867	3,252	2003
168	Huntsville Stars (Brewers)	75	63	.543	5	Frank Kremblas	198,416	2,961	2001
96	Birmingham Barons (White Sox)	73	64	.533	6½	Wally Backman	276,717	4,130	2002
226	Tennessee Smokies (Cardinals)	72	67	.518	8½	Mark DeJohn	256,597	3,888	1978
73	Greenville Braves (Braves)	68	70	.493	12	Brian Snitker	183,564	3,009	1997
161	Jacksonville Suns (Dodgers)	66	73	.475	14½	Dino Ebel	359,979	5,454	2001
255	Orlando Rays (Devil Rays)	65	72	.474	14½	Charlie Montoyo	150,051	2,382	1999
110	Chattanooga Lookouts (Reds)	66	74	.471	15	Phillip Wellman	237,235	3,650	1988
103	West Tenn Diamond Jaxx (Cubs)	65	73	.471	15	Bobby Dickerson	197,226	2,900	2000
234	Mobile BayBears (Padres)	61	77	.442	19	Craig Colbert	219,007	3,221	1998

NOTE: Team's individual batting and pitching statistics can be found on page indicated in lefthand column.

2003 SOUTHERN LEAGUE STATISTICS

CLUB BATTING

	AVG	G	AB	R	H	2B	3B	HR	BB	SO	SB
Birmingham	.270	137	4451	567	1202	227	23	64	466	852	110
Carolina	.267	138	4596	654	1225	264	38	83	496	906	126
Orlando	.265	137	4522	552	1199	253	21	73	402	941	84
Chattanooga	.261	140	4624	660	1209	265	24	104	471	1042	123
Tennessee	.256	139	4595	564	1178	233	22	93	432	924	94
West Tenn	.251	138	4478	517	1125	232	31	70	434	900	98
Greenville	.249	138	4478	571	1116	230	31	81	503	1044	109
Jacksonville	.246	139	4527	554	1113	213	36	94	438	1081	124
Huntsville	.245	138	4556	596	1117	225	24	69	493	1033	174
Mobile	.238	138	4564	547	1085	227	18	96	507	1076	111

CLUB PITCHING

	ERA	G	CG	SHO	SV	IP	H	R	ER	BB	SO
Huntsville	3.16	138	4	12	41	1225	1143	542	431	522	952
Carolina	3.45	138	2	12	41	1198	1085	546	460	524	957
Jacksonville	3.50	139	3	8	29	1218	1185	557	473	405	997
Tennessee	3.58	139	2	13	43	1209	1122	561	481	475	1047
Greenville	3.61	138	6	18	30	1175	1140	549	472	399	903
Birmingham	3.76	137	3	7	45	1185	1158	580	495	506	965
Orlando	3.77	137	6	9	28	1171	1163	604	491	400	870
West Tenn	3.83	138	3	9	35	1190	1186	586	507	454	1064
Mobile	3.88	138	3	6	37	1206	1093	595	520	499	1102
Chattanooga	4.08	140	2	6	41	1214	1294	662	550	458	942

CLUB FIELDING

	PCT	PO	A	E	DP
Tennessee	.976	3627	1452	123	113
Greenville	.975	3525	1416	128	98
West Tenn	.975	3570	1301	127	101
Carolina	.974	3595	1370	131	117
Jacksonville	.972	3653	1415	145	128
Mobile	.970	3618	1300	150	101
Chattanooga	.970	3642	1441	159	105
Huntsville	.969	3676	1517	165	131
Birmingham	.969	3556	1235	153	104
Orlando	.967	3512	1330	164	97

INDIVIDUAL BATTING LEADERS

(Minimum 378 Plate Appearances)

	AVG	G	AB	R	H	2B	3B	HR	RBI	BB	SO	SB
Aguila, Chris, Carolina	.320	93	337	58	108	21	3	11	55	36	67	6
Bikowski, Scott, Birmingham	.312	118	394	53	123	23	3	3	49	50	65	3
Alvarez, Gabe, Birmingham	.310	118	410	60	127	34	0	11	78	58	87	2
Smitherman, Stephen, Chattanooga	.310	105	365	60	113	21	2	19	73	54	95	11
Stenson, Dernell, Chattanooga	.306	101	356	51	109	28	0	14	76	39	74	4
Hart, Corey, Huntsville	.302	130	493	70	149	40	1	13	94	28	101	25
Quintero, Humberto, Mobile	.298	110	386	37	115	26	0	3	52	19	41	0
Jacobsen, Bucky, Tennessee	.298	131	447	84	133	24	1	31	84	56	91	3
Piniella, Juan, Birmingham	.292	115	346	45	101	24	2	4	27	28	82	12
Sadler, Ray, West Tenn	.291	110	412	56	120	31	5	6	42	33	81	17

INDIVIDUAL PITCHING LEADERS

(Minimum 112 Innings)

	W	L	ERA	G	GS	CG	SV	IP	H	R	ER	BB	SO
Hanrahan, Joel, Jacksnonville	10	4	2.43	23	23	1	0	133	117	44	36	53	130
Pacheco, Enemencio, Birmingham	12	2	2.56	30	24	0	0	151	131	51	43	51	116
Martinez, Luis, Huntsville	8	5	2.58	20	20	1	0	115	93	46	33	54	116
Bridges, Donnie, Carolina	10	2	2.81	31	19	1	0	135	85	47	42	70	109
Oxspring, Chris, Mobile	10	6	2.92	40	18	1	0	136	106	47	44	62	129
Nelson, Bubba, Greenville	8	10	3.18	23	20	0	0	119	106	47	42	45	77
Magrane, Jim, Orlando	10	6	3.26	25	24	0	0	144	147	69	52	51	87
Parrott, Rhett, Tennessee	8	9	3.27	21	21	1	0	124	122	52	45	40	112
Mitre, Sergio, West Tenn	7	9	3.34	25	24	0	0	146	162	75	54	41	128
Wainwright, Adam, Greenville	10	8	3.37	27	27	1	0	150	133	59	56	37	128

ALL STAR-TEAM

C—Humberto Quintero, Mobile. **1B**—Bucky Jacobsen, Tennessee. **2B**—Caonabo Cosme, Tennessee. **3B**—Corey Hart, Huntsville. **SS**—J.J. Hardy, Huntsville. **OF**—Matt Diaz, Orlando; Jon Knott, Mobile; Dave Krynzel, Huntsville; Stephen Smitherman, Chattanooga. **DH**—Dernell Stenson, Chattanooga. **Util**—Gabe Alvarez, Birmingham. **RHP**—Joel Hanrahan, Jacksonville. **LHP**—Neal Cotts, Birmingham. **RP**—Rusty Tucker, Mobile.

Most Valuable Player: Corey Hart, Huntsville. **Most Outstanding Pitcher:** Joel Hanrahan, Jacksonville. **Manager of the Year:** Frank Kremblas, Huntsville.

DEPARTMENT LEADERS

BATTING

G	John Nelson, Tennessee	136
AB	John Nelson, Tennessee	506
R	Bucky Jacobsen, Tennessee	84
H	Corey Hart, Huntsville	149
TB	Bucky Jacobsen, Tennessee	252
XBH	Jon Knott, Mobile	59
2B	Corey Hart, Huntsville	40
3B	Dave Krynzel, Huntsville	11
HR	Bucky Jacobsen, Tennessee	31
RBI	Corey Hart, Huntsville	94
SH	Danny Sandoval, Birmingham	14
SF	Josh Wilson, Carolina	10
BB	Jon Knott, Mobile	82
IBB	Bucky Jacobsen, Tennessee	8
HBP	Dan Grummitt, Orlando	22
SO	Reggie Abercrombie, Jacksonville	164
SB	Billy Hall, Carolina	45
CS	Dave Krynzel, Huntsville	21
GIDP	Papo Bolivar, Tennessee	18
OBP	Stephen Smitherman, Chatt.	.402
SLG	Bucky Jacobsen, Tennessee	.564

PITCHING

G	Bryan Gaal, Mobile	62
GS	Heath Totten, Jacksonville	28
CG	Five tied at	2
ShO	Seven tied at	1
GF	Mike Lyons, Tennessee	49
SV	Mike Lyons, Tennessee	31
W	Enemencio Pacheco, Birmingham	12
	Cory Stewart, Mobile	12
L	John Koronka, West Tenn	13
	Pedro Liriano, Huntsville	13
IP	Heath Totten, Jacksonville	181
H	Heath Totten, Jacksonville	196
R	John Koronka, Chatt./West Tenn	88
ER	Nick Stocks, Tennessee	80
HR	Nick Stocks, Tennessee	17
HB	Nick Stocks, Tennessee	13
BB	Donnie Bridges, Carolina	70
SO	Mike Nannini, West Tenn	158
WP	Donnie Bridges, Carolina	11
	Frank Gracesqui, Carolina	11
BK	John Koronka, Chatt./West Tenn	5

FIELDING

C	AVG	Humberto Quintero, Mobile	.995
	PO	Humberto Quintero, Mobile	857
	A	Humberto Quintero, Mobile	93
	E	Three tied at	8
	DP	Yadier Molina, Tennessee	8
		Dane Sardinha, Chattanooga	8
	PB	Mike Kremblas, Huntsville	26
1B	AVG	Brandon Gemoll, Huntsville	.990
	PO	Brandon Gemoll, Huntsville	1025
	A	Brandon Gemoll, Huntsville	77
	E	Bucky Jacobsen, Tennessee	16
		Derek Michaelis, Jacksonville	16
	DP	Brandon Gemoll, Huntsville	100
2B	AVG	Andrew Beattie, Chattanooga	.981
	PO	Caonabo Cosme, Tennessee	253
	A	Caonabo Cosme, Tennessee	373
	E	Jesus Medrano, Carolina	15
	DP	Caonabo Cosme, Tennessee	79
3B	AVG	Corey Erickson, Tennessee	.940
	PO	Corey Hart, Huntsville	74
	A	Brennan King, Jacksonville	223
	E	Corey Hart, Huntsville	32
	DP	Brennan King, Jacksonville	27
SS	AVG	J.J. Hardy, Huntsville	.970
	PO	J.J. Hardy, Huntsville	167
	A	John Nelson, Tennessee	391
	E	John Nelson, Tennessee	23
		Guillermo Reyes, Birmingham	23
	DP	John Nelson, Tennessee	67
OF	AVG	Chip Ambres, Carolina	1.000
	PO	Amado German, Orlando	294
	A	Vince Faison, Mobile	16
	E	Reggie Abercrombie, Jack.	17
	DP	Chad Durham, Birmingham	4

TEXAS LEAGUE

DOUBLE-A

BY MICHAEL POINT

The Texas League's unlikely, but undeniable, new reputation as a paradise for pitching prospects was reinforced by the 2003 season, which saw the most wins by a pitcher in a quarter-century and a batting race that was won by a player who got his last hit in the league on July 1.

Not surprisingly, the team with the best staff—once again pitching-rich San Antonio—claimed the league championship. The Missions, showcasing a rotation of Travis Blackley, Clint Nageotte, Bobby Madritsch and Cha Seung Baek, won both halves of the West before dispatching the first-year Frisco RoughRiders in five games in the league championship series. In keeping with the pitching theme, two of the wins were shutouts.

SPORTS ON FILM

Clint Nageotte

Midland's Rich Harden set the tone for the season with six perfect innings on Opening Day. He went seven perfect innings in his second start before moving upward toward a spot in the Oakland rotation. He was far from the only Texas Leaguer to ascend to such status, as Wichita's Jimmy Gobble moved into the Royals rotation and Tulsa's Chin-Hui Tsao did likewise with the Rockies. Coincidentally, those were the two teams that matched up in an unprecedented major league exhibition series at Round Rock's Dell Diamond the weekend before the regular season began.

Midland's Dan Johnson led the league with 27 home runs and 117 RBIs, and Wichita's Byron Gettis (.302 with 103 RBIs) and Tulsa's Andy Tracy (.299 with 25 home runs) also turned in solid offensive seasons. But the bats were clearly overmatched most of the time.

"There were some good hitters but there were some genuinely great pitchers," Round Rock manager Jackie Moore said. "Every team seemed to have an ace or two."

The only team that didn't was Moore's Express, which after three consecutive playoff seasons went off the rails with a 20-50 first-half record before finishing with the most losses in the league since 1956, when the TL played an expanded schedule.

At the opposite end of the standings was repeat champion San Antonio, which with a 3.04 ERA, the league's best in a decade, dominated both individual and staff pitching statistics. With Nageotte leading the way with 157, San Antonio had three of the top four strikeout pitchers while leading the league with 1,131. No other team had 1,000, but the most impressive aspect of the total was that San Antonio pitchers allowed fewer hits (1,071) than the number of strikeouts they recorded.

Blackley, who finished second to Tsao's 2.46 ERA, posted a 17-3 record, becoming the first to win that many games since Jeff Reardon did so in 1978. The 20-year Australian lefty was named pitcher of the year. San Antonio closer Jared Hoerman, whose 36 saves were twice as many as the entire Round Rock staff, was the league's most successful reliever.

The selection of San Antonio third baseman Justin Leone as player of the year reflected the league's offensive falloff. Leone didn't lead the league in home runs, batting or RBIs, though he was first in runs, on-base percentage and extra-base hits. His consistency, outstanding defense and clutch hitting won him the award.

San Antonio also ran away from the field on the basepaths, amassing 210 stolen bases—more than what five teams compiled in total attempts. Mike Curry led the league with 58, something he also did in 2000 as a member of the Wichita Wranglers.

With 666,977 fans visiting their new stadium in suburban Dallas, the RoughRiders set a Double-A record for first-year attendance, eclipsing the 2000 mark set by Round Rock. But the Express success story rolled on at the turnstiles, despite a 46-94 season on the field. Round Rock averaged 9,800 fans a game, setting a new Double-A season record for the fourth consecutive year. The Express drew 685,973 to Dell Diamond, which will get more seats for 2004 in anticipation of a move to Triple-A in 2005.

The departure of Shreveport in favor of Frisco, which replaced new Rockies affiliate Tulsa as the Rangers affiliate in the league, meant more than a half million new fans, which somewhat disguised five teams that had minor attendance dropoffs in 2003.

STANDINGS: SPLIT SEASON

FIRST HALF					SECOND HALF				
EAST	**W**	**L**	**PCT**	**GB**	**EAST**	**W**	**L**	**PCT**	**GB**
Frisco	40	30	.571	—	Wichita	40	30	.571	—
Tulsa	34	34	.500	5	Tulsa	40	30	.571	—
Arkansas	33	37	.471	7	Arkansas	37	33	.529	3
Wichita	31	39	.443	9	Frisco	33	37	.471	7
WEST	**W**	**L**	**PCT**	**GB**	**WEST**	**W**	**L**	**PCT**	**GB**
San Antonio	47	22	.681	—	San Antonio	41	29	.586	—
El Paso	38	32	.543	9½	Midland	34	36	.486	7
Midland	35	34	.507	12	El Paso	29	41	.414	12
Round Rock	20	50	.286	27½	Round Rock	26	44	.371	15

PLAYOFFS—Semifinals: Frisco defeated Wichita 3-0 in best-of-5 series; San Antonio received a first-round bye. **Final**: San Antonio defeated Frisco 4-1 in best-of-7 series.

STANDINGS: OVERALL

Page		W	L	PCT	GB	Manager	Attendance	Avg.	Last Penn.
248	San Antonio Missions (Mariners)	88	51	.633	—	Dave Brundage	305,235	4,361	2003
126	Tulsa Drillers (Rockies)	74	64	.536	13½	Marv Foley	273,155	4,077	1998
262	Frisco RoughRiders (Rangers)	73	67	.521	15½	Tim Ireland	666,977	9,264	None
154	Wichita Wranglers (Royals)	71	69	.507	17½	Keith Bodie	153,665	2,439	1999
59	Arkansas Travelers (Angels)	70	70	.500	18½	Tyrone Boykin	187,401	2,928	2001
205	Midland RockHounds (Athletics)	69	70	.496	19	Greg Sparks	270,627	3,922	1975
66	El Paso Diablos (Diamondbacks)	67	73	.479	21½	Scott Coolbaugh	224,821	3,212	1994
147	Round Rock Express (Astros)	46	94	.329	42½	Jackie Moore	685,973	9,800	2000

NOTE: Team's individual batting and pitching statistics can be found on page indicated in lefthand column.

2003 TEXAS LEAGUE STATISTICS

CLUB BATTING

	AVG	G	AB	R	H	2B	3B	HR	BB	SO	SB
El Paso	.279	140	4888	689	1364	283	44	81	419	962	91
Wichita	.277	140	4701	665	1304	229	25	78	441	866	137
San Antonio	.276	139	4765	701	1317	261	46	90	403	977	210
Midland	.271	140	4780	710	1293	231	34	87	574	1059	87
Arkansas	.269	140	4774	636	1285	244	43	85	421	882	123
Tulsa	.264	139	4707	668	1245	264	39	134	390	882	82
Round Rock	.256	140	4744	575	1216	186	29	91	407	944	106
Frisco	.254	140	4654	619	1184	202	38	103	475	942	123

CLUB PITCHING

	ERA	G	CG	SHO	SV	IP	H	R	ER	BB	SO
San Antonio	3.03	139	5	14	45	1239	1071	503	417	491	1131
Tulsa	3.85	139	2	8	35	1214	1242	625	519	417	916
Arkansas	3.99	140	6	10	37	1233	1172	654	547	462	987
Wichita	4.11	140	4	9	39	1219	1290	629	557	401	838
Frisco	4.16	140	1	7	43	1237	1267	660	572	455	892
Midland	4.41	140	6	11	38	1225	1348	681	600	377	882
El Paso	4.69	140	4	5	27	1250	1476	758	651	476	887
Round Rock	4.76	140	7	7	18	1224	1342	753	647	451	981

CLUB FIELDING

	PCT	PO	A	E	DP		PCT	PO	A	E	DP
Wichita	.978	3656	1404	114	133	Round Rock	.969	3671	1363	159	123
Frisco	.975	3712	1552	133	113	Arkansas	.969	3700	1392	163	121
Midland	.972	3675	1581	149	134	Tulsa	.968	3642	1421	166	126
San Antonio	.972	3716	1465	147	123	El Paso	.967	3749	1502	182	112

INDIVIDUAL BATTING LEADERS

(Minimum 378 Plate Appearances)

	AVG	G	AB	R	H	2B	3B	HR	RBI	BB	SO	SB
Nivar, Ramon, Frisco	.347	79	317	53	110	17	4	4	37	20	23	9
Weber, Jake, Arkansas	.302	136	539	67	163	31	3	5	66	47	45	12
Green, Andy, El Paso	.302	126	490	70	148	38	2	2	51	38	51	17
Gettis, Byron, Wichita	.302	140	510	80	154	31	4	16	103	55	110	15
Burke, Chris, Round Rock	.301	137	549	88	165	23	8	3	41	57	57	34
Hall, Victor, El Paso	.300	124	490	76	147	13	12	0	45	51	88	23
Sullivan, Cory, Tulsa	.300	135	557	81	167	34	8	5	61	39	83	17
Rouse, Michael, Midland	.300	129	457	75	137	33	3	3	53	63	83	7
Hopper, Norris, Wichita	.300	115	424	56	127	14	2	0	40	27	58	24
Tracy, Andy, Tulsa	.299	106	384	75	115	24	1	25	62	41	116	3

INDIVIDUAL PITCHING LEADERS

(Minimum 112 Innings)

	W	L	ERA	G	GS	CG	SV	IP	H	R	ER	BB	SO
Tsao, Chin-Hui, Tulsa	11	4	2.46	18	18	0	0	113	88	34	31	26	125
Blackley, Travis, San Antonio	17	3	2.61	27	27	0	0	162	125	55	47	62	144
Nageotte, Clint, San Antonio	11	7	3.10	27	27	2	0	154	127	60	53	67	157
Gobble, Jimmy, Wichita	12	8	3.19	22	22	2	0	133	128	57	47	40	100
Moreno, Edwin, Frisco	6	5	3.29	29	15	0	0	112	105	50	41	33	74
Murray, A.J., Frisco	10	4	3.63	27	25	0	0	144	134	68	58	63	90
Madritsch, Bobby, San Antonio	13	7	3.63	27	27	2	0	159	133	75	64	67	154
DiFelice, Mark, Tulsa	7	6	3.72	21	21	0	0	114	121	61	47	24	75
Qualls, Chad, Round Rock	8	11	3.85	28	28	3	0	175	174	85	75	61	132
Ramos, Mario, Frisco	8	7	3.86	19	19	0	0	121	130	59	52	28	103

ALL STAR-TEAM

C—J.D. Closser, Tulsa. **1B**—Dan Johnson, Midland. **2B**—Ramon Nivar, Frisco. **3B**—Justin Leone, San Antonio. **SS**—Jose Lopez, San Antonio. **OF**—Mike Curry, San Antonio; Byron Gettis, Wichita; Tydus Meadows, Wichita; Jake Weber, Arkansas. **DH**—A.J. Zapp, San Antonio. **Util**—Chris Burke, Round Rock. **P**—Travis Blackley, San Antonio; Jimmy Gobble, Wichita; Bobby Madritsch, San Antonio; A.J. Murray, Frisco; Clint Nageotte, San Antonio; Phil Stockman, El Paso; Chin-Hui Tsao, Tulsa.

Player of the Year: Justin Leone, San Antonio. **Pitcher of the Year:** Travis Blackley, San Antonio. **Manager of the Year:** Dave Brundage, San Antonio.

DEPARTMENT LEADERS

BATTING

G	Byron Gettis, Wichita	140
AB	Cory Sullivan, Tulsa	557
R	Justin Leone, San Antonio	103
H	Cory Sullivan, Tulsa	167
TB	Dan Johnson, Midland	271
XBH	Justin Leone, San Antonio	66
2B	Andy Green, El Paso	38
	Justin Leone, San Antonio	38
3B	Victor Hall, El Paso	12
HR	Dan Johnson, Midland	27
RBI	Dan Johnson, Midland	114
SH	Norris Hopper, Wichita	16
SF	Byron Gettis, Wichita	11
	Dan Johnson, Midland	11
BB	Justin Leone, San Antonio	92
IBB	Dan Johnson, Midland	16
HBP	Marco Cunningham, Wichita	17
SO	A.J. Zapp, San Antonio	178
SB	Mike Curry, San Antonio	58
CS	Victor Hall, El Paso	19
GIDP	Jesus Cota, El Paso	17
OBP	Justin Leone, San Antonio	.405
SLG	Andy Tracy, Tulsa	.563

PITCHING

G	Mark Freed, El Paso	67
GS	Chris Buglovsky, Tulsa	28
	Chad Qualls, Round Rock	28
CG	Chad Qualls, Round Rock	3
ShO	Chad Qualls, Round Rock	2
GF	Jared Hoerman, San Antonio	52
	Justin Huisman, Tulsa	52
SV	Jared Hoerman, San Antonio	36
W	Travis Blackley, San Antonio	17
L	Ruddy Lugo, Round Rock	15
IP	Casey Daigle, El Paso	176
H	Casey Daigle, El Paso	219
R	Chris Buglovsky, Tulsa	111
ER	Casey Daigle, El Paso	90
HR	Garrett Lee, Wichita	17
HB	Clint Nageotte, San Antonio	14
BB	Bobby Madritsch, San Antonio	67
	Clint Nageotte, San Antonio	67
SO	Clint Nageotte, San Antonio	157
WP	Casey Daigle, El Paso	14
BK	Six tied at	3

FIELDING

C	AVG	Scott Maynard, San Antonio	.993
	PO	J.D. Closser, Tulsa	670
	A	J.D. Closser, Tulsa	69
	E	J.D. Closser, Tulsa	17
	DP	Chris Tremie, Round Rock	8
	PB	Chris Snyder, El Paso	16
1B	AVG	Dan Johnson, Midland	.992
	PO	A.J. Zapp, San Antonio	1082
	A	A.J. Zapp, San Antonio	113
	E	Corey Myers, El Paso	15
		A.J. Zapp, San Antonio	15
	DP	A.J. Zapp, San Antonio	107
2B	AVG	Chris Burke, Round Rock	.983
	PO	Freddie Bynum, Midland	249
	A	Freddie Bynum, Midland	367
	E	Freddie Bynum, Midland	30
	DP	Freddie Bynum, Midland	75
3B	AVG	Justin Gemoll, Wichita	.952
	PO	Brian Barden, El Paso	80
	A	Justin Leone, San Antonio	251
	E	Adam Morrissey, Midland	21
	DP	Justin Leone, San Antonio	18
SS	AVG	Michael Rouse, Midland	.967
	PO	Brian Specht, Arkansas	204
	A	Michael Rouse, Midland	374
	E	Brian Specht, Arkansas	34
	DP	Michael Rouse, Midland	81
OF	AVG	Marco Cunningham, Wichita	.995
	PO	Cory Sullivan, Tulsa	328
	A	Matt Allegra, Midland	22
	E	Matt Allegra, Midland	12
	DP	Nathan Haynes, Arkansas	4

CALIFORNIA LEAGUE

HIGH CLASS A

BY MICHELLE GARDNER

The Inland Empire 66ers rushed the mound at Stockton's Billy Hebert Field to celebrate. Righthander Emiliano Fruto had just struck out Jason Dill to complete a 1-0 win in Game Three of the 2003 California League championship series.

The Sixers gutted out 2-0 and 3-2 wins over the Stockton Ports in the first two games of the best-of-five series, and the sweep gave the San Bernardino-based team its fourth title in the last nine years (the others coming in 1995, '99 and 2000). This was the most unlikely run of all. Manager Steve Roadcap's team was made up mostly of nondrafted free agents, castoffs from other organizations and veterans who jump-started their careers through independent ball.

"Most of us have had to work hard to get here and we have to keep working harder to stay here," said DH John Castellano, a 66th-round pick whom the Dodgers released after two seasons. "This game weeds out guys that don't work hard. If you don't make it, you don't want it to be because you didn't give it your best."

LARRY GOREN

Josh Barfield

Pitching and defense were the team's foundation all season. The Sixers set two league records for defense, committing just 130 errors and compiling a .97417 fielding percentage to nose out the .97410 of the 1998 San Jose Giants.

Most players singled out an Aug. 18 brawl against Lancaster as the turning point in the season. Second baseman Evel Bastida took a bat to the mound after being hit by a pitch in the 15th inning of a game and took a swing at JetHawks pitcher Josh Kranawetter. The brawl resulted in three-game suspensions for seven players and one coach from Lancaster and nine players from Inland Empire. Bastida, later charged with felony assault, was suspended for the rest of the season by the Mariners.

"It seemed like we played like we were on a mission after that," said scrappy leadoff hitter Dustin Delucchi, who hit .329.

The league went to an unbalanced schedule in 2003, placing greater emphasis on division play. Teams played division foes 27 or 28 times and those in the other division in one series at home and one on the road.

STANDINGS: SPLIT SEASON

FIRST HALF					SECOND HALF				
NORTH	**W**	**L**	**PCT**	**GB**	**NORTH**	**W**	**L**	**PCT**	**GB**
Stockton	41	29	.586	—	Visalia	44	26	.629	—
Bakersfield	38	32	.543	3	Modesto	42	28	.600	2
Visalia	35	35	.500	6	Stockton	36	34	.514	8
Modesto	32	38	.457	9	Bakersfield	32	38	.457	12
San Jose	28	42	.400	13	San Jose	30	40	.429	14
SOUTH	**W**	**L**	**PCT**	**GB**	**SOUTH**	**W**	**L**	**PCT**	**GB**
Rancho Cuca.	40	30	.571	—	Inland Empire	42	28	.600	—
Lancaster	39	31	.557	1	Lake Elsinore	39	31	.557	3
Inland Empire	36	34	.514	4	Rancho Cuca.	34	36	.486	8
Lake Elsinore	36	34	.514	4	Lancaster	34	36	.486	8
High Desert	25	45	.357	15	High Desert	17	53	.243	25

PLAYOFFS—Quarterfinals: Inland Empire defeated Lake Elsinore 2-0 and Visalia defeated Modesto 2-0 in best-of-3 series. **Semifinals:** Inland Empire defeated Rancho Cucamonga 3-1 and Stockton defeated Visalia 3-2 in best-of-5 series. **Final:** Inland Empire defeated Stockton 3-0 in best-of-five series.

Rancho Cucamonga boasted the most talented roster when the season started, as nine of the Angels' top 30 preseason prospects were with the Quakes, including pitcher Ervin Santana, catcher Jeff Mathis, third baseman Dallas McPherson—who homered in five straight games from July 14-18—and first baseman Casey Kotchman.

Santana (10-2, 2.53), Mathis (.323) and McPherson (.308) all earned midseason promotions to Double-A, while Kotchman's season again was interrupted by an injury. He was limited to 57 regular season games because of a pulled hamstring but still hit .357 in the regular season and .428 in the playoffs.

Lake Elsinore second baseman Josh Barfield was a near-unanimous choice as the league's MVP, however. He finished second in the batting race to Jacobs and led all minor leaguers in hits (185) and RBIs (128).

Visalia's Jeff Francis tossed the only no-hitter in the league when he blanked Modesto 6-0 on July 6. It was the first no-hitter in the league since Marcos Castillo of Lake Elsinore threw a perfect game against San Bernardino on June 14, 1999.

Attendance around the league was slow early but picked up in the late summer. Because of planned doubleheaders and weather postponements, the league had 14 fewer openings than 2002. The average attendance was 2,307, down less than 1 percent from the 2,324 in 2002. Six of 10 teams reported increases, with Visalia's 10 percent increase the biggest jump. San Jose posted the highest average attendance in franchise history at 2,312.

STANDINGS: OVERALL

Page		W	L	PCT	GB	Manager	Attendance	Avg.	Last Penn.
127	Visalia Oaks (Rockies)	79	61	.564	—	Stu Cole	62,898	953	1978
248	Inland Empire 66ers (Mariners)	78	62	.557	1	Steve Roadcap	217,866	3,301	2003
263	Stockton Ports (Rangers)	77	63	.550	2	Arnie Beyeler	75,609	1,112	2002
235	Lake Elsinore Storm (Padres)	75	65	.536	4	Jeff Gardner	240,166	3,532	2001
59	Rancho Cucamonga Quakes (Angels)	74	66	.529	5	Bobby Meacham	296,118	4,292	1994
206	Modesto A's (Athletics)	74	66	.529	5	Rick Rodriguez	148,195	2,179	1984
67	Lancaster JetHawks (Diamondbacks)	73	67	.521	6	Mike Aldrete	151,616	2,230	None
256	Bakersfield Blaze (Devil Rays)	70	70	.500	9	Omer Munoz	90,099	1,325	1989
241	San Jose Giants (Giants)	58	82	.414	21	Jack Lind	154,927	2,312	2001
168	High Desert Mavericks (Brewers)	42	98	.300	37	Tim Blackwell	126,705	1,810	1997

NOTE: Team's individual batting and pitching statistics can be found on page indicated in left column.

2003 CALIFORNIA LEAGUE STATISTICS

CLUB BATTING

	AVG	G	AB	R	H	2B	3B	HR	BB	SO	SB
Lancaster	.285	140	4975	810	1420	280	41	136	464	1052	121
Lake Elsinore	.280	140	4874	821	1363	288	41	118	518	1104	162
Inland Empire	.279	140	4759	700	1330	280	50	84	447	752	121
Stockton	.275	140	4791	736	1319	260	40	84	556	1016	130
Rancho Cucamonga	.275	140	4841	685	1330	278	40	122	382	1018	108
Modesto	.273	140	4871	759	1332	273	30	87	581	1007	68
Bakersfield	.271	140	4772	668	1292	256	19	92	386	1183	150
High Desert	.270	140	4860	687	1314	243	49	81	386	903	191
Visalia	.261	140	4782	720	1250	283	32	117	464	1087	87
San Jose	.258	140	4737	620	1224	257	38	91	368	977	132

CLUB PITCHING

	ERA	G	CG	SHO	SV	IP	H	R	ER	BB	SO
Inland Empire	3.77	140	2	8	39	1230	1140	583	515	396	1180
Stockton	3.99	140	0	5	37	1241	1229	684	551	480	1022
Visalia	4.04	140	6	11	31	1231	1280	628	553	410	1021
Bakersfield	4.06	140	4	9	32	1216	1329	665	549	404	957
Modesto	4.22	140	4	4	33	1243	1312	720	583	458	1067
Lake Elsinore	4.35	140	2	3	32	1233	1375	714	596	389	889
Rancho Cucamonga	4.49	140	6	7	42	1234	1287	736	616	469	951
San Jose	4.68	140	3	7	29	1216	1304	740	633	498	1070
Lancaster	4.69	140	4	0	38	1254	1427	777	654	492	904
High Desert	6.34	140	2	2	28	1226	1491	959	864	556	1038

CLUB FIELDING

	PCT	PO	A	E	DP		PCT	PO	A	E	DP
Inland Empire	.974	3689	1214	130	84	Rancho Cuca.	.966	3701	1401	180	119
Visalia	.973	3693	1565	146	155	Stockton	.966	3724	1475	185	120
High Desert	.971	3678	1384	153	107	Bakersfield	.963	3649	1369	192	126
Lancaster	.970	3762	1674	168	125	Lake Elsinore	.963	3698	1532	202	120
San Jose	.968	3649	1331	167	114	Modesto	.962	3730	1322	202	89

INDIVIDUAL BATTING LEADERS

(Minimum 378 Plate Appearances)

	AVG	G	AB	R	H	2B	3B	HR	RBI	BB	SO	SB
Jacobs, Greg, Inland Empire	.357	95	347	67	124	35	7	9	64	42	43	4
Barfield, Josh, Lakeland	.337	135	549	99	185	46	6	16	128	50	122	16
Gathright, Joey, Bakersfield	.324	89	340	65	110	6	3	0	23	41	54	57
Mathis, Jeff, Rancho Cuca.	.323	97	378	73	122	28	3	11	54	35	74	5
Slavik, Corey, Visalia	.321	109	392	66	126	27	1	14	75	40	67	1
Gorneault, Nick, Rancho Cuca.	.321	97	374	67	120	36	2	14	72	20	82	11
Belcher, Jason, High Desert	.320	91	350	43	112	23	3	5	54	26	35	4
Nichols, Kyle, Lancaster	.312	130	484	82	151	34	0	31	108	51	118	0
Castellano, John, Inland Empire	.306	114	461	61	141	34	2	12	80	32	50	11
Ortmeier, Dan, San Jose	.304	115	408	62	124	32	6	8	56	39	89	13

INDIVIDUAL PITCHING LEADERS

(Minimum 112 Innings)

	W	L	ERA	G	GS	CG	SV	IP	H	R	ER	BB	SO
Santana, Ervin, Rancho Cuca.	10	2	2.53	20	20	1	0	125	98	44	35	36	130
Weis, Brad, Modesto	15	7	2.82	30	24	3	0	160	132	66	50	60	145
Bott, Glenn, Inland Empire	7	7	3.16	31	21	0	1	142	131	55	50	38	143
Ketchner, Ryan, Inland Empire	14	7	3.45	31	22	2	1	157	133	63	60	33	159
Thomas, J.T., San Jose	5	12	3.45	33	19	0	3	125	134	64	48	35	104
Francis, Jeff, Visalia	12	9	3.47	27	27	2	0	161	135	66	62	45	153
Andrew, Jason, Stockton	8	7	3.51	31	15	0	1	118	127	66	46	31	94
Pavon, Julio, San Jose	5	4	3.54	41	8	0	2	112	106	48	44	26	103
Hampson, Justin, Visalia	14	7	3.68	26	26	1	0	159	153	73	65	51	150
Esposito, Mike, Visalia	12	6	3.75	27	27	1	0	161	173	83	67	55	116

ALL-STAR TEAM

C—Jeff Mathis, Rancho Cucamonga. **1B**—Kyle Nichols, Lancaster. **2B**—Josh Barfield, Lake Elsinore. **3B**—Dallas McPherson, Rancho Cucamonga. **SS**—J.J. Furmaniak, Lake Elsinore. **OF**—Joey Gathright, Bakersfield; Greg Jacobs, Inland Empire; Gary Thomas, Modesto. **DH**—Corey Slavik, Visalia. **P**—Justin Hampson, Visalia; Ryan Ketchner, Inland Empire; Ervin Santana, Rancho Cucamonga; Brad Weis, Modesto.

Most Valuable Player: Josh Barfield, Lake Elsinore. **Pitcher of the Year:** Ervin Santana, Rancho Cucamonga. **Rookie of the Year:** Joey Gathright, Bakersfield. **Manager of the Year:** Stu Cole, Visalia.

DEPARTMENT LEADERS

BATTING

G	Jayson Nix, Visalia	137
AB	Tommy Murphy, Rancho Cucamonga	565
R	Jayson Nix, Visalia	107
H	Josh Barfield, Lake Elsinore	185
TB	Josh Barfield, Lake Elsinore	291
XBH	Josh Barfield, Lake Elsinore	68
2B	Josh Barfield, Lake Elsinore	46
	Jayson Nix, Visalia	46
3B	Shin-Soo Choo, Inland Empire	13
HR	Kyle Nichols, Lancaster	31
RBI	Josh Barfield, Lake Elsinore	128
SH	Ralph Santana, High Desert	13
SF	Greg Sain, Lake Elsinore	12
BB	Mark Kiger, Modesto	77
IBB	Kyle Nichols, Lancaster	6
HBP	Bryan Carter, San Jose	26
SO	Justin Lincoln, Visalia	151
SB	Chris Morris, High Desert	67
CS	Chris Morris, High Desert	18
GIDP	Mark Teahen, Modesto	19
OBP	Greg Jacobs, Inland Empire	.433
SLG	Greg Jacobs, Inland Empire	.574

PITCHING

G	Jack Cassel, Lake Elsinore	64
GS	Jake Woods, Rancho Cucamonga	28
CG	Brad Weis, Modesto	3
ShO	Jeff Francis, Visalia	2
	Ryan Ketchner, Inland Empire	2
GF	Ryan Speier, Visalia	43
SV	Pete Sikaras, Lancaster	23
W	Brad Weis, Modesto	15
L	John Barnett, Stockton	14
	Dan Hall, High Desert	14
IP	Jake Woods, Rancho Cucamonga	171
H	Dan Kolb, High Desert	194
R	Dan Kolb, High Desert	118
ER	Dan Kolb, High Desert	107
HR	Dan Kolb, High Desert	24
HB	Justin Hampson, Visalia	21
BB	Justin Wechsler, Lancaster	64
SO	Ryan Ketchner, Inland Empire	159
WP	Jeff Bruksch, Modesto	19
BK	Three tied at	4

FIELDING

C	AVG	Luis Oliveros, Inland Empire	.994
	PO	Luis Oliveros, Inland Empire	770
	A	Nick Trzesniak, Lake Elsinore	75
	E	Michael DiRosa, Lancaster	10
		Jed Morris, Modesto	10
	DP	Nick Trzesniak, Lake Elsinore	7
		Jeff Winchester, Visalia	7
	PB	Jed Morris, Modesto	22
1B	AVG	Aaron Clark, Bakersfield	.993
	PO	Aaron Clark, Bakersfield	883
	A	Aaron Clark, Bakersfield	73
	E	Jason Botts, Stockton	16
		Matt Bowser, Modesto	16
	DP	Aaron Clark, Bakersfield	84
2B	AVG	Jayson Nix, Visalia	.972
	PO	Josh Barfield, Lake Elsinore	304
	A	Jayson Nix, Visalia	460
	E	Fernando Cortez, Bakersfield	22
	DP	Jayson Nix, Visalia	120
3B	AVG	Dan Uggla, Lancaster	.941
	PO	Mark Teahen, Modesto	100
	A	Dan Uggla, Lancaster	212
	E	Greg Sain, Lake Elsinore	35
	DP	Justin Lincoln, Visalia	20
		Greg Sain, Lake Elsinore	20
SS	AVG	Eddie Menchaca, Inland Empire	.970
	PO	Angel Chavez, San Jose	213
	A	Tommy Murphy, Rancho Cuca.	375
	E	Tommy Murphy, Rancho Cuca.	36
	DP	Drew Meyer, Stockton	69
		Tommy Murphy, Rancho Cuca.	69
OF	AVG	Melvin Rosario, Visalia	1.000
	PO	Chris Morris, High Desert	324
	A	Melvin Rosario, Visalia	15
	E	Luis Mateo, Bakersfield	13
	DP	Melvin Rosario, Visalia	5

CAROLINA LEAGUE

HIGH CLASS A

BY CHRIS KLINE

The way they played down the stretch, no one expected the first-half Carolina League division champion Winston-Salem Warthogs to be a factor in the race for the 2003 Mills Cup. Not only had they lost their best hitter in Jeremy Reed, but they also stumbled through August with an 11-21 record.

None of that seemed to matter much as the Warthogs swept through Kinston and Lynchburg to capture their first title since 1993, the 11th CL title overall for Winston-Salem.

"We felt like we went in on a roll despite what our record indicated," Warthogs manager Razor Shines said. "We were able to rest some guys down the stretch. We were healthy and had a lot of confidence going in. That was the difference."

MEL BAILEY

Chris Shelton

The Warthogs had two come-from-behind victories to eliminate Kinston in the semifinals, then outslugged Lynchburg in three straight games to complete the Mills Cup sweep. Led by right-hander Kris Honel and closer Josh Fields, the playoff MVP, the Warthogs overmatched their playoff opponents.

"We leaned heavy on Kris and Josh in those playoff games," Shines said. "They're both guys who will fight you even when they don't have their best stuff. They gave us the leadership we needed to put that run together."

Perhaps the most remarkable aspect of the 'Hogs title was that they won it without Reed, who was promoted to Double-A Birmingham in mid-June and went on to lead the minor leagues with a .373 average. Reed batted .333-4-52 for Winston-Salem, but was overshadowed by the accomplishments of Lynchburg's Chris Shelton, who contended for a triple crown and took home league MVP honors.

Shelton batted .359-21-69 and earned a promotion to Double-A Altoona in August. Even with other powerful bats in the lineup—first baseman Walter Young, catcher Ryan Doumit, outfielder Nate McLouth and second baseman Jeff Keppinger—Lynchburg fell short of a second straight title.

While the hitting of Reed and Shelton garnered attention, pitching dominated the league. Touted hurlers Zack Greinke of Wilmington; Lynchburg's John VanBenschoten, Bryan Bullington and Ian Oquendo; Frederick's John Maine; and Myrtle Beach's Macay McBride all impressed in their first high Class A experience. None was tougher than Grienke, however, as the 19-year-old often toyed with CL hitters.

Greinke wasn't the only Wilmington hurler to earn high marks for the Blue Rocks, as a trio of pitchers followed in his footsteps. Kyle Middleton (11-8, 2.41), Brian Bass (9-8, 2.84) and Zach McClellan (8-8, 2.84) helped lead the Rocks to a second-half title after Greinke was promoted to Double-A Wichita in mid-July.

There was pitching in Frederick as well. The Keys showed little pitching prowess in the first half, but the promotion of Maine breathed new life into a downtrodden staff that ranked last in the league. He tossed a seven-inning no-hitter against Winston-Salem July 3 in his second start and finished the season 6-1, 3.07.

Two new affiliates, the Reds in Potomac and the Astros in Salem, did not fare well in their first season in the Carolina League. The Cannons finished with an overall record of 62-77. The Avalanche was the hottest team in the league down the stretch, but like Potomac finished out of the playoffs.

Attendance in the league was also a little short, mostly due to fewer openings because of poor weather. While overall attendance was down, average attendance of 2,900 fans a game was relatively stable. The only team to improve its average attendance was Wilmington, which has established itself as the league's flagship franchise.

STANDINGS: SPLIT SEASON

FIRST HALF					SECOND HALF				
NORTH	**W**	**L**	**PCT**	**GB**	**NORTH**	**W**	**L**	**PCT**	**GB**
Lynchburg	37	28	.569	—	Wilmington	42	28	.600	—
Wilmington	38	32	.543	1½	Lynchburg	39	31	.557	3
Potomac	30	39	.435	9	Frederick	34	35	.493	7½
Frederick	26	40	.394	11½	Potomac	32	38	.457	10
SOUTH	**W**	**L**	**PCT**	**GB**	**SOUTH**	**W**	**L**	**PCT**	**GB**
Win.-Salem	39	29	.574	—	Kinston	39	31	.557	—
Salem	35	33	.515	4	Salem	38	32	.543	1
Kinston	34	35	.493	5½	Win.-Salem	32	38	.457	7
Myrtle Beach	33	36	.478	6½	Myrtle Beach	23	46	.333	15½

PLAYOFFS—Semifinals: Winston-Salem defeated Kinston 2-0 and Lynchburg defeated Wilmington 2-0 in best-of-3 series. **Final**: Winston-Salem defeated Lynchburg 3-0 in best-of-5 series.

STANDINGS: OVERALL

Page		W	L	PCT	GB	Manager	Attendance	Avg.	Last Penn.
155	Wilmington Blue Rocks (Royals)	80	60	.571	—	Billy Gardner	315,134	4,924	1999
219	Lynchburg Hillcats (Pirates)	76	59	.563	1½	Dave Clark	91,935	1,459	2002
148	Salem Avalanche (Astros)	73	65	.529	6	John Massarelli	175,155	2,825	2001
119	Kinston Indians (Indians)	73	66	.525	6½	Torey Lovullo	103,433	1,668	1995
96	Winston-Salem Warthogs (White Sox)	71	67	.514	8	Razor Shines	124,454	2,040	2003
111	Potomac Cannons (Reds)	62	77	.446	17½	Jayhawk Owens	160,238	2,716	1989
81	Frederick Keys (Orioles)	60	75	.444	17½	Tom Lawless	285,048	4,385	1990
74	Myrtle Beach Pelicans (Braves)	56	82	.406	23	Randy Ingle	203,443	3,036	2000

NOTE: Team's individual batting and pitching statistics can be found on page indicated in lefthand column.

2003 CAROLINA LEAGUE STATISTICS

CLUB BATTING

	AVG	G	AB	R	H	2B	3B	HR	BB	SO	SB
Lynchburg	.271	135	4391	670	1190	247	25	93	431	837	109
Frederick	.259	135	4413	541	1144	237	18	79	414	908	59
Wilmington	.256	140	4577	589	1173	211	21	57	529	839	73
Winston-Salem	.256	138	4328	574	1107	237	22	88	443	824	196
Myrtle Beach	.254	138	4494	506	1142	209	25	68	389	914	109
Potomac	.254	139	4475	543	1136	233	21	75	418	909	122
Kinston	.252	139	4448	570	1121	205	25	68	459	991	183
Salem	.249	138	4477	611	1115	220	31	67	480	904	114

CLUB PITCHING

	ERA	G	CG	SHO	SV	IP	H	R	ER	BB	SO
Wilmington	2.92	140	7	16	38	1204	1072	477	391	386	950
Winston-Salem	3.32	138	5	13	36	1153	1049	542	425	491	856
Myrtle Beach	3.63	138	4	11	20	1191	1147	580	480	493	946
Kinston	3.65	139	5	7	43	1187	1170	561	482	440	825
Potomac	3.72	139	5	9	38	1182	1161	579	489	415	955
Lynchburg	3.80	135	5	8	38	1140	1110	585	481	416	909
Salem	4.05	138	6	11	35	1185	1223	612	533	419	782
Frederick	4.40	135	2	11	40	1164	1196	668	569	503	903

CLUB FIELDING

	PCT	PO	A	E	DP		PCT	PO	A	E	DP
Kinston	.975	3562	1467	128	117	Myrtle Beach	.972	3572	1423	144	117
Wilmington	.975	3613	1523	132	129	Win.-Salem	.971	3458	1360	144	93
Salem	.975	3554	1577	134	104	Lynchburg	.970	3421	1313	146	100
Frederick	.973	3493	1407	137	116	Potomac	.966	3545	1453	174	134

INDIVIDUAL BATTING LEADERS

(Minimum 378 Plate Appearances)

	AVG	G	AB	R	H	2B	3B	HR	RBI	BB	SO	SB
Shelton, Chris, Lynchburg	.359	95	315	71	113	24	1	21	69	68	67	1
Self, Todd, Salem	.318	126	431	84	137	27	2	6	57	87	93	2
Cates, Gary, Frederick	.315	92	355	50	112	23	3	3	35	21	40	11
Shanks, James, Wilmington	.301	85	346	54	104	15	2	2	23	28	71	21
McLouth, Nate, Lynchburg	.300	117	440	85	132	27	2	6	33	55	68	40
Bannon, Jeff, Potomac	.295	104	366	45	108	26	2	8	42	35	67	7
Huggins, Mike, Frederick	.293	126	454	66	133	32	0	13	74	55	93	3
Rogers, Omar, Frederick	.292	99	356	49	104	24	0	3	28	42	70	4
Buttler, Vic, Lynchburg	.285	117	382	49	109	18	5	3	44	37	47	22
Marte, Andy, Myrtle Beach	.285	130	463	69	132	35	1	16	63	67	109	5

INDIVIDUAL PITCHING LEADERS

(Minimum 112 Innings)

	W	L	ERA	G	GS	CG	SV	IP	H	R	ER	BB	SO
Middleton, Kyle, Wilmington	11	8	2.41	27	27	1	0	160	155	59	43	35	75
Kleine, Victor, Kinston	6	5	2.56	28	16	0	1	116	114	42	33	35	79
Gothreaux, Jared, Salem	13	4	2.82	29	22	1	1	147	144	54	46	26	85
Bass, Brian, Wilmington	9	8	2.84	26	26	2	0	152	129	59	48	43	119
McClellan, Zach, Wilmington	8	8	2.84	30	23	1	0	133	101	51	42	39	100
McBride, Macay, MB	9	8	2.95	27	27	1	0	165	164	63	54	49	139
Wing, Ryan, Winston-Salem	9	7	2.98	26	26	0	0	145	116	62	48	67	107
Honel, Kris, Winston-Salem	9	7	3.11	24	24	3	0	133	122	51	46	42	122
Oquendo, Ian, Lynchburg	10	3	3.33	20	20	1	0	116	105	46	43	33	122
Lewis, Rommie, Frederick	4	9	3.34	26	20	1	0	113	108	54	42	60	69

ALL-STAR TEAM

C—Ryan Doumit, Lynchburg. **1B**—Walter Young, Lynchburg. **2B**—Ruddy Yan, Winston-Salem. **3B**—Andy Marte, Myrtle Beach. **SS**—Jeff Bannon, Potomac; Andres Blanco, Wilmington. **Util IF**—Todd Self, Salem. **OF**—Trey Dyson, Wilmington/Kinston; Nate McLouth, Lynchburg; Todd Self, Salem. **Util OF**—Woody Cliffords, Frederick. **DH**—Chris Shelton, Lynchburg. **SP**—Zack Greinke, Wilmington. **RP**—Lee Gronkiewicz, Kinston.

Most Valuable Player: Chris Shelton, Lynchburg. **Pitcher of the Year:** Zack Greinke, Wilmington. **Manager of the Year:** Dave Clark, Lynchburg.

DEPARTMENT LEADERS

BATTING

G	Trey Dyson, Wilmington/Kinston	135
	Chris Fallon, Wilmington	135
AB	William Bergolla, Potomac	523
R	Nate McLouth, Lynchburg	85
	Ruddy Yan, Winston-Salem	85
H	William Bergolla, Potomac	142
TB	Andy Marte, Myrtle Beach	217
XBH	Andy Marte, Myrtle Beach	52
2B	Ryan Doumit, Lynchburg	38
3B	Mike Rodriguez, Salem	8
HR	Chris Shelton, Lynchburg	21
RBI	Walter Young, Lynchburg	87
SH	Andres Blanco, Wilmington	21
SF	Brian Becker, Winston-Salem	11
BB	Todd Self, Salem	87
IBB	Trey Dyson, Wilmington/Kinston	9
HBP	Justin Cowan, Wilmington	16
SO	Gregor Blanco, Myrtle Beach	114
SB	Ruddy Yan, Winston-Salem	76
CS	William Bergolla, Potomac	18
GIDP	Jose Salas, Myrtle Beach	16
OBP	Chris Shelton, Lynchburg	.478
SLG	Chris Shelton, Lynchburg	.641

PITCHING

G	Andy Mitchell, Frederick	60
GS	Matt Coenen, Myrtle Beach	28
CG	Zack Greinke, Wilmington	3
	Kris Honel, Winston-Salem	3
ShO	Brian Rodaway, Salem	2
GF	Lee Gronkiewicz, Kinston	47
SV	Lee Gronkiewicz, Kinston	37
W	Jared Gothreaux, Salem	13
L	Kurt Birkins, Frederick	11
	Chris Tierney, Wilmington	11
IP	Macay McBride, Myrtle Beach	165
H	Macay McBride, Myrtle Beach	164
R	Jimmy Barrett, Salem	87
ER	Jimmy Barrett, Salem	82
HR	Brian Rodaway, Salem	16
HB	Kurt Birkins, Frederick	13
BB	Wyatt Allen, Winston-Salem	89
SO	Macay McBride, Myrtle Beach	139
WP	Wyatt Allen, Winston-Salem	21
BK	Ryan Meaux, Winston-Salem	3

FIELDING

C	AVG	Hector Gimenez, Salem	.991
	PO	Hector Gimenez, Salem	574
	A	Hector Gimenez, Salem	77
	E	Chris Stewart, Winston-Salem	14
	DP	Hector Gimenez, Salem	7
		Brian Peterson, Potomac	7
	PB	Ryan Doumit, Lynchburg	23
1B	AVG	Casey Rogowski, Winston-Salem	.997
	PO	Scott Thorman, Myrtle Beach	999
	A	Chris Fallon, Wilmington	82
	E	Walter Young, Lynchburg	15
	DP	Chris Fallon, Wilmington	98
2B	AVG	Aaron Herr, Myrtle Beach	.976
	PO	Ruddy Yan, Winston-Salem	250
	A	William Bergolla, Potomac	380
	E	William Bergolla, Potomac	27
	DP	Ruben Gotay, Wilmington	82
3B	AVG	Tripper Johnson, Frederick	.940
	PO	Tripper Johnson, Frederick	97
	A	Andy Marte, Myrtle Beach	215
	E	Andy Marte, Myrtle Beach	28
	DP	Tripper Johnson, Frederick	21
SS	AVG	Tony Pena, Myrtle Beach	.965
	PO	Ryan Stegall, Salem	203
	A	Ryan Stegall, Salem	354
	E	Andres Blanco, Wilmington	26
	DP	Tony Pena, Myrtle Beach	76
OF	AVG	Mike Spidale, Winston-Salem	.989
	PO	Mike Spidale, Winston-Salem	272
	A	Brandon Caraway, Salem	19
	E	Jeremy Harts, Lynchburg	11
	DP	Fehlandt Lentini, Salem	3

FLORIDA STATE LEAGUE

HIGH CLASS A

BY SEAN KERNAN

St. Lucie shared the Florida State League team ERA lead at 3.09 with the Jupiter Hammerheads. But when it came to the postseason, the Mets weren't sharing anything.

St. Lucie quickly disposed of Jupiter 2-0 in the semifinals, then doused the Dunedin Blue Jays' hopes by winning the championship series 3-1. All three victories were shutouts: 7-0, 4-0 and 10-0.

"From day one, I knew we were going to have good pitching," St. Lucie manager Ken Oberkfell said. "I saw that in spring training. The pitching started from day one and it never stopped."

St. Lucie hurlers dominated a Dunedin club that was second in the league in batting. Oberkfell credited the Mets for making moves to strengthen the team. The most obvious was the July addition of lefthander Scott Kazmir, who won the clinching game while giving up just one hit in 5⅓ innings. Combining his FSL numbers with those from low Class A Capital City, Kazmir had the minor's best strikeouts per nine innings rate (11.94) among starting pitchers.

MORRIS FOSTOFF

Matt Peterson

Matt Peterson, Blake McGinley and Kole Strayhorn combined for a one-hitter in the Mets' second win. McGinley was the team's top pitcher all season, as the lefty went 9-1 with a minuscule 1.02 ERA.

St. Lucie's pitchers also made headlines during the season by throwing three no-hitters. Wayne Ough and Mike Cox combined for the first one against the Tampa Yankees on May 9. Tyler Yates and Chad Elliott combined for a seven-inning job against the Palm Beach Cardinals on May 28. Ken Chenard and Cox made it a trifecta on June 23 against the Brevard County Manatees.

Another pitcher in the league made bigger headlines, for all the wrong reasons. Daytona Cubs righthander Jae-kuk Ryu was in the outfield during batting practice and threw a baseball at an osprey perched about 40 feet above the field. Ryu's throw hit the osprey, affectionately known as Ozzy around Jackie Robinson Ballpark, and it fell to the ground. Ozzy died a week after the incident.

The Cubs suspended Ryu and then demoted him to low Class A Lansing, and later in the season promoted him to Double-A West Tenn so he didn't have to return to Daytona. Ryu eventually entered a no-contest plea to a charge of animal cruelty, agreeing to pay a $500 fine, perform community service and issue a formal apology.

The Cubs promoted righthander Chadd Blasko from Lansing to take Ryu's spot, and he went on to lead the league with a 1.98 ERA.

Fort Myers catcher Joe Mauer spent a little more than half of the season in the FSL before moving up to Double-A. He hit .335 and showed stellar defense on his way to Baseball America's Minor League Player of the Year award. He also got to be a teammate of his older brother, shortstop Jake Mauer.

Dunedin's Kurt Keene was the only FSL player to hit for the cycle. The third baseman did so on May 8 and soon after was promoted to Double-A New Haven.

Daytona lefthander Carmen Pignatiello and closer Jared Blasdell combined to no-hit the Cardinals on July 17. Pignatiello, who went on to lead the league with 140 strikeouts, fanned a season-high 11 batters. Blasdell, who led the FSL with 27 saves, struck out the side to preserve the no-hitter.

STANDINGS: SPLIT SEASON

FIRST HALF

EAST	W	L	PCT	GB
Jupiter	42	28	.600	—
Vero Beach	36	31	.537	4½
Brevard County	35	33	.515	6
St. Lucie	33	37	.471	9
Daytona	32	38	.457	10
Palm Beach	25	43	.368	16
WEST	**W**	**L**	**PCT**	**GB**
Fort Myers	44	26	.629	—
Clearwater	37	31	.544	6
Tampa	38	32	.543	6
Dunedin	38	32	.543	6
Sarasota	31	38	.449	12½
Lakeland	24	46	.343	20

SECOND HALF

EAST	W	L	PCT	GB
St. Lucie	44	25	.638	—
Daytona	34	33	.507	9
Jupiter	34	34	.500	9½
Brevard County	30	33	.476	11
Palm Beach	29	41	.414	15½
Vero Beach	26	38	.406	15½
WEST	**W**	**L**	**PCT**	**GB**
Dunedin	40	30	.571	—
Clearwater	35	30	.538	2½
Sarasota	32	29	.525	3½
Lakeland	31	32	.492	5½
Tampa	30	32	.484	6
Fort Myers	29	37	.439	9

PLAYOFFS—Semifinals: St. Lucie defeated Jupiter 2-0 and Dunedin defeated Fort Myers 2-1 in best-of-3 series. **Final:** St. Lucie defeated Dunedin 3-1 in best-of-5 series.

STANDINGS: OVERALL

Page		W	L	PCT	GB	Manager	Attendance	Avg.	Last Penn.
271	Dunedin Blue Jays (Blue Jays)	78	62	.557	—	Mike Basso	42,752	713	None
198	St. Lucie Mets (Mets)	77	62	.554	½	Ken Oberkfell	81,154	1,230	1998
141	Jupiter Hammerheads (Marlins)	76	62	.551	1	Luis Dorante	90,080	1,344	1991
212	Clearwater Phillies (Phillies)	72	61	.541	2½	Roly deArmas	63,655	1,061	1993
175	Fort Myers Miracle (Twins)	73	63	.537	3	Jose Marzan	110,356	1,698	1985
190	Tampa Yankees (Yankees)	68	64	.515	6	Bill Masse	67,565	1,145	2001
182	Brevard County Manatees (Expos)	65	66	.496	8½	Doug Sisson	83,314	1,602	2001
89	Sarasota Red Sox (Red Sox)	63	67	.485	10	Tim Leiper	49,684	764	1963
104	Daytona Cubs (Cubs)	66	71	.482	10½	Rick Kranitz	97,362	1,521	2000
161	Vero Beach Dodgers (Dodgers)	62	69	.473	11½	Scott Little	57,339	882	1990
134	Lakeland Tigers (Tigers)	55	78	.414	19½	Gary Green	30,832	551	1992
227	Palm Beach Cardinals (Cardinals)	54	84	.391	23	Tom Nieto	68,210	1,003	None

NOTE: Team's individual batting and pitching statistics can be found on page indicated in lefthand column.

2003 FLORIDA STATE LEAGUE STATISTICS

CLUB BATTING

	AVG	G	AB	R	H	2B	3B	HR	BB	SO	SB
Fort Myers	.268	136	4516	607	1211	180	31	49	421	727	91
Dunedin	.264	140	4549	573	1199	239	16	52	422	793	64
Tampa	.257	132	4377	562	1126	233	40	56	398	885	83
Clearwater	.256	133	4368	529	1118	227	26	53	426	845	75
Daytona	.254	137	4521	574	1149	227	26	67	478	955	184
Vero Beach	.250	131	4294	551	1074	213	15	82	395	858	109
St. Lucie	.250	139	4415	566	1104	226	25	60	441	861	216
Lakeland	.250	133	4340	540	1085	215	43	70	457	963	81
Jupiter	.250	138	4420	549	1104	194	32	68	416	959	128
Sarasota	.236	130	4107	480	971	194	30	48	501	901	148
Brevard County	.234	131	4177	466	978	187	30	49	423	938	90
Palm Beach	.226	138	4477	449	1011	185	16	49	489	1010	82

CLUB PITCHING

	ERA	G	CG	SHO	SV	IP	H	R	ER	BB	SO
St. Lucie	3.09	139	4	10	46	1186	998	505	407	490	1050
Jupiter	3.09	138	5	13	42	1193	1112	500	410	414	890
Clearwater	3.25	133	6	13	44	1149	1130	498	415	319	782
Brevard County	3.35	131	5	15	34	1118	1065	490	416	347	745
Dunedin	3.37	140	3	12	41	1188	1081	518	445	471	953
Daytona	3.45	137	4	12	30	1199	1075	549	460	473	1105
Vero Beach	3.49	131	7	7	37	1145	1049	530	444	443	918
Sarasota	3.49	130	3	10	41	1126	1084	535	437	439	783
Tampa	3.54	132	2	8	35	1127.	1023	535	444	480	879
Fort Myers	3.72	136	3	13	34	1181	1123	560	488	483	887
Palm Beach	3.93	138	3	8	34	1205	1189	606	526	465	873
Lakeland	4.17	133	5	8	31	1128	1203	621	522	443	830

CLUB FIELDING

	PCT	PO	A	E	DP		PCT	PO	A	E	DP
Fort Myers	.979	3543	1382	106	121	Sarasota	.971	3377	1364	143	131
Dunedin	.977	3563	1364	117	104	Vero Beach	.970	3436	1334	149	119
Clearwater	.975	3446	1432	126	126	Brevard County	.969	3353	1400	150	103
Jupiter	.973	3580	1509	143	141	St. Lucie	.969	3558	1399	159	124
Tampa	.971	3381	1363	141	108	Palm Beach	.968	3615	1459	167	123
Lakeland	.971	3383	1391	143	140	Daytona	.965	3596	1329	180	106

INDIVIDUAL BATTING LEADERS

(Minimum 378 Plate Appearances)

	AVG	G	AB	R	H	2B	3B	HR	RBI	BB	SO	SB
Howard, Ryan, Clearwater	.304	130	490	67	149	32	1	23	82	50	151	0
Tomlin, James, Fort Myers	.303	122	498	88	151	17	2	2	42	36	51	24
Reed, Eric, Jupiter	.300	134	514	86	154	15	8	0	25	52	83	53
Kubel, Jason, Fort Myers	.298	116	420	56	125	20	4	5	82	48	54	4
Hattig, John, Sarasota	.295	114	400	51	118	29	2	6	70	59	70	9
Maza, Luis, Fort Myers	.290	111	410	70	119	18	6	5	61	34	79	1
Lambin, Chase, St. Lucie	.289	118	401	58	116	27	2	5	49	46	81	13
Granderson, Curtis, Lakeland	.286	127	476	71	136	29	10	11	51	49	91	10
Craig, Matt, Daytona	.285	119	442	56	126	25	2	11	66	46	87	4
Roman, Jesse, Palm Beach	.283	99	364	24	103	27	2	7	53	36	62	1

INDIVIDUAL PITCHING LEADERS

(Minimum 112 Innings)

	W	L	ERA	G	GS	CG	SV	IP	H	R	ER	BB	SO
Blasko, Chadd, Daytona	10	5	1.98	24	24	1	0	136	100	33	30	43	131
Ungs, Nic, Jupiter	8	3	1.99	18	17	1	0	113	92	28	25	14	80
Miller, Greg, Vero Beach	11	4	2.49	21	21	1	0	116	103	40	32	41	111
Harper, Jesse, Dunedin	13	4	2.54	26	24	1	0	131	112	41	37	31	100
Hill, Shawn, Brevard	9	4	2.56	22	21	2	0	127	118	47	36	26	66
Stevenson, Jason, Brevard	9	6	2.62	36	11	0	0	113	88	36	33	33	60
Miller, Colby, Fort Myers	9	6	2.71	26	26	1	0	156	139	58	47	43	114
Nolasco, Ricky, Daytona	11	5	2.96	26	26	1	0	149	129	58	49	48	136
Floyd, Gavin, Clearwater	7	8	3.00	24	20	1	0	138	128	61	46	45	115
Pinto, Renyel, Daytona	3	8	3.22	20	19	0	0	115	91	47	41	45	104

ALL-STAR TEAM

C—Justin Huber, St. Lucie; Joe Mauer, Fort Myers. **1B**—Ryan Howard, Clearwater. **2B**—Luis Maza, Fort Myers. **3B**—David Wright, St. Lucie. **SS**—Don Kelly, Lakeland. **Util IF**—Chase Lambin, St. Lucie. **OF**—Franklin Gutierrez, Vero Beach; Jason Kubel, Fort Myers; Wayne Lydon, St. Lucie. **Util OF**—Eric Reed, Jupiter. **DH**—Jason Stokes, Jupiter. **P**—Ezequiel Astacio, Clearwater; Chadd Blasko, Daytona; Greg Miller, Vero Beach; Nic Ungs, Jupiter. **RP**—Jared Blasdell, Daytona; Kevin Cave, Jupiter.

Most Valuable Player: Ryan Howard, Clearwater. **Most Valuable Pitcher:** Nic Ungs, Jupiter. **Manager of the Year:** Mike Basso, Dunedin.

DEPARTMENT LEADERS

BATTING

G	Mike Snyder, Dunedin	137
AB	Eric Reed, Jupiter	514
R	James Tomlin, Fort Myers	88
H	Eric Reed, Jupiter	154
TB	Ryan Howard, Clearwater	252
XBH	Ryan Howard, Clearwater	56
	David Wright, St. Lucie	56
2B	David Wright, St. Lucie	39
3B	Curtis Granderson, Lakeland	10
HR	Ryan Howard, Clearwater	23
RBI	Jason Stokes, Jupiter	89
SH	Matt Demarco, Jupiter	20
SF	Jason Kubel, Fort Myers	13
BB	David Wright, St. Lucie	72
IBB	Ryan Howard, Clearwater	9
HBP	Luis Maza, Fort Myers	19
	Sean Walsh, Clearwater	19
SO	Ryan Howard, Clearwater	151
SB	Wayne Lydon, St. Lucie	75
CS	Wayne Lydon, St. Lucie	20
GIDP	Vince Vukovich, Clearwater	16
OBP	Dwaine Bacon, Daytona	.392
SLG	Ryan Howard, Clearwater	.514

PITCHING

G	Carmen Cali, Palm Beach	62
GS	Three tied at	26
CG	Nine tied at	2
ShO	Fourteen tied at	1
GF	Jared Blasdell, Daytona	47
SV	Jared Blasdell, Daytona	27
W	Ezequiel Astacio, Clearwater	15
L	Kevin McDowell, Lakeland	12
	Lee Rodney, Lakeland	12
IP	Elizardo Ramirez, Clearwater	157
H	Elizardo Ramirez, Clearwater	181
R	Carmen Pignatiello, Daytona	87
ER	Carmen Pignatiello, Daytona	76
HR	Kevin McDowell, Lakeland	13
	Carmen Pignatiello, Daytona	13
HB	Chance Caple, Palm Beach	19
BB	Joselo Diaz, St. Lucie	73
SO	Carmen Pignatiello, Daytona	140
WP	Donald Levinski, Jupiter	16
	Dave Martinez, Tampa	16
BK	Joselo Diaz, Vero Beach/St. Lucie	6

FIELDING

C	AVG	Tim Whittaker, Dunedin	.996
	PO	Geovany Soto, Daytona	617
	A	Geovany Soto, Daytona	61
	E	Three tied at	10
	DP	Three tied at	6
	PB	Josh Willingham, Jupiter	19
1B	AVG	Garrett Jones, Fort Myers	.994
	PO	Mike Snyder, Dunedin	1055
	A	Ryan Howard, Clearwater	89
		James Loney, Vero Beach	89
	E	Mike Snyder, Dunedin	20
	DP	Ryan Howard, Clearwater	102
		Juan Tejeda, Lakeland	102
2B	AVG	Luis Maza, Fort Myers	.973
	PO	Michael Woods, Lakeland	232
	A	Michael Woods, Lakeland	309
	E	Michael Woods, Lakeland	20
	DP	Michael Woods, Lakeland	74
3B	AVG	Rob Cosby, Dunedin	.957
	PO	Willy Aybar, Vero Beach	87
	A	David Wright, St. Lucie	243
	E	Elvis Corporan, Tampa	25
	DP	Willy Aybar, Vero Beach	29
SS	AVG	Daniel Gonzalez, Clearwater	.964
	PO	Rex Rundgren, Jupiter	204
	A	Rex Rundgren, Jupiter	387
	E	Rex Rundgren, Jupiter	27
	DP	Daniel Gonzalez, Clearwater	85
OF	AVG	Ron Davenport, Dunedin	1.000
	PO	Eric Reed, Jupiter	335
	A	Curtis Granderson, Lakeland	15
		Jason Kubel, Fort Myers	15
	E	Three tied at	8
	DP	Juan Camilo, Clearwater	4
		James Tomlin, Fort Myers	4

MIDWEST LEAGUE

LOW CLASS A

BY J.J. COOPER

In the Midwest League in 2003, Prince was king.

Prince Fielder, the Brewers' first-round pick in 2002, made a run at the league's triple crown, won the league's MVP award and was the league's top prospect. The Beloit Snappers first baseman hit .313-27-112 to finish third in the league in batting, second in home runs and first in RBIs.

"I haven't seen that kind of power since I've been here," said Don Money, Beloit's manager since 1998. "Last year he came here as a raw kid out of high school. This year he came back with a plan. He can hit the ball out of any ballpark to any field. The ball comes off his bat like a big leaguer."

Fielder was joined in Beloit by a number of other top prospects, particularly in the second half when second baseman Rickie Weeks, the Brewers' first-round pick in June, and outfielder Anthony Gwynn came to Beloit.

DAN ARNOLD

Rickie Weeks

One of the highlights of the season came when the Beloit team, full of the hope of better days ahead for the Brewers, played Wisconsin at Milwaukee's Miller Park. A crowd of 14,447 curious Brewers fans turned out for the game.

Beloit went on to meet Lansing in the finals of the MWL playoffs. After blowing a seven-run, ninth-inning lead to Peoria in the last game of the 2002 playoffs, Lansing swept its seven playoff games to win its first league title since 1997. Leading the way were lefthander Andy Sisco, who didn't allow an earned run in either of his starts, and outfielder Felix Pie, who batted .429 in the playoffs. All three wins in the finals were close, as Lansing won a pair of one-run affairs and topped the Snappers 4-2 in a 10-inning game for the title.

The MWL wasn't as balanced as it was in 2002, when Joe Mauer headlined the position players and Dontrelle Willis was the cream of the pitching crop. Outside of Fielder, most of the top talent in the league was found on the mound. In addition to Sisco (6-8, 3.54), the Lugnuts featured lefthander Justin Jones (3-5, 2.28) and righthanders Jae-kuk Ryu (6-1, 1.75) and Anderson Tavarez (12-9, 3.24).

But a crafty lefthander from West Michigan dominated the league. Jon Connolly, the Tigers' 28th-round pick in 2001, was 12-0, 0.78 at the all-star break. While he slowed in the second half, he still finished the season as the league leader in wins and ERA with 16-3, 1.41 numbers.

The league welcomed three new major league affiliates in 2003, with the Rangers in Clinton, the Athletics in Kane County, and the Yankees in Michigan, which changed its name to mark the occasion. The Michigan Battle Cats gave way to the Battle Creek Yankees, and the team's overall attendance increased by about 10,000 fans.

But the real attendance story came in Dayton, where the Dragons drew 590,382 fans to break their own single-season Class A attendance record, set in 2000. League attendance held steady in spite of 71 playing dates lost to unusually cold, wet weather at the beginning of the season.

STANDINGS: SPLIT SEASON

FIRST HALF

EAST	W	L	PCT	GB
Fort Wayne	40	28	.588	—
Lansing	38	27	.585	½
West Michigan	37	33	.529	4
Dayton	35	35	.500	6
Battle Creek	33	35	.485	7
South Bend	28	38	.424	11
WEST	**W**	**L**	**PCT**	**GB**
Kane County	41	29	.586	—
Wisconsin	38	28	.576	1
Beloit	32	35	.478	7½
Quad City	32	36	.471	8
Cedar Rapids	32	37	.464	8½
Clinton	30	36	.455	9
Peoria	30	39	.435	10½
Burlington	29	39	.426	11

SECOND HALF

EAST	W	L	PCT	GB
South Bend	44	26	.629	—
Battle Creek	40	29	.580	3½
Fort Wayne	31	38	.449	12½
Lansing	31	39	.443	13
West Michigan	30	40	.429	14
Dayton	26	43	.377	17½
WEST	**W**	**L**	**PCT**	**GB**
Beloit	43	26	.623	—
Kane County	39	30	.565	4
Clinton	39	30	.565	4
Peoria	35	34	.507	8
Burlington	35	35	.500	8½
Cedar Rapids	34	35	.493	9
Wisconsin	31	38	.449	12
Quad City	27	42	.391	16

PLAYOFFS—Quarterfinals: Lansing defeated South Bend 2-0, Battle Creek defeated Fort Wayne 2-0, Beloit defeated Wisconsin 2-0 and Clinton defeated Kane County 2-1 in best-of-3 series.**Semifinals:** Lansing defeated Battle Creek 2-0 and Beloit defeated Clinton 2-1 in best-of-3 series. **Final**: Lansing defeated Beloit 3-0 in best-of-5 series.

STANDINGS: OVERALL

Page		W	L	PCT	GB	Manager	Attendance	Avg.	Last Penn.
207	Kane County Cougars (Athletics)	80	59	.576	—	Webster Garrison	516,133	7,941	2001
169	Beloit Snappers (Brewers)	75	61	.551	3½	Don Money	96,431	1,439	1995
191	Battle Creek Yankees (Yankees)	73	64	.533	6	Mitch Seoane	93,314	1,458	2000
68	South Bend Silver Hawks (D'backs)	72	64	.529	6½	Von Hayes	203,690	3,134	1993
236	Fort Wayne Wizards (Padres)	71	66	.518	8	Gary Jones	257,013	3,894	None
104	Lansing Lugnuts (Cubs)	69	66	.511	9	Julio Garcia	364,623	5,977	2003
249	Wisconsin Timber Rattlers (Mariners)	69	66	.511	9	Daren Brown	198,001	3,246	1984
264	Clinton LumberKings (Rangers)	69	66	.511	9	Carlos Subero	81,535	1,315	1991
135	West Michigan Whitecaps (Tigers)	67	73	.479	13½	Phil Regan	361,545	5,562	1998
60	Cedar Rapids Kernels (Angels)	66	72	.478	13½	Todd Claus	174,451	2,528	1994
228	Peoria Chiefs (Cardinals)	65	73	.471	14½	Joe Cunningham	246,370	3,623	2002
155	Burlington Bees (Royals)	64	74	.464	15½	Joe Szekely	59,427	900	1999
112	Dayton Dragons (Reds)	61	78	.439	19	Donnie Scott	590,382	8,434	None
176	Quad City River Bandits (Twins)	59	78	.431	20	Jeff Carter	132,983	2,216	1990

NOTE: Team's individual batting and pitching statistics can be found on page indicated in lefthand column.

2003 MIDWEST LEAGUE STATISTICS

CLUB BATTING

	AVG	G	AB	R	H	2B	3B	HR	BB	SO	SB
Cedar Rapids	.265	138	4678	634	1238	202	36	65	384	855	118
South Bend	.261	136	4546	597	1186	224	30	62	429	822	143
Battle Creek	.261	137	4544	628	1185	230	28	98	425	808	76
Beloit	.260	137	4560	639	1185	192	26	67	472	877	172
Quad City	.259	138	4690	573	1215	200	29	54	327	763	94
Wisconsin	.256	136	4635	618	1187	226	27	77	427	1014	158
Lansing	.253	135	4481	554	1133	236	30	74	394	899	131
Burlington	.253	138	4623	628	1168	181	35	47	515	856	123
Kane County	.252	139	4708	636	1188	231	17	81	504	1029	123
Peoria	.249	138	4549	571	1133	194	31	71	393	954	171
Clinton	.247	135	4343	584	1073	208	29	65	560	966	187
West Michigan	.243	140	4527	570	1100	188	50	65	496	965	119
Dayton	.243	139	4593	580	1116	195	17	70	426	1050	93
Fort Wayne	.233	138	4468	520	1043	182	19	47	480	932	75

CLUB PITCHING

	ERA	G	CG	SHO	SV	IP	H	R	ER	BB	SO
Fort Wayne	3.02	138	3	12	43	1204	1081	529	404	373	1064
Lansing	3.18	135	5	15	31	1180	1052	536	417	427	1018
Kane County	3.22	139	13	21	35	1240	1144	519	444	348	966
South Bend	3.29	136	7	16	35	1195	1097	553	437	455	863
Wisconsin	3.34	136	7	9	31	1198	1216	569	445	403	889
Peoria	3.48	138	5	8	36	1200	1185	558	464	396	779
West Michigan	3.54	140	7	12	35	1201	1146	583	472	472	933
Beloit	3.65	137	3	10	34	1210	1195	643	490	470	996
Battle Creek	3.80	137	6	12	33	1184	1118	598	500	448	884
Clinton	3.94	135	1	8	39	1160.	1217	636	508	394	769
Cedar Rapids	3.98	138	2	11	31	1200	1139	656	530	551	864
Dayton	4.05	139	0	5	39	1203	1196	639	541	484	923
Burlington	4.05	138	5	10	30	1215	1149	631	547	492	864
Quad City	4.45	138	3	6	29	1208	1215	682	597	519	978

CLUB FIELDING

	PCT	PO	A	E	DP		PCT	PO	A	E	DP
Kane County	.973	3719	1456	145	83	Cedar Rapids	.966	3599	1377	177	108
Burlington	.971	3644	1464	151	116	Dayton	.965	3609	1477	184	127
Peoria	.971	3600	1670	157	123	Lansing	.963	3541	1469	193	104
Quad City	.970	3625	1426	158	107	Beloit	.962	3629	1387	199	96
Battle Creek	.967	3553	1351	167	124	Wisconsin	.962	3595	1514	204	118
South Bend	.967	3586	1451	172	105	Clinton	.961	3481	1383	200	100
W. Michigan	.967	3603	1391	173	93	Fort Wayne	.960	3611	1404	209	108

INDIVIDUAL BATTING LEADERS

(Minimum 378 Plate Appearances)

	AVG	G	AB	R	H	2B	3B	HR	RBI	BB	SO	SB
Callaspo, Alberto, Cedar Rapids	.327	133	514	86	168	38	4	2	67	42	28	20
Sprowl, Jon-Mark, SB/BC	.321	124	418	77	134	30	3	5	62	71	39	5
Murphy, Don, Burlington	.313	132	504	77	158	29	6	5	98	65	78	15
Fielder, Prince, Beloit	.313	137	502	81	157	22	2	27	112	71	80	2
Aybar, Erick, Cedar Rapids	.308	125	496	83	153	30	10	6	57	17	54	32
Lebron, Hector, Clinton	.305	91	351	40	107	17	4	5	45	24	56	6
Bibbs, Kennard, Beloit	.302	124	497	87	150	14	1	0	40	52	63	55
Oeltjen, Trent, Quad City	.298	123	466	73	139	12	8	4	44	37	57	29
Merchan, Jesus, Quad City	.296	101	392	60	116	16	3	5	53	31	18	8
Romero, Alex, Quad City	.296	120	423	50	125	16	3	4	40	43	43	11

INDIVIDUAL PITCHING LEADERS

(Minimum 112 Innings)

	W	L	ERA	G	GS	CG	SV	IP	H	R	ER	BB	SO
Connolly, Jon, West Michigan	16	3	1.41	25	25	5	0	166	128	37	26	38	104
Whitaker, Brian, Fort Wayne	7	6	2.09	26	26	3	0	164	149	60	38	20	121
Ribas, Gabe, Fort Wayne	13	3	2.25	19	19	0	0	116	86	36	29	26	116
Teekel, Josh, Peoria	6	6	2.36	26	16	0	1	118	107	43	31	39	85
Edwards, Bryan, Fort Wayne	4	7	2.40	39	10	0	2	112	104	41	30	29	79
Toledo, Jean, Cedar Rapids	12	7	2.44	24	24	0	0	136	132	60	37	50	58
Blanton, Joe, Kane County	8	7	2.57	21	21	2	0	133	110	47	38	19	144
Fulmer, T.A., Wisconsin	9	8	2.58	27	27	5	0	168	154	60	48	37	130
Garcia, Jose, Battle Creek	9	8	2.64	21	21	4	0	136	111	46	40	33	90
Parra, Manny, Beloit	11	2	2.73	23	23	1	0	139	127	50	42	24	117

ALL-STAR TEAM

C—Jon-Mark Sprowl, South Bend/Battle Creek. **1B**—Prince Fielder, Beloit. **2B**—Alberto Callaspo, Cedar Rapids. **3B**—Travis Hanson, Peoria. **SS**—Erick Aybar, Cedar Rapids. **OF**—Rudy Guillen, Battle Creek; Kennard Jones, Fort Wayne; Felix Pie, Lansing. **DH**—Jayson Drobiak, Battle Creek; Brian Stavisky, Kane County. **RHP**—Gabe Ribas, Fort Wayne. **LHP**—Jon Connolly, West Michigan. **RHRP**—Dale Thayer, Fort Wayne. **LHRP**—Ian Ostlund, West Michigan.

Most Valuable Player: Prince Fielder, Beloit. **Prospect of the Year:** Prince Fielder, Beloit. **Manager of the Year:** Webster Garrison, Kane County.

DEPARTMENT LEADERS

BATTING

G	Brent Clevlen, West Michigan	138
AB	Jon Nelson, Wisconsin	536
R	Alberto Callaspo, Cedar Rapids	86
H	Alberto Callaspo, Cedar Rapids	168
TB	Jayson Drobiak, Battle Creek	279
XBH	Jayson Drobiak, Battle Creek	69
2B	Jon Nelson, Wisconsin	38
3B	Victor Mendez, West Michigan	11
HR	Jayson Drobiak, Battle Creek	30
RBI	Prince Fielder, Beloit	112
SH	Callix Crabbe, Beloit	18
SF	Four tied at	9
BB	Craig Ringe, Clinton	82
IBB	Prince Fielder, Beloit	16
HBP	Trent Oeltjen, Quad City	20
SO	Jon Nelson, Wisconsin	168
SB	Matt Lemanczyk, Peoria	56
CS	Kennard Jones, Fort Wayne	19
GIDP	Brent Clevlen, West Michigan	16
	Rudy Guillen, Battle Creek	16
OBP	Jon-Mark Sprowl, So. Bend/Battle Creek	.425
SLG	Jayson Drobiak, Battle Creek	.559

PITCHING

G	Jason Wylie, Lancaster	57
GS	Drew Dickinson, Kane County	28
CG	Three tied at	5
ShO	Drew Dickinson, Kane County	3
	Sam Smith, South Bend	3
GF	Jason Wylie, Lancaster	49
SV	Matty Wilkinson, South Bend	30
W	Jon Connolly, West Michigan	16
	Sam Smith, South Bend	16
L	Carlos Vasquez, Lancaster	13
IP	Drew Dickinson, Kane County	191
H	Juan Sandoval, Wisconsin	190
R	Juan Sandoval, Wisconsin	97
ER	Eric Ackerman, Burlington	78
	Juan Sandoval, Wisconsin	78
HR	Tyler Adamczyk, Peoria	15
HB	Four tied at	15
BB	Colt Griffin, Burlington	97
SO	Joe Blanton, Kane County	144
WP	Colt Griffin, Burlington	23
BK	Four tied at	4

FIELDING

C	AVG	Mike Rabelo, West Michigan	.994
	PO	Mike Rabelo, West Michigan	773
	A	Rene Rivera, Wisconsin	114
	E	Jared Abruzzo, Cedar Rapids	14
		Pedro Esparragoza, Beloit	14
	DP	Luis Gonzalez, Burlington	8
		Matt Tupman, Burlington	8
	PB	Four tied at	18
1B	AVG	Sean Luellwitz South Bend	.996
	PO	John Santor, Peoria	1277
	A	John Santor, Peoria	98
	E	Jon Nelson, Wisconsin	21
	DP	John Santor, Peoria	104
2B	AVG	Francis Gomez, Kane County	.977
	PO	Gabe Lopez, Battle Creek	256
	A	Mike McCoy, Peoria	382
	E	Callix Crabbe, Beloit	32
	DP	Gabe Lopez, Battle Creek	90
3B	AVG	Jeff Eure, Beloit	.951
	PO	Randall Shelley, Clinton	104
	A	Travis Hanson, Peoria	268
	E	Matt Hagen, Wisconsin	35
	DP	Matt Hagen, Wisconsin	21
		Travis Hanson, Peoria	21
SS	AVG	Juan Gonzalez, West Michigan	.972
	PO	Jerry Gil, South Bend	225
	A	Joaquin Arias, Battle Creek	415
	E	Buck Coats, Lancaster	51
	DP	Joaquin Arias, Battle Creek	78
OF	AVG	Mel Stocker, Burlington	.992
	PO	Victor Mendez, West Michigan	329
	A	T.J. Bohn, Wisconsin	20
		Juan Senreiso, Clinton	20
	E	Juan Senreiso, Clinton	14
	DP	T.J. Bohn, Wisconsin	5
		Juan Senreiso, Clinton	5

SOUTH ATLANTIC LEAGUE

LOW CLASS A

BY J.J. COOPER

The Lake County Captains came within two games of having the perfect inaugural season.

The Captains drew 437,515 fans in their first season in suburban Cleveland, a giant improvement from the 52,102 fans the team drew in Columbus, Ga., the year before. The fans were rewarded with a talented squad that rolled to a 97-43 record, the most wins in the minors.

But when the playoffs rolled around, another new Sally League city got to celebrate a title, as the Rome Braves beat the Captains three games to one in the best-of-five championship series. It was the second consecutive season the Indians affiliate had fallen in the championship series. The Captains won largely because of a dominating pitching staff. Lake County's 2.67 team ERA led the league, and the Captains also led the league with 22 shutouts. Fausto Carmona came out of nowhere to go 17-4, 2.06, leading the league in wins and ERA.

DAVID SCHOFIELD

Cole Hamels

Carmona was one of a number of top arms as pitching prospects dominated the league. Lefthanders Scott Kazmir (4-4, 2.36) of Capital City and Cole Hamels (6-1, 0.84) of Lakewood both blitzed to high Class A, while righthanders Vince Perkins (3-1, 1.83), Brandon League (2-3, 1.91), Bryan Bullington (5-1, 1.39) and John Maine (7-3, 1.53) also put up big numbers on their way to promotions.

Rome had a standout pitcher of its own, riding Matt Wright (10-2, 1.65) to the title. The young Braves team struggled during the first half, but went 21-9 in the final month to win the second-half title. Rome's move also was a success on the field and at the gate. The Braves drew 246,718 fans, a year after drawing 84,001 in Macon.

The boost from those two franchises helped the Sally League set a record for attendance, with 3,129,212 fans despite a league-record 104 rainouts. It was the first time the league had drawn more than 3 million fans.

The league's other city switch didn't go nearly as well. The South Georgia Waves moved 100 miles from Albany to Columbus, Ga., a week before the season started. The Waves drew the smallest crowds in affiliated baseball—30,565 fans, an average of 509 fans a game.

Attendance was so bad in 2003 that a Waves employee decided to live at the ballpark until a crowd of at least 1,500 showed up. He was there for six weeks, until the team had a promotion welcoming fans from a local army base and freed him.

Hagerstown's Clay Hensley and Kannapolis' Brian Miller each threw seven-inning no-hitters in 2003, but the single-game performance of the season was turned in by Lake County first baseman Matt Knox, who hit a pair of grand slams June 13 against Hagerstown.

STANDINGS: SPLIT SEASON

FIRST HALF					SECOND HALF				
NORTH	**W**	**L**	**PCT**	**GB**	**NORTH**	**W**	**L**	**PCT**	**GB**
Lake County	48	22	.686	—	Lake County	49	21	.700	—
Delmarva	36	32	.529	11	Lexington	43	27	.614	6
Greensboro	36	33	.522	11½	Lakewood	35	34	.507	13½
Hagerstown	35	32	.522	11½	Hagerstown	33	35	.485	15
Lexington	32	35	.478	14½	Greensboro	31	36	.463	16½
Kannapolis	32	36	.471	15	Delmarva	31	39	.443	18
Charleston, W.Va.	27	36	.429	17½	Charleston, W.Va.	30	40	.429	19
Lakewood	22	47	.319	25½	Kannapolis	23	46	.333	25½
SOUTH	**W**	**L**	**PCT**	**GB**	**SOUTH**	**W**	**L**	**PCT**	**GB**
Hickory	42	25	.627	—	Rome	42	28	.600	—
Capital City	39	29	.574	3½	Hickory	40	29	.580	1½
Charleston, S.C.	39	30	.565	4	Charleston, S.C.	38	32	.543	4
Rome	36	33	.522	7	Asheville	38	32	.543	4
Asheville	36	33	.522	7	South Georgia	36	34	.514	6
Savannah	31	38	.449	12	Capital City	34	36	.486	8
South Georgia	28	38	.424	13½	Savannah	27	42	.391	14½
Augusta	24	43	.358	18	Augusta	25	44	.362	16½

PLAYOFFS—Semifinals: Lake County defeated Lexington 2-0 and Rome defeated Hickory 2-1 in best-of-3 series. **Final:** Rome defeated Lake County 3-1 in best-of-5 series.

STANDINGS: OVERALL

Page		W	L	PCT	GB	Manager	Attendance	Avg.	Last Penn.
120	Lake County Captains (Indians)	97	43	.693	—	Luis Rivera	437,515	6,341	None
220	Hickory Crawdads (Pirates)	82	54	.603	11	Tony Beasley	176,366	2,713	2002
75	Rome Braves (Braves)	78	61	.561	18½	Rocket Wheeler	246,718	3,979	2003
256	Charleston, S.C., RiverDogs (Devil Rays)	77	62	.554	19½	Mako Oliveras	259,007	3,754	None
149	Lexington Legends (Astros)	75	63	.543	21	Russ Nixon	370,656	5,372	2001
127	Asheville Tourists (Rockies)	74	65	.532	22½	Joe Mikulik	143,596	2,143	1984
199	Capital City Bombers (Mets)	73	65	.529	23	Tony Tijerina	102,149	1,702	1998
242	Hagerstown Suns (Giants)	68	67	.504	26½	Mike Ramsey	100,865	1,601	None
141	Greensboro Bats (Marlins)	67	69	.493	27½	Steve Phillips	164,589	2,939	1982
82	Delmarva Shorebirds (Orioles)	67	71	.486	29	Stan Hough	228,344	3,460	2000
163	South Georgia Waves (Dodgers)	64	72	.471	31	Dann Bilardello	30,565	509	None
271	Charleston, W.Va., Alley Cats (Blue Jays)	57	76	.429	36½	Mark Meleski	95,590	1,620	1990
183	Savannah Sand Gnats (Expos)	58	80	.420	39	Joey Cora	103,443	1,753	1996
213	Lakewood BlueClaws (Phillies)	57	81	.413	39	Buddy Biancalana	445,838	6,654	None
97	Kannapolis Intimidators (White Sox)	55	82	.401	40½	John Orton	92,321	1,513	None
90	Augusta GreenJackets (Red Sox)	49	87	.360	46	Russ Morman	131,650	2,090	1999

NOTE: Team's individual batting and pitching statistics can be found on page indicated in lefthand column.

2003 SOUTH ATLANTIC LEAGUE STATISTICS

CLUB BATTING

	AVG	G	AB	R	H	2B	3B	HR	BB	SO	SB
Hickory	.267	136	4419	622	1182	202	37	93	426	846	143
Asheville	.265	139	4710	707	1246	259	27	126	511	962	170
Rome	.264	139	4523	577	1192	205	35	71	379	783	150
South Georgia	.262	136	4493	623	1179	211	29	84	417	1003	136
Charleston, S.C.	.258	139	4496	657	1161	227	32	103	549	1020	190
Lake County	.253	140	4527	689	1147	238	39	115	525	966	152
Augusta	.250	136	4290	530	1074	207	23	42	446	879	137
Capital City	.249	138	4411	612	1098	223	25	60	464	1116	203
Savannah	.249	138	4427	568	1101	203	42	63	369	970	153
Delmarva	.243	138	4443	562	1079	236	38	74	474	1029	107
Kannapolis	.240	137	4358	524	1048	218	12	39	432	859	120
Lexington	.238	138	4492	587	1068	222	25	97	501	986	98
Hagerstown	.238	135	4368	505	1038	194	34	44	502	1008	109
Greensboro	.232	136	4366	542	1011	205	27	69	471	1064	128
Charleston, W.Va.	.231	133	4338	490	1003	220	23	50	461	963	57
Lakewood	.217	138	4219	464	916	186	31	54	455	1159	196

CLUB PITCHING

	ERA	G	CG	SHO	SV	IP	H	R	ER	BB	SO
Lake County	2.67	140	5	22	52	1216	1033	440	360	362	1098
Rome	2.95	139	4	16	41	1179	1042	471	387	460	1107
Hagerstown	3.09	135	9	16	34	1167	956	487	401	409	1064
Lexington	3.41	138	1	8	42	1211	1054	555	459	513	1026
Greensboro	3.42	136	7	10	29	1169	1051	563	445	448	954
Delmarva	3.47	138	4	10	46	1191	1057	586	459	460	1148
Hickory	3.52	136	9	13	47	1161	1051	532	454	388	923
Capital City	3.53	138	5	7	31	1179	1092	560	463	463	1078
Charleston, W.Va.	3.58	133	4	10	30	1141	1059	545	454	480	950
Charleston, S.C.	3.61	139	3	7	47	1199	1228	591	481	361	838
Kannapolis	3.81	137	9	7	28	1159	1052	616	490	577	957
Lakewood	3.82	138	5	8	33	1169	1082	599	496	532	911
Asheville	3.83	139	3	4	42	1234	1219	643	525	436	966
Savannah	4.52	138	7	6	31	1154	1175	672	579	509	871
Augusta	4.55	136	0	10	24	1123	1196	673	568	448	825
South Georgia	4.66	136	0	2	33	1163	1196	726	602	536	897

CLUB FIELDING

	PCT	PO	A	E	DP		PCT	PO	A	E	DP
Lake County	.973	3647	1456	143	84	Savannah	.968	3461	1394	159	111
Rome	.972	3538	1260	136	101	Lakewood	.968	3508	1337	160	102
Char., W.Va.	.972	3423	1434	138	131	Char., S.C.	.967	3596	1507	176	125
Hagerstown	.971	3501	1363	144	81	Capital City	.966	3537	1509	178	79
Lexington	.970	3632	1480	159	110	Delmarva	.966	3572	1322	174	74
Hickory	.970	3483	1385	152	105	Greensboro	.965	3507	1344	174	87
Kannapolis	.969	3476	1386	154	52	Augusta	.963	3368	1332	179	97
Asheville	.969	3701	1529	166	115	So. Georgia	.962	3489	1385	194	108

INDIVIDUAL BATTING LEADERS

(Minimum 378 Plate Appearances)

	AVG	G	AB	R	H	2B	3B	HR	RBI	BB	SO	SB
Lytle, Chaz, Hickory	.335	101	364	55	122	11	3	0	42	26	39	22
Cortes, Jorge, Hickory	.325	98	345	55	112	24	2	8	66	56	47	9
Young, Delwyn, South Georgia	.323	119	443	67	143	38	7	15	73	36	87	5
Chop, Chad, Savannah	.322	131	485	55	156	26	5	11	77	32	75	10
Baldiris, Aaron, Capital City	.313	107	393	55	123	19	4	6	68	51	55	13
Spann, Chad, Augusta	.312	116	414	55	129	21	3	5	63	40	64	9
Davis, Rajai, Hickory	.305	125	478	84	146	21	7	6	54	55	65	40
Upton, B.J., Columbia, S.C.	.302	101	384	70	116	22	6	7	46	57	80	38
Joseph, Onil, Rome	.296	120	483	66	143	16	6	4	47	37	89	32
Davis, John-Paul, Columbia, S.C.	.296	97	355	65	105	24	1	15	52	47	59	14

INDIVIDUAL PITCHING LEADERS

(Minimum 112 Innings)

	W	L	ERA	G	GS	CG	SV	IP	H	R	ER	BB	SO
Carmona, Fausto, Lake County	17	4	2.06	24	24	1	0	148	117	48	34	14	83
Valdez, Merkin, Hagerstown	9	5	2.25	26	26	2	0	156	119	42	39	49	166
Habel, Josh, Hagerstown	11	7	2.36	37	16	1	2	122	90	36	32	35	127
Lerew, Anthony, Rome	7	6	2.38	25	25	0	0	144	112	45	38	43	127
Crockett, Ben, Asheville	10	9	2.49	23	23	2	0	152	152	60	42	32	117
Hanson, D.J., Charleston, W.Va.	10	10	2.54	25	25	2	0	138	110	51	39	56	113
Olsen, Scott, Greensboro	7	9	2.81	25	24	0	0	128	101	51	40	59	129
Nin, Sandy, Ccharleston, W.Va.	7	8	2.89	23	23	1	0	131	124	50	42	19	87
Davies, Kyle, Rome	8	8	2.89	27	27	1	0	146	128	52	47	53	148
Prochaska, Mike, Columbia, S.C.	9	7	2.98	29	20	0	0	124	111	49	41	35	76

ALL-STAR TEAM

C—Brian McCann, Rome. **1B**—Larry Broadway, Savannah. **2B**—Delwyn Young, South Georgia. **3B**—Aaron Baldiris, Capital City. **SS**—B.J. Upton, Charleston. **Util IF**—Chad Spann, Augusta. **OF**—Jorge Cortes, Hickory; Jeff Francoeur, Rome; Jeff Salazar, Asheville. **Util OF**—Rajai Davis, Hickory. **DH**—Chad Chop, Savannah. **RHP**—Fausto Carmona, Lake County. **LHP**—Josh Habel, Hagerstown.

Most Valuable Player: Jorge Cortes, Hickory. **Most Outstanding Pitcher:** Fausto Carmona, Lake County. **Most Outstanding Prospect:** B.J. Upton, Charleston. **Manager of the Year:** Luis Rivera, Lake County.

DEPARTMENT LEADERS

BATTING

G	Jon Schuerholz, Rome	135
AB	Jason Pridie, Charleston, S.C.	530
R	Jeff Salazar, Asheville	109
H	Chad Chop, Savannah	156
TB	Jeff Salazar, Asheville	256
XBH	Delwyn Young, South Georgia	60
2B	Bernie Gonzalez, Asheville	38
	Delwyn Young, South Georgia	38
3B	Jason Pridie, Charleston, S.C.	10
HR	Jeff Salazar, Asheville	29
RBI	Jeff Salazar, Asheville	98
SH	Osvaldo Fernando, Lexington	21
SF	Chris Bass, Hickory	10
BB	Jeremy Hermida, Greensboro	80
IBB	Jeff Salazar, Asheville	8
HBP	Jeff Ontiveros, Augusta	20
SO	Brad Eldred, Hickory	142
SB	Chris Roberson, Lakewood	59
CS	Onil Joseph, Rome	22
GIDP	Jeff Francoeur, Rome	21
OBP	Jorge Cortes, Hickory	.427
SLG	Delwyn Young, South Georgia	.542

PITCHING

G	Jentry Beckstead, Asheville	63
GS	Three tied at	28
CG	Jonathan Albaladejo, Hickory	5
ShO	Yorman Bazardo, Greensboro	2
	Clay Hensley, Hagerstown	2
GF	Jentry Beckstead, Asheville	54
SV	Jentry Beckstead, Asheville	29
W	Fausto Carmona, Lake County	17
L	Jailen Peguero, Lexington	13
IP	Doug Johnson, Asheville	167
H	Doug Johnson, Asheville	182
R	Zach Hammes, South Georgia	91
ER	Aaron Heitzman, Lexington	76
	Doug Johnson, Asheville	76
HR	Darren Clarke, Asheville	22
HB	Richard Cartier, Asheville	16
	Doug Johnson, Asheville	16
BB	Daniel Cabrera, Delmarva	78
SO	Merkin Valdez, Hagerstown	166
WP	Omar Anez, Capital City	22
	Brian Bulger, Charleston, S.C.	22
BK	Paulino Reynoso, Kannapolis	5

FIELDING

C	AVG	Mike Nixon, South Georgia	.994
	PO	Brian Munhall, Hagerstown	724
	A	Brian Munhall, Hagerstown	69
	E	Brian Munhall, Hagerstown	18
	DP	German Melendez, Lexington	6
	PB	Mark Obradovich, Lexington	27
1B	AVG	Brad Eldred, Hickory	.990
	PO	Andres Rodriguez, Capital City	1054
	A	John Fagan, Lexington	79
	E	Dustin Yount, Delmarva	20
	DP	Zeph Zinsman, Charleston, W.Va.	91
2B	AVG	Willie Rivera, Charleston, W.Va.	.984
	PO	Victor Mercedes, Hickory	278
	A	Victor Mercedes, Hickory	329
	E	Delwyn Young, South Georgia	32
	DP	Willie Rivera, Charleston, W.Va.	85
3B	AVG	Wes Timmons, Rome	.960
	PO	Wes Timmons, Rome	88
	A	Vince Harrison, Charleston, S.C.	226
	E	Hector Perozo, South Georgia	25
	DP	Three tied at	21
SS	AVG	Luis Hernandez, Rome	.958
	PO	Andy Gonzalez, Kannapolis	236
	A	Osvaldo Fernando, Lexington	355
	E	B.J. Upton, Charleston, S.C.	42
	DP	Luis Hernandez, Rome	58
OF	AVG	Andy Rohleder, Greensboro	.991
	PO	Chris Roberson, Lakewood	323
	A	Frank Diaz, Savannah	21
		Jeff Salazar, Asheville	21
	E	Rodney Medina, Charleston, W.Va.	14
	DP	Ed Montague, South Georgia	4
		Jeff Salazar, Asheville	4

MINOR LEAGUES

NEW YORK-PENN LEAGUE

SHORT-SEASON CLASS A

BY MICHAEL LEVESQUE

It was all Auburn, all year. Almost.

The Doubledays were the most dominant team in the short-season New York-Penn League in 2003 but were swept out of the playoffs by Williamsport, a wild-card entry. The Crosscutters pulled off a first-round upset of Auburn, which compiled a 56-18 record, and swept Brooklyn for their first outright New York-Penn League championship. They shared the title in 2001, after the events of Sept. 11 caused the final series to be canceled.

DAVID SCHOFIELD

Vito Chiaravalloti

After Williamsport defeated Brooklyn 7-2 in Game One, second baseman Michael Cockrell tied Game Two in the late innings with one of his three RBIs in the game. The Crosscutters won it in the 11th when outfielder Milver Reyes singled home outfielder Anthony Bocchino. Speedy outfielder Nyjer Morgan, who led the league in hits and ranked second in batting and steals, led the Cutters' offense, shortstop Javier Guzman anchored the defense and lefties Tom Gorzelanny and Paul Maholm kept opposing hitters at bay.

"We just needed guys to get big hits and we got them," Williamsport manager Andy Stewart said. "This was a great bunch of guys and we won't forget this championship for the rest of the season and the rest of our lives."

The Doubledays dominated the regular season. The Blue Jays stocked the Auburn club with college talent, and it ran away with the league's best record despite the promotions of shortstop Aaron Hill, a first-round pick in June, and righthander Jamie Vermilyea. Auburn set a franchise record for wins and led the league in hitting, pitching and fielding.

Hill pounded NY-P pitchers for a month, hitting .361-4-34 before getting promoted to the high Class A Florida State League. Other promising players on the team included righty Josh Banks, lefty Kurt Isenberg, shortstop Juan Paralta and first baseman Vito Chiaravalloti. Chiaravalloti, a Richmond product drafted by Toronto in the 15th round, became the first NY-P player in 31 years to capture the triple crown. He hit .351-12-67 and led the league in on-base and slugging percentage, making him an easy choice as the league MVP.

"In all my years as a manager on all levels of baseball, I was never associated with a finer bunch of young athletes," Auburn manager Dennis Holmberg said. "This team had the ability and skills to win the championship, but it wasn't to be."

The New York-Penn League enjoyed its share of premium talent, with 10 first-round picks making their pro debuts in the league. Aberdeen lefthander Adam Loewen, the fourth overall pick in 2002, signed as a draft-and-follow in May and debuted with Aberdeen. The 6-foot-6 lefty fanned 25 in 23 innings while allowing only 13 hits, but was shut down early to limit his innings.

Loewen's Aberdeen teammate, outfielder Nick Markakis, was the Orioles' first-round pick in 2003. He hit .283 but missed more than two weeks when he represented Greece at the European Championships in July. He was the league's top prospect, and managers said the two-time Baseball America Junior College Player of the Year had only scratched the surface of his ability.

Plenty of fans got to see Aberdeen's prized prospects, especially on the road, as the team was forced on a 17-day, 16-game road trip in August when the Cal Ripken World Series was being held at their home park.

The league continued to have robust attendance, and the Brooklyn Cyclones again led the way. Overall crowds were down a bit because many teams lost dates to weather, but averages generally held steady. The Cyclones again averaged better than 8,000 fans a game, and their average and overall attendance of 307,383 easily led all short-season teams.

STANDINGS

Page	McNAMARA	W	L	PCT	GB	Manager	Attendance	Avg.	Last Penn.
200	Brooklyn Cyclones (Mets)	47	28	.627	—	Tim Teufel	307,383	8,308	2001
221	Williamsport Crosscutters (Pirates)	46	30	.605	1½	Andy Stewart	83,346	2,253	2003
82	Aberdeen IronBirds (Orioles)	38	38	.500	9½	Joe Almaraz	234,143	6,162	1983
257	Hudson Valley Renegades (Devil Rays)	37	37	.500	9½	Dave Howard	146,613	4,312	1999
229	New Jersey Cardinals (Cardinals)	31	42	.425	15	Tommy Shields	117,220	3,349	1994
192	Staten Island Yankees (Yankees)	29	43	.403	16½	Andy Stankiewicz	163,342	4,807	2002
Page	**STEDLER**	**W**	**L**	**PCT**	**GB**	**Manager(s)**	**Attendance**	**Avg.**	**Last Penn.**
135	Oneonta Tigers (Tigers)	45	30	.600	—	Randy Ready	48,905	1,397	1998
149	Tri-City ValleyCats (Astros)	44	32	.579	1½	Ivan DeJesus	103,984	2,971	1997
91	Lowell Spinners (Red Sox)	39	35	.527	5½	Jon Deeble/Lynn Jones	175,000	5,000	None
184	Vermont Expos (Expos)	19	56	.253	26	Dave Barnett	101,431	2,669	1996
Page	**PINCKNEY**	**W**	**L**	**PCT**	**GB**	**Manager**	**Attendance**	**Avg.**	**Last Penn.**
272	Auburn Doubledays (Blue Jays)	56	18	.757	—	Dennis Holmberg	65,047	1,807	1998
121	Mahoning Valley Scrappers (Indians)	38	36	.514	18	Ted Kubiak	141,889	4,300	None
214	Batavia Muckdogs (Phillies)	30	45	.400	26½	Luis Melendez	42,801	1,157	1963
142	Jamestown Jammers (Marlins)	22	51	.301	33½	Benny Castillo	53,469	1,573	1991

PLAYOFFS—Semifinals: Williamsport defeated Auburn 2-0 and Brooklyn defeated Oneonta 2-1 in best-of-3 series. **Final:** Williamsport defeated Brooklyn 2-0 in best-of-3 series.

NOTE: Team's individual batting and pitching statistics can be found on page indicated in lefthand column.

2003 NEW YORK-PENN LEAGUE STATISTICS

CLUB BATTING

	AVG	G	AB	R	H	2B	3B	HR	BB	SO	SB
Auburn	.283	74	2485	454	703	141	19	56	361	583	46
Mahoning Valley	.267	74	2471	365	659	137	23	48	242	541	61
Williamsport	.265	76	2539	354	673	129	30	20	188	427	65
Oneonta	.261	75	2529	352	661	117	46	25	224	515	73
Tri-City	.251	76	2501	349	629	138	21	31	217	463	70
Lowell	.248	74	2400	348	594	132	20	31	290	597	96
Brooklyn	.241	75	2401	291	579	105	15	25	246	563	103
New Jersey	.239	73	2426	282	579	106	29	15	227	498	81
Jamestown	.236	73	2376	282	561	98	19	31	217	618	87
Staten Island	.235	72	2456	281	576	101	22	29	233	585	83
Hudson Valley	.234	74	2440	281	572	106	25	29	218	607	49
Batavia	.227	75	2497	266	568	107	28	27	237	615	107
Aberdeen	.227	76	2476	294	562	111	27	27	267	537	113
Vermont	.215	75	2392	215	515	81	12	22	229	574	55

CLUB PITCHING

	ERA	G	CG	SHO	SV	IP	H	R	ER	BB	SO
Auburn	2.52	74	0	10	25	650	493	217	182	188	698
Williamsport	2.64	76	1	8	21	662	545	244	194	225	550
Brooklyn	2.97	75	0	11	37	658	547	244	217	214	561
Staten Island	3.12	72	2	4	14	651	613	327	226	251	544
Hudson Valley	3.16	74	1	10	21	645	605	286	227	198	487
Lowell	3.21	74	0	6	17	646	644	313	230	143	482
Aberdeen	3.29	76	1	1	25	680	615	308	249	234	636
Tri-City	3.41	76	0	7	21	662	546	292	251	290	631
Batavia	3.50	75	1	2	15	678	626	333	264	230	513
Oneonta	3.68	75	0	4	22	653	610	318	267	245	532
New Jersey	3.75	73	0	4	17	645	638	331	269	263	509
Mahoning Valley	3.75	74	0	4	15	641	628	330	267	229	536
Vermont	4.61	75	1	1	11	640	625	427	328	338	478
Jamestown	5.61	73	0	1	14	624	696	444	389	348	566

CLUB FIELDING

	PCT	PO	A	E	DP		PCT	PO	A	E	DP
Auburn	.975	1950	727	68	50	Mahoning	.968	1922	783	89	65
Williamsport	.970	1985	794	86	55	Aberdeen	.967	2041	742	94	40
Brooklyn	.970	1975	751	85	55	Jamestown	.967	1871	705	89	59
Oneonta	.969	1958	789	87	62	Lowell	.963	1937	794	105	68
New Jersey	.969	1935	820	88	62	Hudson Valley	.961	1935	803	112	64
Tri-City	.969	1985	769	89	60	Staten Island	.958	1954	792	121	48
Batavia	.968	2034	855	95	66	Vermont	.955	1920	770	126	52

INDIVIDUAL BATTING LEADERS

(Minimum 205 Plate Appearances)

	AVG	G	AB	R	H	2B	3B	HR	RBI	BB	SO	SB
Chiaravolloti, Vito, Auburn	.351	68	228	47	80	20	1	12	67	47	48	0
Morgan, Nyjer, Williamsport	.343	72	268	49	92	7	4	0	23	33	44	26
Giarratano, Tony, Oneonta	.328	47	189	31	62	11	4	3	27	12	22	9
Rodland, Eric, Oneonta	.328	57	244	43	80	15	8	0	27	17	25	13
Bocchino, Anthony, Williamsport	.326	59	215	26	70	13	6	0	29	15	28	5
Cota, Carlo, Auburn	.320	51	169	31	54	13	3	5	34	27	45	3
Ryan, Brendan, New Jersey	.311	53	193	20	60	14	4	0	13	14	25	11
Robinson, Chris, Tri-City	.306	58	209	36	64	8	2	3	29	9	28	4
Kirkland, Kody, Oneonta	.303	67	254	46	77	15	11	4	49	25	60	14
Goleski, Ryan, Mahoning Valley	.296	64	243	39	72	15	2	8	37	21	66	3

INDIVIDUAL PITCHING LEADERS

(Minimum 61 Innings)

	W	L	ERA	G	GS	CG	SV	IP	H	R	ER	BB	SO
Torrealba, Yoann, Williamsport	6	1	2.04	14	14	0	0	75	61	24	17	15	60
Mastny, Tom, Auburn	8	0	2.26	14	14	0	0	64	56	19	16	12	68
Banks, Josh, Auburn	7	2	2.43	15	15	0	0	67	58	21	18	10	81
DeLeon, Joey, Tri-City	5	3	2.47	17	14	0	0	87	67	30	24	26	68
Karstens, Jeff, Staten Island	4	2	2.54	14	10	0	0	67	63	22	19	16	53
Tata, Jordan, Oneonta	4	3	2.58	16	12	0	1	73	64	32	21	20	60
Gangi, Aaron, Hudson Valley	5	2	2.63	14	14	0	0	75	75	33	22	10	59
Plexico, Jeremy, Vermont	3	3	2.69	17	9	0	1	70	59	26	21	16	49
Libey, Justin, Batavia	4	4	2.78	17	9	0	1	68	68	31	21	24	63
Dixon, Zach, Aberdeen	4	3	2.91	14	14	0	0	68	65	26	22	18	70

ALL-STAR TEAM

C—Paul Richmond, Auburn; Danilo Sanchez, Oneonta. **1B**—Vito Chiaravalloti, Auburn. **2B**—Eric Rodland, Oneonta. **3B**—Kody Kirkland, Oneonta. **SS**—Aaron Hill, Auburn. **Util IF**—Tony Giarratano, Oneonta. **OF**—Josh Anderson, Tri-City; Ryan Goleski, Mahoning Valley; Nyjer Morgan, Williamsport; A.J. Porfirio, Auburn. **DH**—Mike Madrid, Williamsport. **RHP**—Brian Bannister, Brooklyn; Matt Lindstrom, Brooklyn. **LHP**—Aaron Gangi, Hudson Valley; Kurt Isenberg, Auburn.

Most Valuable Player: Vito Chiaravalloti, Auburn. **Manager of the Year:** Dennis Holmberg, Auburn. **Most Outstanding Prospect:** Aaron Hill, Auburn.

DEPARTMENT LEADERS

BATTING

G	Josh Anderson, Tri-City	74
	Ian Bladergroen, Brooklyn	74
AB	Josh Anderson, Tri-City	297
R	Juan Peralta, Auburn	62
H	Nyjer Morgan, Williamsport	92
TB	Vito Chiaravalloti, Auburn	138
XBH	Jake Blalock, Batavia	35
2B	Brock Koman, Tri-City	25
	Ryan Mulhern, Mahoning Valley	25
3B	Kody Kirkland, Oneonta	11
HR	Vito Chiaravalloti, Auburn	12
RBI	Vito Chiaravalloti, Auburn	67
SH	Nyjer Morgan, Williamsport	10
SF	Matt Murton, Lowell	7
BB	Kevin Jordan, Lowell	49
IBB	Bryan Hansen, Batavia	5
HBP	Scott Dierks, Jamestown	18
SO	Brad Snyder, Mahoning Valley	82
SB	Javon Moran, Batavia	27
CS	Nyjer Morgan, Williamsport	17
GIDP	Ryan Roberts, Auburn	10
OBP	Vito Chiaravalloti, Auburn	.469
SLG	Vito Chiaravalloti, Auburn	.605

PITCHING

G	Three tied at	30
GS	Four tied at	15
CG	Seven tied at	1
ShO	Jarrod Farrell, Hudson Valley	1
GF	Bubbie Buzachero, Auburn	26
SV	Chris Homer, Oneonta	15
	Bob Paulk, Brooklyn	15
W	Tom Mastny, Auburn	8
L	Anthony Pearson, Vermont	11
IP	Joey De Leon, Tri-City	87
H	Brandon Harmsen, Staten Island	95
R	Nick Long, Vermont	65
ER	Nick Long, Vermont	56
HR	Adam Bostick, Jamestown	9
	Joe Diefenderfer, Batavia	9
HB	Davey Penny, Lowell	11
BB	Anthony Pearson, Vermont	54
SO	Matt Albers, Tri-City	94
WP	Anthony Pearson, Vermont	16
BK	Four tied at	3

FIELDING

C	AVG	Jeff Mackor, Tri-City	.994
	PO	Carlos Rosario, Staten Island	405
	A	Matt Pagnozzi, New Jersey	66
	E	Carlos Rosario, Staten Island	10
	DP	Three tied at	4
	PB	Salomon Manriquez, Vermont	16
1B	AVG	Joe Mather, New Jersey	.994
	PO	Ian Bladergroen, Brooklyn	571
	A	Bryan Hansen, Batavia	56
	E	Gabriel Martinez, Hudson Valley	11
	DP	Ryan Bear, Jamestown	48
		Ian Bladergroen, Brooklyn	48
2B	AVG	Eric Rodland, Oneonta	.970
	PO	Kevin Estrada, New Jersey	123
	A	Melvin Reyes, Lowell	167
	E	Melvin Reyes, Lowell	16
	DP	Eric Rodland, Oneonta	35
3B	AVG	Kevin Kouzmanoff, MV	.964
	PO	Hector Zamora, Staten Island	49
	A	Kevin Kouzmanoff, MV	126
	E	Claudio Arias, Lowell	23
	DP	Brock Koman, Tri-City	15
SS	AVG	David Reaver, Brooklyn	.961
	PO	Bryan Bass, Aberdeen	106
		Aneudi Cuevas, Hudson Valley	106
	A	Aneudi Cuevas, Hudson Valley	197
	E	Bryan Bass, Aberdeen	22
	DP	Aneudi Cuevas, Hudson Valley	40
OF	AVG	Jarod Rine, Aberdeen	1.000
	PO	Mitch Jones, Hudson Valley	162
	A	Matt Rico, Hudson Valley	10
	E	Lorvin Louisa, Vermont	8
	DP	Kory Casto, Vermont	3

NORTHWEST LEAGUE

SHORT-SEASON CLASS A

BY WILL KIMMEY

The Spokane franchise planned a celebration for its 100th anniversary season, but the city had to plan another party before the year was over: a victory celebration. The Indians posted the league's best record at 50-26 to win the Eastern Division by five games, and then finished the job by winning their second league title since 1999.

"This year has been a fun year," said Spokane's Darryl Kennedy, who was named the league's manager of the year. "I'm going to remember it for a long time."

While 2003 started as a season of looking back at the club's history, Spokane opened a new chapter by beginning its first year as a Texas Rangers affiliate after eight years as a Kansas City Royals farm team. That was the only affiliation change in the league from 2002.

BILL MITCHELL

Wes Littleton

Nine of the Rangers' first 12 picks in the June draft found themselves in Spokane at some point during the season. That included a handful of polished college pitchers, led by fourth-round pick Wes Littleton, who helped the club lead the league with a 3.39 ERA. The Cal State Fullerton product got to the league a little late because of his team's trip to the College World Series, and fell eight innings short of qualifying for the ERA title. He went 6-0, 1.56.

Littleton also threw six shutout innings as Spokane blanked Western Division champ Salem-Keizer 10-0 in the first game of the playoffs. The Indians closed out the Volcanoes in three straight games.

Spokane also dominated the league offensively, scoring 52 more runs than any other team while tying Salem-Keizer in batting, at .267. Outfielder Jeremy Cleveland led the league with 64 runs while ranking second in batting to teammate Dane Bubela (.323) by one point. Cleveland, an eighth-round pick out of North Carolina, stayed hot in the finals, going 4-for-11 with a homer, six RBIs and four runs scored.

"(Cleveland) plays with tremendous confidence," Vancouver manager Dennis Rogers said. "The ball sounds different coming off his bat. He might be the sleeper of the league, drafted where he was."

College players drafted in 2003 also populated the rest of the league. Many of them remained in the league for the entire season despite putting up strong numbers that could have warranted promotions.

"It seems like a lot of clubs left their draft choices here," Salem-Keizer manager Joe Strain said. "It was a pretty tough league, and if you don't have older kids, you'll get beat up. But it was very even and no team seemed overmatched."

The Diamondbacks' first- and second-rounders, Conor Jackson and Jamie D'Antona, powered Yakima to the league's second-best record at 45-31. Jackson, named the league MVP, ripped a league-record 35 doubles and paced the circuit with 60 RBIs. D'Antona tied Salem-Keizer's Brad Vericker for the league lead in homers with 15.

Vericker teamed with catcher Todd Jennings and third baseman Nate Schierholtz to lead an impressive Volcanoes offensive attack. Schierholtz, a surprise second-round pick by the Giants, hit .306 and showed plus power potential at age 19. Jennings, also a second-rounder, ranked 10th in the league in average, and managers rated him the best defensive catcher.

Volcanoes teammates Jesse Floyd and Pat Misch formed a solid righty-lefty combination at the front of the rotation and kept hitters off balance with superior command despite less than dominating stuff. Floyd paced the league with a 1.73 ERA, while Misch ranked third at 2.18.

BILL MITCHELL

Nathan Schierholtz

"They throw lots of strikes, neither was overpowering, and both were solid pitchers," Strain said, "but because Misch is left-handed, he gets an extra point."

The league's most dominating pitcher, however, was Everett righthander Felix Hernandez. The 17-year-old Mariners prospect went 7-2, 2.29 with 73 strikeouts in 55 innings before receiving a promotion to low Class A Wisconsin. He ranked as the league's best prospect.

"He's not raw at all," Kennedy said. "The only rawness is that he is 17 years old. He's one of the better young prospects on the mound in this league in a while."

Hernandez' teammate, righthander Troy Cate, produced the league's best single-game pitching efforts with a pair of three-hitters in a year when the Northwest League did not feature a no-hitter.

STANDINGS

Page	EAST	W	L	PCT	GB	Manager	Attendance	Avg.	Last Penn.
265	Spokane Indians(Rangers)	50	26	.658	—	Darryl Kennedy	170,640	4,612	2003
68	Yakima Bears (Diamondbacks)	45	31	.592	5	Bill Plummer	60,037	1,580	2000
128	Tri-City Dust Devils (Rockies)	33	43	.434	17	Ron Gideon	58,976	1,552	None
105	Boise Hawks (Cubs)	27	49	.355	23	Steve McFarland	104,156	2,741	2002
Page	**WEST**	**W**	**L**	**PCT**	**GB**	**Manager**	**Attendance**	**Avg.**	**Last Penn.**
243	Salem-Keizer Volcanoes (Giants)	43	33	.566	—	Joe Strain	119,556	3,146	2001
236	Eugene Emeralds (Padres)	39	37	.513	4	Roy Howell	130,657	3,438	1980
207	Vancouver Canadians (Athletics)	35	41	.461	8	Dennis Rogers	137,026	3,606	None
250	Everett AquaSox (Mariners)	32	44	.421	11	Pedro Grifol	110,043	2,896	1985

PLAYOFFS—Spokane defeated Salem-Keizer 3-0 in best-of-5 final for league championship.

NOTE: Team's individual batting and pitching statistics can be found on page indicated in lefthand column.

MINOR LEAGUES

2003 NORTHWEST LEAGUE STATISTICS

CLUB BATTING

	AVG	G	AB	R	H	2B	3B	HR	BB	SO	SB
Salem-Keizer	.267	76	2638	397	705	126	20	41	291	505	51
Spokane	.267	76	2597	454	694	138	25	44	375	551	45
Everett	.260	76	2565	361	666	109	19	35	244	537	117
Yakima	.257	76	2588	402	664	153	22	39	301	580	96
Vancouver	.256	76	2553	326	654	136	14	22	347	505	54
Eugene	.246	76	2588	346	636	104	22	36	251	610	99
Boise	.233	76	2534	269	590	99	19	54	175	636	73
Tri-City	.228	76	2526	289	575	120	20	36	251	631	42

CLUB PITCHING

	ERA	G	CG	SHO	SV	IP	H	R	ER	BB	SO
Spokane	3.38	76	0	7	26	677	609	289	254	258	513
Eugene	3.69	76	0	3	20	679	605	339	279	307	654
Yakima	3.74	76	0	7	22	676	650	355	281	267	559
Salem-Keizer	3.77	76	0	5	23	680	670	343	285	268	552
Tri-City	3.84	76	0	5	19	676	667	348	288	237	439
Vancouver	4.06	76	0	3	18	671	690	373	303	240	585
Boise	4.13	76	0	6	18	669	625	401	307	319	634
Everett	4.45	76	0	2	19	663	668	396	328	339	619

CLUB FIELDING

	PCT	PO	A	E	DP		PCT	PO	A	E	DP
Spokane	.977	2030	865	69	70	Vancouver	.963	2013	742	105	31
Salem-Keizer	.969	2039	853	93	79	Eugene	.963	2038	719	107	64
Tri-City	.968	2027	874	97	77	Yakima	.959	2029	778	120	62
Everett	.966	1988	740	95	53	Boise	.956	2007	770	128	60

INDIVIDUAL BATTING LEADERS

(Minimum 205 Plate Appearances)

	AVG	G	AB	R	H	2B	3B	HR	RBI	BB	SO	SB
Bubela, Dane, Spokane	.323	62	229	51	74	18	5	4	35	46	62	7
Cleveland, Jeremy, Spokane	.322	64	245	64	79	20	3	7	53	40	50	5
Jackson, Conor, Yakima	.319	68	257	44	82	35	1	6	60	36	41	3
Orlandos, Nick, Everett	.317	69	265	41	84	13	4	2	31	12	22	14
Hornostaj, Aaron, Salem-Keizer	.311	64	257	38	80	9	1	2	33	19	30	10
Kim, Eddie, Vancouver	.305	65	239	26	73	17	0	4	39	35	52	1
Blakeley, Eric, Everett	.303	59	195	31	59	9	2	3	24	19	36	13
Coutlangus, Jon, Salem-Keizer	.301	51	176	34	53	7	3	1	24	25	31	7
Wahlbrink, Brian, Eugene	.300	69	270	45	81	17	4	4	34	28	82	19
Jennings, Todd, Salem-Keizer	.296	59	233	27	69	9	2	3	32	15	36	5

INDIVIDUAL PITCHING LEADERS

(Minimum 61 Innings)

	W	L	ERA	G	GS	CG	SV	IP	H	R	ER	BB	SO
Floyd, Jesse, Salem-Keizer	6	4	1.73	14	14	0	0	83	67	18	16	19	76
Knox, Brad, Vancouver	6	3	2.06	15	12	0	0	70	55	21	16	18	63
Misch, Pat, Salem-Keizer	7	5	2.18	14	14	0	0	87	78	33	21	20	61
Farnum, Matt, Spokane	5	1	2.39	17	13	0	0	75	70	22	20	17	57
Thompson, Sean, Eugene	7	1	2.48	15	15	0	0	80	58	28	22	39	97
Marshall, Sean, Boise	5	6	2.57	14	14	0	0	74	66	31	21	23	88
Wells, Jared, Eugene	4	6	2.75	14	14	0	0	79	77	34	24	32	53
Marsden, Aaron, Tri-City	4	3	2.79	13	10	0	1	61	49	21	19	18	46
Lynch, Brian, Tri-City	4	3	2.84	14	14	0	0	70	66	30	22	20	48
Lo, Ching-Lung, Tri-City	3	7	2.85	14	14	0	0	76	66	27	24	27	48

ALL STAR-TEAM

C—Todd Jennings, Salem-Keizer. **1B**—Brian Dopirak, Boise. **2B**—Nick Orlandos, Everett. **3B**—Jamie D'Antona, Yakima. **SS**—Omar Quintanilla, Vancouver. **OF**—Jeremy Cleveland, Spokane; Conor Jackson, Yakima; Brian Wahlbrink, Eugene. **DH**—Brad Vericker, Salem-Keizer. **RHP**—Felix Hernandez, Everett. **LHP**—Sean Thompson, Eugene. **RHRP**—Eddie Bonine, Eugene; Dustin Glant, Yakima. **LHRP**—Clint Goocher, Yakima.

Most Valuable Player: Conor Jackson, Yakima. **Manager of the Year:** Darryl Kennedy, Spokane.

DEPARTMENT LEADERS

BATTING

G	Peeter Ramos, Eugene	74
AB	Peeter Ramos, Eugene	290
R	Jeremy Cleveland, Spokane	64
H	Nick Orlandos, Everett	84
TB	Jamie D'Antona, Yakima	140
XBH	Conor Jackson, Yakima	42
2B	Conor Jackson, Yakima	35
3B	Sandy Almonte, Tri-City	9
HR	Jamie D'Antona, Yakima	15
	Brad Vericker, Salem-Keizer	15
RBI	Conor Jackson, Yakima	60
SH	Aaron Hornostaj, Salem-Keizer	11
SF	Jeremy Cleveland, Spokane	6
	Josh Kreuzer, Spokane	6
BB	Andrew Wishy, Spokane	54
IBB	Conor Jackson, Yakima	4
HBP	Brian Rose, Yakima	16
SO	Ryan Fox, Tri-City	82
	Brian Wahlbrink, Eugene	82
SB	Steve Garrabrants, Yakima	30
CS	Chris Colton, Everett	9
	Chris Walker, Boise	9
GIDP	Eduardo Cornejo, Vancouver	13
OBP	Dane Bubela, Spokane	.436
SLG	Brad Vericker, Salem-Keizer	.547

PITCHING

G	Leonel Rosales, Eugene	36
GS	Michael McGirr, Vancouver	16
CG	Several tied at	0
ShO	Several tied at	0
GF	Dustin Glant, Yakima	32
SV	Dustin Glant, Yakima	18
W	Rob Corrado, Spokane	8
L	Four tied at	7
IP	Patrick Misch, Salem-Keizer	87
H	Manuel Corpas, Tri-City	98
R	Manuel Corpas, Tri-City	61
ER	Manuel Corpas, Tri-City	54
HR	Five tied at	7
HB	Audy Alcantara, Everett	11
	Tomas Santiago, Tri-City	11
BB	Daniel Portorreal, Salem-Keizer	48
SO	Richard Hall, Boise	99
WP	Stephen Schilsky, Vancouver	11
BK	Henry Perez, Eugene	5

FIELDING

C	AVG	Brian Rose, Yakima	.992
	PO	Brian Rose, Yakima	355
	A	James Sweeney, Tri-City	47
	E	Alan Rick, Boise	8
	DP	Douglas Clark, Spokane	3
		Alan Rick, Boise	3
	PB	Alan Rick, Boise	14
1B	AVG	Christopher Alexander, Spo.	.992
	PO	Travis Ishikawa, Salem-Keizer	589
	A	Travis Ishikawa, Salem-Keizer	55
	E	Travis Ishikawa, Salem-Keizer	11
		Fernando Valenzuela, Eugene	11
	DP	Travis Ishikawa, Salem-Keizer	67
2B	AVG	Abigail Sandoval, Spokane	.980
	PO	Peeter Ramos, Eugene	134
	A	Peeter Ramos, Eugene	215
	E	Peeter Ramos, Eugene	21
	DP	Aaron Hornostaj, Salem-Keizer	48
3B	AVG	Adam Fox, Spokane	.962
	PO	Adam Fox, Spokane	45
	A	Adam Fox, Spokane	160
	E	Jamie D'Antona, Yakima	15
	DP	Adam Fox, Spokane	18
SS	AVG	Oswaldo Navarro, Everett	.937
	PO	Oswaldo Navarro, Everett	118
	A	Adam Haley, Yakima	194
	E	Adam Haley, Yakima	24
	DP	Timothy Hutting, Salem-Keizer	41
OF	AVG	Adam Bourassa, Spokane	.994
	PO	Adam Bourassa, Spokane	146
	A	Adam Bourassa, Spokane	9
		Samuel Bradford, Jr., Everett	9
	E	Trey George, Tri-City	6
	DP	Three tied at	2

APPALACHIAN LEAGUE

ROOKIE

BY BILL BALLEW

The names of legends can be found atop the grandstands at Elizabethton's Joe O'Brien Field. While such players as Kirby Puckett, Kent Hrbek and Gary Gaetti reside in the memories of many Minnesotans, they also have their place in the hearts of fans in the northeast corner of Tennessee, where for the past three decades the Elizabethton Twins have sent minor leaguers to cut their teeth in the professional ranks.

SPORTS ON FILM

Dusty Gomon

More memories were created in 2003, when the E-Twins used one of the minors' best balances of hitting and pitching to post the second-best regular-season record (42-24) in the Rookie-level Appalachian League before defeating Martinsville in the three-game playoffs.

After the Astros won Game One, 4-3, on Lance Koenig's three-run homer in the seventh inning and Elizabethton emerged with Game Two, 4-2, the E-Twins' Brock Peterson took matters into his own hands. Peterson, Minnesota's 49th-round draft pick in 2002, scored the tying run in the ninth inning on J.R. Taylor's sacrifice fly before driving in Dusty Gomon with a game-winning single in the top of the 10th to give Elizabethton a 5-3 triumph.

"We might not have had players like Puckett or Hrbek or even Joe Mauer this year, but we had a group of guys that are fundamentally sound players and never give up," said E-Twins manager Ray Smith, who spent his 16th season on the Elizabethton staff.

Elizabethton led the Appy League with a 3.13 ERA. Righthander Chris Schutt (5-2, 1.98), voted the righthander on the league's year-end all-star team after topping the circuit with 72 strikeouts, headed the rotation, followed by Errol Simonitsch (5-1, 1.76) and Evan Meek (7-1, 2.47), who was rated the league's 11th-best prospect.

All-star first baseman Dusty Gomon recovered from a rough start in the Midwest League to top the charts with 14 home runs in his second stint in the league. Gomon combined with Kyle Phillips, the league leader in RBIs with 49, to give Elizabethton an outstanding one-two punch.

Martinsville, the owners of a league-best 42-23 record, featured its share of talent. The Astros led the league with a team average of .287, 11 points higher than second-place Pulaski. All-stars Ervin Alcantara (.344) and Saul Torres (.324) ranked among the top 10 hitters. The team also had steady starting pitching with Mitch Talbot, ranked the 12th-best prospect; Chance Douglass, who missed the playoffs due to an injured knee; and Ronnie Martinez, one of the league's most consistent pitchers during the season. Righthander Felipe Paulino, the league's 16th-ranked prospect, reached triple digits on the radar gun and could emerge as a premier closer.

While both Martinsville and Elizabethton had solid clubs, no team featured more talented depth on the mound than Burlington.

Reminiscent of what was seen at Burlington Athletic Stadium in 2001, when the B-Tribe sent the likes of J.D. Martin, Travis Foley and Dan Denham to the hill, the Cleveland affiliate continued to stockpile arms with top Appy prospect Adam Miller (0-4, 4.96), Rafael Perez, (9-3, 1.70), Nick Pesco (3-1, 1.82) and Aaron Laffey (3-1, 2.91). Miller was the 31st overall pick in the June draft, while Perez earned league pitcher of the year honors after leading the league in ERA and wins.

CARL KLINE

Adam Miller

A few managers, among them Elizabethton's Smith, thought the overall talent in the league was down in 2003 compared to recent seasons.

Some skippers pointed to Appy League player of the year Tyler Davidson as an example of the lack of complete players in the league. Davidson hit .337-10-35 and easily paced the circuit with a .669 slugging percentage. His defensive shortcomings, however, left most managers wondering where he would play. Gomon, Pulaski catcher Robinzon Diaz (who led the AL with a .374 batting average) and, to a lesser extent, Phillips and Cardinals' first-round pick Daric Barton fell into the same category.

STANDINGS

Page	EAST	W	L	PCT	GB	Manager	Attendance	Avg.	Last Penn.
150	Martinsville Astros (Astros)	42	23	.646	—	Jorge Orta	27,821	897	1999
75	Danville Braves (Braves)	36	30	.545	6½	Kevin McMullan	35,621	1,149	None
122	Burlington Indians (Indians)	37	31	.544	6½	Rouglas Odor	37,380	1,133	1993
83	Bluefield Orioles (Orioles)	23	40	.365	18	Don Buford	22,853	846	2001
258	Princeton Devil Rays (Devil Rays)	23	41	.359	18½	Jamie Nelson	26,339	878	1994
Page	**WEST**	**W**	**L**	**PCT**	**GB**	**Manager**	**Attendance**	**Avg.**	**Last Penn.**
177	Elizabethton Twins (Twins)	42	24	.636	—	Ray Smith	24,004	828	2003
273	Pulaski Blue Jays (Blue Jays)	38	29	.567	4½	Paul Elliott	21,828	728	None
98	Bristol Sox (White Sox)	33	33	.500	9	Jerry Hairston	19,770	732	2002
230	Johnson City Cardinals (Cardinals)	27	36	.429	13½	Ron Warner	31,261	1,158	1976
201	Kingsport Mets (Mets)	25	39	.391	16	Mookie Wilson	19,108	682	1995

PLAYOFFS—Elizabethton defeated Martinsville 2-1 in best-of-3 series for league championship.

NOTE: Team's individual batting and pitching statistics can be found on page indicated in lefthand column.

2003 APPALACHIAN LEAGUE STATISTICS

CLUB BATTING

	AVG	G	AB	R	H	2B	3B	HR	BB	SO	SB
Martinsville	.286	65	2172	335	622	146	12	30	225	440	43
Pulaski	.276	68	2226	372	614	143	15	30	267	491	34
Elizabethton	.265	66	2204	385	585	101	16	47	274	494	83
Johnson City	.262	64	2116	316	555	99	15	44	217	508	32
Bristol	.253	66	2106	303	533	126	20	41	149	491	76
Kingsport	.250	64	2060	259	515	119	21	31	189	482	72
Princeton	.249	64	2011	281	501	76	18	13	209	504	99
Burlington	.244	68	2314	316	565	95	18	30	214	485	70
Danville	.244	66	2138	266	522	107	14	22	202	500	93
Bluefield	.238	63	2037	263	484	90	7	35	201	484	59

CLUB PITCHING

	ERA	G	CG	SHO	SV	IP	H	R	ER	BB	SO
Elizabethton	3.13	66	0	8	12	555	470	244	193	219	581
Danville	3.29	66	0	2	19	576	535	276	211	212	514
Martinsville	3.54	65	0	2	25	556	512	274	219	215	507
Burlington	3.70	68	0	6	15	602	562	293	248	229	592
Bristol	3.99	66	1	8	13	550	536	291	244	218	524
Bluefield	4.00	63	0	4	10	535	540	286	238	196	467
Princeton	4.43	64	1	2	10	525	549	350	258	250	415
Kingsport	4.46	64	0	2	16	536	549	329	266	190	489
Johnson City	4.70	64	3	3	15	536	601	367	280	200	377
Pulaski	4.73	68	1	2	19	572	642	386	301	218	413

CLUB FIELDING

	PCT	PO	A	E	DP		PCT	PO	A	E	DP
Burlington	.964	1807	709	93	41	Elizabethton	.958	1664	675	103	47
Bristol	.964	1651	647	86	46	Bluefield	.957	1606	636	101	49
Danville	.963	1729	683	93	51	Martinsville	.956	1669	699	109	58
Kingsport	.960	1608	543	90	41	Johnson City	.952	1604	702	117	62
Pulaski	.958	1716	784	110	63	Princeton	.946	1574	632	127	49

INDIVIDUAL BATTING LEADERS

(Minimum 184 Plate Appearances)

	AVG	G	AB	R	H	2B	3B	HR	RBI	BB	SO	SB
Diaz, Robinzon, Pulaski	.374	48	182	33	68	20	2	1	44	10	14	1
Alcantara, Ervin, Martinsville	.344	54	195	25	67	18	0	2	33	19	39	1
Davidson, Tyler, Kingsport	.337	50	172	29	58	11	8	10	35	15	36	3
Frisella, Paul, Johnson City	.337	60	175	36	59	13	0	8	37	24	51	1
Perodin, Ron, Elizabethton	.335	50	170	35	57	8	3	0	23	19	34	15
Haerther, Cody, Johnson City	.332	63	226	31	75	12	6	3	39	22	30	2
Torres, Saul, Martinsville	.318	57	214	40	68	19	3	0	25	27	33	3
Brown, Travis, Bluefield	.315	48	165	27	52	11	0	1	15	15	27	15
Valido, Robert, Bristol	.307	58	215	39	66	15	2	6	31	17	28	17
Reiman, Joey, Pulaski	.301	59	206	47	62	18	2	1	35	32	46	1

INDIVIDUAL PITCHING LEADERS

(Minimum 54 Innings)

	W	L	ERA	G	GS	CG	SV	IP	H	R	ER	BB	SO
Perez, Rafael, Burlington	9	3	1.70	13	12	0	0	69	56	23	13	16	63
Pesco, Nick, Burlington	3	1	1.82	13	13	0	0	54	36	16	11	22	55
Schutt, Chris, Elizabethton	5	2	1.98	11	10	0	0	55	37	23	12	21	72
Perez, Carlos, Bluefield	5	5	2.01	12	11	0	0	58	52	23	13	11	58
Petit, Yusmeiro, Kingsport	3	3	2.32	12	12	0	0	62	47	19	16	8	65
Douglass, Chance, Martinsville	5	1	2.34	10	10	0	0	58	50	17	15	10	48
Martinez, Ronnie, Martinsville	6	4	2.39	12	12	0	0	64	61	29	17	11	56
Talbot, Mitch, Martinsville	4	4	2.83	12	12	0	0	54	45	26	17	11	46
Collins, Danny, Danville	1	6	2.87	14	14	0	0	63	63	32	20	19	47
MacLane, Evan, Kingsport	4	1	2.88	14	6	0	0	56	59	20	18	8	57

ALL-STAR TEAM

C—Robinzon Diaz, Pulaski. **1B**—Dusty Gomon, Elizabethton. **2B**—Jeremy Acey, Pulaski; Mike Hanson, Danville. **3B**—Saul Torres, Martinsville. **SS**—Robert Valido, Bristol. **Util IF**—Brandon Pinckney, Burlington. **OF**—Ervin Alcantara, Martinsville; Matt Esquivel, Danville; Chris Young, Bristol. **Util OF**—Sal Frisella, Johnson City. **DH**—Tyler Davidson, Kingsport. **RHP**—Chris Schutt, Elizabethton. **LHP**—Rafael Perez, Burlington. **RP**—Celso Rondon, Kingsport.

Player of the Year: Tyler Davidson, Kingsport. **Pitcher of the Year:** Rafael Perez, Burlington. **Manager of the Year:** Jorge Orta, Martinsville.

DEPARTMENT LEADERS

BATTING

G	Ben Thomas, Danville	66
AB	Brandon Pinckney, Burlington	257
R	Brock Peterson, Elizabethton	53
H	Cody Haerther, Johnson City	75
TB	Dusty Gomon, Elizabethton	120
XBH	Tyler Davidson, Kingsport	29
	Dusty Gomon, Elizabethton	29
2B	Robinzon Diaz, Pulaski	20
3B	Tyler Davidson, Kingsport	8
HR	Dusty Gomon, Elizabethton	15
RBI	Kyle Phillips, Elizabethton	49
SH	Jayce Tingler, Pulaski	7
SF	Robert Valido, Bristol	5
BB	Jayce Tingler, Pulaski	46
IBB	Tyler Davidson, Kingsport	3
HBP	Jeremy Acey, Pulaski	14
SO	Dusty Gomon, Elizabethton	85
SB	Chad Cooper, Princeton	25
CS	Willie James, Danville	10
GIDP	Coltyn Simmons, Princeton	10
OBP	Paul Frisella, Johnson City	.434
SLG	Tyler Davidson, Kingsport	.669

PITCHING

G	Richal Acosta, Bluefield	28
GS	Danny Collins, Danville	14
CG	Six tied at	1
ShO	Miguel Aguero, Johnson City	1
	Tim Tisch, Bristol	1
GF	Dewan Day, Pulaski	24
SV	Dewan Day, Pulaski	12
W	Rafael Perez, Burlington	9
L	Trevor Caughey, Bluefield	7
IP	Miguel Aguero, Johnson City	71
H	Miguel Aguero, Johnson City	76
R	Orlando Rengel, Kingsport	42
ER	Three tied at	32
HR	Chris Neylan, Pulaski	9
HB	Three tied at	8
BB	Dan Mead, Danville	31
SO	Chris Schutt, Elizabethton	72
WP	Chris Schutt, Elizabethton	15
BK	Three tied at	5

FIELDING

C	AVG	Cesar Castillo, Bristol	.993
	PO	Kevin Davidson, Martinsville	291
	A	Kevin Davidson, Martinsville	44
	E	Danilo Reynoso, Kingsport	11
		Ernest Woodruff, Princeton	11
	DP	Jose Acosta, Martinsville	4
		Cesar Castillo, Bristol	4
	PB	Daric Barton, Johnson City	10
		Danilo Reynoso, Kingsport	10
1B	AVG	Dusty Gomon, Elizabethton	.993
	PO	Tim Thurman, Bluefield	441
	A	Dusty Gomon, Elizabethton	32
	E	Tim Thurman, Bluefield	13
	DP	Kevin Vital, Martinsville	38
2B	AVG	Chad Cooper, Princeton	.967
	PO	Mike Hanson, Danville	95
	A	Luis Colina, Johnson City	128
	E	Lance Koenig, Martinsville	14
	DP	Mike Hanson, Danville	27
		Emmanuel Sena, Pulaski	27
3B	AVG	Ben Thomas, Danville	.942
	PO	Melvin Perez, Bristol	40
		Tanner Wootan, Johnson City	40
	A	Saul Torres, Martinsville	118
	E	Brock Peterson, Elizabethton	24
	DP	Ben Thomas, Danville	8
SS	AVG	Brandon Pinckney, Burlington	.953
	PO	Winfield Garcia, Martinsville	94
	A	Brandon Pinckney, Burlington	170
	E	Winfield Garcia, Martinsville	20
	DP	Winfield Garcia, Martinsville	32
OF	AVG	Paul Frisella, Johnson City	1.000
	PO	Jayce Tingler, Pulaski	124
	A	Dominique Partridge, Danville	10
	E	Roberto Solano, Kingsport	11
	DP	Three tied at	3

PIONEER LEAGUE

ROOKIE

BY BILL BALLEW

Talk about your fantastic finishes. The Billing Mustangs and righthander Jim Paduch showed a flair in the Pioneer League's final week by winning the 2003 championship in a most unexpected manner.

Despite finishing in last place in the Northern Division during the second half, the Mustangs earned a wild-card spot on the next-to-last day of the campaign with an overall mark of 41-35. Billings then outlasted Helena, which won both half-season titles, in three games in the semifinals before sweeping the championship series from Provo in two games. Paduch captured the flag for the Mustangs with a no-hitter 3-0 victory over the Angels, giving the Cincinnati affiliate its second PL title in three years and its 10th since 1974.

RODGER WOOD

Habelito Hernandez

The 20-year-old Paduch put together a near-perfect outing in 55-degree weather during the finale. After going 7-1 in 15 regular season starts while ranking second in the circuit with a 1.94 ERA, Paduch faced 28 Provo batters. The righthander walked two, erasing one on a double play, and 76 of his 104 pitches were strikes.

Paduch became the first pitcher to throw a no-hitter in the league since Idaho Falls' Domingo Guzman accomplished the feat on Aug. 15, 1996, and the first to toss a no-hitter in a championship series game since Billings' Peter Grimm whiffed Calgary in the first matchup of the 1983 finals.

Billings posted the lowest winning percentage (.539) for a league champion since the split-season schedule debuted in 1995, defeating a Provo team that tied the record for most regular season wins (54). The Angels also led the league in batting (.304), home runs (70), runs (538) and hits (817).

Pacing Provo was the team's lone member of the year-end all-star team, Warner Madrigal, who led the league in runs (75), hits (103), doubles (28) and extra-base hits (39). Madrigal was the league's seventh-best prospect, three places behind catcher Bobby Wilson, who led the PL with 62 RBIs while battling an ailing wrist.

While Billings led the PL with a team ERA of 3.26, Provo also had its share of pitching. Abel Moreno won all 10 of his decisions to earn a promotion to Class A Cedar Rapids before returning to Utah for the playoffs.

STANDINGS: SPLIT SEASON

FIRST HALF					SECOND HALF				
NORTH	**W**	**L**	**PCT**	**GB**	**NORTH**	**W**	**L**	**PCT**	**GB**
Helena	25	13	.658	—	Helena	23	15	.605	—
Billings	24	14	.632	1	Missoula	18	20	.474	5
Great Falls	20	18	.526	5	Great Falls	18	20	.474	5
Missoula	18	20	.474	7	Billings	17	21	.447	6
SOUTH	**W**	**L**	**PCT**	**GB**	**SOUTH**	**W**	**L**	**PCT**	**GB**
Provo	24	14	.632	—	Provo	30	8	.789	—
Ogden	18	20	.474	6	Ogden	17	21	.447	13
Casper	12	26	.316	12	Casper	16	22	.421	14
Idaho Falls	11	27	.289	13	Idaho Falls	13	25	.342	17

PLAYOFFS—Semifinals: Billings defeated Helena 2-1 and Provo defeated Ogden 2-1 in best-of-3 series. **Final:** Billings defeated Provo 2-0 in best-of-3 final.

Daniel Davidson, the Angels' starter in the finale against the Mustangs' Paduch, led the loop with a 1.64 ERA. Strong-armed reliever Carlos Morban showed after a demotion from the Midwest League that he could have the highest ceiling by displaying a mid-90s fastball and a power curveball.

Among prospects, no one made a more favorable impression than Casper third baseman Ian Stewart. Taken by the Rockies out of a California high school with the ninth overall pick in the June draft, Stewart overpowered the league by lacing line drives to all fields while batting .317-10-43. Righthander Chad Billingsley headed a prospect-laden Ogden club that included outfielder Xavier Paul, lefthander Mike Megrew, shortstop Chin-Lung Hu and righthander Marcos Carvajal.

A couple of other players had their seasons cut short due to injuries, yet still showed promise during their stints in the PL. Helena catcher Lou Palmisano, ranked as the loop's third-best prospect, was named the PL most valuable player after leading the league in average (.391), on-base percentage (.458) and slugging percentage (.592) before breaking his left ankle in mid-August. Billings second baseman Habelito Hernandez, the No. 6 prospect, hit .377-8-32 during the first half of the short-season circuit, only to receive a promotion to the Carolina League after missing a couple of weeks with a separated shoulder.

Two outfielders at Great Falls showed solid promise during brief stints in the league. Brian Anderson and Ryan Sweeney displayed the overall packages that led to their being the White Sox' first two picks in the 2003 draft. Anderson's time was cut short with a wrist injury, while Sweeney got a 10-game taste of the PL in late August and September after making his professional debut in the Rookie-level Appalachian League.

STANDINGS: OVERALL

Page		W	L	PCT	GB	Manager(s)	Attendance	Avg.	Last Penn.
61	Provo Angels (Angels)	54	22	.710	—	Tom Kotchman	56,856	1,672	1981
170	Helena Brewers (Brewers)	48	28	.632	6	Ed Sedar	47,493	1,284	1984
113	Billings Mustangs (Reds)	41	35	.539	13	Rick Burleson/Jay Sorg	122,090	3,213	2001
99	Great Falls White Sox (White Sox)	38	38	.500	16	Chris Cron	114,603	3,183	2002
69	Missoula Osprey (Diamondbacks)	36	40	.474	18	Tony Perezchica	51,236	1,423	1999
163	Ogden Raptors (Dodgers)	35	41	.461	19	Travis Barbary	126,706	3,424	None
129	Casper Rockies (Rockies)	28	48	.368	26	P.J. Carey	51,427	1,390	None
237	Idaho Falls Padres (Padres)	24	52	.316	30	Carlos Lezcano	57,854	1,522	2000

NOTE: Team's individual batting and pitching statistics can be found on the page indicated in lefthand column.

2003 PIONEER LEAGUE STATISTICS

CLUB BATTING

	AVG	G	AB	R	H	2B	3B	HR	BB	SO	SB
Provo	.304	76	2691	538	817	198	22	70	294	598	44
Great Falls	.291	76	2670	468	778	151	25	62	269	636	63
Helena	.288	76	2617	456	755	125	18	33	273	492	142
Billings	.281	76	2640	451	742	143	28	69	256	724	51
Casper	.275	76	2684	389	739	119	31	47	220	643	96
Ogden	.272	76	2603	416	709	144	35	40	246	614	66
Idaho Falls	.254	76	2583	341	655	138	21	33	227	545	68
Missoula	.252	76	2537	347	639	111	21	45	184	513	82

CLUB PITCHING

	ERA	G	CG	SHO	SV	IP	H	R	ER	BB	SO
Billings	3.22	76	0	4	25	662	655	343	237	251	579
Provo	3.62	76	0	4	26	661	693	344	266	196	591
Helena	3.93	76	1	5	27	662	711	373	289	208	600
Ogden	4.58	76	0	1	15	657	715	449	335	275	690
Great Falls	4.89	76	2	3	15	666	759	443	362	228	599
Casper	5.11	76	1	1	15	665	799	513	378	267	544
Missoula	5.12	76	3	3	19	653	733	445	372	262	554
Idaho Falls	5.55	76	0	1	16	652	769	496	402	282	608

CLUB FIELDING

	PCT	PO	A	E	DP		PCT	PO	A	E	DP
Missoula	.963	1959	818	107	55	Ogden	.954	1971	785	134	57
Helena	.960	1987	780	115	66	Great Falls	.952	1998	788	142	69
Provo	.959	1984	822	121	64	Casper	.947	1995	852	160	51
Idaho Falls	.954	1955	735	129	67	Billings	.945	1987	794	162	66

INDIVIDUAL BATTING LEADERS

(Minimum 205 Plate Appearances)

	AVG	G	AB	R	H	2B	3B	HR	RBI	BB	SO	SB
Palmisano, Lou, Helena	.391	47	174	32	68	13	2	6	43	18	29	13
Nanita, Ricardo, Great Falls	.384	47	185	38	71	7	4	5	37	17	28	11
Madrigal, Warner, Provo	.369	70	279	75	103	28	2	9	51	12	58	2
Kendrick, Howie, Provo	.368	63	234	65	86	20	3	3	36	24	28	8
Bolivar, Luis, Billings	.349	55	235	57	82	20	3	9	42	17	32	12
Trofholz, Terry, Helena	.349	68	261	60	91	10	3	0	22	19	39	39
Perez, Miguel, Billings	.339	60	227	46	77	11	2	1	25	18	27	1
Ramirez, Manuel, Helena	.330	63	218	36	72	19	1	11	52	23	48	0
Pali, Matt, Provo	.327	64	223	47	73	15	3	8	43	32	44	2
Bounds, Brandon, Great Falls	.326	72	279	51	91	20	5	9	47	18	58	3

INDIVIDUAL PITCHING LEADERS

(Minimum 61 Innings)

	W	L	ERA	G	GS	CG	SV	IP	H	R	ER	BB	SO
Davidson, Dan, Provo	8	2	1.64	15	13	0	0	71	65	17	13	15	50
Paduch, James, Billings	7	1	1.94	15	15	0	0	79	72	28	17	20	65
Moreno, Abel, Provo	10	0	2.38	13	10	0	0	68	58	23	18	10	79
Knoff, Justin, Billings	7	4	2.83	14	11	0	0	76	76	32	24	19	53
Hawk, Derek, Billings	5	3	2.97	14	12	0	1	70	70	30	23	16	53
Rocha, Angel, Missoula	5	8	3.12	15	15	1	0	92	79	43	32	26	82
Kloosterman, Greg, Helena	6	1	3.28	14	14	0	0	69	68	28	25	23	76
Megrew, Mike, Ogden	5	3	3.40	14	14	0	0	77	64	40	29	24	99
Ramirez, Carlos, Helena	7	3	3.46	15	15	1	0	78	78	34	30	17	60
Arias, Alberto, Casper	4	4	3.58	13	13	1	0	73	69	45	29	23	64

ALL STAR-TEAM

C—Lou Palmisano, Helena. **1B**—Brandon Bounds, Great Falls. **2B**—Habelito Hernandez, Billings. **3B**—Ian Stewart, Casper. **SS**—Luis Bolivar, Billings. **OF**—Warner Madrigal, Provo; Ricardo Nanita, Great Falls; Terry Trofholz, Helena. **DH**—Billy Hogan, Idaho Falls. **RHP**—Abel Moreno, Provo. **LHP**—Daniel Davidson, Provo. **RP**—Dana Eveland, Helena.

Most Valuable Player: Lou Palmisano, Helena. **Pitcher of the Year:** Abel Moreno, Provo. **Manager of the Year:** Ed Sedar, Helena.

DEPARTMENT LEADERS

BATTING

G	Agustin Murillo, Missoula	74
AB	Brandon Bounds, Great Falls	279
	Warner Madrigal, Provo	279
R	Warner Madrigal, Provo	75
H	Warner Madrigal, Provo	103
TB	Warner Madrigal, Provo	162
XBH	Warner Madrigal, Provo	39
2B	Warner Madrigal, Provo	28
3B	Three tied at	6
HR	Casey Fuller, Casper	12
	Walter Olmstead, Billings	12
RBI	Bobby Wilson, Provo	62
SH	Cory Haggerty, Great Falls	14
SF	Three tied at	5
BB	Joey Votto, Billings	56
IBB	Three tied at	3
HBP	Ryan Carter, Ogden	12
SO	Ben Himes, Billings	87
SB	Terry Trofholz, Helena	39
CS	Mike Myers, Great Falls	9
GIDP	Bobby Wilson, Provo	11
OBP	Joey Votto, Billings	.452
SLG	Lou Palmisano, Helena	.592

PITCHING

G	Adam Bright, Casper	33
GS	Larry Robles, Casper	16
CG	Seven tied at	1
ShO	Several tied at	0
GF	Ryan Klatt, Idaho Falls	31
SV	Alex Cremidan, Missoula	15
W	Abel Moreno, Provo	10
L	William Ponce, Idaho Falls	11
IP	Brandon McCarthy, Great Falls	101
H	Larry Robles, Casper	114
R	Juan Morillo, Casper	73
ER	David Cuen, Ogden	58
HR	David Cuen, Ogden	12
	Joel Santo, Idaho Falls	12
HB	Sean Tracey, Great Falls	14
BB	John Allender, Missoula	42
SO	Brandon McCarthy, Great Falls	125
WP	John Allender, Missoula	15
	Jordan Pratt, Ogden	15
BK	Walin Cabrera, Billings	4

FIELDING

C	AVG	Bobby Wilson, Provo	.985
	PO	Miguel Perez, Billings	445
	A	Russ Martin, Ogden	63
	E	Miguel Perez, Billings	17
	DP	Miguel Perez, Billings	7
	PB	Russ Martin, Ogden	27
1B	AVG	Joey Votto, Billings	.979
	PO	Joey Votto, Billings	517
	A	Joey Votto, Billings	36
	E	Brandon Bounds, Great Falls	13
	DP	Joey Votto, Billings	48
2B	AVG	Guilder Rodriguez, Helena	.972
	PO	Guilder Rodriguez, Helena	146
	A	Howie Kendrick, Provo	183
	E	Howie Kendrick, Provo	17
	DP	Guilder Rodriguez, Helena	43
3B	AVG	Agustin Murillo, Missoula	.948
	PO	Agustin Murillo, Missoula	43
		Ian Stewart, Casper	43
	A	Matt Brown, Provo	131
	E	Luis Castillo, Ogden	20
	DP	Matt Brown, Provo	13
SS	AVG	Mike Myers, Great Falls	.935
	PO	Mike Myers, Great Falls	101
	A	Chin-Lung Hu, Ogden	165
	E	Pedro Strop, Casper	29
	DP	Miike Myers, Great Falls	34
OF	AVG	Terry Trofholz, Helena	.989
	PO	Terry Trofholz, Helena	165
	A	Jon Kaplan, Missoula	12
	E	Juan Mosqueda, Casper	12
	DP	Three tied at	3

ARIZONA LEAGUE

ROOKIE

BY ALLAN SIMPSON

When several big league clubs scrambled to align with new affiliates in the traditional short-season leagues after the 2002 season, the resulting game of musical chairs left the Kansas City Royals holding the bag. With no openings elsewhere, it forced them to field two teams in the complex-based Arizona League.

BILL MITCHELL

Mitch Maier

The league granted an exception to the rule that prohibits clubs from having more than eight players that are 20 or older, though the more experienced of the Royals teams (Royals-2) was declared ineligible for post-season play. It hardly mattered as the team went 32-22 and would have failed to qualify for the playoffs any way.

That team—not to mention the entire league—was upstaged by Royals-1, a younger, sleeker outfit that not only won the Arizona League title, beating the Rangers in a one-game playoff, but dominated Baseball America's annual manager's survey of the league's top prospects. Kansas City's pair of first-round picks, outfielder Chris Lubanski and catcher Mitch Maier, both made the top five.

Lubanski hit .326-4-27 and Maier .350-2-45 overall to spark Royals-1 to a 17-7 record in the first half of a split-season schedule. That earned them a spot in the playoffs against the Rangers, who went 20-5 in the second half.

In a one-game showdown, the Royals took an early 4-0 lead and hung on to beat the Rangers 4-2 as lefthander Dustin Hughes and righthander Carlos Sosa combined on a five-hitter. Sosa worked three hitless innings, striking out four, to earn a save. Catcher Adam Donachie and first baseman Brian McFall, the Nos. 7 and 9 hitters in the order, combined for three runs and five hits.

The Rangers were also new to the league in 2003. They shared a new complex in Surprise with both Royals teams. The complex also served as the new spring training home for the parent clubs of both those teams.

The Arizona League fielded seven teams in 2002 and, even with the addition of three clubs, had an odd number of teams again in 2003. The White Sox left the league as the Royals and Rangers moved their complex league operations from the Gulf Coast League.

STANDINGS: SPLIT SEASON

FIRST HALF	W	L	PCT	GB	SECOND HALF	W	L	PCT	GB
Royals-1	17	7	.708	—	Rangers	19	4	.826	—
Cubs	15	9	.625	2	Royals-2	17	9	.654	3½
Rangers	16	10	.615	2	Mariners	15	9	.625	4½
Mariners	14	10	.583	3	Royals-1	14	11	.560	6
Giants	14	10	.583	3	Angels	11	13	.458	8½
Royals-2	15	13	.536	4	Giants	11	14	.440	9
Angels	9	16	.360	8½	Brewers	10	14	.417	9½
Athletics	8	16	.333	9	Cubs	10	15	.400	10
Brewers	5	20	.200	12½	Athletics	7	17	.292	12½

PLAYOFFS—Royals-1 defeated Rangers in one-game playoff.

Overall, the Arizona League was a hitters' league, with several individual records set. As a team, Royals-1 hit .305—the highest team average in the minors.

Mariners outfielder Wladimir Balentien broke the league record for home runs in a season with 16, more than double his closest pursuer. Luis Garcia of the Mexican Baseball Academy held the previous record of 13, set in 1999.

Athletics second baseman Jorge Mejia, a career .247 hitter with five home runs overall in four previous seasons in the A's system, had a breakout season in 2003. He hit .377-7-30 while setting a league record with 84 hits.

Royals-1 shortstop Mike Aviles was named the NCAA Division II Player of the Year in the spring and followed that up by winning Arizona League MVP honors. If the Royals had a more advanced short-season club, the 22-year-old Aviles likely would never have set foot in a complex league. He hit .363-6-39 and led the league in runs and doubles.

Cubs outfielder Ryan Fitzgerald, a Creighton University product, led the league with a .381 average, marking the second year in a row that a Cubs non-drafted free agent topped the league in hitting. In 2002, Matt Creighton paced the league at .361.

While it was a predominantly hitter's league in 2003, Cubs starter Ronald Bay and Giants closer Leslie Nacar worked their way onto the league's top prospect list.

Bay, a 2002 low-round, draft-and-follow from Angelina (Texas) Junior College, led the league with seven wins while finishing second in strikeouts and third in ERA.

Nacar led the league with nine saves while posting a 0.95 ERA. He also struck out 14.9 batters per nine innings.

STANDINGS: OVERALL

Page		Complex Site	W	L	PCT	GB	Manager	Last Penn.
265	Rangers	Surprise	35	14	.714	—	Pedro Lopez	None
156	Royals-1	Surprise	31	18	.633	4	Kevin Boles	2003
251	Mariners	Peoria	29	19	.604	5½	Scott Steinmann	2000
157	Royals-2	Surprise	32	22	.593	5½	Lloyd Simmons	None
244	Giants	Scottsdale	25	24	.510	10	Bert Hunter	None
106	Cubs	Mesa	25	24	.510	10	Carmelo Martinez	2002
62	Angels	Mesa	20	29	.408	15	Brian Harper	None
208	Athletics	Phoenix	15	33	.313	19½	Ruben Escalera	2001
171	Brewers	Phoenix	15	34	.306	20	Hector Torres	1990

NOTE: Teams' individual batting and pitching statistics can be found on page indicated in left column.

2003 ARIZONA LEAGUE STATISTICS

CLUB BATTING

	AVG	G	AB	R	H	2B	3B	HR	BB	SO	SB
Royals-1	.307	55	1979	398	608	114	46	44	168	398	71
Mariners	.289	55	1939	341	561	100	32	31	215	409	71
Rangers	.286	56	1930	357	552	108	31	22	238	440	117
Royals-2	.282	54	1875	310	528	113	25	22	239	406	66
Athletics	.281	55	1942	333	545	104	19	39	201	416	32
Cubs	.276	56	1981	306	546	105	50	15	152	377	44
Brewers	.267	55	1911	284	511	96	27	12	170	447	79
Giants	.266	56	1896	281	505	89	41	14	190	466	81
Angels	.261	56	1944	288	508	86	40	20	182	509	58

CLUB PITCHING

	ERA	G	CG	SHO	SV	IP	H	R	ER	BB	SO
Royals-1	3.98	55	0	2	9	488	507	260	216	146	433
Rangers	4.05	56	0	1	16	506	532	294	228	151	396
Giants	4.33	56	0	3	13	489	496	284	235	222	503
Royals-2	4.42	54	0	1	16	479	508	286	235	150	459
Cubs	4.74	56	0	0	13	500	544	343	263	228	463
Mariners	4.86	55	0	2	12	488	530	329	264	213	381
Brewers	5.23	55	0	0	7	474	556	348	276	202	389
Angels	5.41	56	0	1	8	494	547	366	297	256	441
Athletics	5.73	55	0	2	11	484	644	388	308	187	403

CLUB FIELDING

	PCT	PO	A	E	DP		PCT	PO	A	E	DP
Royals-1	.962	1464	609	81	47	Mariners	.953	1465	655	104	40
Rangers	.960	1519	609	89	54	Brewers	.950	1422	568	105	43
Royals-2	.957	1436	535	88	39	Angels	.950	1481	576	109	49
Giants	.954	1466	560	98	50	Cubs	.949	1499	574	112	37
Athletics	.953	1451	549	98	44						

INDIVIDUAL BATTING LEADERS

(Minimum 151 Plate Appearances)

	AVG	G	AB	R	H	2B	3B	HR	RBI	BB	SO	SB
Fitzgerald, Ryan, Cubs	.381	54	202	37	77	14	8	7	44	18	43	9
Mejia, Jorge, Athletics	.377	50	223	48	84	17	6	7	30	15	46	7
Batista, Alex, Royals-1	.367	48	180	37	66	10	2	1	21	7	30	6
Aviles, Mike, Royals-1	.363	52	212	51	77	19	5	6	39	13	28	11
Maier, Mitch, Royals-1	.350	51	203	41	71	14	6	2	45	18	25	7
Acosta, Gilberto, Brewers	.349	50	189	43	66	8	4	1	26	20	30	30
Springer, Kenard, Royals-1	.346	49	182	35	63	15	1	3	39	10	20	7
Ogando, Alexi, Athletics	.342	48	190	33	65	13	1	7	36	7	42	5
Furtado, Micah, Rangers	.342	49	193	44	66	9	4	0	23	33	33	17
Sutton, Don, Athletics	.333	40	156	33	52	16	0	7	35	18	31	1

INDIVIDUAL PITCHING LEADERS

(Minimum 45 Innings)

	W	L	ERA	G	GS	CG	SV	IP	H	R	ER	BB	SO
Hawk, Tommy, Brewers	2	1	2.31	12	6	0	0	47	47	17	12	17	30
Millikan, Bryan, Giants	5	1	2.35	11	10	0	0	46	42	16	12	22	32
Bay, Ronald, Cubs	7	1	2.50	10	6	0	0	58	51	18	16	9	69
Hughes, Dustin, Royals-1	5	2	2.84	11	6	0	0	51	38	21	16	18	54
Gragg, John, Royals-2	3	2	3.45	13	13	0	0	60	63	27	23	10	55
Palmer, Lucas, Royals-1	6	0	3.62	14	7	0	1	55	55	28	22	17	50
Rosa, Carlos, Royals-1	5	3	3.63	15	11	0	0	69	79	36	28	18	54
Cox, Jason, Angels	3	3	3.81	10	10	0	0	50	58	28	21	11	37
Mullis, Jacob, Royals-2	4	3	3.82	13	13	0	0	64	75	34	27	7	57
Atencio, Greg, Royals-2	2	5	3.91	12	12	0	0	71	62	40	31	17	62

ALL-STAR TEAM

C—Mitch Maier, Royals-1. **1B**—Don Sutton, Athletics. **2B**—Jorge Mejia, Athletics. **3B**—Alexander Batista, Royals-1. **SS**—Michael Aviles, Royals-1. **OF**—Lizahio Baez, Rangers; Wladimir Balentien, Mariners; Ryan Fitzgerald, Cubs. **DH**—Wladimir Balentien, Mariners. **RHP**—Ronald Bay, Cubs. **LHP**—Dustin Hughes, Royals-1. **RHRP**—Leslie Nacar, Giants. **LHRP**—John Gragg, Royals-2.

Most Valuable Player: Michael Aviles, Royals-1. **Manager of the Year:** Pedro Lopez, Rangers.

DEPARTMENT LEADERS

BATTING

G	Michael Mooney, Giants	56
AB	Lizahio Baez, Rangers	223
	Jorge Mejia, Athletics	223
R	Mike Aviles, Royals-1	51
H	Jorge Mejia, Athletics	84
TB	Jorge Mejia, Athletics	134
XBH	Wladimir Balentien, Mariners	33
2B	Mike Aviles, Royals-1	19
3B	Brandon Powell, Royals-1	15
HR	Wladimir Balentien, Mariners	16
RBI	Lizahio Baez, Rangers	55
SH	Johany Abreu, Giants	9
SF	Four tied at	5
BB	Ryan Strain, Giants	41
IBB	Billy Boyer, Angels	2
HBP	Brandon Cashman, Rangers	21
SO	Chris Walston, Angels	88
SB	Gilberto Acosta, Brewers	30
CS	Chris Lubanski, Royals-1	10
GIDP	Four tied at	7
OBP	Micah Furtado, Rangers	.446
SLG	Wladimir Balentien, Mariners	.658

PITCHING

G	Mitchell Arnold, Angels	21
	Dusty Dossett, Royals-2	21
GS	Three tied at	13
CG	Several tied at	0
ShO	Several tied at	0
GF	Mitchell Arnold, Angels	20
SV	Leslie Nacar, Giants	9
W	Ronald Bay, Cubs	7
L	Adiel Sanchez, Athletics	6
	Carlos Villanueva, Giants	6
IP	Braulio Santana, Athletics	74
H	Braulio Santana, Athletics	88
R	Miguel Garcia, Brewers	46
	Pedro Rodriguez, Cubs	46
ER	Pedro Rodriguez, Cubs	39
HR	Cibney Bello, Mariners	8
HB	Karl Gelinas, Angels	10
BB	Ira Brown, Royals-2	50
SO	Carlos Marmol, Cubs	74
WP	Ira Brown, Royals-2	12
BK	Jonathan Ramos, Rangers	4

FIELDING

C	AVG	Dayton Buller, Giants	.992
	PO	Felipe Del Rosario, Royals-2	289
	A	Brett Martinez, Angels	41
	E	Maximo Felix, Giants	11
	DP	Brett Martinez, Angels	4
	PB	Oscar Bernard, Cubs	14
1B	AVG	Brian McFall, Royals-1	.988
	PO	Ian Gac, Rangers	396
	A	Ricky Pijuan, Brewers	29
	E	Billy Zbacnik, Giants	11
	DP	Ian Gac, Rangers	33
		Brian McFall, Royals-1	33
2B	AVG	Jorge Mejia, Athletics	.970
	PO	George Sandel, Mariners	98
	A	Brandon Powell, Royals-1	143
	E	Brandon Powell, Royals-1	10
	DP	Brandon Powell, Royals-1	30
3B	AVG	Lisandro Disla, Giants	.929
	PO	Pedro Ozoria, Mariners	35
	A	Pedro Ozoria, Mariners	101
	E	Alfredo Francisco, Cubs	13
	DP	Pedro Ozoria, Mariners	10
SS	AVG	Carlos Rojas, Cubs	.979
	PO	Mike Aviles, Royals-1	82
	A	Mike Aviles, Royals-1	141
	E	Antonio Pena, Rangers	17
	DP	Three tied at	26
OF	AVG	Lizahio Baez, Rangers	1.000
	PO	Brandon Cashman, Rangers	120
	A	Wladimir Balentien, Mariners	14
	E	Jose Yens, Giants	10
	DP	Adam Mannon, Brewers	3

GULF COAST LEAGUE

ROOKIE

BY ALLAN SIMPSON

The Braves hadn't posted a winning record in the Rookie-level Gulf Coast League in 10 years, but they did a sharp about-face in 2003.

With a roster dominated by early-round picks from the 2003 draft, the Braves went 38-22 to coast to the Eastern Division title. They then won three straight playoff games, beating the Pirates in a best-of-three final, 9-1 and 4-3, to capture their first league championship since 1964—the league's first year of existence. The Braves also placed five players on Baseball America's annual manager's survey of the league's top 20 prospects.

Lefthanders Jo Jo Reyes, Jake Stevens and Matt Harrison—all premium draft picks in June—started the three playoff games for the Braves, but a pair of unheralded southpaws led the team to the title.

RICK BATTLE

Eric Duncan

Dan Smith, who signed with the Braves in June as a non-drafted free agent and worked two innings of the Braves 4-3, 13-inning win over the Red Sox in a sudden-death semifinal, came on in relief of Harrison in the first inning of the deciding game against the Pirates. With his team down 3-0, he worked 6 1/3 scoreless innings, striking out 10, and became the game's winning pitcher when the Braves rallied with two runs apiece in the fourth and seventh innings. Lefty Devin Anderson, a 2002 28th-round draft-and-follow, pitched two scoreless innings to save the 4-3 win.

Stevens, a third-round pick, won the first game of the final series, allowing five hits over the first eight innings. He was the highest-ranking Braves prospect, ranking second overall among the league's 20 best.

Outfielder Steve Doetsch, a 14th-round pick out of Indian River (Fla.) Junior College, was the top offensive player for the Braves. He led the league in hits, total bases and home runs.

Unlike 2002, when players from Latin America occupied 12 of the first 13 spots in the top 20, including the first nine, just three Latin players were recognized a year later. Eleven players from the 2003 draft made the cut, including sweet-swinging third baseman Eric Duncan, the first-round pick of the Yankees who was judged by managers to have the best future in the game.

Duncan, one of only three first-round picks from the June draft to debut in the GCL, hit .278 with two homers in 47 games before being promoted to New York's New York-Penn affiliate at Staten Island, where he hit .373 to finish the year.

"He was the best hitting prospect in this league, by far," said Yankees manager Dan Radison, a former big league coach. "He's got excellent swing mechanics and power to all fields. He just needs a little more discipline with some of the pitches he swings at."

Marlins righthander Jeff Allison, the highest draft pick (16th overall) to play in the league, might have wrestled the No. 1 spot away from Duncan if he had worked enough innings to qualify. But he made just three starts after showing some minor discomfort in his shoulder after laying out for two months while negotiating a $1.85 million contract.

Allison impressed managers with his smooth mechanics, overpowering stuff, command of three pitches and hard-nosed approach.

The league fielded 12 clubs in 2003, down two from 2002. The Texas Rangers and Kansas City Royals moved their complex-based clubs from the GCL to the Arizona League as they opened a complex in Surprise, Ariz.

Marlins lefthander Jon-Michael Nickerson threw the only no-hitter of the season as he blanked the Braves 6-0 in the second game of a doubleheader on Aug. 15.

STANDINGS

Page	EAST	Complex Site	W	L	PCT	GB	Manager	Last Penn.
76	Braves	Kissimmee	38	22	.633	—	Ralph Henriquez	2003
164	Dodgers	Vero Beach	29	31	.483	9	Luis Salazar	1990
143	Marlins	Jupiter	26	32	.448	11	Tim Cossins	None
185	Expos	Melbourne	25	33	.431	12	Bobby Henley	1991
Page	**SOUTH**	**Complex Site**	**W**	**L**	**PCT**	**GB**	**Manager**	**Last Penn.**
91	Red Sox	Fort Myers	33	26	.559	—	Ralph Treuel	None
84	Orioles	Sarasota	32	28	.533	1½	Jesus Alfaro	None
177	Twins	Fort Myers	28	31	.475	5	Rudy Hernandez	None
114	Reds	Sarasota	26	34	.433	7½	Edgar Caceres	None
Page	**NORTH**	**Complex Site**	**W**	**L**	**PCT**	**GB**	**Manager**	**Last Penn.**
222	Pirates	Bradenton	36	20	.643	—	Woody Huyke	None
136	Tigers	Lakeland	28	29	.491	8½	Howard Bushong	None
192	Yankees	Tampa	26	31	.456	10½	Dan Radison	2001
215	Phillies	Clearwater	23	33	.411	13	Ruben Amaro	2002

PLAYOFFS: Semifinal—Braves defeated Red Sox in one-game playoff. **Final**: Braves defeated Pirates 2-0 in best-of-3 series.

NOTE: Teams' individual batting and pitching statistics can be found on page indicated in left column.

2003 GULF COAST LEAGUE STATISTICS

CLUB BATTING

	AVG	G	AB	R	H	2B	3B	HR	BB	SO	SB
Braves	.268	60	2011	291	538	93	20	32	194	398	54
Twins	.266	59	1941	244	516	84	27	9	149	318	68
Pirates	.263	56	1896	286	498	84	19	23	147	354	56
Red Sox	.253	59	1886	251	478	92	25	18	199	403	47
Reds	.251	60	1929	257	485	118	17	17	180	432	77
Dodgers	.249	60	1956	223	488	81	18	12	176	402	79
Phillies	.248	56	1799	241	447	86	24	23	189	496	55
Tigers	.244	57	1833	296	447	78	31	30	181	443	103
Orioles	.243	60	1840	282	448	81	18	16	284	434	79
Yankees	.235	57	1845	241	434	85	11	25	222	428	39
Marlins	.230	58	1825	193	419	71	11	16	174	443	57
Expos	.229	58	1787	205	409	69	9	15	182	399	26

CLUB PITCHING

	ERA	G	CG	SHO	SV	IP	H	R	ER	BB	SO
Dodgers	2.85	60	0	5	16	514	437	217	163	199	418
Red Sox	3.04	59	0	9	19	498	453	223	168	172	370
Braves	3.08	60	1	7	10	528	492	220	181	174	467
Yankees	3.21	57	2	5	7	484	438	224	173	173	494
Orioles	3.25	60	1	8	12	498	471	243	180	196	408
Marlins	3.28	58	2	6	12	496	441	223	181	197	434
Expos	3.52	58	0	4	16	484	484	252	189	156	323
Pirates	3.56	56	4	3	17	485	441	229	192	157	440
Reds	4.04	60	0	4	11	503	508	272	226	198	408
Phillies	4.19	56	2	5	15	463	482	294	216	175	368
Twins	4.22	59	0	4	16	501	495	296	235	246	401
Tigers	4.53	57	3	4	10	475	465	317	239	234	419

CLUB FIELDING

	PCT	PO	A	E	DP						
Braves	.966	1584	612	77	49	Dodgers	.959	1542	679	94	63
Expos	.965	1451	632	76	57	Twins	.958	1503	560	91	49
Orioles	.964	1495	574	78	47	Marlins	.957	1488	562	92	50
Red Sox	.963	1493	662	82	54	Pirates	.956	1456	523	91	57
Yankees	.962	1452	548	78	41	Tigers	.946	1424	552	112	38
Reds	.960	1509	635	90	48	Phillies	.945	1389	517	111	34

INDIVIDUAL BATTING LEADERS

(Minimum 162 Plate Appearances)

	AVG	G	AB	R	H	2B	3B	HR	RBI	BB	SO	SB
Mejia, Gilberto, Tigers	.360	44	175	36	63	11	9	5	29	13	29	23
Rutgers, Paul, Twins	.353	56	201	35	71	12	3	0	21	9	15	16
Apodaca, Luis, Expos	.340	43	156	20	53	7	2	0	19	15	18	1
Klemm, Chris, Phillies	.336	42	143	20	48	8	2	2	23	18	43	3
Gutierrez, Juan, Orioles	.335	55	194	29	65	11	4	4	40	27	27	5
Doetsch, Steve, Braves	.320	60	228	39	73	11	3	8	37	25	49	8
Solano, Solamdi, Pirates	.319	44	166	38	53	4	1	3	20	18	27	12
Loadenthal, Carl, Braves	.310	58	216	41	67	9	1	1	24	31	38	21
Patterson, Tarrence, Twins	.308	49	169	32	52	9	5	2	23	9	19	15
Hughes, Luke, Twins	.305	54	190	22	58	9	4	2	25	15	22	5

INDIVIDUAL PITCHING LEADERS

(Minimum 48 Innings)

	W	L	ERA	G	GS	CG	SV	IP	H	R	ER	BB	SO
Mendez, Wimer, Orioles	5	1	1.52	12	9	0	0	53	42	13	9	17	41
Russ, James, Marlins	1	2	1.63	11	7	0	1	50	33	12	9	15	46
Jackson, Kyle, Red Sox	5	2	1.85	12	12	0	0	58	40	14	12	11	37
Capps, Matt, Pirates	5	1	1.87	10	10	1	0	63	40	16	13	9	54
Nickerson, Jon-Michael, Marlins	5	1	1.87	12	12	1	0	53	36	15	11	23	50
Childs, Ryan, Orioles	5	1	1.99	12	7	0	0	54	46	15	12	11	40
Martinez, Javier, Twins	3	3	2.03	12	10	0	0	62	43	19	14	21	54
Ramirez, Luis, Orioles	6	4	2.12	12	11	0	0	59	45	17	14	14	76
Ochoa, Nehomar, Expos	2	2	2.19	9	9	0	0	49	37	15	12	19	29
Wilson, Joe, Phillies	4	2	2.24	11	9	0	0	52	44	20	13	17	58

ALL STAR-TEAM

C—Juan Gutierrez, Orioles. **1B**—Brad Rea, Pirates. **2B**—Paul Rutgers, Twins. **3B**—Luke Hughes, Twins. **SS**—Gilberto Mejia, Tigers. **OF**—Steve Doetsch, Braves; Chris Klemm, Phillies; Carl Loadenthal, Braves. **SP**—Matt Capps, Pirates. **RP**—Argimiro Guanchez, Red Sox.

Manager of the Year: Woody Huyke, Pirates.

DEPARTMENT LEADERS

BATTING

G	Steve Doetsch, Braves	60
	Carlos Moreta, Braves	60
AB	Steve Doetsch, Braves	228
R	Carl Loadenthal, Braves	41
H	Steve Doetsch, Braves	73
TB	Steve Doetsch, Braves	114
XBH	Gilberto Mejia, Tigers	25
2B	Jeff Urgelles, Reds	20
3B	Gilberto Mejia, Tigers	9
HR	Steve Doetsch, Braves	8
	Carlos Moreta, Braves	8
RBI	Juan Gutierrez, Orioles	40
SH	Martin Padro, Braves	5
	Josh Fulton, Pirates	5
SF	Mike Costello, Orioles	5
BB	Nate Spears, Orioles	40
IBB	Juan Gutierrez, Orioles	5
HBP	Three tied at	8
SO	Kenny Lewis, Reds	66
SB	Kenny Lewis, Reds	37
CS	Three tied at	9
GIDP	Four tied at	7
OBP	Mike Costello, Orioles	.436
SLG	Gilberto Mejia, Tigers	.611

PITCHING

G	Carlos Alvarez, Dodgers	22
GS	Three tied at	12
CG	Luis Munoz, Pirates	2
ShO	Seven tied at	1
GF	Carlos Alvarez, Dodgers	17
	Eulogio Delacruz, Tigers	17
SV	Willy Galvez, Red Sox	9
W	Three tied at	6
L	Scott Mathieson, Phillies	7
IP	Matt Capps, Pirates	63
H	Felipe Garcia, Tigers	66
R	Scott Mathieson, Phillies	42
ER	Scott Mathieson, Phillies	36
HR	Cristhian Martinez, Tigers	9
HB	Isaiah Wright, Expos	11
BB	Alex Merricks, Twins	37
SO	Luis Ramirez, Orioles	76
WP	Alex Merricks, Twins	14
BK	Gabriel Sosa, Expos	6

FIELDING

C	AVG	Jeff Urgelles, Reds	.993
	PO	Jeff Urgelles, Reds	250
	A	Jarrod Saltalamacchia, Braves	35
	E	Jarrod Saltalamacchia, Braves	8
	DP	Three tied at	4
	PB	Gregory Najac, Twins	11
1B	AVG	Victor Hamisevicz, Expos	.993
	PO	David Sutherland, Dodgers	470
	A	David Sutherland, Dodgers	26
	E	Johnny Woodard, Twins	13
	DP	David Sutherland, Dodgers	47
2B	AVG	Cole Seifrig, Marlins	.991
	PO	Martin Prado, Braves	105
	A	Cole Seifrig, Marlins	127
	E	Etanislao Abreu, Dodgers	11
	DP	Cole Seifrig, Marlins	33
3B	AVG	Eric Duncan, Yankees	.898
	PO	John Santiago, Pirates	31
	A	Wilkin Ramirez, Tigers	86
	E	Wilkin Ramirez, Tigers	21
	DP	Jimmy Rohan, Dodgers	14
SS	AVG	Nate Spears, Orioles	.934
	PO	Jonathan Fulton, Marlins	79
	A	Lucas May, Dodgers	143
	E	Jonathan Fulton, Marlins	22
	DP	Jonathan Fulton, Marlins	29
OF	AVG	Steve Doetsch, Braves	1.000
	PO	Steve Doetsch, Braves	139
	A	Wanell Severino, Pirates	9
	E	Timi Moni-Erigbali, Phillies	9
	DP	Four tied at	3

LATIN AMERICA

SUMMER LEAGUES

DOMINICAN SUMMER LEAGUE

Every Pittsburgh Pirates farm club reached post-season play in 2003, and their entry in the Dominican Summer League was no exception.

The Pirates posted the poorest record of the DSL's five division champions, but dispatched the Yankees I in the semifinals and the Diamondbacks in the final to win their first league title. The Yankees (.727) and Diamondbacks (.708) had posted the best records during the regular season.

Manager of the year Ramon Zapata guided the Pirates to a 3-1 win over the Diamondbacks in the best-of-five championship series, but Pirates farm director Brian Graham credited Esteban Beltre, who oversees player development in the Dominican, for most of the organization's turnaround in Latin America.

"He's the guy who's responsible for really getting us a solid core of players there," said Graham of the former major league shortstop for the White Sox, Rangers and Red Sox. "He's really tied it altogether. I give all the credit for our success to Esteban and our scouting department."

Led by all-star shortstop Alexander Peralta (.333-4-35), catcher Kelington Made (.295-3-32) and lefthander Keily Arias (7-3, 2.34), the Pirates finished first in the San Pedro de Macoris Division, one game ahead of the Blue Jays. But the team had plenty of momentum heading into the playoffs.

The Yankees I boasted the league's top pitcher and position player. Lefthander Jonny Cordova dominated the DSL, going 8-0, 0.36 with 66 strikeouts and just two walks in 50 innings. First baseman Raul Dominguez tore through Dominican pitching, leading the league with 46 RBIs.

The league grew from 34 teams in 2002 to to a record 35 in 2003. The Athletics, Braves, Dodgers, Indians, Red Sox and Yankees all fielded two clubs, with the Tribe leading the way with a combined .628 winning percentage. Tampa Bay did not field a team and the Expos shared a team with the Diamondbacks.

The league's third annual all-star game was suspended in the top of the third inning due to torrential rains and was subsequently cancelled.

"We're hoping we can make the all-star game a regular tradition in the Dominican Summer League," league president Freddy Jana said. "It means a lot to the players and the fans here. We've had a great response in the past two games and it's very important to the league to make it an annual event."

—CHRIS KLINE

STANDINGS

SANTO DOMINGO EAST	W	L	PCT	GB
Diamondbacks	46	19	.708	—
Cardinals	38	27	.585	8
Rockies	38	28	.576	8½
Dodgers I	33	31	.516	12½
Giants	34	34	.500	13½
Tigers	29	39	.426	18½
Red Sox I	28	38	.424	18½
Diamondbacks/Expos	17	47	.266	28½
SANTO DOMINGO NORTH	**W**	**L**	**PCT**	**GB**
Athletics II	43	25	.632	—
Dodgers II	38	28	.576	4
Phillies	37	32	.536	6½
Brewers	34	32	.515	8
Athletics I	26	40	.394	16
Red Sox II	23	44	.343	19½
SANTO DOMINGO WEST	**W**	**L**	**PCT**	**GB**
Yankees I	48	18	.727	—
Padres	35	31	.530	13
Twins	33	35	.485	16
Yankees II	29	36	.446	18½
Reds	27	37	.422	20
Mets	26	41	.388	22½
SAN PEDRO de MACORIS	**W**	**L**	**PCT**	**GB**
Pirates	39	25	.609	—
Blue Jays	39	27	.591	1
Angels	34	30	.531	5
Astros	33	33	.500	7
Cubs	31	34	.477	8½
Orioles	28	37	.431	11½
Rangers	24	42	.364	16
CIBAO	**W**	**L**	**PCT**	**GB**
Indians II	41	24	.631	—
White Sox	41	26	.612	1
Braves II	39	27	.591	2½
Indians I	39	29	.574	3½
Braves I	36	28	.563	4½
Mariners	28	36	.438	12½
Royals	20	44	.313	20½
Marlins	18	48	.273	23½

PLAYOFFS: Quarterfinals—Yankees I defeated Athletics II 1-0 in sudden-death series. **Semifinals**—Pirates defeated Yankees I 2-1 and Diamondbacks defeated Indians II 2-0 in best-of-3 series. **Final**—Pirates defeated Diamondbacks 3-1 in best-of-5 series.

ALL-STAR TEAM: C—Pablo Sandoval, Giants. **1B**—Raul Dominguez, Yankees I. **2B**—Hernan Iribarrren, Brewers. **3B**—Maximiliano Ramirez, Braves II. **SS**—Alexander Peralta, Pirates. **OF**—Jose Cruceta, Astros; Eliezer Aguilar, Blue Jays; Gilbert Alcantara, White Sox. **DH**—Ivan Maldonado, Rangers. **RHP**—Jonny Cordova, Yankees I. **LHP**—Rafael Carela, Angels. **RP**—George Delgado, Rockies.

Player of the Year: Raul Dominguez, Yankees I. **Pitcher of the Year:** Jonny Cordova, Yankees I. **Manager of the Year:** Ramon Zapata, Pirates.

INDIVIDUAL BATTING LEADERS

(Minimum 150 At-Bats)

	AVG	AB	R	H	2B	3B	HR	RBI	SB
Aguilar, Eliezer, Blue Jays	**.368**	223	46	82	6	1	2	32	22
Sandoval, Pablo, Giants	.354	209	36	74	16	2	3	33	6
Iribarren, Hernan, Brewers	.344	227	43	78	12	**7**	2	27	17
Cruceta, Jose, Astros	.335	260	41	**87**	17	2	0	43	10
Peralta, Alexander, Pirates	.333	243	36	81	11	3	4	35	2
Rojas, Irwil, Yankees I	.326	178	24	58	12	1	1	29	3
Cabrera, Eduardo, Phillies	.319	188	31	60	6	2	2	34	7
Constanza, Jose, Indians I	.318	239	42	76	9	5	1	32	16
Valdez, Riquelvi, Rangers	.316	193	34	61	9	4	3	29	7
Dominguez, Raul, Yankees I	.316	225	42	71	17	1	5	**46**	1
Rodriguez, Michael, Braves I	.315	216	30	68	**20**	1	4	35	5
Morillo, Franklin, Phillies	.314	188	28	59	5	4	2	30	8
Granadillo, Antonio, Cardinals	.314	204	32	64	10	3	3	33	13
Rojas, Luis, D'backs/Expos	.313	201	31	63	15	0	4	30	6
Silva, Johan, Angels	.313	150	34	47	8	6	0	22	8
Nunez, Jose, Dodgers II	.313	195	25	61	18	0	5	24	0
Pacheco, Joel, Orioles	.312	237	35	74	14	3	3	32	24
Lugo, Henry, Mariners	.312	237	42	74	7	5	0	23	25
Civira, Jonathan, Cardinals	.310	200	31	62	10	6	1	34	16
Guerrero, Ben, D'backs/Expos	.310	155	23	48	10	0	3	19	0
Cordero, Octavio, Blue Jays	.309	256	52	79	5	4	0	21	**56**
Mora, Jesus, Dodgers I	.306	229	37	70	11	5	7	37	13
Ramirez, Maximiliano, Braves II	.305	177	27	54	16	1	5	43	5
Santana. Jeudy, White Sox	.305	233	48	71	9	5	0	22	20
Quinones, Carlos, Cubs	.304	224	37	68	11	2	0	26	6
Hernandez, Francisco, D'backs	.303	175	21	53	8	1	2	21	5
Castillo, Wilkin, D'backs	.301	196	32	59	9	4	1	29	6
Vechionacci, Marcos, Yankees I	.300	200	28	60	10	4	2	30	4
Alcantara, Gilbert, White Sox	.300	217	41	65	16	1	**10**	44	8
Florentino, Johnerys, Astros	.299	197	41	59	10	2	2	20	8
Arrieta, Julio, Brewers	.299	224	34	67	9	4	1	24	18

Vasquez, Juan, Athletics II	.299	204	40	61	7	4	1	24	21
Veintura, Juan Carlo, Indians I	.299	251	46	75	10	1	0	26	35
Feliz, Moises, Rockies	.299	221	31	66	9	1	0	20	3
Rodriguez, Wilkin, Tigers	.298	178	32	53	5	4	2	18	7
Hernandez, Francisco, White Sox	.296	216	34	64	14	0	6	29	9
Minaya, Cesar, Dodgers II	.296	169	22	50	7	1	7	28	5
Made, Kelintog, Pirates	.295	217	25	64	14	4	3	32	5
Rivadeneira, Deivis, Braves I	.295	190	33	56	9	3	1	19	8
Gabino, Gamalier, Indians II	.294	221	46	65	10	2	2	32	19
Almengor, Pedro, Braves II	.293	191	46	56	5	5	0	12	37
Maldonado, Juan, Rangers	.293	246	33	72	7	4	6	40	9
Palmares, Gregory, Cubs	.292	154	19	45	5	2	1	12	2
Herrera, Edgar, Tigers	.292	178	10	52	9	0	0	19	4
Hernandez, Edward, Astros	.291	261	27	76	11	2	1	42	4
Lisson, Mario, Royals	.290	210	26	61	11	1	3	28	9
De los Santos, Jose, White Sox	.290	248	32	72	15	1	1	30	11
Perez, Smerlin, Pirates	.290	224	39	65	6	5	1	18	13
Martinez, Frank, A's I/A's II	.289	218	47	63	16	2	3	35	14
Diaz, Javis, Padres	.286	203	44	58	11	4	0	22	27
Pujols, Kengshil, Dodgers II	.286	213	33	61	8	1	5	28	6
Morales, Saul, Cubs	.286	234	50	67	10	1	1	19	23
Arnedo, Roland, D'backs/Expos	.285	179	31	51	7	1	5	24	4
Perez, Eduardo, Dodgers II	.285	207	30	59	19	3	1	30	3
Perez, Argelis, Phillies	.285	193	22	55	9	2	2	17	7
Espinal, Edward, Red Sox I	.284	176	26	50	11	4	0	18	5
Gonzalez, Alberto, Expos/D'backs	.283	205	38	58	13	2	1	18	15
Arambarris, Manuel, Red Sox I	.282	195	28	55	7	2	0	24	4
Ovalles, Edwards, Twins	.281	221	39	62	10	2	9	37	12
De los Santos, Delby, Dodgers I	.281	221	27	62	18	3	5	37	3
Mijares, Carlos, Cardinals	.280	150	24	42	12	1	1	20	11
Parejo, Freddy, Brewers	.280	218	25	61	6	3	2	29	11
De la Cruz, Julio, Astros	.279	233	37	65	9	1	1	19	14
Valdes, Odannys, Twins	.278	198	41	55	12	1	1	17	14
Manzanillo, Ravelo, Phillies	.277	220	46	61	9	5	6	33	15
Batista, Norberto, Marlins	.277	184	17	51	9	0	0	19	10
Diaz, John, Athletics II	.275	211	40	58	11	1	1	25	29
Insunza, Miguel, Indians II	.275	207	25	57	8	2	0	18	5
Garcia, Jose, Cardinals	.274	197	21	54	5	3	2	20	17
Valdez, Manuel, Rockies	.273	172	26	47	5	1	1	16	11
Lara, Christian, Red Sox I	.273	256	52	70	7	1	0	22	24
Arredondo, Jose, Angels	.273	154	18	42	4	3	0	19	9
Avila, Angel, Orioles	.272	206	36	56	12	5	3	30	10
Rosario, Robinson, Braves I	.272	173	30	47	3	5	0	18	12
Zaranise, Luiz, Reds	.270	152	28	41	10	3	4	16	7
Acuna, Miguel, Red Sox II	.270	215	24	58	7	0	1	13	6
Gil, Jhonathan, Yankees II	.269	160	20	43	5	0	2	16	0
Hernandez, Eddy, Mariners	.269	197	24	53	9	1	0	10	1
Flores, Alexander, Indians II	.268	209	39	56	16	1	4	38	26
Padron, Raul, A's I/A's II	.267	221	35	59	6	5	3	32	2
Benitez, Oscar, Blue Jays	.267	206	24	55	11	2	4	33	0
De la Rosa, Rafael, Brewers	.265	151	34	40	8	1	1	18	15
Silva, Johan, Braves II	.265	219	40	58	8	4	5	34	14
Gonzalez, Adolfo, Dodgers I	.264	208	33	55	9	6	1	28	4
Sanchez, Ivan, Giants	.264	227	31	60	14	2	5	33	8
Garcis, Carlos, Phillies	.264	231	52	61	4	1	0	14	41
Prieto, Michael, Angels	.264	227	26	60	11	0	3	35	4
Cruz, Reynaldo, Mariners	.263	186	22	49	8	4	9	29	4
Cerda, Antonio, Mets	.262	244	23	64	13	0	5	42	1
#Catala, Pedro, Braves II	.229	175	**54**	40	3	5	1	22	34

INDIVIDUAL PITCHING LEADERS

(Minimum 50 Innings)

	W	L	ERA	G	SV	IP	H	BB	SO
Cordova, Jonny, Yankees I	8	0	0.36	11	0	50	17	2	66
Carela, Rafael, Angels	6	1	**0.73**	10	0	74	40	16	93
Rodriguez, Edward, Blue Jays	9	2	0.82	13	0	77	60	29	76
Suero, Nicolas, Pirates	**10**	1	0.86	14	0	63	43	13	46
Maria, Jose, Orioles	5	0	0.92	11	0	68	51	21	55
Valenzuela, Sergio, Braves I	6	2	0.96	11	0	66	34	12	56
Manzueta, Juan, Blue Jays	7	1	1.15	16	2	78	65	15	79
Valdez, Luis Carlos, Indians I	9	3	1.20	13	0	82	55	10	64
Rivas, Carlos, Braves II	7	2	1.25	13	0	65	53	12	34
Cordero, Carlos, Royals	5	3	1.30	12	0	69	61	12	62
Mercedes, Manuel, Padres	5	2	1.32	14	0	61	41	33	86
Valencia, Jose, Angels	5	2	1.45	8	0	56	43	11	47
Mercedes, Milciades, Indians I	7	3	1.46	15	0	92	69	25	67
Peralta, Heriberto, Mets	6	4	1.47	15	0	74	46	21	101
Silva, Sergio, Orioles	4	2	1.48	9	1	61	55	10	57
Peguero, German, Mets	3	2	1.56	12	0	75	44	15	70
#Delgado, George, Rockies	0	1	1.57	28	**20**	29	16	7	33
Abad, Fernando, Astros	6	2	1.61	14	0	78	55	7	87
Valdez, Carlos, Indians II	9	4	1.62	15	0	89	65	20	65
Villa, Kelvin, Braves II	5	1	1.64	13	1	66	40	22	78
Pena, Henry, Angels	7	2	1.64	12	0	82	58	8	53
Galves, Gary, Red Sox I	6	3	1.64	14	2	71	66	10	65
Severino, Sergio, Astros	3	1	1.67	14	1	54	35	33	85
Familia, Antonio, Yankees II	5	1	1.73	10	2	52	42	4	43
Gonzalez, Juan, Astros	5	7	1.81	15	0	80	74	15	62
Moscat, Dalvin, Yankees I	5	2	1.81	12	1	55	40	6	77
Gonzalez, Somer, D'backs	8	0	1.85	11	0	58	37	22	81
Castillo, Jose, Cardinals	4	4	1.87	12	0	77	60	11	49
Mateo, Warner, Mets	3	3	1.88	15	1	77	50	19	84
Torres, Luis, Athletics II	7	2	1.90	13	1	80	59	18	50
Cruz, Santos, Indians II	6	5	1.92	14	0	84	72	20	42
Pena, Mario, Red Sox II	4	5	1.93	16	0	75	59	4	70
Magallanes, Fidel, Giants	**10**	4	1.94	16	0	84	63	39	68
Fernandez, Manuel, Royals	2	5	1.95	13	1	65	56	11	47
Luces, Victor, Athletics II/Athletics I	8	2	1.95	15	0	78	68	23	51
Castillo, Cornelio, Tigers	3	4	1.95	16	1	74	60	25	69
Lugo, Jose, Athletics II/Athletics I	5	2	1.96	14	2	60	45	23	53
Brito, Andres, Cardinals	8	3	1.98	13	0	86	69	23	82
Campos, Jose, Rockies	4	2	1.98	12	0	73	48	13	57
Cordero, Johascar, Blue Jays	3	2	2.00	11	0	54	49	8	49
Garcia, Kelvin, Braves I	4	2	2.01	14	0	72	45	28	76
Pichardo, Kelvin, Phillies	6	6	2.02	13	0	76	50	34	75
Mercado, Arnoldo, Giants	3	2	2.04	19	2	66	55	35	82
Brito, Yunny, Dodgers II	5	3	2.07	14	1	74	65	12	64
Vasquez, Esmerling, D'backs	6	2	2.08	12	0	69	53	19	80
Sanchez, Rafael, Rockies	**10**	2	2.16	14	0	92	76	23	47
Reynoso, Anibal, Athletics II	7	3	2.17	13	0	79	76	10	33
Morales, Franklin, Rockies	9	3	2.18	13	0	78	58	34	69
Duran, Lisandro, Braves II	5	5	2.20	14	0	74	60	19	66
Rodriguez, Noe, White Sox	4	4	2.21	12	0	57	36	34	67
Martinez, Johan, Dodgers I	2	2	2.22	18	3	57	49	27	56
Gomez, Espifanio, Red Sox II	1	3	2.26	15	0	56	48	13	36
Pie, Ecequier, Marlins	1	8	2.26	13	0	72	57	32	73
Remasco, Omar, Padres	3	5	2.30	11	0	55	48	15	59
Castro, Julio, Cardinals	5	3	2.31	24	0	51	39	20	54
Alvarez, Basilio, Pirates	4	4	2.32	13	0	74	70	19	40
Arias, Keily, Pirates	7	3	2.34	13	0	73	53	16	68
Rodriguez, William, Athletics I	1	4	2.34	13	0	58	32	24	43
Pena, Luis, White Sox	5	1	2.35	23	4	61	44	37	52
Sevilla, Wilton, Yankees I	2	4	2.38	12	2	53	61	8	35
Trias, Orlando, Blue Jays	4	0	2.40	13	0	60	59	4	52
Martinez, Franklin, Reds	3	6	2.44	13	0	70	66	18	61
Mercedes, M ichel, Mariners	1	3	2.44	12	0	52	44	19	30
Valverde, Jonathan, Dodgers II	4	4	2.45	17	3	55	43	10	47
De Pena, Ezequiel, Indians I	3	3	2.49	22	2	51	43	13	32
Morales, Angelo, Royals	4	4	2.53	12	0	53	40	16	46
Leyba, Francisco, Twins	6	4	2.56	15	0	84	68	24	76
#Mosquea, Danny, D'backs	8	2	2.86	13	0	79	60	18	**102**

VENEZUELAN SUMMER LEAGUE

After dominating the Venezuelan Summer League for three straight seasons and not having a title to show for its efforts, San Felipe finally got over the hump in 2003. The team of Cleveland Indians farmhands knocked off defending champion Aguirre, winning the best-of-three series 2-1 to lock up the club's second VSL title.

"We definitely wanted to win that one and the players showed that through the way they approached those games," San Felipe manager Henry Centeno said. "We certainly enjoyed winning it all this time. We had been close for the past three years, but the players just seemed to fight more this time around."

San Felipe is a combined 175-58 (.751) over the past four years, something which Indians GM Mark Shapiro attributes to the Indians attention to player development—both in Venezuela and the Dominican Republic.

"Our Latin American operation is a core part of our player acquisition and development philosophy," Shapiro said. "We have spent the resources to implement and grow an operation that is as close as possible to our domestic scouting and development systems."

San Felipe outfielder Kevin Rivas earned MVP honors in the championship series, despite going 1-for-9 in the three games. Rivas' lone hit proved bigger than any other when he delivered a two-run double with two outs in the fourth inning of Game 3 of the series, won by San Felipe 3-2.

The league title might have been won by San Felipe, but no pitcher was more dominant on the mound than Aguirre's Ivan Blanco. The 20-year-old righthander cruised through the VSL, going 7-0, 0.97 with 103 strikeouts and 15 walks in just 74 innings.

"He was tough, probably the toughest pitcher in the league," Centeno said. "His breaking ball improved a lot from last season, but the key to his success this year was location on his fastball which was in the low-90s."

San Felipe figured out Blanco when it counted most, however, touching the young righthander for three earned runs on four hits en route to a 4-0 victory in the first game of the championship series.

Aguirre also boasted the top hitter in the league in third baseman Jesus Guzman, named the league's MVP. Guzman batted .363-5-31 and drew 29 walks while fanning 27 times.

"He's a good hitter," Centeno said. "He might project better as a shortstop in the long run, but he was impressive on the corner. He had a quick bat—very quick hands through the zone. He had the best offensive year in the league this year."

–CHRIS KLINE

STANDINGS

BARQUISIMETO	W	L	PCT	GB
San Felipe (Indians)	45	15	.750	—
Yaritagua (Orioles)	32	28	.575	13
Chivacoa (Pirates)	23	36	.392	21½
Cocorote (Blue Jays/Marlins)	19	40	.325	25½
VALENCIA	**W**	**L**	**PCT**	**GB**
Aguirre (Mariners)	40	17	.695	—
Mariara (Phillies)	34	25	.575	7
Tronconero 2 (Mets)	33	26	.558	8
Venoco (Astros)	31	25	.551	8½
Tronconero 1 (Padres/Twins)	24	35	.408	17
Cagua (Brewers/Reds)	13	47	.217	28½

PLAYOFFS: San Felipe defeated Aguirre 2-1 in best-of-3 series.

ALL-STAR TEAM: C—Jesus Flores, Tronconero 2. **1B**—Yasmil Bucee, Tronconero 2. **2B**—Yilmer Arratia, Tronconero 1 (Twins). **3B**—Jesus Guzman, Aguirre. **SS**—Asdrubal Cabrera, Aguirre. **OF**—Emmanuel Osorio, Mariara; Yamber Rodriguez, Venoco; Manuel Centeno, Mariara. **DH**—Trino Aguilar, Mariara. **SP**—Ivan Blanco, Aguirre. **RP**—Dionny Gaetano, Aguirre.

Most Valuable Player: Jesus Guzman, Aguirre. **Most Outstanding Pitcher:** Ivan Blanco, Aguirre.

INDIVIDUAL BATTING LEADERS

(Minimum 115 At-Bats)

	AVG	AB	R	H	2B	3B	HR	RBI	SB
Guzman, Jesus, Aguirre	**.363**	204	**46**	**74**	14	2	5	31	8
Mora, Effison, San Felipe	.343	198	39	68	17	2	2	**40**	12
Morales, Jaime, Mariara	.333	141	26	47	8	2	1	18	3
Ochoa, Tirzo, Venoco	.328	116	23	38	9	2	2	29	1
Canizalez, Jose, San Felipe	.327	162	40	53	12	6	4	22	16
Lopez, Geomar, Chivacoa	.323	133	17	43	9	1	4	27	4
Oliveros, Ricky, Tronconero 2	.321	215	35	69	15	4	0	19	9
Meza, Javier, Venoco	.318	201	36	64	8	1	1	22	8
Munoz, David, Chivacoa	.317	139	31	44	8	1	3	16	11
Aguilar, Trino, Mariara	.313	166	28	52	10	4	7	39	2
Alayon, Jean Carlos, San Felipe	.311	161	32	50	6	1	2	18	14
Torres, Fredy, San Felipe	.309	149	24	46	10	1	0	22	7
Ramirez, Yorman, San Felipe	.308	133	21	41	12	0	0	18	8
Guevara, Orlando, Mariara	.307	127	21	39	8	1	1	23	7
Osorio, Emmanuel, Mariara	.301	206	31	62	10	1	2	23	11
Arratia, Yilmer, Tronconero 1	.301	206	39	62	9	6	4	26	**29**
Patino, Eduardo, Mariara	.292	168	33	49	8	1	1	17	12
Mendez, Carlos, Yaritagua	.291	165	43	48	12	3	2	17	15
Quesada, Jorge, Aguirre	.288	125	22	36	10	0	3	25	1
Izaguirre, Jose, Yaritagua	.288	177	37	51	13	2	5	31	22
Delgado, Ronny, Cagua	.284	148	22	42	14	4	2	20	6
Cabrera, Asdrubal, Aguirre	.283	198	31	56	12	4	0	29	5
Smolarsky, Freddy, Cocorote	.283	191	29	54	12	5	4	28	7
Colmenarez, Juan, Yaritagua	.280	132	16	37	6	1	0	11	10
Sandez, Jorge, Cocorote	.279	136	26	38	5	0	0	15	14
Pacheco, Livio, Aguirre	.276	174	23	48	7	3	2	36	4
Infante, Ray, Cagua	.275	131	20	36	5	2	1	11	6
Bucce, Yasmil, Tronconero 2	.274	175	26	48	**20**	0	3	32	0
Castillo, Victor, Yaritagua	.271	118	16	32	5	0	2	20	5
Hernandez, Quincy, Cocorote	.268	149	18	40	8	2	0	16	16
Hernandez, Yanko, Tronconero 1	.268	149	20	40	7	3	3	32	4
Rodriguez, Yamber, Venoco	.268	164	34	44	5	2	6	32	19
Sutil, Wladimir, Venoco	.266	154	35	41	11	1	1	21	11
Graterol, Jose, Aguirre	.265	204	43	54	10	2	0	11	12
Garth, Ronald, Aguirre	.264	178	33	47	12	1	3	23	5
Sanchez, Julio, Yaritagua	.262	145	21	38	8	0	2	23	0
Albornoz, Henry, Tronconero 1	.256	168	19	43	9	5	1	23	8
Flores, Jesus, Tronconero 2	.255	165	25	42	16	0	4	32	2
Castanon, Carlos, Chivacoa	.255	153	18	39	9	0	2	15	3
Lopez, Marcos, Mariara	.254	177	31	45	2	3	0	19	15
Garcia, Cristian, Tronconero 2	.254	130	24	33	3	1	1	14	4
Gamboa, Arnaldo, Cocorote	.253	190	24	48	6	0	1	22	14
Rodriguez, Jesus, Cocorote	.252	210	23	53	6	2	1	22	18
Roman, Wilman, Chivacoa	.252	139	16	35	5	1	0	14	4
Cohen, Eleasaib, Tronconero 2	.252	202	27	51	6	6	1	20	6
Hurtado, Marvin, Cocorote	.251	167	24	42	4	1	1	16	4
Gonzalez, Franklin, Yaritagua	.250	152	17	38	9	1	0	15	4
Rodriguez, Christian, Venoco	.250	160	23	40	10	4	4	35	7
Rojo, Billy, Cagua	.249	169	28	42	7	1	0	12	16
Utrera, Jose, Cocorote	.248	137	14	34	2	2	0	14	8
Bermudez, Jose, Tronconero 1	.247	198	15	49	10	2	1	16	7
Hernandez, Jose, Venoco	.245	200	29	49	13	1	0	20	23
Bermudez, Nestor, Cocorote	.241	137	18	33	6	1	1	14	7
Huerta, Luis, San Felipe	.241	174	28	42	4	2	1	17	15
Centeno, Manuel, Mariara	.241	116	16	28	5	1	3	24	4
Lopez, Jose, Mariara	.241	166	31	40	10	1	1	20	11
Rivas, Kevin, San Felipe	.240	179	22	43	2	1	0	17	5
Sandoval, Maikel, Cagua	.237	186	25	44	15	**8**	2	21	14
Moron, Robert, Mariara	.236	165	23	39	7	2	2	20	1

INDIVIDUAL PITCHING LEADERS

(Minimum 46 Innings)

	W	L	ERA	G	SV	IP	H	BB	SO
Blanco, Ivan, Aguirre	7	0	**0.97**	12	0	74	40	15	103
Mijares, Jose, Tronconero 1	2	4	1.05	11	0	52	28	15	58
#Gaetano, Dionny, Aguirre	0	1	1.11	24	**16**	24	16	9	14
Soto, Enyelbert, Venoco	6	4	1.24	16	5	51	47	6	45
Garate, Victor, Venoco	3	1	1.39	12	0	71	39	18	65
Bastardo, Alberto, Yaritagua	5	2	1.48	11	0	67	58	9	51
Gonzalez, Dixon, San Felipe	7	2	1.59	13	0	68	41	21	49
Alvarado, Carlos, San Felipe	4	1	1.68	14	2	48	40	5	41
Santiago, Julio, Aguirre	5	2	1.69	9	0	48	39	19	51
Perdomo, Javier, Tronconero 2	6	4	1.70	13	0	74	44	9	83
Riera, Jorge, San Felipe	2	1	1.76	15	6	46	36	8	31
Zarate, Mauro, Cocorote	5	2	1.79	16	1	95	68	20	**105**
Zambrano, Oscar, Chivacoa	3	4	1.89	15	3	57	38	18	46
Acosta, Jorge, Aguirre	4	0	1.95	11	2	55	38	16	55
Sanchez, Jose, Tronconero 2	**8**	2	2.01	13	0	76	55	20	82
Martinez, Delio, Mariara	4	1	2.18	11	0	58	42	12	51
Mendoza, Robert, Mariara	5	4	2.22	12	0	65	48	24	61
Vargas, Jose, San Felipe	4	2	2.32	13	0	66	41	20	66
Figueroa, Carlos, Aguirre	5	1	2.44	11	1	52	40	13	42
Hurtado, Darwin, Cocorote	1	2	2.45	15	1	48	30	18	53
Martinez, Luis, Tronconero 2	2	3	2.45	9	0	48	47	8	34
Ruiz, Humberto, Yaritagua	2	3	2.89	10	0	53	37	35	46
Escobar, Carlos, Chivacoa	3	4	3.00	12	1	51	41	30	29
Sosa, Oswaldo, Tronconero 1	1	2	3.02	11	0	54	44	18	40
Mendez, Julio Cesar, Tronconero 2	1	3	3.02	16	4	48	44	14	21
Jimenez, Fabian, Tronconero 1	2	2	3.30	16	0	60	48	23	48
Gamez, Marcos, Cagua	0	9	3.45	20	2	76	74	33	70
Salazar, Carlos, Cocorote	1	3	3.48	14	0	52	39	27	45
Olivares, Francisco, Cagua	4	7	3.59	19	0	68	61	39	66
Colina, Ederson, Chivacoa	2	4	3.61	14	1	57	44	38	43
Martinez, Eggly, Yaritagua	4	2	3.61	16	1	52	36	46	40
Rios, Christian, Venoco	2	1	3.70	12	0	49	36	42	45
Marcano, Yorvit, Chivacoa	5	1	3.73	16	0	63	37	44	39
Jimenez, Santos, Cagua	1	5	3.88	25	2	56	58	27	44
Lugo, Victor, Cocorote	3	9	3.93	16	1	69	66	28	44
Reyes, Israel, Chivacoa	2	5	4.08	14	1	53	59	22	30
Mayora, Luis, Yaritagua	3	3	4.12	16	0	72	75	30	28
Correa, Felix, Aguirre	3	1	4.14	12	0	50	44	18	44

Statistics in **boldface** indicate league leader
#League leader but non-qualifier

PROSPECTS

PROSPECT POSITION RANKINGS

BY JOSH BOYD

Following the 2003 season, Baseball America ranked the game's top prospects by position. Only players who have not exceed the major league rookie eligibility standard—130 at-bats for position players and 50 innings for pitchers—were included.

Ages are as of Oct. 1, 2003. The highest level each player reached in 2003 is noted.

RIGHTHANDED STARTERS

If Edwin Jackson's 93-98 mph fastball, hard slider and changeup weren't enough to jump him to the top of the list, his dominant major league debut was. Jackson, 19 at the time, became the youngest player since Dwight Gooden to win his major league debut. While Jackson's stuff is more overpowering than Zack Greinke's, Greinke's pitchability is unmatched by any minor leaguer. A shoulder injury prevented Angel Guzman from ranking higher, while an elbow injury also ended Mike Jones' season.

Rank, Player, Team	Age	Highest Level
1. Edwin Jackson, Dodgers	20	Majors
2. Zack Greinke, Royals	19	Double-A
3. Ervin Santana, Angels	20	Double-A
4. Gavin Floyd, Phillies	20	High A
5. Angel Guzman, Cubs	21	Double-A
6. Chin-Hui Tsao, Rockies	22	Majors
7. Dustin McGowan, Blue Jays	21	Double-A
8. Bobby Jenks, Angels	22	Double-A
9. J.D. Durbin, Twins	21	Double-A
10. John VanBenschoten, Pirates	23	Double-A
11. Taylor Buchholz, Phillies	21	Double-A
12. Joel Hanrahan, Dodgers	21	Triple-A
13. Adam Wainwright, Braves	22	Double-A
14. Kyle Sleeth, Tigers	21	Did not pitch
15. Denny Bautista, Orioles	20	Double-A
16. Kris Honel, White Sox	20	High A
17. Jeremy Guthrie, Indians	24	Triple-A
18. Mike Jones, Brewers	20	Double-A
19. Clint Nageotte, Mariners	22	Double-A
20. Joe Blanton, Athletics	22	Double-A
21. Clint Everts, Expos	19	Low A
22. Merkin Valdez, Giants	21	Low A
23. John Maine, Orioles	22	High A
24. Jeff Allison, Marlins	18	Rookie
25. Bobby Brownlie, Cubs	22	High A

LEFTHANDED STARTERS

Scott Kazmir remains atop the southpaws list for a second year on the heels of his first full-season exposure. He rang up 145 strikeouts in 109 innings with a power breaking ball and 96 mph heater. He is more established than Greg Miller, who skyrocketed to Double-A in his first full year, adding a hard slider and developing a plus changeup to go with his 95 mph fastball and good curveball. Cole Hamels, in his first professional season, used his devastating changeup to limit South Atlantic League hitters to a .136 average before earning a promotion to high Class A Clearwater.

Rank, Player, Team	Age	Highest Level
1. Scott Kazmir, Mets	19	High A
2. Greg Miller, Dodgers	18	Double-A
3. Cole Hamels, Phillies	19	High A
4. Adam Loewen, Orioles	19	Short-season A
5. Mike Hinckley, Expos	20	High A
6. Travis Blackley, Mariners	20	Double-A
7. Sean Burnett, Pirates	21	Double-A
8. Scott Olsen, Marlins	19	Low A
9. Justin Jones, Cubs	19	Low A
10. Dan Meyer, Braves	22	High A
11. Manny Parra, Brewers	20	Low A
12. Brandon Claussen, Reds	24	Majors

LARRY GOREN

At the top of the list among righthanders
Dodgers pitcher Edwin Jackson

Rank, Player, Team	Age	Highest Level
13. Andy Sisco, Cubs	20	Low A
14. Macay McBride, Braves	20	High A
15. John Danks, Rangers	18	Short-season A
16. Neal Cotts, White Sox	23	Majors
17. Jeff Francis, Rockies	22	High A
18. Jorge de la Rosa, Red Sox	22	Triple-A
19. Luke Hagerty, Cubs	22	Did not pitch
20. Chris Narveson, Cardinals	21	High A

RELIEVERS

After establishing a new NCAA Division I standard for strikeouts per nine innings as Houston's closer, Reds first-rounder Ryan Wagner needed just 46 days in the minors before reaching the majors, where he continued to baffle hitters with his darting fastball and unhittable slider. Chad Cordero, another 2003 first-rounder, made quick work of the minors before making a successful major league debut. Brian Bruney didn't allow a hit in his first nine Triple-A outings and could join fellow smokethrower Jose Valverde in a setup role for Arizona in 2004. Acquired from the Dodgers at the trade deadline, Yankees righthander Scott Proctor moved to the pen and was pumping 98-100 mph gas.

Rank, Player, Team	Age	Highest Level
1. Ryan Wagner, Reds	21	Majors
2. Brian Bruney, Diamondbacks	21	Triple-A
3. Derrick Turnbow, Angels.	25	Majors
4. Jesse Crain, Twins	22	Triple-A
5. Todd Wellemeyer, Cubs	25	Majors
6. Chad Cordero, Expos	21	Majors
7. Aaron Taylor, Mariners	26	Majors
8. Royce Ring, Mets	22	Double-A
9. Scott Proctor, Yankees	26	Triple-A
10. Joe Valentine, Reds	23	Majors

CATCHERS

Joe Mauer hit .338 between two levels in 2003 and may have established himself as the best prospect in baseball along the way. He takes a mature, disciplined approach to the plate and drew 49 walks against 49 strikeouts. Behind the plate, he turned in gold glove caliber defense, deterring basestealers with his powerful throwing arm and solid receiving mechanics. Another

PROSPECTS

multi-tooled catcher, Jeff Mathis doesn't lag far behind Mauer, and he has displayed more present power. Guillermo Quiroz has officially shed his defense-only label, as he broke out for a 20 home runs in 2003.

Rank, Player, Team	Age	Highest Level
1. Joe Mauer, Twins	20	Double-A
2. Jeff Mathis, Angels	20	Double-A
3. Guillermo Quiroz, Blue Jays	21	Double-A
4. Kelly Shoppach, Red Sox	23	Double-A
5. Dioner Navarro, Yankees	19	Double-A
6. Justin Huber, Mets	21	Double-A
7. Ryan Doumit, Pirates	22	High A
8. Koyie Hill, Dodgers	24	Majors
9. John Buck, Astros	23	Triple-A
10. Lou Palmisano, Brewers	21	Rookie

FIRST BASEMEN

Kotchman has yet to remain healthy for a full season, but a myriad of injuries hasn't prevented him from raking. He even managed to increase his power production after a torn hamstring wiped out the first half of the 2003 season. Jason Stokes, James Loney and Adrian Gonzalez (who was traded to the Rangers from the Marlins as the centerpiece of the Ugueth Urbina deal) were all hampered by wrist injuries. Prince Fielder slugged 27 bombs and drove in 112 runs during his full-season debut.

Rank, Player, Team	Age	Highest Level
1. Casey Kotchman, Angels	20	High A
2. Jason Stokes, Marlins	21	High A
3. James Loney, Dodgers	19	High A
4. Prince Fielder, Brewers	19	Low A
5. Adrian Gonzalez, Rangers	21	Triple-A
6. Craig Brazell, Mets	23	Triple-A
7. Adam LaRoche, Braves	23	Triple-A
8. Larry Broadway, Expos	22	Double-A
9. Michael Aubrey, Indians	21	Low A
10. Ryan Howard, Phillies	23	High A

SECOND BASEMEN

The rejuvenated Brewers system added another premium talent, Rickie Weeks, with the second pick in the 2003 draft. The all-time Division I batting leader with a .473 career average, Weeks tore up the Midwest League before getting a September callup. Josh Barfield paced the minors with 128 RBIs and tied Jayson Nix with 46 doubles. A back injury in the first half limited Scott Hairston at the plate, though he still put together a solid campaign. Alberto Callaspo's .327 average led the Midwest League, while Delwyn Young's .542 slugging percentage was tops in the South Atlantic League and both emerging second basemen ripped 38 doubles.

Rank, Player, Team	Age	Highest Level
1. Rickie Weeks, Brewers	21	Majors
2. Josh Barfield, Padres	20	High A
3. Scott Hairston, Diamondbacks	23	Double-A
4. Jayson Nix, Rockies	20	High A
5. Robinson Cano, Yankees	20	Double-A
6. Jason Bourgeois, Rangers	21	Double-A
7. Alberto Callaspo, Angels	20	High A
8. Victor Diaz, Mets	21	Double-A
9. Chris Burke, Astros	23	Double-A
10. Delwyn Young, Dodgers	21	Low A

THIRD BASEMEN

Third base has been a productive prospect position in recent years and in a year where rookies Mark Teixeira and Miguel Cabrera (rated Nos. 1 and 2 on this list last year) emerged, Andy Marte, Dallas McPherson, David Wright and Corey Hart maintained the hot corner's high profile in the minors. Edwin Encarnacion bounced back after a slow start in Double-A to have a strong season. Ian Stewart and Eric Duncan, 2003 first-rounders, had impressive debuts and were each named the top prospect in their respective Rookie leagues. Brendan Harris, Chad Tracy and Kevin Youkilis don't have the pop to fit the third base profile, though all boast good hitting approaches.

Rank, Player, Team	Age	Highest Level
1. Andy Marte, Braves	19	High A
2. Dallas McPherson, Angels	23	Double-A
3. David Wright, Mets	20	High A
4. Corey Hart, Brewers	21	Double-A
5. Edwin Encarnacion, Reds	20	Double-A
6. Ian Stewart, Rockies	18	Rookie
7. Brendan Harris, Cubs	23	Double-A
8. Chad Tracy, Diamondbacks	23	Triple-A
9. Kevin Youkilis, Red Sox	24	Triple-A
10. Eric Duncan, Yankees	19	Short-season A

SHORTSTOPS

B.J. Upton struggled during the first month of his pro debut but made adjustments at the plate and quickly established himself as one of the game's most dynamic prospects. He committed a minor league-high 56 errors, a number that should steadily decrease because of his tools and athleticism as he makes his way toward the majors. Coming off his best offensive campaign, Bobby Crosby is set to take over at shortstop for Miguel Tejada, who was eligible to leave the Athletics as a free agent, while Khalil Greene isn't likely to relinquish the Padres job after taking over in September. Some makeup issues may have prevented Hanley Ramirez from showing his true potential in 2003, but when he matures he has the upside to top the list. The best is still to come for Sergio Santos, too.

Rank, Player, Team	Age	Highest Level
1. B.J. Upton, Devil Rays	19	Double-A
2. J.J. Hardy, Brewers	21	Double-A
3. Bobby Crosby, Athletics	23	Majors
4. Aaron Hill, Blue Jays	21	High A
5. Hanley Ramirez, Red Sox	19	Low A
6. Khalil Greene, Padres	23	Majors
7. Sergio Santos, Diamondbacks	20	Double-A
8. Freddy Sanchez, Pirates	25	Majors
9. Jason Bartlett, Twins	23	Double-A
10. Russ Adams, Blue Jays	23	Double-A

OUTFIELDERS

No outfielder posted more impressive stats in 2003 than Jeremy Reed, who hit .409 for Double-A Birmingham in the second half and walked nearly twice as much as he fanned on the season. But it's Alexis Rios' upside that earned him the nod as the top-rated outfield prospect entering 2004. He established career highs with his .352-11-82 performance and a .923 OPS in Double-A, and he projects to add to those power numbers as he continues to mature. The Devil Rays, who turned last year's No. 1 ranked outfield prospect Rocco Baldelli into a star rookie, drafted prep slugger Delmon Young with the first overall pick in June. He made his debut in the Arizona Fall League and projects as one of the minors' most dangerous all-around hitters. Jeff Francoeur and Jeremy Hermida, both 2002 first-rounders, are poised for big seasons in 2004.

Rank, Player, Team	Age	Highest Level
1. Alexis Rios, Blue Jays	22	Double-A
2. Grady Sizemore, Indians	21	Double-A
3. Delmon Young, Devil Rays	18	Did not play
4. Brad Nelson, Brewers	20	Double-A
5. Jeremy Reed, White Sox	22	Double-A
6. Jeff Francoeur, Braves	19	Low A
7. Franklin Gutierrez, Dodgers	20	Double-A
8. Dave Krynzel, Brewers	21	Double-A
9. Chris Snelling, Mariners	21	Triple-A
10. Jeremy Hermida, Marlins	19	Low A
11. Jason Bay, Pirates	25	Majors
12. Gabe Gross, Blue Jays	23	Triple-A
13. Joey Gathright, Devil Rays	21	Double-A
14. Shin Soo-Choo, Mariners	21	High A
15. Ramon Nivar, Rangers	23	Majors
16. Ryan Harvey, Cubs	19	Rookie
17. Felix Pie, Cubs	18	Low A
18. Brent Clevlen, Tigers	19	Low A
19. Mike Restovich, Twins	24	Majors
20. Stephen Smitherman, Reds	25	Majors
21. Lastings Milledge, Mets	18	Rookie
22. Jason Kubel, Twins	21	High A
23. Nick Swisher, Athletics	22	Double-A
24. Reggie Abercrombie, Dodgers	22	Double-A
25. J. J. Davis, Pirates	24	Majors

LEAGUE TOP 20 PROSPECTS

As with most of the prospect lists that appear in Baseball America, the Minor League Top 20 Prospects lists are compiled with long-term major league potential in mind. While we like to see players do well now, what we're really looking for are future major league stars.

These lists do bring a slightly different perspective than Baseball America's traditional organizational Top 10 Prospects lists. Those lists have more of a scouting angle, while our league lists are based on conversations with league managers. Managers and scouts can often view players differently. Both look at a player's tools, but managers give more weight to what a player does on the field, while scouts look at what a player might eventually do. We think both perspectives are useful.

For a player to qualify for a league prospect list, he must have spent at least one-third of the season in a league to qualify. Position players must have one plate appearance per league game. In other words, for a league that plays 140 games, a player is eligible if he has at least 140 plate appearances.

Pitchers must pitch ⅓ inning per league game. Relievers must make at least 20 appearances in a full-season league or 10 appearances in a short-season league (* indicates since traded).

TRIPLE-A

INTERNATIONAL LEAGUE

1. Jose Reyes, ss, Norfolk (Mets)
2. Justin Morneau, 1b, Rochester (Twins)
3. Victor Martinez, c, Buffalo (Indians)
4. Chase Utley, 2b, Scranton/Wilkes-Barre (Phillies)
5. *Freddy Sanchez, ss/2b, Pawtucket (Red Sox)
6. Adam LaRoche, 1b, Richmond (Braves)
7. Brandon Claussen, lhp, Columbus (Yankees)/Louisville (Reds)
8. Cliff Lee, lhp, Buffalo (Indians)
9. Jeremy Guthrie, rhp, Buffalo (Indians)
10. Coco Crisp, of, Buffalo (Indians)
11. Dustin Moseley, rhp, Louisville (Reds)
12. Michael Restovich, of, Rochester (Twins)
13. Ryan Madson, rhp, Scranton/Wilkes Barre (Phillies)
14. Jesse Crain, rhp, Rochester (Twins)
15. Kevin Cash, c, Syracuse (Blue Jays)
16. Gabe Gross, of, Syracuse (Blue Jays)
17. Alex Escobar, of Buffalo (Indians)
18. Grant Balfour, rhp, Rochester (Twins)
19. Cody Ross, of, Toledo (Tigers)
20. Jason Arnold, rhp, Syracuse (Blue Jays)

* Since traded to Pirates

PACIFIC COAST LEAGUE

1. Rich Harden, rhp, Sacramento (Athletics)
2. Rafael Soriano, rhp, Tacoma (Mariners)
3. Bobby Crosby, ss, Sacramento (Athletics)
4. Jerome Williams, rhp, Fresno (Giants)
5. *Jason Bay, of, Portland (Padres)
6. Khalil Greene, ss, Portland (Padres)
7. Chad Tracy, 3b, Tucson (Diamondbacks)
8. Garrett Atkins, 3b, Colorado Springs (Rockies)
9. Jason Young, rhp, Colorado Springs (Rockies)
10. Ryan Ludwick, of, Oklahoma (Rangers)
11. David Kelton, of/3b, Iowa (Cubs)
12. Aaron Taylor, rhp, Tacoma (Mariners)
13. Rodrigo Rosario, rhp, New Orleans (Astros)
14. David DeJesus, of, Omaha (Royals)
15. J.J. Davis, of, Nashville (Pirates)
16. Rene Reyes, of, Colorado Springs (Rockies)
17. Alfredo Amezaga, ss, Salt Lake (Angels)
18. John Buck, c, New Orleans (Astros)
19. Todd Wellemeyer, rhp, Iowa (Cubs)
20. Rett Johnson, rhp, Tacoma (Mariners)

* Since traded to Pirates

DOUBLE-A

EASTERN LEAGUE

1. Joe Mauer, c, New Britain (Twins)
2. Alexis Rios, of, New Haven (Blue Jays)
3. Grady Sizemore, of, Akron (Indians)
4. Guillermo Quiroz, c, New Haven (Blue Jays)
5. Dustin McGowan, rhp, New Haven (Blue Jays)

LARRY GOREN

Casey Kotchman: No. 1 in Cal League

6. J.D. Durbin, rhp, New Britain (Twins)
7. Dioner Navarro, c, Trenton (Yankees)
8. Taylor Buccholz, rhp, Reading (Phillies)
9. Jason Bartlett, ss, New Britain (Twins)
10. John VanBenschoten, rhp, Altoona (Pirates)
11. Jesse Crain, rhp, New Britain (Twins)
12. Kelly Shoppach, c, Portland (Red Sox)
13. Craig Brazell, 1b, Binghamton (Mets)
14. Sean Burnett, lhp, Altoona (Pirates)
15. Kevin Youkilis, 3b, Portland (Red Sox)
16. Jeremy Guthrie, rhp, Akron (Indians)
17. Jorge de la Rosa, lhp, Portland (Red Sox)
18. Fernando Cabrera, rhp, Akron (Indians)
19. Francisco Cruceta, rhp, Akron (Indians)
20. Jose Castillo, 2b/ss, Altoona (Pirates)

SOUTHERN LEAGUE

1. Miguel Cabrera, 3b, Carolina (Marlins)
2. Edwin Jackson, rhp, Jacksonville (Dodgers)
3. Jeremy Reed, of, Birmingham (White Sox)
4. J.J. Hardy, ss, Huntsville (Brewers)
5. David Krynzel, of, Huntsville (Brewers)
6. Joel Hanrahan, rhp, Jacksonville (Dodgers)
7. Dan Haren, rhp, Tennessee (Cardinals)
8. Neal Cotts, lhp, Birmingham (White Sox)
9. Angel Guzman, rhp, West Tenn (Cubs)
10. Mike Jones, rhp, Huntsville (Brewers)
11. Khalil Greene, ss, Mobile (Padres)
12. Adam LaRoche, 1b, Greenville (Braves)
13. Adam Wainwright, rhp, Greenville (Braves)
14. Stephen Smitherman, of, Chattanooga (Reds)
15. Corey Hart, 3b, Huntsville (Brewers)
16. *Denny Bautista, rhp, Carolina (Marlins)
17. Bubba Nelson, rhp, Greenville (Braves)
18. #Adrian Gonzalez, 1b, Carolina (Marlins)
19. Reggie Abercrombie, of, Jacksonville (Dodgers)
20. Humberto Quintero, c, Mobile (Padres)

* Since traded to Orioles
\# Since traded to Rangers

TEXAS LEAGUE

1. Chin-Hui Tsao, rhp, Tulsa (Rockies)
2. Zack Greinke, rhp, Wichita (Royals)
3. Laynce Nix, of, Frisco (Rangers)
4. Ramon Nivar, of/2b, Frisco (Rangers)
5. Jose Lopez, ss, San Antonio (Mariners)
6. Travis Blackley, lhp, San Antonio (Mariners)
7. Bobby Jenks, rhp, Arkansas (Angels)
8. Clint Nageotte, rhp, San Antonio (Mariners)
9. Jimmy Gobble, lhp, Wichita (Royals)
10. Chris Snelling, of, San Antonio (Mariners)
11. Scott Hairston, 2b, El Paso (Diamondbacks)
12. Freddie Bynum, 2b, Midland (Athletics)
13. Cory Sullivan, of, Tulsa (Rockies)
14. Dan Johnson, 1b, Midland (Athletics)
15. Adrian Gonzalez, 1b, Frisco (Rangers)
16. Greg Aquino, rhp, El Paso (Diamondbacks)
17. Chris Burke, 2b, Round Rock (Astros)
18. Juan Dominguez, rhp, Frisco (Rangers)
19. Byron Gettis, of, Wichita (Royals)
20. Rett Johnson, rhp, San Antonio (Mariners)

HIGH CLASS A

CALIFORNIA LEAGUE

1. Casey Kotchman, 1b, Rancho Cucamonga (Angels)
2. Ervin Santana, rhp, Rancho Cucamonga (Angels)
3. Jeff Mathis, c, Rancho Cucamonga (Angels)
4. Dallas McPherson, 3b, Rancho Cucamonga (Angels)
5. Josh Barfield, 2b, Lake Elsinore (Padres)
6. Brad Nelson, 1b/of, High Desert (Brewers)
7. Joey Gathright, of, Bakersfield (Devil Rays)
8. Sergio Santos, ss, Lancaster (Diamondbacks)
9. Juan Dominguez, rhp, Stockton (Rangers)
10. Jayson Nix, 2b, Visalia (Rockies)
11. Jeff Francis, lhp, Visalia (Rockies)
12. Nick Swisher, of, Modesto (Athletics)
13. Shin-Soo Choo, of, Inland Empire (Mariners)
14. Chad Gaudin, rhp, Bakersfield (Devil Rays)
15. Jason Bourgeois, 2b/ss, Stockton (Rangers)
16. Josh Kroeger, of, Lancaster (Diamondbacks)
17. Drew Meyer, ss, Stockton (Rangers)
18. Steven Shell, rhp, Rancho Cucamonga (Angels)
19. Jason Botts, 1b, Stockton (Rangers)
20. Freddy Guzman, of, Lake Elsinore (Padres)

CAROLINA LEAGUE

1. Zack Greinke, rhp, Wilmington (Royals)

2. Jeremy Reed, of, Winston-Salem (White Sox)
3. Andy Marte, 3b, Myrtle Beach (Braves)
4. John VanBenschoten, rhp, Lynchburg (Pirates)
5. Kris Honel, rhp, Winston-Salem (White Sox)
6. Edwin Encarnacion, 3b, Potomac (Reds)
7. John Maine, rhp, Frederick (Orioles)
8. Dan Meyer, lhp, Myrtle Beach (Braves)
9. Ian Oquendo, rhp, Lynchburg (Pirates)
10. Bryan Bullington, rhp, Lynchburg (Pirates)
11. Macay McBride, lhp, Myrtle Beach (Braves)
12. Ryan Doumit, c, Lynchburg (Pirates)
13. Ryan Wing, lhp, Winston-Salem (White Sox)
14. Rommie Lewis, lhp, Frederick (Orioles)
15. Ty Howington, lhp, Potomac (Reds)
16. Hector Gimenez, c, Salem (Astros)
17. Chris Shelton, 1b/c, Lynchburg (Pirates)
18. Jared Gothreaux, rhp, Salem (Astros)
19. Willy Taveras, of, Kinston (Indians)
20. Andres Blanco, ss, Wilmington (Royals)

FLORIDA STATE LEAGUE

1. Joe Mauer, c, Fort Myers (Twins)
2. Greg Miller, lhp, Vero Beach (Dodgers)
3. Gavin Floyd, rhp, Clearwater (Phillies)
4. Franklin Gutierrez, of, Vero Beach (Dodgers)
5. Dioner Navarro, c, Tampa (Yankees)
6. J.D. Durbin, rhp, Fort Myers (Twins)
7. James Loney, 1b, Vero Beach (Dodgers)
8. Dustin McGowan, rhp, Dunedin (Blue Jays)
9. Denny Bautista, rhp, Jupiter (Marlins)
10. David Wright, 3b, St. Lucie (Mets)
11. Brandon League, rhp, Dunedin (Blue Jays)
12. Chadd Blasko, rhp, Daytona (Cubs)
13. Bobby Brownlie, rhp, Daytona (Cubs)
14. Jason Stokes, 1b, Jupiter (Marlins)
15. Ryan Howard, 1b, Clearwater (Phillies)
16. David Bush, rhp, Dunedin (Blue Jays)
17. Jason Kubel, of, Fort Myers (Twins)
18. Robinson Cano, 2b, Tampa (Yankees)
19. Matt Peterson, rhp, St. Lucie (Mets)
20. Justin Huber, c, St. Lucie (Mets)

LOW CLASS A

MIDWEST LEAGUE

1. Prince Fielder, 1b, Beloit (Brewers)
2. Blake Hawksworth, rhp, Peoria (Cardinals)
3. Justin Jones, lhp, Lansing (Cubs)
4. Manny Parra, lhp, Beloit (Brewers)
5. Joe Blanton, rhp, Kane County (Athletics)
6. Joel Zumaya, rhp, West Michigan (Tigers)
7. Andy Sisco, lhp, Lansing (Cubs)
8. Felix Pie, of, Lansing (Cubs)
9. Tom Wilhelmsen, rhp, Beloit (Brewers)
10. Brent Clevlen, of, West Michigan (Tigers)
11. Alberto Callaspo, 2b, Cedar Rapids (Angels)
12. Jae-Kuk Ryu, rhp, Lansing (Cubs)
13. Dennis Sarfate, rhp, Beloit (Brewers)
14. Rafael Rodriguez, rhp, Cedar Rapids (Angels)
15. Erick Aybar, ss, Cedar Rapids (Angels)
16. Donald Murphy, 2b, Burlington (Royals)
17. John Baker, c, Kane County (Athletics)
18. Rudy Guillen, of, Battle Creek (Yankees)
19. Jon Connolly, lhp, West Michigan (Tigers)
20. Colt Griffin, rhp, Burlington (Royals)

SOUTH ATLANTIC LEAGUE

1. B.J. Upton, ss, Charleston, S.C. (Devil Rays)
2. Scott Kazmir, lhp, Capital City (Mets)
3. Cole Hamels, lhp, Lakewood (Phillies)
4. Jeff Francoeur, of, Rome (Braves)
5. Jeremy Hermida, of, Greensboro (Marlins)
6. Hanley Ramirez, ss, Augusta (Red Sox)
7. Fausto Carmona, rhp, Lake County (Indians)
8. Merkin Valdez, rhp, Hagerstown (Giants)
9. Scott Olsen, lhp, Greensboro (Marlins)
10. Mike Hinckley, lhp, Savannah (Expos)
11. John Maine, rhp, Delmarva (Orioles)
12. Larry Broadway, 1b, Savannah (Expos)
13. Brandon League, rhp, Charleston, W.Va. (Blue Jays)
14. Matt Cain, rhp, Hagerstown (Giants)
15. Fernando Nieve, rhp, Lexington (Astros)
16. Delwyn Young, 2b, South Georgia (Dodgers)

B.J. Upton: No. 1 in South Atlantic League

17. Anthony Lerew, rhp, Rome (Braves)
18. Dan Meyer, lhp, Rome (Braves)
19. Michael Aubrey, 1b, Lake County (Indians)
20. Brian McCann, c, Rome (Braves)

SHORT-SEASON CLASS A

NEW YORK-PENN LEAGUE

1. Nick Markakis, of, Aberdeen (Orioles)
2. Aaron Hill, ss, Auburn (Blue Jays)
3. Tony Giarratano, ss, Oneonta (Tigers)
4. Kody Kirkland, 3b, Oneonta (Tigers)
5. Josh Banks, rhp, Auburn (Blue Jays)
6. David Murphy, of, Lowell (Red Sox)
7. Kurt Isenberg, lhp, Auburn (Blue Jays)
8. Nyjer Morgan, of, Williamsport (Pirates)
9. Clint Everts, rhp, Vermont (Expos)
10. Tom Gorzelanny, lhp, Williamsport (Pirates)
11. Brad Snyder, of, Mahoning Valley (Indians)
12. Chris Ray, rhp, Aberdeen (Orioles)
13. Matt Murton, of, Lowell (Red Sox)
14. Paul Maholm, lhp, Williamsport (Pirates)
15. Aneudi Cuevas, ss, Hudson Valley (Devil Rays)
16. Juan Peralta, ss/2b, Auburn (Blue Jays)
17. Claudio Arias, 3b, Lowell (Red Sox)
18. Vincent Blue, of, Oneonta (Tigers)
19. Vito Chiaravalloti, 1b, Auburn (Blue Jays)
20. Javier Guzman, ss, Williamsport (Pirates)

NORTHWEST LEAGUE

1. Felix Hernandez, rhp, Everett (Mariners)
2. Conor Jackson, of, Yakima (Diamondbacks)
3. Nate Schierholtz, 3b, Salem-Keizer (Giants)
4. Wes Littleton, rhp, Spokane (Rangers)
5. Todd Jennings, c, Salem-Keizer (Giants)
6. Jeremy Cleveland, of, Spokane (Rangers)
7. Sean Marshall, lhp, Boise (Cubs)
8. Sean Thompson, lhp, Eugene (Padres)
9. Billy Petrick, rhp, Boise (Cubs)
10. Ching-Lung Lo, rhp, Tri-City (Rockies)
11. Aaron Marsden, lhp, Tri-City (Rockies)
12. Jaime D'Antona, 3b, Yakima (Diamondbacks)
13. Omar Quintanilla, ss, Vancouver (Athletics)
14. Dustin Majewski, of, Vancouver (Athletics)
15. Brian Dopirak, 1b, Boise (Cubs)
16. Oswaldo Navarro, ss, Everett (Mariners)
17. Matt Chico, lhp, Yakima (Diamondbacks)
18. Travis Ishikawa, 1b, Salem-Keizer (Giants)
19. Colt Morton, c, Eugene (Padres)
20. Pat Misch, lhp, Salem-Keizer (Giants)

ROOKIE ADVANCED

APPALACHIAN LEAGUE

1. Adam Miller, rhp, Burlington (Indians)
2. Chris Young, of, Bristol (White Sox)
3. Robert Valido, ss, Bristol (White Sox)
4. James Houser, lhp, Princeton (Devil Rays)
5. Daric Barton, c, Johnson City (Cardinals)
6. Chuck James, lhp, Danville (Braves)
7. Carlos Perez, lhp, Bluefield (Orioles)
8. Matt Esquivel, of, Danville (Braves)
9. Denard Span, of, Elizabethton (Twins)
10. Rafael Perez, lhp, Burlington (Indians)
11. Evan Meek, rhp, Elizabethton (Twins)
12. Mitch Talbot, rhp, Martinsville (Astros)
13. Tim Tisch, lhp, Bristol (White Sox)
14. Charlie Morton, rhp, Danville (Braves)
15. Dusty Gomon, 1b, Elizabethton (Twins)
16. Felipe Paulino, rhp, Martinsville (Astros)
17. Orionny Lopez, rhp, Bristol (White Sox)
18. Robinson Diaz, c, Pulaski (Blue Jays)
19. Kyle Phillips, c/1b, Elizabethton (Twins)
20. Tyler Davidson, dh/of, Kingsport (Mets)

PIONEER LEAGUE

1. Ian Stewart, 3b, Casper (Rockies)
2. Chad Billingsley, rhp, Ogden (Dodgers)
3. Lou Palmisano, c, Helena (Brewers)
4. Bobby Wilson, c, Provo (Angels)
5. Xavier Paul, of, Ogden (Dodgers)
6. Habelito Hernandez, 2b, Billings (Reds)
7. Warner Madrigal, of, Provo (Angels)
8. Mike Megrew, lhp, Ogden (Dodgers)
9. Dana Eveland, lhp, Helena (Brewers)
10. Joey Votto, 1b, Billings (Reds)
11. Abel Moreno, rhp, Provo (Angels)
12. Chin-Lung Hu, ss, Ogden (Dodgers)
13. Howie Kendrick, 2b, Provo (Angels)
14. Carlos Morban, rhp, Provo (Angels)
15. Miguel Perez, c, Billings (Reds)
16. Brandon McCarthy, rhp, Great Falls (White Sox)
17. Marcos Carvajal, rhp, Ogden (Dodgers)
18. Carlos Gonzalez, of, Missoula (Diamondbacks)
19. Ricardo Nanita, of, Great Falls (White Sox)
20. Juan Morillo, rhp, Casper (Rockies)

ROOKIE

ARIZONA LEAGUE

1. Chris Lubanski, of, Royals 1
2. Wladimir Balentien, of, Mariners
3. Ryan Harvey, of, Cubs
4. Mitch Maier, c, Royals 1
5. Alexi Ogando, of, Athletics
6. Ronald Bay, rhp, Cubs
7. Shane Costa, of, Royals 2
8. Adam Jones, ss, Mariners
9. Brandon Wood, ss, Angels
10. Charlie Fermaint, of, Brewers
11. Leslie Nacar, rhp, Giants
12. Lizahio Baez, of, Rangers
13. Mike Aviles, ss, Royals 1
14. Jorge Mejia, 2b, Athletics
15. Don Sutton, 1b, Athletics
16. Brett Martinez, c, Angels
17. Irving Falu, 2b, Royals 2
18. Sean Rodriguez, ss, Angels
19. Gilberto Acosta, ss, Brewers
20. Javier Herrera, of, Athletics

GULF COAST LEAGUE

1. Eric Duncan, 3b, Yankees
2. Jake Stevens, lhp, Braves
3. Jarrod Saltalamacchia, c, Braves
4. Hector Made, ss, Yankees
5. Lorenzo Scott, of, Orioles
6. Blair Johnson, rhp, Pirates
7. Matt Moses, 3b, Twins
8. Tyler Pelland, lhp, Red Sox/Reds
9. Jai Miller, of, Marlins
10. Steve Doetsch, of, Braves
11. Etanislao Abreu, 2b, Dodgers
12. Harvey Garcia, rhp, Red Sox
13. Jo Jo Reyes, lhp, Braves
14. Alexander Smit, lhp, Twins
15. Matt Capps, rhp, Pirates
16. Jay Sborz, rhp, Tigers
17. Estee Harris, of, Yankees
18. Kiel Fisher, 3b, Phillies
19. Paul Bacot, rhp, Braves
20. Kenny Lewis, of, Reds

INDEPENDENT LEAGUES

Indy leagues achieve stability, prove viable source for talent

BY J.J. COOPER

Attendance was down for most of the established independent leagues in 2003, but it's a sign of progress that a minor downturn wasn't a major cause of concern.

Central league champions
Jackson celebrates sweep of Amarillo in Championship Series

Only the Frontier League saw an increase in average attendance per team in 2003, but the big five actually ended up drawing 6,376,618 fans overall, up from 6,015,705 in 2002. That was thanks largely to the addition of two expansion teams in the Central League.

But with the Atlantic, Central, Frontier, Northeast and Northern leagues all averaging more than 1,900 fans per game—the Atlantic and Northern each averaged more than 3,800—the big five have settled into a period of stability.

The Central, Frontier, Northern and Northeast leagues have all been around for more than a decade, while the Atlantic League has six seasons under its belt. All have carved niches in their respective geographic areas, and indy ball has found a successful secondary source of markets by placing teams in the shadow of major league clubs.

While the Professional Baseball Agreement, the document that governs the relationship between major league and affiliated minor league clubs makes it nearly impossible to move an affiliated minor league team into a major league city or suburb without the permission of the major league club, indy teams are under no restrictions.

When the Northern League moved the Duluth-Superior Dukes, an original franchise, to Kansas City for the 2003 season, the T-Bones drew more than 200,000 fans, despite the renewed success of the Royals.

Source Of Talent

Where there are still a sampling of leagues that quickly pop-up, and just as quickly disappear, the big five indy leagues now worry less about franchises folding than developing new markets. And where independent leagues used to be seen as a way station for has-beens and never-will-bes, major league teams are now turning to the leagues as a viable source of additional talent in growing numbers.

The Central League sold a league-record 14 players to big league clubs during the 2003 season, up from four in 2002. The Atlantic League had several players, including outfielders Rickey Henderson and Curtis Pride, and righthander Jose Lima, go from indy ball to the majors within weeks. The Northern League sold 27 players to affiliated teams, which league officials believed was a record, although records on the subject are incomplete.

LARRY LEVANTI

Rickey Henderson

More and more, major league teams are keeping an eye on the independent leagues. After all, it costs very little to purchase an independent league player's contract, which means indy players are a low-cost, low-risk pickup.

"Now more so than two years ago clubs are saying to themselves let's try to get some supplemental coverage. Clubs are being more proactive in saying it's another form of player procurement," said Rockies scout Mike Berger, who covered the Frontier League.

In 2003, plenty of teams took chances on indy players, and in plenty of cases, it paid off.

The Giants signed righthander Chris Begg from the St. Paul Saints and sent him to high Class A. He quickly forced a promotion, as he went 4-1, 1.15 for San Jose before going 2-1, 4.38 at Double-A Norwich.

2003 INDEPENDENT LEAGUE ALL-STARS

Selected by Baseball America

Pos.	Player, Club (League)	AVG	AB	R	H	2B	3B	HR	RBI	SB
C	Kirk Pierce, Schaumburg (Northern)	.305	295	59	90	27	1	15	72	0
1B	Eddie Pearson, Kansas City (Northern)	.362	343	57	124	19	1	14	78	1
2B	Vic Davilla, Allentown (Northeast)	.338	331	58	112	25	1	20	74	2
SS	Elvis Peña, Long Island (Atlantic)	.316	478	104	151	30	6	8	54	45
3B	Jose Amado, Bridgeport (Atlantic)	.317	435	63	138	25	1	10	68	5
OF	Harry Berrios, Winnipeg (Northern)	.312	375	53	117	18	1	15	73	2
OF	Michael Coleman, Newark (Atlantic)	.320	222	53	71	14	0	23	68	2
OF	Buck McNabb, San Angelo (Central)	.350	391	75	137	27	3	10	81	8
DH	Josh Loggins, Washington (Frontier)	.331	290	63	96	13	5	24	72	15
		W	L	ERA	G	SV	IP	H	BB	SO
SP	Rafael Gross, Winnipeg (Northern)	13	2	2.28	18	0	115	102	19	69
SP	John Kelly, North Shore (Northeast)	13	2	2.17	18	0	128	106	25	139
SP	Kenny Rayborn, Jackson (Central)	10	2	2.27	14	0	95	86	21	84
SP	Jason Shelley, Rockford (Frontier)	7	1	0.85	10	0	74	49	21	82
RP	Mike Guilfoyle, Bridgeport (Atlantic)	7	3	1.90	57	40	62	51	20	56

PLAYER OF THE YEAR: Jason Shelley, rhp, Rockford (Frontier).

Relaxed Shelley has breakout year

There were many times when Jason Shelley almost called it quits, times when he thought his dream of becoming a major leaguer was done. But it wasn't until he resigned himself to that fact that his career really took off.

PLAYER of the YEAR

In Shelley's first two years in independent ball, in 2001-02, he spent plenty of time wondering if he'd make it back to affiliated ball. He heard plenty of promises and had plenty of people tell him he was going to be signed by a big league club, only to find himself disappointed.

So he decided to stop worrying about attracting attention from big league clubs. For once, he was going to pitch for the joy of pitching, and leading Rockford to a Frontier League title.

"Once Rockford started, I was happy," Shelley said. "It was my last year in the league and I know all the guys. I just wanted to win and make the playoffs. When I started doing well people kept saying, 'Oh, you might get picked up.' I told them: 'I don't want to hear it. I don't care.' "

Things didn't turn out quite as Shelley had planned as his contract was acquired by the Milwaukee Brewers; he went on to help lead the Brewers' Double-A Huntsville team to the Southern League finals.

But before leaving Rockford in late July, he did enough to be named Baseball America's 2003 Independent League Player of the Year.

Shelley went 7-1, 0.85 for the RiverHawks to win the Frontier League ERA title. He also broke the league's season ERA record and had the third-best ERA in the modern indy ball era. With 82 strikeouts in 74 innings, he was on pace to break his own Frontier League strikeout record before he signed with the Brewers.

"When I was pitching (in Rockford), I didn't think about how well I was doing," Shelley said. "The more I look back on it, it was unbelievable. I wasn't giving up any runs. But at the time, it was no big deal. I was just doing my job."

Shelley's success comes in large part from his split-finger fastball. Originally a shortstop and third baseman, he broke into pro ball as a nondrafted free agent with the Pirates in 1999. A year later, he was converted to the mound but the Pirates

CARL KLINE

Solid as a rock
Rockford's Jason Shelley

asked him to junk his split-finger.

Without his dominant pitch, Shelley went 2-1, 3.92 in 39 innings with the Pirates, and was cut during spring training in 2001.

But he started throwing his splitter again in 2002, and his pitching career turned around. He went 9-5, 3.53 with Rockford in 2002, striking out 156 in 119 innings with seven double-digit strikeout games in 18 starts.

Shelley's second season in Rockford was better than the first. On July 18, the Brewers helped make his dream come into view.

"When I look back at the year, it's funny how fast things can change," he said.

PREVIOUS WINNERS

1996—Darryl Motley, dh, Fargo-Moorhead (Northern)
1997—Mike Meggers, of, Duluth-Superior (Northern)
1998—Morgan Burkhart, 1b, Richmond (Frontier)
1999—Carmine Cappuccio, of, New Jersey (Northern)
2000—Anthony Lewis, 1b, Duluth-Superior (Northern)
2001—Mike Warner, of, Somerset (Atlantic)
2002—Bobby Madritsch, lhp, Winnipeg (Northern)

Coming out of college, no team drafted Justin Olson, as the Illinois product had an unsightly 7.58 ERA as a college senior. But after getting healthy and in better shape, Olson showed off a 91-93 mph fastball that touched 96 for the Frontier League's Rockford RiverHawks. He was quickly signed by the Twins, and he went 3-0, 2.30 with five saves in stops at low and high Class A.

Frontier Posts Big Numbers

The Frontier League, which was formed in 1993, had its most successful year attendance-wise, as the league topped the million mark for the first time in league history. Clubs went from an average of 79,032 fans in 2002 to 92,447 fans per team in 2003.

The biggest reason for the boost was the Gateway Grizzlies. After drawing 92,819 fans in 2002, the Grizzlies led the league with 168,067 fans in 2003. Washington and Kalamazoo also saw healthy attendance increases in 2003.

The league also showed continued growth on the field. While the Atlantic and Northern leagues spend much of their energy on signing minor league veterans, the Frontier League focuses entirely on younger players with no previous professional experience. That's in large measure because it has a 27-year-old age limit. None of the other leagues has such a limitation.

The league sold 16 players to affiliated teams during the season, including league MVP Josh Loggins and ERA leader Jason Shelley.

Struggling Leagues

It's become almost a tradition that an independent league will debut, or fold (or often both). In 2003, it was the Arizona-Mexico League that tried, and failed, to make it through a season.

Poor attendance and financial difficulties led to the four-team league suspending operations only three weeks after Opening Day. The league was attempting to reorganize as the Southwest League for 2004, giving up its goal of having teams located in Mexico.

The Southeastern League had less troubles, as the league did make it through its second season—barely—and actually expanded to six teams, after having only four teams make it through the 2002 season. But the league still had a ways to go to show staying power.

Only Pensacola drew more than 300 fans per game, and two of the six teams played the entire season without permanent homes. And while most indy leagues sold a number of players to affiliated clubs during the season, only two Southeastern League players, infielders Tobin Swope and Heath Kelly, jumped to affiliated ball.

ARIZONA-MEXICO LEAGUE

Like a lot of fledgling independent leagues, the Arizona-Mexico League hoped to bring baseball back to cities in 2003 that had gone without professional baseball for years.

But like several independent leagues over the past decade, the idea fell short in the execution. The ownership group set to run the Nogales, Ariz., franchise fell through before the season began. The Bisbee-Douglas owners tried to foot the bill for both teams, but poor attendance meant that the league's teams quickly ran into financial problems.

Less than three weeks after the season started, league commissioner Bob Lipp decided to suspend the league with the hope of restarting in 2004.

During the league's brief season, it received the most attention when the Bisbee-Douglas Copper Kings allowed a fan to bid on E-Bay for the right to play in a game. Robert Ballinger bid $2,500 to get one at-bat. He struck out in his brief appearance.

STANDINGS

	W	L	PCT	GB
Nogales	8	4	.667	—
Bisbee-Douglas	6	6	.500	2
Tecate	4	4	.500	2
Cananea	2	6	.250	4

League suspended operations on June 17.

INDIVIDUAL BATTING LEADERS

(Minimum 27 Plate Appearances)

	AVG	AB	R	H	2B	3B	HR	RBI	SB
Aracena, Sandy, Tecate	.464	28	7	13	5	0	0	9	0
Alvarez, Juan Carlos, Tec.	.429	35	7	15	3	0	0	6	2
Solano, Benji, Cananea	.423	26	2	11	2	0	0	2	1
Okano, Mark, Tecate	.417	24	9	10	1	0	0	3	3
Spiker, Adam, B-D	.395	38	5	15	3	1	1	12	0
Meza, Peter, B-D	.381	21	2	8	0	0	0	5	3
Johnson, Matt, B-D	.357	28	6	10	3	0	0	6	2
Lopez, Oscar, Nogales	.333	48	9	16	3	2	1	6	1
Perez, Tommy, Nogales	.333	45	10	15	3	0	2	8	3
Garcia, David, Tecate	.333	39	7	13	2	1	0	6	0
Carr, Chuck, B-D	.326	46	9	15	3	1	1	5	10
Thompson, Adam, Can.	.323	31	4	10	1	1	1	3	4
Bruntyn, Brad, Tecate	.318	22	4	7	3	0	0	9	1
Archer, Phil, B-D	.317	41	14	13	2	0	3	9	1
Dorame, Ricky, Nogales	.311	45	6	14	5	1	1	8	3

INDIVIDUAL PITCHING LEADERS

(Minimum 8 Innings)

	W	L	ERA	G	SV	IP	H	BB	SO
Quick, David, Nogales	0	0	0.00	4	0	10	4	4	9
Hall, Brad, B-D	0	0	0.00	4	0	9	10	1	3
Sena, Jason, Cananea	2	0	1.08	4	0	8	7	3	6
Trevino, Chris, B-D	2	0	1.71	3	0	21	11	10	23
Burgess, Rich, Nogales	2	1	1.83	3	0	20	12	7	28
Elias, Rob, Nogales	1	0	1.86	7	1	10	8	3	10
Ross, Brian, Nogales	2	0	2.21	5	0	20	17	10	22
Monterbo, Adam, B-D	2	0	2.25	3	0	20	15	12	8
Kuhlmeyer, Kasey, Tecate	1	1	3.00	2	0	12	9	7	5
Rios, Prentice, Tecate	1	0	3.00	3	0	9	12	5	6

ATLANTIC LEAGUE

The Atlantic League has positioned itself as the independent league of choice for veteran players. The league is the most aggressive at pursuing minor league free agents, and has become an attractive alternative to Triple-A for ex-big leaguers who are trying to work their way back to the majors.

But the success stories of past years paled in comparison to the league's signings in 2003. The league added a future Hall of Famer to the league, and also helped an ex-big leaguer go from a has-been to a major league ace.

The Newark Bears created a ripple of attention when they signed former Astros and Tigers righthander Jose Lima. Lima was released by the Tigers after an ugly 4-6, 7.77 season in 2002. A couple of weeks later, the Bears added outfielder Rickey Henderson, who came to the Atlantic League to stay in shape while he searched for a major league contract.

The two were a perfect pair for the Bears, as Lima went 6-1, 2.33 before signing with the Royals, while Henderson was leading the league in batting (.339) and on-base percentage (.493) when he signed with the Dodgers in July.

After the success Lima and Henderson had, Atlantic League officials hoped that their experiences would help bring more former major leaguers to the league.

Jeff Nettles

"We're getting players who don't want to take a Triple-A job," league executive director Joe Klein said. "A starting pitcher at Triple-A has to wait for one of five guys to get hurt. The agents now realize that for the short term that this may be a better alternative."

Despite Henderson and Lima's success, the Bears were hovering around .500 when the two left. While Newark had the big names, Camden had the best record in the league during the regular season, thanks in part to catcher Angel Peña (.338-16-66), outfielder Brad Strauss (.331-11-55) and righthander Ben Simon (15-6, 2.74).

In the playoffs, Somerset knocked out Camden in two games in the semifinals, then beat Nashua 8-4 in the deciding Game 5 of the championship series for the Patriots second Atlantic League title. Jeff Nettles, the son of former Yankee third baseman Graig Nettles, hit .450 (9-for-20) with a home run and five RBIs to be named playoff MVP.

STANDINGS

FIRST HALF

NORTH	W	L	PCT	GB
Nashua Pride	39	24	.619	—
Bridgeport Bluefish	34	29	.540	5
Long Island Ducks	32	31	.508	7
Pennsylvania Road Warriors	14	49	.222	25
SOUTHERN	**W**	**L**	**PCT**	**GB**
Camden Riversharks	41	22	.651	—
Newark Bears	32	31	.508	9
Somerset Patriots	30	33	.476	11
Atlantic City Surf	30	33	.476	11

SECOND HALF

NORTH	W	L	PCT	GB
Bridgeport Bluefish	39	24	.619	—
Long Island Ducks	35	28	.556	4
Nashua Pride	32	31	.508	7
Pennsylvania Road Warriors	16	46	.258	22½
SOUTH	**W**	**L**	**PCT**	**GB**
Somerset Patriots	37	26	.587	—
Camden Riversharks	37	26	.587	—
Atlantic City Surf	33	30	.524	4
Newark Bears	22	40	.355	14½

PLAYOFFS: Semifinals—Somerset defeated Camden 2-0 and Nashua defeated Bridgeport 2-1 in best-of-3 series. **Finals**—Somerset defeated Nashua 3-2 in best-of-5 series.

MANAGERS: Atlantic City—Mitch Williams. **Bridgeport**— Jose Lind. **Camden**—Wayne Krenchicki. **Long Island**—Don McCormack. **Nashua**—Butch Hobson. **Newark**—Bill Madlock. **Pennsylvania**—Bert Pena. **Somerset**—Sparky Lyle.

ATTENDANCE: Long Island 421,359; Somerset 345,798; Camden 300,130; Bridgeport 231,407; Newark 191,034; Atlantic City 177,723; Nashua 132,278.

ALL-STAR TEAM: C—Damian Sapp, Nashua. **1B**—Oreste Marrero, Bridgeport. **2B**—Alex Eckelman, Camden. **SS**—Elvis Pena, Long Island. **3B**—Brandon Jackson, Atlantic City. **OF**—Rolo Avila, Brideport; Kimera Bartee, Long Island; Derrick Gibson, Long Island. **DH**—Juan Thomas, Atlantic City. **Util**—Dario Delgado, Pennsylvania. **LHP**—Jon Cannon, Long Island. **RHP**—Ben Simon, Camden.

Most Valuable Player: Rolo Avila, Bridgeport. **Pitcher of the Year:** Ben Simon, Camden. **Manager of the Year:** Sparky Lyle, Somerset. **Executive of the Year:** Michael Hirsch, Long Island.

INDIVIDUAL BATTING LEADERS

(Minimum340 Plate Appearances)

	AVG	AB	R	H	2B	3B	HR	RBI	SB
Strauss, Brad, Camden	.331	450	68	149	30	5	11	55	2
Avila, Rolo, Bridgeport	.329	487	80	160	24	5	3	45	20
Francia, Dave, Nashua	.328	396	64	130	24	8	4	37	28
Bartee, Kimera, LI	.328	448	86	147	27	3	8	87	18
Eckelman, Alex, Camden	.321	389	59	125	27	0	4	36	1
Amado, Jose, Bridgeport	.317	435	63	138	25	1	10	68	5
Pena, Elvis, Long Island	.316	478	104	151	30	6	8	54	45
Kilburg, Joe, Nashua	.314	430	59	135	28	2	6	63	22
Jackson, Brandon, AC	.302	434	61	131	26	2	7	64	12
Johnson, Ric, AC	.301	429	78	129	30	1	2	53	19

INDIVIDUAL PITCHING LEADERS

(Minimum101 Innings)

	W	L	ERA	G	SV	IP	H	BB	SO
Cannon, Jon, Long Island	7	6	1.86	38	1	116	69	48	83
Rekar, Bryan, Long Island	9	4	2.12	23	0	140	118	17	101
Chantres, Carlos, Nashua	10	4	2.73	27	2	135	141	52	80
Simon, Ben, Camden	15	6	2.74	24	0	164	144	31	102
Jensen, Justin, Somerset	9	3	2.88	19	0	125	109	36	79
Cornett, Brad, Bridgeport	8	4	3.03	22	0	149	130	34	96
Chavez, Anthony, AC	12	8	3.12	25	0	179	158	51	121
Smith, Brian, Nashua	7	8	3.14	18	0	106	94	23	64
Falteisek, Steve, Somerset	7	7	3.31	25	0	133	135	43	81
Imazeki, Masaru, Bridgeport	10	8	3.39	25	0	151	138	44	95

ATLANTIC CITY

BATTING	AVG	AB	R	H	2B	3B	HR	RBI	SB
Ball, Jeff, 1b	.000	12	1	0	0	0	0	0	0
Batiste, Kim, 3b	.233	43	2	10	1	0	1	6	0
Beamon, Trey, of	.230	139	19	32	7	0	1	10	7
Booth, Jeremy, 1b-c	.200	15	1	3	0	0	0	1	0
2-team (1 Bridgeport)	.211	19	1	4	0	0	0	2	0
Burns, Pat, 1b	.255	149	16	38	5	0	4	21	2
Candelaria, Ben, of	.299	157	25	47	5	4	8	29	2
2-team (70 Bridgeport)	.267	416	53	111	16	5	11	54	4
Deitrick, Jeremy, c	.250	4	1	1	0	0	0	1	0
Denny, John, of	.125	32	3	4	1	0	0	1	2
Felix, Lauro, ss	.244	156	21	38	5	0	1	14	1
Gambill, Chad, of	.264	265	40	70	17	0	11	49	4
Garland, Tim, of	.258	97	20	25	7	0	0	6	2
2-team (73 Nashua)	.265	362	57	96	17	4	1	30	12
Gonzalez, Jimmy, c	.107	28	2	3	0	0	1	3	0
Gubanich, Creighton, c	.256	164	17	42	6	0	5	18	0
Jackson, Brandon, 3b	.302	434	61	131	26	2	7	64	12
Jackson, Brody, of	.286	196	30	56	13	1	3	16	7
Johnson, Ric, of	.301	429	78	129	30	1	2	53	19
Lara, Eddie, 2b	.188	16	1	3	1	0	0	0	0
Maestrales, Pete, 2b-3b	.188	16	1	3	0	0	0	1	0
Marval, Raul, 2b-ss	.284	437	70	124	21	2	12	53	3
Matullo, Joe, c	.190	21	1	4	0	0	0	1	0
Meran, Jorge, c	.246	122	9	30	6	0	5	17	2
Monahan, Shane, of	.197	137	12	27	4	1	2	20	2
Polanco, Enohel, ss	.379	58	15	22	1	1	3	6	4
Ruiz, Willy, ss-2b	.179	168	20	30	1	1	0	19	3
Simmons, Brian, of	.314	35	4	11	1	0	0	5	3
Soto, Emison, c	.238	164	21	39	10	0	6	29	0
Spearman, Vernon, of	.220	50	7	11	2	1	1	5	5
Taylor, Lucas, 2b-of	.056	18	1	1	1	0	0	0	0
Thomas, Juan, dh	.286	304	55	87	16	0	27	84	1
Timmons, Ozzie, dh	.205	44	14	9	0	0	3	8	1
Velazquez, Jose, 1b	.311	251	42	78	17	0	7	33	2

PITCHING	W	L	ERA	G	SV	IP	H	BB	SO
Brown, Tighe	0	2	8.66	5	0	17	22	7	6
Calmus, Lance	2	1	2.68	34	0	37	37	12	25
Carroll, Dave	2	5	4.05	30	0	93	112	41	39
Chavez, Anthony	12	8	3.12	25	0	179	158	51	121
Etler, Todd	2	2	3.93	4	0	18	22	5	14
German, Yon	0	2	27.00	2	0	2	10	1	0
High, Andy	10	8	3.79	24	0	145	122	60	125
Jacome, Jason	3	4	3.62	10	0	64	64	12	38
Mallard, Randi	1	1	3.97	45	24	47	50	15	36
Mattson, Craig	5	2	4.29	32	2	35	41	11	28
Navarro, Scott	1	1	1.74	7	0	10	10	1	4
2-team (15 Somerset)	2	4	4.25	22	0	42	50	10	26
Neil, Dan	0	1	9.00	3	0	2	3	0	2
Nunez, Maximo	1	2	8.49	10	0	29	42	15	16
Rutherford, Mark	4	4	4.23	41	1	87	94	41	55
Searle, Chris	1	2	6.07	9	0	13	16	3	11
Shelby, Anthony	1	1	7.00	12	0	9	14	4	6
Thompson, Travis	6	4	3.94	63	1	105	107	35	87
Vega, Rene	1	1	3.30	18	0	30	25	26	25
Wagner, Matt	2	1	6.27	5	0	33	37	7	23
2-team (18 Newark)	11	6	3.90	23	0	154	143	25	104
Williams, Brian	1	4	7.16	7	0	27	41	16	17
Zwirchitz, Andy	8	7	4.51	21	0	107	96	61	73

BRIDGEPORT

BATTING	AVG	AB	R	H	2B	3B	HR	RBI	SB
Almanzar, Rich, 2b-3b	.195	128	18	25	7	1	2	12	5
Amado, Jose, 3b	.317	435	63	138	25	1	10	68	5
Avila, Rolo, of	.329	487	80	160	24	5	3	45	20
Booth, Jeremy, 1b	.250	4	0	1	0	0	0	1	0
Candelaria, Ben, of	.247	259	28	64	11	1	3	25	2
Devarez, Cesar, c	.249	253	28	63	9	2	4	24	3
Espada, Angel, 2b-ss	.323	285	41	92	9	1	3	30	17
Jenkins, Dee, 3b-2b	.067	30	2	2	1	0	0	0	0
Kuilan, Hector, c	.280	257	28	72	20	1	7	29	0
Lindsey, Rodney, of	.235	243	32	57	5	4	3	14	29
Marrero, Oreste, 1b	.273	341	46	93	23	1	9	63	4
Mota, Tony, of	.223	179	25	40	8	4	0	13	6
Offerman, Jose, 2b-dh	.295	356	55	105	24	5	9	60	5
Otanez, Willis, dh-of	.287	442	55	127	30	0	22	79	1
Pennyfeather, William, of	.200	140	18	28	7	0	2	11	2
Rodriguez, Tony, ss	.245	363	38	89	13	1	5	39	8
Sanchez, Wellington, ss	.167	24	1	4	0	0	0	1	0
Wearing, Mel, dh	.261	46	2	12	1	0	0	7	1

PITCHING	W	L	ERA	G	SV	IP	H	BB	SO
Brownson, Mark	0	1	21.00	1	0	3	10	1	3
Cain, Tim	7	3	4.43	15	0	85	99	21	37
Chouinard, Bobby	5	4	2.17	46	2	49	43	17	43
Cornett, Brad	8	4	3.03	22	0	148	130	34	96
Davis, Keith	4	3	5.17	37	0	54	66	15	45
Forster, Scott	1	1	3.94	24	0	29	28	24	25
Guilfoyle, Mike	7	3	1.90	57	40	61	51	20	56
Henthorne, Kevin	4	2	2.48	10	0	58	52	9	26
Hill, Terrence	3	4	4.37	37	0	47	46	29	22
Imazeki, Masaru	10	8	3.39	25	0	151	138	44	95
Lontayo, Alex	4	5	5.46	10	0	57	66	30	48
Love, Jeff	0	0	9.00	2	0	2	3	0	1
Mangieri, John	0	0	7.27	7	0	8	11	7	5
Martinez, Javier	4	1	4.69	43	0	55	50	35	44
Mathews, T.J.	11	6	4.02	30	0	141	150	37	116
Miranda, Angel	3	3	4.72	15	0	74	86	48	36
Raggio, Brady	0	3	2.93	4	0	27	26	6	25
Rosenkranz, Terry	2	1	2.98	28	0	60	47	39	33

CAMDEN

BATTING	AVG	AB	R	H	2B	3B	HR	RBI	SB
Anderson, Travis, c	.308	133	21	41	12	2	1	17	0
Azuaje, Jesus, ss	.291	237	42	69	16	2	3	22	5
Barbieri, Al, dh	.333	3	0	1	0	0	0	0	0
Benjamin, Al, of	.375	16	3	6	3	0	0	1	0
2-team (24 Newark)	.268	82	13	22	6	0	2	10	2
Briggs, Stoney, of	.257	339	49	87	13	1	15	47	10
Delgado, Alex, c	.333	69	7	23	4	0	2	10	0
Eckelman, Alex, 2b-ss	.321	389	59	125	27	0	4	36	1
Fowler, Maleke, of	.297	64	15	19	5	0	2	10	5
Gainey, Bryon, 1b	.206	378	41	78	15	0	19	61	0
Gibbs, Kevin, of	.000	0	0	0	0	0	0	0	0
Jordan, Kevin, 2b	.286	126	18	36	12	0	1	20	0
Maness, Dwight, of	.259	421	79	109	26	8	18	77	34
Miller, David, of-1b	.232	228	24	53	12	0	3	24	1
Morales, Francisco, dh-c	.264	398	46	105	9	1	10	51	1
Nava, Lipso, 3b-ss	.294	378	56	111	18	1	11	42	0
Nunez, Isaias, of-1b	.209	153	19	32	10	0	1	9	0
2-team (41 Pennsylvania)	.252	290	39	73	18	0	4	24	2
Pena, Angel, c	.338	228	31	77	15	2	16	66	1

Sillup, Pat, ph	.000	1	0	0	0	0	0	0	0
Strauss, Brad, of-3b	.331	450	68	149	30	5	11	55	2
Vopata, Nate, 2b	.276	105	19	29	3	3	0	10	1
Warren, Chris, 2b-3b	.185	108	16	20	2	0	5	16	1

PITCHING	W	L	ERA	G	SV	IP	H	BB	SO
Brown, Derek	5	1	3.41	44	2	60	59	20	34
Carrasco, Troy	1	2	4.36	30	1	53	60	15	36
Davis, Kane	1	0	1.13	9	5	8	3	1	9
Dougherty, Kevin	10	3	3.44	13	0	81	73	29	46
Foster, Cliff	5	1	2.45	29	1	51	36	21	34
Kingrey, Jarrod	0	2	1.55	32	3	46	41	12	46
Maness, Nick	0	4	6.38	10	0	36	44	29	15
Martin, Larry	0	1	6.23	8	0	13	12	11	7
Mathews, Del	5	5	3.03	50	25	59	54	23	33
Mikkelsen, Linc	7	3	3.35	13	0	94	76	20	50
Moraga, David	1	4	8.38	7	0	29	40	9	15
2-team (1 Newark)	1	4	8.10	8	0	30	40	9	15
Nussbeck, Mark	9	3	3.62	21	0	129	132	34	97
Pacheco, Delvis	10	7	3.67	23	0	147	145	47	59
Peters, Chris	1	1	5.68	6	0	6	8	6	5
Rizzo, Todd	0	2	6.35	5	0	5	11	3	4
Schurman, Ryan	3	2	3.49	26	0	69	78	21	48
Simon, Ben	15	6	2.68	24	0	164	144	31	102
Ward, Bryan	5	1	1.84	6	0	44	36	8	39

LONG ISLAND

BATTING	AVG	AB	R	H	2B	3B	HR	RBI	SB
Almonte, Wady, 1b-of	.211	57	7	12	3	1	0	5	3
Baez, Kevin, 3b-ss	.293	304	44	89	17	1	5	39	0
Bartee, Kimera, of	.328	448	86	147	27	3	8	87	18
Caputo, Tom, 3b-1b	.205	146	16	30	5	0	1	15	0
Cardona, Javier, c-1b	.265	294	37	78	12	0	8	48	0
2-team (23 Pennsylvania)	.276	381	46	105	15	0	11	62	1
Davies, Justin, of	.292	439	80	128	8	7	0	37	24
DeLeon, Sandy, c	.216	37	5	8	1	0	0	4	0
2-team (5 Somerset)	.241	54	9	13	2	0	0	4	0
Dorsey, Ryan, 2b	.000	1	1	0	0	0	0	0	0
Escobar, Gustavo, 3b-ss	.274	95	11	26	6	0	0	12	0
2-team (76 Pennsylvania)	.294	377	46	111	14	5	1	38	21
Gibson, Derrick, dh-of	.287	460	72	132	33	0	19	89	14
Hage, Tom, 1b	.246	138	16	34	11	0	5	23	0
2-team (30 Newark)	.238	240	28	57	18	0	6	37	0
Hutchins, Norm, of	.185	65	6	12	2	1	0	5	3
Jennings, Doug, 1b	.366	101	23	37	10	0	2	21	2
Johnson, Jason, of	.305	82	11	25	6	0	1	11	4
Lennon, Pat, dh-1b	.327	171	21	56	11	0	6	40	2
McNamara, Rusty, 2b-3b	.299	461	58	138	26	5	3	53	6
Pena, Elvis, ss-2b	.316	478	104	151	30	6	8	54	45
Pogue, Jamie, c	.255	239	38	61	8	1	3	23	0
Saturria, Luis, of	.235	234	31	55	5	4	6	33	5
Whiten, Mark, of	.212	66	4	14	3	0	2	13	1

PITCHING	W	L	ERA	G	SV	IP	H	BB	SO
Andujar, Luis	3	2	4.58	32	2	37	46	12	18
Borbon, Pedro	5	2	2.08	32	0	69	67	14	50
Burton, Tim	3	1	3.96	25	1	25	30	12	22
2-team (16 Pennsylvania)	3	2	4.74	41	1	49	57	20	33
Cannon, Jon	7	6	1.86	38	1	116	69	48	83
Cerbone, Marc	0	0	1.62	12	0	16	10	10	8
Cotton, Joe	0	4	4.10	54	2	68	70	21	54
Dennis, Jason	0	1	4.15	15	0	30	31	20	17
Devey, Phil	3	2	5.77	16	0	34	43	10	20
Harriger, Denny	5	10	3.79	28	0	133	135	29	66
Henriquez, Oscar	1	3	7.07	27	7	28	31	17	28
Kelley, Rich	0	2	6.57	5	0	12	14	5	8
Kozlowski, Kris	1	1	3.78	19	0	16	13	8	11
2-team (29 Nashua)	3	1	5.79	48	1	42	46	20	31
McGlinchy, Kevin	1	1	9.00	12	0	11	15	1	8
Mix, Greg	4	1	2.63	22	3	24	23	8	13
Navarro, Jason	5	4	3.41	14	0	58	48	12	52
Rekar, Bryan	9	4	2.12	23	0	140	118	17	101
Rodgers, Bobby	8	6	4.63	20	0	105	104	52	81
Sheredy, Kevin	0	1	8.18	15	0	11	16	9	7
Smith, Cam	0	0	6.00	7	0	6	7	6	6
Thompson, Mark	3	2	2.88	8	0	50	51	15	35
Weibl, Clint	4	1	4.44	5	0	26	34	8	23
Whitworth, Brad	5	5	3.79	19	0	92	101	16	44
2-team (7 Pennsylvania)	5	8	4.00	26	0	123	142	23	64

NASHUA

BATTING	AVG	AB	R	H	2B	3B	HR	RBI	SB
Boston, D.J., 1b	.249	402	55	100	18	0	13	71	10
Branin, Ronnie, of-3b	.214	140	17	30	4	0	0	15	2
Francia, Dave, of	.328	396	64	130	24	8	4	37	28
Garland, Tim, of	.268	265	37	71	10	4	1	24	10
Howell, Pat, of-2b	.260	258	41	67	5	4	3	21	8
Kilburg, Joe, 2b-of	.314	430	59	135	28	2	6	63	22
Larkin, Garrett, 3b-ss	.216	153	22	33	6	2	1	17	1
Lofton, James, 2b	.241	79	14	19	6	0	1	12	1
Meluskey, Mitch, dh-c	.333	129	20	43	9	1	1	15	2
Murray, Glenn, of	.252	445	85	112	22	0	23	67	15
Nieves, Melvin, of	.256	172	33	44	10	1	7	28	4
2-team (38 Somerset)	.266	297	55	79	17	1	14	55	11
Petersen, Chris, ss	.267	409	42	109	13	1	3	45	8
Pough, Chop, 3b	.301	346	45	104	21	0	11	54	3
Pride, Curtis, of	.344	61	10	21	5	1	5	25	5
Rodarte, Raul, 3b	.412	17	1	7	0	0	0	3	0
Sapp, Damian, c-1b	.237	359	64	85	21	2	25	62	1
Van Horn, Ryan, c	.212	151	20	32	5	0	6	19	0

PITCHING	W	L	ERA	G	SV	IP	H	BB	SO
Chantres, Carlos	10	4	2.73	27	2	135	141	52	80
Corbin, Archie	8	7	3.60	23	0	142	145	57	91
Crawford, Paxton	12	10	5.34	26	0	155	196	42	62
Darley, Ned	2	1	5.64	21	4	22	28	11	8
Hardwick, Bubba	5	7	4.98	31	1	123	150	29	89
Kozlowski, Kris	2	0	7.11	29	1	25	33	12	20
Looney, Brian	7	2	1.51	19	2	83	68	17	52
Lovingier, Kevin	3	1	6.15	41	3	41	48	33	40
Marquetti, Agustin	0	1	10.13	9	0	10	15	12	5
McGlinchy, Kevin	1	0	4.22	10	0	10	13	3	7
2-team (12 Long Island)	2	1	6.65	22	0	21	28	4	15
Meacham, Rusty	2	3	2.21	30	6	36	46	8	23
Ramirez, Enrique	0	0	1.17	15	1	15	5	5	11
Richards, Dave	2	1	1.88	35	1	38	32	14	34
Ricketts, Chad	0	1	12.27	5	0	3	7	4	2
Rollandini, David	2	1	2.93	16	2	15	21	12	13
Roper, John	0	0	5.89	34	2	44	54	16	18
Ruffin, Johnny	0	1	4.26	9	4	6	4	11	9
Smith, Brian	7	8	3.14	18	0	106	94	23	64
Taylor, Tommy	8	7	4.31	35	4	85	91	23	64

NEWARK

BATTING	AVG	AB	R	H	2B	3B	HR	RBI	SB
Benjamin, Al, of	.242	66	10	16	3	0	2	9	2
Britt, Bryan, 3b-1b	.141	78	10	11	2	0	4	11	0
Clyburn, Danny, of-dh	.248	407	57	101	15	2	21	75	4
Coleman, Michael, of-1b	.320	222	53	71	14	0	23	68	2
DeCinces, Tim, c	.192	120	6	23	8	0	2	14	0
Esposito, Paul, 2b-3b	.249	285	43	71	16	5	0	23	3
Goodwin, Curtis, of	.167	36	5	6	1	0	0	4	1
Hage, Tom, 1b	.225	102	12	23	7	0	1	14	0
Henderson, Rickey, of	.339	171	52	58	15	2	8	33	9
LaFlair, Jay, c-3b	.271	251	31	68	12	0	1	15	2
Lara, Eddie, 2b-1b	.322	205	34	66	10	0	9	30	6
2-team (6 Atlantic City)	.312	221	35	69	11	0	9	30	6
Lebron, Francisco, 1b-dh	.246	191	17	47	14	0	7	23	0
Lorenzo, Juan, ss-2b	.333	114	12	38	5	1	1	12	0
Maestrales, Pete, 3b-2b	.234	278	41	65	14	3	6	18	6
2-team (6 Atlantic City)	.231	294	42	68	14	3	6	19	6
Martinez, Eddy, ss	.263	308	39	81	8	2	6	38	6
Martinez, Hipolito, of	.273	143	16	39	2	0	7	15	1
Minor, Ryan, 1b-3b	.253	91	11	23	4	0	4	11	0
Perez, Koby, c	.182	11	0	2	0	0	0	3	0
Perry, Kyle, c	.167	24	0	4	1	0	0	3	0
Piercy, Mike, of	.319	213	32	68	9	0	0	22	29
Quintana, Wil, of	.256	433	58	111	16	2	24	74	14
Ramirez, Pito, of-1b	.227	128	20	29	6	0	6	12	0
Santora, Jack, 2b	.321	106	20	34	6	3	1	10	5
Torres, Jason, c	.248	133	11	33	7	1	1	12	0

PITCHING	W	L	ERA	G	SV	IP	H	BB	SO
Barrios, Manny	0	1	5.40	14	4	18	25	10	11
Bullinger, Jim	2	4	6.51	7	0	37	48	19	22
Castillo, Alberto	7	8	4.40	28	1	114	112	49	98
Clark, Chris	0	1	24.30	4	0	3	7	5	4
Gagliano, Steve	0	3	5.71	6	0	17	27	4	9
Harris, Reggie	0	1	1.74	18	8	20	13	5	17
Hawkins, Al	2	3	6.99	12	0	47	64	19	23
Hazlett, Andy	1	3	5.47	41	0	54	54	18	50
Keinath, Tim	1	2	5.50	16	0	37	43	12	12
Lima, Jose	6	1	2.33	8	0	54	44	5	52
Maduro, Calvin	1	10	6.78	15	0	70	102	22	50
McClellan, Matt	1	0	4.15	7	0	8	7	1	6
Moraga, David	0	0	0.00	1	0	1	0	0	0
Navarro, Jaime	11	5	3.97	17	0	124	139	26	96
Nina, Elvin	2	2	7.00	6	1	18	21	5	14
Parks, Tommy	0	0	7.36	3	0	3	4	2	1
Pena, Alex	0	2	7.79	14	1	17	23	9	12

Peters, Chris	0	0	11.25	3	0	4	8	6	2
Ponce Deleon, Damon	0	4	5.75	40	9	51	52	20	40
Rodriguez, Juan	1	0	10.13	2	0	2	3	3	1
Smith, Hut	0	5	3.83	29	1	42	45	20	28
Stepka, Tom	8	9	4.29	22	0	123	138	25	72
Viera, Rolando	2	2	3.33	34	0	70	75	27	58
Wagner, Matt	9	5	3.25	18	0	121	106	18	81

PENNSYLVANIA

BATTING	AVG	AB	R	H	2B	3B	HR	RBI	SB
Amador, Jerry, of	.233	429	53	100	16	0	18	68	4
Arroyo, Abner, of	.221	68	5	15	3	0	2	4	1
Ayala, Elio, 2b	.190	21	1	4	2	0	0	1	0
Cafiero, Rob, 1b	.239	180	17	43	9	0	4	14	0
Cancel, Robinson, c	.313	67	7	21	3	0	2	11	3
Cardona, Javier, c	.310	87	9	27	3	0	3	14	1
Delgado, Dario, 3b-1b	.289	391	49	113	20	0	22	47	2
Escobar, Gustavo, ss	.301	282	35	85	8	5	1	26	21
Espino, Jose, 3b-2b	.184	163	9	30	8	0	1	13	4
Giron, Alejandro, of	.200	20	0	4	0	0	0	2	1
Hernandez, Alexis, 3b	.333	9	0	3	1	0	0	2	0
Hutchins, Norm, of	.277	137	21	38	7	1	0	7	10
Johnson, Gary, of	.321	274	39	88	17	1	3	29	9
Lamberg, Joshua, c	.200	5	1	1	1	0	0	0	0
Larned, Drew, c	.133	15	1	2	0	0	1	2	0
Lopez-Cao, Mike, c	.243	383	23	93	13	0	3	31	0
Nunez, Isaias, 1b-of	.299	137	20	41	8	0	3	15	2
Ortiz, Asbel, 2b-3b	.227	229	21	52	13	2	4	26	3
Osuna, Alexis, c	.196	92	8	18	0	0	0	7	1
Pena, Bert, 3b-2b	.188	69	5	13	2	0	0	3	0
Reyes, Deurys, of	.210	100	12	21	1	2	2	8	5
Rodriguez, Juan, 3b-of	.191	141	12	27	2	1	3	9	2
2-team (2 Newark)	.191	141	12	27	2	1	3	9	2
Rosario, Omar, of	.249	181	20	45	9	1	5	23	3
Rosario, Victor, of	.188	138	26	26	5	1	0	5	3
Sanchez, Wellington, ss-2b	.246	378	35	93	17	1	6	25	9
2-team (8 Bridgeport)	.241	402	36	97	17	1	6	26	9
Sein, Javier, 1b	.190	174	15	33	12	0	2	10	1

PITCHING	W	L	ERA	G	SV	IP	H	BB	SO
Batson, Byron	0	3	7.97	10	0	20	34	6	11
Burton, Tim	0	1	5.55	16	0	24	27	8	11
Cly, Jason	0	3	8.82	4	0	16	25	5	10
2-team (4 Somerset)	0	3	10.64	8	0	22	35	7	12
Daneker, Pat	3	10	6.12	20	0	110	144	32	43
Dennis, Jason	1	2	6.06	10	0	32	40	19	18
2-team (15 Long Island)	1	3	5.14	25	0	63	71	39	35
Figueroa, Carlos	0	1	4.70	4	0	7	9	5	0
Gagliano, Steve	4	12	6.37	19	0	87	112	27	49
2-team (6 Newark)	4	15	6.26	25	0	105	139	31	58
Geigel, Rolando	0	1	15.43	4	0	4	12	3	4
Heredia, Julian	1	2	3.91	5	0	23	23	10	22
Lopez, Omar	1	3	6.94	34	0	71	87	42	38
Mangrum, Micah	2	3	5.00	13	0	27	35	5	14
McClain, Kevin	1	9	8.66	36	1	88	126	46	48
Miranda, Angel	1	2	9.00	14	1	21	31	15	16
2-team (15 Bridgeport)	4	5	5.66	29	1	95	117	63	52
Morgan, Shawn	1	5	10.13	12	0	24	36	19	9
Perkins, Mike	2	1	4.01	26	5	33	31	17	28
Peters, Chris	0	4	6.44	8	0	36	42	19	19
3-team (6 Camden, 3 Newark)	1	5	6.75	17	0	46	58	31	26
Pizarro, Melvin	1	4	7.97	19	0	20	24	13	11
Ramos, Eddy	5	6	3.72	44	4	92	90	25	53
Rollandini, David	4	9	4.23	15	0	78	90	26	40
2-team (16 Nashua)	6	10	4.02	31	2	94	111	38	53
Rosado, Hector	0	0	22.09	5	0	3	7	2	1
Rosengren, John	0	1	5.06	23	0	21	24	16	18
Runser, Greg	1	5	4.61	32	6	52	62	24	41
Thomas, Adam	1	3	11.37	4	0	12	20	9	7
Tilton, Ira	0	0	3.86	2	0	2	3	1	1
Tokarse, Brian	1	2	7.90	25	0	41	49	30	30
Whitworth, Brad	0	3	4.65	7	0	31	41	7	20
Wykoff, Jarred	0	0	0.00	1	0	0	1	0	0

SOMERSET

BATTING	AVG	AB	R	H	2B	3B	HR	RBI	SB
Barker, Glen, of	.200	15	3	3	0	2	0	1	2
Blosser, Greg, dh	.182	44	3	8	1	0	2	5	0
Cancel, Robinson, c	.237	236	27	56	3	0	10	38	11
2-team (19 Pennsylvania)	.254	303	34	77	6	0	12	49	14
Clemente, Edgard, of	.331	127	28	42	8	1	9	35	1
DeLeon, Sandy, c	.294	17	4	5	1	0	0	0	0
Dryer, Matt, of-1b	.249	353	53	88	24	2	7	40	8
Escandon, Emiliano, 2b	.298	420	70	125	15	4	6	58	15
Figga, Mike, of	.200	15	2	3	1	0	0	0	0
Gsell, Tony, ss-of	.263	167	29	44	6	0	11	35	4
Hernandez, Alex, of-1b	.281	249	37	70	8	1	3	30	11
Hutchins, Norm, of	.257	284	41	73	13	4	2	26	16
3-team (31 Penn., 15 L.I.)	.280	82	14	23	4	2	2	14	3
Knight, Marcus, of	.196	56	7	11	2	0	0	5	0
Lopez, Luis, 1b	.296	280	28	83	14	0	8	49	0
Luster, Jeremy, 1b-of	.250	188	28	47	8	0	2	25	6
Martins, Eric, ss	.299	402	65	120	17	1	5	43	5
McGee, Tom, c	.221	154	18	34	5	0	1	14	0
Meluskey, Mitch, c-of	.392	102	19	40	9	0	1	19	3
2-team (35 Nashua)	.359	231	39	83	18	1	2	34	5
Nettles, Jeff, 3b	.286	412	68	118	25	2	13	56	1
Nieves, Melvin, of	.280	125	22	35	7	0	7	27	7
Radmanovich, Ryan, of	.282	305	58	86	12	4	21	65	5
Warner, Michael, dh-of	.272	464	81	126	24	2	6	43	29

PITCHING	W	L	ERA	G	SV	IP	H	BB	SO
Aldred, Scott	3	1	1.85	20	7	24	21	6	28
Brea, Lesli	2	1	3.22	35	7	36	26	8	33
Cly, Jason	0	0	15.88	4	0	5	10	2	2
Dace, Derek	0	1	9.00	5	0	4	8	0	0
Dickson, Jason	10	5	3.50	23	0	149	152	41	115
Dodd, Robert	7	7	3.97	18	0	99	100	38	74
Falteisek, Steve	7	7	3.31	25	0	133	135	43	81
Gray, Mike	1	4	1.94	36	0	41	46	21	33
Griffin, Kirk	2	4	5.58	36	1	61	74	20	37
Jensen, Justin	9	3	2.88	19	0	125	109	36	79
Jodie, Brett	12	5	3.78	24	0	135	145	37	88
Krivda, Rick	3	6	6.28	16	0	76	96	24	41
Luce, Rob	2	1	2.12	10	1	17	17	7	5
Navarro, Scott	1	3	5.06	15	0	32	40	9	22
Oquist, Mike	3	6	3.97	33	1	70	83	25	34
Schwager, Matt	5	3	3.33	39	5	51	50	15	36
Smith, Cam	0	2	5.46	21	4	28	24	24	30
2-team (7 Camden)	0	2	5.56	28	4	34	3	30	36

CENTRAL LEAGUE

Give Jackson manager Dan Shwam a choice between adding a hitter in the middle of his lineup or a potential ace for his rotation and he'll choose the pitcher every time.

After the 2003 season the Senators had, it's hard to argue with Shwam. With a team that had few power threats but plenty of pitching, the Senators went 59-37 for the best record in the Central League. The Senators then rode their pitching to the Central League title, sweeping the Amarillo Dillas in the championship series.

Kenny Rayborn

"You've got to put a premium on something. People say that sometimes I go overboard and sometimes I do, but if you pitch you always have a shot," Shwam said.

In the championship series, the Senators allowed five runs in three games, winning the decisive Game Three when Keto Anderson drove in Eric Darjean for the winning run with an infield single with two outs in the tenth in a 4-3 victory. For the season, the Senators set a league record with a 2.91 ERA.

And they did it with an ever-evolving rotation. Righthander Kenny Rayborn dominated the league, going 10-2, 2.27 in 95 innings, before being sold to the Cleveland Indians, and he was in Triple-A Buffalo by the end of the season. Righthander Russ Herbert was 4-4, 3.86 when he decided to retire. The Senators moved Dan Stout out of the bullpen, and he was dominant enough (4-2, 1.50) that the Milwaukee Brewers snapped him up.

Ryan Creek (10-4, 2.66) helped fill the void, as he struck out 127 in 125 innings. Another Senators reclamation project, righthander Marc Persails stepped up to go 8-3, 2.70 and earn the start in the title game.

While Jackson dominated the league with its pitching, San Angelo's Buck McNabb ran away with the MVP award. McNabb hit .350-10-81, leading the league in average, RBIs, hits (137) and runs scored (75).

The league expanded from eight to 10 teams in 2003, adding franchises in Shreveport, La., and Robstown, Texas. Shreveport moved into a long-time Double-A Texas League city when the Captains moved to Frisco, Texas, following the 2002 season.

STANDINGS

FIRST HALF

EAST	W	L	PCT	GB
Jackson Senators	31	17	.646	—
Shreveport Sports	29	19	.604	2
Fort Worth Cats	24	24	.500	7
Springfield/Ozark Mountain Ducks	23	25	.479	8
Alexandria Aces	23	25	.479	8
WEST	**W**	**L**	**PCT**	**GB**
Edinburg Roadrunners	28	20	.583	—
Amarillo Dillas	27	21	.563	1
San Angelo Colts	23	25	.479	5
Coastal Bend Aviators	17	31	.354	11
Rio Grande Valley WhiteWings	15	33	.313	13

SECOND HALF

EAST	W	L	PCT	GB
Fort Worth Cats	27	19	.587	—
Jackson Senators	28	20	.583	—
Shreveport Sports	22	25	.468	5½
Springfield/Ozark Mountain Ducks	17	31	.354	11
Alexandria Aces	17	31	.354	11
WEST	**W**	**L**	**PCT**	**GB**
Edinburg Roadrunners	30	18	.625	—
Coastal Bend Aviators	29	19	.604	1
San Angelo Colts	24	23	.511	5½
Rio Grande Valley WhiteWings	22	26	.458	8
Amarillo Dillas	21	25	.457	8

PLAYOFFS: Semifinals—Amarillo defeated Edinburg 3-2 and Jackson defeated Fort Worth 3-2 in best-of-5 series. **Final**—Jackson defeated Amarillo 3-0 in best-of-5 series.

MANAGERS: Alexandria—R.C. Lichtenstein. **Amarillo**—John Harris. **Coastal Bend**—Les Lancaster. **Edinburg**—Chad Tredaway. **Fort Worth**—Wayne Terwilliger. **Jackson**—Dan Shwam. **Rio Grande Valley**—James Frisbee. **San Angelo**—Steve Maddock. **Shreveport**—Terry Bevington. **Springfield/Ozark**—Phil Wilson.

ATTENDANCE: Fort Worth 161,655; Edinburg 141,900; Coastal Bend 103,134; Jackson 91,571; San Angelo 83,040; Amarillo 85,924; Springfield/Ozark 75,865; Rio Grande Valley 59,130; Shreveport 51,126; Alexandria 37,528 .

ALL-STAR TEAM: C—Jacob Wallis, San Angelo. **1B**—Derek Henderson, Edinburg. **2B**—Alex Llanos, Amarillo. **3B**—Tony Schifano, Shreveport. **SS**—Kevin Polcovich, San Angelo. **OF**—Carlos Adolfo, Alexandria/Coastal Bend; Buck McNabb, San Angelo; Juan Rocha, San Angelo. **DH**—Samone Peters, Alexandria. **RHP**—Rob Averette, Shreveport. **LHP**—Shaun Shiery, Alexandria. **RP**—Brandon Parker, Jackson.

Player of the Year: Buck McNabb, San Angelo. **Rookie Player of the Year:** Matt Mann, Coastal Bend. **Rookie Pitcher of the Year:** Eric Montoya, Edinburg. **Manager of the Year:** Chad Tredaway, Edinburg.

INDIVIDUAL BATTING LEADERS

(Minimum 259 Plate Appearances)

	AVG	AB	R	H	2B	3B	HR	RBI	SB
McNabb, Buck, San Angelo	.350	391	75	137	27	3	10	81	8
Llanos, Alex, Amarillo	.340	391	71	133	30	7	8	68	17
Rocha, Juan, San Angelo	.332	374	72	124	21	1	19	73	7
Adolfo, Carlos, Coastal Bend	.322	323	69	104	28	3	19	62	15
Kofler, Eric, Amarillo	.320	300	48	96	23	8	10	63	1
Langaigne, Selwyn, RGV	.318	255	43	81	15	3	5	40	21
Wallis, Jacob, San Angelo	.313	275	50	86	21	1	12	63	3
Battersby, Eric, Coastal Bend	.313	288	54	90	17	3	10	52	4
Cameron, Stanton, San Angelo	.310	290	67	90	24	1	14	56	3
Angel, Anthony, Edinburg	.309	404	63	125	22	4	7	68	2

INDIVIDUAL PITCHING LEADERS

(Minimum 77 Innings)

	W	L	ERA	G	SV	IP	H	BB	SO
Rayborn, Kenny, Jackson	10	2	2.27	14	0	95	86	21	84
Shiery, Shaun, Alexandria	10	3	2.37	18	0	129	117	27	118
Averette, Rob, Shreveport	13	4	2.42	21	0	153	131	32	103
Langen, Brian, Coastal Bend	7	4	2.48	22	1	131	116	35	67
Stockstill, Jason, Amarillo	10	5	2.49	19	0	134	112	53	119
Valentin, Dan, RGV	10	6	2.51	21	1	129	124	36	123
Aragon, Angel, Fort Worth	8	5	2.57	21	0	116	106	32	91
Thomas, Adam, Amarillo	7	4	2.62	16	0	107	106	27	85
Creek, Ryan, Jackson	10	4	2.66	19	0	125	99	48	127
Persails, Mark, Jackson	8	3	2.70	14	0	90	73	22	79

ALEXANDRIA

BATTING	AVG	AB	R	H	2B	3B	HR	RBI	SB
Adolfo, Carlos, of	.326	264	50	86	22	2	16	56	13
Boyle, Danny, 2b	.250	208	37	52	4	1	1	18	19
Brown, Michael, of-3b	.222	72	15	16	2	1	3	14	7
Ceriani, Matt, c	.294	204	24	60	10	0	7	27	2
Dambach, Ryan, of	.000	4	1	0	0	0	0	0	0
Doggett, Kyndrich, of	.167	12	0	2	0	1	0	0	1
France, Ryan, dh-p	.261	23	2	6	0	0	1	1	0
Granger, Mike, ss-2b	.229	258	43	59	17	2	1	23	18
Hammond, Derry, of	.280	286	52	80	13	2	19	54	9
Harkrider, Kip, ss	.316	117	20	37	9	3	1	15	3
Hewes, Robert, 1b	.361	61	12	22	5	0	0	8	7
Knight, Marcus,of	.000	1	0	0	0	0	0	0	0
2-team (48 Coastal Bend)	.289	173	37	50	14	1	2	8	6
Molidor, David, 3b	.214	14	0	3	0	0	0	2	0
Oropeza, Willie, 3b-c	.282	309	44	87	16	0	7	47	3
Palazzolo, Tony, 1b	.294	109	13	32	5	0	1	13	0
Peters, Samone, dh-of	.275	357	52	98	19	1	20	74	0
Ricard, Toby, of-if	.210	195	24	41	6	0	2	15	7
Ross, Josh, 2b-3b	.226	106	10	24	6	0	0	11	0
Scala, Mickey, 3b	.222	54	10	12	4	0	0	3	0
Schmitt, Brian, 1b-of	.291	282	45	82	19	2	8	45	2
Stewart, Chad, of	.262	267	39	70	9	4	2	19	12
Thompson, Adam, 3b	.256	78	12	20	2	0	3	14	9

PITCHING	W	L	ERA	G	SV	IP	H	BB	SO
Brian, Billy	0	2	13.50	4	0	6	10	12	3
Cordero, Victor	3	2	2.95	30	2	42	33	20	53
Fouts, Nate	2	1	4.43	4	0	20	23	7	21
France, Ryan	1	3	5.87	5	0	23	27	10	22
Freeman, Kai	4	4	7.04	9	0	47	70	9	30
Harrison, Torik	0	0	4.88	14	0	24	28	16	25
Johnson, Casey	4	5	5.45	12	0	66	76	21	54
Joyce, Michael	0	3	3.15	24	3	40	39	17	39
Kramer, Sean	0	1	6.92	6	1	13	14	12	12
Lynn, Kevin	7	9	3.99	22	1	126	137	19	97
Massengale, Chad	1	2	6.59	21	2	28	34	10	31
2-team (17 Shreveport)	1	5	5.51	38	5	49	57	15	46
Peters, Samone	0	0	6.23	11	0	17	20	16	12
Pontifex, Nick	0	0	33.75	1	0	1	6	1	1
Prendes, Alex	0	2	8.20	26	0	26	39	21	17
2-team (6 San Angelo)	0	2	7.75	32	0	36	51	27	24
Rayborn, Kris	1	3	4.25	13	0	36	37	23	28
Renery, Mike	0	3	7.99	13	0	41	56	29	23
Shiery, Shaun	10	3	2.37	18	0	129	117	27	118
Thompson, John	1	5	3.42	16	3	23	21	11	18
Wilkerson, Steven	6	8	4.14	19	0	119	122	57	91

AMARILLO

BATTING	AVG	AB	R	H	2B	3B	HR	RBI	SB
Bell, Derek, 3b	.304	289	38	88	12	2	1	37	0
Brack, Josh, ss	.284	356	57	101	15	5	2	42	3
Craig, Benny, of-dh	.235	323	48	76	12	4	14	51	1
Figueroa, Carlos, 2b-3b	.264	110	24	29	2	0	1	12	3
Gann, Jamie, of	.325	77	12	25	6	2	1	12	3
Hughes, Shawn, c	.282	305	53	86	17	1	5	43	12
Huson, Tim, of	.233	90	10	21	5	1	1	8	0
Kofler, Eric, of	.320	300	48	96	23	8	10	63	1
Lizarraga, Cory, of	.250	208	37	52	4	4	0	22	8
Llanos, Alex, 2b	.340	391	71	133	30	7	8	68	17
McElroy, Travis, of	.158	95	10	15	3	0	0	7	3
McMann, Dallas, c-3b	.216	125	12	27	6	2	0	11	1
Meier, Dan, 1b	.277	332	45	92	23	2	4	52	1
Otis, Trent, 2b	.182	33	6	6	1	1	0	9	2
Ramistella, John, of	.281	57	14	16	2	1	1	3	2
Strickland, Greg, of	.310	100	20	31	4	2	0	16	14
Woods, Blake, 3b	.273	22	4	6	0	0	0	1	1

PITCHING	W	L	ERA	G	SV	IP	H	BB	SO
Bullen, Matt	1	1	4.06	8	0	31	28	13	18
Carter, Ramsey	4	3	3.80	28	2	85	103	38	62
Dobyns, Heath	0	1	5.11	5	0	24	28	8	19
Engels, Jackson	1	0	11.25	2	0	8	14	4	5
Flading, Cameron	5	4	4.23	38	4	38	37	24	48
Frary, Levi	1	1	7.04	8	1	7	11	5	4
Glaser, Nick	0	0	13.50	6	0	9	17	7	4
Grant, Brian	0	1	15.43	3	0	2	3	5	1

	W	L	ERA	G	SV	IP	H	BB	SO
Guess, Scott	0	4	5.30	33	9	35	39	18	30
Morgan, Shawn	2	1	4.11	10	0	15	15	5	11
Newland, Robert	0	2	7.85	7	0	18	27	11	13
Patrick, Jason	0	1	20.25	1	0	2	11	1	1
Percosky, Mark	3	6	4.42	15	0	93	103	30	64
Price, Ryan	1	2	5.25	3	0	12	13	9	13
Rogelstad, Jeremy	0	1	5.00	5	0	9	12	6	8
Ruaz, Enrique	0	1	6.75	6	0	8	11	4	7
Singleton, Steven	2	1	4.23	35	3	44	40	27	43
Stockstill, Jason	10	5	2.49	19	0	133	112	53	119
Thomas, Adam	7	4	2.62	16	0	106	106	27	85
Tomaszewski, Eliot	1	2	6.94	7	2	11	12	4	5
Valles, Rolando	10	5	3.82	21	0	125	145	26	81

COASTAL BEND

BATTING	AVG	AB	R	H	2B	3B	HR	RBI	SB
Adolfo, Carlos, of	.305	59	19	18	6	1	3	6	2
2-team (67 Alexandria)	.322	323	69	104	28	3	19	62	15
Battersby, Eric, of-1b	.313	288	54	90	17	3	10	52	4
Bledsoe, Hunter, 1b	.389	18	5	7	2	0	0	5	0
Bugger, Mark, 2b	.237	317	24	75	13	2	1	49	4
Caston, Bernard, of	.211	38	8	8	1	1	0	2	4
Coffey, Kris, of	.236	157	23	37	2	2	1	12	14
Colon, Cris, 3b-1b	.304	358	40	109	24	1	3	61	5
Correa, Dalphie, ss	.192	229	33	44	5	1	0	7	22
Gonzalez, Eric, 2b	.000	1	0	0	0	0	0	0	0
Hall, Mel, dh	.279	86	9	24	5	0	1	12	1
Hammond, Derry, of	.257	35	5	9	3	0	1	6	1
2-team (75 Alexandria)	.277	321	57	89	16	2	20	60	10
Knight, Marcus, of	.291	172	37	50	14	1	2	8	6
Lucas, Matt, c	.250	8	0	2	0	0	0	0	0
Macchi, Brandon, of	.177	62	4	11	5	2	0	4	0
Maldonado, Edwin, if-of	.262	298	41	78	14	0	8	40	14
Maluchnik, Gregg, c	.241	249	37	60	15	4	4	33	4
Mann, Matt, of	.307	381	49	117	15	3	5	53	11
Merkich, Scott, dh	.265	196	30	52	3	1	3	19	7
Nunez, Rey, c	.204	49	1	10	1	0	1	6	0
Querecuto, Juan, 1b	.267	60	5	16	5	0	0	7	1
Sullivan, Kevin, c	.159	63	4	10	3	0	0	5	1
Swinton, Jermaine, 1b	.277	141	17	39	10	1	5	18	1

PITCHING	W	L	ERA	G	SV	IP	H	BB	SO
Batson, Byron	1	3	5.14	6	0	35	51	8	13
Black, Brett	0	0	5.40	2	1	1	3	0	2
Bolton, Aaron	1	2	5.19	11	0	26	20	26	19
Carney, Jake	4	1	1.41	6	0	38	32	9	22
3-team (5 Ft. Worth, 10 S.A.)	7	3	3.32	21	0	84	92	22	51
Chapa, Rey	4	8	2.91	30	3	65	57	34	59
Corrado, Matthew	0	1	9.00	3	0	14	23	6	11
Council, Gabe	0	0	0.00	1	0	1	0	2	0
Davidson, Andy	0	3	4.81	16	2	24	29	7	21
Dobbins, Aaron	4	6	4.90	20	0	93	100	33	56
Elias, Rob	3	1	3.98	19	4	31	34	12	20
Hooper, Jimmy	0	4	11.32	10	1	10	18	4	6
Landestoy, Gilbert	0	0	4.50	8	5	8	7	7	3
2-team (12 San Angelo)	4	4	4.50	20	7	70	82	35	63
Langen, Brian	7	4	2.48	22	1	130	116	35	67
Lewis, Rickey	7	6	3.79	20	2	116	109	45	88
Lira, James	1	0	0.00	8	5	12	6	1	18
Oksen, Andrew	0	1	5.40	5	0	8	17	4	9
Schuurman, Mark	1	1	4.78	17	0	26	30	13	17
Selmo, Santo	2	3	4.61	8	1	13	16	9	7
Semprun, Chris	0	0	11.88	5	0	8	15	10	5
Smith, Mike	11	4	2.90	22	0	155	130	40	109
Sonnier, Zachary	0	2	4.80	11	0	30	36	8	23

EDINBURG

BATTING	AVG	AB	R	H	2B	3B	HR	RBI	SB
Angel, Anthony, 2b	.309	404	63	125	22	4	7	68	2
Argento, Shaun, c	.354	158	25	56	5	1	1	35	0
Beck, Steven, c	.063	16	2	1	0	0	0	0	0
Coleman, Alph, of	.231	108	16	25	2	2	0	7	4
Contreras, Joe, c	.257	109	12	28	3	0	0	9	1
Cordova, Ben, of	.250	268	54	67	12	1	1	30	4
Fitzpatrick, Eddie, c	.247	81	15	20	3	0	2	9	1
Gonzalez, Eric, 3b-of	.275	302	51	83	22	1	4	42	5
Henderson, Derek, 1b	.296	375	62	111	24	2	8	66	10
Lopez, Manny, of	.248	105	17	26	6	0	2	13	6
McCoy, Jerome, of	.242	128	22	31	5	0	0	11	11
Moore, Vince, of	.250	364	57	91	21	3	4	50	17
Roland, Will, 3b	.261	364	37	95	9	2	2	48	4
Samples, Mike, 2b	.000	1	0	0	0	0	0	0	0
2-team (6 San Angelo)	.048	21	1	1	0	0	0	0	0
Sisk, Aaron, ss	.242	356	55	86	26	2	12	50	16
Strickland, Greg, dh-of	.226	62	10	14	2	1	0	3	1
2-team (23 Amarillo)	.278	162	30	45	6	3	0	19	15
Williams, Peanut, dh-1b	.182	121	8	22	4	2	2	22	7
Wilson, Kevin, ss	.214	14	4	3	1	0	1	2	0

PITCHING	W	L	ERA	G	SV	IP	H	BB	SO
Brown, Chris	3	3	3.03	21	0	89	85	36	51
Colvard, Ron	0	0	10.13	7	0	8	8	8	3
DeSalme, Gene	2	4	6.14	26	0	36	39	29	31
Flores, Pedro	11	4	3.08	21	0	143	111	77	121
Goodmann, Joe	1	0	0.73	8	0	12	6	2	13
2-team (25 Spring./Ozark)	5	1	2.36	33	4	42	35	15	43
Harris, Ryan	9	2	2.81	20	0	137	105	43	110
Merle, Jesen	1	2	9.75	10	0	12	13	5	7
Miller, Kevin	0	1	13.50	2	0	7	11	12	5
Montoya, Eric	14	4	4.27	21	0	147	148	47	143
Mozley, Brandon	1	2	4.62	6	0	37	40	15	24
Ortiz, John	0	1	7.59	8	1	10	14	4	9
Ortiz, Omar	1	3	2.12	34	4	34	23	18	41
Russ, Chris	8	4	2.25	43	17	52	30	22	42
Smith, Clint	7	4	2.77	24	1	110	104	40	71
Vasquez, Tim	0	4	3.15	10	0	20	14	6	22
2-team (13 Spring./Ozark)	1	6	3.54	23	2	48	49	17	47
Wilkerson, Steven	0	0	0.00	5	1	8	4	4	11
2-team (19 Alexandria)	6	8	3.88	24	1	127	126	61	102

FORT WORTH

BATTING	AVG	AB	R	H	2B	3B	HR	RBI	SB
Albertson, Eli, of	.203	59	10	12	3	1	0	6	3
Brown, Kevin, c	.250	8	0	2	1	0	0	1	0
Buckley, Reagan, of	.242	178	20	43	11	5	2	19	5
DeMarco, Tony, 1b	.290	169	18	49	7	1	2	24	0
Essian, Jim, of	.259	317	54	82	19	3	14	50	16
Gomez, Ricky, ss	.255	306	44	78	10	0	1	25	9
Greene, Shawn, 1b	.270	352	45	95	18	0	13	60	1
Guglielmelli, Brad, c	.278	90	11	25	6	1	1	10	2
Hannon, Pat, of	.300	207	33	62	16	3	5	40	3
Hartshorn, Tim, of-2b	.289	187	37	54	9	4	4	30	13
Hill, Jason, dh	.282	131	20	37	7	0	3	21	6
Mejias, Erick, 2b	.260	308	47	80	10	4	2	32	32
Merriman, Terrell, of	.288	146	32	42	11	3	4	19	18
Moon, Brian, c	.278	291	34	81	14	0	5	36	1
Moore, Kevin, of	.125	16	1	2	1	0	0	0	0
Smith, Bryon, 3b	.264	356	51	94	15	4	9	45	13

PITCHING	W	L	ERA	G	SV	IP	H	BB	SO
Aragon, Angel	8	5	2.57	21	0	115	106	32	91
Carney, Jake	0	0	5.40	5	0	6	9	1	2
Carroll, James	1	3	6.19	22	0	36	45	19	33
Cumberland, Chris	1	0	0.00	9	6	11	7	6	9
Franke, Jared	0	0	27.00	1	0	0	1	1	0
Goodrum, Kevin	4	1	4.63	26	0	23	19	24	30
Hahn, Steve	9	4	3.73	25	0	103	123	35	63
Harrington, Matt	2	6	3.64	33	2	71	64	32	81
Hickey, Mark	0	0	9.00	1	0	1	2	2	1
Onley, Shawn	6	10	3.84	21	0	124	125	43	102
Orga, Kevin	1	0	4.80	22	2	30	28	15	23
Outlaw, Mark	1	2	5.06	31	3	37	41	24	26
Thomas, Matt	4	3	2.02	38	6	49	45	28	42
Van Buren, Jermaine	9	4	3.07	18	0	111	107	37	113
Wood, Brandon	5	5	4.77	21	0	103	123	42	93

JACKSON

BATTING	AVG	AB	R	H	2B	3B	HR	RBI	SB
Anderson, Keto, of	.297	364	52	108	14	10	4	42	27
Booth, Jeremy, 1b-3b	.189	37	6	7	2	0	0	2	0
Cameron, Antoine, dh-of	.208	72	9	15	7	0	2	14	0
Campos, Mario, of	.224	152	17	34	7	2	5	27	1
Darjean, Eric, of-3b	.205	185	27	38	4	1	1	8	7
Dettman, Matt, 3b-1b	.145	83	11	12	2	1	1	14	2
Kison, Robbie, ss	.210	138	18	29	8	0	0	15	3
Lombardi, Dominick, c	.229	192	20	44	9	0	1	17	1
Maclin, Lonnie, dh-of	.267	60	14	16	2	0	2	8	0
McCall, Gerard, c	.302	53	7	16	4	1	0	7	1
Oglesby, Travis, dh-1b	.149	47	5	7	1	0	4	9	0
2-team (64 Rio Grande)	.231	251	41	58	16	3	14	45	0
Osilka, Garret, ss-2b	.297	64	15	19	3	0	1	8	7
Palazzolo, Tony, dh	.254	63	7	16	2	0	0	4	1
Patterson, Derek, 3b-2b	.244	217	32	53	9	1	4	23	14
2-team (17 San Angelo)	.228	276	41	63	11	1	5	31	14
Pernell, Brandon, of	.311	219	30	68	16	7	3	25	19
Rojas, Randy, ss	.114	88	13	10	3	0	0	7	1
Ruf, Karl, 2b-ss	.000	7	1	0	0	0	0	1	0
Salinas, Trey, c-1b	.305	59	13	18	0	2	4	13	1
Sanchez, Matt, 2b-3b	.267	281	35	75	16	1	0	29	6
Smith, Sam, 3b	.133	15	3	2	1	0	0	0	0

BATTING	AVG	AB	R	H	2B	3B	HR	RBI	SB
Spearman, Vernon, of	.273	238	47	65	10	5	3	36	14
Todd, Jeremy, 1b	.322	171	20	55	10	1	4	32	3
Tranum, Josh, 1b	.282	149	24	42	16	0	4	35	1
Yamauchi, Hiroshi, of-2b	.257	175	21	45	1	1	0	21	14

PITCHING	W	L	ERA	G	SV	IP	H	BB	SO
Brown, Steve	2	0	1.33	8	0	20	14	13	14
2-team (14 Rio Grande)	3	7	5.68	22	0	84	108	32	50
Camp, Rusty	2	1	1.20	4	0	30	16	9	30
Carroll, Ryan	1	0	4.00	6	0	9	9	3	11
Creek, Ryan	10	4	2.66	19	0	125	99	48	127
Frodsham, Eric	0	0	0.00	1	0	0	1	2	2
Fuqua, David	3	3	3.55	32	1	63	63	16	39
Herbert, Russ	4	4	3.46	8	0	52	40	15	48
Kishita, Kirt	0	1	3.38	17	1	18	12	7	21
2-team (12 San Angelo)	1	2	4.95	29	1	40	42	19	39
Mayi, Leonardo	0	0	5.14	5	0	7	9	4	8
McClain, Jeremy	5	2	3.42	13	0	68	68	22	55
Parker, Brandon	0	4	3.05	37	22	38	24	23	53
Perez, Michelandy	2	3	5.15	8	0	43	48	14	31
Persails, Mark	8	3	2.70	14	0	90	73	22	79
Pribble, Aaron	1	0	6.55	7	1	11	14	0	11
2-team (3 San Angelo)	1	1	7.71	10	1	21	29	5	21
Rayborn, Kenny	10	2	2.27	14	0	95	86	21	84
Ruf, Karl	0	0	6.75	1	0	1	2	0	1
Snyder, Ryan	2	0	2.57	3	0	21	17	5	10
2-team (18 Shreveport)	8	5	3.28	21	1	137	140	31	70
Stout, Dan	4	2	1.50	22	4	60	42	20	63
Vandegriff, Nick	4	8	3.03	30	0	86	93	31	60

RIO GRANDE VALLEY

BATTING	AVG	AB	R	H	2B	3B	HR	RBI	SB
Baker, Jason, of	.306	111	27	34	5	2	0	6	14
Boston, Tyson, of	.267	345	36	92	21	1	2	26	7
Cepeda, Malcolm, 1b	.204	54	7	11	2	0	0	8	2
Figueroa, Carlos, ss	.335	155	27	52	9	3	1	23	6
2-team (33 Armadillo)	.306	265	51	81	11	3	2	35	9
Garcia, Ismael, 3b	.257	35	5	9	1	0	1	4	0
Jaramillo, Tony, 2b-3b	.251	319	32	80	14	1	0	27	5
Langaigne, Selwyn, of	.318	255	43	81	15	3	5	40	21
Magdaleno, Ricky, ss	.284	148	22	42	11	1	3	16	0
Mendoza, Miguel, of	.206	34	5	7	0	0	0	3	3
Murch, Jeremy, of	.278	360	54	100	28	4	10	70	4
Oglesby, Travis, dh-1b	.250	204	36	51	15	3	10	36	0
Querecuto, Juan, 1b	.252	301	31	76	15	0	8	47	4
2-team (15 Coastal Bend)	.255	361	36	92	20	0	8	54	5
Ruf, Karl, 2b-ss	.207	145	15	30	1	0	1	13	2
2-team (5 Jackson)	.197	152	16	30	1	0	1	14	2
Scott, Charlie, c	.232	297	43	69	14	0	5	31	4
Taylor, T.D., 3b-2b	.253	320	41	81	14	2	3	39	4
Williams, Matt, dh	.267	45	8	12	2	0	1	5	0
York, Andrew, c	.172	64	9	11	3	0	0	4	0

PITCHING	W	L	ERA	G	SV	IP	H	BB	SO
Ahearne, Paul	0	1	5.14	6	0	7	4	5	5
2-team (12 San Angelo)	1	2	3.49	18	0	28	33	10	15
Baptist, Travis	1	4	6.43	22	8	28	36	9	42
Bolton, Aaron	0	0	10.13	6	0	5	5	7	3
2-team (11 Coastal Bend)	1	2	6.03	17	0	31	25	33	22
Brown, Steve	1	7	7.07	14	0	63	94	19	36
Estrada, Erik	0	1	4.50	7	0	16	15	8	12
Goure, Sam	10	8	3.02	22	0	155	140	47	138
Gutierrez, Ricky	0	0	3.60	4	0	5	7	1	3
Guzman, Alexis	4	13	6.41	33	4	98	128	23	56
Kuklis, Kevin	2	2	3.43	7	0	44	43	14	27
Martinez, Marcus	0	0	1.29	9	0	7	7	7	5
Moore, Eric	4	3	5.11	34	0	44	58	13	20
Oksen, Andrew	1	7	5.75	15	0	67	78	44	48
2-team (5 Coastal Bend)	1	8	5.71	20	0	75	95	48	57
Perez, Julio	2	2	4.74	17	1	24	24	10	28
Perez, Michelandy	1	3	6.40	5	0	32	40	14	25
2-team (8 Jackson)	3	6	5.68	13	0	76	88	28	56
Preston, George	0	0	3.00	1	0	6	6	5	6
Ramirez, Luis	0	0	3.77	26	3	31	28	10	31
Ruf, Karl	0	0	0.93	7	0	10	10	4	10
2-team (1 Jackson)	0	0	1.64	8	0	11	12	4	11
Valentin, Dan	10	6	2.51	21	1	129	124	36	123
Wilcher, Justin	1	0	6.52	5	0	19	23	11	10
Winkle, Ken	0	2	9.75	6	0	24	36	13	16

SAN ANGELO

BATTING	AVG	AB	R	H	2B	3B	HR	RBI	SB
Buckley, Reagan, c	.155	58	3	9	1	2	1	3	0
2-team (51 Fort Worth)	.220	236	23	52	12	7	3	22	5
Burnham, Jake, 3b	.276	152	26	42	10	3	3	25	1
Burnham, Kendall, 2b	.000	7	0	0	0	0	0	0	0
Cameron, Stanton, of-1b	.310	290	67	90	24	1	14	56	3
Davis, Justin, 2b-ss	.167	12	1	2	0	0	0	2	0
German, Ramon, 3b	.200	25	5	5	0	0	0	3	3
Gilbert, Joe, 3b	.291	79	11	23	5	0	0	9	3
Hanson, Andrew, of	.263	255	53	67	17	5	2	24	5
Joyner, Elliot, c	.167	12	1	2	1	0	0	1	0
Landreth, Jason, of-1b	.277	83	15	23	5	0	1	14	7
McNabb, Buck, of	.350	391	75	137	27	3	10	81	8
Memmert, Gabe, 1b	.277	83	9	23	7	1	0	11	0
Oropeza, Asdrubal, ss	.100	20	2	2	0	0	0	1	0
Patterson, Adam, 1b-3b	.267	318	51	85	22	5	6	49	4
Patterson, Derek, 2b	.169	59	9	10	2	0	1	8	0
Polcovich, Kevin, ss	.289	304	50	88	17	1	8	43	16
Rocha, Juan, of	.332	374	72	124	21	1	19	73	7
Samples, Mike, 2b-ss	.050	20	1	1	0	0	0	0	0
Schumaker, Chris, c	.100	30	0	3	0	0	0	1	0
Tompkins, Jake, of	.000	6	2	0	0	0	0	0	0
Velez, Lanze, 2b-ss	.244	131	13	32	3	0	1	17	0
Wallis, Jacob, c	.313	275	50	86	21	1	12	63	3
Williams, Peanut, of	.238	42	5	10	2	0	0	7	4
2-team (37 Edinburg)	.196	163	13	32	6	2	2	29	11
Wilson, Andy, 2b	.294	231	39	68	13	1	2	23	13

PITCHING	W	L	ERA	G	SV	IP	H	BB	SO
Ahearne, Paul	1	1	2.95	12	0	21	29	5	10
Barnett, Brian	0	0	4.50	1	0	2	4	1	1
Bell, Richard	1	1	7.27	10	3	8	9	6	9
Carney, Jake	3	2	4.85	10	0	39	51	12	27
DePriest, Derrick	3	1	2.05	21	7	22	24	4	22
Dobson, Dwayne	1	0	4.26	9	0	12	14	3	6
Flanagan, Chris	1	1	5.26	27	1	51	62	35	45
Fujii, Satoru	0	1	18.00	1	0	1	0	6	1
Garner, Isiah	0	0	23.14	2	0	2	6	2	2
Jones, Quentin	1	1	3.65	38	2	49	41	23	55
Kishita, Kirt	1	1	6.33	12	0	21	30	12	18
Kizu, Tomoyaki	1	0	5.14	4	0	7	10	2	10
Krivda, Rick	1	1	2.37	3	0	19	21	10	8
Kuiper, David	2	6	4.92	13	0	67	86	22	45
Landestoy, Gilbert	4	4	4.50	12	2	62	75	28	60
Mahan, Dallas	1	4	3.76	6	0	40	41	8	19
Powalski, Rick	1	1	16.20	2	0	6	13	7	5
Prendes, Alex	0	0	6.52	6	0	9	12	6	7
Pribble, Aaron	0	1	9.00	3	0	10	15	5	10
Renteria, Juan	1	1	3.78	4	0	16	19	8	19
Salazar, Luis	10	4	3.63	16	0	109	116	29	74
Sena, Jason	4	4	3.75	12	0	57	52	32	41
Sosebee, Chad	3	3	5.50	32	4	36	36	16	20
Turner, Jess	6	6	5.25	18	0	111	124	42	68
Van Landingham, Jeff	1	2	8.25	6	0	24	41	8	9
Whitfill, Michael	0	2	14.54	2	0	4	12	5	3

SHREVEPORT

BATTING	AVG	AB	R	H	2B	3B	HR	RBI	SB
Alvarez, Jorge, of	.288	371	58	107	32	0	9	56	7
Bragg, Michael, c	.337	92	15	31	7	0	0	12	0
Dusan, Joe, 1b	.298	326	47	97	19	0	7	48	3
Guillen, Jose, ss	.238	277	35	66	7	2	0	24	12
Hicks, Michael, 2b-3b	.245	306	42	75	17	5	6	45	4
Hunter, Herb, 2b	.263	186	27	49	3	4	0	7	3
McClain, Justin, of	.104	48	1	5	1	0	1	5	0
Miles, Thomas, of	.226	106	16	24	6	1	1	14	3
Moore, Kevin, of	.229	131	16	30	4	2	0	12	1
2-team (5 Fort Worth)	.218	147	17	32	5	2	0	12	1
Palazzolo, Tony, dh-1b	.364	22	4	8	2	0	0	1	0
3-team (34 Alex., 15 Jackson)	.289	194	24	56	9	0	1	18	1
Roenicke, Jarett, of	.252	282	27	71	13	1	2	38	0
Rothe, Ryan, of	.242	289	42	70	12	4	6	25	13
Schifano, Tony, 3b-ss	.280	386	49	108	26	2	1	45	25
Stricker, George, 2b-3b	.224	161	17	36	6	1	2	15	1
Webster, Kevin, c	.262	301	35	79	12	1	4	40	1

PITCHING	W	L	ERA	G	SV	IP	H	BB	SO
Averette, Rob	13	4	2.42	21	0	152	131	32	103
Bair, Denny	6	1	4.87	31	7	44	49	20	34
Cowling, Ross	2	0	2.89	4	1	9	10	1	6
2-team (15 Spring./Ozark)	6	5	4.56	19	1	94	106	48	66
Doiron, Ian	3	9	3.89	18	0	90	82	26	43
Ferguson, Levi	0	0	8.31	2	0	4	8	1	1
Gold, Joshua	7	5	3.34	18	0	126	114	41	61
Knox, Jerry	1	5	3.88	17	1	51	52	28	23
Massengale, Chad	0	3	3.98	17	3	20	23	5	15
Moody, Jason	3	2	2.88	37	3	59	61	26	45
Parker, Jonathan	1	1	5.79	5	0	4	9	6	2
Perrucci, Kevin	0	0	6.75	8	0	12	17	7	4
Poland, Trey	0	1	10.38	2	0	8	12	6	9

	W	L	ERA	G	SV	IP	H	BB	SO
Shelton, Lonnie	0	1	13.15	8	0	13	19	13	5
Slanina, Jason	6	4	3.67	16	0	81	77	27	38
Snyder, Ryan	6	5	3.41	18	1	116	123	26	60
Terrell, Jeff	3	2	2.59	7	0	41	37	12	42

SPRINGFIELD/OZARK

BATTING	AVG	AB	R	H	2B	3B	HR	RBI	SB
Ayres, Yancy, c	.097	31	2	3	0	0	0	1	0
Beale, Brad, c	.208	24	4	5	2	0	0	4	0
Buckley, Chris, of	.214	84	11	18	1	2	0	12	2
Cook, Roger, c	.246	134	14	33	3	0	2	14	0
Cummins, Eric, c	.180	150	13	27	3	0	0	12	2
Geffre, Tracy, 1b-3b	.266	139	15	37	9	0	3	19	0
Green, Steve, of	.290	183	26	53	9	1	0	24	5
Green, Terence, ss-3b	.268	377	46	101	19	3	5	57	8
Harriman, Preston, ss-3b	.209	177	27	37	6	0	4	26	10
King, Bryan, 1b-2b	.233	210	32	49	11	2	1	19	5
Koba, Bobby, 2b-3b	.238	172	25	41	4	5	1	20	5
Lang, Eddie, of	.278	223	42	62	12	2	0	18	15
Myers, Rod, dh	.167	6	1	1	0	0	0	1	0
Newson, Steve, of	.333	177	28	59	10	3	4	23	4
O'Sullivan, Patrick, 1b	.276	116	11	32	8	0	2	12	0
Roberts, Damion, 2b	.203	148	18	30	6	0	0	15	0
Sorensen, Nick, of	.252	333	42	84	15	3	2	32	20
Wheeler, Adam, of-3b	.304	204	24	62	13	3	0	20	16
Woody, Dominic, c	.275	69	15	19	4	1	1	8	1
Wright, Bryan, 2b	.155	97	6	15	3	1	0	9	0
Wright, Jonathan, of-dh	.351	151	16	53	11	1	3	21	2

PITCHING	W	L	ERA	G	SV	IP	H	BB	SO
Buchanan, Todd	0	0	27.00	2	0	2	3	10	1
Coleman, Billy	3	7	5.22	12	0	69	69	40	45
Cowling, Ross	4	5	4.75	15	0	85	96	47	60
Dill, Matt	0	4	7.94	10	1	28	48	13	14
Eddie, Derek	3	3	3.59	8	0	47	44	17	31
Evans, Brent	0	0	15.00	1	0	3	5	3	3
Goodmann, Joe	4	1	3.03	25	4	29	29	13	30
Grant, Brian	0	0	13.50	2	0	5	10	4	2
2-team (3 Amarillo)	0	1	14.09	5	0	7	13	9	3
Hall, Gary	3	4	6.97	11	0	50	69	24	34
Hendricks, Thomas	0	0	13.50	3	0	4	11	0	2
Hennessy, Corey	0	1	2.84	4	1	12	8	16	9
Hickey, Mark	1	1	4.00	15	1	36	32	20	23
2-team (1 Fort Worth)	1	1	4.14	16	1	37	34	22	24
Horner, Eric	2	2	2.25	12	0	40	38	14	18
May, Phillip	2	3	7.86	7	0	26	40	7	16
Mayi, Leonardo	0	1	18.56	4	0	5	9	9	7
2-team (5 Jackson)	0	1	10.95	9	0	12	18	13	15
McClaskey, Tim	6	2	1.61	8	0	67	61	2	47
Montarbo, Adam	4	5	3.27	10	0	66	76	20	30
Oelke, Steven	1	6	6.80	9	0	47	53	23	42
Prater, Drew	2	4	6.53	15	0	41	58	21	31
Steinkamp, Matt	2	1	5.05	28	3	41	39	28	31
Sweeney, Paul	0	0	9.14	16	0	21	40	11	13
Thurman, Bryan	0	0	11.12	3	0	5	11	2	2
Vasquez, Tim	1	2	3.81	13	2	28	35	11	25
Wheeler, Adam	2	4	4.57	7	0	41	48	17	29
Wilson, Rick	0	0	5.68	3	0	13	14	5	10

FRONTIER LEAGUE

There was a time when Josh Loggins was a one-dimensional player. He didn't have much power, and he wasn't the speediest baserunner, but the Kentucky product always could hit.

TYLER BOLDEN

Josh Loggins

Loggins had a .297 career average after a three-year minor league career but still got released by the San Diego Padres and New York Yankees. As a first baseman/outfielder, a high batting average wasn't enough.

Even when Loggins hit .347-5-45 for the Frontier League's Washington Wild Things in 2002, he couldn't get a contract to get back into affiliated baseball. So after the season, he and Wild Things manager Jeff Isom talked about ways Loggins could make himself more useful. They decided Loggins would start working behind the plate again—he caught in college—to showcase his versatility and work on pitch recognition.

The result was an MVP season in 2003 for Loggins, as the better pitch recognition led to improved power. He hit .331-24-74 to help lead the Wild Things to a playoff berth.

But while Isom's talk and encouragement helped Loggins develop into a force in the middle of the Wild Things lineup, it did bring one drawback. By the time the playoffs rolled around, Loggins was a Rockies farmhand, as Colorado signed him in mid-August and immediately sent him to their Double-A Tulsa farm club.

In the playoffs, Gateway easily swept Washington in the semifinals in a best-of-three series and swept Evansville in three games in the championship series for their first Frontier League title.

The Grizzlies had two shutouts during the playoffs, as their pitching dominated. Gateway reliever Dave Klahs was named the playoff MVP. He saved Game One of the championship series and picked up the win in Game Three with 2⅔ scoreless innings of relief. For the playoffs, Klahs was 1-0, 1.08 with three saves.

STANDINGS

EAST	W	L	PCT	GB
Chillicothe Paints	54	31	.635	—
Washington Wild Things	54	34	.614	1½
Evansville Otters	51	37	.580	4½
Richmond Roosters	50	39	.562	6
Kalamazoo Kings	33	56	.371	23
Florence Freedom	27	61	.307	28½
WEST	**W**	**L**	**PCT**	**GB**
Gateway Grizzlies	50	38	.568	—
Rockford RiverHawks	48	42	.533	3
Kenosha Mammoths	47	42	.528	3½
River City Rascals	43	47	.478	8
Cook County Cheetahs	42	48	.467	9
Mid-Missouri Mavericks	33	57	.367	18

PLAYOFFS: Semifinals—Gateway defeated Washington 2-0 and Evansville defeated Chillicothe 2-1 in best-of-3 series. **Final**—Gateway defeated Evansville 3-0 in best-of-5 series.

MANAGERS: Chillicothe—Jamie Keefe. **Cook County**—Mike Moore. **Evansville**—Greg Jelks. **Florence**—Chris Sabo. **Gateway**—Danny Cox. **Kalamazoo**—Woody Sorrell. **Kenosha**—Greg Tagert. **Mid-Missouri**—Tony Torchia/Angel Davila. **Richmond**—Chris Mongiardo. **River City**—Marc Hill. **Rockford**—Bob Koopmann. **Washington**—Jeff Isom.

ATTENDANCE: Gateway 168,067; River City 163,114; Washington 156,276; Kalamazoo 127,198; Evansville 116,028; Rockford 88,570; Mid-Missouri 75,589; Cook County 60,481; Chillicothe 58,755; Richmond 51,210; Kenosha 25,449; Florence 18,623.

ALL-STAR TEAM: C—Josh Loggins, Washington. **1B**—Darin Kinsolving, Chillicothe. **2B**—Tony Coyne, Gateway. **3B**—Juan Downing, Evansville. **SS**—Adrian Gascon, Chillicothe. **OF**—Chris Carter, Kalamazoo; Michael Connor, River City; Jake Whitesides, Mid-Missouri. **DH**—Jay Coakley, Washington. **SP**—Chris Spigner, Richmond. **RP**—Matt Schweitzer, Richmond.

Most Valuable Player: Josh Loggins, Washington. **Most Valuable Pitcher:** Chris Spigner, Richmond. **Rookie of the Year:** Amad Stephens, Evansville. **Manager of the Year:** Greg Jelks, Evansville.

INDIVIDUAL BATTING LEADERS

(Minimum 227 Plate Appearances)

	AVG	AB	R	H	2B	3B	HR	RBI	SB
Carter, Chris, Kalamazoo	.364	220	38	80	16	6	5	36	10
Kinsolving, Darin, Chillicothe	.336	295	52	99	19	1	15	76	0
Loggins, Josh, Washington	.331	290	63	96	13	5	24	72	15
Hollingsworth, Josh, Rich.	.324	238	29	77	12	1	2	27	2
Coyne, Tony, Gateway	.313	332	56	104	18	2	6	43	9
Haven, Tory, Rockford	.310	229	41	71	17	2	14	52	0
Miller, Drew, Richmond	.309	311	48	96	15	3	6	36	3
Leathers, Todd, Kenosha	.307	306	46	94	17	0	15	77	0
Gascon, Adrian, Chillicothe	.301	286	51	86	20	1	8	51	8
Greenwell, Bill, Mid-Missouri	.300	330	45	99	21	2	6	78	2

INDIVIDUAL PITCHING LEADERS
(Minimum 67 Innings)

	W	L	ERA	G	SV	IP	H	BB	SO
Shelley, Jason, Rockford	7	1	0.85	10	0	74	49	21	82
Tomsu, Joshua, Rockford	8	5	1.71	17	1	111	81	40	65
Spigner, Chris, Richmond	11	4	2.12	21	0	140	101	54	134
McWatters, David, Kal.	8	4	2.62	17	0	124	124	28	100
Bradley, Dave, Washington	10	5	2.77	17	0	114	97	32	118
Laratta, E.J., River City	6	3	2.78	12	0	74	76	25	43
Patterson, Scott, Gateway	8	3	2.92	20	0	130	119	24	120
Henry, Mike, Richmond	7	6	2.93	24	1	77	58	35	74
Skrukrud, Mark, Chillicothe	4	3	2.94	16	1	67	66	11	56
James, Frank, Rockford	6	4	2.99	13	0	72	71	29	42

CHILLICOTHE

BATTING	AVG	AB	R	H	2B	3B	HR	RBI	SB
Colameco, Joe, of	.244	270	33	66	12	1	4	30	14
Cosentino, Tony, c	.287	261	28	75	12	0	3	41	0
Dreher, Doug, of	.280	304	49	85	21	2	1	36	6
Elrod, Nick, ss-3b	.231	117	22	27	5	0	2	19	1
Epke, Brian, c	.167	84	15	14	2	0	0	3	0
Gascon, Adrian, ss-3b	.301	286	51	86	20	1	8	51	8
Hernandez, Miguel, 3b	.265	245	38	65	12	2	9	37	4
Kinsolving, Darin, 1b	.336	295	52	99	19	1	15	76	0
Loomis, Corey, 2b	.237	232	42	55	9	7	4	30	5
McCay, Matt, of	.295	305	75	90	12	0	6	35	8
Pickens, Scott, c	.188	16	0	3	0	0	0	2	0
Revere, J.R., of	.185	81	18	15	4	0	0	6	7
Swackhamer, Rustin, dh	.259	251	41	65	8	0	12	47	1

PITCHING	W	L	ERA	G	SV	IP	H	BB	SO
Buirley, Kris	3	4	4.39	15	0	67	68	42	46
Burris, Robert	2	0	1.64	2	0	11	10	2	12
Callahan, James	0	0	7.11	7	0	6	9	2	5
Durkee, Jeremy	2	1	2.17	36	4	54	44	16	58
Gits, Mike	7	3	3.16	46	3	62	73	9	27
Gregg, Grant	0	2	2.45	8	4	7	10	4	8
Hansard, Greg	2	0	1.42	6	0	6	2	6	4
Hunter, Jeff	5	3	3.15	15	0	71	67	11	61
Kesten, Michael	0	0	2.84	7	0	6	4	6	9
Lehr, George	0	0	0.00	1	0	1	0	0	2
Mendoza, Frank	0	0	8.59	3	0	7	14	3	6
Moran, Duggan	0	0	8.10	4	0	3	3	7	4
O'Quinn, Mickey	5	3	4.65	26	0	50	53	18	42
Pickens, Scott	0	0	12.60	4	0	5	9	2	5
Rahrer, Josh	8	3	4.30	15	0	81	88	22	53
Royal, Shannon	4	1	3.95	10	0	43	53	18	35
Royce, Ramon	5	1	0.65	16	6	27	18	4	30
Schiml, Tony	5	6	4.21	19	0	109	118	51	79
See, Andrew	2	1	4.26	22	8	25	33	10	14
Skrukrud, Mark	4	3	2.94	16	1	67	66	11	56

COOK COUNTY

BATTING	AVG	AB	R	H	2B	3B	HR	RBI	SB
Archer, Eric, ss	.143	14	0	2	0	0	0	0	1
Barry, Chris, 2b-of	.412	17	5	7	0	1	1	2	0
Bergheger, Jeremiah, ss	.237	38	1	9	0	0	0	3	0
Bischofberger, Sean, 3b	.242	277	54	67	19	0	14	56	4
Brown, Kevin, 1b	.269	308	63	83	27	3	13	57	8
2 Burkhart, Damon, 2b	.220	182	26	40	11	0	4	29	4
2-team (4 Richmond)	.209	196	27	41	11	0	5	31	4
2 Clemente, Rafael, of	.000	1	0	0	0	0	0	0	0
2-team (2 Gateway)	.000	4	0	0	0	0	0	0	0
Gaspar, Warren, of	.278	342	60	95	10	5	5	27	45
2 Gomez, Andre, c	.245	49	10	12	1	1	0	3	0
2-team (38 Mid-Missouri)	.225	173	21	39	3	2	3	21	1
Gontmaher, Nick, of	.128	47	9	6	1	1	0	4	5
Grenda, B.J., ph	1.000	1	1	1	0	0	0	0	0
Harris, Blair, c	.278	36	2	10	2	0	1	5	0
Johnson, Nick, dh	.300	70	7	21	5	0	1	13	0
Jones, Eric, c	.125	8	1	1	1	0	0	1	0
Larson, Ryan, 3b	.287	115	9	33	5	1	1	20	2
Molitor, Paul, ss	.087	23	3	2	0	0	0	0	1
O'Reel, Adam, 1b	.167	36	1	6	0	0	0	3	0
Paciorek, Mack, ss	.314	159	19	50	4	1	0	21	6
Pullins, Tyler, ss	.237	97	15	23	6	0	0	12	5
Reed, Randy, of	.211	109	10	23	3	2	0	13	5
Riera, Zack, dh	.263	57	9	15	4	0	2	10	2
Runnells, T.J., 2b	.111	9	1	1	0	0	0	0	0
Rykaleski, Stuart, of	.255	251	27	64	10	1	1	31	8
Smith, Adonis, 2b	.198	91	15	18	2	1	0	5	2
2-eam (25 River City)	.166	157	21	26	3	1	0	10	5
Spiker, Adam, dh	.083	12	1	1	0	0	0	0	1
Thomas, Josh, 2b	.100	10	1	1	0	0	0	1	1
Van Robays, Chuck, c	.222	221	25	49	8	0	0	17	0
Walker, Mark, of	.278	334	52	93	15	5	5	55	28

PITCHING	W	L	ERA	G	SV	IP	H	BB	SO
Campos, David	6	7	3.78	18	0	104	107	50	61
Clark, Wade	0	0	6.94	7	1	11	11	4	5
Clelland, James	4	1	2.08	5	0	39	28	5	27
Davidson, Tom	0	1	5.06	15	3	21	23	8	10
Grinnell, Tyler	0	0	27.00	1	0	0	2	3	0
Meccage, Justin	0	4	4.61	7	1	13	18	9	9
Ott, Mike	2	3	2.86	23	3	44	49	13	29
Palmer, Adam	6	7	3.20	18	0	115	117	32	47
Quiros, Jaime	0	0	16.20	7	1	6	9	14	3
Regas, Kris	4	7	6.27	15	0	84	109	26	45
Saken, Dan	0	0	5.00	4	0	9	7	3	3
Sokoll, Adam	0	1	23.14	2	0	2	8	1	1
Stephens, Brett	6	5	3.41	17	1	111	117	25	87
Thrasher, Jesse	0	0	6.75	2	0	1	1	4	2
Wells, Dan	1	2	6.23	19	1	30	41	17	11
White, Eric	4	1	3.02	26	1	50	35	32	47
Williams, Grant	9	9	3.88	18	0	116	151	20	76

EVANSVILLE

BATTING	AVG	AB	R	H	2B	3B	HR	RBI	SB
Albert, Steve, ss	.000	14	0	0	0	0	0	0	0
Arishenkoff, Tyson, ss	.253	237	39	60	5	2	3	17	9
Benjamin, Casey, ss	.313	16	1	5	2	0	0	1	0
Brackley, Carlos, of	.278	281	42	78	14	1	14	40	7
Downing, Juan, 3b	.258	325	53	84	7	2	3	33	22
Flynn, Sean, c	.222	45	4	10	2	0	0	3	0
Garza, O.J., of	.276	326	29	90	14	3	9	42	6
Gleaton, Denson, dh-1b	.216	37	4	8	1	0	0	1	0
Griffin, David, 2b-ss	.273	55	10	15	1	1	0	8	2
Hayden, Wes, of	.265	136	8	36	6	0	2	14	2
Johanning, Ben, 1b	.253	166	26	42	8	0	7	22	1
Kohler, Paul, c	.087	23	2	2	0	0	0	0	0
Lee, Gary, c	.303	33	5	10	2	1	0	3	1
McClain, Terrence, of	.268	205	27	55	12	1	3	26	7
Muranishi, Tatsuhiko,ph	.000	1	0	0	0	0	0	0	0
Radwan, Jason, c	.298	292	50	87	22	1	11	61	1
Riggins, Auntwan, of	.244	123	17	30	4	0	0	8	6
Stone, Jon, c	.091	11	2	1	1	0	0	1	0
Stuckey, Denver, 2b	.283	219	25	62	7	0	0	16	5
Swift, Bryan, 2b	.203	118	20	24	5	0	1	10	3
Trujillo, David, 1b	.267	288	40	77	10	0	8	48	6

PITCHING	W	L	ERA	G	SV	IP	H	BB	SO
Ampi, A.J.	2	2	2.48	31	1	36	26	16	31
Bates, Nick	1	1	1.29	7	4	7	9	3	6
Burnau, Ryan	3	1	3.07	29	3	41	36	10	50
Cerminaro, David	4	2	1.53	25	1	58	47	12	38
Crohan, Tom	0	0	3.86	8	0	9	7	6	13
Eppender, James	3	1	3.42	16	0	26	36	4	16
Ewasko, Tod	10	4	3.08	18	0	117	111	25	93
Faigin, Jason	0	0	1.13	5	1	8	8	2	5
2-team (3 Gateway)	0	0	2.25	8	1	12	14	7	10
Faulkner, Steven	5	4	3.66	13	0	71	70	14	65
Good, Logan	0	1	2.70	6	1	6	9	4	3
Incinelli, Matt	6	4	4.19	19	0	101	112	31	63
Lewis, Brett	1	2	5.90	6	0	29	32	14	16
Lewis, Jeremy	3	6	3.49	16	0	87	86	21	71
Simpson, Andre	7	6	3.22	19	0	117	114	41	78
Stephens, Amad	6	1	2.77	31	11	55	44	9	65
Truitt, Derrick	0	2	8.53	2	0	6	11	5	4

FLORENCE

BATTING	AVG	AB	R	H	2B	3B	HR	RBI	SB
Back, Billy, 2b-ss	.203	59	6	12	0	0	0	3	0
Betts, Jason, 1b	.257	101	8	26	2	0	0	6	1
Boggs, Matthew, 2b-of	.200	60	9	12	2	0	0	3	0
Cappucilli, Tony, c	.286	14	4	4	1	0	0	1	0
Combs, Randy, ss	.174	23	1	4	1	0	0	1	0
Creighton, Tom, 2b-3b	.288	205	28	59	15	2	2	29	8
Curnayn, Rocky, 1b	.244	41	3	10	1	0	0	2	0
Fenwick, Ron, 2b-ss	.185	81	3	15	0	0	0	5	2
Hildebrant, Flip, of	.235	230	20	54	7	0	0	16	3
Hudson, Ben, c	.273	132	12	36	3	0	0	13	0
Levengood, Kyle, 1b	.286	112	14	32	4	0	1	11	1
List, Joe, dh	.200	115	7	23	3	0	0	10	2
Macellaro, Nick, 3b	.274	201	24	55	8	1	0	26	4
Muranishi, Tatsuhiko, of	.314	121	15	38	1	1	0	7	13
2-team (1 Evansville)	.311	122	15	38	1	1	0	7	13
O'Neill, Jeremy, ss	.262	42	0	11	1	0	0	3	0
Osterkamp, Chris, ss	.269	201	26	54	6	1	0	24	6
Pfister, Billy, ss-2b	.182	66	7	12	2	0	0	5	4

	AVG	AB	R	H	2B	3B	HR	RBI	SB
Rahschulte, Justin, of	.259	232	30	60	17	1	4	28	9
Rossy, Eric, 3b-1b	.180	50	3	9	2	0	0	3	1
Rucker, Dale, 1b	.037	27	2	1	1	0	0	1	0
Singer, Matt, of-1b	.258	233	26	60	17	3	3	33	3
Stone, Jon, c	.232	125	15	29	6	0	0	10	1
2-team (5 Evansville)	.221	136	17	30	7	0	0	11	1
Taylor, Tony, c	.250	76	7	19	5	0	2	11	0
Tolotti, Jeff, of	.215	65	4	14	4	0	0	5	0
Tuttle, Jason, of	.378	143	31	54	5	3	0	10	16
Ury, Josh, of	.179	56	4	10	1	0	1	10	2

PITCHING	W	L	ERA	G	SV	IP	H	BB	SO
Cercy, Rick	1	0	6.17	10	0	11	9	10	9
Chafey, Hal	3	1	3.11	13	0	46	44	26	48
Christie, Adam	0	2	4.73	10	0	13	16	4	12
Farler, Dan	3	1	4.22	4	0	21	30	13	9
Graves, Bobby	7	10	3.56	20	0	131	114	60	83
Hudson, Ben	0	0	13.50	4	0	2	3	3	5
Hughes, Rocky	0	0	7.04	12	0	15	22	8	14
Jakubauskas, Chris	4	9	5.11	16	0	100	120	38	57
Krugman, John	2	7	6.35	9	0	45	49	29	35
McRoberts, Dennis	0	3	6.08	5	0	23	32	7	15
Mendible, Frank	0	3	4.24	15	0	23	24	15	10
Rinehart, Jeff	0	0	4.15	4	0	4	7	2	2
Rival, Kevin	0	6	4.05	36	6	66	66	38	70
Rogers, Nick	0	0	7.59	7	0	10	19	9	8
Rowland, Nick	3	2	4.10	37	1	52	52	17	29
Schrader, Jesse	2	8	6.19	18	0	72	88	46	48
Zettler, Nate	0	6	6.62	12	0	50	55	31	26
Zizelman, Eric	2	3	2.88	27	5	34	40	13	21

GATEWAY

BATTING	AVG	AB	R	H	2B	3B	HR	RBI	SB
Archer, Eric, ss	.000	6	0	0	0	0	0	1	1
2-team (6 Cook County)	.100	20	0	2	0	0	0	1	2
Astrauskas, Wayne, c	.226	106	11	24	7	0	1	7	0
Bauder, Brad, of	.290	176	28	51	12	0	5	30	5
Bolstad, Joe, of	.231	39	4	9	1	1	1	4	0
Brown, Trevor, c	.270	63	11	17	4	0	2	8	0
Capodieci, Adam, c	.200	10	1	2	0	0	0	0	0
Clemente, Rafael, of	.000	3	0	0	0	0	0	0	0
Coyne, Tony, 2b	.313	332	56	104	18	2	6	43	9
Denischuk, Blake, of	.143	28	1	4	0	0	0	3	0
Fuess, Brian, 3b	.283	99	12	28	3	0	3	12	0
2-team (40 River City)	.286	252	25	72	13	0	5	28	2
Garcia, Jose, of	.182	55	6	10	0	1	1	4	1
Klosterman, Chris, 3b	.245	196	33	48	10	1	5	27	4
Lawrence, Horace, of	.374	107	17	40	9	2	4	19	2
Lee, Gary, c	.190	21	3	4	1	0	0	2	0
3-team (9 Evansville, 5 Wash.)	.261	69	10	18	3	1	0	8	1
Lopez, Damien, 3b	.190	21	2	4	1	0	1	1	0
Lucas, Kevin, ss	.214	56	6	12	1	1	0	6	2
Matuszek, Kevin, ss	.271	59	3	16	5	0	0	6	0
Morris, Mark, of	.000	4	0	0	0	0	0	0	0
2-team (33 Kalamazoo)	.275	102	14	28	6	1	2	6	13
Oetting, Todd, dh	.275	313	47	86	18	0	13	58	7
Piatt, Ben, of	.269	234	26	63	8	6	3	33	3
Reiter, Jimmy, of	.284	275	54	78	9	1	6	39	16
Schutt, Doug, of	.313	16	1	5	0	1	0	1	3
Servais, Eric, c	.171	76	10	13	2	0	1	8	0
Spivey, Brett, of	.222	36	5	8	2	0	0	2	1
Sullivan, Ryan, of-2b	.253	91	23	23	4	2	3	11	0
Talbot, Brandon, c	.158	19	3	3	1	0	0	1	1
Vargas, Oscar, ss	.244	156	21	38	7	0	4	18	3
Warren, Phil, 1b	.295	312	45	92	16	0	13	56	2

PITCHING	W	L	ERA	G	SV	IP	H	BB	SO
Arguello, Carlos	0	0	7.71	3	0	2	3	6	2
Brester, Jason	0	1	4.97	13	0	12	15	7	5
Breuchaud, Ed	0	0	36.00	1	0	1	4	3	2
Buck, Pete	10	8	3.94	20	0	130	133	36	102
Dooley, Joe	6	6	3.69	19	0	95	95	40	94
Faigin, Jason	0	0	4.50	3	0	4	6	5	5
Garrett, Brad	2	1	2.25	6	0	8	7	3	9
Golden, Michael	0	2	3.13	13	1	23	15	8	21
Jahnsen, Adam	5	3	3.96	13	0	72	55	27	71
Klahs, Dave	2	3	2.02	28	8	49	37	12	45
Lane, Josh	6	2	3.82	14	0	77	81	24	65
Matzenbacher, Brian	0	1	6.00	2	0	3	3	2	1
McCool, Ricky	0	0	0.00	1	0	2	1	1	2
Meyer, Layne	2	2	5.40	9	0	26	25	18	26
Newland, Robert	2	2	5.04	9	0	30	28	18	25
Parsons, Brett	1	3	7.04	9	0	23	24	19	17
Patterson, Scott	8	3	2.92	20	0	129	119	24	120
Plancich, Nick	3	1	2.64	22	0	30	30	10	19
Ristau, Adam	0	0	4.50	1	0	2	4	2	2

	W	L	ERA	G	SV	IP	H	BB	SO
Smith, Dan	2	0	2.75	30	15	36	21	14	37
Sullivan, Ryan	1	0	4.32	5	0	8	11	5	8

KALAMAZOO

BATTING	AVG	AB	R	H	2B	3B	HR	RBI	SB
Adair, Dan, 2b	.154	13	1	2	0	0	0	2	2
Archer, Phil, c	.234	77	13	18	4	0	3	15	1
Baird, Chris, of	.237	93	11	22	4	0	2	9	1
Blaze, Darryl, of	.300	210	40	63	4	3	1	15	25
Bottorff, Toby, c	.156	32	4	5	0	0	0	0	0
Burgos, Tino, 2b-ss	.264	246	38	65	8	1	3	28	11
Carter, Chris, of	.364	220	38	80	16	6	5	36	10
Degroote, Casey, dh-3b	.273	44	5	12	1	0	1	5	0
2-team (54 Rockford)	.298	191	26	57	4	2	4	25	5
Ferreira, Brian, of	.274	124	17	34	6	1	1	11	9
Flamont, Sam, of	.457	70	17	32	3	1	3	12	2
Frankhouse, Tim, 3b	.216	250	33	54	10	2	3	16	3
Gunderson, Jeff, 2b-3b	.250	8	0	2	0	0	0	1	1
Haskell, Delvin, 2b-ss	.248	137	14	34	4	1	0	15	8
Haven, Tory, dh	.328	192	35	63	15	2	11	44	0
Hindman, Steve, 1b	.224	241	24	54	9	0	6	21	1
Kent, Matt, c	.284	250	24	71	12	0	5	35	0
Lang, Andy, ss	.288	52	5	15	1	0	0	5	1
Lewis, Damon, 1b	.164	67	6	11	0	0	2	10	0
Morris, Mark, of	.286	98	14	28	6	1	2	6	13
Pearce, Tom, 1b	.189	37	1	7	1	0	0	1	0
2-team (20 Richmond)	.206	97	10	20	4	0	5	15	0
Simmons, Walt, of	.252	278	40	70	8	1	10	44	3
Tully, Jim, 2b-ss	.111	27	1	3	0	0	0	4	0
Uranga, Darren, 3b-ss	.202	84	8	17	1	2	2	12	2
Wilson, Kevin, ss	.273	154	22	42	3	1	3	20	3

PITCHING	W	L	ERA	G	SV	IP	H	BB	SO
Beshears, Joshua	1	0	4.41	17	0	34	36	15	29
Biddlestone, Jason	2	8	4.33	19	0	104	125	51	91
Cartwright, Jim	0	1	4.00	9	0	18	22	12	10
D'Amato, Dan	1	4	5.18	13	0	74	86	24	43
Ferdinand, Brian	0	0	6.23	9	2	13	10	8	6
Fernandez, Julio	2	2	3.66	7	1	19	20	12	15
Huizinga, Jon	1	0	0.79	4	0	11	8	3	10
Kline, Ty	1	2	4.40	6	0	30	34	8	25
Lawson, Scott	0	1	2.61	7	0	10	11	4	7
Marx, Tommy	0	0	0.00	1	0	1	1	1	0
McGee, Denny	5	11	5.31	19	0	95	103	52	59
McWatters, David	8	4	2.62	17	0	123	124	28	100
Naplin, Lee	5	2	4.19	24	0	38	43	18	24
Nawrocki, Keith	1	6	2.98	38	1	60	42	24	49
Olson, David	2	2	4.09	16	0	11	15	7	19
Powell, Jared	2	2	5.79	12	0	18	25	7	8
Schuka, Brad	0	0	10.38	5	0	8	16	5	5
Sheets, Matt	2	6	5.89	11	0	65	83	25	67
Wiltshire, Greg	0	5	4.57	23	9	21	21	18	27

KENOSHA

BATTING	AVG	AB	R	H	2B	3B	HR	RBI	SB
Cisneros, Josh, c	.243	111	14	27	5	0	0	11	1
Goirigolzarri, Raymond, of	.160	188	20	30	8	3	2	16	9
Gontmaher, Nick, of	.200	5	0	1	0	0	0	0	0
2-team (16 Cook County)	.135	52	9	7	1	1	0	4	5
Haake, Steve, of	.297	158	27	47	13	3	3	24	10
Horiguchi, Tommy, of	.268	250	33	67	19	2	2	33	13
Huling, Andrew, of	.287	293	53	84	9	5	0	26	14
King, Matthew, of	.176	17	2	3	0	0	0	3	2
Landon, Josh, 2b	.230	256	32	59	8	0	4	24	2
Leathers, Todd, 1b-3b	.307	306	46	94	17	0	15	77	0
Marshall, Matt, 1b	.043	23	1	1	0	0	1	2	0
Munoz, David, ss	.237	219	25	52	9	1	2	27	8
Pelfrey, Dennis, c	.277	195	31	54	15	0	6	28	18
Spencer, John, c	.302	63	8	19	5	0	1	8	1
Stanley, Aaron, of	.270	270	39	73	4	2	0	23	35
Swerdzewski, Stosh, c	.188	32	4	6	1	0	0	2	0
Townsend, Tanner, 3b-1b	.245	294	27	72	16	1	3	41	12
Uegawachi, Bryce, ss	.238	80	4	19	2	0	0	5	1
Vidal, J.D., 3b-2b	.260	227	34	59	15	1	3	18	12

PITCHING	W	L	ERA	G	SV	IP	H	BB	SO
Bennett, Jamie	6	3	3.69	19	0	112	98	36	87
Cartwright, Jim	2	0	5.40	12	0	26	31	16	20
2-team (9 Kalamazoo)	2	1	4.84	21	0	44	53	28	30
Chenard, Bryan	0	0	4.15	3	0	8	8	1	10
Cooney, Jim	3	2	5.19	25	1	26	28	11	22
Daniels, Zack	2	1	4.91	11	0	25	28	5	14
Davis, Randy	1	1	4.70	2	0	7	7	5	5
Dooley, Jason	6	3	3.44	35	1	52	52	21	31
Esposito, Frank	1	1	5.40	13	0	26	25	12	19

	W	L	ERA	G	SV	IP	H	BB	SO
Fisher, Cody	3	6	4.83	18	0	110	116	31	69
Hardman, Steven	0	1	14.54	4	0	4	8	3	2
Huskey, Matt	5	4	3.96	15	0	84	78	26	52
Linde, Joe	8	5	4.31	18	0	104	112	24	52
Livingston, Brett	3	6	4.29	15	0	56	71	19	35
Lopez, Derek	2	2	2.48	29	16	36	33	10	43
Mau, Ryan	0	0	0.00	1	0	4	6	2	1
Solveson, Saul	3	3	4.29	20	1	50	60	27	30
Stone, Nathan	0	0	1.59	5	0	5	5	1	4
Vanderplow, Randy	2	3	3.10	31	8	49	43	13	36
Wilhite, Matt	0	1	3.18	3	0	5	9	1	4

MID-MISSOURI

BATTING	AVG	AB	R	H	2B	3B	HR	RBI	SB
Blase, Blake, of-1b	.240	250	32	60	21	1	10	42	1
Brown, Seth, 3b	.241	299	36	72	10	3	1	28	4
Carreno, Jose, c	.263	297	27	78	19	0	2	39	0
Doyle, Spencer, 2b-of	.250	28	3	7	1	0	0	1	1
Fewell, Wes, of	.252	226	25	57	8	2	0	13	5
Friedman, Tim, 2b-3b	.179	56	3	10	0	0	0	3	3
Gomez, Andre, c	.218	124	11	27	2	1	3	18	1
Gordon, Eric, of	.136	22	2	3	0	0	1	3	0
Greenwell, Bill, 1b	.300	330	45	99	21	2	6	78	2
Hedgecock, Bryan, of	.200	100	12	20	2	2	2	11	5
Lester, Anthony, of-c	.097	31	1	3	1	0	0	3	1
Lyall, Joe, of	.125	8	0	1	0	0	0	0	0
Nichols, Joe, of	.158	95	11	15	5	1	1	3	1
Prussing, Ric, of	.169	89	9	15	5	0	1	10	3
Rittenhouse, Adam, 2b	.280	311	50	87	18	1	3	32	12
Sinclair, Darrell, c-of	.147	75	6	11	1	0	0	2	1
Vittitow, Cooper, ss	.269	360	64	97	23	3	2	28	15
Whitesides, Jake, of	.298	319	68	95	23	11	4	49	22

PITCHING	W	L	ERA	G	SV	IP	H	BB	SO
Barbettini, Chris	4	6	5.97	37	8	34	39	12	34
Bays, Leonard	6	11	5.50	19	0	104	121	40	58
Bogardus, Ryan	0	0	6.11	25	0	17	22	12	14
2-team (4 River City)	0	0	7.52	29	0	26	30	29	21
Dorn, Grant	6	7	3.74	21	0	127	112	34	107
Hanen, Jake	0	0	11.81	9	0	10	12	11	6
Jensen, Steve	0	2	7.17	9	0	21	27	20	13
Lehr, George	1	4	3.42	35	1	55	55	33	44
2-team (1 Chillicothe)	1	4	3.36	36	1	56	55	33	46
Martin, Kelly	1	3	5.13	19	0	47	56	18	32
2-team (2 River City)	1	3	4.70	21	0	51	58	22	38
McCullem, Ryan	0	0	7.04	5	0	7	11	8	6
Moellering, Dan	2	1	0.95	19	3	28	15	6	27
Reyes, Abimael	0	0	9.69	6	0	13	19	4	5
Reyes, Luis	0	2	4.76	7	0	17	13	13	11
Ross, Brian	1	3	4.76	14	0	39	38	14	32
Stine, Justin	7	6	4.45	18	0	111	133	28	71
Turrell, John	3	1	5.86	35	1	43	49	24	53
Welch, Mark	0	3	6.50	6	0	18	20	13	23
Wood, Jared	2	8	4.66	18	0	75	80	33	55

RICHMOND

BATTING	AVG	AB	R	H	2B	3B	HR	RBI	SB
Apotheker, Joseph, dh	.230	61	9	14	4	0	0	5	0
Burkhart, Damon, dh	.071	14	1	1	0	0	1	2	0
Butler, Matt, 1b	.229	201	14	46	10	1	0	21	1
Frasier, Charlie, dh	.000	2	0	0	0	0	0	0	0
Hall, Trevor, dh-1b	.299	87	12	26	9	1	1	12	0
2-team (48 Rockford)	.294	238	29	70	24	2	3	30	1
Harper, Eddie, of	.267	15	1	4	0	0	0	1	1
Hollingsworth, Josh, 3b-1b	.324	238	29	77	12	1	2	27	2
Johnson, Eric, of	.455	11	3	5	0	0	1	5	1
Klosterman, Jeremiah, c	.220	218	31	48	7	0	4	30	0
Leverett, Blake, 3b	.188	224	22	42	8	0	0	24	2
Marks, Tim, c	.186	97	8	18	5	0	0	8	0
Miller, Drew, of	.309	311	48	96	15	3	6	36	3
Pearce, Tom, dh	.217	60	9	13	3	0	5	14	0
Pirman, Pete, of	.275	287	41	79	14	0	2	45	11
Sandoval, Jose, ss	.277	289	37	80	10	4	3	32	26
Thornton, Rory, of	.233	215	32	50	8	1	1	15	7
Voshell, Key, 2b	.262	301	42	79	12	0	3	39	11
Willingham, Phil, of	.215	261	38	56	8	1	9	27	7
Zacuto, Kris, dh-1b	.221	104	16	23	6	1	2	11	1

PITCHING	W	L	ERA	G	SV	IP	H	BB	SO
Baca, Enriques	0	0	3.00	3	0	3	2	1	6
Barkley, Richard	0	3	3.27	6	0	33	33	14	34
DiFranco, Joseph	0	0	6.75	2	1	1	1	2	1
Ellison, Derrick	0	1	4.38	4	0	12	12	13	10
Gann, Jake	8	1	3.29	27	0	68	73	29	65
Hansen, Josh	0	0	0.00	4	0	3	1	5	5
Henry, Mike	7	6	2.93	24	1	76	58	35	74
Holland, Travis	1	1	4.50	5	0	24	28	10	16
Lawton, Charles	0	1	3.00	3	0	15	16	7	4
Moenter, Curtis	4	1	2.76	8	0	49	50	14	47
Parker, Aaron	0	1	18.00	2	1	1	1	2	1
Phillips, Aaron	1	2	3.57	8	0	40	44	14	20
Richardson, Patrick	1	0	7.88	2	0	8	16	3	5
Robinson, Patrick	0	0	5.40	2	0	3	4	1	1
Samter, Josh	0	1	5.40	9	0	5	5	8	2
Schweitzer, Matt	4	1	1.11	51	3	64	45	15	96
Smetana, Justin	1	2	5.61	21	0	25	33	14	25
Sosebee, Chad	1	1	1.01	16	0	26	16	4	22
Spencer, Chad	1	1	3.48	6	0	20	25	8	19
Spigner, Chris	11	4	2.12	21	0	140	101	54	134
Strohm, Steve	1	2	2.78	12	0	32	26	15	25
Tingley, Pat	0	1	13.50	7	2	9	18	5	9
Troyer, David	0	0	0.00	1	0	0	1	1	0
Vazquez, Vince	0	4	4.96	18	6	16	18	13	9
West, Ryan	4	0	0.90	16	0	20	17	8	26
Williams, Aaron	3	5	1.95	53	11	64	55	16	75
Woychak, Matt	2	0	4.00	4	0	18	13	12	9

RIVER CITY

BATTING	AVG	AB	R	H	2B	3B	HR	RBI	SB
Beckmann, Bryan, 3b	.146	41	4	6	2	0	1	3	1
Bergheger, Jeremiah, ss	.213	61	5	13	1	0	0	7	2
2-team (15 Cook County)	.222	99	6	22	1	0	0	10	2
Caracciolo, Tony, ss	.182	22	4	4	2	0	0	2	3
Christian, Justin, 2b	.301	123	24	37	5	1	1	15	19
Conner, Michael, of	.293	338	64	99	21	2	19	53	39
Critz, Logan, c-of	.180	61	6	11	5	0	0	3	4
Denny, John, of	.200	90	12	18	1	0	0	7	3
Fazio, Adam, of-3b	.224	67	4	15	2	0	0	7	1
Fuess, Brian, 3b	.288	153	13	44	10	0	2	16	2
Gecan, Matthew, 1b	.227	110	13	25	5	0	2	12	1
Hopkins, Brian, of	.232	125	10	29	8	0	2	10	1
Jackson, Brody, of	.270	74	11	20	3	2	1	4	8
Jager, Corey, c-1b	.217	184	23	40	11	0	1	27	4
Kalczynski, Joe, c	.252	222	27	56	12	0	5	36	9
Klosterman, Chris, 3b	.316	117	19	37	11	0	4	25	1
2-team (58 Gateway)	.272	313	52	85	21	1	9	52	5
Molinari, James, 2b	.279	86	15	24	9	0	3	10	6
Morrow, Alvin, of	.146	41	6	6	2	0	3	7	0
Perez, Tomas, 1b	.000	7	0	0	0	0	0	0	0
Riera, Zack, dh-of	.298	124	14	37	3	1	2	16	7
2-team (17 Cook County)	.287	181	23	52	7	1	4	26	9
Saunches, Mike, 1b	.111	18	1	2	0	0	0	0	0
Smith, Adonis, 2b	.121	66	6	8	1	0	0	5	3
Spry, Michael, of	.205	83	14	17	3	0	1	7	4
Taylor, Lucas, of	.272	243	47	66	12	1	0	25	22
Teahen, Matt, 3b	.333	6	1	2	1	0	0	0	0
Ury, Josh, 1b-of	.321	252	35	81	12	1	2	34	17
2-team (17 Florence)	.295	308	39	91	13	1	3	44	19
Vogel, Luke, 1b	.033	30	2	1	0	0	0	2	0
Weiss, Brian, ss	.282	248	36	70	15	0	4	34	5

PITCHING	W	L	ERA	G	SV	IP	H	BB	SO
Beever, James	0	0	6.75	3	0	8	9	3	7
Bogardus, Ryan	0	0	10.38	4	0	8	8	17	7
Dutka, Alex	0	0	3.86	4	1	9	13	1	5
Glassco, Brad	3	4	4.39	10	0	41	39	28	18
Jaillet, Wes	1	4	3.61	21	8	47	35	41	55
Johnson, Kelly	1	4	3.23	20	9	47	38	29	32
Krines, Daniel	7	2	3.73	21	1	89	91	20	34
Laratta, E.J.	6	3	2.78	12	0	74	76	25	43
Ledbetter, Aaron	2	2	2.89	8	0	37	27	6	35
Martin, Kelly	0	0	0.00	2	0	4	2	4	6
Modica, Greg	6	7	4.07	18	0	110	107	28	101
Morgan, Brian	1	2	4.57	22	1	45	43	29	33
Niedbalski, Nick	5	2	2.60	24	1	34	22	15	28
Pennington, Chad	1	0	5.09	10	0	17	22	5	20
Rhue, Mike	0	3	5.94	6	0	33	39	15	29
Rose, John	0	1	4.15	2	0	4	4	7	2
Shabansky, Rob	2	5	5.68	11	0	63	64	28	67
Shippey, Steven	0	2	8.68	3	0	9	13	5	9
Shouse, Dan	5	6	4.11	21	2	72	70	33	38
Soja, Steve	3	0	3.04	12	0	23	20	10	20

ROCKFORD

BATTING	AVG	AB	R	H	2B	3B	HR	RBI	SB
Austin, Richard, of	.249	269	45	67	7	2	6	34	13
Bernstine, Dave, c	.214	159	10	34	8	1	2	18	3
Ciarrachi, Jake, 3b	.000	1	0	0	0	0	0	0	0
Ciarrachi, Kevin, c	.246	57	6	14	7	0	0	4	0
DeGroote, Casey, dh-1b	.306	147	21	45	3	2	3	20	5

DiBlasi, Chris, 3b-1b	.224	67	4	15	2	0	2	10	2
Elkouri, Shaff, 2b	.241	87	9	21	2	1	0	7	5
Fjelland, Ben, 3b-2b	.280	329	38	92	16	0	4	38	8
Floyd, Dan, of-2b	.130	23	1	3	1	0	0	1	2
Fuentes, Fernando, c	.600	5	2	3	0	1	0	0	0
Garner, Mark, ss	.219	233	32	51	9	1	1	17	8
Hall, Trevor, 1b	.291	151	17	44	15	1	2	18	1
Haven, Tory, dh	.216	37	6	8	2	0	3	8	0
2-team (58 Kalamazoo)	.310	229	41	71	17	2	14	52	0
Johnson, Mark, c	.154	13	1	2	0	0	0	1	0
Matthews, Bobby, c-of	.274	223	26	61	4	1	1	31	11
Pigott, Anthony, of	.278	327	44	91	20	4	4	33	27
Ramos, Jan, 1b	.239	188	24	45	15	0	1	27	5
Schutt, Doug, of	.253	217	39	55	7	1	0	17	35
2-team (5 Gateway)	.258	233	40	60	7	2	0	18	38
Sester, Joe, dh	.000	4	0	0	0	0	0	0	0
Urban, Dan, of	.163	86	11	14	1	0	0	3	7
Vaughn, Kiley, 2b-ss	.251	259	33	65	7	2	0	37	4

PITCHING	W	L	ERA	G	SV	IP	H	BB	SO
Badgley, Daniel	0	0	40.50	1	0	0	3	1	1
Barbosa, Joe	1	1	3.82	7	0	30	32	12	23
Barreras, Rene	0	0	18.00	1	0	2	3	4	2
Crowley, Kevin	0	0	9.82	3	0	7	9	2	8
Davidson, Andy	2	1	3.86	8	0	21	21	13	10
Dobyns, Heath	0	1	7.41	7	0	17	30	9	5
Dowdy, Justin	2	1	1.88	17	7	28	19	9	21
Dulkowski, Marc	2	3	6.16	13	2	19	17	15	16
Garza, Alberto	0	0	1.93	3	0	4	4	8	7
Glosser, Jason	3	1	3.33	17	0	27	26	7	16
Hubbel, Travis	0	2	8.68	5	0	9	11	11	6
James, Frank	6	4	2.99	13	0	72	71	29	42
Kincaid, Tyler	0	0	9.00	4	0	5	8	4	5
Kjose, Joe	2	5	6.14	20	4	29	33	10	20
Latimer, Josh	2	2	4.61	24	7	27	26	10	30
Mack, Bobby	0	0	4.05	5	0	6	9	3	6
McCrotty, Wes	0	1	6.75	15	1	14	16	14	16
Olson, Justin	1	1	2.32	8	0	31	19	10	19
Pilkington, Jason	3	0	2.08	5	0	26	24	6	21
Rosengren, Phil	0	0	2.11	12	0	21	18	9	20
Royal, Shannon	0	1	7.50	2	0	6	9	4	5
2-team (10 Chillicothe)	4	2	4.38	12	0	49	62	22	40
Shelley, Jason	7	1	0.85	10	0	74	49	21	82
Sobkowiak, Scott	6	7	3.85	15	0	110	95	42	97
Tomsu, Joshua	8	5	1.71	17	1	110	81	40	65
Troyer, David	0	1	1.23	6	2	14	9	12	5
2-team (1 Richmond)	0	1	1.17	7	2	15	10	13	5
Vaughn, Barton	2	1	2.77	4	0	26	27	7	16
Weel, Mike	0	2	7.27	9	0	26	23	19	20

WASHINGTON

BATTING	AVG	AB	R	H	2B	3B	HR	RBI	SB
Albert, Jeff, 3b-2b	.176	17	2	3	1	0	0	0	0
Bollig, Jake, of	.284	271	46	77	16	4	10	40	4
Buchenauer, Joel, 2b-of	.244	90	14	22	2	2	0	10	1
Cahill, Jon, ss	.287	338	55	97	15	0	4	34	2
Cates, Zach, 1b-3b	.288	302	58	87	10	3	13	48	20
Coakley, Jay, dh-c	.284	331	49	94	13	1	16	57	4
Cowell, John, 2b	.154	26	1	4	0	0	0	1	0
Cruz, Orlando, of	.190	105	10	20	3	0	0	11	5
Cuervo, Joe, of	.157	70	10	11	0	0	1	10	3
Cunningham, Mike, of	.287	101	24	29	3	0	1	6	11
Ellis, Ryan, 2b	.294	102	15	30	8	0	0	14	4
Garcia, Doug, of	.277	289	42	80	10	1	6	32	19
Johnson, Matt, c	.154	26	1	4	0	0	0	1	0
Kane, Jason, 3b	.257	307	42	79	13	4	5	45	7
Lee, Gary, c	.267	15	2	4	0	0	0	3	0
Loggins, Josh, c-of	.331	290	63	96	13	5	24	72	15
McCabe, Tim, dh-1b	.242	33	3	8	1	0	1	11	0
Penberthy, Dan, 1b	.000	10	0	0	0	0	0	0	0
Rini, Marty, ph	.000	1	0	0	0	0	0	0	0
Rollins, Matt, of	.091	22	1	2	1	0	0	2	0
Schmidt, J.P., of	.167	24	4	4	0	1	0	1	3
Tuttle, Chris, of	.348	23	2	8	1	1	0	5	3
Woodrow, Justin, of	.311	45	10	14	2	0	0	6	3
Woods, Blake, 2b	.378	156	34	59	10	3	4	22	14

PITCHING	W	L	ERA	G	SV	IP	H	BB	SO
Aiello, Nick	4	5	4.37	19	0	105	107	25	52
Ally, Ben	9	7	3.02	19	0	134	111	33	124
Bradley, Dave	10	5	2.77	17	0	113	97	32	118
Dorsey, Brian	0	0	3.20	12	0	19	16	14	19
Edwards, Brad	1	0	2.41	9	0	18	14	15	16
Elkins, Jason	3	2	4.03	27	1	38	26	24	57
Ewen, Clayton	1	3	4.09	16	1	44	53	15	33
Heagen, Doug	3	1	2.66	22	2	44	38	17	33
Howton, Jared	7	2	2.60	11	0	65	49	21	41
Kozol, Anthony	3	3	2.62	33	16	34	33	9	25
Leonards, Bake	3	2	1.70	33	0	53	45	14	53
McDonnell, Matt	10	4	2.99	16	0	96	99	30	39
Strickland, Keith	0	0	4.76	6	0	6	7	3	6

NORTHERN LEAGUE

For the first time in five years, the Northern League playoffs did not include a championship series between the traditional Northern League teams and the eight-team Eastern Division, which broke off after the 2002 season and was renamed the Northeast League.

But the Northern League still had plenty of controversy and interest come playoff time. When Winnipeg Goldeyes all-star DH Harry Berrios strained a rib-cage muscle during the Northern League semifinals, the resulting controversy proved to be the story of the playoffs.

Harry Berrios

Commissioner Mike Stone initially decided the Goldeyes could replace Berrios with veteran slugger Bubba Smith, who had just finished playing in the Mexican League. Protests from other clubs involved in the playoffs led to Stone reversing his decision. That led to even more controversy, as Stone had to deal with an angered Goldeyes team and even death threats.

When making his decision, Stone cited league bylaws, which say the commissioner has the authority to rule on any replacement of an injured player within 15 days of the end of the season. The other teams balked, pointing out that in past years teams have not been able to replace injured players during the playoffs, even when key starters were hurt.

It ended up being an inconsequential decision, as Winnipeg reached the championship series without either Berrios or Smith in the lineup. Berrios was healthy enough to play again in the championship series.

But angry Winnipeg fans barraged Stone's office with angry emails and phone calls, including a couple of death threats. Stone ended up not traveling to Winnipeg for the championship series out of concerns for his safety.

Eddie Pearson

Controversy did prove good for business however, as the Winnipeg media covered the story extensively, and more than 6,000 fans attended each of the two championship games in Winnipeg.

On the field, Fargo-Moorhead righthander Todd George proved to be the big story. He beat the Goldeyes twice to earn series MVP honors.

The Kansas City T-Bones, the league's newest team, had a successful debut in 2003. After struggling to draw fans in Duluth-Superior, an original Northern League franchise, the T-Bones drew more than 200,000 fans while designated hitter Eddie Pearson, a former first-round draft pick of the Chicago White Sox, was named the league's MVP.

The league also got an attendance boost when Gary's RailCats Stadium opened. The stadium was originally set to open in 2002 to coincide with the team's entry into the league, but delays meant that the team spent a season as a traveling team.

STANDINGS

FIRST HALF

EAST	W	L	PCT	GB
St. Paul Saints	30	15	.667	—
Winnipeg Goldeyes	26	18	.591	3½
Schaumburg Flyers	25	19	.568	4½
Joliet JackHammers	19	25	.432	10½
Gary Southshore Railcats	15	30	.333	15

WEST	W	L	PCT	GB
Fargo-Moorhead RedHawks	32	13	.711	—
Lincoln Saltdogs	21	24	.467	11
Sioux Falls Canaries	20	24	.455	11½
Kansas City T-Bones	20	25	.444	12
Sioux City Explorers	15	30	.333	17

SECOND HALF

EAST	W	L	PCT	GB
Winnipeg Goldeyes	29	16	.644	—
Schaumburg Flyers	22	22	.500	6½
St. Paul Saints	22	23	.489	7
Joliet JackHammers	21	23	.477	7½
Gary Southshore Railcats	21	24	.467	8

WEST	W	L	PCT	GB
Fargo-Moorhead RedHawks	30	15	.667	—
Kansas City T-Bones	23	21	.523	6½
Lincoln Saltdogs	20	25	.444	10
Sioux City Explorers	18	27	.400	12
Sioux Falls Canaries	17	27	.386	12½

PLAYOFFS: Semifinals—Winnipeg defeated St. Paul 3-2 and Fargo defeated Schaumburg 3-2 in best-of-5- series. **Finals**—Fargo defeated Winnipeg 3-1 in best-of-5 series.

MANAGERS: Fargo-Moorhead—Doug Simunic. **Gary**—Garry Templeton. **Joliet**—Matt Nokes. **Kansas City**—Al Gallagher .**Lincoln**—Tim Johnson. **Schaumburg**—Andy McCauley. **Sioux City**—Jay Kirkpatrick. **Sioux Falls**—Doc Edwards. **St. Paul**—George Tsamis. **Winnipeg**—Hal Lanier.

ATTENDANCE: Winnipeg 300,760; St. Paul 266,804; Lincoln 214,839; Kansas City 204,198; Schaumburg 202,300; Joliet 198,091; Fargo-Moorhead 178,370; Gary 140,310; Sioux Falls 117,937; Sioux City 91,005.

ALL-STAR TEAM: C—Kirk Pierce, Schaumburg. **1B**—Wes Chamberlain, Gary. **2B**—Brian Ward, Fargo-Moorhead. **3B**—Pichi Balet, Sioux City. **SS**—Marc Mirizzi, Sioux Falls. **OF**—Harry Berrios, Winnipeg; Anthony Monegan, Joliet; Rick Prieto, Kansas City; Bryan Warner, Lincoln. **DH**—Eddie Pearson, Kansas City.

Most Valuable Player: Eddie Pearson, Kansas City. **Pitcher of the Year:** Rafael Gross, Winnipeg. **Relief Pitcher of the Year:** Chris Chavez, St. Paul. **Rookies of the Year:** Kris Cox, Winnipeg; Brian Sprout, Fargo-Moorhead. **Rookie Pitcher of the Year:** Chris Begg, St. Paul. **Manager of the Year:** Doug Simunic, Fargo-Moorhead.

INDIVIDUAL BATTING LEADERS

(Minimum 243 Plate Appearances)

	AVG	AB	R	H	2B	3B	HR	RBI	SB
Pearson, Eddie, KC	.362	343	57	124	19	1	14	78	1
Alley, Charles, Winnipeg	.343	233	52	80	17	0	5	35	0
Prieto, Rick, Kansas City	.340	335	63	114	19	7	6	45	11
Delgado, Mario, Schaum.	.340	318	54	108	24	2	9	54	0
Rumfield, Toby, F-M	.332	319	48	106	20	1	8	62	0
Olow, Adam, St. Paul	.327	214	44	70	9	1	5	38	9
Warner, Bryan, Lincoln	.317	378	65	120	19	1	16	69	10
Foley, Steve, Joliet	.317	322	51	102	17	1	3	55	9
Cox, Kris, Winnipeg	.314	255	40	80	12	6	3	22	6
Pagan, Felix, Sioux Falls	.313	336	45	105	15	3	12	58	10

INDIVIDUAL PITCHING LEADERS

(Minimum 72 Innings)

	W	L	ERA	G	SV	IP	H	BB	SO
Gross, Rafael, Winnipeg	13	2	2.28	18	0	115	102	19	69
Thoms, Hank, F-M	6	2	2.42	15	0	108	90	27	78
Foster, Kevin, St. Paul	12	4	2.92	19	0	133	109	64	99
Purcell, Brad, Winnipeg	8	5	2.97	20	0	112	95	49	92
McMurray, Heath, Winnipeg	2	3	3.05	28	2	86	71	31	71
Woodman, Hank, Schaum.	11	5	3.13	19	0	132	106	49	126
Cramblitt, Joey, Winnipeg	11	5	3.15	17	0	120	127	31	72
Hecker, Steven, Joliet	5	5	3.29	34	5	79	68	32	66
O'Donnell, Tony, Gary	5	6	3.39	15	0	85	87	25	55
George, Todd, F-M	9	4	3.41	16	0	90	92	23	53

FARGO-MOORHEAD

BATTING	AVG	AB	R	H	2B	3B	HR	RBI	SB
Argento, Shaun, c	.125	8	1	1	0	0	0	0	0
2-team (6 Gary)	.172	29	1	5	2	0	0	1	0
Burnham, Jake, of	.200	20	0	4	0	0	0	1	0
Byas, Mike, of	.183	60	8	11	2	0	0	1	0
Clark, Jason, of	.194	36	1	7	0	0	0	3	0
Coffie, Ivanon, 3b	.313	16	4	5	0	0	2	4	0
Dormanen, Derek, p	.209	43	6	9	0	0	0	2	0
Fink, Eddie, c-1b	.213	89	10	19	3	0	4	14	0
2-team (39 Joliet)	.217	207	22	45	6	0	7	27	0
Foley, Steve, of	.291	189	32	55	8	1	2	32	4
Franco, Christian, 3b	.273	11	2	3	0	0	0	3	0
Freeman, Ricky, ph	.000	1	0	0	0	0	0	0	0
Garrison, B.J., of	.288	59	12	17	3	0	1	10	2
2-team (69 Schaumburg)	.247	308	48	76	12	2	3	36	7
Gerald, Ed, dh-of	.270	289	44	78	20	2	8	46	7
Goldbach, Jeff, c	.229	109	18	25	4	0	5	21	0
Kirkpatrick, Michael, of	.120	25	2	3	1	1	0	2	1
Leach, Jalal, of	.414	29	4	12	4	0	0	3	0
2-team (24 Winnipeg)	.303	132	20	40	9	1	4	20	3
Mathis, Joe, of	.301	319	64	96	13	9	5	42	19
Mazer, Brad, c	.293	191	31	56	12	1	3	27	4
Melo, Juan, 3b	.387	93	18	36	9	0	5	22	0
Pinto, Rene, c	.205	39	3	8	2	0	1	4	0
Rumfield, Toby, 1b	.332	319	48	106	20	1	8	62	0
Salazar, Ruben, 3b-1b	.292	360	64	105	19	1	8	49	2
Sprout, Brian, ss	.302	361	70	109	21	0	5	45	16
Ward, Brian, 2b	.305	325	60	99	27	2	11	64	3
Weber, Jon, of	.309	204	46	63	8	1	11	48	14

PITCHING	W	L	ERA	G	SV	IP	H	BB	SO
Burch, Matt	0	0	5.01	11	0	32	37	20	23
Dormanen, Derek	2	1	4.20	17	1	40	51	11	18
George, Todd	6	1	2.88	10	0	56	53	14	29
2-team (6 Gary)	9	4	3.41	16	0	89	92	23	53
Hooker, Jon	3	1	5.46	28	1	64	73	29	61
Jamison, Ryan	0	1	15.43	1	0	2	6	2	2
Kennedy, Jodie	10	6	3.64	18	0	118	127	49	62
Moak, Curtus	4	1	3.66	41	0	39	38	17	29
Montgomery, Steve	7	3	3.55	32	11	50	57	15	49
Peschel, Mike	6	3	5.11	19	0	79	85	34	49
Reames, Jay	0	2	8.49	5	0	11	12	10	6
Salvevold, Greg	4	2	4.94	11	0	62	79	19	17
Sander, Richard	4	5	5.22	14	0	79	89	49	57
Sansom, Trevor	8	1	2.09	38	6	56	39	19	47
Sather, Todd	0	1	14.73	2	0	3	7	7	1
Spille, Ryan	2	0	5.51	3	0	16	15	6	15
Thoms, Hank	3	0	3.02	6	0	44	32	9	31
2-team (9 Joliet)	6	2	2.42	15	0	108	90	27	78
Young, Doug	3	0	2.59	29	1	48	35	18	40

GARY

BATTING	AVG	AB	R	H	2B	3B	HR	RBI	SB
Argento, Shaun, c	.190	21	0	4	2	0	0	1	0
Barba, Moises, ss	.238	21	3	5	1	0	0	0	0
Battle, Howard, 3b	.173	98	10	17	3	0	0	8	0
Bonilla, Clemente, ss	.261	69	8	18	1	2	0	2	5
Brown, Billy, of	.282	369	57	104	24	1	8	51	32
Bush, Ron, ss	.179	28	5	5	1	0	0	0	0
Calderon, Henry, 3b	.227	44	2	10	0	1	0	0	0
Carpenter, Bubba, of	.268	112	8	30	8	0	0	5	1
Chamberlain, Wes, 1b	.310	335	47	104	22	0	13	66	3
Cisneros, Josh, c	.182	11	1	2	0	0	0	0	0
Clinton, Ricky, c	.256	43	6	11	3	0	0	2	0
Drumming, Demetrick, 3b	.125	8	0	1	0	0	0	0	0
2-team (15 Joliet)	.217	46	4	10	2	1	0	5	0
Edwards, Dytarious, 2b-ss	.296	294	32	87	9	2	0	23	9
Flaherty, Tim, of-1b	.279	208	32	58	15	1	6	28	3
2-team (29 Sioux City)	.247	316	45	78	18	2	14	49	4
Franco, Christian, 3b	.190	42	4	8	1	0	0	3	4
3-team (20 Joliet, 4 F-M)	.215	121	13	26	3	0	1	12	6
Gontmaher, Nick, of	.260	77	14	20	7	1	1	7	2
Goodman, Scott, dh	.170	106	7	18	7	0	2	8	0
Griffin, Vincent, of	.222	27	1	6	1	0	0	2	0
Hill, Chad, ss	.184	76	9	14	2	1	1	4	0
Hill, Jason, dh-1b	.295	105	18	31	7	1	3	13	3
Kent, Brian, c	.191	47	3	9	0	0	0	5	0
Malone, Billy, 2b	.188	80	7	15	6	0	0	4	3
Murphy, Sean, 3b-2b	.288	156	16	45	12	1	1	15	0
2-team (44 Kansas City)	.281	327	34	92	21	2	3	34	1
Pinto, Rene, c	.287	289	38	83	18	3	8	43	3
2-team (10 F-M)	.277	328	41	91	20	3	9	47	3
Templeton, Garry, 2b-ss	.178	118	14	21	4	2	0	8	2
Thompson, Phil, of	.224	277	26	62	9	3	3	31	13
Urueta, Luis, of	.238	21	2	5	1	0	1	1	0

PITCHING	W	L	ERA	G	SV	IP	H	BB	SO
Andel, Chris	2	0	3.58	16	3	27	24	8	21
Byrdak, Tim	2	4	4.34	10	0	66	60	25	58
2-team (5 Joliet)	4	5	3.78	15	0	100	91	35	76

Callier, Jeremy	0	1	2.45	4	0	3	3	2	0
Coleman, Billy	4	6	5.12	18	0	114	123	29	87
Embry, Byron	0	1	4.19	16	0	19	14	4	20
George, Todd	3	3	4.32	6	0	33	39	9	24
Guthrie, Sazi	9	5	4.00	20	0	108	116	41	53
Harrison, Jim	4	6	4.47	35	0	44	47	16	29
Houdek, Brian	3	6	2.90	14	0	62	48	25	48
Mahan, Dallas	0	1	4.50	3	0	4	2	1	3
Mazur, Graham	0	0	9.82	1	0	3	8	2	3
Miller, Benji	0	3	5.30	34	12	35	49	7	29
O'Donnell, Tony	5	6	3.39	15	0	85	87	25	55
Orr, Benjamin	0	2	9.93	15	0	22	34	14	21
Reid, Aaron	0	0	5.25	8	0	12	17	3	5
Sanchez, Justin	0	0	21.21	2	0	4	8	7	5
Soria, Dan	3	9	5.70	20	0	102	121	32	56
Upwood, Jake	1	1	1.86	30	1	38	38	15	18
2-team (4 Lincoln)	1	1	2.30	34	1	43	46	19	22

JOLIET

BATTING	AVG	AB	R	H	2B	3B	HR	RBI	SB
Bartolucci, Paul, 2b	.000	18	3	0	0	0	0	0	1
Cameron, Troy, 3b-2b	.250	152	28	38	8	3	4	22	3
De los Santos, Eddy, ss	.250	76	3	19	4	2	0	5	2
DeYoung, Peter, 2b-3b	.249	221	20	55	9	1	2	18	3
Drumming, Demetrick, 2b	.237	38	4	9	2	1	0	5	0
Fink, Eddie, c-1b	.220	118	12	26	3	0	3	13	0
Fischer, Rob, of	.118	51	5	6	1	2	1	8	2
Foley, Steve, of	.353	133	19	47	9	0	1	23	5
2-team (51 F-M)	.317	322	51	102	17	1	3	55	9
Franco, Christian, of	.221	68	7	15	2	0	1	6	2
Goldbach, Jeff, c	.231	104	14	24	7	0	4	14	0
2-team (30 F-M)	.230	213	32	49	11	0	9	35	0
Henry, Chad, ss-2b	.313	294	38	92	17	1	2	28	8
2-team (7 Sioux City)	.300	317	40	95	17	1	2	28	8
Kopacz, Derek, of	.264	326	43	86	16	2	5	40	19
Matuszek, Kevin, 2b-3b	.091	22	1	2	0	0	0	0	0
Monegan, Anthony, of	.309	356	61	110	12	4	0	20	50
Norman, Les, dh-of	.359	181	27	65	17	0	3	31	3
Nunez, Hector, of	.182	22	2	4	0	0	0	2	0
Olszta, Eddie, of-3b	.200	145	17	29	2	0	1	15	5
Rose, Pete, 1b-3b	.260	285	29	74	8	0	4	38	1
Sienko, Ryan, c-1b	.216	278	41	60	16	0	14	46	2
Toven, John, 2b	.183	71	5	13	2	0	0	6	1

PITCHING	W	L	ERA	G	SV	IP	H	BB	SO
Brooks, Jake	0	0	0.00	3	0	2	1	0	3
Byrdak, Tim	2	1	2.67	5	0	33	31	10	18
Donlin, Sean	2	2	8.16	24	0	32	55	30	18
Embry, Byron	2	4	2.78	26	0	35	31	14	47
2-team (16 Gary)	2	5	3.27	42	0	55	45	18	67
Franklin, Brent	6	10	4.26	33	5	93	100	32	80
Hecker, Steven	5	5	3.29	34	5	79	68	32	66
Hyde, Rich	9	6	3.63	21	0	139	158	21	99
Jones, Sean	0	1	3.42	14	1	23	18	9	11
Mazone, Brian	5	2	2.89	14	0	71	63	15	72
Montero, Oscar	2	4	3.16	45	9	57	52	25	41
Morales, Alex	0	2	5.14	5	0	14	10	12	12
Saken, Dan	0	0	6.23	6	0	8	12	1	3
Santiago, Derek	2	6	6.65	12	0	65	86	19	34
Thomas, Eric	1	1	6.60	11	1	15	17	9	4
Thoms, Hank	3	2	1.99	9	0	63	58	18	47
Zipser, Mike	1	2	3.92	7	0	39	43	16	18
2-team (9 Lincoln)	3	8	5.10	16	0	83	103	26	41

KANSAS CITY

BATTING	AVG	AB	R	H	2B	3B	HR	RBI	SB
Adams, Skip, 3b	.247	77	16	19	5	0	1	8	4
Brooks, Jeff, 3b	.195	41	3	8	3	0	0	3	0
Brown, Ray, 1b	.279	247	31	69	13	1	6	42	0
Cameron, Stanton, of-1b	.192	26	2	5	0	0	0	3	0
Clifton, Rodney, of	.278	162	23	45	9	0	8	30	4
2-team (28 Schaumburg)	.234	273	32	64	10	0	10	40	6
Ehrnsberger, Chad, of	.331	124	22	41	12	0	7	26	1
Johnson, Eric, of	.071	28	2	2	0	0	0	0	0
Jones, Jack, ss	.237	317	51	75	13	3	7	39	16
Keesee, David, 3b-of	.273	33	6	9	2	1	0	7	0
LePine, Chris, of	.307	215	37	66	7	2	1	13	7
Maier, Taber, 2b-3b	.286	360	67	103	20	3	7	49	6
Murphy, Sean, 3b-2b	.275	171	18	47	9	1	2	19	1
Nelson, Bruce, c	.115	78	2	9	0	0	0	2	0
Pearson, Eddie, dh-1b	.369	290	47	107	16	1	14	72	1
2-team (13 St. Paul)	.362	343	57	124	19	1	14	78	1
Prieto, Rick, of	.340	335	63	114	19	7	6	45	11
Shindle, Chad, c	.254	201	25	51	14	0	3	28	0
Shrum, Allen, c	.184	76	4	14	1	0	0	6	0
Tash, Ryan, 3b	.172	29	1	5	0	0	0	0	0
Teson, Mark, of	.154	13	2	2	1	0	0	0	0
Vinh, Bao, of-2b	.260	227	33	59	8	1	2	26	0
Walker, Jimmy, c	.216	37	8	8	3	0	0	5	0

PITCHING	W	L	ERA	G	SV	IP	H	BB	SO
Bacci, Tony	5	8	4.71	19	0	128	140	44	47
Davis, Jason	3	1	3.24	20	1	25	25	9	13
Felkel, Bryan	0	0	2.89	8	0	9	14	6	5
2-team (22 Sioux Falls)	0	2	5.12	30	1	38	51	22	19
Ford, Brian	2	1	5.26	16	1	25	38	2	20
Franks, Lance	0	2	11.12	4	0	11	18	4	4
Gomes, Tony	3	5	6.11	25	0	53	64	28	29
Grunwald, Erik	5	5	4.25	14	0	78	78	37	48
Hoyt, Michael	0	1	5.60	9	0	27	34	14	16
Johnson, D.J.	7	2	2.45	35	17	47	34	9	47
Koziara, Matt	0	1	5.40	8	0	11	18	9	3
2-team (6 Sioux Falls)	1	4	7.04	14	0	38	66	18	17
Krysa, Jonathan	2	3	3.72	6	0	36	34	13	26
Masterman, Tom	2	1	5.01	14	0	32	41	5	17
Matheny, Brandon	0	0	5.63	2	0	8	9	6	6
McClendon, Tim	0	0	2.70	6	0	10	9	4	7
McDonald, Jon	1	3	5.98	9	0	52	62	18	35
2-team (7 St. Paul)	2	4	6.78	16	1	77	104	31	42
Serrano, Wascar	1	3	7.71	6	0	28	34	10	12
Sevier, Nate	6	7	5.73	23	0	92	112	27	75
Sigley, Jayson	6	3	3.68	20	0	95	106	48	69
Thomas, Tommy	0	0	5.40	3	0	5	2	9	7

LINCOLN

BATTING	AVG	AB	R	H	2B	3B	HR	RBI	SB
Anderson, John, of	.273	22	3	6	0	0	0	2	0
Bell, David, c	.250	8	0	2	1	0	0	0	0
Burke, Mark, 1b	.184	49	5	9	1	0	2	5	0
Carpenter, Bubba, of	.340	103	20	35	10	0	1	8	1
2-team (30 Gary)	.302	215	28	65	18	0	1	13	2
Church, Ian, of	.284	102	7	29	5	0	0	10	3
De los Santos, Eddy, ss	.275	193	14	53	4	0	1	19	5
2-team (23 Joliet)	.268	269	17	72	8	2	1	24	7
Doskocil, Darren, 2b-ss	.281	363	66	102	23	5	10	55	15
Doyle, Spencer, ss-of	.273	33	3	9	2	0	0	2	0
Edge, Dwight, of	.213	80	9	17	2	1	1	9	1
Figga, Mike, dh	.167	24	4	4	1	0	1	3	1
Foreman, JuJu, of	.298	151	33	45	4	0	0	3	15
German, Franklin, of	.163	43	3	7	2	0	1	3	1
Hernandez, Alexis, c	1.000	1	0	1	0	0	0	0	0
Marin, Limberth, ss	.213	61	7	13	1	0	0	5	3
Matos, Francisco, 2b	.281	32	2	9	1	0	0	2	0
Moreno, Jorge, of	.304	125	24	38	9	2	6	27	8
Patton, Josh, 3b	.301	339	56	102	27	3	5	57	8
Powell, Paul, 1b	.274	190	22	52	7	1	2	25	2
Rasmusen, Pete, dh	.000	3	0	0	0	0	0	0	0
Rengifo, Daling, c	.261	88	13	23	2	0	1	7	4
Roberson, Kevin, dh	.297	74	12	22	5	1	2	17	2
Rogers, John, 2b-3b	.182	11	3	2	0	0	0	1	0
Ruiz, Ryan, of	.231	156	26	36	5	2	0	16	10
Shafer, Erik, c	.118	17	1	2	0	0	0	2	0
Smith, Ira, of	.290	176	26	51	8	2	3	22	2
2-tea m (12 Sioux City)	.274	226	29	62	9	2	3	24	2
Smith, Jeremy, 1b	.152	33	6	5	2	0	1	5	0
Smith, Ryan, c	.189	227	16	43	5	0	2	22	0
Sullivan, Jason, ss	.333	24	3	8	0	0	0	2	1
Warner, Bryan, of-1b	.317	378	65	120	19	1	16	69	10

PITCHING	W	L	ERA	G	SV	IP	H	BB	SO
Andrews, Clayton	1	2	4.91	4	0	25	32	9	10
Batson, Byron	0	2	6.75	4	0	20	28	9	11
Beever, James	0	0	6.48	4	0	8	12	3	7
Forbes, Derek	2	2	6.03	6	0	31	40	14	23
Ford, Tom	10	4	3.78	26	0	119	115	45	64
Herz, Jason	1	1	7.08	6	1	20	34	6	8
Johnson, Clark	0	0	7.71	6	0	7	6	5	5
Johnston, Doug	5	6	4.73	18	0	93	85	28	52
Lee, Andy	0	0	5.06	23	0	10	14	3	5
Madrigal, Victor	0	0	6.75	3	0	5	7	3	3
Ochsner, Alan	3	2	2.90	32	1	40	43	9	28
Ott, Thom	0	1	7.71	10	0	11	18	5	10
Pageler, Mick	4	6	2.91	48	12	58	49	9	46
Sawyer, Steve	0	2	7.27	4	0	17	23	4	8
2-team (12 Sioux City)	0	4	5.53	16	0	40	49	9	35
Stoner, Nat	0	0	7.41	15	0	17	25	9	11
2-team (10 Sioux Falls)	0	1	7.33	25	0	27	45	11	16
Thomas, Steve	0	0	2.84	6	0	6	10	1	2
2-team (15 Winnipeg)	0	1	3.15	21	7	20	27	5	5
Truty, Darren	6	6	3.58	17	0	88	82	30	59

	W	L	ERA	G	SV	IP	H	BB	SO
Trytten, Ryan	1	0	1.93	9	1	14	13	4	10
Upwood, Jake	0	0	6.23	4	0	4	8	4	4
Walters, Cory	3	6	4.92	18	0	78	106	18	68
Weast, Skip	3	3	1.34	10	0	53	33	19	30
Weidert, Chris	0	0	0.56	13	6	16	8	4	13
Zipser, Mike	2	6	6.14	9	0	44	60	10	23

ST. PAUL

BATTING	AVG	AB	R	H	2B	3B	HR	RBI	SB
Alfonzo, Eliezer, c	.300	253	46	76	15	1	9	46	0
Brooks, Jeff, 1b-3b	.224	201	26	45	4	0	6	28	1
2-team (11 Kansas City)	.219	242	29	53	7	0	6	31	1
Byas, Mike, of	.250	32	4	8	0	0	0	0	1
Callahan, Dave, 1b	.277	238	28	66	7	0	6	40	1
Fera, Aaron, of	.257	331	49	85	28	1	9	45	3
Hall, Justin, 2b	.310	271	31	84	15	3	1	47	4
Harris, Cory, of	.344	157	38	54	6	2	5	26	7
Jones, Chris, of	.264	163	28	43	14	1	4	30	4
Kane, Ryan, 3b	.233	326	34	76	13	0	3	32	1
Malave, Jose, of	.125	8	0	1	0	0	0	0	0
McKee, Scott, 1b-c	.230	165	11	38	6	0	2	20	0
Minoso, Minnie, dh	.000	0	0	0	0	0	0	0	0
Newson, Warren, of	.306	62	11	19	5	0	0	10	1
Olow, Adam, of	.327	214	44	70	9	1	5	38	9
Pearson, Eddie, dh	.321	53	10	17	3	0	0	6	0
Powell, Paul, of-1b	.220	91	12	20	3	0	1	5	1
2-team (53 Lincoln)	.256	281	34	72	10	1	3	30	3
Shallenberger, Joe, 2b-of	.239	218	36	52	11	0	3	22	2
Swenson, Leland, ss	.237	257	40	61	11	0	1	20	3
Vasquez, Alberto, c	.071	14	2	1	0	0	0	1	0
Wiseman, Jeb, c	.163	43	5	7	1	0	0	3	0

PITCHING	W	L	ERA	G	SV	IP	H	BB	SO
Begg, Chris	7	0	1.50	10	0	66	52	15	63
Buchanan, Brian	4	4	3.82	14	0	75	93	34	58
Chavez, Chris	2	4	2.05	43	22	44	30	19	54
Christman, Tim	5	2	2.70	33	1	50	42	18	49
Cosgrove, Mike	1	1	3.20	40	3	50	43	14	56
Fish, Steve	0	1	4.50	1	0	6	9	1	1
Fleetham, Ben	0	0	6.75	1	0	4	3	3	4
Foster, Kevin	12	4	2.92	19	0	132	109	64	99
Friedman, Jody	1	1	4.08	24	1	39	43	22	24
Goodrum, Kevin	0	0	15.43	2	0	2	6	1	0
McDonald, Jon	1	1	8.51	7	1	24	42	13	7
Mindingall, Wes	2	4	5.59	18	1	37	39	13	25
Takeoka, Kazuhiro	0	0	7.56	2	0	8	12	7	6
Von Haefen, Jason	9	6	4.15	19	0	123	123	34	94
Walters, Cory	2	4	4.10	8	0	26	26	7	19
2-team (18 Lincoln)	5	10	4.71	26	0	105	132	25	87
Whitney, Jake	6	6	3.97	17	0	106	129	31	89

SCHAUMBURG

BATTING	AVG	AB	R	H	2B	3B	HR	RBI	SB
Brown, Brant, 1b	.253	328	55	83	21	6	7	43	16
Campana, Wandel, 2b	.333	39	7	13	2	0	1	4	0
Clifton, Rodney, of	.171	111	9	19	1	0	2	10	2
Delgado, Mario, dh-1b	.340	318	54	108	24	2	9	54	0
Futrell, Michael, c-of	.204	147	14	30	2	1	1	19	2
Garrison, B.J., of	.237	249	36	59	9	2	2	26	5
Gibralter, Dave, of	.157	70	4	11	3	0	1	6	0
Goerdt, Eric, of	.261	138	17	36	7	0	4	16	3
Gomez, Rudy, 2b-ss	.296	297	56	88	27	2	4	37	6
Gray, Josh, of	.000	9	0	0	0	0	0	0	0
Kirkpatrick, Michael, of	.200	40	6	8	2	0	2	6	1
3-team (26 SF, 7 F-M)	.235	162	25	38	13	3	4	19	4
Lundquist, Ryan, 3b	.267	288	35	77	15	0	10	43	2
McCallum, Geoff, ss	.255	325	50	83	11	1	0	21	10
Olson, Chris, 2b	.262	65	5	17	2	0	0	3	4
Pierce, Kirk, c	.305	295	59	90	27	1	15	72	0
Rooke, Brian, of	.136	22	1	3	0	0	0	2	2
Staton, T.J., of	.307	225	47	69	12	1	9	46	12
Van Iderstine, Ben, of	.295	95	7	28	5	1	1	7	5

PITCHING	W	L	ERA	G	SV	IP	H	BB	SO
Cercy, Richard	0	1	7.71	3	0	2	1	6	1
DeHoyos, Gabe	4	0	2.44	38	3	59	44	23	44
Fahrner, Evan	2	0	0.00	17	6	25	10	4	36
Gavelek, Brad	0	0	3.38	5	0	10	17	0	4
Keppen, Dusty	5	4	4.63	25	0	70	87	16	47
Keppen, Jeff	6	7	5.32	19	0	113	125	61	61
Knollin, Chris	0	0	4.50	1	0	2	2	1	2
Martinez, Chris	2	1	3.50	17	0	36	29	6	28
Morgan, Russ	4	2	5.15	15	0	57	73	22	40
Prempas, Lyle	3	4	4.40	25	1	71	73	42	56
Seaton, Chris	0	1	4.26	4	0	6	15	2	6
Therneau, Dave	2	3	4.25	10	0	53	55	17	39
Thomas, Joe	4	9	4.49	19	0	100	102	58	58
Weber, Brett	4	3	2.23	36	6	48	45	18	49
Woodman, Hank	11	5	3.13	19	0	132	106	49	126

SIOUX CITY

BATTING	AVG	AB	R	H	2B	3B	HR	RBI	SB
Baker, Casey, of	.300	250	26	75	7	1	0	14	1
Balet, Pichi, 3b	.359	209	27	75	10	0	4	31	4
Bartolucci, Paul, ss-2b	.255	196	14	50	4	0	0	19	2
2-team (6 Joliet)	.234	214	17	50	4	0	0	19	3
Beamon, Trey, of	.321	56	11	18	4	0	2	8	2
Byas, Mike, of	.239	134	20	32	3	0	1	9	13
Carroll, Justin, c-1b	.260	154	21	40	8	1	10	26	0
Cotton, John, 1b	.297	273	45	81	22	3	8	44	4
Figga, Mike, c-1b	.269	212	22	57	11	0	6	44	0
2-team (6 Lincoln)	.258	236	26	61	12	0	7	47	1
Flaherty, Tim, of-1b	.185	108	13	20	3	1	8	21	1
Foy, Brian, 2b	.000	8	0	0	0	0	0	0	0
Henry, Chad, 2b	.130	23	2	3	0	0	0	0	0
Luther, Ryan, of-2b	.192	167	10	32	7	1	0	11	9
Malave, Jose, dh-of	.281	135	17	38	4	0	0	19	0
2-team (4 St. Paul)	.273	143	17	39	4	0	0	19	0
Nicholas, Darrell, of	.196	56	5	11	2	0	0	2	3
Ruiz, Ryan, of	.270	204	36	55	6	1	0	12	17
2-team (38 Lincoln)	.253	360	62	91	11	3	0	28	27
Santore, Todd, c	.188	112	3	21	2	1	0	8	0
Smith, Ira, of	.220	50	3	11	1	0	0	2	0
Smith, Jeremy, 3b-1b	.338	154	21	52	9	1	0	21	6
3-team (9 Linc., 23 Winn.)	.287	265	35	76	13	1	1	34	7
Sullivan, Jason, 2b	.273	205	27	56	5	0	0	14	4
2-team (6 Lincoln)	.279	229	30	64	5	0	0	16	5
White, Kenny, ss	.256	39	2	10	1	0	0	2	2
Wilson, Andy, of	.176	74	8	13	1	0	0	2	6
Wilson, Desi, of-1b	.315	165	29	52	8	0	1	24	10
2-team (42 Sioux Falls)	.299	328	49	98	13	0	3	45	10
Woodcock, Lance, ss	.235	119	15	28	5	2	0	9	1

PITCHING	W	L	ERA	G	SV	IP	H	BB	SO
Brunswold, John	1	5	4.46	17	0	38	36	22	25
Curran, Joe	0	1	6.55	7	0	11	12	4	6
Duffy, John	1	1	8.06	22	1	25	34	17	17
Faust, Wes	5	10	6.39	17	0	93	130	41	41
2-team (1 Winnipeg)	6	10	6.04	18	0	98	132	43	46
Johnston, Doug	1	1	5.30	3	0	18	19	9	12
2-team (18 Lincoln)	6	7	4.82	21	0	112	104	37	64
Kuklis, Kevin	2	1	1.42	5	1	12	11	1	7
Linares, Ramon	0	0	20.25	2	0	1	2	3	1
Luque, Roger	1	0	1.29	1	0	7	3	4	2
Mabry, Barry	0	1	7.71	3	0	4	7	2	4
McCasland, Ralph	4	5	3.90	19	0	115	144	17	68
Reames, Jay	0	1	7.71	2	0	2	4	8	3
2-team (5 Fargo-Moorhead)	0	3	8.36	7	0	14	16	18	9
Rohlfing, Jon	0	1	4.15	10	2	13	14	5	16
Romero, Jordan	2	3	4.74	22	4	38	41	17	19
Sawyer, Steve	0	2	4.24	12	0	23	26	5	27
Scholten, J.D.	2	0	4.24	8	0	17	19	4	7
Selmo, Santo	0	0	1.29	3	0	7	8	6	3
Shabansky, Rob	0	0	6.43	7	0	7	11	1	7
Shafer, Adam	2	3	5.40	35	2	46	46	26	31
Sido, Wilson	0	0	9.82	1	0	3	5	3	4
Spivey, Melvin	0	6	5.61	7	0	33	42	12	20
Springston, Adam	4	7	5.50	20	0	106	125	35	61
St. Amant, John	0	0	2.70	9	4	10	7	5	9
2-team (29 Sioux Falls)	3	2	4.62	38	5	48	55	20	40
Swiatkiewicz, Chris	8	8	4.20	21	0	141	172	36	87
Yacco, Anthony	0	1	2.84	13	5	12	13	9	7

SIOUX FALLS

BATTING	AVG	AB	R	H	2B	3B	HR	RBI	SB
Anderson, John, of	.133	30	2	4	0	0	0	2	2
2-team (6 Lincoln)	.192	52	5	10	0	0	0	4	2
Bonilla, Clemente, ss	.263	80	7	21	5	1	0	6	4
2-team (21 Gary)	.262	149	15	39	6	3	0	8	9
Bush, Ron, 3b-ss	.266	184	20	49	8	2	0	25	2
2-team (8 Gary)	.255	212	25	54	9	2	0	25	2
Byas, Mike, of	.236	72	12	17	3	0	0	3	9
4-team (16 F-M, 37 SC, 8 St. P)	.228	298	44	68	8	0	1	13	23
Farnsworth, Troy, 3b-1b	.221	68	7	15	2	1	2	6	0
Kirkpatrick, Michael, of	.278	97	17	27	10	2	2	11	2
Lee, Curt, 2b	.255	192	24	49	10	1	2	22	2
Mirizzi, Marc, ss	.286	231	44	66	9	3	12	32	7
Mitchell, Keith, of	.260	96	17	25	8	0	1	12	1
Modami, Ali, 1b	.132	53	2	7	0	0	0	1	0

Pagan, Felix, 3b-of	.313	336	45	105	15	3	12	58	10
Palmer, Cody, dh	.136	22	1	3	1	0	0	1	0
Pendergrass, Tyrone, of	.246	338	48	83	10	9	5	29	31
Pennyfeather, William, of	.261	134	16	35	6	1	2	17	0
Peterson, Charles, dh-of	.289	149	23	43	9	0	6	26	2
2-team (43 Winnipeg)	.278	317	48	88	17	0	10	54	8
Pinkerton, Danny, c	.240	121	18	29	4	0	2	10	1
Rhomberg, Joe, 2b	.106	66	6	7	2	0	0	5	0
Rivero, Eddie, of-1b	.232	155	23	36	7	0	8	19	1
Rodrigues, Rich, c	.234	218	22	51	9	0	6	29	0
Schelhaas, Greg, 1b	.318	179	24	57	13	1	3	22	1
Wilson, Desi, of	.282	163	20	46	5	0	2	21	0

PITCHING	W	L	ERA	G	SV	IP	H	BB	SO
Bright, Nathan	1	3	5.81	6	0	31	38	14	6
Burgess, Richie	5	6	3.84	13	0	84	90	27	44
Dagley, Corey	1	2	7.33	5	0	23	36	8	8
Dickinson, Rodney	1	0	3.38	16	8	16	12	5	10
Felkel, Bryan	0	2	5.83	22	1	29	37	16	14
Holbrook, Shayn	5	3	3.05	32	2	56	45	24	34
Johnson, Chad	7	9	4.79	18	0	118	124	47	61
Koziara, Matt	1	3	7.76	6	0	26	48	9	14
Lajara, Eudy	0	0	27.00	1	0	1	5	0	1
Linares, Ramon	0	3	3.44	30	7	34	21	16	30
2-team (2 Sioux City)	0	3	4.08	32	7	35	23	19	31
Lupul, Ryan	0	0	17.18	2	0	3	7	4	4
Martinez, Marcus	0	0	9.00	1	0	2	1	4	0
Masterman, Tom	0	1	4.30	14	0	23	30	11	8
2-team (14 Kansas City)	2	2	4.72	28	0	55	71	16	25
Matzenbacher, Brian	4	5	5.06	13	0	80	103	31	46
Merrigan, Josh	7	5	3.68	19	0	120	120	46	64
Mincks, Lincoln	2	4	4.20	16	0	45	43	16	23
Prata, Danny	0	2	3.63	5	0	17	19	4	7
St. Amant, John	3	2	5.12	29	1	38	48	15	31
Stoner, Nat	0	1	7.20	10	0	10	20	2	5
Turnrose, Eric	0	0	0.00	5	0	4	3	4	2
Wallace, Shane	0	0	4.05	3	0	6	7	4	5

WINNIPEG

BATTING	AVG	AB	R	H	2B	3B	HR	RBI	SB
Alley, Charles, c	.343	233	52	80	17	0	5	35	0
Bass, Jayson, of	.281	57	7	16	2	0	1	11	2
Berrios, Harry, dh-of	.312	375	53	117	18	1	15	73	2
Boyd, Jared, 3b-ss	.231	108	6	25	4	1	0	18	0
Cox, Kris, of	.314	255	40	80	12	6	3	22	6
Fuess, Brian, 3b	.182	11	1	2	0	0	0	2	0
Gripp, Ryan, 3b	.240	50	8	12	3	0	4	10	0
Jones, Darrick, c	.232	69	7	16	4	0	0	10	0
Keith, Rusty, of	.278	234	41	65	12	3	7	44	10
Leach, Jalal, of	.272	103	16	28	5	1	4	17	3
Lopez, Manny, of	.212	52	8	11	1	0	1	8	1
Morrison, Greg, 1b	.292	353	63	103	20	2	14	53	3
Peterson, Charles, of	.268	168	25	45	8	0	4	28	6
Poulin, Max, ss	.263	274	36	72	8	4	3	39	14
Sachs, Brent, 2b-of	.298	366	71	109	17	4	6	38	22
Scalabrini, Pat, 2b-3b	.300	327	60	98	28	0	4	45	20
Smith, Jeremy, 3b-2b	.244	78	8	19	2	0	0	8	1

PITCHING	W	L	ERA	G	SV	IP	H	BB	SO
Bell, Richard	1	0	1.57	23	1	23	13	8	23
Brooks, Jake	1	0	1.17	3	0	7	4	1	5
2-team (3 Winnipeg)	1	0	0.87	6	0	10	5	1	8
Cramblitt, Joey	11	5	3.15	17	0	120	127	31	72
D'Amato, Dan	0	0	15.19	4	0	5	9	7	3
Dickinson, Rodney	1	0	2.70	17	7	16	12	12	23
2-team (16 Sioux Falls)	2	0	3.03	33	15	32	24	17	33
Faust, Wes	1	0	0.00	1	0	5	2	2	5
Gross, Rafael	13	2	2.28	18	0	114	102	19	69
Hernandez, Ivan	1	1	2.20	21	1	28	16	16	44
Luque, Roger	8	6	3.55	18	0	116	115	33	75
2-team (1 Sioux City)	9	6	3.42	19	0	123	118	37	77
Mazur, Graham	2	2	2.93	19	0	43	43	13	24
2-team (1 Gary)	2	2	3.47	20	0	46	51	15	27
McMurray, Heath	2	3	3.05	28	2	85	71	31	71
Purcell, Brad	8	5	2.97	20	0	112	95	49	92
Sherrill, George	1	0	1.13	16	1	16	8	4	30
Smith, Donnie	2	4	3.98	36	2	31	27	14	38
Thomas, Steve	0	1	3.29	15	7	13	17	4	3
Wagner, Denny	3	5	6.14	12	0	44	59	17	15
Webb, Chris	0	0	14.85	4	0	6	14	4	7

NORTHEAST LEAGUE

Just about everything worked out well for the Brockton Rox in 2003.

When the Late Show With David Letterman was looking for a team to use for a comedy bit with stage manager Biff Henderson, they called the Rox, who managed to get seven minutes of national publicity out of Henderson's strikeout in his only at-bat.

When former Montreal Expos farmhand Craig Lewis was looking to give hitting a try, the Rox offered the ex-pitcher a contract. He responded by being named the Northeast League's rookie of the year, hitting .323-5-40 as a first baseman/outfielder.

Vic Davilla

And when the Northeast League playoffs rolled around, the Rox pounded New Jersey three-games-to-one in the semifinals, then swept North Shore in three games in the championship series

Francisco Matos was named the championship series MVP, as he went 5-for-10 with a double, triple and two RBIs in the three-game series. In the deciding game, Matos' fifth-inning double gave the Rox the lead in the fifth and they went on to win 4-1.

"We knew if we jumped in front right away they were going to be in trouble," Matos said. "We played just great baseball in the playoffs."

Allentown's Vic Davilla almost won the league's triple crown, as he finished second in the league in batting (.338) and home runs (20) while leading the league in RBIs (74). Davilla, who was named the league MVP, also became the Northeast League's career home run leader with 72.

The Northeast League operated under the umbrella of the Northern League prior to 2003, but split off into its own operation.

STANDINGS

FIRST HALF

NORTH	W	L	PCT	GB
North Shore Spirit	25	19	.568	—
Brockton Rox	23	20	.535	1½
Quebec Les Capitales	21	24	.467	4½
Bangor Lumberjacks	21	24	.467	4½
SOUTH	**W**	**L**	**PCT**	**GB**
New Jersey Jackals	28	17	.622	—
Elmira Pioneers	23	21	.523	4½
Berkshire Black Bears	21	25	.457	7½
Allentown Ambassadors	16	28	.364	11½

SECOND HALF

NORTH	W	L	PCT	GB
Quebec Les Capitales	28	16	.636	—
Brockton Rox	27	19	.587	2
North Shore Spirit	26	20	.565	3
Bangor Lumberjacks	21	25	.457	8
SOUTH	**W**	**L**	**PCT**	**GB**
New Jersey Jackals	24	20	.545	—
Berkshire Black Bears	20	26	.435	5
Elmira Pioneers	19	25	.432	5
Allentown Ambassadors	16	30	.348	9

PLAYOFFS: Semifinals—North Shore defeated Quebec 3-0 and Brockton defeated New Jersey 3-1 in best-of-5 series. **Final**—Brockton defeated North Shore 3-0 in best -of-5 series.

MANAGERS: Allentown—Ed Ott. **Bangor**—Kash Beauchamp. **Berkshire**—Darren Bush. **Brockton**—Ed Nottle. **Elmira**—Mitch Lyden. **New Jersey**—Ed Calfapietra. **North Shore**—John Kennedy. **Quebec**—Joe Ferguson.

ATTENDANCE: Quebec 152,153; Brockton 149,738; New Jersey 100,559; North Shore 76,016; Elmira 52,100; Bangor 46,843; Berkshire 43,846; Allentown 40,787.

ALL-STAR TEAM: C—Frank Charles, North Shore. **1B**—Vic Davilla, Allentown. **2B**—Marcos Agramonte, North Shore. **3B**—Eddie Lantigua, Quebec. **SS**—Cleatus Davidson, Elmira. **OF**—Rafael Alvarez, Elmira; Darren Blakely, Brockton/New Jersey; Carlos Rodriguez, Quebec. **DH**—John

Anderson, New Jersey. **RHP**—John Kelly, North Shore. **LHP**—Jordy Alexander, Quebec. **RP**—Conor Brooks, Brockton.

Player of the Year: Vic Davilla, Allentown. **Rookie Player of the Year:** Craig Lewis, Brockton. **Rookie Pitcher of the Year:** Eddie Aucoin, Berkshire. **Manager of the Year:** John Kennedy, North Shore.

INDIVIDUAL BATTING LEADERS
(Minimum 248 Plate Appearances)

	AVG	AB	R	H	2B	3B	HR	RBI	SB
Abreu, Dennis, Elmira	.341	232	35	79	10	1	3	30	13
Davilla, Vic, Allentown	.338	331	58	112	25	1	20	74	2
Lewis, Craig, Brockton	.323	344	54	111	26	9	4	50	9
Anderson, John, New Jersey	.318	277	49	88	11	3	2	26	17
Alvarez, Rafael, Elmira	.318	318	57	101	29	2	14	55	12
Lantigua, Eddie, Quebec	.313	342	51	107	21	1	9	58	8
Garcia, Osmani, Quebec	.311	350	45	109	20	0	7	36	7
Agramonte, Marcos, NS	.309	375	62	116	12	15	3	46	19
Gonzalez, Ender, Allentown	.309	304	51	94	17	0	2	22	10
Jones, Brian, Elmira	.306	310	50	95	26	1	10	39	1

INDIVIDUAL PITCHING LEADERS
(Minimum 74 Innings)

	W	L	ERA	G	SV	IP	H	BB	SO
Aucoin, Eddie, Berkshire	5	0	1.46	38	0	74	50	24	61
Edmondson, Brian, Elmira	8	7	1.95	20	0	148	127	18	114
Kelly, John, North Shore	13	2	2.17	18	0	128	106	25	139
Sugarman, Jeremy, NS	7	1	2.36	18	5	88	76	24	52
Harris, Jeff, Quebec	9	4	2.51	18	0	129	107	22	119
Alexander, Jordy, Quebec	4	7	2.86	17	0	113	102	15	124
Dillinger, John, Allentown	7	8	2.87	19	0	138	138	41	147
Dunn, Keith, Quebec	11	5	2.88	19	0	122	115	30	71
Marchesano, Mike, Brockton	8	7	2.92	18	0	117	100	37	77
Guttormson, Rick, Berkshire	8	8	3.22	20	0	143	133	40	141

ALLENTOWN

BATTING	AVG	AB	R	H	2B	3B	HR	RBI	SB
Acosta, Julio, c	.247	89	11	22	8	0	2	15	0
Adames, Winter, ss	.000	6	0	0	0	0	0	0	0
Bordenick, Ryan, 1b	.247	150	19	37	11	1	2	20	0
Cruz, Tito, ss	.245	53	8	13	6	0	1	6	1
2-team (33 Berkshire)	.217	152	18	33	9	0	3	22	1
Davilla, Vic, 1b-2b	.338	331	58	112	25	1	20	74	2
Diaz, Jorge, 2b-ss	.282	280	42	79	17	4	1	35	28
Doakes, Schuyler, of	.284	67	13	19	4	0	0	14	2
Gonzalez, Ender, 3b-ss	.309	304	51	94	17	0	2	22	10
Hafich, Chris, of	.136	44	5	6	2	0	0	2	1
Harris, Cedrick, of	.249	249	31	62	13	3	1	28	17
2-team (23 New Jersey)	.239	335	41	80	15	4	1	34	21
Karoly, Peter, dh	.000	2	0	0	0	0	0	0	0
Larkin, Garrett, 2b-3b	.256	43	4	11	4	0	1	1	0
Macchi, Brian, of	.283	322	35	91	22	0	3	39	2
Melendez, Luis, c	.154	39	1	6	1	1	0	2	0
3-team (12 Bangor, 3 Quebec)	.172	64	4	11	1	1	0	5	0
Moore, Kevin, c-3b	.238	130	12	31	6	0	0	10	1
Roche, Marlon, of-1b	.286	304	34	87	14	1	3	29	3
Rosenthal, Ben, c	.196	56	7	11	1	0	0	2	0
Schmidt, Greg, 3b-of	.257	296	38	76	20	5	1	33	5
Singletary, Dan, of	.222	90	17	20	5	2	1	12	5
Stevens, Gregory, c	.171	41	6	7	4	0	0	5	0
Tavares, John, ss-2b	.250	12	1	3	0	0	0	1	0
Williams, Jason, ss	.212	85	11	18	3	0	2	5	1

PITCHING	W	L	ERA	G	SV	IP	H	BB	SO
Boker, John	1	4	6.39	27	2	43	58	18	37
Brassington, Phil	0	0	7.11	7	0	6	14	2	2
Clark, Wade	1	2	5.56	19	4	22	34	9	14
Cunningham, Perry	2	1	1.00	5	0	9	7	3	4
Davidson, Tim	1	2	7.62	5	0	28	45	13	26
Dillinger, John	7	8	2.87	19	0	138	138	41	147
Encarnacion, Orlando	1	4	5.74	16	0	26	33	9	23
Fry, Nolan	4	6	5.04	17	0	91	112	28	54
Gannon, Joe	0	0	16.20	1	0	1	4	1	0
Gomez, Carlos	2	2	3.23	36	3	47	46	26	29
Gonzalez, Carlos	1	1	7.13	7	0	17	23	4	13
Guerrero, Jose	1	3	6.11	12	1	17	32	11	14
Harvey, Reed	0	3	9.77	4	0	15	26	8	7
Keeling, Justin	1	0	2.70	12	3	16	13	4	12
Kelly, Chris	2	4	6.84	10	0	48	48	27	20
2-team (4 Berkshire)	4	5	6.86	14	0	63	62	34	30
Klemm, Tom	0	1	12.86	5	0	7	11	7	3
2-team (1 Brockton)	0	1	10.00	6	0	9	11	9	5
Montgomery, Joe	0	0	14.73	4	0	3	8	2	3
Perez, Miguel	6	5	4.41	15	0	96	96	36	112
Perrucci, Kevin	1	2	7.24	3	0	13	23	2	6
Riley, Mike	1	5	6.60	13	0	58	74	21	50
Valdez, Rafael	0	0	1.80	1	0	5	4	0	2
Ward, Chad	0	2	9.00	3	0	16	27	6	12
2-team (14 Brockton)	3	6	4.62	17	0	99	117	36	69
Zallie, Chris	0	3	9.00	7	0	24	36	14	14

BANGOR

BATTING	AVG	AB	R	H	2B	3B	HR	RBI	SB
Blakeney, Mo, of	.219	114	9	25	7	0	0	15	4
Brinkley, Josh, 2b-3b	.269	26	2	7	2	0	0	4	0
Britt, Bryan, 1b-of	.156	45	5	7	3	0	2	7	0
Brock, Todd, 3b-ss	.236	301	39	71	9	1	8	30	11
Burke, Mark, 1b-dh	.330	109	11	36	9	0	3	22	2
Davidson, Aaron, 2b	.192	26	0	5	1	0	0	0	1
De la Cruz, Lorenzo, of	.257	311	47	80	21	2	8	49	11
Doakes, Schuyler, of-2b	.291	206	38	60	11	4	0	12	27
2-team (23 Allentown)	.289	273	51	79	15	4	0	26	29
Dworken, Meisha, c	.143	35	2	5	2	0	1	4	0
2-team (31 New Jersey)	.179	134	14	24	5	0	1	11	0
Groce, Taylor, of	.143	21	2	3	1	0	0	0	0
Hargreaves, Brad, c	.248	278	34	69	6	1	0	20	14
King, Steve, of	.145	69	5	10	1	0	0	4	2
Kobayashi, Mitsuru, ss-2b	.225	89	11	20	1	0	0	10	8
LeBron, Juan, of	.244	168	24	41	11	1	6	26	3
Martinez, Sandy, ss	.269	171	15	46	9	0	0	18	6
Melendez, Luis, c	.227	22	3	5	0	0	0	3	0
Miura, Kenichi, ss-2b	.196	56	8	11	4	0	0	2	1
O'Sullivan, Steve, 2b	.129	70	5	9	0	1	0	6	2
Paulk, Barry, of	.305	82	7	25	1	0	1	10	4
Ross, Donnie, 1b-3b	.253	297	57	75	19	1	13	48	3
Saunders, Nick, 3b-1b	.226	53	4	12	2	0	1	3	0
Silvestre, Juan, of	.224	98	8	22	5	0	0	8	4
Solano, Benji, 2b	.000	8	2	0	0	0	0	0	0
Thompson, Edwin, of	.196	107	9	21	3	1	0	11	2
Tindell, Matt, of	.208	48	6	10	3	0	0	1	2
Voltz, Jude, 1b	.202	89	9	18	0	1	1	9	2

PITCHING	W	L	ERA	G	SV	IP	H	BB	SO
Bowe, Brandon	2	7	4.56	23	1	71	68	24	42
Clark, Chris	0	0	3.18	2	0	5	5	5	6
2-team (7 New Jersey)	1	2	4.82	9	0	37	43	18	32
DeBold, Luke	0	1	15.19	8	0	5	10	5	4
Ford, Brian	0	0	10.13	6	0	5	9	5	2
Gouin, Brian	0	1	12.79	5	0	6	13	3	3
Henry, Santiago	5	5	2.23	36	6	72	61	28	69
Kalinowski, Roger	1	2	3.64	33	0	42	55	12	25
Long, Jerry	2	6	3.61	15	0	84	90	45	54
Miller, Danny	4	10	4.74	18	0	93	93	35	69
Pincavitch, Kevin	7	3	4.04	16	0	93	94	27	68
Rall, Tim	4	0	1.81	9	0	59	45	22	58
Scheuing, Matt	1	1	2.78	8	0	32	34	14	27
Sparks, Jeff	4	1	1.23	17	5	36	25	16	50
Stone, Ashton	0	0	11.57	3	0	4	6	2	0
Thomas, Don	2	3	5.64	24	1	22	30	7	19
Tindell, Matt	0	2	6.35	9	0	11	11	23	10
Vigue, John	5	7	4.55	19	0	118	138	26	82
Woodards, Orlando	5	0	3.07	14	1	14	12	6	13

BERKSHIRE

BATTING	AVG	AB	R	H	2B	3B	HR	RBI	SB
Briones, Chris, c	.228	215	23	49	8	0	5	21	0
Burnett, Mark, 2b	.213	188	18	40	6	0	1	13	3
2-team (29 Quebec)	.222	297	39	66	9	1	1	19	6
Clark, Jason, of	.157	70	11	11	1	0	1	3	3
Crespo, Manny, of-c	.257	303	33	78	19	1	4	36	2
Cruz, Tito, ss	.202	99	10	20	3	0	2	16	0
Forbes, Kevin, of	.241	315	34	76	14	0	1	21	13
Hopper, Shane, of	.282	323	44	91	20	3	8	52	19
Johnston, P.J., 2b-of	.251	275	28	69	8	2	1	17	18
Jones, Ryan, of-1b	.257	304	37	78	18	2	7	41	3
Larned, Drew, c	.152	33	2	5	1	0	0	1	0
Mateo, Jose, ss	.256	203	29	52	6	1	0	14	12
Paciorek, Mack, ss	.185	27	4	5	1	1	0	2	0
Paciorek, Pete, 1b	.276	323	45	89	20	3	6	43	1
Shrum, Allen, c	.239	71	4	17	1	1	1	7	0
Tash, Ryan, 3b	.318	22	4	7	1	1	1	2	0
Valenzuela, Jason, ss	.000	4	0	0	0	0	0	1	0
Williams, Brady, 3b	.221	272	35	60	11	3	9	38	2

PITCHING	W	L	ERA	G	SV	IP	H	BB	SO
Acors, Bo	0	2	21.21	2	0	4	14	5	4
Adams, Daniel	0	0	9.64	4	0	4	12	0	6
Aucoin, Eddie	5	0	1.46	38	0	74	50	24	61
Bailie, Matt	2	1	2.13	31	13	38	39	9	40
Bausher, Tim	0	0	2.25	1	0	4	3	3	8
Dedrick, Jim	0	1	5.79	3	0	14	21	5	1
Dimma, Doug	1	3	6.41	14	0	26	35	11	18

Encarnacion, Orlando	1	0	4.00	9	0	18	16	8	23
2-team (16 Allentown)	2	4	5.04	25	0	44	49	17	46
Etler, Todd	1	2	3.92	3	0	20	17	4	13
Guttormson, Rick	8	8	3.22	20	0	142	133	40	141
Hall, Courtney	2	12	5.60	19	0	101	125	45	58
Harden, Tony	9	4	3.46	19	0	117	110	36	97
Henderson, Dan	4	9	4.76	21	0	87	86	39	47
Kelly, Chris	2	1	6.91	4	0	14	14	7	10
Meyer, Scott	0	1	6.75	7	0	8	11	4	11
2-team (2 Elmira)	0	3	7.15	9	0	11	15	5	12
Minter, Matt	0	1	4.70	3	0	15	24	2	9
O'Connor, Brian	1	2	3.38	3	0	16	21	6	10
Smith, Matt	1	1	2.88	17	3	25	26	14	29
Sparks, Eric	0	0	0.00	1	0	1	1	2	1
Waroff, Shane	4	3	4.61	38	1	66	77	12	69

BROCKTON

BATTING	AVG	AB	R	H	2B	3B	HR	RBI	SB
Arroyo, Abner, of	.241	116	19	28	9	1	2	15	1
Blakely, Darren, of	.286	49	9	14	4	0	2	7	1
2-team (71 New Jersey)	.304	326	53	99	29	5	15	66	16
Booker, Steve, of	.277	65	12	18	2	1	0	5	4
Brown, Bobby, of	.264	148	17	39	10	1	0	12	1
Bustos, Saul, ss	.262	359	48	94	14	1	7	47	14
Daubert, Jake, 3b	.304	312	41	95	16	3	5	45	4
Davis, Mike, 2b-3b	.256	211	32	54	7	1	7	20	8
Edwards, Willie, of	.181	94	13	17	3	0	3	10	1
Henderson, Biff, dh	.000	1	0	0	0	0	0	0	0
Johnstone, Ben,ph	.000	1	0	0	0	0	0	0	0
Landry, Michael, c	.206	68	7	14	0	1	0	4	0
Lewis, Craig, 1b	.323	344	54	111	26	9	4	50	9
Matos, Francisco, dh-2b	.338	145	21	49	8	0	1	14	9
Medina, Junior, of	.246	122	21	30	5	0	2	13	3
Merriman, Terrell, of	.200	5	1	1	0	0	1	1	0
Rosario, Melvin, c	.259	239	27	62	15	0	6	41	9
Smith, Nestor, of	.290	317	51	92	22	0	7	44	15
Swinton, Jermaine, dh	.213	80	10	17	2	0	2	7	1
Torres, Mike, of-2b	.270	319	49	86	21	2	6	48	4

PITCHING	W	L	ERA	G	SV	IP	H	BB	SO
Allen, Rodney	6	6	5.55	14	0	86	103	30	69
Baker, Joey	10	4	4.87	20	0	116	130	19	49
Brooks, Conor	1	4	2.31	44	21	50	45	16	44
Cerbone, Marc	0	0	2.79	4	0	9	10	6	7
Crohan, Tom	4	1	7.96	17	0	26	37	9	15
Faulkner, Steven	0	0	11.57	8	0	7	13	6	5
Guerrero, Jose	0	0	1.80	3	0	5	4	1	5
2-team (12 Allentown)	1	3	5.16	15	1	22	36	12	19
Henry, Mark	0	0	0.00	1	0	1	0	1	0
Jones, Fontella	1	2	4.87	21	0	40	40	20	39
Keinath, Tim	0	0	4.50	1	0	2	3	1	0
Klemm, Tom	0	0	0.00	1	0	2	0	2	2
Lynn, Kevin	1	1	2.45	3	0	11	9	3	4
Marchesano, Mike	8	7	2.92	18	0	117	100	37	77
Martin, Scott	8	5	3.34	20	0	107	105	33	78
Martinez, Marcus	2	0	4.82	7	0	9	12	3	6
Perez, Roberto	0	0	36.00	1	0	1	4	1	0
Salvevold, Greg	2	3	4.04	6	0	35	41	6	11
Sterling, John	1	0	5.40	3	0	5	3	5	4
Stutz, Tony	3	2	3.40	30	0	47	38	17	50
Ward, Chad	3	4	3.78	14	0	83	90	30	57

ELMIRA

BATTING	AVG	AB	R	H	2B	3B	HR	RBI	SB
Abreu, Dennis, 3b-2b	.341	232	35	79	10	1	3	30	13
Alvarez, Rafael, of	.318	318	57	101	29	2	14	55	12
Baker, Jason, of	.194	72	9	14	0	1	0	7	12
Bello, Rolando, 2b	.246	244	33	60	13	0	6	33	5
Davidson, Cleatus, ss	.304	339	56	103	21	4	6	35	15
Hunter, Scott, of	.298	356	47	106	29	0	10	57	13
Jones, Brian, c-1b	.306	310	50	95	26	1	10	39	1
Lehr, Ryan, 1b-3b	.292	336	41	98	27	0	4	45	0
Marconi, Alex, c-1b	.292	274	27	80	20	3	3	32	0
Morton, Rickie, 1b	.250	72	12	18	2	0	4	11	0
Murphy, Sean, 3b	.094	32	4	3	2	0	0	2	1
Rosario, Carlos, 2b	.163	98	11	16	4	0	0	2	12
Valdes, Mike, of	.288	66	4	19	2	0	0	3	0
Wagner, Joe, 3b-2b	.250	4	0	1	0	0	0	0	0
Webb, Ryan, of	.266	271	28	72	9	2	1	30	11
Williams, Matt, 3b	.164	73	7	12	2	1	3	7	0

PITCHING	W	L	ERA	G	SV	IP	H	BB	SO
Corrado, Matthew	0	0	4.50	9	0	14	11	8	11
Edmondson, Brian	8	7	1.95	20	0	148	127	18	114
Head, Daniel	3	5	5.06	15	0	78	93	17	50
Henderson, Ken	2	1	2.89	13	0	28	20	10	21
2-team (13 New Jersey)	4	3	3.55	26	0	58	49	25	40
Kawabata, Kenichiro	1	3	3.93	24	0	36	38	28	27
Keelin, Chris	2	1	4.87	16	5	20	30	9	23
McGee, Chris	3	0	1.57	34	11	46	28	11	48
Mendoza, Geronimo	9	8	4.14	18	0	117	142	26	69
Mendoza, Hatuey	5	9	3.89	18	0	115	125	30	77
Meyer, Scott	0	2	8.10	2	0	3	4	1	1
Perez, Jeffrey	0	2	4.66	13	0	19	29	7	19
Seki, Rentaro	4	0	3.09	28	2	35	24	23	33
Takeuchi, Ryo	1	3	3.89	10	0	39	41	19	16
Tekavec, Nate	0	0	1.80	1	0	5	7	2	2
Vincent, Matt	4	5	4.98	18	0	85	86	24	79

NEW JERSEY

BATTING	AVG	AB	R	H	2B	3B	HR	RBI	SB
Anderson, John, of-dh	.318	277	49	88	11	3	2	26	17
Bailey, Travis, of	.290	345	52	100	28	7	12	59	13
Blakely, Darren, of	.307	277	44	85	25	5	13	59	15
Brinkley, Darryl, of	.405	37	11	15	2	0	1	6	2
Conway, Craig, 2b	.285	302	36	86	15	2	1	32	3
Dworken, Meisha, c	.192	99	12	19	3	0	0	7	0
Glendenning, Mike, of-1b	.228	232	27	53	8	1	9	37	3
Grijak, Kevin, 1b	.408	76	14	31	6	3	2	18	2
Harris, Cedrick, of	.209	86	10	18	2	1	0	6	4
Hernandez, Johnny, of	.143	14	0	2	0	0	0	2	2
Kerrigan, Joe, 3b	.305	328	40	100	10	5	2	33	10
L'Italien, Peter, c	.000	1	0	0	0	0	0	0	0
Law, Jason, of-1b	.233	30	5	7	0	0	0	1	0
Maxwell, Keith, 1b-3b	.240	250	34	60	12	0	9	40	0
McKee, Scott, c-1b	.292	120	12	35	6	0	2	8	0
Pagan, Carlos, c	.244	213	27	52	13	0	10	28	0
Rowan, Chris, ss	.256	317	57	81	13	5	12	38	9
Samuels, Scott, of	.422	64	10	27	8	0	0	9	1
Vasquez, Alberto, c	.200	15	1	3	0	0	0	1	0

PITCHING	W	L	ERA	G	SV	IP	H	BB	SO
Batson, Byron	0	0	12.00	1	0	3	5	0	4
Bennett, Joel	8	1	1.93	12	0	70	62	19	74
Clark, Chris	1	2	5.12	7	0	31	38	13	26
Crowther, Jackson	8	3	3.49	18	0	111	110	28	87
Darcy, Ryan	2	2	6.59	16	0	41	52	9	24
DeSilva, John	1	0	3.60	1	0	5	6	0	4
Grezlovski, Ben	7	4	1.80	36	6	60	44	21	43
Henderson, Ken	2	2	4.15	13	0	30	29	15	19
Keelin, Chris	0	4	4.37	21	1	35	22	24	39
2-team (16 Elmira)	2	5	4.55	37	6	55	52	33	62
Loudon, Gary	1	0	1.26	3	0	14	11	12	13
Magri, Joe	2	4	5.66	20	0	49	61	24	29
Marcotte, Trevor	9	4	3.46	22	0	91	73	39	61
Myers, Aaron	9	8	3.93	20	0	119	119	25	89
Perez, Julio	1	0	0.77	22	10	23	17	3	12
Pike, Matt	0	0	0.00	8	1	10	2	1	16
Powell, Matt	0	1	3.13	22	0	31	28	14	17
Smith, Matt	0	2	3.03	23	1	32	27	32	29
Sneed, John	1	0	3.15	4	0	20	19	6	18

NORTH SHORE

BATTING	AVG	AB	R	H	2B	3B	HR	RBI	SB
Agramonte, Marcos, 2b	.309	375	62	116	12	15	3	46	19
Caruso, Bryan, c	.236	72	8	17	3	0	2	8	1
Castellanos, Jose, of	.175	137	17	24	7	0	3	16	1
Charles, Frank, c	.300	283	25	85	28	3	7	46	0
Espinal, Juan, dh-3b	.194	31	1	6	0	0	0	5	0
Fischer, Robert, of	.293	123	28	36	10	1	7	18	3
German, Ramon, 3b-of	.167	6	0	1	0	0	0	0	0
Malone, Billy, 3b-2b	.333	24	0	8	1	0	0	2	0
Muth, Edmund, of	.245	278	44	68	12	2	7	43	3
Noriega, Kevin, 3b	.000	15	1	0	0	0	0	0	0
Riordan, Fran, 1b	.218	348	34	76	15	2	5	37	0
Sanchez, Yuri, ss	.279	265	37	74	13	9	4	33	4
Schmitt, Brian, dh-1b	.200	20	1	4	0	0	0	2	0
Schmitz, John, of	.273	264	49	72	10	1	3	28	4
Sepulveda, Carlos, of	.285	277	47	79	23	3	9	44	4
Startari, Jason, 3b-ss	.224	313	35	70	14	2	1	35	1
Tejada, Michael, dh-c	.306	173	34	53	9	0	6	23	0

PITCHING	W	L	ERA	G	SV	IP	H	BB	SO
Baez, Miguel	4	4	3.54	9	0	56	47	22	60
Beucler, Nate	2	0	5.44	21	0	51	58	19	38
Bircher, Chad	3	6	3.69	26	5	53	70	12	30
Calvert, Klae	8	5	3.94	17	0	118	120	14	87
Crawford, Wes	4	5	3.03	16	0	71	73	22	62
DePriest, Derrick	1	0	0.64	6	0	14	8	3	15
Hart, Tim	0	0	3.07	8	0	14	13	5	11

	W	L	ERA	G	SV	IP	H	BB	SO
Hoyt, Mike	0	2	7.80	7	0	30	36	23	21
Kelly, John	13	2	2.17	18	0	128	106	25	139
Morse, Bryan	5	5	3.30	16	0	101	100	18	57
Ricciardi, Joe	1	8	3.43	36	11	42	38	16	43
Strickland, Keith	3	1	4.15	9	0	13	18	3	6
Sugarman, Jeremy	7	1	2.36	18	5	87	76	24	52

QUEBEC

BATTING	AVG	AB	R	H	2B	3B	HR	RBI	SB
Ballon, John, of-1b	.300	330	53	99	23	1	11	55	5
Booker, Steve, of	.333	60	8	20	2	1	0	6	4
2-team (31 Brockton)	.304	125	20	38	4	2	0	11	8
Bordenick, Ryan, 1b-c	.167	36	3	6	2	0	0	4	0
2-team (41 Allentown)	.231	186	22	43	13	1	2	24	0
Burnett, Mark, 2b	.239	109	21	26	3	1	0	6	3
Burnham, Jake, of	.176	85	4	15	3	1	1	12	1
Charbonneau, M.A., of	.132	53	6	7	0	1	0	6	2
Deschenes, Pat, 3b-2b	.115	26	3	3	1	0	0	0	2
Emond, Benoit, of	.259	313	41	81	12	1	0	22	7
Garcia, Osmani, 2b-3b	.311	350	45	109	20	0	7	36	7
Gennaro, Brad, of	.133	30	3	4	0	0	0	0	0
Gomez, Galindo, dh-1b	.269	93	16	25	7	2	3	12	0
Hafich, Chris, of	.143	7	1	1	0	0	0	0	0
2-team (15 Allentown)	.137	51	6	7	2	0	0	2	1
Kison, Robbie, ss	.186	102	11	19	6	0	1	8	3
L'Italien, Peter, dh-c	.241	83	9	20	1	0	0	4	1
2-team (2 New Jersey)	.238	84	9	20	1	0	0	4	1
Lang, Andy, 2b	.182	11	0	2	0	0	0	0	0
Lantigua, Eddie, 3b-1b	.313	342	51	107	21	1	9	58	8
Melendez, Luis, c	.000	3	0	0	0	0	0	0	0
Ndungidi, Ntema, dh-of	.233	60	14	14	2	0	4	9	2
Oropeza, Asdrubal, ss	.246	187	25	46	11	0	1	27	8
Pujols, Rafael, c	.285	312	37	89	13	2	2	32	5
Ramirez, Carlos, of	.125	16	2	2	0	0	1	5	0
Rodriguez, Carlos, of	.272	312	51	85	12	1	21	63	16
Todd, Jeremy, 1b	.267	45	7	12	0	0	2	5	0
Tranum, Josh, of	.200	55	7	11	1	0	1	3	0

PITCHING	W	L	ERA	G	SV	IP	H	BB	SO
Alexander, Jordy	4	7	2.86	17	0	113	102	15	124
Allen, Rodney	1	0	0.79	2	0	11	10	3	6
2-team (14 Brockton)	7	6	4.99	16	0	97	113	33	75
Anderson, Antwoine	1	3	5.94	16	0	33	42	8	19
Charron, Eric	1	1	5.88	12	0	26	31	11	11
Cisar, Mark	1	2	4.44	23	7	26	29	11	22
Cly, Jason	7	4	3.31	15	0	87	92	12	56
Dunn, Keith	11	5	2.88	19	0	121	115	30	71
Foss, Brad	3	3	2.91	37	3	52	49	14	38
Franks, Lance	5	4	3.32	12	0	78	78	16	51
Greco, Sam	0	1	27.00	2	0	0	3	1	0
Harris, Jeff	9	4	2.51	18	0	129	107	22	119
Laplante, Michel	1	1	5.56	3	0	11	17	4	7
Marchetti, Dan	3	3	2.32	37	6	50	45	17	42
Perez, Michelandy	1	1	8.10	8	0	13	15	6	15
Plante, Patrice	0	0	15.00	2	0	3	5	3	1
Quintero, Jose	1	0	4.40	9	1	14	16	5	7
Schuurman, Mark	0	0	20.25	2	0	1	2	1	1

SOUTHEASTERN LEAGUE

The second year of the Southeastern League brought a little more stability to the league. But that doesn't mean the league was anywhere close to stable.

Unlike the league's first season, all six teams that started the season finished the 2003 season. And with a full offseason to prepare, the league's most successful franchise, Pensacola, drew nearly 1,000 fans per game, an improvement on 2002.

But the league still had plenty of hurdles to overcome to reach a level of stability, and there were questions about the league's viability for 2004.

Two teams (Macon and Baton Rouge) each had three different managers during the season, and a couple of the league's top players, including former big leaguer Mike Cather, left the league during the season.

The league turned the Selma (Ala.) Cloverleafs into a traveling team when it became clear that the town could not support a team. New teams in Houma and Macon also struggled, as Houma had to play at a high school field 50 miles outside of Houma, while Macon and returning member Baton Rouge struggled with poor attendance.

Heading into 2004, Pensacola was the league's one stable, strong franchise, as Mongtomery, the league's second-strongest team, was facing a move with the arrival of the Double-A Montgomery Biscuits.

On the field, Pensacola easily has the best record in the league during the regular season, but Baton Rouge beat the Pelicans three games to one in the league's championship series. Baton Rouge righthander Mike Meyer went 2-0, 1.69 in the playoffs.

Macon Peaches reliever B.J. Littlefield led the league with an 0.84 ERA in 53 innings, the second best ERA in the modern independent-ball era.

STANDINGS

	W	L	PCT	GB
Pensacola Pelicans	42	23	.646	—
Baton Rouge River Bats	38	31	.551	6
Montgomery Wings	35	32	.522	8
Macon Peaches	33	35	.485	10½
Houma Hawks	28	34	.452	12½
Selma Cloverleafs	23	44	.343	20

PLAYOFFS: Semifinals—Pensacola defeated Macon 2-0 and Baton Rouge defeated Montgomery 2-1 in best-of-3 series. **Final**—Baton Rouge defeated Pensacola 3-1 in best-of-5 series.

MANAGERS: Baton Rouge—Larry Keller/L.J. Dupuy/Ken Parker. **Houma**—Gus Brown III. **Macon**—Al Sontag/Kal Daniels/Todd Hogan. **Montgomery**—Lou Thornton. **Pensacola**—Bernie Carbo. **Selma**—David Angeron.

ATTENDANCE: Pensacola 34,295; Montgomery 13,364; Macon 9,138; Baton Rouge 2,608; Houma 550.

ALL-STAR TEAM: C—Matt Silva, Pensacola. **1B**—Josey Shannon, Baton Rouge. **2B**—Nelson Samboy, Pensacola. **3B**—Kevin Perret, Baton Rouge. **SS**—Jerson Perez, Baton Rouge. **OF**—Chad Campbell, Macon; Rico Santana, Houma; Eric Smallwood, Pensacola; Chris Van Rossum, Macon. **DH**—Blair Borque, Pensacola. **Util**—Jason Williams, Baton Rouge. **SP**—Corey Avrard, Baton Rouge; Jesse Ellison, Montgomery; Mike Meyer, Baton Rouge; Patrick Sexton, Pensacola. **RP**—Bubba Dobson, Pensacola; B.J. Litchfield, Macon. **CL**—Josh Harris, Montgomery.

Manager of the Year: Bernie Carbo, Pensacola.

INDIVIDUAL BATTING LEADERS

(Minimum 194 Plate Appearances)

	AVG	AB	R	H	2B	3B	HR	RBI	SB
Williams, Jason, BR	.346	162	35	56	18	0	7	35	7
Santana, Ricardo, Houma	.337	205	37	69	11	2	4	22	24
Smith, Colby, Mont.	.336	247	43	83	14	1	2	24	33
Campbell, Chad, Macon	.330	218	43	72	19	3	10	48	9
Blackburn, Franco, Mont.	.325	169	18	55	6	0	2	25	2
Harrison, Buck, Pensacola	.324	210	37	68	11	0	6	35	15
Durazo, Ernie, Macon	.322	227	50	73	18	2	7	37	8
Shannon, Josey, BR	.313	240	33	75	15	1	8	42	2
Perez, Jerson, Baton Rouge	.302	252	51	76	12	7	3	33	16
King, Willie, Houma	.299	221	43	66	11	1	2	34	10
Wren, Cliff, Baton Rouge	.295	176	17	52	9	1	2	27	0
Perret, Kevin, Baton Rouge	.291	199	30	58	20	0	5	39	0
Anderson, Melvin, Mont.	.288	198	31	57	18	1	1	21	26
Brown, Eric, Houma	.287	202	25	58	13	1	5	38	16
Riley, Rusty, Montgomery	.283	205	27	58	8	0	3	31	1

INDIVIDUAL PITCHING LEADERS

(Minimum 58 Innings)

	W	L	ERA	G	SV	IP	H	BB	SO
Meyer, Mike, BR	10	2	1.52	13	0	95	76	23	65
Avrard, Corey, BR	9	2	1.73	13	0	88	59	41	79
Roque, Darryll, Pensacola	4	1	2.21	11	0	69	61	16	73
Dunn, Jerry, Pensacola	7	1	2.21	10	0	69	63	24	44
Bourgeos, Steven, Houma	4	4	2.42	10	0	63	48	21	82
Hollis, Bart, Montgomery	6	2	2.44	11	0	63	49	16	38
Sutton, Teddy, Houma	3	4	2.55	20	2	60	67	14	49
McShea, Dan, BR	3	7	2.59	14	0	73	57	19	50
Ellison, Jesse, Mont.	6	4	3.40	13	0	79	67	34	50
Evans, Tony, Selma	2	5	3.55	11	0	58	44	27	57

FOREIGN LEAGUES

Red Devils bounce Tigers again

BY SALO OTERO

The Mexican League championship series is now a best of five series . . . and still counting between two longtime rivals.

For the fifth consecutive year in 2003, the Mexico City Red Devils and the Angelopolis Tigers met for the Mexican League title. It's advantage Reds, three series to two, as the Red Devils beat Angelopolis (previously known as the Mexico City Tigers) for the second consecutive season.

MEXICO

It was the 14th Mexican League title overall for the Reds, who beat Angelopolis four games to one. The Tigers had posted the league's best record in the regular season.

Both teams advanced to the title series with zone titles in six games of a best-of-seven series. The Red Devils knocked off Monterrey for the North Zone title, while the Tigers beat Oaxaca for the South Zone title.

In the fifth and decisive game of the championship series, shortstop Jose Sandoval's bases-loaded single with one out in the 13th inning drove in the winning run in a 7-6 victory. Sandoval was 3-for-6 with a run and two RBIs. Back-to-back doubles by the Tigers' Carlos Gastelum and Matias Carrillo tied the score at 6-6 in the seventh inning, when the game turned into a pitchers' duel. Gus Gandarillas and Santos Hernandez, the league leader in saves, shut down the Red Devils for five-plus innings, while Claudio Moreno and David Sinohui combined for seven scoreless innings of relief for Mexico City.

MORRIS FOSTOFF

Felix Jose

But when Hernandez tired, the Tigers brought in Cecilio Garibaldi in the 13th. He got only one out before allowing back-to-back singles and a walk to load the bases, setting up Sandoval's heroics.

In a league that was dominated by offense, Mexico City and Angelopolis easily had the best hitting clubs.

Mexico City hit .311 as a team, while Angelopolis hit .310. The Red Devils were led by outfielder Felix Jose, who hit .377-19-83 to win his second straight batting title. Seven other Red Devils topped .300. Tigers first baseman Guillermo Garcia led the league in homers (28) and RBIs (95).

Angelopolis' Pablo Ortega went 14-4, 3.21 to be named the pitcher of the year, while teammate Santos Hernandez went 1-1, 1.95 with 36 saves to be named reliever of the year.

Angelopolis' Che Reyes was selected the league's manager of the year, but there were seven managerial changes, including three skippers each for Union Laguna, the Two Laredos, Cordoba and Cancun.

Laguna DH Alejandro Ortiz, 42, hit 10 homers in 2003 and moved to within 21 of all-time Mexican League leader Nelson Barrera's mark of 455.

Barrera, who died at age 44 in 2002 when he was electrocuted, was one of five inductees into the Mexican League Hall of Fame. Also inducted were outfielder Andres Mora, who hit .313 with 419 home runs in a 23-year career and righthander Enrique Romo. All three players played in the major leagues.

STANDINGS

EAST	W	L	PCT	GB
*Mexico City Red Devils	68	40	.630	—
Monterrey Sultans	66	43	.606	2½
+Saltillo Sarape Makers	62	45	.579	5½
Puebla Parrots	62	48	.564	7
Two Laredos Owls	53	56	.486	15½
Monclova Steelers	49	59	.454	19
Reynosa Broncos	43	63	.406	24
Laguna Cowboys	39	71	.355	30
WEST	**W**	**L**	**PCT**	**GB**
*+Angelopolis Tigers	72	35	.673	—
Yucatan Lions	61	45	.575	10½
Oaxaca Warriors	57	52	.523	16
Campeche Pirates	55	51	.519	16½
Veracruz Reds	50	54	.481	20½
Tabasco Cattlemen	49	59	.454	23½
Cancun Lobstermen	44	63	.415	28
Cordoba Coffee Growers	29	75	.265	41½

*First-half champion +Second-half champion

PLAYOFFS—Quarterfinals: Oaxaca defeated Yucatan 4-0; Mexico City Red Devils defeated Puebla 4-3; Tigers defeated Campeche 4-2; and Monterrey defeated Saltillo 4-3 in best-of-7 series. **Semifinals:** Mexico City Red Devils defeated Monterrey 4-2 and Tigers defeated Oaxaca 4-2 in best-of-7 series. **Final:** Mexico City Red Devils defeated Tigers 4-1 in best-of-7 series.

MANAGERS: Angelopolis Tigers—Lee Sigman. **Campeche**—Francisco Estrada. **Cancun**—Lupe Salinas, Ramon Montoya, Enrique Ramirez. **Cordoba**—Eddie Diaz, Lupe Jalabera, Raul Antonio Aguilera. **Laguna**—Alex Taveras, Roberto Mendez, Jose Juan Bellacetin. **Mexico City**—Bernie Tatis. **Monclova**—Derek Bryant. **Monterrey**—Dan Firova. **Oaxaca**—Houston Jimenez. **Puebla**—Enrique Reyes. **Reynosa**—Francisco Rodriguez. **Saltillo**—Raul Cano, Fernando Elizondo. **Tabasco**—Sergio Borges, Gilberto Reyes. **Two Laredos**—Mario Mendoza, Ruben Estrada, Andres Mora. **Veracruz**—Andres Mora, Rolando Camarero. **Yucatan**—Juan Pacho.

ALL-STAR TEAM: C—Noe Munoz, Saltillo. **1B**—Guillermo Garcia, Tigers. **2B**—Jesus Arredondo, Puebla. **3B**—Ramon Orantes, Monterrey. **SS**—Jose Luis Sandoval, Mexico City. **OF**—Luis Garcia, Tigers; Roberto Mendez, Oaxaca; Lorenzo Buelna, Puebla. **RHP**—Pablo Ortega, Puebla. **LHP**—Jesus Guzman, Tigers. **RP**—Santos Hernandez, Tigers. **Manager of the Year**—Enrique Reyes, Puebla.

REGULAR SEASON ATTENDANCE: Saltillo 603,530; Monterrey 511,546; Yucatan 334,066; Monclova 218,866; Laguna 195,724; Puebla 166,341; Mexico 150,278; Cancun 135,416; Oaxaca 133,677; Cordoba 110,382; Reynosa 88,708; Mexico City 85,739; Tabasco 83,133; Veracruz 76,677; Two Laredos 74,290; Campeche 64,913.

INDIVIDUAL BATTING LEADERS

(Minimum 297 Plate Appearances)

	AVG	AB	R	H	2B	3B	HR	RBI	SB
Jose, Felix, Mexico	**.377**	334	82	126	24	1	19	83	10
Villalobos, Carlos, Puebla	.370	281	46	104	25	0	12	63	0
Arredondo, Jesus, Puebla	.352	332	51	117	15	2	0	42	3
Garcia, Luis, Tigers	.349	413	70	**144**	21	1	17	68	20
Sherman, Darrell, Puebla	.347	349	82	121	20	4	5	39	14
Buelna, Lorenzo, Puebla	.346	399	66	138	26	2	7	62	7
Robles, Javier, Tigers	.343	335	69	115	29	2	6	47	11
Garcia, Cornelio, Mex./Oax./Lag.	.342	348	60	119	20	3	3	50	8
Orantes, Ramon, Monterrey	.342	360	54	123	17	0	5	62	1
Brinkley, Darryl, Yucatan	.340	362	62	123	12	0	12	57	22
Rodarte, Raul, Mont./Reynosa	.337	315	49	106	18	2	8	39	13
Garcia, Guillermo, Tigers	.336	390	80	131	21	1	**28**	**95**	3
Iturbe, Pedro, Puebla	.335	385	69	129	30	1	6	56	7
Verdugo, Vincente, Saltillo	.334	341	51	114	14	0	4	42	1
Munoz, Noe, Saltillo	.329	347	70	114	27	1	13	92	0

Kelly, Roberto, Mexico	.328	335	79	110	20	1	10	57	10
Paul, Corey, Saltillo/Tabasco	.327	330	66	108	22	0	11	53	10
Quintero, Christian, Oaxaca	.327	419	67	137	24	4	10	54	12
Gastelum, Carlos, Tigers	.327	303	52	99	9	5	0	33	20
Garcia, Omar, Veracruz/Laredo.	.324	299	49	97	16	1	8	45	0
Pickering, Calvin, Laguna	.323	291	64	94	13	0	25	63	1
Velez, Manuel, Saltillo	.323	316	44	102	15	1	4	41	1
Laya, Rayner, Tabasco	.323	378	50	122	9	4	0	26	25
Bullett, Scott, Reynosa/Monterrey	.323	372	76	120	16	3	14	51	13
Rodriguez, Carlos, Laguna	.321	430	73	138	19	1	0	23	12
Grijak, Kevin, Veracruz	.320	375	46	120	20	1	9	58	3
Guerrero, Sergio, Campeche	.319	329	43	105	20	1	9	40	3
Lucca, Lou, Cordoba/Laguna	.317	265	34	84	10	1	9	47	3
Davis, Jay, Cordoba/Monterrey	.316	399	66	126	**31**	1	11	71	6
Castellano, Pedro, Campeche	.314	328	37	103	18	0	8	52	0
Valencia, Abraham, Laredo	.314	325	45	102	16	0	6	47	5
Smith, Demond, Monterrey	.313	384	80	120	18	3	10	41	**53**
Bass, Jayson, Saltillo	.312	382	**91**	119	29	2	15	71	36
Cervantes, Ivan, Oaxaca	.311	363	43	113	14	2	3	32	4
Morejon, Oswaldo, Yucatan	.311	302	44	94	21	1	4	28	3
Garcia, Amaury, Campeche	.310	397	50	123	16	5	6	31	18
Pemberton, Rudy, Monclova	.309	417	54	129	18	4	10	48	4
Robles, Oscar, Mexico	.309	398	81	123	13	**9**	8	53	6
White, Derrick, Laredo	.305	406	61	124	19	2	19	87	12
Espinosa, Ramon, Yucatan/Laredo	.305	452	57	138	19	3	4	44	18
Sandoval, Jose, Mexico	.305	367	67	112	17	0	22	91	6
Arredondo, Luis, Yucatan	.304	421	62	128	9	1	1	20	23
Hernandez, Vladimir, Cancun	.304	421	51	128	22	2	5	41	15
Fernandez, Dan, Mexico	.303	389	70	118	14	3	1	45	5
Amezcua, Adan, Monterrey	.303	261	40	79	16	1	5	43	3
Vizcarra, Roberto, Tigers	.302	387	52	117	18	1	6	48	3
Martinez, Ramon, Mexico	.302	311	66	94	22	0	13	74	8
Bojorquez, Victor, Mexico	.302	394	58	119	17	5	11	68	10
Meza, Gonzalo, Laguna	.301	382	57	115	12	2	5	45	6
Adriana, Sharnol, Cordoba	.301	299	53	90	21	1	11	49	9
Castillo, Alberto, Mexico/Laguna	.300	303	51	91	13	0	12	61	1
Lara, Idelfonso, Laguna	.300	307	36	92	16	0	9	57	0
Martinez, Enrique, Reynosa	.299	278	43	83	13	0	4	27	5
Fornes, Daniel, Monterrey	.298	302	45	90	13	2	15	71	2
Newson, Warren, Tabasco/Monc	.298	322	49	96	16	0	9	43	12
Hernandez, Julio, Laredo	.298	393	65	117	15	3	9	49	2
Yan, Julian, Puebla	.297	417	63	124	24	0	18	90	3
Garcia, Hector, Tabasco	.296	338	34	100	9	0	1	24	5
Cervantes, Refugio, Cancun	.296	355	43	105	14	2	17	64	0
Ramirez, Oscar, Campeche	.296	406	58	120	16	2	11	45	3
Connell, Lino, Oaxaca/Reynosa	.295	397	57	117	22	2	4	44	18
Mendez, Roberto, Oaxaca	.292	336	75	98	16	1	22	78	5
Soto, Saul, Oaxaca/Mexico	.290	345	53	100	18	1	13	53	2
Mendez, Francisco, Mont./Rey.	.293	290	36	85	15	0	11	45	2
Sanchez, Raul, Cancun	.289	346	46	100	17	0	5	40	4
Carrillo, Matias, Tigers	.288	354	70	102	15	1	15	58	9
Saenz, Ricardo, Monclova/Saltillo	.287	383	49	110	21	0	8	45	4
Magallanes, Ever, Tabasco	.287	300	25	86	11	0	2	25	2
Arredondo, Hector, Cor./Tabasco	.287	289	40	83	15	0	12	43	3
Rios, Eduardo, Cancun/Oaxaca	.282	362	34	102	22	0	6	47	1
Rodriguez, Fernando, Campeche	.280	311	25	87	9	0	9	35	0
Diaz, Edwin, Veracruz	.279	394	61	110	22	1	20	64	7
Ramirez, Omar, Veracruz	.279	420	63	117	20	0	13	50	10
Gomez, Heber, Monterrey	.278	388	65	108	22	0	5	40	6
Ruiz, Juan, Monclova	.277	339	49	94	20	0	10	36	3
Lopez, Raul, Monclova	.276	359	49	99	28	0	5	46	1
Zambrano, Roberto, Laredo	.275	345	77	95	23	0	21	75	1
Guizar, Hector, Cordoba	.275	375	28	103	11	1	1	41	8
LeBron, Juan, Campeche/Oaxaca	.275	320	39	88	12	1	15	52	3
Flores, Miguel, Reynosa/Yucatan	.272	312	37	85	13	1	3	33	13
Romero, Flavio, Saltillo	.271	280	51	76	11	1	4	25	24

Other Select Players

	AVG	AB	R	H	2B	3B	HR	RBI	SB
Martinez, Gabby, Laguna	.465	101	22	47	4	1	1	13	14
Sojo, Luis, Oaxaca	.410	83	17	34	6	0	3	16	0
Leyritz, Jim, Oaxaca	.389	18	4	7	1	0	1	6	0
Perez, Robert. Mexico	.359	181	34	65	12	2	9	33	4
Mejia, Roberto, Oaxaca	.348	210	37	73	9	1	12	36	10
Alcantara, Izzy, Laguna	.341	249	48	85	14	0	14	45	2
Almonte, Wady, Cordoba	.331	178	17	59	5	1	4	25	5
Thompson, Ryan, Oaxaca	.330	106	20	35	6	0	5	14	0
Rodriguez, Boi, Campeche	.321	168	38	54	5	0	8	26	7
Obando, Sherman, Mexico	.315	200	35	63	16	1	8	47	1
Avila, Rolo, Tabasco	.313	16	5	5	2	0	0	2	1
Rojas, Homar, Oaxaca	.305	131	12	40	7	0	3	20	2
Radmanovich, Ryan, Monterrey	.301	156	21	47	12	2	2	20	3
Jones, Chris, Cordoba	.300	70	9	21	3	1	1	22	3
Herrera, Jose, Yucatan	.291	268	28	78	10	4	7	36	4
Cookson, Brent, Oaxaca	.286	119	15	34	4	0	1	16	0

Timmons, Ozzie, Reynosa	.281	121	23	34	9	0	3	25	0
Aguilera, Tony, Cordoba	.279	43	3	12	0	0	1	4	0
Hubbard, Trenidad, Oaxaca	.277	47	6	13	3	0	2	5	3
Rose, Pete, Cordoba	.274	106	13	29	3	0	4	18	0
Carpenter, Bubba, Monclova	.274	84	13	23	8	0	2	12	2
Coleman, Michael, Reynosa	.271	70	14	19	4	0	3	8	3
Raven, Luis, Cancun	.270	244	23	66	12	0	7	40	0
Samuels, Scott, Veracruz	.269	109	18	29	5	0	0	5	10
Salinas, Trey, Cancun	.267	311	44	83	12	0	7	39	6
Melo, Juan, Mexico/Cordoba	.264	106	15	28	2	0	1	9	1
Wilson, Craig, Oaxaca	.261	46	8	12	1	1	1	9	1
Berroa, Geronimo, Monterrey	.258	93	19	24	4	0	6	18	1
Smith, Bubba, Monterrey	.258	357	66	92	15	0	22	70	0
Flores, Kevin, Puebla	.251	171	28	43	10	1	0	22	0
Clemente, Edgard, Cancun	.250	96	13	24	4	1	3	10	0
Martinez, Sandy, Campeche	.250	108	12	27	1	1	2	16	0
Velazquez, Guillermo, Cam./Pueb.	.249	366	38	91	15	0	8	51	0
Rodriguez, Victor, Campeche	.239	67	7	16	2	0	1	3	0
Mouton, James, Reynosa	.236	55	16	13	2	0	1	4	0
Evans, Tom, Tabasco	.227	119	23	27	7	1	3	19	1
Leach, Jalal, Saltillo	.143	28	5	4	2	1	0	7	3

INDIVIDUAL PITCHING LEADERS

(Minimum 88 Innings)

	W	L	ERA	G	SV	IP	H	BB	SO
Serafini, Dan, Monterrey	10	2	**1.59**	16	0	96	70	41	89
Moreno, Angel, Veracruz	8	4	2.27	21	1	127	121	27	42
Manzanillo, Ravelo, Yucatan/Saltillo	10	3	2.36	17	0	118	81	65	81
Campos, Francisco, Campeche	6	4	2.40	12	0	90	85	20	58
Vega, Obed, Cancun	9	4	2.67	21	0	141	135	40	65
Vargas, Joel, Tabasco	7	4	2.69	20	0	124	110	41	61
Romano, Mike, Tabasco	5	4	2.72	38	13	99	100	32	57
Campillo, Jorge, Tigers	12	5	2.79	21	0	119	116	30	63
Nunez, Jose, Laredo	11	5	2.89	21	1	140	148	33	73
Guzman, Jesus, Tigers	10	3	2.92	27	0	99	100	24	47
Rodriguez, Salvador, Yucatan	10	4	3.00	19	0	120	111	37	71
Magee, Bo, Campeche	10	6	3.06	23	0	170	118	109	**155**
Ortega, Pablo, Puebla	13	4	3.14	23	0	161	153	46	98
Esquer, Mercedes, Reynosa	7	7	3.17	20	0	125	128	17	51
Lira, Felipe, Oaxaca	8	9	3.19	23	0	169	188	44	103
Roque, Rafael, Tigers	10	6	3.25	20	0	116	122	54	68
Leyva, Edgar, Monterrey	11	3	3.28	18	0	104	105	32	66
Gandarillas, Gus, Tigers	13	5	3.40	21	0	127	157	37	45
Palafox, Juan, Yucatan	10	8	3.48	18	0	114	121	34	44
Pesqueira, Omar, Cancun/Yucatan	6	7	3.50	19	0	108	116	37	36
Navarro, Hector, Veracruz	8	5	3.56	30	0	119	118	52	71
Delahoya, Javier, Vera./Cam.	5	4	3.70	17	0	97	105	43	56
Hurtado, Edwin, Cancun/Yucatan	9	11	3.70	26	1	175	167	71	124
Leon, Juan, Tabasco	6	7	3.70	25	1	92	82	49	70
Mercedes, Jose, Saltillo	**14**	6	3.71	22	0	160	172	53	114
Giron, Isabel, Laguna	9	9	3.76	23	0	148	150	48	112
Pina, Rafael, Veracruz	6	5	3.77	15	0	93	89	34	36
Navarro, Joel, Oaxaca	6	2	3.97	25	0	95	99	33	62
Loya, Rigoberto, Monterrey	9	6	4.03	22	0	118	123	57	63
Patrick, Bronswell, Mexico	13	2	4.04	23	0	134	153	27	75
Verdugo, Orlando, Reynosa	6	5	4.07	29	0	104	113	40	46
Arroyo, Luis, Monclova	7	8	4.09	24	0	123	124	63	99
Valdez, Efrain, Laguna/Tabasco	4	7	4.12	20	0	111	123	36	52
Mora, Eleazar, Veracruz	5	5	4.23	20	0	106	129	22	42
Sanchez, Efrain, Campeche	4	5	4.27	23	0	97	103	39	32
Alvarez, Octavio, Mexico	11	8	4.35	23	0	165	202	29	88
Huerta, Luis, Laredo	3	8	4.49	21	0	100	125	39	51
Flores, Ignacio, Saltillo	7	6	4.65	24	0	89	99	32	70
Kamar, Emil, Monclova	6	9	4.66	23	0	116	139	60	50
Garcia, Alfredo, Mexico	8	5	4.66	22	0	131	156	64	77
Dominguez, Carlos, Saltillo/Laredo	6	6	4.70	26	0	100	113	55	47
Fernandez, Osvaldo, Mexico	10	4	4.71	19	0	126	157	42	77
Manrique, Alberto, Monterrey	5	7	4.75	20	0	100	124	40	37
Rios, Jesus, Tabasco	0	7	4.86	23	0	93	98	38	45
Kelley, Rich, Puebla	8	8	4.88	35	1	118	123	51	81
Lopez, Emigdio, Cordoba	3	11	4.95	21	0	133	175	48	68

Other Select Players

	W	L	ERA	G	SV	IP	H	BB	SO
Pichardo, Hipolito, Saltillo	0	0	1.05	24	13	26	22	10	17
Garcia, Michael, Yucatan	0	1	1.32	12	7	14	9	5	17
Elvira, Narciso, Campeche	4	2	1.87	8	0	58	37	24	33
Hernandez, Santos, Tigers	1	1	1.95	50	**36**	51	49	15	29
Wallace, Kent, Tabasco	0	1	2.16	7	3	8	9	3	8
DeSilva, John, Reynosa	4	3	2.64	10	0	65	68	21	36
Strong, Joe, Reynosa	6	4	2.71	46	16	66	54	28	44
Mota, Daniel, Campeche	4	2	3.17	14	0	54	49	20	26
Rojas, Mel, Monclova	3	1	3.35	27	2	43	49	18	29
Dingman, Craig, Yucatan/Cancun	4	7	3.53	42	19	43	41	13	37
Heredia, Julian, Campeche	1	1	3.86	8	0	9	7	3	4

Ward, Bryan, Saltillo	4	3	4.14	7	0	37	34	18	21
Sinohui, David, Salt./Tab./Cord./Mex.	2	4	4.21	50	25	47	58	22	34
Parra, Jose, Cordoba	1	3	4.38	29	7	37	37	15	29
Palacios, Vicente, Laredos	0	2	4.43	12	0	20	25	14	11
Harikkala, Tim, Oaxaca	3	7	4.63	12	0	80	98	17	50
Jean, Domingo, Cancun	3	4	4.69	8	0	48	59	14	15
Keppen, Jeff, Laredos	4	5	4.73	10	0	51	59	30	34
Agosto, Stevenson, Tabasco/Oaxaca	5	4	4.88	16	0	72	74	41	63
Martinez, Javier, Saltillo	1	0	6.75	6	0	5	10	3	4
Hasselhoff, Derek, Tigers	0	1	7.04	10	0	8	8	4	2
Dominguez, David, Oaxaca	5	5	7.57	39	3	52	62	24	28
Navarro, Jaime, Oaxaca	1	2	7.85	5	0	29	46	5	14
Preston, George, Reynosa	1	4	8.56	6	0	27	30	25	33
Bones, Ricky, Saltillo	0	1	9.45	3	1	7	7	7	6
Dorame, Randey, Mexico/Laguna	0	2	11.81	16	0	27	35	17	16
Williams, Slim, Cordoba	0	1	13.50	4	3	3	5	1	3

Canadian league folds in first year

CANADA

The Canadian Baseball League always preferred not to be called an independent league, but in the modern tradition of independent baseball, the league did not complete its first season.

The league, composed of eight Canadian cities, suspended play after its all-star game in Calgary on July 23. League chairman Jeff Mallett said he decided that the only way the league would have a chance to return in 2004 was to shut down early in 2003.

"We're really taking a look at what we can do to fix the bleeding," Mallett said. "It's tough enough to start one team, try starting eight. Our execution as an organization was below par."

The league had originally hoped to get started in 2002, but postponed the opening to 2003 to get more organized. The league lined up a national television contract for a game of the week and managed to bring in some recognizable players, such as Francisco Cabrera and Rich Butler, both former big leaguers.

But the league rolled out the gate without a stadium for its Montreal team, which turned into a traveling team. Weather played havoc with the early season schedule, and attendance fell significantly below expectations.

Two of the league's western-based teams, Calgary and Victoria, drew a combined 48,839, with both teams averaging more than 1,000 fans per game. But the other six teams combined to draw less than 25,000 fans, with three of the four Eastern Division teams drawing less than 200 fans per game.

Calgary was named the league champion. The Outlaws had the league's best record of 24-13 when play was suspended.

Calgary's Galindo Gomez was selected the league's MVP. He was leading the league in hitting (.403), home runs (11) and RBIs (42) when it shut down. Outlaws righthander Jesus Matos was named the league's best pitcher after going 5-2, 3.04. He also led the league with 79 strikeouts while walking only seven batters in 80 innings.

Despite the failure of the Canadian League, it was a positive year for Canada on the international level in 2003 as its national team qualified for the Athens Olympics.

Canada secured one of two berths from the Americas in the Olympics by reaching the gold-medal game at the America's qualifier in Panama in November by beating Mexico 11-1 in the semifinals. The Canadians lost to Cuba in the gold-medal game, but their fate was already secured.

—J.J. COOPER

STANDINGS

EAST	W	L	PCT	GB
London (Ont.) Monarchs	20	13	.606	—
Niagara (Ont.) Stars	15	15	.500	3½
Trois-Rivieres (Quebec) Saints	14	17	.452	5
Montreal Royales	10	22	.313	9½
WEST	**W**	**L**	**PCT**	**GB**
Calgary (Alta.) Outlaws	24	13	.649	—
Saskatoon (Sask.) Legends	22	15	.595	2
Kelowna (B.C.) Heat	18	19	.486	6
Victoria (B.C.) Capitals	13	22	.371	10

NOTE: League suspended operations July 20; Calgary crowned champion.

INDIVIDUAL BATTING LEADERS

(Minimum 92 Plate Appearances)

	AVG	AB	R	H	2B	3B	HR	RBI	SB
Gomez, Galindo, Calgary	.403	144	40	58	6	1	11	42	8
Van Iderstine, Ben, Saskatoon	.401	137	30	55	9	0	5	32	4
Uraviola, Carlos, Saskatoon	.375	128	33	48	10	0	0	19	13
Matos, Pascual, Trois Rivieres	.360	125	14	45	8	1	1	21	6
Adams, Skip, Niagara	.359	103	30	37	7	0	5	19	5
Beltran, Denio, Niagara	.358	123	32	44	8	1	1	16	13
Moreno, Jorge, London	.357	112	32	40	9	0	3	19	11
Murphy, Sean, Saskatoon	.354	127	35	45	5	2	6	25	3
Sandoval, Jensy, Calgary	.353	136	29	48	8	2	5	28	20
Arias, Rogelio, Niagara	.352	122	16	43	7	1	3	26	0

INDIVIDUAL PITCHING LEADERS

(Minimum 27 Innings)

	W	L	ERA	G	SV	IP	H	BB	SO
Williams, Shad, Calgary	4	2	1.76	9	0	72	65	18	42
Miller, Matt, Trois Rivieres	3	0	2.12	6	0	30	22	12	17
Collazo, Rafael, Trois Rivieres	3	2	2.37	10	0	30	29	15	25
Tiscareno, Raul, London	3	1	2.53	9	0	43	44	3	37
Etler, Todd, London	4	1	2.80	8	0	45	38	13	44
Koback, Ryan, Saskatoon	2	4	2.98	11	0	51	43	15	14
Felix, Bienvenido, Saskatoon	6	2	3.02	10	0	66	47	14	57
Matos, Jesus, Calgary	5	2	3.04	10	0	80	78	7	79
Alston, Garvin, Montreal	0	3	3.07	8	0	29	29	10	24
LaPlante, Reggie, Trois Rivieres	2	2	3.48	8	0	44	30	31	28

Cuba dominates despite defections

BY MILTON JAMAIL AND KEVIN BAXTER

CUBA

Cuba continued its long history of success in international competition in 2003, but it added another dubious achievement. A year after righthander Jose Contreras, a former national team star, defected and eventually signed a lucrative contract with the New York Yankees, two more Cuban stars defected during the 2003 season.

Righthander Maels Rodriguez and second baseman/outfielder Yobal Dueñas defected in hopes of playing professional baseball in the United States. The pair were reported missing by Cuban authorities at the end of the World Cup, played in Cuba in October.

Rodriguez, 24, would be regarded on a par with Contreras were it not for rumors of back and arm injuries. He has extensive experience in international play and his fastball regularly reached 100 mph in the past. He set the single-season strikeout record in Cuba's Serie Nacional, fanning 263 in 178 innings in 2000. A year later, he struck out 219 in 148 innings, going 14-3, 2.13.

But in the 2002 Cuban playoffs, Rodriguez pitched in 10 of 14 games for his Sancti Spíritus team and pitched complete games in two exhibitions that had been set up for visiting former U.S. President Jimmy Carter. Cuban officials then left him off the Pan American Games, World Cup and Olympic qualifying rosters, blaming arm and back injuries for the sudden loss of 15 mph off his fastball.

IBAF

Yuliesky Gourriel

Rodriguez also may have been left off those rosters for contemplating defection with Contreras in 2002.

"I'll demonstrate (I'm healthy)," Rodriguez said after defecting. "I'm going to demonstrate that I can still throw 100. These are things that they invent to cut a little off the careers of some athletes."

Dueñas, a 6-foot-2, 187-pound second baseman/outfielder from Pinar del Rio, is a former Cuban stolen-base champ who, at 31, is on the downside of a career that saw him debut in the Cuban national league at 17.

Another Cuban player, switch-hitting first baseman Kendry Morales, was sent home from Panama, where he was to play for Cuba in the Olympic qualifier. Morales, 20, was returned to Cuba for improper contact with an American baseball official.

On the field, the Cuban national team won every major tournament it participated in in 2003, including the Pan American Games in August, World Cup in October and the America's Olympic qualifier in November.

Despite the absence of Duenas, Morales, Rodriguez and righthander Pedro Luis Lazo, who were left off the team for disciplinary reasons, Cuba continued its domination of the Pan American Games, played in the Dominican Republic. Cuba defeated the United States 3-1 in the title game for its ninth straight Pan Am gold medal.

Cuba hosted the World Cup and escaped a scare from Brazil to win its 24th gold medal in 27 World Cup outings. After rallying to beat Brazil in the quarterfinals, scoring twice in the bottom of the ninth to win 4-3, the host team cruised past Taiwan in the semifinals and then edged Panama in the finals. With the win, Cuba lifted its overall record in the World Cup to 269-29.

Cuba rode a quartet of young hitters to the gold medal. Third baseman Michel Enriquez, filling the shoes of departed star Omar Linares, hit .424. But it was the bats of 19-year-old second baseman Yuliesky Gourriel, Morales and 23-year-old outfielder Frederich Cepeda that buried opponents during the medal round.

Gourriel's triple launched Cuba's face-saving rally against upset-minded Brazil, and the switch-hitting Morales followed with a homer to clinch one of the biggest comebacks in Cuba's World Cup history. Cepeda's two solo homers were the difference in the gold-medal showdown with Panama, a 4-2 victory that ended on a controversial runner's interference play at second base.

Cuba qualified for the Athens Olympics by reaching the gold-medal game of an Americas qualifying tournament in Panama. The top two finishers, Cuba and Canada, will represent the continent in the '04 Olympics.

In Cuban domestic competition in 2003, the Havana-based Industriales won the 42nd Serie Nacional. The Industriales won Group B with a record-setting 66-23 record and breezed through the playoffs defeating Havana in the quarterfinals 3 games to 1, Pinar del Rio in the semi-finals 4 games to 1 and swept Villa Clara in four games in the championship round.

Las Tunas' outfielder Osmani Urrutia won his third consecutive Serie Nacional batting title, hitting .421. It was Urrutia's third straight year hitting more than .400; he hit .408 in 2002 and .431 in 2001. First baseman, Joan Pedroso, also from Las Tunas, led the league in home runs with 28. But the offensive bursts were of little help to the Las Tunas team, which finished with a 25-65 record, the worst in the league. Adel Palma from Cienfuegos led the league in wins (14) and strikeouts (179), and finished second in ERA with a 2.21 mark.

Cuba's second season—the Super Liga de Béisbol—was won by the Centrales. The league, in its second year, was composed of Cuba's 100 best players, who competed for the 20 positions on Equipo Cuba—the national team. The teams played a 20-game schedule, 10 less than 2002.

STANDINGS

GROUP A	W	L	PCT	GB
Pinar del Rio	56	34	.622	—
Isla de la Juventud	41	48	.461	14½
Matanzas	41	49	.456	15
Metropolitans	41	49	.456	15
GROUP B	**W**	**L**	**PCT**	**GB**
Industriales	66	23	.742	—
Cienfuegos	52	38	.578	14½
Havana	51	39	.567	15½
Sancti Spiritus	49	41	.544	17½
GROUP C	**W**	**L**	**PCT**	**GB**
Villa Clara	56	34	.622	—
Camaguey	44	46	.489	12
Ciego de Avila	37	53	.411	19
Las Tunas	25	65	.278	31
Group D	**W**	**L**	**PCT**	**GB**
Granma	45	45	.500	—
Santiago de Cuba	44	46	.489	1
Holguin	43	47	.478	2
Guantanamo	28	62	.311	17

PLAYOFFS—Quarterfinals: Villa Clara defeated Santiago 3-2; Granma defeated Camaguey 3-1; Industriales defeated Havana 3-1 and Pinar del Rio defeated Cienfuegos 3-2 in best-of-5 series. **Semifinals:** Villa Clara defeated Granma 4-2; Industriales defeated Pinar del Rio 4-1 in best-of-7 division series. **Final:** Industriales defeated Villa Clara 4-0 in best-of-7 series.

INDIVIDUAL BATTING LEADERS

(Minimum 243 At-Bats)

	AVG	AB	R	H	2B	3B	HR	RBI
Urrutia, Osmani, Las Tunas	.421	292	43	123	18	0	13	72
Morales, Kendry, Industriales	.391	202	47	79	13	2	9	42
Macias, Oscar, Havana	.384	279	58	107	20	0	11	69
Issac, Rey, Santiago	.383	269	63	103	22	2	11	66
Suarez, Amaury, Las Tunas	.378	344	77	130	23	2	11	64
Socarras, Yagency, Cienfuegos	.373	292	68	109	15	1	14	87
Ramos, Alexander, IJ	.373	338	67	126	22	1	8	47
Chapelli, Loidel, Camaguey	.367	311	43	114	20	5	7	71
Olivera, Onel, Pinar del Rio	.361	338	54	122	23	2	10	50
Perez, Serguei, Metros	.356	275	43	98	17	1	8	44

INDIVIDUAL PITCHING LEADERS

(Minimum 90 Innings)

	W	L	ERA	G	IP	BB	SO
Soler, Alain, Pinal del Rio	10	4	2.01	18	125	28	102
Palma, Adel, Cienfuegos	14	4	2.21	21	158	49	179
Odelin, Vicohandry, Camaguey	9	4	2.38	19	125	26	102
Aragon, Yovani, Sancti Spiritus	12	3	2.74	21	164	35	147
Garcia, Jose, Havana	7	5	2.82	35	93	58	107
Silva, Reinaldo, Holguin	7	7	2.87	22	113	27	79
Machado, Jorge, Industriales	8	3	2.88	15	94	20	67
Rodriguez, Maels, Sancti Spiritus	8	3	3.11	19	113	87	117
Corrales, Faustino, Pinar del Rio	6	3	3.19	13	90	49	108
Rodriguez, Luis, Holguin	11	6	3.20	20	152	30	102

Fukuoka spoils Hanshin title hopes

BY WAYNE GRACZYK

Until the final game of the Japan Series, the story of the 2003 Japanese season was the championship-starved Hanshin Tigers.

The Tigers, managed by Senichi Hoshino, emerged as the darling of fans, not only in the Tigers' home base of Osaka, but throughout the entire country of Japan. The team had not won a Japan Series, or even a Central League pennant, since 1985 and the nation grew excited as the Tigers built a double-digit lead over the other five teams in the Central prior to the July all-star break. Hanshin coasted to the CL title, winning by 14 ½ games.

JAPAN

But the Pacific League's Fukuoka Daiei Hawks defeated the upstart Tigers four games to three in the 2003 Japan Series, spoiling Hanshin's fans hopes for a title.

The Hawks prevailed in the first seven-game Japan Series since 1993, as home-field advantage played a huge role in determining the winner. The home team ended up winning all seven games of the series.

WAYNE GRACZYK

Tadahito Iguchi

Manager Sadaharu Oh's Daiei club featured a lethal batting attack that included six .300 hitters and four players with more than 100 RBIs. The team's leading hitters were catcher and Pacific League MVP Kenji Jojima (.330-34-119), first baseman Nobuhiko Matsunaka (.324-30-123), second baseman Tadahito Iguchi (.340-27-109) and outfielder Pedro Valdes (.311-26-104).

Leading the charge on the mound for Fukuoka was righthander Kazumi Saito (20-3 with a 2.83 ERA) and lefties Tsuyoshi Wada (14-5, 3.38) and Toshiya Sugiuchi (10-8, 3.38).

The Hawks' Series victory came amid speculation the team might be sold due to the ailing financial situation of its parent company, supermarket operator and retailer Daiei, Inc.

WAYNE GRACZYK

Alex Ramirez

The Tigers were led by Central League MVP Kei Igawa (20-5, 2.80 ERA) and former major leaguer Hideki Irabu (13-8, 3.85). One-time Dodgers lefty Jeff Williams racked up 25 saves in the bullpen.

On offense, the Tigers' big guns were second baseman Makoto Imaoka who led the league in batting at .340, and ex-San Diego Padres infielder George Arias who slammed 38 home runs and had 107 RBIs.

A total of 63 foreigners played in Japan during the 2003 season, with players from the United States, Canada, Australia, Taiwan, Korea, the Dominican Republic, Puerto Rico, Cuba, Venezuela, Panama and Brazil.

The home run titles in both leagues were won by foreign players. Tuffy Rhodes of the Osaka Kintetsu Buffaloes hit 51 to win his third Pacific League crown, edging Seibu Lions' Venezuelan first baseman Alex Cabrera who slammed 50.

The Central League homer crown was shared by Yakult Swallows' leftfielder Alex Ramirez, a former Indians and Pirates minor leaguer, and Yokohama BayStars' first baseman Tyrone Woods, a veteran of the Korean Baseball Organization. Each hit 40 homers. Ramirez also led both leagues with 124 RBIs.

The Pacific League's Nippon Ham Fighters played their last full season in Tokyo under first-year American manager Trey Hillman. Hillman was scheduled to be back in 2004 to lead the team in its first season in Sapporo as the Ham Fighters will move to the northernmost Japanese main island of Hokkaido.

Hillman wasn't the only American manager in 2003, as Leon Lee, father of Florida Marlins first baseman Derrek Lee, took over the Orix BlueWave during the season. When Orix and Nippon met on May 17 at the Tokyo Dome, it was the first Japanese game between American managers in 28 years.

While Lee will not be back at the Orix helm in 2004, Hillman will face another American skipper, former Texas Rangers and New York Mets manager Bobby Valentine. Valentine signed a three-year contract to manage the Pacific League's Chiba Lotte Marines. Valentine returns to the job he held in 1995 when he led the Marines to a second-place finish.

CENTRAL LEAGUE

STANDINGS

	W	L	T	PCT	GB
Hanshin Tigers	87	51	2	.630	—
Chunichi Dragons	73	66	1	.525	14½
Yomiuri Giants	71	66	3	.518	15½
Yakult Swallows	71	66	3	.518	15½
Hiroshima Carp	67	71	2	.486	20
Yokohama BayStars	45	94	1	.324	42½

INDIVIDUAL BATTING LEADERS

(Minimum 434 Plate Appearances)

	AVG	AB	R	H	2B	3B	HR	RBI	SB
Imaoka, Makoto, Tigers	.340	485	67	165	35	1	12	72	1
Ramirez, Alex, Swallows	.333	567	105	189	34	3	40	124	4
Yano, Akihiro, Tigers	.328	433	65	142	25	5	14	79	1
Takahashi, Yoshinobu, Giants	.323	443	85	143	31	1	26	68	3
Suzuki, Ken, Swallows	.317	482	67	153	36	0	20	95	2
Sheets, Andy, Carp	.313	514	77	161	32	1	25	75	3
Fukudome, Kosuke, Dragons	.313	528	107	165	30	11	34	96	10
Akahoshi, Norihiro, Tigers	.312	551	90	172	17	7	1	35	61
Suzuki, Takanori, BayStars	.311	492	67	153	30	0	19	57	6
Kinjo, Tatsuhiko, BayStars	.302	549	78	166	26	1	16	40	4
Fujimoto, Atsushi, Tigers	.301	402	51	121	16	7	0	36	9
Nioka, Tomohiro, Giants	.300	573	88	172	18	1	29	67	14
Ogata, Koichi, Carp	.300	530	75	159	35	0	29	82	8
Ochoa, Alex, Dragons	.294	507	83	149	28	0	21	65	5
Maeda, Tomonori, Carp	.290	427	50	124	14	2	21	71	2
Kanemoto, Tomoaki, Tigers	.289	532	94	154	24	2	19	77	18
Furuta, Atsuya, Swallows	.287	509	69	146	27	1	23	75	2
Betts, Todd, Swallows	.287	408	61	117	24	1	15	52	2

Kimura, Takuya, Carp	.285	473	64	135	19	0	13	38	14
Miyamoto, Shinya, Swallows	.284	543	78	154	20	1	7	44	11
Tatsunami, Kazuyoshi, Dragons	.280	500	52	140	28	2	13	80	2
Hiyama, Shinjiro, Tigers	.278	414	70	115	21	3	16	63	1
Woods, Tyrone, BayStars	.273	479	73	131	17	0	40	87	2
Ibata, Hirokazu, Dragons	.267	386	44	103	14	0	5	27	5
Arias, George, Tigers	.265	464	89	123	25	0	38	107	2
Araki, Masahiro, Dragons	.237	417	42	99	13	5	3	41	16
Arai, Takahiro, Carp	.236	488	58	115	20	2	19	62	2
Ishii, Takuro, BayStars	.231	415	49	96	12	1	6	26	20

Remaining U.S. and Latin Players

	AVG	AB	R	H	2B	3B	HR	RBI	SB
Petagine, Roberto, Giants	.323	331	70	107	17	0	34	81	1
Matsumoto, Daniel, Swallows	.286	14	2	4	1	0	0	0	0
Linares, Omar, Dragons	.229	144	19	33	9	0	6	28	0
Cruz, Ivan, Dragons	.222	225	21	50	8	1	11	34	1
Latham, Chris, Giants	.221	131	21	29	6	1	7	17	4
Hurst, Jimmy, Carp	.207	111	8	23	3	0	5	15	0
Cox, Steve, BayStars	.200	50	5	10	1	0	1	7	0

INDIVIDUAL PITCHING LEADERS

(Minimum 140 Innings)

	W	L	ERA	G	SV	IP	H	BB	SO
Igawa, Kei, Tigers	20	5	2.80	29	0	206	184	58	179
Hirai, Masafumi, Dragons	12	6	3.06	40	0	144	132	25	98
Kuroda, Hiroki, Carp	13	9	3.11	28	0	206	197	45	137
Uehara, Koji, Giants	16	5	3.17	27	0	207	190	23	194
Kisanuki, Hiroshi, Giants	10	7	3.34	25	0	175	168	44	180
Yamamoto, Masahiro, Dragons	9	7	3.58	26	0	156	156	35	121
Takahashi, Ken, Carp	9	8	3.66	24	0	167	174	36	127
Ishikawa, Masanori, Swallows	12	11	3.79	30	0	190	201	33	97
Irabu, Hideki, Tigers	13	8	3.85	27	0	173	186	47	164
Brock, Chris, Carp	8	8	3.94	24	0	144	165	37	88
Noguchi, Shigeki, Dragons	9	11	4.55	29	0	146	154	59	146
Holt, Chris, BayStars	5	14	4.55	24	0	146	175	33	93
Guzman, Domingo, BayStars	8	12	4.69	25	0	154	171	35	123

Remaining U.S. and Latin Players

	W	L	ERA	G	SV	IP	H	BB	SO
Riggan, Jerrod, Tigers	3	0	1.51	29	0	36	29	11	30
Williams, Jeff, Tigers	1	1	1.54	52	25	53	36	13	57
Davey, Tom, Carp	5	2	2.37	15	1	76	68	23	52
Beverlin, Jason, Swallows	8	4	4.08	19	0	106	114	36	94
Gaillard, Eddie, Dragond/Bay Stars	2	3	4.08	36	22	35	29	9	33
Rath, Gary, Giants	3	4	4.14	13	0	63	79	21	42
Moore, Trey, Tigers	10	6	4.35	21	0	112	122	39	94
Valdes, Marc, Dragons	0	3	4.45	37	1	59	54	24	38
Bailey, Cory, Giants	1	0	4.79	30	0	36	41	17	32
Santana, Julio, Giants	2	1	4.94	25	5	27	35	6	21
Hodges, Kevin, Swallows	5	9	5.90	20	0	101	119	39	48
Vargas, Martin, Dragons	0	2	6.65	6	0	22	34	9	15
Whiteside, Matt, BayStars	0	2	7.30	13	2	12	20	6	11
Randel, Matt, Giants	1	1	7.71	3	0	9	12	5	5
Newman, Alan, Carp	0	1	7.77	14	0	22	26	13	16
Lundquist, Dave, Carp	0	0	8.22	6	0	8	14	4	3
Pote, Lou, Tigers	0	1	9.64	8	1	9	16	1	8
Pedraza, Rodney, Giants	1	1	12.00	7	0	6	16	1	0

PACIFIC LEAGUE

STANDINGS

	W	L	T	PCT	GB
Fukuoka Daiei Hawks	82	55	3	.599	—
Seibu Lions	77	61	2	.558	5½
Osaka Kintetsu Buffaloes	74	64	2	.536	8½
Chiba Lotte Marines	68	69	3	.496	14
Nippon Ham Fighters	62	74	4	.456	19½
Orix BlueWave	48	88	4	.353	33½

INDIVIDUAL BATTING LEADERS

(Minimum 434 Plate Appearances)

	AVG	AB	R	H	2B	3B	HR	RBI	SB
Ogasawara, Michihiro, Fighters	.360	445	83	160	34	1	31	100	8
Tani, Yoshitomo, BlueWave	.350	540	86	189	37	1	21	92	9
Wada, Kazuhiro, Lions	.346	468	87	162	34	5	30	89	8
Iguchi, Tadahiro, Hawks	.340	515	112	175	37	1	27	109	42
Shibahara, Hiroshi, Hawks	.333	426	71	142	26	0	4	53	11
Jojima, Kenji, Hawks	.330	551	101	182	39	2	34	119	9
Tsuboi, Tomochika, Fighters	.330	443	70	146	26	3	5	40	13
Muramatsu, Akihito, Hawks	.324	463	85	150	29	13	6	57	32
Matsunaka, Nobuhiko, Hawks	.324	494	99	160	31	1	30	123	2
Cabrera, Alex, Lions	.324	457	85	148	24	0	50	112	2
Valdes, Pedro, Hawks	.311	453	72	141	24	2	26	104	1
Shiotani, Kazuhiko, BlueWave	.307	436	58	134	15	1	8	46	7
Brown, Roosevelt, BlueWave	.307	482	72	148	28	0	28	93	19
Matsui, Kazuo, Lions	.305	587	104	179	36	4	33	84	13
Fukuura, Kazuya, Marines	.304	567	75	172	50	1	21	76	2
Fernandez, Jose, Marines	.303	478	83	145	30	1	32	100	4
Short, Rick, Marines	.303	472	61	143	32	0	12	58	3
Yoshioka, Yuji, Buffaloes	.300	433	63	130	25	1	18	60	3
Omura, Naoyuki, Buffaloes	.300	550	94	165	34	7	16	61	27
Hori, Koichi, Marines	.298	470	78	140	24	0	22	78	3
Kawasaki, Munenori, Hawks	.294	493	78	145	17	9	2	51	30
Abe, Masahiro, Buffaloes	.291	398	58	116	28	1	6	43	6
Isobe, Koichi, Buffaloes	.288	444	56	128	26	3	12	72	9
Oshima, Koichi, BlueWave	.285	369	53	105	20	1	0	20	9
Ozeki, Tatsuya, Lions	.280	397	48	111	12	5	1	33	9
Rhodes, Tuffy, Buffaloes	.276	508	94	140	16	0	51	117	7
Echevarria, Angel, Fighters	.275	429	64	118	24	0	31	84	1
Kosaka, Makoto, Marines	.258	516	67	133	21	7	3	40	27
Ortiz, Jose, BlueWave	.255	470	70	120	29	2	33	86	4
Nakamura, Norihiro, Buffaloes	.236	381	54	90	14	1	23	67	1
McClain, Scott, Lions	.225	418	55	94	19	0	26	69	2

Remaining U.S. and Latin Players

	AVG	AB	R	H	2B	3B	HR	RBI	SB
Zuleta, Julio, Hawks	.266	214	33	57	14	0	13	43	0
Sheldon, Scott, BlueWave	.253	233	27	59	9	0	8	24	4
May, Derrick, Marines	.246	118	13	29	8	0	5	19	0
Nelson, Bryant, Hawks	.228	167	18	38	7	0	3	17	2
Cromer, D.T., Fighters	.201	184	20	37	5	1	7	25	1

INDIVIDUAL PITCHING LEADERS

(Minimum 140 Innings)

	W	L	ERA	G	SV	IP	H	BB	SO
Matsuzaka, Daisuke, Lions	16	7	2.83	29	0	194	165	63	215
Saito, Kazumi, Hawks	20	3	2.83	26	0	194	174	66	160
Shimizu, Naoyuki, Marines	15	10	3.13	28	0	204	200	53	147
Sugiuchi, Toshiya, Hawks	10	8	3.38	27	0	163	148	55	169
Wada, Tsuyoshi, Hawks	14	5	3.38	26	0	189	165	61	195
Iwakuma, Hisashi, Buffaloes	15	10	3.45	27	0	196	201	48	149
Watanabe, Shunsuke, Marines	9	4	3.66	20	0	140	114	31	74
Goto, Mitsutaka, Lions	10	7	3.81	23	0	142	150	34	91
Kobayashi, Hiroyuki, Marines	10	10	3.84	50	0	145	135	36	117
Powell, Jeremy, Buffaloes	14	12	4.13	28	0	196	192	63	165
Kanemura, Satoru, Fighters	10	8	4.24	26	0	157	149	56	103
Minchey, Nate, Marines	14	9	4.54	30	0	192	233	51	96
Mirabal, Carlos, Fighters	16	11	4.65	31	0	194	232	70	103

Remaining U.S. and Latin Players

	W	L	ERA	G	SV	IP	H	BB	SO
Sikorski, Brian, Marines	4	6	3.16	47	1	83	80	23	71
Skrmetta, Matt, Hawks	1	1	3.86	18	11	16	21	6	12
Beirne, Kevin, Buffaloes	8	7	4.37	30	0	130	109	48	107
Knight, Brandon, Hawks	6	4	4.86	16	0	87	105	45	77
Seelbach, Chris, Fighters	2	8	5.61	16	0	79	100	36	33
Rodriguez, Nerio, Buffaloes	3	2	6.61	7	0	33	42	14	13
Phillips, Jason, BlueWave	2	3	6.98	7	0	39	50	15	21
Mallette, Brian, Buffaloes	0	0	14.40	4	0	5	11	1	1

Lee home runs highlight season

KOREA

The 2003 season was considered the greatest ever in Korea as Samsung outfielder Lee Seung-Yeop dominated the season with his home run feats, exciting Korean fans like Barry Bonds and Mark McGwire did in the United States.

Lee, 27, became the youngest player in professional baseball history to reach 300 career home runs. He also broke the Asian single-season home run record of 55, previously held by Japan's Sadaharu Oh. Lee finished with 56, while hitting .301 with 144 RBIs.

Lee's 300th career home run ball was sold for the equivalent of $100,000, so fans with butterfly nets crowded the outfield fence hoping to strike it rich with number 56. In typical dramatic fashion, Lee waited until the last game of the season to hit his 56th. The ball just inched over the outfield wall and was picked up by a worker in a small area between the outfield wall and the bleachers. Lee, a free agent at the end of the season, was expected to play in the major leagues in 2004.

Shim Jong-Soo of league champion Hyundai hit .355-53-142 and was expected to be in a tight race with Lee for MVP honors, but Lee ran away with the voting, winning his fifth award in the last seven seasons. Shim is expected to play in the majors in 2005, when he will be an unrestricted free agent.

THOMAS ST. JOHN
Lee Seung-Yeop

Shim's teammate Chong Min-Tae led the league with a 17-2 record and import Shane Bowers was tops in the league with a 3.01 ERA.

Chong also was the star in Hyundai's third Korean Series title in six seasons. He won Games One, Four and Seven of the series, as Hyundai knocked off the SK Wyverns in seven games. In the deciding game, Chong pitched a complete-game, 7-0 win. Outfielder Cliff Brumbaugh led Hyundai during the Korean Series, hitting .333 with 10 RBIs.

The Wyverns had finished the regular season in fourth place, but swept defending champion Samsung and Kia in the playoffs to earn a spot in the championship series.

—THOMAS ST. JOHN

STANDINGS

	W	L	T	PCT	GB
Hyundai	80	51	2	.611	—
Kia	78	50	5	.609	2
Samsung	76	53	4	.589	4
SK	66	64	3	.508	14
Hanwha	63	65	5	.492	17
LG	60	71	2	.458	20
Doosan	57	74	2	.435	23
Lotte	39	91	3	.300	41

PLAYOFFS—Quarterfinal: SK defeated Samsung 2-0 in best-of-3 series. **Semifinal:** SK defeated Kia 3-0 in best-of-5 series. **Final:** Hyundai defeated SK 4-3 in best-of-7 series.

INDIVIDUAL BATTING LEADERS

	AVG	AB	R	H	HR	RBI
Shim Jong-Soo, Hyundai	.355	460	110	154	53	142
Kim Dong-Joo, Doosan	.342	401	61	137	23	89
Ahn Kyung-Hyun, Doosan	.333	475	65	158	10	72
Yang Joon-Hyuk, Samsung	.329	490	90	161	33	92
Lee Jin-Young, SK	.328	481	81	158	17	70
Park Han-Lee, Samsung	.322	528	113	170	12	59
Kim Tae-Kyun, Hanwha	.319	479	67	153	31	95
Jang Sung-Ho, Kia	.315	476	93	150	21	105
Lee Jeong-Bum, Kia	.315	524	110	165	20	61
Kim Dong-Soo, Hyundai	.308	367	48	113	16	68

Other Foreign Players

	AVG	AB	R	H	HR	RBI
Perez, Roberto, Lotte	.314	194	32	61	9	30
Brumbaugh, Cliff, Hyundai	.303	264	45	80	14	51
Encarnacion, Mario, Lotte	.290	338	45	98	13	45
Diaz, Eddy, SK	.285	439	56	125	22	63
Alcantara, Israel, LG	.281	292	38	82	16	44
Martinez, Manny, LG	.272	483	70	132	17	70
Mejia, Roberto, Hanwha	.259	112	9	29	3	41
Brito, Tilson, Samsung	.255	380	59	97	20	58
Franklin, Micah, Hyundai	.221	136	24	30	10	28
Coolbaugh, Mike, Doosan	.215	149	24	32	10	24
Cookson, Brent, LG	.214	70	6	15	2	5
Rodriguez, Boi, Lotte	.190	21	0	4	0	0

INDIVIDUAL PITCHING LEADERS

	W	L	ERA	SV	IP	H	BB	SO
Bowers, Shane, Hyundai	13	4	3.01	0	144	145	46	85
Lee Seung-Ho, LG	11	11	3.19	0	192	151	103	157
Chong Min-Tae, Hyundai	17	2	3.31	0	177	179	42	122
Kim Jin-Woo, Kia	11	5	3.45	0	169	150	63	146
Lee Sang-Mok, Hanwha	15	7	3.54	1	185	203	29	85
Im Chang-Yong, Samsung	13	3	3.55	1	147	141	44	85
Iriki, Satoshi , Doosan	7	11	3.74	5	159	155	53	87
Kiefer, Mark, Kia/Doosan	8	7	3.79	0	169	160	46	77
Rios, Daniel, Kia	10	13	3.82	0	189	186	62	121
Chong Min-Chul, Hanwha	11	10	4.00	0	140	132	51	73

Other Foreign Players

	W	L	ERA	SV	IP	H	BB	SO
Johnson, Michael, Kia	8	1	3.00	3	69	49	31	53
Picota, Lenin, Hanwha	2	6	3.86	15	56	62	19	43
Smith, Travis, SK	7	10	4.20	0	152	157	61	82
Giron, Emiliano, Hanwha	3	3	4.59	1	65	62	31	49
Estrada, Horacio, Hanwha	1	3	4.71	0	36	30	13	26
Ryan, Glenn, Samsung	1	3	5.02	1	57	65	16	28
Elvira, Narciso, Samsung	1	0	7.06	1	22	20	13	21

Brother wins as leagues merge

TAIWAN

The 2003 Taiwan season emphatically answered one question, but left another unanswered.

The obvious issue resolved was that the caliber of play in the old Taiwan Major League was a class below that of the rival Chinese Professional Baseball League. The 2003 season saw a merger of the bitter rivals as the Taiwanese government brokered a deal to allow the Macoto Gida and First Financial Agan of the TML to be absorbed by the four holdover teams of the CPBL.

The Agan and Gida proved they were mismatched, with First Financial setting a league mark for the worst half season—9-37, .196—in the first half, only to have Macoto match it in the second half.

The two teams' futility was exacerbated by horrendous records compiled by import players on their pitching staffs. A total of 24 foreign pitchers on the two teams combined for only 18 wins during the season.

The question left outstanding was whether any team will ever stop the Brother Elephants, who rolled to their third straight league championship and sixth title overall.

Brother's import duo of Japan's Nakagomi Sin and American Jonathan Hurst combined for 25 wins. Sinon players won top individual honors on the year though. Bulls third baseman Chang Tai-shan (.328-28-94) was named league MVP and teammate Jeff Andra, who went 14-3, 2.01, was voted as the league's top pitcher.

Rookie of the year went to right-hander Pan Wei-lun of Uni-President Lions, who went 13-8, 2.43.

The Elephants won the second half going away with a 36-11 record, and then beat the first half champion Sinon Bulls four games to two in the league championship series. Brother outfielder Chen Chih-yuan earned series MVP honors as he hit .410 with seven RBIs.

The renewed interest in the Taiwan Series pushed average attendance to a record 14,500 per game. When fans left without tickets to the sold out Game Six in Taipei, they vented their anger that scalpers and politicians were able to obtain tickets. Many fans who had camped out overnight in a futile effort to get tickets threw eggs and attacked scalpers. Riot policemen were called in to stop the fighting.

Tempers were hot on the field, as well. In Game Five, Sinon manager Chen Wei-cheng reacted to a controversial call at first base by throwing a punch at one of the umpires. The league socked Chen with a $3,000 fine and an immediate five-game suspension.

–JEFFREY WILSON

STANDINGS

	W	L	T	PCT	GB
#Brother Elephants	63	31	6	.670	—
+Sinon Bulls	62	32	6	.660	1
Uni-President Lions	54	39	7	.581	8½
China Trust Whales	51	43	6	.543	12
Macoto Gida	30	64	6	.319	33
First Financial Agan	20	71	9	.220	41½

+ First-half champion #Second-half champion

PLAYOFFS—Brother Elephants defeated Sinon 4-2 in best-of-7 series.

INDIVIDUAL BATTING LEADERS

(Minimum 270 At-Bats)

	AVG	AB	R	H	2B	3B	HR	RBI	SB
Peng Cheng-min, Brother	.355	369	83	131	25	3	18	83	22
Chen Chih-yuan, Brother	.342	401	84	137	20	6	18	97	31
Yoshimi Hiroaki, Uni-President	.334	368	62	123	19	3	1	47	13
Chen Lien-hung, Uni-President	.333	333	46	111	19	3	10	62	5
Chang Tai-shan, Sinon	.328	396	82	130	21	4	28	94	22
Hung Chi-feng, China Trust	.309	272	45	84	17	2	9	45	2
Tseng Hua-wei, Sinon	.302	367	57	111	19	6	1	57	15
Huang Chung-yi, Sinon	.300	370	50	111	19	2	6	50	9
Lin Hung-yuan, Uni-President	.295	302	42	89	18	2	9	42	1
Chen Huai-shan, Brother	.294	354	50	104	16	3	4	50	6

Other Foreign Players

	AVG	AB	R	H	2B	3B	HR	RBI	SB
Melo, Juan, China Trust	.316	76	11	24	1	0	3	16	2
Ozuna, Rafael, First Financial	.281	96	13	27	5	0	4	12	1
Francois, Manny, First Financial	.214	14	2	3	0	0	0	1	0
Estrada, Omani, Macoto	.200	95	6	19	3	0	1	8	1
Matins, Anthony, First Financial	.000	7	0	0	0	0	0	0	0

INDIVIDUAL PITCHING LEADERS

(Minimum 100 Innings)

	W	L	ERA	G	SV	IP	H	BB	SO
Frascatore, John, Uni-President	8	4	1.80	13	0	100	86	22	82
Andra, Jeff, Sinon	14	3	2.01	25	1	183	158	61	149
Nakayama, Hiroaki, China Trust	13	4	2.20	25	0	180	169	38	106
Pan, Wei-lun, Uni-President	13	8	2.43	26	0	166	143	42	104
Sin, Nakagomi, Brother	13	8	2.53	22	3	163	157	32	129
Hurst, Jonathan, Brother	12	4	2.53	20	0	149	129	38	113
Davenport, Joe, Uni-President	8	4	2.63	16	0	109	102	41	48
Hsieh Cheng-hsun, China Trust	9	5	2.74	37	0	128	116	48	82
Hisanori, Yokota, Brother	16	3	2.90	25	0	164	158	52	162
Martinez, Osvaldo, Sinon	12	11	3.12	32	3	170	144	58	182

Other Foreign Players

	W	L	ERA	G	SV	IP	H	BB	SO
Mallard, Randi, First Financial	0	0	0.00	2	1	6	7	5	5
Morel, Ramon, Sinon	4	2	0.90	48	23	69	47	20	69
Parra, Jose, Uni-President	5	1	1.51	14	1	71	44	20	54
Martinez, Gomez, Brother	4	3	1.69	9	0	58	49	19	52
Pena, Jesus, Macoto	2	1	2.29	8	0	19	18	4	15
Munoz, Bobby, Macoto	0	1	2.65	14	7	17	17	5	14
Burgos, John, Uni-President	5	4	2.76	10	0	65	63	15	51
Galva, Claudio, First Financial	4	6	2.92	18	1	98	85	45	69
Moylan, Peter, Macoto	1	0	3.00	4	0	12	12	4	6
Mikkelsen, Linc, First Financial	1	4	3.15	9	0	54	55	24	30
Guzman, Geraldo, China Trust	1	2	3.42	4	0	23	21	5	20
Rosa, Maximo, China Trust	3	5	3.44	32	9	96	92	43	63
Marchesano, Michael, Macoto	2	13	3.86	7	1	30	32	17	21
Nunez, Maximo, Uni-President	3	0	3.91	12	0	48	50	20	19
Ozuna, Gab, First Financial	0	1	4.19	21	0	111	124	24	73
Lopez, Joan, Macoto	3	0	4.57	4	0	21	22	8	11
Kamar, Emil, Macoto	0	1	4.91	3	0	14	12	16	6
Bicknell, Greg, First Financial	0	8	5.05	13	0	76	85	43	47
Williams, Shad, Macoto	1	6	5.16	9	0	52	54	19	29
Darley, Ned, Macoto	1	4	5.92	8	2	24	37	17	10
Henthrone, Kevin, Macoto	0	3	5.95	5	0	19	32	6	8
Burlingame, Ben, First Financial	2	2	6.18	6	0	27	32	17	12
Bennett, Shayne, Macoto	0	2	7.48	8	2	27	34	15	18
Acosta, John, First Financial	0	1	8.31	13	1	21	37	16	14
Hernandez, Jose, Macoto	0	1	8.78	5	0	13	21	10	6
Hasselhoff, Derek, China Trust	0	1	9.00	3	0	2	4	3	3
Samboy, Javier, First Financial	0	1	13.50	1	0	2	3	4	3
Agosto, Stevenson, U-P	0	0	13.50	1	0	2	3	4	3
Chipperfield, Calvin, FF	0	2	14.85	2	0	6	14	4	3

First season interrupted by SARS

CHINA

As if launching a new professional league wasn't difficult enough, the China Baseball League had to battle through Severe Acute Respiratory Syndrome to complete its first full season in 2003.

The season was originally scheduled to conclude in June, but the government ordered the season suspended for more than a month as part of measures that halted all sports events in China as the country tried to control the spread of the disease.

When play resumed, the Tianjin Lions rolled to the best record, going 18-6, five games better than the second-place Beijing Lions.

But in the playoffs, the Lions pulled off the upset, knocking off Tianjin three games to two with a 4-3 win in the 11th inning in the deciding Game 5. Tianjin starter Linc Mikkelsen took a 2-0 shutout into the eighth, but Beijing rallied, finally edging Tianjin with a run in the 11th off of reliever Ned Darley.

–JEFFREY WILSON

STANDINGS

	W	L	PCT	GB
Tianjin Lions	18	6	.750	—
Beijing Tigers	13	11	.542	5
Guangdong Leopards	9	15	.375	9
Shanghai Eagles	8	16	.333	10

PLAYOFFS: Beijing defeated Tianjin 3-2 in best-of-5 series.

INDIVIDUAL BATTING LEADERS

(Minimum 65 At-Bats)

	AVG	AB	R	H	2B	3B	HR	RBI	SB
Wang Wei, Beijing	.364	66	11	24	5	3	3	14	1
Liu Jianzhong, Tianjin	.350	100	17	35	5	2	0	17	3
Chen Zhe, Beijing	.338	77	10	26	7	1	0	14	0
Li Qinghua, Beijing	.325	77	18	25	8	2	1	12	1
Zhang Hongbo, Guangdong	.318	88	15	28	3	2	2	9	5
Zhang Yufeng, Shanghai	.315	89	11	28	7	2	1	12	2
Luo Yubin, Tianjin	.313	67	13	21	5	1	0	9	2
Hou Fenglian, Tianjin	.300	100	17	30	4	2	0	15	16
Liu Guangbiao, Guangdong	.287	87	14	25	4	2	0	8	14
Jiang Shaoning, Beijing	.280	82	15	23	7	1	0	5	2

Other Foreign Players

	AVG	AB	R	H	2B	3B	HR	RBI	SB
Clemente, Edgard, Tianjin	.277	47	9	13	4	0	0	2	3

INDIVIDUAL PITCHING LEADERS

(Minimum 24 Innings)

	W	L	ERA	G	IP	H	BB	SO
Bai Baoliang, Tianjin	4	1	1.27	10	36	17	11	32
Lai Guojun, Guangdong	1	0	1.46	10	37	30	7	25
Li Peng, Shanghai	1	1	1.65	10	27	20	1	10
Su Zhanglong, Tianjin	3	1	2.33	11	34	26	11	43
Wang Nan, Beijing	2	1	2.35	11	38	27	18	32
Harris, Jeff, Tianjin	4	2	2.47	6	43	34	2	29
Li Zhenhao, Beijing	6	6	2.78	11	68	58	20	50
Ye Mingqiang, Shanghai	2	3	3.00	9	51	46	20	23
Huang Fangwei, Shanghai	4	7	3.03	12	68	61	42	38
Zhu Wanyun, Guangdong	1	1	3.09	9	32	30	5	12

Other Foreign Players

	W	L	ERA	G	IP	H	BB	SO
Darley, Ned, Tianjin	1	0	1.59	4	11	8	4	11
Mikkelsen, Linc, Tianjin	2	0	2.08	3	13	9	5	11
Rain, Steve, Tianjin	1	0	3.60	3	5	3	6	2

Veteran pitchers lead Bologna

Thanks to a couple of aging stars, Bologna managed to shakeup the power structure in Italy's Serie A/1 in 2003.

Behind the pitching of 40-year-old Rolando Cretis and 39-year-old Dan Newman, Bologna knocked off Modena four games to one in the Italy Series for its first title since 1984, and the first that any team but Nettuno, Rimini or Parma had won since 1989.

ITALY

Cretis, a righthander, had the best season of a Serie A/1 career that started in 1979, as he went 13-2, 2.81. Newman, a former minor leaguer who has played in Italy since 1989, went 10-5, 4.45 for his fourth-straight season of double-digit wins—no small accomplishment considering the 54-game Italian League schedule.

Cretis was one of several newcomers on the Bologna roster. Former Seattle farmhand Claudo Liverziani hit three homers in the Italy Series and was among the league leaders in several offensive categories as he hit .368-11-50. The new set of imports included catcher Nelson Antigua, who was chosen as the series MVP.

Modena reached the Italy Series by beating defending champion Rimini in the semifinals. Down three games to two in the best-of-seven series, Modena won the next two games in Rimini, as righthander Cipriano Ventura won three of the four games for Modena.

The Italian national team slumped in the European Championship and finished fifth. But Italy rebounded to win the European Olympic qualifier and earn a berth in the 2004 Summer Games.

—HARVEY SAHKER

STANDINGS

	W	L	PCT	GB
Bologna	42	12	.778	—
Rimini	36	18	.667	6
Modena	36	18	.667	6
Grosseto	35	19	.648	7
Nettuno	31	23	.574	11
Parma	23	31	.426	19
San Marino	23	31	.426	19
Anzio	21	33	.389	21
Reggiana	15	39	.278	27
Firenze	8	46	.148	34

INDIVIDUAL BATTING LEADERS

	AVG	AB	R	H	2B	3B	HR	RBI	SB
Martinez, Greg, Grosseto	.425	214	69	91	13	5	3	21	23
Munoz, Orlando, Modena	.402	204	54	82	19	2	0	32	11
Tavarez, Ramon, Anzio	.380	200	43	76	15	1	5	41	7
Rodriguez, Liubiemthz, Grosseto	.380	137	28	52	13	3	1	34	5
de los Santos, Luis, Nettuno	.370	200	42	74	8	1	13	59	3
Liverziani, Claudio, Bolgona	.368	190	67	70	18	2	11	50	8
Rigoli, David, Bologna	.364	214	55	78	15	3	8	34	24
Schiavetti, Igor, Nettuno	.360	203	38	73	11	4	1	24	0
Frignani, Daniele, Bologna	.358	204	36	73	14	4	7	46	3
Dallospedale, Davide, Bologna	.353	232	82	56	10	4	1	42	21

INDIVIDUAL PITCHING LEADERS

	W	L	ERA	G	SV	IP	H	BB	SO
Vigna, Juan Carlos, Nettuno	9	3	2.25	20	3	100	88	19	100
Cabalisti, Roberto, Rimini	5	3	2.31	17	2	94	79	24	71
Patrone, Sandy, Rimini	9	4	2.86	18	1	104	97	20	88
Ventura, Cipriano, Modena	9	2	2.34	16	0	127	114	20	116
Montine, Ivan, San Marino	7	3	2.59	15	0	90	68	36	99
Sanchez, Martin, Rimini	7	0	2.80	12	0	80	71	17	73
Cretis, Rolando, Bologna	13	2	2.81	18	0	109	104	15	66
Meacham, Russ, Grosseto	5	3	2.91	8	0	59	58	6	52
Heredia, Julian, Bologna	4	2	2.91	8	0	56	38	11	66
Tonkin, Shane, Rimini	5	4	2.97	17	5	64	62	10	36

Neptunas picks up fifth straight

The path was a little more difficult, but the result was the same, as Neptunus picked up its fifth straight Dutch national title in 2003. It beat the Hague Tornados three games to two in a best-of-five semifinal series and then beat HCAW three games to two in the best-of-five final.

HOLLAND

With the victory, Neptunus equaled OVVO of Amsterdam's record for most consecutive titles. OVVO won five straight titles from 1949-1953.

The Neptunus pitching tandem of Rob Cordemans and Eelco Jansen dominated Dutch Major League batters during the regular season. Cordemans won the triple crown of pitching as he went 12-1, 0.93 with 106 strikeouts to lead the league in wins, ERA and strikeouts. Jansen was not far behind in any category, as he was 11-2, 1.40.

Hoofddorp's Glenn Romney hit .367 to win the DML batting crown, edging teammate Aaron Merhoff, who hit .365. Dirk van t' Klooster was third at .350. He was the only Neptunus player in the top 10.

Neptunus also won its fourth straight European Cup. The continental club championship took place in Italy. Neptunus defeated Italy's Rimini in the finale.

There was a continued power shortage in the DML. Home run totals have been drastically lower since the league returned to wood bats a few years ago. Neptunus infielder E.J. t'Hoen, a former Angels farmhand, led the DML with just five homers.

The Netherlands won the 28th European Championship and earned a trip to Athens by finishing second in the continent's Olympic qualification tournament. Both competitions took place on Dutch soil. The national team was managed by former big league skipper Davey Johnson, who was filling in for Robert Eenhoorn.

—HARVEY SAHKER

STANDINGS

PLAYOFF POOL	W	L	T	PCT	GB
Neptunus	33	7	2	.810	—
Hoofddorp Pioniers	31	10	1	.750	2½
HCAW	29	13	0	.690	5
Hague Tornado's	22	19	1	.536	11½
Kinheim	16	24	2	.405	17
Amsterdam Pirates	14	28	0	.333	20

PROMOTION/RELEGATION POOL

	W	L	T	PCT	GB
PSV Eindhoven	18	1	1	.925	—
Almere	12	7	1	.625	6
Oosterhout Twins	10	10	0	.500	8½
Sparta/Feyenoord	8	11	1	.425	10
Quick	6	13	1	.325	12
RCH	4	16	0	.200	14½

WINTER LEAGUES

Dominicans win Caribbean Series; strife derails Venezuelan season

BY ERIC EDWARDS

The Caribbean Series is normally the showcase event in winter baseball, but the 2003 series, played in Carolina, P.R., and 2002-03 season as a whole were overshadowed by a civil strife in Venezuela that forced cancellation of the season in that country.

A national strike, aimed at forcing either the resignation of President Hugo Chavez or a call for early elections, was called in Venezuela on Dec. 2, 2002, paralyzing important sectors such as the oil industry, considered the lifeblood of the South American economy.

The Venezuelan League suspended games for several weeks before electing to cancel the season altogether when the strife continued. The league made its decision because the security of all parties involved, including fans, could not be guaranteed. It had held out hope that a playoff series, which would have qualified a team for the Caribbean Series, could be held but that notion was abandoned.

David Ortiz

Instead of a team from Venezuela, host Puerto Rico was allowed to field a second team in the six-game, double-elimination event.

For the second time in four years, a Caribbean Series title came into focus for Puerto Rico's Mayaguez Indians—until David Ortiz struck a blow that had them seeing double.

The Dominican Republic first baseman, whose two-run double capped an 11th-inning comeback in the decisive game in 1999, was again the scourge of the Puerto Ricans. He led an offensive charge that helped Aguilas win the final two games of the annual four-nation tournament to capture their fifth Series championship in seven years.

Home Away From Home

The Dominicans triumphed on Puerto Rican turf for the second time in a row—this time with an immigrant turnout that had the Puerto Rican champions feeling like the games were being staged in the suburbs of Santo Domingo instead of San Juan.

Ortiz finished the Series with a .462 average (12-for-26), two home runs, 11 RBIs and eight runs scored, edging American League Most Valuable Player and teammate Miguel Tejada (.462-0-7, nine runs) for the MVP award.

Over his team's last three games—all of them do-or-die—Ortiz went 9-for-11 with a home run, six RBIs and four runs scored.

"I thrive in this environment," said Ortiz, who two weeks earlier had signed a contract with the Boston Red Sox after being released by the Minnesota Twins. "There's such a rivalry between the two teams and such passion flowing from our fans. It just gets the juices going a little bit more than normal."

The two-game Dominican barrage

2003 CARIBBEAN SERIES

Carolina, Puerto Rico
Feb. 1-8, 2003

ROUND-ROBIN STANDINGS	W	L	PCT	GB
Dominican Republic (Aguilas)	6	1	.857	—
Puerto Rico-1 (Mayaguez)	5	2	.714	1
Puerto Rico-2 (Caguas)	2	4	.333	3½
Mexico (Los Mochis)	0	6	.000	5½

INDIVIDUAL BATTING LEADERS
(Minimum 16 Plate Appearances)

	AVG	AB	R	H	2B	3B	HR	RBI	SB
Tejada, Miguel, Dom. Rep.	.462	26	9	12	4	2	0	7	1
Ortiz, David, Dom. Rep.	.462	26	8	12	5	0	2	11	0
Valentin, Javier, PR-1	.429	21	2	9	2	0	0	4	0
Ortiz, Hector, PR-2	.385	13	1	5	0	0	1	1	0
Merced, Orlando, PR-2	.375	24	5	9	3	0	3	6	6
Lopez, Luis, PR-1	.375	16	4	6	2	0	1	5	0
Mondesi, Raul, Dom. Rep.	.375	16	1	6	0	0	1	4	0
Orantes, Ramon, Mexico	.364	22	1	8	2	0	0	0	0
Polonia, Luis, Dom. Rep.	.344	32	5	11	4	0	0	3	0
Valentin, Jose, PR-1	.333	24	6	8	4	0	1	3	1
Smith, Bubba, Mexico	.333	21	1	7	1	0	0	1	0
Garcia, Omar, PR-2	.320	25	3	8	2	0	0	0	0

INDIVIDUAL PITCHING LEADERS
(Minimum 6 Innings)

	W	L	ERA	G	SV	IP	H	BB	SO
Calero, Kiko, PR-1	1	0	0.00	1	0	6	2	1	6
Rojas, Chris, PR-1	1	0	0.00	1	0	6	4	0	0
Porzio, Mike, PR-1	1	0	0.00	1	0	6	5	0	2
Navarro, Jaime, PR-2	0	0	1.17	2	0	8	6	2	7
Pichardo, Hipolito, Dom Rep.	2	0	1.42	3	0	6	7	1	7
Cabrera, Fernando, PR-1	0	0	1.50	2	1	6	3	1	8
Acevedo, Jose, Dom. Rep.	1	0	2.38	2	0	11	7	4	15
Patrick, Bronswell, Mexico	0	1	2.57	1	0	7	4	1	7

ALL-TOURNAMENT TEAM: C—Hector Ortiz, Puerto Rico-2. **1B**—David Ortiz, Dominican Republic. **2B**—Rafael Furcal, Dominican Republic. **3B**—Ramon Orantes, Mexico. **SS**—Miguel Tejada, Dominican Repiblic. **OF**—Orlando Merced, Puerto Rico-2; Luis Polonia, Dominican Republic; Jose Valentin, Puerto Rico-1. **DH**—Luis Lopez, Puerto Rico-1. **RHP**—Kiko Calero, Puerto Rico-1. **LHP**—Angel Miranda, Puerto Rico-2. **RP**—Hipolito Pichardo, Dominican Republic. **Manager:** Nick Leyva, Puerto Rico-1.

2002-03 WINTER LEAGUE ALL-STARS

Selected by Baseball America

Pos.	Player, Team (League)	Organization	AVG	AB	H	HR	RBI	SB
C	Eliezer Alfonzo, Oriente (Venezuela)	Cubs	.316	136	43	8	29	0
1B	Ken Harvey, Scottsdale (AFL)	Royals	.479	117	56	7	34	0
2B	D'Angelo Jimenez, Licey (Dominican)	White Sox	.312	138	43	5	31	2
3B	Jose Castillo, Caracas (Venezuela)	Pirates	.327	147	48	8	27	5
SS	Jose Reyes, Gigantes (Dominican)	Mets	.274	190	52	5	22	22
OF	Luke Allen, Azucareros (Dominican)	Rockies	.316	152	48	7	35	0
OF	Ruben Mateo, Escogido (Dominican)	Reds	.308	117	36	11	31	2
OF	Rene Reyes, Caracas (Venezuela)	Rockies	.346	127	44	3	18	5
DH	Julio Zuleta, Guasave (Mexico)	Red Sox	.319	238	76	23	61	0

Pos.	Pitcher, Team (League)	Organization	W–L	ERA	IP	H	BB	SO
SP	Edgar Gonzalez, Hermosillo (Mexico)	Diamondbacks	8–2	2.08	82	68	22	44
SP	Kiko Calero, Mayaguez (Puerto Rico)	Cardinals	7–2	1.73	78	53	27	58
SP	Bobby Jenks, Scottsdale (AFL)	Angels	1–1	1.08	42	33	17	54
SP	Oscar Villarreal, Mexicali (Mexico)	Diamondbacks	9–4	3.87	93	80	41	85
RP	Arnie Munoz, Aguilas (Dominican)	White Sox	4–0	1.83	44	26	12	79

Player of the Year: Arnie Munoz, lhp, Aguilas (Dominican).

Munoz rises to occasion

PLAYER of the YEAR

En route to establishing a Dominican League record for strikeouts by a reliever—ringing up 74 in 41 regular season innings and limiting opponents to a .165 average—Arnie Munoz took home the circuit's pitcher and rookie of the year awards and earned Baseball America's 2002-03 Winter Player of the Year honors.

STEVE MOORE

Arnie Munoz

Some hitters might overlook the diminutive 5-foot-9, 170-pound White Sox left-hander coming out of the bullpen. But his performance for Caribbean World Series champion Aguilas may have finally earned him the recognition he deserved.

"He has a real good feel for his curveball," said Dave Jauss, a Red Sox scout who managed Licey in the Dominican. "He can throw it for a strike or get guys to chase it out of the zone. And he has a nice change and a fastball with at least average velocity and sometimes above. He's short in stature until he takes the mound. Then he's not short anymore."

PREVIOUS WINNERS

1985-1986—Wally Joyner, 1b, Mayaguez (Puerto Rico)
1986-1987—Vicente Palacios, rhp, Mexicali (Mexican Pacific)
1987-1988—Jose Nunez, rhp, Escogido (Dominican Republic)
1988-1989—Phil Stephenson, 1b, Zulia (Venezuela)
1989-1990—Edgar Martinez, 3b, San Juan (Puerto Rico)
1990-1991—Henry Rodriguez, of, Licey (Dominican Republic)
1991-1992—Wilson Alvarez, lhp, Zulia (Venezuela)
1992-1993—Matias Carrillo, of, Mexicali (Mexican Pacific)
1993-1994—John Hudek, rhp, Magallanes (Venezuela)
1994-1995—Carlos Delgado, c, San Juan (Puerto Rico)
1995-1996—Darryl Brinkley, of, Mexicali (Mexican Pacific)
1996-1997—Bartolo Colon, rhp, Aguilas (Dominican Republic)
1997-1998—Jose Hernandez, ss, Mayaguez (Puerto Rico)
1998-1999—Bob Abreu, of, Caracas (Venezuela)
1999-2000—Morgan Burkhart, 1b, Navojoa (Mexican Pacific)
2000-2001—Courtney Duncan, rhp, Caguas (Puerto Rico)
2001-2002—Ramon Hernandez, c, Pastora (Veneuzuela)

broadsided a Mayaguez pitching staff, which had allowed just eight runs in its previous 10 games, all victories.

Heading into the final meeting with the Dominicans in round-robin play, the Puerto Rican champions were 5-0 and had allowed just three earned runs and were closing in on a tournament record in that category. In their first game against the Dominicans, Kiko Calero and Fernando Cabrera allowed just two hits as Mayaguez romped to a 10-0 victory.

In the rematch, the Dominicans surpassed that total in the first inning as they won 6-0. The Dominicans finished the six-game round-robin tied with Mayaguez at 5-1, forcing a tie-breaking game the next night.

The tiebreaker played out in almost identical fashion as the Dominicans scored four times in the opening inning and cruised to a 7-3 victory.

"That first inning killed us," Mayaguez manager Nick Leyva said. "If we can hold them to a run there and take it to the middle innings down just a run or two, with the bullpen we have, I would have liked our chances."

Mayaguez was also handicapped by the absence of Venezuela from the competition. Tournament organizers replaced Venezuela with the Puerto Rican League runners-up, Caguas. Unable to draw from the Criollos' roster as they would have under normal circumstances, the Indians were forced to add two reinforcement pitchers to the starting rotation, righthanders Dicky Gonzalez and Josue Matos, who played for Carolina in the Puerto Rican league but hadn't pitched in more than a month.

Gonzalez was the losing pitcher in the rematch with the Dominicans and Matos took the loss in the tiebreaker.

DOMINICAN LEAGUE

A year after being disappointed in the Dominican League playoffs, Aguilas pulled off a clean sweep in 2002-03.

Aguilas had the best record in the regular season for the fourth year in a row, and swept Escogido for the Dominican League crown. They then rolled to the Caribbean Series title.

Aguilas had seemed to be on a similar path a year earlier, only to be upset by Licey in seven games in the championship series.

This time, that wasn't a concern, as Aguilas rode the league's best hitter and best pitcher to the title.

Second baseman Bernie Castro (Padres) became the first player to lead the league in hitting in his first two seasons, as he won his second straight batting title. He hit .366 for Aguilas while also going a perfect 16-of-16 on steals. Castro built on his strong winter by hitting .309 for Triple-A Portland during the 2003 season.

RODGER WOOD

Bernie Castro

While Castro was leading the league in hitting, 5-foot-9 left-hander Arnie Munoz (White Sox) was playing as big a part in Aguilas' success as a closer. Munoz dominated the league like no reliever ever had, going 4-0, 1.55 with four saves. He won the ERA title and managed to league the league with 74 strikeouts in only 41 innings.

"He has incredible stuff for a little kid and shows outstanding command," Aguilas pitching coach Juan Jimenez said. "He goes after hitters with no fear. The guy surprised veteran hitters using his curve in 3-2 counts. You don't see that very often from young pitchers. He is some kind of a phenom."

The league's best prospects was Gigantes shortstop Jose Reyes (Mets), 19, who displayed outstanding actions in the field, tremendous body control and a plus arm while leading the league in stolen bases (17) and triples (5).

STANDINGS

REGULAR SEASON	W	L	PCT	GB
Aguilas	33	17	.660	—
Estrellas	28	22	.560	5
Gigantes	27	23	.540	6
Escogido Lions	26	24	.520	7
Licey Tigers	20	30	.400	13
Azucareros	16	34	.320	17
PLAYOFFS	**W**	**L**	**PCT**	**GB**
Aguilas	11	5	.688	—
Escogido Lions	10	8	.556	2
Estrelles	8	9	.471	3½
Gigantes	5	12	.294	6½

Championship Series: Aguilas defeated Escogido 4-0 in best-of-7 series.

TOP 10 PROSPECTS: 1. Jose Reyes, ss, Gigantes (Mets). **2.** Ervin Santana, rhp, Estrellas (Angels). **3.** Wilson Betemit, ss, Escogido (Braves). **4.** Franklyn German, rhp, Escogido (Tigers). **5.** Arnie Munoz, lhp, Aguilas (White Sox). **6.** Rafael Soriano, rhp, Escogido (Mariners). **7.** Alfredo Gonzalez, rhp, Azucareros (Dodgers). **8.** Francis Beltran, rhp, Estrellas (Cubs). **9.** Alexis Gomez, of, Aguilas (Royals). **10.** Duaner Sanchez, rhp, Gigantes (Pirates).

Statistics in **bold** indicate league leader.
League leader but non-qualifier

INDIVDUAL BATTING LEADERS
(Minimum 75 At-Bats)

	AVG	AB	R	H	2B	3B	HR	RBI	SB
Castro, Bernie, Aguilas	**.366**	123	22	45	6	1	0	9	16
Felix, Pedro, Gigantes	.363	113	16	41	4	2	3	11	3
Pena, Elvis, Escogido	.354	79	14	28	3	1	0	4	2
Perez, Neifi, Escogido	.329	82	20	27	5	1	3	10	2
Truby, Chris, Estrellas	.329	76	15	25	2	0	3	10	2
Furcal, Rafael, Escogido	.325	83	20	27	3	1	1	10	1
Espinosa, Ramon, Gigantes	.318	110	16	35	4	1	0	8	5
Mateo, Ruben, Escogido	.317	104	18	33	3	0	10	28	2
Allen, Luke, Azucareros	.316	152	19	48	6	2	7	35	0
Veras, Wilton, Escogido	.313	99	12	31	3	0	0	13	1
Betemit, Wilson, Escogido	.312	109	22	34	7	1	1	10	3
Jimenez, D'Angelo, Licey	.312	138	28	43	12	1	5	31	2
Garcia, Guillermo, Aguilas	.311	119	17	37	9	0	9	24	0
McKay, Cody, Licey	.306	147	16	45	**13**	1	1	14	1
Polonia, Luis, Aguilas	.305	128	21	39	8	0	2	14	1
Guerrero, Wilton, Estrellas	.303	152	27	46	3	**5**	1	14	6
Mateo, Henry, Licey	.302	162	26	49	6	2	0	11	14
Martinez, Felix, Aguilas	.301	146	24	44	10	1	1	12	5
Ozuna, Pablo, Estrellas	.301	153	23	46	10	0	0	19	6
Nunez, Raymond, Licey	.297	111	11	33	6	0	3	12	1
Sosa, Juan, Gigantes	.296	81	13	24	4	2	0	9	6
Ruan, Wilkin, Estrellas	.287	94	5	27	4	0	0	10	4
Lombard, George, Escogido	.287	101	9	29	6	1	0	6	4
Garabito, Eddy, Azucareros	.286	199	27	**57**	11	3	3	15	7
Nunez, Abraham, Escogido	.286	84	11	24	4	2	0	3	2
Ramirez, Julio, Gigantes	.281	135	24	38	7	4	4	18	11
Wigginton, Ty, Gigantes	.280	189	23	53	11	2	9	31	0
Mayerson, Manuel, Azu.	.280	75	3	21	2	0	0	3	4
German, Amado, Escogido	.276	98	7	27	4	0	0	11	0
Pena, Angel, Gigantes	.275	120	12	33	8	0	2	9	0
Santos, Deivis, Gigantes	.271	133	8	36	7	1	2	14	5
Reyes, Jose, Gigantes	.270	178	27	48	10	**5**	5	22	**21**
Lopez, Mendy, Aguilas	.269	167	22	45	12	1	7	31	1
Diaz, Juan, Estrellas	.269	160	26	43	9	0	11	27	1
Brumbaugh, Cliff, Azu.	.267	135	13	36	11	0	4	23	1
#Jose, Felix, Estrellas	.264	182	**29**	48	7	0	**13**	**38**	3
#Gomez, Alexis, Aguilas	.263	152	28	40	**13**	1	6	18	6

INDIVIDUAL PITCHING LEADERS
(Minimum 25 Innings)

	W	L	ERA	G	SV	IP	H	BB	SO
Gulin, Lindsay, Estrellas	3	0	1.01	17	1	27	15	10	27
Munoz, Arnie, Aguilas	4	0	**1.55**	20	4	41	23	11	**74**
#Reyes, Alberto, Estrellas	**5**	1	2.25	18	0	20	13	4	28
Morel, Ramon, Gigantes	4	3	2.41	11	0	41	31	10	30
Nunez, Maximo, Estrellas	2	0	2.43	14	0	33	25	7	20
De los Santos, Luis, Est.	4	1	2.49	9	0	43	45	6	10
Acevedo, Jose, Aguilas	4	2	2.53	10	0	53	49	11	44
De la Cruz, Fernando, Azu.	2	4	2.57	17	4	28	25	10	16
Lima, Jose, Escogido	2	1	2.60	6	0	28	26	4	19
Perez, Beltran, Gigantes	1	1	2.84	9	0	38	25	7	26
Gonzalez, Alfredo, Azu.	2	3	2.91	8	0	34	35	9	19
Bernero, Adam, Escogido	4	2	3.02	11	0	42	44	7	31
Perez, Carlos, Licey	3	3	3.07	7	0	29	32	6	22
Serrano, Wascar, Escogido	2	0	3.29	18	0	27	25	5	11
Estrella, Leoncio, Gigantes	2	2	3.30	20	0	30	33	9	14
Ozuna, Gabriel, Azucareros	0	2	3.34	16	0	35	33	8	29
Lopez, Aquilino, Gigantes	2	1	3.35	13	0	48	36	12	54
Wilson, Kris, Gigantes	1	2	3.46	10	0	42	38	5	19
Diaz, Felix, Licey	2	4	3.50	12	0	44	50	4	26
Torres, Salomon, Licey	1	4	3.55	10	0	51	47	14	28
Vargas, Claudio, Aguilas	4	4	3.60	10	0	50	43	17	53
Tavarez, David, Aguilas	3	1	3.86	7	0	26	29	7	19
Davis, Lance, Escogido	2	2	3.92	11	0	39	42	8	31
Coco, Pascual, Escogido	1	1	4.21	10	0	36	37	12	26
Valdez, Efrain, Estrellas	1	5	4.38	14	0	39	43	18	20
#Mercedes, Jose, Estrellas	**5**	3	4.98	12	0	56	77	8	26
#Hill, Jeremy, Gigantes	1	3	5.66	21	**8**	21	16	20	18

MEXICAN PACIFIC LEAGUE

Thanks to the Mexican Pacific League's quirky format in how it picks its league champion, the last finished first during the 2002-03 season.

Los Mochis had the league's worst overall (28-38) record during the regular season, but slipped into the six-team playoffs thanks to their 17-15 record during the second half of the season. Once they made the playoffs, they got on a hot streak, rolling through three rounds of playoffs to win the league title.

Edgar Gonzalez

But the Cinderella run ended there, as they were trounced in the Caribbean Series, going winless in six games. That was a far cry from a year earlier when Culiacan won the 2002 Caribbean Series.

Outfielder Jayson Bass, who hit .238 and led Los Mochis with 12 homers and 42 RBIs, went on a tear in the playoffs, hitting .373-6-18. He had four homers and 13 RBIs in the second round alone as the Sugarcane Growers beat Mazatlan in five games. Righthander Bronswell Patrick went 4-0 in the playoffs after winning just two games in the regular season.

Veteran first baseman Bubba Smith of Mexicali led the league in home runs for the second straight winter. He hit 24.

The emergence of Rodrigo Lopez during the 2001-2002 winter season had scouts watching a little closer for hidden gems. Righthander Edgar Gonzalez wasn't hiding from anyone, though.

The Arizona Diamondbacks' rising prospect dominated by leading the league in ERA with a 1.65 mark while going 8-0. Gonzalez, a Monterrey native, went 14-8, 2.63 between low Class A South Bend and high Class A Lancaster in 2002. He parlayed his success in the league into a callup with the Diamondbacks in 2003.

STANDINGS

REGULAR SEASON	W	L	PCT	GB
*Mexicali Eagles	37	29	.561	—
Hermosillo Orangemen	36	30	.545	1
*Obregon Yaquis	37	31	.544	1
Culiacan Tomato Growers	35	31	.530	2
Mazatlan Deer	31	34	.477	5½
Navojoa Mayos	31	36	.463	6½
Guasave Cottoneers	31	37	.456	7
Los Mochis Sugarcane Growers	28	38	.424	9

*Split-season champions

PLAYOFFS—Quarterfinals: Los Mochis defeated Hermosillo 4-1, Mazatlan defeated Mexicali 4-2 and Obregon defeated Culiacan 4-2 in best-of-7 series. **Semifinals:** Obregon defeated Mexicali 4-3 and Los Mochis defeated Mazatlan 4-1 in best-of-7 series. **Finals:** Los Mochis defeated Obregon 4-1 in best-of-7 series.

TOP 10 PROSPECTS: 1. Edgar Gonzalez, rhp, Hermosillo (Diamondbacks). **2.** Nic Jackson, of, Guasave (Cubs). **3.** Jorge de la Rosa, lhp, Hermosillo (Red Sox). **4.** Oscar Villarreal, rhp, Mexicali (Diamondbacks). **5.** Freddy Sanchez, 2b, Navojoa (Red Sox). **6.** Luis Garcia, of, Obregon (Indians). **7.** David Kelton, 3b, Guasave (Cubs). **8.** Alfredo Amezaga, 2b, Obregon (Angels). **9.** Robb Quinlan, of, Obregon (Angels). **10.** Jason Grabowski, of/1b, Hermosillo (Athletics).

INDIVDUAL BATTING LEADERS
(Minimum 102 At-Bats)

	AVG	AB	R	H	2B	3B	HR	RBI	SB
Gomez, Heber, Mazatlan	**.353**	224	28	79	20	1	4	37	3
Short, Rick, Mexicali	.338	148	26	50	10	0	2	12	2
Lofton, James, Mochis	.333	135	27	45	10	0	4	14	5
Hubbard, Trenidad, Hermosillo	.330	233	40	77	13	4	5	32	14

Quinlan, Robb, Obregon	.328	195	22	64	9	0	3	22	5
Brinkley, Darryl, Mexicali	.323	226	45	73	8	0	14	41	15
Agbayani, Benny, Mochis	.322	171	31	55	11	1	10	33	2
Carrillo, Matias, Mochis	.321	196	26	63	8	1	8	33	1
Doster, Dave, Hermosillo	.321	237	45	76	15	1	9	46	3
Samuels, Scott, Mexicali	.320	175	41	56	11	1	7	33	19
Zuleta, Julio, Guasave	.319	238	43	76	13	0	23	61	0
Garcia, Cornelio, Hermosillo	.315	200	35	63	11	0	3	22	2
Robles, Javier, Obregon	.315	216	33	68	13	0	9	28	3
Orantes, Ramon, Mochis	.312	170	22	53	4	0	7	21	1
Pellow, Kit, Culiacan	.312	231	36	72	18	0	12	50	0
Grabowski, Jason, Hermosillo	.310	171	32	53	6	0	10	30	4
Sanchez, Freddy, Navojoa	.308	133	17	41	6	0	4	19	2
Garcia, Luis C., Obregon	.308	273	38	84	17	2	6	33	9
Bojorquez, Victor, Mochis	.298	188	25	56	6	0	4	15	2
Mendez, Roberto, Guasave	.296	196	36	58	9	0	10	33	5
Robles, Oscar, Navojoa	.294	221	40	65	9	1	4	31	1
Mejia, Roberto, Navojoa	.293	164	22	48	8	0	8	27	8
Velez, Manuel, Obregon	.292	171	16	50	8	0	4	23	4
Saenz, Ricardo, Mexicali	.291	206	29	60	10	0	14	38	2
Smith, Bubba, Mexicali	.285	235	**50**	67	11	0	**24**	**64**	0
Jackson, Nic, Guasave	.283	127	25	36	6	1	6	23	14
Garcia, Luis A., Hermosillo	.282	195	36	55	11	0	11	36	0
Smith, Demond, Guasave	.282	195	31	55	8	0	5	21	26
Morejon, Oswaldo, Guasave	.281	210	30	59	14	1	7	36	5
Coste, Chris, Obregon	.279	129	19	36	7	0	6	16	2
French, Anton, Navojoa	.278	248	44	69	8	2	9	25	**30**
Rodarte, Raul, Navojoa	.277	220	30	61	10	1	3	31	12
Fernandez, Daniel, Mazatlan	.275	193	23	53	8	2	2	12	3
Amezcua, Adan, Culiacan	.273	165	15	45	7	0	3	17	1
Frese, Nate, Guasave	.270	115	14	31	4	1	1	11	0
Alvarez, Gabe, Guasave	.268	142	17	38	8	1	3	18	1
Gil, Geronimo, Obregon	.266	184	22	49	5	0	6	20	1
Grijak, Kevin, Mazatlan	.265	219	26	58	12	1	5	31	1
Sandoval, Jose L., Hermosillo	.265	170	19	45	11	0	4	28	0
Gastelum, Sergio, Mexicali	.264	208	31	55	14	0	2	15	3
Arredondo, Luis, Obregon	.264	140	19	37	0	1	4	11	6
Hessman, Mike, Mazatlan	.264	159	24	42	9	1	6	23	2
Gastelum, Carlos, Hermosillo	.262	130	20	34	9	0	0	10	0
Headley, Justin, Navojoa	.261	226	21	59	6	1	6	27	3
Fornes, Daniel, Mazatlan	.260	146	14	38	10	1	4	20	0
Santana, Mario, Navojoa	.260	173	15	45	7	0	2	16	0
Romero, Flavio, Mazatlan	.259	112	18	29	4	1	1	6	3
Ojeda, Miguel, Mazatlan	.256	160	26	41	7	0	6	29	2

INDIVIDUAL PITCHING LEADERS

(Minimum 34 Innings)

	W	L	ERA	G	SV	IP	H	BB	SO
Garibaldi, Cecilio, Guasave	3	1	1.69	34	7	37	24	23	24
Gonzalez, Edgar, Hermosillo	**8**	1	**1.89**	12	0	76	60	21	41
Campos, Francisco, Mazatlan	3	3	2.25	14	0	84	68	25	**76**
Mendoza, Mario, Navojoa	2	4	2.56	18	0	46	37	21	32
Garcia, Gerardo, Culiacan	4	1	2.57	9	0	42	37	20	23
Blank, Matt, Culiacan	3	2	2.64	7	0	44	42	18	23
DeHart, Rick, Obregon	5	2	2.64	12	0	65	46	15	54
Alvarez, Octavio, Navojoa	7	5	2.81	14	0	**93**	79	34	60
Huerta, Edgar, Culiacan	1	1	2.82	19	0	51	45	18	55
Diaz, Rafael, Mochis	7	3	3.02	15	0	83	60	43	75
Romero, Alejandro, Mexicali	5	6	3.15	14	0	86	67	24	42
Patrick, Bronswell, Mochis	2	2	3.19	7	0	42	39	9	34
Montemayor, Humberto, Navojoa	4	3	3.19	14	0	79	82	16	58
Sinohui, David, Hermosillo	4	2	3.19	29	1	37	32	17	20
Rodriguez, Salvador, Obregon	7	4	3.27	14	0	85	95	31	44
Leyva, Edgar, Guasave	3	2	3.29	8	0	41	41	22	32
#Garcia, Mike, Mexicali	1	2	3.33	26	**17**	27	29	7	32
Nieblas, Mauro, Mochis	0	4	3.34	33	0	35	26	21	34
Rubio, Miguel, Hermosillo	4	3	3.35	29	9	38	30	20	50
Palafox, Juan, Obregon	8	3	3.48	15	0	83	79	30	46
Duarte, Miguel, Obregon	4	5	3.50	27	3	36	34	24	32
Moreno, Angel, Hermosillo	5	4	3.63	13	0	67	71	19	30
Silva, Jose, Culiacan	3	3	3.65	10	0	57	58	19	33
Alvarez, Juan, Mochis	4	4	3.66	12	0	59	54	27	28
Randolph, Stevphen, Herm.	5	4	3.89	13	0	72	51	54	62
Ochoa, Pablo, Mazatlan	2	3	4.00	10	0	45	53	21	25
Quiroz, Aaron, Navojoa	6	3	4.00	13	0	70	69	20	40
Flores, Ignacio, Guasave	3	1	4.05	34	1	47	45	18	44
Garcia, Carlos, Obregon	3	3	4.08	12	0	35	37	13	12
Villarreal, Oscar, Mexicali	7	2	4.10	14	1	64	58	32	54
Campillo, Jorge, Culiacan	2	1	4.11	19	1	35	40	8	25
Galvez, Randy, Guasave	4	6	4.21	14	0	68	80	28	39

PUERTO RICAN LEAGUE

The Puerto Rican League has never been thought of as a place to help a pitcher acclimate to pro baseball.

But when Kansas City Royals righthander Zack Greinke, the club's top pick in the 2002 draft, signed late and got only 12 innings of work before the minor league season wrapped up, the team decided to send its prized prospect to Puerto Rico. Despite worries from some scouts that Greinke, 19, would struggle, the righthander actually handled the transition well, going 0-1, 2.45 in 26 innings for Mayaguez.

"He is the first American player that I'm aware of that came down after he was drafted out of high school," Mayaguez pitching coach Guy Hansen said. "It took a tremendous amount of will and insight to pull that off. It's a very difficult place to play. There is a sprinkling of major leaguers and Double-A and Triple-A players here. You don't get much of a break."

RODGER WOOD

Zack Greinke

Another Royals prospect also shone for league champion Mayaguez, as future Royals closer Mike MacDougal hit 103 mph on the radar gun while striking out 29 in 26 innings.

"He was lights-out," one veteran NL scout said. "Not just velocity, either. He was repeating his delivery and spinning his breaking ball."

It was a sharp improvement for the 6-foot-4, 190-pound righthander, who had walked 91 in 91 innings during the 2002 season.

Dominant pitching was the key for Mayaguez, which led the league with a 2.66 ERA. The Indians finished second to Caguas in the regular season, then rolled through the playoffs, defeating Caguas five games to one in the championship series.

Mayaguez lost 7-3 in the opener, but after that Caguas scored only four runs in the next five games. Jose Valentin, the league's home run leader with nine despite hitting only .214 for the season, hit three home runs during the championship series, while hitting .317-4-10 overall in 11 playoff games.

Though it lost to Mayaguez in the championship series, Caguas was awarded a berth in the Caribbean Series, played in Carolina, P.R., because civil unrest in Venezuela led to that country not sending a team to the tournament.

STANDINGS

REGULAR SEASON	W	L	PCT	GB
Caguas Criollos	32	18	.640	—
Mayaguez Indians	29	21	.580	3
Bayamon Cowboys	27	23	.540	5
Ponce Lions	24	26	.480	8
Carolina Giants	20	30	.400	12
Santurce Crabbers	18	32	.360	14

PLAYOFFS—Semifinals: Caguas defeated Ponce 4-2 and Mayaguez defeated Bayamon 4-1 in best-of-7 series. **Finals:** Mayaguez defeated Caguas 5-1 in best-of-9 series.

TOP 10 PROSPECTS: **1.** Mike MacDougal, rhp, Mayaguez (Royals). **2.** Travis Hafner, 1b, Carolina (Indians). **3.** Zach Greinke, rhp, Mayaguez (Royals). **4.** Joe Borchard, of, Mayaguez (White Sox). **5.** Eric Munson, 1b/3b, Carolina (Tigers). **6.** Andy Pratt, lhp, Mayaguez (Braves). **7.** Fernando Cabrera, rhp, Ponce (Indians). **8.** William Vazquez, rhp, Santurce (Rockies). **9.** Javier Lopez, lhp, Santurce (Red Sox). **10.** Gabby Martinez, ss, Ponce (Devil Rays).

INDIVDUAL BATTING LEADERS

(Minimum 81 At-Bats)

	AVG	AB	R	H	2B	3B	HR	RBI	SB
Martinez, Gabby, Ponce	**.375**	120	20	45	5	1	0	12	**12**
Ortiz, Hector, Caguas	.336	125	13	42	11	2	1	20	0
Roberts, Brian, Ponce	.322	177	31	**57**	7	4	2	22	**12**
Lopez, Luis, Ponce	.319	119	11	38	9	0	5	16	0
Matos, Julius, Mayaguez	.315	165	24	52	8	1	1	15	2
Figueroa, Luis A., Mayaguez	.311	183	25	57	6	4	0	24	1
Molina, Jose, Caguas	.308	130	15	40	3	1	4	22	0
Garcia, Omar, Bayamon	.305	187	23	57	**15**	1	3	29	0
Figueroa, Luis D., Carolina	.304	102	15	31	6	0	0	8	1
Pagan, Angel, Ponce	.298	104	16	31	3	2	1	9	5
Martin, Al, Santurce	.284	148	22	42	10	2	3	15	2
Munson, Eric, Carolina	.283	113	16	32	6	0	4	21	0
Cora, Alex, Caguas	.280	132	15	37	4	1	1	8	2
Espada, Josue, Carolina	.280	125	22	35	3	1	2	13	10
Harris, Willie, Mayaguez	.277	177	26	49	5	**5**	1	17	3
Rivera, Carlos, Ponce	.272	180	22	49	8	0	8	**36**	0
Crespo, Cesar, Carolina	.271	155	24	42	7	4	3	15	4
Guzman, Edwards, Santurce	.270	178	22	48	5	0	7	17	1
Marrero, Oreste, Bayamon	.268	142	14	38	11	0	2	16	3
Clemente, Edgard, Carolina	.264	140	10	37	7	0	1	14	0
Munoz, Jose, Caguas	.264	182	24	48	5	3	1	13	6
Bocachica, Hiram, Ponce	.264	91	16	24	3	0	4	12	4
Chimelis, Joel, Bayamon	.259	147	11	38	3	1	1	9	0
Rios, Armando, Carolina	.256	86	9	22	5	0	1	6	6
Gonzalez, Raul, Bayamon	.255	94	18	24	7	0	1	8	2
Castro, Ramon, Santurce	.255	110	15	28	7	0	4	16	1
Cancel, Robinson, Ponce	.252	103	16	26	4	1	1	5	3
Molina, Izzy, Bayamon	.252	103	7	26	7	0	0	9	1
Valentin, Javier, Mayaguez	.252	127	14	32	5	1	1	14	0
Jones, Jason, Caguas	.252	159	22	40	4	0	8	22	0
Leon, Jose, Bayamon	.250	144	14	36	3	0	4	15	1
Correa, Miguel, Ponce	.250	136	16	34	3	0	3	14	1
Borchard, Joe, Mayaguez	.246	114	16	28	10	1	1	14	0
Sanchez, Agustin, Bayamon	.243	140	12	34	5	1	2	12	2
Diaz, Alex, Mayaguez	.241	191	21	46	8	0	1	23	3
#Valentin, Jose, Mayaguez	.214	192	**33**	41	10	1	**9**	22	1

INDIVIDUAL PITCHING LEADERS

(Minimum 27 Innings)

	W	L	ERA	G	SV	IP	H	BB	SO
Alberro, Jose, Bayamon	2	0	0.60	19	3	30	16	6	19
Albaladejo, Jonathan, May.	2	0	**0.68**	28	1	40	29	9	26
Hackman, Luther, Carolina	3	3	1.38	8	0	46	27	7	29
Small, Aaron, Bayamon	2	0	1.55	18	0	46	37	10	35
Santiago, Jose, Carolina	1	0	1.60	21	6	34	25	4	16
Manning, David, Santurce	2	1	1.67	8	0	43	34	19	33
Lin, Chang, Bayamon	0	2	1.98	6	0	27	24	6	21
Linton, Doug, Bayamon	6	2	2.08	11	0	69	62	13	**56**
Pratt, Andy, Mayaguez	4	1	2.18	10	0	41	38	10	26
Calero, Kiko, Mayaguez	5	2	2.25	12	0	56	42	20	43
#MacDougal, Mike, May.	0	3	2.39	23	**10**	26	17	12	29
Rojas, Chris, Mayaguez	3	2	2.56	14	0	46	33	32	29
Wilson, Jeff, Caguas	**8**	1	2.65	12	0	68	55	21	34
Olivares, Omar, Caguas	5	3	2.72	11	0	73	56	27	36
Childers, Jason, Mayaguez	1	2	2.83	25	1	35	27	7	26
Miranda, Angel, Caguas	3	3	2.95	9	0	43	33	22	18
Oliver, Darren, Bayamon	4	2	2.98	13	0	54	52	36	24
Fernandez, Osvaldo, Ponce	4	1	3.02	11	0	63	56	24	38
McConnell, Sam, Carolina	2	2	3.05	13	0	59	56	10	26
Alvarado, Giancarlo, Ponce	4	1	3.05	17	2	38	31	18	29
Medina, Rafael, Caguas	2	2	3.07	10	0	41	40	16	16
Krivda, Rick, Santurce	0	5	3.12	10	0	40	40	19	17
Gonzalez, Dicky, Carolina	4	4	3.19	13	0	73	67	12	40
Bell, Rob, Santurce	2	1	3.25	7	0	36	32	16	29

VENEZUELAN LEAGUE

Civil unrest throughout Venezuela derailed the 2002-03 Venezuelan League, as the season was cancelled roughly two-thirds of the way through the regular season.

When opponents of Venezuelan president Hugo Chavez called a general strike on Dec. 2, it threw the league into limbo, as protests, a gas crisis and security concerns forced the league to start postponing games. Late in December, Venezuelan League president Guillermo Aveledo decided to cancel the regular season, saying that the league couldn't guarantee the fans and players security.

Of the 248 scheduled games, 88 were lost to cancellation. The league still held out hope of holding the league playoffs, but as the strike continued, the playoffs eventually had to be cancelled as well, and Venezuela did not send a team to the Caribbean Series.

Many Venezuelan major league players had already fled to the United States when the cancellation was announced.

Before the strike forced the season's cancellation, teams did get in enough games for some top prospects to give a sneak peek of future success. The top prospect in Venezuela was Miguel Cabrera, who was also the top prospect in the Florida Marlins organization. He hit .329-4-24 in 140 at-bats and showed a polished hitting approach rarely found in a teenager. Cabrera continued to build on his success during the 2003 season, as he tore up the Double-A Carolina League before joining the Marlins in July.

STANDINGS

DIVISION OCCIDENTE	W	L	PCT	GB
Aragua Tigers	28	11	.718	—
Lara Cardinals	21	20	.512	8
Zulia Eagles	17	23	.425	11½
Occidente Pastora	12	27	.308	16
DIVISION ORIENTAL	**W**	**L**	**PCT**	**GB**
Caracas Lions	23	16	.590	—
La Guaira Sharks	23	17	.575	½
Magallanes Navigators	17	21	.447	5½
Oriente Caribbeans	18	24	.429	6½

PLAYOFFS: None (cancelled due to civil strife).

TOP 10 PROSPECTS: 1. Miguel Cabrera, 3b, Aragua (Marlins). **2.** Jose Castillo, ss, Caracas (Pirates). **3.** Victor Martinez, c, Oriente (Indians). **4.** Lew Ford, of, Aragua (Twins). **5.** Alex Herrera, lhp, Oriente (Indians). **6.** Beau Kemp, rhp, Aragua (Twins). **7.** Rene Reyes, of, Caracas (Rockies). **8.** Miguel Pinango, rhp, Magallanes (Mets). **9.** Alejandro Machado, 2b/ss, Caracas (Royals). **10.** Yoel Hernandez, rhp, Zulia (Phillies).

INDIVDUAL BATTING LEADERS

(Minimum 60 At-Bats)

	AVG	AB	R	H	2B	3B	HR	RBI	SB
Mendoza, Carlos, La Guaira	.383	60	8	23	4	0	2	17	1
Colina, Javier, Occidente	**.355**	110	8	39	9	1	1	13	0
Leach, Jalal, Lara	.353	136	14	48	6	1	4	13	3
Reyes, Rene, Carolina	.346	127	21	44	6	2	3	18	5
Lopez, Jose C., Lara	.345	84	8	29	1	1	1	16	0
Mendez, Carlos, Carolina	.333	102	15	34	5	1	3	25	1
Perez, Robert, Lara	.329	164	26	**54**	4	1	8	**30**	2
Cabrera, Miguel, Aragua	.329	140	17	46	10	0	4	24	0
Wilson, Travis, La Guaira	.329	140	20	46	11	0	4	27	1
Castillo, Jose, Carolina	.327	147	**28**	48	1	**4**	8	27	5
Delgado, Alex, Aragua	.323	99	7	32	6	0	1	7	1
Perez, Tomas, Carolina	.318	110	20	35	7	0	0	11	1
Alfonzo, Eliezer, Oriente	.316	136	16	43	8	2	8	29	0
Landaeta, Luis, Occidente	.314	118	11	37	4	0	4	12	0
Rodriguez, Luis, Oriente	.313	112	17	35	6	0	1	10	4
Querecuto, Juan, Lara	.311	61	3	19	2	0	0	8	0
Soto, Eminson, Occidente	.311	106	8	33	6	2	3	20	0
Ford, Lew, Aragua	.302	149	25	45	12	0	5	15	3
Melian, Jackson, Carolina	.302	116	17	35	5	1	6	21	3
Nava, Lipso, Zulia	.301	93	12	28	8	0	1	12	0
Castro, Ramon, Aragua	.300	60	12	18	4	1	1	8	3
Freire, Alejandro, Zulia	.299	134	18	40	10	0	2	19	1
Martinez, Victor, Oriente	.295	146	25	43	9	1	6	22	1
Duran, Carlos, La Guaira	.294	68	6	20	3	1	2	7	0
Camacho, Juan, Zulia	.287	94	11	27	3	1	2	13	1
Jones, Chris, Zulia	.283	113	20	32	1	2	6	17	1
Blanco, Henry, Carolina	.282	85	14	24	10	0	2	13	0
Rios, Eduardo, Aragua	.282	142	21	40	**13**	0	5	22	0
Canate, William, Occidente	.280	93	12	26	6	0	1	10	3
Freel, Ryan, Magallanes	.279	68	12	19	5	1	0	1	**8**
Gonzalez, Luis, Oriente	.279	104	14	29	3	1	5	18	0
Zambrano, Roberto, Aragua	.269	93	14	25	5	0	2	16	0
Machado, Alejandro, Carolina	.267	86	12	23	3	**4**	0	11	3
Romero, Wilfredo, Carolina	.267	101	17	27	7	2	0	10	2
Velandia, Jorge, La Guaira	.266	79	7	21	3	0	0	3	1
Smith, Nestor, Aragua	.265	83	17	22	2	2	3	8	1
Langaigne, Selwyn, Lara	.264	121	11	32	5	1	0	13	2

Pernalete, Marco, La Guaira	.263	137	21	36	5	2	2	10	4
#Acuna, Ronald, Magallanes	.261	134	11	35	3	**4**	1	17	1
#Ugueto, Luis, Lara	.250	132	19	33	7	0	1	10	**8**
#Nunnally, Jon, Aragua	.214	126	23	27	8	0	5	18	**8**
#Stratton, Rob, La Guaira	.168	101	21	17	1	0	**10**	17	1

INDIVIDUAL PITCHING LEADERS
(Minimum 20 Innings)

	W	L	ERA	G	SV	IP	H	BB	SO
Conde, Argenis, Oriente	2	0	0.44	10	0	21	12	6	10
Murray, Dan, Aragua	5	1	**0.86**	8	0	42	22	13	22
Butto, Francisco, Aragua	1	0	0.90	13	0	20	9	13	20
#Erdos, Todd, Aragua	1	1	0.98	16	**11**	18	9	2	10
Atchison, Scott, Lara	1	2	1.36	16	0	33	26	3	26
Wright, Chris, Occidente	3	2	1.39	9	0	52	39	17	39
Bowers, Cedrick, Aragua	1	0	1.63	6	0	28	20	10	35
Maduro, Calvin, Carolina	4	2	1.75	7	0	36	25	18	15
Torrealba, Yoan, Occidente	0	1	1.75	16	1	26	21	7	15
Ahearne, Pat, Carolina	4	1	1.83	8	0	44	50	5	25
Levrault, Allen, La Guaira	3	1	2.06	8	0	48	40	14	33
Romero, Josmir, Aragua	3	3	2.15	9	0	46	31	6	28
Pulido, Juan, Aragua	5	3	2.24	9	0	52	49	4	45
Silva, Doug, Zulia	2	1	2.37	6	0	30	30	13	18
Chacin, Gustavo, Lara	2	1	2.42	9	0	45	49	19	24
Palki, Jeromy, Aragua	0	1	2.42	13	0	22	23	4	14
Pinango, Miguel, Magallanes	3	4	2.43	9	0	56	41	4	28
Hurtado, Edwin, Lara	3	3	2.45	9	0	62	54	4	**59**
Falteisek, Steve, La Guaira	2	2	2.45	10	2	51	35	16	37
Roach, Jason, Magallanes	3	3	2.45	6	0	37	26	7	15
Pulsipher, Bill, La Guaira	**6**	1	2.47	9	0	47	53	9	39
Campos, Juan, Magallanes	2	1	2.50	10	1	36	27	9	33
Moreno, Victor, Aragua	2	0	2.55	18	0	25	25	8	18
Sweeney, Brian, Lara	3	3	2.57	9	0	49	51	7	34
Serrano, Elio, Oriente	0	1	2.59	21	1	24	24	7	26
Cubillan, Darwin, Carolina	1	2	2.59	18	3	24	17	14	31
Guzman, Alexis, Lara	3	2	2.59	18	0	24	22	3	7
Cedeno, Blas, Zulia	1	1	2.61	15	0	21	18	9	17
Serrano, Alex, Occidente	4	1	2.74	15	0	23	22	9	15
Sequea, Jacobo, Oriente	2	4	3.10	8	0	41	32	12	27
Estrada, Horacio, Occidente	1	5	3.16	8	0	43	48	17	35
Dickey, R.A., Zulia	2	4	3.21	8	0	48	45	8	28

ARIZONA FALL LEAGUE

2002

The 2002 Arizona Fall League season came to an end in anti-climactic fashion as the Peoria Javelinas defeated the Scottsdale Scorpions 7-1, in the league's one-game championship.

Peoria starter Josh Stewart (White Sox), who posted a 0.81 ERA in eight regular-season starts, allowed one unearned run over six innings for the victory.

"I went out there and challenged them and kept our guys in the game," Stewart said, "and it worked out well. I got ground balls when I needed them and we did a pretty good job at the plate, too. I was just trying to keep guys off balance and trying to work out of the zone."

BILL MITCHELL

Ken Harvey

The Arizona Fall League once again gave fans a nice sneak peek at the top rookies of tomorrow, as Mark Teixeira (Rangers) and Rocco Baldelli (Devil Rays) were among the prospects who parlayed successful fall league performances into major league success.

Two long-standing records were toppled in 2002. Scottsdale first baseman Ken Harvey hit .479 to break the record for highest average, set in 1993 by Scott Pose. Peoria first baseman Tagg Bozied eclipsed the single-season record for home runs, with 12. The previous record of 11 was held by five players, most recently Hank Blalock in 2001. With a .752 slugging average, Harvey also broke Blalock's mark of .713, also set in 2001.

STANDINGS

EAST	W	L	PCT	GB
Scottsdale Scorpions	29	15	.659	—
Phoenix Desert Dogs	25	19	.568	4
Mesa Solar Sox	19	24	.442	9½
WEST	**W**	**L**	**PCT**	**GB**
Peoria Javelinas	26	17	.605	—
Grand Canyon Rafters	20	23	.465	6
Maryvale Saguaros	11	32	.256	15

PLAYOFFS: Peoria defeated Scottsdale in one-game playoff.

TOP 10 PROSPECTS: 1. Mark Teixeira, 3b, Peoria (Rangers). **2.** Rocco Baldelli, of, Grand Canyon (Devil Rays). **3.** Brandon Phillips, 2b, Phoenix (Indians). **4.** Bobby Jenks, rhp, Scottsdale (Angels). **5.** Jerome Williams, rhp, Grand Canyon (Giants). **6.** Justin Morneau, 1b, Peoria (Twins). **7.** Hee Seop Choi, 1b, Mesa (Cubs). **8.** Bobby Basham, rhp, Scottsdale (Reds). **9.** Ken Harvey, 1b, Scottsdale (Royals). **10.** Todd Wellemeyer (Cubs), rhp, Mesa.

INDIVIDUAL BATTING LEADERS
(Minimum 65 At-Bats)

	AVG	AB	R	H	2B	3B	HR	RBI	SB
Harvey, Ken, Scottsdale	.479	117	25	56	11	0	7	34	0
Olson, Tim, Scottsdale	.374	107	18	40	8	0	1	18	6
Morrissey, Adam, Phoenix	.371	105	26	39	7	0	4	14	4
Atkins, Garrett, Mesa	.353	116	13	41	6	0	2	14	1
Choi, Hee Seop, Mesa	.345	84	19	29	5	1	8	17	0
Teixeira, Mark, Peoria	.333	99	19	33	5	1	7	23	1
Victorino, Shane, Peoria	.330	109	14	36	6	0	1	10	8
Whiteman, Tommy, Mesa	.330	97	15	32	6	1	2	16	3
Baldelli, Rocco, GC	.316	133	20	42	5	0	1	18	8
Niekro, Lance, GC	.313	96	9	30	5	2	0	16	0
Sardinha, Dane, Scottsdale	.311	106	16	33	8	0	4	24	1
Utley, Chase, GC	.308	130	17	40	6	1	4	23	3
Hill, Koyie, Peoria	.307	75	8	23	5	1	0	8	0
Hummel, Tim, Peoria	.303	89	13	27	3	1	0	7	0
Sitzman, Jay, GC	.303	76	14	23	4	1	1	5	3

INDIVIDUAL PITCHING LEADERS
(Minimum 20 Innings)

	W	L	ERA	G	SV	IP	H	BB	SO
Sanders, Dave, Peoria	6	0	0.75	13	0	24	23	7	17
Stewart, Josh, Peoria	1	0	0.81	9	0	33	23	9	23
Jenks, Bobby, Scottsdale	1	1	1.08	9	0	42	33	17	54
Carrasco, Dan, Phoenix	2	0	1.29	18	2	21	15	7	24
Bong, Jung, GC	3	1	1.50	8	0	30	21	11	23
Griffiths, Jeremy, Phoenix	0	1	1.91	9	0	33	27	5	25
Majewski, Gary, Peoria	3	0	1.96	15	4	23	19	13	18
Basham, Bobby, Scottsdale	3	2	1.98	12	1	36	35	4	35
Williams, Jerome, GC	0	0	2.05	5	0	22	10	7	25
Bowe, Brandon, Mesa	2	0	2.11	16	3	21	21	6	15

2003

The AFL has been providing a sneak peak at future major league stars since its inception in 1992. That was no different in 2003, though it could have been billed as a future Devil Rays showcase.

Tampa Bay's brightest prospects, B.J. Upton, 19, and Delmon Young, 18, were far and away the most promising young talents in the league.

Though they are undoubtedly on a bullet train towards Tampa Bay, Upton and Young will start 2004 in the minors, while righthander Dewon Brazelton—another former Devil Rays first-round pick—made some significant improvements with his breaking ball and should lock up a job in the Devil Rays '04 rotation.

Brazelton topped the league with five wins and saved his best performance for the AFL championship game. He allowed just two hits and a walk over six shutout innings as the Mesa Solar Sox beat the Mesa Desert Dogs 7-2.

Solar Sox outfielder Jason Dubois (Cubs) earned league MVP honors and edged another Devil Rays slugger Jonny Gomes for the home run title. Dubois hit .358-9-29.

Several top prospects scheduled to play in the AFL in 2003 instead joined Team USA for the America's Olympic qualifying tournament. The team played in 12 AFL games as a warmup before departing for Panama. Team USA went 9-3 in Arizona and hit a league-high .351 while averaging nearly nine runs per game.

The 2003 AFL season, however, will be remembered for the tragic death of outfielder Dernell Stenson (Reds). Playing for the Scottsdale Scorpions at the time, he was robbed and kidnapped outside a nightclub and later shot and killed. The following day's games were cancelled and a moment of silence was observed in memory of the 25-year-old former Red Sox first-rounder.

STANDINGS

AMERICAN DIVISION	W	L	PCT	GB
Mesa Solar Sox	20	13	.606	—
Peoria Saguaros	18	16	.529	2½
Scottsdale Scorpions	16	15	.516	3
NATIONAL DIVISION	**W**	**L**	**PCT**	**GB**
Mesa Desert Dogs	18	13	.581	—
Grand Canyon Rafters	13	19	.406	5½
Peoria Javelinas	9	24	.273	10
*Team USA	9	3	.750	

*Ineligible for league championship

PLAYOFFS: Mesa Solar Sox defeated Mesa Desert Dogs in one-game playoff.

TOP 10 PROSPECTS: 1. B.J. Upton, ss, Mesa Solar Sox (Devil Rays). **2.** Delmon Young, of, Mesa Solar Sox (Devil Rays). **3.** David Wright, 3b, Peoria Saguaros (Mets). **4.** Rickie Weeks, 2b, Peoria Saguaros (Brewers). **5.** Jeff Mathis, c, Scottsdale Scorpions (Angels). **6.** Dustin Nippert, rhp, Scottsdale Scorpions (Diamondbacks). **7.** Dallas McPherson, 3b, Scottsdale Scorpions (Angels). **8.** James Loney, 1b, Scottsdale Scorpions (Dodgers). **9.** Sergio Santos, ss, Scottsdale Scorpions (Diamondbacks). **10.** Scott Hairston, 2b, Scottsdale Scorpions (Diamondbacks).

INDIVIDUAL BATTING LEADERS

(Minimum 81 Plate Appearances)

	AVG	AB	R	H	2B	3B	HR	RBI	SB
Lewis, Richard, Solar Sox	.404	89	14	36	4	1	3	19	9
Johnson, Dan, Desert Dogs	.382	110	21	42	11	1	4	30	0
Hairston, Scott, Scorpions	.360	89	20	32	4	0	4	14	3
Dubois, Jason, Solar Sox	.358	120	25	43	12	2	9	29	2
Duffy, Chris, Desert Dogs	.348	89	17	31	2	3	0	18	6
Hankins, Ryan, Javelinas	.347	75	10	26	6	0	3	20	0
Thompson, Rich, Desert Dogs	.346	104	28	36	6	4	1	13	13
Vento, Michael, Rafters	.343	102	17	35	12	2	5	26	1
Wright, David, Saguaros	.341	88	15	30	7	0	2	15	4
House, J.R., Desert Dogs	.338	74	15	25	10	2	5	20	0

INDIVIDUAL PITCHING LEADERS

(Minimum 15 Innings)

	W	L	ERA	G	SV	IP	H	BB	SO
Ramirez, Ramon, Rafters	3	2	1.44	7	0	25	21	2	25
Hebson, Bryan, Desert Dogs	4	0	1.83	14	1	20	12	3	18
Rakers, Aaron, Solar Sox	5	0	1.96	13	2	18	13	4	24
Frasor, Jason, Scorpions	1	1	2.03	8	0	27	21	11	24
Hendrickson, Ben, Saguaros	0	1	2.03	7	0	27	24	2	21
Webb, John, Solar Sox	4	0	2.42	10	0	26	27	6	18
Evans, Kyle, Desert Dogs	3	1	2.45	7	0	29	23	8	18
Francisco, Frank, Saguaros	4	1	2.50	12	0	18	13	10	17
Johnston, Mike, Desert Dogs	0	0	2.55	14	1	18	15	9	14
McClellan, Zach, Javelinas	4	0	2.77	11	0	26	21	4	17

GRAND CANYON RAFTERS

BATTING	AVG	AB	R	H	2B	3B	HR	RBI	SB
Athas, Jamie, 2b	.241	79	14	19	1	2	0	6	3
Bowen, Rob, c	.300	40	9	12	6	1	1	7	0
Boyd, Shaun, of	.219	96	12	21	4	2	1	12	1
Hernandez, Michel, c	.147	34	1	5	0	0	0	2	1
Kelly, Donald, 3b-ss	.213	94	11	20	1	1	2	12	3
Linden, Todd, of	.316	98	21	31	7	1	4	15	1
Logan, Nook, of	.227	97	14	22	4	2	0	9	5
Mauer, Jake, 2b-3b	.306	49	8	15	1	0	0	4	3
Nelson, John, ss	.154	26	2	4	0	0	0	3	0
Niekro, Lance, 1b	.299	77	9	23	3	0	1	9	0
Schumaker, Skip, of	.220	82	8	18	4	1	0	6	4
St. Pierre, Maxim, c	.234	47	6	11	2	0	0	1	0
Tejeda, Ferdin, ss	.242	66	4	16	1	0	0	5	2
Tiffee, Terry, 1b-3b	.305	105	8	32	5	0	1	17	0
Vento, Michael, dh-of	.343	102	17	35	12	2	5	26	1

PITCHING	W	L	ERA	G	SV	IP	H	BB	SO
Anderson, Luke	1	0	1.93	10	0	14	12	4	13
Axelson, Josh	1	3	7.36	9	0	33	48	11	19
Bean, Colter	1	2	6.89	11	1	16	18	11	20
Bonilla, Henry	1	0	3.86	7	0	26	26	8	13
Bonser, Boof	2	3	6.07	7	0	27	32	18	24
Henkel, Rob	0	2	10.38	3	0	8.2	12	3	6
Johnson, Tyler	1	1	4.40	11	0	14	13	5	15
Kinney, Josh	0	1	45.00	2	0	2	8	4	1
Larrison, Preston	2	0	5.03	12	0	20	17	6	7
Lowry, Noah	0	0	9.64	3	0	5	8	1	1
Marsonek, Sam	0	0	4.96	13	1	16	18	3	12
Neshek, Pat	0	1	5.74	11	0	16	15	4	14
Ramirez, Ramon	3	2	1.44	7	0	25	21	2	25
Roney, Matt	0	2	6.43	3	0	7	7	4	1
Thompson, Brad	1	0	1.59	9	1	11	8	2	6
Valdez, Merkin	0	0	3.38	4	0	5	6	0	4
Wolfe, Brian	0	1	4.24	12	1	17	19	3	15
Woodyard, Mark	0	1	5.82	11	2	17	25	3	14

MESA DESERT DOGS

BATTING	AVG	AB	R	H	2B	3B	HR	RBI	SB
Bynum, Freddie, ss-2b	.321	53	17	17	6	2	1	9	1
Chapman, Travis, 1b	.200	25	4	5	0	0	0	2	0
Choy Foo, Rodney, 2b	.243	70	8	17	1	0	0	10	1
Church, Ryan, dh	.400	15	1	6	2	0	0	3	0
Doumit, Ryan, c	.346	26	4	9	3	1	2	7	0
Duffy, Chris, of	.348	89	17	31	2	3	0	18	6
House, J.R., c	.338	74	15	25	10	2	5	20	0
Johnson, Dan, 1b	.382	110	21	42	11	1	4	30	0
Owens, Jeremy, of	.256	86	17	22	5	2	3	16	5
Schrager, Tony, ss-2b	.381	63	16	24	7	0	2	9	1
Scott, Luke, of	.352	71	13	25	6	1	4	16	0
Shoppach, Kelly, c	.281	64	6	18	6	0	3	12	0
Smith, Corey, 3b	.238	105	14	25	6	1	1	7	1
Stotts, J.T., ss-2b	.333	69	8	23	0	0	0	8	1
Swisher, Nick, of	.275	80	14	22	3	2	1	9	0
Thompson, Rich, of	.346	104	28	36	6	4	1	13	13
Wallace, David, c	.192	26	1	5	1	0	0	4	0

PITCHING	W	L	ERA	G	SV	IP	H	BB	SO
Bennett, Jeff	1	1	2.57	10	0	14	15	3	6
Brooks, Frank	2	2	5.79	14	2	19	23	3	22
Bucktrot, Keith	0	1	13.50	1	0	2	3	1	1
Evans, Kyle	3	1	2.45	7	0	29	23	8	18
Fritz, Ben	0	3	5.81	7	0	26	23	14	15
Gamble, Jerome	1	1	6.33	8	0	21	26	6	11
Giese, Dan	1	0	4.50	14	1	16	22	3	14
Hancock, Josh	0	2	3.43	6	0	21	21	9	22
Hebson, Bryan	4	0	1.83	14	1	20	12	3	18
Hernandez, Michael	0	0	9.00	2	0	2	4	3	3
Johnston, Mike	0	0	2.55	14	1	18	15	9	14
Korecky, Bobby	1	0	4.00	12	0	18	16	5	12
Kubes, Greg	1	0	8.56	13	0	14	20	6	5
Mabeus, Chris	0	0	4.50	13	1	18	25	9	15
Pennington, Todd	2	0	5.00	8	0	9	10	5	9
Squires, Matt	1	0	0.00	11	2	12	6	5	9
Zink, Charlie	1	2	4.91	7	0	26	26	13	16

MESA SOLAR SOX

BATTING	AVG	AB	R	H	2B	3B	HR	RBI	SB
Cates, Gary, 2b	.250	24	5	6	1	0	0	4	1
Davis, John Paul, 1b	.229	35	4	8	2	0	1	7	1
Dubois, Jason, of	.358	120	25	43	12	2	9	29	2
Gomes, Jonny, of	.295	88	26	26	10	1	8	22	4
Gredvig, Doug, ph	.000	1	0	0	0	0	0	0	0
Harris, Brendan, 3b	.302	96	19	29	7	0	3	19	2
Hawpe, Brad, of	.276	98	13	27	8	0	4	18	0
Holliday, Matt, of	.333	66	14	22	3	0	3	12	7
Jacobs, Mike, dh-c	.240	25	3	6	1	0	1	5	0
Johnson, Kelly, ss	.303	89	17	27	7	1	5	15	1
Kopitzke, Casey, c	.180	61	10	11	0	0	1	8	0
LaForest, Pete, c	.243	37	5	9	1	0	4	12	0
Lewis, Richard, 2b	.404	89	14	36	4	1	3	19	9
Littleton, B.J., of	.209	43	7	9	0	1	0	3	2
Nix, Jayson, 2b-3b	.226	53	8	12	3	0	1	2	2
Riggans, Shawn, c	.300	10	0	3	0	0	0	1	0
Seestedt, Mike, c	.182	11	0	2	0	0	0	1	0
Shier, Peter, ss-3b	.200	45	6	9	2	0	0	4	1
Stern, Adam, of	.316	57	10	18	4	0	0	2	4
Theriot, Ryan, ss	.240	25	5	6	0	0	0	4	5
Upton, B.J., ss	.214	28	4	6	0	0	0	2	2
Whiteside, Eli, c	.250	4	1	1	1	0	0	1	0
Wilken, Kris, 1b	.330	94	19	31	4	0	1	10	0
Young, Delmon, of	.417	48	6	20	5	1	1	7	1

PITCHING	W	L	ERA	G	SV	IP	H	BB	SO
Barry, Kevin	0	1	5.84	10	0	12	20	7	8
Brazelton, Dewon	4	0	3.27	8	0	33	26	9	36
Buglovsky, Chris	1	0	4.45	9	0	30	44	12	14
Christensen, Ben	0	0	13.50	1	0	1	2	4	2
Corcoran, Tim	0	5	8.88	9	0	25	31	19	12
Dohmann, Scott	1	1	3.86	12	2	16	11	8	17
Evert, Brett	0	1	6.14	8	0	29	34	10	34
Fields, Josh	0	1	12.00	3	0	3	5	2	4
Hines, Carlos	1	2	7.00	12	0	18	24	5	8
Huisman, Justin	0	0	5.00	13	2	18	18	10	11
Ormond, Rodney	0	0	3.95	11	1	14	14	5	16
Rakers, Aaron	5	0	1.96	13	2	18	13	4	24
Szuminski, Jason	0	0	4.19	12	0	19	24	7	19
Veras, Jose	2	1	6.05	12	0	19	27	10	9
Webb, John	4	0	2.42	10	0	26	27	6	18
Zumwalt, Alec	2	1	4.87	13	1	20	26	8	18

PEORIA JAVELINAS

BATTING	AVG	AB	R	H	2B	3B	HR	RBI	SB
Adams, Russ, ss	.272	81	13	22	3	1	0	5	3
Bikowski, Scott, of	.341	41	8	14	3	0	2	10	1
Broadway, Larry, 1b	.230	61	7	14	3	0	2	9	1
Brown, Hunter, 3b	.271	59	9	16	4	1	1	6	1
Bubela, Jaime, of	.301	83	10	25	2	1	1	10	7
DeJesus, David, of	.289	90	20	26	4	3	6	14	6
Gettis, Byron, of	.241	79	9	19	4	0	3	11	3
Godwin, Tyrell, of	.273	66	9	18	4	1	1	6	2
Hankins, Ryan, c-3b	.347	75	10	26	6	0	3	20	0
Horner, James, c	.240	25	4	6	3	1	0	0	0
Labandeira, Josh, ss-3b	.307	75	8	23	3	1	3	8	0
McKinley, Josh, c-2b	.250	44	6	11	5	0	0	2	1
Miles, Aaron, 2b	.271	59	6	16	3	1	0	5	1
Rich, Dominic, 2b	.288	66	11	19	7	2	0	8	2
Santos, Chad, 1b	.219	73	8	16	2	0	2	11	0
Shanks, James, of	.214	42	6	9	1	0	0	1	3
Strong, Jamal, of	.250	72	9	18	4	1	0	7	2
Tonis, Mike, c	.250	60	7	15	4	0	0	9	1

PITCHING	W	L	ERA	G	SV	IP	H	BB	SO
Baek, Cha Sueng	0	1	5.61	7	0	26	28	6	20
Baerlocher, Ryan	1	4	6.65	8	0	23	29	9	19
Bauer, Peter	1	1	5.59	10	1	19	24	2	13
Cotts, Neal	0	2	4.64	6	0	21	24	8	19
DeJong, Jordan	1	0	7.41	13	0	17	12	11	18
DeQuin, Benji	0	1	4.30	11	0	15	17	12	11
Majewski, Gary	0	3	6.43	13	0	14	24	14	11
McClellan, Zach	4	0	2.77	11	0	26	21	4	17
Reimers, Cameron	1	1	4.44	6	0	24	31	3	9
Schroder, Chris	0	3	8.47	11	0	17	22	6	17
Serrano, Jim	1	2	9.00	14	2	13	15	8	10
Sherrill, George	0	0	2.70	13	0	13	14	5	10
Thornton, Matt	0	2	9.22	11	0	14	18	13	10
Wylie, Mitch	0	0	3.22	13	1	22	27	5	14
Young, Chris	0	4	3.75	7	0	24	27	8	15

PEORIA SAGUAROS

BATTING	AVG	AB	R	H	2B	3B	HR	RBI	SB
Aguila, Chris, of	.257	109	21	28	7	3	5	24	2
Bourgeois, Jason, ss-2b	.283	60	14	17	2	0	1	11	4
Furmaniak, J.J., ss	.237	59	6	14	2	0	0	4	2
Gautreau, Jake, 2b	.258	66	5	17	5	0	1	9	0
Gonzalez, Adrian, 1b	.260	77	16	20	4	1	3	16	1
Huber, Justin, c	.233	60	11	14	4	0	0	6	0
Johnson, Kade, c	.395	38	5	15	3	1	0	2	0
Knott, Jon, of	.236	89	11	21	4	0	4	15	2
Krynzel, Dave, of	.233	86	7	20	2	1	1	9	3
Meyer, Drew, of	.333	9	1	3	0	0	0	1	0
Nelson, Brad, of	.220	82	14	18	1	0	0	8	0
Nivar, Ramon, of	.381	63	12	24	3	2	1	8	6
Stokes, Jason, 1b	.145	62	5	9	1	1	2	5	1
Washington, Rico, 3b	.293	41	6	12	0	1	0	6	0
Weeks, Rickie, 2b-ss	.319	72	21	23	5	0	1	15	9
Willingham, Josh, c	.313	64	15	20	2	1	3	11	2
Wright, David, 3b	.341	88	15	30	7	0	2	15	4

PITCHING	W	L	ERA	G	SV	IP	H	BB	SO
Bartosh, Cliff	3	1	7.29	12	1	21	31	6	18
Bausher, Tim	2	0	1.98	9	2	14	14	3	14
Diaz, Joselo	1	1	8.62	12	0	16	18	14	16
Dinardo, Len	2	0	4.50	9	0	18	22	3	27
Echols, Justin	0	3	7.96	8	0	26	36	16	20
Francisco, Frank	4	1	2.50	12	0	18	13	10	17
Hampton, Matt	1	0	2.84	13	1	19	26	2	22
Hendrickson, Ben	0	1	2.03	7	0	27	24	2	21
Holdzkom, Lincoln	1	2	6.11	12	2	18	24	10	20

Hutchinson, Trevor	0	4	7.15	8	0	23	36	8	13
Keppel, Bob	0	0	0.00	1	0	2	0	0	2
Mattox, David	1	0	6.75	11	0	20	28	13	17
Moser, Todd	0	0	8.00	7	0	9	10	5	11
Novinsky, John	0	0	9.00	5	0	6	11	4	3
Peterson, Matt	2	1	6.35	8	0	23	26	11	19
Regilio, Nick	0	1	4.45	8	0	28	27	10	21
Webb, Alan	1	1	11.68	10	0	12	19	12	6

SCOTTSDALE SCORPIONS

BATTING	AVG	AB	R	H	2B	3B	HR	RBI	SB
Abercrombie, Reggie, of	.316	19	2	6	0	0	1	1	3
Aybar, Willy, 3b	.227	22	2	5	0	0	0	1	0
Bruntlett, Eric, 2b	.190	58	4	11	2	0	0	4	1
Gorneault, Nick, of	.233	60	10	14	2	0	0	4	0
Hairston, Scott, 2b	.360	89	20	32	4	0	4	14	3
King, Brennan, 3b	.314	35	5	11	4	0	1	9	1
Kotchman, Casey, 1b	.261	46	7	12	1	0	1	5	0
Kroeger, Josh, of	.253	75	12	19	3	1	1	11	2
Loney, James, 1b	.247	81	16	20	1	3	2	7	1
Mathis, Jeff, c	.180	50	3	9	2	0	0	3	1
McPherson, Dallas, 3b	.218	78	4	17	4	1	1	6	0
Porter, Colin, of	.292	89	9	26	5	1	1	7	4
Santos, Sergio, ss	.250	96	11	24	4	2	3	10	0
Sardinha, Dane, c	.346	52	5	18	7	0	3	9	0
Smitherman, Stephen, of	.295	88	14	26	5	2	3	20	3
Snyder, Chris, c	.235	51	6	12	1	0	2	7	0
Stenson, Dernell, of	.394	66	6	26	4	0	1	9	0
Whiteman, Tommy, ss	.000	9	0	0	0	0	0	1	0

PITCHING	W	L	ERA	G	SV	IP	H	BB	SO
Barzilla, Philip	0	0	12.86	10	0	7	18	5	5
Bittner, Tim	2	0	3.14	7	0	14	17	7	8
Bland, Nate	1	1	6.87	11	0	18	23	7	10
Brunet, Mike	0	0	8.10	2	0	3	5	3	1
Edens, Kyle	0	3	7.43	10	0	13	18	7	7
Farmer, Tom	0	4	11.15	8	0	15	31	6	11
Fischer, Rich	0	0	2.70	4	0	7	10	1	10
Frasor, Jason	1	1	2.03	8	0	27	21	11	24
Gallo, Mike	1	0	0.84	9	0	10.2	10	0	11
Gil, David	1	0	3.72	11	2	19	18	8	10
Medders, Brandon	0	1	1.46	11	2	12	7	7	19
Nall, T.J.	1	1	6.39	8	0	13	17	7	7
Nippert, Dustin	1	2	3.60	8	0	30	26	12	30
Powell, Greg	2	2	3.69	8	0	32	34	1	17
Shackelford, Brian	1	0	4.66	11	0	10	10	6	7
Sikaras, Pete	2	0	8.71	12	1	10	18	11	11
Steffek, Brian	2	0	3.52	11	0	15	15	6	9
Valentine, Joe	1	0	3.46	14	5	13	11	7	16

TEAM USA

BATTING	AVG	AB	R	H	2B	3B	HR	RBI	SB
Atkins, Garrett, 3b	.227	22	4	5	1	0	0	3	0
Burke, Chris, 2b	.212	33	9	7	0	0	1	4	2
Davis, J.J., of	.348	23	4	8	3	0	1	9	1
Gross, Gabe, of	.343	35	13	12	2	2	2	9	1
Hardy, J.J., ss	.219	32	3	7	1	0	1	6	0
Hill, Koyie, c	.238	21	1	5	1	0	0	3	0
Koonce, Graham, 1b	.654	26	7	17	4	1	2	12	0
Laird, Gerald, c	.444	18	5	8	2	0	0	4	0
Lamb, Mike, 1b	.240	25	4	6	1	1	0	2	0
Leone, Justin, 3b	.270	37	12	10	4	0	3	8	0
Mauer, Joe, c	.481	27	7	13	1	1	0	8	0
Reed, Jeremy, of	.250	28	7	7	1	0	1	3	2
Rouse, Mike, ss	.414	29	8	12	2	0	1	7	2
Sizemore, Grady, of	.472	36	11	17	0	2	1	6	0
Sledge, Terrmel, of	.357	28	7	10	1	0	1	7	1
Young, Ernie, 1b	.467	30	5	14	1	0	1	9	0

PITCHING	W	L	ERA	G	SV	IP	H	BB	SO
Bruney, Brian	0	0	0.00	4	0	3	2	0	3
Crain, Jesse	0	0	0.00	5	0	5	3	2	2
Duchscherer, Justin	1	1	4.09	3	0	11	9	2	8
Durbin, J.D.	1	0	4.50	2	0	6	7	3	7
Fikac, Jeremy	0	0	0.00	1	0	1	0	0	2
Grabow, John	0	0	1.69	5	0	5	7	2	5
Madson, Ryan	0	1	3.75	3	0	12	14	1	12
Pratt, Andy	1	0	3.86	3	1	9	11	4	10
Ramirez, Horatio	1	0	0.00	2	0	5	4	0	3
Ring, Royce	2	0	0.00	5	0	6	4	0	4
Stanford, Jason	0	0	3.97	3	0	11	13	2	7
Turnbow, Derrick	1	0	1.42	3	0	6	4	4	3
VanBenschoten, John	1	0	1.80	3	0	10	11	5	1
Wainwright, Adam	1	1	14.85	3	0	7	15	3	3
Williams, Todd	0	0	1.13	5	0	8	7	3	7

COLLEGE BASEBALL

Rice scores one for the underdog as it wins '03 College World Series

BY JOHN MANUEL

Rice University won the 2003 College World Series. Consider that for a moment.

Rice has the smallest enrollment (2,600) of any Division I football school. The school was left out when the old Southwest Conference melted and the Big 12 Conference absorbed what it thought were the SWC's four premium athletic programs. It's also a school with elite academic credentials and a 91 percent graduation rate for its athletes.

But this was also an Owls program making its fourth trip to Omaha since 1997, a team that expected to reach the CWS. The Owls rattled off a 30-game winning streak during the regular season with a pitching staff full of power arms, an airtight defense and a coach whose lineage and legacy are nearly unmatched at any level of baseball.

That coach is Wayne Graham. And he wasn't surprised that Rice won a national championship in baseball—the first for the school in any team sport—by beating Stanford 14-2 in an all-academic finale of the CWS' new best-of-three championship format.

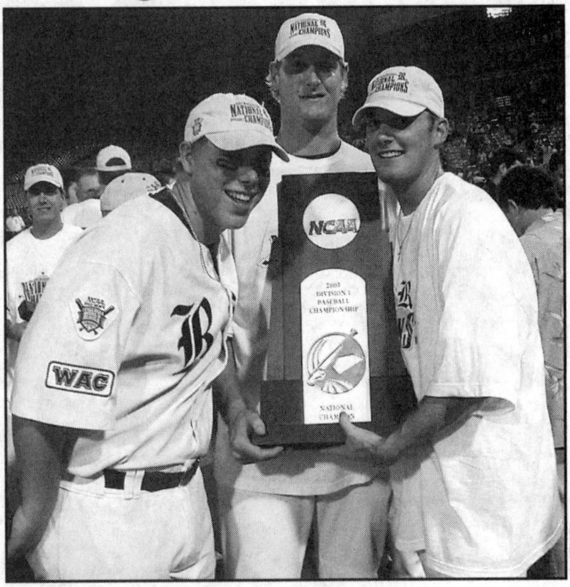
KIRK KENNEY

Trio combines for 39 wins
Rice righthanders Wade Townsend, Jeff Niemann and Philip Humber

It's right there in the Owls' 2003 media guide. He throws the gauntlet down there, when asked, "What's left for Wayne Graham?"

"A national championship for Rice," he responded. "I know it's possible."

His team proved him right with a performance Graham called "a tribute to pitching and defense."

Rice sent Stanford to its third runner-up finish in the last four years on the strength of a trio of sophomore righthanders—Philip Humber, Jeff Niemann and Wade Townsend. They anchored the Owls rotation, combining for 39 victories on the season and 458 of a school-record 653 strikeouts.

At one point, when they did not make an error in 73 straight innings and had committed just 17 in their first 33 games, it looked like the Owls might break the Division I record for fielding average, set by West Virginia in a 27-game schedule in 1971. Still, Rice's .980 fielding average was the best in the country.

JEFF GOLDEN

Wayne Graham

But there were hardships to overcome. The Owls won despite the loss of their projected No. 1 starter, senior righty Steven Herce (13-3, 2.79 in 2002), who missed the first half of the season with a rotator cuff injury. By the time Herce returned to action, he was the team's sixth-best pitcher and became just a bit player.

In Omaha, the Owls were without Jeff Jorgensen, who gamely played once before aggravating the hairline fracture in his right foot that robbed the fleet center fielder—who went to Rice on a track scholarship—of much of his speed. And they had to weather a slump from their top hitter, sophomore first baseman Vincent Sinisi. His two hits in the championship finale doubled his total to that point as he went 4-for-25 (.160) in the series.

To top it off, junior left fielder Chris Kolkhorst dislocated his left kneecap during the first game of the championship series, when he tripped over a bullpen pitcher's mound while chasing a fly ball. "You're not going to get any sympathy from your teammates when you trip and fall like that," he said.

Kolkhorst resolutely played on, making a pair of splendid catches and scoring the winning run in a 4-3, 10-inning win. He went 0-for-5 in the Owls' Game Two loss before keying the offense in the clincher, going 3-for-4 with a pair of doubles, two RBIs, two walks and three runs scored as Rice romped.

Well-Armed Owls

Humber, the third starter on Rice's talented staff, was the story of the finale. At one point, he had won 17 consecutive decisions dating back to his Freshman All-America 2002 season, but lost his last two heading into the CWS, including a super-regional game against Houston.

He also struggled in his first Omaha start, striking out eight but walking five and hitting a CWS-record three consecutive batters against Texas. He lasted just $3\frac{2}{3}$ innings as the Owls rallied to beat the Longhorns, but redemption was clearly on his mind in the championship final—for him and the Owls rotation.

Stanford had stunned Niemann, who was trying to become the NCAA's first pitcher to go 18-0, with three runs in the first inning of the championship opener, but Niemann recovered, as did the Owls. Rice chipped away and won in extra innings when Cardinal reliever Kodiak Quick threw away a routine, two-out grounder off the bat of Austin Davis, scoring Kolkhorst from second.

Stanford's aggressive offense, led by senior catcher Ryan Garko and outfielders Danny Putnam and Carlos Quentin, then attacked Niemann's roommate Townsend, who had won 11 of 12 decisions but suffered the loss in Stanford's 8-2 victory in Game Two. The Cardinal took an early 3-1 lead, then scored five in the seventh as Townsend fell apart and Sinisi, who had made one error all season, made two in the frame.

That set the stage for Humber, with the season on the line. He had two games' worth of notes on how to approach the Cardinal and formulated an excellent game plan. While Humber normally ran his fastball into the low 90s, he relied on his curveball and split-finger fastball in the championship game, keeping Stanford's hitters off balance.

The result was the first complete game in a series clincher since Louisiana State freshman Brett Laxton struck out 16 against Wichita State in 1993. Humber gave up just five hits in going in the distance, and the Owls capitalized on 11 Stanford walks to post the largest margin of victory in championship game history.

"I was overshadowed by those guys for a reason—they're great pitchers," Humber said after the victory. "I was able to throw all my pitches for strikes. Jeff and Wade have carried us all year, and tonight I was able to do my part."

The Cardinal had no defense for the Owls, who jumped to a 4-0 lead as freshman lefthander Mark Romanczuk was unable to find the plate. Romanczuk, a first-team Freshman All-American, was 12-0, 3.39 entering Omaha but was dreadful in two starts, going 0-2, 11.42. He walked six of the 10 batters he faced in the title game, and Stanford never recovered.

The Cardinal's loss did nothing to dim the efforts of junior righthander John Hudgins, who won the Most Outstanding Player trophy after winning three starts. Hudgins beat South Carolina with eight efficient shutout innings in the Cardinal's CWS opener, then beat Cal State Fullerton on four days' rest in the bracket championship. He also won Game Two of the championship series, pitching on three days' rest.

BILL NICHOLS

John Hudgins

His three CWS wins tied a record, as did his four career wins. Hudgins' heavy workload, however, drew national criticism for coach Mark Marquess. Hudgins, a third-round pick of the Texas Rangers, threw 350 pitches in a 10-day span, and the Cardinal still finished second. He also threw 165 innings on the season—28 more than his nearest challenger.

Stanford has now lost to the eventual champion in Omaha in each of the last four years, falling in the title game in 2000 to Louisiana State, 2001 to Miami and 2003 to Rice. It lost in the bracket final to Texas in 2002.

"Losing the title game is the same feeling no matter if you're a freshman, sophomore or junior," said Stanford center fielder Sam Fuld, who broke Keith Moreland's 25-year-old career CWS hits record with 24. "This one is a little harder to get over because when you're a freshman, you feel like you'll be back every year. Now obviously our time is winding down."

COLLEGE WORLD SERIES

Omaha
June 13-23, 2003

STANDINGS

BRACKET ONE	W	L	RF	RA
Rice	3	0	21	8
Texas	2	2	24	20
Miami	1	2	8	25
SW Missouri State	0	2	7	11

Bracket One Final: Rice 5, Texas 4

BRACKET TWO	W	L	RF	RA
Stanford	4	1	38	20
Cal State Fullerton	2	2	22	19
South Carolina	1	2	17	31
Louisiana State	0	2	12	19

Bracket Two Finals: Stanford 5, Cal State Fullerton 3; Stanford 7, Cal State Fullerton 5 (10 innings)

CHAMPIONSHIP SERIES

(Best-of-3)

Rice 4, Stanford 3 (10 innings)
Stanford 8, Rice 2
Rice 14, Stanford 2

INDIVIDUAL BATTING LEADERS

(Minimum 10 Plate Appearances)

	AVG	AB	R	H	2B	3B	HR	RBI	SB
P.J. Pilittere, CS Fullerton	.500	12	4	6	1	1	1	3	0
Brian Buscher, S. Carolina	.455	11	3	5	2	0	1	2	0
Curtis Thigpen, Texas	.438	16	2	7	2	0	0	4	0
Dustin Majewski, Texas	.417	12	3	5	1	0	0	3	1
Justin Turner, CS Fullerton	.417	12	4	5	1	0	1	4	0
Shane Costa, CS Fullerton	.412	17	1	7	2	0	1	5	0
Enrique Cruz, Rice	.409	22	4	9	1	0	0	6	0
Jonny Ash, Stanford	.400	35	7	14	2	1	2	10	0
Steven Tolleson, S. Carolina	.400	10	2	4	0	0	1	4	0
Carlos Quentin, Stanford	.379	29	7	11	1	0	2	8	0

INDIVIDUAL PITCHING LEADERS

(Minimum 7 Innings)

	W	L	ERA	G	SV	IP	H	BB	SO
David O'Hagan, Stanford	1	0	0.00	3	0	8	4	4	6
Matt Campbell, South Carolina	1	0	1.17	3	0	8	4	2	5
Sam LeCure, Texas	1	0	1.17	2	0	8	8	1	3
John Hudgins, Stanford	3	0	1.88	3	0	24	17	6	15
Ryan McCally, Stanford	1	1	2.20	2	0	16	14	7	5
Jeff Niemann, Rice	1	0	2.25	2	0	16	9	3	14
Jason Windsor, CS Fullerton	1	0	3.18	2	0	11	11	4	6
Philip Humber, Rice	1	0	3.55	2	0	13	8	7	12
Wade Townsend, Rice	1	1	4.30	2	0	15	15	6	14
J.P. Howell, Texas	1	0	4.35	2	0	10	12	5	14

ALL-TOURNAMENT TEAM

C—Ryan Garko, Stanford. **1B**—Curtis Thigpen, Texas. **2B**—Enrique Cruz, Rice. **3B**—Jonny Ash, Stanford. **SS**—Justin Turner, Cal State Fullerton. **OF**—Chris Kolkhorst, Rice; Danny Putnam, Stanford; Carlos Quentin, Stanford. **DH**—P.J. Pilittere, Cal State Fullerton. **P**—Jeff Niemann, Rice.

Most Outstanding Player—John Hudgins, rhp, Stanford.

Cagey Veteran

Some would say Graham's time is winding down because of his age, but they'd be sadly mistaken. The 66-year-old is only getting better and has no plans for retirement.

"I've said before, I'll go on a baseball field," he joked after the title was won.

Graham, who became the first coach in years to be ejected from a CWS game after he was tossed in Game Two of the championship series, played for legendary coach Bibb Falk at Texas and for Casey Stengel during one of his brief major league stints. He won five national championships during his tenure at San Jacinto (Texas) Junior College and coached Roger Clemens and Andy Pettitte, but didn't get his first Division I head coaching job until he was 54.

Rice had never made a regional appearance until 1995, Graham's fourth year at the school. It hasn't missed regional play since, producing a stream of big leaguers such as Matt Anderson, Lance Berkman and Jose Cruz Jr. Rice has become the Western Athletic Conference's perennial champion (sharing or winning every league crown since its entry in 1997), an Omaha regular and a consistent stop on the road for pro scouts.

With Humber, Niemann and Townsend, plus rising junior righty Josh Baker (8-0, 3.22), back in 2004, the Owls will be expected to return to the CWS. And now, they'll be expected to win it all. At least Graham thinks so.

"It's redemption, it's validation, it's all those words," he said. "We had a lot to prove, and we still have a lot to prove. We want to do it again."

Garrido Gets Record

Rice beat rival Texas three times in 2003, including twice in Omaha to end the Longhorns' attempt at a repeat national championship. But it was still a year of milestones for the Longhorns' veteran coach, Augie Garrido.

Garrido won his 1,428th career game when the Longhorns swept Florida State in a super-regional at Tallahassee, Fla., to break the Division I record set by his predecessor in burnt orange, Cliff Gustafson. With two

COLLEGE WORLD SERIES CHAMPIONS: 1947-2003

Year	Champion	Coach	Record	Runner-Up	MVP
1947	California*	Clint Evans	31-10	Yale	None selected
1948	Southern California	Sam Barry	40-12	Yale	None selected
1949	Texas*	Bibb Falk	23-7	Wake Forest	Charles Teague, 2b, Wake Forest
1950	Texas	Bibb Falk	27-6	Washington State	Ray VanCleef, of, Rutgers
1951	Oklahoma*	Jack Baer	19-9	Tennessee	Sid Hatfield, 1b-p, Tennessee
1952	Holy Cross	Jack Berry	21-3	Missouri	Jim O'Neill, p, Holy Cross
1953	Michigan	Ray Fisher	21-9	Texas	J.L. Smith, p, Texas
1954	Missouri	Hi Simmons	22-4	Rollins	Tom Yewcic, c, Michigan State
1955	Wake Forest	Taylor Sanford	29-7	Western Michigan	Tom Borland, p, Oklahoma State
1956	Minnesota	Dick Siebert	33-9	Arizona	Jerry Thomas, p, Minnesota
1957	California*	George Wolfman	35-10	Penn State	Cal Emery, 1b-p, Penn State
1958	Southern California	Rod Dedeaux	35-7	Missouri	Bill Thom, p, Southern California
1959	Oklahoma State	Toby Greene	27-5	Arizona	Jim Dobson, 3b, Oklahoma State
1960	Minnesota	Dick Siebert	34-7	Southern California	John Erickson, 2b, Minnesota
1961	Southern California*	Rod Dedeaux	43-9	Oklahoma State	Littleton Fowler, p, Oklahoma State
1962	Michigan	Don Lund	31-13	Santa Clara	Bob Garibaldi, p, Santa Clara
1963	Southern California	Rod Dedeaux	37-16	Arizona	Bud Hollowell, c, Southern California
1964	Minnesota	Dick Siebert	31-12	Missouri	Joe Ferris, p, Maine
1965	Arizona State	Bobby Winkles	54-8	Ohio State	Sal Bando, 3b, Arizona State
1966	Ohio State	Marty Karow	27-6	Oklahoma State	Steve Arlin, p, Ohio State
1967	Arizona State	Bobby Winkles	53-12	Houston	Ron Davini, c, Arizona State
1968	Southern California*	Rod Dedeaux	45-14	Southern Illinois	Bill Seinsoth, 1b, Southern California
1969	Arizona State	Bobby Winkles	56-11	Tulsa	John Dolinsek, of, Arizona State
1970	Southern California	Rod Dedeaux	51-13	Florida State	Gene Ammann, p, Florida State
1971	Southern California	Rod Dedeaux	53-13	Southern Illinois	Jerry Tabb, 1b, Tulsa
1972	Southern California	Rod Dedeaux	50-13	Arizona State	Russ McQueen, p, Southern California
1973	Southern California*	Rod Dedeaux	51-11	Arizona State	Dave Winfield, of-p, Minnesota
1974	Southern California	Rod Dedeaux	50-20	Miami (Fla.)	George Milke, p, Southern California
1975	Texas	Cliff Gustafson	56-6	South Carolina	Mickey Reichenbach, 1b, Texas
1976	Arizona	Jerry Kindall	56-17	Eastern Michigan	Steve Powers, dh-p, Arizona
1977	Arizona State	Jim Brock	57-12	South Carolina	Bob Horner, 3b, Arizona State
1978	Southern California*	Rod Dedeaux	54-9	Arizona State	Rod Boxberger, p, Southern California
1979	Cal State Fullerton	Augie Garrido	60-14	Arkansas	Tony Hudson, p, Cal State Fullerton
1980	Arizona	Jerry Kindall	45-21	Hawaii	Terry Francona, of, Arizona
1981	Arizona State	Jim Brock	55-13	Oklahoma State	Stan Holmes, of, Arizona State
1982	Miami (Fla.)*	Ron Fraser	57-18	Wichita State	Dan Smith, p, Miami (Fla.)
1983	Texas*	Cliff Gustafson	66-14	Alabama	Calvin Schiraldi, p, Texas
1984	Cal State Fullerton	Augie Garrido	66-20	Texas	John Fishel, of, Cal State Fullerton
1985	Miami (Fla.)*	Ron Fraser	64-16	Texas	Greg Ellena, dh, Miami (Fla.)
1986	Arizona	Jerry Kindall	49-19	Florida State	Mike Senne, of, Arizona
1987	Stanford	Mark Marquess	53-17	Oklahoma State	Paul Carey, of, Stanford
1988	Stanford	Mark Marquess	46-23	Arizona State	Lee Plemel, p, Stanford
1989	Wichita State	Gene Stephenson	68-16	Texas	Greg Brummett, p, Wichita State
1990	Georgia	Steve Webber	52-19	Oklahoma State	Mike Rebhan, p, Georgia
1991	Louisiana State*	Skip Bertman	55-18	Wichita State	Gary Hymel, c, Louisiana State
1992	Pepperdine*	Andy Lopez	48-11	Cal State Fullerton	Phil Nevin, 3b, Cal State Fullerton
1993	Louisiana State	Skip Bertman	53-17	Wichita State	Todd Walker, 2b, Louisiana State
1994	Oklahoma*	Larry Cochell	50-17	Georgia Tech	Chip Glass, of, Oklahoma
1995	Cal State Fullerton*	Augie Garrido	57-9	Southern California	Mark Kotsay, of-p, Cal State Fullerton
1996	Louisiana State*	Skip Bertman	52-15	Miami (Fla.)	Pat Burrell, 3b, Miami
1997	Louisiana State*	Skip Bertman	57-13	Alabama	Brandon Larson, ss, Louisiana State
1998	Southern California	Mike Gillespie	49-17	Arizona State	Wes Rachels, 2b, Southern California
1999	Miami*	Jim Morris	50-13	Florida State	Marshall McDougall, 2b, Florida State
2000	Louisiana State*	Skip Bertman	52-17	Stanford	Trey Hodges, rhp, Louisiana State
2001	Miami*	Jim Morris	53-12	Stanford	Charlton Jimerson, of, Miami
2002	Texas*	Augie Garrido	57-15	South Carolina	Huston Street, rhp, Texas
2003	Rice	Wayne Graham	58-12	Stanford	John Hudgins, rhp, Stanford

*Undefeated

more wins in Omaha, Garrido's mark stood at 1,430. The all-time NCAA wins record is held by Division III Ripon (Wis.) coach Gordie Gillespie, who has won 1,630 games in 50 seasons.

Garrido, 64, tried to deflect attention from the record run.

"I've always said, give me more runs than the other team, and I'll give you a win," he deadpanned during the CWS. "As far as specifics go, I don't know. But I know what I can do if you give me more runs."

When he got serious for a moment, Garrido called the record "a number and a moment in time."

"When you dig into it," he said, "it's about relationships."

1,430 and counting
Texas' Augie Garrido

Most of Garrido's were formed at Cal State Fullerton, which he took from a fledgling Division I program in 1974 to Omaha a year later and eventually three national championships, in 1979, '84 and '95. He also coached at Illinois in the interregnum between his two Fullerton stints before replacing Gustafson in 1996.

Garrido wasn't the only college coach to set a career record for wins, as Valdosta State (Ga.) coach Tommy Thomas became Division II's all-time wins leader. His 1,201 wins in 36 seasons bests the mark of 1,198 set over 44 seasons by Cal Poly Pomona's John Scolinos.

Coaching Changes

Garrido lost his top assistant when the 2003 season ended, when Frank Anderson was named head coach at Oklahoma State. He replaced Tom Holliday, who spent more than a quarter-century in Stillwater as an assistant or head coach. Holliday, like Garrido, succeeded a legend when he replaced Gary Ward at Oklahoma State, but he was relieved of his duties when the Cowboys did not advance to NCAA tournament play for the second year in a row. He joined Garrido as pitching coach, filling Anderson's position.

That was one of the more interesting changes in a busy offseason that saw more 20 coaching changes in Division I.

Several veteran coaches left the scene, including Seton Hall's Mike Sheppard, who retired with 998 career victories; Kentucky's Keith Madison, who had been the Southeastern Conference's longest-tenured coach; and Virginia's Dennis Womack, who spent 23 years with the Cavaliers.

Sheppard's son Rob, who led Seton Hall to a regional bid in 2001 when a heart attack sidelined his father, was named the Pirates interim head coach. Madison gave way to former Northwestern State coach John Cohen, who spent the last two seasons as an assistant at Florida. Notre Dame assistant Brian O'Connor, the 2001 Baseball America/American Baseball Coaches Association Assistant Coach of the Year, replaced Womack at Virginia.

Jim Schlossnagle, who in two seasons turned Nevada-Las Vegas from an also-ran into the Mountain West Conference regular-season and tournament champion, took over at Texas Christian for Lance Brown, who resigned after the Horned Frogs narrowly missed a regional bid for the second straight season.

Also of note, 1992 World Series MVP Ed Sprague, his 13-year professional career over, replaced Quincey Noble as head coach at Pacific. It's the first college coaching job for Sprague, a Stockton native who starred for Stanford in the late 1980s. His father, Ed Sr., is a longtime scout and coach.

Frank Sanchez was forced to take a permanent medical leave of absence at Pepperdine after seven years. He was replaced by Steve Rodriguez, a key member of Pepperdine's 1992 College World Series championship team and an assistant with the Waves for four years.

In other coaching milestones:

■ Eight-time National League batting champion Tony Gwynn took over coaching duties at San Diego State, his alma mater, and guided the Aztecs to a 29-32 record. Gwynn's son Anthony played center field and hit .359 while leading the Mountain West Conference with 25 stolen bases. He was later picked in the second round of the draft by the Milwaukee Brewers.

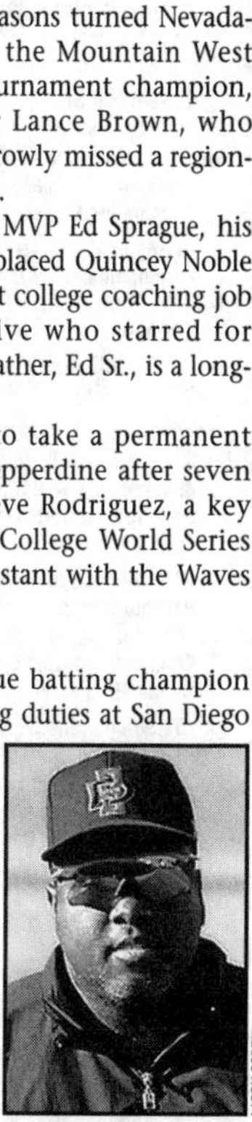

Tony Gwynn

■ Indiana's Bob Morgan became the 12th active coach and 26th overall to win 1,000 games. He reached the milestone in a 4-0 win over Illinois.

■ Don Schaly, who did not have a losing record in 40 years as a head coach at Ohio's Marietta College, announced his retirement, effective at the end of the

RPI RANKINGS

The Ratings Percentage Index (RPI) is a primary tool used by the NCAA in selecting at-large teams for the 64-team Division regional field. The accompanying chart is the final, official 2003 RPI rankings, with records against Division I opponents. Asterisks denote teams that did not get a regional bid; the team's final rank in Baseball America's Top 25 is noted in parentheses. College World Series teams are in boldface.

Team	Record	Team	Record
1. **Stanford** (2)	51-18	26. Richmond	48-15
2. Florida State (6)	54-13	27. Florida	37-21
3. **Miami** (8)	45-17	28. Tulane	44-19
4. **Rice** (1)	58-12	29. Arkansas	34-22
5. **Cal State Fullerton** (3)	50-16	30. Arizona	35-22
6. **Texas** (4)	50-20	31. Virginia Commonwealth	46-13
7. **Louisiana State** (5)	44-22	32. Coastal Carolina	45-18
8. Auburn (18)	42-21	33. Lamar	40-18
9. Georgia Tech (17)	43-18	34. Nevada-Las Vegas (20)	47-17
10. Baylor (11)	45-23	35. Minnesota	37-22
11. North Carolina State (12)	45-18	36. Missouri	32-22
12. Arizona State (7)	53-14	37. UC Riverside	41-17
13. Long Beach State (9)	41-20	38. Mississippi	35-27
14. North Carolina (19)	42-23	39. *West Virginia	36-19
15. Texas A&M (14)	45-19	40. Ohio State (21)	42-21
16. South Alabama	42-19	41. **SW Missouri State** (16)	40-26
17. Clemson	39-22	42. *Southern California	28-28
18. Southern Mississippi (15)	47-16	43. *Georgia	29-26
19. Nebraska (13)	45-18	44. Stetson	41-24
20. Mississippi State (24)	42-20	45. *Fla. International	36-23
21. Alabama (13)	38-23	46. *Texas-Arlington	35-24
22. **South Carolina** (10)	45-22	47. Notre Dame	43-18
23. Houston (22)	37-30	48. UNC Wilmington	40-23
24. Florida Atlantic (23)	47-16	49. Rutgers	37-22
25. *Virginia	29-25	50. *Oklahoma State	33-24

THE ROAD TO OMAHA

SUPER-REGIONALS

June 6-9; 16 teams, eight best-of-3 series (Winners advance to College World Series).

REGIONALS

May 30-June 1; 64 teams, 16 double-elimination tournaments (Winners advance to super-regionals).

*Automatic qualifier

CAL STATE FULLERTON

■ **Super-Regional Site:** Fullerton, Calif. (Cal State Fullerton).
Participants: Arizona State (53-12) at Cal State Fullerton (46-13).
(Cal State Fullerton wins 2-1, advances to College World Series).

□ **Regional Site**: Fullerton, Calif. (Cal State Fullerton).
Participants: No. 1 Cal State Fullerton (43-13), No. 2 Arizona (35-21), *No. 3 Notre Dame (43-16), *No. 4 San Diego (31-28).
Champion: Cal State Fullerton (3-0). **Runner-Up:** Notre Dame (2-2).
Outstanding Player: Chad Cordero, rhp, Cal State Fullerton.

□ **Regional Site**: Tempe, Ariz. (Arizona State).
Participants: No. 1 Arizona State (50-12), *No. 2 Nevada-Las Vegas (45-15), No. 3 New Mexico State (42-16), *No. 4 Central Connecticut State (31-15).
Champion: Arizona State (3-0). **Runner-Up:** Nevada-Las Vegas (2-2).
Outstanding Player: Dustin Pedroia, ss, Arizona State.
(Arizona State advances to meet Cal State Fullerton in super-regional).

LOUISIANA STATE

■ **Super Regional Site:** Baton Rouge, La. (Louisiana State).
Participants: Baylor (44-21) at Louisiana State (43-19).
(Louisiana State wins 2-1, advances to College World Series).

□ **Regional Site**: Baton Rouge, La. (Louisiana State).
Participants: No. 1 Louisiana State (40-19), No. 2 Tulane (43-17), No. 3 UNC Wilmington (38-21), *No. 4 Northeastern (27-22).
Champion: Louisiana State (3-0). **Runner-Up:** UNC Wilmington (2-2).
Outstanding Player: J.C. Holt, of, Louisiana State.

□ **Regional Site**: Hattiesburg, Miss. (Southern Mississippi)
Participants: No. 1 Baylor (41-21), *No. 2 Southern Mississippi (45-14), *No. 3 Southern (43-5), *No. 4 Murray State (25-29).
Champion: Baylor (3-0). **Runner-Up:** Southern Mississippi (2-2).
Outstanding Player: David Murphy, of, Baylor.
(Baylor advances to meet Louisiana State in super-regional).

MIAMI

■ **Super Regional Site:** Coral Gables, Fla. (Miami).
Participants: North Carolina State (45-16) at Miami (42-15).
(Miami wins 2-0, advances to College World Series).

□ **Regional Site**: Coral Gables, Fla. (Miami).
Participants: No. 1 Miami (39-14), No. 2 Florida Atlantic (46-14), No. 3 Florida (34-19), *No. 4 Bethune-Cookman (30-26).
Champion: Miami (3-1). **Runner-Up:** Florida (3-2).
Outstanding Player: J.D. Cockroft, lhp, Miami.

□ **Regional Site**: Wilson, N.C. (North Carolina State).
Participants: No. 1 North Carolina State (42-16), *No. 2 Virginia Commonwealth (45-11), *No. 3 Western Carolina (41-19), *No. 4 Le Moyne (33-15).
Champion: North Carolina State (3-0). **Runner-Up:** Western Carolina (2-2).
Outstanding Player: Colt Morton, c, North Carolina State.
(North Carolina State advances to meet Miami in super-regional).

RICE

■ **Super Regional Site:** Houston (Rice).
Participants: Houston (36-28) at Rice (51-10).
(Rice wins 2-1, advances to College World Series).

□ **Regional Site**: Houston (Rice).
Participants: *No. 1 Rice (48-10), No. 2 Mississippi (34-25), *No. 3 Wichita State (47-25), *No. 4 McNeese State (31-28).
Champion: Rice (3-0). **Runner-Up:** Wichita State (2-2).
Outstanding Player: Chris Kolkhorst, of, Rice.

□ **Regional Site**: College Station, Texas (Texas A&M).
Participants: No. 1 Texas A&M (43-17), *No. 2 Alabama (37-22), No. 3 Houston (32-27), *No. 4 Oral Roberts (41-18).
Champion: Houston (4-1). **Runner-Up:** Texas A&M (2-2).
Outstanding Player: Cole Bruce, 1b, Houston.
(Houston advances to meet Rice in super-regional).

SOUTH CAROLINA

■ **Super Regional Site:** Columbia, S.C. (South Carolina).
Participants: North Carolina (42-21) at South Carolina (42-20).
(South Carolina wins 2-0, advances to College World Series).

□ **Regional Site**: Atlanta (Georgia Tech).
Participants: *No. 1 Georgia Tech (44-16), No. 2 South Carolina (39-20), No. 3 East Carolina (33-25), No. 4 Stetson (39-22).
Champion: South Carolina (3-0). **Runner-Up:** Stetson (2-2).
Outstanding Player: Landon Powell, c, South Carolina.

□ **Regional Site**: Starkville, Miss. (Mississippi State).
Participants: No. 1 Mississippi State (40-18), No. 2 North Carolina (39-21), No. 3 Missouri (35-20), *No. 4 Middle Tennessee State (33-25).
Champion: North Carolina (3-0). **Runner-Up:** Mississippi State (2-2).
Outstanding Player: Sean Farrell, of, North Carolina.
(North Carolina advances to meet South Carolina in super-regional).

SOUTHWEST MISSOURI STATE

■ **Super Regional Site:** Columbus, Ohio (Ohio State).
Participants: Southwest Missouri State (38-24) at Ohio State (44-19).
(Southwest Missouri State wins 2-0, advances to College World Series).

□ **Regional Site**: Lincoln, Neb. (Nebraska).
Participants: *No. 1 Nebraska (44-16), *No. 2 Coastal Carolina (45-16), No. 3 Southwest Missouri State (35-23), *No. 4 Eastern Michigan (32-26).
Champion: Southwest Missouri State (3-1). **Runner-Up:** Nebraska (3-2).
Outstanding Player: Bob Zimmermann, rhp, Southwest Missouri State.

□ **Regional Site**: Auburn, Ala. (Auburn).
Participants: No. 1 Auburn (40-19), No. 2 Clemson (38-20), *No. 3 Ohio State (41-19), *No. 4 Princeton (35-23).
Champion: Ohio State (3-0). **Runner-Up:** Auburn (2-2).
Outstanding Player: Drew Anderson, 2b, Ohio State.
(Ohio State advances to meet Southwest Missouri State in super-regional).

STANFORD

■ **Super Regional Site:** Palo Alto, Calif. (Stanford).
Participants: Long Beach State (41-18) at Stanford (44-15).
(Stanford wins 2-0, advances to College World Series).

□ **Regional Site**: Palo Alto, Calif. (Stanford).
Participants: *No. 1 Stanford (41-15), *No. 2 Richmond (46-13), No. 3 UC Riverside (40-15), *No. 4 Illinois-Chicago (39-16).
Champion: Stanford (3-0). **Runner-Up:** Richmond (2-2).
Outstanding Player: Ryan Garko, c, Stanford.

□ **Regional Site**: Long Beach, Calif. (Long Beach State).
Participants: *No. 1 Long Beach State (38-18), No. 2 Minnesota (39-20), No. 3 Washington (40-16), No. 4 Pepperdine (36-23).
Champion: Long Beach State (3-0). **Runner-Up:** Washington (2-2).
Outstanding Players: Todd Jennings, c, Long Beach State; Jered Weaver, rhp, Long Beach State.
(Long Beach State advances to meet Stanford in super-regional).

TEXAS

■ **Super Regional Site:** Tallahassee, Fla. (Florida State).
Participants: Texas (46-18) at Florida State (54-11).
(Texas wins 2-0, advances to College World Series).

□ **Regional Site**: Austin, Texas (Texas).
Participants: No. 1 Texas (43-17), No. 2 Arkansas (34-20), No. 3 Lamar (37-16), *No. 4 Bucknell (27-14).
Champion: Texas (3-1). **Runner-Up:** Lamar (3-2).
Outstanding Player: Dustin Majewski, of, Texas.

□ **Regional Site**: Tallahassee, Fla. (Florida State).
Participants: No. 1 Florida State (50-10), No. 2 South Alabama (40-17), No. 3 Rutgers (36-20), *No. 4 Jacksonville (32-28).
Champion: Florida State (4-1). **Runner-Up:** South Alabama (2-2).
Outstanding Player: Tony Richie, c, Florida State.
(Florida State advances to meet Texas in super-regional).

2003 season. Schaly guided the Pioneers to three NCAA Division III national titles and seven runner-up finishes. He is one of only five coaches to post more than 1,400 career wins. He finished his career with 1,442 wins.

Tournament Gets Stronger

The NCAA postseason had a new look and gained greater exposure than ever in 2003, and the results were positive. The CWS expanded to 11 days, adding a best-of-three championship series to replace the one-game, winner-take-all championship format in place from 1988-2002. The series drew a record 260,091 fans.

Also, ESPN took over broadcasting duties for the postseason, adding super-regional games (and a pay-per-view package for those who wanted to see all eight super-regionals) and the entire CWS. Previously, CBS had carried two games from Omaha, including the one-game championship.

Ratings for the postseason were robust. Game Three of the championship series drew a 1.8 cable rating, or about 1.567 million households, making it the most-watched CWS game ever on ESPN. (In contrast, about two million fans watched the championship game on CBS in 2002.)

COACHING CAROUSEL

Division I coaching changes since the end of the 2003 season:

School	Former Coach	New Coach	Previous Position
Air Force	Reed Peters	Mike Hutcheon	Bethel (Ind.)
Columbia	Mik Aoki	Paul Fernandes	Associate Athletic Director
Connecticut	Andy Baylock	Jim Penders	Assistant
Creighton	Jack Dahm	Ed Servais	Assistant
Gonzaga	Steve Hertz	Mark Machtolf	Assistant
Iowa	Scott Broghamer	Jack Dahm	Creighton
Kansas State	Mike Clark	Brad Hill	Central Missouri State
Kentucky	Keith Madison	John Cohen	Assistant (Florida)
La Salle	Larry Conti	Lee Saverio	Assistant
Marist	Jim Tyrell	Joe Raccuia	Assistant (George Mason)
Md.-Eastern Shore	Kirkland Hall	Bobby Rodriguez	Baltimore Orioles
McNeese State	Todd Butler	Chad Clement	Assistant
Mercer	Barry Myers	Craig Gibson	Assistant
Nevada-Las Vegas	Jim Schlossnagle	Buddy Gouldsmith	Assistant
Oklahoma State	Tom Holliday	Frank Anderson	Assistant (Texas)
Oral Roberts	Sunny Golloway	Rob Watson	Assistant
Pacific	Quincey Noble	Ed Sprague	Professional player
Pepperdine	Frank Sanchez	Steve Rodriguez	Assistant
St. Mary's	John Baptista	Jedd Soto	Feather River (Calif.) JC
Seton Hall	Mike Sheppard	Rob Sheppard	Assistant
Tennessee Tech	Aaron Carroll	Matt Bragga	Ass't (Birmingham Southern)
Texas Christian	Lance Brown	Jim Schlossnagle	Nevada-Las Vegas
Toledo	Joe Kruzel	Cory Mee	Assistant (Michigan State)
Virginia	Dennis Womack	Brian O'Connor	Assistant (Notre Dame)
Va. Military Institute	Tom Slater	Marlin Ikenberry	Assistant

LARRY GOREN

Ryan Wagner

Weeks Adds To Mark

Southern second baseman Rickie Weeks ran away with Baseball America's College Player of the Year award. Weeks led Division I in hitting for the second year in a row, hitting .479 with 16 homers and 23 stolen bases to lead the Jaguars to a 44-7 record and a regional bid. Weeks finished his career with a Division I-record .467 batting average and was drafted second overall by the Brewers.

Despite Weeks' onslaught at the plate, offense was significantly down in Division I in 2003. The cumulative batting average and ERA for 284 teams were just .291 and 5.23, the lowest marks since 1995. Scoring was down from 6.4 runs per game the previous two years to 6.1, the lowest level since 1993.

Home runs also were down and were nearly 25 percent lower than the record-setting 1998 season. Just 0.74 home runs were hit per team per game, down from 0.83 in 2002 and the '98 record of 1.06.

Another interesting trend was the defensive improvement in college baseball. The national fielding percentage was .958, a record high. Fielding percentages have gone up every year since 1997.

With a drop in offense, some top pitching achievements were recorded in 2003:

■ Righthander Matt DeSalvo, a fifth-year senior for Division III Marietta (Ohio), set NCAA records for career wins (53) and strikeouts (603). The old records were held by Division I players—Wichita State's Don Heinkel set the wins mark at 51 from 1979-82, while Auburn's John Powell struck out 602 from 1991-94. DeSalvo, who entered the year as the Division III career and single-season (205 in 2001) strikeout king, recovered from a knee injury that caused him to red shirt in 2002, by going 13-2, 1.31 in 2003, fanning 157 in 96 innings. He signed with the New York Yankees before the draft.

■ Houston righthander Ryan Wagner, who succeeded Jesse Crain as Houston's closer and gave the Cougars consecutive All-American first-team relievers, struck out 148 in 79 innings for an NCAA Division I record 16.8 per nine innings. The old record of 16.2 was set in 1964 by Murray State's George Dugan. Philadelphia Phillies lefthander Billy Wagner holds the all-time NCAA mark of 19.2, set in 1992 for Division III Ferrum (Va.).

■ Sophomore lefthander Scott Lewis tied Ohio State's single-game strikeouts record with 20 in a 4-1 win against Iowa; the mark had been set by Steve Arlin in the 1965 College World Series. Lewis followed that up with 16 more strikeouts the next weekend in a win against Indiana. After striking out 127 in 84 innings, Lewis was lost for the season when he sustained a tear of his ulnar collateral ligament in his pitching arm. Two days before Lewis struck out 20, Ohio State righthander Greg Prenger pitched a seven-inning perfect game Oakland, winning 2-0.

■ Wake Forest righthander Kyle Sleeth, the third overall pick in the 2003 draft, tied an NCAA record when he ran his streak of consecutive winning decisions to 26. Florida State snapped the streak with a 7-5 Atlantic Coast Conference victory in March, Sleeth's first setback in two years.

TEN-YEAR SNAPSHOT

Offensive numbers in Division I continued to drop in 2003, with batting averages down 15 points and runs per team down more than a full run from 1998, when offense peaked in the college game. Following is a summary of batting averages, run per game, home runs per game and ERA over the last 10 years:

Year	Average	R/Game	HR/Game	ERA
1994	.290	6.24	0.69	5.16
1995	.289	6.20	0.70	5.19
1996	.294	6.48	0.77	5.47
1997	.304	7.00	0.96	5.93
1998	*.306	*7.12	*1.06	*6.12
1999	.303	6.93	0.95	5.94
2000	.297	6.53	0.80	5.56
2001	.296	6.44	0.81	5.50
2002	.296	6.45	0.83	5.49
2003	.291	6.11	0.74	5.23

*NCAA records

2003 COLLEGE ALL-AMERICA TEAM

Selected by Baseball America

Ryan Garko

RICH ABEL

Michael Aubrey

RICH ABEL

Aaron Hill

David Murphy

Brad Snyder

FIRST TEAM

POS	Player, Team	YR	Hometown	AVG	AB	R	H	2B	3B	HR	RBI	SB	Drafted/Round
C	Ryan Garko, Stanford	Sr.	Walnut, Calif.	.402	259	64	104	24	0	18	92	2	Indians (3)
1B	Michael Aubrey, Tulane	Jr.	Shreveport, La.	.420	243	70	102	20	1	18	79	19	Indians (1)
2B	Rickie Weeks, Southern	Jr.	Altamonte Springs, La.	.479	163	82	78	13	7	16	66	28	Brewers (1)
3B	Brian Snyder, Jr., Stetson	Jr.	Wellington, Fla.	.396	227	65	90	23	3	11	55	12	Athletics (1)
SS	Aaron Hill, Louisiana State	Jr.	Visalia, Calif.	.358	265	68	95	27	4	9	67	9	Blue Jays (1)
OF	Dustin Majewski, Sr., Texas	Sr.	Brenham, Texas	.391	274	62	107	22	6	12	85	21	Athletics (3)
OF	David Murphy, Jr., Baylor	Jr.	Spring, Texas	.413	293	84	121	18	4	11	67	3	Red Sox (1)
OF	Brad Snyder, Ball State	Jr.	Bellevue, Ohio	.405	200	68	81	25	3	14	61	20	Indians (1)
DH	Mitch Maier, Toledo	Jr.	Novi, Mich.	.448	194	59	87	16	2	9	61	29	Royals (1)
UT	Scott Beerer, Texas A&M	Jr.	Newport Beach, Calif.	.335	245	44	82	17	1	11	57	5	Rockies (2)
				W	L	ERA	G	SV	IP	H	BB	SO	
SP	David Marchbanks, South Carolina	Jr.	Simpsonville, S.C.	15	3	2.73	21	0	135	148	25	97	Marlins (7)
SP	Jeff Niemann, So., Rice	So.	Houston	17	0	1.70	22	1	137	96	35	156	Not eligible
SP	Wade Townsend, Rice	So.	Dripping Springs, Texas	11	2	2.20	29	5	119	80	46	164	Not eligible
SP	Jered Weaver, Long Beach State	So.	Simi Valley, Calif.	14	4	1.96	19	0	133	87	20	144	Not eligible
RP	Ryan Wagner, Houston	So.	Yoakum, Texas	6	5	1.93	38	15	79	39	21	148	Reds (1)
UT	Scot Beerer, Texas A&M	Jr.	Newport Beach, Calif.	6	1	1.82	27	13	49	32	12	58	

SECOND TEAM

POS	Player, Team	YR	Hometown	AVG	AB	R	H	2B	3B	HR	RBI	SB	Drafted/Round
C	Tony Richie, Florida State	Jr.	Jacksonville	.366	265	60	97	26	0	12	78	5	Cubs (4)
1B	Jeff Larish, Arizona State	So.	Tempe, Ariz.	.372	234	80	87	18	2	18	95	3	Not eligible
2B	Luke Appert, Minnesota	Sr.	Cottage Grove, Minn.	.373	225	53	84	27	0	4	45	15	Athletics (6)
3B	Jamie D'Antona, Wake Forest	Jr.	Trumbull, Conn.	.360	214	59	77	19	1	21	82	1	D'backs (2)
SS	Dustin Pedroia, Arizona State	So.	Woodland, Calif.	.404	297	83	120	34	3	4	52	3	Not eligible
OF	Brian Anderson, Arizona	Jr.	Tucson, Ariz.	.366	232	58	85	12	8	14	62	17	White Sox (1)
OF	Josh Anderson, Eastern Kentucky	Jr.	Eubank, Ky.	.447	237	80	106	21	5	6	53	57	Astros (4)
OF	Carlos Quentin, Stanford	Jr.	Chula Vista, Calif.	.396	265	72	105	24	1	12	65	10	D'backs (1)
DH	Jeremy Cleveland, North Carolina	Jr.	Fairfax Station, Va.	.410	251	74	103	20	1	19	65	8	Rangers (8)
UT	Micah Owings, Georgia Tech	Fr.	Gainesville, Ga.	.307	209	43	64	11	2	15	42	2	Not eligible
				W	L	ERA	G	SV	IP	H	BB	SO	
SP	Abe Alvarez, Long Beach State	Jr.	Fontana, Calif.	11	2	2.35	18	0	123	114	31	102	Red Sox (2)
SP	Scott Lewis, Ohio State	So.	Wash. Court House, Ohio	9	1	1.61	12	0	84	48	24	127	Not eligible
SP	Justin Orenduff, Va. Commonwealth	So.	Chesapeake, Va.	9	3	2.27	18	0	95	70	26	120	Not eligible
SP	Tim Stauffer, Richmond	Jr.	Saratoga Springs, N.Y.	9	5	1.97	15	0	114	87	19	146	Padres (1)
RP	Huston Street, Texas	So.	Round Rock, Texas	8	1	1.33	39	15	74	48	13	69	Not eligible
UT	Micah Owings, Georgia Tech	Fr.	Gainesville, Ga.	9	3	3.99	17	0	88	84	21	58	

THIRD TEAM

POS	Player, Team	YR	Hometown	AVG	AB	R	H	2B	3B	HR	RBI	SB	Drafted/Round
C	Jake Fox, Michigan	Jr.	Greenfield, Ind.	.357	207	44	74	19	3	15	67	2	Cubs (3)
1B	Matt Hopper, Nebraska	Sr.	Golden, Colo.	.382	233	74	89	12	0	22	66	5	Phillies (10)
2B	Lee Curtis, Charleston	Sr.	Greer, S.C.	.399	233	65	93	26	11	11	64	20	Red Sox (8)
3B	Conor Jackson, California	Jr.	Woodland Hills, Calif.	.388	160	53	62	14	1	10	44	2	D'backs (1)
SS	Stephen Drew, Florida State	So.	Valdosta, Ga.	.327	263	83	86	18	8	11	59	33	Not eligible
OF	Jeff Cook, Southern Mississippi	Sr.	Hattiesburg, Miss.	.374	254	71	95	15	3	23	76	16	D'backs (5)
OF	Chris Durbin, Baylor	Sr.	Wylie, Texas	.346	283	94	98	23	4	18	50	9	Red Sox (10)
OF	Clint King, Southern Mississippi	So.	Pearl, Miss.	.394	254	68	100	23	2	23	77	8	White Sox (3)
DH	Billy Becher, New Mexico State	Jr.	Chandler, Ariz.	.420	250	76	105	16	4	32	118	0	Athletics (18)
UT	Ryan Gordon, UNC Greensboro	Jr.	Greenville, N.C.	.416	231	50	96	20	5	5	50	20	Blue Jays (43)
				W	L	ERA	G	SV	IP	H	BB	SO	
SP	Randy Beam, Florida Atlantic	Jr.	Sarasota, Fla.	13	2	2.39	17	0	102	74	17	83	Not drafted
SP	John Hudgins, Stanford	Jr.	Mission Viejo, Calif.	11	3	3.18	19	0	141	121	29	128	Rangers (3)
SP	Paul Maholm, Mississippi State	Jr.	Holly Springs, Miss.	9	2	2.76	15	0	108	102	39	101	Pirates (1)
SP	Tom Mastny, Furman	Sr.	Zionsville, Ind.	11	2	1.09	16	1	124	78	22	103	Blue Jays (11)
RP	Will Fenton, Washington	So.	Kingston, Wash.	2	0	0.00	18	12	32	16	11	49	Not eligible
UT	Ryan Gordon, UNC Greensboro	Jr.	Greenville, N.C.	4	2	2.59	12	0	59	49	21	55	

Record-setter Weeks primed for majors

PLAYER of the YEAR

There wasn't much else Rickie Weeks could have done for Southern University in 2003.

He flirted with .500 all spring, stole 28 bases and hit 16 homers. He led the Jaguars to the postseason, then sparked Southern to an NCAA regional win with a two-run homer. And he finished his junior year with a .463 career average, best in Division I history.

So Weeks will be expected to do a lot to help the Milwaukee Brewers.

The Brewers, trying to dig out from the rubble of 10 straight losing seasons, chose Southern's standout second baseman with the No. 2 overall pick in the 2003 draft. It was nearly as easy for Baseball America to make Weeks its College Player of the Year.

A pick that high brings an enormous amount of pressure, for both the player and the club. After watching Weeks work out under the Brewers' lonely 1982 championship flag at Miller Park, Brewers scouting director Jack Zduriencik had no second thoughts about the second selection.

"He is just a great kid," Zduriencik said. "After getting a chance to spend time with him and his family, I'm sure we made the right pick. We thoroughly enjoyed the visit and I think there was a real camaraderie and closeness that developed between him and our staff. He seemed to take to Milwaukee."

After signing a major league contract with the Brewers in August, Weeks was in the big leagues by September.

Will Milwaukee take to Weeks? Zduriencik has no doubt.

"We've seen the kid play for three years," he said. "His athleticism was always impressive. He can run. He can throw. He's strong. He has great instincts. He's played all three positions in the middle of the field—shortstop, center field and second base. He could realistically play any of those three spots. But he finally settled into one position, and I saw marked improvement as he got comfortable at second base.

"For us, when you think about this organization and where we're heading and what's coming, it's a good fit. He's 20 years old. He's going to get better. Like all young kids, he just needs some fine-tuning of his game. He's going to get that. I just can't wait to get him in a uniform."

While wearing the uniform of the Jaguars, Weeks transformed himself from a skinny, largely unnoticed and underrecruited high school player to a two-time NCAA batting champion. Weeks hit .479 as a junior as he helped his team to a 44-7 record. For his career, he was successful on 66 of 67 stolen base attempts.

Career .463 hitter
Southern's Rickie Weeks broke NCAA record

Brewers general manager Doug Melvin watched Weeks play in Baton Rouge during the spring and met him in the parking lot after the game. "He had a nice, firm handshake," Melvin said. "You like to see that."

Weeks' hands are continually noticed by scouts, who compare his wrist strength to that of home run king Hank Aaron and his bat speed to current major leaguers Gary Sheffield and Alfonso Soriano.

"That blew my mind, right there," Weeks said when asked about the comparison to Sheffield. "I don't pay much attention to that. Hopefully, I'll come out, do my best and turn some heads."

Weeks said his bat speed is just a natural phenomenon. "I have a quick bat, but to tell the truth I don't know where it comes from," he said. "It just comes naturally. You try to work on a few things, but it's pretty much natural."

—DREW OLSON

top FIVE

1. Rickie Weeks, 2b, Southern
2. Jeff Niemann, rhp, Rice
3. Michael Aubrey, 1b, Tulane
4. Ryan Garko, c, Stanford
5. David Murphy, of, Baylor

PREVIOUS WINNERS

1981—Mike Sodders, 3b, Arizona State
1982—Jeff Ledbetter, of-lhp, Florida State
1983—Dave Magadan, 1b, Alabama
1984—Oddibe McDowell, of, Arizona State
1985—Pete Incaviglia, of, Oklahoma State
1986—Casey Close, of, Michigan
1987—Robin Ventura, 3b, Oklahoma State
1988—John Olerud, 1b-lhp, Washington State
1989—Ben McDonald, rhp, Louisiana State
1990—Mike Kelly, of, Arizona State
1991—David McCarty, 1b, Stanford
1992—Phil Nevin, 3b, Cal State Fullerton
1993—Brooks Kieschnick, dh-rhp, Texas
1994—Jason Varitek, c, Georgia Tech
1995—Todd Helton, 1b-lhp, Tennessee
1996—Kris Benson, rhp, Clemson
1997—J.D. Drew, of, Florida State
1998—Jeff Austin, rhp, Stanford
1999—Jason Jennings, rhp, Baylor
2000—Mark Teixeira, 3b, Georgia Tech
2001—Mark Prior, rhp, Southern California
2002—Khalil Greene, ss, Clemson

RICKIE WEEKS at SOUTHERN

Year	AVG	AB	R	H	2B	3B	HR	RBI	BB	SO	SB
2001	.422	185	78	77	13	*12	14	69	30	30	28
2002	*.495	198	82	98	15	*12	20	*96	31	18	10
2003	*.479	163	82	78	13	7	16	66	48	21	28
Totals	**.463**	**546**	**242**	**253**	**41**	**31**	**50**	**231**	**109**	**69**	**66**

*Led nation

Horton thrives in Garrido's shadow

COACH of the YEAR

George Horton walked around Omaha's Rosenblatt Stadium during the 2003 College World Series with a noticeable limp. "It makes you think twice about going out to argue a call with umpires," he joked.

Horton's limp was due to a hip problem that was more painful than the coach would let on, but he was having too much fun to dwell on the negative. While Cal State Fullerton's season ended short of a national championship, it included the best start in the program's proud history at 8-0, a super-regional win against a powerful Arizona State team and a trip to Omaha, the 12th in school history.

Stanford ended the Titans' season with a pair of wins in the CWS, exacting revenge after losing the first four games the teams had played in 2003. The Cardinal sent the Titans packing with a trio of two-run home runs in a come-from-behind 7-5, 10-inning victory in the bracket championship.

LARRY GOREN

Keeps Titans on top
Cal State Fullerton's George Horton

Horton wasn't quite ready to laugh that one off, but he lost with his best—record-setting closer Chad Cordero—on the mound with a lead. The Titans had won 44 consecutive games when they had a lead after seven innings thanks to Cordero, a first-round draft pick. In Horton's mind, winning that game "just wasn't in the cards."

Horton undoubtedly got his philosophical bent on the game from his long association with Augie Garrido, a former Titans coach and the all-time winningest coach in NCAA Division I history. Horton played for Garrido at Cal State Fullerton in the mid-1970s and was his associate head coach for six seasons in the 1990s. Since replacing Garrido after the 1996 season, Horton himself has become one of the top college coaches, leading the Titans to three CWS trips and averaging 44 wins a year.

Horton didn't get the wins he wanted in 2003 in Omaha, but he won a fine consolation prize. He succeeded Garrido again, this time as Baseball America's Coach of the Year. Garrido won the award in 2002 after leading Texas to the national title.

Garrido built the Titans program into a national powerhouse and Horton has continued to keep Fullerton in the national spotlight.

His team had plenty of ammunition, even as things didn't go as planned in 2003. The projected pitching rotation included junior righthanders Wes Littleton, Darric Merrell and Travis Ingle. Because of injuries, ineffectiveness and Littleton's midseason suspension, the Titans went down the stretch with a completely different trio of junior righthander Jason Windsor, freshman lefty Ryan Schreppel and redshirt freshman righty Dustin Miller. That trio combined to go 25-7, 2.63.

"We had a lot of challenges—injuries, incidents, whatever you want to call them," Horton said.

Horton is not afraid to credit others for his success and points to pitching coach and recruiting coordinator Dave Serrano and assistant, Rick Vanderhook, as cogs in Fullerton's efficient machine.

But Horton is most responsible for keeping the Titans on top. Goodwin Field, which played host to both a regional and super-regional in 2003, provides Fullerton with one of the best facilities in the West. It was built on Horton's watch in 1999. And with 11 players drafted in 2003, Horton has kept the talent flowing.

top FIVE

1. George Horton, Cal State Fullerton
2. Wayne Graham, Rice
3. Smoke Laval, Louisiana State
4. Jim Morris, Miami
5. Roger Cador, Southern

PREVIOUS WINNERS

1981—Ron Fraser, Miami
1982—Gene Stephenson, Wichita State
1983—Barry Shollenberger, Alabama
1984—Augie Garrido, Cal State Fullerton
1985—Ron Polk, Mississippi State
1986—Skip Bertman, Louisiana State
Dave Snow, Loyola Marymount
1987—Mark Marquess, Stanford
1988—Jim Brock, Arizona State
1989—Dave Snow, Long Beach State
1990—Steve Webber, Georgia
1991—Jim Hendry, Creighton
1992—Andy Lopez, Pepperdine
1993—Gene Stephenson, Wichita State
1994—Jim Morris, Miami
1995—Rod Delmonico, Tennessee
1996—Skip Bertman, Louisiana State
1997—Jim Wells, Alabama
1998—Pat Murphy, Arizona State
1999—Wayne Graham, Rice
2000—Ray Tanner, South Carolina
2001—Dave Van Horn, Nebraska
2002—Augie Garrido, Texas

Lawler selected top assistant coach

When Mark Johnson was named head coach at Texas A&M in 1985, his first move was to persuade Jim Lawler to join his coaching staff. The two have been together ever since.

Jim Lawler

Lawler, 52, came aboard as pitching coach and recruiting coordinator after stints as head coach at Gonzaga and Texas-El Paso, and was elevated to assistant head coach in 1989.

The 2003 Aggies posted a 45-19 record and narrowly missed winning their first Big 12 Conference title since 1999. Eight members of Lawler's pitching staff were also selected in the draft.

Lawler was named the 2003 winner of the American Baseball Coaches Association/Baseball America Assistant Coach of the Year award.

PREVIOUS WINNERS

1999—Dean Stotz, Stanford
2000—Tim Corbin, Clemson
2001—Brian O'Connor, Notre Dame
2002—Jim Toman, South Carolina

Braun joins illustrious group of UM freshmen

FRESHMAN of the YEAR

Some of the names on Miami's list of freshman record holders are known to fans of college and major league baseball alike.

Pat Burrell has the mark for most total bases. Charles Johnson has the most triples. Kevin Howard, Baseball America's Freshman of the Year in 2000, holds the record for doubles.

Now those storied names need to make way for perhaps the best freshman season in Miami history. Shortstop Ryan Braun, undrafted in 2002 of Granada Hills (Calif.) High, led a young Hurricanes team that had only one player drafted in 2003 back to the College World Series, carrying the team at the plate while taking over shortstop duties midway through the season. For his efforts, he joined Burrell and Howard as 'Canes who have earned Baseball America's Freshman of the Year Award.

"Ryan Braun hit in the three-hole and played shortstop for us the second half of the year, and that's a big reason why we got hot in the second half," Miami coach Jim Morris said. "You break a Pat Burrell record, you've done something right."

Braun hit .364-17-76 and led the Hurricanes in the three triple crown categories. His 76 RBIs tied him for sixth all-time on Miami's single-season list and bettered the freshman record Burrell set with 67 in 1996, when he led the nation in batting at .484.

Like Burrell, Braun turned it up in the postseason, getting his most important RBIs of the year in the super-regional against North Carolina State. Braun slammed a three-run homer in the first inning of the first game, then won it with a walk-off homer in the bottom of the ninth off Wolfpack closer (and fellow Freshman All-American) Joey Devine.

It was the 12th game-winning hit of the season for Braun, and the third walk-off homer, capping a comeback from a 9-3 deficit. Miami won the next day for its eighth trip to Omaha in 10 years.

"I definitely pride myself in that, doing well in pressure situations," Braun said. "I'm confident in myself as a hitter and look forward to hitting in those situations."

Not only did Braun join luminaries like Burrell in Miami lore, but he's also priming himself to join the long line of top shortstops that Morris has coached, which stretches back to Nomar Garciaparra at Georgia Tech. Miami's shortstop legacy indirectly includes Alex Rodriguez, who nearly went to school before signing as the No. 1 pick in the 1993 draft.

"He looks like a Nomar or A-Rod physically," Morris said. "I'm not going to put those kinds of comparisons on him, but he's been a special player for us."

Drove in big runs for Canes
Miami's Ryan Braun

PREVIOUS WINNERS

1982—Cory Snyder, 3b, Brigham Young
1983—Rafael Palmeiro, of, Mississippi State
1984—Greg Swindell, lhp, Texas
1985—Jack McDowell, rhp, Stanford
Ron Wenrich, of, Georgia
1986—Robin Ventura, 3b, Oklahoma State
1987—Paul Carey, of, Stanford
1988—Kirk Dressendorfer, rhp, Texas
1989—Alex Fernandez, rhp, Miami
1990—Jeffrey Hammonds, of, Stanford
1991—Brooks Kieschnick, rhp-dh, Texas
1992—Todd Walker, 2b, Louisiana State
1993—Brett Laxton, rhp, Louisiana State
1994—R.A. Dickey, rhp, Tennessee
1995—Kyle Peterson, rhp, Stanford
1996—Pat Burrell, 3b, Miami
1997—Brian Roberts, ss, North Carolina
1998—Xavier Nady, 2b, California
1999—James Jurries, 2b, Tulane
2000—Kevin Howard, 3b, Miami
2001—Michael Aubrey, of/lhp, Tulane
2002—Stephen Drew, ss, Florida State

top FIVE

1. Ryan Braun, ss, Miami
2. Micah Owings, rhp-dh, Georgia Tech
3. Jeff Clement, c, Southern California
4. Mark Romanczuk, lhp, Stanford
5. Stephen Head, lhp-1b, Mississippi

FRESHMAN ALL-AMERICA TEAM

FIRST TEAM

Pos., Player, School	AVG	AB	R	H	2B	3B	HR	RBI	SB
C Jeff Clement, Southern California	.298	208	53	62	8	1	21	53	1
1B Stephen Head, Mississippi	.337	208	31	70	10	2	6	44	1
2B Justin Turner, Cal State Fullerton	.326	224	40	73	9	1	1	39	13
3B Brad Boyer, Arizona	.351	239	71	84	16	8	5	47	25
SS Ryan Braun, Miami	.364	242	61	88	16	3	17	76	13
OF Daniel Carte, Winthrop	.345	203	56	70	20	1	12	53	9
OF Dan Dorn, Cal State Fullerton	.348	178	47	62	11	3	7	54	5
OF Brent Lillibridge, Washington	.388	183	49	71	16	1	13	47	9
DH Brett Hayes, Nevada	.365	233	48	85	16	2	8	63	8
UT Micah Owings, Georgia Tech	.307	209	43	64	11	2	15	42	2

	W	L	ERA	G	SV	IP	H	BB	SO
SP Mike Pelfrey, Wichita State	10	2	2.49	17	0	105	80	15	98
SP Glen Perkins, Minnesota	10	2	2.91	15	0	105	100	23	117
SP Michael Rogers, N.C. State	12	3	3.02	17	0	125	122	34	113
SP Mark Romanczuk, Stanford	12	2	4.01	23	2	112	97	55	80
RP Joey Devine, N.C. State	6	3	2.19	36	14	66	49	16	78
UT Micah Owings, Georgia Tech	9	3	3.99	17	0	88	84	21	58

SECOND TEAM

C—Taylor Teagarden, Texas (.315-5-41). **1B**—Adam Lind, South Alabama (.349-8-42). **2B**—David Uribes, Pepperdine (.330-2-28). **3B**—Gaby Sanchez, Miami (.328-7-56). **SS**—Tyler Greene, Georgia Tech (.316-8-43, 19 SB). **OF**—Travis Buck, Arizona State (.326-4-46); Jacoby Ellsbury, Oregon State (.330-7-33); Matt Sutton, UNC Wilmington (.317-12-50). **DH**—Ben Zeskind, Richmond (.366-6-40). **Util**—Brian Bogusevic, Tulane (.321-4-36; 3-2, 3.41).

SP—Erik Averill, Arizona State (8-2, 3.66); J.R. Crowel, Tulane (8-1, 3.40); Justin Meier, Louisiana State (8-3, 2.83); Dustin Miller, Cal State Fullerton (9-2, 3.33, 100 IP/97 SO). **RP**—Matt Manship, Stanford (2-4, 3.98, 9 SV).

NCAA DIVISION I LEADERS

TEAM BATTING

BATTING AVERAGE	G	AVG
Southern	51	.351
Arizona State	68	.347
New Mexico	60	.345
UC Riverside	58	.334
West Virginia	55	.334
Eastern Kentucky	53	.332
New Mexico State	61	.330
Brigham Young	54	.330
Minnesota	62	.329
Cal State Fullerton	66	.329

RUNS SCORED	G	R
Arizona State	68	682
New Mexico State	61	602
New Mexico	60	594
Nevada-Las Vegas	64	588
Florida State	68	574
Baylor	68	545
Miami (Fla.)	63	540
Louisiana State	68	524
Arizona	58	521
Southern	51	519
Cal State Fullerton	66	519

DOUBLES	G	2B
New Mexico	60	172
Nevada-Las Vegas	64	168
Baylor	68	167
Florida State	68	161
Cal State Fullerton	66	160
Arizona State	68	160

TRIPLES	G	3B
Arizona	58	50
Texas	70	37
Southern	51	31
Brigham Young	54	31
San Diego State	61	29
Stanford	69	29
Baylor	68	29

HOMERUNS	G	HR
New Mexico State	61	107
Washington	60	96
New Mexico	60	93
Southern Mississippi	63	89
Nevada-Las Vegas	64	85
Louisiana State	68	85
Baylor	68	83
Nevada	56	81
Florida State	68	81

STOLEN BASES	G	SB	ATT
Coastal Carolina	63	155	197
Arizona	58	144	186
Bethune-Cookman	58	138	178
Jackson State	40	134	164
Eastern Kentucky	53	131	167
Northern Iowa	55	130	159
Miami	63	123	165
Texas	70	121	157
Richmond	63	116	135
Tulane	63	116	146
Cal State Fullerton	66	116	160

TEAM PITCHING

WINNING PERCENTAGE	W	L	PCT
Southern	44	7	.863
Rice	58	12	.829
Florida State	54	13	.806
Arizona State	54	14	.794
Virginia Commonwealth	46	13	.780
Richmond	48	15	.762
Cal State Fullerton	51	16	.761
Southern Mississippi	47	16	.746
Florida Atlantic	47	16	.746
Stanford	51	18	.739

EARNED RUN AVERAGE	G	ERA
Virginia Commonwealth	59	2.54
Rice	70	2.74
Cal State Fullerton	66	2.87
Florida State	68	2.96
Long Beach State	61	2.99
Vermont	46	3.12
Illinois-Chicago	57	3.19
Arizona State	68	3.32
Richmond	63	3.32
Marist	54	3.38

TEAM FIELDING

	G	AVG
Long Beach State	61	.980
Rice	70	.980
Washington	60	.978
Purdue	55	.975
Fresno State	59	.975
Mississippi State	63	.974
Wichita State	76	.974
Maine	56	.973
Arizona State	68	.973
Pepperdine	61	.973

INDIVIDUAL BATTING

BATTING AVERAGE

(Minimum 150 At-Bats)

	Yr.	AVG	G	AB	R	H	2B	3B	HR	RBI	BB	SO	SB
Rickie Weeks, Southern	Jr.	.479	51	163	82	78	13	7	16	66	48	21	28
Mitch Maier, Toledo	Jr.	.448	51	194	59	87	16	2	9	61	31	9	29
Josh Anderson, Eastern Ky.	Jr.	.447	53	237	80	106	21	5	6	53	23	15	57
Kelly Hunt, Bowling Green	Sr.	.439	45	171	33	75	18	1	9	61	21	17	4
Adrian Brown, Mississippi Valley	Sr.	.425	50	167	45	71	9	3	1	32	37	19	11
Tim D'Aquila, Central Conn. State	Jr.	.425	50	186	46	79	12	1	2	38	10	15	6
Michael Brown, William & Mary	Sr.	.423	51	201	58	85	13	1	20	66	21	24	11
Ryan Roberts, Texas-Arlington	Sr.	.422	62	230	69	97	21	5	16	69	42	31	13
Jaime Landin, Texas A&M-CC	So.	.421	50	202	62	85	9	9	2	41	21	17	8
Keith Brachold, Marist	So.	.421	54	214	56	90	17	2	8	48	25	27	16
John Gragg, Bethune-Cookman	Sr.	.421	57	214	54	90	18	6	4	62	30	22	23
Billy Becher, New Mexico State	Jr.	.420	61	250	76	105	16	4	32	118	31	37	0
Michael Aubrey, Tulane	Jr.	.420	63	243	70	102	20	1	18	79	34	13	19
Casey Benjamin, Tennessee Tech	Sr.	.418	52	196	54	82	17	3	5	44	32	29	5
Jordan Foster, Lamar	Jr.	.417	58	230	54	96	29	1	7	71	25	18	6
Ryan Gordon, UNC Greensboro	Jr.	.416	60	231	50	96	20	5	5	50	25	24	20
Jeff Van Houten, Arizona	So.	.413	57	213	53	88	10	9	11	72	24	27	9
Josh Phifer, Air Force	Sr.	.413	54	184	50	76	21	3	15	62	20	35	4
David Murphy, Baylor	Jr.	.413	68	293	84	121	18	4	11	67	42	22	3
Vasili Spanos, Indiana	Sr.	.412	54	182	53	75	16	2	11	47	33	27	5
Eddie Kim, James Madison	Sr.	.412	55	204	57	84	16	0	17	67	29	39	4
Ryan Harvey, UC Riverside	Jr.	.411	56	236	65	97	12	3	9	40	10	26	8
Jeremy Cleveland, No. Carolina	Jr.	.410	65	251	74	103	20	1	19	65	37	34	8
Marc Franz, Ball State	So.	.410	51	166	46	68	13	0	3	33	14	19	4
Billy Hess, Columbia	Sr.	.409	45	171	43	70	14	0	7	39	6	24	4
Mike Rozema, St. John's (N.Y.)	Jr.	.408	54	196	44	80	12	4	2	33	16	30	13
Lee Fritz, West Virginia	So.	.407	54	216	40	88	11	2	1	23	11	22	6
Neil Sellers, Eastern Ky.	Jr.	.407	53	231	66	94	24	0	17	85	18	31	14
Brad Snyder, Ball State	Jr.	.405	55	200	68	81	25	3	14	61	49	45	20
Ranger Weins, Brigham Young	Jr.	.405	53	220	50	89	25	4	4	55	20	25	21
Dustin Pedroia, Arizona State	So.	.404	68	297	83	120	34	3	4	52	36	13	3
Mikela Olsen, Sacramento State	Jr.	.404	56	218	50	88	20	2	16	66	19	34	2
Jarod Rine, West Virginia	Jr.	.403	46	186	43	75	12	1	9	34	17	25	14
Josh McCurdy, Niagara	Sr.	.403	51	211	57	85	18	1	12	63	11	18	28
Humberto Aguilar, Texas A&M-CC	Sr.	.402	48	179	43	72	12	0	20	74	25	28	2
Brad Ditter, New Mexico State	Jr.	.402	61	244	84	98	16	8	6	67	36	30	14
Ryan Garko, Stanford	Sr.	.402	69	259	64	104	24	0	18	92	28	17	2
Chad Hauseman, Jacksonville	Sr.	.401	53	187	47	75	11	0	16	37	23	24	10
Brian Hopkins, SE Mo. State	Sr.	.401	51	202	58	81	19	3	18	59	25	48	7
Lee Curtis, Col. of Charleston	Sr.	.399	58	233	65	93	26	11	11	64	28	31	20
Marc Tugwell, Virginia Tech	Sr.	.398	57	226	64	90	17	0	8	59	14	32	16
Tom Shanley, George Washington	Fr.	.398	54	186	48	74	6	1	2	30	20	20	5
Chuck Hickman, Nicholls State	Sr.	.397	54	229	50	91	13	2	3	34	19	29	26
Brian Snyder, Stetson	Jr.	.396	64	227	65	90	23	3	11	55	48	27	12
Carlos Quentin, Stanford	Jr.	.396	68	265	72	105	24	1	12	64	36	28	10
Chris Ard, The Citadel	So.	.396	57	225	49	89	11	1	5	44	10	23	8
Jayce Tingler, Missouri	Sr.	.395	58	215	68	85	11	3	1	49	48	9	19
Scott Dierks, Santa Clara	Sr.	.394	52	170	45	67	14	0	18	42	14	36	1
Clint King, Southern Miss.	So.	.394	63	254	68	100	23	2	23	77	25	48	8
Dan Batz, Rhode Island	Jr.	.393	52	191	32	75	15	2	5	46	19	14	15
Brian Buscher, South Carolina	Sr.	.393	67	270	55	106	19	2	15	66	24	32	5
Eddie Cornejo, Oklahoma	Sr.	.393	54	214	37	84	15	2	2	49	31	11	10
Chris Stanton, Virginia Tech	So.	.392	57	222	61	87	12	6	3	36	18	28	23
Mitch Jones, UAB	Sr.	.392	53	194	40	76	7	1	6	37	16	41	14
Kirk Walters, Eastern Ill.	Sr.	.392	51	189	43	74	8	3	13	56	25	27	7
Matt Wolski, Rutgers	Sr.	.391	57	192	40	75	10	2	1	34	28	29	10
Dustin Majewski, Texas	Sr.	.391	70	274	62	107	22	6	12	85	34	40	21
Dale Mueller, Butler	So.	.391	54	207	43	81	9	1	1	19	14	21	9
Tom Fabrizio, Western Mich.	Sr.	.390	51	187	32	73	18	1	3	38	28	30	8
Ryan Bear, Central Florida	Sr.	.390	56	195	45	76	20	5	5	36	22	18	7
Jesse Schmidt, Sacramento State	Jr.	.389	56	208	53	81	9	0	16	55	29	42	16
Luke Miller, Evansville	Sr.	.388	55	206	42	80	13	2	6	34	14	28	2
Brent Lillibridge, Washington	Fr.	.388	54	183	49	71	16	1	13	47	16	48	9
Ricardo Nanita, Fla. International	Jr.	.388	56	196	54	76	14	3	12	52	39	34	9
Conor Jackson, California	Jr.	.388	48	160	53	62	14	1	10	44	49	22	2

RUNS SCORED	Yr.	G	R
Chris Durbin, Baylor	Sr.	67	94
Brad Ditter, New Mex. State	Jr.	61	84
David Murphy, Baylor	Jr.	68	84
Rickie Weeks, Southern	Jr.	51	83
Stephen Drew, Florida State	So.	65	83
Dustin Pedroia, Arizona State	So.	68	83
Sam Fuld, Stanford	Jr.	69	83
Tim Moss, Texas	Jr.	70	82
Josh Anderson, Eastern Ky.	Jr.	53	80
Jeff Larish, Arizona State	So.	65	80
Alex Borgo, New Mex. State	Sr.	61	77
Chris Kolkhorst, Rice	Jr.	68	77

HITS	Yr.	G	H
David Murphy, Baylor	Jr.	68	121
Dustin Pedroia, Arizona State	So.	68	120
Dustin Majewski, Texas	Sr.	70	107
Josh Anderson, Eastern Ky.	Jr.	53	106
Brian Buscher, So. Carolina	Sr.	67	106
Carlos Quentin, Stanford	Jr.	68	105
Billy Becher, New Mex. State	Jr.	61	105
Ryan Garko, Stanford	Sr.	69	104
Jeremy Cleveland, No. Carolina	Jr.	65	103
Michael Griffin, Baylor	So.	68	103
Michael Aubrey, Tulane	Jr.	63	102
Dusty Young, New Mexico	Sr.	58	101
Shane Costa, CS Fullerton	Jr.	66	101
Clint King, So. Mississippi	So.	63	100

SLUGGING PERCENTAGE

(Minimum 125 At-Bats)	Yr.	G	PCT
Rickie Weeks, Southern	Jr.	51	.933
Billy Becher, New Mexico State	Jr.	61	.900
Humberto Aguilar, TAM-CC	Sr.	48	.804
Josh Phifer, Air Force	Sr.	54	.804
Michael Brown, William & Mary	Sr.	51	.796
Scott Dierks, Santa Clara	Sr.	52	.794
Brian Hopkins, SE Mo. State	Sr.	51	.792
Mike Costello, Towson	Jr.	53	.785
Chris Alexander, New Mexico	Sr.	58	.773
Clint King, So. Mississippi	So.	63	.772
Brad Snyder, Ball State	Jr.	55	.770
Ryan Roberts, Texas-Arlington	Sr.	62	.765
Brian Oakes, La Salle	Jr.	36	.756
Jamie D'Antona, Wake Forest	Jr.	53	.752

ON-BASE PERCENTAGE

(Minimum 125 At-Bats)	Yr.	G	PCT
Rickie Weeks, Southern	Jr.	51	.609
Conor Jackson, California	Jr.	48	.538
Jeff Larish, Arizona State	Jr.	65	.528
Mitch Maier, Toledo	Jr.	51	.525
Jayce Tingler, Missouri	Sr.	58	.525
Brad Snyder, Ball State	Jr.	55	.522
Ryan Roberts, Texas-Arlington	Sr.	62	.514
Jeremy West, Arizona State	Jr.	63	.513
Vasili Spanos, Indiana	Sr.	54	.513
Jeremy Cleveland, No. Car.	Jr.	65	.510
Scooter Jordan, Texas Tech	Sr.	50	.510
Josh Anderson, Eastern Ky.	Jr.	53	.509
Brian Snyder, Stetson	Jr.	64	.505
Michael Aubrey, Tulane	Jr.	63	.505
Matt Hopper, Nebraska	Sr.	62	.505

TOTAL BASES	Yr.	G	TB
Billy Becher, New Mex. State	Jr.	61	225
Clint King, So. Mississippi	So.	63	196
Jeff Cook, So. Mississippi	Sr.	63	185
Chris Durbin, Baylor	Sr.	67	183
Jeremy Cleveland, No. Car.	Jr.	65	182
Ryan Garko, Stanford	Sr.	69	182
David Murphy, Baylor	Jr.	68	180
Michael Aubrey, Tulane	Jr.	63	178
Michael Griffin, Baylor	So.	68	178
Ryan Roberts, Texas-Arlington	Sr.	62	176
Chris Alexander, New Mexico	Sr.	58	174
Lee Curtis, Charleston	Sr.	58	174
Brian Buscher, So. Carolina	Sr.	67	174
Dustin Pedroia, Arizona State	So.	68	172

DOUBLES	Yr.	G	2B
Dustin Pedroia, Arizona State	So.	68	34
Jordan Foster, Lamar	Jr.	58	29
Omar Quintanilla, Texas	Jr.	70	29
Shane Costa, CS Fullerton	Jr.	66	28
Rick Guarno, Ark.-Little Rock	Jr.	56	27
Luke Appert, Minnesota	Sr.	62	27
Adam Pavkovich, Alabama	Jr.	62	27
Aaron Hill, LSU	Jr.	68	27
Lee Curtis, Charleston	Sr.	58	26
Joey Prast, San Diego	Jr.	62	26
Rod Goldston, West. Carolina	Sr.	63	26
Michael Griffin, Baylor	So.	68	26
Tony Richie, Florida State	Jr.	68	26

JEFF GOLDEN

Chris Durbin: 94 runs

TRIPLES	Yr.	G	3B
Lee Curtis, Charleston	Sr.	58	11
Jaime Landin, TAM-CC	So.	50	9
Jeff Van Houten, Arizona	So.	57	9
Sam Fuld, Stanford	Jr.	69	9
Tim Moss, Texas	Jr.	70	9
Evan Tartaglia, Elon	Jr.	53	8
Doug Jackson, BYU	Sr.	54	8
Brad Boyer, Arizona	Fr.	56	8
Brian Anderson, Arizona	Jr.	57	8
Ryan Fitzgerald, Creighton	Sr.	57	8
Brad Ditter, New Mex. State	Jr.	61	8
Stephen Drew, Florida State	So.	65	8
Michael Griffin, Baylor	So.	68	8

HOME RUNS	Yr.	G	HR
Billy Becher, New Mex. State	Jr.	61	32
Chris Alexander, New Mexico	Sr.	58	25
Jeff Cook, So. Mississippi	Sr.	63	23
Clint King, So. Mississippi	So.	63	23
Chad Boudon, Washington	Jr.	57	22
Matt Hopper, Nebraska	Sr.	62	22
Jamie D'Antona, Wake Forest	Jr.	53	21
Jeff Clement, So. California	Fr.	56	21
Humberto Aguilar, TAM-CC	Sr.	48	20
Michael Brown, Wm. & Mary	Sr.	51	20
Ryan Mulhern, So. Alabama	Sr.	59	20
Beau Hearod, Alabama	Sr.	62	20
Ryan Fox, Arkansas	Sr.	57	19
Michael Carlin, Miami (Ohio)	Sr.	60	19
Brett Carroll, Middle Tenn.	So.	60	19
Colt Morton, N.C State	Jr.	62	19
Jeremy Cleveland, No. Carolina	Jr.	65	19
Brian Hopkins, SE Mo. State	Sr.	51	18
Scott Dierks, Santa Clara	Sr.	52	18
Adam Boeve, Northern Iowa	Jr.	55	18
Justin Riley, N.C. State	Sr.	59	18
Michael Aubrey, Tulane	Jr.	63	18
Alan Beck, West. Carolina	Sr.	64	18
Jeff Larish, Arizona State	So.	65	18
Chris Durbin, Baylor	Sr.	67	18
Ryan Garko, Stanford	Sr.	69	18
Drew Moffitt, Wichita State	Jr.	75	18

RUNS BATTED IN	Yr.	G	RBI
Billy Becher, New Mex. State	Jr.	61	118
Jeff Larish, Arizona State	So.	65	95
Chris Alexander, New Mexico	Sr.	58	93
Ryan Garko, Stanford	Sr.	69	92
Neil Sellers, Eastern Ky.	Jr.	53	85
Dustin Majewski, Texas	Sr.	70	85
Jamie D'Antona, Wake Forest	Jr.	53	82
Beau Hearod, Alabama	Sr.	62	82
Michael Aubrey, Tulane	Jr.	63	79
Tony Richie, Florida State	Jr.	68	78
Clint King, So. Mississippi	So.	63	77
Drew Moffitt, Wichita State	Jr.	75	77
Jeff Cook, So. Mississippi	Sr.	63	76
Michael Griffin, Baylor	So.	68	76
Omar Quintanilla, Texas	Jr.	70	76
Fernando Valenzuela, UNLV	Jr.	63	75
Humberto Aguilar, TAM-CC	Sr.	48	74
Ryan Braun, Miami	Fr.	62	74
Jeff Van Houten, Arizona	So.	57	72
Adam Boeve, Northern Iowa	Jr.	55	71
Jordan Foster, Lamar	Jr.	58	71
Alex Borgo, New Mex. State	Sr.	61	71
Jeremy West, Arizona State	Jr.	63	71
Alan Beck, West. Carolina	Sr.	64	71

WALKS	Yr.	G	BB
Jeff Larish, Arizona State	So.	65	78
Michael Johnson, Clemson	Sr.	58	63
Christian Snavely, Ohio State	Jr.	65	62
Graig Badger, Rutgers	Jr.	59	56
Matt Hopper, Nebraska	Sr.	62	53
Ryan McGraw, Co. Carolina	Jr.	63	53
Brian Ingram, Elon	Sr.	55	52
Jeff Baker, Coastal Carolina	Sr.	61	52
Tony McQuade, Fla. State	Jr.	66	52
Andre Ethier, Arizona State	Jr.	68	52

STRIKEOUTS	Yr.	G	SO
Alex Borgo, New Mex. State	Sr.	60	79
Micah Owings, Ga. Tech	Fr.	57	71
Eric Jones, N.C. A&T	Sr.	50	69
Matt Wilkerson, UCSB	So.	53	67
Josh Archer, Middle Tenn.	So.	59	67

TOUGHEST TO STRIKE OUT

(Minimum 125 At-Bats)	Yr.	AB	SO	Ratio
Matt Rogelstad, Ark. State	Jr.	208	5	41.6
Jayce Tingler, Missouri	Sr.	215	9	23.9
Hyung Cho, Houston	Jr.	261	11	23.7
Dustin Pedroia, Ariz. State	So.	297	13	22.8
Larry Wayne York, Liberty	Sr.	196	9	21.8

STOLEN BASES	Yr.	G	SB	ATT
Josh Anderson, Eastern Ky.	Jr.	53	57	65
Sebastien Boucher, B-C	So.	56	48	53
Jon Kaplan, Tulane	Sr.	62	48	56
Ryan McGraw, Co. Car.	Jr.	63	45	57
Graig Badger, Rutgers	Jr.	59	41	48
Danny Figueroa, Miami	So.	63	41	46
Steve Sollmann, Notre Dame	Jr.	61	38	48
Reggie Willits, Oklahoma	Sr.	54	37	44
Kevin Estrada, Pepperdine	Sr.	61	35	40
Carl Loadenthal, Rider	Sr.	48	35	37
Ryan Hubbard, Wake Forest	Sr.	51	35	40
Michael Willis, Prairie View	Jr.	55	35	43
Eric Patterson, Ga. Tech	So.	59	35	41
Evan Tartaglia, Elon	Jr.	53	34	42
Brett Grandstrand, Co. Car.	So.	61	34	43
Stephen Drew, Fla. State	So.	65	33	36
Jordan Czarniecki, Tenn.	Sr.	55	32	39

HIT BY PITCH	Yr.	G	HBP
Cody Rizzo, Notre Dame	Fr.	58	28
Nathan Doyle, James Madison	Sr.	55	26
Chris Kolkhorst, Rice	Jr.	68	25
Brad Frich, Beth.-Cookman	Jr.	56	24
Brandon Baarstad, More. State	Sr.	49	24

BILL NICHOLS

Billy Becher: 32 homers, 118 RBIs

INDIVIDUAL PITCHING

EARNED RUN AVERAGE

(Minimum 60 Innings)

	Yr.	W	L	ERA	G	GS	CG	SV	IP	H	R	ER	BB	SO
Tom Mastny, Furman	Sr.	11	2	1.09	16	15	8	1	124	78	23	15	22	103
Cla Meredith, Va. Common.	So.	6	0	1.19	29	0	0	8	60	44	8	8	16	70
Huston Street, Texas	So.	8	1	1.33	39	0	0	15	74	48	13	11	13	69
Jamie Merchant, Vermont	Sr.	7	2	1.56	11	10	6	1	75	56	21	13	14	81
Chuck Bechtel, Marist	Sr.	8	4	1.59	13	13	7	0	85	65	29	15	26	98
Scott Lewis, Ohio State	So.	9	1	1.61	12	12	3	0	84	48	23	15	24	127
Jeff Niemann, Rice	So.	17	0	1.70	22	18	1	1	137	96	32	26	35	156
Kevin Ool, Marist	Sr.	6	1	1.74	11	9	3	0	72	59	18	14	12	49
Matt Wilhite, Western Ky.	Sr.	8	2	1.78	37	0	0	11	76	49	21	15	20	64
Chris Schutt, Cornell	Jr.	3	5	1.89	10	8	3	1	62	43	24	13	23	89
Ryan Wagner, Houston	So.	6	5	1.93	38	0	0	15	79	39	19	17	21	148
Dewan Day, Southern	Sr.	10	0	1.93	14	13	1	0	70	51	21	15	31	48
Jered Weaver, Long Beach State	So.	14	4	1.96	19	19	3	0	133	87	35	29	20	144
R.J. Swindle, Charleston So.	So.	10	4	1.96	20	17	4	1	119	102	46	26	24	129
Tim Stauffer, Richmond	Jr.	9	5	1.97	15	15	10	0	114	87	35	25	19	146
Jason Windsor, CS Fullerton	Jr.	11	2	1.98	23	12	0	0	95	76	25	21	22	75
Brandon Hankins, SW Texas	Sr.	8	1	2.10	23	11	0	1	94	84	29	22	29	82
Joey Devine, N.C. State	Fr.	6	3	2.19	36	0	0	14	66	49	18	16	16	78
Jessie Corn, Jacksonville State	Jr.	8	6	2.19	15	15	4	0	115	88	40	28	23	119
Wade Townsend, Rice	So.	11	2	2.20	29	13	0	5	119	80	36	29	46	164
James Hoey, Rider	Jr.	6	4	2.24	14	11	3	0	88	71	30	22	44	63
Mike McGirr, Richmond	Sr.	10	1	2.25	16	15	4	0	96	90	38	24	24	91
Taylor McIntyre, Oral Roberts	Fr.	7	2	2.27	20	13	2	1	79	72	36	20	30	59
Justin Orenduff, Va. Common.	So.	9	3	2.27	18	17	1	0	95	70	28	24	26	120
Clayton Jerome, TCU	Jr.	9	4	2.34	16	16	5	0	111	86	38	29	25	106
Abe Alvarez, Long Beach State	Jr.	11	2	2.35	18	18	0	0	123	114	35	32	31	102
Ryan Martin, Ill.-Chicago	Fr.	7	1	2.35	15	11	2	0	73	58	23	19	22	63
Randy Beam, Fla. Atlantic	Jr.	13	2	2.39	17	16	6	0	102	74	30	27	17	83
Justin Verlander, Old Dominion	So.	7	6	2.40	15	15	7	0	116	94	44	31	43	139
Jason Bolinski, Richmond	So.	10	1	2.40	15	11	6	1	82	66	29	22	30	88
Levale Speigner, Auburn	Sr.	10	0	2.42	27	5	0	1	67	58	26	18	20	51
Clark Girardeau, South Alabama	Jr.	6	2	2.43	13	13	1	0	78	59	26	21	46	71
Kevin Shepard, Boston College	So.	8	3	2.44	12	11	0	0	70	72	37	19	28	46
Mike Pelfrey, Wichita State	Fr.	10	2	2.49	17	16	2	0	105	80	30	29	15	98
Jeremy Sowers, Vanderbilt	So.	7	5	2.50	18	16	1	0	115	94	36	32	29	123
J.P. Howell, Texas	So.	10	2	2.52	21	19	1	0	114	97	41	32	43	105
Rich McDevitt, Navy	Sr.	5	5	2.52	12	10	4	0	71	71	29	20	12	59
Aaron Phillips, Butler	Sr.	6	5	2.53	15	15	8	0	103	87	34	29	25	73
Barry Hertzler, Central Conn. State	Jr.	9	3	2.59	14	13	9	0	87	70	34	25	18	72
Matt Durkin, San Jose State	So.	7	6	2.60	16	15	5	1	100	75	36	29	42	110

WINS	Yr.	W	L
Jeff Niemann, Rice	So.	17	0
David Marchbanks, So. Carolina	Jr.	15	3
Tim Alvarez, SE Mo. State	Sr.	14	3
John Hudgins, Stanford	Jr.	14	3
Jered Weaver, Long Beach State	So.	14	4
Randy Beam, Florida Atlantic	Jr.	13	2
Matt Lynch, Florida State	Sr.	13	4
Brad Ziegler, SW Missouri St.	Sr.	12	2
Mark Romanczuk, Stanford	Fr.	12	2
Zac Cline, West Virginia	So.	12	3
Michael Rogers, N.C. State	Fr.	12	3
Vern Sterry, N.C. State	Jr.	11	0
Abe Alvarez, Long Beach State	Jr.	11	2
Tom Mastny, Furman	Sr.	11	2
Wade Townsend, Rice	So.	11	2
Jason Windsor, CS Fullerton	Jr.	11	2
David Austen, South Florida	Sr.	11	3
Steven Carter, Co. Carolina	Jr.	11	3
J.D. Cockroft, Miami	Jr.	11	3
Philip Humber, Rice	So.	11	3
Jeremy Plexico, Winthrop	Sr.	11	3
A.J. Shappi, UC Riverside	So.	11	3
Nate Bumstead, LSU	Jr.	11	4

LOSSES	Yr.	W	L
Jeremy Dracup, Canisius	Sr.	0	12
Kyle Markle, Cincinnati	So.	0	11
Jeremy Mizell, SE Louisiana	Fr.	1	11
Nick Peterson, App. State	Fr.	2	11
Brad Bissell, Char. Southern	So.	4	11

APPEARANCES	Yr.	G
Jarrett Santos, UNC Greensboro	Jr.	41
Chad Cordero, CS Fullerton	Jr.	40
David Aardsma, Rice	Jr.	40
Joey Livingston, South Florida	Sr.	39
Daniel Hodges, Florida State	Sr.	39
Joey Charron, Tulane	Sr.	39
Huston Street, Texas	So.	39

RICH ABEL

Tim Stauffer: 10 complete games

COMPLETE GAMES	Yr.	GS	CG
Tim Stauffer, Richmond	Jr.	15	10
Zac Cline, West Virginia	So.	16	10
Barry Hertzler, Cent. Conn.	Sr.	13	9
Anthony Johnson, Jackson State	So.	10	8
Gregg Pleeter, Fair. Dickinson	Jr.	11	8
David Bayless, Ark.-Pine Bluff	So.	12	8
Ricardo Castillo, Savannah State	Sr.	13	8
Toby Middleton, N.C. A&T	So.	14	8
Kevin Banks, Ark.-Pine Bluff	Sr.	14	8
Tom Mastny, Furman	Sr.	15	8
Aaron Phillips, Butler	Sr.	15	8
John Hudgins, Stanford	Jr.	22	8

LARRY GOREN

Huston Street: 8-1, 1.33, 15 saves

SAVES	Yr.	G	SV
Steven Register, Auburn	So.	33	16
Ryan Wagner, Houston	So.	38	15
Huston Street, Texas	So.	40	15
Mike Dennison, Wichita State	Sr.	27	14
Mark Badgley, No. Illinois	Fr.	28	14
Matt Dalton, Virginia Tech	Sr.	29	14
Matt Davis, Ohio State	So.	33	14
Joey Devine, N.C. State	Fr.	36	14
Stephen Head, Mississippi	Fr.	20	13
Shaun Marcum, SW Mo. State	Jr.	24	13
Scott Beerer, Texas A&M	Jr.	27	13
J.P. Gagne, Notre Dame	Sr.	30	13
Tony Perez, San Diego	Sr.	30	13
Blake Cross, UNC Wilmington	Jr.	35	13
Joey Livingston, South Florida	Sr.	39	13
Will Fenton, Washington	So.	18	12
Will Tucker, Belmont	Jr.	27	12
Brian Reed, Alabama	Sr.	30	12
Carlos Fernandez, Louisville	Sr.	32	12
Brian Marshall, Va. Common.	Jr.	32	12
Joey Charron, Tulane	Jr.	39	12
Daniel Hodges, Florida State	Sr.	39	12
David Aardsma, Rice	Jr.	40	12

INNINGS PITCHED	Yr.	G	IP
John Hudgins, Stanford	Jr.	22	165
Jeff Niemann, Rice	So.	22	137
David Marchbanks, So. Car.	Jr.	21	135
Jered Weaver, Long Beach State	So.	19	133
Steven White, Baylor	Sr.	19	129

WALKS	Yr.	IP	BB
Robbie Van, UNLV	Jr.	104	67
Kevin Banks, Ark.-Pine Bluff	Sr.	96	63
Anthony Tomey, E. Michigan	Sr.	84	62
Toby Middleton, N.C. A&T	So.	101	62

STRIKEOUTS	Yr.	IP	SO
Wade Townsend, Rice	So.	119	164
Casey Abrams, Wright State	Jr.	114	158
Jeff Niemann, Rice	So.	137	156
Brad Sullivan, Houston	Jr.	124	154
Ryan Wagner, Houston	So.	79	148
Tim Stauffer, Richmond	Jr.	114	146
Jered Weaver, Long Beach	So.	133	144
Justin Verlander, Old Dominion	So.	116	139
Philip Humber, Rice	So.	128	138
Steven White, Baylor	Sr.	129	130
R.J. Swindle, Charleston So.	So.	119	129
Scott Lewis, Ohio State	So.	84	127
Vern Sterry, N.C. State	Jr.	116	124
Steve Schmoll, Maryland	Sr.	88	124

STRIKEOUTS/9 INNINGS

(Minimum 50 Innings)	Yr.	IP	SO	AVG
Ryan Wagner, Houston	So.	79	148	16.8
Scott Lewis, Ohio State	So.	84	127	13.7
Chris Schutt, Cornell	Jr.	62	89	12.9
Steve Schmoll, Maryland	Sr.	88	124	12.7
Thomas Diamond, UNO	So.	69	96	12.5
Casey Abrams, Wright St.	Jr.	114	158	12.4
Wade Townsend, Rice	So.	119	164	12.4
Thomas Pauly, Princeton	Jr.	55	74	12.0
Brad Cherry, Ark.-Little Rock	Jr.	82	108	11.8
Tim Stauffer, Richmond	Jr.	114	146	11.5

COLLEGE TOP 25

BATTERS: 10 or more at-bats. **PITCHERS:** 5 or more innings. **Boldface** indicates selected in 2003 draft.

1. RICE

Coach: Wayne Graham — **Record:** 58-12

BATTING	YR	AVG	AB	R	H	2B	3B	HR	RBI	SB
Cruz, Enrique, 2b	Jr.	.352	247	55	87	18	2	10	57	6
Kolkhorst, Chris, of	Jr.	.351	265	77	93	16	4	3	47	8
Davis, Austin, of	Jr.	.344	262	63	90	24	1	6	63	8
Sinisi, Vince, 1b	So.	.338	287	61	97	15	1	10	59	11
Jorgensen, Jeff, of	Jr.	.314	242	42	76	8	2	0	30	18
Stansberry, Craig, 3b	Jr.	.309	272	49	84	12	2	6	56	7
Bubela, Dane, dh-of	Sr.	.302	212	58	64	15	1	7	41	7
Janish, Paul, ss	So.	.294	262	42	77	14	0	4	44	4
Blackinton, Jeff, c	Jr.	.280	100	19	28	2	0	2	11	1
Ueckert, Matt, dh-p	Fr.	.279	43	2	12	0	0	0	8	0
Ruchti, Justin, c	Sr.	.274	164	23	45	5	1	2	19	0
Townsend, Wade, p	So.	.250	16	1	4	1	0	0	4	0
Pendleton, Lance, of-p	Fr.	.193	57	8	11	2	0	1	5	1
Emerson, Matt, dh	Fr.	.103	29	1	3	1	0	0	4	1

PITCHING	YR	W	L	ERA	G	SV	IP	H	BB	SO
Niemann, Jeff, rhp	So.	17	0	1.70	22	1	137	96	35	156
Townsend, Wade, rhp	So.	11	2	2.20	29	5	119	80	46	164
Matheny, Colin, lhp	Fr.	3	1	2.29	15	1	39	19	15	27
Aardsma, David, rhp	Jr.	7	3	2.97	40	12	58	47	19	46
Baker, Josh, rhp	So.	8	0	3.22	19	0	95	89	29	71
Humber, Philip, rhp	So.	11	3	3.30	18	0	128	102	39	138
Ueckert, Matt, lhp	Fr.	0	1	3.86	12	0	14	21	9	11
Pendleton, Lance, rhp	Fr.	0	0	3.93	13	0	18	22	10	19
Herce, Steven, rhp	Sr.	1	2	5.85	10	1	20	26	13	20

2. STANFORD

Coach: Mark Marquess — **Record:** 51-18

BATTING	YR	AVG	AB	R	H	2B	3B	HR	RBI	SB
Garko, Ryan, c	Sr.	.402	259	64	104	24	0	18	92	2
Quentin, Carlos, of	Jr.	.396	265	72	105	24	1	12	64	10
Putnam, Danny, of	So.	.348	230	52	80	17	0	16	66	0
Fuld, Sam, of	Jr.	.321	302	83	97	18	9	4	35	10
Ash, Jonny, 3b-2b	Jr.	.314	194	28	61	11	5	2	33	1
Mayberry, John Jr., 1b	Fr.	.299	194	33	58	6	6	4	33	5
Hall, Brian, 1b-3b	Jr.	.293	266	51	78	17	5	6	44	18
Lowrie, Jed, 2b	Fr.	.292	212	24	62	12	0	0	28	5
Lucy, Donny, dh-c	So.	.291	134	26	39	9	0	2	18	6
Swope, Tobin, ss	Sr.	.263	255	41	67	9	2	1	30	9
Carter, Chris, dh	So.	.241	87	21	21	4	0	7	17	0
Minaker, Chris, 3b	Fr.	.167	12	2	2	0	0	0	0	0
Lewis, Chris, 2b-ss	Fr.	.159	63	12	10	5	1	1	10	1
Hester, John, c	Fr.	.154	13	2	2	0	0	1	1	0

PITCHING	YR	W	L	ERA	G	SV	IP	H	BB	SO
Hudgins, John, rhp	Jr.	14	3	2.99	22	0	165	138	35	143
Paganetti, Billy, rhp	So.	0	1	3.68	8	0	15	10	6	12
Manship, Matt, rhp	Fr.	2	4	3.98	25	9	63	53	27	50
Romanczuk, Mark, lhp	Fr.	12	2	4.01	23	2	112	97	55	80
Quick, Kodiak, rhp	Fr.	2	0	4.25	26	3	36	33	21	34
McCally, Ryan, rhp	Sr.	7	3	4.44	24	2	99	116	28	58
O'Hagan, David, rhp	Jr.	7	1	4.89	27	3	50	51	23	43
Ehrlich, Drew, rhp	Jr.	1	0	5.12	14	0	19	21	3	18
Dyer, Jonny, rhp	So.	2	1	5.14	15	0	21	19	7	11
Jecmen, Mark, rhp	So.	1	0	5.19	9	0	9	9	7	7
Cunningham, Tim, lhp	Sr.	3	3	5.36	12	0	40	40	31	21

3. CAL STATE FULLERTON

Coach: George Horton — **Record:** 50-16

BATTING	YR	AVG	AB	R	H	2B	3B	HR	RBI	SB
Pilittere, P.J., c	Jr.	.380	163	32	62	11	1	3	31	3
Costa, Shane, of	Jr.	.374	270	54	101	28	3	5	59	28
Suzuki, Kurt, c	So.	.350	143	34	50	10	0	2	28	1
Dorn, Danny, of	Fr.	.348	178	47	62	11	3	7	54	5
Prettyman, Ronnie, 3b	So.	.344	250	54	86	17	3	0	37	14
Boyer, Kyle, of	Jr.	.327	245	66	80	18	3	6	49	26
Turner, Justin, 2b-ss	Fr.	.326	224	40	73	9	1	1	39	13
Pedroza, Sergio, dh	Fr.	.325	120	22	39	6	1	4	24	2
Burgos, Richie, 1b	Jr.	.316	250	49	79	25	3	4	51	4
Fischer, David, of-dh	Sr.	.316	76	16	24	2	1	1	13	2
Turgeon, Joe, of	So.	.286	49	11	14	3	1	0	8	1
Corapci, Jason, 2b	Sr.	.285	123	25	35	8	1	0	20	5
Smyres, Justin, ss	Sr.	.284	169	47	48	10	4	4	33	11
Walton, Neil, ss	Fr.	.276	29	6	8	1	0	0	7	1
Scobee, Shawn, of	Fr.	.235	17	2	4	1	0	0	0	0
Mendrin, Jake, 1b	Fr.	.158	19	1	3	0	0	0	1	0
Andrews, Bobby, of	Fr.	.083	12	13	1	0	0	0	2	0

PITCHING	YR	W	L	ERA	G	SV	IP	H	BB	SO
Cordero, Chad, rhp	Jr.	5	1	1.58	40	8	57	41	8	68
Windsor, Jason, rhp	Jr.	11	2	1.98	23	0	95	76	22	75
Tucker, John, rhp	Jr.	2	1	2.39	13	0	26	32	4	18
Schreppel, Ryan, lhp	Fr.	5	3	2.45	11	0	51	41	14	42
Martin, Sean, rhp	Sr.	1	2	2.84	30	1	38	31	4	31
Romero, Ricky, lhp	Fr.	3	0	3.20	23	0	56	48	18	46
Ingle, Travis, rhp	Jr.	3	0	3.21	17	0	34	31	11	36
Miller, Dustin, rhp	Fr.	9	2	3.33	18	0	100	103	25	97
Merrell, Darric, rhp	Jr.	4	1	3.60	13	5	40	48	8	25
Littleton, Wes, rhp	Jr.	7	4	3.89	14	0	86	86	17	67

4. TEXAS

Coach: Augie Garrido — **Record:** 50-20

BATTING	YR	AVG	AB	R	H	2B	3B	HR	RBI	SB
Majewski, Dustin, of	Sr.	.391	274	62	107	22	6	12	85	21
Quintanilla, Omar, ss	Jr.	.348	282	68	98	29	5	6	76	9
Sultemeier, Eric, of	Jr.	.321	237	51	76	16	0	10	56	21
Moss, Tim, 2b	Jr.	.319	276	82	88	18	9	3	33	21
Teagarden, Taylor, c	Fr.	.315	200	26	63	13	3	5	41	0
Thigpen, Curtis, c-1b	So.	.311	196	38	61	8	2	6	38	7
Ferin, Joe, of	Sr.	.307	228	46	70	3	6	4	30	16
Johnston, Seth, 3b	So.	.253	95	13	24	2	1	3	11	6
Reininger, J.D., 1b-3b	So.	.244	193	38	47	9	3	4	27	7
Dodge, Scott, of	So.	.237	97	18	23	5	0	0	11	1
Hollimon, Michael, ss-dh	So.	.236	106	19	25	5	1	3	10	7
Ripper, Stephen, 1b	So.	.231	26	3	6	0	0	1	5	1
Crosta, Nic, dh	So.	.200	30	3	6	2	0	1	10	0
Street, Huston, 3b-p	So.	.176	68	15	12	2	1	0	4	3
Russ, Ryan, dh	Jr.	.100	20	0	2	1	0	0	2	1

PITCHING	YR	W	L	ERA	G	SV	IP	H	BB	SO
Street, Huston, rhp	So.	8	1	1.33	39	15	75	48	13	69
Cody, Buck, lhp	So.	0	0	1.42	9	0	6	6	9	8
Cox, J. Brent, rhp	Fr.	6	0	2.25	27	0	44	36	9	40
Howell, J.P., lhp	So.	10	2	2.52	21	0	114	97	43	105
Gallenkamp, Zach, rhp	Fr.	0	0	2.89	12	1	19	19	7	13
Jordan, Brantley, lhp	Sr.	2	1	3.42	30	0	26	25	10	20
LeCure, Sam, rhp	Fr.	5	0	3.74	16	0	53	59	14	29
Frizzell, Kevin, rhp	Sr.	1	0	3.86	7	0	12	15	2	5
Smith, Josh, rhp	Jr.	2	0	4.21	19	1	36	36	12	23
Simmons, Justin, lhp	Jr.	5	6	4.29	19	0	86	77	26	58
Muegge, Danny, rhp	Sr.	6	6	4.89	15	0	77	85	22	53
Espinelli, Eugene, lhp	Jr.	2	1	5.19	17	0	35	44	14	26
Merle, Jesen, rhp	Sr.	3	3	5.24	26	1	45	54	13	31

5. LOUISIANA STATE

Coach: Smoke Laval — **Record:** 45-22

BATTING	YR	AVG	AB	R	H	2B	3B	HR	RBI	SB
Hill, Aaron, ss	Jr.	.358	265	68	95	27	4	9	67	9
Patterson, Ryan, of-dh	So.	.350	263	59	92	20	1	16	51	3
Zeringue, Jon, of	So.	.339	227	50	77	15	0	13	45	6
Harris, Clay, 1b	So.	.332	211	51	70	16	0	16	62	1
Naccarata, Ivan, 3b-2b	Jr.	.320	256	59	82	14	5	6	53	9
Liuzza, Matt, c	Fr.	.312	192	38	60	8	0	4	26	1
Gill, Blake, 2b-of	So.	.304	260	46	79	13	3	5	54	6
Holt, J.C., of	So.	.299	224	51	67	11	2	5	36	16
Stewart, Quinn, dh	So.	.297	145	26	43	9	1	7	30	1
Sprowl, Bruce, of	So.	.290	262	46	76	8	3	1	33	5
Weaver, Dustin, c	Jr.	.281	32	3	9	0	0	0	5	0
Harris, Will, 1b	Fr.	.233	60	11	14	3	0	2	6	0
Horwath, Matt, 2b	Fr.	.231	26	7	6	2	0	1	6	1
Buteau, Rhett, dh	So.	.200	10	6	2	0	0	0	0	1
French, Shawn, c	Sr.	.167	18	1	3	1	0	0	3	0

PITCHING		W	L	ERA	G	SV	IP	H	BB	SO
Nall, Brandon, rhp	Jr.	0	1	2.45	6	2	7	6	2	3
Meier, Justin, rhp	Fr.	8	3	2.83	16	1	95	95	25	62
Determann, Jason, lhp	So.	7	0	2.94	20	1	67	61	11	51
Wilson, Brian, rhp	Jr.	5	3	3.38	8	0	51	60	13	35
Sadler, Billy, rhp	Jr.	1	2	3.89	28	4	44	36	27	57
Smith, Greg, lhp	Fr.	0	2	4.01	17	1	34	39	7	30
Bumstead, Nate, rhp	Jr.	11	4	4.42	19	0	110	114	28	88
Faircloth, Jordan, rhp	So.	0	0	4.63	8	0	12	12	2	5
Tompkins, Jake, rhp	Sr.	3	5	5.23	18	2	65	69	25	75
Pettit, Bo, rhp	Sr.	9	2	5.90	17	1	104	101	47	99
Vaught, Chad, rhp	Sr.	1	0	7.94	7	0	11	18	6	9

6. FLORIDA STATE

Coach: Mike Martin **Record:** 54-13

BATTING	YR	AVG	AB	R	H	2B	3B	HR	RBI	SB
Martinez-Esteve, Eddy, 3b	Fr.	.371	186	41	69	15	1	9	43	2
Richie, Tony, c	Jr.	.366	265	60	97	26	0	12	78	5
Drew, Stephen, ss	So.	.327	263	83	86	18	8	11	59	33
Balkcom, Blake, of	Jr.	.327	202	39	66	17	2	9	45	2
McQuade, Tony, of	Jr.	.324	256	73	83	15	3	13	56	26
Hart, Chris, 2b-3b	Sr.	.305	200	44	61	19	1	4	35	4
Wardell, Daniel, dh-1b	So.	.304	92	27	28	6	1	7	24	1
Brown, Jerrod, 1b	Sr.	.289	242	70	70	14	0	7	57	3
Cheesman, Aaron, dh-c	So.	.284	109	25	31	7	0	1	22	0
Smith, Derrick, of-dh	Fr.	.280	118	16	33	12	0	1	20	0
Sauls, Matt, of	Jr.	.268	190	46	51	9	2	5	36	14
Zech, Bryan, 2b	So.	.267	150	33	40	11	1	2	25	7
Manasa, Brandon, 3b	Fr.	.175	40	3	7	1	0	0	4	0
Richmond, Kevin, 3b	So.	.143	35	14	5	0	0	0	5	1

PITCHING		W	L	ERA	G	SV	IP	H	BB	SO
LaMacchia, Marc, rhp	Jr.	1	0	0.00	2	0	9	1	3	11
Simon, Glen, rhp	Fr.	3	0	1.57	10	0	29	22	12	23
Hodges, Daniel, lhp	Sr.	5	2	2.08	39	12	52	48	7	38
Jones, Hunter, lhp	Fr.	2	0	2.53	24	0	32	21	11	28
Lynch, Kevin, rhp	So.	3	1	2.59	30	0	31	31	5	32
Davidson, Daniel, lhp	Sr.	10	0	2.63	23	0	86	69	25	77
Peterson, Trent, lhp	Jr.	10	1	2.70	22	0	117	97	37	113
Sauls, Mark, rhp	Fr.	5	0	3.27	15	0	52	60	16	49
James, Rhett, rhp	Jr.	2	4	3.43	36	0	45	37	25	59
Lynch, Matt, lhp	Sr.	13	4	3.53	19	0	112	121	35	89
Cannon, Eddie, rhp	Jr.	0	1	4.58	23	0	35	39	7	37
DiBlasi, Matt, lhp	Fr.	0	0	5.14	14	1	14	15	3	13

7. ARIZONA STATE

Coach: Pat Murphy **Record:** 54-14

BATTING	YR	AVG	AB	R	H	2B	3B	HR	RBI	SB
Pedroia, Dustin, ss	So.	.404	297	83	120	34	3	4	52	3
West, Jeremy, dh-c	Jr.	.381	202	66	77	10	1	17	71	2
Ethier, Andre, of	Jr.	.377	260	75	98	13	4	10	68	7
Larish, Jeff, 1b	So.	.372	234	80	87	18	2	18	95	3
Mesa, Frank, 3b-2b	So.	.364	143	39	52	6	1	1	23	2
Guerrero, Mike, 1b-dh	Jr.	.358	95	23	34	12	2	2	30	0
Walsh, Nick, dh	Jr.	.353	119	37	42	7	1	0	23	3
Wyrick, Dennis, 3b	Sr.	.345	174	36	60	8	4	1	35	7
Gosewisch, Tuffy, c	So.	.340	144	41	49	9	0	2	41	2
Buck, Travis, of	Fr.	.326	239	59	78	13	3	4	46	12
Garrabrants, Steve, 2b	Jr.	.324	213	56	69	16	3	8	59	23
Bocchi, Joel, c	So.	.318	85	17	27	7	0	2	21	1
Allen, Rod, of	Jr.	.305	118	31	36	4	1	6	41	3
Bosch, Ryan, of	Fr.	.209	115	30	24	2	0	5	24	5
Kartler, Bryce, p-1b	Sr.	.053	19	5	1	0	0	0	0	1

PITCHING		W	L	ERA	G	SV	IP	H	BB	SO
Schroyer, Ryan, rhp	Jr.	5	2	1.53	30	9	47	39	19	52
Lopez, Javy, rhp	Jr.	1	0	1.83	16	1	20	23	5	9
Sopko, Mark, rhp	So.	3	2	2.30	25	0	55	52	13	43
Leaf, Matt, rhp	Fr.	0	0	2.70	6	0	7	5	3	4
Thurmond, Ben, rhp	Sr.	8	0	2.73	20	0	79	79	25	58
Liebeck, Jered, rhp	Sr.	8	0	2.88	21	0	78	77	24	54
Bordes, Brett, lhp	Fr.	1	1	3.21	27	0	28	21	28	27
Averill, Erik, lhp	Fr.	8	2	3.66	20	0	86	87	19	61
McClellan, Robbie, rhp	Sr.	7	0	3.70	28	0	58	54	33	57
Vaughan, Beau, rhp	Sr.	10	6	4.68	26	0	92	88	34	105
Arguello, Carlos, lhp	Sr.	3	0	4.88	23	0	24	19	10	23
Kartler, Bryce, lhp	Sr.	0	0	5.03	25	0	20	16	13	25
Beatty, Chris, lhp	Fr.	0	1	7.11	8	0	6	7	5	8

8. MIAMI

Coach: Jim Morris **Record:** 45-17

BATTING	YR	AVG	AB	R	H	2B	3B	HR	RBI	SB
Hooft, Joey, of-2b	So.	.373	126	26	47	8	2	4	28	10
Braun, Ryan, ss-dh	Fr.	.364	242	61	88	16	3	17	76	13
Ricks, Adam, 2b	Jr.	.328	232	50	76	13	1	4	55	5
Figueroa, Danny, of	So.	.328	237	74	77	6	2	3	28	40
Sanchez, Gaby, 3b	Fr.	.328	244	63	80	21	1	7	56	7
Giannotti, Rich, of	So.	.327	107	24	35	11	3	3	28	6
Barton, Brian, of	So.	.325	212	52	69	17	3	7	53	17
San Pedro, Erick, c	So.	.317	180	36	57	13	1	4	43	0
Burt, Jim, 1b	Jr.	.286	238	61	68	10	3	11	40	10
Barket, Matt, of	So.	.279	61	15	17	4	0	2	9	0
Blanco, Alex, 3b-p	So.	.276	29	7	8	2	1	0	7	1
Dini, Greg, c	So.	.270	74	15	20	3	0	2	13	2
Figueroa, Paco, ss	So.	.265	132	38	35	6	1	3	26	9
Shannon, Tom, of	Jr.	.239	71	14	17	4	0	3	15	2
Chirino, Israel, 2b-p	Fr.	.071	14	2	1	0	0	0	1	0

PITCHING		W	L	ERA	G	SV	IP	H	BB	SO
Touchet, Dan, rhp	Jr.	2	0	1.93	3	0	19	21	3	22
Huguet, George, rhp	Jr.	3	2	2.36	24	7	46	36	15	49
Cockroft, J.D., lhp	Jr.	11	3	2.72	22	1	119	116	35	94
Valdes-Fauli, Shawn, rhp	So.	5	0	3.02	36	5	54	52	19	56
Bongiovanni, Vince, rhp	So.	8	4	4.00	14	0	72	71	34	69
Blanco, Alex, rhp	So.	0	0	4.42	14	0	18	18	15	15
Lane, Andrew, lhp	Fr.	2	1	4.50	13	0	18	14	11	10
Camardese, Brandon, lhp	So.	9	2	5.01	18	0	88	90	43	64
Chirino, Israel, lhp	Fr.	2	0	5.31	25	0	20	21	20	20
Perez, Alex, lhp	Jr.	2	2	6.26	11	0	42	49	15	22
Cohn, Andrew, lhp	Jr.	0	0	6.75	11	1	9	9	6	6
Dixon, Ryan, rhp	So.	0	0	7.71	8	0	28	28	26	21
Albir, Marcelo, rhp	Fr.	1	2	8.76	19	0	25	37	18	18
Newman, Brad, rhp	Fr.	0	0	14.40	6	0	5	9	8	1

9. LONG BEACH STATE

Coach: Mike Weathers **Record:** 41-20

BATTING	YR	AVG	AB	R	H	2B	3B	HR	RBI	SB
Heether, Adam, 3b	Jr.	.355	186	55	66	11	0	6	32	7
Bowker, John, of-dh	Fr.	.333	153	27	51	6	2	7	33	2
Hutting, Tim, ss-3b	Sr.	.317	161	20	51	7	1	0	25	4
Davis, Brad, c-of	So.	.306	222	37	68	16	4	3	26	8
Hanson, Chris, dh	Jr.	.304	69	12	21	5	0	0	6	1
Udvarhelyi, Travis, of	Jr.	.303	142	26	43	5	4	1	17	4
Jennings, Todd, c-of	Jr.	.296	213	32	63	8	0	5	33	3
Buhagiar, Josh, of	Jr.	.294	119	18	35	4	3	0	12	2
Hofius, Mike, 1b	Jr.	.290	186	34	54	10	4	4	38	1
Sindlinger, Chuck, 2b	Fr.	.288	125	13	36	7	2	0	21	8
Velazco, Steve, of	So.	.286	133	24	38	5	0	0	12	9
Tulowitzki, Troy, ss-2b	Fr.	.270	196	26	53	10	1	5	44	3
Boatright, Sean, dh	Fr.	.259	58	12	15	4	0	3	9	1
Cruz, Tito, c	Jr.	.217	23	3	5	0	0	0	1	0
Pearce, Bobby, dh	Jr.	.200	25	4	5	1	1	1	4	0
Macaluso, Paul, of	Jr.	.162	37	7	6	2	0	0	4	0

PITCHING		W	L	ERA	G	SV	IP	H	BB	SO
Weaver, Jered, rhp	So.	14	4	1.96	19	0	133	87	20	144
Alvarez, Abe, lhp	Jr.	11	2	2.35	18	0	123	114	31	102
Ashabraner, Bo, rhp	Sr.	1	3	2.51	17	1	32	23	16	35
Baumback, Jeff, rhp	Sr.	0	0	2.70	5	0	7	8	3	6
Ramos, Cesar, lhp	Fr.	6	4	2.85	17	0	88	80	31	33
Muniz, Carlos, rhp	Sr.	0	2	3.14	26	11	29	27	10	30
Jamison, Neil, rhp	So.	5	2	3.43	25	1	45	43	13	35
Shoemaker, Scott, rhp	Jr.	1	1	3.60	13	1	45	42	15	34
Anderson, Brian, rhp	So.	1	0	5.56	10	0	11	13	2	11
Paz, Matt, rhp	Sr.	1	2	7.80	10	0	15	23	6	13
Andrade, Brett, rhp	Fr.	1	0	10.22	11	0	12	22	5	6

10. SOUTH CAROLINA

Coach: Ray Tanner **Record:** 45-22

BATTING	YR	AVG	AB	R	H	2B	3B	HR	RBI	SB
Buscher, Brian, 3b	Sr.	.393	270	55	106	19	2	15	66	5
Harris, Justin, ss	Sr.	.355	276	57	98	14	1	4	33	6
Powell, Landon, c	Jr.	.339	245	46	83	23	0	10	61	3
Melillo, Kevin, 2b	So.	.317	227	59	72	16	0	12	43	6
Coutlangus, Jon, of	Sr.	.317	224	47	71	10	2	3	24	14
Triplett, Bryan, 1b-2b	Jr.	.311	235	39	73	14	1	7	47	7
Tolleson, Steven, of-ss	Fr.	.302	139	23	42	9	1	3	19	3
Campbell, Michael, of	Fr.	.271	221	38	60	11	3	5	32	6
Riddle, Matt, dh	Sr.	.262	65	10	17	5	1	0	12	1
Gardiner, Nick, of	Jr.	.253	79	12	20	2	2	0	11	1
Parks, Hank, dh	Jr.	.226	84	12	19	6	0	3	15	0
McDaniel, Trey, 1b	Fr.	.218	78	15	17	2	0	3	12	1
Smith, Demetric, 1b	Sr.	.192	52	1	10	1	0	1	5	0
Greenwood, Jared, c	So.	.190	21	3	4	1	0	2	6	0
Cafe, Sadry, of	Jr.	.176	17	4	3	0	0	0	3	0
Seaton, Tim, of	Sr.	.161	56	11	9	2	0	0	7	4

PITCHING		W	L	ERA	G	SV	IP	H	BB	SO
Broome, Stephen, rhp	Fr.	1	0	1.59	4	0	6	5	4	7

		W	L	ERA	G	SV	IP	H	BB	SO
Marchbanks, David, lhp	Jr.	15	3	2.73	21	0	135	148	25	97
Lalor, Conor, rhp	Fr.	5	0	2.90	12	0	40	40	8	31
Hernandez, Chris, rhp	Sr.	5	5	3.32	25	2	84	76	27	52
Campbell, Matt, lhp	So.	6	4	3.48	21	2	83	68	47	82
Bravo, Rico, rhp	Sr.	0	0	3.52	7	0	8	8	1	5
Rawl, Aaron, rhp	So.	6	3	3.84	21	6	61	50	24	54
Bondurant, Steven, lhp	Sr.	7	3	4.23	21	0	111	119	32	98
Donald, Cliff, rhp	So.	0	1	4.43	17	1	22	16	10	20
Beverly, Forrest, lhp	Fr.	0	2	4.91	6	0	15	13	9	10
Reeves, Zach, lhp	Fr.	0	1	6.75	15	0	20	31	5	18

11. BAYLOR

Coach: Steve Smith **Record:** 45-23

BATTING	YR	AVG	AB	R	H	2B	3B	HR	RBI	SB
Forestiere, Matt, c	Fr.	.545	11	2	6	1	0	0	3	0
Murphy, David, of	Jr.	.413	293	84	121	18	4	11	67	3
Saccomanno, Mark, 1b-3b	Sr.	.381	194	38	74	16	3	9	44	3
Brees, Reid, of-dh	So.	.356	59	16	21	2	1	2	13	0
Bennett, Ross, dh-1b	Sr.	.354	181	33	64	11	2	4	46	0
Griffin, Michael, of-3b	So.	.350	294	55	103	26	8	11	76	2
Durbin, Chris, of	Sr.	.346	283	94	98	23	4	18	50	9
Ford, Josh, c	So.	.314	283	60	89	19	0	12	63	0
Reynolds, Kyle, 2b	Fr.	.286	185	23	53	8	1	2	33	3
Webb, Trey, ss	Jr.	.284	268	41	76	22	2	5	45	15
Sevigny, Kevin, of	Fr.	.269	52	10	14	4	0	1	7	0
Clements, Jared, 1b-of	Jr.	.267	45	8	12	2	0	1	12	0
Dillon, Zach, c	Fr.	.259	85	15	22	2	0	1	20	0
Witt, Paul, 3b	So.	.255	192	46	49	11	2	4	21	8
Fortenberry, Seth, of	Fr.	.250	60	14	15	2	2	1	7	1
Womble, Blake, of	Fr.	.167	18	3	3	0	0	0	3	0

PITCHING		W	L	ERA	G	SV	IP	H	BB	SO
Carlson, Zane, rhp	Jr.	3	4	2.61	30	11	59	46	14	71
LaMotta, Ryan, rhp	Fr.	7	3	3.48	30	3	75	63	32	62
White, Steven, rhp	Sr.	9	4	4.12	19	0	129	123	49	130
Woody, Abe, rhp	Fr.	6	0	4.22	27	3	60	45	18	41
Walker, Sean, rhp	So.	8	5	4.77	22	1	94	100	39	62
Theodorakos, Jared, lhp	Sr.	1	0	5.00	2	0	9	11	3	6
McCormick, Mark, rhp	Fr.	6	2	5.32	17	0	64	56	50	66
Taylor, Trey, lhp	So.	2	3	5.53	19	0	57	61	32	31
Pape, Andy, rhp	Fr.	3	0	5.65	18	0	29	35	14	22
Reichenbach, Russ, lhp	Fr.	0	0	5.87	9	0	8	8	3	6
Schnizer, Andy, rhp	Jr.	0	0	6.75	7	0	8	9	6	8
Bullock, Tyler, rhp	Fr.	0	1	8.68	17	0	19	28	8	25

12. NORTH CAROLINA STATE

Coach: Elliott Avent **Record:** 45-18

BATTING	YR	AVG	AB	R	H	2B	3B	HR	RBI	SB
Camp, Matt, of-ss	Fr.	.333	228	51	76	7	1	0	29	14
Dutton, Jeremy, 3b	Sr.	.320	197	44	63	13	1	11	48	10
Maynor, Marc, of	So.	.318	217	50	69	16	2	0	30	21
Orvella, Chad, ss-p	Sr.	.314	204	52	64	14	1	5	30	10
Hicks, David, 1b	Jr.	.291	182	29	53	21	0	3	30	1
Riley, Justin, c-1b	Sr.	.274	230	49	63	17	0	18	50	2
Gaetti, Joe, of	Jr.	.270	230	52	62	14	3	14	52	14
Morton, Colt, c	Jr.	.265	238	42	63	14	0	19	54	1
Mezistrano, Lee, dh-of	So.	.262	84	16	22	8	0	0	6	0
Coffield, Tim, dh-of	So.	.250	68	8	17	6	0	3	12	0
Hargrave, Adam, 2b	Sr.	.236	161	19	38	4	0	1	28	10
Knight, Dustin, of-3b	Jr.	.227	75	6	17	4	0	2	8	1
Clougherty, Conor, c	So.	.200	30	6	6	2	0	0	4	0
Murphy, Dustin, 2b	Sr.	.179	28	2	5	1	0	0	3	0

PITCHING		W	L	ERA	G	SV	IP	H	BB	SO
Devine, Joey, rhp	Fr.	6	3	2.19	36	14	66	49	16	78
Rogers, Michael, rhp	Fr.	12	3	3.02	17	0	125	122	34	113
Sterry, Vern, rhp	Jr.	11	0	3.25	17	0	116	99	39	124
Davidson, Phillip, rhp	So.	4	2	4.46	20	0	77	68	29	44
Cretarolo, Nate, lhp	Jr.	5	3	4.78	17	0	79	89	38	68
Brown, Collin, rhp	Fr.	1	1	5.60	8	0	18	15	11	18
Shipwash, Brandon, lhp	So.	1	1	5.86	12	0	28	31	17	25
Hicks, David, lhp	Jr.	2	1	6.88	7	0	17	28	4	15
Orvella, Chad, rhp	Sr.	2	3	8.10	10	2	13	18	4	18
Duncan, Jason, lhp	Fr.	1	1	8.13	17	0	28	36	16	19
Campbell, Jimmy, rhp	Fr.	0	0	8.59	3	0	7	12	8	10

13. NEBRASKA

Coach: Mike Anderson **Record:** 47-18

BATTING	YR	AVG	AB	R	H	2B	3B	HR	RBI	SB
Hopper, Matt, 1b	Sr.	.382	233	74	89	12	0	22	66	5
Ledbetter, Curtis, of	So.	.348	187	42	65	13	2	13	54	3
Leise, Jeff, of	Sr.	.325	271	58	88	10	7	7	37	20
Mullinax, Jake, 2b	Jr.	.320	125	30	40	7	0	0	21	8
Gordon, Alex, 3b	Fr.	.319	216	45	69	13	2	7	48	8
Bruce, Daniel, of	So.	.311	164	33	51	8	2	6	33	8
Grose, John, c-dh	Jr.	.302	149	32	45	3	0	4	22	7
Simokaitis, Joe, ss	So.	.293	239	53	70	7	0	1	39	9
Fusilier, Brandon, of-dh	Jr.	.289	159	29	46	12	2	6	41	4
Steele, Chad, c	Fr.	.278	54	12	15	1	0	0	4	3
Birmingham, Josh, ss	Sr.	.273	11	2	3	0	0	0	5	0
Gullion, Joe, of	Jr.	.250	64	15	16	3	0	1	17	2
Merrill, Bubbs, 2b	Jr.	.241	87	20	21	8	0	1	12	3
Anderson, Drew, of	Jr.	.238	126	17	30	4	0	3	19	7
Odenreider, Chase, 3b	Fr.	.216	37	4	8	1	0	0	6	2
Wells, Matt, c	So.	.196	107	18	21	4	0	5	16	1

PITCHING		W	L	ERA	G	SV	IP	H	BB	SO
Sillman, Mike, rhp	Jr.	1	1	1.82	17	3	25	21	16	22
Duensing, Brian, lhp	Fr.	3	0	2.42	4	0	22	14	6	24
Kroenke, Zach, lhp	Fr.	6	2	2.72	15	0	60	53	19	35
Burch, Jason, rhp	Jr.	4	1	2.89	18	5	28	29	11	32
Marsden, Aaron, lhp	Jr.	8	3	2.90	16	0	115	110	21	113
O'Neil, Patrick, lhp	Jr.	1	1	3.38	22	2	21	18	8	17
Shirek, Phil, rhp	So.	5	3	3.90	18	0	62	48	23	48
Robertson, Quinton, rhp	Jr.	10	2	4.23	16	0	89	95	21	51
Pekarek, Justin, lhp	Jr.	2	1	4.24	9	0	17	19	11	11
Schoeninger, Tim, rhp	Fr.	4	2	4.30	25	6	46	56	5	34
Hale, Steve, rhp	Sr.	2	0	5.64	18	1	30	33	8	26
Becker, Jeremy, lhp	So.	0	1	5.65	15	0	14	14	6	10
Rodrigue, Jamie, lhp	Sr.	1	1	6.81	11	0	37	49	8	34

14. TEXAS A&M

Coach: Mark Johnson **Record:** 45-19

BATTING	YR	AVG	AB	R	H	2B	3B	HR	RBI	SB
Schindewolf, Erik, 2b	Jr.	.351	231	66	81	15	0	2	29	12
Pennington, Cliff, 3b	Fr.	.340	241	54	82	14	2	2	41	12
Beerer, Scott, of-p	Jr.	.335	245	44	82	17	1	11	57	5
Patton, Cory, of	Jr.	.331	257	53	85	15	1	13	58	4
Scheidt, Eric, 1b	Jr.	.330	94	14	31	6	0	2	14	0
Pouk, Justin, c	Jr.	.325	160	33	52	10	0	5	27	3
Ruggiano, Justin, of	Jr.	.322	236	49	76	17	4	10	49	6
Stinson, Craig, c	Fr.	.274	62	10	17	1	0	1	8	2
Mitchell, Jordy, dh	Sr.	.250	168	20	42	10	0	4	20	1
Bowe, Brian, 1b	Jr.	.247	93	11	23	5	0	1	16	0
Infante, John, of	Fr.	.246	69	15	17	7	0	3	9	1
Whelan, Kevin, c	Fr.	.245	49	4	12	2	0	1	6	2
Mavroulis, Coby, of-1b	So.	.231	26	5	6	0	2	0	1	0
Dalton, Parker, ss-2b	Fr.	.231	13	6	3	2	0	0	1	0
Alexander, Matt, ss	Jr.	.229	236	32	54	14	0	4	40	4

PITCHING		W	L	ERA	G	SV	IP	H	BB	SO
Moore, Justin, rhp	Jr.	0	0	1.12	3	0	8	4	4	2
Beerer, Scott, rhp	Jr.	6	1	1.82	27	13	49	32	12	58
Ray, Robert, rhp	Fr.	4	0	2.19	12	0	37	34	12	42
Donaldson, Dan, lhp	Fr.	1	3	3.41	14	1	37	37	13	25
Kensing, Logan, rhp	So.	7	5	3.83	20	1	89	101	22	58
Tacker, Ryne, rhp	Fr.	0	0	4.02	7	0	16	16	14	13
Pollok, Dwayne, rhp	Sr.	2	1	4.07	13	1	24	27	5	16
Farnum, Matt, rhp	Jr.	7	2	4.20	18	1	71	78	20	54
Parcus, Kyle, lhp	Jr.	6	3	4.29	22	1	80	85	26	69
Finch, Brian, rhp	Jr.	6	1	5.40	22	1	65	81	25	57
Dixon, Zach, lhp	Sr.	6	2	5.60	17	0	72	89	31	66
Ramsey, Robert, rhp	So.	0	1	7.11	5	1	6	11	3	10

15. SOUTHERN MISSISSIPPI

Coach: Corky Palmer **Record:** 47-16

BATTING	YR	AVG	AB	R	H	2B	3B	HR	RBI	SB
King, Clint, of	So.	.394	254	68	100	23	2	23	77	8
Cook, Jeff, of	Sr.	.374	254	71	95	15	3	23	76	16
Maddox, Marc, 1b	Fr.	.336	128	30	43	12	1	5	23	1
Willcutt, Brad, c	So.	.325	249	52	81	20	0	12	61	0
Lowery, Jason, of	So.	.322	202	33	65	11	0	2	28	1
Coker, Kevin, c	So.	.316	38	6	12	5	0	0	7	0
Hoffpauir, Jarrett, 2b	So.	.307	238	53	73	13	1	10	53	5
Israel, Griff, 1b-dh	Sr.	.305	177	33	54	15	0	4	31	1
Shepherd, Matt, ss	So.	.296	247	61	73	10	4	3	33	3
Frith, Ryan, of	Jr.	.295	44	6	13	3	1	1	6	0
Benson, Matt, 3b	Sr.	.292	24	6	7	1	0	2	4	0
Smith, Adam, 3b-dh	Jr.	.278	97	17	27	5	2	0	17	1
Griffin, Beau, 3b	So.	.253	174	35	44	4	1	1	20	2
Velasquez, Carlos, of	Jr.	.245	102	25	25	5	0	3	19	3

PITCHING		W	L	ERA	G	SV	IP	H	BB	SO
Tubb, Austin, rhp	Jr.	3	2	1.45	30	10	31	22	9	30
Antonelli, Ray, lhp	Jr.	4	0	2.14	29	5	59	42	23	60
Nicholas, John, rhp	So.	4	1	2.45	24	2	33	31	12	24
Russum, Cliff, rhp	So.	8	5	3.31	17	0	87	60	35	80
Dewitt, Anthony, rhp	Jr.	8	2	3.31	15	0	90	99	19	50

McCrory, Bob, rhp	Jr.	10	3	3.84	18	0	91	94	44	90
Best, Daniel, rhp	Fr.	2	0	4.01	16	1	34	41	13	24
Castleman, Stephen, rhp	Sr.	8	2	4.14	16	0	96	110	36	75
Tritz, Noah, rhp	Fr.	0	1	6.23	11	1	22	27	10	16
Hurley, Brian, rhp	So.	0	0	7.20	2	0	5	3	9	4
Leach, Brent, lhp	So.	0	0	7.27	4	0	9	14	9	7

16. SOUTHWEST MISSOURI STATE

Coach: Keith Guttin **Record:** 40-26

BATTING	YR	AVG	AB	R	H	2B	3B	HR	RBI	SB
Hilgendorf, Jacob, of	So.	.478	23	15	11	2	0	1	8	3
Brinkley, Dant'e, of	Sr.	.345	278	68	96	18	3	8	47	24
Wheeler, Clay, dh	Sr.	.342	202	41	69	7	3	2	35	5
Mathis, Greg, of	Sr.	.323	248	45	80	14	3	5	49	10
Piazza, Tony, c	Sr.	.302	215	51	65	12	0	15	55	2
Pummill, Adam, 2b	Fr.	.297	239	41	71	8	1	0	23	4
Colvin, Brooks, 3b	Jr.	.292	267	51	78	15	1	1	45	5
Rafferty, Tim, 1b	Fr.	.281	121	15	34	1	0	0	19	1
Marcum, Shaun, ss-p	Jr.	.280	246	27	69	13	1	7	44	2
Wilson, Rick, of	Sr.	.272	232	38	63	14	5	3	33	5
Nasby, Scott, c	So.	.209	43	8	9	0	0	1	6	1
Woodmansee, Chad, 1b	Jr.	.198	111	15	22	5	3	2	14	2
DePriest, Justin, dh	Jr.	.107	28	4	3	0	0	0	2	1

PITCHING		W	L	ERA	G	SV	IP	H	BB	SO
Claybrook, Jeff, lhp	Fr.	0	1	1.74	10	0	10	9	5	9
Marcum, Shaun, rhp	Jr.	1	4	2.45	24	13	44	35	13	55
Mulholland, Chad, rhp	Jr.	10	4	3.08	19	0	120	101	31	117
Bader, David, rhp	Sr.	2	2	3.52	17	0	38	37	18	32
Ziegler, Brad, rhp	Sr.	12	2	4.22	17	0	107	115	26	94
Zimmermann, Bob, rhp	Jr.	5	3	4.25	20	1	89	95	26	90
Wilson, Rick, lhp	Sr.	3	4	4.32	13	0	50	43	22	44
Krawczyk, Chris, rhp	Fr.	1	0	4.42	13	0	18	19	6	16
Gray, Jeff, rhp	Jr.	5	3	6.51	13	0	55	73	21	37
Marsala, Paul, rhp	Fr.	1	1	7.71	13	0	28	34	13	28
Brunk, Ryan, lhp	Jr.	0	2	10.29	6	0	7	16	2	5

17. GEORGIA TECH

Coach: Danny Hall **Record:** 44-18

BATTING	YR	AVG	AB	R	H	2B	3B	HR	RBI	SB
Lane, Cameron, of	So.	.417	12	6	5	1	0	0	2	1
Blackwood, Steven, of	Fr.	.353	116	33	41	8	3	5	38	5
Nickeas, Mike, c-3b	So.	.333	219	41	73	16	0	7	44	1
Remole, Clifton, 1b	So.	.323	220	47	71	14	0	4	42	1
Hawranick, Andy, c	Fr.	.321	78	15	25	4	0	0	13	1
Greene, Tyler, ss	Fr.	.316	228	48	72	8	2	8	43	19
Owings, Micah, 1b-p	Fr.	.306	209	43	64	11	2	15	42	2
Murton, Matt, of	Jr.	.301	246	64	74	10	3	13	56	19
Slayden, Jeremy, of	So.	.294	218	44	64	18	4	8	40	2
Hall, Jake, 3b	So.	.292	113	19	33	3	0	0	12	5
Patterson, Eric, 2b	So.	.274	248	56	68	11	4	2	35	35
Boggs, Brandon, of	So.	.246	195	37	48	8	2	9	38	11
Myers, Davis, 3b	Jr.	.120	50	5	6	2	0	1	3	4
Trapani, Mike, ss	Fr.	.095	21	6	2	0	0	2	3	0

PITCHING		W	L	ERA	G	SV	IP	H	BB	SO
Wagner, Nick, rhp	So.	0	0	3.14	13	0	14	15	3	8
Neighborgall, Jason, rhp	Fr.	3	0	3.70	15	0	41	30	36	32
Goodman, Chris, rhp	Sr.	9	3	3.84	17	0	87	85	20	55
Burks, Brian, rhp	Jr.	5	1	3.92	23	8	57	49	13	50
Owings, Micah, rhp	Fr.	9	3	3.99	17	0	88	84	21	58
Schmidt, Kyle, rhp	So.	1	1	4.05	7	0	13	10	11	16
Walker, Aaron, lhp	Jr.	3	2	4.06	22	0	44	50	16	34
Bakker, Kyle, lhp	Jr.	8	3	4.35	18	0	93	97	36	80
Crews, Jordan, rhp	So.	0	0	4.35	10	0	10	10	1	7
Watchko, Jeff, rhp	Sr.	3	3	4.62	29	5	49	50	21	41
Kown, Andrew, rhp	So.	3	2	4.65	18	1	50	55	13	40

18. AUBURN

Coach: Steve Renfroe **Record:** 42-21

BATTING	YR	AVG	AB	R	H	2B	3B	HR	RBI	SB
Hulett, Tug, 2b	So.	.373	249	52	93	25	2	2	39	3
Moran, Javon, of	Jr.	.338	272	53	92	18	7	4	38	26
Amonite, Karl, 1b	Jr.	.330	206	36	68	13	1	12	56	0
Huddleston, Bobby, dh-c	Sr.	.324	219	47	71	19	0	13	64	1
Schade, Scott, 3b	Jr.	.310	239	40	74	17	3	2	35	0
Gamble, Sean, of	So.	.300	243	47	73	8	3	3	33	5
Thomas, Clete, of	Fr.	.297	256	41	76	10	4	2	27	11
Bell, Josh, c-3b	Fr.	.295	200	29	59	15	0	8	35	1
Sain, Derek, of-dh	Fr.	.277	47	4	13	3	0	0	5	0
Bohm, Kyle, c	So.	.250	44	5	11	0	0	1	2	0
Jeroloman, Chuck, ss	So.	.224	219	30	49	10	1	3	36	2
Todd, Josh, 1b	Sr.	.208	24	6	5	0	0	0	1	1
Vines, Doug, of	So.	.115	26	8	3	1	0	0	3	0

PITCHING		W	L	ERA	G	SV	IP	H	BB	SO
Speigner, Levale, rhp	Sr.	10	0	2.42	27	1	67	58	20	51
Register, Steven, rhp	So.	3	3	2.94	33	16	52	42	7	61
Dueitt, Cory, rhp	So.	7	2	3.23	32	1	70	66	10	60
Paxton, Colby, rhp	Jr.	7	3	3.57	16	0	86	91	22	32
Dennis, Chris, rhp	Fr.	3	2	3.80	22	0	45	37	21	42
Miksis, Jim, rhp	Jr.	1	0	3.97	9	0	11	11	6	8
Hughey, Arnold, lhp	So.	6	6	4.15	19	0	102	99	23	85
Brandon, Eric, rhp	Jr.	3	4	6.03	18	1	66	79	21	51
Forrer, Dan, lhp	Fr.	1	0	7.07	8	0	14	17	13	10
Skinner, Andrew, rhp	Jr.	0	0	7.62	11	0	13	19	8	16
Carter, Lee, rhp	So.	1	0	7.90	14	0	14	23	6	8
Sullivan, Josh, rhp	Fr.	0	1	8.59	10	0	15	16	13	11

19. NORTH CAROLINA

Coach: Mike Fox **Record:** 42-23

BATTING	YR	AVG	AB	R	H	2B	3B	HR	RBI	SB
Cleveland, Jeremy, of-1b	Jr.	.410	251	74	103	20	1	19	65	8
Griffin, Mark, c	So.	.364	11	4	4	0	0	0	3	0
Hewitt, Sammy, 3b-dh	Jr.	.355	220	51	78	13	3	10	49	4
Younts, Chase, of	So.	.351	37	8	13	3	0	0	8	1
Farrell, Sean, of	Sr.	.350	266	65	93	19	0	14	61	10
Iannetta, Chris, c-1b	So.	.319	232	44	74	13	2	8	55	2
Waggett, Blair, of	Fr.	.319	138	31	44	10	3	1	16	8
Blake, Ryan, c-1b	Sr.	.318	220	43	70	12	2	5	45	6
Moyer, Wes, of	Jr.	.312	112	24	35	6	1	6	26	4
Mangum, Greg, 2b	So.	.305	239	42	73	9	1	2	34	8
Prosser, Chad, ss	Sr.	.290	283	57	82	14	1	2	40	13
Weaver, Adam, 2b-ss	Fr.	.283	53	10	15	2	0	0	7	1
Cook, Ross, dh	So.	.250	12	3	3	1	0	0	3	0
Daniel, Mike, of	Fr.	.248	137	23	34	5	1	2	22	4
Webb, Justin, 3b-2b	So.	.233	103	21	24	4	0	0	13	5
Zuercher, Zack, dh	Fr.	.231	13	2	3	0	0	0	0	0
Adams, Mell, of	Jr.	.167	30	5	5	1	0	2	5	0

PITCHING		W	L	ERA	G	SV	IP	H	BB	SO
Senatore, Scott, lhp	Jr.	2	1	2.81	32	2	48	43	17	45
Dickerson, Bo, lhp	So.	0	1	3.45	9	0	16	8	10	18
Danford, Matt, rhp	Fr.	3	1	3.47	24	0	47	44	18	38
Benson, Whitley, rhp	Jr.	3	3	3.55	31	4	38	39	12	28
Moore, Daniel, lhp	Jr.	7	3	3.56	17	0	94	102	41	65
Brower, Kevin, rhp	Jr.	4	4	4.05	33	1	40	42	17	28
Kalkhof, Adam, lhp	Fr.	7	2	4.26	17	0	80	82	30	77
Bakker, Garry, rhp	So.	6	3	4.32	16	0	81	82	32	59
Zuercher, Zack, lhp	Fr.	2	1	4.66	23	0	19	23	12	18
Manshack, Scott, rhp	Jr.	4	3	5.40	13	0	48	61	17	40
Hovis, Jonathan, rhp	Fr.	2	1	5.51	19	0	33	32	15	25
Gross, Michael, rhp	Jr.	2	0	6.17	16	1	23	27	8	18
Phillips, Bryan, rhp	So.	0	0	6.75	10	0	15	14	9	14

20. NEVADA-LAS VEGAS

Coach: Jim Schlossnagle **Record:** 47-17

BATTING	YR	AVG	AB	R	H	2B	3B	HR	RBI	SB
Nielsen, Eric, of	So.	.365	197	54	72	17	1	7	41	6
Dobson, Patrick, of-3b	Jr.	.358	240	71	86	20	2	12	66	7
Johnson, Brent, 3b-of	Jr.	.350	274	70	96	19	3	6	55	13
Valenzuela, Fernando, 1b	Jr.	.337	243	60	82	20	0	14	75	0
White, Peter, ss	Jr.	.336	232	72	78	13	1	10	49	5
Gill, Eddie, of-dh	Jr.	.323	189	43	61	17	2	8	54	1
Shitanishi, Garett, 2b	Sr.	.319	163	49	52	9	1	3	30	17
Ghutzman, Stephen, c	Sr.	.303	132	40	40	16	0	4	35	2
Ruiz, Ryan, 2b	Jr.	.296	169	28	50	8	2	9	41	8
VanKirk, Robert, c	Sr.	.285	172	37	49	12	0	8	43	1
D'Angelo, Andrew, of	Jr.	.279	136	36	38	7	1	3	12	6
Uriegas, Johnny, of	Jr.	.278	36	10	10	2	2	1	13	1
Wickman, Joe, of-dh	So.	.271	96	17	26	8	0	0	14	2

PITCHING		W	L	ERA	G	SV	IP	H	BB	SO
Braun, Ryan, rhp	Sr.	5	3	3.44	28	7	37	37	18	53
Luca, Matthew, rhp	Fr.	5	0	4.17	15	0	58	55	25	49
Clatterbuck, Shane, rhp	Jr.	1	0	4.24	17	0	17	14	9	17
Wagner, Matt, rhp	Fr.	1	0	4.40	14	1	29	29	13	20
Van, Robbie, lhp	Jr.	9	4	4.51	21	1	104	101	67	97
Seccombe, David, rhp	Jr.	3	1	5.14	7	0	28	33	8	36
Vose, Jake, lhp	Jr.	8	4	5.20	19	0	99	117	34	89
Pupo, Giovanni, lhp	Sr.	5	1	6.30	17	0	50	56	18	28
Watts, Donnie, rhp	Sr.	0	0	6.43	5	0	7	11	0	6
Guerra, Jason, rhp	Jr.	2	0	7.15	26	3	23	29	18	22
Thompson, James, rhp	So.	3	0	7.34	19	0	34	47	16	19
Scheinbaum, Ben, lhp	Jr.	5	1	7.77	23	2	44	63	16	36
Lesko, Adam, rhp	Jr.	0	3	10.70	19	0	35	63	15	39

21. OHIO STATE

Coach: Bob Todd **Record:** 44-21

BATTING	YR	AVG	AB	R	H	2B	3B	HR	RBI	SB
Snavely, Christian, of-3b	Jr.	.335	200	55	67	12	3	16	55	8
Caravati, Steve, of-dh	So.	.333	204	39	68	11	2	8	50	12
Garrard, Brett, ss	Jr.	.308	208	46	64	11	4	9	33	5
Anderson, Drew, 2b	So.	.307	251	51	77	13	4	12	34	17
Kinnear, Derek, c	Jr.	.298	181	23	54	8	0	5	41	5
Farinacci, Paul, 1b	So.	.291	203	30	59	11	0	7	33	1
Rabin, Mike, of	So.	.291	234	47	68	6	1	2	18	17
Caughenbaugh, Cody, of	Fr.	.288	146	20	42	6	2	1	20	0
Pettorini, Terry, 3b-dh	Jr.	.286	126	17	36	7	0	3	18	1
Houser, Kelly, c	Fr.	.242	33	6	8	1	0	0	3	0
Schirtzinger, Wes, of	Fr.	.237	76	13	18	3	2	1	8	3
Stephen, Jedidiah, 3b	Fr.	.233	116	19	27	4	1	6	20	2
Larason, Doug, c-dh	Jr.	.175	40	4	7	3	0	0	6	0
Thomas, Drew, of	Fr.	.143	49	5	7	0	0	0	1	1

PITCHING	YR	W	L	ERA	G	SV	IP	H	BB	SO
Myers, Justin, rhp	Fr.	1	0	1.42	4	0	6	4	0	4
Lewis, Scott, lhp	So.	9	1	1.61	12	0	84	48	24	127
Luyster, Trent, lhp	So.	3	1	3.30	19	0	44	45	13	28
Madsen, Mike, rhp	So.	8	1	3.31	19	0	65	60	25	45
Brown, Kyle, rhp	Jr.	3	0	3.50	18	2	44	40	15	40
Prenger, Greg, rhp	Sr.	3	1	4.57	15	0	41	56	7	25
Newman, Josh, lhp	Jr.	8	6	4.64	16	0	99	103	22	70
Smith, Nate, rhp	Sr.	2	6	5.80	11	0	54	67	16	43
Davis, Matt, rhp	So.	3	1	6.05	33	14	39	42	11	39
Hanners, Chris, lhp	So.	4	4	6.63	18	0	56	65	22	37

22. HOUSTON

Coach: Rayner Noble **Record:** 37-30

BATTING	YR	AVG	AB	R	H	2B	3B	HR	RBI	SB
Sullivan, Brad, p-2b	Jr.	.367	30	7	11	4	0	0	1	2
Cho, Hyung, 3b-ss	Jr.	.360	261	54	94	19	0	14	66	5
Tully, Travis, of-dh	Fr.	.350	180	30	63	9	0	0	28	12
Bourn, Michael, of	Jr.	.330	182	44	60	1	5	1	16	23
Cooley, Brett, 1b	Sr.	.286	42	3	12	0	0	1	6	2
Bruce, Cole, 2b-dh	Jr.	.278	158	24	44	10	1	8	28	7
Farrington, Matt, of	Fr.	.277	188	27	52	17	3	1	23	7
Martin, Brian, dh-of	So.	.276	58	8	16	4	0	2	7	1
Lucas, Gabe, of	Jr.	.272	206	30	56	7	0	4	23	10
Mitchell, Sam, of	Jr.	.264	87	13	23	0	1	1	9	6
Musslewhite, Stuart, ss-2b	So.	.261	245	27	64	19	1	1	26	5
Papavasiliou, Thanos, 1b	Jr.	.255	216	27	55	12	2	4	34	4
Bott, Nick, c	Jr.	.231	173	22	40	7	0	2	23	2
Roberts, Kevin, 2b	Fr.	.203	64	8	13	1	0	0	4	2
Logan, Brett, c	Fr.	.149	114	14	17	3	0	1	14	1
Buchanan, Greg, 2b	Fr.	.122	49	6	6	0	0	0	5	1
Bluhm, Adam, of-1b	Jr.	.071	14	1	1	0	0	0	1	0

PITCHING	YR	W	L	ERA	G	SV	IP	H	BB	SO
Mays, Travis, lhp	Fr.	0	0	1.69	7	0	5	7	2	0
Wagner, Ryan, rhp	So.	6	5	1.93	38	15	79	39	21	148
Roberts, Kevin, rhp	Fr.	1	0	2.63	14	0	14	8	12	15
Sullivan, Brad, rhp	Jr.	6	8	2.91	20	0	124	90	44	154
Zell, Danny, lhp	Jr.	9	5	3.34	18	0	113	118	34	79
Henderson, Brian, lhp	Jr.	5	5	4.43	25	0	61	69	21	59
Mock, Garrett, rhp	So.	5	4	4.50	18	0	86	69	44	66
Harris, Bryan, rhp	Jr.	2	0	5.09	19	0	23	16	22	19
Putman, Rickey, rhp	Jr.	0	1	5.87	17	0	15	14	10	16
Flores, Gene, rhp	Jr.	3	2	6.70	18	1	42	49	24	24
Gartz, Taylor, lhp	So.	0	0	9.64	14	0	14	25	13	11
Vaclavik, Justin, rhp	Fr.	0	0	14.09	8	0	8	17	6	3
Martin, Brian, lhp	So.	0	0	15.09	9	0	11	16	12	8

23. FLORIDA ATLANTIC

Coach: Kevin Cooney **Record:** 47-16

BATTING	YR	AVG	AB	R	H	2B	3B	HR	RBI	SB
Fiorentino, Jeff, of	So.	.382	233	71	89	14	0	15	49	14
Brown, Rusty, 1b	Jr.	.368	231	58	85	17	0	11	66	0
Pali, Matt, of	Sr.	.345	220	61	76	15	3	10	46	8
Mascia, Tim, of	Fr.	.344	93	19	32	3	1	2	14	2
O'Connor, Shaen, dh-c	Sr.	.328	131	19	43	12	1	4	26	0
Murray, Mike, c	Jr.	.305	118	24	36	5	0	0	23	1
Hutton, Derek, 2b-ss	So.	.295	193	39	57	9	0	7	39	8
Brannon, Evan, ss	Jr.	.293	167	33	49	9	2	1	27	3
Horst, Rob, of-dh	Sr.	.283	159	27	45	14	0	7	36	1
Orton, Robbie, c	Jr.	.276	123	28	34	4	0	3	23	2
Cox, Mike, 3b	Sr.	.273	216	49	59	13	1	11	46	7
Gilmore, Marc, c	Sr.	.263	19	3	5	1	0	0	5	0
Fonseca, Alex, 3b	Fr.	.247	73	13	18	4	0	0	8	4
Ryan, Matt, of	Jr.	.240	75	23	18	0	0	0	9	19
Yeager, Joe, 3b	Fr.	.133	15	10	2	1	0	0	1	1

PITCHING	YR	W	L	ERA	G	SV	IP	H	BB	SO
Beam, Randy, lhp	Jr.	13	2	2.39	17	0	102	74	17	83
O'Brien, Matt, rhp	Jr.	1	1	2.49	23	1	43	37	10	38
Saxton, Chris, rhp	Jr.	4	4	2.70	25	5	57	50	15	44
Knight, Allen, rhp	Fr.	0	0	2.70	9	0	7	2	5	6
Callahan, James, lhp	Sr.	2	0	3.04	22	0	24	15	7	20
Core, Danny, rhp	Sr.	10	2	3.31	16	0	106	91	34	98
Mann, Will, rhp	Fr.	0	0	3.55	9	0	13	16	5	12
NeSmith, Travis, lhp	Jr.	7	2	3.92	16	0	67	71	22	36
Della Rocco, Chris, rhp	Jr.	2	1	4.26	15	1	19	25	8	22
Ingwell, Brad, lhp	Sr.	0	0	4.76	5	0	6	7	5	3
Pillsbury, Chris, rhp	Jr.	8	4	4.85	21	5	69	75	24	59
Miller, Aaron, rhp	Fr.	0	0	13.50	6	0	5	6	9	5

24. MISSISSIPPI STATE

Coach: Ron Polk **Record:** 42-20

BATTING	YR	AVG	AB	R	H	2B	3B	HR	RBI	SB
Goodson, Robby, dh	Jr.	.358	95	18	34	7	1	1	22	0
Maniscalco, Matthew, ss	Sr.	.338	278	57	94	15	4	7	42	20
Gendron, Steve, 3b	Jr.	.333	264	48	88	14	0	1	35	13
Corley, Brad, of-p	Fr.	.321	224	40	72	15	0	1	36	4
Pearson, Winston, of	So.	.320	25	9	8	3	1	0	4	2
Butts, Jeff, of	Fr.	.313	134	18	42	11	1	0	14	4
Tucker, J.B., c	So.	.312	96	17	30	5	0	2	20	1
Brinson, Matthew, 1b	Jr.	.311	241	50	75	20	1	8	49	2
Lewis, Brent, dh	Jr.	.309	94	14	29	8	1	3	18	0
Tatum, Craig, c	Fr.	.302	192	35	58	8	0	6	33	0
Jones, Brad, 1b-of	Fr.	.296	27	4	8	2	0	0	7	0
Hunter, Joseph, of	Fr.	.274	124	25	34	6	4	4	24	1
Berkery, Thomas, 2b	Fr.	.269	193	26	52	6	0	6	34	3
Mungle, Jon, of	So.	.260	204	38	53	10	2	7	35	4
Scarbrough, Tyler, 2b	Jr.	.228	57	10	13	1	0	3	7	2
Thoms, Josh, 2b-ss	So.	.100	10	2	1	0	0	0	0	0

PITCHING	YR	W	L	ERA	G	SV	IP	H	BB	SO
Gant, Jamie, rhp	Fr.	6	1	1.15	21	1	55	37	21	39
Papelbon, Jon, rhp	Jr.	6	2	2.28	25	7	47	41	14	54
Owens, Brian, lhp	Sr.	1	0	2.70	16	0	13	9	9	11
Maholm, Paul, lhp	Jr.	9	2	2.76	15	0	108	102	39	101
Ramsey, Saunders, rhp	So.	0	1	3.38	23	1	37	28	14	38
Cleveland, Brett, rhp	Fr.	0	0	3.38	7	0	13	13	6	12
Lacher, Jeff, rhp	Jr.	6	0	3.61	15	0	67	67	17	46
Corley, Brad, rhp	Fr.	0	2	4.32	8	0	33	33	21	19
Nicholas, Todd, lhp	So.	5	4	4.47	12	0	52	50	31	40
Blakeney, Jacob, rhp	Sr.	3	0	4.50	11	0	30	26	16	33
Johnson, Alan, rhp	So.	5	5	4.77	16	0	83	81	24	58
Goodson, Robby, rhp	Jr.	0	3	7.07	12	1	14	17	12	23
Dunn, Brooks, lhp	Fr.	1	0	7.71	11	0	14	19	4	12

25. WASHINGTON

Coach: Ken Knutson **Record:** 42-18

BATTING	YR	AVG	AB	R	H	2B	3B	HR	RBI	SB
Ramsey, Steve, of-1b	Jr.	.407	27	7	11	3	0	2	5	0
Lillibridge, Brent, of-ss	Fr.	.388	183	49	71	16	1	13	47	9
Hathaway, Aaron, c	So.	.350	203	38	71	12	2	5	38	3
Batkoski, Nick, 2b	So.	.346	81	12	28	6	0	3	18	1
Isaacson, Greg, 2b	Jr.	.322	208	54	67	10	2	9	38	9
Drake, Justin, of	Jr.	.318	66	7	21	1	1	2	12	2
Wagner, Mike, of	Jr.	.308	201	45	62	11	0	15	48	3
Reynolds, Tila, ss	Sr.	.299	241	47	72	15	2	3	36	12
Otness, John, 3b	Jr.	.298	218	41	65	16	4	6	36	2
Reynolds, Simi, of	Fr.	.289	38	6	11	2	0	0	2	2
Boudon, Chad, of-dh	Jr.	.287	209	49	60	9	2	22	58	4
Larsen, Kyle, 1b	So.	.274	219	44	60	8	0	8	41	0
Johnson, Taylor, of	So.	.264	163	38	43	6	0	6	25	6
Johnson, Ben, c	Jr.	.154	39	7	6	2	0	1	5	0
Thiel, Jefferson, c	Jr.	.100	10	1	1	0	0	0	0	1

PITCHING	YR	W	L	ERA	G	SV	IP	H	BB	SO
Fenton, Will, rhp	So.	2	0	0.00	18	12	32	16	11	49
Baysinger, Trent, lhp	Jr.	4	1	3.02	24	3	51	45	20	48
Conover, Josh, rhp	So.	4	0	3.46	14	0	39	36	15	33
Hawkins, Jamie, lhp	So.	0	0	3.72	5	0	10	9	6	9
Gibson, Trevor, rhp	Jr.	3	0	4.02	9	1	31	23	18	29
Robertson, Scott, rhp	Sr.	0	0	4.26	14	3	25	25	6	21
Petersen, Jeff, rhp	Jr.	6	6	4.65	17	0	89	92	43	66
Carter, Brian, lhp	Jr.	1	1	4.72	23	5	34	31	19	19
White, Sean, rhp	Sr.	8	4	4.76	16	0	91	88	38	70
Dowling, David, lhp	So.	7	2	5.11	19	1	56	66	29	58
Johnson, Clay, rhp	Jr.	6	4	6.05	13	0	58	71	24	40
Kasser, Matt, rhp	Fr.	1	0	6.57	9	0	12	14	12	16

CONFERENCE STANDINGS & LEADERS

*Won conference tournament
Boldface: NCAA regional participant/conference department leader

#Conference department leader who is a non-qualifier

AMERICA EAST CONFERENCE

	Conference		Overall	
	W	L	W	L
Vermont	17	5	32	14
Maine	17	7	38	18
Stony Brook	15	9	33	21
***Northeastern**	12	10	27	24
Albany	10	14	20	32
Hartford	7	15	9	34
Binghamton	2	20	10	40

ALL-CONFERENCE TEAM: C—Ed Kull, Sr., Stony Brook. **1B**—Barry Chamberland, Jr., Vermont. **2B**—Brett Ouellette, Sr., Maine. **3B**—Joe Drapeau, Sr., Maine. **SS**—Bobby Tewksbary, So., Vermont. **OF**—Jeff Barry, Sr., Vermont; T.J. Kowalchuk, Jr., Binghamton; Simon Williams, Jr., Maine. **DH**—Alain Picard, Sr., Maine. **P**—Jamie Merchant, Sr.,Vermont; Mike Collar, Jr., Maine.

Player of the Year: Bobby Tewksbary, Vermont. **Pitcher of the Year:** Jamie Merchant, Vermont. **Rookie of the Year:** Greg Norton, Maine. **Coach of the Year:** Bill Currier, Vermont.

INDIVIDUAL BATTING LEADERS
(Minimum 125 At-Bats)

	AVG	AB	R	H	2B	3B	HR	RBI	SB
Tewksbary, Bobby, Vermont	**.357**	157	45	56	11	3	5	30	4
Bush, Tim, Northeastern	.353	139	31	49	10	2	4	37	1
Chamberland, Barry, Vermont	.346	159	36	55	11	1	11	41	9
Ouellette, Brett, Maine	.340	188	44	**64**	13	0	10	45	6
Emanuele, Chris, Northeastern	.335	176	36	59	12	1	5	31	13
Cuscovitch, Ryan, Hartford	.333	144	29	48	8	0	3	30	5
Topp, Josh, Hartford	.333	126	11	42	3	0	1	18	3
Kull, Ed, Stony Brook	.327	159	21	52	14	1	2	22	0
Martin, Jason, Albany	.327	150	20	49	11	0	1	22	0
Sidhu, Arman, Northeastern	.325	166	27	54	14	0	2	20	2
Russo, Mike, Stony Brook	.325	160	**51**	52	12	2	10	43	0
Picard, Alain, Maine	.321	196	42	63	12	1	6	**50**	9
Cicatelli, Cole, Stony Brook	.318	129	27	41	7	1	7	31	1
Costello, Joe, Binghamton	.313	163	21	51	14	1	6	35	5
McCurdy, Jim, Stony Brook	.312	176	34	55	11	2	5	41	5
Balback, Jay, Binghamton	.312	160	45	50	10	1	**13**	26	1
#Barry, Jeff, Vermont	.311	161	39	50	9	1	1	21	**29**
#Devins, Matt, Stony Brook	.307	192	42	59	**20**	1	5	46	0
#Pena, Omar, Northeastern	.304	161	30	49	15	2	6	26	10
#Renner, Garrett, Stony Brook	.259	143	37	37	9	**4**	3	23	6

INDIVIDUAL PITCHING LEADERS
(Minimum 50 Innings)

	W	L	ERA	G	SV	IP	H	BB	SO
Merchant, Jamie, Vermont	7	2	**1.56**	11	1	75	56	14	81
Dixon, Jeff, Vermont	**9**	0	1.93	14	2	56	47	9	34
Norton, Greg, Maine	7	1	2.97	11	0	67	62	17	57
Collar, Mike, Maine	8	3	3.14	12	0	83	75	10	**98**
MacDonald, Mike, Maine	7	5	3.28	13	0	82	73	17	82
Restivo, Mike, Stony Brook	6	4	3.34	24	4	57	49	15	49
Miller, Derek, Vermont	4	4	3.34	10	0	59	52	18	61
Hedrick, Justin, Northeastern	7	2	3.47	12	0	70	56	42	89
Lewis, Jonathan, Stony Brook	5	3	3.49	12	0	67	73	29	58
Emmerthal, Steve, Albany	5	6	3.94	14	0	75	75	24	73
Robinson, Brian, Vermont	3	1	4.50	11	0	54	54	33	60
Wood, David, Stony Brook	4	5	4.66	14	0	66	57	30	54
#Dobens, Brett, Vermont	0	3	6.28	16	**5**	14	14	4	12

ATLANTIC COAST CONFERENCE

	Conference		Overall	
	W	L	W	L
Florida State	19	5	54	13
***Georgia Tech**	17	7	44	18
North Carolina State	15	9	45	18
Clemson	15	9	39	22
North Carolina	13	11	42	23
Virginia	11	12	29	25
Wake Forest	8	15	29	24
Maryland	6	17	20	33
Duke	2	21	18	36

ALL-CONFERENCE TEAM: C—Colt Morton, Sr., North Carolina State. **1B**—Michael Johnson, Sr., Clemson. **2B**—Eric Patterson, So., Georgia Tech. **3B**—Jamie D'Antona, Jr., Wake Forest. **SS**—Stephen Drew, So., Florida State. **OF**—Adam Bourassa, Sr., Wake Forest; Jeremy Cleveland, Jr., North Carolina; Tony McQuade, Jr., Florida State. **DH**—Joe Koshansky, Jr., Virginia. **Util**—Micah Owings, Fr., Georgia Tech. **P**—Joey Devine, Fr., North Carolina State; Vern Sterry, Jr., North Carolina State; Trent Peterson, Jr., Florida State; Kyle Sleeth, Jr., Wake Forest.

Player of the Year: Jamie D'Antona, Wake Forest. **Rookie of the Year:** Micah Owings, Georgia Tech. **Coach of the Year:** Elliot Avent, N.C. State.

INDIVIDUAL BATTING LEADERS
(Minimum 125 At-Bats)

	AVG	AB	R	H	2B	3B	HR	RBI	SB
Cleveland, Jeremy, No. Carolina	**.410**	251	74	**103**	20	1	19	65	8
Martinez-Esteve, Eddy, Fla. State	.371	186	41	69	15	1	9	43	2
Johnson, Ryan, Wake Forest	.369	187	46	69	9	0	9	52	3
Richie, Tony, Florida State	.366	265	60	97	**26**	0	12	78	5
D'Antona, Jamie, Wake Forest	.360	214	59	77	19	1	**21**	**82**	1
Hewitt, Sammy, North Carolina	.355	220	51	78	13	3	10	49	4
Farrell, Sean, North Carolina	.350	266	65	93	19	0	14	61	10
McCann, Brad, Clemson	.347	251	44	87	21	1	9	67	2
Johnson, Michael, Clemson	.338	198	54	67	11	0	12	51	1
Triplett, Russell, Clemson	.335	233	54	78	14	0	7	32	5
Bourassa, Adam, Wake Forest	.335	239	63	80	12	0	3	28	29
Camp, Matt, N.C. State	.333	228	51	76	7	1	0	29	14
Nickeas, Mike, Ga. Tech	.333	219	41	73	16	0	7	44	1
Slevin, David, Clemson	.330	191	28	63	10	0	5	30	0
Patrick, Brian, Duke	.329	210	42	69	13	3	6	42	1
Drew, Stephen, Florida State	.327	263	**83**	86	18	**8**	11	59	33
Balkcom, Blake, Florida State	.327	202	39	66	17	2	9	45	2
Sweet, Chris, Virginia	.326	215	33	70	9	1	0	28	17
Green, Zane, Clemson	.326	172	39	56	12	0	0	14	6
McQuade, Tony, Florida State	.324	256	73	83	15	3	13	56	26
Remole, Clifton, Ga. Tech	.323	220	47	71	14	0	4	42	1
Frank, Kyle, Clemson	.322	236	38	76	9	0	9	48	3
Koshansky, Joe, Virginia	.320	178	43	57	10	3	9	36	2
Dutton, Jeremy, N.C. State	.320	197	44	63	13	1	11	48	10
Iannetta, Chris, North Carolina	.319	232	44	74	13	2	8	55	2
Waggett, Blair, North Carolina	.319	138	31	44	10	3	1	16	8
Blake, Ryan, North Carolina	.318	220	43	70	12	2	5	45	6
Maynor, Marc, N.C. State	.318	217	50	69	16	2	0	30	21
Hubbard, Ryan, Wake Forest	.318	192	62	61	10	0	4	26	**35**
Maxwell, Justin, Maryland	.317	189	37	60	12	1	10	43	11
Ingold, Ben, Wake Forest	.317	199	34	63	5	0	1	34	4
Greene, Tyler, Ga. Tech	.316	228	48	72	8	2	8	43	19
Street, Matt, Virginia	.315	235	38	74	14	0	1	23	16
LaFaivre, Steve, Wake Forest	.315	127	24	40	9	1	3	29	0
Orvella, Chad, N.C. State	.314	204	52	64	14	1	5	30	10
Evans, Garrick, Clemson	.311	132	27	41	11	1	2	15	8
Caradonna, Troy, Duke	.309	204	19	63	14	0	3	38	3
Constantino, Mike, Maryland	.309	188	30	58	15	2	3	17	1
Buffone, Anthony, Maryland	.308	214	28	66	12	0	1	25	3
Zimmerman, Ryan, Virginia	.308	221	28	68	13	1	0	36	2
Owings, Micah, Ga. Tech	.306	209	43	64	11	2	15	42	2
Mangum, Greg, North Carolina	.305	239	42	73	9	1	2	34	8
Hart, Chris, Florida State	.305	200	44	61	10	1	4	35	4
Getz, Chris, Wake Forest	.305	187	36	57	11	2	2	19	5
Murray, Adam, Duke	.302	212	39	64	6	0	0	15	11
Gemmill, Ray, Maryland	.301	156	31	47	12	2	8	29	0
Murton, Matt, Georgia Tech	.301	246	64	74	10	3	13	56	19
#Patterson, Eric, Ga. Tech	.274	248	56	68	11	4	2	35	**35**

INDIVIDUAL PITCHING LEADERS
(Minimum 50 Innings)

	W	L	ERA	G	SV	IP	H	BB	SO
Hodges, Daniel, Florida State	5	2	**2.08**	39	12	52	48	7	38
Devine, Joey, N.C. State	6	3	2.19	36	**14**	66	49	16	78
Koshansky, Joe, Virginia	7	2	2.31	9	0	58	43	19	54
Davidson, Daniel, Florida State	10	0	2.63	23	0	86	69	25	77
Peterson, Trent, Florida State	10	1	2.70	22	0	117	97	37	113
Sleeth, Kyle, Wake Forest	7	3	2.81	14	0	96	78	29	102
Rogers, Michael, N.C. State	12	3	3.02	17	0	125	122	34	113
Berken, Jason, Clemson	4	2	3.19	19	0	59	58	25	41
Sterry, Vern, N.C. State	11	0	3.25	17	0	116	99	39	**124**
Sauls, Mark, Florida State	5	0	3.27	15	0	52	60	16	49
Schmoll, Steve, Maryland	4	5	3.49	18	4	88	72	25	**124**

	W	L	ERA	G	SV	IP	H	BB	SO
Lynch, Matt, Florida State	**13**	4	3.53	19	0	112	121	35	89
Moore, Daniel, North Carolina	7	3	3.56	17	0	94	102	41	65
Hahn, Jeff, Clemson	5	7	3.57	20	0	58	57	19	39
Lumsden, Tyler, Clemson	8	2	3.77	16	0	86	82	31	72
Dobies, Andrew, Virginia	6	3	3.84	14	0	80	90	31	72
Goodman, Chris, Ga. Tech	9	3	3.84	17	0	89	85	20	55
Bach, Brian, Wake Forest	5	2	3.89	15	0	69	66	28	40
Burks, Brian, Georgia Tech	5	1	3.92	23	8	57	49	13	50
Owings, Micah, Ga. Tech	9	3	3.99	17	0	88	84	21	58
Kalkhof, Adam, North Carolina	7	2	4.26	17	0	80	82	30	77
Jackson, Steven, Clemson	7	3	4.27	13	0	78	81	32	38
Hogan, Patrick, Clemson	3	2	4.30	17	3	59	54	24	49
Bakker, Garry, North Carolina	6	3	4.32	16	0	81	82	32	59
Bakker, Kyle, Georgia Tech	8	3	4.35	18	0	93	97	36	80
Davidson, Phillip, N.C. State	4	2	4.46	20	0	77	68	29	44
Alleva, Jeff, Duke	4	7	4.62	16	0	78	95	16	62
Kown, Andrew, Ga. Tech	3	2	4.65	18	1	50	55	13	40
Gale, Chris, Virginia	3	4	4.68	12	0	67	76	15	35
Cretarolo, Nate, N.C. State	5	3	4.78	17	0	79	89	38	68
Hanson, Adam, Wake Forest	5	4	5.02	25	3	61	78	23	48
Walker, Blake, Duke	3	1	5.37	31	2	52	53	20	34

ATLANTIC SUN CONFERENCE

	Conference		Overall	
	W	L	W	L
Florida Atlantic	25	8	47	16
Stetson	21	12	41	24
Jacksonville State	19	14	32	26
Belmont	19	14	29	23
Gardner-Webb	18	15	33	23
***Jacksonville**	17	16	32	30
Troy State	16	17	27	27
Georgia State	16	17	25	29
Central Florida	14	16	31	25
Campbell	14	19	22	28
Samford	7	23	17	34
Mercer	6	21	11	34

ALL-CONFERENCE TEAM: C—Rusty Bennett, So., Georgia State. **1B**—Rusty Brown, Jr., Florida Atlantic. **2B**—Sal Deanda, Sr., Campbell. **3B**—Brian Snyder, Jr., Stetson. **SS**—Sean Fitzgerald, Sr., Georgia State. **OF**—Ryan Bear, Sr., Central Florida; Jeff Fiorentino, So., Florida Atlantic; Chad Hauseman, Sr., Jacksonville. **DH**—Dustin Phillips, Sr., Georgia State. **P**—Randy Beam, Jr., Florida Atlantic; Jessie Corn, Jr., Jacksonville State; Ronnie Robinson, Sr., Georgia State. **RP**—Will Tucker, Jr., Belmont.

Player of the Year: Chad Hauseman, Jacksonville. **Freshman of the Year:** Gordie Gronkowski, Jacksonville. **Coach of the Year:** Dave Jarvis, Belmont.

INDIVIDUAL BATTING LEADERS

(Minimum 125 At-Bats)

	AVG	AB	R	H	2B	3B	HR	RBI	SB
Hauseman, Chad, Jacksonville	**.401**	187	47	75	11	0	**16**	37	11
Snyder, Brian, Stetson	.396	227	65	**90**	**23**	3	11	55	12
Bear, Ryan, Central Florida	.390	195	45	76	20	**5**	5	36	7
Fiorentino, Jeff, Fla. Atlantic	.382	233	**71**	89	14	0	15	49	14
Brown, Rusty, Fla. Atlantic	.368	231	58	85	17	0	11	**66**	0
Gronkowski, Gordie, Jack.	.366	145	26	53	13	0	6	39	1
Soukup, Dan, Belmont	.364	187	35	68	15	1	7	40	9
Deanda, Sal, Campbell	.364	163	26	52	6	0	2	21	6
Warpool, Jason, Belmont	.361	183	31	66	18	0	5	25	14
Timpner, Clay, Central Florida	.347	202	40	70	13	3	1	35	22
Pali, Matt, Fla. Atlantic	.341	220	61	75	15	3	10	45	8
Bradford, Sam, Gardner-Webb	.337	202	41	68	9	1	12	41	9
Evans, Sae, Samford	.335	179	30	60	13	1	7	34	6
Quirello, Ryan, Gardner-Webb	.335	182	29	61	7	3	7	37	2
Church, Ian, Stetson	.333	198	38	66	12	0	8	34	4
Knagt, Nathan, Central Fla.	.333	138	34	46	6	0	1	19	7
Evans, Robert, Samford	.329	164	28	54	10	2	6	29	5
Phillips, Dustin, Georgia State	.328	195	43	64	22	1	3	43	13
Ruckdeschel, Matt, JSU	.328	183	31	60	15	1	0	30	7
O'Connor, Shaen, Fla. Atl.	.328	131	19	43	12	1	4	25	0
Destefano, John, Stetson	.327	220	57	72	10	2	3	28	2
Zenchyk, Bryan, Stetson	.322	180	32	58	11	0	8	53	1
Mann, David, Central Florida	.321	162	39	52	2	2	0	13	17
Hicks, Bobby, JSU	.320	203	31	65	11	1	5	35	12
Haskins, Brian, JSU	.318	151	27	48	10	0	4	24	2
Fitzgerald, Sean, Georgia State	.317	167	35	53	6	1	0	24	0
Burroughs, Stephen, Ga. State	.316	174	26	55	11	1	2	28	10
Howard, Chad, Troy State	.315	168	31	53	9	1	7	27	16
Blick, Jeff, Campbell	.315	181	31	57	6	2	2	15	16
Futrelle, David, Gardner-Webb	.314	194	36	61	11	3	12	39	9
McKoy, Jonathan, Gard.-Webb	.312	173	24	54	7	0	2	16	6
Kawasaki, Kevin, Ga. State	.309	194	52	60	6	2	1	19	16
Rispoli, Tom, Campbell	.309	191	34	59	14	2	4	32	8
Barrows, Derek, Campbell	.309	162	25	50	9	2	**7**	40	2
Butera, Drew, Central Florida	.305	128	18	39	6	0	1	30	0
Cox, Trent, Troy State	.304	161	26	49	4	0	0	12	4
Peterson, Clay, Belmont	.304	161	33	49	6	2	6	28	8
O'Quinn, Casey, Troy State	.301	193	27	58	9	1	5	28	1
Wallace, Rich, Central Fla.	.300	140	21	42	8	0	4	34	2
Bennett, Rusty, Georgia State	.299	187	30	56	16	0	10	62	0
Sundstrom, Stephen, Belmont	.296	159	28	47	7	2	2	17	7
Sheffield, Brad, Troy State	.295	146	21	43	6	3	1	28	6
Brannon, Evan, Fla. Atlantic	.293	167	33	49	9	2	1	27	3
Glueckert, Jim, Gardner-Webb	.293	140	19	41	10	0	2	12	1
#Hart, Clint, Jacksonville	.286	189	37	54	9	**5**	3	27	18
#Best-Berfet, Larry, Jacksonville	.283	205	39	58	11	0	1	26	**27**

INDIVIDUAL PITCHING LEADERS

(Minimum 50 Innings)

	W	L	ERA	G	SV	IP	H	BB	SO
Corn, Jessie, Jacksonville State	8	6	**2.27**	15	0	115	86	23	**119**
Beam, Randy, Florida Atlantic	**13**	2	2.39	17	0	102	74	17	83
Saxton, Chris, Florida Atlantic	4	4	2.68	25	5	57	50	15	44
Michael, Mark, Central Florida	7	6	3.13	14	0	83	76	25	71
Robinson, Ronnie, Ga. State	9	2	3.18	14	0	93	81	33	77
Kleweno, Matt, Campbell	3	7	3.22	17	0	95	91	25	49
Stovall, Jeff, Campbell	6	5	3.31	15	0	73	74	15	39
Haas, Shane, Belmont	9	4	3.39	14	0	66	61	23	47
Core, Danny, Florida Atlantic	10	2	3.40	16	0	106	91	34	98
Blades, Josh, Campbell	5	2	3.67	16	1	61	66	15	35
Blair, Adam, Stetson	3	2	3.73	15	0	70	69	28	47
Winters, Mal, Troy State	3	7	3.74	15	0	84	83	24	45
Long, Jeff, Gardner-Webb	4	5	3.74	12	1	67	71	26	55
Martin, Josh, Gardner-Webb	6	5	3.77	14	0	76	71	22	54
NeSmith, Travis, Fla. Atlantic	7	2	3.92	16	0	67	71	22	36
McCuen, Cy, Stetson	9	5	3.95	21	0	96	112	21	64
Wiley, Mike, Stetson	5	2	4.06	21	0	69	79	30	50
Eason, Justin, Troy State	3	5	4.07	16	1	73	83	16	41
Ward, Zachary, Gardner-Webb	5	1	4.14	18	2	50	41	23	51
Buckley, Allen, JSU	2	4	4.22	17	1	70	72	33	69
Destefano, John, Stetson	5	3	4.24	16	0	68	87	16	29
Cobb, Taylor, Central Florida	4	3	4.39	16	1	53	52	33	41
Brickle, Donald, Jacksonville	3	4	4.41	15	1	63	61	19	28
Stertzbach, Von, Central Florida	4	5	4.43	19	0	85	83	25	74
Wikstrom, Eric, Troy State	7	3	4.52	15	0	100	108	23	73
#Tucker, Will, Belmont	3	2	4.58	27	**12**	39	50	18	33
Abel, Cameron, Stetson	3	0	4.58	19	0	53	48	25	39
Deel, Josh, Jacksonville	4	5	4.65	20	4	50	50	24	49
Artz, Stephen, Samford	1	6	4.67	21	2	89	103	26	67
Palmer, C.R., Jacksonville State	7	5	4.67	19	0	79	90	21	60
Lincoln, Roger, Stetson	5	8	4.68	38	9	75	86	15	73
Blackard, Cody, Belmont	6	4	4.69	15	1	86	101	20	74

ATLANTIC-10 CONFERENCE

	Conference		Overall	
EAST	W	L	W	L
Massachusetts	14	7	26	19
Rhode Island	16	8	26	26
St. Bonaventure	9	11	22	19
Temple	10	14	20	27
St. Joseph's	10	14	17	31
Fordham	8	15	16	27
WEST	**W**	**L**	**W**	**L**
***Richmond**	19	4	48	15
Duquesne	15	9	25	29
Xavier	13	8	25	26
George Washington	12	9	37	18
LaSalle	6	17	11	30
Dayton	4	20	16	36

ALL-CONFERENCE TEAM: C—Brian Oakes, Jr., LaSalle. **1B**—Jim Fasano, So., Richmond. **2B**—Travis Crowder, Sr., George Washington. **3B**—Mike Walls, Sr., St. Joseph's. **SS**—David Reaver, Sr., Richmond. **OF**—Vito Chiaravalloti, Sr., Richmond; Mark Andres, Sr., Xavier; Chad Williams, Sr., Duquesne. **DH**—Ryan Roberson, So., George Washington. **P**—Mike McGirr, Sr., Richmond; Tim Stauffer, Jr., Richmond. **RP**—Scott Ratliff, So., Massachusetts.

Player of the Year: Jim Fasano, Richmond. **Pitcher of the Year:** Tim Stauffer, Richmond. **Rookie of the Year:** Tom Shanley, George Washington. **Coach of the Year:** Frank Leoni, Rhode Island.

INsDIVIDUAL BATTING LEADERS

(Minimum 125 At-Bats)

	AVG	AB	R	H	2B	3B	HR	RBI	SB
Shanley, Tom, Geo. Wash.	**.398**	186	48	74	6	1	2	30	5
Batz, Dan, Rhode Island	.393	191	32	75	15	2	5	46	15
Roberson, Ryan, Geo. Wash.	.383	196	43	75	14	1	8	**68**	9

	AVG	AB	R	H	2B	3B	HR	RBI	SB
Oakes, Brian, LaSalle	.370	135	32	50	14	1	12	39	7
Zeskind, Ben, Richmond	.366	213	49	**78**	13	3	6	40	17
Quigley, John, Temple	.361	144	40	52	11	1	14	39	10
Kemmer, Kris, Dayton	.358	151	22	54	10	0	5	38	1
Rapacioli, Mike, St. Bonaventure	.355	152	40	54	14	0	8	40	9
Williams, Chad, Duquesne	.350	137	29	48	8	3	2	24	15
Wilson, Eric, St. Bonaventure	.345	139	34	48	12	2	5	29	2
Cucinotta, Rob, Temple	.345	168	41	58	11	0	10	25	5
Wilson, Sean, Duquesne	.345	145	37	50	7	0	0	32	8
Fasano, Jim, Richmond	.344	218	40	75	16	0	**16**	**68**	0
Boulanger, Matt, Mass.	.343	140	28	48	13	1	4	26	1
Walls, Mike, St. Joseph's	.340	150	23	51	10	2	3	27	3
Athas, Mike, Massachusetts	.339	168	37	57	9	1	2	20	7
Snyder, John, LaSalle	.338	139	24	47	14	0	1	17	4
Thomas, Kurt, Fordham	.338	142	31	48	13	1	4	24	9
Morgan, Chris, Massachusetts	.336	149	29	50	14	0	7	32	1
Johnson, Jay, Xavier	.333	198	33	66	9	0	1	30	19
Landahl, Matt, St. Bonaventure	.333	135	28	45	13	1	2	28	3
Bourgeois, Jeremy, Fordham	.333	129	27	43	6	0	9	34	8
Raglani, Anthony, Geo. Wash.	.331	181	48	60	**19**	1	6	40	12
Pritz, Bryan, Richmond	.328	195	49	64	15	2	5	30	23
Andres, Mark, Xavier	.328	177	30	58	10	1	4	44	7
Reaver, David, Richmond	.328	232	**53**	76	12	2	1	32	28
Crowder, Travis, Geo. Wash.	.327	165	48	54	10	0	6	31	16
Kokol, John, St. Joseph's	.327	159	29	52	12	2	6	23	3
Flynn, Patrick, Dayton	.325	200	39	65	5	2	7	37	5
Sullivan, Matt, Rhode Island	.315	181	27	57	9	1	1	37	21
#LeNoir, Bobby, Richmond	.299	187	42	56	9	3	1	24	**29**
#Bourassa, Jeff, Dayton	.262	141	22	37	6	**4**	1	17	8

INDIVIDUAL PITCHING LEADERS

(Minimum 50 Innings)

	W	L	ERA	G	SV	IP	H	BB	SO
Stauffer, Tim, Richmond	9	5	**1.97**	15	0	114	87	19	**146**
McGirr, Mike, Richmond	**10**	1	2.25	16	0	96	90	24	91
Bolinski, Jason, Richmond	**10**	1	2.40	15	1	82	66	30	88
Gunesch, Matt, St. Bonaventure	3	2	2.52	10	1	50	45	17	29
Jahnsen, Adam, Xavier	5	1	2.79	15	0	84	75	31	58
Sullivan, Dan, Geo. Wash.	4	1	2.96	13	0	70	65	19	54
Crane, Mike, Massachusetts	4	0	3.08	10	0	53	53	12	48
Wiggers, Greg, Xavier	4	6	3.50	17	0	75	83	18	58
Baco, John, Fordham	3	6	3.60	10	0	60	64	14	47
Kelly, Bryan, Fordham	3	4	3.64	13	2	54	45	27	47
#Ratliff, Scott, Massachusetts	2	2	3.70	18	**7**	24	23	15	27
Wilkie, Josh, Geo. Washington	6	2	3.75	14	0	58	59	15	64
Conden, Greg, Geo. Wash.	7	6	3.77	15	0	91	81	36	93
Haun, Adam, Duquesne	5	4	3.81	14	1	78	78	28	66
Sues, Jarret, Xavier	7	5	3.91	18	2	78	79	27	54
Trout, Jared, Rhode Island	6	3	3.97	12	0	79	79	43	93
McCormack, Mike, St. Bonaventure	6	1	4.09	10	0	51	55	24	45
Pfau, Dan, Geo. Washington	6	0	4.13	19	1	61	68	20	59
Reifschneider, Bob, Duquesne	6	5	4.19	13	0	82	68	42	51
Chown, Eric, Massachusetts	7	4	4.25	14	1	72	76	21	49
#Koken, Nick, Geo. Washington	4	4	5.28	23	**7**	29	35	21	18

BIG EAST CONFERENCE

	Conference W	Conference L	Overall W	Overall L
Rutgers	19	6	37	22
West Virginia	18	6	36	19
***Notre Dame**	16	7	45	18
Virginia Tech	15	10	34	23
Boston College	13	11	33	21
Pittsburgh	13	13	36	20
St. John's	12	14	29	27
Seton Hall	11	14	23	24
Connecticut	10	15	24	23
Villanova	6	19	14	32
Georgetown	4	22	14	33

ALL-CONFERENCE TEAM: C—Wyatt Toregas, So., Virginia Tech. **1B**—Matt Edwards, So., Notre Dame. **2B**—Marc Tugwell, Sr., Virginia Tech. **3B**—Chris Stanton, So., Virginia Tech. **SS**—Mike Rozema, Jr., St. John's. **OF**—Jeff Frazier, So., Rutgers; Casey Grimm, Sr., Seton Hall; Jarod Rine, Jr., West Virginia. **DH**—Matt Wolski, Sr., Rutgers. **Util**—Peter Soteropoulos, Sr., Connecticut. **P**—Chris Lambert, So., Boston College; Chris Niesel, So., Notre Dame; Matt Dalton, Sr., Virginia Tech.

Co-Players of the Year: Jarod Rine, West Virginia; Marc Tugwell, Virginia Tech. **Pitcher of the Year:** Chris Niesel, Notre Dame. **Rookie of the Year:** Stan Posluszny, West Virginia. **Coach of the Year:** Greg Van Zant, West Virginia.

INDIVIDUAL BATTING LEADERS

(Minimum 125 At-Bats)

	AVG	AB	R	H	2B	3B	HR	RBI	SB
Rozema, Mike, St. John's	**.408**	196	44	80	12	4	2	33	13
Fritz, Lee, West Virginia	.407	216	40	88	11	2	1	23	6
Rine, Jarod, West Virginia	.403	186	43	75	12	1	9	34	14
Tugwell, Marc, Virginia Tech	.398	226	64	90	17	0	8	59	16
Stanton, Chris, Virginia Tech	.392	222	61	87	12	**6**	3	36	23
Wolski, Matt, Rutgers	.391	192	40	75	10	2	1	34	10
Sollmann, Steve, Notre Dame	.384	255	**67**	**98**	16	5	4	40	38
Soteropoulos, Peter, UConn	.381	176	38	67	10	4	3	43	10
Edwards, Matt, Notre Dame	.376	229	40	86	16	2	8	**69**	2
Spamer, Bryan, Pittsburgh	.375	184	50	69	15	3	4	45	17
Lombardi, Michael, Georgetown	.374	174	36	65	16	0	2	34	0
Grimm, Casey, Seton Hall	.370	154	40	57	13	1	10	34	2
Serfass, Jake, West Virginia	.357	157	49	56	17	0	10	37	6
Locke, Drew, Boston College	.354	161	33	57	14	2	4	29	9
Maler, Bryan, UConn	.348	132	26	46	8	0	2	15	6
Pahuta, Tim, Seton Hall	.345	148	28	51	13	0	5	37	6
McCabe, Tim, West Virginia	.344	209	48	72	14	0	11	43	0
Rykaceski, Stuart, Pittsburgh	.342	199	49	68	18	3	2	45	14
Cleary, Andrew, Georgetown	.338	157	45	53	12	1	12	47	1
Folmar, Scott, Pittsburgh	.337	169	36	57	12	0	0	17	10
Clinton, Kurtis, West Virginia	.335	206	44	69	12	0	**13**	50	2
Normane, Steve, Rutgers	.335	200	43	67	14	3	8	53	6
Scanzano, Mike, Pittsburgh	.332	193	36	64	4	4	2	31	16
Esposito, Vinny, Rutgers	.328	201	47	66	16	2	4	43	5
Cashman, Tom, Pittsburgh	.328	186	38	61	15	1	6	36	3
D'Argento, Russ, UConn	.326	181	49	59	9	2	5	25	9
Toregas, Wyatt, Virginia Tech	.319	216	41	69	14	2	10	60	5
Badger, Graig, Rutgers	.318	214	61	68	10	3	1	34	**41**
DiScipio, Josh, Boston College	.317	199	35	63	10	2	2	20	13
Burnham, Brett, UConn	.317	161	44	51	8	2	7	47	12
Grimm, Eric, West Virginia	.316	209	45	66	14	2	10	55	2
Leahy, Ryan, Boston College	.316	187	33	59	12	0	2	24	17
Frazier, Jeff, Rutgers	.315	213	56	67	**19**	0	8	54	7
Graiser, Billy, St. John's	.315	178	39	56	7	3	1	14	25
Quinn, Billy, Georgetown	.315	178	33	56	8	2	10	42	6
Rizzo, Cody, Notre Dame	.314	191	53	60	11	1	4	38	1
DeRosa, Anthony, St. John's	.312	176	42	55	13	2	6	34	4

INDIVIDUAL PITCHING LEADERS

(Minimum 50 Innings)

	W	L	ERA	G	SV	IP	H	BB	SO
#Dalton, Matt, Virginia Tech	3	1	0.76	29	**14**	36	16	6	28
Thornton, Tom, Notre Dame	5	1	**1.81**	15	0	55	54	14	29
Shepard, Kevin, Boston College	8	3	2.44	12	0	70	72	28	46
Noonan, Chris, Seton Hall	3	2	2.61	33	9	59	46	33	65
Kennedy, Ryan, Virginia Tech	6	2	2.62	11	1	55	45	25	37
Niesel, Chris, Notre Dame	9	1	2.65	15	0	98	86	19	87
Gagne, J.P., Note Dame	4	6	2.70	30	13	60	55	21	45
Lambert, Chris, Boston College	8	2	2.71	13	0	80	61	38	88
O'Donnell, Matt, Boston College	4	4	2.82	13	0	67	61	14	46
Rhoten, Don, Pittsburgh	4	2	3.30	14	1	60	45	36	40
Evangelista, Nick, Pittsburgh	8	5	3.32	14	0	89	85	20	76
Kalita, Ryan, Notre Dame	7	1	3.42	13	0	76	71	31	64
Cline, Zac, West Virginia	**12**	3	3.44	16	0	126	125	31	**101**
Klemm, Tom, St. John's	5	4	3.58	25	0	50	50	19	38
Reid, Joe, St. John's	3	3	3.74	15	0	77	73	42	68
Santmyer, Mike, Seton Hall	5	2	3.83	20	1	54	65	26	46
Elfeldt, Matt, Boston College	3	4	3.93	16	1	50	51	22	35
Egbert, Jack, Rutgers	8	5	3.95	15	0	87	94	21	72
Miller, Shawn, West Virginia	6	3	4.00	12	0	72	69	35	53
Laird, Matt, Notre Dame	3	1	4.22	20	1	53	46	20	48
Axford, John, Notre Dame	9	3	4.31	14	0	71	63	50	69
Yeager, John, Villanova	3	7	4.57	11	0	63	82	9	31
DiAngelo, Jason, West Virginia	8	5	4.64	14	0	87	82	50	72
Parker, Shaun, Rutgers	4	3	4.78	16	0	85	87	56	59
Varvaro, Anthony, St. John's	4	6	4.83	15	0	63	71	29	56
Wells, Andrew, Virginia Tech	4	4	4.92	15	0	68	85	19	36

BIG SOUTH CONFERENCE

	Conference W	Conference L	Overall W	Overall L
Winthrop	15	4	35	22
***Coastal Carolina**	12	7	45	18
Elon	12	7	34	23
UNC Asheville	12	9	27	28
Charleston Southern	9	12	19	37
Liberty	7	12	17	37
High Point	5	12	14	37
Radford	5	14	13	28

ALL-CONFERENCE TEAM: C—Grant Rembert, So., UNC Asheville. **1B**—Chad Bryan, Sr., Liberty. **2B**—Matt Matkovich, Jr., Winthrop. **3B**—David Scoggin, Jr., Winthrop. **SS**—Brian Ingram, Sr., Elon. **OF**—Jordan Haar, So., Charleston Southern; Ryan McGraw, Jr., Coastal Carolina; Daniel Carte, Fr., Winthrop. **DH**—Mike Fratoe, Jr., Elon. **P**—R.J. Swindle, Charleston

Southern; Jeremy Plexico, Winthrop.

Most Valuable Player: R.J. Swindle, Charleston Southern. **Freshman of the Year:** Daniel Carte, Winthrop. **Coach of the Year:** Matt Myers, UNC Asheville.

INDIVIDUAL BATTING LEADERS

(Minimum 125 At-Bats)

	AVG	AB	R	H	2B	3B	HR	RBI	SB
Matkovich, Matt, Winthrop	**.388**	183	54	71	14	2	8	34	5
Powell, Brandon, Co. Carolina	.364	253	48	**92**	**22**	3	5	46	30
Bryan, Chad, Liberty	.349	166	24	58	8	0	6	29	4
York, Larry Wayne, Liberty	.347	196	28	68	8	1	0	21	26
Carte, Daniel, Winthrop	.345	203	56	70	20	1	**12**	53	9
McGraw, Ryan, Co. Carolina	.339	245	58	83	16	4	6	41	**45**
Scoggin, David, Winthrop	.333	201	36	67	12	1	9	**64**	1
Roberson, Kyle, Winthrop	.329	219	44	72	12	0	2	28	17
Rembert, Grant, UNC-A	.323	192	38	62	15	4	7	45	2
Dempsey, Jacob, Winthrop	.320	128	38	41	12	1	7	27	4
Costanzo, Mike, Co. Carolina	.318	173	31	55	9	0	8	43	1
Fratoe, Mike, Elon	.318	129	17	41	6	0	6	32	1
Haar, Jordan, Charleston So.	.316	209	48	66	7	1	**12**	36	5
Thacker, Scott, Charleston So.	.312	173	21	54	7	0	3	35	0
Ingram, Brian, Elon	.311	193	43	60	11	2	7	50	12
Cloninger, Erich, Liberty	.311	132	15	41	8	3	2	22	4
Sherman, Steve, UNC-A	.305	164	33	50	9	2	3	25	7
Neidenfeuhr, Grant, Winthrop	.305	164	34	50	12	1	3	24	0
Repec, Matt, Winthrop	.304	194	32	59	13	0	5	38	5
Ritchie, Stuart, Radford	.303	155	29	47	7	1	0	21	19
Tartaglia, Evan, Elon	.299	204	50	61	7	**8**	0	22	34
Grandstand, Brett, Co. Car.	.298	225	**63**	67	11	1	6	44	34
McConiga, Jake, UNC-A	.298	191	39	57	16	1	1	30	20
Kolhagen, Jeff, Charleston So.	.298	188	26	56	10	0	3	23	5
Sandri, Drew, UNC-A	.298	131	22	39	5	0	7	25	0

INDIVIDUAL PITCHING LEADERS

(Minimum 50 Innings)

	W	L	ERA	G	SV	IP	H	BB	SO
Swindle, R.J., Charleston So.	10	4	**1.96**	20	0	119	102	24	**129**
#Lieberman, Bret, Radford	0	2	2.38	19	**8**	23	17	12	21
Waack, Brian, Co. Carolina	4	2	2.90	31	3	78	72	31	70
Plexico, Jeremy, Winthrop	**11**	3	2.90	17	1	109	86	26	99
Bechtold, David, Liberty	4	4	3.07	12	0	70	62	26	57
Binda, Byron, Co. Carolina	6	1	3.21	29	3	62	47	33	65
Garner, Matt, Elon	7	5	3.27	15	0	85	75	32	62
Sturge, Justin, Co. Carolina	10	3	3.27	17	0	99	92	33	92
Hurry, Jake, Co. Carolina	6	1	3.42	20	1	53	41	25	48
Burch, Kevin, High Point	4	7	3.51	14	0	95	104	22	53
Williams, Stephen, Liberty	2	3	3.68	21	2	51	52	19	32
Blocker, Tyson, Elon	5	4	3.84	15	0	75	71	20	53
Donovan, Seamus, Co. Carolina	4	7	3.86	18	1	86	89	34	71
Hensen, Brian, Elon	5	2	3.91	21	1	78	95	17	51
Slowey, Kevin, Winthrop	6	2	3.98	17	1	86	86	18	90
#Carter, Stephen, Co. Carolina	**11**	3	4.06	20	0	115	109	33	110

BIG TEN CONFERENCE

	Conference W	Conference L	Overall W	Overall L
Minnesota	24	6	40	22
***Ohio State**	20	12	44	21
Michigan	16	14	30	27
Penn State	17	15	29	28
Northwestern	15	14	25	25
Indiana	16	15	34	22
Purdue	13	18	29	26
Illinois	12	19	27	26
Michigan State	10	19	21	34
Iowa	10	21	18	29

ALL-CONFERENCE TEAM: C—Jake Fox, Jr., Michigan. **1B**—Andy Schutzenhofer, Sr., Illinois. **2B**—Luke Appert, Sr., Minnesota. **3B**—Vasili Spanos, Sr., Indiana. **SS**—Scott Welch, Sr., Minnesota. **OF**—Sam Steidl, Jr., Minnesota; Christian Snavely, Jr., Ohio State; Daniel Underwood, Sr., Purdue. **DH**—Mike Sokol, Sr., Michigan. **P**—Drew Taylor, So., Michigan; Glen Perkins, Fr., Minnesota; Scott Lewis, So., Ohio State; J.A. Happ, So., Northwestern. **RP**—Matt Davis, Jr., Ohio State.

Player of the Year: Luke Appert, Minnesota. **Pitcher of the Year:** Scott Lewis, Ohio State. **Freshman of the Year:** Glen Perkins, Minnesota. **Coach of the Year:** John Anderson, Minnesota.

INDIVIDUAL BATTING LEADERS

(Minimum 125 At-Bats)

	AVG	AB	R	H	2B	3B	HR	RBI	SB
Spanos, Vasili, Indiana	**.412**	182	53	75	16	2	11	47	5
Burrill, Brady, Michigan State	.381	155	27	59	11	0	3	23	2
Underwood, Daniel, Purdue	.377	199	44	75	16	2	12	57	8
Appert, Luke, Minnesota	.373	225	53	84	**27**	0	4	45	15
Heckman, Corby, Indiana	.372	183	44	68	15	0	4	29	2
Gulick, Travis, Michigan State	.370	211	**60**	78	13	3	13	43	9
Koman, Brock, Michigan	.368	220	47	81	21	0	8	55	0
Steidl, Sam, Minnesota	.367	237	45	**87**	10	0	0	33	10
Eymann, Eric, Illinois	.359	198	37	71	15	2	5	32	6
Fox, Jake, Michigan	.357	207	44	74	19	3	15	**67**	2
Thousand, Kyle, Iowa	.355	166	42	59	17	1	2	16	20
Welch, Scott, Minnesota	.351	222	43	78	19	0	5	46	6
Smithlin, Zack, Penn State	.347	170	31	59	6	4	0	28	**24**
Fritz, Ben, Purdue	.345	142	36	49	13	0	0	19	7
Hunter, Andy, Minnesota	.344	154	18	53	13	2	4	44	0
Sokol, Mike, Michigan	.340	203	38	69	19	0	3	35	1
Snavely, Christian, Ohio State	.335	200	55	67	12	3	**16**	55	8
Caravati, Steve, Ohio State	.333	204	39	68	11	2	8	50	12
Warchal, Adam, Penn State	.331	127	26	42	7	1	5	25	1
Lollio, Gino, Michigan	.329	219	58	72	16	2	7	37	9
Bensko, Dusty, Illinois	.326	141	27	46	9	0	5	29	0
Hrncirik, David, Minnesota	.324	222	36	72	11	2	1	29	6
Cashman, Brandon, Illinois	.324	176	34	57	11	1	8	38	9
Davidson, Drew, Illinois	.324	170	29	55	9	4	3	26	2
Klink, Simon, Purdue	.321	193	37	62	21	2	1	27	2
Evans, Nick, Indiana	.321	134	18	43	7	0	3	40	1
Reohr, Wes, Penn State	.319	213	45	68	15	2	11	43	6
Rudden, Nick, Michigan	.318	154	37	49	6	0	1	17	11
Mikrut, Jon, Northwestern	.317	180	28	57	14	3	4	29	1
Schutzenhofer, Andy, Illinois	.316	187	38	59	11	1	1	36	3
McIntyre, Nick, Purdue	.315	203	42	64	9	1	11	45	8
Koerber, Scott, Michigan State	.315	143	24	45	9	1	1	27	1
Gremley, Jeff, Iowa	.313	166	27	52	16	2	3	32	8
Gresky, David, Northwestern	.313	179	35	56	13	1	9	43	7
Pattee, Ben, Minnesota	.312	240	48	75	24	1	4	33	3
Barr, Derrick, Penn State	.312	205	33	64	7	0	0	39	5
Morris, Erik, Michigan State	.311	177	24	55	7	0	1	30	7
Johnston, Tyler, Purdue	.310	158	34	49	5	2	1	17	12
Rempel, Andy, Purdue	.310	171	31	53	8	2	1	25	**24**
Garrard, Brett, Ohio State	.308	208	46	64	11	4	9	33	5
Anderson, Drew, Ohio State	.307	251	51	77	13	4	12	34	17
#Guyer, Lance, Iowa	.289	152	30	44	7	**5**	7	23	8

INDIVIDUAL PITCHING LEADERS

(Minimum 50 Innings)

	W	L	ERA	G	SV	IP	H	BB	SO
Lewis, Scott, Ohio State	9	1	**1.61**	12	0	84	48	24	**127**
Perkins, Glen, Minnesota	**10**	2	2.91	15	0	105	100	23	117
Konecny, Dan, Northwestern	4	7	3.24	14	0	89	91	30	57
Madsen, Mike, Ohio State	8	1	3.31	19	0	65	60	25	45
Johnson, Nathan, Iowa	6	2	3.38	16	1	59	66	9	53
Farrell, Jim, Penn State	7	3	3.47	15	0	70	67	26	60
Gale, Bryan, Michigan State	7	6	3.48	13	0	96	83	21	53
Brauer, Dan, Northwestern	5	3	3.50	12	2	54	50	32	44
Happ, J.A., Northwestern	7	6	3.58	14	0	83	85	33	94
Tognetti, Phil, Michigan	6	5	3.76	14	0	69	77	20	29
Ziemba, Joe, Illinois	7	2	3.77	12	0	62	65	12	36
Taylor, Drew, Michigan	9	1	3.97	16	0	95	104	25	51
Lane, Josh, Illinois	5	2	4.15	14	0	65	67	25	39
Rowe, Ted, Illinois	3	6	4.19	14	0	82	90	28	51
Ori, Mark, Northwestern	3	1	4.22	14	0	53	56	20	32
Woodrow, C.J., Minnesota	8	3	4.34	15	0	85	95	12	74
Behrens, Chris, Indiana	5	4	4.50	14	0	64	65	37	42
Lewis, Josh, Indiana	5	2	4.55	14	0	61	54	33	35
Garza, Bobby, Michigan	5	4	4.60	16	1	78	84	35	56
Newman, Josh, Ohio State	8	6	4.64	16	0	99	103	22	70
Pruemer, Mitch, Purdue	5	4	4.74	11	0	63	65	17	54
Day, Tim, Michigan State	3	7	4.91	14	0	84	97	21	49
Penn, Michael, Michigan	2	8	5.11	17	1	76	80	33	51
Loberg, Matt, Minnesota	6	2	5.14	14	0	70	89	20	35
Byrnes, Scott, Purdue	4	5	5.29	12	0	63	74	21	44
Cary, Jacob, Indiana	7	3	5.40	14	0	82	99	26	49
#Davis, Matt, Ohio State	3	1	6.05	33	**14**	39	42	11	39

BIG 12 CONFERENCE

	Conference W	Conference L	Overall W	Overall L
***Nebraska**	20	7	47	18
Texas A&M	19	8	45	19
Texas	19	8	50	20
Missouri	15	11	36	22
Baylor	15	12	45	23
Oklahoma State	14	13	34	24
Oklahoma	10	17	23	31
Kansas	9	18	35	28
Texas Tech	8	18	30	25
Kansas State	5	22	15	37

ALL-CONFERENCE TEAM: C—Jason Jaramillo, So., Oklahoma State. **1B**—Matt Hopper, Sr., Nebraska. **2B**—Eddie Cornejo, Sr., Oklahoma. **3B**—Josh Fields, So., Oklahoma State. **SS**—Omar Quintanilla, Jr., Texas. **OF**—Chris Durbin, Sr., Baylor; David Murphy, Jr., Baylor; Jayce Tingler, Sr., Missouri; Jose Virgil, Sr., Oklahoma State; Dustin Majewski, Sr., Texas. **DH**—Curtis Ledbetter, So., Nebraska. **P**—Aaron Marsden, Jr., Nebraska; J.P. Howell, So., Texas; Quinton Robertson, Jr., Nebraska; Scott Baker, Jr., Oklahoma State. **RP**—Huston Street, So., Texas; Scott Beerer, Jr., Texas A&M.

Player of the Year: Matt Hopper, Nebraska. **Pitcher of the Year:** Aaron Marsden, Nebraska. **Newcomer of the Year:** Scott Beerer, Texas A&M. **Freshman Player of the Year:** Taylor Teagarden, Texas. **Coach of the Year:** Mike Anderson, Nebraska.

INDIVIDUAL BATTING LEADERS

(Minimum 125 At-Bats)

	AVG	AB	R	H	2B	3B	HR	RBI	SB
Murphy, David, Baylor	**.413**	293	84	**121**	18	4	11	67	3
Tingler, Jayce, Missouri	.395	215	68	85	11	3	1	49	19
Cornejo, Eddie, Oklahoma	.393	214	37	84	15	2	2	49	10
Majewski, Dustin, Texas	.391	274	62	106	22	6	12	**85**	21
Jaramillo, Jason, Okla. State	.385	213	44	82	18	1	9	42	0
Spanish, Casey, Kansas	.383	230	58	88	15	7	12	55	14
Hopper, Matt, Nebraska	.382	233	74	89	12	0	**22**	66	5
Saccomanno, Mark, Baylor	.381	194	38	74	16	3	9	44	3
Jordan, Scooter, Texas Tech	.381	160	46	61	11	3	1	30	14
Virgil, Jose, Okla. State	.381	239	63	91	23	2	11	54	15
Willits, Reggie, Oklahoma	.379	206	55	78	16	1	3	19	**37**
Baty, Ryan, Kansas	.377	257	50	97	23	2	10	57	13
Colonel, Christian, Texas Tech	.373	169	34	63	13	1	6	45	11
Soto, Ty, Kansas State	.360	125	23	45	8	0	6	29	2
Fields, Josh, Okla. State	.358	229	50	82	10	3	12	55	4
Bennett, Ross, Baylor	.354	181	33	64	11	2	4	46	0
Schindewolf, Erik, Texas A&M	.351	231	66	81	15	0	2	29	12
Griffin, Michael, Baylor	.350	294	55	103	26	8	11	76	2
Urick, John, Okla. State	.348	210	52	73	10	2	13	53	1
Ledbetter, Curtis, Nebraska	.348	187	42	65	13	2	13	54	3
Quintanilla, Omar, Texas	.348	282	68	98	**29**	5	6	76	9
Durbin, Chris, Baylor	.346	283	**94**	98	23	4	18	50	9
Pennington, Cliff, Texas A&M	.340	241	54	82	14	2	2	41	12
Haney, Josh, Texas Tech	.338	207	53	70	15	4	6	50	6
Doty, Tim, Kansas State	.338	195	45	66	8	1	9	39	2
Baty, Matt, Kansas	.336	131	23	44	3	0	0	17	14
Tribble, Matt, Kansas	.335	242	50	81	17	3	5	41	8
Beerer, Scott, Texas A&M	.335	245	44	82	17	1	11	57	5
Kinsler, Ian, Missouri	.335	194	54	65	13	4	6	45	16
Flanders, Brad, Missouri	.332	196	39	65	13	0	6	43	4
Patton, Cory, Texas A&M	.331	257	53	85	15	1	13	58	4
Baldwin, Ryan, Kansas State	.328	204	30	67	16	0	7	52	0
Fuller, Cody, Texas Tech	.326	190	47	62	8	2	2	30	29
Pouk, Justin, Texas A&M	.325	160	33	52	10	0	5	27	3
Leise, Jeff, Nebraska	.325	271	58	88	10	7	7	37	20
Kirby, Scott, Okla. State	.325	166	29	54	9	0	11	42	2
Ruggiano, Justin, Texas A&M	.322	236	49	76	17	4	10	50	6
Bruce, T.J., Texas Tech	.321	209	44	67	11	1	3	38	8
Sultemeier, Eric, Texas	.321	237	51	76	16	0	10	56	21
Mullinax, Jake, Nebraska	.320	125	30	40	7	0	0	21	8
Moss, Tim, Texas	.319	276	82	88	18	**9**	3	33	21
Gordon, Alex, Nebraska	.319	216	45	69	13	2	7	48	8
Price, Ritchie, Kansas	.319	235	44	75	11	0	0	17	10
Wheeler, Kevin, Kansas	.319	210	45	67	7	2	10	45	0
Teagarden, Taylor, Texas	.315	200	26	63	13	3	5	41	0
Ford, Josh, Baylor	.314	283	60	89	19	0	12	63	0
Maloney, Pat, Kansas State	.314	204	42	64	13	0	10	32	3
Taylor, Zane, Missouri	.312	192	42	60	6	0	1	37	4
Bruce, Daniel, Nebraska	.311	164	33	51	8	2	6	33	8
Thigpen, Curtis, Texas	.311	196	38	61	8	2	6	38	7
Beck, Doug, Texas Tech	.310	200	48	62	7	3	4	38	6
Ferin, Joe, Texas	.307	228	46	70	3	6	4	30	16
Matulich, Mario, Okla. State	.305	187	33	57	7	1	9	45	0

INDIVIDUAL PITCHING LEADERS

(Minimum 50 Innings)

	W	L	ERA	G	SV	IP	H	BB	SO
Street, Huston, Texas	8	1	**1.33**	39	**15**	74	48	13	69
McAuliff, Jarod, Oklahoma	2	5	2.04	35	9	53	54	16	38
Howell, J.P., Texas	**10**	2	2.52	21	0	114	97	43	105
Carlson, Zane, Baylor	3	4	2.61	30	11	59	46	14	71
Kroenke, Zach, Nebraska	6	2	2.72	15	0	60	53	19	35
Mardsen, Aaron, Nebraska	8	3	2.90	16	0	115	109	21	113
Hawk, Shane, Okla. State	7	3	3.06	22	2	53	62	23	49
LaMotta, Ryan, Baylor	7	3	3.48	30	3	75	63	32	62
LeCure, Sam, Texas	5	0	3.74	16	0	53	59	14	29
Baker, Scott, Okla. State	**10**	5	3.79	17	0	112	117	29	97
Kensing, Logan, Texas A&M	7	5	3.83	20	1	89	101	22	58
Shirek, Phil, Nebraska	5	3	3.90	18	0	62	48	23	48
Gooch, Steve, Texas Tech	4	5	4.00	16	0	106	120	24	58
James, Justin, Missouri	7	6	4.03	17	0	114	110	26	92
White, Steven, Baylor	9	4	4.12	19	0	129	123	49	**130**
Farnum, Matt, Texas A&M	7	2	4.20	18	1	70	78	20	54
Woody, Abe, Baylor	6	0	4.22	27	3	60	45	18	41
Robertson, Quinton, Nebraska	**10**	2	4.23	16	0	89	95	21	51
Parcus, Kyle, Texas A&M	6	3	4.29	22	1	79	85	26	69
Simmons, Justin, Texas	5	6	4.29	19	0	86	77	26	58
Karstens, Jeff, Texas Tech	8	4	4.29	24	6	63	70	14	39
Buck, Dusty, Texas Tech	5	3	4.34	18	2	77	90	16	46
Smart, Chris, Kansas	2	5	4.35	20	3	72	93	12	32
Walker, Sean, Baylor	8	5	4.77	22	1	94	100	39	62
Muegge, Danny, Texas	6	6	4.89	15	0	77	85	22	53
Holmes, Pat, Kansas	4	1	4.91	15	0	51	54	28	33
Roberts, Mark, Oklahoma	5	7	5.07	15	0	99	116	32	81
Grogan, Spencer, Okla. State	3	5	5.09	17	0	76	95	26	48
Blair, Buddy, Oklahoma	5	6	5.09	15	0	88	98	36	63
Knippschild, Ryan, Kansas	8	5	5.16	22	0	113	134	24	63
Purcey, David, Oklahoma	3	3	5.20	26	1	73	72	41	67
Shipman, Andy, Missouri	9	4	5.26	26	1	65	80	19	48
Wheeler, Kevin, Kansas	6	6	5.30	17	0	110	126	23	72
McCormick, Mark, Baylor	6	2	5.32	17	0	64	56	50	66
Finch, Brian, Texas A&M	6	1	5.40	22	1	65	81	25	57

BIG WEST CONFERENCE

	Conference		Overall	
	W	L	W	L
Long Beach State	16	5	41	20
Cal State Fullerton	15	6	50	16
UC Riverside	14	7	41	17
Cal Poly	9	12	27	28
Cal State Northridge	8	13	14	42
UC Irvine	8	13	21	35
UC Santa Barbara	8	13	25	28
Pacific	6	15	27	27

ALL-CONFERENCE TEAM: C—Todd Jennings, Jr., Long Beach State. **1B**—Kevin Mangels, Jr., UC Riverside. **2B**—Adam Leavitt, Jr., Cal Poly. **3B**—Tony Festa, Jr., UC Riverside. **SS**—Randy Blood, Sr., UC Riverside. **OF**—Shane Costa, Jr., Cal State Fullerton; Ryan Harvey, Jr., UC Riverside; Brian Wahlbrink, Sr., UC Riverside. **DH**—Cory Lake, Sr., Pacific. **Util**—Brad Davis, So., Long Beach State. **SP**—Abe Alvarez, Jr., Long Beach State; Jered Weaver, So., Long Beach State; Jaymie Torres, Jr., UC Riverside. **RP**—Chad Cordero, Jr., Cal State Fulerton.

Player of the Year: Shane Costa, Cal State Fullerton. **Co-Pitchers of the Year:** Abe Alvarez, Long Beach State; Jered Weaver, Long Beach State. **Coach of the Year:** Mike Weathers, Long Beach State.

INDIVIDUAL BATTING LEADERS

(Minimum 125 At-Bats)

	AVG	AB	R	H	2B	3B	HR	RBI	SB
Harvey, Ryan, UC Riverside	**.411**	236	65	97	12	3	9	40	8
Pilittere, P.J., CS Fullerton	.380	163	32	62	11	1	3	31	3
Costa, Shane, CS Fullerton	.374	270	54	**101**	**28**	3	5	**59**	**28**
Wahlbrink, Brian, UC Riverside	.368	258	**68**	95	19	4	**12**	41	6
Blood, Randy, UC Riverside	.368	223	44	82	17	3	5	51	0
Heether, Adam, Long Beach	.355	186	55	66	11	0	6	32	7
Festa, Tony, UC Riverside	.352	219	56	77	14	1	5	52	6
Suzuki, Kurt, CS Fullerton	.350	143	34	50	10	0	2	28	1
Dorn, Danny, CS Fullerton	.348	178	47	62	11	3	7	54	5
Cunningham, Matt, UCR	.348	201	38	70	11	5	5	42	6
Herbert, Sam, Cal Poly	.346	240	49	83	20	3	2	30	13
Prettyman, Ron, CS Fullerton	.344	250	54	86	17	3	0	37	14
Powis, Scott, UC Riverside	.344	131	30	45	9	1	1	18	6
Aguailar, Drew, CS Northridge	.339	127	21	43	7	0	1	21	0
Saul, Billy, Cal Poly	.333	177	31	59	19	0	2	33	2
Bowker, John, Long Beach	.333	153	27	51	6	2	7	33	2
Lake, Cory, Pacific	.329	158	35	52	11	0	0	32	3
Leavitt, Adam, Cal Poly	.327	217	42	71	10	3	0	26	21
Boyer, Kyle, CS Fullerton	.327	245	66	80	18	3	6	49	26
Headley, Chase, Pacific	.326	193	35	63	13	2	3	26	3
Turner, Justin, CS Fullerton	.326	224	40	73	9	1	1	39	13
McCauley, Mark, CS Northridge	.323	155	16	50	5	3	2	18	2
Breen, Pat, Cal Poly	.320	175	36	56	15	4	10	49	6
Klemm, Chris, UC Irvine	.319	207	35	66	11	**6**	5	27	8
Sutton, Nate, UCSB	.318	214	42	68	8	3	4	28	9
Hutting, Tim, Long Beach	.317	161	20	51	7	1	0	25	4
Burgos, Richie, CS Fullerton	.316	250	49	79	25	3	4	51	4
Harper, Aaron, Pacific	.311	196	32	61	10	1	2	31	2
Mangels, Kevin, UC Riverside	.310	213	35	66	9	1	10	49	1
Fulton, Josh, UCSB	.310	155	27	48	3	1	1	19	8
Voita, John, CS Northridge	.309	152	25	47	9	1	4	24	1
Davis, Brad, Long Beach	.306	222	37	68	16	4	3	25	8
Emmons, Brian, UC Riverside	.305	154	35	47	9	0	7	36	1

	AVG	AB	R	H	2B	3B	HR	RBI	SB
Udvarhelyi, Travis, Long Beach	.303	142	26	43	5	4	1	17	4
Snook, Josh, Pacific	.301	193	37	58	12	1	4	32	8

INDIVIDUAL PITCHING LEADERS

(Minimum 50 Innings)

	W	L	ERA	G	SV	IP	H	BB	SO
Cordero, Chad, CS Fullerton	5	1	1.58	40	8	57	41	8	68
Weaver, Jered, Long Beach	**14**	4	**1.96**	19	0	133	87	20	**144**
Windsor, Jason, CS Fullerton	11	2	1.98	23	0	95	76	22	75
Alvarez, Abe, Long Beach	11	2	2.35	18	0	123	114	31	102
Schreppel, Ryan, CS Fullerton	5	3	2.45	11	0	51	41	14	42
Ramos, Cesar, Long Beach	6	4	2.85	17	0	88	80	31	33
Muniz, Carlos, Long Beach	0	2	3.14	26	**11**	29	27	10	30
Romero, Ricky, CS Fullerton	3	0	3.20	23	0	56	48	18	46
Miller, Dustin, CS Fullerton	9	2	3.33	18	0	100	103	25	97
Torres, Jaymie, UC Riverside	10	2	3.59	17	0	110	116	24	74
Swanson, Glenn, UC Irvine	2	9	3.67	15	0	91	98	23	68
Koehler, Michael, UC Irvine	1	4	3.68	25	1	59	57	19	36
Smith, Brett, UC Irvine	8	4	3.71	17	0	102	108	39	87
Shappi, AJ, UC Riverside	11	3	3.74	17	0	113	100	30	92
Littleton, Wes, CS Fullerton	7	4	3.89	14	0	86	86	17	67
Olson, Garrett, Cal Poly	5	3	4.37	18	0	82	78	27	67
Hoff, Brian, UC Riverside	3	5	4.76	19	3	62	86	23	42
Rosales, Leo, CS Northridge	5	7	4.82	20	2	108	116	29	117
Stanford, James, Pacific	2	7	5.06	18	0	84	108	26	53
Moser, Nolan, Cal Poly	3	2	5.08	19	1	51	59	13	34
Vasquez, Matt, UCSB	4	4	5.11	15	0	93	105	28	71
Silva, Sergio, Pacific	5	7	5.16	20	1	84	113	28	71
Thompson, Sean, UCSB	6	6	5.18	18	0	104	137	18	60
French, Paul, UC Irvine	2	7	5.20	21	1	73	80	20	65

COLONIAL ATHLETIC ASSOCIATION

	Conference		Overall	
AMERICAN	**W**	**L**	**W**	**L**
UNC Wilmington	15	6	40	23
James Madison	13	7	29	27
Towson	11	9	28	25
Old Dominion	5	15	18	33
Drexel	3	17	12	34
COLONIAL	**W**	**L**	**W**	**L**
***Virginia Commonwealth**	17	3	46	13
William & Mary	12	4	31	20
George Mason	9	8	31	20
Delaware	7	13	21	32
Hofstra	5	15	12	35

ALL-CONFERENCE TEAM: C—Jeff Parrish, So., Virginia Commonwealth. **1B**—Eddie Kim, Sr., James Madison. **2B**—Nick Jones, Jr., Virginia Commonwealth. **3B**—Nick Shimer, Jr., George Mason. **SS**—Brian McKenna, Jr., Towson. **OF**—Michael Brown, Sr., William & Mary; Jamie Hemingway, Sr., UNC Wilmington; Mike Butia, So., James Madison. **DH**—Mike Costello, Jr., Towson. **P**—Justin Orenduff, So., Virginia Commonwealth; Justin Verlander, So., Old Dominion. **RP**—Cla Meredith, So., Virginia Commonwealth.

Player of the Year: Eddie Kim, James Madison. **Rookie of the Year:** Forrest Cory, William & Mary. **Coach of the Year:** Paul Keyes, Virginia Commonwealth.

INDIVIDUAL BATTING LEADERS

(Minimum 125 At-Bats)

	AVG	AB	R	H	2B	3B	HR	RBI	SB
Brown, Michael, Wm. & Mary	**.423**	201	**58**	85	13	1	**20**	66	11
Kim, Eddie, James Madison	.412	204	57	84	16	0	17	**67**	4
Costello, Mike, Towson	.387	186	49	72	21	1	17	63	2
Hemingway, Jamie, UNC-W	.363	237	52	**86**	22	1	11	60	**31**
Butia, Mike, James Madison	.362	199	48	72	12	2	8	43	9
Grawey, Chip, UNC Wilmington	.358	229	55	82	12	1	5	37	22
Jones, Nick, VCU	.355	214	39	76	**23**	2	7	51	11
Baldwin, Bruce, George Mason	.354	209	38	74	17	0	1	42	5
Metheny, Brent, James Madison	.353	204	56	72	14	2	6	43	20
Mattison, Justin, VCU	.351	205	51	72	17	2	6	39	8
Shimer, Nick, George Mason	.349	189	42	66	19	2	9	41	5
Jones, Tim, William & Mary	.346	214	38	74	16	1	2	37	4
Denson, Brad, UNC-W	.345	148	40	51	10	1	3	18	5
Looze, Chris, George Mason	.343	198	52	68	13	1	15	56	1
Justis, Shane, Towson	.342	190	39	65	9	1	3	28	16
Chipman, Evan, Old Dominion	.340	159	30	54	4	0	2	17	25
Latura, Eric, VCU	.333	213	48	71	8	3	1	32	17
Parrish, Jeff, VCU	.332	196	36	65	17	1	8	50	5
Wechter, J.P., Hofstra	.328	189	30	62	17	1	3	35	4
Paduano, Bobby, Towson	.325	197	44	64	9	2	5	35	2
LeNoir, Brandon, Old Dominion	.324	145	24	47	3	0	3	25	3
Wright, Matt, UNC Wilmington	.323	220	51	71	17	4	11	49	9
McKenna, Brian, Towson	.322	205	39	66	12	1	8	38	3
Walk, Mitch, William & Mary	.319	160	36	51	10	1	9	28	4
Ebaugh, Travis, James Madison	.318	201	47	64	15	1	4	28	7
Sutton, Matt, UNC Wilmington	.317	227	43	72	16	2	12	50	11
Stewart, Josh, Hofstra	.317	161	40	51	11	1	3	23	9
Yocum, Josh, Drexel	.316	136	26	43	10	1	4	19	7
Trela, Tom, Towson	.315	168	35	53	10	2	2	18	3
Heaberlin, Brent, Drexel	.314	137	21	43	7	1	3	30	1
Palumbo, Jeff, George Mason	.310	203	43	63	8	0	5	36	7
Stifler, Jeremy, Towson	.309	165	38	51	6	0	14	40	4
Schindler, Jason, UNC-W	.308	130	18	40	10	0	3	23	5
Cosentino, Ryan, Hofstra	.305	131	25	40	7	0	3	22	1
Lentz, John, William & Mary	.303	198	46	60	12	1	8	36	4
#Cooksey, Matt, Geo. Mason	.255	149	40	38	9	**5**	1	14	18

INDIVIDUAL PITCHING LEADERS

(Minimum 50 Innings)

	W	L	ERA	G	SV	IP	H	BB	SO
Meredith, Cla, VCU	6	0	**1.19**	29	8	60	44	16	70
Cross, Blake, UNC Wilmington	4	4	2.04	35	**13**	53	36	16	52
Orenduff, Justin, VCU	**9**	3	2.27	18	0	95	70	26	120
Verlander, Justin, Old Dominion	7	6	2.40	15	0	116	94	43	**139**
Marshall, Sean, VCU	7	2	2.62	15	0	86	77	29	95
Prendergast, Matt, VCU	8	1	2.64	12	0	72	58	28	62
Leishman, Michael, VCU	5	1	2.66	12	0	61	45	15	55
Marshall, Brian, VCU	5	5	2.81	32	12	51	36	22	77
Overton, Brad, UNC Wilmington	7	2	2.99	16	0	96	71	38	75
Mihalik, Mike, Delaware	4	3	3.44	12	0	68	72	21	65
Ray, Chris, William & Mary	6	5	3.52	16	0	95	87	22	87
Sterling, John, George Mason	6	5	3.80	14	0	97	90	21	75
Mullis, Jake, UNC Wilmington	8	5	3.81	20	0	106	96	30	98
Rogers, Jason, Delaware	2	8	3.90	13	0	83	99	26	65
Dagenhart, Jeff, Wm. & Mary	5	3	3.99	14	1	68	59	29	61
Shefka, Ricky, Old Dominion	6	8	4.10	14	0	90	106	28	52
Shaver, Chris, William & Mary	4	1	4.13	22	2	57	52	25	45
Coughlin, Chris, UNC-W	6	3	4.16	21	1	89	87	27	87
Caslin, John, Towson	6	3	4.57	12	0	65	78	31	24
Merson, Stephen, Towson	4	4	4.72	13	0	61	68	15	42
Cochran, Chris, James Madison	**9**	3	4.80	17	1	96	127	27	72
Glanzmann, Jake, Geo. Mason	4	5	4.96	11	0	65	72	35	59
Murray, Chris, George Mason	3	6	4.98	13	0	85	93	26	56
Hill, Ronald, UNC Wilmington	7	2	5.10	20	0	72	81	25	55

CONFERENCE USA

	Conference		Overall	
	W	**L**	**W**	**L**
***Southern Mississippi**	23	7	47	16
Texas Christian	22	8	35	22
Tulane	20	10	44	19
Houston	18	12	37	30
East Carolina	17	13	34	27
South Florida	14	14	31	27
Louisville	14	15	34	23
Charlotte	11	15	21	28
Alabama-Birmingham	12	17	27	26
Memphis	11	18	21	33
Cincinnati	7	22	15	39
St. Louis	6	24	18	32

ALL-CONFERENCE TEAM: C—Devin Ivany, So., South Florida. **IF**—Michael Aubrey, Jr., Tulane; Hyung Cho, Jr., Houston; Tony Giarratano, Jr., Tulane; Mike Settle, Sr., Texas Christian. **OF**—Jon Kaplan, Sr., Tulane; Jeff Cook, Sr., Southern Mississippi; Clint King, So., Southern Mississippi. **DH**—Chris Neuman, Jr., Texas Christian. **P**—Clayton Jerome, Jr., Texas Christian; Brad Sullivan, Jr., Houston.

Player of the Year: Michael Aubrey, Tulane. **Pitcher of the Year:** Clayton Jerome, Texas Christian. **Freshman of the Year:** J.R. Crowel, Tulane. **Coach of the Year:** Corky Palmer, Southern Mississippi.

INDIVIDUAL BATTING LEADERS

(Minimum 125 At-Bats)

	AVG	AB	R	H	2B	3B	HR	RBI	SB
Aubrey, Michael, Tulane	**.420**	243	70	**102**	20	1	18	**79**	19
King, Clint, Southern Miss	.394	254	68	100	**23**	2	**23**	77	8
Jones, Mitch, UAB	.392	194	40	76	7	1	6	37	14
Cook, Jeff, Southern Miss	.374	254	71	95	15	3	**23**	76	16
Duncan, Jake, Texas Christian	.368	220	53	81	11	1	12	47	11
Bolen, Josh, Louisville	.364	236	61	86	16	4	8	54	11
Braun, Ron, Louisville	.363	179	27	65	9	1	7	41	0
Ivany, Devin, South Florida	.362	224	30	81	18	2	4	46	5
Cho, Hyung, Houston	.360	261	54	94	19	0	14	66	5
Settle, Mike, Texas Christian	.360	214	52	77	18	2	6	58	1
Kaplan, Jon, Tulane	.358	265	**76**	95	19	2	11	44	**48**
Baisley, Jeff, South Florida	.355	242	46	86	18	2	6	46	8
Tully, Travis, Houston	.350	180	30	63	9	0	0	28	12
Meeks, Chris, Texas Christian	.349	212	49	74	17	**7**	5	33	10
Haley, Nick, Louisville	.346	188	37	65	8	2	1	25	4

	AVG	AB	R	H	2B	3B	HR	RBI	SB
Leon, Kyle, UAB	.346	191	44	66	6	1	14	57	11
Manzella, Tommy, Tulane	.343	236	50	81	20	1	6	44	4
Martin, Ryan, Memphis	.338	133	18	45	9	0	7	19	3
Leslie, Myron, South Florida	.338	213	56	72	17	4	3	35	16
Lewis, Will, Texas Christian	.337	193	37	65	15	3	6	44	8
Maddox, Marc, Southern Miss	.336	128	30	43	12	1	5	23	1
Giarratano, Tony, Tulane	.336	274	66	92	17	3	8	42	22
Hatcher, Justin, Texas Christian	.333	192	40	64	14	2	4	41	11
Lawhorn, Darryl, East Carolina	.332	232	49	77	15	1	14	49	4
Sandel, George, Charlotte	.330	194	46	64	11	2	3	31	19
Bourn, Michael, Houston	.330	182	44	60	1	5	1	16	23
Trofholz, Terry, Texas Christian	.328	204	50	67	15	3	1	31	19
Willcutt, Brad, Southern Miss	.325	249	52	81	20	0	12	61	0
Poplin, Randy, Charlotte	.323	192	36	62	8	1	7	48	1
Hill, Daniel, UAB	.322	211	33	68	10	1	10	47	2
Lowery, Jason, Southern Miss	.322	202	33	65	11	0	2	28	1
Bogusevic, Brian, Tulane	.321	193	35	62	10	4	4	36	2
Erwin, Brad, Charlotte	.321	134	24	43	7	0	6	27	1
Brown, Travis, South Florida	.318	220	33	70	19	3	6	40	9
Lawson, Corey, Saint Louis	.317	167	34	53	14	0	8	39	10
Rogers, Don, Saint Louis	.316	158	35	50	10	1	8	27	4
Rodriguez, Eugene, UAB	.316	152	18	48	6	0	2	17	3
LaFountain, J.T., Louisville	.313	217	52	68	16	0	8	47	2
Cunningham, Mike, So. Florida	.310	226	47	70	20	4	1	17	20
Paige, Jamie, East Carolina	.307	231	42	71	8	2	3	33	5
House, Kevin, Memphis	.307	202	34	62	11	4	5	34	9
Hoffpauir, Jarrett, So. Miss	.307	238	53	73	13	1	10	53	5
Israel, Griff, Southern Miss	.307	177	33	54	15	0	4	31	1
Martin, Steve, UAB	.304	148	34	45	7	0	1	13	25
Norwood, Ryan, East Carolina	.298	235	28	70	9	0	13	46	1
Bowker, Tommy, Charlotte	.298	178	42	53	7	2	8	31	19

INDIVIDUAL PITCHING LEADERS

(Minimum 50 Innings)

	W	L	ERA	G	SV	IP	H	BB	SO
Fernandez, Carlos, Louisville	5	1	**1.21**	32	12	59	42	14	57
Wagner, Ryan, Houston	6	5	1.93	38	**15**	79	39	21	148
Antonelli, Ray, Southern Miss	4	0	2.14	29	5	59	42	23	60
Livingston, Joey, South Florida	0	4	2.14	39	13	55	44	8	41
Jerome, Clayton, Texas Christian	9	4	2.34	16	0	112	86	25	106
Charron, Joey, Tulane	4	7	2.36	39	12	62	39	27	68
Findlay, Robbie, Texas Christian	6	1	2.74	14	2	69	67	27	58
Penny, Davey, East Carolina	4	3	2.82	10	0	61	54	18	59
Tucker, Glenn, East Carolina	5	4	2.82	26	3	89	87	16	86
Cillo, Cody, UAB	6	5	2.90	23	4	68	54	28	87
Sullivan, Brad, Houston	6	8	2.91	20	0	124	90	44	**154**
Gibson, Scott, UAB	6	2	3.03	13	0	77	70	12	49
Hahn, Cory, Tulane	9	1	3.07	16	0	88	91	28	70
Rios, Travis, South Florida	6	1	3.07	12	0	59	44	27	63
Reel, Rob, Cincinnati	2	1	3.27	29	2	52	63	7	23
Russum, Cliff, Southern Miss	8	5	3.31	17	0	87	60	35	80
Dewitt, Anthony, Southern Miss	8	2	3.31	15	0	90	99	19	50
Zell, Danny, Houston	9	5	3.34	18	0	113	118	34	79
Crowel, J.R., Tulane	8	1	3.40	17	0	106	106	33	73
Austen, David, South Florida	**11**	3	3.45	19	0	115	111	26	106
Shoemaker, Kyle, TCU	7	3	3.50	15	0	80	75	34	50
Rowan, Brandon, Memphis	2	3	3.63	20	2	62	70	22	51
Grube, Jarrett, Memphis	5	5	3.68	15	0	73	73	32	66
McCrory, Bob, Southern Miss	10	3	3.84	18	0	91	94	44	90
Uhl, Jon, South Florida	6	5	3.90	15	0	106	104	35	88
Trotter, Lucas, UAB	5	3	4.01	16	0	85	82	23	98
Gostkowski, Stephen, Memphis	4	5	4.13	17	0	65	77	36	46
Castleman, Stephen, So. Miss	8	2	4.14	16	0	96	110	36	75
Borsa, B.J., Cincinnati	4	7	4.25	14	0	102	98	20	78
Jackson, Zach, Louisville	7	6	4.31	21	0	113	121	29	75

HORIZON LEAGUE

	Conference		Overall	
	W	L	W	L
***Illinois-Chicago**	15	6	39	18
Butler	16	8	34	27
Wisconsin-Milwaukee	13	10	25	25
Youngstown State	12	11	27	28
Wright State	10	13	21	34
Detroit Mercy	8	12	15	32
Cleveland State	4	18	13	39

ALL-CONFERENCE TEAM: C—Adam Cox, Jr., Youngstown State. **1B**—Tim Poley, Jr., Detroit. **2B**—Bryan Russo, Sr., Illinois-Chicago. **3B**—Nelson Gord, Jr., Illinois-Chicago. **SS**—Jared Lowe, Sr., Butler. **OF**—Dale Mueller, So., Butler; Chuck Peters, Sr., Illinois-Chicago; Mike Hughes, Jr., Illinois-Chicago. **DH**—Bryan Vickers, So., Wright State. **Util**—Troy Doering, Sr., Wisconsin-Milwaukee. **P**—Ryan Gehring, So., Illinois-Chicago; Mikel Schaefer, Sr., Wisconsin-Milwaukee.

Player of the Year: Chuck Peters, Illinois-Chicago. **Pitcher of the Year:** Mikel Schaefer, Wisconsin-Milwaukee. **Newcomer of the Year:** Ryan Martin, Illinois-Chicago. **Coach of the Year:** Mike Dee, Illinois-Chicago.

INDIVIDUAL BATTING LEADERS

(Minimum 125 At-Bats)

	AVG	AB	R	H	2B	3B	HR	RBI	SB
Mueller, Dale, Butler	**.391**	206	43	**81**	9	1	1	19	9
Hughes, Mike, Illinois-Chicago	.381	194	**52**	74	14	2	8	30	11
Lowe, Jared, Butler	.377	204	41	77	**17**	2	4	33	4
Tuttle, Chris, Wright State	.370	216	40	80	**17**	**6**	0	31	20
Schultz, Charles, YSU	.356	188	42	67	10	4	2	30	5
Peters, Chuck, Illinois-Chicago	.343	178	38	61	10	1	11	**56**	1
DeVoir, Jordan, Illinois-Chicago	.341	223	45	76	15	4	2	29	6
Moran, J.P., Illinois-Chicago	.338	207	40	70	10	1	2	38	4
Marks, Tim, Butler	.326	190	22	62	6	0	3	29	3
Pudlosky, Dave, UWM	.326	178	40	58	15	0	4	29	3
Caipen, Brandon, YSU	.321	193	35	62	12	4	3	33	6
Gord, Nelson, Illinois-Chicago	.318	192	40	61	12	1	2	34	5
Wechter, Roger, Detroit	.318	170	32	54	14	0	5	26	3
Poley, Tim, Detroit	.315	165	22	52	13	1	2	30	0
Nelson, Kevin, Illinois-Chicago	.311	180	27	56	15	0	4	33	0
#Chapieski, Jason, Detroit	.282	163	30	46	3	2	0	16	**21**
#Vickers, Bryan, Wright State	.262	202	26	53	9	1	**13**	41	0

INDIVIDUAL PITCHING LEADERS

(Minimum 50 Innings)

	W	L	ERA	G	SV	IP	H	BB	SO
Martin, Ryan, Illinois-Chicago	7	1	**2.35**	15	0	73	58	22	63
Phillips, Aaron, Butler	6	5	2.53	15	0	103	87	25	73
Gehring, Ryan, Illinois-Chicago	**8**	5	2.73	16	0	99	104	16	64
Abrams, Casey, Wright State	2	7	2.76	19	3	114	96	51	**158**
Schaefer, Mikel, UWM	7	2	2.77	12	0	81	53	34	73
Haehnel, David, Illinois-Chicago	6	1	2.93	28	**9**	55	60	17	53
Astrauckas, Keith, Detroit	2	8	3.16	14	1	80	77	27	34
Rudolfi, Josh, Butler	4	4	3.38	11	0	51	48	17	40
Braden, Aaron, Wright State	5	6	3.40	15	1	79	86	18	48
Jung, J.P., Wright State	4	6	3.54	19	2	81	78	19	83
Flood, John, Illinois-Chicago	6	2	3.68	13	0	71	74	15	38
Sobecki, Kyle, YSU	6	4	3.80	13	1	64	74	17	56

IVY LEAGUE

	Conference		Overall	
GEHRIG	**W**	**L**	**W**	**L**
***Princeton**	15	5	27	23
Pennsylvania	12	8	22	17
Cornell	9	11	16	20
Columbia	9	11	21	27
ROLFE	**W**	**L**	**W**	**L**
Harvard	11	9	20	23
Dartmouth	10	10	17	19
Brown	8	12	18	28
Yale	6	14	16	24

ALL-CONFERENCE TEAM: C—Brian Lentz, Sr., Harvard. **1B**—Trey Hendricks, Jr., Harvard. **2B**—Nick Italiano, Sr., Pennsylvania. **3B**—Mike Gulker, So., Yale. **SS**—Ed Lucas, Jr., Dartmouth. **OF**—Matt Kutler, Jr., Brown; Nate Moffie, So., Pennsylvania; Scott Shirrell, Jr., Dartmouth. **DH**—Dave Fortenbaugh, Sr., Yale. **Util**—Andrew McCreery, Sr., Pennsylvania. **P**—Chris Schutt, Jr., Cornell; Brian Doveala, Jr., Columbia. **RP**—Thomas Pauly, Jr., Princeton; Barry Wahlberg, Sr., Harvard; Brian Winings, So., Pennsylvania.

Player of the Year: Andrew McCreery, Pennsylvania. **Pitcher of the Year:** Chris Schutt, Cornell. **Rookie of the Year:** Zak Farkes, Harvard.

INDIVIDUAL BATTING LEADERS

(Minimum 100 At-Bats)

	AVG	AB	R	H	2B	3B	HR	RBI	SB
Hess, Billy, Columbia	**.395**	162	39	64	14	0	6	37	4
Hendricks, Trey, Harvard	.387	106	19	41	10	0	5	29	1
Lentz, Brian, Harvard	.386	145	29	56	16	1	1	26	10
Italiano, Nick, Penn	.371	132	28	49	8	0	4	30	2
Kutler, Matt, Brown	.369	179	28	**66**	14	0	5	**44**	14
Baxter, Mike, Columbia	.368	152	41	56	12	2	0	30	12
Shirrell, Scott, Dartmouth	.367	150	41	55	12	3	6	41	10
Fortenbaugh, Dave, Yale	.363	113	12	41	7	2	1	18	4
Moffie, Nate, Penn	.355	141	39	50	9	1	3	24	5
Deeb, Robert, Brown	.354	178	**44**	63	12	3	4	18	**22**
Lucas, Ed, Dartmouth	.347	144	25	50	11	1	3	33	9
DaCosta, Jason, Dartmouth	.346	127	31	44	8	1	0	29	**22**
Salsgiver, Lance, Harvard	.340	159	23	54	6	0	4	25	13
McCreery, Andrew, Penn	.338	136	31	46	9	1	7	36	5
Miller, Jon, Princeton	.336	146	32	49	12	0	2	29	2
Glass, Steve, Penn	.333	141	43	47	5	2	2	15	2
Livermore, Jorge, Columbia	.331	160	41	53	7	3	0	15	11

	AVG	AB	R	H	2B	3B	HR	RBI	SB
Schmidt, Ryan, Columbia	.331	142	29	47	14	2	6	42	3
Szymanski, B.J., Princeton	.329	158	37	52	8	**6**	2	27	13
Nichols, Jeff, Brown	.329	155	34	51	**20**	1	5	22	7
Gulker, Mike, Yale	.328	131	16	43	12	3	2	25	5
Eldridge, Ryan, Princeton	.327	104	10	34	6	0	2	19	0
Farkes, Zak, Harvard	.322	146	42	41	11	2	8	18	7
#Lahey, Tim, Princeton	.242	128	23	31	6	1	**11**	25	1

INDIVIDUAL PITCHING LEADERS

(Minimum 40 Innings)

	W	L	ERA	G	SV	IP	H	BB	SO
#Pauly, Thomas, Princeton	**5**	1	0.92	15	5	39	25	14	60
Schutt, Chris, Cornell	3	5	**1.89**	10	1	62	43	23	**89**
Hendricks, Trey, Harvard	2	1	2.86	6	0	44	45	5	37
Collis, Rocky, Cornell	3	2	3.26	11	1	47	46	14	36
Quillian, Ryan, Princeton	**5**	4	3.26	9	0	58	53	12	42
Doveala, Brian, Columbia	**5**	2	3.27	9	0	55	56	9	44
Hearin, Tim, Columbia	2	4	3.71	10	0	51	61	11	19
Faiola, Joshua, Dartmouth	3	3	3.93	9	0	50	50	15	48
Baysinger, Dan, Cornell	**5**	2	3.93	8	0	50	52	11	35
Boehle, David, Princeton	4	2	3.96	9	0	52	67	13	42
Priede, Jason, Brown	1	1	4.07	14	0	42	44	14	46
Cramphin, James, Brown	4	3	4.13	10	0	52	54	25	45
McCreery, Andrew, Penn	3	2	4.17	8	0	54	53	17	37
Sowers, Josh, Yale	**5**	3	4.18	11	0	60	52	30	48
Grant, Tim, Dartmouth	4	3	4.22	9	0	64	66	23	46
#Winings, Brian, Penn	1	0	4.70	15	**8**	15	15	12	19

METRO ATLANTIC CONFERENCE

	Conference W	Conference L	Overall W	Overall L
***Le Moyne**	22	3	33	17
Marist	19	8	33	20
Niagara	16	10	26	25
Manhattan	15	10	26	26
Iona	15	11	21	24
Siena	15	11	17	35
Rider	14	13	22	27
Saint Peter's	6	20	7	34
Fairfield	5	21	7	34
Canisius	3	23	4	38

ALL-CONFERENCE TEAM: C—Mike Sidoti, Sr., Marist. **1B**—John McGorty, Sr., Marist. **2B**—Vince Ircandia, So., Niagara. **3B**—Mike Affronti, Fr., Le Moyne. **SS**—Travis Garcia, Jr., Iona. **OF**—Josh McCurdy, Sr., Niagara; Rob Fortner, Jr., Iona; Keith Brachold, So., Marist. **DH**—John Fitzpatrick, Fr., Manhattan. **Util**—Ryan Knapp, Sr., St. Peter's. **P**—Ryan Bitter, Jr., Siena; Chuck Bechtel, Sr., Marist.

Player of the Year: Josh McCurdy, Niagara. **Pitcher of the Year:** Chuck Bechtel, Marist. **Rookie of the Year:** James Avery, Niagra. **Coach of the Year:** Mike McRae, Niagara.

INDIVIDUAL BATTING LEADERS

(Minimum 125 At-Bats)

	AVG	AB	R	H	2B	3B	HR	RBI	SB
Brachold, Keith, Marist	**.421**	214	56	**90**	17	2	8	48	16
McCurdy, Josh, Niagara	.403	211	57	85	18	1	**12**	**63**	28
Justice, Jeff, Le Moyne	.377	167	36	63	6	**6**	3	36	9
Cucurullo, Matt, Manhattan	.365	137	23	50	9	3	2	36	15
Fortner, Rob, Iona	.358	159	21	57	12	0	4	40	7
Harper, Eddie, Le Moyne	.356	191	**60**	68	12	2	2	32	26
Ircandia, Vince, Niagara	.345	174	39	60	11	5	4	46	19
Parkins, Sam, Le Moyne	.345	148	35	51	10	2	7	32	6
Sidoti, Mike, Marist	.344	209	37	72	18	1	3	33	0
Lewandowski, Jesse, St. Peter's	.340	159	19	54	9	2	2	24	7
Aquilino, Anthony, Le Moyne	.339	180	36	61	15	3	3	34	16
Pesaresi, Erinn, Rider	.339	180	40	61	11	4	1	18	18
Brown, Kyle, Le Moyne	.338	139	39	47	11	2	4	26	25
Loadenthal, Carl, Rider	.337	175	51	59	9	2	6	43	**35**
Garcia, Travis, Iona	.323	167	37	54	14	0	5	18	7
Pineiro, Josh, St. Peter's	.320	153	30	49	9	5	0	16	5
Board, Jimmy, Marist	.321	190	27	61	10	0	3	29	1
Whalen, Sean, Rider	.318	151	22	48	5	1	4	21	1
Long, Casey, Rider	.315	168	28	53	11	2	4	34	5
Rich, Scott, Iona	.314	175	27	55	18	3	2	28	2
Pecchia, Mike, Le Moyne	.314	156	21	49	8	1	3	31	4
Fitzpatrick, John, Manhattan	.312	170	30	53	11	0	3	28	4
Bomar, Marc, Niagara	.309	139	25	43	6	1	4	33	4
Affronti, Mike, Le Moyne	.305	131	27	40	5	3	0	21	8
Allen, Tim, Marist	.304	217	37	66	17	0	10	48	3
#McGorty, John, Marist	.293	208	38	61	**20**	4	4	36	3

INDIVIDUAL PITCHING LEADERS

(Minimum 50 Innings)

	W	L	ERA	G	SV	IP	H	BB	SO
#Weimer, Andy, Le Moyne	7	1	0.95	24	**7**	47	23	15	48
Sullivan, Ryan, Iona	6	2	**1.21**	22	4	52	45	12	25
Bechtel, Chuck, Marist	8	4	1.59	13	0	85	65	26	**98**
Ool, Kevin, Marist	6	1	1.74	11	0	72	59	12	49
Hoey, James, Rider	6	4	2.24	14	0	88	71	44	63
Hand, Marty, Iona	3	1	2.24	13	0	56	42	19	27
Mattoon, Brian, Le Moyne	**10**	4	2.95	14	0	101	91	17	79
Tracz, Chris, Marist	9	2	3.19	13	0	90	104	18	69
Darcy, Ryan, Manahttan	6	6	3.32	14	0	98	107	18	80
Bitter, Ryan, Siena	6	6	3.51	14	0	95	98	30	77
Weiner, Eric, Rider	5	3	3.51	14	0	67	67	19	54
Avery, James, Niagara	7	2	3.64	13	0	82	69	28	63
Scherer, Matt, Le Moyne	4	4	3.76	13	0	67	74	21	41
Parisi, Mike, Manhattan	3	6	3.87	15	0	77	74	38	87
Cody, Chris, Manhattan	5	2	4.27	14	0	65	66	33	50
Haggerty, Sean, Niagara	5	6	4.30	14	0	90	92	33	62
Rakoczy, Mike, Rider	4	5	4.83	13	0	60	66	29	34
Gorra, Paul, Fairfield	1	9	5.15	12	0	58	66	34	48

MID-AMERICAN CONFERENCE

	Conference W	Conference L	Overall W	Overall L
EAST				
Kent State	20	4	36	18
Miami (Ohio)	19	9	36	24
Ohio	15	11	35	23
Akron	12	15	22	30
Marshall	11	16	22	31
Buffalo	5	21	16	37
WEST	**W**	**L**	**W**	**L**
Ball State	17	10	36	21
***Eastern Michigan**	16	11	33	28
Northern Illinois	15	11	34	24
Western Michigan	16	12	25	26
Central Michigan	9	15	25	28
Bowling Green State	9	18	17	28
Toledo	8	19	22	29

ALL-CONFERENCE TEAM: C—Mitch Maier, Jr., Toledo. **1B**—Kelly Hunt, Sr., Bowling Green. **2B**—Taylor Eckel, Sr., Toledo. **3B**—Adam Fox, Jr., Ohio. **SS**—Chris Welsch, Sr., Kent State. **OF**—Brad Snyder, Jr., Ball State; Michael Carlin, Sr., Miami; Tom Fabrizio, Sr., Western Michigan. **DH**—Adam Crowder, Jr., Kent State. **Util**—Ben Crabtree, So., Ohio. **P**—Frank Mendoza, Sr., Akron; Dirk Hayhurst, Sr., Kent State; Marc Cornell, Jr., Ohio; Keith Perez, Sr., Western Michigan. **RP**—Gus Hlebovy, Jr., Kent State.

Player of the Year: Brad Snyder, Ball State. **Pitcher of the Year:** Dirk Hayhurst, Kent State. **Freshman of the Year:** Graham Taylor, Miami. **Coach of the Year:** Rick Rembielak, Kent State.

INDIVIDUAL BATTING LEADERS

(Minimum 125 At-Bats)

	AVG	AB	R	H	2B	3B	HR	RBI	SB
Maier, Mitch, Toledo	**.448**	194	59	87	16	2	9	61	**29**
Hunt, Kelly, Bowling Green	.439	171	33	75	18	1	9	61	4
Franz, Marc, Ball State	.410	166	46	68	13	0	3	33	4
Snyder, Brad, Ball State	.405	200	68	81	**25**	3	14	61	20
Fabrizio, Tom, West. Michigan	.390	187	32	73	18	1	3	38	8
Crabtree, Ben, Ohio	.387	235	40	**91**	17	0	10	53	7
Buck, Bryan, Ohio	.379	132	41	50	3	0	0	13	10
Peterson, Derrick, EMU	.377	212	50	80	16	0	5	49	0
O'Bryan, Corie, Marshall	.376	202	45	76	15	1	10	45	5
Simon, Scott, Northern Illinois	.370	192	25	71	11	1	6	40	1
Crowder, Adam, Kent State	.368	152	39	56	11	1	13	44	3
Dobson, Sean, Toledo	.367	210	60	77	13	**4**	3	30	19
Fox, Adam, Ohio	.366	238	51	87	21	1	14	61	4
Ferris, Mike, Miami	.360	175	51	63	16	1	5	43	1
Mazzuca, Joe, Northern Illinois	.357	213	52	76	13	3	10	57	20
Busch, Jeremy, No. Illinois	.353	170	41	60	6	2	5	30	8
Lunsford, Dan, Ohio	.351	208	53	73	13	3	8	39	3
Frederick, Adam, Marshall	.350	137	24	48	7	0	4	14	6
Grubb, Tommy, Cent. Michigan	.349	192	46	67	15	1	3	39	17
Slone, John, Miami	.349	195	39	68	14	0	1	33	27
Barkholz, David, Bowling Green	.348	181	44	63	13	2	6	27	7
Cook, David, Miami	.345	252	**70**	87	17	1	15	61	21
Mihalics, Joe, Buffalo	.344	189	32	65	4	**4**	2	31	3
Kinyon, Chad, Kent State	.341	205	52	70	18	0	16	51	2
Schroeder, Ben, Ball State	.340	206	55	70	15	**4**	2	24	10
Sabatini, Phil, Ohio	.339	233	48	79	12	3	7	52	14
Victor, Israel, Akron	.337	181	35	61	18	2	2	23	6
Arnett, Ryan, Eastern Michigan	.335	215	55	72	11	3	12	44	15
Carlin, Michael, Miami	.332	217	59	72	10	2	**19**	**68**	7
Welsch, Chris, Kent State	.332	214	55	71	23	0	11	53	8
Metzler, Adam, Ball State	.332	214	33	71	12	2	9	60	1
Ford, Ryan, Eastern Michigan	.329	167	30	55	10	3	2	29	5
Fry, Lucas, Ball State	.329	152	27	50	12	0	5	26	1
Reimold, Nolan, Bowl. Green	.329	140	29	46	6	0	1	17	5

	AVG	AB	R	H	2B	3B	HR	RBI	SB
Larmore, Francois, Marshall	.329	207	46	68	18	1	14	43	7
Dygert, Kyle, Bowling Green	.328	174	30	57	10	0	3	21	5

INDIVIDUAL PITCHING LEADERS

(Minimum 50 Innings)

	W	L	ERA	G	SV	IP	H	BB	SO
Peet, Shaun, Ohio	5	0	**2.77**	17	1	65	65	23	60
Hayhurst, Dirk, Kent State	6	2	3.10	14	0	93	95	23	74
Perez, Keith, West. Michigan	7	3	3.10	15	0	81	69	31	77
Lynch, Bryan, Ball State	**8**	4	3.21	15	0	93	94	24	**80**
Mendoza, Frank, Akron	7	3	3.22	12	0	78	72	19	70
Mumma, Brad, West. Michigan	6	4	3.27	15	2	85	76	35	79
Duffey, J.R., Toledo	4	2	3.29	11	0	79	85	21	64
Bellacose, Nick, Buffalo	3	5	3.31	12	0	65	70	28	30
Knoblauch, Kyle, Bowl. Green	2	6	3.48	12	0	83	85	18	51
Minor, Zach, Northern Illinois	6	4	3.63	19	0	79	81	40	62
Lorenzo, Matt, Kent State	6	5	3.64	13	0	72	56	34	78
Taylor, Graham, Miami	7	4	3.83	22	2	99	106	28	67
Saneholtz, Tyler, Bowling Green	4	3	3.83	12	0	52	55	36	53
Cornell, Marc, Ohio	7	3	3.84	13	0	59	49	24	69
LeMieux, David, Central Michigan	5	2	3.88	26	10	56	55	30	55
Skrukrud, Mark, Northern Illinois	6	4	4.01	14	0	101	114	10	77
Bova, Chris, Ohio	4	4	4.01	18	3	90	100	22	75
Gangi, Aaron, Akron	5	5	4.02	15	0	63	64	21	32
Ziroli, Steve, Marshall	4	3	4.08	19	2	53	55	16	30
Gardner, Michael, Miami	7	4	4.09	32	8	51	46	21	55
Shorts, Sam, Miami	6	3	4.12	16	0	79	99	24	42
Paul, Jason, Ball State	7	3	4.31	14	0	79	85	21	69
#Badgley, Mark, Northern Illinois	2	4	5.29	28	**14**	34	41	20	24
#Tomey, Anthony, East. Michigan	4	5	5.57	21	2	84	91	62	**80**

MID-CONTINENT CONFERENCE

	Conference W	Conference L	Overall W	Overall L
***Oral Roberts**	19	1	41	20
Southern Utah	11	9	21	29
Western Illinois	10	10	25	38
Valparaiso	9	11	22	33
Oakland	7	13	20	34
Chicago State	4	16	9	47

ALL-CONFERENCE TEAM: C—David Castillo, Jr., Oral Roberts. **1B**—Andy Hargrove, Jr., Oral Roberts. **2B**—Ryan Cougill, Jr., Western Illinois. **3B**—Scott Campbell, Sr., Oral Roberts. **SS**—Grant Plumley, Jr., Oral Roberts; Ryan Schmidgall, Fr., Western Illinois. **OF**—Jake Reynolds, Sr., Southern Utah; Blake Schultz, Jr., Western Illinois; Will Tollison, So., Oakland. **DH**—Dennis Bigley, So., Oral Roberts; Marc Boggio, Sr., Valparaiso. **Util**—Matt VanDerBosch, Jr., Oral Roberts. **P**—Dennis Bigley, So., Oral Roberts; Dallas Martin, Sr., Oral Roberts; Tom Starck, Jr., Valparaiso. **RP**—Kyle Boehm, So., Oakland.

Player of the Year: David Castillo, Oral Roberts. **Co-Pitchers of the Year:** Dallas Martin, Oral Roberts; Tom Starck, Valparaiso. **Newcomer of the Year:** Blake Schultz, Western Illinois. **Coach of the Year:** Stan Hyman, Western Illinois.

INDIVIDUAL BATTING LEADERS

(Minimum 125 At-Bats)

	AVG	AB	R	H	2B	3B	HR	RBI	SB
VanDerBosch, Matt, ORU	**.373**	225	**61**	84	5	4	1	26	27
Schultz, Blake, Western Illinois	.366	246	52	**90**	**25**	4	7	56	11
Cougill, Ryan, Western Illinois	.361	202	39	73	12	2	1	38	13
Shelby, Troy, Western Illinois	.357	143	21	51	15	0	3	28	0
Boggio, Marc, Valparaiso	.347	193	33	67	10	4	4	37	7
Plumley, Grant, Oral Roberts	.345	229	60	79	15	2	4	51	13
Castillo, David, Oral Roberts	.344	212	57	73	11	1	**17**	**70**	5
Reynolds, Jake, Southern Utah	.331	169	41	56	12	**6**	0	29	27
Schmidgall, Ryan, West. Illinois	.329	207	35	68	11	0	3	27	7
Dufour, Gerry, Oakland	.321	134	24	43	4	0	0	10	5
Tollison, Will, Oakland	.315	168	37	53	15	3	9	41	8
Milliken, Aaron, West. Illinois	.315	130	19	41	6	1	1	14	7
Peickert, Sean, Valparaiso	.310	216	40	67	18	2	4	30	6
Buchen, Clint, Western Illinois	.310	187	53	58	14	5	1	34	11
Campbell, Scott, Oral Roberts	.309	207	52	64	14	0	4	32	4
Hynes, Spencer, Oakland	.296	125	20	37	6	0	3	13	0
#Welborn, Ryan, Oral Roberts	.281	217	52	61	5	3	1	33	**28**

INDIVIDUAL PITCHING LEADERS

(Minimum 50 Innings)

	W	L	ERA	G	SV	IP	H	BB	SO
McIntyre, Taylor, Oral Roberts	7	2	**2.27**	20	1	79	72	30	59
Martin, Dallas, Oral Roberts	8	7	2.83	25	2	92	93	22	77
Ramsey, Justin, Oral Roberts	5	0	3.04	29	5	50	46	16	45
Bigley, Dennis, Oral Roberts	**10**	3	3.06	15	0	94	75	13	**85**
Starck, Tom, Valparaiso	4	2	3.44	13	0	71	50	32	76
Carmosino, Dominic, Oakland	3	10	3.95	16	0	82	75	49	82
Schmieder, Billy, Oakland	4	5	4.35	13	0	70	78	17	40
#Paetznick, Adam, Valparaiso	2	2	4.74	25	**8**	25	29	16	29
Miller, Nathan, W. Illinois	4	6	5.34	19	2	91	108	25	60
Boggio, Marc, Valparaiso	6	5	5.38	13	0	74	78	29	49
Brown, Brent, Oakland	2	5	5.67	15	0	54	52	43	65
Sorrow, Sean, Oral Roberts	4	1	5.71	21	2	58	76	21	37

MID-EASTERN CONFERENCE

NORTH	Conference W	Conference L	Overall W	Overall L
Delaware State	9	0	27	25
Coppin State	7	4	12	27
Maryland-Eastern Shore	1	13	5	33
SOUTH	**W**	**L**	**W**	**L**
***Bethune-Cookman**	11	5	30	28
Florida A&M	12	6	29	21
North Carolina A&T	6	10	13	36
Norfolk State	5	13	18	28

ALL-CONFERENCE TEAM: C—Eugene Goodson, Sr., Norfolk State. **IF**—Frank Scott, Sr., Florida A&M; Bret Underwood, Jr., Delaware State; Quincy Jones, Sr., North Carolina A&T; Brad Frick, Jr., Bethune-Cookman. **OF**—John Gragg, Sr., Bethune-Cookman; Sebastien Boucher, So., Bethune-Cookman; Scott Martin, Sr., Delaware State. **DH**—Adam Figueroa, Sr., Coppin State. **P**—John Gragg, Sr., Bethune-Cookman; Eugene Goodson, Sr., Norfolk State.

Player of the Year: John Gragg, Bethune-Cookman. **Rookie of the Year:** Colin Irvine, Bethune-Cookman. **Coach of the Year:** Joe Durant, Florida A&M.

INDIVIDUAL BATTING LEADERS

(Minimum 100 At-Bats)

	AVG	AB	R	H	2B	3B	HR	RBI	SB
Gragg, John, Beth.-Cookman	**.421**	214	54	**90**	18	**6**	4	**62**	23
Norvell, Brandon, Norfolk State	.385	156	34	60	10	0	0	27	2
Martin, Scott, Del. State	.378	188	53	71	**19**	1	**15**	47	9
Spann, Mike, Coppin State	.361	133	36	48	8	4	1	18	24
Underwood, Bret, Del. State	.356	180	39	64	11	0	10	46	9
Morgan, Ben, Florida A&M	.349	166	28	58	14	1	3	45	5
Goodson, Eugene, Norfolk State	.343	172	34	59	12	4	3	40	4
Bernier, Eric, Florida A&M	.342	114	31	39	3	3	1	21	10
Scott, Frank, Florida A&M	.341	170	52	58	12	3	1	21	18
Stevens, Price, N.C. A& T	.340	150	32	51	10	2	1	21	7
Boucher, Sebastien, B-C	.333	192	**58**	64	11	3	1	47	**48**
Frick, Brad, Bethune-Cookman	.333	183	56	61	9	4	1	18	15
Miranda, Juan, Coppin State	.328	125	25	41	7	0	4	25	6
King, Jeffrey, N.C. A&T	.323	155	33	50	8	0	5	26	7
Wilson, Eddie, Coppin State	.323	130	29	42	8	1	3	25	10

INDIVIDUAL PITCHING LEADERS

(Minimum 40 Innings)

	W	L	ERA	G	SV	IP	H	BB	SO
#Johnson, Carl, Florida A&M	4	1	2.22	16	**5**	24	17	7	20
Phillips, Shawn, Del. State	5	7	**2.84**	16	0	101	86	20	82
Irvine, Colin, Beth.-Cookman	3	2	3.46	18	3	55	53	18	46
Rivera, Mumba, Beth.-Cookman	6	5	3.51	15	0	87	85	55	67
Gragg, John, Beth.-Cookman	**9**	4	3.64	16	0	94	80	20	**93**
Middleton, Tony, N.C. A&T	4	8	3.95	15	0	98	82	56	76
Batton, Derek, Del. State	5	3	4.07	15	0	73	71	15	57
Patrick, A.J., Florida A&M	5	6	4.17	13	0	64	55	44	40
Tim Vaillancourt, Del. State	6	4	4.19	14	0	68	58	48	75
Sills, Mike, Florida A&M	8	2	4.61	15	2	72	72	29	53
#Goodson, Eugene, Norfolk St.	3	4	5.88	16	**5**	49	56	26	50

MISSOURI VALLEY CONFERENCE

	Conference W	Conference L	Overall W	Overall L
Southwest Missouri State	19	11	40	26
***Wichita State**	19	13	49	27
Southern Illinois	17	13	30	25
Northern Iowa	16	15	27	28
Indiana State	15	17	36	22
Creighton	14	17	20	37
Illinois State	14	17	23	29
Bradley	12	17	23	30
Evansville	12	20	24	31

ALL-CONFERENCE TEAM: C—Toby Barnett, Sr., Southern Illinois. **1B**—Luke Miller, Sr., Evansville; Logan Sorensen, Jr., Wichita State. **2B**—Phil Napolitan, So., Wichita State. **3B**—Tyson Hanish, Sr., Northern Iowa. **SS**—Jeremy Accardo, Jr., Illinois State. **OF**—Dant'e Brinkley, Sr., Southwest Missouri State; Drew Moffitt, Jr., Wichita State; Adam Boeve, Jr., Northern Iowa. **DH**—Clay Wheeler, Sr., Southwest Missouri State. **Util**—Wes Davis, Sr., Evansville. **P**—Mike Pelfrey, Fr., Wichita State; Brad Ziegler, Sr.,

Southwest Missouri State; Jake Alley, Sr., Southern Illinois. **RP**—Mike Dennison, Sr., Wichita State; Shaun Marcum, Jr., Southwest Missouri State.

Player of the Year: Adam Boeve, Northern Iowa. **Pitcher of the Year:** Brad Ziegler, Southwest Missouri State. **Newcomer of the Year:** Chad Mulholland, Southwest Missouri State. **Freshman of the Year:** Mike Pelfrey, Wichita State. **Coach of the Year:** Keith Guttin, Southwest Missouri State.

INDIVIDUAL BATTING LEADERS

(Minimum 125 At-Bats)

	AVG	AB	R	H	2B	3B	HR	RBI	SB
Miller, Luke, Evansville	**.388**	206	42	80	13	2	6	34	2
Boeve, Adam, Northern Iowa	.368	212	**68**	78	18	4	**18**	71	**29**
Hanish, Tyson, Northern Iowa	.359	217	55	78	17	2	4	45	26
Hall, Chris, Indiana State	.350	217	30	76	20	0	2	30	5
Brinkley, Dant'e, SMS	.345	278	**68**	**96**	18	3	8	47	24
Wheeler, Clay, SMS	.342	202	41	69	7	3	2	35	5
Accardo, Jeremy, Illinois State	.333	183	32	61	9	1	6	31	7
Barnett, Toby, Southern Illinois	.332	193	36	64	11	2	10	43	2
Napolitan, Phil, Wichita State	.330	267	55	88	4	5	3	35	27
Morelock, Jason, Bradley	.330	176	18	58	6	0	1	24	0
Lis, Erik, Evansville	.327	171	25	56	13	2	2	29	6
Molina, Jay, Illinois State	.327	165	29	54	15	0	4	37	5
Hatler, Jereme, Indiana State	.326	193	31	63	9	0	0	25	5
Emrick, Nathan, Southern Illinois	.324	139	17	45	9	1	1	21	3
Mathis, Greg, SMS	.323	248	45	80	14	3	5	49	10
Blasi, Nick, Wichita State	.321	234	49	75	15	1	1	31	12
Clark, Cody, Wichita State	.320	269	49	86	16	**6**	8	55	4
Egli, Kevin, Indiana State	.320	194	49	62	10	2	7	35	8
Vannatter, Ben, Indiana State	.319	163	30	52	13	1	12	40	0
LaCoste, Sean, Northern Iowa	.316	206	40	65	15	0	6	41	13
Boldt, Nathan, Southern Illinois	.315	184	29	58	7	0	1	25	3
Norquist, Dan, Creighton	.315	178	29	56	11	3	3	28	6
Pickrel, Jeremy, Illinois State	.313	201	42	63	17	1	12	39	14
Frisella, Sal, Southern Illinois	.312	189	45	59	10	0	10	30	9
Aqueron, Rene, Bradley	.312	141	28	44	7	3	3	17	12
Heath, Nate, Northern Iowa	.309	204	41	63	6	0	1	28	19
Albano, Anthony, Evansville	.309	188	38	58	10	0	7	40	2
Sorensen, Logan, Wichita State	.306	242	54	74	**23**	2	8	61	25
Piazza, Tony, SMS	.304	214	51	59	12	0	15	55	2
Purdom, John, Indiana State	.303	194	30	59	7	1	12	43	5
Moffitt, Drew, Wichita State	.302	262	58	79	18	2	**18**	**77**	7
Johnson, Mark, Wichita State	.301	136	22	41	7	0	2	21	10
Erstad, Bryan, Wichita State	.300	150	18	45	11	1	2	22	1
McCoola, Nick, Wichita State	.300	253	50	76	13	0	2	27	4
#Miller, Michael, Indiana State	.295	237	45	70	11	3	0	25	**29**
#Fitzgerald, Ryan, Creighton	.294	214	41	63	15	**8**	10	39	8

INDIVIDUAL PITCHING LEADERS

(Minimum 50 Innings)

	W	L	ERA	G	SV	IP	H	BB	SO
Pelfrey, Mike, Wichita State	10	2	**2.49**	17	0	105	80	15	98
Mulholland, Chad, SMS	10	4	3.08	19	0	120	101	31	**117**
Dennison, Mike, Wichita State	1	3	3.10	27	**14**	41	29	11	46
Alley, Jake, Southern Illinois	7	4	3.22	14	0	95	87	38	72
Daneff, Jeff, Creighton	4	3	3.32	12	0	60	60	22	52
Woods, Brian, Indiana State	5	4	3.35	15	0	86	87	18	57
Kerbs, Reuben, Wichita State	5	4	3.58	16	0	73	79	28	58
Walker, Collin, Bradley	5	5	3.65	13	0	94	106	15	69
Garrett, Brad, Bradley	3	8	3.80	15	0	71	78	29	38
Grasley, Steve, Creighton	2	7	3.86	28	7	56	51	13	60
Rueger, Bryan, Southern Illinois	6	2	3.88	12	0	58	61	25	28
McDonald, Dave, Illinois State	2	0	3.93	20	2	50	50	16	14
Bloom, Kyle, Illinois State	4	5	3.94	13	0	78	73	40	79
Zaleski, Matt, Indiana State	6	5	4.02	14	0	81	71	21	53
Davis, Wes, Evansville	3	5	4.20	19	8	64	62	27	43
Samuels, Matt, Indiana State	4	4	4.21	14	0	88	95	24	72
Ziegler, Brad, SMS	**12**	2	4.22	17	0	107	115	26	94
Uhlmansiek, Steve, Wichita State	8	3	4.23	16	0	81	80	50	58
Zimmermann, Bob, SMS	5	3	4.25	20	1	89	95	26	90
Jakubowski, Mike, Bradley	6	5	4.32	16	1	58	70	14	28
Wilson, Rick, SMS	3	4	4.32	13	0	50	43	22	44
Oldham, Tom, Creighton	5	7	4.67	15	0	91	103	27	79
Hawkins, Craig, Bradley	2	3	5.02	10	0	52	58	23	29
Jakubov, Matt, Wichita State	5	4	5.11	15	0	62	61	21	32

MOUNTAIN WEST CONFERENCE

	Conference W	Conference L	Overall W	Overall L
***Nevada-Las Vegas**	24	6	47	17
Brigham Young	18	12	30	24
San Diego State	18	12	29	32
New Mexico	17	13	34	26
Utah	10	20	24	32
Air Force	3	27	15	39

ALL-CONFERENCE TEAM: C—Josh Allen, Sr., San Diego State. **1B**—Fernando Valenzuela, Jr., Nevada-Las Vegas. **2B**—Jared Pena, Jr., Utah. **3B**—Josh Mader, So., New Mexico. **SS**—Dusty Young, Sr., New Mexico. **OF**—Matt Ciaramella, So., Utah; Anthony Gwynn, Jr., San Diego State; Doug Jackson, Sr., Brigham Young. **DH**—Joe Salas, Jr., New Mexico. **P**—Paul Jacinto, Jr., Brigham Young; Matt Luca, Fr., Nevada-Las Vegas; Jamie Vermilyea, Jr., New Mexico. **RP**—Ryan Braun, Sr., Nevada-Las Vegas.

Player of the Year: Fernando Valenzuela, Nevada-Las Vegas. **Pitcher of the Year:** Paul Jacinto, Brigham Young. **Coach of the Year:** Jim Schlossnagle, Nevada-Las Vegas.

INDIVIDUAL BATTING LEADERS

(Minimum 125 At-Bats)

	AVG	AB	R	H	2B	3B	HR	RBI	SB
Phifer, Josh, Air Force	**.413**	184	50	76	21	3	15	62	4
Wiens, Ranger, Brigham Young	.405	220	50	89	**25**	4	4	55	21
Murray, Sean, New Mexico	.383	222	58	85	20	1	7	60	5
Young, Dusty, New Mexico	.378	267	**75**	**101**	**25**	4	8	66	6
Lizarraga, Cory, New Mexico	.374	230	67	86	21	4	9	50	16
Rose, Mike, Air Force	.371	175	44	65	9	3	6	32	8
Chevalier, Eric, Utah	.371	175	35	65	14	4	6	29	17
Stonard, Peter, San Diego St.	.368	136	28	50	9	3	1	29	8
Jackson, Doug, Brigham Young	.367	218	71	80	12	**8**	4	34	10
Salas, Joe, New Mexico	.366	238	59	87	21	1	16	56	0
Nielsen, Eric, UNLV	.365	197	54	72	17	1	7	41	6
Obrey, Kainoa, Brigham Young	.362	199	50	72	24	0	11	65	0
Alexander, Chris, New Mexico	.360	225	62	81	18	0	**25**	**93**	1
Petro, Daniel, Air Force	.360	175	30	63	18	2	4	43	2
Gwynn, Anthony, San Diego St.	.359	270	50	97	15	7	0	38	**25**
Dobson, Patrick, UNLV	.358	240	71	86	20	2	12	66	7
Mader, Josh, New Mexico	.357	241	55	86	16	5	7	49	10
Ciaramella, Matt, Utah	.354	212	54	75	16	1	6	42	9
Johnson, Brent, UNLV	.350	274	70	96	19	3	6	55	13
Howes, Adam, Air Force	.340	215	56	73	16	4	7	38	17
Kasel, Derck, Air Force	.339	168	31	57	14	1	5	33	2
Valenzuela, Fernando, UNLV	.337	243	60	82	20	0	14	75	0
Burt, Landon, San Diego State	.337	178	45	60	12	2	1	30	7
Pena, Jared, Utah	.337	184	35	62	16	1	7	36	5
#Young, Matt, New Mexico	.327	220	**75**	72	14	2	1	23	10

INDIVIDUAL PITCHING LEADERS

(Minimum 50 Innings)

	W	L	ERA	G	SV	IP	H	BB	SO
#Martinez, Brady, Utah	4	3	3.02	21	**7**	42	41	8	55
#Braun, Ryan, UNLV	5	3	3.44	28	**7**	37	37	18	53
Jacinto, Paul, Brigham Young	**10**	5	**4.14**	18	0	113	101	38	83
Luca, Matt, UNLV	5	0	4.17	15	0	58	55	25	49
Vermilyea, Jamie, New Mexico	7	4	4.27	20	0	126	147	26	**112**
Moat, Mike, San Diego State	6	6	4.50	18	0	108	125	24	72
Van, Robbie, UNLV	9	4	4.51	21	1	104	101	67	97
Carque, Joe, San Diego State	5	5	4.89	18	0	107	108	33	61
Vose, Jake, UNLV	8	4	5.20	19	0	99	117	34	89
Bergeron, Michel, Brigham Young	6	3	5.37	16	2	54	74	18	45
Price, Jason, Utah	4	1	5.40	19	1	63	73	19	50
Coon, Ben, San Diego State	5	5	5.68	16	0	90	106	19	65
MacKay, Doug, Utah	4	6	5.99	15	0	83	100	55	70
Gravley, Ken, Brigham Young	4	2	6.09	17	0	78	114	25	29
Pupo, Giovanni, UNLV	5	1	6.30	17	0	50	56	18	28

NORTHEAST CONFERENCE

	Conference W	Conference L	Overall W	Overall L
***Central Connecticut State**	19	6	31	17
St. Francis (N.Y.)	17	10	21	21
Monmouth	15	11	24	27
Maryland-Baltimore County	15	12	20	27
Quinnipiac	14	13	17	24
Fairleigh Dickinson	12	15	14	25
Long Island	11	15	16	24
Mount St. Mary's	9	14	14	23
Wagner	10	16	11	36
Sacred Heart	7	17	13	29

ALL-CONFERENCE TEAM: C—Tim D'Aquila, Jr., Central Connecticut State. **1B**—Phil Rothkugel, So., Central Connecticut State. **2B**—Lance Koenig, Sr., Monmouth. **3B**—Nick Macellaro, Sr., Central Connecticut State. **SS**—Mike Kelly, Jr., Monmouth. **OF**—Stephen Echevarria, Jr., Long Island; Rob Hosgood, Jr., Central Connecticut State; Chris Yetter, Maryland-Baltimore County. **DH**—Anthony Esposito, Sr., St. Francis (N.Y.). **P**—Anthony Esposito, Sr., St. Francis (N.Y.); Barry Hertzler, Jr., Central Connecticut State.

Player of the Year: Tim D'Aquila, Central Connecticut State. **Pitcher of the Year:** Barry Hertzler, Central Connecticut State. **Rookie of the Year:** Marc Weres, Monmouth. **Coach of the Year:** Charlie Hickey, Central Connecticut State.

INDIVIDUAL BATTING LEADERS
(Minimum 125 At-Bats)

	AVG	AB	R	H	2B	3B	HR	RBI	SB
D'Aquila, Tim, Cent. Conn.	**.425**	186	46	**79**	12	1	2	38	6
Echevarria, Stephen, LIU	.374	147	31	55	11	1	1	17	7
Thompson, Mike, Long Island	.365	126	30	46	14	2	4	31	6
Stegbauer, Keith, Cent. Conn.	.360	172	46	62	10	1	3	35	7
Yetter, Chris, UMBC	.358	162	27	58	13	0	2	21	0
Macellaro, Nick, Cent. Conn.	.355	166	31	59	5	0	0	25	1
Kosmicky, Scott, UMBC	.345	168	25	58	12	1	7	27	0
Rothkugel, Phil, Cent. Conn.	.345	171	42	59	13	0	8	**44**	1
Hosgood, Rob, Cent. Conn.	.343	175	37	60	11	**6**	6	42	15
Dick, Chris, Wagner	.338	145	28	49	13	0	**10**	35	1
Koenig, Lance, Monmouth	.337	193	**47**	65	**20**	1	5	28	21
Marano, Albert, Quinnipiac	.329	140	31	46	11	1	7	29	4
Muldoon, Brad, Cent. Conn.	.324	204	45	66	14	0	0	21	16
Pezzello, Tom, Cent. Conn.	.319	138	19	44	6	2	1	31	1
Nugent, Matt, Fair. Dickinson	.319	135	22	43	6	0	4	16	5
Geroni, Pat, Fair. Dickinson	.316	133	23	42	8	0	9	29	1
Weres, Marc, Monmouth	.314	175	29	55	12	3	5	35	0
Papa, Nick, Wagner	.314	140	19	44	5	4	2	17	12
Schilkowski, Jamie, S. Heart	.312	141	10	44	9	1	1	27	0
Molinini, Mike, St. Francis	.311	151	25	47	10	1	2	31	10
Giudice, Anthony, St. Francis	.308	146	38	45	2	0	1	16	**22**
D'Elia, Charles, Quinnipiac	.305	154	22	47	10	1	4	22	2
Furst, Kane, Wagner	.305	151	28	46	9	0	1	17	6
Boles, Jesse, St. Francis	.304	125	18	38	11	2	0	25	11
Magee, Brien, Quinnipiac	.304	135	18	41	10	0	0	15	0

INDIVIDUAL PITCHING LEADERS
(Minimum 50 Innings)

	W	L	ERA	G	SV	IP	H	BB	SO
Hertzler, Barry, Cent. Conn.	**9**	3	**2.59**	14	0	87	70	18	72
Bengel, Buddy, Quinnipiac	6	3	2.66	13	0	68	65	22	57
#Kelly, Mike, Monmouth	0	4	2.70	12	**6**	17	18	3	14
Herrick, Zachary, Cent. Conn.	6	3	2.82	12	0	73	70	37	34
Palmieri, Andrew, Monmouth	6	4	2.89	12	0	72	62	35	34
Anziano, Jesse, Fair. Dickinson	3	4	3.09	10	0	64	57	20	79
Esposito, Anthony, St. Francis	6	2	3.24	12	0	67	60	25	49
#Garrison, Chuck, Monmouth	1	1	3.32	22	**6**	43	48	15	26
Ristano, Charles, S. Heart	3	4	3.38	10	0	61	64	13	50
Santo, Brian, Mt. St. Mary's	2	6	3.45	12	1	70	69	26	81
Butkiewicz, Eric, UMBC	4	7	3.95	17	1	84	94	22	60
Carone, Jim, Monmouth	4	5	4.05	13	0	80	102	30	32
Pappariella, Lewis, Cent. Conn.	7	4	4.17	12	0	73	77	33	49
Pleeter, Greg, Fair. Dickinson	5	6	4.24	12	0	76	65	54	**86**
Zadina, Scott, Monmouth	4	6	4.74	13	0	63	72	32	42
Leahy, Francis, Long Island	4	4	4.76	10	0	59	52	36	61
Scott, Dan, S. Heart	2	9	4.80	12	0	66	70	30	66

OHIO VALLEY CONFERENCE

	Conference W	Conference L	Overall W	Overall L
Austin Peay State	14	5	27	27
Southeast Missouri State	14	6	31	20
Tennessee Tech	13	6	27	25
***Murray State**	9	11	25	31
Eastern Kentucky	8	11	24	29
Eastern Illinois	8	12	26	31
Tennessee-Martin	6	13	17	30
Morehead State	6	14	16	33

ALL-CONFERENCE TEAM: C—A.J. Ellis, Sr., Austin Peay. **1B**—Aaron Shelbourne, Sr., Eastern Illinois. **2B**—Justin Christian, Sr., Southeast Missouri State. **3B**—Neil Sellers, Jr., Eastern Kentucky. **SS**—Casey Benjamin, Sr., Tennessee Tech. **OF**—Josh Anderson, Jr., Eastern Kentucky; Brian Hopkins, Sr., Southeast Missouri State; Ron Bethke, Jr., Austin Peay. **DH**—Scott Terry, Jr., Tennessee Tech. **Util**—Cole Helms, So., Tennessee Tech. **SP**— Tim Alvarez, Sr., Southeast Missouri State; Ben Downs, Sr., Tennessee Tech. **RP**—Jeff Mault, Jr., Austin Peay.

Player of the Year: Josh Anderson, Eastern Kentucky. **Pitcher of the Year:** Tim Alvarez, Southeast Missouri State. **Rookie of the Year:** Justin Christian, Southeast Missouri State. **Coach of the Year:** Gary McClure, Austin Peay.

INDIVIDUAL BATTING LEADERS
(Minimum 125 At-Bats)

	AVG	AB	R	H	2B	3B	HR	RBI	SB
Anderson, Josh, E. Kentucky	**.447**	237	**80**	**106**	21	**5**	6	53	**57**
Benjamin, Casey, Tenn. Tech	.418	196	54	82	17	3	5	44	5
Sellers, Neil, E. Kentucky	.407	231	66	94	**24**	0	17	**85**	14
Hopkins, Brian, SE Missouri	.401	202	58	81	19	3	**18**	59	7
Walters, Kirk, Eastern Illinois	.392	189	43	74	8	3	13	56	7
Bethke, Ron, Austin Peay	.385	187	49	72	15	0	7	32	14
Christian, Justin, SE Missouri	.376	197	55	74	12	3	13	48	18
Borowiak, Zach, SE Missouri	.372	199	40	74	19	0	15	59	2
Carter, Stephen, E. Kentucky	.361	133	42	48	6	2	4	30	11
Nighswonger, Brady, UT-Martin	.357	182	43	65	10	1	6	26	4
Seasor, Lance, Morehead State	.349	169	39	59	7	1	10	36	10
Hay, Ryan, Tennessee Tech	.340	188	46	64	13	0	6	45	0
Haines, Kyle, Eastern Illinois	.340	212	49	72	13	1	10	47	8
Martin, Carlos, Tenn. Tech	.339	186	37	63	13	0	10	49	2
Stuckey, Denver, SE Missouri	.338	216	55	73	17	3	6	31	16
Ellis, A.J., Austin Peay	.337	199	31	67	12	0	7	38	5
Kirksey, Geoff, Murray State	.335	197	27	66	10	1	8	41	1
Price, Robby, E. Kentucky	.333	180	33	60	13	2	7	42	7
Turner, Loren, Tenn.-Martin	.333	129	31	43	10	0	6	33	0
Jones, Bryant, Tenn.-Martin	.332	184	32	61	8	1	3	32	4
Uhle, Chris, Eastern Illinois	.329	231	63	76	19	2	8	36	13
Beech, Travis, Austin Peay	.329	219	41	72	18	1	4	43	13
Woodard, Jonathan, E. Ky.	.329	207	48	68	12	0	3	33	5
Gentry, Roy, Morehead State	.324	142	32	46	10	2	7	25	15

INDIVIDUAL PITCHING LEADERS
(Minimum 50 Innings)

	W	L	ERA	G	SV	IP	H	BB	SO
Alvarez, Tim, SE Missouri	**14**	3	**2.74**	21	1	108	86	33	79
#Mault, Jeff, Austin Peay	3	2	3.52	24	**10**	31	30	11	25
Smith, Dustin, Austin Peay	6	6	3.70	14	0	97	89	31	**81**
Kraus, Craig, Murray State	3	6	3.95	15	1	57	75	22	44
Ringwald, Craig, Murray State	5	4	4.04	16	0	71	88	23	61
Downs, Ben, Tennessee Tech	9	2	4.19	19	1	92	93	27	**81**
White, Damon, Eastern Illinois	4	4	4.62	15	0	86	104	34	77
Vincent, Doug, Tennessee Tech	4	4	4.66	17	2	73	74	45	63
Perry, Kyle, Murray State	8	4	4.82	17	0	80	97	31	79
Eubanks, Dusty, Tennessee Tech	6	2	5.00	15	0	76	101	16	59
Thomas, Devin, Austin Peay	9	3	5.05	17	0	77	94	28	53
Forsyth, Ryan, SE Missouri	5	2	5.14	20	0	68	76	26	49
Marshall, Jared, Eastern Illinois	7	2	5.34	12	0	56	57	18	26
Bryant, Justin, Tenn.-Martin	4	3	5.43	16	0	63	82	24	29
Nourie, Jon, SE Missouri	2	3	5.90	16	0	56	57	18	26
Corey, Donnie, Tenn.-Martin	4	5	5.95	15	0	65	82	31	54

PACIFIC-10 CONFERENCE

	Conference W	Conference L	Overall W	Overall L
Stanford	18	6	51	18
Arizona State	16	8	54	14
Washington	15	9	42	18
Arizona	13	11	35	23
Southern California	11	13	28	28
UCLA	11	13	28	31
California	10	14	28	27
Washington State	7	17	19	37
Oregon State	7	17	25	28

ALL-CONFERENCE TEAM: C—Jeff Clement, Fr., Southern California. **1B**—Conor Jackson, Jr., California; Jeff Larish, So., Arizona State. **2B**—Steve Garrabrants, Jr., Arizona State. **3B**—Brad Boyer, Fr., Arizona. **SS**—Anthony Lunetta, Sr., Southern California. **OF**—Jeff Van Houten, So., Arizona; Brian Anderson, Jr., Arizona; Andre Ethier, Jr., Arizona State; Sam Fuld, Jr., Stanford; Brent Lillibridge, Fr., Washington; Danny Putnam, So., Stanford; Carlos Quentin, Jr., Stanford. **DH**—Chad Boudon, Jr., Washington. **Util**—Wes Whisler, So., UCLA. **P**—Richie Gardner, Jr., Arizona; Jake Postlewait, Jr., Oregon State; Mark Romanczuk, Fr., Stanford. **RP**— Will Fenton, So., Washington; Ryan Schroyer, Jr., Arizona State.

Co-Players of the Year: Ryan Garko, Stanford; Dustin Pedroia, Arizona State. **Pitcher of the Year:** John Hudgins, Stanford. **Freshman of the Year:** Jeff Clement, Southern California. **Coach of the Year:** Mark Marquess, Stanford.

INDIVIDUAL BATTING LEADERS
(Minimum 125 At-Bats)

	AVG	AB	R	H	2B	3B	HR	RBI	SB
Van Houten, Jeff, Arizona	**.413**	213	53	88	10	**9**	11	72	9
Pedroia, Dustin, Arizona State	.404	297	**83**	**120**	**34**	3	4	52	3
Garko, Ryan, Stanford	.402	259	64	104	24	0	18	92	2
Quentin, Carlos, Stanford	.396	265	72	105	24	1	12	64	10
Lillibridge, Brent, Washington	.388	183	49	71	16	1	13	47	9
Jackson, Conor, California	.388	160	53	62	14	1	10	44	2
West, Jeremy, Arizona State	.381	202	66	77	10	1	17	71	2
Ethier, Andre, Arizona State	.377	260	75	98	13	4	10	68	7
Larish, Jeff, Arizona State	.372	234	80	87	18	2	18	**95**	3
Anderson, Brian, Arizona	.366	232	58	85	12	8	14	62	17
Mesa, Frank, Arizona State	.364	143	39	52	6	1	1	23	2
Calderon, Tony, Oregon State	.362	199	48	72	24	1	4	43	2
Hundley, Nick, Arizona	.361	133	37	48	12	2	2	25	8
Biles, Chris, Oregon State	.357	154	36	55	23	1	3	31	4

Boyer, Brad, Arizona	.351	239	71	84	16	8	5	47	**25**
Hathaway, Aaron, Washington	.350	203	38	71	12	2	5	38	3
Lunetta, Anthony, USC	.349	215	46	75	22	0	7	31	5
Pietsch, Seth, Oregon State	.348	224	54	78	11	4	12	40	6
Putnam, Danny, Stanford	.348	230	52	80	17	0	16	66	0
Horwitz, Brian, California	.347	170	28	59	10	2	6	47	3
Wyrick, Dennis, Arizona State	.345	174	36	60	8	4	1	35	7
Grossman, Chris, California	.341	211	32	72	16	0	8	45	0
Miller, Jay, Wash. State	.341	214	40	73	21	0	2	36	4
Gosewisch, Tuffy, Arizona State	.340	144	41	49	9	0	2	41	2
Hart, Justin, Wash. State	.338	139	19	47	5	2	2	13	6
Ellsbury, Jacoby, Oregon State	.330	206	56	68	10	3	7	33	14
McMillan, Brett, UCLA	.330	203	42	67	16	1	8	35	1
Reilly, Pat, Arizona	.329	161	36	53	11	5	2	23	15
Averill, Brandon, UCLA	.329	149	31	49	11	3	10	33	0
Jarvis, Andy, Oregon State	.327	217	42	71	10	1	7	49	2
Buck, Travis, Arizona State	.326	239	59	78	13	3	4	46	12
Mercado, Richard, Arizona	.324	145	32	47	7	1	4	31	3
Garrabrants, Steve, Arizona State	.324	213	56	69	16	3	8	59	23
Isaacson, Greg, Washington	.322	208	54	67	10	2	9	38	9
Fuld, Sam, Stanford	.321	302	**83**	97	18	**9**	4	35	10
Metropoulos, Joey, USC	.321	209	34	67	15	1	11	41	6
Denove, Chris, UCLA	.319	141	23	45	6	0	6	26	0
Richardson, Grant, Wash. State	.318	195	35	62	7	1	13	50	2
Crowe, Trevor, Arizona	.316	187	34	59	14	2	2	35	13
Ash, Jonny, Stanford	.314	194	28	61	11	5	2	33	1
Susdorf, Billy, UCLA	.310	216	40	67	12	0	10	40	1
Whisler, Wes, UCLA	.310	226	44	70	4	1	9	39	1
Brewster, Jon, USC	.310	197	30	61	14	0	4	27	6
Wagner, Mike, Washington	.308	201	45	62	11	0	15	48	3
Holder, James, California	.305	187	32	57	15	0	6	38	0
McAndrews, Travis, USC	.304	207	36	63	12	2	5	32	2
Decater, Derek, Arizona	.299	127	32	38	9	3	4	32	7
Mayberry, John, Stanford	.299	194	33	58	6	6	4	33	5
Thayer, Matt, UCLA	.299	194	46	58	13	1	5	37	9
Reynolds, Tila, Washington	.299	241	47	72	15	2	3	36	12
Otness, John, Washington	.298	218	41	65	16	4	6	36	2
Clement, Jeff, USC	.298	208	53	62	8	1	21	53	1
Bruce, Derek, Wash. State	.294	221	43	65	14	4	6	29	6
#Boudon, Chad, Washington	.287	209	49	60	9	2	**22**	58	4

INDIVIDUAL PITCHING LEADERS

(Minimum 50 Innings)

	W	L	ERA	G	SV	IP	H	BB	SO
#Fenton, Will, Washington	2	0	0.00	18	**12**	32	16	11	49
Sopko, Mark, Arizona State	3	2	2.30	25	0	55	52	13	43
Thurmond, Ben, Arizona State	8	0	**2.73**	20	0	79	79	25	58
Liebeck, Jered, Arizona State	8	0	2.88	21	0	78	77	24	54
Hudgins, John, Stanford	**14**	3	2.99	22	0	165	138	35	**143**
Baysinger, Trent, Washington	4	1	3.02	24	3	51	45	20	48
Postlewait, Jake, Oregon State	5	1	3.43	15	0	63	68	28	37
Averill, Erik, Arizona State	8	2	3.66	20	0	86	87	19	61
McClellan, Robbie, Arizona State	7	0	3.70	28	0	58	54	33	57
Manship, Matt, Stanford	2	4	3.98	25	9	63	53	27	50
Romanczuk, Mark, Stanford	12	2	4.01	23	2	112	97	55	80
McCally, Ryan, Stanford	7	3	4.44	24	2	99	116	28	58
Gardner, Richie, Arizona	9	3	4.49	16	0	108	120	39	93
Bannister, Brian, USC	6	5	4.53	18	0	93	105	24	56
Butler, Bret, USC	1	5	4.56	33	8	51	65	17	52
Cordeiro, Chris, UCLA	1	2	4.62	21	4	51	55	8	42
Todoroff, Joe, California	5	2	4.64	21	1	64	71	21	43
Petersen, Jeff, Washington	6	6	4.65	17	0	89	92	43	66
Rummonds, Josh, USC	5	3	4.66	30	2	66	76	17	60
Vaughan, Beau, Arizona State	10	6	4.68	26	0	92	88	34	105
White, Sean, Washington	8	4	4.76	16	0	91	88	38	70
Guyette, Kevin, Arizona	3	3	4.80	16	2	51	65	10	34
Dowling, David, Washington	7	2	5.11	19	1	56	66	29	58
Rierson, Sean, Arizona	9	3	5.38	18	0	104	126	19	66
Little, Joe, Arizona	4	4	5.40	18	0	75	87	44	62
Paschal, Bobby, USC	3	7	5.43	16	0	70	73	30	67
McKenzie, Aaron, Wash. State	5	5	5.56	18	1	92	95	41	81
Montalbo, Brian, California	4	3	5.61	17	0	61	65	43	43
Anderson, Kenny, Oregon State	3	3	5.65	22	0	51	53	30	38

PATRIOT LEAGUE

	Conference W	Conference L	Overall W	Overall L
***Bucknell**	15	5	27	16
Navy	12	8	21	24
Lehigh	9	11	19	23
Army	9	11	17	25
Holy Cross	8	12	13	23
Lafayette	7	13	16	24

ALL-CONFERENCE TEAM: C—Schuyler Williamson, So., Army. **1B**—Walker Gorham, So., Army. **2B**—Jeff Rodgers, Jr., Lafayette. **3B**—Jesse Novalis, Jr., Lehigh. **SS**—Ben Stoll, Jr., Bucknell. **OF**—Adam Rosenberg, Jr., Lafayette; Craig Candeto, Jr., Navy; Pete Curnow, So., Navy. **DH**—Matt Foster, Sr., Navy. **P**—Kevin Miller, Jr., Bucknell; Rich McDevitt, Sr., Navy. **RP**—Phil Futrick, Fr., Bucknell.

Player of the Year: Jesse Novalis, Lehigh. **Pitcher of the Year:** Kevin Miller, Bucknell. **Rookie of the Year:** Phil Futrick, Bucknell. **Coach of the Year:** Gene Depew, Bucknell.

INDIVIDUAL BATTING LEADERS

(Minimum 100 At-Bats)

	AVG	AB	R	H	2B	3B	HR	RBI	SB
Stoll, Ben, Bucknell	**.376**	133	29	50	9	1	0	17	17
Rodgers, Jeff, Lafayette	.371	105	20	39	4	1	0	15	2
Candeto, Craig, Navy	.370	138	25	**51**	**14**	4	6	31	11
Rosenberg, Adam, Lafayette	.359	142	32	**51**	7	1	5	28	11
Hoffman, Eric, Lehigh	.353	116	26	41	9	0	0	13	4
Bucci, Adam, Lafayette	.341	129	23	44	4	2	4	26	2
Novalis, Jesse, Lehigh	.333	138	31	46	13	1	**9**	**35**	7
Curnow, Pete, Navy	.331	148	26	49	8	3	0	16	19
Moss, Sam, Bucknell	.318	110	22	35	2	1	2	13	11
Schell, Mike, Holy Cross	.318	129	18	41	8	0	2	18	1
Holden, Josh, Army	.318	148	**34**	47	4	3	1	11	**27**
Asinhurst, Chris, Navy	.315	149	29	47	5	1	0	16	3
Boyd, Jason, Lafayette	.311	132	28	41	11	1	6	31	16
Walter, Kyle, Bucknell	.308	133	30	41	7	2	3	24	4
Foster, Matt, Navy	.302	106	22	32	6	5	0	14	5
Stone, Nate, Army	.300	150	23	45	**14**	1	2	27	11
Potvin, Tom, Holy Cross	.300	120	23	36	6	1	1	8	7
#Hirschberg, Brian, Bucknell	.278	133	23	37	4	**6**	6	27	3

INDIVIDUAL PITCHING LEADERS

(Minimum 40 Innings)

	W	L	ERA	G	SV	IP	H	BB	SO
McDevitt, Rich, Navy	5	5	**2.52**	12	0	71	71	12	**59**
Lyons, Jack, Lehigh	3	4	2.56	9	0	56	59	19	27
Allen, Zachery, Bucknell	6	3	2.56	10	0	53	42	18	44
Muscalus, Jack, Lehigh	6	4	2.70	12	0	73	62	16	46
Froistad, Andy, Navy	6	0	2.76	12	0	59	49	12	43
Kashner, Justin, Army	1	6	2.91	12	0	59	55	15	44
#Futrick, Phil, Bucknell	0	1	2.93	16	**11**	15	11	2	15
Lucey, D.J., Holy Cross	2	2	3.38	10	0	51	52	19	34
Burns, Kevin, Bucknell	5	1	3.48	9	0	44	56	9	16
Foster, Matt, Navy	4	5	3.67	10	0	54	56	15	50
Miller, Kevin, Bucknell	**8**	2	3.68	11	0	64	65	19	50
Saporetti, Joe, Lafayette	3	5	3.81	8	0	50	57	7	22

SOUTHEASTERN CONFERENCE

EAST	Conference W	Conference L	Overall W	Overall L
South Carolina	19	11	45	22
Vanderbilt	14	16	27	28
Florida	13	16	37	21
Tennessee	13	17	31	24
Georgia	10	20	29	26
Kentucky	9	20	24	32
WEST	**W**	**L**	**W**	**L**
Louisiana State	20	9	45	22
Auburn	18	12	42	21
Mississippi State	17	12	42	20
Mississippi	17	13	35	27
***Alabama**	14	16	38	24
Arkansas	14	16	35	22

ALL-CONFERENCE TEAM: C—Landon Powell, Jr., South Carolina. **1B**—Clay Harris, So., Louisiana State. **2B**—Tug Hulett, So., Auburn. **3B**—Brian Buscher, Sr., South Carolina. **SS**—Aaron Hill, Jr., Louisiana State. **OF**—Jordan Czarniecki, Sr., Tennessee; Ryan Fox, Sr., Arkansas; Beau Hearod, Sr., Alabama. **DH**—Ryan Patterson, So., Louisiana State. **P**—Paul Maholm, Jr., Mississippi State; David Marchbanks, Jr., South Carolina. **RP**—Steven Register, So., Auburn.

Player of the Year: Aaron Hill, Louisiana State. **Pitcher of the Year:** David Marchbanks, South Carolina. **Freshman of the Year:** Stephen Head, Mississippi. **Coach of the Year:** Smoke Laval, Louisiana State.

INDIVIDUAL BATTING LEADERS

(Minimum 125 At-Bats)

	AVG	AB	R	H	2B	3B	HR	RBI	SB
Buscher, Brian, So. Carolina	**.393**	270	55	**106**	19	2	15	66	5
Hulett, Tug, Auburn	.373	249	52	93	25	2	2	39	3
Garner, Travis, Alabama	.365	241	64	88	15	4	2	29	19
Harrison, Ben, Florida	.362	224	59	81	16	2	11	61	14
Dowdy, Brett, Florida	.361	244	67	88	18	3	4	40	14

Hill, Aaron, LSU	.358	265	**68**	95	**27**	4	9	67	9
Rose, Brian, Florida	.357	182	52	65	9	1	16	59	1
Harris, Justin, South Carolina	.355	276	57	98	14	1	4	33	6
Coffey, David, Georgia	.354	212	50	75	9	4	9	40	7
Patterson, Ryan, LSU	.354	263	59	93	20	1	16	52	3
Garza, Mario, Florida	.349	195	52	68	18	1	13	66	2
Armitage, Jon, Georgia	.347	202	36	70	14	1	3	39	4
Hearod, Beau, Alabama	.346	231	64	80	18	4	**20**	**82**	8
Moran, Javon, Auburn	.339	271	53	92	18	**7**	4	38	26
Zeringue, Jon, LSU	.339	227	50	77	15	0	13	45	6
Powell, Landon, So. Carolina	.339	245	46	83	23	0	10	61	3
Smith, Josh, Georgia	.338	198	33	67	11	1	1	26	6
Maniscalco, Matthew, Miss. State	.338	**278**	57	94	15	4	7	42	20
Pavkovich, Adam, Alabama	.338	240	64	81	**27**	1	11	56	6
Smith, C.J., Florida	.337	202	53	68	11	1	17	63	2
Head, Stephen, Mississippi	.337	208	31	70	10	2	6	44	1
Gendron, Steve, Miss. State	.333	264	48	88	14	0	1	35	13
Welch, Zac, Alabama	.333	228	38	76	15	1	4	49	2
Smith, Seth, Mississippi	.333	222	42	74	13	2	5	35	6
Harris, Clay, LSU	.332	211	51	70	16	0	16	62	0
Goodwin, Clay, Arkansas	.332	184	34	61	13	3	2	31	5
Amonite, Karl, Auburn	.330	206	36	68	13	1	12	56	0
Crowe, Nick, Tennessee	.327	159	32	52	12	0	2	29	9
Tucker, Jonathan, Florida	.326	227	63	74	17	0	0	26	11
Huddleston, Bobby, Auburn	.324	219	47	71	19	0	13	64	1
Pickrell, Brad, Kentucky	.322	177	25	57	10	0	8	33	3
Corley, Brad, Miss. State	.321	224	40	72	15	0	1	36	4
Wishy, Andrew, Arkansas	.319	210	45	67	25	1	8	50	1
Melillo, Kevin, So. Carolina	.317	227	59	72	16	0	12	43	6
Naccarata, Ivan, LSU	.316	256	59	81	14	5	6	52	9
Kaye, John, Vanderbilt	.316	174	22	55	8	0	3	21	1
Butts, Jeff, Mississippi State	.316	133	18	42	11	1	0	14	4
Coutlangus, Jon, So. Carolina	.316	225	47	71	10	2	3	24	13
Breyman, Mike, Kentucky	.315	203	39	64	11	2	13	42	0
Nicolas, Cesar, Vanderbilt	.313	201	28	63	12	0	7	33	2
Alley, Josh, Tennssee	.313	131	20	41	2	1	1	21	10
Corsaletti, Jeff, Florida	.313	211	46	66	20	2	6	44	6
Liuzza, Matt, LSU	.312	192	38	60	8	0	4	26	1
Brinson, Matthew, Miss. State	.311	241	50	75	20	1	8	49	2
Czarniecki, Jordan, Tennessee	.311	209	54	62	12	0	4	30	**32**
Triplett, Bryan, So. Carolina	.311	235	39	73	14	1	7	47	7
Pratt, Haas, Arkansas	.310	232	45	72	15	0	10	48	1
Schade, Scott, Auburn	.310	239	40	74	17	3	2	35	0
Jones, Warner, Vanderbilt	.307	228	22	70	10	2	3	28	2
Stewart, Caleb, Kentucky	.306	173	29	53	10	0	4	25	1
Szabo, Marshall, Georgia	.305	210	35	64	10	4	4	33	8
Waite, Charlie, Mississippi	.304	207	35	63	11	2	4	28	1
Toops, Brady, Arkansas	.304	161	35	49	8	0	4	24	5
Holmes, Justin, Georgia	.304	181	34	55	8	1	1	16	8
Gill, Blake, LSU	.304	260	46	79	13	3	5	54	6
McClain, Justin, Georgia	.303	198	33	60	15	2	5	36	4
Tolleson, Steven, So. Carolina	.302	139	23	42	10	1	3	19	3
Tatum, Craig, Mississippi State	.302	192	35	58	8	0	6	33	0
Hecklinski, Al, Alabama	.301	186	41	56	15	1	11	49	6
Tolbert, Matt, Mississippi	.301	193	34	58	11	4	1	22	8

INDIVIDUAL PITCHING LEADERS

(Minimum 50 Innings)

	W	L	ERA	G	SV	IP	H	BB	SO
Gant, Jamie, Miss. State	6	1	1.15	21	1	55	37	21	39
Head, Stephen, Mississippi	4	1	1.40	20	13	58	40	16	43
Speigner, Levale, Auburn	10	0	**2.42**	27	1	67	58	20	51
Sowers, Jeremy, Vanderbilt	7	5	2.50	18	0	115	94	29	**123**
Marchbanks, David, So. Carolina	**15**	3	2.73	21	0	135	148	25	97
Maholm, Paul, Mississippi State	9	2	2.76	15	0	108	102	39	101
Meier, Justin, LSU	8	3	2.83	16	1	95	95	25	62
Cupps, Anthony, Mississippi	4	3	2.92	19	2	65	65	17	32
Beam, T.J., Mississippi	8	2	2.94	16	0	101	92	33	91
Determann, Jason, LSU	7	0	2.94	20	1	67	61	11	51
Register, Steven, Auburn	3	3	2.94	33	**16**	52	42	7	61
Lewis, Jensen, Vanderbilt	3	6	3.00	26	8	57	50	20	62
Johnson, Dusty, Tennessee	6	1	3.04	16	0	56	57	15	41
Dueitt, Cory, Auburn	7	2	3.23	32	1	70	66	10	60
Carter, Brent, Alabama	10	5	3.30	19	0	123	115	19	105
Hoyman, Justin, Florida	8	6	3.31	16	0	111	100	30	77
Hernandez, Chris, So. Carolina	5	5	3.32	25	2	84	76	27	52
Wilson, Brian, LSU	5	3	3.38	8	0	51	60	13	35
Sawatski, Jay, Arkansas	3	3	3.44	23	3	55	62	13	42
Mullins, Ryan, Vanderbilt	3	**8**	3.48	15	0	88	96	19	64
Riley, Ben, Tennessee	3	6	3.48	15	0	93	70	51	63
Boyce, Charley, Arkansas	6	5	3.48	17	0	93	97	18	59
Campbell, Matt, So. Carolina	6	4	3.48	21	2	83	68	47	82
Wright, Brae, Mississippi	4	4	3.49	19	1	70	75	22	36
Castle, Heath, Kentucky	6	5	3.54	15	0	86	89	40	60
Paxton, Colby, Auburn	7	3	3.57	16	0	86	91	22	32
Brannon, Clint, Arkansas	3	1	3.59	13	0	53	58	21	34
Lacher, Jeff, Mississippi State	6	0	3.61	15	0	67	67	17	46
Holliman, Mark, Mississippi	4	7	3.84	18	0	89	76	46	60
Falkenbach, Connor, Florida	4	2	3.86	26	3	58	64	8	54
Reed, Brian, Alabama	2	2	3.90	30	12	55	55	20	41
Tharpe, Derek, Tennessee	6	6	3.95	15	0	93	101	25	88
Lubrano, Paul, Georgia	5	3	3.96	15	0	52	53	15	44
Rawl, Aaron, So. Carolina	6	3	3.98	21	6	61	50	24	54
Fowler, Eric, Mississippi	3	2	4.05	18	0	60	78	16	47
Ransom, Robert, Vanderbilt	4	3	4.08	15	0	93	90	32	74
Hughey, Arnold, Auburn	6	6	4.15	19	0	102	99	23	85
Bondurant, Steven, So. Carolina	7	3	4.23	21	0	111	119	32	98
Pete, Mike, Florida	5	2	4.29	25	1	71	84	11	39
Startup, Will, Georgia	3	4	4.36	21	1	66	67	20	56

SOUTHERN CONFERENCE

	Conference		Overall	
	W	L	W	L
***Western Carolina**	22	8	43	21
Georgia Southern	19	10	39	21
The Citadel	19	11	32	25
UNC Greensboro	17	13	39	21
Furman	17	13	32	24
College of Charleston	17	13	31	27
Virginia Military Institute	16	14	24	28
Davidson	12	17	18	27
East Tennessee State	9	20	15	36
Appalachian State	8	22	14	36
Wofford	7	22	9	40

ALL-CONFERENCE TEAM: C—Matt Lauderdale, Sr., Charleston. **1B**—Chip Cannon, Jr., The Citadel. **2B**—Lee Curtis, Sr., Charleston. **3B**—Chris Ard, So., The Citadel. **SS**—Andy Howdeshell, Jr., East Tennessee State. **OF**—Alan Beck, Sr., Western Carolina; Rod Goldston, Sr., Western Carolina; Brendan Gilligan, Sr., Georgia Southern. **DH**—Ryan Gordon, Jr., UNC Greensboro. **P**—Tom Mastny, Sr., Furman; Jarrett Santos, Jr., UNC Greensboro. **RP**—David Mitchell, Fr., Furman.

Player of the Year: Alan Beck, Western Carolina. **Pitcher of the Year:** Tom Mastny, Furman. **Freshman of the Year:** Kelly Sweppenhiser, Virginia Military. **Coach of the Year:** Tom Slater, Virginia Military.

INDIVIDUAL BATTING LEADERS

(Minimum 125 At-Bats)

	AVG	AB	R	H	2B	3B	HR	RBI	SB
Gordon, Ryan, UNC-G	**.416**	231	50	**96**	20	5	5	50	20
Curtis, Lee, Charleston	.399	233	65	93	**26**	**11**	11	64	20
Ard, Chris, Citadel	.396	225	49	89	11	1	5	44	8
Howdeshell, Andy, ETSU	.354	209	40	74	14	3	10	33	9
Dantzler, Brook, Citadel	.354	212	43	75	14	2	2	39	3
Goldston, Rod, West. Carolina	.348	247	61	86	**26**	1	6	58	9
Burruss, Grant, Ga. Southern	.348	204	44	71	20	0	6	47	4
Casey, Steve, Wofford	.341	176	31	60	11	0	6	25	1
Cannon, Chip, Citadel	.337	205	50	69	15	3	12	60	0
Sarvis, Jason, UNC-G	.333	225	56	75	11	3	4	37	6
Love, Carlos, Ga. Southern	.333	183	40	61	7	0	2	29	2
Davis, Chris, Western Carolina	.331	181	24	60	10	0	1	34	3
Smith, Derek, Appalachian St.	.331	163	27	54	14	0	8	32	0
Kilmer, Wayne, West. Carolina	.329	258	62	85	10	3	3	33	26
Navarro, Sam, Davidson	.329	167	23	55	15	2	2	27	1
Gilligan, Brendan, Ga. Southern	.329	216	49	71	13	3	4	32	12
Payne, James, Ga. Southern	.328	192	41	63	10	4	0	34	18
Saltalamacchia, Justin, UNC-G	.327	217	45	71	14	3	5	48	11
Holloway, Scott, Wofford	.326	184	33	60	15	0	4	16	2
Frankey, Dominic, Furman	.324	213	32	69	16	2	4	46	3
Spivey, Brett, Charleston	.322	208	45	67	11	3	9	45	16
Beck, Alan, Western Carolina	.321	249	**68**	80	15	0	**18**	**71**	15
Thomas, Justin, Appalachian St.	.321	184	29	59	14	1	2	39	3
McLain, Sam, Furman	.320	150	20	48	12	0	3	32	2
Maule, Jay, UNC Greensboro	.318	148	41	47	11	2	9	38	8
Barden, Andy, Virginia Military	.318	148	30	47	5	2	7	30	7
Buchanan, Todd, West. Car.	.317	243	54	77	19	1	12	61	10
Baker, Rocky, Ga. Southern	.315	241	50	76	21	1	4	44	18
Casey, Brian, Wofford	.315	181	28	57	12	0	5	29	0
Long, Brandon, Ga. Southern	.315	143	38	45	12	1	2	31	13
Thomas, Allen, UNC-G	.314	229	61	72	6	1	0	24	23
Nelson, Matt, West. Carolina	.313	166	34	52	15	2	2	28	8
Briggs, Justin, Virginia Military	.312	157	22	49	7	0	5	27	0
#Gardner, Brett, Charleston	.284	215	56	61	9	0	2	29	**28**

INDIVIDUAL PITCHING LEADERS

(Minimum 50 Innings)

	W	L	ERA	G	SV	IP	H	BB	SO
Mastny, Tom, Furman	**11**	2	**1.09**	16	1	124	78	22	103
Gordon, Ryan, UNC Greensboro	4	2	2.59	12	0	59	49	21	55
Hawk, Derrick, Western Carolina	10	2	2.86	28	4	63	51	22	49

	W	L	ERA	G	SV	IP	H	BB	SO
Soale, Matt, Charleston	8	2	2.93	17	1	86	85	23	58
Basner, Ryan, Western Carolina	8	3	2.95	22	0	125	122	28	91
Cannon, Chip, Citadel	3	4	2.95	11	0	55	49	17	38
Hamer, Matt, Citadel	5	1	3.00	27	1	72	70	18	45
Tolbert, Scott, Georgia Southern	7	2	3.03	16	0	68	49	33	60
Stallsmith, Jon, Furman	4	6	3.18	19	2	88	83	22	62
Santos, Jarrett, UNC-G	**11**	5	3.30	41	3	101	90	28	106
McDowell, Brandon, West. Carolina	7	2	3.42	13	0	68	54	28	45
Michael, Scooter, UNC-G	6	5	3.49	17	0	101	112	14	85
Metzger, Jay, UNC Greensboro	8	3	3.58	15	0	75	73	21	63
Egelton, Ken, Citadel	6	3	3.61	16	0	72	76	31	73
Price, Reid, Charleston	6	5	3.66	18	0	96	111	28	75
Falcon, Ryan, UNC Greensboro	3	3	3.69	16	0	54	46	19	52
Carroll, John, Georgia Southern	7	2	3.75	18	1	82	78	20	101
Acors, Duke, Virginia Military	6	5	3.78	15	0	88	74	39	74
Josey, Brad, Western Carolina	7	2	3.81	19	1	104	107	17	62
Hendrix, Phil, Virginia Military	7	4	3.87	15	0	98	115	30	77
Harper, Jeremy, Virginia Military	4	4	4.07	16	0	77	69	36	70
#Mason, Chris, UNC Greensboro	4	2	4.12	30	**8**	59	58	16	63
Dove, Dennis, Georgia Southern	7	2	4.52	17	0	94	84	48	**118**
Ellis, John, Citadel	5	5	4.79	15	0	83	99	19	58

SOUTHLAND CONFERENCE

	Conference W	Conference L	Overall W	Overall L
Lamar	**20**	**6**	**40**	**18**
Southwest Texas State	19	7	30	28
Texas-Arlington	18	9	37	25
Northwestern State	16	11	35	22
Louisiana-Monroe	12	14	29	28
***McNeese State**	12	15	31	30
Texas-San Antonio	12	15	29	27
Sam Houston State	9	18	20	33
Southeastern Louisiana	8	18	18	35
Nicholls State	7	20	22	32

ALL-CONFERENCE TEAM: C—Joey Wolfe, Sr., Louisiana-Monroe. **1B**—Ben Jones, So., Louisiana-Monroe. **2B**—Blake Justice, Sr., Lamar. **3B**—Ryan Roberts, Sr., Texas-Arlington. **SS**—Chuck Hickman, Sr., Nicholls State. **OF**—Josh Boop, Sr., Northwestern State; Jordan Foster, Jr., Lamar; Hunter Pence, So., Texas-Arlington. **DH**—John Allen, Jr., Lamar. **P**—Jesse Floyd, Sr., Lamar; Brandon Hankins, Sr., Southwest Texas State; Matt Overman, Sr., Nicholls State.

Player of the Year: Ryan Roberts, Texas-Arlington. **Pitcher of the Year:** Jesse Floyd, Lamar. **Newcomer of the Year:** Anthony Garibaldi, Southeastern Louisiana. **Freshman of the Year:** Ryan Crew, Texas-San Antonio. **Coach of the Year:** Jim Gilligan, Lamar.

INDIVIDUAL BATTING LEADERS

(Minimum 125 At-Bats)

	AVG	AB	R	H	2B	3B	HR	RBI	SB
Roberts, Ryan, UT-Arlington	**.422**	230	**69**	**97**	21	5	**16**	69	13
Foster, Jordan, Lamar	.417	230	54	96	**29**	1	7	**71**	6
Hickman, Chuck, Nicholls State	.397	229	50	91	13	2	3	34	26
Tano, David, Nicholls State	.378	193	25	73	11	2	1	33	10
Boop, Josh, NW State	.374	227	47	85	21	4	4	45	28
Kasparek, Andrew, Sam Hous.	.368	209	33	77	17	2	12	47	0
Garibaldi, Anthony, SE La.	.366	172	45	63	9	3	15	49	6
Pirkle, Wade, Lamar	.352	165	30	58	14	1	3	40	2
Dantonio, Brad, Nicholls State	.351	205	43	72	14	2	6	45	22
Taylor, Chris, UT-Arlington	.348	250	53	87	18	1	8	56	6
Foster, Brandon, Sam Houston	.348	207	44	72	15	2	1	24	9
Pence, Hunter, UT-Arlington	.347	239	53	83	15	6	8	42	7
Baker, Kasey, UT-Arlington	.344	241	54	83	22	2	3	33	12
Prince, Dooley, McNeese State	.340	241	43	82	11	0	4	32	25
James, Bryan, Nicholls State	.340	197	35	67	15	3	3	50	8
Justice, Blake, Lamar	.340	203	60	69	8	0	0	22	**29**
Garcia, Don, Sam Houston	.340	156	24	53	10	0	5	39	1
Wolfe, Joey, La.-Monroe	.338	207	47	70	18	0	5	41	6
Jones, Ben, La.-Monroe	.333	222	44	74	13	0	9	55	1
Spencer, Jacob, SW Texas	.329	228	32	75	11	2	4	44	3
Chance, Andy, La.-Monroe	.322	171	47	55	10	4	5	35	19
Gray, Jeremy, Lamar	.320	231	53	74	15	1	3	48	10
Larsen, Robert, SE Louisiana	.319	210	43	67	8	0	2	25	7
Ferrell, Lou, Sam Houston	.318	223	46	71	15	**7**	4	50	5
Finan, Ryan, Lamar	.317	205	33	65	12	2	6	34	0
Bruder, Paul, UT-Arlington	.316	152	29	48	13	2	3	32	4
Covert, Cory, SW Texas	.315	149	25	47	5	2	8	35	0
Palermo, Michael, NW State	.315	181	39	57	8	1	0	38	7
Eubanks, Tommy, McNeese St.	.313	252	48	79	14	4	13	55	6
Crew, Ryan, UT-San Antonio	.313	217	37	68	14	2	5	34	4
Preston, Darrell, UT-Arlington	.313	195	46	61	14	0	3	39	3
Mayard, Lenny, SE Louisiana	.312	128	14	40	11	3	0	15	2
#Lyles, Tigger, NW State	.287	160	38	46	10	2	1	31	**29**

INDIVIDUAL PITCHING LEADERS

(Minimum 50 Innings)

	W	L	ERA	G	SV	IP	H	BB	SO
Hankins, Brandon, SW Texas	**8**	1	**2.10**	23	1	94	84	29	82
Robbins, Tom, SW Texas	7	4	2.70	20	1	73	63	15	74
Delage, William, Lamar	5	0	2.82	21	3	51	50	17	35
Dencausse, Josh, NW State	4	2	3.12	17	0	61	51	8	47
Begnaud, Rusty, McNeese State	**8**	4	3.14	21	1	117	114	33	86
Gravis, Aaron, NW State	6	4	3.21	20	3	73	74	22	47
Nolen, Walt, McNeese State	1	3	3.23	28	4	56	68	21	41
Sanches, Zach, NW State	2	4	3.24	23	3	58	64	14	31
Gray, Josh, Lamar	**8**	6	3.42	21	0	92	111	17	59
Floyd, Jesse, Lamar	**8**	2	3.52	15	1	84	84	14	61
Loveless, Pierce, UT-Arlington	5	3	3.74	19	1	55	61	15	35
Marceaux, Jacob, McNeese State	2	4	3.77	17	0	62	74	36	36
McConnell, Caleb, La.-Monroe	**8**	3	3.83	26	3	101	105	29	74
Keener, Cory, NW State	5	2	3.88	15	2	51	46	30	50
Perkins, Michael, NW State	5	2	3.96	12	0	50	59	12	33
Stutes, Kyle, Lamar	3	3	4.07	26	4	55	47	20	65
Boehme, Klae, UT-San Antonio	4	1	4.15	21	2	52	66	15	33
Adkisson, Zach, Sam Houston	2	0	4.18	16	1	71	77	20	41
Pullin, Aaron, UT-Arlington	**8**	2	4.23	18	0	106	119	42	56
Rice, Trey, UT-San Antonio	5	6	4.24	14	0	76	58	40	55
Overman, Matt, Nicholls State	**8**	3	4.27	17	0	110	107	44	**99**
#Stewart, Lucas, UT-San Antonio	5	2	5.08	19	**8**	39	33	20	16

SOUTHWESTERN ATHLETIC CONFERENCE

EAST	Conference W	Conference L	Overall W	Overall L
Mississippi Valley State	22	6	29	29
Jackson State	18	12	20	20
Alcorn State	14	18	20	28
Alabama A&M	13	18	15	32
Alabama State	8	21	11	28
WEST	**W**	**L**	**W**	**L**
***Southern**	31	1	44	7
Texas Southern	19	13	22	30
Grambling State	16	16	22	25
Prairie View A&M	7	23	10	45
Arkansas-Pine Bluff	5	25	12	38

ALL-CONFERENCE TEAM: C—Brian McGinty, Jr., Prairie View. **1B**—Kevin Vital, Sr., Southern. **2B**—Rickie Weeks, Jr., Southern. **3B**—Antoin Gray, Sr., Southern. **SS**—Fernando Puebla, Jr., Southern. **OF**—Joseph Vaughn, Jr., Prairie View; Adrian Brown, Sr., Mississippi Valley State; Andrew Toussaint, So., Southern. **DH**—Nathan Purvis, Jr., Mississippi Valley State. **P**—Dewan Day, Sr., Southern; Aaron Simms, Sr., Alabama A&M; Damien Ursin, Jr., Southern; David Bayless, Fr., Arkansas-Pine Bluff.

Player of the Year: Rickie Weeks, Southern. **Outstanding Pitcher:** Dewan Day, Southern. **Newcomer of the Year:** Andrew Toussaint, Southern. **Freshman of the Year:** Tory Bates, Alcorn State; Jonathan Kohn, Southern.

INDIVIDUAL BATTING LEADERS

(Minimum 100 At-Bats)

	AVG	AB	R	H	2B	3B	HR	RBI	SB
Weeks, Rickie, Southern	**.479**	163	**83**	**78**	12	**7**	**16**	**66**	23
Vaughn, Joseph, Prairie View	.429	119	34	51	17	1	4	20	10
Brown, Adrian, Miss. Valley	.425	167	45	71	9	3	1	32	11
Bruce, Jerry, Ark.-Pine Bluff	.390	105	17	41	7	2	0	20	11
Mouton, Joey, Southern	.389	108	36	42	5	3	6	34	2
Cooper, James, Grambling	.386	158	43	61	15	5	5	33	11
May, Michael, Alabama A&M	.368	133	34	49	7	4	2	23	14
Alexander, Cory, Tx. Southern	.364	118	43	43	8	1	11	35	12
Townsend, Marcus, Southern	.363	157	51	57	13	3	7	45	18
Gray, Antoin, Southern	.356	191	72	68	18	0	6	50	8
Purvis, Nathan, Miss. Valley	.356	188	47	67	10	1	7	43	4
Deleon, Mario, Tx. Southern	.355	107	25	38	8	1	3	32	9
Williams, Kenji, Jackson State	.354	130	42	46	10	**7**	3	37	27
Walton, Thurman, Ark.-Pine Bluff	.352	108	22	38	9	2	1	18	6
Toussaint, Andrew, Southern	.351	168	44	59	10	**7**	7	56	8
Puebla, Fernando, Southern	.351	174	45	61	10	2	2	32	8
Reynolds, Robert, Miss. Valley	.351	188	44	66	12	5	4	45	14
Bilokur, Stephen, Miss. Valley	.350	183	38	64	**22**	1	5	51	4
Murray, Andrew, Grambling	.350	100	23	35	5	0	1	18	7
Galloway, Tim, Alcorn State	.347	101	18	35	10	2	1	15	5
Thomas, Tee, Miss. Valley	.347	199	49	69	10	6	3	38	18
Hebert, Herman, Tx. Southern	.338	145	35	49	9	0	3	30	5
#Willis, Michael, Prairie View	.258	159	50	41	3	0	6	24	**35**

INDIVIDUAL PITCHING LEADERS

(Minimum 40 Innings)

	W	L	ERA	G	SV	IP	H	BB	SO
Sims, Aaron, Alabama A&M	4	2	**1.41**	8	0	51	37	16	44
Day, Dewan, Southern	**9**	0	2.01	12	0	67	51	30	45

	W	L	ERA	G	SV	IP	H	BB	SO
Khon, Jonathan, Southern	5	0	2.77	8	0	42	40	6	27
#Ursin, Damien, Southern	2	1	3.34	29	**5**	35	27	19	41
Johnson, Corey, Alcorn State	5	7	3.95	14	0	82	99	22	55
Bayless, David, Ark.-Pine Bluff	4	8	4.35	18	1	89	90	43	67
Johnson, Anthony, Jackson State	6	4	4.40	12	0	77	61	41	79
Poret, Corey, Southern	8	0	4.18	13	0	60	69	24	56
Floyd, Kori, Jackson State	6	3	4.65	11	0	60	65	45	55
Banks, Kevin, Ark.-Pine Bluff	6	5	5.05	17	0	96	96	63	68
Davis, Vince, Southern	8	2	5.40	14	0	46	48	21	25
Hailey, Josh, Miss. Valley	7	3	5.44	16	0	92	98	20	**93**
McFarland, Kennedy, Grambling	3	7	5.49	11	0	59	71	17	20
Smith, Dan, Alcorn State	2	6	5.74	10	0	51	64	39	34
Liberto, Joseph, Miss. Valley	6	5	5.95	13	1	65	74	24	64
Guerra, Jesus, Texas Southern	5	6	6.02	14	0	73	84	36	43

SUN BELT CONFERENCE

	Conference		Overall	
	W	L	W	L
South Alabama	17	7	42	19
New Mexico State	15	9	43	18
Louisiana-Lafayette	15	9	30	30
Western Kentucky	12	11	34	22
Florida International	12	12	36	23
***Middle Tennessee State**	10	13	33	27
Arkansas-Little Rock	9	14	30	26
Arkansas State	9	14	24	31
New Orleans	7	17	23	32

ALL-CONFERENCE TEAM: C—Rick Guarno, Jr., Arkansas-Little Rock. **1B**—Billy Becher, Jr., New Mexico State. **2B**—Brad Ditter, Jr., New Mexico State. **3B**—Brett Carroll, So., Middle Tennessee State. **SS**—Brett Parker, Sr., South Alabama. **OF**—Corey Coles, Jr., Louisiana-Lafayette; Ryan Mulhern, Sr., South Alabama; Alex Borgo, Sr., New Mexico State. **DH**—Bryan Pullin, Fr., Florida International. **Util**—Chad Cooper, Sr., Middle Tennessee State. **P**—Josh Banks, Jr., Florida International; Jordy Templet, Jr., Louisiana-Lafayette. **RP**—Matt Wilhite, Sr., Western Kentucky.

Player of the Year: Billy Becher, New Mexico State. **Pitcher of the Year:** Matt Wilhite, Sr., Western Kentucky. **Newcomer of the Year:** Billy Becher, New Mexico State. **Freshman of the Year:** Luis Rivera, Florida International. **Coach of the Year:** Steve Kittrell, South Alabama.

INDIVIDUAL BATTING LEADERS

(Minimum 125 At-Bats)

	AVG	AB	R	H	2B	3B	HR	RBI	SB
Becher, Billy, New Mexico State	**.420**	250	76	**105**	16	4	**32**	**118**	0
Ditter, Brad, New Mexico State	.402	244	**84**	98	16	**8**	6	67	14
Nanita, Ricardo, Fla. Int.	.388	196	54	76	14	3	12	52	9
Pietro, Joe, New Orleans	.385	221	45	85	10	3	2	19	15
Cooper, Chad, Mid Tennessee	.374	195	52	73	14	2	7	35	19
Coles, Corey, La.-Lafayette	.371	240	56	89	18	7	9	45	13
Craig, Cole, South Alabama	.371	210	52	78	14	3	6	41	10
Parker, Brett, South Alabama	.365	208	48	76	23	2	4	45	12
Haefele, Aaron, UALR	.362	174	37	63	12	0	2	34	6
Borgo, Alex, New Mexico State	.361	252	77	91	17	4	17	71	8
Trevizo, Gabe, New Orleans	.358	229	41	82	10	3	10	48	2
Lind, Adam, South Alabama	.349	209	50	73	15	2	8	42	1
Guarno, Rick, UALR	.344	209	54	72	**27**	1	5	48	6
Sytko, Kevin, South Alabama	.344	183	51	63	9	1	7	51	11
Rogelstad, Matt, Arkansas State	.341	208	34	71	12	2	8	41	7
Rivera, Luis, Fla. International	.337	246	47	83	15	1	0	41	14
Mulhern, Ryan, South Alabama	.335	230	62	77	19	4	20	67	3
Mercer, Joe, UALR	.335	173	44	58	16	0	5	43	5
Nuckles, Mike, New Orleans	.331	136	20	45	8	1	5	23	0
Carroll, Brett, Mid Tennessee	.330	221	54	73	18	0	19	52	1
Diaz, Dennis, Fla. International	.328	177	36	58	11	1	1	24	**26**
Julo, Chris, UALR	.328	229	52	75	22	0	9	65	7
Shipley, Zach, Arkansas State	.325	166	21	54	11	0	1	27	3
Lopez, Michael, Fla. International	.325	154	39	50	9	0	5	24	7
Pullin, Bryan, Fla. International	.322	149	29	48	8	0	1	23	6
Hayes, Brad, Arkansas State	.321	209	36	67	10	1	8	25	5
Touchstone, Josh, South Alabama	.319	235	62	75	11	1	10	39	3
Jaggers, Nate, Mid Tennessee	.319	182	29	58	15	0	8	37	3
Towns, Antone, Western Ky.	.318	195	31	62	9	1	5	36	5
Pittullo, Clay, UALR	.317	167	51	53	10	4	6	32	11
Touchstone, T.J., South Alabama	.316	215	43	68	11	1	1	31	11
Land, Tim, South Alabama	.314	194	44	61	14	2	9	42	1
Bisnett, Hal, New Mexico State	.309	236	71	73	14	2	9	45	4
Beachum, Jeff, Mid Tennessee	.309	220	34	68	11	2	0	27	2
Jenkins, Keith, New Mexico State	.308	130	33	40	10	1	4	22	1

INDIVIDUAL PITCHING LEADERS

(Minimum 50 Innings)

	W	L	ERA	G	SV	IP	H	BB	SO
Wilhite, Matt, Western Ky.	8	2	**1.78**	37	**11**	76	49	20	64
Garretson, Andrew, New Mex. St.	8	2	2.25	20	3	52	46	13	46
Girardeau, Clark, South Alabama	6	2	2.43	13	0	78	59	46	71
Trammell, Travis, UALR	3	3	3.08	29	9	53	54	17	54
Petty, Jody, Arkansas State	5	6	3.39	17	0	109	124	24	60
DeCarlo, Derek, Fla. International	6	0	3.39	20	4	80	60	33	80
Diamond, Thomas, New Orleans	3	5	3.39	21	5	69	50	42	96
Neiser, Evan, UALR	2	1	3.45	19	2	57	68	14	47
Banks, Joshua, Fla. International	8	3	3.50	17	1	105	95	25	**114**
Neal, Tony, South Alabama	**10**	5	3.62	28	8	99	90	41	100
Martinez, J.P., New Orleans	5	3	3.63	25	3	69	61	32	78
Swing, Chase, Mid Tennessee	2	4	3.68	27	**11**	51	41	20	53
Schambough, Kraig, La.-Lafayette	4	1	3.79	25	4	62	57	16	58
Santos, Arthur, Fla. International	4	7	3.80	18	0	69	79	25	58
Gros, Andy, La.-Lafayette	8	6	3.94	16	0	103	112	23	70
Baldwin, Andy, Western, Kentucky	6	6	3.97	18	0	102	93	44	66
Templet, Jordy, La.-Lafayette	6	5	4.02	16	0	96	93	30	83
Ardoin, Kevin, La.-Lafayette	5	5	4.03	21	3	92	92	21	73
Faircloth, J.C., Western Kentucky	6	3	4.15	15	0	82	86	23	37
Carter, Aaron, UALR	3	4	4.16	16	0	67	70	24	57
Hamilton, Ryan, Arkansas State	3	4	4.18	30	2	56	57	29	65
Cromer, Bennett, UALR	6	3	4.28	17	0	76	76	42	79
Vertz, Karnie, Arkansas State	4	8	4.42	18	0	100	106	19	59
Church, B.J., Mid Tennessee	4	1	4.58	13	1	55	50	23	58

WEST COAST CONFERENCE

	Conference		Overall	
WEST	W	L	W	L
***San Diego**	**18**	**12**	**32**	**30**
San Francisco	17	13	25	31
Loyola Marymount	13	17	26	30
Portland	5	24	9	45
COAST	W	L	W	L
Pepperdine	**23**	**7**	**36**	**25**
Santa Clara	21	9	31	26
Gonzaga	14	16	26	25
Saint Mary's	8	21	18	37

ALL-CONFERENCE TEAM: C—Jon Higashi, Jr., Loyola Marymount. **1B**—Gordon Corder, Jr., Gonzaga. **2B**—David Uribes, Fr., Pepperdine. **3B**—Bryan Byrne, Fr., Saint Mary's. **SS**—Kevin Estrada, Sr., Pepperdine. **OF**—Scott Dierks, Sr., Santa Clara; Josh Hansen, Jr., San Diego; Joey Prast, Jr., San Diego. **DH**—Ryan Sittauer, Sr., San Francisco. **Util**—Tony Perez, Sr., San Diego. **P**—Jacob Barrack, Jr., Pepperdine; Joe Diefenderfer, Sr., Santa Clara; Greg Ramirez, Sr., Pepperdine.

Co-Players of the Year: Scott Dierks, Santa Clara; Kevin Estrada, Pepperdine. **Pitcher of the Year:** Greg Ramirez, Pepperdine. **Freshman of the Year:** Bryan Byrne, Saint Mary's. **Coach of the Year:** Frank Sanchez, Pepperdine.

INDIVIDUAL BATTING LEADERS

(Minimum 125 At-Bats)

	AVG	AB	R	H	2B	3B	HR	RBI	SB
Dierks, Scott, Santa Clara	**.394**	170	45	67	14	0	**18**	42	1
Corder, Gordon, Gonzaga	.382	217	50	83	22	0	14	**57**	3
Byrne, Bryan, Saint Mary's	.358	218	42	78	15	2	5	46	2
Perez, Tony, San Diego	.356	233	**66**	83	11	1	7	35	6
Higashi, Jon, LMU	.349	209	39	73	7	1	0	40	13
Sittauer, Ryan, San Francisco	.349	152	31	53	13	2	1	28	2
Prast, Joey, San Diego	.346	260	60	**90**	**26**	1	12	**57**	15
Whitesell, Josh, LMU	.340	162	40	55	19	0	15	47	1
Evans, Danny, Gonzaga	.339	168	29	57	6	0	4	23	3
Casto, Kory, Portland	.338	195	42	66	18	0	13	55	2
Kelly, Chris, Pepperdine	.336	247	42	83	23	1	15	54	2
Thompson, Will, Santa Clara	.335	167	33	56	15	2	11	31	1
Conte, Nick, Saint Mary's	.335	167	20	56	13	1	3	36	0
Headley, Jack, Santa Clara	.335	218	39	73	17	3	3	30	19
Lockin, Billy, LMU	.333	231	44	77	14	1	2	31	19
Uribes, David, Pepperdine	.330	230	45	76	11	1	2	28	7
Culpepper, Jeff, Gonzaga	.330	200	26	66	13	3	1	40	7
Frazee, Joe, Loyola Marymount	.330	197	38	65	11	**4**	1	30	11
Hanson, Ryan, San Francisco	.329	170	19	56	7	0	2	31	1
Pettit, Chris, Loyola Marymount	.328	189	36	62	18	2	2	29	17
Estrada, Kevin, Pepperdine	.327	269	53	88	16	2	4	30	**35**
Harper, Ty, Pepperdine	.326	129	22	42	5	1	1	21	3
Gaerlan, Armand, San Francisco	.325	157	34	51	7	3	8	34	2
Sandoval, Freddy, San Diego	.319	216	38	69	20	2	9	41	7
#Stoeber, Carl, Loyola Marymount	.275	160	23	44	6	**4**	1	30	5
#Sansoe, Mike, Saint Mary's	.273	132	25	36	4	**4**	1	10	8
#Tarbat, Nick, San Francisco	.270	174	40	47	8	**4**	3	18	11

INDIVIDUAL PITCHING LEADERS

(Minimum 50 Innings)

	W	L	ERA	G	SV	IP	H	BB	SO
Boesch, Brandon, Pepperdine	7	5	**2.83**	16	0	99	105	35	55
Ramirez, Greg, Pepperdine	**9**	3	2.88	16	0	**122**	117	26	**98**

	W	L	ERA	G	SV	IP	H	BB	SO
Dworkis, Eric, Gonzaga	8	5	2.88	16	1	91	91	34	81
McConnell, Kellan, Santa Clara	4	4	3.18	14	0	51	45	17	46
Diefenderfer, Joe, Santa Clara	8	3	3.40	17	0	87	94	12	69
Annis, Kevin, San Francisco	7	3	3.41	19	2	69	57	29	62
Barrack, Jacob, Pepperdine	**9**	3	3.44	16	0	99	110	37	82
Clelland, Ed, Gonzaga	4	5	3.51	16	2	90	90	24	58
Collins, Kyle, San Diego	**9**	5	3.61	16	0	102	98	43	73
Huddy, Kyle, Loyola Marymount	5	6	3.81	22	4	90	83	42	84
Fillinger, Chad, Santa Clara	2	0	4.08	25	0	53	50	19	49
Cordova, Vince, Loyola Marymount	6	6	4.21	15	0	98	135	22	81
Wilson, Aaron, San Diego	6	6	4.30	17	0	88	117	34	53
Muecke, Josh, Loyola Marymount	3	3	4.38	26	2	62	59	38	64
#Perez, Tony, San Diego	2	5	4.50	30	**13**	48	44	13	41
Blaine, Justin, San Diego	4	5	4.64	21	0	76	85	46	52
Travis, Matt, Santa Clara	5	7	4.89	17	0	99	117	22	58
Abreu, Justin, Loyola Marymount	5	4	5.04	15	0	91	111	32	42
Williams, Bryan, San Francisco	5	5	5.42	17	2	98	115	27	39
Bowden, Eric, Saint Mary's	7	8	5.52	17	0	106	144	21	74

WESTERN ATHLETIC CONFERENCE

	Conference		Overall	
	W	L	W	L
***Rice**	**25**	**5**	**58**	**12**
Nevada	19	10	32	24
Fresno State	14	16	30	29
Hawaii	11	19	30	26
San Jose State	10	19	25	32
Louisiana Tech	10	20	18	34

ALL-CONFERENCE TEAM: C—Brett Hayes, Fr., Nevada. **1B**—Vincent Sinisi, So., Rice. **2B**—Enrique Cruz, Jr., Rice. **3B**—Kevin Kouzmanoff, Sr., Nevada. **SS**—Chris Patrick, Jr., Fresno State. **OF**—Scott Beshears, Sr., Fresno State; Austin Davis, Jr, Rice; Chris Gimenez, So., Nevada; Jeff Jorgensen, Jr., Rice; Chris Kolkhorst, Jr., Rice. **DH**—Dane Bubela, Sr., Rice. **Util**—Brent Cook, Sr., Hawaii. **P**—Matt Durkin, So., San Jose State; Philip Humber, So., Rice; Jeff Niemann, So., Rice. **RP**— Wade Townsend, So., Rice.

Player of the Year: Kevin Kouzmanoff, Nevada. **Pitcher of the Year:** Jeff Niemann, Rice. **Freshman of the Year:** Brett Hayes, Nevada. **Co-Coaches of the Year:** Wayne Graham, Rice; Gary Powers, Nevada.

INDIVIDUAL BATTING LEADERS

(Minimum 125 At-Bats)

	AVG	AB	R	H	2B	3B	HR	RBI	SB
Butler, Jacob, Nevada	**.367**	147	26	54	11	2	9	37	3
Hayes, Brett, Nevada	.365	233	48	85	16	2	8	63	8
Kouzmanoff, Kevin, Nevada	.361	233	55	84	12	0	**17**	**67**	3
Cruz, Enrique, Rice	.352	247	55	87	18	2	10	57	6
Beshears, Scott, Fresno State	.351	188	32	66	12	0	9	38	6
Kolkhorst, Chris, Rice	.351	265	**77**	93	16	**4**	3	47	8
McGehee, Casey, Fresno State	.346	234	37	81	14	0	3	32	5
Davis, Austin, Rice	.344	262	63	90	**24**	1	6	63	8
Gimenez, Chris, Nevada	.340	156	37	53	9	2	12	44	2
Sinisi, Vincent, Rice	.338	287	61	**97**	15	1	10	59	11
Frandsen, Kevin, San Jose State	.332	220	40	73	15	0	4	30	5
Robinson, Wade, La. Tech	.332	205	30	68	13	3	2	28	8
Strain, Ryan, Nevada	.328	137	32	45	7	0	1	17	5
Streelman, Erick, Nevada	.325	191	44	62	8	0	8	31	6
Jorgensen, Jeff, Rice	.314	242	42	76	8	2	0	30	18
Bergstrom, Jordan, San Jose St.	.313	179	27	56	16	1	3	33	0
Stansberry, Craig, Rice	.309	272	49	84	12	2	6	56	7
Bubela, Dane, Rice	.302	212	58	64	15	1	7	41	7
Marcial, Robert, Nevada	.299	177	35	53	7	0	1	20	8
Omura, Isaac, Hawaii	.297	158	20	47	10	2	1	28	2
Bates, Aaron, San Jose State	.297	145	17	43	8	0	2	23	1
Janish, Paul, Rice	.294	262	42	77	14	0	4	43	4
Cook, Brent, Hawaii	.288	208	41	60	9	**4**	4	32	14
#Allen, Fairon, La. Tech	.255	141	35	36	10	2	2	14	**19**

INDIVIDUAL PITCHING LEADERS

(Minimum 50 Innings)

	W	L	ERA	G	SV	IP	H	BB	SO
Niemann, Jeff, Rice	**17**	0	**1.70**	22	1	137	96	35	156
Townsend, Wade, Rice	11	2	2.20	29	5	119	80	46	**164**
Durkin, Matt, San Jose State	7	6	2.60	16	1	100	75	42	110
Aardsma, David, Rice	7	3	2.97	40	**12**	57	47	19	46
Bauer, Ricky, Hawaii	3	5	3.12	15	0	84	96	7	47
Baker, Josh, Rice	8	0	3.22	19	0	95	89	29	71
Humber, Philip, Rice	11	3	3.30	18	0	128	102	39	138
Lockwood, Jon, La. Tech	4	3	3.79	17	1	78	73	26	81
Wolfenbarger, Bryan, Fresno State	5	3	4.24	30	7	51	54	16	54
Smith, Cody, Fresno State	8	5	4.26	18	0	101	115	24	52
Rawlins, Keahi, Hawaii	5	5	4.27	16	0	65	55	34	45
Winck, Matthew, San Jose State	1	3	4.61	21	1	55	60	16	33
George, Chris, Hawaii	8	6	4.80	15	0	96	99	34	89
Cayetano, Justin, Hawaii	2	2	4.83	18	0	60	83	22	50
Varner, Matt, La. Tech	3	7	4.83	18	2	60	66	30	43
Esposito, Frank, San Jose State	2	4	4.89	16	0	85	119	17	63
Miramontes, Mateo, Nevada	9	5	4.97	17	0	100	100	56	79
Sherman, Justin, Nevada	8	5	5.11	17	0	111	136	21	79
Glynn, Josh, Fresno State	3	6	5.30	21	1	71	86	23	37
Bonine, Eddie, Nevada	5	6	5.84	17	0	91	115	30	79

INDEPENDENTS

	Overall	
	W	L
Miami	45	17
Savannah State	34	15
Texas A&M-Corpus Christi	33	17
#Birmingham-Southern	33	18
Cal State Sacramento	33	24
Centenary	23	33
Texas-Pan American	21	33
Indiana-Purdue-Fort Wayne	17	33
#Lipscomb	16	31
New York Tech	15	32
Hawaii-Hilo	9	38
Pace	9	39

#Provisional NCAA Division I in 2003

INDIVIDUAL BATTING LEADERS

(Minimum 125 At-Bats)

	AVG	AB	R	H	2B	3B	HR	RBI	SB
Landin, Jaime, TAM-CC	.421	202	62	85	9	9	2	41	8
Olsen, Mikela, CS Sacramento	.404	218	50	88	20	2	16	66	2
Aguilar, Humberto, TAM-CC	.402	179	43	72	12	0	20	74	2
Schmidt, Jesse, CS Sacramento	.389	208	53	81	9	0	16	55	16
Robertson, Connor, BSU	.389	157	37	61	9	0	11	52	1
Alamia, Louie, Texas-Pan Am	.382	178	37	68	15	3	1	26	15
Garanzuay, Hector, TAMU-CC	.379	190	60	72	14	3	4	39	2
Cline, Michael, Birm-South.	.379	190	52	72	16	2	6	50	24
Hooft, Joey, Miami	.373	126	26	47	8	2	4	28	10
Beale, Patrick, Centenary	.371	205	54	76	19	1	4	24	20
Parker, Chris, Lipscomb	.367	166	24	61	10	0	1	24	13
Braun, Ryan, Miami	.364	242	61	88	16	3	17	76	13
Cardone, Tony, Centenary	.347	199	39	69	7	1	0	35	6
Schlekewy, Mike, TAM-CC	.347	176	58	61	13	4	11	53	16
Cleveland, Clay, Savannah State	.346	162	53	56	15	1	8	53	18
Lonnon, Thomas, Sav. State	.345	139	42	48	4	1	0	31	12
Jolley, Patrick, Centenary	.344	128	26	44	12	4	7	35	2
Remer, Doug, Savannah State	.342	146	45	50	14	0	6	42	16
Urgelles, Jeffrey, Sav. State	.340	153	49	52	14	3	8	53	3
Ortiz, Tony, Texas-Pan Am	.336	211	40	71	18	5	0	37	7
Garza, Marco, Texas-Pan Am	.336	220	43	74	16	6	4	48	11
Armstrong, Brandon, IPFW	.333	150	26	50	12	0	4	22	1
McCorkle, Nathan, Lipscomb	.331	157	25	52	13	1	2	32	10
Sanchez, Gaby, Miami	.328	244	63	80	21	1	7	56	7
Ricks, Adam, Miami	.328	232	50	76	13	1	4	55	5
Figueroa, Danny, Miami	.325	237	74	77	6	2	3	28	40
Barton, Brian, Miami	.325	212	52	69	17	3	7	53	17
Blanco, Rafael, Savannah State	.325	151	40	49	17	4	2	27	10
Acha, John, CS Sacramento	.322	177	34	57	9	3	2	24	6
Griffith, Ryan, Birm-Southern	.322	180	31	58	13	0	11	42	1

INDIVIDUAL PITCHING LEADERS

(Minimum 50 Innings)

	W	L	ERA	G	SV	IP	H	BB	SO
Cockroft, J.D., Miami	11	3	2.72	22	1	119	116	35	94
Walker, Scott, TAM-CC	7	5	2.88	15	1	75	66	28	55
Markyna, Carlos, Savannah State	6	2	2.96	12	1	55	58	18	39
Valdes-Fauli, Shawn, Miami	5	0	3.02	36	5	54	52	19	56
Griffith, Derek, Birm.-Southern	7	3	3.09	11	0	67	57	20	70
Britnell, Josh, Birm.-Southern	6	1	3.10	16	1	52	39	28	38
Karkoulas, Andrew, NY Tech	5	6	3.12	12	0	75	77	33	50
Letson, Wes, Birmingham-Southern	6	3	3.91	14	0	69	66	30	63
Bongiovanni, Vince, Miami	8	4	4.00	14	0	72	71	34	69
Plouffe, Marshall, CS Sacramento	6	3	4.01	16	0	76	83	21	51
Hamon, Jimmy, TAM-CC	9	2	4.06	16	0	100	90	46	107
Cassidy, Kevin, Centenary	7	5	4.12	15	0	87	91	19	81
Martanovic, Eric, TAM-CC	4	1	4.24	14	1	57	64	18	43
Kinsey, Chris, CS Sacramento	7	6	4.25	21	3	95	85	30	98
Ayre, David, Lipscomb	3	3	4.40	14	0	57	67	21	25
Marshall, Kellen, IPFW	4	4	4.43	13	0	63	75	26	61
Crew, John, Birmingham-Southern	2	2	4.47	18	2	52	47	13	39
Castillo, Ricardo, CS Sacramento	9	4	4.70	14	0	84	81	29	67
Garcia, Angel, CS Sacramento	6	3	4.70	10	0	54	65	17	32
Ruffing, David, Centenary	3	6	4.81	15	0	67	70	17	56

Mules trot to second Division II title

13 and counting
Lewis-Clark State claims another NAIA World Series crown

NCAA DIVISION II

Central Missouri State completed an unbeaten run through the bracket with an 11-4 victory over Tampa in the title game, earning its second national championship and first since 1994 at the NCAA Division II World Series in Montgomery, Ala.

Down 4-3 in the fifth inning against a Tampa squad that also advanced to the title game without a loss, the Mules (51-7) rallied with eight unanswered runs to break open a nail-biter. The barrage was led by third baseman Zach Norman, who launched a three-run homer in the eighth, and outfielder Danny Guidry, who went 2-for-4 with two runs scored and three RBIs. Both were named to the all-tournament team.

Tampa outfielder Jay Hyland had a two-run home run in the losing cause, finishing off a stellar week that earned him most outstanding player honors. Hyland went 9-for-20 with three homeruns and 13 RBIs in the tournament.

After leading his team to a championship season, Central Missouri coach Brad Hill left to take the head coaching job at Kansas State.

■ Chuck Anderson, who compiled an 843-251 record in 19 years as coach at Florida Southern before being forced to retire in 2002, died in 2003 after a long battle with colon and liver cancer. Anderson led the Moccasins to Division II titles in 1985, 1988 and 1995.

FINAL POLL

NCAA Division II

1.	Central Missouri State	51-7
2.	Tampa	45-18
3.	Kennesaw State (Ga.)	40-18
4.	Delta State (Miss.)	51-10
5.	North Florida	39-18
6.	Florida Southern	44-13
7.	Franklin Pierce (N.H.)	32-17
8.	Abilene Christian (Texas)	45-20
9.	Armstrong Atlantic (Ga.)	36-15
10.	Central Oklahoma	44-13

Chapman: Back With A Vengeance

NCAA DIVISION III

Chapman (Calif.) fought back through the loser's bracket in a big way, routing previously unbeaten Christopher Newport (Va.) twice on the final day to surge to its first Division III national championship in Appleton, Wis. Chapman also won a title in 1968, but the team competed in Division II at the time.

By defeating Christopher Newport 15-2 in the first game and 15-7 in the clincher, the Panthers earned revenge. After winning its opening-round game, Chapman was knocked into the loser's bracket when it lost to Christopher Newport, 6-4. The Panthers recovered to post four consecutive victories, the final two in convincing fashion.

In bashing 40 combined hits on the final day, Chapman received contributions from up and down the lineup. Outfielder Shaun Donahue went 7-for-11 on the day, with five runs scored and four RBIs, while shortstop Brian Sanders posted six hits in 10 at-bats, scored three runs, and knocked in five.

The tournament's most outstanding player award went to Chapman second baseman Alex Taylor, who finished off a strong tournament by going 5-for-11 on the final day with three runs scored and four RBIs.

■ Salve Regina (R.I.) outfielder Damian Constantino set an NCAA record with a 60-game hitting streak, breaking Robin Ventura's 16-year-old mark set in 1987. Constantino, 24, set the record over parts of three seasons after his career was delayed by a stint in the army.

■ Texas Lutheran opened the 2003 season by winning its first 26 games to extend its streak over a two-year period to 31. But the Bulldogs, 37-6 on the season, didn't even qualify for post-season play.

FINAL POLL

NCAA Division III

1.	Chapman (Calif.)	39-12
2.	Christopher Newport (Va.)	35-9
3.	Eastern Connecticut State	43-9
4.	Anderson (Ind.)	35-16
5.	Wisconsin-Oshkosh	37-8
	Emory (Ga.)	37-15
7.	Trinity (Conn.)	27-12
8.	DeSales (Pa.)	30-13
9.	Cortland State (N.Y.)	35-11
10.	Carthage (Wis.)	35-8

Warriors Triumph Again

NAIA

Host Lewis-Clark State continued its dominance of NAIA baseball by winning its 13th national championship, the school's second consecutive title and fourth in five years. In a rematch of the 2002 title game, the Warriors defeated Oklahoma City twice on the final day, 6-5 and 7-5, to atone for a loss to the Stars earlier in the tournament. It marked the second consecutive year that Lewis-Clark defeated Oklahoma City twice on the tournament's final day.

Warriors righthander Marc Kaiser went the distance in the title game, earning both the victory and the tournament's MVP award. He finished the series 2-0, 3.93 with 21 strikeouts in 18 innings. The former Arizona pitcher was drafted in the 10th round by the Rockies.

■ Ripon's Gordie Gillespie coached his 50th year and extended his record for coaching wins to 1,630-830 by guiding his team to a 32-6 record. Gillespie led teams to four NAIA titles in previous coaching stints at Lewis (Ill.) and St. Francis (Ill.).

■ Spalding (Ky.) senior third baseman Jake Ford set an NAIA record by hitting five home runs in an 18-4 win against Tennessee Wesleyan in a regional tournament game. Ford went 6-for-6 with 11 RBIs. The previous NAIA record for homers in a game was four, held by 15 players.

First Time's The Charm

In its first appearance in the National Christian College Athletic Association national championship, Dallas Baptist hung on for a 4-3 over three-time champion and No. 1 seed Spring Arbor (Mich.) in the deciding game in Celina, Ohio. Tournament MVP Drew Holder, a freshman, preserved the win by making a diving catch of a sinking fly ball and gunning out the potential tying run at the plate.

NCCAA

Southern Nevada Wins Crown

After losing its opening game, the Community College of Southern Nevada bounced back with five consecutive victories at the Junior College World Series in Grand Junction, Colo., completing a championship run in only the team's fourth year of existence. The Coyotes defeated No. 1-ranked San Jacinto (Texas) 4-1 in the final.

JUNIOR COLLEGE

Josh Bolingbroke gave the Coyotes all the offense they needed when he crushed a three-run home run in the third inning. Freshman lefthander Tyler Coon took care of the rest, limiting San Jacinto to seven hits and one run and striking out nine in his complete game victory. Coon's Herculean effort, in which he threw 148 pitches, earned him most outstanding player honors.

San Jac's Clint Goocher, who started against Coon in the final, was named tournament's outstanding pitcher. He pitched three complete games, going the distance in the final game on two days rest. He won two previous outings.

■ Tournament MVP Justin McKenzie had three hits as Grand Rapids (Mich.) rallied from an opening-round loss to win six straight games and capture the Division II JUCO title, played in Millington, Tenn. The Raiders beat Iowa Central 9-2 in the final, pounding out 19 hits.

PLAYERS OF THE YEAR

Matt DeSalvo

Nick Markakis

Small College: Matt DeSalvo, rhp, Marietta (Ohio)

DeSalvo closed out a spectacular five-year career (including one red shirt season) at Division III power Marietta by setting NCAA records for career wins (53) and strikeouts (603). As a senior, he went 13-2, 1.31 with a national-best 157 strikeouts in 96 innings. DeSalvo signed with the New York Yankees as a free agent prior to the 2003 draft.

Junior College: Nick Markakis, lhp-of, Young Harris (Ga.) JC

Markakis was honored for the second year in a row as he enjoyed one of the greatest two-way seasons in junior college history. He led the country in RBIs (92) and strikeouts (160), while hitting .439 with 21 homers and going 12-0, 1.68. He elevated his stock from a 23rd-round pick in 2002 to the seventh overall selection in the 2003 draft.

■ Richland (Texas) won the Division III JUCO title for the second year in a row, going undefeated in an eight-team tournament, played in Batavia, N.Y. The Thunderducks beat Gloucester County (N.J.) 7-0 in the final, with Ryan Dreibelbis throwing a complete-game, four-hitter. Dreibelbis (13-3 on the season) was named the tournament MVP. Demarcus Coats homered in the deciding game, his fourth of the tournament.

■ Tournament co-MVP Felipe Garcia hit two home runs and pitcher Justin Keadle tossed a complete game with eight strikeouts, leading Cypress College to a 13-3 victory over Saddleback in the 2003 California Community College Baseball Championship title game. Cypress won three straight games, outscoring its opponents 42-5. Garcia went 8-for-12 with two doubles, two homers and six RBIs.

COLLEGE BASEBALL

SMALL COLLEGE ALL-AMERICA TEAM 2003

Selected by Baseball America

POS	Player, College	Division	YR	AVG	AB	R	H	2B	3B	HR	RBI	SB	Drafted
C	Matt Houston, Oklahoma City	NAIA	Jr.	.451	204	16	92	20	1	14	60	0	Orioles (11)
1B	Chad Fox, SE Oklahoma State	Division II	Sr.	.421	171	66	72	22	3	17	65	5	Not drafted
2B	Ben Zobrist, Olivet Nazarene (Ill.)	NAIA	Jr.	.409	186	65	76	13	5	10	65	12	Not drafted
3B	Jake Ford, Spalding, Ky.	NAIA	Sr.	.436	259	82	113	26	0	31	110	12	Tigers (21)
SS	Mike Aviles, Concordia, N.Y.	Division II	Sr.	.500	190	83	95	20	6	22	65	6	Royals (7)
OF	Vince Mancuso, Wisc.-Oshkosh	Division III	Sr.	.465	155	67	72	13	4	17	70	5	Not drafted
OF	Jerry Owens, The Master's	NAIA	Jr.	.451	184	73	83	11	6	6	31	30	Expos (2)
OF	Ben Himes, Oklahoma City	NAIA	So.	.392	194	65	76	16	3	23	59	17	Reds (9)
DH	Jose Cortez, Pomona-Pitzer	Division III	Sr.	.446	130	62	58	10	0	18	59	0	Phillies (14)
UT	Greg Kloosterman, Bethel	NAIA	Jr.	.423	156	44	66	12	2	15	49	4	Brewers (9)

POS	Player, College	Division	YR	W	L	ERA	G	SV	IP	H	BB	SO	Drafted
SP	Brandon DeJaynes, Quincy (Ill.)	Division II	Sr.	10	1	0.71	15	2	88	39	22	126	Cardinals FA
SP	Matt Weagle, Franklin Pierce	Division II	Jr.	9	2	1.99	13	0	100	70	19	103	Cardinals (6)
SP	Eric Beattie, Tampa	Division II	So.	15	3	2.55	20	0	134	124	23	105	Not eligible
SP	Matt DeSalvo, Marietta, Ohio	Division III	Sr.	13	2	1.31	18	1	96	46	40	157	Yankees FA
SP	Ryan France, Chapman, Calif.	Division III	Sr.	10	1	1.38	16	0	111	73	24	100	A's (17)
UT	Greg Kloosterman, Bethel	NAIA	Jr.	7	2	2.61	12	0	62	52	23	74	

SMALL COLLEGES

NCAA DIVISION II

WORLD SERIES

Site: Montgomery, Ala.

Participants: Franklin Pierce, N.H. (30-15); Slippery Rock, Pa. (48-11); Central Missouri State (47-7); Grand Valley State, Mich. (40-12); Kennesaw State, Ga. (38-16); UC Davis (35-22); Tampa, Fla. (42-17); Abilene Christian, Texas (45-18).

Champion: Central Missouri State (4-0). **Runner-Up**: Tampa (3-1).

Outstanding Player: Jay Hyland, of, Tampa.

DIVISION II ALL-AMERICA TEAM

Pos.	Player, School	Yr.	AVG	HR	RBI
C	Joey Rieman, Grand Canyon (Ariz.)	Sr.	.395	6	48
1B	Chad Fox, Southeastern Oklahoma State	Sr.	.421	17	65
2B	Brad Church, Mount Olive (N.C.)	Sr.	.429	5	54
3B	Ben Tinius, Fort Hays State (Kan.)	Sr.	.396	19	77
SS	Mike Aviles, Concordia (N.Y.)	Sr.	.500	22	65
IF	Guy O'Connell, Tusculum (Tenn.)	Jr.	.403	21	67
OF	Ashley Farr, South Carolina-Aiken	So.	.483	10	64
	Tim Battaglia, Minnesota-Duluth	Jr.	.455	15	65
	Jeff Millsaps, North Florida	Jr.	.401	5	47
	Jud Thigpen, Delta State (Miss.)	Jr.	.379	15	76
DH	Tracy Geffre, Southern Arkansas	Sr.	.385	18	50

		Yr.	W	L	ERA
SP	Brandon DeJaynes, Quincy (Ill.)	Sr.	10	1	0.71
	Matt Weagle, Franklin Pierce (N.H.)	Jr.	9	2	1.99
	Jon Dobyns, Armsrong Atlantic (Ga.)	Jr.	12	2	3.07
	Eric Beattie, Tampa	So.	15	3	2.55
RP	Jeremy Noegel, West Florida (10 SV)	Sr.	3	3	1.72

Player of the Year: Mike Aviles, Concordia. **Pitcher of the Year**: Brandon DeJaynes, Quincy.

NATIONAL LEADERS

BATTING AVERAGE
(Minimum 100 At-Bats)

Player, School	Yr.	AB	H	AVG
Mike Aviles, Concordia (N.Y.)	Sr.	190	95	.500
T.J. Shimizu, Salem International	Jr.	144	72	.500
Ashley Farr, South Carolina-Aiken	So.	207	100	.483
Greg Annino, C.W. Post (N.Y.)	Sr.	135	65	.481
Brian Foy, Wayne State (Neb.)	Sr.	143	68	.476
Milton Redd, Shaw (N.C.)	Sr.	121	56	.463
Hasani Whitfield, Caldwell	So.	119	55	.462
William Sanders, Shaw (N.C.)	So.	120	55	.458
Tim Battaglia, Minnesota-Duluth	Jr.	156	71	.455
Joe Cantone, New Haven (Conn.)	Jr.	156	71	.455
Mike Spry, Shepherd (W.Va.)	Sr.	151	68	.450
John Rogers, Central Oklahoma	Sr.	163	73	.448
Ryan White, Arkansas Tech	So.	168	75	.446
Shane Roberts, Northern Colorado	Jr.	208	92	.442

Department Leaders: Batting

Dept.	Player, School	Yr.	G	Total
R	Mike Aviles, Concordia (N.Y.)	Sr.	45	83
H	Ashley Farr, South Carolina-Aiken	So.	54	100
TB	Mike Aviles, Concordia (N.Y.)	Sr.	45	193
2B	Barrett Whitney, Central Oklahoma	Sr.	57	32
3B	Four tied at 9			
HR	Mike Aviles, Concordia (N.Y.)	Sr.	45	22
RBI	Zach Norman, Central Missouri	Jr.	56	87
SB	Clint Keown, South Carolina-Aiken	Sr.	53	52
BB	Trevor Allen, Northern Colorado	Jr.	55	50

EARNED RUN AVERAGE
(Minimum 50 Innings)

Player, School	Yr.	IP	ER	ERA
Brandon DeJaynes, Quincy (Ill.)	Sr.	88	7	0.71
Anthony Zambotti, Indiana (Pa.)	Sr.	64	8	1.12
Mike Sikorski, Slippery Rock (Pa.)	Sr.	77	13	1.51
Tony Watkins, Columbia Union (Md.)	Sr.	67	12	1.61
Billy Sittig, Stonehill (Mass.)	Fr.	52	10	1.72
Chris Wright, St. Rose (N.Y.)	Sr.	57	11	1.73
Matthew Vanfleet, Florida Tech	So.	65	13	1.79
Steve Norris, Slippery Rock (Pa.)	Jr.	75	15	1.81
Juston Olson, Western Oregon	Sr.	59	12	1.83
Greg Tucker, Pfeiffer (N.C.)	So.	63	13	1.86

Department Leaders: Pitching

Dept.	Player, School	Yr.	G	Total
W	Eric Beattie, Tampa	So.	20	15
SV	Don Clement, Colo. State-Pueblo	Jr.	28	13
SO	Tyrell Moore, Albany State (Ga.)	So.	15	126
	Brandon DeJaynes, Quincy (Ill.)	Sr.	15	126

NCAA DIVISION III

WORLD SERIES

Site: Appleton, Wis.

Participants: Eastern Connecticut State (41-7); DeSales, Pa. (30-12); Emory, Ga (36-13); Anderson, Ind. (33-14); Trinity, Conn. (27-10); Christopher Newport, Va. (31-7); Wisconsin-Oshkosh (36-6); Chapman, Calif. (34-11).

Champion: Chapman (5-1). **Runner-Up**: Christopher Newport (4-2).

Outstanding Player: Alex Taylor, 2b, Chapman.

DIVISION III ALL-AMERICA TEAM

Pos.	Player, Team	YR	AVG	HR	RBI
C	Jose Cortez, Pomona-Pitzer (Calif.)	Sr.	.446	18	59
1B	Eric Bell, Georgia Fox (Ore.)	Sr.	.390	17	61
2B	Kurt Piantek, Trinity (Conn.)	Sr.	.514	18	62
3B	Jacob Frank, Wooster (Ohio)	So.	.434	6	45
SS	Chad Cambra, Bridgewater State (Mass.)	Sr.	.483	5	52
	Ian Hauze, DeSales (Pa.)	So.	.418	7	51
OF	Vince Mancuso, Wisconsin-Oshkosh	Sr.	.465	17	70
	Matt Turner, Christopher Newport (Va.)	Sr.	.371	15	59
	Jeremy Elliot, Christopher Newport (Va.)	Sr.	.402	2	22
UT	Tyler Mott, Ohio Wesleyan	Jr.	.408	8	57
	Nick Johnson, Ripon (Wis.)	Sr.	.545	14	63

			W	L	ERA
SP	Matt DeSalvo, Marietta (Ohio)	Sr.	13	2	1.31
	Jordan Timm, Wisconsin-Oshkosh	Jr.	11	0	2.09
	Ryan France, Chapman (Calif.)	Sr.	10	1	1.38
	Dan Grybash, Carthage (Wis.)	Jr.	8	0	1.27
UT	Tyler Mott, Ohio Wesleyan	Jr.	12	1	2.07
	Nick Johnson, Ripon (Wis.)	Sr.	8	1	3.25

Player of the Year: Vince Mancuso, Wisconsin-Oshkosh.

NATIONAL LEADERS

BATTING AVERAGE
(Minimum 100 At-Bats)

Player, School	Yr.	AB	H	AVG
Nick Johnson, Ripon (Wis.)	Sr.	145	79	.545
Miguel Jaquez, John Jay (N.Y.)	So.	124	66	.532
Kurt Piantek, Trinity (Conn.)	Sr.	138	71	.514
Mark Roth, Delaware Valley (Pa.)	Jr.	111	56	.505
Adam Best, Penn State-Behrend	Jr.	144	71	.493
Luke Wilson, Fontbonne (Mo.)	Jr.	123	60	.488
Matt Moore, Rose-Hulman (Ind.)	Jr.	130	63	.485
Chad Cambra, Bridgewater State (Mass.)	Sr.	151	73	.483
Adam Mandel, Denison (Ohio)	Jr.	152	72	.474
Jeremy Collins, East Texas Baptist	Sr.	138	65	.471
Pat Marsh, Augsburg (Minn.)	Sr.	102	48	.471
Luke Hagel, Ripon (Wis.)	Sr.	149	70	.470
Pat Ryan, Westfield State (Mass.)	Jr.	124	58	.468
Vince Mancuso, Wisconsin-Oshkosh	Sr.	155	72	.465

Department Leaders: Batting

Dept.	Player, School	Yr.	G	Total
R	Mike Maguire, Suffolk (Mass.)	So.	40	67
	Vince Mancuso, Wisconsin-Oshkosh	Sr.	44	67
	Brent Hodges, Anderson (Ind.)	Sr.	51	67
H	Andrew Pinckney, Emory (Ga.)	So.	50	85
TB	Vince Mancuso, Wisconsin-Oshkosh	Sr.	44	155
2B	Andy Kucek, Hendrix (Ark.)	So.	40	27
3B	Miguel Jaquez, John Jay (N.Y.)	So.	35	11
HR	Jose Cortez, Pomona-Pitzer (Calif.)	Sr.	39	20
RBI	Aaron Giza, Benedictine (Ill.)	Jr.	46	71
	Troy Loyd, Anderson (Ind.)	Sr.	51	71
SB	Jeremy Elliot, Christopher Newport (Va.)	Sr.	44	54
BB	Jose Cortez, Pomona-Pitzer (Calif.)	Sr.	39	45

EARNED RUN AVERAGE
(Minimum 40 Innings)

Player, School	Yr.	IP	ER	ERA
Chad Cosby, Worcester State (Mass.)	Sr.	56	6	0.96
Mike Luzim, St. Joseph's (N.Y.)	Jr.	61	7	1.04
Derrick Rawlings, Virginia Wesleyan	Jr.	52	6	1.04
Joey Serfass, Eastern Conn. State	Jr.	68	8	1.08
Matt DeSalvo, Marietta (Ohio)	Sr.	96	14	1.31
Paul Basdekis, Mount St. Mary's (N.Y.)	Sr.	81	12	1.33
Jason Jarrett, Virginia Wesleyan	Jr.	80	12	1.35
Dan Grybash, Carthage (Wis.)	Jr.	66	10	1.37
Ryan France, Chapman (Calif.)	Sr.	111	17	1.38

Department Leaders: Pitching

Dept.	Player, School	Yr.	G	Total
W	Matt DeSalvo, Marietta (Ohio)	Sr.	18	13
SV	Teddy Grothe, Augustana (Ill.)	Sr.	23	12
SO	Matt DeSalvo, Marietta (Ohio)	Sr.	96	157

NAIA

WORLD SERIES

Site: Lewiston, Idaho.

Participants: Ohio Dominican (39-16); Olivet Nazarene, Ill. (45-8); LSU-Shreveport (49-22); Indiana Tech (40-18); Bellevue, Neb. (45-20); Biola, Calif. (41-15); Lewis-Clark State, Idaho (43-12); Spalding, Ky. (51-18); Embry-Riddle, Fla. (43-13); Oklahoma City (59-6).

Champion: Lewis-Clark State (5-1). **Runner-Up**: Oklahoma City (4-2).

Outstanding Player: Marc Kaiser, rhp, Lewis-Clark State.

NAIA ALL-AMERICA TEAM

Pos.	Player, School	Yr.	AVG	HR	RBI
C	Matt Houston, Oklahoma City	Jr.	.435	15	62
	Wilfredo Colon, Ohio Dominican	Sr.	.456	14	57
1B	Brandon Kaye, Oklahoma City	Sr.	.383	25	82
2B	Ben Zorbrist, Olivet Nazarene (Ill.)	Fr.	.409	10	65
3B	Jake Ford, Spalding (Ky.)	Sr.	.436	31	110
SS	Sam Orr, Biola (Calif.)	So.	.407	24	74
UT	Chili Miranda, Cumberland (Tenn.)	Sr.	.393	22	73
OF	Jerry Owens, The Master's (Calif.)	Jr.	.451	6	31
	Ben Himes, Oklahoma City	Jr.	.381	25	65
	Tavaris Gary, Cumberland (Tenn.)	Jr.	.372	18	72
	Aaron Lewis, Wilmington (Del.)	Jr.	.399	6	43
DH	Carl Galloway, Biola (Calif.)	So.	.360	19	53

			W	L	ERA
SP	Justin Hahaj, Spring Arbor (Mich.)	Sr.	15	1	1.65
	Brad Davis, Spalding (Ky.)	So.	15	2	1.98
	E.J. Shanks, Oklahoma City	Jr.	14	1	3.16
	Brian Anderson, Embry-Riddle (Fla.)	Sr.	12	3	2.22
RP	Justin Hennington, William Carey (13 SV)	Jr.	4	3	1.78

Player of the Year: Jake Ford, Spalding.

NATIONAL LEADERS

BATTING AVERAGE
(Minimum 100 At-Bats)

Player, School	Yr.	AB	H	AVG
Andrew Belcher, King (Tenn.)	Jr.	168	85	.506
Lenny Henriquez, Bellevue (Neb.)	So.	141	67	.475
Josh Keister, Goshen (Ind.)	Jr.	139	65	.468
Ted Ledbetter, Oklahoma City	So.	239	109	.456
Ryan Koerner, Judson (Ill.)	Sr.	145	66	.455
Nick Miller, Sterling (Kan.)	Sr.	158	70	.443
Erick Perez, Culver-Stockton (Mo.)	Sr.	190	84	.442
Jeff Wilson, Indiana Tech	Sr.	215	95	.442
Keith Waller, Marian (Ind.)	Jr.	150	66	.440
Jake Ford, Spalding (Ky.)	Sr.	259	113	.436
Matt Houston, Oklahoma City	Jr.	230	100	.435
Tim Burris, Huntington (Ind.)	So.	143	62	.434

Department Leaders: Batting

Dept.	Player, School	Yr.	G	Total
R	Ryan Howell, St. Xavier (Ill.)	Jr.	60	83
H	Jake Ford, Spalding (Ky.)	Sr.	72	113
2B	Andrew Belcher, King (Tenn.)	Jr.	52	28
	Jeff Wilson, Indiana Tech	Sr.	61	28
3B	Ben Colling, Olivet Nazarene (Ill.)	Sr.	54	10
HR	Jake Ford, Spalding (Ky.)	Sr.	72	31
RBI	Jake Ford, Spalding (Ky.)	Sr.	72	110
SB	Carlos Ramirez, Tennessee Wesleyan	So.	49	49

EARNED RUN AVERAGE
(Minimum 50 Innings)

Player, School	Yr.	IP	ER	ERA
Ryan Lupul, William Penn (Iowa)	Sr.	62	8	1.16
Tony Casoli, Georgia Southwestern	Sr.	87	13	1.34
Justin Hahaj, Spring Arbor (Mich.)	Sr.	126	23	1.65
Justin Henington, William Carey (Miss.)	Jr.	61	12	1.78
Craig Harvey, Husson (Maine)	So.	59	12	1.83
David Feliscian, Avila (Mo.)	Jr.	51	11	1.90
Brad Davis, Spalding (Ky.)	So.	132	29	1.98
Eric Evans, William Penn (Iowa)	Sr.	58	13	2.03
Rick Long, St. Francis (Ill.)	Jr.	88	20	2.05
Ismael Casillas, Benedictine (Kan.)	So.	93	22	2.12
Brooks McNiven, British Columbia	Sr.	90	22	2.20

Department Leaders: Pitching

Dept.	Player, School	Yr.	G	Total
W	Jon Kars, Missouri Baptist	Jr.	24	16
SO	Brad Davis, Spalding (Ky.)	So.	14	138

JUNIOR COLLEGE

DIVISION I WORLD SERIES

Site: Grand Junction, Colo.

Participants: San Jacinto, Texas (48-11); Indian Hills, Iowa (37-21); Spartanburg Methodist, S.C. (48-14); Neosho County, Kan. (42-13); Seminole, Fla. (41-19); Southern Nevada (50-9); Grayson County, Texas (52-13); Connors State, Okla. (46-15); Walters State, Tenn. (44-11); Meridian, Miss. (38-17).

Champion: Southern Nevada (5-1). **Runner-Up**: San Jacinto (4-2).

Outstanding Player: Tyler Coon, lhp, Southern Nevada.

ALL-AMERICA TEAM

C—Nick Stavinoha, San Jacinto (Texas). **INF**—Ian Baldergroen, Lamar (Colo.); Ryan Nelson, Seward County (Kan.); Chris Cunningham, South Suburban (Ill.); Josh Forbus, Central Alabama. **OF**—Pat Miller, Crowder (Mo.); Andy Scholl, Lamar (Colo.); Nick Bohnenstichl, Southwestern Illinois. **DH**—Ryan Rohlinger, Clarendon (Texas). **P**—Nick Markakis, Young Harris (Ga.); Jeff Morgan, Seminole State (Okla.); Jake Beard, Southern Nevada.

NATIONAL LEADERS

BATTING AVERAGE
(Minimum 100 At-Bats)

Player, School	AB	H	AVG
Chris Cunningham, South Suburban (Ill.)	149	78	.523
Emory Davies, John A. Logan (Ill.)	110	57	.518
Luis DeJesus, New Mexico	133	65	.489
J.R. Towles, Collin County (Texas)	155	75	.484
Nathan Thurber, NE Oklahoma A&M	111	53	.477
Andy Scholl, Lamar (Colo.)	212	100	.472
Ryan Nelson, Seward County (Kan.)	153	72	.471
Nick Ewen, Triton (Ill.)	179	84	.469
Mike Stice, Cloud County (Kan.)	150	69	.460
Eric Horstman, Cloud County (Kan.)	144	66	.458

Department Leaders: Batting

Dept.	Player, School	G	Total
HR	Ian Bladergroen, Lamar (Colo.)	61	32
RBI	Nick Markakis, Young Harris (Ga.)	63	92
SB	Joey Friddle, Young Harris (Ga.)	64	52

EARNED RUN AVERAGE
(Minimum 50 innings)

Player, School	IP	ER	ERA
Lino Valenzuela, Central Arizona	65	8	1.10
Cesar Lopez, Arizona Western	69	9	1.18
Clint Goocher, San Jacinto (Texas)	71	11	1.39
Jason Fellows, Georgia Perimeter	75	12	1.43
Jason Urquidez, Central Arizona	79	14	1.59
Jeremy King, Hanceville (Ala.)	62	11	1.60
Grant Varnell, North Central	78	14	1.61
Ryan Garmon, Georgia Perimeter	66	12	1.63

Department Leaders: Pitching

Dept.	Player, School	G	Total
W	Nick Markakis, Young Harris (Ga.)	19	12
	Chris Johns, Lamar (Colo.)	16	12
SO	Nick Markakis, Young Harris (Ga.)	19	160
SV	Brent Marsh, Tallahassee (Fla.)	27	14

DIVISION II WORLD SERIES

Site: Millington, Tenn.

Participants: Itawamba, Miss. (45-9); Parkland, Ill. (48-12); Iowa Central (36-16); Baltimore County, Md. (29-14); Bevill State, Ala. (35-23); Glendale, Ariz. (31-29); Mercer County, N.J. (23-10); Grand Rapids, Mich. (35-18).

Champion: Grand Rapids (6-1). **Runner-Up**: Iowa Central (3-2).

Outstanding Player: Justin McKenzie, inf, Grand Rapids.

DIVISION III WORLD SERIES

Site: Batavia, NY.

Participants: Richland, Texas (33-20); Ridgewater, Minn. (33-7); Columbus State, Ohio (40-16); Dutchess, N.Y. (40-13); Gloucester County, N.J. (34-13); Erie, N.Y. (32-13); Quinsigamond, Mass. (19-8); Montgomery, Md. (26-24).

Champion: Richland (4-0) **Runner-Up**: Gloucester County (3-2)

Outstanding Player: Ryan Dreibelbis, rhp, Richland.

CALIFORNIA CC CHAMPIONSHIP

Site: Fresno.

Participants: Saddleback (33-15); Cypress (35-14); San Mateo (39-8); Feather River (36-11).

Champion: Cypress (3-0). **Runner-Up**: Saddleback (2-2).

Most Valuable Player: Felipe Garcia, c, Cypress.

HIGH SCHOOL
BASEBALL

California finally pushes through as Chatsworth wins national title

BY ALAN MATTHEWS

The 2003 high school season had a California team atop the national rankings at the beginning, two Texas schools jockeying for the top spot in the middle and a new but familiar California club claiming the No. 1 spot at the end.

Perennial power Chatsworth High became the first California team in the 11-year history of the Baseball America/National High School Baseball Coaches Association poll to finish No. 1. The Chancellors went 33-1, winning their first 20 and final 13 games. They also won the California Interscholastic Federation Southern Section Los Angeles City championship. California is the only state that does not have a state championship.

Chatsworth was ranked 20th to start the season and steadily climbed toward No. 1 with a veteran roster that included 10 seniors and six juniors. Three Division I signees highlighted Chatsworth's lineup, but the only player drafted was righthander Justin Cassel, who went in the 30th round to the Athletics.

While the Chancellors were gaining national acclaim, coach Tom Meusborn made a point to let the fans and media talk, and the players just play.

"I think the key for our guys was that we stayed focused on the task at hand, on winning a sectional title and continuing to get better every day," Meusborn said. "We played with a lot of enthusiasm and a lot of determination every day.

"We try and keep our players grounded. We knew we were near the top, but we didn't talk about it at all. Not once did we mention it in the clubhouse. We felt the best way to approach it was not to address it, just let those things take care of themselves."

That's what happened, as the teams ranked ahead of Chatsworth fell while the Chancellors kept winning.

Chatsworth's lone setback came in a 3-0 decision at an April tournament in Durango, Nev., to Sabino High of Tucson. The Chancellors also found themselves in trouble in their first conference game less than a week later as they trailed 6-0 after three innings. But Chatsworth got its bats going and pulled out a 9-8 victory.

"That really gave our guys the confidence, regardless of any situation," Meusborn said. "There was an air of confidence from that point forward. Whenever we were down there was not a sense of panic but of assurance that we could come back."

The Chancellors needed that confidence in the postseason. Following 12-0 and 2-0 wins in the first two rounds, Chatsworth trailed Wilmington's Banning High 2-0 before junior outfielder/righthander Jason Dominguez laced a two-run double. He later added a solo homer while working five strong innings on the hill and departed with a 4-3 lead. Cassel saved the game with two shutout innings of relief.

Cassel came back with a shutout in the finals, even carrying a no-hitter into the seventh against Carson High at Dodger Stadium. Cassel surrendered a one-out single in the seventh but nothing more as Chatsworth claimed its third sectional title in five years and its first national title with a 3-0 win.

BASEBALLRESOURCE.COM

Celebrating a national championship
Chatsworth coach Tom Meusborn

"We had a group of players that had a common goal, and we had the intangible things. There were no distractions," Meusborn said. "We went 6-6 after USA Today ranked us No. 1 (in 2002), and we did a pretty good job of figuring out what happened at that point and doing things differently this year."

PREVIOUS WINNERS

Previous No. 1 teams in the year-end Baseball America/National High School Baseball Coaches Association poll:

1992—Westminster Christian HS, Miami
1993—Greenway HS, Phoenix
1994—Sarasota (Fla.) HS
1995—Germantown (Tenn.) HS
1996—Westminster Christian HS, Miami
1997—Jesuit HS, Tampa
1998—Vestavia Hills (Ala.) HS
1999—Lassiter HS, Marietta, Ga.
2000—Gloucester Catholic HS, Gloucester City, N.J.
2001—Seminole (Fla.) HS
2002—Elkins HS, Missouri City, Texas

Cassel completed the season with a 15-0, 1.13 record and didn't allow a run in 20 postseason innings on his way to securing first-team All-America honors. Dominguez was outstanding as well, going 11-0, 5.60 and batting .449-9-47. Senior catcher Jordan Sisson hit .385-9-42 to help Chatsworth set a school record for home runs in a season with 41.

"When you've got guys that are able to swing the bat, you feel you can score at any time," Meusborn said. "This team had the ability to score runs with two outs as well, more so than any team I've coached in the past.

"To win 33 of 34, with all the competition in California is truly remarkable. What a fabulous feeling, for our school, kids and community. It's a thrill, there's no question, to have our high school finish No. 1."

ANDREW WOOLLEY

Round Rock ace
First-rounder John Danks

HIGH SCHOOL TOP 50

Baseball America's final 2003 Top 50, selected in conjunction with the National High School Baseball Coaches Association.

Rank, Team, City	Record	Accomplishment
1. Chatsworth (Calif.) HS	33-1	CIF Los Angeles section champion
2. Farragut HS, Knoxville, Tenn.	48-1	Tennessee 3-A champion
3. La Quinta HS, Westminster, Calif.	30-2	CIF Southern section champion
4. Riverside HS, Greer, S.C.	29-1	South Carolina 3-A champion
5. La Costa Canyon HS, Carlsbad, Calif.	32-1	CIF San Diego section champion
6. Round Rock (Texas) HS	36-4	Texas 5-A runner-up
7. St. Paul's Episcopal HS, Mobile, Ala.	41-4	Alabama 5-A champion
8. La Cueva HS, Albuquerque, N.M.	29-0	New Mexico 5-A champion
9. Seton Hall Prep, West Orange, N.J.	30-1	New Jersey Parochial A champion
10. Rose HS, Greenville, N.C.	26-2	North Carolina 4-A champion
11. New Hope HS, Columbus, Miss.	34-4	Mis.sissippi 4-A champion
12. Owasso (Okla.) HS	36-4	Oklahoma 6-A champion
13. Chaparral HS, Scottsdale, Ariz.	32-3	Arizona 4-A champion
14. Elkins HS, Missouri City, Texas	31-8	Texas 5-A champion
15. A&M Consolidated HS, College Station, Texas	30-3	Lost in state playoffs
16. Florida Christian HS, Miami	31-3	Lost in state playoffs
17. Taylorsville HS, Salt Lake City	25-3	Utah 5-A runner-up
18. Lakewood Ranch HS, Bradenton, Fla.	28-6	Florida 5-A champion
19. Columbus HS, Miami	26-7	Florida 6-A champion
20. Tottenville HS, Staten Island, N.Y.	35-2	New York public school champion
21. Milford (Ohio) HS	30-3	Ohio Group I runner-up
22. Clay-Chalkville HS, Pinson, Ala.	36-5	Alabama 6-A champion
23. Rancho Bernardo HS, San Diego	27-6	CIF San Diego section runner-up
24. Brownsburg (Ind.) HS	27-2	Indiana 4-A runner-up
25. East Ascension HS, Gonzales, La.	29-4	Louisiana 5-A champion
26. Liberty (Mo.) HS	29-2	Lost in state playoffs
27. Clovis (Calif.) HS	23-7	CIF Central section champion
28. Apopka (Fla.) HS	30-6	Florida 6-A runner-up
29. Westside HS, Omaha	32-3	Nebraska state champion
30. Paul Dunbar HS, Lexington, Ky.	36-3	Kentucky champion
31. Horizon HS, Scottsdale, Ariz.	32-4	Arizona 5-A runner-up
32. Wolfson HS, Jacksonville	28-3	Lost in state playoffs
33. Oviedo (Fla.) HS	27-3	Lost in state playoffs
34. DeMatha HS, Hyattsville, Md.	25-3	Maryland Catholic school champion
35. Flower Mound (Texas) HS	32-5	Lost in state playoffs
36. John Curtis HS, New Orleans	35-2	Lost in state playoffs
37. Midway HS, Hewitt, Texas	35-4	Texas 4-A champion
38. Capistrano Valley HS, Mission Viejo, Calif.	25-4	Lost in sectional playoffs
39. Buchanan HS, Clovis, Calif.	27-5	CIF Central section runner-up
40. Reno (Nev.) HS	36-2	Nevada 4-A runner-up
41. Colquitt County HS, Moultrie, Ga.	30-9	Georgia 4-A champion
42. Fuquay-Varina (N.C.) HS	24-3	Lost in state playoffs
43. Great Bridge HS, Chesapeake, Va.	22-5	Virginia 3-A champion
44. Bishop Hendricken, Warwick, R.I.	27-2	Rhode Island state champion
45. Veterans Memorial HS, Peabody, Mass.	20-2	Lost in state playoffs
46. Barbe HS, Lake Charles, La.	32-6	Lost in state playoffs
47. Lyons HS, La Grange, Ill.	32-6	Illinois large school champion
48. South Kitsap HS, Port Orchard, Wash.	21-4	Washington 4-A champion
49. Parkview HS, Lilburn, Ga.	24-4	Lost in state playoffs
50. Marina HS, Huntington Beach, Calif.	24-7	CIF Southern section champion

Texas Schools Have Their Day

Round Rock (Texas) High, which would have three players selected in the top five rounds of the 2003 draft, entered postseason play ranked first in the BA/NHSBCA poll. The Dragons sailed through the Texas 5-A playoffs until the finals when it met 2002 state and national champion Elkins High of Missouri City.

Elkins (31-8) had opened the 2003 season with five losses in its first 13 games, due in part to injuries to key players and a rugged early schedule. But the Knights finished the season with a flurry and knocked off the highly-rated Dragons 5-4 in the final. The Knights pushed across five runs in the first three innings off Round Rock ace John Danks, who was drafted in the first round by the Rangers, and hung on behind Mike Susaneck (10-1), who went the distance and scattered nine hits.

Round Rock ended the season ranked sixth while Elkins jumped to 14th.

A&M Consolidated High of College Station (30-3) also occupied the No. 1 spot for a time at midseason but its season came to a premature end as it was ousted early in the Texas 5-A playoffs. The Tigers were ranked 15th in the final poll.

■ Both Round Rock and A&M Consolidated lost their veteran head coaches to retirement following the season.

Round Rock head coach John Langerhans announced he would step down after compiling a 613-200 record in 27 years. Rex Sanders gave up his post after 31 years at A&M Consolidated.

"I wanted to have more time and less responsibility," said Langerhans, who played at the University of Texas from 1969-1972 and was a second-round draft pick of the Cleveland Indians in 1972. "But I'm not getting out of it, just getting out of the high school level and some of the stress and pressures of teaching (U.S. history) and coaching. I will still work with the kids because I haven't lost (the interest for) that. I still enjoy being around the kids."

Langerhans twice was named Texas coach of the year and won a Texas 5-A state title in 1997. "It's very gratifying," he said. "I guess what means the most to me are all the great players I've been blessed with. They deserve all the credit."

Langerhans coached 72 players at Round Rock who went on to play Division I or professional baseball, including his son Ryan, an outfielder in the Atlanta Braves organization. Langerhans' final team featured Danks (10-3, 1.61 and 173 strikeouts), righthander Matt Nachreiner (14-0, 0.78) and shortstop Travis Schlichting (.413-4-46), who were all premium picks in the 2003 draft.

Sanders announced his retirement late in the regular season. He said the standout season his team was enjoying and his decision to retire were completely unrelated.

"I had really kind of thought two or three years ago that this would be my final season and my wife became ill last fall and that solidified the decision," Sanders said. "It was the right time to do it. It's a good time for her and I to spend some time together."

Sanders, 53, spent 23 of his 31 years in coaching as

Allison goes 9-0, 0.00, wins top honor

PLAYER of the YEAR

Young athletes growing up in the Northeast most often gravitate to hockey, basketball or football. Summers are short and winters bitterly cold, making baseball a less attractive option and ensuring fewer blue-chip baseball prospects than other regions.

But Massachusetts' Jeff Allison shattered those stereotypes with a senior season that earned him Baseball America's 2003 High School Player of the Year Award. It didn't hurt his cause that the Massachusetts Interscholastic Athletic Association voted to ban metal bats for the 2003 regular season and tournament.

The 6-foot-2, 195-pound righthander from Veterans Memorial High of Peabody, Mass., had already dominated hitters armed with aluminum as a junior. He was downright devastating in 2003 against those wielding wood.

DENIS BANCROFT

Dominated Massachusetts hitters
Righthander Jeff Allison

Allison, drafted in the first round by the Florida Marlins, tossed 64 innings without allowing an earned run. He was 9-0, 0.00 with 142 strikeouts and nine walks, surrendering just 13 hits and one unearned run. He also hit .441 with two homers and 29 RBIs.

"A number of times after Allison won a game all the reporters went and talked to the players that got hits," coach Ed Nizwantowski said. "That's how good he was, they wanted to talk to the guy who (reached base) against him. I've coached for 34 years and this was something special. Rarely do you run into something like this."

As electric as his arm is, Allison offers an equally overpowering attitude. He pitches with ferocity, trying to overpower opponents with both his stuff and his will.

"I don't care where you're from," Allison said. "I know where I'm from and I'm going to dominate you. It's a different mentality I've had all my life."

Allison projected as a top 10 pick in the 2003 draft, but he fell to 16th overall because of speculation he would be tough to sign. Marlins scouting director Stan Meek was optimistic Allison would sign—he did on July 22 for $1.85 million—and felt strongly enough about Allison's tools and makeup to take him.

"He usually brings good stuff to the park and his competitiveness sets him apart," Meek said. "You could call it a little bit of a chip on his shoulder, and a good chip. It's helped him become more determined, to work harder, and we like that."

top FIVE

1. Jeff Allison, rhp, Veterans Memorial HS, Peabody, Mass.
2. Chris Lubanski, of, Kennedy-Kenrick HS, Schwenksville, Pa.
3. Brandon Wood, ss, Horizon HS, Scottsdale, Ariz.
4. Ian Stewart, 3b, La Quinta HS, Garden Grove, Calif.
5. Eric Duncan, 3b, Seton Hall Prep, Florham Park, N.J.

PREVIOUS WINNERS

1992—Preston Wilson, of-rhp, Bamberg-Ehrhardt (S.C.) HS
1993—Trot Nixon, of-lhp, New Hanover HS, Wilmington, N.C.
1994—Doug Million, lhp, Sarasota (Fla.) HS
1995—Ben Davis, c, Malvern (Pa.) Prep
1996—Matt White, rhp, Waynesboro Area (Pa.) HS
1997—Darnell McDonald, of, Cherry Creek HS, Englewood, Colo.
1998—Drew Henson, 3b-rhp, Brighton (Mich.) HS
1999—Josh Hamilton, of-lhp, Athens Drive HS, Raleigh, N.C.
2000—Matt Harrington, rhp, Palmdale (Calif.) HS
2001—Joe Mauer, c, Cretin-Derham Hall, St. Paul, Minn.
2002—Scott Kamir, lhp, Cypress Falls HS, Houston

A&M Consolidated's head coach. He won 463 career games while compiling a .658 career winning percentage.

La Quinta Falls Twice

A&M Consolidated temporarily claimed the top spot in the national poll in late April after preseason No. 1 La Quinta High of Westminster, Calif., suffered back-to-back losses in the National Classic, the nation's most prestigious in-season tournament. La Quinta (30-2) never lost again while winning its 11th consecutive league title and the CIF Southern Section Division IV championship.

La Quinta head coach Dave Demarest was left wondering what might have been.

"To be 30-2 and only have (Ian) Kennedy for part of the season, I can't complain," he said. "People lose kids all the time so it's not an excuse. But there's not too many teams who can lose a kid of his caliber and be 30-2."

Kennedy, a second-team All-American, rebounded from a knee injury that sent him to the sidelines for several weeks to go 8-0, 0.83. Teammate Ian Stewart was a first-team All-American selection. A third baseman, he hit .462-16-61 and was drafted by the Colorado Rockies in the first round.

Taylorsville High of Salt Lake City handed La Quinta its first loss of the season, in the second round of the National Classic. The Warriors (25-3) went on to win the prestigious event and would have been ranked higher than 17th in the final poll had they not been swept in the Utah 5-A championship series in two straight games by Bingham High. Taylorsville lost the second game of the best-of-3 series 12-10 when ace pitcher Chad Barben was lifted after three innings and Bingham scored 11 runs in the sixth. Barben, MVP of the National Classic, was removed to rest him for a potential third and deciding game.

■ Rarely does a high school team push the 50-win plateau but Farragut High of Knoxville, Tenn., capped a 48-1 campaign by winning a Class 3-A state title in 2003.

The second-ranked Admirals secured their place as one of the most prolific teams in state history, eclipsing the previous state record for wins in a season of 41.

STATE HIGH SCHOOL CHAMPIONS, 2003

ALABAMA. 6-A: *Clay-Chalkville HS, Pinson (36-5). **5-A:** *St. Paul's Episcopal HS, Mobile (41-4). **4-A:** Hokes Bluff HS, Gadsden (28-4). **3-A:** Ashville HS (28-8). **2-A:** Gordo HS (29-5). **1-A:** Holy Spirit HS (26-8).

ALASKA. Douglas HS, Juneau (15-2).

ARIZONA. 5-A: Hamilton HS, Chandler (27-10). **4-A:** *Chaparral HS, Paradise Valley (32-3). **3-A:** Seton Catholic HS, Chandler (22-11). **2-A:** Phoenix Christian HS (18-11). **1-A:** Joseph City HS (18-8).

ARKANSAS. 5-A: Fayetteville HS (25-8). **4-A:** Sylvan Hills HS, Sherwood (22-10). **3-A:** Pulaski Academy, Little Rock (29-2). 2-A: Norphlet HS (26-8). **1-A:** Concord HS (26-0).

CALIFORNIA. No state championship

COLORADO. 5-A: Pomona HS, Arvada (22-4). **4-A:** Golden HS (20-7). **3-A:** Eaton HS (25-2). **2-A:** Paonia HS (20-1).

CONNECTICUT. LL: Norwich Free Academy (21-2). **L:** North Haven HS (18-7). **M:** Notre Dame Catholic HS, Fairfield (22-2). **S:** Immaculate HS, Danbury (18-7).

DELAWARE. St. Mark's HS, Wilmington (16-8).

FLORIDA. 6-A: *Columbus HS, Miami (26-7). **5-A:** *Lakewood Ranch HS, Bradenton (28-6). **4-A:** St. Thomas Aquinas HS, Fort Lauderdale (23-12). **3-A:** Eustis HS (22-10). **2-A:** Pensacola Catholic (29-5). **1-A:** Providence Christian HS, Jacksonville (27-2).

GEORGIA. 5-A: *Colquitt County HS, Moultrie (30-9). **4-A:** Marist School, Atlanta (26-12). **3-A:** Cartersville HS (29-4). **2-A:** Vidalia HS (31-4). **1-A:** Clinch County HS, Homerville.

HAWAII. Kamehameha HS, Honolulu (19-3).

IDAHO. 5-A: Eagle HS. **4-A:** Jerome HS. **3-A:** Wood River HS, Hailey. **2-A:** New Plymouth HS.

ILLINOIS. 2-A: *Lyons Township HS, La Grange (36-6). **1-A:** Wilmington HS (37-5). **Summer:** Schaumburg HS (22-6).

INDIANA. 4-A: McCutcheon HS, Lafayette (30-5). **3-A:** Norwell HS, Ossian (23-11). **2-A:** Triton Central HS, Fairland (26-2). **1-A:** Tecumseh HS, Lynnville (16-12).

IOWA. 4-A: West Des Moines Valley HS (38-7). **3-A:** Harlan Community HS (29-7). **2-A:** Carlisle HS (32-5). **1-A:** Van Meter HS (29-5).

KANSAS. 6-A: Maize HS (21-4). **5-A:** Topeka West HS (23-2). **4-A:** Bishop Ward HS, Kansas City (22-4). **3-A:** Baxter Springs HS (21-2). **2-A/1-A:** Sacred Heart HS, Salina (23-2).

KENTUCKY. *Paul Dunbar HS, Lexington (40-3).

LOUISIANA. 5-A: East Ascension HS, Gonzales (29-4). **4-A:** DeRidder HS, DeRidder. **3-A:** Parkview Baptist HS, Baton Rouge (29-4). **2-A:** Newman HS, New Orleans (20-12). **1-A:** Country Day HS, Metairie (26-7). **B:** Pine Prairie HS. **C:** Hicks HS, Leesville.

MAINE. A: Deering HS, Portland (18-2). **B:** Oak Hill HS, Sabattus (18-3). **C:** George Stevens Academy, Blue Hill (18-2). **D:** North Yarmouth Academy, Yarmouth (19-0).

MARYLAND. 4-A: Old Mill HS, Millersville (20-3). **3-A:** Severna Park HS (21-4). **2-A:** Walkersville HS (16-5). **1-A:** South Hagerstown HS, Hagerstown. **A:** St. Paul's HS, Brooklandville (23-6). **B:** Chapelgate Christian Academy, Marriottsville. **Private:** *DeMatha Catholic HS, Hyattsville (25-3).

MASSACHUSETTS. I: Malden Catholic HS, Malden (18-8). **II:** Athol HS. **III:** Marian HS, Framingham (19-6).

MICHIGAN. I: West Ottawa HS, Holland (31-4). **II:** St. Mary's Prep, Orchard Lake (22-11). **III:** Blissfield HS (31-10). **IV:** Decatur HS (28-6).

MINNESOTA. 3-A: Century HS, Rochester (24-5). **2-A:** Cathedral HS, St. Cloud (22-6). **1-A:** Howard Lake-Waverly-Winstead HS, Howard Lake (18-9).

MISSISSIPPI. 5-A: Oak Grove HS, Hattiesburg (30-6). **4-A:** *New Hope HS< Columbus (34-4). **3-A:** Greene County HS, Leakesville (32-6). **2-A:** Eupora HS (21-9). **1-A:** Mize HS (31-4).

MISSOURI. 4-A: Francis Howell HS, St. Charles (25-6). **3-A:** North County HS, Bonne Terre (28-3). **2-A:** Valley Park HS (23-4). **1-A:** Sparta HS (21-1).

NEBRASKA. *Westside HS, Omaha (32-3).

NEVADA. 4-A: Green Valley HS, Henderson (28-8). **3-A:** Bishop Manogue HS, Reno. **2-A:** Faith Lutheran HS, Las Vegas. **1-A:** Wells HS.

NEW HAMPSHIRE. L: Salem HS. **M:** Bow HS. **I:** Sougegan HS, Amherst. **S:** Derryfield HS.

NEW JERSEY. IV: Shawnee HS, Medford (23-7). **III:** South HS, Tom's River (24-4). **II:** Raritan HS, Hazlet (24-5). **I:** Pennsville Memorial HS, Pennsville (26-4). **Parochial A:** *Seton Hall Prep, West Orange (30-1). **Parochial B:** Gloucester Catholic HS, Gloucester City (26-5).

NEW MEXICO. 5-A: *La Cueva HS, Albuquerque (29-0). **4-A:** St. Pius X HS, Albuquerque (21-7). **3-A:** St. Michael's HS, Santa Fe (21-8). **2-A:** Loving HS (20-5).

NEW YORK. A: Half Hollow Hills West HS, Dix Hills. **B:** Marlboro Central HS, Marlboro. **C:** Dobbs Ferry HS. **D:** Schenevus Central HS, Schenevus.

NORTH CAROLINA. 4-A: *J.H. Rose HS, Greenville (26-2). **3-A:** Ashbrook HS, Gastonia (27-4). **2-A:** East Rutherford HS, Forest City. **1-A:** South Stokes HS, Walnut Cove.

NORTH DAKOTA. A: Bismarck (29-4). **B:** Cavalier HS.

OHIO. I: St. Xavier HS, Cincinnati (24-9). **II:** Purcell Marian HS, Cincinnati (23-9). **III:** St. Henry HS (30-3). **IV:** Newark Catholic HS, Newark (28-5).

OKLAHOMA. 6-A: *Owasso HS (36-4). **5-A:** Claremore HS (33-10). **4-A:** Weatherford HS (35-9). **3-A:** Henryetta HS (32-4). **2-A:** Latta HS, Ada (34-5). **A:** Rattan HS. **B:** Buffalo Valley HS, Talihina.

OREGON. 4-A: Newberg HS (23-7). **3-A:** Mazama HS, Klamath Falls (26-5). **2-A/1-A:** Regis HS, Stayton (26-1).

PENNSYLVANIA. 3-A: East HS, West Chester (24-2). **2-A:** Ellwood City HS (21-6). **1-A:** Bellwood-Antis HS, Bellwood (22-4).

RHODE ISLAND. A: *Bishop Hendricken HS, Warwick (27-2). **B:** Barrington HS.

SOUTH CAROLINA. 4-A: Summerville HS (23-12). **3-A:** *Riverside HS, Greer (29-1). **2-A:** Bishop England HS, Charleston. **1-A:** Lamar HS.

TENNESSEE. 3-A: *Farragut HS, Knoxville (48-1). **2-A:** Ripley HS (35-11). **II:** Baylor School, Chattanooga (32-13).

TEXAS. 5-A: *Elkins HS, Missouri City (31-8). **4-A:** *Hewitt Midway HS, Hewitt (35-4). **3-A:** Lorena HS (31-0). **2-A:** Weimar HS (28-6). **1-A:** Colmesneil HS (26-4).

UTAH. 5-A: Bingham HS, South Jordan (20-7). **4-A:** Springville HS (23-3). **3-A:** Pine View HS, Saint George (24-1). **2-A:** Juan Diego HS, Draper (17-6).

VERMONT. I: Champlain Valley Union HS, Hinesburg (18-2). **II:** Lyndon Institute, Lyndon Center (17-3). **III:** Enosburg Falls HS (20-0). **IV:** Richford HS (17-3).

VIRGINIA. 3-A: *Great Bridge HS, Chesapeake (22-5). **2-A:** Amherst County HS, Amherst (18-6). **1-A:** Essex HS, Tappahannock (20-0).

WASHINGTON. 4-A: *South Kitsap HS, Port Orchard (21-4). **3-A:** Liberty HS, Renton (21-7). **2-A:** Othello HS. **1-A:** Colfax HS. **B:** De Sales Catholic HS, Walla Walla.

WASHINGTON, D.C. Woodrow Wilson HS.

WEST VIRGINIA. 3-A: Cabell Midland HS, Ona (28-4). **2-A:** Lincoln HS, Shinnston (27-3). **1-A:** Matewan HS (25-10).

WISCONSIN. I: Middleton HS (21-6). **II:** Lutheran HS, Milwaukee (19-7). **III:** Pacelli HS, Stevens Point (24-3). **Summer:** Oak Creek HS (28-9).

*** Ranked in Baseball America/National High School Baseball Coaches Association poll**

Farragut had finished as state runners-up three times in the previous four years but closed out its record season with a 6-0 win over Munford High.

"This is what you play for," coach Tommy Pharr said. "We had a great group of seniors, and I'm glad they finally got one."

Farragut hit .402 as a team, averaged 11 runs per game and posted a team ERA of 1.27. Senior righthander Craig Cobb was 13-0, 0.36 while junior first baseman Kyle Waldrop led the team with a .513 average.

■ Lakewood Ranch High of Bradenton got a major shot in the arm when outfielder Lastings Milledge, who never hit less than .500 at Northside Christian High in St. Petersburg, transferred for his senior year. The Mustangs went on to capture the Florida 5-A crown in the school's fifth year of existence.

The season looked bleak in mid-April when the Mustangs (28-6) dropped three in a row, while scoring just four runs. Opposing teams began pitching around Milledge, who was drafted in the first round by the New York Mets, and it wasn't until late in the season that others in the lineup picked up the slack consistently.

"After about three-quarters of the season it became apparent Milledge wasn't going to see anything down the middle of the plate," Lakewood Ranch coach Dave Moats said. "We moved Milledge to leadoff and he did a great job of getting on (base). Guys down the lineup really fed off that and picked it up."

Top Pitcher Struggles

Entering the 2003 prep season, lefthander Andrew Miller was the nation's most ballyhooed high school pitcher. But Miller closed out his high school career unceremoniously as Buchholz High of Gainesville, Fla., was bounced by Tallahassee's Lincoln High 11-1 in a Florida regional final.

Miller was lifted with two outs in the fourth inning after walking four and allowing three runs. The 6-foot-6, 192-pound lefthander struggled with his command throughout the final month of the season and slipped from his prospect perch. He was drafted in the third round by Tampa Bay but became the highest draft pick not to sign when he elected to attend the University of North Carolina.

His place as the nation's best pitching prospect was assumed by Massachusetts righthander Jeff Allison, who went 9-0 and didn't give up an earned run all season. He was named Baseball America's High School Player of the Year.

■ The debate between wood and metal bats, a controversial subject at the college level for several years, made headlines on the high school level in 2003.

Citing safety concerns, the Massachusetts Interscholastic Athletic Association's baseball committee voted to ban metal bats for the 2003 regular season and state tournament, only to reverse the ruling after one season.

The MIAA's original decision made Massachusetts the first state to ban aluminum bats. The momentum for a change was prompted by a pair of incidents in 2001 when Massachusetts high school pitchers suffered head injuries from balls hit back up the middle.

GATORADE AWARD WINNERS

Outfielder Chris Lubanski was named winner of the 2003 Gatorade national high school player of the year award, given annually to a top high school player who excelled in the classroom and community. Lubanski, drafted fifth overall by the Kansas City Royals, had a remarkable high school career, hitting .405 as a freshman, .467 as a sophomore, .592 as a junior and .528 as a senior at Kennedy-Kenrick Catholic High in Schwenksville, Pa.

The Gatorade state-by-state 2003 winners (juniors noted by *):

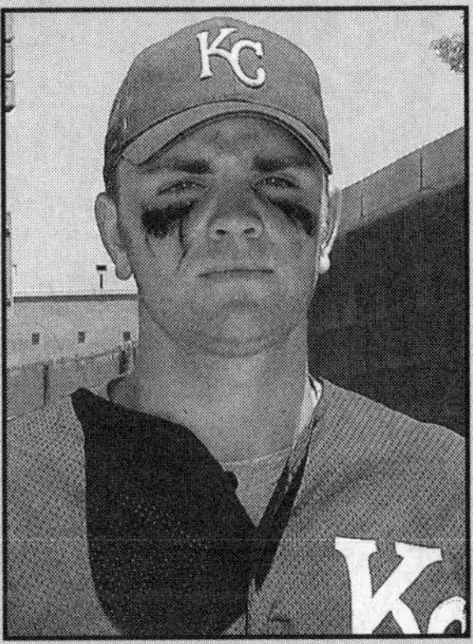

BILL MITCHELL

Chris Lubanski

Alabama—Chris Vines, rhp, Pelham HS. **Alaska**—Anton Maxwell, lhp, East HS, Anchorage. **Arizona**—Brandon Wood, ss, Horizon HS, Scottsdale. **Arkansas**—Derik Drewett, rhp, Watson Chapel HS, Sherrill. **California**—Greg Reynolds, rhp, Terra Nova HS, Pacifica. **Colorado**—Mark Melancon, rhp, Golden HS, Arvada. **Connecticut**—Chris Fournier, ss, Fairfield HS. **Delaware**—Adrian Santiago, rhp, Dickinson HS, Wilmington. **Florida**—Andrew Miller, lhp, Buchholz HS, Gainesville. **Georgia**—C.J. Bressoud, c, North Cobb HS, Kennesaw.

Hawaii—Kala Kaaihue, c, Iolani HS, Kahua. **Idaho**—Zach Simmons, 1b-lhp, Glenns Ferry HS. **Illinois**—George Kontos, rhp, Niles West HS, Lincolnwood. **Indiana**—Robbie Wooley, rhp, Taylor HS, Kokomo. **Iowa**—Ryan Sweeney, of-lhp, Xavier HS, Cedar Rapids. **Kansas**—Matt Foust, rhp, Blue Valley West HS, Overland Park. **Kentucky**—John Shelby, ss, Tates Creek HS, Lexington. **Louisiana**—Xavier Paul, of, Slidell HS. **Maine**—*Mark Rogers, rhp, Mt. Ararat HS, Orr's Island. **Maryland**—*Nick Adenhart, rhp, Williamsport HS, Hagerstown.

Massachusetts—Jeff Allison, rhp, Veterans Memorial HS, Peabody. **Michigan**—Dan Kapala, rhp, Shrine Catholic HS, Royal Oak. **Minnesota**—Sean Kommerstead, of, Minnetonka HS. **Mississippi**—Cliff Davis, rhp, Eupora HS. **Missouri**—Jonathan Barratt, lhp, Hillcrest HS, Springfield. **Montana**—No formal program. **Nebraska**—*Alex Hale, c, Creighton Prep, Omaha. **Nevada**—Steve Lerud, c, Galena HS, Reno. **New Hampshire**—Zach Piccola, lhp, Phillips Exeter HS, Manchester. **New Jersey**—Eric Duncan, 3b, Seton Hall Prep, Florham Park.

New Mexico—Griffin Phelps, lhp, Farmington HS. **New York**—Estee Harris, Islip HS, Central Islip. **North Carolina**—Paul Bard, rhp, Charlotte Christian Academy. **North Dakota**—Bo Stanley, ss, Bismarck HS. **Ohio**—Chad Billingsley, rhp, Defiance HS. **Oklahoma**—Mike Rogers, lhp-of, Del City HS. **Oregon**—Jordan Pratt, rhp, Central HS, Independence. **Pennsylvania**—Chris Lubanski, of, Kennedy-Kenrick HS, Schwenksville. **Rhode Island**—*Jay Rainville, rhp, Bishop Henricksen HS, Warwick. **South Carolina**—Nick Mershon, ss, St. Joseph's HS, Taylors. **South Dakota**—No formal program.

Tennessee—Brendan Murphy, 1b, Grace Baptist Academy, Chattanooga. **Texas**—John Danks, lhp, Round Rock HS. **Utah**—Aaron Jensen, rhp, Springville HS. **Vermont**—Kyle Henry, Brattleboro Union HS. **Virginia**—Matt Moses, 3b, Mills Godwin HS, Richmond. **Washington**—Tim Lincecum, rhp, Liberty HS, Issaquah. **West Virginia**—Anthony Whittington, lhp, Buffalo HS, Putnam. **Wisconsin**—Ryan Zink, rhp, Lafollette HS, Madison. **Wyoming**—No formal program.

After eight months of debate, research and discussion, the MIAA voted against a proposal to ban aluminum bats from state high school games in 2004, reversing course after the previous ruling.

Prep All-Star Games Debut

The 2003 summer season saw the debut of two high school all-star games—one for graduating seniors in Little Falls, N.J., the other for rising seniors in Fort Myers, Fla.

The All-American Baseball Game, played in June, featured several top high school picks from the 2003 draft. Righthander Jay Sborz of Langley High in Great Falls, Va., struck out five in two shutout innings and Eric Duncan of Seton Hall Prep in West Orange, N.J., went 3-for-3 as the East beat the West 8-4. Sborz was drafted in the second round by the Tigers, Duncan in the first by the Yankees.

In August, the top members of the class of 2004 were assembled to play in the first-ever AFLAC All-American High School Classic.

RICK BATTLE

Chris Nelson

Righthanders Nick Adenhart (Willamsport High, Hagerstown, Md.), Jay Rainville (Bishop Hendricken High, Pawtucket, R.I.), Andy Gale (Philips Exeter Academy, Durham, N.H.) and Mark Rogers (Mount Ararat High, Orr's Island, Maine) combined to strike out 16 batters as the East defeated the West 5-3. All four pitchers are considered possible first-round picks in 2004.

Shortstop Chris Nelson (Redan High, Decatur, Ga.) was named the event's MVP. He went 2-for-3 with three runs, a walk, a stolen base and a solo homer.

2003 HIGH SCHOOL ALL-AMERICA TEAM

Selected by Baseball America

*Junior

MEL BAILEY

Ian Stewart

BILL MITCHELL

Brandon Wood

MORRIS FOSTOFF

Lastings Milledge

Jeff Manship

RICK BATTLE

Matt Bush

FIRST TEAM

POS	Player, School	School, Hometown	AVG	AB	R	H	2B	3B	HR	RBI	SB	Drafted (Round)
C	Steve Lerud	Galena HS, Reno, Nev.	.466	103	54	48	11	1	21	64	2	Pirates (3)
1B	Mark Hamilton	Episcopal HS, Bellaire, Texas	.500	96	48	48	7	2	14	60	7	Not drafted
INF	Eric Duncan	Seton Hall Prep, Florham Park, N.J.	.536	97	42	52	11	4	12	60	18	Yankees (1)
INF	Ian Stewart	La Quinta HS, Garden Grove, Calif.	.462	104	52	48	13	0	16	61	9	Rockies (1)
INF	Brandon Wood	Horizon HS, Scottsdale, Ariz.	.500	116	65	58	18	0	20	58	15	Angels (1)
OF	Chris Lubanski	Kennedy-Kenrick HS, Schwenksville, Pa.	.528	72	36	38	3	10	6	38	20	Royals (1)
OF	Lastings Milledge	Lakewood Ranch HS, Bradenton, Fla.	.414	99	41	41	4	3	10	35	43	Mets (1)
OF	Delmon Young	Camarillo (Calif.) HS	.523	65	40	34	4	0	7	28	6	Devil Rays (1)
UT	Michael Rogers	Del City (Okla.) HS	.608	74	28	45	10	2	6	16	12	Twins (16)
			W	L	ERA	G	SV	IP	H	BB	SO	
P	Jeff Allison	Veterans Memorial HS, Peabody, Mass.	9	0	0.00	9	1	64	13	9	142	Marlins (1)
P	Justin Cassel	Chatsworth (Calif.) HS	15	0	1.13	17	1	99	57	22	119	Athletics (30)
P	Wade LeBlanc	Barbe HS, Lake Charles, La.	16	1	0.45	20	0	109	43	20	184	Devil Rays (36)
P	Jeff Manship	Ronald Reagan HS, San Antonio	13	2	0.58	17	0	85	40	18	146	Diamondbacks (50)
P	Adam Miller	McKinney (Texas) HS	10	2	0.49	18	4	86	48	16	128	Indians (1)
P	Stuart Pomeranz	Houston HS, Collierville, Tenn.	13	1	0.52	16	2	94	28	15	165	Cardinals (2)
UT	Michael Rogers	Del City (Okla.) HS	5	1	1.23	6	0	40	22	22	75	

SECOND TEAM

POS	Player, School	Class	AVG	AB	R	H	2B	3B	HR	RBI	SB	Drafted (Round)
C	Raul Rodriguez	Florida Christian School, Miami	.546	94	32	51	18	0	14	57	0	Giants (20)
1B	Brendan Murphy	Grace Baptist Acad., Chattanooga	.630	54	35	32	2	3	13	44	3	Expos (37)
INF	Jason Donald	Buchanan HS, Clovis, Calif.	.534	127	52	55	12	0	11	31	19	Angels (20)
INF	Jeff Flaig	El Dorado HS, Placentia, Calif.	.591	88	38	52	13	0	7	41	13	Mariners (2)
INF	Philip Stringer	Klein Oak HS, Spring, Texas	.523	72	39	38	7	2	9	29	26	Not drafted
OF	Adam Hale	Bellaire (Texas) HS	.460	87	40	40	12	2	4	46	19	Not drafted
OF	Mickey Hall	Walton HS, Marietta, Ga.	.392	74	20	29	7	2	7	35	6	Red Sox (2)
OF	Xavier Paul	Slidell HS, New Orleans	.391	69	31	27	4	0	9	17	18	Dodgers (4)
UT	*Matt Bush	Mission Bay HS, San Diego	.458	118	50	54	9	2	8	34	21	Not eligible
			W	L	ERA	G	SV	IP	H	BB	SO	
P	Chad Billingsley	Defiance (Ohio) HS	7	2	1.21	13	1	69	29	21	138	Dodgers (1)
P	John Danks	Round Rock (Texas) HS	10	3	1.61	18	2	100	59	27	173	Rangers (1)
P	Cliff Davis	Eupora (Miss.) HS	11	1	0.94	15	0	89	27	33	194	Astros (6)
P	Ian Kennedy	La Quinta HS, Huntington Beach, Calif.	8	0	0.43	12	3	49	19	7	76	Cardinals (14)
P	Keith Weiser	Talawanda HS, Hamilton, Ohio	8	0	0.00	13	0	78	39	8	97	Braves (18)
P	Anthony Whittington	Buffalo (W.Va.) HS	13	2	0.80	15	0	82	20	18	187	Angels (2)
UT	Matt Bush	Mission Bay HS, San Diego	8	2	1.34	13	0	68	37	21	86	

THIRD TEAM

POS	Player, School		AVG	AB	R	H	2B	3B	HR	RBI	SB	Drafted (Round)
C	C.J. Bressoud	North Cobb HS, Kennesaw, Ga.	.440	91	30	40	10	0	7	36	12	Braves (26)
1B	Brandon Lowe	Vidalia HS, Mt. Vernon, Ga.	.460	100	61	46	9	0	22	56	11	White Sox (30)
INF	Sean Rodriguez	Braddock HS, Miami	.413	80	30	33	9	0	8	21	9	Angels (3)
INF	Jonathan Fulton	George Washington HS, Danville, Va.	.476	63	23	30	4	6	1	18	10	Marlins (3)
INF	Travis Schlichting	Round Rock (Texas) HS	.413	121	41	50	13	6	4	46	11	Devil Rays (4)
OF	Chris Errecart	Lincoln HS, Stockton, Calif.	.531	96	41	51	11	3	12	41	20	Not drafted
OF	Estee Harris	Islip HS, Central Islip, N.Y.	.431	58	27	25	6	5	6	18	21	Yankees (2)
OF	Alex Presley	Neville HS, Monroe, La.	.434	99	42	43	11	2	15	41	7	Not drafted
UT	*James Parr	La Cueva HS, Albuquerque	.573	96	52	55	14	2	14	61		Not eligible
			W	L	ERA	G	SV	IP	H	BB	SO	Drafted
P	Daniel Bard	Charlotte (N.C.) Christian School	11	1	0.78	14	1	70	43	22	103	Yankees (20)
P	Jon Barratt	Hillcrest HS, Springfield, Mo.	6	1	0.14	10	1	55	13	7	111	Devil Rays (5)
P	James Houser	Sarasota (Fla.) HS	11	1	1.40	13	0	75	48	21	118	Devil Rays (2)
P	Scott Maine	Dwyer HS, Palm Beach Gardens, Fla.	5	2	0.10	12	1	64	23	16	110	Mariners (15)
P	Matt Nachreiner	Round Rock (Texas) HS	14	0	0.78	19	1	99	36	45	118	White Sox (5)
P	Robbie Wooley	Taylor HS, Kokomo, Ind.	11	1	0.90	14	0	78	34	22	149	Brewers (6)
UT	James Parr	La Cueva HS, Albuquerque	8	0	1.94	10	0	54	51	17	69	

AMATEUR BASEBALL

Team USA Olympic hopes foiled as Cuba, Canada win qualifying event

BY JOHN MANUEL

Canadian baseball fans will always be able to point to the 2003 Olympic qualifying tournament in Panama as a shining moment in the country's long baseball history. Their nation earned a spot in the Olympics for the first time since 1988.

Cuban fans will point to the tournament and their preceding World Cup victory as further proof that their nation remains virtually unbeatable in international baseball, despite defections by key players, the introduction of wood bats and the inclusion of professionals.

STAN DENNY

Rigo Beltran

Canada and Cuba qualified as the two teams that will represent the Americas at the 2004 Olympics. They were the last two teams standing at the qualifying event, played in November.

Cuba won the qualifier with three shutouts in the medal round, capped by a 5-0 victory over Canada in the final. Lefthander Adiel Palma, the only lefthander on Cuba's pitching staff, threw a two-hitter with 11 strikeouts in eight innings to beat Canada for the second time in the tournament. Cuba outscored its opponents 20-0 in the medal round.

For the United States, the 2003 Olympic qualifier will go down as one of the country's darkest moments in international baseball. A 2-1 loss to Mexico in the quarterfinal round meant that the 2000 Olympic champion would not get a chance to defend its title.

Three former big league pitchers, led by lefthander Rigo Beltran, shut down Team USA's offense in the quarterfinal upset, and Luis A. Garcia (Indians) hit a tiebreaking home run in the ninth inning as Mexico eliminated Team USA. Garcia, a former Red Sox and Cardinals farmhand, said he came to the plate against American reliever Brian Bruney (Diamondbacks) looking for a fastball he could handle. He got one on the second pitch.

"I had seen him on television and noticed he threw a lot of fastballs," Garcia said. "I got one on the inside part of the plate, a pitch I could drive."

Garcia also caught the final popup to end the game. "It's an incredible feeling pulling this off," he said. "No one believed it could happen but us."

The loss was a sour pill for a U.S. team that had run through pool play with a perfect 3-0 record and hadn't allowed its opposition a run, outscoring Nicaragua, Colombia and host Panama 20-0. Mexico had failed to win a game in three pool play games, but none of that mattered in the quarterfinal.

Team USA manager Frank Robinson (Expos) said he didn't fault the tournament format. The event was scheduled to have 13 teams, but four nations—Aruba, the Bahamas, the Dominican Republic and Venezuela—never showed up. Instead of changing the format, tournament organizers had nine teams play a round robin to eliminate only one nation—Nicaragua. Then the other eight teams played a straight one-and-done tournament. That was the perfect formula for an upset of out one of the favorites, and it happened to Team USA.

"Everyone is playing under the same system," Robinson said. "It's just as fair for us as everyone else."

For Canada, an Olympic berth was payback for 1999, when it was the host of the Pan American Games—the qualifier that year—and posted the tournament's best record. Like Team USA in 2003, the Canadians suffered a loss at the wrong time, losing 3-2 in the semifinal to Cuba.

Not this time. Canada sported the event's most powerful offense, led by young sluggers Pete LaForest (Devil Rays) and Justin Morneau (Twins). Morneau hit his fifth home run of the tournament as Canada beat Mexico 11-1 in the semifinal to earn the Olympic berth.

Cuba showed up for the qualifier without its ace starter and top reliever from the recent past, as Jose Contreras and Maels Rodriguez both had defected. Moreover, the stalwarts of the lineups for the last 15 years—players such as Antonio Pacheco, Orestes Kindelan, Luis Ulacia and the great Omar Linares—had given way to a new generation of Cuban players.

Frank Robinson

On the mound, Cuba lacks its past depth, but is still stout at the top. Ace righty Norge Vera blanked Brazil in the quarterfinals, and No. 2 starter Vicyoandri Odelin followed suit with a 10-0 shutout of Puerto Rico in the semifinal, clinching another Olympic berth. Palma added another shutout in the finale.

The Cubans have not lost in international competition since losing to Ben Sheets and Team USA in the gold-medal game of the 2000 Olympics. In the process, Cuba won the 2001 and 2003 World Cups, the 2002 Americas Series and now the 2003 Pan Ams and the Olympic qualifier. Is there any question as to who the favorite will be in Athens in 2004?

2004 OLYMPICS

Eight-team field set

With the exception of a series between South Africa and the Oceania champion to determine the eighth and final berth, the field for the 2004 Olympics baseball competition has been determined. The Olympics are set for Aug .13-29 in Athens, Greece,

The field is more noteworthy for teams that did not qualify. It does not include the United States, the 2000 Olympic gold medallist, or Korea, the bronze medallist. The U.S. failed to advance out of the America's qualifying tournament in Panama in November, while Korea failed to finish among the top two at the Asian qualifying event in Japan, also in November.

Canada and Cuba will represent the Americas, while Japan and Taiwan will represent Asia.

Despite an undistinguished track record in international baseball, Europe will field three teams—host Greece (composed mainly of Americans of Greek descent), Italy and the Netherlands. The latter two qualified at the European qualifier in July 2003.

2003 INTERNATIONAL CHAMPIONSHIPS/PROFESSIONAL

XXXV WORLD CUP
Cuba, Oct. 12-25, 2003

STANDINGS

POOL-PLAY STANDINGS

POOL A	W	L	RF	RA	POOL B	W	L	RF	RA
Cuba	6	0	52	5	Japan	7	0	74	16
Nicaragua	4	2	31	23	United States	5	1	42	11
Taiwan	3	3	29	23	Panama	5	2	67	36
Korea	3	3	51	25	Brazil	4	3	27	34
Canada	3	3	26	40	Netherlands	3	3	35	26
Italy	1	5	23	28	Mexico	2	5	35	30
Russia	1	5	12	80	China	1	6	14	63
					France	0	7	13	91

SEMI-FINALS: Panama 4, Japan 1; Cuba 6, Taiwan 3. **GOLD-MEDAL GAME:** Cuba 4, Panama 2. **BRONZE-MEDAL GAME:** Japan 7, Taiwan 3.

INDIVIDUAL BATTING LEADERS
(Minimum 20 At-Bats)

	AVG	AB	R	H	2B	3B	HR	RBI	SB
Tabares, Carlos, Cuba	.478	23	7	11	2	0	1	4	1
Sachs, Brent, USA	.478	23	8	11	3	0	0	4	1
Enriquez, Michel, Cuba	.424	33	11	14	1	1	0	10	0
Ward, Bryan, USA	.423	26	8	11	3	0	1	2	0
Saenz, Olmedo, Panama	.410	39	8	16	0	0	1	7	0
Coffie, Ivanon, Neth.	.409	22	6	9	3	0	2	3	1
Cepeda, Drederich, Cuba	.406	32	7	13	4	0	4	9	0
Ito, Yuki, Japan	.400	25	10	10	1	1	2	8	0
Cruz, Luis, Mexico	.400	25	5	10	3	0	2	4	0
Yoshida, Hiroshi, Japan	.391	23	9	9	2	0	1	3	1
Adriana, Sharnol, Neth.	.391	23	6	9	3	0	4	10	0
Yoshiura, Takashi, Japan	.387	31	7	12	0	0	5	17	3
Shimizu, Asihide, Japan	.387	31	11	12	5	0	0	3	0
Fera, Aaron, Canada	.381	21	4	8	0	0	0	2	0
Kingsale, Eugene, Neth.	.381	21	7	8	1	1	2	4	0

INDIVIDUAL PITCHING LEADERS
(Minimum 10 Innings)

	W	L	ERA	G	SV	IP	H	BB	SO
Pena, Mario, Nicaragua	2	0	0.00	3	0	11	10	1	7
Tanimura, Itsuro, Japan	2	0	0.00	4	1	10	3	2	8
Nomaguchi, Takahiro, Japan	2	0	0.50	4	0	18	9	0	15
Marchesano, Michael, Italy	1	1	0.71	2	0	13	12	3	11
Woodman, Harold, USA	1	0	0.82	2	0	11	5	0	10
Brooks, Conor, USA	1	2	0.93	4	0	10	8	0	8
Vega, Norge, Cuba	3	0	1.19	4	0	23	11	2	23
Yamada, Carlos, Brazil	2	1	1.29	3	0	21	16	6	19
Cannon, Jon, USA	2	0	1.50	3	0	18	9	7	12
Sevilla, Wilton, Nicaragua	1	0	1.54	3	1	12	4	4	8

TEAM USA
Tournament Statistics

BATTING	AVG	AB	R	H	2B	3B	HR	RBI	SB
Sachs, Brent, 2b-ss	.478	23	8	11	3	0	0	4	1
Ward, Brian, 2b	.423	26	8	11	3	0	1	2	0
Patton, Josh, ss	.375	24	7	9	1	0	2	9	0
Warner, Bryan, of	.353	34	7	12	6	0	2	11	0
Avila, Rolo, of	.345	29	7	10	1	0	0	2	7
Berrios, Harry, dh	.333	36	9	12	2	0	3	9	1
Eckelman, Alex, 3b	.312	16	1	5	0	0	0	2	0
Davilla, Vic, 1b	.250	24	5	6	2	0	1	8	0
Kison, Robbie, 3b	.231	13	5	3	1	0	0	1	0
Rumfield, Toby, c	.222	9	1	2	1	0	0	1	0
Blakely, Darren, of	.219	32	5	7	0	0	3	7	0
Goldbach, Jeff, c	.176	17	4	3	1	0	2	4	0
Jones, Brian, 1b	.067	15	2	1	0	0	0	1	0

PITCHING	W	L	ERA	G	SV	IP	H	BB	SO
Christman, Tim	0	0	0.00	4	0	3	0	1	7
Sansom, Trevor	0	0	0.00	3	0	3	2	0	5
Woodman, Hank	1	0	0.82	2	0	11	5	0	10
Brooks, Conor	1	2	0.93	4	0	10	8	0	7
Johnson, D.J.	0	0	1.42	6	1	6	6	0	7
Cannon, Jon	2	0	1.50	3	0	18	9	7	12
Thoms, Hank	1	0	1.50	1	0	6	4	0	7
Guilfoyle, Mike	1	0	1.80	5	0	5	1	3	7
Whitney, Jake	1	0	3.09	2	0	12	12	1	13
McMurray, Heath	0	0	4.91	3	0	4	3	4	2
Creek, Ryan	0	0	99.00	1	0	0	4	1	0

AMERICA'S QUALIFIER
Panama City, Panama, Nov. 1-10, 2003

STANDINGS

POOL-PLAY STANDINGS

POOL A	W	L	RF	RA	POOL B	W	L	RF	RA
Cuba	3	0	16	8	United States	3	0	20	0
Canada	2	1	18	14	Panama	3	1	28	9
Puerto Rico	1	2	12	13	Colombia	2	2	11	23
Mexico	0	3	7	18	Brazil	1	2	8	16
					Nicaragua	0	4	8	27

QUARTERFINALS: Cuba 5, Brazil 0; Puerto Rico 5, Panama 3; Canada 14, Colombia 6; Mexico 2, United States 1. **SEMI-FINALS:** Cuba 10, Puerto Rico 0; Canada 11, Mexico 1. **GOLD-MEDAL GAME:** Cuba 5, Canada 0.

TEAM USA
Tournament Statistics

BATTING	AVG	AB	R	H	2B	3B	HR	RBI	SB
Young, Ernie, dh	.455	11	2	5	1	0	1	4	0
Koonce, Graham, 1b	.364	11	3	4	2	0	1	3	0
Rouse, Michael, ss	.308	13	3	4	3	0	0	1	1
Leone, Justin, 3b	.286	14	4	4	0	0	3	3	0
Mauer, Joe, c	.273	11	0	3	1	0	0	2	0
Sizemore, Grady, of	.231	13	3	3	0	0	0	1	2
Reed, Jeremy, of	.231	13	2	3	0	1	0	0	1
Burke, Chris, 2b	.214	14	1	3	2	0	0	1	0
Holliday, Matt, of	.143	7	0	1	0	0	0	1	0
Gross, Gabe, of	.125	8	2	1	1	0	0	1	0
Laird, Gerald, c	.000	5	0	0	0	0	0	0	0
Hardy, J.J., ss	.000	3	0	0	0	0	0	0	0
Lamb, Mike, 3b	.000	0	1	0	0	0	0	0	0

PITCHING	W	L	ERA	G	SV	IP	H	BB	SO
Madson, Ryan	1	0	0.00	1	0	5	2	1	7
Ramirez, Horacio	1	0	0.00	1	0	5	1	3	2
Durbin, J.D.	0	0	0.00	2	0	3	2	1	5
VanBenschoten, John	0	0	0.00	1	0	3	2	1	4
Ring, Royce	0	0	0.00	1	0	1	1	0	1
Crain, Jesse	0	0	0.00	1	0	3	1	0	4
Williams, Todd	0	0	0.00	1	0	1	1	0	1
Stanford, Jason	1	0	0.75	2	0	12	5	1	6
Bruney, Brian	0	1	3.00	3	0	3	1	1	5

Cubans Survive Scare In World Cup

Cuba continued its dominance of World Cup play in 2003, escaping a scare from Brazil to win its 24th gold medal in 27 World Cup outings. The 16-team tournament was played in Cuba in October.

After rallying to beat Brazil in the quarterfinals, the host team cruised past Taiwan in the semifinals and then edged Panama 4-2 in the finals. With the win, Cuba lifted its overall record in the World Cup to 269-29.

Cuba rode a quartet of young hitters to the gold medal. Third baseman Michel Enriquez, filling the shoes of departed star Omar Linares, hit .424. But it was the bats of 19-year-old second baseman Yuliesky Gourriel, 20-year-old first baseman Kendry Morales and 23-year-old outfielder Frederich Cepeda that buried opponents during the medal round.

Gourriel's triple launched Cuba's face-saving rally against upset-minded Brazil, and the switch-hitting Morales followed with a homer to clinch one of the biggest comebacks in Cuba's World Cup history. Cepeda's two solo homers were the difference in the gold-medal showdown with Panama, a 4-2 victory that ended on a controversial runner's interference play at second base.

While Cuba soared, Team USA's team of independent leaguers finished a disappointing fifth.

TEAM USA AMATEUR

BY JOHN MANUEL AND ALAN MATTHEWS

By nearly any measure, the summer of 2003 was a successful one for USA Baseball's college national team. But it was one with a familiar ending for Team USA—a loss to Cuba in its most important game.

Coach Ray Tanner (South Carolina) led the team to a 27-2 record, the best for a college-level club in Team USA history, just edging the 27-3-1 mark set by the 2000 outfit coached by Mike Gillespie (Southern California).

Ray Tanner

Team USA won its first 25 games (22 on its domestic Red, White and Blue tour) before losing twice in the Pan American Games in the Dominican Republic, including a 3-1 defeat by Cuba in the gold-medal game.

Led by Olympic veterans Arial Pestano and Norge Vera, the Cubans extended their Pan Am gold streak that began in 1967—the last time the U.S. won gold. Team USA earned the silver medal at the Pan Ams, which are contested every four years, for the second straight time.

Vera, who in the wake of Jose Contreras' defection could be the island nation's top starting pitcher, dominated a U.S. lineup of college freshmen and sophomores with a two-hit complete game.

"We thought it was going to be a duel between the pitchers and it turned out to be that," said Team USA coach Ray Tanner (South Carolina). "Vera was just outstanding for Cuba. Jered Weaver (Long Beach State) battled his heart out for us, but we just weren't able to muster enough offense to get to Vera."

For Tanner, who was in his fifth tour of duty with USA Baseball but his first as head coach, the silver medal was still plenty of a reward for a summer of success.

"It was a really special summer," said Tanner, who called his fifth tour with Team USA his best. "To play 29 games and to lose only two is impressive. That doesn't mean we're satisfied, though, because we all wanted to go undefeated and win the gold medal. That's what we thought we would do.

"But we had a great time. We had a special group of players and a great coaching staff. When you spend 55 days together day and night, you have to just have a special group to be that successful."

Despite the disappointing finish, the Pan Ams were not without their share of highlights for the American team, especially on the mound. Righthander Justin Orenduff (Virginia Commonwealth) started two of the team's four shutouts in the tournament, bringing the program record to 13 for the summer.

RICH ABEL

Huston Street

Weaver and reliever Huston Street (Texas) combined on a two-hit shutout of the host Dominicans in the round-robin, beating a team that had 13 former big leaguers on the roster. Former Yankees and Athletics outfielder Luis Polonia had both Dominican hits.

After a 3-0 loss to Nicaragua relegated the U.S. to a No. 2 seed in its pool, the Americans opened medal-round play by blanking Brazil 7-0. Street then turned in an outing for the ages in Team USA's 14-inning, 3-2 semifinal win against previously-undefeated Mexico, which also used a roster full of veterans from its professional league. Already having tied Team USA's single-season and career saves marks, Street assured his place in USA Baseball lore with a 94-pitch, 8⅔-inning scoreless relief outing to squeeze out the win against Mexico.

Street gave up just three hits and wouldn't come out of the game, dealing to the end. His last pitch registered 94 mph, and he got the win as Paul Janish (Rice) plated the game-winner with a sacrifice fly in the 14th.

"What a performance by Huston Street," Tanner said. "There aren't enough adjectives to describe his performance. I kept asking him between innings if he was OK, and he kept saying 'I'm good, I'm good.' We planned to use him for about four innings but more if we needed to. He deserved to decide that ballgame."

Street finished the summer with a 29-inning scoreless streak, but he wasn't available or even needed in the gold-medal contest. Weaver entered the game with a 40-inning scoreless stretch of his own and held Cuba scoreless for five more innings.

But Cuba got to Weaver with a two-out RBI single in the sixth inning by Yulieski Gourriel, ending his scoreless

TEAM USA: COLLEGE 2003

Season Statistics (27-2)

HEAD COACH: Ray Tanner (U. of South Carolina)

BATTING	AVG	AB	R	H	2B	3B	HR	RBI	SB	College	Class
Tyler Greene, 3b-ss	.431	65	16	28	3	0	4	21	3	Georgia Tech	Fr.
Seth Smith, of	.322	87	17	28	4	0	4	9	3	Mississippi	So.
Danny Putnam, of	.321	112	21	36	8	2	2	22	4	Stanford	So.
Mike Nickeas, c	.303	66	8	20	5	0	1	10	1	Georgia Tech	So.
Dustin Pedroia, ss	.294	102	22	30	5	0	1	12	4	Arizona State	So.
Jeff Clement, c	.256	78	19	20	5	1	4	16	0	Southern California	Fr.
Jeff Larish, 1b	.255	102	19	26	3	1	8	23	1	Arizona State	So.
Brent Lillibridge, of	.253	99	15	25	7	0	4	19	3	Washington	Fr.
Eric Patterson, 2b	.245	110	28	27	6	3	1	17	13	Georgia Tech	So.
Michael Griffin, of	.211	38	8	8	1	0	0	2	1	Baylor	So.
Stephen Head, 1b-p	.211	38	4	8	2	0	1	8	0	Mississippi	Fr.
Paul Janish, 3b	.105	38	1	4	0	0	0	2	1	Rice	So.
Micah Owings, p	.000	15	1	0	0	0	0	0	0	Georgia Tech	Fr.

PITCHING	W	L	ERA	G	SV	IP	H	BB	SO	College	Class
Huston Street	1	0	0.00	14	7	29	13	4	33	Texas	So.
Jered Weaver	4	1	0.38	7	0	48	21	11	36	Long Beach State	So.
Mark Romanczuk	5	0	0.75	6	0	36	25	8	34	Stanford	Fr.
Steven Register	1	0	1.23	11	0	15	11	4	15	Auburn	So.
Justin Orenduff	6	0	1.31	6	0	41	24	13	40	Va. Commonwealth	So.
Justin Verlander	5	1	1.34	7	0	40	25	17	41	Old Dominion	So.
Stephen Head	3	0	1.50	9	0	18	13	2	17	Mississippi	Fr.
Matt Campbell	0	0	3.31	10	1	16	12	7	28	South Carolina	So.
Micah Owings	2	0	5.28	6	0	15	19	6	18	Georgia Tech	Fr.

TEAM USA: JUNIOR 2003

Pan Am Cup, Willemstad, Curacao (7-1/Silver Medal).

HEAD COACH: Doug Wabeke (Grand Rapids, Mich., CC).

BATTING	AVG	AB	R	H	2B	3B	HR	RBI	SB	High School
Brad Chalk, of	.542	24	13	13	0	0	0	3	2	Riverside HS, Greer, S.C.
Sean Henry, 3b	.481	27	12	13	3	2	0	4	1	Armijo HS, Suisun, Calif.
Billy Butler, 1b	.414	29	12	12	5	0	1	10	0	Wolfson HS, Jacksonville
Chris Valaika, 2b	.385	26	6	10	2	0	2	10	0	Hart HS, Valencia, Calif.
Chuck Lofgren, of-p	.375	32	11	12	4	1	0	15	0	Serra HS, Burlingame, Calif.
Nathan Faulkner, of	.360	25	10	9	0	0	2	11	1	Temecula Valley HS, Temecula, Calif.
Matt Bush, ss-p	.333	27	7	9	2	1	0	7	2	Mission Bay HS, San Diego
Neil Walker, dh	.310	29	10	9	5	0	0	7	0	Pine Richland HS, Gibsonia, Pa.
C.J. Bressoud, c	.278	18	5	5	2	0	0	4	0	North Cobb HS, Kennesaw, Ga.
Seth Garrison, inf	.200	5	1	1	0	0	0	1	0	Coppell (Texas) HS
Billy Killian, c	.167	6	1	1	1	0	0	3	0	Chippewa Hills HS, Stanwood, Mich.
Jon Willard, dh	.000	3	3	0	0	0	0	0	0	Green Hope HS, Morrisville, N.C.

PITCHING	W	L	ERA	G	SV	IP	H	BB	SO	High School
Erik Davis	2	0	0.00	3	0	13	3	4	18	Mountain View (Calif.) HS
Matt Bush	0	0	0.00	2	0	2	2	2	3	Mission Bay HS, San Diego
Eric Berger	0	0	0.00	2	0	2	0	1	4	Woodcreek HS, Roseville, Calif.
Armando Carrasco	0	0	0.00	1	0	1	1	0	0	Mater Dei HS, Santa Ana, Calif.
Jonathan Barratt	2	0	0.69	3	0	13	9	8	26	Hillcrest HS, Springfield, Mo.
Jeff Manship	1	0	0.84	2	0	11	6	5	20	Ronald Reagan HS, San Antonio
Eric Hurley	1	0	1.08	4	0	8	5	2	10	Wolfson HS, Jacksonville
Daniel Bard	1	1	1.59	2	0	11	8	6	11	Charlotte Christian HS, Charlotte
Blake Holler	0	0	99.00	1	0	0	0	3	0	North Vigo HS, Terre Haute, Ind.

string at 45⅔ frames. Pestano, a veteran of Cuban international clubs like the 1999 Pan Am gold-medal winners and the 2000 Olympic team, went 3-for-4 in the championship game, including a go-ahead RBI single in the seventh inning during a three-hit rally. He also added an insurance solo homer in the ninth off reliever Steven Register.

Weaver went eight innings, giving up eight hits and striking out seven while allowing two runs. He finished the summer with a 0.42 ERA in 48 innings.

"You can't do much about what happened tonight," said Weaver. "I felt great, but they just kept hitting good pitches.

"This is a once-in-a-lifetime opportunity; not everybody gets to wear USA across their chest. It has been a fabulous journey. Pitching against the Dominican and here in the gold medal game against Cuba has been the experience of my life. I wouldn't change it for the world."

This was the fifth straight year that Team USA and Cuba met in the gold medal game of a major international event, and Team USA's only win remained the complete game shutout by Ben Sheets that earned the U.S. the gold medal at the 2000 Olympics in Sydney. Cuba now leads the series of all games played between the two nations since 1987, 56-27.

Juniors Take Home Silver

USA Baseball's junior national team (18-and-under) captured a silver medal at the COPABE Junior Pan Am Cup in Willemstad, Curacao, successfully qualifying for the 2004 International Baseball Federation's World Junior Championships, to be held in Taiwan.

The juniors won seven straight games in the 12-nation competition before dropping an 8-4 decision to reigning World champion Cuba in the gold-medal game.

Cuba (8-0) took advantage of some sloppy American defense in the bottom of the fifth that allowed five runs to score, snapping a 3-3 tie. Cuban righthander Frank Montiet (2-0) worked 7⅔ innings of relief, striking out 17.

"We did start to swing the bats at the right time and it was a great experience," Team USA coach Doug Wabeke (Grand Rapids, Mich., CC) said. "Unfortunately we didn't get the job done in the championship game. We ran into a pretty good pitcher and had some defensive lapses that made for a tough night."

Team USA had outscored its seven previous opponents 86-11 but struggled against Montiet.

"He had excellent command and excellent velocity, and he shut down a group that had led the tournament in hitting," Team USA coach Doug Wabeke said. "(Montiet) threw two different curveballs that he could throw on any count and his fastball was in the 90-94 range."

Though Team USA settled for silver, a handful of rising high school seniors elevated their prospect status during the event, notably outfielders Chuck Lofgren (Serra High, Burlingame, Calif.), who hit .375 with a team-leading 15 RBIs, and Brad Chalk (Riverside High, Greer, S.C.), who led the team with a .711 on-base percentage and the tournament with a .542 average.

The pitching staff posted a 1.03 ERA overall. Lefthander Jonathan Barratt, an unsigned

TEAM USA: YOUTH 2003

World Youth Championships, Kaohsiung, Taiwan (7-1/Gold Medal)

HEAD COACH: Don Freeman (Prairie, Wash.)

BATTING	AVG	AB	R	H	2B	3B	HR	RBI	SB	High School, Hometown
Anthony Perez, p	.667	3	2	2	0	0	0	2	0	Pace HS, Hialeah, Fla.
Jarred Bogany, of	.619	21	8	13	4	0	0	2	1	Fort Bend Bush HS, Houston
Justin Bristow, ss	.516	31	9	16	2	0	3	11	2	Mills Godwin HS, Richmond, Va.
Danny Espinosa, 2b	.483	29	10	14	1	1	0	5	1	Mater Dei HS, Santa Ana, Calif.
Ike Davis, 1b	.464	28	8	13	7	0	0	10	0	Chaparral HS, Scottsdale, Ariz.
Aaron Luna, of-3b	.423	26	10	11	3	1	1	7	0	Carroll HS, Southlake, Texas
Landon Hernandez, c	.400	20	8	8	3	1	2	10	2	Desert Christian HS, Cathedral City, Calif.
Josh Zeid, p-3b	.400	5	0	2	1	0	0	5	0	Hamden Hall County HS, New Haven, Conn.
Sean O'Sullivan, of-p	.379	29	9	11	3	0	2	9	1	Valhalla HS, El Cajon, Calif.
Jason Codiroli, p-of	.364	11	3	4	1	0	0	3	0	Archbishop Mitty HS, San Jose
Lammar Guy, of	.353	17	6	6	3	1	1	5	0	Lake Brantley HS, Sanford, Fla.
Brandon Laird, 3b-of	.323	31	7	10	4	0	0	3	0	La Quinta HS, Garden Grove, Calif.
Joseph Parigi, p	.333	6	3	2	1	0	0	3	0	Monterey (Calif.) HS
Jay Ponciano, c	.250	8	4	2	1	0	0	2	1	Hudson Bay HS, Vancouver, Wash.
Mark Ortega, 2b-of	.231	13	1	3	2	0	0	2	1	King's Academy, Palm Beach, Fla.

PITCHING	W	L	ERA	G	SV	IP	H	BB	SO	High School, Hometown
Jeremy Hellickson	2	0	0.00	2	0	14	8	1	17	Hoover HS, Des Moines
Josh Zeid	1	0	0.00	2	0	6	6	1	9	Hamden Hall County HS, New Haven, Conn.
Kyle Thebeau	0	0	0.00	1	0	4	1	1	4	Carroll HS, Corpus Christi, Texas
Ike Davis	1	0	0.00	1	0	3	0	1	4	Chaparral HS, Scottsdale, Ariz.
Brandon Laird	0	0	0.00	1	0	2	1	1	4	La Quinta HS, Garden Grove, Calif.
Justin Bristow	0	0	0.00	1	0	1	0	1	2	Mills Godwin HS, Richmond, Va.
Kasey Kiker	0	0	2.45	3	1	7	11	4	9	Russell County HS, Phenix City, Ala.
Anthony Perez	1	0	2.57	2	0	7	9	1	7	Pace HS, Hialeah, Fla.
Joseph Parigi	1	1	6.23	2	0	9	5	5	11	Monterey (Calif.) HS
Sean O'Sullivan	1	0	6.75	2	1	7	9	3	6	Valhalla HS, El Cajon, Calif.
Jason Codiroli	0	0	11.37	1	0	6	8	2	7	Archbishop Mitty HS, San Jose

2003 INTERNATIONAL CHAMPIONSHIPS/AMATEUR

PAN AMERICAN GAMES
Santo Domingo, Dominican Republic
August 1-15, 2003

POOL-PLAY STANDINGS

POOL A	W	L	RF	RA
Mexico	2	1	18	15
Cuba	2	1	10	7
Brazil	1	2	10	18
Panama	1	2	11	9

POOL B	W	L	RF	RA
Nicaragua	4	0	19	1
United States	3	1	24	3
Dominican Republic	2	2	25	5
Gautemala	1	3	10	29
Bahamas	0	4	2	42

GOLD-MEDAL GAME: Cuba 3, United States 1.

COPABE PAN AM CHAMPIONSHIP
2004 World Junior Qualifier
Willemstad, Curacao
July 14-24, 2003

POOL-PLAY STANDINGS

POOL A	W	L
United States	5	0
Panama	3	2
Netherlands Antilles	3	2
Brazil	2	3
Dominican Republic	1	4
Guatemala	1	4

POOL B	W	L
Cuba	5	0
Venezuela	4	1
Colombia	3	2
Canada	2	3
Mexico	1	4
Aruba	0	5

GOLD-MEDAL GAME: Cuba 8, United States 4.

WORLD YOUTH CHAMPIONSHIP
Kaohsiung, Taiwan
August 8-17, 2003

POOL-PLAY STANDINGS/Preliminary Phase

POOL A	W	L	RF	RA
United States	4	0	52	6
Taiwan	3	1	58	10
Japan	2	2	26	21
Czech Republic	1	3	22	70
South Africa	0	4	10	61

POOL B	W	L	RF	RA
Cuba	3	0	52	7
Australia	2	1	60	16
Korea	1	2	31	11
Indonesia	0	3	2	111

POOL-PLAY STANDINGS/Final Phase

POOL C	W	L	RF	RA
Taiwan	2	0	23	10
United States	1	1	25	18
Cuba	1	1	22	24
Australia	0	2	6	24

SEMI-FINALS: Taiwan 6, Australia 3; United States 2, Cuba 1. **GOLD-MEDAL GAME:** United States 11, Taiwan 7. **BRONZE-MEDAL GAME:** Cuba 10, Australia 9.

FINAL STANDINGS: 1. United States. 2. Taiwan. 3. Cuba. 4. Australia. 5. Korea. 6. Japan. 7. Czech Republic. 8. South Africa. 9. Indonesia.

Most Valuable Player: Justin Bristow, ss, United States.

fifth-round pick of the Devil Rays at the time (he later signed), and rising senior Erik Davis (Mountain View, Calif., HS) both went 2-0. Barratt struck out 26 in 13 innings while Davis didn't allow a run in 13 innings.

Youth Team Wins Gold

USA Baseball's youth national team earned its third consecutive title in the International Baseball Federation's 2003 World Youth Championship in Kaohsiung, Taiwan. Team USA defeated host Taiwan 11-7 in the championship game, adding a third gold medal to those earned in 1998 and 2001, and improving the youth team's record to 40-5 in its six years of international competition.

RICK BATTLE

Pitching aces for Team USA medal winners
Erik Davis, left, and Jeremy Hellickson

Catcher Landon Hernandez (Desert Christian High, Cathedral City, Calif.) slammed a three-run home run to cap a four-run fifth inning that put the U.S. ahead 10-4. Lefthander Kasey Kiker (Russell County High, Phenix City, Ala.) successfully secured the lead with 3⅔ innings of relief, allowing an unearned run on four hits. Outfielder Jarred Bogany (George Bush High, Houston) went 4-for-4, scored twice and stole a base for the 18-member American 16-and-under squad.

"Our players appeared relaxed and confident throughout the day and warmups," Team USA coach Don Freeman said. "We felt what we had to do was go out and play the way we had been playing during the week."

The victory against Taiwan came a day after Team USA defeated Cuba in the semifinals, an accomplishment American teams at other levels struggled to manage. Righthander Jeremy Hellickson (Hoover High, Des Moines) dealt a complete-game six-hitter, striking out 12 in the 2-1 decision.

"Jeremy did an absolutely phenomenal job," Freeman said. "He was in total command. The importance of his pitching job can't be expressed enough."

The 6-foot, 185-pound Hellickson was 2-0 over 14 scoreless innings with 17 strikeouts and one walk in the tournament. Perhaps the most promising U.S. prospect at the event, Hellickson threw between 88-90 mph consistently, touching 92.

Shortstop Justin Bristow (Mills Godwin High, Richmond), who led the team with 16 hits in 31 at-bats (.519) and 11 RBIs, was named the tournament's MVP. He had a key two-run single in the seventh inning of the gold-medal game.

The team was selected from a 33-player pool at trials in Los Angeles comprised of the top talent from Team USA's youth national championships held earlier in Tucson and Jupiter, Fla.

The U.S. won the gold medal despite playing without three of the nation's top players in the 16-and-under age bracket. Outfielder Austin Jackson (Ryan High, Denton, Texas) and shortstop Justin Upton (Great Bridge High, Chesapeake, Va.) opted to stay stateside because of health concerns surrounded by the SARS epidemic that gripped Taiwan much of 2003. Righthander Ryan Mitchell (Magnolia High, Tomball, Texas) backed out, citing other travel-related concerns.

Adenhart named top youth player

When the Maryland Orioles found themselves facing elimination in the 21-and-under All-American Amateur Baseball Association World Series in Johnstown, Pa., they did what any other team would do: They turned to their best pitcher.

PLAYER of the YEAR

It's just that not many such teams' best pitcher is a 16-year-old.

After the Orioles lost the first game of the double-elimination event, coach Dean Albany knew only one of his players could take the mound in the high-pressure situation and deliver. Nick Adenhart didn't disappoint.

"I hadn't planned on pitching Nick in the second game but we needed a lift," Albany said. "I knew we'd be in the ballgame if we had him on the mound."

Adenhart, a rising senior righthander at Williamsport High in Hagerstown, Md., shut out Philadelphia through four innings as the Orioles took a 5-0 lead. He allowed two runs and had 11 strikeouts in six innings, and the Orioles went on a six-game winning streak to take the 2003 AAABA title.

Adenhart stood out in a league consisting almost entirely of college-age players. His standout summer featured stellar performances on the biggest stages following a dominant high school season, making him Baseball America's 2003 Youth Player of the Year.

One of the top prospects in the class of 2004 and a probable first-round pick in June, Adenhart went 7-1, 1.00 as a junior at Williamsport High. At 6-foot-3, 185 pounds, he has a projectable body and an effortless delivery with sound mechanics, part of the reason he was ranked as the top prospect at the 2003 East Coast Professional Showcase in Wilmington, N.C.

RICK BATTLE

Nick Adenhart

Adenhart proved he was more than a high school kid looking to gain experience against older competition. He went 8-1, 1.65 with 75 strikeouts and 16 walks, surrendering just 38 hits in 52 innings for the Orioles.

"He has tremendous mound presence," said Albany, who is also a scout with the Baltimore Orioles. "He was the youngest player on the team, but he handled himself very well. He looks like a guy who is always in control when he's on the mound."

Many of those who have seen Adenhart pitch compare him to another high-profile righthander from Maryland. Scouting reports on Phillies prospect Gavin Floyd as a senior in high school are almost identical to those on Adenhart.

Floyd was the fourth overall pick in 2001 as a 6-foot-5, 200-pounder from Mount St. Joseph High in suburban Baltimore. Floyd was lauded for a plus breaking ball and outstanding makeup, as is Adenhart.

"It's not hard to figure out that they both have great arms and their curveballs are comparable and they played on the same summer and fall league teams," said Albany, who also coached and scouted Floyd.

YOUTH TOP 5

1. Nick Adenhart, rhp, Hagerstown, Md. (16)
2. Chris Nelson, ss-rhp, Decatur, Ga. (17)
3. Matt Bush, ss-rhp, San Diego (17)
4. Justin Upton, ss, Chesapeake, Va. (15)
5. Ryan Klem, rhp-of, Chandler, Ariz. (12)

Weeks wins Spikes award

USA Baseball tabbed one of its own as the 2003 Golden Spikes Award winner.

GOLDEN SPIKES AWARD

Southern second baseman Rickie Weeks, who spent the summers of 2001 and 2002 in the red, white and blue uniform of Team USA, was named the award's winner. The Golden Spikes Award goes to the top amateur player in the country.

BILL MITCHELL

Rickie Weeks

Weeks, whom the Milwaukee Brewers selected second overall in the 2003 draft, was also Baseball America's College Player of the Year after winning his second consecutive NCAA Division I batting title. He hit .479 in 2003 with 16 home runs and 66 RBIs, on the heels of his .495-20-96 season in 2002. He finished his career as Division I's career batting leader with a record .473 average.

"Growing up as a little kid, I always wanted to be considered one of the best players in the country, so I'm very elated to win the Golden Spikes Award," Weeks said. "It's the Heisman Trophy of baseball."

The other finalists were Tulane first baseman Michael Aubrey; Stanford outfielder Carlos Quentin; Wake Forest righthander Kyle Sleeth; and Richmond righthander Tim Stauffer.

Weeks joins an exclusive club as the 26th recipient of the award. Every winner since Alabama's Dave Magadan in 1983 has played in the major leagues except for recent winners such as South Carolina's Kip Bouknight (2000), a Rockies farmhand.

PREVIOUS **WINNERS**

1978—Bob Horner, 3b, Arizona State
1979—Tim Wallach, 1b, Cal State Fullerton
1980—Terry Francona, of, Arizona
1981—Mike Fuentes, of, Florida State
1982—Augie Schmidt, ss, New Orleans
1983—Dave Magadan, 1b, Alabama
1984—Oddibe McDowell, of, Arizona State
1985—Will Clark, 1b, Mississippi State
1986—Mike Loynd, rhp, Florida State
1987—Jim Abbott, lhp, Michigan
1988—Robin Ventura, 3b, Oklahoma State
1989—Ben McDonald, rhp, Louisiana State
1990—Alex Fernandez, rhp, Miami-Dade CC
1991—Mike Kelly, of, Arizona State
1992—Phil Nevin, 3b, Cal State Fullerton
1993—Darren Dreifort, rhp-dh, Wichita State
1994—Jason Varitek, c, Georgia Tech
1995—Mark Kotsay, of-lhp, Cal State Fullerton
1996—Travis Lee, 1b, San Diego State
1997—J.D. Drew, of, Florida State
1998—Pat Burrell, 3b, Miami
1999—Jason Jennings, rhp-dh, Baylor
2000—Kip Bouknight, rhp, South Carolina
2001—Mark Prior, rhp, Southern California
2002—Khalil Greene, ss, Clemson

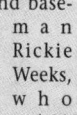

Weaver enjoys record summer

BY JOHN MANUEL

As Team USA righthander Jered Weaver walked off the mound at *Estadio Quisqueya* in Santo Domingo, the capital of the Dominican Republic, he wondered what kind of ovation he would get from the Dominican fans.

PLAYER of the YEAR

It was the eighth inning of his team's 2-0 victory against the host nation in pool play at the 2003 Pan American Games. Weaver was handing the ball and the game over to closer Huston Street for the final five outs. He jogged toward the dugout, and that's when he heard the cheers.

Around 20,000 fans had overwhelmed the ballpark to see the Americans—a team of college freshmen and sophomores like Weaver—play their national club, which had 13 former big leaguers on the roster. They had been loud and passionate the entire game, but when Weaver came out they were in full throat once more, standing to acknowledge his two-hit shutout performance.

"That might be the best experience of my life," Weaver said after returning to the United States, ready to begin his junior year at Long Beach State. "There were about 20,000 people and they were all rooting against us, and to leave the game ahead and for us to win it, it was pretty exhilarating. I was pretty pumped for that one."

It showed on the radar gun. Team USA coaches say Weaver hit 96 mph with his fastball and was in the mid-80s with his power slider while shutting down the Dominicans. Big league veteran Luis Polonia, 38, had both hits off Weaver, who extended his scoreless innings streak for the summer to 40.

Weaver ran the streak to 45⅔ before giving up a run to Cuba in the Pan Am gold medal game. Weaver ended up giving up two runs in seven frames as the Cubans won 3-1 and handed the 6-foot-6, 200-pounder his first defeat of the summer in five decisions.

That did little to dim Weaver's accomplishments, however. He started five of a team-record 13 shutouts by the staff, which compiled a 1.29 ERA, best in Team USA history. His 0.38 ERA broke Dewon Brazelton's program record, set in 2000, and Weaver allowed just 21 hits in 48 innings—a .135 opponents batting average. For his efforts, Weaver earned Baseball America's 2003 Summer Player of the Year award.

Better known as the younger brother of New York Yankees righthander Jeff Weaver, Jered resembles his brother physically and in his pitching motion.

He was a first-team All-American for the 49ers in the spring of 2003, going 14-4, 1.96 with 144 strikeouts and just 20 walks in 133 innings.

RICH ABEL

Scoreless streak reached 45⅔ innings
Team USA's Jered Weaver

PREVIOUS WINNERS

1984—Will Clark, 1b, Team USA
—Rafael Palmeiro, of, Hutchinson (Jayhawk)
1985—Jeff King, 3b, Team USA
—Bob Zupcic, of, Liberal (Jayhawk)
1986—Jack Armstrong, rhp, Wareham (Cape Cod)
—Mike Harkey, rhp, Fairbanks (Alaska)
1987—Cris Carpenter, rhp, Team USA
1988—Robin Ventura, 3b, Team USA
—Ty Griffin, 2b, Team USA
1989—John Olerud, 1b-lhp, Palouse (Alaska)
1990—Calvin Murray, of, Anchorage Bucs (Alaska)
1991—Chris Roberts, of, Team USA
1992—Jeffrey Hammonds, of, Team USA
1993—Geoff Jenkins, of, Team USA
1994—Steve Carver, 1b, Anch. Glacier Pilots (Alaska)
1995—Travis Lee, 1b, Team USA
1996—Seth Greisinger, rhp, Team USA
1997—Pat Burrell, 3b, Team USA
1998—Bobby Kielty, of, Bourne (Cape Cod)
1999—Xavier Nady, 3b, Team USA
2000—Mark Teixeira, 3b, Team USA
2001—Bobby Brownlie, rhp, Team USA
2002—Brad Sullivan, Team USA

top FIVE

1. Jered Weaver, rhp, Team USA
2. Huston Street, rhp, Team USA
3. Thomas Diamond, rhp, St. Cloud (Northwoods)
4. Tyler Greene, 3b, Team USA
5. J.C. Holt, of, Brewster (Cape Cod)

SUMMER LEAGUE ALL-AMERICA TEAM

Selected by Baseball America

FIRST TEAM

Pos.	Player	Club/League	College	AVG	AB	R	H	HR	RBI
C	Brett Hayes	Santa Barbara (Cal. Coast.)	Nevada	.340	156	33	53	0	18
1B	Adam LaRoche	Wareham (Cape Cod)	Grayson (Texas) CC	.326	92	15	30	6	18
2B	Hyung Cho	Yar.-Dennis (Cape Cod)	Houston	.336	137	17	46	4	22
3B	Tyler Greene	Team USA	Georgia Tech	.431	65	16	28	4	21
SS	Dustin Pedroia	Team USA	Arizona State	.294	102	22	30	1	12
OF	Sam Fuld	Hyannis (Cape Cod)	Stanford	.361	119	28	43	1	14
	J.C. Holt	Brewster (Cape Cod)	Louisiana State	.388	134	25	52	11	9
	Danny Putnam	Team USA	Stanford	.321	112	21	36	2	22
DH	Hunter Pence	Liberal (Jayhawk)	UT Arlington	.427	143	48	61	7	39

Pos.	Player	Club/League	College	W	L	ERA	IP	H	BB	SO
SP	Eric Beattie	Bourne (Cape Cod)	Tampa	4	0	0.39	46	23	6	51
	Thomas Diamond	St. Cloud (Northwoods)	New Orleans	6	1	1.63	72	43	21	103
	Justin Orenduff	Team USA	Va. Commonwealth	6	0	1.31	41	24	13	40
	Jered Weaver	Team USA	Long Beach State	4	1	0.38	48	21	11	36
RP	Huston Street	Team USA	Texas	1	0	0.00	29	13	4	33

SECOND TEAM

C—Erick San Pedro, Staunton/Valley (Miami). **1B**—Jeff Larish, Team USA (Arizona State). **2B**—Chris Malec, Yarmouth-Dennis/Cape Cod (UC Santa Barbara). **3B**—Van Pope, Danville/Central Illinois (Meridian, Miss., CC). **SS**—Grant Psomas, Pittsburgh/Great Lakes (West Virginia). **OF**—Marshall Hubbard, Outer Banks/Coastal Plain (North Carolina); Kyle Keen, Keene/New England (Georgia); Jeff Van Houten, Harrisonburg/Valley (Arizona). **DH**—Daniel Carte, Columbus/Great Lakes (Winthrop).

SP—Ryan Mullins, Riverpoint/New England (Vanderbilt); Mark Romanczuk, Team USA (Stanford); Jeremy Sowers, Wareham/Cape Cod (Vanderbilt); Justin Verlander, Team USA (Old Dominion). **RP**—David Haehnel, El Dorado/Jayhawk (Illinois-Chicago).

SUMMER LEAGUES

BY JOHN MANUEL

For the first time since Nomar Garciaparra was their shortstop, Orleans claimed the Cape Cod League's Arnold Mycock trophy in 2003, sweeping a two-game championship series against Bourne. The Cardinals won their first series by sweeping Brewster (including a 14-inning 1-0 victory) and became the first team to go undefeated in the Cape's postseason since Wareham in 1997.

Righthander Ryan Schroyer (Arizona State) won the first game out of the bullpen for Orleans and struck out five of the six batters he faced in the clincher to earn the save. First baseman Cesar Nicolas (Vanderbilt) was named the playoffs MVP after totaling three home runs and four RBIs in four playoff games. Nicolas also won the league's home run derby during the all-star game festivities.

Despite losing in the first-round of the playoffs, Brewster walked away with most of the league's top individual awards. Outfielder J.C. Holt (Louisiana State) won the batting title at .388 and was named the league's MVP; Jarrett Santos (UNC Greensboro) was named the top reliever after going 2-1, 1.42 with 11 saves; and Bob Macaluso earned manager of the year honors for leading the Whitecaps to the Eastern Division title.

Northwoods League star St. Cloud's Thomas Diamond

Two-time defending champion Wareham had entered the 2003 season as the league favorite on the strength of an unprecedented assemblage of pitching talent. Once Rice righthanders Josh Baker and Wade Townsend arrived from the College World Series, the Gatemen had at least a half-dozen pitchers who threw their fastballs comfortably in the 90s, plus smooth, efficient lefthander Jeremy Sowers (Vanderbilt), an unsigned 2001 first-round pick.

Freshman righthanders Mark McCormack (Baylor) and Jason Neighborgall (Georgia Tech) were unmatched in terms of pure velocity. Despite all the pitching talent, the Gatemen would have finished with the league's poorest record if their final game hadn't been washed out. Wareham went just 4-13 in one-run games.

After pitching Rice to the College World Series championship, Philip Humber, Jeff Niemann and Townsend weren't in peak form in the Cape Cod League but continued to establish themselves as prime draft picks for 2004. Humber didn't fare as well as Niemann and Townsend, the league's top two talents, but didn't hurt his stock.

"I've ranked Niemann, Townsend and Humber in every possible order the last two years," an American League scouting director said. "They could all go in the top five picks next year."

Taiwan Wins NBC Championship

Taiwan's national team became the first foreign entry in the 69-year history of the National Baseball Congress World Series to win the title as it beat the Santa Barbara (Calif.) Foresters in the championship game 5-0.

Righthander Chang-Wei Tu, 21, stopped the Foresters on one hit while pitching to only 28 hitters—one more than the minimum. Overall, he went 3-0 with two saves in the 16-day tournament and didn't allow an earned run in 23 innings. He spun two shutouts and was named the tournament's MVP.

Taiwan went 9-1 in the 44-team, double-elimination tournament. It was forced to come back through the loser's bracket after suffering a 4-3, third-round loss to the defending champion Alaska Goldpanners, who promptly lost their next two games—in 15 innings to Havasu, Ariz., and then to Santa Barbara.

Taiwan used just six pitchers in its 10 games and they combined to post a 1.25 ERA, allowing only 52 hits in 86 innings. None was better than Tu, a 6-foot-2, 185-pound righthander.

"I learned a lot in the United States, and I'd like to pitch here someday," Tu said. "The hitters are so strong here. We don't see hitters like that back home."

Tu took a no-hitter into the sixth inning against Santa Barbara before it was broken up by shortstop Nick McCoola (Wichita State), who was erased on a double play.

All-tournament shortstop Yung-Chi Chen, who led Taiwan with a .405 average and 11 RBIs in the tournament, had three hits in the deciding game. His first-inning single started a three-run uprising that put the game out of reach early.

The Goldpanners, six-time NBC champions, earned a return engagement to Wichita by winning the Alaska League regular season title. Alaska's second team, Athletes in Action, also made an early exit after drawing the No. 2 seed.

In other summer league highlights:

■ The Arlington Senators won their sixth consecutive Clark Griffith League title with a 7-0 win over Fauquier, their third shutout of the postseason tourney, but were unable to defend their title at the All-American Amateur Baseball Association World Series in Johnstown, Pa. The Senators won the tournament four of the previous five seasons but Youse's Maryland Orioles won the 2003 title, beating the host Johnstown team 19-0 in the deciding game.

■ St. Cloud righthander Thomas Diamond (New Orleans) had an outstanding season in the Northwoods League, going 6-1, 1.63 with 103 strikeouts in 72 innings. He gave up just 43 hits, holding opponents to a .171 average. In his best start against Alexandria, he threw a no-hitter and struck out 17. St. Cloud lost in the playoffs to Wisconsin, which posted the league's best regular-season record.

■ In their first season in the league, the Lehigh Valley Catz won the Atlantic Collegiate League championship with a 10-7 victory against the two-time defending champion New Jersey Colts.

■ Outfielder Fernando Perez (Columbia) provided the winning margin with a two-run homer to lead Columbus to a 2-1 win against Delaware in the Great Lakes League championship game. Perez was named the postseason MVP while righthander Josh Newman (Ohio State) got the win, striking out 11 in 8⅔ innings. Columbus won its seventh championship in the league's 17-year history.

COLLEGE SUMMER LEAGUES

NCAA-CERTIFIED

CAPE COD LEAGUE

EAST	W	L	T	PCT	Pts
Brewster Whitecaps	24	17	3	.585	51
Orleans Cardinals	25	18	1	.581	51
Chatham A's	22	21	1	.512	45
Yarmouth-Dennis Red Sox	21	22	1	.488	43
Harwich Mariners	21	22	1	.488	43
WEST	**W**	**L**	**T**	**PCT**	**Pts**
Bourne Braves	23	19	1	.548	47
Hyannis Mets	21	19	4	.525	46
Cotuit Kettleers	20	21	2	.488	42
Wareham Gatemen	17	25	1	.405	35
Falmouth Commodores	16	26	1	.381	33

PLAYOFFS—Semifinals: Bourne defeated Hyannis 2-1 and Orleans defeated Brewster 2-1 in best-of-3 series. **Final:** Orleans defeated Bourne 2-0 in best-of-3 series.

ALL-STAR TEAM: C—Curtis Thigpen, Yarmouth-Dennis (Texas). **1B**—Joey Metropoulos, Falmouth (Southern California). **2B**—Hyung Cho, Yarmouth-Dennis (Houston). **3B**—Warner Jones, Wareham (Vanderbilt). **SS**—Ryan Klosterman, Chatham (Vanderbilt). **IF**—Cesar Nicolas, Orleans (Vanderbilt). **OF**—Sam Fuld, Hyannis (Stanford); J.C. Holt, Brewster (Louisiana State); Justin Maxwell, Bourne (Maryland); Eric Neilsen, Cotuit (Nevada-Las Vegas). **DH**—Sean Gamble, Yarmouth-Dennis (Auburn). **SP**—Eric Beattie, Bourne (Tampa); Jeremy Sowers, Wareham (Vanderbilt); Jarrett Santos, Brewster (Alabama). **RP**—Zane Carlson, Chatham (Baylor).

Most Valuable Player: J.C. Holt, of, Brewster (Louisiana State). **Outstanding Pitcher:** Eric Beattie, rhp, Bourne (Tampa). **Manager of the Year:** Bob Macaluso, Brewster.

TOP 20 PROSPECTS: 1. Jeff Niemann, rhp, Harwich (Rice). **2.** Wade Townsend, rhp, Wareham (Rice). **3.** Andy LaRoche, ss/1b, Wareham (Grayson County, Texas, CC). **4.** Jeremy Sowers, lhp, Wareham (Vanderbilt). **5.** John Mayberry Jr., of/1b, Yarmouth-Dennis (Stanford). **6.** Mark McCormick, rhp, Wareham (Baylor). **7.** Philip Humber, rhp, Yarmouth-Dennis (Rice). **8.** David Purcey, lhp, Orleans (Oklahoma). **9.** Chris Lambert, rhp, Chatham (Boston College). **10.** Jason Neighborgall, rhp, Wareham (Georgia Tech). **11.** Eric Beattie, rhp, Bourne (Tampa). **12.** Jonathan Zeringue, of, Orleans (Louisiana State). **13.** Justin Maxwell, of, Bourne (Maryland). **14.** Garrett Mock, rhp, Yarmouth-Dennis (Houston). **15.** Kyle Schmidt, rhp, Bourne (Georgia Tech). **16.** Zach Jackson, lhp, Hyannis (Louisville). **17.** Garry Bakker, rhp, Cotuit (North Carolina). **18.** Jeremy Slayden, of, Falmouth (Georgia Tech). **19.** Matt Macri, 3b, Brewster (Notre Dame). **20.** Luke Hochevar, rhp, Cotuit (Tennessee).

INDIVIDUAL BATTING LEADERS

(Minimum 119 Plate Appearances)

	AVG	AB	R	H	2B	3B	HR	RBI	SB
Holt, J.C., Brewster	.388	134	25	52	6	1	1	9	13
Fuld, Sam, Hyannis	.361	119	28	43	7	0	1	14	10
Jones, Warner, Wareham	.344	186	20	64	11	2	1	12	6
Cho, Hyung, Y-D	.336	137	17	46	7	0	4	22	0
Nielsen, Eric, Cotuit	.333	150	25	50	11	2	2	23	4
Gamble, Sean, Y-D	.319	113	20	36	3	1	1	7	9
Maxwell, Justin, Bourne	.307	153	18	47	5	1	2	17	9
Patterson, Ryan, Brewster	.288	118	13	34	8	1	2	24	3
McCann, Brad, Harwich	.283	127	17	36	10	1	2	16	0
Zeringue, Jonathan, Orleans	.283	127	21	36	8	1	3	22	4
Crowe, Trevor, Y-D	.283	159	23	45	6	4	1	18	12

INDIVIDUAL PITCHING LEADERS

(Minimum 35 Innings)

	W	L	ERA	G	SV	IP	H	BB	SO
Beattie, Eric, Bourne	4	0	0.39	7	0	46	23	6	51
Schmidt, Kyle, Bourne	2	2	0.55	8	0	49	28	18	63
Gogal, Jeff, Falmouth	3	1	0.60	8	0	45	31	7	46
Grant, Tim, Bourne	3	0	0.74	14	4	37	26	7	30
Butler, Bret, Brewster	2	2	0.75	6	0	36	20	8	26
Bigley, Dennis, Bourne	3	1	0.77	5	0	35	20	5	30
Yates, Adam, Chatham	2	1	0.96	19	0	38	20	10	30
Startup, Will, Orleans	1	2	1.19	17	2	38	23	7	37
Rawl, Aaron, Brewster	5	0	1.20	7	0	45	40	4	41
Sowers, Jeremy, Wareham	4	3	1.20	9	0	67	47	17	64

KEN BABBITT

Part of a deep, talented staff
Wareham lefthander Jeremy Sowers

BOURNE

BATTING	AVG	AB	R	H	2B	3B	HR	RBI	SB
Bush, Tim, 1b-3b	.000	2	1	0	0	0	0	0	1
Butia, Michael, of	.230	122	11	28	3	0	2	12	3
Dobson, Sean, of	.227	150	17	34	5	1	1	8	6
Gunther, Barry, c	.134	82	6	11	0	0	0	3	1
Ivany, Devin, c	.243	107	12	26	3	1	0	13	1
Johnson, Taylor, of	.190	63	3	12	0	0	0	5	2
Maxwell, Justin, of	.307	153	18	47	5	1	2	17	9
Mercurio, Matt, 2b	.178	73	7	13	3	0	1	2	1
Morgan, Ryan, dh	.233	103	11	24	8	0	3	15	0
Palumbo, Jeff, 2b-3b	.224	125	12	28	2	0	1	7	6
Remole, Clifton, 1b	.238	143	16	34	6	0	3	12	3
Tolbert, Matt, ss	.215	149	13	32	7	1	0	11	6
Toussaint, Andrew, 3b	.231	117	13	27	4	1	2	14	1

PITCHING	W	L	ERA	G	SV	IP	H	BB	SO
Bakker, Kyle	0	1	20.25	2	0	3	7	6	1
Beattie, Eric	4	0	0.39	7	0	46	23	6	51
Bigley, Dennis	3	1	0.77	5	0	35	20	5	30
Bongiovanni, Vince	3	2	2.89	6	0	28	25	12	32
Bush, Tim	0	0	4.50	2	0	2	2	1	3
Dagenhart, Jeff	4	2	2.52	9	0	50	40	13	41
Glanzmann, Jake	1	4	4.74	10	0	44	51	11	30
Grant, Tim	3	0	0.74	14	4	37	26	7	30
Layden, Tim	0	0	13.50	1	0	1	1	0	1
Morgan, Ryan	1	0	0.60	10	1	15	9	2	13
Schmidt, Kyle	2	2	0.55	8	0	49	28	18	63
Shapiro, Scott	1	2	2.75	11	1	20	14	13	10
Shaver, Chris	1	3	2.91	8	1	34	38	14	25
Slorp, Andrew	0	2	2.79	12	3	19	16	5	23
Thatcher, Joe	0	0	2.25	3	0	4	4	0	2

BREWSTER

BATTING	AVG	AB	R	H	2B	3B	HR	RBI	SB
Bixler, Brian, ss-2b	.120	108	7	13	2	0	0	7	3
Broderick, Ryan, of	.214	70	5	15	3	1	0	2	0
Burt, Jim, of	.213	75	11	16	6	0	0	6	2
Crabtree, Ben, c	.215	130	4	28	7	0	0	16	0

AMATEUR BASEBALL

	AVG	AB	R	H	2B	3B	HR	RBI	SB
Figueroa, Paco, 2b-ss	.250	116	14	29	4	0	0	6	12
Hathaway, Aaron, c-of	.206	141	17	29	4	0	0	10	5
Hendricks, Trey, 1b-dh	.216	116	8	25	4	0	2	10	0
Himes, Ben, of	.200	15	1	3	0	0	1	1	0
Holt, J.C., of-2b	.388	134	25	52	6	1	1	9	13
Larsen, Kyle, 1b	.286	105	15	30	3	0	3	19	0
Lemieux, Jared, of	.000	1	0	0	0	0	0	0	0
Macri, Matt, 3b	.172	122	23	21	4	1	7	16	8
Manzella, Tommy, ss-2b	.164	134	12	22	3	1	0	6	4
Patterson, Ryan, of	.288	118	13	34	8	1	2	24	3
Rice, Toby, of	.273	11	0	3	0	0	0	1	0
Twomley, Jason, of	.345	29	5	10	0	0	3	7	0

PITCHING	W	L	ERA	G	SV	IP	H	BB	SO
Bauer, Ricky	3	2	3.66	9	0	52	54	6	23
Butler, Bret	2	2	0.75	6	0	36	20	8	26
Davidson, Phillip	2	3	3.57	8	0	45	34	14	32
Dayley, James	0	0	9.00	4	0	3	5	3	1
Krise, Kris	1	4	2.81	13	1	32	36	12	28
Lalor, Conor	3	1	3.57	10	0	23	28	8	26
Meagher, Michael	1	0	1.80	1	0	5	4	1	3
Noonan, Chris	0	3	3.75	19	1	24	21	11	13
Ransom, Robert	2	0	0.47	4	0	19	8	4	15
Rawl, Aaron	5	0	1.20	7	0	45	40	4	41
Rummonds, Josh	2	1	2.03	9	0	44	36	6	27
Santos, Jarrett	2	1	1.42	23	11	32	20	12	27
Thomson, Jordan	1	0	3.38	17	0	32	33	15	25

CHATHAM

BATTING	AVG	AB	R	H	2B	3B	HR	RBI	SB
Anderson, Matt, 1b	.215	144	10	31	3	0	0	12	1
Delaney, Jason, 1b-dh	.183	93	9	17	3	0	2	8	1
Dillion, Zack, c	.168	95	7	16	5	0	1	6	1
Frazier, Jeff, of	.250	180	15	45	11	1	2	22	4
Getz, Chris, 2b	.206	97	9	20	4	1	0	6	1
Green, Zane, of-dh	.233	86	8	20	2	0	0	4	4
Hackney, Matt, c	.222	9	1	2	0	0	0	0	0
Ingold, Ben, 3b-ss	.171	123	9	21	6	1	0	20	1
Klosterman, Ryan, ss	.279	154	29	43	8	1	4	15	13
Lahey, Tim, c	.179	67	4	12	3	0	1	7	0
Pritz, Bryan, of	.254	142	17	36	7	0	4	15	3
Raglani, Anthony, of	.258	128	18	33	4	2	6	15	5
Scioletti, Brad, 3b-2b	.214	14	1	3	1	0	0	1	0
Witt, Paul, 2b-3b	.182	99	14	18	1	2	0	4	7

PITCHING	W	L	ERA	G	SV	IP	H	BB	SO
Avery, James	4	5	3.46	10	0	55	44	22	42
Carlson, Zane	0	2	1.35	18	10	20	18	5	29
Davidson, Dan	0	1	4.30	9	0	15	15	11	12
Jamison, Neil	1	0	1.13	20	1	32	23	8	41
Lambert, Chris	3	3	2.12	9	0	51	23	23	56
Ohlendorf, Ross	0	2	6.26	13	0	27	23	20	28
Ramirez, Edgar	0	0	32.40	2	0	2	6	2	0
Rice, Tim	3	3	1.50	10	0	48	38	29	31
Rogers, Jason	1	1	3.20	7	0	20	22	9	14
Swanson, Glenn	5	1	2.14	9	0	55	58	19	54
Tucci, Nick	3	2	3.00	11	0	33	30	14	28
Yates, Adam	2	1	0.96	19	0	38	20	10	30

COTUIT

BATTING	AVG	AB	R	H	2B	3B	HR	RBI	SB
Baisley, Jeff, 3b	.253	154	12	39	6	0	2	19	7
Bocchi, Joel, c	.145	55	5	8	3	0	0	4	1
Diaz, Dennis, 2b	.190	21	4	4	0	0	0	0	4
Fiorentino, Jeff, of	.188	133	9	25	5	0	2	10	6
Gill, Blake, 2b-of	.225	120	14	27	1	1	2	6	5
Hardy, John, ss	.268	142	19	38	10	0	2	12	12
Nielsen, Eric, of-1b	.333	150	25	50	11	2	2	23	4
Parraz, Zeke, 2b-ss	.229	105	13	24	3	0	0	9	5
Sammons, Clint, c-1b	.208	106	10	22	5	0	0	10	2
Smith, C.J., 1b	.254	142	18	36	10	2	5	20	0
Suarez, Alex, of	.114	44	4	5	1	0	0	3	3
Timpner, Clay, of	.238	143	14	34	10	1	0	12	8
Wickman, Joe, of	.221	77	10	17	2	0	0	4	2

PITCHING	W	L	ERA	G	SV	IP	H	BB	SO
Axford, John	1	0	9.00	7	0	9	4	16	8
Bakker, Garry	2	0	1.76	9	0	51	36	21	48
Brickle, Donald	1	1	1.59	6	0	17	17	2	6
Brower, Kevin	1	2	4.82	12	1	19	21	10	14
Cobb, Taylor	0	1	7.88	4	1	8	7	8	11
Deel, Josh	3	3	1.59	13	0	45	24	14	47
Espineli, Eugene	2	2	1.48	20	2	30	30	13	35
Hochevar, Luke	1	1	1.10	11	6	16	16	3	21
Holmen, Ian	0	1	6.75	1	0	4	5	2	1
Hyle, Michael	1	4	3.72	11	0	46	46	15	30
Layden, Tim	0	0	2.08	4	0	4	6	1	3
Little, Joe	3	2	3.26	7	0	30	25	19	30
Lubrano, Paul	1	2	3.53	9	0	51	46	16	43
Phillips, Shawn	0	0	0.00	1	0	0	1	1	0
Valdes-Fauli, Shaun	1	0	4.76	3	1	6	8	1	2
Worrell, Mark	3	2	4.80	9	0	45	44	15	40

FALMOUTH

BATTING	AVG	AB	R	H	2B	3B	HR	RBI	SB
Anderson, Doug, 3b	.000	9	0	0	0	0	0	0	0
Anderson, Drew, 2b	.209	148	11	31	9	0	2	8	7
Eastman, Collin, of	.000	2	0	0	0	0	0	0	0
Eck, Brian, c	.000	6	0	0	0	0	0	0	0
Hernandez, Brian, c	.088	114	8	10	0	0	0	4	0
Johnson, Brent, of	.199	141	14	28	3	0	2	17	7
Lawhorn, Darryl, ss	.204	157	10	32	10	0	5	19	3
LaFontain, J.T., 3b	.176	17	1	3	1	0	0	2	0
Lewis, Chris, 3b	.211	123	14	26	2	0	1	8	6
LeFaivre, Steve, of	.128	94	13	12	6	0	1	4	0
Mahoney, Collin, c	.220	91	7	20	2	0	2	7	1
Metropoulos, Joey, 1b	.243	148	25	36	4	0	11	21	2
Ruiz, Ryan, if-of	.138	58	6	8	2	0	0	2	3
Slayden, Jeremy, of	.231	121	14	28	4	1	5	13	1
Towns, Antone, of	.143	35	1	5	2	0	0	0	1
Wirth, Rob, of	.172	58	6	10	1	0	1	4	0

PITCHING	W	L	ERA	G	SV	IP	H	BB	SO
Gale, Chris	1	0	9.00	3	0	4	7	2	3
Gogal, Jeff	3	1	0.60	8	0	45	31	7	46
Gomes, Brandon	0	2	5.87	11	0	15	22	4	14
Hahn, Jeff	1	6	4.24	9	0	47	43	18	35
Jerome, Clayton	0	1	4.15	2	0	9	12	1	9
Lewis, Jensen	0	1	3.80	15	3	21	20	7	34
Mahoney, Collin	0	0	3.00	3	0	3	0	3	4
Mohl, Billy	3	2	1.62	6	0	39	21	4	35
Niesel, Chris	1	4	7.18	13	7	26	24	11	33
Quick, Kody	0	0	5.00	12	0	18	22	12	14
Reeves, Zack	0	0	6.75	2	0	4	6	2	6
Ruhlman, Jayson	2	3	4.06	8	0	44	38	16	34
Sues, Jeff	0	3	3.00	7	0	36	24	23	38
Tracz, Chris	4	3	4.29	9	0	57	68	9	39
Varner, Matt	1	0	12.60	5	0	5	8	4	7

HARWICH

BATTING	AVG	AB	R	H	2B	3B	HR	RBI	SB
Akers, Chuck, of	.196	97	10	19	1	0	0	7	6
Archer, Josh, 1b	.175	120	4	21	5	0	3	12	0
Davidson, Drew, of	.200	15	1	3	0	0	0	1	1
Dragicevich, Jeff, ss-2b	.219	146	16	32	5	0	2	16	1
Festa, Tony, 1b-3b	.183	153	13	28	3	0	0	14	0
Hulett, Tug, 2b	.207	116	25	24	6	0	0	6	13
Jeroloman, Chuck, ss	.315	92	6	29	9	0	0	8	2
Leonard, Mike, c	.198	96	11	19	3	0	1	7	2
McCann, Brad, 3b	.283	127	17	36	10	1	2	16	0
Newman, Cory, of	.233	120	9	28	2	0	1	9	4
Reynolds, Mark, of-2b	.304	23	3	7	0	1	0	1	0
Toregas, Wyatt, c	.236	140	12	33	5	2	2	15	1
Van Note, Steven, of	.218	142	18	31	6	0	3	9	7
Weathers, Trent, of	.143	91	8	13	0	0	0	3	3

PITCHING	W	L	ERA	G	SV	IP	H	BB	SO
Acors, Duke	1	3	3.08	11	1	26	30	15	25
Field, Kevin	0	1	5.40	1	0	5	5	1	5
Frost, Michael	1	1	2.49	8	1	25	20	5	26
Happ, James	2	1	2.61	9	0	48	45	20	52
Hedrick, Justin	3	2	1.96	9	0	60	39	18	68
James, Mike	3	1	3.27	13	1	22	21	6	20
Lynch, Kevin	1	2	2.28	13	1	24	23	6	22
Niemann, Jeff	2	0	0.00	4	0	19	17	8	19
Paxton, Colby	1	2	5.63	7	0	32	45	7	12
Reid, Joe	0	1	6.30	6	0	20	21	16	23
Shirek, Phil	0	2	1.67	10	0	32	23	20	43
Sprouse, Shannon	1	3	1.69	20	10	21	21	9	22
Swindle, R.J.	6	3	3.29	9	0	63	65	7	53

HYANNIS

BATTING	AVG	AB	R	H	2B	3B	HR	RBI	SB
Athas, Mike, 2b-1b	.147	68	6	10	1	1	0	4	1
Baty, Ryan, 1b	.274	135	15	37	6	0	0	19	5
Cleary, Andrew, 1b-c	.200	5	0	1	1	0	0	1	0
D'Argento, Russ, of	.222	9	1	2	0	0	0	2	0
Dlugach, Brent, 3b	.077	13	1	1	0	0	0	1	0
Fuld, Sam, of	.361	119	28	43	7	0	1	14	10

Hall, Brian, 3b	.248	109	16	27	4	1	1	16	11
Harrison, Ben, of	.322	59	7	19	2	1	0	12	5
Horwitz, Brian, of	.132	53	3	7	1	0	0	4	4
Klink, Simon, 3b	.125	32	1	4	0	0	0	2	0
Lucy, Donny, c	.262	122	10	32	2	0	1	12	5
Mann, David, of	.000	10	1	0	0	0	0	0	0
McCauley, A.J., of	.211	109	12	23	1	0	0	4	9
McMillan, Brett, dh-1b	.158	19	1	3	0	0	0	1	0
Mercado, Richard, c	.214	145	10	31	4	1	0	16	1
Sauls, Matt, of	.240	125	15	30	3	1	0	9	3
Tordi, Justin, ss	.184	141	13	26	4	0	0	11	4
Tucker, Jonathan, 2b	.259	170	24	44	5	1	1	11	16

PITCHING	W	L	ERA	G	SV	IP	H	BB	SO
Cassidy, Kevin	0	1	3.00	2	0	6	8	0	4
Doveala, Brian	0	2	4.97	10	0	25	27	8	19
Jackson, Zach	6	0	1.88	8	0	53	42	10	48
Jecmen, Mark	0	0	8.10	2	0	3	3	3	5
King, Travis	0	0	7.71	1	0	2	4	1	2
Lewis, Jon	1	1	6.14	9	0	22	26	7	12
Miller, Chandler	0	0	1.69	4	0	5	6	4	3
Morley, Tim	3	1	1.75	13	0	26	16	11	24
Sabo, Tim	4	3	3.33	8	0	49	35	26	36
Sauls, Mark	1	2	2.38	13	0	45	29	25	49
Shappi, A.J.	3	1	2.65	8	0	51	44	11	36
Simmons, Justin	1	4	4.81	6	0	34	34	12	20
Taylor, Graham	2	0	1.14	7	0	24	16	7	17
Tubb, Austin	0	1	1.40	16	10	19	11	1	11
Walker, Sean	0	3	3.57	11	3	23	27	9	17

ORLEANS

BATTING	AVG	AB	R	H	2B	3B	HR	RBI	SB
Allen, Rodney, of	.213	136	10	29	5	0	1	10	5
Boggs, Brandon, of	.216	125	15	27	3	0	0	8	8
Buffone, Anthony, c-if	.146	96	5	14	3	0	0	4	3
Cooksey, Matt, of	.248	105	28	26	3	0	1	7	16
Harris, Clay, 3b-1b	.157	89	5	14	3	0	1	5	0
Itri, Rob, 2b-3b	.156	32	1	5	1	0	0	3	0
Jaramillo, Jason, c	.210	100	14	21	5	0	2	13	4
Leslie, Myron, ss-3b	.269	156	26	42	9	0	4	19	13
LeNoir, Bobby, 2b-3b	.188	85	5	16	3	0	0	8	2
Lockin, Billy, 2b-ss	.238	126	11	30	4	0	0	8	14
Nicolas, Cesar, 1b	.243	152	20	37	11	1	5	28	2
Roberson, Ryan, of	.212	99	9	21	2	0	3	10	0
Zeringue, Jonathan, of	.283	127	21	36	8	1	3	22	4
Zickgraf, A.J., c	.143	14	0	2	1	0	0	1	0

PITCHING	W	L	ERA	G	SV	IP	H	BB	SO
Bray, Bill	2	1	1.44	18	4	25	22	2	29
Camardese, Brandon	3	1	1.08	6	0	33	20	16	26
Edsall, Steve	0	1	6.00	2	0	3	3	0	1
Estrada, Jesse	0	6	4.42	9	0	39	40	14	28
James, Rhett	7	1	2.60	14	0	55	32	21	65
Metzger, Jay	1	3	3.94	6	0	32	36	4	18
Purcey, David	4	1	1.88	9	0	53	27	28	60
Schroyer, Ryan	1	0	1.42	13	3	19	10	4	24
Smith, Brett	3	1	2.92	9	0	49	46	16	52
Startup, Will	1	2	1.19	17	2	38	23	7	37
Swindell, Mike	2	1	2.45	11	1	26	19	13	27
Weaver, Joe	0	0	3.00	3	0	6	4	3	2
Woody, Abe	1	0	0.77	17	0	23	17	10	28

WAREHAM

BATTING	AVG	AB	R	H	2B	3B	HR	RBI	SB
Armitage, Jon, of	.255	145	17	37	3	0	4	12	7
Emanuele, Chris, of	.248	125	15	31	6	0	0	12	3
Ford, Josh, c	.188	138	11	26	6	0	2	12	3
Hollimon, Michael, ss	.197	117	11	23	8	0	2	13	6
Holmes, Justin, 2b	.095	21	1	2	2	0	0	1	0
Jones, Warner, 3b	.344	186	20	64	11	2	1	12	6
Kazmar, Sean, 2b	.231	13	2	3	0	0	0	2	1
Kutler, Matt, of	.228	145	15	33	6	0	0	9	4
LaRoche, Andy, ss-1b	.326	92	15	30	4	0	6	18	3
Lind, Adam, 1b	.269	104	11	28	5	0	2	11	0
Locke, Drew, of	.262	42	4	11	2	0	0	2	3
Pendleton, Lance, of-p	.170	47	6	8	3	0	1	3	1
Relihan, Paddy, of	.000	3	0	0	0	0	0	0	0
Reynolds, Kyle, 2b	.227	119	12	27	3	0	2	10	4
Rodgers, Adam, c-1b	.264	91	13	24	6	1	3	11	1
Sipp, Tony, of	.000	1	0	0	0	0	0	0	0
Stavinoha, Nick, c	.111	36	2	4	1	0	1	3	0

PITCHING	W	L	ERA	G	SV	IP	H	BB	SO
Baker, Josh	1	1	3.04	11	1	27	23	7	38
Guyette, Kevin	3	2	3.21	8	0	48	39	13	25
Howell, J.P.	0	4	3.68	9	0	29	24	20	39
McCormick, Mark	2	1	2.12	7	2	34	20	18	41
Monds, Devin	0	0	2.70	5	0	3	2	5	1
Neighborgall, Jason	0	5	3.81	12	0	28	15	29	37
Newsom, Randy	0	0	20.25	3	1	1	4	0	0
Pendleton, Lance	0	0	0.00	2	0	1	2	1	3
Shepard, Kevin	2	1	1.72	12	0	31	20	14	25
Sowers, Jeremy	4	3	1.20	9	0	67	47	17	64
Sowers, Josh	0	1	5.40	3	0	5	7	1	9
Stewart, Clayton	0	0	7.36	2	0	4	3	3	4
Taylor, Drew	1	1	1.53	7	0	18	13	10	9
Taylor, Trey	3	3	2.13	8	0	51	44	8	38
Townsend, Wade	1	3	1.82	5	1	30	21	9	39

YARMOUTH-DENNIS

BATTING	AVG	AB	R	H	2B	3B	HR	RBI	SB
Carter, Chris, dh-of	.197	61	9	12	2	0	1	5	0
Cho, Hyung, 3b-ss	.336	137	17	46	7	0	4	22	0
Ciaramella, Matt, of	.203	79	3	16	1	0	0	5	0
Crowe, Trevor, of-if	.283	159	23	45	6	4	1	18	12
Finigan, P.J., ss	.083	12	2	1	0	0	0	0	0
Gamble, Sean, of	.319	113	20	36	3	1	1	7	9
Hundley, Nick, c	.153	72	5	11	2	1	1	5	1
Johnson, Rob, c-of	.213	80	6	17	2	0	1	9	5
Kungl, Jake, 3b-1b	.281	32	6	9	1	0	0	0	0
Malec, Chris, 2b-of	.280	143	18	40	4	1	2	14	3
Mansolino, Tony, 3b	.254	71	10	18	2	0	0	9	2
Mayberry Jr., John, of-1b	.370	73	6	27	5	1	0	10	1
Nicholson, David, ss-of	.274	95	16	26	5	1	1	8	10
Szabo, Marshall, 2b	.206	63	8	13	2	1	0	8	1
Thigpen, Curtis, c-of	.280	100	14	28	6	0	0	13	3
Whisler, Wes, 1b-p	.162	99	10	16	2	0	1	13	2

PITCHING	W	L	ERA	G	SV	IP	H	BB	SO
Ardoin, Kevin	0	0	9.00	2	0	6	10	2	3
Brauer, Jim	5	3	2.26	9	0	56	48	14	43
Finigan, P.J.	2	0	3.48	13	1	31	27	7	19
Graham, Sam	1	0	2.08	2	0	9	7	8	4
Humber, Phil	1	4	5.28	6	0	31	27	14	35
Keadle, Justin	4	4	2.83	10	0	64	46	27	66
McLoughlin, Matt	0	0	0.00	1	0	1	0	1	1
Meier, Justin	1	1	1.19	14	6	23	13	4	42
Meloan, John	1	0	1.93	13	2	23	19	6	25
Mock, Garrett	2	3	4.17	7	0	37	26	17	48
Moore, Justin	0	1	18.56	4	0	5	11	8	4
Templet, Jordy	4	3	1.97	7	0	46	30	13	46
Tisone, Nick	0	1	2.96	11	1	27	29	19	22
Walker, Aaron	0	0	13.50	4	0	4	4	4	3
Whisler, Wes	0	2	2.63	7	0	14	14	3	9

OTHER NCAA-CERTIFIED LEAGUES

ATLANTIC COLLEGIATE LEAGUE

WOLFF	W	L	PCT	GB
Lehigh Valley Catz	29	11	.725	—
Quakertown Blazers	25	17	.595	5
Scranton Red Soxx	17	25	.405	13
Berkshire Red Sox	15	27	.357	15
Jersey Pilots	14	28	.333	16

KAISER	W	L	PCT	GB
New Jersey Colts	30	12	.714	—
Metro New York Cadets	28	12	.700	1
Long Island Collegians	20	22	.476	10
New York Generals	14	23	.378	13½
Stamford Robins	10	27	.270	17½

PLAYOFFS: **Semifinals**—Lehigh Valley defeated Quakertown 2-1 and New Jersey defeated Long Island 2-0 in best-of-3 series. **Final**—Lehigh Valley defeated New Jersey in one-game championship.

Most Valuable Player: Graig Badger, New Jersey (Rutgers). **Outstanding Pitcher**: Donnie Smith, rhp, Lehigh Valley (Old Dominion).

TOP 10 PROSPECTS: 1. Shaun Parker, lhp, Jersey (Rutgers). **2.** Donnie Smith, rhp, Lehigh Valley (Old Dominion). **3.** Alex Perez, lhp, Miami (New Jersey). **4.** Ryan Mahoney, c, New Jersey (South Carolina). **5.** Jordan Foster, 3b, Stamford (Lamar). **6.** Erik Ruff, 1b/rhp, Lehigh Valley (West Chester, Pa.). **7.** Tom Sgueglia, 2b, Metro N.Y. (Rockland, N.Y., CC). **8.** Milton Feliciano, rhp, Metro N.Y. (Okaloosa-Walton, Fla., CC). **9.** Anthony Varvaro, rhp, Metro N.Y. (St. John's). **10.** Kevin Wright, of, Jersey (Kean, N.J.).

INDIVIDUAL BATTING LEADERS

(Minimum 100 Plate Appearances)

	AVG	AB	R	H	2B	3B	HR	RBI	SB
Foster, Jordan, Stamford	.385	117	16	45	9	0	4	25	0

Burke, Joe, Metro NY	.368	133	35	49	10	3	1	26	18
DeSiena, Joseph, Metro NY	.366	93	15	34	5	0	0	13	6
Molinini, Mike, Metro NY	.353	116	30	41	6	0	0	21	11
Badger, Graig, New Jersey	.349	109	30	38	7	2	0	13	38
Kiesel, Evan, Quakertown	.342	161	37	55	11	1	5	21	9
Schultz, Eddie, Jersey	.341	132	24	45	14	1	5	27	2
Ledbetter, Ted, LV	.330	106	15	35	10	0	0	19	3
Wright, Kevin, Jersey	.324	102	23	33	2	3	5	13	14
Ruff, Eric, Lehigh Valley	.323	130	20	42	7	1	4	28	6
Echevarria, Steve, NJ	.322	121	18	39	9	2	0	21	3
Leitgeb, Jim, Quakertown	.317	126	25	40	6	0	0	15	6
Dennis, Bernie, NJ	.311	90	15	28	5	0	0	13	1
Hehner, Doug, Metro NY	.311	90	16	28	9	0	1	20	3
Kuklick, Clay, Quakertown	.309	97	19	30	4	1	2	21	0

INDIVIDUAL PITCHING LEADERS

(Minimum 30 Innings)

	W	L	ERA	G	SV	IP	H	BB	SO
Smith, Donnie, Lehigh Valley	5	0	0.66	10	0	41	23	12	60
Legiadre, Chris, NJ	4	1	1.07	10	1	42	33	4	20
Beecher, Nic, Scranton	4	2	1.24	8	1	51	34	9	58
Feliciano, Milton, Metro NY	3	1	1.54	8	2	35	29	9	32
Perez, Alex, New Jersey	5	1	1.57	8	1	34	28	14	34
Reedy, Ted, New Jersey	3	0	1.78	9	0	35	31	11	31
Parker, Shaun, Jersey	4	2	1.95	8	0	51	30	22	61
Varvaro, Anthony, Metro NY	2	1	2.13	7	1	38	27	22	38
Watzek, Kurt, Lehigh Valley	4	2	2.15	10	0	50	32	21	50
Luzim, Mike, Long Island	4	1	2.21	8	0	37	34	10	23

CENTRAL ILLINOIS COLLEGIATE LEAGUE

EAST	W	L	PCT	GB
Danville Dans	28	16	.636	—
Decatur Blues	22	22	.425	6
Twin City Stars	17	27	.386	11
WEST	**W**	**L**	**PCT**	**GB**
Quincy Gems	23	21	.523	—
Bluff City Bombers	22	22	.500	1
Springfield Rifles	20	24	.455	3

POSTSEASON TOURNAMENT: Danville (4-1) defeated Bluff City (3-2) in championship game of four-team, double-elimination tournament.

Player of the Year: Logan Hughes, 3b, Bluff City (Missouri-St. Louis). **Pitcher of the Year**: None; Danville staff.

TOP 10 PROSPECTS: 1. Van Pope, 3b, Danville (Meridian, Miss., JC). **2.** Matt Daley, rhp, Danville (Bucknell). **3.** Kyle Bloom, lhp, Twin City (Illinois State). **4.** Anthony Albano, of, Quincy (Evansville). **5.** Reid Brees, of, Danville (Baylor). **6.** Justin Blaine, lhp, Danville (San Diego). **7.** Jose Tadeo, rhp, Quincy (Culver Stockton, Mo.). **8.** Jeremy Pickrel, of, Twin City (Illinois State). **9.** Jesse Krause, rhp, Springfield (Purdue). **10.** Grover Benton, of, Springfield (Webber, Fla.).

INDIVIDUAL BATTING LEADERS

(Minimum 100 Plate Appearances)

	AVG	AB	R	H	2B	3B	HR	RBI	SB
Benton, Grover, Springfield	.364	99	19	36	5	2	0	12	8
Hughes, Colby, Bluff City	.331	169	30	56	14	2	3	29	6
Landi, Joe, Twin City	.314	118	20	37	3	1	0	9	9
Reynolds, Kevin, Bluff City	.311	90	11	28	4	3	0	12	6
Blaesing, Greg, Twin City	.303	119	10	36	12	0	0	17	2
Pope, Van, Danville	.290	169	22	49	10	1	4	26	6
Negron, Jason, Decatur	.286	126	13	36	3	0	0	7	4
Brees, Reid, Danville	.284	151	23	43	4	1	6	32	13
Coles, Mike, Decatur	.284	116	18	33	7	0	1	14	8
Munoz, Dan, Bluff City	.278	115	14	32	7	1	5	17	2
Albano, Anthony, Quincy	.278	162	27	45	6	2	5	20	6
Desmond, Geoff, Danville	.277	155	19	43	13	1	2	16	3
Howell, Ryan, Decatur	.275	149	20	41	10	2	2	28	11
Barnes, Eric, Bluff City	.274	95	11	26	2	0	0	7	2
Geisler, Neil, Decatur	.268	149	21	40	12	1	0	16	5

INDIVIDUAL PITCHING LEADERS

(Minimum 30 Innings)

	W	L	ERA	G	SV	IP	H	BB	SO
Daley, Matt, Danville	3	0	0.00	18	2	32	14	5	39
Blaine, Justin, Danville	5	3	1.13	10	0	48	29	13	42
Spurgeon, Steve, Danville	0	1	1.41	20	2	32	13	9	20
Huffman, Ben, Danville	6	3	1.45	12	0	68	50	18	59
Borgmann, Brian, Danville	7	2	1.76	12	0	61	51	6	31
Stewardson, Will, Spring.	0	1	1.85	16	0	34	30	12	29
Bloom, Kyle, Twin City	3	1	2.01	8	0	54	36	13	71
Tadeo, Jose, Quincy	4	2	2.12	17	2	47	36	23	37
Dunn, Brooks, Danville	5	1	2.18	10	0	54	37	24	32
Keating, Brian, Bluff City	4	3	2.26	10	0	68	48	12	93

COASTAL PLAIN LEAGUE

NORTH	W	L	PCT	GB
+*Petersburg Generals	32	16	.667	—
Outer Banks Daredevils	28	21	.571	4½
Peninsula Pilots	23	23	.500	8
Edenton Steamers	12	34	.261	19
SOUTH	**W**	**L**	**PCT**	**GB**
+Florence RedWolves	28	19	.596	—
Wilmington Sharks	29	22	.569	1
*Durham Americans	25	23	.521	3½
Fayetteville Swampdogs	21	24	.467	6
Wilson Tobs	19	28	.404	9
WEST	**W**	**L**	**PCT**	**GB**
+*Thomasville Hi-Toms	32	16	.667	—
Asheboro Copperheads	23	21	.523	7
Spartanburg Stingers	19	26	.422	11½
Gastonia Grizzlies	14	32	.250	17

+First-half champion. *Second-half champion

PETTIT CUP TOURNAMENT: Outer Banks (3-0) defeated Florence (2-1) in championship game of eight-team, single-elimination tournament.

Player of the Year: Marshall Hubbard, of, Outer Banks (North Carolina). **Pitcher of the Year**: Brian Hensen, Wilmington (Elon).

TOP 10 PROSPECTS: 1. Marshall Hubbard, of, Outer Banks (North Carolina). **2.** Ryan Gordon, of/lhp, Thomasville (UNC Greensboro). **3.** Chip Cannon, 3b, Thomasville (The Citadel). **4.** Juan Figueroa, 1b/lhp, Petersburg (Bethune-Cookman). **5.** Ryan Zimmerman, 3b/ss, Peninsula (Virginia). **6.** Jake Hurry, lhp, Florence (Coastal Carolina). **7.** Mike Davern, rhp, Wilson (UC Irvine). **8.** Stephen Tolleson, ss, Spartanburg (South Carolina). **9.** Josh Cribb, rhp, Florence (Clemson). **10.** Brett Harker, rhp, Peninsula (Charleston).

INDIVIDUAL BATTING LEADERS

(Minimum 100 Plate Appearances)

	AVG	AB	R	H	2B	3B	HR	RBI	SB
Figueroa, Juan, Petersburg	.355	152	27	54	12	1	5	30	6
Shimizu, T.J., Petersburg	.339	124	23	42	4	0	0	13	9
Hubbard, Marshall, OB	.337	166	29	56	15	1	7	37	5
Howard, Jason, Florence	.333	156	20	52	10	0	1	24	2
Zimmerman, Ryan, Pen.	.331	142	12	47	8	1	1	19	3
Triplett, Bryan, Asheboro	.330	94	19	31	6	1	1	23	8
Grove, Jeremiah, Spart.	.323	99	23	32	9	1	0	7	25
Deeb, Bobby, OB	.322	143	32	46	9	0	0	17	8
Gregg, Davy, Florence	.318	179	37	57	6	2	0	10	16
Tolleson, Steve, Spart.	.313	99	20	31	9	2	0	12	12
Tartaglia, Evan, Asheboro	.311	135	37	42	2	0	0	7	31
Griffin, Kevin, Wilson	.306	144	14	44	4	0	1	14	1
Frazier, Will, Durham	.304	171	19	52	10	0	6	34	9
Davison, Todd, OB	.297	192	34	57	3	2	0	23	6
Thomas, Allen, Fayetteville	.294	170	28	50	4	0	0	20	16

INDIVIDUAL PITCHING LEADERS

(Minimum 30 Innings)

	W	L	ERA	G	SV	IP	H	BB	SO
Senatore, Scott, Wilm.	2	2	0.52	17	2	34	21	13	31
Ruwe, Kyle, Peninsula	3	0	0.87	5	0	41	23	2	34
Fish, Josh, Spartanburg	2	2	0.87	16	6	31	16	19	22
Mobley, Chris, Florence	4	4	1.01	10	0	53	40	31	46
Hensen, Brian, Wilmington	9	1	1.03	13	0	79	60	3	51
Falcon, Ryan, Durham	5	1	1.04	11	0	61	38	22	72
Hurry, Jake, Florence	4	0	1.05	12	0	60	41	16	37
Norfleet, Matt, Florence	2	4	1.15	25	13	39	21	16	40
Hill, Ronald, Wilmington	4	1	1.36	7	0	40	21	5	31
Carter, Andy, Fayetteville	4	3	1.37	13	0	79	56	26	69

GREAT LAKES LEAGUE

	W	L	T	PCT	Pts
Northern Ohio Baseball	32	9	0	.780	64
Columbus All-Americans	28	14	0	.667	56
Lima Locos	26	12	0	.684	52
Delaware Cows	26	15	0	.634	52
Southern Ohio Copperheads	19	20	1	.487	39
Grand Lake Mariners	19	17	0	.527	38
Stark County Terriers	17	23	1	.425	35
Pittsburgh Pandas	17	22	0	.435	34
Indianapolis Servants	14	28	0	.327	28
Youngstown Express	11	28	0	.267	22
Murrysville Maulers	9	29	0	.237	18

PLAYOFFS: Columbus defeated Delaware in championship game of four-team, double elimination tournament.

ALL-STAR TEAM: **C**—Grant Neidenfeuhr, Columbus (Winthrop). **1B**—Anthony Gressick, Southern Ohio (Ohio). **IF**—Ed Lucas, Columbus (Dartmouth); Matt Miller, Columbus (Wooster, Ohio); Grant Psomas, Pittsburgh (West Virginia). **3B**—Bryan Byrne, Northern Ohio (St. Mary's, Calif.); Jake Frank, Grand Lake (Wooster, Ohio). **UT**—Mark Abro, Lima (Western Michigan); Mike Martinez, Northern Ohio (Cal State Fullerton). **OF**—Daniel Carte, Columbus (Winthrop); Danny Dorn, Northern Ohio (Cal State Fullerton); Davey Johnson, Northern Ohio (Gonzaga); Dan Lunsford, Delaware (Ohio); Adam Witter, Stark County (East Carolina). **DH**—Nick Cadena, Northern Ohio (Arizona State). **P**—Burke Badenhop, Stark County (Bowling Green); Chris Bova, Stark County (Ohio); Ryan Doherty, Delaware (Notre Dame); Eric Dworkis, Northern Ohio (Gonzaga); Eli Friedman, Pittsburgh (Pittsburgh); Tyler Mott, Columbus (Ohio Wesleyan); Brian Osmogrosso, Pittsburgh (Indiana State); Seth Stanley, Delaware (Kentucky).

Player of the Year: Daniel Carte, of, Columbus. **Pitcher of the Year**: Tyler Mott, Columbus.

TOP 10 PROSPECTS: **1.** Ricky Romero, lhp, Northern Ohio (Cal State Fullerton). **2.** Eric Dworkis, rhp, Northern Ohio (Gonzaga). **3.** Grant Psomas, ss, Pittsburgh (West Virginia). **4.** Daniel Carte, of, Columbus (Winthrop). **5.** Ryan Doherty, rhp, Delaware (Notre Dame). **6.** Mark Jecmen, rhp, Stark County (Stanford). **7.** Chris Bova, rhp, Stark County (Ohio). **8.** Chris Gutierrez, ss, Delaware (Oklahoma State). **9.** Andrew Butera, c, Northern Ohio (Central Florida). **10.** Mike Martinez, 3b-rhp, Northern Ohio (Cal State Fullerton).

INDIVIDUAL BATTING LEADERS
(Minimum 100 Plate Appearances)

	AVG	AB	R	H	2B	3B	HR	RBI	SB
Carte, Daniel, Columbus	.419	124	34	52	16	3	2	35	1
Lunsford, Dan, Delaware	.402	122	22	49	6	0	2	27	1
Buck, Bryan, Delaware	.389	108	25	42	3	0	0	11	12
Frank, Jake, Grand Lake	.379	103	21	39	5	1	1	17	3
Lucas, Ed, Columbus	.376	133	19	50	9	1	0	27	5
Psomas, Grant, Pittsburgh	.373	126	12	47	6	4	1	20	3
Gressick, Anthony, So. Ohio	.353	136	22	48	10	2	1	22	2
Warnock, Jeff, Grand Lake	.352	105	21	37	4	2	0	15	10
Getty, Bobby, Southern Ohio	.348	115	16	40	9	1	1	18	5
Ketron, Brandon, Indianapolis	.331	130	19	43	12	1	5	21	1
Bynum, Seth, Southern Ohio	.328	122	23	40	13	2	4	23	4
Karkoulas, Andrew, Lima	.357	112	16	40	4	0	0	16	3
Caple, Tom, Northern Ohio	.311	116	25	36	8	1	0	23	0
Martinez, Mike, No. Ohio	.303	109	23	33	10	0	2	25	2

INDIVIDUAL PITCHING LEADERS
(Minimum 30 innings)

	W	L	ERA	G	SV	IP	H	BB	SO
Mott, Tyler, Columbus	4	0	0.28	6	0	32	20	7	24
Cowden, Cam, Lima	4	0	0.75	8	0	36	24	8	27
Bova, Chris, Stark County	1	1	0.76	6	0	36	21	19	31
Stanley, Seth, Delaware	3	1	0.93	8	0	39	29	5	27
Miller, Kevin, Columbus	4	1	1.11	6	0	32	16	7	29
Geiersbach, Ken, Delaware	3	0	1.17	8	0	30	19	9	26
Newman, Josh, Columbus	4	2	1.45	7	0	37	19	8	51
Benjamin, Robert, Columbus	3	1	1.56	8	0	35	25	6	28
Friedman, Eli, Pittsburgh	6	1	1.86	9	0	58	43	16	47
Penn, Ryan, Youngstown	2	2	1.95	8	1	37	28	4	39

NEW ENGLAND COLLEGIATE LEAGUE

NORTH	W	L	PCT	GB
Sanford Mainers	28	13	.683	—
Keene Swamp Bats	27	14	.659	1
Concord Quarry Dogs	20	20	.500	7½
North Adams SteepleCats	17	24	.415	11
Vermont Mountaineers	15	26	.366	13
Mill City All-Americans	13	28	.317	15

SOUTH	W	L	PCT	GB
Torrington Twisters	30	10	.750	—
Newport Gulls	25	15	.625	5
Danbury Westerners	22	17	.564	7½
Middletown Giants	18	23	.439	12½
Manchester Silkworms	16	24	.400	14
Riverpoint Royals	16	24	.400	14
Thread City Tides	16	25	.390	14½

PLAYOFFS: Quarterfinals—Sanford defeated North Adams 2-0, Keene defeated Concord 2-0, Torrington defeated Middletown 2-0 and Newport defeated Danbury 2-1 in best-of-3 series. **Semifinals**—Keene defeated Sanford 2-0 and Torrington defeated Newport 2-0 in best-of-3 series. **Final**—Keene defeated Torrington 2-0 in best-of-3 series.

ALL-STAR TEAM: **C**—Chris Iannetta, Newport (North Carolina). **1B**—Greg Dowling, Sanford (Georgia Southern). **2B**—Josh DiScipio, Concord (Boston College). **3B**—Jason Armstrong, Newport (Trinity, Texas). **SS**—Armand Gaerland, Torrington (San Francisco). **OF**—Steve Blackwood, Keene (Georgia Tech); Kyle Keen, Keene (Georgia); Kyle Brown, Sanford (Le Moyne). **DH**—Jeff Natale, Torrington (Trinity, Conn.). **P**—Adam Kalkhof, North Adams (North Carolina); Ryan Mullins, Riverpoint (Vanderbilt); Dennis Robinson, Torrington (Jacksonville).

Most Valuable Player: Steve Blackwood, of, Keene (Georgia Tech). **Outstanding Pitcher:** Ryan Mullins, Riverpoint (Vanderbilt).

TOP 10 PROSPECTS: **1.** Ryan Mullins, lhp, Riverpoint (Vanderbilt). **2.** Kyle Keen, of, Keene (Georgia). **3.** Adam Kalkhof, lhp, North Adams (North Carolina). **4.** Jason Berken, rhp, Keene (Clemson). **5.** Matt Torra, rhp, Torrington (Massachusetts). **6.** Kyle Brown, of, Sanford (Le Moyne). **7.** Dennis Robinson, rhp, Torrington (Jacksonville). **8.** Andy Sonnastine, rhp, Sanford (Kent State). **9.** Wes Swackhamer, of, Danbury (Tulane). **10.** Neil Walton, ss, North Adams (Cal State Fullerton).

INDIVIDUAL BATTING LEADERS
(Minimum 100 Plate Appearances)

	AVG	AB	R	H	2B	3B	HR	RBI	SB
Keen, Kyle, Keene	.384	151	32	58	6	0	3	21	22
Armstrong, Jason, Newport	.349	149	27	52	10	0	1	14	12
Finan, Ryan, Manchester	.349	86	11	30	7	1	1	14	1
Balster, Scott, Thread City	.347	150	19	52	7	2	1	20	11
Blackwood, Steve, Keene	.340	162	33	55	7	1	6	28	4
Isaacson, Greg, Newport	.339	112	21	38	10	0	3	20	4
Julien, Eugene, Thread City	.337	104	19	35	3	0	0	7	22
Hoffpauir, Jarrett, Danbury	.327	153	30	50	9	0	6	25	5
Natale, Jeff, Torrington	.322	87	16	28	12	1	0	11	6
Izaryk, Aaron, Sanford	.321	109	8	35	1	0	0	5	1
Bogusevic, Brian, Danbury	.320	128	22	41	8	1	2	18	4
Brown, Kyle, Sanford	.317	101	21	32	5	2	0	12	31
Looze, Chris, Concord	.316	155	20	49	10	1	3	40	1
DiScipio, Josh, Concord	.316	155	30	49	10	1	1	16	13
Pahuta, Tim, Newport	.315	143	21	45	9	1	3	21	1
Defendis, John, Danbury	.309	110	11	34	4	1	0	5	2

INDIVIDUAL PITCHING LEADERS
(Minimum 35 innings)

	W	L	ERA	G	SV	IP	H	BB	SO
Kalkhof, Adam, North Adams	3	1	0.65	8	0	55	34	19	69
Cody, Chris, Manchester	4	2	0.91	7	0	49	30	13	56
Long, Jeff, Danbury	3	2	1.33	7	0	54	33	18	52
Torra, Matt, Torrington	5	1	1.37	7	0	46	34	8	53
Sonnanstine, Andy, Sanford	4	1	1.40	8	0	58	28	9	57
Frederick, Dan, Mill City	3	4	1.43	9	0	69	64	19	44
Rowe, Ben, Torrington	3	1	1.54	9	0	35	26	13	31
Duffey, J.R, Newport	4	2	1.57	8	0	46	43	9	43
Saneholtz, Tyler, Sanford	3	1	1.59	8	0	40	30	17	37
Robinson, Dennis, Torrington	6	1	1.60	9	0	45	37	7	33
Mullins, Ryan, Riverpoint	6	2	1.70	9	0	69	53	10	89

NEW YORK COLLEGIATE LEAGUE

EAST	W	L	PCT	GB
Amsterdam Mohawks	31	11	.738	—
Watertown Wizards	26	16	.619	5
Plattsburgh Thunder	25	17	.595	6
Ithaca Classics	12	30	.286	17
Mohawk Valley Cobras	8	34	.190	23

WEST	W	L	PCT	GB
Hornell Dodgers	30	12	.714	—
Geneva Red Wings	28	14	.667	2
Athletes In Action-Alfred	22	20	.524	8
Allegany County Nitros	21	21	.500	9
Wayne County Raptors	7	35	.167	23

PLAYOFFS: Semifinals—Hornell defeated Geneva 2-0; Amsterdam defeated Watertown 2-0 in best-of-3 series. **Final**—Amsterdam defeated Hornell 2-1 in best-of-3 series.

INDIVIDUAL BATTING LEADERS
(Minimum 100 Plate Appearances)

	AVG	AB	R	H	2B	3B	HR	RBI	SB
Zimniewicz, Kirt, Amsterdam	.374	107	30	40	10	3	5	32	7
Hammond, Matt, Plattsburgh	.353	119	16	42	11	2	0	19	4
Shanley, Tom, Amsterdam	.350	117	27	41	8	1	1	23	7
Baker, Eric, Hornell	.347	121	29	42	3	2	0	9	14
Stewart, Trey, Hornell	.341	88	12	30	5	1	0	18	5
Lamb, Joe, Amsterdam	.339	121	30	41	3	0	1	17	9
Didsbury, Stephen, Mohawk	.336	113	18	38	4	0	0	14	3
Van Allan, Ned, Ithaca	.331	124	17	41	6	0	0	19	2
Scott, Brian, Hornell	.321	109	22	35	8	1	3	14	4
Regan, Chris, Allegany	.320	103	16	33	7	0	0	7	0
Landahl, Matt, Geneva	.318	110	20	35	5	2	0	13	3

	AVG	AB	R	H	2B	3B	HR	RBI	SB
Edmondson, Jarod, Ithaca	.315	124	20	39	4	5	1	16	6
McLin, Anthony, Hornell	.314	118	18	37	4	1	1	14	7
King, Craig, Geneva	.309	136	24	42	10	1	3	20	6
Mariano, Joe, Amsterdam	.302	116	17	35	4	0	0	12	4

INDIVIDUAL PITCHING LEADERS

(Minimum 35 innings)

	W	L	ERA	G	SV	IP	H	BB	SO
Boutilier, Logan, AIA	4	2	0.33	7	0	55	39	9	42
Tatlock, Ryan, Amsterdam	5	0	1.49	7	0	42	29	13	20
Messina, Mark, Geneva	4	2	1.64	7	0	49	41	10	45
Braden, Dallas, Hornell	7	1	1.65	8	0	60	37	11	79
Scott, Matthew, AIA	6	1	1.73	7	0	52	56	7	28
Shone, Jason, Watertown	5	2	1.73	8	0	52	41	10	54
Lightsey, Brad, Hornell	3	2	1.98	8	0	45	36	12	37
Drechsler, Alan, Wayne County	1	2	1.99	8	0	45	36	12	37
Pacella, J.J., Amsterdam	4	2	2.09	7	0	43	29	22	33
Karas, Russell, Allegany	3	1	2.15	11	0	38	35	18	33

NORTHWOODS LEAGUE

NORTH	W	L	PCT	GB
+*St. Cloud River Bats	38	25	.603	—
Alexandria Beetles	32	31	.508	6
Thunder Bay Border Cats	31	33	.484	7½
Mankato MoonDogs	27	37	.422	11½
Duluth Huskies	24	39	.381	14
SOUTH	**W**	**L**	**PCT**	**GB**
+Wisconsin Woodchucks	41	22	.651	—
Rochester Honkers	40	23	.635	1
*Madison Mallards	37	27	.578	4½
La Crosse Loggers	27	36	.429	14
Waterloo Bucks	20	44	.313	21½

* First-half champion. +Second-half champion.

PLAYOFFS—Semifinals: Wisconsin defeated Madison 2-1, St. Cloud defeated Alexandria 2-1 in best-of-3 series. **Final**: Wisconsin defeated St. Cloud 2-1 in best-of-3 series.

ALL-STAR TEAM: C—Baron Frost, Alexandria (Southern California); Ned Yost, Wisconsin (Georgia). **1B**—David Schultz, La Crosse (Creighton). **2B**—Stephen Barton, Rochester (Florida). **3B**—Chris Nowak, Rochester (South Carolina-Spartanburg). **SS**—Ben Zobrist, Wisconsin (Olivet Nazarene, Ill.). **IF**—Jeremiah Piepkorn, Mankato (North Dakota State). **OF**—Jesse Boyer, Rochester (Nebraska); Chase Gerdes, Wisconsin (Baylor); Aaron Grant, Mankato (UC Riverside); Mike Pankratz, Wisconsin (Baylor); Joe Pietro, St. Cloud (New Orleans). **DH**—Kyle Bohm, Wisconsin (Auburn). **P**—Cory Cabral, Madison (San Jose State); Jimmy Conroy, Rochester (Illinois); Thomas Diamond, St. Cloud (New Orleans); Jason Driscoll, Rochester (Purdue); Steve Grasely, Wisconsin (Creighton); Jake Hansen, Madison (Northern Iowa); Jesse Ingram, Alexandria (California); Will Krout, Mankato (Sonoma State, Calif.); J.P. Martinez, St. Cloud (New Orleans); Chris Nicoli, Alexandria (UC Irvine); Adam Rowe, Wisconsin (Mount Vernon Nazarene, Ohio); Ben Stanczyk, La Crosse (Wisconsin-Milwaukee).

Most Valuable Player: Mike Pankratz, Wisconsin (Baylor).

TOP 10 PROSPECTS: **1.** Thomas Diamond, rhp, St. Cloud (New Orleans). **2.** Mike Pankratz, of-1b, Wisconsin (Baylor). **3.** J.P. Martinez, rhp, St. Cloud (New Orleans). **4.** Joe Pietro, of, St. Cloud (New Orleans). **5.** Adam Rowe, lhp, Wisconsin (Mount Vernon Nazarene, Ohio). **6.** Justin Sokol, rhp, Thunder Bay (Iowa Central CC). **7.** Ben Zobrist, ss, Wisconsin (Olivet Nazarene, Ill.). **8.** Ben Stanczyk, 3b-rhp, La Crosse (Wisconsin-Milwaukee). **9.** Jeremiah Piepkorn, if-of, Mankato (North Dakota State). **10.** Daniel Mocny, 3b, Alexandria (Santa Rosa, Calif., JC).

INDIVIDUAL BATTING LEADERS

(Minimum 150 Plate Appearances)

	AVG	AB	R	H	2B	3B	HR	RBI	SB
Pankratz, Mike, Wisconsin	.372	156	40	58	13	1	12	35	2
Gerdes, Chase, Wisconsin	.335	161	31	54	5	0	5	20	12
Wiedewitsch, Pete, Wis.	.324	136	11	44	7	0	1	22	1
Zobrist, Ben, Wisconsin	.319	226	53	72	11	1	3	25	17
Einspahr, Matt, La Crosse	.311	222	37	69	11	0	2	15	10
Grant, Aaron, Mankato	.310	171	26	53	4	1	1	26	12
Camp, Matt, Thunder Bay	.305	167	29	51	9	0	0	21	10
Morris, Eric, St. Cloud	.303	201	26	61	11	0	2	24	9
Barton, Stephen, Rochester	.303	175	31	53	10	1	1	31	26
Frost, Baron, Alexandria	.301	219	32	66	15	1	5	43	5
Rozema, Mike, Madison	.300	213	42	64	10	3	2	23	32
Long, Wes, St. Cloud	.300	223	34	67	14	2	3	33	10
Bohm, Kyle, Wisconsin	.299	187	44	56	10	0	7	32	2
Boyer, Jesse, Rochester	.299	117	34	35	6	0	0	9	20
Dalton, Brett, Alexandria	.297	148	31	44	6	0	1	18	9
Wettlaufer, Josh, Madison	.297	165	23	49	8	2	2	14	11

INDIVIDUAL PITCHING LEADERS

(Minimum 50 Innings)

	W	L	ERA	G	SV	IP	H	BB	SO
Hansen, Jake, Madison	5	1	1.23	11	0	59	37	36	59
Nicoll, Chris, Alexandria	5	2	1.46	9	0	56	48	8	53
Krout, Will, Mankato	8	3	1.50	12	0	96	78	15	52
Stanczyk, Ben, La Crosse	6	4	1.51	16	1	84	58	19	93
Diamond, Thomas, St. Cloud	6	1	1.63	12	1	72	43	21	103
Cabral, Corey, Madison	5	2	1.72	9	0	58	45	7	44
Driscoll, Jason, Rochester	6	2	1.76	30	11	51	38	9	33
Rowe, Adam, Wisconsin	9	1	1.98	12	0	91	59	30	92
Conroy, Jimmy, Rochester	7	1	1.98	13	0	77	45	24	67
McGinn, Brendan, St. Cloud	5	4	2.14	9	0	59	46	16	59

VALLEY LEAGUE

NORTH	W	L	PCT	GB
Winchester Royals	30	10	.750	—
New Market Rebels	26	14	.650	4
Luray Wranglers	15	25	.375	15
Front Royal Cardinals	12	28	.300	18
SOUTH	**W**	**L**	**PCT**	**GB**
Staunton Braves	27	14	.658	—
Harrisonburg Turks	26	15	.634	1
Waynesboro Generals	14	26	.350	12
Covington Lumberjacks	11	29	.275	15

PLAYOFFS: **Semifinals**—Winchester defeated Harrisonburg 3-0 and New Market defeated Staunton 3-1 in best-of-5 series. **Final**—Winchester defeats New Market 3-2 in best-of-5 series.

ALL-STAR TEAM: C—Erick San Pedro, Staunton (Miami). **1B**—Donnie Burkhalter, Luray (Seminole, Fla., CC). **2B**—Moises Duran, Harrisonburg (Arizona). **3B**—David Marlett, Harrisonburg (Oklahoma City). **SS**—Dennis Diaz, Luray (Florida International). **IF**—Tyler Scarbrough, Covington (Mississippi State). **OF**—Antoan Richardson, Winchester (Palm Beach, Fla., CC); Worth Scott, Staunton (Vanderbilt); Jeff Van Houten, Harrisonburg (Arizona); Kevin White, New Market (Presbyterian, S.C.) **DH**—Brett Showalter, Winchester (Penn State). **SP**—Phil Bartleski, New Market (William & Mary); Andrew Dobies, Staunton (Virginia); E.J. Shanks, Harrisonburg (Oklahoma City). **RP**—Grant Hansen, Harrisonburg (Oklahoma City); Chase Swing, Staunton (Middle Tennessee State).

Most Valuable Player: Jeff Van Houten, Harrisonburg (Arizona).

TOP 10 PROSPECTS: **1.** Jeff Van Houten, of, Harrisonburg (Arizona). **2.** Andrew Dobies, lhp, Staunton (Virginia). **3.** Erick San Pedro, c, Staunton (Miami). **4.** Worth Scott, of, Staunton (Vanderbilt). **5.** Philip Bartleski, rhp, New Market (William & Mary). **6.** Antoan Richardson, of, Winchester (Palm Beach, Fla., CC). **7.** Gaby Sanchez, 3b, Staunton (Miami). **8.** Joe Koshansky, 1b, Staunton (Virginia). **9.** Kevin White, of, New Market (Presbyterian, S.C.). **10.** E.J. Shanks, rhp, Harrisonburg (Oklahoma City).

INDIVIDUAL BATTING LEADERS

(Minimum 100 Plate Appearances)

	AVG	AB	R	H	2B	3B	HR	RBI	SB
Van Houten, Jeff, Harrisonburg	.391	138	27	54	19	5	4	37	5
Scarbrough, Tyler, Covington	.357	98	16	35	10	0	2	7	3
Scott, Worth, Staunton	.339	165	26	56	11	2	4	26	6
Brooks, Daniel, Harrisonburg	.331	136	16	45	10	0	1	18	2
Diaz, Dennis, Luray	.326	135	29	44	6	1	0	10	37
Gord, Nelson, Winchester	.325	160	23	52	8	0	0	25	5
White, Kevin, New Market	.315	181	36	57	11	4	11	40	2
Showalter, Brett, Winchester	.314	102	18	32	7	1	1	19	9
Davis, Julian, Luray	.314	118	18	37	7	0	5	22	2
Spatafora, Matt, Winchester	.310	126	19	39	7	2	0	20	2
Marlett, David, Harrisonburg	.295	132	14	39	14	1	5	25	0
Richardson, Antoan, Winchester	.291	134	40	39	6	3	1	9	31
San Pedro, Erick, Staunton	.291	117	18	34	8	0	4	16	13
Gardner, Brett, New Market	.288	177	40	51	7	5	2	24	23
Stavinoha, Nick, Front Royal	.287	94	18	27	5	0	6	17	2
Sanchez, Gaby, Staunton	.286	119	16	34	5	1	2	18	14
Duran, Moises, Harrisonburg	.282	156	36	44	10	1	3	21	12

INDIVIDUAL PITCHING LEADERS

(Minimum 40 Innings)

	W	L	ERA	G	SV	IP	H	BB	SO
Bartleski, Philip, New Market	5	3	1.38	9	0	65	46	7	64
Egbert, Jack, Winchester	6	1	1.75	9	0	62	50	13	75
Phillips, Shawn, Waynesboro	2	4	1.99	9	0	59	45	4	68
Rohrbaugh, Robert, Winchester	6	1	2.07	9	0	61	41	8	59
Ramsey, Justin, Waynesboro	2	3	2.17	8	2	46	42	10	45
Cromer, Bennett, Winchester	4	1	2.17	8	0	50	34	18	63
Sayre, Joel, New Market	3	3	2.17	16	4	50	39	23	63
Dobies, Andrew, Staunton	4	1	2.25	8	0	56	43	8	92
Shanks, E.J., Harrisonburg	6	1	2.33	8	0	58	35	16	50
Hamilton, Clayton, Winchester	5	1	2.45	9	0	51	52	13	37

ALASKA LEAGUE

	W	L	PCT	GB	Overall W	Overall L
Fairbanks Goldpanners	22	13	.629	—	37	19
Athletes In Action	19	15	.559	2½	28	20
Anchorage Glacier Pilots	18	17	.514	4	25	26
Kenai Peninsula Oilers	17	18	.486	5	25	26
Mat-Su Miners	16	19	.457	6	24	23
Anchorage Bucs	12	22	.353	9½	17	30

ALL-STAR TEAM: C—Tyler Best, Goldpanners (Lewis-Clark State, Idaho). **1B**—Jeff Culpepper, Goldpanners (Gonzaga). **2B**—Joe Holland, Oilers (Blinn, Texas, JC). **3B**—Cody Montgomery, Athletes In Action (Dallas Baptist). **SS**—Josh Mader, Miners (New Mexico). **OF**—Nick Blasi, Goldpanners (Wichita State); Michael Cline, Athletes In Action (Birmingham Southern); Jacoby Ellsbury, Pilots (Oregon State). **DH**—John Bowker, Pilots (Long Beach State). **P**—Ricky Fairchild, Pilots (Tulane); Andrew Kown, Pilots (Georgia Tech); Wes Letson, Athletes In Action (Birmingham Southern); Jake Postlewait, Oilers (Oregon State); Sean Timmons, Goldpanners). **RP**—Jon McCaslin, Goldpanners (Lower Columbia, Wash., CC).

Player of the Year: Sean Timmons, rhp, Goldpanners.

TOP 10 PROSPECTS: 1. Mike Pelfrey, rhp, Glacier Pilots (Wichita State). **2.** Jeremy Accardo, rhp, Athletes In Action (Illinois State). **3.** Ricky Fairchild, rhp, Glacier Pilots (Tulane). **4.** Travis Buck, of, Oilers (Arizona State). **5.** Jacoby Ellsbury, of, Glacier Pilots (Oregon State). **6.** Andrew Kown, rhp, Bucs (Georgia Tech). **7.** Wes Letson, lhp, Athletes In Action (Birmingham-Southern). **8.** Emerson Frostad, c-3b, Alaska Goldpanners (Lewis-Clark State, Idaho). **9.** Steve Uhlmansiek, lhp, Glacier Pilots (Wichita State). **10.** Jake Postlewait, lhp, Oilers (Oregon State).

INDIVIDUAL BATTING LEADERS
(Minimum 110 Plate Appearances)

	AVG	AB	R	H	2B	3B	HR	RBI	SB
Best, Tyler, Goldpanners	.352	108	26	38	7	1	0	10	6
Bowker, John, Pilots	.344	125	17	43	11	0	3	19	1
Ellsbury, Jacoby, Pilots	.338	145	24	49	3	3	1	13	16
Culpepper, Jeff, Goldpanners	.323	167	27	54	8	1	3	27	5
Blasi, Nick, Goldpanners	.306	160	25	49	5	1	3	20	4
Cline, Michael, AIA	.291	165	30	48	8	3	2	31	26
Davis, Brad E., Goldpanners	.291	172	30	50	5	1	0	16	5
Accardo, Jeremy, AIA	.290	138	21	40	2	0	2	21	7
Young, Matt, Mat-Su	.286	168	24	48	3	1	0	13	7
Montgomery, Cody, AIA	.285	151	16	43	7	1	0	21	4
Bruce, Derek, Goldpanners	.280	182	17	51	9	0	2	25	4
Uribes, David, Oilers	.279	136	21	38	1	2	1	9	10
Frostad, Emerson, Goldpanners	.278	169	24	47	15	4	3	28	1
Holland, Joe, Oilers	.276	152	23	42	9	1	1	10	4
Bogue, Matthew, AIA	.276	174	30	48	9	4	0	14	18
Butts, Jeff, Mat-Su	.270	178	22	48	6	2	2	16	8
Streelman, Erick, AIA	.260	154	25	40	9	2	3	23	3

INDIVIDUAL PITCHING LEADERS
(Minimum 35 innings)

	W	L	ERA	G	Sv	IP	H	BB	SO
Postlewait, Jake, Oilers	2	3	1.21	10	0	52	49	17	39
Timmons, Sean, Goldpanners	5	1	1.50	9	0	66	56	15	51
Hall, Ladd, Oilers	4	0	1.54	11	0	53	36	21	31
Welch, Kevin, Goldpanners	4	2	1.56	10	0	58	53	16	37
Davis, Brad A., Goldpanners	4	0	1.64	10	0	55	45	15	37
Hanson, Jeff, AIA	4	1	1.73	13	0	42	28	14	27
Ambriz, Hector, Pilots	0	4	1.95	12	2	51	44	9	44
Kolberg, Koley, Mat-Su	6	3	1.99	9	0	59	40	22	34
Kown, Andrew, Bucs	3	3	2.17	10	0	54	47	17	50
Timm, Jordan, Bucs	2	3	2.30	8	0	58	38	22	41
Zaleski, Kyle, AIA	4	1	2.35	10	0	46	40	9	33
Beam, Randy Oilers	1	2	2.41	8	0	56	43	7	39
Kline, Steve, Mat-Su	4	2	2.61	10	0	62	63	6	37

CLARK GRIFFITH LEAGUE

	W	L	PCT	GB
Arlington Senators	30	10	.750	—
Fauquier Gators	25	15	.625	5
Silver Spring-Takoma Thunderbolts	24	16	.600	6
Vienna Mustangs	23	17	.575	7
Bethesda Big Train	22	18	.550	8
Herndon Braves	20	20	.500	10
Germantown Black Rox	17	23	.425	13
Reston Hawks	10	30	.350	20
Baltimore Pride	9	31	.225	21

PLAYOFFS: Arlington (3-1) defeated Fauquier (3-2) in championship game of four-team, double-elimination tournament.

INDIVIDUAL BATTING LEADERS
(Minimum 100 Plate Appearances)

	AVG	AB	R	H	2B	3B	HR	RBI	SB
Southard, Nathan, Arlington	.359	131	24	47	15	1	0	13	9
Calderone, Adam, Vienna	.341	126	23	43	5	1	0	16	15
Outman, Josh, Fauquier	.340	100	20	34	4	4	6	13	1
Costanzo, Mike, Bethesda	.340	103	25	35	11	0	3	17	1
Hendrix, Scott, Fauquier	.327	153	30	50	9	3	9	37	2
Bailey, Josh, Germantown	.322	118	20	38	4	0	0	11	7
Milsom, Geoff, Vienna	.319	91	11	29	5	5	2	15	1
Rhymes, Will, Arlington	.314	102	18	32	4	0	0	5	3
Mignogna, Steve, Vienna	.301	103	16	31	2	1	0	18	14
Waddell, Kenny, Arlington	.299	87	20	26	2	0	0	12	9
Sluder, Matt, Herndon	.296	98	11	29	13	0	0	10	0
Speights, Jeff, Germantown	.294	136	11	40	7	0	1	25	0
Cowgill, Michael, Fauquier	.294	109	16	32	9	1	0	17	4

INDIVIDUAL PITCHING LEADERS
(Minimum 35 innings)

	W	L	ERA	G	SV	IP	H	BB	SO
Link, Jon, Herndon	3	2	1.32	7	0	48	31	10	50
Reeder, Jonathan, Fauquier	4	2	1.50	10	2	48	47	11	38
Billek, Michael, SS-T	6	0	1.74	8	0	57	49	12	51
Horseman, Shay, Bethesda	4	1	1.80	9	0	40	26	15	46
Meredith, Cla, Arlington	5	2	1.86	11	1	39	24	9	59
Daniels, Adam, Arlington	3	1	2.06	7	0	39	29	14	50
Clark, Scott, Fauquier	4	0	2.06	7	0	44	29	22	35
Kantakevich, Joe, Germantown	2	2	2.09	6	0	39	31	15	25
Covington, Tristen, SS-T	4	1	2.25	8	1	40	33	8	28

JAYHAWK LEAGUE

	W	L	PCT	GB	Overall W	Overall L
Hays Larks	23	6	.790	—	43	12
El Dorado Broncos	15	11	.580	6½	38	19
Liberal BeeJays	13	14	.480	9	22	18
Nevada Griffons	13	16	.450	10	34	23
Topeka Capitals	11	18	.380	12		
Elkhart Dusters	8	18	.310	13½		

ALL-STAR TEAM: C—Clay Blevins, El Dorado (Cowley County, Kan., CC). **1B**—Cody Ehlers, Hays (Missouri). **2B**—Aaron Battle, Hays (Texas-Arlington). **3B**—Dan Rogers, El Dorado (Saint Louis). **SS**—Dan Schwartzbauer, Hays (Duquesne). **IF**—Jared Clements, Liberal (Baylor). **OF**—Craig Cooper, Hays (Notre Dame); Hunter Pence, Liberal (Texas-Arlington); Chad Steele, Nevada (Nebraska). **DH**—Eric Thornton, El Doprado (Cowley County, Kan., CC). **SP**—Tom Hottovy, Hays (Wichita State); Rusty Jones, El Dorado (Butler County, Kan., CC); Chris Ofat, Hays (Ohio Dominican). **RP**—Dave Haehnel, El Dorado (Illinois-Chicago).

TOP 10 PROSPECTS: 1. Dave Haehnel, lhp, El Dorado (Illinois-Chicago). **2.** Cory Patton, of, Liberal (Texas A&M). **3.** Robert Ray, rhp, Liberal (Texas A&M). **4.** Joe Ness, rhp, Elkhart (Ball State). **5.** Mike Sillman, rhp, Nevada (Nebraska). **6.** Hunter Pence, of, Liberal (Texas-Arlington). **7.** Josh Asanovich, ss, Elkhart (Arizona State). **8.** Kevin Whelan, rhp, Liberal (Texas A&M). **9.** Craig Cooper, of, Hays (Notre Dame). **10.** Josh Wahpepah, rhp, Elkhart (Cowley County, Kan., CC).

INDIVIDUAL BATTING LEADERS
(Minimum 75 Plate Appearances)

	AVG	AB	R	H	2B	3B	HR	RBI	SB
Steele, Chad, Nevada	.410	78	19	32	6	0	1	19	1
Pence, Hunter, Liberal	.389	90	23	35	8	3	5	21	5
Battle, Aaron, Hays	.368	95	19	35	6	0	2	16	1
McConnell, Kirk, Nevada	.333	78	19	26	4	1	0	8	3
Jones, Ben, Elkhart	.328	67	14	22	3	0	4	14	0
Green, Brandon, Nevada	.321	78	16	25	1	1	2	16	0
Cooper, Craig, Hays	.321	78	19	25	4	0	3	18	14
Schwarzbaugh, Danny, Hays	.317	82	19	26	7	0	1	15	12
Ehlers, Cody, Hays	.310	87	17	27	4	0	5	23	0
Lilly, Ryan, Elkhart	.290	69	15	20	3	0	4	12	2
Horstman, Eric, Nevada	.276	98	23	27	7	1	1	10	8
Cox, Adam, Hays	.265	68	18	18	7	1	1	8	2

INDIVIDUAL PITCHING LEADERS
(Minimum 20 Innings)

	W	L	ERA	G	SV	IP	H	BB	SO
Ofat, Chris, Hays	4	0	0.91	7	2	40	23	6	31
Haehnel, Dave, El Dorado	5	0	1.41	10	0	32	16	13	51
Valdes-Fauli, Shawn, Topeka	2	1	1.80	4	1	20	14	8	18
Brownell, John, El Dorado	1	1	2.05	4	0	22	18	4	14
Jones, Rusty, El Dorado	3	1	2.52	5	0	25	17	7	21
Ness, Joe, Elkhart	2	1	2.79	6	0	42	34	15	30
Harper, Landon, Hays	5	1	2.79	7	0	42	40	11	32
Hottovy, Tommy, Hays	5	1	2.85	7	0	41	35	10	36

YOUTH BASEBALL

BY ALLAN SIMPSON

Japan broke open a fourth-inning, scoreless tie in the championship game of the 2003 Little League (11-12) World Series, played in Williamsport, Pa., by erupting for eight runs as it beat East Boynton Beach, Fla., 10-1. Japan, represented by Musashi-Fuchu Little League of Tokyo, won six straight games to win the championship.

It marked the third Little League World Series title in five years for Japan and the eighth time in Series history that a team from Florida lost in the championship game. In 2001, Japan defeated Apopka, Fla., 2-1 in the final.

LITTLE LEAGUE BASEBALL

Hokuto Nakahara

Japan and Boynton Beach were deadlocked 0-0 when Japan suddenly scored eight times with two outs in the top of the fourth. The big blow was a grand slam by Hokuto Nakahara. Winning pitcher Yuutaro Tanaka (2-0) helped his own cause by drilling a two-run homer in the inning and he went on to throw a four-hitter, striking out 14. It was his second win of the 16-team event.

Japan also scored eight times in the fourth inning of a 14-6 win over Curacao in the semifinals.

Mexico Claims Ripken Title

Just like in the Little League World Series, Mexico broke open a scoreless game by scoring seven runs in the fourth inning on its way to a 13-2 victory over Hilo, Hawaii, in the championship game of the Cal Ripken (11-12) World Series, played for the first time in Aberdeen, Md., the hometown of the former Orioles star.

Both teams entered the final with perfect 6-0 records, but a two-run homer by tournament MVP Nestor Lopez started Mexico's fourth-inning assault and he went on to pitch the final 4⅓ innings to earn his third victory of the 15-team tournament. Lopez allowed four hits and struck out 10 in the deciding game, while going 3-for-4 with four RBIs.

The tournament featured a record five no-hitters, three of which were pitched against the host Aberdeen team.

East Cobb Rolls Again

The East Cobb Yankees from Marietta, Ga., captured their third Connie Mack (18 and under) World Series title in five years by defeating the Cincinnati Midland Redskins 5-4 in the championship game. The Yankees went undefeated in the eight-team, double-elimination event, played in Farmington, N.M..

Georgia Tech-bound first baseman Whit Robbins delivered the big blow in the deciding game, a two-run double in the fifth inning that put his team ahead 4-1. All-tournament righthander Dustin Evans, a 28th-round pick of the Reds headed for Georgia Southern, pitched the first five innings for the win—his second of the tournament.

East Cobb center fielder Danny Payne, a rising senior at Sequoyah High in Woodstock, Ga., was named the tournament MVP. He hit .438 overall, made a game-saving catch in the seventh inning of East Cobb's first win against Midland and pitched three scoreless innings in an opening-round game. East Cobb won four of its five games by one run.

■ The East Cobb Astros continued their mastery of AAU's Junior Olympic (16 and under) baseball championship by winning nine straight games to capture the title for the seventh time in eight years. The Astros beat Florida's Chet Lemon's Juice 6-5 in the deciding game in a showdown of the nation's top 16-year-old teams, breaking a 5-5 in their final at-bat on a run-scoring single by shortstop Gordon Beckham.

On the summer, East Cobb went 81-11 and won its final 36 games. The Astros also won the Continental Amateur Baseball Association 16-year-old title in Marietta, Ga., for the second year in a row, beating the Bayside (N.Y.) Yankees 7-4 in the final.

The loss was the only one on the summer for Lemon's team, which went 44-1 overall. Earlier in the summer, Lemon's team won 10 straight games in Team USA's Junior Olympic 72-team tournament in Jupiter, Fla.

TOP-RANKED YOUTH TEAMS

2003

Compiled by USA Sports Rankings

12	Mac N Seitz (Mo.) Indians (74-3)
13	Utah Hitmen (71-11)
14	Florida Elite (44-2)
15	Georgia Stars (42-9)
16	Ohio Warhawks (48-9)

Back In The Winner's Circle

Baltimore's Maryland Orioles rallied from a first-round loss to blitz the host Johnstown, Pa., entry 19-0 in the final to win the 59th annual All-American Amateur Baseball Association (21 and under) World Series. It was the 21st title by a team from Baltimore, but only the first since 1996.

The Orioles broke open the deciding game in the first inning by scoring seven runs. Tournament MVP Kevin Hart had a grand slam and drove in five runs in the game.

The Arlington (Va.) Senators of the Clark Griffith League had won four of the previous five tournaments, but they lost to the Orioles.

Mason's Efforts Not Enough

Despite the heroic two-way efforts of UNC Greensboro righthander Chris Mason, Rochester, Minn., won the 2003 American Legion World Series, beating Cherryville, N.C., 5-2 in the championship game. The tournament was played in Bartlesville, Okla.

Rochester (53-5) scored three times in the third inning to overcome an early 2-0 deficit and Aaron Craig and Michael Badger made the lead stand up as they combined on a six-hitter. Craig (12-0) worked the first eight innings.

Mason (15-1 on the season) was the individual star of the tournament and earned MVP honors. He went 2-0, 0.86 with 36 strikeouts in 21 innings while hitting .550 with three homers. A day after striking out 15 in six innings and hitting two homers against previously-unbeaten Corvallis, Ore., in a semi-final game, he came on to pitch the final six innings of the championship game, striking out 10 while allowing only an unearned run.

In regional and national competition combined, Mason went 5-0, 0.43 with 69 strikeouts in 42 innings. His 69 strikeouts shattered the Legion record of 55 set in 1980 by Honolulu's Sid Fernandez, who went on to pitch 15 years in the big leagues.

AMATEUR/YOUTH CHAMPIONS 2003

TEAM USA

COLLEGE TEAM	Site	Champion	Runner-up
Pan American Games	Santo Domingo, D.R.	Cuba	United States

JUNIOR TEAM (18 & Under)	Site	Champion	Runner-up
COPABE Pan Am Cup	Willemstad, Aruba	Cuba	United States

YOUTH TEAM (16 & Under)	Site	Champion	Runner-up
World Youth Championship	Kaohsiung, Taiwan	United States	Taiwan
USA Junior Olympics—East	Jupiter, Fla.	Chet Lemon's (Fla.) Juice	Perfect Game (Iowa)
USA Junior Olympics—West	Tucson, Ariz.	San Diego Sharks	Arizona Monsoon

ALL-AMERICAN AMATEUR BASEBALL ASSOCIATION (AAABA)

Event	Site	Champion	Runner-up
World Series (21 & Under)	Johnstown, Pa.	Youse's Maryland Orioles	Johnstown (Pa.) Delweld

AMATEUR ATHLETIC UNION (AAU)

Event	Site	Champion	Runner-up
9 & Under	Orlando	Central Florida Express	Tampa Cannons
10 & Under (60-foot)	Des Moines	Ocala (Fla.) Blaze	Manasota (Fla.) Stingrays
10 & Under (65-foot)	Knoxville	Carolina Angels	Virginia Storm
11 & Under	Orlando	Greenville (S.C.) Gators	San Diego Stars
12 & Under	Burnsville, Minn.	Tampa Bay Crush	Carolina Mariners
13 & Under (90-foot)	Kinston, N.C.	Central Florida Cyclones	N.C. Lumber and Lightning
13 & Under (80-foot)	Amarillo, Texas	Texas Blackhawks	East Cobb (Ga.) Stallions
14 & Under (90-foot)	Sarasota, Fla.	Florida Elite	Bay Area (Calif.) Starmakers
15 & Under	Kingsport, Tenn.	Greensboro (N.C.) BB Club	Florida Hitmen
Junior Olympics/16 & Under	Detroit	East Cobb (Ga.) Astros	Chet Lemon's (Fla.) Juice
17 & Under	Orlando	Diamond (S.C.) Travelers	Knoxville Thunder
18 & Under	Fort Myers, Fla.	Tallahassee (Fla.) BB Club	Chain (Ga.) BB Club

AMERICAN AMATEUR BASEBALL CONGRESS (AABC)

Event	Site	Champion	Runner-up
Willie Mays (10 & Under)	Catano, P.R.	Puerto Rico	California Bandits
Pee Wee Reese (12 & Under)	Toa Baja, P.R.	Puerto Rico Mariners	Dallas Tigers
Sandy Koufax (14 & Under)	Gurnee, Ill.	Seattle	Morrow/Lake City, Ga.
Mickey Mantle (16 & Under)	McKinney, Texas	Dallas	California
Connie Mack (18 & Under)	Farmington, N.M.	East Cobb (Ga.) Yankees	Midland (Ohio) Redskins
Stan Musial (open)	Battle Creek, Mich.	Atlanta Yankees	Canton, Ohio

AMERICAN LEGION BASEBALL

Event	Site	Champion	Runner-up
World Series (19 & Under)	Bartlesville, Okla.	Rochester, Minn.	Cherryville, N.C.

BABE RUTH BASEBALL

Event	Site	Champion	Runner-up
Cal Ripken (10 & Under)	Williamsburg, Va.	Lexington, Ky.	Jupiter, Fla.
Cal Ripken (11-12)	Aberdeen, Md.	Mexico	Hilo, Hawaii
13	Pine Bluff, Ark.	Bronx, N.Y.	Jefferson Parish, La.
14	Quincy, Mass.	Youngstown, Ohio	Willamette Valley, Ore.
13-15	Williston, N.D.	Taylorsville, Utah	Jefferson Parish, La.
16	Jamestown, N.Y.	Syracuse, N.Y.	Columbus, Ga.
16-18	Weimar, Texas	Hammond, Ind.	Mobile, Ala.

CONTINENTAL AMATEUR BASEBALL ASSOCIATION (CABA)

Event	Site	Champion	Runner-up
9 & Under	Charles City, Iowa	Kansas City (Kan.) Wildcats	Omaha Pacesetters
10 & Under	Aurelia, Iowa	Oak Forest, Ill.	Northwest Iowa
11 & Under	Marion, Ohio	Mansfield, Ohio	Caguas, P.R.
12 & Under	Cincinnati	Knoxville (Tenn.) Stars	Tennessee Thunder
13 & Under	Broken Arrow, Okla.	Brazil	Oklahoma City Indians
14 & Under	Dublin, Ohio	Seattle Stars	Kansas Royals
15 & Under	Crystal Lake, Ill.	Seattle Stars	East Cobb (Ga.) Hurricanes
16 & Under	Marietta, Ga.	East Cobb (Ga.) Astros	Bayside (N.Y.) Yankees
High school age	Euclid, Ohio	Brooklyn, N.Y.	Kansas City, Mo.
18 & Under	Houston	Houston Heat Black	Bayside (N.Y.) Yankees
College	Schenectady, N.Y.	Schenectady (N.Y.) Jays	Electric City (N.Y.) Giants

DIXIE BASEBALL

Event	Site	Champion	Runner-up
Dixie Youth (9-10) Majors	Florence, S.C.	Montgomery, Ala.	Louisiana
Dixie Youth (12 & Under)	Florence, S.C.	Nacogdoches, Texas	Bedford, Va.
Dixie 13	Jackson, Tenn.	Opelika, Ala.	Sumter, S.C.
Dixie Boys (13-14)	Jackson, Tenn.	Columbia County, Ga.	Dentsville, S.C.
Dixie Pre-Majors (15-16)	Thomasville, Ala.	Monroe, La.	Alabama AUM
Dixie Majors (15-18)	Laurel, Miss.	Monroe, La.	Chester County, Tenn.

DIZZY DEAN BASEBALL

Event	Site	Champion	Runner-up
Minors (10 & Under)	Huffman, Ala.	Brent, Fla.	Belle Chasse, La.
11 & Under	Coal Mountain, Ga.	St. John's, La.	Kenner, La.
Freshman (11-12)	Barton County, Ga.	Kenner (La.) Eagles	Northport (Ala.) Blue
13 & Under	Southaven, Miss.	Baton Rouge (La.) Raiders	Cullman, Ala.
Sophomore (13-14)	Southaven, Miss.	Lufkin, Texas	Baton Rouge (La.) Rockies
Junior (15-16)	Southaven, Miss.	Brent, Fla.	Maryland Yankee Rebels

AMATEUR/YOUTH CHAMPIONS 2003

Senior (17-18)	Southaven, Miss.	Over the Mountain, Ala.	Boynton, Ga.
High school	Hixson, Tenn.	Lufkin, Texas	Walker Valley, Tenn.

HAP DUMONT BASEBALL/National Baseball Congress

Event	Site	Champion	Runner-up
9 & Under	Bartlett, Tenn.	Tennessee Travelers	Tennessee Tigers
11 & Under	Oklahoma City	Wichita Sluggers	Oklahoma City Gladiators
12 & Under	Harrison, Ark.	Texas Mudbugs	Tennessee Travelers
13 & Under	Tunica, Miss.	Alabama	Arkansas Lasers
14 & Under	Brainerd, Minn.	Rolling Meadows, Ill.	Cincinnati
15 & Under	Greenfield, Ind.	Tennessee Hornets	Louisiana Tigers
16 & Under	Oklahoma City	Wichita Sluggers	Wichita Metros
18 & Under	Wichita	Wichita Sluggers	Wichita Jets

LITTLE LEAGUE BASEBALL

Event	Site	Champion	Runner-up
Little League (11-12)	Williamsport, Pa.	Japan	Boynton Beach, Fla.
Junior League (13-14)	Taylor, Mich.	La Mirada, Calif.	Santiago, Panama
Senior League (15-16)	Bangor, Me.	Hilo, Hawaii	Chesterfield, Va.
Big League (17-18)	Easley, S.C.	South Carolina	Thousand Oaks, Calif.

NATIONAL AMATEUR BASEBALL FEDERATION (NABF)

Event	Site	Champion	Runner-up
Freshman (12 & Under)	Hopkinsville, Ky.	Harford (Md.) Sox	Funacho (Ohio) Flames
Sophomore (14 & Under)	Joplin, Mo.	Nashville Sabers	Indiana Bulls
Junior (16 & Under)	Northville, Mich.	Fairfield (Ohio) Diamond Stars	Huntington (W.Va.) Hounds
High School (17 & Under)	Millington, Tenn.	Christian Brothers HS, Memphis	Indiana Bulls
Senior (18 & Under)	Welland, Ontario	Pa. Batting Practice	Florida Scorpions
College (22 & Under)	Springfield, Ohio	Fenton, Mo.	Cincinnati Stars
Major (open)	Louisville	New Haven, Conn.	Fort Wayne, Ind.

PERFECT GAME/WORLD WOOD BAT ASSOCIATION

Event	Site	Champion	Runner-up
Summer Championship/Senior	Marietta, Ga.	Florida Bombers	Bill Hood (La.) Broncos
Summer Championship/Junior	Marietta, Ga.	East Cobb (Ga.) Braves	NorCal
Summer Championship/Freshman	Marietta, Ga.	East Cobb (Ga.) Aztecs	NorCal
Fall Underclassmen	Fort Myers, Fla.	Chet Lemon's (Fla.) Juice	East Cobb (Ga.) Astros
PG/BA Fall World Championship	Jupiter, Fla.	East Cobb (Ga.) Astros	Dallas Tigers

PONY BASEBALL

Event	Site	Champion	Runner-up
Mustang (9-10)	Irving, Texas	Tamiami, Fla.	Irving, Texas
Bronco (11-12)	Monterey, Calif.	Levittown, P.R.	Tamiami, Fla.
Pony (13-14)	Washington, Pa.	Lakewood, Calif.	Humacao, P.R.
Colt (15-16)	Lafayette, Ind.	Tampa Town & Country	Levittown, P.R.
Palomino (17-18)	Santa Clara, Calif.	Orange County, Calif.	Houston Kyle Chapman

REVIVING BASEBALL IN INNER CITIES (RBI)

Event	Site	Champion	Runner-up
Junior (13-15)	Houston	Los Angeles	Houston
Senior (16-18)	Houston	Los Angeles	Fort Worth, Texas

TRIPLE CROWN BASEBALL

Event	Site	Champion	Runner-up
9 & Under	Steamboat Springs, Colo.	Santa Clarita (Calif.) Hurricanes	West Covina (Calif.) Bandits
10 & Under	Steamboat Springs, Colo.	Texas Sports	Plano (Texas) Young Guns
11 & Under	Steamboat Springs, Colo.	Chino Hills (Calif.) Storm	Murrieta (Calif.) Muddogs
12 & Under	Steamboat Springs, Colo.	Spanish Fork (Utah) Mariners	Wisconsin Diamond Kings
13 & Under	Steamboat Springs, Colo.	West Covina (Calif.) Rebels	Southern Nevada Bulldogs
14 & Under	Steamboat Springs, Colo.	Houston Warriors	Corona (Calif.) Dodgers
15 & Under	Steamboat Springs, Colo.	Palm Desert (Calif.) Tigers	Oklahoma Stix
16 & Under	Steamboat Springs, Colo.	Ann Arbor (Mich.) Braves	Austin Slam Braves
18 & Under	Steamboat Springs, Colo.	Dallas Mets	Taylorsville (Utah) Warriors

U.S. AMATEUR BASEBALL ASSOCIATION (USABA)

Event	Site	Champion	Runner-up
10 & Under	Sequim, Wash.	Compton, Calif.	Sequim, Wash.
12 & Under	Sequim, Wash.	Vacaville, Calif.	Kingston, Wash.
14 & Under	Pasco, Wash.	Bend (Ore.) Elks	Seattle Southside Sox
15 & Under	Mianer, Nev.	Clovis (Calif.) Twin City	Langley, B.C.
16 & Under	Richland, Wash.	Pasco (Wash.) Sun Devils	Seattle Triple Play

U.S. SPECIALTY SPORTS ASSOCIATION (USSSA)

Event	Site	Champion	Runner-up
9 & Under/Majors	Baton Rouge, La.	Team Atlanta, La.	Houston Colt .45s
10 & Under/Majors	Henderson, Nev.	Georgia Seminoles	Texas Stars
11 & Under/Majors	Gulfport, Miss.	Texas Rattlers	Texas Thunder
12 & Under/Majors	Chino Hills, Calif.	San Diego Stars	So Cal Twisters
13 & Under/Majors	High Point, N.C.	No Fear Astros (Calif.)	Tamiami (Fla.) Rangers
14 & Under/Majors (80-foot)	San Antonio	Louisiana Tigers	Houston Banditos
14 & Under/Majors (90-foot)	Orlando	East Cobb (Ga.) Aztecs	Columbus (Ga.) Young Guns
15 & Under/Majors	Murfreesboro, Tenn.	Georgia Stars	North Carolina Cardinals
16 & Under/Majors	Orlando	Maryland Orioles	Florida Bombers
18 & Under/Majors	Nicholasville, Ky.	Cedar City (Tenn.) Curve	Midwest (Mo.) Prospects

BASEBALL FOR THE AGES

Baseball America's annual Baseball For the Ages selections brings together players from every age, every level and every region. But they share one thing in common: They're the best baseball players in the country—if not the world—at their ages.

The universal youth baseball cutoff date of Aug. 1 is used to establish a player's age for the 2003 winners.

12 Ryan Klem, rhp/of, Chandler, Ariz.

As a member of the Chandler Express travel team, Klem put up eye-popping numbers. He led the Express to victory in one of Cooperstown Dreamspark's weekly tournaments, hitting .840 and slamming 14 home runs in 12 games. He beat Missouri's Mac-N-Seitz, then the nation's No. 1-ranked 12-year-old team, in the championship game 2-0 on a one-hitter, striking out 10. Klem was recruited to play for California's Say Hey Kids in Cooperstown's National Tournament of Champions and hit 11 more homers and had 17 strikeouts while throwing a no-hitter against the North Alabama Vipers. His fastball was clocked at 84 mph. Klem played in 120 games overall, mostly against players a year or two older and won 35 games, posted a 0.60 ERA and struck out 360 in 145 innings. As a hitter, he had a .606 average and 71 home runs. "He's a phenom, a freak of nature," said Express coach Larry High, who also scouts for the Cardinals.

Ryan Klem

13 Robert Stock, c/rhp, Agoura, Calif.

The 5-foot-11, 170-pound Stock narrowly missed winning his age group as a 12-year-old. With bigger fields, 13 is a more difficult age to dominate, but there was no denying Stock. He played for three different teams—the 13-year-old West Coast Rebels, the 14-year-old California Eagles and his local 17-and-under American Legion team. With a fastball that touched 89 mph, Stock led the Rebels to a second straight Triple Crown World Series title. With Stock in the lineup over a two-year period, the Rebels posted a 120-3 record.

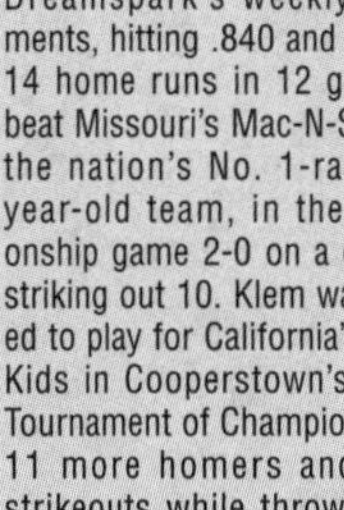

Robert Stock

"He was by far the best player in every tournament he played," Rebels coach David Whetstone said.

14 John Tolisano, 3b, Sanibel, Fla.

Tolisano played on two premium youth teams in 2003, the Florida Elite and East Cobb (Ga.) Aztecs, and between them won the AAU 14 national title, Triple Crown spring nationals, USSSA 14 title and inaugural World Wood Bat Association Freshman championship. In 103 games, the 6-foot, 180-pound Tolisano, a ninth-grader at Estero High, hit .679 with 13 home runs. He hit at least .600 in every tournament he played, including a lofty .842 average while leading the Elite to the AAU title. "He's as accomplished a 14-year-old hitter as I've ever seen," Aztecs coach Earl Newalu said.

WINNERS AGES 20-25

20. Miguel Cabrera, 3b-of, Marlins
21. Dontrelle Willis, lhp, Marlins
22. Mark Prior, rhp, Cubs
23. Albert Pujols, of, Cardinals
24. Vernon Wells, of, Blue Jays
25. Alfonso Soriano, 2b, Yankees

15 Justin Upton, ss, Chesapeake, Va.

Upton isn't eligible for the draft until 2005, but he was the No. 1 player on the Major League Scouting Bureau's follow list in the summer of 2003. As a high school sophomore, Upton led Great Bridge High to the Virginia 3-A title, hitting .458-7-39 with 11 stolen bases. He split his summer between tournaments and showcase events. He earned a spot on Team USA's national youth squad off his performance in June at USA Baseball's Junior Olympics, but he decided not to make the trip to Taiwan in the aftermath of the SARS epidemic.

Justin Upton

16 Nick Adenhart, rhp, Hagerstown, Md.

Armed with a mid-90s fastball and a knee-buckling curve, Adenhart went 7-1, 1.00 as a junior at Hagerstown's Williamsport High. He then pitched at the top of the rotation for the 21-and-under Maryland Orioles and led that team to the All-American Amateur Baseball Association title in Johnstown, Pa.

17 Felix Hernandez, rhp, Mariners

Hernandez rolled through the college-dominated, short-season Northwest League with a 7-2, 2.29 record and 73 strikeouts in 53 innings for Everett. He was named the league's top prospect. Signed out of Venezuela in 2002, Hernandez led the league in wins, ERA and strikeouts for most of the summer, before allowing four earned runs over five innings in his final start prior to a promotion to low Class A Wisconsin, where he went 0-0, 1.93 with 18 K's in 14 innings.

"He more or less dominated every time he took the mound," Tri-City manager Ron Gideon said. Hernandez throws his overpowering fastball at 94-95 mph. It topped out at 97, and could easily reach 100 as he matures and adds strength.

18 Greg Miller, lhp, Dodgers

Miller's fastball reached the mid-80s as a high school junior, but few pitchers have improved as much since. The 31st overall pick in the 2002 draft. Miller's fastball now reaches the mid-90s. He blew through the high Class A Florida State League despite having just 38 innings of prior experience. In 116 innings, he went 11-4, 2.49 and struck out 11. "It's pretty rare to do what Greg is doing," Dodgers scouting director Logan White said after Miller's promotion to Double-A, where he went 1-1, 1.01 and struck out 40 while walking seven in 27 innings. "He's come farther (since being drafted) than any kid I've ever seen."

19 Zack Greinke, rhp, Royals

Greinke, a first-round pick in 2002, pitches with the savvy and poise of a major league veteran. His fastball can touch 94 mph, but he prefers to work between 88-91 mph, adding or taking a little off to keep hitters off balance. He also can alter the speed on a nasty curveball and has a slider and changeup that project as major league pitches.

"He's as close to what you'd call a sure thing as I've seen," Class A Kinston manager Torey Lovullo said. "Sometimes you look at him and it's hard to believe he's only 19. It doesn't make sense." Greinke went 11-1, 1.14 at Wilmington of the Carolina League and earned a promotion to Double-A Wichita, where he went 4-3, 3.23.

DRAFT

MLB pressure to cut back bonuses results in sharp decline in 2003

BY JIM CALLIS

During the 2002-03 offseason, most free agents not named Jim Thome struggled to maintain the status quo. Lucrative multiyear offers were few and far between, as the median salary and the number of big leaguers making $1 million slid slowly backward for the second straight season.

But compared to 2003 first-round draft picks, those free agents were wined and dined and swimming in cash.

Collusion is prohibited by baseball's collective bargaining agreement, but draftees aren't covered by that pact. So starting in 2000, Major League Baseball has cajoled teams into keeping draft bonuses down.

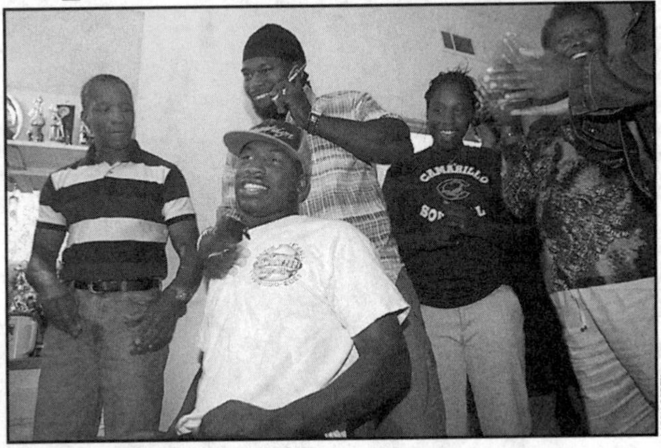
LARRY GOREN

Big brother offers his congratulations
Delmon Young, the No. 1 pick in the 2003 draft, and big leaguer Dmitri

MLB has conducted negotiating seminars, rightfully realizing that agents had more experience in that regard. The commissioner's office now suggests bonuses for each pick in the first 10 rounds, and pressures clubs not to step out of line.

These efforts had an immediate effect, as first-round bonuses rose just 3.5 percent from 1999 to 2000, the smallest gain since Baseball America began tracking them in 1989 (not counting 1996, when the figures were affected by loophole free agency).

First-round bonuses jumped by 15.0 percent in 2001, thanks mostly to a historically strong draft that featured Joe Mauer, Mark Prior, Mark Teixeira and five bonuses of at least $4 million in the first five picks. But MLB was really able to clamp down in 2002, as bonuses decreased (by 2.2 percent) for the first time on record.

And that was just a warmup. In 2003, the average first-round pick signed for $1,766,667, the cheapest cost since 1998 and down a whopping 16.2 percent from 2002. That even exceeded MLB's hopes and dreams, as its predraft guidelines for the first round averaged $1,855,833.

"If you're not willing to sign for slot money," one agent said, "you're going to start sliding through the draft."

Just six first-rounders exceeded their predraft slots. They were the top three picks and three players who could have gone in the first 6-10 choices based solely on ability and were paid accordingly: Tulane first baseman Michael Aubrey (Indians, No. 11), Florida high school outfielder Lastings Milledge (Mets, No. 12) and Massachusetts prep righthander Jeff Allison (Marlins, No. 16).

No. 1 overall pick Delmon Young received the highest bonus, $3.7 million from the Devil Rays as part of a five-year major league contract worth a guaranteed $5.8 million and as much as $6.2 million. That was the lowest top bonus since 1998, when Corey Patterson signed a two-sport deal with the Cubs for the same amount. The last three drafts combined for eight bonuses of $4 million or more.

Despite the tight budgeting, teams found it easier to sign draftees than ever before. For the first time, every player selected in the first two rounds came to terms. Florida high school pitcher Andrew Miller, the first pick in the third round (Devil Rays, No. 68 overall), turned down a backloaded big league contract worth more than $2 million and opted to attend the University of North Carolina.

Just 16 of the 307 players from the first 10 rounds went unsigned, which also was unprecedented. The previous low was 24 in 2000.

BONUS ESCALATION

First-round bonuses showed the most dramatic decrease on record in 2003, with bonuses dropping 16.2 percent from 2002. The year-by-year, first-round average with the resulting annual increase or decrease (bonuses rounded to nearest thousand).

Year	Average	Change
1989	$176,000	—
1990	246,000	39.7%
1991	355,000	44.3%
1992	482,000	35.8%
1993	611,000	26.8%
1994	790,000	29.3%
1995	913,000	15.6%
1996*	924,000	1.2%
1997	1,326,000	43.5%
1998	1,638,000	23.5%
1999	1,810,000	10.5%
2000	1,873,000	3.5%
2001	2,154,000	15.0%
2002	2,107,000	-2.2%
2003	1,766,000	-16.2%

*Average doesn't include four loophole free agents who didn't sign with the teams that drafted them.

Rays Take Young Over Weeks

Tampa Bay finalized its decision to make Young the first pick overall the night before the June 3 draft. But Young, a Camarillo (Calif.) High outfielder, didn't learn his fate until he heard his name called on MLB.com's internet draft broadcast shortly after 1 p.m. ET. His father Larry knew beforehand but kept it a secret.

Young said he had thought the Devil Rays were going with Southern second baseman Rickie Weeks. He had the requisite Tampa Bay cap and T-shirt on hand for photo opportunities, but he also had Brewers paraphernalia on hand in case he lasted until the second pick.

Though the Devil Rays had lengthy discussions about Young, Weeks and, to a lesser extent, Florida high school outfielder Ryan Harvey, Tampa Bay general manager Chuck LaMar said they kept coming back to Young.

"We thought he was one of the best players long before the draft," LaMar said. "But we're in a critical situation, having the No. 1 pick in the country and not winning as many games as we hoped. We made sure we asked all the questions to make sure we got the best player in the country. He was awfully high on our list for a while. We went through everything to see if anyone could unseat Delmon, and the answer was no."

Few teams had any questions about Young, the most accomplished high school hitter in the draft. Already 6-foot-3 and 205 pounds, he projects as a slugging right fielder. He set a U.S. junior national team record with 16 homers in 2002, when he topped all players at the World Junior Championships with nine homers and 18 RBIs in seven games.

"He is one of the finest power hitters our scouts have evaluated, not only this year but over the years," Devil Rays scouting director Cam Bonifay said. "He's the kind of guy that you don't get out of your seat and go buy a hot dog when you know he's coming to the plate. You want to stay there and watch him hit. He lights up your eyes."

The only negatives on Young were a couple of minor injuries during the spring, neither of which is remotely a long-term concern. He missed Camarillo's first five games after spraining his right ankle in a pickup basketball game, and he didn't pitch after coming down with shoulder tendinitis. His fastball had been clocked up to 95 mph in the past.

Young and his brother Dmitri, a Tigers outfielder, became the highest drafted siblings in draft history. Dmitri, who went fourth overall to the Cardinals in 1991, also had been drafted by the Devil Rays. Tampa Bay selected him in the November 1997 expansion draft, then traded him to Cincinnati in a prearranged deal.

Because the Tigers were in San Diego to play the Padres, Dmitri was able to surprise his brother by arriving via limousine for the draft-day celebration. Delmon sounded relaxed and confident afterward, saying he wasn't going to put pressure on himself and comparing his game to Vladimir Guerrero's. He also said he hoped to reach Tampa Bay by 2005.

"That gives me two years. I want to be there as quick as possible, like Andruw Jones, Ken Griffey Jr. and A-Rod," Young said. "I'm trying to be just like them, to get to the big leagues as quick as possible and be dominant like they are."

BILL MITCHELL

Brewers settle for odd man out
Southern's record-setting Rickie Weeks

The start of his pro career was delayed by negotiations. The last of the 30 first-round picks to sign, Young finalized his contact with Tampa Bay on Sept. 9.

Three To The Majors

Young may have edged Weeks for the honor of being the No. 1 pick, but Weeks already has beaten him to the majors.

After the Brewers took him second, Weeks also held out for most of the summer. On Aug. 5 he accepted a deal that set the stage for Young's: a five-year big league contract worth at least $4.8 million and as much as $5.5 million, including a $3.6 million bonus.

Baseball America's 2003 College Player of the Year, Weeks won NCAA Division I batting titles in 2002 and 2003 and left Southern as the all-time leading hitter (.473) in NCAA history. He hit .358 in 21 minor league games before Milwaukee recalled him when rosters expanded in September.

Weeks popped out to second base in his first big league at-bat, against the Cardinals' Brett Tomko on Sept. 15. He went 2-for-12 in seven games, then headed for the Arizona Fall League.

Weeks was just the third 2003 draftee to reach the big leagues. The first was University of Houston righthander Ryan Wagner, chosen 14th overall by the Reds. Wagner, who broke a 39-year-old NCAA Division I record by averaging 16.8 strikeouts per nine innings during the spring, retired all five batters he faced against the Astros on July 19.

Wagner's debut came just 46 days after the draft, making his the swiftest trip to the majors since Ariel Prieto went from the independent Western League to No. 5 overall pick to the Athletics in 28 days in 1995. Among non-professionals, Wagner was the fastest since Jerry Don Gleaton moved from the Texas Longhorns to the Texas Rangers in a 36-day

CINCINNATI REDS

MORRIS FOSTOFF

Reaching for the top
Ryan Wagner, left, and Chad Cordero made the majors in first season

span in 1979.

Wagner's dastardly slider proved to be just as unhittable in the majors as it was in college. He went 2-0, 1.66 in 17 appearances with Cincinnati, putting himself in the club's closer mix for 2004.

The Expos surprised other teams by taking Cal State Fullerton righthander Chad Cordero with the 20th overall choice, but he fit two important criteria for a team with an uncertain future. He signed quickly for below-slot money ($1.35 million) and was close to being ready for the big leagues.

Cordero pitched a scoreless inning against the Marlins in his Aug. 30 debut. In 12 games, he went 1-0, 1.64 with one save.

The last draft to send this many players to the majors in their draft year was 1978, when five players made the jump. No. 1 overall pick Bob Horner (Braves), first-rounders Mike Morgan and Tim Conroy (Athletics) and seventh-round Brian Milner (Blue Jays) all went straight to the majors, while Britt Burns (third round) arrived in August. Horner and Burns were fast-tracked on merit, while Morgan and Conroy were publicity stunts by Oakland owner Charlie Finley and Milner's callup was part of a deal to entice him away from college football.

MAJOR LEAGUE CONTRACTS

Three more players were signed to major league contracts in 2003, including 2002 draft-and-follow Adam Loewen, who signed with Baltimore less than an hour before he would have re-entered the 2003 draft. Such contracts require players to be placed immediately on the selecting team's 40-man roster. The 2003 signings increased the number of major league contracts to 22 since Bo Jackson agreed to a major league deal with the Royals in 1986 as a condition of his being pried away from a promising NFL career. Here's the full list, including the bonus the player received as well as the amount guaranteed in major league salaries and roster bonuses.

Year	Club (Round)	Player, Pos.	Bonus	Guar. Amount
1986	Royals (4)	Bo Jackson, of	$100,000	$1,066,000
1989	Orioles (1)	Ben McDonald, rhp	350,000	824,000
	Blue Jays (3)	John Olerud, 1b	575,000	800,000
1990	Athletics (1)	*Todd Van Poppel, rhp	500,000	1,200,000
1993	Mariners (1)	*Alex Rodriguez, ss	1,000,000	1,300,000
1998	Phillies (1)	Pat Burrell, 1b-of	3,150,000	8,000,000
	Cardinals (1)	J.D. Drew, of	3,000,000	7,000,000
	Cardinals (2)	Chad Hutchinson, rhp	2,300,000	3,400,000
1999	Marlins (1)	*Josh Beckett, rhp	3,625,000	7,000,000
	Tigers (1)	Eric Munson, c	3,500,000	6,750,000
2000	Reds (1)	*David Espinosa, ss	None	2,950,000
	Reds (2)	Dane Sardinha, c	None	1,950,000
	Padres (2)	Xavier Nady, 3b	1,100,000	2,850,000
	Devil Rays (5)	Jace Brewer, ss	450,000	1,200,000
2001	Cubs (1)	Mark Prior, rhp	4,000,000	10,500,000
	Devil Rays (1)	Dewon Brazelton, rhp	4,200,000	4,800,000
	Rangers (1)	Mark Teixeira, 3b	4,500,000	9,500,000
2002	+Orioles (1)	Adam Loewen, lhp	3,200,000	4,020,000
	Indians (1)	Jeremy Guthrie, rhp	3,000,000	4,000,000
	Rockies (4)	Jeff Baker, 3b	200,000	2,000,000
2003	Devil Rays (1)	*Delmon Young, of	3,700,000	5,800,000
	Brewers (1)	Rickie Weeks, 2b	3,600,000	4,790,000

* High school signee
+ Draft-and-follow, signed the following year

Loewen Shatters DFE Record

Lefthander Adam Loewen, the fourth overall pick by the Orioles in 2002, became the highest-drafted player ever to go through the draft-and-follow process. When negotiations broke down with Baltimore that summer, he opted to attend Chipola (Fla.) JC, which gave the team another chance to sign him after his spring season ended in 2003.

RODGER WOOD

Adam Loewen

The Orioles had until midnight on the evening of May 26 to finalize a deal, and did so with minutes to spare. The key was giving him a major league contract that provided for a $3.2 million bonus and a $4.02 million guarantee over five years. That obliterated the previous record for a draft-and-follow, which was the $1.701 million Sean Henn got from the Yankees in 2001.

Baltimore had offered Loewen $2.5 million before he went to Chipola, while Loewen had sought $3.9 million at that time. Had he re-entered the 2003 draft, he likely would have been the first or second pick.

"We're feeling awfully good about it," Orioles vice president of baseball operations Mike Flanagan said. "There was a lot of hard work that went into it from the scouts to the front office. Talent is talent, and we thought Adam was a talent."

Baltimore wound up with both of the top draft-and-follows from the 2002 draft when the Reds couldn't land Young Harris (Ga.) JC's Nick Markakis, whom they had selected in the 23rd round. Markakis, Baseball America's Junior College Player of the Year in both 2002 and 2003, led all national junior college players in victories and strikeouts as pitcher and RBIs as a hitter in the latter season.

Markakis turned down a $1.5 million offer from Cincinnati to re-enter the draft. Looking to conserve money after signing Loewen, the Orioles tried to get Tulane first baseman Michael Aubrey to accept a below-slot bonus for their No. 7 pick. When he declined, they took Markakis and signed him for $1.85 million, $450,000 less than MLB's recommendation.

While Baltimore's decision to take Markakis wasn't surprising, its choice for his future was. Most teams preferred him as a pitcher and some clubs were split, but the Orioles liked his bat more and made him a full-time outfielder. He hit .455-17-74 as a freshman and .439-21-92 as a sophomore, and impressed Baltimore at the plate during a workout the day before the draft.

"We think he's going to develop into a fine power hitter," Orioles scouting director Tony DeMacio said. "We're not looking at him as a fallback-type player. We think he's going to hit. He's got a nice swing. He centers the ball consistently, and we like that as well."

BONUSES BY ROUND

The change in bonuses, by round, from 2002 to 2003:

Round	2002 Avg	2003 Avg	Change
1	$2,106,810	1,765,667	-16.2%
S-1	849,091	975,357	+14.9%
2	680,964	759,233	+11.5%
3	461,018	415,981	-9.8%
4	260,383	280,466	+7.7%
5	184,636	185,893	+0.7%
6	107,827	138,685	+28.6%
7	110,320	96,450	-12.6%
8	81,920	71,964	-12.2%
9	69,700	49,345	-29.2%
10	44,537	47,704	+7.1%

Honest To A Fault

Scouts determined early in the spring that Wake Forest's Kyle Sleeth and Richmond's Tim Stauffer were the top two college pitchers available. The Tigers took Sleeth third overall, and the Padres followed by selecting Stauffer.

San Diego scouting director Bill Gayton said Stauffer's makeup was one of the deciding factors in the club's decision. Stauffer's character became evident during the negotiating process, when he and his agent, Ron Shapiro, told the Padres that he had weakness in his shoulder.

MLB recommended $2.8 million for the fourth slot, and the Padres initially offer $2.6 million. After Stauffer's revelation, he signed for $750,000. Sleeth received $3.35 million from the Tigers.

"Quite honestly, this is a special family and a special kid with a lot of integrity," Gayton said. "They came to us and they disclosed there was possibly something in the shoulder. Their honesty and integrity is second to none. They didn't have to do that. That's one of the things that's so attractive about him. We tested over 30 potential first-round fits and Tim Stauffer rated No. 1. That is the separator."

RICH ABEL

Good-faith gesture
Padres pick Tim Stauffer

Stauffer said his shoulder felt sore for longer than normal after his final college start, a 10-8 loss to UC Riverside in the NCAA regional at Stanford on May 30. Stauffer took the loss, allowing five runs (three earned) on 11 hits and three walks while striking out 11.

An MRI in July didn't reveal any tears, but Stauffer's shoulder joint was weak from wear on his labrum and rotator cuff. He worked with Padres trainers at high Class A Lake Elsinore and planned to throw in instructional league, with the goal of being 100 percent by spring training after rest and rehabilitation.

MIKE JANES

Kyle Sleeth

He said he had no reservations about telling the Padres about the condition of his shoulder.

"It was going to be found out eventually," Stauffer said. "I wanted to tell them personally. They were pretty shocked, as shocked as we were. They had no idea. Even the last game of the season, I was throwing as hard or harder as I had all year."

Stauffer's situation recalled three similar cases over the previous decade where first-round pitchers received low bonuses because of their medical condition. UCLA righthander Pete Janicki, who sustained a stress fracture in his elbow in a regional against Mississippi State just days after the Angels selected him eighth overall in 1992, signed a big league contract with a $90,000 bonus and only $215,000 guaranteed.

In 1996, University of Tennessee righthander R.A. Dickey was about to sign with the Rangers for $810,000 as the no. 18 pick before a Rangers doctor discovered Dickey had no ulnar collateral ligament in his elbow during a routine physical. The Rangers reduced their offer to $75,000.

Loyola Marymount lefty Billy Traber, the 16th overall selection in 2000, had a $1.7 million bonus pulled off the table by the Mets when doctors found abnormalities in his elbow that suggested damage to his medial collateral ligament. His bonus was scaled down to $400,000.

Controversial Selection

As the Mets and Milledge were getting close to a deal in early August, talks were suddenly suspended by the club after allegations surfaced that he had sexual relations with underage girls while at Northside Christian School (St. Petersburg, Fla.) during the 2001-02 school year.

After the Mets had a private investigator look into the charges, they signed the 12th overall pick on Aug. 19 for a $2.075 million bonus, which will be spread over five years per the draft rule governing two-sport athletes. Though Milledge hadn't played football since emerging as a top baseball prospect in 2001, Mississippi Gulf Coast CC offered him the chance to play both sports.

The allegations first surfaced in an unsigned letter sent to Northside Christian in the fall of 2001. The letter asserted that Milledge, then 16, had sex with girls as young as 12 and 13.

The Pinellas County Sheriff's Department conducted its own investigation and never brought charges. Northside Christian expelled him on May 17, 2002—three days after Milledge and his teammates lost in the state 1-A finals—but rescinded the expulsion three weeks later.

Milledge attended Lakewood Ranch High (Bradenton, Fla.) as a senior, leading his team to the 2003 state 5-A championship before the Mets selected him 12th overall. At the time, the Mets acknowledged they were aware of the reason for his expulsion, characterizing it as improper behavior with a female minor.

Others described it as Milledge admitting to having consensual sex with his 15-year-old girlfriend when he was 16. Because he could have been prosecuted, Milledge voluntarily entered a juvenile arbitration program that included community service, an essay and a tour of a jail.

On the day the club drafted Milledge, Gary LaRocque, its assistant general manager for scouting operations, said

HISTORICAL SIGNIFICANCE

First-round bonuses took a pronounced drop in 2003, and predictably no significant bonus records were set. Below are the 10 largest bonuses for players who signed with the teams that drafted them (for those players who signed major league contracts, only the cash bonus is noted):

Player, Pos.	Club, Year (Round)	Bonus
1. Joe Borchard, of	White Sox '00 (1)	$5,300,000
2. Joe Mauer, c	Twins '01 (1)	5,150,000
3. B.J. Upton, ss	Devil Rays '02 (1)	4,600,000
4. *Mark Teixeira, 3b	Rangers '01 (1)	4,500,000
5. *Dewon Brazelton, rhp	Devil Rays '01 (1)	4,200,000
Gavin Floyd, rhp	Phillies '01 (1)	4,200,000
7. *Mark Prior, rhp	Cubs '01 (1)	4,000,000
Bryan Bullington, rhp	Pirates '02 (1)	4,000,000
9. Josh Hamilton, of	Devil Rays '99 (1)	3,960,000
10. Corey Patterson, of	Cubs '98 (1)	3,700,000
*Delmon Young, of	Devil Rays '03 (1)	3,700,000

*Signed major league contract

DRAFT '03 TOP 100 PICKS

Signing bonuses do not include scholarships, incentive bonus plans or salaries from a major league contract.
*Highest level of professional baseball attained #Signed major league contract +College Senior

Rank. Team, Player, Pos.	School	Hometown	Bonus	Birthdate	B-T	Ht.	Wt.	AVG	AB	H	HR	RBI	SB	*'03 Assignment
1. #Devil Rays. Delmon Young, of	Camarillo HS	Camarillo, Calif.	$3,700,000	9-14-85	R-R	6-3	205	.523	65	34	7	28	6	DNP—Signed late
2. #Brewers. Rickie Weeks, 2b	Southern U.	Altamonte Springs, Fla.	3,600,000	9-13-82	R-R	6-0	195	.479	163	78	16	66	28	Milwaukee
5. Royals. Chris Lubanski, of	Kennedy-Kenrick HS	Schwenksville, Pa.	2,100,000	3-24-85	L-L	6-3	185	.528	72	38	6	38	20	AZL Royals (R)
6. Cubs. Ryan Harvey, of	Dunedin HS	Palm Harbor, Fla.	2,400,000	8-30-84	R-R	6-5	215	.463	41	19	4	14	4	AZL Cubs (R)
7. Orioles. Nick Markakis, lhp	Young Harris (Ga.) JC	Woodstock, Ga.	1,850,000	11-17-83	L-L	6-2	185	.439	223	98	21	92	—	Aberdeen (A)
10. Rockies. Ian Stewart, 3b	La Quinta HS	Garden Grove, Calif.	1,950,000	4-5-85	L-R	6-3	200	.462	104	48	16	61	9	Casper (R)
11. Indians. Michael Aubrey, 1b	Tulane U.	Shreveport. La.	2,010,000	4-15-82	L-L	6-1	195	.420	243	102	18	79	19	Lake County (A)
12. Mets. Lastings Milledge, of	Lakewood Ranch HS	Palmetto, Fla.	2,075,000	4-5-85	R-R	6-0	185	.414	99	41	10	35	43	Kingsport (R)
13. Blue Jays. Aaron Hill, ss	Louisiana State U.	Visalia, Calif.	1,675,000	3-21-82	R-R	6-0	200	.358	265	95	9	67	9	Dunedin (A)
15. White Sox. Brian Anderson, of	U. of Arizona	Tucson	1,600,000	3-11-82	R-R	6-2	205	.366	232	85	14	62	17	Great Falls (R)
17. Red Sox. David Murphy, of	Baylor U.	Spring, Texas	1,525,000	10-18-81	L-L	6-3	185	.413	293	121	11	67	3	Sarasota (A)
18. Indians. Brad Snyder, of	Ball State U.	Bellevue, Ohio	1,525,000	5-25-82	L-R	6-3	210	.405	200	81	14	61	20	Mahoning Valley (A)
19. D'backs. Conor Jackson, 3b	U. of California	Woodland Hills, Calif.	1,500,000	5-7-82	R-R	6-3	210	.388	160	62	10	44	2	Yakima (A)
21. Twins. Matt Moses, 3b	Mills Godwin HS	Richmond, Va.	1,450,000	2-20-85	L-R	6-0	210	.421	57	24	3	14	4	GCL Twins (R)
23. Angels. Brandon Wood, ss	Horizon HS	Scottsdale, Ariz.	1,300,000	3-2-85	R-R	6-2	175	.500	116	58	20	58	15	Provo (R)
26. A's. Brian Snyder, 3b	Stetson U.	Wellington, Fla.	1,325,000	3-17-82	R-R	6-0	195	.396	227	90	11	55	12	Vancouver (A)
27. Yankees. Eric Duncan, 3b	Seton Hall Prep	Florham Park, N.Y.	1,250,000	12-7-84	L-R	6-1	205	.536	97	52	12	60	18	Staten Island (A)
28. Cardinals. Daric Barton, c	Marina HS	Huntington Beach, Calif.	975,000	8-16-85	L-R	5-11	195	.372	78	29	10	27	8	Johnson City (R)
29. D'backs. Carlos Quentin, of	Stanford U.	Chula Vista, Calif.	1,100,000	8-28-82	R-R	6-2	215	.396	265	105	12	64	10	DNP—Injured
30. Royals. Mitch Maier, c	U. of Toledo	Novi, Mich.	900,000	6-30-82	L-R	6-1	185	.448	194	87	9	61	29	AZL Royals (R)
32. Red Sox. Matt Murton, of	Georgia Tech	McDonough, Ga.	1,010,000	10-3-81	R-R	6-1	225	.301	246	74	13	56	19	Lowell (A)
33. A's. Omar Quintanilla, ss	U. of Texas	El Paso, Texas	992,500	10-24-81	L-R	5-9	185	.348	282	98	6	76	9	Modesto (A)
36. Braves. Jarrod Saltalamacchia, c	Royal Palm Beach HS	West Palm Beach, Fla.	950,000	5-2-85	B-R	6-4	195	.431	65	28	4	21	26	GCL Braves (R)
37. Mariners. Adam Jones, ss	Morse HS	San Diego	925,000	8-1-85	R-R	6-2	185	.348	66	23	2	18	16	AZL Mariners (R)
39. Brewers. Anthony Gwynn, of	San Diego State U.	Poway, Calif.	875,000	10-4-82	L-L	6-0	185	.359	270	97	0	38	25	Beloit (A)
42. Royals. Shane Costa, of	Cal State Fullerton	Visalia, Calif.	775,000	12-12-81	L-R	6-1	200	.371	264	98	5	59	28	Wilmington (A)
46. Rangers. Vince Sinisi, 1b	Rice U.	The Woodlands, Texas	2,070,000	11-7-81	L-L	6-0	195	.338	287	97	10	59	11	Stockton (A)
48. Indians. Javy Herrera, c	U. of Tennessee	Miami	710,000	10-8-81	R-R	6-2	190	.296	199	59	9	32	5	Lake County (A)
52. White Sox. Ryan Sweeney, of	Xavier HS	Cedar Rapids, Iowa	785,000	2-20-85	L-L	6-5	200							Great Falls (R)
54. Red Sox. Mickey Hall, of	Walton HS	Marietta, Ga.	800,000	5-20-85	L-L	6-0	180	.392	74	29	7	35	6	GCL Red Sox (R)
55. Giants. Todd Jennings, c	Long Beach State U.	New Castle, Calif.	620,000	12-10-81	R-R	6-0	190	.296	213	63	5	33	3	Salem-Keizer (A)
56. Mariners. Jeff Flaig, 3b	El Dorado HS	Placentia, Calif.	710,000	3-3-85	R-R	6-2	180	.591	88	52	7	41	13	DNP—Signed late
57. Expos. Jerry Owens, of	The Master's College	Newhall, Calif.	600,000	2-16-81	R-R	6-3	190	.451	184	83	6	31	30	Vermont (A)
62. A's. Andre Ethier, of	Arizona State U.	Glendale, Ariz.	580,000	4-10-82	L-L	6-3	200	.377	260	98	10	68	7	Kane County (A)
63. Giants. Nathan Schierholtz, 3b	Chabot (Calif.) JC	Danville, Calif.	572,000	2-15-84	L-R	6-2	205	.400	180	72	18	60	4	Salem-Keizer (A)
64. Yankees. Estee Harris, of	Central Islip HS	Islip, N.Y.	725,000	1-8-85	L-R	6-0	170	.431	58	25	6	18	21	GCL Yankees (R)
66. D'backs. Jamie D'Antona, 3b	Wake Forest U.	Trumbull, Conn.	560,000	5-12-82	R-R	6-2	215	.360	214	77	21	82	1	Yakima (A)
69. Brewers. Lou Palmisano, c	Broward (Fla.) CC	Fort Lauderdale, Fla.	500,000	9-16-82	R-R	6-1	205	.438	128	56	5	39	17	Helena (R)
70. Tigers. Tony Giarratano, ss	Tulane U.	Marlboro, N.J.	500,000	11-29-82	B-R	6-0	180	.336	274	92	8	42	22	Oneonta (A)
71. Padres. Colt Morton, c	North Carolina State U.	Loxahatchee, Fla.	500,000	4-10-82	R-R	6-5	225	.265	238	63	19	54	1	Fort Wayne (A)
72. Royals. Brian McFall, 1b	Chandler-Gilbert JC	Flagstaff, Ariz.	385,000	3-17-84	R-R	6-3	205	.313	198	62	8	42	16	AZL Royals (R)
73. Cubs. Jake Fox, c	U. of Michigan	Greenfield, Ind.	500,000	7-20-82	R-R	5-10	210	.357	207	74	15	67	2	Lansing (A)
75. Pirates. Steve Lerud, c	Galena HS	Reno, Nev.	512,500	10-13-84	L-R	6-1	205	.466	103	48	21	64	2	DNP—Injured
78. +Indians. Ryan Garko, c	Stanford U.	Walnut, Calif.	270,000	1-2-81	R-R	6-1	220	.402	259	104	18	92	2	Mahoning Valley (A)
81. Reds. Jose Ronda, ss	Gabriela Mistral HS	San Juan, P.R.	440,000	6-8-85	B-R	6-2	175	No high school team						Billings (R)
82. White Sox. Clint King, of	U. of So. Mississippi	Pearl, Miss.	440,000	8-6-82	L-R	5-11	205	.394	254	100	23	77	8	Great Falls (R)
83. Marlins. Jonathan Fulton, ss	George Washington HS	Danville, Va.	440,000	12-1-83	R-R	6-4	200	.476	63	30	1	18	10	GCL Marlins (R)
85. Phillies. Tim Moss, 2b	U. of Texas	Lancaster, Texas	440,000	1-26-82	R-R	5-11	180	.319	276	88	3	33	21	Batavia (A)
87. Expos. Kory Casto, of	U. of Portland	Aurora, Ore.	410,000	12-8-81	L-R	6-0	190	.338	204	69	14	57	2	Vermont (A)
88. Twins. John Woodard, 1b	Cosumnes River JC	Fairfield, Calif.	425,000	9-15-84	L-L	6-4	190	.374	147	55	7	28	—	GCL Twins (R)
89. Astros. Drew Stubbs, of	Atlanta HS	Atlanta, Texas	Did not sign	10-4-84	R-R	6-5	190	.429	84	36	5	20	22	Did not sign
90. Angels. Sean Rodriguez, ss	Braddock HS	Miami	400,000	4-26-85	R-R	6-0	175	.413	80	33	8	21	9	AZL Angels (R)

DRAFT '03 TOP 100 PICKS

Signing bonuses do not include scholarships, incentive bonus plans or salaries from a major league contract.
*Highest level of professional baseball attained #Signed major league contract

Rank. Team, Player, Pos.	School	Hometown	Bonus	Birthdate	B-T	Ht.	Wt.	AVG	AB	H	HR	RBI	SB	*'03 Assignment
92. +A's. Dustin Majewski, of	U. of Texas	Brenham, Texas	220,000	8-16-81	L-L	5-11	190	.391	274	107	12	85	21	Kane County (A)
93. +Giants. Brian Buscher, 3b	U. of South Carolina	Jacksonville, Fla.	215,000	4-18-81	L-R	6-0	185	.393	270	106	15	66	5	Hagerstown (A)
94. Yankees. Tim Battle, of	McIntosh HS	Riverdale, Ga.	425,000	9-10-85	R-R	6-1	180	.406	64	26	7	23	22	GCL Yankees (R)
98. Devil Rays. Travis Schlichting, ss	Round Rock HS	Round Rock, Texas	400,000	10-19-84	R-R	6-4	190	.413	121	50	4	46	11	Princeton (R)
99. Brewers. Charlie Fermaint, of	Jose S. Alegria HS	Vega Alta, P.R.	295,000	10-11-85	R-R	5-10	170	No high school team						AZL Brewers (R)

Rank. Team, Player, Pos.	School	Hometown	Bonus	Birthdate	B-T	Ht.	Wt.	W-L	ERA	IP	H	BB	SO	*'03 Assignment
3. Tigers. Kyle Sleeth, rhp	Wake Forest U.	Westminster, Colo.	$3,350,000	12-20-81	R-R	6-5	205	7-3	2.81	96	78	29	102	DNP—Signed late
4. Padres. Tim Stauffer, rhp	U. of Richmond	Saratoga Springs, N.Y.	750,000	6-2-82	R-R	6-2	205	9-5	1.97	114	87	19	146	DNP—Signed late
8. Pirates. Paul Maholm, lhp	Mississippi State U.	Holly Springs, Miss.	2,200,000	6-25-82	L-L	6-3	215	9-2	2.76	107	102	39	101	Williamsport (A)
9. Rangers. John Danks, lhp	Round Rock HS	Round Rock, Texas	2,100,000	4-15-85	L-L	6-2	190	10-3	1.61	100	59	27	173	Spokane (A)
14. Reds. Ryan Wagner, rhp	U. of Houston	Yoakum, Texas	1,400,000	7-15-82	R-R	6-4	210	6-5	1.93	79	39	21	148	Cincinnati
16. Marlins. Jeff Allison, rhp	Veterans Memorial HS	Peabody, Mass.	1,850,000	11-7-84	R-R	6-2	195	9-0	0.00	64	13	9	142	GCL Marlins (R)
20. Expos. Chad Cordero, rhp	Cal State Fullerton	Chino, Calif.	1,350,000	3-18-82	R-R	6-0	195	5-1	1.34	54	38	7	67	Brevard County (A)
22. Giants. David Aardsma, rhp	Rice U.	The Woodlands, Texas	1,425,000	12-27-81	R-R	6-5	200	7-3	2.97	58	47	19	46	San Jose (A)
24. Dodgers. Chad Billingsley, rhp	Defiance HS	Defiance, Ohio	1,375,000	7-29-84	R-R	6-2	195	7-2	1.21	69	29	21	138	Ogden (R)
25. A's. Brad Sullivan, rhp	U. of Houston	Nederland, Texas	1,360,000	9-12-81	R-R	6-1	190	6-8	2.91	124	90	44	154	Kane County (A)
31. Indians. Adam Miller, rhp	McKinney HS	McKinney, Texas	1,025,000	11-26-84	R-R	6-4	180	10-2	0.49	86	48	16	128	Burlington (R)
34. Giants. Craig Whitaker, rhp	Lufkin HS	Lufkin, Texas	975,000	11-19-84	R-R	6-4	180	8-2	1.12	63	22	28	105	AZL Giants (R)
35. Braves. Luis Atilano, rhp	Gabriela Mistral HS	San Juan, P.R.	950,000	5-10-85	R-R	6-3	180	No high school team						GCL Braves (R)
38. Devil Rays. James Houser, lhp	Sarasota HS	Sarasota, Fla.	900,000	12-15-84	L-L	6-5	185	11-1	1.40	75	48	21	118	Princeton (R)
40. Tigers. Jay Sborz, rhp	Langley HS	Great Falls, Va.	865,000	1-24-85	R-R	6-4	200	6-2	0.71	59	26	17	116	GCL Tigers (R)
41. Padres. Daniel Moore, lhp	U. of North Carolina	Spencer, N.C.	800,000	6-24-82	R-L	6-6	215	7-3	3.56	94	102	41	65	Eugene (A)
43. Braves. Jo Jo Reyes, lhp	Poly HS	Riverside, Calif.	800,000	11-20-84	L-L	6-2	215	7-2	1.91	51	24	15	76	GCL Braves (R)
44. Orioles. Brian Finch, rhp	Texas A&M U.	Brazoria, Texas	750,000	9-27-81	R-R	6-4	195	6-1	5.40	65	81	25	57	Aberdeen (A)
45. Pirates. Tom Gorzelanny, lhp	Triton (Ill.) JC	Orland Park, Ill.	775,000	7-12-82	B-L	6-3	200	7-2	2.47	66	54	26	91	Williamsport (A)
47. Rockies. Scott Beerer, rhp	Texas A&M U.	Newport Beach, Calif.	725,000	7-4-82	R-R	6-1	200	6-1	1.82	49	32	12	58	Casper (R)
49. Red Sox. Abe Alvarez, lhp	Long Beach State U.	Fontana, Calif.	700,000	10-17-82	L-L	6-3	185	11-2	2.35	123	114	31	102	Lowell (A)
50. Blue Jays. Josh Banks, rhp	Florida International U.	Arnold, Md.	650,000	7-18-82	R-R	6-3	195	8-3	3.50	105	95	25	114	Auburn (A)
51. Reds. Thomas Pauly, rhp	Princeton U.	Atlantic Beach, Fla.	660,000	7-28-81	R-R	6-1	195	6-2	1.46	55	37	25	74	Dayton (A)
53. Marlins. Logan Kensing, rhp	Texas A&M U.	Boerne, Texas	675,000	7-3-82	R-R	6-1	185	7-5	3.83	89	101	22	58	Greensboro (A)
58. Twins. Scott Baker, rhp	Oklahoma State U.	Shreveport, La.	600,000	9-19-81	R-R	6-4	190	10-5	3.79	111	117	29	97	Quad City (A)
59. Astros. Jason Hirsh, rhp	Cal Lutheran U.	Burbank, Calif.	625,000	2-20-82	R-R	6-8	250	9-1	3.68	100	92	22	126	Tri-City (A)
60. Angels. Anthony Whittington, lhp	Buffalo HS	Buffalo, W.Va.	650,000	10-9-84	L-L	6-5	225	13-2	0.80	82	20	18	187	AZL Angels (R)
61. Dodgers. Chuck Tiffany, lhp	Charter Oak HS	Covina, Calif.	1,100,000	1-25-85	L-L	6-1	200	7-1	0.66	53	30	17	78	Ogden (R)
65. Cardinals. Stuart Pomeranz, rhp	Houston HS	Collierville, Tenn.	570,000	12-17-84	R-R	6-7	220	13-1	0.52	94	28	15	165	Johnson City (R)
67. Braves. Paul Bacot, rhp	Lakeside HS	Atlanta	550,000	8-16-84	R-R	6-6	193	7-3	1.72	69	53	13	109	GCL Braves (R)
68. Devil Rays. Andrew Miller, lhp	Buchholz HS	Gainesville, Fla.	Did not sign	5-21-85	L-L	6-6	175	10-3	1.79	70	17	63	136	Did not sign
74. Orioles. Chris Ray, rhp	Coll. of William & Mary	Tampa	485,000	1-12-82	R-R	6-2	190	6-5	3.52	95	87	22	87	Aberdeen (A)
76. Rangers. John Hudgins, rhp	Stanford U.	Mission Viejo, Calif.	490,000	8-31-81	R-R	6-2	195	14-3	2.99	165	138	35	143	Clinton (A)
77. Rockies. Aaron Marsden, lhp	U. of Nebraska	Grand Forks, N.D.	462,500	11-18-81	L-L	6-5	225	8-3	2.90	115	110	21	113	Tri-City (A)
79. Braves. Jacob Stevens, lhp	Cape Coral HS	Cape Coral, Fla.	475,000	3-15-85	L-L	6-3	220	8-1	1.96	60	32	18	116	GCL Braves (R)
80. Blue Jays. Shaun Marcum, rhp	SW Missouri State U.	Excelsior Springs, Mo.	449,000	12-14-81	R-R	6-1	180	1-4	2.45	44	35	13	55	Auburn (A)
84. +Red Sox. Beau Vaughan, rhp	Arizona State U.	Glendale, Ariz.	250,000	6-4-81	B-R	6-4	225	10-6	4.68	92	88	34	105	Lowell (A)
86. Mariners. Ryan Feierabend, lhp	Midview HS	Grafton, Ohio	437,500	8-22-85	L-L	6-4	200	4-3	0.79	44	30	11	86	AZL Mariners (R)
91. Dodgers. Cory Van Allen, lhp	Clements HS	Sugar Land, Texas	Did not sign	12-24-84	L-L	6-2	180	12-3	1.50	93	67	20	130	Did not sign
95. Cardinals. Dennis Dove, rhp	Georgia Southern U.	Ocilla, Ga.	400,000	8-31-81	R-R	6-4	200	7-2	4.52	94	84	48	118	New Jersey (A)
96. D'backs. Matt Chico, lhp	Palomar (Calif.) JC	Fallbrook, Calif.	365,000	6-10-83	L-L	5-11	190	Did not play						Yakima (A)
97. Braves. Matt Harrison, lhp	South Granville HS	Stem, N.C.	395,000	9-16-85	L-L	6-3	190	8-1	0.74	47	14	16	103	GCL Braves (R)
100. Tigers. Josh Rainwater, rhp	DeRidder HS	DeRidder, La.	300,000	4-9-85	R-R	6-1	220							GCL Tigers (R)

the Mets had followed Milledge throughout his scholastic and summer league career and were confident they knew him well. They said they were secure in their understanding of the alleged incident that prompted his expulsion.

LaRocque said Milledge had been investigated in 2002 and noted charges never were filed. He said the Mets were confident the allegations were unsubstantiated and added, "We are confident of his makeup and character."

In a statement released Aug. 5, however, the Mets said, "These allegations are not at all consistent with what we understood to be the case when we drafted Lastings Milledge. These new allegations are far more serious and warrant further investigation to assess their validity. Until we know what the facts are, we will reserve judgment and any further comment."

Two teams told Baseball America they knew of the unsubstantiated charges involving the 12- and 13-year-olds well before the 2003 draft.

Milledge, now 18, was considered one of the most dynamic athletes in the 2003 draft crop. His bat speed, foot speed and arm strength are all exceptional tools. He lasted until the 12th pick for a variety of reasons: the incident at Northside, his past difficulties with wood bats and his struggles against breaking pitches. He batted .414-10-35 with 42 steals as a senior after hitting more than .500 each season through his junior year at Northside Christian.

MORRIS FOSTOFF

Lastings Milledge

"He has the potential to hit for power and for average," LaRocque said. "We see him staying as a center fielder, not a position change. He runs exceptionally well. We see him as an offensive player with power to the gaps, an aggressive baserunner and a player with passion for the game."

Heart Condition Briefly Stalls Moses

After agreeing to a $1.45 million bonus on July 7, first-round pick Matt Moses headed to the Twins' complex in Fort Myers, Fla. He was set to make his debut in the Rookie-league Gulf Coast League after a few workouts and a routine physical.

Except the physical turned out to be anything but routine. The doctor heard a subtle, unusual sound when he listened to Moses' heart. A subsequent EKG turned up an abnormality.

Suddenly, Moses' career was on hold.

"I was pretty shocked," said Moses, a third baseman chosen 21st overall out of Mills Godwin High in Richmond, Va. "I didn't really know what to think about it."

"When I got the news, I couldn't believe it was his heart," Twins scouting director Mike Radcliff said. "It was just mind-boggling. This guy has a heart problem? He looks as healthy as any human being I've ever seen. Our first concern was his life, not baseball."

Fortunately for Moses, doctors quickly discovered that neither his life nor his career was in jeopardy. He had a

NO. 1 PICKS, 1965-2003

Year	Club, Player, Pos.	School	Hometown	Highest Level (G#)	2003 Team	Bonus
1965	A's. Rick Monday, of	Arizona State U.	Santa Monica, Calif.	Majors (1,996)	Out of Baseball	$104,000
1966	Mets. Steve Chilcott, c	Antelope Valley HS	Lancaster, Calif.	Triple-A (2)	Out of Baseball	75,000
1967	Yankees. Ron Blomberg, 1b	Druid Hills HS	Atlanta	Majors (461)	Out of Baseball	75,000
1968	Mets. Tim Foli, ss	Notre Dame HS	Sherman Oaks, Calif.	Majors (1,696)	Out of Baseball	75,000
1969	Senators. Jeff Burroughs, of	Wilson HS	Long Beach, Calif.	Majors (1,689)	Out of Baseball	88,000
1970	Padres. Mike Ivie, c	Walker HS	Decatur, Ga.	Majors (857)	Out of Baseball	80,000
1971	White Sox. Danny Goodwin, c	Central HS	Peoria, Ill.	Majors (252)	Out of Baseball	DNS
1972	Padres. Dave Roberts, 3b	U. of Oregon	Corvallis, Ore.	Majors (709)	Out of Baseball	60,000
1973	Rangers. David Clyde, lhp	Westchester, HS	Houston	Majors (84)	Out of Baseball	125,000
1974	Padres. Bill Almon, ss	Brown U.	Warwick, R.I.	Majors (1,236)	Out of Baseball	90,000
1975	Angels. Danny Goodwin, c	Southern U.	Peoria, Ill.	Majors (252)	Out of Baseball	125,000
1976	Astros. Floyd Bannister, lhp	Arizona State U.	Seattle	Majors (431)	Out of Baseball	100,000
1977	White Sox. Harold Baines, of	St. Michaels HS	St. Michaels, Md.	Majors (2,830)	Out of Baseball	40,000
1978	Braves. Bob Horner, 3b	Arizona State U.	Glendale, Ariz.	Majors (1,020)	Out of Baseball	175,000
1979	Mariners. Al Chambers, of	Harris HS	Harrisburg, Pa.	Majors (57)	Out of Baseball	60,000
1980	Mets. Darryl Strawberry, of	Crenshaw HS	Los Angeles	Majors (1,583)	Out of Baseball	152,500
1981	Mariners. Mike Moore, rhp	Oral Roberts U.	Eakly, Okla.	Majors (450)	Out of Baseball	100,000
1982	Cubs. Shawon Dunston, ss	Jefferson HS	New York	Majors (1,750)	Out of Baseball	100,000
1983	Twins. Tim Belcher, rhp	Mt. Vernon Naz. Coll.	Sparta, Ohio	Majors (362)	Out of Baseball	DNS
1984	Mets. Shawn Abner, of	Mechanicsburg HS	Mechanicsburg, Pa.	Majors (392)	Out of Baseball	150,000
1985	Brewers. B.J. Surhoff, c	U. of North Carolina	Rye, N.Y.	Majors (2,122)	Orioles	150,000
1986	Pirates. Jeff King, 3b	U. of Arkansas	Colorado Springs	Majors (1,201)	Out of Baseball	160,000
1987	Mariners. Ken Griffey Jr., of	Moeller HS	Cincinnati	Majors (1,924)	Reds	169,000
1988	Padres. Andy Benes, rhp	U. of Evansville	Evansville, Ind.	Majors (403)	Out of Baseball	235,000
1989	Orioles. Ben McDonald, rhp	Louisiana State U.	Denham Springs, La.	Majors (211)	Out of Baseball	*350,000
1990	Braves. Chipper Jones, ss	The Bolles School	Jacksonville	Majors (1,405)	Braves	275,000
1991	Yankees. Brien Taylor, lhp	East Carteret HS	Beaufort, N.C.	Double-A (27)	Out of Baseball	1,550,000
1992	Astros. Phil Nevin, 3b	Cal State Fullerton	Placentia, Calif.	Majors (838)	Padres	700,000
1993	Mariners. Alex Rodriguez, ss	West. Christian HS	Miami	Majors (1,275)	Rangers	*1,000,000
1994	Mets. Paul Wilson, rhp	Florida State U.	Orlando, Fla.	Majors (132)	Reds	1,550,000
1995	Angels. Darin Erstad, of	U. of Nebraska	Jamestown, N.D.	Majors (1,002)	Angels	1,575,000
1996	Pirates. Kris Benson, rhp	Clemson U.	Kennesaw, Ga.	Majors (106)	Pirates	2,000,000
1997	Tigers. Matt Anderson, rhp	Rice U.	Louisville, Ky.	Majors (245)	Tigers	2,505,000
1998	Phillies. Pat Burrell, 3b	U. of Miami	Boulder Creek, Calif.	Majors (569)	Phillies	*3,150,000
1999	Devil Rays. Josh Hamilton, of	Athens Drive HS	Raleigh, N.C.	Double-A (23)	Did not play	3,960,000
2000	Marlins. Adrian Gonzalez, 1b	Eastside HS	Chula Vista, Calif.	Triple-A (39)	Rangers (AA)	3,000,000
2001	Twins. Joe Mauer, c	Cretin-Derham Hall	St. Paul, Minn.	Double-A (73)	Twins (AA)	5,150,000
2002	Pirates. Bryan Bullington, rhp	Ball State U.	Fishers, Ind.	Class A (25)	Pirates (A)	4,000,000
2003	Devil Rays. Delmon Young, of	Camarillo HS	Camarillo, Calif.	Has not played	None	*3,600,000

*Received major league contract with guaranteed incentives #No. of games at that level DNS—Did not sign

UNSIGNED PICKS

A record number of players drafted in the first 10 rounds of the 2003 draft were signed. Of 307 such players selected, only 16 did not sign. The previous record was 24 in 2000. Teams control the rights to players attending junior college and may sign them between the completion of their junior college season and the start of the closed period (one week before the 2004 draft). A list of the players selected in the first 12 rounds of the 2003 draft who didn't sign, and the college they're attending. Players denoted with an asterisk are collegians returning to the same school.

THIRD ROUND	
68. Devil Rays. Andrew Miller, lhp	North Carolina
89. Astros. Drew Stubbs, of	Texas
91. Dodgers. Cory Van Allen, lhp	Baylor
FOURTH ROUND	
108. Indians. Ben Harrison, of	*Florida
124. Yankees. Steven White, rhp	Eligibility expired
FIFTH ROUND	
141. Reds. Marc Cornell, rhp	*Ohio
148. Twins. Brandon McArthur, ss	Florida
SIXTH ROUND	
161. Padres. Cory Patton, of	*Texas A&M
165. Pirates. C.J. Smith, 1b	*Florida
175. Phillies. Jordan Parraz, rhp	CC of Southern Nevada
EIGHTH ROUND	
220. Tigers. Adam Trent, rhp	Young Harris (Ga.) JC
224. Orioles. Nathan Nery, lhp	Stetson
NINTH ROUND	
248. Devil Rays. Billy Buckner, rhp	South Carolina
10th ROUND	
280. Tigers. Sean Henry, of	Diablo Valley (Calif.) JC
282. Royals. Luis Cota, rhp	South Mountain (Ariz.) CC
291. Reds. Andy D'Alessio, 1b	Clemson
11th ROUND	
322. White Sox. Ricky Brooks, rhp	East Carolina
325. Phillies. Myron Leslie, 3b	*South Florida
328. Twins. Ryan Schroyer, rhp	San Diego State
329. Astros. Nick Green, rhp	*Darton (Ga.) JC
331. Dodgers. Tony Harper, c	Frank Phillips (Texas) JC
12th ROUND	
352. White Sox. Donald Veal, lhp	Arizona
361. Dodgers. Cody White, lhp	Texarkana (Texas) JC
365. Cardinals. Calvin Beamon, of	*CC of Southern Nevada
367. Braves. Casey Spanish, of	Eligibility expired

tiny hole in his heart, which caused it to pump more blood on its right side and into his lungs than was needed.

Dr. Evan Zahn, the director of cardiology at Miami Children's Hospital, put a patch of sorts on the hole during a 20-minute procedure on July 25. Zahn attached a small device that will help Matt's heart grow cells that it should have developed on its own.

Moses was back working out with the GCL Twins three days later, got into his first game on July 31 and batted .385 in 16 contests. He said that having his heart abnormality discovered and repaired would benefit him from a health standpoint and a baseball standpoint.

Sinisi Cashes In From Second Round

Unlike in past years, most players who dropped because of their price tags didn't break the bank. Three exceptions were Rangers second-rounder Vince Sinisi, Astros 13th-rounder Jimmy Barthmaier and Dodgers 39th-rounder Andy LaRoche.

Sinisi was considered the third-best college hitter, trailing only Weeks and Aubrey. But he had three signability strikes against him: he was a sophomore-eligible who could re-enter the 2004 draft without compromising his leverage; he was at Rice, a school where it's often difficult to get players to come out early; and he was advised by Scott Boras. A first baseman/outfielder who could have been a top-10 pick based solely on ability, he signed for $2.07 million after going 46th overall.

Barthmaier, a Georgia high school righthander, made a late push for the first round after throwing a 91-95 mph fastball and 80-83 mph slider in a mid-May playoff game. But he was also a quarterback prospect recruited by several Southeastern Conference colleges and was vague about his willingness to give up football. He committed to baseball when the Astros signed him for a $750,000 bonus that was to be spread over five years.

The Padres tried to sign LaRoche as a 21st-round draft-and-follow from 2002, and when they failed teams assumed he'd make good on his intention to transfer from Grayson County (Texas) CC to Rice. The Dodgers took a flier on him in the 39th round, and he headed to the Cape Cod League for the summer.

A shortstop, LaRoche established himself as the best position-player prospect on the Cape and a first-rounder for the 2004 draft. At that point, Los Angeles stepped in and signed him for $1 million, the highest bonus in the 2003 draft after the second round.

Rule Changes Still On Hold

■ When major league owners and players agreed on a new Basic Agreement on Aug. 30, 2002, narrowly averting a strike, they agreed to adjust the draft rules. But they later failed to agree on what they had agreed to when it came down to put those changes in writing, so alterations were tabled. A joint committee of officials from both sides has held meetings without resolving anything. Among the changes that have been discussed are: the elimination of draft-pick compensation for top free agents; awarding teams that fail to sign first-round picks a bonus choice immediately following the corresponding pick in the next year's draft (the existing rule gives clubs a supplemental first-rounder); extending the draft to cover the entire globe rather than just the United States, Puerto Rico and Canada; shortening the draft to between 20 and 38 rounds from the current 50; and allowing teams to trade draft picks.

■ Besides the Young brothers, the draft had its usual assortment of selections with baseball connections. The most notable was outfielder Anthony Gwynn (second round, Brewers), the son of eight-time National League batting champion Tony Gwynn, his coach at San Diego State. Righthander Brian Bannister's (seventh, Mets) father Floyd was the No. 1 overall pick by the Astros in the 1976 draft.

DAN ARNOLD

Anthony Gwynn

■ A total of 1,480 players were selected in 2003. Arizona State led all colleges with 12 draftees, starting with outfielder Andre Ethier (Athletics, second round). Cal State Fullerton had 11, including Cordero in the first round. Texas A&M also had a noteworthy draft as it had eight pitchers selected, including three in the second round.

Miami's Brito Private High, with an enrolment of just over 100, tied a prep record set by Seminole (Fla.) High in 2001 with six draftees, none higher than 23rd-round catcher Danny Santin (Mariners). While Seminole won the 2001 national title, Brito went 30-6 and finished the season unranked.

DRAFT 2003

CLUB-BY-CLUB SELECTIONS

Order of selection indicated in parentheses ■ **Boldface** indicates player signed

ANAHEIM ANGELS (23)

1. Brandon Wood, ss, Horizon HS, Scottsdale, Ariz.
2. Anthony Whittington, lhp, Buffalo HS, Putnam, W.Va.
3. Sean Rodriguez, ss, Braddock HS, Miami
4. Bob Zimmermann, rhp, Southwest Missouri State U.
5. Blake Balkcom, of, Florida State U.
6. Jesse Smith, rhp, Illinois Valley CC
7. Reggie Willits, of, U. of Oklahoma
8. Josh Cowles, rhp, East Valley HS, Redlands, Calif.
9. Von Stertzbach, rhp, U. of Central Florida
10. Patrice Lepage, c, Edouard Montpetit College HS, Montreal
11. Adam Pavkovich, ss, U. of Alabama
12. Andy Hill, rhp, Brewster (Wash.) HS
13. Daniel Davidson, lhp, Florida State U.
14. Kelly Shearer, lhp, Elkins HS, Missouri City, Texas
15. David Austen, rhp, U. of South Florida
16. Stantrel Smith, of, North Florida CC
17. Matt Pali, of, Florida Atlantic U.
18. Fernando Rodriguez, rhp, El Paso (Texas) CC
19. Billy Boyer, 2b, Enumclaw (Wash.) HS
20. Jason Donald, ss, Buchanan HS, Clovis, Calif.
21. Josh Land, of, Milton (Fla.) HS
22. B.J. Brown, lhp, Oakland (Mich.) U.
23. Brett Douglas, rhp, Westminster (Calif.) HS
24. Chad Hauseman, of, Jacksonville U.
25. Justin Brashear, c, Barbe HS, Lake Charles, La.
26. Joseph Rowe, rhp, Central Alabama CC
27. Jimmy Durette, lhp, Ahuntsic College HS, Matine, Quebec
28. Nick Roxby, 2b, North Florida JC
29. Andrew Fiorenza, rhp, Okaloosa-Walton (Fla.) CC
30. Adam Frank, c, Lamar (Colo.) CC
31. David Huff, lhp, Edison HS, Huntington Beach, Calif.
32. Keith Williams, of, Gulf Coast (Fla.) CC
33. Ricky Bambino, c, Foothill HS, Redding, Calif.
34. Jason Blackey, rhp, Malaspina (B.C.) CC
35. Jay Mattox, of, Chipola (Fla.) JC
36. Brandon Doddo, 3B, Broward (Fla.) CC
37. Tommy Baumgardner, lhp, Indian River (Fla.) CC
38. Ronald Lowe, lhp, Pasco-Hernando (Fla.) CC
39. Nate Boman, lhp, Patrick Henry HS, San Diego
40. Brandon Morrow, rhp, Rancho Cotate HS, Rohnert Park, Calif.
41. Chris Hunter, rhp, Utah Valley State JC
42. Cody Nelson, ss, Chabot (Calif.) JC
43. Caleb Hatfield, rhp, Red Bluff (Calif.) HS
44. John Mariotti, rhp, Chaminade College HS, Toronto
45. Chris Noonan, lhp, Seton Hall U.
46. Hank Lanto, c, Modesto (Calif.) HS
47. Ryan Anderson, lhp, St. Petersburg (Fla.) CC
48. Jeremy Labigano, lhp, Westwood HS, Fort Pierce, Fla.
49. Evan Bailey, rhp, Westsyde SS, Kamloops, B.C.
50. Kris Johnson, lhp, Blue Springs (Mo.) HS

ARIZONA DIAMONDBACKS (29)

1. Conor Jackson, 1b, U. of California (Choice from Mariners—19th—as compensation for Type B free agent Greg Colbrunn).
1. Carlos Quentin, of, Stanford U.
2. Jamie D'Antona, 3b, Wake Forest U.
3. Matt Chico, lhp, Palomar (Calif.) JC
4. Chris Kinsey, rhp, Sacramento State U.
5. Jeff Cook, of, U. of Southern Mississippi
6. Orlando Mercado, c, Antonio Luchetti HS, Arecibo, P.R.
7. Dustin Glant, rhp, Purdue U.
8. Robbie Van, lhp, U. of Nevada-Las Vegas
9. Steve Garrabrants, 2b, Arizona State U.
10. Adam Bass, rhp, U. of Alabama-Huntsville
11. Tila Reynolds, ss, U. of Washington
12. Jon Kaplan, of, Tulane U.
13. Todd Buchanan, 1b, Western Carolina U.
14. Brian Rose, c, U. of Florida
15. Ben Krantz, rhp, U. of Pennsylvania
16. Ruben Kerbs, lhp, Wichita State U.
17. Jayson Santiago, of, Maestro Ladi HS, Vega Alta, P.R.
18. Chris Coghlan, c, East Lake HS, Tarpon Springs, Fla.
19. Danny Muegge, rhp, U. of Texas
20. Joe Carque, rhp, San Diego State U.
21. Chad Clark, rhp, Azusa Pacific U.
22. Walt Novosel, lhp, Ohio U.
23. Travis McAndrews, of, U. of Southern California
24. Allen Mottram, c, U. of Massachusetts-Lowell
25. Kellen Raab, lhp, U. of Wisconsin-Parkside
26. Travis Van Zile, of, U. of Wisconsin-Whitewater
27. Jason McStoots, ss, Missouri Baptist College
28. Brian Viafore, 1b, Central Washington U.
29. Tony Festa, 3b, UC Riverside
30. Greg Mathis, of, Southwest Missouri State U.
31. Tim Vaillancourt, rhp, Delaware State U.
32. Andrew McCreery, 3b, U. of Pennsylvania
33. Brandon Belcher, lhp, Ruston (La.) HS
34. Gabe Rio, lhp, Florida Southern College
35. Alex Cremidan, rhp, UC San Diego
36. Derik Nippert, rhp, Ohio Valley (W.Va.) College
37. Ryan LaCross, lhp, Lakewood Ranch HS, Bradenton, Fla.
38. Shane Dove, lhp, Spartanburg Methodist (S.C.) JC
39. Cristobal Melendez, of, Missouri Baptist College
40. Connor Rapkoch, c, Bellarmine Prep, Tacoma, Wash.
41. Kevin Stiehl, lhp, West Torrance HS, Torrance, Calif.
42. Mike Guerrero, of, Arizona State U.
43. Matt Mammen, lhp, St. Charles (Mo.) CC
44. Jacob Coash, lhp, JC of the Canyons (Calif.)
45. Joshua Terrell, 1b, Lurleen B. Wallace State (Ala.) JC
46. Lester Contreras, ss, Champagnat Catholic HS, Hialeah, Fla.
47. Brody Taylor, lhp, Louisburg (N.C.) JC
48. Ben Colton, rhp, Reno (Nev.) HS
49. Juan Velazquez, rhp, Grossmont (Calif.) CC
50. Jeff Manship, rhp, Ronald Reagan HS, San Antonio

ATLANTA BRAVES (30)

1. (Choice to Royals as compensation for Type B free agent Paul Byrd).
1. Luis Atilano, rhp, Gabriela Mistral HS, San Juan, P.R. (Supplemental pick—35th—for Type A free agent Tom Glavine)
1. Jarrod Saltalamacchia, c, Royal Palm Beach HS, West Palm Beach, Fla. (Supplemental pick—36th—for Type A free agent Mike Remlinger)
2. Jo Jo Reyes, lhp, Riverside Poly HS, Riverside, Calif. (Choice from Cubs—43rd—as compensation for Remlinger)
2. Paul Bacot, rhp, Lakeside HS, Atlanta, Ga.
3. Jacob Stevens, lhp, Cape Coral (Fla.) HS (Choice from Mets—79th—as compensation for Glavine)
3. Matt Harrison, lhp, South Granville HS, Stem, N.C.
4. Jamie Romak, 3b, A.B. Lucas SS, London, Ontario
5. Chris Vines, rhp, Pelham (Ala.) HS
6. Asher Demme, rhp, South Lakes HS, Reston, Va.
7. Ryan Basner, rhp, Western Carolina U.
8. Sean White, rhp, U. of Washington
9. Adam Stanley, lhp, Garner (N.C.) HS
10. Brad Nelson, rhp, Lenoir (N.C.) CC
11. Glenn Tucker, rhp, East Carolina U.
12. Casey Spanish, of, U. of Kansas
13. Mark Jurich, of, U. of Louisville
14. Steven Doetsch, of, Indian River (Fla.) CC
15. Ben Thomas, 3b, Midland (Texas) JC
16. Cole Armstrong, c, Chipola (Fla.) JC
17. Keith Eichas, 1b, Temple (Texas) JC
18. Keith Weiser, lhp, Talawanda HS, Hamilton, Ohio
19. Andy Barden, c, Virginia Military Institute
20. Kyle Bakker, lhp, Georgia Tech
21. Brooks Brown, rhp, Portal (Ga.) HS
22. Jacob Blakeney, rhp, Mississippi State U.
23. Jamie Hemingway, of, UNC Wilmington
24. Brandon Jones, of, Tallahassee (Fla.) CC
25. Quintin Berry, of, Morse HS, San Diego
26. C.J. Bressoud, c, North Cobb HS, Kennesaw, Ga.
27. Brandon Berdoll, lhp, Temple (Texas) JC
28. Kyle Perry, rhp, Ball HS, Galveston, Texas
29. Drew Shetrone, rhp, Apopka (Fla.) HS
30. Jonny Benters, lhp, Lake Brantley HS, Altamonte Springs, Fla.
31. Jon Schaus, rhp, East Lake HS, Palm Harbor, Fla.
32. Larry Williams, 1b, Hawthorne HS, Lawndale, Calif.
33. Daniel Stange, rhp, Elsinore HS, Wildomar, Calif.

34. Michael Gibbs, rhp, Chipola (Fla.) JC
35. Daniel Rios, 1b, Mt. Whitney HS, Visalia, Calif.
36. Justin Phillips, ss, Louisburg (N.C.) JC
37. Cody Pyle, 3b, Smithson Valley HS, Spring Branch, Texas
38. Eric Chown, rhp, U. of Massachusetts
39. Eugene Edwards, 1b, Mayfair HS, Bellflower, Calif.
40. Joey Doan, rhp, Baker HS, Mobile, Ala.
41. John Ray, c, Monarch HS, Louisville, Colo.
42. Marcus Covington, rhp, East Rutherford HS, Forest City, N.C.
43. Zechry Zinicola, rhp, Arlington HS, San Bernardino, Calif.
44. Tony Portugal, rhp, Northeast HS, Fort Lauderdale, Fla.
45. David Crook, lhp, Monte Vista HS, Spring Valley, Calif.
46. Lyall Foran, c, Delta SS, Ladner, B.C.
47. Joe Northrup, rhp, West Covina (Calif.) HS
48. Tony Harris, lhp, Surry (N.C.) CC
49. Kyle Price, 2b, Green Valley HS, Henderson, Nev.
50. John Scaglione, rhp, Palm Beach Gardens HS, Lake Park, Fla.

BALTIMORE ORIOLES (7)

1. **Nick Markakis, of, Young Harris (Ga.) JC**
2. **Brian Finch, rhp, Texas A&M U.**
3. **Chris Ray, rhp, College of William & Mary**
4. **Bob McCrory, rhp, U. of Southern Mississippi**
5. **Nate Spears, ss, Charlotte HS, Port Charlotte, Fla.**
6. **Eric Sultemeier, of, U. of Texas**
7. **Justin Azze, lhp, U. of Hawaii**
8. Nathan Nery, lhp, Moon Area HS, Moon Township, Pa.
9. **Jarod Rine, of, West Virginia U.**
10. **Jacob Duncan, of, Texas Christian U.**
11. **Matt Houston, c, Oklahoma City U.**
12. **Matt Pulley, 3b, Woodland (Calif.) HS**
13. **James Hoey, rhp, Rider U.**
14. **Brian Bock, c, U. of Hawaii**
15. Jordan Timm, lhp, U. of Wisconsin-Oshkosh
16. **Alan Beck, of, Western Carolina U.**
17. **Lorenzo Scott, of, Ball State U.**
18. **Jason Furrow, lhp, Judson (Texas) HS**
19. Matt Tolbert, 2b, U. of Mississippi
20. **Tony Neal, rhp, U. of South Alabama**
21. David Cash, ss, Northside Christian HS, St. Petersburg, Fla.
22. **Zach Dixon, lhp, Texas A&M U.**
23. **Dennis Wyrick, 3b, Arizona State U.**
24. **Josh McCurdy, of, Niagara U.**
25. **Richard Hummell, of, Tombstone HS, Sierra Vista, Ariz.**
26. Brian LeClerc, of, Northside Christian HS, Clearwater, Fla.
27. **Travis Brown, ss, Western Kentucky U.**
28. **Russ Brocato, rhp, U. of Pennsylvania**
29. Jason Ward, rhp, Utah Valley State JC
30. **Chris Osentowski, rhp, Texas Christian U.**
31. **Ryan Brnardic, rhp, Southeastern Oklahoma State U.**
32. **Landon Wareham, 2b, Mesa State (Colo.) College**
33. Jake Muyco, c, Columbia Basin (Wash.) CC
34. **Brad Wiggins, of, Howard (Texas) CC**
35. Richard Orange, of, Greenville (Texas) HS
36. Danny Martin, of, Dunedin (Fla.) HS
37. David Smith, rhp, Chrysler HS, New Castle, Ind.
38. Matthew Garnett, lhp, Stockdale HS, Bakersfield, Calif.
39. Shaun Corning, lhp, Madison Area (Wis.) Tech JC
40. Joe Welsh, lhp, Grand Rapids (Mich.) ~~CC~~
41. Aaron Feterl, rhp, Crescenta Valley HS, La Crescenta, Calif.
42. **Chad Boudon, of, U. of Washington**
43. **Kyle George, ss, U. of Maryland**
44. Scott Houin, of, Rampart HS, Colorado Springs
45. Brett Jensen, rhp, Iowa Central CC
46. Gregory Young, of, Old Mill HS, Millersville, Md.
47. Roy Irle, rhp, Rend Lake (Ill.) JC
48. Cameron McGuire, c, McLennan (Texas) JC
49. Casey Janssen, rhp, UCLA
50. Adam Ricciardulli, of, Mission Bay HS, San Diego

BOSTON RED SOX (17)

1. **David Murphy, of, Baylor U.**
1. **Matt Murton, of, Georgia Tech** (Supplemental choice—32nd—for loss of Type A free agent Cliff Floyd)
2. **Abe Alvarez, lhp, Long Beach State U. (Choice from Mets—49th—as compensation for Floyd)**
2. **Mickey Hall, of, Walton HS, Marietta, Ga.**
3. **Beau Vaughan, rhp, Arizona State U.**
4. **Jon Papelbon, rhp, Mississippi State U.**
5. **Brian Marshall, lhp, Virginia Commonwealth U.**
6. **Jessie Corn, rhp, Jacksonville State U.**
7. **Jeremy West, c, Arizona State U.**
8. **Lee Curtis, 2b, College of Charleston**
9. **John Wilson, rhp, Northeastern (Colo.) JC**
10. **Chris Durbin, of, Baylor U.**
11. **Barry Hertzler, rhp, Central Connecticut State U.**
12. **Justin Sturge, lhp, Coastal Carolina U.**
13. **Zach Basch, rhp, U. of Nevada**
14. **Zach Borowiak, ss, Southeast Missouri State U.**
15. **Chris Turner, of, Texarkana (Texas) JC**
16. **Kevin Ool, lhp, Marist College**
17. William Newton, lhp, Mountain View HS, Orem, Utah
18. **Tom Cochran, lhp, Middle Georgia JC**
19. **Jarrett Gardner, rhp, U. of Arkansas**
20. Josh Morris, of, Cartersville (Ga.) HS
21. **Mike Dennison, rhp, Wichita State U.**
22. Kala Kaaihue, c, Iolani HS, Kailua, Hawaii
23. **David Coffey, of, U. of Georgia**
24. **Ignacio Suarez, ss, Southwest Texas State U.**
25. Drew Moffitt, of, Wichita State U.
26. **Jason Ramos, ss, St. Petersburg (Fla.) JC**
27. Andrew Sharpe, ss, Los Angeles Pierce JC
28. **Davey Penny, rhp, East Carolina U.**
29. **Doug Fink, rhp, Manatee (Fla.) JC**
30. **David Sanders, lhp, Wichita State U.**
31. Greg Schilling, lhp, Taravella HS, Coral Springs, Fla.
32. Matt Pike, rhp, Centennial HS, Pueblo, Colo.
33. **Scooter Jordan, of, Texas Tech**
34. **Arthur Santos, rhp, Florida International U.**
35. **Erich Cloninger, c, Liberty U.**
36. Ben Sosebee, rhp, Truett McConnell (Ga.) JC
37. Chris Johnson, ss, Bishop Verot HS, Fort Myers, Fla.
38. Michael McBryde, of, Palm Beach Gardens HS, North Palm Beach, Fla.
39. Jeffrey Culpepper, of, Gonzaga U.
40. Michael Rutledge, ss, Cullman (Ala.) HS
41. **Lance Shartz, c, Garden City (Kan.) CC**
42. Dallas Williams, of, Pike HS, Indianapolis
43. Scott Thomas, c, Chaminade College Prep, St. Louis
44. Tom Caple, of, U. of San Diego
45. Terrence Cramer, rhp, Palm Beach (Fla.) JC
46. Victor Rodriguez, c, Cape Coral (Fla.) HS
47. A.J. Loyd, of, Bishop Carroll HS, Wichita, Kan.
48. Adam Davis, rhp, Middle Georgia JC
49. **Jason Smith, rhp, Bourne (Mass.) HS**
50. Mitch Stachowsky, c, JC of Southern Idaho

CHICAGO CUBS (6)

1. **Ryan Harvey, of, Dunedin (Fla.) HS**
2. (Choice to Braves as compensation for Type A free agent Mike Remlinger)
3. **Jake Fox, c, U. of Michigan**
4. **Tony Richie, c, Florida State U.**
5. **Darin Downs, lhp, Santaluces HS, Boynton Beach, Fla.**
6. **Sean Marshall, lhp, Virginia Commonwealth U.**
7. **Kyle Boyer, of, Cal State Fullerton**
8. **Matt Lincoln, lhp, Santa Ana (Calif.) JC** (selection voided)
9. **Drew Larsen, ss, Salt Lake CC**
10. **Casey McGehee, 3b, Fresno State U.**
11. **Nick Jones, 2b, Virginia Commonwealth U.**
12. **Chuck Hickman, ss, Nicholls State U.**
13. Ryan Coultas, ss, UC Davis
14. Matt LaPorta, c, Charlotte HS, Port Charlotte, Fla.
15. **Tony McQuade, of, Florida State U.**
16. **Matt Weber, rhp, Boylan Catholic HS, Rockford, Ill.**
17. **Ryan Kalita, rhp, U. of Notre Dame**
18. **Trey Johnston, 3b, Schaumburg (Ill.) HS**
19. **Brian Carter, lhp, U. of Washington**
20. **Lance Dawkins, ss, McNeese State U.**
21. **Reid Willett, rhp, U. of Rhode Island**
22. **Craig Green, rhp, Bakersfield (Calif.) JC**
23. **Robert Ransom, rhp, Vanderbilt U.**
24. Sam Fuld, of, Stanford U.
25. Landon Powell, c, U. of South Carolina
26. Barret Browning, lhp, Middle Georgia JC
27. **Jose Rios, ss, Barranquitas, P.R.**
28. **Adam Tidball, c, U. of Richmond**
29. Matt Brown, rhp, U. of California
30. Corteze Armstrong, of, Hiwassee (Tenn.) JC
31. Chris Ortmeier, rhp, Marcus HS, Flower Mound, Texas
32. Adam Tobler, rhp, Rochelle (Ill.) HS
33. **Jasha Balcom, of, U. of Georgia**
34. Adam Harvey, c, Grayson County (Texas) CC
35. **Sean Overholt, rhp, U. of Utah**
36. Jason Fellows, 1b, Georgia Perimeter JC
37. Chris Ericksen, lhp, South Suburban (Ill.) CC
38. Skyler Southwick, rhp, Dixie (Utah) JC
39. **David Gresky, of, Northwestern U.**
40. **Danny Lopaze, 1b, Virginia Commonwealth U.**

41. Doug Low, c, Foothill HS, Henderson, Nev.
42. Danny Calvert, rhp, Grain Valley HS, Blue Springs, Mo.
43. Brandon Harmon, rhp, Shadle Park HS, Spokane, Wash.
44. Cyle Hankerd, 1b, South Hills HS, Covina, Calif.
45. Jose Sanchez, c, West Covina (Calif.) HS (selection voided)
46. Jefferies Tatford, 3b, St. Thomas Moore HS, Lafayette, La.
47. Justin Simmons, lhp, U. of Texas
48. Tim Lincecum, rhp, Liberty HS, Renton, Wash.
49. Brian Cleveland, ss, U. of Tennessee
50. Kris Rochelle, c, Mills Godwin HS, Richmond, Va.

CHICAGO WHITE SOX (15)

1. Brian Anderson, of, U. of Arizona
2. Ryan Sweeney, of, Xavier HS, Cedar Rapids, Iowa
3. Clint King, of, U. of Southern Mississippi
4. Robert Valido, ss, Coral Park HS, Miami
5. Matt Nachreiner, rhp, Round Rock (Texas) HS
6. Chris Kelly, of, Pepperdine U.
7. James Casey, rhp, Azle (Texas) HS
8. John Russ, rhp, Frank Phillips (Texas) JC
9. David Cook, of, Miami (Ohio) U.
10. Fraser Dizard, lhp, U. of Southern California
11. Ricky Brooks, rhp, North Tonawanda (N.Y.) HS
12. Donald Veal, lhp, Buena HS, Hereford, Ariz.
13. Wes Hodges, ss, The Baylor School, Ooltewah, Tenn.
14. Ricardo Nanita, of, Florida International U.
15. Greg Moviel, lhp, St. Ignatius HS, Cleveland
16. Cody Dickens, rhp, Surry (N.C.) CC
17. Guillermo Martinez, ss, Coral Park HS, Miami
18. Cory Haggerty, 2b, Cortland State (N.Y.) U.
19. Mike Moat, rhp, San Diego State U.
20. Jeff Schmidt, ss, Mira Mesa HS, San Diego
21. Matt Lenderman, c, Plano (Texas) East HS
22. Travis Doyle, lhp, Grand Rapids (Mich.) CC
23. John Hurd, rhp, JC of Southern Idaho
24. Burke Baldwin, lhp, Neuqua Valley HS, Naperville, Ill.
25. Antoin Gray, 3b, Southern U.
26. Logan Williamson, lhp, Penscola (Fla.) Catholic HS
27. Dwayne Pollok, rhp, Texas A&M U.
28. Van Pope, 3b, Meridian (Miss.) CC
29. Gerardo Cabrera, of, Miami-Dade CC South
30. Brandon Lowe, 1b, Vidalia HS, Mt. Vernon, Ga.
31. Robbie Grinestaff, c, Jeffersonville (Ind.) HS
32. Josh Morgan, of, Meridian (Miss.) CC
33. Alex Acevedo, ss, Dr. Carlos Gonzales HS, Aguada, P.R.
34. Scott Martin, of, Delaware State U.
35. Sean Thompson, lhp, UC Santa Barbara
36. Paul Moviel, rhp, Kishwaukee (Ill.) JC
37. Neil Giesler, 1b, Okaloosa-Walton (Fla.) JC
38. Michael Mendrin, lhp, Central HS, Fresno, Calif.
39. Jason Sullivan, rhp, Joplin (Mo.) HS
40. Matt Deuchler, c, James Madison U.
41. Rolando Acosta, ss, Pima (Ariz.) CC
42. Eric Everly, lhp, Olney Central (Ill.) JC
43. Dustin Shafer, ss, Russell HS, Flatwoods, Ky.
44. Brandon Johnson, 2b, Crowder (Mo.) JC
45. Mitchell Woolf, rhp, JC of Southern Idaho
46. Greg Del George, ss, Monsignor Farrell HS, Staten Island, N.Y.
47. Richard O'Brien, c, Catholic HS, Little Rock, Ark.
48. Mike Alvarez, rhp, Monsignor Pace HS, Opelika, Fla.
49. Tim Edmeades, 3b, Buena Regional HS, Weymouth, N.J.
50. Sean Gaston, c, Brownsburg (Ind.) HS

CINCINNATI REDS (14)

1. Ryan Wagner, rhp, U. of Houston
2. Thomas Pauly, rhp, Princeton U.
3. Jose Ronda, ss, Gabriela Mistral HS, San Juan, P.R.
4. Kenny Lewis, of, George Washington HS, Danville, Va.
5. Marc Cornell, rhp, Ohio U.
6. Richie Gardner, rhp, U. of Arizona
7. Carlos Guevara, rhp, St. Mary's (Texas) U.
8. Damian Ursin, rhp, Southern U.
9. Ben Himes, of, Oklahoma City U.
10. Andy D'Alessio, 1b, Barron Collier HS, Naples, Fla.
11. Blake Hendley, rhp, Oklahoma City U.
12. James Paduch, rhp, Concordia (Ill.) U.
13. Matt Gray, of, Butler County (Kan.) CC
14. Marcus Townsend, of, Southern U.
15. Jo Jo Batten, of, Telfair County HS, McRae, Ga.
16. Chris Dickerson, of, U. of Nevada
17. Brock Till, rhp, Bradley U.
18. Kyle Smith, of, Houston Baptist U.
19. Charles Benoit, lhp, Carroll HS, Southlake, Texas
20. Dennis Dixon, of, San Leandro (Calif.) HS

First of Indians three first-rounders
Tulane first baseman Michael Aubrey

21. Todd Nicholas, lhp, Mississippi State U.
22. Brian Barr, rhp, Southern Arkansas U.
23. Chad Ziemendorf, c, UC Santa Barbara
24. Matt Harrington, rhp, Fort Worth (Central League)
25. Jack Harris, 3b, Ronald Reagan HS, San Antonio
26. Jeff Urgelles, c, Savannah State U.
27. Zac Stott, rhp, Dixie (Utah) JC
28. Dustin Evans, rhp, Adairsville HS, Taylorsville, Ga.
29. Philip Gentry, of, U. of Texas-San Antonio
30. Michael Brown, rhp, Grayson County (Texas) JC
31. Josh Newman, lhp, Ohio State U.
32. German Duran, ss, Paschal HS, Fort Worth
33. David Talamantez, rhp, Lamar U.
34. Evan Conley, c, Jacksonville State U.
35. Matt Trepkowski, lhp, Incarnate Word (Texas) College
36. Nick Vaughn, rhp, Oak Ridge HS, Dorado Hills, Calif.
37. Bart Braun, lhp, Southeastern Louisiana U.
38. Adam Hicks, 3b, Scottsdale (Ariz.) CC
39. Clay Cleveland, 1b, Savannah State U.
40. Jake McCarter, rhp, Tivy HS, Kerrville, Texas
41. Jordan Belcher, of, Augusta (Ga.) Christian HS
42. David Scott, c, Northside Christian HS, Pinellas Park, Fla.
43. Nick Devito, 1b, Hingham (Mass.) HS
44. Carlyle Holliday, of, U. of Notre Dame
45. Rusty Beale, ss, Stetson U.
46. Brian Wyatt, rhp, Vernon Regional (Texas) JC
47. Dane Mason, rhp, Gloucester County (N.J.) JC
48. Johntavis Character, of, McNair HS, Decatur, Ga.
49. Jordan Mayer, 1b, Alexandria (La.) HS
50. Colin Curtis, of, Issaquah (Wash.) HS

CLEVELAND INDIANS (11)

1. Michael Aubrey, 1b, Tulane U.
1. Brad Snyder, of, Ball State U. (Choice from Phillies—18th—as compensation for Type A free agent Jim Thome)
1. Adam Miller, rhp, McKinney (Texas) HS (Supplemental pick—31st—for loss of Thome)
2. Javi Herrera, c, U. of Tennessee
3. Ryan Garko, c, Stanford U.
4. Ben Harrison, of, U. of Florida
5. Juan Valdes, of, Fernando Callejo HS, Manati, P.R.
6. Kevin Kouzmanoff, 3b, U. of Nevada
7. Matt Davis, rhp, Ohio State U.
8. Bo Ashabraner, rhp, Long Beach State U.
9. Anthony Lunetta, ss, U. of Southern California
10. Scott Roehl, rhp, U. of Arkansas
11. Ryan Mulhern, of, U. of South Alabama
12. Brandon Pinckney, ss, Sacramento CC
13. Steven Reinhold, 2b, Tuscola HS, Waynesville, N.C.
14. Denton Williams, of, A&M Consolidated HS, College Station, Texas
15. Ryan Spilman, c, Mt. Vernon (Ind.) HS

16. Aaron Laffey, lhp, Allegany HS, Foxburg, Md.
17. Jeff Pry, rhp, Franklin HS, Portland, Ore.
18. Dusty Barnard, rhp, Connors State (Okla.) JC
19. Joseph Huskins, c, Cypress (Calif.) JC
20. Shane Mathews, rhp, St. Stephens HS, Conover, N.C.
21. Adam Brandenburg, lhp, Kennesaw State (Ga.) U.
22. Matt Elliot, rhp, Dixie (Utah) JC
23. Tim Montgomery, of, U. of Hawaii
24. Ryan Goleski, 1b, Eastern Michigan U.
25. Travis Debondt, lhp, Bakersfield (Calif.) JC
26. Andrew Johnston, rhp, Jefferson (Mo.) JC
27. Michael Felix, rhp, Rutherford HS, Panama City, Fla.
28. Jason James, of, Kishwaukee (Ill.) JC
29. Brett Parker, ss, U. of South Alabama
30. James Smith, rhp, Merced (Calif.) JC
31. Mark Harris, rhp, College of William & Mary
32. Steven Jackson, rhp, Clemson U.
33. Joe Reid, rhp, St. John's U.
34. Roger Lincoln, lhp, Stetson U.
35. Bart Babineaux, of, El Camino (Calif.) JC
36. Jared Goedert, 3b, Concordia (Kan.) HS
37. Zach Wallis, lhp, Enid (Okla.) HS
38. Neall French, c, Grand Rapids (Mich.) CC
39. Jim Rapoport, of, Chaminade Prep, Westlake Village, Calif.
40. Adrian Schau, rhp, Villanova U.
41. Robert Leonhardt, rhp, Cypress Fairbanks HS, Cypress, Texas
42. Adam Hanson, rhp, Wake Forest U.
43. Joe Weaver, rhp, Oklahoma State U.
44. Kyle Muschara, rhp, Lassiter HS, Marietta, Ga.
45. Rafael Cotto, of, Miguel Such HS, Rio Piedras, P.R.
46. James O'Neill, lhp, Milford HS, Highland, Mich.
47. Chad Corona, 3b, San Diego State U.
48. Jordan Karnofsky, of, Christian Brothers HS, Sacramento
49. David Horlacher, rhp, Dixie (Utah) JC
50. Seth Button, of, Elk Lake HS, Meshoppen, Pa.

COLORADO ROCKIES (10)

1. Ian Stewart, 3b, La Quinta HS, Garden Grove, Calif.
2. Scott Beerer, rhp, Texas A&M U.
3. Aaron Marsden, lhp, U. of Nebraska
4. Richard Guarno, c, U. of Arkansas-Little Rock
5. Christian Colonel, ss, Texas Tech
6. Randy Blood, 2b, UC Riverside
7. Larry Robles, rhp, Cal State Dominguez Hills
8. Darric Merrell, rhp, Cal State Fullerton
9. Gene Reynolds, ss, U. of Tampa
10. Marc Kaiser, rhp, Lewis-Clark State (Idaho) College
11. John Restrepo, of, Santa Ana (Calif.) JC
12. Joe Gaetti, of, North Carolina State U.
13. Matt Brinson, 1b, Mississippi State U.
14. J.P. Gagne, rhp, U. of Notre Dame
15. Mark Ion, rhp, Lamar U.
16. Mike Wiley, lhp, Stetson U.
17. Jim Brauer, rhp, U. of Michigan
18. Friedel Pinkston, rhp, Chipola (Fla.) JC
19. Ryan Mattheus, rhp, Sacramento CC
20. Scott Anderson, ss, Cal Poly San Luis Obispo
21. Ryan Fox, of, U. of Arkansas
22. Adam Daniels, lhp, Eastern Oklahoma State JC
23. Brian Lynch, rhp, Ball State U.
24. Jeff Watchko, rhp, Georgia Tech
25. Jordan Czarniecki, of, U. of Tennessee
26. Cole Garner, of, La Quinta HS, Westminster, Calif
27. Jason DiAngelo, rhp, West Virginia U.
28. Ricardo Rivas, rhp, El Paso (Texas) CC
29. David Hernandez, rhp, Elk Grove (Calif.) HS
30. Eric Young, 2b, Piscataway (N.J.) HS
31. Aaron George, rhp, Scottsdale (Ariz.) CC
32. Kyle Allen, lhp, Orange Coast (Calif.) JC
33. Garret Baker, 3b, Modesto (Texas) JC
34. Stoney Stone, rhp, Texarkana (Texas) JC
35. Kyle Wright, rhp, Columbia Basin (Wash.) CC
36. Derek Patterson, lhp, Northeast Texas JC
37. Jesse Litsch, rhp, Dixie Hollins HS, St. Petersburg, Fla.
38. Ryan Snell, rhp, Skyline HS, Sammamish, Wa.
39. Don Powers, rhp, Seminole State (Okla.) JC
40. David Hurst, lhp, Florida CC
41. Brandon Anderson, of, Wayland (Mass.) HS
42. Carlos Moreno, rhp, Odessa (Tex.) CC
43. Justin Jameson, of, Creekside HS, Fairburn, Ga.
44. Robert Rose, rhp, Cleveland State (Tenn.) CC
45. Joshua Banda, c, Artesia HS, Lakewood, Calif.
46. Jason Van Kooten, ss, Regis Jesuit HS, Aurora, Colo.
47. Jose Cardona, lhp, San Juan, P.R.
48. Ryan Flavell, c, Clarendon (Texas) JC
49. Jason Martinez, lhp, Mesa State (Colo.) College
50. Michael Jenkins, 3b, Hiwassee (Tenn.) CC

DETROIT TIGERS (3)

1. Kyle Sleeth, rhp, Wake Forest U.
2. Jay Sborz, rhp, Langley HS, Great Falls, Va.
3. Tony Giarratano, ss, Tulane U.
4. Josh Rainwater, rhp, DeRidder (La.) HS
5. Danny Zell, lhp, U. of Houston
6. Cody Collet, c, Newbury Park (Calif.) HS
7. Matt Vasquez, rhp, UC Santa Barbara
8. Adam Trent, rhp, Ooltewah (Tenn.) HS
9. Eric Rodland, 2b, Gonzaga U.
10. Sean Henry, of, Armijo HS, Suisun City, Calif.
11. Brian Rogers, rhp, Georgia Southern U.
12. Jeremy Laster, of, Hunters Lane HS, Nashville, Tenn.
13. Michael Brown, of, College of William & Mary
14. Luis Sabino, of, Wabash Valley (Ill.) JC
15. Andy Baldwin, rhp, Western Kentucky U.
16. Jordan Tata, rhp, Sam Houston State U.
17. Ronnie Martin, lhp, St. Mary's HS, St. Louis, Mo.
18. Josh Wahpepah, rhp, Cowley County (Kan.) CC
19. Andrew Graham, c, Armstrong Atlantic State (Ga.) College
20. Nick McIntyre, 2b, Purdue U.
21. Jacob Ford, 3b, Spalding (Ky.) U.
22. Richie Burgos, 1b, Cal State Fullerton
23. Bobby Huddleston, c, Auburn U.
24. Chris Homer, rhp, Marist College
25. Nathan Doyle, ss, James Madison U.
26. Lavon Lewis, rhp, Northeastern Oklahoma A&M JC
27. Aaron McRae, c, LSU-Shreveport
28. Steven Alexander, 1b, Rocklin (Calif.) HS
29. Kelly Hunt, 1b, Bowling Green State U.
30. Anthony Tomey, rhp, Eastern Michigan U.
31. Justin Justice, of, Tavares HS, Leesburg, Fla.
32. Justin Barnes, c, U. of Alabama-Huntsville
33. Kenon Ronz, lhp, Harvard U.
34. Chaz Schilens, of, Highland HS, Mesa, Ariz.
35. Ryan Muller, rhp, Live Oak HS, Morgan Hill, Calif.
36. John McGorty, 1b, Marist College
37. Cirilo Cruz, 3b, Chandler (Ariz.) HS
38. John Juergens, c, Bradley Bourbonnais HS, Bourbonnais, Ill.
39. Dustin Richardson, lhp, Cowley County (Kan.) CC
40. Emmanuel Vasquez, rhp, Nicholas Rodriguez HS, Corozal, P.R.
41. Ezequiel Perez, rhp, Missouri Baptist College
42. Daniel Spring, rhp, Brown U.
43. Brian Santo, rhp, Mount St. Mary's (Md.) College
44. Kurt Piantek, 1b, Trinity (Conn.) College
45. Joshua Tarnow, c, Carona del Sol HS, Chandler, Ariz.
46. Clay Britton, of, Canyon HS, Canyon Country, Calif.
47. Travis Simmons, 3b, Cleveland State (Tenn.) CC
48. Dusty Ryan, c, Merced (Calif.) JC
49. Reese Baez, rhp, Northwood (Texas) U.
50. Brandon McCormick, rhp, Spartanburg Methodist (S.C.) JC

FLORIDA MARLINS (16)

1. Jeff Allison, rhp, Veterans Memorial HS, Peabody, Mass.
2. Logan Kensing, rhp, Texas A&M U.
3. Jonathan Fulton, ss, George Washington HS, Danville, Va.
4. Jai Miller, of, Selma (Ala.) HS
5. Cole Seifrig, 3b, Heritage Hills HS, Lincoln City, Ind.
6. Lee Mitchell, 3b, U. of Georgia
7. David Marchbanks, lhp, U. of South Carolina
8. Tanner Rogers, c, Columbine HS, Littleton, Colo.
9. David Humen, rhp, Bethel (Ind.) College
10. J.T. Restko, 3b, Marist HS, Tinley Park, Ill.
11. Zach McCormack, lhp, Sacramento CC
12. Joe Mazzuca, ss, Northern Illinois U.
13. Chris Pillsbury, rhp, Florida Atlantic U.
14. Scott Nestor, rhp, Chaffey (Calif.) JC
15. Mikela Olsen, of, Sacramento State U.
16. Jon Nickerson, lhp, Stanhope Elmore HS, Millbrook, Ala.
17. Kurt Koehler, rhp, Sacramento CC
18. Craig Lybarger, lhp, Jefferson State (Ala.) CC
19. Nathan Nowicki, rhp, Colorado State U.
20. Seferino Encarnacion, of, Orange Park, Fla.
21. Brandon Tripp, of, Los Alamitos (Calif.) HS
22. Ryan Blake, c, U. of North Carolina
23. Tony Watson, lhp, Dallas Center-Grimes HS, Grimes, Iowa
24. Scott Dierks, of, Santa Clara U.
25. Alex Hinshaw, lhp, Chaffey (Calif.) JC
26. Ben Schroeder, of, Ball State U.
27. Toddric Johnson, of, Provine HS, Jackson, Miss.

28. **Greg Bartlett, lhp, Pheonix JC**
29. Stuart Alexander, rhp, Windsor (Calif.) HS
30. **Ryan Bear, of, U. of Central Florida**
31. **Spencer Wyman, c, U. of Oklahoma**
32. **Kris Thedorf, of, Elgin (ill.) CC**
33. **Roy Friesen, rhp, Columbia Basin (Wash.) CC**
34. **Antonio Orozco, rhp, California Baptist College**
35. **Justin Mattison, of, Virginia Commonwealth U.**
36. Rodney Rutherford, of, Shaw HS, Columbus, Ga.
37. **Nick Lovato, lhp, Cal State Fullerton**
38. Chris Bodishbaugh, rhp, Freedom HS, Oakley, Calif.
39. Neal Warchol, rhp, Triton (Ill.) JC
40. Geoff Rottmayer, of, Countryside HS, Clearwater, Fla.
41. Randall Clay, ss, Rattan (Okla.) HS
42. **Jim Adducci, of, Evergreen Park (Ill.) HS**
43. Jared Johnson, rhp, Kelowna, B.C.
44. Ben Hodges, ss, Allan Hancock (Calif.) JC
45. Chris Allen, c, South Williamsport Area HS, Duboistown, Pa.
46. Angel Flores, c, Petra Corret O'Neill HS, Manati, P.R.
47. Chilion Stapleton, rhp, Mississippi Delta JC
48. Ashkelon Stapleton, rhp, Mississippi Delta JC
49. Kyle Dickson, rhp, Sacramento CC
50. George Otero, ss, Hialeah (Fla.) HS

HOUSTON ASTROS (22)

1. (Choice to Giants as compensation for Type A free agent Jeff Kent)
2. **Jason Hirsh, rhp, California Lutheran U.**
3. Drew Stubbs, of, Atlanta (Texas) HS
4. **Josh Anderson, of, Eastern Kentucky U.**
5. **Josh Muecke, lhp, Loyola Marymount U.**
6. **Cliff Davis, rhp, Eupora (Miss.) HS**
7. **Jeff Jorgensen, of, Rice U.**
8. **Mike Collar, rhp, U. of Maine**
9. **Brock Koman, 3b, U. of Michigan**
10. **Beau Hearod, of, U. of Alabama**
11. Nick Green, rhp, Darton (Ga.) JC
12. **Wade Robinson, ss, Louisiana Tech**
13. **Jimmy Barthmaier, rhp, Roswell (Ga.) HS**
14. Mike Dunn, of, Cimarron Memorial HS, Las Vegas, Nev.
15. **Bo Edmiston, rhp, Mississippi College**
16. **Jamie Merchant, rhp, U. of Vermont**
17. **Pat O'Brien, c, Kent State U.**
18. **Kevin Vital, 1b, Southern U.**
19. **Edwin Maysonet, 2b, Delta State (Miss.) U.**
20. **Brian Skaug, 2b, California Lutheran U.**
21. **Kerri Fair, of, Jacksonville State U.**
22. **Lance Koeing, 2b, Monmouth U.**
23. **Mark Saccomanno, 3b, Baylor U.**
24. **Ryan Yurek, rhp, Loyola Marymount U.**
25. **Mario Garza, c, U. of Florida**
26. **Robert Ramsey, rhp, Texas A&M U.**
27. Omar Arif, lhp, Poteet HS, Mesquite, Texas
28. **Chad Prosser, ss, U. of North Carolina**
29. **Jason Corapci, 2b, Cal State Fullerton**
30. Scott Bradley, 2b, Chabot (Calif.) JC
31. Brandon McDougall, ss, Diablo Valley (Calif.) CC
32. Justin O'Bannon, rhp, Kingwood (Texas) HS
33. **Michael Walls, 3b, St. Joseph's U.**
34. Shawn Burris, lhp, North Central Texas JC
35. John Slusarz, rhp, U. of Connecticut-Avery Point JC
36. Logan Ondrusek, rhp, St. Paul HS, Shriner, Texas
37. Ethien Santana, of, Laredo (Texas) JC
38. Victor Ferrante, rhp, Benicia HS, Vallejo, Calif.
39. Josh Smith, rhp, Riverside (Calif.) CC
40. David Roberts, of, The Woodlands (Texas) HS
41. Ray Stokes, 2b, San Leandro (Calif.) HS
42. Shane Buschini, 1b, California HS, San Ramon, Calif.

KANSAS CITY ROYALS (5)

1. **Chris Lubanski, of, Kennedy-Kenrick HS, Schwenksville, Pa.**
1. **Mitch Maier, c, U. of Toledo** (Choice from Braves—30th—as compensation for Type B free agent Paul Byrd)
2. **Shane Costa, of, Cal State Fullerton**
3. **Brian McFall, 1b, Chandler-Gilbert (Ariz.) JC**
4. **Miguel Vega, 3b, Carmen B. Huyke HS, Arroyo, P.R.**
5. **Chris Goodman, rhp, Georgia Tech**
6. **Ryan Braun, rhp, U. of Nevada-Las Vegas**
7. **Michael Aviles, ss, Concordia (N.Y.) College**
8. **Brandon Powell, 2b, Coastal Carolina U.**
9. **John Gragg, lhp, Bethune-Cookman College**
10. Luis Cota, rhp, Sunnyside HS, Tucson
11. **Dustin Hughes, lhp, Delta State (Miss.) U.**
12. **Robbie McClellan, rhp, Arizona State U.**
13. **Mike Gaffney, ss, New York Tech**
14. **Steve Bray, rhp, U. of New Haven**
15. **Jake Mullis, rhp, UNC Wilmington**
16. **Bryan Graham, of, William Paterson U.**
17. Keoni Ruth, ss, Kamehameha HS, Honolulu
18. **Jeff Barry, of, U. of Vermont**
19. Nick Tisone, rhp, Pearl River (Miss.) CC
20. Michael Hernandez, of, Daytona Beach (Fla.) CC
21. **Irving Falu, 2b, Indian Hills (Iowa) CC**
22. Phillip Andersen, rhp, Chandler-Gilbert (Ariz.) CC
23. Pat Bresnehan, rhp, Dover Sherborn HS, Dover, Mass.
24. Wayne Daman, rhp, Forks (Wash.) HS
25. Jim West, rhp, River Valley HS, Fort Mohave, Ariz.
26. Mitch Goins, rhp, New Mexico JC
27. Kendall Thurman, rhp, Angelina (Texas) JC
28. Derrick Thomas, rhp, Captain Shreve HS, Shreveport, La.
29. William Arnold, ss, Tallahassee (Fla.) CC
30. Austin Pride, c, Lake Mary (Fla.) HS
31. D'Antonio Warren, rhp, Woodham HS, Pensacola, Fla.
32. Darrell Qualls, 3b, Lake City (Fla.) CC
33. Adam Miller, rhp, Knoxville (Iowa) HS
34. **Walter Sevilla, 2b, U. of Tennessee**
35. John Sokoll, lhp, Solon (Iowa) HS
36. Chris Malone, rhp, San Joaquin Delta (Calif.) CC
37. Clay Young, lhp, St. Francis HS, La Canada, Calif.
38. Jeff Ostrander, lhp, Louisburg (N.C.) JC
39. **Eddie Solis, 3b, Eastlake HS, San Diego**
40. Todd Redmond, rhp, Northside Christian HS, St. Petersburg, Fla.
41. Andy Underwood, rhp, Madera (Calif.) HS
42. Josh Hernandez, 2b, El Paso (Texas) CC
43. Matt Mallory, rhp, Central HS, Grand Junction, Colo. HS
44. Vince Berry, of, Triton (Ill.) JC
45. Andrew Groves, rhp, John Glenn HS, Walkerton, Ind.
46. Robert Coello, c, Lake Region HS, Winter Haven, Fla.
47. Jimmy Wallace, rhp, Bossier Parish (La.) CC
48. Zach Weidenaar, of, Bozeman (Mont.) HS
49. Gered Mochizuki, ss, Baldwin HS, Wailuku, Hawaii
50. Keven Whalen, 3b, Mid-Pacific Institute, Kanoehe, Hawaii

LOS ANGELES DODGERS (24)

1. **Chad Billingsley, rhp, Defiance (Ohio) HS**
2. **Chuck Tiffany, lhp, Charter Oak HS, Covina, Calif.**
3. Cory Van Allen, lhp, Clements HS, Sugar Land, Texas
4. **Xavier Paul, of, Slidell (La.) HS**
5. **Jordan Pratt, rhp, Central HS, Independence, Ore.**
6. **Matthew Kemp, of, Midwest City (Okla.) HS**
7. **Wesley Wright, lhp, Goshen (Ala.) HS**
8. **Lucas May, 3b, Parkway West HS, Chesterfield, Mo.**
9. **Brett Dowdy, 2b, U. of Florida**
10. **Phil Sobkow, rhp, Central Missouri State U.**
11. Tony Harper, c, Oak Creek HS, South Milwaukee
12. Cody White, lhp, Pleasant Grove HS, Texarkana, Texas
13. Derik Olvey, rhp, Pelham (Ala.) HS
14. David Pfeiffer, lhp, Lincoln Park Academy, St. Lucie, Fla.
15. **Russ Mitchell, ss, Cartersville (Ga.) HS**
16. **James Peterson, 1b, Indian Hills (Iowa) CC**
17. **Steven Sapp, of, West Torrance HS, Los Angeles**
18. **A.J. Ellis, c, Austin Peay State U.**
19. Matt Antonelli, ss, St. John's Prep, Danvers, Mass.
20. Chad Barben, 3b, Taylorsville (Utah) HS
21. **Travis Denker, 2b, Brea Olinda HS, Brea, Calif.**
22. Doug Frame, lhp, Tomball (Texas) HS
23. **Taylor Slimak, c, California Lutheran U.**
24. Ben Snyder, lhp, Bellevue (Ohio) HS
25. Kevin Skogley, lhp, Hermiston (Ore.) HS
26. **Thomas Piazza, c, Palm Beach Atlantic (Fla.) College**
27. Jesus Castillo, rhp, Tuscon (Ariz.) HS
28. Adam Moore, c, Northeast Texas CC
29. Adam Parliament, of, Pentiction (B.C.) SS
30. Mark Melancon, rhp, Golden HS, Arvada, Colo.
31. Garrett Kohler, rhp, Cimarron-Memorial HS, Las Vegas, Nev.
32. Kyle Reichert, rhp, Porterville (Calif.) JC
33. Ryan Zaft, rhp, Yuba (Calif.) CC
34. Brett Lawler, 1b, A&M Consolidated HS, College Station, Texas
35. Antonio Anderson, of, Greene County HS, Leakesville, Miss.
36. Drew Jeffcoat, lhp, Martin HS, Arlington, Texas
37. **Michael Ludwig, 1b, St. Olaf (Minn.) College**
38. Justin Ferreira, of, Stoneman Douglas HS, Parkland, Fla.
39. **Andy LaRoche, ss, Grayson County (Texas) CC**
40. D.J. Lewis, 1b, San Fernando (Calif.) HS
41. Matt Votaw, 3b, Brea-Olinda HS, Brea, Calif.
42. Cory Vanderhook, c, Golden West (Calif.) JC
43. Clayton Van Hook, ss, Brenham (Texas) HS
44. Travis Check, c, Logan HS, La Crosse, Wis.
45. Cass Rhynes, c, Bluefield HS, Cornwall, P.E.I.

46. Steven Paddock, of, Milford (Mass.) HS
47. Matt Chase, rhp, Naaman Forest HS, Garland, Texas
48. Kyle Rapp, of, Milford HS, Cincinnati
49. Clarence Farmer, of, U. of Arizona
50. Curtis Hudson, c, Yuba (Calif.) JC

MILWAUKEE BREWERS (2)

1. **Rickie Weeks, 2b, Southern U.**
2. **Anthony Gwynn, of, San Diego State U.**
3. **Lou Palmisano, c, Broward (Fla.) CC**
4. **Charlie Fermaint, of, Jose S. Alegria HS, Dorado, P.R.**
5. **Bryan Opdyke, c, Catalina Foothills HS, Tucson**
6. **Robbie Wooley, rhp, Taylor HS, Kokomo, Ind.**
7. **Brian Montalbo, rhp, U. of California**
8. **Ryan Marion, rhp, Glenn HS, Kernersville, N.C.**
9. **Greg Kloosterman, lhp, Bethel (Ind.) College**
10. **Tyler Morrison, rhp, Glendora (Calif.) HS**
11. **Adam Heether, 3b, Long Beach State U.**
12. **Carlos Corporan, 1b, Lake City (Fla.) CC**
13. Daniel Cannon, of, North Central Texas CC
14. Garrett Bussiere, c, Northglenn HS, Thornton, Colo.
15. Joel Rivera, of, Hoboken (N.J.) HS
16. **Mitch Stetter, lhp, Indiana State U.**
17. **Tommy Hawk, rhp, Cabrillo HS, Lompoc, Calif.**
18. **Oscar Montes, rhp, Flanagan HS, Cooper City, Fla.**
19. **Ty Taubenheim, rhp, Edmonds (Wash.) CC**
20. **Nick Slack, rhp, Lake City (Fla.) CC**
21. Taylor Meier, rhp, Orangewood Christian HS, Maitland, Fla.
22. **Terry Trofholz, of, Texas Christian U.**
23. Jon Mungle, of, Mississippi State U.
24. **Drew Anderson, of, U. Nebraska**
25. Jared Theodorakos, lhp, Baylor U.
26. Hasan Rasheed, of, Lake City (Fla.) CC
27. **Daniel McKenna, rhp, Rutgers-Camden U.**
28. **Kenny Durost, rhp, Lubbock Christian U.**
29. **Ricky Stover, lhp, U. of Texas-Arlington**
30. **Robby Deevers, of, U. of Texas-Arlington**
31. Sheldon Catchot, lhp, North Shore HS, Slidell, La.
32. **Will Lewis, 2b, Texas Christian U.**
33. Chad Miller, 1b, Mesquite HS, Gilbert, Ariz.
34. **Dan Grybash, rhp, Carthage (Wis.) College**
35. **Phil Hendrix, rhp, Virginia Military Institute**
36. Joe Ayers, ss, Juneau (Alaska) HS
37. Justin Wilson, lhp, Chandler-Gilbert (Ariz.) CC
38. Brent Weaver, rhp, Midwest City (Okla.) HS
39. Wes Yeary, rhp, Leon HS, Tallahassee, Fla.
40. Robert Hinton, rhp, Riverview HS, Sarasota, Fla.
41. Evan Baubles, c, Wall HS, Wall Township, N.J.
42. Zach Kohan, ss, Juneau-Douglas HS, Juneau, Alaska
43. Daryl Maday, rhp, Westocha Central HS, Bristol, Wis.
44. Raynel Robles-Encarnacion, 2b, Florida Air Academy, Melbourne, Fla.
45. Tim Grubbs, rhp, Lake City (Fla.) CC
46. Clay Blevins, c, Cowley County (Kan.) CC
47. Ryan Zink, rhp, La Follette HS, Madison, Wis.
48. Calvin Thompson, of, Shaw HS, East Cleveland, Ohio
49. Justin Sarka, rhp, Englewood HS, Jacksonville, Fla.
50. Luis Pardo, rhp, Westminster Christian HS, Miami

MINNESOTA TWINS (21)

1. **Matt Moses, 3b, Mills Godwin HS, Richmond**
2. **Scott Baker, rhp, Oklahoma State U.**
3. **Johnny Woodard, 1b, Cosumnes River (Calif.) JC**
4. **David Shinskie, rhp, Mt. Carmel Area HS, Kulpmont, Pa.**
5. Brandon McArthur, ss, Armwood HS, Seffner, Fla.
6. **Errol Simonitsch, lhp, Gonzaga U.**
7. **Chris Schutt, rhp, Cornell U.**
8. **Brandon McConnell, rhp, Foothill HS, Red Bluff, Calif.**
9. **Kevin Culpepper, lhp, Georgia Southern U.**
10. **Chris Marini, lhp, Glendale (Ariz.) CC**
11. Ryan Schroyer, rhp, Arizona State U.
12. **Steven Duguay, rhp, Gulf Coast (Fla.) CC**
13. **David Winfree, 1b, First Colonial HS, Virginia Beach, Va.**
14. **Levale Speigner, rhp, Auburn U.**
15. Trey Shields, rhp, Gulf Coast (Fla.) CC
16. **Michael Rogers, lhp, Del City (Okla.) HS**
17. Danny Vais, rhp, Seward County (Kan.) CC
18. **Eli Tintor, c, Hibbing (Minn.) HS**
19. **Jon Uhl, rhp, U. of South Florida**
20. **Gregory Najac, c, Mons, Belgium**
21. Scott Leffler, c, Dunedin (Fla.) HS
22. **Joe Gault, rhp, Canyon HS, Canyon Country, Calif.**
23. Charles Smith, rhp, Casa Roble HS, Orangevale, Calif.
24. **Patrick Ortiz, ss, Alfonso Casta Martinez HS, Maunabo, P.R.**
25. John Gaub, lhp, South St. Paul (Minn.) HS
26. **Jason Bowlin, rhp, Volunteer State (Tenn.) CC**
27. Peter Taraskevich, rhp, American Heritage HS, Sunrise, Fla.
28. Josh Oslin, rhp, Mora (Minn.) HS
29. **Bo Pettit, rhp, Louisiana State U.** (selection voided)
30. **Josh Gray, lhp, Lamar U.**
31. **Kris Lankford, rhp, Western Oklahoma State JC**
32. Nicholas Bleau, lhp, St. Elizabeth-Anne HS, Mercier, Quebec
33. Yvenson Bernard, of, Boca Raton (Fla.) Community HS
34. Quentin Andes, rhp, Cibola HS, Albuquerque, N.M.
35. Phillip Utley, rhp, Central-Merry HS, Jackson, Tenn.
36. Marquez Smith, 3b, Forest HS, Ocala, Fla.
37. **Heath Anderson, c, Pensacola (Fla.) JC**
38. Travis Metcalf, 3b, U. of Kansas
39. **Jesse Collins, c, U. of North Florida**
40. Adam Hawes, rhp, Connors State (Okla.) JC
41. **John Rumsey, of, San Diego Mesa JC**
42. **Mitchell Zamojc, of, U. of British Columbia**
43. **Travis Kalin, ss, Bishop Moore HS, Orlando, Fla.**
44. **Larry Jones, of, Baldwin County HS, Minette, Ala.**
45. Steve Pearce, ss, Indian River (Fla.) CC
46. Brant Rustich, rhp, Grossmont HS, San Diego
47. Clayton Trenary, of, Central Florida CC
48. Jared Swart, rhp, Cimmarron HS, Ames, Okla.
49. Michael Hollimon, ss, U. of Texas
50. Andrew Delagarza, lhp, Norwell HS, Ossian, Ind.

MONTREAL EXPOS (20)

1. **Chad Cordero, rhp, Cal State Fullerton**
2. **Jerry Owens, of, The Masters (Calif.) College**
3. **Kory Casto, of, U. of Portland**
4. **Edgardo Baez, of, Jose S. Alegria HS, Dorado, P.R.**
5. **Trey Webb, ss, Baylor U.**
6. **Josh Whitesell, 1b, Loyola Marymount U.**
7. **Devin Perrin, rhp, Grand Canyon U.**
8. **Daryl Thompson, rhp, La Plata HS, Mechanicsville, Md.**
9. **Gabriel Sosa, lhp, Lino Padron Rivera HS, Vega Baja, P.R.**
10. **Victor Hamisevicz, 1b, Gonzaga College HS, Dunn Loring, Va.**
11. **A.J. Wideman, lhp, Streetsville HS, Mississauga, Ontario**
12. **Mike St. Martine, c, Monmouth U.**
13. **Brad Ditter, 2b, New Mexico State U.**
14. **Larry York, 2b, Liberty U.**
15. **Brett Reid, rhp, Avila (Mo.) College**
16. **Ricky Jenkins, rhp, U. of South Carolina-Aiken**
17. **Luke Montz, c, Hill (Texas) JC**
18. **Eduardo Nunez, ss, American Military Academy, Guaynabo, P.R.**
19. **Jeremy Plexico, lhp, Winthrop U.**
20. Terry Engles, rhp, St. Peters Boys HS, Staten Island, N.Y.
21. Joe Bisenius, rhp, Iowa Western CC
22. **Gus Hlebovy, rhp, Kent State U.**
23. Brett Cooley, rhp, U. of Houston
24. Jonathan Hunton, rhp, Hutchinson (Kan.) JC
25. **James Russell, rhp, Villanova U.**
26. **James Henderson, rhp, Tennessee Wesleyan College**
27. **Bret Pignatiello, c, Eastern Illinois U.**
28. **Oscar Bernazard, 2b, Lindenwood (Mo.) U.**
29. **James Lehman, rhp, Notre Dame HS, Brampton, Ontario**
30. Matt Buck, lhp, Cactus Shadows HS, Cave Creek, Ariz.
31. Chris Hufft, rhp, West Hills HS, Santee, Calif.
32. B.J. Weidenbach, of, Fresno CC
33. Gabe Suarez, ss, Arcadia HS, Scottsdale, Ariz.
34. Matt Montgomery, rhp, Watkins Mill HS, Gaithersburg, Md.
35. **Doug Vroman, of, U. of New Haven**
36. Konrad Thieme, rhp, Westlake HS, Westlake Village, Calif.
37. Brendan Murphy, 1b, Grace Baptist Academy, Chattanooga, Tenn.
38. Seth Bynum, ss, Indiana U.
39. Trent Kline, c, West York Area HS, York, Pa.
40. Jacob Cook, lhp, Lee Davis HS, Mechanicsville, Va.
41. Jonathan Kalkau, rhp, Holy Trinity HS, Hicksville, N.Y.
42. Scott Rogowski, rhp, White County HS, Doyle, Tenn.
43. Anthony Savio, rhp, American River (Calif.) JC
44. Mike Ambort, c, South Side HS, Rockville Centre, N.Y.
45. Sean O'Brien, 1b, Horace Greeley HS, Chappaqua, N.Y.
46. **Alexis Morales, rhp, Oakton (Ill.) CC**
47. Steven Romero, rhp, Mt. San Antonio (Calif.) JC
48. Lance Zawadski, ss, St. John's HS, Ashland, Mass.
49. Kyle Nicholson, rhp, A&M Consolidated HS, College Station, Texas
50. Michael James, rhp, U. of Connecticut

NEW YORK METS (12)

1. **Lastings Milledge, of, Lakewood Ranch HS, Palmetto, Fla.**
2. (Choice to Red Sox as compensation for Type A free agent Cliff Floyd)
3. (Choice to Braves as compensation for Type A free agent Tom Glavine)
4. **Shane Hawk, lhp, Oklahoma State U.**
5. **Corey Coles, of, U. of Louisiana-Lafayette**

6. **Mateo Miramontes, rhp, U. of Nevada-Reno**
7. **Brian Bannister, rhp, U. of Southern California**
8. **Seth Pietsch, of, Oregon State U.**
9. **Vince Cordova, rhp, Loyola Marymount U.**
10. **David Reaver, ss, U. of Richmond**
11. **Andy Sides, rhp, De Soto (Mo.) HS**
12. **Tony Piazza, c, Southwest Missouri State U.**
13. **Carlos Muniz, rhp, Long Beach State U.**
14. **Stacy Bennett, 3b, Armstrong Atlantic State (Ga.) U.**
15. Harold Mozingo, rhp, Essex HS, Tappahannock, Va.
16. **David Smith, lhp, Pfeiffer U.**
17. **Ryan Meyers, rhp, Round Valley HS, Springerville, Ariz.**
18. Kyle McCulloch, rhp, Bellaire HS, Houston
19. **Ryan Harvey, of, UC Riverside**
20. Trip Mealor, rhp, Oconee County HS, Bishop, Ga.
21. **Travis Garcia, ss, Iona College**
22. **Greg Ramirez, rhp, Pepperdine U.**
23. **Dante Brinkley, of, Southwest Missouri State U.**
24. **Troy Fry, rhp, Berry (Ga.) College**
25. **Evan MacLane, lhp, Feather River (Calif.) CC**
26. **Kevin Rios, ss, Concordia (Calif.) U.**
27. Deunte Heath, rhp, Newton County HS, Decatur, Ga.
28. **Cory Wells, of, Plant City (Fla.) HS**
29. Justin Valdes, rhp, Dunedin (Fla.) HS
30. Adam Carr, rhp, West Valley (Calif.) JC
31. Jordan Newton, c, Larue County HS, Hodgenville, Ky.
32. **Humberto Gonzalez, ss, Feather River (Calif.) JC**
33. Abel Newton, rhp, Arkansas-Fort Smith JC
34. Drew Johnson, rhp, Wylie (Texas) HS
35. Patrick Howe, lhp, Faith Baptist HS, Longmont, Colo.
36. **Jim Wallace, c, Santa Clara U.**
37. Alex Turner, of, Catonsville (Md.) CC
38. Simon Gagnon, lhp, Montmorency (Quebec) College
39. Garrett Young, 3b, Edison HS, Fountain Valley, Calif.
40. Dan Fischer, rhp, Los Angeles Pierce JC
41. Mike Bartley, rhp, Alleghany HS, Covington, Va.
42. Brian Baugher, rhp, Brunswick HS, Frederick, Md.
43. Mike Chambless, c, Round Rock (Texas) HS
44. Tom Sgueglia, 3b, Rockland (N.Y.) CC
45. Jean-Michael Rochon-Salvas, rhp, Edouard Montpettit College HS, Longeuil, Quebec
46. Joel Thorney, rhp, Leaside HS, Toronto
47. **David Torres, rhp, U. of Central Florida**
48. Jon Malo, ss, Miami-Dade JC
49. Grover Benton, of, Webber (Fla.) College
50. Lester Aragon, c, Brito Private HS, Miami

NEW YORK YANKEES (27)

1. **Eric Duncan, 3b, Seton Hall Prep, Florham Park, N.J.**
2. **Estee Harris, of, Islip HS, Central Islip, N.Y.**
3. **Tim Battle, of, McIntosh HS, Peachtree City, Ga.**
4. Steven White, rhp, Baylor U.
5. **Cory Stuart, rhp, U. of British Columbia**
6. **Jason Stephens, rhp, Tallmadge (Ohio) HS**
7. **Jose Perez, of, Oceanside (Calif.) HS**
8. **Josh Smith, rhp, U. of Texas**
9. **Tyler Clippard, rhp, J.W. Mitchell HS, Trinity, Fla.**
10. **T.J. Beam, rhp, U. of Mississippi**
11. **Bryce Kartler, lhp, Arizona State U.**
12. **Brad Blackwell, rhp, North Carolina State U.**
13. **Michael Gardner, rhp, Miami (Ohio) U.**
14. **Enrique Cruz, 2b, Rice U.**
15. **Elvys Quezada, rhp, Seton Hall U.**
16. **Heath Castle, lhp, U. of Kentucky**
17. David Purcey, lhp, U. of Oklahoma
18. Michael Wagner, lhp, Lincoln Park Academy, Fort Pierce, Fla.
19. **Jeff Karstens, rhp, Texas Tech**
20. Daniel Bard, rhp, Charlotte Christian HS, Charlotte, N.C.
21. Richard Brindle, rhp, Peru (Ind.) HS
22. **John Urick, 1b, Oklahoma State U.**
23. Josh Smith, rhp, Central Arizona JC
24. Jeremiah Shepherd, rhp, Kilgore (Texas) HS
25. Kevin Smith, 3b, Cypress (Calif.) JC
26. Ryan Aldridge, rhp, Middle Georgia JC
27. Andrew Edwards, rhp, Florida International U.
28. Scott Kelly, rhp, St. Louis CC-Forest Park
29. **Adam Unger, 2b, Great Neck (N.Y.) South HS**
30. Grant Duff, rhp, JC of the Sequoias (Calif.)
31. Joe Larman, c, Purcell (Okla.) HS
32. Jeff Jacobsen, rhp, CC of Southern Nevada
33. Gary Keithley, rhp, Cleburn (Texas) HS
34. Robbie Widlansky, 3b, Taravella HS, Coral Springs, Fla.
35. **Hector Gonzalez, 2b, Brito Private HS, Miami**
36. Jose Hernandez, rhp, Oceanside (Calif.) HS
37. Blake Murphy, c, Tuscola HS, Waynesville, N.C.
38. David Welch, lhp, Texarkana (Texas) CC
39. Mikel McIntyre, of, Antioch (Calif.) HS
40. Brandon Kintzler, rhp, Pasadena (Calif.) CC
41. Carleton Hargrove, lhp, San Diego CC
42. **Taylor Mattingly, 1b, Central HS, Evansville, Ind.**
43. Justin Berg, rhp, Indian Hills (Iowa) CC
44. Mike Martinez, rhp, Cal State Fullerton
45. **Andre Randolph, 2b, Felecian (N.J.) College**
46. Jonathan Bertschinger, of, Fossil Ridge HS, Keller, Texas
47. Dan McCutchen, rhp, Grayson County (Texas) JC
48. Eric Schaler, rhp, Cherry Creek HS, Englewood, Colo.
49. David Ferazza, c, American River (Calif.) JC
50. Mike Muscato, c, Glendale (Ariz.) CC

OAKLAND ATHLETICS (25)

1. **Brad Sullivan, rhp, U. of Houston**
1. **Brian Snyder, 3b, Stetson U.** (Choice from Giants—26th—as compensation for Type A free agent Ray Durham)
1. **Omar Quintanilla, ss, U. of Texas** (Supplemental pick—33rd—for Durham)
2. **Andre Ethier, of, Arizona State U.**
3. **Dustin Majewski, of, U. of Texas**
4. **Eddie Kim, 1b, James Madison U.**
5. **Trent Peterson, lhp, Florida State U.**
6. **Luke Appert, 2b, U. of Minnesota**
7. **David Castillo, c, Oral Roberts U.**
8. **Mike McGirr, rhp, U. of Richmond**
9. **Grant Reynolds, rhp, Kennesaw State U.**
10. **Matt Lynch, lhp, Florida State U.**
11. **Vasili Spanos, 3b, Indiana U.**
12. **Brian Ingram, ss, Elon U.**
13. **Eddie Cornejo, ss, U. of Oklahoma**
14. **Anthony Zambotti, rhp, Indiana (Pa.) U.**
15. **Steve Bondurant, lhp, U. of South Carolina**
16. Vern Sterry, rhp, North Carolina State U.
17. **Ryan France, rhp, Chapman (Calif.) U.**
18. Billy Becher, 1b, New Mexico State U.
19. Graham Harrison, c, Tulare Union HS, Tulare, Calif.
20. **Gordon Corder, 1b, Gonzaga U.**
21. Braedyn Pruitt, ss, King's Academy, West Palm Beach, Fla.
22. Brian Peacock, c, Palmetto (Fla.) HS
23. Justin Towles, c, Collin County (Texas) CC
24. Cory Hahn, rhp, Tulane U.
25. **Sean Farrell, of, U. of North Carolina**
26. Brian Horwitz, of, U. of California
27. **James Heuser, lhp, Illinois Valley CC**
28. **Jared Trout, rhp, U. of Rhode Island**
29. Alex Woodson, lhp, Stella Marquez HS, Salinas, P.R.
30. Justin Cassel, rhp, Chatsworth (Calif.) HS
31. Joel Fountain, rhp, Feather River (Calif.) CC
32. Steve Sollmann, 2b, U. of Notre Dame
33. **Eric Macha, 3b, Case Western Reserve (Ohio) U.**
34. Broc Coffman, lhp, Rainier (Ore.) HS
35. Mike Mitchell, rhp, St. Charles (Mo.) CC
36. Matt Ryals, rhp, Wilson HS, Hacienda Heights, Calif.
37. Sean Kazmar, ss, CC of Southern Nevada
38. Zachary Simons, rhp, Glenns Ferry (Idaho) HS
39. Josh Rodriguez, 2b, South Houston HS, Houston
40. Chris Westervelt, c, Stetson U.

DENTON HANNA

BILL MITCHELL

Twin Athletics first-rounders
Brad Sullivan, left, and Brian Snyder

PHILADELPHIA PHILLIES (18)

1. (Choice to Indians as compensation for Type A free agent Jim Thome)
2. (Choice to Giants as compensation for Type B free agent David Bell)
3. **Tim Moss, 2b, U. of Texas**
4. **Michael Bourn, of, U. of Houston**
5. **Javon Moran, of, Auburn U.**
6. Jordan Parraz, rhp, Green Valley HS, Henderson, Nev.
7. **Kyle Kendrick, rhp, Mount Vernon (Wash.) HS**
8. **Matt Linder, rhp, Winston Churchill HS, Thunder Bay, Ontario**
9. **Jason Crosland, 3b, Lamar (Colo.) CC**
10. **Matt Hopper, 1b, U. of Nebraska**
11. Myron Leslie, 3b, U. of South Florida
12. **Kyle Parcus, lhp, Texas A&M U.**
13. **Joe Wilson, lhp, U. of Maryland-Baltimore County**
14. **Jose Cortez, c, Pomona-Pitzer (Calif.) College**
15. **Joe Brunink, 1b, Grand Valley State (Mich.) U.**
16. **Nate Cabrera, rhp, Trinidad State (Colo.) JC**
17. **Derek Griffith, lhp, Birmingham-Southern College**
18. Rob Johnson, c, Saddleback (Calif.) JC
19. **Joe Diefenderfer, lhp, Santa Clara U.**
20. **Brad Ziegler, rhp, Southwest Missouri State U.**
21. **Caleb McConnell, rhp, U. of Louisiana-Monroe**
22. **Marc Tugwell, 2b, Virginia Tech**
23. **Charlie Waite, c, U. of Mississippi**
24. **Justin Foust, of, U. of Toledo**
25. **C.J. Woodrow, rhp, U. of Minnesota**
26. **Dan Hodges, lhp, Florida State U.**
27. **Brad Overton, rhp, UNC Wilmington**
28. Blair Erickson, rhp, Jesuit HS, Fair Oaks, Calif.
29. **Justin Cerrato, rhp, U. of North Florida**
30. Ryan Harris, ss, Eisenhower HS, Rialto, Calif.
31. **Matt Padilla, rhp, America River (Fla.) CC**
32. Jake Tompkins, rhp, Louisiana State U. (contract voided)
33. **Justin Libey, rhp, Manchester (Ind.) College**
34. **Justin Riley, c, North Carolina State U.**
35. **Jason Pritchard, rhp, Baylor U.**
36. Brett Amyx, 3b, Coppell (Texas) HS
37. **Jesse Torborg, of, Suffolk County (N.Y.) CC-Ammerman**
38. Edgar Mercado, ss, Stoneman Douglas HS, Parkland, Fla.
39. Edward Romero, lhp, Central Union HS, Fresno
40. Andy Barb, c, Juanita HS, Kirkland, Wash.
41. Greg Reynolds, rhp, Terra Nova HS, Pacifica, Calif.
42. Matt Lambeth, of`, Mesa (Ariz.) CC
43. Cole Buchanan, lhp, Santiago HS, Corona, Calif.
44. Cal Stanke, rhp, St. Mary Central HS, Neenah, Wisc.
45. Jerod Estey, of, Moffat County HS, Craig, Colo.
46. Ryan Tabor, lhp, Green Valley HS, Henderson, Nev.
47. Michael Crotta, rhp, Martin County HS, Stuart, Fla.
48. Kyle Nash, rhp, Mater Dei HS, Huntington Beach, Calif.
49. Adam Sorgi, ss, Capistrano Valley HS, Mission Viejo, Calif.
50. Tad Reida, ss, Western HS, Kokomo, Ind.

PITTSBURGH PIRATES (8)

1. **Paul Maholm, lhp, Mississippi State U.**
2. **Tom Gorzelanny, lhp, Triton (Ill.) JC**
3. **Steve Lerud, c, Galena HS, Reno**
4. **Kyle Pearson, rhp, Mosley HS, Panama City, Fla.**
5. **Craig Stansberry, 3b, Rice U.**
6. C.J. Smith, 1b, U. of Florida
7. **Russell Johnson, rhp, Benjamin Russell HS, Alexander City, Ala.**
8. **Sergio Silva, rhp, U. of the Pacific**
9. **Kent Wulf, 2b, Quartz Hill HS, Lancaster, Calif.**
10. **John Peabody, of, Rancho Bernardo HS, San Diego**
11. **John Santiago, 3b, Nuestra Senora Del Carmen HS, Trujillo Alta, P.R.**
12. **Adam Boeve, of, U. of Northern Iowa**
13. Lee Land, rhp, Riverside HS, Durham, N.C.
14. **Jake Cuffman, rhp, Butler Area HS, Butler, Pa.**
15. **Dustin Molleken, rhp, Lethbridge (Alberta) CC**
16. **Justin Harris, ss, U. of South Carolina**
17. **Steven Herce, rhp, Rice U.**
18. **Pedro Powell, of, Middle Georgia JC**
19. Dallas Buck, rhp, Newberg (Ore.) HS
20. **Brett Holmes, of, Auburn U.-Montgomery**
21. Clay Hamilton, rhp, Penn State U.
22. **Chris Hernandez, rhp, U. of South Carolina**
23. Gregory Picart, ss, Adela Brenes Texidor HS, Guayama, P.R.
24. **Josh Sharpless, rhp, Allegheny (Pa.) College**
25. Matt Downs, rhp, Shelton State (Ala.) CC
26. Owen Williams, lhp, Edmonds (Wash.) CC
27. Clegg Snipes, rhp, Lincoln HS, Tallahassee, Fla.
28. Matthew Creighton, lhp, Meridian (Miss.) CC
29. James Van Ostrand, of, Allan Hancock (Calif.) JC
30. Joey Friddle, ss, Young Harris (Ga.) JC
31. Cody Doonan, rhp, Kirkwood (Iowa) CC
32. Sean Coughlin, c, Golden (Colo.) HS
33. Nicholas Palmisano, 1b, Broward (Fla.) CC
34. Jeremy Horst, lhp, Des Lacs-Burlington HS, Des Lacs, N.D.
35. Nick Colborn, rhp, Blue Mountain (Ore.) CC
36. Andy Mudd, of, Scotland HS, Laurinburg, N.C.
37. Daniel Brown, lhp, Bakersfield (Calif.) CC
38. Robert Felmy, of, Georgia Perimeter JC
39. Peter Wiggins, rhp, Patterson HS, Morgan City, La.
40. Christian Romple, c, West Valley HS, Yakima, Wash.
41. Chandler Miller, rhp, Young Harris (Ga.) JC
42. Tony Snow, rhp, Edmonds (Wash.) CC
43. Lance Scoggins, lhp, Bolton HS, Memphis, Tenn.
44. Troy Harrington, rhp, Palmdale (Calif.) HS
45. Domingo Reyes, lhp, Brito Private HS, Miami
46. Cody Lovejoy, c, Cypress (Calif.) HS
47. Bryan Henry, rhp, Florida HS, Tallahassee, Fla.
48. Antonio Westfield, of, Cleveland (Tenn.) HS
49. Raul Torres, rhp, Puerto Rico Advance College HS, Bayamon, P.R.
50. Ryhne Hughes, 1b, Pearl River (Miss.) CC

ST. LOUIS CARDINALS (28)

1. **Daric Barton, c, Marina HS, Huntington Beach, Calif.**
2. **Stuart Pomeranz, rhp, Houston HS, Collierville, Tenn.**
3. **Dennis Dove, rhp, Georgia Southern U.**
4. **Mark Michael, rhp, U. of Delaware**
5. **Brandon Yarbrough, c, Richmond HS, Ellerbe, NC**
6. **Matt Weagle, rhp, Franklin Pierce (N.H.) College**
7. **Brendan Ryan, ss, Lewis-Clark State (Idaho) College**
8. **Matt Pagnozzi, c, Central Arizona JC**
9. **Justin Garza, rhp, Seminole State (Okla.) JC**
10. **Buddy Blair, lhp, U. of Oklahoma**
11. **Nathan Kopszywa, rhp, Crichton (Tenn.) College**
12. Calvin Beamon, of, CC of Southern Nevada
13. **Kainoa Obrey, 3b, Brigham Young U.**
14. Ian Kennedy, rhp, La Quinta HS, Huntington Beach, Calif.
15. **Anthony Reyes, rhp, U. of Southern California**
16. **Omar Pena, ss, Northeastern U.**
17. **Kevin House, of, U. of Memphis**
18. **Jose Virgil, of, Oklahoma State U.**
19. **Jason Motte, c, Iona College**
20. **Jordan Pals, rhp, Eastern Illinois U.**
21. **Jason Burch, rhp, U. of Nebraska**
22. Derik Drewett, rhp, Watson Chapel HS, Sherrill, Ark.
23. **Matt Blanton, lhp, Hendrix (Ark.) College**
24. **Temetric Thomas, 2b, Mississippi Valley State U.**
25. **Tavaris Gary, of, Cumberland (Tenn.) U.**
26. **Levi Webber, of, Oregon State U.**
27. **Jason John, rhp, Grayson County (Texas) JC**
28. **Tanner Wootan, 2b, Chandler-Gilbert (Ariz.) JC**
29. **Brantley Jordan, lhp, U. of Texas**
30. Matt Lane, rhp, Iowa Western CC
31. **Mike Tamulionis, rhp, St. John's U.**
32. **Derek Roper, rhp, U. of Missouri**
33. **Casey Grimm, of, Seton Hall U.**
34. Kevin Mulvey, rhp, Bishop Ahr HS, Edison, N.J.
35. **Peter Eberhardt, rhp, Cerritos (Calif.) JC**
36. **John Powell, rhp, Carl Albert State (Okla.) JC**
37. **Sal Frisella, of, Southern Illinois U.**
38. Brent Sinkbeil, rhp, Charles Page HS, Sand Springs, Okla.
39. Thomas Brewer, rhp, Bloomington South HS, Bloomington, Ind.
40. **Peter Soteropoulos, lhp, U. of Connecticut**
41. Ryan Castellanos, 3b, Silverado HS, Las Vegas, Nev.
42. Roydrick Merritt, of, Nimitz HS, Houston
43. Max Scherzer, rhp, Parkway Central HS, St. Louis, Mo.
44. Ryan Reichelderfer, 1b, Arkansas-Fort Smith JC
45. **Joshua Markham, lhp, Riverdale HS, Murfreesboro, Tenn.**
46. Kameron Micholio, rhp, Eastern Utah CC
47. Tobirus Bell, of, John Wood (Ill.) CC

SAN DIEGO PADRES (4)

1. **Tim Stauffer, rhp, U. of Richmond**
2. **Daniel Moore, lhp, U. of North Carolina**
3. **Colt Morton, c, North Carolina State U.**
4. **Peter Stonard, ss, San Diego State U.**
5. **Billy Hogan, ss, Chandler-Gilbert (Ariz.) JC**
6. Cory Patton, of, Texas A & M U.
7. **Clark Girardeau, rhp, U. of South Alabama**
8. **Dirk Hayhurst, rhp, Kent State U.**
9. **Matt Lauderdale, c, College of Charleston**
10. **Fernando Valenzuela Jr., 1b, U. of Nevada-Las Vegas**
11. **Justin Smyres, ss, Cal State Fullerton**
12. **Jeff Leise, of, U. of Nebraska**

DRAFT

13. **Ryan Johnson, of, Wake Forest U.**
14. Steve Gendron, ss, Mississippi State U.
15. **Chuck Bechtel, rhp, Marist College**
16. Zane Carlson, rhp, Baylor U.
17. Justin Sokol, rhp, Iowa Central CC
18. **Greg Conden, rhp, George Washington U.**
19. Jesse Estrada, rhp, Grayson County (Texas) CC
20. **Leo Rosales, rhp, Cal. State Northridge**
21. **Brett Burnham, ss, U. of Connecticut**
22. **Brandon Kaye, 1b, Oklahoma City U.**
23. **Eddie Bonine, rhp, U. of Nevada**
24. **Ronnie Robinson, rhp, Georgia State U.**
25. Chuckie Caufield, of, Seminole State (Okla.) JC
26. Steven Wright, rhp, Valley View HS, Moreno Valley, Calif
27. John Banach, 3b, Los Angeles Harbor (Calif.) JC
28. Corey McCoy, of, Arkansas-Fort Smith JC
29. Steven Delabar, rhp, Volunteer State (Tenn.) CC
30. Ben Cox, rhp, San Jacinto (Texas) JC
31. Alan Tungate, rhp, St. Catharines (Ky.) JC
32. Chad Catalano, rhp, Pearl River (Miss.) CC
33. Colin Carter, lhp, Liberty Christian HS, Frisco, Texas
34. Chris Rayborn, rhp, Meridian (Miss.) CC
35. Dean Turner, rhp, Bellevue (Wash.) CC
36. Josh Sawatzky, rhp, W.C. Miller Collegiate HS, Altona, Manitoba
37. Thomas Skipper, of, Sandy Union (Ore.) HS
38. **Ryan Klatt, rhp, Biola (Calif.) U.**
39. Ryan McGraw, of, Coastal Carolina U.
40. Zach Shadle, rhp, Bethel HS, Spanaway, Wash.
41. Pat Warfle, of, Eau Gallie HS, Melbourne, Fla.
42. Nigel Goodwin, rhp, Spokane Falls (Wash.) CC
43. **Nathan Rogers, lhp, Connors State (Okla.) JC**
44. Justin Wichert, rhp, Cowley County (Kan.) CC
45. Clay Collier, c, Edmond North HS, Edmond, Okla.
46. **Brian Edwards, of, Metro State (Colo.) College**
47. Bryan Eubanks, rhp, Meridian (Miss.) CC
48. **Tom Vincent, of, McKellar, Australia**
49. Nate Simms, c, Central HS, Grand Junction, Colo.
50. Sean Rierson, rhp, U. of Arizona

SAN FRANCISCO GIANTS (26)

1. **David Aardsma, rhp, Rice U.** (Choice from Astros—22nd—as compensation for Type A free agent Jeff Kent)
1. (Choice to Athletics as compensation for Type A free agent Ray Durham)
1. **Craig Whitaker, rhp, Lufkin (Texas) HS** (Supplemental pick—34th—for loss of Kent)
2. **Todd Jennings, c, Long Beach State U.**
2. **Nate Schierholtz, 3b, Chabot (Calif.) JC**
3. **Brian Buscher, 3b, U. of South Carolina**
4. **Brooks McNiven, rhp, U. of British Columbia**
5. **Mike Wagner, of, U. of Washington**
6. **Billy Sadler, rhp, Louisiana State U.**
7. **Pat Misch, lhp, Western Michigan U.**
8. **Tim Hutting, ss, Long Beach State U.**
9. **Kellen Ludwig, rhp, Chipola (Fla.) JC**
10. **Jesse Schmidt, of, Cal State Sacramento**
11. **Jeff Petersen, rhp, U. of Washington**
12. **Ryan Sadowski, rhp, U. of Florida**
13. **Nick Conte, c, St. Mary's (Calif.) U.**
14. **Sean Martin, rhp, Cal State Fullerton**
15. **Ben Thurmond, rhp, Arizona State U.**
16. **Mike Mooney, of, JC of San Mateo (Calif.)**
17. Marcus Sanders, ss, Sarasota (Fla.) HS
18. **Patrick Dobson, of, U. of Nevada-Las Vegas**
19. **Jon Coutlangus, of, U. of South Carolina**
20. Raul Rodriguez, c, Florida Christian HS, Miami
21. Sean Watson, rhp, Florida Christian HS, Miami
22. Nathan Fogle, rhp, Mt. Hood (Ore.) CC
23. **Mike Kunes, lhp, UCLA**
24. **Brian Wilson, rhp, Louisiana State U.**
25. Nolan Mulligan, rhp, Chaminade-Madonna Prep, Hollywood, Fla.
26. Tyler Coon, lhp, CC of Southern Nevada
27. Omar Aguilar, rhp, Livingston (Calif.) HS
28. Roberto Gonzalez, of, Sunny Hills HS, Fullerton, Calif.
29. Danny DeSouza, of, Connors State (Okla.) JC
30. **Derek Barrows, 3b, Campbell U.**
31. Eduardo Baeza, rhp, Mission (Calif.) JC
32. O.D. Gonzalez, of, American HS, Miami
33. **Travis NeSmith, lhp, Florida Atlantic U.**
34. Cody McAllister, rhp, Edmonds (Wash.) CC
35. Tyson Brummett, rhp, Spanish Fork (Utah) HS
36. **Tim Alvarez, lhp, Southeast Missouri State U.**
37. Shannon Wirth, lhp, Mt. Hood (Ore.) CC
38. Jordan Hafer, 1b, Deerfield Beach (Fla.) HS
39. Mike Pierce, c, Fresno CC
40. Dylan Gonzalez, rhp, American Heritage HS, Plantation, Fla.
41. Mike Johnston, lhp, Ball State U.
42. Luis Martinez, c, Coral Park HS, Miami
43. Mike Bell, c, Red Bluff (Calif.) HS
44. John Odom, rhp, Tallahassee (Fla.) CC
45. James Braden, rhp, Manatee (Fla.) JC
46. Brandon Federici, lhp, Polk (Fla.) CC
47. Thomas Correa, ss, Florin HS, Sacramento, Calif.
48. Matt Berezay, of, Modesto (Calif.) JC
49. Doug Fister, rhp, Merced (Calif.) JC
50. Jim Popp, rhp, Duquesne U.

SEATTLE MARINERS (19)

1. (Choice to Diamondbacks as compensation for Type B free agent Greg Colbrunn)
1. **Adam Jones, ss/rhp, Morse HS, San Diego** (Supplemental pick—37th pick—as compensation for failure to sign 2002 first-round pick John Mayberry Jr.
2. **Jeff Flaig, 3b, El Dorado HS, Placentia, Calif.**
3. **Ryan Feierabend, lhp, Midview HS, Grafton, Ohio**
4. **Paul Fagan, lhp, Bartram Trail HS, Jacksonville**
5. **Casey Abrams, lhp, Wright State U.**
6. **Eric O'Flaherty, lhp, Walla Walla (Wash.) HS**
7. **Jeremy Dutton, 3b, North Carolina State U.**
8. **Tom Oldham, lhp, Creighton U.**
9. **Justin Ruchti, c, Rice U.**
10. **Mike Cox, 3b, Florida Atlantic U.**
11. **Joe Woerman, rhp, San Diego CC**
12. **Ruben Flores, rhp, El Paso (Texas) CC**
13. **Shawn Nottingham, lhp, Jackson HS, Canton, Ohio**
14. **Tim Dorn, rhp, East Los Angeles JC**
15. Scott Maine, lhp, Dwyer HS, Palm Beach Gardens, Fla.
16. **Brian Schweiger, c, Cal State San Bernardino**
17. Jason Snyder, rhp, Dixie (Utah) JC
18. **James Hymon, ss, Rust (Miss.) College**
19. **Aaron Jensen, rhp, Springville (Utah) HS**
20. Carroll Gaddis, of, Hoke County HS, Raeford, N.C.
21. **Casey Craig, of, Granite Hills HS, La Mesa, Calif.**
22. **Sam Bradford, of, Gardner-Webb U.**
23. Danny Santin, c, Brito Private HS, Miami
24. **Kenneth Falconer, rhp, U. of Kansas**
25. Jason Cable, lhp, Palmdale (Calif.) HS
26. Dwayne Lynah, of, Spartanburg Methodist (S.C.) JC
27. Richard Breshears, rhp, Hutchinson (Kansas) CC
28. Daniel McDonald, lhp, Theodore (Ala.) HS
29. Chris Garcia, rhp, Brooklyn, N.Y.
30. Steve Santos, rhp, Los Medanos (Calif.) JC
31. Doug Mathis, rhp, Central Arizona JC
32. Adam Poole, lhp, Lincoln Trail (Ill.) JC
33. Blake Rampy, rhp, Tomball (Texas) HS
34. Paul Keck, c, Sacramento CC
35. Andy Reichard, rhp, State College (Pa.) HS
36. Alex Baboulas, lhp, Birchmount Park Collegiate Institute, Toronto
37. Joel Allin, lhp, Stockbridge (Ga.) HS
38. Yusuf Carter, c, Canarsie HS, Brooklyn, N.Y.
39. Trevor Heid, of, Dixie (Utah) JC
40. Mark Tournangeau, rhp, Queen Elizabeth Park HS, Scarborough, Ontario
41. Dane Awana, lhp, Saddleback (Calif.) CC
42. Danny Santiesteban, of, Brito Private HS, Miami
43. Harold Williams, rhp, Cerritos (Calif.) CC
44. Edwin Totesault, ss, Brito Private HS, Miami
45. McCay Green, rhp, Lake Sumter (Fla.) CC
46. Mike Hofius, 1b, Long Beach State U.
47. Dan Kapala, rhp, Shrine HS, Royal Oak, Mich.
48. Markus Roberts, ss, Deer Valley HS, Antioch, Calif.
49. Jose Laffitte, of, Miami Senior HS
50. Tim Turner, of, East Tennesee State U.

TAMPA BAY DEVIL RAYS (1)

1. **Delmon Young, of, Camarillo (Calif.) HS**
2. **James Houser, lhp, Sarasota (Fla.) HS**
3. Andrew Miller, lhp, Buchholz HS, Gainesville, Fla.
4. **Travis Schlichting, 3b, Round Rock (Texas) HS**
5. **Jon Barratt, lhp, Hillcrest HS, Springfield, Mo.**
6. **Christian Lopez, c, Hialeah HS, Miami Lakes, Fla.**
7. **Brian Henderson, lhp, U. of Houston**
8. **Matthew Maniscalco, ss, Mississippi State U.**
9. Billy Buckner, rhp, Young Harris (Ga.) JC
10. **Shaun Cumberland, of, Pace (Fla.) HS**
11. **Chad Cooper, 2b, Middle Tennessee State U.**
12. **John Jaso, c, Southwestern (Calif.) JC**

13. Chad Orvella, rhp, North Carolina State U.
14. Aaron Gangi, lhp, U. of Akron
15. Andy Weimar, rhp, LeMoyne College
16. Jared Hughes, rhp, Santa Margarita HS, Laguna Niguel, Calif.
17. Chris Gustafson, of, Kamiak HS, Granite Falls, Wash.
18. Jason Cayton, rhp, Cerritos (Calif.) JC
19. Joshua Geer, rhp, Navarro (Texas) JC
20. Mark Schleicher, 2b, Pfeiffer (N.C.) U.
21. Casey Hudspeth, rhp, Sarasota (Fla.) HS
22. Rod Allen, of, Arizona State U.
23. Ryan McCally, rhp, Stanford U.
24. Chris Shaver, lhp, College of William & Mary
25. Stephen Jones, of, U. of Alabama-Birmingham
26. Joe Little, lhp, U. of Arizona
27. Adam Roos, 3b, Hamarskjeld HS, Thunder Bay, Ontario
28. Andrew Swanson, rhp, Galesburg (Ill.) HS
29. Fernando Puebla, ss, Southern U.
30. Adam Ottavino, rhp, Berkeley Carroll HS, Brooklyn, N.Y.
31. Tom Lagreid, c, Everett (Wash.) CC
32. Matt Travis, lhp, Santa Clara U.
33. Jordan Olson, lhp, U. of Southern California
34. Travis Fuller, lhp, Hayesville (N.C.) HS
35. Gus Jacobson, rhp, Cactus Shadows HS, Cave Creek, Ariz.
36. Wade Leblanc, lhp, Barbe HS, Lake Charles, La.
37. Kris Medlen, ss, Garh HS, Cerritos, Calif
38. Kris Dufner, ss, U. of Delaware
39. Kevin Allen, of, West Henderson HS, Hendersonville, N.C.
40. Graham Baxter, rhp, McQueen HS, Reno, Nev.
41. Leon Johnson, of, Thatcher (Ariz.) HS
42. Travis Beech, 2b, Austin Peay State U.
43. Grant Theophilus, lhp, Ocean View HS, Huntington Beach, Calif.
44. Josh Kendrick, 1b, U. of Mobile (Ala.)
45. Brandon Rousseve, ss, Meridian (Miss.) CC
46. Josh Bolen, of, U. of Louisville
47. Brad Matthews, 2b, Surry (N.C.) CC
48. Derrick Shaw, ss, Benton HS, Bossier City, La.
49. Lars Davis, c, Grand Prairie Composite HS, Grande Prairie, Alberta
50. Brent Speigner, rhp, Vestavia Hills, Ala.

TEXAS RANGERS (9)

1. John Danks, lhp, Round Rock (Texas) HS
2. Vince Sinisi, 1b, Rice U.
3. John Hudgins, rhp, Stanford U.
4. Wes Littleton, rhp, Cal State Fullerton
5. Matt Lorenzo, rhp, Kent State U.
6. Adam Bourassa, of, Wake Forest U.
7. Matt Farnum, rhp, Texas A&M U.
8. Jeremy Cleveland, of, U. of North Carolina
9. Tim Cunningham, lhp, Stanford U.
10. Adam Fox, 3b, Ohio U.
11. Cody Clark, c, Wichita State U.
12. Andrew Wishy, of, U. of Arkansas
13. Emerson Frostad, 3b, Lewis-Clark State (Idaho) College
14. Brian Mattoon, lhp, LeMoyne College
15. Chris Alexander, 1b, U. of New Mexico
16. Kevin Altman, rhp, Rubidoux HS, Riverside, Calif.
17. Ian Kinsler, ss, U. of Missouri
18. Cain Byrd, rhp, Southwood HS, Shreveport, La.
19. Charles Bowman, rhp, Jacksonville U.
20. Micah Furtado, 2b, Lewis-Clark State (Idaho) College
21. Marc LaMacchia, rhp, Florida State U.
22. Dane Bubela, of, Rice U.
23. Jonathan Ramos, rhp, Tomas C Ongay HS, Bayamon, P.R.
24. Ben Rowe, rhp, Oregon State U.
25. Justin Hatcher, c, Texas Christian U.
26. Ian Gac, 1b, Edmonds-Woodway HS, Seattle
27. Johnny Washington, ss, Mt. San Jacinto (Calif.) JC
28. Brad Lincoln, rhp, Brazoswood HS, Clute, Texas
29. Chris Cordeiro, rhp, UCLA
30. Scott Feldman, rhp, San Mateo (Calif.) JC
31. Rosalino Valenzuela, rhp, Central Arizona JC
32. Colby Paxton, rhp, Auburn U.
33. Scott Welch, ss, U. of Minnesota (contract voided)
34. Sammy Hewitt, 3b, U. of North Carolina
35. Austin Faught, lhp, U. of Louisiana-Lafayette
36. Dwayne White, of, Cowley County (Kan.) CC
37. Loren Deans, of, Capistrano Valley HS, Mission Viego, Calif.
38. Paul Sandoval, rhp, Saddleback (Calif.) JC
39. Josh Lansford, 3b, St. Francis HS, Santa Clara, Calif.
40. Matt Vogel, 2b, East Los Angeles JC
41. Francisco Mora, rhp, Eastlake HS, Chula Vista, Calif.
42. Charles Hesseltine, lhp, Maloney HS, Meriden, Conn.
43. Hunter Harrigan, c, Cowley County (Kan.) CC
44. Curtis White, lhp, U. of Oklahoma

RICK BATTLE

Blue Jays first-rounder
Louisiana State shortstop Aaron Hill

TORONTO BLUE JAYS (13)

1. Aaron Hill, ss, Louisiana State U.
2. Josh Banks, rhp, Florida International U.
3. Shaun Marcum, rhp, Southwest Missouri State U.
4. Kurt Isenberg, lhp, James Madison U.
5. Justin James, rhp, U. of Missouri
6. Christian Snavely, of, Ohio State U.
7. Danny Core, rhp, Florida Atlantic U.
8. Chad Mulholland, rhp, Southwest Missouri State U.
9. Jamie Vermilyea, rhp, U. of New Mexico
10. Jayce Tingler, of, U. of Missouri
11. Tom Mastny, rhp, Furman U.
12. Jayson Rodriguez, rhp, Indian River (Fla.) CC
13. Matt Foster, lhp, U.S. Naval Academy
14. Jeremy Harper, rhp, Virginia Military Institute
15. Vito Chiaravalloti, 1b, U. of Richmond
16. Joey Reiman, c, Grand Canyon U.
17. Jordy Templet, rhp, U. of Louisiana-Lafayette
18. Ryan Roberts, 3b, U. of Texas-Arlington
19. Adrian Martin, rhp, South Fork HS, Stuart, Fla.
20. Brad Depoy, rhp, The Woodlands (Texas) HS
21. Mark Sopko, rhp, Arizona State U.
22. Vinny Esposito, 3b, Rutgers U.
23. Jeremy Acey, 2b, Skyline (Calif.) JC
24. Nick Evangelista, rhp, U. of Pittsburgh
25. Brian Patrick, 2b, Duke U.
26. Kyle Thousand, of, U. of Iowa (selection voided)
27. Brian Reed, rhp, U. of Alabama
28. Patrick Breen, of, Cal Poly San Luis Obispo
29. Chris Nieto, lhp, Riverside (Calif.) CC
30. Billy Wheeler, rhp, South Suburban (Ill.) JC
31. Joaquin Canizal, rhp, Union (Ky.) College
32. Brad Mumma, lhp, Western Michigan U.
33. Joey Wolfe, c, U. of Louisiana-Monroe
34. Jeremy Noegel, rhp, U. of West Florida (selection voided)
35. Jim Burt, 1b, U. of Miami
36. Matt Trink, rhp, Horizon HS, Scottsdale, Ariz.
37. Aric Van Gaalen, lhp, St. Petersburg (Fla.) JC
38. Jack Ryser, of, Santa Ana (Calif.) JC
39. William Blackmon, lhp, Arlington Heights HS, Fort Worth, Texas
40. Jimmy Coker, lhp, Spartanburg (Methodist (S.C.) JC
41. Scott Tolbert, rhp, Georgia Southern U. (selection voided)
42. Jeremy Knicely, c, Longwood (Va.) College
43. Ryan Gordon, lhp, UNC Greensboro
44. Brent Johnson, of, U. of Nevada-Las Vegas
45. Paul Franko, 1b, Horizon, HS, Scottsdale, Ariz.
46. Paul Marlow, rhp, Elgin Park HS, White Rock, B.C.
47. Jeff Walker, lhp, Vernon Regional (Texas) JC
48. Bryan Hansen, lhp, Kishwaukee (Ill.) JC
49. Michael Rider, rhp, Cosumnes River (Calif.) JC
50. Angel Hernandez, of, Champagnat Catholic HS, Hialeah, Fla.

OBITUARIES

OBITUARIES

NOVEMBER 2002-OCTOBER 2003

Ed Albosta, a righthander who had brief stints in the majors in 1941 and 1946, died Jan. 7 in Saginaw, Mich. He was 84. Albosta led the Class B Piedmont League in ERA (1.83) in 1941 while going 15-5, which earned him a two-game stint with the Brooklyn Dodgers, where he went 0-2, 6.23. Albosta missed the 1943-45 seasons in military service but went straight back to the majors, going 0-6, 6.08 in 17 games with the Pirates in 1946.

Chuck Aleno, a third baseman who spent parts of four seasons with the Reds, died Feb. 10 in Deland, Fla. He was 84. Aleno hit .243-1-18 as a bench player with the Reds in 1941, got 14 at-bats in 1942 and 10 more in 1943. He played a full season for Cincinnati in 1944, hitting .165-1-15 in 127 at-bats.

Chuck Anderson, who was part of Division II power Florida Southern's baseball program for more than 43 years, died April 3 from cancer. He was 63. Anderson played for the Moccasins in the late 1950s and joined the coaching staff in 1963. He became head coach in 1984. He posted a career 843-251 record (including 1967, when he served as interim coach) in 20 years, placing him 12th all-time in D-II victories. His .770 winning percentage ranks second in D-II history. His Mocs teams won national championships in 1985 and 1995.

Hank Arft, a first baseman for the St. Louis Browns from 1948-52, died Dec. 14, 2002, at the age of 80. In 1951, Arft hit .261-7-42, his most productive season in the major leagues.

Toby Atwell, a catcher who spent five seasons in the majors, died Jan. 25 in Purcellville, Va. He was 78. Atwell broke into the majors in 1952, hitting .290-2-31 in 395 at-bats. He split his major league time between the Cubs, Pirates and Braves.

Red Barbary, who got one at-bat with the Washington Senators in 1943, died Sept. 27 in Simpsonville, S.C. He was 83.

Ralph Beard, a righthander who went 0-4, 3.72 in 13 games for the Cardinals in 1954, died on Feb. 10 in West Palm Beach, Fla. He was 74.

Steve Bechler, a righthander who spent five years in the Orioles minor league system and played briefly in Baltimore in 2002, died Feb. 17 after collapsing at a spring training workout. He was 23.

Emil Belich, a long-time scout for the Phillies and Brewers, died Sept. 3. He was 83. Paul Molitor and Jim Gantner, two of his key signings, were part of the Brewers' pennant-winning team in 1982.

Greg Biagini, who had a 10-year minor league playing career and an 11-year minor league managerial career, died of kidney cancer Oct. 3 in Oklahoma City. He was 51. Biagini broke into pro ball as an outfielder in 1973. He spent most of his final five pro seasons in the Mexican League, hitting .348-17-90 for Juarez in 1981, his best season. After his playing career ended, Biagini managed mostly in the Rangers organization, peaking at Triple-A Oklahoma City, where he won (346) and managed (716) more games than anyone in Oklahoma City's 92-year professional baseball history. His team won the American Association championship in 1996.

Dick Bogard, the Athletics' scouting director from 1984-94, died Aug. 29. He was 66. Bogard's playing career ended in 1962, and he began scouting for the Astros from 1963-1972. He also managed for three seasons. After working as an area scout for the Brewers and a national crosschecker for the Major League Scouting Bureau, he was hired as A's scouting director in 1984 and oversaw the drafting and signing of Walt Weiss, Jason Giambi and Ben Grieve, among others.

Bobby Bonds, a speedy outfielder who was a frequent member of the 30-30 club long before it was recognized, died Aug. 23 in San Francisco. He was 57. By the time he passed away, Bonds was best known as Barry Bonds' father, but Bonds was a formidable talent himself. He hit a grand slam in his first at-bat in 1968 and led the National League in runs (120) a season later. In 1971, he became the fourth player to hit 30 home runs and steal 30 bases in the same season. Bonds hit at least 20 home runs in 10 of 11 seasons from 1969-79, and he stole more than 40 bases seven different times. Bonds came within one home run of becoming the first member of the 40-40 club in 1973, when he hit .283-39-96 with 43 steals. Bonds was a three-time Gold Glove winner and MVP of the 1971 All-Star Game. He finished his career with 332 home runs and 461 stolen bases.

BILL NICHOLS

Bobby Bonds

Sam Bowens, an outfielder who spent seven seasons in the majors, died March 28 in Wilmington. N.C. He was 64. Bowens played for the Nashville Elite Giants in 1957 and '58, one of the final Negro League teams. He signed with the Orioles and broke into the majors in 1963.

Bobby Bragan Jr., the general manager of the Double-A Jacksonville Suns and owner of the independent Elmira Pioneers, died Feb. 7 in Las Vegas. He was 59.

Josh Brinkley, the hitting coach for the Bangor Lumberjacks of the independent Northeast League, died Oct. 16 in Wallace, N.C. He was 30. Brinkley was jogging when he was struck and killed by a passing automobile.

Jack Bruner, a lefthander who spent parts of two seasons in the American League, died June 24 in Lincoln, Neb. He was 88. Bruner had a short stint in 1949 with the White Sox, where he went 1-3, 7.88 in eight innings. The next season Bruner split the year between the White Sox and Browns, going 1-2, 4.40 in 47 innings.

Bill Buhler, the trainer for the Dodgers for 36 years, died May 17. He was 75. Buhler served as the Dodgers' lead trainer from 1960-1995. He helped develop several innovations, including a throat guard for catchers and equipment to help rehabilitation after Tommy John surgery.

George Bullard, who had one at-bat for the Tigers in 1954, died in Lynn, Mass., on Dec. 23, 2002. He was 74.

Randall Burden, a righthander in the Angels system, died in his sleep on Dec. 6, 2002, at his Suffolk, Va., home. He was 23. Burden was 0-0, 7.45 for Rookie-level Provo in 10 appearances in 2002.

Wally Burnette, a righthander with the Kansas City Athletics from 1956-58, died Feb. 12 in Danville, Va. He was 73. Burnette went 14-21, 3.56 in his major league career.

Joe Buzas, a longtime minor league baseball owner who also had a long minor league career and a brief major league career as an infielder, died March 19 in Salt Lake City, Utah. He was 83. At the time of his death, he owned the Pacific Coast League's Salt Lake franchise.

Dick Case, the former executive director of USA Baseball, died Nov. 20, 2002. He was 73. Case was instrumental in baseball becoming an official Olympic sport.

Eddie Chandler, a righthander who went 0-1, 6.30 in 30 innings for Brooklyn in 1947, died July 6 in Las Vegas. He was 81.

Slick Coffman, a righthander who spent four seasons in the American League from 1937-40, died May 8 in

APPENDIX

Birmingham. He was 92. Coffman was 15-12, 5.60 overall for the Tigers and Browns.

Alta Cohen, who hit .194-0-2 in 67 at-bats for the Brooklyn Dodgers and Phillies from 1931-33, died March 11. He was 94.

Al Corwin, a righthander for the New York Giants from 1951-55, died Oct. 23 in Geneva, Ill. He was 76. Corwin pitched in 117 games, going 18-10, 3.98.

Claude Crocker, who pitched five innings and compiled a 6.75 ERA for the Brooklyn Dodgers in 1944-45, died Dec. 19, 2002, in Clinton, S.C. He was 78.

Dave DeBusschere, one of the few athletes to successfully play two professional sports, died May 14 in New York. He was 62. DeBusschere was a National Basketball Association hall of famer. As a righthanded pitcher, DeBusschere made the majors in 1962, his first pro season. He threw 18 innings for the White Sox in 1962, going 0-0, 2.00. A year later, he went 3-4, 3.11 with the White Sox in 84 innings. He spent the next two seasons in the minors before giving up baseball as his NBA career developed.

Joe Decker, who pitched for the Cubs, Twins and Mariners in a nine-year career from 1969-79, died March 2 at age 55. Decker went 36-44, 4.17 overall.

Charlie Devens, a righthander who was the last living member of the 1932 Yankees, died Aug. 13 in Milton, Mass. Devens signed with the Yankees in 1932 and made one start late in the season. He picked up a complete-game victory, allowing two runs. A year later, Devens went 3-3, 4.35 in 62 innings. He made one more start with the Yankees in 1934.

Larry Doby, the first black player in the American League, died June 18 in Montclair, N.J. He was 79. Doby, an all-state high school player in football, basketball and baseball at East Side High in Paterson, N.J., joined the Negro Leagues' Newark Eagles in 1942, playing second base and shortstop for two seasons. After missing two years serving in the Navy during World War II, Doby returned to the Eagles in 1946, helping them to a Negro League World Series title. After he hit .414 for the Eagles in 1947, the Indians signed Doby and immediately put him in the big leagues. He hit .156 in 32 at-bats as an infielder, but by 1948 he earned a starting job in the outfield and hit .301-14-66. Doby was one of the better players in the American League for the next decade, twice leading the league in homers and in RBIs once. He was an all-star for seven straight seasons, from 1949-55. Doby wrapped up his career in 1959 with 1,515 hits, 253 home runs and 970 RBIs. He later managed the White Sox in 1978.

MEL BAILEY

Larry Doby

Harry Eisenstat, a lefthander who spent parts of seven seasons in the majors, died March 21 in Beachwood, Ohio. He was 87. Eisenstat broke into the majors with the Brooklyn Dodgers in 1935 and went on to compile a 25-27, 3.84 career record.

Al Epperly, a righthander who had a long minor league career, died April 14 in McFarland, Wis. He was 84. Epperly made it to the majors for nine games in 1938, going 2-0, 3.67 with the Cubs, but he didn't make it back for another 12 seasons. He had a 5.00 ERA in five games with the Dodgers in 1950 in his only other major league stint. Epperly won 167 games in the minors, reaching double-digits in wins in nine different seasons.

Dottie Ferguson, an outfielder in the All-American Girls Baseball League for 10 seasons, died May 8. Ferguson, also known as Dottie Key after she married in 1949, was a fixture in Rockford throughout her decade in baseball. Speed was Ferguson's forte; she stole 91 bases in 1951 and more then 50 bags in three other seasons.

Hilly Flitcraft, a lefthander who went 0-0, 3.00 for the Phillies in 1942, died April 2 in Boulder, Colo. He was 79.

Eddie Freed, an outfielder who played for the Phillies in 1942, died on Nov. 11 in Rock Hill, S.C. He was 83. Freed made his mark in his debut against the Reds, going 4-for-5 off Johnny Vander Meer.

Jim Fridley, an outfielder who spent parts of three seasons in the majors, died Feb. 28 in Port Charlotte, Fla. He was 78. Fridley played 152 games in the majors over three different seasons. He hit .251-4-16 for the Indians in 1952, .246-4-36 for the Orioles in 1954 and .222 in limited action with the Reds in 1958.

Jim Garland, a scout for 28 years, died Dec. 8 in Wake Forest, N.C. He was 86. Garland scouted for four years for the Royals and another 24 years for the Dodgers. With the Dodgers, he signed Sid Bream, Franklin Stubbs, Tracy Woodson, Brian Holton, Wayne Kirby and Darren Holmes.

Greg Garrett, a lefthander who spent parts of two seasons in the majors, died June 7 in Santa Clara, Calif. He was 55. Garrett spent the entire 1970 season with the Angels, going 5-6, 2.64. The next season, he made two appearances with the Reds, going 0-1, 1.00.

Stephen Gates, who worked in media relations and broadcasting in the minor leagues, died Oct. 4 in Hillsborough, N.C. He was 27. Gates died in a hit-and-run accident after he pulled off an interstate near Hillsborough, N.C., to check a flat tire. He had been the media-relations director for the independent Northeast and Central leagues and the radio play-by-play voice for the Burlington Indians (Appalachian) in 2002-03.

Rodger George, the Wayne State (Mich.) baseball coach for 14 years, died Oct. 15. He was 63. With 272 career victories, George was the winningest coach in school history. He led Wayne State to the 1998 Great Lakes Athletic Conference title.

Al Gionfriddo, an outfielder who robbed the Yankees Joe DiMaggio of a home run with a spectacular catch in the 1947 World Series, died on March 14. He was 81. Gionfriddo played for the Pirates and Brooklyn Dodgers from 1944-47, hitting .256-2-58 overall.

Dick Hanlon, a former minor league pitcher and longtime scout, died Sept. 27. He was 70. Hanlon spent eight years as a minor league righthander with his biggest success coming on April 27, 1958, when he pitched a seven-inning no-hitter for Spokane (Pacific Coast) against Vancouver. His best season came in 1951, when he went 19-11, 3.32 for Santa Barbara (California). After he retired as a player, Hanlon worked as a scout for the Dodgers from 1975-96.

Red Hardy, a righthander who pitched two games for the New York Giants, died Aug. 15 in Phoenix. He was 80. Hardy spent most of seven seasons in the minors before getting a taste of the big leagues in 1951. Hardy made two appearances.

Sid Hatfield, the most outstanding player at the 1951 College World Series, died in late January. He was 78. Playing for runner-up Tennessee, Hatfield had a homer and two runs scored while pitching a complete-game shutout in a 2-0 win over Springfield, Mass. He came back to pitch six innings of relief in Tennessee's loss to Oklahoma in the title game.

Jack Hays, a scout, minor league coach and minor league pitcher, died in February in Lake Oswego, Ore. He was 48. Hays had most recently worked as a scout for the Tigers. He also had a five-year career as a pitcher, beginning in 1976.

Stokes Hendrix, who pitched in the Negro Leagues for the Nashville Elite Giants, died on Feb. 4. He was 89.

Earl Henry, who pitched for the Indians in 1944 and 1945, died on Dec. 10, 2002, in Zanesville, Ohio. He was 85. Henry pitched 39 innings and finished his career 1-4, 5.03.

Johnny Hopp, a first baseman who spent 14 seasons in the majors, died June 1 in Scottsbluff, Neb. He was 86. Hopp was an all-star in 1946 for the National League's

Boston Braves, when he hit .333-3-48 with 21 steals. He also played on four different World Series champions. He was a member of the 1942 and '44 Cardinals teams and the 1950 and '51 Yankees squads. Hopp's best major league season was 1950, when he hit .340-8-47 with 43 walks for the Pirates before being dealt to the Yankees.

Art Houtteman, a righthander who spent 12 seasons in the American League, died May 6 in Rochester Hills, Mich. He was 75. Houtteman went 87-91, 4.14 as a major leaguer. His best season was in 1950, when he went 19-12, 3.54 while leading the league in shutouts.

Bob Kammeyer, a righthander who had two short stints with the Yankees, died Jan. 27 in Sacramento, Calif. He was 52. Kammeyer made it to the majors in 1978, after a 12-2, 4.59 season for Tacoma (Pacific Coast) earned him a callup for seven games. He made it back to New York in September 1979 for one inauspicious outing. Kammeyer allowed eight earned runs, including two home runs, without recording an out. After the game, manager Billy Martin gave him and fellow pitcher Paul Mirabella (who allowed three runs in two-thirds of an inning) $100 each and told them to go out and have a good time to forget their outings. It was Kammeyer's last major league appearance.

Harry Kinzy, a righthander who went 0-1, 5.03 in 34 innings with the White Sox in 1934, died June 22 in Fort Worth. He was 92.

John Klippstein, a righthander who spent 18 seasons in the majors as a spot starter and reliever, died Oct. 10 in Elgin, Ill. He was 75. Klippstein reached the majors in 1950, but had only one season, 1956, where he made more than 25 starts. He recorded saves in 16 of his 18 seasons, and led the American League in saves in 1960, when he went 5-5, 2.91 with 14 saves for the Indians. Klippstein also went 10-11, 4.83 for the Cubs in 1953 and 12-11, 4.09 for the Reds in 1956. He played for eight different major league clubs during his career, finishing with a 101-118 career record, 4.24 ERA and 66 saves.

David Koch, the president of New Era Cap Co., died Dec. 13, 2002, in Pittsburgh. He was 66. Koch spent his lifetime working for New Era, the exclusive provider of caps for major league teams since 1993. As a salesman he helped the company build from a small family operation into a company that produces more than 15 million caps a year.

Mike Kosman, who appeared in one game for the Reds, died on Dec. 10, 2002, in Lafayette, Ind. He was 85. On April 20, 1944, Kosman entered a game as a pinch-runner and was thrown out at the plate to end his major league career. He never registered a major league at-bat.

Makoto Kozuru, who holds the Japanese baseball single-season record for RBIs (161) and runs scored (143), died June 2 in Tokyo. He was 80.

Mickey Kreitner, a catcher who played 42 games in the majors, died March 6 in Nashville. He was 80. Kreitner hit .375 in eight at-bats for the Cubs in 1943 and .153 in 85 at-bats a year later.

Joan Kroc, the widow of McDonald's founder Ray Kroc, died Oct. 12 at age 75 after a battle with brain cancer.She inherited the Padres when her husband died in 1984 and sold the team in 1990 to a group led by Los Angeles TV producer Tom Werner.

Don Landrum, an outfielder who spent seven seasons in the majors, died Jan. 9 in Pittsburgh, Calif. He was 66. Landrum made it to the majors for a brief two-game stint with the Phillies in 1957. He didn't return until 1960 after an all-star season for Buffalo (International) in which he hit .292-18-75 while leading the league in games, at-bats, runs, hits, total bases and doubles earning him a late-season call from the Cardinals.

Johnny Lazor, an outfielder who spent four seasons with the Red Sox, died Dec. 9, 2002, in Renton, Wash. He was 90. Lazor didn't begin playing professional baseball until he was 25 and it took him another seven seasons to make it to the majors. He debuted with the Red Sox in 1943, hitting .226-0-13 in 83 games. Lazor hit .310-5-45 season in 1945, but hit just .138 for the Red Sox in 1946 in his final season.

Al Libke, a pitcher/outfielder who spent two seasons in the majors, died March 7 in Wenatchee, Wash. He was 84. Libke initially broke into pro ball as a pitcher, but became an outfielder in 1944, hitting .307-5-51 for Seattle (Pacific Coast) while also going 2-2, 4.00 in limited action as a pitcher. The next season, he broke into the war-depleted major leagues, where his versatility was an asset. Libke hit .283-4-53 for the Reds, while also pitching four scoreless innings. A year later, he hit .253-5-42 for the Reds in his final major league action.

Vince Lloyd, a broadcaster of Cubs games for WGN-TV and WGN Radio, died July 3 in Green Valley, Ariz. He was 86. Lloyd joined Jack Brickhouse on the first Cubs telecast in 1948. He later served as the Cubs' radio voice for 23 years.

Bob Loane, an outfielder who made it to the majors for three games with the Washington Senators in 1939 and 13 with the Boston Braves in 1940, died Dec. 11, 2002, in Monterey, Calif. He was 88.

George Maloney, an American League umpire from 1969-84, died July 29 in Barstow, Calif. He was 75. Maloney worked the 1975 World Series and three AL Championship Series. Maloney also spent 18 seasons working in the minors. After he retired as an umpire, Maloney spent eight seasons as the commissioner of the South Florida College Baseball Umpire Association and served as an area observer for the Professional Baseball Umpire Corporation since 1997.

Frank McCormack, a trainer and scout, died Oct. 9 in Bakersfield, Calif. He was 84. McCormack served as a trainer for Ventura (California) in 1947-1949. He later became a scout for the Yankees in the 1950s. But while he was a Yankees' scout, McCormack never lost his love of the Brooklyn Dodgers. A longtime member of the Society For American Baseball Research, McCormack wrote a trivia column for the Dodgers fan newsletter. He was buried in a Dodgers cap and t-shirt with a bat and a copy of Baseball America. His headstone reads "This Ain't Dodger Stadium."

Phil McCullough, a righthander who made it to the majors for one game with the Washington Senators in 1942, died Jan. 16 in Decatur, Ga. He was 85.

Mickey McDermott, a lefthander who spent 12 seasons in the majors, died Aug. 7 in Phoenix. He was 74. McDermott made it to the majors after three seasons in the minors, but it took another three seasons for him to settle in with the Red Sox for good. After going 5-4, 4.05 in limited action with the Red Sox in 1949, McDermott stuck in 1950 for the full season. A year later, he was 8-8, 3.35 as a member of the Sox' rotation. In 1953, he went 18-10, 3.01 in his best season. He also reached double digits in wins in 1952 and 1955.

Mickey McGowan, who pitched in three games for the New York Giants in 1947, died March 8.

DIAMOND IMAGES

Dave McNally

Dave McNally, one of the top pitchers in the early 1970s and a key figure in overturning baseball's reserve clause, died Dec. 1, 2002, in Billings. Mont. He was 60. McNally won at least 20 games in four consecutive seasons, including a league-leading 24 in 1970. He was the first pitcher inducted into the Orioles hall of fame and had a career record of 184-119, 3.24. McNally spent all but one of his 14 major league seasons as an Oriole. He was on two Baltimore World Series winners, and he pitched a four-hit shutout in Game

APPENDIX

Four of the 1966 World Series as the Orioles swept the Dodgers. He also pitched in the World Series in 1969 and '70, and his grand slam in 1970 is the only World Series grand slam ever by a pitcher. But it was his role in the groundbreaking lawsuit that overturned the reserve clause that may be McNally's lasting legacy. He played the 1975 season without signing his contract, declaring that by not signing it he would become a free agent at the end of the season. The owners asserted the reserve clause tied a player to his team in perpetuity, but an arbitrator ruled for McNally and fellow pitcher Andy Messersmith, declaring them free agents. That paved the way for the free agency rules that have led to greatly increased player freedom and higher salaries. McNally never got to enjoy the benefits of the decision, however. After a 3-9 season in 1975, he retired during the offseason when he became a free agent.

Norm McRae, a righthander who spent parts of two seasons with the Tigers, died July 25 in Garland, Texas. He was 55. McRae went 10-5, 2.83 for Daytona Beach (Florida State) in his minor league debut in 1966. Three years later he was in the majors, going 0-0, 6.00 in three innings with the Tigers. A year later, he had a longer run and had a 2.90 ERA in 31 innings.

Durwood Merrill, an American League umpire for 23 years, died Jan. 11 in Texarkana, Texas. He was 64. Merrill worked three All-Star Games and the 1988 World Series. But he was probably better known for his sense of humor and outlandish persona. He wrote a book about his experiences as an umpire entitled, "You're Out and You're Ugly Too".

Jim Mertz, a righthander who went 5-7, 4.62 for the Washington Senators in 1943 in his lone season in the majors, died Feb. 4 in Waycross, Ga. He was 86.

Bud Metheny, a former coach and athletic director at Old Dominion who hit .247-31-156 in a four-year career with the Yankees from 1943-46, died Jan. 2. He was 87.

Dutch Meyer, a second baseman who spent parts of six seasons in the majors, died Jan. 19 in Fort Worth, Texas. He was 87. As a 22-year-old, Meyer made a brief debut in the majors, pinch-running in one game for the Cubs in 1937. Meyer made it back to the majors in 1940, hitting .259 in 58 at-bats for the Tigers. He spent the next two seasons shuttling between the minors and Detroit before missing the 1943 and '44 seasons because of military service. When he returned from the war, Meyer settled in for his best big league season. After being sent to the Indians for Roy Cullenbine before the 1945 season, Meyer hit .292-7-48 in 524 at-bats.

Bill Miller, a lefthander who spent four seasons in the American League, died July 1 in Lititz, Pa. He was 80. Miller went 4-6, 3.48 for the Yankees in 1952, his best season.

Deacon Murray, a catcher who had a six-year major league career, died April 9 in Fort Worth. He was 85. Murray reached the majors in 1948, getting four at-bats for the Indians. Two years later, he was up with the Indians to stay, hitting .273-1-13. He spent the next five seasons with the Indians, Athletics, and Orioles.

Joe Ostrowski, a lefthander who played with the St. Louis Browns and Yankees from 1948-52, died Jan. 3 in Wilkes-Barre, Pa. He was 87. Ostrowski went 23-25, 4.54 with 15 saves in his career.

George Plimpton, a gentleman editor, literary patron and most notably participatory journalist, died Sept. 25 in New York. He was 76. Plimpton had achievements in a variety of pursuits but was best known for participating in various sports and writing about it. One of his earliest forays in the sporting world came when he pitched against several all-stars at Yankee Stadium in 1960, which inspired the book "Out of My League." His best-known baseball work, however, came in the April 1, 1985 edition of Sports Illustrated. "The Curious Case of Sidd Finch" described a mysterious Mets rookie who was said to throw his fastball up to 168 mph. The April Fool's Day hoax gained national attention, and SI received more than 2,000 letters in response to the story. Plimpton later developed the story into a novel.

Billy Parker, a middle infielder who spent three seasons in the majors, died Feb. 9 in Sun City West, Ariz. He was 56. Parker made it to the majors in his third professional season with his speed helping him rocket through the Angels minor league system. Parker stole 67 games in his debut at Davenport (Midwest) in 1969. A year later, he stole 71 bases while hitting .287 for El Paso (Texas). After hitting .306 and stealing 115 bases in 1971 for Salt Lake (Pacific Coast), Parker made it to the majors for a 70 at-bat stint, but he hit only .229.

Claude Passeau, a righthander who was one of the best pitchers in the majors in the early 1940s, died Aug. 30 in Lucedale, Miss. He was 94. Passeau was a four-time all-star and led the National League with 137 strikeouts in 1939 while reaching double-digits in wins in 10 straight seasons from 1936-45. He broke into the majors with the Pirates in 1935 and spent parts of four seasons with the Phillies, but it was with the Cubs that Passeau did his greatest work. His best season came in 1940, when he went 20-13, 2.50 with four shutouts and five saves. He also led the NL in innings (292) in 1937 and shutouts (five) in 1945, when he was a key member of the last Cubs teams to appear in the World Series. He went 1-0, 2.70 in the series.

Rusty Peters, a middle infielder who spent a decade in the majors, died Feb. 21 in Harrisonburg, Va. He was 82. The versatile Peters was capable of playing anywhere in the infield, but a suspect bat limited his opportunity. He finished his career with a .236 batting average. His best seasons was 1937, when he hit .260-3-43 in a career-high 339 at-bats.

Jim Pruett, a catcher who played nine games in the majors in 1944-45, died July 29 in Waukesha, Wis. He was 85. Pruett hit .250 in three games with the Philadelphia Athletics in 1944 and .222 in six games a year later.

Ken Raffensberger, a lefthander for the Reds and Phillies who reached double digits in wins in five straight seasons, died Nov. 10 in York, Pa. He was 85. Raffensberger spent 15 seasons in the majors in a career that stretched from 1937-1957. In his first pro season at Cambridge, he led the Class D Eastern Shore League in innings while going 18-6. A 15-10, 2.91 season at Triple-A Rochester (International) in 1938 got Raffensberger noticed, and he earned a one-game callup to the Cardinals in 1939. He also pitched for the Cubs and Phillies before his career surged when he was traded to Cincinnati in 1947. Raffensberger was a solid pitcher who finished his career with a 119-154 record. His best season was 1952, when he went 17-13, 2.81 and led the National League with six shutouts. He also led the league in saves (six) in 1946.

Frank Reiber, a catcher who played in 44 games for the Tigers from 1933-1936, died on Dec. 26, 2002, in Bradenton, Fla. He was 93.

Bob Rinker, a catcher who hit more than .300 in three different minor league stops and a brief major league appearance, died Dec. 19, 2002, in Hazleton, Pa. He was 81. Rinker hit a career-high .381-5-36 for Class C Youngstown (Middle Atlantic) in 1950, earning him a three-game callup to the Phillies, where he hit .333 in three games.

John Ritchey, a catcher in the Negro Leagues in the 1940s, died on Jan. 14 in Chula Vista, Calif. He was 80. Ritchey led the Negro American League in batting in 1947 as a member of the Chicago American Giants.

Billy Rogell, a slick-fielding shortstop who spent 14 seasons in the majors, died Aug. 9 in Sterling Heights, Mich. He was 98. Rogell led American League shortstops in fielding percentage three consecutive years (1935-37). His best season offensively came in 1934, when he hit .293-3-100 while stealing 13 bases for the Tigers. Rogell spent all but the final season of his major league career in the American League, retiring after hitting .136 for the Cubs in 1940.

John Royster, a Baseball America staff member from 1988-2002 died June 29 in Raleigh, N.C. He was 43. Royster spent 14 years working for the magazine, serving as an editor while also covering high school baseball, coordinating international baseball coverage and editing a variety of Baseball America books.

Ernie Rudolph, a righthander who reached the majors for seven games in 1945, died Jan. 13 in Black River Falls, Wis. Rudolph's best season was in 1944, when he was 14-14, 2.88 for the American Association's St. Paul Saints. The next season he made seven appearances with the Brooklyn Dodgers, going 1-0, 5.00.

Henry Santos, a lefthander who spent seven seasons in the minors, died June 27 in Union City, N.J. He was 30. Santos was signed by the Tigers out of the Dominican Republic in 1989. He reached Triple-A Toledo for one appearance in 1995, but spent all of the 1996 season with Double-A El Paso in the Brewers organization. After going 7-7, 6.10, he was released.

Steve Shilling, owner of the independent Atlantic League's Camden Riversharks, died of cancer May 7 at his Medford, N.J., home. He was 44. Shilling was instrumental in getting Camden's 6,500-seat Campell Field built. Under his leadership, the Riversharks went from an expansion team to the playoffs in only two seasons.

Pete Sivess, a righthander who spent three years with the Phillies, died June 1 in Candler, N.C. He was 89. Sivess went directly to the majors after playing college ball, going 3-4, 4.57 for the Phillies in 1936.

Lefty Sloat, a righthander who spent parts of two seasons in the National League, died April 18 in St. Paul. He was 84. It took Sloat 11 years to make it to the majors. After he went 17-9 with a league-leading 1.99 ERA for the Double-A Fort Worth Cats (Texas) in 1947, he finally got noticed, earning a seven-inning stint with the Brooklyn Dodgers.

Harry Smith, a longtime scout, died Jan. 3. He was 75. Smith spent 18 years as a part-time scout for the Dodgers and Orioles before becoming a full-time scout in 1978. He spent the next 14 years working for the Brewers, and also scouted for the Angels (1991-1994) and Red Sox (1995-2000) before retiring.

Bob "Riverboat" Smith, who pitched for the Red Sox, Cubs and Indians in 1958-59, died on June 23 in Clarence, Mo. He was 76. Smith pitched 97 innings, going 4-4, 4.75.

J.B. Spencer, who played for three Negro Leagues championship teams, died on May 17. He was 83. Spencer won titles from 1943-1945 as a member of the Homestead Grays and the Birmingham Barons.

Homer Spragins, a righthander who led the Class B Southeastern League in ERA in 1950, died Dec. 10, 2002, in Minter City, Miss. He was 81. Spragins had a four-game stint with the Phillies in 1947, going 0-0, 7.20.

Dernell Stenson, a promising young outfielder for the Reds, was shot and killed in Chandler, Ariz., Nov. 5. He was 25. Stenson batted .247-3-13 in 37 games for the 2003 Reds, who claimed him off waivers from the Red Sox in spring training. Stenson was hitting .394-1-9 in 18 games in the Arizona Fall League at the time of his death.

Bragg Stockton, a righthander who had a short stint in the Cocoa Rookie League in the early 60s, died Jan. 21, 2003, in Pasadena, Texas. He was 64. After his playing career was over, Stockton coached at Jones High in Houston, San Jacinto (Texas) Junior College and the University of Houston. He was a volunteer pitching coach at Houston at the time of his death.

Dick Stuart, a first baseman who became well known for his powerful bat and misadventures as a fielder, died Dec. 15, 2002. He was 70. Stuart was aptly known as "Dr. Strangeglove" because of his troubles in the field. He committed 29 errors as a first baseman for the Red Sox in 1963 and never had a fielding percentage higher than .986 in 10 major league seasons. But while Stuart had trouble with the glove, he always could hit. In 1956, he put together one of the great years in minor league baseball history, hitting 66 homers and driving in 158 runs for Class A Lincoln of the Western League. He made it to the majors two seasons later with Pittsburgh. In eight full major league seasons, Stuart hit more than 30 homers on four occasions, including 42 homers and a league-leading 118 RBIs for Boston in 1963.

Haywood Sullivan, a former major league player, manager, general manager and owner, died on Feb. 12 in Fort Myers, Fla. He was 72. Sullivan debuted as a player in 1955 with the Red Sox and also played for the Kansas City Athletics. His most productive season came in 1961 when he batted .242-6-40 for the A's. In 1965, he managed the Athletics for 136 games, finishing with a 54-82 record. At the end of that season, he joined the Red Sox as director of player personnel. Sullivan, Jean Yawkey and Buddy LeRoux became part owners of the Red Sox in 1978, with Sullivan adding responsibilities as the the team's general manager. He held the job until 1983.

Haywood Sullivan

Jug Thesenga, a righthander who went 0-0, 5.25 for the Washington Senators in 1944, died Dec. 3, in Wichita, Kansas. He was 88.

Ben Wade, the scouting director for the Dodgers from 1973-1990, died Dec. 2, 2002. He was 80. Wade spent five years as a pitcher for the Brooklyn Dodgers, Cardinals, Cubs and Pirates from 1948-55, going 19-17, 4.34 overall. He began scouting for the Dodgers from 1962-73 and it was his work as the team's scouting director that will be most remembered. During Wade's tenure, the Dodgers consistently produced strong drafts, signing such players as Rick Sutcliffe, Dave Stewart, Mike Scioscia, Steve Sax, Steve Howe, Orel Hershiser, John Franco, John Wetteland, Mike Piazza and Eric Karros. During Wade's tenure, the Dodgers won the World Series in 1981 and 1988.

John Welaj, an outfielder who spent four years in the majors, died Sept. 13 in Arlington, Texas. He was 89. Welaj hit .274-1-33 with 13 steals in 201 at-bats as a rookie with the Washington Senators in 1939. He played parts of the next two seasons with the Senators and returned to the bigs with the Philadelphia A's in 1943, batting .242-0-15.

Jim Westlake, a first baseman whose major league career consisted of one at-bat, died Jan. 3 in Sacramento, Calif. He was 72. Westlake spent nine years in the minors, including a .291-5-122 season for Yakima (Western International) in 1950. After missing three seasons because of military service, Westlake hit .285-5-70 for San Francisco (Pacific Coast) in 1954. The next season, he failed to get a hit in his one pinch-hit appearance for the Phillies during the first week of the season, and was quickly sent to Syracuse (International).

Dick Whitman, an outfielder who spent six seasons with the Brooklyn Dodgers and Phillies, died Feb. 12 in Peoria, Ariz. He was 82. Whitman broke into the majors in 1946, hitting .260-2-31 in 265 at-bats.

Chris Zachary, a righthander who was one of the first Houston Colt .45s, died April 19 in Knoxville, Tenn. He was 59. Zachary was one of the many prospects the Colt .45s signed to 1963 contracts early in 1962 as part of a huge spending spree to try to stock the expansion team with young talent. Zachary impressed enough in instructional league in 1962 that the Colt .45s put him on the major league roster for the 1963 season. He went 2-2, 4.89 in his debut, the only season Zachary did not spend time in the minors. Zachary went 16-6, 3.20 for San Antonio the next season, leading the Double-A Texas League in complete games and winning percentage before getting a brief callup back to Houston.

APPENDIX